DUBLIN BUSINESS SCHOOL
LIBRARY

KU-305-820

THE YEAR'S WORK 2003

DBS Library
22436

The Year's Work in English Studies
Volume 84

Covering work published in 2003

Edited by
WILLIAM BAKER
and
KENNETH WOMACK

with associate editors

JANET BEER
KIRSTIE BLAIR
JOHN BRANNIGAN
DOREEN D'CRUZ
OLGA FISCHER
LISA HOPKINS
STEVEN PRICE
MARY SWAN

DUBLIN BUSINESS SCHOOL
LIBRARY
RECEIVED
1 7 JAN 2006

Published for
THE ENGLISH ASSOCIATION
by

OXFORD JOURNALS
OXFORD UNIVERSITY PRESS

OXFORD
UNIVERSITY PRESS

Great Clarendon Street, Oxford OX2 6DP, UK

Oxford University Press is a department of the University of Oxford.
It furthers the University's objective of excellence in research, scholarship,
and education by publishing worldwide in

Oxford New York

Athens Auckland Bangkok Bogotá Buenos Airez Cape Town
Chennai Dar es Salaam Delhi Florence Hong Kong Istanbul Karachi
Kolkata Kuala Lumpur Madrid Melbourne Mexico City Mumbai Nairobi
Paris São Paulo Shanghai Taipei Tokyo Toronto Warsaw

Oxford is a registered trade mark of Oxford University Press
in the UK and in certain other countries

Published in the United States
by Oxford University Press Inc., New York

© The English Association 2005

The moral rights of the author have been asserted
Database right Oxford University Press (maker)

First published 2005

All rights reserved. No part of this publication may be reproduced,
stored in a retrieval system, or transmitted, in any form or by any means,
without the prior permission in writing of Oxford University Press,
or as expressly permitted by law, or under terms agreed with the appropriate
reprographics rights organization. Enquires concerning reproduction
outside the scope of the above should be sent to the Rights Department.
Oxford University Press, at the address above

You must not circulate this publication in any other binding or cover
and you must impose this same condition on any acquirer

British Library Cataloguing in Publication Data
Data available

ISSN 0084 4144

ISBN 9780199299201

1 3 5 7 9 10 8 6 4 2

Typeset in Europe by the Alden Group, Oxford

Printed in Great Britain
on acid-free paper by
Biddles Ltd., King's Lynn

The English Association

The object of The English Association is to promote the knowledge and appreciation of English language and its literatures.

The Association pursues these aims by creating opportunities of co-operation among all those interested in English; by furthering the recognition of English as essential in education; by discussing methods of English teaching; by holding lectures, conferences, and other meetings; by publishing several journals, books, and leaflets; and by forming local branches overseas and at home. English Association Fellowship recognize distinction and achievement in the field of English worldwide. The Association will celebrate its centenary in 2006.

Publications

The Year's Work in English Studies. An annual narrative bibliography which aims to cover all work of quality in English studies published in a given year. Published by Oxford University Press.

The Year's Work in Critical and Cultural Theory. An annual narrative bibliography which aims to provide comprehensive cover of all work of quality in critical and cultural theory published in a given year. Published by Oxford University Press.

Essays and Studies. A well-established series of annual themed volumes edited each year by a distinguished academic. The 2005 volume is *Literature and the Visual Media* edited by Professor David Seed, University of Liverpool and published by Boydell & Brewer.

English. This internationally-known journal of the Association is aimed at teachers of English in universities and colleges, with articles on all aspects of literature and critical theory, an extensive reviews section and original poetry. Three issues per year.

Use of English. The longest-standing journal for English teachers in schools and colleges. Three issues per year.

English 4–11. Designed and developed by primary English specialists to give practical help to primary and middle school teachers. Three issues per year.

English Association Studies. A new monograph series published in association with Boydell & Brewer.

Issues in English. Occasional pamphlet series.

Membership

Membership information can be found at http://www.le.ac.uk/engassoc or please write to The English Association. University of Leicester, University Road, Leicester LE1 7RH, UK or email: engassoc@le.ac.uk.

The Year's Work in English Studies

Subscriptions for Volume 84

Institutional (combined rate to both *The Year's Work in English Studies* and *The Year's Work in Critical and Cultural Theory*) print and online: £228/$376.

Personal rates: as above.

Please note: £ Sterling rates apply in Europe, US$ elsewhere. All prices include postage, and for subscribers outside the UK delivery is by Standard Air. There may be other subscription rates available. For a complete listing, please visit www.ywes.oxfordjournals.org/subinfo.

Online Access

For details please email Oxford University Press Journals Customer Services on: jnls.cust.serv@oxfordjournals.co.uk.

Order Information

Full prepayment, in the correct currency, is required for all orders. Orders are regarded as firm and payments are not refundable. Subscriptions are accepted and entered on a complete volume basis. Claims cannot be considered more than FOUR months after publication or date of order, whichever is later. All subscriptions in Canada are subject to GST. Subscriptions in the EU may be subject to European VAT. If registered, please supply details to avoid unnecessary charges. For subscriptions that include online versions, a proportion of the subscription price may be subject to UK VAT. Personal rate subscriptions are only available if payment is made by personal cheque or credit card and delivery is to a private address.

Methods of payment. Payment may be made by cheque (payable to Oxford University Press) in £ Sterling drawn on a UK bank or in US$ drawn on a US bank, bank transfer (£ Sterling–Barclays Bank plc, Oxford City Office, PO Box 333, Oxford, OX1 3HS, UK. Bank sort code: 20-65-18, Account No. 70299332, IBAN number GB89BARC20651870299332, Swift code BARCGB22), or by credit card (Mastercard, Visa, Switch or American Express).

Back Issues

The current plus two back volumes are available from Oxford University Press. Previous volumes can be obtained from the Periodicals Service Company, 11 Main Street, Germantown, NY 12526, USA. Email: psc@periodicals.com; tel: +1 (518) 537 4700; fax +1 (518) 537 5899.

Further information. Journals Customer Service Department, Oxford University Press, Great Clarendon Street, Oxford OX2 6DP, UK. Email: jnls.cust.serv@oxfordjournals.org; tel (and answerphone outside normal working hours): +44 (0) 1865 353907; fax: +44 (0) 1865 353485. *In the US, please contact:* Journals Customer Service Department, Oxford University Press, 2001 Evans Road, Cary, NC 27513, USA. Email: jnlorders@oxfordjournals.org; tel (and answerphone outside normal working hours): 800 852 7323 (toll-free in USA/ Canada); fax: 919 677 1714. *In Japan, please contact:* Journals Customer Services, Oxford University Press, 1-1-17-5F. Mukogaoka, Bunkyo-ku, Tokyo, 113-0023, Japan. Email: okudaoup@po.iijnet.or.jp; tel: (03) 3813 1461; fax: (03) 3818 1522.

The Year's Work in English Studies (ISSN 0084 4144) is published annually by Oxford University Press, Oxford, UK. Annual subscription price is £228/$376. *The Year's Work in English Studies* is distributed by Mercury International, 365 Blair Road, Avenel, NJ 07001, USA. Periodicals postage paid at Rahway, NJ and at additional entry points.

US Postmaster: send address changes to *The Year's Work in English Studies*, c/o Mercury International, 365 Blair Road, Avenel, NJ 07001, USA.

The Table of Contents email alerting service allows anyone who registers their email address to be notified via email when new content goes online. Details are available at http://ywes.oxfordjournals.org/cgi/alerts/etoc.

Permissions

For permissions requests, please visit www.oxfordjournals.org/permissions.

Advertising

Inquiries about advertising should be sent to Helen Pearson, Oxford Journals Advertising, PO Box 347, Abingdon OX14 1GJ, UK. Email: helen@oxfordads.com; tel/fax: +44 (0) 1235 201904.

Disclaimer

Statements of fact and opinion in the articles in *The Year's Work in English Studies* are those of the respective authors and contributors and not of the English Association or Oxford University Press. Neither Oxford University Press nor the English Association make any representation, express or implied, in respect of the accuracy of the material in this journal and cannot accept any legal responsibility or liability for any errors or omissions that may be made. The reader should make his/her own evaluation as to the appropriateness or otherwise of any experimental technique described.

© The English Association 2005. All rights reserved; no part of this publication may be reproduced, stored in a retrieval system, or transmitted in any form of by any means, electronic, mechanical, photocopying, recording, or otherwise without the prior written permission of the Publishers, or a licence permitting restricted copying issued in the UK by the Copyright Licensing Agency Ltd, 90 Tottenham Court Road, London W1P 9HE, or in the USA by the Copyright Clearance Center, 222 Rosewood Drive, Danvers, Massachusetts 01923, USA.

Contents

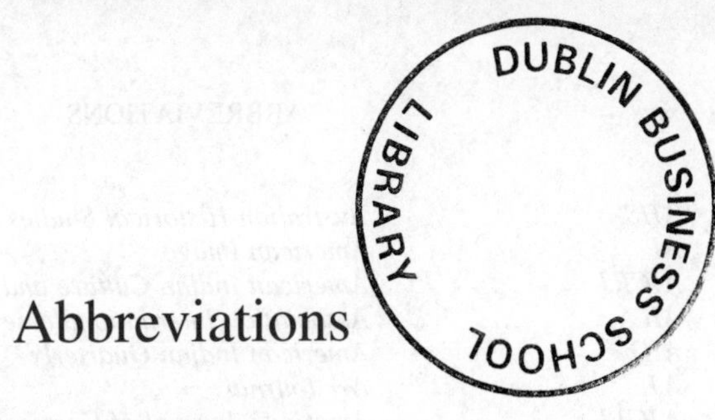

Abbreviations

1. Journals, series and reference works

1650–1850	*1650–1850 Ideas, Aesthetics, and Inquiries in the Early Modern Era*
A&D	*Art and Design*
A&E	*Anglistik und Englishunterricht*
AAA	*Arbeiten aus Anglistik und Amerikanistik*
AAAJ	*Accounting, Auditing and Accountability Journal*
ABäG	*Amsterdamer Beiträge zur Älteren Germanistik*
ABC	*American Book Collector*
ABELL	*Annual Bibliography of English Language and Literature*
ABM	*Antiquarian Book Monthly Review*
ABQ	*American Baptist Quarterly*
ABR	*American Benedictine Review*
ABSt	*A/B: Auto/Biography Studies*
AC	*Archeologia Classica*
Academy Forum	*Academy Forum*
AcadSF	Academia Scientiarum Fennica
ACar	*Analecta Cartusiana*
ACF	*Annuli, Facolta di Lingue e Litterature Straniere di Ca' Foscari*
ACH	*Australian Cultural History*
ACLALSB	*ACLALS Bulletin*
ACM	*Aligarh Critical Miscellany*
ACR	*Australasian Catholic Record*
ACS	*Australian–Canadian Studies: A Journal for the Humanities and Social Science*
Acta	Acta (Binghamton, NY)
AdI	*Annali d'Italianistica*
ADS	*Australasian Drama Studies*
AEB	*Analytical and Enumerative Bibliography*
Æstel	*Æstel*
AF	*Anglistische Forschungen*
AfricanA	*African Affairs*
AfrSR	*African Studies Review*
AgeJ	*Age of Johnson: A Scholarly Annual*
Agenda	*Agenda*
Agni	*Agni Review*
AH	*Art History*
AHR	*American Historical Review*

Year's Work in English Studies, Volume 84 (2005) © The English Association; all rights reserved. For permissions, please email: journals.permissions@oxfordjournals.org

AHS	*Australian Historical Studies*
AI	*American Imago*
AICRJ	*American Indian Culture and Research Journal*
AILA	*Association Internationale de Linguistique Appliqué*
AIQ	*American Indian Quarterly*
AJ	*Art Journal*
AJGLL	*American Journal of Germanic Linguistics and Literatures*
AJIS	*Australian Journal of Irish Studies*
AJL	*Australian Journal of Linguistics*
AJP	*American Journal of Psychoanalysis*
AJPH	*Australian Journal of Politics and History*
AJS	*American Journal of Semiotics*
AKML	Abhandlungen zur Kunst-, Musik- and Literaturwis-senschaft
AL	*American Literature*
ALA	African Literature Association Annuals
ALASH	*Acta Linguistica Academiae Scientiarum Hungaricae*
Albion	*Albion*
AlexS	Alexander Shakespeare
ALH	*Acta Linguistica Hafniensia; International Journal of Linguistics*
Alif	*Journal of Comparative Poetics* (Cairo, Egypt)
ALitASH	*Acta Literaria Academiae Scientiarum Hungaricae*
Allegorica	*Allegorica*
ALR	*American Literary Realism, 1870–1910*
ALS	*Australian Literary Studies*
ALT	*African Literature Today*
Alternatives	*Alternatives*
AmasJ	*Amerasian Journal*
AmDram	*American Drama*
AmerP	*American Poetry*
AmerS	*American Studies*
AmLH	*American Literary History*
AmLS	American Literary Scholarship: An Annual
AMon	*Atlantic Monthly*
AmPer	*American Periodicals*
AmRev	*Americas Review: A Review of Hispanic Literature and Art of the USA*
Amst	*Amerikastudien/American Studies*
AN	Acta Neophilologica
Anaïs	*Anaïs*
AnBol	*Analecta Bollandiana*
ANF	*Arkiv för Nordisk Filologi*
Angelaki	*Angelaki*
Anglia	*Anglia: Zeitschrift für Englische Philologie*
Anglistica	*Anglistica*

Anglistik	*Anglistik: Mitteilungen des Verbandes Deutscher Anglisten*
AnH	*Analecta Husserliana*
AnL	*Anthropological Linguistics*
AnM	*Annuale Mediaevale*
Ann	*Annales: Économies, Sociétés, Civilisations*
ANQ	*ANQ: A Quarterly Journal of Short Articles, Notes and Reviews* (formerly *American Notes and Queries*)
AntColl	*Antique Collector*
AntigR	*Antigonish Review*
Antipodes	*Antipodes: A North American Journal of Australian Literature*
ANZSC	*Australian and New Zealand Studies in Canada*
ANZTR	*Australian and New Zealand Theatre Record*
APBR	*Atlantic Provinces Book Review*
APL	*Antwerp Papers in Linguistics*
AppLing	*Applied Linguistics*
APR	*American Poetry Review*
AQ	*American Quarterly*
Aquarius	*Aquarius*
AR	*Antioch Review*
ArAA	*Arbeiten aus Anglistik und Amerikanistik*
ARAL	*Annual Review of Applied Linguistics*
Arcadia	*Arcadia*
Archiv	*Archiv für das Stadium der Neueren Sprachen und Literaturen*
ARCS	*American Review of Canadian Studies*
ArdenS	Arden Shakespeare
ArielE	*Ariel: A Review of International English Literature*
ArkQ	*Arkansas Quarterly: A Journal of Criticism*
ArkR	*Arkansas Review: A Journal of Criticism*
ArQ	*Arizona Quarterly*
ARS	Augustan Reprint Society
ARSR	*Australian Religion Studies Review*
ArtB	*Art Bulletin*
Arth	*Arthuriana*
ArthI	*Arthurian Interpretations*
ArthL	*Arthurian Literature*
Arv	*Arv: Nordic Yearbook of Folklore*
AS	*American Speech*
ASch	*American Scholar*
ASE	*Anglo-Saxon England*
ASInt	*American Studies International*
ASoc	*Arts in Society*
Aspects	*Aspects: Journal of the Language Society* (University of Essex)
AspectsAF	*Aspects of Australian Fiction*
ASPR	*Anglo-Saxon Poetic Records*

ASSAH	*Anglo-Saxon Studies in Archaeology and History*
Assaph	*Assaph: Studies in the Arts* (Theatre Studies)
Assays	*Assays: Critical Approaches to Medieval and Renaissance Texts*
ASUI	*Analele Stiintifice ale Universitatii 'Al.I. Cuza' din lasi(Serie Noua), e. Lingvistica*
ATQ	*American Transcendental Quarterly: A Journal of New England Writers*
AuBR	*Australian Book Review*
AuFolk	*Australian Folklore*
AuFS	*Australian Feminist Studies*
AuHR	*Australian Humanities Review*
AuJL	*Australian Journal of Linguistics*
AUMLA	*Journal of the Australasian Universities Language and Literature Association*
AuS	*Australian Studies*
AuSA	*Australian Studies* (Australia)
AusCan	*Australian-Canadian Studies*
AusPl	*Australian Playwrights*
AusRB	*Australians' Review of Books*
AuVSJ	*Australasian Victorian Studies Journal*
AuWBR	*Australian Women's Book Review*
AvC	*Avalon to Camelot*
AY	*Arthurian Yearbook*
BakhtinN	*Bakhtin Newsletter*
BALF	*Black American Literature Forum*
BAReview	*British Academy Review*
BARS Bulletin	*British Association for Romantic Studies Bulletin & Review*
BAS	*British and American Studies*
BASAM	*BASA Magazine*
BathH	*Bath History*
BayreuthAS	Bayreuth African Studies
BB	*Bulletin of Bibliography*
BBCS	*Bulletin of the Board of Celtic Studies*
BBCSh	*BBC Shakespeare*
BBN	*British Book News*
BBSIA	*Bulletin Bibliographique de la Société Internationale Arthurienne*
BC	*Book Collector*
BCan	*Books in Canada*
BCMA	*Bulletin of Cleveland Museum of Art*
BCS	*B.C. Studies*
BDEC	*Bulletin of the Department of English* (Calcutta)
BDP	*Beiträge zur Deutschen Philologie*
Belfagor	*Belfagor: Rassegna di Varia Umanità*
Bell	*Belgian Essays on Language and Literature*
BEPIF	*Bulletin des Itudes Portugaises et Brésiliennes*

BFLS	*Bulletin de la Faculté des Lettres de Strasbourg*
BGDSL	*Beiträge zur Geschichte der Deutschen Sprache and Literatur*
BHI	*British Humanities Index*
BHL	*Bibliotheca Hagiographica Latina Antiquae et Mediae Aetatis*
BHM	*Bulletin of the History of Medicine*
BHR	*Bibliothèque d'Humanisme et Renaissance*
BHS	*Bulletin of Hispanic Studies*
BI	*Books at Iowa*
Biblionews	*Biblionews and Australian Notes and Queries: A Journal for Book Collectors*
Bibliotheck	*Bibliotheck: A Scottish Journal of Bibliography and Allied Topics*
Biography	*Biography: An Interdisciplinary Quarterly*
BIS	*Browning Institute Studies: An Annual of Victorian Literary and Cultural History*
BJA	*British Journal of Aesthetics*
BJCS	*British Journal of Canadian Studies*
BJDC	*British Journal of Disorders of Communication*
BJECS	*British Journal for Eighteenth-Century Studies*
BJHP	*British Journal for the History of Philosophy*
BJHS	*British Journal for the History of Science*
BJJ	*Ben Jonson Journal*
BJL	*Belgian Journal of Linguistics*
BJPS	*British Journal for the Philosophy of Science*
BJRL	*Bulletin of the John Rylands* (University Library of Manchester)
BJS	*British Journal of Sociology*
Blake	*Blake: An Illustrated Quarterly*
BLE	*Bulletin de Littérature Ecclésiastique*
BLJ	*British Library Journal*
BLR	*Bodleian Library Record*
BN	*Beiträge zur Namenforschung*
BNB	*British National Bibliography*
BoH	*Book History*
Bookbird	*Bookbird*
Borderlines	*Borderlines*
Boundary	*Boundary 2: A Journal of Postmodern Literature and Culture*
BP	*Banasthali Patrika*
BPMA	*Bulletin of Philadelphia Museum of Art*
BPN	*Barbara Pym Newsletter*
BQ	*Baptist Quarterly*
BRASE	*Basic Readings in Anglo-Saxon England*
BRH	*Bulletin of Research in the Humanities*
Brick	*Brick: A Journal of Reviews*

BRMMLA	*Bulletin of the Rocky Mountain Modern Language Association*
BRONZS	*British Review of New Zealand Books*
BS	*Bronte Studies*
BSANZB	*Bibliographical Society of Australia and New Zealand Bulletin*
BSE	*Brno Studies in English*
BSEAA	*Bulletin de la Société d'Études Anglo-Américaines des XVIIe et XVIIIe Siècles*
BSJ	*Baker Street Journal: An Irregular Quarterly of Sherlockiana*
BSLP	*Bulletin de la Société de Linguistique de Paris*
BSNotes	*Browning Society Notes*
BSRS	*Bulletin of the Society for Renaissance Studies*
BSSA	*Bulletin de la Société de Stylistique Anglaise*
BST	*Brontë Society Transactions*
BSUF	*Ball State University Forum*
BTHGNewsl	*Book Trade History Group Newsletter*
BTLV	*Bijdragen tot de Taal-, Land- en Volkenhunde*
Bul	*Bulletin* (Australia)
Bullán	*Bullán*
BunyanS	*Bunyan Studies*
BuR	*Bucknell Review*
BurlM	*Burlington Magazine*
BurnsC	*Burns Chronicle*
BWPLL	Belfast Working Papers in Language and Linguistics
BWVACET	*Bulletin of the West Virginia Association of College English Teachers*
ByronJ	*Byron Journal*
CABS	Contemporary Authors Bibliographical Series
CahiersE	*Cahiers Élisabéthains*
CAIEF	*Cahiers de l'Association Internationale des Études Françaises*
Caliban	*Caliban* (Toulouse, France)
Callaloo	*Callaloo*
CalR	*Calcutta Review*
CamObsc	*Camera Obscura: A Journal of Feminism and Film Theory*
CamR	*Cambridge Review*
CanD	*Canadian Drama / L'Art Dramatique Canadienne*
C&L	*Christianity and Literature*
C&Lang	*Communication and Languages*
C&M	*Classica et Medievalia*
CanL	*Canadian Literature*
CAnn	*Carlyle Annual*
CanPo	*Canadian Poetry*
CapR	*Capilano Review*
CARA	*Centre Aixois de Recherches Anglaises*

Carib	*Carib*
Caribana	*Caribana*
CaribW	*Caribbean Writer*
CarR	*Caribbean Review*
Carrell	*Carrell: Journal of the Friends of the University of Miami Library*
CASE	*Cambridge Studies in Anglo-Saxon England*
CathHR	*Catholic Historical Review*
CaudaP	*Cauda Pavonis*
CBAA	*Current Bibliography on African Affairs*
CBEL	*Cambridge Bibliography of English Literature*
CCL	*Canadian Children's Literature*
CCRev	*Comparative Civilizations Review*
CCrit	*Comparative Criticism: An Annual Journal*
CCTES	*Conference of College Teachers of English Studies*
CCV	*Centro de Cultura Valenciana*
CDALB	*Concise Dictionary of American Literary Biography*
CDCP	Comparative Drama Conference Papers
CDIL	*Cahiers de l'Institut de Linguistique de Louvain*
CdL	*Cahiers de Lexicologie*
CE	*College English*
CEA	*CEA Critic*
CEAfr	*Cahiers d'Études Africaines*
CE&S	*Commonwealth Essays and Studies*
CentR	*Centennial Review*
Cervantes	*Cervantes*
CF	*Crime Factory*
CFM	*Canadian Fiction Magazine*
CFS	*Cahiers Ferdinand de Saussure: Revue de Linguistique Générale*
CH	*Computers and the Humanities*
Chapman	*Chapman*
Chasqui	*Chasqui*
ChauR	*Chaucer Review*
ChauS	*Chaucer Studion*
ChauY	*Chaucer Yearbook*
ChH	*Church History*
ChildL	*Children's Literature*
ChiR	*Chicago Review*
ChLB	*Charles Lamb Bulletin*
CHLSSF	*Commentationes Humanarum Litterarum Societatis Scientiarum Fennicae*
CHR	*Camden History Review*
CHum	*Computers and the Humanities*
CI	Critical Idiom
CILT	Amsterdam Studies in the Theory and History of the Language Sciences IV: Current Issues in Linguistic Theory

Cinéaste	*Cinéaste*
CinJ	*Cinema Journal*
CIQ	*Colby Quarterly*
CISh	Contemporary Interpretations of Shakespeare
Cithara	*Cithara: Essays in the Judaeo-Christian Tradition*
CJ	*Classical Journal*
CJE	*Cambridge Journal of Education*
CJH	*Canadian Journal of History*
CJIS	*Canadian Journal of Irish Studies*
CJL	*Canadian Journal of Linguistics*
CJR	*Christian–Jewish Relations*
CK	*Common Knowledge*
CL	*Comparative Literature* (Eugene, OR)
CLAJ	*CLA Journal*
CLAQ	*Children's Literature Association Quarterly*
ClarkN	*Clark Newsletter: Bulletin of the UCLA Center for Seventeenth- and Eighteenth-Century Studies*
ClassW	*Classical World*
CLC	*Columbia Library Columns*
CLE	*Children's Literature in Education*
CLIN	*Cuadernos de Literatura*
ClioI	*Clio: A Journal of Literature, History and the Philosophy of History*
CLQ	*Colby Library Quarterly*
CLS	*Comparative Literature Studies*
Clues	*Clues: A Journal of Detection*
CMCS	*Cambridge Medieval Celtic Studies*
CML	*Classical and Modern Literature*
CN	*Chaucer Newsletter*
CNIE	*Commonwealth Novel in English*
CogLing	*Cognitive Linguistics*
Cognition	*Cognition*
ColB	*Coleridge Bulletin*
ColF	*Columbia Forum*
Collections	*Collections*
CollG	*Colloquia Germanica*
CollL	*College Literature*
Com	*Commonwealth*
Comitatus	*Comitatus: A Journal of Medieval and Renaissance Studies*
Commentary	*Commentary*
Comparatist	*Comparatist: Journal of the Southern Comparative Literature Association*
CompD	*Comparative Drama*
CompLing	*Contemporary Linguistics*
ConfLett	*Confronto Letterario*
ConL	*Contemporary Literature*
Connotations	*Connotations*

ConnR	*Connecticut Review*
Conradian	*Conradian*
Conradiana	*Conradiana: A Journal of Joseph Conrad Studies*
ContempR	*Contemporary Review*
Coppertales	*Coppertales: A Journal of Rural Arts*
Cosmos	*Cosmos*
Costume	*Journal of the Costume Society*
CP	*Concerning Poetry*
CQ	*Cambridge Quarterly*
CR	*Critical Review*
CRCL	*Canadian Review of Comparative Literature*
CRev	*Chesterton Review*
CRevAS	*Canadian Review of American Studies*
Crit	*Critique: Studies in Modern Fiction*
CritI	*Critical Inquiry*
Criticism	*Criticism: A Quarterly for Literature and the Arts*
Critique	*Critique* (Paris)
CritQ	*Critical Quarterly*
CritT	*Critical Texts: A Review of Theory and Criticism*
CrM	*Critical Mass*
CRNLE	*CRNLE Reviews Journal*
Crossings	*Crossings*
CRUX	*CRUX. A Journal on the Teaching of English*
CS	*Critical Survey*
CSASE	Cambridge Studies in Anglo-Saxon England
CSCC	*Case Studies in Contemporary Criticism*
CSELT	Cambridge Studies in Eighteenth-Century Literature and Thought
CSLBull	*Bulletin of the New York C.S. Lewis Society*
CSLL	*Cardozo Studies in Law and Literature*
CSML	Cambridge Studies in Medieval Literature
CSNCLC	Cambridge Studies in Nineteenth-Century Literature and Culture
CSPC	Cambridge Studies in Paleography and Codicology
CSR	Cambridge Studies in Romanticism
CSRev	*Christian Scholar's Review*
CStA	*Carlyle Studies Annual* (previously *CAnn*)
CTR	*Canadian Theatre Review*
Cuadernos	*Cuadernos de Literatura Infantil y Juvenil*
CulC	*Cultural Critique*
CulS	*Cultural Studies*
CulSR	*Cultural Studies Review*
CUNY	*CUNY English Forum*
Current Writing	*Current Writing: Text and Reception in Southern Africa*
CV2	*Contemporary Verse 2*
CVE	*Cahiers Victoriens et Edouardiens*
CW	*Current Writing: Text and Perception in Southern Africa*

CWAAS	*Transactions of the Cumberland and Westmorland Antiquarian and Archaeological Society*
CWS	*Canadian Woman Studies*
DA	*Dictionary of Americanisms*
DAE	*Dictionary of American English*
DAEM	*Deutsches Archiv für Erforschung des Mittelalters*
DAI	*Dissertation Abstracts International*
DAL	*Descriptive and Applied Linguistics*
D&CN&Q	*Devon and Cornwall Notes and Queries*
D&S	*Discourse and Society*
Daphnis	*Daphnis: Zeitschrift für Mittlere Deutsche Literatur*
DC	*Dickens Companions*
DerbyM	*Derbyshire Miscellany*
Descant	*Descant*
DFS	*Dalhousie French Studies*
DHLR	*D.H. Lawrence Review*
DHS	*Dix-huitième Siècle*
Diac	*Diacritics*
Diachronica	*Diachronica*
Dialogue	*Dialogue: Canadian Philosophical Review*
Dickensian	*Dickensian*
DicS	*Dickinson Studies*
Dictionaries	*Dictionaries: Journal of the Dictionary Society of North America*
Dionysos	*Dionysos*
Discourse	*Discourse*
DisS	*Discourse Studies*
DLB	*Dictionary of Literary Biography*
DLN	*Doris Lessing Newsletter*
DM	*Dublin Magazine*
DMT	Durham Medieval Texts
DNB	*Dictionary of National Biography*
DOE	*Dictionary of Old English*
Dolphin	*Dolphin: Publications of the English Department* (University of Aarhus)
DOST	*Dictionary of the Older Scottish Tongue*
DownR	*Downside Review*
DPr	*Discourse Processes*
DQ	*Denver Quarterly*
DQR	*Dutch Quarterly Review of Anglo-American Letters*
DQu	*Dickens Quarterly*
DR	*Dalhousie Review*
Drama	*Drama: The Quarterly Theatre Review*
DrS	*Dreiser Studies*
DS	*Deep South*
DSA	*Dickens Studies Annual*
DSNA	*DSNA Newsletter*

DU	*Der Deutschunterricht: Beiträge zu Seiner Praxis und Wissenschaftlichen Grundlegung*
DUJ	*Durham University Journal*
DVLG	*Deutsche Viertejahrsschrift für Literaturwissenschaft und Geistesgeschichte*
DWPELL	*Dutch Working Papers in English Language and Linguistics*
EA	*Études Anglaises*
EAL	*Early American Literature*
E&D	*Enlightenment and Dissent*
E&S	*Essays and Studies*
E&Soc	*Economy and Society*
EAS	*Essays in Arts and Sciences*
EASt	*Englisch Amerikanische Studien*
EBST	*Edinburgh Bibliographical Society Transactions*
EC	*Études Celtiques*
ECan	*Études Canadiennes/Canadian Studies*
ECCB	*Eighteenth Century: A Current Bibliography*
ECent	*Eighteenth Century: Theory and Interpretation*
ECF	*Eighteenth-Century Fiction*
ECI	*Eighteenth-Century Ireland*
ECIntell	*East-Central Intelligencer*
ECLife	*Eighteenth-Century Life*
ECN	*Eighteenth-Century Novel*
ECon	*L'Époque Conradienne*
ECr	*L'Esprit Créateur*
ECS	*Eighteenth-Century Studies*
ECSTC	*Eighteenth-Century Short Title Catalogue*
ECW	*Essays on Canadian Writing*
ECWomen	*Eighteenth-Century Women: Studies in their Lives, Work, and Culture*
EDAMN	*EDAM Newsletter*
EDAMR	*Early Drama, Art, and Music Review*
EDH	*Essays by Divers Hands*
EdL	*Études de Lettres*
EdN	*Editors' Notes: Bulletin of the Conference of Editors of Learned Journals*
EDSL	*Encyclopedic Dictionary of the Sciences of Language*
EEMF	*Early English Manuscripts in Facsimile*
EF	*Études Francaises*
EHR	*English Historical Review*
EI	*Études Irlandaises* (Lille)
EIC	*Essays in Criticism*
EinA	*English in Africa*
EiP	*Essays in Poetics*
EIRC	*Explorations in Renaissance Culture*
Éire	*Éire-Ireland*

EiTET	*Essays in Theatre / Études Théâtrales*
EJ	*English Journal*
EJES	*European Journal of English Studies*
ELangT	*ELT Journal: An International Journal for Teachers of English to Speakers of Other Languages*
ELet	*Esperienze Letterarie: Rivista Trimestrale di Critica e Cultura*
ELH	*English Literary History*
ELing	*English Linguistics*
ELL	*English Language and Linguistics*
ELN	*English Language Notes*
ELR	*English Literary Renaissance*
ELS	*English Literary Studies*
ELT	*English Literature in Transition*
ELWIU	*Essays in Literature (Western Illinois University)*
EM	*English Miscellany*
Embl	*Emblematica: An Interdisciplinary Journal of English Studies*
EMD	*European Medieval Drama*
EME	*Early Modern Europe*
EMedE	*Early Medieval Europe* (online)
EMLS	*Early Modern Literary Studies* (online)
EMMS	*Early Modern Manuscript Studies*
EMS	*English Manuscript Studies, 1100–1700*
EMu	*Early Music*
EMW	*Early Modern Englishwomen*
Encult	*Enculturation: Cultural Theories and Rhetorics*
Encyclia	*Encyclia*
English	*English: The Journal of the English Association*
EnT	*English Today: The International Review of the English Language*
EONR	*Eugene O'Neill Review*
EPD	*English Pronouncing Dictionary*
ER	*English Review*
ERLM	*Europe-Revue Littéraire Mensuelle*
ERR	*European Romantic Review*
ES	*English Studies*
ESA	*English Studies in Africa*
ESC	*English Studies in Canada*
ESQ	*ESQ: A Journal of the American Renaissance*
ESRS	*Emporia State Research Studies*
EssaysMedSt	*Essays in Medieval Studies*
EST	*Eureka Street*
ET	*Elizabethan Theatre*
EuroS	*European Studies: A Journal of European Culture, History and Politics*
EWhR	*Edith Wharton Review*

EWIP	*Edinburgh University, Department of Linguistics, Work in Progress*
EWN	*Evelyn Waugh Newsletter*
EWPAL	*Edinburgh Working Papers in Applied Linguistics*
EWW	*English World-Wide*
Excavatio	*Excavatio*
Exemplaria	*Exemplaria*
Expl	*Explicator*
Extrapolation	*Extrapolation: A Journal Science Fiction and Fantasy*
FC	*Feminist Collections: A Quarterly of Women's Studies Resources*
FCEMN	*Mystics Quarterly* (formerly *Fourteenth-Century English Mystics Newsletter*)
FCS	*Fifteenth-Century Studies*
FDT	Fountainwell Drama Texts
FemR	*Feminist Review*
FemSEL	*Feminist Studies in English Literature*
FFW	*Food and Foodways*
FH	*Die Neue Gesellschaft / Frankfurter Hefte*
Fiction International	*Fiction International*
FilmJ	*Film Journal*
FilmQ	*Film Quarterly*
FiveP	*Five Points: A Journal of Literature and Art* (Atlanta, GA)
FJS	*Fu Jen Studies: Literature and Linguistics* (Taipei)
FLH	*Folia Linguistica Historica*
Florilegium	*Florilegium: Carleton University Annual Papers on Classical Antiquity and the Middle Ages*
FMLS	*Forum for Modern Language Studies*
FNS	*Frank Norris Studies*
Folklore	*Folklore*
FoLi	*Folia Linguistica*
Forum	*Forum*
FranS	*Franciscan Studies*
FreeA	*Free Associations*
FrontenacR	*Revue Frontenac*
Frontiers	*Frontiers: A Journal of Women's Studies*
FS	*French Studies*
FSt	*Feminist Studies*
FT	*Fashion Theory*
FuL	*Functions of Language*
Futures	*Futures*
GAG	Göppinger Arbeiten zur Germanistik
GaR	*Georgia Review*
GBB	*George Borrow Bulletin*
GBK	*Gengo Bunka Kenkyu: Studies in Language and Culture*
GEGHLS	*George Eliot-George Henry Lewes Studies*

GeM	*Genealogists Magazine*
Genders	*Genders*
Genre	*Genre*
GER	*George Eliot Review*
Gestus	*Gestus: A Quarterly Journal of Brechtian Studies*
Gettysburg Review	*Gettysburg Review*
GG@G	*Generative Grammar in Geneva* (online)
GHJ	*George Herbert Journal*
GissingJ	*Gissing Journal*
GJ	*Gutenberg-Jahrbuch*
GL	*General Linguistics*
GL&L	*German Life and Letters*
GlasR	*Glasgow Review*
Glossa	*Glossa: An International Journal of Linguistics*
GLQ	*A Journal of Lesbian and Gay Studies* (Duke University)
GLS	*Grazer Linguistische Studien*
GR	*Germanic Review*
Gramma	*Gramma: Journal of Theory and Criticism*
Gramma/TTT	*Tijdschrift voor Taalwetenschap*
GrandS	*Grand Street*
Granta	*Granta*
Greyfriar	*Greyfriar Siena Studies in Literature*
GRM	*Germanisch-Romanische Monatsschrift*
GSE	Gothenberg Studies in English
GSJ	*Gaskell Society Journal*
GSN	*Gaskell Society Newsletter*
GURT	*Georgetown University Round Table on Language and Linguistics*
HamS	*Hamlet Studies*
H&T	*History and Theory*
HardyR	*Hardy Review*
Harvard Law Review	*Harvard Law Review*
HatcherR	*Hatcher Review*
HBS	Henry Bradshaw Society
HC	*Hollins Critic*
HCM	*Hitting Critical Mass: A Journal of Asian American Cultural Criticism*
HE	*History of Education*
HEAT	*HEAT*
Hecate	*Hecate: An Interdisciplinary Journal of Women's Liberation*
HEdQ	*History of Education Quarterly*
HEI	*History of European Ideas*
HeineJ	*Heine Jahrbuch*
HEL	*Histoire Épistémologie Language*
Helios	*Helios*
HEng	*History of the English Language*

Hermathena	*Hermathena: A Trinity College Dublin Review*
HeyJ	*Heythrop Journal*
HFR	*Hayden Ferry Review*
HistJ	*Historical Journal*
History	*History: The Journal of the Historical Association*
HistR	*Historical Research*
HJEAS	*Hungarian Journal of English and American Studies*
HJR	*Henry James Review* (Baton Rouge, LA)
HL	*Historiographia Linguistica*
HLB	*Harvard Library Bulletin*
HLQ	*Huntingdon Library Quarterly HLSL* (online)
HLSL	(online)
HNCIS	Harvester New Critical Introductions to Shakespeare
HNR	Harvester New Readings
HOPE	*History of Political Economy*
HPT	*History of Political Thought*
HQ	*Hopkins Quarterly*
HR	*Harvard Review*
HRB	*Hopkins Research Bulletin*
HSci	*History of Science*
HSE	*Hungarian Studies in English*
HSELL	*Hiroshima Studies in English Language and Literature*
HSJ	*Housman Society Journal*
HSL	*University of Hartford Studies in Literature*
HSN	*Hawthorne Society Newsletter*
HSSh	*Hunganan Studies in Shakespeare*
HSSN	*Henry Sweet Society Newsletter*
HT	*History Today*
HTR	*Harvard Theological Review*
HudR	*Hudson Review*
HumeS	*Hume Studies*
HumLov	*Humanistica Lovaniensia: Journal of Neo-Latin Studies*
Humor	*Humor: International Journal of Humor Research*
HUSL	*Hebrew University Studies in Literature and the Arts*
HWJ	*History Workshop*
HWS	History Workshop Series
Hypatia	*Hypatia*
IAL	*Issues in Applied Linguistics*
IAN	*Izvestiia Akademii Nauk SSSR* (Moscow)
I&C	*Ideology and Consciousness*
I&P	*Ideas and Production*
ICAME	*International Computer Archive of Modern and Medieval English*
ICS	*Illinois Classical Studies*
IEEETrans	*IEEE Transactions on Professional Communications*
IF	*Indogermanische Forschungen*

IFR	*International Fiction Review*
IGK	*Irland: Gesellschaft and Kultur*
IJAES	*International Journal of Arabic-English Studies*
IJAL	*International Journal of Applied Linguistics*
IJB	*International Journal of Bilingualism*
IJBEB	*International Journal of Bilingual Education & Bilingualism*
IJCL	*International Journal of Corpus Linguistics*
IJCT	*International Journal of the Classical Tradition*
IJECS	*Indian Journal for Eighteenth-Century Studies*
IJES	*Indian Journal of English Studies*
IJL	*International Journal of Lexicography*
IJPR	*International Journal for Philosophy of Religion*
IJSL	*International Journal of the Sociology of Language*
IJSS	*Indian Journal of Shakespeare Studies*
IJWS	*International Journal of Women's Studies*
ILR	*Indian Literary Review*
ILS	*Irish Literary Supplement*
Imago	*Imago: New Writing*
IMB	*International Medieval Bibliography*
Imprimatur	*Imprimatur*
Indexer	*Indexer*
IndH	*Indian Horizons*
IndL	*Indian Literature*
InG	*In Geardagum: Essays on Old and Middle English Language and Literature*
Inklings	*Inklings: Jahrbuch für Literatur and Ästhetik*
Ioc	*Index to Censorship*
Inquiry	*Inquiry: An Interdisciplinary Journal of Philosophy*
Interlink	*Interlink*
Interpretation	*Interpretation*
Interventions	*Interventions: The International Journal of Postcolonial Studies*
IowaR	*Iowa Review*
IRAL	*IRAL: International Review of Applied Linguistics in Language Teaching*
Iris	*Iris: A Journal of Theory on Image and Sound*
IS	*Italian Studies*
ISh	*Independent Shavian*
ISJR	*Iowa State Journal of Research*
Island	*Island Magazine*
Islands	*Islands*
Isle	*Interdisciplinary Studies in Literature and Environment*
ISR	*Irish Studies Review*
IUR	*Irish University Review: A Journal of Irish Studies*
JAAC	*Journal of Aesthetics and Art Criticism*
JAAR	*Journal of the American Academy of Religion*
Jacket	*Jacket*

JADT	*Journal of American Drama and Theatre*
JAF	*Journal of American Folklore*
JafM	*Journal of African Marxists*
JAIS	*Journal of Anglo-Italian Studies*
JAL	*Journal of Australian Literature*
JamC	*Journal of American Culture*
JAmH	*Journal of American History*
JAmS	*Journal of American Studies*
JAPC	*Journal of Asian Pacific Communication*
JArabL	*Journal of Arabic Literature*
JAS	*Journal of Australian Studies*
JASAL	*Journal of the Association for the Study of Australian Literature*
JAStT	*Journal of American Studies of Turkey*
JBeckS	*Journal of Beckett Studies*
JBS	*Journal of British Studies*
JBSSJ	*Journal of the Blake Society at St James*
JCAKSU	*Journal of the College of Arts* (King Saud University)
JCanL	*Journal of Canadian Literature*
JCC	*Journal of Canadian Culture*
JCF	*Journal of Canadian Fiction*
JChL	*Journal of Child Language*
JCL	*Journal of Commonwealth Literature*
JCP	*Journal of Canadian Poetry*
JCPCS	*Journal of Commonwealth and Postcolonial Studies*
JCSJ	*John Clare Society Journal*
JCSR	*Journal of Canadian Studies / Revue d'Études Canadiennes*
JCSt	*Journal of Caribbean Studies*
JDECU	*Journal of the Department of English* (Calcutta University)
JDHLS	*D.H. Lawrence: The Journal of the D.H. Lawrence Society*
JDJ	*John Dunne Journal*
JDN	*James Dickey Newsletter*
JDTC	*Journal of Dramatic Theory and Criticism*
JEBS	*Journal of the Early Book Society*
JEDRBU	*Journal of the English Department* (Rabindra Bharati University)
JEGP	*Journal of English and Germanic Philology*
JEH	*Journal of Ecclesiastical History*
JELL	*Journal of English Language and Literature*
JEn	*Journal of English* (Sana'a University)
JEngL	*Journal of English Linguistics*
JENS	*Journal of the Eighteen Nineties Society*
JEP	*Journal of Evolutionary Psychology*
JEPNS	*Journal of the English Place-Name Society*

JES	*Journal of European Studies*
JETS	*Journal of the Evangelical Theological Society*
JFR	*Journal of Folklore Research*
JGE	*Journal of General Education*
JGenS	*Journal of Gender Studies*
JGH	*Journal of Garden History*
JGL	*Journal of Germanic Linguistics*
JGN	*John Gower Newsletter*
JH	*Journal of Homosexuality*
JHI	*Journal of the History of Ideas*
JHLP	*Journal of Historical Linguistics and Philology*
JHP	*Journal of the History of Philosophy*
JHPrag	*Journal of Historical Pragmatics*
JHSex	*Journal of the History of Sexuality*
JHu	*Journal of Humanities*
JHuP	*Journal of Humanistic Psychology*
JIEP	*Journal of Indo-European Perspectives*
JIES	*Journal of Indo-European Studies*
JIL	*Journal of Irish Literature*
JIPA	*Journal of the International Phonetic Association*
JIWE	*Journal of Indian Writing in English*
JJ	*Jamaica Journal*
JJA	*James Joyce Annual*
JJB	*James Joyce Broadsheet*
JJLS	*James Joyce Literary Supplement*
JJQ	*James Joyce Quarterly*
JKS	*Journal of Kentucky Studies*
JL	*Journal of Linguistics*
JLH	*Journal of Library History, Philosophy and Comparative Librarianship*
JLLI	*Journal of Logic, Language and Information*
JLP	*Journal of Linguistics and Politics*
JLS	*Journal of Literary Semanitcs*
JLSP	*Journal of Language and Social Psychology*
JLVSG	*Journal of the Longborough Victorian Studies Group*
JMemL	*Journal of Memory and Language*
JMEMS	*Journal of Medieval and Early Modem Studies*
JMGS	*Journal of Modern Greek Studies*
JMH	*Journal of Medieval History*
JMJS	*Journal of Modern Jewish Studies*
JML	*Journal of Modern Literature*
JMMD	*Journal of Multilingual and Multicultural Development*
JMMLA	*Journal of the Midwest Modern Language Association*
JModH	*Journal of Modern History*
JMRS	*Journal of Medieval and Renaissance Studies*
JMS	*Journal of Men's Studies*
JNLH	*Journal of Narrative and Life History*
JNPH	*Journal of Newspaper and Periodical History*

JNT	*Journal of Narrative Theory* (formerly *Technique*)
JNZL	*Journal of New Zealand Literature*
Jouvert	*Jouvert: A Journal of Postcolonial Studies*
JoyceSA	*Joyce Studies Annual*
JP	*Journal of Philosophy*
JPC	*Journal of Popular Culture*
JPCL	*Journal of Pidgin and Creole Languages*
JPhon	*Journal of Phonetics*
JPJ	*Journal of Psychology and Judaism*
JPrag	*Journal of Pragmatics*
JPRAS	*Journal of Pre-Raphaelite and Aesthetic Studies*
JPsyR	*Journal of Psycholinguistic Research*
JQ	*Journalism Quarterly*
JR	*Journal of Religion*
JRAHS	*Journal of the Royal Australian Historical Society*
JRH	*Journal of Religious History*
JRMA	*Journal of the Royal Musical Association*
JRMMRA	*Journal of the Rocky Mountain Medieval and Renaissance Association*
JRSA	*Journal of the Royal Society of Arts*
JRUL	*Journal of the Rutgers University Libraries*
JSA	*Journal of the Society of Archivists*
JSaga	*Journal of the Faculty of Liberal Arts and Science* (Saga University)
JSAS	*Journal of Southern African Studies*
JScholP	*Journal of Scholarly Publishing*
JSem	*Journal of Semantics*
JSoc	*Journal of Sociolinguistics*
JSSE	*Journal of the Short Story in English*
JSTWS	*Journal of the Sylvia Townsend Warner Society*
JTheoS	*Journal of Theological Studies*
JVC	*Journal of Victorian Culture*
JWCI	*Journal of the Warburg and Courtauld Institutes*
JWH	*Journal of Women's History*
JWIL	*Journal of West Indian Literature*
JWMS	*Journal of the William Morris Society*
JWSL	*Journal of Women's Studies in Literature*
KanE	*Kansas English*
KanQ	*Kansas Quarterly*
KB	*Kavya Bharati*
KCLMS	King's College London Medieval Series
KCS	*Kobe College Studies* (Japan)
KDNews	*Kernerman Dictionary News*
KJ	*Kipling Journal*
KN	*Kwartalnik Neoflologiczny* (Warsaw)
KompH	*Komparatistische Hefte*
Kotare	*Kotare: New Zealand Notes and Queries*

KPR	*Kentucky Philological Review*
KR	*Kenyon Review*
KSJ	*Keats-Shelley Journal*
KSR	*Keats-Shelley Review*
Kuka	*Kuka: Journal of Creative and Critical Writing* (Zaria, Nigeria)
Kunapipi	*Kunapipi*
KWS	*Key-Word Studies in Chaucer*
L&A	*Literature and Aesthetics*
L&B	*Literature and Belief*
L&C	*Language and Communication*
L&E	*Linguistics and Education: An International Research Journal*
Landfall	*Landfall: A New Zealand Quarterly*
L&H	*Literature and History*
L&L	*Language and Literature*
L&LC	*Literary and Linguistic Computing*
L&M	*Literature and Medicine*
L&P	*Literature and Psychology*
L&S	*Language and Speech*
L&T	*Literature and Theology: An Interdisciplinary Journal of Theory and Criticism*
L&U	*Lion and the Unicorn: A Critical Journal of Children's Literature*
Lang&S	*Language and Style*
LangF	*Language Forum*
LangQ	*USF Language Quarterly*
LangR	*Language Research*
LangS	*Language Sciences*
Language	*Language* (Linguistic Society of America)
LanM	*Les Langues Modernes*
LATR	*Latin American Theatre Review*
LaTrobe	*La Trobe Journal*
LB	*Leuvense Bijdragen*
LBR	*Luso-Brazilian Review*
LCrit	*Literary Criterion* (Mysore, India)
LCUT	*Library Chronicle* (University of Texas at Austin)
LDOCE	*Longman Dictionary of Contemporary English*
LeedsSE	*Leeds Studies in English*
Legacy	*Legacy: A Journal of Nineteenth-Century American Women Writers*
L'EpC	*L'Epoque Conradienne*
LeS	*Lingua e Stile*
Lexicographica	*Lexicographica: International Annual for Lexicography*
Lexicography	*Lexicography*
LFQ	*Literature/Film Quarterly*
LH	*Library History*

LHY	*Literary Half-Yearly*
Library	*Library*
LibrQ	*Library Quarterly*
LIN	*Linguistics in the Netherlands*
LingA	*Linguistic Analysis*
Ling&P	*Linguistics and Philosophy*
Ling&Philol	*Linguistics and Philology*
LingB	*Linguistische Berichte*
LingI	*Linguistic Inquiry*
LingInv	*Linvisticæ Investigationes*
LingP	*Linguistica Pragensia*
Lingua	*Lingua: International Review of General Linguistics*
Linguistics	*Linguistics*
Linguistique	*La Linguistique*
LiNQ	*Literature in Northern Queensland*
LingRev	*Linguistic Review*
LIT	*LIT: Literature, Interpretation, Theory*
LitH	*Literary Horizons*
LitI	*Literary Imagination: The Review of the Association of Literary Scholars and Critics*
LitR	*Literary Review: An International Journal of Contemporary Writing*
LittPrag	*Litteraria Pragensia: Studies in Literature and Culture*
LJCS	*London Journal of Canadian Studies*
LJGG	*Literaturwissenschaftliches Jahrbuch im Aufrage der Görres-Gesellschaft*
LJHum	*Lamar Journal of the Humanities*
LMag	*London Magazine*
LockeN	*Locke Newsletter*
LocusF	*Locus Focus*
LongR	*Long Room: Bulletin of the Friends of the Library* (Trinity College, Dublin)
Lore&L	*Lore and Language*
LP	*Lingua Posnaniensis*
LPLD	*Liverpool Papers in Language and Discourse*
LPLP	*Language Problems and Language Planning*
LR	*Les Lettres Romanes*
LRB	*London Review of Books*
LSE	Lund Studies in English
LSLD	Liverpool Studies in Language and Discourse
LSoc	*Language in Society*
LSp	*Language and Speech*
LST	Longman Study Texts
LTM	Leeds Texts and Monographs
LTP	*LTP: Journal of Literature Teaching Politics*
LTR	*London Theatre Record*
LuK	*Literatur und Kritik*

LVC	*Language Variation and Change*
LWU	*Literatur in Wissenschaft und Unterricht*
M&Lang	*Mind and Language*
MÆ	*Medium Ævum*
MAEL	Macmillan Anthologies of English Literature
MaComere	*MaComère*
MagL	*Magazine Littéraire*
Mana	*Mana*
MAS	*Modern Asian Studies*
M&H	*Medievalia et Humanistica*
M&L	*Music and Letters*
M&N	*Man and Nature / L'Homme et la Nature: Proceedings of the Canadian Society for Eighteenth-Century Studies*
Manuscripta	*Manuscripta*
MAR	*Mid-American Review*
Margin	*Margin*
MarkhamR	*Markham Review*
Matatu	*Matatu*
Matrix	*Matrix*
MBL	*Modern British Literature*
MC&S	*Media, Culture and Society*
MCI	Modern Critical Interpretations
MCJNews	*Milton Centre of Japan News*
McNR	*McNeese Review*
MCRel	*Mythes, Croyances et Religions dans le Monde Anglo-Saxon*
MCV	Modern Critical Views
MD	*Modern Drama*
ME	*Medieval Encounters*
Meanjin	*Meanjin*
MED	*Middle English Dictionary*
MedFor	*Medieval Forum* (online)
MedHis	*Media History*
Mediaevalia	*Mediaevalia: A Journal of Mediaeval Studies*
MedPers	*Medieval Perspectives*
MELUS	*MELUS: The Journal of the Society of Multi-Ethnic Literature of the United States*
Meridian	*Meridian*
MESN	*Mediaeval English Studies Newsletter*
MET	*Middle English Texts*
METh	*Medieval English Theatre*
MFF	*Medieval Feminist Forum* (formerly *Medieval Feminist Newsletter*)
MFN	*Medieval Feminist Newsletter* (now *Medieval Feminist Forum*)
MFS	*Modern Fiction Studies*
MH	*Malahat Review*
MHL	Macmillan History of Literature

MHLS	*Mid-Hudson Language Studies*
MichA	*Michigan Academician*
MiltonQ	*Milton Quarterly*
MiltonS	*Milton Studies*
MinnR	*Minnesota Review*
MissQ	*Mississippi Quarterly*
MissR	*Missouri Review*
Mittelalter	*Das Mittelalter: Perspektiven Mediavistischer Forschung*
MJLF	*Midwestern Journal of Language and Folklore*
ML	*Music and Letters*
MLAIB	*Modern Language Association International Bibliography*
MLing	*Modelès Linguistiques*
MLJ	*Modern Language Journal*
MLN	*Modern Language Notes*
MLQ	*Modern Language Quarterly*
MLR	*Modern Language Review*
MLRev	*Malcolm Lowry Review*
MLS	*Modern Language Studies*
M/M	*Modernism/Modernity*
MMD	Macmillan Modern Dramatists
MMG	Macmillan Master Guides
MMisc	*Midwestern Miscellany*
MOCS	*Magazine of Cultural Studies*
ModA	*Modern Age: A Quarterly Review*
ModET	*Modern English Teacher*
ModM	*Modern Masters*
ModSp	*Moderne Sprachen*
Mo/Mo	*Modernism/Modernity*
Monist	*Monist*
MonSP	*Monash Swift Papers*
Month	*Month: A Review of Christian Thought and World Affairs*
MOR	*Mount Olive Review*
Moreana	*Moreana: Bulletin Thomas More* (Angers, France)
Mosaic	*Mosaic: A Journal for the Interdisciplinary Study of Literature*
MoyA	*Moyen Age*
MP	*Modern Philology*
MPHJ	*Middlesex Polytechnic History Journal*
MPR	*Mervyn Peake Review*
MQ	*Midwest Quarterly*
MQR	*Michigan Quarterly Review*
MR	*Massachusetts Review*
MRDE	*Medieval and Renaissance Drama in England*
MRTS	*Medieval and Renaissance Texts and Studies*
MS	*Mediaeval Studies*
MSC	Malone Society Collections
MSE	*Massachusetts Studies in English*

DUBLIN BUSINESS SCHOOL LIBRARY

MSEx	*Melville Society Extracts*
MSh	Macmillan Shakespeare
MSNH	Mémoires de la Société Néophilologique de Helsinki
MSpr	*Moderna Språk*
MSR	Malone Society Reprints
MSSN	*Medieval Sermon Studies Newsletter*
MT	*Musical Times*
MTJ	*Mark Twain Journal*
Multilingua	*Multilingua: Journal of Cross-Cultural and Interlanguage Communication*
MusR	*Music Review*
MW	*Muslim World* (Hartford, CT)
MysticsQ	*Mystics Quarterly*
Mythlore	*Mythlore: A Journal of J.R.R. Tolkein, C.S. Lewis, Charles Williams, and the Genres of Myth and Fantasy Studies*
NA	*Nuova Antologia*
Names	*Names: Journal of the American Name Society*
NAmR	*North American Review*
N&F	*Notes & Furphies*
N&Q	*Notes and Queries*
Narrative	*Narrative*
Navasilu	*Navasilu*
NB	*Namn och Bygd*
NCaS	*New Cambridge Shakespeare*
NCBEL	*New Cambridge Bibliography of English Literature*
NCC	*Nineteenth-Century Contexts*
NCE	Norton Critical Editions
NCFS	*Nineteenth-Century French Studies*
NCL	*Nineteenth-Century Literature*
NConL	*Notes on Contemporary Literature*
NCP	*Nineteenth-Century Prose*
NCS	New Clarendon Shakespeare
NCSR	New Chaucer Society Readings
NCSTC	Nineteenth-Century Short Title Catalogue
NCStud	*Nineteenth-Century Studies*
NCT	*Nineteenth-Century Theatre*
NDQ	*North Dakota Quarterly*
NegroD	*Negro Digest*
NELS	*North Eastern Linguistic Society*
Neoh	*Neohelicon*
Neophil	*Neophilologus*
NEQ	*New England Quarterly*
NERMS	*New England Review*
NewA	*New African*
NewBR	*New Beacon Review*
NewC	*New Criterion*

New Casebooks	New Casebooks: Contemporary Critical Essays
NewComp	*New Comparison: A Journal of Comparative and General Literary Studies*
NewF	*New Formations*
NewHR	*New Historical Review*
NewR	*New Republic*
NewSt	*Newfoundland Studies*
NewV	*New Voices*
NF	*Neiophilologica Fennica*
NfN	*News from Nowhere*
NFS	*Nottingham French Studies*
NGC	*New German Critique*
NGS	*New German Studies*
NH	*Northern History*
NHR	*Nathaniel Hawthorne Review*
NIS	*Nordic Irish Studies*
NJL	*Nordic Journal of Linguistics*
NL	*Nouvelles Littéraires*
NLAN	*National Library of Australia News*
NL<	*Natural Language and Linguistic Theory*
NLH	*New Literary History: A Journal of Theory and Interpretation*
NLitsR	*New Literatures Review*
NLR	*New Left Review*
NLS	*Natural Language Semantics*
NLWJ	*National Library of Wales Journal*
NM	*Neuphilologische Mitteilungen*
NMAL	*NMAL: Notes on Modern American Literature*
NMer	New Mermaids
NMIL	*Notes on Modern Irish Literature*
NMS	*Nottingham Medieval Studies*
NMW	*Notes on Mississippi Writers*
NN	*Nordiska Namenstudier*
NNER	*Northern New England Review*
Nomina	*Nomina: A Journal of Name Studies Relating to Great Britain and Ireland*
NoP	*Northern Perspective*
NOR	*New Orleans Review*
NorfolkA	*Norfolk Archaeology*
NortonCE	Norton Critical Edition
Novel	*Novel: A Forum on Fiction*
NOWELE	*North-Western European Language Evolution*
NPS	New Penguin Shakespeare
NR	*Nassau Review*
NRF	*La Nouvelle Revue Française*
NRRS	*Notes and Records of the Royal Society of London*
NS	*Die neuren Sprachen*

NSS	New Swan Shakespeare
NTQ	*New Theatre Quarterly*
NVSAWC	*Newsletter of the Victorian Studies Association of Western Canada*
NwJ	*Northward Journal*
NWR	*Northwest Review*
NWRev	*New Welsh Review*
NYH	*New York History*
NYLF	New York Literary Forum
NYRB	*New York Review of Books*
NYT	*New York Times*
NYTBR	*New York Times Book Review*
NZB	*New Zealand Books*
NZJAS	*New Zealand Journal of Asian Studies*
NZListener	*New Zealand Listener*
OA	Oxford Authors
OB	*Ord och Bild*
Obsidian	*Obsidian II: Black Literature in Review*
OBSP	Oxford Bibliographical Society Publications
OED	*Oxford English Dictionary*
OEDNews	*Oxford English Dictionary News*
OENews	*Old English Newsletter*
OET	Oxford English Texts
OH	*Over Here: An American Studies Journal*
OHEL	Oxford History of English Literature
OhR	*Ohio Review*
OLR	*Oxford Literary Review*
OnCan	*Onomastica Canadiana*
OPBS	*Occasional Papers of the Bibliographical Society*
OpenGL	Open Guides to Literature
OpL	*Open Letter*
OPL	Oxford Poetry Library
OPLiLL	*Occasional Papers in Linguistics and Language Learning*
OPSL	*Occasional Papers in Systemic Linguistics*
OralT	*Oral Tradition*
Orbis	*Orbis*
OrbisLit	*Orbis Litterarum*
OS	Oxford Shakespeare
OSS	Oxford Shakespeare Studies
OT	*Oral Tradition*
Outrider	*Outrider: A Publication of the Wyoming State Library*
Overland	*Overland*
PA	*Présence Africaine*
PAAS	*Proceedings of the American Antiquarian Society*
PacStud	*Pacific Studies*
Paideuma	*Paideuma: A Journal Devoted to Ezra Pound Scholarship*

PAJ	*Performing Art Journal*
P&C	*Pragmatics and Cognition*
P&CT	*Psychoanalysis and Contemporary Thought*
P&L	*Philosophy and Literature*
P&P	*Past and Present*
P&R	*Philosophy and Rhetoric*
P&SC	*Philosophy and Social Criticism*
PAPA	*Publications of the Arkansas Philological Association*
Papers	*Papers: Explorations into Children's Literature*
PAPS	*Proceedings of the American Philosophical Society*
PAR	*Performing Arts Resources*
Parabola	*Parabola: The Magazine of Myth and Tradition*
Paragraph	*Paragraph: The Journal of the Modern Critical Theory Group*
Parergon	*Parergon: Bulletin of the Australian and New Zealand Association for Medieval and Renaissance Studies*
ParisR	*Paris Review*
Parnassus	*Parnassus: Poetry in Review*
PastM	Past Masters
PaterN	*Pater Newsletter*
PAus	*Poetry Australia*
PBA	*Proceedings of the British Academy*
PBerLS	*Proceedings of the Berkeley Linguistics Society*
PBSA	*Papers of the Bibliographical Society ofAmerica*
PBSC	*Papers of the Biographical Society of Canada*
PCL	*Perspectives on Contemporary Literature*
PCLAC	*Proceedings of the California Linguistics Association Conference*
PCLS	*Proceedings of the Comparative Literature Symposium* (Lubbock, TX)
PCP	*Pacific Coast Philology*
PCRev	*Popular Culture Review*
PCS	*Penguin Critical Studies*
PEAN	*Proceedings of the English Association North*
PE&W	*Philosophy East and West: A Quarterly of Asian and Comparative Thought*
PELL	*Papers on English Language and Literature* (Japan)
Pequod	*Pequod: A Journal of Contemporary Literature and Literary Criticism*
Performance	*Performance*
Peritia	*Peritia: Journal of the Medieval Academy of Ireland*
Persuasions	*Persuasions: Journal of the Jane Austen Society of North America*
Philosophy	*Philosophy*
PHist	*Printing History*
Phonetica	*Phonetica: International Journal of Speech Science*

PHOS	Publishing History Occasional Series
PhRA	*Philosophical Research Archives*
PhT	*Philosophy Today*
PiL	*Papers in Linguistics*
PIMA	*Proceedings of the Illinois Medieval Association*
PinterR	*Pinter Review*
PJCL	*Prairie Journal of Canadian Literature*
PLL	*Papers on Language and Literature*
PLPLS	*Proceedings of the Leeds Philosophical and Literary Society, Literary and Historical Section*
PM	Penguin Masterstudies
PMHB	*Pennsylvania Magazine of History and Biography*
PMLA	*Publications of the Modern Language Association of America*
PMPA	*Proceedings of the Missouri Philological Association*
PNotes	*Pynchon Notes*
PNR	*Poetry and Nation Review*
PoeS	*Poe Studies*
Poetica	*Poetica: Zeitschrift fur Sprach- und Literaturwissenschaft* (Amsterdam)
PoeticaJ	*Poetica: An International Journal of Linguistic-Literary Studies* (Tokyo)
Poetics	*Poetics: International Review for the Theory of Literature*
Poétique	*Poétique: Revue de Théorie et d'Analyse Littéraires*
Poetry	*Poetry* (Chicago)
PoetryCR	*Poetry Canada Review*
PoetryR	*Poetry Review*
PoetryW	*Poetry Wales*
POMPA	*Publications of the Mississippi Philological Association*
PostS	*Past Script: Essays in Film and the Humanities*
PoT	*Poetics Today*
PP	Penguin Passnotes
PP	*Philologica Pragensia*
PPA	*Philosophical Perspectives Annual*
PPMRC	*Proceedings of the International Patristic, Mediaeval and Renaissance Conference*
PPR	*Philosophy and Phenomenological Research*
PQ	*Philological Quarterly*
PQM	*Pacific Quarterly* (Moana)
PR	*Partisan Review*
Pragmatics	*Pragmatics: Quarterly Publication of the International Pragmatics Association*
PrairieF	*Prairie Fire*
Praxis	*Praxis: A Journal of Cultural Criticism*

Prépub	*(Pré)publications*
PRev	*Powys Review*
PRIA	*Proceedings of the Royal Irish Academy*
PRIAA	Publications of the Research Institute of the Abo Akademi Foundation
PRMCLS	*Papers from the Regional Meetings of the Chicago Linguistics Society*
Prospects	*Prospects: An Annual Journal of American Cultural Studies*
Prospero	*Prospero: Journal of New Thinking in Philosophy for Education*
Proteus	*Proteus: A Journal of Ideas*
Proverbium	*Proverbium*
PrS	*Prairie Schooner*
PS	*Prose Studies*
PSt	*Prose Studies*
PsyArt	*Psychological Study of the Arts* (hyperlink journal)
PsychR	*Psychological Reports*
PTBI	Publications of the Sir Thomas Browne Institute
PubH	*Publishing History*
PULC	*Princeton University Library Chronicle*
PURBA	*Panjab University Research Bulletin (Arts)*
PVR	*Platte Valley Review*
PWC	*Pickering's Women's Classics*
PY	*Phonology Yearbook*
QDLLSM	*Quaderni del Dipartimento e Lingue e Letterature Straniere Moderne*
QI	*Quaderni d'Italianistica*
QJS	*Quarterly Journal of Speech*
QLing	*Quantitative Linguistics*
QQ	*Queen's Quarterly*
QR	*Queensland Review*
QRFV	*Quarterly Review of Film and Video*
Quadrant	*Quadrant* (Sydney)
Quarendo	*Quarendo*
Quarry	*Quarry*
QWERTY	*QWERTY: Arts, Littératures, et Civilisations du Monde Anglophone*
RadP	*Radical Philosophy*
RAL	*Research in African Literatures*
RALS	*Resources for American Literary Study*
Ramus	*Ramus: Critical Studies in Greek and Roman Literature*
R&C	*Race and Class*
R&L	*Religion and Literature*
Raritan	*Raritan: A Quarterly Review*
Rask	*Rask: International tidsskrift for sprong og kommunikation*

RB	*Revue Bénédictine*
RBPH	*Revue Belge de Philologie et d'Histoire*
RCEI	*Revista Canaria de Estudios Ingleses*
RCF	*Review of Contemporary Fiction*
RCPS	*Romantic Circles Praxis Series* (online)
RDN	*Renaissance Drama Newsletter*
RE	*Revue d'Esthétique*
Reader	*Reader: Essays in Reader-Oriented Theory, Criticism, Reader and Pedagogy*
ReAL	*Re: Artes Liberales*
REALB	*REAL: The Yearbook of Research in English and American Literature* (Berlin)
ReAr	*Religion and the Arts*
RecBucks	*Records of Buckinghamshire*
RecL	*Recovery Literature*
RECTR	*Restoration and Eighteenth-Century Theatre Research*
RedL	*Red Letters: A Journal of Cultural Politics*
REED	Records of Early English Drama
REEDN	*Records of Early English Drama Newsletter*
ReFr	*Revue Française*
Reinardus	*Reinardus*
REL	*Review of English Literature* (Kyoto)
RELC	*RELC Journal: A Journal of Language Teaching and Research in Southeast Asia*
Ren&R	*Renaissance and Reformation*
Renascence	*Renascence: Essays on Values in Literature*
RenD	*Renaissance Drama*
Renfor	*Renaissance Forum* (online)
RenP	*Renaissance Papers*
RenQ	*Renaissance Quarterly*
Rep	*Representations*
RePublica	*RePublica*
RES	*Review of English Studies*
Restoration	*Restoration: Studies in English Literary Culture, 1660–1700*
Rev	*Review* (Blacksburg, VA)
RevAli	*Revista Alicantina de Estudios Ingleses*
Revels	Revels Plays
RevelsCL	Revels Plays Companion Library
RevelsSE	Revels Student Editions
RevR	Revolution and Romanticism, 1789–1834
RFEA	*Revue Française d'Études Américaines*
RFR	*Robert Frost Review*
RG	*Revue Générale*
RH	*Recusant History*
Rhetorica	*Rhetorica: A Journal of the History of Rhetoric*
Rhetorik	*Rhetorik: Ein Internationales Jahrbuch*

RHist	*Rural History*
RHL	*Revue d'Histoire Littéraire de la France*
RHT	*Revue d'Histoire du Théâtre*
RIB	*Revista Interamericana de Bibliografia: Inter-American Reviews of Bibliography*
Ricardian	*Ricardian: Journal of the Richard III Society*
RL	Rereading Literature
RLAn	*Romance Languages Annual*
RLC	*Revue de Littérature Comparée*
RLing	*Rivista di Linguistica*
RLit	*Russian Literature*
RLM	*La Revue des Lettres Modernes: Histoire des Idées des Littératures*
RLMC	*Rivista di Letterature Moderne e Comparate*
RLT	*Russian Literature Triquarterly*
RM	*Rethinking Marxism*
RMR	*Rocky Mountain Review of Language and Literature*
RM	*Renaissance and Modern Studies*
RMSt	*Reading Medieval Studies*
Romania	*Romania*
Romanticism	*Romanticism*
RomN	*Romance Notes*
RomQ	*Romance Quarterly*
RomS	*Romance Studies*
RoN	*Romanticism on the Net*
ROO	*Room of One's Own: A Feminist Journal of Literature and Criticism*
RORD	*Research Opportunities in Renaissance Drama*
RPT	*Russian Poetics in Translation*
RQ	*Riverside Quarterly*
RR	*Romanic Review*
RRDS	Regents Renaissance Drama Series
RRestDS	Regents Restoration Drama Series
RS	*Renaissance Studies*
RSQ	*Rhetoric Society Quarterly*
RSV	*Rivista di Study Vittoriani*
RUO	*Revue de l'Université d'Ottawa*
RUSEng	*Rajasthan University Studies in English*
RuskN	*Ruskin Newsletter*
RUUL	*Reports from the Uppsala University Department of Linguistics*
R/WT	*Readerly/Writerly Texts*
SAC	*Studies in the Age of Chaucer*
SAD	*Studies in American Drama, 1945–Present*
SAF	*Studies in American Fiction*
Saga-Book	*Saga-Book (Viking Society for Northern Research)*
Sagetrieb	*Sagatrieb: A Journal Devoted to Poets in the Pound–H.D.–Williams Tradition*

SAIL	*Studies in American Indian Literatures: The Journal of the Association for the Study of American Indian Literatures*
SAJL	*Studies in American Jewish Literature*
SAJMRS	*South African Journal of Medieval and Renaissance Studies*
Sal	*Salmagrundi: A Quarterly of the Humanities and Social Sciences*
SALCT	*SALCT: Studies in Australian Literature, Culture and Thought*
Salt	*Salt: An International Journal of Poetry and Poetics*
S&S	*Sight and Sound*
SAntS	*Studia Anthroponymica Scandinavica*
SAP	*Studia Anglica Posnaniensia*
SAQ	*South Atlantic Quarterly*
SAR	*Studies in the American Renaissance*
SARB	*South African Review of Books*
SASLC	Studies in Anglo-Saxon Literature and Culture
SatR	*Saturday Review*
SB	*Studies in Bibliography*
SBHC	*Studies in Browning and his Circle*
SC	*Seventeenth Century*
Scan	*Scandinavica: An International Journal of Scandinavian Studies*
ScanS	*Scandinavian Studies*
SCel	*Studia Celtica*
SCER	*Society for Critical Exchange Report*
Schuylkill	*Schuylkill: A Creative and Critical Review* (Temple University)
SCJ	*Sixteenth Century Journal*
SCL	*Studies in Canadian Literature*
ScLJ	*Scottish Literary Journal: A Review of Studies in Scottish Language and Literature*
ScLJ(S)	*Scottish Literary Journal Supplement*
SCLOP	*Society for Caribbean Linguistics Occasional Papers*
SCN	*Seventeenth-Century News*
ScottN	*Scott Newsletter*
SCR	*South Carolina Review*
Screen	*Screen* (London)
SCRev	*South Central Review*
Scriblerian	*Scriblerian and the Kit Cats: A Newsjournal Devoted to Pope, Swift, and their Circle*
Scripsi	*Scripsi*
Scriptorium	*Scriptorium: International Review of Manuscript Studies*
ScTh	*Scottish Journal of Theology*
SD	*Social Dynamics*
SDR	*South Dakota Review*

SECC	*Studies in Eighteenth-Century Culture*
SECOLR	*SECOL Review: Southeastern Conference on Linguistics*
SED	*Survey of English Dialects*
SEDERI	*Journal of the Spanish Society for Renaissance Studies (Sociedad Española de Estudios Renacentistas Ingleses)*
SEEJ	*Slavic and East European Journal*
SEL	*Studies in English Literature, 1500–1900* (Rice University)
SELing	*Studies in English Linguistics* (Tokyo)
SELit	*Studies in English Literature* (Tokyo)
SELL	*Studies in English Language and Literature*
Sem	*Semiotica: Journal of the International Association for Semiotic Studies*
Semiosis	*Semiosis: Internationale Zeitschrift für Semiotik und Ästhetik*
SER	*Studien zur Englischen Romantik*
Seven	*Seven: An Anglo-American Literary Review*
SF&R	*Scholars' Facsimiles and Reprints*
SFic	*Science Fiction: A Review of Speculative Literature*
SFNL	*Shakespeare on Film Newsletter*
SFQ	*Southern Folklore Quarterly*
SFR	*Stanford French Review*
SFS	*Science-Fiction Studies*
SH	*Studia Hibernica* (Dublin)
ShakB	*Shakespeare Bulletin*
ShakS	*Shakespeare Studies* (New York)
Shandean	*Shandean*
Sh&Sch	*Shakespeare and Schools*
ShawR	*Shaw: The Annual of Bernard Shaw Studies*
Shenandoah	*Shenandoah*
SherHR	*Sherlock Holmes Review*
ShIntY	*Shakespeare International Yearbook*
Shiron	*Shiron*
ShJE	*Shakespeare Jahrbuch* (Weimar)
ShJW	*Deutsche Shakespeare-Gesellschaft West Jahrbuch* (Bochum)
ShLR	*Shoin Literary Review*
ShN	*Shakespeare Newsletter*
SHR	*Southern Humanities Review*
ShS	*Shakespeare Survey*
ShSA	*Shakespeare in Southern Africa*
ShStud	*Shakespeare Studies* (Tokyo)
SHW	*Studies in Hogg and his World*
ShY	*Shakespeare Yearbook*
SiAF	*Studies in American Fiction*

SIcon	*Studies in Iconography*
SidJ	*Sidney Journal*
SidN	*Sidney Newsletter and Journal*
Signs	*Signs: Journal of Women in Culture and Society*
SiHoLS	*Studies in the History of the Language Sciences*
SIL	*Studies in Literature*
SiM	*Studies in Medievalism*
SIM	*Studies in Music*
SiP	*Shakespeare in Performance*
SiPr	*Shakespeare in Production*
SiR	*Studies in Romanticism*
SJS	*San José Studies*
SL	*Studia Linguistica*
SLang	*Studies in Language*
SLCS	*Studies in Language Companion Series*
SLI	*Studies in the Literary Imagination*
SLJ	*Southern Literary Journal*
SLRev	*Stanford Literature Review*
SLSc	*Studies in the Linguistic Sciences*
SMART	*Studies in Medieval and Renaissance Teaching*
SMC	*Studies in Medieval Culture*
SMed	*Studi Medievali*
SMELL	*Studies in Medieval English Language and Literature*
SMLit	*Studies in Mystical Literature* (Taiwan)
SMRH	*Studies in Medieval and Renaissance History*
SMRT	*Studies in Medieval and Renaissance Teaching*
SMS	*Studier i Modern Språkvetenskap*
SMy	*Studia Mystica*
SN	*Studia Neophilologica*
SNNTS	*Studies in the Novel* (North Texas State University)
SO	*Shakespeare Originals*
SOA	*Sydsvenska OrtnamnssällskapetsÅrsskrift*
SoAR	*South Atlantic Review*
SoC	*Senses of Cinema* (online)
Sociocrit	*Sociocriticism*
Socioling	*Sociolinguistica*
SocN	*Sociolinguistics*
SocSem	*Social Semiotics*
SocT	*Social Text*
SohoB	*Soho Bibliographies*
SoQ	*Southern Quarterly*
SoR	*Southern Review* (Baton Rouge, LA)
SoRA	*Southern Review* (Adelaide)
SoSt	*Southern Studies: An Interdisciplinary Journal of the South*
Soundings	*Soundings: An Interdisciplinary Journal*
Southerly	*Southerly: A Review of Australian Literature*
SovL	*Soviet Literature*

SP	*Studies in Philology*
SPAN	*SPAN: Newsletter of the South Pacific Association for Commonwealth Literature and Language Studies*
SPAS	*Studies in Puritan American Spirituality*
SPC	*Studies in Popular Culture*
Spectrum	*Spectrum*
Speculum	*Speculum: A Journal of Medieval Studies*
SPELL	*Swiss Papers in English Language and Literature*
Sphinx	*Sphinx: A Magazine of Literature and Society*
SpM	*Spicilegio Moderno*
SpNL	*Spenser Newsletter*
Sprachwiss	*Sprachwissenschalt*
SpringE	*Spring: The Journal of the e.e. cummings Society*
SPub	*Studies in Publishing*
SPWVSRA	*Selected Papers from the West Virginia Shakespeare and Renaissance Association*
SQ	*Shakespeare Quarterly*
SR	*Sewanee Review*
SRen	*Studies in the Renaissance*
SRSR	*Status Report on Speech Research* (Haskins Laboratories)
SSEL	Stockholm Studies in English
SSELER	Salzburg Studies in English Literature: Elizabethan and Renaissance
SSELJDS	Salzburg Studies in English Literature: Jacobean Drama Studies
SSELPDPT	Salzburg Studies in English Literature: Poetic Drama and Poetic Theory
SSELRR	Salzburg Studies in English Literature: Romantic Reassessment
SSEng	*Sydney Studies in English*
SSF	*Studies in Short Fiction*
SSL	*Studies in Scottish Literature*
SSLA	*Studies in Second Language Acquisition*
SSR	*Scottish Studies Review*
SSt	*Spenser Studies*
SStud	*Swift Studies: The Annual of the Ehrenpreis Center*
Staffrider	*Staffrider*
StaffordS	*Staffordshire Studies*
STAH	*Strange Things Are Happening*
STGM	Studien und Texte zur Geistegeschichte des Mittelalters
StHR	*Stanford Historical Review*
StHum	*Studies in the Humanities*
StIn	*Studi Inglesi*
StLF	*Studi di Letteratura Francese*
StQ	*Steinbeck Quarterly*
StrR	*Structuralist Review*
StTCL	*Studies in Twentieth-Century Literature*

StTW	*Studies in Travel Writing*
StudWF	*Studies in Weird Fiction*
STUF	*Sprachtypologie und Universalienforschung*
Style	*Style* (De Kalb, IL)
SUAS	*Stratford-upon-Avon Studies*
SubStance	*SubStance: A Review of Theory and Literary Criticism*
SUS	*Susquehanna University Studies*
SussexAC	*Sussex Archaeological Collections*
SussexP&P	*Sussex Past & Present*
SVEC	*Studies on Voltaire and the Eighteenth Century*
SWPLL	*Sheffield Working Papers in Language and Linguistics*
SWR	*Southwest Review*
SwR	*Swansea Review: A Journal of Criticism*
Sycamore	*Sycamore*
Symbolism	*Symbolism: An International Journal of Critical Aesthetics*
TA	*Theatre Annual*
Tabu	*Bulletin voor Taalwetenschap, Groningen*
Takahe	*Takahe*
Talisman	*Talisman*
T&C	*Text and Context*
T&L	*Translation and Literature*
T&P	*Text and Performance*
TAPS	*Transactions of the American Philosophical Society*
TCBS	*Transactions of the Cambridge Bibliographical Society*
TCE	*Texas College English*
TCL	*Twentieth-Century Literature*
TCS	*Theory, Culture and Society: Explorations in Critical Social Science*
TCWAAS	*Transactions of the Cumberland and Westmorland Antiquarian and Archaeological Society*
TD	*Themes in Drama*
TDR	*Drama Review*
TEAS	*Twayne's English Authors Series*
Telos	*Telos: A Quarterly Journal of Post-Critical Thought*
TennEJ	*Tennessee English Journal*
TennQ	*Tennessee Quarterly*
TennSL	*Tennessee Studies in Literature*
TeReo	*Te Reo: Journal of the Linguistic Society of New Zealand*
TSLL	*Texas Studies in Language and Literature*
Text	*Text: Transactions of the Society for Textual Scholarship*
TH	*Texas Humanist*
THA	*Thomas Hardy Annual*
Thalia	*Thalia: Studies in Literary Humor*
ThC	*Theatre Crafts*

Theater	*Theater*
TheatreS	*Theatre Studies*
Theoria	*Theoria: A Journal of Studies in the Arts, Humanities and Social Sciences* (Natal)
THES	*Times Higher Education Supplement*
Thesis	*Thesis Eleven*
THIC	*Theatre History in Canada*
THJ	*Thomas Hardy Journal*
ThN	*Thackeray Newsletter*
ThoreauQ	*Thoreau Quarterly: A Journal of Literary and Philosophical Studies*
Thought	*Thought: A Review of Culture and Ideas*
Thph	*Theatrephile*
ThreR	*Threepenny Review*
ThS	*Theatre Survey: The American Journal of Theatre History*
THSLC	*Transactions of the Historic Society of Lancashire and Cheshire*
THStud	*Theatre History Studies*
ThTop	*Theatre Topics*
THY	*Thomas Hardy Yearbook*
TiLSM	*Trends in Linguistics: Studies and Monographs*
Tip	*Theory in Practice*
Tirra Lirra	*Tirra Lirra: The Quarterly Magazine for the Yarra Valley*
TJ	*Theatre Journal*
TJS	*Transactions* (Johnson Society)
TJAAWP	*Text: Journal of the Australian Association of Writing Programs*
TkR	*Tamkang Review*
TL	*Theoretical Linguistics*
TLR	*Linguistic Review*
TLS	*Times Literary Supplement*
TMLT	*Toronto Medieval Latin Texts*
TN	*Theatre Notebook*
TNWSECS	*Transactions of the North West Society for Eighteenth Century Studies*
TP	*Terzo Programma*
TPLL	*Tilbury Papers in Language and Literature*
TPQ	*Text and Performance Quarterly*
TPr	*Textual Practice*
TPS	*Transactions of the Philological Society*
TR	*Theatre Record*
Traditio	*Traditio: Studies in Ancient and Medieval History, Thought, and Religion*
Transition	*Transition*
TRB	*Tennyson Research Bulletin*

TRHS	*Transactions of the Royal Historical Society*
TRI	*Theatre Research International*
TriQ	*TriQuarterly*
Trivium	*Trivium*
Tropismes	*Tropismes*
TSAR	*Toronto South Asian Review*
TSB	*Thoreau Society Bulletin*
TSLang	Typological Studies in Language
TSLL	*Texas Studies in Literature and Language*
TSWL	*Tulsa Studies in Women's Literature*
TTR	*Trinidad and Tobago Review*
TUSAS	Twayne's United States Authors Series
TWAS	Twayne's World Authors Series
TWBR	*Third World Book Review*
TWQ	*Third World Quarterly*
TWR	*Thomas Wolfe Review*
Txt	*Text: An Interdisciplinary Annual of Textual Studies*
TYDS	*Transactions of the Yorkshire Dialect Society*
Typophiles	*Typophiles* (New York)
UCrow	*Upstart Crow*
UCTSE	*University of Cape Town Studies in English*
UCWPL	*UCL Working Papers in Linguistics*
UDR	*University of Drayton Review*
UE	*Use of English*
UEAPL	*UEA Papers in Linguistics*
UES	*Unisa English Studies*
Ufahamu	*Ufahamu*
ULR	*University of Leeds Review*
UMSE	*University of Mississippi Studies in English*
Untold	*Untold*
UOQ	*University of Ottawa Quarterly*
URM	*Ultimate Reality and Meaning: Interdisciplinary Studies in the Philosophy of Understanding*
USSE	*University of Saga Studies in English*
UtopST	*Utopian Studies*
UTQ	*University of Toronto Quarterly*
UWR	*University of Windsor Review*
VCT	Les Voies de la Création Théâtrale
VEAW	Varieties of English around the World
Verbatim	*Verbatim: The Language Quarterly*
VIA	*VIA: The Journal of the Graduate School of Fine Arts* (University of Pennsylvania)
Viator	*Viator: Medieval and Renaissance Studies*
Views	*Viennese English Working Papers*
VIJ	*Victorians Institute Journal*
VLC	*Victorian Literature and Culture*
VN	*Victorian Newsletter*
Voices	*Voices*

VP	*Victorian Poetry*
VPR	*Victorian Periodicals Review*
VQR	*Virginia Quarterly Review*
VR	*Victorian Review*
VS	*Victorian Studies*
VSB	*Victorian Studies Bulletin*
VWM	*Virginia Woolf Miscellany*
WAJ	*Women's Art Journal*
WAL	*Western American Literature*
W&I	*Word and Image*
W&L	*Women and Literature*
W&Lang	*Women and Language*
Wasafiri	*Wasafiri*
WascanaR	*Wascana Review*
WBEP	Wiener Beiträge zur Englischen Philologie
WC	World's Classics
WC	*Wordsworth Circle*
WCR	*West Coast Review*
WCSJ	*Wilkie Collins Society Journal*
WCWR	*William Carlos Williams Review*
Wellsian	*Wellsian: The Journal of the H.G. Wells Society*
WEn	*World Englishes*
Westerly	*Westerly: A Quarterly Review*
WestHR	*West Hills Review: A Walt Whitman Journal*
WF	*Western Folklore*
WHASN	*W.H. Auden Society Newsletter*
WHR	*Western Humanities Review*
WI	*Word and Image*
WLA	*Wyndham Lewis Annual*
WL&A	*War Literature, and the Arts: An International Journal of the Humanities*
WLT	*World Literature Today*
WLWE	*World Literature Written in English*
WMQ	*William and Mary Quarterly*
WoHR	*Women's History Review*
WolfenbütteleB	*Wolfenbüttele Beiträge: Aus den Schätzen der Herzog August Bibliothek*
Women	*Women: A Cultural Review*
WorcesterR	*Worcester Review*
WORD	*WORD: Journal of the International Linguistic Association*
WQ	*Wilson Quarterly*
WRB	*Women's Review of Books*
WS	*Women's Studies: An Interdisciplinary Journal*
WSIF	*Women's Studies: International Forum*
WSJour	*Wallace Stevens Journal*
WSR	*Wicazo Sa Review*

WstA	*Woolf Studies Annual*
WTJ	*Westminster Theological Journal*
WTW	*Writers and their Work*
WVUPP	*West Virginia University Philological Papers*
WW	*Women's Writing*
WWR	*Walt Whitman Quarterly Review*
XUS	*Xavier Review*
YCC	*Yearbook of Comparative Criticism*
YeA	*Yeats Annual*
YER	*Yeats Eliot Review*
YES	*Yearbook of English Studies*
YEuS	*Yearbook of European Studies/Annuaire d'Études Européennes*
YFS	*Yale French Studies*
Yiddish	*Yiddish*
YJC	*Yale Journal of Criticism: Interpretation in the Humanities*
YLS	*Yearbook of Langland Studies*
YM	*Yearbook of Morphology*
YNS	York Note Series
YPL	*York Papers in Linguistics*
YR	*Yale Review*
YULG	*Yale University Library Gazette*
YWES	*Year's Work in English Studies*
ZAA	*Zeitschrift für Anglistik and Amerikanistik*
ZCP	*Zeitschrift für celtische Philologie*
ZDA	*Zeitschrift für deutsches Altertum und deutsche Literatur*
ZDL	*Zeitschrift für Dialektologie und Linguistik*
ZGKS	*Zeitschrfit für Gesellschaft für Kanada-Studien*
ZGL	*Zeitschrift für germanistische Linguistik*
ZPSK	*Zeitschrift für Phonetik Sprachwissenshaft und Kommunikationsforschung*
ZSpr	*Zeitschrift für Sprachwissenshaft*
ZVS	*Zeitschrift für vergleichende Sprachforschung*

Volume numbers are supplied in the text, as are individual issue numbers for journals that are not continuously paginated through the year.

2. Publishers

AAAH	Acta Academiae Åboensis Humaniora, Åbo, Finland
AAH	Australian Academy of Humanities
A&B	Allison & Busby, London
A&R	Angus & Robertson, North Ryde, New South Wales
A&U	Allen & Unwin (now Unwin Hyman)

A&UA	Allen & Unwin, North Sydney, New South Wales
A&W	Almqvist & Wiksell International, Stockholm
AarhusUP	Aarhus UP, Aarhus, Denmark
ABC	ABC Enterprises
ABC CLIO	ABC CLIO Reference Books, Santa Barbara, CA
Abbeville	Abbeville Press, New York
ABDO	Association Bourguignonne de Dialectologie et d'Onom-astique, Dijon
AberdeenUP	Aberdeen UP, Aberdeen
Abhinav	Abhinav Publications, New Delhi
Abingdon	Abingdon Press, Nashville, TN
ABL	Armstrong Browning Library, Waco, TX
Ablex	Ablex Publishing, Norwood, NJ
Åbo	Åbo Akademi, Åbo, Finland
Abrams	Harry N. Abrams, New York
Academia	Academia Press, Melbourne
Academic	Academic Press, London and Orlando, FL
Academy	Academy Press, Dublin
AcademyC	Academy Chicago Publishers, Chicago
AcademyE	Academy Editions, London
Acadiensis	Acadiensis Press, Fredericton, New Brunswick, Canada
ACarS	Association for Caribbean Studies, Coral Gables, FL
ACC	Antique Collectors' Club, Woodbridge, Suffolk
ACCO	ACCO, Leuven, Belgium
ACLALS	Association for Commonwealth Literature and Language Studies, Canberra
ACMRS	Arizona Center for Medieval and Renaissance Studies
ACP	Another Chicago Press, Chicago
ACS	Association for Canadian Studies, Ottawa
Adam Hart	Adam Hart Publishers, London
Adam Matthew	Adam Matthew, Suffolk
Addison-Wesley	Addison-Wesley, Wokingham, Berkshire
ADFA	Australian Defence Force Academy, Department of English
Adosa	Adosa, Clermont-Ferrand, France
AEMS	American Early Medieval Studies
AF	Akademisk Forlag, Copenhagen
Affiliated	Affiliated East–West Press, New Delhi
AFP	Associated Faculty Press, New York
Africana	Africana Publications, New York
A–H	Amold–Heinemann, New Delhi
Ahriman	Ahriman-Verlag, Freiburg im Breisgau, Germany
AIAS	Australian Institute of Aboriginal Studies, Canberra
	Ajanta Ajanta Publications, Delhi
AK	Akadémiai Kiadó, Budapest
ALA	ALA Editions, Chicago
Al&Ba	Allen & Bacon, Boston, MA

Albatross	Albatross Books, Sutherland, New South Wales
Albion	Albion, Appalachian State University, Boone, NC
Alderman	Alderman Press, London
Aldwych	Aldwych Press
AligarhMU	Aligarh Muslim University, Uttar Pradesh, India
Alioth	Alioth Press, Beaverton, OR
Allen	W.H. Allen, London
Allied Publishers	Allied Indian Publishers, Lahore and New Delhi
Almond	Almond Press, Sheffield
AM	Aubier Montaigne, Paris
AMAES	Association des Médiévistes Angliciste de l'Enseignement Supérieur, Paris
Amate	Amate Press, Oxford
AmberL	Amber Lane, Oxford
Amistad	Amistad Press, New York
AMP	Aurora Metro Press, London
AMS	AMS Press, New York
AMU	Adam Mickiewicz University, Posnan
Anansi	Anansi Press, Toronto
Anderson-Lovelace	Anderson-Lovelace, Los Altos Hills, CA
Anma Libri	Anma Libri, Saratoga, CA
Antipodes	Antipodes Press, Plimmerton, New Zealand
Anvil	Anvil Press Poetry, London
APA	APA, Maarssen, Netherlands
APH	Associated Publishing House, New Delhi
APL	American Poetry and Literature Press, Philadelphia
APP	Australian Professional Publications, Mosman, New South Wales
Applause	Applause Theatre Book Publishers
Appletree	Appletree Press, Belfast
APS	American Philosophical Society, Philadelphia
Aquarian	Aquarian Press, Wellingborough, Northants
ArborH	Arbor House Publishing, New York
Arcade	Arcade Publishing, New York
Archon	Archon Books, Hamden, CT
ArchP	Architectural Press Books, Guildford, Surrey
Ardensh	Arden Shakespeare
Ardis	Ardis Publishers, Ann Arbor, MI
Ariel	Ariel Press, London
Aristotle	Aristotle University, Thessaloniki
Ark	Ark Paperbacks, London
Arkona	Arkona Forlaget, Aarhus, Denmark
Arlington	Arlington Books, London
Arnold	Edward Arnold, London
ArnoldEJ	E.J. Arnold & Son, Leeds
ARP	Australian Reference Publications, N. Balwyn, Victoria
Arrow	Arrow Books, London
Arsenal	Arsenal Pulp Press

Artmoves	Artmoves, Parkdale, Victoria
ASAL	Association for the Study of Australian Literature
ASB	Anglo-Saxon Books, Middlesex
ASchP	Australian Scholarly Publishing, Melbourne
ASECS	American Society for Eighteenth-Century Studies, c/o Ohio State University, Columbus
Ashfield	Ashfield Press, London
Ashgate	Ashgate, Brookfield, VT
Ashton	Ashton Scholastic
Aslib	Aslib, London
ASLS	Association for Scottish Literary Studies, Aberdeen
ASP	Australian Scholarly Publishing
AStP	Aboriginal Studies Press, Canberra
ASU	Arizona State University, Tempe
Atheneum	Atheneum Publishers, New York
Athlone	Athlone Press, London
Atlantic	Atlantic Publishers, Darya Ganj, New Delhi
Atlas	Atlas Press, London
Attic	Attic Press, Dublin
AuBC	Australian Book Collector
AucklandUP	Auckland UP, Auckland
AUG	Acta Universitatis Gothoburgensis, Sweden
AUP	Associated University Presses, London and Toronto
AUPG	Academic & University Publishers, London
Aurum	Aurum Press, London
Auslib	Auslib Press, Adelaide
AUU	Acta Universitatis Umensis, Umeå, Sweden
AUUp	Acta Universitatis Upsaliensis, Uppsala
Avebury	Avebury Publishing, Aldershot, Hampshire
Avero	Avero Publications, Newcastle upon Tyne
A-V Verlag	A-V Verlag, Franz Fischer, Augsburg, Germany
AWP	Africa World Press, Trenton, NJ
Axelrod	Axelrod Publishing, Tampa Bay, FL
BA	British Academy, London
BAAS	British Association for American Studies, c/o University of Keele
Bagel	August Bagel Verlag, Dusseldorf
Bahri	Bahri Publications, New Delhi
Bamberger	Bamberger Books, Flint, MI
B&B	Boydell & Brewer, Woodbridge, Suffolk
B&J	Barrie & Jenkins, London
B&N	Barnes & Noble, Totowa, NJ
B&O	Burns & Oates, Tunbridge Wells, Kent
B&S	Michael Benskin and M.L. Samuels, Middle English Dialect Project, University of Edinburgh
BAR	British Archaelogical Reports, Oxford
Barn Owl	Barn Owl Books, Taunton, Somerset

Barnes	A.S. Barnes, San Diego, CA
Barr Smith	Barr Smith Press, Barr Smith Library, University of Adelaide
Bath UP	Bath UP, Bath
Batsford	B.T. Batsford, London
Bayreuth	Bayreuth African Studies, University of Bayreuth, Germany
BBC	BBC Publications, London
BClarkL	Bruccoli Clark Layman
BCP	Bristol Classical Press, Bristol
Beacon	Beacon Press, Boston, MA
Beck	C.H. Beck'sche Verlagsbuchandlung, Munich
Becket	Becket Publications, London
Belin	Éditions Belin, Paris
Belknap	Belknap Press, Cambridge, MA
Belles Lettres	Société d'Édition les Belles Lettres, Paris
Bellew	Bellew Publishing, London
Bellflower	Belflower Press, Case University, Cleveland, OH
Benjamins	John Benjamins, Amsterdam
BenjaminsNA	John Benjamins North America, Philadelphia
BennC	Bennington College, Bennington, VT
Berg	Berg Publishers, Oxford
BFI	British Film Institute, London
BGUP	Bowling Green University Popular Press, Bowling Green, OH
BibS	Bibliographical Society, London
Bilingual	Bilingual Press, Arizona State University, Tempe
Bingley	Clive Bingley, London
Binnacle	Binnacle Press, London
Biografia	Biografia Publishers, London
Birkbeck	Birkbeck College, University of London
Bishopsgate	Bishopsgate Press, Tonbridge, Kent
BL	British Library, London
Black	Adam & Charles Black, London
Black Cat	Black Cat Press, Blackrock, Eire
Blackie	Blackie & Son, Glasgow
Black Moss	Black Moss, Windsor, Ontario
Blackstaff	Blackstaff Press, Belfast
Black Swan	Black Swan, Curtin, UT
Blackwell	Basil Blackwell, Oxford
BlackwellR	Blackwell Reference, Oxford
Blackwood	Blackwood, Pillans & Wilson, Edinburgh
Bl&Br	Blond & Briggs, London
Blandford	Blandford Press, London
Blaue Eule	Verlag die Blaue Eule, Essen
Bloodaxe	Bloodaxe Books, Newcastle upon Tyne
Bloomsbury	Bloomsbury Publishing, London

Blubber Head	Blubber Head Press, Hobart
BM	Bobbs-Merrill, New York
BMP	British Museum Publications, London
Bodleian	Bodleian Library, Oxford
Bodley	Bodley Head, London
Bogle	Bogle L'Ouverture Publications, London
BoiseSUP	Boise State UP, Boise, Idaho
Book Enclave	Book Enclave, Jaipur, India
Book Guild	Book Guild, Lewes, E. Sussex
BookplateS	Bookplate Society, Edgbaston, Birmingham
Boombana	Boombana Press, Brisbane, Queensland
Borealis	Borealis Press, Ottawa
Borgo	Borgo Press, San Bernardino, CA
BostonAL	Boston Athenaeum Library, Boxton, MA
Bouma	Bouma's Boekhuis, Groningen, Netherlands
Bowker	R.R. Bowker, New Providence, NJ
Boyars	Marion Boyars, London and Boston, MA
Boydell	Boydell Press, Woodbridge, Suffolk
Boyes	Megan Boyes, Allestree, Derbyshire
Br&S	Brandl & Schlesinger
Bran's Head	Bran's Head Books, Frome, Somerset
Braumüller	Wilhelm Braumüller, Vienna
Breakwater	Breakwater Books, St John's, Newfoundland
Brentham	Brentham Press, St Albans, Hertfordshire
Brepols	Brepols, Turnhout, Belgium
Brewer	D.S. Brewer, Woodbridge, Suffolk
Brewin	Brewin Books, Studley, Warwicks
Bridge	Bridge Publishing, S. Plainfield, NJ
Brill	E.J. Brill, Leiden
BrillA	Brill Academic Publishers
Brilliance	Brilliance Books, London
Broadview	Broadview, London, Ontario and Lewiston, NY
Brookside	Brookside Press, London
Browne	Sinclair Browne, London
Brownstone	Brownstone Books, Madison, IN
BrownUP	Brown UP, Providence, RI
Brynmill	Brynmill Press, Harleston, Norfolk
BSA	Bibliographical Society of America
BSB	Black Swan Books, Redding Ridge, CT
BSP	Black Sparrow Press, Santa Barbara, CA
BSU	Ball State University, Muncie, IN
BuckUP	Bucknell UP, Lewisburg, PA
Bulzoni	Bulzoni Editore, Rome
BUP	Birmingham University Press
Burnett	Burnett Books, London
Buske	Helmut Buske, Hamburg
Butterfly	Butterfly Books, San Antonio, TX
BWilliamsNZ	Bridget Williams Books, Wellington, New Zealand

CA	Creative Arts Book, Berkeley, CA
CAAS	Connecticut Academy of Arts and Sciences, New Haven
CAB International	Centre for Agriculture and Biosciences International, Wallingford, Oxfordshire
Cadmus	Cadmus Editions, Tiburon, CA Cairns Francis Cairns, University of Leeds
Calaloux	Calaloux Publications, Ithaca, NY
Calder	John Calder, London
CALLS	Centre for Australian Language and Literature Studies, English Department, Universty of New England, New South Wales
Camden	Camden Press, London
CamdenH	Camden House (an imprint of Boydell and Brewer), Rochester, NY
C&G	Carroll & Graf, New York
C&W	Chatto & Windus, London
Canongate	Canongate Publishing, Edinburgh
Canterbury	Canterbury Press, Norwich
Cape	Jonathan Cape, London
Capra	Capra Press, Santa Barbara, CA
Carcanet	Carcanet New Press, Manchester, Lancashire
Cardinal	Cardinal, London
CaribB	Caribbean Books, Parkersburg, IA
CarletonUP	Carleton UP, Ottawa
Carucci	Carucci, Rome
Cascadilla	Cascadilla Press, Somerville, MA
Cass	Frank Cass, London
Cassell	Cassell, London
Cavaliere Azzurro	Cavaliere Azzurro, Bologna
Cave	Godfrey Cave Associates, London
CBA	Council for British Archaeology, London
CBS	Cambridge Bibliographical Society, Cambridge
CCEUCan	Centre for Continuing Education, University of Canterbury, Christchurch, New Zealand
CCP	Canadian Children's Press, Guelph, Ontario
CCS	Centre for Canadian Studies, Mount Allison University, Sackville, NB
CDSH	Centre de Documentation Sciences Humaines, Paris
CENS	Centre for English Name Studies, University of Nottingham
Century	Century Publishing, London
Ceolfrith	Ceolfrith Press, Sunderland, Tyne and Wear
CESR	Société des Amis du Centre d'Études Supérieures de la Renaissance, Tours
CETEDOC	Library of Christian Latin Texts
CFA	Canadian Federation for the Humanities, Ottawa

CG	Common Ground
CH	Croom Helm, London
C–H	Chadwyck–Healey, Cambridge
Chambers	W. & R. Chambers, Edinburgh
Champaign	Champaign Public Library and Information Center, Champaign, IL
Champion	Librairie Honoré Champion, Paris
Chand	S. Chand, Madras
ChelseaH	Chelsea House Publishers, New York, New Haven, and Philadelphia
ChLitAssoc	Children's Literature Association
Christendom	Christendom Publications, Front Royal, VA
Chronicle	Chronicle Books, London
Chrysalis	Chrysalis Press
ChuoUL	Chuo University Library, Tokyo
Churchman	Churchman Publishing, Worthing, W. Sussex
Cistercian	Cistercian Publications, Kalamazoo, MI
CL	City Lights Books, San Francisco
CLA	Canadian Library Association, Ottawa
Clarendon	Clarendon Press, Oxford
Claridge	Claridge, St Albans, Hertfordshire
Clarion	Clarion State College, Clarion, PA
Clark	T. & T. Clark, Edinburgh
Clarke	James Clarke, Cambridge
Classical	Classical Publishing, New Delhi
CLCS	Centre for Language and Communication Studies, Trinity College, Dublin
ClogherHS	Clogher Historical Society, Monaghan, Eire
CLUEB	Cooperativa Libraria Universitaria Editrice, Bologna
Clunie	Clunie Press, Pitlochry, Tayside
CMAP	Caxton's Modem Arts Press, Dallas, TX
CMERS	Center for Medieval and Early Renaissance Studies, Binghamton, NY
CML	William Andrews Clark Memorial Library, Los Angeles
CMST	Centre for Medieval Studies, University of Toronto
Coach House	Coach House Press, Toronto
Colleagues	Colleagues Press, East Lansing, MI
Collector	Collector, London
College-Hill	College-Hill Press, San Diego, CA
Collins	William Collins, London
CollinsA	William Collins (Australia), Sydney
Collins & Brown	Collins & Brown, London
ColUP	Columbia UP, New York
Comedia	Comedia Publishing, London
Comet	Comet Books, London
Compton	Compton Press, Tisbury, Wiltshire
Constable	Constable, London

Contemporary	Contemporary Books, Chicago
Continuum	Continuum Publishing, New York
Copp	Copp Clark Pitman, Mississuaga, Ontario
Corgi	Corgi Books, London
CorkUP	Cork UP, Eire
Cormorant	Cormorant Press, Victoria, BC
Cornford	Cornford Press, Launceston, Tasmania
Cornup	Cornell UP, Ithaca, NY
Cornwallis	Cornwallis Press, Hastings, E. Sussex
Coronado	Coronado Press, Lawrence, KS
Cosmo	Cosmo Publications, New Delhi
Coteau	Coteau Books, Regina, Saskatchewan
Cowley	Cowley Publications, Cambridge, MA
Cowper	Cowper House, Pacific Grove, CA
CPP	Canadian Poetry Press, London, Ontario
CQUP	Central Queensland UP, Rockhampton
Crabtree	Crabtree Press, Sussex
Craftsman House	Craftsman House, Netherlands
Craig Pottoon	Craig Pottoon Publishing, New Zealand
Crawford	Crawford House Publishing, Hindmarsh, SA
Creag Darach	Creag Durach Publications, Stirling
CreativeB	Creative Books, New Delhi
Cresset	Cresset Library, London
CRNLE	Centre for Research in the New Literatures in English, Adelaide
Crossing	Crossing Press, Freedom, CA
Crossroad	Crossroad Publishing, New York
Crown	Crown Publishers, New York
Crowood	Crowood Press, Marlborough, Wiltshire
CSAL	Centre for Studies in Australian Literature, University of Western Australia, Nedlands
CSLI	Center for the Study of Language and Information, Stanford University
CSP	Canadian Scholars' Press, Toronto
CSU	Cleveland State University, Cleveland, OH
CTHS	Éditions du Comité des Travaux Historiques et Scientifiques, Paris
CUAP	Catholic University of America Press, Washington, DC
Cuff	Harry Cuff Publications, St John's, Newfoundland
CULouvain	Catholic University of Louvain, Belgium
CULublin	Catholic University of Lublin, Poland
CUP	Cambridge UP, Cambridge, New York, and Melbourne
Currency	Currency Press, Paddington, New South Wales
Currey	James Currey, London
CV	Cherry Valley Edition, Rochester, NY
CVK	Cornelson-Velhagen & Klasing, Berlin
CWU	Carl Winter Universitätsverlag, Heidelberg
Da Capo	Da Capo Press, New York

Dacorum	Dacorum College, Hemel Hempstead, Hertfordshire
Daisy	Daisy Books, Peterborough, Northampton
Dalkey	Dalkey Archive Press, Elmwood Park, IL
D&C	David & Charles, Newton Abbot, Devon
D&H	Duncker & Humblot, Berlin
D&M	Douglas & McIntyre, Vancouver, BC
D&S	Duffy and Snellgrove, Polts Point, New South Wales
Dangaroo	Dangaroo Press, Mundelstrup, Denmark
DavidB	David Brown Books
Dawson	Dawson Publishing, Folkestone, Kent
DawsonsPM	Dawsons Pall Mall
DBAP	Daphne Brasell Associates Press
DBP	Drama Book Publishers, New York
Deakin UP	Deakin UP, Geelong, Victoria
De Boeck	De Boeck-Wesmael, Brussels
Dee	Ivan R. Dee Publishers, Chicago, IL
De Graaf	De Graaf, Nierwkoup, Netherlands
Denoël	Denoël S.A.R.L., Paris
Dent	J.M. Dent, London
DentA	Dent, Ferntree Gully, Victoria
Depanee	Depanee Printers and Publishers, Nugegoda, Sri Lanka
Deutsch	André Deutsch, London
Didier	Éditions Didier, Paris
Diesterweg	Verlag Moritz Diesterweg, Frankfurt am Main
Dim Gray Bar Press	Dim Gray Bar Press
Doaba	Doaba House, Delhi
Dobby	Eric Dobby Publishing, St Albans
Dobson	Dobson Books, Durham
Dolmen	Dolmen Press, Portlaoise, Eire
Donald	John Donald, Edinburgh
Donker	Adriaan Donker, Johannesburg
Dorset	Dorset Publishing
Doubleday	Doubleday, London and New York
Dove	Dove, Sydney
Dovecote	Dovecote Press, Wimborne, Dorset
Dovehouse	Dovehouse Editions, Canada
Dover	Dover Publications, New York
Drew	Richard Drew, Edinburgh
Droste	Droste Verlag, Düsseldorf
Droz	Librairie Droz SA, Geneva
DublinUP	Dublin UP, Dublin
Duckworth	Gerald Duckworth, London
Duculot	J. Duculot, Gembloux, Belgium
DukeUP	Duke UP, Dublin
Dundurn	Dundurn Press, Toronto and London, Ontario
Duquesne	Duquesne UP, Pittsburgh
Dutton	E.P. Dutton, New York

DWT	Dr Williams's Trust, London
EA	English Association, London
EAS	English Association Sydney Incorporated
Eason	Eason & Son, Dublin
East Bay	East Bay Books, Berkeley, CA
Ebony	Ebony Books, Melbourne
Ecco	Ecco Press, New York
ECNRS	Éditions du Centre National de la Recherche Scientifique, Paris
ECW	ECW Press, Downsview, Ontario
Eden	Eden Press, Montreal and St Albans, VT
EdinUP	Edinburgh UP, Edinburgh
Edizioni	Edizioni del Grifo
Educare	Educare, Burnwood, Victoria
EEM	Eastern European Monographs, Boulder, CO
Eerdmans	William Eerdmans, Grand Rapids, MI
EETS	Early English Text Society, c/o Exeter College, Oxford
1890sS	Eighteen-Nineties Society, Oxford
Eihosha	Eihosha, Tokyo
Elephas	Elephas Books, Kewdale, Australia
Elibank	Elibank Press, Wellington, New Zealand
Elm Tree	Elm Tree Books, London
ELS	English Literary Studies
Ember	Ember Press, Brixham, South Devon
EMSH	Editions de la Maison des Sciences de l'Homme, Paris
Enitharmon	Enitharmon Press, London
Enzyklopädie	Enzyklopädie, Leipzig
EONF	Eugene O'Neill Foundation, Danville, CA
EPNS	English Place-Name Society, Beeston, Nottingham
Epworth	Epworth Press, Manchester
Eriksson	Paul Eriksson, Middlebury, VT
Erlbaum	Erlbaum Associates, NJ
Erskine	Erskine Press, Harleston, Norfolk
EscutchP	Escutcheon Press
ESI	Edizioni Scientifiche Italiane, Naples
ESL	Edizioni di Storia e Letteratura, Rome
EUFS	Editions Universitaires Fribourg Suisse
EUL	Edinburgh University Library, Edinburgh
Europa	Europa Publishers, London
Evans	M. Evans, New York
Exact Change	Exact Change, Boston
Exile	Exile Editions, Toronto, Ontario
Eyre	Eyre Methuen, London
FAB	Free Association Books, London
Faber	Faber & Faber, London
FAC	Federation d'Activites Culturelles, Paris
FACP	Fremantle Arts Centre Press, Fremantle, WA
Falcon Books	Falcon Books, Eastbourne

FALS	Foundation for Australian Literary Studies, James Cook University of North Queensland, Townsville
F&F	Fels & Firn Press, San Anselmo, CA
F&S	Feffer & Simons, Amsterdam
Farrand	Farrand Press, London
Fay	Barbara Fay, Stuttgart
F–B	Ford–Brown, Houston, TX
FCP	Four Courts Press, Dublin
FDUP	Fairleigh Dickinson UP, Madison, NJ
FE	Fourth Estate, London
Feminist	Feminist Press, New York
FictionColl	Fiction Collective, Brooklyn College, Brooklyn, NY
Field Day	Field Day, Derry
Fifth House	Fifth House Publications, Saskatoon, Saskatchewan
FILEF	FILEF Italo–Australian Publications, Leichhardt, New South Wales
Fine	Donald Fine, New York
Fink	Fink Verlag, Munich
Five Leaves	Five Leaves Publications, Nottingham
Flamingo	Flamingo Publishing, Newark, NJ
Flammarion	Flammarion, Paris
FlindersU	Flinders University of South Australia, Bedford Park
Floris	Floris Books, Edinburgh
FlorSU	Florida State University, Tallahassee, FL
FOF	Facts on File, New York
Folger	Folger Shakespeare Library, Washington, DC
Folio	Folio Press, London
Fontana	Fontana Press, London
Footprint	Footprint Press, Colchester, Essex
FordUP	Fordham UP, New York
Foris	Foris Publications, Dordrecht
Forsten	Egbert Forsten Publishing, Groningen, Netherlands
Fortress	Fortress Press, Philadelphia
Francke	Francke Verlag, Berne
Franklin	Burt Franklin, New York
FreeP	Free Press, New York
FreeUP	Free UP, Amsterdam
Freundlich	Freundlich Books, New York
Frommann-Holzboog	Frommann-Holzboog, Stuttgart
FS&G	Farrar, Straus & Giroux
FSP	Five Seasons Press, Madley, Hereford
FW	Fragments West/Valentine Press, Long Beach, CA
FWA	Fiji Writers' Association, Suva
FWP	Falling Wall Press, Bristol
Gale	Gale Research, Detroit, MI
Galilée	Galilée, Paris
Gallimard	Gallimard, Paris

G&G	Grevatt & Grevatt, Newcastle upon Tyne
G&M	Gill & Macmillan, Dublin
Garland	Garland Publishing, New York
Gasson	Roy Gasson Associates, Wimbourne, Dorset
Gateway	Gateway Editions, Washington, DC
GE	Greenwich Exchange, UK
GIA	GIA Publications, USA
Girasole	Edizioni del Girasole, Ravenna
GL	Goose Lane Editions, Fredericton, NB
GlasgowDL	Glasgow District Libraries, Glasgow
Gleerup	Gleerupska, Lund
Gliddon	Gliddon Books Publishers, Norwich
Gloger	Gloger Family Books, Portland, OR
GMP	GMP Publishing, London
GMSmith	Gibbs M. Smith, Layton, UT
Golden Dog	Golden Dog, Ottawa
Gollancz	Victor Gollancz, London
Gomer	Gomer Press, Llandysul, Dyfed
GothU	Gothenburg University, Gothenburg
Gower	Gower Publishing, Aldershot, Hants
GRAAT	Groupe de Recherches Anglo-Américaines de Tours
Grafton	Grafton Books, London
GranB	Granary Books, New York
Granta	Granta Publications, London
Granville	Granville Publishing, London
Grasset	Grasset & Fasquelle, Paris
Grassroots	Grassroots, London
Graywolf	Graywolf Press, St Paul, MI
Greenhalgh	M.J. Greenhalgh, London
Greenhill	Greenhill Books, London
Greenwood	Greenwood Press, Westport, CT
Gregg	Gregg Publishing, Surrey
Greville	Greville Press, Warwick
Greymitre	Greymitre Books, London
GroC	Grolier Club, New York
Groos	Julius Groos Verlag, Heidelberg
Grove	Grove Press, New York
GRP	Greenfield Review Press, New York
Grüner	B.R. Grüner, Amsterdam
Gruyter	Walter de Gruyter, Berlin
Guernica	Guernica Editions, Montreal, Canada
Guilford	Guilford, New York
Gulmohar	Gulmohar Press, Islamabad, Pakistan
Haggerston	Haggerston Press, London
HakluytS	Hakluyt Society, c/o British Library, London
Hale	Robert Hale, London
Hall	G.K. Hall, Boston, MA

Halstead	Halstead Press, Rushcutters Bay, New South Wales
HalsteadP	Halstead Press, c/o J. Wiley & Sons, Chichester, W. Sussex
Hambledon	Hambledon Press, London
H&I	Hale & Iremonger, Sydney
H&L	Hambledon and London
H&M	Holmes & Meier, London and New York
H&S	Hodder & Stoughton, London
H&SNZ	Hodder & Stoughton, Auckland
H&W	Hill & Wang, New York
Hansib	Hansib Publishing, London
Harbour	Harbour Publishing, Madeira Park, BC
Harman	Harman Publishing House, New Delhi
Harper	Harper & Row, New York
Harrap	Harrap, Edinburgh
HarrV	Harrassowitz Verlag, Wiesbaden
HarvardUP	Harvard UP, Cambridge, MA
Harwood	Harwood Academic Publishers, Langhorne, PA
Hatje	Verlag Gerd Hatje, Germany
HBJ	Harcourt Brace Jovanovich, New York and London
HC	HarperCollins, London
HCAus	HarperCollins Australia, Pymble, New South Wales
Headline	Headline Book Publishing, London
Heath	D.C. Heath, Lexington, MS
HebrewUMP	Hebrew University Magnes Press
Heinemann	William Heinemann, London
HeinemannA	William Heinemann, St Kilda, Victoria
HeinemannC	Heinemann Educational Books, Kingston, Jamaica
HeinemannNg	Heinemann Educational Books, Nigeria
HeinemannNZ	Heinemann Publishers, Auckland (now Heinemann Reed)
HeinemannR	Heinemann Reed, Auckland
Helm	Christopher Helm, London
HelmI	Helm Information
Herbert	Herbert Press, London
Hermitage	Hermitage Antiquarian Bookshop, Denver, CO
Hern	Nick Hem Books, London
Heyday	Heyday Books, Berkeley, CA
HH	Hamish Hamilton, London
Hilger	Adam Hilger, Bristol
HM	Harvey Miller, London
HMSO	HMSO, London
Hodder, Moa, Beckett	Hodder, Moa, Beckett, Milford, Auckland, New Zealand
Hodge	A. Hodge, Penzance, Cornwall
Hogarth	Hogarth Press, London
HongKongUP	Hong Kong UP, Hong Kong
Horsdal & Schubart	Horsdal & Schubart, Victoria, BC

Horwood	Ellis Horwood, Hemel Hempstead, Hertfordshire
HoughtonM	Houghton Mifflin, Boston, MA
Howard	Howard UP, Washington, DC
HREOC	Human Rights and Equal Opportunity Commission, Commonweath of Australia, Canberra
HRW	Holt, Reinhart & Winston, New York
Hudson	Hudson Hills Press, New York
Hueber	Max Hueber, Ismaning, Germany
HUL	Hutchinson University Library, London
HullUP	Hull UP, University of Hull
Humanities	Humanities Press, Atlantic Highlands, NJ
Huntington	Huntington Library, San Marino, CA
Hurst	C. Hurst, London
Hutchinson	Hutchinson Books, London
HW	Harvester Wheatsheaf, Hemel Hempstead, Hertfordshire
HWWilson	H.W. Wilson, New York
Hyland House	Hyland House Publishing, Victoria
HyphenP	Hyphen Press, London
IAAS	Indian Institute of Aveanced Studies, Lahore and New Delhi
Ian Henry	Ian Henry Publications, Homchurch, Essex
IAP	Irish Academic Press, Dublin
Ibadan	Ibadan University Press
IBK	Innsbrucker Beiträge zur Kulturwissenschaft, University of Innsbruck
ICA	Institute of Contemporary Arts, London
IHA	International Hopkins Association, Waterloo, Ontario
IJamaica	Institute of Jamaica Publications, Kingston
Imago	Imago Imprint, New York
ImperialWarMuseum	Imperial War Museum Publications, London
IndUP	Indiana UP, Bloomington, IN
Inkblot	Inkblot Publications, Berkeley, CA
IntUP	International Universities Press, New York
Inventions	Inventions Press, London
IonaC	Iona College, New Rochelle, NY
IowaSUP	Iowa State UP, Ames, IA
IOWP	Isle of Wight County Press, Newport, Isle of Wight
IP	In Parenthesis, London
Ipswich	Ipswich Press, Ipswich, MA
IrishAP	Irish Academic Press, Dublin
ISI	ISI Press, Philadelphia
Italica	Italica Press, New York
IULC	Indiana University Linguistics Club, Bloomington, IN
IUP	Indiana University of Pennsylvania Press, Indiana, PA
Ivon	Ivon Publishing House, Bombay
Jacaranda	Jacaranda Wiley, Milton, Queensland

JadavpurU	Jadavpur University, Calcutta
James CookU	James Cook University of North Queensland, Townsville
Jarrow	Parish of Jarrow, Tyne and Wear
Jesperson	Jesperson Press, St John's, Newfoundland
JHall	James Hall, Leamington Spa, Warwickshire
JHUP	Johns Hopkins UP, Baltimore, MD
JIWE	JIWE Publications, University of Gulbarga, India
JLRC	Jack London Research Center, Glen Ellen, CA
J-NP	Joe-Noye Press
Jonas	Jonas Verlag, Marburg, Germany
Joseph	Michael Joseph, London
Journeyman	Journeyman Press, London
JPGM	J. Paul Getty Museum
JT	James Thin, Edinburgh
Junction	Junction Books, London
Junius-Vaughan	Junius-Vaughan Press, Fairview, NJ
Jupiter	Jupiter Press, Lake Bluff, IL
JyväskyläU	Jyväskylä University, Jyväskylä, Finland
Kaibunsha	Kaibunsha, Tokyo
K&N	Königshausen & Neumann, Würzburg, Germany
K&W	Kaye & Ward, London
Kangaroo	Kangaroo Press, Simon & Schuster (Australia), Roseville, New South Wales
Kansai	Kansai University of Foreign Studies, Osaka
Kardo	Kardo, Coatbridge, Scotland
Kardoorair	Kardoorair Press, Adelaide
Karia	Karia Press, London
Karnak	Karnak House, London
Karoma	Karoma Publishers, Ann Arbor, MI
Katha	Katha, New Delhi
KC	Kyle Cathie, London
KCL	King's College London
KeeleUP	Keele University Press
Kegan Paul	Kegan Paul International, London
Kenkyu	Kenkyu-Sha,Tokyo
Kennikat	Kennikat Press, Port Washington, NY
Kensal	Kensal Press, Oxford
KentSUP	Kent State University Press, Kent, OH
KenyaLB	Kenya Literature Bureau, Nairobi
Kerosina	Kerosina Publications, Worcester Park, Surrey
Kerr	Charles H. Kerr, Chicago
Kestrel	Viking Kestrel, London
K/H	Kendall/Hunt Publishing, Dubuque, IA
Kingsley	J. Kingsley Publishers, London
Kingston	Kingston Publishers, Kingston, Jamaica
Kinseido	Kinseido, Tokyo
KITLV	KITLV Press, Leiden

Klostermann	Vittorio Klostermann, Frankfurt am Main
Kluwer	Kluwer Academic Publications, Dordrecht
Knopf	Alfred A. Knopf, New York
Knowledge	Knowledge Industry Publications, White Plains, NY
Kraft	Kraft Books, Ibadan
Kraus	Kraus International Publications, White Plains, NY
KSUP	Kent State UP, Kent OH
LA	Library Association, London
LACUS	Linguistic Association of Canada and the United States, Chapel Hill, NC
Lake View	Lake View Press, Chicago
LAm	Library of America, New York
Lancelot	Lancelot Press, Hantsport, NS
Landesman	Jay Landesman, London
L&W	Lawrence & Wishart, London
Lane	Allen Lane, London
Lang	Peter D. Lang, Frankfurt am Main and Berne
LehighUP	Lehigh University Press, Bethlehem, PA
LeicAE	University of Leicester, Department of Adult Education
LeicsCC	Leicestershire County Council, Libraries and Information Service, Leicester
LeicUP	Leicester UP, Leicester
LeidenUP	Leiden UP, Leiden
Leopard's Head	Leopard's Head Press, Oxford
Letao	Letao Press, Albury, New South Wales
LeuvenUP	Leuven UP, Leuven, Belgium
Lexik	Lexik House, Cold Spring, NY
Lexington	Lexington Publishers
LF	LiberFörlag, Stockholm
LH	Lund Humphries Publishers, London
Liberty	Liberty Classics, Indianapolis, IN
Libris	Libris, London
LibrU	Libraries Unlimited, Englewood, CO
Liguori	Liguori, Naples
Limelight	Limelight Editions, New York
Lime Tree	Lime Tree Press, Octopus Publishing, London
LincolnUP	Lincoln University Press, Nebraska
LITIR	LITIR Database, University of Alberta
LittleH	Little Hills Press, Burwood, New South Wales
Liveright	Liveright Publishing, New York
LiverUP	Liverpool UP, Liverpool
Livre de Poche	Le Livre de Poche, Paris
Llanerch	Llanerch Enterprises, Lampeter, Dyfed
Locust Hill	Locust Hill Press, West Cornwall, CT
Loewenthal	Loewenthal Press, New York
Longman	Addison Longman Wesley, Harlow, Essex
LongmanC	Longman Caribbean, Harlow, Essex

LongmanF	Longman, France
LongmanNZ	Longman, Auckland
Longspoon	Longspoon Press, University of Alberta, Edmonton
Lovell	David Lovell Publishing, Brunswick, Australia
Lowell	Lowell Press, Kansas City, MS
Lowry	Lowry Publishers, Johannesburg
LSUP	Louisiana State UP, Baton Rouge, LA
LundU	Lund University, Lund, Sweden
LUP	Loyola UP, Chicago
Lutterworth	Lutterworth Press, Cambridge
Lymes	Lymes Press, Newcastle, Staffordshire
Lythrum	Lythrum Press, Adelaide
MAA	Medieval Academy of America, Cambridge, MA
Macleay	Macleay Press, Paddington, New South Wales
Macmillan	Macmillan Publishers, London
MacmillanC	Macmillan Caribbean
Madurai	Madurai University, Madurai, India
Maecenas	Maecenas Press, Iowa City, Iowa
Magabala	Magabala Books, Broome, WA
Magnes	Magnes Press, The Hebrew University, Jerusalem
Mainstream	Mainstream Publishing, Edinburgh
Maisonneuve	Maisonneuve Press, Washington, DC
Malone	Malone Society, c/o King's College, London
Mambo	Mambo Press, Gweru, Zimbabwe
ManCASS	Manchester Centre for Anglo-Saxon Studies, University of Manchester
M&E	Macdonald & Evans, Estover, Plymouth, Devon
M&S	McClelland & Stewart, Toronto
Maney	W.S. Maney & Sons, Leeds
Manohar	Manohar Publishers, Darya Gan, New Delhi
Mansell	Mansell Publishing, London
Manufacture	La Manufacture, Lyons
ManUP	Manchester UP, Milwaukee, WI
Mardaga	Mardaga
Mariner	Mariner Books, Boston, MA
MarquetteUP	Marquette UP, Milwaukee, WI
Marvell	Marvell Press, Calstock, Cornwall
MB	Mitchell Beazley, London
McDougall, Littel	McDougall, Littel, Evanston, IL
McFarland	McFarland, Jefferson, NC
McG-QUP	McGill-Queen's UP, Montreal
McGraw-Hill	McGraw-Hill, New York
McIndoe	John McIndoe, Dunedin, New Zealand
McPheeG	McPhee Gribble Publishers, Fitzroy, Victoria
McPherson	McPherson, Kingston, NY
MCSU	Maria Curie Sk³odowska University
ME	M. Evans, New York

Meany	P.D. Meany Publishing, Port Credit, Ontario
Meckler	Meckler Publishing, Westport, CT
MelboumeUP	Melbourne UP, Carlton South, Victoria
Mellen	Edwin Mellen Press, Lewiston, NY
MellenR	Mellen Research UP
Menzies	Menzies Centre for Australian Studies
MercerUP	Mercer UP, Macon, GA
Mercury	Mercury Press, Stratford, Ontario
Merlin	Merlin Press, London
Methuen	Methuen, London
MethuenA	Methuen Australia, North Ryde, New South Wales
MethuenC	Methuen, Toronto
Metro	Metro Publishing, Auckland
Metzler	Metzler, Stuttgart
MGruyter	Mouton de Gruyter, Berlin, New York, and Amsterdam
MH	Michael Haag, London
MHRA	Modern Humanities Research Association, London
MHS	Missouri Historical Society, St Louis, MO
MI	Microforms International, Pergamon Press, Oxford
Micah	Micah Publications, Marblehead, MA
MichSUP	Michigan State UP, East Lansing, MI
MidNAG	Mid-Northumberland Arts Group, Ashington, Northumbria
Mieyungah	Mieyungah Press, Melbourne University Press, Carlton South, Victoria
Milestone	Milestone Publications, Horndean, Hampshire
Millennium	Millennium Books, E.J. Dwyer, Newtown, Australia
Millstream	Millstream Books, Bath
Milner	Milner, London
Minuit	Éditions de Minuit, Paris
MIP	Medieval Institute Publications, Western Michigan University, Kalamazoo
MITP	Massachusetts Institute of Technology Press, Cambridge, MA
MLA	Modern Language Association of America, New York
MIM	Multilingual Matters, Clevedon, Avon
MLP	Manchester Literary and Philosophical Society, Manchester
Modern Library	Modern Library (Random House), New York
Monarch	Monarch Publications, Sussex
Moonraker	Moonraker Press, Bradford-on-Avon, Wiltshire
Moorland	Moorland Publishing, Ashbourne, Derby
Moreana	Moreana, Angers, France
MorganSU	Morgan State University, Baltimore, MD
Morrow	William Morrow, New York
Mosaic	Mosaic Press, Oakville, Ontario
Motilal	Motilal Books, Oxford
Motley	Motley Press, Romsey, Hampshire

Mouton	Mouton Publishers, New York and Paris
Mowbray	A.R. Mowbray, Oxford
MR	Martin Robertson, Oxford
MRS	Medieval and Renaissance Society, North Texas State University, Denton
MRTS	MRTS, Binghamton, NY
MSUP	Memphis State UP, Memphis, TN
MtAllisonU	Mount Allison University, Sackville, NB
MTP	Museum Tusculanum Press, University of Copenhagen
Mulini	Mulini Press, ACT
Muller	Frederick Muller, London
MULP	McMaster University Library Press
Murray	John Murray, London
Mursia	Ugo Mursia, Milan
NAL	New American Library, New York
Narr	Gunter Narr Verlag, Tübingen
Nathan	Fernand Nathan, Paris
NBB	New Beacon Books, London
NBCAus	National Book Council of Australia, Melbourne
NCP	New Century Press, Durham
ND	New Directions, New York
NDT	Nottingham Drama Texts, c/o University of Nottingham
NEL	New English Library, London
NELM	National English Literary Museum, Grahamstown, S. Africa
Nelson	Nelson Publishers, Melbourne
NelsonT	Thomas Nelson, London
New Endeavour	New Endeavour Press
NeWest	NeWest Press, Edmonton, Alberta
New Horn	New Horn Press, Ibadan, Nigeria
New Island	New Island Press
NewIssuesP	New Issues Press, Western Michigan University
NH	New Horizon Press, Far Hills, NJ
N-H	Nelson-Hall, Chicago
NHPC	North Holland Publishing, Amsterdam and New York
NicV	Nicolaische Verlagsbuchhandlung, Berlin
NIE	La Nuova Italia Editrice, Florence
Niemeyer	Max Niemeyer, Tübingen, Germany
Nightwood	Nightwood Editions, Toronto
NIUP	Northern Illinois UP, De Kalb, IL
NUSam	National University of Samoa
NLA	National Library of Australia
NLB	New Left Books, London
NLC	National Library of Canada, Ottawa
NLP	New London Press, Dallas, TX
NLS	National Library of Scotland, Edinburgh

NLW	National Library of Wales, Aberystwyth, Dyfed
Nodus	Nodus Publikationen, Münster
Northcote	Northcote House Publishers, Plymouth
NortheastemU	Northeastern University, Boston, MA
NorthwesternUP	Norhwestem UP, Evanston, IL
Norton	W.W. Norton, New York and London
NorUP	Norwegian University Press, Oslo
Novus	Novus Press, Oslo
NPF	National Poetry Foundation, Orono, ME
NPG	National Portrait Gallery, London
NPP	North Point Press, Berkeley, CA
NSP	New Statesman Publishing, New Delhi
NSU Press	Northern States Universities Press
NSWUP	New South Wales UP, Kensington, New South Wales
NT	National Textbook, Lincolnwood, IL
NUC	Nipissing University College, North Bay, Ontario
NUP	National University Publications, Millwood, NY
NUSam	National University of Samoa
NUU	New University of Ulster, Coleraine
NWAP	North Waterloo Academic Press, Waterloo, Ontario
NWP	New World Perspectives, Montreal
NYPL	New York Public Library, New York
NYUP	New York UP, New York
OakK	Oak Knoll Press, New Castle, DE
O&B	Oliver & Boyd, Harlow, Essex
Oasis	Oasis Books, London
OBAC	Organization of Black American Culture, Chicago
OberlinCP	Oberlin College Press, Oberlin, OH
Oberon	Oberon Books, London
O'Brien	O'Brien Press, Dublin
OBS	Oxford Bibliographical Society, Bodleian Library, Oxford
Octopus	Octopus Books, London
OdenseUP	Odense UP, Odense
OE	Officina Edizioni, Rome
OEColl	Old English Colloquium, Berkeley, CA
Offord	John Offord Publications, Eastbourne, E. Sussex
OhioUP	Ohio UP, Athens, OH
Oldcastle	Oldcastle Books, Harpenden, Hertfordshire
Olms	Georg Ohms, Hildesheim, Germany
Olschki	Leo S. Olschki, Florence
O'Mara	Michael O'Mara Books, London
Omnigraphics	Omnigraphics, Detroit, MI
Open Books	Open Books Publishing, Wells, Somerset
Open Court	Open Court Publishing, USA
OpenUP	Open UP, Buckingham and Philadelphia
OPP	Oxford Polytechnic Press, Oxford

Orbis	Orbis Books, London
OregonSUP	Oregon State UP, Corvallis, OR
Oriel	Oriel Press, Stocksfield, Northumberland
Orient Longman	Orient Longman, India
OrientUP	Oriental UP, London
OriginalNZ	Original Books, Wellington, New Zealand
Ortnamnsarkivet	Ortnamnsarkivet i Uppsala, Sweden
Orwell	Orwell Press, Southwold, Suffolk
Oryx	Oryx Press, Phoenix, AR
OSUP	Ohio State UP, Columbus, OH
OTP	Oak Tree Press, London
OUCA	Oxford University Committee for Archaeology, Oxford
OUP	Oxford UP, Oxford
OUPAm	Oxford UP, New York
OUPAus	Oxford UP, Melbourne
OUPC	Oxford UP, Toronto
OUPI	Oxford UP, New Delhi
OUPNZ	Oxford UP, Auckland
OUPSA	Oxford UP Southern Africa, Cape Town
Outlet	Outlet Book, New York
Overlook	Overlook Press, New York
Owen	Peter Owen, London
Owl	Owl
Pace UP	Pace University Press, New York
Pacifica	Press Pacifica, Kailua, Hawaii
Paget	Paget Press, Santa Barbara, CA
PAJ	PAJ Publications, New York
Paladin	Paladin Books, London
Palgrave	Palgrave, NY
Pan	Pan Books, London
PanAmU	Pan American University, Edinburgh, TX
P&C	Pickering & Chatto, London
Pandion	Pandion Press, Capitola, CA
Pandora	Pandora Press, London
Pan Macmillan	Pan Macmillan Australia, South Yarra, Victoria
Pantheon	Pantheon Books, New York
ParagonH	Paragon House Publishers, New York
Parnassus	Parnassus Imprints, Hyannis, MA
Parousia	Parousia Publications, London
Paternoster	Paternoster Press, Carlisle, Cumbria
Patten	Patten Press, Penzance
Paulist	Paulist Press, Ramsey, NJ
Paupers	Paupers' Press, Nottingham
Pavilion	Pavilion Books, London
PBFA	Provincial Booksellers' Fairs Association, Cambridge
Peachtree	Peachtree Publishers, Atlanta, GA
Pearson	David Pearson, Huntingdon, Cambridge
Peepal Tree	Peepal Tree Books, Leeds

Peeters	Peeters Publishers and Booksellers, Leuven, Belgium
Pelham	Pelham Books, London
Pembridge	Pembridge Press, London
Pemmican	Pemmican Publications, Winnipeg, Canada
PencraftI	Pencraft International, Ashok Vihar II, Delhi
Penguin	Penguin Books, Harmondsworth, Middlesex
PenguinA	Penguin Books, Ringwood, Victoria
PenguinNZ	Penguin Books, Auckland
Penkevill	Penkevill Publishing, Greenwood, FL
Pentland	Pentland Press, Ely, Cambridge
Penumbra	Penumbra Press, Moonbeam, Ontario
People's	People's Publications, London
Pergamon	Pergamon Press, Oxford
Permanent	Permanent Press, Sag Harbor, NY
Permanent Black	Permanent Black, Delhi, India
Perpetua	Perpetua Press, Oxford
Petton	Petton Books, Oxford
Pevensey	Pevensey Press, Newton Abbot, Devon
PH	Prentice-Hall, Englewood Cliffs, NJ
Phaidon	Phaidon Press, London
PHI	Prentice-Hall International, Hemel Hempstead, Hertfordshire
PhilL	Philosophical Library, New York
Phillimore	Phillimore, Chichester Phoenix Phoenix
Piatkus	Piatkus Books, London
Pickwick	Pickwick Publications, Allison Park, PA
Pilgrim	Pilgrim Books, Norman, OK
PIMS	Pontifical Institute of Mediaeval Studies, Toronto
Pinter	Frances Pinter Publishers, London
Plains	Plains Books, Carlisle
Plenum	Plenum Publishing, London and New York
Plexus	Plexus Publishing, London
Pliegos	Editorial Pliegos, Madrid
Ploughshares	Ploughshares Books, Watertown, MA
Pluto	Pluto Press, London
PML	Pierpont Morgan Library, New York
Polity	Polity Press, Cambridge
Polygon	Polygon, Edinburgh
Poolbeg	Poolbeg Press, Swords, Dublin
Porcepic	Press Porcepic, Victoria, BC
Porcupine	Porcupine's Quill, Canada
PortN	Port Nicholson Press, Wellington, NZ
Potter	Clarkson N. Potter, New York
Power	Power Publications, University of Sydney
PPUBarcelona	Promociones y Publicaciones Universitarias, Barcelona
Praeger	Praeger, New York
Prakash	Prakash Books, India

Prestel	Prestel Verlag, Germany
PrestigeB	Prestige Books, New Delhi
Primavera	Edizioni Primavera, Gunti Publishing, Florence, Italy
Primrose	Primrose Press, Alhambra, CA
PrincetonUL	Princeton University Library, Princeton, NJ
PrincetonUP	Princeton UP, Princeton, NJ
Printwell	Printwell Publishers, Jaipur, India
Prism	Prism Press, Bridport, Dorset
PRO	Public Record Office, London
Profile	Profile Books, Ascot, Berks
ProgP	Progressive Publishers, Calcutta
PSUP	Pennsylvania State UP, University Park, PA
Pucker	Puckerbrush Press, Orono, ME
PUF	Presses Universitaires de France, Paris
PurdueUP	Purdue UP, Lafayette, IN
Pushcart	Pushcart Press, Wainscott, NY
Pustet	Friedrich Pustet, Regensburg
Putnam	Putnam Publishing, New York
PWP	Poetry Wales Press, Ogmore by Sea, mid-Glamorgan
QED	QED Press, Ann Arbor, MI
Quarry	Quarry Press, Kingston, Ontario
Quartet	Quartet Books, London
QUT	Queensland University of Technology
RA	Royal Academy of Arts, London
Rainforest	Rainforest Publishing, Faxground, New South Wales
Rampant Lions	Rampant Lions Press, Cambridge
R&B	Rosenklide & Bagger, Copenhagen
R&L	Rowman & Littlefield, Totowa, NJ
Randle	Ian Randle, Kingston, Jamaica
RandomH	Random House, London and New York
RandomHAus	Random House Australia, Victoria
Ravan	Ravan Press, Johannesburg
Ravette	Ravette, London
Ravi Dayal	Ravi Dayal, New Delhi, India
Rawat	Rawat Publishing, Jaipur and New Delhi
Reaktion	Reaktion Books, London
Rebel	Rebel Press, London
Red Kite	Red Kite Press, Guelph, Ontario
Red Rooster	Red Rooster Press, Hotham Hill, Victoria
Red Sea	Red Sea Press, NJ
Reed	Reed Books, Port Melbourne
Reference	Reference Press, Toronto
Regents	Regents Press of Kansas, Lawrence, KS
Reichenberger	Roswitha Reichenberger, Kessel, Germany
Reinhardt	Max Reinhardt, London
Remak	Remak, Alblasserdam, Netherlands
RenI	Renaissance Institute, Sophia University, Tokyo
Research	Research Publications, Reading

RETS	Renaissance English Text Society, Chicago
RH	Ramsay Head Press, Edinburgh
RHS	Royal Historical Society, London
RIA	Royal Irish Academy, Dublin
RiceUP	Rice UP, Houston, TX
Richarz	Hans Richarz, St Augustin, Germany
RICL	Research Institute for Comparative Literature, University of Alberta
Rivers Oram	Rivers Oram Press, London
Rizzoli	Rizzoli International Publications, New York
RobartsCCS	Robarts Centre for Canadian Studies, York University, North York, Ontario
Robinson	Robinson Publishing, London
Robson	Robson Books, London
Rodopi	Rodopi, Amsterdam
Roebuck	Stuart Roebuck, Suffolk
RoehamptonI	Roehampton Institute London
Routledge	Routledge, London and New York
Royce	Robert Royce, London
RS	Royal Society, London
RSC	Royal Shakespeare Company, London
RSL	Royal Society of Literature, London
RSVP	Research Society for Victorian Periodicals, University of Leicester
RT	RT Publications, London
Running	Running Press, Philadelphia
Russell	Michael Russell, Norwich
RutgersUP	Rutgers UP, New Brunswick, NJ
Ryan	Ryan Publishing, London
SA	Sahitya Akademi, New Delhi
Sage	Sage Publications, London
SAI	Sociological Abstracts, San Diego, CA
Salamander	Salamander Books, London
Salem	Salem Press, Englewood Cliffs, NJ
S&A	Shukayr and Akasheh, Amman, Jordon
S&D	Stein & Day, Briarcliff Manor, NJ
S&J	Sidgwick & Jackson, London
S&M	Sun & Moon Press, Los Angeles
S&P	Simon & Piere, Toronto
S&S	Simon & Schuster, New York and London
S&W	Secker & Warburg, London
Sangam	Sangam Books, London
Sangsters	Sangsters Book Stores, Kingston, Jamaica
SAP	Scottish Academic Press, Edinburgh
Saros	Saros International Publishers
Sarup	Sarup, New Delhi, India
SASSC	Sydney Association for Studies in Society and Culture, University of Sydney, New South Wales

Saur	Bowker-Saur, Sevenoaks, Kent
Savacou	Savacou Publications, Kingston, Jamaica
S-B	Schwann-Bagel, Düsseldorf
ScanUP	Scandinavian University Presses, Oslo
Scarecrow	Scarecrow Press, Metuchen, NJ
Schäuble	Schäuble Verlag, Rheinfelden, Germany
Schmidt	Erich Schmidt Verlag, Berlin
Schneider	Lambert Schneider, Heidelberg
Schocken	Schocken Books, New York
Scholarly	Scholarly Press, St Clair Shores, MI
ScholarsG	Scholars Press, GA
Schöningh	Ferdinand Schöningh, Paderbom, Germany
Schwinn	Michael Schwinn, Neustadt, Germany
SCJP	Sixteenth-Century Journal Publications
Scolar	Scolar Press, Aldershot, Hampshire
SCP	Second Chance Press, Sag Harbor, NY
Scribe	Scribe Publishing, Colchester
Scribner	Charles Scribner, New York
Seafarer	Seafarer Books, London
Seaver	Seaver Books, New York
Segue	Segue, New York
Semiotext(e)	Semiotext(e), Columbia University, New York
SePA	Self-Publishing Association
Seren Books	Seren Books, Bridgend, mid-Glamorgan
Serpent's Tail	Serpent's Tail Publishing, London
Sessions	William Sessions, York
Seuil	Éditions du Seuil, Paris
7:84 Pubns	7:84 Publications, Glasgow
Severn	Severn House, Wallington, Surrey
SF&R	Scholars' Facsimiles and Reprints, Delmar, NY
SH	Somerset House, Teaneck, NJ
Shalabh	Shalabh Book House, Meerut, India
ShAP	Sheffield Academic Press
Shaun Tyas	Paul Watkins Publishing, Donington, Lincolnshire
Shearwater	Shearwater Press, Lenah Valley, Tasmania
Sheba	Sheba Feminist Publishers, London
Sheed&Ward	Sheed & Ward, London
Sheldon	Sheldon Press, London
SHESL	Société d'Histoire et d'Épistemologie des Sciences du Langage, Paris
Shinozaki	Shinozaki Shorin, Tokyo
Shinshindo	Shinshindo Publishing, Tokyo
Shire	Shire Publications, Princes Risborough, Buckinghamshire
Shoal Bay Press	Shoal Bay Press, New Zealand
Shoe String	Shoe String Press, Hamden, CT
SHP	Shakespeare Head Press
SIAS	Scandinavian Institute of African Studies, Uppsala

SIL	Summer Institute of Linguistics, Academic Publications, Dallas, TX
SIUP	Southern Illinois University Press
Simon King	Simon King Press, Milnthorpe, Cumbria
Sinclair-Stevenson	Sinclair-Stevenson, London
SingaporeUP	Singapore UP, Singapore
SIUP	Southern Illinois UP, Carbondale, IL
SJSU	San Jose State University, San Jose, CA
Skilton	Charles Skilton, London
Skoob	Skoob Books, London
Slatkine	Éditions Slatkine, Paris
Slavica	Slavica Publishers, Columbus, OH
Sleepy Hollow	Sleepy Hollow Press, Tarrytown, NY
SLG	SLG Press, Oxford
Smith Settle	Smith Settle, W. Yorkshire
SMUP	Southern Methodist UP, Dallas, TX
Smythe	Colin Smythe, Gerrards Cross, Buckinghamshire
SNH	Société Néophilologique de Helsinki
SNLS	Society for New Language Study, Denver, CO
SOA	Society of Authors, London
Soho	Soho Book, London
SohoP	Soho Press, New York
Solaris	Solaris Press, Rochester, MI
SonoNis	Sono Nis Press, Victoria, BC
Sorbonne	Publications de la Sorbonne, Paris
SorbonneN	Publications du Conseil Scientifique de la Sorbonne Nouvelle, Paris
Souvenir	Souvenir Press, London
SPA	SPA Books
SPACLALS	South Pacific Association for Commonwealth Literature and Language Studies, Wollongong, New South Wales
Spaniel	Spaniel Books, Paddington, New South Wales
SPCK	SPCK, London
Spectrum	Spectrum Books, Ibadan, Nigeria
Split Pea	Split Pea Press, Edinburgh
Spokesman	Spokesman Books, Nottingham
Spoon River	Spoon River Poetry Press, Granite Falls, MN
SRC	Steinbeck Research Center, San Jose State University, San Jose, CA
SRI	Steinbeck Research Institute, Ball State University, Muncie, IN
SriA	Sri Aurobindo, Pondicherry, India
Sri Satguru	Sri Satguru Publications, Delhi
SSA	John Steinbeck Society of America, Muncie, IN
SSAB	Sprakförlaget Skriptor AB, Stockholm
SSNS	Scottish Society for Northern Studies, Edinburgh
StanfordUP	Stanford UP, Stanford, CA

Staple	Staple, Matlock, Derbyshire
Starmont	Starmont House, Mercer Island, WA
Starrhill	Starrhill Press, Washington, DC
Station Hill	Station Hill, Barrytown, NY
Stauffenburg	Stauffenburg Verlag, Tübingen, Germany
StDL	St Deiniol's Library, Hawarden, Clwyd
Steel Rail	Steel Rail Publishing, Ottawa
Steiner	Franz Steiner, Wiesbaden, Germany
Sterling	Sterling Publishing, New York
SterlingND	Sterling Publishers, New Delhi
Stichting	Stichtig Neerlandistiek, Amsterdam
St James	St James Press, Andover, Hampshire
St Martin's	St Martin's Press, New York
StMut	State Mutual Book and Periodical Source, New York
Stockwell	Arthur H. Stockwell, Ilfracombe, Devon
Stoddart	Stoddart Publishing, Don Mills, Ontario
StPB	St Paul's Bibliographies, Winchester, Hampshire
STR	Society for Theatre Research, London
Strauch	R.O.U. Strauch, Ludwigsburg
Streamline	Streamline Creative, Auckland, New Zealand
Stree	Stree/Bhatkal and Sen, Kolkata, India
Studio	Studio Editions, London
Stump Cross	Stump Cross Books, Stump Cross, Essex
Sud	Sud, Marseilles
Suhrkamp	Suhrkamp Verlag, Frankfurt am Main
Summa	Summa Publications, Birmingham, AL
SUNYP	State University of New York Press, Albany, NY
SUP	Sydney University Press
Surtees	R.S. Surtees Society, Frome, Somerset
SusquehannaUP	Susquehanna UP, Selinsgrove, PA
SussexAP	Sussex Academic Press
SussexUP	Sussex UP, University of Sussex, Brighton
Sutton	Alan Sutton, Stroud, Gloucester
SVP	Sister Vision Press, Toronto
S–W	Shepheard–Walwyn Publishing, London
Swallow	Swallow Press, Athens, OH
SWG	Saskatchewan Writers Guild, Regina
Sybylla	Sybylla Feminist Press
SydneyUP	Sydney UP, Sydney
SyracuseUP	Syracuse UP, Syracuse, NY
Tabb	Tabb House, Padstow, Cornwall
Taishukan	Taishukan Publishing, Tokyo
Talonbooks	Talonbooks, Vancouver
TamilU	Tamil University, Thanjavur, India
T&F	Taylor & Francis Books
T&H	Thames & Hudson, London
Tantivy	Tantivy Press, London

Tarcher	Jeremy P. Tarcher, Los Angeles
Tartarus	Tartarus Press
Tate	Tate Gallery Publications, London
Tavistock	Tavistock Publications, London Taylor Taylor Publishing, Bellingham, WA
TaylorCo	Taylor Publishing, Dallas, TX
TCG	Theatre Communications Group, New York
TCP	Three Continents Press, Washington, DC
TCUP	Texas Christian UP, Fort Worth, TX
TEC	Third Eye Centre, Glasgow
Tecumseh	Tecumseh Press, Ottawa
Telos	Telos Press, St Louis, MO
TempleUP	Temple UP, Philadelphia
TennS	Tennyson Society, Lincoln
TexA&MUP	Texas A&MUP, College Station, TX
Text	Text Publishing, Melbourne
TextileB	Textile Bridge Press, Clarence Center, NY
TexTULib	Friends of the University Library, Texas Tech University, Lubbock
The Smith	The Smith, New York
Thimble	Thimble Press, Stroud, Gloucester
Thoemmes	Thoemmes Press, Bristol
Thornes	Stanley Thornes, Cheltenham
Thorpe	D.W. Thorpe, Australia
Thorsons	Thorsons Publishers, London
Times	Times of Gloucester Press, Gloucester, Ontario
TMP	Thunder’s Mouth Press, New York
Tombouctou	Tombouctou Books, Bolinas, CA
Totem	Totem Books, Don Mills, Ontario
Toucan	Toucan Press, St Peter Port, Guernsey
Touzot	Jean Touzot, Paris
TPF	Trianon Press Facsimiles, London
Tragara	Tragara Press, Edinburgh
Transaction	Transaction Publishers, New Brunswick, NJ
Transcendental	Transcendental Books, Hartford, CT
Transworld	Transworld, London
TrinityUP	Trinity UP, San Antonio, TX
Tsar	Tsar Publications, Canada
TTUP	Texas Technical University Press, Lubbock
Tuckwell	Tuckwell Press, East Linton
Tuduv	Tuduv, Munich
TulaneUP	Tulane UP, New Orleans, LA
TurkuU	Turku University, Turku, Finland
Turnstone	Turnstone Press, Winnipeg, Manitoba
Turtle Island	Turtle Island Foundation, Berkeley, CA
Twayne	Twayne Publishing, Boston, MA
UAB	University of Aston, Birmingham

UAdelaide	University of Adelaide, Australia
UAlaP	University of Alabama Press, Tuscaloosa
UAlbertaP	University of Alberta Press, Edmonton
UAntwerp	University of Antwerp
UArizP	University of Arizona Press, Tucson
UArkP	University of Arkansas Press, Fayetteville
UAthens	University of Athens, Greece
UBarcelona	University of Barcelona, Spain
UBCP	University of British Columbia Press, Vancouver
UBergen	University of Bergen, Norway
UBrno	J.E. Purkyne University of Brno, Czechoslovakia
UBrussels	University of Brussels
UCalgaryP	University of Calgary Press, Canada
UCalP	University of California Press, Berkeley
UCAP	University of Central Arkansas Press, Conway
UCapeT	University of Cape Town Press
UChicP	University of Chicago Press
UCDubP	University College Dublin Press
UCL	UCL Press (University College London)
UCopenP	University of Copenhagen Press, Denmark
UDelP	University of Delaware Press, Newark
UDijon	University of Dijon
UDur	University of Durham, Durham, UK
UEA	University of East Anglia, Norwich
UErlangen-N	University of Erlangen-Nuremberg, Germany
UEssex	University of Essex, Colchester
UExe	University of Exeter, Devon
UFlorence	University of Florence, Italy
UFlorP	University of Florida Press
UFR	Université François Rabelais, Tours
UGal	University College, Galway
UGeoP	University of Georgia Press, Athens
UGhent	University of Ghent
UGlasP	University of Glasgow Press
UHawaiiP	University of Hawaii Press, Honolulu
UIfeP	University of Ife Press, Ile-Ife, Nigeria
UIllp	University of Illinois Press, Champaign
UInnsbruck	University of Innsbruck
UIowaP	University of Iowa Press, Iowa City
UKanP	University of Kansas Press, Lawrence, KS
UKL	University of Kentucky Libraries, Lexington
ULavalP	Les Presses de l'Université Laval, Quebec
ULiège	University of Liège, Belgium
ULilleP	Presses Universitaires de Lille, France
ULondon	University of London
Ulster	University of Ulster, Coleraine
U/M	Underwood/Miller, Los Angeles
UMalta	University of Malta, Msida

UManitobaP	University of Manitoba Press, Winnipeg
UMassP	University of Massachusetts Press, Amherst
Umeå	Umeå Universitetsbibliotek, Umeå
UMichP	University of Michigan Press, Ann Arbor
UMinnP	University of Minnesota Press, Minneapolis
UMirail-ToulouseP	University of Mirail-Toulouse Press, France
UMIRes	UMI Research Press, Ann Arbor, MI
UMissP	University of Missouri Press, Columbia
UMP	University of Mississippi Press, Lafayette
UMysore	University of Mysore, India
UNancyP	Presses Universitaires de Nancy, France
UNCP	University of North Carolina Press, Chapel Hill, NC
Undena	Undena Publications, Malibu, CA
UNDP	University of Notre Dame Press, Notre Dame, IN
UNebP	University of Nebraska Press, Lincoln
UNevP	University of Nevada Press, Reno
UNewE	University of New England, Armidale, New South Wales
UnEWE, CALLS	University of New England, Centre for Australian Language and Literature Studies
Ungar	Frederick Ungar, New York
Unicopli	Edizioni Unicopli, Milan
Unity	Unity Press, Hull
UnityP	Unity Press Woollahra
Universa	Uilgeverij Universa, Wetteren, Belgium
UNMP	University of New Mexico Press, Albuquerque
UNorthTP	University of North Texas Press
UNott	University of Nottingham
UNSW	University of New South Wales
Unwin	Unwin Paperbacks, London
Unwin Hyman	Unwin Hyman, London
UOklaP	University of Oklahoma Press, Norman
UOslo	University of Oslo
UOtagoP	University of Otago Press, Dunedin, New Zealand
UOttawaP	University of Ottawa Press
UPA	UP of America, Lanham, MD
UParis	University of Paris
UPColardo	UP of Colorado, Niwot, CO
UPennP	University of Pennsylvania Press, Philadelphia
UPittP	University of Pittsburgh Press, Pittsburgh
UPKen	University Press of Kentucky, Lexington
UPMissip	UP of Mississippi, Jackson
UPN	Université de Paris Nord, Paris
UPNE	UP of New England, Hanover, NH Uppsala Uppsala University, Uppsala
UProvence	University of Provence, Aix-en-Provence
UPSouth	University Press of the South, NO
UPValéry	University Paul Valéry, Montpellier

UPVirginia	UP of Virginia, Charlottesville
UQDE	University of Queensland, Department of English
UQP	University of Queensland Press, St Lucia
URouen	University of Rouen, Mont St Aignan
URP	University of Rochester Press
USalz	Institut für Anglistik and Amerikanstik, University of Salzburg
USantiago	University of Santiago, Spain
USCP	University of South Carolina Press, Columbia
USFlorP	University of South Florida Press, Florida
USheff	University of Sheffield
Usher	La Casa Usher, Florence
USPacific	University of the South Pacific, Institute of Pacific Studies, Suva, Fiji
USQ, DHSS	University of Southern Queensland, Department of Humanities and Social Sciences
USydP	University of Sydney Press
USzeged	University of Szeged, Hungary
UtahSUP	Utah State UP, Logan
UTampereP	University of Tampere Press, Knoxville
UTas	University of Tasmania, Hobart
UTennP	University of Tennessee Press, Knoxville
UTexP	University of Texas Press, Austin
UTorP	University of Toronto Press, Toronto
UTours	Université de Tours
UVerm	University of Vermont, Burlington
UVict	University of Victoria, Victoria, BC
UWalesP	University of Wales Press, Cardiff
UWAP	University of Western Australia Press, Nedlands
UWarwick	University of Warwick, Coventry
UWashP	University of Washington Press, Seattle
UWaterlooP	University of Waterloo Press, Waterloo, Ontario
UWI	University of the West Indies, St Augustine, Trinidad
UWIndiesP	University of West Indies Press, Mona, Jamaica
UWiscM	University of Wisconsin, Milwaukee
UWiscP	University of Wisconsin Press, Madison
UWoll	University of Wollongong
UYork	University of York, York
Valentine	Valentine Publishing and Drama, Rhinebeck, NY
V&A	Victoria and Albert Museum, London
VanderbiltUP	Vanderbilt UP, Nashville, TE
V&R	Vandenhoeck & Ruprecht, Göttingen, Germany
Van Gorcum	Van Gorcum, Assen, Netherlands
Vantage	Vantage Press, New York
Variorum	Variorum, Ashgate Publishing, Hampshire
Vehicule	Vehicule Press, Montreal
Vendome	Vendome Press, New York

Verdant	Verdant Publications, Chichester
Verso	Verso Editions, London
VictUP	Victoria UP, Victoria University of Wellington, New Zealand
Vieweg	Vieweg Braunschweig, Wiesbaden
Vikas	Vikas Publishing House, New Delhi
Viking	Viking Press, New York
VikingNZ	Viking, Auckland
Virago	Virago Press, London
Vision	Vision Press, London
VLB	VLB Éditeur, Montreal
VP	Vulgar Press, Carlton North, Australia
VR	Variorum Reprints, London
Vrin	J. Vrin, Paris
VUUP	Vrije Universiteit UP, Amsterdam
Wakefield	Wakefield Press
W&B	Whiting & Birch, London
W&N	Weidenfeld & Nicolson, London
Water Row	Water Row Press, Sudbury, MA
Watkins	Paul Watkins, Stanford, Lincsolnshire
WB	Wissenschaftliche Buchgesellschaft, Darmstadt
W/B	Woomer/Brotherson, Revere, PA
Weaver	Weaver Press
Webb&Bower	Webb & Bower, Exeter
Wedgestone	Wedgestone Press, Winfield, KS
Wedgetail	Wedgetail Press, Earlwood, New South Wales
WesleyanUP	Wesleyan UP, Middletown, CT
West	West Publishing, St Paul, MN
WHA	William Heinemann Australia, Port Melbourne, Victoria
Wheatsheaf	Wheatsheaf Books, Brighton
Whiteknights	Whiteknights Press, University of Reading, Berkshire
White Lion	White Lion Books, Cambridge
Whitston	Whitston Publishing, Troy, NY
Whittington	Whittington Press, Herefordshire
WHP	Warren House Press, Sale, Cheshire
Wiener	Wiener Publishing, New York
Wildwood	Wildwood House, Aldershot, Hampshire
Wiley	John Wiley, Chichester, New York and Brisbane
	Wilson Philip Wilson, London
Winter	Carl Winter Universitätsverlag, Heidelberg, Germany
	Winthrop Winthrop Publishers, Cambridge, MA
WIU	Western Illinois University, Macomb, IL
WL	Ward Lock, London
WLUP	Wilfrid Laurier UP, Waterloo, Ontario
WMP	World Microfilms Publications, London
WMU	Western Michigan University, Kalamazoo, MI
Woeli	Woeli Publishing Services

Wolfhound	Wolfhound Press, Dublin
Wombat	Wombat Press, Wolfville, NS
Wo-No	Wolters-Noordhoff, Groningen, Netherlands
Woodstock	Woodstock Books, Oxford
Woolf	Cecil Woolf, London
Words	Words, Framfield, E. Sussex
WP	Women's Press, London
WPC	Women's Press of Canada, Toronto
WSUP	Wayne State UP, Detroit, MI
WVUP	West Virginia UP, Morgantown
W-W	Williams-Wallace, Toronto
WWU	Western Washington University, Bellingham
Xanadu	Xanadu Publications, London
YaleUL	Yale University Library Publications, New Haven, CT
YaleUP	Yale UP, New Haven, CO and London
Yamaguchi	Yamaguchi Shoten, Kyoto
YorkP	York Press, Fredericton, NB
Younsmere	Younsmere Press, Brighton
Zed	Zed Books, London
Zell	Hans Zell, East Grinstead, W. Sussex
Zena	Zena Publications, Penrhyndeudraeth, Gwynedd
Zephyr	Zephyr Press, Somerville, MA
Zomba	Zomba Books, London
Zwemmer	A. Zwemmer, London

3. Acronyms

AAVE	African-American Vernacular English
AmE	American English
AusE	Australian English
BrE	British English
DP	Determiner Phrase
ECP	Empty Category Principle
EFL	English as a Foreign Language
EIL	English as an International Language
ELT	English Language Teaching
eModE	early Modern English
ENL	English as a Native Language
EPNS	English Place-Name Society
ESL	English as a Second Language
ESP	English for Special Purposes
HPSG	Head-driven Phrase Structure Grammar
LF	Logical Form
LFG	Lexical Functional Grammar
ME	Middle English

MED	Middle English Dictionary
NZE	New Zealand English
ODan	Old Danish
OE	Old English
OED	Oxford English Dictionary
OF	Old French
ON	Old Norse
OT	Optimality Theory
PDE	Present-Day English
PF	Phonological Form
PP	Prepositional Phrase
SABE	South African Black English
SAE	South African English
TMA	Tense, Mood and Aspect
UG	Universal Grammar

Preface

The Year's Work in English Studies is a narrative bibliography that records and evaluates scholarly writing on English language and on literatures written in English. It is published by Oxford University Press on behalf of the English Association.

The Editors and the English Association are pleased to announce that this year's Beatrice White Prize has been awarded to Simon Horobin for his work on *The Language of the Chaucer Tradition* published by D.S. Brewer (ISBN 0 8599 1780 0).

The authors of *YWES* attempt to cover all significant contributions to English studies. Writers of articles can assist this process by sending offprints to the journal, and editors of journals that are not readily available in the UK are urged to join the many who send us complete sets of current and back issues. These materials should be addressed to The Editors, *YWES*, The English Association, The University of Leicester, University Road, Leicester LEI 7RH, UK.

Our coverage of articles and books is greatly assisted by the Modern Language Association of America, who annually supply proofs of their *International Bibliography* in advance of the publication of each year's coverage.

The views expressed in *YWES* are those of its individual contributors and are not necessarily shared by the Editors, Associate Editors, or the English Association.

We would like to acknowledge a special debt of gratitude to Gill Mitchell for her efforts on behalf of this volume.

The Editors

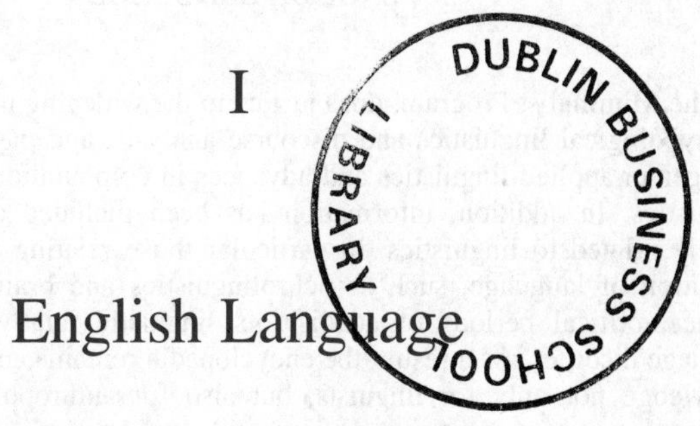

I

English Language

EVELIEN KEIZER, JEROEN VAN DE WEIJER, BETTELOU LOS, WIM VAN DER WURFF, BEÀTA GYURIS, JULIE COLEMAN, EDWARD CALLARY, LIESELOTTE ANDERWALD, ANDREA SAND, PETRA BETTIG AND CLARA CALVO

This chapter has eleven sections: 1. General; 2. Phonetics and Phonology; 3. Morphology; 4. Syntax; 5. Semantics; 6. Lexicography, Lexicology and Lexical Semantics; 7. Onomastics; 8. Dialectology and Sociolinguistics; 9. New Englishes and Creolistics; 10. Pragmatics and Discourse Analysis; 11. Stylistics. Section 1 is by Evelien Keizer; section 2 is by Jeroen van de Weijer; sections 3 and 4 are by Bettelou Los and Wim van der Wurff; section 5 is by Beàta Gyuris; section 6 is by Julie Coleman; section 7 is by Edward Callary; section 8 is by Lieselotte Anderwald; section 9 is by Andrea Sand; section 10 is by Petra Bettig; section 11 is by Clara Calvo.

1. General

As far as general reference books are concerned, neither 2002 nor 2003 had any major new publications to offer. We were, however, treated to second editions of two landmark works. The first of these, Frawley, ed., *The International Encyclopedia of Linguistics*, is easily the more comprehensive. Its four volumes cover every known language, as well as a wide range of areas in language research, including historical linguistics, language philosophy, sociolinguistics, computational linguistics, psycholinguistics, behavioural linguistics and applied linguistics. Despite its size, the encyclopedia is easy to handle, reader-friendly and accessible to scholars and students alike. In the new edition, each of the more than 900 articles, all written by experts in the field, have been either updated or completely rewritten, while 15 per cent of them are entirely new. The changes reflect new developments in the field: where the first edition was especially strong on language description and social and anthropological approaches to language, the second edition, while maintaining these strengths, gives attention to new directions in language research, such as OT

Year's Work in English Studies, Volume 84 (2005) © The English Association; all rights reserved. For permissions, please email: journals.permissions@oxfordjournals.org

doi: 10.1093/ywes/mai001

and the Minimalist Program, does justice to the widening influence of functional and typological linguistics and discourse analysis, and pays attention to recent changes in applied linguistics and advances in computational and mathematical linguistics. In addition, information has been included on areas of research closely related to linguistics, in particular those relating to the subject of the evolution of language, such as neurolinguistics and brain imaging, cognitive science, critical periods of acquisition, linguistic relativity, learnability and language disorder. As a result, the encyclopedia remains an invaluable source of knowledge not only for linguists, but also for anthropologists, semioticians, computer scientists, literary critics, philosophers and cognitive, social and behavioural scientists.

The other truly impressive work of reference that appeared in a second edition is David Crystal's *The Cambridge Encyclopedia of the English Language*. Dealing with the English language specifically, this work is necessarily of a different scope than Frawley's international encyclopedia. Another important difference, however, is in the intended readership: whereas Frawley's work is aimed primarily at linguists or scholars from related fields, Crystal's encyclopedia is intended for a much more general readership. This is clearly reflected both in its physical appearance—it is presented in full colour and contains numerous illustrations, charts, tables and maps—and in its highly accessible and entertaining style of writing. In this respect the second edition, which apart from being revised has also been redesigned, can be said to be even more successful than the first. In addition, it contains a large amount of updated information, as well as new material on such subjects as machine translation and language teaching, acoustics, physiological concepts of language and World English. All in all, it remains a delightful book to consult—a varied and comprehensive work of reference, which includes not only expected, but in many cases also unexpected, odd pieces of information which lend it extra charm and make it difficult to put down.

Looking at the new publications in 2002 and 2003, one is struck by two things: first of all, by the fact that none of the major publications deals specifically with the English language; secondly, by the growing interest in the evolution of language, or, more generally, in issues of language and mind. Interdisciplinary research, whether on evolution or any other topic in linguistics, is clearly the key word; this, it will appear, has an interesting influence on both the form and the content of many of these publications, as it inspires a need to make information accessible not only to experts in the field, but also to scholars with little knowledge of the subject. Points in case are two new publications in the (relatively new) OUP series Studies in the Evolution of Language: Wray, ed., *The Transition to Language*, and Christiansen and Kirby, eds., *Language Evolution*. In her introductory chapter to *The Transition to Language*, Alison Wray describes the future of language evolution research as one of cross-disciplinary collaboration, stressing the need for researchers from different fields (anthropology, archaeology, artificial intelligence, biology, genetics, primatology, psychology and linguistics) to find ways of fitting their own individual accounts into a larger, joined-up theory. The practical way to construct such a joined-up theory, according to Wray, is to place different hypotheses, from different disciplines, into a 'focal position' and subsequently to find out, through a process of comparison and testing, which proposals are the most tolerant of evidence from elsewhere. These are then the accounts that deserve most attention. To make such cross-disciplinary comparisons possible, the book is organized around a number of themes, each of which is approached from different angles. Part 1, 'Making Ready for Language', discusses the various physical and cognitive pre-adaptations needed for the evolution of language, such as the descent of the larynx and the development of serial expertise (contributions by W. Tecumseh Fitch, Kazuo Okanoya, and H.S. Terrace). Part 2 deals with the internal triggers to transition and considers the role of genes (T.J. Crow), processing (Alison Wray), culture (Chris Knight), gesture (Michael Corballis) and technology (Iain Davidson). Part 3 is devoted to possible external triggers to transition, such as the environment, population and social context (contributions by Derek Bickerton, Bradley Tonkes and Janet Wiles, L. Steels et al., and Sonia Ragir). Part 4, 'The Onward Journey', discusses later stages in the shaping of language, characterized by the adoption of syntactic structure (contributions by Robbins Burling, James Hurford, Morten Christiansen and Michelle Ellefson, Frederick Newmeyer, and Bernd Heine and Tania Kuteva).

In Christiansen and Kirby's *Language Evolution* by and large the same issues are taken up. How did humans come to have language? Where did language come from? How did it change? This volume, however, is more specifically concerned with the question of whether language evolved by natural selection, and, if so, whether language resulted from the adaptation of an innate language faculty or emerged as a manifestation of more general cognitive abilities, such as general intelligence, a symbolic capacity, social cognition or cultural learning. The first contribution, by Steven Pinker, is an update of the highly influential paper by Pinker and Bloom, 'Natural Language and Natural Selection' [1990], which revived interest in the evolution of language. Pinker and Bloom proposed the theory that language is an adaptation in the biologist's sense of the word, i.e. a trait whose genetic basis was shaped by natural selection. In the present volume, Pinker evaluates this theory in the light of new kinds of analysis and evidence and concludes that the only plausible explanation for the complexity of the biological adaptations is still one that involves natural selection, whereby language is seen as having evolved as an innate specialization to code propositional information for the purpose of social information-gathering and exchange. Although, according to Pinker, this claim might seem self-evident, it has proved to be highly controversial, and several alternative points of view have been presented. One of these alternatives is based on the idea that language itself is not an adaptation, but that it has emerged through cultural transmission after the adaptation of more general cognitive processes. This is the position taken by Michael Tomasello in his chapter on the different origins of symbols and grammar. According to the scenario proposed by Tomasello, there is no specific adaptation for symbolic or linguistic communication; instead the adaptation was for a particular kind of social cognition. Symbols then developed as a natural consequence of this adaptation, while at a later stage grammar emerged from discourse patterns. Most of the other contributions seem to follow either the innate grammar position (e.g. Derek Bickerton, Robin Dunbar, Ted Briscoe) or the cultural transmission position (e.g. James Hurford, Iain Davidson, Michael Arbib). A notable exception is the contribution by Terrence Deacon, who, in his chapter on the origin of language universals, argues that certain core language universals are of neither biological nor cultural origin. Instead, Deacon maintains, these universals reflect semiotic constraints, originating from within the linguistic symbol itself.

Two other publications on the subject of language evolution are Talmy Givón's *Bio-linguistics: The Santa Barbara Lectures* (discussed elsewhere in this volume) and Givón and Malle, eds., *The Evolution of Language out of Pre-Language*. The latter volume once again contains contributions from a large number of disciplines, including linguistics, psychology, neuroscience, primatology and anthropology. Unlike in Christiansen and Kirby's book, however, all the contributors to this volume share the broad assumption that the human mind and brain as well as language and culture are the products of adaptive evolution. Accordingly, the rise of human knowledge is not viewed as a serendipitous mutation that gave birth to an utterly unique language organ, but as a gradual, adaptively driven elaboration and extension of pre-existing mental capacities and brain structures. The evolution of human language thus follows the same route of gradual, adaptive extension that is found elsewhere in biology (p. viii).

The book is organized around a number of different themes. The first of these, language and the brain, looks at possible links between earlier stages of the brain system and the evolution of language (contributions by Talmy Givón, Don Tucker and Charles Li). Part 2 is concerned with the relation between language and cognition and includes chapters on the relation between the hierarchical organization of language and temporal structure (Joan Bybee), the evolution of the syllable from constraints on jaw movement (Barbara Davis and Peter MacNeilage), and two different perspectives on linguistic processing rates (by Marjorie Baker and Talmy Givón, and Gertraud Fenk-Oczlon and August Fenk, respectively). The third theme, the interface between language and social cognition, is explored by Brian MacWhinney, Bertram Malle and Dare Baldwin, who discuss various aspects of the conceptual framework known as theory of mind. Finally, part 4 deals with language development and consists of a chapter by Michael Tomasello on a possible analogy between language ontogeny and language learning; two chapters, by Jill Morford and Susan Golin-Meadow respectively, on the spontaneous emergence of sign language in children and the possible analogies with the emergence of certain linguistic properties; and a chapter by Dan Slobin arguing against possible contributions of child language study to questions of diachronic change or the evolution of language.

Let us finish our discussion of publications on the evolution of language by having another look at Jackendoff's *Foundations of Language*, in particular chapter 8 (for a review of the whole book, see *YWES* 83[2004] 11). In this chapter, Jackendoff argues that the nativist claim of generative grammarians that the capacity to learn language must have emerged at some point in the evolution of the human species does not seem very plausible, given the immense complexity of the language capacity. Another problem for the nativist claim is the fact that in generative grammar UG is usually seen as an undecomposable grammar box, no part of which can function without all the rest, which seems to exclude the possibility of an evolutionary process. Jackendoff, instead, argues in favour of an incremental evolution of the language capacity, an approach for which the parallel model introduced in the previous chapters of his book offers attractive possibilities. Thus, unlike in generative grammar, where only syntax is assumed to be generative, Jackendoff's parallel model offers a framework in which phonology, syntax and semantics are all equally generative. These generative components communicate with each other through 'interface' components, resulting in a parallel architecture. This decomposition of the language capacity into many semi-independent parts makes it possible for these different parts to have emerged independently or in sequence and for little pieces to have been added incrementally. Jackendoff points out that his proposal is entirely in line with earlier suggestions that language has evolved in two incremental steps, i.e. that modern language (language as it is) has developed from an earlier stage, protolanguage (language without syntax). This protolanguage, Jackendoff continues, is still very much present in the modern human brain, surfacing in early child language, pidgin languages, and possible agrammatic aphasia. Jackendoff thus accounts for the critical period in language acquisition and the fact that not all parts of language display critical period effects by assuming that language can only by fully acquired during the critical period; after that, we can only acquire protolanguage.

Another area of research with a strong interdisciplinary tradition is that of language and mind. Research in this area typically combines insights from linguistics and psychology or psycholinguistics. Examples can be found in Nooteboom, Weerman and Wijnen, eds., *Storage and Computation in the Language Faculty*, which explores the relative roles of computation (the rule-driven manipulation of symbols) and storage of lexical (or other linguistic) information in the mind. Over the last couple of decades the attention for the computational nature of language has assigned a major role to the rule- and variable-governed capacities of the language faculty, at the expense of the storage component of the language system. In computational theories such as Bloomfieldian structuralism and Chomskian generative grammar, the role of storage is limited to listing irregularities in language. More recently, however, linguists and psycholinguists have come to question the plausibility of such an approach. On the basis of linguistic, psycholinguistic and brain-imaging evidence concerning a wide range of language phenomena, they argue that storage is not restricted to irregular forms, but is also used for regular forms. The most radical position in this respect is that taken by the connectionists, who deny the need for a computational component, claiming that the linguistic productivity can be wholly accounted for by pattern association. One problem for such a view, however, is that it cannot explain the fact that humans behave as if they use rules, not only in their production of language, but also in other aspects of their behaviour. The question, therefore, does not so much seem to be whether the language system contains a rule component, but rather what (how much) is computed by rule, and what (how much) is stored in the lexicon. Other issues addressed in this volume concern the nature of the rules governing the use of language and the question of whether the two components are located in different parts of the brain. After a preface by Steven Pinker, an introductory chapter by the editors and another general chapter on the partition between storage and computation by Ray Jackendoff, the remaining chapters address such issues as accessing regular and irregular word forms (contributions by Harald Baayen et al. and by Tessa Say and Harald Clahsen), changing the rules (contributions by Geert Booij and Pieter Muysken), pronouncing spoken words (Ardi Roelofs), buffering and computing (Peter Ackema and Ad Neeleman, and by Edith Kaan and Laurie Stowe), and computing and storing aspects of discourse (Nicholas Asher).

Banich and Mack, eds., *Mind, Brain and Language*, offers a multidisciplinary perspective on the relationships between mind, brain and language. Contributions from linguistics, philosophy, psychology and neuroscience address such topics as language emergence, influence, and development; models of language and language-processing; the neurological bases of language; language disruption and loss; and dual-language systems. More specifically, the book seeks to answer such fundamental questions as how language evolved (in a contribution by Philip Lieberman); how it is acquired by the child language learner (Peter W. Jusczyk); how culture influences language (Giovanni Bennardo); how the brain processes linguistic information and how that information is represented at the psycholinguistic and neurolinguistic levels (chapters by Marta Kutas and Barbara M. Schmitt; Robert J. Zatorre; Christine Chiarello); how computational models provide insights into mind and brain (chapters by Neil Smith; Geoffrey Pullum and Barbara Scholz; David Plaut); what are some of the neurolinguistic and psycholinguistic consequences of brain injury (Eleanor Saffran; Marie Banich and Piage Scalf); and what we know about dual language systems, such as language representation in the two cerebral hemispheres, and language representation in “the bilingual brain” (contributions by Molly Mack and Michael Paradis). Each of the chapters has been written to be accessible to scholars from different backgrounds, as well as to generally educated readers interested in an interdisciplinary approach to the issues addressed. The overall readability of the book also makes it suitable for use as a textbook, possibly at the undergraduate, but certainly at the graduate, level.

Gentner and Goldin-Meadow, eds., *Language in Mind*, is concerned with the relation between language and thought, taking up a hypothesis which, for the last two decades, has been in serious disrepute: the Whorfian hypothesis that language can influence thought. Criticism has, however, mainly been directed at the strong version of the hypothesis, which states that (1) languages vary in their semantic partitioning of the world; (2) the structure of one’s language influences the manner in which one perceives and understands the world; and therefore (3) speakers of different languages will perceive the world differently (p. 4). In its weaker form, however, the hypothesis has never quite lost its appeal; and now, with the emergence of new evidence from a variety of sources, including cognitive psychology, linguistics, anthropology and animal cognition, the relation between language and thought has once more become a subject of debate. Rather than trying to settle the questions raised in the debate, the editors try to convince the reader that these questions are worth asking, an attitude necessitated by the fact that the various chapters present mixed results, making a clear yes or no answer to the Whorfian thesis as a whole unlikely. Interesting new insights are offered into a large number of more specific topics, including space, number, motion, gender, theory of mind, thematic roles and the ontological distinction between objects and substances. The first three contributions, by Eve Clark, Stephen Levinson, and Michael Tomasello, serve to introduce the relevant questions from different perspectives. Further contributors include Melissa Bowerman, Jill de Villiers, Peter de Villiers, Giyoo Hatano, Stan Kuczaj, Barbara Landau, John Lucy, Barbara Malt, Dan Slobin, Steven Sloman and Elizabeth Spelke, whose papers fall into three broad (and overlapping) categories based on the questions addressed and the methods used. The first category, 'language as a lens', poses the question whether the language we acquire influences how we see the world; the second theme, that of 'language as a toolkit', addresses the question whether the language we acquire augments our capacity for representation and reasoning; while the third theme, 'language as a category maker', deals with the question whether the language we acquire influences where we make our category distinctions. Together, these contributions do not merely revive the old language and thought debate; by asking new questions, using new methods and considering new evidence, they succeed in offering new perspectives and defining new research questions, and in encouraging scholars from a variety of backgrounds to take up these questions.

A different kind of interdisciplinarity can be found in Tomasello, ed., *The New Psychology of Language: Cognitive and Functional Approaches to Language Structure*, volume 2—a volume of papers about language and linguistic theory, written by linguists, but aimed primarily (though certainly not exclusively) at an audience of psychologists, cognitive scientists, psycholinguists and developmental linguists. Just like the first volume (published in 1998), the chief purpose of the book is to present, in an accessible (non-technical) style, current work in linguistics which may be of interest to psychologists and psycholinguists. All contributions are from leading functional and/or cognitive linguists, because, as Tomasello explains in his introductory chapter, these linguists tend to define and explain their analyses in the kind of usage-based terminology that cognitive scientists are often familiar with. Five of the ten chapters in this book deal exclusively with English: Leonard Talmy's contribution on concept-structuring systems in language, John Du Bois on discourse and grammar, the chapter by Cecilia Ford, Barbara Fox and Sandra Thompson on the relation between social interaction and grammar, that by Karen van Hoek on the cognitive principles of coreference and the final chapter, by Charles Fillmore, Paul Kay and Mary Catherine O'Connor, on the regularity and idiomaticity of *Let alone*. What all ten chapters have in common is that they deal with the cognitive and social interactional processes of linguistic communication, whereby a number of related themes can be distinguished, such as the role of grammaticalization in language history and the idea that grammar arises (over time) from discourse use (chapters by Joan Bybee and Karen van Hoek), and the claim that universals are cognitive in nature (are conceptual structures) rather than specific linguistic items or constructions (chapters by Leonard Talmy, Suzanne Kemmer, Martin Haspelmath, and Bernard Comrie). A final point of interest concerns the relation between written and spoken language, the idea being that spoken language does not fit in to what is often perceived as the (core) grammar, and requires a different approach (as exemplified in the chapter by Fillmore et al.).

Apart from these rather general and largely non-technical publications, the cognitive aspects of language are also discussed in two volumes dedicated to one of the central research areas in the study of language and cognition, that of spatial relations. In the first of these, *Space in Language and Cognition: Explorations in Cognitive Diversity*, Stephen Levinson describes and categorizes various spatial coordinate systems in language and cognition, indicating also the general implications for a number of general issues, such as the question of what is universal and what is language-specific, the evolution of human cognition, and the relation between language and human thinking. After an introductory chapter, chapter 2 introduces a typology of spatial coordinate systems in language and cognition which distinguishes three major frames of reference: the intrinsic frame (found in a sentence like *He's in front of the house*), the relative frame (as in *He's left of the house*) and the absolute frame (as in *He's north of the house*). In chapter 3, Levinson shows how different languages encode the three major frames in different ways, while the cross-linguistic and cross-cultural studies recorded in chapters 4 and 5 provide further evidence not only of linguistic variation, but also of the fact that not all languages use all types of frame. In addition—and this is what Levinson himself describes as the major discovery of the book—these linguistic differences are taken not only to correlate with, but also to induce differences in spatial cognition across human groups. Chapter 6 is concerned with non-linguistic frames of reference, which are claimed to mirror the systems available in the linguistic system of a particular group. Levinson concludes that, whereas the three major frames of reference are universally available, languages vary according to the selection they make of these frames and the ways in which they instantiate them. He takes this as evidence against a view of 'simple nativism' (the idea that both the form and the content of language are essentially innate) and in favour of a theory of co-evolution (the idea that the mind is pre-structured, but that cognitive patterns can also be induced by the cultural environment). This leads to a neo-Whorfian stance, according to which language influences how people memorize and reason about spatial relations and directions (chapter 7).

Another contribution to the fast-developing interdisciplinary research area of language and space is van der Zee and Slack, eds., *Representing Direction in Language and Space*. Like Levinson's book, it is concerned with such issues as how directions in language are represented in the brain, how such directions are expressed in different languages, and which constraints (both universal and language-specific) there are on linguistic directional encoding. Nevertheless, the result is an entirely different kind of publication. First of all, the book is more restricted in scope, as most contributions focus on a subset of spatial relations, direction, which comprises (at times rather confusingly) orientation, location in a specific area relative to another entity, and direction of movement. Secondly, since the contributors are from widely different backgrounds—including linguistics, psychology, computer science, cognitive science and neuroscience—it is not surprising that the thirteen contributions differ widely in the kind of representations used (from cognitive to formal), in method (from deductive to empirical—though the book offers very little original empirical work) and in accessibility (from reasonably general to highly technical). What most authors have in common is that the primitives they use to encode direction are spatial entities such as vectors and axes; the models they propose, however, are very different, and sometimes (seemingly, at least) contradictory. Although evidence is drawn for a number of different languages, English is by far the most prominent (e.g. chapters by Barbara Landau; Joost Zwarts; John O'Keefe; Laura Carlson, Terry Regier and Eric Covey; Barbara Tversky; Kenny Coventry); other languages discussed include French, German, Finnish and Dutch. All in all, the book provides an interesting overview of current issues in spatial language and cognition, as well as useful reviews of earlier work in this area.

Yet another contribution to the subject of language and mind, this time from a philosophical perspective, is a volume entitled Language and Mind edited by James E. Tomberlin (*PPA* 16[2002]). In this volume the contributions are organized around four themes. Part 1 deals with demonstratives and anaphora, and contains papers by James Higginbotham on competence with demonstratives, Kent Johnson and Ernie Lepore on the question of whether the syntax of complex demonstratives reveals their semantics, and R.M. Sainsbury on reference and anaphora. In part 2, Kent Bach offers a 'Nominal Description Theory' of proper names, Anne Bezuidenhout writes about truth-conditional pragmatics, David Chalmers deals with sense and intention, while Marga Reimer is concerned with the question of whether adjectives conform to compositionality. Part 3 is dedicated to the subject of belief and privileged access. Michael McKinsey defends the claim that semantic externalism is incompatible with the principle of privileged access; Kenneth Taylor challenges one of the consequences of most current applications of the De Re/De Dicto distinction, arguing that the truth value of an ascription should be dependent not on the ascribee, but on the ascriber; and Ralph Wedgwood qualifies the claim that beliefs aim at the truth, proposing to interpret it as a normative claim instead. In part 4, on modality, concepts, and time, Bob Hale discusses the source of (absolute) necessity; Jason Stanley discusses the relation between modality and what is said; Neil Tennant offers a reformulation of Christopher Peacocke's account of concepts as abstract objects; and James Van Cleve assesses Jorge Luis Borges's two proofs of the unreality of time, and offers a new objection to David Lewis's Patchwork principle. Finally, in part 5, Bernard Linsky, and Kirk Ludwig and Greg Ray concern themselves with paradox: Linsky with the resolution of Russell's paradox in *Principia Mathematica*; Ludwig and Ray with vagueness and the Sorites paradox. All these contributions, although no doubt of interest to linguists working in these areas, are clearly intended for a specialized audience and as such may not always be accessible to the uninitiated.

An entirely different issue in the field of linguistics is taken up in two otherwise rather different publications: Gustafsson and Hertzberg, eds., *The Practice of Language*, and Moore and Polinsky, eds., *The Nature of Explanation in Linguistic Theory*. Both books concentrate on the question of the validity of the arguments and methods employed in linguistic research. *The Practice of Language* takes a very critical attitude towards linguistic practice. Its main concern is with the relation between language as it is used in real life and the treatment of linguistic phenomena as objects of theoretical study; more specifically it addresses such questions as 'What do theoretical models tell us about real-life use?' and 'Are there any limits to what such theoretical notions and models can reasonably be taken to accomplish?' The contributors conclude that linguists and language philosophers from different backgrounds have tended to give theoretical considerations precedence over the practical dimension—even to the extent that it has become common practice, in those cases where actual language use does not fit the theory, to postulate deeper levels to which the theory can consistently be applied. In other words, the main aspiration of these scholars has been to achieve explanatory adequacy within the model, often at the expense of describing the actual practice of language. Part 1 comprises three historically oriented discussions. Sören Stenlund offers new perspectives on what brought about the linguistic turn (from a mentalist to a logical or structuralist approach) in twentieth-century philosophy, Olav Gundersen discusses the work of Wilhelm von Humboldt, while Michael Gustavsson reinterprets Ferdinand de Saussure's notions *langue*, language and *parole*. Part 2 is concerned with notions of language within linguistics and feminist epistemology. Sven Öhman discusses the confusion that arises from the fact that, on the one hand, spoken language is assumed to be primary to written language, while on the other linguists tend to treat all language as though it were graphically represented. Saara Haapamäki describes how Swedish grammarians, believing Chomsky's generative linguistics to constitute a direct reflection of concrete linguistic phenomena, have tried to implement this framework in Swedish grammar textbooks. Sharon Rider examines feminist approaches to epistemology, criticizing the tendency of feminist philosophers of science to conflate their own theoretical perspective with that of working scientists. Part 3 consists of two papers dealing with conceptions of meaning, truth and linguistic practice in the works of Hilary Putnam and Charles Travis, by Frederick Stoutland and Martin Gustaffson, respectively. Finally, in part 4, Per Segerdahl, Thorsten Johansson, Juan Wilhelmi, Gudmundur Steingrímsson and Lars Hertzberg all discuss themes from Wittgenstein.

A different treatment of more or less the same issue can be found in *The Nature of Explanation in Linguistic Theory*, which concentrates on the question of what precisely renders a linguistic account explanatorily adequate. Ever since Chomsky's [1962] definition of the goals of linguistic theory, explanation has been at the heart of every linguistic model. By now the basic requirements for attaining explanatory adequacy—defining the linguistic phenomenon to be investigated, adequately describing this phenomenon, linking it to independently motivated generalizations, and making testable predictions about related phenomena—are well established, and following this procedure has proved successful in a great many cases. Nevertheless, this approach leaves a number of questions unanswered, questions which, Moore and Polinsky argue in their introductory chapter, can be defined in terms of three oppositions. The first of these, the opposition between language-universal and language-particular explanation, forces a linguist to choose a position on a scale at one end of which is the idea that all languages are manifestations of a single UG and all diversity can either be relegated to the lexicon or explained in terms of parametric differences in the grammar, and at the other end of which is the idea that languages can differ from each other without limit and in unpredictable ways. The second opposition is that between internal and external explanation, i.e. between an explanation that is valid within the context of a specific linguistic theory, and based on the principles of that theory, and an explanation which tries to account for linguistic phenomena on the basis of principles outside the domain of grammar (e.g. more general cognitive or functional principles). The third opposition is that between synchronic and diachronic explanation. All the contributions to this volume address one (or more) of these oppositions. The opposition between internal and external explanation is taken up by Hagit Borer, Greg Carlson, Robert Kluender, S.-Y. Kuroda, Ronald Langacker, Frederick Newmeyer and Robert van Valin; the papers by John Haiman and Edward Keenan deal with the diachronic approach of explanation. John Hawkins stresses the need to take processing factors into consideration, while Peter Culicover, Andrzej Nowal and Wojciech Borkowski use language change phenomena to argue in favour of external explanation.

In his impressive two-volume study *Structure and Function: A Guide to Three Major Structural-Functional Theories*, Christopher Butler also pays ample attention to such notions as the goals of linguistic theory and the nature of explanation, in functionalist theories in general, and in the structural-functionalist theories of Functional Grammar (FG), Role and Reference Grammar (RRG) and Systemic Functional Grammar (SFG) in particular. Volume 1, *Approaches to the Simplex Clause*, starts with a brief discussion of the functionalist approach by listing seven defining characteristics, including its view of language as an instrument for communication, its object of study (language in context), its position on the role of syntax (and its relation to semantics and pragmatics, discourse and the cognitive dimension), the nature of its explanations, and its views on innateness and language acquisition. Chapter 2 then discusses six approaches which, on the basis of these characteristics, can be regarded as part of the functionalist enterprise. Chapters 3, 4 and 5 present preliminary discussions of FG, RRG and SFG, respectively, each chapter beginning with a section on the underlying goals of the model in question, before giving a summary of how each model deals with simplex clauses. Chapter 6 subsequently offers an interim critical comparison of these three approaches, offering an evaluation in terms of overall approach, levels of description, treatment of syntagmatic and paradigmatic relationships and the question of layering. The other chapters present cross-theoretical discussions of three specific areas of the grammar: the structure and meaning of phrasal units, the representation of situations, and the treatment of tense, aspect, modality and polarity. Volume 2, *From Clause to Discourse and Beyond*, looks beyond the simple clause and gradually moves towards a discussion of the way in which the three theories deal with discourse-oriented aspects of the grammar. The first three chapters still concentrate on the (complex) clause, dealing with illocution, information structure and clause combining respectively, while chapter 4 is devoted to wider discourse phenomena (context, cohesion, processing). Chapter 5 subsequently describes functionalist approaches to such issues as language learning, and considers applications of structural-functional models to computational linguistics, stylistics, translation and comparative studies, and language pathology. Chapter 6 offers a final assessment of the three theories with respect to the goals they set themselves. The chapter ends with the outline of an integrated model and the possible contributions that the three theories reviewed might make to such an approach. Entirely in line with the objectives of the functional approach, examples throughout the book are authentic, taken from a number of English, Spanish and multilingual corpora. Despite the vast amount of detail, the book is very readable, and of interest to anyone interested in functionalist approaches in general, any—or all—of the three theories discussed, or a cross-theoretical discussion of any particular area within the grammar.

Works of a more or less general character have also appeared in other theoretical traditions. The Dušková, ed., *Dictionary of the Prague School of Linguistics*, provides the first English version of a text out of print for more than forty years, thereby marking a general revival of the Prague School of Linguistics (founded in 1926), and more specifically of the work by one of its leading advocates, Josef Vachek (1909–1997). The book begins with an introduction by František Čermák and Eva Hajičová, which provides a brief characterization of some of the main concepts of the Prague School, describing the influence—up to the very present—of these concepts on the work of (structural-functional) linguists all over the world. This is followed by a foreword to the dictionary by the editors and translators, which traces the history of the dictionary and gives an account of the choices made in translating. Next, we find Josef Vachek's preface to the original edition [1959], followed by a list of the more than 160 sources (and their abbreviations) employed by Vachek. The dictionary itself consists of an alphabetized summary of the key theoretical notions of the Prague School, given in the form of quotations. Each headword is provided with its French, German and Czech equivalents; alphabetical lists of these equivalents can be found in the index. It will be clear that the book will be of interest to both historiographers of linguistics and theoretical linguists working with the concepts of the Prague School.

Within the Chomskian tradition, Neil Smith has published an amusing little book entitled *Language, Bananas and Bonobos: Linguistic Problems, Puzzles and Polemics*, which consists of revised and updated versions of a number of columns and reviews, written mainly for Glot International, addressing facts and observations that struck the author as 'inherently interesting or surprising' (p. vii). Smith addresses 'problems' such as 'What do bananas have to do with autism?', 'Is it normal to hear colours and see sounds?' and 'Do noises have complex internal structure?', and attempts to shed light on 'puzzles' like 'Why do children make certain pronunciation mistakes?' and 'What is it that makes people funny?'. The sketches are written from a generative point of view (as indeed pointed out by the author in the preface); nevertheless, most sections are accessible to a more general readership—especially with the help of the glossary of technical terms at the back of the book. In the section called 'Polemics', the author's linguistic prejudices are (understandably) more strongly expressed. Here he defends the generativist stance on issues within language acquisition (innateness, critical period) and reference, occasionally lashing out at other approaches (particularly connectionism). Although the author never fails to intrigue and engage, reading these sketches one after the other gives one the impression of the author as a 'defender of the faith'. This does not, however, detract from the overall accomplishment of the book, which, despite its modest size, succeeds in bringing together different facets of language and situating them in wider social and cognitive contexts, and in inviting the reader to join the author in speculating about the issues raised.

Within cognitive linguistics, two successful works benefited from a second edition. The first of these, Ronald Langacker's *Concept, Image, and Symbol: The Cognitive Basis of Grammar* is an anniversary edition of the original monograph [1991]. The book is a reissue rather than a revision, since nothing has been changed in or added to the body of the text. What has been added is a preface to the new edition (pp. ix–xiii). Here the author comments on the continued success of cognitive linguistics, as attested by the formation of new national cognitive linguistics societies, as well as by the large number of dissertations, publications, conferences and workshops devoted to aspects of cognitive linguistics. One reason for reissuing the monograph is to make the basic claims and principles of the theory accessible to a wider audience—especially since there are as yet no textbooks available. The reason that a ten-year-old manuscript has been chosen to fill this gap shows that, although cognitive grammar has certainly developed and expanded over the time, its underlying principles, core notions and basic architecture have not altered. The preface also includes a brief overview of the most important publications since 1991.

The other second edition within cognitive grammar is *Metaphors We Live By*, by George Lakoff and Mark Johnson. The book is an updated version of the by now classic first edition [1980] and contains an extensive afterword by the authors, in which they explain that what was intended as a modest contribution to the understanding and use of (everyday) metaphorical thought has had great impact not only on linguistics, cognitive science and philosophy, but also on literary studies, politics, law, clinical psychology, religion, mathematics. The reason for this success, the authors suggest, may well have been the fact that it offered a new approach to the study of metaphor—an approach which, first, was based on empirical study, and second, assumed the existence of conceptual metaphor. The second point, in particular, turned out to be of crucial importance. Unlike former approaches, that of Lakoff and Johnson saw metaphor as a natural phenomenon, conceptual metaphor as a natural part of human thought, and linguistic metaphor as a natural part of human language. In addition, there was the idea of embodiment, i.e. the idea that the metaphors we use and what they mean depends on the nature of our bodies, our interactions in the physical environment, and our social and cultural practices. Finally, the authors provide a summary of recent developments in metaphor theory, discussing both new additions to the theory and applications in a large number of different fields.

Let us now turn our attention to the large number of handbooks, practical guides and textbooks published in 2002 and 2003. First of all, 2003 saw two new additions to the Blackwell Handbooks in Linguistics series. Both volumes, one on language and gender, the other on second language acquisition, are of a highly interdisciplinary character, offering contributions by scholars from different backgrounds and presenting discussions of key issues in the two fields from a variety of (sometimes conflicting) points of view. In their introductory chapter to

The Handbook of Language and Gender, editors Janet Holmes and Miriam Meyerhoff describe the purpose of the volume as being to provide 'an authoritative, comprehensive and original collection of articles representing the richness and diversity of contemporary research in the area' (p. 1). The first of these aims has been achieved by inviting contributions by leading specialists, including Mary Bucholtz, Deborah Cameron, Penelope Eckert, Robin Lakoff, Suzanne Romaine, Mary Talbot and Deborah Tannen. The scope of the book is also impressive: not only do the twenty-nine chapters (plus introduction and epilogue) address a multitude of topics; in addition, their authors come from a range of different backgrounds, representing many different points of view, theoretical frameworks and methodologies. Finally, originality has been achieved by a focus on recent trends and developments. Much attention has also been given to the organization of the volume. The chapters have been divided over five areas of research (history and theoretical background, negotiating relations, authenticity and place, stereotypes and norms, and institutional research), with an overall progression from highly theoretical issues to practical applications of language and gender research. Moreover, accessibility is enhanced by having the first chapter of each section serve as a preparation for the discussions to follow, the idea being that all papers ought to be accessible for readers without too much background in the field. As a result, the handbook is a valuable resource for both students and scholars, and for readers interested in theoretical matters as well as for those with more applied interests.

The other volume is *The Handbook of Second Language Acquisition*. In their introductory chapter, editors Catherine Doughty and Michael Long explain that in second language acquisition research a multidisciplinary approach is inevitable in view of the broad scope of second language acquisition, which, in turn, has inevitably led to a large variety of research methods, as well as a proliferation of theories. The remaining twenty-two contributions to the handbook reflect this diversity, representing several of these theories and employing different methodologies. They are divided over six categories (capacity and representation, environments for SLA, processes in SLA, biological and psychological constraints, research methods, and the state of SLA), and address such diverse topics as grammatical nativism, general nativism, emergentism and connectionism, implicit and explicit learning, incidental and intentional learning, automaticity, attention and memory, (individual) variation, language-processing, cross-linguistic influence, and fossilization. What most of the contributions to the volume have in common, however, is their ultimate goal—to identify the nature and sources of the underlying L2 knowledge system and to explain developmental success and failure—as well as their strongly cognitive orientation. That this shared cognitive dimension is not a coincidence becomes clear from the afterword, in which Doughty and Long convincingly argue in favour of regarding SLA as a branch of cognitive science. The overall result is an excellent overview of the field—the central ideas, the major approaches, the range of research methods—and an invaluable resource for students and scholars from a variety of backgrounds.

A more practical publication on the subject of second language acquisition is Carol Chappelle's *English Language Teaching and Technology*, which discusses recent developments in technologies used in second language teaching and assessment, language analysis and language use, and their implications for applied linguistics. More specifically, it addresses such questions as how learning can benefit from the use of technology; how research on SLA can help to inform the design of technology-based language learning; how the learning accomplished through technology can be evaluated; and how technology-based practices can be used as tools for applied linguistics research. The chapters are based on material from lectures given by the author, whereby the recurrent theme is the need for a constructive relationship between technology and second language acquisition research. Chapter 1 describes recent changes in language technology and the new opportunities these offer to language teachers; moreover, the discussion is meant to encourage applied linguists to take a more direct interest in the complex language-technology reality. Chapter 2 explores this reality by examining how computer-assisted language learning can be informed by professional knowledge about SLA. In chapter 3 Chapelle argues that, instead of still justifying the use of computers in language learning, the focus should by now be on developing effective software for CALL, and on ensuring that effective use is made of this software. Chapter 4 points out the need to develop basic principles for dealing with data on the processes used by learners in working on technology-mediated language learning tasks, and outlines such principles by employing the three research perspectives of description, interpretation, and evaluation. Chapters 5 and 6 defend the view that technology should not only be seen as a practical tool, but also as a means to influence and advance SLA research. Chapter 5 concentrates on the ways in which technology can raise theoretical issues that may be of interest to SLA, while chapter 6 concentrates on what computer-aided language assessment can do to enhance understanding of assessment issues in general. Chapter 7 summarizes the main points, once again stressing the need for research in CALL to move away from efficiency comparisons with classroom teaching to finding innovative ways of informing SLA research.

Also exploring the relation between theory and practice, but tending more towards the practical side, are three new publications in the field of translation. The first of these, Eugene Nida's *Contexts in Translating*, emphasizes how a good understanding of the different kinds of context of a discourse is essential for comprehending that discourse and reproducing its meaning in another language. Context here is given a very broad interpretation: it includes the phonological, lexical and grammatical features of a text, its history, its past interpretations and, perhaps most importantly, its cultural embeddedness. In addition, the role of some more external features of a discourse is considered, such as its audience and the concerns of those commissioning the translation. Although, in itself, the message is not always original, the many examples (in the form of translations into English from French, Spanish and German) and practical tips given in the first five chapters of the book make it a useful resource for both beginning and practising translators. The book ends with two chapters describing a number of theoretical treatments of translation: chapter 6 provides a summary of some lesser known treatments, while chapter 7 discusses the three major types of theory of translation in terms of philological, sociolinguistic and socio-semiotic principles.

A very practical volume on translation is Somers, ed., *Computers and Translation: A Translator's Guide*, a guide for (would-be) translators and professional linguists (technical writers, language teachers) who are interested to know how the computer can help them, and what the computer can and cannot do to make their job easier and more satisfying. It is not a book in computer science, nor does it have much to offer in the area of translation theory. Instead, it is a book written by a team of experts (teachers and researchers in language and linguistics, especially computational linguistics and translation theory, employees of software companies and translators) dealing with such practical matters as the translator's workstation, computer-based resources for translators (terminology tools, translation memory systems, corpora), as well as computer-aided translation and machine translation. One of the book's objectives is to set the record straight by dispelling some of the prevailing myths and prejudices and by offering a realistic picture of the past, present and future of translation and the computer.

For anyone interested in screen translation, it will be interesting to know that there is a special issue of *Translator* (9:ii[2003]), edited by Yves Gambier, which is entirely devoted to the three fundamental issues in the field of screen translation: the relationship between verbal output and pictures and soundtrack, the relationship between a foreign language/culture and the target language/ culture, and the relationship between the spoken code and the written one. In the introduction the editor provides an overview of the state of the art in screen studies, including types of audiovisual translation, the terminology used, recent developments in the field and topics for future research. The remaining seven articles address such subjects as the use of multimodal transcription as a methodological tool in the analysis of audio-visual text; the main strategies by which cultures which are distant in time and space are depicted in a selection of Disney animated films produced in the 1990s; the way in which subtitles in Flanders strengthen mainstream film stories' already streamlined narratives, enhancing their underlying ideology while censoring a few critical voices in the process; developing a research methodology for testing the effectiveness of intralingual subtitling for the deaf and hard of hearing; the pragmatic, semiotic and communicative dimensions of puns and plays on words in *The Simpsons*; and the reception of translated humour in the Marx Brothers' film *Duck Soup*.

Finally, quite a number of textbooks appeared in 2002 and 2003, both new publications and revised editions. In the latter category we find a third, updated edition of John Taylor's outstanding introduction to the field of cognitive linguistics, *Linguistic Categorization*. The purpose of the textbook is to introduce students to prototype theory and its role in linguistic categorization, i.e. in the categorization of non-linguistic entities by means of language, as well as in the categorization of linguistic units (grammatical categories, syntactic constructions). Using the theme of linguistic categorization as the organizing principle, Taylor's book introduces the reader to all the key notions and basic principles of cognitive linguistics. The third edition is fully revised, with new material reflecting recent developments in the field (e.g. an additional chapter on polysemy). In addition, study questions and suggestions for further reading have been added to each chapter. The book, which is suitable for those without any prior knowledge of prototype theory as well as for the more advanced student, is written in a lucid style, and throughout discussion is elucidated by many well-chosen examples.

Another third edition, also in the area of language and cognition, is *Words in the Mind: An Introduction to the Mental Lexicon* by Jean Aitchison. The book, which is meant as an introduction for undergraduate students as well as for the interested layman, presents a theoretical background to the mental lexicon, addressing such questions as how words are learned, understood, stored, retrieved and produced. The chapters are all relatively short, and designed to present information in an attractive and approachable manner (with examples from poems and popular literature, and using visual props in the form of graphs, comic strips and diagrams). This edition contains new material reflecting recent findings in the study of the mental lexicon.

Paul Hopper and Elizabeth Traugott's *Grammaticalization* also benefited from a new (second) edition. In this textbook, which discusses the ways in which lexical terms and constructions, having first developed grammatical functions in certain linguistic contexts, may grammaticalize and then continue to develop new grammatical functions, the authors present a state-of-the-art overview of the most important research findings in this area. The new edition is fully updated to reflect recent developments (both theoretical and methodological), which has resulted in the addition of a chapter on grammaticalization in situations of extreme language contact.

For those interested in a very general introduction to the field of linguistics, there is the new edition of *How To Study Linguistics: A Guide To Understanding Language*, by Geoffrey Finch. The book was originally aimed at newcomers to the subject (at undergraduate or even sixth-form level), but now also includes material intended for the more advanced reader; it includes a glossary, but, unfortunately, no exercises. There are two more or less introductory chapters, followed by three separate chapters introducing the areas of phonology, syntax and semantics, respectively. Chapter 6 offers a further discussion of these three subjects, as well as short sections on sociolinguistics, stylistics and psycholinguistics. The book ends with a very useful chapter full of practical advice on how to write a linguistic essay. The style is relaxed and engaging; on the whole, the book can perhaps best be seen as an invitation to students to take up the study of linguistics, rather than as an attempt to actually teach them linguistics.

As far as new publications are concerned, let us begin with Elly van Gelderen's *An Introduction to the Grammar of English: Syntactic Arguments and Socio-Historical Background*. This very concise textbook is described by the author as belonging to the tradition of the 'Quirk family of grammars', examples of which would be the work of Aarts and Wekker, Burton-Roberts, and Huddleston, as well as, of course, that of Quirk, Greenbaum, Leech and Svartvik. The book, however, moves beyond the descriptive approach, also using concepts from generative grammar (X-bar theory, Inflection Phrase, extraposition, trace, UG, etc.). The chapters cover such standard topics as categories (lexical, grammatical), phrases, functions and clauses (finite and non-finite). Each chapter ends with a special topic giving a prescriptive rule relevant to the topic discussed in that chapter (rules banning e.g. comma splice, contracted forms, split infinitives, stranded prepositions and dangling participles); this is followed by a discussion of the sociolinguistic and historical backgrounds behind these rules. The book is written in a clear and pleasant style and contains numerous examples in the form of puns and cartoons. Each chapter contains exercises (with keys) and a brief section with suggestions for further reading; chapters 6, 8 and 11 are followed by a review of the two or three preceding chapters, offering more exercises (without keys). The book also includes a comprehensive glossary. All in all, it is a very accessible introduction to English syntax for students at the undergraduate level.

No fewer than five new textbooks appeared in the Routledge English Language Introductions series: *Grammar and Vocabulary*, by Howard Jackson (discussed elsewhere in this volume); *Pragmatics and Discourse*, by Joan Cutting; *World Englishes*, by Jennifer Jenkins; *Practical Phonetics and Phonology*, by Beverley Collins and Inger Mees (with CD-ROM); and *Psycholinguistics*, by John Field. Like all other publications in this series, each of these textbooks is intended as a one-stop resource for students without any prior knowledge of the subject, providing an accessible overview, with activities throughout the book, commentaries and key readings. All five books display the 'two-dimensional' structure characteristics of the series, whereby chapters are divided into four sections—introduction, development, exploration and extension—each of which contains chapters on the same set of topics. *Pragmatics and Discourse*, for instance, addresses six main topics—context, co-text, speech acts, conversation, the cooperative principle and politeness—each of which is discussed in each of the four sections. As a result, the textbooks can be read vertically—simply from beginning to end—as well as horizontally—chapters on the same topic in the four sections, enabling the reader to explore a specific topic in increasing depth. In all cases, the extension section contains key readings from work by leading experts in the field. On the whole, this approach seems to work very well: it allows for a large number of issues to be covered in a short space, while at the same time offering increasing insight into a number of core issues. In some cases, however, the two-dimensional set-up perhaps leads to too much fragmentation, as in the case of *Psycholinguistics*, which contains as many forty-eight chapters (with an average length of only four pages).

An entirely different kind of textbook on psycholinguistics is Timothy Jay's *The Psychology of Language*. Also aimed at undergraduate students, this textbook offers a much more detailed and in-depth discussion not only of the classic paradigms and standard issues but also of cutting-edge research. Interestingly, it also includes separate chapters on the emotional and cultural aspects of language—aspects which, according to the author, belong in an outline of traditional language phenomena. The book consists of two parts. Part 1 resembles most other textbooks on psycholinguistics in terms of scope and design. Thus, the first seven chapters cover the traditional material, thereby creating a basis for the rest of the book. Part 2 is devoted to applied linguistics and includes chapters on discourse, figurative speech and thought, language development (including a controversial discussion on emergence, emotion and embodiment), language and thought in a social context, as well as further applications of psycholinguistics to everyday life. Each chapter opens with a set of questions meant to stimulate enquiry into the topic at hand; in addition, (boxed) discussion questions, special topics and review questions can be found throughout each chapter. Each chapter ends with a list of recommended websites, and an extensive glossary can be found at the back of the book. Although intended for undergraduate students, the book is certainly not suitable for students with no prior knowledge of the subject. At the same time, the comprehensive treatment of the material, the detailed discussion and the impressive bibliography make it an extremely useful reference book for any scholar interested in the subject of psycholinguistics.

Also dealing with language and the mind is *A Glossary of Language and Mind* by Jean Aitchison. The book forms an easy-to-read reference guide intended for both undergraduate and postgraduate students in (developmental) linguistics or psycholinguistics. It consists of an introductory chapter, introducing the reader to the field of psycholinguistics, a glossary of key terms used in the study of language and mind, complete with examples and cross-references, and a section with suggestions for further reading.

Finally, having started with the most ambitious and comprehensive publication in the field of language and linguistics, let us end with the smallest and most modest book of all: *Linguistics: A Very Short Introduction*, by P.H. Matthews. Though of an introductory nature, this delightful little book is not strictly speaking a textbook, as it is geared to a general readership with an interest in language and linguistics, intended to raise the interest of the reader rather than provide detailed discussions. Matthews succeeds in doing so by asking a number of seemingly simple questions (What is linguistics? What is meaning? What is a word?) and by hinting at the problematic areas rather than addressing them. The book discusses such subjects as evolution, language variation (diachronic and synchronic), language families, systematicity and rules, phonetics, and language and the brain. It will be clear that a book this size cannot but oversimplify—nevertheless, it is both informative and entertaining, full of fascinating facts and figures presented in an engaging and utterly accessible style.

2. Phonetics and Phonology

With respect to varieties of English in general, Edgar W. Schneider, 'The Dynamic of New Englishes: From Identity Construction to Dialect Birth' (*Language* 79[2003] 233–81), presents a general model of how New Englishes develop and applies this model to case studies of seven different countries (Fiji, Hong Kong, Malaysia, the Philippines, Singapore, Australia and New Zealand). With regard to phonology and phonetics, there is a vast amount of material, literally from all around the world. Within Britain, Wales is represented by two articles by J. Roderick Walters. In 'On the Intonation of a South Wales "Valleys Accent" of English' (*JIPA* 33[2003] 211–38), he presents an investigation of the typical, 'tuneful' intonation of a Welsh dialect, also drawing attention to the meaning in discourse which tone movements (or the absence thereof) are intended to convey. The same author, in '"Celtic English": Influences on a South

Wales Valleys Accent' (*EWW* 24[2003] 63–87), investigates Rhondda Valleys English and, in particular, the degree to which it is influenced by Welsh, and finds some direct transfers (especially in intonation), but also notes that these are recessive. Jonathan Marshall's 'The Changing Sociolinguistic Status of the Glottal Stop in Northeast Scottish English' (*EWW* 24[2003] 89–108), investigates the occurrence of /ʔ/ as a variant of /t/. A short description of the salient phonetic characteristics of Tyneside English is given by Dominic Watt and William Allen in 'Tyneside English' (*JIPA* 33[2003] 267–71).

JIPA should in fact be mentioned as a wonderful source for work on English phonetics and phonology. The journal regularly has articles on the phonetics of particular varieties of English, as well as reviews which will be important to English phonetics and phonology instructors, and discussion and illustration of the International Phonetic Alphabet. In this year's volume, Michael J. Clark and James M. Hillenbrand, in 'Quality of American English front vowels before /r/' (*JIPA* 33[2003] 1–16), report on acoustic measurements and listening tests of the vowels in words such as *beer*, *bear*, *hear* and *hair*. They find that pre-/r/ vowels are acoustically intermediate between /i e/ and /I E/ but are generally closer to the former category. In the same issue, James M. Hillenbrand, 'American English: Southern Michigan' (*JIPA* 33[2003] 121–6), provides a characterization of the phonetics of southern Michigan English especially concerned with the vocalic segments of that variety.

Also in America, there is a review by Matthew J. Gordon (*LSoc* 32[2003] 131–4) of Erik R. Thomas's *An Acoustic Analysis of Vowel Variation in New World English* (DukeUP [2001]) which reports on acoustic measurements of vowel realization of 192 North American speakers, including Native Americans. Renée Blake and Meredith Josey in 'The /ay/ Diphthong in a Martha's Vineyard Community: What Can We Say 40 Years after Labov?' (*LSoc* 32[2003] 451–85), tell the famous story of how William Labov (in the 1960s and 1970s) observed that the first element of the /ay/ diphthong was raised towards a central position in the speech of many Martha's Vineyarders. The present authors find much less centralization today, and relate this to changes in the socioeconomic fabric of the community: speakers are nowadays much less prone to adopt a linguistic marker in order to differentiate themselves from non-locals. Sylvie Dubois and Barbara M. Horvath's 'The English Vernacular of the Creoles of Louisiana' (*LVC* 15[2003] 255–88) studies the English spoken by Creole Africans in southern Louisiana. One interesting phonological aspect of their speech is a high rate of absence of glides in vowels and diphthongs like *ai*, *au* and *u*. The authors suggest that the absence of a glide in these vowels was part of the English brought to the area by native speakers in the early nineteenth century. A general phonological article by Stuart Davis and Mi-Hui Cho, 'The Distribution of Aspirated Stops and /h/ in American English and Korean: An Alignment Approach with Typological Implications' (*Linguistics* 41[2003] 607–52), accounts for the observation that in English the distribution of aspirated stops (e.g. initially in *putrid*, *candour*) parallels that of /h/ (e.g. *hatred*, *harbour*) while non-aspirated stops appear where /h/ is absent (cf. *rapid*, without aspiration, and *vehicle*, without [h]). The account is cast in an OT framework where the feature that is used to represent both aspiration and the sound [h], [+ spread glottis], is aligned with the left boundary of a stress foot.

On the other side of the globe, Bao Zhiming, 'Social Stigma and Grammatical Autonomy in Nonnative Varieties of English' (*LSoc* 32[2003] 23–46), analyses the innovative phonological features of Singapore English. Among the more noteworthy of these, voiced obstruents become voiceless at the end of the syllable (as in *rob*, *live*, *rose*, *judge*). This is widely accepted within the speech community in both formal and informal speech and carries little or no social stigma. It is also interesting that word stress falls more consistently on the penultimate syllable (as in *industry*, *broccoli*, *phonology*). David Deterding, 'An Instrumental Study of the Monophthong Vowels of Singapore English' (*EWW* 24[2003] 1–16), notes that, although in this variety the distinction between /i:/ and /I/ and /e/ and /æ/ are not maintained, this does not contribute to much loss of intelligibility.

The *Australian Journal of Linguistics* 23:ii[2003] is a special issue on Australian English, with an informative general background article by the late A.G. Mitchell (based on a lecture given in 1993), and a specific article on AusE pronunciation by Colin Yallop, 'A.G. Mitchell and the Development of Australian English' (*AuJL* 23:ii[2003] 129–41). Davis Bradley, in 'Mixed Sources of Australian English' (*AuJL* 23:ii[2003] 143–50), points out some Irish English characteristics of AusE, including, for instance, the use of schwa rather than /I/ in words like *naked*. Barbara M. Horvath and Ronald J. Horvath, 'A Closer Look at the Constraint Hierarchy: Order, Contrast and Geographical Scale' (*LVC* 15[2003] 143–70), offer a close investigation of /l/ vocalization in Australian as well as New Zealand English.

Finally, Lothar Peter, Hans-Georg Wolf and Augustin Simo Bobda's 'An Account of Distinctive Phonetic and Lexical Features of Gambian English' (*EWW* 24[2003] 43–61) sketches the linguistic situation in The Gambia and places this within the context of other national varieties of West African English. Outstanding features are the replacement of /ʃ/ by /s/ in *ship*, *shop*, *conclusion* (and, inversely, hypercorrect /ʃ/ in *soup*, *sauce*), cluster reduction (even as in [krɛt] for *scratch*, etc. Other articles on African English, by Augustin Simo Bobda, 'The Formation of Regional and National Features in African English Pronunciation: An Exploration of Some Non-Interference Factors' (*EWW* 24[2003] 17–42), and Inyang Udofot, 'Stress and Rhythm in the Nigerian Accent of English: A Preliminary Investigation' (*EWW* 24[2003] 201–20), can be found in the same issue.

With regard to regular phonological topics, T.A. Hall's 'Phonetics in Phonology: The Markedness of the Rhotic + Palatal Glide Sequence in English' (*FL* 37[2003] 249–67) shows and accounts for the fact that the sequence /rj/ never occurs as an onset and rarely occurs as a syllable contact (e.g. in *erudite*, *garrulous*). Constraints militating against this sequence are grounded in the phonetics. Gregory K. Iverson and Joseph C. Salmons, 'Legacy Specification in the Laryngeal Phonology of Dutch' (*JGL* 15[2003] 1–26), make a specific proposal on specification of the voice contrast which seems to function like an aspiration contrast in languages like English and German, and as a real voice contrast in languages like Dutch and French. One of the sources of evidence is

Yorkshire English devoicing (*bedtime* with medial [tt], *live performance* with medial [fp]).

Phonetic studies on segmental topics are concerned with /r/—Michiko Hashi, Kiyoshi Honda and John R. Westbury, 'Time-Varying Acoustic and Articulatory Characteristics of American English [r]"A Cross-Speaker Study' (*JPhon* 31[2003] 3–22)—and with /t/—Isaiah WonHo Yoo and Barbara Blankenship, 'Duration of Epenthetic [t] in Polysyllabic American English Words' (*JIPA* 33[2003] 153–64). The latter report on a phenomenon which has received attention before in *YWES*: stop insertion between nasal and fricative as in a realization [prInts] for *prince*. They examined stop duration in four different environments in which stress and position in the word of the target cluster were systematically varied, contrasting, for instance, *intense* and *intents*. Their finding is that underlying /t/ is not significantly longer than epenthetic [t], although earlier work did find a significant difference. A study on schwa is David Patteson, Paul C. LoCasto and Cynthia M. Connine's 'Corpora Analyses of Frequency of Schwa Deletion in Conversational American English' (*Phonetica* 60[2003] 45–69), who show that schwa deletion is not very frequent in American conversational speech, though more frequently so in post-stress environment (e.g. in *corporate*) than in pre-stress environment (e.g. *suppose*, *semester*). Finally, there is a short note on *wanna*-contraction from a syntactic point of view in Peter Ackema and Ad Neeleman's 'Context-Sensitive Spell-Out' (*NL<* 21[2003] 681–735).

With respect to prosodic issues, Susan G. Guion, J.J. Clark, Tetsuo Harada and Ratree P. Wayland show, in 'Factors Affecting Stress Placement for English Nonwords Include Syllabic Structure, Lexical Class, and Stress Patterns of Phonologically Similar Words' (*L&S* 46[2003] 403–27), that phonological theories of English word stress need to allow for multiple, competing, probabilistic factors in accounts of main stress placement. Paul Bauschatz, 'Rhyme and the Structure of English Consonants' (*ELL* 7[2003] 29–56), investigates 'off-rhyming', i.e. the use of words such as *cease* and *seize* in poetry which do not quite (but almost) rhyme, on the basis of an investigation of English poetry in the course of three centuries (from Spenser to Yeats). He shows that little has changed during this time with respect to this phenomenon and offers an analysis in terms of distinctive features.

An original article on orthography is Andrew Rollings's 'System and Chaos in English Spelling: The Case of the Voiceless Palato-Alveolar Fricative' (*ELL* 7[2003] 211–33). Rollings investigates the orthographic complexities concerning the phoneme /ʃ/ (which besides *sh* and *ti* include *sch* (*schedule*), *ss* (*assume* for some speakers), *c* (*appreciate*), *ce* (*ocean*), etc.).

The textbook by Linda Shockey, *Sound Patterns of Spoken English* (reviewed by David Deterding in *JIPA* 33[2003] 252–4), will make excellent reading material for students who have covered the basic notions in phonetics and phonology and are looking to increase their knowledge concerning fast speech phenomena in English or are preparing for phonetics–phonology interface investigation of particular dialects of English, including American English (see also Section 9 below). A more introductory textbook is *Pronunciation of English—A Course Book*, by Charles W. Kreidler, which, however, is quite solid and comprehensive in its scope, covering basic articulatory phonetics up to phonological rules, with practice material, questions and exercises.

3. Morphology

Over the years we have seen many studies arguing that, if only you look at morphology carefully enough, what you see is syntax. This is also the message of Marit Julien's *Syntactic Heads and Word Formation*. The model assumed has lexical insertion of morphemes, at Spell-Out. Words are not necessarily grammatical terminals—they are merely sequences of morphemes that regularly appear in adjacent positions, because one morpheme has undergone head movement to another one, or is its specifier or its complement. Morphology proper is then only concerned with the shape of allomorphs, as determined by their environment. Data to flesh out these ideas come from morphemes conveying tense and aspect in 530 languages. It turns out that position and nature (as free or bound morphs) correlate with the verb-initial or -final nature of the language in question, which is clear evidence of their syntactic status. Nevertheless, once a wider range of facts is taken into account, the difficulty of maintaining that morphology is (nearly) all syntax becomes obvious. Plenty of such facts are described and discussed in Ingo Plag's *Word-Formation in English*, an excellent textbook for beginning morphologists. Striking a balance between description and analysis, and supposing very little prior linguistic knowledge on the part of the student, Plag manages to successfully convey the interest and riches of the field. There are chapters on basic morphological concepts, the study of complex words, productivity (one of Plag's own special areas), affixation, affixless derivation, compounding, and theoretical issues in modelling word-formation. Each chapter is followed by a set of exercises (simple and more advanced), with a key being provided at the back of the book. Although of course the study of morphology could not exist without the use of cross-linguistic data and theoretical models, it is refreshing to read a textbook which is not at all simplistic yet gets by with using data from English only and without committing itself to a specific theory.

Marcin Krygier offers 'A Re-Classification of Old English Nouns' (*SAP* 38[2002] 311–19). He shows that the traditional Germanic division (with strong and weak classes, vocalic, consonantal and root nouns) makes little sense for the synchronic OE data, and instead proposes the following three inflectional categories: the *-es* type (e.g. *stan*, *scip*), the *-e* type (e.g. *talu*, *lar*) and the *-an* type (e.g. *hunta*, *tunge*). Adjectival inflection is found in Piotr Jakubowski's 'West Midland and Southwestern Adjectival Systems in Early Middle English: A Reanalysis' (*SAP* 38[2002] 271–8), where it is shown that these varieties generalized originally feminine *-re* as a case marker for dative. Alternations like *spring-vernal* and *horse-equine* are examined by Tetsuya Koshiishi in 'Collateral Adjectives, Latinate Vocabulary, and English Morphology' (*SAP* 37[2002] 49–88); one of their distinctive properties is argued to be their status as a social class divider, due to the need for memorization of each individual item.

Verbal inflection has received some attention as well. Elzbieta Adamczyk's 'Reduplication and the Old English Strong Verb Class VII' (*SAP* 38[2002]

23–34) attributes the marginalization of this pattern to the Germanic stress shift, followed by reduction and simplification. The new ablaut in this verbal class is argued to come from Frankish, a prestigious variety around the fifth century AD. Gary Miller has investigated 'The Origin and Diffusion of English 3 Sg *-s*' (*SAP* 38[2002] 353–61). He argues that *-s* is not due to Norse influence (either directly or indirectly) but originated in the 2nd singular, from there spread to the 2nd plural, then to all plurals and finally to the 3rd singular. Joanna Bugaj's 'Verbal Morphology of South-Western Middle Scots' (*SAP* 38[2002] 49–59) provides several corrections to LALME's profile of the area; in particular, it is shown that there is less variability in the verbal endings than LALME suggests. Richard Hogg's paper 'Regular Suppletion' (in Hickey, ed., *Motives for Language Change*, pp. 71–81) discusses instances of suppletive variation, both verbal and nominal, in the history of English, and argues that suppletive forms are no mere fossils; the language system apparently favours suppletion over regularity with highly frequent items.

The history of the affix *-ly* is examined in Ewa Ciszek's 'ME *-lich*(e)/*-ly*' (*SAP* 38[2002] 105–29). The loss of the final consonantal element is attributed not to Scandinavian influence but to a process of simplification in allegro speech, especially in preconsonantal position. The question why English has adopted the marker *-ly* for adverbs while German has not similarly adopted *-lich* (although it was used to mark adverbs in earlier German) is addressed by Amanda Pounder in 'Adverb-Marking in German and English: System and Standardization' (*Diachronica* 18[2001] 301–58). Her answer consists of three parts: German *-lich* but not English *-ly* had a heavy functional load in deriving adjectives; without adverb marking, a phrase like *a disgraceful late reply* would be ambiguous in English but not in German, which inflects prenominal adjectives; and standardization promoted consistency, also in contexts where the first two factors would not play a significant role.

Finally, there is a handful of studies on derivation, compounding and other issues. 'Derived Nominalizations in *-Ee*: A Role and Reference Grammar Based Semantic Analysis' by Carmen Portero Muñoz (*ELL* 7[2003] 129–59) argues that *-ee* derivations as in *examinee* cannot be predicted on the basis of the argument structure of the verb but have a semantic motivation, which she identifies as the notion of Undergoer as defined in Role and Reference Grammar. Thomas Berg, in 'Right-Branching in English Derivational Morphology' (*ELL* 7[2003] 279–307), examines the trimorphemic words in the English CELEX database and discusses their branching structure on the basis of six (phonological, morphological, lexical and semantic) criteria. Familiar facts often explained by positing the existence of Level 1 and Level 2 affixes are re-examined by Jennifer Hay in 'From Speech Perception to Morphology: Affix Ordering Revisited' (*Language* 78[2002] 527–55). She argues that facts like **kind-ness-ical* and **hope-less-ity* depend on ease of parsability of the morphemes in question, which in turn depends not on level ordering but on phonotactics and relative frequency of base and derived forms. John Anderson's 'On the Structure of Names' (*FoLi* 37 [2003] 347–98) discusses the syntax of (English) names and the role of (classes of) names in lexical derivation. On compounds, there is Stanislav Kavka's 'On the Idiomatic Status of English Compounds' (*SAP* 37[2002] 119–29), a rather discursive piece, which includes many examples (e.g. *woman doctor* 'gynaecologist') that are all idiomatic to various degrees. Pavol Štekauer writes 'On the Theory of Neologisms and Nonce-Formations' (*AuJL* 22[2002] 97–112). After reviewing the scanty earlier literature on this topic, the author distinguishes between the two types, with a nonce-formation being odd because of some deviation from pragmatic knowledge and experience (*ultra-alphabetically*, *unmurder*) or the use of low-frequency or low productivity-rules (*oidy*).

4. Syntax

(a) Modern English

Rodney Huddleston and Geoffrey K. Pullum have produced a magnificent opus in *The Cambridge Grammar of the English Language*. This is not just a descriptive grammar of what they term 'general-purpose standard Present-day English' but also incorporates the progress that has been made in our understanding of English grammar. This shows itself throughout the book in the discussions of the (in)appropriateness of some traditional definitions and in upfront discussions of issues of definition and analysis, but also in linguistic background comments such as 'auxiliaries tend to express the same kinds of meaning as inflections, but are syntactically separate words', in the discussion of the relation between locative complements and predicative complements, in the analysis of particles as intransitive prepositions, or in the classification of relative *that* as a complementizer (rather than a relative pronoun on a par with *who/which*). The volume also goes beyond standard descriptive grammars in that it incorporates and explains/defines so many linguistic notions: *Aktionsart* (achievements etc.), telicity, backshift, external and internal arguments, valency, selection restrictions, factivity, etc. Where such linguistic commentary could be regarded as too specialist for the more general reader, because it basically contains linguistic argumentation justifying the analysis of or approach to that particular topic, this has been shown by a smaller font and shading. It is impossible here even to simply list the topics covered in this mega-book—let the reader be assured that (almost) everything s/he is likely to be interested in is there.

At a much more basic level, the second edition of Ronald Wardhaugh's *Understanding English Grammar: A Linguistic Approach* has appeared. This is an excellent introduction which presupposes no initial linguistic knowledge at all but nevertheless manages to address the central issues of the various linguistic levels. Its structure is slightly unorthodox in that it starts with syntax (chapters 1–8), then deals with phonology (chapters 9–10), morphology (chapter 11), and prosody (chapter 12), and closes with syllable structure and intonation (chapter 13). The phonology section itself is similarly unorthodox in that phonology (phonemes, allophones, etc.) is discussed first and phonetics second. Though unorthodox, the ordering works because students do indeed find word classes easier than, say, morphology, because the little linguistic knowledge they initially possess will tend to be of word classes and simple syntax. Phonology, too, is often felt to be easier than phonetics, because the former requires fewer features to be distinguished.

Penelope Eckert and Sally McConnell-Ginet have written an interesting textbook on the relation between *Language and Gender*. Although the book is not primarily about syntax and morphology, there are some interesting findings in chapter 2, 'Linking the Linguistic to the Social', on the pervasiveness of gender even at these fairly abstract levels of grammar (for further review see Section 8 below). Feminine suffixes often derive from diminutives, and attract additional meanings beyond that of indicating gender. The suffix *-ette*, for instance, as in Ray Charles's Raylettes, suggests that these background singers are small and cute; more insidiously, in an example like *Barbie—the consumerette*, and also originally in *suffragette*, the *-ette* suffix appears to have a trivializing effect. Chapter 6, 'Saying and Implying', features aspects of syntax. Passives constitute another area that may reveal the hidden mores of a society. They are a useful device to demote or obscure the agent of a violent act, and even transfer the burden of guilt to others. A headline such as 'Girl 7 murdered while mum drank at the pub' appears to put the blame squarely on the victim's carousing mother rather than on the murderer. Other studies show that defendants accused of acts of (sexual) violence use passives and impersonals to make it appear that they were not responsible for their actions: *it became increasingly sexual*, *it started to heat up*, etc. The theme throughout the book is that research into gender and the use of language raises at least as many questions as it answers, and that results need to be interpreted very carefully, always with an eye for the social situation in which talk takes place. More about gender and language is to be found in 'The Role of Epistemic Modality in Women's Talk' by Jennifer Coates (in Facchinetti, Krug and Palmer, eds., *Modality in Contemporary English*, pp. 331–48), which discusses the use of epistemic modals in combination with typical hedges like *perhaps*, *I think*, *sort of* and *probably*.

Marc C. Baker, in *Lexical Categories: Verbs, Nouns and Adjectives*, has set himself the difficult task of trying to define these major lexical categories. Every theory uses them as primitives, but it has never become clear in what respects they differ from each other. Baker's theory uses insights particularly from Distributed Morphology (DM), but unlike DM, in which the concept 'category' is not a given primitive but is determined by the category of the functional projection of which it is the complement, Baker's idea of category is more akin to the earlier notion of categories as lexical primitives. One of his findings that argues against category being determined by a higher functional head is that syntactic operations are more particular as to what category they operate on than morphological ones. Morphological compounds do not care about the category of the first element—any combination goes (N + N, A + N, V + N, but also A + A, N + A); elements that are combined syntactically do not exhibit this freedom. The crucial difference setting verbs apart from nouns and adjectives is that only verbs are true predicates, licensing and theta-marking specifiers; the other categories require a functional category Pred to function as predicates. Nouns are set apart from the other two categories by the fact that only nouns can bear a referential index and can bind anaphors, traces and the theta-roles of verbs. Adjectives are not inherently predicative or inherently referential; adjective is essentially a default category. That they make good modifiers—which is often claimed to be their basic characteristic—follows from this. The author also explores the idea that all verbs are derived from adjectives, which would reduce the inventory of primitive categories to just noun and adjective. There is an appendix, 'Adpositions as Functional Categories', in which adpositions (postpositions and prepositions), often taken to be the fourth lexical category, are argued to belong to the functional categories. This is a well-written, thought-provoking book, by no means an easy read but extremely rewarding, particularly for anyone interested in the morphology–syntax interface.

We next turn to corpus work. Jacqueline Monschau, Rolf Kreyer and Joybrato Mukherjee, in 'Syntax and Semantics at Tone Unit Boundaries' (*Anglia* 121[2003] 581–609), explore the interaction of syntax and prosody in a corpus-based experiment. 'The ISLE Corpus: Italian and German Spoken Learners', by Eric Atwell, Peter Howarth and Clive Souter (*ICAME* 27[2003] 5–18), reports on the ISLE (Interactive Spoken Language Education) project, which exploits available speech recognition technology to improve the performance of computer-based English language learning systems. Göran Kjellmer, in 'Synonymy and Corpus Work: On *Almost* and *Nearly*' (*ICAME* 27[2003] 19–28), shows that a corpus study can bring out the subtle difference in usage of these words with respect of text types (*almost* occurs more in literary than in popular styles of writing) and collocations (*almost* is characteristically followed by adverbs, adjectives, pronouns and prepositional phrases, whereas *nearly* tends to be followed by numerals). 'What's the Real Thing? Paradoxes and Prototypes of an English Adjective', by Ulf Magnusson (*ICAME* 27[2003] 29–50), presents a preliminary corpus survey of the adjective *real*, and its collocational properties. The meaning of *real* appears to vary in a paradoxical manner, sometimes referring to natural and sometimes to unnatural things. 'A Corpus-Based Study of Connectors in Student Writing: Research from the International Corpus of English in Hong Kong (ICE-HK)', by Kingsley Bolton, Gerald Nelson and Joseph Hung (*IJCL* 7[2003] 165–82), compares the frequency of connectors in this sub-corpus with that in professional academic writing, and shows that, measured in this way, both groups of students—native speakers and non-native speakers alike—overuse a wide range of connectors.

In 'Automatic Retrieval of Syntactic Structures: The Quest for the Holy Grail' (*IJCL* 7[2003] 183–214), Gaëtanelle Gilquin argues that even in unparsed and/or untagged corpora it is possible to retrieve complex syntactic structures; she provides various alternative strategies that can be used to this effect. 'Two Quantitative Methods of Studying Phraseology in English', by Michael Stubbs (*IJCL* 7[2003] 215–44), proposes two independent methods of studying frequent phrases in English to illustrate how systematic observation of large datasets can allow generalizations about phraseology. 'Short Term Diachronic Shifts in Part-of-Speech Frequencies: A Comparison of the Tagged LOB and F-LOB Corpora', by Christian Mair, Marianne Hundt, Geoffrey Leech and Nicholas Smith (*IJCL* 7[2003] 245–64), presents a comparison of tag frequencies in two matching one-million-word reference corpora of British standard English in order to evaluate claims about the prevalence of a nominal style in present-day written English. 'Today's Corpus Linguistics: Some Open Questions', by František Cermák (*IJCL* 7[2003] 265–82), evaluates the present status of corpora and corpus linguistics in general. Some of the reported shortcomings are problems of methodology, while others are inherent in natural language, for example the fuzzy border between grammar and lexicon. 'From Translational Data to Contrastive Knowledge: Using Bi-Text for Bilingual Lexicons Extraction', by Olivier Kraif (*IJCL* 8[2003] 1–29), proposes a redefinition of lexical aligning and concludes that adapted statistical filters allow the accurate extraction of significant regularities. In 'SPAACy—A Semi-Automated Tool for Annotating Dialogue Acts' (*IJCL* 8[2003] 63–74), Martin Weisser reports on a pilot project to create a speech-act annotated training corpus for service dialogue systems. 'Automatic Extraction of Meaningful Units from Corpora: A Corpus-Driven Approach Using the Word Stroke', by Pernilla Danielsson (*IJCL* 8[2003] 109–27), proposes that, in an information- and meaning-carrying system, the unit of analysis should be a 'unit of meaning' rather than a word. In 'Collostructions: Investigating the Interaction of Words and Constructions' (*IJCL* 8[2003] 209–43), Anatol Stefanowitsch and Stefan Th. Gries introduce a method of collocational analysis that can be applied to linguistic expressions at various levels of abstraction (words, semi-fixed phrases, argument structures, tense, aspect and mood). 'A Multifactorial Corpus Analysis of Adjective Order in English', by Stefanie Wulff (*IJCL* 8[2003] 245–82), presents a model of the (predominantly semantic) factors that determine adjective order on the basis of a large corpus.

From corpora we turn to specific theories. Anyone who wants to keep abreast of Noam Chomsky's thinking on general issues in the theory of generative grammar can now read his *New Horizons in the Study of Language and Mind* and his *On Nature and Language*. The former work—reviewed here somewhat belatedly—contains seven papers written in the period 1992–9, focusing on the study of language viewed in relation to the history of scientific development and the philosophy of language. As in earlier work, Chomsky argues cogently for an internalist-individualist approach to language, without any further a priori requirements being imposed; among the issues dealt with are the role of innateness in semantics and the basic elements of the Minimalist Program. The latter work arose from a stay at the University of Siena in 1999. It is edited by Luigi Rizzi and Adrina Belletti, who provide an 'Editors' Introduction: Some Concepts and Issues in Linguistic Theory', sketching the basic elements in Chomsky's approach to language; they have also done 'An Interview on Minimalism', in which Chomsky talks about various topics related to the shift from parameters to minimalism. The book also contains an article on 'Perspectives on Language and Mind' (pp. 45–60), setting the study of language in the tradition of Galileo, Newton, Descartes and Darwin and emphasizing the notion that linguistic enquiry is a search for understanding, an article on 'Language and the Brain', exploring the possible connections between the two, and a political piece. Together, these two works form an accessible continuation of Chomsky's general reflections on the topic of language.

The structure of clauses and nominal phrases is investigated from a generative perspective in Cinque, ed., *The Cartography of Syntactic Structures*, vol. 1: *Functional Structure in DP and IP*. Cinque provides an introduction on 'Mapping Functional Structure: A Project', in which he sketches the background to the work and discusses the different diagnostics that can be used to identify functional projections (such as word-order facts, functional morphemes, and the nature and order of elements like topic and focus). In the volume such diagnostics are applied to demonstratives, to elements making DPs definite, to verbs and clitics in verb-second languages, and to the clausal categories of tense, aspect, agreement and negation. Most chapters are on other languages, but facts from English are in focus in Gary-John Scott's 'Stacked Adjectival Modification and the Structure of Nominal Phrases', which surveys earlier accounts of sequences like *a red Russian ball* and *a small round table*, and proposes a hierarchy of functional projections for them (SubjectiveCommentPhrase > SizePhrase > LengthPhrase > ColourPhrase, etc.). One wonders whether such a hierarchy could be integrated with Stephany Wulff's semantic account of adjectival ordering. The volume's other chapter drawing on English facts is Maria Teresa Guasti and Luigi Rizzi's 'Agreement and Tense as Distinct Syntactic Positions', which uses the discrepancy in child English between *Robin don't play* and unattested *Do Robin play?* to argue that AgrP is higher than TP.

Once we have a multitude of functional projections, we also have plenty of scope for moving elements into them. The questions that then arise (What moves? Where does it move? Why does it move?) are addressed in the contributions to Alexiadou, Anagnostopoulou, Barbiers, and Gaertner, eds., *Dimensions of Movement: From Features to Remnants*. The editors provide a useful introduction, in which they discuss the general issues involved and describe the trend from analyses in terms of feature movement towards analyses postulating remnant movement. The overall impression arising from the volume is that the field is in a state of flux, with some defending feature movement, others arguing for remnant movement (which may come in two different types), and yet others allowing both, the choice varying from construction to construction and language to language. The volume as a whole is squarely cross-linguistic; the only piece that focuses on a specific instance of movement in English is Howard Lasnik's 'Feature Movement or Agreement at a Distance?' in which he argues, on the basis of pseudo-gapping and sluicing facts, that sentences like *There is a woman here* have feature movement (with subsequent deletion). While on movement, we also mention some further contributions to this topic. Justin Fitzpatrick writes 'On Minimalist Approaches to the Locality of Movement' (*LingI* 33[2002] 443–63). A survey shows that none of the present approaches to locality is fully successful; what becomes clear is that simple concepts like dominance and c-command seem best suited to theories of locality. Mark Baltin claims that, in pseudo-gapping, 'Movement to the Higher V is Remnant Movement' (of VP) (*LingI* 33[2002] 653–9). Evidence comes from sentences like *Although he didn't try to persuade Sally, he did Martha.*

A different aspect of the structural architecture of the clause is examined in Hale and Keyser's *Prolegomenon to a Theory of Argument Structure*. Proceeding from the idea that all syntactic configurations are binary branching (having a specifier, head, and complement) and there is no iteration, the authors are led to various different analyses of items that look similar on the surface (e.g. intransitives of various kinds, transitives, light verb constructions). To convey the flavour of the approach, we give the example of the sentence *he saddled a horse*—its structure would be [$_{V}$ he [$_{V}$ V [$_{P}$ [$_{DP}$ a horse] [$_{P}$ P [$_{N}$ saddle]]]]]. To arrive at the surface forms, a great deal of incorporation or conflation takes place. Among the specific constructions and verb classes discussed in detail are the *splash* verbs, middles, the double object construction, *there* unaccusatives, the *spray* and *load* alternations, and particle verbs. A different approach to some of these facts is taken by John Bowers in 'Transitivity' (*LingI* 33[2002] 183–224). He postulates a functional category Tr between small *v* and V in all transitive clauses, offering plentiful evidence from the behaviour of VP adverbs, exceptional case-marking structures, expletives, inversion processes, passives, and middles.

While Hale, Keyser and Bowers concentrate on predicates, there is also a collection of generative papers on *Subjects, Expletives, and the EPP*, edited by Peter Svenonius. The editor's introduction provides an overview of the state of the art; further chapters consider the issues in much greater detail. The data analysed are all cross-linguistic, but the results invite application also to subject-related phenomena in English (especially, we would suggest, historical ones). From a theoretical perspective, the main lesson is that the Extended Projection Principle (EPP) is becoming increasingly important as a factor triggering movement. This lesson is also evident from Željko Bošković's 'A-Movement and the EPP' (*Syntax* 5[2002] 167–218), which pays special attention to the relation between the EPP, on the one hand, and semantics, successive cyclicity, and case on the other. Inger Rosengren considers 'EPP: A Syntactic Device in the Service of Semantics' (*SL* 56[2002] 145–90). She proposes that the EPP requires the presence of an expletive in SpecFin (leading to an existential reading) or a subject in SpecT (yielding a specific of generic reading); whether the EPP applies or not is subject to parametric variation.

Several articles explore general issues in generative syntax. Thus, Vivian Cook, in 'Poverty-of-the-Stimulus Argument and Structure-Dependency in L2 Users of English' (*IRAL* 41[2003] 201–21), reports on experimental evidence showing that L2 learners draw not just on their knowledge of their L1, but also on their knowledge of UG. Geoffrey K. Pullum and Barbara C. Scholz provide 'Empirical Assessment of Stimulus Poverty Arguments' (*LingRev* 19:i[2002] 9–50) in a special issue of *LingRev* entirely devoted to this topic. Pullum and Scholz argue that reports of the poverty of the stimulus have been greatly exaggerated, and come to the conclusion that 'the APS [argument from poverty of stimulus] still awaits even a single good supporting example' (p. 47). These claims are responded to in the seven articles that follow (by Geoffrey Sampson, Janet Dean Fodor and Carrie Crowther, Howard Lasnik and Juan Uriagereka, and others), which consider the different aspects of the problem from various angles and with varying results. Paul Postal casts a critical eye in '(Virtually) Conceptually Necessary' (*JL* 39[2003] 599–620) on the rhetoric employed in generativist literature used as a persuasive device to forestall any closer enquiries into the value of the assumptions underlying theoretical work. Guillermo Lorenzo and Victor M. Longa, in 'Minimizing the Genes for Grammar: The Minimalist Program as a Biological Framework for the Study of Language' (*Lingua* 113[2003] 643–57), argue that Chomsky's Minimalist Program is in line with recent findings about brain development in that it conceives of a minimal initial state of the faculty of language and relies for its subsequent development on general properties of complex organic systems for self-organization. In 'Innateness, Internalism and Input: Chomskyan Rationalism and its Problems' (*LangS* 25[2003] 615–35), Philip Carr contributes to the ongoing debate about the philosophical strengths and weaknesses of Chomsky's conception of the human language faculty. In 'Goodman, Quine, and Chomsky: From a Grammatical Point of View', Marcus Tomalin (*Lingua* 113[2003] 1223–53) assesses the influence of Nelson Goodman and W.V. Quine on Chomsky's ideas about economy in language.

At a more technical level, Hisatsugu Kitahara offers 'Some Notes on Minimalist Theorizing' (in Ukaji, Ike-Uchi and Nishimura, eds., *Current Issues in English Linguistics*, pp. 1–17), explaining the goals of the Minimalist Program and discussing some of its specific proposals. Masayuki Oishi's 'When Linearity Meets Bare Phrase Structure' (in Ukaji et al., eds., pp.18–41) discusses the different views of language design offered by Richard Kayne's Antisymmetry Hypothesis, on the one hand, and Chomsky's Bare-Phrase-Structure on the other. 'Rightward Positionings in Antisymmetric Syntax', by Yuji Takano (in Ukaji et al., eds., pp. 42–66) attempts to reconcile the notion that antisymmetry is deeply embedded in UG with apparent rightward movement (of adjuncts and heavy NPs) without resorting to moving other elements. Richard S. Kayne addresses some points raised in these three chapters in 'Some Remarks on Agreement and on Heavy-NP Shift' (in Ukaji et al., eds., pp. 67–86).

Further exploration of Minimalist theory is found in Noam Chomsky's 'Derivation by Phase' (in Kenstowicz, ed., *Ken Hale: A Life in Language*, pp. 1–52). Chomsky's focus here is on the precise status of movement, for which he suggests a privileged status of the domains of CP and vP (they are phases); among the phenomena discussed are head movement (which may take place at PF), object shift, and expletives. David Pesetsky and Esther Torrego examine 'T-to-C Movement: Causes and Consequences' (in Kenstowicz, ed., pp. 355–426). Their Minimalist analysis of T-to-C embraces phenomena like *that*-trace, *that*-omission and the ungrammaticality of *who did buy the book?*. Joachim Sabel offers 'A Minimalist Analysis of Syntactic Islands' (*LingRev* 19[2002] 271–315), relying mainly on the minimal link condition, supplemented by some effects due to Merge and theta-theory. Vikki Janke, in 'A PRO-less Theory of Control' (*UCWPL* 15[2003] 213–42), presents an alternative account of control. Mark Baltin, in 'The Interaction of Ellipsis and Binding: Implications for the Sequencing of Principle A' (*NL<* 21[2003] 215–46), argues from the evidence of pseudo-gapping that Principle A must operate relatively late in derivations. Principle C effects in free relatives (*we will ignore whatever pictures of Hans$_i$ he$_i$ displays*) are used by Barbara Citko, ('(Anti)reconstruction Effects in Free Relatives: A New Argument against the Comp Account' (*LingI* 33[2002] 507–11), to argue that free relatives are similar to ordinary relatives and therefore do not have the *wh*-phrase in COMP. In 'When Minimalism Isn't Enough: An Argument for Argument Structure' (*LingI* 33[2002] 172–82), Jeffrey Runner considers sentences like *John wondered which picture of himself Bill took* (where, in the meaning 'photographed', *himself* must be bound by *Bill*). Runner argues that the binding takes place not at LF (as assumed in Minimalism) but at the level of argument structure. Marcel den Dikken and Anastasia Giannakidou go 'From *Hell* to Polarity: "Aggressively Non-D-Linked" *Wh*-Phrases as Polarity Items' (*LingI* 33[2002] 31–61), examining the behaviour and status of phrases like *why on earth*, *what the hell*, and *where the dickens*. They suggest these items are licensed under c-command and, in root questions, are in SpecFocusP rather than SpecCP. Heidi Harley has looked at the initials 'WCO, ACD, and QR of DPs' (*LingI* 33[2002] 659–64). She shows that antecedent-contained deletion triggers weak cross-over (**his$_i$ mother loves the boy$_i$ that Sue does*), which suggests that such deletion involves A-bar movement (with definite DPs undergoing quantifier raising). Similar in outlook is Danny Fox's 'Antecedent-Contained Deletion and the Copy Theory of Movement' (*LingI* 33[2002] 63–96), which considers better-known cases like *John likes every boy Mary does*. To make quantifier raising compatible with the copy theory, Fox suggests that the relative clause is merged late. Uli Sauerland and Paul Elbourne examine 'Total Reconstruction, PF Movement, and Derivational Order' (*LingI* 33[2002] 283–319). They argue that in sentences like *a doctor with any reputation is likely not to be available*, there is PF-movement of the subject, with the base site being interpreted at LF.

For students of Optimality Theory, there is Sells, ed., *Formal and Empirical Issues in Optimality Theoretic Syntax*. The editor's introduction explains the basic elements of the theory (e.g. the notions of input and candidates, the use of violable generalizations, and constraint ranking reflecting cross-linguistic variation) and then homes in on a possible operationalization of the theory in a lexical-functional grammar framework. Here the input could consist of underspecified f-structures, while the candidates might be pairings of f-structure with c-structure. The further chapters in the volume mostly deal with other languages, but three engage crucially with English facts. Hye-Won Choi contributes 'Phrase Structure, Information Structure, and Resolution of Mismatch'; here, English–German–Catalan differences with respect to the word order of [±new] and [±prominent] constituents are derived from different constraint rankings. Computational issues in the development of an optimality-theoretic lexical-functional grammar are addressed in Jonas Kuhn's 'Generation and Parsing in Optimality Theoretic Syntax: Issues in the Formalization of OT-LFG'. Finally in the Sells volume, there are Anette Frank, Tracy Holloway King, Jonas Kuhn and John T. Maxwell III with 'Optimality Theory Style Constraint Ranking in Large-Scale LFG Grammars'; they propose the use of (dis)preference marks for individual constructions, reflecting their status as being well established or rare, and discuss possible approaches to the problem of syntactic and lexical ambiguity. Another optimal paper 'On the Nature of the Input in Optimality Theory' is co-authored by Fabian Heck, Gereon Müller, Ralf Vogel, Silke Fischer, Sten Vikner, and Tanja Schmid (*LingRev* 19[2002] 345–76); the authors argue that, unlike phonology, syntax does not need an input but can get by with constraints on output.

There are a number of interesting contributions in the area of cognitive and functional grammar. The cognitive notion of conceptual overlap, in which, for example, different grammatical structures may invoke the same conceptual components and have essentially the same semantic structure, is discussed in Ronald W. Langacker's 'Conceptual Overlap in Reference Point Constructions' (in Ukaji et al., eds., pp. 87–117), which focuses on the overlap between locative and possessive constructions. Kawai Chui, in 'Is the Correlation between Grounding and Transitivity Universal?' (*SLang* 27 [2003] 221–44), demonstrates that there is a gap between written and spoken language in that it is only in the former that the correlation appears to hold, and concludes that grounding is independent of the morpho-syntactic and semantic manifestations of transitivity. Cliff Goddard, in 'Whorf Meets Wierzbicka: Variation and Universals in Language and Thinking' (*LangS* 25[2003] 393–432), explores the similarities and differences between Wierzbicka's 'Natural Semantic Metalanguage' approach and the linguistic theory of Benjamin Lee Whorf. 'Linguistic Metatheory', by Keith Allan (*LangS* 25[2003] 533–60), discusses two macro-paradigms in linguistic meta-theory: the inductivist and the deductivist approaches, exemplified here by Bloomfieldian and Chomskian linguistics. It concludes that neither approach can justifiably exclude the other. In 'Terms, Clauses and Constructions in Functional Grammar' (*LangS* 25[2003] 515–30), Javier Martín Arista offers a critical evaluation of Dik's Functional Grammar by focusing on the main theoretical constructs of the theory, namely clauses, term phrases (NPs) and complex constructions. For a brief sketch of Hallidayan functional grammar, students can turn to Peter H. Fries's 'Systemic Functional Linguistics: A Close Relative of French Functional Linguistics?' (*Linguistique* 37:ii[2001] 89–100). For anyone wanting more functionalism, both in terms of data analysis and in terms of different theoretical approaches, the work to turn to is Christopher Butler's two-volume *Structure and Function: A Guide to Three Major Structural-Functional Theories* (for an extensive review, see Section 1 above).

We have now arrived at the individual elements of the clause, beginning with the NP. 'Uniqueness in Definite Noun Phrases', by Craige Roberts (*Ling&P* 26[2003] 287–350), argues that this uniqueness is both semantic, in that it is a conventional presupposition, and pragmatic, in that it refers to uniqueness with respect to the overall information of the discourse participants. Phoevos Panagiotidis, in 'Empty Nouns' (*NL<* 21[2003] 381–432), argues that phonologically null nouns are not instances of *pro* but should be analysed as semantically empty nouns like *one*. Michaela Mahlberg, in 'The Textlinguistic Dimension of Corpus Linguistics: The Support Function of English General Nouns and its Theoretical Implications' (*IJCL* 8[2003] 97–108), investigates nouns such as *man*, *move* and *thing* in three aspects of the support function: 'giving emphasis', 'adding information in passing' and 'providing an introduction'. Lieselotte Brems, in 'Measure Noun Constructions: An Instance of Semantically-Driven Grammaticalization' (*IJCL* 8[2003] 283–312), reviews the possible analyses for measure nouns like *acre* and *kilo*, including the less specific ones in phrases like *heaps of* or *bunches of* on the basis of corpus findings. Chu-Ren Huang and Kathleen Ahrens, in 'Individuals, Kinds and Events: Classifier Coercion of Nouns' (*LangS* 25[2003] 353–73), suggest that classifiers coerce nouns to refer to kinds and events as well as exclusively to individuals. Rolf Kreyer, in 'Genitive and *Of*-Construction in Modern Written English: Processability and Human Involvement' (*IJCL* 8[2003] 169–207), argues on the basis of a corpus study that the variation of genitive and *of*-construction can be explained with regard to two major underlying factors, namely 'processability' and 'degree of human involvement'. Carl Vikner and Per Anker Jensen propose 'A Semantic Analysis of the English Genitive: Interaction of Lexical and Formal Semantics' (*SL* 56[2002] 191–226). Using a Pustejovskyan lexical semantic approach, they argue that the genitive only combines with relational nouns (which can be of different types), and may in fact coerce a noun into adopting such a meaning. Judith Aissen, in 'Differential Object Marking: Iconicity vs. Economy' (*NL<* 21 [2003] 435–83), argues that cross-linguistic case-marking on objects reveals tension between two poles: an iconic principle according to which the more marked a direct object is *qua* object, the more likely it is to be overtly case-marked, and an economy principle that favours an absence of case-marking. C. Brisson, in 'Plurals, *ALL*, and the Nonuniformity of Collective Predication' (*Ling&P* 26 [2003] 129–84), rejects the claim that the sentence *The girls jumped in the lake* implies universal quantification (*Every girl jumped in the lake*) and proposes a meaning for *all* that explains why *all* but not *every* can combine with collectives.

Turning from nouns to pronouns we arrive at Michael Cysouw's *The Paradigmatic Structure of Person Marking*, an impressive typological and comparative study on person marking based on data from some 400 languages. The notion 'plural' is problematic: *we* is not the plural of *I*, not morphologically (the plural person markers are rarely derived from the singular categories) but also not semantically, as *we* is not speakers speaking in unison but a group of people, only one of whom is currently speaking. In this respect, *we* is more like an associative: 'I and my associates'. The first person plural has an additional opposition of inclusive/exclusive that the term 'plural' similarly fails to capture. The term 'group' would therefore be a more adequate term than 'plural'. Of the seven possible combinations of participants, two are not attested as a grammatical category: the choral-*we*, i.e. *we* as mass speakers (1 + 1) and the plural-*you* addressing present audience only, i.e. *you-all* (2 + 2). The five remaining group categories are 1 + 2 ('minimal inclusive'), 1 + 2 + 3 ('augmented inclusive'), 1 + 3 ('exclusive'), 2 + 3 ('second person plural') and 3 + 3 ('third person plural'). These, with the three singular categories, represent a cross-linguistically viable grid of person marking. Strong typological generalizations about the preferred paradigmatic structures of person among the world's languages prove impossible, although there are strong tendencies, which in turn allow the formulation of a number of hierarchies which state which oppositions will be marked by separate pronouns and which will not; the absence of special marking is expressed in terms of homophony. An example of such a hierarchy is the Explicitness Hierarchy: singular homophony ≥ vertical homophony ≥ unified-*we* ≥ inclusive/exclusive ≥ minimal/augmented. In other words, the first opposition to give way in the first person complex are minimal inclusive (1 + 2) and augmented inclusive (1 + 2 + 3); the next one to give way will be that between this cluster and the exclusive (1 + 3) to yield a unified *we*. This hierarchy also proves to be a valid hypothesis for diachronic change.

More about pronouns can be found in Philippe Schlenker's 'A Plea for Monsters' (*Ling&P* 26[2003] 29–120), which argues, contrary to accepted thinking, that indexicals (like the pronoun *I*) do not have a fixed value; there are languages in which *John*$_i$ *says that I*$_i$ *am a hero* is OK. 'HE and THEY in Indefinite Anaphora in Written Present-Day English', by Mikko Laitinen (*IJCL* 7[2003] 137–64), explores the trend to use *they/their* instead of normative *he/him* when referring back to earlier indefinites like *someone*. Bengt Jacobsson contributes to the ongoing debate on the *It is I/me* puzzle in 'Notes on Pronominal Case' (*SN* 75[2003] 21–31) by presenting a careful examination of the other contexts in which there is variation between the object and the subject form. That there are pronouns and pronouns is the thesis of Rose-Marie Déchaine and Martina Wiltschko's 'Decomposing Pronouns' (*LingI* 33[2002] 409–42). They argue that, for example, *one* is a pro-NP, *I* and *you* are DPs, *they* is a PhiP, and *them* is a combination of determiner *th-* and a clitic phi-morpheme *-em*. More on 'Anaphoric *One* and NP-Ellipsis' has been written by Amàlia Llombart-Huesca (*SL* 56[2002] 59–89). After reviewing earlier analyses, she proposes that *one* is a last-resort filler of the head Num, if this element is not licensed by agreement.

We now turn to the internal elements of the NP. R.M.W. Dixon, in 'Demonstratives: A Cross-Linguistic Typology' (*SLang* 27[2003] 61–112), presents a survey of demonstratives and proposes a checklist of questions that are relevant for an investigation of the demonstratives in a given language. Holger Diessel, in 'The Relationship between Demonstratives and Interrogatives' (*SLang* 27[2003] 635–55), argues that the two word classes encode the same semantic features because of the similarity of their pragmatic function: both initiate a search for information. Mariangela Spinillo, in 'On *Such*' (*ELL* 7[2003] 195–210), argues that *such* is best analysed as an adjective and that a dual treatment, as a determiner and a pronoun, is unwarranted. Such a unified analysis is not what Johanna L. Wood proposes: in 'Much about *Such*' (*SL* 56[2002] 91–115) she argues that there is an intensifying *such* (which occupies Num^0) and an identifying *such* (which may be a predicate raised from a small clause, or a base-generated SpecNumP). In 'Adjectives of Comparison: The Grammaticalization of their Attributive Uses into Postdeterminer and Classifier Uses', Tine Breban and Kristin Davidse (*FoLi* 37[2003] 269–317), examine Cobuild examples of adjectives such as *same, identical, equal, comparable, similar, related, other, different, further* and *additional* and conclude that their postdeterminer and classifier uses result from the grammaticalization of the lexical notions of likeness and non-likeness. John R. Taylor, in 'Near Synonyms as Co-Extensive Categories: "High" and "Tall" Revisited' (*LangS* 25[2003] 263–84), examines the near synonyms *high* and *tall*, and argues that the words offer different construals of an entity's verticality, with *high* designating the dominant vantage, *tall* the recessive vantage. 'Vantages on the Category of Vertical Extent: John R. Taylor's "High" and "Tall"', by Robert E. MacLaury (*LangS* 25[2003] 285–8), provides a postscript, outlining further possibilities of Taylor's 'vantage theory'. 'Testing the Sub-Test: An Analysis of English *-ic* and *-ical* Adjectives', by Stefan Th. Gries (*IJCL* 8[2003] 31–61), shows that some *-ic/-ical* pairs are virtually synonymous while others are strongly differentiated, and reviews the statistical methods that are most relevant here. Henk Pander Maat, in 'Graadadjectieven, Subjectificatie en Argumentatie [Gradable Adjectives, Subjectification, and Argumentation]' (*Gramma/TTT* 10 [2003] 60–92), concludes that the properties of gradable or degree adjectives fall out naturally if they are viewed as subjectified counterparts of the correlative grading construction *so X that Y*.

From NPs we turn to subjects. 'On the Syntactic and Semantic Status of Anticipatory *it*', by Gunther Kaltenböck (ELL 7[2003] 235–55), discusses the status of anticipatory *it* (semantically empty dummy, referential pronoun or cataphoric element?) in e.g. *It is surprising that John went to London*, on the basis of a corpus study. Ana E. Martinez Insua and Ignacio M. Palacios Martinez, in 'Non-Concord in Existential *There*-Constructions' (*ES* 84[2003] 262–83), investigate the occurrence of examples like *There's six of the best*, which are a feature of spoken rather than written speech and are restricted to present tense forms of *be*. They are particularly likely with long, structurally complicated post-verbal sequences. Paul Kay looks at 'English Subjectless Tagged Sentences' (*Language* 78[2002] 453–81). He discusses the properties of sentences like *Fooled us, didn't they*, and proposes a constructional account for them, making use of multiple inheritance. Ilse Depraetere, in 'On Verbal Concord with Collective Nouns in British English' (*ELL* 7 [2003] 85–127), presents a corpus-based classification of which collective nouns may combine with single or plural verbs (*cast, government, crowd, crew*, etc.) and shows that the selection of number in the corpus examples can often not be accounted for by the semantic/ pragmatic motivations suggested in the literature. The default option appears to be the singular.

We have now reached the verb. The study of *Modality in Contemporary English* is this year boosted by an entire volume on the subject, edited by Roberta Facchinetti, Manfred Krug and Frank Palmer. The work is introduced by Frank Palmer (Mr Modality) in 'Modality in English: Theoretical, Descriptive and Typological Issues', which presents a survey of various issues in the study of English modality, such as *can't* as the suppletive form of negative epistemic *must*, the deontic functions of *mustn't* and the role of *will* in interrogatives with second person subjects. 'Irrealis, Past Time Reference and Modality', by Paul Larreya, claims that all past tense forms express some type of presupposed (implicit) unreality. Richard Matthews's 'Modal Auxiliary Constructions, TAM and Interrogatives' discusses the interaction of grammaticalized modality as expressed by the English modals with the temporal properties of finite clauses and the illocutionary properties of interrogatives. In 'A Pragmatic Analysis of the Epistemic *Would* Construction in English', Gregory Ward, Betty J. Birner and Jeffrey P. Kaplan discuss the pragmatics of the use of *would* in e.g. *That would be J.K. Rowling* as a possible response to *Who's the British woman over there?* 'Towards a Contextual Micro-Analysis of the Non-Equivalence of *Might* and *Could*', by Stéphane Gresset, shows that the basic meaning of *could* is one of 'unilateral possibility' vs. the 'bilateral possibility' of *might*. 'On Two Distinct Uses of *Go* as a Conjoined Marker of Evaluative Modality', by Philippe Bourdin, discusses examples like *This disease goes generally undetected until its later, more dangerous stages* and *Whenever I let him cook, he goes burning everything.* Keith Mitchell's '*Had Better* and *Might as Well*: On the Margins of Modality?' demonstrates that each of these two expressions is the inverse of the other: *had better* consists of a necessity verb + a comparative of superiority, whereas *might as well* consists of a possibility verb + a comparative of equality. Geoffrey Leech, in 'Modality on the Move: The English Modal Auxiliaries 1961–1992', offers a quantitative study of how and why central modals are declining in both BrE and AmE. More evidence of the same change in progress is presented by Nicholas Smith in 'Changes in the Modals and Semi-Modals of Strong Obligation and Epistemic Necessity in Recent British English'; *must* is being replaced by *have (got) to*. Both authors see shifts in the perception of power ('democratization') as a possible cause. Maurizio Gotti, in '*Shall* and *Will* in Contemporary English: A Comparison with Past Uses', presents evidence that *shall* in current spoken texts is mainly used to express prediction, while in written texts it also expresses obligation. The prediction use of *shall* is increasingly being taken over by *will*. Stephen J. Nagle's 'Double Modals in the Southern United States: Syntactic Structure or Syntactic Structures?' argues that the first modal in such sequences (e.g. *might could*) typically refers to the speaker's views on possibility or probability of the remainder of the predication, whereas the second scopes over the predicated state or action. Nagle proposes a biclausal analysis of such cases. Graeme Trousdale, in 'Modal Verbs in Tyneside English: Evidence for (Socio)linguistic Theory', discusses non-standard uses of modals and their patterns of sociolinguistic variation (age, gender). 'Pragmatic and Sociological Constraints on the Functions of *May* in Contemporary British English', by Roberta Facchinetti, teases out the factors governing the distribution of this modal across different text types. Some more articles from this volume will be discussed below, where appropriate.

Further modal matters can be found in 'A Minimalist Treatment of Modality' (*Lingua* 113[2003] 967–96), where Jonny Butler argues that there are two scope positions for English modals, corresponding to root and epistemic meanings. Göran Kjellmer, in 'A Modal Shock Absorber, Empathiser/Emphasiser and Qualifier' (*IJCL* 8[2003] 145–68), investigates the use of *can* in *I can promise that you'll like it* in the CobuildDirect Corpus and concludes that it carries a number of important functions to which he gives the labels mentioned in his title. '*Be Going to* versus *Will/Shall*: Does Syntax Matter?', by Benedikt Szmrecsanyi (*JEngL* 31[2003] 295–323), suggests that the choice between these two future markers is sensitive to four factors: (1) contexts of negation, (2) contexts of subordination, (3) IF-clause environments, and (4) syntactic complexity. Gordon Tucker writes about the uses and meanings of the non-verbal modal item *possibly* in 'Possibly Alternative Modality' (*FuL* 8[2001] 183–216), comparing it with *may*, *might*, and *perhaps*. Another non-verbal item is examined by Angela Downing in '"Surely you knew!" *Surely* as a Marker of Evidentiality and Stance' (*FuL* 8[2001] 253–85). This word sometimes has modal overtones, though its main function is to express a wide range of interpersonal attitudes, ranging from surprise, disbelief and disapproval to persuasion and invitation to share beliefs (the choice depending on such factors as its position and the nature of the subject). Timothy Jowan Curnow, in 'Nonvolitionality Expressed through Evidentials' (*SLang* 27[2003] 39–59), demonstrates that evidentials, which normally indicate a speaker's source of information, sometimes develop into markers of nonvolitionality.

We now turn to aspect and aspectuality. John Newman's paper 'A Cross-Linguistic Overview of the Posture Verbs "Sit", "Stand" and "Lie"' (in Newman, ed., *The Linguistics of Sitting, Standing, and Lying*, pp. 1–24) argues that the posture verbs, all indicating states in which the human body is 'at rest', are often extended to refer to the location and orientation of inanimates, and from this use they may go on to become locational or existential verbs or participles, functioning, in effect, like classifiers. Another major pattern of extension is that posture verbs tend to evolve into aspectual auxiliaries, most commonly with progressive or habitual meaning. John Newman and Toshiko Yamaguchi, in 'Action and State Interpretations of "Sit" in Japanese and English' (in Newman, ed., pp. 43–59), investigate the way in which each of these languages differentiates between sitting as a state as opposed to the action of getting into the sitting posture ('sitting down'). Fritz Hamm and Michiel van Lambalgen, in 'Event Calculus, Nominalisation, and the Progressive' (*Ling&P* 26[2003] 381–458), present an event calculus computation of nominalization, *Aktionsart* and aspect. Kate Kearns, in 'Durative Achievements and Individual-Level Predicates on Events' (*Ling&P* 26[2003] 595–635), looks at achievements such as *miscount, break a promise* and *cure the patient* and argues that they lack process progressives despite being durative.

Next we look at tense. 'Insularity and Linguistic Endemicity', by Daniel Schreier (*JEngL* 31[2003] 249–72), reports on the usage of past tense forms in combination with the English quasi-modal *useta* (from *used to*) in the variety of English spoken on the island of Tristan da Cunha, as in e.g. *My father-in-law useta came in every morning before he go down to work.* Paul Portner, in 'The (Temporal) Semantics and (Modal) Pragmatics of the Perfect' (*Ling&P* 26[2003] 459–510), proposes an analysis of the English perfect based on the Extended Now theory (as e.g. in R.W. McCoard's *The English Perfect: Tense-Choice and Pragmatic Inferences* [1978]). Sabine Iatridou, Elena Anagnostopoulou, and Roumyana Izvorski present some 'Observations about the Form and Meaning of the Perfect' (in Kenstowicz, ed., pp. 189–238). Focusing on the universal and experiential perfect (which they argue to be semantically different from each other) and drawing on data from English, Greek and Bulgarian, they make several points about the temporal extension of the situation described by a perfect, the need for the presence of specific adverbials with specific types of perfect, and the status of anteriority in the meaning of the perfect. Göran Kjellmer, in 'On Nonoccurring Perfective *Have* in Modern English' (*SN* 75[2003] 11–20), discusses the status of the occasional missing form of the auxiliary *have*, both in finite (*he shown me*) and in non-finite contexts (*he must been born*): performance error or genuine change?

Laura Rupp, *The Syntax of Imperatives in English and Germanic: Word Order Variation in the Minimalist Framework*, looks at the positioning of imperatives at the left edge of the clause. In spite of its title, the book mainly deals with English; imperatives in Dutch, German, West Flemish and Danish are briefly dealt with in chapter 7. The author rejects previous claims that the NPs optionally accompanying imperatives are vocatives or any other 'special' category, and argues instead that they are subjects; another popular claim, that *don't* in imperatives should be analysed as a lexical unit, a negative particle, is similarly rejected: it is simply dummy *do* with negation. Dummy *do* is not possible in affirmative imperatives (**Do you try again!*) for the same reason as in non-emphatic declaratives. The supposed link with interrogatives is illusionary: the inverted subject-aux order is not due to I to C movement as in interrogatives, but to the fact that the subject in imperatives, if present, optionally stays lower in the structure and does not need to rise to SpecIP. This explains the much-discussed contrast with negative interrogatives seen in **Do you not try again!* With *do* inserted into the INFL head, and with *not* in NegP immediately below, there is no way in which such a sentence could be derived. The unacceptability of **Do not you desert me!* versus the acceptability of *Do not all of you desert me!* is argued to be due to the fact that the latter is an instance of constituent negation rather than clausal negation: *not* is part of the subject, *not all of you*, which means that there is no NegP. In the case of the former, with clausal negation, there is a Neg-head intervening between the subject and *do* and this blocks agreement between the two, so that this order is out. The fact that the former order is OK when the negation is cliticized onto *do* (*Don't you desert me!*) apparently points to *auxn't* forms being unitary lexical items, inserted into INFL directly, not only in negative imperative contexts but also elsewhere, witness the contrast between **there is not anyone waiting outside* and *There isn't anyone waiting outside.* The final chapter tentatively identifies the lower subject position as SpecAsp(ect)P. It also offers intriguing speculations on the motivation of the presence or absence of imperative subjects, of imperative subjects not rising to SpecIP and on the interpretative difference between pre-*do*(*n't*) and post-*do*(*n't*) subjects.

The complementation patterns of a number of individual verbs and verb classes have received special attention this year. 'A Usage-Based Approach to Argument Structure: "Remember" and "Forget" in Spoken English', by Hongyin Tao (*IJCL* 8[2003] 75–95), shows that both *remember* and *forget* disprefer complements. *Forget* lacks the placement flexibility of *remember* but allows more tense options; *remember*, on the other hand, is becoming a discourse particle. Gaëtanelle Cilquin, in 'Causative *Get* and *Have*: So Close, So Different' (*JEngL* 31[2003] 125–48), presents a corpus-based study of the similarities and differences of these two causatives in a frame semantics framework. Heidi Verplaetse, in 'What You and I Want: A Functional Approach to Verb Complementation of Modal *Want to*' (in Facchinetti et al., eds., pp. 151–89), focuses on the private character of the type of volition in this modal; it is used typically with first and second person subjects. Yoko Iyeiri, in '"God Forbid!" A Historical Study of the Verb *Forbid* in Different Versions of the English Bible' (*JEngL* 31[2003] 149–62), tries to account for the fact that *forbid* can be complemented by a finite clause only as part of the phrase *God forbid*. In all its other uses, we find non-finite clauses. An Laffut and Kristin Davidse's 'English Locative Constructions: An Exercise in Neo-Firthian Description and Dialogue with Other Schools' (*FuL* 9[2002] 169–207) is a study of *load*-verbs (*load hay on the wagon, load the wagon with hay*). It offers a Hallidayan–Sinclairean analysis of the syntax and semantics of the alternation, with some glances at Government-Binding and Cognitive Grammar accounts. Seizi Iwata asks 'Does MANNER Count or Not? Manner-of-Motion Verbs Revisited' (*Linguistics* 40[2002] 61–110). Noting facts like *He rolled/?bounced/*skidded the doll into a blanket*, the author proposes a lexical constructional account in which two levels of meaning are distinguished (lexical and phrasal). Toshiaki Oya addresses 'Reflexives and Resultatives: Some Differences between English and German' (*Linguistics* 40[2002] 961–86). Oya argues that German reflexives are weak while English ones are strong, and uses this distinction to derive contrasts such as *er legte sich hin* vs. **he lay himself down* and *er stand sich müde* vs. **he stood himself tired*. We also include here

You-Mee Sohn on 'The Interpretation of English Middle Constructions' (*HEng* 14[2002] 147–65), who finds that their function is to describe a general distinguishing property of the subject, singling it out from other entities.

Copulas have also attracted some attention. D.J. Allerton and Itsuki Koya, in '"Prepositional Predicatives" in English' (*ES* 84[2003] 80–91), examine PPs in the complement of copulas as in *Bill remained in a bad mood* and conclude that they warrant the adoption of a new grammatical category, i.e. that of prepositional predicatives. Ora Matushansky has been working on 'Tipping the Scales: The Syntax of Scalarity in the Complement of *Seem*' (*Syntax* 5[2002] 219–76). It is shown that a small-clause (but not a full-clause) complement to *seem* must contain a Degree Phrase, which has various consequences for syntactic behaviour. Gerhard Jäger, in 'Towards an Explanation of Copula Effects' (*Ling&P* 26[2003] 557–93), discusses semantic contrasts between the copula *be* and the preposition *as*. The former forces a type coercion from (partial) situations to (total) possible worlds, whereas the latter is a type-lowering device shifting the meaning of its complement NP from the type of generalized quantifiers to the type of properties. Regina Pustet, *Copulas: Universals in the Categorization of the Lexicon*, is an extensive cross-linguistic study of the use and non-use of copulas in some 160 languages. Copulas have been claimed to be semantically empty elements that only serve as carriers of tense and agreement, but a detailed look at the languages sample reveals that this cannot be the whole story. The use or non-use of copulas in any one language appears to be predictable to some extent from the semantic features of the predicate, e.g. for the features of dynamicity, transience, transitivity and dependency. None of these semantic parameters, however, ever reaches the point of a perfect statistical convergence with copula use. Some generalizations are possible, however. Copula distribution can be described in terms of the implicational scale nominals ≥ adjectivals ≥ verbals: in any one language, adjectivals may behave either like nominals or like verbals with respect to copularization, but nominals and verbals never display uniform behaviour which contrasts with the behaviour of adjectivals. In many languages, for instance, nominals require copulas, unlike adjectivals and verbals; if, in another language, nominals do not require copulas, then neither will adjectivals and verbals.

Adverbs and adverbials feature next. 'Between Epistemic Modality and Degree: The Case of *Really*', by Carita Paradis (in Facchinetti et al., eds., pp. 191–220) identifies three uses of this adverb: as a marker of evidentiality, of subjective emphasis and of degree (compare Magnusson on the adjective *real* above). In 'Trouble on the Left Periphery' (*Lingua* 113[2003] 607–42), Richard Hudson investigates how best to capture the ban on adjunct preposing in embedded interrogatives, as in *I told you (*tomorrow) what we shall do*, even though such adjuncts are fine in main clause interrogatives: *Tomorrow what shall we do?* Liliane Haegeman examines 'Sentence-Medial NP-Adjuncts in English' (*NJL* 25[2002] 79–108). She notes that sentences like *He yesterday published his version of the story* are especially frequent in journalistic prose and proposes an analysis whereby the adjunct is to the left of VP and to the right of the subject position; usually, the entire VP moves to the left of the adjunct, but this sometimes fails to happen in journalese.

We've come to subordinate clauses. Pride of place here must be given to *Subordination* by Sonia Cristofaro, a functional-typological study of subordination systems based on an eighty-language sample. The author first discusses the problems of definition: cross-linguistically, the same semantic/pragmatic relationships are not coded by the same construction types. Defining subordination on the basis of formal parameters like embedding leads to the inevitable conclusion that some languages have no subordination at all. Dependency as a criterion also poses problems. Defining subordination in cognitive/functional terms avoids these problems by looking at which of the two states of affairs in the complex sentence is an assertion scoping over the other one (e.g. in *I know she left* the state of affairs expressed by *she left* is embedded in the assertion *I know*); the relevant generalization is then that a subordinate clause is defined as a non-asserted state of affairs. This may mean that clauses are designated 'subordinate' that do not conform to the morpho-syntactic profile for subordination, but it at least ensures that no language type is excluded. If the assumption that there is a motivated connection between the form and function of linguistic expressions is valid, defining subordination in this way should still yield generalizations, and this prediction turned out to be correct: there is a significant connection between the cross-linguistic distribution of individual morpho-syntactic phenomena across different types of subordination relation and the semantic features of these relations. The motivation behind this connection is argued to be best accounted for by the cognitive distinction between processes and things. Processes are prototypically coded by verbs, and processual properties are reflected by verbal properties such as TAM distinctions. The lack of TAM distinctions often found in subordination (think of non-finite clauses) reflects suspension of the processual properties of dependent states of affairs. The fact that subordination is often signalled by nominal properties on the dependent verb is also a reflection of the processes-and-things distinction. This is a very solid and clearly argued work. More about functional/cognitive views on subordination can be found in 'Conceptual Overlap in Complex Sentence Constructions: A Cognitive Grammar Account', by Masuhiro Nomura (in Ukaji et al., eds., pp. 142–64).

Richard Hudson, in 'Gerunds without Phrase Structure' (*NL<* 21[2003] 579–615), attempts to reconcile the dual nature of the gerund (simultaneously clausal and nominal) by adopting an analysis in which a node can inherit categorial characteristics from two supercategories. Liesbet Heyvaert analyses 'Nominalization as an "Interpersonally-Driven" System' (*FuL* 8[2001] 287–329). Using a Hallidayan framework, she analyses gerunds and other factive subordinate clauses (as well as formations in *-er* like *baker*, *computer* and *can opener*) as down-ranked clauses and examines the relation between them and their corresponding full clauses. Idan Landau investigates '(Un)interpretable Neg in Comp' (*LingI* 33[2002] 465–92), which is found after verbs like *refrain*, *stop*, and *prevent*. The analysis proposed results in structures like *we prevented* $[_{CP}$ *him*$_i$ $[_C$ *from* $]$ $[_{IP}$ t_i $[_{VP}$ t_i *going there* $]]]$. Patrick J. Duffley, in 'The Gerund and the *To*-Infinitive as Subject' (*JEngL* 31[2003] 324–52), argues that the two structures show considerable overlap and that they should not be regarded as representing a binary opposition. Their basic meanings are more subtle than has been proposed in the literature.

Michael Hegarty, in 'Semantic Types of Abstract Entities' (*Lingua* 113[2003] 891–927), explores the differences between clauses denoting propositions, facts, reasons, and situations and clauses denoting events, and offers an explanation based on semantic types. Mark de Vries, in 'Three-Dimensional Grammar' (*LIN* 20[2003] 201–12), argues that paratactic constructions such as coordination and parentheses cannot be dealt with satisfactorily in a binary branching framework and proposes instead a grammar which, in addition to traditional generative terms like *dominance* and *precedence*, makes use of the notion *behindance*. Philippe Schlenker, in 'Clausal Equations (A Note on the Connectivity Problem)' (*NL<* 21[2003] 157–214), addresses the problems of the pseudo-cleft *What John likes is himself*, which is grammatical and should therefore show the same c-command relations as *John likes himself*—which it does not. Alexander Grosu, in 'A Unified Theory of "Standard" and "Transparent" Free Relatives' (*NL<* 21[2003] 247–331), argues for a common configurational analysis for sentences like *I'll sing what/whichever songs/however silly a song you want me to sing* and *He made what may appear to be a radically new proposal.* Göran Kjellmer's writes 'On Relative *Which* with Personal Reference' (*SAP* 37[2002] 17–38). Interestingly, it turns out that the 56 million-word Cobuild Corpus yields enough examples of this usage to recognize it as a real option; the frequency of *which* is found to decline along the following scale: concrete inanimate ≥ abstract nouns relating to humans (*decisions which*) > companies and firms (*publisher Penguin, which*) ≥ bodies of people (*the militia which*) ≥ human groups (*these people, which*) ≥ human posts (*a registrar which*) ≥ babies/children ≥ human individuals (*my brother, which*). Susanna Murcia-Bielsa and Judy Delin examine the various methods of 'Expressing the Notion of Purpose in English and Spanish Instructions' (*FuL* 8[2001] 79–108). The choice among the English variants (*to* + infinitive, *for* + NP, *for* + V-*ing*, *so that* …, and *in order to* + infinitive) is found to depend on eight factors, such as the semantic relation involved, scope, the nature of the goal of the action, possible contrast, and the (non)overtness of the agent.

Isabel Gómez Txurruka, in 'The Natural Language Conjunction *And*' (*Ling&P* 26[2003] 255–85), argues that inter-clausal *and* is not semantically equivalent to a logical conjunction and has no temporal semantics. *And* is best analysed from a discourse-based perspective. Ljiljana Progovac, in 'Correlative Conjunctions and Events: A Reply to a Reply' (*Syntax* 5[2002] 277–83), responds to criticism of her earlier analysis of sentences like *Both Maria and Pete will bring a bottle*; she argues that her two-event analysis can stand if we allow two grammatically encoded events to coincide in a single real-world occurrence. Rajesh Bhatt, in 'Locality in Correlatives' (*NL<* 21[2003] 485–541), argues that there are locality effects in correlatives: a correlative clause must be merged as closely as possible to the phrase that it modifies.

We end this section with some work on clausal phenomena. Tae-Sook Park discusses 'Discourse Familiarity and English Word Order' (*HEng* 13[2002] 227–51), coming to the conclusion that both inverted and canonical orders in English usually have old information before new (with the category of 'inferable' counting as old). Monika Doherty, in 'Topikalisierungsstrategien aus der Perspektive diskursadäquater Übersetzungen' (*LingB* 194[2003] 183–212), shows that German and English have similar strategies to deal with complex information structures which go beyond the straightforward 'given before new' maxim, but these strategies are subject to different syntactic conditions, as one language is a 'freely' variable language with a right peripheral VP and the other a rigidly ordered language with a left peripheral VP. Torben Thrane, in 'Breakstructures' (*JL* 39[2003] 327–72), argues that the difference between structural and rhetorical topicalization can be captured by positing movement of CP to the specifier of TopP. Daniel Büring, in 'On D-Trees, Beans, and B-Accents' (*Ling&P* 26[2003] 511–45), presents a pragmatic theory of contrastive topic and its relation to focus in English. Caterina Donati and Marina Nespor, in 'From Focus to Syntax' (*Lingua* 113[2003] 1119–42), argue that the more prominence may move around within an intonational phrase, the more the language is characterized by rigid word order properties. Seizi Iwata, in 'Echo Questions are Interrogatives? Another Version of a Metarepresentational Analysis' (*Ling&P* 26[2003] 185–254), fine-tunes existing ideas about echo questions. William D. Davies and Stanley Dubinsky, in 'On Extraction from NPs' (*NL<* 21[2003] 1–37), look at *wh*-extraction out of object NPs and conclude that the conditions for such extractions are largely semantic: only NPs that are participants may extract. Paolo Acquaviva considers 'The Morphological Dimension of Polarity Licensing' (*Linguistics* 40[2002] 925–59), and attributes the difference between *A/*Any child hasn't been born in this clinic for two years* to the fact that *any* needs a preceding overt licenser at the level of morphological structure.

(b) Early Syntax

We begin with a textbook on OE. Although the student-friendly tone of the preface that opens Peter S. Baker's *Introduction to Old English* may at first suggest otherwise, this is in fact a very solid and comprehensive textbook. Student-friendliness is also much to the fore in the fourteen 'minitexts', little practice texts scattered throughout the book's sixteen chapters, the accompanying exercises on the internet ('Old English Aerobics') and the extremely useful appendix A on 'Common Spelling Variants'. But there are no compromises on the fact that learning OE involves sustained effort. A brief 'Sermonette' in chapter 2 warns against sloppiness in looking up words and word forms, and urges students not to let the amount of scribal variation in spelling tempt them to think that 'anything goes' in OE, an attitude that easily leads them to blithe equations of, say, *biddan* 'pray, ask' and *bīdan* 'wait'. Students are also urged to familiarize themselves with the more distinctive endings, and are offered guidelines on which endings to look for. It is refreshing to find that the phonological origin of the alternations in morphological paradigms is given less prominence than in more traditional OE grammars, but the information is there nonetheless, briefly but accurately presented. After twelve chapters on grammar, there are a further four on metre, poetic style, the grammar of poetry and the reading of OE manuscripts. The second part of the book is an anthology of OE texts. There is a glossary covering not only the anthology and the 'minitexts' but also the many short passages illustrating grammar points. This is an excellent introduction.

Joseph and Janda, eds., *The Handbook of Historical Linguistics*, presents a survey of the field with sections on 'Methods for Studying Language Change' (part 2), 'Phonological Change' (part 3), 'Morphological and Lexical Change' (part 4), 'Syntactic Change' (part 5), 'Pragmatico-Semantic Change' (part 6), and 'Explaining Linguistic Change' (part 7). We will concentrate in what follows on parts 4 and 5. Raimo Anttila introduces part 4 with a chapter on analogy as an abstract concept: 'Analogy: The Warp and Woof of Cognition'. Anttila views analogy as a pervasive cognitive human property, powerful enough to account for the human language faculty all by itself. Hans Henrich Hock's contribution, 'Analogical Change', presents a survey of the different morphological processes that rely on analogy ('four-part analogy', 'levelling', 'contamination' and 'blending') and reviews the various ways in which analogy has been defined over the years. Wolfgang U. Dressler's 'Naturalness and Morphological Change' explains the theory of Natural Morphology and language change. The idea is that it is possible to formulate the most natural, optimal setting for various linguistic parameters, but that these options may conflict. Language types (analytic/synthetic/fusional, etc.) represent different responses to naturalness conflicts. The agglutinating type, for instance, has the advantages of form-meaning transparency, but the length of the resulting word represents a sacrifice of the optimal shape of morphological words. Brian D. Joseph has written a chapter on 'Morphologization from Syntax'. There are two directions for morphologization: either something in syntax can turn into morphology ('desyntacticization'), or something in phonology can morphologize ('dephonologization'). Both processes reflect a preference on the part of the speakers for a local rather than global solution. 'Grammatical Approaches to Syntactic Change', by David Lightfoot, views syntactic change as a change in the setting of a parameter during language acquisition. Susan Pintzuk, in 'Variationist Approaches to Syntactic Change', presents a more statistically oriented account of syntactic change, with changes in the position of the finite verb in OE as its case study. 'Cross-Linguistic Perspectives on Syntactic Change', by Alice C. Harris, presents some universal tendencies in diachronic syntax, with an examination of the processes by which biclausal constructions become monoclausal as a case study. 'Functional Perspectives on Syntactic Change', by Marianne Mithun, is a fine chapter illustrating the functional motivation of syntactic changes with examples primarily from the Eskimo–Aleut language family.

Several excellent discussions about the locus of language change have appeared this year, most prominently in *Syntactic Change: A Minimalist Approach to Grammaticalization* by Ian Roberts and Anna Roussou. In a formal theory like the Minimalist Program, the loss of lexical content and the concomitant gain in the functional domain which is typically found in grammaticalization translates as the heads of lexical projections becoming reanalysed as heads of functional projections. Once items have come to express functional rather than lexical information, there are various ways in which they can become associated with certain functional heads, with various consequences for their morphological status (bound, clitic, or free). In Roberts and Roussou's system, these ways are represented as parameter settings. Parameters are a finite set of syntactic options made available by UG. The PDE modals, for instance, are base-generated in the 'Mood' head ('Merge'; let's call it setting 1). A syntactic affix, like the subjunctive ending in OE, is not only merged in Mood but also requires movement to become attached to the verb ('Merge and Move'; setting 2). If it is not expressed by some designated overt element, material from elsewhere may have to move to Mood, typically the verb ('Move'; setting 3); an example of this is the pre-modals in ME, where the subjunctive mood started to be encoded by modal verbs which moved to Mood and were not yet base-generated there. It is of course also possible that a language gets away with not expressing this particular bit of functional information overtly at all, by neither a free nor a bound form—and as R&R's model assumes that the functional architecture of human language is invariant, i.e. that all possible functional projections are present in all languages, this seems to be a parameter of a higher order, with two settings, 'yes' or 'no': is this functional category expressed in this language or not? It is of course only if the answer is 'yes' that the three settings above come into play. It is the task of the language learner to determine from the input he or she is exposed to which settings are the ones that are compatible with the input received from this particular language. The examples in chapters 2, 3 and 4 contain eighteen case studies from the grammaticalization literature analysed along these lines: Romance future markers that start out as lexical verbs (e.g. French *chanterai*, ultimately derived from the Latin periphrasis *cantare habeo*), the modal particles *na* in Greek and *mu* in Calabrian, infinitival *to* deriving from a preposition, the complementizer *that* deriving from a demonstrative, etc. Chapter 5, 'Theoretical Consequences', recapitulates the formal similarities of the cases of the previous chapters and discusses the contribution of a formal framework to grammaticalization theory. Roberts and Roussou argue that syntactic change always represents structural simplification. Typical grammaticalization phenomena, such as phonological reduction and semantic bleaching, are reduced to the generalization that functional categories are defective at the interfaces of form and meaning (PF and LF): the lexical item loses all of its non-logical content, including its argument structure (LF interface) and is prosodically subminimal (PF interface). It is this latter feature that allows them to cliticize; a clitic is a phonologically bound element, which allows it to be re-analysed further into an affix, a morphologically bound element.

Here, too, we should mention Fuyo Osawa's 'Syntactic Parallels between Ontogeny and Phylogeny' (*Lingua* 113[2003] 3–47), which argues that the same mechanism of functional category maturation is at work in both diachrony and language acquisition. These approaches, which firmly identify the locus of language change in language acquisition, have nothing to say about the initial motivation (like greater expressivity) behind the first emergence of, say, modal verbs, but focus on the point when such forms acquire a momentum of their own when systematized by subsequent generations of learners, i.e. when there is a change in the 'I(nternal)-language'. Other scholars attach greater importance to 'E(xternal)-language' changes: Peter Matthews expresses doubt about the need for a deeper level of abstraction in explaining language change in 'On Change in "E-Language"' (in Hickey, ed., pp. 7–17). Frederick Newmeyer discusses the pros and cons of the two sides in the debate in 'Formal and Functional Motivation for Language Change' (in Hickey, ed., pp. 18–36). In 'Bringing Speakers Back In? Epistemological Reflections on Speaker-Oriented Explanations of Language Change', Ana Deumert (*LangS* 25[2003] 15–76), in a discussion of the strengths and limitations of speaker-oriented models, asks to what extent speakers can be said to be free agents. Here, too, belong James Milroy's 'On the Role of the Speaker in Language Change' (in Hickey, ed., pp. 143–57), which discusses the issues involved from a sociolinguistic viewpoint, and Markku Filppula's 'The Quest for the Most "Parsimonious" Explanations: Endogeny vs. Contact Revisited' (in Hickey, ed., pp. 161–73), which argues that a number of changes in some English varieties are due to a Celtic substrate rather than to independent internal developments. Jean Aitchison, in 'Metaphors, Models and Language Change' (in Hickey, ed., pp. 39–53) provides an inventory of the metaphors which have been employed to describe language change and how they may have influenced our thoughts on the subject. David Denison, in 'Log(ist)ic and Simplistic S-Curves' discusses the reality of the phenomenon of the S-curve in linguistic change (in Hickey, ed., pp. 54–70), which is such a pervasive image in language change that it is even implicitly implied to the history of English, with OE and PDE regarded as relatively invariant (slow parts of the curve) and ME as changing rapidly (steep part of the curve). Raymond Hickey looks at the emergence of NZE in 'How Do Dialects Get the Features They Have? On the Process of New Dialect Formation' (in Hickey, ed., pp. 213–39) and links migration patterns and family structure of the immigrant groups to the extent to which features from the input varieties 'made' it into the new dialect. Bernd Heine and Tania Kuteva, in 'On Contact-Induced Grammaticalization' (*SLang* 27 [2003] 529–72), argue that grammaticalization and language contact can work together to trigger grammatical change. More on grammaticalization can be found in David Lightfoot's 'Grammaticalization: Cause or Effect?' (in Hickey, ed., pp. 99–123), which argues against grammaticalization as an independent phenomenon; it is the result of the interplay between chance (i.e., local changes which make the input of the new generation slightly different from that of earlier ones) and necessity (UG constraining the child's choices in the construction of his/her grammar). Elizabeth Closs Traugott's 'From Subjectification to Intersubjectification' (in Hickey, ed., pp. 124–39) describes this grammaticalization path—where items go from expressing the speaker's cognitive stance to expressing that of the addressee—with examples taken from Japanese and English.

Although their main focus is on modern German, the following two papers are also relevant for the study of early English syntax, where many questions regarding the interaction between syntax and discourse (e.g. optionality) have long remained unaddressed. The first one is Cedric Boeckx's 'Free Word Order in Minimalist Syntax' (*FoLi* 37[2003] 77–102). In his quest for the best syntactic description of non-configurational languages, Boeckx summarizes and rejects previous analyses of scrambling in favour of an analysis that makes use of structures involving null resumptive elements. The second paper, 'Free Constituent Order: A Minimalist Interface Account' (*FoLi* 37[2003] 191–231), by Gisbert Fanselow, argues against incorporating discourse into syntax by trying to explain word order optionality in terms of attraction by 'pragmatic' features to a local specifier. Surface word order is also influenced by extra-syntactic principles, and from this it follows that it is not necessarily true that it is the frequent, 'unmarked' word order that reflects underlying structure. More work on Germanic that might be relevant to early syntax can be found in Dirk Bury's 'Selection and Head Chains' (*UCWPL* 15[2003] 177–211), which compares theories of phrase structure with and without categorial projection, and in this discussion offers an explanation of Sten Vikner's generalization that optional complementizers are only found in languages that lack obligatory verb movement (V2).

A general question about the history of English is asked by John McWhorter in 'What Happened to English?' (*Diachronica* 19[2002] 217–72). His answer is that in the Danelaw its transmission from one generation to the next was 'diluted', resulting in not exactly simplification, but less semantic overspecification and less syntactic overcomplexification in modern English than in other Germanic languages. The examples given concern inherently reflexive predicates, affected datives, gender, verbal prefixes, the auxiliaries of the perfect and passive, verb-second, second-person pronouns, and others. Merja Kytö and Terry Walker, in 'The Linguistic Study of Early Modern English Speech-Related Texts: How "Bad" Can "Bad" Data Be?' (*JEngL* 31[2003] 221–48), conclude that records that are contemporaneous with the speech event (trial transcriptions, witness depositions), though far from perfect, are still more revealing for the purposes of linguistic research than later printings and editions. Linda Georgianna, in 'Periodization and Politics: The Case of the Missing Twelfth Century in English Literary History' (*MLQ* 64[2003] 153–68), discusses the historical interpretation and reinterpretation of the Norman Conquest, and its consequences for periodization. Bruce Mitchell and Susan Irvine present 'A Critical Bibliography of Old English Syntax: *Supplement* 1993–1996, Parts I–III' (*NM* 103[2002] 3–32, 179–204, 275–304). They list 1,740 items, greatly facilitating the work of specialists trying to identify prior work on specific topics. A brief summary is provided of each item, and some have the honour (not always to be envied) of being singled out for further comment (a representative example being: 'These findings cannot be accepted as conclusive, given the slender evidence on which they are based and the vague terms in which they are couched', p. 195).

We now turn to individual elements of the clause. Hee-Cheol Yoon reflects on 'Economy Considerations and the Derivation of DP in Old English' (*HEng* 13[2002] 201–226). Using a Minimalist approach, the author proposes that demonstratives are merged in SpecDP but genitives can also move there; if both processes take place, the result is GEN-DEM-N order. Cynthia L. Allen's 'Deflexion and the Development of the Genitive in English' (*ELL* 7[2003] 1–28) discusses the history of the group genitive (as in *The King of England's daughter*) and the separated genitive (as in *my seid lorde Bysshop of Exeter is commaundement*). She presents evidence against the claim that the genitive could not remain as a morphological case once the other case distinctions had disappeared. Agata Rozumko offers 'Countable, Uncountable and Collective Nouns in the Early Eighteenth Century in English: An Overview' (*SAP* 37[2002] 131–59); many examples are given that would be unusual today (e.g. *an entertainment, assistances, six horse*), but no general tendencies emerge from them.

Dagmar Haumann, in 'The Postnominal "*and* Adjective" Construction in Old English' (*ELL* 7[2003] 57–83), argues that this construction (*Soðfæstne man & unscyldigne* 'a righteous person and guiltless') should be analysed as an instance of DP coordination with an empty nominal element in the second conjunct, which she identifies as *pro*. Isabel Moskowich considers 'The Adjective in English: The "French" Type and its Place in the History of the Language' (*FLH* 23[2002] 59–71). After a rather outdated discussion of some historical aspects of adjectives in general, she presents data on the postposing of French-derived adjectives in the period 1420–1500. Changes in the expression of the comparative form of the adjective—from a bound morpheme *-er* to a free form *more*—are charted by Jun Terasawa in 'A Sociohistorical Study of Periphrastic Comparison in English: Foreign Influence, Text Type and Individual Style' (in Ukaji et al., eds., pp. 191–207).

Subjects and verbs have inspired just a handful of studies. In 'The Change That Never Happened: The Story of Oblique Subjects' (*JL* 39[2003] 439–72), Jóhanna Barðdal argues that the syntactic status of oblique subjects (such as *me* in *methinks*) in the Germanic languages had always been that of subject, rather than object, *contra* certain standard claims in the literature, though the counterclaim has in fact been made before, in particular by Cynthia Allen in 1986 (*JL* 22) and 1995 (in her book on *Case Marking and Reanalysis*, OUP). Rafał Molencki writes about 'The Status of *Dearr* and *Þearf* in Old English' (*SAP* 38[2002] 363–80). These verbs coalesced in ME, but were clearly distinct in OE, as Molencki's full description testifies. The auxiliary of the future is studied by Merja Kytö and the late Andrei Danchev in 'The *Go*-Futures in English and French as an Areal Feature' (*NOWELE* 40[2002] 29–60). After considering the historical evidence, their conclusion is that futurate uses of *go* may well have diffused from French into English (as well as southern Dutch and Luxembourg German) but that their reception was eased because late ME was developing various types of verbal periphrasis anyway. Michiko Ogura, in '*Have Do Make* and *Have Do and Make* in the *Paston Letters*' (*N&Q* 248[2003] 8–10), suggests that *and* in the latter construction makes it less causative, while *do* in the former construction is possibly a forerunner of later periphrastic *do*.

We move on to adverbial elements of various types. Bélen Méndez-Naya, in 'On Intensifiers and Grammaticalization: The Case of *Swiþe*' (*ES* 84[2003] 372–91), tracks the development of this adverb from 'to a strong extent' to a scalar intensifier 'very' and suggests a possible grammaticalization path: adverb in adjunct function associated with verbs like *feohtian* 'fight' where its original meaning of 'strong' is still in evidence ≥ degree reading with these verbs ≥ degree reading with any verb ≥ degree reading with predicative participles ≥ intensifier. Alfred Bammesberger considers 'The Syntactic Analysis of *Beowulf*, Lines 750–754' (*Neophil* 86[2002] 303–6); he proposes that the crucial word *sona* (usually taken to be short for *sona swa* 'as soon as') is actually an adverb, meaning 'immediately'. Diana M. Lewis studies 'Rhetorical Motivations for the Emergence of Discourse Particles, with Special Reference to English *Of*

Course' (*BJL* 16[2002] 79–91), tracing the historical development of *of course* from VP adverb to S' adverb. Luis Iglesias-Rábade, in 'A Semantic Study of *On*-Phrases in Middle English' (*SN* 75[2003] 104–18), tabulates the spatial and temporal uses of prepositional phrases with *on* in the Helsinki Corpus. Hanna Rutkowska, in 'Toward a More Analytic Expression of Grammatical Relationships: The Use of Prepositions and Adverbs in Early English Correspondence' (*SAP* 38[2002] 411–32), provides examples of prepositions and adverbs of various types in various constructions in the *Cely Letters*—the factor unifying them is that they could be said to express meaning analytically rather than synthetically. Marion Elenbaas, in 'Particle Verbs in Early Middle English: The Case of *Up*' (*LIN* 20[2003] 45–57), concludes that this particle was still a secondary predicate (i.e. a phrase) in OE and eME, rather than a particle (a head), as it subsequently became.

We now come to phenomena that affect the clause as a whole. Richard Ingham, in 'Negated Subjects and Objects in 15th-Century Nonliterary English' (*LVC* 14[2002] 291–322), shows that these elements are found in two contexts where their non-negative counterparts do not occur: in transitive expletive constructions (*There has no-one asked about it*) and in preverbal position (*They could nothing say*). In both cases, Ingham argues, the negative element has moved to the specifier of the functional projection NegP. The decline of verb-second is investigated by Bjørg Bækken in her *Word Order in 17th Century English: A Study of the Stabilisation of the XSV Pattern*, based on all declarative main clauses not starting with the subject in *circa* 2,500 pages of prose texts. Among the many findings are: that negative initial elements increasingly trigger inversion, while non-negative elements do so less and less often; that inversion clauses often have a nominal subject and an intransitive or passive verb; that the length of the initial element does not have a very clear effect on inversion rates; that the subject in inverted clauses often conveys new information; that affirmative declarative *do* is frequent in inverted clauses; that there is considerable intertextual and intratextual variability in the occurrence of verb-second; and that the eventual stabilization of word order progresses by leaps and bounds. Anna Bondaruk and Magdalena Charzyńska-Wójcik, in 'Expletive *pro* in Impersonal Passives in Irish, Polish and Old English' (*LingB* 195[2003] 325–62), present a typological comparison of these languages and argue that impersonal passives in OE, in contrast to the other two, are genuinely subjectless: there is never a nominative subject and the past participle is never inflected for subject agreement. Scholars of English historical linguistics might also find James P. Blevins's 'Passives and Impersonals' (*JL* 39[2003], 473–520) of interest, in spite of the fact that his data are taken from German, Finnic, Slavic and Celtic, as he presents a survey of the properties of passive versus impersonal constructions that are also very relevant to the study of OE and ME. 'On the Development of English Adverbial Connectives', by Matti Rissanen (in Ukaji et al., eds., pp. 229–47) tries to account for the increase in the inventory of connectives like *as long as, save, except, unless* in ME. Masamoto Ukaji's ' Subject Zero Relatives in Early Modern English' (in Ukaji et al., eds., pp. 248–77) looks at sentences of the type *There is nobody loves me*. 'The Relationship between the Decline of

Multiple Negation and the Development of Non-Assertive *Any* in Later Middle English', by Yoko Iyeiri (in Ukaji et al., eds., pp. 208–28) charts the decline of sentences like *None of you shall have no part of her* and the rise of *None of you shall have any part of her*.

5. Semantics

Peregrin, ed., *Meaning: The Dynamic Turn*, is an excellent new collection in the Current Research in the Semantics/Pragmatics Interface series by Routledge. Its aim is to take a look at the conceptual foundations of dynamic semantics, one of the most important current theoretical approaches to the formal study of meaning, which parts with the conception of language as a static system and takes meanings as involving context-change potentials. The contributors are leading authorities in the field, who, instead of concentrating on technical details, take a look at some fundamental issues of the theory, with the aim of investigating the nature of meaning. The contributions to the first part of the collection concentrate on foundational questions like why we should think that meaning is dynamic, what dynamicity of meaning means and what it implies for the methodology. 'Structural Properties of Dynamic Reasoning', by Johan van Benthem, investigates the nature of dynamic inference. Noor van Leusen and Reinhard Muskens argue, in 'Construction by Description in Discourse Representation', that important parts of the Discourse Representation Theory construction algorithm (cf. Kamp 1981, Kamp and Ryle 1993), which is highly procedural, can be given a purely declarative, logical formulation. Richard Breheny, 'On the Dynamic Turn in the Study of Meaning and Interpretation', takes stock of linguistic phenomena that have been argued to provide empirical motivation for dynamic semantics, and shows about one of them—the fact that semantic content is underdetermined by static linguistic meaning—that it cannot adequately be handled by dynamic theories either. Lastly, Wolfram Hitzen's 'Real Dynamics' investigates the status of semantic theory in the study of language. The chapters in the second part illustrate the application of dynamic approaches to the analysis of different domains of phenomena. In 'Growth of Logical Form: The Dynamics of Syntax', Ruth Kempson, Wilfried Meyer-Viol and Masayuki Otsuka suggest, by presenting analyses of anaphora, relative clauses and quantifier construal, that syntax might be the only place where the dynamics of language is grounded. Klaus von Heusinger presents a dynamic semantic analysis of definite descriptions ('The Double Dynamics of Definite Descriptions'), and Petr Sgall, 'Dynamics in the Meaning of the Sentence and of Discourse', discusses the interplay of semantics and the workings of discourse in the process of identifying coreferential antecedents of definite NPs and anaphoric pronouns. Two chapters are concerned with the semantics of imperatives: Berislav Žarnić's 'Imperative Negation and Dynamic Semantics' argues for a dynamic approach to the meaning of negative imperatives, which can incorporate the thesis that an atomic sentence and its negation belong to the same category, whereas the chapter by Timothy Childers and Vladimír Svoboda puts forth a dynamic analysis 'On the Meanings of Prescriptions'. The third part of the book discusses dynamic extensions of the classical game-theoretical approach to semantics, featuring essays by Tapio Janasik and Gabriel Sandu ('Dynamic Game Semantics'), Manuel Rebuschi ('About Games and Substitution'), and Louise Vigeant ('In Defense of Some Verificationism: Verificationism and Game-Theoretical Semantics').

The aim of Schwabe and Winkler, eds., *The Interfaces: Deriving and Interpreting Omitted Structures*, is to contribute to the study of the set-up of the interfaces between phonology, syntax and semantics, discourse, and the information structural component of grammar by investigating new evidence from the research of ellipsis and omitted elements. The contributions address questions related to the representation and interpretation of ellipsis and the role of focusing and information structure in the latter. They fall into three categories depending on the nature of the answer they provide to these questions. The first type of approach is to consider ellipsis a PF-deletion. Christopher Kennedy's 'Ellipsis and Syntactic Representation' shows, by investigating various types of constructions (VP-ellipsis, attributive comparative deletion, pseudogapping), that ellipsis constructions are sensitive to configurational constraints on syntactic representations. Further representatives of the approach are Jason Merchant's 'Subject-Auxiliary Inversion in Comparatives and PF Output Constraints', an analysis of subject-auxiliary inversion with VP-ellipsis in comparative constructions, as in *Abby knows more languages than does her father* as deletion at PF, Chris Wilder's investigation of 'Antecedent Containment and Ellipsis', and Katharina Hartmann's 'Background Matching in Right Node Raising Constructions', which formulates a pragmatic well-formedness condition that serves as a licensing condition on ellipsis at PF. A second group of essays accounts for various kinds of ellipsis in terms of syntactic displacement, such as the one by Caterina Donati ('Merge Copy'), which puts forward the proposal that movement and ellipsis should be considered the same operation, the essay by Winfried Lechner on 'Phrase Structure Paradoxes, Movement and Ellipsis', arguing for the sameness of VP-fronting and VP-deletion, the contribution by Uli Sauerland ('Unpronounced Heads in Relative Clauses'), defending the view that matching relative clauses involve ellipsis and not movement, and the study by Luis López and Susanne Winkler ('Variation at the Syntax-Semantics Interface'), which provides additional support for the view proposed by Kyle Johnson [1997] that gapping does not involve deletion but across-the-board movement of the verb. A third group of essays explores the semantic properties of silent elements. Daniel Hardt, 'Ellipsis and the Structure of Discourse', proposes that possible readings of clauses containing some form of ellipsis do not only have to show structural parallelism with some antecedent clause, but the two have to stand in a discourse relation as well. Maribel Romero, 'Correlate Restriction and Definiteness Effects in Ellipsis', and Kerstin Schwabe, 'Focus Marking and Specificity in Sluicing Constructions', argue that the semantic restrictions on the well-formedness of sluicing constructions and reduced conditionals can be accounted for in terms of the semantics of questions and focus. Petra Gretsch, in 'Omission Impossible: Topic and Focus in Focal Ellipsis', investigates a less studied construction, one in which the focus exponent is included in the omitted part of the structure.

Kühnlein, Rieser and Zeevat, eds., *Perspectives on Dialogue in the New Millennium*, contains essays concerned with the formal modelling of dialogue.

With the growth of the market for human–machine interfaces, not only representatives of the humanities but also computer scientists and artificial intelligence experts have begun to take an interest in the formal regularities of inter-human interaction. The volume, which has grown out of the proceedings of one instalment of a workshop series on the formal semantics and pragmatics of dialogue (BI-DIALOG [2001]), reports results of new theoretical work as well as implementations in formal and technical systems. The essays in the volume most relevant to the semanticist include the written version of Alex Lascarides and Nicholas Ascher's keynote presentation at the conference, 'Imperatives in Dialogue', which proposes an account of the semantics and the logical properties of imperative utterances in terms of Segmented Discourse Representation Theory. Etsuko Oishi's 'Semantic Meaning and Four Types of Speech Act' proposes to redefine the domain of semantics to include, in addition to truth-conditional meaning, social meaning as well as the meaning of performatives.

The aim of Francis and Michaelis, eds., *Mismatch: Form-Function Congruity and the Architecture of Grammar*, is to investigate the general implications of form-function mismatch phenomena for the general architecture of grammatical theory. The contributions to the volume concentrate on four problem areas: mismatch in complex predicates, categorial mismatch, mismatch and coercion, and mismatch in grammar. Complex predication is considered as an instance of mismatch since it involves multiple elements on at least one level of representation that at some other level behave like a single lexical verb, (contributions by Alex Alsina, Farrell Ackerman and Adele Goldberg). Categorial mismatch involves an unusual mapping between syntactic category information and semantic information, which seems to necessitate separating syntactic category information from other kinds of information in grammar, as argued by Frederick J. Newmeyer, Etsuyo Yuasa and Elaine J. Francis. Coercion takes place when there is a mismatch between the semantic type required by a given operator and the semantic type with which that operator is actually combined. Henriëtte de Swart's 'Coercion in a Cross-Linguistic Theory of Aspect' shows how coercion operators can solve aspectual mismatches cross-linguistically. Laura A. Michaelis, in 'Headless Constructions and Coercion by Construction', argues for a constructional approach as opposed to the modular one exemplified by de Swart's contribution, to account for cases of coercion in nominal syntax, in cases of mismatch between the event type denoted by the head verb and the event type denoted by the sentence, as well as for aspectual coercion. Maria Mercedes Piñango discusses coercion effects from a psycholinguistic and neurolinguistic perspective, whereas the contributions by Jerrold M. Sadock, Richard Hudson and Robert Malouf concentrate on the theoretical side of the problem of mismatch.

Barss, ed., *Anaphora: A Reference Guide*, is concerned with the study of linguistic expressions which receive part or all of their semantic interpretation via a dependency upon an antecedent, rather than from their internal lexical content. Andrew Barss's own contribution, 'Timing Puzzles in Anaphora and Interpretation', presents a new model of the syntax-semantics mapping according to which the logico-semantic representation of the sentence is built up parallel with the syntactic derivation, in which anaphoric reconstruction is seen as an instance of a formation of syntactically constrained semantic relations in the middle of an ongoing derivation. In 'Tense and Anaphora: Is There a Tense-Specific Theory of Coreference?', Karen Zagona proposes a new theory of anaphoric relations between tenses. She argues that temporal anaphora is non-existent, and observed interactions between tenses can all be accounted for on the basis of Condition A of the binding theory and relations between aspect and mood in a hierarchical syntactic structure, there being no distinction between temporal arguments and standard arguments. D. Terence Langendoen and Joël Magloire's 'The Logic of Reflexivity and Reciprocity' proposes an account of the logical properties of simple reflexive and reciprocal sentences, which is based on the assumption that these properties result from the interaction of the 'plural properties of the predicate', the core meanings of reflexivity and reciprocity, and from whether reflexivity and reciprocity is expressed overtly by an anaphor or covertly by incorporation into a corresponding one-place predicate.

Gutiérrez-Rexach, ed., *Semantics: Critical Concepts in Linguistics*, is a large-scale six-volume undertaking by Routledge to collect the most influential papers to have shaped the development of semantic theory in the last thirty years, together with a few classics (see below). The six volumes in this largest-ever published compilation devoted to semantics contain more than a hundred papers grouped around several descriptive topics. They fall into two categories: they either appeared originally in leading journals, already having generated a lot of discussion, or they originate from less known conference proceedings or collections of papers, and have been included in the volume so that they could receive more attention. The latter group also includes papers which can be considered a summary of the main ideas expressed in book-length studies: for example, Henriëtte de Swart's 'Quantification Over Time', Terence Parsons's 'Underlying Events in the Logical Analysis of English', Henk Verkuyl's 'Aspectual Asymmetry and Quantification', or Sjaak de Mey's 'Generalized Quantifier Theory and the Semantics of Focus', or sections from dissertations, such as the papers by Kai von Fintel and Enric Vallduví.

Volume 1 is devoted to foundational issues in the conceptual and methodological development of the discipline, i.e. papers discussing the relation between truth and denotation, by Gottlob Frege, Bertrand Russell, Peter F. Strawson, and Rudolph Carnap, and studies investigating the architecture of the semantics component of grammar, by Jerrold Katz and Paul Postal, Richard Montague, David Lewis, Noam Chomsky, George Lakoff, Barbara Partee, Robert May, Richard Larson and Gabriel Segal, and a recent, still unpublished paper by Carlos P. Otero. The second volume contains papers discussing noun phrase semantics, particularly the interpretation of quantificational NPs in terms of Generalized Quantifier Theory and cross-linguistic phenomena of scope interaction, by Jon Barwise and Robin Cooper, William Ladusaw, Johan van Benthem, Franciska de Jongh and Henk Verkuyl, Dag Westerståhl, Barbara Partee, Edward Keenan, Gila Sher, Donka Farkas, Fengh-Hsi Liu, Dorit Ben-Shalom and Anna Szabolcsi. Continuing with noun phrase semantics, volume 3 concentrates on two ways of classifying NPs. The papers by David Lewis, Lauri Karttunen, Gary Milsark, Janet Fodor and Ivan Sag, Irene Heim, Edward Keenan, Alessandro Zucchi, Mürvet Enç, Molly Diesing, Veerle van Geenhoven, and Yoad Winter are concerned with the interpretation of indefinite versus definite NPs, and the exceptional semantic properties of indefinite NPs, namely (1) that when they appear in the restriction of an adverb of quantification they get their quantificational force from this quantifier, (2) that they can occur in the post-copular position of existential sentences, and (3) that they can also have specific readings. The contributions by Greg Carlson, Remko Scha, Godehard Link, Brendan Gillon, Peter Lasersohn, Roger Schwarzschild, Almerindo Ojeda and Gennaro Chierchia discuss the interpretation of plurals and mass nouns. These papers represent different points of view in the debate whether collective and distributive readings of sentences containing plural NPs should be located in the verb or in the noun phrase. Volume 4 contains papers discussing predicate semantics, falling into two categories: those by Zeno Vendler, Terence Parsons, Emmon Bach, Henk Verkuyl, James Pustejovsky, Greg Carlson, Malka Rappaport and Beth Levin, and David Dowty are concerned with events, aspect and thematic roles, whereas those by Hans Reichenbach, David Dowty, Mürvet Enç, Dorit Abusch, Marc Moens and Mark Steedman, Dorit Abusch, Toshiyuki Ogihara, Henriëtte de Swart, Angelika Kratzer, Donka Farkas, and Paul Portner investigate problems of tense and modality. Volume 5 has the subtitle *Operators and Sentence Types*, and contains studies on adjectival modification (by Hans Kamp, Max J. Cresswell, Jean-Yves Lerner and Manfred Pinkal, and Christopher Kennedy) as well as contributions on the issue of negation and negative polarity (by Gilles Fauconnier, Jack Hoeksema, Nirit Kadmon and Fred Landman, Frans Zwarts, and William Ladusaw). The sub-collection on questions includes papers by Lauri Karttunen, James Higginbotham and Robert May, Jeroen Groenendijk and Martin Stokhof, Stephen Berman, Utpal Lahiri, Jonathan Ginzburg, Veneeta Dayal, James Higginbotham and Javier Gutiérrez-Rexach. The last volume, entitled *Discourse and Dynamics*, comprises a discussion of phenomena such as topic-focus articulation, and the interpretation of pronouns across fragments of discourse, which 'push the standard "static" semantic theory to its limits' (p. 1). Topic and focus are discussed by Barbara Partee, Manfred Krifka, Sjaak de Mey, and Daniel Büring, pronouns and anaphora by Peter Geach, Gareth Evans, Hans Kamp, Craige Roberts, Paul Dekker, Gennaro Chierchia, Jeroen Groenendijk, Martin Stokhof and Frank Veltman, and Chris Barker, whereas the collection on the semantics/pragmatics interface includes contributions by Robert Stalnaker, David Lewis, Enric Vallduví, Kai von Fintel, Dov Gabbay and Ruth Kempson, and by Nicholas Asher. Although the system of selection for inclusion in the volume may be debatable (most papers represent the American linguistic tradition), the result is definitely a must-read for anyone wishing to start research on any of the topics listed above.

The monograph *The Semantics of Incorporation: From Argument Structure to Discourse Transparency* by Donka F. Farkas and Henriëtte de Swart is concerned with the semantics of incorporated nominals, i.e. those nominals that 'form a particularly tight unit with the predicate they are arguments of' (p. 1). Although the primary aim of the authors is to account for nominal incorporation in Hungarian, a language which makes a syntactic and semantic distinction between morphologically singular versus plural incorporated nominals (the former being number neutral, syntactically restricted, and exhibiting reduced discourse visibility, while the latter are semantically plural, syntactically free, and fully discourse-transparent), the study has wide-ranging implications for the cross-linguistic study of incorporation as well as discourse anaphora. The above regularities, well known in the literature, are explained in a version of Discourse Representation Theory, in which discourse referents and thematic arguments are separated from each other. Whereas thematic arguments are part of the predicative conditions contributed by lexical predicative expressions such as nouns, verbs and adjectives, discourse referents are introduced by determiners, proper nouns and pronouns. The authors then claim that singular incorporated nominals are predicative, i.e., contribute a predicative condition involving a thematic argument but introduce no discourse referent, whereas bare plurals introduce a discourse referent into the presuppositional structure of the sentence. The authors argue that the present framework can successfully be extended to the analysis of other languages involving incorporation, such as Hindi, Chamorro and West Greenlandic.

A volume from the Outstanding Dissertations in Linguistics series, published by Routledge, deserves attention this year. Yael Greenberg's *Manifestations of Genericity* takes a new look at two kinds of generic sentence in English, which at first sight appear to be almost synonymous: those containing indefinite singular subjects (IS sentences), such as *A dog has four legs*, and those with bare plural subjects, such as *Dogs bark* (BP sentences). Although the differences between the semantic, pragmatic and distributional features of these two types of generic sentence have already been observed in the literature, they have never been incorporated into a formal theory of genericity. This is the task undertaken by Greenberg in this book. She argues that the basic underlying reason for the differences is that, whereas IS sentences can only express 'in virtue of' generalizations—i.e. the fact that 'the generalization is nonaccidentally true in virtue of some inherent property or factor, associated with the denotation of the subject'—BP sentences can express both 'in virtue of' and 'descriptive' generalizations, asserting that 'the generalization is simply non-accidentally true, without specifying any factor in virtue of which it is true' (p. xxii). The author claims that both kinds of generalization should be represented as quantified, modalized tripartite structures, which, however, differ in the kind of modality they involve, i.e. in the characterization of the set of accessible worlds relative to which the universal statement is evaluated.

Turning to work related to semantics and its interfaces, Robyn Carston's *Thoughts and Utterances: The Pragmatics of Explicit Communication*, which investigates the semantics/pragmatics interface, is worth mentioning. The central thesis of the book is that the linguistic semantics of an utterance underdetermines the proposition expressed by it, and the hearer has to use processes of pragmatic inference to work out not only what the speaker is implying but also what proposition she is directly expressing, and, therefore, that linguistic undeterminacy is an essential feature of natural languages. Carston argues that the relation between the encoded linguistic meaning and the proposition explicitly communicated is mediated through a variety of pragmatic processes. This general proposal is illustrated by means of a Relevance Theoretic analysis of the semantics/pragmatics of three types of construction: 'and'-conjunctions, negation, and loose (including metaphorical) uses of linguistically encoded meaning. As to the first one, the author rejects semantic approaches that attribute the various possible temporal and cause–consequence relations between conjuncts to the meaning of 'and' itself, and argues for a position in which they are considered cases of enrichment, contributing to the proposition expressed by the utterance. Negation can also be given a univocal, truth-functional semantics, claims the author, in which the negative operator is assumed to have a maximally wide scope, and all other interpretations (narrow-scope understanding, constituent negation, the presupposition-preserving meaning, objection to some echoed material) are the result of enrichment at the level of the proposition expressed by the sentence. Loose use (including certain kinds of figurative use such as metaphor and hyperbole), however, is accounted for in terms of the complementary processes of loosening or broadening of the encoded conceptual content. It is argued that processes of pragmatic narrowing and broadening of encoded lexical meaning are the norm in understanding utterances.

A collection investigating issues of interest both to linguists and philosophers is Richard, ed., *Meaning*. The volume contains a representative sample of philosophical work on meaning produced in the last hundred years, most of which can be considered as a reaction to Gottlob Frege's work on meaning, the most important inventions of which are discussed in the essay 'On Sense and Reference', the opening piece of the collection. Further contributions include classic essays and excerpts from longer work by Saul A. Kripke, Hilary Putnam, W.V. Quine, and Donald Davidson, as well as more recent reactions to this work by Paul Horwich, Scott Soames, Jody Azzouni, James Higginbotham, John Perry, Frank Jackson, and Mark Wilson, on topics such as analyticity, translational indeterminacy, theories of reference, meaning as use, the nature of linguistic competence, truth and meaning, and relations between semantics and metaphysics. The collection is supplemented by an introduction by the editor, providing the philosophical context for the works to follow.

Per Hasle, Peter Øhrstrøm, Torben Braüner, and Jack Copeland have provided a new edition of the collection of papers by Arthur N. Prior, *Papers on Time and Tense*. This collection, together with Prior's two previous works, *Time and Modality* and *Past, Present and Future*, form the core of Prior's modern temporal logic, which until the present day has constituted a reference point for investigations into the meaning of tense in natural languages. As the editors emphasize in their introduction, this collection, as opposed to Prior's other two studies, which introduce the basic ideas of temporal logic, suggests a number of open issues and establishes connections to other philosophical topics; it should therefore be viewed as work in progress. This new edition was already planned by the author himself one year after the first edition in 1969, but his untimely death meant that he was not able to carry it through. The papers in the second edition are exactly those that Prior intended to include himself, but the editors have changed the logical notation from a Polish into a Russellian one. They have added 'Editors' Notes', which contribute to a better understanding of the text. Also included are an interview with Dr Mary Prior, the wife of the late philosopher, on his life and his philosophical and logical views, and a bibliography of Prior's work.

Marcus Kracht's acclaimed textbook, *The Mathematics of Language*, is a must for those who have solid foundations in mathematics and intend to understand the formal structure of language, i.e. the principles underlying the description of language with mathematical methods. The main emphasis is on the formal foundations of syntax and semantics; issues related to the latter include the basic concepts of algebraic logic, boolean semantics, questions of intensionality, binding and quantification, the possibilities and limitations of Montague semantics and questions of partiality and presupposition.

Theoretical Linguistics devotes its third issue to a critical discussion of the Natural Semantics Metalanguage (NSM) approach developed by Anna Wierzbicka and her colleagues. NSM theory rejects the use of any formal language for the description of meanings. It proposes that the meaning of all natural language expressions can be described with the help of paraphrases, all of which involve a minimal set of linguistic items ('the alphabet of human thoughts'), regarded as universal semantic primitives. Consequently, a semantic explication consists of sentence-like expressions in ordinary language. In the target article, 'The Natural Semantic Metalanguage Approach to Linguistic Meaning' (*TL* 29[2003] 157–200) Uwe Durst provides an overview about the history of the theory, summarizes the theoretical basis of the NSM model, which includes the indefinability of the semantic primitives, their universality, indispensability, and combinability, illustrates the method of how semantic explications are prepared, and mentions some fields of linguistics where this approach proves particularly useful. Cliff Goddard's comment in 'Natural Semantics Metalanguage: Latest Perspectives' (*TL* 29[2003] 227–36) aims to supplement Durst's exposition by elaborating on the syntax of the NSM metalanguage. The other comments on the target article concentrate on the difficulties this approach faces when applied to the characterization of the meaning of particular domains of phenomena. Chris Barker's 'Paraphrase Is Not Enough' (*TL* 29[2003] 201–9) identifies, among the challenges to this kind of approach, the treatment of names, natural kind terms, and cases where meanings interact with linguistic structure, i.e. the treatment of indexicals, presuppositions, and performatives. Jürgen Bohnemeyer's 'NSM Without the Strong Lexicalization Hypothesis' (*TL* 29[2003] 211–22) discusses the non-verifiability of the hypotheses of the NSM approach. Bart Geurts, in 'Semantics as Lexicography' (*TL* 29[2003] 223–6), expresses his scepticism about the enterprise by stressing that it is not in the position to make any claims about some of the most central issues in semantics such as quantification, pronouns and their antecedents, and non-lexical semantics, and by questioning the validity of its philosophical approach to meaning and its methodology. Paul Kay, in 'NSM and the Meaning of Color Words' (*TL* 29[2003] 237–45), criticizes the theory for the obscurity of the semantic explications, by investigating its treatment of colour words. Maria Koptjevskaja-Tamm and Inger Ahlgren's 'NSM: Theoretical, Methodological and Applicational Problems' (*TL* 29[2003] 247–61) elaborates on the theoretical and methodological problems of determining what counts as a semantic primitive, on the issue of whether semantic universals have to be lexical, and on an applicational problem: to what extent does the idea of a monolingual dictionary carried out in accordance with NSM principles make sense? Lisa Matthewson, in 'Is the Meta-language Really Natural?' (*TL* 29[2003] 263–74), argues that the primitives of NSM do not in fact correspond directly to English lexical items, and are not directly translatable into other languages either; she also comments on the lack of transparency in NSM explications arising from the avoidance of referential indices. Laura A. Michaelis, 'NSM and Cognitive-Functional Models of Grammar' (*TL* 29[2003] 275–81), claims that the NSM approach has no way of capturing the contribution of syntax to interpretation. Finally, Nick Reimer, in 'Servant of Two Masters' (*TL* 29[2003] 283–94), comments on the impossibility of co-ordinating the pedagogical aims of NSM with its aspiration to be considered a semantic theory, and the controversies arising from its aspiration to simplicity.

Among journal articles discussing the interaction of information structure with meaning, H. Bernhard Drubig's 'Toward a Typology of Focus and Focus Constructions' (*Linguistics* 41[2003] 1–50) argues in favour of considering focus a syntactic feature assigned freely to word-level categories at numeration, licensed by integration into a wider domain (presentational focus) or by overt/covert movement to a functional projection headed by a polarity formative (focus operator constructions). Hanneke van Hoof's 'The Rise in the Rise–Fall Contour: Does it Evoke a Contrastive Topic or a Contrastive Focus?' (*Linguistics* 41[2003] 515–63), and Daniel Büring's 'On D-Trees, Beans, and B-Accents' (*Ling&P* 26[2003] 511–45), represent two contrasting views in an ongoing debate about the semantics/pragmatics of sentences containing a constituent pronounced with a B-accent and one with an A-accent in English (cf. Bolinger [1965], Jackendoff [1972]), and their cross-linguistic counterparts. The former argues for the position that sentences of the above type are multiple-focus constructions, on the basis of data indicating that they are natural answers to matching questions. The latter study arrives at an opposite conclusion from the same data, arguing that such sentences never constitute complete answers to matching questions, and therefore the B-accent should be viewed as a means to signal the presence of a discourse structure in which the main question under consideration is not answered in one go, but via a division into sub-questions. Daniel Glatz and Ralf Klabunde analyse the factors that determine focusing in language production by examining retellings of stories by speakers, in 'Focus as Perspectivation' (*Linguistics* 41[2003] 947–77). They claim that minimal foci, identifiable on the basis of prosodic information, and maximal foci, derived with the help of the percolation rules (as proposed for German in Günther [1999]) serve different functions: minimal foci express contrast, whereas maximal foci express newness. David Beaver and Brady Clark, in '*Always* and *Only*: Why Not All Focus-Sensitive Operators are Alike' (*NLS* 11[2003] 323–62), show that, for *only*, it is the lexical meaning of the word that encodes a dependency on focus marking, whereas the focus sensitivity of *always* is a result of its dependency on context. In 'Additive Particles and Polarity' (*JSem* 20[2003] 329–401), Hotze Rullmann discusses the semantics of the additive focus particles *too* and *either* and the factors governing the alternation between the two.

Among studies on the semantics of verbal expressions, we should mention Paul Portner's monosemous account of the English present perfect, 'The (Temporal)

Semantics and (Modal) Pragmatics of the Perfect' (*Ling&P* 26[2003] 459–510), which is based on the claim that the English present perfect involves two fundamental concepts of meaning: a truth-conditional one involving temporal notions and a current relevance presupposition best expressed in terms drawn from the analysis of modality. Yael Sharvit argues, in 'Trying to be Progressive: The Extensionality of Try' (*JSem* 20[2003] 403–45), that the semantics of *try* is different from that of the other attitude verbs and should be captured on the pattern of the interpretation of the progressive. Fritz Hamm and Michiel van Lambalgen's 'Event Calculus, Nominalisation, and the Progressive' (*Ling&P* 26[2003] 381–458) combines the event calculus familiar from Artificial Intelligence with Soloman Feferman's theory of truth to treat a group of phenomena including nominalization, *Aktionsart* and the progressive.

Regarding the interpretation of tenses and temporality, Silvia P. Gennari takes a new look at the interpretation of embedded tenses in 'Tense Meanings and Temporal Interpretation' (*JSem* 20[2003] 35–71), and proposes a mechanism by which the interpretation of the latter can be derived on the basis of the interaction of tense meanings and general facts of the grammar such as *Aktionsart* properties, and without relying on a sequence of tense rule or other specific mechanisms. In 'Temporal Adjectives and the Structure of Possessive DPs' (*NLS* 11[2003] 217–47), Richard Larson and Sungeun Cho take the ambiguity of temporal adjectives such as *former* in *John's former car* to suggest that the structure of possessive nominals matches that of possessive clauses, which, furthermore, supports recent work pointing towards parallels between nominal and clausal structure.

Moving on to nominal semantics, Edward E. Keenan's study 'The Definiteness Effect: Semantics or Pragmatics?' (*NLS* 11[2003] 187–216) deserves particular attention. It proposes a semantic account of the distribution of DPs in existential *there*-sentences in English, using only generalized quantifiers and relying only on judgements of truth conditions and entailment, and defends it against the pragmatic analysis of Zucchi [1995]. Malte Zimmermann's 'Pluractionality and Complex Quantifier Formation' (*NLS* 11[2003] 289–321) investigates two constructions in which an adjective takes scope out of its embedding DP as in *The occasional sailor strolled by* and *Individual students entered the room.* He argues that in the former case the adjective incorporates into the determiner of its DP, forming a complex quantifier, which then has to be analysed as a pluractionality quantifier in the sense of Lasersohn [1995], whereas the latter involves a movement of the adjective to [Spec,DP]. Rick Nouwen looks at 'Complement Anaphora and Interpretation' (*JSem* 20[2003] 73–113). The term refers to the phenomenon where, given a quantificational sentence of the structure D(A)(B), a subsequent anaphor refers back to the set corresponding to $A \cap -B$. For example, *they* in *Few students came to the talk, they went to the movies* is an anaphor of the above type if it refers back to the students who did not come to the talk. The starting point for Philippe Schlenker's 'A Plea for Monsters' (*Ling&P* 26[2003] 29–120) is David Kaplan's 1989 theory, according to which indexicals are directly referential: they pick out their referents directly from the context of utterance, and, consequently, the value of an indexical is fixed once and for all by the context of utterance, and cannot be affected by the logical operators in the scope of which they appear. The value of indexicals could therefore be shifted only with the help of operators which shift the context of evaluation of an indexical. Whereas Kaplan does not believe that such operators, 'monsters', could exist in natural language, Schlenker claims that they do: we use one each time we report somebody's speech or thought.

Kai von Fintel and Sabine Iatridou's 'Epistemic Containment' (*LingI* 34[2003] 173–98) investigates a constraint on the interaction of quantifier phrases and epistemic modals, referred to as the Epistemic Containment Principle: a quantifier cannot have scope over an epistemic modal. The authors argue that this condition should be considered an LF-intervention effect, where a quantifier-trace chain cannot cross an epistemic modal. In 'Presuppositions and Implicatures in Counterfactuals' (*NLS* 11[2003] 145–86), Michela Ippolito offers a semantic account of past subjunctive conditionals that talk about the future, as in *If Charlie had taken his Advanced Italian test tomorrow, he would have passed*. Gerhard Jäger's 'Towards an Explanation of Copula Effects' (*Ling&P* 26[2003] 557–93) explains the semantic contrast between the copula *be* and the preposition *as*, both heading elementary predication structures as in *We saw John as a priest* versus *John is a priest*. Robert van Rooy offers a genuine analysis of 'Negative Polarity Items in Questions: Strength as Relevance' (*JSem* 20[2003] 239–73) by proposing that NPIs are used in a question to increase the average informativity of its answers. In the twin articles 'Questioning to Resolve Decision Problems' (*Ling&P* 26[2003] 727–63) and 'Asserting to Resolve Decision Problems' (*JPrag* 35[2003] 1161–79), he argues for the use of decision-theoretic tools to make some pragmatic inferences possible.

6. Lexicography, Lexicology and Lexical Semantics

Piet van Sterkenburg's *A Practical Guide to Lexicography* is a collection of excellent essays covering many different aspects of dictionary production. They are divided into seven chapters (foundations, descriptive lexicography, special types of dictionaries, corpora for dictionaries, design of dictionaries, realization of dictionaries and examples of design and production criteria for major dictionaries), though the placement of individual essays is sometimes open to question. As the preface emphasizes, the volume provides a range of perspectives from academics and professional lexicographers. It concentrates on monolingual general-purpose dictionaries, though other dictionaries are covered in individual essays. Although the style and readability of each essay vary, the volume is generally accessible to an interested but non-expert audience. It is only possible to cover a sample of the essays here. Van Sterkenburg's own contribution '"The" Dictionary: Definitions and History' includes an interesting account of the development of dictionaries for various European languages. František Čermák's 'Source Materials for Dictionaries' provides a useful summary of methods employed for collecting usage evidence. John Simpson develops this strand in 'The Production and Use of Occurrence Examples'. In 'Meaning and Definition', Dirk Geeraerts considers the choices facing a lexicographer dealing with semantic information in dictionaries, while Fons Moerdijk looks at 'The Codification of Semantic Information'. Stanisław Prędota writes on dictionaries of proverbs, Mike Hannay on bilingual dictionaries and Lynne Bowker on specialized dictionaries. John Sinclair describes the processes involved in constructing and processing a dictionary corpus in 'Corpora for Lexicography' and 'Corpus Processing'. The inclusion of essays on the design and production of dictionaries is a particularly useful contribution to the field from commercial lexicography. Because this is an account of current lexicographic practice, the volume concentrates on recent technological developments, particularly in dictionary construction and design.

This is also a subject taken up by a number of periodical articles this year. In 'Lexicographers' Dreams in the Electronic-Dictionary Age' (*IJL* 16[2003] 143–99), Gilles-Maurice de Schryver examines how far computers have revolutionized lexicography and how near that revolution has come to earlier predictions. David Jost and Win Carus look at how computational and statistical techniques can revolutionize lexicographical practices in 'Computing Business Multiwords: Computational Linguistics in Support of Lexicography' (*Dictionaries* 24[2003] 59–83). Charles M. Levine considers 'The Coming Boom in English Lexicography—Reconsidered (Part Two)' (*KDNews* 11[2003] 1–5) and argues that, despite corporate problems, dictionary sales have remained stable in the face of increasing online reference. Janice McAlpine's 'The Warp and Woof of an Electronic Dictionary; or, Beyond the Full-Text Search' (*Dictionaries* 24[2003] 84–96) shows how the new ways in which electronic dictionaries can be searched are altering what is put into these dictionaries in the first place. The September issue of *IJL* was devoted to the FrameNet project. Charles J. Fillmore, Christopher R. Johnson and Miriam R.L. Petruck provide a 'Background to FrameNet' (*IJL* 16[2003] 235–50), which 'extracts information about the linked semantic and syntactic properties of English words from large electronic text corpora, using both manual and automatic procedures' (p. 235). Articles include discussions of the selection of information from corpus evidence, the structure of the FrameNet database, FrameNet in action and the contributions that FrameNet could make to practical lexicography. Gilles-Maurice de Schryver and D.J. Prinsloo propose a methodology for 'Compiling a Lemma-Sign List for a Specific Target User Group: The Junior Dictionary as a Case in Point' (*Dictionaries* 24[2003] 28–58), and argue that this approach produces a dictionary with a number of unique characteristics.

Several recent and current dictionary projects were discussed this year. Paul Bogaards provides a thorough and thoughtful review of the *Macmillan English Dictionary for Advanced Learners* in 'MEDAL: A Fifth Dictionary for Learners of English' (*IJL* 16[2003] 43–55), and concludes that it compares favourably with dictionaries currently available. Wendalyn Nichols explores why British monolingual learners' dictionaries are still more innovative than their American counterparts in 'English Dictionary Making in America Today' (*KDNews* 11[2003] 6–9). John Algeo reports briefly on the progress of Allen Walker Read's historical dictionary of Briticisms (*DSNA* Spring[2003] 5). Anatoly Liberman provides 'a Description and Progress Report' on his *Dictionary of English Etymology* (*DSNA* Fall[2003] 5). To ensure that 'the author [does not] die in the middle of the letter F', Liberman is currently concentrating on words without cognates outside English.

Besides projects discussed, there are also some noteworthy new dictionaries. Chris Lewis's *The Dictionary of Playground Slang* is a fascinating book, not least because of its origins as a website. Lewis posted 'a nucleus of words', which was expanded and corrected by millions of visitors to the site. The site (http://www.odps.org) currently lists 3,213 entries for playground slang and 269 for 'ghastly games' and invites submissions amending or supplementing what is already there. The entries are clearly edited before going online, but it is not clear what the filtering process is, or what criteria were adopted for transferring the online version to paper. Nevertheless, this is an absorbing update of the Opies' work on children's games, and provides a valuable insight into a register that is usually entirely overlooked by dictionaries more reliant on documentary evidence. Carl Sifakis's *The Dictionary of Crime Terms* begins with a lively introduction to the American mob, but provides little information about the language or about how the dictionary was compiled. The implication is that all entries are for current terms, but several are clearly obsolete or now used too widely to be functional as cant. Definitions are discursive and anecdotal.

Two monographs this year reflect on the compilation of familiar dictionaries. Simon Winchester's *The Meaning of Everything* is a lively account of the history of the *OED* and is written for a non-specialist audience. Its content is most usefully compared with K.M. Elisabeth Murray's *Caught in the Web of Words* [1977], which it updates and, to a point, supplants. Murray's work is a biographical account of James Murray's experience as editor of the *OED*, and consequently other editors and contributors are discussed only in so far as they came into contact with or provide a comparison with Murray. Winchester's scope is much broader, in that it is a biography of the dictionary itself rather than of the people involved in its production. It also makes more of sensational elements in the dictionary's history, as is to be expected from the author of *The Surgeon of Crowthorne*. Colourful information is given about many of the contributors, which builds up to provide a striking impression of the scope of the enterprise. In less detail, and with less personal information about those involved, for obvious reasons, an epilogue covers the production of the supplements and later editions. It is a shame that this section was not longer. The production of the first supplement merits only four pages of text, the second only two, and the second and third editions only three between them. Still on the topic of the *OED*, Greg Crosson notes, in 'Unnoticed Words in Beddoes for *OED*' (*N&Q* 248 [2003] 446–53), that existing *OED* citations from Thomas Lovell Beddoes are all from two poems, and sets out to rectify this with '250 or so' additions.

Damian Atkinson's edition of *The Correspondence of John Stephen Farmer and W.E. Henley on their Slang Dictionary, 1890–1904* provides an interesting insight into the production of a little studied but often used dictionary, *Slang and its Analogues*, and gives much useful information about its editors. The letters show an extensive correspondence between the compilers and the editors of the *OED*. It seems that all saw it as a supplement to the *OED*, covering for subscribers those areas of the lexis for which a squeamish public was not yet ready. The letters, which are mainly those written by Farmer, reveal the practical problems involved in compiling the dictionary, including finance, obtaining suitable texts, and printers' concerns about obscenity. The letters appear to reveal that Farmer compiled the dictionary and Henley read over his work and provided detailed comments and supplementary material. Henley also provided welcome financial assistance and some influential contacts. This volume will also be of interest to scholars of early English drama, because it provides a detailed account of Farmer's work in that field. Allen Walker Read's 'The Beginning of English Lexicography', originally written in 1935, was revised for posthumous publication in *Dictionaries* (24[2003] 187–226). It argues that six main streams influenced the development of the English dictionary: the 'schoolmaster's help'; dictionaries of classical languages; glosses and interlingual dictionaries; the scientific study of language; antiquarian and etymological dictionaries; and specialist dictionaries. Read examines the contribution of each in turn, highlighting some works that have remained neglected in studies of this area.

Word and field studies are presented here chronologically. As the title suggests, C.P. Biggam's *From Earth to Art. The Many Aspects of the Plant-World in Anglo-Saxon England* considers much more than just the lexical evidence for Anglo-Saxon plant names, but about half of the twelve essays are of lexicological interest. These include Carole Hough's 'Place-Name Evidence for Anglo-Saxon Plant-Names', which looks particularly at plant names not otherwise attested. Peter Bierbaumer considers plant names found in OE glossaries, and attempts to determine which of them are 'real' and not glossarial errors. Hans Sauer analyses 'The Morphology of Old English Plant-Names', which were largely produced by compounding. Biggam's own essay is a detailed account of the term *æspe* in OE, which, she argues, was applied to all of the poplars growing in Anglo-Saxon England. Anthony Esposito's 'Medieval Plant-Names in the *Oxford English Dictionary*' compares coverage in the first and third editions, and demonstrates that the new edition will be 'more comprehensive, consistent, and authoritative' (p. 247), as might be expected.

A number of journal entries are also concerned with the OE period. In '*Grendel*: Another Dip into the Etymological Mere' (*ELN* 40[2003] 1–13), Felicia Jean Steele discusses the etymological interpretations that have been made of both *Grendel* and *Beowulf*. She asserts that *Grendel* is a metathesized form of **drengel,* meaning 'a blood-drinking creature from the watery depths'. Dennis Cronan's 'Poetic Meanings in Old English Poetic Vocabulary' (*ES* 84[2003] 397–425) looks at terms labelled 'poetic' in OE dictionaries and glossaries, arguing that, of the sixty-two words thus labelled, only thirty-six actually do have distinct poetic meanings, as do a further six not noted by the dictionaries. Cronan concludes that the inherent flexibility of OE vocabulary resulted in the production of poetry that did not require its own register. Alfred Bammesberger's 'The Entry *Henna* in Dictionaries of Old English' (*N&Q* 248[2003] 258) argues that *henna* does not deserve an entry of its own, and should be treated as the nominative plural of *henn* 'hen'.

In 'A Second Adjective *dern(e)* or *dearn(e)* in Middle and Early Modern English' (*N&Q* 248[2003] 162–72), T.M. Smallwood supplements and amends Wright's coverage of *dern* adj^1, adj^2 and adj^3 or adv in the *English Dialect Dictionary*, by offering ME and eModE antecedents. E.G. Stanley's 'Middle English *Neotsum*' (*N&Q* 248[2003] 276–7) casts doubt on *OED* and *MED* etymologies. Heli Tissari's *Lovescapes: Changes in Prototypical Senses and Cognitive Metaphors since 1500* explores the relationship between world-view and language. The book is divided into two main parts: an introductory setting and research articles. The articles have largely been published elsewhere and their format is not standardized, nor are their contents unified here, but much of the rest of the volume is new. The introduction is a useful account of recent developments in lexical semantics, lexicography and particularly the various fields of research into the emotions. Although Tissari's research was influenced and inspired by the *Historical Thesaurus of English* (*HTE*), her study is based on seven corpora, providing a good coverage of the sixteenth and seventeenth centuries for comparison with her twentieth-century material. The research articles are all quite different in scope, though there is inevitably some overlap between them. For example, in 'Five Hundred Years of LOVE', Tissari uses prototype theory to make a diachronic comparison between the eModE and PDE 'semantic microfield' of LOVE. 'LOVE Shakes the Spheres' concentrates on Shakespeare's use of *love*. 'AFFECTION, FRIENDSHIP, PASSION and CHARITY' looks at the history of four related lexemes since the fifteenth century. I found 'Metaphors We Love By' particularly interesting in its consideration of the cognitive metaphors of love, ranging from the dubious (to me) 'love is a container' to 'love is food' and 'love is heat'. 'LOVE in Words' is a detailed consideration of the *HTE* classification of LOVE. The final chapter looks at the implications of this study for various related areas of research.

In 'Getting Hitched or Shacking Up and Other Domestic Arrangements' (*Verbatim* 28:i[2003] 12), Devorah Stone looks at the vocabulary available to describe marriage and cohabitation. Nick Shearing considers 'Raving Bonkers, Much! Radio, Film, and Television Scripts in the *OED*' (*OEDNews* 2:xxvi[2003] 3–4). In 'Speak of the Devil: Dangerous Names' (*Verbatim* 28:iv[2003] 5–6), Jessy Randall considers words that are considered dangerous to speak aloud. Tim Kane considers 'Teacherese' (*Verbatim* 28:iv[2003] 15–16), including some terms apparently restricted to the US, and others also familiar to teachers in the UK.

A selection of articles this year considered the origins of words formed from within the resources of English. In 'Blog This' (*Verbatim* 28:iii[2003] 8–9), Steve Lawson discusses the use of *blog*, noun, verb and compounds, with reference to frequently updated webpages, which are commonly diaries or comments on current affairs. Larry Tritten's 'Let There Be Light' (*Verbatim* 28:iii[2003] 19–20) is an account of respellings used by manufacturers and advertisers, such as ⟨lite⟩ for *light*. Allison Whitehead also considers advertisers' language in 'Words That Sell' (*Verbatim* 28:iv[2003] 25). Orin Hargraves discusses the use of the suffix *pre-* in 'Prewarned is Prearmed' (*Verbatim* 28:i[2003] 25–7). Melanie Falcon's paper 'Everything You Always Wanted To Know About Pig Latin But Were Afraid To Ask' (*Verbatim* 28:i[2003] 9–10) covers pig Latin and similar invented languages. Gordon S. Jones follows on with an account of what he calls Horse Latin in 'Ersatz Languages' (*Verbatim* 28:iii[2003] 12).

Words from outside English were not neglected either. Sarah Ogilvie and Joanna Tulloch consider exotic loans into English in 'Exotic Words in the *OED:*

Or Why Won't Anybody Play Us at Scrabble?' (*OEDNews* 2:26[2003] 1–2). *OEDNews* (2:xxvii[2003] 3–4) also includes a piece on words with interesting etymologies: 'Words of Choice: John Simpson's Selection of Words with Unusual Origins'. In 'Such a Fine Pot of Curry: South Asian Influences on the English Lexicon' (*Verbatim* 28:ii[2003] 12–15), Mike Youngblood looks at recent and ancient loans from South Asian languages. Dave Wilton also looks at food terms in 'A Hoagie By Any Other Name' (Verbatim 28:iii[2003] 1–5). David Shirt makes 'a foray into the world of bird names' in 'Muffies, Moreporks, and Ooaas' (*OEDNews* 2:xxiv[2003] 1–2). William Young discusses bird names and the sounds made by birds in 'Translating the Language of Birds' (*Verbatim* 28:i[2003] 1–5).

The contribution that English has made to other languages is not neglected. Manfred Görlach's *English Words Abroad* is a collection of accounts and analyses of research for the *Dictionary of European Anglicisms*, which was published in 2001. The papers were published and presented at conferences during the course of the project, but this volume sees them edited and unified. Together, they consider the effects of English on other world languages, concentrating particularly on the period after 1945. Careful distinctions are made between groups of terms included and excluded. Neoclassical terms, for example, are excluded, on the grounds that it is often impossible to determine where they were originally coined. The difficulties of determining which loans are permanent and which merely ephemeral are also discussed, and one chapter considers in details the problem of marginal lexis: 'quotation words, foreignisms, technical terms, and archaisms' (p. 64). Calques are only listed 'where at least one of the languages has the loanword and others have a translation' (p. 101). Chapter 6 is an interesting account of the incorporation of English loans into languages using different alphabets, such as Russian, Bulgarian and Greek. Chapter 7 considers, among other morphological features, the integration of English loans into the German system of gender. Chapter 8 discusses the problem of assigning meaning across sixteen separate languages, since languages using an English loan may not all use it synonymously. Reviews of recent dictionaries of Anglicisms are provided in chapter 11, providing interesting parallels with early English attitudes towards foreign loans. Chapter 12 considers other dictionaries that would be useful: of Gallicisms, Germanisms and neoclassic diction. All in all, this is a fascinating volume, containing considerable quantities of useful information for readers of all the languages considered. Cristano Furiassi picks up the theme in considering pseudo-loans or 'False Anglicisms in Italian Monolingual Dictionaries: A Case Study of Some Electronic Editions' (*IJL* 16[2003] 121–42).

7. Onomastics

The most significant publication in onomastics in 2003 was undoubtedly the monumental *Dictionary of American Family Names* (*DAFN*), edited by Patrick Hanks. *DAFN* is not only a major achievement in onomastic lexicography, it also provides a novel and very promising methodological approach in ascertaining the etymology of personal names. Everything about *DAFN* is on a grand scale: three volumes, 100 pages of outstanding introductory material, nearly 2,000 pages of text, and consideration of more than 70,000 American surnames, which the editor claims include about 85 per cent of the American population. A major theoretical contribution of *DAFN* is the way given names are used to suggest the source of surnames whose language or culture of origin is uncertain or unknown. Hanks, in collaboration with Ken Tucker, devised a classification scheme by which given names can be rated relative to their association with particular surnames. For instance, *Declan* is strongly associated with (or is 'diagnostic for' in *DAFN*'s terminology) Irish names, while *Patrick*, although originally Irish, is now so generally used that it is 'non-diagnostic' for Irish. This system brings some surprises. The surname *Dam*, for instance, traditionally classified as a shortening of Dutch *Van Dam*, was reclassified in *DAFN* as primarily Vietnamese on the basis of the given names which occurred with it. Hanks and Tucker found US telephone listings for *Hung Dam, Ngoc Dam, Vinh Dam* and *Hoa Dam*, among others. The introductory material in *DAFN* is excellent and provides a valuable reference for anyone interested in personal names. Ken Tucker has a substantial essay on 'Surnames, Forenames, and Correlations' (pp. xxiii–xxvii), which sets out the basis for using given names to suggest the origins of surnames, and there are a number of often brief but highly informative essays on surnaming in many of the cultures which have provided American surnames. Especially welcome are the essays on naming in less familiar cultures such as Arabic and Chinese. A typical *DAFN* entry includes the frequency of the surname (drawn from the INFOUSA ProCD Select Phone pack which lists just under 89 million US telephone subscribers), the language or culture in which the name originated, its etymology, and, for some entries, historical notes on famous bearers of the name. Many of the entries as well carry specific information about the diagnostic given names associated with the surname. There is a great deal more which could be said about the wealth of onomastic information which is contained in *DAFN*. For elaborations on the points made above and for additional information, see the review by Edward Callary (*Onoma* 38[2003] 349–53).

In addition to *DAFN*, several other notable onomastics reference works were published in 2003. Adrian Room's *Penguin Dictionary of British Place Names* is a compact but valuable guide to some 10,000 British place names, including the names of communities, districts, such as Latchford, ruins, such as Bewley Castle, and natural features such as The Manacles and Malvern Hills. Rarely does one find so much authoritative information packed into such a small space. This is arguably the best compact guide to British place names currently available. For details and a general appraisal of the book, see the review by Ken Tucker (*Names* 51[2003] 139–45). Adrian Room's *Placenames of the World* is not new, but 2003 saw the very welcome publication of a paperback edition. The price of the hardback original put this volume out of the reach of most individual onomasts, who had to make do with a library or borrowed copy, but this paperback edition, which lists at US$ 49.95, but can be found online for considerably less, makes this highly valuable reference work available to an audience previously denied it.

Jill Bourne's *Understanding Leicestershire and Rutland Place-Names* is a brief but handy guide to 500 or so place names of Leicestershire and 120 or so place names of Rutland. Bourne has relied on standard sources, such as the publications of the English Place-Name Society, the work of Margaret Gelling and Kenneth Cameron, etc., so the information is reliable. The entries are interestingly written, devoid of jargon, and should appeal to general readers.

The last volume on our reference shelf from 2003 is the seventh edition of *Oregon Geographic Names* (*OGN*), by Lewis A. McArthur, revised and enlarged by his son, Lewis L. McArthur, who has prepared every edition since the third. At 1,074 pages and weighing more than three and a half pounds in paperback, *OGN* is more an encyclopedia than a dictionary and it sets the standard for a detailed, authoritative, and indeed near exhaustive study of the place names of an individual state. McArthur relates the sources and history of Oregon's names with wit, grace, and often barbed comments. The entry for 'Whorehouse Meadow' provides a classic illustration. The meadow was named after a secluded valley where self-employed young women provided cattlemen and miners with (some of) the comforts of home. In the 1960s the name was changed to appease local self-appointed guardians of morality to 'Naughty Girl Meadow', which McArthur calls 'a namby-pamby name'. With unrestrained satisfaction, McArthur announces that 'Naughty Girl Meadow' is once again officially 'Whorehouse Meadow'. His riposte: 'O tempora! O mores!' For an expanded description and evaluation of *OGN*, see Edward Callary's review (*OnCan* 86[2004] 55–8).

Two notable anthologies were published in 2003. Demsky, ed., *These are the Names*, volume 4 of the Studies in Jewish Onomastics series, is a 'Festschrift in Honor of Edwin D. Lawson on the Occasion of his 80th Birthday'. Several articles in this collection deserve special mention. Stanley Lieberson, in 'Jewish Names and the Names of Jews', notes a reversal in what had become an increasing overlap of popular names given by Jewish and non-Jewish parents in the US, a trend which was apparent into the 1970s. Lieberson offers several possible reasons for the new divergence, including the potential attractiveness of Israeli names and the recognition that the general popularity of biblical names (or any other names for that matter) does not impact social groups equally. Rather, in this instance their popularity is seen first in the Jewish community and only several years later does it begin to show up among non-Jews. Of theoretical importance to onomastics in general is Alexander Beider's 'Methodological Principles for Determining Etymologies of Ashkenazic Given Names'. The principles established by Beider can be applied to both the etymologizing and the classifying of given names, whatever their origin, and they also provide a basis for classifying names which is more rigorous than that found in many, if indeed not most, current onomastic studies. Beider notes that a name may go through up to five 'life-cycle stages', all optional except, obviously, the first: appearance, derivation, variation, conjunction (Beider calls this 'joining with other names'), and disappearance. In order to determine the complete etymology of a name one needs to consider the reporter's five questions: what, how, why, where, and when. What was the source of the name? How did this non-name become a name? Why did naming occur? Where did it occur? When did it occur? Beider goes on to flesh out this skeletal structure in the remainder of this substantial article, which is recommended reading for anyone seriously interested in the study of the origins and development of a particular set of given names (and these principles are probably applicable as well to family names, hypocorisms, bynames and the like). I will mention one additional article in this collection (although many others are worthwhile and offer rewarding reading as well), and that is Rita Bredefeldt's 'Naming Customs as an Indication of Assimilation'. Bredefeldt studied the names of two congregations of Swedish Jews, an Orthodox Congregation in Malmö and a Liberal congregation in Stockholm, during the period 1895–1921 and noted a decline in the incidence of Jewish names soon after the period of greatest immigration in both congregations but especially in the more liberal Stockholm congregation.

The second anthology is Finke and Ashley, eds., *A Garland of Names*, a compilation marking the fortieth anniversary of the Names Institute of presentations held annually each spring at Baruch College in New York. This volume is dedicated to the memory of E. Wallace McMullen, a past president of the American Name Society and founder of the Names Institute, who died in 2002. The lead article, 'Uses of Names in Fictional Narratives', by W.F.H. Nicolaisen, is both a rationale for and an introduction and guide to studying names and naming in narrative literature, a field which has become known as literary onomastics, a term coined several decades ago by Grace Alvarez-Altman, who annually hosted a conference on names in literature. Using narrative works by Robert Louis Stevenson, Sir Walter Scott, Chaim Bermant, and others, Nicolaisen attempts to show how the study of names in literature can (and should) go beyond such simple and trivial questions as 'What are the connotations of such and such a name?' and 'Why did the author choose this name and not another?' Nicolaisen very neatly contrasts authors' use of 'fictionalized fact', i.e. of 'real' places such as London or Edinburgh, and 'factualized fiction', i.e. an author's creation of a name and a place from whole cloth. This is a profound apology for literary onomastics but it is a tough read, especially for beginners. The sentences are long and complex (Nicolaisen never met a subordinate clause he didn't like) and much of the terminology is confusing. Nicolaisen's arguments are much clearer the second, and especially the third, time through, but I doubt that most readers will have the stamina necessary to get this far. For summaries of this and other articles in the anthology, see Robert Rennick's review (*Names* 52[2004] 45–51).

Articles in journals will be our next concern. We will start with *Names*. In 'Naming with Lewis and Clark' (*Names* 51[2003] 3–11), Thomas Gasque gives an overview of the geographical naming of Meriwether Lewis and William Clark, in keeping with the celebration of the bicentennial of the remarkable expedition of the Corps of Discovery. The captains named features after members of the party (e.g. Floyd's River), after descriptions (Milk River), after national figures of the time (Madison, Gallatin, and Jefferson rivers), after friends and family (Judith's River, Maria's River), and even after Clark's dog, Seaman. Herbert Barry and Aylene S. Harper, in 'Final Letter Compared with Final Phoneme in Male and Female Names' (*Names* 51[2003] 13–33), continue their investigation into the linguistic features which distinguish names given to males from those given to females. In this account of the orthography of male and female names, the final letter proved crucial, with final spelled b, c, d, g, k, l, m, o, p, r, s, t, w, and x suggesting male names and final a, e, and i suggesting female names. Susan

Petit's 'Proper Names and Improper Meanings in Thomas Hardy's *Far From the Madding Crowd*' (*Names* 51[2003] 35–53) argues that Hardy chose the names Bathsheba Everdene, Francis Troy, and Fanny Robin in order to raise these characters to classical or even biblical status, in effect turning Wessex into a pagan land, despite its appearance of Christianity. In 'On the Birthday and Etymology of the Placename Missouri' (*Names* 51[2003] 111–25), Michael McCafferty gives a comprehensive account of the origins, etymology and historiography of 'Missouri'. The name is from the Illinois language meaning 'big boat' or, as McCafferty says in a later 'correction', more likely 'wooden boat', in other words a dugout canoe. The Illinois morpheme *mihs* 'big' is homophonous with 'wood'. The article by Ibrahim Aksu (Graham Lee), 'The Sultan's Journey and Other Turkish Placename Stories' (*Names* 51[2003] 163–92) gives an overview of Turkish place-naming and a rich selection of place names which carry with them naming stories, as often as not fanciful, popular etymologies but which are well known and have been repeated for generations. John Cross's 'Amish Surnames, Settlement Patterns, and Migration' (*Names* 51[2003] 193–213) shows how surnames can be used to plot, geographically and socially, the distribution of cultures. In this case the distribution of names is used to show the rapid increase in the number of Amish dairy farmers in certain locations in Wisconsin in the 1990s and the in-migration to new communities where certain surnames are largely confined, often to a single community. Finally, in 'The Culture of Shaker Placenames: Sacred Geography and Communal Biography' (*Names* 51[2003] 215–39), Christine De Vinne argues that, even though Shaker communities are now spread over a wide area, their names maintain associations of purity, unity, simplicity, equality, and industry, virtues which are reflected in such names as 'Chosen Land', 'Lovely Vinyard', and 'Wisdom's Paradise'.

Onomastica Canadiana also has a number of articles of interest, including the following. In 'Names of the Seven Days of the Week in the Languages of Western Europe' (*OnCan* 85[2003] 43–57), Michael Falk notes that the numerical and religious names (first day, second day, etc.) were established by the Church. However, the planetary names, which survive largely in Germanic areas, are reflexes of Latin names, which were maintained in spite of the fact that the Church did its best to eradicate them. In a second article, 'Lunenburg *Dutch* and the Use of *Dutch* for *German* in Nova Scotia' (*OnCan* 85[2003] 81–8), Michael Falk clarifies the meaning of the word 'Dutch' as used in Nova Scotia (and also in parts of the US) where it is an archaism referring to Germans rather than people from the Netherlands.

Also deserving of mention is Michael McCafferty's 'A Fresh Look at the Place Name Chicago' (*JISHS* 96[2003] 116–29). In this article McCafferty summarizes scholarship of the etymology of 'Chicago', a name which continues to fascinate historians and etymologists. McCafferty explains not only the origin of the name (from Illinois for 'striped skunk', 'wild leek'), but also, ingeniously, many of the thirty or so different spellings of the name, from the first known, ⟨Checagou⟩, recorded by La Salle about 1680. Finally, Patxi Salaberri notes in 'On Hypocoristic Formation in Basque' (*FLV* 35[2003] 329–36), that in Basque, at least from the Middle Ages, hypocoristics have been formed mainly by palatalization, suffixation, and general shortening, often in combination, for example, 'Maria', by palatalization and suffixation becomes 'Txariako', 'Domingo', by palatalization and shortening becomes 'Txomin', and 'Josefina', by shortening and suffixation becomes 'Finatxo'.

8. Dialectology and Sociolinguistics

This year we are almost swamped by the number of books that have appeared in the field of sociolinguistics and dialectology, not to mention journal articles and several special issues of journals that were published. This overview therefore starts with a look at the general publications before moving on to more specialist and regional ones.

The first new 'old' textbook to be mentioned is a substantial reworking of Lesley Milroy's *Observing and Analysing Natural Language* [1987], with Matthew Gordon as co-author, well known to sociolinguists and dialectologists from his work on the Northern Cities Chain Shift. The book is now called *Sociolinguistics: Methods and Interpretation* and is probably unique in that it can serve as a manual for young sociolinguists, but at the same time makes explicit the various theoretical assumptions that often lie hidden in 'apparently innocuous methods' (p. xii). Practical steps, from locating informants and collecting speech to analysing and interpreting data, are discussed in great detail and with many examples—also from outside of the authors' own work. The volume also discusses matters 'Beyond Phonology', such as morphological and syntactic variation and the important topics of style-shifting and code-switching. The epilogue gives an interesting overview of how the field of sociolinguistic studies has changed over the last twenty-odd years, with large-scale urban surveys giving way to smaller-scale studies often much more varied in methodology.

Another important textbook published this year is the second edition of J.K. Chambers's *Sociolinguistic Theory: Linguistic Variation and its Social Significance*, improving on the first edition [1995] 'in countless details' (p. xxii) and thoroughly updating it. Despite the abundance of recent alternative approaches to language variation and change, this book remains firmly rooted in the Labovian tradition, which makes it the ideal textbook of classic sociolinguistic work. Nevertheless, it is not always uncontroversial, for example when Chambers traces gender differences in language to biologically determined differences, or when he speculates on the adaptive significance of dialect variation by having recourse to variation in bird songs.

An interesting—and hopefully useful—little book is *A Glossary of Sociolinguistics* by Peter Trudgill. Although only a paperback of less than 150 pages, it contains a wealth of information in its entries, ordered alphabetically and written in simple, clear prose. Trudgill explains the central technical terms and concepts of sociolinguistics, dialectology and creolistics, presents the classic studies conducted in Labov's and other frameworks (accessible by author as well as by place name), and also includes descriptions of many varieties, not just from the English-speaking world (although these do make up the greatest part of this book). Thus he also has entries on 'Serbo-Croat' or Norwegian 'Bokmål', as well as many creole languages. In many cases, descriptions of less well known varieties are complemented by a map, and many entries include some salient examples from the language in question. In contrast to Chambers above, Trudgill also acknowledges new approaches like the 'community of practice', which for example is cross-referenced to Penelope Eckert's work on 'Belten High'. Trudgill even includes some central concepts from pragmatics and discourse analysis; thus there are entries on 'performatives', 'J.L. Austin' and 'speech act theory' as well as 'turn-taking', 'adjacency pairs' and 'face-to-face interaction'. Although the individual entries are short, this book can serve as the ideal little reference book sitting on your desk in case you happen to have forgotten where the Miskito Coast is, who exactly the Arvanitika are, or where the slang expression *yob* comes from.

Much less entertaining and somewhat dry is the German language textbook *Dialektologie: Eine Einführung* by Heinrich Löffler. After a brief overview of the history of the field of (German) dialectology, Löffler discusses data collection, description and interpretation in much detail. The clear order of his exposition is remarkable, and Löffler deals with something missing from the host of English-language textbooks: he always links back data and data investigation to the main theoretical frameworks in the respective fields. Thus he has short sub-chapters on acoustic and generative phonology, on structuralist, generative and comparative morphology, and on lexical field vs. structuralist semantics. In this respect this short book is much needed, filling a gap often deplored. Unfortunately it is only available to a German-reading audience.

Christina Bratt Paulston and G. Richard Tucker have edited the rather monumental *Sociolinguistics: The Essential Readings* of around 500 pages. Needless to say, all contributions have appeared before and will thus not be reviewed in detail here. The collection is divided into eleven(!) parts and is based on a very wide concept of sociolinguistics. After the initial section on the 'History of Sociolinguistics' (both American and European), we find introductions to the 'Ethnography of Speaking', and to 'Pragmatics' (which is in fact discourse analysis), sections on the more narrowly sociolinguistic topics of 'Language and Gender', 'Language and Variation' and 'Pidgins and Creoles', as well as five sections on multilingualism: 'Individual Bilingualism', 'Diglossia', 'Group Multilingualism', 'Language Policy and Planning', and 'Multilingualism, Policies, and Education'. Contributors range from the very well known (William Labov, Dell Hymes, Walt Wolfram, Charles Ferguson, Joshua Fishman, Einar Haugen, John Gumperz, Janet Homes, Robin Lakoff, Deborah Tannen) to the not so well known. Every part starts off with a detailed—and rather informal—editorial introduction to the contributions, often situating them in their historical context, and is rounded off with discussion questions based on the texts, which will make this reader (or parts of it, considering its size) very suitable for class use.

A rather informal introduction to some sociolinguistic issues is provided by Donna Jo Napoli in *Language Matters: A Guide to Everyday Thinking About Language*. As the title implies, this book is geared more towards a general reading public, although it might be useful as rather basic introductory reading for undergraduate students. Especially the second part of the book ('Language in

Society') is relevant to sociolinguistics, as it deals with such questions as 'Whose Speech is Better?' discussing matters of prestige, attitudes and variation, 'Why Do Dialects and Creoles Differ from Standard Language?' (including a short list of purported 'universals' of creoles), and of course the classic gender topos 'Do Men and Women Talk Differently? And Who Cares?', where Napoli discusses—briefly—the sociological vs. biological basis of gender differences, but comes to the conclusion that many other factors may also play a role. Napoli also asks: 'Should the United States Adopt English as the Official Language and Overhaul the Educational System Accordingly?', discussing possible motives of the 'English First' movement and making a strong point for bilingual education.

It is sometimes said by critics that dialect data are compared to an abstract notion of 'Standard English' (usually equated with the written standard), without taking account of general processes of spoken language. For phonetics, this situation can now be remedied, as Linda Shockey, in *Sound Patterns of Spoken English*, gives a concise overview of 'the casual pronunciation of everyday English as compared to formal citation forms' (blurb). Shockey also cites data from Edinburgh, Stockport, Coventry, Norwich, east London and Kent, so that her compendium can serve as a useful (realistic) foil against which dialect data can be tested (see also Section 2 above).

Another reader published this year is more specific in scope, Harris and Rampton, eds., *The Language, Ethnicity and Race Reader*. As the editors acknowledge, the topic is 'rather contentious', and indeed they try to show in their collection of essays the 'range of different ways in which language has been involved in arguments about race and ethnicity' and to capture 'the major lines of disagreement' (p. 1). The contributions are divided into three sections, 'Colonialism, Imperialism and Global Process', 'Nation-States and Minorities', and 'Language, Discourse and Ethnic Style'. Some contributions go back to the 1920s and 1930s (Otto Jespersen, Edward Sapir, Benjamin Lee Whorf), some date from the 1970s, but most are relatively recent (1990–2003). Very helpful are diagrams locating the authors on a scale from tradition via modernity to post-modernity, also indicating nicely the internal structure of the individual sections and cross-classifying the contributions according to geographical focus and institutional focus. With the help of these various metatextual tables and diagrams, it should become possible to use this reader in the classroom or for an initial overview of this field. However, as all extracts are heavily edited (also containing numerous editorial footnotes as well as cross-references to similar or contrasting texts), any in-depth studies of individual texts cannot be recommended on the basis of this reader.

If anything, 2003 is the year of books on gender. Although of course this topic has been around for quite a while now, this year sees the publication of its first textbook, *Language and Gender* by Penelope Eckert and Sally McConnell-Ginet. Firmly rooted in constructionist theories, in particular the community of practice framework, they investigate at length—and persuasively—how gender is constructed in our everyday life from very early on, they link the linguistic to the social, and look at how talk is organized, i.e. who has access to the floor and when (chapters 1–3). Chapter 4 traces how speech acts accomplish gender, and chapter 5 investigates how women and men come to position their ideas and subjects, as well as themselves. The authors further investigate how gender is implied and sustained overtly and covertly; they look at gendered categorizations of the world, and study the use of gender varieties in the linguistic marketplace (chapters 6–8). In a final chapter, the link of language to style is considered, and the performance of the self. Throughout, the authors discuss a wide range of studies from all over the world, in a clear and accessible style that supposes no previous knowledge of the subject. They manage to present the often controversial discussions clearly and fairly, and draw their own, persuasive conclusions. All in all, this is a highly welcome and much needed addition to the field (see also Section 4 above).

This textbook is complemented by yet another handbook in the Blackwell series, Holmes and Meyerhoff, eds., *The Handbook of Language and Gender*, whose editors also give an excellent overview of 'Different Voices, Different Views: An Introduction to Current Research in Language and Gender'. All articles are of course relevant to Gender Studies, but not all of them are equally relevant for English linguistics. For this reason, not all contributions will be mentioned here. The handbook is divided into five parts, starting with the 'History and Theoretical Background to the Study of Language and Gender'. Here, Bonnie McElhinny, in 'Theorizing Gender in Sociolinguistics and Linguistic Anthropology', stresses in particular that assuming a clear dichotomy in gender is problematical. Mary Bucholtz traces the emergence of feminist theories of gender in discourse analysis in 'Theories of Discourse as Theories of Gender: Discourse Analysis in Language and Gender Studies'. Sally McConnell-Ginet contributes a very interesting chapter on gendered naming practices in different cultures in '"What's in a Name?" Social Labeling and Gender Practices', while Suzanne Romaine gives an overview of 'Variation in Language and Gender', perhaps the contribution most centrally relevant to variationist sociolinguistics. Don Kulick calls for the study of 'Language and Desire' instead of language and sexuality, and Anna Livia investigates gender in literary texts in '"One Man in Two is a Woman": Linguistic Approaches to Gender in Literary Texts'.

Part 2 deals with 'Negotiating Relations'. Starting off the section, Robin Lakoff discusses 'Language, Gender, and Politics: Putting "Women" and "Power" in the Same Sentence' in three case studies: in the academic world (Emanuel Schegloff's attempt at redefining the field of conversation analysis), in arts (the debate about the play *Oleanna*) and in politics (reactions to Hilary Clinton). Lakoff shows how the power struggle in these male-dominated domains is reflected in the asymmetrical discourse that views full female participation as 'incompetent, inappropriate, or unintelligible' (p. 176), but ends on the hopeful note that 'change is coming' (p. 177), which is the reason why these debates can now take place at all. Trying to close a gap in research so far, Deborah Tannen examines 'Gender and Family Interaction', where she argues, from her 'difference' perspective, that family interactions as well as gender interactions are not only negotiations of power, but also of 'connection' (closeness). The new media are under investigation in 'Gender and Power in On-line Communication', by Susan C. Herring, as the internet has been claimed (or hoped) to lead to greater gender equality. Contrary to what is often believed, Herring finds that gender is by no means invisible on the internet: gendered linguistic features tend to be the same in text messages as in face-to-face interactions, and the real power (access to technology etc.) is still wielded by men. Marjorie Harness Goodwin discusses 'The Relevance of Ethnicity, Class, and Gender in Children's Peer Negotiations', the site of children's informal social learning. Looking beyond white middle-class children at African American, Latina and lower-class white girls, she calls into question the widespread assumption that girls are 'fundamentally interested in cooperative, face-saving interaction' (p. 243), as this may be due to the ethnic/cultural bias in earlier studies. Closing this section, Susan U. Philips examines 'The Power of Gender Ideologies in Discourse' in anthropology.

In part 3, on 'Authenticity and Place', many contributions deal with rather exotic places (Tonga, Vanuatu, Guyana) not directly relevant here. Kira Hall addresses a fundamental question, namely what to do with 'Exceptional Speakers: Contested and Problematized Gender Identities', tracing their treatment through the history of the field. Penelope Eckert gives an excellent overview of 'Language and Gender in Adolescence', stressing that the movement from the family into the heterosexual peer social order (or 'hetero-sociability') makes gender a highly salient category during this time. At the same time, she problematizes the concept of 'adolescence' as being an ideological construct and calls for the study of gender in life stages, rather than as an absolute attribute.

Part 4, on 'Stereotypes and Norms', starts off with Deborah Cameron's 'Gender and Language Ideologies', which claims that, although we can never 'transcend' ideology, we should be reflexive about where our ideology comes from, and what we do with it. Mary Talbot looks at 'Gender Stereotypes: Reproduction and Challenge', in particular stereotypes about over-talkative women. Although in academic circles this stereotype has been challenged, it has become widespread in folk linguistic perceptions. Ann Weatherall and Cindy Gallois examine 'Gender and Identity: Representation and Social Action' in two models: the social-cognitive perspective, which holds cognition to be prior to language, and the discursive psychology perspective, which emphasizes the study of language over mind. In one of the few contributions concentrating on male language, Scott Fabius Kiesling discusses 'Prestige, Cultural Models, and Other Ways of Talking about Underlying Norms and Gender' linking objective and subjective norms through the notion of *stance*, the 'local instantiations of a personal style, performed in a particular speech event' (p. 516).

Part 5, finally, discusses 'Institutional Discourse', with some contributions based on Dutch, German and New Zealand data again not directly relevant here. Shari Kendall examines 'Creating Gendered Demeanors of Authority at Work and at Home' in the case study of one woman (a manager at work, parent at home). Ironically, this woman draws on more face-saving strategies (typically associated with the behaviour of mothers) when issuing directives to her subordinates than in her role as mother. Joan Swann looks at the shifts in research in educational settings in 'Schooled Language: Language and Gender in Educational Settings', and Susan Ehrlich investigates gender ideologies in institutional discourse in 'Coercing Gender: Language in Sexual Assault Adjudication Processes', showing how the dominant discourse constrains even the complainant's own linguistic practices. In the 'Epilogue: Reflections on

Language and Gender Research', Alice F. Freed takes the reader through the historical development of the study of gender in sociolinguistics, stressing the shift to constructionist views that has taken place in the field, and discussing the breakdown of the binary system 'male–female'. Freed concludes on the positive note that 'women are not being silenced in the same fashion as was true just ten years ago' (p. 717), a perfect conclusion to this highly welcome and accessible handbook. An important article on gender by Bonnie McElhinny, Marijke Hols, Jeff Holtzkener, Susanne Unger and Claire Hicks as a meta-topic has already been reviewed last year: see *YWES* 83[2004] 63.

Another volume that takes recent theoretical developments into account is *Language and Power in the Modern World* by Mary Talbot, Karen Atkinson and David Atkinson. On the basic tenet that 'power is exercised through language in ways which are not always obvious' (p. 5), they deal with 'Language and the Media', looking in particular at how 'common sense' is constructed in the media, and how this can lead, for example, to the perpetuation of racist discourse. Other chapters deal with 'Language and Organizations', which investigates the language of social welfare; 'Language and Gender', which on the one hand discusses gender construction in childhood, looking at the topos of 'father knows best', and on the other looks at the language of violent men. The chapter on 'Language and Youth' investigates adolescents' strategies of either using AAVE (as the in-group code), adopting it (white students, to sound cool), or rejecting it (nerds, resulting in 'hyperwhite' super-standard speech). 'Multilingualism, Ethnicity and Identity', finally, discusses the language situation in Hong Kong, and discusses the 'English only' movement in the US. All chapters contain an up-to-date introduction to important studies in the field—written from a constructionist perspective, which makes it useful as an advanced textbook—followed by extensive readings of those studies already discussed in the text (up to five), which always include a large amount of data and careful analyses by the original authors. In this way, *Language and Power in the Modern World* is an interesting (probably not uncontroversial) combination of a textbook and a reader, which should spark off useful classroom discussion.

Moving now to reflections on language change, in 'Social and Linguistic Dimensions of Phonological Change: Fitting the Pieces of the Puzzle Together' (in Britain and Cheshire, eds., *Social Dialectology: In Honour of Peter Trudgill*, pp. 155–71) Lesley Milroy reanalyses a number of recent studies in terms of local ideology, claiming that 'changing local ideologies shape trajectories of linguistic change' (p. 163), which cut across traditional distinctions of internally and externally motivated change. Jim Milroy asks: 'When is a Sound Change? On the Role of External Factors in Language Change' (in Britain and Cheshire, eds., pp. 209–21), drawing in particular on data on TH-fronting in Derby. Relating this to other well-known changes in the English language, Milroy suggests that perhaps long-term changes in the history of English should better be viewed as longstanding variability, and that, while internal factors are involved in innovations, only external factors are decisive in explaining 'how and why any particular linguistic change takes place at any particular time' (p. 220). In another collection, Milroy specifically deals with 'The Role of the Speaker in Language Change' (in Hickey, ed., *Motives for Language Change*, pp. 143–57), arguing against the traditional discourse of historical linguistics of endogenous changes. Drawing on some recent research on AAVE in Detroit, Milroy argues that, at least in this case, social explanations are necessary, and they may well be necessary in others as well. Markku Filppula takes up Roger Lass's explicit formulation that, in language change, endogeny must in all cases be preferred to contact explanations, in 'The Quest for the Most "Parsimonious" Explanations: Endogeny vs. Contact Revisited' (in Hickey, ed., pp. 161–73). While taking Lass's principle as a useful starting point, Filppula argues that, to obtain a complete picture, every aspect of the construction in question must be investigated, and that multiple causation should not be ruled out from the beginning.

Another strong point this year is publications on historical sociolinguistics. In the vanguard of this new field is the first report in book form from the Helsinki CEEC project (the Corpus of Early English Correspondence), namely *Historical Sociolinguistics* by Terttu Nevalainen and Helena Raumolin-Brunberg. CEEC consists of over 6,000 letters, totalling 2.7 million words, by both women and men (although the women are necessarily under-represented), whose social and regional background is known. The time span covered is the fifteenth to seventeenth centuries. The authors trace fourteen(!) morpho-syntactic changes and relate them to 'classic' variationist variables such as age, gender, region and social class (each of which is treated in a separate chapter). Although readers interested in a particular morpho-syntactic phenomenon might be disappointed because individual treatments are relatively short, the more general picture that emerges from these pilot studies in historical sociolinguistics is fascinating. Thus the authors show that most changes do in fact follow the well-known S-curve, or that gender differences can be traced back to times before the standardization and codification of English. Women can in fact be shown to be leading the majority of morpho-syntactic changes (e.g. the replacement of *ye* by *you*, *mine/thine* by *my/thy* or third person singular *-th* by *-s*). Only three changes are consistently promoted by men (the decline of multiple negation, inversion after negators and the use of the relative pronoun *which*). These are typically supra-local changes that are channelled through 'learned and professional usage' (p. 130)—something to which women at the time simply had no access.

Another publication straddles the boundary of historical sociolinguistics and literary criticism, Tim Machan's monograph *English in the Middle Ages*. Machan tries to apply the concept of 'linguistic ecology' to literary and governmental texts from the thirteenth to fifteenth centuries. Particularly relevant to this overview is his chapter 3, 'Language, Dialect and Nation', where he argues that the language situation in England was diglossic, but that variation in English was not sociolinguistically stratified. In chapter 4, Machan tries to answer the question 'What's a Dialect Before It's a Dialect?' by analysing Chaucer's *The Reeve's Tale* and *Sir Gawain and the Green Knight* and comes to the conclusion that linguistic variation is employed to signal social instability and/or social ambition of the characters. The standardization of 'English' is also the topic of Terttu Nevalainen (in Deumert and Vandenbussche, eds., *Germanic Standardizations: Past to Present*, pp. 127–56). Using Haugen's four dimensions of standardization, Nevalainen gives an overview of norm selection, acceptance, codification and elaboration of English, providing one of the best concise overviews of the topic published so far. In the process, she also gives the socio-historical background of the rise of English, presents the four major waves of immigration to North America and gives information on grammars of English to the present day.

Starting the regional overview, a very brief introduction to dialects, accents, and regional identity in Britain is provided by Robert Penhallurick in chapter 11 of his *Studying the English Language*, where he discusses in particular cultural stereotypes and attitudes towards a number of varieties. A somewhat fuller overview of *World Englishes* is given by Gunnel Melchers and Philip Shaw (for full details see Section 10 below). Both Melchers and Shaw and Penhallurick might be useful as very short introductions to the topic of regional variation in the undergraduate classroom.

Anyone interested in Scots should take note of Corbett, McClure and Stuart-Smith, eds., *The Edinburgh Companion to Scots*, a compilation of up-to-date essays that is designed to help younger scholars 'identify key topics of research' into Scots, both historical and contemporary. The editors set out to define Scots and give 'A Brief History of Scots' by way of introduction. Margaret Scott gives evidence for early Scots in onomastics in 'Scottish Place-Names' while Carole Haugh does the same for 'Scottish Surnames'. Caroline Macafee, in her 'Studying Scots Vocabulary', claims that 'over much of the Lowlands, Scots is now at an advanced stage of language death' (p. 50). Jim Miller presents 'Syntax and Discourse in Modern Scots', which, despite the title, also includes distinctive features of morphology. Jane Stuart-Smith gives an outline of 'The Phonology of Modern Urban Scots', more precisely of Glaswegian working-class speakers. Moving back historically, Caroline Macafee contributes 'The Phonology of Older Scots', also drawing on material by the late A.J. Aitken. She claims that this chapter should give the student the ability to pronounce older Scottish texts, for this purpose also including some sample transcriptions. In the good Helsinki tradition of corpus linguistics, Anneli Meurman-Solin introduces the 'Corpus-Based Study of Older Scots Grammar and Lexis'. 'The Language of Older Scots Poetry' is the subject of Jeremy J. Smith. J. Derrick McClure moves us back to modern Scots in 'The Language of Modern Scots Poetry'. Linking Scotland with Ulster and North America, Michael Montgomery introduces the reader to 'The Scots Language Abroad'. Finally, John Corbett discusses 'Language Planning and Modern Scots', citing for example the 'Thirteen Principles for the Scots Language' by the Cross-Party Group, among them the demand that 'Naebody shuid be penalized or pitten doun for speakin Scots' (p. 257). One more detailed case study on Scots was also published this year. In 'The Changing Sociolinguistic Status of the Glottal Stop in Northeast Scottish English' (*EWW* 24[2003] 89–108), Jonathan Marshall confirms the rapid spread of the glottal stop across Scotland also to the traditional dialect area of Aberdeenshire.

Ireland is the subject of Karen P. Corrigan in 'The Ideology of Nationalism and its Impact on Accounts of Language Shift in Nineteenth Century Ireland' (*AAA* 28[2003] 201–29). Corrigan argues that events in the decline of Gaelic have been mythologized, especially the establishment of National Schools, and the great potato famine (the traditional scapegoats of the shift from Gaelic to English).

This year also sees a number of publications on Wales, otherwise a dialect area about which relatively little is published. Peter Garrett, Nikolas Coupland and Angie Williams have collected various articles published since 1995 from their attitudes-to-Welsh-dialects study and turned them into a coherent little book, *Investigating Language Attitudes: Social Meanings of Dialect, Ethnicity and Performance*. The authors start off by giving a very detailed overview, discussing the pros and cons of 'Direct Approaches' and 'Indirect Approaches' to eliciting language attitudes, a discussion which will also be useful beyond the immediate context of Welsh English. The study involved teachers and teenage students as informants. Teachers were surveyed by way of questionnaires, and the results are detailed in two chapters: 'Mapping and Labelling' and 'Attitude Scales and "Social Advantage" Items'. Teenagers first produced narratives and both teachers and students were then asked to evaluate the (Welsh English) narratives (with one RP/Standard English control), or rather their speakers, and the results are reported in 'The Narratives Study: Performances, Responses and Evaluations' and 'Keyword Responses'. Informants were also tested on the 'Recognition of Dialects'. Moving away from attitudes to Welsh English, J. Roderick Walters investigates this variety as a '"Celtic English: Influences on a South Wales Valleys Accent' (*EWW* 64[2003] 63–87). In the Rhondda Valleys, those phonological features that might be a direct transfer from Welsh can be shown to be recessive, whereas prosodic features are more likely to endure, since these 'suprasegmental features seem more pervasive' (p. 63).

Paul Kerswill discusses 'Dialect Levelling and Geographical Diffusion in British English' (in Britain and Cheshire, eds., pp. 223–43), arguing that accommodation can only occur 'where there is high mobility within a relatively compact area' (p. 239), whereas over a large area (such as the whole of Great Britain) other mechanisms, such as geographical diffusion, have to be considered. What seems to be different today from earlier changes is the extremely rapid spread of some changes, and in contrast to earlier studies Kerswill holds the 'spoken media' at least partly responsible. The north of England features in two articles by Graeme Trousdale, one reviewed in Section 4(*a*) above, the other entitled 'Simplification and Redistribution: An Account of Modal Verb Usage in Tyneside English' (*EWW* 24[2003] 271–84). In this north-eastern dialect of England, Trousdale finds a trend towards monosemy (either root or epistemic modality are dominant): thus *might* and *must* are overwhelmingly used to indicate epistemic modality, while *can* is almost exclusively used to express the permission sense only. Finally, Rika Ito and Sali Tagliamonte discuss the use and the history of intensifiers in York, already reported on in *YWES* 83[2004] 68.

Several studies have been published this year that concentrate on the (otherwise rather neglected) south-east of England. Thus, Peter Trudgill gives a popular (and personal) introduction to *The Norfolk Dialect*, both its linguistic background and its vocabulary, grammar and pronunciation, in the process noting interesting phenomena which have not been discussed elsewhere (at least not to this reviewer's knowledge), such as the use of *do* or *time* as conjunctions (*don't take these off, do you'll get rheumatism*; *Go you and have a good wash time I get tea ready*). Ulrike Altendorf presents a book-length study of that much-maligned south-eastern accent, *Estuary English: Levelling at the Interface of RP and South-Eastern British English*. Drawing on elicited data from female sixth-formers from several schools in London, Colchester and Canterbury, Altendorf describes a group of phonetic variants that can be considered part of EE, many of them (especially the vowel variants) being intermediate between Cockney and RP. She therefore situates EE on a continuum between Cockney and RP, claiming that EE is a 'social upgrade' of features formerly not available to non-working-class speakers. Interestingly, many non-EE speakers use the pool of variants (in particular T-Glottalling, TH-Fronting and L-Vocalization) occasionally and selectively (Altendorf suggests the term 'flirting with EE', p. 160), in order to profit from the positive image (Cockney down-to-earthness) without being hindered by the negative prestige of Cockney (lack of education, etc.). Also on the subject of EE, the second edition of Lynda Mugglestone's *Talking Proper: The Rise of Accent as Social Symbol* includes a new chapter on very recent developments in the area of accent levelling or new prestige accents arising, 'The Rise (and Fall?) of Received Pronunciation' (pp. 258–88). Mugglestone here traces a trend towards more regionalization of voices even in the BBC going back to the 1960s, claiming that 'fashion has apparently continued to downshift' (p. 275), with RP increasingly being viewed as 'snobbish' or 'too posh'. Mugglestone even reports—anecdotal—patterns of 'Pygmalion in reverse' (people who grew up speaking RP trying, or managing, to acquire a more regional accent). In this way, EE might indeed become the new way of 'talking proper'.

On a more theoretical topic, David Britain 'Explor[es] the Importance of the Outlier in Sociolinguistic Dialectology' (in Britain and Cheshire, eds., pp. 191–208). In his own material from the British Fens, Britain cites two outliers (in terms of their phonology and morphology), whose linguistic behaviour can be explained by their social or geographical isolation. Jenny Cheshire investigates some 'Social Dimensions of Syntactic Variation: The Case of When-Clauses' (in Britain and Cheshire, eds., pp. 245–61), in particular twenty-eight lone *when*-clauses in her data from adolescent Reading speakers, and finds that most of them have the function of initiating 'an extended turn, usually a narrative of personal experience' (p. 250), and that almost all of them were used by male speakers.

Linking Britain and North America, Orin Hargraves moves back and forth across the Atlantic in his book *Mighty Fine Words and Smashing Expressions: Making Sense of Transatlantic English*. The differences between the British and American varieties are embedded in narrative chapters on the extra-linguistic background of many distinct expressions, with helpful tables that summarize specialist vocabulary and the differences in question. The book starts off with a general chapter on grammatical differences, and then proceeds to chapters arranged by topic. Most topics relevant to everyday life are covered (money matters, the government, education, health, food and clothing, transport and sports). An interesting chapter is 'What You Don't Say', which concentrates on obscenities and taboo vocabulary, surely vital for surviving in either society. While this book is not intended for the specialist, it makes highly entertaining reading whatever the subject, and may indeed serve to provide interesting research ideas as to where, when and why these differences came into existence. Interest in this book is not limited to the comparative perspective. If you have ever wondered about the exact hierarchy of ranks in the British Royal Navy and its equivalents in the RAF (say), look no further than page 237.

We begin our overview of English in North America with William Labov's 'Pursuing the Cascade Model' (in Britain and Cheshire, eds., pp. 9–22), which comprises a small study on the spread of the term *hoagie* vs. *submarine* (i.e. a 'sandwich on a long roll, split in half') from Philadelphia to Pittsburgh. As already noted in our review last year (*YWES* 83[2004] 70), Renée Blake and Meredith Josey have continued one of Labov's original investigation in a follow-up study on the /ay/ diphthong in a community on Martha's Vineyard (*LSoc* 32[2003] 451–85). Dennis R. Preston sets out to characterize the elusive Midland region, in his words the 'now-you-see-it-now-you-don't region of North American English', in 'Where Are the Dialects of American English At Anyhow?' (*AS* 78[2003] 235–54), finding both morpho-syntactic and phonological differences (as well as perceptual salience), advocating the look at systems (rather than individual factors), but admitting that really the Midland area is a 'pretty puny little critter' (p. 239). Erica J. Benson links 'Folk Linguistic Perceptions and the Mapping of Dialect Boundaries' (*AS* 78[2003] 307–30) in her discussion of the dialect affiliation of Ohio. Interestingly, informants from southern Ohio 'perceived fewer dialect differences than those from central and northwestern Ohio' (p. 323), which Benson links to their linguistic insecurity. Dennis R. Preston also examines '"Systemic Accommodation" to the Northern Cities Chain Shift [NCCS]' (in Britain and Cheshire, eds., pp. 39–58). African American and white Appalachian immigrants to Michigan show markedly different behaviour, despite having very similar vowel inventories to start with: while first-generation Appalachians slightly modify their vowel system, second-generation Appalachians accommodate rapidly to the NCCS. African Americans, however, accommodate very little; instead they keep 'alignment of the back vowel system for ethnic identity' (p. 55).

Southern US English certainly wins this year's trophy for being the variety written about the most. This is due on the one hand to a special issue of *American Speech* (78:ii[2003]) devoted to 'Language Variation in the American South', edited by Walt Wolfram, and to the collection of articles in Nagle and Sanders, eds., *English in the Southern United States*, as well as to a host of independent publications. Contributions will be discussed in thematic (regional) order, rather than by publication. Walt Wolfram gives a useful overview of the study of Southern English in the introduction to the special volume (*AS* 78[2003] 123–9), calling it 'a proving ground for examining principles of language change and variation' (p. 127). William A. Kretzschmar Jr. takes the interested reader on a tour of 'Mapping Southern English' (*AS* 78[2003] 130–49), dividing maps of Southern English into whether they display or interpret variation, and whether they are based on linguistic production or perception. Interestingly, even purely descriptive maps can be shown to have an interpretative element, especially when they use isoglosses, which, as Kretzschmar shows, are ultimately based on subjective perceptions—a feature clearly relevant beyond studies of Southern US English. The late Donald M. Lance investigates 'The Pronunciation of *Missouri*:

Variation and Change in American English' at length (*AS* 78[2003] 255–84), finding that the traditional pronunciation (ending in schwa) shows 'drastic loss'.

In *English in the Southern United States*, editors Stephen Nagle and Sara Sanders present a well-balanced introduction to the latest research, concentrating mainly on the White Vernacular of this region. About half of the (original) contributions concentrate on the history of this variety. Thus, John Algeo briefly discusses 'The Origins of Southern American English' from multiple lines of descent (discarding the family tree metaphor on the way), namely the English core, the Scots–Irish stratum, the African stratum and even the American and Polynesian stratum, which has left words like *raccoon* or *moccasin*. Edgar W. Schneider tries to find 'Shakespeare in the Coves and Hollows? Toward a History of Southern English' introducing the new Southern Plantation Overseers' Corpus by Michael Montgomery and Schneider himself (covering letters from 1794 to 1876). The SPOC can help to show which features were present in 'Traditional Southern English' (like the Northern Subject Rule) and which only evolved after the Civil War, and are thus part of what Schneider terms 'New Southern', a very useful distinction that is taken up by Bailey (discussed below). While Schneider found only a small number of lexical or morphological correspondences between Southern (US) English and south-east (British) English, Laura Wright investigates 'Eight Grammatical Features of Southern United States Speech Present in Early Modern London Prison Narratives'—the reason being that many sixteenth-century London prisoners were subsequently sentenced to transportation to the new colonies, many in fact going directly to Virginia. Dialect features like invariant *be*, third-person zero, the Northern Subject Rule or precursors of *liketa*, all documented in these court narratives, could thus well have been part of the linguistic input of at least some Southern states. Salikoko Mufwene looks in some more detail at the demographic background of settlement in 'The Shared Ancestry of Southern Englishes', invoking in particular the founder principle to explain similarities between AAVE and Southern White Vernacular English (SWVE). Mufwene claims that 'both varieties can be traced back to the tobacco and cotton plantations' (p. 69), where white indentured servants and black slaves worked side by side and where both took part in the restructuring processes *before* widespread segregation. Features of these founder populations have a much better chance of becoming deeply entrenched if colonial populations grew by moderate increments, which explains the differences between the coastal plains (where Gullah developed) and the hinterland (where it did not). 'The Complex Grammatical History of African-American and White Vernaculars in the South' is taken up by Patricia Cukor-Avila. Based on apparent-time data from Springville, Texas, covering a century, she finds that, of the thirty-two grammatical features investigated, the vast majority are or have been shared between AAVE and SWVE. Those features that are different can in many cases be traced back to recent developments (post-Second World War), leading Cukor-Avila to conclude that 'it is only over the last few decades that change has caused an independent development in the grammar of AAVE' (p. 93). In 'Urbanization and the Evolution of Southern American English', Jan Tillery and Guy Bailey claim that Southern US English is characterized by rapid and widespread change, rather than being a conservative variety. Especially after the Civil War and after the Second World War (major periods of urbanization), changes gathered momentum, shown not only in the rise of well-known features (the *pen–pin* merger), but also in the rapid decline of others (perfective *done*, loss of /hw/ and of long off-glides, etc.). Interestingly, even features like *r*-lessness seem to be affected, as the South can be seen to become more rhotic.

A number of further articles in the Nagle and Sanders volume are synchronic rather than diachronic in nature. Cynthia Bernstein investigates three (stereo)typical Southern features in more depth in 'Grammatical Features of Southern Speech: *Yall, Might Could*, and *Fixin To*', claiming that they map onto gaps in the standard and convey (nuances of) meanings that cannot be communicated satisfactorily using other means. Barbara Johnstone investigates 'Features and Uses of Southern Style', unfortunately mostly relying on literary representations. She identifies the usual stereotypes of white southerners being 'more polite, more easygoing, less direct in speech … more verbose' (p. 190) and shows how 'sounding southern' is employed to varying degrees by four women in their performance of 'self'. Several contributions deal with phonological matters. George Dorrill introduces the reader to 'Sounding Southern: A Look at the Phonology of English in the South'. Interestingly, he finds that 'there is no single set of features that distinguishes S[outhern] A[merican] E[nglish] phonology from the rest of the United States' (p. 122), although the general perception is certainly different. Crawford Feagin proceeds with a more detailed look at 'Vowel Shifting in the Southern States', a change in progress that is almost exclusively found in the white community. Feagin discusses a number of projects that have found evidence for the Southern Vowel Shift (Labov's Atlas of North American English, work in Charleston, Memphis and Alabama) and gives some reasons for seeming divergences, among them the fact that the front shift may be associated with local (also rural) identity. The Southern shift is also the subject of Erik R. Thomas's 'Secrets Revealed by Southern Vowel Shifting' (*AS* 78[2003] 150–70), which specifically looks at glide weakening and/or monophthongization of /ai/, /oi/ and /au/. Walt Wolfram examines and in fact defines 'Enclave Dialect Communities in the South', of interest to dialectologists on the assumption that enclaves are linguistically more conservative and might thus provide a 'window' on the past. Wolfram comes to the conclusion that the dialects under consideration are defined more by 'differential combinations of dialect structures … than the existence of unique structures' (p. 157) and provides comparative profiles of their grammar, phonology and lexis.

Walt Wolfram and Natalie Schilling-Estes take up one of these grammatical variants in 'Language Change in Conservative Dialects: The Case of Past Tense *Be* in Southern Enclave Communities' (*AS* 78[2003] 208–27), and investigate its apparent time distribution in a number of Southern enclave communities (Ocracoke, Harkers Island, Smith Island, and Hyde County). This data is further compared to data from the British Fens in their otherwise very similar 'Parallel Development and Alternative Restructuring: The Case of *Weren't* Intensification' (in Britain and Cheshire, eds., pp. 131–53). Wolfram and Schilling-Estes claim in particular that the longstanding existence of this non-standard pattern has led to parallel (but independent) developments in these disconnected communities.

The winter issue of *AS* (78:iv[2003]), edited by Connie Eble, concentrates on the Louisiana Purchase exactly 200 years before (in December 1803). Eble gives historical background information on 'The Louisiana Purchase and American English' (*AS* 78[2003] 347–52), claiming that it was an 'event of rare linguistic consequence' (p. 349) as it paved the way for the English-speaking nation. Richard Bailey looks at the historical language situation in Louisiana in 'The Foundation of English in the Louisiana Purchase: New Orleans 1800–1850' (*AS* 78[2003] 363–84), which he characterizes as the 'most compactly multilingual place in the country' (p. 365). Moving west a little (but still dealing with an area part of the original Louisiana purchase), Lamont Antieau presents data on 'Plains English in Colorado' (*AS* 78[2003] 385–403), collected for the *Linguistic Atlas of the West*. Antieau gives some phonological features and also notes some grammatical features for this dialect area such as positive *anymore, was/wasn't* regularization, non-standard past tense forms, *a*-prefixing on participles and the use of double modals. Finally, Michael D. Picone suggests that 'Anglophone Slaves in Francophone Louisiana' (*AS* 78[2003] 404–33) hastened the switch from French and/or Creole to English by exerting pressure from 'below'.

Connie Eble also looks at something that has received surprisingly little linguistic attention so far, 'The Englishes of Southern Louisiana' (in Nagle and Sanders, eds., pp. 173–88). She considers in particular popular and linguistic descriptions of Cajun English and New Orleans English and finds that 'speakers of regional varieties of English are preserving, and perhaps even exaggerating, at least some local features of their dialect' (p. 183). Sylvie Dubois and Barbara Horvath investigate the source of 'Verbal Morphology in Cajun Vernacular English: A Comparison with Other Varieties of Southern English' (*JEngL* 31[2003] 34–59) and find that this vernacular originated in the Cajun community rather than being imported from other dialects, from which it differs quantitatively and qualitatively. Incidentally, Louisiana Creole is the subject of Thomas A. Klingler's monumental study, *If I Could Turn My Tongue Like That: The Creole Language of Pointe Coupee Parish, Louisiana*. Although the Creole in question is a French Creole and as such not directly relevant to this section on English varieties, Klingler also discusses the Creole–English language situation, finding that this language community at the periphery of Francophone Louisiana is diglossic and that Creole is reserved for intimate situations. As Eble (above) pointed out, 'the traces of French language and heritage are evident in all the Englishes of southern Louisiana' (p. 175), and Klingler's in-depth study of this one French variety should thus makes excellent complementary reading to any envisaged study of Louisiana English(es). The switch from French to English is the subject of Sylvie Dubois and Barbara Horvath in 'Creoles and Cajuns: A Portrait in Black and White' (*AS* 78[2003] 192–207), *Creoles* representing blacks of French-speaking ancestry, and *Cajuns* white Acadians. Dubois and Horvath find that for two phonetic features (realization of *th* as /d/, and glide absence in /ai/), all Creole African Americans keep the local pronunciation, while, in the Cajun population, middle-aged speakers move to the English norm. The youngest speakers, however, have 'recycled' the local norm, using it more frequently than even the older speakers, and employ it to signal their membership in this ethnic group.

Moving further west, a state previously little written about is Utah. David Bowie changes this situation with his article on the 'Early Development of the Card–Cord Merger in Utah' (*AS* 78[2003] 31–51), using data from the Early Utah English Project. In Utah, both *card* and *cord* are pronounced as *card*. Drawing on radio broadcasts recordings of upper-class white male speakers born between 1850 and 1890, Bowie finds a striking rise in the merger from 1870 onwards.

An ethnolect that has so far received very little attention is Chicano English (the English spoken by Hispanics). Carmen Fought tries to redress this imbalance in her monograph *Chicano English in Context*. She presents an in-depth study of this English dialect, investigating mostly young adults of Mexican descent (although some older speakers are also interviewed for the sake of comparison) in Culver City, Los Angeles. Combining quantitative with qualitative analyses, she finds that this ethnic minority—contrary to received sociolinguistic wisdom—does in fact take part in at least some Anglo (Californian) sound changes. In particular, female middle-class non-gang members show /u/ fronting much like their 'white' counterparts. A syntactic variable like negative concord, however, patterns slightly differently. Very interesting is her qualitative analysis of Spanish language competence as most of these speakers grew up learning Spanish first, but now show widely differing competence (from native-like fluency to hardly any knowledge of the language at all). Fought argues for a process of language acquisition with subsequent attrition; the critical age here seems to be around 8–9 years of age. This much-needed piece of research answers some important initial questions, but of course raises many more, and, as Fought helpfully points out, this book is also a good place to go to for anyone interested in promising areas of research on this important English dialect.

AAVE (apart from featuring in some contributions on Southern English above) is not exactly neglected this year. Makoni, Smitherman, Ball and Spears, eds., *Black Linguistics: Language, Society, and Politics in Africa and the Americas*, firmly sets the study of AAVE in an African context, as the title indicates. Relevant to English linguistics is the article by Donald Winford on 'Ideologies of Language and Socially Realistic Linguistics', written for a non-specialist audience. Winford stresses that 'linguistic prejudice … is simply race or class or ethnic prejudice a subtle guise' (p. 35), and shows how the media and the educational system are responsible for the misrepresentation of AAVE, and for denying its speakers access to power and privilege. H. Samy Alim studies the syntax of hiphop lyrics and artists in '"We are the Streets": African American Language and the Strategic Construction of a Street Conscious Identity', investigating in particular copula absence in the lyrics and in interviews of two female hiphop artists. Alim claims that 'one can find every feature of African American Language represented in Hip Hop lyrics' (p. 46) and that copula absence in particular is used to construct a street-conscious identity.

Nathaniel Norment has edited a reader on AAVE, *Readings in African American Language: Aspects, Features and Perspectives*, collected from a firmly Creolist perspective. It contains contributions on 'The Scope of African

American Language' ('scope' here referring to 'perspectives that document the emergence of African American language, which are traceable to Africans' presence in the United States in the early seventeenth century', p. 2); on (linguistic) 'Aspects of African American Language' (containing contributions on intonation, invariant *be*, auxiliaries and semi-auxiliaries, and verbal *-s*); and 'African American Pedagogy and Writing', with two contributions on students' writing and one on teaching. Contributors include John Baugh, Walt Wolfram, John Myhill, Ronald Butters, Ralph Fasold, Arthur Spears, Lisa Green, Edgar Schneider (mis-cited here as Edgard), Arnetha Ball and many others, and publication times span from the 1970s to the very recent. As all contributions have appeared before, they will not be reviewed again in detail. This collection will be useful in that it contains many papers not readily accessible to a wider audience, but its clear Creolist bias should be taken into account.

A more careful, but still clearly Creolist, stance is taken by Tracy L. Weldon in 'Revisiting the Creolist Hypothesis: Copula Variability in Gullah and Southern Rural AAVE' (*AS* 78[2003] 171–91). Comparing these two varieties, Weldon finds that Gullah is more similar to Southern rural AAVE than to other Creoles and may thus well have been the model for AAVE. A new source in the origins debate has been uncovered by Stuart Davis, who asks: '"Is This Negroish or Irish?" African American English, the Antebellum Writings of Francis Lieber, and the Origins Controversy' (*AS* 78[2003] 285–306). In the nineteenth century, this liberal academic, a student of Wilhelm von Humboldt, described black speech occasionally in his writing, reporting influences from English dialects on the speech of black slaves on the one hand, but also documenting the use of some Creole, especially in the language of 'untutored' field slaves. Also related to the origins debate is Walt Wolfram's contribution 'Reexamining the Development of African American English: Evidence from Isolated Communities' (*Language* 79[2003] 282–316). Data from three bi-ethnic enclave communities in North Carolina suggest that widespread accommodation to white vernaculars characterized earlier African American speech. However, some persisting dialect features such as consonant cluster reduction, absence of third person singular *-s*, or copula absence may hint at substrate influence. Today, younger speakers orient more towards a national AAVE norm.

Moving to present-day AAVE, Dan Beckett stresses the role dialect has in the construction of 'self' in 'Sociolinguistic Individuality in a Remnant Dialect Community' (*JEngL* 31[2003] 3–33). In the speech of fourteen adolescent AAVE speakers in Hyde County, North Carolina, he finds massive linguistic variation (inside the bounds of the dialect) and concludes that speakers employ sociolinguistic variables to construct their identity: 'individual variation is a function of system-constrained speaker creativity' (p. 26). Valerie Fridland connects 'Network Strength and the Realization of the Southern Vowel Shift Among African Americans in Memphis, Tennessee' (*AS* 78[2003] 3–30). While the Southern Vowel Shift affects both black and white speakers, Fridland does not take this as a sign of convergence but argues instead that 'these changes assert engagement in a locally bound identity and its associated values' (p. 23), both ethnic groups displaying a Southern regional identity and marking ethnic identity by other means. A similar topic is also enlarged upon in Fridland's article '"Tie,

Tied and Tight": The Expansion of /ai/ Monophthongization in African-American and European-American Speech in Memphis, Tennessee' (*JSoc* 7[2003] 279–98). African Americans can in fact be shown to lead the monophthongization of this glide even in pre-voiceless position, something that Fridland again links to a 'Southern' identity. Finally, in a very personal account, Alice Ashton Filmer discusses 'African American Vernacular English: Ethics, Ideology and Pedagogy in the Conflict Between Identity and Power' (*WEn* 22[2003] 253–70), calling into question her own belief that bidialectalism should be the goal of school education.

9. New Englishes and Creolistics

As in 2002, there was a wealth of publications on English as a world language or international English. The globalization of English was a recurring theme this year. David Crystal has published a revised and expanded second edition of *English as a Global Language* (cf. *YWES* 78[1999] 110–11), which also contains footnotes and a comprehensive bibliography, both sadly lacking in the first edition. The book traces the spread of English around the world and presents factors which led to the predominance of English worldwide. Crystal provides a new section on the linguistic features of the New Englishes, including lexical, grammatical and supra-segmental features, and he addresses MacArthur's prediction of the development of English into a family of related sub-languages (cf. *YWES* 79[2000] 2–3), pointing out that, in international settings, a 'World Standard of Spoken English' is already in the making, which would prevent the disintegration of English.

Jennifer Jenkins's *World Englishes: A Resource Book for Students* is designed as a textbook for classroom use. The first section introduces the key terms in the study of World Englishes, including the socio-historical background of the spread of English. The next section addresses issues such as colonialism, the development of pidgins and creoles, standardization, and the native vs. non-native speaker. The third section introduces some current debates, for example on teaching World Englishes, on English as a 'killer language' and core approaches to English as an international language. The final section is in the form of a reader, including important text extracts by Alastair Pennycook, Henry Widdowson, Chinua Achebe, Leslie Milroy and David Graddol among others. The book contains many linguistic examples, student activities and suggestions for further reading. A textbook with a different approach is Gunnel Melchers and Philip Shaw's *World Englishes*. After a brief survey of the development and spread of English and the introduction of some important concepts concerning linguistic variation, the authors present a large number of countries in which English is spoken, beginning with 'inner circle' countries such as Great Britain, Ireland, the USA, Canada, Australia, and New Zealand. Lamentably short descriptions of South Africa, Liberia and the Caribbean are also included in this chapter, although the status of English in these countries is hardly comparable to that in countries like in the USA or Canada, apart from the fact that some L1 speakers of English live there. But that is also true of countries such as Singapore or India, which are discussed in the next chapter, 'The Outer Circle'. This chapter includes an introduction to the socio-historical background and some common linguistic features of the New Englishes as well as more detailed descriptions of English in South Asia, Africa, and South-East Asia, as well as Gibraltar, Cyprus, Puerto Rico, the Seychelles, Mauritius, Papua New Guinea and the South Pacific. For each region, the history of the spread of English and its present situation are given before the reader is presented with a list of features and suggestions for further reading. The next chapter deals with 'The Expanding Circle', which is a topic that sets this book apart from other textbooks on World Englishes. Melchers and Shaw discuss the rise of English as a lingua franca in international communication; they look at the role of English in the European Union and other countries, and its use in subcultures such as hiphop or graffiti. They further consider the domains of English in the expanding circle, some of its linguistic features and lectal variation, as well as the effects of English on other languages. The chapters are accompanied by pre- and post-reading questions, and there is a CD (to be ordered separately) containing seventeen interviews with speakers from all the different parts of the English-speaking world. With its focus on the expanding circle, this book is definitely more suited to the demands of EFL students than, for example, Jennifer Jenkins's book, but on the other hand it lacks the richness of actual linguistic data and student tasks Jenkins offers in hers.

Mair, ed., *The Politics of English as a World Language: New Horizons in Postcolonial Cultural Studies*, contains both linguistic and literary publications on World Englishes. I will point out contributions of general interest to linguists here and discuss several other papers dealing with individual Englishes in the sections below. Alastair Pennycook's 'Beyond Homogeny and Heterogeny: English as a Global and Worldly Language' examines the use of English in popular culture around the world. Tove Skutnabb-Kangas discusses 'Linguistic Diversity and Biodiversity: The Threat from Killer Languages', taking an ecolinguistic approach to the spread of English. Similarly, Peter Mühlhäusler's contribution, 'English as an Exotic Language', seeks to point out the ill-suitedness of English in many places, using the ecological development of Pitcairn Island after the advent of English as an example. Photis Lysandrou and Yvonne Lysandrou develop a model of 'Proregression and Dynamic Stasis: The Ambivalent Impact of English as Reflected in Postcolonial Writing' within the framework of Two-Space Theory. Jenny Price reports on the policy of 'The Recording of Vocabulary from the Major Varieties of English in the Oxford English Dictionary', providing detailed appendices containing sample entries from the second and third edition. Finally, Barbara Seidlhofer and Jennifer Jenkins discuss 'English as a Lingua Franca and the Politics of Property', reporting previous research on the phonology and lexico-grammar of English as a world language and English as a foreign language.

An issue of *JSoc* (7:iv[2003]), edited by Nikolas Coupland, is devoted to 'Sociolinguistics and Globalization', containing articles by Monica Heller on 'Globalization, the New Economy, and the Commodification of Identity' (*JSoc* 7[2003] 473–92), by Alastair Pennycook on 'Global Englishes, Rip Slyme and Performativity' (*JSoc* 7[2003] 513–33), which is concerned with the role of rap and hiphop in the globalization of English, and by Juliane House on 'English as a Lingua Franca: A Threat to Multilingualism?' (*JSoc* 7[2003] 556–78). Finally, Tom McArthur addresses the question of 'World English, Euro-English, Nordic English?' (*EnT* 73:i[2003] 54–8), discussing the kinds of English emerging worldwide and specifically in the European Union.

Two monographs are devoted to language contact phenomena. Donald Winford's *An Introduction to Contact Linguistics* is devised as a comprehensive textbook for advanced students of linguistics which covers all aspects of lexical borrowing, various types of structural diffusion in situations of language maintenance, social and linguistic aspects of code-switching, the development of mixed languages, individual and group SLA, language shift, first language attrition, and language death, as well as pidginization and creole formation, in great detail. The textbook character is enhanced by many examples, exercises, chapter summaries and an ample bibliography. In most chapters, Winford critically evaluates previous research in the field and presents his readers with different approaches to each topic, for example Shana Poplack's Interacting Grammars and Carol Myers-Scotton's Matrix Language Frame (MLF) model in the case of code-switching. His book is thus a well-rounded overview of all the issues relevant in the field of contact linguistics. Michael Clyne takes a different approach in the *Dynamics of Language Contact: English and Immigrant Languages*, using data from bilingual and trilingual immigrants in Australia (and their descendants) to evaluate the theoretical models (e.g. language shift, code-switching, transference, convergence, transversion) used in contact linguistics. His informants speak a range of languages, including German, Dutch, Spanish, Italian and Hungarian, and he also uses data from previous studies of speakers of Greek, Croatian, Vietnamese and various Chinese dialects. Supplementing the chapters on the linguistic features of language contact, there is also a chapter on the role of cultural values in contact discourse, which explores aspects of politeness, the use of modal particles and English discourse markers. Clyne identifies the social and linguistic factors leading to transference and transversion and points out that, while none of the theoretical models can accommodate all his data, a number have proven very useful, such as Carol Myers-Scotton's MLF model, Joshua Fishman's Graded Intergenerational Disruption Scale and Pim Levelt's model of Speaking/Processing.

A 'Symposium on World Englishes Today' was held in 2002 at the University of Illinois and is now published in a special issue of *WEn* (22:iii[2003]), edited by Larry E. Smith. The contributions, which all approach the topic from an applied linguistics perspective, include Robert J. Baumgardner and Kimberly Brown's 'World Englishes: Ethics and Pedagogy' (*WEn* 22[2003] 245–51), Edwin Thumboo's 'Closed and Open Attitudes to Globalized English: Notes on Issues' (*WEn* 22[2003] 233–43), Ayo Bamgbose's 'A Recurring Decimal: English in Language Policy and Planning' (*WEn* 22[2003] 419–31), Michael A.K. Halliday's 'Written Language, Standard Language, Global Language' (*WEn* 22[2003] 405–18) and Ruqaiya Hasan's 'Globalization, Literacy and Ideology' (*WEn* 22[2003] 433–48).

Finally, a number of articles specifically address the New Englishes rather than English as a global language. Edgar Schneider presents 'The Dynamics of New Englishes: From Identity Construction to Dialect Birth' (*Language* 79[2003]

233–81), proposing a cyclical model to accommodate the formation and development of all New Englishes. This comprises five consecutive phases (Foundation, Exonormative Stabilization, Nativization, Endonormative Stabilization and Differentiation), which are illustrated by a number of case studies ranging from Fiji to New Zealand, which were chosen to reflect different stages of this more or less uniform development. Andrea Sand looks at 'The Definite Article in Irish English and Other Contact Varieties of English' (in Tristram, ed., *The Celtic Englishes*, pp. 413–30), pointing out that many features previously attributed to Gaelic substrate influence in Irish English can be found in many New Englishes as well. Yamuna Kachru reports 'On Definite Reference in World Englishes' (*WEn* 22[2003] 497–510), drawing on insertion task experiments in her EIL classroom and previous research on article use in the New Englishes to suggest new pedagogical approaches to teaching article use in an ESL environment.

Outside the sphere of the New Englishes, but nevertheless important for the study of English as a world language, a special issue of *WEn* (22:i[2003]) deals with English in South America. In their introduction, 'English in South America, the Other Forgotten Continent' (*WEn* 22[2003] 83–90), the editors Patricia Friedrich and Margie Berns discuss the role of English in the linguistic and ethnic diversity of many developing nations on this continent and trace the political developments in South America. Most of the contributions are concerned with issues of education and language planning, but Paul Maersk Nielsen's study of 'English in Argentina: A Sociolinguistic Profile' (*WEn* 22[2003] 199–209) is also of interest to linguists working on the New Englishes.

Moving on the southern hemisphere, we note that the majority of publications are concerned with NZE. Koenraad Kuiper's 'Studying New Zealand English' (*EnT* 75:iii[2003] 31–4) gives a brief overview of recently completed and ongoing research, especially with regard to the history of NZE. Publications from the major projects include Margaret Maclagan and Elizabeth Gordon's report on 'Variation and Sound Change in New Zealand' (in Britain and Cheshire, eds., *Social Dialectology*, pp. 69–80), in which they support Trudgill's hypotheses about individual internal variation on the basis of data collected within the Origins of New Zealand English project (ONZE), especially concerning the TRAP and DRESS vowels and the merger of the NEAR and SQUARE vowels. Daniel Schreier, Elizabeth Gordon, Jennifer Hay and Margaret Mclagan also look at 'The Regional and Sociolinguistic Dimension of /hw/ Maintenance and Loss in Early 20th Century New Zealand English' (*EWW* 24[2003] 245–70), identifying the demographic, social and linguistic factors leading to the retention or loss of this feature in Otago, Canterbury and North Island. Another study of 'Linguistic Archaeology: The Scottish Input to New Zealand Phonology' (*JEngL* 31[2003] 103–24), by Peter Trudgill, Margaret Mclagan and Gillian Lewis, identifies the—rather indirect—Scottish input to the phonology of NZE based on the ONZE data. Daniel Schreier reports on 'Convergence and Language Shift in New Zealand: Consonant Cluster Reduction in 19th Century Maori English' (*JSoc* 7[2003] 378–91) on the basis of ONZE data, showing that the Maori informants in the early database display consonant cluster reduction frequencies on a par with L2 speakers of English, but the feature did not fossilize and disappeared around the First World War. Miriam Meyerhoff and Nancy Niedzielski's study of 'The Globalisation of Vernacular Variation' (*JSoc* 7[2003] 534–55) is concerned with more recent changes in NZE, namely the adoption of a flap for intervocalic /t/ or the adoption of lexical items such as *truck* or quotative *be like*. Donna Starks and Scott Allan investigate 'What Comes Before *t*? Nonalveolar *s* in Auckland' (*JEngL* 31[2003] 273–80) on the basis of elicited speech data from over 600 Pakeha speakers from the Auckland area, finding that fronted /s/ is socially conditioned and mainly found in the speech of younger female professionals. Janet Holmes, Maria Stubbe and Meredith Marra look at 'Language, Humour and Ethnic Identity Marking in New Zealand English' (in Mair, ed., pp. 431–56), pointing out features which mark Maori ethnicity, such as syllable-timed rhythm, the use of the pragmatic particle *eh*, the borrowing of Maori lexical items into English discourse and the use of humour to mark the ethnic boundary between Maori and Pakeha speakers. Robert B. Kaplan and Richard B. Baldauf Junior's *Language and Language-in-Education Planning in the Pacific Basin* gives detailed information about the linguistic situation and 'Language Planning in New Zealand: A Window of Opportunity' (pp. 167–84), as well as on 'Language Planning Australia: From Indigenous to International Multiculturalism?' (pp. 143–66). Finally, Barbara M. Horvath and Ronald J. Horvath take 'A Closer Look at the Constraint Hierarchy: Order, Contrast and Geographical Scale' (*LVC* 15[2003] 143–70) by examining five constraint hierarchies involved in the vocalization of /l/ in Australian and NZE across a number of geolinguistic scales in order to differentiate between universal constraints and geolinguistically conditioned constraints.

Daniel Schreier has published extensively on Tristan da Cunha English this year. Tristan da Cunha English, together with the other south Atlantic varieties, Falkland Islands English and St Helena English, belongs to the least studied native varieties of English, hence new research in this area is highly welcome. In his monograph, *Isolation and Language Change*, he addresses the question of language development in the 'remotest inhabited island in the world' (p. 5): whether the features found in this linguistic enclave can be attributed to retention from nineteenth-century dialects, to linguistic innovation, or whether they were transplanted from varieties spoken elsewhere. After outlining the linguistic and extra-linguistic history of the tiny speech community on Tristan da Cunha, the author proceeds to analyse present tense concord, the regularization of the present and past tense forms of BE to *is* and *was*, completive *done* and the construction *useta went* in great detail. He comes to the conclusion that a combination of language contact and dialect contact have led to the present-day variety. A brief description of the phonetic and phonological features of Tristan da Cunha English can be found in the appendix. This pioneering study is of great importance to the study of varieties of English, since all previous descriptions of Tristan da Cunha English are based on data collected while the inhabitants of the island were evacuated in England and could thus not be recorded in familiar surroundings. Schreier compares the conditions on the island to a 'linguistic Petri dish', which can shed light on language change in progress with minimal outside influence. He has also published an adapted version of chapter 8 of his book as an article entitled 'Insularity and Linguistic Endemicity' (*JEngL* 31[2003] 249–72), in which he discusses the origins of the construction in which *used to* is combined with the past tense, as in *useta went*, which he attributes to the influence of SLA on the island. Schreier also wonders whether there is 'An East Anglian in the South Atlantic? Interpreting Morphosyntactic Resemblances in Terms of Direct Input, Parallel Development, and Linguistic Contact' (in Britain and Cheshire, eds., pp. 81–96), interpreting irregular third person singular *-s* in Tristan da Cunha English and other varieties of English, and arguing in favour of an independent development based on language contact and dialect levelling.

Tom McArthur's 'English as an Asian Language: Some Observations on Roles and Realities in the World's Largest Continent' (*EnT* 74:ii[2003] 19–22) may serve as an introduction to the topic of English in Asia since it provides a very brief survey of the use of English in this area. Kaplan and Baldauf provide a much more detailed description of the current situation in their volume *Language and Language-in-Education Planning* concerning the situation in countries such as Singapore (pp. 123–42), Malaysia and Brunei Darussalam (pp. 103–22), Indonesia (pp. 83–102), the Philippines (pp. 63–82), Taiwan (pp. 47–62), the two Koreas (pp. 31–46) and Japan (pp. 17–30). Several contributions in Ahrens, Parker, Stiersdorfer and Tam, eds., *Anglophone Cultures in Southeast Asia*, deal with issues of linguistic identity in South-East Asia. Braj. B. Kachru concentrates on India in his report 'On Nativizing *Mantra:* Identity Construction in Anglophone Englishes' (pp. 55–72), while Anne Pakir's discussion of 'Which English? The Nativization of English' (pp. 73–84) and Kwok-kan Tam's 'Negotiating the Self Between Cultures and Nation' (pp. 85–96) deal with Singapore English and its role in the construction of linguistic and non-linguistic identity.

China receives a lot of attention again this year. Kingsley Bolton presents *Chinese Englishes: A Sociolinguistic History*, the most comprehensive treatment of the topic so far. After an introduction discussing New Englishes and World Englishes, Bolton begins his study in the recent past with 'The Sociolinguistics of English in Late Colonial Hong Kong, 1980–1997', in which he discusses the demographics and socio-economic contexts for English in Hong Kong, as well as language attitudes and language ideology (e.g. the myth of the falling standard). The chapter on 'The Archaeology of "Chinese Englishes", 1637–1949' sheds light on the spread of English in China. Bolton makes use of a large number of early sources, such as the diary of Peter Mundy from the seventeenth century, or early accounts of Canton jargon or Chinese Pidgin English, the *Monograph of Macao* from 1751 and a glossary of *The Common Foreign Language of the Redhaired People* (i.e. the English) from the mid-nineteenth century. The next chapter, 'The Emergence of Hong Kong English as a "New English"', is traced within Braj Kachru's framework of the three concentric circles; it gives a survey of Hong Kong English phonology and lexicon, and reports earlier research on attitudes towards Hong Kong English. In the final chapter on 'Hong Kong, China and Chinese Englishes' the most recent developments since the handover in 1997 are covered, as well as the history of teaching English in mainland China. The appendix contains many maps and illustrations, as well as reproductions of *The Common Foreign Language of the Redhaired People,* a glossary of present-day Hong Kong English lexemes and a comprehensive bibliography. This monograph will without doubt become the standard reference work on the Chinese Englishes, despite the fact that the coverage of the linguistic (especially the morpho-syntactic) features remains sketchy at best.

Jiang Yajun looks at 'English as a Chinese Language' (*EnT* 74:ii[2003] 3–8), describing the increasing use of English in China and the government policies concerning the teaching of English. Niu Qiang and Martin Wolff write about 'China and Chinese, or Chingland and Chinglish?' (*EnT* 74:ii[2003] 9–11), and are deeply concerned that China's new English-oriented language policy will adversely affect its autonomy. Wei Yun and Fei Jia's article 'Using English in China' (*EnT* 74:ii[2003] 42–7) is more feature-oriented, and traces the linguistic development from Chinese Pidgin English to Chinglish, a more recent nativized variety called 'China English' and a modern version of pidgin English called 'New Chinese Pidgin English'. Terence T.T. Pang discusses 'Hong Kong English: A Stillborn Variety?' (*EnT* 74:ii[2003] 12–18), pondering whether Hong Kong English is a variety of its own on linguistic grounds. Stephen Evans and Christopher Green report on 'The Use of English by Chinese Professionals in Post-1997 Hong Kong' (*JMMD* 24[2003] 386–412), giving detailed evidence on who speaks or listens to English in the workplace and who reads or writes English emails, faxes, memos or letters. According to their questionnaire data, English is used most in the fields of engineering, construction/real estate and manufacturing, and it is largely individuals in the highest positions who also speak English rather than just write or read in it.

There are also a large number of publications on English in Singapore and Malaysia. Unfortunately, Deterding, Ling and Brown, eds., *English in Singapore: Research on Grammar*, was unavailable for review. According to the publisher's homepage, the volume contains a large number of contributions, of which nine are concerned with descriptive analyses of Singapore English grammar, for example null subjects, plural marking, tense-marking, and relative clauses, while the remaining chapters are concerned with issues of language and grammar teaching in Singapore. David Deterding also presents 'An Instrumental Study of the Monophthong Vowels in Singapore English' (*EWW* 24[2003] 1–16), comparing the formants of conversational vowels of ten Singapore English speakers with measurements of British speakers. He comes to the conclusion that there are fewer vowel contrasts in Singapore English and that the remaining contrasts are smaller than in British English, but that this does not impair intelligibility. David Gil shows how 'English Goes Asian: Number and (In)definiteness in the Singlish Noun Phrase' (in Plank, ed., *Noun Phrase Structure in the Languages of Europe*, pp. 467–514), looking at determiners and possessives and different ways of expressing definiteness in Colloquial Singapore English (CSE). Mary Besemeres and Anna Wierzbicka take a closer look at 'The Meaning of the Particle *lah* in Singapore English' (*P&C* 11[2003] 3–38), giving a number of meanings and paraphrases for this discourse particle. Lionel Wee observes 'The Birth of a New Particle: *know* in Colloquial Singapore English' (*WEn* 22[2003] 5–13), claiming that *know* has developed away from *you know* in CSE and now falls into the same category as the Singaporean discourse markers *lah, lor* or *meh.* Bao Zhiming is concerned with 'Social Stigma and Grammatical Autonomy in Nonnative Varieties of English' (*LSoc* 32[2003] 23–46), using innovative phonological features in CSE as an example and showing that some of these features originate in the phoneme system, while others are associated with specific lexemes. He further claims that the social stigma attached to such features poses a barrier to the autonomous development and stabilization of the variety. Shanta Nair-Venugopal discusses 'Malaysian English, Normativity and Workplace Interaction' (*WEn* 22[2003] 15–29), illustrating the fact that a local non-standard variety of Malaysian English is indeed used widely in business and training contexts, along with code-switching and code-mixing (mainly to Malay), although the official policy calls for standard English in formal business contexts. Yeok-hwa Ngeow, Keng-soon Soo and Avon Chrismore also look at 'Workplace Perceptions and Attitudes Toward Standard English Use' (*JAPC* 13[2003] 231–67), showing that, while many civil service and private sector employees prefer standard English to Malaysian English, it is not necessarily available to them due to changes in language and education policy since independence. Subra Govindasamy and Mohana Nambiar study 'Social Networks: Applicability to Minority Communities in Multilingual Settings' (*IJSL* 161[2003] 25–45) in the immigrant community of the Malayalees, where, despite close-knit community interaction, a language shift from Malayalam to English is presently taking place.

Moving on to the Indian subcontinent, Eugenia Olavarría de Ersson and Philip Shaw study the 'Verb Complementation Patterns in Indian Standard English' (*EWW* 24[2003] 137–61) of nine different verbs on the basis of online newspapers from India and Great Britain. They show that patterns like *He provided them money* are more frequent in Indian English, while British writers prefer prepositional constructions such as *He provided them with money*. Raja Ram Mehrotra gives 'A British Response to Some Indian English Usages' (*EnT* 75:iii[2003] 19–25), in which he examines the intelligibility of various Indian English expressions, such as *face-cut* 'facial profile' or *tempo* 'three-wheeled motorized vehicle'. Finally for the Indian subcontinent, Rajiva Wijesinha reports on 'Bringing Back the Bathwater: New Initiatives in English Policy in Sri Lanka' (in Mair, ed., pp. 367–74), discussing language attitudes and language policy concerning the use of English since Sri Lanka's independence fifty years ago.

Roger M. Thompson provides an in-depth study of *Filipino English and Taglish: Language Switching from Multiple Perspectives*. The first part of the book is dedicated to the history, status and functions of English in the Philippines, the rise of Tagalog as 'rival to English' and the development of a mixed code, Taglish. The second part is concerned with a questionnaire-based analysis of the social functions of English in Manila and some of the remoter provinces of the Philippines, while the third part is a data-based analysis of the use of English, Tagalog and Taglish in the media. Thompson shows that English remains the language of the elite and that Tagalog and Taglish media portray English as a negative, corrupting force in the Philippines. Because of this, his forecast for the future of English is rather bleak, with the prediction that once a version of Filipino suited for the domains of science and business is accepted, English will disappear from the Philippines.

In contrast to some previous years, African Englishes received a fair amount of attention in 2003. Sinfree Makone and Ulrike H. Meinhof are the editors of the *AILA Review* (16[2003]), entitled *Africa and Applied Linguistics*. Gibson

Ferguson provides a survey of research on 'Classroom Code-Switching in Post-Colonial Contexts: Functions, Attitudes and Policies' (*AILA Review* 16[2003] 38–51) not restricted to African settings, and proposes a number of ways of using code-switching effectively in bi- or multilingual classrooms. Yisa Kehunde Yusuf analyses 'Dysphemisms in the Language of Nigeria's President Olusegun Obasanjo' (*AILA Review* 16[2003] 104–19). The bulk of the contributions, however, are concerned with South Africa, such as Ian Bekker's article 'Using Historical Data to Explain Language Attitudes: A South African Case Study' (*AILA Review* 16[2003] 62–77), in which he compares language attitude data from the apartheid period with more recent data. Pulie Thetala writes on 'Discourse, Culture and the Law: The Analysis of Crosstalk in the South African Bilingual Courtroom' (*AILA Review* 16[2003] 78–88), especially with regard to the role of court interpreters and the importance of cultural repertoires in a courtroom setting. Vivian de Klerk looks at 'Language and the Law: Who Has the Upper Hand?' (*AILA Review* 16[2003] 89–103), discussing the features of legal English in the South African court system and its implications for professional and non-professional participants in court cases. Another publication also concerned with more than one variety of English in Africa is Augustin Simo Bobda's article, 'The Formation of Regional and National Features in African English Pronunciation: An Exploration of Some Non-Interference Factors' (*EWW* 24[2003] 17–42), in which he points out possible sources of phonetic and phonological features in a large number of African Englishes, which cannot be traced to L1 interference. These sources include feature dissemination through migration or geographical vicinity (as in West Africa), colonial or post-colonial influence, and the pressures of a national standard, among others.

Turning to the Englishes of East Africa, we welcome the publication of a volume on Kenyan English. The title of Paul Skandera's monograph, *Drawing a Map of Africa: Idiom in Kenyan English*, already contains one of the idiomatic features he discusses, since 'drawing a map of Africa' refers to the foot movements of embarrassed girls when talking to a boy they are interested in. Skandera combines several methodological approaches, including casual observation, corpus analysis and elicitation tests, to identify idioms which are typical of Kenyan English. While the first four chapters are devoted to introductory topics such as definitions, previous research, and the sociolinguistic make-up of Kenyan English, chapters 5 to 10 present various types of idioms, ranging from those which only differ in frequency with regard to StE (e.g. *medicine man*) and those whose form or meaning have changed in comparison to StE (e.g. *fuelwoods*) to new coinages (e.g. *talk nicely* 'bribe'), borrowings (e.g. *polepole* 'slowly'), and loan translations (e.g. *to have eaten much salt* 'be old'). Skandera presents his material in a straightforward and transparent way and manages to correct a number of mistaken assumptions and incorrect citations found in previous studies. In his conclusions, he carefully places his study within the wider context of the New Englishes and correctly points out that not all of the over 300 idioms discussed in his book are restricted to Kenyan usage. Skandera provides a very thorough and careful discussion of a topic which has so far been mainly treated on the basis of anecdotal evidence. Kembo-Sure describes 'The Democratization of Language Policy:

A Cultural-Linguistic Analysis of the Status of English in Kenya' (in Mair, ed., pp. 247–66), suggesting that the incorporation of local varieties like Sheng in official language policy could bridge the gap between those Kenyans who unquestioningly hold English in highest esteem and those who resent it on the grounds of postcolonial cultural dominance. Safari T.A. Mafu investigates 'Postcolonial Language Planning in Tanzania: What Are the Difficulties and What Is the Way Out?' (in Mair, ed., pp. 267–78), showing that the political ideals of the immediate post-independence period which led to a language policy strongly in favour of Swahili are now being replaced by the economic aspirations of the elite in favour of English.

The majority of publications are concerned with South Africa. Kay McCormick's account of *Language in Cape Town's District Six* is a detailed sociolinguistic study of language use in a working-class neighbourhood of Cape Town. The study is based on data collection in the 1980s and 1999–2000, including informant interviews, observation and written records. McCormick provides ample background information on the history of language contact in the Cape Town area and the socio-economic make-up of the Chapel Street neighbourhood. The linguistic codes available in this speech community are Afrikaans and English, both in more standard and local non-standard varieties. McCormick discusses code choices in the family and neighbourhood, the workplace, and social institutions such as the rugby club, the church guild and schools. This is followed by a detailed analysis of code-mixing and code-switching, both in adult and children's interactions. In her conclusions, she traces the development of language contact in the area, pointing out changes in language attitudes leading to a more positive evaluation of the local vernacular, and a complete language shift in the school system, from Afrikaans and English to English-only education. A detailed appendix provides concise grammatical descriptions of the local varieties. Nkonko M. Kamwangamalu is concerned with the 'Globalization of English, and Language Maintenance and Shift in South Africa' (*IJSL* 164[2003] 65–81), discussing the recent trend towards English monolingualism in South Africa and suggesting ways to preserve the indigenous languages. Along similar lines, he discusses 'When 2 + 9 = 1: English and the Politics of Language Planning in a Multilingual Society' (in Mair, ed., pp. 235–46) and 'Social Change and Language Shift: South Africa' (*ARAL* 23[2003] 225–42). Vivian de Klerk is working 'Towards a Norm in South African Englishes: The Case for Xhosa English' (*WEn* 22[2003] 463–81), analysing twenty linguistic features on the basis of her Xhosa English corpus which have previously been attested for SABE in order to find out whether they are widespread enough to be accepted as linguistic norms for SABE. Along similar lines, de Klerk writes on 'Xhosa English as an Institutionalized Variety of English: In Search of Evidence' (*EWW* 24[2003] 221–43), providing linguistic features which may be regarded as part of the emerging standard of Xhosa English or even SABE. Sharita Bharuthram studies 'Politeness Phenomena in the Hindu Sector of the South African Indian English Speaking Community' (*JPrag* 35[2003] 1523–44) on the basis of informant interviews and completion tasks. Finally, Gregory Kamwendo asks 'Is Malawi Guilty of Spoiling the Queen's Language? The Past and Present of a Distinctive English in Southern Africa'

(*EnT* 74:ii[2003] 30–3), discussing the status of English in Malawi since the end of the colonial period and new policies to remedy the lack of competence in English on the part of some Malawi speakers of the language.

Moving on to West Africa, Inyang Udofot examines 'Stress and Rhythm in the Nigerian Accent of English: A Preliminary Investigation' (*EWW* 24[2003] 201–20) on the basis of reading and spontaneous speech data from sixty Nigerians and a native speaker of British English. Udofot proceeds to show that the non-standard speech of Nigerians is indeed characterized by syllable-timing, but the results for the more standard speakers are inconclusive and require further research. Lothar Peter, Hans-Georg Wolf and Augustin Simo Bobda provide 'An Account of Distinctive Phonetic and Lexical Features of Gambian English' (*EWW* 24[2003] 43–61), which distinguish Gambian English from other West African varieties. Finally, Jean-Paul Kouega reports on 'Camfranglais: A Novel Slang in Cameroon Schools. An Account of an Intricate Hybrid Use by Young People in West Africa' (*EnT* 74:ii[2003] 23–9), also providing a sample text and a glossary of terms used in Camfranglais.

From Africa to the Caribbean. Jeannette Allsopp has published *The Caribbean Multilingual Dictionary of Flora, Fauna and Foods in English, French, French Creole and Spanish*, which supplements *The Dictionary of Caribbean English Usage* compiled by Richard Allsopp (cf. *YWES* 77[1998] 96). Although the dictionary is organized according to Caribbean English entries, lexemes from the other languages can easily be accessed through the index. The dictionary also gives the scientific Latin terms for plants and animals to help identify items for which many different terms have been coined or which are used differently in the Caribbean, e.g. *almonds* are the fruits of the tree *Terminalia catappa*, while those seeds known as *almonds* in Europe are called *almond nuts* in the Anglophone Caribbean. Hubert Devonish discusses two instances of 'Language Advocacy and "Conquest" Diglossia in the "Anglophone" Caribbean' (in Mair, ed., pp. 157–78), reflecting the consequences of linguistic expertise on the status of Caribbean Creoles in the political, legal and educational system. Hazel Simmons-McDonald ponders the implications of 'Decolonising English: The Caribbean Counter-Thrust' (in Mair, ed., pp. 179–202), analysing changing language attitudes towards various varieties of English in the Caribbean and opening perspectives for a critical language pedagogy in the region.

Turning our attention to creolistics, we note a number of publications addressing central questions about the nature of creoles in general. The collection of papers on the *Phonology and Morphology of Creole Languages* edited by Ingo Plag presents the results of a conference aimed at redressing the imbalance of research in creolistics, which is largely concerned with morpho-syntax but tends to ignore stress, intonation or inflectional morphology. Most contributions to this volume deal with one particular creole and will be discussed below. On a more general level, Christian Uffmann writes on 'Markedness, Faithfulness and Creolization: The Retention of the Unmarked' (in Plag, ed., pp. 2–23). He examines the vowel inventories of Haitian Creole and Ndyuka and their African substrate languages on the basis of OT. Marlyse Baptista looks at 'Inflectional Plural Marking in Pidgins and Creoles: A Comparative Study' (in Plag, ed., pp. 315–32), considering pluralization strategies in six Atlantic and Pacific P/C languages and determining the linguistic triggers for pluralization. Alain Kihm examines 'Inflectional Categories in Creole Languages' (in Plag, ed., pp. 333–63) from the theoretical angle of Distributed Morphology, concluding that, while creole languages do display some inflectional morphology, its role is generally limited while the role of syntax is maximized. Three further papers presented at the same conference on creole morphology are included in the *Yearbook of Morphology 2002*, namely Peter Bakker's discussion of 'Pidgin Inflectional Morphology and its Implications for Creole Morphology' (*YM* [2002] 3–33) and two papers concerned with the Suriname creoles which are reviewed below.

Kouwenberg, ed., *Twice as Meaningful: Reduplication in Pidgins, Creoles and Other Contact Languages*, is the first comprehensive treatment of the morphological process of reduplication, which is often cited as typical for P/C languages. The book contains over thirty contributions, both longer articles and shorter notes on individual varieties, which cannot all be reviewed in detail here. Silvia Kouwenberg and Darlene LaCharité explain 'The Meanings of "More of the Same": Iconicity in Reduplication and the Evidence for Substrate Transfer in the Genesis of Caribbean Creole Languages', teasing apart the various meanings of reduplication and suggesting that any claims of substrate transfer must pass a test of similar degrees of markedness in substrate and recipient language. This is taken up by Mikael Parkvall's chapter on 'Reduplication in the Atlantic Creoles', in which he looks at different types of reduplication found in the Atlantic Creoles and possible connections with their African substrates. However, Peter Bakker highlights 'The Absence of Reduplication in Pidgins', concluding that for the majority of non-expanded pidgins, reduplication is absent despite its presence in the substrate languages. This would suggest a connection between reduplication and creolization. The remaining contributions are concerned with reduplication in individual varieties, such as Guyanese Creole, Jamaican Creole, the Suriname Creoles, Limonese Creole, Krio, Ghanaian Pidgin English, Bislama, Pitkern-Norfolk, the Pacific Pidgins, Hawai'ian Creole English and a large number of P/C languages with French, Spanish, Portuguese and Dutch lexifiers. The book thus provides an excellent survey of the various processes studied under the heading of 'reduplication', of their presence or absence in a large range of P/C languages and their possible origins, as well as different methodological approaches to the topic.

For those interested in recent developments in creolistics, John H. McWhorter's article 'Pidgins and Creoles as Models of Language Change: The State of the Art' (*ARAL* 23[2003] 202–12) is a good starting point since it addresses recent findings and controversies on topics such as the Language Bioprogram Hypothesis, the nature of creole continua, grammaticalization in P/C languages, new findings by creolists working within the framework of generative grammar and the latest controversies over the definition of *creole*. Sarah G. Thomason's column 'What Motivates Changes that Occur in Emerging Pidgins and Creoles?' (*JPCL* 18[2003] 107–20) also addresses issues of language change, showing that it is very difficult to separate language change due to pidgin or creole formation from 'ordinary' language change. Salikoko S. Mufwene's note on 'Genetic Linguistics and Genetic Creolistics: A Response to Sarah G. Thomason's "Creoles and Genetic Relationships"' (*JPCL* 18[2003] 273–88), and Sarah Thomason's 'Response to Mufwene's Response' (*JPCL* 18[2003]

289–98), once again debate whether P/C languages are simply varieties or genetic descendants of their lexifier languages or represent a special type of language. Along similar lines, Michel de Graff argues 'Against Creole Exceptionalism' (*Language* 79[2003] 391–410) in favour of 'postcolonial creolistics', in which creole languages could be studied just like postcolonial literature and culture. Robert Chaudenson examines 'Creolistics and Sociolinguistic Theories' (*IJSL* 160[2003] 123–46), looking at historical sociolinguistic approaches to creolization as well as synchronic sociolinguistic studies, such as research on creole continua, diglossia and language appropriation. Silvia Kouwenberg and Peter L. Patrick are the editors of a special volume of *SSLA* (25[2003] 175–306) on creolistics and SLA. In their introduction, they are 'Reconsidering the Role of SLA in Pidginization and Creolization' (*SSLA* 25[2003] 175–84), tracing the history of the relationship between SLA and creolistics and pointing out areas that have not been addressed in previous research. Jeff Siegel looks at 'Substrate Influence in Creoles and the Role of Transfer in Second Language Acquisition' (*SSLA* 25[2003] 185–209), showing that transfer in L2 acquisition and use play a role in the emergence of pidgins and creoles, which can help us understand substrate influence and the origins of particular creole features. Rena Helms-Park is concerned with 'Transfer in SLA and Creoles' (*SSLA* 25[2003] 211–44), using data produced by native speakers of Vietnamese. J. Clancy Clements compares 'The Tense-Aspect System in Pidgins and Naturalistically Learned L2' (*SSLA* 25[2003] 245–81) on the basis of data produced by a Chinese speaker of English. Angelika Becker and Tonjes Veenstra discuss 'The Survival of Inflectional Morphology in French-Related Creoles' (*SSLA* 25[2003] 283–306) with regard to SLA.

Carla L. Hudson and Inge-Marie Eigsti propose 'The Lexical Competence Hypothesis: A Cognitive Account of the Relationship between Vernacularization and Grammatical Expansion in Creolization' (*JPCL* 18[2003] 1–79), providing fascinating experiment-based research on the relationship between the lexical competence of speakers of a newly created language and the ability to use complex sentence structures. Finally, Valerie Youssef examines 'How Perfect is Perfective Marking? An Analysis of Terminological Problems in the Description of Some Tense-Aspect Categories in Creoles' (*JPCL* 18[2003] 81–105), showing that the different meanings ascribed to the labels *perfective, imperfective* and *perfect* have prevented a clear analysis of creole TMA and pointing out a range of features central to these categories on the basis of typological and descriptive work on Caribbean creoles.

A number of publications dealing with individual Atlantic creoles have also appeared this year. Aceto and Williams, eds., *Contact Englishes of the Eastern Caribbean*, is especially welcome since the contributions offer insights on the lesser-known varieties spoken in the region. Becky Childs, Jeffrey Reaser and Walt Wolfram start by 'Defining Ethnic Varieties in the Bahamas: Phonological Accommodation in Black and White Enclave Communities' on Great Abaco Island, looking especially at consonant cluster reduction, *h*-deletion and insertion, /w/ and /v/ alternation and the vowels. Helean McPhee studies 'The Grammatical Features of TMA auxiliaries in Bahamian Creole', such as *bin*, *did*, *go*, *musi*, *da/ a*, *-in*, *does*, *useta* and *done*. Cecilia Butler provides the first account of 'English in the Turks and Caicos Islands: A Look at Grand Turk' on the basis of informant interviews, describing its phonology and morpho-syntax, while the short section on the lexicon is purely anecdotal. Robin Sabino, Mary Diamond and Leah Cockcroft examine 'Language Variety in the Virgin Islands: Plural Marking' on the basis of four corpora consisting of folktales recorded in the 1930s and 1980s as well as a political forum broadcast from the 1980s. Jeffrey P. Williams reports on 'The Establishment and Perpetuation of Anglophone White Enclave Communities in the Eastern Caribbean: The Case of Island Harbour, Anguilla', providing the socio-historical background and the linguistic features of the 'Webster Dialect' (p. 108). Michael Aceto discusses 'What Are Creole Languages? An Alternative Approach to the Anglophone Atlantic World with Special Emphasis on Barbudan Creole English', and suggests a classification into 'Immigrant Creole Varieties' (as spoken in Panama or Trinidad), 'Dialect Creole Varieties' (as spoken on the Bahamas or the Cayman Islands) and 'Autonomous or Deep Creole Varieties' (as spoken in Jamaica or Barbuda). Beverley Bryan and Rosalind Burnette study 'Language Variation and Language Use among Teachers in Dominica', where English, French-based Kwéyòl and two creolized varieties of English are spoken. Paul B. Garrett has found 'An "English Creole" That Isn't: On the Sociohistorical Origins and Linguistic Classification of the Vernacular English of St. Lucia', concluding that many non-standard features in the vernacular on St. Lucia are due to influence from French-based Kwéyòl. Ronald Kephart reports on 'Creole English on Carriacou: A Sketch and Some Implications', describing some of its most salient structural features. Gerard van Herk looks at 'Barbadian Lects: Beyond Meso' based on informant interviews, pointing out some of the creole features of Bajan. David Sutcliffe describes 'Eastern Caribbean Suprasegmental Systems: A Comparative View with Particular Reference to Barbadian, Trinidadian and Guyanese', in which he gives examples of lexical and grammatical tone in these varieties. In another volume, Hubert Devonish provides a survey article on 'Caribbean Creoles' (in Deumert and Vandenbussche, eds., *Germanic Standardizations*, pp. 41–67), looking at issues of socio-historical history, norm selection, creole standardization, codification and norm acceptance for Standard Caribbean English and English-lexicon creoles.

Turning to individual varieties, we find a number of publications on the Suriname creoles. Bettina Migge examines *Creole Formation as Language Contact: The Case of the Suriname Creoles*. She traces the early development of the Suriname creoles using data on the socio-economic situation in Suriname at the time of the earliest forms of creole development in the seventeenth and eighteenth centuries. Following Thomason and Kaufman's approach to language contact, Migge examines the European input, such as bound morphology and the retention of free grammatical morphemes, as well as the African input, such as lexical and structural retentions and language internal change. In her final chapter, Migge discusses possible implications of her findings for the theoretical framework of creolistics, claiming that the evidence from Suriname points to strong parallels between L2 acquisition and creole formation. Several contributions in Plag, ed., *Phonology and Morphology of Creole Languages*, deal with early forms of the Suriname creoles. Sabine Lappe and Ingo Plag compare 'Rules vs. Analogy: Modelling Variation in Word-Final Epenthesis in Sranan' (pp. 71–90), arguing that both factors play a role in the development from eighteenth-century to modern Sranan. Norval Smith looks at 'New Evidence from the Past: To Epenthesize or Not to Epenthesize? That Is the Question' (pp. 91–107) in the eighteenth-century creoles Sranan, Ndyuka and Aluku showing that the three types of liquid consonant cluster were originally divided by epenthetic vowels. Margot van den Berg's contribution is concerned with an example of derivational morphology, namely 'Early 18th Century Sranan *-man*' (pp. 231–51), which could be used in compounds but also in gender-neutral noun derivations. Elsewhere, Maria Braun and Ingo Plag examine 'How Transparent is Creole Morphology? A Study of Early Sranan Wordformation' (*YM* [2002] 81–104) and Jeff Good reports on 'Tonal Morphology in a Creole: High-Tone Raising in Saramaccan Serial Verb Constructions' (*YM* [2002] 105–34).

Angela Bartens provides *A Contrastive Grammar Islander–Caribbean Standard English–Spanish*, in which she presents the structures of the English-based creole spoken in San Andrés and Providence in contrast to Caribbean Standard English and Spanish to suit the educational needs of the speech community, in which those are the official languages. All examples from Islander are thus translated into English and Spanish. The grammar, which comprises word classes, phrases, and clauses as well as simple and complex sentences, is rounded off by a description of the phonetic and graphemic system of Islander and an appendix containing African lexical retentions. Peter Snow reports on 'Talking with Tourists in a Panamanian Creole Village: An Emerging Site of Production' (*JPCL* 18 [2003] 299–309) in Old Bank on the island of Bastimentos, where due to an influx of English-speaking tourists the locally spoken English-based creole is maintained as an alternative code to the official language, Spanish. Winford James examines 'The Role of Tone and Rhyme Structure in the Organisation of Grammatical Morphemes in Tobagonian' (in Plag, ed., pp. 165–92), especially with regard to auxiliaries, negators, determiners and suffixes, showing that there is grammatical tone in Tobagonian Creole as well as emphatic tone, and that rhyme plays an important role in the selection of allomorphs. Similarly, Shelome Gordon provides examples of 'Prosodic Contrast in Jamaican Reduplication' (in Plag, ed., pp. 193–208), in which the intensifier meaning is distinguished from the distributive meaning by means of pitch patterns.

Two articles stress the connections between Caribbean creoles and AAVE. David Sutcliffe studies 'African American English Suprasegmentals: A Study of Pitch Patterns' (in Plag, ed., pp. 147–62), pointing out similarities in grammatical pitch between AAVE and many Atlantic creoles, which he proposes to classify on a cline of tonality. Tracey L. Weldon discusses 'Copula Variability in Gullah' (*LVC* 15[2003] 37–72), pointing out connections between Gullah, AAVE and the Atlantic creoles on the basis of copula distribution patterns.

Let us turn to Africa. Anne Schröder has published a pioneering study of the *Status, Functions, and Prospects of Pidgin English: An Empirical Approach to Language Dynamics in Cameroon*, in which she combines qualitative and quantitative methods to shed light on actual language use and attitudes towards Cameroon Pidgin English (CamP)—a language generally neglected by language planners in Cameroon—in eight of the ten provinces, including some areas traditionally not considered pidgin-speaking. Schröder conducted sixty-six semi-structured interviews at a large number of educational institutions with students and staff, both Anglophone and Francophone, and evaluated almost 2,000 questionnaires to determine the actual language use, variability of forms and mutual intelligibility of the CamP spoken by a wide range of Cameroonians. She concludes that CamP is used much more widely than previously attested and that variability with regard to morpho-syntax is low. Thus the prospects of CamP as at least a regional lingua franca if not a national language are high. The book is accompanied by a CD-ROM containing maps, questionnaires, SSPS cross-tabulations for the questionnaire items, a few CamP sample texts and the transcriptions of all interviews. One French and one English interview are also available as sound files, which reveal that the orthographic transcriptions of the interviews are probably not always as faithful as one would wish, but since the interviews are only analysed in terms of their content these faults are minor. Unfortunately, no samples of spoken CamP are given, since the interviews were conducted in the official languages English and French. Despite these small shortcomings, Schröder's study fills a large gap in research on CamP, which has been mainly concerned with its linguistic features and so far has not covered its actual functions and status.

Jean-Paul Kouega looks at 'Word Formative Processes in Camfranglais' (*WEn* 22[2003] 511–38), a mixed code combining elements of French, Cameroon Pidgin English, Cameroon English and indigenous languages spoken by Cameroonian secondary students. Dagmar Deuber and Patrick Oloko report on the 'Linguistic and Literary Development of Nigerian Pidgin: The Contribution of Radio Drama' (in Mair, ed., pp. 289–304), providing the results of a survey rating the acceptability and appropriateness of a number of extracts from various text types using pidgin English, such as radio news, radio drama, conversations and interviews, and illustrating the most successful strategy of handling the codes available in Nigeria with extracts from the serial *Rainbow City*. And finally, Joan M. Fayer examines the role of 'African Interpreters in the Atlantic Slave Trade' (*AnL* 45[2003] 281–95) in the formation of the Atlantic creoles, claiming that their continued presence counts as evidence for gradual rather than abrupt creolization.

To round off the section on creolistics, there are a number of publications dealing with Pacific P/C languages. Peter Mühlhäusler's survey article 'Pacific Pidgins and Creoles' (in Deumert and Vandenbussche, eds., pp. 355–81) covers aspects of language planning and standardization for Torres Strait Creole, Norfolk, Hawai'ian Creole, Solomon Island Pijin, Papuan Pidgin English, Kanaka English, Kriol, Chinese Pidgin English, Tok Pisin, Bislama and Pitcairn. Mühlhäusler, Dutton and Romaine, eds., *Tok Pisin Texts: From the Beginning to the Present*, appeared in the text collection sub-series of *VEAW*. As in the other volumes of this series, a chapter (written by Peter Mühlhäusler) on the socio-historical background and the main linguistic features (phonology, morphology, syntax and lexicon) of the variety is followed by a selection of sample texts which have been annotated, glossed, translated and commented on by the editors. The collection contains 100 sample texts spanning the period from the earliest records of pidgin English in New Guinea from the 1840s to the present, including a variety of text types such as government and missionary writing, transcriptions of traditional storytelling, translations into Tok Pisin, spoken and written urban creolized Tok Pisin, newspaper texts, correspondence and advertising, among others. The texts have been collected by the three editors over a long period of time and this is unfortunately reflected in varying transcription conventions; for example, it is not clear whether the preposition *bilong* is always fully pronounced unless the short form *blo* is used or whether the short form is only used by some transcribers while the pronunciation is always *blo*. The book is clearly not intended as a textbook, but rather as a data supplement to publications such as Geoff P. Smith [2002] (see *YWES* 83[2004] 85–6) and Stephen A. Wurm and Peter Mühlhäusler's *Handbook of Tok Pisin* [1985].

Two publications deal with the morphosyntax of Hawai'ian Creole English (HCE). Jeff Siegel and Kent Sakoda's *Pidgin Grammar: An Introduction to the Creole Language of Hawai'i* is a grammar written primarily for a lay audience who still believe that HCE—called *Pidgin* by its speakers—is just 'broken English'. The first chapter traces the origins of HCE and its current situation. In the second chapter, the pronunciation and the writing system are explained, without referring to phonetic symbols. This is followed by a detailed description of word classes, phrases and sentence types. The appendix also contains a word list and a selection of references. The book is written in a very accessible style which makes it useful to non-linguists and beginning students as well. The other publication, Viveka Velupillai's *Hawai'i Creole English: A Typological Analysis of the Tense-Mood-Aspect System* targets an academic audience. The author uses a cross-linguistic framework to assess the present state of TMA in HCE on the basis of a large corpus of spoken and written sources and a questionnaire. Velupillai's use of a well-known framework and terminology, in combination with her careful and detailed analysis, make this an excellent contribution to the field, especially since she is able to show that present-day HCE does not conform to Bickerton's Language Bioprogram Hypothesis, which, ironically, was originally conceived on the basis of HCE data, and that most features of its TMA system are cross-linguistically common.

10. Pragmatics and Discourse Analysis

Taavitsainen and Jucker, eds., *Diachronic Perspectives on Address Term Systems*, is a collection of papers on the use of address terms in more or less distant historical periods of several European languages. In most of the articles, address terms used in the English language, and especially in the early modern period, are examined; the remainder are investigations of the Anglo-Norman, Czech, Finnish, German, and Spanish address term systems. David Burnley studies the use of 'The T/V Pronouns in Later Middle English Literature' (T refers to the second person singular pronoun and its case forms, V refers to the second person plural). Burnley first presents a diagram showing Chaucer's use of the T and V pronouns, in which genre (courtly and non-courtly) and interpersonal relations (e.g. age and social status) are identified as possible factors influencing the choice. The model also accounts for cases of switching between T- and V-forms. The author points out, however, that no single system can explain all occurrences of the pronominal address terms because of the unreliability of sources and variation on different levels: diachronic, regional, personal. Thomas Honegger's '"And if ye wol nat so, my lady sweete, thanne preye I thee ...": Forms of Address in Chaucer's Knight's Tale' is a plea not to restrict research into forms of address to pronominal forms only but to take the complete situational context into account. This includes linguistic features, such as nominal forms of address and terms of self-reference, as well as non-linguistic ones, such as gaze and gesture. All these features are comprised in the concept of 'adversion'. Honegger analyses passages containing dialogue and prayers which show switching between T- and V-forms and identifies combinations of various elements of adversion in these passages. The combinations, which are shown to form five distinctive patterns, illustrate the relations between the protagonists. In 'Family First: Address and Subscription Formulae in English Family Correspondence from the Fifteenth to the Seventeenth Century', Minna Nevala uses a selection of family letters written by members of the gentry or royalty as her data, taken from the Corpus of Early English Correspondence. Nevala focuses on the recipient-oriented address formulae and the subscription formulae, which are more writer-oriented and show the relation between writer and recipient. Placing the formulae found in the letters on a scale which ranges from positive to negative politeness, she finds an overall increase in the use of expressions denoting positive politeness and a general simplification of address forms. Shakespeare's plays provide the data for the next three papers. Ulrich Busse investigates 'The Co-occurrence of Nominal and Pronominal Address Forms in the Shakespeare Corpus: Who Says *Thou* or *You* to Whom?'. The nominal forms included in his analysis are grouped into six categories: titles of courtesy, occupational terms, terms of family relationship, generic terms such as *boy*, *friend*, terms of endearment, and terms of abuse. Although none of the address terms occurs exclusively with either a T-form or a V-form, they usually show a clear preference for one pronoun or the other. There are differences in the use of address terms within the individual categories as well as differences across categories. Titles of courtesy co-occur most regularly with *you*, followed by terms of address indicating occupation. Terms of abuse and terms of endearment co-occur most regularly with *thou*. Busse also finds that the use of pronouns is influenced by literary genre, with comedies showing the highest proportion of V-forms. In 'Pronouns and Nominal Address in Shakespearean English: A Socio-Affective Marking System in Transition', Gabriella Mazzon analyses *Othello, King Lear* and *Hamlet*, focusing in particular on the relationships between protagonists, which are categorized as either family or official ones. Mazzon goes on to show patterns of pronoun usage within individual relationships, correlating these patterns with the use of nominal forms of address. She next discusses deviations from these patterns, which, according to her, reflect the varying social relations between the characters and also the changing degrees of distance versus intimacy and power versus solidarity. Dieter Stein, 'Pronominal Usage in Shakespeare: Between Sociolinguistics and Conversation Analysis', analyses the use of pronominal address forms in *King Lear* and *As You Like It*. After dividing all speakers and addressees into six groups according to their social standing and identifying the unmarked choice of pronoun for the various social relations, he turns to instances of pronoun switching, which he shows to be determined by changes in the speakers' emotional states. In '*You* and *Thou* in Early Modern English Dialogues: Patterns of Usage', Terry Walker studies the use of the second person in twenty-four text samples taken from the computerized Corpus of English Dialogues 1560–1760. The texts are taken from two sub-periods, 1560–1600 and 1680–1720, and are organized into two different categories, namely authentic dialogue, comprising the text types trials and witness depositions, and constructed dialogue, comprising comedy drama and handbooks. In addition to this text type-based approach Walker presents an investigation of the influence of gender on the choice of pronominal address terms. The loss of number distinction in second person pronouns serves as the starting point of Raymond Hickey's 'Rectifying a Standard Deficiency: Second-Person Pronominal Distinction in Varieties of English'. In varieties of English spoken around the world, but not in the standard language, the resulting gap has been filled. Hickey examines these developments in varieties spoken in Newfoundland, the United States, the Caribbean, South Africa, Australia, New Zealand, and the Pacific area. He suggests the following sources for the plural forms found in these varieties: dialect input from the British Isles, substrate languages, restructuring of English input or independent developments.

Gabriele Kasper and Kenneth Rose investigate *Pragmatic Development in a Second Language*. The authors begin with the presentation and assessment of theoretical and methodological approaches employed in investigations of L2 pragmatic development, followed by a discussion of findings reported on in the literature. Topics discussed are the development of pragmatic comprehension and pragmatic production, as well as the relationship between pragmatic transfer and development. Kasper and Rose also pay attention to the relationship between inter-language pragmatic and grammatical development, finding evidence for both the primacy of pragmatics and the primacy of grammar in the literature. A reason for this might be that the tasks that the learner faces change in the course of the learning process, so that, in the early stages, pragmatic competence precedes grammatical competence whereas later the opposite pattern can be observed. The influence of the environment on the development of L2 pragmatics is next examined, with the authors addressing the following issues: length of the learner's residence in the target speech community, access to L2 pragmatic input, and pragmatic development in second and foreign language learning contexts. They also consider individual differences in the acquisition of L2 pragmatics. In the concluding chapter, Kasper and Rose outline three thematic areas to which further research should be directed.

Anne Barron presents a study of *Acquisition in Interlanguage Pragmatics: Learning How To Do Things with Words in a Study Abroad Context*. She investigates the development of the L2 pragmatic competence of Irish learners of German. The participants spent one academic year in the target speech community, and their pragmatic competence was assessed on three separate occasions (prior to, during and towards the end of their stay abroad). Barron uses (free) discourse completion tasks, role-play, and meta-pragmatic assessment questionnaires to elicit data. She follows a speech-act-based approach, focusing on requests, offers and refusals of offers. Barron finds that changes in the learners' L2 pragmatic competence are mostly, although not exclusively, developments towards the target norm. She also identifies several factors which influence the amount of pragmatic transfer, for instance the learners' perceptions of transferability, increasing pragmatic ability, or the learners' willingness to transfer. Besides transfer from English to German, there is also evidence of transfer in the opposite direction.

Bettina Heinz investigates 'Backchannel Responses as Strategic Responses in Bilingual Speakers' Conversations' (*JPrag* 35[2003] 1113–42). The paper contains a contrastive analysis of the backchannel behaviour of monolingual German and American speakers in telephone conversations, finding that German speakers produce fewer backchannel responses. The types of responses, however, coincide, and also the most and least frequently used types are the same for both groups of speakers. The backchannel behaviour of bilingual native German speakers living in the United States is also examined. Bilingual German speakers produce more backchannel responses than German monolingual speakers but not as many as American monolingual speakers. The same is true for the number of responses occurring in overlapping positions. Heinz suggests that a combination of biological, psychological and sociological factors determines the production of backchannel behaviour. Another comparative study of German and English is an investigation by Caroline L. Rieger into 'Repetitions as Self-Repair Strategies in English and German Conversations' (*JPrag* 35[2003] 47–69). The main function of these repetitions is 'to delay the production of the next lexical item and/or to postpone a possible transition-relevance place' (p. 58). The author reports that some types of repetition occur equally frequently in both languages (e.g. repetition of conjunctions or definite articles), but that there are significant differences in the usage of other types: demonstrative pronouns are repeated more frequently in German, whereas repetitions of personal pronouns are significantly more frequent in English. She argues that choice of repetition strategies is dependent on the structure of the language used.

Helen Spencer-Oatey and Wenying Jiang present an attempt at 'Explaining Cross-Cultural Pragmatic Findings: Moving from Politeness Maxims to Sociopragmatic Interactional Principles (SIPs)' (*JPrag* 35[2003] 1633–50). SIPs are defined as 'socioculturally-based principles, scalar in nature, that guide or influence people's productive and interpretive use of language' (p. 1635). The authors prepared questionnaires for the British and the Chinese participants in the study, in which they were asked to rate the importance that concerns such as 'avoiding imposition' or 'avoiding negative evaluation by the hearer' had for them in various situations. In their analysis they identify several SIPs and propose that some of these principles are universal but subject to cultural and situational influences. Another cross-cultural topic is examined by Anne-Marie Barraja-Rohan in 'Past Troubles: Talk in Nonnative–Native Interviews' (*JPrag* 35[2003] 615–29). She finds that the interviewers, non-native speakers of English, and the interviewees influence the way in which past troublesome events in the lives of the interviewees are recounted. For the non-affiliative behaviour frequently displayed by the interviewers, Barraja-Rohan suggests various reasons, such as the type of interaction, failure to recognize contextualization cues, or lack of instruction in the treatment of sensitive matters in conversation.

Janet M. Fuller investigates the use of the discourse markers *oh, well, you know/y'know, like*, and *I mean* in two separate studies. For 'The Influence of Speaker Roles on Discourse Marker Use' (*JPrag* 35[2003] 23–45), she collected data from two speech contexts: interviews, in which interviewer and interviewee were relative strangers, and casual conversations between close friends or family members. Only the use of *oh* and *well* shows significant differences in the two speech contexts, both occurring more frequently in conversation. As *oh* and *well* function primarily as reception markers, they are used relatively infrequently by the interviewees, whose role is that of the speaker rather than the listener. Fuller identifies a wider range of functions for the other discourse markers, which explains why their rates of occurrence are similar across the speech contexts. Fuller extended this study to investigate 'Discourse Marker Use Across Speech Contexts: A Comparison of Native and Non-Native Speaker Performance' (*Multilingua* 22[2003] 185–208). She finds that non-native speakers use fewer discourse markers overall. Their use of *oh* and *well*, but not of *y'know, like*, and *I mean* mirrors the native speakers' use of these markers. Fuller suggests that the reason for this might be that *oh* and *well* serve primarily as reception markers, whereas the functions of the other markers are more varied, and thus their usage patterns are more difficult to acquire. Discourse markers are also the centre of interest in two more articles. Max M. Louwerse and Heather Hite Mitchell work 'Towards a Taxonomy of a Set of Discourse Markers in Dialog: A Theoretical and Computation Linguistic Account' (*DPr* 35[2003] 199–239). Their data source is the Santa Barbara Corpus of Spoken AmE. The analysis is restricted to the 196 between-turn markers which occur at the beginning of a turn. Louwerse and Mitchell conduct a substitution test to identify the (synonymous, hypernymous, hyponymous, or exclusive) relations between the discourse markers. The resulting network of markers is then further analysed to establish categories of relations. This analysis generates the categories' direction, polarity, acknowledgement, and emphatics, which the authors correlate with the different levels in conversation at which discourse markers operate. Hansung Zhang Waring investigates '*Also* as a Discourse Marker: Its Use in Disjunctive and Disaffiliative Environments' (*DisS* 5[2003] 415–36). She uses data from graduate seminars and from television round-table discussions and finds that, in disjunctive environments, speakers employ 'also' to legitimize their speaking rights, whereas in disaffiliative environments 'also' may function as either a mitigator or an upgrader.

The contributions in Prevignano and Thibault, eds., *Discussing Conversation Analysis: The Work of Emanuel A. Schegloff*, are structured around an interview in two parts with Schegloff, which was conducted by Světla Čmejrková and Carlo L. Prevignano, and at a later moment continued by Prevignano and Paul J. Thibault. In the first part of the interview, Schegloff describes his current research projects, for instance his work on 'other-initiated repairs' and his endeavour to produce an overview of conversation analytic work. In this context, Schegloff also mentions his interest in a dialogue with other disciplines. The interviewers then direct their questions to Schegloff's career, especially to its early stages and to the development of conversation analysis (CA). Other issues addressed are the kind of data that CA focuses on, the claim by critics that conversation analytic work is formalistic, and the relationship between CA and cognitively oriented research. In a brief first chapter, 'Presenting Emanuel Schegloff', John Heritage covers basically the same ground: the development of CA, influences, uses and criticisms. In 'The Power of Schegloff's Work', Charles Goodwin recalls his first encounter with CA and the impact it had, and still has, on his own research, for example on his study of how people with aphasia participate in conversation. The authors of the next two papers (Rick Iedema, 'Putting Schegloff's Principles and Practices in Context', and Pär Segerdahl, 'Conversation Analysis as Rigorous Science') take a critical stance towards Schegloff's CA. Iedema first comments on aspects of methodology criticizing the focus of CA on 'context-free constants of talk' and the organization of turn-taking to the neglect of other resources for structuring communication. He next questions the usefulness of the distinctions between 'ordinary' and 'non-ordinary' interaction and between 'internal' and 'external' context. Segerdahl rejects a claim he attributes to Schegloff, namely that the research tools used in CA (e.g. those of repair, turn-taking, and adjacency pair) are relevant to the participants in interaction. The author contends that Schegloff is in effect claiming that these tools are 'making' the participants 'do what they do, or hear what they hear' (p. 99), i.e. that these tools are operative within conversation as well as being used as analytical devices. Pirkko Raudaskoski, 'Users' Interpretations at a Computer Tutorial: Detecting (Causes) of Misunderstandings', reports on a case study of how users interpret electronic texts. Two participants in the study were asked to go through a computer tutorial with Raudaskoski applying CA to an instance of misunderstanding. The author examines the encounter between user and computer as well as the interaction between the two users. In 'When Conversation Is Not Normal: The Role of Conversation Analysis in Language Pathology', Ruth Lesser offers a survey of research, in which conversation analysis was applied to the speech of persons with aphasia or dementia. She also briefly presents a conversation analysis profile she developed together with co-researchers to be used in therapy. Referring to Lesser's paper, Schegloff reiterates his interest in interaction with other disciplines which he declared in the interview. As Schegloff has concerned himself with neurologically oriented research, he particularly welcomes Lesser's article. He questions, however, the applicability of CA in Raudaskoski's study, pointing out, for instance, that the use of a computer does not involve interaction as understood in CA and that a computer cannot take turns. Schegloff's response to Iedema's and Segerdahl's contributions is relatively brief. He dismisses their critique of CA as based on misunderstandings and a misreading of the interview and/or of his work in general. The main purpose of the second part of the interview, which follows Schegloff's response, is to clarify the notion of 'turn'. The book is rounded off with a bibliography of Schegloff's work edited by Susan L. Eerdmans.

Gene H. Lerner investigates methods of 'Selecting Next Speaker: The Context-Sensitive Operation of a Context-Free Organization' (*LSoc* 32[2003] 177–201). He focuses on forms of addressing employed by a current speaker in sequence-initiating actions to select the next speaker and distinguishes between explicit and tacit addressing. Lerner argues that gaze as a method of explicit addressing can only be successful if the intended recipient (and often also the other participants in the conversation) notice it. Address terms, another form of explicit addressing, appear to be used not only to indicate the next speaker, but may simultaneously fulfil other functions, such as demonstrating the current speaker's attitude towards the next speaker. Tacit addressing, i.e. designing a sequence-initiating action for a single recipient, can only be successful if the other participants in the conversation manage to determine who is eligible to speak next from details of the content and context of the action.

Anssi Peräkylä and Sanna Vehviläinen propose a dialogue between 'Conversation Analysis and the Professional Stocks of Interactional Knowledge' (SIKs) (*D&S* 14[2003] 727–50). SIKs are defined as 'organized knowledge (theories or conceptual models) concerning interaction, shared by particular professions or practitioners' (p. 730). The authors point out that conversation analytic research may provide a valuable link between SIKs and the professional practices they inform. They present analyses of several instances of professional–client interaction and assign two main tasks to conversation analysis: the identification of simplified or empirically unsustainable assumptions of SIKs (the 'critical task'), and the description of new practices or functions as well as the enrichment of existing descriptions of practices (the 'complementary task'). 'Conversational Techniques Used in Transferring Knowledge between Medical Experts and Non-Experts' (*DisS* 5[2003] 235–63) are examined by Elisabeth Gülich. Gülich does not only deal with the procedures employed by medical experts to convey illness-related information to their patients (the focus here is on techniques of illustration) or vice versa (here she draws attention to the speaker's use of descriptive means and placement of relevance); she also comments on the practices of establishing expert and non-expert roles. Guiomar E. Ciapuscio's paper on 'Formulation and Reformulation Procedures in Verbal Interactions between Experts and (Semi-)Laypersons' (*DisS* 5[2003] 207–33) is structured somewhat similarly. It is based in part on previous work by Gülich, and investigates the same procedures, namely reformulation and illustration procedures. However, the data used in this study are taken from interviews with specialists from several disciplines. The purpose of the interviews was to obtain information about current research projects, which the interviewer would then use to write a newspaper article targeted at the lay public.

Maria Stubbe, Chris Lane, Jo Hilder, Elaine Vine, Bernadette Vine, Meredith Marra, Janet Holmes, and Ann Weatherall present 'Multiple Discourse Analyses of a Workplace Interaction' (*DisS* 5[2003] 351–88). They provide five interpretations of the same set of data (a passage of spontaneous workplace interaction), which are the results of analyses that made use of five different approaches to discourse analysis: conversation analysis, interactional sociolinguistics, politeness theory, critical discourse analysis, and discursive psychology. The authors give an introduction to the individual approaches before they proceed with the analyses and conclude with a discussion of the common and the distinctive features of the approaches which the analyses revealed.

In *Analysing Discourse*, Norman Fairclough aims to provide a framework for textual analysis for social research. As the book is intended for researchers with little or no knowledge of linguistic analysis, Fairclough first presents an overview of the theoretical background to his approach to textual analysis and of the key concepts he employs. He also discusses the interrelation between texts and the social world as well as the internal relations of texts (e.g. grammatical or lexical relations). In parts 2 to 4, the focus is on 'Genres and Action', 'Discourses and Representations', and 'Styles and Identifications' respectively. The structure of the book is designed to facilitate the reader's understanding of the author's approach to discourse analysis. Fairclough begins the individual chapters with a list of the text analysis issues and social research issues to be addressed, and ends them with a brief summary. There is an appendix of the texts which are used for analysis in the book, and there are glossaries of key terms and key theorists. In the conclusion, the various aspects of textual analysis that have been introduced in the book are brought together and applied to one of the texts in the appendix. Textual analysis is then shown as part of a more extensive analytical framework, and Fairclough attaches to the conclusion a 'manifesto' for critical discourse analysis as a resource in social scientific research.

This resource is made use of by Rebecca Rogers in *A Critical Discourse Analysis of Family Literacy Practices: Power In and Out of Print*, a study in which she explores literacy practices in different contexts. The participants in the study were a student in adult basic education and her daughter, who was 11 years old at the beginning of the research project. Rogers collected her data over a period of more than two years, focusing on the participants' literate proficiencies in the context of their home, the community, and school. She finds that the participants deal with the demands for literacy in their private lives competently and efficiently, whereas their achievements in school are low. In the institutional setting, the mother is assessed as low-literate, the daughter judged to be speech-impaired and multiply disabled. Rogers pays particular attention to the process of placing the daughter in special education, a development resisted by both mother and daughter at home, but accepted in meetings with the committee in charge of the process. To explain this inconsistency, she analyses the data from these meetings as well as the wider context in which the meetings take place and the personal background of the two participants in the study. She points out that mother and daughter do not value their home/community literacy, an attitude they adopted in the institutional setting of the school, where these literacy skills are not recognized. Rogers claims that it is this acceptance of the school's judgement of what counts as literacy, together with the determination to let her daughter have the best education available, that makes the mother consent to the placement of her daughter in special education.

In *Critical Discourse Analysis and Language Cognition*, Kieran O'Halloran is concerned with mystification, a particular type of language manipulation. He analyses news texts to see in which ways they mystify, i.e. reduce the reader's understanding of the participants and events they describe. In the first section of the book, O'Halloran provides introductions to critical discourse analysis (CDA) and symbolicism, going on to show how symbolic assumptions underlie mystification analysis in CDA. The second section is dedicated to language cognition. The author discusses connectionism, cognitive linguistics, and psycholinguistic evidence for inference generation with regard to the conflicts between these approaches and symbolicism. He points out that the new approaches to language cognition challenge the symbolic assumptions adopted in CDA. In the last section, an idealized reader framework is developed. The type of reader envisaged by O'Halloran is largely unfamiliar with the events reported in the news text and is reading for the gist of the matter. Incorporated in the framework are elements from the approaches to language cognition that were discussed in the second part as well as elements from relevance theory. The focus of the framework is on causal relations in news texts. O'Halloran applies his idealized framework to the analysis of a sample news text (and of three other newspaper reports of the same event) to show its usefulness for mystification analysis. He then presents the sample text again, but in an adapted form, adding information that is relevant to the reader but which was absent from the original version. His purpose is to demonstrate how the potential of the text for mystification can be reduced.

In 'Habitus as the Principle for Social Practice: A Proposal for Critical Discourse Analysis' (*LSoc* 32[2003] 143–75), Jann Scheuer addresses one of the criticisms directed at CDA, namely that analysts' interpretations of linguistic data in political contexts are influenced by political agendas. He proposes the use of socio-historical analysis to address social contexts. This method is based on Pierre Bourdieu's work and incorporates his concepts of 'field', 'capital', 'trajectory', 'habitus' and 'taste'. After an introduction to the analytical framework, Scheuer demonstrates how socio-historical analysis can be applied to discourse. His data are taken from a corpus of job interviews which includes not only the interviews as such but also the committee's talk before and discussions after each interview, its final evaluation of the interviews, and retrospective interviews with the applicants. In his analysis of one of the job interviews, the author focuses on the interviewee's intertextual and interdiscursive recontextualizations. The interpretation of the findings involves an analysis of the interviewee's habitus. The data needed for this are taken from the retrospective interview. Finally, Scheuer briefly discusses the strengths of his analytic approach and its compatibility with CDA.

The two publications which conclude this section are concerned with politeness theory. Michael Haugh investigates 'Anticipated versus Inferred Politeness' (*Multilingua* 22[2003] 397–413). The basis for this distinction is provided by the notion of 'expectation as an estimation of the probability that a certain behaviour will occur' (p. 400). Haugh argues that politeness is anticipated when the behaviour of the speaker that gives rise to politeness coincides with the behaviour the hearer expected. If the hearer had no such expectations, politeness must be inferred. Haugh provides some examples to illustrate the distinction between anticipated and inferred politeness before he turns to a discussion of theoretical approaches which might usefully be employed to investigate this distinction, preferring discourse politeness theory to relevance theory in this respect. Jonathan Culpeper, Derek Bousfield, and Anne Wichmann's focus is on impoliteness rather than politeness, in 'Impoliteness Revisited: With Special Reference to Dynamic and Prosodic Aspects' (*JPrag* 35[2003] 1545–79). They argue for the establishment of an impoliteness framework, as impoliteness strategies cannot be convincingly accommodated within politeness theory. After clarifying their notion of impoliteness, the authors identify impoliteness strategies within passages of conflictive talk. They find that interactants usually employ combinations of impoliteness strategies, typically either combinations of different strategies or repetitions of a particular strategy (or of combinations of strategies). The authors point out that the study of impoliteness phenomena must also take account of responses to impoliteness, and they outline a number of response options. In addition, they emphasize the role of prosody, focusing in the last part of their paper on the components of pitch and loudness.

11. Stylistics

The single most important addition to the linguistic study of literature this year has no doubt been Jonathan Hope's much-anticipated *Shakespeare's Grammar*. Born out of an Arden Shakespeare commission aiming to replace a Victorian grammar of Shakespeare's language (Abbott's *A Shakespearean Grammar*, whose third edition dates from 1870), it is addressed to at least two different types of user: students and editors of Shakespeare. As the author explains in his introduction, no prior linguistic knowledge is required, since concepts and terms are explained at several points in the course of the book: when they are first introduced, when they are dealt with extensively, and in a glossary. For the volume's structure, Hope follows the syntax of the English sentence, establishing thus a binary division: part 1 deals with the NP and part 2 with the VP. He is nevertheless aware of the drawbacks of a division that, on the one hand, mirrors syntax and, on the other, misrepresents it, since NPs are often embedded in VPs and vice versa. He counteracts these shortcomings with two sections preceding each part where he provides overviews of the NP and VP that account for their stylistic use and grammatical structure. In the overview dealing with the stylistics of the NP, Hope analyses Macbeth's first soliloquy at the end of Act I to show that linguistic choice matters in literary texts. Macbeth's discourse is full of NPs filled by pronominal *it* (lacking clear reference) and abstract nouns; such vague NPs perfectly convey his wavering mind, his doubts and misgivings. Hope also shows convincingly how Shakespeare handles given and new information with a clever deployment of modification in *The Winter's Tale* (V.ii.20–40), when Perdita's royal identity is discovered and profusely described through post-modification. The stylistic use of the VP is illustrated with the help of Iago's artful discourse, where he manipulates a narrative about a street brawl (*Othello* II.iii) through specific verbal choices that suppress agency (covering up his role in provoking the fight) and plays with temporal and deictic reference, achieving control of Othello's mind. Hope is particularly good at this kind of micro-stylistics, exposing hidden linguistic marvels otherwise missed by the bare eye (or ear, since Shakespeare's language, as Hope reminds us, was mostly oral and aural). Even though his intention—and his commission—is to produce a 'grammar' and not a stylistic study of Shakespeare's works, his considerable effort to present Shakespeare's language in a user-friendly way, highlighting its peculiarities and its differences from present-day English, would have been even more valuable if the two stylistic overviews had given students, lecturers, editors and scholars a firmer idea of how powerful a stylistic analysis of the Shakespearian text proves to be as a key to interpretation. Hope has nevertheless provided readers of Shakespeare with an indispensable tool. It is difficult to see why the *Grammar* has only been produced in hardback, given that it is aimed at students. This grammar may build up their confidence in approaching the Shakespearian text and could make itself very useful in both secondary and higher education environments.

Soledad Pérez de Ayala's monograph on parliamentary language, *Cortesía e imagen en el parlamento británico: Question Time*, contains a very thorough and detailed analysis of the aggressive use of face and politeness strategies in the parliamentary weekly sessions that allow politicians to question the prime minister. 'Question Time' constitutes a challenge for the discourse analyst because it consists of both spoken and written language: before each session, MPs hand in written questions which they later read aloud; they receive previously written answers delivered orally, which may then be followed by an impromptu verbal debate. A yet further dimension is added to this, since Question Time is then transcribed into the *Hansard* report. Pérez de Ayala offers a comparative analysis of three politeness models (those of Geoffrey Leech, Robin Lakoff, and Penelope Brown and Stephen Levinson) and then settles for a combination of Brown and Levinson's framework, discourse analysis and conversation analysis for her study of parliamentary politeness. She applies the concept of 'negative public face' to the peculiar discourse situation Question Time occasions, as it invites MPs to attack their colleagues to their face. This aggressive use of face-work is kept under check by the Erskine–May code of parliamentary behaviour, which is in fact a series of rules about linguistic politeness. This study reveals, as could be expected, that parliamentary language has a very high frequency of both face-threatening acts and negative politeness strategies: the first are used to attack a member of a different party, the second to comply with the Erskine–May code. Pérez de Ayala also shows that politeness fulfils a discourse function in the register of Question Time, as many MPs avail themselves of politeness strategies to endow their speeches with a rhetorical structure. Beside the specific findings about parliamentary language, this study offers an interesting exploration of the benefits of linguistic cross-breeding: politeness studies can be more rewarding if combined with discourse or conversation analysis.

Cognitive stylistics has now established itself as one of the major trends in the field. Gavins and Steen, eds., *Cognitive Poetics in Practice*, is a collection of studies with contributions by leading practitioners, aiming to introduce students to its practice. It also shows that there is still interesting practical analytical work to look forward to from this area of stylistics. In the introduction, the editors address the relationship between cognitive poetics and cognitive linguistics, between cognitive poetics and other kinds of poetics and between the two different kinds of cognitive poetics represented in their collection. The editors' voice is also heard at the beginning of every chapter, directing the reader's attention towards crucial issues, and pointing out connections between the different contributions. The editors also conceived the volume as a companion piece to Peter Stockwell's *Cognitive Poetics: An Introduction* (see *YWES* 83[2004] 90), aiming to provide a practical analysis to complement Stockwell's introduction. Stockwell himself is one of the contributors, and in 'Surreal Figures' deploys the cognitive understanding of figure and ground to explain how stylistic foregrounding works in a literary text. In 'Prototypes in Dynamic Meaning Construal', Raymond W. Gibbs Jr. questions the validity of prototypes to explain the cognitive processes taking place as readers construe meaning during the process of reading literary texts. Reuven Tsur, one of the first to apply cognitive science to literary works, offers an analysis of the deictic configurations in the poetry of Shakespeare, Marvell, Wordsworth and two Hebrew poets, Nathan Alterman and Abraham Shlonsky, in 'Deixis and Abstractions: Adventures in Space and Time', and explains students' responses to given texts through scientific knowledge about the different ways in which the right and left sides of the brain work. Craig Hamilton, in 'A Cognitive Grammar of "Hospital Barge" by Wilfred Owen' provides an analysis of Owen's poem with Ronald Langacker's 1980s cognitive grammar to show how the reader's attention is drawn to the scene depicted in the poem by means of specific grammatical constructions. Gerard Steen's '"Love Stories": Cognitive Scenarios in Love Poetry' argues that readers of love poetry need to activate scenarios to understand the text they face, no matter if it is a poem by Shakespeare, Robert Graves or A.E. Housman or a non-canonical text obtained from contemporary rock and pop love songs. In 'Possible Worlds and Mental Spaces in Hemingway's "A Very Short Story"', Elena Semino combines possible worlds theory and the cognitive framework of mental space theory to assess their respective benefits and shortcomings in helping us to understanding Hemingway's story. Peter Crisp, in 'Conceptual Metaphor and its Expressions' chooses a poem by D.H. Lawrence and a passage from Keats's *The Fall of Hyperion* to discuss how conceptual metaphors that originate in everyday language are given a new lease of life by poets. Michael Burke, in 'Literature as Parable', introduces Mark Turner's notion of 'parabolic projection', by means of which readers use their everyday knowledge to interpret texts and then project the interpretation thus obtained back onto their own everyday lives, and applies it to Shakespeare's sonnet 2. Joanna Gavins, like Catherine Emmott, is interested in providing a discourse approach that deals with the cognitive poetics of whole texts, and in 'Too Much Blague? An Exploration of the Text Worlds of Donald Barthelme's *Snow White*' undertakes a text world theory analysis of Barthelme's novel to show how readers build and maintain complex mental representations when reading a narrative. In 'Reading for Pleasure: A Cognitive Poetic Analysis of "Twists in the Tale" and Other Plot Reversals in Narrative Texts', Catherine Emmott applies her 'contextual frame theory' to several prose fiction texts by Roald Dahl, Ian Rankin and Deborah Moggach to see how readers make head or tail out of plots reversals in narratives. Keith Oatley, in 'Writingandreading', brings the collection to an end with a series of thoughts on the future of cognitive poetics, identifying three roads under construction: mimesis, emotions and the uses of literature.

This year's output of pedagogical stylistics also witnessed another addition, a new item in the Intertext series. In *The Language of Comics*, Mario Saraceni dissects the peculiarities of this language variety, paying attention to its non-verbal elements too. In fact, much of the book, and hence its value, is dedicated to exploring the relationship between the linguistic and the visual elements in comics. Unit 1 examines the main components: panel, gutter, balloon and caption. Unit 2 shows how images and words interact in comics, as well as in other media, to create meaning. Unit 3 deals with the sequential organization of panels and how cohesion is achieved, while unit 4 deals with 'voice' in comics: how speech and thought are represented. Unit 5 discusses the importance of the angle of seeing and explores the construction of point of view. The final unit shows how computers make use of comics while at the same time comics may benefit from the enhanced graphic quality of computers. The book is profusely illustrated and will no doubt increase students' awareness and enjoyment of linguistic analysis.

The New Critical Idiom series, still with John Drakakis at the steering-wheel as general editor, continues to produce volumes that, although not strictly of a stylistic nature, will no doubt be of interest to readers of this section, and this is particularly true of Glennis Byron's *Dramatic Monologue*, if only for the attention it pays to reader–audience interplay and the psychological revelation of character through verbal self-portraits. Written in a bright, stimulating, witty and, at times, deliciously subtle tone, this new volume is a very thoughtful and conscientious exploration of the term 'dramatic monologue'. Byron explores the origins of the form and the difficulties involved in attempts to establish a uniform categorization for it as a genre. She questions the received definition of the dramatic monologue that takes Browning's 'My Last Duchess' as paradigm, and shows how canonical poets and their texts (Browning, Tennyson) have to make room for non-canonical poets and their non-canonical texts in the use of this poetic form. She also ventures that, although Browning has been credited with its invention, Romantic women poets such as Felicia Hemans were already experimenting with similar poetic forms. Byron's reassessment of the dramatic monologue enables her to show how it now enjoys a new life in the work of contemporary poets such as Carol Ann Duffy, Ai and Ken Smith. Lecturers will surely find the book very useful for teaching purposes, but its greatest asset is that its smooth, gliding prose makes it a very easy, and surprisingly pleasant, read.

The scarcity of stylistics monographs this year is amply redressed by the number of journal articles. Michael Toolan's takeover as editor of *Journal of Literary Semantics* has turned out to be more than a mere skin-deep face-lift. The articles in this year's volume offer a wide, diverse and stimulating sample of topics and issues that range from point of view to postcolonial narrative and the semantics of gender. The journal as a whole caters for many of the areas of interest which are now current in stylistics and brings together empirical studies of literature, semantics and discourse, cognitive and functional linguistics and philosophy and critical theory. It is to be hoped that it will continue to exist as a forum for such diverse approaches to literary texts. The two studies on speech and thought presentation in this volume testify to this. Stefan Oltean's 'On the Bivocal Nature of Free Indirect Discourse' (*JLS* 32[2003] 167–76) offers an interesting study of the dual voice in relation to Free Indirect Discourse, approaching this frequently debated concept from both truth-conditional semantics and possible world semantics points of view. In 'How to Manipulate

Tenses to Express a Character's Point of View' (*JLS* 32[2003] 85–112), Renaat Declerck argues for the need to differentiate between three subtypes of point of view (communicative, experiencer's and narrative) through a grammatical analysis of the mechanics of the English tense system. Studies of poetic texts are particularly plentiful in this volume. Rukmini Bhaya Nair, in 'Sappho's Daughters: Postcoloniality and the Polysemous Semantics of Gender' (*JLS* 32[2003] 113–32), discusses how a polysemous literary semantics can be the natural ally of a pluralist postcolonial feminist theory and shows the plurality of voices existing in the work of contemporary women poets on the Indian subcontinent, who reject established binary divisions (male/female, Western/Eastern, colonial/postcolonial). In 'Linguistic Thinking; Or the Poet, his Beloved and the Outsider' (*JLS* 32[2003] ??), Flip G. Droste uses the first quartet of Shakespeare's sonnet 18 ('Shall I compare thee to a summer's day?') to perform an exercise in description that takes off with an analysis of the conceptual, as opposed to the formal, level in order to show that interpretation works in a 'feed-forward and feed-back movement, comparable to the way a Turing machine works' (p. 1). The processing of poetic text is also the topic of Iris Yaron's 'Mechanisms of Combination in the Processing of Obscure Poems' (*JLS* 32[2003] 151–66), as it addresses the question of how readers process contemporary obscure poems that violate communicational norms and, after conducting two experimental studies, suggests that readers can deal with this problem because obscurity in texts triggers mechanisms of combination. Donald E. Hardy, in '*Face* and the Middle Voice in Flannery O'Connor's Fiction' (*JLS* 32[2003] 133–50), dissects the syntax and semantics of the middle voice in relation to the body in O'Connor's work and offers a contrastive analysis of the use of the lexeme *face* in her fiction and the Brown Corpus. In '"By any other name": Kripke, Derrida and an Ethics of Naming' (*JLS* 32[2003] 35–47), Carrol Clarkson, using Ondaatje's *The English Patient* as an example, questions Christopher Norris's influential work regarding the difference between Derridean deconstruction and Saul Kripke's *Naming and Necessity* [1972], given that Derrida's and Kripke's accounts of proper names broach the divide between these two lines of philosophical enquiry. Cognitive linguistics inform Ning Yu's 'Synesthetic Metaphor: A Cognitive Perspective' (*JLS* 32[2003] 19–34), a study of this kind of metaphor in the narrative of the contemporary Chinese novelist Mo Yan, praised for his innovative style, showing that even unusual metaphors follow tendencies found in ordinary language and that both kinds of language, poetic and ordinary, are constrained by the human body and how it functions. In 'More Features of the Mythic Spacetime Algebra' (*JLS* 32[2003] 49–72), Michael Griffin applies an algebraic set notation to mythic motifs and develops his notion of mythic space-time as a mathematical concept, using elementary operations of mathematics, such as multiplication and equation, to relate mythology, literature, language and psychology.

The interface between the linguistic study of literary text, on one hand, and sociology, critical theory and empirical study on the other is quite successfully managed in several articles published in this year's volume of *Poetics*. Gabriel Ignatow, in '"Idea Hamsters" on the "Bleeding Edge": Profane Metaphors in High Technology Jargon' (*Poetics* 31[2003] 1–22), reveals that profane metaphors are currently abundant in the language register of the American high technology industry and makes a case for the benefits of studying metaphors in connection with sociological and cultural issues. Metaphor is also the concern of 'Aptness Is More Important than Comprehensibility in Preference for Metaphors and Similes' (*Poetics* 31[2003] 51–68), by Dan L. Chiappe, John M. Kennedy and Penny Chiappe, who ask themselves about the factors determining the choice between metaphor and simile when a speaker decides to establish a comparison. They conclude that 'aptness' (the capacity to capture important features of a topic) is of greater consequence than 'comprehensibility' (to be easy to understand) when choosing between metaphors and similes. Malcolm Hayward, in 'Are Texts Recognizably Gendered? An Experiment and Analysis' (*Poetics* 31[2003] 87–101), presents the results of an experiment suggesting that readers can frequently guess the gender of an author whose text is presented to them anonymously since subjects in his experiment identified gender correctly 61 per cent of the time.

Those interested in empirical stylistics will welcome the special issue on reading research (*Poetics* 31:ii[2003]), dedicated to articles that propose and test specific hypotheses about reading. Although mostly concerned with Dutch readership, since the articles are by Dutch social scientists and scholars, the issue's editorial claims that the theoretical perspectives and the findings discussed will be of interest to a broad range of disciplines in the social sciences and humanities spectrum. Readers will decide for themselves whether this is an accurate assessment, but it is nevertheless true that many of these articles are concerned with the reading of fiction, so readers of this section working on empirical approaches to literature will know better than to give it a miss. Even those whose concern is not primarily empirical might be interested in the reasons E. Van Schooten and K. de Glopper give for negative responses to literary reading in 'The Development of Literary Response in Secondary Education' (*Poetics* 31[2003] 155–87) or in the findings of H.W.J.M. Miesen regarding reading behaviour and attitudes towards reading fiction in 'Predicting and Explaining Literary Reading: An Application of the theory of Planned Behavior' (*Poetics* 31[2003] 189–212). Wim Knulst and Andries van den Broek discuss the decline in fiction reading in 'The Readership of Books in Times of De-reading' (*Poetics* 31[2003] 213–33), whereas Gerbert Kraaykamp deals with reading promotion and the stimulation of reading amongst young people in 'Literary Socialization and Reading Preferences: Effects of Parents, the Library, and the School' (*Poetics* 31[2003] 235–57). This issue on reading ends with an article by Marc Verbood that proposes to eschew the notion of literary canon and replace it with the concept of literary prestige ('Classification of Authors by Literary Prestige' *Poetics* 31[2003] 259–81) and another one by Mac Verbood and Kees van Rees on reading socialization with the self-explanatory title 'Do Changes in Socialization Lead to Decline in Reading Level? How Parents, Literary Education, and Popular Culture Affect the Level of Books Read' (*Poetics* 31[2003] 283–300). Given the influence of Pierre Bourdieu's work on studies of discourse and language, readers of this section may want to be alerted to the publication of another special issue of *Poetics* in this year's volume, wholly dedicated this time to work stemming from Bourdieu's critical and theoretical legacy.

Cognitivism and cognitive poetics is the subject of a special issue of this year's volume of *Poetics Today* (24:ii[2003]), which has been given the questioning title 'The Cognitive Turn? A Debate on Interdisciplinarity'. Alan Richardson and Francis F. Steen head the issue with 'Reframing the Adjustment: A Response to Adler and Gross' (*PoT* 24[2003] 151–9), a reply to Hans Adler and Sabine Gross's 'Adjusting the Frame: Comments on Cognitivism and Literature' (*PoT* 23[2002] 195–220), who had taken issue with some of the notions and ideas contained in Richardson and Steen's special issue of *Poetics Today*, entitled 'Literature and the Cognitive Revolution' (*PoT* 23:i[2002]). Ellen Spolsky also replies to Adler and Gross in 'Cognitive Literary Historicism: A Response to Adler and Gross' (*PoT* 24[2003] 161–83) and so does Paul Hernadi in 'On Cognition, Interpretation, and the Survival of Literature: A Response to Hans Adler and Sabine Gross' (*PoT* 24[2003] 185–9). The debate mostly centres on the, for some difficult, for others joyful, marriage of cognitive literary theory and literary criticism and shows how the impact of cognitive science on the humanities extends far beyond the theory of cognitive metaphor. Meir Sternberg, in two very lengthy articles, 'Universals of Narrative and their Cognitivist Fortunes I and II' (*PoT* 24[2003] 297–395, 518–638), addresses the relationship between a field that favours inbreeding and self-containment, such as narratology, and cognitive science. Richard van Oort, in 'Cognitive Science and the Problem of Representation' (*PoT* 24[2003] 237–95), argues that the notion of 'representation' is the crucial issue in any discussion of the relationship between literary studies and a cognitive model of research for the humanities.

Cognitive metaphor *per se* is also the concern of two further articles. David S. Danaher, in 'A Cognitive Approach to Metaphor in Prose: Truth and Falsehood in Leo Tolstoy's "The Death of Ivan Il'ich"' (*PoT* 24[2003] 439–69), offers an analysis of everyday metaphorical expressions for the domains of Truth and Falsehood in contemporary Russian and in a novella by Tolstoy. Brent Wood, in 'Robert Hunter's Oral Poetry: Mind, Metaphor, and Community' (*PoT* 24[2003] 35–63), approaches Hunter's song lyrics through Ruth Finnegan's work on oral poetics, Aldous Huxley's views on altered states of mind brought about by drug consumption, and George Lakoff's theory of metaphor.

Narratology has been the object of another lively debate in the pages of *Poetics Today* (24:iii[2003]), involving Monika Fludernik, Tom Kindt and Hans-Harald Müller and David Darby. Fludernik, in 'History of Narratology: A Rejoinder' (*PoT* 24[2003] 405–11) takes issue with David Darby's article ''Form and Context: An Essay in the History of Narratology' (*PoT* 22[2001] 829–52), in which he had compared German narratological studies (*Erzähltheorie*) with structuralist narratology to the detriment of the former, arguing that German narrative theory is less narrow and more far-reaching than Darby's picture of it. Kindt and Müller join forces with Fludernik in 'Narratology and Interpretation: A Rejoinder to David Darby' (*PoT* 24[2003] 413–21) to criticize Darby's proposal to turn narratology into a contextualized theory of interpretation and question his use of Wayne C. Booth's notion of the 'implied author'. Darby responds to both these articles in 'Form and Context Revisited' (*PoT* 24[2003] 423–37), even though he seems to think that Kindt and Müller accuse him of perpetrating a crime, casting him as the contextualist aggressor of 'classical' German narratology, whereas Fludernik takes him to task for not being criminal enough, since she thinks he plays down the contextualist elements in 'post-classical' German narratological scholarship.

Language and Literature continues to devote monographic issues to a given theme or field, as shown by 'Special Issue: Science Fiction and Literary Linguistics' (*L&L* 12:iii[2003]). The issue's editor, Peter Stockwell, has provided a brief but stimulating introduction (*L&L* 12[2003] 195–8), which begins with the question: 'Why should literary linguistics be interested in science fiction?' and ends with the answer 'Because it is fundamentally concerned with us', arguing that science fiction offers a holistic view of experience and knowledge and rejecting the division between the arts and science, just like literary linguists. Sylvia Hardy, in 'A Story of the Days to Come: H.G. Wells and the Language of Science Fiction' (*L&L* 12[2003] 199–212), argues that Wells is more concerned with language and linguistic issues than are other science fiction writers, and shows this to be the case through the role played by failures in communication in some of his early novels, *The Time Machine* and *The Island of Dr Moreau*, but also in the later utopias *The World Set Free* and *The Shape of Things to Come*, in which English is a necessary ingredient of social cohesion and human cognition. Using Catherine Emmott's framework for narrative comprehension, Mary Ellen Ryder dissects two short stories by the American science fiction writer Robert Heinlein, in 'I Met Myself Coming and Going: Co(?)-Referential Noun Phrases and Point of View in Time Travel Stories' (*L&L* 12[2003] 213–32) to illustrate how authors can avail themselves of devices to help or obstruct the reader's identification of characters. Clare Walsh, in 'From "Capping" to Intercision: Metaphors/Metonyms of Mind Control in the Young Adult Fiction of John Christopher and Philip Pullman' (*L&L* 12[2003] 233–51), compares two science fiction trilogies addressed to a young adult readership, John Christopher's *Tripods* and Philip Pullman's *His Dark Materials* and concludes that, contrary to expectations, both trilogies are highly metaphorical and display a tendency to blur the boundaries between the metaphorical, the metonymic and the literal. The monograph issue is rounded off by Stockwell himself, who contributes an essay to the volume on 'Schema Poetics and Speculative Cosmology' (*L&L* 12[2003] 252–71) showing why schema poetics is of use to the reading of science fiction, with a particular focus on the work of Australian science fiction author Greg Egan.

Studies of narrative texts continue to be proportionally more numerous, in the pages of *Language and Literature* at least, than studies of other text types. Luc Herman, Robert Hogenraad and Wim van Mierlo, in 'Pynchon, Postmodernism and Quantification: An Empirical Content Analysis of Thomas Pynchon's *Gravity's Rainbow*' (*L&L* 12[2003] 27–41), compare Pynchon's postmodern novel with Conrad's *Heart of Darkness* and Joyce's *Ulysses*, propose a framework that enables them to quantify postmodernism and thus offer a means of distinguishing empirically between modernism and postmodernism. In 'Feminist Narratology? Literary and Linguistic Perspectives on Gender and Narrativity' (*L&L* 12[2003] 43–56), Ruth E. Page examines, from a critical but also integrative stance, the existing work in the developing field of feminist narratology and analyses a short story by Michèle Roberts, *Une Glossaire/A Glossary*, to show that no direct correlation can be established between narrative form and *écriture feminine*. In 'Chronology, Time, Tense and Experientiality in Narrative' (*L&L* 12[2003] 117–34), Monika Fludernik argues that in literary texts the grammatical category of tense can fulfil functions that are literary rather than syntactic, such as foregrounding or backgrounding, and uses Michael Ondaatje's *The English Patient* to illustrate these specifically literary uses of tense. Yanna Popova looks into the representation of smell through verbs of perception in '"The Fool Sees with his Nose": Metaphoric Mappings in the Sense of Smell in Patrick Süskind's *Perfume*' (*L&L* 12[2003] 135–51), exploring the cognitive and experiential motivations behind metaphorical mappings related to smell and showing how, since SMELL IS VISION and UNDERSTANDING IS SEEING, in the phenomenological world of the novel's hero UNDERSTANDING IS SMELLING. Celia Wallhead addresses the relation between narrative and biography in 'Metaphors for the Self in A.S. Byatt's *The Biographer's Tale*' (*L&L* 12[2003] 291–308) and applies Lakoff and Johnson's body-based linguistic model of metaphor to one of Byatt's latest novels to show the correspondence between metaphors for the self from everyday language deployed by Byatt and the artistic, structural metaphors which conform *The Biographer's Tale*.

This year's issues of *Language and Literature* also contain some articles on poetry and poetic texts. Dennis Sobolev, in 'Hopkins' Rhetoric: Between the Material and the Transcendent' (*L&L* 12[2003] 99–115), studies how religious meaning is inscribed into poetic descriptions of the material world and existential experience in the poetry of Gerard Manley Hopkins, partly with the aid of metaphors that have a double referential field, and enable Hopkins to bridge the separation between two worlds, the material and the transcendental, with the help of his rhetoric of 'nowness' that creates a poetic space beyond empirical time. In 'Towards a Theory of Poetic Change' (*L&L* 12[2003] 5–25), C.B. McCully proposes a diachronic and conceptual framework for the study of structural change in poetic forms, which provides four general categories: adaptive change, assimilative change, typological change and reactive change. Kristin Hanson, in 'Formal Variation in the Rhymes of Robert Pinsky's *The Inferno of Dante*' (*L&L* 12[2003] 309–37), explores the variations used by Pinsky in his slant-rhyme translation of the *Inferno* and identifies practices that are shared by other English poets, supporting suggestions made by Paul Kiparsky and Roman Jakobson about the similarity of the constraints affecting poetic form and grammatical choice. Attention given to poetry in this year's volume also includes a debate on English metre between Derek Attridge and Nigel Fabb stemming from Fabb's article on 'The Metres of "Dover Beach"' (see *YWES* 83[2004] 96). In 'The Rules of English Metre: A Response to Nigel Fabb' (*L&L* 12[2003] 71–2), Attridge questions the validity of the 'stress maximum' principle proposed by Morris Halle and Samuel Jay Keyser and deployed by Fabb, since it would render a large proportion of English iambic pentameters in well-known poetic texts unmetrical. Fabb replies in 'Metrical Rules and the Notion of "Maximum": A Reply to Derek Attridge' (*L&L* 12[2003] 73–80), explaining why he finds the notion of 'maximum' useful and suggesting that their debate rests on differing views of metricality. He attributes to Attridge an understanding of metricality as 'the experience of rhythm' (p. 79) whereas his proposal aims to account for the regular features of metricality through counting. Attridge replies in ' Maxima and Beats: A Response to Nigel Fabb's Reply' (*L&L* 12[2003] 81–2), denouncing the uselessness of any theory that divides lines between metrical and unmetrical and defending his preference for beat prosody against any theory of generative metrics.

Non-literary texts have also received some attention this year. Marina Lambrou studies a collection of oral narratives by native speakers of English from the Greek Cypriot community in London in 'Collaborative Oral Narratives of General Experience: When an Interview Becomes a Conversation' (*L&L* 12[2003] 153–74), showing that narrating can be a highly social, interactive act that demands the use of both implicit and explicit collaborative strategies, particularly 'prompts' and 'requests for clarification'. In 'The Historical Composition of the Lexicon as a Stylistic Factor in a Text-Oriented Culture: A Case-Study from Modern Hebrew' (*L&L* 12[2003] 57–70), Yael Reshef undertakes the stylistic analysis of modern Hebrew texts from the perspective of a historical lexical study of two very different linguistic genres, administrative discourse and folk song; it is of interest to students of English stylistics in that it shows how historical factors can be used to account for stylistic choice. To round off their 2003 volume, *Language and Literature* prints a very thought-provoking article by Urszula Clark and Sonia Zyngier, 'Towards a Pedagogical Stylistics' (*L&L* 12[2003] 339–51), and the by now indispensable review by Geoff Hall, 'The Year's Work in Stylistics: 2002' (*L&L* 12[2003] 353–70). Clark and Zyngier review the work carried out since the 1997 PALA conference held in Nottingham by the PEDSIG (a special interest group for pedagogical stylistics, one of whose aims is to construe a theoretical dimension for stylistic practice in L1 and L2 language classrooms) and after a section devoted to an attempt to define pedagogical stylistics itself, they offer a typology of pedagogical activities and a pilot study of a text by the American poet Langston Hughes. Geoff Hall's review, as readers of *Language and Literature* know, is much more than an annotated reference list and it is cleverly divided into five distinctly labelled sections for Cognitive Poetics, Metaphor, Narrative, Discourse Analysis and Textuality, and Poetry and Poetics, which in themselves almost constitute a state of the art summary of the discipline: cognitive poetics and metaphor leading at the front, narrative at its centre, discourse analysis still lagging behind and a miscellaneous section to serve as ragbag. No sign of drama and dramatic texts, but to readers of this section this will not come as a surprise.

Books Reviewed

Aceto, Michael, and Jeffrey P. Williams, eds. *Contact Englishes of the Eastern Caribbean*. VEAW G30. Benjamins. [2003] pp. xx + 320. €120 ISBN 9 0272 4890 7, $120 ISBN 1 5881 1363 9.

Ahrens, Rüdiger, David Parker, Klaus Stiersdorfer, and Kwok-kan Tam, eds. *Anglophone Cultures in Southeast Asia: Appropriations, Continuities, Contexts*. Winter. [2003] pp. 316. €40 ISBN 3 8253 1508 8.

Aitchison, Jean. *A Glossary of Language and Mind*. EdinUP. [2003] pp. 131. pb £6.99 ISBN 0 7486 1824 4.

Aitchison, Jean. *Words in the Mind: An Introduction to the Mental Lexicon*, 3rd edn. Blackwell. [2002] pp. xiv + 314. pb £18.99 ($36.95) ISBN 0 6312 3244 3.

Alexiadou, Artemis, Elena Anagnostopoulou, Sjef Barbiers, and Hans-Martin Gaertner, eds. *Dimensions of Movement: From Features to Remnants*. Linguistik Aktuell/Linguistics Today 48. Benjamins. [2002] pp. vi + 342. €110 ISBN 9 0272 2769 1.

Allsopp, Jeanette. *The Caribbean Multilingual Dictionary of Flora, Fauna and Foods in English, French, French Creole and Spanish*. Arawak Publications. [2003] pp. lvi + 184. hb £45 ($70) ISBN 9 7681 8914 2, pb £33 ($50) ISBN 9 7681 8909 6.

Altendorf, Ulrike. *Estuary English: Levelling at the Interface of RP and South-Eastern British English*. Language in Performance. Narr. [2003] pp. xiv + 187. pb €48 ISBN 3 8233 6022 1.

Atkinson, Damian. *The Correspondence of John Stephen Farmer and W.E. Henley on their Slang Dictionary, 1890–1904*. Mellen. [2003] pp. xxxxv + 164. £69.95 ISBN 0 7734 6612 6.

Bækken, Bjørg. *Word Order in 17th Century English: A Study of the Stabilisation of the XSV Pattern*. Studia Anglistica Norvegica 12. Novus. [2003] pp. xiii + 220. pb €32.90 ISBN 8 2709 9377 8.

Baker, Mark C. *Lexical Categories: Verbs, Nouns, and Adjectives*. Cambridge Studies in Linguistics 102. CUP. [2003] pp. xvi + 353. hb £50 ISBN 0 5218 0638 0, pb £ 19.95 ISBN 0 5210 0110 2.

Baker, Peter S. *Introduction to Old English*. Blackwell. [2003] pp. xv + 332. hb £55 ISBN 0 6312 3453 5, pb £17.99 ISBN 0 6312 3454 3.

Banich, Marie T., and Mack Molly, eds. *Mind, Brain and Language*. Erlbaum. [2003] pp. xxii + 394. hb $89.95 ISBN 0 8058 3327 7, pb $45 ISBN 0 8058 3328 5.

Barron, Anne. *Acquisition in Interlanguage Pragmatics: Learning How To Do Things with Words in a Study Abroad Context*. Pragmatics & Beyond NS 108. Benjamins. [2003] pp. xviii + 403. €115 ISBN 9 0272 5350 1, $138 ISBN 1 5881 1342 6.

Barss, Andrew, ed. *Anaphora: A Reference Guide*. Explaining Linguistics. Blackwell. [2002] pp. xi + 288. hb £55 ISBN 0 6311 9571 8, pb £18.99 ISBN 0 6312 1118 7.

Bartens, Angela. *A Contrastive Grammar: Islander–Caribbean Standard English–Spanish*. Finnish Academy of Science and Letters. [2003] pp. 176. €25 ISBN 9 5141 0940 6.

Biggam, C.P. *From Earth To Art: The Many Aspects of the Plant-World in Anglo-Saxon England*. Rodopi. [2003] pp. 342. €70 ISBN 9 0420 0807 5.

Bolton, Kingsley. *Chinese Englishes: A Sociolinguistic History*. CUP. [2003] pp. xvi + 360. £45 ISBN 0 5218 1163 5.

Booij, Geert, and Jaap van Marle, eds. *Yearbook of Morphology 2002*. Kluwer/Springer. [2003] pp. 336. €139.10 ISBN 1 4020 1150 4.

Bourne, Jill. *Understanding Leicestershire and Rutland Place-Names*. Heart of Albion Press. [2003] pp. 124. pb £6.95 ISBN 1 8728 8371 0.

Britain, David, and Jenny Cheshire, eds. *Social Dialectology: In Honour of Peter Trudgill*. Impact: Studies in Language and Society 16. Benjamins. [2003] pp. viii + 343. €85 ISBN 9 0272 1854 4, $102 ISBN 1 5881 1403 1.

Butler, Christopher S. *Structure and Function: A Guide to Three Major Structural-Functional Theories,* vol. 1: *Approaches to the Simplex Clause*. SLCS. Benjamins. [2003] pp. xx + 570. hb €140 ISBN 9 0272 3069 2, pb €70 ISBN 9 0272 3070 6.

Butler, Christopher S. *Structure and Function: A Guide to Three Major Structural-Functional Theories,* vol. 2: *From Clause to Discourse and Beyond*. SLCS. Benjamins. [2003] pp. xiii + 576. hb €140 ISBN 9 0272 3071 4, pb €70 ISBN 9 0272 3072 2.

Byron, Glennis. *Dramatic Monologue*. The New Critical Idiom. Routledge. [2003] pp. viii + 167. hb £45 ISBN 0 4152 2936 7, pb £10.99 ISBN 0 4152 2937 5.

Carston, Robyn. *Thoughts and Utterances: The Pragmatics of Explicit Communication*. Blackwell. [2002] pp. x + 418. hb £60 ($69.95) ISBN 0 6311 7891 0, pb £19.99 ($34.95) ISBN 0 6312 1488 7.

Chambers, J.K. *Sociolinguistic Theory: Linguistic Variation and its Social Significance*. 2nd edn. Blackwell. [2003] pp. xxi + 320. hb (not in print) ISBN 0 6312 2881 0, pb £17.99 ISBN 0 6312 2882 9.

Chapelle, Carol A. *English Language Teaching and Technology*. Benjamins. [2003] pp. xvi + 213. hb €95 ($114) ISBN 9 0272 1703 3, pb €33 ($39.95) ISBN 9 0272 1704 1.

Chomsky, Noam. *New Horizons in the Study of Language and Mind*. CUP. [2000] pp. 248. hb £40 ISBN 0 5216 5147 6, pb £14.95 ISBN 0 5216 5822 5.

Chomsky, Noam, edited by Belletti Adriana, and Rizzi Luigi. *On Nature and Language*. CUP. [2002] pp. 180. hb £40 ISBN 0 5218 1548 7, pb £13.95 ISBN 0 5210 1624 X.

Christiansen, Morten H., and Simon Kirby, eds. *Language Evolution*. OUP. [2003] pp. xviii + 395. hb £63 ISBN 0 1992 4483 9, pb £21.99 ISBN 0 1992 4484 7.

Cinque, Guglielmo, ed. *The Cartography of Syntactic Structures,* vol. 1: *Functional Structure in DP and IP*. Oxford Studies in Comparative Syntax. OUP. [2002] pp. vii + 233. hb £65 ISBN 0 1951 4879 7, pb £28.99, ISBN 0 1951 4880 0.

Clyne, Michael. *The Dynamics of Language Contact: English and Immigrant Languages*. CUP. [2003] pp. xv + 282. hb £47.50 ISBN 0 5217 8136 1, pb £16.95 ISBN 0 5217 8648 7.

Collins, Beverley, and Inger M. Mees. *Practical Phonetics and Phonology*. Routledge. [2003] pp. xx + 267. hb £55 ISBN 0 4152 6133 3, pb £15.99 ISBN 0 4152 6134 1.

Corbett, John, J. Derrick McClure, and Jane Stuart-Smith, eds. *The Edinburgh Companion to Scots*. EdinUP. [2003] pp. xiii + 304. pb £16.99 ISBN 0 4786 1596 2.

Cristofaro, Sonia. *Subordination*. Oxford Studies in Typology and Linguistic Theory. OUP. [2003] pp. xvi + 355. £55 ISBN 0 1992 5279 3.

Crystal, David. *The Cambridge Encyclopedia of the English Language*. 2nd edn. CUP. [2003] pp. vii + 499. hb £55 ($75) ISBN 0 5218 2348 X, pb £25 ($39.99) ISBN 0 5215 3033 4.

Crystal, David. *English as a Global Language*. 2nd edn. CUP. [2003] pp. xv + 212. hb £32.50 ISBN 0 5218 2347 1, pb £10.99 ISBN 0 5215 3032 6.

Cutting, Joan. *Pragmatics and Discourse*. Routledge. [2002] pp. xii + 187. hb £50 ISBN 0 4152 5357 8, pb £15.99 ISBN 0 4152 5358 6.

Cysouw, Michael. *The Paradigmatic Structure of Person Marking*. Oxford Studies in Typology and Linguistic Theory. OUP. [2003] pp. xiv + 375. £50 ISBN 0 1992 5412 5.

Demsky, Aaron, ed. *These Are the Names*. Bar-Ilan UP. [2003] pp. 350. £? ISBN 9 6522 6267 6.

Deterding, David, Ee Ling Low, and Adam Brown, eds. *English in Singapore: Research on Grammar*. McGraw-Hill (Asia). [2003] pp. ? $12.95 ISBN 0 0712 3103 X.

Deumert, Ana, and Wim Vandenbussche, eds. *Germanic Standardizations: Past to Present*. Impact: Studies in Language and Society 18. Benjamins. [2003] pp. vi + 479. €115 ISBN 9 0272 1856 0, $138 ISBN 1 5881 1437 6.

Doughty, Catherine J., and Michael H. Long, eds. *The Handbook of Second Language Acquisition*. BHLS. Blackwell. [2003] pp. x + 888. £99.99 ($149.95) ISBN 0 6312 1754 1.

Dušková, Libuše, ed. *Dictionary of the Prague School of Linguistics*. translated from the French, German, and Czech sources. Benjamins. [2003] pp. x + 216. €85 ($102) ISBN 9 0272 1559 6.

Eckert, Penelope, and Sally McConnell-Ginet. *Language and Gender*. CUP. [2003] pp. xii + 366. hb £47.50 ($70) ISBN 0 5216 5283 9, pb £17.99 ($25.99) ISBN 0 5216 5426 2.

Facchinetti, Roberta, Manfred Krug, and Frank Palmer, eds. *Modality in Contemporary English*. Topics in English Linguistics 44. Mouton. [2003] pp. xvi + 396. €98 ISBN 3 1101 7686 6.

Fairclough, Norman. *Analysing Discourse: Textual Analysis for Social Research*. Routledge. [2003] pp. vii + 270. hb £60 ISBN 0 4152 5892 8, pb £16.99 ISBN 0 4152 5893 6.

Farkas, Donka F., and Henriëtte de Swart. *The Semantics of Incorporation: From Argument Structure to Discourse Transparency*. Stanford Monographs in Linguistics. CSLI. [2003] pp. xi + 178. hb $65 ISBN 1 5758 6419 3, pb $20 ISBN 1 5758 6420 7.

Field, John. *Psycholinguistics*. Routledge. [2003] pp. xvii + 231. hb £50 ISBN 0 4152 7599 7, pb £14.99 ISBN 0 4152 7600 4.

Finch, Geoffrey. *How To Study Linguistics: A Guide to Understanding Language*. 2nd edn. Palgrave. [2003] pp. x + 249. pb £11.99 ISBN 1 4039 0106 6.

Finke, Wayne H., and Leonard R.N. Ashley, eds. *A Garland of Names*. Cummings & Hathaway. [2003] pp. viii + 158. £? ISBN 1 5798 1048 9.

Fought, Carmen. *Chicano English in Context*. Macmillan. [2003] pp. xi + 253. pb £18.99 ISBN 0 3339 8638 5.

Francis, Elaine J., and Laura A. Michaelis, eds. *Mismatch: Form-Function Congruity and the Architecture of Grammar*. CSLI Lecture Notes. CSLI. [2003] pp. x + 430. hb $75 ISBN 1 5758 6383 9, pb $30 ISBN 1 5758 6384 7.

Frawley, William J., ed. *International Encyclopedia of Linguistics*. 2nd edn. 4 vols. OUP. [2003] pp. 2,218. $495 ISBN 0 1951 3977 1.

Fry, John. *Ellipsis and Wa-Marking in Japanese Conversation*. Outstanding Dissertations in Linguistics. Routledge. [2003] pp. xiii + 204. £50 ISBN 0 4159 6764 3.

Gambier, Yves, ed. *Screen Translation: The Translator,* vol. 11(2): *Special Issue: St Jerome*. [2003] pp. 323. pb £25 ISBN 1 9006 5071 1.

Garrett, Peter, Nikolas Coupland, and Angie Williams. *Investigating Language Attitudes: Social Meanings of Dialect, Ethnicity and Performance*. UWalesP. [2003] pp. x + 251. £40 ISBN 0 7083 1803 7.

Gavins, Joanna, and Gerard Steen, eds. *Cognitive Poetics in Practice*. Routledge. [2003] pp. xii + 188. hb £65 ISBN 0 4152 7798 ?, pb £18.99 ISBN 0 4152 7799 X.

Gentner, Dedre, and Goldin-Meadow Susan, eds. *Language in Mind*. MITP. [2003] pp. x + 528. pb $38 (£24.95) ISBN 0 2625 7163 3.

Givón, Talmy, and Bertram F. Malle, eds. *The Evolution of Language Out of Pre-Language*. Benjamins. [2002] pp. x + 394. hb €90 ($108) ISBN 9 0272 2959 7, pb €44 ($52.95) ISBN 9 0272 2960 0.

Görlach, Manfred. *English Words Abroad*. Benjamins. [2003] pp. xii + 188. €70 ISBN 9 0272 2331 9.

Greenberg, Yael. *Manifestations of Genericity*. Outstanding Dissertations in Linguistics. Routledge. [2003] pp. xxvi + 323. £60 ISBN 0 4159 6777 5.

Gustafsson, Martin, and Lars Hertzberg, eds. *The Practice of Language*. Kluwer. [2002] pp. viii + 273. £66 (€95) ISBN 1 4020 0691 8.

Gutiérrez-Rexach, Javier. *Semantics: Critical Concepts in Linguistics*. 6 vols. Routledge. [2003] pp. ? €675 ISBN 0 4152 6632 7.

Hale, Ken, and Samuel Jay Keyser. *Prolegomenon to a Theory of Argument Structure*. Linguistic Inquiry Monograph 39. MITP. [2002] pp. x + 281. hb £41.50 ISBN 0 2620 8308 6, pb £16.95 ISBN 0 2625 8214 7.

Hanks, Patrick, ed. *Dictionary of American Family Names*. 3 vols. OUP. [2003] vol. 1: pp. cviii + 615; vol. 2: pp. 685; vol. 3: pp. 671. $295 the set; ISBN 0 1951 6557 8 (vol. 1), 0 1951 6558 6 (vol. 2), 0 1951 6559 4 (vol. 3).

Hargraves, Orin. *Mighty Fine Words and Smashing Expressions: Making Sense of Transatlantic English*. OUP. [2003] pp. xiii + 305. £16.99 ISBN 0 1951 5704 4.

Harris, Roxy, and Ben Rampton. *The Language, Ethnicity and Race Reader*. Routledge. [2003] pp. x + 357. hb £65 ISBN 0 4152 7601 2, pb £17.99 ISBN 0 4152 7602 0.

Hickey, Raymond, ed. *Motives for Language Change*. CUP. [2003] pp. ix + 286. £40 ISBN 0 5217 9303 3.

Holmes, Janet, and Miriam Meyerhoff, eds. *The Handbook of Language and Gender*. BHLS. Blackwell. [2003] pp. xvi + 759. hb £85 ($131.95) ISBN 0 6312 2502 1, pb £24.99 ($44.95) ISBN 0 6312 2503 X.

Hope, Jonathan. *Shakespeare's Grammar*. Arden. [2003] pp. xiv + 210. hb £47 ISBN 1 9034 3636 2.

Hopper, Paul J., and Elizabeth Closs Traugott. *Grammaticalization*. 2nd edn. CUP. [2003] pp. xx + 276. hb £50 ISBN 0 5210 0948 0, pb £18.99 ISBN 0 5218 0421 3.

Huddleston, Rodney, and Geoffrey K. Pullum. *The Cambridge Grammar of the English Language*. CUP. [2002] pp. 1,864. £100 ISBN 0 5214 3146 8.

Jackendoff, Ray. *The Foundations of Language*. OUP. [2002] pp. xix + 477. hb £40 ISBN 0 1982 7012 7, pb £17.50 ISBN 0 1992 6437 6..

Jay, Timothy. *The Psychology of Language*. Pearson. [2002] pp. xviii + 604. £31.99 ISBN 0 1302 6609 4.

Jenkins, Jennifer. *World Englishes: A Resource Book for Students*. Routledge. [2003] pp. xvi + 233. hb £55 ISBN 0 4152 5805 7, pb £ 14.99 ISBN 0 4512 5806 5.

Joseph, Brian D., and Richard D. Janda, eds. *The Handbook of Historical Linguistics*. BHLS. Blackwell. [2003] pp. xviii + 881. £95 ISBN 0 6311 9571 8.

Julien, Marit. *Syntactic Heads and Word Formation*. Oxford Studies in Comparative Syntax. OUP. [2002] pp. viii + 407. hb £60 ISBN 0 1951 4950 5, pb £35 ISBN 0 1951 4951 3.

Kaplan, Robert B., and Richard B. Baldauf, Jr. *Language and Language-in-Education Planning in the Pacific Basin*. Kluwer. [2003] pp. viii + 276. €103 (£66) ISBN 1 4020 1062 1.

Kasper, Gabriele, and Kenneth R. Rose. *Pragmatic Development in a Second Language*. Language Learning Monograph Series 3. Blackwell. [2003] pp. 300. pb £21.99 ISBN 0 6312 3430 6.

Kenstowicz, Michael, ed. *Ken Hale: A Life in Language*. Current Studies in Linguistics 36. MITP. [2001] pp. xiii + 480. hb $75 ISBN 0 2621 1257 4, pb $30. ISBN 0 2626 1160 0.

Klingler, Thomas A. *If I Could Turn My Tongue Like That: The Creole Language of Pointe Coupee Parish, Louisiana*. LSUP. [2003] pp. xxxv + 627. £57.50 ISBN 0 8271 2779 5.

Kouwenberg, Silvia, ed. *Twice as Meaningful: Reduplication in Pidgins, Creoles, and Other Contact Languages*. Battlebridge. [2003] pp. vi + 330. pb £25 ISBN 1 9032 9202 6.

Kracht, Marcus. *The Mathematics of Language*. Studies in Generative Grammar 63. MGruyter. [2003] pp. xvi + 589. €98 ISBN 3 1101 7620 3.

Kreidler, Charles W. *Pronunciation of English: A Course Book*. Blackwell. [2003] pp. xvi + 328. pb $34.95 ISBN 1 4051 1336 7.

Kühnlein, Peter, Rieser Hannes, and Zeevat Henk, eds. *Perspectives on Dialogue in the New Millennium*. Pragmatics and Beyond ns 114. Benjamins. [2003] pp. xii + 395. €115 ISBN 9 0272 5356 0, $138 ISBN 1 5881 1404 X.

Lakoff, George, and Johnson Mark. *Metaphors We Live By*. 2nd edn. UChicP. [2003] pp. xiv + 276. pb $14 ISBN 0 2264 6801 1.

Langacker, Ronald W. *Concept, Image, and Symbol: The Cognitive Basis of Grammar*. 2nd edn. MGruyter. [2002] pp. xvi + 395. pb €29.95 ($29.95) ISBN 3 1101 7280 1.

Levinson, Stephen C. *Space in Language and Cognition: Explorations in Cognitive Diversity*. CUP. [2003] pp. xxiv + 389. hb £47.50 0 5218 1262 3, pb £17.99 ISBN 0 5210 1196 5.

Lewis, Chris. *The Dictionary of Playground Slang*. Allison and Busby. [2003] pp. 304. pb £6.99 ISBN 0 7490 0607 2.

Löffler, Heinrich. *Dialektologie: Eine Einführung*. Narr. [2003] pp. xiv + 158. pb €18.90 ISBN 3 8233 4998 8.

Machan, Tim William. *English in the Middle Ages*. OUP. [2003] pp. x + 205. £45 ISBN 0 1992 6268 3.

Mair, Christian, ed. *The Politics of English as a World Language: New Horizons in Postcolonial Cultural Studies*. ASNEL 7. Rodopi. [2003] pp. xxi + 797. hb €110 ($143) ISBN 9 0420 0876 8, pb €55 ($72) ISBN 9 0420 0866 0.

Makoni, Sinfree, Smitherman Geneva, Arnetha F. Ball, and Arthur K. Spears, eds. *Black Linguistics: Language, Society, and Politics in Africa and the Americas*. Routledge. [2003] pp. xii + 228. hb £60 ISBN 0 4152 6137 6, pb £16.99 ISBN 0 4152 6138 4.

Matthews, P.H. *Linguistics: A Very Short Introduction*. OUP. [2003] pp. 152. pb £9.95 ISBN 0 1928 0148 1.

McArthur, Lewis A. *Oregon Geographic Names*. 7th edn. Revised and enlarged by Lewis L. McArthur, includes CD-ROM. Oregon Historical Society. [2003] pp. xiv + 1070. hb $60 ISBN 0 8759 5278 X, pb $30 ISBN 0 8759 5277 1.

McCormick, Kay. *Language in Cape Town's District Six*. OUP. [2003] pp. 288. $85 ISBN 0 1982 3554 2.

Melchers, Gunnel, and Philip Shaw. *World Englishes*. The English Language Series. Arnold. [2003] pp. x + 229. hb £40 ISBN 0 3407 1887 0, pb £14.99 ISBN 0 3407 1888 9.

Migge, Bettina. *Creole Formation as Language Contact: The Case of the Suriname Creoles*. CLL 25. Benjamins. [2003] pp. x + 149. €85 ISBN 9 0272 5247 5, $85 ISBN 1 5881 1397 3.

Milroy, Lesley, and Matthew Gordon. *Sociolinguistics: Methods and Interpretation*. Blackwell. [2003] pp. xv + 261. hb (not in print) ISBN 0 6312 2224 3, pb £16.99 ISBN 0 6312 2225 1.

Moore, John, and Maria Polinsky, eds. *The Nature of Explanation in Linguistic Theory*. UChicP. [2003] pp. 320. hb $80 ISBN 1 5758 6453 3, pb $27.50 ISBN 1 5758 6454 1.

Mugglestone, Lynda. *Talking Proper: The Rise of Accent as Social Symbol*. 2nd edn. OUP. [2003] pp. 362. hb £35 ISBN 0 1992 5061 8, pb £17.99 ISBN 0 1992 5062 6.

Mühlhäusler, Peter, Thomas E. Dutton, and Suzanne Romaine, eds. *Tok Pisin Texts: From the Beginning to the Present*. VEAW T9. Benjamins. [2003] pp. x + 286. €115 ISBN 1 5881 1456 2, $115 ISBN 9 0272 4718 8.

Nagle, Stephen J., and Sara L. Sanders, eds. *English in the Southern United States*. Studies in English Language. CUP. [2003] pp. xiii + 244. £42.50 ISBN 0 5218 2264 5.

Napoli, Donna Jo. *Language Matters: A Guide to Everyday Thinking About Language*. OUP. [2003] pp. vii + 198. pb £12.99 ISBN 0 1951 6048 7.

Nevalainen, Terttu, and Helena Raumolin-Brunberg. *Historical Sociolinguistics*. Longman. [2003] pp. xvi + 266. pb £31.99 ISBN 0 5823 1994 3.

Newman, John, ed. *The Linguistics of Sitting, Standing, and Lying*. Typological Studies in Language 51. Benjamins. [2002] pp. xii + 407. €120 ISBN 9 0272 2957 0.

Nida, Eugene A. *Contexts in Translating*. Benjamins. [2002] pp. x + 127. €70 ($84) ISBN 9 0272 1647 9.

Nooteboom, Sieb, Fred Weerman, and Frank Wijnen, eds. *Storage and Computation in the Language Faculty*. Kluwer. [2002] pp. xiv + 342. hb £90 (€130) ISBN 1 4020 0526 1, pb £34 (€49) ISBN 1 4020 0527 X.

Norment, Nathaniel. *Readings in African American Language: Aspects, Features and Perspectives*. Lang. [2003] pp. xv + 356. pb £22 ISBN 0 8204 5797 3.

O'Halloran, Kieran. *Critical Discourse Analysis and Language Cognition*. EdinUP. [2003] pp. 280. pb £18.99 ISBN 0 7486 1828 7.

Paulston, Christina Bratt, and G. Richard Tucker, eds. *Sociolinguistics: The Essential Readings*. Blackwell. [2003] pp. xviii + 502. hb £60 ISBN 0 6312 2716 4, pb £18.99 ISBN 0 6312 2717 2.

Penhallurick, Rob. *Studying the English Language*. Macmillan. [2003] pp. xii + 249. pb £13.99 ISBN 0 3337 2740 1.

Peregrin, Jaroslav, ed. *Meaning: The Dynamic Turn*. Current Research in the Semantics/Pragmatics Interface 12. Elsevier. [2003] pp. x + 277. €81($81) ISBN 0 0804 4187 4.

Pérez de Ayala, and Soledad. *Cortesía e imagen en el parlamento británico: Question Time*. Congreso de los Diputados. [2003] pp. 342. pb €11 ISBN 8 4794 3215 2.

Plag, Ingo, ed. *Phonology and Morphology of Creole Languages*. Niemeyer. [2003] pp. xi + 376. €98 ISBN 3 4843 0478 2..

Plag, Ingo. *Word-Formation in English*. Cambridge Textbooks in Linguistics. CUP. [2003] pp. xiii + 240. hb £45 ISBN 0 5218 1959 8, pb £17.95 ISBN 0 5215 2563 2.

Plank, Frans, ed. *Noun Phrase Structure in the Languages of Europe*. MGruyter. [2003] pp. xxi + 845. €188 ($244) ISBN 3 1101 5748 9.

Prevignano, Carlo, and Paul J. Thibault, eds. *Discussing Conversation Analysis: The Work of Emanuel A. Schegloff*. Benjamins. [2003] pp. xiv + 192. €60 ISBN 9 0272 2599 0, $72 ISBN 1 5881 1354 X.

Prior, Arthur N., new edn. Per Hasle, Øhrstrøm Peter, Braüner Torben, and Copeland Jack. *Papers on Time and Tense*. OUP. [2003] pp. ix + 331. hb £45 ISBN 0 1992 5606 3, pb £18 ISBN 0 1992 5607 1.

Pustet, Regina. *Copulas: Universals in the Categorization of the Lexicon*. Oxford Studies in Typology and Linguistic Theory. OUP. [2003] pp. xiv + 262. £50 ISBN 0 1992 5850 3.

Richard, Mark, ed. *Meaning*. Blackwell Readings in Philosophy. Blackwell. [2003] pp. x + 341. pb £17.99 ISBN 0 6312 2223 5.

Roberts, Ian, and Anna Roussou. *Syntactic Change: A Minimalist Approach to Grammaticalization*. Cambridge Studies in Linguistics 100. CUP. [2003] pp. xi + 275. £45 ISBN 0 5217 9056 5.

Rogers, Rebecca. *A Critical Discourse Analysis of Family Literacy Practices: Power In and Out of Print*. Erlbaum. [2003] pp. 232. hb $69.95 ISBN 0 8058 4226 8, pb $27.50 ISBN 0 8058 4784 7.

Room, Adrian. *Penguin Dictionary of British Place Names*. Penguin. [2003] pp. xxxix + 549. pb £9.99 ISBN 0 1405 1453 8.

Room, Adrian. *Placenames of the World*. McFarland. [2003] pp. 441. $49.95 ISBN 0 7864 1814 1.

Rupp, Laura. *The Syntax of Imperatives in English and Germanic: Word Order Variation in the Minimalist Framework*. Palgrave. [2003] pp. ix + 204. £45 ISBN 0 3339 9342 X.

Saraceni, Mario. *The Language of Comics*. Intertext. Routledge. [2003] pp. x + 110. hb £40 ISBN 0 4152 8670 0, pb £12.99 ISBN 0 4152 1422 X.

Schreier, Daniel. *Isolation and Language Change: Contemporary and Sociohistorical Evidence from Tristan da Cunha English*. Palgrave. [2003] pp. 256. £50 ($78) ISBN 1 4039 0407 3.

Schröder, Anne. *Status, Functions, and Prospects of Pidgin English: An Empirical Approach to Language Dynamics in Cameroon*. LiP 27. Narr. [2003] pp. 284 + CD-ROM. €58 ISBN 3 8233 5821 9.

Schwabe, Kerstin, and Susanne Winkler. *The Interfaces: Deriving and Interpreting Omitted Structures*. Linguistik Aktuell/Linguistics Today 61. Benjamins. [2003] pp. vi + 399. €120 ISBN 9 0272 2784 5, $120 ISBN 1 5881 1330 2.

Sells, Peter, ed. *Formal and Empirical Issues in Optimality Theoretic Syntax*. CSLI. [2001] pp. ix + 420. hb £42.50 ISBN 1 5758 6243 3, pb £15.95 ISBN 1 5758 6244 1.

Shockey, Linda. *Sound Patterns of Spoken English*. Blackwell. [2003] pp. vii + 156. hb £45 ISBN 0 6312 3079 3, pb £14.99 ISBN 0 6312 3080 7.

Siegel, Jeff, and Kent Sakoda. *Pidgin Grammar: An Introduction to the Creole English of Hawai'i*. Bess Press. [2003] pp. 126. pb $11.95 ISBN 1 5730 6169 7.

Sifakis, Carl. *The Dictionary of Crime Terms*. Facts on File. [2003] pp. xvi + 272. £44 ISBN 0 8160 4548 8, Also published as *Mobspeak*. Checkmark. [2003] pp. xvi + 272. pb $17.95 ISBN 0 8160 4548 6.

Skandera, Paul. *Drawing a Map of Africa: Idiom in Kenyan English*. LiP 26. Narr. [2003] pp. xv + 238. €54 ISBN 3 8233 5820.

Smith, Neil. *Language, Bananas and Bonobos: Linguistic Problems, Puzzles and Polemics*. Blackwell. [2002] pp. x + 150. hb £45 ($62.95) ISBN 0 6312 2871 3, pb £14.99 ($21.95) ISBN 0 6312 2872 1.

Somers, Harold, ed. *Computers and Translation: A Translator's Guide*. Benjamins. [2003] pp. xvi + 351. €115 ($138) ISBN 9 0272 1640 1.

Svenonius, Peter, ed. *Subjects, Expletives, and the EPP*. Oxford Studies in Comparative Syntax. OUP. [2002] pp. viii + 245. hb £47.50 ISBN 0 1951 4224 1, pb £22.50 ISBN 0 1951 4225 X.

Taavitsainen, Irma, and Andreas H. Jucker, eds. *Diachronic Perspectives on Address Term Systems*. Pragmatics and Beyond ns 107. Benjamins. [2003] pp. viii + 446. €115 ISBN 9 0272 5348 X, $138 ISBN 1 5881 1310 8.

Talbot, Mary, Karen Atkinson, and David Atkinson. *Language and Power in the Modern World*. EdinUP. [2003] pp. ix + 342. hb £45 ISBN 0 7486 1539 1, pb £16.99 ISBN 0 7486 1538 5.

Taylor, John R. *Linguistic Categorization*. 3rd edn. OUP. [2003] pp. xvi + 308. pb £18.99 ISBN 0 1992 6664 6.

Thompson, Roger M. *Filipino English and Taglish: Language Switching from Multiple Perspectives*. VEAW G31. Benjamins. [2003] pp. xiv + 288. €99 ISBN 9 0272 4891 5, $99 ISBN 1 5881 1407 4.

Tissari, Heli. *Lovescapes: Changes in Prototypical Senses and Cognitive Metaphors since 1500*. Mémoires de la Société Néophilologique de Helsinki. [2003] pp. xvi + 470. €45 ISBN 9 5190 4018 8.

Tomasello, Michael, ed. *The New Psychology of Language: Cognitive and Functional Approaches to Language Structure*. vol. 2. Erlbaum. [2003] pp. vi + 278. hb $69.95 ISBN 0 8058 3428 1, pb $32.50 ISBN 0 8058 3429 X.

Tomberlin, James E., ed. *Language and Mind*. Philosophical Perspectives 16. Blackwell. [2002] pp. viii + 462. £19.99 ($36.95) ISBN 0 6312 3409 8.

Tristram, Hildegard L.C., ed. *The Celtic Englishes III*. Winter. [2003] pp. xiv + 478. €78 ISBN 3 8253 1241 0.

Trudgill, Peter. *A Glossary of Sociolinguistics*. EdinUP. [2003] pp. 148. £6.99 ISBN 0 7486 1623 3.

Trudgill, Peter. *The Norfolk Dialect*. Poppyland. [2003] pp. 103. £8.95 ISBN 0 9461 4863 5.

Ukaji, Masatomo, Masayuki Ike-Uchi, and Yoshiki, eds. *Currents Issues in English Linguistics*. Special Publications of the English Linguistic Society of Japan 2. Katakusha. [2003] pp. viii + 277. pb. £? ISBN 4 7589 2117 2.

van Gelderen, Elly. *An Introduction to the Grammar of English: Syntactic Arguments and Socio-Historical Background*. Benjamins. [2002] pp. xxiv + 200. hb €75 ($90) ISBN 9 0272 2588 5, pb €33 ($39.95) ISBN 9 0272 2586 9.

van Sterkenburg, Piet. *A Practical Guide to Lexicography*. Benjamins. [2003] pp. xi + 460. €65 ISBN 9 0272 2330 0.

van der Zee, Emile, and Jon Slack, eds. *Representing Direction in Language and Space*. OUP. [2003] pp. xvi+ 282. hb £68.50 ISBN 0 1992 6018 4, pb £25.50 ISBN 0 1992 6019 2.

Velupillai, Viveka. *Hawai'i Creole English: A Typological Analysis of the Tense-Mood-Aspect System*. Palgrave. [2003] pp. xv + 216. £45 ($69.95) ISBN 0 3339 9340 3.

Wardhaugh, Ronald. *Understanding English Grammar: A Linguistic Approach*. 2nd edn. Blackwell. [2003] pp. xi + 279. hb £55 ISBN 0 6312 3291 5, pb £16.99 ISBN 0 6312 3292 3.

Winchester, Simon. *The Meaning of Everything: The Story of the Oxford English Dictionary*. OUP. [2003] pp. xxv + 260. hb £12.99 ISBN 0 1986 0702 4.

Winford, Donald. *An Introduction to Contact Linguistics*. Blackwell. [2003] pp. xvii + 416. hb £55 ($69.95) ISBN 0 6312 1250 7, pb £17.99 ($34.95) ISBN 0 6312 1251 5.

Wray, Alison, ed. *The Transition to Language*. OUP. [2002] pp. xii +410. hb £65 ISBN 0 1992 5065 0, pb £19.99 ISBN 0 1992 5066 9.

II

Old English Literature

STACY S. KLEIN AND MARY SWAN

This chapter has ten sections: 1. Bibliography; 2. Manuscript Studies, Palaeography and Facsimiles; 3. Social, Cultural and Intellectual Background; 4. Literature: General; 5. The Exeter Book; 6. The Poems of the Vercelli Book; 7. The Junius Manuscript; 8. The *Beowulf* Manuscript; 9. Other Poems; 10. Prose. Sections 1, 2, 3 and 10 are by Mary Swan; section 4 is by Stacy S. Klein with contributions by Mary Swan; sections 5–9 are by Stacy S. Klein.

1. Bibliography

OENews 34:ii[2001] and 35:ii[2002] were published in 2003. They contain, respectively, the year's work in Old English Studies 1999 and 2000. Volume 36:iii[Spring 2003] includes news of conferences and publications. The eighteenth progress report of the Fontes Anglo-Saxonici project (*OENews* 36:iii[2003] 9–10) is contributed by Peter Jackson, and the fourth annual report on the Anglo-Saxon Plant Name Survey by C.P. Biggam (*OENews* 36:iii[2003] 11–12). Carmen Acevedo Butcher reports on 'Recovering Unique Ælfrician Texts Using the Fiber Optic Light Cord: Pope XVII in London, BL Cotton Vitellius C. v' (*OENews* 36:iii[2003] 13–22), and on her discovery that Pope's reconstructions and conjectures in his 1967–8 edition match almost exactly the readings obtainable with fibre optic light. This volume also contains abstracts of papers in Anglo-Saxon Studies. Volume 36:iv[Summer 2003] contains the Old English bibliography for 2002 and the research in progress listings. Volume 37:i[Fall 2003] includes notes on forthcoming conferences, news of publications, reports on the International Society of Anglo-Saxonists 2003 meeting at Scottsdale, the *Dictionary of Old English* and the Friends of the *DOE* fundraising campaign, the Durham *Liber Vitae* Project, and the Alfredian Boethius Project, and instructions on how to acknowledge the *Fontes Anglo-Saxonici* database. Ute Schwab writes on 'More Anglo-Saxon Runic Graffiti in Roman Catacombs' (*OENews* 37:i[2003] 36–9), Thomas A. Bredehoft on 'Anglo-Saxonists and eBay' (*OENews* 37:i[2003] 40–5), and Martin K. Foys contributes his annual article on digital resources: '*Circolwyrde 2003*: New Electronic Resources for

Year's Work in English Studies, Volume 84 (2005) © The English Association; all rights reserved. For permissions, please email: journals.permissions@oxfordjournals.org

doi: 10.1093/ywes/mai002

Anglo-Saxon Studies' (*OENews* 37:i[2003] 46–53). *ASE* 32[2003] 307–406 contains the bibliography for 2002.

2. Manuscript Studies, Palaeography and Facsimiles

Helmut Gneuss publishes 'Addenda and Corrigenda to the *Handlist of Anglo-Saxon Manuscripts*' (*ASE* 32[2003] 293–305), which stands as a first supplement to his immensely useful *Handlist* (*YWES* 82[2003] 116).

Celia Chazelle examines in detail 'Ceolfrid's Gift to St Peter: The First Quire of the *Codex Amiatinus* and the Evidence of its Roman Destination' (*EME* 12[2003] 129–57). Through careful analysis of the likely original arrangement of the preliminary quire of the manuscript, Chazelle argues that this quire was intended from the start as part of a gift to the holy see, and she interprets the manuscript's Ezra portrait as a reflection of the papal office.

Michelle P. Brown's important new research on the Lindisfarne Gospels is presented in *The Lindisfarne Gospels: Society, Spirituality and the Scribe*, which offers a richly illustrated, wide-ranging and closely argued study of the genesis of the manuscript, its provenance, text, codicology and art, and the impetus behind its production. Brown presents a careful case for the influence of Monkwearmouth-Jarrow on the manuscript, and for a probable date of production in the second decade of the eighth century. In addition to a wealth of scrupulous analysis of the Lindisfarne Gospels, Brown offers new comparative interpretations of the dating and provenance of other manuscripts, including the Durham Gospels, the Books of Durrow and Kells, and the Echternach Gospels. The volume's appendices provide an analysis of the pigments used in the manuscript and (in the form of a CD-ROM), a tabulation of the manuscript contents. The very reasonable price of this volume will make it accessible to students of Anglo-Saxon culture at all levels. Lawrence Nees also publishes on the Lindisfarne Gospels this year. In 'Reading Aldred's Colophon for the Lindisfarne Gospels' (*Speculum* 78[2003] 333–77) he sets out a case for reading the colophon in the tenth-century context in which it was composed, rather than as an unproblematic record of the manuscript's production, and also suggests that the date of production of the manuscript might be the second quarter of the eighth century.

Birgit Ebersperger's 'BSG, MS 2409 + Arsenal, MS 933, ff. 128–334: An Anglo-Saxon Manuscript from Canterbury?' (in Kornexl and Lenker, eds., *Bookmarks from the Past*, pp. 177–93) examines the palaeographical and codicological aspects of this once single manuscript, to show that it may have been made in close proximity to Bibliothèque Sainte-Geneviève 2410 + Bibliothèque de l'Arsenal 903, fos. 1–52, which have already been demonstrated to date from *c.*1000, and to have been written in Canterbury.

Anne Lawrence-Mather's *Manuscripts in Northumbria in the Eleventh and Twelfth Centuries* includes discussions of the influence of the Anglo-Saxon past on post-Conquest Durham, as evidenced by pictorial narrative produced there, the continued promotion of the cult of Cuthbert, the continuing importance of Bede, and the significance of all of these for regional identity.

Elaine Treharne's analysis of Leofric's making of a library in Exeter, and Mechthild Gretsch's study of Cambridge, Corpus Christi College MS 57 are reviewed in Section 3 of this chapter. For the discussion of Anglo-Saxon manuscripts in Mary C. Olsen, *Fair and Varied Forms*, see Section 1 of Chapter 3 of this volume.

3. Social, Cultural and Intellectual Background

Work on Anglo-Saxon intellectual and religious culture continues to deepen our understanding of the conditions for textual production and dissemination. Joyce Hill surveys 'Learning Latin in Anglo-Saxon England: Traditions, Texts and Techniques' (in Rees-Jones, ed., *Learning and Literacy in Medieval England and Abroad*, pp. 7–29) through the whole of the period, and with a focus on the particular challenges brought about by the conversion to Christianity and by Germanic first-language speakers learning Latin. Hill's most detailed case study is the works of Ælfric, in particular his *Grammar* and *Colloquy*, and the function of the latter in language-teaching. Stephen Lake offers a very useful examination of 'Knowledge of the Writings of John Cassian in Early Anglo-Saxon England' (*ASE* 32[2003] 27–41). He surveys Anglo-Saxon works which might use Cassian as a source, in particular the Leiden Glossary and Alcuin's *De Virginitate* and several works by Bede, all of which clearly draw on Cassian, and the anonymous *Life of Cuthbert* and Augustine of Canterbury's *Responsio IX*, whose use of Cassian Lake judges to be less certain. Lake deduces from this overview that more than one manuscript of the works of Cassian circulated in Anglo-Saxon England between the later seventh and mid-eighth centuries, and notes evidence for earlier knowledge of the works of Cassian in Ireland and Brittany, and also additional, more extensive manuscript evidence from England in the late Anglo-Saxon and early Anglo-Norman period.

In 'York, Bede's Calendar and a Pre-Bedan English Martyrology' (*AnBol* 121[2003] 329–55), Donald Bullough argues that the consecration of the *Alma Sophia* basilica in York in 780 lies behind a double entry in a mid-ninth-century Carolingian calendar from Prüm, and that relics might have been transferred from Rome on the occasion of the consecration. Bullough proposes the existence of a breviate version of the Hieronyman Martyrology, enlarged in Northumbria in the late seventh or early eighth century, which served as a model for the York metrical Martyrology.

Marilyn Dunn's *The Emergence of Monasticism*, first published in 2000, but not reviewed in *YWES*, is issued in paperback this year. Its broad-ranging overview of the development of monastic life from late antiquity to the early Middle Ages is of great use to Anglo-Saxonists seeking to understand English monasticism in an international context, and the final chapter, 'England in the Seventh Century', provides a focused discussion of the introduction of the Benedictine Rule; the liturgy of Monkwearmouth-Jarrow; pastoral care; royal, aristocratic and women's monasteries; and an interesting argument for the composition of Gregory's *Dialogues* in seventh-century Northumbria.

Royal and female monastic life in Anglo-Saxon England are also the subject of Barbara Yorke's important new study, *Nunneries and the Anglo-Saxon Royal*

Houses. Chapters cover foundation in the conversion period, the late eighth and ninth centuries, and the tenth and eleventh centuries, nunneries as royal ecclesiastical foundations, abbesses and nuns as members of royal houses, and nunneries, royal families and power, and the appendix provides an annotated list of nunneries founded by *c*.735. Yorke shows how royal nunneries are embodiments of the crucial relationship between church and state, and intricately bound up with the ways in which 'new dynasties coming to power sought to legitimize their rule' (p. 195).

Thacker and Sharpe, eds., *Local Saints and Local Churches in the Early Medieval West*, contains several essays on Anglo-Saxon topics. Alan Thacker's '*Loca Sanctorum*: The Significance of Place in the Study of the Saints' (pp. 1–43) includes a section on 'The "Age of Saints" in the British Isles'; Thacker's other contribution to the volume, 'The Making of a Local Saint' (pp. 45–73), studies the translations at Ely and Lindisfarne in the 690s and their connections with Rome, pointing to more likely influence from Gaul. Richard Sharpe's 'Martyrs and Local Saints in Late Antique Britain' (pp. 75–154) deals with the relative paucity of evidence for the Romano-British Church from the fourth to sixth centuries, the question of discerning discontinuity or continuity, information which can be derived from the work of Gildas, and evidence for martyr cults, and concludes by stressing the importance of recognizing links between Gaul, Britain and Ireland. John Crook's 'The Enshrinement of Local Saints in Francia and England' (pp. 189–224) examines the Roman background to the cult of saints, Roman and Merovingian influence on Anglo-Saxon relic cults, and the relatively few examples of Carolingian influence on English cult architecture, in the form of Anglo-Saxon ring crypts. O.J. Padel's 'Local Saints and Place-Names in Cornwall' (pp. 303–60) highlights differences between English-and Celtic-speaking area, and between local and universally culted saints, and in an appendix edits and annotates William Worcester's late fifteenth-century Notices of Cornish Saints' Bodies. Catherine Cubitt's 'Universal and Local Saints in Anglo-Saxon England' (pp. 423–53) examines Oswald as an example of a figure of popular sanctity, cults of heads of monasteries, and the role of liturgical and other texts and of liturgical practice in promoting cults. John Blair contributes two sections of the collection: 'A Saint for Every Minster? Local Cults in Anglo-Saxon England' (pp. 455–94) draws on the data set out in his extremely useful 'A Handlist of Anglo-Saxon Saints' (pp. 495–565) and includes maps of the sites of Anglo-Saxon saints' cults included in the handlist. Blair establishes four categories of cult for the seventh to ninth centuries—lay founders, heads and members of communities, bishops, and hermits—discusses a range of examples, and concludes that there is evidence for similarity of local cult practices in Brittonic and English societies. The appendices to the article are an edition of John Leland's Resting-Place List (probably from a manuscript no earlier than the twelfth century), and a discussion and argument that translation into raised shrines was not universal in Anglo-Saxon England.

Martin Grimmer's 'The Early History of Glastonbury Abbey: A Hypothesis Regarding the "British Charter"' (*Parergon* 20[2003] 1–20) scrutinizes this grant included in William of Malmesbury's *De antiquitate Glastonie ecclesie* and concludes that the reference to land at '*Ineswitrin*' is West Saxon in form, and that the charter cannot be used as evidence for a pre-Saxon foundation for Glastonbury Abbey. Hardy, Dodd and Keevill, eds., *Ælfric's Abbey: Excavations at Eynsham Abbey, Oxfordshire 1989–92*, is an impressively thorough report on the archaeological campaign in question, set in context with an introductory chapter by Alan Hardy and John Blair which charts the foundation and development of the abbey and previous archaeological work on the site, and has a substantial set of discussions of each phase of evidence.

Joanna Story's *Carolingian Connections* offers a rich and valuable account of influence between England and Francia between *c.* 750 and 870. Story draws on detailed analysis of a range of evidence, in particular chronicles and coinage, to track a complex set of connections and interdependences which provides a powerful reminder of the importance of situating Anglo-Saxon studies in a comparative European context. Two of the essays in Smith, ed., *Early Medieval Rome and the Christian West*, focus on internationally influenced Anglo-Saxon ecclesiastical developments. Nicholas Brooks examines 'Canterbury, Rome and the Construction of English Identity' (pp. 221–46) with a focus on the conversion of King Æthelberht's people and the presentation of Canterbury as the English Church site approved by Rome, and suggests that 'Canterbury's prolonged campaign of *imitatio Romae* was an essential element in the process of English ethnogenesis' (p. 222) for a British and Anglo-Saxon population. Alan Thacker goes 'In Search of Saints: The English Church and the Cult of Roman Apostles and Martyrs in the Seventh and Eighth Centuries' (pp. 247–77), and argues that early post-Augustine conversion Anglo-Saxon England followed Roman rather than Gallic models for saints' cults because Roman missionaries brought to England forms of cult and the cults of Roman patronal saints which were only replaced with Gallic-influenced cults of Anglo-Saxon saints a century later.

Two of the essays in Goetz, Jarnut and Pohl, eds., *Regna and Gentes: The Relationship between Late Antique and Early Medieval Peoples and Kingdoms in the Transformation of the Roman World*, consider Anglo-Saxon ethnicity. Patrick Wormald's 'The *Leges Barbarorum*: Law and Ethnicity in the Post-Roman West' (pp. 21–53) includes a discussion of Æthelberht's lawcode as an example of Germanic feud-based law established in emulation of Roman traditions. Barbara Yorke's 'Anglo-Saxon *Gens* and *Gentes*' (pp. 381–407) reassesses assumptions about developments in fifth-and sixth-century eastern Britain, through an examination of textual and archaeological evidence, a consideration of the role of the king, the ongoing influence of Roman administration, and the formation of Anglo-Saxon *regna*. Yorke concludes that there are parallels in the formation of *gentes* and *regna* between Anglo-Saxon England and other former Roman provinces.

Scandinavian connections are explored in two articles in *LeedsSE* 34[2003]. Susanne Kries, '"Westward I Came Across the Sea": Anglo-Scandinavian History Through Scandinavian Eyes' (pp. 47–76), focuses on Egill Skallagrímsson's *Aðalsteinsdrápa* as 'a poetic statement that served as a demarcation between Scandinavian and English claims to power in England' (p. 67). Magnús Fjalldal's 'Anglo-Saxon History in Medieval Iceland: Actual and Legendary Sources' (pp. 77–108) re-examines whether Icelandic historians can be shown to have known twelfth-century English writings on Anglo-Saxon history, and whether they might have also had access to now lost texts or documents. Fjalldal concludes that no firm evidence exists to support the likelihood of Icelandic historians using sources other than Latin anthologies of international history for information on Anglo-Saxon England.

A long-awaited, and major, contribution to the study of Anglo-Saxon saints' cults and their products is published this year in the form of the latest volume in part 4(ii) of the Winchester Studies series, The Anglo-Saxon Minsters of Winchester: *The Cult of St Swithun*, by Michael Lapidge, with contributions by John Crook, Robert Deshman and Susan Rankin. Part 1 of the volume contains a full and detailed analysis of all aspects of the cult of Swithun in Anglo-Saxon Winchester, a survey of its development elsewhere in Europe, the hagiographical tradition, liturgical texts, medieval historical writings on Swithun, and Swithun's place in medieval art, and liturgical music. Part 2 presents a set of edited texts—Latin and Old English Lives, and Latin poems—with full introductions, textual and manuscript discussions, notes, and translations. In gathering together its detailed analysis of the cult and its edited and translated texts, the volume will both act as an essential point of reference for work on other Anglo-Saxon cults and facilitate more new work on Swithun. It is a shame that its very high price means that it will mostly function as a library reference book.

Anglo-Saxon England this year includes two articles which serve to deepen our understanding of the Benedictine Reform, and in particular of its use of the Rule of St Benedict. The first, 'Cambridge, Corpus Christi College 57: A Witness to the Early Stages of the Benedictine Reform in England?', by Mechthild Gretsch (*ASE* 32[2003] 111–46), is an example of materialist philology: a holistic examination of the manuscript's physical features and contents as evidence for the impetus behind the production of Corpus 57 and its ultimate exemplar. Gretsch uses her assembled evidence and hypotheses to show that 'in England the texts of the Anianian reforms and the Aachen legislation played a role far more decisive than has generally been assumed' (p. 146). In 'The Old English Benedictine Rule: Writing for Women and Men' (*ASE* 32[2003] 147–87), Rohini Jayatilaka suggests that the surviving manuscript evidence reveals 'at least three interrelated attempts … to adapt and revise a male version for use in female communities' (p. 150), and that the female-adapted versions refer to the existence of non-Benedictine women's communities.

In 'King Athelstan and St John of Beverly' (*NH* 40[2003] 5–23), Susan E. Wilson examines the tradition that Athelstan established a college of canons at Beverly, and endowed the minster with privileges. Wilson shows how this tradition began at the time of Athelstan, and was embellished at later points in order to reinforce the positions of both Athelstan and Beverly.

In 'Negotiating Gender in Anglo-Saxon England (in Farmer and Braun Pasternack, eds., *Gender and Difference in the Middle Ages*, pp. 107–42), Carol Braun Pasternack looks at tensions between aristocratic and Christian constructions of gender in the early period, with detailed reference to the laws of Æthelberht and the Penitential of Theodore, and draws out the negotiable and provisional status of differentiations of masculine and feminine in different situations.

New interpretations of archaeological evidence from Anglo-Saxon England continue to enrich our understanding of the contexts for culture and textual production. Hamerow and MacGregor, eds., *Image and Power in the Archaeology of Early Medieval Britain: Essays in Honour of Rosemary Cramp* (published in 2001 but not available for review until now) offers a wide range of important new work: Martin Carver's 'Why That? Why There? Why Then? The Politics of Early Medieval Monumentality', Peter Hill's 'Whithorn, Latinus and the Origins of Christianity in Northern Britain', Deirdre O'Sullivan's 'Space, Silence and Shortages on Lindisfarne: The Archaeology of Asceticism', Nancy Edwards's 'Monuments in a Landscape: The Early Medieval Sculpture of St David's', Christopher Loveluck's 'Wealth, Waste and Conspicuous Consumption: Flixborough and its Importance for Mid-and Late Saxon Settlement Studies', and Catherine Hills's 'From Isidore to Isotopes: Ivory Rings in Early Medieval Graves'. Three items related to its dedicatee—Richard Bailey's preface, Christopher Morris's 'From Beowulf to Binford: Sketches of an Archaeological Career', and 'Rosemary Cramp: An Interim Bibliography' by Derek Craig—frame the collection.

Helena Hamerow's *Early Medieval Settlements: The Archaeology of Rural Communities in North-West Europe 400–900* is partly aimed at introducing the mainland European settlement evidence to an Anglophone audience, so that Anglo-Saxon settlement studies can be seen in this context. Hamerow surveys archaeological approaches, houses and households, settlement structure and social space, land and power, crop and animal husbandry, rural centres, trade and non-agrarian production, and emphasizes 'the great potential of settlement archaeology to reflect the changing relationships between individuals, households, and communities' (p. 193).

Clare Downham's study of 'The Chronology of the Last Scandinavian Kings of York, AD 937–54' (*NH* 40[2003] 25–51) reviews other recent work on the topic, re-examines evidence, including the D-text of the *Anglo-Saxon Chronicle*, and argues for the largely accurate nature of the received chronology of Northumbrian history for this period. Timothy Graham writes on 'King Cnut's Grant of Sandwich to Christ Church, Canterbury: A New Reading of a Damaged Annal in Two Copies of the Anglo-Saxon Chronicle' (in Amodio and O'Brien O'Keeffe, eds., *Unlocking the Wordhord*, pp. 172–90). From a careful re-examination of the relevant Old English entries in manuscripts A and F, Graham argues that both annals are the work of the same scribe. The article concludes with a facing-page edition of the two annals.

Kathryn A. Lowe examines 'Sawyer 1070: A Ghost Writ of King Edward the Confessor' (*N&Q* 50[2003] 150–2), and shows that this charter does not provide proof of a relationship between the charters in Cambridge, University Library, Ff. 2.33, British Library, Add. 14847, and the Northwold Register. 'The Use of Writs in the Eleventh Century' is studied by Richard Sharpe (*ASE* 32[2003] 247–91), with a particular focus on the writ-charter, and the archive of Bury St Edmunds. Sharpe gives the text of, and detailed notes on, four series of documents from the archive, and shows that 'a writ-charter was not considered to be a permanent testimony to the grant of rights' (p. 284), and that a community needed documentation showing that the current king had approved the continued holding of the rights.

Anglo-Saxon courtly culture is the subject of new research this year. David Pratt explores 'Persuasion and Invention at the Court of King Alfred the Great' (in Cubitt, ed., *Court Culture in the Early Middle Ages*, pp. 189–221), first by assessing Alfred's purposes in the composition of texts, and then by evaluating the potential links between Alfredian artefacts with the king's thought as expressed in the texts. James Campbell's study of 'Anglo-Saxon Courts' (in Cubitt, ed., pp. 155–69) reviews archaeological and textual evidence for the sites of Anglo-Saxon royal courts and for attendance at them, and considers a number of potential continental European parallels. G.W.S. Barrow studies 'Companions of the Atheling' (*Anglo-Norman Studies* 25[2003] 35–45) from 1016 to the early twelfth century.

Eric Stanley asks: 'Did the Anglo-Saxons Have a Social Conscience Like Us?' (*Anglia* 212[2003] 238–64). Through an examination of religious writings, laws and charitable provisions, he argues that there is evidence for an Anglo-Saxon social conscience, but that it is significantly different in direction and emphasis from related modern concepts.

New work on manuscript art continues to appear. 'Illustrations of Damnation in Late Anglo-Saxon Manuscripts' are the subject of Sarah Semple's discussion (*ASE* 32[2003] 231–45). Semple focuses on the assorted artists of the Harley Psalter, and on the image of Mambes at the mouth of hell in London, British Library, Cotton Tiberius B.v, in order to identify a distinctively Anglo-Saxon landscape of damnation which combines Christian teachings, burial practices and popular beliefs. Two of the essays in Powell and Scragg, eds., *Apocryphal Texts and Traditions in Anglo-Saxon England*, deal with manuscript art. Elizabeth Coatsworth shows the connections between 'The Book of Enoch and Anglo-Saxon Art' (pp. 135–50) through a detailed analysis of the illustrations in the Old English Hexateuch and Junius 11. Coatsworth argues that the Anglo-Saxon illustrations show a familiarity with the book of Enoch which implies access to a wider range of sources than those encompassed by surviving Anglo-Saxon texts. Catherine E. Karkov examines 'Judgement and Salvation in the New Minster Liber Vitae' (pp. 151–63) to show that this unusual representation of the Last Judgement combines popular textual sources and Winchester iconography, architecture and history.

Material culture, with and without connections to matters textual, is the subject of some interesting new publications. 'An Anglo-Saxon Runic Coin and its Adventures in Sweden' are charted by Margaret Clunies Ross (*ASE* 32[2003] 79–88): first through an account of the correspondence between Edward Lye and the Swedish scholar Eric Benzelius, about a coin owned by Benzelius, secondly by identifying the coin under discussion as that now in the Royal Coin Cabinet (Kungl. Myntkabinettet) in Stockholm, and thirdly by a comparison with the other Anglo-Saxon coin from the reign of Offa whose runic inscription names Botred as its moneyer. Clunies Ross concludes with a tentative life-story of the coin, from its minting in East Anglia in around 790 to its acquisition by the Royal Coin Cabinet in the mid-eighteenth century.

Elisabeth Okasha and Susan Youngs describe 'A Late Saxon Inscribed Pendant from Norfolk' (*ASE* 32[2003] 225–30), transcribe and reconstruct as much of the inscription as is retrievable, date the pendant to the tenth or eleventh century, and suggest that its purpose was protective and/or devotional. Elisabeth Okasha's study of 'Anglo-Saxon Inscribed Rings' (*LeedsSE* 34[2003] 29–45) lists and describes the twenty-two known examples, examines their inscriptions, shows that eight of them are explicitly religious, considers the possible functions for the inscription of personal names on rings, and contrasts the relatively small number of surviving Anglo-Saxon rings with the frequent references to them in Old English poetry. Gaby Waxenberger's 'The Intriguing Inscription of the Gandersheim Runic Casket Revisited' (in Kornexl and Lenker, eds., pp. 143–76) sets out a very detailed description of the inscription, accompanied by photographs and transcriptions, and a proposed new reading, which allows Waxenberger to conclude that the carver of the inscription was from a learned ecclesiastical background.

Howard Williams explores 'Material Culture as Memory: Combs and Cremation in Early Medieval Britain' (*EME* 12[2003] 89–128), with reference to several early Anglo-Saxon cremation cemeteries. He argues for the mnemonic significance of combs as markers of the 'reconstruction of the deceased's personhood in death' (p. 89). Tyler, ed., *Treasure in the Medieval West* (published in 2000, but not available until now for review), includes several essays of relevance. Anglo-Saxon treasure, and attitudes to it, are amongst the examples discussed by Dominic Janes in 'Treasure, Death and Display from Rome to the Middle Ages' (pp. 1–10); by Timothy Reuter in '"You can't take it with you": Testaments, Hoards and Movable Wealth in Europe, 600–1100' (pp. 11–24); and Pauline Stafford in 'Queens and Treasure in the Early Middle Ages' (pp. 61–82). Anglo-Saxon England is the central subject of Martin Carver, 'Burial as Poetry: The Context of Treasure in Anglo-Saxon Graves' (pp. 25–48); Leslie Webster, 'Ideal and Reality: Versions of Treasure in the Early Anglo-Saxon World' (pp. 49–59); and Elizabeth M. Tyler, '"When wings incarnadine with gold are spread": The *Vita Ædwardi Regis* and the Display of Treasure at the Court of Edward the Confessor' (pp. 83–107).

Jane Hawkes published *The Sandbach Crosses: Sign and Significance in Anglo-Saxon Sculpture* in 2002, providing a detailed and perceptive description of the monuments and their setting, possible functions, dating and cultural contexts. Karkov and Orton, eds., *Theorizing Anglo-Saxon Stone Sculpture*, gathers papers from sessions at the International Medieval Congress at Leeds in 1998, all of which offer significantly new approaches to understanding their subject-matter. Richard N. Bailey's introduction to the volume gives a focused overview of its contents and of the impact and importance of its new directions, and perceptive notes on directions for future work, concluding that 'there is still obviously much to do, and this collection, in its admirably argumentative fashion, urges us to get on with it' (p. 4). Jane Hawkes, in 'Reading Stone' (pp. 5–30), addresses the question of the 'story-telling' involved in responding to the Sandbach Crosses at different moments in the history of the study of Anglo-Saxon stone sculpture. Hawkes gives examples of nineteenth-and twentieth-century interpretations of the monuments, demonstrates how the modern iconographer of sources and the iconographer of significances might interpret them differently, and then turns to an assessment of how we might imagine the experience of Anglo-Saxon viewers, offering an important reminder of the limitations of assuming that readings of such monuments are unchanged over time. Hawkes also provides a set of four interesting plates, showing how different schemes for painting the east face of the North Sandbach Cross produce dramatically different results. Catherine E. Karkov explores 'Naming and Renaming: The Inscription of Gender in Anglo-Saxon Stone Sculpture', with reference to early grave-slabs from Northumbrian religious houses and what they reveal about lack of gender segregation in the associated cemeteries, the Ruthwell monument's inclusion of and allusion to female figures and names, and the inscription on the monument Hackness 1 and its commemoration of those it names. Karkov suggests that all these examples deploy a 'degendered difference' (p. 31), which might be an attempt to break down traditional gendered roles and images, and that this might itself be a feminine strategy. Fred Orton's 'Rethinking the Ruthwell and Bewcastle Monuments: Some Strictures on Similarity; Some Questions of History' continues his critique of the limitations of 'corpus scholarship', as exemplified by the ongoing Corpus of Anglo-Saxon Stone Sculpture (CASS) project: 'It classifies and lists what can be seen to be the case on the basis of similarity or by valuing similarity over difference' (p. 67). Here, Orton offers a theorization of the Ruthwell and Bewcastle monuments which insists on difference. Richard N. Bailey's own essay, '"Innocent from the Great Offence"', is a response to Orton's which sets out a different rationale for and description of the CASS project, critiques some details of Orton's reading of Ruthwell and Bewcastle, but welcomes the use of a variety of theoretical approaches in understanding the monuments. Ian Wood's 'Ruthwell: Contextual Searches' opens with a detailed account of the sequence of scenes and inscriptions on the main faces of both of the stages of the monument, considers the case for Ruthwell as a monastic community, explores the possibility that the monument's political function might be to mark 'Northumbrian spiritual aggression' (p. 127), and closes with an important reminder of 'the need to recognize the impermanence of any single context' (p. 130). Éamonn Ó Carragáin's 'Between Annunciation and Visitation: Spiritual Birth and the Cycles of the Sun on the Ruthwell Cross' argues that the second stage was added at an early period, *c.*730–60, when the monument was still outdoors, because the upper stone 'was particularly designed to relate to the sun's daily course' (p. 135), and gives a very detailed reading of the subjects and sequence of panels on the monument as celebrating the victory of Christ.

In their introduction to *Anglo-Saxon Styles*, Catherine E. Karkov and George Hardin Brown define its central subject as '"the ordering of forms" (verbal and visual)' (p. 3). The essays that follow duly treat a range of primary materials, genres and techniques, from stone and ivory carving to scriptorium practice, manuscript production, poetry, hagiography and language, and in some cases relate to pieces in *Theorizing Anglo-Saxon Stone Sculpture*. Essays on literary topics are reviewed in the appropriate sections of this chapter. Those which deal with non-literary artistic and textual culture are: 'Encrypted Visions: Style and Sense in the Anglo-Saxon Minor Arts, A.D. 400–900' (pp. 11–30), by Leslie Webster; 'Rethinking the Ruthwell and Bewcastle Monuments: Some Deprecation of Style; Some Consideration of Form and Ideology' (pp. 31–67), by Fred Orton; '*Iuxta Moren Romanorum*: Stone and Sculpture in Anglo-Saxon England' (pp. 69–99), by Jane Hawkes; 'Beckwith Revisited: Some Ivory Carvings from Canterbury' (pp. 101–13), by Perette E. Michelli; 'Style in Late Anglo-Saxon England: Questions of Learning and Intention' (pp. 115–30), by Carol Farr; 'House Style in the Scriptorium, Scribal Reality, and Scholarly Myth' (pp. 131–50), by Michelle P. Brown; 'Style and Layout of Anglo-Saxon Manuscripts' (pp. 151–68), by William Schipper; 'Aldhelm's Jewel Tones: Latin Colors Through Anglo-Saxon Eyes' (pp. 223–38), by Carin Ruff; and 'Rhythm and Alliteration: Styles of Ælfric's Prose up to the *Lives of Saints*' (pp. 25–69), by Haruko Momma.

Post-Conquest attitudes to Anglo-Saxon England continue to generate a good deal of new work. In a study of a bishop whose career spans the Conquest, Elaine Treharne discusses 'Producing a Library in Late Anglo-Saxon England: Exeter, 1050–1072' (*RES* 54[2003] 155–72). Through a meticulous examination of surviving vernacular manuscripts, she is able to chart a 'wholesale shift in the scriptorium's activity in the second half of the eleventh century' (p. 169), and to build a convincing case for Leofric's construction of a collection which reflected his needs as bishop and for a systematic programme of acquiring exemplars for copying.

In 'The Fables of the Bayeux Tapestry: An Anglo-Saxon Perspective' (in Amodio and O'Brien O'Keeffe, eds., pp. 192–216), Gail Ivy Berlin examines the cultural work performed by the images from Aesop's Fables in the borders of the Bayeux tapestry, and argues that they represent the production by English artisans of 'a covert Anglo-Saxon commentary upon the events leading to their subjugation' (p. 192). Williams and Martin, eds., *Domesday Book: A Complete Translation*, will be of great use as a convenient reference work to scholars working on Anglo-Saxon communities, although some errors in the page numbers given in its index of places will hamper those wishing to search it. Two of the essays in *Anglo-Norman Studies* 25[2003] focus on post-Conquest views of things Anglo-Saxon. Julia Crick studies 'St Albans, Westminster and Some Twelfth-Century Views of the Anglo-Saxon Past' (*Anglo-Norman Studies* 25[2003] 65–83), starting with the observation that 'The extent of the indebtedness of twelfth-century monastic historians to earlier written tradition is easily underestimated' (p. 65), and then examining spurious pre-Conquest charters produced at Westminster and St Albans in the twelfth century by setting out the pre-Conquest evidence for the claims they contain, and noting that the generations immediately after the Benedictine Reform mark a third period of rupture which provoked the production of charters. In the appendix to the article, Crick supplies a comparative table giving the text of an interpolation in a St Albans diploma of 1005 and the matching passages from four Westminster documents. Bruce O'Brien's 'The *Instituta Cnuti* and the Translation of English Law' (*Anglo-Norman Studies* 25[2003] 177–97) examines this example of the twelfth-century translation into Latin of a pre-Conquest legal text. O'Brien comments on the study of this text by Liebermann, identifies errors in his readings from the manuscripts, and offers his own analysis of the textual transmission process and the method of its translator.

Elaine Treharne considers 'The Form and Function of the Twelfth-Century Old English *Dicts of Cato*' (*JEGP* 102[2003] 465–85), which survives in three independent versions in manuscripts Cambridge, Trinity College, R.9.17, London, British Library, Cotton Vespasian D. xiv, and Cotton Julius A. ii. Treharne shows, through detailed analysis of the texts and their manuscript contexts, that the Old English *Dicts* do not have the same function as their Latin analogues, and are less pedagogical and more devotional in character. In 'The Tremulous Hand of Worcester and the Nero Scribe of the *Ancrene Wisse*' (*MÆ* 12[2003] 13–31), Christine Franzen makes another important addition to her study of this thirteenth-century annotator of Old English manuscripts. Through careful comparative analysis, Franzen demonstrates that the earliest work of the Tremulous Hand is very close to that of the Nero *Ancrene Wisse* scribe, and argues that the two scribes 'may have had a common training in the writing of English', and that 'somewhere in Worcestershire (probably in Worcester itself) in the first half of the thirteenth century (very likely after 1215 and possibly in the second quarter), there may have been a centre for the production of vernacular manuscripts in which scribes were trained to produce, perhaps among other things, up-to-date English books in the local dialect from older, and sometimes much older, English material' (p. 28).

Two new, wide-ranging overviews of the period are published this year in the Short Oxford Histories of the British Isles series. Charles-Edwards, ed., *After Rome*, includes an introduction by Thomas Charles-Edwards, and also an opening essay, 'Nations and Kingdoms: A View from Above'; 'Society, Community, and Identity', by John Hines; 'Conversion to Christianity', by Charles-Edwards; 'The Art of Authority', by Jennifer O'Reilly; 'Latin and the Vernacular Languages: The Creation of a Bilingual Textual Culture', by Andy Orchard; 'Texts and Society', by Robin Chapman Stacey; and a Conclusion by Charles-Edwards. In Davies, ed., *From the Vikings to the Normans*, editor Wendy Davies contributes the introduction and conclusion to the volume; Pauline Stafford covers 'Kings, Kingships, and Kingdoms'; Barbara E. Crawford 'The Vikings'; David Griffiths 'Exchange, Trade and Urbanization'; Robin Fleming 'Lords and Labour'; Huw Pryce 'The Christianization of Society'; Dàibhi Ó Cróinín 'Writing'; John Gillingham 'Britain, Ireland, and the South', and the conclusion is by Davies. Sections on further reading, a chronology, glossary and index make these two volumes very useful informed introductions for students of Anglo-Saxon culture.

The second edition of Peter Brown's *The Rise of Western Christendom: Triumph and Diversity A.D. 200–1000* is published this year, and will be of great interest to all working on the Anglo-Saxon period. Brown describes the second edition as 'substantially revised and rewritten' as a result of the 'veritable "dam burst" in the study of late antiquity and of the early Middle Ages which has taken place in the last five years' (p. 1). The book contains two entirely new chapters, and its introduction sets out an engaged and analytical account of scholarly work on the topic.

4. Literature: General

Stephen J. Harris's study of *Race and Ethnicity in Anglo-Saxon Literature* is an important contribution to our understanding of pre-modern attitudes towards racial and ethnic identities. Harris investigates the complex intersections between racial models and literary categorization in order to help us understand 'what makes Old English literature *English*' (p. 2). Through close readings, theoretical work, and historical analysis, Harris demonstrates that 'ethnicity is also a narrative phenomenon' (p. 1), and that racial models play a central role in shaping social attitudes towards literature. Individual chapters consider Bede's discussions of ethnic identity in the *Historia Ecclesiastica*, the Old English Bede's adaptation of these ideas, the historical validation of a Germanic Christendom in the Old English *Orosius*, Wulfstan's efforts to construct Englishness as a product of legal and moral rather than ethnic identity, and the European story of Trojan origins as told by Geoffrey of Monmouth.

Katharine Scarfe Beckett provides a thorough study of *Anglo-Saxon Perceptions of the Islamic World*. Through a survey of Anglo-Saxon contact with Islam, and an examination of references to Arabs and Arabia, Ismaelites and Saracens in Latin and in Old English, Scarfe Beckett shows that 'new information about the religion and empire of Islam did reach England before the Norman Conquest, but it arrived in a context dominated by older, inherited images of the Arabs, Saracens and Ismaelites' (p. 9), and that Saracens were presented in less complex terms in the vernacular than in Latin. [MS]

John Edward Damon's *Soldier Saints and Holy Warriors: Warfare and Sanctity in the Literature of Early England* sheds new light on competing ideals of Christian heroism in early medieval England. Focusing on a range of hagiographical narratives, Damon explores how Anglo-Saxon and post-Conquest writers worked to bridge the seemingly unbridgeable gulf between the pious and peace-loving martyrs of late antiquity and the chivalric warrior saints of the Middle Ages. Beginning with Bede's *Historia Ecclesiastica*, moving through the works of Felix, Cynewulf, Alcuin, Abbo, and Ælfric, and concluding with the *South English Legendary*, Damon charts the development of the Anglo-Saxon ideal of the martyred warrior-king, its transplantation to Carolingian culture, and its re-emergence on English soil. *Soldier Saints and Holy Warriors* helps us to understand the subtle evolution in Christianity from the pacifist saint to a new kind of holy warrior—one who not only died for Christ but also fought for him.

R.D. Fulk and Christopher M. Cain's *A History of Old English Literature* is well suited to scholars and teachers who are particularly interested in the relationship between literature and culture. Beginning from the belief that 'The renewed emphasis on historicism and the decline of formalist aestheticism in medieval studies have rendered it desirable to have a literary history that attends more singularly to the material and social contexts and uses of Old English texts' (p. vii), Fulk and Cain offer a wide-ranging introduction to Old English literature, with an emphasis on prose texts. Individual chapters discuss 'The Chronology and Varieties of Old English Literature'; 'Literature of the Alfredian Period'; 'Homilies'; 'Saints' Legends' (this chapter is by Rachel S. Anderson); 'Biblical Literature'; 'Liturgical and Devotional Texts'; 'Legal, Scientific, and Scholastic

Works'; 'Wisdom Literature and Lyric Poetry'; 'Germanic Legend and Heroic Lay'; and 'Making Old English New: Anglo-Saxonism and the Cultural Work of Old English Literature'. Although devoted mainly to vernacular texts, this study is nevertheless attuned to the close relationship between Latin and vernacular literary production.

Scragg, ed., *Textual and Material Culture in Anglo-Saxon England: Thomas Northcote Toller and the Toller Memorial Lectures*, brings together for the first time a selection of the annual Toller Memorial Lectures, with supplementary material added by the authors to bring them up to date. The collection also contains the 2002 Toller Lecture, Peter Baker's study of Toller, commissioned specially for this volume, as well as several new essays on Toller's life and work, and his influence on the development of Old English lexicography. The volume's contents are: 'Manuscript Layout and the *Anglo-Saxon Chronicle*', by Janet Bately; 'Scyld Scefing and the Dating of *Beowulf*—Again', by Audrey L. Meaney; 'The Study of Language in Anglo-Saxon England', by Helmut Gneuss; 'Textual Criticism and the Literature of Anglo-Saxon England', by Michael Lapidge; 'The Search for the Anglo-Saxon Oral Poet', by Roberta Frank; 'Source, Method, Theory, Practice: On Reading Two Old English Verse Texts', by Katherine O'Brien O'Keeffe; 'The Dynamics of Literacy in Anglo-Saxon England', by George Hardin Brown; '"What mean these stones?" Some Aspects of Pre-Norman Sculpture in Cheshire and Lancashire', by Richard Bailey; 'Translating the Tradition: Manuscripts, Models and Methodologies in the Composition of Ælfric's *Catholic Homilies*', by Joyce Hill; 'Anglo-Saxon Smiths and Myths', by David A. Hinton; 'Toller at School: Joseph Bosworth, T. Northcote Toller and the Progress of Old English Lexicography in the Nineteenth Century', by Peter Baker; 'T. Northcote Toller and the Making of the *Supplement* to the *Anglo-Saxon Dictionary*', by Dabney Anderson Bankert; 'Items of Lexicographical Interest in the Toller Collection, John Rylands University Library of Manchester', by Alexander Rumble; and 'Thomas Northcote Toller: "This fearless and self-sacrificing knight of scholarship"', by Joana Proud.

Several essays in Karkov and Brown, eds., *Anglo-Saxon Styles*, have broad relevance to Old English literary studies. Nicholas Howe investigates 'What We Talk about When We Talk about Style' (pp. 169–78). Howe offers a useful overview of scholarship on Anglo-Saxon style, and finds that literary scholars have tended to view style simply as a matter for linguistic or philological analysis, unlike art historians, who have embraced a more expansive understanding of style as historically and culturally driven. Howe urges us to view history, culture, and ideology as central to the study of aesthetics and to understand the study of style as itself a historical and cultural act. In this same collection, Roberta Frank examines 'The Discreet Charm of the Old English Weak Adjective' (pp. 239–52). Focusing on the weak adjective as one wrongly neglected aspect of Anglo-Saxon style, Frank analyses weak adjective constructions in Old English poetry, and considers their possible effects on contemporary readers. Andy Orchard also offers insight into Anglo-Saxon styles in his 'Both Style and Substance: The Case for Cynewulf' (pp. 271–305), with emphasis on the formulaic phrases in Cynewulf's four signed poems. Orchard provides a concordance of these phrases, and analyses formulaic diction that is shared by

Cynewulf's poems as well as by poems outside the Cynewulfian corpus. Orchard concludes that the *Andreas*-poet most likely knew and borrowed from Cynewulf's works, and that 'In Cynewulf's case, as with Aldhelm ... the style is the substance, and the formulaic diction is the framework on which the individual poet's own poetic art depends' (p. 296).

Amodio and O'Brien O'Keeffe, eds., *Unlocking the Wordhord*, contains several essays that deal with the complexities of Old English poetic genres. John Miles Foley examines 'How Genres Leak in Traditional Verse' (pp. 76–108). Beginning from the observation that the same four-stress alliterative verse form serves as the underpinning for all Old English poetic genres, Foley argues that this metrical continuity allows for an easy migration of phraseology, narrative structures, and motifs from one genre to another. By way of comparison, Foley examines genre leakage in South Slavic and ancient Greek oral poetry, and concludes that Old English verse exhibits the most widespread movement between and among its traditional genres. Sarah Larratt Keefer's '"Ic" and "We" in Eleventh-Century Old English Liturgical Verse' (pp. 123–46) also focuses on genre, with a particular interest in liturgical verse. Noting that 'Virtually all of the liturgical verse from Anglo-Saxon England is preserved in manuscripts that date from around or after 960', Keefer suggests that 'the reinvigorated monastic and educational practices of Dunstan's period and the tenth-century Reform proper provided the necessary impetus to writings of this kind' (p. 127). After exploring the social conditions that may have inspired this genre of Old English verse, Keefer analyses the different kinds of poetic voice found within it: communal voices, which Keefer terms 'Liturgical' or 'Devotional', and the private, single voice, which she calls the 'Meditational'.

Several other essays in Amodio and O'Brien O'Keeffe, eds., offer valuable lexicographical studies that contribute to our understanding of Anglo-Saxon language and culture. Antonette diPaolo Healey's 'Questions of Fairness: Fair, Not Fair, and Foul' (pp. 252–73) focuses on the senses that 'fair' and its related terms have in Old English, and traces the transformations that these terms have undergone over the past thousand years. Healey's careful work in lexicography is interwoven with insights regarding the complex relations between Anglo-Saxon language and culture. In this same collection, Janet Bately investigates 'Bravery and the Vocabulary of Bravery in *Beowulf* and the *Battle of Maldon*' (pp. 274–301). By analysing the words used to describe heroic deeds and valorous acts in these two texts, Bately shows that modern English terms such as 'bravery' and 'courage' cannot accurately capture the culturally specific resonances of the Old English words that they purport to translate. This collection also includes Roberta Frank's study of 'Sex in the *Dictionary of Old English*' (pp. 302–12). Turning her attention to some of the 'four-letter Anglo-Saxonisms' preserved in Old English writings, Frank considers the challenges attendant upon the *Dictionary of Old English* editors as they try to render modern translations for these terms: modern readers neither want nor need euphemistic translations, yet to offer blunt no-nonsense translations of sexual vocabulary is to depart from how such terms were used by Anglo-Saxon writers, who tended to prefer indirectness over explicitness. Kazutomo Karasawa also uses a lexicographical approach to investigate 'Christian Influence on OE *Dream*: Pre-Christian and Christian Meanings'

(*Neophil* 87[2003] 307–22). By tracing the numerous occurrences of *dream* in Old English poetry, Karasawa shows that 'under the influence of Christianity, the word enlarged its semantic range, weakening the connotation it originally carried' (pp. 307–8), i.e., 'joy at a feast or in an ideal society'. Karasawa proposes that as *dream* became increasingly linked with the joys of heaven as an ideal society, and was also used to articulate a Christian dichotomous world-view of the vast divide between earthly and heavenly life, the term, paradoxically, acquired the new meaning of 'joy on earth [as a man]'.

Withers and Wilcox, eds., *Naked Before God*, contains several essays that focus on Anglo-Saxon attitudes towards the body. John M. Hill studies 'The Sacrificial Synecdoche of Hands, Heads, and Arms in Anglo-Saxon Heroic Story' (pp. 116–37), with the intent of showing that heroic poetry's obsessive interest in fragmented hands, heads, and arms cannot be explained as a straightforward result of the fact that such body parts wield swords or become vulnerable in battle. Hill contends that the mutilated heroic body served a variety of complex symbolic functions in Anglo-Saxon society, most notably to outline the contours of culturally constructed oppositions, or, to '[assert] definitive differences between good man and beast, between hero and coward, between commitment and fear, renown and infamy, lawful warfare or what is right and terror' (p. 117). This collection also contains Jonathan Wilcox's valuable study, 'Naked in Old English: The Embarrassed and the Shamed' (pp. 275–309). Wilcox's main concern is to find a productive way to explore Anglo-Saxon attitudes towards nudity and sexuality, topics that tend to receive short shrift or to be avoided altogether in Old English texts. By focusing on nudity's relationship to embarrassment and shame and, more specifically, on the homiletic motif of a shameful sinner at the Last Judgement who stands before Christ as if naked before the people, Wilcox provides 'a useful key in opening up an understanding of an Anglo-Saxon sense of bodily self' (p. 309).

Scholars interested in the intersections between language and verse will find that 2003 offered a small but noteworthy amount of new reading material. Donka Minkova's foundational study, *Alliteration and Sound Change in Early English*, uses evidence from alliterative verse to reconstruct important phonological changes in the history of the English language. Beginning from the premise that 'the history of poetry is also in part a history of the language in which it was created', Minkova argues that 'the patterns found in early English alliterative compositions provide a valuable resource for the reconstruction of the contemporary language' (p. xv). Individual chapters discuss the social and linguistic setting of alliterative verse in Anglo-Saxon and post-Conquest England, the history of the velars, the structure and history of vowel-initial syllable onsets, and cluster alliteration. As Minkova examines the linguistic properties of early English verse, she reflects on the complex relationship between orality and literacy in the evolution of English poetry. Thomas A. Bredehoft also takes up the topic of alliterative verse in his 'The Three Varieties of Old English Hypermetric Versification' (*N&Q* 248[2003] 153–6). Observing that scholars often characterize hypermetric verses simply as 'normal verses with something extra added or combinations of two normal verses' (p. 153), Bredehoft argues that we ought to recognize no fewer than three hypermetric versification systems in surviving Old English poems. After outlining these three systems, Bredehoft shows that 'the key differences between the various varieties of hypermetric versification lie in the restrictions on where various hypermetric forms can fall in the poetic line' (p. 153).

The question of whether and/or how Old English poetry might shed light on the physical realities and social practices of Anglo-Saxon England is taken up in two essays this year. Jennifer Neville investigates 'Leaves of Glass: Plant-Life in Old English Poetry' (in Biggam, ed., *From Earth to Art: The Many Aspects of the Plant World in Anglo-Saxon England*, pp. 287–300) in order to determine whether representations of plant life in the Old English poetic corpus may yield insight into plant names and species as they existed in Anglo-Saxon England. Noting that plants are not commonly featured in Old English poems, and that representations of the natural world tend to appear mainly in discussions about human limitations, divine power, and social interactions between humans and God, Neville argues that Old English poetry is at best a poor source for understanding plant life in Anglo-Saxon England. John D. Niles considers 'The Myth of the Anglo-Saxon Oral Poet' (*WF* 62[2003] 7–61). Beginning from the premise that representations of scops in Old English literature 'can tell us something about how the Anglo-Saxons conceived of their art of poetry', Niles argues that these scenes ought to be considered as 'part of the Anglo-Saxons' mental modeling of their ancestral past' (p. 12). Through close readings of Bede's story of Cædmon, Æthelweard's *Chronicon*, *Widsith*, and *Deor*, Niles seeks to call attention to 'the way that oral and literate modes of thought, which were quite separate in Bede's day, came to merge in the work of late Anglo-Saxon authors' (p. 14). He concludes by urging that 'The Anglo-Saxon search for the oral poet can be viewed as one aspect of a cultural myth that was in the process of formation as the English-speaking peoples of Britain developed from a state of primary orality in their native tongue to a state of sophisticated orality-plus-literacy in both Latin and the vernacular' (p. 12).

Dennis Cronan studies 'Poetic Meanings in the Old English Poetic Vocabulary' (*ES* 84[2003] 397–425). Beginning from the premise that scholars have tended to neglect studies of the Old English poetic vocabulary and to simply assume that numerous words carry figurative force via synecdoche, Cronan argues that words with figurative meanings play a very limited role in Old English verse.

Homiletic prose, scriptural and liturgical texts and poetry are all considered by Sarah Larratt Keefer in 'In Closing: Amen and Doxology in Anglo-Saxon England' (*Anglia* 121[2003] 210–37). Through a comparison of these different types of text, Keefer argues for a range of uses of and responses by Anglo-Saxon authors to 'amen', which indicate varying degrees of understanding of its literal significance. [MS]

Catherine A.M. Clarke examines 'Envelope Pattern and the *Locus Amoenus* in Old English Verse' (*N&Q* 248[2003] 263–4). Clarke points out that critics have long recognized the envelope pattern as a recurring feature in Old English descriptions of landscape. She argues that 'these examples of uses of envelope patterns do suggest that a sense of "enclosure" is part of the English conception and representation of the delightful place' (p. 264).

5. The Exeter Book

The Exeter Book riddles are the subject of a number of new pieces of work this year. Michael Korhammer investigates 'The Last of the Exeter Book Riddles' (in Kornexl and Lenker, eds., pp. 69–80). This final riddle (Riddle 95) has proven notoriously difficult to solve or even to understand, and has generated a variety of different solutions. In recent years, scholars have suggested that Riddle 95 deals with writing and textual production, and Korhammer works to corroborate Helga Göbel's suggestion in 1980 that the riddle is about a holy text, perhaps the Holy Scriptures. Several essays in Withers and Wilcox, eds., *Naked Before God*, investigate the riddles for insight into Anglo-Saxon attitudes towards the body and sexuality. Sarah L. Higley's 'The Wanton Hand: Reading and Reaching into Grammars and Bodies in Old English Riddle 12' (pp. 29–59) takes the sexual activities of the dark-haired Welsh servant woman in Riddle 12 as a point of departure for investigating the nuances of the Old English verb *swifeð*. Higley investigates the grammar and possible solutions of the riddle, and shows how the riddles shed light on modern critical desires and reading practices. Mercedes Salvador writes on 'The Key to the Body: Unlocking Riddles 42–46' (pp. 60–96). Focusing on a group of riddles that comprise some of the most sexually explicit texts in the extant corpus of Old English writings, Salvador argues that these riddles were intended to be read less as individual pieces of pornographic material than as a cohesive series with allegorical import providing instruction regarding the dangers of the body.

Textual difficulties continue to provoke new work on the Exeter Book elegies. John D. Niles considers 'The Trick of the Runes in *The Husband's Message*' (*ASE* 32[2003] 189–223). Niles revisits the thorny question of how readers ought to interpret the special characters which appear in the poem's final four lines. After careful intertextual work on runes, with an emphasis on Cynewulf's signed poems, Niles demonstrates that the special characters in *The Husband's Message* constitute a deliberate challenge to readers, and also serve to lend an air of secrecy to the issue at hand, namely, the identity of the speaker and the message he/it seeks to convey. Niles contends that the speaker of the poem is neither a living person nor a personified rune-stick but rather the wooden ship itself, or, more precisely, the ship's personified mast, which symbolizes the man's unchanging *treow* to his wife. Niles concludes by proposing that *The Husband's Message* ought to be read in conjunction with *The Wife's Lament*, and that the two poems may form a kind of 'Lost Husband Mini-Group'. Niles also writes on 'The Problem of the Ending of *The Wife's Lament*' (*Speculum* 78[2003] 1107–50) in order to help us understand the poem's enigmatic final lines. Critics have long debated whether lines 42–52a ought to be read as the speaker's gnomic reflection on the sorrows of her life or as an outright curse on her lover. Through careful philological work and through historical analysis of cursing as both a social institution and a literary theme, Niles argues for the latter view, and contends that 'The Wife's curse challenges modern readers to rethink their assumptions regarding what emotional responses are to be regarded as a feminine norm' (p. 1150). Carole Hough examines 'The Riddle of *The Wife's Lament* Line 34b' (*ANQ* 16[2003] 5–8), with a focus on the much-debated crux *leger weardiað*. Reminding us that *The Wife's Lament*, along with the other Exeter Book elegies, uses rhetorical strategies similar to those found in the Exeter Book riddles, Hough argues that modern readers ought to recognize the 'artful ambiguity' that informs the poem and accept that the poet constructed line 34b to be read as both 'they inhabit graves' and 'they share a bed'.

The complex gender dynamics of the Exeter Book elegies continue to inspire new work. Anne L. Klinck studies 'Poetic Markers of Gender in Medieval "Woman's Song": Was Anonymous a Woman?' (*Neophil* 87[2003] 339–59) in order to determine whether there might be any other devices besides grammatical markers that point to the gender of either author or speaker in medieval poetry. Her study focuses on five pairs of 'woman's voice love-lyrics', each drawn from a different cultural context; one of these pairs is *Wulf and Eadwacer* and *The Wife's Lament*. Klinck concludes that, while nothing can be regarded as a reliable test of authorial gender, female-authored love-lyrics nevertheless exhibit a higher degree of self-assertiveness than anonymous or male-authored ones, perhaps because 'women authors may have had more to say about the complexities of women's feelings and more incentive to see the positive as well as the negative elements in their situation' (p. 354). Patricia Clare Ingham investigates the cultural transition 'From Kinship to Kingship: Mourning, Gender, and Anglo-Saxon Community' (in Vaught, ed., *Grief and Gender, 700–1700*, pp. 17–31). Ingham reads the lamenting women in *The Wife's Lament* and *Wulf and Eadwacer* alongside the queens in *Beowulf*, and demonstrates that female grief 'underwrite[s] the cultural transition from "kinship to kingship," from the Anglo-Saxon *comitatus* as a kin-based brotherhood to an English sovereign community of exogamous foreign alliance' (p. 19).

Several essays in Jaritz and Moreno-Riaño, eds., *Time and Eternity: The Medieval Discourse*, focus on representations of time in the Exeter Book elegies. John Dennis Grosskopf examines 'Time and Eternity in the Anglo-Saxon Elegies' (pp. 323–30), with particular interest in using *The Wanderer* and *The Seafarer* to shed light on Anglo-Saxon attitudes towards time and all things temporal. Grosskopf sees the Wanderer as 'trapped within time, lamenting past losses and seeking to recreate the past for his future' (p. 324), unlike the Seafarer, who has 'effectively escaped the lure of temporal things and the passage of time' and thus begun to move toward a kind of 'Augustinian state of perfection' (p. 326). Grosskopf concludes that 'each of these poems provides an extreme example of the possible strategies for dealing with time' (p. 324). Juan Camilo Conde-Silvestre's 'Discourse and Ideology in the Old English *The Wanderer*: Time and Eternity' (pp. 331–53) engages similar issues, yet focuses less on the thematics of time than on its use as a narrative device for structuring fictions and conveying different points of view. Drawing on methodologies employed by critical linguists and modern narratologists allows Conde-Silvestre to distinguish between the fictive or real time of the act of narrating *The Wanderer* and the time of the narrative itself and to show that this split 'allows the audience to discern different ways of perceiving time prevalent in the early Middle Ages' (p. 352).

R.M. Liuzza writes on 'The Tower of Babel: *The Wanderer* and the Ruins of History' (*SLI* 36[2003] 1–35). Beginning from the familiar premise that representations of ruins in Old English literature are intended to be read as an evocation of the topos of mutability, Liuzza examines the 'ruin motif' in a variety of Old English texts to demonstrate its imbrication in a far larger set of cultural concerns, including divine punishment, migration history, and the cultural specificity of language. Through sensitive close readings of the Tower of Babel story in *Genesis A*, *The Ruin*, and *The Wanderer*, Liuzza reveals that Anglo-Saxon writers drew on the 'ruin motif' in order to express their nostalgia for a past that was becoming increasingly inarticulable and unknowable as a result of changing technologies of writing and recording history. Liuzza's study of historiography, memory, and nostalgia among the Anglo-Saxons concludes with a brief meditation on how modern desires structure our understanding of these issues.

Jorge Luis Bueno Alonso's '"Less epic than it seems": *Deor*'s Historical Approach as a Narrative Device for Psychological Expression' (*RCEI* 46[2003] 161–72) considers the *Deor*-poet's use of historical and/or legendary events as a means of foregrounding personal experiences of psychological suffering. Alonso argues that the *Deor*-poet glosses over well-known historical events in an attempt to subordinate historical accounts of suffering to individual experiences of misfortune. This emphasis on personal grief and psychological suffering places *Deor* less in the epic than in the elegiac tradition.

Barbara Raw offers an important study of 'Two Versions of Advent: The Benedictional of Æthelwold and *The Advent Lyrics*' (*LeedsSE* 34[2003] 1–28). Although the Benedictional and *The Advent Lyrics* were both likely to have been composed during the tenth-century monastic revival, Raw shows that these texts present strikingly different interpretations of the season of Advent. While the Benedictional reveals a clear sense of the passing of time, *The Advent Lyrics* position their audience in a world in which Christ is both awaited and has already come; while the Benedictional focuses on the coming judgement, *The Advent Lyrics* focus on the hope of heaven; while the Benedictional emphasizes the gulf between the divine and the human, *The Advent Lyrics* establish a sense of intimacy and dialogue between the poet and Christ and Mary.

Michael Lapidge examines 'Cynewulf and the *Passio S. Iulianae*' (in Amodio and O'Brien O'Keeffe, eds., pp. 147–71). Beginning from the observation that studies of *Juliana* have long been hindered by our inability to identify the precise redaction of the *Passio* that Cynewulf used as his Latin source, Lapidge argues that Cynewulf relied on a text very similar to the *Passio* contained in Paris, Bibliothèque Nationale de France, lat. 10861. After detailing the transmission history of the *Passio*, Lapidge outlines similarities and differences between the Latin and Old English texts. The essay concludes with an appendix in which Lapidge prints the text of the *Passio* as found in the Paris manuscript, 'with the intention of providing students of Cynewulf with a secure base from which to study the poet's handling of the legend' (p. 155).

Several essays this year focus on Anglo-Saxonism, with particular interest in nineteenth- and twentieth-century writers who reimagine Old English poems for contemporary purposes. Robert E. Bjork writes on 'N.F.S. Gruntvig's 1840 Edition of the Old English *Phoenix*: A Vision of a Vision of Paradise' (in Amodio and O'Brien O'Keeffe, eds., pp. 217–39). Focusing on the various literary and historical contexts that inform this first edition of the Old English *Phoenix*, Bjork establishes Gruntvig's edition as 'an intricate blending of Gruntvig's nationalistic, aesthetic, religious, and scholarly interests' (p. 219), and concludes that 'the book becomes an embodiment of a coherent view of history and the place of the Anglo-Saxons and the Danes within it even as it celebrates a new era of the spirit of Denmark' (p. 231). Miranda Wilcox studies 'Exilic Imagining in *The Seafarer* and *The Lord of the Rings*' (in Chance, ed., *Tolkien the Medievalist*, pp. 133–54). Reminding us that Tolkien read, studied, and intended to produce an edition of *The Seafarer*, Wilcox traces the theme of exile in *The Seafarer* and the Elvish poems in *The Lord of the Rings*, and identifies striking similarities in theme, style, and symbolism between the main characters and events in these two texts. Wilcox concludes that, in both texts, the sea functions as a 'transcendent bridge' between the mortal and immortal worlds, but that the sailors in both texts fail to cross this bridge and thus remain forever 'caught in a poignant gap between the past pains of mortality and future expectations of joy' (p. 152). For other new work on post-Conquest reappropriations of the Anglo-Saxon past, see Section 3 of this chapter.

Alexandra H. Olsen's 'Subtractive Rectification and the Old English *Riming Poem*' (*InG* 24[2003] 57–66) urges us to consider the potentially negative effects of editing on the Old English *Riming Poem*. Focusing on emendations that appear in O.D. Macrae-Gibson's modern edition of the text, Olsen argues for restoring numerous manuscript readings in order to highlight the poem's thematic interest in loss, and to reflect accurately its shared world-view with such texts as *The Ruin* and *The Wanderer*.

E.G. Stanley re-examines 'Old English *The Fortunes of Men*, Lines 80–84' (*N&Q* 248[2003] 265–8), with particular attention to possible interpretations of the manuscript's *neome cende* in line 84a. Stanley rejects C.W.M. Grein's long-accepted emendation *neomegende* and argues that the phrase is correctly understood as either *neome cende* or as *neoman cende*, with *nægl* as the subject, and that the half-line thus reads 'the plectrum brought forth (or proclaimed) the sound (or melody)' (p. 268).

6. The Poems of the Vercelli Book

Stacy S. Klein writes on 'Reading Queenship in Cynewulf's *Elene*' (*JMEMS* 33[2003] 47–89). Klein's main concern is to explore the poem's complex depiction of queenship and to help us understand the kind of cultural work that *Elene* might have performed for both its author and contemporary audiences. Focusing on key changes that Cynewulf makes to his source text, Klein shows that Cynewulf encases Elene in the linguistic, social, and material trappings that were particular to Anglo-Saxon discourses of queenship. She argues that 'Such transformations enhance the queen's ability to function as a exemplar, but one impelled by ideological goals that reach far beyond the mere fashioning of model roles for royal women' (p. 52). Klein concludes that Cynewulf attempts to use Elene to perpetuate his own highly conservative vision of social hierarchy but in fact 'creates a female figure whose renewed, culturally specific potentiality and own capacity to revise history implicitly destabilize his own poetic vision of social hierarchy' (p. 52).

Two essays in Karkov and Brown, eds., *Anglo-Saxon Styles*, focus on poems in the Vercelli Book. Sarah Larratt Keefer writes on '"Either/And" as "Style" in Anglo-Saxon Christian Poetry' (pp. 179–200) by investigating the idea of an Anglo-Saxon poetic style characterized by ambiguity and by the coexistence of opposing world-views and cultural realities. Beginning from the long-noted tensions between Germanic action and Christian self-control that underwrite *The Dream of the Rood*, Keefer extends this dualism to consider the fact that 'Anglo-Saxon culture fixes readily on neither the one nor the other, but instead on the perceived *process* by which the two are related, and by which the one changes into the other, deepening the meaning of both as a result' (p. 181). Keefer concludes that the poetic actualization of this process is driven by dramatic articulations of the power of God. This same volume also contains Jonathan Wilcox's 'Eating People Is Wrong: Funny Style in *Andreas* and its Analogues' (pp. 201–22). Noting that critics have tended to overlook the more humorous moments in *Andreas*, Wilcox identifies the 'comic violence' that underlies the poem and its prose cognate. Focusing on the ways in which humour may proceed from irony, incongruity, and tensions between different viewpoints allows Wilcox to show that comedy is a crucial aspect of hagiographical style, and one that encourages readers to probe the opposing world-views of the saint and his or her torturers.

7. The Junius Manuscript

Interest in interdisciplinary scholarship and cultural studies keeps the Junius 11 manuscript at the centre of much exciting new work. Nicholas Howe's 'Falling Into Place: Dislocation in the Junius Book' (in Amodio and O'Brien O'Keeffe, eds., pp. 14–37) is a deeply nuanced study of the geographical poetics that inform the Junius manuscript. Howe identifies two distinct voices of exile in Old English poetry, namely the voice of the individual *anhaga* and that of the displaced *folc*, and explores how the four poems in the Junius manuscript imagine the displacement of a people as a phenomenon that 'imperils the poetic voice by which a people praises God and locates its place in His creation' (p. 14). By analysing these four poems as 'books of religious history … [that form] parts of an improvised but necessary quadrateuch' (p. 18), Howe extends his earlier groundbreaking study, *Migration and Mythmaking in Anglo-Saxon England*, to show that 'this logic of place was used not simply to inscribe the transformative migration of the Germanic tribes to Britain, but also to denote a larger pattern of human history within the fallen world: that of movement, of the restless search for a place to call home' (p. 18).

Several essays from Withers and Wilcox, eds., *Naked Before God*, focus on the Junius 11 manuscript. Catherine E. Karkov examines 'Exiles from the Kingdom: The Naked and the Damned in Anglo-Saxon Art' (pp. 181–220). Her essay is a rich interdisciplinary study that brings together depictions of male genitalia that appear on the fallen angels in Junius 11 and on demons in the Harley Psalter, discussions of fallen male bodies in legal and penitential writings, and archaeological evidence from late Anglo-Saxon execution ceremonies. Pointing out that the Junius 11 manuscript is marked by ambivalence towards and an effort to erase the exposed female form, Karkov argues that the manuscript 'places our attention on the naked male body as the primary site of sin and damnation ... [and is] but one manifestation of the way in which the Anglo-Saxons came to equate demonic actions with human actions, and to unite both in the image of the damned male body' (p. 184). Mary Dockray-Miller writes on 'Breasts and Babies: The Maternal Body of Eve in the Junius 11 *Genesis*' (pp. 221–56). Focusing on the new interpretative possibilities generated by studying *Genesis A* and *B* in conjunction with the Junius 11 illustrations, Dockray-Miller points to the use of the breast, especially the nipple, as the Junius 11 artist's main criteria for distinguishing sexual difference in the prelapsarian bodies of Adam and Eve. She concludes that the nipple calls attention to Eve's role as a mother, thus urging closer attention to the numerous other mothers depicted in the manuscript. Janet S. Ericksen studies 'Penitential Nakedness and the Junius 11 *Genesis*' (pp. 257–74). By investigating the *Genesis*-poet's discussions of the unclothed bodies of Adam and Eve in the light of anonymous homilies and penitentials that use the naked body as a metaphor for the unconfessed and unrepentant soul, Ericksen shows that 'nakedness itself ... is a sign of sin and a demonstration of the clothing that confession and penance might provide' (pp. 257–8). For Coatsworth's study of the Junius 11 illustrations, see Section 3 of this chapter.

Jun Terasawa examines 'Old English *Exodus* 118a: The Use of Wolf Imagery' (*N&Q* 248[2003] 259–61), and calls into question the generally accepted phrase *har hæðbroga* 'gray heath-terror'. Pointing out that the Old English *Exodus* frequently associates the Egyptians with wolves, Hough suggests emending *har hæðbroga* to *har hæðstapa* and reading the latter phrase as a metaphorical reference to Pharaoh, the pursuing Egyptian king.

Alfred Bammesberger offers 'A Note on *Genesis A*, Line 22a' (*N&Q* 248[2003] 6–8). Concurring with earlier readings offered by both Thomas Cockayne and Julius Zupitza, Bammesberger proposes emending *weard* (line 22a) to *wearð*, thus rendering lines 20b–23a 'In the heavens they did not perform anything except what was right and true, before a part of the angels [= some of the angels] fell into error because of pride' (p. 8).

8. The *Beowulf* Manuscript

The *Beowulf* manuscript typically generates a good deal of new criticism and this year is no exception. 2003 marked the publication of Andy Orchard's much-awaited *A Critical Companion to Beowulf*. Orchard claims to have 'often felt the need for a *Companion* to steer me towards subsequent research ... and to assure me that ... there remains much work to be done' (p. 11). His book is designed to help scholars negotiate the vast array of *Beowulf* scholarship and to point students in productive directions for future work. After a brief introduction to the history of *Beowulf* criticism, Orchard offers eight substantial chapters which 'can be seen to be roughly arranged to reflect a range of perspectives on *Beowulf*' (p. 11).

Chapters 2 and 3 examine the visual and verbal aspects of the poem, with particular attention to its manuscript context and its patterns of repetition and variation. Chapters 4 and 5 focus on the poem's literary and cultural contexts, with discussions of Germanic myth and legend as well as the Latinate world of Christian learning. Chapters 6 and 7 are devoted to narrative themes and techniques, and offer consideration of major and minor characters, and of the use of speeches in different parts of the poem. Chapter 8 and the 'Afterward' outline past and future critical approaches to *Beowulf* scholarship. There are three appendices: one gives a key to the poem's foliation and the other two chart repeated formulae within *Beowulf*. Orchard's book promises to significantly enhance our understanding of *Beowulf* and to inspire much future work on the poem.

Two essays in Amodio and O'Brien O'Keeffe, eds., *Unlocking the Wordhord*, focus on *Beowulf*. A.N. Doane writes on '"Beowulf" and Scribal Performance' (pp. 62–75). Beginning from the fairly well-accepted premise that scribal activity ought not to be seen as 'damaging' to texts but rather as a crucial part of the process of textual reception and transmission, Doane argues that a scribe's writing should be understood as 'a performance of a specialized kind, which in its physicality and uniqueness is an analog to oral performance' (p. 63). He then turns to a close examination of the different kinds of variance present in the work of the two scribes responsible for producing the *Beowulf* manuscript. Doane concludes that Scribe A is more literate, visual, and iconic, while Scribe B is more firmly rooted in a tradition of oral or 'vocalic' writing. This same collection also contains Jane Roberts's study of 'Hrothgar's "Admirable Courage"' (pp. 240–51). Focusing on recent interpretations of the noun *aglæca*, Roberts argues that scholars ought to reject earlier translations of this term as 'monster' or 'demon' and follow the editors of the *Dictionary of Old English*, who translate it by such phrases as 'awesome opponent' or 'fearsome fighter'. By embracing these more flexible definitions of *aglæca*, Roberts believes that modern readers will ultimately reach a more sophisticated understanding of both Hrothgar's and Beowulf's courage.

Frederick M. Biggs has produced two important essays on *Beowulf* this year. In 'Hondscioh and Æshere in *Beowulf*' (*Neophil* 87[2003] 635–52), Biggs investigates the *Beowulf*-poet's complex attitude towards kinship ties. Pointing out that Hondscioh's death appears not to matter to the Geats while Æshere's does to the Danes, Biggs argues that this contrast functions as a means of distinguishing the respective importance of kin loyalties within the two communities. Biggs then turns to various problems within the Danish court created by failed kin relations, and argues that in *Beowulf* we see 'a poet reshaping the Scandinavian past through fiction to explore a theme central to understanding a significant issue of his own day, the role of kin structure in succession' (p. 635). In '*Beowulf* and Some Fictions of the Geatish Succession' (*ASE* 32[2003] 55–77), Biggs revisits the difficult issue of Anglo-Saxon succession practices. Through close examination of Beowulf's laments for the son he never had, the anonymous female mourner at Beowulf's funeral, the cup theft as a sign of sexual deviance, and the dragon as a symbol for the dying royal line, Biggs argues that 'As fictions ... these characters and monsters contribute to a discussion of succession ... [and] provide rare evidence of an Anglo-Saxon author meditating on this issue' (p. 76).

The *Beowulf*-poet's complex treatment of Christianity and Germanic paganism continues to intrigue scholars. Judy King's 'Launching the Hero: The Case of Scyld and Beowulf' (*Neophil* 87[2003] 453–71) examines the Scyld Scefing portrait at the poem's opening as 'the first panel of a diptych to be completed with the portrait of the hero' (p. 453). Contrasting Scyld's aggressive violence with Beowulf's efforts to avoid war, King argues that the poet offers readers two different models of kingship, and seeks to associate Beowulf's reign with Christian ethics through a strong contrast to Scyld's reign via heroic ideals. Ron Stein examines 'Royal Name, Hero's Deeds: A Pattern in *Beowulf*' (in Finke and Ashley, eds., *A Garland of Names*, pp. 127–39). Stein argues that the *Beowulf*-poet created an epic poem with two different parallel stories: one that could be understood as Christian, the other as pagan. He suggests that Christians and pagans might have listened to *Beowulf* together, perhaps in a royal court, and thus 'learn[ed] to confront their differences openly and peacefully' (p. 128) through shared appreciation for Beowulf as a hero. Raymond P. Tripp, Jr. writes on 'The Role of God in the Semantics of *Þryðswyð*: *Beowulf* 131a and 736b' (*InG* 24[2003] 67–80). Tripp challenges conventional readings of the term *þryðswyð* 'mighty one' as applying to the earthly kings Hrothgar (131a) and Beowulf (736b), and argues that in both cases *þryðswyð* refers to 'Almighty God'. Tripp's proposed reading 'sheds positive light on God's pro-active role in the poem [and on] the poet's habit of commenting upon it' (p. 80). Nicholas Wallerstein revisits 'The *Ubi Sunt* Problem in *Beowulf*'s Lay of the Last Survivor' (*InG* 24[2003] 41–55). Reminding us that the Lay of the Last Survivor lacks the *ubi* 'where' question found in classic examples of *ubi sunt* writings, Wallerstein argues that 'the Lay's lack of the rhetorical question "where?" can be seen as *emblematic* of the Last Survivor's spiritual condition' (p. 54). Wholly pagan and thus spiritually destitute, the Last Survivor is unable to ask where in the world permanence might lie, for the answer to that question for him would be not 'with God' but rather 'nowhere'. Ron Fischer writes on 'The Loved and the Honored: The Medieval Altars of Atonement' (in Sauer, ed., *Proceedings of the 11th Annual Northern Plains Conference on Early British Literature*, pp. 218–31). Fischer's goal is to consider whether textual representations of atonement reflect specific social and cultural contexts, and he offers a brief consideration of Beowulf's three battles.

R.D. Fulk writes 'On Argumentation in Old English Philology, with Particular Reference to the Editing and Dating of *Beowulf*' (*ASE* 32[2003] 1–26). Fulk's main goals are to show that 'probabilism is the foundation on which the edifice of philological inquiry is constructed' and to demonstrate 'the extent to which philological argumentation in Old English studies suffers because of neglect of, or mistaken notions about, probability' (p. 2). For Fulk, probabilism plays an especially crucial role in translation and textual editing, both of which, he contends, raise philological questions that 'cannot be decided in any rational way without recourse to probabilities' (p. 9). Focusing on Kevin Kiernan's *Electronic Beowulf* and Roy M. Liuzza's study of metrical disruption caused by scribal change, 'On the Dating of *Beowulf*' [1995], Fulk argues that both of these works are rendered faulty by an inadequate understanding and use of probability.

Felicia Jean Steele writes on '*Grendel*: Another Dip into the Etymological Mere' (*ELN* 40[2003] 1–13). Reminding us that no critic to date has been able to formulate an entirely satisfactory etymology based on Old English words with the root structure [* grVnd], Steele suggests that *Grendel* is the product of a process of taboo word formation involving the verb *drencan* 'to give to drink' or 'to drown', and that Grendel's name was 'originally a euphemism for a terrifying, blood-thirsty water-monster living at the edges of society' (p. 1).

James D. Thayer's 'Fractured Wisdom: The Gnomes of *Beowulf*' (*ELN* 41[2003] 1–18) is a fascinating study of the *Beowulf*-poet's experiments with the genre of the gnome. Thayer challenges earlier reading of the gnomes as conventional statements of timeless truths or as evidence of the poet's desire to uphold social norms, and argues that many of the gnomes illustrate the limitations of the wisdom they contain, making it 'appear inadequate or inappropriate to govern the lives of the poet's audience or even the poem's characters' (p. 17).

William Perry Marvin investigates 'Heorot, Grendel, and the Ethos of the Kill' (*InG* 24[2003] 1–39), and 'seek[s] the meaning(s) of "Heorot" in the context of Germanic hunting culture' (p. 2). Marvin uses discussions of hunting in both Tacitus's *Germania* and Anglo-Saxon law codes to establish that hunting carried strong symbolic resonances in Germanic culture, particularly regarding the redistribution of wealth via shared hunting spoils. He concludes: 'When the Scylding dynasts institute their house-order under the aegis of the hart, they create a representational space that seeks ideally to justify dominion through a ceremonial and lavish circulation of wealth' (pp. 22–3).

Two essays this year consider modern responses to *Beowulf*. Edward Christie's 'The Image of the Letter: From the Anglo-Saxons to the *Electronic Beowulf*' (*Culture, Theory & Critique* 44[2003] 129–50) analyses the digital manuscript facsimile as both an image and a textual object. In a densely theorized study that focuses on the *Electronic Beowulf*, Christie shows how Anglo-Saxon writers, early modern printers, and modern users of digital technology all subscribe to the same impossible fantasy that the letter can provide unmediated access to the past. Christie's essay provides a valuable model for scholars interested in using contemporary theory to illuminate Old English texts. Inge B. Milfull and Hans Sauer write on 'Seamus Heaney: Ulster, Old English, and *Beowulf*' (in Kornexl and Lenker, eds., pp. 81–141). Beginning from the belief that Heaney's translation has brought *Beowulf* into the midst of popular culture and is thus deserving of closer attention, Milfull and Sauer argue that Heaney's *Beowulf* is deeply linked to his work as a whole, and thus must be studied in relation to his earlier and later writings. Their essay begins with an overview of *Beowulf*, *Beowulf* translations, and Heaney's career, and then turns to his preoccupation with Anglo-Saxon themes in earlier works, such as 'Bone Dreams'. They offer detailed discussions of the style, syntax, layout, metre, and vocabulary of Heaney's translation, and also consider its use in his later works.

As in past years, Alfred Bammesberger offers helpful textual notes on difficult lines. In a study of 'The Sequence *sib ge mænum* in *Beowulf* Line 1857a' (*ANQ* 16[2003] 3–5), Bammesberger urges us to reject Sievers's emendation to *gemæne* and to view the word instead as *gemænū*, a scribal abbreviation of *gemænum*. In 'OE *Befeallen* in *Beowulf*, line 1126a' (*N&Q* 248[2003] 156–8),

Bammesberger argues that we ought to delete the editorial comma after *befeallen* in line 1126a and translate lines 1125–6 as 'Then warriors went to seek their dwellings, to visit a Friesland deprived of friends'. Other brief analyses of difficult lines and phrases have also appeared. William Cooke offers 'Two Notes on *Beowulf* (with Glances at *Vafþrúðnismál*, Blickling Homily 16, and *Andreas*, Lines 839–46)' (*MÆ* 72[2003] 297–301). Cooke argues that *Guðrinc astah* (1118b) does not refer to Hnaef being lifted onto the funeral pyre but rather to his spirit rising or, more likely, to a male relative lighting Hnaef's pyre. Cooke also shows that the various *hare stanas* in *Beowulf* are correctly understood not simply as ancient stones but as boundary markers between human and non-human worlds. In 'Three Notes on Swords in *Beowulf*' (*MÆ* 72[2003] 302–7), Cooke uses evidence from the *Lacnunga*, the *Nine Herbs Charm*, and archaeological studies to offer fresh insight into the weaponry in *Beowulf*.

Two important essays on *Judith* have appeared this year. Heide Estes's 'Feasting with Holofernes: Digesting *Judith* in Anglo-Saxon England' (*Exemplaria* 15[2003] 325–50) offers new insight into the complexities of Anglo-Saxon attitudes towards Judaism. Contextualizing the Old English Judith's dietary practices, curly hair, and ready acceptance of material wealth in the light of other Anglo-Saxon texts that link these phenomena to Hebrews and Judaism, Estes shows that, for all the poet's efforts to transform the biblical Judith into a chaste Christian heroine, he nevertheless 'repeatedly interrupts the narrative with reminders that Judith's power … is derived not just from her chastity in widowhood, but from her devout observance of Jewish law' (p. 330). Estes concludes by pointing to Holofernes' bloody head as a kind of indigestible meal that 'symbolize[s] the Old English poem's ultimate incapacity to transform the biblical figure of Judith into a fully acceptable Anglo-Saxon Christian heroine' (p. 350). Haruko Momma writes on 'Epanalepsis: A Retelling of the Judith Story in the Anglo-Saxon Poetic Language' (*SLI* 36[2003] 59–73). Reminding us that the *Judith*-poet eliminates numerous characters who appear in the biblical source, Momma shows how these omissions result in new parallelisms, symmetries, and contrasts between the Hebrews and Assyrians, and within the narrative as a whole. Momma's study significantly expands our understanding of epanalepsis to encompass not only the repetition of individual words and phrases but also of concepts and scenes.

9. Other Poems

From this year onwards, work on Anglo-Latin poetry will be included in this section.

Donald Scragg offers 'A Reading of *Brunanburh*' (in Amodio and O'Brien O'Keeffe, eds., pp. 109–22) in order to show how the poem's manuscript context sheds light on its contemporary social functions. Scragg argues that critics have tended to judge *Brunanburh* mainly for its stylistic merits as verse and to overlook the poem's 'clear signs of political consciousness' (p. 114). Through close study of the thematic, formal, and stylistic similarities between *Brunanburh* and *Five Boroughs*, another verse text in the *Anglo-Saxon Chronicle*, Scragg concludes that the two poems are the product of a single writer and that both are part of a written tradition designed to establish the successors of Edward as legitimate and effective rulers of Britain and as kings of all the English.

Daniel Anlezark examines 'The Fall of the Angels in *Soloman and Saturn II* (in Powell and Scragg, eds., pp. 121–33). While the fall of the angels is a recurrent motif in Old English poetry, little attention has been paid to the version that appears in *Soloman and Saturn II*. Anlezark identifies some of the more unusual aspects of this account of the fall, most notably the poet's description of demonic procreation, of the manufacture of weapons, and of hell as a place filled with both fire and water. He then examines other texts that share some of these features, such as the book of Enoch and *Beowulf*, and concludes that these similarities point to a closer literary association between *Beowulf* and *Soloman and Saturn II* than has previously been supposed.

Andrew Breeze studies 'A Welsh Crux in an Æthelwoldian Poem' (*N&Q* 248[2003] 262–3) in order to discover the meaning of the term *iornum* which appears in the opening lines of the tenth-century poem *Altercatio Magistri et Discipuli* in Cambridge, University Library, MS Kk.5.34. Breeze argues that *iornum* was originally *diornum* 'blameless, faulty' and was emended by a scribe who did not understand Welsh.

Marijane Osborn offers a fascinating study of '*Tir* as Mars in the Old English *Rune Poem*' (*ANQ* 16[2003] 3–13). Osborn begins by introducing the runelist and placing the rune *Tir* in its Anglo-Saxon and Scandinavian contexts. She concludes that lines 48–50 in the *Rune Poem* do indeed describe Mars, but only in a carefully limited sense, and that the poet 'depaganizes' Mars in order to 'realign a native cultural artifact to an acceptable belief system' (p. 9).

Andrew Breeze re-examines 'The Date of the Ruthwell Cross Inscription' (*ANQ* 16[2003] 3–5). Breeze reminds us that life in late ninth-century Ruthwell was disturbed by Viking attacks and settlement, and that the early tenth century witnessed the invasion of troops from Strathclyde. He thus concludes that the Ruthwell Cross inscription was most likely commissioned during the late ninth century, when Ruthwell was free from Viking and British attacks, and a patron might have had the means and desire to initiate artistic work.

John DuVal's 'The First Author' (*Metamorphoses* 11[2003] 222–6) offers brief reflections on Cædmon as the first English author and on various modern translations of *Cædmon's Hymn*.

10. Prose

Powell and Scragg, eds., *Apocryphal Texts and Traditions*, includes important new studies of Anglo-Saxon prose. The collection opens with Frederick M. Biggs's 'An Introduction and Overview of Recent Work' (pp. 1–25). Then follows Charles D. Wright's '*The Apocalypse of Thomas*: Some New Latin Texts and their Significance for the Old English Versions' (pp. 27–4), which gives a clear and detailed account of the relationship of the various versions in the Latin tradition, and identifies a thirteenth-century copy in Oxford, Bodleian Library, Hatton 26, part II, as the only known English manuscript of that tradition. Wright draws on his analytical reconstruction of the tradition to establish a composite approximation of the lost immediate sources of the four Old English versions of the *Apocalypse*. The appendix to the article gives a parallel-column edition of six new Latin texts of the work.

Thomas N. Hall examines 'Ælfric and the Epistle to the Laodiceans' (in Powell and Scragg, eds., pp. 65–83), with reference to the *Letter to Sigeweard*, in which Ælfric includes the apocryphal epistle to the Laodiceans in a list of the Pauline epistles. Hall proposes that Ælfric's conception of the numerical integrity of the canon leads him to include the epistle to the Laodiceans. The appendix to the article edits the epistle from the 'Royal Bible' (London, British Library, Royal I.E.VII). Patrizia Lendinara's 'The *Versus Sibyllae de die iudicii* in Anglo-Saxon England' (pp. 85–101) discusses the influence of the Sibylline acrostic in Anglo-Saxon England and its relationship to the tradition of the signs of judgement, where it overlaps in content with part of the *Apocalypse of Thomas* tradition. Aideen O'Leary's 'Apostolic *Passiones* in Early Anglo-Saxon England' (pp. 103–19) traces the Anglo-Latin traditions of the *Passiones* and their connections to Anglo-Saxon apostles' cults. The final essay in the collection is Joyce Hill's 'The Apocrypha in Anglo-Saxon England: The Challenge of Changing Distinctions' (pp. 165–8); a reflection on the contents of the volume which proposes that Anglo-Saxon definitions of the apocryphal depended on 'tradition, authority, perception, and polemic' (p. 165). The essays in this collection by Anlezark, Coatsworth and Karkov are reviewed in the appropriate sections of this chapter.

Rhonda L. McDaniel's 'An Unidentified Passage from Jerome in Bede' (*N&Q* 50[2003] 375) shows that in *In Epistolas VII Catholicas* Bede adapts a quotation from Jerome's *Adversus Jovinianum*. In 'Sticks or Stones? The Story of Imma in Cambridge, Corpus Christi College, MS 41 of the *Old English Bede*, and Old English *tān* ('twig')' (*MÆ* 72[2003] 1–12), Peter Orton offers a response to R.I. Page's analysis of the different Old English versions of Bede's account of Imma, and in particular the reference in all versions except that in CCCC 41 to 'þa stafas' ('the letters'), which has been understood as meaning runic magic, where CCCC 41 has 'þa stanas' ('the stones'). Orton proposes that 'þa stanas' is a misreading for 'þas tanas', which he argues means 'the inscribed twigs' (pp. 6–7).

Several studies of Alfredian prose are published this year. Susan Irvine's 'Wrestling with Hercules: King Alfred and the Classical Past' (in Cubitt, ed., pp. 171–88) surveys and compares representations of Hercules in the literature of Alfred's court, in other Anglo-Saxon texts, and in Carolingian literature. Irvine argues that Alfred wishes to deploy Hercules as 'a prototype for the ideal Christian Roman ruler such as existed in the Carolingian Empire from the time of Charlemagne' (p. 185). Malcolm Godden examines 'Text and Eschatology in Book III of the Old English *Soliloquies*' (*Anglia* 121[2003] 177–209), and offers a disentangling of the confused, and only surviving, manuscript of this book. Godden constructs a revised rearrangement of the manuscript, and draws on this to analyse Alfred's eschatology, which he characterizes as traditional in some respects, but radical on the issue of knowledge after death. The appendix to the article gives a modern English translation of the text of Book III, following the revised rearrangement. For another study of Alfredian prose, see David Pratt,

'Persuasion and Invention at the Court of King Alfred the Great', in Section 3 of this chapter.

Hagiographic prose generates new research this year. Christine Rauer gives a new appraisal of 'The Sources of the *Old English Martyrology*' (*ASE* 32[2003] 89–109), in order to clarify our understanding of earlier ninth-century Anglo-Saxon literary culture. A thorough survey of current knowledge of the martyrologist's sources, working habits, and possible aims, is set out, and the appendix to the article, 'The Library of the Old English Martyrologist: A Handlist of Sources', offers a very useful checklist of texts which are apparently or possibly sources or analogues, with notes on the nature of additional possible, but so far unidentified, sources. Scott DeGregorio's '*Þegenlic* or *flæsclic*: The Old English Prose Legends of St. Andrew' (*JEGP* 102[2003] 449–4) compares the Ælfrician and anonymous Andrew narratives in order to argue that Ælfric makes careful and informed choices about which version of the legend to translate, and that his 'unease over *gedwyld*' (p. 462) might be partly rooted in an anxiety about presenting sanctity to an unlettered audience. In 'Is the Barnacle Goose Selfish, and Is It Harold?' (*N&Q* 50[2003] 10–11), Rhona Beare adds a fourth to her series of short articles on a passage in the earliest Life of Edward the Confessor.

Mark Atherton studies Old English homiletic prose up to the time of Ælfric in 'Quoting and Re-Quoting: How the Use of Sources Affects Stylistic Choice in Old English Prose' (*SN* 72[2000] 6–17), to show how the language, style and discourse structure of the texts in question are affected by quotation.

More Ælfric studies appear this year. Paul Szarmach's 'Ælfric Revises: The Lives of Martin and the Idea of the Author' (in Amodio and O'Brien O'Keeffe, eds., pp. 38–1) compares Ælfric's treatments of Martin's life in the *Catholic Homilies* and *Lives of Saints* to show 'that Ælfric has taken up at least a semi-independent position in the matter of prose style at the end of the tenth century' (p. 55). Miranda Hodgson's 'Impossible Women: Ælfric's Sponsa Christi and "La Mystérique"' (*MFF* 33[2002] 12–20) focuses on 'the self-styled *sponsa Christi*' (p. 13) in Ælfric's works, in particular his Life of St Agnes. Through an analysis of speech and boundaries in these texts, Hodgson reveals 'the genre's intersection between feminine utterance and patriarchal desires' (p. 19). For Momma's article on Ælfric's *Lives of Saints*, and for the publication of the Eynsham excavations by Hardy, Dodd and Keevill, see Section 3 of this chapter.

Books Reviewed

Amodio, Mark C., and Katherine O'Brien O'Keeffe, eds. *Unlocking the Wordhord: Anglo-Saxon Studies in Memory of Edward B. Irving, Jr.* UTorP. [2003] pp. x + 359. £48 ($78) ISBN 0 8020 4822 6.

Biggam, C.P., ed. *From Earth to Art: The Many Aspects of the Plant World in Anglo-Saxon England.* Proceedings of the First ASPNS Symposium, University of Glasgow, 5–7 April 2000. Costerus ns 148. Rodopi. [2003] pp. 342. pb €70 ($94) ISBN 9 0420 0807 5.

Brown, Michelle P. *The Lindisfarne Gospels: Society, Spirituality and the Scribe.* BL. [2003] pp. xvi + 479; 177 plates. pb £19.95 ISBN 0 7123 4807 7.

Brown, Peter. *The Rise of Western Christendom: Triumph and Diversity, A.D. 200–1000*. 2nd edn. Blackwell. [2003] pp. x + 625. pb £16.99 ISBN 0 6312 2138 7.

Chance, Jane, ed. *Tolkien the Medievalist*. Routledge. [2003] pp. xiv + 295. $114.95 ISBN 0 4152 8944 0.

Charles-Edwards, Thomas, ed. *After Rome*. OUP. [2003] pp. xvii + 342. pb £15.99 ISBN 0 1992 4982 2.

Cubitt, Catherine, ed. *Court Culture in the Early Middle Ages: The Proceedings of the First Alcuin Conference*. Brepols. [2003] pp. xiv + 290. €75 ISBN 2 5035 1164 3.

Damon, John Edward. *Soldier Saints and Holy Warriors: Warfare and Sanctity in the Literature of Early England*. Ashgate. [2003] pp. ix + 327. £47.50 ($94.95) ISBN 0 7546 0473 X.

Davies, Wendy, ed. *From the Vikings to the Normans*. OUP. [2003] pp. xvi + 276. pb £15.50 ISBN 0 1987 0051 2.

Dunn, Marilyn. *The Emergence of Monasticism: From the Desert Fathers to the Early Middle Ages*. Blackwell. [2003] pp. viii + 280. pb £19.99 ISBN 0 4051 0641 7.

Farmer, Sharon, and Carol Braun Pasternack, eds. *Gender and Difference in the Middle Ages*. UMinnP. [2003] pp. xxvii + 354. pb £17.50 ISBN 0 8166 3894 2.

Finke, Wayne H., and Leonard R.N. Ashley, eds. *A Garland of Names: Selected Papers of the Fortieth Names Institute*. Cummings & Hathaway. [2003] pp. viii + 158. price na ISBN 1 5798 1048 9.

Fulk, R.D., Christopher M. Cain, with Rachel S. Anderson. *A History of Old English Literature*. Blackwell. [2003] pp. viii + 346. £50 ($66.95) ISBN 0 6312 2397 5.

Goetz, H.-W., J. Jarnut and W. Pohl, eds. *Regna and Gentes: The Relationship Between Late Antique and Early Medieval Peoples and Kingdoms in the Transformation of the Roman World*. Brill. [2003] pp. xi + 705. €162 ($232) ISBN 9 0041 2524 8.

Hamerow, Helena. *Early Medieval Settlements: The Archaeology of Rural Communities in North-West Europe 400–900*. OUP. [2002] pp. xiii + 225. pb £17.99 ISBN 0 1992 7318 9.

Hamerow, Helena, and Arthus MacGregor, eds. *Image and Power in the Archaeology of Early Medieval Britain: Essays in Honour of Rosemary Cramp*. Oxbow. [2001] pp. xii + 180. £35 ISBN 1 8421 7051 1.

Hardy, Alan, Anne Dodd and Graham D. Keevill. *Ælfric's Abbey: Excavations at Eynsham Abbey, Oxfordshire, 1989–92*. Oxford Archaeology. [2003] pp. xxv + 636. £49.95 ISBN 0 9478 1691 7.

Harris, Stephen J. *Race and Ethnicity in Anglo-Saxon Literature*. Routledge. [2003] pp. xvii + 297. $96.95 ISBN 0 4159 6872 0.

Hawkes, Jane. *The Sandbach Crosses: Sign and Significance in Anglo-Saxon Sculpture*. FCP. [2002] pp. 192. €45 (£30) ISBN 1 8518 2659 9.

Jaritz, Gerhard, and Gerson Moreno-Riaño, eds. *Time and Eternity: The Medieval Discourse*. Brepols. [2003] pp. viii + 535. €80 ISBN 2 5035 1312 3.

Karkov, Catherine E., and George Hardin Brown, eds. *Anglo-Saxon Styles*. SUNYP. [2003] pp. viii + 320. hb $71.50 ISBN 0 7914 5869 5, pb $23.95 ISBN 0 7914 5870 9.

Karkov, Catherine E., and Fred Orton, eds. *Theorizing Anglo-Saxon Stone Sculpture*. WVUP. [2003] pp. xi + 219. $45 ISBN 0 9370 5879 3.

Kornexl, Lucia, and Ursula Lenker, eds. *Bookmarks from the Past: Studies in Early English Language and Literature in Honour of Helmut Gneuss*. Lang. [2003] pp. xxxiii + 319. pb €65 (£43, $94) ISBN 3 6315 1692 4.

Lapidge, Michael, with contributions by John Crook, Robert Deshman and Susan Rankin. *The Cult of St Swithun*. Winchester Studies 4(ii): The Anglo-Saxon Minsters of Winchester. Clarendon. [2003] pp. xxvi + 811; 17 plates. £225 ISBN 0 1981 3183 6.

Lawrence-Mathers, Anne. *Manuscripts in Northumbria in the Eleventh and Twelfth Centuries*. Brewer. [2003] pp. xii + 303. £60 ($110) ISBN 0 8599 1765 7.

Minkova, Donka. *Alliteration and Sound Change in Early English*. CUP. [2003] pp. xix + 400. £60 ISBN 0 5215 7317 3.

Orchard, Andy. *A Critical Companion to Beowulf*. Brewer. [2003] pp. xix + 396. £45 ($75) ISBN 0 8599 1766 5.

Powell, Kathryn, and Donald Scragg, eds. *Apocryphal Texts and Traditions in Anglo-Saxon England*. Brewer. [2003] pp. x + 170. £50 ($85) ISBN 0 8599 1774 6.

Rees Jones, Sarah, ed. *Learning and Literacy in Medieval England and Abroad*. Brepols. [2003] pp. x + 222. €55 ISBN 2 5035 1076 0.

Sauer, Michelle M., ed. *Proceedings of the 11th Annual Northern Plains Conference on Early British Literature*. Minot State University Printing Services. [2003] pp. xxvi + 247. price na ISBN not given.

Scarfe Beckett, Katharine. *Anglo-Saxon Perceptions of the Islamic World*. CUP. [2003] pp. viii + 276. £45 ISBN 0 5218 2940 2.

Scragg, Donald, ed. *Textual and Material Culture in Anglo-Saxon England: Thomas Northcote Toller and the Toller Memorial Lectures*. Brewer. [2003] pp. xx + 345. £75 ($150) ISBN 0 8599 1773 8.

Smith, Julia. *Early Medieval Rome and the Christian West: Essays in Honour of Donald A. Bullough*. Brill. [2000] pp. xv + 446. €117 ($158) ISBN 9 0041 1716 4.

Story, Joanna. *Carolingian Connections: Anglo-Saxon England and Carolingian Francia, c.750–870*. Ashgate. [2003] pp. xvii + 311. £57.50 ($109.95) ISBN 0 7546 0124 2.

Thacker, Alan, and Richard Sharpe, eds. *Local Saints and Local Churches in the Early Medieval West*. OUP. [2002] pp. xiii + 581. £90 ISBN 0 1982 0394 2.

Tyler, Elizabeth M., ed. *Treasure in the Early Medieval West*. Boydell, York Medieval Press. [2000] pp. xi + 174. £50 ($90) ISBN 0 9529 7348 0.

Vaught Jennifer C., with Lynne Dickson Bruckner., *Grief and Gender, 700–1700*. Palgrave. [2003] pp. xii + 310. hb £42.50 ISBN 0 3122 9382 8, pb £15.99 ISBN 0 3122 9381 X.

Williams, Ann, and G.H. Martin. *Domesday Book: A Complete Translation*. Penguin. [2002] pp. x + 1436. pb £22.50 ISBN 0 1414 3994 7.

Withers, Benjamin C., and Jonathan Wilcox, eds. *Naked Before God: Uncovering the Body in Anglo-Saxon England*. WVUP. [2003] pp. xii + 315; 40 pp. plates. pb $45 ISBN 0 9370 5868 8.

Yorke, Barbara. *Nunneries and the Anglo-Saxon Royal Houses*. Continuum. [2003] pp. x + 229. £75 ISBN 0 8264 6040 2.

III

Middle English: Excluding Chaucer

DORSEY ARMSTRONG, JENNIFER BROWN, NICOLE CLIFTON, KENNETH HODGES, JURIS LIDAKA, MARION TURNER AND GREG WALKER

This chapter has ten sections: 1. General and Miscellaneous; 2. Women's Writing; 3. Alliterative Verse and Lyrics; 4. The *Gawain*-Poet; 5. *Piers Plowman*; 6. Romance; 7. Gower, Lydgate, Hoccleve; 8. Malory and Caxton; 9. Middle Scots Poetry; 10. Drama. Sections 1 and 7 are by Juris Lidaka; section 2 is by Marion Turner; sections 3 and 5 are by Nicole Clifton; section 4 is by Dorsey Armstrong; section 6 is by Kenneth Hodges and Juris Lidaka; section 8 is by Kenneth Hodges; section 9 is by Jennifer Brown; section 10 is by Greg Walker.

1. General and Miscellaneous

Among new texts edited—and this year there are quite a few—Laura Ashe discusses and presents 'The "Short Charter of Christ": An Unpublished Longer Version, from Cambridge University Library, MS Add. 6686' (*MÆ* 72[2003] 32–48). The 'Short Charter' is more legal in diction, while the 'Long' one is more affective and thereby less charter-like. The new version is internally complete and in three parts, the latter two unpublished and unrecorded: first, the 'Short Charter'; second, appointing St John Christ's attorney, witnessed by the apostles and Mary; and third, guaranteeing grace, showing the necessity of the offer, and witnessing by angels and people as to the sealing of the agreement, complete with the drawing of a seal. The manuscript is a composite put together in the first quarter of the fifteenth century, perhaps by the Carthusians of Mount Grace. Veronica O'Mara believes that *Four Middle English Sermons: Edited from British Library MS Harley 2268* were written between 1414 and 1421 by Thomas Spofford, abbot of St Mary's Abbey in York. The manuscript is an interesting compilation including Petrarchan items, Salernitan texts, these sermons plus two in Latin, and a catalogue of the abbey's library. The sermons are fascinating reading, bearing allusions to contemporary issues and events that help place and date them, as well as demonstrating concerns over the schism and the Lollards, in a style that varies from erudite to popular. O'Mara discusses the complicated

Year's Work in English Studies, Volume 84 (2005) © The English Association; all rights reserved. For permissions, please email: journals.permissions@oxfordjournals.org

doi: 10.1093/ywes/mai003

relations between written sermons and oral preaching with ease, and the introduction alone is highly recommended for all who wish to understand a major aspect of medieval culture. One should note, however, that Anne Hudson makes two 'Notes on the Sources of the Sermons of MS British Library Harley 2268' (*N&Q* 51[2004] 122–4), showing use of the *Flores Bernardi* and apparent recollection of the lost broadside *Twelve Conclusions of the Lollards.*

The 'Ancrene Wisse': A Four-Manuscript Parallel Text, Preface and Parts 1–4, edited by Tadao Kubouchi and Keiko Ikegami, with a number of other contributors, is evidently preparatory to some forthcoming edition, for, instead of presenting the manuscript texts in blocks for smoother reading with comparison, they present the texts as if upon collation cards: a short line from Corpus Christi College, Cambridge, 402 is followed by the text as British Library Cotton Cleopatra C.vi, then Cotton Nero A. xiv, and finally the Vernon manuscript, with folio and line references for the first and last and folio references (when they change) for the two in the middle. The first three are taken from the EETS editions but were checked against the manuscripts; the Vernon text is from the facsimile and is more diplomatic in its presentation, including renderings of paraphs and *punctus elevatus*. However, there is no explanation of the purpose of this edition or of any larger project of which it may be a part. See also Yoko Wada's *Companion to 'Ancrene Wisse'*, below, which refers to a 'variorum-edition' involving Bella Millett and Richard Dance, who are said to be working on the stemma (p. 23). Actually, Millett's edition will be a critical one, with glossary and some notes by Dance, the first volume probably to be published in 2005 as EETS OS 325; a prototype EETS digital edition of this may be found at http://www.tei-c.org.uk/Projects/EETS/

Ruth Kennedy's EETS edition of *Three Alliterative Saints Hymns: Late Middle English Stanzaic Poems* contains Richard Spalding's hymn on St Katherine of Alexandria and anonymous ones on John the Evangelist and John the Baptist, revised from a thesis. The three are gathered not just because they alliterate and are hymns on saints, but because they also rhyme and are in fourteen-line stanzas split into metrically distinct octaves and sestets; they are also in unique copies dated *c.*1400 from the north and east Midlands (a Bodley roll and the Thornton and Wheatley manuscripts). The effusive introduction covers the usual materials of EETS introductions: manuscript descriptions, metre, language, provenance, and editorial treatment; after the text appear notes and a glossary. There is one novelty, however, which may not be taken well: the *wynn* graph is used frequently throughout the introduction to represent the graph used identically for <þ > and < y >. In much of the discussion, it is explicitly labelled as such or as representing one or the other, but often enough it is simply used in surprising ways, so, for example, the title 'Of Sayne John þe Euaungelist' is given so in the text, but is transcribed in the introduction as 'Of Sawne John w^{e} eu*aun*gelist' (*wynn* appearing there for < w >), guaranteed to give scholars pause. It can be handy to note the use of an identical graph for <þ > and < y > , but we seem to have done quite well over the decades simply noting the fact and dealing with problem instances as they arrive. Normally the EETS is quite careful, so this is surprising, as is the fact that plates III and IV are reversed and mislabelled.

Ralph Hanna and David Lawton's *The Siege of Jerusalem* is an exemplary version of an EETS edition; highly compact yet dealing with a difficult textual tradition with clarity. The introduction covers the usual ground of manuscript descriptions (already including linguistic analyses), authorship (dialect around Barnoldswick in West Yorkshire, date probably in 1370s or 1380s), sources, dissemination (mainly the textual tradition and the thorny problem of internal divisions), and style. These sections, with abbreviations before and a bibliography following, come to a full hundred pages. After this comes the text, which is only 1,340 lines long. A novelty of the text is the use of the ' + ' sign to indicate editorial removal of letters or words from the base text; this and other editorial symbols are not included among the abbreviations at the front, but a short note right before the text itself would have clarified, since many would go the text first and not browse through the introduction to find it on page lxxxviii. The foot of each page provides a full corpus of variants deemed substantive, though one can always quibble: if 'Iewes' for 'Iewen' is a variant in line 1232, is 'Withouten' for 'Without' in MS V in line 1224 not a variant only because it is in the a-verse (see p. lxxxix)? Because there are so many variants, the editors have worked hard to compress the corpus, yet it still often takes up more than half the page even though it is in a smaller font and is given the full margin width. The textual commentary includes some explanatory information concerning history, versification, and language, as well as textual matters. The appendices are labelled at the beginning as being edited versions of the sources, but actually include only relevant bits from the *Vindicta Salvatoris* and Higden's *Polychronicon* and the evidence for manuscript affiliations. The glossary seems thorough, including concordance-like varying forms with line references, as well as the usual parts of speech and short definitions, but it also provides some helpful cross-references from selected forms (e.g. '*hem* see *þei*, *þey*' but nothing for *here*).

Another secular text is Frank Schaer's edition of a previously unpublished version of *The Three Kings of Cologne, Edited from London, Lambeth Palace MS 491*, with an excerpt in the same hand in Huntington 114, the hand being Hand 1 of *Troilus and Criseyde* in Harley 3943. The introduction includes the usual abbreviated manuscript descriptions, a note on the language by Manfred Görlach, discussion of authorship and date, summary, legend and sources, the English versions, and editorial matters. There is some difficulty in reading the introduction, for it seems to introduce more abbreviations as it proceeds, and their significance is not easily found for those scanning quickly because they are not listed among the abbreviations at the start and may not be explained until after they are used, such as 'T' for the manuscript of the Latin text most resembling the Lambeth text, which is first mentioned as just 'T' at the top of page 30 but is given no manuscript designation until a footnote at the bottom of page 39: Copenhagen, Thott 518 4o (no doubt 4°). Further allusiveness is not difficult to find: we are informed of a hypothesized 'innovative technique of textual reproduction' (p. 30) footnoted with no more information than a quoted 'this mediaeval rapid-copy device', sending curious readers off to a library in hopes the source will explain what the technique or device was. But on the whole the introduction is otherwise succinct, readable, and informative. One interesting feature is that the Latin text underlying this Lambeth English version can be reconstructed, given the Thott manuscript as a working base. Thus, the text is presented with the Middle English on the top of each page (with corrections indicated below) in a serif font and the Latin below it (with substantive readings below which 'supply the more original readings of O, the archetypal text of *HTR* [as given in Hm.]', p. 47) in a sans serif font. The two are not coordinated in matters such as paragraphing, however. Commentary notes cover a wide range of ground, including variants from '*PsM* witnesses AB' as relevant to the Latin and hence Middle English text; these are followed by selected variants to the reconstructed Latin text presented and by a short glossary.

James Hogg's *'The Rewyll of Seynt Sauioure' and 'A Ladder of Foure Ronges by the Which Men Mowe Clyme to Heven': Edited from MSS Cambridge University Library Ff.6.33 and London Guildhall 25524* is a very different edition from the two preceding, perhaps because of the prolific editor's retirement (the back cover sports a colour photograph of him with his blue parrot, 'relaxing with Oscar Hogg from his labours on the Middle English manuscripts'). The introduction is a swift discussion of Syon Abbey's need for translations of the Brigittine Rule and then the manuscripts used here. The two texts—translations of the Regula Salvatoris and the Scala Paradisi or Scala Claustralium—are edited fairly diplomatically and with extensive textual apparatus, but the actual presentation is a facsimile of the Cambridge Rule followed by the edition, then a facsimile of the Guildhall Rule and its edition; thereafter come a facsimile of the Latin Rule in Harley MS 612 and a text edited from several manuscripts, and a facsimile of the Latin in Syon Abbey MS 7. Next are facsimiles of the Rule of St Austin (a translation of Augustine's *Regula ad servos Dei*) in the Cambridge and Guildhall manuscripts, with no edited text, and finally the *Ladder* in facsimile from the Cambridge manuscript and an edited text using two additional manuscripts, with its own brief introduction and bibliography. The quality of the facsimiles varies, many appearing to be photocopies of manuscripts or from microfilms, but their presence is welcome for palaeographic study and for those who may have some doubt about the text's readings. One hopes the haste of this edition does not mark the end of the Analecta Cartusiana, but it seems as though it well may.

Thomas G. Duncan and Margaret Connolly have edited the first part of *The Middle English 'Mirror': Sermons from Advent to Sexagesima*, this portion being the prologue and first twelve of some sixty sermons. These are translations and adaptations of an Anglo-Norman *Miroire* composed by one Robert de Gretham in the thirteenth century, who may also have written the treatise *Corset* on the seven sacraments. The *Miroire* survives in some six manuscripts, none of which is the translator's copy, plus two fragments and extracted in two more; the *Mirror* also survives in six, with one split between two libraries, and a partial derivative. Four manuscripts added further materials for a total of seventeen more texts. The English and Anglo-Norman texts are presented *en regarde*, each based on one representative manuscript, with minimal apparatus, though the English text has more. The *Mirror* was probably made about 1375–80 in the greater London area, in Samuels' Type II Language, as in the main hand of the Auchinleck manuscript. The introduction briefly describes the manuscripts and their relationships, based on the exempla rather than a full collation, then discusses the passage from the Anglo-Norman to the Middle English translation, following this with an overview of the structure; mainly the Sunday gospel pericopes in Sarum use. It concludes with the base manuscript, its language, and editorial principles. After the text are brief commentary notes on the text, language, and sources (using a Clementine version of the Bible), a short glossary, and the bibliography.

Alternatively, for those not wishing to wait for all the volumes of this edition to appear, the full text can be read in Kathleen Marie Blumreich's edition, *The Middle English 'Mirror': An Edition Based on Bodleian Library, MS Holkham misc. 40*. The introduction is short: a little on Gretham, some notes on the translation and contents, summaries of the seventeen exempla, longer descriptions of the base manuscript and of Pepys 2498 (with which it was collated), very short descriptions of the four other manuscripts, a brief rationale for using the two manuscripts chosen, a dialect analysis provided by Lister M. Matheson (acknowledged in a footnote), and editorial practices. The Middle English text is presented in good size with generous white space, and textual notes and substantive collational variants are at the foot, with some notes on Vulgate readings (we are not told which Vulgate); at the end are a brief glossary, an index of scriptural citations, and a bibliography. This makes the edition serviceable for ready access, with references to previously published work, by Duncan and others, serving for more fulsome exposition; nevertheless, given the size of the volume, the brevity may well be preferable. It could be useful to have both editions, especially when that by Duncan and Connolly is finished.

Another large volume is also a mirror: Robert R. Raymo, Elaine E. Whitaker, and Ruth E. Sternglantz's edition of *The Mirroure of the Worlde: A Middle English Translation of 'Le Miroir du Monde'*. The sole copy is a well decorated manuscript Bodley 283, but the only illustration in the edition is on the dust-jacket. A typical manual of moral instruction, the *Mirroure* is based on *Le Miroir du Monde* and *La Somme le Roi*, both developed from William Peraldus. The translation was made in the north Midlands, perhaps 1440–50—the editors suggest by Stephen Scrope—and this manuscript was copied probably 1470–5. The editors used ten manuscripts of the French to help correct the text, and provide detailed textual notes in compact form and explanatory notes in more expansive, but still tight, form, before a good glossary and bibliography.

If these were not mirrors enough, we must add Albert C. Labriola and John W. Smeltz's *The Mirror of Salvation* [*Speculum Humanæ Salvationis*]: *An Edition of British Library Blockbook G. 11784*. This is really a translation with commentary, rather than an edition, since it presents only the images with their captions and replaces the text column with a translation. Aimed at the general reader, the introduction concerns the general purpose and related interests but omits a detailed description of the blockbook itself and its history. This one was produced in Holland probably around 1470, but whether it was intended for export to England is not discussed, nor do the editors reveal when or how the British Library acquired it. The interpretative commentary makes observations on iconographic details but also at times discusses sources, even referring readers to Comestor's *Historia scholastica* but curiously leaving the reference '*PL*, CXCVIII, 1414' unexpanded and explained; thus the commentary is poised between the general and the scholarly. Also for the general reader, but perhaps useful in a classroom, is Richard Barber's *Myths and Legends of the British Isles*, with original translations or paraphrases, some previously published. It is broadly divided into sections on origins, early history, 'marvels and magic', 'heroes and saints', and 'history and romance', with the individual tales ranging from the giants of Albion, through the Taliesin, the voyage of St Brendan, Joseph of Arimathea, Richard the Lionhearted, and Robin Hood to Lady Godiva. All are told freely and easily, and there is a wealth of pleasurable reading, even for scholars who have been too busy to catch up on so many stories they should know.

Eve Salisbury's *The Trials and Joys of Marriage* conveniently gathers a number of texts otherwise widely dispersed in various editions, such as Furnivall's *Jyl of Breyntford's Testament*, which is quite difficult to find. These range from *Dame Sirið* and the related *Interludium de clerico et puella* through *The Wright's Chaste Wife*, *A Talk of Ten Wives on their Husbands' Ware*, Lydgate, Dunbar, several tales from the *Gesta Romanorum*, a short Wyclifite treatise, and both *How the Goode Wife Taught Hyr Doughter* and *How the Goode Man Taght Hys Sone* to a few lyrics from the fourteenth and fifteenth centuries. The selection is interesting and useful, giving various approaches to help students see that there was not a monolithic, unanimous concept of the relationship between men and women. However, the discussion and notes seemed to need more work. Do the encyclopedias by Alexander Neckam and Bartholomaeus Anglicus really 'resemble the *Gesta Romanorum* in form' (p. 16 n. 42)? The apparently unfinished nature of the *Ballad of a Tyrannical Husband* is mentioned, but not the fragmentary nature of the *Interludium*. Linguistic matters also needed a firmer hand, given the glossary and comments such as '"to wifeth" or "to weave" in Old English becomes "to wife"' (p. 80, note on l. 43). The texts seem fairly accurate, though one should not rely upon this edition for scholarly rigour; for example, *How the Goode Man Taght Hys Sone* (*Wise Man* in five of the six manuscripts, but not all were collated) is said to use Ashmole 61 as its base on page 239 (it does not) but Cambridge University Library Ff.2.38 on page 241 (close, but not exact unless the notes are missing many variants, including editorial emendations). For general student use these drawbacks may not matter.

Another student edition of texts previously edited but now presented anew is Julia Boffey's *Fifteenth-Century English Dream Visions*, including five Chaucerian works: Lydgate's *Temple of Glass*, James I of Scotland's *Kingis Quair*, Charles d'Orléans' *Love's Renewal*, *The Assembly of Ladies*, and John Skelton's *Bouge of Court*. Orthography is also somewhat modernized, and possibly difficult words are glossed at the foot of the page only (there is no glossary, and a very few glosses seem excessive), keyed to line numbers, together with occasional explanatory comments and references. Textual matters are taken more seriously than usual in student editions. For example, variants in collated manuscripts precede each text, and the *Temple of Glass* is based on Shirley's copy British Library Additional 16165 rather than the previous editions' Bodleian Tanner 346, precisely because Shirley's is the earliest complete copy and its errors seem transparent and thus easy to emend. There is no such choice for the *Kingis Quair*, of course, and the textual discussions for both suffer from the obvious lack of explicit dates, given that they are addressed to students who will not know them. Introductions to individual texts reflect Boffey's wide knowledge of fifteenth-century literature and its background; though the source citations may seem overwhelming at times, they are well worth having.

A third student text is the second edition of Elaine Treharne's *Old and Middle English c.890–c.1400: An Anthology*. It is just over fifty pages longer than the first (published in 2000) because of added selections from Langland (Passus I and V–VI), Chaucer (the *General Prologue* and *Wife of Bath's Prologue* and *Tale*), and *Sir Gawain and the Green Knight* (Fitts I and IV). To help make room for these, a number of items have been omitted: *The Proverbs of Alfred* from Oxford Jesus College 29, *History and Invention of the True Cross* and *Saint Quiriac* from the South English Legendary, Robert Mannyng of Brunne's *Handlyng Synne*, *The Four Foes of Mankind* from the Auchinleck Manuscript, *Kyng Alisaunder*, and the textual emendations. The additions cause me to wonder what Blackwell will do with 'companion' textbooks that would include the fifteenth century, such as Derek Pearsall's 2002 *Poetry from Chaucer to Spenser*, which begins with Chaucer, Langland, and *Sir Gawain and the Green Knight*, with some overlap of selections, though otherwise Pearsall included only some Henryson and Dunbar works before moving to the sixteenth century.

Julia Boffey and A.S.G. Edwards produced 'Unrecorded Middle English Verse Texts in a Canterbury Cathedral Library Manuscript' (*MÆ* 72[2003] 49–62), MS Add. 46, a collection of paper leaves from the late fifteenth century, perhaps in Kent. The fragmentary texts include 'Gregory's Trental', prose recipes, prayers, and notes, some verse that has appeared in both love and religious lyrics, some Latin notes, the 'Long Charter of Christ', and a poem on the Seven Deadly Sins. Elsewhere, A.S.G. Edwards asserts that we have a 'A New Version of Part of Chaucer's "Lak of Stedfastnesse"' (*Archiv* 240[2003] 106–8) in BL MS Additional 37049, for *IMEV* 558 includes a variant version of the third stanza, with the rhyme royal turned to couplets and with some textual displacement.

George R. Keiser edits and discusses a few 'Verse Introductions to Middle English Medical Treatises' (*ES* 84[2003] 301–17), concluding that they were indeed decorative and evidently a French-inspired vogue, though he stops short of commenting on their penchant for drasty rhyming. Monica H. Green edits and discusses 'Masses in Remembrance of "Seynt Susan": A Fifteenth-Century Spiritual Regimen' (*N&Q* 50[2003] 380–4), before a Middle English gynaecological treatise in Sloane 249. The text has some similarity to 'charms found on so-called birth girdles' (p. 382), but its location in a pamphlet with a medical text does indicate how physical and spiritual health were joined.

Simone Marshall edits an instructional text for novices, '"An abstracte owte of a boke þat is callid *Formula nouiciorum*": Edited from London BL MS Arundel 197' (*MysticsQ* 29[2003] 71–139), a translation of *De exterioris et interioris hominis compositione* by David of Augsberg. The Latin text was written *c.*1240 and survives in over 370 manuscripts, not including extracts; the English, however, is in only two complete versions: this manuscript with just part one of the text, and two more short extracts. The scribe of the Arundel text was probably also the translator and was actively revising it at various times in the second half of the century. Marshall posits a female readership, this being perhaps a personal copy, and reports suggestions of a connection with Syon Abbey. In 'Yorkist Propaganda and *The Chronicle from Rollo to Edward IV*' (*SP* 100[2003] 401–24), Raluca Radulescu presents the previously unedited text from British Library Manuscript Harley 116 (written in 1461 or later) with variants from another copy, pasted into Harley 326, possibly by the same scribe but with corrections and additions by another. The text seems to support Edward IV's ancestry and claim to the throne, with the justification aimed at the gentry. Margaret Connolly discusses the complicated textual tradition of several prayers such as 'A Prayer to the Guardian Angel and Wynken de Worde's 1506 Edition of *Contemplations of the Dread and Love of God*' (*Manuscripta* 45–6[2001–2] 1–17), which also occurs in several manuscripts. She edits and translates several prayers from a Nijmegen manuscript.

Manuscript studies begin this year with Cotton Nero A. xiv. In 'The Tremulous Hand of Worcester and the Nero Scribe of the *Ancrene Wisse*' (*MÆ* 72[2003] 13–31), Christine Franzen argues that 'the earliest work of the tremulous scribe has a great many similarities to the unknown scribe'. Most of the glosses have been unpublished, largely because they had been erased, but Franzen retrieved quite a few thanks to ultraviolet light. The earliest D English glosses show he was 'updating vocabulary, spellings, and inflections' (p. 17); B and M glosses have more archaic spellings. Both scribes modernize older texts, use a similar dialect, and even employ a similar hand, perhaps in the first half of the thirteenth century. Thus, Frantzen hypothesizes a training centre for such activities, but admits we have no real evidence for one. The manuscripts has other texts, too, we are reminded by Caroline Cole in a short but interesting study of the 'Wooing Group' in 'The Integrity of Text and Context in the Prayers of British Library, Cotton MS Nero A.XIV' (*NM* 104[2003] 85–94); the manuscript shows them more tightly related than editions do, and it even displays a careful thematic development through the contents. A.S.G. Edwards and Alexandra Gillespie describe 'A Manuscript of Robert of Gloucester's *Chronicle* Copied by John Stow' (*N&Q* 50[2003] 384–5), now Guildhall MS 34125. And despite the general lack of manuscripts surviving from there, Jane Chedzey is able to show good evidence for 'Manuscript Production in Medieval Winchester' (*RMSt* 29[2003] 1–18) using records of personal and street names, other documentary evidence, and archaeological finds.

Ralph Hanna takes 'Yorkshire Writers' (*PBA* 121[2003] 91–109) to task in several elliptical respects, exploring several manuscripts, their scribes, their texts, and the complicated interrelationships ranging further afield, remarking on the liveliness of Yorkshire literary culture until it ebbed early in the fifteenth century. The breadth of information contained here is belied by the apparent brevity of the Gollancz lecture, and students of many texts will profit from the article and its valuable notes—on the *Prick of Conscience*, *Northern Homily Cycle*, *Cursor Mundi*, Nicholas Love, and, of course, Rolle. Of perhaps greater import will be the many comments on manuscript features, layout, and related matters. As Ralph Hanna III, he also briefly describes 'A New Fragment of the *Speculum Vitae*' (*JEBS* 6[2003] 137–42), found by Thorlac Turville-Petre in the Staffordshire Record Office in binding wrappers, from a lost Leicestershire manuscript. Linne R. Mooney describes and edits 'A Fragment of the *Cursor Mundi* in the Sutherland Collection on Deposit in the National Library of Scotland' (*JEBS* 6[2003] 143–7), found in binding strips from *c.*1400, produced in North Lincolnshire or Yorkshire.

Linne R. Mooney and Lister M. Matheson's 'The Beryn Scribe and His Texts: Evidence for Multiple-Copy Production of Manuscripts in Fifteenth-Century England' (*Library* 4[2003] 347–70) describe palaeographic and linguistic (south-central Essex) evidence, as well as provenance and inscriptions, and textual relationships to pose a commercial scriptorium in London for a limited number of popular texts. The unique copy of the *Tale of Beryn* was written by a scribe who also produced five copies of the prose *Brut* chronicle, one of Lydgate's *Life of Our Lady*, and a manuscript of three booklets with the *Prick of Conscience*, a fifteenth-century chronicle of London, Chaucer's *Parliament of Fowls*, and Henry V's statutes for the army at Mantes (1419). This 'Beryn Scribe' apparently supervised the copying of *Brut* manuscripts using a single exemplar, and had a small collection of other works that would also find a paying audience. Elisabeth Dutton discusses 'Textual Disunities and Ambiguities of *mise-en-page* in the Manuscripts Containing Book to a Mother' (*JEBS* 6[2003] 149–59), by which the scribes' physical presentations create or hide textual divisions of the work, thereby leading one to read it quite differently. Lisa H. Cooper's 'The "Book of Oure Charges": Constructing Community in the Masons' Constitutions' (*JEBS* 6[2003] 1–39) works with two manuscripts of the constitutions—one in prose, the other verse, both roughly 1400 and of very portable size—which trace masons back to Old Testament patriarchs, showing how the texts embracing history, method, and behaviour to instruct masons and enhance their sense of unity within the guild.

Manuscript descriptions have also been produced by Betty Hill. First, her 'Oxford, Jesus College MS 29, Part II: Contents, Technical Matters, Compilation, and its History to *c.*1695' (*N&Q* 50[2003] 268–76) is not a continuation of some lost part I but a description of the second part of MS 29, whose part I is a fifteenth-century Latin chronicle. Best known for containing *The Owl and the Nightingale*, the manuscript has twenty-five items of English verse, four of Anglo-Norman, and one apiece of English prose, Latin prose, French verse, and macaronic Anglo-Norman and English verse. Ten items are shared with MS Cotton Caligula A.ix, and four of these appear in the library catalogue of the Premonstratensian abbey of Titchfield. Hill argues that the manuscript, written *c.*1285–1300 in one hand, was compiled by a member of the familia of Richard Swinfield, bishop of Hereford 1283–1317. Second, her 'A Manuscript from Nuneaton: Cambridge Fitzwilliam Museum MS McLean 123' (*TCBS* 12:iii[2002] 191–205) would little concern us but for its inclusion of the *Poema morale* preceded by two lines from 'Sinners Beware!' (*IMEV* 1272 and 3607, respectively) and a brief text on the names and forms of '*thorn*, *wen*, *yogh*, *and*, with illustrations of their use in initial and final position'; the manuscript (*c.*1300) and its history are described here. She briefly notes that 'A Couplet from the *Conduct of Life* in Maidstone MS A 13' (*N&Q* 50[2003] 377) works itself into a Latin sermon, showing the text had wider dissemination than its extant manuscripts might suggest.

In *Fair and Varied Forms: Visual Textuality in Medieval Illuminated Manuscripts*, Mary C. Olson looks at manuscripts from a different angle:

graphic design. The study works from an investigation based on schemata, which are generic forms used to represent particular figures, together with metaphor and spatiality. The opening chapter sets the theoretical grounds for what follows, and the second extends the theory into looking for evidence concerning attitudes about writing and especially imaging, in so far as such evidence can be found in written discussions or as indicated through the work of artisans; schemata are easily found, with attributes provided to particularize specific individuals (a generic human with a harp must be David), and spatial displays could present concepts of time, as well as relationships. The next three chapters concern Anglo-Saxon manuscripts of varying 'genres'—the Harley Psalter (devotion), the Illustrated Hexateuch (narrative), and *Marvels of the East* in the Nowell Codex (science)—and the fourth concerns the Ellesmere Chaucer. It is argued that the genre is important to page layout, spatial relationships, and schemata, so that the Psalter frequently displays tripartite divisions mirroring the religious universe, the Hexateuch allegorizes its subjects and shows narrative time, and the monsters in the *Marvels* are isolated from narrative and relationships but are still schemata with key attributes to identify them. However, with the passing of centuries methods of production have changed; the 'bookish' Ellesmere foregrounds the orality of the *Tales*, with Chaucer's portrait having a problematic tension.

Among tools we could consider Daniel T. Kline's 'Web Spotlight: Medieval Portal Sites' (*Medieval Forum* 2[March 2003] http://www.sfsu.edu/~medieval/Volume2/Klin_D.html, home), with links to and brief notes on the Labyrinth (http://labyrinth.georgetown.edu/),the ORB (http://orb.rhodes.edu/), NetSERF (http://www.netserf.org/), and the Voice of the Shuttle (http://vos.ucsb.edu/). If Kline's article looks a bit funny on a high-resolution monitor and has peculiar line breaks, this is because the *Medieval Forum* uses a table format which forces narrow columns that become very tedious with the longer articles. In *Middle English Literature: A Historical Sourcebook* Matthew Boyd Goldie presents background material (in Middle English or modern English translation) for students of Chaucer, his contemporaries, and followers, heavily directed towards Chaucer. The materials are divided into seven broad areas of unequal weight and clearly questionable categorization, as will be clear from the first category's subdivisions: 'Conventions and Institutions' (comprising the 'Benedictine Rule', 'Friars', 'Humors', 'Marriage', 'Pilgrimage', and 'Prioresses'), 'Force and Order', 'Gender, Sexuality, and Difference', 'Images' (the shortest, with twelve small grey-scale images, four of them being images of Chaucer or of *Canterbury Tales* manuscripts), 'Labor and Capitol', 'Style and Spectacle', and 'Textualities'. There is a very short appendix of currency, income, prices, and measures, followed by a quick glossary of Middle English, a four-page bibliography, and an index of just over thirteen pages). While we are on the subject of websites, we could also add Bella Millett's *Wessex Parallel WebTexts* at http://www.soton.ac.uk/~wpwt/. The site contains some Middle English lyrics (especially from Harley 2253), translations of some longer poems, and some additional materials, including a descriptive introduction to 'traditional grammar' because students are generally not taught the terms and concepts they need for working on understanding and even translating Middle English texts. For graduate students in medieval studies, there is a peer-reviewed online journal

Hortulus at http://www.hortulus.net/. The first issue should appear in January 2005.

The Yearbook of English Studies 33[2003] is a special issue on 'Medieval and Early Modern Miscellanies and Anthologies', guest-edited by Philippa Hardman and reaching chronologically from the thirteenth century until after the Restoration. Andrew Taylor's 'Manual to Miscellany: Stages in the Commercial Copying of Vernacular Literature in England' (*YES* 33[2003] 1–17) displays a number of manuscripts with Anglo-Norman works as evidence for commercial production of booklets starting by the middle of the thirteenth century. John Scahill shows how the languages of works at the same time influenced the selection and organization of manuscripts in 'Trilingualism in Early Middle English Miscellanies: Languages and Literature' (*YES* 33[2003] 18–32). Neil Cartlidge restores the Latin works to their manuscript context, usually described as vernacular or English, in 'Festivity, Order, and Community in Fourteenth-Century Ireland: The Composition and Contexts of BL MS Harley 913' (*YES* 33[2003] 33–52), leading to a new evaluation of all the manuscript's works, particularly 'The Land of Cockaygne'. Jason O'Rourke's 'English and Latin Texts in Welsh Contexts: Reflections of a Multilingual Society in National Library of Wales MS Peniarth 12' (*YES* 33[2003] 53–63) continues the theme but jumps to the sixteenth century, with a thriving trilingual literary community in Denbighshire.

Next we turn to authority with Marilyn Corrie discussing how the manuscript context implies an undermining of the authority of 'Kings and Kingship in British Library MS Harley 2253' (*YES* 33[2003] 64–79). Ardis Butterfield's 'Articulating the Author: Gower and the French Vernacular Codex' (*YES* 33[2003] 80–96) considers how the concept of an (or the) author is presented in the *Confessio amantis* and in *Le Roman de la Rose*, Chaillou de Pestain's alteration of *Fauvel*, and briefly selected aspects of Machaut, Froissart, and the *Trésor amoureux*. But are these anthologies or miscellanies? An author's anthology is summarized nicely by Susanna Fein in 'Good Ends in the Audelay Manuscript' (*YES* 33[2003] 97–119), where the two scribes' compiling of Audelay's and others' works is neatly shown to maintain the author's emphasis on finality.

Instead of an anthology or miscellany, Julia Boffey surveys '*The Charter of the Abbey of the Holy Ghost* and its Role in Manuscript Anthologies' (*YES* 33[2003] 120–30) as it relates to the *Abbey* in numerous manuscripts and Wynken de Worde's printed editions, and offers observations on the importance of female readership on their circulation. This theme continues in A.S.G. Edwards' 'Fifteenth-Century English Collections of Female Saints' Lives' (*YES* 33[2003] 131–41), hypothesizing a relationship among small books, books of hours, verse written as prose, and women owners, and surveying related works—with an eye on St Margaret, Bokenham, and Lydgate's *Life of Our Lady*—and manuscripts, adding a few notes on the circulation of literary works in East Anglia.

This is followed by several pieces focusing on manuscripts, beginning with Ralph Hanna on John Dygon's 'Producing Magdalen College MS lat. 93' (*YES* 33[2003] 142–55), previously described by Siegfried Wenzel for its macaronic materials and including *Pore Caitif*; cataloguing Magdalen manuscripts, Hanna finds this miscellany hard to describe properly within the limits of a catalogue, and here presents a codicological reconstruction of the manuscript's creation and assembly. Amanda Moss reviews what is known about Westminster School MS 3 in 'A Merchant's Tales: A London Fifteenth-Century Household Miscellany' (*YES* 33[2003] 156–69), containing numerous pious vernacular works. Margaret Connolly surveys 'Books for the "helpe of euery persoone þat þenkiþ to be saued": Six Devotional Anthologies from Fifteenth-Century London' (*YES* 33[2003] 170–81), whose similarity of content argues for wide interest in texts of religious instruction across the century. At the close of this section, Linne R. Mooney gathers together material pertaining to the scribes who might in a literary sense be called 'John Shirley's Heirs' (*YES* 33[2003] 182–98).

Turning to the transition from script to print, Martha Driver again reviews the almanac in 'When Is a Miscellany Not Miscellaneous? Making Sense of the *Kalender of Shepherds*' (*YES* 33[2003] 199–214), with its texts and illustrations. Alternatively, some printed books served as exemplars for manuscripts, as Alexandra Gillespie shows in '"These proverbes yet do last": Lydgate, the Fifth Earl of Northumberland, and Tudor Miscellanies from Print to Manuscript' (pp. 215–32), this case working in favour of the 'stigma' of print, within a 'paratextual' polarity of courtliness versus commodity, the 'bespoke' manuscript versus the printed book for purchase.

The volume then turns fully to the period of print with Elizabeth Heale's well-exampled argument that Tottel's and others' miscellanies removed women from the universe of courtly verse, 'Misogyny and the Complete Gentleman in Early Printed Miscellanies' (*YES* 33[2003] 233–47). This is followed by Randall L. Anderson on 'Metaphors of the Book as Garden in the English Renaissance' (*YES* 33[2003] 248–61), with some emphasis on the self-conscious selection of 'flowers' in anthologies. Adam Smyth turns to audience in '"Such a general itching after book-learning": Popular Readers of "the most eminent Wits"' (*YES* 33[2003] 262–72), in that the miscellanies purported to display courtly eloquence and etiquette but were directed to and read by *hoi polloi*, who used the material to their own ends. Taking the authors' view in '"A Storm of Lamentations Writ": *Lachrymae Musarum* and Royalist Culture After the Civil War' (*YES* 33[2003] 263–89), John McWilliams sees the elegies for Henry Hastings more broadly—mourning the lost past but aiming to prevail over this loss. Cedric C. Brown makes a case for a connection between the 'Recusant Community and Jesuit Mission in Parliament Days: Bodleian MS Eng. poet. b. 5' (*YES* 33[2003] 290–315), with the contents reflecting Jesuit indoctrination; the scribe was not Thomas Fairfax but someone close to the mission, perhaps a member. Finally, Victoria E. Burke discusses 'Contexts for Women's Manuscript Miscellanies: The Case of Elizabeth Lyttelton and Sir Thomas Browne' (*YES* 33[2003] 316–28), placing it in an environment consisting of her extended family and friends.

The theme of this year's *New Medieval Literatures*, edited by David Lawton, Wendy Scase, and Rita Copeland, is the metaphorical 'Mapping Performance', which is where it does begin and end, with quite a bit in between; Lawton's introduction is keen on 'interdisciplinary' but more so on 'antidisciplinary'. Daniel Birkholz's 'Vernacular Map: Re-Charting English Literary History' (pp. 11–77) begins with a mid-sixteenth-century scientific commonplace miscellany containing a map that is odd because it seems closely related to be Gough map but was drawn or copied at a time when maps were more representative than metaphorical, just as the Gough map apparently was in its time—he does not explain, but one may consider the difference between T-O maps and nautical portolan charts. Thomas Butler, scribe and owner of the manuscript and woollen-draper, has a cultural value useful as a springboard to discussing provenance, interests of owners, and middle-class values in the contents of the miscellanies, which allows a bit of theorizing about literary history. Suzanne M. Verderber's 'Refiguring the Veil: The Transvaluation of Human History in Marie de France's *Yonec*' (pp. 79–106) won the $1,000 prize in the second essay contest for doctoral candidates and recent Ph.D.s; her essay uses a different springboard, the hawk-lover's shadow, to merge sacred and secular history and claim the latter is as true as the former, using Lacan in support.

Alastair Minnis's 'Chaucer and the Queering Eunuch' (in Lawton, Scase, and Copeland, eds., pp. 107–28) is interesting: modern queer theory relies upon modern not medieval notions of sexuality, so a different explanation must be found for how Chaucer and his audience would have understood the Pardoner. Given humoral theory and medical doctrine about sexual origins depending on right/left settlement in the uterus (and origin from the testicles), and more, five possible explanations make the Pardoner a ball-less hetero; 'geldyng' and 'mare' are insults, not descriptions. Also on Chaucer is Larry Scanlon's 'What's the Pope Got To Do With It? Forgery, Didacticism, and Desire in the *Clerk's Tale*' (pp. 129–65), whose opening gambit is playing theory against theory against theory and eschewing the anecdote, and who wishes to explain that Chaucer had Walter get a fake papal dispensation for divorcing Griselda because the Church largely regulated marriage and particularly kept an eye on royalty; of course, it must in fact be more complicated because it is the Clerk who tells the tale and because of the envoy. In 'A Political Pamphleteer in Late Medieval England: Thomas Fovent, Geoffrey Chaucer, Thomas Usk, and the Merciless Parliament of 1388' (pp. 167–98), Clementine Oliver shows Fovent was not a Lancastrian partisan but more like a Grub Street hack; where Chaucer was a moderate who avoided factional traps, Usk fell into them, and Fovent seemed interested in royal politics only in so far as they represented reform by the people of corruption by the powerful.

The people can also be called the 'commonalty', and Emily Steiner's 'Commonalty and Literary Form in the 1370s and 1380s' (pp. 199–221) sees Usk and Langland dealing with the voice of the commonalty's political clamour after the Good Parliament of 1376. Turning to a more private reaction to society, Jeremy Tambling muses on 'Allegory and the Madness of the Text: Hoccleve's *Complaint*' (pp. 223–48), taking off from comments by C.S. Lewis and travelling the thickets of Shoshana Felman, Walter Benjamin, Lacan, Deleuze and Guattari, and Freud. Slightly marginal to our literary purview is Mark Gregory Pegg '"Catharism" and the Study of Medieval Heresy' (pp. 249–69). The volume closes with the review article 'Analytical Survey 6: Medieval Literature and Cultures of Performance' by Bruce W. Holsinger (pp. 271–311), including topics such as oral/aurality, the book, the 'rhetorical turn', genre and ritual, liturgy, and drama, and covering only the last two decades or so of publications.

In *Chaucer and the Challenges of Medievalism: Studies in Honor of H.A. Kelly*, Donka Minkova and Theresa Tinkle have gathered new offerings from Andy's students and others, grouped under six headings. 'Text, Image, Script' opens with Christopher Baswell's 'King Edward and the Cripple' on Matthew Paris's verse life of St Edward the Confessor (pp. 15–29). V.A. Kolve inspects Criseyde's dream of the white eagle and Troilus's of Criseyde and the boar in 'Looking at the Sun in Chaucer's *Troilus and Criseyde*' (pp. 31–71), placing them in the traditions of the bestiary and art of memory before locating love in the context of Antigone's song. Gordon Kipling describes 'Lydgate: The Poet as Deviser' in that seven of his mummings or disguises are not scripts but 'devices' for artisans to turn into realities of performance (pp. 73–101).

'Text and Meter' has two pieces. Martin Duffell looks at how French versification changed Castilian verse from a stress-counting line somewhat like Germanic lines to French models, in 'French Symmetry, Germanic Rhythm, and Spanish Metre' (pp. 105–27). Donka Minkova and Robert Stockwell's 'Emendation and the Chaucerian Metrical Template' (pp. 129–39) is a different perspective on Jill Mann's recent article (see *YWES* 82[2003] 202), arguing, basically, that Chaucer did write iambic pentameter, if we allow for syncopation, elision, headless lines, and compression of small words into one unstressed position.

'Reception' starts with Glending Olson's 'A Franciscan Reads the *Facetus*' (pp. 143–55), on Gerard of Odo's commentary on the *Nicomachean Ethics*, which draws on the *Facetus* among other works; this is one example of how the *Facetus* influenced perceptions of social affability. Theresa Tinkle finds male bonding through 'Cupid' poems in 'The Imagined Chaucerian Community of Bodleian MS Fairfax 16' (pp. 157–74). John Ganim's 'Mary Shelley, Godwin's *Chaucer* and the Middle Ages' (pp. 175–91) looks at Romantic and early Victorian medievalism.

'Chaucer'—a section not including four earlier relevant pieces—is restricted to four items itself, beginning with Edward I. Condren's explication 'The Disappointments of Criseyde' (pp. 195–204), a pleasure to read not least because the author relies only upon the text (the sole source credited being *The Riverside Chaucer*) and upon his contemplation of the ramifications of I.124–6. John V. Fleming reviews rosaries and Chaucer's reliance upon the *Roman de la Rose* in 'Madame Eglantyne: The Telling of the Beads' (pp. 205–33), most notably her echoes of Astenance Constrainte and even the syntax of *Amor vincit omnia*, with related excursus. Matthew Brosamer's 'The Cook, the Miller, and Alimentary Hell' (pp. 235–51) takes those characters into the common visual depiction of the mouth of hell and extends the coverage to human ingestion and how its many aspects were associated with sin, death, and the infernal. And Eric Jager looks again at the satire between values of this world and the next, in 'The Shipman's Tale: Merchant's Time and Church's Time, Secular and Sacred Space' (pp. 253–60).

'Hagiography' includes George Hardin Brown on the honoree's namesake, St 'Ansgar, Pragmatic Visionary' (pp. 263–73), a ninth-century missionary in northern Europe. Margaret Bridges seems to have the longest title, with 'Uncertain Peregrinations of the Living and the Dead: Writing (Hagiography) as Translating (Relics) in Osbern Bokenham's Legend of St. Margaret' (pp. 275–87), which is an exploratory inception touching upon the trope of writer as traveller, Bokenham's admission that he is but a 'translatour', some saints in his *Legendys of Hooly Wummen* having had their relics translated, the uncertainty of his translation of Margaret's relics, the *Legendys* as a compilation not a planned work, and more. Anita Obermeier traces 'Joachim's Infertility in the St. Anne's Legend' (pp. 289–307) from Old Testament analogues through the *Protoevangelion*, *Legenda aurea*, and Bokenham, to show that Joachim became marginalized while Anne became a sort of medieval fertility goddess.

Finally, 'Lay Piety and Christian Diversity' begins with Joseph Nagy's marshalling allusions and tales affirming a motif of 'A Pig for *Samhain*?' (pp. 311–25). Michael Hanly looks at treatments of three related motifs by three unrelated authors in 'Marriage, War, and Good Government in Late-Fifteenth-Century Europe: The *De regimine principum* Tradition in Langland, Mézières, and Bovet' (pp. 327–49). In '"I xal excusyn þe & ledyn þe a-geyn in safte": Liturgy and Authority in *The Book of Margery Kempe*' (pp. 351–67), Terri Bays works out how Margery uses the imagery and liturgy of the Corpus Christi procession as a defensive support against opposing authority on her pilgrimage to Wilsnack and as an argument towards the ideal represented in a procession. And Thomas Hahn discusses 'Christian Diaspora in Late Medieval, Early Modern Perspective: A Transcription of the Treatise *Decem nationes Christianorum*' (pp. 369–87), based mostly on one early printed text, which he also translates, briefly naming and describing Christian groups in Europe, Africa, and the Near and Far East (who could ignore Prester John?). The volume ends with brief author and subject indices.

We now turn to more focused publications. According to Stefan Jurasinski in 'The *Rime of King William* and its Analogues' (*Neophil* 88[2004] 131–44), the rhyming entry in the Peterborough Chronicle for 1087 was probably an original work and began a tradition of anti-Forest polemic. The text, here conveniently reproduced, has three difficult passages that twelfth-century analogues help to clarify: the 'frith' as a forest, excessive love of beasts as a stock motif, and the free running of hares as alluding to the conflict between hunting and agriculture. John P. Brennan asks more literally than we might suspect 'The Nightingale's Forum: A Privy Council?' (*ChauR* 38[2004] 376–82). That is, he lays out the possibility that the poet overheard *The Owl and the Nightingale* while sitting in an outhouse. The argument, brief as it is, is an attractive complement to the poem's humour. Rüdiger Spahl's 'Richard and William, or To Whom was Richard Rolle's *Emendatio vitae* Dedicated?' (*Revue d'Histoire des Textes* 32[2002] 301–12) proposes an interesting, careful argument that the work was not dedicated to any William: the address is borrowed from the *Form of Living*, it is in only six of 108 manuscripts, the name appears in only two of those six, and of those two one addresses William with plural verbs and pronouns while the other corrects the concord errors as well as much of the text otherwise.

Nicholas Perkins compares 'Reading the Bible in *Sawles Warde* and *Ancrene Wisse*' (*MÆ* 72[2003] 207–37), with the former using direct citation but relying on allusive use, more in the style of *ruminatio*, thus allowing more silent biblical support for its main theme, and the latter has more of a dialogue between the Latin and English, favours the Psalms, and uses thirteenth-century exegetical tools a bit more. A broader survey of material is Wada, ed., *A Companion to 'Ancrene Wisse'*, a collection of essays by various hands, with peculiar lacks of capitalization, as will appear shortly, and an apparent compulsion to repeat the subject work's title as if the essays were reprinted from previous publications or otherwise commissioned. The editor opens by asking 'What is *Ancrene Wisse*?' (pp. 1–28) and covering much of what a 'companion' would be expected to: content summary, style, original purpose, later readership, language, textual relationships, date, and authorship. Bella Millett concludes that 'The Genre of *Ancrene Wisse*' (pp. 29–44) is not really a Rule but simply the broader genre of 'religious writing'. Anne Savage argues for 'The Communal Authorship of *Ancrene Wisse*' (pp. 45–55) in the sense that the author had close contact and experience with his target audience and thus was responding to their real, presumably expressed, needs and interests. Richard Dance reviews the AB language and places it into a larger culture with 'The AB Language: the Recluse, the Gossip and the Language Historian' (pp. 57–82). Turning to a different language (and shifting from footnotes to parenthetical citations) is D.A. Trotter's 'The Anglo-French Lexis of *Ancrene Wisse*: a Re-evaluation' (pp. 83–101), looking at the status and function of loanwords, their number, and hybrid loanwords. A.S.G. Edwards concisely summarizes information about 'The Middle English Manuscripts and Early Readers of *Ancrene Wisse*' (pp. 103–12), and we return to footnotes for the rest of the volume (though Watson uses both).

Investigations into readership continue in the next few articles, beginning with Elizabeth Robertson, who looks again at the textual history, author's target audience, provenance, and more, with fresh eyes, in 'Savoring "Scientia": the Medieval Anchoress Reads *Ancrene Wisse*' (pp. 113–44). Catherine Innes-Parker's 'The Legacy of *Ancrene Wisse*: Translations, Adaptations, Influences and Audience, with Special Attention to Women Readers' (pp. 145–73) also looks again at the manuscripts, with forays into select themes and even reading circles. Christina von Nolcken focuses on one such adaptation in 'The *Recluse* and its Readers: Some Observations on a Lollard Interpolated Version of *Ancrene Wisse*' (pp. 175–96), extant in a unique copy previously published but insufficiently discussed; her comments on how Lollards read should be consulted in a wider context. Pulling back to look again at adaptations and particularly influences (and acknowledging the volume and at least one other article in it), Nicholas Watson looks at '*Ancrene Wisse*, Religious Reform and the Late Middle Ages' (pp. 197–226). Finally, Roger Dahood ranges about to discover one person's perceived historicity in '*Ancrene Wisse* and the Identities of Mary Salome' (pp. 227–43), Though each article has its own bibliography, there is a short 'Select Bibliography' at the end, followed by a peculiar two-page 'Index of Middle English Words' of fewer than 200 words and not going past page 97; one of manuscripts; and a short general index.

Anne. B. Thompson's *Everyday Saints and the Art of Narrative in the South English Legendary* begins by placing the *South English Legendary* in the context of roughly contemporary works of religious instruction, such as the *Ormulum*, *Cursor mundi*, and *Handlyng Synne*, and then looks at the poetic mode with a focus on how John the Baptist is handled. Since romances were a popular type of narrative, she turns to them, in the form of Mary Magdalen and Eustace (the versions in Digby 86 and the *Northern Homily Cycle* are not compared); then the liturgy and the very idea of a collection are discussed, with special attention to All Souls and the buried miner, with the *Legenda aurea* and *Handlyng Synne*. Finally, she turns to depictions of everyday women to elucidate Julian the Hospitaller and Clement, before closing with observations on social bonds as shown in scattered passages, science (St Michael, of course), and a passage in Petronella that implies the story surpasses its explication.

Joyce Coleman's 'Strange Rhyme: Prosody and Nationhood in Robert Mannyng's *Story of England*' (*Speculum* 78[2003] 1214–38) addresses some old issues about the *Chronicle* in new ways, though raising some straw men on the way. The prologue's complaint about hard language is that contemporary performers cannot handle complicated poetic forms, which Mannyng enjoys (including tail-rhyme, known as *couwee*, but see p. 1221 n. 30). If his audience were Lincolnshire gentry, these concerns and his subject would make sense as a commission where English-language texts from Scotland provided an alternative native literary venue, for which Coleman adduces some support. She shows him more pro-Scots than previously thought, clashing with his commission, just as his 'literary ambitions' clashed with its 'stylistic restraints' (p. 1235). The argument seems strained at times but should be considered thoughtfully, and it would be good to have such genius in pre-Chaucerian Middle English literature.

David Moses explains that it is Aristotelian thinking that places 'the feminine' in Book XVIII ('On Animals') of 'John Trevisa's Translation of Bartholomaeus Anglicus' *De Proprietatibus Rerum*' (*N&Q* 50[2003] 11–13). That is, a defining feature of animals is their reproductive ability; this being a corporeal element of female animals, Bartholomaeus supplied a discussion of 'the female' amid the chapters on diverse animals. Curiously, A.S.G. Edwards also returns to 'The Text of John Trevisa's Translation of Bartholomaeus Anglicus' *De Proprietatibus Rerum*' (*Text* 15[2003] 83–96), admitting a 'froideur' with its general editor long ago (p. 84). Here, he questions the choice of copy-text on the limited linguistic grounds provided and returns to the problem of matching Trevisa's translation with the Latin in only two witnesses. Reviewing how Trevisa might have been involved with the Wyclifite Bible translation, but not with how the Early and Late versions of that were made, he points out that two manuscripts (D and E) resemble an earlier, more literal translation of Bartholomaeus' Latin text, which was then revised into a smoother version, represented by the other manuscripts, though apparently with further degradation in the textual tradition. The evidence for such revision seems supported by the state of the unique manuscript of Trevisa's translation of Aegidius Romanus' *De regimine principum*.

More new work is published this year on literature and its relationships with legal or documentary environments. First, Michael Hanrahan's 'Defamation as Political Contest during the Reign of Richard II' (*MÆ* 72[2003] 259–76) looks at the uses and claims of slander in several political conflicts with an eye on literary occurrences in Thomas Usk's *Testament of Love*, and, briefly, Richard

Maidstone's *Concordia* and the 'quyting contest' in Fragment 1 of Chaucer's *Canterbury Tales*. Second, Emily Steiner's *Documentary Culture and the Making of Medieval English Literature* takes a simple observation and expands it in various directions: since documents of legal and other business natures had become familiar aspects of life by the middle of the fourteenth century, she looks at how they appear in, are reflected in, and influence the shape or content of a variety of works. Charters, related to grants and wills, as treated by Henry de Bracton's *On the Laws and Customs of England*, informed Guillaume de Deguileville's trilogy of dream visions, two of which were translated into English—the first anonymously and by Lydgate, the second by Hoccleve. The same background manifests also in the various *Charters of Christ*, some of which were done up visually to resemble charters, as a number of illustrations show. Langland's *Piers Plowman* is known to have extensive legal and documentary references, not least the Pardon, which is here read as Augustine's *chirographum dei* in his commentary on Psalm 144. The testaments, charters, and patents in Langland are met by the Langlandian works, such the letters of John Ball and *Mum and the Sothsegger*. While indulgences and letters of fraternity confirmed status within orthodoxy, the Lollards preferred to find salvation outside the institution via the Charter of Christ, which prompted orthodox responses, including Langland. But the Lollards and sympathizers continued to reject received documentary culture and even used it to further their own ends in undermining it, as Margery Baxter and William Thorpe strove to do. In contrast, Margery Kempe seems to have sought out and collected letters from the establishment not only for protection against charges of heterodoxy, but also to help establish her identity.

Lawrence M. Clopper answers 'No' to his question 'Is the *Tretise of Miraclis Pleyinge* a Lollard Tract against Devotional Drama?' (*Viator* 34[2003] 229–71), in a wide-ranging article, seemingly a reply to Ruth Nissé's 'Reversing Discipline: The *Tretise of Miraclis Pleyinge*, Lollard Exegesis, and the Failure of Representation' (*YLS* 11[1997] 163–94). The author, a secular cleric, was instead simply objecting to *ludi inhonesti*, perhaps using a Dominican preaching manual.

Material of more historical bent includes Anne Hudson's 'Notes of an Early Fifteenth-Century Research Assistant, and the Emergence of the 267 Articles against Wyclif' (*EHR* 118[2003] 684–97) on Magdalen College MS lat. 99 and the development and early history of the Articles. In 'The Island of England in the Fifteenth Century: Perceptions of the Peoples of the British Isles' (*JMH* 29[2003] 177–200), Ralph Griffiths surveys outside views of insular inhabitants, largely by Spaniards and frequently of the Scots, whose women seemed to control the household and the budget. Paul Battles finds a critique of courtly culture when comparing poems of similar themes in 'In Folly Ripe, in Reason Rotten: *The Flower and the Leaf* and the "Purgatory of Cruel Beauties"' (*MÆ* 72[2003] 238–58); the poem draws upon the *Lai du Trot*, Andreas Capellanus, and Gower's 'Tale of Rosiphelee', which present the 'PurgatoryCoss' as punishment for neglect of *carpe diem*. *The Flower and the Leaf* opposes this attitude and finds value in worthy love, not sensuality.

Coss and Keen, eds., *Heraldry, Pageantry and Social Display in Medieval England*, may seem too historical to be of literary relevance, but pageantry and social display are of obvious relevance if we just think of Lydgate's many occasional pieces. The papers find their source in a Cardiff conference. After an introduction by Maurice Keen, re-emphasizing our lip-service to visual aspects of culture and ritual because of our strong bias towards the written word, David Crouch treats the sociological study of family and how primogeniture was not a hard rule, since heraldry may well follow a matriarchal lineage to show parage, or high status via ancestors and among peers, in 'The Historian, Lineage and Heraldry, 1050–1250' (pp. 17–37). Peter Coss discusses the displays of arms—mostly in churches—and their demonstrations of lineage and relation across most of the thirteenth century, in 'Knighthood, Heraldry and Social Exclusion in Edwardian England' (pp. 39–68). Caroline Shenton surveys uses of emblematic and live big cats in 'Edward III and the Symbol of the Leopard' (pp. 69–81). Adrian Ailes provides a wealth of examples to show the use of and reaction to arms, banners, livery, and badges showing 'Heraldry in Medieval England: Symbols of Politics and Propaganda' (pp. 83–104). Frédérique Lachaud reviews 'Dress and Social Status in England before the Sumptuary Laws' (pp. 105–23), which began with Edward III, despite evidence such as the poem *On the Follies of Fashion*, to point out that social fluidity and fashion were always ahead of attempts to control dress, as they remain today.

Marian Campbell shifts the topic to 'Medieval Founders' Relics: Royal and Episcopal Patronage at Oxford and Cambridge Colleges' (pp. 125–42)—and to goldsmiths' work and textiles. Brian and Moira Gittos wonder about the causes of tomb monuments in 'Motivation and Choice: The Selection of Medieval Secular Effigies' (pp. 143–67), using a few cases to present preliminary conclusions. Nigel Saul's 'Bold as Brass: Secular Display in English Medieval Brasses' (pp. 169–94) reviews the larger questions about brasses, particularly their social distribution. In an embracive manner, Fionn Pilbrow's 'The Knights of the Bath: Dubbing to Knighthood in Lancastrian and Yorkist England' (pp. 195–218) investigates who was knighted, how, their relation to the king, and relevant social display. In 'Chivalry, Pageantry and Merchant Culture in Medieval London' (pp. 219–41), Caroline Barron links tournaments, pageants, and other displays to both religious sentiments and romance reading, but notes that the merchants were interested in the trappings of chivalry, not in becoming knights. Finally, John Watts's 'Looking for the State in Later Medieval England' (pp. 243–67) queries what the state was and how it was visually apprehended: buildings and their decor; pageantry (the argument that *Wynnere and Wastour* was for a 1352 Christmas play is repeated; Lydgate is brought up); officers and their dress; and coins, seals, and badges.

In *Mandeville's Medieval Audiences: A Study on the Reception of the Book of Sir John Mandeville (1371–1550)*, Rosemary Tzanaki reviews readers' interests and reactions to the wildly popular work, following the themes they did: pilgrimage, geography, romance, history, and theology. Verisimilitude was enhanced by apparently personal comments, insertion of details of daily life, denials of some marvels or inconsistencies, and other devices. The sources are the versions (textual and scribal), translations, selections in other works, manuscript environment, and owners and donors, and particularly the manuscript marginalia, symbols, and mark-up, such as underlining. Authorial intention evidently was not matched by later audience interest: Jerusalem was a devotional centre of pilgrimage, but the focus shifted from crusades towards missions and even simple tourism; an interest in 'a unified religious geography' (p. 20) led instead to encyclopedic lore and mounting curiosity about circumnavigating the globe; didactic interludes were borrowed for their romance elements, sacred history led to mere chronicle, and ecumenical tolerance was replaced by obsession over an 'other'. A brief discussion of the manuscripts in the various traditions is provided, with notes on marginalia and how many of each type were used for the study.

Including other medieval literatures is Theodore L. Steinberg's slim *Reading the Middle Ages: An Introduction to Medieval Literature*, which seems aimed at undergraduate students beginning a multicultural course in medieval literature and thus to correct their misconceptions, even as it often reinforces a good number. A very short introduction approaches religion and literacy briefly, including poetry, and then the book moves on to *Beowulf*, with examples of and digressions upon digressions, and a plot summary with commentary. This is followed by similar chapters on Chrétien de Troyes, Marie de France (who is immediately placed in the context of 'Medieval Women Writers' and is allotted $12\frac{1}{2}$ pages), the *Romance of the Rose* ('A Medieval "Best-Seller"'), the *Tale of Genji*, 'Jewish Literature', sagas, Dante ($15\frac{1}{2}$ pages), *Pearl* and *Sir Gawain and the Green Knight* together (a tad over 17 pages), and Chaucer (beginning with 'Chaucer's Contemporaries' and reaching 20 pages). There is much energy here and much effusiveness, as well as a wide range in reading. Another broad approach is Joel T. Rosenthal's *Telling Tales: Sources and Narration in Late Medieval England*, but this is really a group of three essays, only one being literary in character, and only because the Paston letters are often considered among late medieval English literary texts. Rosenthal actually provides a close look at three bodies of texts for social purposes: proofs of age during Richard II and Henry IV, brief legal records of usually a dozen witnesses attesting to a person's having come of age; depositions on behalf of Scrope in the Scrope-Grosvenor controversy, which arose when both appeared with the same coat of arms, and it was thus necessary to decide who had prior or more legitimate claim to those arms; and Margery Paston's letters—among the few sets of letters and documents remaining from the English Middle Ages, the Pastons' are the largest and happily have a large number from Margery: 107 out of 379 (over 28 per cent, and 21 more than her son John II, over 22 per cent). He briefly surveys her 'output', the scribes, salutations, style, closings (including signatures, postscripts, etc.), delivery, contents—how many people she corresponded with and how many she mentioned, subject material—and her will. The disparate kinds of documents, Rosenthal points out at the end, let us snoop a little on how people's lives went on, but they also showed a kind of us/them dichotomic thought process we still share; however, of the documents selected for these essays, if it were not for Margery Paston's letters the documents would show only a male world.

Elizabeth Fowler's *Literary Character: The Human Figure in Early English Writing* endeavours to detail and clarify ways to deal with literary character, working from a historically conventional understanding of how individuals act and represent various social roles, sometimes more than one at a time, and how these multiple roles can be contradictory depending on the perspectives brought to bear upon them. She has a four-part argument, each illustrated by a separate chapter on one work or figure: 'habituation' of the reader in Chaucer's Pardoner (keyed to intention), by which reading introduces the reader to various 'social persons' and their intentions; 'social bonds' on *Piers Plowman* (keyed to agency), by which the political, economic, and other relationships are laid out; 'historical time' on Skelton's 'Tunnyng of Elynour Rummynge' (keyed to value), by which a text's actions upon readers over time are examined, emphasizing how changes of social conventions over time alter the readings; and 'the polity' on Spenser's *Faerie Queene* (keyed to dominion), which seeks to link social persons with political space with geographical space. The reading of individual works is wide and deep, but the overall argument often seems allusive rather than integrated (for example, it is the reader who must figure out what 'habituation' means, after reading the introduction and a good portion of the first chapter); also, substantial portions appeared earlier as articles or parts of articles, and their integration is not complete, as evidenced by the peculiar first footnotes to the third and fourth chapters, referencing the introduction as if it were a separate work.

Several perspectives on reading medieval texts in later times are offered this year. Seth Lerer's 'Medieval Literature and Early Modern Readers: Cambridge University Library Sel. 5.51–5.63' (*PBSA* 97[2003] 311–32) reviews thirteen early printed editions of works ranging from chronicles and books of manners to Lydgate, Anthony Woodville (Earl Rivers), and Hawes from the collection of John Moore, bishop of Ely, bound together when donated in the early eighteenth century. His interest lay in the early owners and their marginalia, which provide clues to recusant readers' use more of the books than the texts, especially by the young, though for Moore the *Sammelband* was probably of collection interest for publications by Caxton and his successors. Seth Lerer continues this study of this *Sammelband* in 'English Literature and the Idea of the Anthology' (*PMLA* 118[2003] 1251–67), putting it in the context of Harley 2253 to find similarities of interpretative thought between medieval and contemporary literary thought, considering what provides a notion of a canon. Stephen Knight's *Robin Hood: A Mythic Biography* is not a fictional biography of the hero but a historical survey of the myth in its various forms. Thus the first chapter surveys the bold, doughty outlaw as found in the early ballads, plays, and references. The second views the fallen aristocrat, first depicted in the sixteenth century. In the third, the two myths are united in the eighteenth and nineteenth centuries, thanks to Ritson, and the romantics make more space for women. Finally, there are Hollywoodization, child and adolescent homosocialization, a bit of feminist fictionalization, and, inevitably, academic investigation. Helen Phillips's '"This Mystique Show": Dryden and *The Flower and the Leaf*' (*RMSt* 29[2003] 51–70) places the motifs and translation of the work in the time of the translation. And J.A. Burrow asks 'Should We Leave Medieval Literature to Medievalists?' (*EIC* 53[2003] 278–83), a retrospect of his fifty years since graduating at Oxford, noticing how the academy has separated medieval from English literature and gone on to specialize, so that a new historical approach seems to have supplanted literary criticism.

A broad look at more than just English is Brian Murdoch's *The Medieval Popular Bible: Expansions of Genesis in the Middle Ages*, originally a series of

Speaker's Lectures at Oxford in 2001–2. Covering the whole Bible in its various manifestations would be too much, but since Genesis provided a large number of stories that appeared in many popular forms Murdoch could focus upon it alone in a manageable space. Accordingly, the first chapter/lecture looks at the serpent in the Garden of Eden and at the fallen Lucifer, who were and are connected with each other in the popular imagination, despite the lack of a biblical relationship. Next is the obvious question: what did Adam and Eve do after the expulsion? This is partly answered in the many versions of the *Vita Adae et Evae*, as well as related texts. Then, there are the two Lamechs—or possibly one Lamech—henpecked, bigamist, Cain-killing, and patriarchal. Noah is known for the ark (and however many animals of whatever kind) and for wine-drunken exhibitionism, but also for his wife and even the ark-borne devil in medieval biblical texts; Murdoch stops short of treating Ham's curse in detail, since that would be too much. Can we ignore the Tower of Babel and Nimrod? Not at all, given the interesting twists in medieval versions. If pride were not enough, we could not stop without looking at trickery, typified by the tale of Jacob and Joseph and extending to the related women and stories, involving Potiphar and his wife. This is a wide-ranging book with a knack for pouncing on key passages in many works, reminding us how necessary it is to maintain a multilingual and effectively multicultural mindset.

Larger issues based on medieval England's trilingual nature are brought to the fore. First, Linda Georgianna 'Periodization and Politics: The Case of the Missing Twelfth Century in English Literary History' (*MLQ* 64[2003] 153–68) explains some of her contributions to the forthcoming first volume of the new *Oxford English Literary History*, which will embrace more of the trilingual nature of post-Conquest England. She discusses the political interpretations that used the English language to determine literary history—best typified by Scott's *Ivanhoe*, implicitly contradicted by Ker's *English Manuscripts in the Century after the Norman Conquest*—and then employs William of Monmouth's *Gesta Regum Anglorum* to reveal a different notion of English history. This article may seem short, but it is well worth the read and should foster further thought on culture in the early Middle English period. A different but related argument lies in Jeremy Catto's 'Written English: The Making of the Language 1370–1400' (*PP* 179[2003] 24–59). The multilingual skills of English writers cannot and should not be ignored, even as Latin and French influenced their style and vocabulary, but written late Middle English, he argues, 'was effectively the artificial construct of a single generation of writers' (p. 25). The learned nature of works by Chaucer, Gower, Langland, the *Gawain*-poet, Trevisa, and the Wyclifite translators implies also the learnedness of their primary readers. Catto is certain the authors were quite aware of this, which can be detected in the texts, the manuscripts, and their owners. Because the northern writers lacked the 'Westminster' and Oxonian learning, their works bore much less fruit; similarly, England's remote and provincial status delayed Continental reception and appreciation until much later. Two relevant articles also appeared in Somerset and Watson, eds. *The Vulgar Tongue: Medieval and Postmedieval Vernacularity*: first, in 'Using the *Ormulum* to Redefine Vernacularity' (pp. 19–30) Meg Worley uses an old point from Kenneth Sisam to argue that Orm's orthography is prescriptive, not linguistically descriptive, to help Anglo-Norman preachers read aloud correctly, especially emphasizing features in great flux in contemporary French; second, in '"Moult Bien Parloit et Lisoit le Franchois", or Did Richard II Read with a Picard Accent?' (pp. 132–44) Andrew Taylor uses Froissart's gift to Richard of BN fr. 831 in the context of French dialects to pose that Richard probably would have been aware of the dialectal difference.

To put English into a larger historical perspective, it may be necessary to reconsider the Statute of Pleading, as does W.M. Ormrod in 'The Use of English: Language, Law, and Political Culture in Fourteenth-Century England' (*Speculum* 78[2003] 750–87). The text differs in wording between its version in the Parliament roll and that in the statute roll, and other information implies that the source may well have been a political move in celebration of Edward III's fiftieth birthday, not petitions based on desire for change. Alternatively, judicial changes had extended civil and criminal hearings into the shires where the judicial elite of the central courts had less influence and thus could not well enforce legal French (whose date of origin is still unclear, and which is not a result of the Norman Conquest); given the need for local enforcement of peace, where 'an ostentatious use of French ... not only prevented those beyond the bench from comprehending proceedings, but also, equally significantly, undermined the authority and credibility of the county-based commissioners', English 'represented the most suitable language' (p. 771). Ormrod emphasizes that 'pleading' embraces both documentary and oral forms, and that the documentary form was expressed more precisely in French or Latin while oral debate would at times require legal precision in those languages but was otherwise easily conducted in English; indeed, French as the written language of government seems to have lasted only from the thirteenth into the early fifteenth century, but as the spoken language it seems to have been perceived as problematic. This is similar to how sermons were preached in the vernacular but were written up in Latin, in England and France. Ormrod also characterizes the Statute as part of Edward III's national policy just after a major Anglo-French war. Until the shift from French to Latin was completed, structural obstacles maintained the status quo.

Having touched on language already, we may continue briefly with a few articles more specifically on language in literary texts. Alexandra Barratt displays 'Dame Eleanor Hull: The Translator at Work' (*MÆ* 72[2003] 277–96) on the Prayers and Meditations (Meditations on the Days of the Week), published only in excerpts and in a dissertation. After summarizing what is known about Hull, Barratt carefully compares Hull's version with several Anglo-Norman texts and reveals Hull to have been sensitive, thoughtful, and evidently experienced as a translator. Mary Catherine Davidson, 'Code-Switching and Authority in Late Medieval England' (*Neophil* 87[2003] 473–86), provides a few examples of how code-switching can work to ethnic purposes, as in Pierre de Langtoft's *Chronicle*, but more frequently to establish a more authoritative identity for a speaker, as in the *Canterbury Tales* and *Piers Plowman*. Adam Miyashiro identifies as a double-bladed axe 'The Middle English Term *Bipen* in *Castleford's Chronicle*' (*N&Q* 50[2003] 5–6), from the Latin *bipennis*. And Carole Hough offers a simple and reasonable gloss for the 'papeiai in pyn' in 'A Note on Harley Lyric No. 3 Line 21' (*RES* 54[2003] 173–7): 'a parrot in a pine tree'. Previously taken as 'pain', 'pyn' as 'pine' is not really an *OED* antedating and is driven by alliteration as well as the romantic image of pines. Asking '"Aluen swiðe sceone": How Long Did OE *ælfen/elfen* Survive in ME?' (*ELN* 41[2003–4] 1–6), William Cooke examines the passages posed for 'a female elf' and concludes that all are from *elf* but for one in Layamon (line 14278).

John Frankis, in 'Layamon or the Lawman? A Question of Names, a Poet and an Unacknowledged Legislator' (*LeedsSE* 34[2003] 109–32), reviews the literary traditions for addressing people by given names, surnames, and bynames, and adds some discussion of what duties a parish priest might have actually performed, in order to note that if the poet were active early in the thirteenth century this could have been his given name, but later in that century it would have been his byname and he would have hidden his given name. James R. Sprouse describes 'The Scribal Dialect of the Bodleian Manuscript Ashmole 42' (*NM* 104[2003] 95–113), containing the Northern Homily Cycle, as coming from the north-west tip of the West Riding. Isabel de la Cruz Cabanillas briefly studies 'The Language of the Extant Versions of Rolle's *Ego Dormio*' (*ES* 4[2003] 511–19), surviving in thirteen copies in English of which she analyses eleven, to see if the scribes could be localized. Unremarkably, the manuscripts seem northern or from nearby in the Midlands, none coming from the south, perhaps due to the location of centres of book production. And Peter Grund, in 'Golden Formulas: Genre Conventions of Alchemical Recipes' (*NM* 104[2003] 455–75), analyses the linguistic components of recipes, mainly the unpublished ones in MS Corpus Christi College, Oxford, 226.

Items not seen include *RCEI* 47[2003], which contains, among other works, Graham Caie's '"New Corn from Old Fields": The *Auctor* and *Compilatour* in Fourteenth-Century English Literature', Andrew Taylor's 'Was Grosseteste the Father of English Literature?', Nicholas Watson's 'Vernacular Apocalyptic: On *The Lanterne of Liȝt*', and Jordi Sánchez Marti's 'Manchester Chetham's Library MS 8009 (Mun.A.6.31): A Codicological Description'. Unavailable for review were Jeffrey J. Cohen's *Medieval Identity Machines* and Kathy Lavezzo, ed., *Imagining a Medieval English Nation* (both UMinnP).

2. Women's Writing

The publication this year of Dinshaw and Wallace, eds., *The Cambridge Companion to Medieval Women's Writing*, marked a watershed in the study of texts associated with medieval women. This volume includes seventeen essays plus an introduction, a very detailed and useful chronology covering the years 425–1505, suggestions for further reading for each chapter, and a guide to relevant resources on the web. It is an affordable and accessible volume that will prove an invaluable teaching resource. The articles are easily digestible but are dense with scholarship. Unlike many 'companion' volumes, this book contains some high-quality, theoretically engaged research, as well as providing overviews and contextual information. As a result, it is that rare and wonderful book: a volume that undergraduate students and academics alike will find useful and stimulating. This companion is also properly interdisciplinary, with several chapters penned by historians, and a consistent awareness of the blurred boundary between history and literature. The first five chapters, grouped under the heading 'Estates of Women', cover 'Female Childhoods' (Daniel T. Kline), 'Virginities' (Ruth Evans), 'Marriage' (Dyan Elliott), 'Widows' (Barbara A. Hanawalt), and 'Between Women' (Karma Lochrie). These opening chapters discuss a wide variety of texts, both by and about women, and more generally set the scene by placing medieval women's writing in social and historical contexts. Elliott's essay, for example, draws on examples from texts such as the Paston letters, the *Canterbury Tales*, legal cases, bestiaries, the *Life of Christina of Markyate*, and *Handlyng Synne*.

Most interestingly, this volume encourages readers to consider 'women's writing' in inclusive and creative ways, by emphasizing a sense of 'women's involvement with textual culture' (introduction by Dinshaw and Wallace, p. 1). Chapter 6, for example, asks us to consider what a medieval author is, and discusses networks of textual production that included scribes, patrons, and readers. This thought-provoking essay by Jennifer Summit argues that we need to revise our sense of what constitutes 'authorship' in order to comprehend the range and diversity of women's authorial roles in the Middle Ages. This essay ('Women and Authorship') begins section 2, 'Texts and Other Spaces'. This section continues with an exceptionally sophisticated and elegant meditation on 'Enclosure', an essay that brings together Julian of Norwich's *Showings*, the idea of subjection, Hegel's *Phenomenology*, the *Ancrene Wisse*, and the work of Judith Butler. Chris Cannon focuses on the connections between enclosure and the idea of the construction of the self, producing a fascinating essay on subjectivity and anchoritic literature. The final section of the book, 'Medieval Women', also contains an essay on Julian of Norwich by Nicholas Watson, providing an excellent companion piece to 'Enclosure'. This essay on Julian also touches on ideas of self-knowledge in the text, and makes a case for her writings as some of the most ambitious and daring texts extant from this period. In addition, the essay functions as an introduction to the texts, their theology, and the context in which they were produced. Taken together, these two pieces should become central to any reading list on Julian of Norwich.

Dinshaw's essay on Margery Kempe also provides a lucid introduction to an influential woman writer, covering some of the central issues in Kempe's Book, and setting her in a variety of contexts—Lollardy, Continental women, and the writings of Julian herself. Controversially, this essay raises the possibility of reading Kempe's work in profoundly personal ways, using the 1994 novel by Robert Gluck as an example of such reading. Sarah Salih's 'At Home: Out of the House' discusses Kempe in the context of examining medieval women and their households, and this essay also includes discussion of Margaret Paston's letters. 'Beneath the pulpit', by Alcuin Blamires, sets Kempe in her relationship to the Church and to institutions, while also focusing on medieval Lollard women such as Margery Baxter and Hawisia Moon. Further expanding the perimeters of what constitutes women's writing, Sarah McNamer's chapter looks at 'Lyrics and Romances', both discussing lyrics known to have been penned by women (such as those by Elizabeth Woodville and Eleanor Percy), and also considering the possibility of female authorship of anonymous poems. The volume also includes five articles that take Continental women as their principal subject—'Heloise' (Chris Baswell), 'Marie de France' (Roberta L. Krueger), 'The *Roman de la Rose*, Christine de Pizan and the *Querelle des Femmes*' (David F. Hult), 'Continental Women Mystics and English Readers' (Alexandra Barratt), and 'Joan of Arc' (Nadia Margolis)—articles that do much to reveal the difficulties inherent in looking at medieval Englishwomen without considering their European counterparts. Overall, this volume shows a breadth of vision in its consideration of medieval women's engagement with textuality, opens up new avenues of interest, and should prompt an upsurge of interest in teaching medieval women's writing in all its diversity.

The increasing critical engagement with medieval women's letters noted here over the last two years has continued in 2003. Joel Rosenthal's *Telling Tales*, a monograph concerned with the 'concept of community and the role and construction of collective or social memory' (p. xiii), is divided into three parts that focus on 'Proofs of Age', the Scrope–Grosvenor depositions, and Margaret Paston. Rosenthal is interested in the anatomy of Margaret's letters, examining their structure and the patterns that underpin them as he seeks to reconstruct her views of her own identity. The chapter ('Margaret Paston: The Lady and the Letters') provides an interesting consideration of Margaret herself and her self-fashioning, as well as describing the style and conventions of the letters in detail. In addition, Rosenthal provides useful apparatus for studying the Pastons, as he includes a Paston genealogy and various tables about the Pastons and their letters, such as a table of 'Margaret's Letters in the Context of "Current Events" and Family Matters'.

The writing style of the Pastons is the focus of a short piece by Michiko Ogura, '*Have Do Make* and *Have Do and Make* in the Paston Letters' (*N&Q* 50[2003] 8–10) a note that compares the use of certain forms by different writers within the Paston letters. Brian W. Gastle discusses Margaret Paston in detail in his 'Breaking the Stained Glass Ceiling: Mercantile Authority, Margaret Paston, and Margery Kempe' (*SLI* 36[2003] 123–47). Gastle is concerned with the idea of the 'businesswoman' and examines a range of fascinating texts, including guild returns and wills. He suggests that Margaret Paston and Margery Kempe both use mercantile experiences to define themselves through their texts. He also points out that the two women have different strategies for their self-fashioning: one (Paston) turns to other women while the other (Kempe) turns to God. One of the moments in Margaret's letters on which he focuses is her reference to her pregnancy and to the ring she has given her husband, a moment that is also foregrounded by Carol Rawcliffe in 'Women, Childbirth and Religion in Later Medieval England' (in Wood, ed., *Women and Religion in Medieval England*, pp. 91–117). Rawcliffe also comments on Margery Kempe in her exploration of childbirth, discussing the mini-Christ dolls to which Kempe refers and also mentioning her interest in visiting the relic of Mary's smock, an item that was supposed to give relief in childbirth.

One of the most original discussions of Margery Kempe published this year is Martin L. Warren's *Asceticism in the Christian Transformation of Self in Margery Kempe, William Thorpe, and John Rogers*. A truly diachronic book, it places Kempe in fresh and interesting contexts. Intersecting with Cannon's

'Enclosure', this book argues that cenobitic asceticism produces a technology of the self that ultimately creates rather than annihilating it. Warren himself points out that 'Discussing the Book of Margery Kempe as an example of cenobitic asceticism with its emphasis on obedience, may seem unlikely at first sight' (p. 38). However, he goes on to emphasize Margery's obedience, arguing that she constructs her identity through self-emptying, masochism, and *imitatio*, ultimately finding power through obedience and subjection.

Somewhat similar concerns with examining Margery Kempe and the technology of the self can also be discerned in two articles that discuss Kempe's knowledge of Augustine's *Confessions*. In 'Did Medieval English Women Read Augustine's *Confessions*?' (in Rees Jones, ed., *Learning and Literacy in Medieval England and Abroad*, pp. 69–96), Linda Olson focuses on a particular nun's knowledge of Augustine, but also comments on Julian and Margery's engagement with the *Confessions*. Mary Morse's 'Tak and Bren Hir': Lollardy as Conversion Motif' (*MysticsQ* 29[2003] 24–41) also compares Margery with Augustine in her discussion of the idea of conversion in the *Book*. The article focuses on Lollardy as a condition that enables Margery to construct her identity, as accusation allows Margery to assert both her orthodoxy and her authority. Morse explores the way that Margery portrays herself as bringing others to Christ through her own example and through her responses to persecution. She also sets Margery in context, discussing matters such as East Anglian Lollardy and Continental beguines. The reported writings of Lollard women themselves are briefly discussed by Margaret Aston, in 'Lollard Women' (in Wood, ed., pp. 166–85), and by Ann E. Nichols in 'The East Anglian Lollards Revisited: Parochial Art in Norfolk' (*Ricardian* 13[2003] 359–70). In this interdisciplinary piece, Nichols includes some comparison of Margery Baxter's comments on icons with actual icons that she may have seen.

Margery Kempe's involvement with a decidedly non-Lollard practice, pilgrimage, is a concern of two articles published this year. Darlene M. Juschka's '"Whose Turn Is It to Cook?" Communitas and Pilgrimage Questioned' (*Mosaic* 36[2003] 189–204) contains only a little discussion of Margery herself and is more concerned with a general critique of Victor Turner's theories of liminality and pilgrimage. Leigh Ann Craig's '"Stronger than men and braver than knights": Women and the Pilgrimages to Jerusalem and Rome in the Later Middle Ages' (*JMH* 29[2003] 153–75) sets the treatment of Margery Kempe while on pilgrimage alongside evidence for the way that other fifteenth-century female pilgrims were treated. This interesting comparison involves an examination of a fifteenth-century pilgrimage account by a German friar, who comments extensively on the position of female pilgrims. The hostility experienced by Kempe and her difficulties while on pilgrimage are set in a context that allows us to see her treatment as fairly typical. The rebukes suffered by Margery, and her own rebuking of others, are the subject of Edwin D. Craun's chapter, '*Fama* and Pastoral Constraints on Rebuking Sinners: *The Book of Margery Kempe*' (in Fenster and Smail, eds., *Fama: The Politics of Talk and Reputation in Medieval Europe* pp. 187–209). Craun explains the difference between fraternal correction, and correction by superiors, arguing that Margery engages in proper fraternal correction when she reproves others, such as

Arundel's men. In contrast, the abuse that she undergoes is destructive slander, intended to attack her 'fama'.

Several other articles published this year also deal with Margery and her text. R.N. Swanson's 'Will the Real Margery Kempe Please Stand Up' (in Wood, ed., pp. 141–65) aims to fit Kempe into her contemporary spiritual world, and includes some discussion of often overlooked material such as the accounts of Lynn priory. Swanson also discusses the spirituality of the marginalized John Kempe. Henrietta Leyser's 'Women and the Word of God' (in Wood, ed., pp. 32–45) sets Margery and Julian into a *longue durée* of bookish women, discussing Anglo-Saxon women such as Leoba and Huneberc, and also commenting on women readers and book-owners. She characterizes the piety of both Margery and Julian as 'deeply bookish' (p. 42). Sarah Salih's 'When Is a Bosom Not a Bosom? Problems with Erotic Mysticism' (in Bernau, Evans, and Salih, eds., *Medieval Virginities*, pp. 14–32) questions the glib use of the word 'erotic' in a timely interrogation of critics' easy use of this term when discussing figures such as Margery Kempe. In 'Margery Kempe: An Exemplar of Late Medieval English Piety' (*CathHR* 89[2003] 1–23), Raymond A. Powell suggests that modern interpretations 'ignore Kempe's context' and her religiosity. He concludes that she is a 'typical product of late medieval English religious life'.

Another (abridged) translation of *The Book of Margery Kempe* has been published this year, edited and translated by Liz Herbert McAvoy. Margery also turns up in Rigby, ed., *A Companion to Britain in the Later Middle Ages*, in the chapters by Judith M Bennett, 'England: Women and Gender' (pp. 87–106) and by Matthew Groom, 'England: Piety, Heresy, and Anti-Clericalism' (pp. 381–95), the latter of which also mentions Julian. An article by Kim Jaehyun that focuses on Julian of Norwich and other European female mystics, 'Medieval Women Theologians' (*MEMES* 11[2003]) has appeared in Korean and has not been reviewed for *YWES*. For Terri Bays's essay on *The Book of Margery Kempe*, see Section 1 of this chapter.

Diverse medieval women writers are discussed by Felicity Riddy in 'Looking Closely: Authority and Intimacy in the Late Medieval Urban Home' (in Erler and Kowaleski, eds., *Gendering the Master Narrative*, pp. 212–28). Her fascinating examination of the household and the circumstances of urban domestic living draws on examples from texts by Julian of Norwich, Margery Kempe, Margery Baxter, and Margaret Paston. One of her most insightful points of comparison is a discussion of the fact that Baxter, Kempe, and Julian all write about defecation. Riddy links this shared specific concern with women's general involvement with tasks related to the management of the body, an intimate involvement that can implicate them in a dethronement of the patriarch. A related point is made by Liz Herbert McAvoy in her 'Monstrous Masculinities in Julian of Norwich's *A Revelation of Love* and *The Book of Margery Kempe*' (in Bildhauer and Mills, eds., *The Monstrous Middle Ages*, pp. 55–74). McAvoy here discusses the incontinence and abjection of John Kempe as something that gives Margery power. This article argues that, in both Julian's and Margery's texts, the masculine is made monstrous, and feminine 'monstrosity' is triumphant. In the same volume, Bob Mills also explores the idea of monstrosity in these two texts, suggesting that the hybridity of Christ's identity and body in both works blurs the boundary between divinity and monstrosity ('Jesus as Monster', pp. 28–54). Similar interests in the body underpin Ruth Evans's essay, 'The Jew, the Host, and the Virgin Martyr: Fantasies of the Sentient Body' (in Bernau, Evans, and Salih, eds., pp. 254–88). In the context of an article that examines the connections between host desecration stories and virgin martyr stories, Evans probes the queerness of the virgin and of the Jew, and explores aspects of Margery's *Book* such as the archbishop of York's suggestion that she might be a Jew herself.

Alongside the redoubtable new *Cambridge Companion*, other articles published this year might also encourage us to think further about the boundaries of what we consider to be women's writing. Ann L. Klinck's 'Poetic Markers of Gender in Medieval "Women's Song": Was Anonymous a Woman?' (*Neophil* 87[2003] 339–59) examines women's songs in a variety of languages, including Middle English, comparing anonymous songs with songs where the gender of the author is known. In 'The Women Readers in Langland's Earliest Audience: Some Codicological Evidence' (in Rees Jones, ed., pp. 121–31), Kathryn Kerby-Fulton discusses the six manuscripts of *Piers Plowman* that contain women's signatures or the names of women owners/readers, and also examines Digby 145, a manuscript annotated by a husband and wife team, Sir Adrian and Lady Anne Fortescue. Such work adds to our general knowledge of medieval women's complex and extensive involvement in textuality, an area that we are only just beginning to conceptualize in its richness and variety.

3. Alliterative Verse and Lyrics

Julia Boffey and A.S.G. Edwards report on 'Unrecorded Middle English Verse Texts in a Canterbury Cathedral Library Manuscript' (*MÆ* 72[2003] 49–62). Following a palaeographical description, they transcribe versions of 'St Gregory's Trental', the B-text of the 'Long Charter of Christ', and some lines of verse, portions of which appear elsewhere, as *IMEV* 1120 and *IMEV* 3805 (a secular and a religious lyric). More difficult to categorize are religious fragments of either verse or prose; the final item is *IMEV* 2523, on the Seven Deadly Sins. Boffey and Edwards consider the manuscript to be 'evidence of a modest kind of vernacular piety' (p. 60), possibly from Kent.

Ralph Hanna also presents new fragments of verse in 'Middle English Verses from a Bodleian Binding' (*BLR* 17[2002] 488–92). Some of the snippets that appear on this parchment strip are 'reminiscent' of the South English Legendary, though not from any known version of it (p. 489). One selection reminds Hanna of the Auchinleck manuscript story of the Virgin's appearance to a clerk. Linguistic analysis connects these verses to the South English Legendary, which may prove useful for studies of its 'editorial procedures' (p. 492).

George Keiser studies three sets of 'Verse Introductions to Middle English Medical Treatises' (*ES* 84[2003] 310–17). One set consists of both prologue (*IMEV* 3422) and epilogue, both ending with prayers for the salvation of pagan medical authorities, which for Keiser recalls the endings of medieval English romances: 'The writer … perceives the relation between sickness and the sick person as equivalent to that of the foe and the hero of medieval combat narratives' (p. 309). In general, these verses 'assert the value and purpose of the prose texts that follow them' (p. 316) and attest to an 'English tradition … behind … verse prologues and epilogues' in English incunabulae, rather than these simply following French models.

4. The *Gawain*-Poet

This year's contribution to scholarship on the *Gawain*-poet includes articles on *Pearl* and *Sir Gawain and the Green Knight*, and one book-length study of all four of the poems in the manuscript designated Cotton Nero A.x., Art. 3.

In 'The Axe in *Sir Gawain and the Green Knight*' (*ANQ* 16[2003] 13–18), Kathryn Walls suggests that the significance of the Green Knight's axe has not been sufficiently examined, and that it 'cries out for interpretation' (p. 13). Using an approach that combines biblical exegesis with Augustinian interpretation of Scripture, Walls argues that, although the axe is the last mentioned of all the Green Knight's accessories, it is the most important of his *accoutrements*. She contends that because it would have resonated strongly with the fourteenth-century audience of the poem, especially as an allusion to Matthew 3:10 and 12:33, the axe 'governs the action of the poem as a whole' (p. 13). In its initial appearance in the poem, the axe suggests the iconographical tradition associated with Matthew 3, in which John's warning is variously represented as a woodcutter chopping down a tree or as an axe placed next to, or hanging from, a tree. At the close of the poem, the Green Knight's third strike with the axe—that which nicks Sir Gawain's neck—suggests Augustine's interpretation of Matthew 12:33, a reading that describes men as trees and which urges men not to 'murmur against Him that chasteneth him' (*Sermons* 201). Interpreting the nick on Gawain's neck as 'chastening', Walls suggests that the two scenes including the Green Knight's axe are symbolic of Old Testament 'types' and their New Testament 'antitypes', and thus sees the logic of the entire poem as governed by the symbolism of the axe.

In 'Textual Studies, Feminism, and Performance in *Sir Gawain and the Green Knight*' (*ChauR* 38[2003] 158–77), Sharon M. Rowley focuses on an oft-explored topic in *Gawain* criticism: the interrelationship of performance and gender identity in the text. Rowley, however, contends that 'Most such analyses of performance and identity in the text … have been quietly compromised by editorial interventions in the first bedroom scene, at lines 1283–7' (p. 158). Her argument hinges specifically on various critical emendations made to line 1283, which reads in the manuscript 'Þaȝ I were burde bryȝtest þe burde in mynde hade' ('Even if I were the brightest lady, the lady thought'). Rowley argues that the majority of editorial interventions in this line function to suppress any hint that Lady Bertilak is contemplating the situation at hand, and thus render the lines that follow a comment from the narrator, rather than the inward musings of the Lady. Such an alteration calls into question whether or not Lady Bertilak has clear knowledge of the situation involving her husband and Gawain; in addition, it casts the Lady's attempted seduction of Gawain as an act that is more sincere than subterfuge. Rowley contends that many of these past editorial changes have been based on essentializing gender stereotypes. If the manuscript at line 1283 is allowed to stand without emendation, she argues, then the tension in the bedroom scenes is heightened and the audience will see the actions of both the lady and Gawain as 'convincing performances … inviting the reader to wonder all along whether either of them can really "be" who s/he claims to be' (p. 167).

Gender concerns are also present in Rhonda Knight's 'All Dressed Up with Someplace to Go: Regional Identity in *Sir Gawain and the Green Knight*' (*SAC* 25[2003] 259–84). Making use of recent intersections between postcolonial criticism and medieval studies, Knight explores how ideas about geographical place and borders inform *Sir Gawain and the Green Knight*. Using as her starting point arguments by recent critics such as Patricia Clare Ingham that *Sir Gawain* is a poem that strategically seeks to erase differences—particularly those signified by the border—Knight offers an interpretation that is the inverse: she contends that 'the poem challenges the very idea of homogeneity and … the figure of the Green Knight/Bertilak aggressively disrupts Camelot's attempts to create such an illusion' (p. 262). She goes on to examine carefully the geographical specificity of the regions described by the poet in *Sir Gawain*, particularly the Welsh border of the north-west Midlands, reading the Green Knight/Bertilak as a figure that performs the hybridity of the borderlands by deliberately juxtaposing elements of wildness and courtliness in his physical make-up. In this sense, Knight sees the courtly aspects of the Green Knight's appearance as a kind of 'drag' that both performs courtliness and calls into question courtly identity by 'overdoing' that performance. As the argument progresses, Knight pays special attention to the arming and bedroom scenes and the significance of objects like the girdle; in the end she contends that '*Sir Gawain and the Green Knight* advertises its own identity as a border text in order to show that all identities are constituted through what remains outside the borders that peoples draw or imagine around themselves' (p. 284).

David Baker's 'The Gödel in *Gawain*: Paradoxes of Self-Reference and the Problematics of Language in *Sir Gawain and the Green Knight*' (*CQ* 32[2003] 349–66) is the prize-winning essay from the 2003 Cambridge University graduate English honours examination. In this article, Baker argues that paradox is central to *Sir Gawain and the Green Knight*, and that the *Gawain*-poet deliberately introduces and cultivates paradox within the poem as part of an investigation into the ability of language to communicate. After beginning with a carefully laid foundation that explores the philosophy of a 'hierarchy in language' in the fourteenth century, Baker moves to the poem itself, examining how symbols (such as the girdle and pentangle) and language (especially self-reference and the concept of metalanguage) are used by the poet to create paradoxes, some of which the poet chooses to leave unresolved. Baker suggests that the *Gawain*-poet's 'maintenance of paradox and refusal fully to resolve it is a literary refusal to submit to medieval philosophy, and a demonstration of the problems and potential of language which impedes understanding even as it communicates truth' (p. 365).

In 'The *Pearl*-Maiden's Two Lovers' (*SP* 100[2003] 1–21) Jane Beal takes issue with the long-held assumption on the part of most critics that *Pearl* is the elegiac lament of a man (the Dreamer) for his young daughter; Beal contends that the *Pearl*-Maiden is in fact the Dreamer's lover, and furthermore, that she is also represented within the poem as the lover of Christ. Beal revisits the lines of the poem that have traditionally been read as indicating a father–daughter relationship between the Dreamer and the Maiden, arguing that the evidence for such an interpretation is at best ambiguous. She then examines two illustrations that accompany *Pearl* in the manuscript and analyses the poem in the light of Song of Songs imagery which is often found in Marian hymns; her interpretative conclusion from these investigations is that *Pearl* is a poem about a lover mourning his beloved. Beal then rereads the poem, seeing in the Dreamer's attempt to cross the stream 'a jealous act motivated by a desire to possess his beloved Pearl-Maiden, an act that is forestalled by Christ himself' and thus she concludes that 'While the Dreamer may love the Pearl-Maiden, he is compelled through his encounter with her to learn about the love of God … [and t]his knowledge transforms him from a suitor to a servant' (p. 21).

In 'Body and Soul: *Pearl* and Apocalyptic Literature' (in Jaritz and Moreno-Riano, eds., *Time and Eternity: The Medieval Discourse*, pp. 355–62), Cynthia Kraman also makes use of the Song of Songs and Marian hymns in her analysis as she tackles the question of *Pearl* and genre, noting that the poem has been variously categorized as elegy, *consolatio*, dream vision, and *disputatio*, to name just a few. Kraman argues that these generic designations are misidentifications and then sets out to prove that *Pearl* should be understood as belonging to the tradition of apocalyptic literature. Contending that the poem exists in both romance and apocalyptic time, Kraman suggests that this 'double frame gives the poem power, derived from its insistent dualism of body and soul in time rubbing against the world of unity' and further argues that an identification of *Pearl* as apocalyptic literature 'both simplifies the genre discussion and permits the reader to recognize the author's originality and skill' (p. 362).

Ann R. Meyer devotes two chapters to *Pearl* in *Medieval Allegory and the Building of the New Jerusalem*, a book that explores medieval representations of the New Jerusalem through examination of liturgy, architecture, and literature. Beginning with an investigation of the philosophical and theological foundations of the idea of the New Jerusalem (particularly the work of Plotinus and Augustine), Meyer then moves to an examination of the medieval liturgy of the Royal Abbey of Saint-Denis near Paris, a study of the architecture of private chapels, and a discussion of the effects of the chantry movement in England; she then concludes her work with an examination of *Pearl*, taking care to engage it individually and in relationship to the other poems in the Cotton Nero manuscript. In the section on *Pearl*, she argues that the *Gawain*-poet 'attempted to push the boundaries of literature beyond the spoken and the written word, to move literature aggressively into the realm of the visual, the liturgical, and the architectural' (p. 10). In chapter 5, 'Taking Allegory Seriously: Ornament as Invitation in *Pearl*', Meyer examines how the *Gawain*-poet uses poetry to display the 'mechanism' of philosophical allegory and thus creates a poem that is 'architectural' in nature. In chapter 6, '"þe new cyté o Jerusalem": *Pearl* as Medieval Architecture', Meyer treats *Pearl* as a 'literary edifice', linking it to the chantry movement and the architecture of private chapels. She argues that ultimately '*Pearl* is a "nexus" between architecture, goldsmithing, and literature, but it is at the same time a dramatization of an action that derives its eschatological force from the liturgical commemoration of the dead and a concern with the fate of the soul after death' (p. 186).

In *The Numerical Universe of the Gawain–Pearl Poet: Beyond Phi*, Edward I. Condren examines Cotton Nero A.x., Art. 3 from the perspective of medieval theories of mathematics, arguing that the manuscript 'is not an anthology of four unrelated poems. It is a single, tightly constructed artefact with four movements, each of them connected to the others by precise links that represent and attempt to resolve the central problem facing humanity' (p. 2). Condren begins by explaining the theory of the Divine Proportion (also called the Golden Mean, the Golden Section, and *phi* [ϕ]), in which when $a + b = c$, then $a : b \approx b : c \approx 1.61803$ or *phi*; Condren goes on to demonstrate how the Divine Proportion may be applied to the *Gawain*-poet's manuscript, arguing that a complex numerical design serves as the foundation and structure of each of the four poems in the codex, and explains their relationship to one another. Carefully situating his argument in terms of the disciplines of the medieval *quadrivium*, Condren examines the manuscript from a variety of perspectives, offering several charts and equations that explore the numerically structured nature of the manuscript in terms of the order of the poems, line numbers, stanzas, decorated capitals, and geometrical patterns. Condren contends that Cotton Nero A.x., Art. 3 deliberately represents two concentric rings: *Purity* and *Patience*, the two poems in the inner ring, represent the Old Testament era, while *Pearl* and *Sir Gawain and the Green Knight*, in the outer ring, represent the New Testament era. After the introductory chapters he works through the manuscript poem by poem, explicating the particular numerical structure of each and then relating these findings back to the manuscript as a whole. His text is accompanied by three appendices and a glossary to help readers negotiate what may be foreign territory for many who are more accustomed to literary analysis by means of historical context or critical theory.

5. Piers Plowman

In *Arts of Possession: The Middle English Household Imaginary*, D. Vance Smith revisits *Piers Plowman* and *Wynnere and Wastour*. Apparently an offshoot of *The Book of the Incipit*, *Arts of Possession* forms a long meditation on the ideas of possession, goods, surplus and value, rooted in literal and objective details but far-reaching in its abstract implications. The alliterative works are considered alongside romances and household accounts in order to argue that all these works show the influence of 'a particular set of problems having to do with the household' (p. 6), including calculations of capital and stock on hand, which lead to the problem of deciding 'when need is satisfied' (p. 18), a central question in *Piers*. Though references to both alliterative works appear throughout the book, chapter 3, 'The Visible Investments of Winning and Wasting', and chapter 4, 'Merchants in the Margin: Writing and the National Domestic of *Piers Plowman*', deal with them directly. In chapter 3, Smith focuses on display of status, through heraldry, clothing, and other signs of wealth and social standing, read against the backdrop of fourteenth-century Cheshire, to argue that the poem 'not only demonstrates the discursive insistence on establishing limits, boundaries, distinctions, it thematizes the very centrality of gestures of possession and their ambivalent nature' (p. 76). Chapter 4 explores Langland's problems with excess, surplus, exchange, 'chaffare', and economies, looking not at Meed but at the poet's account of his own life, Hunger's appearance in Passus VIII of the C-text, and the pardon scene.

The *Yearbook of Langland Studies* 17[2003] opens with a special section on Langland and Lollardy, with a brief introduction by Andrew Cole and articles by Derek Pearsall, Cole, David Aers, Fiona Somerset and Anne Hudson. In 'Langland and the Lollardy: From B to C' (*YLS* 17[2003] 7–23), Pearsall returns to the study of Langland's revisions, considering possible Wyclifite-influenced changes, though acknowledging that there are problems with dating 'Lollard' writings. He suggests that Langland adapted his lines on confession so as not to be thought a Lollard. Andrew Cole studies the question of what 'Lollard' means both in general and to Langland, suggesting that Lollardy and Wyclifism are two different things, in 'William Langland's Lollardy' (*YLS* 17[2033] 25–54). He proposes that the movement be known as 'Wyclifite' while 'Lollard', as a 'deeply ideological' term, should be kept for 'the complex, contradictory, yet overtly generic identities constructed by medieval witnesses' (p. 52). 'John Wyclif: Poverty and the Poor', by David Aers (*YLS* 17[2033] 55–72) begins with close consideration of Margaret Aston's 1993 essay in order to qualify her conclusions by offering nine points about Wyclif's political theology. While 'evangelical poverty' is central to Wyclif's theory of discipleship, he uses various strategies to de-emphasize this doctrine; his aim with 'evangelical discipleship' was clerical reform, which secular elites were to enforce, thus strengthening themselves 'politically and economically'. Moreover, Thomas Netter's observation that a Wyclifite reformation would 'produce … [a] "caesarean" clergy' was correct. Though Wyclif aims to improve the lot of 'poor tenants and peasants', this would happen by a 'trickle-down effect', and Wyclif did not support an end to villeinage (pp. 67–8).

Fiona Somerset argues that Langland's influence on Lollard writings shows in their use of Latin quotation, translations from Latin, and commentary on learning and 'clergy', in 'Expanding the Langlandian Canon: Radical Latin and the Stylistics of Reform' (*YLS* 17[2033] 73–92). She studies three texts to make this point: the *Lanterne of Light*, *Omnis Plantacio*, and *De Oblacione Iugis Sacrificii*. All three make their own translations from patristic writings and commentaries on the Bible, all show deep familiarity with both canon and civil law, they all use or even show their audiences how to use academic styles of argument, and they all 'have literary qualities that might surprise critics who think Wycliffite writings are strident and boring' (p. 75). Anne Hudson poses the question 'Langland and Lollardy?' (*YLS* 17[2033] 93–105). She lays out approaches that might further the investigation of this combination: an enquiry into dating 'without an underlying interpretive argument to support' (p. 94), which should be coupled with queries such as that of Cole in the same volume as to the meaning of 'loller(e)' for Langland. Only texts from the 1380 s that are not subsequently revised will be useful, Hudson warns. She considers that Langland's use of the term is 'not sect-specific' (p. 100).

Following this grouping come four more essays on *Piers*. In 'Becket and the Hopping Bishops' (*YLS* 17[2033] 107–34), Lawrence Warner reconstructs the ur-B text of XV.523–32 in order to explore Langland's association of 'titular bishops' (those ostensibly responsible for Near Eastern sees) and friars, relying on the 'rhetorical register' of his citations and language to make that connection (p. 111). Langland's admiration for Becket draws attention to his interest in '*episcopal martyrdom*, stress on both terms' (p. 115). Warner considers parallels with 'The Simonie' and the South English Legendary. Matthew Giancarlo addresses '*Piers Plowman*, Parliament and the Public Voice' (*YLS* 17[2033] 135–74), rejecting the Donaldsonian view of *Piers* as interested only in 'commune' as community rather than as the Commons of Parliament; he aims to recuperate Jusserand's reading of the significance of Langland's parliament. Giancarlo begins with Thomas Hoo's vision, invoking problems of money's proper owners and wielders; he also considers the Parliament Rolls' references to Alice Perrers; but he reads both as commenting on *Piers*, not the other way round: 'contemporary politics were performing ... what Langland had also or already scripted' (p. 164). He argues that the Meed trial must take place in parliament as a court of law, as in the fourteenth century it was.

'Retaining a Court of Chancery in *Piers Plowman*', by Kathleen E. Kennedy (*YLS* 17[2033] 175–89), looks at the trial of Peace v. Wrong to explore the 'maintenance networks' of these characters and Meed. Kennedy follows Aers in questioning what 'characters ... *need* to do ... to survive' (p. 177; emphasis Kennedy's), not just what they might wish to do. Peace, Kennedy argues, wants and receives monetary satisfaction for wrongs done him, Wrong appears to be Meed's purveyor, and the king may retain Meed along with Reason and Conscience. In 'Wasting Time, Wasting Words in *Piers Plowman* B and C' (*YLS* 17[2003] 191–202), J.A. Burrow discusses Wit's different characterizations of Dobet in Passus IX, the first of which refers to wasting speech, though the second does not. In C, references to not wasting speech or time apply to Dowel, rather than Dobet, and Langland also adds Imaginatif's warning to put aside idleness. Treatises on sloth emphasize good use of time. *Pace* Le Goff's views on the mercantilization of time in religious thought, Burrow thinks Langland has a 'theological reason' for his indictment of wasting time and words (p. 201). In *YLS*'s Forum, Traugott Lawler responds to Míceál Vaughan's criticisms of his essay in *YLS* 16 (*YWES* 83[2003] 168).

"Biddeth Peres Ploughman go to his werk": Appropriation of *Piers Plowman* in the Nineteenth and Twentieth Centuries', by Paul Hardwick, appears in Shippey, ed., *Film and Fiction: Reviewing the Middle Ages* (pp. 171–95). Hardwick briefly reviews early appreciation of *Piers Plowman* for its historical rather than literary value, then turns to a study of Langland's influence on William Morris, particularly in *News from Nowhere*. Hardwick also discusses *Long Will*, a 1903 novel by Florence Converse for older children, which portrays Chaucer, Gower, John Ball and his cronies, Langland and his daughter, Calote, in a plot organized around the Rebellion of 1381. Langland's vision offers a model for Christian socialism, 'a competitive medievalism that may challenge dominant medievalist ideology' (p. 185).

Douglas Wurtele's 'The Bane of Flattery in the World of Chaucer and Langland' (*Florilegium* 19[2002] 1–25) notes that flattery was taken much more seriously as a sin in the Middle Ages, and surveys its treatment in the Bible, Christian and Jewish biblical commentaries, and patristic writings before discussing Mede, Haukyn the Active Man, and Penetrans-Domus in the Barn of Unity (Passus II–III, XIII, and XIX). Wurtele places greatest emphasis on the last, saying that his 'mischief lies deeper than ignorance or carelessness or mere venality' (p. 9). Considering that Chaucer may have known Langland's work, he uses these explorations to explain aspects of flattery in the *Nun's Priest's Tale*. Wurtele also published 'The Importance of the Psalms of David in William Langland's *The Vision of Piers Plowman*' (*Cithara* 42:ii[2003] 15–24). Here, noting that Will earns his living by his 'seuen psalmes', he examines the passages that refer to any of the penitential psalms; six references each to psalms 31 and 50 receive most attention. Giving the line 'non intres in iudicium', originally a sinner's plea, to Christ in Passus XVIII shows Langland's 'perceptiveness into the heart of the Christological sense' of these words (p. 16); Wurtele concludes that, like David, Langland shows that 'tears of contrition can flow simultaneously with songs of joy' (p. 21).

Mary Catherine Davidson uses linguistic theory to study 'Code-Switching and Authority in Late Medieval England' (*Neophil* 87[2003] 473–86), looking at how Langland (among others) uses Latin to define in-groups. Though Mede attempts to assert her authority through Latin quotation, Conscience 'out-maneuvers' her 'by constructing her code-switch as inferior' to his own (p. 477–9). Will manages this technique more effectively in Passus XI; it can also be used to assert one's position 'against an outgroup member who is a social superior' (p. 480), as Davidson shows by examining Reason's use of Latin words and phrases in B.IV.143–5.

6. Romance

Comedy is the theme of Busby and Dalrymple, eds., *Arthurian Literature XIX*, many of the articles having been presented at the nineteenth international congress of the International Arthurian Society, in Toulouse [1999]. Two of the articles concern Malory. First, Donald L. Hoffman's 'Malory and the English Comic Tradition' (pp. 177–88) surveys many comic and possibly comic moments in Malory, from the confusing line when a crying lady is carried away by a knight—'whan she was gone the kynge was gladde, for she made such a noyse'—to its end in the 'Book of Sir Tristram' because jokes in the quest for the Grail would be indecorous. Second, Elizabeth S. Sklar's '"Laughyng and smylyng": Comic Modalities in Malory's *Tale of Sir Launcelot du Lake*' (pp. 189–98) traces Lancelot's development from fully heroic knight to the apogee of knighthood, a comic development as opposed to a tragic one. Within this movement are at least three episodes of low comedy: Sir Phelot catches Lancelot nearly naked up a tree, for which our hero must batter the lout with a branch, before scurrying off; Sir Pedyvere directs Lancelot to look the other way while he swipes off his wife's head; and Sir Belleus begins making love to Lancelot, having mistaken him for his paramour. The low comedy starkly contrasts the elegance and skill of the best of knights, mocking his perfection and drawing the almost inhuman Lancelot back towards the earth.

Most of the articles concern French romances: Elizabeth Archibald's 'Comedy and Tragedy in Some Arthurian Recognition Scenes' (pp. 1–16), mainly on French romances, but also Malory, *De Ortu Waluuanii*, German romances, and briefly *Ipomedon* and the alliterative *Morte*; Christine Ferlampin-Acher's 'Merveilleux et comique dans les romans arthuriens français (XIIe–XVe siècles)' (pp. 17–47); Angelica Rieger's 'La Bande dessinée virtuelle du lion d'Yvain: Sur le sens de l'humeur de Chrétien de Troyes' (pp. 49–64); Norris J. Lacy's 'Convention, Comedy, and the form of *La Vengeance Raguidel*' (pp. 65–75); Peter S. Noble's 'La Comique dans *Les merveilles de Rigomer* et *Hunbaut*' (pp. 77–86); Karen Pratt's 'Humour in the *Roman de Silence*' (pp. 87–103); Bénédicte Milland-Bove's 'La Pratique del "disconvenance" comique dans le *Lancelot en prose*: Les Mésaventures amoureuses de Guerrehet' (pp. 105–15); Frank Brandsma's '*Lancelot* Part 3' (pp. 117–33); and Marilyn Lawrence's 'Comic Functions of the Parrot as Minstrel in *Le Chevalier du Papegau*' (pp. 135–51). A few extend to other countries: Francesco Zambon's 'Dinadan en Italie' (pp. 153–63); Marjolein Hogenbirk's 'A Comical Villain: Arthur's Seneschal in a Section of the Middle Dutch *Lancelot* Compilation' (pp. 165–75); and Linda Gowans's 'The *Eachtra an Amadáin Mhóir* as a Response to the *Perceval* of Chrétien de Troyes' (pp. 199–20). Sadly, the volume dispenses with an index. [JL]

Geraldine Heng's *Empire of Magic: Medieval Romance and the Politics of Cultural Fantasy* is likely to be a major work in the field, which makes it a pity her writing style is not more inviting. She argues that romance was a way of dealing with cultural anxieties concerning Eastern, often Muslim, cultures. Her usual approach is to begin with a passage in a text and then open out ever more widely into cultural history. Her first chapter looks at cannibalism and giants in Geoffrey of Monmouth's *Historia Regum Britanniae*, arguing that these episodes respond to episodes of Christian cannibalism during the Crusades, which seemed fundamentally to taint Christian ideals. The next chapter looks at Richard the Lion-Hearted in romance, arguing that episodes of cannibalism have been transformed into triumphant superiority over the Islamic enemies. She then moves to the alliterative *Morte Arthure*, talking about ideals of manhood as crusading waned and commerce, even with the enemy, became more prominent (hence the giants of Genoa that fight with the pagan Romans). The last chapter looks at versions of the Custance story as ways of romancing the East which had proved unconquerable. She thus makes a valuable contribution to the study of romance, medieval colonialism, and the ways in which European authors imagined other peoples around them.

Also looking east is Carol F. Heffernan's *The Orient in Chaucer and Medieval Romance*. Invoking Said's concept of Orientalism (with surprisingly little discussion of whether it fits the medieval world) and generally treating the Islamic world as the 'Orient', she analyses both images of the East and Islamic analogues of Western works. After discussing several Chaucerian pieces from *The Canterbury Tales* and *The Legend of Good Women*, she argues that the spectre of incest haunts *Floris and Blancheflour* and that there are Eastern analogues for *Bone Florence of Rome*. A conclusion and an afterword look at East–West contacts in the Middle Ages and the Renaissance.

Richard Moll's *Before Malory: Reading Arthur in Later Medieval England* is a welcome study of English writings about Arthur, especially in the chronicle tradition, and how writers debated which parts of the Arthurian tradition were genuinely historical and which were fabrications. He looks at works including Robert Mannyng's chronicle, Sir Thomas Gray's *Scalacronica*, John Trevisa's *Polychronicon,* Andrew Wyntoun's *Gret Gest of Arthure*, the alliterative *Morte Arthure*, *The Awntyrs of Arthure*, *Sir Gawain and the Green Knight*, John Hardyng's and Robert of Gloucester's chronicles, and the prose *Brut*.

D. Vance Smith looks at questions of ownership in *Arts of Possession*. He argues that managing awkward surpluses, from greedy accumulation to multiplying liveries provided by ambitious lords to concealing wealth to evade the distraint of knighthood, was a prevalent social concern reflected in romances. He consistently invokes both Marxist and Freudian analyses of excess and surplus to look at a variety of social phenomena, from heraldry and merchants' marks to household management. Medieval works studied include *Wynnere and Wastour*, *Piers Plowman*, *Sir Launfal*, and the alliterative *Morte Arthure*.

Laura D. Barefield examines the role of gender in historiography and associated romances in *Gender and History in Medieval Romance and Chronicle*. Her basic argument (often oversimplified) is that plain, paratactic history (which includes fabulous histories) is held together by a simple genealogical succession of father to son. Romances, or inserted sections tending toward romance, deal with interruptions or complications of this easy scheme and can highlight the role of women, good or bad, and the stylistic tendency towards hypotaxis reflects the complications. Chapters deal with Geoffrey of Monmouth's *Historia Regum Britanniae*; Nicholas Trevet's *Les Chronicles*, female patronage, and the Custance tale; and *Sir Gawain and the Green Knight* and the prose *Brut*.

Derek Pearsall provides a summary of the Arthurian literary tradition in *Arthurian Romance: A Short Introduction*. Concerned with background rather than analysis, the book has chapters on the early British tradition through Layamon; Chrétien de Troyes; the European tradition, including the Vulgate Cycle, Wolfram von Eschenbach, Hartman von Aue, and Gottfried von Strassburg; Arthur in Ricardian England; Sir Thomas Malory; Arthur in England from the Renaissance through Victoria; and American versions of the legend.

Scott Kleinman, 'The Legend of Havelok the Dane and the Historiography of East Anglia' (*SP* 100[2003] 245–77). Gaimar based some elements of the story on local historical literature, including Scandinavian, and later writers used the same tactic in turning Havelok into a local legend. [JL]

K.S. Whetter uses *Havelok* to explore the problems of defining romance in '*Gest* and *Vita*, Folktale and Romance in *Havelok*' (*Parergon* 20[2003] 21–46). He argues that a series of adventures strongly influenced by love is enough to characterize romance, and that aristocratic chivalry is not a necessary component of the definition.

Alison Wiggins '*Guy of Warwick* in Warwick? Reconsidering the Dialect Evidence' (*ES* 84[2003] 219–30. Whatever the Earls of Warwick may have wished, the A-redaction evidently had its origins in London, though the early textual tradition seems to have had a Warwickshire or Shropshire influence. [JL]

In 'Laȝamon or the Lawman? A Question of Names, a Poet, and an Unacknowledged Legislator' (*LeedsSE* 34[2003] 109–32), John Frankis argues that the possibility that Laȝamon is a professional name rather than a personal one cannot be ruled out. In consequence, one candidate for authorship is William, rector of Areley, suggesting a slightly later date and different social milieu for the poem than usually ascribed. Tamar Drukker's 'Thirty-three Murderous Sisters: A Pre-Trojan Foundation Myth in the Middle English Prose *Brut* Chronicle' (*RES* 54[2003] 449–63) surveys themes such as subjugation, liberty, just rule, female founders, and giants in homelands to be gained in the *Brut*'s prologue and other works. Married to kings they feel are beneath their station, Albina and her younger sisters kill their husbands, are exiled, found Albion, and produce the giants Brutus must later overcome. Drukker is also at pains to discuss why the narrator does not blame them for what could have been taken as various offences.

Stephen Kelly and Jason O'Rourke lay out the beginnings of an ambitious project to analyse the history of the *Brut* chronicles in 'Culturally Mapping the English *Brut*: A Preliminary Report from the "Imagining History" Project' (*JEBS* 6[2003] 41–60). Interested in exploring medieval senses of ethnic and national identity, especially with regard to relations between England and Ireland, the members of the project are analysing the *Brut* tradition to see where manuscripts were produced, who read them, who copied them, and how the texts helped shape regional identities. They hope to achieve book and article publications as well as a scholarly website making this information generally available (http//www.qub.ac.uk/en/trads/imagining-history/index.htm).

Sarah McNamer lays out the evidence for female readership of romances in the chapter 'Lyrics and Romances,' (in Dinshaw and Wallace, eds., 195–209), arguing that, while noble women remained interested in French romances, later romances in English show a shift toward increasingly masculine audiences. Noting that *gestes* might be sung as well as read or recited, Karl Reichl tries to estimate what kind of performances such singing might involve in 'Comparative Notes on the Performance of Middle English Popular Romance' (*WF* 62[2003] 63–81). Drawing on the scanty medieval evidence and observation of modern Kirghiz and Turkoman performances, he speculates that the melodies would have been simple but that the music would be important, not merely emphasizing parts of the action, and that bad poetry could nonetheless have been part of good performances. In '*The Awntyrs off Arthure at the Terne Wathelyne*: Reliquary for Romance' (*ArthL* 20[2003] 103–22) Krista Sue-Lo Twu argues that the poem is unified by King Arthur's attempt to regulate violence, from hunting to duelling, and the ultimate failure his kingdom faces as human passions and displacements cannot be held in check for ever.

Andrew R. Walkling's 'The Problem of "Rondolesette Halle" in *The Awntyrs off Arthure*' (*SP* 100[2003] 105–22) accepts the identification of this as the medieval 'Randulph Seat' (now just Seat), and discusses its use in the poem as a literary and structural device, with 'Halle' meaning the temporary structure, pavilion, or even tent, not a modern hall. [JL]

Dinah Hazell's 'The Blinding of Gwennere: Thomas Chestre as Social Critic' (*ArthL* 20[2003] 123–43) argues that *Sir Launfal* is a social critique highlighting the moral responsibilities (especially *trouthe*) of individuals in a just society, and that Gwennere's blinding is a necessary response to a woman who will not see others' worth or her own faults. Richard Horvath looks at the social consequences of speech in 'Romancing the Word: *Fama* in the Middle English *Sir Launfal* and *Athelston*' (in Fenster and Smail, eds., pp. 165–86). Both poems show the importance of language as constituted of speech acts, creating and shaping events instead of simply reporting them. The awareness of the power of language is not just social commentary but an awareness of the literary powers of romance.

In 'Rebelling Daughters and Rotten Chickens: Gender and Genre in Caxton's *Paris and Vienne*' (*M&H* 29[2003] 81–102), Harriet Hudson continues the recent trend of examining how romances appealed to female readers. In this one, though Paris is the one who falls in love first, it is Vienne who acts assertively, not he. Her behaviour does not wholly contrast the paradigms of obedience and chastity evidenced in other works and in the Paston women, yet her independence and initiative set her apart from the usual passivity. She is able to overcome her father's objections to her marriage to a man of lower social class, suffering imprisonment and his banishment until he returns, disguised as a Moor now in her father's favour. Until Paris reveals himself, she has forestalled marriage by placing rotten hens' parts in her armpits, using the tactic to claim she is severely diseased. These ruses and even their speech habits employ and subvert various conventions of gender and genre. [JL]

Nicole Clifton considers '*Of Arthour and Merlin* as Medieval Children's Literature' (*Arth* 13[2003] 9–22) in part because of the editorial changes from the Old French original, but mostly for how the adaptations are designed to appeal to children, even with parental oversight. That is, it prefers action to thought in shortened form, its repetition helps them learn, and its themes treat issues of families, inheritance, fairness, unselfishness, and the ability to prevail when not expected to. Nicole Dentzien traces the German Arthurian literary tradition of a bridge that causes dishonourable men and women to fall in 'Hans Sachs's Arthurian Chastity Test' (*Arth* 13[2003] 43–65). She argues that a later, 'Renaissance', version emphasizes the personal over the collective, and she includes a translation of Sachs's poem.

John William Sutton interprets literally 'Mordred's End: A Reevaluation of Mordred's Death Scene in the Alliterative *Morte Arthure* (*ChauR* 37[2003] 280–5), in that the *fente* Arthur raises to stab Mordred is a flap in the armour covering his backside. The stab, then, parallels that traditionally given to Edward II, and is an emasculating retribution for Mordred's having children with Gaynor and symbolically castrating Arthur by wounding him in the *felettes*. [JL]

James T. Bracher has found 'A Mexican Analogue of *The Carl of Carlisle*' (*ChauR* 37[2003] 286–92). Though the tale is more like an exemplary

Bildungsroman, both share elements such as the Imperious Host, who is or seems supernatural, tests of self-control, and the display of the skeletons of those disobeying the host. Helen Cooper discusses medieval English (and Scottish) translations from the *Lancelot–Grail Cycle* in 'The *Lancelot–Grail Cycle* in England: Malory and his Predecessors' (in Dover, ed., *A Companion to the 'Lancelot–Grail Cycle'*, pp. 147–62). A complementary chapter in the same book is Roger Middleton's 'Manuscripts of the *Lancelot–Grail Cycle* in England and Wales: Some Books and their Owners' (pp. 219–35), focusing on manuscripts in French.

Finally, though the text is not in English, Ad Putter restores an amazing story in 'King Arthur at Oxbridge: Nicholas Cantelupe, Geoffrey of Monmouth, and Cambridge's Arthurian Foundation Myth' (*MÆ* 72[2003] 63–81). In the early fifteenth century, Nicholas Cantelupe (d. 1441) composed a 'prodigiously fantastical' *Historiola de antiquitate et origine almae et immaculatae Universitatis Cantebrigiae*: outside Athens, Cambridge has the oldest institution of higher learning, given liberties and privileges by many ancient popes and kings, including King Arthur, whose charter was also invented. Putter lays out the situation underlying the plausibility of such a concept—we must remember that Geoffrey of Monmouth was considered a reliable historian, for example (and there is a Spanish connection). In 529, King Arthur appoints one Kynot as Proctor (Geoffrey has a Kinocus promoted to a higher dignity), and on 7 April 531 sends him a charter via Gawain (who also delivered Arthur's challenge to Lucius Hiberius). Sadly, after Arthur's death the barbarians sack Cambridge, but it is restored by King Æthelbert of Kent. The *Historiola* was copied for the university's records, Lydgate mined it for his 'Verses on Cambridge', and Oxford was keen to prove itself the elder. Our understanding of facts and proper argumentation have changed, so what Cantelupe, his contemporaries, and early followers believed simply is not shared by us. [JL]

7. Gower, Lydgate, Hoccleve

(a) Gower

The second volume of the *Confessio Amantis*, edited by Russell A. Peck, with Latin translations by Andrew Galloway, contains Books 2, 3, and 4 (see *YWES* 81[2000] 204 for the first volume). The text is presented with unkeyed marginal glosses for difficult words or phrases and footnotes for translations of the Latin verses and occasional difficult passages in the vernacular. However, Gower's Latin marginalia are relegated to the explanatory notes at the end, so the text read is still not quite what Gower intended; at least their location is signalled by a pointing hand. Changes of speaker are indicated by bold face in the line-numbering columns (so **Confessor**, **Amans**, **Opponit Confessor**, and **Confessio Amantis**); lapses in signalling changes are supplied in brackets. The introduction discusses the structural aspects but also devotes space to dramaturgy, setting, and rhetorical patterning, followed by a selected bibliography and an enlargement of Bodley 902's miniature with Amans confessing. The textual notes are minimal, as seems normal in editions for student use.

Martin J. Duffell and Dominique Billy's 'From Decasyllable to Pentameter: Gower's Contribution to English Metrics' (*ChauR* 38[2004] 383–400) analyses Gower's ten-syllable lines and places them in the context of French *vers de dix*, Italian *endecasillabo*, and Chaucer's iambic pentameter to conclude that Gower was experimenting with iambic pentameter before Chaucer and went further after Chaucer brought news of the *endecasillabo* back from his Italian trip. Since Gower's verse was much more regular than Chaucer's, it is clearer that the origins of iambic pentameter belong to the fourteenth century, and Gower's contribution is as great as Chaucer's.

We may assume we know how Gower was read, but do we have any evidence for our assumptions? In 'Lay Readers and Hard Latin: How Gower May Have Intended *Confessio Amantis* To Be Read' (*SAC* 24[2002] 209–35), Joyce Coleman begins by reviewing how the apparently most likely audience would not have been able to get through the Latin verses and glosses, if we assume private reading. The English is patently transparent, the Latin glosses moralize and summarize, and the Latin verses resemble those created for public displays of virtuosity; therefore, if Gower were assuming a public reading by a skilled clerk, that clerk would have an easy text to read, along with sufficient commentary material and occasional shifts from low or middle style to the high style of the Latin, which the reader might translate to show his skill. The reading could change from one time to another, following the reader's and the audience's thoughts on a script prepared for multiple performances. A different approach to his Latinity and its purpose is Sîan Echard's 'Gower's "bokes of Latin": Language, Politics, and Poetry' (*SAC* 25[2003] 123–56), which looks primarily at how the *Vox clamantis* and *Cronica tripertita* display his stance towards language and how his use of Latin is a considered one rather than a reliable stand-by, and which suggests that an evolutionary assumption that his English was the crowning development misses the mark. That is, his language is closely related to his political intentions, and both intertwine with poetics.

Two further interpretative articles have appeared. First, Diane Watt's 'Oedipus, Apollonius, and Richard II: Sex and Politics in Book 8 of John Gower's *Confessio Amantis*' (*SAC* 24[2002] 181–208) is a complicated enquiry into why Gower revealed himself to Amans and why the work ends with incest. Her answer involves seeing both Amans and Apollonius as representing Richard II, who has not sufficiently learned from counsel about abuse of power. By identifying himself thus as adviser to the king, Gower reveals his own failure. The need to contain female desire is contrasted with the unnatural, uncontrolled lusts that lead to incest, a failure of the male to rule his passions or follow external counsel. Second, Candace Barrington looks at a renaissance reader in '"Misframed Fables": Barclay's Gower and the Wantonness of Performance' (*Medievalia* 24[2003] 195–225). He declined a commission to revise the *Confessio Amantis* not because of the content of some of the tales, but because in the whole 'Some processes appere replete with wantonnes', referring to the aspect of performance, specifically age acting like youth or a priest acting like a courtier or soldier, and suggesting that his patron's exemplary life should match the verse. Taking the Field of Cloth of Gold as the most visible instance of ostentatious display, Barrington reviews contemporary criticism of it and presents Alyngton

(Barclay's instigator) and Richard Grey (earl of Kent and the 'instance' of Pynson's publishing Barclay) as positive and negative exempla for Barclay's argument.

Unavailable for review was Diane Watt's *Amoral Gower: Language, Sex, and Politics* (UMinnP).

(b) Lydgate

It was not a busy year for the Monk of Bury. In 'The Art of History Writing: Lydgate's *Serpent of Division*' (*Speculum* 78[2003] 99–127), Maura B. Nolan argues that the problem with the poem is 'its attempt to use art to think history' (p. 101). Surveying Lydgate's actual and allusive sources, she finds him struggling among choices for varied facts, choosing to present his moral argument through the esteem bestowed upon his auctors. The concept of the world divided and seen as such through historical retrospective is taken from Gower's *Confessio Amantis*, best seen in Nebuchadnezzar's dream. When Lydgate adds to his sources, he does so to moralize through making the tale of Caesar relevant to the British (the duke of Cornwall betrays his king by allowing Caesar to land) and by discussing philosophically three causes for the destruction of Rome, although two of them are contradictory.

Robert R. Edwards's 'Translating Thebes: Lydgate's *Siege of Thebes* and Stow's Chaucer' (*ELH* 70[2003] 319–41) makes the point that Stow's 1561 editorial treatment of the *Siege* enhances it as a political statement about 'the persistent, unresolved claims of succession and process' lying beneath 'a myth of urban harmony' (p. 329), emphasizing the legitimacy of power in the nation, outside the state and ruler. Placing the Monk of Bury's work alongside Chaucer's even implicitly legitimized it for perusal.

Robert Epstein, 'Lydgate's Mummings and the Aristocratic Resistance to Drama' (*CompD* 36[2002–3] 337–58), principally uses the *Mumming at Hertford* to point out that the mummings were more like masques than dramatic texts, and that their relationship with the audience (here, mainly the 5-year-old Henry VI) is key to understanding them. Drama may have been too base and playful for the aristocratic circle, but the political subject allowed for some self-aggrandizement. It is not clear how a rustics' battle of the sexes 'could be dangerous if it fell into the wrong hands' (p. 353), but the nature of the mumming made it 'impossible to restage' because of how their original performances are built into their texts.

(c) Hoccleve

It was a also poor year for our mad beggar. Rather than place him with Lydgate or Chaucer, Robert Epstein's 'Prisoners of Reflection: The Fifteenth-Century Poetry of Exile and Imprisonment' (*Exemplaria* 15[2003] 159–98) places him together with Ashby in a contrast with James I and Charles d'Orléans to examine how identity or subjectivity are rendered by poets of different classes who were subjected to physical or mental constraint. The *Kingis Quair*, Charles's poems, and even those ascribed to the duke of Suffolk show their aristocratic authors as autonomous, with a unified subjectivity, while that of the non-aristocratic servants is more clearly contingent and far less autonomous. In '"I this book shal make": Thomas Hoccleve's Self-Publication and Book Production' (*LeedsSE* 34[2003] 133–60) David Watt reminds us that Hoccleve was involved in book production, and then uses that information to indicate how Hoccleve's experience affected his creative work, notably 'Learn to Die' as in the *Series*. See also Jeremy Tambling's 'Allegory and the Madness of the Text: Hoccleve's *Complaint*' (in Lawton, Scase, and Copeland, eds., pp. 223–48), briefly described in Section 1 of this chapter.

8. Malory and Caxton

Two books on Sir Thomas Malory's *Le Morte Darthur* were published in 2003. Raluca Radulescu's *The Gentry Context of Malory's 'Morte Darthur'* argues that Malory's work grew out of the gentry communities of fifteenth-century England, and thus that it must be looked at specifically in a gentry (as opposed to a generalized aristocratic) context. By analysing chivalric miscellanies and collections of letters (such as the Pastons'), she establishes certain characteristic attitudes towards notions of honour, fellowship, and love that also appear in Malory. Rather than an attempt to provide a new interpretation of *Le Morte Darthur* as a whole, she is instead interested in views of good behaviour and appropriate political structure as they appear in sections of the text, especially the 'Trystram' and later.

Dorsey Armstrong's *Gender and the Chivalric Community in Malory's 'Morte d'Arthur'* reads Malory's work as a whole, arguing that evolving gender dynamics connect the various sections. Her focus is on gender, understood not simply as analysing individual male or female characters but rather as abstract, mutually dependent abstractions of what masculinity and femininity should be. The Round Table oath establishes a pattern in which a vigorous, heroic masculinity is motivated by and thus dependent on a defence of a weak, vulnerable feminine—knights need damsels to rescue. At first successful, this model of gender relations causes increasing conflicts as it is unable to handle assertive women, some forms of masculine rivalry, and even marriage, which can remove much of a knight's motivation for adventure and thus for masculine self-assertion. Armstrong works her way systematically through the *Morte Darthur*, showing how gender dynamics change as the book progresses. Her focus on gender is thus valuable not only in its own right but as a fresh angle on the old debate over unity.

Similar in argument is Armstrong's 'Gender, Marriage, and Knighthood: Single Ladies in Malory' (in Amtower and Kehler, eds., *The Single Woman in Medieval and Early Modern England: Her Life and Representation*, pp. 41–61). She argues that, while the ostensible purpose of courtship is marriage, marriage ends a knight's career, while trying to win a lady enhances it. Launcelot's service of an already-married woman provides one way out this dilemma, but because his prowess provokes him to serve other ladies, growing tensions result.

Susan E. Murray argues, in 'Women and Castles in Geoffrey of Monmouth and Malory' (*Arth* 13[2003] 17–41), that castles symbolically anchor literary landscapes, and that, despite their mainly masculine inhabitants, they are often strongly associated with female bodies that reflect social values, values violated in the rape of Igrayne and the story of the sick lady who must receive blood from a royal virgin to be healed.

Arthuriana has had two special issues on Malory. In 'Rhetorical Approaches to Malory's *Le Morte Darthur*' (*Arth* 13:?[2003]), after the introduction by Ann Dobyns and Anne Laskaya urging rhetorical study of Malory (*Arth* 13[2003] 3–9), Lisa Robeson analyses Malory's rhetorical approaches to violence in 'Noble Knights and "Mischievous War": The Rhetoric of War in Malory's *Le Morte Darthur*' (*Arth* 13[2003] 10–35). She argues that, like many other late medieval texts, there is a tension in the *Morte Darthur* between recognition that war, viewed as combat among masses of men, is horrible and destructive and deep appreciation of the courage and glory of individual men in honourable combat. While through most of the book Malory focuses on the individual, obscuring the links that lead from personal chivalry to war, in the story of Arthur's fall Malory makes visible how personal concerns lead to war in all its horror.

In 'Malory and Fifteenth-Century Political Ideas" (*Arth* 13[2003] 36–51), Radulescu argues that fifteenth-century chronicles praise kings for listening to council, resolving disputes among his subjects, and rewarding faithful service, and that Malory draws on this to show Arthur at his most successful, ruling accordingly but falling away from this, failing to resolve key disputes and then lashing out at Guinevere and Launcelot despite the advice of senior counsellors.

D. Thomas Hanks turns away from the familiar binary of romance and chronicle to suggest that Malory's 'Gareth' draws on the rhetorical patterns of folk tales. In 'The Rhetoric of the Folk Fairy Tale in Sir Thomas Malory's *Tale of Sir Gareth*' (*Arth* 13[2003] 52–67), he lays out the case for regarding the *Gareth* this way and then extends his argument to suggest that Malory's treatment of the whole work, especially Arthur's death, is likewise influenced by folk tale and thus concerned with individual men gaining perfect success (as opposed to more generalized political and social commentary).

In 'Elaine's Epistolarity": The Fair Maid of Astolat's Letter in Malory's *Morte Darthur*' (*Arth* 13[2003] 68–82), Georgiana Donovin uses medieval letters and theories of letter-writing to look at Elaine's deathbed letter to Launcelot, arguing that the letter, different in certain respects from the letters knights send each other, is crucial in developing a sense of Elaine's character and a feminine view of a largely masculine world.

The final essay in this issue is Kenneth J. Tiller's '"So precyously coverde": Malory's Hermeneutic Quest of the *Sankgreal*' (*Arth* 13[2003] 83–97). In it, he argues that Malory deliberately mixes several modes of interpretation, from the most secular chivalric systems to sophisticated allegorical modes, to show how much experience depends on the ways in which individuals interpret signs, texts, and experiences. He privileges neither the secular nor the allegorical to complicate his source's confident exclusion of knightly hermeneutics in favour of allegory. Instead of simply revealing religious doctrine, therefore, Malory's Grail quest explores ways of knowing.

The second special issue dedicated to Malory, 'Reading Malory Aloud, Then and Now' (*Arth* 13:iv[2003]), includes a CD of Malory being read aloud. Karen

Cherewatuk's introduction, 'An Introduction to Aural Malory: Sessions and Round Tables' (*Arth* 13[2003] 3–13) explains the process that led to the recording and the special issue.

Jeanette Marshall Denton's 'An Historical Linguistic Description of Sir Thomas Malory's Dialect' (*Arth* 13[2003] 14–47) both discusses the characteristic orthographic forms of Malory's dialect and reconstructs how he was likely to have pronounced what he wrote. Since he wrote seventy years after Chaucer and was raised to the north and west of London, Malory's dialect differs substantially from Chaucerian English.

In 'Reading Malory in the Fifteenth Century: Aural Reception and Performance Dynamics' (*Arth* 13[2003] 48–70), Joyce Coleman argues that *Le Morte Darthur* would probably have been read aloud within households. She does her best to reconstruct the details of such readings and how they might have affected the reception of Malory's work.

Malory's style functions better aurally than visually, Rosamund Allen claims in 'Reading Malory Aloud: Syntax, Gender, and Narrative Pace' (*Arth* 13[2003] 71–85). While Malory's style is predominantly paratactic, he controls the rhythm and speed of reading, often switching to a more subordinated style in speech (especially reflective speech), and such speeches are often in the mouths of women.

Janet Jesmok focuses more on sound than on syntax in her 'Reading Malory Aloud: Poetic Qualities and Distinctive Voice' (*Arth* 13[2003] 86–102). Malory consistently uses sound effects, from alliteration to onomatopoeia, and reading aloud heightens appreciation of these effects. His dialogue—both its words and its silences—characterizes his protagonists effectively when read aloud, particularly when read by more than one reader.

Michael W. Twomey argues, in 'The Voice of Aurality in the *Morte Darthur*' (*Arth* 13[2003] 103–18), that the uniformity of Malory's style is related to being read aloud; while it sacrifices technique to the sharp distinguishing of characters, the repetition of word and structure aids memory and holds a long work together in the hearer's mind. D. Thomas Hanks, one of those responsible for beginning the project on reading Malory aloud, ends the issue with an epilogue, 'Malory's *Morte Darthur* and "the Place of the Voice"' (*Arth* 13[2003] 119–33), in which he reiterates all that is to be learned from reading Malory aloud and urges readers to hear and speak the text as well as simply looking at it.

Rebutting attempts to find explicit political passages in *Le Morte Darthur* is Edward Donald Kennedy's 'Malory's *Morte Darthur*: A Politically Neutral Adaptation of the Arthurian Story' (*ArthL* 20[2003] 145–69). While comfortable imagining the imprisoned Malory trying to please Edward IV, who had shown a taste for chivalric histories, Kennedy points out that in uncertain times a prisoner would have been foolish to comment on current disputes, and he shows that many of the references, geographical and otherwise, that have been suggested as references to current events are in fact found in Malory's sources well before those events had occurred.

Jane Bliss examines the tension between human will and destiny in 'Prophecy in the *Morte Darthur*' (*Arth* 13[2003] 1–16). She argues that the multiple prophetic voices, coupled with the removal of some of the allegorical and theological structure of the prophecies about Arthur being punished for sin, result in prophecies that serve less to illuminate a clear divine plan and more to highlight the human struggle against forces that may be irresistible, that might be divine, or that might simply be fate.

Felicia Ackerman writes on philosophical and practical elements of the Round Table oath as a warrior code in '"Never to do outrageousity nor murder": The World of Malory's *Morte Darthur*' (in French, ed., *The Code of the Warrior: Exploring Warrior Values Past and Present*, pp. 115–37). Although not completely logically consistent (for instance, the commands to serve justice and to protect ladies are contradicted in cases of evil women), and although the knights that follow it are impetuous, emotional, and not very analytical, the code proves to do well enough, she argues. Kenneth Hodges, in 'English Knights, French Books, and Malory's Narrator' (*FCS* 28[2003] 148–72), argues that Malory uses a naive narrator and dramatizes differences in genre and style among his sources to reveal disagreements over chivalric values among the various chronicles and romances.

Bonnie Wheeler focuses on masculine grief and failure in 'Grief in Avalon: Sir Palomydes' Psychic Pain' (in Vaught and Bruckner, eds. *Grief and Gender, 700–1700*, pp. 65–77). Instead of lamenting comrades' deaths or misfortunes, Palomides laments his status, rare in *Le Morte Darthur*, of a good knight who frequently loses, falling short of complete victory, romantic triumph, and religious fulfilment. Unlike Kay or Dinadan, he is not unworthy or comic; but he must mourn his own state of being almost great.

Malory scholars will probably be interested in Dover, ed., *A Companion to the 'Lancelot–Grail Cycle'*. The work has twenty-one essays (including one select bibliography) divided into three sections: 'The *Lancelot–Grail Cycle* in Context', 'The Art of the *Lancelot–Grail Cycle*', and 'Posterity'. The last section includes an essay by Helen Cooper, 'The *Lancelot–Grail Cycle* in England: Malory and his Predecessors' (pp. 148–62). The first half of the essay lists translators before Malory, pointing out that they chose material early in the cycle, generally excluding both Lancelot and the Grail to focus on Merlin or Joseph of Arimathea as an apostle. Having established that Malory's translation was therefore new, she briefly documents what and how he translated, and discusses the cumulative effect of his changes.

Finally, two articles deal with the publication history of *Le Morte Darthur*. Manabu Agari's 'Linguistic Layers in Caxton's Malory' (*PoeticaJ* 59[2003]), building on the well-tested hypothesis that Caxton edited an earlier version of Malory to produce his printed edition, tries to distinguish the linguistic habits of the compositors from Malory's practice and Caxton's editing. An increase in Latinized spellings towards the end suggests that compositors drifted towards their own usage, which was similar to Caxton's. Yu-Chiao Wang provides an interesting analysis of the woodcuts of St George on the title pages of William Copland's and Thomas East's editions of Malory (1557 and 1582, respectively). In 'William Copland's and Thomas East's Promotional Strategies for the *Morte Darthur*: A Study of the Origins, Forms, and Contexts of their Title Pages' (*JEBS* 6[2003] 77–92), Wang argues that Copland used the St George as part of a strategy to survive Mary's re-establishment of Catholicism by printing pre-Reformation texts with religious overtones. George was an obvious candidate, not only for his martial and national associations, but because Edward VI had opposed his cult. East, printing during Elizabeth's reign, used a similar woodcut not for Catholic sympathizers but because the queen had made Garter ceremonies very public, and George was the patron saint of the Order of the Garter.

9. Middle Scots Poetry

This section covers work published in 2002 and 2003. In Michael Cornelius's article 'Robert Henryson's Pastoral Burlesque "*Robene and Makyne*"' (*FCS* 28[2002] 80–96), Cornelius argues that Henryson's *Robene and Makyne* is not, as some critics have argued, an anomaly in his canon of work. Despite its somewhat bawdy subject matter, the poem can be reconciled with Henryson's more moralistic poetry if seen as a 'literary experiment' of Henryson's, one that attempts to both 'burlesque' and 'satirize' different genres. Cornelius goes on to argue that the poem is a burlesque of five separate poetic genres: the courtly romance, the *pastourelle*, the *carpe diem* poem, the elegy, and the 'popular medieval convention of women wanting to rule men'. While Cornelius does a good job explaining the poem in the light of the first three genres, he seems to force it into the category of 'elegy', and while his last category is certainly an important trope in some medieval literature, Cornelius does not convince his audience that it can be considered a 'genre' worth exploiting. Overall the article is an interesting overview of the genres and how they may intersect with *Robene and Makyne*, but ultimately Cornelius falls a bit short of his stated goal 'to show the full spectrum of the poet's potential'.

Thomas Rutledge's article 'Robert Henryson's *Orpheus and Eurydice*: A Northern Humanism?' (*FMLS* 35[2002] 396–411) examines Henryson's influences and independent development of a kind of humanism at the same time as humanism was growing and gaining ground in Italy. He rejects the notion, first put forward by R.D.S. Jack, that Angelo Poliziano's *Favola di Orfeo* influenced Henryson's *Orpheus and Eurydice*, citing R.J. Lyall's arguments against such a connection. Instead, Rutledge suggests, 'these two works, both composed in the last quarter of the fifteenth century and in the vernacular, share more than has generally been recognized and may cast considerable light upon each other and upon the purposes to which their writers have put the inherited Orpheus material'. Rutledge further argues that perhaps the terms 'renaissance and medieval, humanist and scholastic' are false dichotomies, and that pigeonholing Henryson's text serves only to cloud the actual intellectual mechanisms at work in the piece. Rutledge's article is provocative and persuasive, laying out Henryson's probable influences and explaining how together these lead to, if not exactly a 'northern humanism', then a new kind of morality and poetry at work in fifteenth-century Scotland.

Like Thomas Rutledge, Alessandra Petrina argues, in '"Aristeus Pastor Adamans": The Human Setting in Henryson's *Orpheus and Eurydice* and its Kinship with Poliziano's *Fabula di Orpheo*' (*FMLS* 38[2002] 382–96), that, while Henryson was probably not influenced directly by Poliziano, there is clearly a similar relationship between the two poems as both '[part] from classical models, and [introduce] motifs belonging to courtly literature conventions'.

R.J. Lyall's article 'Henryson's *Fabillis* and Steinhöwel' in *Forum for Modern Language Studies* (*FMLS* 38[2002] 362–81) does a thorough, if somewhat laborious, job of looking at Henryson's *Fabillis* and its possible sources. To this end, Lyall compares passages from Baldo, Steinhöwel, Macho, Leeu, Caxton and Biel with Henryson's take on the same aspect of his fables to conclude that Henryson ultimately relied on the Steinhöwel tradition as a major source.

The 2002 and 2003 issues of *Scottish Studies Review* surprisingly only yield one article on Middle Scots literature. Nicola Royan writes about Scottish representations of the British hero King Arthur in '"Na les vailyeant than ony uthir princis of Britane": Representations of Arthur in Scotland 1480–1540' (*SSR* 3[2002] 9–20). Royan does a great service by drawing together 'the historiographical representations and the romance representations of Arthur in the reigns of the middle Jameses and … consider[ing] whether a pattern emerges in relation to the political situation of the period, before the Reformation but at the beginning of the Renaissance'. Royan writes that Arthur's place in late medieval Scotland has been ignored at the expense of his more prominent role in the British writings and court culture of the time. She focuses on two Scottish Arthurian romances that were written at the end of the fifteenth century—*Galagros and Gawain* and *Lancelot of the Laik*—as well as two pieces of Scottish historiography that deal with Arthur at some length—those by John Mair and Hector Boece. Her article will be informative and interesting to any student of Scottish medieval literary history or of Arthurian studies in general.

A new publication by the Scottish Text Society will undoubtedly be helpful for scholars of Middle Scots Poetry, even though it does not directly address the poets: A.J. Aitken, *Older Scottish Vowels: A History of The Stressed Vowels of Older Scots from the Beginnings to the Eighteenth Century*, edited by Caroline Macafee.

Finally, Theo van Heignsbergen and Nicola Royan have edited an important volume, *Literature, Letters and the Canonical in Early Modern Scotland.* While many of the essays presented therein will be of interest to scholars covering Middle Scots, a few are worth noting specifically: Keely Fisher's 'The Contemporary Humour in William Stewart's *The Flytting betuix þe Sowtar and the Tailyour*', Janet Hadley Williams's 'The Earliest Surviving Text of Lyndsay's *Trageide of the Cardinall*: An English Edition of a Scottish Poem', and David J. Parkinson's 'Dreams in the Clear Light of Day: Older Scots Poetry in Modern Scotland'. Each of these essays in some way engages the work of Middle Scots poetry and will be useful for those scholars whose work bridges the Middle Ages and the early modern period in Scotland.

An important addition to Middle Scots studies came out in 2003: the TEAMS edition of *The Wallace*, which contains major selections from the fifteenth-century verse biography of the Scottish national hero William Wallace. Edited by Anne McKim, the TEAMS version will be helpful for students and scholars alike with its thorough glossing in the margins and comprehensive editing. The Scottish Text Society republished in 2003 *The Shorter Poems of Gavin Douglas*, edited by Priscilla Bawcutt. This second edition updates the 1965 original, with expansion to the supplement and corrections to the introduction, texts, and apparatus. The supplement now contains a 'review of scholarship since 1967'. The book contains three critically edited poems: *The Palice of Honour* (which Bawcutt states unequivocally is by Douglas), *Conscience* (which Bawcutt surmises is probably Douglas's), and *King Hart* (whose authorship is questionable but which is usually considered to be Douglas's work).

Lisa Perfetti includes a chapter on William Dunbar in her book *Women and Laughter in Medieval Comic Literature*. In '"A bowrd about bed": Women's Community of Laughter and the Woes of Marriage in Dunbar's *The Tretis of the Tua Maritt Wemen and the Wedo*', Perfetti describes the gendered humour and laughter that Dunbar presents in his comedic description of women complaining about their men and their marriages in what they assume is the privacy of a garden. Perfetti makes much of the voyeuristic male narrator, and how this alters the politics of the laughter for the audience—both medieval and modern—of Dunbar's *Tretis*. The chapter reads well on its own, but is even more illuminating when linked to the chapter preceding it on women's wit in Boccaccio's *Decameron*, where the women laugh in mixed company. Perfetti posits that the women's laughter about male deficiency is a mixture of both the fear and the fantasy of the male narrator/author/audience that lays bare the mechanisms of a society where women's choices are limited when it comes to marriage, and where laughter may be the only recourse.

Robert Epstein writes about 'Prisoners of Reflection: The Fifteenth-Century Poetry of Exile and Imprisonment' (*Exemplaria* 15[2003] 159–99), examining the effect that imprisonment and exile had on the poets James I of Scotland and Charles d'Orléans. Unlike previous critics, Epstein argues that the imprisonment is not what lends a destabilized sense of self to these poets but rather that they are working from an inherited poetic tradition, 'in which conventions of imprisonment are constitutive to subjectivity, and in which their sense of self is only further confirmed by their aristocratic status'. His analysis of James I through a Chaucerian lens is particularly interesting.

Additionally useful to students of Scottish poetry is Boardman and Ross, eds., *The Exercise of Power in Medieval Scotland c.1200–1500*. This collection of essays covers many aspects of Scottish political and cultural history.

10. Drama

The latest volume in the distinguished Records of Early English Drama series is James Gibson's magnificent three-volume collection based on the records of Kent. Like its predecessors, Gibson's text is a meticulous work of scholarship attesting to many years of diligent work in the archives allied to careful thought about the status and implications of the records uncovered. In keeping with the REED house style, the collection begins with an overview of the geographical, administrative, and religious history of the diocese and the county of Kent, its towns and other administrative divisions. Further introductory sections discuss dramatic, musical and ceremonial customs, the activities of amateur and professional musicians and acting troupes, civic ceremonies, sports, and games, and the urban and rural spaces in which these were produced. Then come the records themselves, drawn from an astonishing range of sources, each carefully described in the introduction, and arranged by borough and parish from Alkham to Wormshill, and by religious house from Boxley to Wye. Smaller bodies of records are drawn from aristocratic household accounts and archiepiscopal records, chiefly visitation articles. The third volume consists entirely of appendices, including an excellent section concerning playwrights and producers with Kentish connections (from John Bale to Christopher Marlowe), English translations of the Latin documents, and extensive scholarly notes for each record printed in the previous volumes. The collection is rounded off with helpful lists of patrons and companies mentioned in the records, a Latin glossary, and an analytical index. Given the centrality of the archdiocese to English ecclesiastical culture, and the position and prosperity of Kent throughout the late medieval and early modern periods, it is somewhat disappointing to find that there is not more extensive evidence of major religious drama productions surviving from the county. Perhaps the most interesting evidence here is for the New Romney Passion Play, which Gibson persuasively reconstructs on the basis of the available accounts. But even in the absence of a plethora of major cycle plays, these volumes offer copious evidence of a rich and varied ceremonial and ludic culture on a smaller scale throughout the pre-modern period. Gibson, and the team of other REED researchers, whose labours he generously acknowledges, have completed a huge undertaking. These three volumes are a magnificent achievement for which future generations of literary and cultural historians will be deeply grateful.

On a similarly monumental scale is the massive, two-volume edition of *The Oxford Encyclopedia of Theatre and Performance*, edited by Dennis Kennedy. Aiming to cover the whole range of world theatre and drama from the classical period to the present day, the book can devote limited space to the early drama, but there are substantial entries on subjects such as biblical plays (pp. 154–6), Corpus Christi (pp. 315–16) and Cycle Plays (pp. 341–20), Miracle (pp. 861–2) and Morality Plays (pp. 881–3). There are also brief—and not always particularly informative—biographies of individuals such as John Bale, John Heywood, Hildegard of Bingen, Lydgate and Skelton. Avowedly for the first-time enquirer rather than the scholar in search of new directions, the book offers a valuable sense of the breadth and depth of dramatic activity across cultural and historical divides. Another book with a comprehensive scope that nonetheless has considerable potential value for students of early drama is *The Drama Handbook: A Guide to Reading Plays*, by John Lennard and Mary Luckhurst. Accessibly written and characterized by an understated dry wit, the book provides a very brief history of the Mystery, Saints' and Cycle plays in the course of an introduction to the generic conventions and contexts of drama from ancient Greece to twenty-first-century Britain and America. More useful perhaps are the excellent sections that problematize the value of the printed text as evidence of performance, describe the physical and cultural processes by which a text is turned from an original idea into both a theatrical production and a printed text, and introduce the various elements at work in any theatrical production, from theatre space and prevailing codes of censorship to the roles of dramaturg, front of house staff and critics. Anyone looking for a good single-volume introduction to both the complexities and the pleasures to be found in studying 'the drama' need look no further.

A number of the essays in McGee, ed., *Improvisation in the Arts of the Middle Ages and Renaissance*, relate directly to the drama. Clifford Davidson's 'Improvisation in Medieval Drama' (pp. 193–221) is the most substantial, offering an interesting overview of the potential for improvised playing in both scripted plays and non-scripted games, dances, and other entertainments, drawing useful analogies with other forms, including Indian dance and performance traditions. In 'Shakespeare's Rhetorical Riffs' (pp. 247–72), Jane Freeman examines that potentially oxymoronic concept, 'scripted improvisation'. Again reaching over long distances for illuminating analogies—here to modern jazz improvisational techniques—Freeman provides detailed readings of semi-improvised, witty exchanges in Shakespeare's work in the light of humanist schoolroom techniques, an approach that would illuminate a good deal of the early drama too. Finally, David Klausner's brief but suggestive essay, 'The Improvising Vice in Renaissance England' (pp. 273–85), offers a tentative taxonomy of modes of improvisation employed by the Vices on the professional stage, both those that are scripted and those more obviously ad-libbed interventions which provoked Hamlet to demand that, in Elsinore at least, clowns should speak no more than is set down for them.

There are a number of challenging and informative essays on gender and its representations in Bernau, Evans, and Salih, eds., *Medieval Virginities*. None of the authors addresses the drama consistently, but all valuably map out the territory for future work on the 'performance' of virginity in a more literal sense. Equally stimulating for the inadvertent insights it provides for study of the drama is Christiania Whitehead's excellent study *Castles of the Mind: A Study of Medieval Architectural Allegory*. Although it does not consider *The Castle of Perseverence* or the various depictions of urban spaces in the passion plays directly (it focuses instead of Chaucer's *House of Fame*, the temples of the *Knight's Tale*, and other non-dramatic representations of architectural features), the book nonetheless offers some exemplary readings of imaginative and physical space and of the implications of using architecture to think through ideas, that are highly suggestive for study of the drama.

Students with interests in John Lyly's drama will be grateful for the appearance of Leah Scragg's single-volume modern-spelling edition of his prose works, *Euphues: The Anatomy of Wit* and *Euphues and his England*. In addition to clear and thorough texts of the two works and a full scholarly introduction, the edition prints a translation of Lyly's Latin poem 'Jupiter's Elizabeth' as an appendix. It is also good to see a revised edition of David Bergeron's groundbreaking study *English Civic Pageantry, 1558–1642* published by the Medieval and Renaissance Text Society. First published in 1971, this classic study made the case for the specific and significant links between civic ceremonial such as royal entries, progresses, and lord mayor's shows and the playhouse drama, drawing out the cross-fertilization of personnel, ideas, and methodologies between the two forms of spectacle. It is good to have the book back in print again, and to share its author's new ideas about and continued enthusiasm for this fascinating topic.

There is the usual excellent mixture of breadth and depth to the essays published in the most recent issues of *European Medieval Drama*. Volume 6, published in 2003 for 2002, but actually full of papers from the tenth colloquium of the Société Internationale pour l'Étude du Théâtre Médiéval held in Groningen in July 2001, has material on Parisian, Livonian, Spanish, French, and Middle Eastern drama and spectacle as well as two pieces of more direct interest to students of the British drama. In 'The Morphology of the Parade' (*EMD* 6[2003 for 2002] 1–30), Tom Pettitt draws upon both historical and anthropological approaches to illuminate the Corpus Christi plays and other 'promenade' forms, a subject also covered by Peter Happé in 'Procession and the Cycle Drama in England and Europe: Some Dramatic Possibilities' (*EMD* 6[2003 for 2002] 31–48), in which the use of procession in both pageant wagon and place-and-scaffold productions is thoughtfully examined.

European Medieval Drama 7 was also published in 2003, but reassuringly does what it says on the label, containing as it does pieces submitted for publication in that year. There is a strong French theme to this edition, with articles focusing on drama and spectacle in, among other places, Rouen, Dijon, Orléans, and the Abbey of Origney-Sainte-Benoîte. But England does again gain two notable mentions. We are once more indebted to Tom Pettitt for '"I am here, Syre Cristesmasse": Dramatic Aspects of Early Poetry and Songs' (*EMD* 7[2003] 1–28), which argues for the survival of evidence of (and in some cases even scripts for) medieval performances in the texts of lyrics, songs, and games of later periods. In 'The Bodley *Christ's Burial* and *Christ's Resurrection*: Vernacular Dramas for Good Friday and Easter' (*EMD* 7[2003] 51–68), C. Davidson looks closely at the somewhat neglected texts contained in Oxford, Bodleian Library, MS e Museo 160, speculating about their likely origins, the auspices of performance, and their wider cultural significance.

The two issues of *Medieval English Theatre* published since the last *YWES* also contain much of interest. In *METh* 23[2002 for 2001], Margaret Rogerson's 'Rediscovering Richard Eurich's "York Festival Triptych"' (*METh* 23[2002 for 2001] 3–16) is a fascinating discussion of a panoramic painting completed in 1954/5 by Eurich, a celebrated Royal Navy war artist, depicting the presentation of the Mystery Plays in the 1954 York Festival. A similar modern focus on medieval performance issues characterizes Olga Horner's essay, 'The Law That Never Was: A Review of Theatrical Censorship in Britain' (*METh* 23[2002 for 2001] 34–96), which also looks at the York Festival Mysteries, especially the anxieties concerning the blasphemy laws and the dangers of representing God onstage that exercised the producers of the 1951 production. In 'Devils of Baltic Towns in the Context of Late-Medieval German Tradition' (*METh* 23[2002 for 2001] 17–33) Anu Mänd traces the traditions associated with the *schoduvel* or 'festival devil' in the culture of medieval Livonia. A brief intervention by Henk Gras, 'Theatre By the Book? Some Thoughts on Kipling's Fouquet' (*METh* 23[2002 for 2001] 97–9), continues the running debate prompted by an article by Gordon Kipling in the 1997 issue (*METh* 19) concerning what the Fouquet miniature, *The Martyrdom of Saint Apollonia*, exactly depicts. Gras argues against Kipling's suggestion that the scene represents an imaginative reconstruction of a martyrdom play performed in a Roman theatre as described in the *Etymologiae* of Isidore of Seville, suggesting that the theatre depicted probably reflected contemporary rather than classical theatre architecture. This debate seems likely to run and run.

Equally popular with *METh* readers has been the ongoing discussion about the nature of the jousting game 'farte pryke in cule' played by the characters 'A' and 'B' in Henry Medwall's interlude *Fulgens and Lucrece*. The latest chapter in a saga begun by Peter Meredith as early as 1984 is the alluringly entitled '"Farte pryke in cule": The Pictures' (*METh* 23[2002 for 2001] 100–21), by Meg Twycross, with Malcolm Jones and Alan Fletcher. Here the authors detail their own experiments in trying to stage the game during modern productions, and cite textual and visual representations of analogous medieval and modern scatological jousting 'games', including photographs of grandly moustached gentlemen engaging in 'Norwegian Cockfighting' aboard the SS *Norman Castle* in the 1890 s. Somewhat less surreal is the final article in the volume, 'Prompting in Full View of the Audience: The Groningen Experiment' (*METh* 23[2002 for 2001] 122–71), written up as a report on practical theatre research in action by Philip Butterworth. The central research question here is the effect that the presence of an active 'prompter' figure onstage has on the dynamics of a production and the responses of audience members, Butterworth discusses the various medieval accounts of such 'visible' interventions by prompter or expositor figures in the drama, recounts the practical experiences of a student production that tried out the idea in practice, and prints the responses of various scholars to both the idea and the performance itself during an international drama conference in Groningen.

METh 24[2003 for 2002] is equally rich in stimulating articles. '"My Lady Tongue": Thomas Tomkis's *Lingua*', by Sarah Carpenter (*METh* 24[2003 for 2002] 3–14), examines *Lingua: Or The Combat of the Tongue and the Five Senses for Superiority*, an interlude performed in Cambridge *c.*1607 and first published in that year. Exploring the symbolic values of spoken language and the various senses in the play, Carpenter subtly draws out the issues related to the representation of language and related concepts such as memory and imagination in the play, and in the period as whole. John McGavin's essay, '"That thin skin": Skipper Lindsay and the Language of Record' (*METh* 24[2003 for 2002] 15–31), is equally thought-provoking. It focuses on a dramatic intervention by a 'known frenetic man', the eponymous Skipper Lindsay, into an arena prepared for the performance of a play before James VI in St Andrews in 1580. In an intellectual tour de force, McGavin explores the various levels of artifice and improvisation in both Lindsay's seemingly impromptu oration and the subsequent written account of it in the diary of the Reverend James Melville, drawing out their implications for our understanding of the chronicler's art, for the study of dramatic performance from written records, and for the study of history itself as an intellectual exercise. In 'The Valencian *Misteri Del Rey Herodes*: Misogyny, Politics, and Caste Conflict' (*METh* 24[2003 for 2002] 32–43) Ronald E. Surtz examines the possible reception of the Valencian play of Herod in the fifteenth and early sixteenth centuries, suggesting the complex series of 'messages' it might have carried for different sections of society.

Two articles look at ecclesiastical texts of considerable significance for the drama. Sue Niebrzydowski's 'Encouraging Marriage *In Facie Ecclesiae*: The Mary Play "Betrothal" and the Sarum *Ordo ad faciendum Sponsalia*' (*METh* 24[2003 for 2002] 44–61) draws out the use of the Sarum *Ordo* in the N-Town play's representation of the marriage of Mary and Joseph; while 'The Corpus Christi Bull, 1264: Latin Text with Modern English Translation', by Lynette R. Muir and Peter Meredith (*METh* 24[2003 for 2002] 62–78) valuably prints the founding document of the feast associated with the urban plays with scholarly apparatus and translation. 'Medieval Fools in Biblical Iconography', by Sandra Pietrini (*METh* 24[2003 for 2002] 79–103) looks primarily at manuscript illuminations of fools and simpletons, while in '"The law that never was": A Codicil. The Case of *The Just Vengeance*' (*METh* 24[2003 for 2002] 104–16), Olga Horner revisits the subject of theatre, blasphemy, and censorship covered in the earlier article mentioned above, adding further first-hand testimony concerning the 1951 production of the York Mysteries and the analogous case of Dorothy L. Sayer's play, performed five years earlier. In 'The Dating of Bale's King Johan' (*METh* 24[2003 for 2002] 116–37), Jeffrey Leininger steers the reader through the curious tangle that is the surviving text of Bale's polemical play. Finally, Pam King's '*La Festa D'Elx* Revisited' (*METh* 24[2003 for 2002] 138–40) and David Mills's 'Chester Mystery Plays' (*METh* 24[2003 for 2002] 141–5) review the Elche *Festa* of August 2003 and the revival of the Chester Cycle on Cathedral Green in June and July 2003 respectively.

Books Reviewed

Aitken, A.J. *The Older Scottish Vowels: A History of the Stressed Vowels of Older Scots from the Beginnings to the Eighteenth Century*. 5th series. Scottish Text Society. [2002] pp. xxxii + 225. £30 ISBN 1 8979 7618 6.

Amtower, Laurel, and Dorothea Kehler, eds. *The Single Woman in Medieval and Early Modern England: Her Life and Representation*. Arizona Center for Medieval and Renaissance Studies. [2003] pp. xx + 242. £30 ($35) ISBN 0 8669 8306 6.

Armstrong, Dorsey. *Gender and the Chivalric Community in Malory's 'Morte d'Arthur'*. UFlorP. [2003] pp. viii + 272. $59.95 (£44.50) ISBN 0 8130 2686 5.

Barber, Richard. *Myths and Legends of the British Isles*. Boydell. [1999] pp. xx + 572. pb £24.95 ISBN 0 8511 5748 3.

Barefield, Laura D. *Gender and History in Medieval Romance and Chronicle*. Lang. [2003] pp. 135. $53.95 (£66.95) ISBN 0 8204 6184 9.

Bawcutt, Priscilla, ed. *The Shorter Poems of Gavin Douglas*. 5th series. Scottish Text Society. [2003] pp. lxxxvii + 347. £30 ISBN 1 8979 7619 4.

Bergeron, David. *English Civic Pageantry, 1558–1642*. revised edn. MRTS 267. [2003] pp. 313. £42 ISBN 0 7083 1762 6.

Bernau, Anke, Ruth Evans and Sarah Salih, eds. *Medieval Virginities*. UWalesP. [2003] pp. xiv + 296. hb £40 ($53) ISBN 0 7083 1763 4, pb £16.99 ($24.95) ISBN 0 7083 1762 6.

Bildhauer, Bethina, and Robert Mills, eds. *The Monstrous Middle Ages*. UWalesP. [2003] pp. xiv + 236. hb £40 ($64.95) ISBN 0 7083 1821 5, pb £16.99 ($21.95) ISBN 0 7083 1822 3.

Blumreich, Kathleen Marie, ed. *The Middle English 'Mirror': An Edition Based on Bodleian Library, MS Holkham misc. 40*. MRTS 182; Arizona Studies in the Middle Ages and the Renaissance 9. ASU/Brepols. [2002] pp. xlviii + 558. £48 ($55) ISBN 0 8669 8224 8, ISBN 2 5035 1438 3.

Boardman, Steve, and Alasdair Ross, eds. *The Exercise of Power in Medieval Scotland*. FCP. [2003] pp. 240. €65 (£50, $55) ISBN 1 8518 2749 8.

Boffey, Julia, ed. *Fifteenth-Century English Dream Visions: An Anthology*. OUP. [2003] pp. x + 284. hb £47 ($70) ISBN 0 1992 6397 3, pb £18 ($24.95) ISBN 0 1992 6398 1.

Busby, Keith, and Roger Dalrymple, eds. *Arthurian Literature XIX: Comedy in Arthurian Literature*. Brewer. [2003] pp. viii + 232. £45 ($70) ISBN 0 8599 1745 2.

Condren, Edward I. *The Numerical Universe of the Gawain–Pearl Poet: Beyond Phi*. UFlorP. [2003] pp. 205. £40.95 ($59.95) ISBN 0 8130 2554 0.

Coss, Peter, and Maurice Keen, eds. *Heraldry, Pageantry and Social Display in Medieval England*. Boydell. [2002] pp. x + 278. pb £19.99 ($35) ISBN 1 8438 3036 1.

Dinshaw, Carolyn, and David Wallace, eds. *The Cambridge Companion to Medieval Women's Writing*. CUP. [2003] pp. xx + 292. hb £45 ($65) ISBN 0 5217 9188 X, pb £16.99 ($24.99) ISBN 0 5217 9638 5.

Dover, Carol, ed. *A Companion to the 'Lancelot-Grail Cycle'*. Brewer. [2003] pp. xii + 267. $85 (£50) ISBN 0 8599 1783 5.

Duncan, Thomas G., and Connolly Margaret, eds. *The Middle English 'Mirror' Sermons from Advent to Sexagesima*. MET 34. Winter. [2003] pp. lxxii + 190. €46.30 ISBN 3 8253 1537 1.

Erler, Mary C., and Maryanne Kowaleski, eds. *Gendering the Master Narrative*. CornUP. [2003] pp. ix + 269. hb £38.95 ($52.50) ISBN 0 8014 4112 9, pb £14.50 ($19.95) ISBN 0 9014 8830 3.

Fenster, Thelma, and Daniel Smail Lord, eds. *Fama: The Politics of Talk and Reputation in Medieval Europe*. CornUP. [2003] pp. vii + 227. hb £28.95 ($49.95) ISBN 0 8014 3939 6, pb £11.50 ($19.95) ISBN 0 8014 8857 5.

Fowler, Elizabeth. *Literary Character: The Human Figure in Early English Writing*. CornUP. [2003] pp. xii + 263. £27.50 ($45) ISBN 0 8014 4116 1.

French, Shannon E., ed. *The Code of the Warrior: Exploring Warrior Values Past and Present*. [2003].

Gibson, James M., ed. *Records of Early English Drama: Kent. Diocese of Canterbury*. 3 vols. BL/UTorP. [2002] pp. ccxxiv + 301. $500 ISBN 0 7123 4803 4, inc. maps (vol. 1); iii + 641 (vol. ii); iii + 719 (vol. iii).

Goldie, Matthew Boyd, ed. *Middle English Literature: A Historical Sourcebook*. Blackwell. [2003] pp. xxxviii + 301. hb £55 ISBN 0 6312 3147 1, pb £19.99 ISBN 0 6312 3148 X.

Hanna, Ralph, David and Lawton, eds. *The Siege of Jerusalem*. EETS os 320. OUP. [2003] pp. c + 224. £50 ISBN 0 1972 2323 0.

Heffernan, Carol F. *The Orient in Chaucer and Medieval Romance*. Brewer. [2003] pp. x + 160. £40 ($70) ISBN 0 8599 1795 9.

Heng, Geraldine. *Empire of Magic: Medieval Romance and the Politics of Cultural Fantasy*. ColUP. [2003] pp. xii + 521. hb $45 (£28.50), pb $22.50 (£15) ISBN 0 2311 2527 5.

Hogg, James, ed. *'The Rewyll of Seynt Sauioure' and 'A Ladder of Foure Ronges by the Which Men Mowe Clyme to Heven'. Edited from MSS Cambridge University Library Ff.6.33 and London Guildhall 25524*. Analecta Cartusiana 183. USalz. [2003] pp. xxvi + 327. €40 ISBN 3 9019 9582 X.

Jaritz, Gerhard, and G. Moreno-Riano, eds. *Time and Eternity: The Medieval Discourse*. Brepols. [2003] pp. vii + 535. £65 ($100) ISBN 2 5035 1312 3.

Kennedy, Dennis, ed., *The Oxford Encyclopedia of Theatre and Performance*, vol. 1: *A–L*, vol. 2: *M–Z*. OUP. [2003] pp. li + 776 (vol. 1), v + 1559 (vol. 2). £175 ISBN 0 1986 0672 9 (vol. 1), ISBN 0 1986 0671 0 (vol. 2).

Kennedy, Ruth, ed. *Three Alliterative Saints Hymns: Late Middle English Stanzaic Poems*. EETS os 321. OUP. [2003] pp. cx + 120. £40 ISBN 0 1972 2324 9.

Knight, Stephen. *Robin Hood: A Mythic Biography*. CornUP. [2003] pp. xxiv + 248. $25 ISBN 0 8014 3885 3.

Kubouchi, Tadao, and Keiko Ikegami, eds. *The 'Ancrene Wisse': A Four-Manuscript Parallel Text, Preface and Parts 1–4*. Lang. [2003] pp. xvi + 564. £64 (€97.50, $108.95) ISBN 3 6315 1599 5.

Labriola, Albert C., John W. and Smeltz, eds. *The Mirror of Salvation [Speculum Humanæ Salvationis]: An Edition of British Library Blockbook G. 11784*. Clarke. [2002] pp. x + 194. £45 ISBN 0 2276 7969 5.

Lawton, David, Wendy Scase and Rita Copeland, eds. *New Medieval Literatures 6*. OUP. [2003] pp. viii + 318. £65 ISBN 0 1992 5251 3.

Lennard, John, and Luckhurst Mary. *The Drama Handbook: A Guide to Reading Plays*. OUP. [2002] pp. xii + 416. £16.99 ISBN 0 1987 0070 9.

McAvoy, Elizabeth Herbert, ed. and trans. *The Book of Margery Kempe: An Abridged Translation*. Boydell. [2003] pp. 160. pb £15.99 ($27.95) ISBN 0 8599 1791 6.

McGee, Timothy J., ed. *Improvisation in the Arts of the Middle Ages and Renaissance*. Early Drama, Art, and Music Monograph Series 30. MIP. [2003] pp. xii + 331. hb $35 ISBN 1 5804 4044 4, pb $17.50 ISBN 1 5804 4045 2.

McKim, Anne, ed. *The Wallace: Selections*. TEAMS Middle English Texts. MIP. [2003] pp. vii + 285. $20 ISBN 1 5804 4076 2.

Meyer, Ann R. *Medieval Allegory and the Building of the New Jerusalem*. Brewer. [2003] pp. x + 214. £40 ($70) ISBN 0 8599 1796 7.

Minkova, Donka, and Theresa Tinkle, eds. *Chaucer and the Challenges of Medievalism: Studies in Honor of H.A. Kelly*. Studies in English Medieval Language and Literature 5. Lang. [2003] pp. xxii + 404. €55.90 (£36 $66.95) pb ISBN 3 6315 1377 1.

Moll, Richard. *Before Malory: Reading Arthur in Later Medieval England*. UTorP. [2003] pp. ix + 368. $63 (£40) ISBN 0 8020 3722 4.

Murdoch, Brian. *The Medieval Popular Bible: Expansions of Genesis in the Middle Ages*. Brewer. [2003] pp. x + 210. £50 ($85) ISBN 0 8599 1776 2.

Olson, Mary C. *Fair and Varied Forms: Visual Textuality in Medieval Illuminated Manuscripts*. Medieval History and Culture 15. Routledge. [2003] pp. xviii + 232. £50 ($80.95) ISBN 0 4159 4267 5.

O'Mara, Veronica, ed. *Four ME Sermons: Edited from British Library MS Harley 2268*. Middle English Texts 33. Winter. [2002] pp. 216. pb €42 ISBN 3 8253 1463 4.

Pearsall, Derek. *Arthurian Romance: A Short Introduction*. Blackwell. [2003] pp. vii + 182. $22.95 (£12.99) ISBN 0 6312 3320 2.

Peck, Russell A., and Andrew Galloway, eds. *Confessio Amantis*. by John Gower. Vol. 2. MIP. [2003] pp. viii + 416. $20 ISBN 1 5804 4047 9.

Perfetti, Lisa. *Women and Laughter in Medieval Comic Literature*. UMichP. [2003] pp. xiii + 286. $60 ISBN 0 4721 1321 6.

Radulescu, Raluca L. *The Gentry Context of Malory's 'Morte Darthur'*. B&B. [2003] pp. 176. 75 (£45) ISBN 0 8599 1785 1.

Raymo, Robert R., Whitaker Elaine E. and Sternglantz Ruth E., eds. *The Mirroure of the Worlde: A Middle English Translation of 'Le Miroir du Monde'*. Medieval Academy Books 106. UTorP for MAA. [2003] pp. x + 644. £55 ($85) ISBN 0 8020 3613 9.

Rees Jones, Sarah, ed. *Learning and Literacy in Medieval England and Abroad*. Brepols. [2003] pp. x + 222. €55 ISBN 2 5035 1076 0.

Rigby, S.H., ed. *A Companion to Britain in the Later Middle Ages*. Blackwell. [2003] pp. xxx + 665. £85 ($138.95) ISBN 0 6312 1785 1.

Rosenthal, Joel T. *Telling Tales: Sources and Narration in Late Medieval England*. PSUP. [2003] pp. xxv + 217. £42.95 ($49.95) ISBN 0 2710 2304 X.

Salisbury, Eve, ed. *The Trials and Joys of Marriage*. MIP. [2002] pp. x + 276. $18 ISBN 1 5804 4035 5.

Schaer, Frank, ed. *The Three Kings of Cologne. Edited from London, Lambeth Palace MS 491*. Middle English Texts 31. Winter. [2000] pp. 208. €46 ISBN 3 8253 1122 8.

Scragg, Leah, ed. *Euphues: The Anatomy of Wit and Euphues and his England*. RevelsCL. by John Lyly. MUP. [2003] pp. 358. £47.50 ISBN 0 7190 6458 9.

Shippey, Tom, ed. *Film and Fiction: Reviewing the Middle Ages*. Studies in Medievalism 12. Brewer. [2003] pp. 257. $70 ISBN 0 8599 1772 X.

Smith D, Vance. *Arts of Possession: The Middle English Household Imaginary*. UMinnP. [2003] pp. xviii + 319. $68.95 ISBN 0 8166 3950 7.

Somerset, Fiona, and Nicholas Watson, eds. *The Vulgar Tongue: Medieval and Postmedieval Vernacularity*. PSUP. [2003] pp. xvi + 277. $55 ISBN 0 2710 2310 4.

Steinberg, Theodore L. *Reading the Middle Ages: An Introduction to Medieval Literature*. McFarland. [2003] pp. viii + 188. $32 ISBN 0 7864 1648 3.

Steiner, Emily. *Documentary Culture and the Making of Medieval English Literature*. CUP. [2003] pp. xvi + 268. £45 ($60) ISBN 0 5218 2484 2.

Thompson, Anne B. *Everyday Saints and the Art of Narrative in the South English Legendary*. Ashgate. [2003] pp. xii + 224. £45 ($79.95) ISBN 0 7546 3293 8.

Treharne, Elaine. *Old and Middle English c.890–c.1400: An Anthology*. 2nd edn. Blackwell. [2003] pp. xxx + 678. hb £75 (–78.95) ISBN 1 4051 1312 X, pb £19.99 ($39.95) ISBN 1 4051 1313 8.

Tzanaki, Rosemary, ed. *Mandeville's Medieval Audiences: A Study on the Reception of the Book of Sir John Mandeville (1371–1550)*. Ashgate. [2003] pp. xvi + 302. £47.50 ($84.95) ISBN 0 7546 0846 8.

van Heignsbergen, Theo, and Ryan Nicola, eds. *Literature, Letters and the Canonical in Early Modern Scotland*. Tuckwell. [2002] pp. xxx + 158. £20 ($32.95) ISBN 1 8623 2270 8.

Vaught, Jennifer C., and Lynne Dickson Bruckner, eds. *Grief and Gender, 700–1700*. Palgrave. [2003] pp. xii + 310. hb $55 ISBN 0 3122 9382 8, pb $18.95 ISBN 0 3122 9381 X.

Wada, Yoko, ed. *A Companion to 'Ancrene Wisse'*. Brewer. [2003] pp. xii + 258. £60 ($110) ISBN 0 8599 1762 2.

Warren, Martin L. *Asceticism in the Christian Transformation of Self in Margery Kempe, William Thorpe, and John Rogers*. Mellen. [2003] pp. 172. £64.95 ($99.95) ISBN 0 7734 6772 6.

Whitehead, Christina. *Castles of the Mind: A Study of Medieval Architectural Allegory*. UWalesP. [2003] pp. x + 324. £45 ISBN 0 7083 1794 4.

Wood, Diana, ed. *Women and Religion in Medieval England*. Oxbow. [2003] pp. xiv + 185. £20 ISBN 1 8421 7098 8.

IV

Middle English: Chaucer

VALERIE ALLEN AND MARGARET CONNOLLY

This chapter has four sections: 1. General; 2. *Canterbury Tales*; 3. *Troilus and Criseyde*; 4. Other Works. The ordering of individual tales and poems within the sections follows that of the Riverside Chaucer edition.

1. General

Mark Allen and Bege K. Bowers continue to oversee the production of 'An Annotated Chaucer Bibliography 2001' (*SAC* 25[2003] 459–546); for the electronic version see the New Chaucer Society webpage: http://artsci.wustl.edu/~chaucer/ or http://uchaucer.utsa.edu.

Chaucer's language and Chaucer's politics prove to be two subjects of most vibrant scholarly enquiry this year. Although Tim Machan's sociolinguistic study of *English in the Middle Ages* is not primarily concerned with literature, he gives a detailed reading of *The Reeve's Tale* in his fourth chapter, which asks the question: 'What's a dialect before it's a dialect?' (p. 111). Noting that Chaucer's use of language is usually fairly homogeneous, Machan tries to explain the presence of dialect in the tale and to demonstrate how the status of a language can figure in cultural activity; there is also passing reference to other parts of *The Canterbury Tales* and the dream poems in this chapter, as well as a detailed analysis of *Sir Gawain and the Green Knight*. Elsewhere in this thought-provoking book Machan explores the relationship between languages, dialects, and nations, using Henry III's issue of two English letters in 1258 (nicely presented in a fold-out facsimile) as his starting point when attempting to determine how the status of a language such as Middle English comes into being.

Another monograph study, this time wholly devoted to the subject of *The Language of the Chaucer Tradition*, is presented by Simon Horobin. The first introductory chapter offers useful thumbnail sketches of recent developments in Chaucer manuscript studies and Middle English dialectology. Chapter 2 considers the place of Chaucer's language within the London dialect of Middle English in the fourteenth and fifteenth centuries, and how scribes responded to this Type III London English. Chapters 3 and 4 focus on the manuscripts of

Year's Work in English Studies, Volume 84 (2005) © The English Association; all rights reserved. For permissions, please email: journals.permissions@oxfordjournals.org

doi: 10.1093/ywes/mai004

The Canterbury Tales. Horobin evaluates the evidence offered by the Hengwrt and Ellesmere manuscripts for Chaucer's own linguistic practices, and also localizes all of the fifty-four complete manuscripts of the *Tales*, affording provincial products the same respect as metropolitan ones, and compiling a wealth of information about provenance. The three final chapters look, in different ways, at the history of Chaucer's verse after his own time: chapter 5 surveys the Chaucer printed tradition from Caxton to the Riverside edition, noting editorial strategies that maintain linguistic accessibility; chapter 6 shows how changes in English grammar affected scribal understanding of metre and rhyming practices; and chapter 7 charts the influence of Chaucer's language on later English poets such as Hoccleve and Lydgate, and on the Scottish scribes who copied Chaucer's work. Earlier versions of parts of chapters 3 and 4 have previously appeared in article form (see *YWES* 81[2002] 249; 82[2003] 205–6), but otherwise this clearly written and wide-ranging study is wholly new. This is a brilliant analysis of Chaucer's language that shows up—in the nicest possible way—the inadequacies of former studies. Some of the scaffolding of the argument betrays the book's origins as a thesis, but this also contributes to its clarity. At fewer than 200 pages this is not a big book, but it comes to some big conclusions. Horobin identifies three major areas, all pertinent to Chaucerians, which require renewed attention: the development of the London dialect needs to be reconsidered; traditional assumptions regarding the authorship of certain works need to be revisited (essentially, the *Equatorie* may be out of the canon, and the whole of the *Romaunt* may be in, on which see also his article 'Pennies, Pence and Pans' below); and finally the vexed question of dating Hengwrt and Ellesmere, as well as the consequences of this for the editing of *The Canterbury Tales*, rears its head again. An even bigger issue, and one that Horobin is not afraid to confront, is our ever-increasing reliance on the Riverside Chaucer, which, with its hybrid text, provides a convenient but lazy and inaccurate touchstone. Throughout this book Horobin argues for the crucial importance of seeing Chaucer's work and language within the context of its manuscripts; his attention to precisely this matter has produced a rare study that will interest both linguists and literary critics, whether or not they are Chaucerians.

There is also the usual clutch of articles treating aspects of Chaucer's language. Chaucer's usage of *ye* and *thou* forms is analysed in a posthumously published essay by David Burnley, 'The T/V Pronouns in Later Middle English Literature' (in Taavitsainen and Jucker, eds., *Diachronic Perspectives on Address Term Systems*, pp. 27–45). Burnley warns that we cannot be certain that pronoun choice belongs to the author's original text, and that our knowledge of the socio-historical factors that influenced linguistic usage is incomplete. Nevertheless he concludes that pronominal address forms tend to collocate with specific lexical items, and finds that the plural pronoun *ye* as an address form for a singular addressee is restricted to courtly genres; in other types of discourse, including learned, religious, and unsophisticated, speakers used the singular pronoun to address a singular addressee. In the courtly genre the plural address form was further restricted to non-intimate addressees of greater age or higher status. Switches between *ye* and *thou* may be explained on the basis of affection, rhetoric and genre. In another essay in the same volume, '"And if ye wol nat so, my lady sweete, thanne preye I thee …": Forms of Address in Chaucer's *Knight's Tale*' (in Taavitsainen and Jucker, eds., pp. 61–84), Thomas Honegger discusses the seemingly arbitrary variation between *ye* and *thou* in the ritualistic addresses to deities in this tale. Honegger argues that pronominal forms must be investigated within a broader context that takes account of the situational status of the interactants, and incorporates not just linguistic but non-linguistic elements of adversion such as self-reference, gesture, and spatial position. Elsewhere Verena Jung and Angela Schrott examine speech act shift in *The Wife of Bath's Prologue* in 'A Question of Time? Question Types and Speech Act Shifts from a Historical-Contrastive Perspective: Some Examples from Old Spanish and Middle English' (in Jaszczolt and Turner, eds, *Meaning Through Language Contrast*, vol. 2, pp. 345–71). Combining historical pragmatics with translation studies, they take two of the Wife's most infamous statements and note whether the sentence focus of the original is maintained or altered in two intralingual translations of the text (modern English versions by Coghill and Lumiansky) and two translations into modern German (by Kemmler and Lehnert).

Mary Catherine Davidson writes on 'Code-Switching and Authority in Late Medieval England' (*Neophil* 87[2003] 473–86) using approaches adapted from studies of multilingualism in linguistics to investigate patterns of mixed-language speech in *The Canterbury Tales*, *Piers Plowman*, and *The Chronicle of Pierre de Langtoft*. She finds that choice of language is bound up with social motivation, and that mixed-language speech can be used to construct authority. R.D. Eaton writes on 'Gender, Class and Conscience in Chaucer' (*ES* 84[2003] 205–18), comparing occurrences of the term *conscience* in *The Canterbury Tales* (principally in *The Second Nun's Tale*), *The Legend of Good Women*, and *Troilus*, and concluding that the perceived diversity in Chaucer's use of this term is linked to factors of gender and class. Simon Horobin builds an interesting case on the word *panne* in 'Pennies, Pence and Pans: Some Chaucerian Misreadings' (*ES* 84[2003] 426–32). Far from meaning 'dish' or 'pan', as has been suggested for various contexts in *The Reeve's Tale* and *The Friar's Tale*, Horobin argues that the form 'panne' is a common variant of the form 'penny' in Middle English, particularly in the Essex and London dialects; the discovery of an attestation of the form in a London Guild Return of 1389 makes his argument compelling, and carries some implications for critical interpretation. Horobin further argues that if we are to accept the greater linguistic variety found in London English of this period then the evidence for Chaucer's authorship of the later part of the *Romaunt* needs to be reconsidered.

Turning to Chaucer's politics, not one shred of positive evidence exists to suggest that Chaucer was bumped off nor does this book produce any, but in *Who Murdered Chaucer? A Medieval Mystery* Terry Jones and his team of researchers (Terry Dolan, Juliette Dor, Alan Fletcher, and Robert Yeager) spin a 400-page yarn of circumstantial evidence arguing that in the paranoia of the new Lancastrian regime Chaucer's work appeared ideologically suspect, and that the poet and his work were actively suppressed by the real villain of the moment, who was not Henry IV but Thomas Arundel, reinstated archbishop of Canterbury. The first six chapters focus on Richard II, and piece by piece dismantle the edifice, constructed in the chronicles after 1399, that portrays Richard as the unpopular, irresponsible, luxurious tyrant who sold England down the river in the Hundred Years' War. The chronicles' picture of a loyal Bolingbroke who returns to reclaim his birthright and unwillingly accepts the mantle of power thrust upon him by the nation is also contested. Instead, Bolingbroke is presented as having come under the influence of Arundel while on the Continent in exile; usurpation seems intended from the beginning. In light of the need of Henry's administration for court poets to write serious propaganda, Chaucer's *Complaint to his Purse* looks measly at best in comparison to Gower's self-serving hyperboles. Arundel embarks on a systematic elision of treason with heresy, and things that could be debated and written in the 1380s become a death warrant in 1400.

Seen thus, Chaucer's anti-ecclesiastical satire acquires a dangerously subversive edge, and the Parson seems increasingly to look like everything Arundel is not. The earliness of Hengwrt is accepted, and the authors suggest that its occasional hastiness in composition indicates Chaucer's efforts to leave behind a full corpus of his poem. Early damage to the manuscript also suggests that it was hidden during the early years of Henry's reign. Ellesmere, on the other hand, appears to have been appropriated by Henry after careful censorship; the illustrations of the Monk and Friar have been over-washed to remove signs of the luxury and vice of the pilgrims. Where Chaucer survived the political crisis of 1387 by lying low, he moves into the eye of the storm in 1399 by his association with Westminster Abbey, a focal point of opposition to Henry. The *Retraction* is reconsidered as a possible forced confession elicited by Arundel. Evidence for 1402 as Chaucer's real death date is seriously considered, and the case closes with the chilling picture of Chaucer dying, not peacefully in a Westminster garden with birds twittering, but starving to death in Arundel's prison, Saltwood Castle, or meeting a sticky end in a back-street alley.

Cast as a law suit, the case assembled by Jones and his team, which is not uniformly convincing but in places intriguingly so, reminds us that to allow our imaginations to be circumscribed by such positive evidence as propagandist policies, chance, and the mice have left us is to impoverish history. Absolute reliance on empirical verification asks 'Why?' This book asks 'Why not?' This is a great read, revisionist history at its cheekiest and most instructive.

Worth mentioning alongside the book is Alan Fletcher's long article, 'Chaucer the Heretic' (*SAC* 25[2003] 53–121), so closely connected are the thoughts of both. Fletcher's premise is that Chaucer's poetry appears much more contentious than it now seems when considered in light of contemporary religious radicalism. He begins by examining the theological resonances of *errour* in the *ABC* and of *heresye* in *The Legend of Good Women*. Fletcher then considers the religious pilgrims systematically in light of contemporary anti-mendicant writings; the Pardoner, who has a good innings this year, emerges as not a regular reprobate but a dangerously ambivalent character. Although there is no evidence to suggest a direct alignment between Chaucer and Lollardy, the poet nonetheless raises the very same questions that the Lollards ask explicitly. He could certainly have been suspected in his time of Lollard sympathies, and the rising climate of conservative reaction at the turn of the century could not have improved his standing with Arundel. Considering Alcuin Blamires' choice of title from an essay published in 2000, 'Chaucer the Reactionary' (*YWES* 81[2002] 248), it is clear that current criticism is doing some serious re-evaluation of the political commitments of this poet of many masks, and that opinion is not unanimous. The 'Chaucer of the margin' who so dominated the thinking of the late 1980s and 1990s is transforming into a figure of more dangerous and colourful extremity.

Elizabeth Fowler revisits the theoretical status of *Literary Character: The Human Figure in Early English Writing*. To distinguish the object of her enquiry from the usual nomenclature of 'type' or 'character', she adopts the phrase 'social person', by which term we understand the inscription of the individual figure into an implied cluster of cultural conventions and expectations. 'Character' offers too individualistic an understanding of the person, and 'type' too discrete a cultural category, for persons cut across different types in conflicting and contradictory ways. Taking the Knight and Prioress as illustration, Fowler considers the various categories by which they are interpreted: in the Knight's case, pilgrim and crusader; in the Prioress's, pilgrim, nun, and lady. It is telling that the characters worth Fowler's consideration cause us 'to feel a density in the character' (p. 9); modern distaste for the purely conventional and typical, which so mark medieval characterization, still shows. Unless an ideal contains 'internal contradictions' (p. 15), it does not hold our interest.

In this early part of Fowler's discussion, it is hard to see what was new, the theoretical framework is unclear, and the difference not apparent between Fowler's new vocabulary of character analysis and that of, for example, Jill Mann in *Chaucer and Medieval Estates Satire* (*YWES* 54[1975] 113), despite the author's claims to the contrary. All this changes once Fowler turns to legal distinctions between 'natural person', 'juridical person', which designates a corporation or institution, and *persona*, which inhabits both terms by referring to both a real person and a legal status. In the sphere of legal *persona*, the modern individual fades out of relevance, leaving new avenues of exploration in the authors Fowler discusses. Although legal thought is only one of a number of aspects of Fowler's social person, it is the one that most productively speaks to literary analysis. In her first chapter, she analyses the social, commercial, and institutional habits of the Pardoner as social person. She ably shows how pardoners in general summed up the Church's contradictory position on need for funds and contempt for wealth. In the Pardoner 'we see a monstrous production of the divided structure of the canon law itself' (p. 54). Fowler's interest is essentially in psychological interiority, and she locates its most radical and insightful analysis within (Chaucer's) poetry rather than theological or penitential discourse, within the 'superior resources of fiction' (p. 87).

Caroline M. Barron's substantial study of *London in the Later Middle Ages: Government and People 1200–1500* contains surprisingly little specific reference to Chaucer, but provides detailed information about the urban context of his writings. Equally brief in its treatment of Chaucer is Anthony Low's monograph *Aspects of Subjectivity: Society and Individuality from the Middle Ages to Shakespeare and Milton*, where it is surprising, given the study's wide-ranging nature, to find only the Pardoner and the Parson represented in the appended 'Further Considerations on Penance' (pp. 203–9).

In a clearly written and logically ordered study of *The Orient in Chaucer and Medieval Romance*, Carol F. Heffernan aims to show how the Orient and its people are represented in late medieval romance. After an initial chapter in which she introduces her thesis that there is a remarkable Oriental influence in medieval romance, and canters through various concepts of obvious relevance such as the Crusades, pilgrimage, and trade, Heffernan begins her literary analysis with a chapter on *The Man of Law's Tale*. Here she demonstrates how faith and commerce intersected in the medieval eastern Mediterranean. She also explores evidence of Christian–Muslim tensions within the narrative, and pays attention to the analogues written by Gower and Boccaccio. Chapter 3 focuses on the representation of Cleopatra and Dido in *The Legend of Good Women*, showing that these two North African queens are depicted as purveyors of sexual excess, while ostensibly being praised as models of true love; their claim to sainthood is thus deeply ambiguous. In the next chapter, on *The Squire's Tale*, Heffernan stands back slightly from her thesis, suggesting that, although the content of the tale is Oriental, its structure is firmly European, and that any structural resemblances between Western interlace and Eastern frame narratives are merely coincidental, not indications of particular influence. Two further chapters treat *Floris and Blancheflour* and *Le Bone Florence of Rome*, before a brief conclusion, and an afterword that gestures towards the appearance of the Orient in Elizabethan literature and drama, and in Johnson's *The History of Rasselas: Prince of Abyssinia*. Earlier versions of chapters 4 and 6 have already been published (see *YWES* 78[1999] 249–50). Overall this is an East-meets-West study which manages to be both concise and comprehensive, and which contains useful surveys of previous scholarship on each topic. However, its conclusion is too tame, and Heffernan's statement that Western writers of imaginative literature were inspired by Eastern culture seems unlikely to inspire a reaction to her call for a reconsideration of textual and cultural links between medieval European literature and the East.

Glenn Burger brings together much of his earlier work and more in *Chaucer's Queer Nation*. Earlier work appeared in (*YWES* 74[1995] 163–4, 78[1999] 244, 79[2000] 217, and 82[2003] 209, 212). The nation at issue is less the political entity, although that is certainly addressed, than community in its broadest social sense. Between the binary poles of essentialist and social constructionist views of identity, Burger finds a third way in queer theory, which, in employing laboured terms such as 'antihomophobia', aims by means of the double negative in the term to resist lapsing into counter-essentialism. Thinking 'queerly' entails thinking 'impurely and productively' (p. xviii). A strong theme in his consideration of the community is marriage, which he portrays as an emerging category that is 'good to think with' for the middling group of society, the lower gentry. Some time is spent on the historical background of medieval marriage, especially the Gregorian reform of the eleventh century, which helped fix the lines of distinction between lay marriage and clerical celibacy. The growing emphasis, however, on individual consent helped to unsettle fixed essential identities by enabling figures such as the Wife of Bath to disturb gender hierarchies. *The Merchant's Tale* and *The Franklin's Tale* are also seen to undo traditional notions of masculine agency. In many ways the book is about subjectivity rather than nation or community, though clearly the terms imply each other, and Burger threads his discussion of subjectivity through the tales, ending with a consideration of the final tales, where the poem's unfinished state illustrates the performative and ongoing manner in which identity is constructed.

Almost all of the essays in Lawton, Scase, and Copeland, eds., *New Medieval Literatures* 6, are relevant either to Chaucer or to the context of his works. Daniel Birkholz's lengthy essay, 'The Vernacular Map: Re-Charting English Literary History' (pp. 11–77), is about cartography and manuscripts, specifically the thirteenth-century Gough map and Thomas Butler's sixteenth-century copy of it in Yale University Beinecke Library MS 558. This wide-ranging discussion is also about astrology, geography, and commonplace books; it is not about Chaucer, but its suggestion that English literary history might be re-charted means that 'the name of the master (Our Father of English Literature)', must necessarily be invoked (p. 71). Clementine Oliver offers a richly historical study of 'A Political Pamphleteer in Late Medieval England: Thomas Fovent, Geoffrey Chaucer, Thomas Usk, and the Merciless Parliament of 1388' (pp. 167–98). She questions the identity and affiliation of Thomas Fovent, the author of the late fourteenth-century polemical tract, *Historia mirabilis parliamenti*, arguing that he was not, as has been believed, a pro-Appellant propagandist. She finds some similarities between Fovent's career and Chaucer's, and compares both authors' astuteness in dealing with factionalism and with the political failures of Thomas Usk. Although she discusses the pamphlet only briefly, she offers a revisionist account of its impact, and uses it to explore historiographical issues related to the way in which historians have read later medieval English political writings. Oliver's essay is followed by another historically informed piece, 'Commonalty and Literary Form in the 1370s and 1380s' (pp. 199–221), in which Emily Steiner discusses the Good Parliament of 1376 and *Piers Plowman*. This essay is not about Chaucer, but, as Steiner herself points out, its argument could easily be expanded to include *The Parliament of Fowls*. Similarly Jeremy Tambling's study of 'Allegory and the Madness of the Text: Hoccleve's *Complaint*' (pp. 223–48) draws analogies between Hoccleve's melancholia and that of Arcite in *The Knight's Tale*. *The Canterbury Tales* also feature briefly in Bruce W. Holsinger's 'Analytical Survey 6: Medieval Literature and Cultures of Performance' (pp. 271–311). The issue also contains essays on the Pardoner and *The Clerk's Tale*, reviewed below.

Voaden, Tixier, Sanchez Roura, and Rytting, eds., *The Medieval Translator*, contains twenty-eight essays on medieval translation, four of which take Chaucer as their principal focus. In the first of these David Wallace considers 'Chaucer and Deschamps, Translation and the Hundred Years' War' (pp. 179–88), arguing that Deschamps's acclamatory ballade (no. 285) to Chaucer must be read in the context of Anglo-French relations and conflict rather than in isolation. Maria K. Greenwood explores 'What Dryden Did to Chaucer's *The Knight's Tale*, or Translation as Ideological Input' (pp. 189–200), finding that Dryden's 'improvements' in *Palamon and Arcite* result in distortions of Chaucer's text, with a consequent loss of meaning and quality. Thomas G. Duncan compares different senses of translation between *Troilus* and *The Testament of Cresseid* in 'Calculating Calkas: Chaucer to Henryson' (pp. 215–22), arguing that Henryson's reconstructions serve to promote a charitable and compassionate reading of Cresseid. And Michael Alexander brings the benefits of practical experience translating medieval verse to an evaluation of 'Dante and *Troilus*' (pp. 201–13). Describing Dante as a 'concentrated ingredient' (p. 202) in Chaucer's poetry, he looks briefly at three areas of *Troilus* (the Invocations to each book, the lore of Hell, and ideas about Love), providing a list of the parallel passages from Dante's *Commedia* in an appendix. Alexander repeats some of his more general points about Chaucer and Dante in another short piece, 'Poets in Paradise: Chaucer, Pound, Eliot' (*PNR* 29[2003] 6–7).

Benson and Ridyard, eds., *New Readings of Chaucer's Poetry*, contains ten essays, introduced very briefly and in characteristically urbane manner by Derek Brewer (pp. 1–6). Most of Chaucer's poetry is represented in this collection, though *The Canterbury Tales*, unsurprisingly, receives most attention. The first two essays are both by Helen Cooper. She discusses first 'Chaucerian Representation' (pp. 7–29), and then 'Chaucer's Poetics' (pp. 31–50). In the first piece she argues that poetry for Chaucer was above all a matter of imitating other authors, rather than imitating life. In the second essay she considers why Chaucer aligned himself with English rather than French, comparing the status of fourteenth-century English to that of modern-day Welsh, and then offering readings of the dream poems in which she suggests a much later date for *The House of Fame* than is usually assumed. Chaucer's learning is praised by John V. Fleming in 'The Best Line in Ovid and the Worst' (pp. 51–74), who also charts various (surely well-known?) influences on *The Wife of Bath's Tale*. The next piece, by Traugott Lawler, 'Delicacy vs. Truth: Defining Moral Heroism in *The Canterbury Tales*' (pp. 75–90), is a lexical study which notes Chaucer's use of terms connected with *delit* in *The Canterbury Tales*, and argues that these words are used to convey a sense of decadence. William Provost looks closely at five of 'Chaucer's Endings' (pp. 91–105), namely those of *An ABC*, *Book of the Duchess*, *House of Fame*, *Troilus and Criseyde*, and *The Canterbury Tales*, finding that the endings of the earlier poems are better constructed than their beginnings, whereas in his later works Chaucer has a tendency to begin strongly and then run into trouble with his conclusions.

Three further contributions on *The Canterbury Tales* follow. In the first, '"Beth fructuous and that in litel space": The Engendering of Harry Bailly' (pp. 107–18), John Plummer speculates about the Host's interest in the sexuality of some of his fellow pilgrims, in particular the Nun's Priest, the Monk, and the Pardoner. William E. Rogers and Paul Dower have been 'Thinking about Money in Chaucer's *Shipman's Tale*' (pp. 119–38), wondering whether Chaucer is praising or blaming money, and suggesting that it is our own modern problematic relationships with money and language that complicate our understanding of the tale. And thirdly, Celia Lewis writes about the medieval preoccupation with mortality in 'Framing Fiction with Death: Chaucer's *Canterbury Tales* and the Plague' (pp. 139–64), looking closely at the tales of the Physician and the Pardoner, and ultimately proposing that Chaucer's work rejects any notion that fiction can order and prolong life. John Hill's essay on 'Aristocratic Friendship in *Troilus and Criseyde*: Pandarus, Courtly Love and Ciceronian Brotherhood in Troy' (pp. 165–82) contends that the friendship between Troilus and Pandarus is to be understood in terms of Cicero's *De amicitia*. Finally in the briefest contribution to the collection R. Barton-Palmer looks at 'Chaucer's *Legend of*

Good Women: The Narrator's Tale' (pp. 183–94), arguing that this poem should be seen as part of Chaucer's work in the French tradition, and outlining the way in which its most important structural features depend upon Guillaume de Machaut's *Jugement dou roy de Navarre*. Overall this is a worthy, if rather unexciting, collection of essays whose new readings are not those of current theoretical fashions.

The university presses of both Oxford and Cambridge offer companions to Chaucer this year. *The Oxford Companion to Chaucer*, edited by Douglas Gray, is a brand new, attractively packaged, and weighty addition to the reference shelf. Organized alphabetically in the manner of a mini-encyclopedia, this volume offers succinct and informative assessments of all aspects of Chaucer's life and writing, including his works, their characters, main themes and influences; language and metre; discussion of contemporary authors, genres, and philosophies; and details of Chaucer's critical reception over six centuries. Adorned with sixteen illustrations, the volume comes complete with maps, a chronology, and ample pointers to further reading, and is copiously (occasionally irritatingly), cross-referenced. Though it is churlish to complain about what is omitted from an offering as rich as this, it is surprising to find no entries on 'scribe' and 'translation', and to be redirected in a search for 'manuscripts' ('see book', p. 309). There are individual entries on Ellesmere and Hengwrt, but other important codices go unmentioned, and the representation of modern editors, printers, and illustrators is patchy: Skeat and Furnivall are afforded entries, as is William Morris, but not Manly and Rickert nor Mary Haweis. However these quibbles should not detract from Gray's achievement; with over two thousand entries this volume will surely achieve its stated aim to be a practical guide to readers of Chaucer at every level.

Boitani and Mann, eds., *The Cambridge Companion to Chaucer* is the other type of literary companion, comprising a set of critical essays. This volume first appeared in 1986 (*YWES* 67[1988] 169–70) and has become a true staple of undergraduate bibliographies, so its revamped reappearance is most welcome. Although the structure of the book remains essentially the same, the original contributors have rewritten and updated their essays, and there are some new commissions that take into account recent trends in literary theory as well as in Chaucer studies. There are now seventeen essays, some orientated towards specific texts, and others of a more general and contextual nature; a handy chronology has also been added. The opening piece by Paul Strohm sets 'The Social and Literary Scene in England' (pp. 1–19). This is followed by twin studies of Chaucer's European background: Ardis Butterfield outlines 'Chaucer's French Inheritance' (pp. 20–35), and David Wallace does the same service for 'Chaucer's Italian Inheritance' (pp. 36–57).

Piero Boitani's elegant discussion of Chaucer's bookish world, 'Old Books Brought to Life in Dreams: *The Book of the Duchess*, *The House of Fame*, *The Parliament of Fowls*' (pp. 58–77), is the first of the text-specific essays. This is followed by two studies of *Troilus*: Mark Lambert's account of 'Telling the Story in *Troilus and Criseyde*' (pp. 78–92) focuses on the poem's narrative techniques and the figure of the poet-narrator, while Jill Mann compares 'Chance and Destiny in *Troilus and Criseyde* and *The Knight's Tale*' (pp. 93–111).

The complexities of 'The *Legend of Good Women*' are highlighted by Julia Boffey and A.S.G. Edwards (pp. 112–26) in a newly commissioned discussion that is underpinned by reference to the poem's manuscript context. Five essays on *The Canterbury Tales* follow. In the first, '*The Canterbury Tales*: Personal Drama or Experiments in Poetic Variety?' (pp. 127–42), C. David Benson offers an overview of the dynamic diversity of the fictional pilgrims and the doubly fictional figures who populate their stories. The generic variety of Chaucer's story collection is then explored in four successive essays that treat romance (by J.A. Burrow, pp. 143–59), comedy (by Derek Pearsall, pp. 160–77), pathos (by Robert Worth Frank, Jr, pp. 178–94), and exemplum and fable (by A.C. Spearing, pp. 195–213). The final essays, which are mostly new, resume a more general approach. Barry Windeatt surveys 'Literary Structures in Chaucer' (pp. 214–32), while Christopher Cannon offers an appreciation of 'Chaucer's Style' (pp. 233–50). In 'Chaucer's Presence and Absence, 1400–1550' (pp. 251–69), James Simpson considers aspects of the reception of Chaucer's poetry, particularly in the early modern era. A final substantial chapter, by Carolyn Dinshaw, offers a selective survey of 'New Approaches to Chaucer' (pp. 270–89), concentrating on feminist, queer, and postcolonial readings of the medieval poet. The collection concludes with 'Further Reading: A Guide to Chaucer Studies' (pp. 290–306), a discursive bibliography compiled and thoroughly updated by Joerg O. Fichte.

Another useful addition to general undergraduate reading lists that comes from the same stable is Dinshaw and Wallace, eds., *The Cambridge Companion to Medieval Women's Writing*. References to Chaucer's works are to be found *passim*, as in Daniel T. Kline's survey of 'Female Childhoods' (pp. 13–20), which is heavily dependent upon literary examples drawn from *The Canterbury Tales* and *Pearl*. More sustained discussion is offered by Barbara Hanawalt, whose legalistic essay on 'Widows' (pp. 58–69) summarizes the varied options open to women such as Criseyde, Alison, and the poor peasant widow of *The Nun's Priest's Tale*, and by Alcuin Blamires, who begins his chapter, 'Beneath the Pulpit' (pp. 141–58), a summary of the rights, limitations, rituals and contributions of women in relation to the Church, with the narrative of Mabel in *The Friar's Tale*.

Matthew Boyd Goldie has made a range of historical texts, cultural documents, and images available in *Middle English Literature: A Historical Sourcebook*. Both well-known and less familiar writings are included: parliamentary and local acts and trials, letters and testimonies, moral, homiletic and educational tracts—items otherwise difficult to access, chosen for their intrinsic significance and for the light that they can shed on the context of Middle English literature. Documents are translated or glossed as necessary, and furnished with useful introductions; other supporting materials (a timeline, map, bibliographies, explanations of currency, prices, measures), are present in abundance. The collection has some weaknesses: the selection is self-confessedly narrowly English, excluding material on Ireland, Wales and Scotland, and the illustrations, principally from manuscripts, are perhaps the least exciting offerings to students of Chaucer since they comprise the most obvious and frequently reproduced images (from Ellesmere, the Hoccleve portrait, the *Troilus* frontispiece). Despite this, students will find this a helpful compendium when attempting to understand the realities of life in later medieval England.

Editor Wendy Harding's *Drama, Narrative and Poetry in the 'Canterbury Tales'* brings together essays that consider the poem's aesthetic organization. C. David Benson opens the first section, dealing with general aesthetic issues, with 'Trust the Tale, Not the Teller' (pp. 21–33), in which he seeks to de-emphasize the influence of the pilgrims and their alleged naturalism in understanding their tales as poetry. Pasolini's *I racconti di Canterbury* is becoming an ongoing interest (see *YWES* 83[2004] 210), and in 'Narrative Play and the Display of Artistry in Chaucer's *Canterbury Tales* and Pasolini's *I racconti di Canterbury*' (pp. 35–50), Agnès Blandeau finds that the mannered fictionality of the film's stories enables a fresh consideration of the irony and narrativity of Chaucer's poem. Leo Carruthers reminds us of the ongoing and controlling presence of Harry Bailly in 'Narrative Voice, Narrative Framework: The Host as "Author" of *The Canterbury Tales*' (pp. 51–67). Despite obvious differences between the Host's aesthetic sensibility and that of Chaucer, whether as poet or pilgrim, the Host does much of the work of an author, makes insightful enough criticisms of the tales, and adds complexity and resonance to Chaucer's artistic intention. John M. Ganim borrows a phrase from Northrop Frye in 'Drama, Theatricality and Performance: Radicals of Presentation in *The Canterbury Tales*' (pp. 69–82). The term indicates the multiple meanings at work in 'audience', which refers equally to the audience of a performance and to the readership of a book. When we consider that Chaucer may have read aloud to listeners, the inadequacy of our terminology becomes evident, and, in a revision of Kittredge's conception of the pilgrimage as roadside drama, Ganim speaks of the theatricality of Chaucer's poetry.

In 'Linking *The Canterbury Tales*: Monkey-Business in the Margins' (pp. 83–98), Laura Kendrick conceives of the verbal tomato-throwing between pilgrims as a textual example of the kind of rude humour that exists between the text and the illustrated margin, such as we see in the Rutland Psalter (British Library MS Add. 62925). The high point of such marginal slapstick illumination was a century before Chaucer, and thus Chaucer's playful narrative represents the textual internalization of the illuminated page. In its reduction of everything to 'discourse', contemporary criticism largely and wrongly overlooks the difference between poetry and prose, argues Derek Pearsall in 'Towards a Poetics of Chaucerian Narrative' (pp. 99–112). Colette Stévanovitch takes this point to heart and concludes the section on general aesthetics in an accessible and informative consideration of 'Polysyllabic Words in End-of-Line Position in *The Franklin's Tale*' (pp. 113–24). Polysyllabic words, being largely of French extraction, are frequently placed at the end of lines by Chaucer, and offer considerable flexibility and nuance not only in metrical but also in semantic terms, for polysyllabic nouns are frequently abstract. Her prosodic analysis neatly highlights the thematic centrality of *gentilesse*.

Derek Brewer opens the book's second section, which treats of individual tales, with 'Knight and Miller: Similarity and Difference' (pp. 127–38). The two tales represent Chaucer at his two extremes, and the close juxtaposition of the extremities reveal the gothic aesthetic of his verse. In 'The Wife of Bath's

"Wanderynge by the Weye" and Conduct Literature for Women' (pp. 139–55) Juliette Dor shows how Alison's considerable failings act out many of the warnings of conduct books, a genre often ignored in consideration of her make-up. Lesley Lawton writes about the various levels at which language works in '"Glose whoso wole": Voice, Text and Authority in *The Wife of Bath's Prologue*' (pp. 157–74). The misogynist convention that women are natural manipulators of language is both confirmed and undone by Alison, yet at the same time, Lawton argues, the Wife is not so much an 'ontologically conceived character' as a textual composite (p. 170). Noting a certain ambivalence in fourteenth-century marriages on the subject of female agency, Elizabeth Robertson nonetheless finds Chaucer a sympathetic proponent of it in 'Marriage, Mutual Consent, and the Affirmation of the Female Subject in *The Knight's Tale*, *The Wife of Bath's Tale*, and *The Franklin's Tale*' (pp. 175–93). Susanna Fein traces philosophical patterns of contrariety, crisis, and union in 'Boethian Boundaries: Compassion and Constraint in *The Franklin's Tale*' (pp. 195–212). In 'Poetry and Play in *The Nun's Priest's Tale* and *The Pardoner's Tale*' (pp. 213–26) David Raybin notes the many voices of Chaucer: in the case of *The Pardoner's Tale* it is direct and sentential; in that of *The Nun's Priest's Tale* it is multiple and playful. Together, the narrative range enacts the philosophical requirement that poetry should offer both *sentence* and *solaas*. André Crépin notes the correlations between Chauntecleer, the Nun's Priest, and Chaucer as expositors of the text in 'The Cock, the Priest, and the Poet' (pp. 227–36). Finally, Hélène Dauby notes the presence of—but comes to no clear conclusion about—'The Generation Gap in *The Canterbury Tales*' (pp. 237–41).

John C. Hirsh's new anthology *Medieval Lyric: Middle English Lyrics, Ballads, and Carols*, is predominantly a collection of anonymous lyric texts, but Chaucer is granted an appendix where five of his shorter poems appear, along with two embedded lyrics from *The Canterbury Tales*. The topic of Chaucer's metrics has attracted little scholarship this year. An exception is Michael Redford's investigation of word stress in 'Middle English Stress Doubles: New Evidence from Chaucer's Meter' (in Fikkert and Jacobs, eds., *Development in Prosodic Systems*, pp. 159–95). Focusing on 'stress doubles' in *The Canterbury Tales*, that is, words that sometimes have initial, and sometimes final, stress, Redford asks whether these provide evidence for Middle English stress or for Chaucer's metrical style. He demonstrates that the distribution of stress doubles is very regular—Strong-Weak line internally and Weak-Strong at line-internal phrase boundaries and at the end of a line—and concludes that word stress in Middle English was initial, except at the end of phrases, where both syllables were prominent. In the same volume Wim Zonneveld's essay, 'Constraining S and Satisfying Fit' (pp. 197–247) is focused mainly on *The Life of St Lutgart* and the metrics of Middle Dutch poetry, but his analysis involves numerous comparisons with Chaucer's works.

Glenn Burger and Steven F. Kruger advocate more extensive pedagogical use of queer theory in their essay 'Queer Chaucer in the Classroom' (in Agathocleous and Dean, eds., *Teaching Literature: A Companion*, pp. 31–40). They begin with a brief survey of the impact that gay/lesbian/queer studies have had on medieval literary criticism, noting that queer theory has now extended to emphasize the unstable relations between normative social categories and complexly lived experiences. They propose that attention be shifted away from the usual focus on the Pardoner to other aspects of *The Canterbury Tales*, including the marriage group and the idea of Chaucer the pilgrim. In this way, they hope, queer theory may be used to call into question the set of relations between our current position as readers of Chaucer and medieval constructions of sexuality and identity.

A different type of teaching aid is surveyed by Teresa P. Reed in 'Overcoming Performance Anxiety: Chaucer Studio Products Reviewed' (*Exemplaria* 15[2003] 245–61). The Chaucer Studio's recordings emerge very favourably from this review. Reed offers anecdotal evidence of her own use of various audio tapes in the classroom, and is obviously more pleased with their effects than were the other reviewers she cites. William F. Woods puts Chaucer and freshmen writing composition together in 'The Chaucer Foundation: Composition, Social History, and *The Canterbury Tales*' (*SMART* 10[2003] 51–85). Freshman composition aims to train the student in techniques of research, argumentation, and exposition, and content is thus secondary. Woods speaks of his experiences of using social history and Chaucer as the occasion for freshman writing training: what works and what does not. There are many good topic ideas and useful references in the article, although the narrative never rises above the anecdotal to achieve a thesis as such. A detailed syllabus concludes the piece. In 'Teaching *The Squire's Tale* as an Exercise in Literary History' (*SMART* 10[2003] 5–18), Alan Ambrisco notes the popularity of the tale up to the eighteenth century, and the waning in critical acclaim since then, despite recent consideration of its interest in the exotic and national otherness. He poses the tale to the students as an unsolved problem in reception, thereby dispatching them as critical detectives to do their homework on new-critical reception (the Squire's use of rhetoric and the tale's unfinished state), pre-modern reception (Hengwrt and early commentary on the tale), and modern concerns (Orientalism).

Discussed here rather than along with other critical essays on the Wife of Bath is Merrill Black's 'Three Readings of the Wife of Bath' (in Freedman and Frey, eds., *Autobiographical Writing across the Disciplines: A Reader*, pp. 85–95). The three readings refer not to different critical stances but to the three times Black encountered the *Prologue* and *Tale* in her reading experience, as a high-school student, undergraduate, and postgraduate. The autobiographical note is sounded of course in the volume's title, and the author proceeds to weave a connection between Alice and her own experiences as a former battered wife: Alice's deafness and Black's ruptured spleen, what women want, split consciousness, etc. The essay cuts clean across the divide between creative and critical discourse in a way that raises important questions for the convention of objectivity in academe—an effect that is clearly the aim of the entire collection. Taking the editors' challenge seriously will surely affect not only what we require of ourselves when writing but also what we expect of our students.

The presidential address at the 2002 New Chaucer Society conference was given by Helen Cooper and is printed, more or less verbatim, in this year's *Studies in the Age of Chaucer* (25 [2003] 3–24). Entitled 'After Chaucer', this essentially comprises a few thoughts on Chaucer's various later translations and adaptations in verse and drama, and, more recently, film. Cooper begins with an extended and rather unedifying account of the design that adorned the 2002 advance programme cover (not even, it turns out, the programme that was actually distributed at the conference), before moving on to plead for a rehabilitation of the fifteenth century, still, she insists (despite mountains of recent work), the Cinderella of Chaucer studies. She concludes by offering the full text of the broadside ballad, 'The Wanton Wife of Bath' (*c.*1600), lightly annotated but otherwise without comment, aside from her judgement that this is 'one of the most delightful translations ever made After Chaucer' (p. 20). Thinking broadly along the same lines, A.E.B. Coldiron writes about 'Paratextual Chaucerianism: Naturalizing French Texts in Early Printed Verse' (*ChauR* 38[2003] 1–15), discussing the translator's prologue to *The Fyftene Joyes of Maryage* printed by Wynkyn de Worde in 1509. The translator uses rhyme royal and a number of recognizably Chaucerian conventions, presumably to enhance the perceived value of the work, a translation of the anonymous *Les Quinze Joyes de mariage*, and to help it gain an English literary citizenship. And as part of an examination of 'Fifteenth-Century English Collections of Female Saints' Lives' (*YES* 33[2003] 131–41), A.S.G. Edwards suggests that Chaucer's *Second Nun's Tale* may have been the earliest influential model of the separately circulating female saint's life in Middle English verse, a tradition shaped and extended especially within East Anglia by Bokenham, Lydgate, and Capgrave.

Chaucer's afterlife in the sixteenth century continues to attract increasing amounts of critical attention. Robert Costomiris attempts to throw 'Some New Light on the Early Career of William Thynne, Chief Clerk of the Kitchen of Henry VIII and Editor of Chaucer' (*Library* 4[2003] 3–15). He notes that some of Thynne's official appointments were postponed 'for years and sometimes for his entire career' (p. 14), a fact that has previously been overlooked. Thynne therefore had more time to indulge in editing and publishing, and may have seen these activities as an alternative means of self-advancement. Sarah A. Kelen examines what she terms the 'Tudorization' of Chaucer in 'Climbing up the Family Tree: Chaucer's Tudor Progeny' (*JEBS* 6[2003] 109–23). Her essay focuses on the full-page engraving that occurs in Thomas Speght's 1598 edition of Chaucer's *Works* depicting Chaucer's lineage and explicitly associating this with that of the Tudor royal family; she suggests that this may have been a ploy to increase Chaucer's apparent relevance to the Elizabethan reader. If Cambridge University Library, Peterborough B.6.13 is anything to go by, Tudor readers of Chaucer were particularly inept, observes Seth Lerer in 'Unpublished Sixteenth-Century Arguments to *The Canterbury Tales*' (*N&Q* 50[2003] 13–17). Lerer judges the annotations to this printed copy of part of Chaucer's works both banal and an important personal response to the poetry, as in, for example, the reader's fascination with the magic gadgets in *The Squire's Tale*; he also notes the emergence of the 'argument' or plot summary as a publishing phenomenon in the sixteenth century, and finds them valuable for the evidence they reveal about the changing nature of post-medieval English vocabulary.

In 'Translating Thebes: Lydgate's *Siege of Thebes* and Stow's Chaucer' (*ELH* 70[2003] 319–41), Robert R. Edwards deftly charts the relocation of Lydgate's work of Lancastrian propaganda about kingship in Stow's early Elizabethan discourse of monarchy, nationhood, and debated political authority. Finally, in his study of 'Robert Henryson's Pastoral Burlesque "Robene and Makyne" (*c.*1470)' (*FCS* 28[2003] 80–96) Michael G. Cornelius compares Makyne to the Wife of Bath, and claims that Henryson's poem represents an overwhelming satirical complication of popular literary conventions.

Chaucer's influence on modern literature also continues to provoke critical attention. Julie Carlson gives a few nods towards the importance of Chaucer and the romance revival for the Romantic movement in her account of 'Fancy's History' (*ERR* 14[2003] 163–76). Solomon Sallfors and James Duban propose a connection between *The Miller's Tale* and *Moby-Dick* in 'Chaucerian Humor in *Moby-Dick*: Queequeg's "Ramadan"' (*Leviathan* 5[2003] 73–7). Melville, who is known to have enjoyed Chaucer, creates a Chaucerian subtext in his novel by making Ishmael in the image of John the husband (both characters share a number of plot details). Although his resemblance is closest to the superstitious carpenter, Ishmael also possesses Nicholas's scholasticism.

In an issue of *SAIL* dedicated to Carter Revard, Osage poet and medievalist, Peter Beidler, in 'Louise Erdrich's Lulu Nanapush: A Modern-Day Wife of Bath?' (*SAIL* 15[2003] 92–103), attempts to free American Indian literature from misconceptions of it as a body of work sealed from the influence of other cultures. In Erdrich's *Tales of Burning Love*, Beidler suggests the Chaucerian inspiration of the frame-tale structure, and in Erdrich's *Love Medicine*, he sees a connection between Lulu Nanapush Morrisey Lamartine and the Wife of Bath. Warren Edminster writes about 'Fairies and Feminism: Recurrent Patterns in Chaucer's *The Wife of Bath's Tale* and Brontë's *Jane Eyre*' (*VN* 104[2003] 22–8). In both stories the passing of fairies and elves is bemoaned, and in each case the nostalgia represents both an idealization of the past, and a lost world of feminine power that gives way to masculine rule. Both stories feature rape, in Chaucer's case literal, in Brontë's symbolic, when Rochester intends to wed Jane illegally. And both men must ultimately learn the feminine power of faery. Charlotte Brontë could well have encountered *The Canterbury Tales* in Pope's modernized version of the poem, despite the fact that she never mentions Chaucer by name.

Meanwhile Patricia Ingham's chapter 'Contrapuntal Histories' (in Ingham and Warren, eds., *Postcolonial Moves: Medieval Through Modern*, pp. 47–70) charts recent uses of categories of historicist and cultural alterity in medieval cultural studies. Giving first a medievalist reading of the tropes of medieval Britain in Conrad's *Heart of Darkness*, and then an analysis of the various histories and geographies enshrined within *The Man of Law's Tale*, Ingham proposes that the contrapuntal histories of her title offer a more mobile historicist method for assessing the complex repetitions of colonial instability and oppositional agency. Larry Scanlon writes on 'Poets Laureate and the Language of Slaves: Petrarch, Chaucer, and Langston Hughes' (in Somerset and Watson, eds., *The Vulgar Tongue: Medieval and Postmedieval Vernacularity*, pp. 220–56), offering a rich theoretical discussion of the strange parallels between Middle English studies and African American studies, in their deep but apparently unrelated current engagement with the issue of vernacularity.

Finally, in a piece received too late for inclusion in last year's review, "Glorie of Spayne": Juan Ruiz through the Eyes of an Englishman' (*RCEI* 45[2002] 233–44), Eugenio M. Olivares Merino seeks to revive the notion that Chaucer may have been familiar with medieval Spanish literature, in particular the *Libro de Buen Amor*. Various possible channels of transmission are identified, based on the patronage of John of Gaunt and his Iberian familial connections, in order to suggest that the perceived similarities between the *Libro de Buen Amor*, *Troilus*, and *The Canterbury Tales* were more than the result of shared authorial temperament and contemporary environment.

2. The Canterbury Tales

Perhaps the largest body of work done this year is on the illustrations through the ages of *The Canterbury Tales*. Mary Olson's *Fair and Varied Forms: Visual Textuality in Medieval Illuminated Manuscripts* considers the double aspect of medieval manuscripts as objects both to be read and looked at, and Ellesmere is a chosen example of such doubleness. Given that her previous chapters are devoted to earlier medieval manuscripts, Olson spends some time considering the historical developments of book production to carry her discussion into the early fifteenth century. The general cultural shift is traced towards private reading, which results in a certain bookishness of late medieval manuscripts, a literary self-reflexivity that is clear in such features as the visually distinctive shape of *Thopas*'s tail rhymes, and the Ellesmere glosses, the letters of which are the same size as the main text. For Olson, Ellesmere stands between two cultural modes, oral and literate, telling and writing, and the tension is mirrored in the relationship between the marginal illuminations and text. The portrait of Chaucer himself and his two tales demonstrate the tension at its strongest. Where *Thopas* calls into question his poetic abilities, his portrait gives him an added air of authority. The portraits display both signature motifs that render them types, such as the Physician's urinal, and individuating details from the poet's description. In this respect, Ellesmere stands in contrast to the workmanlike Hengwrt, whose lack of adornment invites a studious reading of text rather than an admiring gaze at images.

Olson's discussion reappears as the opening chapter, 'Marginal Portraits and the Fiction of Orality: The Ellesmere Manuscript' of Finley and Rosenblum, eds., *Chaucer Illustrated: Five Hundred Years of 'The Canterbury Tales' in Pictures* (pp. 1–35). This is a hefty volume, and remarkably good value considering its number of illustrations and spacious layout. It takes us from the Ellesmere portraits to the twentieth-century illustrations of Rockwell Kent and Eric Gill. The presentation of material tends more towards description and historical context than interpretation. Philippa Hardman discusses the relative dearth of pictorial illustration in the manuscript tradition of Chaucer's poem in 'Presenting the Text: Pictorial Tradition in Fifteenth-Century Manuscripts of *The Canterbury Tales*' (pp. 37–72). Some were there but have been excised, as is the case with Cambridge University Library MS Gg.4.27, but Hardman argues that the illuminators of both the Cambridge and the Ellesmere manuscripts drew from a common tradition, where the intention was to have presented the tales as an ordered series of differing narrative voices, each one marked with its own portrait at the beginning of its tale. Her survey leads her to affirm conclusions reached by

Joyce Coleman (*YWES* 77[1998] 216–17) that the manuscripts were read aloud as a social performance to a group of listeners. The portraits function as visual cues to the reader. Next David R. Carlson considers 'The Woodcut Illustrations in Early Printed Editions of Chaucer's *Canterbury Tales*' (pp. 73–119). The series that really counts is Caxton's second edition of 1483, where, Carlson argues, Caxton aimed for something new, sparing no expense and reproducing the woodcuts twice in the volume, once in *The General Prologue* and again in the body of tales. Even so, the woodcuts show less individuation than do the Ellesmere portraits. Subsequent reproductions were increasingly parsimonious, and Pynson's woodcut series of 1492 is effectively a reprint of Caxton's, done to supply demand for more issue rather than to achieve any new artistic agenda.

In the same volume, Betsy Bowden continues her work on eighteenth-century representations of Chaucer (*YWES* 72[1993] 255) in 'Tales Told and the Tellers of Tales: Illustrations of *The Canterbury Tales* in the Course of the Eighteenth Century' (pp. 121–90). The pictures are wonderful, and amongst the treasures reproduced are the portrait sequence of James Jefferys, thought lost, but found by Bowden in the Houghton Library. The work of 'visionary artist' John Mortimer (p. 126) and 'hard-working artisan' Thomas Stothard (p. 126) are also presented in detail. The pilgrim portraits of the John Urry edition of *The Canterbury Tales* [1721] have been unattributed, but Bowden proposes John Vanderbank as the artist.

In 'From Canterbury to Jerusalem: Interpreting Blakes's *Canterbury Pilgrims*' (pp. 191–209), Warren Stevenson briefly considers Blake's pilgrims in light of his accompanying *Descriptive Catalogue*, which is reproduced in full as an appendix. 'Thomas Stothard's *The Pilgrimage to Canterbury* (1806): A Study in Promotion and Popular Taste' (pp. 211–31) has been wrongly overshadowed by Blake's pilgrim portraits, argues Dennis M. Read. In its time it was greatly praised for its natural simplicity and lack of mannerism. Judith L. Fisher and Mark Allen fill in the gap between Stothard and Blake at one end of the nineteenth century and the Kelmscott Chaucer of 1896 at the other with 'Victorian Illustrations to Chaucer's *Canterbury Tales*' (pp. 233–73). Here they trace various kinds of Victorian medievalism in the depictions—antiquarian, romantic, popular, etc.—that despite their differing emphases all regard the medieval as a stable cultural order with a genial 'old Dan Chaucer'.

The medieval nonetheless felt distinctly modern to the Victorians. 'The Kelmscott Chaucer' is considered by Duncan Robinson (pp. 274–310), who includes many engaging excerpts from Burne-Jones as he recorded his work on the project: 'I have put myself wholly aside, trying to see things as Chaucer saw them. Not once have I invaded his kingdom with one hostile thought' (p. 285), and, most feelingly, 'I wish Chaucer could once and for all make up his unrivalled and precious mind' (p. 287). Two final essays bring us into the twentieth century: Jake Milgram Wien on 'Rockwell Kent's Canterbury Pilgrims' (pp. 311–25) and Peter Holliday on 'The Golden Cockerel Press, *The Canterbury Tales*, and Eric Gill: Decoration and the *Mise-en-page*' (pp. 326–67). Both bring a distinctively modern sensibility to the portraits. Kent's pilgrims are characteristically depicted off their horses and in motion; hence the Friar sits and plays a fiddle. Gill's are stylized, and devoid of both sentiment and historical sensibility. Two other appendices conclude this tome: Maria McGarrity's edition of William Paulet Carey's *Critical Description of the Procession of Chaucer's Pilgrims to Canterbury* by Stothard, and William K. Finley's 'Chaucer at Home: The Canterbury Pilgrims at Georgian Court'.

The same editors have had a busy year. Joseph Rosenblum with William K. Finley, in 'Chaucer Gentrified: The Nexus of Art and Politics in the Ellesmere Miniatures' (*ChauR* 38[2003] 140–57), contend that, while Chaucer's language could not be changed, the artists of Ellesmere steered away from the anti-establishment satire endemic in his text and deliberately toned down their subjects, probably in response to the wishes of a conservative patron. Their suggestion seems to corroborate Jones's thesis above that Ellesmere is a study in ideological appropriation. Charlotte Morse's survey, 'Popularizing Chaucer in the Nineteenth Century' (*ChauR* 38[2003] 99–125), is ostensibly a study of three men, Charles Cowden Clarke, Charles Knight, and John Saunders, who promoted Chaucer's readership before it became the object of university study. Her article includes detailed discussion of nineteenth-century illustrations of *The Canterbury Tales*, especially *The Clerk's Tale*. She also draws comparisons with the later twentieth century, and eventually her essay turns into a plea that twenty-first-century academics should keep Chaucer on the syllabus.

In the first chapter of *Chaucer and the 'Canterbury Tales': A Short Introduction*, John C. Hirsh asks 'Who was Geoffrey Chaucer?'. The answer is not simply a question of data, and Hirsh attempts to convey something of the atmosphere of the poet's London, paralleling its diversity with the multi-ethnic modern city. The portrait he draws of Chaucer imputes guilt for the rape of Cecily Chaumpaigne, and reminds us that, according to Thomas Speght, Chaucer was supposed to have beaten up a Franciscan friar. In the short chapter on 'Gender and Religion, Race and Class', Hirsh hedges his bets, commenting that Chaucer treats masculinity with as much ambiguity as he does femininity. By way of illustration, Hirsh first demonstrates the similarity between the Shipman and Chaucer's notorious contemporary, John Hawley, and then considers the paradox of such a manly man telling a tale that was originally assigned to the Wife of Bath. For Hirsh, 'gender' concerns never occur as the single focus of interest in Chaucer, but are consistently mediated through other categories—race, class, religion. Hirsh admits to an uncertainty with which we are all familiar: whether Chaucer ironically distances himself from some representation or just describes things the way he sees them. The uncertainty is acute in relation to hot topics such as anti-feminism and anti-Semitism, although we can be fairly sure that Chaucer was not a modern democrat on such matters. One notable feature of the book is his explicit discussion of recent critical classics and the critical opinions they espouse: for example, he discusses how the Knight has never looked quite the same again since Terry Jones finished with him. Although this helps readers to situate themselves in relation to those opinions, it runs the danger of dating the discussion. A third chapter, entitled 'Others', argues against any neat us/them treatment of alterity and includes in its discussion the tales of the Canon Yeoman and Squire. As this and subsequent chapters progress (chapter 4 on love, chapter 5 on God), his categories become so vague that one ends up feeling that any of the tales could have been made to fit into any chapter. The analysis is thoughtful, however and, as student introductions go, this one has its uses.

The second edition of Winthrop Wetherbee's student guide, *Chaucer: The 'Canterbury Tales'*, does not show significant changes from its first edition in 1989. The three-page 'Guide to Further Reading' at the end of the book is updated, but since the annotation is minimal, a search through a library catalogue might produce as much information. In contrast to Hirsh, who situates his ideas in relation to current critical opinion, Wetherbee never incorporates recent criticism explicitly into his discussion. The short section on Chaucer's language, for example, would have been an ideal place to discuss the originality or otherwise of Chaucer's English in light of Christopher Cannon's discussion (*YWES* 79[2000] 204–5). N.S. Thompson continues his features on Chaucer in Jay Parini's British Writers series, *Classics*, volume 1, with an overview of 'Geoffrey Chaucer's *The Canterbury Tales*' (pp. 41–63). The background to the poem is considered: the pilgrimage industry and its possibilities for satire; the mendicant orders and anti-mendicant protest; Lollardy; the Hundred Years War; the inspiration of Boccaccio's *Decameron*. Thompson works through the poem fragment by fragment, building up a picture of a world of lost ideals, portrayed ironically by Chaucer's narrator, who describes the pilgrims' faults as if they were virtues. In this fast-disappearing world of communal good, encroached on by a new ethic of private interest, Chaucer emerges as one of the first 'modern' authors (p. 59).

Marie Borroff brings together new and previously published work in *Traditions and Renewals: Chaucer, the Gawain-Poet, and Beyond*; for her previous work, see *YWES* 79[2000] 222. In the main it is the first two chapters that comprise the new material. In chapter 1 she argues that the main sin of friar Thomas in *The Summoner's Tale* is blasphemy, and notes that 'savour' in the text puns on both flavour and smell, a point already brought to our attention by Thomas D. Hanks. Connection is made between the Pardoner and anti-mendicancy, and this is set into a long and dilatory consideration of the first anti-mendicant work, William of St Amour's *De Periculis novissimorum temporum*, of Jean de Meun's *Fals Semblant* (Jean de Meun and William of St Amour being possible colleagues in Paris), John Wyclif, and Richard Fitzralph. The argument is slow to build up, and unsatisfying when it arrives; ultimately it does not justify the extended consideration of background material. In chapter 2, Borroff defends the crudity of 'in he throng' in *The Merchant's Tale*, on the grounds that, in the story, January is impotent and May pregnant by Damian. Chaucer exacts revenge on January in an oblique manner, and this 'silent retribution' is his *modus operandi* when dealing with any politically charged material such as laws of inheritance. Chaucer points the way to interpretation, but leaves it to the reader to make the final connections.

Two of Chaucer's women, Constance and the Wife of Bath, feature among the five female characters used as templates by Teresa P. Reed in *Shadows of Mary: Reading the Virgin Mary in Medieval Texts*. This short study analyses the figure of Mary, variously defined as virgin, mother, daughter, and wife, in medieval theological, philosophical, and literary texts, in order to show that stories about her were influential in the creation of other female characters. Thus in the first chapter Reed discusses narratives of Mary's birth and death, linking these to the preoccupation with death and legality that is foregrounded in *The Man of Law's Tale*. In the second chapter Reed contends that, although Mary is nominally absent from *The Wife of Bath's Tale*, she is nevertheless very much a part of it; aspects of the annunciation and incarnation are brought to bear on this reading of Chaucer's text. Two further chapters focus on the *English Trotula*, the legend of St Margaret of Antioch, and *Pearl*. Reed's approach is one that combines careful contextual close reading with post-structuralist theories of language, subjectivity, and gender; the result is interesting, but not altogether convincing, and her discussion would have benefited from more rigorous organization and the provision of a separate conclusion. Previous versions of chapters 1 and 4 have already appeared (see *YWES* 81[2002] 182).

The *Canterbury Tales* project has generated a cluster of articles this year. Peter Robinson provides an overview of 'The History, Discoveries, and Aims of the *Canterbury Tales* Project' (*ChauR* 38[2003] 126–39), in which he reminds us of the contention that all of the extant copies of the poem descend from a small number of manuscripts produced by a group of scribes within a few years before and after Chaucer's death. He dodges the perennial question, 'Hengwrt or Ellesmere?' ('our research suggests that the relationship between the two manuscripts cannot be simply categorized', p. 132), but is clear about the presentation of results, noting the danger that supposedly all-inclusive editions can simply become accumulations of material. The project is now using an electronic publishing program, the Anastasia system, to organize its output, which is proving more flexible than the DynaText software used in earlier publications. The two most recent CD-ROM publications to issue from the project, Bordalejo, ed., *Caxton's Canterbury Tales: The British Library Copies*, and Lloyd-Morgan, ed., *The Hengwrt Chaucer: Standard Edition*, are examples of what this program can achieve. Bordalejo's work is notable for containing the first ever full-colour facsimiles of any copies of William Caxton's first and second editions of *The Tales*, and the first electronic publication of the full text of any copy of these editions. Lloyd-Morgan's CD-ROM offers full-colour digital images and full text transcripts of every page of Hengwrt, and presents images and text of the Merthyr fragment as well; unusually, the editor's introduction is written in English and Welsh. Barbara Bordalejo notes an inaccuracy in 'The Collational Formula of Caxton's Second Edition of *The Canterbury Tales*' (*ANQ* 16[2003] 8–10). The particular copy of which she speaks, held at St John's College Library, Oxford, is often thought of as the only perfect edition of the thirteen extant copies. The current 312 leaves should in fact have been 314, and the copy is missing the first and last leaves, which have been cut. There are, then, no fully intact surviving copies of Caxton's second edition.

Orietta da Rold offers a detailed analysis of 'The Quiring System in Cambridge University Library MS Dd.4.24 of Chaucer's *Canterbury Tales*' (*Library* 4[2003] 107–28), which includes a complete collation of the manuscript keyed to its contents, and illustrations of the watermarks. Her research posits a close relationship between the quiring system and the text, and prompts speculation about the role that the early scribe or supervisor may have played in establishing the ordering of the tales. She also suggests that, far from being a provincial product, Dd may be the work of a skilful scribe working in the Westminster area of London. Another discussion of tale order, 'Analyzing the Order of Items in Manuscripts of *The Canterbury Tales*', jointly authored by Matthew Spencer, Barbara Bordalejo, Li-San Wang, Adrian C. Barbrook, Linne R. Mooney, Peter Robinson, Tandy Warnow and Christopher J. Howe (*CH* 37[2003] 97–109), confirms the idea that there was no established order when the first manuscripts were written. These scholars have used gene order analysis to construct a stemma for *The Canterbury Tales*; the resulting stemma shows relationships predicted by earlier scholars, reveals new relationships, and shares features with a word variation stemma.

Meanwhile the HUMI (Humanities Media Interface) project of Keio University in Japan, in conjunction with the British Library, has digitized Caxton's two editions of *The Canterbury Tales*, which is a great advance for typographical research. Satoko Tokunaga outlines the variety of Caxton's typefaces in 'A Digital Approach to the History of the Book: The Case of Caxton' (*PoeticaJ* 60[2003] 65–76), and calls for the outdated classification of William Blades and G.I.F. Tupper to be revised.

In *Signs and Circumstances: A Study of Allegory in Chaucer's 'Canterbury Tales'*, Alan Hughes takes a stance against what he sees as misguided literal criticism of Chaucer's poem, proposing instead that only a thoroughly allegorical reading of the text can expose its true meaning. His thesis is that *The Canterbury Tales* constitutes a political account of Richard II's reign, offering an exploration of Richard's personality, and a figurative description of his later descent into tyranny. The book opens with a brief review of some salient historical facts, and cites *Lak of Stedfastnesse* as other evidence of Chaucer's criticism of the monarch. Hughes then aligns all of the pilgrims mentioned in *The General Prologue* with three historical individuals: Richard II, Isabelle of France, and Chaucer himself. Various aspects of Richard's character are personified by different pilgrims; so, for example, the Squire represents the young Richard of the 1380s. As it turns out, Richard is represented by pilgrims as diverse as the Yeoman, the Monk, the Merchant, the Physician, the Miller, the Host himself, and several more (most, in fact, relate to him); Isabelle, unsurprisingly, is represented by all the female pilgrims. Turning to the tales, and following his own version of their order (p. viii), Hughes contends that each may be read as criticism of Richard. Allusions to Richard's unpopular second marriage apparently lie throughout: Hughes reads *The Merchant's Tale* as an implicit charge of paedophilia against Richard in marrying the 7-year-old pre-pubescent Isabelle; the 'litel clergeon' of *The Prioress's Tale* is another figuration of the princess, while Griselda is taken as representative of Richard's first wife, Anne of Bohemia. In an appendix Hughes further applies his approach to the *Lenvoy de Chaucer a Scogan* and the *Lenvoy de Chaucer a Bukton*. He argues that such a sustained historical reading of the text would be impossible were it not authorially intended, but is all too aware that his claim for an allegorical Chaucer may not meet with the approval of the academy. His book at least has the virtues of newness and honesty. It is accompanied by a CD recording 'Geoffrey and Me', a BBC Radio 4 interview between Hughes and Tony Robinson broadcast on 21 February 2003, during which the two participants engage in their own pilgrimage to Canterbury and London.

In 'Changing Chaucer' (*SAC* 25[2003] 27–52) Richard Firth Green links Chaucer's strange term *elvysshe* with fairy craft and alchemy: both promise fabulous wealth and preternaturally long life; both are occult and mysterious. Although many of Firth Green's references allude to *The Canon Yeoman's Tale*, the discussion is more generally about the discourse of fairyland and medieval alchemy, the technicalities of which clearly awakened Chaucer's curiosity. The harsh satire of the tale is not so much a measure of (regressive) reaction against (progressive) alchemy than it is disenchantment with the abuse of a genuine endeavour. Elvishness emerges as an interesting thread this year, in view of the discussions of Firth Green, Elizabeth Robertson and Warren Edminster. W.W. Allman and D. Thomas Hanks Jr. consider Chaucer's representation of the sex act in 'Rough Love: Notes Toward an Erotics of *The Canterbury Tales*' (*ChauR* 38[2003] 36–65), finding it a far cry from any association with jolly rogering and honest appetite. Rather, the imagery throughout is of cutting, piercing, and bleeding. References to knives and blood in a surprising range of tales provide a highly violent context in which copulation occurs. The authors begin their discussion with the biographical detail of the Cecily Chaumpaigne rape case, and argue that violence permeates the poet's representation of all sex, even consensual and marital. Michael P. Kuczynski invites us to rethink the famous Chaucerian disclaimers in '"Don't Blame Me": The Metaethics of a Chaucerian Apology' (*ChauR* 37[2003] 315–28). Rather than being a disingenuous apology for what's about to come, 'blameth nat me' is actually a fair translation of two of the penitential psalms (6 and 37 in the Vulgate). Normative ethics involves prescription and proscription, but Chaucer emerges as more a spokesman of metaethics, in which he indirectly accepts moral responsibility for what he has written.

Gerald Morgan finds Chaucer no bleeding-heart liberal in his consideration of 'Moral and Social Identity and the Idea of Pilgrimage in *The General Prologue*' (*ChauR* 37[2003] 285–314). Not that Chaucer is a snob or a bigot; rather, the 'master poet' emerges as a man of tolerance, who, although he despises vice, leaves judgement to God. Morgan traces a grand encyclopedic scheme in the sequence of portraits, and delineates a basic bipartite division of the portraits into gentles and commons. For him, Chaucer's sympathies are largely stacked on the side of the gentles, leading Morgan to the questionable assertion that, while the commons generally display a 'certain vulgarity in the flaunting of material prosperity', the 'class of gentles as a whole is unified by the subtle discrimination of dress' (p. 297). Where does that leave the Prioress? In 'Chaucer's Prioress: *Et Nos Cedamus Amori*' (*ChauR* 38[2003] 199–202) Joseph P. McGowan discusses the absent half-line of the Latin tag 'amor vincit omnia'. The full line of Virgil's *Eclogue* was well known in Chaucer's time, and we can thus be sure the omission was meaningful. In noting the ambiguity of *amor*—whether it means celestial or erotic love—McGowan does not seem to add anything new to the debate.

Robert Stretter considers the bonds of sworn brotherhood in 'Rewriting Perfect Friendship in Chaucer's *Knight's Tale* and Lydgate's *Fabula Duorum Mercatorum*' (*ChauR* 37[2003] 234–52). In Chaucer's tale, Emily's feminine presence unwittingly destroys the male friendship of the two knights, and the overwhelming consequences of erotic love undercut homosocial bonds of affection. In its opposition between friendship and love, the *Fabula Duorum Mercatorum* can be seen as Lydgate's response to Chaucer's tale, but the outcome is different, and Lydgate has *amicitia perfecta* survive the destructive effects of erotic love.

Film renditions of Chaucer and the Middle Ages continue to gather momentum as a continuous thread of serious critical study. In 'Reinventing Chaucer: Helgeland's *A Knight's Tale*' (*ChauR* 37[2003] 253–64), Kathleen Forni exposes the film as a 'vulgar capitalist myth' (p. 254) where a low-born but motivated boy can change his stars. In sharp contrast to Chaucer's story, the film's *summum bonum* is materialist. This much admitted, the essay demonstrates the many ways in which the film reinvents Chaucer, often ingeniously, often crudely. Either way, 'popular' and 'modern' reappropriation of our subject productively scrutinizes the value of the past.

Robin's propensity for wrestling has usually been interpreted as yet another sign of his boorishness, but Gregory M. Colón Semenza, 'Historicizing "Wrastlynge" in *The Miller's Tale*'(*ChauR* 38[2003] 66–82), argues otherwise in a persuasive piece that supplies useful contemporary documentation and explanation. Proclamations forbidding idle sports were common throughout the period, and the general absence of wrestling from the blacklist of time-wasting activities leads Semenza to suggest that it was considered a legitimate sport useful in one-on-one combat and national defence. He notes the presence of wrestling as a courtly sport, and speculates that the Knight himself wrestled; for Semenza this possibility emphasizes the threat the Miller poses to his social superior as rival. The wrestling circle becomes the only social site where the two can have a fair fight. In 'Gerveys Joins the Fun: A Note on *Viritoot* in *The Miller's Tale*' (*ChauR* 37[2003] 275–9), James Ortego notes the ambiguity of *upon the viritoot*, of which the most usually accepted meaning is 'on the move'. Linking the phrase to two other points in Gerveys's whole sentence, *gay gerl* and the oath to St Neot, Ortego understands *viritoot* as a slang corruption of Latin *virtutis*, genitive of *virtus*, which means 'manhood, courage, virility'. St Neot's shortness of stature further emphasizes Gerveys's general meaning: that Absolom has failed to rise to the occasion with some wanton wench. His exit from the blacksmith's carrying the burning hot poker comically visualizes his failure to get lucky.

Elizabeth Robertson offers a revised version of her excellent former essay (*YWES* 82[2003] 213) in 'Nonviolent Christianity and the Strangeness of Female Power in Geoffrey Chaucer's *Man of Law's Tale*' (in Farmer and Pasternack, eds. *Gender and Difference in the Middle Ages*, pp. 322–51).

Amtower and Kehler present a collection of eleven essays on *The Single Woman in Medieval and Early Modern England: Her Life and Representation*, and the Wife of Bath features in two of these, with some reference to Criseyde also. Amtower's own contribution is 'Chaucer's Sely Widows' (pp. 119–32), in which she links Chaucer's sympathetic portrayal of the widow to his interrogation of the rules of discourse. Despite medieval society's demand that widows be humble and chaste, the concept of widowhood remains sexually charged; a figure such as the Wife of Bath easily becomes the target of the bawdy imagination, and Criseyde also has stereotypes of widowhood forced upon her. Amtower argues that these women are unable to rebut such jokes or slander because they are silenced and, in Pauline terms, 'unheaded' by their widowhood. In a second discussion of imaginary widowhood, Jeanie Grant Moore explores '(Re)creations of a Single Woman: Discursive Realms of the Wife of Bath' (pp. 133–46), observing that despite her designation the Wife is essentially a single woman. She argues that Alice neutralizes the gendered force of the various medieval roles that intervene in women's lives—the *auctor*, husband, hero-knight and king; and that, in the newly conceived fictional world of her tale, the voices of single women are heard and respected. This achievement is only temporary however, and is problematized by the hag's marriage to the rapist-knight.

Tison Pugh ponders why the Wife of Bath tells a romance and not a fabliau in 'Queering Genres, Battering Males: The Wife of Bath's Narrative Violence' (*JNT* 33[2003] 115–42). Queering is not so much about uncovering homosexuality any more as about resisting the normative and celebrating whatever destabilizes and makes polymorphous within discourse. Pugh argues that Alice queers romance and strikes a radically feminist blow against heteronormative maleness by stripping the masculinist genre of romance of male agency and by putting wives on top. Her concluding curse against niggardly husbands further undercuts the genre. In Susan Carter's 'Coupling the Beastly Bride and the Hunter Hunted: What Lies Behind Chaucer's *Wife of Bath's Tale*' (*ChauR* 37[2003] 329–45), we also have a defence of the radical sexual agenda of the Wife in her tale, which, argues Carter, is essentially about liberation from the constraints of gender roles. In contrast, Gower's *Tale of Florent* in *Confessio Amantis* centres on the theme of kingship. Carter sets her study in the context of the Irish Sovranty Hag tales, in which the hero must be tested by a loathly lady in order to prove his worth as king. Wherever Chaucer gained his acquaintance with the loathly lady tradition, his interest in it is less in kingship *per se* than in the feminization of Arthur's court and the psychically liberating possibilities of the loathly lady's role.

Larry Scanlon's detailed study of Walter and Griselda's marriage asks: 'What's the Pope Got To Do with It? Forgery, Didacticism, and Desire in *The Clerk's Tale*' (in Lawton, Scase and Copeland, eds., pp. 129–65). Arguing that the didactic can only be properly understood as a diachronic problem, Scanlon notes Griselda's longevity in the English literary tradition, invoking her appearance in Caryl Churchill's play *Top Girls* [1982], and her similarities with its protagonist Marlene. His discussion focuses on three moments in the tale: the espousal scene and its metaphor of translation; the forged papal letter granting Walter a divorce; and the tale's conclusion with its ironic appeal to the Wife of Bath. In rereading these sections Scanlon also explores two prominent features of medieval society: the widespread forgery of official documents, and the papal regulation of princely marriage. The gender politics of *translatio* as the exchange of (feminized) bodies between (masculine) authors has long been noted. Drawing on the work of Judith Butler, Emma Campbell considers the subversive side of 'Sexual Poetics and the Politics of Translation in the Tale of Griselda' (*CL* 55[2003] 191–216). She traces the various translations of Griselda from Boccaccio, to Petrarch, to Chaucer. In the semiotic play between her clothing and her body, Campbell finds Griselda systematically dematerialized and rematerialized, as if embodying the very principle of translation itself. As such, feminine gender emerges as a performance achieved through repeated acts of translation and retranslation. 'Source or Hard Analogue? *Decameron* X.10 and *The Clerk's Tale*' (*ChauR* 37[2003] 346–64) returns Thomas J. Farrell to the question of the relationship of the Italian story to Chaucer's poem. Borrowing his categories from those laid out by Peter Beidler (*YWES* 81[2002] 245), in which he distinguishes systematically between source, hard analogue, and soft analogue, Farrell argues that *Decameron* X.10 is not a source, which denotes a text available to and used by Chaucer as he wrote, but a hard analogue, which denotes a text known to Chaucer but not used directly by him at the time of composition. It is thus a mistake, cautions Farrell, to place too much weight on textual differences between the two accounts.

Carl Falvo Heffernan identifies 'Three Unnoticed Links between Matthew of Vendôme's *Comedia Lidie* and Chaucer's *Merchant's Tale*' (*N&Q* 50[2003] 158–62). The intermediary text between Chaucer and Vendôme is Boccaccio's *Decameron*, in particular the ninth tale told on day seven, but on the strength of three points of linguistic comparison Heffernan suggests a more immediate acquaintance on the part of Chaucer with the *Comedia Lidie*. One particular manuscript is suggested as possible candidate: MS Florence, Biblioteca Medicea-Laurenziana, Pluteus 33.31, which was for Boccaccio's personal use, and which might have been available to Chaucer on his extended visit to Genoa and Florence in 1372–3.

Holly A. Crocker discusses 'Performative Passivity and Fantasies of Masculinity in *The Merchant's Tale*' (*ChauR* 38[2003] 178–98). Feminine passivity, she notes, is an act, and it is May's agency in the tale that exposes and discredits masculine agency, which itself depends upon the fiction of feminine passivity. January entirely believes in this fiction, with the result that he fails to act (on his wedding night). The embittered narrator sees straight through May's apparent passivity, and has thus been insulated by critics from the failure of masculine agency that characterizes January. Crocker, however, argues for Chaucer's implication in his own stories, and thus for his inability to assert any more masculine control over feminine passivity than can January.

Chaucer's *Franklin's Tale* exhibits a strange preference for desire over fulfilment, argues John A. Pitcher in '"Word and Werk" in Chaucer's *Franklin's Tale*' (*L&P* 49[2003] 77–109). Desire figures in the tale less by means of explicit statement of appetite than through various retreats from satisfaction enacted most obviously by Aurelius. His adulterous wish is to replace Arveragus in secret liaison with Dorigen, but her unwilling submission to him with Arveragus's full knowledge derails satisfaction in a resolution that has Oedipal overtones. In the condition Dorigen imposes on Aurelius and in her subsequent lament, where she identifies herself with victims of rape, we see a repressed desire that can only be admitted as prescription and prohibition. Colin Wilcockson discusses Y-forms and T-forms of address in 'Thou and Tears: The Advice of Arveragus to Dorigen in Chaucer's *Franklin's Tale*' (*RES* 54[2003] 308–12). He supports a sympathetic reading of Arveragus, observing that he uses the 'plural of respect' form of address (*ye*) to Dorigen. The one exception, where he forbids her to tell anyone of his decision, has a parallel in *The Clerk's Tale*; Walter switches to the T-form (*thou*) when allowing her to return home in her original smock. Both such instances, argues Wilcockson, reveal intimacy and intense emotion on the part of the speakers. A contrary position is assumed by M.C. Bodden in 'Disordered Grief and Fashionable Afflictions in Chaucer's *Franklin's Tale* and *The Clerk's Tale*' (in Vaught and Bruckner, eds., *Grief and Gender, 700–1700*, pp. 51–63), who argues that Walter's grief is underplayed in comparison to Chaucer's Latin and French sources. Male grief arises from loss or failure of power over women, female grief from loss of power over self. Male grief finds an outlet in the formal rituals of courtly romance and is an enabling emotion, for it leads to acts of *fredom*; but female grief, articulated in Dorigen's 'excessive', 'incoherent', and 'inappropriate' lament, finds no acceptable outlet and offers no sublimation into noble action.

In the first of his two essays appearing this year on the Pardoner, 'Chaucer and the Queering Eunuch' (in Lawton, Scase, and Copeland, eds., pp. 107–28), Alastair Minnis disagrees with the conclusions of previous critics, notably Monica McAlpine, suggesting that we leave the Pardoner himself as the mystery he feels sure Chaucer intended him to be. He prefers to further the debate by appealing to some of the core principles of queer theory itself. He focuses on the range of conditions covered by 'eunuchry' in Chaucer's day, and notes that disparaging references to the Pardoner's sexuality may be employed simply as a means of registering disapproval. Further thoughts by Alastair Minnis appear in 'Reclaiming the Pardoners' (*JMEMS* 33[2003] 311–34), in which he spends the larger part of the article defining the ticklish criteria by which and conditions upon which the indulgence 'industry' operated: the phrase *a pena et culpa* ('from punishment and guilt') caused particular problems, for it implied that, the indulgence once procured (by means of charitable donation), the soul upon death went immediately to heaven. Minnis notes the extent of the concern and debate over indulgences in Chaucer's time, and the ways in which the Pardoner egregiously oversteps the limits of his remit. He does not come up with any new reading of the Pardoner as such, save to argue that such secret sexual sins he may harbour are of less importance than the ones that lie on the surface, namely, his greed and fraudulence. In 'Transgressive Word and Image in Chaucer's Enshrined *Coillons* Passage' (*ChauR* 37[2003] 365–84) Marijane Osborn notes that the *coilles* passage in the *Roman de la Rose*, Chaucer's inspiration for the Host's crude wish that the Pardoner's testicles be enshrined in a hog's turd, only appears in some manuscripts of the French poem. Where others found the passage objectionable, Chaucer found special significance. He also exaggerates the crudity by introducing scatological imagery. Noting Reason's reference to *integumentum* in the *Roman*, Osborn suggests that Chaucer's insult alludes to the famous fruit/chaff or kernel/husk metaphor of biblical hermeneutics, and obscenely inverts it by rendering the kernel in this case a pair of testicles that we are not sure the Pardoner even possesses. Gudrun Richardson detects shades of ambiguity in medieval attitudes towards suicide in 'The Old Man in Chaucer's *Pardoner's Tale*: An Interpretative Study of his Identity and Meaning' (*Neophil* 87[2003] 323–37). Her discussion encompasses Judas and Gregorius (in the version by Hartman von Aue), along with the related themes of incest and Oedipus. Although suicide is most frequently castigated as the final act of despair, certain sermon versions allude to Judas having died in hope of forgiveness, suggesting the possibility of the redemption of suicides. For Richardson the Pardoner has turned from God and despaired of grace, and the Old Man represents the pilgrim's wandering soul, which seeks but cannot attain oblivion.

Stephen G. Moore urges the reader to 'Apply Yourself: Learning While Reading *The Tale of Melibee*' (*ChauR* 38[2003] 83–97). The performative nature of the narrative structure of the tale, he claims, has not been fully appreciated. It is essentially recursive in structure, continually doubling back to judge present events in the light of past experience. The ultimate learner of the tale is not Melibee but the reader, who is provoked throughout to recognize the general principle of sentential wisdom within the specific instance of Melibee's circumstances.

Studies in the Age of Chaucer includes a 'Colloquium: *The Manciple's Tale*' (25 [2003] 287–337). Marianne Børch, in 'Chaucer's Poetics and *The Manciple's Tale*' (*SAC* 25 [2003] 287–97), presents the tale as Janus-faced, looking back on the Canterbury poetics and forward to the spiritual principles of *The Parson's Tale*. On the one hand the tale is a nightmare version of Chaucer's own poetic, and it spleenfully glosses that of the Knight, to which it is similar; where Arcite's name lives on after his death, the wife's is obliterated in her murder by Phoebus. On the other hand, it problematizes the tale of the Parson, who attempts to displace it with his homiletic and penitential discourse. In '"For sorwe of which he brak his minstralcye": The Demise of the "sweete noyse" of Verse in *The Canterbury Tales*' (*SAC* 25[2003] 299–308) John Hines suggests that Chaucer aligns himself with courtly and conservative principles by satirizing the Manciple, who is strongly linked to urbanity, and thus to the incipient republicanism of the bourgeois guild movement. The Manciple as narrator is embroiled in self-contradiction by his castigation of adultery and simultaneous admonition to 'kepe wel thy tonge'. Eve Salisbury fixes upon points where legal reality intrudes upon narrative fiction in 'Murdering Fiction: The Case of *The Manciple's Tale*' (*SAC* 25[2003] 309–16). Comparing the Parson's treatment of sin with Henry Bracton's definitions of homicide in *De Legibus et Consuetudinibus Angliae*, she shows how both find damage done to a pregnant woman reprehensible. Chaucer omits the detail of Coronis's pregnancy from his Ovidian source, leaving both Manciple and Parson chillingly silent on the question of the murder of an adulterous wife.

Peter W. Travis takes a psychoanalytic turn in 'The Manciple's Phallic Matrix' (*SAC* 25[2003] 317–24), noting the tale's oral fixation, the bestialization of female nature, the narrator's self-contradictions, and the castration rituals for both Apollo and the crow. The Manciple, he concludes, is negative, infantilized, and self-castrating, and remains an integral part of Chaucer, however much one would want to separate them. The tale as aetiological fable relates the origins of the self played out in the domain of language. Stephanie Trigg draws two axes of male relationship in 'Friendship, Association and Service in *The Manciple's Tale*' (*SAC* 25[2003] 325–30): a vertical axis of service to a master and a horizontal one of friendship. The tale sends a cautionary message to courtiers as servants, yet also asserts male solidarity against female perfidy. Trigg detects a certain anxiety in the tale, which has to do with Chaucer's own uncertainty about how to write and speak as a court poet. Warren Ginsburg wraps up the sequence with a 'Response' (*SAC* 25[2003] 331–7), commending the range and variety of critical approach demonstrated by the five essays, and noting his own response to the tale's connection between homicidal fury and maternal teaching, a theme also evident in *The Prioress's Tale*.

3. Troilus and Criseyde

Troilus and Criseyde is discussed in the third chapter of Sylvia Federico's new book, *New Troy: Fantasies of Empire in the Late Middle Ages*, where she assesses Chaucer's response to the problematic history of Troy. Her central assertion is that representations of the matter of Troy were of vital importance in the formation of authorial, regnal, and national identity in late medieval England, and her discussion reflects on the ways in which Trojan-ness was invoked in the service of national memory and literary history. She begins by showing how, during the Peasants' Revolt of 1381 and the financial quarrel with Richard II in 1392, London (the New Troy) was imagined as a sexually misbehaving woman in the contemporary writing of Gower and Richard Maidstone. In her second chapter she focuses on the treason of Aeneas, giving readings of *Sir Gawain and the Green Knight* and *The House of Fame*; along the way she raises questions about transmission and translation, relating these both to ancient stories and the historical reputations of Chaucer and Richard II. Her chapter on 'Chaucer's Troy Book' (pp. 65–98), is followed by a discussion of Gower's and Lydgate's reconstructions of the Ricardian era. Throughout the book there is a focus on Trojan and post-Trojan women, and the significance of gender is brought to the fore in a brief conclusion. In its coverage this study offers a rare combination of Arthurian and Chaucerian literary criticism, using the central methodologies of historicism and pyschoanalysis. Earlier versions of chapters 1 and 3 have already appeared (see *YWES* 80[2001] 204).

In 'Chaucer's *Troilus and Criseyde*' (*Expl* 61[2003] 69–71) Roy J. Pearcy notes a change of detail in Chaucer's poem from his Boccaccian source, *Il Filostrato*. Where Boccaccio's lovers smother each other in kisses, Troilus kisses only Criseyde's eyes. Pearcy notes the only other reference in Chaucer's work, namely, Absolom's kissing of Alison's *nether ye*, and the absence of the motif among his English contemporaries. The motif was, however, popular in French secular literature of the thirteenth century, especially early Arthurian verse romances. Pearcy suggests that Chaucer uses it to depict the antique manner of Trojan love.

Troilus and Criseyde is the Chaucerian text interrogated by Richard E. Zeikowitz in his study *Homoeroticism and Chivalry: Discourses of Male Same-Sex Desire in the Fourteenth Century*, which otherwise draws its examples mostly from romance narratives. Zeikowitz is concerned to distinguish his own approach from that of other recent queer studies, and to investigate both positive and negative discourses of male same-sex desire, dividing his discussion into two parts to achieve this. In the longer first part he begins by surveying the political motivation for promoting male homosocial intimacy, alluding to various treatises on chivalry and mentioning the formation of the Order of the Garter. He also sketches the classical ideas of male friendship articulated by Aristotle and Cicero and reformulated in the Middle Ages by Aelred and Jean de Meun. He finds that in *Amis and Amylion* and the *Prose Lancelot* key concepts such as loyalty are homoeroticized, and in *Troilus* the hero's relationship with Pandarus is privileged above all others. In the two final chapters of this first section Zeikowitz analyses male–male spectatorial acts in chivalric texts, particularly in the *Stanzaic Morte Arthur*, and draws upon medieval theories of vision to try to understand various visual acts in *Troilus* and *Sir Gawain and the Green Knight*. In the second part of the book a negative stance is assumed. Zeikowitz briefly surveys the political capital that could be made out of false accusations of sodomy, and then examines some instances where this seems to occur in historical and literary texts. He concludes that, although there are attempts to taint Troilus's friendship with Pandarus with sodomy, the poem as a whole affirms the cultural normativity of male homosocial intimacy.

Marion Turner's essay '*Troilus and Criseyde* and the "Treasonous Aldermen" of 1382: Tales of the City in Late Fourteenth-Century London' (*SAC* 25[2003] 225–57) profitably combines textual analysis with a close knowledge of late medieval English history. Turner focuses on documentary sources relating to the Peasants' Revolt, highlighting the case of three aldermen who were accused—probably falsely, and for factional reasons—of facilitating the rebels' entry to the city. This is linked to the way in which blame is apportioned in *Troilus*: bona fide Trojans such as Calchas and Criseyde are depicted as faith-breaking traitors, while the Greeks, the actual aggressors, are sidelined. Turner's reading succeeds in situating *Troilus* within contemporary discourses of treason and urban fragmentation, but results in the bleak conclusion that society is divided, dysfunctional, and irredeemable.

Sealy Gilles underlines the connections between 'Love and Disease in Chaucer's *Troilus and Criseyde*' (*SAC* 25[2003] 157–97), beginning with the paradox that Criseyde's body is both cause and cure of Troilus's sickness, and noting that, though her physical removal to the Greek camp sends Troilus into a decline, the use of her body in this exchange constitutes an attempted cure for the ills of Troy. The discussion ranges from the courtly science of lovesickness to a contemplation of the realities of bodily disease in the fourteenth century; Gilles can find few direct references to plague in Chaucer's works, but claims that *Troilus* is medicalized through a sustained use of the language of contagion and death. The evidence of contemporary plague tracts is enlisted in this discussion, notably the account of the siege of Caffa given by Gabriele de' Mussis in the *Historia de Morbo*. The realities of a city under siege are wisely considered by Carl Grey Martin in '"Bitraised thorugh false folk": Criseyde, the Siege, and the Threat of Treason' (*ChauR* 37[2003] 219–33). He reminds us that siege warfare necessarily draws in ordinary people who are otherwise unversed in military practice, and also notes that the outcome of a successful siege brings sudden and violent changes of fortune to both sides. Reading Criseyde's actions in the light of this situation, he views her acquiescence in the exchange as a great act of self-sacrifice—one that allows Troilus to remain a Trojan hero rather than become a deserter.

In her discussion of 'Criseyde's Prudence' (*SAC* 25[2003] 199–224), Monica E. McAlpine confronts the problem of Criseyde's perceived passivity. She analyses Criseyde's final private meeting with Troilus in Book IV as a scene of prudential female counsel, and highlights the importance of the 'prudence' stanza in Book V (ll. 744–9); Criseyde's rejection of violent action, her patient acceptance of exchange, and her dissuasion of Troilus from elopement, are all viewed as evidence of her prudence. McAlpine thus regards Criseyde as conforming to the model of active suffering delineated by Jill Mann, and an anticipation of the wifely eloquence displayed by the prudent women of *The Canterbury Tales*. Dabney Anderson Bankert suggests that we should read *Troilus* as a kind of parable in 'Secularizing the Word: Conversion Models in Chaucer's *Troilus and Criseyde*' (*ChauR* 37[2003] 196–217). The protagonists' different experiences of falling in love remind her of the varied experiences of religious converts: the conversion of Troilus (to the religion of love) is compared to the abrupt and radical conversion of Paul, whereas the paradigm for Criseyde's more gradual psychological transformation is Augustinian.

Jamie C. Fumo displays a detailed knowledge of Ovid's text in a long essay, '"Little *Troilus*": *Heroides* 5 and its Ovidian Contexts in Chaucer's *Troilus and Criseyde*' (*SP* 100[2003] 278–314). Fumo outlines the general relevance of this section of the *Heroides*, Oenone's letter to Paris, to *Troilus*, and claims that Chaucer makes sustained and allusive use of *Heroides* 5 in the design and structure of the poem. Similarly, in 'Boethius and Pandarus: A Source in Maximian's *Elegies*' (*N&Q* 50[2003] 377–80), J. Allan Mitchell proposes that Maximian's third elegy may have been the source of inspiration for Chaucer's unique development of a Boethian pander. In 'Marginal Presence, Lyric Resonance, Epic Absence: *Troilus and Criseyde* and/in *The Shepheardes Calender*' (*SSt* 18[2003] 25–39), Clare R. Kinney proposes that the nearest thing to epic that Spenser could find within English literary history was Chaucerian narrative. While acknowledging that Spenser's debt to Chaucer is well known, Kinney makes a special case for the influence of *Troilus and Criseyde* on Spenser's pastoral poem, noting verbal echoes and finding parallels in the Petrarchan posturing of the unhappy lovers, Troilus and Colin Clout. She further suggests that Spenser's archaic diction in *The Shepheardes Calender* and *The Faerie Queene* constitutes a gesture of literary solidarity with the idiolect of Chaucer.

Finally, Jeff Massey's essay, '"The *Double Bind* of Troilus to Tellen": The Time of the Gift in Chaucer's *Troilus and Criseyde*' (*ChauR* 38[2003] 16–35), claims that the fourteenth-century atypical romance anticipates modern theories about gift-giving propounded by Derrida and Cixous. Working from Derrida's assertion that if a gift results in reciprocity then it is really no more than a commodity, Massey contends that in courtly love there can be no gift, since the system explicitly expects reciprocity. However, Troilus is so ignorant of love that he does not hope for consummation; unlike Diomede, who is a real courtly lover, driven solely by personal gain, Troilus is an ideal—and feminized—lover. To complete this reading, Massey sees Criseyde as a masculinized woman who operates within a commodity economy, and the go-between Pandarus as a counterfeiter who can translate Troilus's gift (love) into non-gift terms, and Criseyde's non-gift into gift terms. This reading may not convince all readers, but it does help to make sense of some of the gender inversions in Chaucer's romance.

4. Other Works

Chaucer's other works seem to be experiencing a critical lull. An exception is a lengthy study 'Ecofeminism and the Father of English Poetry: Chaucer's *Parliament of Fowls*' (*Isle* 10[2003] 97–114), in which Lesley Kordecki claims that the poem is early evidence of the tendency in English literature to exclude women (and animals) from traditions of subjectivity. Kordecki tries to distinguish the effects of the establishment of an exclusionary human subjectivity in a discourse populated by talking non-humans, praising Chaucer for considering other voices, but gloomily noting that his championing of female supremacy turns out to be ephemeral, with male (and human) priorities quickly reasserted.

Anne Worthington Prescott offers *Imagining Fame: An Introduction to Geoffrey Chaucer's 'The House of Fame'* for the general reader, which comprises a dual-text original and translation of excerpts punctuated with short introductions. The edition presupposes no knowledge of either Chaucer or the period, and its overview is at best sketchy, rendering it suitable really only for the young school student. This said, Chaucer's lines are rendered in lively fashion, while a short section of study questions at the end of the book encourages some critical thought about the text.

Hi Kyung Moon questions the validity of Chaucer's title in '"The Legend of False Men"? Chaucer's *Legend of Good Women* Re-titled' (*MEMES* 11[2003] 117–30), arguing that the stories presented in this collection are as much about men's misdeeds as women's goodness.

Finally, Catherine Eagleton is to be congratulated on her discovery of 'A Previously Unnoticed Fragment of Chaucer's *Treatise on the Astrolabe*' (*JEBS* 6[2003] 161–73) in the library of the Royal College of Physicians, London (MS 358), which illuminates some aspects of the work's authorship and readership.

Books Reviewed

Agathocleous, Tanya, and Ann C. Dean. *Teaching Literature: A Companion*. Palgrave. [2003] pp. xvi + 197. hb£50 ISBN 0 3339 8792 6, pb£16.99 ISBN 0 3339 8793 4.

Amtower, Laurel, and Dorothea Kehler, eds. *The Single Woman in Medieval and Early Modern England: Her Life and Representation*. Arizona Center for Medieval and Renaissance Studies. [2003] pp. xx + 242. £30 ($35) ISBN 0 8669 8306 6.

Barron, Caroline M. *London in the Later Middle Ages: Government and People 1200-1500*. OUP. [2003] pp. xvi + 472. £50 ISBN 0 1992 5777 9.

Benson, Robert G., and Susan J. Ridyard, eds. *New Readings of Chaucer's Poetry*. Chaucer Studies 31. Brewer. [2003] pp. 200. £30 ($50) ISBN 0 8599 1778 9.

Boitani, Piero, and Jill Mann, eds. *The Cambridge Companion to Chaucer*. 2nd edn. CUP. [2003] pp. xiv + 317. hb £45 ISBN 0 5218 1556 8, pb £15.99 ISBN 0 5218 9467 0.

Bordalejo, Barbara, ed. *Caxton's Canterbury Tales: The British Library Copies*. Scholarly Digital Editions. [2003] Individual licence. £20 ($29.95) ISBN 1 9046 2802 8, institutional licence £40 ($70) ISBN 1 9046 2803 6.

Borroff, Marie. *Traditions and Renewals: Chaucer, the Gawain-Poet, and Beyond*. YaleUP. [2003] pp. xii + 275. $35 ISBN 0 3000 9612 7.

Burger, Glenn. *Chaucer's Queer Nation*. Medieval Cultures 34. UMinnP. [2003] pp. xxv + 264. $68.95 ISBN 0 8166 3805 5, pb $22.95 ISBN 0 8166 3806 3.

Dinshaw, Carolyn, and David Wallace, eds. *The Cambridge Companion to Medieval Women's Writing*. CUP. [2003] pp. xix + 289. hb £45 ISBN 0 5217 9188 X, pb £16 ISBN 0 5217 9638 5.

Farmer, Sharon, and Carol Braun Pasternack, eds. *Gender and Difference in the Middle Ages*. Medieval Cultures 32. UMinnP. [2003] pp. xxvii + 354. $74.95 ISBN 0 8166 3893 4, pb $24.95 ISBN 0 8166 3894 2.

Federico, Sylvia. *New Troy: Fantasies of Empire in the Late Middle Ages*. Medieval Cultures 36. UMinnP. [2003] pp. xxiv + 207. hb $65.95 ISBN 0 8166 4166 8, pb $21.95 ISBN 0 8166 4167 6.

Fikkert, Paula, and Haike Jacobs, eds. *Development in Prosodic Systems*. Studies in Generative Grammar 58. MGruyter. [2003] pp. viii + 463. €88 ($114) ISBN 3 1101 6684 4.

Finley, William K., and Joseph Rosenblum, eds. *Chaucer Illustrated: Five Hundred Years of 'The Canterbury Tales' in Pictures*. OakK and BL. [2003] pp. xxxiii + 445. £45 ISBN 0 7123 4816 6, $75 ISBN 1 5845 6102 5.

Fowler, Elizabeth. *Literary Character: The Human Figure in Early English Writing*. CornUP. [2003] pp. xii + 263. £27.50 ($45) ISBN 0 8014 4116 1.

Freedman, Diane P., and Olivia Frey, eds. *Autobiographical Writing across the Disciplines: A Reader*. DukeUP. [2003] pp. xviii + 487. hb $84.95 ISBN 0 8223 3200 0, pb $23.95 ISBN 0 8223 3213 2.

Goldie, Matthew Boyd, ed. *Middle English Literature: A Historical Sourcebook*. Blackwell. [2003] pp. xxxviii + 301. hb£55 ISBN 0 6312 3147 1, pb£19.99 ISBN 0 6312 3148 X.

Gray, Douglas, ed. *Oxford Companion to Chaucer*. OUP. [2003] pp. xxvii + 526. £65 ISBN 0 1981 1765 5.

Harding, Wendy, ed. *Drama, Narrative and Poetry in the 'Canterbury Tales'*. PUM. [2003] pp. 246. €23 ISBN 2 8581 6705 2.

Heffernan, Carol F. *The Orient in Chaucer and Medieval Romance*. Brewer. [2003] pp. x + 160. £40 ($70) ISBN 0 8599 1795 9.

Hirsh, John C. *Chaucer and the 'Canterbury Tales': A Short Introduction*. Blackwell. [2003] pp. x + 175. $22.95 ISBN 0 6312 2562 5.

Hirsh, John C., ed. *Medieval Lyric: Middle English Lyrics, Ballads, and Carols*. Blackwell. [2003] pp. xiv + 220. hb£50 ($64.95) ISBN 1 4051 1481 9, pb£17.99 ($29.95) ISBN 1 4051 1482 7.

Horobin, Simon. *The Language of the Chaucer Tradition*. Chaucer Studies 32. Brewer. [2003] pp. x + 179. £45 ($75) ISBN 0 8599 1780 0.

Hughes, Alan. *Signs and Circumstances: A Study of Allegory in Chaucer's 'Canterbury Tales'*. AlaNia. [2003] pp. ix + 160. £20 ISBN 0 9544 4910 X. With accompanying CD 'Geoffrey and Me', Tony Robinson and Alan Hughes, BBC Radio 4 [21 Feb. 2003].

Ingham, Patricia Clare, and Michelle R. Warren, eds. *Postcolonial Moves: Medieval Through Modern*. Palgrave. [2003] pp. x + 264. £40 ISBN 1 4039 6073 9.

Jaszczolt, K.M., and Ken Turner, eds. *Meaning Through Language Contrast*. 2 vols. Benjamins. [2003] pp. xii + 383 (vol. 1), vii + 491 (vol. 2). Set: €263 ISBN 9 0272 5349 8, $316 ISBN 1 5881 1332 9. Individual volumes: vol. 1, €125 ISBN 9 0272 5119 3, $150 ISBN 1 5881 1206 3; vol. 2, €138 ISBN 9 0272 5120 7, $166 ISBN 1 5881 1207 1.

Jones, Terry, et al., *Who Murdered Chaucer? A Medieval Mystery*. Methuen. [2003] pp. 408. $38.22 ISBN 0 4137 5910 5.

Lawton, David, Scase Wendy and Rita Copeland, eds. *New Medieval Literatures 6*. OUP. [2003] pp. vi + 317. £75 ISBN 0 1992 5251 3.

Lloyd-Morgan, Ceridwen, ed. *The Hengwrt Chaucer Standard Edition on CD-ROM*. Scholarly Digital Editions. [2003] Individual licence. £16 ($27.95) ISBN 1 9046 2800 1, institutional licence ISBN 1 9046 2801 X.

Low, Anthony. *Aspects of Subjectivity: Society and Individuality from the Middle Ages to Shakespeare and Milton*. Duquesne. [2003] pp. xxi + 242. $60 ISBN 0 8207 0337 0.

Machan, Tim W. *English in the Middle Ages*. OUP. [2003] pp. x + 205. £45 ISBN 0 1992 6268 3.

Olson, Mary. *Fair and Varied Forms: Visual Textuality in Medieval Illuminated Manuscripts*. Studies in Medieval History and Culture 15. Routledge. [2003] pp. xxv + 232. $80.95 ISBN 0 4159 4267 5.

Parini, Jay, ed. *British Writers: Classics*. vol. 1. Scribner. [2003] pp. xiii + 393. $145 ISBN 0 6843 1253 0.

Prescott, Anne Worthington. *Imagining Fame: An Introduction to Geoffrey Chaucer's 'The House of Fame'*. Fithian Press. [2003] pp. 126. $12.95 ISBN 1 5647 4404 3.

Reed, Teresa. *Shadows of Mary: Reading the Virgin Mary in Medieval Texts*. UWalesP. [2003] pp. 171. hb£35 ISBN 0 7083 1798 7, pb£15.99 ISBN 0 7083 1797 9.

Somerset, Fiona, and Nicholas Watson, eds. *The Vulgar Tongue: Medieval and Postmedieval Vernacularity*. PSUP. [2003] pp. xvi + 277. $55 ISBN 0 2710 2310 4.

Taavitsainen, Irma, and Andreas H. Jucker, eds. *Diachronic Perspectives on Address Term Systems*. Benjamins. [2003] pp. vii + 441. $138 ISBN 9 0272 5348 X.

Vaught, Jennifer C., and Lynne Dickson Bruckner, eds. *Grief and Gender, 700-1700*. Palgrave. [2003] pp. xii + 310. hb $55 ISBN 0 3122 9382 8, pb $18.95 ISBN 0 3122 9381 X.

Voaden, Rosalynn, René Tixier, Teresa Sanchez Roura and Jenny Rebecca Rytting, eds. *The Medieval Translator*. Traduire au Moyen Age 8. Brepols. [2003] pp. xxvi + 350. €60 ISBN 2 5035 1016 7.

Wetherbee, Winthrop. *Chaucer: The 'Canterbury Tales'*. 2nd edn. CUP. [2003] pp. 125. hb $43 ISBN 0 5218 3249 7, pb $14.99 ISBN 0 5215 4010 0.

Zeikowitz, Richard E. *Homoeroticism and Chivalry: Discourses of Male Same-Sex Desire in the Fourteenth Century*. Palgrave. [2003] pp. xi + 216. £42.50 ISBN 1 4039 6042 9.

V

The Sixteenth Century: Excluding Drama after 1550

ROS KING AND JOAN FITZPATRICK

This chapter has three sections: 1. General; 2. Sidney; 3. Spenser. Section 1 is by Ros King; sections 2 and 3 are by Joan Fitzpatrick.

1. General

The year 2003 being the 400th anniversary of the death of Elizabeth I, a major exhibition on her life, curated by David Starkey, was staged at the National Maritime Museum in Greenwich. The handsome catalogue of the exhibition, edited by Susan Doran, with full colour photographs of many of the items shown, leaves us with a useful pictorial resource of art and artefacts from the reign. It also includes short essays by scholars including David Starkey on 'Elizabeth: Woman, Monarch, Mission', Patrick Collinson on 'The Mongrel Religion of Elizabethan England' and Susan Frye on 'Entertainments at Court'. A large number of other contributors provide useful descriptions of the items illustrated, citing more extensive literature. While many items are familiar, others are not. One in particular, the arms board from the parish church of Preston St Mary in Suffolk, constitutes a revealing combination of mythology and utility that exemplifies the reign. An extremely rare example of the only type of decoration allowed in the reformed English church, it provides a genealogy for the Tudors, incorporating emblems and heraldic devices that denote the most significant turning points in British history right back to the legendary Trojan Brutus himself. Edward the Confessor, Cadwallader, and even the Roman occupation are thus all represented as contributing to the inexorable providentiality of the Tudor dynasty's right to rule not only England but also France and Ireland. Originally constructed to celebrate Edward VI's leadership of the church, it was over-painted with Elizabeth's name, presumably (and reasonably) in the pursuit of economy. As a postscript to the catalogue, the exhibition and also to the reign, Michael Dobson and Nicola Watson contribute a final section on 'Elizabeth's Legacy'. This gives a brief taster of their witty, wide-ranging, extensively illustrated and often

Year's Work in English Studies, Volume 84 (2005) © The English Association; all rights reserved. For permissions, please email: journals.permissions@oxfordjournals.org

doi: 10.1093/ywes/mai005

surprising volume *England's Elizabeth: An Afterlife in Fame and Fantasy*, which examines Elizabeth's appearance in novels and films, pageants and propaganda—both separately and in combination—for which, too often, humour should indeed be the only serious mode of discourse. It is a mark of the finesse with which they approach their material that the authors also treat seriously those items, like the TV series *Blackadder II*, that are meant to be funny.

Susan Doran, with Thomas S. Freeman, has also edited a collection of essays, *The Myth of Elizabeth*, which with the exception of a final essay by Thomas Betteridge concerning Elizabeth on film, all deal with the manufacture of Elizabeth myths during and immediately after her lifetime. The first of these, by Freeman, is a product of the British Academy John Foxe project. He shows how Foxe's description of Elizabeth's imprisonment in the Tower in the *Acts and Monuments* immediately inspired a range of popular ballads and plays, and later encouraged a uniform judgement by scholars that 'Foxe's objectives were: the glorification of Elizabeth as a means of securing the Elizabethan settlement' (p. 28). The British Academy-funded research, however, has enabled the systematic study of the many alterations to Foxe's book, which are best explained by changes in politics and doctrine during the reign. Alexandra Walsham ('A Very Deborah?') also explores the fine line between 'panegyrical praise and stinging reproof' drawn in the sermons of the period, while Patrick Collinson ('William Camden and the Anti-Myth of Elizabeth') examines the clever politicking that accompanied the signing of the death warrant of Mary Queen of Scots and the perhaps even cleverer description of it in Camden's *Annales*. Written in the form of a rhetorical essay in Latin on the very nature of history, and entitled *Ars Historica*, Collinson concludes that it is not Camden himself but his English translators who 'are responsible for the warm post-Elizabethan glow in which the subject is, so to speak, gift-wrapped' (p. 85). Andrew Hadfield ('Duessa's Trial and Elizabeth's Error') performs a similar exercise on *The Faerie Queene*, pointing out that since Spenser's letter to Ralegh draws attention to the fact that the queen is represented in a variety of allegorical ways in the poem, it follows that 'the queen may be shadowed in ways that are as often critical as they are celebratory or flattering' (p. 57). Doran too presents a sophisticated rereading of canonical work—this time the iconographical portraits of Elizabeth—stressing the Protestant Tudor or otherwise imperial aspects of the rose and phoenix motifs that we have long been taught were merely virginal.

The anniversary of the death of Elizabeth has also encouraged re-examination of the succession crisis—with more books to follow in 2004. But as Kevin Dunn points out ('Gorboduc', *ELR* 33[2003] 279–308), this issue had been a problem since the 1530s. He explores the play *Gorboduc* not only as it was no doubt intended—as a metaphor for discussing the problem itself—but also as an illustration of the growth, and growing self-consciousness, of the Privy Council, seeing it as a 'representation of counsel, and of the Council, *to itself*'. As he points out, although the play was given at court, its first performance was for the members of the Inns of Court, 'the group that was rapidly becoming a distinct conciliar class' (p. 282). He begins and ends with Cecil's self-effacing but leading role in the dangerous politics arising from both Henry VIII's and Edward VI's wills regarding the succession. As he tellingly says, 'With sovereignty contested, all action becomes private' (p. 281), but whether Cecil's 'uncomfortable sense of his subjectivity' was indeed 'not revealed, but created, by conflicts within sovereignty itself—that his subjectivity was vestment rather than essence' (p. 307) is perhaps not proven and relies on a currently fashionable notion of sixteenth-century understanding of identity and its presentation.

This problem also underlies two books that look from opposite angles at the contested issue of the meaning and consciousness of authorship in sixteenth-century literature. Marcy L. North (*The Anonymous Renaissance*) explores the different reasons as to why and how writing might be presented anonymously, whether in manuscript or in print, while Elizabeth Heale (*Autobiography and Authorship in Renaissance Verse*) considers how poetry could be a way of chronicling 'the self'. Starting from the observation that the production and circulation of manuscript collections of poetry occur within the domestic sphere, North's underlying agenda is to try to identify more lost women's voices in the discreetly anonymous verse of the period. This is a project which, she regretfully confirms, is probably a lost cause, but (perhaps as a result) she takes seriously those examples of anonymous verse that have a female voice—although, as she also observes, there is also a not inconsiderable number of female-voiced poems with male signatures. Nevertheless, her discussions usefully complicate our understanding of male–female relations during the period. Perhaps more significantly, her first chapter seeks to restore something of the original anonymity that attached to works that are now firmly authored in modern editions. While, for example, we can now never not know that Robert Burton wrote *The Anatomy of Melancholy*, it is important to recognize that this work initially appeared under the pseudonym Democritus Junior. The assignation is mysterious both in itself and because it forces comparison with Democritus (whose works covered almost every scientific, technical and philosophical field but which are now almost entirely lost), and because it borrows Democritus's presumed link with Pythagoras and therefore pre-Hellenistic knowledge. Despite the 'Junior' it is a bold claim, and must affect the way we read Burton. Thus while some work becomes anonymous by accident (a copyist's negligence, for instance) and other anonymity is a studied attempt to preserve gentlemanly (and perhaps gentlewomanly) decorum, sometimes anonymous or pseudonymous work can display, ironically enough, a consciously authored identity.

Elizabeth Heale's article 'Misogyny and the Complete Gentleman in Early Elizabethan Printed Miscellanies' (*YES* 33[2003] 233–47) likewise acknowledges that women were an active force in manuscript circulation, but details a number of examples in which poems with a female voice are given a male voice in print, arguing that 'anxiously masculine self-formation of the gentleman poet in most mid-century printed miscellanies depends on the rewriting of women's centrality to the genre of courtly verse at court and in country houses' (p. 246). She develops this theme in her book, which begins by examining the 'flurry of single-author verse miscellanies that appeared in print in the 1560s and 1570s' and which had the intention of making the author's 'self to be known of many'. In so doing, she argues that, in the work of Gascoigne and Turberville, 'amorous verse sequences expose anxieties about a dangerous, feminized, instability in language that calls into question the inscription of the well-framed, masculine authorial self' (p. 11). As befits her subject, Heale writes in an elegant style, although I wonder whether she is not too keen to prove the perceived dangerousness of the feminine. The quotation from Ascham's *The Scholemaster* that she cites in order to substantiate the requirement that a 'well-ordered male' should control 'the disorderly feminine world of his own passions' actually refers to the 'filthie taulke' that will cause him to 'vomet and cast vp, all the holesome doctrine, that he receiued in childhoode' and, if anything, rather suggests to me the dangers of unbridled 'masculinity'. Perhaps the main problem of the book, however, is its unexamined, shorthand use of the term 'Protestant' throughout, and the tendency, common amongst writers on literature, to assume that the excessive, rabid opinions of some extremists in print reflected authorized or at least widespread belief. Heale seems in any case more concerned with the tensions within the self than in society and does not, therefore, really develop the possibility that the contradictions she discerns in the miscellanies between a strict morality and more urbane, lightly humorous courtliness may be an attempt to negotiate, whether on a personal level or as part of the search for preferment, the contradictions that reformation had unleashed.

Catharine Davies's *A Religion of the Word*, however, is devoted to the complexity of English Protestantisms and is a detailed, carefully written study of the Edwardian reformation through analysis of its published writings. She argues that the dichotomizing of Christianity into the true and false religion, and most importantly the notion of a clerical conspiracy that had led the people astray, 'allowed protestants to disassociate themselves completely from popery', exonerate the mass of the people from blame for former erroneous belief, and avoid the charge of schism (p. 21). A succession of chapters deal with the threat to the reformed church of religious radicalism, the realization that the danger of allowing the mass of the people to read the Bible for themselves could only be contained through greater efforts to produce a learned ministry of recognized preachers, and with instigation of the idea that 'True order was the corollary of true religion' (p. 140). Although order as described in the homily on obedience implies strict hierarchy, the Lord's Prayer was the 'great leveller of Christian society', while charity 'provided a rationale for almsgiving which had nothing to do with merit or "works' righteousness"'; indeed 'God permitted inequality in order to provide opportunity for practical charity' (p. 163). Davies helpfully provides an introduction and a conclusion to each chapter to steer her readers through the multiplicity and changeability of the points of view under discussion.

Ethan H. Shagan (*Popular Politics and the English Reformation*) also addresses the multiplicity of viewpoints in sixteenth-century England. He has mined the National Archives (formerly the PRO) for deposition records, which even at this distance let us hear a welter of voices as parishioners argue about the keeping of feast days and other aspects of ritual observance. But we can also hear their personal animosities and jealousies so that the extent to which these disputes actually reflect difference of belief remains still unclear. Many sound like the normal day-to-day squabbles of village life. As fewer of us live in villages—and fewer still work in them—we may be too tempted to take such disputes at face value.

Elizabeth Vandiver, Ralph Keen and Thomas D. Frazel (*Luther's Lives*) perform the invaluable task of bringing together and making readily available in an affordable edition two important contemporary accounts of the life of Martin Luther, both in English translation and with short informative introductions. Philip Melanchthon, Luther's lifelong supporter, published his short Latin *History of the Life and Acts of Dr Martin Luther* in Heidelberg in 1548. It was published in English translation in 1561 and later incorporated into Foxe's *Acts and Monuments*. The much longer *Commentaria de Actis et Scriptis Martini Luther* by Johannes Cochlaeus, Luther's life-long opponent, is a virulent attack and was published in Latin in Mainz in 1549 but has never before been translated into English. The styles of the two writers are strikingly different: Melanchthon calm and methodical; Cochlaeus vehement. Both, however, incorporate the direct speech and quoted writing of others, including Luther himself, so that, albeit in a modern translation, the book gives a valuable impression of the passionately held differences of belief amongst those leading the arguments for and against reformation.

Alastair Fowler's *Renaissance Realism: Narrative Images in Literature and Art* is a search for a definition of mimesis in the Renaissance, and correlates literature with developments in the visual arts: 'The possibility of single-point perspective brought a new integration to picturing and to narrative alike.' He finds that the uses of perspective at this period were neither a matter of metaphysics or, contrastingly, of geometrical technique—the terms in which the debate has been commonly constructed—but rather 'part of a complex change in visualizing, psychological as well as perceptual'. While the plays of Shakespeare achieve a consistent and extended topographical and realistic *mise-en-scène* 'centuries before it becomes possible in the novel', Renaissance narrative 'was discontinuous' with 'multiple viewpoints' that 'commonly broke into relatively short segments'. This contributed to a 'participatory' realism that made it 'possible to integrate different viewpoints and tackle the problem of combining a character's "outside" and "inside"'. The effect is quite different from the discontinuities of postmodern fiction, and therefore demands a very different mode of reading (pp. 121–2). Fowler describes his relatively short but generously illustrated book as 'no more than an essay' (intending the original meaning of that word), and says himself that the way in which perspective came to be 'part of our mental set' still 'remains to be written' (p. 10).

An even more interdisciplinary approach to understanding the Renaissance artistic mindset is taken by a collection of essays edited by Timothy McGee (*Improvisation in the Arts of the Middle Ages and Renaissance*). All the performing arts are covered in this fascinating and groundbreaking book, including dance, music, theatre and even performance poetry—often in combination. As Dominico Pietropaolo points out in the opening essay in the collection, we misunderstand the performing arts of this period if we do not appreciate the extent to which they routinely involved improvisation, by which is meant the rule-bound, convention-exploiting, but nevertheless imaginatively free activity which skilled performers were expected to be able to exhibit to a greater or lesser extent both in work that was notated and for occasions or events in which no prior writing was involved. Although now an activity which is generally thought of as belonging solely to music, and particularly to jazz, it originally denoted 'only the art of impromptu verse-making'. Apart from the obvious difficulty of talking about an art form that exists only in the moment and, if it is written down at all, represented either by a mere skeleton designed to be fleshed out by the performer, or a report of a previously entirely unscripted performance, there is a problem concerning analysis of the form: 'A performance that is not the execution of a notated text, which precedes it in time and logic but is a self-sustaining creative act, remains always in danger of being radically altered by the theoretical categories through which it is examined if these categories were originally developed for the analysis of a scripted or notated work' (p. 3). We know from the *Decameron* that fourteenth-century Florentine aristocrats might be expected to know how to improvise a melody for poetry (p. 32), but the authors point out that improvised poetry, song and theatre were not always intended purely for entertainment. Being unscripted, improvisation could be a powerful tool for political commentary since it was impossible to censor in advance and almost impossible to prosecute afterwards. It might also have an official function. McGee tells us that the post of civic herald in many Italian communities required someone adept in *cantare all'improvviso* in order to welcome visiting dignitaries and celebrate military victory. But this figure would also be called upon to entertain government officials at dinner. Like an English court jester he was the town's 'civic conscience...free to comment on all important matters' (p. 34). While there is now a long tradition of scholarly research into the historical performance of music, which has been used to feed back into the modern performance of historical music, such activity has been strongly resisted by modern literary critics and theatre performers alike. Even in music, according to Randall A. Rosenfeld ('Performance Practice, Experimental Archaeology and the Problem of the Respectability of Results' also in this collection), the theory for evaluating experiment in performance practice 'has yet to be written' and a 'textual citation alone seems to carry far more weight in scholarly circles than does an insight gained from a performance'. He therefore asks whether the methodologies and 'criteria for degrees of proof' of experimental archaeology can be applied to the study of improvisation in performance practice. The collection also includes two essays which explore the extent to which improvisation is in fact simulated in carefully wrought later sixteenth-century drama. Jane Freeman ('Shakespeare's Rhetorical Riffs') uses the concept of improvisation to discuss Shakespeare's habit of making his characters pun. Both essays cite Hamlet's instruction to player clowns to play 'no more than is set down for them', but David N. Klausner ('The Improvising Vice in Renaissance England') sees this instruction not so much as voicing Shakespeare's own demands as constructing an idea of Hamlet as an 'overwrought and not very experienced theater director attempting to micro-manage his troupe for a very specific effect' (p. 273). He notes stage directions from a range of dramatists in which characters—as in the following example from John Cooke's play *Greene's Tu Quoque*—are called upon to 'talk and rail what they list'.

A parallel-text translation of an early Renaissance treatise on music and poetry, which ends with a defence of improvised song, was recently published by Ann Moyer. Raffaele Brandolini's *De Musica et Poetica* [1513], written for Giovanni de Medici, insists on music's social importance. A product of the high Renaissance, it is filled with allusion to classical mythology and history, but confirms the theoretical stance taken by the contributors to McGee's collection that improvisation needs to be judged on its own criteria and not those drawn up for fully scripted work.

Another neglected and under-theorized phenomenon affecting the creation and transmission of texts and works of art is plagiarism. This is explored in an interdisciplinary collection of essays edited by Paulina Kewes, *Plagiarism in Early Modern England*, which again includes contributions from the field of dance as well as of sermon and of printers' ornament. Despite the rigour with which we attempt to combat plagiarism when we find it for instance in undergraduate essays, defining what it is and when it first arose has proved more difficult than one might at first suppose. This is perhaps partly because of the flattening effect of the ubiquitous term 'appropriation'. When does something borrowed become something new? When is it actually theft? And when, if ever, does plagiarism slide into infringement of copyright? The term *plagiarius*, an abductor of slaves, was first applied in a literary context by Martial, although his use of it—concerning as it does the material theft of the only copy of a work—also constitutes a clear material loss and therefore implies theft in the conventional sense. He can no longer sell the piece, as someone else has now done so. If on the other hand the plagiarism (in the modern sense) consists only of the unacknowledged use of published work, can it properly be called theft at all? Christopher Ricks, whose British Academy lecture on this theme forms the first chapter of the collection, is quite clear as to the answers to these questions. The other contributors explain why they have proved so problematic in practice despite the undeniable moral case. Together they make an often witty and entertaining volume.

Robert Cockcroft's *Rhetorical Affect and Early Modern Writing* explores the notorious problem of how to evaluate the emotional effect of historical texts. He approaches this through an evaluation of rhetoric, looking not only at the classical theories of rhetoric and of natural philosophy available to sixteenth- and early seventeenth-century writers, but also at the arts of persuasion utilized by some of the more influential 1980s and 1990s critics. And very black arts they turn out to have been too. The approach is surely correct. The very first book on human psychology to be written in England, *The Passions of the Mind in General* [1601] by Thomas Wright, ostensibly a treatise on how to deliver an effective and affecting speech, follows an ancient tradition in arguing that an orator needs a detailed understanding of human behaviour in order to mimic certain emotions in oratorical delivery and play on the emotions of his auditors. As a recusant, he presumably had ample motive to try to discern the 'mind's construction in the face'. Cockcroft does not mention that book, but his careful dissection of both literature and criticism according to the Aristotelian terms *ethos*, *pathos* and *logos* makes for some useful readings of the early modern texts and some polite but devastating analyses of the techniques of some postmodern criticism.

The metaphor underpinning David Glimp's *Increase and Multiply: Governing Cultural Reproduction in Early Modern England* is by contrast a lesson in what has given rhetoric a bad name. Curiously, the effect of the relentless repetition of the reproductive metaphor is both to kill it dead and to make one over-aware of certain bodily functions. Recourse to Foucault in order to make 'legible' a late sixteenth-century writer's description of the ordering of a state in terms of the ordering of a household (p. 8) seems an unnecessary reversal of history, and there is also an unfortunate tendency to rely on false dichotomies. This is a shame since the basic idea, which was to explore the dynamic between a growth in the efficiency and scope of government and the new techniques of recording and counting people (through the institution of parish and other registers), is promising. Whether this amounts to 'tools to render people into discourse' (p. 12), however, is another question.

Alex Davis's *Chivalry and Romance in the English Renaissance* likewise betrays its origins as a PhD thesis. It contains a mass of useful and interesting material but tends simply to cite rather than to synthesize and develop its secondary sources. It is also unnecessarily difficult to read—showing perhaps both the overwhelming pressure on young scholars to publish, and the lack of attention paid by teachers to writing by students of all ages. As a result, critical disagreements are rehearsed and positions tentatively endorsed without the problem being fully critiqued by reference either to much in the way of analysis of the literary texts or to in-depth discussion of the political history. The final chapter contributes to the theme of Elizabethan afterlives by exploring the way in which sixteenth-century appropriation of medieval chivalry, in particular the entertainments at Kenilworth during the queen's progress in 1575, were in turn repeatedly revisited and romanticized in the eighteenth and nineteenth centuries, even while medievalism itself was so frequently characterized as the product of a 'dark age'. Davis demonstrates the remarkable ability of chivalry to 'sustain repeated—indeed innumerable—deaths and rebirths' and shows that there is scope for further study.

Randall L. Anderson, 'Metaphors of the Book as Garden in the English Renaissance' (*YES* 33[2003] 248–61), is a survey of STC items—in particular poetic miscellanies—that incorporate metaphors of the book as a flower or garden, and of the compiler as florist or bee within their text. Perhaps appropriately, it is itself almost a miscellany of extracts on this theme.

At this period of course, poetry can be found in more places than mere poetry books. Guillaume Coatalen, 'Unpublished Elizabethan Sonnets in Legal Manuscripts in the Cambridge University Library' (*RES* 54[2003] 551–65) acknowledges J.H. Baker's *Catalogue of Legal Manuscripts in Cambridge University Library* for pointing him to a manuscript compiled by Ralph Stawell of the Middle Temple, which squeezes ten sonnets and some extra stray couplets, all with Petrarchan and French influences, into the margins of his legal notes. While the poems are conventional and amateurish in content and execution, the manuscript provides telling evidence for Inns of Court culture and lifestyle.

Sarah M. Dunnigan, however, demonstrates that Petrarchan poetry of desire can have both far-reaching and deadly consequences once it is both written and read in a political context. Her book *Eros and Poetry at the Courts of Mary Queen of Scots and James VI*, like those by Heale and North mentioned earlier, deals with the generic themes of female unruliness and the problem of authorial identity, but the specific, known historical contexts give the story a chilling edge.

In the circumstances it is a shame that she too feels that she needs to resort to a circuitous critical style. This is a short book. It would have been considerably shorter—though much more powerful—without the repetitions, which seem particularly frequent in the first chapter on the so-called 'casket sonnets'. These were supposedly written by Mary Queen of Scots as expressions of overt desire for Bothwell, seemingly while they were still both married to other people. These suppositions acquired the status of fact at the time and as such were used to demonstrate her failure to protect the body politic through her readiness to allow access to her body corporeal. But dirty tricks campaigns—and this one in itself is no different from many we have seen, even quite recently, in which the public figure is gendered male—need to be described with the same level of sceptical pragmatism as is used by those who orchestrate them. The second section of the book opens with a chapter devoted to the poetry of the young James VI: a body of love lyrics, including some addressed to Anne of Denmark, and *A Tragedie called Phoenix* [1584], concerning his distress at the banishment of his French cousin (and favourite) Esmé Stewart, which 'crosses the threshold of politics in ways which travesty the king's own literary prescriptions for a poetics immured from political intrusion or "contamination"' (p. 97). Other chapters deal with the collection of poetry made by the Edinburgh merchant George Bannantyne during Mary's time, as well as work by John Stewart, Alexander Montgomerie and William Fowler from the Jacobean period.

In the light of the topics considered this year with regard to writing by women, it is helpful to move just across the channel to consider *Women and the Book Trade in Sixteenth-Century France* by Susan Broomhall—not so much, perhaps, as a subject area but as a methodology. Just as with the approaches to improvisation considered earlier, Broomhall argues that different criteria need to be used in order adequately to acknowledge the different circumstances in which women wrote and published. She picks up on David R. Carlson's work to argue that 'publication' must include the circulation of manuscripts amongst peers and the submission of deluxe copies to patrons, but goes on to argue that it is proper to include the likes of the illiterate convicted murderer Marguerite Haldebois in the category of published authors since her scaffold speech was transcribed for circulation. Broomhall's discussion is usefully nuanced by an awareness of class: 'it is problematic to speak of categories of "men" and "males" when a small subset of the entire male population of early modern France disproportionately influenced that society' (p. 10). Her first chapter looks at women of all classes as different types of reader, and usefully distinguishes between the two very different skills, reading and writing: 'Female literacy was designed to promote absorption of ideas through reading, but not to encourage composition' (p. 16). But the Lutheran Reformation had a positive effect: women had a 'moral status as wives and mothers' (as opposed to the sinfulness that attached even to married non-celibates). The duty women thus acquired to educate their children encouraged female literacy. Clearly written and immensely readable, the book is crammed with detail, not only of translators and authors, but also of named women readers, patrons, scribes and printers—in a trade which, contrary to the situation in England, was unregulated by a guild. Broomhill always soberly assesses the evidence both for and against women's involvement in these roles.

Charlotte Guillard, for instance, a printer for over fifty years (including two short periods of marriage to other printers) includes a preface in one of her volumes as a 'defence of her public working role', showing 'a clear awareness of both the uniqueness of her position as a female publisher and contemporary hostility to her business actions' (p. 66). The difficulties, bravely confronted and strategically coped with, are inspiring.

2. Sidney

Two valuable monographs on Sidney appeared in 2003. Elizabeth Mazzola presents a comprehensive picture of the way in which changing notions of the family in the early modern period influenced the writings of Philip Sidney, his sister Mary, his brother Robert, and his niece, Lady Mary Wroth (*Favourite Sons: The Politics and Poetics of the Sidney Family*). At the core of Mazzola's study is her assertion that 'the fledgling English literary tradition…offers a "hot-house" atmosphere similar to the one provided by the early modern family, crowded with patrons and offshoots and by near and far-flung members of the Sidney circle' (p. 7). Drawing upon the work of the historians Lawrence Stone and Peter Laslett and the psychoanalysts Sigmund Freud, Melanie Klein, and D.W. Winnicott, Mazzola considers the impact of the Sidney family upon Philip's cultural legacy and the extent to which his writings and image informed their ideas about fiction. Chapter 1, which is a reprint of '"Natural" Boys and "Hard" Stepmothers: Sidney and Elizabeth' (in Corinne S. Abate, ed., *Privacy, Domesticity, and Women in Early Modern England* [2003]), considers the relationship between Philip and Queen Elizabeth, which Mazzola views in terms of that between early modern mothers and children, an identification positively encouraged by Elizabeth and which Sidney enjoyed but also sought to subvert. Chapter 2 considers the influence of Philip upon his siblings Mary, who completed his psalm translations, and Robert, who composed poetry inspired by *Astrophil and Stella*, and the degree to which both were inspired by the same somewhat misleading image of Philip that influenced English poets outside the family circle. The first part of the book is focused on poetry, but part 2 shifts to prose, with chapter 3 reading Sidney's *Old Arcadia* as a literary investigation of the benefits and defects of early modern families via the romance genre and its preoccupations with rape and incest anxieties. Chapter 4 reconsiders the critical notion that Lady Mary Wroth is overwhelmed by the reputation of her famous uncle, arguing, rather, that she consciously drew upon his work, in particular his 'interest in the family as a source of romance problems and their solutions' (p. 88). Mazzola's book offers an insightful study of the Sidney family dynamic which emphasizes the role of reputation, influence and myth upon those who followed its favourite son.

Charles Ross's *Elizabethan Literature and the Law of Fraudulent Conveyance: Sidney, Spenser, and Shakespeare* is a well-researched and thought-provoking study of recurrent literary references to the practice of fraudulent conveyancing. Fraudulent conveyancing occurs when 'someone in debt places his or her property out of reach of his or her creditors' process' (p. 1), and each of the writers considered by Ross had a specific approach to the issue. Philip Sidney is discussed in the context of his father Henry, Lord Deputy of Ireland between 1565 and 1571, where fraudulent conveyancing 'has an eventful history' (p. 5). The lack of provision against fraudulent conveyancing in an Irish statute drafted by Henry against Shane O'Neill in 1569 indicates Henry's ambivalence towards the practice, a view seemingly shared by his son Philip; both father and son experienced financial difficulties and thus recognized the necessity for a degree of moral dissembling, even amongst the virtuous. In the *Arcadia* Philip developed a plot 'that could represent the moral ambiguity of fraudulent conveyances', representing the tension between 'the interests of creditors, including the state, who sought to counter fraud with the desire of men in varied circumstances to retain control of their lives and property' (p. 56). The separate ravishments (the sexual aspect of moving 'property') committed by Philip's heroes in the story indicate his openness to conveyancing and, as Ross shows, this plot innovation influenced Spenser and Shakespeare in their construction of literary elopements.

In a compelling article which, understandably, won the South-Central Renaissance Conference Louis L. Martz Essay Prize for 2003, Derek B. Alwes argues that Sidney's *New Arcadia* is a defence of poetry, with Sidney viewing the composition of poetry as a social duty: '"To Serve Your Prince By…an Honest Dissimulation": The *New Arcadia* as a Defense of Poetry' (*EIRC* 29[2003] 147–69). Using the stories of Zopyrus and Abradatas, who pretend to be in disgrace with their king to infiltrate the enemy, Sidney distinguishes between two forms of serving one's monarch: extreme self-sacrifice (Zopyrus had cut off his own ears and nose to convince the enemy) and fiction (Abradatas was merely rumoured to be in disgrace). In a probable swipe at Queen Elizabeth herself, Sidney recommends poetry as 'an alternate form of service' but crucially, that service is conceived of as public service to the state rather than private service to the monarch. In his revision of the *Old Arcadia* Sidney 'reveals a serious literary commitment that he had been at pains previously to deny' (p. 150), thus contradicting Fulke Greville's view that Sidney's 'end was not writing even while he wrote'. Using a range of examples from the text, Alwes shows that the *New Arcadia* is filled with fictions (disguises, feigned executions), and there is 'no question that the ability to fictionalize is a source of genuine power in the world of Arcadia'. Where the *Old Arcadia* focused on the pastoral genre, the revision 'takes all fiction as its subject, examining both the proper, strategic uses of fiction as well as the destructive power of mere deception' (p. 154). Although in Arcadia fiction is not always in the service of truth and virtue, the ability to see truth through fiction is necessary because nothing is as it seems.

Sidney's *Arcadia* also forms the focus of a short piece by John Considine, who takes issue with Wendy Gibson's explanation of two riddles that appear in the *Old Arcadia*: 'Two Riddles By Sir Philip Sidney and Their Solutions' (*ELN* 41[2003] 32–6). Gibson traced the first of the two riddles to a contemporary manuscript source, and although Considine agrees that this was indeed a source he argues persuasively that both of Sidney's riddles and that which appears in the source refer not to pregnancy, as Gibson suggested, but rather to coition.

In 'Sidney's *Defence of Poetry*: Ethos and the Ideas' (*BJJ* 10[2003] 101–15) Travis Curtright argues that Sidney's ideas should be explained in the rhetorical context of Aristotelian *ethos*, rather than universals and forms. In his *Defence of*

Poetry Sidney's innovative use of Aristotle's teachings, on character from the *Poetics* and the *Rhetoric*, provides the *Defence*'s response to the Platonic attacks upon poetry. In his modification of Aristotle's teaching, in particular that good character persuades audiences, Sidney 'does not simply reproduce a classical source' but 'freely discovers, innovates, and synthesizes' (p. 112), working Aristotelian thought into a thoroughly modern discourse.

George Gömöri, 'A Poem By Sir Philip Sidney in a Seventeenth-Century *Album Amicorum*' (*Renfor* 6:ii[2003]), traces what is probably the first known reference indicating German interest in Sidney's poetry to a seventeenth-century travel album, known also by the German name *Stammbuch* or by the Latin *Album amicorum*, which belonged to a German-speaking Bohemian scholar Daniel Stolz von Stolzenberg, a medical doctor and editor of alchemistic texts. The poem that appears in the album, currently located in the British Library in London, was inscribed by Johannes Rhenanus, also a doctor and a poet, on 7 March 1623. The poem, number 34 from the *Old Arcadia*, contains an almost illegible insertion by Rhenanus, deciphered here by Gömöri, and the version ends with an alchemistic formula and a Latin commendation to Stolz. Although the opening of Sidney's poem was known in Germany via an earlier publication by John Dowland, it was not clear that Sidney was the source of his couplet, and Gömöri doubts 'any direct influence of Dowland on Rhenanus'. As Gömöri points out, Stolz's album is important as 'a unique, early document of the appreciation of English poetry on the continent' and demonstrates the specific influence of Sidney's poetry.

In this year's *Sidney Journal* Julie Eckerle's engaging essay, '"With a tale forsooth he cometh unto you": Sidney and the Storytelling Poet', focuses on the importance of stories and reading in Sidney's theoretical work *A Defence of Poetry* and the *New Arcadia* (*SJ* 21[2003] 41–65). Poetry should entertain and instruct, and Sidney located the power of the poet in the narrative, especially the narrative example; he differs from his classical predecessors, who did not think exemplum could be expanded into a lengthy narrative. The story in the *Defence* about the great horseman John Pietro Pugliano functions as a fable and a rhetorical exemplum and provides an important lesson about effective reading. There is an assumption, however, that only those readers 'with access to the same kind of superior education that Sidney himself received' (p. 49) would be able to decipher the multiple layers of meaning embedded in the narrative. If the reader cannot decipher the moral message then poetry might only delight and so fail in its more important didactic purpose. Two kinds of reader are evident in the *New Arcadia*: the aristocratic Pamela, who can read properly, and the peasant Mopsa, who does not understand. For Sidney, pleasure is generally associated with the feminine and instruction with the masculine and he praises a very specific kind of story: that connected with the male world of masculine heroes. The ideological power of poetry, a power gained through the act of reading, is thus limited to a male and upper-class world.

Critics have commented on Sidney's debt to Francesco Colonna's *Hypnerotomachia: The Strife of Love in a Dreame* when composing the *Arcadia*, but in a persuasively argued essay Hester Lees-Jeffries, 'Sidney's Zelmane and the *Songe de Poliphile*', suggests a specific influence to the text in its original Italian and French translation (*SJ* 21[2003] 67–75). Lees-Jeffries concentrates on the description of Pyrocles, one of the *Arcadia*'s two heroes, when first he disguises himself as the Amazon Zelmane and identifies hitherto unnoted parallels between the description of Zelmane and description of the apparel of the Cytherean nymphs in the *Hypnerotomachia*, parallels which are even closer in the shorter French translation, known as the *Songe de Poliphile*. Sensitive to those readers who are not proficient in foreign languages, Lees-Jeffries provides the relevant passages from Sidney, then the Italian, followed by Joscelyn Godwin's 1999 translation, the French text, and her own translation of the *Songe*, which has never been translated into English. Sidney knew the original Latin text but, as Lees-Jeffries shows, used its French version. The passages from the *Hypnerotomachia/Song* which attracted him are all beautifully illustrated, suggesting that he may have been drawn to these passages by their illustrations.

3. Spenser

Spenser is considered alongside his predecessors and contemporaries in two important books published this year. Elizabeth Fowler's monograph, *Literary Character: The Human Figure in Early English Writing*, is specifically concerned with the development of literary figures extricated from social persons (for example the pilgrim, the conqueror, the maid, the narrator) in works by Chaucer, Langland, Skelton and Spenser. The chapter on Spenser considers the marriage of the Thames and the Medway from Book IV of *The Faerie Queene* and the two cantos of Mutabilitie. Fowler regards Spenser as 'the first poet in English to theorize the architectonic nature of fictional characterization' which allowed him to use characters as a means of 'assessing and reimagining the very foundations of social life' (p. 179). The portrait of the Thames 'evokes various kinds of political entities' (p. 202) and the principles reinforcing them suggest that the source of England's power lies not in royal succession but rather in its landed gentry and citizens (p. 204). The figure of Mutability is also considered in terms of social persons, some of them surprisingly positive. Legal issues, which dominate Fowler's thesis, are crucial also to the understanding of Mutability, who is involved not in a criminal trial but a legal suit which has important ramifications for debates over the ownership of place in early modern Ireland.

Charles Ross's monograph *Elizabethan Literature and the Law of Fraudulent Conveyance*, considering the representation of fraudulent conveyancing in the work of Philip Sidney, is reviewed in Section 2 above. Ross also investigates the practice as represented by Spenser and argues that, although Spenser condemns fraudulent conveyancing in his political prose and minor poetry, like Sidney he 'creates a more liberal or balanced view of this legal issue in his narrative poetry' (p. 72). That Spenser took a more severe line in the *View* than either of the Sidneys regarding the need to stamp out the practice was presumably also due to personal circumstances, his own estate being founded on lands escheated to the queen after the attainder of the earl of Desmond. *The Faerie Queene* contains various episodes where the process is less straightforward, amongst them that featuring the magician Busirane, 'the deceitful conveyor of women', in Books III and IV of *The Faerie Queene*. In contrast to the situation in Arcadia, where conveyance is pardoned, Spenser's Busirane 'is forced to give up his prize' (p. 72) but he goes unpunished, and in Book IV Venus is implicated in Amoret's capture. Ross also considers the episode featuring Aemylia in Book IV as a reflection of contemporary debates over the issue, and Arthur's seizure and redistribution of a malefactor's property in Book V as a reflection of the experience of the Munster settlers, in particular Spenser's personal disputes with Lord Roche over land. In the Ruddymane episode from Book II of the poem, 'Three separate types of conveyance attend the baby's stains: ravishment, inheritance, and theft' (p. 90), and Guyon's predicament is considered with the kind of attention to detail evident throughout this study.

In the introduction to their study of death in Spenser and Milton, the editors Elizabeth Jane Bellamy, Patrick Cheney and Michael Schoenfeldt rightly point out that it is an under-investigated topic (*Imagining Death in Spenser and Milton*, p. 2). There is a particular focus on Spenserian and Miltonic epic and 'what it means to trace a literary continuum' between the two, with John Dryden's famous claim that Spenser was Milton's original underpinning the impetus behind many of the comparative essays herein. Milton's debt to Spenser, specifically in the depiction of death and holiness, is explored by Roger Kuin and Anne Lake Prescott in chapter 5 ('"After the first death, there is no other": Spenser, Milton, and (Our) Death'), and in chapter 6 ('Anatomizing Death') Linda Gregerson considers representations of death by Spenser and Milton via anatomy and the act of creation as a means of writing against death. Welcome attention is given to Spenser's *Epithalamion* which, Gregerson argues, 'celebrates the work of generation' as well as 'the flesh's strict entailment, which is death' (p. 114). In chapter 7 Marshall Grossman ('Reading Death and the Ethics of Enjoyment in Spenser and Milton') considers the 'qualitative difference between the representations of death in *The Faerie Queene* and in *Paradise Lost*', identifying what he terms 'pleasures of anticipation and deferral' in the former and 'the terrible fascination of retrospection' in the latter (p. 117), locating the implications of reading both texts firmly in the present. Three essays deal specifically with Spenser: in chapter 2, 'Spenser and the Death of the Queen', which draws upon some of the ideas evident in 'Duessa's Trial and Elizabeth's Error: Judging Elizabeth in Spenser's *Faerie Queene*' (in Freeman and Doran, eds., *The Myth of Elizabeth*), Andrew Hadfield reads Spenser's epic as a poem 'haunted by an imminent death that has not happened' (p. 36), that of Elizabeth, the ageing monarch. In chapter 3, 'Psychic Deadness in Allegory: Spenser's House of Mammon and Attacks on Linking', Theresa M. Krier argues that, in Guyon's descent into the underworld in Book II, Spenser 'represents and critiques the discourse of punitive moral-exemplum allegory', frustrating the reader's attempt to force links, and presenting an allegory that makes the reader uncomfortable because, as well as witnessing the character's suffering, 'we are asked to think, but then refused either the modal or generic features that invite further venturing on a path of thought or an open interpretive matrix that makes thinking generative and genial' (p. 54). Gordon Teskey (chapter 4, 'Death in an Allegory') also considers Spenser's approach to allegory, arguing that death functions differently in this genre than, say, the novel. Focusing on the episode from *FQ* Book II featuring the brothers Cymocles and Pyrocles, Teskey contends that, paradoxically, 'an allegorical character's death is the moment when that character is most alive as meaning' (p. 65). Although at times clarity is sacrificed as a result of esoteric theorizing, this collection provides some thoughtful explorations of the topic under consideration.

Three essays are of interest to Spenserians in Jennifer C. Vaught, ed., *Grief and Gender: 700–1700*, a study which claims that 'in England and Europe during the Middle Ages and Renaissance, representations of grief were profoundly shaped by gender' (p. 1), and expressions of grief 'vary according to time and place' (p. 3). Spenser is considered in part 4, 'Elizabethan Loss and Regeneration', with essays by Donald Cheney, Theresa M. Krier, and Judith H. Anderson. Cheney's contribution ('Grief and Creativity in Spenser's *Daphnaida*'), a welcome study of what William Oram termed one of Spenser's 'most experimental and least-loved works', considers Spenser's adaptation of Chaucer's *Book of the Duchess* via 'both poets' negotiations with Ovid and his post-Classical transmission…to reconsider the vexed question of whether and how Spenser's poem criticizes or distances itself from a widower's excessive, unmanly grief' (p. 125). For Cheney, Spenser's poem 'is at once a criticism and an endorsement of Alcyon's relentless grieving', for although the narrator urges community, 'he is intent on the solitary brooding that is essential to his art' (pp. 128–9). In 'Mother's Sorrow, Mother's Joy: Mourning Birth in Edmund Spenser's Garden of Adonis', Theresa M. Krier focuses on the episode's 'celebration of generativity, maternity, gestation, and filiation' in the context of Luce Irigaray's comments about our sense of loss upon being born and the mourning that attends being separated from the body of our mother. Krier argues that Spenser is keen to show that 'birth, in its attendant losses as well as its evident joys, *needs* to be represented, and draws the reader into the Garden itself, which compounds recognition of maternal loss even as it celebrates generation' (p. 142). One of the episodes considered by Krier involves the goddess Venus, who also features in Judith H. Anderson's essay '*Venus and Adonis*: Spenser, Shakespeare, and the Forms of Desire'. Anderson traces Shakespeare's debt to Spenser in his gendered depiction of passion and grief, noting Shakespeare's allusions to Spenser's Garden of Adonis in his narrative poem, allusions also evident in *Richard III*. Anderson also detects Shakespeare's debt to Book III's 'cast of Venerian refractions' (p. 159) which informs Shakespeare's Venus and Cleopatra, the poem and play presenting more 'fully fleshed-out' versions of Spenser's allegorical figures (p. 160). This is an impressive collection, but one small criticism is the decision to place notes at the back of the volume instead of after each chapter, headed only by chapter numbers, not the author's name or title.

Vince P. Redder's entertaining essay, '"The reliques and ragges of popish superstition": The Effect of Richard Hooker's *Of the Lawes of Ecclesiastical Polity* on Book V of *The Faerie Queene*' (in Michelle M. Sauer, ed., *Proceedings of the 11th Annual Northern Plains Conference on Early British Literature*) argues that the difference in tenor between the first part of Spenser's *Faerie Queene*, published in 1590, and the second part, published in 1596, specifically regarding the depiction of Catholicism, can be explained via Spenser's reading of Richard Hooker's theology. In *FQ* Book I, Catholic priests are represented by the demonic magician Archimago and the False Una who, like the foxes in

The Shepheardes Calender, deceives her victims 'by trickery and illusion, not by force' (p. 137). Where Book I urges Protestants 'to beware of the sophistry of the mission priests and their leader', Book V depicts their tricks as 'something much more sinister: rebellion and regicide' (p. 138). Redder provides a convincing argument that the episode where Britomart narrowly escapes from a disappearing bed in the House of Dolon is not a comment on marriage and fidelity, as put forward by critics such as A.C. Hamilton, but rather alludes to the failure of the Babington plot and the remaining threat posed by papists. Redder identifies Dolon, once a faithful knight, as Robert Persons, Jesuit in charge of the English mission who had once been a good Protestant and became one of group of exiled Catholic clergy who believed it permissible to remove Elizabeth and replace her with the Catholic Mary Queen of Scots. Redder provides close analysis of Hooker's work, which he notes must have angered Spenser and other progressive Protestants as 'a dangerous collusion at the highest levels of the church with the missionary priests' (p. 144), since it was welcomed by Elizabeth and the archbishop of Canterbury, who urged compromise.

Most of the points raised by Andrew Hadfield in 'Duessa's Trial and Elizabeth's Error: Judging Elizabeth in Spenser's *Faerie Queene*' (in Freeman and Doran, eds.) will be familiar to Spenserians, but provide a useful introduction to those less informed about his writings, in particular *The Faerie Queene* and the complexities surrounding Spenser's representation of Queen Elizabeth. As Hadfield points out, Spenser's poem offers criticism of Elizabeth as well as encomium, and she is figured in the poem's bad queens as well as those who are good. Although Spenser's earlier works suggest radical Protestant leanings, with his criticism of Elizabeth focusing on her political and religious policy, *The Faerie Queene* offers specific criticism of her refusal to marry and is concerned with the succession question.

The issue of succession also interests Catherine G. Canino, who reads Spenser's *Faerie Queene* not in terms of women's rule in general but specifically Queen Elizabeth's virginity and the power it gave her to determine England's future monarch: '"Thy weaker novice to perform thy will": Female Dominion Over Male Identity in *The Faerie Queene*' (in Abate, ed., *Privacy, Domesticity, and Women in Early Modern England*). That Elizabeth could choose her own successor, and thus shape the future of English men, is reflected in Spenser's reference to 'fashioning a gentleman' and the whole trajectory of *The Faerie Queene*, which is 'the story of men whose identities are forged, and whose destinies are decided, by women' (p. 114). Although female dominance over male identity is evident throughout the poem, Canino's focus is on Book I (space apparently not allowing for a fuller study) and in particular the control that Una, Duessa, and Lucifera assert over Redcrosse.

Two volumes of *Spenser Studies* were published this year and the first of these saw an especially eclectic mix. In M.L. Donnelly's 'The Life of Vergil and the Aspiration of the "New Poet"' (*SSt* 17[2003] 1–35) recent critical opinion surrounding Spenser's alleged Virgilian ambitions is taken to task. Especially targeted is Richard Rambuss who, according to Donnelly, does not take into account 'the actual Vergilian model as known to Spenser and his contemporaries from the *Life* of the poet' which depicts him as laureate but also as 'counsellor at the elbow of power, the definer and inspirer of the course of empire' (p. 3). Making close reference to Virgil's biography, available in Renaissance editions of the *Princeps poetarum* and usually attributed to Aelius Donatus, Donnelly argues that the classical poet 'would have been a powerful spur to emulation for young Edmund Spenser' since, like Spenser, Virgil was 'poor, without place or status, modest, but widely and usefully learned…adept at making the right connections and attracting the interest of potential patrons…[who were] wealthy, powerful, complaisant and liberal but…requiring advice and counsel for which there is a rich reward, and which only the poet can provide' (p. 8). Crucially for Donnelly, Rambuss and other critics focus on the Virgilian career as 'exclusively literary and aesthetic' (p. 10), ignoring the early modern view of his work as 'a virtual handbook and guide to statecraft, policy, and military arts' (p. 7). Although Donnelly makes no explicit connection between Spenser's admiration for Virgil and his opinion of the influential Irish bards, Spenser's envious acknowledgement in *A View of the Present State of Ireland* of the respect afforded the Irish poets by their rulers reinforces Donnelly's argument for Spenser's emulation of Virgil and the focus in Donatus on 'the good poet's merited rewards of fame, wealth, and political influence' (p. 18). This informative and nicely written essay, accompanied by five illustrations for Renaissance editions of Virgil, is a corrective to the notion that Spenser's literary ambitions were somehow distinct from his desire for power.

Religion forms the focus of Benedict Robinson's essay, 'The "Secret Faith" of Spenser's Saracens' (*SSt* 17[2003] 37–73), which argues that *The Faerie Queene* assimilates Catholicism to Islam by fusing medieval crusade narratives against Saracens with Protestant apocalyptic histories, thus emphasizing Islam and Catholicism as manifestations of false belief. This assimilation is perhaps most clearly seen in the poem's depiction of Philip II as a sultan. The romance genre is particularly suitable for Spenser's purpose and Robinson outlines what she terms its 'crusading impulse' (p. 41). She also traces the connections made between Islam and the Christian enemy by commentators from either side of the Christian divide: Thomas More compared Protestantism to Islam while Luther compared the pope to Mohammed. John Bale, who constantly mentions Islam in his reading of Revelation, believed in its complicity with Catholicism and rejected the medieval romance form for its Catholic associations, but Spenser revitalized the genre for Protestant England, incorporating 'Bale's apocalyptic vision', especially in Book I of his poem. As Robinson points out, Saracens have been somewhat neglected by Spenserians, with no articles on Saracens, Turks or Islam in the usually thorough *Spenser Encyclopedia* (p. 38), but the point that pagans in *The Faerie Queene* represent Catholics was made by Richard A. McCabe, 'The Fate of Irena: Spenser and Political Violence' (in Patricia Coughlan, ed., *Spenser and Ireland: An Interdisciplinary Perspective* (Cork: CorkUP [1989])), a work not cited in an otherwise thorough study.

Staying with religion, Andrew Escobedo reads specific episodes from Spenser's *Faerie Queene* in the light of ideas about Protestant despair in the work of the nineteenth-century philosopher Søren Kierkegaard: 'Despair and the Proportion of the Self' (*SSt* 17[2003] 75–90). Escobedo's essay is one of two linked pieces with the thesis that 'despair functions simultaneously as a transparent manifestation of God's dispensation and as a kind of joint or pivot between paradoxes inherent in Protestant Christianity' (p. 77). For both Escobedo and Beth Quitslund, who wrote the accompanying essay 'Despair and the Composition of the Self' (*SSt* 17[2003] 91–106), Spenser's epic poem is one of the most complex investigations of despair to emerge in the sixteenth century. Escobedo regards Redcrosse's experience on the mount of Contemplation in I.x, which carries echoes of the Despair episode in I.ix, a comment on the dangers of 'abstraction of self from world' (p. 86) and the opposite of Malbecco's fate who, being obsessed with worldliness, forgets he is a man. Quitslund's focus is similarly on Book I, and she identifies a link between medical and devotional writings, where sin was treated as sickness and wounded conscience as disease, and the episodes featuring Despair and House of Holiness. Quitslund concludes that, 'Rather than separating the spiritual and the physical aspects of despair, Spenser's allegory fuses them in such a way that they are simultaneous expressions of the same problem' (p. 103), the difficulties facing all Christians who are both physically and spiritually weak.

In a clearly argued and imaginative essay, '"Just time expired": Succession Anxieties and the Wandering Suitor in Spenser's *Faerie Queene*' (*SSt* 17[2003] 107–32), Ty Buckman interrogates Spenser's treatment of the tension between the succession issue and the generic imperative that epic should celebrate dynastic ambitions. He agrees with Richard McCabe that Merlin's silent trance, which concludes his prophecy in *FQ* Book III, suggests 'unsettled succession', but adds that this silence is '*by royal decree*' (p. 109) since Elizabeth would not allow open discussion of the issue. Spenser resolves the problem of having no Tudor future to praise and the danger of incurring the wrath of Elizabeth by arranging his dynastic project via Britomart and Artegall, who 'function as founding dynasts', after his classical and Italian sources, and Arthur and Gloriana, whose courtship 'holds out the possibility of a fruitful marriage and a peaceful succession' replacing 'the celebration of an endless Tudor dynasty' (p. 118). Buckman explains the erotic nature of Arthur's dream in Book I via Spenser's *Letter to Ralegh*: the queen is virginal in her private capacity, represented by Belphoebe, but the tradition of 'amorous fairy mistress' better suits 'her official capacity as queen' (p. 120). He also identifies in the dream scene 'the rudiments of a troth-plighting ceremony or a secret marriage pact', the nine months Arthur has sought her in vain being 'the gestation period of the Faery Queen's long awaited heir' (p. 120). Having the relationship occur within a dream allows Spenser to abstract events, thus providing protection from criticism. Their 'infinitely deferred union becomes a structural metaphor for Spenser's unfinished and unfinishable *Faerie Queene*' but might also refer to the desire for stability in a constantly changing world.

Focusing on sources, Judith H. Anderson, 'Busirane's Place: The House of Rhetoric', (*SSt* 17[2003] 133–50), argues that Spenser's House of Busirane, recently discussed by critics in Petrarchan terms, is specifically Ovidian and that its rooms would have been familiar to early modern readers as rhetorical places. Spenser's use of the story of Arachne's weaving contest with Pallas Athena, here and elsewhere in his poetry, 'bear[s] on art and the role of the artist…in sinister or "daungerous," eroticized contexts' (p. 139). Cupid's masquers, who parade in

Busirane's house, are 'impostors of the living and every bit as artificial, as "personified", hence metaphorized, as the "carkasse dead" of the False Florimell' (p. 140). Anderson adds to Thomas Roche's definition of Busirane as *abuse*, meaning 'imposture, ill-usage, delusion', or the archaic *abusion* meaning a 'perversion of the truth, deceit, deception, imposture' by suggesting *abusio*: 'the familiar Renaissance word for catachresis, a wrenching of metaphor or an extravagant use of it', most clearly apparent in 'the masquers' dead likenesses'. The figure of Busirane himself 'primarily represents the radical constructedness of the entire place' and Amoret is his creation, 'the cultural subject par excellence', pleading for his life in order to preserve her own (p. 141). Busirane represents a fantasy and perhaps a culture of rape, but it is crucial that he is unsuccessful because he represents 'a peculiarly rhetorical form of abuse' (p. 142) in his treatment of both women.

For Mary B. Bowman, 'Distressing Irena: Gender, Conquest, and Justice in Book V of *The Faerie Queene*' (*SSt* 17[2003] 151–82), gender forms the focus for Spenser's ethos of justice outlined in *FQ* Book V. Bowman contends that Artegall's success as a dispenser of justice depends 'on the effacement of women's autonomy' (p. 160), with early cantos of the book depicting 'elision of women's agency and a tendency to treat women as property' (p. 159). Later in the book, the figure of Radigund 'raises disturbing questions about the nature of the justiciar's authority': how to distinguish between female tyrants and the divinely anointed exception represented by Elizabeth (p. 166). In the final cantos of the book 'the female figures are neither central nor complex' (p. 166) and, for Bowman, this reduction in female power is related to the ethos of justice since 'both help to naturalize an aggressive policy in Ireland' (pp. 167–8). This is focused on the figure of Irena, who serves to naturalize the poem's depiction of a dependent and passive population. She represents 'peace as defined by the victor' (p. 173) and Elizabeth's power in Ireland, but the fact that she is defeated by Artegall raises awkward questions about Spenser's attitude to his female monarch.

Lin Kelsey, 'Spenser, Ralegh, and the Language of Allegory' (*SSt* 17[2003] 183–213), considers Spenser's use of allegory in *Colin Clouts Come Home Againe* by contrasting the fairly obvious allusions to Ralegh's loss of royal favour, lamented by the Shepheard of the Ocean, with the more subtle allusions evident in Colin's song. Specifically, Kelsey identifies the devious figure of Bregog with Spenser himself and the poet's ability to 'sing whatever he pleases undetected' (p. 195), especially by Burghley, whose wrath Spenser had previously incurred with *Mother Hubberds Tale*.

Alan Stewart and Garrett A. Sullivan Jr., '"Worme-eaten and full of canker holes": Materializing Memory in *The Faerie Queene* and in *Lingua*' (*SSt* 17 [2003] 215–38), focus on the last four cantos of *FQ* Book II, which involve memory's operations in the House of Alma. In doing so they revisit Thomas Tomkis's play *Lingua* [*c.*1604] which, as M.P. Tilley noted in 1927, contains material drawn from Spenser's Alma episode. Spenser's depiction of Eumnestes' chamber, with its old books full of worm-holes, is expanded upon in *Lingua*, which attacks 'the new antiquarianism that was perceived as taking hold of scholarly life in the last years of the sixteenth century' (p. 226). Tomkis follows

Spenser in viewing antiquarianism as 'disabling the proper functioning of memory' which is to 'present evidence of "honorable, and true heroycall actions"' (p. 227). Guyon's encounter with Acrasia in her bower is indebted to his memory of heroic, rather than trivial, exemplars.

In a brilliantly argued piece, 'Republicanism, Nostalgia, and the Crowd' (*SSt* 17 [2003] 253–73; in a section entitled 'Forum'), David Scott Wilson-Okamura disputes the view, most recently put forward by Andrew Hadfield, that Spenser was a republican. Wilson-Okamura takes issue with the four points that make up Hadfield's case: that Spenser praised the Venetian republic in a sonnet, that Spenser moved in republican-inspired circles, that Spenser called for a more republican distribution of power at the end of the *View*, and that the distributive justice advocated by the Giant with the scales in *FQ* V.ii.30–54 has a sound basis in Aristotle's *Ethics*. Identifying substantial holes in Hadfield's argument (as Hadfield himself graciously acknowledges in his response to Wilson-Okamura, 'Was Spenser Really a Republican After All? A Reply to David Scott Wilson-Okamura' (*SSt* 17[2003] 275–290)) a persuasive case is made for Hadfield having misidentified Spenser's conservative response to what he perceived was the decline of the English aristocracy as evidence of his republican sympathies. Spenser, it seems, was not opposed to monarchy but rather its abuse of power.

In the journal's 'Gleanings' section, Richard McNamara, 'Spenser's Dedicatory Sonnets to the 1590 *Faerie Queene*: An Interpretation of the Blank Sonnet' (*SSt* 17[2003] 293–5), contends that the blank space under dedicatory sonnet 15 is a deliberate tribute to the deceased poet Philip Sidney which echoes the 'universal ritual' of laying an extra place for the dead at formal dinners. McNamara claims that, since Sidney was dead, 'all Spenser was able to do was to give him a "blank" space, not among the men, but among the women', Sidney's sister Mary, Elizabeth Carey, and the ladies of the court. Unfortunately McNamara does not give us any indication why poems could not be dedicated to the deceased (presumably because the dedicator could not benefit from their patronage). This reviewer also wonders why, given that sonnet 15, dedicated to Mary, is the only one that 'does not directly praise the recipient' but is a 'eulogy of her dead brother', Spenser should feel the need to repeat himself.

Also in the 'Gleanings' section, Andrew Hadfield, 'Robert Parsons/Richard Verstegen and the Calling in of *Mother Hubberds Tale*' (*SSt* 17[2003] 297–300), points out the irony of Spenser being best known in continental Europe as a source of Catholic propaganda via his attack on William Cecil, Lord Burghley in *Mother Hubberds Tale*. Spenser's poem is referred to in a polemical pamphlet entitled *A Declaration of the True causes of the Great Troubles, Presupposed to be Intended against the Realme of England*, published in Antwerp in 1592. Hadfield contends that the tract was probably written either by Robert Parsons, a prominent English Jesuit and rector of the English College in Rome, or Richard Verstegen, a Catholic antiquarian and polemicist who lived in Paris and Antwerp. The pamphlet's reference to 'fox's cubs' in Spenser poem indicates that the author was not familiar with the poem itself (since no cubs appear) but was informed about events in England and aware that the poem was an important source for English readers regarding Cecil's villainy.

The second volume of *Spenser Studies* includes selected papers from an international conference held at Spenser's alma mater, Pembroke College, Cambridge in 2001. Elizabeth J. Bellamy, 'Wind in Spenser's Isis Church' (*SSt* 18[2003] 9–23), reads the ceremonial mysteries of Spenser's Isis Church episode (*FQ* V.ii) in the context of a forty-five-year-old study in Neoplatonism by Edgar Wind, *Pagan Mysteries in the Renaissance*. Although Wind's focus is on Italian paintings, woodcuts, engravings, emblems, and medals, he also considers the dance of the Graces witnessed by Calidore in *FQ* Book VI. Outlining Wind's definition of a pagan mystery, Bellamy considers why the Isis Church episode didn't measure up and wonders whether Spenser deliberately presented the episode as a failed mystery, but thinks it more likely that, given the influence of Plutarch, the episode 'is perhaps best read as *The Faerie Queene*'s performance of Wind's own methodological concern over the blurred meanings of the term "mysteries" in antiquity' (p. 21).

Although Spenser's debt to Chaucer is widely acknowledged, Clare R. Kinney, 'Marginal Presence, Lyric Resonance, Epic Absence: *Troilus and Criseyde* and/in *The Shepheardes Calender*' (*SSt* 18[2003] 25–39), makes a convincing case for the particular influence of *Troilus and Criseyde* upon Spenser's shift from pastoral to epic. Engaging with Spenser's numerous allusions to Chaucer's poem, Kinney demonstrates the parallel between Troilus and Colin, both betrayed lovers in Petrarchan mode, and argues that, although Chaucer 'explicitly refuses to be "heroic"' (p. 34), privileging instead the romance narrative, Spenser 'will not only find room for Chaucerian romance within his epic, he will also discover epic possibilities within Chaucerian romance' in his tribute to the poet who, even in the sixteenth century, was considered too alien for most tastes.

In an important contribution to our understanding of Spenser's attitude to the Catholic religion John Watkins, 'Polemic and Nostalgia: Medieval Crosscurrents in Spenser's Allegory of Pride' (*SSt* 18[2003] 41–57), explores the tension between Spenser's Reformation polemic and his nostalgia for medieval sacramentalism, arguing that he had a more complex attitude to the older representational order than critics have hitherto recognized. This ambivalence, claims Watkins, is most evident in his treatment of the Seven Deadly Sins in *FQ* Book I. Watkins traces the relationship between Lucifera's House of Pride, which is indebted to the medieval allegorical tradition, and the Orgoglio episode, which draws on the later genre of Italian romance, specifically that of Ariosto's *Orlando Furioso*. The movement from Lucifera to Orgoglio is from one kind of pride to another and also from 'an optimistic belief in human perfectibility and perseverance to a skepticism about humanity's ability to achieve anything of moral value through its own efforts' (p. 45). Although Spenser retains the old sins 'he presents them in a novel way' since, unlike the medieval analogues, 'his procession is heavily disciplined and self-contained' (p. 46) and Spenser's sins 'never confront their corresponding virtues and they do not engage in battle' (p. 47). Redcrosse's battle with Sans Joy and his escape from Lucifera recall medieval conventions but they are drained of moral force and representational vigour. In Ariosto's romance Ruggiero is defeated but his valour remains, whereas the moral power of Redcrosse is entirely defeated by Orgoglio, the fusion of Ariosto's Orca and giant, thus creating an allegory of pride 'that overgoes even

Ariosto in its pessimism about humanity's ability to redeem itself through its own efforts' (p. 50). As Watkins reminds us, critics have traditionally read these two episodes as a supersession, and although the oppositions between good and evil in Book I can be read in terms of its apocalyptic theology they also constitute 'a reaffirmation of a moral dialectic' (p. 54) that began in a much earlier period.

In a well-observed and tightly argued piece Andrew King, 'Lines of Authority: The Genealogical Theme in *The Faerie Queene*' (*SSt* 18[2003] 59–77), interrogates the critical tendency to provide an unproblematic reading of Arthur as Elizabeth's ancestor in *The Faerie Queene*. Rather than endorsing Tudor dynastic claims, argues King, Spenser is 'increasingly aware...that certain narratives that presume to derive objective authority from God (such as royal genealogy) may be in fact human constructs, and as such mutable and lacking in divine authority' (p. 61), an insight which King relates to the poem's epic ambitions. The 'Briton moniments' read by Arthur in Book II end abruptly and so Arthur is 'not so much a figure of promise as the emblem of time's tyranny, of things cut off' (p. 63), a contrast to the Fairy Chronicle and its idealized genealogy ending with Gloriana. Merlin's prophecy, detailing Britomart's marriage to Artegall and lineage down to Elizabeth, is also interrupted and Elizabeth functions as Arthur's double rather than his descendant: crucially, she too is without a legitimate heir. King notes that Arthur is a strange choice for an epic hero, and it is Artegall who emerges as Elizabeth's ancestor, producing an heir before his untimely demise. Artegall thus occupies 'a false historical space in which the known historical failing of Arthur can be rewritten in providential terms' (p. 68) and the use of this unhistorical character makes the poem's status as epic questionable. The Garden of Adonis, central to Book III and 'the great regenerative engine-room of the entire cosmos' (p. 68), presents reproductive creativity as a solution to mutability, but its elusive nature (the narrator does not know its exact location) is reflected in the lack of regeneration in the genealogy of Arthur and Elizabeth; it is fitting that the garden is home to Amoret, not Belphoebe, the Elizabeth figure. Genealogy is under attack in *The Faerie Queene* by time and mutability, and so too are the poem's epic ambitions when Britomart's chastity is represented in the context of Paridell's seduction of Hellenore, an episode undercutting the seriousness of epic by recalling Chaucer's fabliaux. The parody of Paris and Helen problematizes the notion of Britain's providential origin and politically stable future, and though Britomart 'fights to define *The Faerie Queene* as epic' (p. 73), the figure of Paridell presents a serious challenge to her aims and the poem's ambitions.

In 'Wring Out the Old: Squeezing the Text, 1951–2001' (*SSt* 18[2003] 81–121) Harry Berger Jr. provides what is essentially a lengthy survey of Spenser criticism on the Bower of Bliss episode, informed by his discovery of feminist politics, and although the essay provides a useful overview it would perhaps be more at home in a case-book study or an undergraduate textbook than a leading journal. As stated above, this volume of *Spenser Studies* includes selected papers from an international conference held at Pembroke College, Cambridge in 2001 which, as the introduction to the volume informs us, 'brought together 200 Spenserians from around the world' (p. 3). It is therefore surprising that space should have been given to the publication of two very personal essays, one from

A.C. Hamilton, remembering his time as an undergraduate at Cambridge in the 1940s ('Reminiscences of the Study of Spenser in Cambridge in the Late 1940s' (*SSt* 18[2003] 275–86)), and a similar entry by Thomas P. Roche, Jr., 'Spenser, Pembroke, and the Fifties' (*SSt* 18[2003] 287–93), which is described in its abstract as 'An anecdotal reminiscence about the year that Roche spent in Pembroke College, Cambridge, at the point when he became a Spenserian' (p. 287). These pieces are broadly interesting as nostalgia—and thus better suited to the section headed 'Spenser Fashioning a Past: Nostalgia and Irony' than 'Spenser Opening to the Future'—but they hardly constitute a contribution to knowledge and the editors' comment that there were 'far too many [papers] to fill one volume' makes one wonder what was excluded.

Gordon Braden's essay, 'Pride, Humility, and the Petrarchan Happy Ending' (*SSt* 18[2003] 123–42), is a keen analysis of the traditional Petrarchan juxtaposition of the woman's pride and humility as depicted in Spenser's *Amoretti* with specific attention to sonnets 58, 45, and 75. Although the woman in the *Amoretti* is sometimes resentful, as was traditional, there are times when 'the language seems to be reaching for new extremes' (p. 128), and Braden believes that the woman's pride pleases the lover who, unlike in other sequences, recognizes marriage as his goal with wooing as a mutual test. The woman wants to know if the lover will take the trouble to win her and he wants to know 'her potential faithfulness as a wife', if she's worth winning (p. 132). Wooing is also 'the means by which the pride that makes the woman admirable is reconciled with the dependence that comes with accepting love' (p. 133). Braden considers the 'odd textual issue' of the superscription that comes with sonnet 58: 'By her that is most assured to herself'. This could indicate that the poem is spoken by the woman, so the pride being attacked is the speaker's pride, or it could constitute a printing-house mistake with the superscription intended to accompany sonnet 59, but Braden disagrees with both views, arguing that sonnet 59 'reaffirms the perspective clearly established in sonnets 5 and 6' (p. 135). Sonnet 45, Spenser's revision of Petrarch's poem on Laura's narcissism, is 'fully in line with the goal of the sequence that the lady is being asked not to give up the pleasure of admiring herself in a mirror, but rather to relocate that pleasure in a way that makes the man an intimate collaborator' (p. 137). In sonnet 75 the woman is told that she will be immortalized in verse, and the arrangement proposed by the speaker 'has, against almost all Petrarchan precedent, been accepted' so that 'the static Petrarchan posture of worshipful frustration has relaxed into a transaction between the two of them' (p. 139) when she entrusts her pride to him.

Patrick C. Cheney, editor of the study of death in Spenser and Milton reviewed above, stays with this under-explored aspect of Spenser's writing and considers it in the context of English Renaissance tragedy in 'From Dido to Daphne: Early Modern Death in Spenser's Shorter Poems' (*SSt* 18[2003] 143–63). Cheney challenges Jonathan Dollimore's claim that Spenser desires death, arguing rather that he seems to fear that 'desire is death' (p. 147), especially in the *Epithalamion*. Cheney contends that Spenser 'is rarely content to represent death as annihilation' (p. 147), but rather that he 'seems attracted to narratives in which characters miraculously survive death' (p. 148) and it is the 'external agents of divine grace sent directly by God' (p. 149) rather than the hero's confrontation with death which primarily concerns him. Spenser's focus is on marriage, death, and resurrection and in his writing death is 'socialized', 'Christianized', and usually 'eroticized and familialized' (p. 150). In many of Spenser's poems what Cheney terms 'the closure of transcendent consolation' (p. 150) is evident, but not in *Daphnaida*, which suggests not criticism of a husband's intemperate grief, as some critics have supposed, so much as the notion that loss 'can create useful poetry' (p. 152), as noted by Ellen M. Martin. This is a useful analysis of Spenser's attitude to the inevitable since, as Cheney points out, Spenser is one of the period's most important commentators on death and what comes after.

Joining the debate between Andrew Hadfield and David Scott Wilson-Okamura regarding Spenser's republican tendencies, Graham Hammill, in '"The thing/which never was": Republicanism and *The Ruines of Time*' (*SSt* 18[2003] 165–83), considers the question of the author's political opinions less important than the 'encoding of political thought and political history' (p. 166) in his poetry. Hammill reads Spenser's dedicatory sonnet to Lewkener's translation of Contarini's *De magistratibus*, one of the first two republican treatises published in English, alongside *The Ruines of Time* and *FQ* Book V, specifically the Belge episode, in order to show that, in the 1590s, 'Spenser became increasingly frustrated with Elizabethan domestic and foreign policy', engaging in 'alternative forms of political thought like republicanism...[which] intensified its readers' responsibilities for political and historical thought' (p. 170). In the sonnet and in *Ruines* Spenser 'shows an interest in republican temporal paradigms of virtue and corruption' (p. 170) and his attack on Burghley suggests that such an administrator 'threatens the freedom of the entire state' (p. 171). Hammill takes issue with William R. Orwen's reading of *Ruines* as a nationalist response to the problem of succession, arguing, rather, that 'with its focus on Sidney's death at Zutphen, *The Ruines of Time* takes on a more trans-European historical content: England's failed intervention in the Low Countries' (pp. 172–3). In the *Ruines* Spenser 'presents republican civic virtue in combination with Christian figuration in order to propose Sidney, exemplar of the virtuous citizen soldier, as a cultural solution to the historical problem of Protestant devolution that England's failure in the Low Countries was coming to represent' (p. 173). In Sidney can be found the republican model of the *vita activa*, a strategy Spenser continued in *FQ* Book V, and which can be contrasted with the cowardice of certain members of the English court.

In a well-researched and engaging essay, providing further evidence of Spenser's eclecticism and his ability to appeal to a wide range of readers, Mary Ellen Lamb, 'The Red Crosse Knight, St George, and the Appropriation of Popular Culture' (*SSt* 18[2003] 185–208) traces the changing signification of St George in the early modern period via public representations of him in performance which she relates to his appearance in *The Faerie Queene*. During the reign of Queen Elizabeth, St George, formerly a military and patriotic figure associated with royalty, was denounced by Protestant reformers since he was a figure of festivity as well as a Catholic saint; in this period 'elite and middling groups became increasingly alienated from a once-shared common culture' (p. 186). Lamb contends that the response by Spenser's readers to St George in *FQ* Book I 'would have varied widely, depending on their age, geographical location, and religious sensibilities' (p. 197) and his narrative could engage readers 'at several levels simultaneously' (p. 198). The Redcrosse knight is a 'clownishe' rustic, as Spenser makes clear in the *Letter to Ralegh*, but his aristocratic lineage would have appealed to less humble readers. That Redcrosse is a 'fallen man subject to flesh, as are all humans' (p. 199) allows certain readers to perceive the flesh as suggestive of the common culture that should be left behind, but at the same time suggests 'an inner form of nobility residing within any Christian chosen as God's elect' (p. 199). Redcrosse's associations with the performed St George are most evident in his encounters with the Saracens and the dragon, and for Lamb Sansjoy might represent either 'self-alienation from physical pleasures', something that could apply to the critics of the traditional pastimes, or the 'emptiness of such pleasures without spiritual grace' (p. 201). The Sansjoy episode parodies its classical source and thus appeals to classically educated readers but at same time casts doubt on the value of this knowledge, since the pagan Aesculapius cannot heal the soul. Furthermore, Spenser puts a twist on the fall and resuscitation of St George's opponent, a key aspect of the mumming ritual, since here it is George who falls and is given spiritual, specifically Christian, assistance.

Bart Van Es, '"The streame and currant of time": Land, Myth, and History in the Works of Spenser' (*SSt* 18[2003] 209–29), considers Spenser's debt to Camden and his fellow chorographers who presented a narrative focusing on the landscape and alert to history and myth. This debt is most apparent in the marriage of the Thames and Medway in *FQ* Book IV and, although the political detail that attends the description of the Irish rivers is evident also in the Irish section of Camden's *Britannia*, the meeting of Irish and English rivers originates with Spenser. Van Es compares the river marriage canto to *Colin Clouts Come Home Againe* and situates the latter in the tradition of chorographic poetry, asserting that it is 'about a transition from Irish to English land' (p. 218). According to Van Es, *Colin Clouts Come Home Againe* attaches stories to rivers in an effort to forge a place for Ireland and make it a valid subject for future chorographers, and in this poem and the river marriage canto, land, myth, and history combine in the poet's attempt at myth-making.

Memory, the focus of the essay by Alan Stewart and Garrett A. Sullivan Jr. in this year's other volume of *Spenser Studies*, is also discussed by Grant Williams in 'Phantastes's Flies: The Trauma of Amnesic Forgetting in Spenser's Memory Palace' (*SSt* 18[2003] 231–52), which, like the essay by Stewart and Sullivan, is concerned with the depiction of memory in *FQ* Book II, in particular the problem of Guyon's inauthentic subjectivity. Many critics, amongst them Stephen Greenblatt, have argued that Guyon 'represses libidinous urges', but Williams contends that, although the book 'does indeed flesh out Guyon's subjectivity with desire', it is 'a desire more representative of early modern mnemonic culture than of modernity's preoccupation with repressed libidinal energy: Guyon embodies the desire to remember' (p. 232). Early moderns believed that forgetting induced degeneracy, a state most evident in the bestial Grill who, as Richard McCabe noted, stands for the perceived degeneration of English colonizers in Ireland. What Williams terms Guyon's 'introspective odyssey' allows self-knowledge which results in 'mastering the corporeal other' (p. 240), essential for the proper functioning of temperance.

Staying with Book II, Elizabeth D. Harvey's 'Sensational Bodies, Consenting Organs: Helkiah Crooke's Incorporation of Spenser' (*SSt* 18[2003] 295–314) considers the seventeenth-century physician Helkiah Crooke, who used Spenser's body allegory as a structural model for his influential anatomical treatise, the *Microcosmographia*, published in 1615. Informed by Luce Irigaray's objections to Freudian and Lacanian ideas about the female body, Harvey argues that Crook's inclusion of the sexual and reproductive organs omitted by Spenser carries 'an intensity of pleasure that produces an ecstasy very much like the one Irigaray describes' (p. 297). Crooke used Spenser's allegory because it allowed him to borrow its 'metaphorizing and idealizing mechanisms ... at the moment that he ostensibly exposes the secrets of the female body and the origins of life itself' (p. 299). Spenser's reluctance to describe the sex organs in his body allegory—instead portraying sexuality and generation more subtly and throughout his narrative—conformed to 'cultural imperatives of modesty' (p. 309) and an established tradition in medical literature which echoed John Banister's 1578 English anatomical treatise *The Historie of Man*. In Banister and Spenser we see evidence of 'the medical tradition that replicates the inherent secrecy of the female body' (p. 302), a tradition from which Crooke departs.

Irigaray comes up again in 'Daemonic Allegory: The Elements in Late Spenser, Late Shakespeare, and Irigaray' (*SSt* 18[2003] 315–42), Theresa Krier's analysis of the depiction of the elements in Spenser's Mutabilitie Cantos and Shakespeare's *The Tempest* via Irigarayan delineations of elemental mobility. Krier identifies Spenser's debt to ancient Stoic allegory and Shakespeare's debt to Spenser's narrative, in particular its treatment of justice and dominion. As Krier notes, both Spenser and Shakespeare 'create characters who move from one element to another, characters with other than natural lineages and capacities, and freely adapt Graeco-Roman myth to this end' (p. 328).

The link between Spenser and Shakespeare, and specifically *Hamlet*, is also explored by Gordon Teskey in '"And therefore as a stranger give it welcome": Courtesy and Thinking' (*SSt* 18[2003] 343–59). As well as considering *Hamlet* in the context of claims made by Martin Heidegger, Teskey makes two assertions about Spenser: firstly that he 'is not primarily a narrative poet but a poet whose concern is to think' (p. 347) and that 'thinking is an encounter with the strange to which courtesy is the key' (p. 348). In contrast to Milton, whom Teskey considers primarily didactic, not thinking but teaching what has already been taught, Spenser is a poet who 'proceeds by wandering, non-deliberate procedures into original, and often radical thoughts' (p. 350).

Galina Yermolenko's engaging essay, '"That troublous dreame": Allegory, Narrative and Subjectivity in *The Faerie Queene*' (*SSt* 18[2003] 253–71), reads two dream passages from *The Faerie Queene* in the context of medieval dream vision allegories: Redcrosse's sleep at Archimago's Hermitage in Book I and Scudamour's sleep at Care's Cottage in Book IV. The focus is on the difficulty in distinguishing between that which is external (reality) and that which is internal (the dream), a distinction crucial to the perception of both protagonist and reader. Yermolenko relates this aspect of the vision to the 'nonlinear, entangled' (p. 267) structure of the narrative which, it is suggested, interferes with the protagonist's ability to understand themselves and the reader's ability to understand the allegory.

Moving on to the other journals which contained essays on Spenser this year but staying with sources for the time being, Lee Piepho, 'Edmund Spenser and Neo-Latin Literature: An Autograph Manuscript on Petrus Lotichius and His Poetry' (*SP* 100[2003] 123–34), considers transcriptions by Spenser which indicate his interest in European Latin literature. The texts transcribed appear on the last leaf of a collection of verse and prose by the German neo-Latin poet Georgius Sabinus that was probably bound with and preceded a copy of a poem by Petrus Lotichius Secundus when Spenser was in possession of the volume. The texts are a letter by Erhard Stibar, pupil of Lotichius and nephew of his patron, and two poems, one by Artifex Athensis (apparently not his real name) and the other by Joannes de Silva (Jean du Bois). The Sabinus collection contains letters by Erasmus, Pietro Bembo and others who are associated with the German poet as well as an appendix of letters by him. Although Spenser was especially interested in Lotichius, who has been judged the most accomplished of the German neo-Latin poets, Sabinus and Lotichius both wrote eclogues and Peipho suggests their influence on Spenser's composition of *The Shepheardes Calender* but also on *The Faerie Queene*. Moreover, Stibar's letter 'expresses an ideal of patronage that haunted Spenser throughout his career' (p. 128). Peipho usefully provides a transcription of Spenser's autograph as well as images from it.

In 'Spenser's Parody' (*Connotations* 12[2003] 1–13) Donald Cheney considers Spenser's complex relationship to his sources by reference to what he terms 'sympathetic parody' (p. 1). Several episodes from *The Faerie Queene* are explored by Cheney, who notes that Spenser's engagement with Ariosto's *Orlando Furioso* in particular is in conflict with his claims that he will moralize his source material and, indeed, Spenser's 'relationship to Ariosto's mode of chivalric romance becomes increasingly sympathetic, as the limitations of his moralized song become more complex' (p. 8). In 'The Death of the "New Poete": Virgilian Ruin and Ciceronian Recollection in Spenser's *The Shepheardes Calender*' (*RenQ* 56[2003] 723–56) Rebecca Helfer considers Virgilian imitation in Spenser's *Shepheardes Calender* via commentary by E.K., the poem's first critic, and suggests that Spenser's engagement with Virgil is more nuanced than that put forward by E.K. or, indeed, the shepherds in the poem. While these figures 'look for a new Virgil to repair England's ostensible cultural ruin, Spenser looks to Ciceronian dialogue for England's cultural formation, for building new memorial edifices from ruin' (p. 726).What Helfer refers to as a 'desire to cast Spenser within a Virgilian mold' extends to modern critics, even those 'who pursue Spenser's evident deviations from Virgilian paradigms' (p. 731). Although Spenser clearly imitates Virgil by writing pastoral eclogues, this is only the first step in the poem, argues Helfer, and Virgil's ideal of permanently repairing the ruins of the past in poetic or imperial monuments gives way to ruins as sites for building anew.

Spenser and his influence upon others is explored by Sung-Kyun Yim, '"Thy temperance invincible": Humanism in Book II of *The Faerie Queene* and *Paradise Regained*' (*EMLS* 9:i[2003]), whose focus is the tension between humanism and Christianity in the writings of Spenser and Milton, writers who shared a humanist educational background and Protestant ethical codes. The essay considers Spenser's view of humanism through Guyon's visit to Mammon's cave and his destruction of the Bower of Bliss, and Milton's depiction of it through Jesus's battle with Satan in the wilderness. For Spenser, 'The virtue of temperance is not opposed to that of Christians but protected by God' and Spenser is concerned not with 'revealing the shortcomings of classical virtue', as some critics have argued, 'but in the encouragement of it within the Christian viewpoint'. Milton takes rather a different stance and makes clear the hierarchy at work: as Sung-Kyun puts it, 'No matter how highly portrayed and elaborated, classicism cannot maintain its value against Christian virtue.'

The view espoused by Richard Helgerson that Spenser was exclusively devoted to a poetical calling and Richard Rambuss's more recent claim that his bureaucratic ambitions were of equal importance are interrogated by Jeffrey Knapp in 'Spenser the Priest' (*Rep* 81[2003] 61–78), who claims that both critics overlook Spenser's 'focus on the profession of pastor or clergyman' in *The Shepheardes Calender* and later works, including *The Faerie Queene* and the *View*. According to Knapp, critics have commented little on Spenser's views on the clergy because 'they share Helgerson and Rambuss's anachronistically restricted notion of Spenser's profession' (p. 62). Although Spenser was reluctant to identify himself as poet, preacher, or secretary, a reluctance Helgerson and Rambuss interpret as a curb (either internal or external) on his ambitions, Knapp argues that it represents a divinely inspired choice for someone who 'regarded an ecclesiastical career as a limitation on the sort of ministry he valued' (p. 63). Via discussion of the 'Marprelate' controversy, Knapp shows that religion helped define the role of the poet in the period, and in his *Letter to Ralegh* Spenser 'contrasted his own poetry to the less engaging efforts of preachers' (p. 68). For Spenser, as for Thomas Nashe, 'poets edify better than sermonizers do by making their lessons congenial to the flesh and therefore convenable to their audience' (p. 69). In the *View* Spenser makes the same point as Nashe, criticizing 'the implicit elitism of those who would divorce religion from delightful shows' and, allowing the laity involvement in religious sacraments, suggests that they can do the same work as clergymen. *The Faerie Queene* 'differentiates the power to preach from professional clergymen' (p. 70), and indeed two of the positive preachers in Book of Holiness are women: Una and Fidelia. In *Colin Clouts Come Home Againe* Colin is referred to as a 'priest', a term not exclusive to Catholicism in the period, and a reference to the poet as pastor first encountered in *The Shepheardes Calender*. Although the ministerial role of the poet is emphasized throughout Spenser's oeuvre, Knapp concludes that Spenser only explicitly highlighted 'his ministerial ambitions through Colin' (p. 71) because he was apparently concerned that he might undermine the established clergy.

Memory, considered in both volumes of *Spenser Studies* this year, is also of interest to Jennifer Summit in 'Monuments and Ruins: Spenser and the Problem of the English Library' (*ELH* 70[2003] 1–34), who reads Guyon's behaviour in the Bower of Bliss via the castle of Alma and the library of Eumnestes ('Good Memory'), noting that the episodes are related to the establishment of post-Reformation libraries. Summit provides a detailed and engrossing history of the Protestant collectors who, 'in an effort to preserve the nation's past', reinvented the library 'from an ecclesiastical receptacle of written tradition to a state-sponsored centre of national history' (p. 2). Only some books were deemed worth keeping, specifically those dealing with matters of national and ecclesiastical history which could be interpreted as supporting the newly reformed state. Spenser's engagement with the post-Reformation book collectors is evident in the books contained in Eumnestes' library, *Briton moniments* and *Antiquitie of Faerie lond*, since after the Dissolution the terms 'monument' and 'antiquity' 'inspired and justified the project of rescuing and preserving medieval books' (p. 6). The act of reading itself was part of the process, with annotation denouncing and dismissing any Catholic aspects of a specific text. The main aim was to distinguish 'the fabulous from the true' (p. 13), something that underlines Spenser's defensiveness about his use of allegory which could be interpreted as obfuscation. In Alma's castle the library is situated in the interior of the brain and the imagination, associated with idolatry by reformers, located in the chamber of Phantastes, which explains why the library is incomplete. Guyon learns his lesson in Alma's Castle and enacts it in the Bower of Bliss, which 'embodies the very qualities of Imagination that are excluded from the library of memory' (p. 23). Guyon's destruction of the bower is 'an act of violent remembering' and Spenser's knight can be compared to the post-Reformation readers and library-makers, 'who sought to recuperate England's lost origins in its "monuments of antiquity" by purifying those monuments of the corrosive accretions of monastic influence' (pp. 25–6), a clever and convincing explanation of Guyon's otherwise seemingly inexplicable aggression.

Although Ireland has recently played a prominent role in Spenser criticism there is still much to be said about Spenser's connections with the colony, and Judith Owens, 'Professing Ireland in the Woods of Spenser's *Mutabilitie*' (*EIRC* 29[2003] 1–22), presents a thoughtful and nuanced assessment of what she regards to be Spenser's ambivalent attitude towards Ireland's landscape, in particular its woodland. For Owens, Ireland's woods 'approximate more closely than does cartography the English 'indwellers' experience of Ireland as a country that both allures…and harbours perils real and imagined', which might explain the 'dream of easy movement' underwriting Spenser's poem (p. 3). Owens disputes Julia Lupton's argument that Spenser maps Ireland as a wasteland in order to defend further wasting, arguing instead that he displays 'more amplitude of political and moral mind than Lupton allows' (p. 3). In the Mutabilitie Cantos, Faunus' 'wooded voyeurism' upon Diana plays out 'English fears that Irish invisibility undermines the English presence in Ireland', but what Owens refers to as the 'low-keyed register' of the Faunus episode suggests that Spenser plays down the Irish threat 'while registering apprehension' (p. 6). She thus identifies a tension between the colonial desire to control, via English forest law and the eradication of dangerous wooded areas, and Spenser's 'contesting or slighting' of this desire (p. 6). Owens makes it clear that she is not suggesting that Spenser supported rebellion, merely that that his use of the forest trope reveals ambivalent philosophical and political positions by tapping into long-standing forest associations: the early modern reader would have known that forest law 'admitted ambiguous effects in execution' and that in folklore the forest 'generates more justice than does the law' (p. 10). Adding to the evidence for

Spenser's ambivalence is 'the considerable appeal' of Mutability, the deflationary image of Diana as a housewife, and the 'generally humorous tone of the Diana-Faunus interlude' (pp. 10–11) which indicate a challenge to the sovereignty of Cynthia/Elizabeth by Faunus and Spenser, who writes from the relative autonomy of colonial Ireland.

William A. Oram's imaginative and thought-provoking essay considers Spenser's rhetorical ambitions and detects in his writings an important shift in attitude during the eighteenth months he spent in England, having returned there from Ireland where he had lived for nine years ('Spenser's Audiences, 1589–91', *SP* 100[2003] 514–33). He engages with Richard Helgerson's theory that Spenser saw himself as a poet with the patriotic importance of Virgil but argues that Helgerson gave inadequate focus to the epic poet's responsibility to advise princes. Spenser initially dramatizes the relation he desires with queen and the court in the proems and dedicatory sonnets in the first edition of *The Faerie Queene* [1590], assuming that what he has to offer 'will be seen and welcomed' (p. 517). The proems suggest an intimacy of shared humour, understanding, and acquaintance with the queen, while the sonnets seem to be 'announcing his triumphant homecoming', the sheer number of them signalling 'exuberant arrival' (p. 519). The dedicatees represent an ideal audience that is 'overwhelmingly aristocratic and very largely male' (p. 521) and the sonnets 'quietly assert both his authority and his centrality to the English court' (p. 522) as a poet who can fashion his audience. Oram compares this 'self-assured and exuberantly self-promoting installment of *The Faerie Queene*' with *The Complaints* which were published a year later and which represent a 'considerable shift of scope and attitude' (p. 523). The latter work is dedicated to far fewer and less powerful figures and its major poems 'focus on the deterioration of the cultural and political climate of Elizabeth's court' (p. 523) where the poet is under pressure to please. Oram suggests that Spenser, having achieved success in Ireland and having fulfilled his laureate ambitions, would have been sorely disappointed by not being accepted as Elizabeth's adviser, especially in relation to Ireland.

In 'The Place of Arthur in Children's Versions of *The Faerie Queene*' (*Arthuriana* 13:ii[2003] 23–37) Matthew Woodcock provides a welcome analysis of what tends to be a rather neglected area in Spenser studies, adaptations of *The Faerie Queene*, in particular those aimed at young readers. Woodcock shows that nineteenth- and early twentieth-century adaptations of the poem focused on the figure of Arthur, considered especially suitable as a model of virtue as evident in the emergence of youth groups built on a chivalric model, amongst them the British Boy Scout movement. Adaptations of *The Faerie Queene* considered by Woodcock share a tendency towards moral instruction, with sex, though not violence, being 'a frequent site for censorship' (p. 27). As Woodcock points out, cutting all references to sex from the episodes involving Arthur interferes with 'the character's principal structural function [which] is inexorably connected to the erotic quest that forms the underlying ur-narrative of the poem itself' (p. 31). In many cases the quest for Gloriana is removed entirely and, perhaps unsurprisingly, Victorian versions of the poem tend to emphasize marriage, Britomart's quest for Artegall and the invented unions of other eligible couples in the poem becoming the main concern of the narrative.

In 'Materialist History of the Publication of Spenser's *Faerie Queene*' (*RES* 54[2003] 1–26) Jean Brink takes Spenserians to task for assuming that Spenser had more control over the printing of *The Faerie Queene* than the evidence suggests. That assumption was first made by J. C. Smith in his 1909 edition of the poem, a view repeated by subsequent scholars who have not re-examined the situation in the light of work by New Bibliographers who, as Brink points out, 'began to make us aware that sixteenth-century printing practices would have discouraged authorial supervision' (p. 2). The notion that Spenser was allowed to correct proofs while printing was in progress does not explain why 'uncorrected and corrected sheets were indiscriminately bound together in the *Faerie Queene*, as was common practice' (p. 3). The presence of two sets of dedicatory sonnets in the 1590 printing of *The Faerie Queene*, the second repeating some names from the first and so calling attention to those originally omitted, must have caused considerable embarrassment to Spenser. As Brink put it, the 1590 *Faerie Queene* was 'not a printing success' (p. 15) and, noting the tendency towards a conflation of biography with bibliography in Spenser studies, Brink dismisses the anecdote usually offered to explain the 'jumbled repetition' (p. 8), that Spenser's friends urged a hasty addition to the dedications so as not to offend Burghley. This is unlikely, claims Brink: 'Since the type for the sonnets from the first issue was not redistributed before the second set was printed, there was, practically speaking, little time for consultation with friends and for the composition of additional sonnets' (p. 9), and it is more plausible that 'all of the sonnets were given to the printer, but that the leaves of the manuscript were mixed up and hastily reassembled' (p. 10). Brink observes that Spenser may have intended the printed sonnets to accompany presentation copies of his text, but 'the printer and binder bungled the handling of the dedications', the appearance of both sets together at the conclusion of Book III undercutting the 'dignified dedication to Elizabeth at the front of the volume' (p. 15). Spenser was involved in the presentation of introductory and concluding matter in the 1596 edition of the poem, and the dedicatory sonnets were not reprinted. Brink complains that in modern editions of *The Faerie Queene* the dedications from the 1590 edition are 'silently offered as a preface and context for the poem', thus refashioning Spenser 'as a court poet' (p. 19), something he may not have been at all happy about.

Charlotte Artese, in 'King Arthur in America: Making Space in History for *The Faerie Queene* and John Dee's *Brytanici Imperii Limites*' (*JMEMS* 33[2003] 125–41), considers the manner in which Spenser and John Dee emphasized and at the same time exploited distinctions between the literary and non-literary in an effort to legitimize their historical projects relating to the New World. Dee wrote several texts claiming that England 'had a better claim to America than other European nations' (p. 126) because the English had got there first, with King Arthur amongst the many unlikely figures reaching the New World before the fifteenth century. Although Dee insisted on the veracity of his claims, Spenser classified such stories as fiction: his story of Arthur is placed in the *Antiquitie of Faerie lond* not the chronicle history of Britain. But in writing about Arthur, Spenser similarly used America 'to effect a confusion of fiction and history'

(p. 134), utilizing the gaps in knowledge about Arthur and the New World to 'transmute his poem into a history' (p. 135). So, Dee and Spenser share a similar approach to the instability of genre and, as Artese shows, both used it to their advantage.

Harry Berger Jr., 'Archimago: Between Text and Countertext' (*SEL* 43[2003] 19–64), takes a while to get to the analysis of Archimago suggested by the title of the essay, first providing the reader with a lengthy section focusing only on signs and signifiers, and another on ways of reading *The Faerie Queene*. Berger suggests that Archimago is ineffective as a character and makes connections between the magician and the poem's narrator, noting that 'their two methods and projects sinuously intertwine' (p. 48), which helps explain how Archimago functions in the narrative.

Hester Lees-Jeffries, in 'From the Fountain to the Well: Redcrosse Learns to Read' (*SP* 100[2003] 135–76), argues that in *FQ* Book I Spenser uses fountains not merely as topographical features but as a means of exploring textual issues such as genre and Protestant polemic. Lees-Jeffries traces the depiction of fountains in Book I via the influence of religious writings, including the Bible and Erasmus's *Enchiridion* [1533], the literary conventions of courtly romance, and Ovid. Although it is not entirely convincing to read Errour as 'a parodic fountain' (p. 14), much of what Lees-Jeffries presents in this essay is persuasive, and in general the study provides a welcome expansion upon the religious sources and analogues provided by Naseeb Shaheen's invaluable *Biblical References in 'The Faerie Queene'*.

There were only two pieces pertaining to Spenser in this year's *Notes and Queries*. Whether or not one is convinced by Shohachi Fukuda's essay, 'The Numerological Patterning of the *Mutabilitie Cantos*' (*N&Q* 50[2003] 18–20), which finds structures and patterns in the Cantos, depends on whether or not one is convinced by numerology as an intellectually rigorous means by which to elucidate Spenser's writings. Although Fukuda's argument that patterns from the Mutabilitie Cantos echo those used in earlier books of *The Faerie Queene* is not incorrect, 'evidence' used to support it tends to be presented without explanation: for example we are not told why 8 is 'the number of rebirth' nor why, for Spenser, 19 should be the 'number of evil' (p. 19). Ultimately, the difficulty with this approach to poetry is perhaps best summed up by Fukuda's statement that 'All this may be a mere coincidence' (p. 20).

Matthew Woodcock, a leading authority on Spenser and fairies, usefully clarifies Spenser's connections with the spelling of the word *faerie* in 'The First Sightings of Spenser's *Faeries*' (*N&Q* 50[2003] 390–1). Woodcock disputes the *OED*'s assertion that the spelling can be first attributed with any certainty to Spenser's first edition of *The Faerie Queene*, published in 1590, noting that it appears three times in *The Shepheardes Calender*, published in 1579. Moreover, correspondence between Spenser and Gabriel Harvey, published in 1580, refers to Spenser's work in progress as the 'Faery Queene'. Woodcock rightly notes that the importance of establishing an early date for the spelling undermines attempts to establish 'any form of special ontological status' to Spenser's fairies, 'an implicit feature of many early commentators' frustrated responses to the differences between Spenser's and Shakespeare's representations of fairy lore'

(p. 391). Lack of distinction between 'fairy' and 'faerie' is reinforced by the fact that Spenser uses these words and the word 'elf' interchangeably. The *OED* noted that the spelling 'faerie' probably existed in Middle English, and Woodcock concurs that Spenser was most likely influenced by Anglicized variants of French sources found in Middle English texts, using the word 'as a conscious archaism' in *The Faerie Queene* as he did in the earlier *Shepheardes Calender*.

Books Reviewed

Bellamy, Elizabeth Jane, Cheney Patrick and Michael Schoenfeldt, eds. *Imagining Death in Spenser and Milton*. Palgrave Macmillan. [2003] pp. 240. £45 ISBN 0 3339 8398 X.

Brandolini, Raffaele. *On Music and Poetry (De Musica et Poetica, 1513)*. Trans. Ann Moyer. Arizona Center for Medieval and Renaissance Studies. [2001] pp. xxxv + 124. £31 ISBN 0 8669 8274 4.

Broomhall, Susan, ed. *Women and the Book Trade in Sixteenth-Century France*. Ashgate. [2002] pp. viii + 282. £40 ISBN 0 7546 0671 6.

Cockcroft, Robert. *Rhetorical Affect and Early Modern Writing*. Palgrave. [2003] pp. ix + 209. £47.50 ISBN 0 3338 0252 7.

Davies, Catharine. *A Religion of the Word: The Defence of the Reformation in the Reign of Edward VI*. ManUP. [2003] pp. xxiv + 264. £49.99 ISBN 0 7190 5730 2.

Davis, Alex. *Chivalry and Romance in the English Renaissance*. Brewer. [2003] pp. 263. £50 ISBN 0 8599 1777 0.

Dobson, Michael and Nicola Watson. *England's Elizabeth: An Afterlife in Fame and Fantasy*. OUP. [2003] pp. 360. hb £19.99 ISBN 0 1981 8377 1, pb £12.99 ISBN 0 1992 6919 X.

Doran, Susan, ed. *Elizabeth: The Exhibition at the National Maritime Museum*. C&W. [2003] pp. xiii + 287. £25 ISBN 0 701 17476 5.

Doran, Susan and Thomas S. Freeman, eds. *The Myth of Elizabeth*. Palgrave. [2003] pp. xv + 276. hb £52.50 ISBN 0 3339 3083 5, pb £16.99 0 3339 3084 3.

Dunnigan, Sarah M. *Eros and Poetry at the Courts of Mary Queen of Scots and James VI*. Palgrave. [2003] pp. 232. $85 ISBN 0 3339 1875 4.

Fowler, Alastair. *Renaissance Realism: Narrative Images in Literature and Art*. OUP. [2003] pp. xvii + 221. £58 ISBN 0 1992 5958 5.

Fowler, Elizabeth. *Literary Character: The Human Figure in Early English Writing*. CornUP. [2003] pp. 263. £25.95 ISBN 0 8014 4116 1.

Glimp, David. *Increase and Multiply: Governing Cultural Reproduction in Early Modern England*. UMinnP. [2003] pp. xxviii + 230. hb $65.95 ISBN 0 8166 3990 6, pb $21.95 0 8166 3991 4.

Heale, Elizabeth. *Autobiography and Authorship in Renaissance Verse: Chronicles of the Self*. Palgrave. [2003] pp. viii + 206. £47.50 ISBN 0 3337 7397 7.

Kewes, Paulina, ed. *Plagiarism in Early Modern England*. Palgrave. [2003] pp. xv + 276. £50 ISBN 0 3339 9841 3.

Mazzola, Elizabeth. *Favourite Sons: The Politics and Poetics of the Sidney Family*. Palgrave Macmillan. [2003] pp. 150. £30 ISBN 1 4039 6321 5.

McGee, Timothy J., ed. *Improvisation in the Arts of the Middle Ages and Renaissance*. Early Drama, Art and Music Monograph Series 30. Medieval Institute Publications, Western Michigan University. [2003] pp. xii + 331. hb $30 ISBN 1 5804 4044 4, pb $15 ISBN 1 5804 4045 2.

North, Marcy L. *The Anonymous Renaissance: Cultures of Discretion in Tudor–Stuart England*. UChicP. [2003] pp. xi + 309. $37.50 ISBN 0 2265 9437 8.

Ross, Charles. *Elizabethan Literature and the Law of Fraudulent Conveyance: Sidney, Spenser, and Shakespeare*. Ashgate. [2003] pp. 300. £37.50 ISBN 0 7546 3263 6.

Sauer, Michelle M., ed. *Proceedings of the 11th Annual Northern Plains Conference on Early British Literature*. Minot State University Printing Services. [2003].

Shagan, Ethan H. *Popular Politics and the English Reformation*. CUP. [2003] pp. xiii + 331. hb £39 ISBN 0 5218 0846 4, pb £19.99 ISBN 0 5215 2555 1.

Vandiver, Elizabeth, Ralph Keen, and Thomas D. Frazel. *Luther's Lives*. ManUP. [2003] pp. 416. £15.99 ISBN 0 7190 6802 9.

Vaught, Jennifer C., ed. *Grief and Gender: 700–1700*. Palgrave Macmillan. [2003] pp. 310. £15.99 ISBN 0 3122 9381 X.

VI

Shakespeare

GABRIEL EGAN, PETER J. SMITH, LUCY MUNRO,
DONALD WATSON, JAMES PURKIS, ANNALIESE CONNOLLY,
ANDREW HISCOCK, STEPHEN LONGSTAFFE, JON ORTEN
AND CLARE MCMANUS

This chapter has four sections: 1. Editions and Textual Matters; 2. Shakespeare in the Theatre; 3. Shakespeare on Screen; 4. Criticism. Section 1 is by Gabriel Egan; section 2 is by Peter J. Smith; section 3 is by Lucy Munro; section 4(a) is by Donald Watson, section 4(b) is by James Purkis, section 4(c) is by Annaliese Connolly, section 4(d) is by Andrew Hiscock, section 4(e) is by Stephen Longstaffe, section 4(f) is by Jon Orten; section 4(g) is by Clare McManus.

1. Editions and Textual Matters

This year saw over seventy items touching on what an editor has done, or exhorting what an editor should do, or announcing a discovery about evidence that might shape what an editor will do. The burgeoning subject of how the different early versions of what we used to think of as a single play might differ in their performance potentialities bears only indirectly on what an editor should do and it has grown too large to be contained within a section of this book that is properly reserved for matters textual. Of the fine essays in Hardin L. Aasand's collection *Stage Directions in Hamlet: New Essays and New Directions*, all but two fall into this category and are ignored here.

It was a busy year for Shakespearian textual studies with three landmark monographs appearing, but only one new substantial edition: Michael Taylor's *Henry VI, Part One* for the Oxford Shakespeare. The only authoritative early printing of this pla is the 1623 Folio, so Taylor's relatively short introduction (seventy-seven pages) naturally has much more to say about the meanings and reception of the play than about the textual situation. Taylor first attends to the year 1592, when Thomas Nashe famously alluded to the play in performance, contrasting the heroic English past it presented with his own Puritan-ridden, usurious present (p. 2). Treating that year's *Greene's Groatsworth of Wit* as

Year's Work in English Studies, Volume 84 (2005) © The English Association; all rights reserved. For permissions, please email: journals.permissions@oxfordjournals.org

doi: 10.1093/ywes/mai006

though it were simply Greene's work, Taylor finds it betraying a 'rancid … anxiety of influence' that in a footnote he glosses as 'mutual stimulation' and by which he clearly means to imply mental masturbation (p. 5). This seems somewhat unfair to Harold Bloom, whose notion of 'anxiety of influence' can often refer to a positive and indeed productive relation between present and preceding writers. Also somewhat misrepresented is one of Andrew Gurr's admittedly difficult essays, 'The Chimera of Amalgamation' (*TRI* 18[1993] 85–93), in which Taylor thinks Gurr opposed the whole idea that 'in the early 1590s companies amalgamated' (p. 6) whereas in fact Gurr was specifically referring to the oft-alleged Strange's/Admiral's men's amalgamation.

In a section about 'The "Henry VI" Plays in 1592' (pp. 10–14) that discusses the sequentiality of *1*, *2*, and *3 Henry VI*, Taylor surprisingly neglects to mention the problem that the allusion to *3 Henry VI* in *Greene's Groatsworth* suggests that *3 Henry VI* was at least written—and presumably, in fact, in performance—before *Groatsworth*'s Stationers' Register entry on 20 September 1592, and yet *1 Henry VI* was apparently 'new' (according to most people's reading of Henslowe's Diary) on 3 March 1592. There seems, on this evidence, insufficient time for parts 1, 2, and 3 being written in that order. Taylor's compressed account of the debate about the order is written from the point of view of someone who knows the data and does not need them repeated. Taylor fails to mention that B.J. Sokol has presented strong evidence that *1 Henry VI* cannot have been written before 25 April 1591 because its 'garden' scene alludes to the refurbishment of the Inner Temple Garden completed by that date ('Manuscript Evidence for an Earliest Date of *Henry VI Part One*', *N&Q* 47[2000] 58–63). A much more serious error, however, is Taylor's claim that because the first printings of *2 Henry VI* and *3 Henry VI* do not name Shakespeare as the dramatist, there is nothing to link these plays to Shakespeare until the 1623 Folio firmly located them in his oeuvre (p. 11). In fact, there appeared in 1619 a printing of both plays in one volume called *The Whole Contention between the Two Famous Houses Lancaster and York*, and its title page named 'William Shakespeare, Gent' as the dramatist.

Taylor treats the multiple authorship of the play as a matter of 'problems and anomalies', not just the way drama was usually made, and observes that if, as Gary Taylor argued, Nashe wrote Act I of *1 Henry VI* then it was surprisingly reticent of him to praise the Talbot scenes so lavishly in his *Pierce Pennilesse* without mentioning his own contribution. If *1 Henry VI* was written before *2 Henry VI* and *3 Henry VI*, as some have recently claimed, it is odd, remarks Taylor, that *2 Henry VI* does not follow up many of its leads and that *1 Henry VI* is more like *3 Henry VI* than like *2 Henry VI*. On the other hand, *1 Henry VI* coming first would explain its weaknesses: they are beginner's flaws (p. 12). If *1 Henry VI* is a prequel, why did Shakespeare collaborate on it and so produce something inferior (p. 13)? Here again, Taylor perhaps unconsciously deems collaboration a sign of weakness, an anomaly. In a footnote (p. 14 n. 1), Taylor characterizes Marlowe's *Tamburlaine* as a 'daring venture' in being a two-parter. In fact there were many two-parters and Marlowe's play might well have not been conceived as one: the second part simply continues the story (extending an unexpected dramatic success?) and negates the first part's radical innovation by having the anti-hero eventually get his come-uppance.

Shakespeare inherited rather than invented the history play genre, which collection of plays (mostly not by Shakespeare) Taylor sees as constituting 'a critical response to Marlowe's glorification of ruthless foreign individualism' (p. 19). *1 Henry VI* is a piece of patriotic propaganda in a time of national crisis—post-Babington plot, post-Armada—but despite its patriotic elements it is not quite the kind of story one would tell to stiffen the national sinews (pp. 21–4). Taylor thinks the second tetralogy 'infinitely superior in every way' to the first—it is refreshing to have an editor not extol his play as an undervalued masterpiece—yet the first is also vastly (if not infinitely) superior to the other history plays around at the time (p. 25). At this point, Taylor starts to write using sentence fragments that make sense only in relation to the antecedent subject of the previous sentence, as in 'A pleasure we now take for granted' (p. 29 n. 1) referring to Elizabethan audiences' pleasure in being made familiar with great ones. In this case the antecedent subject is in the body text and the fragment in a footnote, which is quite a stretch. This habit gets severely irritating in Taylor's section on the plays in recent performance: '[It was] A clear shape, we may recall, [formed] principally at the expense of *Henry VI, Part One*' and '[It was] Epic for theatregoers too as the three Henries were performed on the same day on eight occasions, outlasting the Terry Hands 1977 marathon by over an hour' (p. 36). In parts the introduction is repetitive: on page 41 is repeated from page 21 n. 21 the claim that the encounter of Talbot and the countess of Auvergne looks forward to the 'sharp-edged dialogue' between men and women in Shakespeare's romantic comedies; true, but presumably it also looks back to the same in *The Taming of the Shrew*. Taylor cites two critics (David Riggs and E. Pearlman) who refer to *Tamburlaine* playing at the Fortune, without mentioning that that theatre was built at least ten years after the play opened at the Rose.

Taylor's sections on 'The Text' (pp. 75–7) and his 'Editorial Procedures' are remarkably brief, acknowledging no scholarship since the Textual Companion to the Oxford *Complete Works* and offering no discussion of what effect it might have upon editing certain parts of the play to think that Nashe, not Shakespeare, wrote them. There is, indeed, no acknowledgement of the New Textualism: 'Loose ends, inconsistencies, contradictions, misplaced stage directions, changeable speech prefixes combine, with other irregularities in the Folio text, to make it very unlikely that the manuscript came from the playhouse' (p. 76). Taylor finds some theatrically unnecessary details that would suggest foul paper copy lying behind the Folio text, but too many irregularities for the foul papers to be those of one author, so he goes along with the Textual Companion's view that F's copy was 'collaborative foul papers'. (The date of the Oxford *Complete Works* itself, to which the Textual Companion is companion, is wrongly given here as 1988 rather than 1986.) Taylor confesses himself 'somewhat eclectic' in choosing names for his characters, preferring historically correct names for minor figures but Folio names for major ones (p. 80).

In the text of the play itself there are more signs of incomplete proofing: the note to Talbot's entry in the dramatis personae has a cross-reference to 'Introduction, pp. 00–00' (p. 92). Thankfully, Joan of Arc gets her right name,

Joan la Pucelle, rather than the name Joan Puzel used by Edward Burns for the rival Arden 3 edition of the play published three years ago. Likewise Taylor has Bedford say 'Our isle be made a marish of salt tears' (I.i.50), sensibly following Alexander Pope, C.J. Sisson and the Oxford *Complete Works* and rejecting Burns's retention of 'nourish of salt tears' from the Folio. At I.ii.21.1 Taylor comments that 'Oxford [*Complete Works*] begins a new scene here, but this adherence to the letter of the dramatic law—an unwritten one—that a new scene begins each time the stage is cleared seems pedantic in this case'. Actually, we know that Shakespeare did not mark scene breaks and that theatrical scribes did not add them, so they are only editorial markers anyway; that being the case, it does make sense to consistently follow the rule. Throughout the third scene (I.iii.19, 36, 42, 49, 56, 79, and 84) Taylor retains F's repeated insistence that Winchester is a cardinal even though subsequent scenes show him to be only a bishop and that he is made a cardinal in V.i. This generates an anomaly, but Taylor thinks that 'there is simply too much dramatic fall-out here from the Cardinal appearing as a Cardinal—his scarlet hat and his robes for instance—to allow us to correct F's contradictory chronology at the expense of the scene's colour and flair'. This decision risks being tyrannized by the copy-text, which presumably had to be corrected before performance. And yet, having accepted that F's inconsistency should stand, Taylor nonetheless emends F's '*Here Glosters men beat out the Cardinalls men*' to '*Here Gloucester's men beat out the Bishop's men*' (I.iii.56.1), which suggests that he thinks that Winchester really *is* only a bishop at this point. If the colourfulness of the error in F is worth preserving when it made real trouble (by being in contradiction with what is said about him elsewhere) it is surely then worth retaining when it does not create trouble within a scene in which the editor has decided that Winchester is a cardinal.

At I.v.11 Taylor has Talbot say 'Rather than I would be so vile-esteemed', which is essentially Pope's emendation of F's 'pil'd esteem'd' for his edition of 1723–5, although the Textual Companion and Taylor himself credit Lewis Theobald in 1733. In support of 'vile-esteemed' is sonnet 121's ''Tis better to be vile than vile esteemed', although this does not mean quite the same thing. The Folio has Mortimer absurdly likening death or locks of hair to Nestor: 'And these gray Locks, the Pursuiuants of death, | Nestor-like aged, in an Age of Care, | Argue the end of Edmund Mortimer', which Taylor (like the Oxford *Complete Works*) sensibly reorders to make it clear that Mortimer is comparing himself to Nestor: 'And these grey locks, the pursuivants of death, | Argue the end of Edmund Mortimer, | Nestor-like agèd in an age of care' (II.v.5–7). Likewise Taylor follows the Oxford *Complete Works*'s assignment of one of Warwick's lines to Gloucester: 'WINCHESTER Rome shall remedy this. [GLOUCESTER] Roam thither then. | [WARWICK] (*to Winchester*) My lord, it were your duty to forbear. | SOMERSET Ay, so the bishop be not overborne' (III.i.51–3), whereas F has Warwick say 'Roame thither then. | My Lord it were your dutie to forbeare', which Sisson (*New Readings in Shakespeare*, pp. 69–70) defended as being said in two tones: first he taunts ('off you go then') and then he softens to remind the bishop of his duty. Following a suggestion made but not enacted by Michael Hattaway in his New Cambridge Shakespeare edition of the play, Taylor reorders

F's 'Looke on thy Country, look on fertile France, | And see the Cities and the Townes defac't, | By wasting Ruine of the cruell Foe, | As lookes the Mother on her lowly Babe, | When Death doth close his tender-dying Eyes'. F makes (albeit awkward) sense as it is, but is better rearranged as Taylor has it: 'JOAN Look on thy country, look on fertile France, | As looks the mother on her lowly babe | When death doth close his tender-dying eyes, | And see the cities and the towns defaced | By wasting ruin of the cruel foe' (III.iii.44–8).

A footnote gloss ought to be something one could substitute for the tricky word or phrase being glossed, but for '*Alarum. Enter the Earl of Suffolk with Margaret in his hand*' Taylor offers the footnote gloss '0.1 **in** led by the'. To be grammatical this should of course read '**in his** led by the', else the substituted phrase would read 'led by the his hand', but more importantly still Taylor's gloss switches whose hand it is: in F it is Suffolk's hand, in Taylor's edition it is Margaret's hand. Like many editors since Edward Capell, Taylor finds disorder in Suffolk's Folio lines 'For I will touch thee but with reuerend hands, | I kisse these fingers for eternall peace, | And lay them gently on thy tender side' (V.iv.3–5). Like Sisson, I cannot see what the problem is. In the famous scene of Suffolk and Margaret making lengthy asides (V.iv.17–63), Taylor repeatedly has one or other speak '(*To himself*)' or '(*To herself*)'. It has been a while since anyone concerned with staging wanted to be quite so specific that an aside is self-communion rather than making the less restrictive assertion that it merely is not to be clearly heard by, or directly addressed to, the other character. Finally, at V.iv.148 Taylor deletes 'Mad' from Suffolk's 'Mad naturall Graces that extinguish Art' on the grounds that it is superfluous and that Burns suggested it was merely a false start in the underlying manuscript that was imperfectly deleted and hence set by the printer. Yet Burns did not just delete the word as Taylor had done. As with Hattaway's suggestion about France as a dead baby (III.iii.44–8), Taylor follows another editor's suggestion even though that editor was insufficiently convinced on the point to enact it for himself in his edition.

Easily the most important contribution to the field this year—indeed the most important contribution for a long time—is Lukas Erne's *Shakespeare as Literary Dramatist*, which aims to overturn the oft-repeated orthodoxy that Shakespeare took no interest in the publication of his plays. That Shakespeare might in fact have worked with a readership in mind was the subject of an essay by Richard Dutton seven years ago ('The Birth of the Author', in R.B. Parker and S.P. Zitner, eds., *Elizabethan Theater: Essays in Honor of S. Schoenbaum* [1996]) and of an article by Erne in *SQ* reviewed last year. In the book-length study Erne sets out his case in full. In recognition of the importance of the arguments, the University of Lancaster convened a two-day conference on the subject in July 2004, nominally entitled 'New Shakespeare: A Writer and his Readers: The Return of the Author in Shakespeare Studies' but effectively 'The Erne Debate'. Erne begins by getting right the fine detail of Thomas Heywood's letter appended to his *Apology for Actors* that explains that it was William Jaggard the printer's fault that a couple of Heywood's poems (from Heywood's *Troia Britannica*) were described as Shakespeare's in the 1612 edition of the miscellany *The Passionate Pilgrim*. Heywood thought that people might mistakenly assume that Shakespeare put his name to them because Heywood had tried to steal them, which he had not: they were not Shakespeare's in the first place. Since the title page of *The Passionate Pilgrim* was reset, we may reasonably assume that Shakespeare got it changed, and this presents us with a Shakespeare concerned about his literary property and about publication (p. 2). (Since Heywood clearly objected to the misattribution too, I cannot see why he could not be the agent of change.) Erne thinks that the *Greene's Groatsworth* attack on Shakespeare, alluding to *3 Henry VI*, is about his temerity in outdoing Marlowe and Kyd (writers of two-parters) with a three-parter. Erne twice calls the Henry VI series an 'ambitious project' (pp. 2, 5) but of course the likeliest scenario is that it was a two-parter that grew into a three-parter, which shows not ambition but mere opportunism.

Erne reminds us that twenty-eight of the *sonnets* are about 'poetry as immortalization' (p. 5), although it is worth recalling (as Robert Wilcher does in a forthcoming book) that Sonnet 17 refers to 'my papers' not pages, suggesting manuscript survival. The view about writing yourself into posterity that we get from the Sonnets is incompatible with the publication-indifferent Shakespeare we get elsewhere, and Erne asserts that in late sixteenth-century England it became a real possibility for a poet to enter posterity (p. 6). An increasing amount of literary work was printed, and although it is true that printers, not authors, held legal copyright, it was nonetheless widely recognized that writers had a moral claim to their own works. Erne gives examples of authors complaining that the Stationers' Company monopoly of printing gave these men unjust power over authors' work, and indeed there were royal patents granted that allowed particular authors 'to a derive a profit from the sale of their books' (p. 9). Of course, that is not quite the issue: a share in the profits is not the same as control over the material. Thomas Bodley, it is true, kept printed plays out of his library, but Erne insists that he was not typical in that, witness Sir John Harington, and Francis Bacon's grandson Sir Roger Townshend, and others, who took printed plays seriously. Certainly in the first years of the theatrical period (say, 1567 to 1589) plays were primarily for performance only, but thereafter they took on a dual life, just as Shakespeare got going in the early 1590s. The peak of play publication in the twenty years of 1594–1613 exceeded (indeed was double) the combined total for the ten years before and the ten years after this 'spike'. That is, it was not simply a matter of ongoing increase: those years were special (p. 15). What we would call literature was only about a quarter of all publishing in these years, but within that literary segment drama was fully a seventh. Drama's share today is much less. Erne notices that particular men—Thomas Creede, Edward Allde, and Valentine Simmes—were especially active in play printing (p. 16 n. 50), which point might usefully be cross-referenced with Gary Taylor's plenary paper at the Lancaster conference, which made the point that publishers might over-compensate for their low-life reputation by publishing uncommercial material. This provides a useful counterbalance to Peter W.M. Blayney's empirical demonstration that, in general, play printing was not lucrative ('The Publication of Playbooks', in John D. Cox and David Scott Kastan, eds., *A New History of Early English Drama* [1997]).

Material form showed drama's place: printed plays adopted Roman typefaces before other genres did, and hence were 'catering to an educated and progressive readership' (p. 17). The anthology *England's Parnassus* [1600] puts an extract illustrating 'care' from Edmund Spenser's *The Faerie Queen* (a clear piece of high culture) next to Friar Laurence on 'care', so Shakespeare was not thought of as low-culture in his own time. As an avid reader, Shakespeare must have seen this. Whereas freelance dramatists got their income primarily from selling the play to the company, Shakespeare's income was primarily from box office (p. 19). And whereas the freelancers (we infer from Henslowe's Diary) wrote just enough to fulfil their commissions, Shakespeare habitually wrote more than was needed, because he could afford to write for the page as well (p. 20). This argument could usefully be nuanced with consideration of Tiffany Stern's work on dramatists' 'benefit days' that were an additional source of income beyond the flat fee for delivery of a playbook. Erne surveys the rise of performance-centred thinking in Shakespeare studies, which he dates as starting in the late 1970s, and dismisses the idea that we only 'overhear' Shakespeare via his scripts, the detritus of performance, as nonsense (pp. 20–5). The publishers, he points out, thought them coherent and whole enough to publish. Erne is explicitly against returning us to the New Critical position that drama is poetry, but he wants to push the pendulum back a little from the current obsession with performance only. The Romantics were not entirely wrong to say that Shakespeare is more suitable to be read than performed, but our view has been skewed by the fact that Shakespeare has been performed from the over-long reading texts that he produced rather than the short theatrical ones. Erne's view of Shakespeare's literariness has amongst its many merits the fact that it solves the long-standing mystery that his dramatic poetry whizzes by one in performance, seeming to demand close attention that it cannot, in the moment, be given.

Usually Jonson is named as the first man to insist that plays were literature, either in his 1616 *Workes*, or in more tentative ways in the printings of *Every Man Out of His Humour* [1600] and *Sejanus* [1605] that mark a gap between the book and the performance text. For Erne, the gap between performance and print opened up at least as early as the 1590 printing of *Tamburlaine* and plays became literary artefacts part-way through Shakespeare's career and did so at the behest of publishers not playwrights (pp. 31–3). Pushing back by ten years (1590 instead of 1600) the date when printed playbooks began to legitimize themselves by stressing their non-theatrical features and their authorial (as opposed to theatrical) origins is important for the case of Shakespeare, because it puts him inside this trend. Erne rightly objects to Jeffrey Masten's erroneous assertion that play title pages in the late sixteenth and early seventeenth centuries generally did not mention authors, and insists rather that there was a palpable tension between performance and reading marked in the title pages. In the 1590s, naming the author became a way to detach printed plays from the taint of the playhouse, but of course collaborative dramatic composition was a hindrance to this detachment. Nearly 60 per cent of the plays written for the Admiral's men from autumn 1597 to summer 1600 were collaborative, yet not a single one of the plays printed in that period mentions multiple authorship on its title page: either a single author is named or no author is named. (Erne should be careful here of taking the Admiral's men as the norm of collaborative writing: perhaps unattached dramatists (from whom this company got its drama) were more likely to collaborate than the attached dramatists who supplied other companies.) Overall, from 1584 to 1623, fewer than 12 per cent of title pages that mentioned playwrights mentioned multiple playwrights. So, it seems that collaboratively written drama is under-represented in publication, either by being not selected or by being printed without mention of the dramatists. Playbills, it seems from John Dryden's evidence, did not name the author until the end of the seventeenth century, while title pages started to do so a hundred years earlier, so the theatre and the printing industry were not treating authors in the same way (pp. 43–4). In *England's Parnassus*, John Allot attributed collaboratively written material to one playwright only, as though writers were supposed, in their very natures, to be loners.

Non-commercial plays (translations and Latin plays for example) were in the mid-sixteenth century published with their authors'/editors'/translators' names on the title pages and even appeared in collections of 'Works', but the commercial theatre play printings remained mostly anonymous until the 1590s. However, by the 1610s it was the norm to name the dramatist, so during the span of Shakespeare's career drama went from almost always anonymous in print to almost always attributed (pp. 45–7). The Jonsonian distinction between great dramatic matter to be studied in print by the learned, and the dross that the actors threw in to please the multitude, is already apparent in the preface to the reader in the 1590s printing of *Tamburlaine* that 'left out some fond and friuolous Iestures'. It is not clear whether the material excluded was Marlowe's work or actors' interpolations, but the point is that already, by 1590, there was a sense of what suits the stage and what suits the page, and this sense is coming from a publisher, not an author (pp. 48–9). Did publishers perhaps carve out the sense of 'dramatic author' that the authors then took up? As well as creating the 'author', publishing might well have helped stabilize genre indeterminacy: Shakespeare's *Troilus and Cressida* was variably called a comedy (Q-1609 address), a tragedy (F1), and a history (Q-1609 title page). Likewise, the 1590 printing of *Tamburlaine* refers to the removal of comic bits and its Stationers' Register entry calls it 'commical'. Histories and tragedies seem to have been more respectable reading matter than comedies (certainly, Shakespeare's comedies were not reprinted half so often as his histories and tragedies), and thus our modern genre expectations (for example, that *Tamburlaine* is a tragedy) might themselves have been shaped by the publishers (pp. 50–1). When Richard Jones published *Tamburlaine* there was not yet an established market for printings of plays from the commercial theatre, and he trod carefully in how he addressed his readers. This care was emulated by others. When *The Spanish Tragedy* was printed, its multi-lingual inset play was turned into English for the benefit of readers (hence it is not a record of performance), apparently by Kyd who thus wrote the same thing twice, once for the stage and once for the page. Around the same time the same stationer (Edward White) published Kyd's full version of the inset play, *Soliman and Perseda*, and it is conceivable that the miniature version in *The Spanish Tragedy* was a taster for the full one (pp. 53–5).

Turning to Shakespeare's printed output in particular, Erne counts that by 1600 he had written twenty plays, of which fifteen had been printed. (When the facts are stated baldly like that, it is easy to share Erne's impatience with the orthodoxy that Shakespeare was print-indifferent.) Erne's impatience is heightened by Douglas Brooks's repeated assertion (in *From Playhouse to Printing House*) that the 1600 quarto of *2 Henry IV* was the first printed play to name Shakespeare on its title page, made as part of an argument that this fact is extraordinary since *1 Henry IV* caused such a fuss. For Brooks, Shakespeare's authorship was constructed (as Michel Foucault would say) in an act of transgression and as a response to the Oldcastle controversy. Of course, this is nonsense since earlier printings of *Love's Labour's Lost*, *1 Henry IV*, *Richard III*, and *Richard II* had all named Shakespeare. Brooks's mistake was to look only at first printings and ignore reprints. What is truly odd (almost unique, in fact) about the Shakespearian cases is that an anonymous edition gets replaced by one that names the author (pp. 57–8). For Erne, 1598 is the year that Shakespeare gets invented as an author, and around the turn of the century a lot of authors were invented in this way. That is, they cease to get anonymously published and start to get named on title pages. Shakespeare leads the way. At this point in an extraordinarily detailed argument, Erne makes the first slip that I can find: 'the Pavier quarto of *1 Contention* was said to be "Written by W. Shakespere, Gent"' (p. 65). In fact it was called *The Whole Contention* and its title page reads 'William Shakespeare, Gent' (a different spelling and an unabbreviated first name).

In 1598 Falstaff had just become a popular character and Shakespeare had become a gentleman, but Erne does not think these things account for his emergence as an author. Rather, what mattered was his being canonized by Francis Meres and put amongst the acknowledged great writers (pp. 66–7). This seems to be why reprints of Shakespeare suddenly, thereafter, name him where the first editions had not: now, post-Meres, Shakespeare's name sells. This might also be why *The Passionate Pilgrim* [1599], a collection with a few bits of Shakespeare in it, is attributed to Shakespeare on its title page, and might also explain why four non-Shakespearian plays (*Cromwell*, *London Prodigal*, *Puritan Widow*, and *Yorkshire Tragedy*) were printed with his name on their title pages. Thus 'the social *cachet* of printed playbooks increased well before the advent of Ben Jonson and the publication of his *Workes* in folio in 1616' (p. 71). Allot's selection for his collection *England's Parnassus* was strongly influenced by non-anonymous publication: most excerpts were from printed plays and of those most were from printings with named authors. Identifiable playwrights, then, already qualified for inclusion amongst 'the choicest flowers of our modern poets' as the collection called them. Another compilation is A.M.'s (probably Anthony Munday's) *Belvedere, or the Garden of the Muses* [1600], which gives much shorter snippets (a couple of lines) and does not attribute them, although Charles Crawford was able to identify more than half of them by hand in the early twentieth century. The situation with *Belvedere* is like that with *England's Parnassus*: plays are given place amongst the literary, and Shakespeare most of all. So, we must review our standard history and stop saying that plays were, before the big dramatic folios, sub-literary, and we must stop thinking of the publishers as the enemies of the dramatists. To a considerable extent, the publishers made the dramatic authors. By 1600 Shakespeare had a substantial body of published work and must have expected that what he wrote next would also appear in print. The remarkable fact is that mostly it did not, and only five more of his plays—*Merry Wives of Windsor*, *Hamlet*, *King Lear*, *Troilus and Cressida*, and *Pericles*—were printed in his lifetime.

This fact structures Erne's next two chapters, which examine in detail Shakespeare's publication career up to and after the fulcrum year 1600. The gist of these chapters appeared as Erne's *SQ* article reviewed last year and need not detain us too long. Erne examines the first twelve plays that Shakespeare wrote for the Chamberlain's men. *Romeo and Juliet*, *The Merry Wives of Windsor*, *Henry V*, and perhaps *Love's Labour's Lost* first appeared in 'bad' quartos. Perhaps because subsequent printings were 'good', we can say that players did care about the quality of their plays in print and intervened. For Q1 *Romeo and Juliet* John Danter got licence but not Stationers' Register entry before printing it, but by 1599 Cuthbert Burby seems to have acquire the rights to *Romeo and Juliet* and owned a 'good' manuscript that he went on to print. It is hard to be certain what happened, but if the company sold a good manuscript to Burby, it might well have done this before Q1 appeared. (True, but equally it might not have.) That the good manuscript underlying Q2 *Hamlet* changed hands before Q1 *Hamlet* appeared is evidenced by the fact that James Roberts, who went on to print Q2, entered his copy in the Stationers' Register before Q1 was printed for Nicholas Ling and John Trundle. Presumably Roberts, pointing out the unintentional breach of the publishers of Q1, resolved the potential dispute by selling Ling and Trundle his good manuscript and having them pay him to print it. Q1 *Love's Labour's Lost* calls itself 'Newly corrected and augmented', implying the existence of an earlier, lost 'bad' quarto; but there are other cases where such claims about correcting and augmenting are demonstrably false and Paul Werstine showed that Q1 *Love's Labour's Lost* was probably set up from printed copy, in which case the lost Q0 was good too.

So, it is likely that, rather than responding to 'bad' publication, the company sale of manuscripts to publishers *preceded* the bad publication. The 'bad' *Henry V* and *Merry Wives of Windsor* were not superseded by good ones in Shakespeare's lifetime, but the latter did not sell well (no reprint until 1619) so the players would not have been able to get a good text printed if they wanted to, for the publisher would have wanted to shift his existing copies first. Here Erne repeats the jumping from list to list that marred his *SQ* article: 'Of eight other plays Shakespeare is likely to have written for his company from 1594 until close to the turn of the century' (p. 82), *Love's Labour's Won* might be the same as *Much Ado About Nothing* or might be another play since lost, and *King John* could not be printed because *Troublesome Reign*'s publication blocked it. (It would be doing the reader a service if, every time a list of plays is referred to, the items in the list were spelled out. A little wasted space would save a lot of readerly guesswork.) Of the remaining six plays—*Richard II*, *A Midsummer Night's Dream*, *The Merchant of Venice*, *1 Henry IV*, *2 Henry IV*, and *Much Ado About Nothing*—we are now more sceptical than ever about our ability to tell the nature of the underlying copy from the printed text. Still, it remains quite possible that these plays were printed from good manuscripts supplied by the company. As a rule, two years seem to elapse between composition and Stationers' Register entry, although Erne has to dodge around a little amongst the critics for his dates of composition in order to make this all fit; there is a faint sense of shoehorning the evidence to fit the theory. To his credit, Erne admits the danger of circularity:

some of the datings of plays are based on the idea that they would not get printed soon after composition because that would hurt performance income.

The people involved in publishing the good texts of Shakespeare were a tightly knit group of primarily just three men: the publisher of playbills James Roberts, plus Andrew Wise (with whom Roberts worked) and Cuthbert Burby. Why wait two years before selling the manuscript to the publisher? Perhaps to keep up the income from scribal dissemination (which was certainly more costly per book than print) to discerning aristocrats, or perhaps to get publicity for a revival (pp. 87–91). A few performances (including revivals) that we can date—*Titus Andronicus* June 1594, *The Taming of the Shrew* June 1594, *A Knack to Know an Honest Man* October 1594 to November 1596, and *Massacre at Paris* June–September 1594—coincide with printed texts being published. Of Shakespeare's pre-Chamberlain's men's plays the evidence is generally hazy, and it is no surprise that a clear pattern cannot be determined. Although Erne does not explicitly make the connection, it follows from his argument that once the two main companies have what Andrew Gurr called 'settled practices' resulting from their state-enforced duopoly of London playing (*The Shakespearian Playing Companies*, pp. 78–104), settled practices in publication also emerged.

Then, suddenly, Shakespeare playbook publishing fell off after 1600, with just five plays appearing from 1601 to 1616. The decline was in new editions and in reprints, and only two new plays, *Hamlet* and *Pericles*, went into a second edition. This is harder to explain than the fairly straightforward pattern of the pre-1600 years, which was clearly one of intended company publication (p. 100). One possible explanation is that there was a glut of playbooks around 1600–1 and supply outstripped demand; this would make publishers reluctant to take on new books. Another explanation would be competition from the newly re-formed Paul's and Blackfriar's boys: their plays got into print and hurt the adult players' publications. The Stationers' Register 'staying' order of *Much Ado About Nothing* and *2 Henry IV* (not *Henry V* as usually thought), *As You Like It*, and *Every Man In His Humour* was not an attempt to block publication but rather an acknowledgement that the licence lacked ecclesiastical authorization; otherwise, how come three of the four plays were regularly entered within twenty days and published the same or the next year? Looked at this way, *As You Like It* failed to get published, rather than being blocked (p. 103). Dutton suggested that the prefatory address to the *Troilus and Cressida* quarto about the play never being performed refers to the readerly, long text of that edition, just as Q2 *Hamlet* boasts of being longer and new in the sense of being newly available in this long version. James Roberts entered *Troilus and Cressida* in the Stationers' Register on 7 February 1603, the entry recording that he still needed 'sufficient authority' (that is, ecclesiastical approval). This does not mean that there was anything wrong: Roberts entered several plays that had not been allowed, but as he seems to have been trading in manuscripts (entering them and then selling his rights to let someone else publish them) he did not need to pay the 10 pence to have the plays allowed, since he was not going to publish them. So, we do not have to imagine two different *Troilus and Cressida* manuscripts, an acting version that was not allowed and a reading version that was.

Tracing Stationers' Register entry of Shakespeare plays, there is a big gap from *Troilus and Cressida* on 7 February 1603 to *King Lear* on 26 November 1607 (after a steady flow before then), and *King Lear* is the most badly printed of the 'good' quartos. This Erne admits presents a problem for his argument that Shakespeare cared about its publication (p. 107). The same is also true of the next but one Stationers' Register entry in respect of Shakespeare: *Pericles* on 20 May 1608 by Edward Blount, which was followed in 1609 by Henry Gosson's publication of the 'bad' quarto without a transfer of rights from Blount to Gosson. That Gosson was not contravening Blount's rights seems indicated by the fact that he printed a second edition in 1609. Erne rather cryptically here asserts that, if Gosson got his manuscript and his rights from Blount, it is unlikely that the company was involved. (Why? Because *Pericles* is textually so bad? If so, that stands as an objection no matter what Gosson or Blount did.) If the *King Lear*, *Antony and Cleopatra* and *Pericles* entries in the Stationers' Register did originate in the playing company passing its manuscripts to publishers, then there was at least a trickle of the old flood after 1600. But since we cannot assume that, we must see what else might account for the Stationers' Register entry gaps from 1603 to 1607. Plague closure of the theatre would have hurt everyone, and it is only Shakespeare's printed output that dwindles. Erne has no certain answer, but wonders if there was a collected works of Shakespeare being planned, or perhaps the company chose to limit its print output in order to favour patrons, especially William Herbert, who probably got it royal patronage, probably is the dedicatee of *Sonnets*, and certainly is, with his brother, joint dedicatee of the 1623 Folio, and almost certainly stopped Pavier's collected works in 1619. (In an article to be reviewed here next year, Gary Taylor argues that Shakespeare's dramatic powers failed him and he simply did not have a hit until *Pericles*; that would explain the gap).

The history of Shakespeare printing duly (and largely convincingly) rewritten, Erne moves to the consequences of his ideas. Regarding the players' alleged opposition to print (pp. 115–28) Erne can build on existing knowledge with which his narrative is compatible. That printing did not lead to other companies playing a company's play is indicated by companies paying for new plays on subjects about which printed plays already existed: the Master of the Revels' licence did not allow just anybody to perform a play, only the company that licensed it. There is no evidence—just the tradition started by A.W. Pollard—that printing a play reduced its box office. Contrary to the usual explanation that players sometimes sold their plays to publishers when they were hard up, the amount given by publishers (Blayney reckons 30 shillings) was trivial when compared with the cost of costumes; it would have been better to sell those to raise cash. Richard Brome's deal with Queen Henrietta's men, come to court in 1640, prevented him from getting his plays published. G.E. Bentley extrapolated from this that Shakespeare was bound by the same rule, but in fact Brome's contract prevented him only from printing his plays without company agreement, which suggests that in fact companies did support publication. Heywood's address to the reader in *The English Traveller* seems to imply that actors were against publication and that he has no such ambitions, but needs to be read in the context of his frustration that his *Age* plays did not come out as a collection, as he had been promised, so he was making a virtue of non-publication necessity. Likewise, the Articles of Agreement amongst the Whitefriars sharers seem to prohibit publication, but only by individuals: collectively the company could print its plays. Moreover, the Articles most particularly protect the 'playbook' (the copy with the all-important performance licence) currently being used, rather than any copy of any of its plays. All the mistakes about publication of plays in Shakespeare's time stem, as Blayney pointed out, from the failure to look at it from the publisher's point of view. Once we get that straight, we can deal with such questions as why Shakespeare wrote over-long plays, how performance relates to published text, what is a 'socialized' text in this context, and what lies behind the 'bad' quartos. These matters occupy the rest of Erne's book.

Erne detects a neat irony in performance-centred study of early modern drama: the very fact that we have the plays relies on someone not thinking that the scripts existed only to be performed (p. 131). Since we have only the printings, it is delusional to think we can achieve performance-centred criticism in any meaningful sense. (Here Erne makes another of his rare errors, referring to 'Elizabethan groundlings standing in the pit of the Globe' (p. 136); he means of course standing in the yard.) We can, however, detect a wide gap between performance and printing in the excessive length of many Shakespeare printed plays; even a company specializing in speedy delivery such as the Shenandoah Shakespeare Express cannot get through *Hamlet* or *Richard III* in under three hours. (This reviewer's telephone call to Barrie Rutter of the Northern Broadsides company revealed that, with the cutting of about one-sixth of the Arden 2 *Richard III*, about 600 lines, the remaining text of 3,400 lines was routinely performed in under $2\frac{1}{2}$ hours. There may well be truth in Rutter's claim that the southern regional accent draws out Shakespeare's lines and makes them tedious.) It is indeed hard to see why playwrights would have written hundreds of lines that could not be performed, and Alfred Hart's counts in the 1930s showed that Shakespeare and Jonson were unusual in writing such long plays as they did. Erne twice (pp. 139, 144) refers to the belief that abridgement was done for provincial touring while full texts were performed in London, without commenting on whether he accepts this idea about provincial touring and without noting Scott McMillin's demonstration that abridgement often increases rather than reduces the number of actors needed by reducing the opportunities for doubling. Shakespeare's comedies average around 2,500 lines, which would be performable in just a few minutes over two hours, while the histories and tragedies are markedly longer, averaging around 3,000 lines. The most heavyweight plays (in subject matter and sources) are also the longest: *Hamlet*, *Richard III*, *Troilus and Cressida*, and *Coriolanus*. Contemporary accounts also seem to suggest that comedies were thought lightweight and not much worth reading, while tragedies had readerly gravity.

Erne notes that the printings of Webster's *The Duchess of Malfi* [1623] and of Brome's *The Antipodes* [1640] explicitly refer to the printing being longer than what was performed. (True, but the latter says that the printing included extra material from 'the allowed original', meaning the licensed playbook, so that is still a theatrical rather than a readerly, origin.) Of course, with the introduction of musical act intervals performance took longer for the same total number of lines, so line counts might go down if performance duration were to be kept the same. Erne makes much of the strongest piece of evidence of cutting for performance: Humphrey Moseley's publisher's address to the reader in the 1647 Beaumont and Fletcher folio. Moseley claims that whole scenes were cut from the plays for performance and that the private transcripts that circulated were of the cut texts, so the folio is the first opportunity to see the uncut versions. The plays in the folio are not particularly long, averaging about 15 per cent fewer lines than those in the Shakespeare Folio; so, if these shortish Beaumont and Fletcher plays had to be cut for performance, much more cutting would have been needed to perform Shakespeare plays. Moseley's claim about cutting was rejected by W.W. Greg but is borne out by the fact that the plays Moseley did not initially enter in the Stationers' Register (presumably because he did not have manuscript copies) are indeed much shorter than the others, perhaps because printed from those private, post-cutting transcripts (p. 153). In particular, the private transcript of *The Woman's Prize* seems to give the cut version of what the folio has in full, albeit minus what the censor removed in 1633. Likewise the manuscript from which the folio's *Beggar's Bush* is printed seems to have had restored to it some things that were originally cut for performance, to judge from repetitions and metrical lines split in two. Erne's own counts of lines in manuscript playbooks from 1576 to 1642 confirm the general picture that plays of under 2,500 lines are left virtually uncut and those with substantially more than that number are cut down to about that number (pp. 158–64). The only indirectly applicable evidence of the post-Restoration stage points the same way: the long Shakespeare plays were not performed in their entirety.

What are the implications of all this for editorial policy? At the height of New Bibliography, Erne's conclusion that plays were cut for performance would not have mattered much for editors because their aim was to recover the play as it would have stood in the author's manuscript as he handed it over to the players. However, for the stage-centred new New Bibliography (most obviously manifested in the 1986 Oxford *Complete Works*) that tries to recover the play as it was first performed, routine cutting for performance is devastating (p. 175). The underlying rationale for new New Bibliography that Shakespeare's intentions extended only so far as performance (and hence that the performed text is primary) has been buttressed by the idea that he was indifferent to print; this latter has fallen in the first half of this book, so the former is vulnerable. In other words, perhaps Shakespeare's ideals for his works were fully realized by him in the print versions. From this point of view, Greg's seeking after the authorial manuscript before the players got hold of it is a less distorting ideal than the Oxford *Complete Works*' seeking after the first performance. Gurr's New Cambridge Shakespeare edition of *Henry V* argued that Q1 shows us that the choruses were omitted in performance, so an edition done according to the principles of new New Bibliography would have to omit them.

Folio *Hamlet* might well reflect some of the cuts made to make the play performable: it has absences in common with Q1. On a couple of occasions, F omits some things that are in Q2 and at that point where the extra material is in Q2 there is a lost half-line: presumably there was a mark for a theatrical cut in the manuscript underlying Q2 that the compositor took for a half-line deletion.

Because printers printed everything in their copy, 'no printed text allows us to recover how much would have been marked for omission in its copy text and, consequently, would have been cut in performance' (pp. 180–1). How come Folio *Hamlet* contains some of the cuts (from Q2) that Q1 shows, but not all? Because it is based on a preliminary abridgement. The history of *The Honest Man's Fortune* by Fletcher, Massinger, and Field provides a parallel: the play was 'lost' in 1625 so the censor Henry Herbert relicensed a transcript of the author's foul papers for performance. The play was printed in the Beaumont and Fletcher folio of 1647 from the author's foul papers. Thus, the folio shows the play-as-written before cuts and whatever the folio has that the manuscript has not (primarily one scene, V.iii, and a different version of another, V.iv) are things that the players cut or changed before sending the play for relicensing. However, the manuscript also has marginal bars showing further cutting, so is itself another example of a 'preliminary abridgement' because already reduced from its copy and marking more reduction to be made, just like Folio *Hamlet*. It follows from this that, since there was cutting before licensing, Gurr's Maximal/Minimal textual model—that they licensed the most text they could ('Maximal and Minimal Texts: Shakespeare v. the Globe', *ShSurv* 52[1999] 68–87)—is not corroborated (p. 182 n. 31). One might well respond to this that the circumstances of *Honest Man's Fortune*, with the licensed playbook being lost, are scarcely typical.

In this view, neither Q2 nor F *Hamlet*, nor editions based on them, show us the play as performed. Equally, Q1 *Othello*'s being 160 lines shorter than F might be explained by its deriving from a preliminary abridgement, since 160 lines is not enough to bring it down to the performable length. The argument that the revision of *King Lear* caused the loss of the mock-trial scene simply because it was artistically ineffective is strained, and we would have to factor in the certainty that the play as represented in Q1 is unperformably long. The idea that Q1 *Richard III* was produced by collective, company memorial reconstruction while on tour (because the company lost its licensed playbook) is inherently implausible: if you know your parts (which is what a memorial reconstruction presupposes) there is no point recreating the playbook when what you really need is the licence. Also, at 3,400 lines, Q1 *Richard III* is too long to represent performance. Here Erne might usefully have acknowledged John Jowett's brilliant demonstration, by entirely independent means, that Q1 *Richard III* cannot be a memorial reconstruction ('"Derby", "Stanley", and Memorial Reconstruction in Quarto *Richard III*', *N&Q* 47[2000] 75–9). *Macbeth* is short (about 2,000 lines) and if it does indeed, as many suspect, derive from a posthumous theatrical adaptation, we should have to accept that in performance the other long tragedies might have lost more than about a third of their lines too. Concluding this section, Erne asserts that once we admit revision as an agent that separates versions that have competing authority, we have accepted an artistically self-conscious Shakespeare and we should go the extra mile to accept that not everything he did was driven by the exigencies of live performance (p. 189).

There follows a chapter on the origins of the so-called 'bad' quartos for which there are also over-long 'good' companion texts (*Romeo and Juliet*, *Henry V*, and *Hamlet*), which chapter adds little that is new to the debate and largely echoes the best of the work of the New Textualists. Erne's intention is not to show that the 'bad' quartos are really 'good' (p. 194) but that they do nonetheless yield important evidence about performance. McMillin's point about the absurdity of cutting for a smaller cast (because in fact cutting often removes opportunities for doubling) finally appears here (p. 207). Kathleen O. Irace pointed out that certain alleged memorial reconstruction texts retain characters' parts disproportionately—as in Q1 *Henry V* retaining 84 per cent of Exeter's part as represented in F, although Q1 is only half the length of F overall, and Q1 *Hamlet* retaining 92 per cent of Marcellus's part, although it is only 60 per cent as long as F—and she thought this incompatible with the claim that the actors were remembering a text already abridged for provincial performance. After all, would not Exeter's and Marcellus's parts have been cut with something approaching the severity that the entire play was cut? Erne thinks not: Marcellus's lines are largely unscathed in Q1 *Hamlet* because they are necessary to the plot (p. 208). Taking F *Henry V*'s part for Exeter and cutting it by 16 per cent (or rather, taking the combined reporter's parts for Exeter, Pistol, and Gower, which overall are cut by 20 per cent) is a process we can imagine being done to the whole play, and if the choruses were entirely removed too (as Gurr thinks happened in performance) this would put the play that the reporters were trying to reconstruct at around 2,500 lines. The point that Erne is making (and it is not easy to keep sight of it in all this detail) is that the memorial reconstruction was indeed aiming to reproduce a text that had been cut (relative to F in each case), but not drastically for regional performance but by the usual amount necessary to make a play performable. The short quartos are performance texts, and their long companions are essentially literary works not for performance.

Pursuing this claim about literariness further, Erne attempts to show that the short quartos are speakerly and rely on performance showing things to the audience while the long texts are readerly and have things described. Thus Q2 *Romeo and Juliet* has Juliet say that she is kneeling to beseech her father while Q1 simply has a stage direction for it. Rather illogically Erne runs the same kind of evidence the other way too: Q2 *Hamlet* (but not Q1) gives a stage direction for the cock crowing that startles the Ghost in the first scene (pp. 222–4). One might well respond to this by pointing out that stage directions can be readerly and theatrical at once: after all, someone in the theatre needs to know that a cock crowing noise is to be made. Erne surveys other passages in the long texts (absent from the short ones) that seem gauged to please a reader and, although performable, would probably be the first to go when cutting for length. For Erne, Friar Laurence's 'grey-eyed morn' speech in Q2 *Romeo and Juliet* is 'purple'—surely that is too strong a word—and appears in two places because Shakespeare was planning where to drop this detachable, literary bit of anthologizable writing. Risking a charge of ethnocentricity, Erne quotes Walter Ong using E.M. Forster's notion of 'rounded' character to argue that oral culture cannot produce characters that challenge our expectations, only ones that fulfil them. (By this logic, we would have to accept the implausible notion that the complexity of Odysseus's character in *The Odyssey* was something absent in all the oral retellings and that emerged only once it got written down.) Erne is quite serious on this concluding point, and suggests that criticism based on a better understanding of 'the cultural contingency of characterization' might take its proper place in Shakespeare studies (p. 243).

Erne provides three appendices. The first ('The Plays of Shakespeare and his Contemporaries in Print, 1584–1623') provides useful tables of all the first editions of all the plays (abbreviated by using Greg's numbering in the *Bibliography of English Printed Drama*). These are marred by attempts at typographical distinctions—such as solid or dashed underlining to show how firmly Shakespeare's authorship is advertised on the title page—that in the review copy were almost impossible to see. In the second appendix Erne ponders whether the 'stolen and surreptitious' copies of Shakespeare plays that the 1623 Folio preliminaries refer to could have been Thomas Pavier's quartos of 1619; they might, but Erne has no new evidence to offer. In the third appendix Erne gives reasons to believe in the circulation of dramatic manuscripts of successful plays well before the phenomenon is referred to in the Beaumont and Fletcher folio of 1647. Greg observed that we have no surviving examples before 1624, but Erne notes that the publisher's epistle to the 1619 printing of Beaumont and Fletcher's *A King and No King* refers to Sir Henry Nevill having one, and the printer's address to the 1620 printing of *The Two Merry Milk-Maids* refers to 'false Copies' travelling abroad. Also, Gabriel Harvey's reference to *Hamlet*, written into his copy of Chaucer, sounds like a reference to a reading copy, yet is pre-Essex's execution and hence pre-Q1 *Hamlet*.

The year 2003 certainly was a landmark one for monographs, and Andrew Murphy's extraordinary *Shakespeare in Print: A History and Chronology of Shakespeare Publishing* will remain the standard single-volume reference work for a long time. Murphy covers the entire timespan from first printings to the present, and geographically he covers English, Scottish, Irish, and American editions, but thankfully for our purposes he gives equal space to each period covered so that the material relevant to this review is only a small part of the whole. Murphy's introduction attends to the matter of balance and observes that some editions that are not distinguished as textual scholarship are nonetheless important for their place in the struggle over Shakespeare as intellectual property, or for sheer numbers sold (pp. 6–7). To complement his scrupulous scholarship Murphy has a fine feeling for a good anecdote, as shown in his account of the publishing house Macmillan's employment of an imperfect mechanical process to copy their outgoing correspondence. The images turned out to be impermanent, and Murphy has us picture him in the British Library receiving to his desk bound volume after bound volume of carefully stored and respectfully handled material, the pages of which were, upon opening, entirely blank (p. 11).

Murphy's first chapter ('The Early Quartos') is a fine work of print history but adds nothing to our knowledge of matters textual. As with Erne's book reviewed above, Murphy seldom makes a slip, but I am sure that when he twice uses the formula 'X published Y for Z' he really means 'X printed Y for Z' (pp. 24–5). If not, I do not understand what 'publishing for' someone might mean. In his second chapter ('Early Collected Editions') Murphy gives a potted history of the Pavier quartos, with a useful summary table, and likewise for F1, F2, F3, F4, and the putative F5. Chapters 3 and 4 cover the Tonson era from Nicholas Rowe to Edmond Malone and are helpful to have to hand when examining one of the many multi-volume Shakespeare editions produced in the eighteenth century (often republished with alterations) and trying to work out what it is. Murphy credits Samuel Johnson as the first to articulate the principle that derivative texts must be given lower authority than the texts they derive from, from which they 'only deviate … by the printer's negligence' (p. 82), and he, correctly in my view, demurs from Margreta de Grazia's Foucauldian view that Malone's edition was a whole new way of doing things. Following Simon Jarvis, Murphy prefers to see it within the developing tradition (p. 97). In chapters 5 and 6 Murphy breaks off the historical narrative to consider the matter of copyright disputes amongst English, Scottish, and Irish publishers that emerged because of the legal differences across the (only fictionally 'united') kingdom. Murphy describes the eighteenth-century price war between Tonson and the publisher Robert Walker, who between them flooded the market with cheap editions (4 pence per play, and under) and drove a boom in Shakespeare appreciation generally (pp. 107–10). There was some confusion about whether English law applied in Scotland after the union of 1707, and it certainly did not apply in Ireland, so the copyright situation in those places was unclear in a way that favoured printing and exporting to England books previously printed in England. These editions' original English publishers believed them to be subject to perpetual, rather than time-limited, copyright, and after a test case of 1774 rejected this interpretation Shakespeare printing doubled in rate.

Murphy's chapter 7 on American editions is especially interesting on the genesis and development of the Furness Variorum, and his surveys of nineteenth-century popular (chapter 8) and scholarly (chapter 9) editions are exemplary condensations of his extensive work in archives, but fall outside our scope here. In chapter 10 ('The New Bibliography') Murphy covers the faltering Oxford Shakespeare (under R.B. McKerrow and then Alice Walker) and the rival ('New') Cambridge Shakespeare (under Arthur Quiller-Couch and John Dover Wilson). Murphy has not much to say about the principles of New Bibliography itself, although he makes the important observation that Wilson's series was the first to be completed (albeit very late, in 1966) along New Bibliographical lines. Discussing the later twentieth century, Murphy too cautiously (as we shall shortly see) remarks that *Pericles* 'may have been co-authored' (p. 250). In his conclusion ('Twenty-First Century Shakespeares') Murphy repeats the familiar line about hypertext as a new configuration that decentres the author because of the capacity for movement from one place to another. Actually, a print library itself can be seen as a hypertext with the individual works' footnotes as the links; electronic media just make the jumps from text to text that we all do anyway a little less time-consuming. To my mind, focusing on the links misses the truly important differences between paper and e-text, which have to do with alterability (in postmodern terminology, 'textual stability') and copyability.

Murphy ends with an anecdote about printed Shakespeare crossing class boundaries and with an implied prediction that print will survive a long time for certain kinds of reader. Murphy contrasts such a printed book with the electronic text that is 'dispersed' and not so much for reading as 'surfing' (p. 275). Such terminology taints the medium, e-text, by association with allegedly mindless recreations (surfing television channels, surfing the internet) and sounds rather like the pre-web pseudo-theoretical mistakings of the nature of e-text, which could see no further than the 'magic' of hypertext. Quite possibly the relative advantages of the printed book will soon disappear with the mass production of e-paper: illuminated or reflective electronic displays capable of showing as much detail as paper and consuming power only when changing the image, and flexible enough to be folded (or rolled into a tube) when not in use. About a third of Murphy's book is an appendix—a substantial work of scholarship in itself, that lists all the major Shakespeare editions to date and provides multiple indices sorted on such fields as 'publisher name' and 'editor name'. In a revealing footnote (p. 412 n. 4) Murphy cites Erne's demurral from the general consensus that Shakespeare was indifferent to publication, which Murphy announces is forthcoming in a book called *Lines to Time: Shakespeare and Literary Drama*. This must have been an earlier title for Erne's book *Shakespeare as Literary Dramatist* reviewed above, and it is worth knowing that, like Wilcher, Erne alighted on sonnet 18 ('Shall I compare thee to a summer's day?') for his exploration of the potential for immortality through art.

MacDonald P. Jackson's *Defining Shakespeare: Pericles as Test Case* is rather like Brian Vickers's *Shakespeare, Co-author*, reviewed last year, in its subject matter and its deprecation of certain aspects of modern theory's application to dramatic authorship. More focused than Vickers's book, however, Jackson's aims for one target and hits its squarely: to show that George Wilkins wrote *Pericles* with Shakespeare. Indeed, Jackson hits his mark many times over from multiple new angles, taking the demonstration of his correctness far beyond the limits of anyone's reasonable scepticism. Unusually for our subject, we may truly say that the case is now closed. Jackson begins by quoting Jeffrey Masten's *Textual Intercourse* to disagree with the view that, when collaborating, dramatists submerged their personal distinctiveness (p. 6), and instead cites Vickers's book on collaboration being done 'by acts or scenes or other large units dominated by differing plot lines or sets of characters'. As noted last year, that was one of the weakest points of Vickers's book since there is not as much evidence to support the claim as Vickers's rhetoric suggests. Happily, however, Jackson adds to the evidence that collaboration was not done at the level of the line but something larger by showing Middleton's preference for the shortening *I've* and Rowley's absolute avoidance of it, across many sole-authored plays 'with their diverse textual histories'. When they collaborate on a play, each section (be it Middleton's or Rowley's, determined on other grounds) betrays its author's particular preference for or against *I've* (p. 7). Jackson makes the important point that every act of 'disintegration' (say, splitting off a part of a play from Shakespeare) is simultaneously an act of 'integration' (say, giving that part to the rest of the Middleton canon). This is worth saying because there is a current mistaken orthodoxy (articulated by Masten amongst others) that an author-based approach to drama is anachronistically post-Enlightenment. In fact, as Jackson (like Vickers) points out, the ancient Greek dramatic authorship contests, and the pre-Christian canonizing of Aeschylus, Sophocles, and Euripides, show otherwise (p. 12).

The ground cleared of theoretical objections, Jackson turns to the necessary preliminary matter of statistics, stylishly addressed via the opening scene of Tom Stoppard's *Rosencrantz and Guildenstern Are Dead* concerning the strangeness of a tossed coin coming up heads ninety-two times in a row (p. 23). Everyone uses statistics, asserts Jackson, even those who attribute something on the basis of verbal parallels with a work of known authorship, because there the implied reasoning is that chance could not produce those parallels with work by a different known author. In truth, chance often can produce the unexpected, and Jackson promises that when verbal parallels are used in his argument there will be also 'a search for similarities with other playwrights' and that statistics will be used to test what chance can do (p. 22). Jackson thinks the clincher for Wilkins's prose narrative *Painful Adventures* being based on the play is that it has Lychorida bring the newborn Marina up on deck to show Pericles: this utterly implausible event (Marina is just a few minutes old) happens in the play because Pericles cannot leave the deck without leaving the Globe stage bare. Had Wilkins not been copying the performance, he would have written the scene differently. (I would not have thought plausibility a reasonable criterion in relation to this story and would also object that Marina's association with the sea cannot be formed in a scene set below decks. Indeed, it is not dramatic practice that prevents Pericles going below deck: Shakespeare could have written a new scene or written the existing scene differently; he did not have to have Lychorida come on deck.)

Jackson traces Ernest Schanzer's and then Gary Taylor's demolition of Philip Edwards's claim that the whole of the quarto is by Shakespeare, but that Acts I–II had a different (and worse) reporter than Acts III–V. Were this so, Wilkins's *Painful Adventures* and the *Pericles* quarto would be independent witnesses to the play as performed, and hence where they agree they must be right since chance could hardly make them agree in error. And yes, they agree on five lines in II.iii that are too bad to be Shakespeare and are typical of the first half of the play. The obvious inference is that the offending lines are by Wilkins, which is why his novel has them right (pp. 27–8). Also, if Acts III–V of the *Pericles* quarto are simply a more accurately reported account of the play as performed than Acts I–II were, these last three acts should be more similar to the corresponding parts of Wilkins's novel than the first two acts were, since in Edwards's theory Wilkins's novel is just a uniformly good/bad account of the performance. In fact, Acts III–V of the *Pericles* quarto diverge from rather than converge upon the novel (p. 29). More speculatively, Jackson insists that, if *Pericles* had been Shakespeare's solo work, Heminges and Condell would not have left it out of F1; the only other play they left out was the undisputedly collaborative *The Two Noble Kinsmen*. *Pericles* was in the company repertory around 1623, so they had a playbook of it (hence availability of copy was not the problem), and Blount (one of the F1 publishers) had a Stationers' Register entry proving his copyright priority over Gosson; thus Blount could have printed the play if he had wanted. Indeed, claims Jackson, printing the play would have established a text 'which would have differed sufficiently from Gosson's quarto to be exempt from any copyright claim Gosson's successors might have made' (p. 31). This is not right: stationers were protected from another stationer publishing the same story even if it was from a different text, as Blayney pointed out in relation to *King Lear* and *King Leir* ('The

Publication of Playbooks', in John D. Cox and David Scott Kastan, eds., *A New History of Early English Drama* [1997]). From Blayney's view it seems to follow that Blount had effectively conceded the right to print *Pericles*, or even privately agreed to it, by not objecting to Gosson's 1609 quarto, for, as Blayney showed, it was printing that firmly established ownership of copy. Jackson claims that the 'problem' with *Troilus and Cressida* in F1 seems to have been overcome 'in this way' (that is, by printing a good text) and cites the Oxford Textual Companion p. 425 (p. 31), but in fact the Companion at that point makes no mention of how 'difficulties over copyright' in respect of Folio *Troilus and Cressida* were overcome, only that we can presume they existed because F1's printing of the play was interrupted. Jackson is assuming that getting a manuscript to supplement the *Troilus and Cressida* quarto—to substantially alter its readings—was how the F1 publishers got around the copyright problem, but that is not what Taylor is arguing at the place cited.

Finally, the idea that *Pericles* Acts I–II are early Shakespeare material that he reused at the end of his career can be dismissed because, whereas everything else he wrote can, by certain independent tests, be shown to belong to a particular phase in his career, these two acts have some kinds of stylistic links with early Shakespeare, some other kinds of links with mid-career Shakespeare, and other kinds of links still with late Shakespeare. (Actually, that is what I would expect to find if it were reworked juvenilia—a mix of old and new characteristics—but Jackson clearly means to imply that it belongs to no definite stage of Shakespeare's career because it does not belong to Shakespeare at all.) To refute the late Eric Sams's claim that *Pericles* is, in part at least, a Shakespeare play from the 1580s, Jackson shows that the alleged early allusions to it are weak or simply mistaken, and usefully lists all the clear allusions to it that cluster after 1609, appearing in the plays *Pimlico, or Run Red-Cap*, Robert Tailor's *The Hog Hath Lost His Pearl*, and (via a plot echo) in Robert Armin's *The Two Maids of Moreclacke* (pp. 34–9). Perhaps seeing Gower's tomb in St Saviour's church during the burial of his brother Edmund on 31 December 1607 gave Shakespeare the idea for the play, Jackson wonders. Having established that the sole-authorship claim cannot stand, Jackson turns to the particular evidence for dual authorship, which is where the hard matter of this book begins.

The key to Eliot Slater's work in this field is rare-word usage, which is also what interested the most famous stylometrician Donald Foster and for which he was soundly excoriated in Vickers's other book reviewed last year, *'Counterfeiting' Shakespeare*. The principle followed by Slater and Jackson is that 'works written by the same author at about the same time are apt to have more of their low-frequency words in common than works whose dates of composition are separated by many years' (p. 40). Low-frequency means that the writer concerned does not use them often, and hence they are for him or her (but not necessarily anyone else) 'rare' words. Slater's precise criterion was words used in at least two plays and a total of fewer than ten times overall in the canon, and he counted how many such words should be common between play *X* and other plays in the canon on the basis of expectation derived simply from play *X*'s total vocabulary. Jackson reckons that Slater should have derived his expectation from the proportion of rare words in *X* compared to the total number of rare words in the canon. This notion of 'expectation' is the ground upon which stylometricians start to leave the rest of literary scholarship behind, primarily because the stylometricians can put a number on it. The numbers generally refer to how unlikely a given event is, a matter about which non-specialists are apt to be wildly mistaken in their assumptions. Unless they are extremely careful with phrasing, stylometricians tend to make claims that non-specialists find either wholly persuasive or absurd. Here (p. 41) Jackson writes of the link between *The Tempest* and Acts III–V of *Pericles* in the form of rare words that 'the possibility of this discrepancy [between expected links and found links] being due to chance is infinitesimal'. In fact he means that, were random chance all that connected rare-word choice in *The Tempest* and *Pericles* Acts III–V—the whole of Shakespeare's career considered as a single word-pool with no chronological forces shaping his selection of words—then the likelihood of this high linkage (way above 'expectation') occurring by chance alone were infinitesimal. A little logic, however, shows that this does not necessarily link *The Tempest* and *Pericles* III–V directly by shared authorship. Imagine a world in which all dramatists were choosing their rare words according to the seasons (words beginning with the letters A–B in January, C–D in February, and so on): then the same results might occur if *The Tempest* and *Pericles* III–V were written at the same time of the year. The high-sounding mathematics ('infinitesimal') does not tell us that we are on to the *right* connection between *The Tempest* and *Pericles* Acts III–V, only that the chance of there being no causal connection is small.

In a footnote (p. 41 n. 2) Jackson explains his method for linking *The Tempest* and *Pericles* III–V. *The Tempest* contains about 2.4 per cent of the rare words in all Shakespeare and *Pericles* III–V contains 1,228 Shakespearian rare words itself, so we would expect about thirty of these words (2.4 per cent of 1,228) to be in common, that is to be the same words, were a writer's changing habits over time not a factor. But a writer's changing habits over time *are* a factor—plays written about the same time tend to share rare words because the writer is favouring those words at that moment—and indeed *The Tempest* and *Pericles* III–V have sixty-two rare words in common, more than twice what we would otherwise expect. Jackson uses a procedure called chi-square to give a sense of how big a difference from expectation this is (and explains it well), and cautions that it is not really an index of probability (a comparison with random chance) being tested, but of alleged association (of rare words with phases in a writer's career). That is, a high chi-square indicates that two variables are unlikely to be randomly associated and likely to be causally linked somehow, but it does not (despite some popular misuse) tell you how likely something is. Rather, it tells you how *unlikely* the result you got would be *if* the variables were linked only by random chance, which is to say it tells you how infrequently chance alone will produce the result obtained. In Great Britain, a 1 in 14 million unlikelihood happens to someone about every other week in the National Lottery: the chance of a particular person winning is tiny, but the chance of someone winning is about 1 in 2. The likelihood that the phenomenon 'winning' will emerge from these events needs to be closely defined with qualifiers before we can put numbers on it. This objection to terminological slippage applies throughout Jackson's book: he repeatedly makes claims of the kind 'the odds of this being by chance are 1 in

100' (which sounds like 'it almost certainly is not chance') which strictly means the same as, but has different rhetorical force from, 'by chance this will happen 1 time in a 100 anyway' (so, eventually chance alone does it).

Returning to Jackson's main argument, it emerges that if the same rare word tests are repeated with *Pericles* Acts I–II, the association with the last phase of Shakespeare's career disappears. One can also do the same tests for the absence of rare-word linkages between plays since chance operates equally on the non-selection of the same rare words in two plays. I would have thought this no more illuminating than the test for present links, since non-selection is selection's mathematical complement, but Jackson seems to think it highly significant. At this point, I suspect most non-mathematical readers will become lost. Jackson admits that *Pericles* I–II has above-expectation links with *Antony and Cleopatra* and *Coriolanus*, but rejects the obvious conclusion that this makes *Pericles* I–II likely to be Shakespeare's too with the assertion that this can happen by verbal osmosis from one's collaborator. That is, when working on *Antony and Cleopatra* and *Coriolanus* the rare words of the other man's work in *Pericles* were in Shakespeare's mind. I cannot see how this can be accepted without it diminishing the significance of the claimed links of *Pericles* III–V with other plays: might not they too be explained this way? Jackson anticipates this objection by pointing out that *Pericles* III–V's departures from random chance are way above those of *Pericles* I–II, and indeed taking the Shakespeare canon together, the links of *Pericles* I–II are within what random chance would be expected to produce (p. 42). Better still, taking the canon in four sections, *Pericles* III–V has a strong association with the plays from *King Lear* to *All Is True* and against the three earlier sections, while *Pericles* I–II has no significantly strong associations with any period. The pattern looks much the same if one considers the even more rare words, those occurring two to six times rather than two to ten times (p. 43), although there emerges a hint of connection between *Pericles* I–II and *Titus Andronicus* and *1 Henry VI*. Jackson does not think that this supports the idea of *Pericles* I–II being early Shakespeare because the evidential base becomes so small—in that case (I would say) he should draw no conclusions from it either way—and in any case *Titus Andronicus* and *1 Henry VI* were probably collaborative and in any case early Shakespeare is less idiosyncratic (uses more common words) so will have more links with what other men do than later Shakespeare will (p. 44). (Here Jackson sails closest to special pleading for his case.)

Jackson 'proves' the insignificance of *Pericles* I–II having links with early Shakespeare by showing that a sole-authored Wilkins play, *The Miseries of Enforced Marriage*, or at least a random sample of its rare words, has links with early Shakespeare too. Jackson here brings in the fact that *Pericles* III–V has fewer than 'expected' rare-word links with *1 Henry VI* and *Titus Andronicus*, but by this point the exhausted reader has surely forgotten that 'expected' means 'were only chance operating' and that in fact Jackson believes that changing authorial preference is what he is tracking. That is, we *would* expect old Shakespeare to have given up rare words he favoured as a young man, and hence falling below 'expectation' also confirms the 'changing tastes' hypothesis. Yet if that is so—if dropping words over time is as important as acquiring new ones—we should expect Jackson to be presenting all the evidence of non-linking between chronologically separated plays too (p. 44). At this point Jackson introduces a fundamental principle that so many attributers have neglected: the importance of negative testing. It is one thing to show that writing X is like writing Y in certain respects, but for authorship attribution you have also to show that lots of other writings are not like writing Y in those respects (pp. 45–6). This will become important later in Jackson's argument.

Karolina Steinhäuser's work on Shakespearian rare words in each scene of *Pericles* (including the choruses) can be used to show that the choruses in Acts I–II are like the scenes in Acts I–II (and like early Shakespeare) and those in Acts III–V are like the scenes in Acts III–V (and like late Shakespeare); so again the play is internally divided and hence probably not all by Shakespeare. Even if he were, in the choruses, imitating an archaic style, then Shakespeare would have to have dropped this imitation part-way through. Steinhäuser's more finely reticulated counting of rare words (by scene) allows Jackson to rank the scenes in terms of rare words per thousand words even though the scenes differ in length. When he does this, not all the seventeen scenes of Acts III–V come ahead (in terms of Shakespearian rare-word richness) of all the eleven scenes of Acts I–II, but most of them do, and that is not likely by chance distribution of rare words (pp. 47–9). Gregor Sarrazin's work on very rare words confirms the foregoing: there are far fewer of these (expressed in lines per rare word) in *Pericles* I–II and Middleton's part of *Timon of Athens* and Fletcher's part of *All Is True* than is normal for all the other Shakespeare plays (pp. 51–3). While it is admittedly much more subjective, poetic parallels (such as calling eyelashes the 'fringes' of the eye) between *Pericles* I–II and the rest of the Shakespeare canon and between *Pericles* III–V and the rest of the canon confirm what has already been found: the latter is much more Shakespearian (parallels occur twice as often) than the former. This also makes unlikely the possibility that *Pericles* I–II are early Shakespeare later reworked (pp. 56–9).

Metrical features such as extra syllables over the usual ten, various degrees of enjambment, and absence of a caesura, can all be measured (pp. 59–68), and Karl Wentersdorf produced a table showing how a single indexical figure derived from these features rises steadily over Shakespeare's career. The figure for *Pericles* III–V takes its expected place amongst the late plays, but the figure for *Pericles* I–II is more like the figures for Shakespeare's late sixteenth-century plays. Jackson describes Ants Oras's work on where the caesura falls, which shows that increasingly over his career Shakespeare put the pause in the second half of a verse line; the figure for *Pericles* III–V matches the late plays and the figure for *Pericles* I–II again matches the late sixteenth-century plays. Charles A. Langworthy's work on rates at which sentences start at a verse-line beginning and/or end at a verse-line end—in early plays they usually do, in late plays usually not—confirms the preceding work. Marina Tarlinskaja's works on rates at which 'slots' for unstressed and stressed syllables in iambic pentameter verse (1, 3, 5, 7, and 9, and 2, 4, 6, 8, and 10 respectively) are actually filled by stressed or unstressed syllables shows that over his career Shakespeare decreasingly put stressed syllables in slots 1 and 4 and increasingly put stressed syllables in slots 3, 6, and 9. Into this trend of changing habits *Pericles*

III–V fits well as late Shakespeare and *Pericles* I–II looks more like late sixteenth-century Shakespeare. Also, in the second half of his career, Shakespeare increasingly allowed polysyllabic words to be the cause of loss of stress in a slot where we would expect it, compared to how often he allowed monosyllabic words to do this work of taking away stress.

As well as summarizing these mutually supportive (and under-recognized) works, Jackson has done his own fresh work on elision. In early Shakespeare *we/you/they are* and *I/we/you/they/to have* are rarely best spoken as monosyllables (such as *we're* and *they've*) and frequently are best spoken as disyllables if one wants to follow strict iambic pentameter. Jackson does not make it clear whether he means this claim regardless of how the words are spelt, but in fact he is confining himself to cases where they are fully spelt out, since he uses only Marvin Spevack's concordance entries for *are* and *have* and these do not include the elisions, which get listed under the first word (so under *they* for *they're*). Of course, one would want to check whether the edition Spevack used, the Riverside edited by Gwynne Blakemore Evans, had ever changed non-elided to elided spelling for the sake of metre. Evans's introduction (*The Riverside Shakespeare*, p. 40) refers to his regularization of *-ed* and *-'d* endings (all made *-'d*) in prose passages on the assumption that mere compositorial convenience might be the determinant; Evans might also, on that basis, have wondered whether convenience shaped practice in full-width verse lines where the compositor faced the same pressure in justifying the line of type. Evans's saying nothing of *are* and *-'re* and *have* and *-'ve* implies that he left them as he found them, but it would be reassuring to know and Jackson's argument is not complete without this information. *Pericles* I–II, it turns out, has a much higher proportion of fully spelt out *we/you/they are* and *I/we/you/they/they have* being pronounced monosyllabically (if we want to preserve iambic pentameter) than ought to be the case were it early Shakespeare (p. 71). Shakespeare's use of rhyme fell (albeit unevenly) over his career and was low by 1607; rhyme use is high in *Pericles* I–II (1 in 4 lines) while it is low in *Pericles* III–V (1 in 33 lines), and the particular kinds of rhyme in *Pericles* I–II (especially the pattern *aabcc*) are unlike what Shakespeare does elsewhere (pp. 72–3).

To conclude this section on why *Pericles* simply cannot be the work of one writer, Jackson touches briefly on Barron Brainerd's tests, which relied mostly on usage of certain words across the career (*unto*, *because*, and *with* decreased over time while *might*, *more*, and *most* increased over time) and the tests of the Claremont McKenna College Shakespeare Clinic that pass *Pericles* III–V as Shakespearian but *Pericles* I–II as not (pp. 75–9). Jackson does not give much detail about the Claremont McKenna tests, but criticizes their method of 'badges and flukes'. This method relies on Shakespeare's most commonly used and least commonly used words, relative to the dramatists Marlowe, Greene, Kyd, and Munday. The problem with this is that Shakespeare started writing in a style that was like everyone else and got distinctive over time, and the Shakespeare plays chosen to form a baseline of his style were about ten or more years later than the plays from Marlowe, Greene, Kyd, and Munday. Thus by this test the early plays of Shakespeare tend to look non-Shakespearian because they sound too much like Marlowe, Greene, Kyd, and Munday.

Having established that someone other than Shakespeare wrote *Pericles* I–II, Jackson turns to identifying the writer, paying most attention to the likeliest candidate, George Wilkins. The only known sole-authored play by Wilkins is *The Miseries of Enforced Marriage*, so that is not much to go on for establishing if the Wilkins oeuvre shares features with *Pericles* I–II. We can also see if things unique to *Miseries* and *Pericles* I–II crop up in Wilkins's share of Wilkins, Day, and Rowley's *The Travels of the Three English Brothers*. Of course, most of the stylometricians so far discussed never thought to look at Wilkins's work, but F.G. Fleay and H. Dugdale Sykes found that *Miseries* has metrical affinities with *Pericles* I–II (pp. 83–6). Jackson has not done Langworthy's or Tarlinskaja's kind of analysis on Wilkins's play, but he has repeated Oras's work on where the caesura falls (how often after the first syllable, how often after the second syllable, and so on) and finds that *Miseries* is much like *Pericles* I–II and unlike *Pericles* III–V and *Coriolanus*. This result Jackson submits to a series of comparisons between *Pericles* I–II, *Pericles* III–V, *Miseries* and all the Shakespeare plays, with statistical computation to show how likely it is that the result achieved could happen by random chance (pp. 88–94). Consistently *Pericles* I–II is like *Miseries* and *Pericles* III–V is like the rest of Shakespeare around 1607. Likewise, repeating the *we/you/they are* and *I/we/you/they have* as monosyllable or disyllable test for *Miseries* shows it to be like *Pericles* I–II, and so on for the Wilkins share of *Travels* too. Jackson reports David J. Lake's work on rhymes, especially assonantal near-rhymes (such as ship/split, sung/come), and finds *Pericles* I–II's high frequency of them to be like Wilkins's work and not like Shakespeare's or anyone else's (pp. 95–6). Jackson's fresh work on rhymes (of the direct, *law/awe* kind) shows that, where *Miseries* and *Pericles* have a rhyme in common, it is almost always in *Pericles* I–II and not in *Pericles* III–V, and that three of the rhymes that *Miseries* and *Pericles* I–II share (*consist/resist*, *him/sin*, *impudence/offence*) occur nowhere in the Shakespeare canon (pp. 97–9). Comparison of all the rhymes in *Miseries* with the rhymes in all the Shakespeare works shows that the Shakespeare works have far fewer rhymes in common with *Miseries* than *Pericles* I–II has rhymes in common with *Miseries*, and indeed that after *Pericles* I–II the text with the next greatest number of rhymes in common with *Miseries* is Wilkins's share of *Travels*. But what if the rhyming links between *Pericles* I–II and *Miseries* are due to them both being full of commonplace rhymes? To exclude this possibility Jackson ran a couple of unShakespearian rhymes that appear in *Pericles* I–II and in *Miseries* (*consist/resist* and *impudence/offence*) through Chadwyck-Healey's Literature Online (LION) database and found that they are extremely rare (pp. 100–4).

To show that the counting of function words (articles, conjunctions, pronouns, prepositions, auxiliary verbs, and so on) can be a stylometric tool, Jackson quotes passages from Marlowe's *Tamburlaine* (full of *of* ... *the* constructions), Kyd's *The Spanish Tragedy* (full of *and*s), and Middleton's *Women Beware Women* (full of *it* ... *a* constructions), which features, were they typical of the plays at large, would make for good general discriminators of authorship (pp. 105–6). Jackson touches on analysis of the so-called *Federalist* papers from the mid-eighteenth century and the Pauline New Testament using function-word frequency—in the latter case the analysis is now considered suspect—and Thomas Merriam's application of function-word analysis to *Sir Thomas More*. The *Federalist* work was especially good because the researchers produced their discriminators using just half the available material, reserving the other half (of known authorship) for the unbiased testing of the efficacy of their discriminators (p. 107). Jackson reports M.W.A. Smith's function-word analysis of *Pericles* I–II and *Pericles* III–V compared to the works of Shakespeare, Chapman, Middleton, Jonson, Webster, Tourneur, and Wilkins, in which *Pericles* III–V comes out as consistently (over different kinds of test) closest to Shakespeare and *Pericles* I–II gets inconsistent results, with some tests favouring Shakespeare and other tests favouring other dramatists (pp. 109–13). Jackson describes his own function-word analysis done by hand in the 1960s and 1970s, in which he counted the frequencies (relative to one another) of the occurrences of *a*, *and*, *but*, *by*, *for*, *from*, *in*, *if*, *of*, *that*, *the*, *to*, and *with* in Shakespeare. Unsurprisingly, amongst a group of contemporary dramatists chosen, the work of Wilkins is closest in function-word frequencies to *Pericles* I–II and the work of Shakespeare closest to *Pericles* III–V (pp. 113–18). Here again Jackson slips into unhappy phrasing about chance: 'the probability [of *Revenger's Tragedy* sharing the discovered function-word frequencies with a set of Middleton plays] being considerably less than one in ten thousand that it was due to chance' (pp. 114–15), when in fact he means that, were chance responsible for the rates at which function-words are chosen in the test texts, we would get this result one time in ten thousand. Even chance can produce these results on rare occasions, and there are lots of other factors to consider in real writing, such as one writer imitating another.

When one puts the twenty-seven scenes of *Pericles* in descending order of the frequency with which they use 'to + verb infinitive' (such as the opening line's 'To sing a song'), seven of the top eight scenes are from *Pericles* I–II, the interloper being IV.iv, which, for other reasons, people have long suspected is not by Shakespeare (pp. 118–22). This distribution into two distinct populations is most unlikely if all the scenes were by one hand and the use of the 'to + verb infinitive' usage were randomly distributed amongst the scenes. There are about twenty such uses per thousand words in *Pericles* I–II (close to the Wilkins norm and unlike almost all other writers) and about ten such uses per thousand words in *Pericles* III–V, which is close to the Shakespeare norm. Simply counting how often the function word *to* is used corroborates Wilkins's writing of *Pericles* I–II, and so do unusual uses of *which*, such as *the which*, favoured by Wilkins and no one else and occurring in *Pericles* I–II (pp. 122–9). Jackson reports that Jonathan Hope's sociolinguistic approach says little about *Pericles*, because for most of the things he measures Acts I–II are like Acts III–V, although in the detail there are some things that indicate Wilkins for *Pericles* I–II; examples are use of non-personal *who* and 'non-restrictive zero forms', which means the dropping of relative pronouns, as in 'all the examples [that] I can think of' (pp. 129–34). Early in his career Shakespeare over-used the word *unto*, and late in his career he over-used the word *most*. *Pericles* III–V has few *unto*s and many *most*s, while *Pericles* I–II and Wilkins's other work has more *unto*s than *most*s (pp. 136–8). Jackson also surveys certain kinds of analysis begun by Cyrus Hoy and used successfully to determine what Middleton wrote, but which is of limited value in relation to *Pericles* because Acts I–II and Acts III–V are not unalike in this regard (pp. 138–42). (This should, of course, have been counted amongst the evidence against dual authorship rather than listed as non-evidence.)

A bridge to chapter 5 ('A Literary-Critical Approach to Style in *Pericles*') appears at the end of chapter 4 where Jackson reports some interesting verbal parallels and collocations between Wilkins's work and *Pericles* I–II (pp. 142–8). Chapter 5 itself is old-fashioned literary criticism and is the least successful part of this book simply because it is subjective. If one cannot hear the difference between Acts I–II and Acts III–V—and this reviewer confesses that he cannot—then literary criticism is not likely to make good the deficiency. Chapter 6 is devoted to summarizing and defending the case for Wilkins as the co-author of *Pericles*, and refuting the claims for Shakespearian sole authorship made by James O. Woods (based on imagery that is in fact commonplace), Karen Csengeri (likewise for diction), and A.Q. Morton (bad stylometry, especially for measuring the placing of words at sentence boundaries, which in fact is editorially not authorially made). Jackson points out that the consistent use of the two main sources in the play (Gower's *Confessio Amantis* and Laurence Twine's *The Pattern of Painful Adventures*) is not of itself evidence for a single shaping hand across Acts I–II and Acts III–V, because collaborating writers simply agree about these things. J.C. Maxwell (in the Cambridge New Shakespeare) pointed out that in Wilkins's *Painful Adventures* Marina does not know of her parentage (that Cleon and Dionyza are only foster-parents) until the dying Lychorida tells her, which is how Twine has it, and hence thought that Wilkins did not have anything to do with the play in which, of course, Marina knows her parentage all along. Jackson points out that this shows only that Wilkins did not know the second half of the play well: he had presumably seen it in performance but not having written these scenes it would be easier to plagiarize Twine on this point than follow what happened in performance (pp. 180–1). Jackson mocks the New Cambridge Shakespeare editors Doreen DelVecchio and Anthony Hammond's absurd adherence to all the errors in the *Pericles* quarto and their strained attempts to defend the misreadings, and hence he justifies the use of Wilkins's prose novella to help patch the deficiencies in the quarto (pp. 183–9).

Jackson's final chapter explains his 'New Technique for Attribution Studies', which turns out to be fairly obvious in principle and novel only in exploiting new technology. The idea is to look in LION for words/phrases (using 'near to' proximity searching for phrases) in the passage under investigation amongst the known works of the rival contenders for authorship, and to count the hits. One has to make the corpora of the rival candidates roughly equal in size, otherwise getting a hit amongst, say, Shakespeare plays means little if the rival is Kyd whose entire corpus is just *The Spanish Tragedy* (pp. 193–203). In the case of *Pericles*, the corpus of Wilkins is already tiny (just *Miseries of Enforced Marriage*) and to match this the Shakespeare corpus is reduced to just *The Tempest*. Unsurprisingly, *Pericles* I–II has many more words/phrases in common with *Miseries* than with *The Tempest*, and for *Pericles* III–V the reverse is true. Turning to the detail, Jackson reports that *Pericles* scenes IV.ii, IV.v, and IV.vi, which he expected to be more like *The Tempest* than like *Miseries*, are in fact more like *Miseries* so perhaps Wilkins had a hand in them (p. 206). When, as a test of the methodology, the words/phrases that *The Tempest* and *Miseries* share with *Antony and Cleopatra*, *The Winter's Tale*, and Wilkins's supposed part of *The Travels of the Three English Brothers* are counted, *Antony and Cleopatra* gives 'ambiguous results', *The Winter's Tale* shows up more *Tempest* connections than *Miseries* connections, and the *Travels* bit shows more *Miseries* connections than *Tempest* connections (p. 207). Jackson seems to think his test has come out rather well, but he is calling 'ambiguous results' the fact that *Antony and Cleopatra* (which is definitely Shakespeare's) has fewer links with *The Tempest* (definitely Shakespeare's) than it has with *Miseries* (definitely Wilkins's), in the ratio of 2:3. That is to say, 40 per cent of *Antony and Cleopatra*'s links are to *The Tempest* and 60 per cent of them are to Wilkins's writing. I would have thought this to be devastating evidence of the insufficiency of this discriminator: it finds a known Shakespeare play to be, if anything, unShakespearian.

At this point Jackson starts to (rightly) fret over the *Antony and Cleopatra* results and wonders whether the test is skewed by *Miseries* being almost half as long again as *The Tempest*. If we adjust the figures for this (by making more of the Shakespeare connections, proportionally) then *Antony and Cleopatra* comes out as Shakespearian again, but of course if Jackson really thinks that *The Tempest*'s being short has skewed the test he should go back and recalculate all the figures on the previous page: presumably the things that looked Wilkinsian should now seem a bit less Wilkinsian in the light of the greater weight to be placed on the (numerically fewer) links to Shakespeare (p. 208). Clearly still worried, Jackson turns to a subset of his *Pericles/Miseries* links to focus on just those that are unlike anything elsewhere in the entire Shakespeare canon. He produces a pretty extensive and impressive list of fifty-nine links, of which forty-seven are in *Pericles* I–II and twelve are in *Pericles* III–V, hence the former is by Wilkins. The ones in Acts III–V cluster in tiny bits of that part of the play (such as part of a brothel scene) that might also be by Wilkins; this might explain why the brothel scene is contradictory about Lysimachus's intentions in going to the brothel: Shakespeare toned down, but did not entirely eliminate, Lysimachus's vice (pp. 208–12).

Using Sarrazin's rare-word links (from chapter 3) it emerges that the bits of the brothel scenes that seem, on the new evidence, to be Wilkins's have links with the four periods of Shakespeare (*Two Gentlemen of Verona* to *A Midsummer Night's Dream*, *Romeo and Juliet* to *Julius Caesar*, *As You Like It* to *Timon of Athens*, and *King Lear* to *All is True*) that are distributed much like the links between *Pericles* I–II and those four periods are distributed. And conversely, the bits of the brothel scenes that do not, on the new evidence, seem to be Wilkins's have links with the four periods that are distributed much like the links between *Pericles* III–V and those four periods are distributed. Thus, although the sample of data is too small to prove much, the bits of Wilkins that we seem to have found in the brothel scenes are like the work of Wilkins in *Pericles* I–II (p. 213). If, as seems to be emerging, Wilkins had a hand in the brothel scenes, then the versions of those scenes in his prose novella have added usefulness in supplementing the *Pericles* quarto versions of those scenes. The important conclusion of the book, of course, is that Wilkins wrote *Pericles* I–II. There is no reason to suppose he ever wrote more than that (say, a full play), from which Shakespeare just extracted two acts.

Renaissance theatre was more economical with revision than that, and the likeliest collaborative scenario is that Shakespeare and Wilkins worked together as collaborators with an agreed division of labour (pp. 215–16).

His main claim effectively (indeed, multiply) proven—my quibbles notwithstanding—Jackson offers a couple of appendices. In the first he defends the view that Pericles says 'till she be married … all unscissored shall this hair of mine remain' instead of 'vnsisterd … heyre' (as the play quarto has it) on the grounds of the unemended text making no sense of 'till she be married'; it is not as if Marina would get a sister on her marriage day. (Actually, Pericles could plausibly be saying that he will not produce another heir, to whom Marina would be sister, until Marina is married. It is a wonder Jackson could not see that.) Jackson points out that *Painful Adventures*, which was unknown when the 'unscissored' emendation was first proposed by George Steevens, independently confirmed the emendation, and Gower and Twine's versions of the story also confirm the hair-growing vow. Although it is never going to be explained with complete satisfaction, Jackson surveys the theories about the manuscript underlying the *Pericles* quarto and concludes that Gary Taylor's account (in the Oxford Textual Companion) is the best overall. Jackson reconsiders the brothel scenes (especially in their repetitiveness and contradictions) in the *Pericles* quarto, in Wilkins's prose novella, and in the sources, in the light of the 'discovery' that Wilkins had a hand in them. In the second appendix Jackson gives the LION data showing words/phrases that each scene of *Pericles* shares with *The Tempest* or *Miseries* but not both.

Richard Proudfoot is a general editor of the Arden Shakespeare, and at an age when others might be thinking of winding down he launched its third series (the current one) in 1995. In a large collection of fairly short essays called *In Arden: Editing Shakespeare. Essays in Honour of Richard Proudfoot*, edited by Ann Thompson and Gordon McMullan, twenty-one Arden editors, past and present, pay tribute to the generosity with which Proudfoot gives away ideas that others turn into books of their own. 'In all fairness', write Thompson and McMullan, 'the name of Richard Proudfoot should be on the cover of every volume, not just as general editor but as, in effect, co-editor' (p. xii). Proudfoot's work has brought stage-centred thinking to prominence in Shakespeare scholarship, via Arden and as textual adviser to the Oxford *Complete Works* that so dramatically (in both senses) altered the scene in 1986. The second Arden was not stage-centred, but the third is, and indeed George Walton Williams argues that editing is itself a kind of performance directing 'for the page' (p. xv). For Thompson and McMullan, after years of division between editing and theory, suddenly they have come together (pp. xvi–xvii). The essays in the book are divided into five categories: 'Bibliography/Theory of Editing', 'Editing and Feminism', 'Editing and Stage Practice', 'Annotation and Collation', and 'The Playwright and Others'. Not all the essays are relevant to this review. A.L. Braunmuller ('Shakespeares Various'), starts with early twentieth-century comments on editorial notes and collations from E.M.W. Tillyard and Stephen Potter, but is primarily concerned with eighteenth- and nineteenth-century variorum editions.

In the next chapter, Giorgio Melchiori asserts 'The Continuing Importance of New Bibliography' but has nothing substantial with which to support that (entirely reasonable) claim. Melchiori rightly comments that Werstine 'could hardly be more unfair' for claiming that New Bibliography did not take account of the multiple, non-authorial inputs that could get registered in early printed texts (p. 19). Something goes awry in Melchiori's quotation of Stanley Wells: 'There is no doubt that Stanley Wells is right in stating that "The primary surviving texts of Shakespeare's plays represent those plays in various states of composition" and that none of these texts "necessarily represents in anything but in a definitive state the words that Shakespeare wished to be spoken or a larger action that he wished to be bodied forth" (in Elam, 340)' (p. 24). This is such an odd thing to claim—surely Wells meant that a definitive state was not available to us—that I followed Melchiori's footnote. 'Elam, 340' is supposed to refer to an article by Keir Elam but is in fact an article by Melchiori himself ('What Did Shakespeare Write?', *Textus: English Studies in Italy* 9[1996] 339–56) and in it Wells is indeed quoted thus, and the quotation cited as a letter to the *Times Literary Supplement* on 18 January 1986. There was no issue of the *TLS* on 18 January that year, and a glance at the previous and following years' issues shows that Wells's letter actually appeared on 18 January 1985. And, unsurprisingly, Wells wrote that we should not expect to find the plays in 'anything like a definitive state' ('Editing Shakespeare', *TLS* 4268[1985] 63) rather than the opposite as Melchiori's quotation has it. Melchiori concludes his essay by giving his views on the provenance of all the plays that exist in quarto form, without bothering to explain how he came to these opinions (pp. 26–9).

The next essay, 'Correct Impressions: Editing and Evidence in the Wake of Post-Modernism', is much better, and in it Anthony B. Dawson argues that we do not have to give up entirely our notions of the authorial ideal, only to moderate them. *Troilus and Cressida* at IV.iv.47 (Folio TLN 2434) F, but not Q, has '*Enter Aeneas*' and then both texts have '*Aeneas within*. My lord, is the lady ready?'. Is he within or not? This '*Enter*' could be the bookkeeper's reminder to himself to have the actor ready, and is not likely to be an authorial revision: it is unlikely to be Shakespeare saying, no, let us have him come in there, since the whole point of the scene is 'the pressure exerted by Aeneas's invisible presence' (p. 34). For the Oxford *Complete Works*, Gary Taylor argued that the '*Enter*' had to be purposeful, while the '*within*' might be a failed deletion, so perhaps he just stands in the doorway, making a kind of half-entrance. (In fact, work by the scholar who has spent the longest considering Shakespearian entrances and exits, Mariko Ichikawa, shows that an actor being 'within' did not necessarily mean he could not be seen by the audience ('"Acting Spaces" in English Renaissance Drama: An Unpublished Research Report' [2003]).) Later in the scene there is an '*Exit*' after Cressida's last line, which cannot be her exit as she needs to be silently onstage for what happens next. Taylor took this as an exit for Paris whom he also, like Aeneas, imagines 'at the door' rather than 'within' even though he speaks lines marked 'within' in Q and F. The trouble is that this staging makes awkward Troilus's line 'come you hither' to Paris, which is more easily spoken to someone offstage ('come on, get on stage') than someone in the doorway. Dawson thinks that perhaps this '*Exit*' is an error made by a bookkeeper looking quickly over the text, seeing that Cressida has nothing more to say, and so erroneously giving her an exit (p. 35). The scene, Dawson argues, needs Aeneas and the others to be offstage not loitering in doorways; perhaps the actors were keen to show themselves and so spoilt Shakespeare's design. Or perhaps, and the mistaken entry stage direction '*Enter the Greekes*' supports this, the manuscript underlying F was imperfectly annotated by a bookkeeper—who did not care that there is actually only one Greek, Diomedes, in the group that enters, only that a group enters—and the '*Enter Aeneus*' was him warning himself to have the actor ready and the '*Exit*' after Cressida's last line was him noticing that she had finished her speeches in the scene (p. 36). Sensibly, Dawson advises that, just because performance never quite conforms to a given manuscript (there are always the little flourishes not scripted), it does not mean we cannot reasonably treat it as though it does (p. 37).

Surveying how these matters have been theorized, Dawson relates that, for Jerome McGann, there is the 'text' (the 'literary product … as a lexical event'), the 'poem' (the place where this happens in 'a specific process of production … and consumption'), and the 'work' (the superset containing 'all the texts and poems which have merged in the literary production and reproduction processes'). For W.B. Worthen in *Shakespeare and the Authority of Performance* a performance is like McGann's 'poem', which can never be authentic because the 'poem' in this sense is utterly tied to Shakespeare's own time: there are only performance events in their own specific times, each of which is different because the time is different. McGann argues that the contingency of meaning—its being the result of collaborative forces (and, I should argue, conflictual ones such as censorship)—makes the author's final intention unsuitable as a guiding criterion for selecting one's copy-text (p. 39). In *Unediting the Renaissance*, Leah Marcus attacked the New Bibliography, but as Michael Bristol argued (and Dawson agrees) there is a difference between veridical and circumstantial evidence. The New Bibliographers were not trying to establish a single coherent history of the texts (what veridical evidence helps with), only a set of plausible explanations for the texts (for which there is only circumstantial' evidence; this is what Marcus misunderstood) (p. 40). Dawson points out the problems with Marcus's view—most importantly that a commitment on principle to 'discontinuity and rupture' is as ideological as a commitment to continuity and order—and insists that McGann's terminology does not give enough space for the idea, the non-material version, of the created artefact: there has to be a 'work' that is not simply Q or F *Troilus and Cressida* (p. 41). Where is it? Dawson answers: 'The text is born in the brain of its comically talented author, but when it grows up it becomes a book' (p. 42). With ideas like this in circulation, 2003 really was a good year for literary approaches to Shakespeare. The 'work', Dawson goes on, is a dialectic of the immaterial idea and the physical embodiment, and without some element of the immaterial in one's conceptual framework for editing you could not even fix the grossest errors (p. 42). Quite right. Just because Shakespeare is not the single author of his plays (they are indeed collaborative in a number of ways) does not mean that he is not the 'primary' author; he is, and his 'initiating authorial act', even though not wholly recoverable, is not wholly lost either: pluralizing authority does not undermine it completely (p. 43). And that, as Dawson observes, is one of the concerns of *Troilus and Cressida* too.

H.R. Woudhuysen's 'Early Play Texts: Forms and Formes' explores the peculiar phenomenon that printed plays had unnecessary blank pages at the front and the back despite this being an expensive waste. Generally the versos of title pages were left blank to prevent show-through, but that was expensive: Blayney reckons that when making 800 copies of a quarto about half the cost was the paper. We do not know who made book-design decisions. Compositors were paid by printers by the page, so the non-labour of setting a blank page was 'fat work' (as it was called), yet printers seem to have liked leaving a blank page, or even a whole leaf of two pages, at the end of a book to protect it when unbound. Such a blank end-leaf could be folded round to protect the title page at the front, and there developed in the eighteenth century the half-title to protect the title page proper. It is possible that blank pages and even whole leaves were there to make a short play seem bulkier in print than it really was, for the phenomenon is more common in plays under 2,000 lines long such as the first quartos of Shakespeare's *Henry V*, *Hamlet*, and *The Merry Wives of Windsor* than it is in longer plays. This would suggest that plays were not quite the ephemera we have thought (the point made also by Erne above). The practice that Greg called 'continuous printing'—not starting a new line for a new speech but printing it on the same line as the end of the preceding speaker's speech—looks like a compositorial trick to save paper (and so correct for casting-off errors) but it appears in Q1 *King Lear*, which was set seriatim. Here the effort seems to be to leave the final verso unprinted upon, since there is much 'continuous printing' on the last three pages (p. 57). That leaving the final verso unprinted was considered important is witnessed by books such as Q2 *Romeo and Juliet*, which increases its lines-per-page rate towards the end, but has an unprinted final verso. Ultimately, having described the phenomenon in detail, Woudhuysen admits that he has not solved the puzzle that, even though paper was expensive and worth saving, pointless blank pages were considered worth including in books.

Easily the richest and most intellectually stimulating section of the book is the second one, 'Editing and Feminism'. It begins with a demonstration by Suzanne Gossett (whose Arden 3 edition of *Pericles* will be reviewed next year) that, in the absence of hard evidence, editing *Pericles* is a critical, not a scientific, matter. In the play, Cleon asks Dionyza what she will say to Pericles about Mariana's disappearance, and in Q1 Dionyza replies 'That shee is dead. Nurses are not the fates to foster it, not euer to preserue, she dide at night, I'll say so' (sig. G2^{r}). H.H. Vaughan suggested emending to 'That she is dead. Nurses are not the fates. To foster is not ever to preserve', which posits minimal error (*is* to *it*) and some repointing, and mirrors the repartee in the previous scene about bastards being brought up and down in the brothel (p. 65). Gossett thinks that 'to foster is not always to preserve' is a good editorial aphorism. The Oxford *Complete Works* emended and patched the play wholesale while the New Cambridge Shakespeare edition bent over backwards to trust Q1, finding 'To foster it' acceptable because *it* can be the indefinite object of the verb *to foster*, as in Lear 'I cannot daub it further', and ignoring the problem of 'not ever to preserve'. The New Cambridge Shakespeare editors thought the *Pericles* quarto to be printed from foul papers because it is like the *King Lear* quarto (which probably was). However, Werstine has deconstructed the category 'foul papers', showing it to be metaphysical, and what is worse the New Cambridge Shakespeare's unemended lines of *Pericles* are often just gibberish. On the other hand, Taylor's solution for the Oxford *Complete Works* was vastly over-confident in the face of indeterminability and according to Gossett what the text needs is 'a post-modern, post-structuralist approach' that takes each decision locally (p. 67).

As an example of how feminism affects editing, Gossett notes that editors often have Lychorida exit after giving Pericles his baby as though she were too low-status to stay while Pericles welcomes his daughter to the world, but in fact midwives were well thought of. Equally, Pericles is often made to hand over his baby while bewailing his wife's death, as though 'a man cannot emote with a baby in his arms' (p. 68). Another example is Marina's startled response to Leonine's commission from Dionyza: 'Why would she haue mee kild now? as I can remember by my troth, I neuer did her hurt in all my life' (sig. F3^{r}), which editors since Malone alter the punctuation of to make 'Why would she have me killed? Now, as I can remember ... '. but the point is indeed 'why now?' after fostering her all these years. The answer (that Marina does not know) is the recent unfavourable comparisons that people have drawn between her biological and her adopted daughter, and the subtext of their being now pubescent (p. 69). A common substitution of a passage from Wilkins's novella for what seems a faulty bit of the quarto—Cerimon's speech about the cold and apparently dead being revived (sig. E4^{r})—is unnecessary and apparently motivated by a concern that the Egyptian should be male and hence should be the agent, not the recipient, of a reviving. In fact, there was much interest in cold, apparently (but not really) dead women in the period (p. 70). The peculiar repetition of Pericles' vow about cutting his hair (first said after Thaisa's apparent death, 13.29, and repeated after hearing about Marina's death, 18.28) is the consequence of an emendation of the first one, which reads: 'till she [Marina] be maried, | Madame, by bright *Diana*, whom we honour, | All vnsisterd shall this heyre of mine remayne, | Though I shew will in't' (sig. E4^{r}), which usually gets changed to 'all, | Unscissored shall this hair of mine remain, | Though I show ill in 't'. That is, *unsistered* becomes *unscissored* and *will* becomes *ill*, both of which are easy mishearings (p. 71). And yet, Gossett argues, a *wil*ful Pericles refusing to remarry and produce another heir makes sense when one considers the play's concern with dynasty and sisterhood. Regarding sisterhood, the quarto says that Philoten 'Would euer with *Marina* bee. Beet when they weaude the sleded silke, | With fingers long, small, white as milke, | Or when she would with sharpe needle would ... ' (sig. F1^{v}). This speech goes on about Marina, not Philoten, so editors often have changed 'they' to 'she' so only Marina weaves with attractive long white fingers. In fact, later needlework again comes up in connection with sisterhood ('her art sisters the natural roses', 20.7) and as in *A Midsummer Night's Dream* and *The Two Noble Kinsmen* the point is about 'the quasi-identity of young girls' being 'destroyed by competition for men', as Gossett brilliantly puts it (pp. 72–3).

The brothel scene of Lysimachus's conversion is often patched with lines from Wilkins because Marina just does not seem to say enough for the miracle to happen; to bring in Wilkins's version is to make Lysimachus actually a brothel-frequenter (he confesses it), while in Q he could be just a tester like the Duke in *Measure for Measure*. Gary Taylor's use of Wilkins here on the grounds of corruption in Q is inconsistent: the actor playing Marina is supposed to be a reporter, and she is in this scene, so the actor ought to have known the scene well. Taylor thought also that perhaps the censor cut the scene, but since George Buc began censoring printed plays from 1607 and Edmund Tilney continued censoring performances until 1610, who would have done it? (Actually, that uncertainty does not of itself make the censorship less likely.) More significantly, Shakespeare's *Measure for Measure*, and Beaumont and Fletcher's *Philaster* and *The Maid's Tragedy*, also have randy men of authority and yet these plays escaped apparently unscathed. Our modern objection to Q's version of the scene is its sexual double standard—Lysimachus is a brothel visitor, we suspect, yet Marina apparently does not mind—while Wilkins at least gives Marina a quasi-feminist resistance in her long speeches. Unfortunately, but unavoidably, argues Gossett, that double standard does seem to be the period's norm (pp. 75–6). Alterations in the brothel scene can be made on the grounds of strengthening Marina's resolve and resistance, and of weakening Lysimachus's integrity, and we have really nothing hard in the way of evidence to go on. It has, finally, to be a critical decision, not a purely bibliographical one (p. 77).

In the next essay, 'Editing Desdemona', Lois Potter argues that Desdemona is innocent yet sexual and that the Q/F differences can be seen as an attempt to get that tricky balance right. For his stories, the quarto has Desdemona give Othello 'a world of sighs' (as Brabantio says, a 'maiden never bold') but in the Folio she gives the much more sexually active 'world of kisses'. Editors generally prefer the demure Desdemona of Q even when using F as their control text. Alice Walker preferred F overall, but her views were couched in extraordinarily moralist language. To use Jowett's handy terminology, Walker thought MSQ a debased version of MSF; Potter reports this as Walker believing that 'the Quarto is a perversion of the Folio', which taken literally is absurd since of the two the quarto was printed first. (This demonstrates why everyone should use Jowett's terminology.) For Arden 3 Honigmann also thought MSF better, but because it was a revision of MSQ and not the uncorrupted source, and Honigmann held that in this revision Desdemona was 'protected', made less forward (p. 83). Certainly, a number of small Q/F differences (detailed by Potter) seem to show the Folio toning down the sensuality and loquaciousness of Desdemona, although Cassio's speech on Othello arriving in Cyprus and making 'loues quicke pants in *Desdemonaes* Armes' (F) is stronger than the same moment in Q: 'swiftly come to *Desdemona's* armes' (pp. 84–5). Annoyingly, Walker (one of the few women to do a major edition in her age) was less feminist than M.R. Ridley (the Arden 2 editor), and indeed editors have consistently been irritated by Desdemona's partial failure to be the demure girl they want her to be: she understands Iago's bawdy banter, and (in their eyes), should not (p. 86). The line 'O, fie upon thee, slanderer!' (II.i.113) is the moment Desdemona enters into dialogue with Iago, but although indented (to indicate a new speaker) in Q, it lacks a speech prefix so it might be Emilia or Desdemona saying it; F gives it to Desdemona. If Emilia says it, it is just one more example of her and Iago's marital bickering, but if Desdemona says it then she knows what Iago has been talking about (sex) and encourages him by responding. Honigmann ingeniously argued that Desdemona intervenes and 'places herself in the firing line' (by asking how Iago would praise her, II.i.117) in order to stop the marital bickering. The really tricky scene is IV.iii (the Willow Scene), especially as Q lacks Desdemona's song, and much of the dialogue, including Emilia's long final speech, while F has Desdemona say, with no prompting, 'This Lodovico is a proper man' (IV.iii.34), which might indicate that she is tempted to infidelity. For this reason, some editors have transferred it to Emilia. Desdemona's twice asking Emilia (in F) whether she would commit adultery for all the world might, Honigmann suggested, be due to a faintly marked deletion by Shakespeare of his first stab (pp. 87–8).

Potter wonders (without much supporting evidence) if the same thing happened with Cassio's hyperbolic speeches about Desdemona before she landed in II.i, and Montano's question, à propos of nothing, 'is your general wived?'. Editorial emendations tend, for later readers, to smack of their own times, as when Charles Jennens solved Iago's puzzling comment that Cassio is 'A fellow almost damned in a fair wife' (I.i.20) by changing it to the caddish 'A fellow's almost damned in a fair wife!' (p. 89). Honigmann's emendations too may seem dated to future generations. Although F seems a building-up of Q, there are places where Q must represent a cutting-down of F since there are lines in Q that do not make sense without the context for them, context that only F provides. An example that Potter draws from Honigmann is Desdemona's prayer ('God [Heauen] me such vsage [vses] send' at the end of IV.iii in (Q and F) that relies upon Emilia's preceding 'Then let them vse vs well' that is only in F (p. 89). If the song and Emilia's long speech were cut out to make Q, this might again be a sign of embarrassment: women should not talk so much about potential infidelity. Q2, like F, sometimes makes Desdemona more sensual and sometimes less, and Potter wonders if this might be 'the result of a general male inability to come to terms with female sexuality' (p. 92). It is fair to consider Q and F as two differing 'takes' on how to balance the sexuality and innocence of Desdemona, and although the sum total of Q/F differences is small, so is Desdemona's part. A few changes can greatly alter the characterization.

Barbara Hodgdon's essay, 'Who is Performing "in" These Text(s)?; Or, *Shrew-ing Around*', argues that modern editions of *The Taming of the Shrew* have much in them from the masculinist theatrical tradition and that the Folio text itself has potential for feminist reinterpretation of the play. Hodgdon begins with some fairly trivial objections to the editing principles of Gary Taylor (who, unlike Jeffrey Masten, seeks authorial origin) and Stanley Wells, whose model of the 'general reader', for whom one makes up stage directions, does not really match anyone. Then she gets specific about Arden 3's guidelines, which 'bracket off performance *as* performance', separating it 'physically and spatially as part of the Introductory matter', and which presume an '"original" theatrical life' that 'lies at the heart of textual editing'. These observations are true, but it is rather annoyingly vague to write that 'X presumably implies Y' without explicitly stating what you think about X or Y themselves (pp. 96–7). Like a lot of modern books that begin as documents created with Microsoft's Word software, this one has possessive apostrophes that point the wrong way (pp. 98–9). Overly prescriptive stage directions, Hodgdon complains, make impossible certain mental stagings that a reader might otherwise have entertained. For example, adding 'Servant spills some water' to gloss Petruchio's 'Will you let it fall?'

removes the possibility that Petruchio spilt it himself and is blaming the servant unreasonably; that is, it makes Petruchio less mad. Similarly, as H. J. Oliver pointed out, sending off a servant because Petruchio says 'bid my Cousin Ferdinand come hither' suggests that there actually is a Cousin Ferdinand to be fetched when the point might well be that there is not and that Petruchio and the servant know it. Just because dialogue implies an action does not necessarily mean that there should be an action.

Importantly, F has no stage directions for Petruchio hitting people: he is verbally, not physically, abusive. Many modern editions distort his character by inventing stage directions for him assaulting his servants, and even Ann Thompson's feminist Cambridge edition of the play has a cover illustration of Petruchio with a whip. This property comes from John Philip Kemble's much later performance of the role, and got into editions from the performance tradition. Indeed, the play's problematical reputation comes largely from the performance history, and as Stephen Orgel puts it, 'actors are the original poststructuralists, assuming … that the author does not control the play, the interpreter does' (pp. 100–2). Virtually all modern editions have Petruchio and Kate exit together at the end of the play, but in fact F has an exit only for him, leaving her behind. It is hard to see this as error since all preceding stage directions have them leaving together, even when it was hard to crowd this information on the line ('*Exeunt P.Ka*'). Since we have been importing material from seventeenth- to nineteenth-century theatrical tradition to our editions, why not do it consciously, asks Hodgdon, imagining use of the ending from David Garrick's adaptation *Catherine and Petruchio* [1754]. Then she imagines a performance following F—rather than importing *A Shrew*'s end-frame that too smoothly closes down the narrative as a 'masculinist power fantasy'—and leaving Kate onstage as a object of wonder (as though in a 'domestic' masque) who might or might not be thought to have been tamed (pp. 103–5).

Taking quite the opposite approach, George Walton Williams, 'To Edit, To Direct?—Ay, There's the Rub', argues that editors should intervene to fix faulty stage directions, even to show simply what they believe is the most likely staging. Like Peter Holland (and unlike Harold Jenkins), Williams thinks that the editor is a director, the page his stage; after all, directors always presume to edit, not least by cuts (p. 112). An editor simply has to fix faulty stage directions such as '*Enter Clarence, and Brakenbury, guarded*' (Folio *Richard III*) because it is clearly wrong: the latter guards the former, as the ensuing dialogue makes clear. Why privilege the dialogue? Because 'All editors will agree that the dramatist's dialogue is primary'. (Actually, they will not.) Williams surveys moments when an editor obviously needs to think up entrance and exit stage directions, and then startlingly asserts that 'The term "aside" appears in Folio directions only some seventeen times, of which about half are in one play, *Pericles*; the direction is clearly not something that Shakespeare thought necessary to include in his text' (p. 117). *Pericles* is not in the 1623 Folio; I wonder if he means F3 or F4. Williams declares that he is not going to get into the debate about whether editors have been over-prescribing 'aside' markers (the ones that make a character speak to the audience) and whether more of them should be removed to make speeches be given aloud, which makes the reader wonder why he raised the matter in the first place. Of the other kind of 'aside', where members of one faction on the stage talk amongst themselves, Williams notes that the term 'apart' could usefully be employed, as in III.ii of *All Is True*, where three factions form and multiple 'aside' markers would be confusing (p. 118).

Williams raises but does not settle the trickier problem of placing the kiss(es) in the sonnet spoken by Romeo and Juliet when they first meet (pp. 119–20). Most alarmingly, Williams quotes an article by M.J. Kidnie, 'Text, Performance, and the Editors: Staging Shakespeare's Drama' (*SQ* 51[2000] 456–73), in a way that shows that he entirely mistakes her to be taking his side when he claims that: 'The very difficulty, however, of the decision-making process implicitly validates the editorial activity, and behind assertions of the editorial responsibility to the author and the reader lies the conviction that the intellectually—even morally—upstanding editor is the busy editor'. Williams precedes this with the claim that, when editors are convinced about the need for a particular emendation, they are 'obliged to print that choice', and writes that Kidnie 'phrased this necessity well' (p. 121). In fact, Kidnie's entire article is concerned to make the case that this obligation does not exist; her tone is ironic and she does not think that making these difficult choices is 'intellectually—even morally—upstanding', quite the opposite. Whereas Kidnie demands that editors leave matters open, Williams insists that editors must print 'the instruction that they think "most likely"'. I am with Williams and, according to him, Proudfoot agrees, but the cause is not helped by again glancing at Kidnie with the remark that 'One critic wants editors ... to be morally upstanding' (p. 122). Would that she did.

Continuing the theme of stage directions, R.A. Foakes, 'Raw Flesh/Lion's Flesh: A Cautionary Note on Stage Directions', also thinks that we should not slavishly follow those in early printed texts, for the little evidence we have from playhouse 'plots' and the one surviving actor's 'part' shows that the different manuscripts involved in a performance could differ greatly in this regard. As research by Alan Dessen and Leslie Thomson has shown, there was a standard vocabulary for stage directions and there were special, unusual terms for particular effects. Foakes argues, *contra* Dessen, that editors should 'expand and explain more than is customary in such scholarly editions as the Arden Shakespeare' (pp. 125–6). Manuscript playbooks are sparsely and inconsistently marked up with stage directions, but that is because the performers had the 'plot' to supplement it in the theatre. The plot for *The Battle of Alcazar* has staging detail for the dumbshows that is not in Q, except the first and (because missing from the damaged plot) the last. Whereas Greg thought Q represented a 'drastically cut down' version of the play represented by the plot, Bernard Beckerman showed that in fact they agree structurally and in the number of actors needed. The plot is more precise in naming properties and actions than Q, specifying Q's 'murderous iron' as a 'Chopping knife' and 'raw flesh' for Q's 'lyons flesh' (pp. 128–9). Beckerman thought he could distinguish authorial (literary) from playhouse (practical) stage directions in Q, indeed he mapped this onto the two typefaces (roman and italic) used for Q's stage directions, but Foakes finds this unconvincing. Over his career, Marlowe's stage directions got sparser and less descriptive, as if in learning his trade he came to trust a kind of theatrical shorthand that he knew the players would understand. It may well be that authorial texts are more extensive and complete in their stage directions than theatrical ones, but we should not assume that these authorial stage directions show us what the players actually did: they might have chosen other means to the same effect. Edward Alleyn's part for *Orlando Furioso* omits and shortens Q's stage directions, but adds others.

The relationship between playbook, plot, and part 'seems to have been complex' and although William Long might well be right that 'nothing was done to the author's directions unless the players felt it to be necessary', that does not mean they followed those directions, for the plot and/or part might have something different (p. 134). Amidst all this uncertainty, Foakes wants editors to be bold 'in suggesting possible action' and to use Dessen and Thomson's new dictionary of stage directions to distinguish those directions that are the conventional, widely used, vocabulary and 'those that seem special to the author or play'. After all, the only actor's part we have shows directions not in Q, so editors might 'go further and look constantly for possible stage business'. Foakes gives the example of how he wishes he had dealt with the opening stage direction of *King Lear*: 'Sennet [or flourish of trumpets introducing a formal processional entry]. Enter one bearing a coronet, then Lear [in majesty, crowned], then the Dukes of Albany and Cornwall, Goneril, Regan, Cordelia, and attendants' (p. 136). I suspect that second word 'or' might mislead someone into thinking that Foakes is presenting alternatives rather than a gloss, so perhaps an ' = ' sign would be better. The point of the additions is to indicate the formality of the scene (which 'may not be obvious to laid-back readers of the twenty-first century') and to indicate that a 'coronet' (a detail from Q1 only) is less than a crown (p. 137).

Lynette Hunter and Peter Lichtenfels, 'Reading in the Moment: Theatre Practice as a Guide to Textual Editing', certainly agree that a feeling for the theatre is necessary for an editor, but like Hunter's work on *Romeo and Juliet* reviewed here two years ago, there are considerable problems with their essay giving detail about how the theatrical sense should operate. Hunter describes herself as a bibliographer, but gives an extraordinary (and pointedly non-bibliographical) reason for deciding to base the Arden 3 edition of *Romeo and Juliet* on Q2: 'Because we are interested in the social and political relations of the early modern period and how they have laid grounds for current liberal nation state democracies … ' (pp. 138–9). Apparently there is more of that sort of thing in Q2 than Q1 or F1. With a conceitedness that must offend several senior editors sharing the same covers as themselves, Hunter and Lichtenfels bemoan the fact that 'there is so little previous scholarly work that has wholeheartedly used the theatre' (p. 139). Contrary to preceding contributions to this book, Hunter and Lichtenfels think that directing a play 'is completely different to the process of editing' and give a very woolly account of directing that includes 'making possible the rhythms of the interaction of the production elements'; that sounds more like stage managing, having little to do with ideas and much to do with organizing people (p. 140). Hunter and Lichtenfels decided to mount productions of Q1 and Q2 *Romeo and Juliet* as if they were new plays, and in describing what this achieved they leave comprehensible English far behind: 'This made possible an experience rarely realized on the modern stage: productions that used a text with little editorial input, except as a physical object, after 1623'. It gets worse:

'We were struck by the inexorable power of working on collation, during which one follows the historical logic of particular decisions, and how this generates a physical musculature of acceptance' (p. 141). Such gibberish is itself in need of a firm editorial hand.

One of the abiding limitations of Hunter's editorial work is her absolute disbelief in the existence of error, which leads to such problems as the assertion that collation 'precisely locates the historical specificity of decision-making' (p. 142). Of course, collation should merely report difference regardless of cause, and such difference *might* be due to someone's decision (in which case a collation might help locate the decision historically), or it might just be random error. Hunter and Lichtenfels are quite right to describe how actors have managed to find meanings in things that editors have excised as error, but that should not be understood as a demonstration that the meanings really are there; actors habitually construe meanings from scraps (p. 143). The repetition of 'The grey-eyed morn' speech Hunter and Lichtenfels defend as implying 'an overlap of time that impels us from one scene to the other, constructing the illusion of haste'. Thankfully they admit defeat with the repetition of 'O true apothecary | Thy drugs are quick' in Q2's version of V.iii (sig. L3^{r}), since even the best actor cannot convincingly die twice (p. 141). Hunter and Lichtenfels think that keeping to Q2's punctuation can help in performance, as when Capulet tells Peter to 'find those persons out | Whose names are written there, and to them say | My house and welcome on their pleasure stay' (the end of I.i), which in Q2 is 'and to them say, | My house and welcome, on their pleasure stay'. Hunter and Lichtenfels think that the comma after 'welcome' makes the line mean 'They are welcome to my house. Wait to find out whether they can come'. Of course, it does not since no one can convincingly utter 'My house and welcome' as an invitation on its own.

Hunter and Lichtenfels admit that punctuation has changed its meaning, and they return to good sense with the observation that, in response to the Nurse's ambiguous 'He's dead', Juliet's 'Brief sounds determine of my weal or woe' might be a piece of swearing: 'sounds' could be 'zounds', which is spelt this way in Mercutio's dying speech: 'a plague a both your houses, sounds a dog, a rat' (Q2 sig. F3^{v}). This reading is strengthened by the fact that the Nurse uses 'wounds' (the origin of swounds) in the next line (p. 146). A couple of nine-syllable lines in Q2 Hunter and Lichtenfels found to be capable of 'a provoking instability' that 'could generate all manner of signification' (p. 147), but they decline to disclose any of these possible significations. Q2 has Juliet exclaim against Romeo (hearing that he has killed Tybalt): 'Rauenous douefeatherd raue<n>, woluishrauening lamb', which Hunter and Lichtenfels report the actors finding significantly irregular (p. 148). (It is pretty clearly an undeleted first thought; the first word should just go.) Hunter and Lichtenfels claim that 'Recent editions' claim to be based on Q2 but have 'few qualms about using Q1 where they prefer it' (p. 149), which is entirely unfair to the most recent edition—the one that their Arden 3 will be directly competing with in the marketplace—Jill Levenson's Oxford Shakespeare (reviewed here three years ago). Levenson refused to do this and edited Q1 and Q2 as separate states of the play-in-production in Shakespeare's lifetime, and reproduced both in her edition. Fittingly, Hunter and Lichtenfels close with a sample of their choicest gibberish:

'Reconstructive readings are specific to a cultural materiality; they depend on the ability to negotiate, to net together new grounds between oneself, one's context and the text, that will delineate the materiality of difference' (p. 154).

John Russell Brown, 'Annotating Silence', wants editors to think about the theatrical importance of silent action and to annotate for it where they can. Brown knows that this is a counsel of perfection—scarcely achievable in many instances—but he takes some recent editors to task for not commenting on (or for only commenting reductively on) the performance of the final battle between Richard and Richmond in *Richard III* (pp. 161–2). There is, he admits, simply too much to say about performance possibilities in the most interesting of Shakespeare's lines (such as Lear's dying 'Never, never, never, never, never') yet he maintains that simply sending the reader to a secondary text (as Stanley Wells does for the Oxford Shakespeare) is an abdication of editorial responsibility. Unreasonably, Brown thinks that an incomplete verse line implies silence before or after it (p. 165), which is a claim that crops up periodically without evidence to support it. The rest of the essay is not about editing at all but about directorial choices (especially concerning moments of silence) in performance and has some clear misprints: an impossible comma after 'father's' (p. 167) and 'chose' for 'choose' (p. 171). An experienced practitioner, Brown has definite views about acting: 'action and words [should] seem to spring from unspoken thoughts and feelings in such a way that the persons of the play seem to be alive in their innermost beings' (p. 172). That there are other ways to do it is clear from Bertolt Brecht's ideas, of course.

By this point, around half-way through the book, it becomes clear that not everyone gave McMullan and Thompson their best work. G.K. Hunter, 'The Social Function of Annotation', offers a pedestrian tour of 400 years of printed Shakespeare, with some fairly garbled assertions about annotation within that tradition. In a rather strained comparison, Hunter argues that actors were 'the first annotators' of Shakespeare's text, for 'they determined, by voice, by gesture, by pause and speed of utterance, the focus of significance for the words they spoke' (p. 178). A little misleadingly Hunter refers to the theatre company's 'copyright' on the plays passing to the printers in 1623, when in fact there was no such concept: the Stationers' Company rules simply protected stationers. Hunter summarizes the seventeenth- and eighteenth-century publishing history using the ideas of people such as Margreta de Grazia and Michael Dobson, which is all very well but unnecessary (pp. 181–8). As in previous essays, errors that should have been spotted remain ('honours' is spelt two ways in one sentence on page 189) and the contributor should have been saved from gibberish such as 'The gap between what the Cowden Clarkes' annotations offer as a representation of what Shakespeare was trying to communicate is particularly obvious in a modern world in which the vocabulary they use can no longer be taken, any more than can the neoclassical strictures, as an objective expression of what is there for us in the play' (p. 191). A gap can only exist between an A and a B, and Hunter's sentence has no B. Still lower in aim and execution is Helen Wilcox's 'The Character of a Footnote … Or, Annotation Revisited', which contains failed witticisms such as the 'character' of a footnote being dwarfish and low (like Hermia) because confined to the bottom of the page. Wilcox explains how (and using which types of footnote) she would annotate the 'virginity' banter between Helena and Parolles in the first scene of *All's Well That Ends Well* (pp. 199–204) before returning to irritatingly unfunny characterizations of footnotes as butlers to a longstanding house, or guides to a newly opened one. Ernst Honigmann, 'To Be or Not To Be', keeps his contribution brief: Hamlet's phrase comes from Cicero's *Tusculan Disputations* ('aut esse aut non esse') and is really, as Honigmann has argued elsewhere, about Hamlet's own death.

Eric Rasmussen, 'Richly Noted: A Case for Collation Inflation', argues that, although it is often unwieldy, historical collation is a good thing that editors should do more of. Rasmussen is working on a full historical collation for the New Variorum *Hamlet*, so the matter is in his mind, and recently completed the Arden *3 Henry VI* with John D. Cox (reviewed here two years ago). In the Folio text of *3 Henry VI*, the eyewitness to York's murder has the stage direction '*Enter one blowing*' (TLN 697, II.i.42), which many editors have interpreted as a reference to blowing a horn, hence he is a post. But it just means 'out of breath', so that is what Cox and Rasmussen gloss it as in their text, yet because they did not do a historical collation—they recorded only departures from their control text—it was not obvious that they were overturning decades of editorial error. Another example is that Victorian editors favoured '*the Queene embracing him*' (F's version) in the dumbshow in *Hamlet*, rather than Q2's more mutual '*embracing him, and he her*'; such things are of interest to historians of patriarchy.

John J.M. Tobin, 'Sources and Cruxes' (pp. 221–38), is still finding fresh examples of Shakespeare borrowing from Thomas Nashe, and thinks that we can use Nashe's writing to find solutions to cruxes in Shakespeare: if there is a Nashean analogue to the crux in the vicinity of the part that Shakespeare borrowed, Shakespeare probably borrowed that too. Taking just *King Lear*, there are within three pages of Nashe's *Pierce Pennilesse*: 'Hell … stench … darknesse' (like *King Lear* IV.vi.123–5), 'Fortune turnes her wheele' (like *King Lear* II.ii.171), 'Dover Clyffes', 'We, that' (like *King Lear* V.iii.324–5), and 'flyes plaie' (like *King Lear* IV.i.38–9) (p. 227). Those are Tobin's strongest candidates, and he has some rather weaker parallels between *King Lear* and Nashe's *Summer's Last Will and Testament*, *Have With You to Saffron Walden* and *Lenten Stuffe*. This last has 'a trundle-taile tike' so Q's 'tyke or trundle-tail' is preferable to F's meaningless 'tight or troudle-taile' (*King Lear* III.vi.67). Tobin goes on to detail *Hamlet*'s borrowings from Nashe's *Pierce Penilesse*, *Christ's Tears over Jerusalem*, *Have With You to Saffron Walden*, and *Lenten Stuffe* and then *Othello*'s memorable 'O beware my Lord of *Jealousy*! | It is the green-eyed *monster*, which doth mock | The meat it *feeds on*' (III.iii.167–9), which comes from *Pierce Penilesse*: '*Envie* [is] a crocodile that weepes when he kils, and fights with none but he *feedes on*. This is the nature of this quick-sighted *monster*' (p. 233). In the same book Nashe writes about the ignorance of Indians (not Judeans) about the value of gems, so that solves a longstanding problem about Othello's last words. Tobin ends with some examples of Nashe in *Macbeth*.

Things get sharply better with the penultimate essay in the book, 'Topical Forest: Kemp and Mar-text in Arden', in which Juliet Dusinberre argues that Will Kemp, not Robert Armin, played Touchstone in the first performances of *As You*

Like It and that Sir Oliver Mar-text is brought on simply so Kemp can have some of his usual fun at the expense of the Martinists. Unfortunately this essay is beyond the scope of this review. The same is true of John Pitcher's typically learned 'Some Call Him Autolycus', in which he argues that Shakespeare inserted a representation of himself into this character from *The Winter's Tale*. Overall, Thompson and McMullan's collection is an uneven affair. The best work—in the feminist section—is groundbreaking, but many of the more established editorial scholars are, to use a theatrical expression, merely 'phoning it in.

A couple of other books of essays contained material relevant to this review. Adrian Kiernander, in '"Betwixt" and "Between": Variant Readings in the Folio and First Quarto Versions of *Richard III* and W. W. Greg's Concept of Memorial Reconstruction', reckons that oral dictation was used in the copying of manuscripts in the theatre, and that this could be the origin of Q/F differences in *Richard III* (in Davis, ed., *Shakespeare Matters: History, Teaching, Performance*). Kiernander tracks the arguments over what kind of manuscript underlay Q1, up to the point where Laurie Maguire declared that it is not a memorial reconstruction. As mentioned above in relation to Lukas Erne's book, the latest work is Jowett's proof that Q1 *Richard III* cannot be based on a memorial reconstruction, reviewed here three years ago. So what is it? Part of the puzzle is the variety of small differences between F and Q such as *slew/kill'd*, *King/Sovereign*, *betwixt/between*. Printing generally destroyed the manuscript copy, so it is unlikely that the players sent a theatrical manuscript that they were using unless they never wanted to perform the play again or they had a spare one for some reason. Most likely, a special transcript was made for the purpose of printing, and it might well contain the latest changes initiated by the actors, 'even if it were being transcribed by the author' (p. 243). In an imagined world of proliferating manuscript copies of the play—the model the New Bibliographers tried to resist—innumerable small variants are not surprising, especially if a system of shorthand were used that recorded not sound but meaning. In the system described in Timothy Bright's *Characterie* [1588], a synonym might easily be substituted for a word not in the list of signs. (Painful as it is to admit, I suppose that early modern theatrical practitioners might indeed have been sufficiently barbarous as to put dramatic poetry through the mangle of such a shorthand system.) Of course, use of stenography was rejected by most New Bibliographers when it was a means of explaining what was thought to be piracy—memorial reconstruction being the preferred explanation—but as we no longer believe there was piracy we should reconsider stenography afresh.

The idea (perpetuated, for example, by Peter Thomson) that a scribe chopped a single copy of the play into individual speeches and then glued all the speeches for one role together to make an actor's part is not borne out by the only surviving part, Alleyn's for *Orlando Furioso*. It does not have a glue join between each speech, but only between sheets, on each of which is a collection of speeches that must, therefore, have been copied out together (p. 246). Kiernander rightly points out that it is hard to imagine a single scribe managing to do what we see in Alleyn's part for a whole play: there would be just too many heaps of papers, one for each of forty or fifty parts. It would have been much easier to do the copying by oral dictation from a master text with each of several scribes recording the lines for a few characters (say, one major and a handful of minor). During this dictation, slight revisions arising from the thoughts of the author–dictator, or indeed of actors acting as scribes for their own parts, might easily have emerged and been accepted (p. 247). Kiernander finds evidence of oral dictation in Alleyn's part: there are gaps where words (mostly unusual proper nouns) have been left out and filled in later by another hand. If the part were made by scribal copying of another document, then where the scribe left a gap because he could not read the word in his master text he would certainly have left a gap big enough for what he could see. But in the part many of the gaps left are too small for the necessary words to be fitted in, and this sort of thing is only likely to occur during oral dictation in which the scribe knows that he has not caught the word or words needed, but fails to leave enough room (p. 248).

A new book on stage directions in *Hamlet* produced three essays of relevance here. In the first, 'Variable Texts: Stage Directions in Arden 3 *Hamlet*', Ann Thompson and Neil Taylor survey some of the problems in those directions and give hints how their Arden 3 edition will treat them (in Aasand, ed., *Stage Directions in Hamlet: New Essays and New Directions*). Because they will be doing separate Q1, Q2, and Folio versions of their play, Thompson and Taylor are free to have each play's stage directions apply only to that version. For their main text (based on Q2), Thompson and Taylor will retain an act interval at III.iv/IV.i that they do not really believe in but which it would too greatly inconvenience readers (and those following citations from criticism) to change (pp. 29–31). This is too timid: if Arden editors were to go with what they think is right, others would follow. For their Q1 text they will use sequential scene-numbering only, and in their F text they will move the Act III/IV interval to where they think it really belongs: beginning Act IV with Ophelia's mad scene, traditionally called IV.v. Actually, they write 'IV.iv', but it is clear that they mean IV.v when they go on to write that '[traditional] IV.v becomes [our] IV.i' (p. 31).

In the second chapter of relevance from this book, 'Explicit Stage Directions (Especially Graphics) in *Hamlet*', Bernice Kliman (like Carl D. Atkins in the article reviewed below) finds the punctuation in the early printed texts to be meaningful and seems not to accept the principle that it is just printer's work and not authorial. Or rather, Kliman acknowledges the point but proceeds as though she had not. Kliman insists on reading line-end commas as a sign that the speaker is being interrupted, for which we might use a dash. She has certainly found some cases where interruption is plausible ('*Bar*. Long liue the King, | *Fran*. Barnardo' *Hamlet* Q2 I.i.3–4), but that does not make all such cases interruptions, and Kliman insists that some examples are clearly interruptions when they do not have to be. For example there is '*Bar*. Welcome *Horatio*, welcome good *Marcellus*, | *Hora*. What, ha's this thing appeard againe to night?' (Q2 I.i.29–30), about which Kliman writes: 'Horatio eagerly interrupts Bernard's salutations' (p. 79). Well, he might, but the text does not demand it. Abandoning all logic, Kliman goes on to claim that no punctuation at all at the line-end might also indicate interruption. The final chapter of relevance, '"… *and Laertes*": The Case against Tidiness', is by Pamela Mason and trumps this run of silliness by arguing that editions need not tidy up absurd stage directions (such as Q2 *Hamlet* requiring Osric to enter twice in the final scene without an intervening exit), nor variable speech-prefixes, because pondering these things can stimulate readers and performers to explore interesting corners of the play.

Turning to articles in journals, there were four items of relevance in *Shakespeare Quarterly* this year. In the first, 'Pancakes and a Date for *As You Like It*' (*SQ* 54[2003] 371–405), Juliet Dusinberre gets a new date and venue for the first performance of *As You Like It*—20 February 1599 at court—by means of a flawed elimination of the alternative candidate plays that might have preceded a surviving epilogue from that date and venue, assisted by acres of speculation. *As You Like It* is absent from Francis Meres's list of 1598, so it must be after that date—unless he forgot it, I suppose—and it cannot be later than 4 August 1600 when its printing was stayed (pp. 371–2). Dusinberre surveys internal evidence for the date, including Jaques' 'All the world's a stage' speech and the alleged allusion to the Bishops' Order for book-burning on 1 June 1599; she finds them unconvincing. There is an unsupported nineteenth-century claim that a letter once existed that named Shakespeare as being at court at Wilton in December 1603 and hence that *As You Like It* probably played there that season, but the only hard evidence for early performance is the document that grants Thomas Killigrew 108 old Blackfriars plays for his new Theatre Royal in 1669, including *As You Like It* amongst twenty-one Shakespeare plays. An epilogue to a play performed before the queen at Shrovetide 1599 turned up in the 1960s and Dusinberre agrees with its finders (and with Brian Vickers) that it is Shakespeare: it has the trochaic couplets that he favoured for epilogues (Robin Goodfellow's, Prospero's), and it was found copied into the commonplace book of Henry Stanford, tutor in the household of the second Baron Hunsdon, the lord chamberlain (and Shakespeare's patron) from 1597 (pp. 375–7).

Looking for which play the epilogue was for, Dusinberre decides at this point to exclude as candidates certain of 'the non-Shakespearian plays for which the Stanford epilogue might have been written' on the basis that we know that a couple of them (Dekker's *Old Fortunatus* and *The Shoemaker's Holiday*) were performed at court around new year 1599/1600, in which case they were probably not also performed at Shrovetide 1599. (They might have been, though, might they not?) Jonson's *Every Man In His Humour* was described as performed at court and 'new' in a letter dated 20 September 1598, but Dusinberre wrongly reports this letter as indicating that the play was performed *on* 20 September, which is not what her cited source—the Oxford edition by C.H. Herford and Percy and Evelyn Simpson—actually claims. As with the Dekker plays, Dusinberre too quickly excludes the possibility that it could have been performed again at Shrovetide 1599. Dusinberre's exclusion of *A Warning for Fair Women* and *A Larum for London* really is sloppy: she claims that they are 'too late for the new epilogue', citing the epilogue's finders. In fact those finders, William M. Ringler and Steven May, do not exclude the plays, noting only that 'there is no evidence that they were performed as early as February 1599' ('An Epilogue Possibly By Shakespeare', *MP* 70[1972] 138–9). It is not reasonable to date first performance solely from Stationers' Register entry dates, which is where Dusinberre gets the dates of 1599 and 1600 that she puts in brackets after these last two plays—although you need to read Ringler and May to discover that—because register entry gives only a *terminus ad quem*. Moreover, earlier in the article Dusinberre dated *As You Like It* itself by using Erne's suggestion that register entry usually followed eighteen to twenty-four months after first performance, and by this same reckoning *A Warning for Fair Women* (entry 17 November 1599) and *A Larum for London* (entry 29 May 1600) were performed too early to be Stanford's play, not too late. Dusinberre also seems to think that *Every Man Out Of His Humour* being performed in the autumn of 1599 at the Globe precludes its being performed earlier that year at court, without saying why and without mentioning (yet, it comes later) her position on the relationship between public performance and court performance, the possibilities for repeat court performance, and the notion of newness in relation to court performance. This whole paragraph of Dusinberre's is an evidential and logical mess and should not have been published (p. 378).

Having cleared away the non-Shakespearian candidates, we get the real reason why Dusinberre thinks it is a court epilogue to *As You Like It*: Touchstone makes a joke about pancakes (I.ii.61–3) and that is what the court would have been eating at Shrovetide (p. 379). It being 20 February 1599, in this performance Touchstone would have been Kemp not Armin. Ganymede had a special association with Shrovetide, and the new epilogue fits nicely on the end of *As You Like It* once you take Rosalind's epilogue off. The epilogue's references to a 'dial' (like the pocket sun-dial that Touchstone is supposed to have) suit the play, and also link with Shakespeare via Sir John Harington, who possessed such a rare dial and whose translation of Ariosto's *Orlando Furioso* is a major source for *As You Like It*; Richmond Palace, where the performance took place, had a famous enormous dial that was spruced up for the occasion (pp. 383–4). Perhaps having not entirely convinced herself, Dusinberre returns to the other candidates for the play that preceded this epilogue and, despite the epilogue's likeness to some things by Jonson, she excludes him again on the grounds of his being in prison from the end of January 1599 and hence not around on 20 February 1599. (Might he not have written it before going to prison?) Dusinberre closes with some loosely argued links between the court occasion and the play, including the idea that the Globe theatre could thereby open in autumn 1599 with a play that already had royal approval. (The whole official excuse for having theatres, of course, was to get plays ready for the court, and we know that public performance did indeed precede court performance.)

The next article from *SQ*, 'From Strange's Men to Pembroke's Men: *2 Henry VI* and *The First Part of the Contention*' (*SQ* 54[2003] 253–87), is much better, and in it Lawrence Manley argues that *The Contention of York and Lancaster* and *2 Henry VI* differ regarding the presentation of Eleanor Cobham, duchess of Gloucester, in ways consistent with the latter being essentially the earlier, Strange's men's, version of the play that was revised (perhaps when it came into the hands of Pembroke's men) to reduce the ambiguity about her guilt; the revised version is what lies under *The Contention*. Strange's men is the first company we know of that tried to have a permanent (or at least long-term) residency in London, staying four months at the Rose in Spring 1592 during which it gave 105 performances; the company was somewhat maverick and said to be defiant of authority. The editorial consensus (although Manley footnotes the dissenters and their range of views) is that MSQ is not merely a report of MSF but a report of a revised, perhaps abridged, version of the play as represented in F. *The Contention of York and Lancaster* gets associated with Pembroke's men because its sequel *Richard Duke of York* was printed in an octavo of 1595 mentioning Pembroke's men on the title page. It is not clear which company first owned *The Contention*, but there is 'a substantial body of opinion' that Folio *2 Henry VI* was based on a script written for Strange's men and edited/censored over the next thirty years. There is also a 'growing consensus', to which Manley will add, that *The Contention* quarto represents a Pembroke's men's adaptation of this Strange's men's play (the one visible in F *2 Henry VI*) (p. 256). The nub of this is what happens to Eleanor Cobham in the two versions, which reflects some topical matters. Ferdinando Strange's mother was herself accused of using witchcraft to predict the monarch's future. Folio *2 Henry VI* has Eleanor Cobham sent into banishment on the Isle of Man, the witch Jordan burnt, and the priests and Bullingbrooke hanged, while *The Contention* omits what happens to her accomplices and just has Eleanor Cobham banished (pp. 257–8).

Scott McMillin showed that the differences between the versions regarding Eleanor Cobham's sentencing (and indeed her earlier scene of conjuring) are consistent with alteration to suit a reduced cast. But also, Manley notes, in F she is condemned for witchcraft (which Exodus 22:18 says must be punished by death) while in Q she is condemned for the lesser crime of treason (p. 259). According to Foxe's *Acts and Monuments* (1563 edition), Eleanor Cobham suffered from the same anti-Lollard prejudice that killed her kinsman John Oldcastle and she was falsely accused of heresy. A Catholic response claimed that Foxe was inventing martyrs and that Eleanor Cobham was in fact banished not for heresy but for treason, and in subsequent editions Foxe back-pedalled, but insisted that false charges of heresy were the sort of thing that sixteenth-century papists habitually made up (pp. 260–1). Hall and Holinshed have Eleanor Cobham accused of making a kind of wax voodoo doll of Henry VI and harming it, rather than of foretelling the future; of course, the latter (with a devil and with prophecies) makes better theatre. In at least one version of the Eleanor Cobham story, she admits trying to foretell the future but without harmful intent. Topically, the law against prophesying about the life of the monarch (whether or not for harmful purpose) was reinstated as capital treason in 1581 after a period when the penalties had been lower (p. 262). In 1591, amid the Martin Marprelate controversy, a Presbyterian called William Hacket was executed for prophesying about the monarch, clearly as part of an attempt to crack down on Puritanism generally (p. 263). In propaganda it was alleged that Hacket had done voodoo-like harm to a picture of queen Elizabeth, which, the propaganda pointed out, was not what he had been charged with. This might be why the play turned Eleanor Cobham's voodoo into prophecy, but although that would reduce the topicality somewhat it also would have the dangerous effect of making her, like Hacket, someone who is tried for the merely heretical (not actually homicidal) act of prophesying, which nonetheless now was a capital offence (p. 264).

It was the real, historical, Eleanor's trial that set the precedent that witchcraft against the monarch was capital treason, although she was tried by an ecclesiastical court and hence got banishment instead of execution. F's version of the play has Eleanor committing essentially a spiritual crime and getting a (possibly unjust) political punishment, while Q's version has her committing treason. That is to say, Q accepts the new principle that her prophecy was itself a state crime and not just a spiritual one, and thus Q eliminates the possibility that mere papist superstition was what lay behind Eleanor's condemnation (p. 265). Persuasive as Manley's historical narrative is, this is rather a lot of weight to put on a few words of F/Q difference: 'Sinne, | Such as by Gods Booke are adiudg'd to death' (F) and 'Treasons … committed against vs, our States and Peeres' (Q). But this is not the only means by which 'Q follows the government's line' (p. 266). As well as the difference in wording of the accusation Q has Eleanor be more active in the preparations for the conjuring and makes it less possible for an audience to see her as entrapped by others: she has already written the questions, and she is more eager to get on with it, and more devious in taking advantage of everyone's else's being away at St Albans. F has the bishop of Winchester (as well as Suffolk) be behind Hume's temptation of Eleanor, and has Hume say more about his trickery of her; this makes her downfall more a political conspiracy than Q has it. Comparing the two versions of the conjuring scene itself (pp. 268–72), Q has Eleanor be an active instigator while F has her aloft and something of a spectator, and Q has Jordan ('a surrogate for the duchess herself') be active and culpable, and likewise when Buckingham makes public the arrest of Eleanor, in Q she is guiltier and more treasonous than in F. The bit of paper on which are written the questions and answers is clearly tracked in Q's version of the story, and it is the paper that constitutes proof of Eleanor's guilt; F, by contrast, allows hearsay to condemn Eleanor. Manley thinks all these F/Q differences show what Pembroke's men did to the play once it entered their repertory. Manley recounts the story of Ferdinando Stanley's mother, the countess of Derby, falling from grace for seeking prophecies about the monarch's life, and he wonders if that is why the F version (the Strange's men's version) is softer on Eleanor—so like the countess of Derby—than Q's version (the Pembroke's men's). Ferdinando Strange himself had a claim to the throne, and potentially was the object for a Catholic succession (or even a coup), but was inscrutable about his own ambitions, managed to alienate the Crown and his own people, and died on 16 April 1594. When did the play that became Folio *2 Henry VI* get revised into the play that became *The Contention of York and Lancaster*? A good time would have been after the anti-alien riots that closed the playhouses in June 1592, which seem connected, somehow, with the formation of Pembroke's men.

Timothy Billing, 'Caterwauling Cataians: The Genealogy of a Gloss' (*SQ* 54[2003] 1–28) shows that the word Cataians being glossed as a derogatory term in Shakespeare is just a piece of eighteenth-century racism (especially by George Steevens) being projected back to the Elizabethans, with whom it does not belong. The two Shakespearian uses are 'PAGE (*aside*) I will not believe such a Cathayan though the priest o' th' town commended him for a true man' (*Merry Wives of Windsor* II.i.136–7) and 'SIR TOBY My lady's a Cathayan, we are politicians' (*Twelfth Night* II.iii.72). Steevens's racist gloss—that Cataian means thief/cheat—has stuck, even though it hardly fits the context (would Toby call Olivia this?) and despite the fact that Cathayans were not so characterized by John Mandeville, Marco Polo, and Frère Hayton. It was an Elizabethan error (that we must not replicate) to call China by the name Cataia, which was in fact a Mongolian and outdated name for it: 'we must treat *Cataia* as a distinct discursive construction' (p. 5). Indeed, there was much confusion about whether China and Cataia were the same place, and not until the mid-seventeenth century was it decided that they were; thus it is anachronistic to treat the word Cataia from before this time as if it meant China: it did not. What Cataian actually meant to the Elizabethans was a person whose threats or boasts were not to be believed, and it came from (1) the exaggerations of European travellers about such places as the mythically wonderful Cataia, and (2) Ludovico Ariosto's Cataian princess Angelica in *Orlando Furioso* who was not to be believed, and a lost Elizabethan play called *Sir John Mandeville* that Henslowe's Diary shows was popular in early 1593 and which presumably popularized that traveller's stories (pp. 7–8). Billings traces Cataian in the glosses to various editions, and especially how Lewis Theobald's, Thomas Hanmer's, and William Warburton's insight that it meant an unreliable European's report of the East got displaced by Steevens's racist explanation that it meant an unreliable person from the East (pp. 9–17), and thence through the words chosen by translators of Shakespeare into a foreign language, including (ironically) those translating into Chinese (pp. 18–20). Finally for *SQ*, John Considine, '"Thy bankes with pioned, and twilled brims": A Solution to a Double Crux' (*SQ* 54[2003] 160–6), solves a crux in *The Tempest*: the correct reading is 'bankes with pioned, and twigged brims' (IV.i.64). *Pioning* is excavating (what a pioneer does) and it produces sloping banks of earth, hence it is suitable to the banks in the form of an adjective, *pioned*. *Twilled* should be *twigged* because it suits the needed sense and occurs in Arthur Golding's translation of Ovid's *Metamorphoses* (one of the play's sources) and in the same context of plants growing by water. Forced to explain how *-gg-* got mistaken for *-ll-*, Considine strains a little but does not push his claim beyond the bounds of possibility.

Unusually, an article in *Poetics Today* was relevant to this review. In 'Gadamer and the Mechanics of Culture' (*PoT* 24[2003] 673–94), Douglas A. Brooks links Shakespeare to Hans-Georg Gadamer via a basic misreading of the Folio preliminaries. After ten pages of asserting that Gadamer anticipated where we are now in matters textual, Brooks writes that the Folio title-page phrase 'Published according to the true originall copies' is a claim 'not employed on the title page of any other collection of plays published in early modern London' (p. 685). Actually, the title page of the 1647 Beaumont and Fletcher folio claims that its contents are 'published by the authours originall copies'. If Brooks sees a difference between those, he declines to mention it. Equally slippery is Brooks's claim that the printed page was 'essentially unstable' because no two pages of a given printed edition 'are identical' (p. 687). Well, strictly speaking no two things of any kind are exactly identical, but plenty of books appeared in editions containing pairs of copies in which page after page have the same letters and punctuation marks in the same order. I suspect that Brooks is referring to variants within print runs caused by stop-press correction, but he is wildly overestimating the frequency of variants if he thinks that every page of every copy routinely differed from its fellows. Brooks reads Heminges and Condell's exhortation to the Folio peruser to buy ('what ever you do, Buy') as being self-interested, worrying about 'their purse' (p. 689). There is in fact no reason to suppose that Heminges and Condell stood to gain from sales: the publisher's money was at stake, not theirs (p. 689). As happens so often that she must have considered changing it, Katharine Eisaman Maus's name is repeatedly misspelled as 'Katherine' (pp. 691, 693).

Edward Pechter, 'What's Wrong with Literature?' (*TPr* 17[2003] 505–26), argues that, due to misguided ideas about radicalism and theatrical anti-elitism, the New Textualism undervalues the literary in relation to theatre. In essence this, like Erne's, is an argument for a revaluation of Shakespeare's literariness, although like Brooks's it is marred by misspelling (Nevill Coghill becomes 'Neville', p. 509). The argument that the short quartos are theatricalized (cut for a fast pace, losing the wordy stuff not needed in the theatre) is, Pechter claims, based on an impoverished sense of what the theatre can do. Fourth acts are often reflective (and female) acts, and cutting there (as many shortened versions do) does not just increase the pace, it changes the gender balance (pp. 509–15). Thus we should not be afraid to laud the plays' literary qualities. Politics also gets in the way: we are supposed to reject the literary as conservative and elitist and the theatrical as radical and demotic, but in many cases to support Q because you think it more radical than F is to give up F's more interesting political material such as the complexities of Henry V's heroism and Desdemona and Emilia's discussion of the gender double standard. Moreover, the claimed Romantics' idealization of solitary authorship just is not true: they did not so idealize it (pp. 520–1).

Carl D. Atkins, 'The Application of Bibliographical Principles to the Editing of Punctuation in Shakespeare's Sonnets' (*SP* 100[2003] 493–513), argues that we should not treat punctuation as less important than the words when modernizing Shakespeare's *Sonnets*). The argument begins with a contradiction that mars the whole thing, for Atkins is not 'denying … [the] assumption' that punctuation might be scribal/compositorial and yet he thinks that editors should be just as careful 'about emending accidentals as they are about substantives' (p. 493). If one accepts that they are accidental, there is no sense in respecting them. Atkins points out that for the *Sonnets* the 1609 quarto is all we have to go on regarding the punctuation, and he rightly observes that, if an author expected a printer to put his punctuation right for him, an authorial manuscript might, paradoxically, be further from the author's intention than a printed text made from that manuscript (p. 494). The punctuation we find in Shakespearian early printed texts might be following a logic of its own that we do not necessarily need to disrupt, such as marking for breath rather than logic. This is clearly mistaken: we must disrupt that logic if we are to put Shakespeare into good modern English that uses punctuation for sense, not breathing. Atkins cannot believe that compositors would put punctuation in at random—actually, they might to justify a line—but of course he accepts that they made random errors, and he holds that we should apply the same standards to punctuation as to other parts of the text: firstly deciding if what we have is in error (in relation to contemporary usage, not ours), and if it is we must decide how the error came about. Atkins insists that we should never emend where to do so would be to assume that the compositor added punctuation where none was in his copy (pp. 497–9). It would be interesting to hear what Atkins thinks compositors did with authorial copy like Hand D of

Sir Thomas More, which is almost entirely unpunctuated, although Atkins's knowledge of printing generally is weak. For example, in a footnote (p. 499 n. 27) Atkins tells the reader to 'remember that the compositor set his work in his stick upside-down and backwards', which would be quite a trick if anyone could do it. The truth, of course, is that the letters are upside-down but nonetheless left-to-right. Atkins (or his printer) also consistently misspells 'forme' as 'form'.

Atkins dismisses MacDonald P. Jackson's compositor attributions on the grounds that they require changes of shift within a forme, which he (citing Philip Gaskell's primer on bibliography) thinks unlikely; in fact if the compositors were doing other work at the time such a change would not be surprising at all. Atkins decides that it is impossible for a compositor to choose punctuation marks during setting, so they must have been written into the copy during 'proofreading or casting off' (p. 502). Certainly they could be added during casting off, but not during proof-reading; I suspect that Atkins mistakenly thinks this means the reading of copy but in fact it means the reading of what has been printed. In another mistaken footnote (pp. 501–2 n. 37) Atkins thinks he can tell that the outer forme of C was printed before the inner forme, as it has an 'error' (an unwanted comma in the running head on one page) that is not on the inner forme. His principle is that such an error could not be introduced during skeleton reuse, only corrected, and thus C-outer with the error was printed before C-inner without the error. This is not so: error can be introduced during skeleton reuse because the type easily pies. Since a period was a perfectly acceptable mark to end the running head with (since it appears on others in the book) a comma could have been introduced to replace a space lost when the skeleton's type was partially pied. Atkins suggests some emendations of *Sonnets* that editors have overlooked but that are strengthened by an assumption that the punctuation is as reliable as the substantives; none is unreasonable, nor are any especially better than what other editors have done with the problems (pp. 503–13). The two blank lines within parentheses after sonnet 126, Atkins thinks, arose because the casting-off was made on the assumption that a sonnet has fourteen lines, and when the compositor came to set this one he found it had only twelve lines, so he added the two parenthesized blank lines rather than have 'an ugly blank space' (p. 512). I should have thought this a splendid means to draw attention to the supposed printing error rather than a device to conceal it.

Kenji Go, 'The Bawdy "Talent" to "Occupy" in *Cymbeline*, *The Complaint of Rosamond*, and the Elizabethan Homily for Rogation Week' (*RES* 54[2003] 27–51), argues that in *Cymbeline* I.vi.79–81 the word 'talent' means vagina. In this case, Iachimo says (and Go interprets) 'yet heaven's bounty towards him [that is, the big penis that Posthumus has] might | Be used more thankfully [rather than putting it in whores of Rome, as he does]. In himself 'tis much; | In you [that is, your delightful vagina], which I count his, beyond all talents' (pp. 29–31). In Samuel Daniel's *The Complaint of Rosamond* (published 1592) 'talent' means vagina, and in the context of an argument about how sexual sinning with a king is not really sinning at all—because he is God-like—that alludes to Isaiah 1:18, which speaks of God making red sins white again. Also, the Daniel reference uses 'author' to mean king (or God), just as does, many times over, 'The Homily for the Days of Rogation Week', which also refers to the biblical Parable of the Talents. Daniel's poem has the collocation 'author … redeem … sanctifies', which would have reminded readers of the Anglican catechism for the confirmation ceremony ('who hath made … redeemed … sanctifies') (pp. 32–5). In the collocation of 'lot … cast into … lap' Daniel's poem echoes Proverbs 16:33, and what follows is an allusion to Jove's showering gold into Danae's lap that strongly suggests that the good fortune that befalls Rosamond (the king fancying her) is the work not of untrustworthy Fortune but of sanctified Providence. The same point about distinguishing Fortune from Providence is the point of the second part of the homily for Rogation Week (pp. 36–8). Daniel's poem also alludes to the importance of seizing the moment, which is the subject of the third part of the homily for Rogation Week, which quotes the Pauline exhortation in Ephesians 5:16 to 'redeem the time'; this same phrase appears in Daniel's poem. Furthermore, 'the world' gets used in the poem just as it does in the homily, as something not to be thought of by godly Christians. The homily goes on to allude to the Parable of the Talents in connection with adultery, implying (again) that 'talent' means vagina (pp. 39–41). In the Bibles of Daniel's and Shakespeare's time, the servant who traded the five talents to make five more 'occupied with' them (the King James has 'traded with'), and this word 'occupy' was of course also a bawdy term. Yet 'occupy' was also in the homily for Rogation Week: 'we shall make account for that which God gives us to occupy' and so get the praise that befell the good servant in the Parable of the Talents. With the recent change in the meaning of the last word *occupy* (mentioned in the 1600 quarto of *2 Henry IV*, sig. D4^{v}), this threatens to become an extended pun since what God gives us are our talents, our sexual organs. The 1611 Authorized Version of the Bible changed 'occupy' to something else wherever it might be misconstrued as having a human person as its object (pp. 45–51).

Just one article from *PBSA* is relevant to this review, 'What *I Will*: Mediating Subjects; Or, Ralph Crane and the Folio's *Tempest*' (*PBSA* 97[2003] 43–56), and in it Vernon Guy Dickson finds a sliver of evidence about spelling from which he makes just a little capital. Dickson begins with the uncertainties that currently dominate textual studies, and responding to Werstine's work on distinguishing Ralph Crane's habits from compositors' habits reviewed here two years ago, Dickson hopes to offer a little certainty regarding elisions of the phrase *I will*: more than 1,600 times the Folio has *Ile*, 1,200 times it is *I will*, *I'll* only three times and only in *Measure for Measure*, and *I'le* twenty-seven times, of which twenty-one are in *The Tempest* plus two in *The Two Gentlemen of Verona*, two in *Measure for Measure*, one in *The Winter's Tale*, and one in *Henry VIII* (pp. 44–5). This list almost matches the list of plays printed from Crane manuscript: *The Tempest*, *The Two Gentlemen of Verona*, *The Merry Wives of Windsor*, *Measure for Measure*, and *The Winter's Tale*. *Henry VIII* Dickson discounts as an aberration: the words there means *isle* not *I will*. (So, contrary to his terminology, it is not the same word at all, just the same string of letters.) Dickson does not know why *The Merry Wives of Windsor* has no uses of *I'le*.

After the Folio was published, *I'll*, which was pretty rare before, became the standard shortening (according to the 'Helsinki Corpus', which admittedly misses much of the evidence), and thus *I'le* in Crane Folio plays might be his own *Ile* on its way to becoming *I'll* (pp. 46–8). When one analyses *I'll* and *I'le* usage by compositor, the man Taylor calls 'D?(F?)' has by far the highest usage of *I'le* over *Ile* (16 against 39 times) and compositor C is also pretty high (7 against 175), while the other men massively favour *Ile* over *I'le*. Confusingly, Dickson calls these 'higher ratios of *Ile* to *I'le* use' (p. 49) but they are not, they are *relatively low* ratios of *Ile* to *I'le*, being ratios of about 2:1 and 25:1 against their fellow compositors' ratios of about 300:1 and some infinities (that is, never using *I'le*). Dickson decides to confine himself to *The Tempest*, which was set by compositors B, C, and D?(F?). They all use all three variants (*Ile*, *I'le*, and *I will*) although D?(F?) is responsible for the majority of the play's *I'le* occurrences. Compositors B and C seem, on other evidence, to deviate from copy, while D?(F?) seems likely to follow copy, which here would seem (this is all tentative) to be copy that contains Crane's (relative) preference for *I'le* (pp. 49–50). Werstine showed that the distinction of compositor D from compositor D?(F?) might just be an effect of different copy on one man, and indeed it is likely that (as Werstine showed) Crane's practice itself has produced 'the recent scholarly splintering of Compositor D' (p. 52).

Last year was noticed the first volume of a new annual book, the *Shakespearean International Yearbook*, which had a cover date of 1999. Abstracting services show that two more volumes (volumes 2 and 3, dated 2002 and 2003 respectively) have appeared, but I have been able to get hold only of volume 2 [2002]; the third volume will be noticed next year if it is received. Stop-go production of volumes is not sufficiently confusing to defeat well-trained librarians, cataloguers, and indexers, so the periodical's editors invented a new confusion-inducing anomaly by giving volume 2 [2002] the same volume title ('Where Are We Now in Shakespearean Studies?') as volume 1 [1999]; such ingenuity warrants a peculiar kind of admiration. An entire section ('Text, Textuality and Technology') yields only two articles of interest. In the first, '"And stand a comma": Reinterpreting Renaissance Punctuation for Today's Users:-' (*SIY* 2[2002] 111–26), Ros King exhorts editors to pay more respect to the punctuation and lineation of early Shakespeare printings because they might not in fact be corrupt. After a longish disquisition on the biblical origins of punctuation systems, King remarks (as she did in a book chapter reviewed here three years ago) that the colon joined as well as separated clauses and should not be modernized to a period (p. 115). Even line-endings are punctuation of a kind, since Shakespearian actors are trained to stress the last word of a line. (True, but should they be?) King inveighs against editorial relining to fit Shakespeare into strict iambic pentameter, and cites David Bevington objecting to it, but ignoring Werstine's demonstration that interesting, non-metrical lineation is usually not Shakespeare's but his compositors' ('Line Division in Shakespeare's Dramatic Verse: An Editorial Problem', *AEB* 8[1984] 73–125). King takes an exchange between Antony and Caesar (III.i.28–36) and attempts to show that the unmetrical short lines in F are better than the editorially relined versions because they are in fact not incomplete but 'completed by silence' (p. 120). There follow more, fairly convincing, examples of how King would preserve F's lineation while altering the punctuation to convey what was originally meant by the lines (pp. 121–4), but the problem here is subjectivity. King is entitled to think certain editorial choices are not as good as the ones she makes—and she certainly has a good ear—but not to complain about those choices unless she has a method for making better choices, and she has not. Indeed, that here King records her work as dramaturg to an English Shakespeare Company production of *Antony and Cleopatra* indicates that the possibilities she is exploring are not closed down to practitioners. More power to her elbow.

In the second of the new periodical's two relevant articles, 'New Conservativism and the Theatrical Text: Editing Shakespeare for the Third Millennium' (*SIY* 2[2002] 127–42), Richard Proudfoot surveys the situation in Shakespeare editing from an Arden perspective, with particular reference to editors' engagement with theatricalization and what the New Textualism (which he calls 'new textual fundamentalism', suggesting dogmatism) is bringing about. Proudfoot claims that for his landmark Folio facsimile Charlton Hinman chose pages to show 'only the corrected states of variant formes' (p. 130), which is true, but he chose not by forme but by page. Hinman, Proudfoot notices, missed one: d2d^{v} shows a turned 'll' in 'hollow' in *Titus Andronicus* (TLN 1223) that got corrected. For some reason, having given the correct date of Hinman's book on the previous page, Proudfoot wrongly gives is as 1967. There is no equivalent to the Folio facsimile for the quartos, of course, because Kenneth Muir and Michael Allen's collection does not give a proper collation and they chose texts not by textual status but by convenient place of custody, and the Malone Society's series is as yet incomplete. Proudfoot is undoubtedly right to remind us that we have New Bibliography to thank for all the great facsimile books of the twentieth century (p. 131). These days, editors by and large do not establish 'the text' from the early textualizations; rather, they accept one of those textualizations *in toto* (p. 133).

Proudfoot surveys key moments regarding theatricalization that Arden 3 editors have had to address in a range of plays (pp. 135–9), including the questions 'Does Lavinia stoop to using "thee" when taunting Tamora?' ('to try [thy] experiments', *Titus Andronicus* II.iii.69); 'Does Juliet stoop to using 'zounds' when asking her Nurse to make it clear who has died?' ('Brief sounds' or 'Brief, zounds', *Romeo and Juliet* III.ii.51); and 'Does Miranda call Caliban "Abhorred slave" in reference to his rape attempt?' (*Tempest* I.ii.353). For the last, Proudfoot outlines the circularity of arguing from character (giving or not giving her this speech *makes* her character and to a lesser extent makes Prospero's too) and gives his reasons for thinking that the lines do actually belong to Prospero. However, as Proudfoot points out, our current gender politics make us want Miranda to say the lines just as previous generations' gender politics made them want Miranda not to say the lines. Proudfoot ends with a suggestion for a new kind of edition (based on what Stephen Booth did with his *Sonnets* edition): each opening has a facsimile page on one side and modernization on the other, so that less explaining of the alterations would have to be done. Ironically, the New Textualism (with its insistence on making an edition of an existing textualization) makes this possible even for multi-text plays, because each early textualization would be done separately rather than picked from eclectically. Also, rather than giving editors' names in the historical collation, Proudfoot suggests using date of publication in order to show what changed from age to age (pp. 140–1).

In respect of *Studies in Bibliography*, the slippage between cover date and date of actual delivery to libraries remains wide, and the volume for 2001 has just been delivered. It has one article of interest, '*A Funerall Elegye* … Not … *by W.S.* After All' (*SB* 54[2001] 157–72), in which Jill Farringdon uses what is called cusum analysis to confirm that *Funerall Elegye* is not by Shakespeare but by John Ford, and to announce that the dedication to it is by someone else again. Farringdon makes the absolutist claim that hers is an objective method of analysis that can show that *Funerall Elegye* is 'certainly by one author' (p. 158). Anyone not blinded by the mists of stylometry can see the absurdity of this claim: any writer might ask a friend to supply the odd word, and no test can hope to catch this. As is often the case in print, the URL for a web-based introduction to Farringdon's work is wrongly given as 'http://members.aol.com.qsums' when it should be 'http://members.aol.com/qsums' (p. 160 n. 14). Anticipating incredulity, Farringdon rather embarrassingly brags that the cusum analysis that she is using was invented by A.Q. Morton, 'Fellow of the Royal Society of Edinburgh and a Retired Minister in the Church of Scotland', and that it has been used in court (pp. 160–1). So indeed has the 'ear-print' evidence left behind at the scene of a burglary, and its 'forensic' champions talked a judge and jury into believing that it was as distinctive as a fingerprint; the poor innocent they convicted, Mark Dallagher, has since been released without an apology. Farringdon's cusum method is based on the proportions of function words that constitute a large part of what we say and write and yet are a tiny fraction of our total vocabulary (she offers *the*, *and*, *of*, *in*, *I*, *a*, *to*, *you*, *my*, *is*, *that*, and *he* as examples) and she thinks that, because writers as different as Dylan Thomas and Henry Fielding have more or less the same words as their most frequently used, 'This surely confirms the usefulness of using these vocabulary items for recognizing authorship' (p. 161). No, it does not confirm that: there are punctuation marks that are even more widely shared, but that does not make them distinguishing items. That all humans have ears does not mean that 'ear-prints' are distinctive.

Farringdon's tone gets increasingly tense as she goes on to describe media moments of triumph and disaster for the cusum method. She reveals that the tests rely on frequency of function words and on sentence length, but is rather sparing of the details. Importantly, she does not address the problem that a peculiar class of writers called dramatists are highly developed in their ability to invent the characteristic speaking of persons whose existences they have imagined for the purposes of entertainment. A dramatist writing a scene between a wordy pedant and a simpleton will write a mix of long and short sentences and sentences with lots of hard words and sentences with lots of easy words; the 'habits' of this writer are not his own but those of this creations. Having decided that the dedications to *Venus and Adonis* and *The Rape of Lucrece* are 'authentic Shakespeare', and having asserted again that cusum has nothing to do with style, Farringdon admits that she had to leave 'What I have done is yours; what I have to do is yours, being part in all I have, devoted yours' (from the dedication to *Lucrece*) out of the process because it is 'an anomaly' in that it 'departs so far from natural utterance' and so upsets the graphs (p. 164). I wonder if Farringdon thinks the dedication's first sentence is closer to what she calls 'natural utterance': 'The love I dedicate to your lordship is without end, whereof this pamphlet without beginning is but a superfluous moiety' (p. 164).

Farringdon talks the reader through her graphs, but she does not actually describe the cusum technique at all. It works like this: find the average sentence length (in number of words) for the block of text. For each sentence, take the actual sentence length from the average, thus giving a positive number for short sentences and a negative number for long sentences. This produces a series of positive and negative numbers (S_1 to S_n), of which the cusum series is (S_1), ($S_1 + S_2$), ($S_1 + S_2 + S_3$), up to ($S_1 \ldots + S_n$). Say one takes a block of seven sentences whose sentence lengths are, in turn, 8 words, 8 words, 9 words, 5 words, 6 words, 7 words, and 6 words. There are 49 words in total, so the average sentence length is 7 words (49 words divided into 7 sentences). The differences from the average are, in turn, -1, -1, -2, 2, 1, 0, and 1. Adding these cumulatively gives -1 (= first number), -2 (= first two numbers added together), -4 (= first three numbers added together), -2 (= first four numbers added together), -1 (= first five numbers added together), -1 (= first six numbers added together), and 0 (= all seven numbers added together). A cusum series always ends with zero because the total of differences from the average must sum to zero, since that is how an average is defined.

A cusum graph, then, is a trace showing how much variation there is in particular writing habit (here, sentence length) across the text, but presented so that at any one point the *total variation so far* from the block's eventual norm is visible. This is not, it should be noted, a new stylometric method—it depends on the old technique of counting sentence length, word length, and so on—only a new way of presenting the numbers that the counts produce. The same counting can be repeated for any habit, such as use of two-, three-, and four-letter words. Farringdon's claim (based on Morton's) is that for a single writer the plot of *total variation so far* of one habit (say, sentence length) should be the same shape as the plot of *total variation so far* of another habit (say, use of two-, three-, and four-letter words), allowing for rescaling of the Y axis between the two plots. In other words, one writer's pattern of deviation from her own norm in one feature should be the same as her pattern of deviation from her own norm in the other. If the pattern of *total variation so far* in respect of one feature does not have the same shape as the pattern for the other feature, Farringdon says that 'the sample may be safely assumed to the [*sic*] "mixed" utterance, or non-homogeneous'. I cannot tell if she means that the sample may be assumed to *be* 'mixed', nor whether 'or' is used here to mean 'also known as'; or is non-homogeneity an alternative explanation for the difference between the patterns? Stylometry stands generally accused of failing to explain itself in plain English, and this sort of thing shows why. Next Farringdon attaches the four sentences of the *Venus and Adonis* dedication to the four sentences of the *Rape of Lucrece* dedication to make an eight-sentence block. (She wrote earlier that she was excluding one sentence as anomalous. That would leave seven sentences, but the chart clearly shows that she used eight.) Farringdon shows the cusum charts for this combined block and indeed the sentence length and the '3 and 4 letter words and words starting with a vowel' habits do vary from their own norms in ways that have the same shape. That the two habits change together is, claims Farringdon, a sign that the author of the combined block is one person (p. 165).

Next Farringdon puts bits of *Funerall Elegye* into the blocks of Shakespeare, and shows that this makes the charts (of cusum sentence length and another chosen habit) diverge. It must be remembered that even when the text is wholly by Shakespeare the charts' lines only sit on top of one another when you rescale the *Y* axis for one of the charts and not the other; a mismatch might only be a failure to rescale properly. Indeed, in Farringdon's Figure 4 the two lines do indeed look like they would match up if only one had its *Y* axis rescaled. Moreover, this figure shows the lines for a block of four sentences from *Venus and Adonis* followed by four sentences from *Lucrece* followed by five sentences from the *Funerall Elegye* dedication, and the noticeable mismatch occurs *before* the *Funerall Elegye* part (p. 166). That is, the mismatch happens within the purely Shakespearian section. Did Farringdon (or the journal's editors) think the reader would not notice? More convincing is Figure 5, where the obvious mismatch happens in the *Funerall Elegye* bit, but nonetheless the mismatch has certainly started by the end of the twenty-fourth sentence (that is, within the Shakespearian block) and thereafter the mismatch is not great (p. 167). Likewise Figure 6 (for fifteen sentences of *Funerall Elegye* followed by thirty sentences of *The Tempest*) shows clear mismatch *before* the end of the *Funerall Elegye* part. Trying *Funerall Elegye* with Ford's known work, Farringdon finds a clear match and hence her primary conclusion that the Ford attribution is correct (p. 168). The problem of Farringdon's dodgy charts gets worse as she now starts inserting the foreign material not at the end of the block but in the middle. (No explanation for this change of method is given, nor how it relates to the overall stylometric rationale.) Farringdon's Figure 9, showing 'Ten sentences of the *Elegye* with its dedication inserted at sentence 6', is labelled (at sentence 6) 'insertion causes separation', which is why she claims that the dedication was not by Ford. Yet anyone looking at the chart can clearly see there was separation at sentence 4 and at sentence 5 and that the lines come together again thereafter so that at sentences 8 (the inserted dedication), 9 (the inserted dedication), and 12 (back to the poem) they are united (p. 17). The conclusions of this article should not, on this evidence, be trusted, and the whole thing brings no credit to *Studies in Bibliography*.

David M. Bergeron, '*All's Well That Ends Well*: Where Is Violenta?' (*EIRC* 29[2003] 171–84), argues that excising the character Violenta from *All's Well That Ends Well* is a decision that editors should at least defend with an argument. The opening stage direction of III.v in the Folio text is '*A Tucket afarre off* | *Enter old Widdow of Florence, her daughter Violenta and Mariana, with other Citizens*' (TLN 1602). There are no lines for Violenta in the scene, but there are for a character called Diana who is not mentioned as entering, so one might simply think that Violenta equals Diana. Bergeron surveys the editorial treatment of Violenta (usually, simple removal) and argues that her being silently present can be in itself an important function. After all, if we are removing silent figures, why not remove 'the whole army' who troop across the stage in this scene (pp. 171–7)? The obvious answer is that their stage direction gives them something to do—troop across the stage—while Violenta has nothing to do or say. Bergeron has one piece of real argument to offer (pp. 178–9). We know that the group of women that begins III.v is Old Widow, Mariana, Diana, and (entering to them after a few dozen lines) Helen, because they all talk, and perhaps there is a silent Violenta with them. Near the end of the scene the Old Widow invites Helen to eat with her and Helen asks that 'this Matron, and this gentle Maide' should join them too and '*Both*'. answer 'Wee'l take your offer kindly' (TLN 1729). Who is meant by '*Both*'? As Bergeron points out, the Old Widow and her daughter Diana do not need permission to dine at their own house, so the 'both' has to be two other people: therefore, it is Mariana and another, and hence Violenta is present. Fatally, Bergeron has mistaken the nature of Helen's offer, which is not just to pay for everyone's dinner but also to bestow 'some precepts' on 'this Virgin' (that is, Diana), so Mariana ('this Matron') may be saying thanks for the dinner invitation and Diana ('this gentle Maide') for the offer of words of wisdom from a pilgrim. Bergeron thinks that Violenta highlights the limitations of New Bibliography, with its Platonic ideals of textual purity. I would respond that this is not Platonism: editors who remove Violenta hold that Shakespeare himself would have removed her had he realized what he had done. The ideal is not in an ethereal realm but in potential reality. Bergeron says that the authorial manuscript by reference to which Stanley Wells and Gary Taylor for the Oxford *Complete Works* edited the play is one 'that the editors have imagined' (p. 181). They imagined its particularities, for sure (since it is lost), but not its existence: that there once was one is a certainty.

The 2003 issues of *The Library* contained nothing of interest to this review. It is difficult to track the output of the journal *TEXT: An Interdisciplinary Annual of Textual Studies*, the subtitle of which is needed to distinguish it from a journal of the same name in a sister discipline. Volumes 12 and 13 of the journal *TEXT* are dated 1999 and 2000 on the title pages and their copyright notices, but volume 14 is dated 2002 on its title page and its copyright notice and volume 15 is dated 2002 on its title page and 2003 on its copyright notice. Presumably, volume 14 should have been dated 2001 ('2002' being simply an error) and volume 15 was meant to appear in 2002 but actually slipped out a little late; one can put what one likes on a title page but a copyright notice has legal force and must needs admit what really happened. The two latest volumes—14 [2001] and 15 [2002]—contain no articles of interest noticed here; volume 16 [2003] will be noticed when it appears. In *Shakespeare Newsletter*, Bernice Kliman, '"Cum notis variorum": A Nineteenth-Century "Restorer" of Shakespeare's True Text: David Maclachlan's *Hamlet*' (*ShN* 53[2003] 15–16), reports on the fairly wild emendations made by editor David Maclachan in his 1888 edition of *Hamlet*, presumably arising from her work on the New Variorum edition of that play.

In the *Times Literary Supplement*, Brian Vickers argues (under a cryptic title) that *A Lover's Complaint* is not by Shakespeare but by John Davies of Hereford ('A Rum "Do"', *TLS* 5253[2003] 13–15). The poem just does not sound Shakespearian—there is some poetic ineptness unlike him—and its only connection with Shakespeare is that Thomas Thorpe printed it in the 1609 *Sonnets* quarto that may or may not have been authorized. The poem does have certain rather Spenserian things about it, including the setting, particular images, and the form, and especially pleonastic *do* (hence this article's title?). Vickers ran some words and phrases from *A Lover's Complaint* through LION: *maund*, *forbod*, *affectedly*, *rocky heart*, and *fell rage*. The only person who uses all five is John Davies of Hereford (1564–1618). A Spenser imitator, Davies was fond of pleonastic *do* and (like the *Lover's Complaint* poet) had a host of almost risible tricks to make a rhyme work. Davies was an avid coiner of words that no one took up, and certain overdone images such as love-letters in blood are common to *A Lover's Complaint* and Davies and are not found elsewhere. A Stationers' Register entry for 3 January 1600 has a book called '*Amours* by JD.' entered at the same as '*certen oy*[r] [other] *sonnetes* by WS.' entered to Eleazor Edgar, which initials might be for J[ohn] D[avies] and W[illam] S[hakespeare], although Vickers wisely does not press this point else he would have to explain Edgar's possession of copy for Shakespeare's *Sonnets*.

Finally, to *Notes and Queries*. Paul Hammond, 'Sources for Shakespeare's Sonnets 87 and 129 in *Tottel's Miscellany* and Puttenham's *The Arte of English Poesie*' (*N&Q* 50[2003] 407–10), finds where Shakespeare got certain poetical phrases and rhymes. Sonnet 129 owes a debt to a sonnet by Lord Vaux in *Tottel's Miscellany* [1557], sharing language about infection, and about the dissatisfaction that ensues upon the consummation of hotly pursued lust, expressed by figures of asyndeton or brachylogia (both meaning the suppression of conjunctions, so list-making) such as 'perjured, murd'rous, bloody, full of blame, | Savage, extreme, rude, cruel, not to trust'. There is a similar poem (a response? a copy?) in George Puttenham's *The Arte of English Poesie* [1589] that seems to have given Shakespeare the adjectival phrase 'not to trust', which occurs in sonnet 129—in both poems it is at a line ending—and nowhere else in contemporary literature. Shakespeare copied Puttenham's *deserving/swerving* rhyme for his sonnet 87 (it occurs nowhere else in poetry of the time), and also seems to be showing that he can do the verse form tricks that Puttenham is illustrating. In the first of four articles this year, Thomas Merriam, 'Correspondences in *More* and *Hoffman*' (*N&Q* 50[2003] 410–14), claims that the stylometry in Vickers's book *Shakespeare, Co-author* (reviewed here last year) concerning the hands in *Sir Thomas More* was flawed by his failure to do the proper 'negative check'. Vickers was wrong to endorse the claim that one can distinguish Henry Chettle's part of *Sir Thomas More* from Munday's on the basis of its use of *twixt*, *nere*, *yond*, and *for to* that Chettle was supposed to prefer and others not. In fact, in the only certain Chettle play, *The Tragedy of Hoffman*, there is no *twixt*, four *nere*, no *yond*, and one *for to*. But there is a *for to* in Munday's *John a Kent*, so the evidence is just that use of *nere* (p. 410). Vickers picked up the four words he thought were markers of Chettle from Jowett's work on what Chettle (presumed by Jowett on other evidence to be the writer at this point) does in *Sir Thomas More*, so the argument is circular.

Likewise, Jowett's hunch that Chettle's liking of the words *hurt* and *remedy* could be a possible way to distinguish him from Munday becomes, in Vickers's hands, a much stronger distinguisher than Jowett meant it to be. Also, some of *Sir Thomas More*'s uses of *hurt* and *remedy* come directly from Holinshed and should be discounted (p. 411). Merriam agrees with Jowett's view that many of these allegedly distinguishing traits (and others including certain rhyme pairs) are useless because others writers have them too; like poor Dallagher's 'ear-print' they are common to many. Merriam points out that 'negative checking' (making sure an alleged similarity between known-author-text-A and unknown-author-text-B is not simply a commonplace) using LION is frustratingly awkward because of original spelling, using as his illustration the fourteen ways that *to thee* could appear (p. 414). In this, Merriam is mistaken, since the search 'to? FBY.1 th??' would catch all of these because the wildcard character '?' stands for '0 or 1 occurrences of any character'. To be fair, the online documentation provided with LION is also wrong on this point, claiming that '?' stands for just one occurrence of any character. That is not what computer programmers (to whom such things are everyday affairs) would expect the character to mean and it is not indeed what the LION database software (written by programmers) actually does with this term. To illustrate this, one might try a LION search for 'm??n', which according to the documentation should return only four-letter words but in fact returns three-letter words (such as *man*, *men*) as well as four-letter words (such as *mean*, *moan*). The only flaw in my suggestion for Merriam's search would be that one would have to eliminate the false positive *to them*, but that is easily accomplished with a logical NOT. Merriam includes *ye* as a form of *thee* which in fact one might want to isolate, but if not it could easily be incorporated with a logical OR.

Horst Breur, in 'Hamlet's "Dram of Eale" Reconsidered' (*N&Q* 50[2003] 416–19), thinks that Hamlet's 'dram of eale' should be 'dram of gall'. Whatever it is a dram of, it should be a concrete noun not an abstract thing like evil (because 'dram' suggests concreteness). The speech is about slander, and what is used to slander? The tongue. That is what makes humans serpent-like, and their equivalent of a serpent's poison is their gall, so the solution to the 'dram of eale' crux is 'dram of gall'. Breuer decides to 'leave it to the handwriting specialists' (p. 419) whether that is a likely misreading, but one does not have to be a specialist to see that with most hands it is a pretty unlikely confusion. It requires *g* to be misread as *e* and *l* to be misread as *e* too. The latter is not too hard in many secretary or italic hands, but in both the former error (*g* to *e*) is most unlikely as the descending loop of *g* is pretty clear, and to read such differing letters as *g* and *l* as both being *e* is hard to do too. It would, I suppose, have been a little less hard if for some reason the *g* were a capital. Thomas Merriam's second note, 'Taylor's Method Applied to Shakespeare and Fletcher' (*N&Q* 50[2003] 419–23), argues that Gary Taylor's function-word tests to discriminate Shakespeare from Fletcher can be refined, and the refinement used to more accurately apportion their shares in *Henry VIII*. Taylor's ten function words used in the Textual Companion to the Oxford *Complete Works* do not distinguish Fletcher from Shakespeare particularly well. When you have two known authors, you can pick your function words to be ones that their habits diverge over and that each dramatist is personally consistent about. For Shakespeare and Fletcher the good words are *all, dare, hath, in, must, sure*, and *too*. Once you know the standard deviation—how often Shakespeare himself will use a function word unusually often (for him) or unusually infrequently (for him)—you can say how likely it is that the frequency observed in a particular play will be a normal occurrence within the work of the given writer, and hence how likely that in fact it is not that writer's (anticipated) unusual behaviour, but the behaviour of another writer (p. 420). Doing the function word frequency testing for the thirty-six Shakespeare Folio plays, and a handful of Fletcher's, the Fletcher ones often show frequencies that would be highly anomalous for Shakespeare (p. 421). So much so, in fact, that by far the most plausible explanation is that they are not by Shakespeare (and indeed we know that they are Fletcher plays). Dividing *Henry VIII* up the way that James Spedding does and testing each separately by this function-word method, the Shakespeare parts come out like Shakespeare and the Fletcher parts come out mostly not like Shakespeare, so that is a confirmation of Spedding's division. Readjusting the boundaries between Shakespeare's and Fletcher's parts of *Henry VIII*, however, we can get Shakespeare's parts to come out like Shakespeare and Fletcher's to come out *totally* unlike Shakespeare, so this division of the shares is even better than Spedding's (p. 422). Merriam gives his usual Principal Component Analysis (PCA) diagram showing how the populations (Shakespeare plays and Fletcher plays) occupy different regions of the grid, and as usual he does not explain PCA well (p. 423).

Merriam's next note, 'Though This be Supplementarity, Yet There is Method In't' (*N&Q* 50[2003] 423–6), also makes slight adjustments to the boundaries of the Fletcher and Shakespeare shares in *Henry VIII*, but by a different method. Merriam starts by citing Gordon McMullan's Arden 3 edition of the play in order to mock the editor's closing statement about the two dramatists' 'supplementarity', and to claim that the use of the word *conscience* challenges McMullan's position. *Conscience* occurs twenty-four times in the play, the highest in the canon and twice as high as the count for the next highest use, *Henry V*. Charting usage of *all*, *are*, *conscience*, *did*, *'em*, feminine endings, *find, from*, *hath*, *in*, *is*, *it*, *little*, *-ly*, *must*, *now*, *sure*, *they*, *'tis*, *too*, and *elsewhere*, Merriam is able to produce a chart in which positive slopes roughly correspond to Shakespeare sections and negative slopes correspond to Fletcher sections. Merriam calls the chart a 'cumulative sum' graph, which sounds like the technique described above in relation to Farringdon's article, but it appears to be simpler than that: Merriam seems to have divided the current total count for all the features being watched for by the current line number, so that the slope is always either going up (when there is a hit) or down (for every line where there is not) (p. 423). Looking at each use of *conscience* and whether it is ironic, there is a good fit between the ironic/non-ironic distinction and the Shakespeare/Fletcher distinction as attributed by Spedding and Jonathan Hope. That is, it looks like Shakespeare is almost always ironic in his use of *conscience* in this play, and Fletcher is almost always non-ironic. Using the chart that Merriam thinks shows Shakespeare's preference for the twenty-one features listed above, Merriam proposes that Shakespeare was always ironic with *conscience* in this play (we know he used it to mean *vagina*, because of the *con-/cunt* pun) and Fletcher never was, and hence that the dividing lines between the two dramatists' shares of the play need to be altered slightly to accommodate this (p. 434). The alternative is for criticism of the play to interpret the evidence conceptually (as McMullan has)—to give Fletcher some ironic moments that really belong to Shakespeare—and thereby in fact, according to Merriam, blunt the sharp Shakespearian wit (p. 435).

Charles Cathcart's amusing note, '*Histriomastix*, *Hamlet*, and the "Quintessence of Duckes"' (*N&Q* 50[2003] 427–30), claims that the play *Histriomastix* alludes to Hamlet's 'quintessence of dust' speech with one about the 'quintessence of ducks'. In *Every Man Out of His Humour*, Jonson has Fastidius give a speech that uses 'apprehension', 'angellical', 'quintessence', 'the verie christall crowne of the skie', and 'delights', and hence sounds like it is making fun of Hamlet's 'I have of late … quintessence of dust' speech. We know that *Every Man Out of His Humour* is complexly linked to *Histriomastix*, and the simplest explanation for what seems to be two-way traffic between those plays is that *Every Man Out* was first performed, then *Histriomastix* mocked it, then extra material was written for *Every Man Out* to mock *Histriomastix* in turn. In *Histriomastix* Velure and Lyon-rash enter 'with a water-spaniel and a duck' and Vourchier says 'One of the goodliest Spaniels I have seene' to which Lyon-rash responds 'And heer's the very quintessence of Duckes', which is an allusion to Hamlet's talk about man as the paragon of animals. Cathcart ends by trying to work out how this might fit into Marston's career, if he did indeed write *Histriomastix* (p. 430). Katherine Duncan-Jones, '"Three partes are past": The Earliest Performances of Shakespeare's First Tetralogy' (*N&Q* 50[2003] 20–1), has evidence that *1*, *2*, and *3 Henry VI* were in performance before the mid-1592 playhouse closure, and that *Richard III* was not. In 1593 Giles Fletcher's *Licia, or Poems of Love* was published, and it included a poem about Richard III that begins 'The Stage is set, for stately matter fitte, | *Three partes* are past, which Prince-like acted were, | To play *the fourth*, requires a Kingly witte, Else shall my muse, their muses not come nere. | Sorrow sit downe, and helpe my muse to sing, | For weepe he may not, that was cal'd a King'. Duncan-Jones thinks this must refer to the three Shakespearian Henry VI plays and an anticipated play (set up for in *3 Henry VI*) about Richard III (the fourth). 'Their muses' indicates (as we already suspected) that the works were not all by one dramatist. The book is dated in its epistles to September 1593. The 'clouds that loured over our house' in *Richard III* could allude to clouds of pestilence that had so long loured over (and kept closed) the playhouse.

Adrian Streete, 'Chrysostom, Calvin, and Conscience: More on *King Richard III*, I.iii.222' (*N&Q* 50[2003] 21–2), thinks that Queen Margaret's 'The worm of conscience still begnaw thy soul' (*Richard III* I.iii.222) contains an idea (the 'worm of conscience', which is not proverbial) from the work of John Chrysostom, but in phrasing from John Calvin's *Institutes* of 1561. Specifically, it is Book 1, chapter 2: 'the worm of conscience gnaweth them'. That chapter is about how one cannot entirely blot out one's feeling for the Godhead, not matter how sinful one is, which suits Richard III who wakes from his sleep crying 'Jesu!' and speaking of the 'coward conscience'. J.J.M. Tobin, 'Dr Pinch and Gabriel Harvey' (*N&Q* 50[2003] 23–5), has evidence that in *The Comedy of Errors* Shakespeare borrowed from Nashe. *The Comedy of Errors* IV.iv has 'Heart and good will … not a rag of money', which is in Nashe's *Strange News* [1592] as a phrase used by Gabriel Harvey's dead brother. Tobin puts this together with some other collocations from the same two places (the nearby pages of *Strange News* and the scene from *The Comedy of Errors*) to argue that, although Dr Pinch in *The Comedy of Errors* is not necessarily supposed to evoke Gabriel Harvey, the play draws on Nashe's *Strange News* and Pinch might have been performed 'with voice, grimace, posture, and even perhaps clothing to suggest Harvey' (p. 25). R.W. Maslen, '*The Taming of the Shrew* and *The Image of Idleness*' (*N&Q* 50[2003] 25–7), notes that Petruchio's particular means of subduing his wife in *The Taming of the Shrew* is not the usual one in stories of taming, and that Shakespeare may have got it from the wife-taming story *The Image of Idleness* [1556], which advises treating wives like falcons. The trick is to let them think they are doing their own bidding, and wives also can be tamed by the husband feigning madness made to seem consequent upon the failure to follow a special diet ordered by a physician (as Petruchio claims to be under when he throws his food away).

Thomas Merriam's final note, '*More* and *Woodstock*' (*N&Q* 50[2003] 27–31), argues that the feminine-ending evidence in *Sir Thomas More* has not been sufficiently recognized in the debate about the play's authorship and date. The play has a strikingly high proportion of lines with feminine endings: between about 15 per cent and 25 per cent of all lines, depending on how strict you are in what counts as a feminine ending. An average of 21 per cent is a reasonable figure, and only *The Merry Wives of Windsor* (dated 1597–8, at 22 per cent) and *Woodstock* (date uncertain, at 21 per cent) come close it to. If MacDonald P. Jackson is right in dating *Woodstock* to the early seventeenth century, then *Sir Thomas More* is 'isolated and anomalous' regarding its high proportion of feminine endings in the early 1590s. The data from the Shakespeare Authorship Clinic at Claremont McKenna College might help here, for they give the rate of feminine endings (plus fifty-six other linguistic variables) in 112 plays. Of the linguistic variables, seventeen seem to be significantly correlated to the date of play composition (that is, they fairly consistently get more common or less common as time goes on), so we can *assume* that these variables (or rather, the first principal components of them taken together) form a continuum and let the dates be derived from them (p. 29). This should give an independent check on the dating. This confirms that *Sir Thomas More* dates from about 1593 and *Woodstock* from about 1605. Supporting this conclusion is a graph that suffers from a familiar Merriam problem identified in previous years: the horizontal axis must be incorrectly labelled since it rises, left to right, in steps of 0.2 until it gets close to zero, then it skips one step. Also, moving in steps of 0.2 it cannot be right for the central label to be 0.5 (must be 0.4 or 0.6). Merriam uses 'can not' where he means 'cannot'. The former has the sense of 'it is possible not to', as might be said by cricketers sent to Zimbabwe and considering their options ('we can not play the game') whereas the latter has the sense 'it is impossible to', as black cricketers used to find in racist South Africa ('we cannot play the game'). Merriam ends with the observation that if the Additions to *Sir Thomas More* are ten years or so later than the original composition, it is odd that Addition 1, in Hand A (Chettle's), has a low proportion of feminine endings (2 per cent) that is generally characteristic of the early 1590s, not the early 1600s (p. 31).

A.B. Taylor, 'Golding and the Myth Underlying Hermia's Dream' (*N&Q* 50[2003] 31–2), thinks that the serpent that Hermia dreams is at her breast (*A Midsummer Night's Dream* II.ii.151–6) comes from Arthur Golding's translation of Book 4 of Ovid's *Metamorphoses*, the punishment of Ino by Juno and the Furies. Hermia's dream is obviously phallic—Lysander tried to sleep with her (near her, I would say)—and the dream is of penetration and represents her entry into the adult world. Shakespeare's using the word 'serpent' (where Golding has 'snake') gives the moment also a biblical connotation. The play also draws on Nashe's *Have With You to Saffron-Walden*, according to J.J.M. Tobin,

'Have with You to Athens' Wood' (*N&Q* 50[2003] 32–5). Tobin finds a collection of words and phrases the texts share, including 'the short and long [of it]', jokes about bare French crowns, and some others that might just be commonplaces. *Saffron-Walden* was dedicated to the Master Barber of Trinity College, and is full of barber references that link it with *A Midsummer Night's Dream*, such as Bottom's hairy face, Flute's beard, and the barber's pole that Nashe calls a 'painted may-pole', just as Hermia calls Helena. Nashe has a scene in which musk, sugar and honey are personified and addressed much as Bottom addresses the fairies Cobweb, Peaseblossom, and Mustardseed. Tobin discounts, without giving reason, the possibility that Nashe echoes Shakespeare, and observes that the dependence puts *A Midsummer Night's Dream* no earlier than 1596. The late I.A. Shapiro, in 'Wedding- or Weeding-Knives?' (*N&Q* 50[2003] 35), notes that the word 'wedding-knives' in *Edward III* does not mean anything and must be a misprint for 'weeding-knives'. In a second note on the same play, 'The Text of *The Raigne of Edward III*' (*N&Q* 50[2003] 35–6), Shapiro observes that the countess inappropriately addresses the king using 'thee', 'thou', 'thyself', and 'thy' even before she decides to repulse him, so the dramatist apparently did not know court protocol. Also, the king and countess speak in rhyming couplets, which is an early dramatic device that later writers dropped, so probably this part of the play was written by Shakespeare more or less as soon as he arrived in London, which would also explain some similarity in ideas and images in this play and others by Shakespeare. J.C. Ross, 'Stephen Gosson and *The Merchant of Venice* Revisited' (*N&Q* 50[2003] 36–7), hears in Shylock's 'stop my house's ears' (*The Merchant of Venice* II.v.34) an echo of Stephen Gosson's *The School of Abuse* in the context of not being seduced by sounds ('stoppe your ears') and finds a couple of other (fairly common, it must be said) phrases that Shakespeare and Gosson share.

Steve Sohmer, in 'Shakespeare's Posthumous Apology to Lord Cobham: *Henry V* (II.iii.8–14)' (*N&Q* 50[2003] 39–42), points out that 'Oldcastle died martyr, and this is not the man' (epilogue to *2 Henry IV*) is not really an apology to anyone, and hence not to William Brooke, seventh Lord Cobham, as is usually claimed. But the death of Falstaff between midnight and 1 a.m. as the tide turned (*Henry V* II.iii.9–16) fits William Brooke's death on 5–6 March 1597, and the Book of Common Prayer reading for 5 March was Psalm 23 ('rest in grene pasture') hence ''a babbled of green fields'. Falstaff's death is Protestant (no priest, no sacrament, yet he goes to heaven), which suits Brooke, and hence Shakespeare's death of Falstaff is a eulogy to William Brooke. Sohmer points out a few other uses of material from Psalms in Shakespeare, on just the right days as given by the calendar. Steve Roth, '*Hamlet*, II.ii.332: "Their inhibition comes by the means of the late innovation"' (*N&Q* 50[2003] 43–6), thinks that the 'late innovation' that Rosencrantz refers to (*Hamlet* II.ii.334) means Fortinbras's uprising that makes the whole of Denmark so edgy. Edginess (specifically, fear of civil unrest) Roth illustrates from across the play. Claudius seems glad to see the players, so presumably it was Polonius (who is not) who banned them. Where Q2 and F have (more or less) 'POLONIUS Seneca cannot be too heavy, nor Plautus too light. For the law of writ and the liberty, these are the only men' (II.ii.401–3), Q1 has 'For the law hath writ those are the onely men'. The latter sounds like a statement about 'allowed' players and hence the memorial reconstructor of Q1 associates Polonius with what players are allowed do, which suits him being the official who banned them.

Tobin pops up again, in 'How Drunk Was Barnadine?' (*N&Q* 50[2003] 46–7), to argue that *Measure for Measure* is indebted to Nashe's *Strange News*, not least in its reference to 'Barnadines', which R.B. McKerrow glossed as referring to Barnard's Law, a means of cheating at cards by working with a confederate who feigns drunkenness. Thus Barnardine in the play is probably faking intoxication to avoid execution. In 'Nashe and Iago' (*N&Q* 50[2003] 47–50), Tobin finds in Nashe's *Christ's Tears over Jerusalem* the source of a number of words and phrases in Iago's part in *Othello*, especially 'nonsuits' (I.i.5), 'cashiered' (I.i.48), and 'put money' (I.iii.339, 341, 351), and there are some parallel themes. Following Garry Wills's suggestion, Matthew Baynham, 'The Naked Babe and Robert Southwell', *N&Q* 50[2003] 55–6), thinks that Robert Southwell's poetry was the source for the naked babe image in *Macbeth* (I.vii.21–5), but not the poem 'The burning babe' but rather 'New heaven, new war' (published in the same book of 1602), which has certain verbal parallels with *Macbeth*. In *Coriolanus* the tribunes say that Martius is happy to be commanded by Cominius in war because if it goes well he will get the credit and if badly Cominius will get the blame. For this David George, 'The Tribunes' Envy: *Coriolanus*, I.i.245–60 (*N&Q* 50[2003] 56–7), finds a source in John Hayward's 1599 prose *Life of Henry IV*. It is well known that in the King James Bible, the 46th psalm has 'shake' as its 46th word from the beginning and 'spear' as its 46th word from the end, and that Shakespeare was aged 46 when the book was completed. R.H. Robbins, 'Shakespeare and Psalm 46: An Accumulation of Coincidences', *N&Q* 50[2003] 58–60), shows that this is just a coincidence: the agents and texts involved, surveyed by Robbins, admit no opportunity for deliberate rigging of the text.

2. Shakespeare in the Theatre

Robert Smallwood's *Players of Shakespeare* series is still going strong, reaching its fifth volume and including discussion of fourteen performances, in twelve productions between 1999 and 2002. The focus of the discussion is, as usual, firmly on the RSC (all but one of the productions featured took place in Stratford), which allows a conspicuously controversial element to Smallwood's introduction. Project Fleet—the proposal to demolish the Royal Shakespeare Theatre and develop Waterside—is roundly attacked. Smallwood writes of the 'devastating RSC reorganisation of 2000–1, the Thatcherite version of a "Cultural Revolution"' (p. 3). He goes on to condemn the closure of the company's studio space, and so it is fitting that the first essay in the volume details the last production to take place before The Other Place went dark. Philip Voss describes playing Prospero in James MacDonald's 2000–1 touring production. There are some refreshingly unsentimental opinions: 'I don't believe Prospero makes that vital self-healing leap of real forgiveness' (p. 16); 'I think he renounces magic to face up to the awfulness of life' (p. 27). Indeed Voss is bracingly candid about the disadvantages of playing opposite a weak Miranda (though he is adamant that Nikki Amuka-Bird is far from poor): 'So often work is spoiled by an actor, crucial to one's own performance, being inadequate—unable to speak the verse, or playing for laughs, or in some other way inappropriate' (p. 19). One wonders how popular Voss is amongst other members of the company. Such supercilious reserve is swapped for a faux comic banter in Ian Hughes's account of playing Dromio of Syracuse in Lynne Parker's 2000 *Comedy of Errors*. His essay ends with the typically gauche summary: 'Simple story-telling, well-drawn characters—the fundamental things apply … as time goes by. Play it again, Bill!' (p. 42). Perhaps this is explainable (though hardly excusable) in the light of the production's reliance on and allusions to *Casablanca*, *The Third Man*, *The Maltese Falcon* as well as Abbott and Costello, Groucho Marx, Bob Hope and Bing Crosby, all of whom are listed as influences. But this ebullience is tested when Hughes opines that 'One of the problems of pre-designing a show before rehearsals start is that new ideas that spring up from the creative process cannot always be accommodated' (p. 36). Writing of her Hermione in Gregory Doran's 1998 production of *The Winter's Tale*, Alexandra Gilbreath explains why: 'the design and concept … always has to be in place as rehearsals start, for the sets and costumes are built and made in six weeks, simultaneously with the average rehearsal time at the RSC' (p. 76). This cuts no ice with Aden McArdle, who insists on the tyranny of the designer in his account of playing Puck and Philostrate: '*A Midsummer Night's Dream* in the modern theatre is such a design-based play that actors are more or less at the designer's mercy' (p. 43). The essay goes on to argue for a crude humanity in this magical character: 'Puck may come from the fairy world, but what makes audiences love him are the qualities of mischievous humanity that he constantly evinces' (p. 44), 'Puck is rough and ready; there is an essential *rudeness* about him' (p. 51). The essay also contains some interesting insights on the doubling of Puck and Philostrate—comparing the former to the ego and the latter to the id (p. 47). The symbiosis between the roles of Viola and Olivia makes the joint authorship of Zoë Waites and Matilda Ziegler's essay on their performances in Lindsay Posner's 2001 *Twelfth Night* entirely appropriate. There is a particularly incisive account of I.v, in which Viola, sent by Orsino, is required to praise Olivia's beauty. Olivia and Maria (and occasionally other waiting women) are veiled as Viola enters. Waites and Ziegler write: Viola 'immediately blunders, launching into an unrestrained eulogy of Olivia's "unmatchable beauty" (I.v.164). Too late she realizes the irony of praising the beauty of someone whose face she cannot see: the veil has successfully disempowered her and given Olivia the upper hand, a situation that Olivia builds upon by remaining silent and unforthcoming whilst an increasingly desperate Viola tries to coax forth some hint as to which is "the lady of the house"' (p. 63). For all the sensitivity of this reading, the production's closure seemed to baffle its performers: 'The play culminates in a series of revelations and resolutions in Act Five which, in our experience of playing them, can be either completely joyful or tortuously extended, depending on the evening!' (p. 71). Unfortunately, it sounds as though the press was in on one of the latter occasions: 'The production received some criticism on all fronts and we did suffer feelings of acute disappointment and sorrow that we seemed to be failing to serve up the brilliance that is undoubtedly in the play' (p. 73).

Antony Sher played Leontes in 1998 and Macbeth in 1999. Both productions were directed by Gregory Doran. His account of the roles is book-ended by clumsy references to Doran as his 'partner' (pp. 92 and 112)—as though we didn't already know that. It also contains the by now standard condemnation of academics (here contemptuously referred to as 'scholars', p. 99) who read rather than speak the lines. The most interesting part of the essay comes in the conclusion, in which Sher compares the two protagonists in terms of their mental health: 'Macbeth's "diseased" mind is nothing like that of Leontes. Leontes is afflicted with temporary madness. Macbeth is tortured by sanity, by clarity, by both consciousness and conscience' (p. 111). Then he goes on, 'If I were to choose an artist to portray each, I would say that Leontes' imagination is like something painted by Bosch—it teems with horrid little sticky pink nudes—while Macbeth's imagination is by Dali—elegant, epic pictures of lonely figures in empty landscapes: a newborn baby carried on the wind, one bloody hand turning the oceans red'. In comparison to this acute analogy the rest of the essay is disappointing, though nowhere near as banal as David Tennant on Romeo (for Michael Boyd's 2000 production). His description of Mercutio as 'a "high maintenance" personality' (p. 118) and talk of scenes which 'we found came to life fairly easily' (p. 127) are not atypical. By contrast Michael Pennington's account of Timon (which he played for Gregory Doran in 1999) is a model of clarity and eloquence. Of Timon's mysterious death, Pennington writes, 'Shakespeare has sustained his metaphor so thoroughly that he doesn't trouble with a cause … Something similar happens to the broken-hearted Enobarbus … written at much the same time' (p. 142). The longest, most detailed essay in the volume is also its most bewildered. Simon Russell Beale's account of playing Hamlet in John Caird's 2000 National Theatre production opines at its conclusion, 'more than any other character I have ever played, the person called Hamlet does not exist'—hard to see how he can exist *less* than other characters, but let that pass. In fact this laborious account is peppered with the kinds of anxieties and hesitations which can only be described as Hamletic: 'if I am incoherent, it is because there is simply too much to say' (p. 154); 'It is difficult for me to write anything remotely coherent about the last act of *Hamlet*. It is … a mystery that is insoluble. I cannot, therefore, *precisely* express my thoughts and feelings in playing it' (p. 174). Indeed, paradoxically, the only thing Beale is insistent on and definite about is the one thing that he considers to be totally inappropriate to the performance of a Shakespearian role: 'It is important that anyone playing Hamlet should invent or construct a series of events that took place before the play began—the good old (and very un-Shakespearean) "Method"!' (p. 149). That a consummate Shakespearian actor should insist on such an anomalous technique is astounding. No explanation is offered, but that way, perhaps, madness lies.

In his last stage role before his death, Nigel Hawthorne played King Lear in Yukio Ninagawa's RSC production. His account of the experience is not a happy one. Having had his arm twisted by Adrian Noble to accept the role, 'I was soon to discover that our director didn't speak English' (p. 180). The rest of the essay is glumly insistent on the ways in which the actor is hamstrung without the benefit of a communicative director: 'It was maddening not having the director at the end of a phone' (p. 182); 'I felt frustrated at not being able to discuss these matters with the director' (p. 183); 'For the entire time I worked with him [Ninagawa] on Lear, I never had a single note, never had a single discussion with him about the character I was playing'; '[I] met with stubborn resistance and quite a little hostility'; 'Ninagawa-san was not going to be a huge amount of help' (p. 186); 'The rest of the story … is tinged with disappointment'; 'there was little or no guidance' (p. 189). This is one of the most downhearted contributions to the *Players of Shakespeare* series to date and it is all the more melancholic considering that this frankly disappointing production was Hawthorne's swan song.

Richard McCabe's account of Iago, which he played for Michael Attenborough's 1999 production of *Othello*, though sober and intelligent, is sanguine by comparison. He is interesting on the character's 'obsession with sexuality' which 'colours so much of his language' (p. 194). McCabe set great store by Iago's precise military bearing and he is intriguing on the physical demands of the role: 'I wore five-pound ankle weights on each foot to root me to the ground and gained nearly thirty pounds in weight to contrast my appearance with Othello's muscular physique [played by Ray Fearon]' (p. 200). In contrast to McCabe's precise account of a precise character, the final essay of the volume is an over-the-top account of an over-the-top character. Frances de la Tour details her performance of Cleopatra in Steven Pimlott's 1999 production (opposite Alan Bates). Call me an old cynic or—even more likely—a patriarchal monster, but the essentialism of this contribution both mystified and irritated me: 'Any woman knows when a man has fallen [for her]; keeping him is a far bigger issue' (p. 215). At points we were dangerously close to *Bridget Jones's Diary*.

Shakespeare in Performance [2003] contains the proceedings of a 1999 conference at Drew University and is edited by Frank Occhiogrosso. The volume is a consolidation of things we know so far rather than representing anything radically new. John Russell Brown's 'Shakespeare in Performance, Study, and Criticism' is unsurprisingly insistent on the importance of … well … *performance*: the texts 'were not written to be read, either silently or aloud; they were meant to be part of entire plays acted by actors on a stage before audiences' (p. 15). Actors, it seems, are the most reliable authorities; indeed, Brown cites the *Players of Shakespeare* series and lauds its 'new self-awareness and openness among actors and directors' (p. 19). But as well as this rather predictable adoration of those that tread the boards, Brown is candid about the problems that beset performance specialists—not least the difficulties of defining what it is they actually do: 'Perhaps the most serious problem in convincing others to study Shakespeare in the theater has been a lack of widely recognized standards of judgment' (p. 21). Two essays on *The Merchant of Venice* follow. James C. Bulman's 'Shylock, Antonio, and the Politics of Performance' takes the indeterminacy of Brown's essay and demonstrates with reference to readings of several productions of *The Merchant* the cultural contingency of each of its incarnations. As he says, 'Making meaning in a theater is … a collaborative and historically particular enterprise' (p. 27). Henry Irving's late nineteenth-century performances (he played the role over a thousand times) insisted on both his familial bonds and the vehemence of his persecution. Irving's Shylock was 'a noble Jew victimized by an insular, hypocritical society' (p. 33). Bulman proceeds with rather broad brushstrokes to describe Jonathan Miller's 1971 production (with Olivier) as a production about economics rather than about race; Bill Alexander's 1987 version as inflected by AIDS (though much more evidence is needed from the production rather than newspaper reactions); and Andrei Serban's American Repertory Theater production in 1998, which prioritized Antonio as 'an unfulfilled gay man whose inner torment the audience was encouraged to probe even as Shylock performed a comic schtick that made him far less sympathetic' (p. 41). While Bulman's multiple readings of the play are illustrated by the variety of the productions cited here, Ralph Berry (in '*The Merchant of Venice*') suggests that the most successful way of maintaining what he sees as the 'essential ambivalence' of the play is best achieved by returning it 'to its historical origins, a Venice where the uneasy collaboration of Christians and Jews offers something to all parties' (p. 56)—though words like 'essential' and 'something' ought to alert us to the uncertainty of his conclusion. Tim Luscombe's English Shakespeare Company production of 1991, set in 1930s Italy, is pedantically rejected for historical inaccuracy, while David Thacker's 1993 RSC version is too concerned with the ethics of the city and the forces of a market economy to be relevant. On the other hand, Gregory Doran's 1997 RSC production (with Antony Sher), which set the play in Renaissance Venice, gets the thumbs-up, though in the light of Berry's patrician pronouncement, one can't help wondering whether this selection offers a case in point of what Brown has already called 'a lack of widely recognized standards of judgment' (p. 21).

Jay L. Halio offers a straightforward stage history of '*Romeo and Juliet* in Performance'. Given the textual plurality of the play and the variety of its stage manifestations, the essay makes the unarguable if unremarkable argument for a 'reconsideration of the concept of authenticity as a criterion for Shakespearean performance' (p. 67). In '"I have done the deed": *Macbeth* II.ii', James P. Lusardi and June Schlueter detail the various performance solutions to the murder scene. Though lacking a rigorous argument, the essay does raise a couple of intriguing problems—first, why does the murder take place offstage, and, secondly, why does it take Lady Macbeth so long to see the daggers? Several possibilities are advanced. H.R. Coursen's 'Disguise in Trevor Nunn's *Twelfth Night*' is frankly bewildering, as its closing sentences illustrate: 'A recent Subaru commercial shows a beautiful woman subduing the representative of an evil empire, and making her escape in what looks like a Subaru. Another car—was that a Honda?—fails to make it through the closing doors of the warehouse. The masculine does not feminize the feminine here. That's Crocodile Dundee under the rubber mask! The feminine has been the site whereon surprise is enacted. The revelation of the masculine subtext is, by 1999, unnecessary' (p. 92). Your guess is as good as mine.

In 'Storm, Fire, and Blood: Patterns of Imagery in Stuart Burge's *Julius Caesar*', Harry Keyishian notes the presence of these three motifs in this film version and their origins in Shakespeare's text. A more telling point occurs during his comparison of the relative freedom of a spectator in the theatre over the cinema-goer: 'the camera's ability to determine the vantage point of each audience member stabilizes the cinematic experience' (p. 94). Alan C. Dessen, in 'Teaching What's Not There', examines various lacunae in film versions both verbally (cuts from the text) and visually (are Banquo's or Old Hamlet's ghosts visible or not?). Dessen is alert not only to the various possibilities contained in his texts but also to the eminently pragmatic responses of his students, who are considerably more visually (than textually) competent: they 'often approve of directors who take liberties with the original words and … streamline the original playscripts and invoke various television or cinematic conventions with which they are familiar. To such students playing pedagogical games linked to "What's not there?" can seem artificial or, in a pejorative sense, "academic"' (p. 111). Pauline Kiernan makes various interesting, though unrelated, points about the dynamics of playing at 'The New Globe'—which I suppose was still relatively new in 1999. Among these for instance, is the difficulty of using the central opening as a discovery space 'because a large part of the audience, and playgoers' [*sic*] in the lords' room above the stage, cannot see what is happening' (p. 115). But any essay on the Globe wouldn't be complete without the mystical musings of its Artistic Director, and Kiernan cites a choice bit of Rylance lunacy: 'the emotional experience for an audience is both individual and collective at the same time … The physical activeness of the body whether standing or seated at the new Globe is a quite different state for the heart and mind. The elements add to an awakened, sometimes drenched, sense of the physical body' (p. 116). In 'Tracking Performance Criticism of Shakespeare', Marvin Rosenberg roundly asserts that early modern 'playwrights were mainly aiming at a lifelike, poetical natural "realism"' (p. 124). Those 'scare quotes' around realism ought to alert us to the tendentious nature of such an assertion, and indeed the evidence is thin. Rosenberg cites the Prologue from *Henry VIII* (ll. 25–7): 'Think ye see | The very persons of our noble story | As they were living'. Of course what he doesn't say is that the very invocation is just as likely to undermine the mimetic quality of the drama as reinforce it, that is, that far from erasing the stagecraft of the play, this insistence on metadrama militates against the creation of 'a lifelike, poetical natural "realism"'. (Unsurprisingly, Rosenberg doesn't mention the repetitively intrusive Chorus of *Henry V*.) Most interesting about this essay is Rosenberg's crediting himself with the discontented Isabella, who turns her back on the Duke's proposal of marriage at the end of *Measure for Measure*: 'I urged such rejection in a paper to the International Shakespeare Association conference at Stratford; two years later the *Measure for Measure* staging there by the Royal Shakespeare Company used my ending—the first time known in the theater'. Would that the world of Shakespeare scholarship were that noteworthy!

A Companion to Shakespeare's Works is a four-volume set edited by Richard Dutton and Jean E. Howard. The first and third volumes contain essays of relevance to this section. Volume 3 is dedicated to the comedies and contains the intriguing 'Rhetoric and Comic Personation in Shakespeare's Comedies' (pp. 200–22), in which Lloyd Davis stresses the 'rhetorical sense of selfhood' (p. 202) which is quite different from modern psychobiographical notions of character. For the early modern period (and hence the early modern theatre), there is, rather, 'an interaction between rhetoric and identity' (p. 202). Davis evinces this prioritization of rhetoric by citing literary theorists of the period, including Philip Sidney, George Puttenham, Abraham Fraunce, Henry Peacham, Francis Bacon, Thomas Wilson and, of course, Ben Jonson. Davis then goes on to examine how such a rhetorical sense of self is manifest and deployed in a wide range of Shakespearian comedies. Admirable here is a fluency with the material and the apposite nature of Davis's examples. For instance, Davis finds that '*The Comedy of Errors* careers through the complications of self-personation' (p. 214), deconstructing the process to make it all the more visible. He also notes the importance of family relationships, arguing, in relation to Jessica and Hermia, that the family is 'an institution which both provides and denies their identity' (p. 216). In the case of *Much Ado* Davis proposes that the play shows how 'a community's personal discourse is for better or worse organized through definitions of character and conduct provided by its ruling figures, Don Pedro and Don John' (p. 219). Based on a careful and thorough reading of contemporary theorists of rhetoric and a wide sample of Shakespearian comedy, Davis's conclusion is unassailable: 'the plays use the comic genre to reiterate and reassess major points about social relations and ethical identity that rhetorical discourse had always sought to explain and define' (p. 220). This is a subtle and sophisticated essay.

Volume 1, dedicated to the tragedies, contains Bernice W. Kliman's '*Hamlet* Productions Starring Beale, Hawke, and Darling from the Perspective of Performance History' (pp. 134–57). Kliman asserts that, more than any other play, *Hamlet* is open-ended and 'may be the best worst play in the world; the possibilities for artists, readers, and audience to fill in the gaps are what make it the play most performed and written about in dramatic literature' (p. 135). By way of potted histories of David Garrick, Edwin Booth and John Barrymore, Kliman works her way to the contemporary, turning her attentions to the Hamlets of Simon Russell Beale (directed by John Caird, National Theatre, 2000–1: this is the performance Beale himself writes about in Smallwood, see above), Ethan Hawke (directed by Michael Almereyda, film, 2000) and Peter Darling (directed by Robert Lepage, 1996–7). Kliman, well versed in the play, is an astute critic of its recent performances and her admiration for Beale's 'intelligent, sensitive, gentle, and sweet-tempered Hamlet' (p. 143) is seasoned with one or two gentle digs. He is, she writes, an unlikely hero being 'Above average in girth and below average in height' and she goes on mischievously, 'Hamlet should be nasty and brutish (but not short)' (p. 143). For all this, she rightly admires Beale's detailed performance: 'most of the effects Beale depends on are supertextual, developed not only on the lines but also in the spaces between words, communicated through enactment on stage' (p. 146). Kliman contrasts Beale's romantic Prince with the disaffected youth portrayed by Ethan Hawkes. She suggests that Almereyda's film offers 'an opportunity to comment on society' (p. 148). She goes on to note how the film engages with a capitalist economy and particularly the ways in which 'Almereyda engages in aggressive product display, making his film fully complicit in corporate society' (p. 149). Moreover, the film is full of videocameras and tapes—one scene taking place in a Blockbuster video store—and this, Kliman contends, is responsible for the film's 'metafilmic impulses' (p. 151). It is this meta-quality that Kliman highlights in Robert

Lepage's *Elsinore* (which ran for four hours in its 1996 version but was cut to ninety minutes in 1997): 'Lepage's work is not so much *Hamlet* as it is a play about playing Hamlet' (p. 153). This one-man show, starring Peter Darling, is a combination of 'Spectacle, movement, music, design, vocal and instrumental sound effects' (p. 153). This multi-media text allows Kliman to conclude her essay by asserting that Shakespeare's play transcends any particular genre: 'little is to be gained by sorting out current *Hamlet* productions into film, video, or stage versions' (p. 155). The work of these three directors, she concludes, 'can sweep out of our heads the preconceived notions we have of Hamlet and the play and marshal us towards the diverse paths productions will take in the future'.

3. Shakespeare on Screen

This was something of a vintage year for Shakespeare on screen. Although only one monograph was published, a wealth of material, much of it of an extremely high standard, was published in collections and journals. As usual, some plays and films received more attention. Recent films such as Almereyda's *Hamlet* and Taymor's *Titus* continued to be popular among critics, while Branagh's ill-fated *Love's Labour's Lost* and Kristian Levring's *The King is Alive* have begun to move from review to scholarly analysis. Substantial work was also published on the various adaptations of *Othello*, *Macbeth* and *A Midsummer Night's Dream*, and there were welcome clutches of essays on animated and silent Shakespeare.

A useful review article, Elsie Walker's 'Shakespeare on Film: Early Modern Texts, Postmodern Statements' (*Literature Compass* 1[2003]), critiques Shakespeare film criticism's frequent dependence on notions of authorial intention (often displaced onto the figure of the *auteur*) and questions of fidelity to the 'original' text. Although these preconceptions are often reflected in the films themselves—Branagh's *Hamlet*, as Walker notes, promises 'without irony' to present 'the most fully authentic version of the play'—they are intrinsically problematic in relation to the plays' collaborative, textually unstable, and intertextual character. Following scholars such as Andrew Murphy, she calls for a more theoretically aware critical practice, which would pay greater attention to the collaborative nature of Shakespearian films and to the cultural contexts in which they are produced and circulated. The best of the essays under review this year already partake in such a critical practice, interrogating in their various ways the films' complex relationships with the nations and cultures that produced them and their relationships with other media.

The year's monograph is Samuel Crowl's *Shakespeare at the Cineplex: The Kenneth Branagh Era*, a survey of Shakespearian adaptations produced during the 'long decade' 1989–2001. Crowl's focus is on direct adaptations rather than appropriations, those films which are 'directly committed to reproducing a Shakespearian text in the traditional language of the narrative film'. Even within this group there is, however, considerable variation. Films range from Hoffman's wholeheartedly starry *Midsummer Night's Dream* to Edzard's determinedly marginal *Children's Midsummer Night's Dream*, from Parker's glossy thriller *Othello* to Taymor's avant-garde extravaganza *Titus*. Especially useful is Crowl's clear explication of the cultural contexts in which these films were produced, the complex interaction of artistic and commercial factors which led to the 1990s explosion of Shakespearian films after a barren period in the 1970s and 1980s. Branagh-era Shakespeare is marked, he argues, by a willingness to engage with Hollywood genres, tropes, technical innovations and casting practices, whether the films are produced in Hollywood itself or on the margins of the film industry. Important exceptions are Edzard's Shakespearian films, *As You Like It* and *The Children's Midsummer Night's Dream*, produced on London's Bankside and financially and aesthetically removed from Hollywood, which instead use Shakespeare to interrogate and create communities.

Crowl is a lucid and perceptive guide, with a winning turn of phrase (the squeals of a high-school audience for *William Shakespeare's Romeo + Juliet*, for instance, sound 'like weasels in heat'). He is good on Branagh's attempt to fuse language and image in his Shakespearian films, although his regard for the director's achievements leads him to a slightly strenuous defence of *Love's Labour's Lost*, but even better on some of the non-Branagh films. In particular, his analysis of Zeffirelli's *Hamlet*, where he draws on Janet Adelman's *Suffocating Mothers*, published around the same time as *Hamlet* was released, is an illuminating exploration of the film's maternally centred narratives, which centre on the casting of Glenn Close as Gertrude. Similarly, his analyses of the metacinematics of Almereyda's *Hamlet*, and of the contradictions inherent in the *Midsummer Night's Dream*s of Hoffman and Adrian Noble (one produced by a Hollywood veteran with little prior experience in Shakespeare, the other by a Stratford veteran with little prior experience in film), are entertaining and informative. This book will be particularly useful for students who are beginning their work in Shakespeare on film, who will be introduced to a range of concepts and approaches without being frightened off by overly technical vocabulary.

Three essay collections are relevant to Shakespeare on screen, and I will comment briefly now, returning to look at individual essays in more detail below. One collection focuses entirely on filmic Shakespeare, Richard Burt and Linda E. Boose's inspiringly entitled *Shakespeare, the Movie II: Popularizing the Plays on Film, TV, Video, and DVD*, a sequel to *Shakespeare, the Movie* (1997, reviewed in *YWES* 78[1999] 302–3). Like Hollywood sequels, it mixes old and new. Some essays are reprinted from *Shakespeare, the Movie*, notably two influential pieces: James Loehlin's '"Top of the World, Ma": *Richard III* and Cinematic Convention' and Sue Wiseman's 'The Family Tree Motel: Subliming Shakespeare in *My Own Private Idaho*'. The majority are newly writtten, however, and they encompass recent additions to the 'Shakespeare on film' canon, such as Kristian Levring's *The King is Alive* and the *Midsummer Night's Dreams* of Edzard, Hoffman and Noble. As a whole, the collection aims to consider how film and television have changed in the wake of digitalization and globalization. Accordingly, in 'Introduction: Editors' Cut' (in Burt and Boose, eds., pp. 1–13) Burt considers two issues relating to the proliferation of Shakespearian films: the circulation and alteration of the films in media such as DVD and the shift from national to transnational cinemas.

Two further collections also contain a substantial amount of material for scholars interested in screen Shakespeare: Aebischer, Esche and Wheale, eds., *Remaking Shakespeare: Performance Across Media, Genres and Cultures*, and Reynolds, *Performing Transversally: Reimagining Shakespeare and the Critical Future*. *Remaking Shakespeare* valuably juxtaposes essays on film and other modes of performance; of particular note are essays by Jean Chothia, Barbara Hodgdon, Catherine Silverstone and Robert Shaughnessy, which integrate analysis of various modes. *Performing Transversally* is another beast altogether. Framed as a monograph, it is in fact a collaborative effort, in which Reynolds co-writes each chapter with one or more co-authors. The unifying factor is Reynolds's 'transversal' theory, a new methodology which aims to create a politically and theoretically engaged critical practice. It is all too easy to make fun of Reynolds's compulsively self-referential transversalism, which is simultaneously ill defined and strictly limiting. The essays in *Performing Transversally* are, accordingly, frequently thought-provoking and stimulating but often maddeningly opaque and allusive.

A general essay, 'Nudge, Nudge, Wink, Wink, Know What I Mean, Know What I Mean? A Theoretical Approach to Performance for a Post-Cinema Shakespeare' (in Reynolds, pp. 137–70), written by D.J. Hopkins, Catherine Ingman and Bryan Reynolds, serves to illustrate many of the book's virtues and failings. The authors suggest that a supposed 'absence of invention' inherent in cinema's constant recourse to Shakespeare is the product less of failings in screenwriting, than of failures in direction and acting. They therefore aim to interrogate the relationship between written texts and the performances of the actors in film adaptations of those texts, and, drawing on Patrice Pavis's model of the 'actor-dramaturg', they focus on the agency of the 'self-aware, self-referential' actor. Given that audiences are always self-conscious when watching Shakespeare on screen, Hopkins, Ingram and Reynolds argue that Shakespearian film acting should resist realism, and accommodate in a knowing manner the 'contrived' nature of filmic representation. The analysis focuses on *Shakespeare in Love*, *Never Been Kissed*, *10 Things I Hate About You* and Almereyda's *Hamlet*, and much of it is extremely illuminating. This is at times, however, in spite rather than because of transversal theory, which often serves to distract the reader from the essay's more valuable theoretical and analytical material.

Much of Hopkins, Ingman and Reynolds's essay is built on foundations laid by Richard Burt, so it is only fit to move next to look at two general essays by Burt himself, both published in *Shakespeare, the Movie II*. In 'Shakespeare, "Glo-Cali-Zation", Race, and the Small Screens of Post-Popular Culture' (in Burt and Boose, eds., pp. 14–36), Burt considers in more detail some of the issues raised in the collection's introduction. He argues that the heterogeneity of popular culture and its manifestations in mass media call into question assumptions about the relationship between Shakespeare and popular and elite culture which have been shared by left and right alike. Typically, his argument is encapsulated in a punning neologism: 'glo-cali-zation'. 'Glocal' is the collapse of the local and the global, while 'cali' is retained to represent the continued importance of Hollywood as the centre of the film industry. One of the strengths of Burt's analysis is, as always, his omnivorous appetite for a vast range of Shakespearian adaptations deriving from disparate cultures and locations. They here include the films *Orange County* [2002], *The Street King* [2002] and *Maybe Baby* [2000], the television series *Blackadder* and *South Park*, and adverts for Barclays Bank. Burt's second essay, 'Shakespeare and Asia and Postdiasporic Cinema: Spin-Offs and Citations of the Plays from Bollywood to Hollywood' (in Burt and Boose, eds., pp. 265–303) is similarly wide-ranging, examining a plethora of Shakespearian films featuring or emanating from Asia and the Asian diaspora. In particular, he is interested in the disparity between national culture and the transnational marketing of films, interrogating the 'belatedness' of criticism in general and postcolonial criticism in particular.

Similar issues meet with different treatment in two essays in *Remaking Shakespeare*, Paromita Chakravarti's 'Modernity, Postcoloniality and *Othello*: The Case of *Saptapadi*' (in Aebischer, Esche and Wheale, eds., pp. 39–55) and Catherine Silverstone's '*Othello*'s Travels in New Zealand: Shakespeare, Race and National Identity' (in Aebischer, Esche and Wheale, eds., pp. 74–92). Chakravarti's essay focuses on *Saptapadi* [1961], a film set in the colonial India of the 1940s featuring the staging of a production of *Othello* in which a young Bengali actor plays the Moor opposite a white Desdemona. This 'revolutionary' stage image is analysed in the context of a colonial project which used Shakespeare as a vehicle of disseminating 'modern' and 'civilized' values to a 'benighted' nation. By the 1960s, post-independence India was as focused on gender issues as on racial ones, and these concerns are reflected in *Saptapadi*, in which the performance of *Othello* becomes emblematic of the way in which Shakespeare can create space for an otherwise unavailable dialogue between cultures. Silverstone's analysis, meanwhile, attempts to expand the 'postcolonial *Othello* archive' by looking at two recent appropriations in New Zealand: a school performance of *Othello* in the soap-opera *Shortland Street* and Theatre at Large's controversial *Manawa Taua* (*Savage Hearts*). She aims to explore what happens when a racially loaded text such as *Othello* comes into contact with New Zealand's postcolonial settler culture. While *Shortland Street* attempts to defuse the potential relationship between *Othello* and often fraught race relations in New Zealand, *Manawa Taua* foregrounds the connection by embedding Shakespeare's play in a history of colonialization and miscegenation.

Another stimulating essay on *Othello*, Barbara Hodgdon's 'Race-ing *Othello*, Re-Engendering White-Out, II' (in Burt and Boose, eds., pp. 89–104) examines three recent adaptations of the play, Parker's *Othello* [1995], Andrew Davies's ITV *Othello* [2001] and Tim Blake Nelson's *O* [2001]. Although deriving from the same play, each film is an example of a different genre: the Shakespeare remake; the television docudrama; and the Shakespeare high-school film. Exploring specific cultural contexts for each film—the aftermath of the O.J. Simpson trial, the Stephen Lawrence case and the Columbine-era wave of high-school violence—Hodgdon examines their engagement with interrelations of race and power, and with the problems of white paranoia and blindness.

Staying with adaptations of the tragedies, issues concerning national identity are also central to Amy Scott-Douglas's 'Dogme Shakespeare 95: European Cinema, Anti-Hollywood Sentiment, and the Bard' (in Burt and Boose, eds., pp. 252–64), which focuses on Lars Von Trier's *Festen* (*The Celebration*) and Kristian Levring's *The King is Alive*. Characterizing Dogme as a 'retrolutionary' approach, she suggests that the engagements of films with Shakespeare—*Festen* with *Hamlet*, *The King is Alive* with *King Lear*—are symptomatic of their relationship with wider film culture. Shakespeare films create a space which is simultaneously engaged with commodity and culture, and with entertainment and art. Dogme sets itself in opposition to Hollywood—as culture to its commodity, art to its entertainment—but it cannot help engaging with commercial film, if only in its over-strenuous rejection of it.

As I mentioned above, the largest group of articles this year focuses on Almereyda's *Hamlet*. Many of them are concerned with the film's employment of technology and its metacinematic aspects. For instance, Katherine Rowe's '"Remember me": Technologies of Memory in Michael Almereyda's *Hamlet*' (in Burt and Boose, eds., pp. 37–55), meditates on media and memory, arguing that Almereyda's film provides an example of what Michel Serres might term the 'polychronic' nature of various kinds of technology. She argues that Almereyda adapts *Hamlet*'s allegory of earlier memory technologies: multimedia practices relating to early modern memory, as displayed in texts such as John Willis's *The Art of Memory* [1621], are transformed into the restless cutting and splicing of Ethan Hawke's *Hamlet*. The essay concludes by raising questions relating to the forms of quotation used by academics in print and online.

Taking a rather different approach to similar questions, Mark Thornton Burnett's '"To hear and see the matter": Communicating Technology in Michael Almereyda's *Hamlet* (2000)' (*CinJ* 42:iii[2003] 48–69), focuses on the influence of the 'late capitalist mindset' on Almereyda's film, which he sees as addressing specifically fin-de-siècle, millennial anxieties. Situating the film in terms of postmodern culture and theory, Burnett suggests that, while the surface of *Hamlet* focuses on a postmodern corporate dystopia, an alternative, transgressive energy can be grasped through invocations of a counter-culture. Through a self-conscious emphasis on the processes of film-making, Almereyda's Hamlet paradoxically finds his tragic subjectivity and integrity.

In 'Re-Incarnations' (in Aebischer, Esche and Wheale, eds., pp. 190–209), Barbara Hodgdon ponders the utility of reincarnation as a possibly useful metaphor for thinking about 'Shakespearian repetition compulsions' evident in late twentieth- and early twenty-first-century performance culture. Almereyda's *Hamlet* is juxtaposed with two contemporaneous theatrical productions: Peter Brook's *Hamlet*, featuring Adrian Lester as the Prince, and Simon Russell Beale's performance as Hamlet in John Caird's National Theatre production. She aims to read *Hamlet* 'Hamletically, which is to say, provisionally', and focuses on the body of the performer, in particular its embodiment of Hamlet's paradoxical claim that meaning can be read from others' bodies, but that he himself possesses 'that within which passes show'.

Branagh's *Hamlet* is the subject of Iska Alter's '"To see or not to see": Interpolations, Extended Scenes, and Musical Accompaniment in Kenneth Branagh's *Hamlet*' (in Aasand, ed., *Stage Directions in Hamlet*, pp. 161–9). Alter focuses on three aspects of the directors' transformation of *Hamlet* for the screen: interpolation, which includes visual articulation of verbal imagery, extratextual material, alterations to accommodate the nineteenth-century setting and flashbacks; extension ('or bloat, if one were to be unkind'), the amplification of scenes beyond what is present in the text; and musical accompaniment which aims to signal, define or intensify audience response. She argues that ultimately these techniques serve to oversimplify the film, but that this may be inherent in the differences between film epic, based on spectacle, and *Hamlet*, based on 'Words, words, words.'

Another tragedy, *Macbeth*, is the subject of two fine essays. Susanne Greenhalgh's '"Alas poor country!": Documenting the Politics of Performance in Two British Television *Macbeths*' (in Aebischer, Esche and Wheale, eds., pp. 93–114), examines Penny Woolcock's *Macbeth on the Estate* (BBC2 [1997]) and Greg Doran's television version of his acclaimed RSC production (Channel 4 [2001]) and seeks to examine the ways in which Shakespeare is retextualized in television. In particular, she is interested in how a 'turn' to documentary affects these two adaptations: while Woolcock's film has much in common with her previous documentaries, Doran uses a documentary style to authenticate the fiction of the play, heightening its 'reality'. This difference in style suggests various ways in which the two films recontextualize the performance of television Shakespeare, and its local and global politics, in an age of video and digital media.

Questions of nation and culture are also central to Courtney Lehmann's 'Out Damned Scot: Dislocating *Macbeth* in Transnational Film and Media Culture' (in Burt and Boose, eds., pp. 231–51). Lehmann examines a flurry of *Macbeth* adaptations in the 1990s, including Allison LiCalsi's *Macbeth: The Comedy* [2001], Stuart Canterbury's porn film *In the Flesh* [1999], and Billy Morrissette's *Scotland, PA* [2002]. Analysing the problematic representation or non-representation of Scotland in films as disparate as the heritage movies *Braveheart* [1995] and *Rob Roy* [1995], and the postmodern *Shallow Grave* [1994] and *Trainspotting* [1996], she argues that the 'Scottish play' on film is 'post-Scottish'. The dislocated 'Scotland' which figures prominently in adaptations of the play 'suggests a compelling metaphor for the transnational playground where the challenges and possibilities of globalization may be traversed'. Sticking with *Macbeth* for a moment, Bryan Reynolds's 'Untimely Ripped: Mediating Witchcraft in Polanski and Shakespeare' (reviewed in *YWES* 79[2000] 268 and *YWES* 83[2004]) makes another reappearance in *Performing Transversally* (pp. 111–35).

Julie Taymor's *Titus* continues to receive attention from critics, resulting in three valuable essays. The most provocative is Courtney Lehmann, Bryan Reynolds and Lisa Starks's jargon-heavy '"For such a sight will blind a father's eye": The Spectacle of Suffering in Taymor's Titus' (in Reynolds, pp. 215–43). Taymor demonstrates, they argue, a 'transversal aesthetic' which goes beyond mixed modes, media and cultures, and beyond graphic realism, to create a revolutionary transformation in its audience, who become involved in the suffering depicted on the screen. In '"A tiger's heart wrapped in a player's hide": Julie Taymor's War Dances' (*ShakB* 21:iii[2003] 61–9), Lisa Hopkins uses the play's tiger imagery, which is translated and amplified in Taymor's film, as a starting point from which to analyse the film's intersection of nature and violence. Violence takes on, she argues, a ritual and purgative function; rather than being merely sentimental, the final shots of Young Lucius and Aaron's baby son provide the film with a kind of catharsis, rather than mere anarchy. Taymor's Brechtian depiction of stylized rather than realistic violence allows her to assert in the film's final scenes that 'nothing—not even the most monolithic-seeming, ritual-bedecked form of political cruelty—is irresistible'. The year's final *Titus* essay, Virginia Mason Vaughan's 'Looking at the "Other" in Julie Taymor's *Titus*' (*ShakB* 21:iii[2003] 71–80), focuses on the film's complication of categories of the 'other'. Rather than simply focusing on Aaron as a racial 'other'—a categorization found in the play which is broken down in Taymor's film—she also looks at gender issues and, most strikingly, those relating to the 'slippery space' between youth and age, demonstrated in the handling of Chiron, Demetrius and Young Lucius.

As usual, film versions of *Romeo and Juliet* were also popular subjects for analysis. Michael Anderegg's 'James Dean Meets the Pirate's Daughter: Passion and Parody in *William Shakespeare's Romeo + Juliet* and *Shakespeare in Love*' (in Burt and Boose, eds., pp. 56–71), begins with an account of a 1954 episode of CBS Television's *You Are There*, which presented a documentary account of 'The First Command Performance of *Romeo and Juliet*'. The programme opens up, he suggests, issues central to his consideration of *Romeo + Juliet* and *Shakespeare in Love*: the popularity of *Romeo and Juliet* in Shakespeare offshoots and the way in which Shakespeare functions in contemporary film as at once highbrow and lowbrow, 'a sign of culture and a vehicle for puncturing cultural pretension'. Both films negotiate the problematic relationship between a desire to make Shakespeare 'relevant' and a desire for cinematic novelty. Chris Palmer's '"What tongue shall smooth thy name?": Recent Films of *Romeo and Juliet*' (*CQ* 32:i[2003] 61–76) also focuses on *William Shakespeare's Romeo + Juliet* and *Shakespeare in Love*, and adds to the mix Zeffirelli's *Romeo and Juliet*. Palmer suggests that the films' strategies regarding names and naming intersect with the wider cultural significance of the Romeo and Juliet story, based as it often is on a tangible difference between Montague and Capulet which is absent from Shakespeare's play.

'Fever | I'm afire | Fever yea I burn forsooth'. The words ascribed to Romeo in Peggy Lee's 'Fever' are the starting point for Robert Shaughnessy's entertaining essay '*Romeo and Juliet*: The Rock and Roll Years' (in Aebischer, Esche and Wheale, eds., pp. 172–89). In the 1950s, spurred by new ideas about the nature of adolescent experience and the emergence of new forms of youth culture, Romeo and Juliet become teenagers. Examining the implications of this shift, Shaughnessy focuses on the complex dialogue which developed between different kinds of appropriation of *Romeo and Juliet* in the second half of the twentieth century. His discussion encompasses stage productions (Zeffirelli's 1960 Old Vic production), film adaptations (*West Side Story*; Zeffirelli's film, memorably described by one critic as 'a Renaissance *Graduate*'), scholarly editions (J. Dover Wilson benignly dedicating his 1955 edition to his former students), and popular music ('Fever'; the 'Love Theme' from *Romeo and Juliet*, later featured in the Radio 1 DJ Simon Bates's appalling catalogue of listeners' heartbreak, *Our Tune*).

Two essays focused on *Julius Caesar*. In a complex and rewarding study, '*Julius Caesar* in Interesting Times' (in Aebischer, Esche and Wheale, eds., pp. 115–33), Jean Chothia compares Orson Welles's 1937 stage adaptation, *Caesar*, with Joseph L. Mankiewicz's 1953 film. The two adaptations are located in their specific historical and political contexts. While Welles's production was overtly political, Mankiewicz's film, made at the height of McCarthyism, deliberately tried to avoid such questions. She concludes by considering the fact that Welles proposed a modern-dress screen version of *Julius Caesar* in 1949, plans which were only abandoned when he heard about Mankiewicz's film. The other *Julius Caesar* essay, Harry Keyishian's 'Storm, Fire, and Blood: Patterns of Imagery in Stuart Burge's *Julius Caesar*' (in Occhiogrosso, ed., pp. 93–103), takes as its subject Burge's little-studied adaptation. Keyishian focuses on the film's cinematography and its representation of certain key strands of imagery present in Shakespeare's film: storm, fire and blood. He aims to open up the critical resources available to students, encouraging them not to neglect close-reading techniques, which he suggests can be stimulated through the analysis of film.

Adaptations of Shakespeare's history plays also garnered attention. Barbara Korte's 'Elizabethan History Play into Postmodernist Screen/Play: McKellen and Loncraine's *Richard III*' (*ZAA* 51[2003] 371–85), argues that the film's intertextual engagement with popular film undermines its historical engagement. Rather than presenting 'history' it instead presents ahistorical pastiche, and its dependence on postmodern 'double access' to not only Shakespearian high culture but also the low culture of popular film limits its scope. Thomas Cartelli's 'Shakespeare and the Street: Pacino's *Looking For Richard*, Bedford's *Street King* and the Common Understanding' (in Burt and Boose, eds., pp. 186–99), meanwhile, takes as its starting point the performance of Shakespeare in a parking lot on New York's Lower East Side. Investigating the nationalistic implications of Shakespeare's performance in the USA, he shifts its focus to consider the street and, specifically, Al Pacino's attempt to assimilate Shakespeare to the sounds, rhythms and emotions of the American street in *Looking for Richard*. He then moves to analyse briefly *The Street King*, a different kind of dislocation of *Richard III*, in which Shakespeare is relocated to southern California and his language replaced by a site-specific and ethnically hybridized vernacular.

Appropriations of Shakespeare's histories also feature in Ton Hoenselaars's fascinating essay '"Out-ranting the enemy leader": *Henry V* and/as World War II Propaganda' (in D'haen, Liebregts, Tigges and Ewen, eds., *Configuring Romanticism*, pp. 215–34). Hoenselaars examines Olivier's *Henry V* in the context of both Olivier's autobiographical writings and biographical writings about him, including a 1990 novel, Philip Purser's *Friedrich Harris: Shooting the Hero*. The film interacts in important ways with mid-twentieth-century questions concerning Anglo-Irish and Anglo-German relations, and in its Second Word War context is related to a range of ideas concerning 'charismatic authority, hero worship and movie stardom'. Also focusing on an adaptation of *Henry V*, Deborah Vukovitz's 'Shakespeare on Film: *Henry V* Rendered in Music' (*ShakB* 21:i[2003] 42–3) analyses Paddy Doyle's music for Branagh's film, tracing the relationship between music and dialogue.

Adaptations of Shakespearian comedy featured more strongly this year than in recent years. An extremely useful bibliography was published: José Ramón Díaz

Fernández's 'Shakespeare's Comedies on Film, 1990–2001: A Checklist of Criticism' (*ShN* 52:iv[2002–3] 99–100, 102, 104, 108, 114, 116, 120). The year's most substantial critical essays focused on *Love's Labours Lost* and *A Midsummer Night's Dream*. In 'Putting Bottom on Top: Gender and the Married Man in Michael Hoffman's *Dream*' (*ShakB* 21:iv[2003] 40–56), Megan M. Matchinske examines the film's foregrounding of Bottom, as played by Kevin Kline—'this time around, it's Bottom's story, and Bottom has a wife'. Although critics should welcome a film version of *A Midsummer Night's Dream* which is prepared to take Bottom and his fellow workers seriously, Kline and Bottom's centrality effaces some of the problematic aspects of the mechanicals' presentation in Shakespeare's play. In place of the play's class tensions, Hoffman substitutes gender tensions. While Bottom's liaison in the play is a moment of wish-fulfilment focused on service as much as sex, the film instead gives Bottom an unhappy marriage and views his liaison with Titania as just another one-night stand. Social transformation, she concludes, is impossible in Hoffman's film, and it may even be undesirable; gender politics remain static.

Sarah Mayo's '"A Shakespeare for the people"? Negotiating the Popular in *Shakespeare in Love* and Michael Hoffman's *A Midsummer Night's Dream*' (*TPr* 17[2003] 295–315) uses two popularist Shakespeare films to investigate the problematic notion of 'Shakespeare for the people' and interrelated notions of high and popular culture. She first explores the way in which these films 'entertain the popular' by insisting on a continuity between Shakespeare's plays and Hollywood's romantic love narratives, and then moves to compare the 'cultural branding exercise' of Hoffman's *Midsummer Night's Dream* with the apparently postmodern entertainment of *Shakespeare in Love*. 'Both films', she concludes, 'finally and tellingly rely on the modernist paradigm which insists that art will redeem the masses, and that Shakespeare, as art, has that transcendent power to redeem.'

Finally, Douglas Lanier's 'Nostalgia and Theatricality: The Fate of the Shakespearean Stage in the *Midsummer Night's Dreams* of Hoffman, Noble, and Edzard' (in Burt and Boose, eds., pp. 154–72) examines the three films' engagement with the play's insistent theatricality, suggesting that a theatrical kernel resists the 'concerted mediatization' of Shakespeare's plays in the 1990s and 2000s. He concludes that Hoffman's *Dream* displays an ambivalent concern with the consequences of modern mediatization for the theatre, but that the *coup de théâtre* in the mechanicals' play—Thisbe's realistic pain on the death of Pyramus—aims to please an audience in the multiplexes by purging theatricality. Noble and Edzard, however, are more fully engaged in their films with the 'distinctively British question' of how to produce a popular Shakespeare in the theatre.

Questions regarding Britain and Shakespeare were also prominent in discussions of *Love's Labours Lost*. Ramona Wray's complex and multi-layered essay, 'The Singing Shakespearean: Kenneth Branagh's *Love's Labour's Lost* and the Politics of Genre' (in Aebischer, Esche and Wheale, eds., pp. 151–71), suggests that the 'animating logic' of Branagh's film was its generic transformation, an aspect which was continually stressed in the film's marketing and which led, she argues to its notorious commercial failure. Stressing the culturally contingent nature of genre, she suggests that the reception of *Love's Labours Lost* produces a version of the play far removed from the *auteur*'s original conception, destabilizing its narrative and the disclosing the limitations of the screen musical. *Love's Labours Lost* also set up a disjunction between genre and nation: a peculiarly British sensibility, tinged with nostalgia and implicit patriotism, was finally at odds with the film's American-orientated generic aspirations. A more fitting context, she suggests, can perhaps be traced not in the heyday of Hollywood, but in the heyday of British television and the musical experimentation of Dennis Potter in series such as *Pennies from Heaven* and *The Singing Detective*.

Similar concerns can be traced in Katherine Eggert's 'Sure Can Sing And Dance: Minstrelsy, the Star System, and the Post-Postcoloniality of Kenneth Branagh's *Love's Labour's Lost* and Trevor Nunn's *Twelfth Night*' (in Burt and Boose, eds., pp. 72–88). Eggert suggests that in a 'post-postcolonial' world, Britain is now subject to the cultural imperialism of the USA. The result, she argues, is a range of contradictory responses: nostalgia (the desire to make Shakespeare 'English' again), mockery (the parodic imitation of Hollywood), and affection and desire (a genuine love for and homage to Hollywood). These responses are exhibited in Branagh's *Love's Labour's Lost* and Nunn's *Twelfth Night*, and they serve to create a deeply ambiguous relationship between British and American Shakespeare.

In the same collection, Diana E. Henderson's 'A *Shrew* for the Times, Revisited' (in Burt and Boose, eds., pp. 120–39) revisits the concerns of an essay originally published in *Shakespeare, the Movie* (reviewed in *YWES* 78[1999] 302–3) to look at spin-offs such as *10 Things I Hate About You*. She concludes that *10 Things* 'continues to remind one of the recalcitrance of Shakespeare's story' in its movement from farce to marriage. A single essay on *Much Ado About Nothing*, William Brugger's 'Sins of Omission: Textual Deletions in Branagh's *Much Ado about Nothing*' (*Journal of the Wooden O Symposium* 3[2003] 1–11), details the changes made by Branagh to the Shakespearian text, which he suggests lead to underdeveloped characters, and to loss of thematic development, wit and humour, poetry and 'even truth'. He is prepared, however, to consider some possible excuses for these 'sins'. 'Like Claudio', he writes, 'Branagh has never really sinned; he just made some mistakes, with no lasting harm.' Finally, H.R. Coursen's 'Disguise in Trevor Nunn's *Twelfth Night*' (in Occhiogrosso, ed., pp. 84–5) focuses on the problematic nature of Viola's disguise and its handling in Nunn's film, comparing it with the treatment of Viola de Lesseps's male disguise in *Shakespeare in Love* and with that of Dustin Hoffman's female disguise in *Tootsie* [1982].

The year also featured some strong work on silent Shakespeare. In 'Two Silent Shakespeares: *Richard III* and *Othello*' (*Cinéaste* 28:ii[2003] 48–51), Russell Jackson reviews two silent films newly available on DVD (though only in North America), James Keane's 1912 *Richard III*, starring Frederick Warde, which has a claim to being the first American 'feature', and Dmitri Buchowetski's *Othello* [1922], which featured Emil Jannings and Werner Krauss in the leading roles. Whereas Warde's Richard clearly preserves a theatrical tradition of performance on film, Buchowetski's film demonstrates a range of performance registers, none of which corresponds to the older stylized methods, but instead represents a 'new continental European blend of naturalism and stylization'.

Cary DiPietro's 'Shakespeare in the Age of Mechanical Reproduction: Cultural Discourse and the Film of Tree's *Henry VIII*' (*NTQ* 19[2003] 352–65) discusses the film of *Henry VIII* made by producer William Barker and actor-manager Herbert Beerbohm Tree. Based on scenes from Tree's then current stage production, *Henry VIII* was first shown in March 1911; six weeks later, when the film had been shown around the country, all twenty prints were called in and burned. Tracing the film's fascinating history, DiPietro suggests that its manufacture and, more importantly, its destruction, can be associated with early twentieth-century debates about the nature and function of film and theatrical performance.

Similar concerns on the other side of the Atlantic animate Eddy Von Mueller's 'The Shakespeare Stratagem: Legitimacy, Legality and the Nickelodeon Shakespeare Boom' (*Journal of the Wooden O Symposium* 3[2003] 60–9), which discusses the ways in which silent Shakespeare mediated between high and low culture, displacing middle-class anxieties about the Nickelodeon boom while simultaneously attracting a new middle-class audience to the cinema. Detailed discussion focuses on J. Stewart Blackton's *A Midsummer Night's Dream* [1909], a species of film which aimed to retain conventional crowd-pleasers—'costume melodrama, sword-play, and camera magic'—within a pseudo-high-culture package, and Warde's *Richard III* [1912], a film dependent on the reputations of actor and dramatist.

Three essays took Disney's engagement with Shakespeare as their subject, and all are interested in how the appropriation of Shakespeare intersects with the cultural politics of the corporation. In 'Shakespeare and Company: *The Lion King* and the Disneyfication of *Hamlet*' (in Ayres and Hines, eds., *The Emperor's Old Groove: Decolonizing Disney's Magic*, pp. 117–29), Stephen M. Buhler examines the way in which *The Lion King* not only transforms and re-presents *Hamlet* but also reworks several critical modes of understanding Shakespeare. He links *The Lion King* with criticism and modes of teaching prevalent from the early 1960s to the mid-1980s, suggesting that *The Lion King* might equally well be entitled 'Disney's The African World Picture'. In particular, the film's presentation of father–son relationships effaces the problematic aspects of Shakespeare's own treatment of these relationships.

Also concerned with *The Lion King* is Jan Hollm's 'Streamlining Multicultural Feminism: Shakespearean Traits in Disney's *The Lion King*' (in Carroll, Pretzsch and Wagner, eds., *Framing Women: Changing Frames of Representation from the Enlightenment to Postmodernism*, pp. 283–94). Drawing on Gabriel Gutiérrez's critique of Disney, Hollm suggests that the incorporation of seemingly countercultural ideas into the company's films—in particular those connected with feminist and gay demands for gender relations to be restructured—masks the way in which their edge is simultaneously blunted. Although *The Lion King* seems to endorse demands for sexual equality and acceptance of non-conventional relationships, a deeper reading shows that it ultimately defends a patriarchal status quo.

Disney's representation of gender is also examined in Richard Finkelstein's 'Disney's Tempest: Colonizing Desire in *The Little Mermaid*' (in Ayres and Hines, eds., pp. 131–47). Finkelstein argues that, through the representation of Ariel and Ursula, and in particular their struggle over Ariel's voice, the film works hard to regulate the female body. Following *The Tempest*, Disney's *Little Mermaid* replaces the matriarchal structures of Anderson's story with the rule of a Prospero-like patriarchal father/king; the role of the women in the story is reduced, but the villainous Ursula becomes a combined Sycorax/Caliban, a locus for anxieties about the desiring and maternal female body. Disney's essentially conservative project is reified through the Shakespearian narrative. Staying with animated Shakespeare, Laurie Osborne's 'Mixing Media and Animating Shakespeare Tales' (in Burt and Boose, eds., pp. 140–53) is a revised and updated version of 'Mixing Media in Shakespeare: Animating Tales and Colliding Modes of Production' (*PostScript* 17:ii[1998] 73–89, reviewed in *YWES* 79[2000] 268). Osborne analyses the second series of *Shakespeare: The Animated Tales*, discussing its relationship with the first series and its provocative use of different modes of animation.

Finally, from what's there on screen, to what's not. As is clear from the discussion above, *Shakespeare in Love* continues to feature strongly in discussions of Shakespeare on screen, even though no articles focused on it exclusively. Another Shakespearean bio-pic is, however, the subject of Kay H. Smith's '*Will!* or Shakespeare in Hollywood: Anthony Burgess's Cinematic Presentation of Shakespearean Biography' (in Aebischer, Esche and Wheale, eds., pp. 134–50). Smith takes as her subject the surviving manuscripts of Anthony Burgess's 1968 screenplay for a fictional musical biography of Shakespeare (the genre apparently prompted by Warner Brothers' desire to encompass both Shakespeare and the then popular British musical). Examining the screenplay in the context of late 1960s cinema culture, commercial negotiations, and Burgess's own works, Smith is particularly illuminating on its connections with Burgess's novel *Nothing Like the Sun*, another fictional account of Shakespeare's life.

Similarly concerned with the absent, Alan C. Dessen's 'Teaching What's Not There' (in Occhiogrosso, ed., pp. 104–12) focuses on how questions relating to omissions in films—such as Brutus's desire to bathe the conspirators' hands in Caesar's blood, Romeo's killing of Paris, or Shylock's asides—can generate discussion in the undergraduate classroom. He concludes by asking, 'On a spectrum that ranges from the second quarto of *Romeo and Juliet* to *West Side Story*, at what point does one move from interpretation to translation or rewriting? Should we, as teachers and students, care about such matters? If not us, then who?' Discuss.

4. Criticism

(a) General

The known facts and the existing documents continue to attract biographers to the enigmatic gaps in the life of William Shakespeare, eliciting conjecture and speculation about the lost years, the 'fair youth', the 'Dark Lady', the correlation of the contours of the playwright's career and his personal fortunes and misfortunes, and prompting scholars to recycle old theories with new arguments or offer new rearrangements of Elizabethan contexts and connections. The BBC four-part television series went *In Search of Shakespeare* to promise a fresh perspective upon this familiar territory, and Michael Wood provides a handsome, oversized, lavishly illustrated companion volume of the same title. Wood handles the narrative extremely well. He opens the story a year before William's birth, with his father's assignment from the town corporation to whitewash and otherwise deface the Catholic images of the Guild Chapel in Stratford, a project that John apparently carried out with ambivalence if not reluctance and only partially completed. This sets the stage for Wood's 'revolution of the times', a complex opposition of the old Catholic beliefs and the new Protestantism of Elizabeth's religious programme of instituting her father's break from Rome, of the rural market town and the urban commerce of London, of the festive customs of an agricultural province and the mercantile future of England, of the small, marginally important island nation—Elizabeth standing so large on the tiny Britannia of the Ditchley portrait—and the powerhouse of trade England would soon become, the late medieval traditions and the early modern iconoclasm. Shakespeare was born, therefore, at this significant conjunction of change in an environment which accentuated the 'revolution' and provided him with an unusual and dramatic perspective.

The next few chapters thoroughly examine the Shakespeare family's farming and Catholic connections in Warwickshire, with the pre-Reformation and rural background making their reappearances often in Wood's narrative of Shakespeare's many recreations of the 'lost worlds' of his youth and his family's pre-Reformation society. The world of Elizabethan and Jacobean England was becoming 'global' as our world is now, as 'humanity's encoded memories are being erased everywhere across the planet', concludes Wood in his Epilogue (p. 344), our own 'revolution of the, as by 'its very nature, of course, modernity destroys tradition' (p. 343). One must appreciate Wood's sense of the turbulence surrounding Shakespeare's life in Stratford and London and his ability to illustrate the dynamics of conflict and change, presenting some seldom-noted archival evidence, some nineteenth-century photographs of no longer standing Tudor buildings, and maps of the Shoreditch and Bishopsgate theatre districts (pp. 119 and 125), all of which helpfully locate the playwright in the bustling life of 1590s London. Even if his story often seems to explain less than he assumes it does, he develops his approach with assurance and conviction in a very accessible style, scholarly without being threateningly academic. When there exists only mystery, Wood admits defeat in his search, but he doesn't hesitate to take a stand about most of the vexed questions a biographer faces, though, given his perspective, his identification of the 'fair youth' of the *sonnets* as William Herbert (p. 179) seems a surprising preference over the 'beautiful, bisexual' and Catholic Southampton (p. 147). He appears somewhat puzzled by the juxtaposition of the Lutheran Wittenberg and the purgatorial Ghost in *Hamlet* and comments: 'the pre-Reformation past is beginning to recede, and now Shakespeare can dramatize it, exorcising the ghosts' (p. 240). The volume's 'search' precludes the extensive analysis of the plays that would slow down the narrative and take it other directions than its televised series could accommodate.

An additional or alternative choice might be another oversized, well-illustrated volume by prolific editor and scholar Stanley Wells, *Shakespeare: For All Time*. In the first hundred or so pages, Wells summarizes what can be safely known about Shakespeare's biography and about his career 'in his time', and the next three hundred or so pages on the steady rise in the interest in and performance of the plays in later centuries until the present. Wells's summary of the life stays close to the known facts and documents, providing an accessible, well-written narrative; while more 'conservative' than Wood, Wells is not reticent in dismissing a number of conjectures as wishful fictions, such as the 'Shakeshaft' explanation of the 'lost years'.

Though something of a hybrid, the biography's emphasis on the man of the theatre and the fortunes and misfortunes of performance connects the parts. Wells includes a variety of representations of Shakespeare, his plays, and his characters in what transcends a stage history of four centuries of performance, though the theatre remains his main interest. Illustrations are plentiful—paintings, photographs, playbills—and along with Wells's scholarly but not intimidating writing keep the reader's interest in the narrative. Shakespeare made the fortunes of many actors, directors, and entrepreneurs, and Wells seems more willing to offer his opinions, especially about recent productions he has experienced, when he arrives at recent decades of Shakespeare's 'afterlife'. Generous attention to Shakespearian productions beyond English-speaking countries develops the 'title', as does the inclusion of the plays' centrality in educational and cultural politics, though Wells seldom insists upon the ideological appropriations of Shakespeare, as some of his scholarly colleagues have. Even more often than with Wood's volume, the reader will meet contexts, connections, and suggestions about how to interpret a scene or an entire play and wish Wells could slow down and develop the analysis, but for neither author is this the main goal.

In its size and ambition, Frank Kermode's *The Age of Shakespeare* cannot rival Wood's or Wells's volumes. A small book of less than two hundred pages, it begins with several chapters on the England of Elizabeth and the 'greater world of national politics' to set the stage for its primary focus on 'the development of a professional drama' and Shakespeare's place in and contributions to the literary and economic rise of the theatres as cultural institutions of importance. Pre-Reformation England and the accession of Elizabeth get a brief chapter, as Kermode takes the reader from the 1558 to 1603 in three pages, with the survival of Catholic sympathies, expression of 'popular religion' in the Corpus Christi mystery plays and festivals, and the ascendancy of Protestantism. The chapters that follow bring Shakespeare to London and trace his career with various companies and theatres, locating important productions along a chronological line of development.

The reader will find that, even after so much devotion to Shakespeare, Kermode in his eighties resolutely refuses to speculate about the enigmas of the biography: that 'Herbert was the Fair Youth of the Sonnets is an opinion that still has its adherents' (p. 158); 'Chapman, who is thought by some to be the Rival Poet' (p. 115); 'perhaps, as the story goes, Southampton gave him what he needed' to become a sharer in the Lord Chamberlain's Men' (p. 105). Kermode is equally cautious about the identity of the Dark Lady, and more than content to allow Shakespeare in the 'lost years' to have 'quite a long spell of life that remains completely private' (p. 41).

Perhaps such speculations merely distract from the accomplishments of the dramatist. Kermode's narrative moves swiftly through the plays, commenting upon their literary fashions, the popularity, and the political relevance; he offers concise suggestions about the maturation of the verse, suggestions that leave the reader wanting further analysis. For example, comparing the 'orations' of the early history plays with Macbeth's soliloquies, he asks: 'What has happened between 1594 and 1606, the date of *Macbeth*? It is hardly too much to call it a revolutionary change in dramatic language, even a transformation of English itself, now alive to a whole new range of poetic possibilities' (p. 69). Kermode's *Shakespeare's Language* [2000] provides a fuller exploration, but still one can welcome this compact survey of Shakespeare's dramatic development.

Early in *The Age of Shakespeare*, after doubting the 'fictions' that take an aspiring actor and playwright from Stratford to London, Kermode offers his own suggestion: perhaps Shakespeare went to London 'as a poet seeking a patron, somehow having got wind of one' (p. 41). Kermode does not pursue the thought, but it seems plausible to locate literary ambitions in the young Shakespeare, who may have already been working on the long narratives *Venus and Adonis* and *The Rape of Lucrece*, compositions later in search of Southampton as patron and poems carefully prepared for the printer. Given the centrality of Shakespeare's works in the literature curriculum and the years scholars have lectured and written about them as well as guiding students to think about them *as* literature, Lukas Erne's *Shakespeare as Literary Dramatist* might seem inevitable. Not only does Erne face the long-held notion that Shakespeare cared not at all about the publication of his plays (a notion the prominent Wells shares) but he also swims against the tide of growing body of criticism that bases all interpretation upon 'performance'. The 'evidence' for the former is based partly upon the idea that companies kept plays out of print to avoid other players from profiting by acting them, partly upon the fact that the price for a playscript could be a little as a few pounds, and partly upon the 'bad' quartos and the absence of many printed plays before the collected Folio edition of 1623. Erne persuasively shows that the Lord Chamberlain's men from 1594 to 1603 consistently saw Shakespeare's plays published, usually about two years after their first performance. From the length of most of Shakespeare's plays, he argues that they would have been too long for performance in the public playhouse and that—as they are today—they would have been shortened, sometimes radically, in the theatre. *Richard III* in its Folio version, for example, would in his estimation take five hours for Elizabethan actors to perform. His supporting arguments are too complex to be examined here, and many are better left to the reviewer of textual criticism (see Section 1 above), as they involve theories of memorial reconstruction and revision and as he spends his final chapters on detailed comparisons of various editions of *Romeo and Juliet*, *Hamlet*, and *Henry V*. But his overall conclusion is relevant here as affecting a 'general' assessment of Shakespeare: the quartos were representations of theatrical performances, while longer versions were written for readers, for the page rather than the stage. Further research might enhance Erne's argument, perhaps by textual comparisons, perhaps by further exploring the practices of the ninety or so Elizabethan printers whose economics may have dictated a shorter version for their quartos. The factors that might mediate between the theatre and the printing house probably render any explanation tenuous. But if Kermode's speculation is given some credence, Shakespeare may have first thought of himself as a poet, and certainly his writing the two *four*-part sequences of English history plays in the 1590s reveal an ambitious playwright if not also a 'literary dramatist'. With Erne's documentation of the growing respectability of printed plays as they were now being collected in private libraries and mentioned with more traditionally 'literary' works by contemporaries, Shakespeare's reputation among readers prepared for the kind of advice with which Heminge and Condell preface the First Folio: 'Read him again, and again'. Scholars will have to reckon with this book.

Stephen Orgel would presumably have dismissed Erne's argument if he had had access to it. In *Imagining Shakespeare: A History of Texts and Visions*, he writes that 'Shakespeare never conceived, or even re-conceived, his plays as texts to be read. They were scripts, not books; the only readers were the performers, and the function of the script was to be realized on the stage' (p. 1). Oddly enough, Orgel and Erne use many of the same sources and facts to support opposing approaches, and ironically Erne several times uses Orgel's earlier essays, which raise the issue of the disparity between time needed for performance and length of text and the unexplored theatrical implications of those differences, to advance his argument for theatrical and reading versions of the plays. Orgel's view, however, insists that performance almost always trumps text. An early chapter asks what drama is, and offers some competing, some complementary answers. In Shakespeare's own time drawings such as Henry Peacham's of a scene from *Titus Andronicus* or the engraving from the 1615 edition of Kyd's *Spanish Tragedy* illustrate no equivalent passages in those plays. The history of Shakespearian representations is full of such indifference to the 'text', and many of the hundred black and white and sixteen colour plates underscore the secondary importance of the printed play and sometimes its irrelevance. In one chapter he explores the increasing emphasis in the eighteenth century on the plays as a window to history, as the elaborate spectacles in the theatre almost rendered not only words but actors inessential to the performance. In another chapter, exploring the representations of Shakespeare himself, he asks 'why, given the unquestionable credentials of the folio frontispiece and the Stratford bust [in Holy Trinity], did the Chandos portrait, which looks so little like them, become the standard portrait of Shakespeare' (p. 76)? Though these are more limited in focus than Wells' 'history' of the highs and lows of adaptation and performance, Orgel's chapters raise many of the same questions about modern scruples about 'recovering' the text of the play as performed in the public playhouse, a concern which he would share with Erne's challenge of Wells and Taylor's claim in the Oxford edition to present texts of the plays 'as they were acted in the London playhouses' (Erne, p. 135). He sees that and the quest for a 'modern definitive biography' as fantasies: 'The mind, the character, the personality, are expressed in the plays and poems' (p. 83). So Orgel turns to 'the interrelations of script, performance, text and interpretation' (p. 85) to examine several plays.

After two truly remarkable chapters on the implications of the 'patriarchal ideology' of *Midsummer Night's Dream* and the ambivalence of audience response to Shylock and a rather meandering chapter about Giulio Romano's pornographic imagination and *The Winter's Tale*, a one-page Epilogue concludes: 'Having begun with scripts and performers, here is where we must conclude: the essence of drama, and theater's life and soul, is finally the audience' (p. 163). These are challenging readings of the *Dream* and the *Merchant*, though one will not miss the irony that they depend upon printed texts rather than scripts for performance.

Douglas Bruster's *Shakespeare and the Question of Culture* concerns itself more with the culture of contemporary criticism than with Shakespeare or his culture. Bruster's elaborate and complex argument with critical trends and practice takes place over three related parts. In the first he finds that the 'thick description' of recent criticism reads too much 'culture' from too little evidence. The reliance on anecdote and narrative, he admits, can be rich and informative, but often leads to untenable conclusions about Renaissance 'culture' based upon a rather small number of 'literary texts'. He argues the necessity of a 'thin description'—'reading widely' to 'aggregate evidence, to gather available information before coming to any conclusions about the culture toward which that evidence may gesture' (p. 42), to 'capture foreground and background not sequentially but simultaneously' as the 'deep focus' of the cinematographer does (p. 59).

Bruster uses film metaphors and analogies throughout to show how texts need to be seen through concentric circles of larger and larger cultural contexts and longer temporal stretches. Though one may agree that the wider and deeper the scholarly immersion in literary and other texts, the more secure the analysis of early modern culture, in part 2, when Bruster provides examples of 'thin description', it is difficult to measure the gains it offers. His 'aggregate of evidence' demonstrates that from the 1580s to the 1630s the number of stage properties steadily declined (chapter 4) and that female characters on stage were 'increasingly objectified, manipulated, and disempowered' (p. 143). The better literary and cultural historians have been reading widely even before the demise of New Criticism. Part 3 takes on the limitations of a variety of current practitioners of cultural criticism, adding the 'new formalists' and the 'new materialists' to the 'new historicists'. He thoroughly examines the questions of what counts as 'culturally significant' and what counts as 'evidence', and challenges the trendiness of Renaissance studies. That our own 'criticism' is mediated by our own cultural lenses, by 'academic entrepreneurship', by the market forces of universities' 'bureaucratic emphasis on productivity', and by the declining value of 'culture' in today's world (p. 209) no doubt well underscores the ways in which scholarship can be skewed. As a searching critique of the current state of Renaissance (or is it now 'early modern'?) studies, Bruster's book provides a thorough examination of many of the ways literary criticism can go wrong.

Somewhat more specialized are the three volumes—one collection and two monographs—that will conclude this section.

Linda Woodbridge, ed., *Money and the Age of Shakespeare: Essays in the New Economic Criticism*, may be the newest trend in 'cultural criticism', though interest in the 'nascent capitalism' and the dramatic representations of merchants, entrepreneurs, confidence men, prostitutes, and all other manner of financial profit and exchange has long concerned students of Elizabethan, and especially Jacobean, theatre. This collection assembles sixteen essays, most from the 2001 annual meeting of the Shakespeare Association of America. Many of them focus on single works—not surprisingly five on *The Merchant of Venice* and two on *Measure for Measure*, as well as essays on George Herbert's poetry, Deloney's *Jack of Newbury*, and Ben Jonson's 1624 'Elegy'. Three others take on other individual Shakespeare plays. The introduction by Woodbridge sets the larger context of an increasingly intense interest in mathematics, accounting, and commerce, an interest that produced private schools in which 'reckonmasters' taught such new topics as 'double-entry bookkeeping' and 'an explosion of mathematical and commercial publishing' (p. 4). She provides a list of about forty such titles published from 1519 to 1614, a suggestive context for all the language and metaphors that circulate through almost every play by Shakespeare and his contemporaries. Money, debt, commodity, and exchange value have been unavoidable in our reading of Shakespeare for a long time, but the essays often provide a fresh approach and valuable research from perspectives influenced by materialist, feminist, and New Historicist angles. The 'new economic criticism' is a 'big tent', Douglas Bruster says in one of the few general essays; again, he warns against the 'slippery' meanings of 'economy': is 'economy' the formal financial system of credit, debt, profit, and so forth or the metaphor that describes any loosely organized collection of themes and behaviours (as in the 'economies of race and gender', for example)?

B.J. and Mary Sokol continue their investigation of the laws of Elizabethan England (begun in *Shakespeare's Legal Language* [2000]) in *Shakespeare, Law and Marriage*. One might immediately think of the multiple marriages that conclude the festive comedies, but marriage, law, and property issues arise often in other plays. The Sokols have exhaustively studied the legal and historical documents of dowries, dowers, 'jointure', and property rights in the legal and social history of Shakespeare's England and applied those contexts to the vexed issues that arise in the plays. The legal establishment could disagree about when a marriage was valid, about the legal rights of widows, and about a variety of other matters controversial and confusing. Arranged, enforced, and broken marriages receive attention, as do the confusion and uncertainty in the law itself. They apply their research to the plays—the *Taming of the Shrew*, *Measure for Measure*, and many others—to address the issues of marriage, law and property, sometimes to show how Shakespeare shares the confusion with his legal contemporaries. The authors' interdisciplinary approach unites literary study with cultural history and social practices that involve class status, religion and gender issues.

Finally, readers may be interested in Suzanne Lord's *Music from the Age of Shakespeare: A Cultural History*. The references to Shakespeare are brief and scattered, but her thorough survey of the diversity of music and dance in the English Renaissance covers the various genres and practices among the aristocracy and commons, the Londoners and those at the country fairs and elsewhere. Though Lord never really elaborates upon the presence of music in Shakespeare's plays, she is fully aware of its contexts, and delineates the musical culture in which the theatre thrived. She provides us with helpful illustrations of Elizabeth instruments, and in a final chapter thumbnail biographies of the more important composers of the English Renaissance, including Thomas Morley, who lived near Shakespeare and set a 'song' from *As You Like It* to music. The organization and writing are at best workmanlike, but the information is useful.

(b) Comedies

The Merchant of Venice proved to be last year's most popular play, in part through its dominating presence in a collection of essays on economic criticism of early modern English Literature, Woodbridge, ed., *Money and the Age of Shakespeare*. In this collection, Eric Spencer, 'Taking Excess, Exceeding Account: Aristotle Meets The Merchant of Venice' (pp. 143–58), turns to Aristotle's *Nichomachean Ethics* to develop an exploration of (in)commensurability and excess in the play. Spencer argues that the play stages an impasse between, on the one hand, the indispensable nature of money and merchandizing and, on the other hand, the liberating excess of love, judicial equity, and grace. Mark Netzloff's 'The Lead Casket: Capital, Mercantilism, and *The Merchant of Venice*' (pp. 159–76) from the same volume argues for a more complex and historically nuanced notion of the relationship between capitalism and mercantilism than previous readings have offered. In particular, Netzloff traces the manner in which tensions between representative currency and material currency emerge in the play, epitomized in the values of the caskets. Steven Mentz's 'The Fiend Gives Friendly Counsel: Launcelot Gobbo and Polyglot Economics in *The Merchant of Venice*' (pp. 177–87) argues for the importance of Gobbo to the play's economic interests, and in so doing offers a critique of prevalent features of New Economic Criticism. Mentz argues that Gobbo, a middle-man, destabilizes the ideological binaries commonly read in the play, and in particular that between Portia's fantasy of abundance and Shylock's mercantilism or usury, offering a third economic position that he interprets as a pluralist urge to exchange at the heart of emergent capitalism. In our final contribution from the collection, 'Freeing Daughters on Open Markets: The Incest Clause in *The Merchant of Venice*' (pp. 189–200), Robert F. Darcy explores the duplicity of Venice, and in particular Belmont, in seeming to offer fairness to all while implicitly and fraudulently privileging insiders. Darcy reads Portia's adherence to her dead father's will as a form of incestuous compliance whereby the dead patriarch is able to withhold his daughter from outsiders until an endogamous match may be found for her.

John Klause explores Shakespeare's special pains to introduce religion into the play in 'Catholic and Protestant, Jesuit and Jew: Historical Religion in *The Merchant of Venice*' (in Taylor and Beauregard, eds., *Shakespeare and the Culture of Christianity in Early Modern England*, pp. 180–221). Klause maps what he identifies as the key religious issues traversed by the play through connecting it with the Jesuit missionary and martyr Robert Southwell's poetry, and points to a number of passages where Southwell's vocabulary has seemingly 'seeped' into Shakespeare's text (p. 189). The essay ends with the proposal that we read Shylock as a puritan Protestant confronted by two Southwells, the mercy-giving Portia and the martyr Antonio. In 'Portia and the Prince of Morocco' (*ShakS* 31[2003] 89–126), Gustav Ungerer traces a number of points of contact between Saadian-dynasty Morocco and England in the early modern period, foremost amongst which are trade links, political and diplomatic relations, and literary representations of the sexuality of Saadian and Muslim rulers. Ungerer argues that the Prince of Morocco's mistaken choice of the golden casket represents a contemporary fear of miscegenation, and the cultural and racial incompatibility between Morocco and an England shaped by the duplicity of merchant capitalists towards their Muslim partners. Filomena Mesquita's 'Royal and Bourgeois Translators: Two Late-Nineteenth-Century Portuguese Readings of *The Merchant of Venice*' (in Pujante and Honselaars, eds., *Four Hundred Years of Shakespeare in Europe*, pp. 145–60) compares King D. Luís's 1879 translation with that of Bulhão Pato, which followed two years later. Mesquita reads the latter translation as a response to the monarch's earlier work, and focuses on a number of divergent single words between the translations that are significant in terms of the contemporary economic, cultural, and political context. James O'Rourke reads the play as 'an antiracist response' to the execution of Rodrigo Lopez in 'Racism and Homophobia in *The Merchant of Venice*' (*ELH* 70[2003] 375–97). Against the setting of the Lopez execution, O'Rourke explores the manner in which the play complicates the distinction between Jews and Christians, principally by making the Christian faction Italian Catholics, the object of much contemporary invective for moneylending as well as for accusations of sodomy. The article ends with some brief reflections on later stagings of the play, considering performances that side with either Shylock or the Christians, and O'Rourke sees in Charles Macklin's performance a reading that complicates the terms of this opposition.

J.C. Ross, 'Stephen Gosson and *The Merchant of Venice* Revisited' (*N&Q* 50[2003] 36–7), notes an echo of Gosson's *Schoole of Abuse* in Shylock's advice to Jessica, 'But stop my house's ears—I mean my casement' (II.v.34), an association that casts both Shylock and Gosson as 'narrow-spirited killjoys' (p. 37). In 'Shylock's Unpropped House and the Theatre in Shoreditch' (*N&Q* 50[2003] 37–9), Gabriel Egan argues that, contrary to claims that the play was performed after the Chamberlain's men had left the theatre, *The Merchant of Venice* was probably first produced as the players considered the coming loss of their playhouse as they continued to use it after their first lease expired. Rafel Major's '*The Merchant of Venice*' (*Expl* 61[2003] 198–200) reflects upon how the gossipy form taken by the reporting of events by Salerio and Solano influences our reading of Shylock and the presumed loss of Antonio's argosies.

Woodbridge's collection also included work on *The Comedy of Errors*. Curtis Perry reads the play in relation to the developing commodity culture of early modern England in 'Commerce, Community, and Nostalgia' (in Woodbridge, ed., pp. 39–51). The play's early scenes, Perry argues, present an insistent interrelation between the familial and the economic, while the farcical action of the central scenes also relates human relations through commercialization, in this case through complex relations of credit and reputation. The climax of the play sees the repudiation of the interpersonal commerce of the earlier scenes for the re-establishment of familial bonds. Richard Dutton's '*The Comedy of Errors* and *The Calumny of Apelles*: An Exercise in Source Study' (in Taylor and Beauregard, eds., pp. 26–43) reads the repeated slanders in the play in the light of Shakespeare's use of Lucian's *Calumny*, or 'On not believing rashly in slander'. Shakespeare's recourse to Lucian's text, which was readily understood as a metaphor for religious heresy in the period, invokes within the play religious slanders between Protestants and Catholics. In the play's reconstructive ending—where the family riven by symbolic differences in faith is unified under the aegis of an abbess at Ephesus, a place symbolically associated with the Virgin Mary—we see an inclusiveness that reaches towards an undivided, and perhaps Catholic, Christendom. J.J.M. Tobin's note on 'Dr. Pinch and Gabriel Harvey' (*N&Q* 50[2003] 32–5) discusses the Nashean content of Shakespeare's play, and reflects upon whether Dr Pinch may even have been presented on stage as an immediately recognizable caricature of Gabriel Harvey. Martine Van Elk's 'Urban Misidentification in *The Comedy of Errors* and the Cony-Catching Pamphlets' (*SEL* 43[2003] 323–46) develops intertextual relations between Shakespeare's play and the pamphlets through a cultural fascination with misidentification. The mutability of the trickster and the identity confusions in the play occasioned by the twins both expose the precarious nature of social identity, leaving the audience with a disconcerting insight into a world in which cultural expectations only serve to further disorder.

Thomas Moisan's 'Deforming Sources: Literary Antecedents and their Traces in *Much Ado About Nothing*' (*ShakS* 31[2003] 165–83) also turns to our understanding of Shakespearian intertexts. Moisan argues that the play repeatedly appears to summon its heroic romance sources—particularly the work of Ariosto and *La Prima Parte de la Novelle del Bandello*—only to then distance itself from them, leaving their presences in the play as parodic and ironic allusions, out of place in the decidedly unheroic Messina. Kathryn Walls, in a note on '*Much Ado About Nothing* III.v.17–26' (*Expl* 61[2003] 200–2), proposes that Leonato's impatient expostulation that Verges and Dogberry are 'tedious' (III.v.17) is taken by the latter as a compliment on his verbal facility, as Dogberry understands the comment in the sense of 'copious' as 'Having a plentiful command of language' (p. 201).

Carol Enos, 'Catholic Exiles in Flanders and *As You Like It*; Or, What if You Don't Like It At All?' (in Dutton and Findlay, eds., *Theatre and Religion: Lancastrian Shakespeare*, pp. 130–42) connects the exiles in Arden with the plight of Catholics who sought refuge abroad during the latter years of the sixteenth century. Enos proposes that the play's idyllic representation of exile might be seen as a rebuttal of English government propaganda that proclaimed the bleakness and hardship suffered by those who fled to Spain and Flanders, and, leaning upon some theories of how Shakespeare spent the 'lost years', speculates on some of the figures and situations that may have shaped Shakespeare's writing. In 'Pancakes and a Date for *As You Like It*' (*SQ* 54[2003] 371–405), Juliet Dusinberre argues that a short poem in the commonplace book of Henry Stanford is Shakespeare's prologue for the performance at Richmond of the play on Shrove

Tuesday, 20 February 1599. Establishing a date and location for the play, Dusinberre suggests, gives us a special insight into its relation to its world and the conditions of its performance, and she speculates on topical allusions to pancakes and Ganymede, the play's casting, the performance venue, its audience, the playing of music, and a number of court connections, including Shakespeare's relationship to the composer Thomas Morley. Dusinberre's second offering on the play, 'Rival Poets in the Forest of Arden' (*ShJE* 139[2003] 71–83) also has matters at court in the background. Endeavouring to move beyond both traditional forms of source study and more recent forms of intertextuality, Dusinberre proposes that the numerous poets and writers conjured into the play—Lodge, Sidney, and Marlowe, but also John Heywood, Virgil, Chaucer—should be understood not in terms of rivalry, as her title suggests, but as 'co-mates and brothers in exile' (p. 83). The conciliatory relationship between the poets, argues Dusinberre, may be seen as a looking forward to future harmony in the light of the factious events of the Irish crisis and Essex's struggle for mastery with Elizabeth.

'Wrangling Pedantry: Education in *The Taming of the Shrew*' (in Davis, ed., *Shakespeare Matters*, pp. 191–208) sees Kim Walker interrogate the gender- and class-specific issues of education in the play. Walker exposes the contradiction within humanist pedagogical discourse that at once sees education as the appropriate acquisition of a gentlewoman and as something both dangerously erotic and a source of potential disorder; foregrounding education as a troubling issue from the beginning, the play in effect presents education as a potential 'shrew-making' school. Walker ends with a reflection upon the transformation of class and gender issues in Marowitz's version of the play and *Kiss Me Kate*. 'Neither a Tamer Nor a Shrew Be: A Defense of Petruchio and Katherine' (in Abate, ed., *Privacy, Domesticity, and Women in Early Modern England*, pp. 31–44) sees Corinne S. Abate drawing upon theories of the private and the public, including the thought of Habermas, to argue that Petruchio's unconventional wooing of Katherine allows her to create a sense of private self within her marriage that eschews public acceptance. Katherine's final speech is thus revealed as an 'inessential speech act', empty of any real meaning because it is divorced from her private self and the bond that she shares with her unconventional and appreciative husband (p. 39). Holly Crocker's 'Affective Resistance: Performing Passivity and Playing A-Part in *The Taming of the Shrew*' (*SQ* 54[2003] 142–59) disrupts the conflation of female virtue with passivity. Rather, Crocker argues, Katherine's submission may be revealed as something deeply performative, a taking on of an ideology, that reveals that 'active/passive binary meant to represent gender difference is really only a ruse' (p. 158). R.W. Maslen's note on '*The Taming of the Shrew* and *The Image of Idleness*' (*N&Q* 50[2003] 25–7) ponders whether Petruchio's shrew-taming techniques may have found a hint in the advice given by Bawdin Bachelor, the protagonist of *A little treatyse called the Image of Idleness*.

Regina M. Buccola's 'Shakespeare's Fairy Dance with Religio-Political Controversy in *The Merry Wives of Windsor*' (in Taylor and Beauregard, eds., pp. 159–79) argues that the presence of fairies in the play sees Shakespeare engaging with some weighty contemporary religious controversies through these spiritually ambivalent creatures. In particular, Buccola sees in Hugh Evans an embodiment of the Welsh Anglican John Penry's fears that the Welsh clergy were jeopardizing the salvation of their parishioners through persistent loyalty to both the Catholic Church and fairy lore, the two often being conflated. Still with fairies, J.P. Conlon suggests, in 'Puck's Dread Broom' (*ELN* 40[2003] 33–41), that when Puck comes onstage with a broom he is a frightening prospect for those sitting upon the stage, as he threatens to sweep away herbs or flowers laid around to prevent the spread of disease. Conlon speculates upon the different manners in which fearful reactions of the elite would register to the rest of the audience, including appearing as a rebuke to the authorities that used fear of infection to close down the theatres. J.J.M. Tobin's 'Have With You to Athens' Wood' (*N&Q* 50[2003] 32–5) notes with mild surprise the extent to which Nashe's *Have With You to Saffron Walden* appears to have influenced the play, and in particular the adventures of Bottom.

Back to the Woodbridge collection, Valerie Forman, in 'Material Dispossessions and Counterfeit Investments: The Economies of *Twelfth Night*' (in Woodbridge, ed., pp. 113–27), contends that the play consistently disavows not only the mercantile nature of its literary source *Gl'Ingannati* and the nascent capitalism of early modern England, but reality itself. This '*anti-topic*' emphasis of disavowal simultaneously sees the play's characters needing to assert their autonomy from the objects circulating within the Illyrian economy, and yet unavoidably finding themselves investing, and invested, in them. Lisa Marciano's 'The Serious Comedy of *Twelfth Night*: Dark Didacticism in Illyria' (*Renascence* 56[2003] 3–19) explores the looming presence of death throughout the play in terms of a form of didacticism. *Twelfth Night*, like many of Shakespeare's comedies, Marciano argues, sees characters responding to mortality with the recognition that because life is transient it must be lived well, and that this truth must be communicated to others. The essay focuses on the work of the play's two primary educators, Feste and Viola. 'Caterwauling Cataians: The Genealogy of a Gloss' (*SQ* 54[2003] "My Lady's a Cataiain" (II.iii.124) that reflects upon a succession of editors' confused conflations of Cathay and China. The essay's main focus is the history of the gloss itself, but Timothy Billings also offers a more contemporary possibility that the term Cataian might be read as 'someone whose speech is not to be trusted' (p. 7). Jami Ake's 'Glimpsing a "Lesbian" Poetics in *Twelfth Night*' (*SEL* 43[2003] 347–74) offers an argument that the play sees an emergent language of female–female erotic desire through the transformation of conventional heteroerotic discourse. Focusing on the interview scene (I.v), Ake argues that the failure of Orsino's heteroerotic Petrarchanism gives way to a 'pastoral poetics of female desire' between Viola and Olivia, characterized in terms of presence by way of contrast to the Petrarchan discourse of absence.

'Oxford University and *Love's Labour's Lost*' (in Taylor and Beauregard, eds., pp. 80–102), by Clare Asquith, argues that a number of topical allusions converging on Oxford University reveal the play as an appeal for a more liberal approach to learning in the universities. The oath undertaken by the play's academics thus evokes the Oath of Supremacy required of those entering Oxford; the male lovers, once forsworn, become humanist scholars; while Don Armado echoes John Donne's Oxford tutor Antonio de Corro. More than a romantic comedy, Shakespeare's play, argues Asquith, is a comment on the pressing issues of education and religion.

(c) Problem Plays

This was a bumper year for work produced on the problem plays. This was due in part to the publication of *A Companion to Shakespeare's Works*, edited by Richard Dutton and Jean E. Howard. The fourth volume in this series covers the poems, problem comedies, and late plays, with seven articles relating to the problem plays.

The essay which focuses exclusively on *Measure for Measure* from this collection is Karen Cunningham's 'Opening Doubts upon the Law: *Measure for Measure*' (pp. 316–32). Cunningham reads the play's concern with the law and its methods of attempting to resolve the various disputes in the light of the contemporary legal ritual of mooting. Moots were the imaginary cases performed by trainee lawyers at the Inns of Court, but which had also became a popular form of debate. A moot placed greater emphasis upon speculation and imagining situations which would present challenges to the law. Cunningham argues persuasively for the influence of moots on *Measure for Measure*, and cites examples from contemporary moots, which looked to biblical stories such as that of Jacob and Esau for their inspiration. The play's concern with pregnancy and the necessary bed trick reflects the legal interest in paternity, while its apparently arbitrary ending is an example of the moot's concern with exploring and raising problems, rather than the emotional considerations required for their resolution.

Another important publication for Shakespeare's problem plays was Taylor and Beauregard, eds., *Shakespeare and the Culture of Christianity*, which contained essays on both *Measure for Measure* and *All's Well*. In 'Shakespeare on Monastic Life: Nuns and Friars in *Measure for Measure*' (pp. 311–35), David Beauregard considers Shakespeare's treatment of monastic life, particularly the Franciscans, to counter the arguments of those critics who suggest that the nuns and friars in the play are used primarily for satirical or demystifying purposes. Beauregard carefully details Shakespeare's comparatively favourable presentation of monastic life by locating the play in the context of other anti-fraternal drama, while also considering the changes Shakespeare makes to his sources to support his argument. In attempting to redress the imbalance of secular responses or those based on Reformed theology to the monks and nuns in *Measure for Measure*, Beauregard's own essay adopts an oppositional position, which despite providing a useful vantage point from which to view the play, overlooks the subtleties of its handling of the multiple religious perspectives in England at that time.

The *Journal of the Wooden O Symposium* offered a collection of articles on *Measure for Measure* from its annual conference, hosted by Southern Utah University. The first is Stephanie Chamberlain's 'Capitalising on the Body: *Measure for Measure* and the Economics of Patrilineal Worth' (*Journal of the Wooden O Symposium* 3[2003] 12–22), in which she examines the loss of Mariana's dowry and the delay in the payment of Juliet's in order to argue that the play is concerned with 'the persistent problem of funding marriage portions in

Shakespeare's early modern England'. David Crosby, in 'Shakespeare's Use of Examination in *Measure for Measure*' (*Journal of the Wooden O Symposium* 3[2003] 23–35), argues that examination scenes in Shakespeare's plays, such as Othello's appearance before the Venetian senate and the opening scene of *King Lear*, have their origins in Protestant polemical literature. Crosby then offers a reading of the examination scenes in *Measure for Measure*, particularly that in Act II, scene iv between Angelo and Isabella, to suggest the influence of famous printed accounts of the examinations of Protestant martyrs on the play. The third essay, by Tom Flanigan, 'What To Do About Bawds and Fornicators: Sex and Law in *Measure for Measure* and Tudor/Stuart England' (*Journal of the Wooden O Symposium* 3[2003] 36–49), reads the play's depiction of sexual transgression against early modern laws, particularly the Church laws that dealt with bawds and prostitutes, to examine repeated attempts during the sixteenth and early seventeenth centuries to suppress sexual misconduct. The final essay from the conference, 'A Case of Psychological Impotence: Diagnosing Angelo though Montaigne and Freud' (*Journal of the Wooden O Symposium* 3[2003] 79–94), by Carole Schuyler, offers a study of Angelo's character and behaviour using Montaigne's 'Of the Force of Imagination' and Freud's 'Contributions to the Psychology of Love' in order to construct a response to Walter Pater's question of whether Angelo is 'indeed psychologically possible'.

Other articles on *Measure for Measure* included J.J.M. Tobin's note 'How Drunk Was Barnadine?' (*N&Q* 50[2003] 46–7). Tobin argues that Shakespeare's name for the prisoner Barnadine was taken not, as some editors have suggested, from Marlowe's *The Jew of Malta*, but from Nashe's pamphlet *Strange News*. In the epistle dedicatory to his pamphlet Nashe addresses his friend William Beestine as 'Maister Apis Lapis', who he remarks was 'never of the order of Barnadines' (p. 46). R.B. McKerrow, the editor of *The Works of Thomas Nashe*, glosses 'Barnadines' as 'a jesting allusion to the order of St. Bernard and at the same time to the so-called "Barnard's law", a method of cheating at cards by the aid of a confederate who feigns drunkenness and who is called Barnard' (p. 47). Tobin concludes that Barnadine's name points to this confidence trick, which Barnadine himself practises. In this case, however, Barnadine feigns drunkenness to the Duke disguised as the Friar to prevent his execution. Barnadine believes that the Friar will support his argument that a drunken man is in no spiritual state for execution.

Andrew Hadfield's note, 'Shakespeare's *Measure for Measure*' (*Expl* 61[2003] 71–3), suggests that James I's homosexuality would have been known to a contemporary theatre audience from the rumours about his relationships with his favourites. Hadfield points to the exchange between Lucio and the Duke in Act III, scene ii, when the Duke, in disguise as the Friar, responds to Lucio's remarks about his licentious reputation with 'I have never heard the absent Duke much detected for women; he was not inclined that way', to suggest that Shakespeare is deliberately alluding to the king's sexuality. While the evidence from the play certainly supports Hadfield's position, his suggestion that the 'duke is the only major character in the play who does not have a relationship with anyone of the opposite sex' (pp. 71–3), does, however, raise questions about the Duke's proposal to Isabella at the end of the play.

In her article 'Which Model? Whose Measure? Sexuality, Morality and Power in *Measure for Measure* and *Basilicon Doron*' (*Philament* 1[2003]), Alison O'Hare examines the treatment of political authority, power and gender in both texts, to argue that *Measure for Measure* offers a response to James's treatise in which the mythology of authority is deconstructed. Finally for *Measure for Measure* is Barbara Everett's article, 'A Dreame of Passion' (*LRB* 25[2003] 23–6), in which she offers a reading of the play, beginning with its reputation as flawed, an assertion which she counters by examining the ways in which it draws attention to its own strangeness, particularly in Act V, when what has really been happening is finally revealed.

All's Well That End's Well seemed to be the most popular of the problem plays this year, with a number of important articles. Several come from the collection *Shakespeare and the Culture of Christianity*. The first, Lisa Hopkins's 'Paris Is Worth a Mass: *All's Well That Ends Well* and the Wars of Religion' (in Taylor and Beauregard, eds., pp. 369–81), argues that the play is concerned with looking back to the old world of classical myth and fairytale as a strategy for responding to the future. Hopkins explains that the past is then juxtaposed to references to contemporary French history, namely the marriage of Catherine de' Medici to Henry II and the French wars of religion. Despite the play's concern with religious conflict, its vision for the future is positive, as it looks to Helena and her association with the miraculous to suggest that healing lies in the 'reversion to a much older, quasi-magical mode of thought and worship that preceded the splitting of the faiths and the theological controversies that consequently ensued'.

The second essay from the collection, Maurice Hunt's 'Helena and the Reformation Problem of Merit in *All's Well That Ends Well*' (pp. 336–67), complements Hopkins's reading of the religious conflict in *All's Well* by focusing on the contentious issue of merit. Hunt argues that the play explores the problematic idea of the heresy of merit; the Protestant belief in faith as opposed to the Catholic belief in deeds, suggesting that, through Helena's cure for the King of France's fistula and the bed trick, Shakespeare 'introduces into his play Catholic as well as Protestant contexts for positively appreciating merit' (p. 341).

In 'Sick Desires': *All's Well That Ends Well* and the Civilising Process' (in Davis, ed., *Shakespeare Matters*, pp. 89–102), Lloyd Davis examines Bertram's behaviour in the light of educational manuals by Ascham, Elyot and Erasmus. Davis suggests that the play, with its prescribed codes of behaviour, is 'a vivid illustration of the social pressures that strongly impinge upon male identity and desire' (p. 97). Bertram is unable to adapt the codes of conduct he has learned as he moves between familial, courtly and military circles. This leaves him caught between conforming with expected behaviour and pursuing his own ambitions and sexual desires.

Barbara Howard Traister's scholarly essay, '"Doctor She": Healing and Sex in *All's Well that Ends Well*' (in Dutton and Howard, eds., vol. 4, pp. 333–47), looks at Helena's role as a healer in the context of the contemporary medical hierarchy of licensed physicians and unlicensed empirics and their respective practices. Traister explores the way in which Helena's adoption of the roles of physician and wooer, roles usually reserved for men, challenges both the medical and social hierarchy. As a physician Helena is not only able to cure the king, but her fee bargaining for Bertram as her husband ensures that she is also able to cure herself of her love sickness. The anxiety that Helena's success generates within the play is ultimately vanquished in its final scene. Traister argues that Helena is contained by placing her within the narrative of folklore, where she is no longer a physician, but a 'clever wife who wins a husband' (p. 345). The expertise required to cure the king is tainted by sexual innuendo and her prize is to be Bertram's wife. 'There is no suggestion that she will ever practise the healing arts again; the troubling female empiric has been erased and replaced by the licensed reproductive wife' (p. 345).

Meanwhile David M. Bergeron's essay, '*All's Well That Ends Well*: Where is Violenta?' (*EIRC* 29[2003] 171–84), is concerned with a textual matter, namely consideration of editors' treatment of Violenta, the play's silent character. Bergeron offers an insightful account of the way in which modern editors have often excised Violenta from the play, without explanation. He goes on to suggest that her presence in Act III, scene v as a silent woman is important as she contributes thematically to the play's concern with male and female relationships. Bergeron argues that Violenta can be seen to speak through Mariana's description of male infidelity: 'Violenta can give mute testimony to men's violence, a silent but gripping example of the wreckage of relationships, the victim of promises' (p. 176).

Work this year on *Troilus and Cressida* came exclusively from volume 4 of *A Companion to Shakespeare*. The first, 'The Two-Party System in *Troilus and Cressida*' (pp. 302–15), by Linda Charnes, discusses the war between the Greeks and the Trojans in terms of the two-party system of American politics. Using the example of the party system and the discrepancies with the elections in 2000, Charnes argues that the responses to these events offer parallels with the strategies and attitudes adopted by Greeks and Trojans to the war. In each case both sides are aware of the 'consequences and implications of knowing what's going on and subscribing to it anyway' (p. 306). Charnes demonstrates this attitude with a reading of the Trojan debate about 'value' in Act II, scene ii, in which, she argues, their discussion about honour and the importance of keeping Helen is less about 'how they are going to proceed but rather about consolidating and reaffirming their commitment to a shared ideological fantasy in which no one actually believes' (p. 309).

Bruce Boehrer's 'The Privy and its Double: Scatology and Satire in Shakespeare's Theatre' (pp. 69–88), places *Troilus and Cressida* with two later Jacobean plays, Jonson's *The Alchemist* and Middleton's *A Game at Chess*. Each of the plays, performed by the King's men, is informed by the discourse of scatology, with each play employing a range of doubling devices to examine the relationship between bodily fluids and the world, and in particular to establish the binary themes of baseness and gentility.

There are three essays from *A Companion to Shakespeare* which deal with the problem plays collectively. The first is Paul Yachnin's 'Shakespeare's Problem Plays and the Drama of his Time: *Troilus and Cressida*, *All's Well That Ends Well*, *Measure for Measure*' (in Dutton and Howard, eds., vol. 4, pp. 46–68). Yachnin begins by addressing the use of the title 'problem plays', and suggests that the 'problem' with the plays is that they are radical experiments by

Shakespeare and as such 'can be understood best against the background of the competitive field of dramatic writing in the decade from approximately 1595 to 1605' (p. 47). To this end the plays are considered chronologically, with *Troilus and Cressida* discussed in relation to a new style of playwriting initiated by Chapman and Jonson, with the emphasis on satire and the movement away from narrative-based drama. *All's Well That Ends Well* is then considered alongside Dekker's *The Shoemaker's Holiday* to examine their treatment of the issues of romantic love and rank. The essay concludes with an examination of the political perspectives available in *Measure*, which is grouped with Middleton's *The Phoenix* [1604] and Heywood's *If You Know Not Me, You Know Nobody* [1605]. Yachnin describes these as accession plays, arguing that Middleton and Heywood offer an ideal of an absolutist monarchy; in *Measure for Measure*, however, Shakespeare works around the model of absolutist rule under James to present a Vienna where the Duke relies upon a series of individuals to effect his plans, so that there is the suggestion of a 'governmental structure that effectively shares power with the ruler' (p. 65).

In a lively and wide-ranging discussion of dynastic and companionate marriages during the early modern period, Theodora Jankowski, in 'Hymeneal Blood, Interchangeable Women, and the Early Modern Marriage Economy in *Measure for Measure* and *All's Well That Ends Well*' (in Dutton and Howard, eds., vol. 4, pp. 89–105), focuses on the importance of virginity for marriage and on what she calls 'the fetishization of the hymen' (p. 89). Jankowski explores the bed tricks in *Measure for Measure* and *All's Well* to ask 'How can we resolve the bizarre grotesquerie of the interchangeable hymen with the notion of the couple (and later the family) created by love and further creating love in the children who will be produced?' (p. 101). The article suggests that, while such resolution may be impossible, the bed tricks in fact deconstruct the concept of the companionate marriage based on love to question the very nature of marriage within a patriarchal society.

The third and final essay from volume 4 of *A Companion to Shakespeare* is John Jowett's 'Varieties of Collaboration in Shakespeare's Problem Plays and Late Plays' (pp. 106–28). In this stimulating essay Jowett begins by addressing the Folio's presentation of its author as a dramatist who did not collaborate and the influence this has had on critical responses to Shakespeare's plays and the role of those collaborators. The essay explores the different methodologies of attribution studies and the difficulties that can be encountered, using *Henry VIII*, *Timon of Athens* and *Pericles* as test cases. The essay concludes with an examination of *Measure for Measure*, in which Jowett returns to the Folio to highlight that the text derives from a revival of the play put on by Middleton in 1621. Jowett highlights the inclusion of a song for Mariana, as well as political references to foreign affairs, such as to the king of Hungary, which James's government was trying to suppress. Finally, a book I have been unable to see is *Four Hundred Years of Shakespeare in Europe*, edited by Luis A. Pujante and Ton Hoenselaars.

(d) Poetry

There were two main publications in 2003 which focused on Shakespeare's poetic output as a whole. The first was Peter Hyland's *An Introduction to Shakespeare's*

Poems. This is in many ways a very attractive volume which will offer students new to this field a wide-ranging critical overview. Hyland is keen to stress that Shakespeare's poems were written for a quite different market of consumption to that of the drama and he contends at several junctures that 'underlying all of his major non-dramatic poems is a fierce scepticism about aristocratic power and values'. Hyland's initial discussions of the early modern literary marketplace, court culture, patronage and Shakespeare's portrayal of poets, for example, are welcome additions to an introductory volume of this kind and clearly respond to the needs of undergraduates trying to make sense of the nasty and brutish environment of early modern writers. The introduction to early modern poetics and Ovidian influence is rather too brief by comparison, and would need to be supplemented by reading elsewhere by the student. In the section devoted to *Venus and Adonis* the discussion is particularly lively when appreciating the narrative triangulation between character, narrator and reader. Moreover, the emphasis on rhetorical tropes in the close reading of the text will surely be of assistance to the student struggling with reading strategies for the poem. However, this section might have been enriched with a more ambitious critical overview which would have offered more possibilities for interpretation for Hyland's reader. Moreover, the attention afforded to Adonis is disappointing. In the section devoted to *The Rape of Lucrece*, the discussion is valuable once again in pointing up the significance of narrative voices in the poem and the ways in which this story might be politicized by early modern readers. However, in general, the poem is dispatched rather too quickly to make way for the altogether more animated and ambitious discussion of the sonnets. Here the volume is responding keenly to student requirements, giving introductory accounts of the development of the sonnet and the sonnet sequence, and the publication of Shakespeare's collection. There is some repetition here and there (stressing Dubrow's point that we should question more rigorously the addressee's identity in many sonnets), but in general the combination of close reading of a few sonnets with more general critical lines of attack (drawing upon important studies of recent decades) works well. The accompanying section dealing with 'A Lover's Complaint' is particularly welcome in an introductory volume of this kind, as it draws the reader's attention not only to the existence of the poem but to recent critical scholarship on the relationships of this complaint with the preceding sonnets. The closing section, 'Various Poems', might have been more vigorous, especially in the account of *The Phoenix and the Turtle*; but perhaps the brevity of this discussion reflects the fact that these texts rarely surface onto university syllabuses.

Sasha Roberts's *Reading Shakespeare's Poems in Early Modern England* is not an introductory volume specifically targeting an undergraduate readership. It aims to open up for students and scholars alike a refreshing emphasis upon early modern reading practices when dealing with writing from the period. Close attention to publishing histories and contemporary references to the poems persuasively serves to make Roberts's point that, despite being 'relegated to the margins of the Shakespearean canon (the narrative poems, for example) commanded a much more significant presence in early modern England'. In concentrating upon the transmission and consumption of Shakespeare's texts in the late sixteenth and early seventeenth centuries, this volume joins a growing number of studies questioning the supposedly 'finished' nature of printed texts in the period. Roberts demonstrates the dynamic engagement which early modern readers could have with these texts in terms of marginalia, non-verbal notations (such as underlining), copying, commonplacing, emending, excising and reworking. She carefully maps out the robust nature of manuscript culture in this period (in which Shakespeare, unlike Donne, Jonson and Ralegh, for example, 'wielded only a minor presence'). Like other scholars working in this area (Orgel, Marotti and Bristol, for example), she cautions against the anachronistic critical fixation with the integrity of the 'true copy'. The discussion of *Venus and Adonis* carefully combines an acknowledgement of recent critical angles of vision on the poem with detailed attention to surviving early modern documents which reference the text. The first chapter is brought to a close with an emphasis upon the woman reader in the period. She focuses on two short case studies of contemporary women readers of the poem: Anne Southwell (1573–1636) and Frances Wolfreston (1607–77). In the following chapter, the poem is culturally contextualized, with an account of the epyllion as a sub-genre, and this is combined with an account of references to *Venus and Adonis* in contemporary dramatic and poetic texts. The second half of Roberts's work deals, in two chapters, with *The Rape of Lucrece* and the sonnets. In the first of these discussions Roberts stresses that Shakespeare's second narrative poem did not share the notoriety of the first amongst contemporary readers, but that it appears nonetheless to have been subject to a great deal of commonplacing during the seventeenth century. Here, the evidence of early modern responses is clearly more sketchy and the discussion extends to the later seventeenth century and to modern critical evaluations. In the final chapter Roberts makes the interesting point that modern critical fascination with Shakespeare's sonnets is not mirrored in surviving documents from the early modern period. Much of the discussion at this point concentrates upon print culture and textual transmission—most particularly the peculiarities of Benson's 1640 edition of the sonnets. In general, this is a lively and refreshing study which may hope to go some way to reinvigorate the figure of the early modern reader for more modern eyes.

In 'Rehearsing the Absent Name: Reading Shakespeare's Sonnets through Anonymity' (in Griffin, ed., *The Faces of Anonymity: Anonymous and Pseudonymous Publication from the Sixteenth to the Twentieth Century*, pp. 19–38), Marcy L. North focuses on the meanings surrounding unattributed texts in publications and manuscripts in early modern culture. In an illuminating way she outlines how anonymity may link to questions of genre, publishing medium, legality and patronage. She emphasizes that, even in an age when 'popular names could sell books', anonymity remained an extremely common form of publication. Clearly building upon the scholarship in this field of such critics as Marotti and de Grazia, North stresses that the modern habit of associating anonymity and anonymous circulation in early modern textual culture with expectations of missing data, error and ignorance are at best unhelpful and at worst fallacious in relation to a period when the author's name was still not established as 'the deciding marker of intellectual property'. In her discussion, the practices of anonymous publication in the early modern period emerge as a 'legitimate and practical alternative' to (mis)attribution, and she analyses a number of Shakespeare's sonnets in the latter stages of the discussion, focusing on themes of identification, attribution and anonymity. Katherine Duncan-Jones also reviews Shakespeare's poetic output, drawing to some degree upon the testimonies of early modern readers, in 'Playing Fields or Killing Fields: Shakespeare's Poems and Sonnets' (*SQ* 54[2003] 127–41). The earlier phases of her discussion concentrate upon plague and its metaphors, and Duncan-Jones stresses that the years in which the poetry was first published (1593, 1594, and 1609) were years of plague in the capital. The metropolitan booksellers at St Paul's were in rather close proximity to the graveyard in which at least six parishes of the capital buried their plague dead, and during such times the 'eternizing' lines of Shakespeare's productions may have been apotropaic for the elite readership being targeted—a means of keeping death at bay. Duncan-Jones then focuses centrally upon the destructive energies involved in killing and loving in Shakespeare's poems—giving special attention to sonnets 126, 63 and 104. By way of conclusion, the loved one of the sonnets is found by Duncan-Jones to be held captive by Shakespeare's lines—'embalmed like a corpse or speared like a butterfly'. Even if the poetry persists across the centuries, the 'lovely boy', Lucrece and Adonis are destined to die.

In *Bawdy and Soul: A Revaluation of Shakespeare's Sonnets*, Frank Erik Pointner prosecutes his thesis that Platonic and non-Platonic interpretations of the collection are not necessarily mutually exclusive. Pointner declares himself early on in the study to be more sympathetic to a 'dramatic' than a 'lyric' reading of the collection, and at points is in danger of novelizing the poetic relationships which Shakespeare's texts delineate. However, the main emphasis of the first phase of discussion is upon a very thorough critical overview of critical responses to the sonnets, with particular reference to eroticization and/or Platonizing idealism. While Pointner is keen to maintain both angles of vision on the poems simultaneously in his analyses ('In my opinion the poet is as serious a Platoniser as he is a craver for sexual satisfaction'), much of the liveliest discussion in this volume focuses on the grammatical and phonological ambiguities which may shed light on early modern discourses of desire rather than upon those which point up 'the Platonic story', as he terms it. While the first half of Pointner's study is mostly concerned with scholarly evaluations and the contextualization of early modern understandings of 'passion', the themed chapters which follow involve a sequence of close readings which acknowledge strategically the contributions of recent key studies and editions (e.g. Pequigney, Kerrigan, Duncan-Jones, Dubrow and Vendler) and stress once again for the reader the ways in which quite different interpretations of Shakespeare's collection may be seen to compete with each other for attention. Bruce R. Smith's 'Shakespeare's Sonnets and the History of Sexuality: A Reception History' (in Dutton and Howard, eds., vol. 4, pp. 4–26) initially examines modern critical formulations of sexual identity and early modern understandings of 'passion'. He gives an interesting analysis of the ways in which the sonnets were responded to and reworked in manuscript circulations of the time, and stresses the discomfort which Benson felt with the sonnets as he proceeded to 'censor the homoeroticism of the 1609 Quarto'. In this historical overview, Smith underlines that such discomfort appears to have been shared by many in succeeding generations, including George Steevens, who refused to print the sonnets in his 1793 Shakespeare edition. The final phases of Smith's introductory discussion map out the more recent critical studies which have concentrated upon the sexual politics of Shakespeare's sequence. Valerie Traub's 'The Sonnets: Sequence, Sexuality, and Shakespeare's Two Loves' (in Dutton and Howard, eds., vol. 4, pp. 275–301) again concentrates attention upon the expectations of successive generations of readers concerning the sexual personas deployed in Shakespeare's collection. Using the 1998 film *Shakespeare in Love* as a framing device for the discussion, Traub illuminatingly stresses critical desires to narrativize, indeed to novelize, the sonnets, and underlines the asymmetry in the amount of critical attention afforded to the Young Man in comparison with that given to the Dark Lady. Traub invites her reader to complicate and diversify the possibilities of gender and erotic identification in these poems in order to appreciate the competing meanings of gender and sexuality which separate the twenty-first from the sixteenth and seventeenth centuries.

In 'Sources for Shakespeare's Sonnets 87 and 129 in Tottel's *Miscellany* and Puttenham's *The Arte of English Poesie*' (*NQ* 50[2003] 407–10), Paul Hammond identifies a model for sonnet 129 in one attributed to Lord Vaux in Tottel's collection—'The frailtie and hurtfulness of beautie'. Hammond contrasts the thematic emphasis on the fatal attractions of beauty in Vaux's sonnet with the fatal compulsions of lust described in Shakespeare's poem, as well as comparing rhetorical tropes in both. He also brings in Puttenham's 'Brittle beauty blossome daily fading' as potentially a source for Shakespeare's sonnet, and draws attention also to the 'swerving/deserving' rhyme in Puttenham's 'The smoakie sighes, the bitter teares' as having influenced sonnet 87. In general, Hammond indicates that Shakespeare's sonnets may be conducting a dialogue with such poems from an earlier Tudor generation. In 'The Application of Bibliographical Principles to the Editing of Punctuation in Shakespeare's *Sonnets*' (*SP* 100[2003] 493–513), Carl D. Atkins argues that, while modern editors are eager to stress that spelling was not standardized at the time of the collection's publication in 1609, much less debate is being devoted to early modern practices of punctuation. He gives some detailed analysis of sonnets 115, 58, 16, 29 and 136, and contends that, while examples of errors in spelling and punctuation may be in evidence in the *sonnets*, modern editors should attend more closely to the *modus operandi* of the compositors in the area of punctuation and consider Shakespearian usage elsewhere in the canon when proposing amendments. In 'Shakespeare's Sonnet 73' (*Expl* 62[2003] 3–4), Bernhard Frank details the ways in which this sonnet reverses the expectations of sequential logic and relies instead upon the 'logic of pathos' in order to create its poetic effects. In this reading the final couplet is characterized by 'anti-climactic redundancy' in contrast to the poignancy of the preceding three quatrains. Robert E. Jungman's 'Trimming Shakespeare's Sonnet 18' (*ANQ* 16:i[2003] 18–19) proposes a nautical meaning for 'untrimmed' in line 8 of the sonnet. Rudolf Schmid's *Shakespeare's Beloved: The Solution to the Riddle of Shakespeare's Sonnets* is not an exercise in detection as the title might suggest, but instead emerges as an extremely idiosyncratic narrative in which the citations of the sonnets operate mostly as opportunities for personal meditation.

Dympna Callaghan's 'The Book of Changes in a Time of Change: Ovid's *Metamorphoses* in Post-Reformation England and *Venus and Adonis*' (in Dutton and Howard, eds., vol. 4, pp. 27–54) clearly establishes the central importance of Ovid's place in pedagogical and literary culture of late sixteenth-century England and most particularly in the evolution of epyllia. The first part of the discussion emphasizes that the frank eroticism of the Latin poet continued to pose considerable moral problems for the post-Reformation culture of Tudor Britain and generated significant opposition from those hungry for explicitly didactic literature in the closing decades of the century following Golding's translation. Callaghan continues her investigation of secular and religious early modern aesthetics in the second half of the discussion, in which she points up some more modern disapproving critical voices who have treated Elizabethan epyllia. Callaghan is timely in her stress that the emphasis on excess and process which recurs so frequently in these poems proves to be among their more enduring sources of interest. Another of her discussions of the poem, 'Comedy and Epyllion in Post-Reformation England' (*ShS* 56[2003] 27–38), has many similar emphases, linking the growing interest in racy Ovidian verse in the closing decades of the sixteenth century to the emergence of a secular aesthetic in post-Reformation society. Here, Callaghan pays rather more attention to Golding, to the medieval reception of Ovid and to the pedagogical uses to which his poetry was subjected in the early modern period. The discussion closes with a consideration of the finale of *Venus and Adonis*, in which she identifies a 'comic transformation of the sacred' as Venus emerges as a parody of the *mater dolorosa*. Her final submission on the poem for 2003 was '(Un)natural Loving: Swine, Pets and Flowers in *Venus and Adonis*' (in Berry and Tudeau-Clayton, eds., *Textures of Renaissance Knowledge*, pp. 58–78). Here, Callaghan changes her angle of vision on the poem rather radically, and focuses on the encounter between Adonis and the boar: 'nuzzling in his flank, the loving swine | Sheath'd unaware the tusk in his soft groin'. This episode leads to a wide-ranging discussion of early modern perceptions of 'sexual congress with brute creation'. Drawing upon familiar critical material establishing that 'in legal and religious discourse of the period, bestiality and homosexuality were often contiguously positioned', Callaghan nonetheless leads a lively discussion reflecting upon the cultural anxieties generated by transgression of 'certain foundational categories': man/beast, hunter/victim, culture/nature. Richard Rambuss's 'What It Feels Like For a Boy: Shakespeare's *Venus and Adonis*' (in Dutton and Howard, eds., vol. 4, pp. 240–58) concentrates upon the continuing critical fascination with reversals of gender expectations in Shakespeare's narrative poem and yet challenges the normative pressures at work in some scholarship which evaluate relationships in the poem solely in terms of 'a heterosexual template'. Acknowledging critical estimations of the effeminacy and passivity of Adonis, Rambuss chooses nevertheless to render the boar hunt as an erotic arena, and argues that Adonis's passion for it renders him neither deviant nor misogynistic. Judith H. Anderson's '*Venus and Adonis*: Spenser, Shakespeare, and the Forms of Desire' (in Vaught, ed. *Grief and Gender: 700–1700*, pp. 149–59) reflects initially upon the movement from aggression to pathos in Shakespeare's account of Venus. Most centrally, however, Anderson is interested in plotting textual echoes between

Richard III, *Venus and Adonis* and the 1590 *Faerie Queene*, with especial reference to the Garden of Adonis episode and the Giantess Argante in Book III.

Coppélia Kahn's 'Publishing Shame: *The Rape of Lucrece*' (in Dutton and Howard, eds., vol. 4, pp. 259–74) initially concentrates upon the ways in which the cultural narrative (as it circulated down the centuries) was exploited by patriarchal ambitions. Subsequently, particular emphasis is given to early contextualizations of the crimes of rape and suicide. However, it is in the final discussion of political revolution that Kahn stresses the ways in which Lucrece is prevented from authoring her own meaning by the political ambitions of the Roman menfolk who surround her. In *Rape and Religion in English Renaissance Literature* Anna Swärdh draws together *Titus Andronicus*, *The Rape of Lucrece*, Drayton's *Matilda* and Middleton's *The Ghost of Lucrece* to reflect upon the ways in which they may be seen as engaging with post-Reformation culture. Swärdh initially focuses on an episode in which one Anne Bellamy (previously imprisoned for her Catholicism) assists the Catholic persecutor Richard Topcliffe to capture Southwell in 1592. At the close of that year she gave birth to a child who may have been fathered by Topcliffe himself. Surveying more modern expectations surrounding the terms seduction and/or rape, Swärdh then turns to early modern understandings of 'rape' in terms of robbery, abduction and sexual violation, and how in early modern England rape and abduction were viewed as being crimes against the property of the woman's family. The deployment of the Bellamy–Topcliffe story throughout this study is not always persuasive, but it testifies to Swärdh's determination to explore the potential topicality of her selected texts as being 'engaged in religious controversies of the day'. In the discussion of Shakespeare's narrative poem the heroine is viewed variously as a saint-like figure, Marian image and holy statue in a shrine-like chamber. When the false worshipper Tarquin enters this shrine he becomes both idolater and iconoclast in his subsequent words and actions. It is when the Tarquin–Topcliffe and Bellamy–Lucrece equation surfaces in the following discussion that a sense of strain is most keenly felt. From Swärdh's angle, the poem concludes with an emphasis upon 'tolerance and inclusive religious politics to replace the contemporary situation'.

In his lively and stimulating discussion 'Shakespeare and Republicanism: History and Cultural Materialism' (*TPr* 17[2003] 461–83), Andrew Hadfield argues that the politicization of early modern criticism might usefully take more account of issues which dominated political debate in the period: for example, the possibility of resistance to tyranny; the effectiveness of hereditary monarchy as a political system; the legitimacy of female sovereignty; access to political office; and the most appropriate political representation of the populace. His discussion ranges across the *Henry VI* plays and *Titus Andronicus*, but when he comes to focus on *The Rape of Lucrece* particular emphasis is given to the ways in which the heroine's actions allow others to formulate a response to tyranny—in this poetic world the abuse of a single individual triggers a process of political transformation. Barbara Bowen returns to *The Rape of Lucrece* in 'Beyond Shakespearean Exceptionalism' (in Davis, ed., *Shakespeare Matters*, pp. 209–21). She begins in a telling manner, lamenting the academic isolationism which has beleaguered critical approaches to Shakespeare: here she underlines that

Shakespearians, for example, all too often fail to consider women writers 'seriously as producers of knowledge', while even distinguished scholars of early modern women's writing 'have too often had recourse to biography as a touchstone for criticism in a way they seldom allow themselves when writing about men'. In a bid to challenge such conventions Bowen deploys Lanyer's 'Eve's Apologie' as in part a critical response and counter-narrative to Shakespeare's narrative poem. She acknowledges that this study is 'still at a preliminary stage', and the juxtaposition is not always persuasive in this brief discussion, but the resolve to reinscribe Shakespeare's poetry into its textual culture of production and consumption generates many lively and potentially exciting avenues of enquiry.

In *The Shakespeare Game: The Mystery of the Great Phoenix*, Ilya Gililov publishes in English his complete thesis concerning not only the identities of the Phoenix and the Turtle, but indeed the true identity behind the 'mask' of Shakespeare. The finger of suspicion points to Roger Manners, fifth earl of Rutland, with his consort Elizabeth as co-actor in Shakespeare's most cryptic poem, who took her own life some ten days after the death of her husband in 1612. Elizabeth was Philip Sidney's daughter and appears to have entered into a 'chaste' marriage with her husband for much of their life together. Robert Chester, whose *Love's Martyr* collection includes Shakespeare's poem, was a distant relative of Rutland, and Gililov compares watermarks across all the known copies of *Love's Martyr* to establish that the collection should be dated to the 1612–13 period—thus, the aftermath of Manners's death and, significantly, the end of Shakespeare's career in the theatre. The vast majority of this book is, however, focused on prosecuting the thesis that Rutland is the presence behind the quill of Shakespeare. Gililov advances his ideas with brio, noting, among other details, that the first voices to recognize Shakespeare's playwriting genius were Rutland's Cambridge University compatriots; that 'nearly all the books' used by Shakespeare as sources were part of the Manners library at Belvoir Castle; that Manners studied in Padua with Danish students called Rosencrantz and Guildenstern; and that it was in 1613 that Shakespeare and Burbage received from Francis Manners forty-four gold shillings for the preparation of his late brother's *impreso*. This large volume resuscitates the Rutland thesis, which was first submitted in the twentieth century by C. Bleibtrau and Celestin Demblon. However, some of the greatest interest in this volume is not only in the 'refashioning' of Shakespeare but also in its overview of the developing narrative of Russian Shakespeare scholarship across the twentieth century.

(e) Histories

In a bumper year for criticism of the histories, the politics of *Henry V* in particular has attracted a great deal of attention. Jeffrey Knapp's *Shakespeare's Tribe: Church, Nation and Theater in Renaissance England* develops a novel thesis regarding the nationalism of the histories, and *King John* and *Henry V* in particular. This is that the various civil wars shown in the histories may have been intended not as a critique of internal divisions but as a critique of English insularism (p. 84). The key to this is the deployment of historical memory of the Crusades (a 'determinative issue for the understanding of "imagined communities" in Renaissance England') in conjunction with what Knapp memorably calls 'rogue nationalism', predicated upon an Erasmian openness to the 'morally questionable fellowship' of the lawless presented most fully by Shakespeare in the *Henry IV* plays. Knapp presents the histories as critiques, claiming Shakespeare as a deliberate commentator through the histories. Thus, John's 'apparently mixed polemical signals' 'point to Shakespeare's hope that religious corruption in Protestant England as well as Catholic Christendom might ultimately lead to a reformation of Christianity in fact' (p. 95). The anti-prelatism of the histories, along with the pro-theatricalism of some of the plays, seems to suggest a broadening out of the post-Reformation sacramental, though Knapp's analysis of *Henry V*'s concern with communion 'broadened from clergy to congregation' must first be 'sanctified by violence'.

Hugh Grady seeks, in *Shakespeare, Machiavelli, and Montaigne*, to trace 'a dialectic of Machiavellian power and Montaignean subjectivity' through the second tetralogy and *Hamlet*. The world of *Richard II* is modern, in the sense that its view of politics as 'the value-free logic of power at work' is an early example of the instrumental reason Machiavelli critically theorized, and which the Frankfurt school characterizes as a determinant of the modern. Richard is a (failed) Machiavel rather than Machiavellian, as Bolingbroke is; but in the crisis preceding his death he explores, in Montaignean fashion, the possibility of multiple identities. Later plays in the tetralogy relocate such subjectivity from the prison to communal and public spaces. Falstaff's subjectivity is fuelled by desire, a constitutive element which is 'the ultimate double-edged sword'; in critical dialogue with the instrumental reason successful elsewhere in the *Henry IV* plays, he stands between (aesthetic) modernity and its (carnival) predecessor. In *1 Henry IV* Hal and Hotspur, too, show complex subjectivities, the latter divided between domestic and public selves, while Henry IV 'is represented to us as the shaken, careworn outcome of reduction to a Machiavellian self' (p. 164). Both the prince and Falstaff inhabit the Machiavellian world more fully in the sequel, though the Gloucestershire scenes are readable as both proleptic mourning for and counter-memory of the Hal we have lost. In contrast, *Henry V*'s 'exposure of the calculation and instrumentalization behind the heroics does not really undermine them' (p. 204). Here a 'positive Machiavellianism' comes into play, whose source, Grady argues, is the Essex faction. The positivity Grady identifies is located in Henry's once again unfixed subjectivity—he is 'warrior, dutiful son, playful jokester, and plebeian empathizer, as well as hero-king' (p. 225)—though the plebeian world of the play is virtually extinct, replaced 'by the militaristic, multinational fellowship' of the four captains. But, despite the play's overt Machiavellianism, there remains a 'political unconscious' of dissonant moments which is not effaced by Henry's quasi-Machiavellian victory.

David Ruiter covers much of the same ground in his *Shakespeare's Festive History: Feasting, Festivity, Fasting and Lent in the Second Henriad*, which focuses on the second tetralogy. Like Grady, he seeks to recover the plays from overly schematic (and pessimistic) Foucauldian readings, focusing on the relationship between festivity and order. Like Grady, though without Grady's deployment of theory, he insists that the seemingly subordinate term (here, festivity) is never completely defeated. The term is somewhat slippery, however.

In the discussion of *Richard II*, festivity seems to mean community, so that Richard's use of banishment and disinheritance shows his 'disregard for community ritual and festivity' (p. 57). In *1Henry IV* Hal constructs 'the socio-political Feast of Falstaff' through food imagery and through his own participation in Falstaff's world. It is not clear just what this feast is. Ruiter reminds us that Hal sees in Falstaff's court the image of fellowship and festivity he aspires to command, but he also tells us that the feast remains a metaphor. The underdeveloped nature of this figure can be seen in the discussion of *2 Henry IV*, where Bardolph's reference to Falstaff as 'Harry Monmouth's brawn, the hulk Sir John' is glossed as 'a character outside of the prince's immediate circle [picking] up on the idea of the Feast of Falstaff' (p. 106). The slippage is even more apparent later in the chapter when Ruiter claims that Bardolph's reference indicates he, with others, 'participates in a metaphorical feast'. In the light of this, the book's claim that the politics of festivity is central to the play seems strained.

John Roe's *Shakespeare and Machiavelli* allows Machiavelli's texts more subtlety than Grady's deployment of Machiavelli as an early, and critical, theorist of instrumental reason. It begins its engagement with the histories by discussing *Richard III*. Richard's wooing of Anne enacts a Machiavellian dominance over *fortuna* in his redeployment of Petrarchan victimhood to efface his own guilt and advance his own eroto-political project. Subsequent chapters investigate *Richard II*, *Henry V* and *King John*. Characters' political Machiavellism is a familiar topic; Roe adds to it, however, a comparison between Shakespeare and Machiavelli as 'tacticians of presentation', and in particular their use of the rhetorical device of paradiastole (whereby what initially seems bad comes to seem good) in their representations of historical examples. Examples include the way in which Henry's ordering the execution of French prisoners is contextualized so that this battlefield war crime comes to seem less barbaric, and how 'his clear-headedness on the battlefield seems retrospectively to underline the clarity of judgement with which he renounces Falstaff' (p. 92). The chapter on *King John* compares the play directly with *Il Principe*, as negotiations with competing concepts of legitimacy, *virtù*, and patriotism.

Cyndia Susan Clegg's 'Feared and Loved: *Henry V* and Machiavelli's Use of History' (*BJJ* 10[2003] 179–207) sees the play as interrogating both Machiavellian *virtù* and the humanist conviction that good rhetoric and the good man are inseparable. For her, the play's indebtedness to Machiavellian rhetoric does not lead to the kind of resolution Roe implies; rather, it 'reinscribes the generally antithetical concepts within the terms of its opposite' (p. 194), staging a world 'in which human affairs are indeed contingent and politics ironic' (p. 199). This approach is also identified as Machiavellian.

Dominique Goy-Blanquet's *Shakespeare's Early History Plays: From Chronicle to Stage* provides exhaustive readings of the ways in which the first tetralogy dramatizes its sources as a basis for an investigation of 'the mark of a conscious artist'. The focus is sometimes upon craft—matters of construction or selection—and sometimes upon art—the way in which chronicle themes are developed or critically rewritten. Goy-Blanquet's remit extends to explorations of the ways in which verbal elements in Shakespeare's reading are the basis for a characterization or a theme. Her broad conclusion is that *2 Henry VI* sees

Shakespeare at his most interventionist regarding his sources, notably in his travesty of the Cade rising. The value of the book, however, is not in its arguing a particular thesis regarding the relationship between plays and chronicles, but in its painstaking and lucid comparative accounts of both. Unusually for a book committed to detailed exposition of others' detailed expositions, it is critically sophisticated and written with panache.

Dermot Cavanagh's *Language and Politics in the Sixteenth-Century History Play* builds bridges between Shakespeare's histories and their predecessors, using both to develop a theory of the relationship between language and politics in the sixteenth century, and in particular the attempts of centralizing political projects to define and proscribe deviant language use. *King John* does not merely represent rumour's operation; it shares some of rumour's functions, including 'scurrile invention, the deflation of authority, and an impulse to expose the disparity between public and private realities' (p. 82). Reversing the typical characterizations of Tudor apologists, rumour here is allied to scepticism rather than credulity, and the play's representations of a variety of scepticisms, and of the necessity for them, reimagines the usefulness of rumour (or, at least, the rumouresque) to a capaciously imagined body politic. Cavanagh argues that the political world depicted in *Richard II* is consistently reflexive, especially regarding 'the shifting configuration of treason' (p. 105). Conflicting registers of speech are staged as mutually qualifying; in particular, the concept of treason, centred upon the monarch, is dialectically twinned with the de- or un-centred one of betrayal. Contrariwise, *Henry V* displays an attempted 'reformation of the word', beginning from an absolute confidence in the royal word as the locus not only of charismatic oratory but also of the regulation and chastisement of 'deficient speech'. Commons or French do not, however, simply function as foils, for Cavanagh insists that 'the play's dramatic language is not simply a supplement to the king's speech, but a discourse that exceeds his power to regulate it' (p. 143). The same breadth of perspective is present in Marsha Robinson's *Writing the Reformation: Actes and Monuments and the Jacobean History Play*, on Foxe and the Jacobean history play, which does not engage at length with *Henry VIII*, but productively recontextualizes elements of it, including plotting, prophecy, and apocalyptic history.

Harry Berger, Jr., returns to the histories again in 'Harrying the Stage: *Henry V* in the Tetralogical Echo Chamber' (*SIY* 3[2003] 131–55). He develops the thesis that performance delivers less than reading in terms of 'intralocutory' language, which he glosses as 'what goes on within speech rather than between speakers'. Further, Shakespeare knew and was frustrated by this 'detextualization', and attempted to pre-empt the process by including metatheatrical allusions. *Henry V*'s Chorus is an obvious element to consider here; Berger proceeds to produce a 'Folio' reading of the play linking it to its three predecessors, claiming that 'the performances that make for good theatre and effective politics are represented as opportunities for strategic displacements of responsibility and culpability' (p. 153). I was unconvinced by Berger's general argument, which, after criticizing performance for its intralocutory poverty, praises a tetralogical reading for adding 'specificity to the protagonist's motivation'. The article, however, makes some persuasive points about the Chorus's inadequacy as a guide to the play, and on the French war as a displacement of (royal) English anxieties. Marvin Krims investigates 'Prince Hal's Aggression' (*PsyArt* [2002]), arguing that in the *Henry IV* plays 'his ready acceptance of thuggery as his royal prerogative is as central to his character as his often cited plucky leadership qualities and keen intelligence'. Krims provides a clear analysis of the Prince, focusing on matters Oedipal and Falstaff.

Within *Henry V* criticism there was a particular confluence of interest in the play's final scene. Donald Hedrick's 'Advantage, Affect, History, *Henry V*' (*PMLA* 118[2003] 470–87) argues that 'Shakespeare entangles the problematic of history with the analogous problematic of love' (p. 471). Affect is not as remote from 'history' as materialist critics sometimes claim. Henry's pre-Agincourt characterization of the battle's historical afterlife places it in terms of its affective labour (as does the Chorus). The counter-memory of Falstaff is equally placed, though this time in opposition to Henry. The final scene with all its undercuttings and ironies exemplifies the reach and limitations of this consideration of history. Tom McAlindon writes on 'Natural Closure in *Henry V*' (*SIY* 3[2003] 156–71), arguing that Henry is heroic in his 'capacity to unite opposites both in himself and the world he has inherited' (p. 156). This 'transforming power' is identified as his ability to persuade, as exemplified in the final wooing scene. The language of this scene—itself an example of eloquent inarticulacy—is full of 'puns, paradoxes, antitheses, parallelisms and antimetaboles' which embody *discordia concors*. For McAlindon these are 'clear signs of thinking in terms of resolved opposites'; however, his account also gives due weight to those elements of the scene which mitigate against this resolution, without explaining how they contribute to or are effaced by the elements of closure he explores. Ernst Honigmann's revised edition of his *Shakespeare: Seven Tragedies Revisited* includes a new chapter on *Henry V*. Honigmann lucidly covers post-Rabkin debate over the play, concluding that 'the dominant response is favourable, that it coexists with one less favourable, and that the interaction of the two is the question with which criticism should concern itself' (p. 194). Like McAlindon, he finds the wooing scene's 'double double vision' crucial; like McAlindon, he finally comes down on the side of a favourable response.

Richard Hillman's *Shakespeare, Marlowe and the Politics of France* considers all the histories apart from *Henry VIII* and is particularly concerned with exploring their intertextuality with French sixteenth-century writings on history and politics. It thus deploys a Lacan-inflected resistance to simple binary imaginings of France as Other, pointing out how many of the situations and themes of the plays echo elsewhere. *King John* refuses the mythic intertext connoted by the name of Arthur, turning to a historical and inward-looking nationalism. The chapter on the first tetralogy explores how they 'might have been inflected in their reception by images of incoherence and disfunctionality' originating in France. Hillman sees the reign of Henry VI in these plays as evoking the 'disastrous reign of Henri III'. More specifically, France's representation in *1 Henry VI* as England's Other shows the instability of discourses of 'England'.

Lisa Dickson explores self-fashioning in *2 Henry VI* in '"Tent him to the quick": Vision, Violence and Penalty in Shakespeare's *2 Henry VI*' (*RenD*

32[2003] 69–93). Beginning from the construction of York's interiority through dramatic irony, and the paradox of an interiority on display, she explores representations of violence and wounding. Gloucester while alive is subject to competing readings; it is only over his dead body that a stable characterological narrative emerges. This fixity does not transfer into a general epistemological (and, where treason is the issue, political) stability, however, as Horner and Eleanor prove unreadable by the judicial gaze. John Brett Mischo focuses on 'The Rhetoric of Poverty and the Poverty of Rhetoric: Shakespeare's Jack Cade and the Early Modern Rhetorical Manual' (*ELN* 41[2003] 32–43). He reads the rising as first dramatizing the destabilizing appropriation of rhetoric by the commons, and then the reappropriation of rhetoric by the aristocracy. Cade's appropriation of rhetoric is most obvious when he uses blank verse, but he also shows 'an incongruously sophisticated knowledge of fine points in current rhetorical theory' (p. 36).

Kathryn Schwarz, in 'A Tragedy of Good Intentions: Maternal Agency in *3 Henry VI* and *King John*' (*RenD* 32[2003] 225–54), suggests that characters such as Margaret and Constance are unsettling because they seek not to promote themselves but their children. Schwartz proposes that, 'rather than challenging patrilineality or male sovereignty, each of these mothers defends those imperatives to the death. The death in question, however, is not her own; maternal intervention proves fatal to its object' (p. 228). Paradoxically, in these cases the 'good enough mother' must not perform her 'vanishing act' but give 'a hands-on shove into patrilineal knowledge'. Mothers, through buying in so completely to patriarchy, make a social rather than sexual link with their sons, which in turn exposes patriarchy itself as a construct.

Madhavi Menon writes on '*Richard II* and the Taint of Metonymy' (*ELH* 70[2003] 653–73). Menon suggests reading the language of the garden scene as metonymic rather than metaphorical. Metonymically, the language insists on 'the sexual nature of Richard's state rather than the stately nature of England's garden' (p. 669). Stephen Marche investigates Shakespeare's generic experimentation in 'Mocking Dead Bones: Historical Memory and the Theater of the Dead in *Richard III*' (*CompD* 37[2003] 37–58), but adds little new to existing work. Michael Harrawood's 'Overreachers: Hyperbole, the "circle in the water", and Force in *1 Henry VI*' (*ELR* 33[2003] 309–27) investigates the performance of power, principally through an exhaustive analysis of Joan's speech in Act I, scene ii. This power is crucially instantiated in language, but the expression of this force is also its exhaustion. Joan's hyperbole undoes itself, in part through its making clear the circumstances of its own production. Harrawood cites Tamburlaine in contrast, where material power is identical to linguistic power.

R.J.C. Watt's Longman Critical Reader on *Shakespeare's History Plays* is squarely aimed at the undergraduate market. After a preface introducing the reader to such terms as 'ideology', it reprints twelve essays, sometimes excerpted, each with a very short introduction. Two-thirds concern the second tetralogy. The essays date from the mid-1980s to the mid-1990s, and include many classic pieces by the likes of Patterson, Dollimore and Sinfield, Holderness, Ryan and Rackin, and Howard. The selection is sound, though the commentary is pitched a little low. Elsewhere, Stanley Wells and Lena Cowen Orlin have produced

Shakespeare: An Oxford Guide. This lucid and up-to-date work focuses on readings of plays applying approaches previously introduced. Thus, Phyllis Rackin follows her short but incisive introduction to the histories with a reading of *Henry V*, Inga-Stina Ewbank provides a close reading of *Richard III*, and Jonathan Gil Harris models materialist criticism in his account of *1 Henry IV*.

Essays from Dutton and Howard, eds., *A Companion to Shakespeare's Works*, vol. 2: *The Histories*, will be reviewed next year.

(f) Tragedies

The study of Shakespeare's tragedies is continually enriched through the publication of a multiplicity of articles and books that reveal much creativity and learning and contribute significantly to steadily revitalizing the field. Critics tend to focus on their particular subject, rather than devoting their energies to finding fault with others' approaches.

Thus the contributions from 2003 represent a variety of critical views, from more traditional approaches, such as textual criticism, to studies influenced by psychoanalysis, cultural materialism, feminism, and New Historicism. Of the tragedies, *Hamlet* continues to be the play that attracts most attention and an impressive amount of creative effort. Of the other dramas, *Othello* and *King Lear* inspire much fine criticism. It is interesting to note that *Titus Andronicus*, and not least *Timon of Athens*, have received critical treatment, while *Antony and Cleopatra* is still awaiting a renewal of interest. The following survey of publications within the field initially focuses on studies of a more general nature before turning to specific plays. In the discussion of each play, books dealing with the specific play, if a book is listed, are placed before the treatment of articles.

Lukas Erne's *Shakespeare as Literary Dramatist* is well written and wide-ranging. Erne attacks many of the most cherished assumptions of the New Bibliography, especially memorial reconstruction and the origin of the 'bad' quartos. Erne argues well, but relies heavily on the research findings of Peter Blayney, especially as summarized in his article, 'The Publication of Playbooks'(in John D. Cox and David Scott Kastan, eds., *A New History of Early English Drama*). Like Blayney, Erne views the publication of playbooks in the late sixteenth and early seventeenth centuries from the point of view of London stationers, publishers, and booksellers rather than from that of actors and dramatists. Erne rejects, with Blayney, the unfounded myth that acting companies considered publication to be against their best interests. It seems to have been the regular practice of Shakespeare's company to sell plays to the printers about two years after they were first performed. Erne's last four chapters deal with the length of plays. Using statistics from Alfred Hart, Erne in fact presents a two-text system: the longer printed play was intended for readers, while the play presented in the theatre was a reduced version designed for audiences. Erne is strongly opposed to the Oxford editors' view that plays such as *Hamlet* and *King Lear* were performed in their entirety. Consequently, he maintains that the so-called 'bad' quartos, especially of *Romeo and Juliet, Henry V*, and *Hamlet*, were acting versions of longer texts intended for readers. In Erne's view, the bad quartos were neither memorial reconstructions nor early drafts, and they were not abridged texts for provincial performance. These views are in accordance with Erne's belief that 'The literariness of Shakespeare's long dramatic texts emerges quite clearly from some of the passages that entirely disappear from the short, theatrical texts, of the bad quartos' (p. 226). From the viewpoint of printing and publishing, Erne makes a vigorous argument for the 'literary' Shakespeare.

In 'Shakespeare, Geography, and the Work of Genre on the Early Modern Stage'(*MLQ* 64[2003] 299–322) Jean E. Howard observes that Shakespeare set most of his tragedies outside England. *Titus Andronicus* and *Julius Caesar*, for example, take place in Rome, *Romeo and Juliet* in Verona, *Hamlet* at Elsinore, *Othello* in Venice and Cyprus, *Antony and Cleopatra* in the eastern Mediterranean, primarily oscillating between Rome and Egypt, *Coriolanus* chiefly in Rome, Corioli, and Actium, while *Timon of Athens* is obviously set in Athens. *Macbeth* unfolds in Scotland, with a brief detour to England but, as Howard observes, 'Scotland to the English was very much a foreign country'. Of all the plays today identified as part of Shakespeare's tragic canon, only *King Lear* is set in England, albeit in its distant past. As Howard points out, 'temporal distance in *Lear* replaces the spatial distance from England that characterizes the other tragedies'. Howard asks whether the pattern of locating tragedy outside England is unique to Shakespeare, and whether it is of critical significance or just a random curiosity. While answering these questions, Howard meditates on the links among genre, geography, and 'the class and gender investments' of particular kinds of plays on the early modern stage. She observes that Shakespeare wrote comedies throughout his career. The geography of the comedies changes over time. But his English history plays definitely belong to the first half of his writing career. After the writing of *Hamlet* in 1601, his involvement with tragedy accelerated. Shakespeare changed to tragedy just as many of his fellow playwrights, from 1599 on, started exploring London city comedy, a localized dramatic genre that Shakespeare never extensively worked with.

As Howard observes, all the great Jacobean tragedies, from Marlowe's *Dr Faustus* to Middleton's *Women Beware Women*, are overwhelmingly set within Europe but outside England. This provides a sense of familiarity, as well as distance and difference. Secondly, many tragedies are set on a border between two eras or places. Shakespeare set his Roman plays, at the crux of epochal transitions, for example at the moment when the Christian era is dawning (in *Antony and Cleopatra*). In *Hamlet* there is a sense that an old order cannot be retrieved or restored. Thirdly, 'the articulation of crisis and loss enables the tragedy to create the illusion, partly through soliloquy, of a fractured self, a riven interiority that nonetheless exposes the cracks in an entire cultural edifice'. In the exploration of explosive social and political matters, early modern tragedy depends on borderline geographies and temporalities, according to Howard. To illustrate this she chooses *Macbeth*. Shakespeare's tragedies are set not so close as London or (except for *Antony and Cleopatra*) so far as Africa but in Scotland, France or Italy, appropriate venues for the anatomization of the collapse of a ruling order. London, and the periphery, 'belong to the men of money and wit, to the future and to the commercial classes that will dominate it'.

Peter Holbrook considers 'Shakespeare as a Force for Good' (*ShS* 56[2003] 203–14). Holbrook notes that for two decades Shakespeare scholars have been busy exposing the use of the dramatist in the legitimation of various oppressive regimes to the extent that the World's Most Canonical Author 'has become synonymous with the Establishment'(p. 203). Referring to, for example, J.S. Mill's *On Liberty*, and the work of Nietzsche and Herder, Holbrook addresses the question of how notions of Shakespeare's life, times and works inform Victorian culture critique. In this regard he refers to A.C. Bradley's *Shakespearean Tragedy* [1904], and suggests that Bradley's book, like Mill's *On Liberty*, entertains the notion that some individualities, although immoral, are desirable because original. Holbrook indicates that Shakespeare's plays are used in a self-liberating project. For Bradley, the essence of the plays is personality: each play's 'action is essentially the expression of character' (*Shakespearean Tragedy*, p. 19). The nature of this character is exceptional, but it is necessary that he should have sufficient greatness that in his fall we may be conscious of the possibilities of human nature. L.C. Knights ridiculed the Bradleyan stress upon 'personality', advocating that a Shakespeare play is above all a poetic structure. But, in Holbrook's view, Knights failed to see that Bradley's Shakespeare criticism does not simply intend to 'get it right' but to 'make a difference'. Knights did not look behind Bradley's stress on personality to his dissenting cultural agenda.

Björk, Knutsen and Vestli, eds., *Modi operandi*, a study offering different perspectives on crime in literature, has an article by Jon D. Orten, '"That perilous stuff": Crime in Shakespeare's Tragedies', a discussion of the concept of crime in relation to Shakespeare's drama. In *Fantasies of Female Evil: The Dynamics of Gender and Power in Shakespearean Tragedy* Cristina León Alfar discusses, from the standpoint of cultural materialist, psychoanalytic, and feminist theoretical investigation, what has been left out of Western scholarly tradition on Shakespeare's 'evil' women. Focusing on *Romeo and Juliet, King Lear, Macbeth, Antony and Cleopatra*, and *The Winter's Tale*, she argues that, by adhering to the socio-political basis of the tragedies, women characters traditionally identified as evil might rather be understood as pressing against early modern popular beliefs about female nature. If so, the tragedies represent a complex illustration and investigation of the dynamics of gender and power. Alfar places *King Lear* and *Macbeth* at the centre of the study. She sees the female characters of these plays as women whose relationship to state power is placed on a masculinist and violent foundation. Accordingly, naturalized categories of femininity prove to be incongruous measurements for the judgement of their actions. Alfar's book focuses on the pressures, tensions, and constraints women confront in a culture in which definitions of gender and power are in a state of negotiation. In Shakespeare's tragedies the distinctions between good and evil femininity become decidedly artificial, deeply political, moralized constructs.

Lausund and Olsen, eds., *Self-Fashioning and Metamorphosis in Early Modern English Literature*, is a collection of essays derived from a conference at the University of Oslo. Of particular relevance to this section are the essays by Kirsti Minsaas, on 'Metamorphic Marvels: Shakespeare and Tragic Wonder', and Robin Headlam Wells, on 'The Metamorphosis of Othello'. The former asks what are the deeper moral and aesthetic concerns that underlie the metamorphoses of Shakespeare's tragic heroes. What the article explores is related to the Renaissance fascination with the idea of the 'marvellous' or the 'wondrous'.

Minsaas finds that Shakespeare's tragic art forges a close link between tragic metamorphosis and the effect of wonder. In Shakespeare's hands, wonder becomes a useful vehicle for the exploration of man's unstable moral nature. Ultimately, it is the 'wonder-wounding' paradox that constitutes the centre of Shakespeare's tragic vision. Headlam Wells's essay on Othello's transformation makes clear that the hero we see in the first act of *Othello* may give the impression of being a noble savage, but as he degenerates from respected general and loving husband to embittered avenger it becomes evident that the passions that drive him are savage rather than noble. According to Headlam Wells, the point of Shakespeare's deflation of the ideal of primitive nobility is to suggest the barbaric nature of pre-civilized heroic values. The connection between savagery and the heroic in *Othello* suggests Shakespeare's scepticism about those values.

Shakespeare's earliest tragedy is approached in an article by Stefan D. Keller, 'Shakespeare's Rhetorical Fingerprint: New Evidence on the Authorship of *Titus Andronicus*' (*ES* 84[2003] 105–18). Keller observes that there is a variety of evidence today indicating that *Titus Andronicus* was the work of two authors, George Peele and William Shakespeare. His article gives the results of his study of rhetorical techniques in the play, showing that a possible reason why many have felt that Act I of *Titus* does not 'sound' like Shakespeare is that its rhetoric deviates sharply from that of his other early works. Comparing Shakespeare's verse to that of George Peele, Keller notes that much of what we admire about his dramas lies in a uniquely imaginative use of classical rhetoric. Keller also stresses that rhetorical analysis may be a helpful tool in authorship studies. A compilation of all rhetorical figures in Shakespeare would be very helpful, Keller suggests. In the field of comparative rhetoric studies a great deal is left to be done.

Romeo and Juliet appeared in the series of volumes on Shakespeare's plays in performance in 2003, written by Russell Jackson and published by the Arden Shakespeare in association with the Shakespeare Birthplace Trust. It is a representative volume in the series, which discusses and analyses a wide range of theatrical interpretation. In this volume Jackson addresses a great many issues concerning the dilemmas faced, the poetic force of the characters, the portrayal of the two households, how to play the Capulets, Mercutio, the lovers. (Are they adolescents or idealized? Is Juliet convincingly youthful? How is Romeo's moody changeability dealt with?) All in all, the book opts for a variety of interpretations.

Alberto Cacicedo discusses 'Shakespeare's *Romeo and Juliet*' (*Expl* 61[2003] 134–6), with special reference to the sexual innuendo of the opening scene, involving Samson and Gregory. As Cacicedo notes, most of the bawdiness is directed against women, but he finds that it sometimes gestures towards sexual violence as Samson affirms that women, 'being the weaker vessels, are ever thrust to the wall' (pp. 15–16). He notes that just as typical of the scene's, and also of the play's, presentation of male friendship is the badinage directed by each servant at his interlocutor. This word 'play' parallels the imagined swordplay of the violent bawdiness.

'*Goodnight Desdemona* (*Good Morning Juliet*): From Shakespearian Tragedy to Postmodern Satyr Play' by Igor Djordjevic (*CompD* 37[2003] 89–115) considers Ann-Marie MacDonald's postmodern work, which revisits

Shakespeare's *Othello* and *Romeo and Juliet*. The article is interesting for our purposes for taking Aristotle as an example of generic theory concerning drama, observing that this resonates with Horace's *Art of Poetry*, and considering Northrop Frye's work in this respect. He also comments on the fact that numerous critics have discovered the presence of both comedy and tragedy in *Romeo and Juliet* and *Othello*. For example, the first two acts of *Romeo and Juliet* promise romantic comedy, but the action and the characters are then transformed to compose the pattern of tragedy. The 'comical' beginning of *Othello* is not as festive as that of *Romeo* but, according to Djordjevic, the text contains just as many comic elements and easily reverts to comedy.

Katalin Tabi has written about 'Editing Shakespeare for the Stage: A Comparative Analysis of Act I, scene iv of *Romeo and Juliet*' (*AnaChronisT* 6[2003] 1–28). Tabi points out that, after the text-based editorial approach of the seventeenth and eighteenth centuries, from the end of the nineteenth century, and even more from the middle of the 1970s, an increasing number of scholars turned towards the study of stage directions. Shakespeare criticism could no longer limit itself to literature but had to involve disciplines such as cultural studies and theatre history. The traditions of Elizabethan theatre and the relationship between theatre and literature came into focus. Tabi's paper presents a comparative analysis of stage directions in the ballroom scene of *Romeo and Juliet* (I.iv), as they appear in six prominent twentieth-century editions. It is Tabi's contention that nearly all the problems an editor has to face are theatrical in nature. It is therefore necessary to re-establish the relation between page and stage and to make performance-based editions that are useful to theatrical personnel as well as academics.

Among studies of *Julius Caesar* we find Maurice Hunt considering 'Cobbling Souls in Shakespeare's *Julius Caesar*' (*CahiersE* 64[2003] 19–28). He mentions that many commentators, including David Kaula, Marshall Bradley, and Steve Sohmer, have previously noted that Christian values inform Shakespeare's description of a famous moment in Roman history. For example, the fact that both Julius Caesar and Christ have names beginning with the same initials has been used to underscore the connection. Also, it has been noted that Shakespeare has changed Plutarch's reference to Caesar's body having twenty-three wounds to thirty-three mortal wounds (V.i.51–4), possibly a reference to Christ's age at the time of his crucifixion. In his article, Hunt suggests that Shakespeare's association of Caesar and Christ is at times positive rather than parodic. He does so by starting with what he considers unexplored Christian overtones in play-opening dialogues of minor characters, when they partly talk of 'cobbling souls'. Hunt suggests that this phrase becomes important later in the play, when Caesar precipitates soul cobbling—the mending of souls—among Romans influenced by his revolutionary presence, in the flesh and then in spirit. This pagan soul-making is imperfect, but it acquires Christian resonance when Brutus and Cassius form a soulful brotherhood when forced to react to Caesar's mobilizing spirit. In Hunt's view, Brutus and Cassius's soul-cobbling represents the culmination of a concept lightly introduced by a cobbler in Act I, scene i.

Lloyd Davis considers 'Embodied Masculinity in Shakespeare's *Julius Caesar*' (*EnterText* 3[2003] 161–82). He finds that Julius Caesar exemplifies a complex response to classical narrative, in that it dramatizes the problematic effects of a world controlled by aristocratic men. They experience the triumphs and failures of their own dominance and submit to the system they command. This allows a culture of male authority to continue. As Davis observes, Shakespeare's drama unravels the costs of the system for masculine selfhood, but it does not stage in detail its consequence for those outside the focal group, such as women and men from different classes. The play demonstrates theatrical, historical, and contemporary attraction to the powerful aristocratic male, while the critical perspective is circumscribed. To Davis *Julius Caesar* reproduces a bodily rhetoric of superior masculinity whose universal acceptance is assumed.

An edition of *Hamlet*, updated from the 1985 edition of the New Cambridge Shakespeare, and edited by Philip Edwards, introduces the section on *Hamlet* studies. The changes from the previous New Cambridge Shakespeare edition are apparent not least in the valuable long introduction, which has been made to include references to New Historicism and cultural materialism. In addition, recent stage, film, and critical interpretations are a valuable part of the updating. The bibliography now includes some few more recent works. The volume has several illustrations, a handy format, and an appealing exterior, and will no doubt be useful to students of the play.

Modern Hamlets and their Soliloquies, by Mary Z. Maher, first published in 1992, appears in an expanded edition. Maher examines how modern actors such as Gielgud, Guinness, Olivier, Burton, David Warner, and Derek Jacobi have chosen to perform Hamlet's soliloquies, and how they made their particular choices. In the expanded edition two new interviews, one with Kenneth Branagh and one with Simon Russell Beale, have been added. The book includes Hamlet's seven soliloquies.

In 'Black *Hamlet*: Battening on the Moor' (*ShakS* 31[2003] 127–64), Patricia Parker explores aspects associated with the Moor. She refers to the closet scene of *Hamlet*, when the Prince forces his mother to look upon the portraits of her husbands in lines that draw the familiar contrast between the two, 'Looke heere upon this Picture … And batten on this Moore …?' (Q2). The passage foregrounds one of the many polarities constructed in this play, between an idealized Old Hamlet and his usurping brother, who appears here as a 'Moore'. Dover Wilson's suggestion in the first New Cambridge edition of the play (that 'batten on this Moore' simultaneously evokes the figure of a black 'Moor') is noted in the fine print of some modern editions. But it has not yet penetrated the consciousness of most critics, readers, and audiences. Moors are assumed to belong only to *Titus Andronicus, Antony and Cleopatra, The Merchant of Venice*, or *Othello*. The appearance of a 'Moore' in Hamlet's contrast of a 'faire' dead father to his mother's present husband is underscored, as Harold Jenkins notes, by the corresponding lines of the first quarto's version of this scene: 'Looke you now, here is your husband, | With a face like *Vulcan* … What Diuell thus hath cosoned you at hob-man blinde?' (TTH 166, 168). Parker points out that 'Face like Vulcan' (with 'hell-bred eie') explicitly invokes an infernal blackness for this second husband, in lines whose 'dull dead hanging look' summons the combination of dullness, death, and Moors reflected in the 'dull Moor' of *Othello*. The identification of Vulcan with the 'blackness' of devil and Moor was routinely applied to the blacksmith hurled from heaven, like Lucifer himself, transformed from angel of light to prince of darkness. 'Face like *Vulcan*' simultaneously evokes the darkening of a white actor's face with soot, cosmetic counterpart to the racialized figure of blackness as sullied, 'besmear'd' or 'smirch't'. The soot or coal associated with blackface, colliers, and Vulcan produces the 'coal-black' hue of Aaron the Moor in *Titus Andronicus*, joined by the 'sooty bosom', 'begrim'd' face, and 'collied' judgement of Othello. Smearing, sullying, or blackening the face with soot to produce a 'face like Vulcan' or a Moor was familiar from the mumming, morris dancing, and carnival that the early texts of *Hamlet* repeatedly invoke, associating the present king of Denmark with the black face not only of the collier but of carnival misrule—the 'King of shreds and patches' (Q2 and F) that criticism has long linked to a carnival reversal or *mundus inversus*. The sooty Vulcan and the black face associated with a carnival 'Moore' is thus part of all three early texts of the closet scene. As in the case of the Lucifer who was once an angel of light, Parker notes, Hamlet's polarized contrast of 'faire' and 'Moore' posits an original white or light as the point of departure for his mother's decline, echoing the Ghost's 'what a falling off was there' (Q2/F).

Parker argues that this summoning of a 'Moore' enables us to reconsider these early texts of *Hamlet*, rereading their preoccupation with blackness, soiling, sullying, and dulling, in relation to both contemporary discourses of blackness and the 'tropical' reversibility or indistinguishability of white and black, angel and devil. The early texts of *Hamlet* repeatedly construct oppositions of white and black, heaven and hell, angel and devil, and they simultaneously undo these polarities, as Parker points out. Hamlet's opposition of 'faire' and 'Moore' iterates the polarizations of its culture, foregrounding its material 'foils', in a context in which empire itself is ironized. Returning to these early texts enables us to re-examine what has been lost in the conflation. As Parker notes, it may also enable us to read them against the rhetoric of their time.

'Writing, Revision, and Agency in *Hamlet*' is the subject addressed by Thomas Deans in *Exemplaria* (15:i[2003] 223–43). He asks in what way attending to acts of writing in *Hamlet* shades our understanding of the play and what Hamlet's uses of literacy tell us about him and his context. While there is a flood of spoken discourse in *Hamlet*, the written texts in the drama are given only passing attention. According to Deans, this oversight merits attention, for a careful study of those moments when characters write something down or when stage documents change hands reveals that Hamlet's agency is partly linked to his capacity to manipulate written text. His transactions with writing contribute to unfolding his character as well as influencing the action of the play. Hamlet's faculty for reading and writing has received some critical attention, Deans observes, while his capacity to appropriate and revise material texts of others, specifically their relation to personal agency, continues to be largely unexamined. Deans argues that 'acts of writing and rewriting in *Hamlet* not only reveal key dimensions of Hamlet's character but also showcase humanistic literacy practices associated with the Renaissance commonplace book' (p. 223). Deans sees writing as a lever to action in *Hamlet*, points to places in the play where writing serves as a means to power, and maintains the constructive function of writing in Hamlet's development.

Bernice W. Kliman comments on a special commentator's work in 'Cum Notis Variorum: A Nineteenth-Century "Restorer" of Shakespeare's True Text: David Maclachlan's *Hamlet*' (*ShN* 53:i[2003] 15–16). She views Maclachlan as a minor Dover Wilson, bringing less knowledge but similar assumptions to his task. Kliman's attitude to such commentators is fairly sceptical, for they tend to be certain that they can see beyond the error to Shakespeare's perfection. But the adjustment often sounds far worse than the obscure patch that led to it. In the same publication Robert F. Fleissner writes on 'Celebrating a Milestone: *HSt* 53[2003] (*ShN* 53:i[2003] 73, 96, 98), in which he deplores the fact that *Hamlet Studies* has ceased publication after twenty-five years of service. He suggests that subjectivity has been a leading concern among Hamleteans over the years, the prevalent question being how far one can go interpreting issues in the play. One question that has occupied commentators has been the concern about whether Ophelia is a virgin or whether she has been seduced by the Prince. Another issue that has received much attention is the matter of piracy. Fleissner concludes his survey of the journal by pointing out that it afforded space for all considerations and speculations that were not possible in journals such as *Shakespeare Quarterly* or *The Shakespeare Newsletter*.

'Speaking Daggers' is Bruce Danner's contribution to *SQ* (54[2003)] 29–62). Danner points to the fact that Hamlet chooses to 'speak daggers … but use none' (III.ii.387). He thus relies on language when he should rather act. Why he should become distracted in the speaking of daggers evades scholarly consensus, Danner notes. This and related questions have led to comparisons between Hamlet's distraction from his revenge and the metadramatic elements that undermine the play's pretensions to mimesis. Hamlet's move from violence to language carries a futility and desperation that bear little resemblance to the comic. It is in the context of the play's tragic form that Danner tries to connect what he refers to as 'its metatheatrical self-consciousness' with the ethical imperatives of Hamlet's dilemma. Theatricality is asked to stabilize ambiguity and to authorize Hamlet's call to action.

Andrew Hadfield writes about 'The Power and Rights of the Crown in *Hamlet* and *King Lear*: "The King—the King's to blame"' (*RES* 54[2003] 566–86). Addressing the question of hereditary monarchical succession, he observes that this issue is commented on and analysed by much drama written before and after the accession of James I. Comparing the political comments, themes, and images found in *Hamlet* and *King Lear* reveals that such concerns were central to Shakespeare's dramatic imagination. It also shows how abruptly the political universe changed in England after Queen Elizabeth's death. According to Hadfield, *Hamlet* shows a corrupt, vulnerable, and beleaguered nation which can be considered a representation of the worst elements of England and Scotland in combination. Hadfield further states that the plot can be regarded as a variation on the foundational republican story of the rape of Lucrece and the banishment of the Tarquins. Also, the play engages with monarchomach ideas expressed in treatises such as *Vindiciae, Contra Tyrannos*, but there are no straightforward answers in the play to the questions that it poses. *King Lear*, like *Hamlet*, shows the consequences of an undesirable succession, but in the case of *King Lear*, the concentration is on what needs to be corrected rather than whether the monarch can be removed. As Hadfield observes, *King Lear* can be seen in a tradition of 'mirror for princes' literature, advising and correcting a monarch. *Hamlet*, on the other hand, suggests the possible disaster of the impending Stuart succession. As a cure, some might turn to assassination. According to Hadfield, Shakespeare never loses sight of political manoeuvres that might have prevented the catastrophe. He finds *King Lear* an optimistic work, unlike *Hamlet*, 'because the ways and means of avoiding tragedy are explicit within the play'.

Horst Breuer tries to reopen the discussion about the 'dram of eale' in *Hamlet* (I.iv.36) (*N&Q* 50[2003] 416–19), observing that the passage, followed by the equally unintelligible phrase 'of a doubt' in the next line, has been 'among the most widely commented on textual corruptions in the canon' (p. 416). While many read 'dram of evil' as the most plausible emendation, Breuer chooses to take into account Shakespearian collocations and image clusters accompanying the slander motif. Concluding that the collocational field slander-tongue-venom-poison-gall-bitterness allows a novel conjecture for the 'dram of eale' crux, Breuer ends up suggesting dram of gall. In his reading, the 'dram of eale' characterizes 'not the small defect of the gossiped-about-grandee (evil), but the spitefulness of the backbiters (gall)' (p. 419). Hamlet's utterance may then suggest first the little deficiency of the exalted person, then the slander fastening upon that weak point, and the resulting blackening of the whole character.

Kathryn Dent comments on 'Reading Stage Directions in the Fourth Act of the Second Quarto and First Folio Versions of *Hamlet*' (*N&Q* 50[2003] 414–16). Noting that Shakespearian textual criticism has increasingly come to accept the existence of multiple substantive texts as a treasure to be enjoyed, she points out that much ink has been spilt over Hamlet's famous soliloquy in IV.iv, which exists only in Q2. Rather than examining this scene directly, Dent discusses elements of the scenes that adjoin it (IV.i, iii, and v), because, in her view, these scenes show a process of revision that makes dramatic sense of the loss of Hamlet's soliloquy and may convincingly help to explain the disappearance of these lines from F. If we accept that this part of the drama has been altered from Q2 to F in order to shift the focus from Hamlet and onto the King and Queen and their increasing dilemma as the reactions to Polonius' death become strongly felt, then the reasons for reducing much of the scene that interrupts these developments become apparent, according to Dent. To switch the drama back to Hamlet at this point in the play, in a long soliloquy that focuses on Hamlet and his situation and thoughts, would break the tension building up in the Danish court. Instead, F cuts this scene to a minimum, and we are left to assume that Hamlet is on his way to England. In Dent's view, Hamlet's meeting with Fortinbras's army can be left out with no loss of meaning. Accordingly, Q2 and F have different dramatic structures. The loss of this large piece of Q2's text makes perfect aesthetic sense and is far from being detrimental to F.

'Through Hamlet's Eyes …' is a short article by Timothy Harris (*PNR* 30[2003] 10–12). Essentially a comment on Peter Brook's version of *Hamlet*, it adds interest by referring to Harley Granville Barker's remark about the play, quoted from his Preface on *Hamlet*: 'Hamlet so dominates the play that we are too apt to see things through his eyes.' Countering Peter Brook's assertion that 'many, many great authorities have said that *Hamlet* is an artistic failure', and that the reason was that Shakespeare did not conceive of the play as a whole since he was reworking a 'not very good ... melodrama', Harris allows that Granville Barker thought that Shakespeare had not managed to 'so assimilate character and story that no incongruities appear'. But, as Harris emphatically states, 'he did not judge the play an artistic failure' (p. 10). The main problem for any director of the play lies in ensuring that Hamlet's antagonist is a worthy one, for it is not only through Hamlet's eyes that we should see the play's events.

Steve Roth comments on '*Hamlet*, II.ii.332: "Their inhibition comes by the means of the late innovation"' (*N&Q* 50[2003] 43–6). Roth notes that many commentators have discussed what 'inhibition' Rosencrantz's utterance refers to. Practically all annotations in critical editions assume a contemporary allusion to a change in playing practices or some rebellious activity in 1600 or 1601, more specifically to an inhibition of one or more of the playing companies. By contrast, Roth suggests that the passage refers to the rising of Fortinbras and his lawless resolutes. In Roth's view, the inhibition was in response to that rising and to the general atmosphere of rebellion in Denmark.

A.D. Cousins comments on 'Shakespeare's *Hamlet*, I.ii.153' (*Expl* 62[2003] 5–7). He notes that, on returning home from university, Hamlet finds that his father's absence and his uncle's pre-eminence have changed the pattern of relationships that he was used to. In order to make sense of unfamiliar circumstances, Hamlet borrows materials from Graeco-Roman myth. In doing so, he creates a duplicitous map that falsifies both past and present. According to Cousins, Hamlet responds to his sense of displacement with a nostalgia that misrepresents the new as well as the old home. His ambiguous association of his father with Hercules at I.ii.153 'betrays and epitomizes the falsehood of his politics of nostalgia' (p. 5). When read in the context of the other mythological references Hamlet makes use of, we see that already in line 140 Hamlet compares his father to Hyperion and his uncle to a satyr. The comparison to Hyperion suggests that King Hamlet was the centre of his son's world, while the second analogy portrays the successor as a creature of uncontrolled appetite and degraded rationality. The hyperbole exemplified here as well as in the description of the Danish court as an 'unweeded garden' where things are 'rank and gross in nature' (ll. 136–7) is a warning to the reader that it can hardly be taken at face value.

In another commentary in *Explicator*, Daniel Shapiro considers 'Shakespeare's *Hamlet* III.i.88–9' (*Expl* 61[2003] 130–1), the scene in which Hamlet delivers his soliloquy 'To be or not to be'. He sees Ophelia, who is apparently praying. After having interrupted himself, saying, 'Soft you now, the fair Ophelia!', he approaches her, saying 'Nymph, in thy orisons be all my sins remembered'. The issue here is whether Hamlet is being sincere or ironic. John Dover Wilson, for example, was solidly on the side of irony, Shapiro observes. He suggests another possibility, namely that Hamlet does not speak the line directly to Ophelia but out of her hearing before he approaches her. If this is the case, critics can have it both ways: those who want it can have it, Shapiro says, but it would then be a less hard-edged irony.

In *Shakespeare Survey* 56, which is devoted to 'Shakespeare and Comedy', Ann Thompson considers 'Infinite Jest: The Comedy of *Hamlet, Prince of Denmark*' (*ShS* 56[2003] 93–104). She starts out by referring to a cartoon by Patrick Blower, published in the *London Evening Standard* on 16 March 2001, with the subtitle 'To run on May 3rd or not to run on May 3rd', stating that *Hamlet* is being used because it has such a high recognition factor. She notes that we are sometimes told that *King Lear* has overtaken *Hamlet* as the play acknowledged as 'Shakespeare's greatest tragedy' (referring to R.A. Foakes in *Hamlet versus Lear*), but stating that no single image from *King Lear* has the same recognition factor. In the article she discusses aspects of comedy in *Hamlet*, with special reference to such characters as Yorick, the Gravedigger, Osric, and Polonius, and commenting on stage tradition. She mentions, for example, that the performance Thomas Platter saw of *Julius Caesar* on 21 September 1599 ended with a jig, and when *Hamlet* was performed at the reconstructed Globe in 2000, the audience were baffled to see it end with a jig as well.

Sarah Beckwith presents an interesting discussion of 'Stephen Greenblatt's *Hamlet* and the Forms of Oblivion' (*JMEMS* 33[2003] 261–80). She notes at the outset that Greenblatt has explored *Hamlet* in relation to the Eucharist and the institution of purgatory. Greenblatt has long been criticized for adopting an overly synchronic approach. Placing two texts, usually a canonical one and a more exotic or esoteric one, side by side, he has provided fascinating readings without explaining their interrelationships. What are his principles of selection and juxtaposition?, she asks. Implicitly their link is their synchronicity, meaning that change over time is not applicable. In the article Beckwith examines Greenblatt's New Historicism, which she finds compelling and brilliant, and notes that Greenblatt is followed by critics such as Michael Neill, Michael O'Connell, Huston Diehl, Peter Womack, and Anthony Dawson in reconsidering Elizabethan and Jacobean theatre. She examines first of all Greenblatt's essay '"The Mousetrap" on *Hamlet*' (in *Practicing New Historicism*), which focuses on the Eucharist in reformed culture. She highlights Greenblatt's functionalism, which has contributed to mystifying the relations between the medieval and the early modern periods, and then notes his choice of and isolation of purgatory as a stand-in for religion and as an absolute loss. In Beckwith's view, Greenblatt fails to see the centrality of performance to medieval and Reformation religious practice in both theological and theatrical senses. 'By ignoring the ritual and liturgical settings of eucharist practice … Greenblatt dehistoricizes and thus absolutizes a distinction between appearance and reality' (p. 273).

'Hamlet and the Genders of Grief' by Marshall Grossman appears in Vaught, ed., *Grief and Gender* (pp. 177–93). In order to find the truth of Hamlet's grief, Grossman traces the figure of chiasmus as the channel in which madness, pity, anger, and grief circulate in the play. He explores the ability of chiasmus to mediate rhetorically the impasse between representation and affect. Finally he explores the extension of rhetoric across the mirroring (chiasmic) boundary between stage and audience. Grossman finds that pursuing the peregrinations of this figure will take us along a path in which gender is mapped by following alternative trails from grief to anger, madness, action, and performance.

Grace Tiffany notes in 'Hamlet and Protestant Aural Theatre' that over the past half-century many Shakespearians have argued that either Protestantism or Catholicism informs the Christian ethos of Hamlet (*C&L* 52[2003] 307–23). She observes that John Dover Wilson, Raymond Waddington, and Roland Mushat Frye, among others, consider Claudius a Lutheran. Tiffany agrees with David Daniell's view that Shakespeare's plays declare their author's allegiance to neither faith to the exclusion of the other. She argues the influence of what Daniell calls Shakespeare's 'Protestant inheritance' on Hamlet. According to Tiffany, the play, as well as its hero, seem constructed to display views on theatre's potential for good or for evil. Such ideas were expressed in much English Protestant discourse near the time of the play's creation, she points out. In Tiffany's view Hamlet's paradoxical anti-theatrical drama may be described as 'aural theatre'.

An edition of *Othello* appeared in an updated edition in 2003, edited by Norman Sanders and issued in the New Cambridge Shakespeare series. It was originally published in 1984. The new edition has been brought up to date, both by adding some new works to the bibliography and by updating the extensive and insightful introduction with reference to criticism and productions of the play since 1984. New Historicism, feminism, and cultural materialism are part of the discussion, together with references to recent film and television productions and a section on critical responses and the issue of casting. The volume contains several illustrations. It will no doubt be of good use to students of the play.

In 'Psychoanalysis and the Problem of Evil: Debating *Othello* in the Classroom' (*AI* 60[2003] 481–99), Barbara A. Schapiro sets out to explore the psychic meaning and origin of the word 'evil'. As Schapiro points out, the text of *Othello* forces us to consider the nature and problem of evil, and it also makes us reflect on our own destructiveness. She also observes that the play is currently enjoying a kind of renaissance, as it has been the theme of several films and television adaptations. While *Othello* proves especially timely and relevant, it also presents us with alternatives, according to Schapiro, because it demonstrates other levels of psychic functioning and other versions of self. The text includes, for example the unidealized and pragmatic Emilia, a combination of basic goodness and flawed humanity, who could not exist in a strictly paranoid-schizoid universe. And although Othello might not recognize it, Iago's demonic destructiveness belongs to Othello 'just as Othello's narcissistic rage over betrayal and abandonment belongs to Iago—they are of a piece, along with the idealized/denigrated woman' (p. 497). While Othello never fully takes responsibility and identifies Iago's destructiveness as his own, the language and metaphors of the play recognize such an identification. Schapiro holds the belief that in discussing the play, the classroom becomes a space for tolerating and holding in tension various feelings and contrasting points of view. Because the classroom is a place for conflict and difference, it acts against destructive, narcissistic defences and may serve as a goal of psychic development.

Given the fact that Shakespeare frequently returned to Nashe's *Christ's Tears over Jerusalem* for vivid imagery and witty phrasing while writing his major tragedies, J.J.M. Tobin, in 'Nashe and Iago' (*N&Q* 50[2003] 47–50), finds it likely that *Othello*, too, should show signs of Nashean incorporation. He notes that some expressions in *Christ's Tears* are paralleled by words and phrases in

Othello. Dealing with Iago, Tobin finds several thematic parallels of frustrated promotion, and observes that Iago's envious and contrastive judgement of Cassio seems to come from Nashe's discussion of envy. As a creative recidivist, Shakespeare would have turned to *Christ's Tears* during the composition of *Othello* for usable motifs and phrases, not only in the case of the protagonist, but also in the motivation and expression of the antagonist.

Ágnes Matuska discusses 'An Ontological Transgression: Iago as Representation in its Pure Form' (*AnaChronisT* 6[2003] 46–64). She takes various approaches to Iago's function and position in *Othello* so as to show different cultural-dramatic levels and layers of contrasting interpretations present in the play. She suggests that the peculiar ontology of Iago can be explained by the late Renaissance epistemological crisis and the basic change in the logic of representation that took place at the beginning of the seventeenth century. A parallel to Iago's paradoxical existence is a painting by Velazquez, *Las Meninas*, which upon examination likewise reflects and comments on the changed modes of representation of the age.

R.F. Fleissner's concern in 'Othello as "Faire" and Aaron's Child as "base": Analogous Problems in Consulting the *Oxford English Dictionary*' (*ANQ* 16[2003] 5–9) is with the meaning of the two adjectives 'faire' (I.iii.292–3: 'Your Son-in-law is farre more faire then Blacke') and 'base' (IV.ii.73: 'is black so base a hue?'). He finds that the basic problem with 'faire' as meaning light-skinned is that it sounds vaguely racist, which the Duke would hardly have meant, for 'although Brabantio's daughter married a dark Moor, the latter was not sub-Saharan' (p. 6). With regard to 'base', the point is that the force of Aaron's remark is lost if *base* here means only *lowly*. The point is certainly not that Aaron is questioning whether his child is racially black, for he knows that it is. Fleissner finds the textual problem arising again in the play when the Moor, in contrast, compares himself with a 'base Indian' (V.ii.437). Here the adjective seems to connote both *dark-skinned* and *lowly* (*OED*, adj., 2.6).

Dennis Kezar discusses 'Shakespeare's Addictions' (*CritI* 30[2003] 31–62). He wants to show that *Othello* is all about addiction, for which he offers Iago and the critical approach for which he stands as synecdoche and model. In Kezar's view, 'technological innovation, epistemic disruption, dubiously reified agency, and the conversion of contiguity into causality provide the methodological urges of materialist and New Historicist readings' (p. 33). They have already provided the scapegoating tactics of Iago and King James, according to Kezar. Iago and James enact and embody a kind of cultural criticism that many readers of the play emulate. It is, as Kezar considers it, an interpretative mode that the play prescribes and pathologizes. The play refuses the historicist and materialist conflation of culture with cultivation. Iago finds another way, proving that the worst kinds of abuse can involve very little substance. All that is necessary for his abuse is a submission to addiction.

Steve Cassall discusses honour in 'Shakespeare's *Othello*' (*Expl* 61[2003] 131–4). He commences by referring to the final scene of the play, where the title character asks, 'But why should honour outlive honesty?' (V.ii.245). According to William Empson (in *The Structure of Complex Words*), this question sums up the play: the play's references to 'honour' almost always associate the term with

Othello. Othello's question is then another way of asking: 'Why should Othello, the personification of honour, outlive Desdemona, the personification of chastity?' Cassall counters that the question cannot be dealt with so tidily. He quotes the glossing of 'honour' as 'personal prowess and courage, and one's reputation for them', and 'honesty' as 'inward integrity'. The question is thus defined in terms of the contrast between what society knows about an individual and what he knows about himself. From this point of view, Othello's question would be: 'Why should my reputation for prowess and courage outlive Desdemona's inward virtue?' If so, Othello seems to finally look beyond socially constructed truths to inner truths. In this sense, his question may represent a reordering of his personal values. The references to 'honesty' hardly have Iago in mind late in the play. What Cassall suggests is that Emilia may be the new symbol of honesty. For at the end of the play she speaks her mind publicly. She has the final word on female sexual honesty, as she exonerates Desdemona with her final words: 'Moor, she was chaste' (V.ii.249). It is Emilia who redefines 'honesty' for women in the play, giving it the meaning 'not only a case of chastity, but one of being "truthful", "loyal", "loving toward friends which bring honor", and "one who takes up the cause of another as if it were her own"' (p. 134).

King Lear has also attracted much attention. Nina Taunton and Valerie Hart have written an interesting article on '*King Lear*, King James and the Gunpowder Treason of 1605' (*RS* 17[2003] 695–715). They point to King James's failure to keep the hearts and minds of his English subjects, in spite of a scramble to produce new editions of his writings following his accession. In this respect, James's account of the Gunpowder Plot treason achieved some success as opposed to his other writings. The argument in this article is that issues in the early years of James's reign inform the first quarto (Q1) of *King Lear*, published in 1608, but first performed in 1606 before the king at Whitehall. The striking correspondences support the evaluation of Q1 as a historical text with a special relationship to its immediate cultural and political context. Shakespeare must be careful to pay sufficient homage to Stuart idealism, on the one hand, and to suggest the injustices and tensions of a divided society foregrounded by the Gunpowder Plot, on the other.

Taunton and Hart note that the dating of *King Lear* has created much critical debate. E.K. Chambers argued for an early dating around the winter of 1604/5, while the case for a later dating of 1606/7, presented by Gary Taylor and Annabel Patterson, does not remain uncontested. But by considering the connection between the play and the events surrounding 5 November 1605 this essay keeps the debate open by assuming the later dating. As Taunton and Hart observe, *King Lear* presents rebellion as a complex issue. In the text Lear's despotic banishment of Kent and Cordelia is viewed with dismay. This also goes for Lear's insistence on being maintained and courted as monarch. But the play discourages active rebellion and recoils from the actions of Cornwall, Goneril, and Regan in plotting against Lear's life. Through their action, sympathy is restored to Lear. However, his reinstatement is through the agency of 'foreign' powers. Taunton and Hart also note a clear indication of the play's engagement with the events of November 1605 in the early exchanges between Edmund and Gloucester (Q1, 80–1), pointing to the delivery of a letter to Lord Monteagle on 26 October 1605, an event that contributed to foiling the plotters. Like the letter Gloucester receives, the Monteagle letter was also delivered anonymously. Taunton and Hart also consider the system of justice, pointing out that, in the first part of the play, injustice seems to emanate from the king down through an inherently corrupt system. In the absence of all legal and moral checks and balances, all order dissolves into chaos when Cornwall exacts his brutal revenge upon Gloucester (Q1, 123). On the one hand, this double-edged scene represents the wronged king bringing his persecutors to book. On the other hand, the mock-trial could be seen as a sharp critical comment on the judiciary. To conclude, *King Lear* reveals a keen interest in the personality and policies of the new king while struggling with his basically autocratic and absolutist form of government.

Another aspect of *King Lear* is addressed by Dan Brayton in 'Angling in the Lake of Darkness: Possession, Dispossession, and the Politics of Discovery in *King Lear*' (*ELH* 70[2003] 399–426). Brayton notes that issues of space and territory in Elizabethan and Jacobean drama have received considerable attention recently. In this connection Lear's map, as well as more general questions of territory and space, have been considered. What he finds missing from these discussions is 'an account of the relationship between the map as a visible token of the king's will (as bequest and desire) and the misogynist thematics of female will and deception that permeate the play' (p. 403). Brayton tries to offer a reading of Lear's map as an emblematic key to the text by focusing on the blurred area between two thematic constants in the play, namely the visual mastery of political space and the imputation of the monstrous in feminized somatic space. He points out that historicist readings have helped illuminate the rhetoric of demonism that saturates the play and shed light on the close relationship of kingship and the demonic. In this respect he refers to Stephen Greenblatt's essay 'Shakespeare and the Exorcists', but notes that, while the understanding of *King Lear* as second-order theatre of exorcism is very compelling, Greenblatt fails to notice 'the extent to which the play is invested in making metaphorical and nonmetaphorical links between the rhetoric of demonic possession and the status of territorial and somatic space' (p. 406).

Marc Berley's chapter on 'Reading the Renaissance: The "Idea" of *King Lear*' (in Berley, ed., *Reading the Renaissance: Ideas and Idioms from Shakespeare to Milton*, pp. 27–56), observes that for his *King Lear* Shakespeare would want none of the redemption celebrated by his sources. He chose to make *Lear* not only tragic but brutal. Berley sees the source of Shakespeare's refusal of a happy ending in Sidney's *Apology*, especially in its discussion of 'fore-conceit', and argues that he turned it into the chief dramatic principle of *King Lear*. Berley describes *Lear* as a brutally didactic play, its chief lesson being that fore-conceits work for poets but not for people shaping lives, even kings. He argues that this play about the loss of its protagonist's mastery and his repression of it reveals too much mastery of the audience. The audience is mastered and rendered passive, and both men and women dislike it.

Exemplaria contains an article by Paula Blank on 'Shakespeare's Equalities: Checking the Math of *King Lear*' (*Exemplaria* 15:ii[2003] 473–508). She notes that Shakespeare and his contemporaries were the heirs of a philosophical tradition, attributed ultimately to Pythagoras, which identified numbers and numerical relations as the essential and underlying cause of all phenomena. There was also a Judaeo-Christian analogue to this tradition. Although it is doubtful that Shakespeare had formal training in 'higher' mathematics such as algebra, he seems to have known the basic operations of addition, multiplication, and division, as taught to schoolchildren from the 1540s. But, according to Blank, Shakespeare seems to have known more than the general terms for computing with numbers (note the frequent occurrence of 'account', 'cast', 'count', and 'figure'). 'In *King Lear*, especially, mathematics supplied him with a more specialized discourse, and with a mode of reasoning crucial to his estimates of self and other' (p. 476). *King Lear* dramatizes Recorde's idea (from *Ground of Artes*) that arithmetic is the ground of the arts of justice. From the start, Lear tries to weigh 'equalities' among his children, but, as Blank observes, his mathematics is not very good. He makes the fateful error regarding Cordelia's true value, having already miscalculated by giving 'equalities' to Albany and Cornwall, then divides Cordelia's 'third more opulent share', and further miscalculates what will be left to him as 'remainders' (I.iv.250). The problem is that Lear divides up everything and yet claims he will retain 'the name, and all th'addition to a king' (I.i.136).

Representations contains an article by Richard C. McCoy on '"Look upon me, Sir": Relationships in *King Lear*' (*Representations* 81[2003] 46–60). Inspired in part by ideas from Paul J. Alpers's article '*King Lear* and the Theory of the Sign Pattern', which appeared in *In Defense of Reading* [1963], McCoy builds on some of the issues raised in Alpers's article. His main concern is to examine further the source of that play's vitality and force. He observes that literary criticism's basic premises have changed dramatically since Alpers's article. Feminism and queer theory have demonstrated how the bond of love can become a form of bondage in the traditional family, deconstruction has attacked our fictive impressions of wholeness, presence, and contact and replaced them with a sense of fragmentation, absence, and loss, and New Historicism has undercut our sense of connection to the past by emphasizing disjunction and strangeness over intellectual continuity. In his article McCoy draws on a variety of critics in his discussion of *King Lear*. Much of his study deals with relations among characters, especially between Lear and Cordelia, and, as McCoy puts it, 'Relationships are the comparably simple but supreme achievement of Shakespeare's drama' (p. 55). The play's most powerful moments are those that involve some form of physical contact, not those that signify some scheme of things absent.

JEP publishes an article by Martha J. Craig on 'The Rise of the Mother: Violation and Retribution of the Maternal Body in King Lear' (*JEP* 24[2003] 73–92). Craig maintains that Shakespeare's synecdochal use of the womb is nowhere so pronounced as in *King Lear*. She notes that in all versions of the Leir legend the question of Lear's power, age, and foolishness is considered, as well as the responses of his daughters, but it is Shakespeare's contribution to show the deep development of the passionate and destructive undercurrents of power and family and of the archetypal attack on feminine potential and sexuality. Craig discusses the problematics of filial sexuality and asks how it changes our view of the play to think about Lear symbolically raping his own family and crawling towards death over their bodies. In her view, Shakespeare is reflecting on the inevitability of the sexual nature of the father's relationship with the daughter when she comes of age and the eerie continuum from sex to death. Craig joins several critics in having long felt sympathy for Lear, and maintains that the play reveals that man's need for mercy does not mitigate patriarchal sin and self-subversion.

Stephen Orgel introduces papers on *Othello* with a discussion of '*Othello* and the End of Comedy' (*ShS* 56[2003] 105–16). He observes that *Othello* starts where comedies end, with a happy marriage. Also, it begins where *The Merchant of Venice* and *Twelfth Night* leave off, with the question of ethnic or social outsiders as the catalyst for the destructive elements within society. The case in *Othello* is not that the dangerous alien is now the hero, while the mysterious villain is the insider. The insider/outsider dichotomy is really a false one, Orgel notes, for the tragedy is not that Othello is essential to Venice, but that Iago is essential to Othello. While historically we have focused on the interracial marriage as the crucial source of tension and tragedy in the play, the larger issue in *Othello*, as Orgel sees it, centres on the tragic implications of patriarchy, on the one hand, and patronage or gender bonding on the other. He discusses the patriarchal imperatives in different comedies and states that it is on the defeat of the fathers that the comedy depends. In the case of *Othello*, the patriarchy of Desdemona's father conflicts with the patriarchy of her husband. In Orgel's view, Othello may be considered the next step after comedy. Regarded as a comedy, *Othello* might have come out as 'husband and wife are reconciled, and Othello promises not to be jealous any more'. Orgel asks what kind of tragic satisfaction *Othello* delivers, and he aptly answers that by stating that frustration clearly constitutes a substantial part of the play's dramatic force. He refers to Thomas Rymer's attack on the play from 1693, but misses a consideration of Iago in Rymer's account. Iago is the play's villainous schemer, but the principal scheme, the deceptive time-scheme in the play, inherent in Rymer's criticism, is being practised on us by Shakespeare, the real villain.

Approaching *Macbeth*, we find the discussion 'Was Macbeth Lying? The "Be-All", the "End-All", and the Ethics of Time' (*EJES* 7[2003] 137–49). Géza Kállay points out that Macbeth thematizes time explicitly after his crux 'And nothing is, but what is not' (I.iii.142), and then relinquishes authority over it: 'Come what come may, | Time and the hour runs through the roughest day' (I.iii.148). Kállay notes that much work has been done on the relations between ethics and literature, but the significance of the temporal dimension has often been overlooked. This intersection between time and the ethical is particularly important for drama, he contends, because it brings to light the relation between the 'dramatic moment' and the wider narrative of drama, as well as the ethical implications of this relationship. In this connection *Macbeth* is especially central, as it is a play obsessed with time. In discussing the 'dramatic moment', Kállay describes the relations between the dramatic and narrative and finds that the dramatic 'always aims at containing and possessing it own end, at being the "be-all" and the "end-all" at the same time, at embracing the "after" into itself, at controlling temporality by not yielding to the "and then" in the sweep of narrative' (p. 146). He emphasizes that the dramatic moment, through its immediacy, its being always 'the present', in a performance situation happens before interpretation: the moment is the rehearsal, the preparation for the beginning of the meaningful and the interpreted.

'The Entrances and Exits of *Macbeth*' is the theme of David Farley-Hills' article (*N&Q* (50[2003] 50–5), in which he maintains that the entrances and exits of the one authentic text we have of *Macbeth*, that of the First Folio, follow an un-Globe-like fashion. Furthermore, he notes that there are other aspects of the play that seem to imply a version to be played in a space other than a popular theatre such as the Globe, particularly the extensive use of night scenes and the need for elaborate machinery that the Globe is not known to have possessed. His conclusion is that *Macbeth* was most likely written for a covered hall such as that used for performances at the royal palaces. The stagecraft, he points out, is not inconsistent with H.N. Paul's contention (in *The Royal Play of Macbeth*) that Shakespeare wrote the play for performance at the Great Hall of Hampton Court.

Timon of Athens has prompted several studies. In '*Timon of Athens* and Jacobean Politics' (*ShS* 56[2003] 215–26), Andrew Hadfield asks what is the relationship between Shakespeare's plays and their political significance. He observes that Shakespeare's history plays deal extensively with the question of the monarch's legitimacy and the problem of the succession. After 1603 he produced several plays that deal with the matter of Britain, for example *King Lear* and *Macbeth*, suggesting that Shakespeare's use of history had changed with the new issues of James's reign. In this essay Hadfield argues that Shakespeare accepted the legitimacy of King James, in spite of the fact that he had feared his accession while Elizabeth was still on the throne. But supporting the right of the monarch does not mean uncritically celebrating his reign, so to Hadfield the political significance of Shakespeare's plays lies in their frequently critical representations of the monarch. These plays then become part of the tradition of humanist works that try to advise and correct the monarch through the counsel provided, or at least represent on stage how the monarch might be advised. Hadfield suggests that James used the tradition of literature of counsel at court, that he encouraged lively debate, and that he sponsored performances and texts that he considered of political value. A culture of lively critical debate existed in England at the time.

According to Hadfield, *Timon of Athens* illustrates many of the issues relating to the practice of James's reign. Many of the plays produced at the court for James illustrate occasions when the behaviour of one of the central characters resembles that of the king. James refused to attend to matters of state when he could go hunting, for example. Shakespeare's reference to hunting in *Timon of Athens* is therefore quite pointed, since it is made clear in the second act that Timon dislikes returning from the hunt when pressing business is waiting. Hadfield further suggests that the image of the undignified, prostrate James sorting out his displayed wealth might well be signalled in Shakespeare's stage image of Timon digging for roots and finding gold. By this time Timon's wealth is/has been dissipated, and he has left Athens and is searching for the most basic metal but finds gold, exactly what he has left Athens to avoid. Timon's riches fuel careless and dangerous profligacy, just as James's assumption that the financial structures placed on him as king of Scotland would be ended when he got his hands on 'englands bounty', and this earned him the enmity of some of his subjects.

Timon can be read as a play which represents the political world. Athens, for all its philosophical sophistication, lurches chaotically from one extreme to another. But *Timon* is not wholly negative in its implications, although it has usually proved somewhat relentless as a piece of theatre. The play ends with Alcibiades about to conquer Athens, an uncertain moment which presages disaster in the short term, but in the longer term the audience knows that Athens will become the bedrock of European thought. People can learn from their mistakes.

Timon is also the subject of Sara Hanna's 'The Trial of Alcibiades in Shakespeare's *Timon of Athens*' (*CML* 23:i[2003] 77–94). She notes that Plutarch presents Alcibiades as a vivid character impelled by one great desire, ambition. The Athenians tended to excuse Alcibiades' faults because of his ancestry, physical beauty, military skills, and marvellous oratory. Hanna finds that Shakespeare changed an important detail in his portrait of Alcibiades, in that he made him a poor man sharing the common lot of soldiers. This might be considered a dramatic necessity, since a second spendthrift could upstage the hero Timon, she points out. Also, a poor Alcibiades contrasts effectively with the affluent flatterers at the banquet and the corrupt senators in later scenes. Poverty makes Alcibiades more sympathetic, a man of the people, aspiring to being a favourite among Shakespeare's military leaders. The change also helps Shakespeare focus on one dominant feature, ambition for conquest.

Tanya Pollard writes about '"A thing like death": Sleeping Potions and Poisons in *Romeo and Juliet* and *Antony and Cleopatra*' (*RenD* 32[2003] 95–121). She notes that these two plays are Shakespeare's only double tragedies, and, like *Othello*, they are his only tragedies of love. The plays represent a hybrid genre, divided between the domain of tragedy (death) and that of comedy (erotic desire). Accordingly, *Romeo and Juliet*, as well as *Antony and Cleopatra*, toys with genres. Critics have noticed the generic ambivalence characterizing these plays, Pollard remarks, but its significance has not received much discussion. This may be partly due to lack of attention to the strange potions that correspond to the plays' many oppositions. In her view, the narcotic, soporific drink, ambiguously positioned between medicine and poison, reflects the plays' uncertain generic status. While the promise of pleasure, ease, and reawakening might link sleeping potions with the realm of comedy, their implicit threat of death ties them to tragedy. In *Romeo and Juliet* the device of the sleeping potion is placed at a crucial intersection between the poles of desire and death, as well as between the genres of comedy and tragedy, Pollard argues. But it is in *Antony and Cleopatra* that the ambivalent interweaving of sleep, potions, and poisons is most fully dramatized. For while Romeo and Juliet are almost accidental consumers of the disturbing potions that pervade the play, Cleopatra is the font of her play's poisons, and she exerts an intoxicating influence on her audiences, including Antony.

Turning to Shakespeare's last play, we find an article by Jon D. Orten that compares the versification of that play and Shakespeare's first one in 'Facets of Shakespeare's Versification: *Titus Andronicus* versus *Coriolanus*' (in Bäckman, Hansson, and Lilja, eds., *Rytm och dialog* (pp. 228–40)). 'Coriolanus and the paradox of Rome in Shakespeare and Calderón' is the title of an article by Ali Shehzad Zaidi (*Hispanofila: literature, ensayos* 137[2003] 1–17). To Zaidi,

Rome in Shakespeare's *Coriolanus* and Calderón's *Las armas de la hermosura* represents the city *par excellence*; the dramatic tension in these plays comes from opposing attitudes to the city. Rome's mythical past overshadows its present in the paradoxical relationship of the ideal and the actual. According to Zaidi, the victorious military heroes, the protagonists of Shakespeare's and Calderón's plays, 'at once embody and challenge a legacy of reflexive caste violence which eclipses love as the animating mission of empire' (p. 1). In Shakespeare's version of the Coriolanus myth, anachronisms (such as the allusion to Galen in II.i.119–20, or the Roman aqueducts) serve to create a composite image of Rome. Shakespeare's sparing use of anachronisms brings the past to life for, as Aristotle observed, the truth of poetry is not factual accuracy but verisimilitude. Zaidi refers to the conflict-ridden years immediately preceding the first performance of *Coriolanus* in 1609, when England underwent a severe social crisis. The coherence of the English state, based on what Mervyn James terms a synthesis of honour, humanistic wisdom and Protestantism, started to fall apart under the Stuarts. For example, the contempt for the poor, so evident in *Coriolanus*, was the norm, Zaidi asserts. *Coriolanus* and *Las armas* are conceived in times of inflated words, egos and prices, and they both highlight the growing social injustice and cultural repression that threatened critical self-reflection in Spain and England. Rome's efforts to establish a universal commonwealth failed to lay a stable foundation and achieved a balance of privileges and corruptions. This is the reason for the underlying discord in *Las armas* and *Coriolanus*.

Finally, David George looks into 'The Tribunes' Envy: *Coriolanus*, I.i.245–60' (*N&Q* 50[2003] 56–7). Observing that in the eyes of the new tribunes of the Roman plebeians, Brutus and Sicinius, Caius Martius is a political threat, and that their defaming tongues will greatly impair his achievements in the war, George finds that the detraction smacks more of Elizabethan England than early republican Rome. In George's view, Shakespeare seems to have remembered a passage in John Hayward's *The Firste Parte of the Life and Raigne of King Henrie III* [1599], a book primarily devoted to Richard II's reign. The book was burned and Hayward imprisoned because of the suspicion that it mirrored the contemporary political situation, namely that the earl of Essex might be seen as a potential Bolingbroke. As George notes, Essex interested Shakespeare, and Coriolanus might be reminiscent of Essex. Both men were vigorous commanders who faced infamy and degradation on their return to their native country.

(g) Last Plays

Alison Thorne's contribution to the Palgrave Macmillan New Casebooks series, *Shakespeare's Romances*, raises and explores many pressing critical issues surrounding these plays. The collection is carefully named to allow it to focus on *Cymbeline*, *Pericles*, *The Winter's Tale* and *The Tempest*, while avoiding the thorny problems of accommodating *The Two Noble Kinsmen*, *Henry VIII* and *Cardenio*, so allowing the reader to focus in more detail on the four plays in question. Dealing with criticism from the last decade of the twentieth century, the book is admirable for its balanced representation of these four plays, redressing the skewed (if not obsessive) focus on *The Tempest* in recent work. Following a careful introduction and Kiernan Ryan's wide-ranging essay on the nature of

Shakespearian romance, Thorne provides two essays on each play, moving primarily between historicist approaches (David Scott Kastan, James Ellison, Margaret Healy, Jodi Mikalachki) and psychoanalytic modes of criticism (Ruth Nevo, Janet Adelman), in the broadest senses of each term. These broad distinctions, though, are carefully negotiated by Thorne, and the reader is asked to discriminate on the basis of subtle critical differences rather than of broad schools of thought. The editor's introduction is a good grounding for this rather challenging task, since it is particularly strong in drawing these fine distinctions and in clarifying their implications for interpretations of the plays. For instance, Thorne's description of the limitations and possibilities of the early New Historicist model would be particularly illuminating for an upper-level undergraduate or postgraduate audience, although the level of knowledge of recent debates over the plays does suggest that the book has a more scholarly audience in mind. As Thorne herself acknowledges, several surveys of criticism of the late plays (and, of course, *The Tempest* in particular) are available, and her arrangement is careful to carve out its own niche. It is both successful in doing so and sophisticated in its approach, and is especially useful for those who are fully up to date on the issues raised in recent years.

Prime among the concerns raised by these essays is that of gender. This is expressed in varying ways within the collection, but it rarely dips out of sight. It is evident, for example, in Mikalachki's astute reading of the 'delivery of one of the great nationalist speeches in Shakespeare' (p. 121) by the supposedly evil Queen of *Cymbeline*; or in Singh's absorbing exploration of the ways in which later appropriations of Shakespeare's play replicate their source's patriarchal hierarchies while looking to disrupt those of race, ethnicity and colonial oppression. In this way, the reader is faced not with a reading of gender and romance alone, but with the intersection of gender with other critical paradigms (in the case of the two above examples, with national identity and colonialism). One of the oldest selections of the book is also one of its strongest pieces: while there are perhaps some difficulties with the neat Shakespearian trajectory from tragedy to 'romance' which Janet Adelman's *Suffocating Mothers* tries to establish, the extract on *The Winter's Tale* included here unravels the particularly knotty interplay of perceptions of masculinity and 'the full maternal body' (p. 149) and, revealing much about the dynamics of the play, fully deserves its description in Thorne's notes as 'magisterial' (p. 163).

As far as *The Tempest* is concerned, however, perhaps the main concern of the collection is the contestation between the 'New World' focus (itself—as Singh shows—cut across by gendered and sexual considerations) and what David Scott Kastan's essay (taken from *Shakespeare After Theory*) sees as its European contexts. This is complemented by Constance C. Relihan's exploration of the classical, New Testament and Ottoman geographies of *Pericles*. Relihan shows clearly how both the play and its critical interpretations can move between various geographies and, in doing so, offers a productive model for readings of other plays (*The Tempest* included) which exploit such rich settings. Returning to *The Tempest*, the collection ends with this 'last' play and discusses its place within creative rewritings and critical appropriation. Indeed, Kastan's essay, the final one in the book, resituates the critic within the world in a way that challenges any avoidance of responsibility for one's own critical actions. Kastan, agreeing with Jerry Brotton's 1998 argument that *The Tempest* is fascinating to American academics for its reappropriation of a British source, suggests that 'the Americanisation of *The Tempest* may itself be an act of cultural imperialism' (p. 231). This is, certainly, a very appealing notion to British academics, and perhaps one, for that reason, of which we should be particularly wary. What is more, the fight over this ground is certainly at the centre of critical considerations of the play, and is further taken up by Jonathan Goldberg's *Tempest in the Caribbean* ([2004]; to be reviewed next year): the conversation continues.

Goldberg's theorized editorial work on the textuality of *The Tempest* recurs in *Shakespeare's Hand*—a retrospective set of essays written on Shakespeare from the early 1980s on—this time in a reprinted chapter entitled 'Under the Covers with Caliban', which is itself reworked in *Tempest in the Caribbean*. Sitting alongside Goldberg's reprinted essays on textuality, character and inscription (for example, 'Hamlet's Hand', 'Shakespearean Characters' and 'Textual Properties'), 'Under the Covers with Caliban' takes two textual cruxes as its central focus. The first is the masculine pronoun used by Prospero in I.ii to describe Sycorax as she gives birth to Caliban, the second is the better-known and far more controversial 'wife/wise' variant of IV.i. Working from the bibliographic coda to Stephen Orgel's influential essay 'Prospero's Wife' and his assertion that 'wife' is a 'reading whose time has come' (p. 300), Goldberg assesses the approach of editors past and present to this variant (although even the use of that term is contentious in this context) and finds many lacking. However, perhaps more interestingly, Goldberg acutely reveals the utopian tendency of feminist readings of the crux, which see the choice of 'wife' as giving representation to Miranda and so a presence to Shakespeare's female characters. Goldberg cogently shows how eighteenth-century editors chose 'wife' above 'wise' in ways that may speak more immediately to a concern to police the male–male relationships between Prospero and Ferdinand by reinserting Miranda in her functional position as wife, a more legitimate outlet for certain passions. After all, as Goldberg points out, Prospero's 'Sweet, now, silence!' (IV.i) suggests a distinctly non-heteronormative relationship between father and future son-in-law. The collection as a whole is a fiercely committed polemic, assertively addressing issues of deconstruction, postmodernism, historicism, feminism and their relationships to a Shakespearian studies which Goldberg reads as innately conservative and doggedly 'anti-theoretical'. In the main, the author is committed to introducing an analysis of sexuality into Shakespearian studies, and to acting on Eve Kosofsky Sedgwick's identification of heteronormativity as a confining paradigm which must be deconstructed in order to understand our own ways of thought and representation. Goldberg himself, ever witty, ever persuasive, is open to his own critical developments and changes of trajectory, while engaging in heated and ongoing conversations.

One of those debates, that over the 'wife/wise' crux of *The Tempest*, also rears its head in Dutton and Howard, eds., *A Companion to Shakespeare's Works, volume 4: The Poems, Problem Comedies, Late Plays*, part of a four-volume *Companion* set. This collection, drawing on the cutting edge of current Shakespearian criticism and including contributions by Dympna Callaghan,

Coppélia Kahn, Bruce R. Smith and Valerie Traub among others, aims to offer 'a uniquely comprehensive snapshot of current Shakespearean criticism' (p. 1). John Jowett, one of the targets of Jonathan Goldberg's criticism over his editorial decisions in the Oxford Shakespeare, returns to the issue in a brief section of his 'Varieties of Collaboration in Shakespeare's Problem Plays and Late Plays'. In contrast to Goldberg's theorization, Jowett invokes the objectivity and scientific dispassion of 'an electron microscope' to support his interpretation of the controversial letter (p. 122), which he refers to as a 'pseudo-variant' (p. 123). Stephen Orgel's provocative—as it turns out—statement that this reading's time 'has come' now looks less like an announcement of a critical certainty than the stimulus for a whole range of ongoing critical conversations. Jowett's chapter is not wholly devoted to this crux, however, and his discussion of collaboration attempts the difficult task of bringing the work of editors, textual scholars and critics closer together for the mutual benefit of all.

The contributions focusing on Shakespeare's late plays offer a wide variety of critical approaches to these works, and the editors are careful to ensure that essays range beyond the usual suspects, including work on *The Two Noble Kinsmen* and *Henry VIII*. This is not a textbook in the conventional sense, and these newly solicited essays are, according to the editors, intended for scholars and graduate students, and certainly deal with some of the most pressing of critical preoccupations. Canon formation comes under investigation in Russ McDonald's pithy essay 'Fashion: Shakespeare and Beaumont and Fletcher' which—comparing several of the less fashionable playwrights' works to those of Shakespeare—makes a persuasive case for the rehabilitation of a collaborative team which the twentieth century found 'superficial, trivial, meretricious, sensational, shallow' (pp. 154–5), a verdict McDonald convincingly shows to be that of fashion rather than of substance. Barbara A. Mowat takes the generic categorization of the plays to task in '"What's in a name?" Tragicomedy, Romance, or Late Comedy'; John Gillies deals with 'Space and Place in Three Late Plays'; and Valerie Wayne's '*Cymbeline*: Patriotism and Performance' unpacks the historical circumstances of the play's conversations about Britishness in the light of the current pressures bearing upon that concept and the theatrical afterlife of Shakespeare's play. Continuing the work on subdued representations of Anna of Denmark (here called 'Anne') in *Henry VIII* that she began in her essay in James Daybell's *Women and Politics in Early Modern England, 1450–1700*, Susan Frye offers a rather straightforward reading of the connections between the Jacobean moment of the play's composition and the role of the Tudor queen consort. In 'Queens and the Structure of History in *Henry VIII*', she reads the play in the light of the competition between Anna of Denmark and the male favourites of James VI and I, suggesting that, unlike previous consorts, Anna found 'ways to move beyond the court of the king' (p. 441). Diana E. Henderson contributes a sparkling consideration of critical allegories, productions, reproductions and appropriations of *The Tempest* to consider its resonances in performance; David M. Bergeron reads the political and theatrical significance of spectacle in the late plays, rejecting conventional literary interpretations which align 'spectacle' with 'sensation', to read it instead as endowed with meaning. Suzanne Gossett's contribution, '"You not your child well loving": Text and Family Structure in *Pericles*', takes the play's notoriously problematic textual status as its starting point. Reiterating the conviction that *Pericles* is a collaborative work, in all likelihood the outcome of collaboration between Shakespeare and George Wilkins, Gossett goes on to point out that 'Little notice has been taken of Cleon and his invisible daughter' (p. 352), and suggests that the relationships within the Tarsian family are more illuminating of the play as a whole than has hitherto been granted. In '"Imagine me, gentle spectators": Iconomachy and *The Winter's Tale*', Marion O'Connor considers the nature of iconoclasm and the impact of Shakespeare's representation of the icon in his play. Daniel Vitkus's essay, '"Meaner ministers": Mastery, Bondage, and Theatrical Labor in *The Tempest*' stands as a corrective to readings of the play which assert that it has one single focus to the exclusion of all others. Vitkus considers the status of colonialist and 'Old World' readings of the play, seemingly so much in opposition to each other in many of the materials featuring in this review, and sees them as 'mutually reinforcing, not mutually exclusive' (p. 411). Inspired by Douglas Bruster's essay 'Local *Tempest*', Vitkus unpicks the play's depiction of theatrical labour in its distinct forms. In particular, he reads Ariel as a character who is bound to Prospero much as a player would be bound to a company and to a script. The volume's final essay is by Julie Sanders. In 'Mixed Messages: The Aesthetics of *The Two Noble Kinsmen*', she considers what she describes as 'Shakespeare's late accommodation with the genre of tragicomedy' through the idea of the margin as a motif of the genre and of the play in particular—a play in which major events take place offstage—and links its generic structures to the political moment of 1613 and to the structures and concerns of aristocratic house entertainments to round out the play's contexts and meanings. All in all, this companion achieves its aims, raising important debates and critical concerns for its intended audience and offering an important chance (in the editors' own words) 'to think again about the utility and theoretical coherence of the terms by which both Shakespeare's contemporaries and generations of subsequent critics have attempted to understand the conventionalized means through which his texts can meaningfully be distinguished and grouped.' (p. 2).

Bryan Reynolds's *Performing Transversally: Reimagining Shakespeare and the Critical Future* is emphatically and ebulliently a 'different' kind of book. Employing a collaborative model of writing, Reynolds has, with his co-authors, created something which is neither single-author monograph nor edited collection. While it is a pleasure to see the possibilities beyond the RAE-bound 'outcomes' currently defining British academic writing, one's image of this book depends on one's perspective. When considered from a utopian angle, as in Janelle Reinelt's foreword, it is a work of collaboration, an expansive and inclusive monograph by 'Bryan Reynolds and friends'; when read more negatively (perhaps with a sense of the institutional pressures of academia), it is haunted by the suspicion that this is an edited collection in which the editor has a presence in every chapter, and in which there is a hierarchy of contributors—'Bryan Reynolds and friends'. Although there is only one chapter in this book dealing with a late Shakespeare play, the fact that it is *The Tempest* and the high profile that Reynolds has gained for the transversal 'brand' (I adapt this term from

Paul Yachnin's cover blurb) mean that it is worth considering how one of the most contested of Shakespeare's plays is read through this new critical paradigm.

I begin, though, with a few comments on the underpinnings and methods of transversal theory itself. Reynolds's chapter, 'Transversal Performance: Shakespace, the September 11 Attacks, and the Critical Future', lays out some of the groundwork of the theory, which seems partly to build on a utopian notion of the potential of empathy, since one's selfhood (in Reynolds's term 'subjective territory') can be altered through the experience of 'border-crossings' (p. 4) into the territory of the other through empathy, even if that empathy and its resulting identifications are themselves only ever imaginary. Reversing the critical centrality of difference to identity and political praxis while not eliding difference itself, Reynolds suggests that even an imagined point of contact between others can release what he calls 'transversal energies'. This has many resonances and many practical ramifications, and I, for one, find the ideas that it outlines very attractive and its political project admirable and inclusive. It is also refreshing to find in Reynolds and his collaborators critics who place so great an emphasis and a philosophical weight on performance, and in particular, the concept of embodied performance. This book reaffirms the centrality of performance (whether filmed or theatrical) to critical consideration. More importantly, though, the theoretical model for this book is not a naively utopian construction, but a self-conscious opening of the mind to wider, variant, broader aspects of culture which works against the idea of stable states or meanings as a kind of *mauvaise foi* that must be resisted.

Inevitably, I also have reservations concerning the critical methods of *Performing Transversally*. On a fundamental level, there is a difficulty with the utopian deployment of empathy, since empathy itself—the finding (or imagined finding) of the same in the other—can itself be read as the colonization, appropriation and elision of the experience of the other and so of difference. Secondly, there is a particularly simplistic section dealing with the work of clinical psychologists which reads them only as part of 'the society's monitoring mechanisms', claiming that they seek to 'normalize' a patient's 'subjective territory' and so 'cure' them (p. 5) to reinsert them into the 'state machinery' (p. 2). In omitting to mention that this very topic is the issue of a long-standing debate between psychologists, Reynolds's partial summary misrepresents that discipline and renders it an unsophisticated monolith. Reynolds's misunderstanding of clinical psychology extends to the claim that the aim of such clinicians is to 'manipulate [patients who have experienced the transversality emanating from traumatic moments] with psychology, behavioral therapy, and/or medication into snapping back emotionally and conceptually, and finally physically' (p. 6) 'thus restoring them to their prescribed subjective territories' (p. 5). Reynolds counters that such a restoration is not in fact possible: 'Once exposed to alternative thoughts and feelings, one can never return to the way one used to think and feel' (p. 6). Although it is presented as a new idea, this realization is in fact the fundamental premise of a clinical psychologist's practice: while psychologists certainly attempt to lessen symptoms and restore function (and in that sense they are indeed part of the state machinery), they do not attempt to remove or deny formative experiences, but instead work to accommodate and adapt in order to build something new from that experience, rather than aiming for Reynolds's restorative and retrograde 'snapping back'. Change, therefore, coexists with the restoration of function at the basis of clinical practice rather than as the radically new departure which Reynolds suggests. This realization, which implies the value of such change while also emphasizing the simultaneous workings of psychology to restore function and therefore to reinsert the individual into society, would perhaps be valuable for Reynolds since it demonstrates the impossibility of the state machinery's total control over the individual who has experienced what he terms 'transversality'.

While being sympathetic to the grand claims of Reynolds' project, I do worry that, despite its radical foundations, it does not seem to differ greatly in its results from an eclectic and wide-ranging version of cultural materialism, and in some senses (as my discussion of clinical psychology suggests) its findings are quite obvious. For instance, one goal seems to be the 'subversion' of what Reynolds calls the 'state machinery' to allow for a more radical questioning of the self and its social construction. Further, although the book ranges widely for its materials, it is perhaps its centring upon Shakespeare, or 'Shakespace'—a term 'for the particular articulatory space through which discourses, adaptations, and uses of Shakespeare have suffused the cosmopolitan landscape transhistorically' (p. 9)—that reveals its firmly Western and ultimately canonical focus. Mentioning the potential other spaces of 'Freudspace' and 'Marxspace', Reynolds reveals the underpinning of this project by the hallowed works of a Western cultural canon. I would like to see a utopian vision such as Reynolds's brought to bear on the object choice of his work, and to allow it to consider other subjects of investigation. Perhaps though, this is a wish that really belongs outside the reality of present-day academia: after all, as Reynolds writes, 'Because Shakespeare is taught regularly in schools across the country [the United States], it is more likely that on September 11 Americans were thinking about life in Elizabethan England than in contemporary Southwest Asia [more specifically, Afghanistan]' (p. 18).

Further, Reynolds's handling of both the concept of empathy and the 'transversal power' it creates is totalizing: 'Transversal power … can be found in anything from terrorist acts to natural catastrophes to heart-wrenching poetry to philosophical inquiry' (p. 5). Despite the fact that it can seemingly be found almost everywhere and in every kind of upheaval, this totality, it turns out, is peculiarly North American, and it is perhaps no coincidence that all Reynolds's contributors and co-authors are based in North American institutions. To a certain extent, this may be entirely positive (see my comments above about the RAE and its constraints on such experimental and collaborative work), but there are moments in which the American focus of Reynolds's readings betrays the wider project he wishes to outline. One such instance is in the proposed investigation of 11 September 2001, which—rather than affecting some, affecting others to a lesser degree or not at all, and affecting all differently—is seen as not *a* but *the* defining cultural moment, a 'gateway' into 'different kinds of learning and evolution' (p. 1), 'which continues to impact all areas of critical inquiry' (p. 2). Although dealing with a model which itself (as Jonathan Gil Harris's afterword points out) deals in the terminology of space and territory, and while raising the pertinent (and witty) question 'When was the last time you forgot what space you were in?' (p. 8), Reynolds's opening salvo does not break out beyond this American focus, and his consideration of the attacks on New York and Washington, DC, seems itself trapped within a contained system of thought from which perhaps, after all, it is not yet possible to escape.

The problem recurs when Reynolds defines what he calls 'Osamaspace'. The apparent glibness of the phraseology might itself be one ground for objection here, since it seems to simplify the issues at stake, but it may perhaps also be part of an important, jarring irreverence on the part of American academia regarding a cultural bugbear. The author outlines the significance of Osama bin Laden to those in the Middle East and then—too quickly—asserts that the American response to the attacks on the World Trade Center and the Pentagon is more important than non-American responses to bin Laden (p. 12), so simplifying a far more complex set of cultural and political issues. Further, at the end of a lengthy explanation, Reynolds's suggestion is that Americans should try 'to understand the Taliban's ideology and goals', empathizing 'with our attackers and/or asking ourselves subjunctively "what if we were them?"' (p. 21)—the use of 'our' betraying the writing's allegiance. This, while wholly of a piece with transversal readings as outlined in the collection, is not such a new or radical goal and does not seem to merit such a lengthy explanation. Perhaps here, though, I should admit the possibility that I may myself be trapped within a Eurocentric mindset, and I should in fact take the chance to attempt to empathize with that section of the US community for whom, Reynolds implies, a consideration of Afghanistan and its former rulers would be a leap. Whatever the case, Reynolds's argument is eloquent testimony to contemporary America's insular mindset.

Turning to Shakespeare and *The Tempest*, the eighth chapter of this book, Reynolds and Ayanna Thompson's 'Inspriteful Ariels: Tranversal Tempests' takes the play as its subject and offers the chance to see the workings of transversal theory in practice. If the object of investigation is perhaps not radical the aim is certainly political, since the authors trace the production of Ariel from Shakespeare's original, through Dryden and Davenant's *The Tempest, or the Enchanted Island*, through Césaire, Fernandez Retámar and Rodó, seeking ways in which racialized essentialism might be challenged and short-circuited. Tracing the shift from Shakespeare's ambiguous and ambivalent play, the authors state that 'Mixed meanings have come to characterize *The Tempest*'s ideological coordinates, for which it serves as a magnetic sociopolitical conductor, attracting its opposites and propelling those with strong similarities into perhaps more confusing territories' (p. 190). Their investigation of these 'mixed meanings' centres on the character of Ariel, of whom they write that the 'sylph's gender, sexuality, humanity, birth, origin, and future existence all evade exact terms within the play, and its nebulous presence has gone on to inform a variety of discourses through Shakespearean criticism, adaptation and production' (p. 190). By contrast, they position Caliban as wholly explained in terms of 'gender, sexuality, family lineage, and physicality' (p. 190), a claim which would benefit from exposure to Goldberg's more sophisticated consideration of family lineage and sexuality in *Tempest in the Caribbean* and perhaps cannot be stated as straightforwardly as Reynolds and Thompson do here.

Through a sequence of often apparently contradictory arguments—the fact that Dryden and Davenant had Ariel as a breeches role at one point renders Ariel into 'a clearly defined (male) gender' (p. 195) and at other points allows the character to take on the gendered *frisson* of the actress playing the part (p. 198)—the authors trace the deployment of Ariel in adaptations of *The Tempest*. They conclude that the only consistent characteristic of the character's representation has been its race, finding that, although shifting in gender, history, future and sexuality, the role is always depicted on stage and in art as white. This, they suggest, is one reason why the character is not useful for anti-colonialist rewritings, in that there is no ambiguity there to be literalized, as these texts literalize the racial debates of their cultures. However, in line with the utopian transversal method, Reynolds and Thompson suggest that 'the successful appropriation of Ariel, as a symbol of racial and political freedom, offers the ability to deconstruct the assumption that indeterminacy (or, more to the point, unspecificity) equates whiteness' (p. 207). This, they argue, highlights and begins to address the problems of essentialism, and this they see as the realization of a 'transversal *Tempest*'. In this very moment of realization, however, the reading shows the problems caused by its unacknowledged local (i.e. American) focus: Reynolds and Thompson suggest that, in order to release the transversal power of Ariel on stage, one would have to represent the character with extreme care. So far, so good. But they then write that 'by reproducing Ariel as a non-gendered and non-racialized physical presence … an unspecified, *in*human (within the human) form, such as a non-gendered nude whose body was painted in a non-racially coded color, say orange—Ariel could retain its indeterminable "otherness"' (p. 207). Entirely circumstantially, very unluckily, but nonetheless importantly, the authors' choice reveals the seeming impossibility of indeterminate signification, since they have selected a colour which, for a reader in Northern Ireland and perhaps the rest of Ireland and Britain, is—if not 'racialized'—certainly sectarian and inescapably tied not to a utopian indeterminability, but to concrete political meanings. Once again, as in Goldberg's analysis of *The Tempest* in the Caribbean, this points up the ways in which colonialism and its aftermath is not only projected by Europeans onto America, but which, far from being over, at the start of the twenty-first century exists both within Europe and as an American production. If my objection to an orange Ariel may seem trivial and overly localized, I would also maintain that it would be almost impossible to find a colour that was not—for someone, somewhere—politically determined. This perhaps goes to show how particular the seemingly indeterminable can look from somewhere else.

Reynolds's book is enjoyable and admirable for some of its ways of thought—in outline if not always in detail. However, while it is certainly different, and while there should be room for this kind of experimentation and the sheer intellectual pleasure which Reynolds et al. take in this project, this book is perhaps not as different as it believes itself to be.

The concepts of sameness and difference which are so integral to Reynolds's transversal readings significantly recur in Laurie Shannon's stimulating book *Sovereign Amity: Figures of Friendship in Shakespearean Contexts*. Shannon, remarking that 'The critical reputation of *likeness* has probably never been lower, associated, as it now is, with practices ranging from narcissism to political exclusion' (p. 17), considers the idea of friendship in its early modern manifestation, seeing Renaissance friendship as 'privileging … (erotic and non-erotic) same-sex bonds over (presumptively erotic) heterosexual relations' (p. 1). Claiming that 'Likeness in both sex and status *is* (the only) political equality in period terms' (p. 3), this carefully historicized study, which does not seek to suggest a transhistorical essence to friendship, investigates the idea of selfhood and the trope of sameness as means of overcoming the difference in 'kind' between those of differing degrees, between ruler and ruled, and in so doing offers new ways of considering the distinctions between public and private people and personages. In particular, Shannon is concerned with the intersection of the monarch (usually the king) as a private person and public figure, and with the impact of such a cultural figurehead on the idea and practicalities of friendship. One form that this takes in the book is the examination of *mignonnerie* and the investigation of the royal favourite, and the ways in which friendship becomes intertwined with the erotic as a denigratory principle, and leads to the fascinating suggestion that *1* and *2 Henry IV* in fact ironically reverse the trajectories of friendship and dethroning that preoccupy Marlowe in *Edward II*. Shannon's analysis is also keen to take the impact of gender into account for the dynamics of friendship: in her reading of Elizabeth Cary's *Tragedy of Mariam*, the author relates the rhetorics of female chastity to male friendship, which is itself a strategy of resistance against tyranny (something which Cary suggests is impossible under Herod's rule) and reads this into an interpretation of friendship in *The Two Noble Kinsmen*, taking on the analogy 'between female friendship and what we might call male political chastity' (p. 12). Shannon's reading of *The Winter's Tale* challenges conventional heteronormative readings of this play in favour of 'the enormous and shaping power of friendship forms' (p. 14).

In its reconsideration of interpersonal relationships, and Shannon's stimulating reconsideration of notions of the erotic and the sexual, this books sits interestingly next to Goldberg's energetic rereadings of Shakespearian texts and contexts. Indeed, Shannon is very clear in claiming political agency and individual gains for the dynamics of friendship: 'in Renaissance friendship we see certain forms of agency and capacity imagined that would only later be justified by more abstract arguments entitling political subjects to exercise them' (p. 18), but she is careful to assert that this equality is maintained within the couple rather than between couples. She is also careful to show the collision of friendship with the heterogeneous logic of marriage, and her reading of early modern perceptions of marriage as difficult precisely because of its conjunction of the heterogeneous brings the problematic and unfamiliar into sharp focus. This collision forms an integral aspect of the author's consideration of *The Two Noble Kinsmen*, in which the depiction of Palamon and Arcite's friendship is read as an ironizing parody of the ideal, in contrast to the straightforward male friendships of Cary's *Mariam*. Recognizing that there are many forms of licit discourse, which may collide with and contradict other legitimate epistemes, Shannon discusses the collision between the discourse of friendship and homoeroticism in Fletcher and Shakespeare's play. As Shannon writes, 'Shakespeare and Fletcher collaborate to construct a female voice as the pre-eminent advocate of a tyranny-resisting, same-sex principle of friendship' (p. 95), one that allows sexuality as part of its make-up. Shannon argues that the play genders friendship as feminine, voicing friendship's discontent and opposition to domestic and political tyranny through the Amazon Emilia's recalling of a utopian same-sex friendship in the face of the threat of the marital institution, itself depicted as 'a (brutally) political institution' (p. 100). That institution she considers to be wielded by Theseus, the tyrant of the play, the keeper of both the kinsmen and the amazons as prisoners of war, and much of her argument is concerned with the opposition of friendship to tyranny, and tyranny's counter-investment in heteronormativity. Emilia's very constancy is a significant part of this opposition, and Shannon reveals previously unconsidered aspects of the character in a sophisticated, engaging and persuasive interpretation of the play. She rather exaggerates the critical neglect of the erotic dialogue between Emilia and her woman as they walk in the garden in II.i, but her reading of Emilia's characterization as offering 'a rebuttal to Renaissance commonplaces about the impossibility of female friendship' (p. 120) is shrewd and perceptive.

Developing her reading of *mignonnerie* and continuing her focus on the political ramifications of her subject, Shannon moves from a consideration of the varyingly inappropriate friendships in Marlowe's *Edward II* and Shakespeare's *1* and *2 Henry IV* to consider *The Winter's Tale*, which compounds the dynamics of royal friendships by establishing a relationship between two kings. Shannon reads Polixenes' famous speech in I.ii as a nostalgic lament for a time before the monarch's self-division between the realms of public and private. This she sees as being implicated in the play's depiction of both masculine fantasies of parthenogenesis (as unravelled by Janet Adelman) and of the process of denigration and eventual acceptance of women: she suggests that the play's terms of friendship, in 'imagining forms of relation beyond heterosexual reproductive ones' (p. 190), in fact offers a less misogynistic picture than might otherwise be found, one which bases its acceptance of women in something other than reproduction or eroticism. Significantly, Shannon makes clear that the play dramatizes a universe in which 'family metaphors in particular are incapable of sustaining dynastic integrity' (p. 201) and in which the rhetorics of friendship and counsel become the operating political language. This is a particularly important observation for scholars engaged in the reading of the political and its linguistic embodiment, and reveals much that is new about a well-read play.

Interest in *The Tempest*, of course, remains high, and 2002 saw the timely paperback reissue of a volume of *Shakespeare Survey* (first published in 1991) dedicated to the play and its afterlives. Inga-Stina Ewbank's essay gives the volume its title, and several of its interpretations of the term 'after': the volume takes a liberal interpretation of the term, with essays dealing with both the afterlives and appropriations of Shakespeare's play, with its place in the canon of Shakespearian activity, and with those plays which Shakespeare wrote after *The Tempest*. So, in addition to Michael Dobson's reading of eighteenth-century appropriations and adaptations of Shakespeare's 'original' and Matthew H. Wikander's reading of the representation of royalty and royalism in Dryden and Davenant's *The Tempest, or the Enchanted Island*, the collection includes contributions by Camille Wells Slights and Peter L. Rudnytsky on *Henry VIII* and by Richard Hillman on *The Two Noble Kinsmen*. In dealing with these plays, issues of collaboration inevitably crop up: Rudnytsky deals with Fletcher's and Shakespeare's parts in *Henry VIII*, offering a reading which now seems rather out of step with recent criticism; Hillman considers Fletcher's and Shakespeare's contributions to *The Two Noble Kinsmen*; and Stephan Kukowski returns to the issue of authorship attribution and adaptation in 'The Hand of John Fletcher in *The Double Falsehood*', suggesting the more profitable course of looking for Fletcher rather than for Shakespeare. Meanwhile, Martin Scofield interrogates the place of *The Tempest* in T.S. Elliot's poetry.

The volume usefully shows its allegiances to an earlier critical moment, in that the beginnings of a sophisticated critique of New Historicist and cultural materialist readings, the limitations of which approaches are now accepted in the critical mainstream, are in evidence. Russ McDonald's 'Reading *The Tempest*' is perhaps the clearest and most useful example: centring on the play's poetry, verse and dramatic structure and identifying a fundamental self-consciousness and ambiguity in its constructs and language, McDonald combines political sensitivity with close attention to the detail and effects of the play's narrative and language to attempt to 'reassert the value of textuality in a nontextual phase of criticism and … contribute to the reconciliation of text and context, the aesthetic and the political' (p. 15). Seeing 'much criticism of *The Tempest*, like much political reading in general, [as] deliberately anti-aesthetic' (p. 17), McDonald writes insightfully that 'Pleas for interpretative caution are often attacked as retrogressive politics, but the recognition that this is one of the most knowing, most self-conscious texts in the canon should warn us about pretensions to ideological certainty' (p. 27). All in all, this is a useful and well-timed reprint for this set of essays.

Shakespeare and Violence, R. A. Foakes's study of the cultural effects of violence in their Shakespearian representations, comments on the nature of violence in Shakespeare's late plays. He investigates what he calls the 'primary act of violence' (p. 16) and aims, it seems, to establish a trajectory from Shakespeare's early drama in which, as in *Titus Andronicus*, violence tips over into a near-hysterical laughter, through to the mature tragedies in which violence and the emotions it creates are more carefully controlled and channelled, and into the seeming resolution of the late plays. This, he suggests 'helps to account for important aspects of Shakespeare's growth as a dramatist' (p. 10). Working through the histories, tragedies and 'Roman' plays, short sections are devoted to each play, with the exception of *Hamlet* which warrants a chapter to itself and in which he considers Polonius's murder as an act releasing Hamlet from introspection into action. As this structure suggests, this is very much a survey, and each individual play is dealt with at pace and as part of the overall Shakespearian 'whole'. During his analysis, Foakes considers the assignment after the fact of meaning to 'unmotivated or inadequately motivated' violence (p. 61). He then moves on to discuss violence in Shakespeare's romances, centring his argument around *The Tempest* which, he feels, 'seems in many ways a kind of summing up' (p. 10) since it deals with natural violence, Prospero's struggle for control of his own violent impulses, and the violence of power struggles in the repeated patterns of successful and attempted usurpations and rebellions dramatized within the play. Indeed, he sees the romances as finding new ways of handling the idea of violence and its effects: 'Shakespeare's late plays accept violence as an inescapable part of the natural world and of human society, and are more interested in ways to moderate, control or atone for it' (p. 183).

Beginning with *Pericles*, Foakes's investigation of violence in the romances starts with a consideration of the symbolic meanings of natural violence, in this case, the violence of the storm. These he sees as connected to the fickleness of Fortune, and to the romance genre itself, and only retrospectively do they fit into a pattern of 'divine dispensation' (p. 186). However, not much is made of institutional violence in this short section, such as the deaths of the suitors and the display of their severed heads in Act I, and Foakes prefers to centre on the idea of romance and the violence of the natural world. In *Cymbeline*, in contrast, Foakes identifies an 'estrangement from ordinary expectations' (p. 187) which he sees as closely tied to our reading of the play's violent episodes and in particular the laughter at the treatment of Cloten's severed head. Approaching *The Winter's Tale*, Foakes makes a rather sweeping dismissal of any and all psychoanalytic approaches to Leontes' jealousy, without mentioning Janet Adelman's extremely persuasive reading of the play's opening scenes. Moving on finally to *The Tempest*, he sees the opening storm as 'an appropriate beginning for a play in which a barely suppressed violence threatens always to break through the veneer of civilization' (p. 197). At the heart of the play, he states, are power relations and Prospero's vigilance in command of his own, potentially violent, impulses. Along these lines, Prospero's famous assertion (discussing Caliban) that 'this thing of darkness I | Acknowledge mine' (V.i.275–6) becomes an acceptance of the speaker's own violence, and, the author extrapolates, of the darkness that is 'in everyone' (p. 203).

Violence, for Foakes, is the product of the authorizing structures of patriarchy, in war and punishment, and this is especially clear in his investigation of the uses of violence in Shakespeare's history plays. This is not, however, the kind of rationale or phrasing which the author himself would use, as he neglects to interrogate the gendering of violence or the assumptions underlying his particular focus on violence between men and within masculine institutions. This focus itself cannot be faulted, but the assumptions underpinning this choice are tendentious. Foakes describes violence as the natural property of men, emanating from men and directed at men while only occasionally being directed towards women, and always in circumstances which are defined solely as sexual. The anxiety generated by these unquestioned assumptions is perhaps signalled in the frequent repetition of the idea that violence is particularly male, and the following is one of its more revealing manifestations: 'Violence has always been associated chiefly with masculinity, and although Shakespeare created some remarkably tough and violent female characters in his history plays and in Lady Macbeth, for example, I am inevitably much more concerned with his male figures' (p. 10). This inevitability, I would suggest, needs to be questioned in order for a more clear-sighted investigation of the dramatic representation of violence to be undertaken, since to assay the examination based on such shaky foundations is to simplify the nature of violence and its effects, and to marginalize and sexualize women.

Foakes writes expertly and engagingly about Shakespeare and Shakespearian literature, but especially at the outset the book often finds itself sidetracked into rather sweeping statements about the concept of violence and about human nature which are rather less convincing than his analyses of the individual plays. As with so much current criticism, Foakes partakes in attacks against deconstructionist and materialist criticism and wishes to see a reinstatement of Shakespeare as an authorial personality and authority: however, he bases this claim at least partly on commonsense, with little actual explanation or argument. This leads to some moments of anachronism, as when Foakes uses the sensationalist term 'terrorism' to describe the 1605 Gunpowder Plot (p. 1) and as in the suggestion that new technologies have not altered perceptions of warfare or violence in any substantial manner since the early modern period. This commitment to a transhistorical Shakespeare in touch with an essential human nature and relationship to violence seems aimed at ensuring a continued consideration of Shakespeare and his plays. Given the ongoing pre-eminence of Shakespeare studies in educational curricula and other cultural realms, this seems slightly redundant.

Given the usual focus of attention on *The Tempest*, it is gratifying to see a monograph centring on *Pericles*, a play which is often neglected but is currently attracting increased critical interest, with the publication of both Suzanne Gossett's Arden 3 edition in 2004 and MacDonald P. Jackson's *Defining Shakespeare: Pericles as Test-Case*. Jackson returns to the problematic attribution of the play, with the aim of showing 'how minor playwright George Wilkins can be identified as Shakespeare's collaborator in *Pericles* and the shares of the two men determined' (p. xii). This, in a year in which the play has been re-edited, is a thorny subject and a timely reconsideration of a perennial problem. Providing a charming introduction, via David Lodge, to this potentially dusty subject, Jackson traces his own engagement with *Pericles* and his involvement in and considerations of the Oxford Shakespeare's 'reconstructed text' of the play, in which he and Gary Taylor drew heavily on George Wilkins's *Painful Adventures of Pericles Prince of Tyre* (published 1608), to defend the attribution of the play to 'William Shakespeare and George Wilkins'.

This project is carefully and methodically undertaken. Running through the textual history of *Pericles*, documenting its corrupt 1609 quarto and its omission from the First Folio, Jackson asserts that 'the verse of the play's two first acts is unlike anything else associated with the Shakespeare canon' (p. 11), and it is on this claim and its substantiation that his argument rests. Jackson provides a wealth of detail both in the main body of the book and in its two appendices, the first of which deals with the text of *Pericles* while the second documents the evidence Jackson has unearthed from his use of the Chadwick-Healey Literature Online database (he spends some time outlining the potential pitfalls of the use of such a database). Jackson's work is perhaps particularly interesting for embracing new technologies while adhering to a scholarly idiom and ethic that seeks to revive past interests and—he claims—lost skills. For instance, Jackson is clear in his desire to rescue the discipline of metrics from its current oblivion, countering David Bergeron's claim in *Practicing Renaissance Scholarship* that 'No one today would likely give much credence to this "evidence", although it had its believers 100 years ago' (cited p. 94). In order to do this, he provides a wealth of evidence concerning metrics, rhyme, prosody, 'stylometry', verbal echoes and so on to build his claim, while freely admitting to the unfashionable nature of his work. He feels that the reason, why—for instance—metrics is so denigrated in today's academy is because of 'a preference for broad theorizing over the painstaking accumulation of data' (p. 95). He is especially disapproving of the work of Jeffrey Masten, who is described as indulging in 'quasi-metaphysical thought' (p. 8), a designation which, it could be countered, might restrict the wealth of thought that can emerge from textual studies in favour of more cautious hypotheses. Even given Jackson's painstakingly gathered cumulative and often minute detail, though, the claim to objectivity is always inherently problematic, and several of his assertions depend on what he terms the 'quality' and 'value' of Shakespeare's work. One interesting outcome of this is that a near-bardolatrous (although not naive) appreciation of Shakespeare sits comfortably here with an acceptance of Shakespeare as a collaborative dramatist in ways that do manage to avoid using the idea of collaboration as a means of 'saving' Shakespeare from deficiencies of style or taste.

While Jackson does not avoid the theoretical paradigms of recent years, he does occasionally use a dismissive style of argument to bypass the arguments they raise. Further, there are moments when an unconsidered conservatism seeps through. This is notable in Jackson's comment that 'The plays that still seem worth staging are mostly by men of acknowledged individual talent' (pp. 14–15), which, in its eliding of gendered considerations (and the existence of women's dramatic writing) and in a sweeping universalization, seems to imply that the choice of what is worthwhile would somehow be the same in 2004 as it was in 1609.

However, the real scholarly conversation going on in this book is between Jackson and the Cambridge editors. Doreen DelVecchio and Anthony Hammond's assertion that 'We as editors don't really care who wrote *Pericles*' (cited p. 2) is the point of departure for this book, and Jackson is firm in his belief that we should indeed care, asserting that an effort to solve the authorship problem is 'simply sound scholarly procedure' (p. 3). Accepting this principle (and recognizing that it is curmudgeonly to complain that a book containing quite so much sheer hard work and scholarship as *Defining Shakespeare* does might not go quite far enough), one might prefer more precise consideration of exactly why authorship issues remain important to current criticism than Jackson gives here. (A result of this slight neglect also allows one to indulge in the gripe that the book does not really do what it suggests in its title, being, as it is, concerned with defining Wilkins and his contribution to *Pericles* rather than with Shakespeare). Although he states that issues of authorship show that 'our sense of Shakespeare's evolution as a dramatist is at stake' (p. 3), in fact Jackson does not offer many thoughts on what we may gain from this redefinition of *Pericles* and its place in the Shakespearian canon, being content to raise questions of his discipline's importance rather than to follow those ideas through to their ends. This is left for Gossett's introduction to the Arden 3 edition [2004], which is far fuller in its consideration of the meanings of collaboration and attribution, and far firmer in its conclusion that a refusal to countenance collaboration is 'simple bardolatry, which dies hard' (Gossett, p. 68). While it is certainly justifiable to feel that such analysis may be best left to another book, this omission leaves Jackson's rationale and his claims for *Pericles* itself (beyond the issue of authorship) rather nebulous. On the other hand, Jackson is scrupulous in his care throughout to admit to any shortcomings of stylistic analysis, and this care is reflected in the distinction drawn in his final conclusion: 'one thing we can claim for the first time, not to *know*, certainty being unattainable in these affairs, but to have very solid grounds for believing, is that *Pericles* is, as the Oxford Shakespeare labelled it, "by William Shakespeare and George Wilkins"' (p. 217).

Lori Humphrey Newcomb's wide-ranging study *Reading Popular Romance in Early Modern England* centres on the production and history of Robert Greene's *Pandosto* and contains much of interest about the relationship between this prose romance both in its own right and as it concerns Shakespeare's *Winter's Tale*. Far more than simply a source study, Newcomb's book ranges throughout the early modern period and into the eighteenth and nineteenth centuries, interrogating the nature and critical perception of popular reading, authorship and publication through a consideration of the intersections of class, gender, literacy and self-fashioning, claiming that the 'making of popular literature … turns out to be an essential, but mostly suppressed, element in the making of English elite literature' (p. 2). In tracing the reception and history of *Pandosto*, Newcomb is in a position to undermine some extremely persistent literary preconceptions surrounding the categories of 'high' and 'low' art as they connect with Shakespeare's reputation and—far more importantly to the author—with issues of popular reading practices: as she accurately concludes, Restoration and eighteenth-century Shakespearians 'were faced with the dual problem of assimilating *The Winter's Tale*, so unapt to neoclassical tastes, into the Shakespearean canon, and of dissociating the play from *Pandosto*, still embarrassingly available in cheap editions' (p. 2). Further, she stresses that this embarrassing connection between the poles of English national poet and hack writer of low-grade romance emerged slowly during the post-publication lives of both works rather than being clearly and immediately apparent to early modern readers, the result of 'as complex a relationship between Shakespeare and his precursors as between Shakespeare and his [later] appropriators' (p. 14).

Newcomb's first chapter places Greene's prose romance alongside Philip Sidney's *Arcadia* to reread both texts, their moment of production and their afterlives. As she writes, 'Although we should have moved beyond seeing Sidney as a golden poet-prince and Greene as the envious mocker of Shakespeare, Sidney scholarship still tends to isolate the *Arcadia* from other works of vernacular prose romance' (p. 30), and she argues persuasively against this artificial separation. The book's second chapter approaches *Pandosto*'s seventeenth-century fortunes, and the growing attack on romance as a form of ephemeral print. In particular, Newcomb examines what she terms scenes of 'romance consumption' (p. 79) on stage and in prose writings, tracing the boundaries such scenes placed around this reading to assess the changing fortunes and perceptions of the genre. However, her focus on *The Winter's Tale* is revealing. Insisting on inverting the usual order of things by reading Shakespeare's play as part of the reception history of *Pandosto* rather than vice versa (p. 117), she reads *The Winter's Tale* as articulating 'class-specific relationships to the "truth" of mimetic narrative' and suggests that, in its anxiety over romance and its ability to speak truly, '*The Winter's Tale* contributed to the gradual segregation of reading practices' (p. 109).

Newcomb traces the emergence of Shakespeare's reputation—and the problem of Greene's—with wit and eloquence, connecting each phenomenon firmly to its cultural milieu and to the varying fortunes of popular printed literature and stage plays through the material history of the book and the printing trade. Sections of *Reading Popular Romance in Early Modern England* are devoted to the intertwined history of the two texts from 1623 into the Restoration and the early eighteenth century, investigating the status of the text of *The Winter's Tale* in the First Folio, reading the printed text and its live performance as two means of reproducing narrative, and unlocking the political significances of adaptations and rewritings of both stage play and romance. With direct reference to *The Winter's Tale*, Newcomb sees its 'narratological self-consciousness' and the departure from Greene's source in the introduction of the ballad-seller Autolycus as results of the play's negotiation with its source: 'these two features respond subtly to *Pandosto* and to its place as representative popular cultural commodity' (p. 117). Newcomb goes on to unpick the relationship between seemingly lower-class oral and printed narrative and the elite characters of the play, Paulina and Mamillius in particular, and the relationship of the play's narrative structures and the ways in which it represents them to print. Newcomb also provides a particularly significant epilogue, in which she unravels the issues surrounding the use of romances to teach literacy in Irish schools during the nineteenth century, and documents the horror this aroused in observers. As she concludes: 'Every elite condemnation confirmed that popular reading was analogous to other popular freedoms, and that in choosing their reading material, popular audiences were engaged in political acts' (p. 260).

Of the various essays written in 2003, several discussed Shakespeare's late plays. Peter A. Parolin's astute 'Anachronistic Italy: Cultural Alliances and National Identity in *Cymbeline*' (*ShakS* 30[2003] 188–215) argues for the discussion of British civility and the early modern relationship of England to continental European sites of power through the play's appropriation of 'the mantle of Roman civilization' (p. 189) and the anachronistic, underlying presence of Italy and what Parolin sees as the resulting necessary hybridization of culture. Michael Mack's 'The Consolation of Art in the *Aeneid* and *The Tempest*' (in Berley, ed., *Reading the Renaissance: Ideas and Idioms from Shakespeare to Milton*, pp. 57–77) considers, among the relationships between Shakespeare's play and Virgil's epic, their shared focus on the artifice of art and the distinct treatment of art's renunciation and embrace respectively. Significantly, in the light of many readings of the play over the past twenty-five years, Mack cogently suggests that the Epilogue represents Prospero's political victory—the recovery of his dukedom—as a penance rather than a triumph. Susan Frye, 'Incest and Authority in *Pericles, Prince of Tyre*' (in Barnes, ed., *Incest and the Literary Imagination*, pp. 39–58), returns to the representation of incest in *Pericles* and its connections to the construction of authority and national identity. Frye reads the crossing of internal familial boundaries and taboos as closely related to the constitution of royal and institutional power through the metaphor of the family unit. Finally, in her introductory survey book *Shakespeare's Daughters*, Sharon Hamilton provides a thematized close reading of a range of Shakespeare's plays, focusing on the relationship between fathers and daughters. This relationship, which she mistakenly asserts has not previously been studied from the child's perspective, is constructed around groups of plays, moving from a comparison of *The Tempest* and *Romeo and Juliet* to conclude with a reading of healing daughters in *Pericles*, *The Winter's Tale*, and *King Lear*.

Books Reviewed

Aasand, Hardin L., ed. *Stage Directions in Hamlet: New Essays and New Directions*. AUP. [2003] pp. 234. $42.50 ISBN 0 8386 3946 1, with Eric Rasmussen.

Abate, Corinne S., ed. *Privacy, Domesticity, and Women in Early Modern England*. Ashgate. [2003] pp. ix + 204. £40 ISBN 0 7546 3043 9.

Aebischer, Pascale, Edward J. Esche and Nigel Wheale, eds. *Remaking Shakespeare: Performance Across Media, Genres and Cultures*. Palgrave. [2003] pp. 323. £45 ISBN 1 4039 1266 1.

Alfar, Cristina León. *Fantasies of Female Evil: The Dynamics of Gender and Power in Shakespearean Tragedy*. UDelP. [2003] pp. 256. £31.95 ISBN 0 8741 3781 0.

Ayres, Breanda, ed. and introd., and Susan Hines, introd. *The Emperor's Old Groove: Decolonizing Disney's Magic Kingdom*. Lang. [2003] pp. 216. $24.95 ISBN 0 8204 6363 9.

Bäckman, Sven, M. Hansson and Eva Lilja, eds. *Rytm och Dialog*. Papers from the 8th Nordic Conference on Metrics. Göteborg, Centrum för metriska studier. [2003] pp. 281. ISBN 9 1879 8811 9.

Barnes, Elizabeth, ed. *Incest and the Literary Imagination*. UFlorP. [2002] pp. 382. £48.50 ISBN 0 8130 2540 0.

Berley, Marc, ed. *Reading the Renaissance: Ideas and Idioms from Shakespeare to Milton*. DuquesneUP. [2003] pp. 278. $60 ISBN 0 8207 0336 2.

Berry, Philippa and Margaret Tudeau-Clayton, eds. *Textures of Renaissance Knowledge*. ManUP. [2003] pp. 240. £45 ISBN 0 7190 6465 3.

Björk, Eva Lambertsson, Karen Patrick Knutsen and Elin Nesje Vestli, eds. *Modi Operandi: Perspektiver på Kriminallitteratur*. Högskolen i Östfold. [2003] pp. 347. NOK200 ISBN 8 2782 5125 8.

Bruster, Douglas. *Shakespeare and the Question of Culture*. Palgrave. [2003] pp. 256. pb £13.99 ISBN 0 3122 9439 5.

Burt, Richard and Lynda E. Boose, eds. *Shakespeare, the Movie II: Popularizing the Plays on Film, TV, Video, and DVD*. Routledge. [2003] pp. 352. pb £60 ISBN 0 4152 8298 5, pb £15.99 ISBN 0 4152 8299 3.

Carroll, Sandra, Birgit Pretsch and Peter Wagner, eds. *Framing Women: Changing Frames of Representation from the Enlightenment to Postmodernism*. Niemeyer. [2003] pp. 346. pb €62 ISBN 3 4844 0143 5.

Cavanagh, Dermot. *Language and Politics in the Sixteenth-Century History Play*. Palgrave. [2003] pp. ix + 197. £45 ISBN 1 4039 0132 5.

Crowl, Samuel. *Shakespeare at the Cineplex: The Kenneth Branagh Era*. OhioUP. [2003] pp. 296. $34.95 ISBN 0 8214 1494 1.

Davis, Lloyd. *Shakespeare Matters: History, Teaching, Performance*. UDelP. [2003] pp. 330. £37.50 ISBN 0 8741 3790 X.

D'haen, Theo, Peter Liebregts, Wim Tigges and Colin Ewen, eds. *Configuring Romanticism*. Rodopi. [2003] pp. 306. €60 ISBN 9 0420 1055 X.

Dutton, Richard and Alison Findlay, eds. *Theatre and Religion: Lancastrian Shakespeare*. ManUP. [2003] pp. xiii + 267. pb £16.99 ISBN 0 7190 6363 9.

Dutton, Richard and Jean E. Howard, eds. *The Companion to Shakespeare's Works,* vol. i: *The Tragedies*. Blackwell. [2003] pp. x + 491. £80 ISBN 0 6312 2632 X.

Dutton, Richard and Jean E. Howard, eds. *The Companion to Shakespeare's Works,* vol. iii: *The Comedies*. Blackwell. [2003] pp. x + 464. £80 ISBN 0 6312 2634 6.

Dutton, Richard and Jean E. Howard. *A Companion to Shakespeare's Works,* vol. iv: *The Poems, Problem Comedies and Late Plays*. Blackwell. [2003] pp. xi + 482. £80 ISBN 0 6312 2635 4.

Dutton, Richard and Jean E. Howard. *A Companion to Shakespeare's Works*, 4-volume set, Blackwell. [2003] . £295 ISBN 1 4051 0730 8.

Edwards, Philip, ed., *Hamlet*. CUP. [2003] pp. 270. pb £6.95 ISBN 0 5215 3252 3.

Erne, Lukas. *Shakespeare as Literary Dramatist*. CUP. [2003] pp. 300. £45 ISBN 0 5218 2255 6.

Foakes, R.A. *Shakespeare and Violence*. CUP. [2003] pp. xiii + 224. hb £47.50 ISBN 0 5221 52743 0, pb £16.95 ISBN 0 5218 2043 X.

Gililov, Ilya. *The Shakespeare Game: The Mystery of the Great Phoenix*. Algora. [2003] pp. xvii + 482. £40 ISBN 0 8758 6182 2.

Goldberg, Jonathan. *Shakespeare's Hand*. UMinnP. [2003] pp. xx + 371. hb $68.95 ISBN 0 8166 4148 X, pb $22.95 ISBN 0 8166 4149 8.

Goy-Blanquet, Dominique. *Shakespeare's Early History Plays: From Chronicle to Stage*. OUP. [2003] pp. 312. £63 ISBN 0 1981 1987 9.

Grady, Hugh. *Shakespeare, Machiavelli, and Montaigne: Power and Subjectivity From Richard II to Hamlet*. OUP. [2002] pp. 286. £47 ISBN 0 1992 5760 4.

Griffin, Robert J., ed. *The Faces of Anonymity: Anonymous and Pseudonymous Publication from the Sixteenth to the Twentieth Century*. Palgrave. [2003] pp. 272. £40 ISBN 0 3122 9530 8.

Hamilton, Sharon. *Shakespeare's Daughters*. McFarland. [2003] pp. vii + 184. $32 ISBN 0 7864 1567 3.

Hillman, Richard. *Shakespeare, Marlowe and the Politics of France*. Palgrave. [2002] pp. vii + 260. £50 ISBN 0 3336 9454 6.

Honigmann, Ernst. *Shakespeare: Seven Tragedies Revisited*. Palgrave. [2002] pp. 288. ph £55 ISBN 0 3339 9754 9, pb £19.99 ISBN 0 3339 9582 1.

Hyland, Peter. *An Introduction to Shakespeare's Poems*. Palgrave. [2003] pp. vii + 231. £40 ISBN 0 3337 2592 1.

Jackson, MacDonald P. *Defining Shakespeare: Pericles as Test Case*. OUP. [2003] pp. 256. £52.50 ISBN 0 1992 6050 8.

Jackson, Russell. *Romeo and Juliet*. Shakespeare at Stratford series. ArdenS. [2003] pp. xiv + 241. $25.99 ISBN 1 9034 3614 1.

Kermode, Frank. *The Age of Shakespeare*. W&N. [2003] pp. 210. £12.99 ISBN 0 2978 4881 X.

Knapp, Jeffrey. *Shakespeare's Tribe: Church, Nation and Theater in Renaissance England*. UChicP. [2002] pp. xvi + 227. £25 ISBN 0 2264 4569 0.

Lausund, Olav and Stein Haugum Olsen, eds. *Self-Fashioning and Metamorphosis in Early Modern English Literature*. Novus. [2003] €32.80 pp. xix + 259. ISBN 8 2709 9386 7.

Lord, Suzanne. *Music from the Age of Shakespeare A Cultural History*. Greenwood. [2003] pp. 236. £25.99 ISBN 0 3133 1713 5.

Maher, Mary Z. *Modern Hamlets and their Soliloquies*. UIowaP. [2003] pp. 288. £13.95 ISBN 0 8774 5826 X.

Murphy, Andrew. *Shakespeare in Print: A History and Chronology of Shakespeare Publishing*. CUP. [2003] pp. xiii + 503. £55 ISBN 0 5217 7104 8.

Newcomb, Lori Humphrey. *Reading Popular Romance in Early Modern England*. ColUP. [2002] pp. xiv + 332. £40 ISBN 0 2311 2378 7.

Occhiogrosso, Frank, ed., *Shakespeare in Performance: A Collection of Essays*. AUP. [2003] pp. 147. $37.50 ISBN 0 8741 3776 4.

Orgel, Stephen. *Imagining Shakespeare: A History of Texts and Visions*. Palgrave. [2003] pp. 192. £25 ISBN 1 4039 1177 0.

Pointner, Frank Erik. *Bawdy and Soul: A Revaluation of Shakespeare's Sonnets*. Winter. [2003] pp. 223. £36 ISBN 3 8253 1504 5.

Pujante, Luis A, Ton Honselaars, eds. *Four Hundred Years of Shakespeare in Europe*. UDelP. [2003] pp. 274. £35.95 ISBN 0 8741 3812 4.

Reynolds, Bryan, with Janelle Reinelt and Jonathan Gil Harris. *Performing Transversally: Re-Imagining Shakespeare and the Critical Future*. Palgrave. [2003] pp. 288. £40 ISBN 0 3122 9331 3.

Roberts, Sasha. *Reading Shakespeare's Poems in Early Modern England*. Palgrave. [2003] pp. xi + 254. £47.50 ISBN 0 3337 4014 9.

Robinson, Marsha. *Writing the Reformation: Actes and Monuments and the Jacobean History Play*. Ashgate. [2002] pp. xxiii + 192. £42.50 ISBN 0 7546 0614 7.

Roe, John. *Shakespeare and Machiavelli*. Brewer. [2002] pp. xiii + 218. £40 ISBN 0 8599 1764 9.

Ruiter, David. *Shakespeare's Festive History: Feasting, Festivity, Fasting and Lent in the Second Henriad*. Ashgate. [2003] pp. vii + 204. £40 ISBN 0 7546 0626 0.

Sanders, Norman, ed. *Othello*. CUP. [2003] pp. 236. pb £7.99 ISBN 0 5215 3517 4.

Schmid, Rudolf. *Shakespeare's Beloved: The Solution to the Riddle of Shakespeare's Sonnets*. 1st Books Library. [2003] pp. 136. £7.40 ISBN 1 4107 2047 0.

Shannon, Laurie. *Sovereign Amity: Figures of Friendship in Shakespearean Contexts*. UChicP. [2002] pp. xiii + 240. pb $19 ISBN 0 2267 4967 3.

Smallwood, Robert, ed. *Players of Shakespeare 5*. CUP. [2003] pp. x + 234. £30 ISBN 0 5218 1131 7.

Sokol, B.J. and Mary Sokol. *Shakespeare, Law and Marriage*. CUP. [2003] pp. 264. £45 ISBN 0 5218 2263 7.

Swärdh, Anna. *Rape and Religion in English Renaissance Literature*. Academitryck Uppsala. [2003] pp. 254. $52.50 ISBN 9 1554 5690 1.

Taylor, Dennis and David Beauregard, eds. *Shakespeare and the Culture of Christianity in Early Modern England*. FordUP. [2003] pp. viii + 451. hb £48.50 ISBN 0 8232 2283 7, pb £14.65 ISBN 0 8232 2284 5.

Taylor, Michael, ed., *Henry VI, Part One*. OUP. [2003] pp. ix + 256. £53 ISBN 0 1981 8392 5.

Thompson, Ann and Gordon McMullan, eds. *In Arden: Editing Shakespeare. Essays in Honour of Richard Proudfoot*. Thomson Learning. [2003] pp. xxiv + 288. £25 ISBN 1 9042 7131 6.

Thorne, Alison, ed. *New Casebooks: Shakespeare's Romances*. Palgrave. [2003] pp. xii + 255. hb £45 ISBN 0 3336 7974 1, pb £14.99 ISBN 0 3336 7975 X.

Vaught, Jennifer C., ed. *Grief and Gender: 700–1700*. Palgrave. [2003] pp. xii + 310. £42.50 ISBN 0 3122 9382 8.

Watt, R.J.C., ed. *Shakespeare's History Plays*. Longman. [2002] pp. 246. £20.99 ISBN 0 5824 1831 3.

Wells, Stanley W. *Shakespeare: For All Time*. OUP. [2003] pp. 480. $40 ISBN 0 1951 6093 2.

Wells, Stanley and Lena Cowen Orlin, eds. *Shakespeare: An Oxford Guide*. OUP. [2003] pp. 713. £19.99 ISBN 0 1992 4522 3.

Wood, Michael. *In Search of Shakespeare*. BBC Books. [2003] pp. 352. £20 ISBN 0 5635 3477 X.

Woodbridge, Linda, ed. *Money and the Age of Shakespeare: Essays in the New Economic Criticism*. Palgrave. [2003] pp. xiii + 281. £40 ISBN 1 4039 6307 X.

VII

Renaissance Drama: Excluding Shakespeare

SARAH POYNTING, PETER J. SMITH, MATTHEW STEGGLE AND DARRYLL GRANTLEY

This chapter has three sections: 1. Editions and Textual Scholarship; 2. Theatre History; 3. Criticism. Section 1 is by Sarah Poynting; section 2 is by Peter J. Smith; sections 3(a) and (c) are by Matthew Steggle; and section 3(b) is by Darryll Grantley.

1. Editions and Textual Scholarship

Eight years after the publication of the first volume of *The Works of John Webster*, it is a pleasure to welcome the second and (at least as far as drama is concerned) final volume, which contains the tragicomedy *The Devil's Law-Case* and the collaborative plays *A Cure for a Cuckold* and *Appius and Virginia*. Other collaborative plays in which Webster is believed to have been involved (*Sir Thomas Wyatt, Northward Ho, Westward Ho*, and *The Fair Maid of the Inn*) are not to be included in this collected edition, as having been recently published in old-spelling editions of Dekker and of Beaumont and Fletcher. As before, David Gunby and David Carnegie are primarily responsible for the critical and theatrical discussion of the plays respectively, while MacDonald P. Jackson has taken over as textual editor following the death in 1996 of Antony Hammond, who is credited as having carried out a great deal of work on the texts in the volume, and especially on the problematic lineation of *The Devil's Law-Case*. The principles adopted in the editing of the texts have shifted slightly, partly in response to problems concerning the use of verse and prose not found in the plays in volume 1, but also as regards the extent of intervention in the punctuation of the copy-texts (all departures from which are collated). Jackson is theoretically and practically readier than Hammond to help readers—and more particularly directors and actors, who the editors hope will make use of *The Works*—by clarifying longer speeches through the shaping provided by modern standards of punctuation. Intelligibility is regarded, rightly in my opinion, as more important

 © The English Association; all rights reserved. For permissions, please email: journals.permissions@oxfordjournals.org

doi: 10.1093/ywes/mai007

than adhering to the exact usage of seventeenth-century compositors, while the collation shows that this intervention has been carried out with a light hand. Concern for the theatrical qualities of the plays (a strength of both volumes) has also led the editors to go further in the provision of stage directions than has been the case in previous editions of Webster, including their own first volume, to enable readers to visualize the on-stage action more easily. Indeed, given that changes to lineation are supplied in an appendix, a good deal of the collation is taken up with the stage directions.

It is *The Devil's Law-Case*, the 1623 quarto of which contains at times 'severe mislineation' (p. 70) of the play's free versification, that presents most difficulties in terms of distinguishing verse from prose, with the sharing of possibly metrical lines between different speakers being an especial problem. Jackson clearly lays out the questions any editor of the text faces, the solutions found in earlier significant editions, and the thinking behind the decisions taken in *The Works*. In doing so, he also addresses the provenance of the manuscript behind the quarto, examining how, between author, scribe and compositor, such faults may have arisen. Gunby's substantial critical introduction considers the historical and social context within which the exploration in *The Devil's Law-Case* of contemporary attitudes to the position of women and to duelling is based, before focusing on the play's structure and genre, and the ways in which these influence characterization. He argues strongly for greater coherence in the former, through the use of parallel actions and speeches, than earlier critics have often found, and defends the sudden and surprising denouement as carefully prepared for by earlier pointers concerning the characters. The presence, or otherwise, of divine intervention in this outcome is also examined. Gunby sees the play's 'tonal instability' (p. 33), particularly as regards the figure of Romelio and the sympathy shown for Leonora, as making it interestingly impossible to categorize. Carnegie's theatrical introduction looks at ways in which lighting and music might be used to handle these generic shifts within the play, as well as discussing in detail the likely costumes, sets, and properties that would have been used in its original production. As this suggests, this introduction faces in two directions, looking back at Jacobean staging and forward to the possibilities for the modern theatre. The consideration of the emblematic use of props is particularly helpful and suggestive. As the only one of the plays in the volume to have had relatively recent professional revivals, its theatrical potential for a modern audience is considered in the light of directorial decisions taken concerning its staging, and of reviews of those productions.

A Cure for a Cuckold, an entertaining and improbable mix of romantic tragicomedy and broad comedy written in collaboration with Heywood and Rowley, receives rather less critical attention, as has always been the case. Gunby surveys such criticism as there has been, looking at the problems of lack of coherence and unconvincing characterization that have been found within the play. He concentrates his discussion on the central and problematic figures of Lessingham and Clare and finds greater consistency in their motivation and actions than is entirely persuasive, suggesting ways in which the play is held together by strands of metaphor, while recognizing that the 'reversals of Act V have about them too much contrivance' (p. 276). Carnegie has considerably less material of interest to discuss in his theatrical introduction, though once again he is particularly good on the use and significance of props. A production by his own students in New Zealand apparently showed that the play is eminently stageworthy, and with the proviso that it would require a really good Lessingham, I am inclined to agree.

The last play in the volume, *Appius and Virginia*, a Roman tragedy by Heywood and Webster, is another matter. Gunby may be right that the characters are deliberately not individuated by the writers in order to focus on ideas concerning public service and honour. This does not, however, in general make for good drama: although the play's neoclassicism made it popular in the Restoration, and David Carnegie's students again proved it to be worth performing, this seems the least likely of the three plays to win over a modern audience. With nothing known of the original production, Carnegie concentrates on the likely mix of Roman and contemporary costumes that might have been used in it, though it is slightly confusing to find him referring to 'Jacobean' dress immediately after Gunby's discussion of dating which, on the basis of possible topical allusions to the duke of Buckingham, places *Appius and Virginia* in about 1626. Gunby considers these references in detail, linking them to the exploration of the theme of honour central to the play. His examination of its development within the drama is detailed and enlightening.

In Jackson's textual introductions to the two collaborative plays, he considers the question of authorship, drawing on linguistic evidence discovered through the method he himself devised (noted in reviews in past volumes of *YWES*) using the LION database, according to which he attributes scenes to the dramatists involved with a reasonable degree of confidence, while also pointing out why these conclusions might need qualification. The copy-texts are described in detail, and subsequent editions briefly noted; departures from the copy-text, other than changes in lineation, are recorded at the foot of each page (there is no historical collation). All other notes are to be found following the text of the play to which they refer, and they are admirably full and informative. I would, though, recommend the use of a spare book-mark, as it is easy to lose track of them.

I owe an apology to Peter Corbin and Douglas Sedge for missing their edition of *Thomas of Woodstock* last year, when I firmly, and wrongly, declared my disappointment at there being only one single edition in 2002 (in excuse, my copy was mis-shelved when I moved house). It is all the more regrettable since *Thomas of Woodstock: or King Richard the Second, Part One*, to give it the full title assigned to it by the editors, fills a significant gap; given critical interest in the play in the last decade or more, it is only surprising that it has not been filled sooner. Very little is known about the play, which exists only in one manuscript that has clearly deteriorated badly and lacks a final sheet or sheets. This edition is, as it must be, a transcription of the manuscript, while also drawing on the scrupulous and detailed Malone Society edition of 1929, and occasionally on even earlier variant readings and conjectures, made at a time when it appears that some parts of the manuscript were more legible than when it was seen by Corbin and Sedge. All of these are recorded in the collation. I assume that the Malone edition contains a full physical description of the manuscript, which is presumably now too fragile to examine closely, but I would still have appreciated more technical information on its make-up and paper.

The editors accept arguments, based on linguistic grounds, that the manuscript is an early Jacobean copy, probably made for a revival of a play that was by then about ten years old, originally pre-dating Shakespeare's *Richard II*. If this is the case, then the marginal directions that may indicate official censorship must be read in the context of the demands of the Jacobean rather than the Elizabethan censor. Corbin and Sedge are, though, properly cautious as to how these mark-ups should be understood.

The modernized text is meticulously presented, with a very careful collation that records variants from previous editions as well as problematic readings in the manuscript. Extracts from Chronicle sources are printed in appendices, and a further appendix examines all the marginal interventions found in the manuscript, which range from pencil crosses through additional stage directions for music and props to Christian names, presumably of actors. The commentary is genuinely helpful, though sometimes it could be more generous, especially in relation to language and imagery: a note on the emblematic significance of elephants leaning on oak trees, for example, would have been useful. In the introduction, in addition to consideration of the manuscript and possible specific reasons for censorship of the play, the editors explore *Thomas of Woodstock* in the context of other 'Richard II' plays of the 1590s—not merely Shakespeare's, but *The Life and Death of Jack Straw* and Sir John Hayward's *The First Part of the Life and Reign of Henry IIII*. Perhaps surprisingly, however, there is no real comparison of the anonymous playwright's treatment of the politically dangerous material with that of Shakespeare (who, in the brief section on authorship, is the only name very tentatively put forward, with no other candidates considered). The discussion focuses more on the response generated by the plays than on their relative content. The style, structure and imagery of the play are considered, with an interesting focus on its similarities to, and sophisticated departures from, the morality play tradition. Its possible stage history is explored, and in a final section Corbin and Sedge speculate (in an informed way) on what the action of the missing ending of the play might have consisted of. While I would sometimes have appreciated more by way of criticism and commentary, this is a very welcome edition.

By coincidence, another 'Richard II' play escaped me last year (though in this case lack of marketing by the publishers was responsible). *A Critical Edition of the Life and Death of Jack Straw, 1594*, edited by Stephen Longstaffe, is the first annotated edition for a century—so another, if not quite so large, gap is filled. This is a near-diplomatic edition of the first quarto publication of the play, with occasional corrections supplied from the second quarto of 1604. Despite the problematic nature of the copy-text (discussed in detail in the introduction), its lineation and punctuation have been retained, with suggested emendations by earlier editors noted in the commentary. Drama editions are a new departure for the publishers, and the layout they have adopted makes for some slightly distracting oddities in the presentation. Footnote rather than line numbers are used for the critical apparatus, although the text has been numbered by lines, and information that would usually be presented in a collation is supplied in note form. Otherwise the commentary provides information on the Chronicle sources (of which generous extracts are provided in an appendix), and the play's departures from them, as well as on echoes of other plays and explanations of problematic passages. The long critical and textual introduction challenges previous critics of the play both as to the kind of text presented in the quarto, and the quality of the play itself. Longstaffe argues, interestingly but not altogether convincingly, that the play's repetitiousness and irregular metre should not necessarily be seen as signs of either a poor text or a poor play. Drawing on the history of the fourteenth century as refracted through sixteenth-century eyes, he examines the play's positioning in the debate on rebellion, seeing it as countering tropes used to vilify popular risings. Longstaffe argues that elements of the carnivalesque (in the Bakhtinian sense) within the play make the portrayal of the commons, for an audience consisting largely of the same class, 'not merely unpatronising, but … celebratory'.

To return to this year's output and the first sighting of Jonson, Richard Dutton has produced a substantial new edition of *Epicene* with an exceptionally full introduction, which would, however, have benefited from being more logically organized, as well as better proof-read, or at least spell-checked. The text is based on the version in the 1616 Folio (the only authoritative copy-text), the presence of press corrections in some copies being the only real textual complication. Dutton analyses the different kinds of corrections that occur and differentiates those that are likely to be authorial from those that could be the work of a careful printer, touching briefly on the contentious question of the extent of Jonson's involvement in the printing of the Folio. The commentary is thorough and helpful.

The critical and theatrical introduction focuses on a number of key areas: the original staging of *Epicene* by the boys at the Whitefriars and the history of its revivals; gender; the specific social geography of the play's setting in the Strand; and acquisitive materialism. The manifestations of the latter in the play are illuminated by *The Entertainment at Britain's Burse*, written by Jonson and presented to the king and court at the opening in 1609 of this 'high-class shopping and residential centre' in the Strand (p. 279), which is printed as an appendix, introduced and edited from manuscript by James Knowles. Dutton's major interest, though, emerges in a question he raises quite late in the introduction: 'Where is Jonson in this text?' (p. 59). He sees *Epicene* as 'an acutely autobiographical play', and a good part of the criticism is devoted to rather speculative discussion on Jonson's own attachment to boys and young men, as to whether the young wits might be based on Donne and Sir Edward Herbert, and the possible identification of Morose as a Jesuit in hiding. These threads weave through and tie together considerations of religion, pederasty, misogyny and the Gunpowder Plot. It is fascinating stuff, but needs to be approached with a degree of caution.

The final Revels edition this year in fact turned out to be a reprint. It is good to have Andrew Gurr's edition of *Philaster* available again, but ManUP's publication details both in the book and particularly on their website are misleading, a problem that is common to a number of their reprints. This is the original edition from 1969, and good as it is, it of course takes no account of the last thirty-five years of criticism, nor, in its textual details, of Bowers's *Dramatic Works in the Beaumont and Fletcher Canon*.

The year's Malone Society volume is a near-diplomatic transcription by Grace Ioppolo of the Portland manuscript of Middleton's *Hengist, King of Kent*. Substantive variants from the other remaining manuscript of the play are recorded in the textual apparatus, and the relationship between the manuscripts, and between them and the quarto edition of 1661 (its first appearance in print despite being entered in the Stationers' Register in 1646) is analysed in the introduction. Ioppolo also discusses the probable provenance and dating of the manuscript, and the possible reasons behind a copy of the play having been commissioned. In addition to the usual very full and precise physical description of the manuscript, she also considers issues of authorship and performance, with an especially interesting examination of revisions made to *Hengist* between manuscript and print.

Christopher Marlowe: The Complete Plays, edited by Frank Romany and Robert Lindsey, is a survivor of the short-lived foray by Penguin into the publication of old-spelling editions of early modern drama, although it now appears with a modernized text. Lindsey is responsible for the preparation of the texts from the earliest printed editions of Marlowe's plays, providing also a brief introduction to the principles behind their presentation. The modernization has been conservatively and sensitively carried out, though I dislike the substitution—common in modern-spelling editions—of 'and' (meaning 'if') with 'an': students (who are the most likely users of editions where this has been done) ought, I think, to be able to cope with the dual use of 'and'. At least, though, it has been pointed out here and not simply substituted silently as it sometimes is. There is little further textual information other than notes on the A- and B-texts of *Dr Faustus* (the first of which is the text chosen for this edition), and on the problematic text of *The Massacre at Paris*. The accompanying commentary, mainly by Romany, succinctly clarifies difficulties and allusions within the plays. He has also written the general critical introduction, as well as headnotes for the individual plays that examine their meaning. While these are necessarily brief, they are all enlightening: no equivalent introduction this year has given me such a strong sense of the sheer excitement of early modern drama, and particularly of the exhilaration that can be generated by language.

Finally, there is another collection aimed firmly at the undergraduate market, *The Routledge Anthology of Renaissance Drama*. The works included are *The Spanish Tragedy*, *Arden of Faversham*, *Edward II*, *A Woman Killed with Kindness*, *The Tragedy of Mariam*, *The Masque of Blackness*, *The Knight of the Burning Pestle*, *Epicoene*, *The Roaring Girl*, *The Changeling* and *'Tis Pity She's a Whore*, brought together for the first time, as the editors, Simon Barker and Hilary Hinds, tell us (though almost all of these appeared in the previous year's Norton collection along with a number of even more generally unavailable plays). There is a useful introduction that examines the place of theatre within early modern society and looks at the expanding geographical sense of the London audience, as well as exploring the ways in which religious, ideological and political developments were reflected in the theatre as part of a debate about national identity. Questions concerning gender, marriage and family are also considered in relation to the plays in the volume. A tabular 'Chronology of English Culture and Society 1558–1642' lists significant events in the theatre and the wider world, as well the publication of non-dramatic texts. This is not without its idiosyncrasies: William Prynne's mutilation and imprisonment in 1637 is listed, but not his massive attack on the theatre in 1632–3 in *Histriomastix*, for which his ears first suffered; the Anglocentricity suggested by the heading is avoided with entries for Ireland, Europe and the New World, but Scotland, even in the late 1630s, might as well not exist.

Each play in the volume is preceded by a short critical introduction and list of further reading, including suggestions for other dramatic works that students could find interesting to read alongside it, and has explanatory notes (footnotes rather than endnotes) to elucidate words, phrases and allusions, as well as occasionally giving information about textual variants. Students should, though, be extremely cautious about accepting the dates confidently assigned to the first performance of each play. It is slightly unnerving to find *The Spanish Tragedy* assigned (without explanation or qualification) to 1585.

Jonson, as so often, dominates the most significant articles this year. In 'The Final Stages of Printing Ben Jonson's *Workes*, 1640–1' (*PBSA* 97[2003] 57–68) Eugene Giddens departs from the more usual concentration on the quartos and 1616 Folio to examine the legal dispute that disrupted the printing by Thomas Walkley of the third volume of the second collection of Jonson's *Workes*, and in particular how this affected the accuracy of the printing of *Discoveries* and *The Sad Shepherd*. Using the evidence provided by headlines, he questions the assumption that these texts were hastily printed after printing had been resumed. He suggests that, on the contrary, much of the text of the former, and roughly a quarter of the latter, had been finished before the sheets were seized by a rival printer in a dispute over rights. Moreover, Giddens argues that there is nothing to suggest they were completed in haste, and that these texts should be regarded as no less authoritative than the rest of the Folio. Martin Butler, in 'The Riddle of Jonson's Chronology Revisited' (*Library* 4[2003] 49–63), takes us back to earlier periods in Jonson's printing history to examine the difficulty of establishing the correct year for the first performance of certain plays and masques. Jonson used incompatible dating systems in his published works for plays and masques performed between 1 January and 24 March, sometimes using old-style English legal dating, whereby the year began on 25 March, and at other times the modern calendrical system found in almanacs (and already used in Scotland). Greg, in an article in 1926, argued that in the 1616 Folio Jonson applied the latter system, shifting to a preference for legal dating in about 1620. However, by examining contextual evidence, especially for masques, to establish dates, Butler finds that Jonson was by no means so consistent, either in the Folio or in later quartos. No uniform pattern or rationale can be discerned, and particular problems are presented by *Sejanus*, *Volpone*, and *Epicene*, where the contextual evidence is unhelpful. A useful appendix supplies a table listing all the dates occurring in Jonson's printed texts and manuscripts, with corrected calendrical dates where these can be shown to differ.

Another challenge to conclusions reached by Greg comes in 'Press Corrections in Fulke Greville's *Mustapha* (1609)' by G. A. Wilkes (*RES* 54[2003] 473–8).

This focuses on the typesetting of the Chorus Tartarorum in Act III, printed with the heading only in italic in some copies and wholly in italic in others. Greg's belief that the former presented the corrected state of the forme is shown persuasively by Wilkes to be mistaken, on the basis of other corrections to the text on the sheet bearing the italicized version, and backed up by the evidence of the catchwords. Printing puzzles recur in Chiaki Hanabusa's 'Shared Printing in Robert Wilson's *The Cobbler's Prophecy* (1594)' (*PBSA* 97[2003] 333–49). Hanabusa finds that the final sheet of the play, the rest of which was printed by John Danter, was probably printed by Thomas Scarlet. However, he suggests that this is more likely to have been the result of simple pressure of work than of political caution or censorship, the evidence for which he believes is unconvincing.

The remainder of this year's articles are largely concerned with source identification. Brock Cameron MacLeod, in 'An Unacknowledged Debt to Seneca in the Quarto *Sejanus*' (*N&Q* 50[2003] 427), suggests that the final line of Jonson's play is drawn from the third choral ode of Seneca's *Thyestes*. He sees the playwright's failure to cite this in his marginal notes as a sign of Jonson's deliberate construction of the material form of the quarto. In 'A New Source for *'Tis Pity She's a Whore*' (*N&Q* 50[2003] 443–4), Lisa Hopkins argues that details of the plot and dramatis personae of the anonymous *Fair Maid of Bristow* [1603–5] make it an important source not only for Ford's play, but also for the Frank Thorney plot in *The Witch of Edmonton*. The name of the heroine, the return of a wronged challenger as a doctor, and attempts made to corrupt by female characters all indicate that Ford may have seen and remembered a performance of the play at the Globe when he was a young man at the Middle Temple. Luciano Garcia, in a rather more tenuous piece, 'The Motif of Reluctance to See the King in Lope de Vega's *El villano en su rincón* and James Shirley's *The Royal Master*' (*RES* 54[2003] 365–85), proposes a strong parallel between the two plays. This he sees as manifested in the attempt of a character in each to escape the attention of the king, though he also notes that this functions very differently in the two plays, being central to de Vega's and marginal in Shirley's. While, as he shows, a relationship has already been demonstrated between other of Shirley's plays and works by de Vega, as well as by Tirso de Molina, this particular parallel is not wholly persuasive, but it is undoubtedly the case that many of us ought to be more familiar with Spanish drama of the period. In '*Histriomastix*, *Hamlet*, and the "Quintessence of Duckes"' (*N&Q* 50[2003] 427–30) Charles Cathcart investigates the line in the first of these plays, 'And heer's the very quintessence of Duckes'. In a tightly argued article which looks at the connections between *Histriomastix*, *Every Man Out of His Humour*, and *Hamlet*, he traces the theatrical lineage of the joke, noting Marston's parody of the same speech from *Hamlet* in *The Malcontent*. The identification, he says, remains precarious, as this is the only such verbal connection between the two plays. It is not, however, impossible, given the uncertain composition history of *Histriomastix*, for which Cathcart suggests a slightly later date than the *c.*1599 to which it is normally assigned. On the whole, I am only surprised that the connection has not been proposed before, as the article would appear to indicate. David Nicol has two notes on sources this year. In the first, 'The Name "Lilia

Guida" in William Rowley's *The Thracian Wonder*' (*N&Q* 50[2003] 437), he offers as a source for the play George Wilkins's pamphlet *The Three Miseries of Barbary* [1606], which refers to a wife of the emperor of Barbary named Lilia Ageda, 'a blacke woman', with 'Lilia' apparently used as a title. Rowley seems to have borrowed the name, but used its similarity to 'lily' to create the character of a 'white moor'. This derivation makes the explanation of the name by the most recent editor of *The Thracian Wonder* as coming from 'lilium' and the Italian for 'guide' unlikely. Another play by Rowley figures in '*A Shoemaker A Gentleman*: Dates, Sources and Influence' (*N&Q* 50[2003] 441–3). Nicol suggests that Rowley's primary sources were Thomas Fortescue's translation of Pedro Mexia's *The Forest* [1571] and Deloney's *The Gentle Craft* [1597], from which Rowley conflated two stories. Harbage's dating of the play to 1607–9 cannot, he argues, be upheld: it could have been written any time between 1607 and 1626, though probably before 1620, as Nicol sees it as having had a direct influence on Dekker and Massinger's *The Virgin Martyr* of that year. Naming is again the subject of Rodney Stenning Edgecombe's 'The Nomenclature of the King's Counsellors in Lyly's *Midas*' (*N&Q* 50[2003] 401), in which he proposes Ovid's *Heroides* XVI as a possible source as well as the previously recognized *Metamorphoses*. He challenges the meaning put forward by Hunter and Bevington of the name 'Eristus' as 'matter for contest', as well as their explanation of 'Mellacrites' as 'judging by sweetness': the first he sees as a conflation of 'eros' and 'aristos' to mean 'love is best', while the second he argues should be aligned with 'Melicertes', a name for Moloch.

Finally, Lucy Munro, in an article concerned with the very large subject of how the study of early modern drama should be approached, touches briefly on the issue of editing (*RORD* 42[2003] 1–33). She proposes that we should move 'beyond the usual authorial intention paradigm' to a repertory-based approach, and that in support of this editors of early modern drama should be less inclined to privilege the individual playwright in ways that disguise the theatrical framework of dramatic texts. She cites Fredson Bowers's edition of *Barnavelt* in *The Dramatic Works in the Beaumont and Fletcher Canon* as an example of how editorial choices can skew the experience of a play for readers towards seeing it as the literary product of an author rather than the theatrical product of a playhouse. Bowers is, though, an extreme example to pick. To take an example from this year's reviews, in his edition of *Epicene* (by that most self-consciously authorial of authors), Richard Dutton, alongside his strong biographical interest in Jonson, also discusses the play within the context of the repertoire of the Children of the Whitefriars. Editors are generally more aware of the issues raised by Munro than she gives them credit for.

2. Theatre History

Catherine Richardson's account of the table in Heywood's domestic drama has much wider implications for early modern, and indeed contemporary, stagecraft. In 'Properties of Domestic Life: The Table in Heywood's *A Woman Killed With Kindness*' (in Harris and Korda, eds., *Staged Properties in Early Modern English*

Drama, pp. 129–52), Richardson examines the 'intricate web of meaning in this play that connects properties, stage space, action and characterization' (p. 137). This is an intriguing and forceful essay which sees the table in scene viii as a 'crucial symbol which gives meaning to the actions of the play as a whole' (p. 130). This occurs in a number of ways. Most obviously the table stands metonymically for the domestic sphere of Frankford's house, but its being laid twice (once for dinner and once for the playing of cards) suggests a domestic ritual which implies, Richardson argues, the presence of 'the regular, the predictable, and the routine' (p. 135). As she carefully demonstrates, dining itself, with its implications of commensality, 'has connotations of bounty and of Christian charity through such imperatives as the corporal acts of mercy, and is related to Christ's actions at the Last Supper' (p. 138). Moreover, she goes on, 'Protestantism had strengthened and drawn attention to these meanings through the altered form of the Eucharist with its "table" and "cup" in place of altar and chalice'. In all these ways Richardson shows how such an innocuous prop can take on multiple significations. Perhaps most important of all, in the context of Heywood's play, is that the '*normality* of the domestic environment' makes Anne's infidelity all the more shocking. Although Richardson refers to it as 'Anne and Wendoll's crime' (p. 146), it is clearly, both in terms of the domestic setting and the patriarchal discourse of the day, a female fault. The only failing of this fine essay is that Richardson seems squeamish about declaring it to be so. Jeanne Addison Roberts has no such qualms. Her 'Types of Crone: The Nurse and the Wise Woman in English Renaissance Drama' (*RenP 2000* [2001] 71–86) suggests the overwhelming power of patriarchy: 'Nurses are simple-minded, dangerously sex-obsessed, potentially destructive rather than nurturing, and finally powerless. Wise women are rare. Where they seem to appear they may be fraudulent, or turn out to speak in ventriloquized voices of male culture. In any case they too are usually powerless' (p. 85). While the Nurse may occasionally threaten patriarchal order by 'regularly facilitating female regression to the wild' (p. 80), such subversion is only ever temporary. Indeed, 'It is no surprise that they are frequently killed off by resentful or desperate males.'

'"As from the Waste of Sophonisba"; or, What's Sexy about Stage Directions?' (*RenD* 32[2003] 3–31) is an ingenious essay in which Genevieve Love sets the play-goer and the reader alongside one another. Marston's plays, noted for their plethoric stage directions, must leave the reader disappointed since the very wealth of detail implies the poverty, in comparison, of the reading experience. Love demonstrates how both *The Malcontent* and *The Fawn* appear to prioritize performance over the reading of the playtexts. However, she asserts that *Sophonisba* is, in this respect, atypical since it 'is a text specially tailored to readers' (p. 15). In spite of this, she maintains that Marston 'thinks … that theatrical effects are not transferable to the scene of reading' (p. 17). This paradox underlies *Sophonisba*, a play, Love proposes, that 'not only elucidates but also exhibits an absence at the heart of the theatrical' (p. 20). Love goes on to demonstrate that these moments of absence are frequently sexual in nature—such as erotic encounters staged upon a curtained bed or within a 'canopy' (or concealed space). Thus, she concludes, 'audience and readers come together not because they relate similarly to the seen but because they relate similarly to the unseen' (p. 25).

3. Criticism

(a) General

One should begin this year with a series of monographs which range widely across early modern drama. Daniel Vitkus's *Turning Turk: English Theater and the Multicultural Mediterranean 1570–1630* argues that 'the binary opposition of colonizer and colonized, so familiar in recent scholarship informed by postcolonial identity politics, cannot be maintained in a properly historicized description of England's early modern culture' (p. 3). In practice, he contends, the details of English dealings with other cultures, especially with respect to the powerful states around the Mediterranean, show a much more complex process of cultural exchange at work. Vitkus then proceeds to apply this framework to a range of texts including *Tamburlaine, The Jew of Malta*, and *Othello*, Daborne's *A Christian Turned Turk*, and Massinger's *The Renegado*. Vitkus also reads Heywood's two *The Fair Maid of the West* plays in terms of English trade, exchange, and captivity in the East.

An alternative reading of *The Fair Maid of the West* plays is to be found in another of the year's monographs, Jennifer A. Low's *Manhood and the Duel: Masculinity in Early Modern Drama and Culture*. For Low, the play's heroine Bess Bridges is one of a group of female dramatic characters, including Moll Cutpurse and Aspatia in *The Maid's Tragedy*, who undertake duels while dressed as men. Low's concern is the social codes which surround the 'ritualized violence' (p. 5) of early modern duelling. She offers a social history of the duel and of fencing technique, argues that duelling offers an important and useful terminology for masculine ideas of personal space, and considers different ideas of personal honour. Hence her interest in those stage representations of female duellists, since they provide particularly interesting cases for examining how ideas of gender and ideas of the duel overlap. Low's study also pays particular attention to plays including Shakespeare's *Much Ado about Nothing*, Middleton and Rowley's *A Fair Quarrel*, Chapman's *Bussy D'Ambois* plays, and the anonymous *Swetnam the Woman-Hater*.

Nora Johnson's *The Actor as Playwright in Early Modern Drama* provides comparative analysis of the careers and works of four actor/playwrights: Robert Armin, Nathan Field, Anthony Munday, and Thomas Heywood. Johnson is interested in their self-fashioning as authorial figures, and their approaches to the playwright's art. Lurking throughout in the background is the figure of Shakespeare, who is given special consideration in a coda. William E. Engel's *Death and Drama in Renaissance England: Shades of Memory* speeds through several Renaissance tragedies in its first eighty-five pages, including those of Kyd, Marlowe, Webster, and Ford. Engel is interested in their staging of memory, with particular relation to the mnemonic arts and the idea of memory theatres. One obvious reference point is Engel's earlier book *Mapping Mortality*, and another is Michael Neill's *Issues of Death*, with which Engel is in dialogue.

Ronald Huebert's *The Performance of Pleasure in English Renaissance Drama* should also be mentioned here, a wide-ranging study of stage figurations of pleasure both aesthetic and erotic, in plays by Marlowe, Marston, Jonson, Webster, Ford, and others. Ina Habermann's *Staging Slander and Gender in Early Modern England* looks to historicize early modern drama's treatment of slander. In particular, Habermann is interested in early modern attempts legally to define slander, given the slipperiness of all linguistic utterances. She pays attention to representations of slander in a range of plays including *Othello*, *The Devil's Law-Case*, Jonson's *The Devil is an Ass*, Tomkis's *Lingua*, and Cary's *Mariam*, as well as in non-dramatic texts, from legal treatises to psalm translations.

Moving on to article-length studies, this chapter will proceed in a very loosely chronological sweep through a field notable this year for its fascination with Thomas Middleton. Still awaiting a definitive edition, Middleton's plays are attracting ever greater interest. But this survey begins well before his birth, with Sackville and Norton's *Gorboduc*.

Gorboduc is the subject of an article by Kevin Dunn, 'Representing Counsel: *Gorboduc* and the Elizabethan Privy Council' (*ELR* 33[2003] 279–308). Dunn investigates the problems of representing counsel, that most self-effacing of political processes: in the case of *Gorboduc*, he argues, this 'unrepresentable centrality of counsel' (p. 295) goes some way towards explaining one of the strangest structural features of the play, the fact that Act V goes on even though the king and all his family are dead before it starts.

Dramatic texts by Lyly and Peele feature in Jeanne H. McCarthy's 'Elizabeth I's "Picture in Little": Boy Company Representations of a Queen's Authority' (*SP* 100[2003] 425–62). She offers a historical account of Elizabeth's support, over the years, for the boy companies, and relates the companies to Patricia Fumerton's concept of an 'Elizabethan aesthetics of the miniature' (p. 440), in particular as it concerns their representations of queenship in plays including Lyly's *Endymion* and Peele's *The Arraignment of Paris*. Lyly is also considered by Rodney Stenning Edgecombe in 'The Names of the King's Counsellors in Lyly's *Midas*' (*N&Q* 50[2003] 401), suggesting etymologies for the names of Midas's counsellors Eristus and Mellacrites.

It has been a quieter year on Kyd. Arthur Freeman, in a brief note, 'Thomas Hawkins, Richard Farmer, and the Authorship of *The Spanish Tragedy*' (*N&Q* 50[2003] 214–15), reapportions the credit for first attributing the play to Kyd away from Hawkins and towards Farmer.

Ian McAdam's 'Protestant Manliness in *Arden of Faversham*' (*TSLL* 45[2003] 42–72) considers the anonymous tragedy (which one might help electronic searchers to find by also naming here as *Arden of Feversham*). McAdam's concern is the central importance of religion to all aspects of Renaissance thought: indeed, distancing himself from the materialist frame of reference of many recent commentators, he goes so far as to argue that religion inflects all aspects of the play, most of all the marriage of the protagonists. The play, argues McAdam, 'reveals an inability in early modern society to envisage purely secular forms of human relationships' (p. 67).

Whenever modern texts depict Robin Hood as an aristocrat in disguise, rather than merely a disaffected peasant, they propagate a tradition that was started by

Anthony Munday's two plays, *The Downfall of Robert Earl of Huntington* and *The Death of Robert Earl of Huntington*. Munday's contribution to the Robin Hood mythos, and in particular the crucial change he made to Robin Hood's social class, have generally been thought of in the context of Robin Hood history, but in 'Anthony Munday's Gentrification of Robin Hood' (*ELR* 33[2003] 155–80), Meredith Skura puts the plays in the context of Munday's London, and measures Munday's Robin Hood against other fictional figures such as Dekker's Simon Eyre and Deloney's Jack of Newbury. Skura's surprising conclusion is that Munday makes Robin Hood into a disguised aristocrat not exactly as part of an elite appropriation of a vernacular figure, but rather in order to make him fit the stories of social mobility favoured by a self-confident, aspirational middle class.

That troublesome play *Lust's Dominion*, recently linked with the Marston canon, is discussed by Ian Smith in 'White Skin, Black Masks: Racial Cross-Dressing on the Early Modern Stage' (*RenD* 32[2003] 33–68). Modifying the terminology of Frantz Fanon, Smith compares the play to *Othello* in terms of its interest in 'the prosthetics of race' (p. 42), in particular the use of black cloth as a representation of black skin. Smith relates this to ideas of cosmetics, and, intriguingly, to the textile trade from England to the East.

A series of articles by Charles Cathcart constitutes most of the year's periodical literature on Marston. In 'Borrowings and the Authorial Domain: Gostanzo, Polonius, and Marston's Gonzago' (*CompD* 27[2003] 159–74), Cathcart considers Marston's *Parasitaster, or the Fawn*, drawing attention to its extensive borrowings from *Hamlet* and its links to Chapman's *All Fools*. *The Fawn*, Cathcart argues, is full of 'insistent verbal obeisance to the plays of the Lord Chamberlain's Men' (p. 172). Cathcart's note, '*Histriomastix*, *Hamlet*, and the "Quintessence of Duckes"' (*N&Q* 50[2003] 427–30), offers a reading of a crux in *Histriomastix*, whose status in the Marston canon continues to be debated (with more work on the attribution question to be reported next year). Another note by Cathcart, 'Lodge, Marston, and the Family of Love' (*N&Q* 50[2003] 68–70), explicates references to the Familist sect in Marston's *The Dutch Courtesan* and *The Malcontent*, linking them to Lodge's *Wit's Miserie*. In another article, Cathcart writes on '*The Insatiate Countess*: Date, Topicality, and Company Appropriation' (*MRDE* 16[2003] 81–100). He argues that two layers of composition can be discerned in the play as we have it: the first, Marston's original work 'in or soon after 1601, probably during the time of Marston's connection with the Children of Paul's', and the second, a revision of that work prepared by William Barksted and Lewis Machin with a view to performance at Whitefriars by the Children of the King's Revels. Cathcart is persuasive when linking *The Insatiate Countess* to Marston, and in particular to earlier rather than later Marston: the Marston of the War of the Theatres.

That Marston features too in James Bednarz's article, 'Dekker and Marston's Coactive Drama' (*BJJ* 10[2003] 209–34). Bednarz offers a comparative study of these two authors, the differences between whom have often been elided in the light of their joint controversy with Jonson. But Bednarz writes interestingly about the interplay of themes between the two writers, a dialogue at its most explicit and obvious in the *Ho!* plays. He is also illuminating on the relationship between *The Dutch Courtesan* and the *Honest Whore* plays.

Also on the *Honest Whore* plays, Ken Jackson's 'Bethlem and Bridewell in the *Honest Whore* Plays' (*SEL* 43[2003] 395–414) takes as its starting point a recent book by Jonathan Andrews et al., *History of Bethlem*. This book is keen to emphasize the distance between the literary representation of Bethlem in the two *Honest Whore* plays, and the historical reality; Jackson, by contrast, looks to emphasize the similarities between the fictional institution and the historical one. In particular, Bethlem is now notorious for its use of the mad as a form of public entertainment, and Bridewell a byword for authority turned evil, but Jackson argues that it is a mistake to read these plays in terms of such a sensationalist view of these institutions: 'Dekker and Middleton did not use these institutions ironically. These institutions were used because they were figures for a humble charity in early modern London that engaged and integrated many elements of the city' (p. 410).

Dekker and Middleton's *The Roaring Girl* is perhaps the central text in another wide-ranging article, Leslie Thomson's '"As proper a woman as any in Cheap": Women in Shops on the Early Modern Stage' (*MRDE* 16[2003] 145–61). Thomson locates around twenty plays which use the convention of displaying a shopwoman in her shop, and relates them to contemporary concerns about the morality of shopwomen: in particular, the idea that they might potentially be as purchasable as the goods they sell. Thomson's survey seems to have missed Brome's *The New Academy*, which is a pity, as it supplies further supporting evidence for the argument. Mario diGangi's 'Sexual Slander and Working Women in *The Roaring Girl*' (*RenD* 32[2003] 240–88) has points of contact with both Thomson's article and Habermann's book discussed above, since it is interested in the 'economic and erotic agency' of Mistress Openwork and Mistress Gallipot (p. 248), and the ways in which their social position as shopwomen leaves them vulnerable to slander. Heather Hirschfeld, in contrast, examines the eponymous heroine of the play, in 'What Do Women Know? *The Roaring Girl* and the Wisdom of Tiresias' (*RenD* 32[2003] 123–46). She argues that the play is concerned not merely with ontology—what Moll *is*—but with epistemology: how might an observer know what she is? Hirschfeld demonstrates that the play is full of imagery of knowing, and that Moll herself seems both unknowable and yet always in the know.

A group of articles deal with the drama of Webster. Aspasia Velissariou writes about 'Class and Gender Destabilization in Webster's *The Devil's Law-Case*' (*CahiersE* 63[2003] 71–88). Velissariou argues that that play uses elements of city comedy to reward female desire and to destabilize patriarchal structures, most of all in the trial scene. She sees the play as a celebration of 'defiant individualism' (p. 85), and of sexual desire, treated in this play as the most important form of human agency.

Webster's *The White Devil* and *The Duchess of Malfi*, together with *Hamlet*, are the main concern of Thomas Rist in 'Religion, Politics, Revenge: The Dead in Renaissance Drama' (*EMLS* 9:i[2003]). Rist is interested in the religio-political import of these plays' differing representations of the gap between the living and the dead, and interrogating Stephen Greenblatt's famous analysis of *Hamlet* by comparing Webster's two tragedies. Like Rist, Lara Bovilsky compares Webster and Shakespeare. In 'Black Beauties, White Devils: The English Italian in Milton and Webster' (*ELH* 70[2003] 625–51), Bovilsky considers *The White Devil*, taking her cue from the moment in *The Merchant of Venice* when Portia, dressed as a man, takes on the name of the African king Balthazar. This is the basis for an examination of racial imagery in Milton's sonnets and Webster's play, particularly as regards the slippage between racial and sexual disguise, and the slippage between Italianness and blackness.

Also partly on Webster is Philip D. Collington's 'Pent-Up Emotions: Pity and the Imprisonment of Women in Renaissance Drama' (*MRDE* 16[2003] 162–91). Collington considers female imprisonment in plays by Dekker, Heywood, Marlowe, and Shakespeare, as well as Webster's *The Duchess of Malfi*, exploring the political resonances of such pictures of wrongly imprisoned women meeting their imprisonment with Stoic resolve. Lisa Hopkins's 'With the Skin Side Inside: The Interiors of *The Duchess of Malfi*' (in Abate, ed., *Privacy, Domesticity, and Women in Early Modern England*, pp. 21–30), explores the play's interest in the category of 'inside': inside a house, inside a body, inside a mind, culminating in the 'private hell' (p. 27) of Ferdinand's interiority. Hopkins traces the play's fascination with such images of containment. Perhaps, then, she argues, the Duchess can dominate the play even after her death because she, uniquely among its characters, is able to understand 'a radical divorce between external body and internal mind' (p. 29).

Reina Green writes on the subject of '"Ears prejudicate" in *Mariam* and *Duchess of Malfi*' (*SEL* 43[2003] 459–74), considering the two plays as examinations of 'the gendered power dynamic between listeners and speakers' (p. 470). In particular, Green argues, women's listening is constructed as a problematic and sexualized activity. All this, she further argues, is particularly loaded in the case of Webster's play, designed for performance as an auditory event in a public theatre. Additionally, Cary's play features in two other articles this year. Marguérite Corporaal, '"Thy speech eloquent, thy wit quick, thy expressions easy": Rhetoric and Gender in Plays by English Renaissance Women' (*Renfor* 6:ii[2003]), considers, as it were, the other side of the equation, looking at Mariam's silent rhetoric relative to gendered ideas of rhetoric in the period, and comparing Cary's practice with Margaret Cavendish's heroines in *The Unnatural Tragedy* and *Youth's Glory*.

Cary's play is also discussed in William Hamlin's 'Elizabeth Cary's *Mariam* and the Critique of Pure Reason' (*EMLS* 9:i[2003]). Hamlin explores the play relative to contemporary attitudes to Pyrrhonism, arguing that it displays a Montaigne-like scepticism towards the conventional Stoic distinction between reason and feeling. This is also a convenient place to mention Anne Russell's 'The Politics of Print and *The Tragedy of Antonie*' (*RORD* 42[2003] 92–100), which meditates on the decision of Mary Sidney Herbert, countess of Pembroke, to print her translation of Garnier in 1592. Reviewing recent work on the cultural valencies of different forms of publication, Russell observes that there is an indirect political agenda at work in the play, echoing as it does the instabilities of Elizabeth's reign.

It is a pleasure to be able to report two useful notes on William Rowley, both written by David Nicol. The first glosses 'The Name "Lilia Guida" in William Rowley's *The Thracian Wonder*' (*N&Q* 50[2003] 437). In Rowley's play, this name is given to a daughter of the King of Africa, and the name has previously been interpreted as some sort of reference to lilies: but Nicol notes that 'Lilia Ageda' is named as a wife of the emperor of Barbary in George Wilkins's pamphlet *The Three Miseries of Barbarie* [1606]. The second note is entitled '*A Shoemaker a Gentleman*: Dates, Sources, and Influence' (*N&Q* 50[2003] 441–3). Nicol argues for a much wider date range than has previously been assumed, shows that Rowley used as sources Thomas Fortescue's translation of Pedro Mexia, and Deloney's *The Gentle Craft*, and links the play to Dekker and Massinger's *The Virgin Martyr*.

EMLS 8:iii is devoted to Middleton. By a curious coincidence, three of the articles are mainly concerned with one play: Rick Bowers's 'Comedy, Carnival, and Class: *A Chaste Maid in Cheapside*', Pier Paolo Frasinelli's 'Realism, Desire and Reification: Thomas Middleton's *A Chaste Maid in Cheapside*', and Alizon Brunning's '"O, how my offences wrestle with my repentance!": The Protestant Poetics of Redemption in Thomas Middleton's *A Chaste Maid in Cheapside*'. Brunning reads the religious tensions in the play in terms of its sacramental overtones, and the wider confusions between signifier and signified in the London it describes. Whorehound, she argues, who achieves genuine penitence, is thus, paradoxically, excluded from the play's comic ending. Bowers describes the play as 'urban grotesque', using Bakhtinian and feminist analysis to read its dialogic and ironic structures. He even invokes *nu shu*, the Chinese tradition of women's secret writing, as a useful reference point for thinking about the interaction of the women which we see through the eyes of the exploitative Allwit. 'Everything within the comical urban grotesque of *A Chaste Maid in Cheapside* goes "right"', concludes Bowers, 'but only because it's wrong to begin with.' Frasinelli's article sits interestingly with the other two, building on recent work on Middleton's critiques of commodification and of market systems. Although *A Chaste Maid in Cheapside* and its ilk describe a world which seems to be 'claustrophobically materialistic', Frasinelli argues, 'as they expose their satirical object in its most ludicrously grotesque expressions, Middleton's comedies offer a leverage to transfigure it into the subject for a releasing, potentially liberating laughter'. It is a mistake to limit readings of Middleton either to ideas of photographic social realism, or to formal generic traditions: his plays are more transformative than that.

Also in this issue, Lisa Hopkins writes on '*A Yorkshire Tragedy* and Middleton's Tragic Aesthetic' (*EMLS* 8:iii[2003]). While this play is generally now attributed to Middleton, its treatment of religion is not exactly what one would expect from a dramatist generally constructed as having strong Puritan sympathies: Hopkins explores this paradox, reading the play not as a confessional document but as a piece of aesthetics. The issue also contains '"Today, Vindici returns": Alex Cox's *Revengers Tragedy*', a discussion by Ben Spiller of Cox's splendid film of Middleton's play; and a useful introductory essay to the whole collection by Mathew Martin reviewing the current state of Middleton criticism.

Elsewhere on Middleton, a short note by A.A. Bromham, '*Women Beware Women*, Danaë, and Iconographic Tradition' (*N&Q* 50[2003] 74–6), examines the ways in which Middleton's tragedy alludes to the Danaë story, culminating in a cruel visual parody of it when Isabella is killed by a shower of gold. The female body is violated again in Kathryn R. Finin's 'Re-membering Gloriana: "Wild Justice" and the Female Body in *The Revenger's Tragedy*' (*Renfor* 6:ii [2003]), which studies the presence of the female and especially the maternal body in Middleton's play, arguing that Vindice's creation of the revenge plot is driven by his response to that gendered body.

In a not dissimilar vein, Kevin Crawford's '"All his intents are contrary to man": Softened Masculinity and Staging in Middleton's *The Lady's Tragedy*' (*MRDE* 16[2003] 101–29) reads Middleton's lurid tragedy in the light of Bruce Smith's recent work on early modern constructions of masculinity, and in the light of Crawford's own experience of staging the play. Crawford gives detailed discussion to the practicalities of staging necrophilia, and argues that the effect is to make the Tyrant an interestingly conflicted figure rather than a cipher, and Govianus a weak and ultimately unmanly revenger. Jennifer Panek contributes an article entitled 'The Mother as Bawd in *The Revenger's Tragedy* and *A Mad World, My Masters*' (*SEL* 43[2003] 415–37). Panek argues that the motif of mother as bawd taps into early modern anxieties about maternal authority, even if *A Mad World, My Masters* finally rejects the idea that the commodification of virginity is a problem caused by mothers. Especially good is Panek's account of how Middleton amusingly makes Frank Gullman's status as a 'professional virgin' (p. 428) resemble at once both whoredom and chastity.

Frances Teague considers *The Changeling*, alongside other early modern plays, in '"What about our hands?": A Presentational Image Cluster' (*MRDE* 16[2003] 218–27). Teague renews Caroline Spurgeon's terminology of 'image clusters', applying it to stage business instead and tracing in five plays 'the association of woman's sexualized hand, inappropriate suitor, and mutilated man' (p. 223). Teague argues that this isn't, as Spurgeon would have argued, an involuntary process reflecting something about the collective subconscious of the early modern theatre: in plays like *The Knight of the Burning Pestle*, which seems consciously to travesty this image cluster, she finds evidence that this may be something approaching a stage convention.

Paul Yachnin's 'Reversal of Fortune: Shakespeare, Middleton, and the Puritans' (*ELH* 70[2003] 757–86), compares *Twelfth Night* with *The Puritan Widow* [1606], a play now attributed to Middleton and linked to Shakespeare not merely in its treatment of Puritans but by the fact that an early printing credited the play to 'W.S.'. Yachnin's concern is not to restore *The Puritan* to the Shakespeare apocrypha, nor to revive the contention of Margot Heinemann that it cannot be by Middleton as it attacks, rather than celebrates, Puritanism; rather, it is to point out the similarities of style and register between this play and its more famous Shakespearian cousin. Also on the edge of the Middleton canon one finds *The Family of Love*, although this attribution has been challenged in recent years in favour of Lording Barry. In '*Club Law*, the *Family of Love*, and the Familist Sect' (*N&Q* 50[2003] 65–8), Charles Cathcart explores the significance of the name Nicholas Nebulo in *The Family of Love*, linking it back to Nicholas Niphle in the anonymous university comedy *Club Law*, and contextualizing both plays as attacks on the Familists.

Plays by Shakespeare, Jonson, Marston, Middleton, and Dekker are illuminated in an interdisciplinary article by Louis F. Qualtiere and William

W.E. Slights, 'Contagion and Blame in Early Modern England: The Case of the French Pox' (*L&M* 22[2003] 1–24). Qualtiere and Slights argue that dramatic representations of syphilis offer a exemplary instance of a conflict between 'the older idea of disease as divine punishment' and 'new understandings of how pathology and human agency function in disease transmission'.

Work on Ford includes Susannah B. Mintz, 'The Power of "Parity" in Ford's *'Tis Pity She's a Whore*' (*JEGP* 102[2003] 269–91). Mintz takes issue with Bruce Boehrer's account of the play, in which incest is a symptom of an absence of centralized rule. Rather, suggests Mintz, there is altogether too much and too effective rule in Ford's Parma, with its 'firmly entrenched patriarchal order' (p. 275), reflected even in the way Giovanni tends to apply patriarchal power dynamics to his incestuous 'marriage' to his sister. It is Annabella, Mintz argues, who is the really subversive character, since her quest for pleasure constitutes a much more profound rejection of patriarchal authority. Mintz's reading is subtler than this summary would suggest, but it does have the strange consequence of almost entirely suppressing Annabella's conversion at the end, seeing her as merely 'cowed' by the Friar (p. 290). Also on this play, Lisa Hopkins proposes 'A New Source for *'Tis Pity She's a Whore*' (*N&Q* 50[2003] 443–4), in the anonymous Jacobean comedy *The Fair Maid of Bristow*, with which *'Tis Pity* shares several proper names and plot twists. Nancy A. Gutierrez writes on 'Trafficking in Ford's *The Broken Heart*' (in Abate, ed., pp. 65–81). Reading closely the arranged marriages in the play, and relating them to early modern practice around arranged marriages in particular, Gutierrez argues that Penthea's refusal of food is not a marker of her passive victimhood but rather an active and symbolically loaded decision to withhold her participation in the community within which her forced marriage was arranged. Gutierrez develops these ideas at greater length in her book, *'Shall she famish then?' Female Food Refusal in Early Modern England*, which contains, among other things, a case study of the death by self-starvation of Elizabeth's lady-in-waiting Margaret Ratcliffe, a study of the phenomenon of 'miracle maidens', and a careful analysis of Thomas Heywood's *A Woman Killed With Kindness*. Arbitrating between recent interpretations of the play, Gutierrez argues that Anne Frankford's food refusal constitutes both religious salvation and a form of political resistance.

Returning to the Caroline, there is an article by Richard A. Cave considering 'The Playwriting Sons of Ben: Nathan Field and Richard Brome' (in Woolland, ed., *Jonsonians: Living Traditions*, pp. 69–92). Cave relates Field and Brome to Jonson both biographically and in terms of their use of the conventions of urban comedy, arguing that both the later writers are ripe for rediscovery. Matthew Steggle's note, 'C.G.: A Member of the Brome Circle' (*N&Q* 50[2003] 175–7), reconsiders and tentatively identifies C.G., who contributed commendatory verse to the printed texts of Caroline playwrights including Brome, Nabbes, and Rawlins.

Melinda J. Gough, '"Not as myself": The Queen's Voice in *Tempe Restored*' (*MP* 101[2003] 48–67), considers the masque written by Inigo Jones and Aurelian Townsend in 1632 for Queen Henrietta Maria, distinctive in that it included female singers. While it has generally been written off as a self-indulgent performance of no literary merit, Gough sets it in a European tradition of court performances featuring female singers, and argues that there is a coherent intellectual agenda at work. She presents the case for seeing the masque as both an assertion of Henrietta Maria's prerogatives and power as queen consort and as 'a defence of beauty instantiated in art but also in artful performing women' (p. 52). The same masque forms the subject of Axel Stähler's 'Inigo Jones's *Tempe Restored* and Alessandro Piccolomini's *Della Institution Morale*' (*SC* 18[2003] 180–210). Jones's personal annotated copy of Piccolomini's moral manual survives, and Stähler traces Jones's use in *Tempe Restored* of Piccolomini's philosophical ideas. A second article by Stähler concerns *The Temple of Love*, the masque written by Jones and William Davenant for Henrietta Maria, in which she danced the role of Indamora, queen of Narsinga. In 'The Arduous Path to the Temple of Love' (*RORD* 42[2003] 34–61), Stähler relates this masque's temple to sources including the Temple of Venus Physiozoa from Colonna's *Hypnerotomachia Poliphili*.

Yet a third entertainment for Henrietta Maria forms the subject of an enjoyable and well-illustrated article by C.E. McGee, '*The Presentment of Bushell's Rock*: Place, Politics and Theatrical Self-Promotion' (*MRDE* 16[2003] 39–80). In 1636 Charles and Henrietta went to Enstone, near Woodstock, to see an unusually shaped ten-foot-high rock on the estate of one Thomas Bushell. Bushell celebrated this rock in garden design and specially commissioned entertainment, tied in to a number of personal concerns and business interests. McGee's article reconstructs the pleasingly eccentric entertainment, and includes an edition of the documents involved.

(b) Marlowe

After 2002's bumper crop, no book-length critical works on Marlowe appeared this year, apart from *Marlowe*, a collection edited by Avraham Oz, which brings together in one volume a range of important Marlowe criticism of recent years. After an introduction by the editor that interweaves commentary on Marlowe's life and work and introduces the essays in the volume, the first item is Emily Bartels's 'Strange and Estranging Spectacles: Strategies of State and Stage', giving an overview of Marlowe's work from her 1993 book *Spectacles of Strangeness: Imperialism, Alienation and Marlowe*. As this and other items are likely to have been covered in previous issues of *YWES*, they will simply be noted here. Bartels's essay is followed by Michael Hattaway, 'Christopher Marlowe: Ideology and Subversion' (from Darryll Grantley and Peter Roberts, eds., *Christopher Marlowe and English Renaissance Culture* [1996]); Avraham Oz, 'Faces of Nation and Barbarism: Prophetic Mimicry and the Politics of *Tamburlaine the Great*' (revised from his edited volume *Strands Afar Remote: Israeli Perspectives on Shakespeare* [1998]); Stephen Greenblatt, 'Marlowe, Marx and Anti-Semitism' (from *Critical Enquiry* 5[1978]); Sara Munson Deats and Lisa S. Starks, '"So neatly plotted, and so well performed": Villain as Playwright in Marlowe's *The Jew of Malta*' (from *Theatre Journal* 44[1992]); David H. Thurn, 'Economic and Ideological Exchange in Marlowe's *Jew of Malta*' (from *Theatre Journal* 46[1994]); Jonathan Dollimore, '*Dr Faustus*: Subversion Through Transgression' (from his *Radical Tragedy: Religion, Ideology and Power in the Drama of Shakespeare and his Contemporaries*

[1989]); Catherine Belsey, 'Doctor Faustus and Knowledge in Conflict' (from her *The Subject of Tragedy: Identity and Difference in Renaissance Drama* [1985]); Alan Sinfield, 'Reading Faustus's God' (from *Faultlines: Cultural Materialism and the Politics of Dissident Reading* [1992]); Dympna Callaghan, 'The Terms of Gender: "Gay" and "Feminist" Edward II' (from Valerie Traub, M. Lindsay Kaplan, and Dympna Callaghan, eds., *Feminist Readings of Early Modern Culture* [1996]); and Thomas Cartelli, '*Queer Edward II*: Postmodern Sexualities and the Early Modern Subject' (from Paul Whitfield White, ed., *Marlowe, History and Sexuality* [1998]). The volume is rounded off with a briefly annotated list of further reading and a chronology of Marlowe's life and times.

It is Marlowe's life and times that are more fully explored in the only other book-length study to emerge during the year, Roy Kendall's *Christopher Marlowe and Richard Baines: Journeys through the Elizabethan Underground*, a manifestation of the enduring interest in the biography of the playwright. Kendall looks at Marlowe's life and works from the perspective of the life of Richard Baines, a picture of which is constructed partly speculatively and partly with reference to documents, some of which are new to Marlowe studies. The 'underground' of the title refers to the covert world of religious dissent and espionage, though other 'tunnels' are referred to: 'homosexuals, criminals and theological freedom fighters'. The book is divided into four broadly chronological sections focused on the Rheims and Flushing episodes and the periods between and after these, including Marlowe's death, and there is speculative discussion about the identity of Baines, the accusations against Marlowe of counterfeiting—for which the tentative explanation is offered that it could have been to fund his supposed book against the Trinity—and the intrigue and politics surrounding the playwright's death. At several points connections are suggested between the utterances and actions of Marlowe's dramatic characters and the documented or putative events from the biographical narrative that Kendall presents, and he later extends these allusive connections to instances in works of several of Marlowe's contemporaries which might possibly refer to the playwright's life. This tends to push the search for contemporary significance of textual content rather too far at times, but the main problem with a study of this type is that it is largely conjectural and that its arguments either can never be verified, or await possible future proof. However, the available data has been energetically sifted through and various interpretations proposed at all points, while the adduction of new bits of material, no matter how small, is always welcome. In addition to this, Jeffrey Meyers in 'Marlowe's Lives' (*MQR* 42:iii[2003] 468–95) offers an examination of the twentieth-century biographical interest in Marlowe. He considers first the small body of bare factual evidence on the playwright's life—peppered with violent or near-violent incident—and reflects also on what is not known about him. He then focuses on four mysterious aspects of his biography: homosexuality, atheism, involvement with espionage, and the circumstances of his death, noting the problematic nature of evidence about these four areas, and the contradictions in Marlowe's posthumous reputation. The second and substantive part of the article consists of a critical review of nineteen biographical works on the playwright, both historical and fictional, from 1904 to 1992.

Situating Marlowe's writing within its literary, historical, or theatrical contexts is the thrust of several of the smaller contributions, with a slightly greater interest being evident in the Tamburlaine plays and *Edward II* than in the other work. Charles Whitney, in '*Tamburlaine* and Self-Shattering, 1605: Applying the New Reception Theories' (*RORD* 42[2003] 79–91), notes some recent studies that explore the way the early modern stage's representation of self-conscious characters both stimulates and articulates the growth of inwardness and individuality, and the ways in which the early modern audience's desire for violent representations suggests an impulse to negate the autonomous self. He goes on to focus on John Davies's *Wittes Pilgrimage*, specifically a sonnet on *Tamburlaine* and a verse essay in the collection, in respect of the way in which they reveal the theatre's capacity to allow the play-goer to reflect on his place in the world and its hierarchy. In considering Davies's response to Marlowe's play, Whitney concludes that it provided at once the opportunity for a sadomasochistic *jouissance*, an identification with Tamburlaine's aggression, and a reflective distance from the experiences represented on stage. Daniel Vitkus looks at possible perspectives on religion and international politics of the Tamburlaine plays in 'Marlowe's Mahomet: Islam, Turks and Religious Controversy in *Tamburlaine, Parts I and II*', the third chapter of his *Turning Turk: English Theater and the Multicultural Mediterranean* (pp. 45–75). Vitkus argues that, in the context of early modern religious conflicts about claims to know God's will, Marlowe's drama lays open to questioning the providentialist approach to history invoked by both Reformation and Counter-Reformation polemicists. In the play the variety of appellations to a deity on the one hand, and divine unresponsiveness on the other, contribute to destabilizing the identity of God, while Marlowe's writing also parodies religious rhetoric that lays claim to divine authority and support. While pleasure is provided for the audience in the spectacle of Tamburlaine's conquest of the perceived enemy, the Turks, he suggests that at the same time Marlowe undermines the idea of a holy war by making might victorious, and insinuates notions of atheism which are endowed with acceptability by being placed in an Islamic context. Vitkus also discusses the play's anti-providentialism in the context of the complicating dual threat of Turkish power and papal power, and points to Tamburlaine as an anamorphic figure, being both a conquering hero articulating English imperial ambitions and a terrifying tyrant. Corinne S. Abate suggests, in 'Zenocrate: Not Just Another "Fair Face"' (*ELN* 41:i[2003] 19–32), that Zenocrate is an empowered character who provides Tamburlaine with a more compassionate approach to ruling, which he adopts towards the end of the play. She points out that Tamburlaine does not subordinate Zenocrate and that, valuing her for her social position, he rather seeks her approval. His marriage to her legitimizes him and subsumes him into the society he challenges, while she is also instrumental in his eventual advocacy of peace. In a note, 'Tamburlaine as the "Scourge of God" and *The First English Life of King Henry the Fifth*' (*N&Q* 50:iv[2003] 399–400), Andrew Hadfield reflects on the term 'the scourge of God' as applied to Tamburlaine and suggests that Marlowe may have found this in the earlier manuscript play that was in John Stowe's possession, and to which the playwright could possibly have had access. Bruce Brandt, 'The Art of War: Shakespeare and Marlowe' (in Brandt, and Sauer, eds., *The Art of War: Shakespeare and Marlowe*, pp. 65–70), compares the representation of war and warriors in Shakespeare and Marlowe, suggesting that Shakespeare raises questions about the reasons a king may go to war but ultimately does not challenge the status quo, while Marlowe does not primarily probe the motives for war in *Edward II* and the Tamburlaine plays, much of this drama's attraction being the martial imagery that contributes to the representation of the protagonist as a romantic warrior hero.

Edward II is the other major focus of interest in the 2003 batch of Marlowe scholarship. Niall Richardson's essay, 'The Queer Performance of Tilda Swinton in Derek Jarman's Edward II' (*Sexualities* 6:iii–iv[2003] 427–42), remarks on the critical perception that in much gay male writing women are represented as grotesque or abject, and that many critics have cited Derek Jarman's films as examples of this misogyny. Richardson attempts to refute this by arguing that an important element of the film's gay sensibility is the camp performance of Tilda Swinton as Isabella, which takes on the quality of a Brechtian deconstruction of images and conventions of femininity, while it is Gaveston and Edward who are at times abject. Even in her vampiric assault on Kent, it is his body that is abject rather than her female one. Isabella offers considerable pleasure to queer spectators while also, as a form of female vampire, challenging gender boundaries and stereotypes, and Richardson concludes that the film requires the spectator to reconsider the cliché of gay male misogyny. Boldizsár Fejérvári, 'Rosencrantz and Guildenstern Meet Edward II: A Study in Intertextuality' (*AnaChronisT* 6[2003] 173–96), attempts unconvincingly to posit an intertextual relationship between Stoppard's *Rosencrantz and Guildenstern are Dead* and *Edward II* in a rambling essay that comes to no conclusion and has little apparent point. Charles R. Forker, 'Regime Change at Shakespeare's Globe' (*ShN* 53:iii[2003] 71 and 82), reviews productions of two of the three productions of the Globe's 'regime change' season, *Edward II* and *Richard II*, commending the clarity imposed by the director on Marlowe's crowded plot. While impressed by most of the performances, he is less so by Liam Brennan's speaking of verse as Edward, which he regards as lacking in poignancy. The final offering on *Edward II* is Agnès Lafont's 'Le Corps nu de Diane ou les égarements du coeur et de l'esprit dans *Doctor Faustus* et *Edward II*' (*Anglophonia* 13[2003] 69–82). After noting several instances of the Diana and Actaeon myth in early English literature and drama, Lafont considers the references to it in these two Marlowe plays. In *Edward II*, she argues, it suggests forbidden and perverted pleasures, with some blurring of gender in sexual desire, while in *Doctor Faustus* it represents the enslavement of Faustus to his desires, and she maintains that the central figures of both plays are thrown off their aspiration to power and control by physical beauty. The significance of the body of Diana remains comprehensible and interpretable to the audience, but not the tragic heroes it ensnares.

Curiously, the only other essay on *Doctor Faustus* is Eric C. Brown's 'Shakespeare's Anxious Epistemology: *Love's Labour's Lost* and Marlowe's *Doctor Faustus*' (*TSLL* 45:i[2003] 20–41). Brown investigate parallels between *Love's Labours Lost* and *Doctor Faustus*, including the ironic quest for knowledge, the frustrations of love, and the imminence of death, and also contends that Shakespeare's work subverts many of Marlowe's constructions. He argues especially from the point of view of Shakespeare's ridicule of academic learning in his play, as well as the themes of the breaking of contracts and the undermining of authority, concluding that the play reveals a self-consciousness about its own identity and cultural contexts.

There are two essays and a note on *The Jew of Malta*, the most substantial of which is B.R. Menpes's 'The Bondage of Barabas: Thwarted Desire in *The Jew of Malta*' (*Parergon* 20:i[2003] 65–84). Menpes suggests that the actions of Barabas are bound entirely by and to the policy of his dramatic world, and that the limitations this imposes on him violate his identity as a successful merchant when he exchanges his mercantile endeavours for activities of revenge. As his stratagems fail, he thus becomes the victim of a morally bankrupt world and an image of the dysfunction of man. In another essay that refers to Barabas's occupation, 'A Society of One: Reading *The Jew of Malta* through Serres's Theory of Exchange' (*Exemplaria* 15:ii[2003] 419–50), Shawn Smith contends that a theme of exchange is central to the play, growing out of the main character's own mercantile vocation, and that the violence and intrigues of the plot proceed from the wilful blocking of this process of exchange by Barabas. He sees the play's representation of a greedy Barabas as drawing on a tradition of anti-Judaism in England to create an anti-hero who can be read in terms of Serres's theory, being one who refuses the reciprocity of exchange. By becoming self-contained and excluding himself from the social economy, Barabas is isolated from the society around him, even though theatrically he is in interaction with it. J.J.M. Tobin's note, 'How Drunk Was Barnardine?' (*N&Q* 50[2003] 46–7) speculates on various possible derivations of the character of Barnardine in Shakespeare's *Measure for Measure* in order partly to dismiss an association with Marlowe's Friar in *The Jew of Malta*.

On *Dido, Queen of Carthage* there are two brief notes. Tom Carroll's 'Marlowe's *Dido, Queen of Carthage*' (*ShN* 53:ii[2003] 60) concludes that the Globe's production failed to give the play the 'local habitation' it deserved and that the frivolous approach did not do justice to the seriousness of the work, despite some success of the Dido–Aeneas plot, while Mike Pincombe, in '"Gloomy Orion": Eliot, Marlowe, Virgil' (*N&Q* 50[2003] 329–30), suggests that Eliot's reference in 'Sweeney Among the Nightingales' echoes a line in *Dido, Queen of Carthage*, a play that Pincombe contends was a favourite of the poet's, and he also argues for possible influence on the poem of *The Jew of Malta*.

The only work on the poetry was three items, each only partially on *Hero and Leander*. In the context of an examination of elements of paganism in early modern thought, Philippa Berry, 'Renewing the Concept of Renaissance: The Cultural Influence of Paganism Reconsidered' (in Berry, and Tudeau-Clayton, eds., *Textures of Renaissance Knowledge*, pp. 17–34), offers a brief discussion of the temple in the poem, before going on to a consideration of Spenser's *The Faerie Queene*. The copiously polysemic quality of the temple is, she argues, also reflected in the syntax of the poem, something which suggests that any cultural structure that includes such images of mutability will itself be transformed by them. Nathalie Rivère de Carles, with reference to the myth of Minerva/Athene and Arachne and noting the importance of tapestries in elite Tudor interiors, discusses the arras in early literature and drama in respect of parallels between weaving a tapestry and weaving a text, in 'Tenture et théâtre, de Minerve à Thespis' (*Anglophonia* 13[2003] 83–96). The bulk of the essay focuses on plays by Shakespeare and Lyly, but there is a brief discussion of 'Hero and Leander' in relation to the fusion of the visual and the textual. Finally, in 'The Analysis of Culture Revisited: Pure Texts, Applied Texts, Literary Historicisms, Cultural Histories' (*JHI* 64:iii[2003] 173–87), an essay exploring the relationship between the study of canonical texts and broader social history, Warren Boutcher considers *Hero and Leander* as an 'applied text' for an enquiry into early modern intellectual history. After reviewing the twentieth-century history of critical theory and practice in relation to social history, he uses the poem as a case study, focusing on its connections with early modern English annotations of Boscán's *Leandro*, noting and resisting institutional pressures to make this principally a means to interpret the Marlowe text.

I would like to include here reports on two brief notes from 2002 that I was unable to see in time for inclusion last year. Rodney S. Edgecombe, in 'Skeptical Moments in *As You Like It* and their Possible Connection with Marlowe' (*ShakB* 20:iv[2002] 45–6), sees echoes of Marlowe's work in *As You Like It*, other than those that have hitherto already been proposed, and focuses on Jacques' 'Ducdame' refrain in Act II, scene v, which by a complicated set of arguments involving reference to Marlowe's writing is read as a possible encrypted sceptical perspective on Christian asceticism. Charles Marowitz gives an account, in 'Marlowe's Murderer Revealed!' (*ShakB* 20:iv[2002] 31–2), of the writing of his play in Elizabethan blank verse, *Murdering Marlowe*, based on the idea that Shakespeare's early work was heavily influenced by Marlowe and the fictional notion of Shakespeare, as an aspiring playwright suffering from the competition of his then more famous contemporary, finding a murderous solution to his problem. I have not been successful in getting hold of another essay from 2002, Vasiliki Markidou's 'The "Floating Island": Malta in Marlowe's *Jew of Malta*' (in Stephanides and Bassnett, eds. *Beyond the Floating Islands: An Anthology*).

(c) Jonson

This year marks the tenth birthday of the *Ben Jonson Journal*, many articles from which are discussed below. Published from Las Vegas (a city that would have fascinated Jonson) *BJJ* has established itself as a leading player in this area of scholarship, both for its articles and for its reviews, and long may it continue. Its influence is apparent from, for instance, the entries in Douglas A. Brooks's useful bibliography, 'Recent Studies in Ben Jonson (1991–mid-2001)' (*ELR* 33[2003] 110–52).

Books devoted to Jonson this year include Woolland, ed., *Jonsonians: Living Traditions*. This collection of essays, all informed, broadly speaking, by an interest in performance studies approaches to Jonson, picks up on topics raised in an earlier collection, Richard Cave, Elizabeth Schafer, and Brian Woolland, eds., *Ben Jonson and Theatre*. The book is divided into three parts: part 1 contains essays on particular Jonson plays in performance, which are discussed individually in the main body of this piece. Part 2, 'Sons and Daughters of Ben', consists of three essays, by Richard A. Cave, Carolyn D. Williams, and Alison Findlay, examining Jonson's reception in later seventeenth-century playwrights including Nathan Field, Richard Brome, and Margaret Cavendish. Part 3, the most substantial section of the volume, comprises six essays on twentieth-century inheritors of Jonson, including John Arden, Joe Orton, Peter Barnes, Caryl Churchill, Alan Ayckbourn, and American cinema. Together they paint a persuasive picture of Jonson's continuing power and importance.

One should mention here Rocco Coronato's monograph *Jonson Versus Bakhtin: Carnival and the Grotesque*, which situates Jonson on the side of Carnival rather than of Lent. Much of the book is devoted to *Sejanus* and *Catiline*, read relative to ideas of popular festivity, although Coronato also pays attention to *Epicoene*, *Bartholomew Fair*, *The Staple of News*, and masques, including *Pleasure Reconciled to Virtue* and *Neptune's Triumph*.

In terms of critical attention in article-length studies, this has been a particularly good year for Jonson's early comedies. The co-ordinates of John Mulryan's 'Tradition and the Individual Talent: Shakespeare's and Jonson's Appropriation of the Classics' (*BJJ* 10[2003] 117–37), are provided by Plautus and Terence, *The Case is Altered* and the *Comedy of Errors*, Plutarch and Tacitus, and *Julius Caesar* and *Sejanus*. While this summary captures something of the antithetical method of Mulryan's argument, it doesn't do justice to the subtlety of its observation, and it contains a particularly good discussion of the differing function of props in *The Case is Altered* and *The Comedy of Errors*.

From *Every Man Out of His Humour* to *A Tale of a Tub*, Peter Happé analyses 'Jonson's On-Stage Audiences: *Spectaret populum ludis attentius ipsis*' (*BJJ* 10[2003] 23–41). Happé offers three categories of on-stage audience: largely choric, as with Mitis and Cordatus in *Every Man Out*; associated with plays-within-a-play, as in the audience for Crites' masque in *Cynthia's Revels*; and 'problematic', where an on-stage audience is watching something other than a formal dramatic performance, of which the paradigmatic instance is the audience watching Virgil read to Augustus in *Poetaster*. Happé considers how Jonson uses and shifts these categories. The epigraph quoted in Happé's title, and taken from Horace via *Bartholomew Fair*, translates as '[Democritus] would watch the audience more intently than the entertainments themselves', a fitting comment, Happé argues, for Jonson's technique in this regard.

Jason Scott-Warren's 'When Theaters Were Bear-Gardens; Or, What's at Stake in the Comedy of Humors' (*SQ* 54[2003] 63–82) examines the connections between early modern drama and early modern blood sports, most obviously the fact that they were often located in the same physical space. Scott-Warren pursues imagery of bear-baiting through *Twelfth Night*, *Epicoene*, and late Elizabethan humours comedy, particularly as it pertains to the War of the Theatres, arguing the overlap was not just an adventitious matter of location, but rather a sign of 'converging spatial practices' (p. 82).

This interest in the early comedies extends even to *Cynthia's Revels*, one of the most neglected items in the Jonson canon, which received some welcome attention this year. In 'A New Allusion by Jonson to Spenser and Essex?' (*N&Q* 50[2003] 63–5), Hester Lees-Jeffries draws attention to the fact that the famous lyric 'Queen and Huntress', clearly a commentary of some sort on the fate of Essex, is sung by an otherwise supernumerary character named Hesperus, and that Spenser's *Prothalamion* had praised Essex with reference to Hesperus. Lees-Jeffries explores the implications of this for the interpretation, and for the date, of the play. In 'Casting the Prelude in *Cynthia's Revels*' (*N&Q* 50[2003] 62–3), Matthew Steggle revisits the allusion in the Prologue to 'Sal'—Salomon Pavy—arguing that it reveals a different allocation of parts from that usually conjectured. I have not yet seen Cécile Mauré's 'Mythe et moralité dans *Cynthia's Revels* de Ben Jonson (1600)' (*Anglophonia* 13[2003] 113–24). *Poetaster*, too, is considered at length, in an article by Richard A. Cave, '*Poetaster*: Jonson and his Audience' (in Woolland, ed., pp. 13–26). Cave argues that *Poetaster* is a play very interested in audiences: how they are constituted, how they react as a collective, and what constitutes a good audience. Cave reads *Poetaster* as an element in Jonson's ongoing campaign to develop a discriminating audience.

By contrast, Jonson's middle comedies attracted only a handful of articles. Whereas Stephen Greenblatt identifies the turning-point of *Volpone* as the end of Act IV, Murray Roston, in '*Volpone*: Comedy or Mordant Satire?' (*BJJ* 10[2003] 1–22), argues that the crucial moment is Volpone's attempted rape of Celia. Roston makes some cogent points in pursuing the argument that the tone of the play is deceptively sunny before this point, and uses Machiavelli's *La Mandragola* as a point of reference. The analysis of what lies behind this swerve in tone—a calculated burst of morality 'placating the dons' of Oxford and Cambridge universities (p. 16)—is more problematic. An entirely different approach to the play is taken by Michael P. Jensen in 'Volpone Meets Matt Dillon: Jonson's Play Adapted for *Gunsmoke*' (*BJJ* 10[2003] 235–8). Jensen shows that a 1961 episode of the television series set in the Wild West used the legacy-hunting plot from Jonson's play.

Bruce Boehrer's 'The Classical Context of Ben Jonson's "other youth"' (*SEL* 43[2003] 439–58) takes as its starting point a single line in *Epicoene*, the description of a female critic who will evaluate authors comparatively, 'DANIEL with SPENSER, JONSON with the tother youth, and so forth'. While this passage seems to invite biographical speculation about the identity of Jonson's rival, Boehrer reads it instead in terms of the Renaissance reception of classical ideas about the intersection of youth and maturity. This, in turn, is a set of ideas highly relevant to *Epicoene*, a play 'very much about intergenerational conflict' (p. 442). In particular, Boehrer reviews the classical concept of *iuventus*, and the ways in which it functions in this play.

Also concerning the nature of male maturity, one might mention Jennifer A. Low's *Manhood and the Duel* for the sake of the eight pages it devotes to duelling in *The Alchemist*. In its ritualized body language and spoken language, duelling functions as a system for creating meaning, Low argues, and in particular for affirming masculinity: the play shows this discursive system creating meaning, even in the chaotic world presented in the play.

Work on *Bartholomew Fair* this year includes Margaret Tudeau-Clayton's '"I do not know my selfe": The Topography and Politics of Self-Knowledge in Ben Jonson's *Bartholomew Fair*' (in Berry and Tudeau-Clayton, eds., pp. 177–98). Her argument is that the play depicts the fair as a Neoplatonic underworld, filled with characters, of whom Cokes is the paradigmatic example, who are defined by their lack of self-knowledge. This yields a rich collection of insights, since Tudeau-Clayton has an acute ear for a Virgilian tag, and also writes interestingly about the play's connection with *The Tempest*. For this reviewer, at least, Jonson's idea of wisdom seems more provisional, more plural, and more forgiving than Tudeau-Clayton's model would suggest, but nonetheless this is a strong and thought-provoking article. A complete contrast in approach and reference points is provided by Peter Barnes's piece '*Bartholomew Fair*: All the Fun of the Fair' (in Woolland, ed., pp. 43–50), an exuberant account of Barnes's involvement in productions of the play. Barnes is very good on *Bartholomew Fair*'s energy, language, and inclusiveness, and on how it works as a piece of theatre: for instance, his observation that Trouble-All, relatively invisible on the page, proves to be a pivotal character in performance as he 'zigzags through the fair like a demented ferret' (p. 44).

Work on Jonson's tragedies includes an article by Brian Woolland, '*Sejanus His Fall*: Does Arruntius Cry at Night?' (in Woolland, ed., pp. 27–41). This develops from a workshop production of *Sejanus* at the University of Reading, investigating in particular the ensemble effect of the play: '*Sejanus* ... is as interested in the social and political environment as it is in the man himself' (p. 27). Arruntius, who on the page seems to be the most sympathetic character, is strangely impotent and ineffective when the play is fully performed: Woolland argues for an almost Brechtian interpretation of the play, in which Arruntius's detachment is displayed as a negative rather than a positive example. Brock Cameron McLeod's note, 'An Unacknowledged Debt to Seneca in the Quarto *Sejanus*' (*N&Q* 50[2003] 427), finds a Senecan source for the play's final couplet: 'For whom the morning saw so great, and high, | Thus low, and little, 'fore the Even doth lie.'

Timothy J. Burbery's 'John Milton, Blackfriars Spectator? *Elegia prima* and Ben Jonson's *The Staple of News*' (*BJJ* 10[2003] 57–75) is worth mention here for anyone interested in *The Staple of News*. Milton's Latin *Elegia prima* contains an allusion to enjoying theatre. Burbery, reading it closely, argues that it is specifically alluding to the Blackfriars, and indeed that the drama described is certainly very close in content to *The Staple of News*. In a compact and intriguing article, Burbery starts to explore the implications of this for the Milton canon, and also for the Jonson play. Catherine Rockwood unearths 'Topicality and Dissent in Jonson's *A Tale of a Tub*' (*BJJ* 10[2003] 77–100), arguing that 'one of the remarkable things about *A Tale of a Tub* is how closely Jonson's representation of the plight of local officials hews to seventeenth-century English debates about the rights of the subject' (p. 79). In particular, Rockwood argues that the play's representations of the constable system, and its intertextual reference to the story of Appius and Virginia, give *A Tale of a Tub* a striking political bite. Julie Sanders's '*The New Inn* and *The Magnetic Lady*: Jonson's Dramaturgy in the Caroline Context' (in Woolland, ed., pp. 51–66), is interested in the ways in which Jonson creates domestic spaces in the late comedies: the 'backroom spaces of an early modern household' (p. 55) in *The Magnetic Lady*, and the public house of *The New Inn*. Using evidence from recent productions, and comparisons with modern dramatists including Arden and Ayckbourn, Sanders argues that Jonson's late plays can be read as meditations on social space.

Work on Jonson's masques approaches them from a variety of directions. D. Heyward Brock, in 'Ben Jonson's First Folio and the Textuality of his

Masques at Court' (*BJJ* 10[2003] 43–55), discusses strategies by which Jonson's First Folio seeks to elevate the literary status of the masques which conclude the volume. Brock's evidence includes the paratexts, and the rearrangement of chronological order and indeed of the masque's internal structure that ensures that the last speech in the whole volume is Astraea's declaration of a Golden Age under King James. William N. West's 'Talking the Talk: Cant on the Jacobean Stage' (*ELR* 33[2003] 228–51) relates the canting scenes in Jonson's *Gypsies Metamorphosed* to professional theatre, including Dekker and Middleton's *The Roaring Girl* and Beaumont and Fletcher's *Beggar's Bush*, as part of an argument that cant represents a purified form of ludic language, which reveals 'the work that words do, purified of reference to things' (p. 250). Russell West's 'Perplexive Perspectives: The Court and Contestation in the Jacobean Masque' (*SC* 18[2003] 25–43) examines a range of Jonson's Jacobean masques and entertainments in the course of an argument that the Jacobean masque was 'a multifaceted work of art in which perspective, as one element of the theatrical ensemble, appears to have been riddled by contradictions which made it a less than assured mode of asserting spatial control' (p. 25).

There is an important account of masques by Jonson, as well by Daniel and Campion, in Clare McManus's *Women on the Renaissance Stage: Anna of Denmark and Female Masquing in the Stuart Court*. McManus's interest is in the codes and traditions of female aristocratic performance, with Jonson's *The Masque of Blackness* as a paradigmatic example. Anyone interested in Jonson's masques will want to consult this book, and also Mary Floyd-Wilson's *English Ethnicity and Race in Early Modern Drama*, which puts *The Masque of Blackness* alongside texts including *Othello*, *Cymbeline*, and Marlowe's *Tamburlaine* as examples of English interest in the strange and complex ramifications of geohumoralism—the theory of a relationship between geographical conditions and humoral complexion. Finally, Gabriel Heaton and James Knowles report an interesting archival recovery in '"Entertainment Perfect": Ben Jonson and Corporate Hospitality' (*RES* 54[2003] 587–600). It is known that Jonson wrote an entertainment to be performed at the Merchant Taylors' Hall in Threadneedle Street on 16 July 1607, when the king visited them. Heaton and Knowles argue that three mariners' songs preserved among the papers of Jonson's patron Robert Cecil in the Hatfield House archives can be linked to this lost entertainment, which also featured (according to an eyewitness) songs sung by mariners. They print the text of the songs, and contextualize this new evidence, linking it to the rediscovery of Jonson's *Entertainment at Britain's Burse* in 1995. Jonson's civic entertainments, they argue, were a centrally important element of his career, although they have been largely overlooked in subsequent scholarship and criticism.

The last items in this year's survey are two articles of biographical importance. Martin Butler's 'The Riddle of Jonson's Chronology Revisited' (*Library* 4[2003] 49–63), deals with the question of Jonson's own practice in recording dates. W.W. Greg had argued that he used the calendrical system early in his career, and the legal system in his later years, but Butler shows that Jonson's practice is much less consistent than this. Finally, there is a new biographical detail concerning Jonson and the Sidneys. In 'Robert Sidney, "Mr Johnson", and the Education of

William Sidney at Penshurst' (*N&Q* 50[2003] 430–36), Michael G. Brennan and Noel J. Kinnamon reconsider a letter written by Robert Sidney on 25 July 1611 which alludes to a 'Mr Johnson' acting as tutor to William Sidney. Brennan and Kinnamon argue the case for this being Jonson the poet, and put the letter in the context of Jonson's other known links with the Sidneys, most obviously, *Forest* 14, 'Ode to Sir William Sidney on his Birth-Day'.

Books Reviewed

Abate, Corinne S. ed. *Privacy, Domesticity, and Women in Early Modern England*. Ashgate. [2003] pp. ix + 204. £40 ISBN 0 7546 3043 9.

Barker, Simon and Hilary Hinds, eds. *The Routledge Anthology of Renaissance Drama*. Routledge. [2003] pp. x + 458. £16.99 ISBN 0 4151 8734 6.

Berry, Philippa and Margaret Tudeau-Clayton, eds. *Textures of Renaissance Knowledge*. ManUP. [2003] pp. 240. £45 ISBN 0 7190 6465 3.

Brandt, Bruce and Michelle M. Sauer, eds. *The Art of War: Shakespeare and Marlowe*. Minot State University Printing Services. [2003] pp. xxvi + 247, Proceedings of the 11th Annual Northern Plains Conference on Early British Literature.

Corbin, Peter and Douglas Sedge, eds. *Thomas of Woodstock, or King Richard the Second, Part One*. Revels. ManUP. [2002] pp. xvi + 230. £45 ISBN 0 7190 1563 4.

Coronato, Rocco. *Jonson Versus Bakhtin: Carnival and the Grotesque*. Rodopi. [2003] pp. 275. $60 ISBN 9 0420 1174 2.

Dutton, Richard, ed. *Epicene, or The Silent Woman*, by Ben Jonson. Revels. ManUP. [2003] pp. xiv + 338. £47.50 ISBN 0 7190 5543 1.

Engel, William E. *Death and Drama in Renaissance England: Shades of Memory*. OUP. [2003] pp. 200. $52 ISBN 0 1992 5762 0.

Floyd-Wilson, Mary. *English Ethnicity and Race in Early Modern Drama*. CUP. [2003] pp. 275. $70 ISBN 0 5211 8105 6.

Gunby, David, David Carnegie and MacDonald P. Jackson, eds. *The Works of John Webster*, vol. ii. CUP. [2003] pp. xxxii + 644. £110 ISBN 0 5212 6060 4.

Gurr, Andrew, ed. *Philaster*, by Francis Beaumont and John Fletcher. Revels. ManUP. [1969/2003] pp. lxxxiv + 142. £11.99 ISBN 0 7190 6485 6.

Gutierrez, Nancy A. *'Shall she famish then?': Female Food Refusal in Early Modern England*. Ashgate. [2003] pp. vii + 146. £40 ISBN 1 8401 4240 5.

Habermann, Ina. *Staging Slander and Gender in Early Modern England*. Ashgate. [2003] pp. 206. $94.95 ISBN 0 7546 3384 5.

Harris, Jonathan Gil and Natasha Korda, eds. *Staged Properties in Early Modern English Drama*. CUP. [2002] pp. x + 347. £45 ISBN 0 5218 1322 0.

Huebert, Ronald. *The Performance of Pleasure in English Renaissance Drama*. Palgrave. [2003] pp. 256. $85 ISBN 0 3339 5557 0.

Ioppolo, Grace, ed. *Hengist, King of Kent, or The Mayor of Queenborough*, by Thomas Middleton. Malone. OUP. [2003] pp. xxvi + 84. £25 ISBN 0 1972 9043 4.

Johnson, Nora. *The Actor as Playwright in Early Modern Drama*. CUP. [2003] pp. 216. £65 ISBN 0 5218 2416 8.

Kendall, Roy. *Christopher Marlowe and Richard Baines: Journeys through the Elizabethan Underground*. FDUP. [2003] pp. 453. $75 ISBN 0 8386 3974 7.

Longstaffe, Stephen, ed. *A Critical Edition of the Life and Death of Jack Straw*. Mellen. [2002] pp. xviii + 296. £74.95 ISBN 0 7734 7118 9.

Low, Jennifer A. *Manhood and the Duel: Masculinity in Early Modern Drama and Culture*. Palgrave. [2003] pp. 256. £75 ISBN 1 4039 61301.

McManus, Clare. *Women on the Renaissance Stage: Anna of Denmark and Female Masquing in the Stuart Court*. MUP. [2002] pp. 276. $24.95 ISBN 0 7190 6250 0.

Romany, Frank and Robert Lindsey, eds. *Christopher Marlowe: The Complete Plays*. Penguin. [2003] pp. xliv + 702. £9.99 ISBN 0 1404 3633 2.

Oz, Avraham, ed. *Marlowe*. Palgrave. [2003] pp. 224. hb. £45 ISBN 0 3336 2498 X, hb. £14.99 ISBN 0 3336 2499 8.

Stephanides, Stephanos and Susan Bassnett, eds. *Beyond the Floating Islands: An Anthology*. Bologna: COTEPRA Reader Series [2002] pp. 206. ISBN 9 9638 7580 7.

Vitkus, Daniel. *Turning Turk: English Theater and the Multicultural Mediterranean, 1570–1630*. Palgrave. [2003] pp. xiv + 244. £42.50 ISBN 0 3122 9452 2.

Woolland, Brian, ed. *Jonsonians: Living Traditions*. Ashgate. [2003] pp. 264. $94.95 ISBN 0 7546 0610 4.

VIII

The Earlier Seventeenth Century: General, Prose, Women's Writing

HELEN VELLA BONAVITA AND LISA WALTERS

This chapter has two sections: 1. General and Prose; 2. Women's Writing. Section 1 is by Helen Vella Bonavita and section 2 is by Lisa Walters.

1. General and Prose

The year 2003 appears to have been that of the essay collection. Writings on women, law, colonialism and politics have brought together collections which span a broad range of genres, authors and disciplines in one volume. While this means that the year offers a particularly fruitful diversity of criticism, there are very few single-author works, still less works focusing only on prose texts. For this reason I have chosen to address the General and Prose sections as one section rather than two.

Writings by and about royalty form a major element of earlier seventeenth-century publications in 2003, beginning with Rhodes, Richards and Marshall, eds., *King James VI and I: Selected Writings*, an edition which draws together a broad and representative range of his works, poems as well as prose. The introduction offers a valuable overview of his writing, emphasizing James's view of himself as the physician to his kingdom and his overriding need to communicate with his subjects. The texts are complete, with a comprehensive glossary as well as footnotes for terms requiring explanation, and the select bibliography provides a useful starting point for further reading. Though not an author in her own right, the authority and patronage of Anna of Denmark as a major player in court culture and politics is the subject of discussion in Louis H. Roper's essay, 'Unmasquing the Connections between Jacobean Politics and Policy: The Circle of Anna of Denmark and the Beginning of the English Empire, 1614–18' (in Levin, Barrett-Graves and Carney, eds., *'High and Mighty Queens' of Early Modern England: Realities and Representations*, pp. 45–60). Beginning with the performance of Inigo Jones and Ben Jonson's masque *A Vision of Desire* at court in January 1617, Roper demonstrates that the queen and her circle appear

Year's Work in English Studies, Volume 84 (2005) © The English Association; all rights reserved. For permissions, please email: journals.permissions@oxfordjournals.org

doi: 10.1093/ywes/mai008

to have had a clear interest in promoting the interests of the Virginia Company. He points out that, during James's return to Scotland in 1617, Anna ruled jointly with her son Prince Charles, and that during that time a fresh wave of support for the company swept the country, with a list of investors whose names are those of Anna's associates. While Anna herself may not have invested in this particular venture, the interest of her supporters would seem to indicate that she was not the 'feather-brained backer of expensive and frivolous court entertainments' but rather a woman fully engaged in the political, economic and colonial issues of the day.

A similar position is adopted in McManus, ed., *Women and Culture at the Courts of the Stuart Queens*. This wide-ranging and extremely interesting collection takes as its template the concept of the 'Queen's Court' as Anna and James led increasingly separate lives. James Knowles's essay, '"To enlight the darksome night, pale Cinthia doth arise": Anna of Denmark, Elizabeth I and the Images of Royalty', discusses Anna's appropriation of Elizabethan iconography to establish herself as a powerful figure in her own right, diverging both politically and aesthetically from her husband's court. Mara R. Wade's essay from the same collection, 'The Queen's Courts: Anna of Denmark and her Royal Sisters—Cultural Agency at Four Northern European Courts in the Sixteenth and Seventeenth Centuries', considers Anna's Danish birth and upbringing, and demonstrates the influence of the 'festival culture' of the court of Copenhagen on Anna's later contribution to the culture of her own court. Wade's emphasis on Anna's family, and her northern European background, provide a valuable insight into the 'reciprocal cultural exchange' that took place within the courts of Anna and her three sisters and serves to locate Jacobean court culture within a broad international context. Clare McManus, in 'Memorialising Anna of Denmark's Court: *Cupid*'s Banishment at Greenwich Palace', focuses on the same key year of 1617 during James's progress to Scotland, during which time Anna appropriated James's position as privileged royal spectator of the masque. The masque as a subject for political and artistic investigation is taken up by Sarah Poynting, '"In the name of all the sisters": Henrietta Maria's Notorious Whores', in which she develops a discussion of Walter Montagu's play *The Shepherd's Paradise* into an investigation of the careers of the ladies of Henrietta Maria's court. Karen Britland, 'An Under-Stated Mother-in-Law: Marie de Médicis and the Last Caroline Court Masque', traces the influence on William Davenant's *Salmacida Spolia,* the last masque of the Caroline reign, of Marie de Médicis and her friend Marie, duchess of Chevreuse, also visiting England in 1640.

Caroline writing and its reception is the subject of Derek Hirst's article, 'Reading the Royal Romance; or, Intimacy in a King's Cabinet' (*SC* 18:ii[2003] 211–29). In this study of the 1645 publication by parliament of the letters of Charles I to Henrietta Maria, following the capture of the letters after the Battle of Naseby, Hirst demonstrates the association of uxoriousness with misrule used to attack Charles I. In marked contrast to James's control over his writings, publishers such as Marchamont Nedham used the king's letters to his wife to demonstrate his shortcomings as a monarch. The downfall of kings is also the subject of Curtis Perry, 'Yelverton, Buckingham and the Story of Edward II in the 1620s' (*RES* 54[2003] 313–35). The article examines the competing appropriations of Sir Henry Yelverton's comparison of George Villiers, marquis of Buckingham, to one of the most notoriously corrupt and corrupting favourites of Edward II, Hugh Spencer. The transcription of a manuscript account of Yelverton's tirade forms an interesting and useful conclusion to the article. Doran and Freeman, eds., *The Myth of Elizabeth*, contains essays addressing the iconic status of Elizabeth in her time to the present age, with the middle section concentrating on Jacobean perspectives on James's predecessor. Patrick Collinson, Lisa Richardson, and Teresa Grant investigate the differing images of Elizabeth promoted at this time by Camden, Fulke Greville, and Heywood in his play *If You Know Not Me, Then You Know Nobody*. Drawing on a wide range of textual and non-textual evidence from stained-glass windows to monuments and verse, Alexandra Walsham demonstrates the mix of elite and popular culture which maintained the cult of Elizabeth as Protestant heroine and warrior queen.

Concerns over authority and rulership are a key feature of one of the significant publications of the year, Sim and Walker's *The Discourse of Sovereignty: Hobbes to Fielding*. The book focuses on the fears of social disorder that existed throughout the seventeenth century, and the various strategies to address that fear that were employed by political and literary authors. The changing definitions of and attitudes towards the law of nature and natural law form a structure for the book and the choice of texts. The book is readable and interesting; it would be highly accessible to students for its careful explanations of key concepts and their development throughout the century. The range of authors discussed is particularly broad, with chapters focusing on key political texts and literary works such as Harrington's *Oceana*, Neville's *Isle of Pines*, and Behn's *Oroonoko.* Particularly useful is the careful analysis of the political debate that went on over the period, as this enables the establishment of a genealogy of political and literary texts, giving works such as the *Isle of Pines* a much-needed literary and political context.

The study of cultural production is the subject of David Glimp, who in *Increase and Multiply: Governing Cultural Reproduction in Early Modern England* has produced a highly readable book that covers a broad range of texts and issues. Glimp's use of Foucault and Barthes, in particular, provides him with a theoretical framework which he uses to address issues of population growth and change, and the way in which the legitimacy or otherwise of an action, whether it be humanist education, theatrical performance, religious observance or government of the state, was represented and contested in terms of its capacity to 'make' people, whether in a literal or a figurative sense. The first half of the book offers an interesting juxtaposition of texts such as *Apologie for Poetry*, Thomas Smith's *Discourse of the Commonweal* and Richard Mulcaster's *Positions*, a 1581 book of educational advice, before moving to a broad discussion of the late sixteenth- and early seventeenth-century theatre as a dangerously fecund place with the potential to generate disruptive citizens. Chapter 4 explores the anxieties about the reproductive effects associated with educational reform. While Glimp focuses on Milton's tract *Of Education*, the main thrust of the chapter is towards the ways in which the education of children was incorporated into a specific plan of national reform, with all the anxieties and dynamics that surround that subject. The final chapter, 'Paradisal Arithmetic:

Paradise Lost and the Genesis of Populations', continues the issue of demographic anxiety and national reform. While providing specific readings of several Shakespeare plays and Milton's writings, the book as a whole offers a broadly materialist critique of late sixteenth- and early seventeenth-century expressions of national consciousness in dramatic, poetic and non-fictional writing.

Much of the year's work in 2003 has a focus on literature as one form of cultural production, with other types of cultural artefact also being read as 'texts'. One such work is Julian Yates, *Error, Misuse, Failure: Object Lessons from the English Renaissance*. This lively and entertaining book offers a semiotic reading of diverse artefacts ranging from the textual to the architectural: the printed page, the portrait miniature, the relic, the privy, and the priest hole, and their participation in human existence. Specifically, he discusses the ramifications of these objects ceasing to perform their designated functions and their consequent intrusion into the known environment. Of particular interest in this respect is Yates's analysis of the priest hole and its function in the building, pointing out that it is only visible and known when it ceases to function effectively. Arguing that Catholic houses themselves were designed to conceal within their fabric the signs of Catholicism—the chalice and other items used for the Mass as well as the priest himself—Yates shows that the house itself becomes inscribed with the identifying marks of Catholic belief. Once it has ceased to function, made itself 'known' through smell or other give-away, the priest hole thus becomes a key player in Protestant narratives of tracing and capturing Catholic priests such as the 1606 text, *The Apprehension of Henrie Garnet, Provinciall of the Jesuites, at the house of Mr. Thomas Abbington in Worcester Shire*. The relationship between literary forms of communication and the social and political framework in which they are embedded is, in one sense or another, the concern of much of the general writing on earlier seventeenth-century studies; it is therefore useful to have Ingo Berensmeyer's article, 'No Fixed Address: Pascal, Cervantes, and the Changing Function of Literary Communication in Early Modern Europe' (*NLH* 34[2003] 623–37), which focuses precisely on this point. Using Cervantes' *Don Quixote* to demonstrate that the concept of fictionality should be located earlier than has previously been considered, Berensmeyer discusses the methodological problems of conceiving fictionality in ahistorical terms and proposes an alternative model of discursive virtualization to describe the changing function of literary communication in the early seventeenth century.

Rhetoric, and its function in the early modern period, is the subject of several publications this year, and Alastair Fowler's article, 'The Formation of Genres in the Renaissance and After' (*NLH* 34[2003] 185–204) is a particularly useful contribution since it provides a clear and useful study of the range of genres and their origins used in the Renaissance and later English literature. Fowler examines the changing uses of certain rhetorical forms, and traces their relationship with the social, cultural and political driving forces of the period: the exploration of the New World, the development of print culture, and changes in the mode and purpose of country houses, to name but a few. Jennifer Richards's edition, *Early Modern Civil Discourses*, concentrates on the related concept of civility and its multiple meanings. The collection of essays ranges across all forms of writing, from diaries to dramas. David Norbrook's essay, '"Words more than civil": Republican Civility in Lucy Hutchinson's "The Life of John Hutchinson"', examines Hutchinson's use of language and how her rhetoric affirms and spiritualizes civic institutions, while Thomas Healy's exploration of representations of Ireland and the ostensibly civilizing impact of its Anglicization ('Drama, Ireland and the Question of Civility') demonstrates the process by which claims to civility were confirmed by ascribing incivility to the Other. The examples that he uses range from Spenser's *A View of the State of Ireland* to John Speed's *Theatre of the Empire of Great Britain* [1611], and show the depictions of Ireland, particularly later ones, as being liminal, indicative of the fluid boundary between savagery and civilization.

Sheen and Hutson, eds., *Literature, Politics and Law in Renaissance England*, is a collection of essays focusing on the dynamic relationship between the law's 'rhetorical possibilities' and literary discourse. The collection draws to the reader's attention the contiguous 'cultural spaces' of law and literature, and notes the high number of writers who either trained or indeed practised as lawyers. All ten essays contained in this work are valuable contributions to our recognition of the simultaneously theatrical and legal discourse which shaped much of sixteenth- and early seventeenth-century writing. In particular Ina Habermann's essay, '"She has that in her belly will dry up your ink": Femininity as Challenge in the "Equitable Drama" of John Webster', considers Webster's three major plays in the light of forensic drama, foregrounding the issues of female characters and thereby investigating the related notions of equity and Christian charity. Her work demonstrates in some detail the links between the law and the theatre already mentioned by Sheen and Hutson in their introduction, before moving on to the function of equity in *The Devil's Law Case*, *The White Devil* and *The Duchess of Malfi*. While Habermann sees the female body as a site which draws the law into an untenable position that can only be resolved through the application of the principle of equity in Webster's plays, Subha Mukherji discusses the female body in terms of property in '"Unmanly indignities": Adultery, Evidence and Judgement in Heywood's *A Woman Killed with Kindness*'. Her investigation of issues of privacy, evidence and invasion leads us to the female body of Anne, exposed to public gaze first as an adulteress caught *in flagrante* and secondly as the repentant, self-starved female. *A Woman Killed With Kindness* features also in Nancy A. Gutierrez, *'Shall she famish, then?': Female Food Refusal in Early Modern England*, an interesting work which uses colonialist discourse within the context of the early modern domestic household. Beginning with an analysis of the death and state funeral of Margaret Ratcliffe, she goes on to consider other depictions of the starving female, including *A Woman Killed* and John Ford's *The Broken Heart*. Chapter 3 provides a fascinating analysis of the various 'miracle maidens' celebrated in pamphlets, ballads and broadsheets, who were able to survive without food. In her argument the body of the starving woman is constructed as one element of the colonial dialogue, a means whereby the oppressed and silenced colonial object is able to express its own protest even when that protest is made through the voice of the male authors.

Sandra Clark's *Women and Crime in the Street Literature of Early Modern England* forms another valuable contribution to the corpus of gender-oriented work published over the year. The first chapter offers an introduction to early modern sensationalist and news writing, providing a useful introduction to the subject. The second focuses more closely on the concept of crime in general, and its relation to the broader field of morality. The careful focus on literary representations of the female protagonists, rather than attempting to establish factual accuracy, enables the author to demonstrate the ways in which the female figure was shaped by early modern popular culture, while the discussion of the history of pamphleteering and print houses gives the book a broad historical interest. Clark uses the figure of the female to shape a more general discussion of the subject of 'ephemeral' print culture such as ballads and pamphlets to depict the ways in which women were made to acknowledge their crimes and the justice of their punishment, forcing them to become willing participants in the spectacle of punishment and hence uphold the ideology which has condemned them. Her chapter on domestic drama discusses the genre as a whole before turning to women in the drama, and the book concludes with a discussion of the news pamphlet. This focus on 'ephemeral' street literature and its liminal position within the intersecting categories of political and literary writing is taken up by Joshua B. Fisher, '"He is turned a ballad-maker": Broad-side Appropriations in Early Modern England' (*EMLS* 9:ii[2003]). His study of the broadside ballad and its social, political and literary implications attests to the value of this highly mobile and protean form. *Pamphlets and Pamphleteering in Early Modern Britain*, by Joad Raymond, is another valuable study of 'ephemeral' print culture, tracing the rise of the pamphlet as a complex literary form that encompassed a range of political, religious and cultural genres. The relationship between manuscript and print culture and the tensions that it generated between authors, stationers and booksellers is explored by Katherine Perry in '"I do it onely for the printers sake": Commercial Imperatives and Epigrams in the Early Seventeenth Century' (*EnterText* 3:i[2003] 204–26). Her study of five collections of epigrams linked by a common use of animal imagery enables a broader exploration of authors' anxiety to control their readership, and the impossibility of doing so. Samuel Glen Wong, 'Constructing a Critical Subject in *Religio Medici*' (*SEL* 43[2003] 117–36) also focuses on authorial issues as he considers *Religio Medici* in the light of Sir Kenelm Digby's *Observations on Religio Medici*, and argues for a redefinition of *Religio Medici* as participating in the history of authorial struggle over precedence and reception.

The issue of print culture and its development in the seventeenth century is also the concern of Harold Love, 'Early Modern Print Culture: Assessing the Models' (*Parergon* 20:i[2003] 45–64), which provides a concise and enlightening explanation of the various interpretations of the concept of 'print culture' before arguing that neither print culture nor other media of communication can be viewed as monumental; rather, they are 'accumulations of subcultures' and must be considered as such. In a similar vein, Marcy L. North considers the question of anonymity in *The Anonymous Renaissance*: *Cultures of Discretion in Tudor–Stuart England.* North takes issue with the 'story' of the figure Anon. and his demise to define the boundaries between the Middle Ages and the Renaissance. Instead, she provides a study in which the author's name, or lack of name, is foregrounded as an important interpretative tool which continued to be used as the point of intersection between the framework for the primary text and the secondary, accompanying text well into the early modern period. Citing Foucault, who suggests that 'the author's name functions as a crucial interpretive frame for the primary text more often than readers acknowledge', North argues that this 'interpretive frame' should be extended to acknowledge the complexities of authorship, anonymity, and pseudonymity. In doing so she is able to argue for a revised understanding of authorship, one which emphasizes the theoretical instability of the concept in early modern culture.

Control of Religious Printing in Early Stuart England by S. Mutchow Towers offers a meticulous and informative study of the religious press and its publications between 1603 and 1640. This work of detailed and precise scholarship begins with a comparative analysis of the publication patterns of the evangelical Calvinist Thomas Taylor and the Arminian Thomas Jackson. Towers uses this discussion to approach the concepts of censorship, resistance to regulations on religious printing and the fluctuating freedom of the press. Further to her study of Taylor and Jackson, Towers samples the output of the religious press in 1607, 1617, 1627 and 1637 in an effort to chart the changing controls arising from the interaction of different regimes with religious developments in the church. Religious authorship and interpretation is also the subject of Henry M. Knapp, 'John Owen's Interpretation of Hebrews 6: 4–6, Eternal perseverance of the Saints in Puritan Exegesis' (*SJC* 34:i[2003] 29–52), which examines Owen's interpretative strategy and methodology.

The task of re-examining boundaries and emphasizing their fluidity is taken up by Margaret Ferguson, *Dido's Daughters: Literacy, Gender and Empire in Early Modern England and France*, in her analysis of the 'gendered theories and practices of literacy within the context of late medieval and early modern nation-building'. This significant work begins with three chapters on the theoretical and historical considerations surrounding the concepts of literacy and nationhood, engaging with the relationship between national languages and issues of political and economic dominion before moving on to case studies of Christine de Pizan, Marguerite de Navarre, Elizabeth Cary and Aphra Behn. In common with Marcy North, she challenges the still influential distinction between the medieval and Renaissance worlds as being feminine, oral and communal (medieval) and masculine, individualistic and written (even printed) (Renaissance). Her discussion of literacy reclaims it from a single, monumental construct and foregrounds its different forms relating to female literacy and partial literacy. In so doing, Ferguson uses the responses of 'relatively privileged European women' to try and formulate an answer to the question of how classes (or races) classified as illiterate or subliterate responded to this classification in an imperial context. Ferguson's multifaceted and indeed magisterial work takes key issues of gender, literacy and empire and provides a meticulously detailed interdisciplinary discussion of their relationships. Moving from Ferguson's work on literacy as a gendered issue, Corinne S. Abate's collection of essays, *Privacy, Domesticity, and Women in Early Modern England*, focuses on private space as an equally gendered location. Lisa Hopkins's study of interiority in the *Duchess of Malfi* offers a reading that enables us to see the Duchess's death in the fourth act as one which enables her to conclude her search for secure enclosure and escape from those who would study her (exterior) body ('The Interiors of the *Duchess of Malfi*'). Corinne S. Abate deals with the problematic play *The Taming of the Shrew*, arguing that Petruchio and Katherine establish a companionate marriage which celebrates inner space and privacy for both parties. Abate addresses the misogynistic elements of Petruchio's speeches by showing how many of them are given in public, to an audience of male onlookers whose opinion of and influence on Petruchio's marriage are alike inessential. Referring to the increasing distinction between private and public space within the early modern household, Abate argues that, in a similar vein, Petruchio and Katherine succeed in establishing their own private space within marriage, free from the public gaze.

Mihoko Suzuki's *Subordinate Subjects: Gender, the Political Nation, and Literary Form in England, 1588–1688* should be considered in conjunction with *Dido's Daughters*, since it is also concerned with the imaginative creation of a political entity—the nation—that incorporates the voices of the disenfranchised elements of society, namely women and apprentices throughout the seventeenth century. Her discussion of the development of a distinctive political identity for apprentices enables her to address the similar, but more problematic, efforts of women to establish for themselves a distinct public voice.

As opposed to seeing the female voice as being aggressively silenced or in other ways marginalized, Anne Cotterill, in *Digressive Voices in Early Modern English Literature*, demonstrates the value of a female or effeminate character in assisting writers such as Browne, Marvell, and Dryden in their efforts to establish a voice for themselves, as a mode of deflecting the demands of their patrons and society's expectations and establishing a private, independent voice instead. One result of this is to see that 'the narrative tactics of digression and excess, conventionally (if misogynistically) viewed as female, may in fact be read as a subversive response to hegemonic dictates which transcends issues of class and of gender'. Following an introduction that offers a clear and readable explanation of key rhetorical terms and their wider significances, Cotterill turns to six different authors, Donne, Marvell, Browne, Milton, Dryden and Swift, to demonstrate the different strategic uses to which digression could be put. Of particular interest to this section is chapter 3, discussing Thomas Browne's *Garden of Cyrus* [1658] as a response to a fragmented age, one which celebrates elaborate order in nature, in mysticism and in rhetoric. The place of the garden in sixteenth- and seventeenth-century culture is examined in detail by Rebecca Bushnell in *Green Desire: Imagining Early Modern English Gardens* in which debates of class, art and gender are viewed through the medium of the gardening manuals of the period.

Christopher Hendrick's article, 'The Imperial Laboratory: Discovering form in *The New Atlantis*' (*ELH* 70[2003] 1021–42) focuses, unusually for this year, on a single prose text. The essay considers whether Bacon's *New Atlantis* should be termed an ideal Commonwealth rather than a Utopia, before discussing the ways in which it presents itself as an imperialist narrative through its depiction of different models of learning and knowledge. Bacon's work features again in Willy Maley, *Nation, State and Empire in English Renaissance Literature*, in an analysis of his little-known work *Certain Considerations Touching the Plantation in Ireland* [1606, 1657] as part of a study of the development of national consciousness in Britain and the consequent need to integrate Ireland

and Scotland into that imperialist narrative. Maley's discussion of the concept of Britain as the 'first empire' challenges the focus of both new historicism and cultural materialism on Ireland as the site of contest and anxiety, arguing instead that 'Britain was the great problem', and that the concept of Britain masked a multinational state with complex internal tensions and debates. Bringing together issues of Anglo-Scottish union and the Ulster Plantation, Maley argues that Bacon's treatise forms an important contribution to the formation of a concept of 'Britishness'. In addition to Bacon's *Certain Considerations*, Maley uses Ford's *Perkin Warbeck* [1633] and Milton's *Observations upon the Articles of Peace with the Irish Rebels*, as well as Shakespeare's *Cymbeline*, to develop his study of the British state as an 'entity made up of four nations and many nationalities'. In a similar vein, Mark Netzloff, *England's Internal Colonies: Class, Capital, and the Literature of Early Modern English Colonialism*, focuses on the 'internal colonies' of Scotland, Ireland and early modern England. Netzloff discusses the fusion of class concerns and foreignness into an 'exclusionary discourse', one which incorporates issues of piracy, gypsies, the displacement of the poor and colonial resettlement in areas of England, Scotland and Ireland. Netzloff employs a variety of texts in his study of colonialism and industrialization, primarily Shakespeare's *The Merchant of Venice* and *The Tempest*, Heywood's *Fortune by Land and Sea*, Jonson's masque *The Gypsies Metamorphosed* and John Speed's atlas, *The Theatre of the Empire of Great Britain*. In addition to these he refers to a wide range of archival research, for example into correspondence and prose treatises from the State Papers.

Issues of colonialism, national identity and cartography are also reflected in several articles published this year: Ken MacMillan's '"Sovereignty more plainly described": Early English Maps of North America, 158–1625' (*JBS* 42[2003] 413–47) discusses maps as 'texts' that allude to English sovereignty and Crown authority at the same time as expressing the area's potential for colonization. For this reason, he argues, the most accurate maps of the Americas tended to remain in manuscript while printed maps of 'newfound lands' were used as a form of propaganda to demonstrate English sovereignty. Jerome De Groot turns to the political landscape of England itself in the civil war in 'Chorographia, Newcastle and Royalist Identity in the late 1640s' (*SC* 18:i[2003] 61–75). He begins, usefully, by defining 'chorography' as the art or practice of delineating particular regions or districts on a map, as opposed to geography, taken as dealing with the earth in general, and (less distinctly) topography, which deals with particular places. With this definition in mind, de Groot demonstrates how this form of cartography was used to re-map and describe political landscapes in royalist writings.

The Variorum collection of David Cressy's articles, *Society and Culture in Early Modern England*, is a valuable assembly of this distinguished scholar's work. The articles contained within the edition span a broad range of subjects, but of particular relevance to this section are two articles, the first on transvestism in early modern England. Cressy begins his discussion of cross-dressing and anxieties surrounding gender roles with a survey of writers such as Stubbes, Gosson and Gascoigne, and goes on to discuss a court case in which a man was accused of having entered a birthing chamber disguised as a woman. Drawing on the court records for this case and other similar ones, as well as later literary examples in Jonson, Massinger and Fletcher to name but a few, Cressy challenges our understanding of cross-dressing either as 'eroticized transgression' or subversion, calling instead for room to be made for an understanding of the act as one of festive jest. 'Books as Totems in Seventeenth-Century England and New England' explores the cultural significance of books as non-literary or symbolic objects in both countries, while 'Francis Bacon and the Advancement of Schooling' traces Bacon's interest in education through a particular legal dispute over the fabulously wealthy Thomas Sutton's will. Cressy argues that in Bacon's efforts to halt Sutton's bequest of £8,000 a year to found a 'hospital or college' at Charterhouse, and to reassign it to other educational purposes, Bacon's early thoughts concerning a 'Great Instauration' may be discerned.

A fascinating contribution to new historicist studies and comparative literature is Hilaire Kallendorf, *Exorcism and its Texts: Subjectivity in Early Modern Literature of England and Spain.* Kallendorf adopts elements of structuralism and new historicism to provide a comprehensive study of the paradigm of demonic possession, both beneficial and malignant. The book begins with a survey of instances of possession in Spanish and English literature between 1550 and 1700, in which she provides a brief but detailed exegesis of a number of key texts, including Jonson's *The Devil is an Ass* and *Volpone*, Ruggle's *Ignoramus* and Shadwell's *The Lancashire Witches*, before discussing issues of exorcism, satire and tragedy. Kallendorf displays an impressive breadth of research in her use of literature and literary theory (both contemporary and early modern) throughout the book, and her theoretical approach both employs new historicism to good effect and challenges it to encompass phenomena such as possession and exorcism in its accounts of the marvellous in literature.

2. Women's Writing

(a) Books

This year saw an increased interest in understanding early modern women in relation to popular culture and non-literary forms of discourse. Focusing on non-hegemonic and popular literature, Mihoko Suzuki examines the construction of the early modern political subject through the discursive practices of both apprentices and women in her significant book *Subordinate Subjects: Gender, the Political Nation, and Literary Form in England, 1588–1688*. Interestingly, there were many legal and social similarities between the roles of apprentices and wives, and the aim of the book is to demonstrate how both groups positioned themselves in the political sphere. Chapter 3 focuses on how Aemilia Lanyer presents women's perspectives and subjects in the Bible to redefine misogynist interpretations of biblical history, while Rachel Speght emphasizes the historical context of biblical injunctions, questioning their universal authority. Both challenge patriarchy by reinterpreting the authoritative texts of their culture and revising the ideology of history. Chapter 4 discusses how both apprentices and women used the form of petition, exploring the reactions these groups provoked. Though scholarship often perceives female petitioners as accepting their status, women repetitively assert that they are not included in their husband's legal and political persons, challenging a fundamental tenet of patriarchy. 'Royalist' women are the subject of chapter 5, which examines the caskets embroidered by aristocratic young women, and the political writings of Margaret Cavendish. Suzuki argues that these women complicate gender, adopting subject positions that do not entirely correlate with a royalist understanding of monarchism. Cavendish, in particular, safely voices radical parliamentarian ideas through a multi-voiced text.

Though more historical in nature, Laura Gowing's excellent book, *Common Bodies: Women, Touch and Power in Seventeenth-Century England*, discusses understandings of gender and the body in relation to 'common people', the poor, the servants and the labourers. Providing the first in-depth analysis of how ordinary women understood and experienced their bodies, Gowing demonstrates how the most apparently natural processes of the body can be understood as products of cultural and economic conditions. Deriving many of her sources from ecclesiastical courts, popular print, jokes and common cultural practices, Gowing also illustrates how women often actively contributed to maintaining the patriarchal order. Chapter 1 discusses how popular medical discourses held conceptions of sexual difference and reproduction that were uncertain and in debate. Though female bodies were ideologically secret, they were also, ironically, public, subject to official regulation and informal surveillance. However, married women had their own distinct authority over female bodies. Chapter 2 explores how young single women in service were particularly vulnerable to invasive social regulation and sexual abuse. Though marriage formally alienated women from their own bodies, it brought them status, authority and protection. However, becoming elderly simultaneously caused a loss of social autonomy and a degree of corporeal authority. Chapter 3 discusses the complex understandings of consent and desire and their practical implications. Examining numerous testimonies regarding fornication, adultery and rape, Gowing demonstrates how the limits of female consent could result in undermining female desire, effacing women's agency and validating male sexual violence. Perceptions of pregnancy, along with infanticide and illegitimacy, are the topic of chapter 4. Gowing argues that, though married and single women would have experienced pregnancy in radically different ways, pregnancy always provoked many uncertainties, and all women faced anxieties about monstrous births and miscarriages, often believed to be caused by their own emotions or imaginations. Though early modern childbirth rituals are often understood to have taken place in an empowering, harmonious all-female environment, chapter 5 explains that they were often the source of conflicts, tensions, fears and confrontations. Single women were particularly vulnerable to regulation, punishment and torturer-like interrogations during labour. Chapter 6 demonstrates the precariousness that illegitimacy, adultery and poverty introduced into notions of stable parenthood. Gowing discusses the problematic nature of establishing paternity and how this affected lower-class women, who were regularly whipped for illegitimacy and were likely to end up destitute.

Female deviancy in the context of popular culture is also discussed in Sandra Clark's *Women and Crime in the Street Literature of Early Modern England*, which explores the ideological context of early modern news and crime writing, along with perceptions of women's crimes. Clark examines literary representations in broadside ballads, domestic plays and pamphlets, the media used to present news before the age of newspapers. Though the material analysed is generally written by men or anonymous authors, the section on witchcraft in chapter 5 is specifically relevant to the field of women's writing. In discussing the various crimes recorded in pamphlets, Clark argues that depictions of witchcraft cases provide a unique opportunity to hear women's voices since they relied heavily on the witch's own confession. Though the texts are placed within a male-authored narrative, women scripted their own stories, revealing powerful fantasies about their psychic lives, and anxieties regarding their role as women.

Pamphlets are also explored in Joad Raymond's *Pamphlets and Pamphleteering in Early Modern Britain*. Raymond devotes chapter 7 specifically to women's participation in the pamphlet form. Examining the *querelle des femmes*, prophetic and political pamphlets, and women's involvement in almanacs and newsbooks, Raymond demonstrates that, although the pamphlet was often a form used to prescribe codes on gender behaviour, the 1640s significantly enhanced opportunities for women's publications.

The unique relationship that early modern women had with death is explored in Lucinda M. Becker's *Death and the Early Modern Englishwoman*. The concept of dying well in early modern culture included 'masculine' virtues such as strength, determination and pious public speaking. In order to have a 'good' death women were to exhibit masculine characteristics within the parameters of acceptable female behaviour. Using literary and non-literary sources, Becker draws her information from spiritual conduct manuals, funeral sermons, ballads, broadsheets, poetry, contemporary accounts and commemorative writing. The book also represents various faiths such as Catholicism, Protestantism and Quakerism, while examining a range of class positions, in order to demonstrate that, although there were diverse rituals of death, there was nonetheless an identifiably female form of dying. Becker traces early modern representations of death from both men and women writers, not only discussing 'good' female deaths, but also exploring 'bad' deaths and their ideological and practical functions. The last section specifically focuses on female expression, examining how women sometimes contributed towards their own funeral sermon, funeral arrangements and posthumous representation, while further considering what these representations meant to the individual and others. Identity in relation to writing wills and gift-giving at the deathbed is also analysed, discussing how such acts could secure relations. Becker further explores numerous posthumous literary legacies, arguing that such texts particularly demonstrate how death served as a powerful catalyst for female creativity. Though the book is interesting, scholars may be disappointed, not only by the focus on print, but also because claims are sometimes incorrect or problematic; for example Becker states that Cavendish wrote her biography as a widow, that women often led 'sheltered' lives, and that early modern society had little 'understanding of, the possibilities of individuality as opposed to conformity'.

An interesting aspect of early modern culture, slander, is analysed in *Staging Slander and Gender in Early Modern England* by Ina Habermann. Examining early modern legal understandings of slander, along with literary texts by authors such as Shakespeare, Wroth, Mary Sidney, Webster, Jonson and Cary, Habermann traces representations and meanings of slander, particularly sexual defamation, in relation to gender. Chapter 5 discusses how plays that were presented as innovative works of art, such as *Il Pastor Fido* by Guarini and Jonson's *The Devil is an Ass*, situate male authorship as intrinsically linked with a construction of femininity bound between praise and slander. In contrast, Wroth's *Love's Victory* negotiates a more equitable, comprehensive depiction of gender relations. Chapter 8 explores the 'slandered heroine', or the virtuous woman wrongly defamed, who signifies an ideologically charged fantasy of femininity. Comparing *Othello* to *The Tragedy of Miriam*, Habermann argues that, as Cary presents notions of female and human honour as contradictory, she uses the convention of the slandered woman for a powerful political vision of female agency.

Literacy, gender and empire are explored in Margaret W. Ferguson's significant book, *Dido's Daughters: Literacy, Gender, and Empire in Early Modern England and France*. The first part discusses the problems with defining and valuing literacy in medieval and early modern imperial nations such as England and France. Part 2 applies these ideas to four women writers, Christine de Pizan, Marguerite de Navarre, Elizabeth Cary and Aphra Behn. Grouping these authors under the title 'Dido's daughters', Ferguson argues that they resemble the legendary Dido who was often perceived as a perpetrator of lies and who became a focus of enduring debate regarding history and fiction, empire, sexuality, gender roles and the dangers of speaking and listening. Ferguson perceives Dido's daughters as exemplifying her central argument that literacy is often constituted by 'interesting lies'. For example, chapter 6 examines female literacy as equivocation in Elizabeth Cary's *Tragedy of Mariam*. Cary uses forms of equivocation to articulate, while also disguise, a critique on imperial England. Contextualizing the play in relation to Catholic and Protestant debates, and the views of both Jews and Catholics, Ferguson argues that *Tragedy of Miriam* critically explores censorship and politics. Judgement of morality becomes problematic in a story where signs and meanings are highly unstable, when there are conflicting interpretations amongst different social groups and when martyr-like characters are never clearly ethical from other characters' perspectives. The idea of truth, along with social, gender and racial hierarchies, is destabilized and complicated, rendering it difficult to discern who is a persecutable group. Though there is no stable outcome, the text critically explores the problems of language, meaning, and identity, and the problems of any state founded on patriarchal marriage.

The politics of the early modern family are discussed in relation to the literature of the Sidney family in Elizabeth Mazzola's *Favorite Sons: The Politics and Poetics of the Sidney Family*. The understanding of family defined from the Middle Ages was changing in the early modern period, and this new family structure consequently affected politics, culture and psychology. Examining not only the texts of Philip Sidney but also the literature of his family members,

Mazzola argues that the Sidney family represented themselves through their famed lineage, yet repeatedly used poetry and literature to analyse and comment on family values and politics. Using both history and psychology, she demonstrates how Philip Sidney's poetics and figure as poet contained many contradictions and problems. Through this problematic poetic legacy and unstable image, family members such as Mary Wroth and Robert and Mary Sidney appropriated or corrected his example, creating a new representation of Sidney that consequently gave him literary significance. Chapter 2 discusses how both Robert and Mary Sidney attempt to subdue Philip Sidney's flaws while establishing more stable and coherent worlds. Mary Sidney redefines the vocation of poetry and uses the Psalmist's rhetoric of anonymity to channel her own poetic authority and expression. Using theories of the novel, chapter 4 examines how Mary Wroth's *Urania* questions the fundamental values and perspectives of the romance genre. She particularly challenges the politics of family through focusing upon members, such as younger brothers, who were on the margins of the aristocratic family. Not only are siblings equal in the text, the non-linear structure further disrupts notions of coherent family history and lineage.

The Sidney family is also the focus of *A Sidney Chronology, 1554–1654* by Michael G. Brennan and Noel J. Kinnamon. Using the Julian calendar, the aim of the chronology is to document the century following the birth of Sir Philip Sidney in 1554 till the death of Lady Mary Wroth in 1653. The chronology begins with a brief family history before 1554 and then offers a calendar, not only of historical events relevant to the lives of the Sidneys, but also containing family information. Each year is categorized, and at the end of each year are three sections. The first is a list of select literary works, including printed volumes, manuscript and correspondence, which includes Short-Title Catalogue and Wing Catalogue numbers. The second section includes a select list of manuscript and printed texts dedicated to the Sidneys, and the third section documents references to literary matters relating to the Sidney family. For example, select references to which books the Sidneys purchased or received as gifts are listed, along with brief outside references to members of the family. The vast amount of Sidney correspondence, dedications and references means that the chronology cannot provide all of the sources, but it has nonetheless included a wide range of samples.

(b) Editions

Scholars will be very disappointed this year by the surprisingly sharp decline in editions of early modern women's writing. However, there has been an increase in facsimile reproductions, demonstrating that there is still an interest in expanding the developing canon. The series 'The Early Modern Englishwoman: A Facsimile Library of Essential Works' provides 'carefully chosen copies' of texts and has produced five facsimile publications this year. Each text has a brief introduction that includes an overview of the life and work of the writer. In his introduction to *Elizabeth Major*, Jeffrey Powers-Beck claims that little is known about this middle-class woman. Her religious text, *Honey on the Rod*, published in 1656, has similarities with the work of George Herbert and Francis Quarles in its emphasis upon utter submission to God. The very Word-centred text contains a long prose meditation in the form of a dialogue and a sequence of pentameter couplet poems expressing Calvinistic themes. Religion is also the focus of *An Collins*, whose mysterious identity is as uncertain as her religious stance. Though critics disagree about the social, political and religious views in Collins's *Divine Songs and Meditacions*, published in 1653, it is one of the earliest volumes of collected poems by a seventeenth-century English woman. Robert C. Evans notes that Collins, who claimed she was chronically ill, produced poetry that is highly varied in form. Though she often demonstrates a strong conviction of the inevitable sinfulness of humanity, some of her poetry is also overtly political. Religion and problematic authorship are also discussed by L.E. Semler in the introduction to '*Eliza*'. In 1642 this anonymous author published *Eliza's Babes*, a collection containing prose meditations along with devotional and political verse. Semler argues that the piece is particularly significant in its response to four Protestant literary traditions that are intermixed into a complex whole. Covering a wide variety of forms, the text contains an 'ostentatious spiritual brashness and overtly pro-woman stance', that also exemplifies the Puritan plain style.

The same series has also produced two translations. In *Elizabeth Evelinge, II* Jos Blom and Frans Blom explain that Evelinge, who was a nun, then an abbess, wrote two translations, most likely from French. However her third translation, *The Declarations and Ordinances,* which is the one presented in this facsimile reproduction, may have been translated from Latin. The original is by two Franciscan general ministers who were creating a set of rules for the sisters of the Order of St Clare, a vegetarian order devoted to poverty. The original text was an attempt for the order to correspond more closely to St Clare's original radical ideal of communal poverty.

Unlike Evelinge's text, the other translation in the series, *Judith Man*, is not religious, but a sensational and popular romance. Introducing Man, Amelia A. Zurcher claims that nothing is known about her except the details she provides in the prefatory material of her rare translation of *An Epitome of the History of Faire Argenis and Polyarchus*. The text, which was printed in 1640 and translated from French, was a mixture of fiction and political allegory, demonstrating an assertion of monarchical power in politically troubled times.

In *Almanacs*, Alan S. Weber explains that the almanac was the most inexpensive form of print in the early modern period and exerted much influence on popular opinion. Almanacs included astrology, medicine, astronomy and prophecy, which could be political or scientific in nature. The writings in the edition contain almanacs from various women, while also including *The Prophesie of Mother Shipton* by Richard Lownd and the satirical anti-Welsh works by the pseudonymous Shinkin ap Shone. Weber argues that almanacs are particularly important for understanding women's participation in popular culture, astrology, medicine and prophecy.

(c) Edited Volumes

Three interesting collections were published this year covering a range of subjects from consort queens and domesticity to violence. The neglected history of the Stuart queen consorts and their influences on performance, writing and patronage is explored in McManus, ed., *Women and Culture at the Courts of the Stuart Queens*. This wide-ranging interdisciplinary collection attempts to uncover the nature of the role of the queen consort, her court and how they symbolically created spaces for women's cultural agency. Part 2 of the collection specifically focuses on the queen's court in relation to female authorship. In the significant essay, 'Reflected Desire: The Erotics of the Gaze in Aemilia Lanyer's *Salve Deus Rex Judaeorum*' Suzanne Trill argues that, although criticism generally understands Lanyer as an essentialist and separatist writer, her poetry instead challenges binary oppositions. Using a psychoanalytical interpretative model while illustrating the limitations of essentialist readings, Trill examines how both Christ and the countess of Cumberland are figured as objects of homo- and hetero-erotic desire. In 'Playing By and With the Rules: Genre, Politics, and Perception in Mary Wroth's *Love's Victorie*', Alexandra G. Bennett argues that Wroth's play demonstrates femininity as a performance. Though the text actively engages in the patriarchal system, it nonetheless reveals some of its implicit flaws, providing a wry commentary upon the underlying realities of the Stuart court and its gender anxieties. Mary Wroth is also the subject of Rebecca Lemon's 'Indecent Exposure in Mary Wroth'. Lemon argues that, in *Urania* and *Pamphilia to Amphilanthus*, Wroth radically engages with the Petrarchan genre, challenging gender boundaries and negotiating privacy and female desire. Wroth's sonnets compare with Queen Anna's masque productions, in which Wroth participated, since both position the female body within a performative courtly space.

In *Privacy, Domesticity, and Women in Early Modern England* editor Corinne S. Abate explains that her collection attempts to offer a broader picture of female culture and authority as it explores the confines of women's private and domestic space. Using a range of critical approaches, including feminist, historicist and psychoanalytical methods, the essays examine authors such as Webster, Wroth, Shakespeare, Ford, Cavendish, Spenser and Sidney. Kathryn Pratt's '"Wounds still curelesse": Estates of Loss in Mary Wroth's *Urania*', examines how Wroth's use of the word 'estate' signifies both a state of being and material possession, contradictory meanings which mirror the status of women. Through the imagery of a tree, the character Pamphilia takes possession of her own body and the realm of romance, allowing Wroth to assert 'her right to literary estate'. Wroth is also discussed in Sheila T. Cavanagh's 'Mystical Sororities: The Power of Supernatural Female Narratives in Lady Mary Wroth's *Urania*'. Cavanagh argues that the supernatural in *Urania* establishes a space that allows women significant power and authority. Women's visions regularly prove effective, dramatically altering the lives of numerous men. As women craft mystical spaces, even the most powerful men's destinies are shaped by the will of women.

Violence in relation to gender is discussed in Woodbridge and Beehler, eds., *Women, Violence, and English Renaissance Literature: Essays Honoring Paul Jorgensen*. Though most of the collection provides articles about male authors, two essays address women writers. In 'Female Selfhood and Male Violence in English Renaissance Drama: A View from Mary Wroth's *Urania*' Akiko Kusunoki argues that Wroth and Cary portray female identity as split between a conventional social performance and a private selfhood not subject to male control. In contrast, plays by Shakespeare and Webster depict women's secrets or their private selves as violently punished in grotesque ways, a pattern also visible in Japanese kabuki plays. In 'Blood in the Kitchen: Violence and Early Modern

Domestic Work', Wendy Wall innovatively discusses how recipe books, particularly those by women, demonstrate that cooking instructions smacked of creative, aggressive and licensed violence. Cookbooks also linked medicine and butchery, not only endowing the housewife with shaman-like qualities, but creating associations between eating and the anatomist's dissection theatre. Plays such as *The English Traveller* link anxieties regarding everyday culinary violence with transgressive domestic subordinates.

(d) Journal Articles

Aemilia Lanyer featured in three articles this year. In 'Prophecy and Gendered Mourning in Lanyer's *Salve Deus Rex Judaeorum*' (*SEL* 43:i[2003] 101–16), Elizabeth M.A. Hodgson discusses Lanyer's strategic use of post-Reformation ideologies of gendered grief. In appropriating the trope of womanly grief combined with the use of a passive prophetic dream state, praise of Mary Sidney, and conflating biblical women, Lanyer constructs her own complex self-authorization. Lanyer's representation of religion is also discussed in Micheline White's '"A Woman with Saint Peter's Keys?": Aemilia Lanyer's *Salve Deus Rex Judaeorum* (1611) and the Priestly Gifts of Women' (*Criticism* 45:iii[2003] 323–41). White argues that, in her praise of female dedicatees, Lanyer uses orthodox religious imagery. However, she simultaneously uses clerical language, which radically suggests that these women wielded priestly powers that were normally only allotted to men. Lanyer further suggests that women are the true disciples and founders of Christ's church. In 'Aemilia Lanyer and Queen Elizabeth at Cookham' (*CahiersE* 63[2003] 17–32) Roger Prior argues that Elizabeth I may have instigated Lanyer to write the *Salve Deus Rex Judaeorum*. Examining the text along with historical evidence, Prior discusses the reasons why Elizabeth would have taken an interest in the penniless, illegitimately pregnant Lanyer, and how this possible relationship may have been part of an actual female community.

Mary Wroth's sonnets are examined in Susan Lauffer O'Hara's 'Sonnets as Theater: The Performance of Ideal Love and the Negation of Marriage in Mary Wroth's Masque' (*EIRC* 29:i[2003] 59–99). O'Hara argues that the sonnets in *Pamphilia to Amphilanthus* adhere closely to masque conventions. Not only does this indicate that they could be staged, but perceiving them as a masque is crucial to understanding how they significantly question love and the institution of marriage. Rather than masques, epithalamium is the focus of Elizabeth M.A. Hodgson's 'Katherine Philips: Agent of Matchlessness' (*WW* 10:i[2003] 119–36). Hodgson argues that Philips's view of women's agency in marriage is fundamental to the epithalamic form. As Philips engages with questions of real or performative gender roles raised by the genre, her portrayals of marriage are flexible, various and strategic, rendering it difficult to ascribe to her a single, clear authorial voice. In 'Dressed as Esther: The Value of Concealment in Ester Sowernam's Biblical Pseudonym' (*WW* 10:i[2003] 153–67), Erin Henriksen contextualizes Sowernam's choice of her biblical pseudonym, Ester, which provides an enabling strategy for her defence of women and may suggest a proto-feminist 'imagined community' mobilized by print. Sowerman also complicates her role of author and legitimates her defence as she doubles her words with those of Christ.

Carolyn Sale discusses Arbella Stuart's letters in 'The "Roman Hand": Women, Writing and the Law in the Att.-Gen. v. Chatterton and the Letters of the Lady Arbella Stuart' (*ELH* 70:iv[2003] 929–61) . Examining Stuart's self-fashioned authorial persona, Sale argues that Stuart's letters subvert dominant ideology and 'unwrite' legal narratives injurious to women, questioning scholarly understandings of her work and the critical framework which interprets early modern women's writing in general. The developing critical model for analysing the early modern female canon is also discussed in Sarah M. Dunnigan's 'Undoing the Double Tress: Scotland, Early Modern Women's Writing, and the Location of Critical Desires' (*FSt* 29:ii[2003] 299–319). Dunnigan argues that Scotland's paradoxical status and the problematic relation between women and nationalism contributes to the invisibility of early modern Scottish women's writing. Dunnigan examines how such texts challenge fixed identities of language and culture while providing strategies by which this double exclusion may be overcome. Scottish women's canonical status is also explored in Dunnigan's other article 'Sacred Afterlives: Mary, Queen of Scots, Elizabeth Melville and the Politics of Sanctity' (*WW* 10:iii[2003] 401–24). Dunnigan argues that both Mary Queen of Scots and Elizabeth Melville could receive greater recognition through exploring the political and personal selfhoods found in their representation of sanctity and devotion. Both women demonstrated a desire to influence their posthumous representation while providing politically motivated defences of their respective faiths.

This year also saw three articles about Elizabeth Cary. William M. Hamlin explores Cary's emphasis on epistemology in 'Elizabeth Cary's *Mariam* and the Critique of Pure Reason' (*EMLS* 9:i[2003]). Placing Cary in the context of Montaigne's philosophical ideas of doubt, credulity and certainty, Hamlin argues that Cary challenges the distinction between reason and emotion. *The Tragedy of Mariam* consequently demonstrates that human judgement and desire are not merely founded on reason alone. Cary's epistemology is also explored in 'Insurgent Flesh: Epistemology and Violence in *Othello* and *Mariam*' (*WS* 32:iv[2003] 393–410). Elizabeth Gruber discusses how metaphors of violence against women were routinely evoked to discuss the 'masculine' pursuit of knowledge. Both *Mariam* and *Othello* correspond to this axiom as women's violent deaths prove crucial to their husbands' discovery of knowledge; such investigations also 'expose a necrophilic logic at the root of epistemology'. Cary's drama is also discussed by Marguérite Corporaal in '"Thy Speech eloquent, thy wit quick, thy expressions easy": Rhetoric and Gender in Plays by English Renaissance Women' (*Renfor* 6:ii[2003]). Corporaal discusses plays by both Elizabeth Cary and Margaret Cavendish, examining the problematic ways in which gender, genre and rhetoric interact. However, both authors ultimately negotiate and justify women's use of rhetorical strategies, representing female rhetoric as a necessary tool for survival.

(e) Margaret Cavendish

Scholars of Margaret Cavendish will undoubtedly be pleased by the abundant amounts of innovative and exciting work published this year. Not only are there two edited volumes, one book, a biography, and numerous journal articles about Cavendish, there also is a new edition containing *The Blazing World*. The edition is entitled *Margaret Cavendish: Political Writings*, edited by Susan James for the series Cambridge Texts in the History of Political Thought. The edition includes the first contemporary publication of *Divers Orations*, which provides much commentary on seventeenth-century English social and political life, while also including a student-friendly rendition of *A New World called the Blazing World* with modern spellings and some alterations in punctuation. Not only does James include the explanatory notes from the 1992 Penguin edition of *The Blazing World*, but she significantly elaborates on the commentary, including many explanations of the references to the intellectual debates of the time and the ways in which Cavendish engages with these debates. Although *Divers Orations*, by contrast, does not provide extensive notes, the edition as a whole includes a helpful index locating where historical and intellectual figures are mentioned. James argues that the two pieces demonstrate how Cavendish's political theories uphold a conservative political and social order yet simultaneously challenge and destabilize it.

Cavendish's political thought is also the focus of Emma L.E. Rees's *Margaret Cavendish: Gender, Genre, Exile*. Rees argues that, through a strategic and complex use of genre, Cavendish formulates controversial politics that are 'softened' or made to appear unthreatening within their genre types. Cavendish was in triple exile since she was a woman and a royalist, and since her husband was later banished from courtly culture. Genre is a means of articulating her powerlessness from triple exile. It is through her engagement with genres and the departures from their normative structures that their full subversive impact can be understood. For example, since drama, performance and ceremony were associated with royalist activities, Cavendish manipulates the genre of drama to express subversive, royalist political ideas while simultaneously critiquing the Puritan legislation that censored dramatic production. Cavendish's adaptation of Lucretius's model of theorizing science in a poetic form in *Poems and Fancies* is used to blur distinctions between fact and fiction, to convey royalist sympathies, and to authorize her own act of publishing as a woman. Cavendish further invokes Platonic theories of generic ideals and literary structure that critique the Interregnum regime and Puritan ideology. Using conventions from Homer, Cavendish creates a dynamic mixture of epic and romance in *Assaulted and Pursued Chastity* that reworks the cultural definitions of feminine virtue while allowing her heroine to display 'masculine' characteristics such as ability in oratory, public action and epic heroism. In *The Animall Parliament* Cavendish also employs the ancient trope of the body as kingdom combined with contemporary scientific theories of human physiology, particularly blood circulation, to create a criticism of the Puritan parliament while arguing that monarchy is natural. Finally, in *Orations of Divers Sorts* oration allows Cavendish to express diverse gender positions, yet curtails other women's engagement with the genre. Though Cavendish's attitude to genre changed after the Restoration, she does not create a generic hierarchy, but instead argues that interdependence is necessary.

In *A Princely Brave Woman: Essays on Margaret Cavendish, Duchess of Newcastle*, editor Stephen Clucas claims that, although scholars should be aware of Cavendish's libertine singularity, it is nonetheless beneficial to place Cavendish in the context of contemporary philosophical and literary norms. Thus, this significant collection of essays contributes to understanding Cavendish's engagement with the intellectual figures and concepts of her time. Scholars researching Cavendish's philosophy and science will be particularly interested in the many articles that address her scientific thought. In part 1 of the collection, 'Prose Fictions', Kate Lilley argues in her essay 'Contracting Readers: "Margaret Newcastle" and the Rhetoric of Conjugality' that Cavendish strategically presents her writing, reading, conversing and publishing as the effect of chaste and noble matrimony. Using the rhetoric of the marriage contract, and portraying her husband as an exemplary male type, she authorizes her own intellectual independence. Women's writing is also placed in the context of family structures in '"How Great is Thy Change:" Familial Discourses in the Cavendish Family'. Marion Wynne-Davies traces a line of female authorship within the Cavendish family, arguing that the connection between these women is derived from family bonds and shared discourses. Though the aristocratic family provided a secure space for female writing, the disruption of this stability was also a stimulus to women's literary productivity. In Nicole Pohl's '"Of Mixt Natures": Questions of Genre in Margaret Cavendish's *The Blazing World*', Pohl argues that Cavendish, through her unique blending of science, romance and fancy, genres which had specific gender associations, deconstructs gender binaries and develops her own critical baroque exploration of a transgressive hermaphroditism. Her utopian narrative does not give either/or choices, but allows continuity, multiplicity, variation and inclusion. In 'Autobiography, Parody and the Sociable Letters of Margaret Cavendish' James Fitzmaurice demonstrates the autobiographical and biographical elements of *Sociable Letters*. Using new manuscript evidence of William Cavendish's flirtations before he married Margaret, he shows how cryptic characters such as Lady M.L. and Mr. N.N. in *Sociable Letters* express Cavendish's anxieties about her husband's promiscuous past while also parodying her own self.

Drama is the focus of part 2, and in 'Writing for the Brain and Writing for the Boards: the Producibility of Margaret Cavendish's Dramatic Texts', Judith Peacock compares the drama of Cavendish and Aphra Behn, persuasively arguing that it was the extremely subversive content of Cavendish's plays, rather than their 'untheatrical nature', that obstructed their performance. Analysing Restoration theatre production, she claims that Cavendish's dramatic form was not as unusual as critics assume and that, unlike those of Behn, Cavendish's texts never received the extensive editing and alteration of the theatre management. Rebecca D'Monté's '"Making a Spectacle": Margaret Cavendish and the Staging of the Self' argues that Cavendish and her female characters deliberately display themselves to a male audience in such a way that they control the spectacle, transferring sexuality into textuality and creating spaces of potential power. Consequently, Cavendish transgresses boundaries, redirects the male gaze and reappropriates the female body. Julie Sanders demonstrates that closets were significant to Cavendish's drama and public self-construction in '"The Closet

Opened": A Reconstruction of "Private" Space in the Writings of Margaret Cavendish'. Sanders questions traditional concepts of privacy, closets and closet drama, arguing that the supposed privacy of the closet was overtly performative. Consequently, closets were a public place in 'real' early modern households and an empowering space in writings by women.

In part 3, 'Poetry', Jay Stevenson's significant article 'Imagining the Mind: Cavendish's Hobbesian Allegories' demonstrates that Cavendish's theory of the mind not only parallels Hobbes's philosophy, but paradoxically contains both empiricism and rationalism with their epistemological 'menaces' enthusiasm and atheism. Since the self-ordered, conflicted mind is material and everything is thought itself, the mind is a central literary strategy for Cavendish as she uses it to authorize herself and her texts. Cavendish's acquaintance with the most advanced mathematical concepts of her age is discussed by B.J. Sokol in 'Margaret Cavendish's *Poems and Fancies* and Thomas Harriot's Treatise on Infinity'. Sokol argues that Cavendish represented through poetry the mathematical theories of Thomas Harriot, who anticipated the ideas which led to the development of infinitesimal calculus and conundrums of infinity that have only recently been resolved and are still partly in question. Rather than science, Emma L.E. Rees discusses Cavendish's appropriation of the Homeric Penelope in 'A Well-Spun Yarn: Margaret Cavendish and Homer's Penelope'. Through manipulating domestic images connected with needlework and the chaste figure of Penelope, Cavendish redefined gender and femininity. Consequently, she renegotiated her position as a woman writer so that her act of publication would be acceptable rather than transgressive.

In part 4, 'Natural Philosophy, in 'Margaret Cavendish and Henry More', Sarah Hutton discusses how Cavendish inverts Henry More's Platonism. Hutton demonstrates how Cavendish's 'Nature' proves a material universe that is the direct opposite of More's philosophy. In understanding Cavendish's critique of More in *Philosophical Letters*, it becomes evident that More 'the great Cabalist' becomes a prominent target of satire in *The Blazing World*. In 'Variation, Irregularity and Probabilism: Margaret Cavendish and Natural Philosophy as Rhetoric', Stephen Clucas examines Cavendish's philosophy in the context of seventeenth-century epistemological tendencies towards probabilism and provisionality. The insistence on the probability of her theories and her claims of artlessness are not caused by insecurity, but are a sophisticated engagement with contemporary intellectuals such as Boyle, Charleton and Glanvill and are the foundation of her philosophical libertinism. Cavendish's medical thought is examined in Susan Fitzmaurice's 'Margaret Cavendish, the Doctors of Physick and Advice to the Sick'. Fitzmaurice compares the functions and effects of medical advice in *Sociable Letters* to the work of contemporary seventeenth-century professional physicians. Borrowing from the conventions of both laymen's familial letters and the work of physicians, Cavendish implicitly claims expertise with a less dogmatic approach than that of the medical authorities. In 'Paradigms and Politics: Hobbes and Cavendish Contrasted', Neil Ankers argues that, although there are many links between Cavendish's and Hobbes's political philosophy, her theories are actually a counter-thrust to his mechanist understanding of human politics. Cavendish offers an alternative approach that relies on a willing, nonconformist compliance, as opposed to Hobbes's competitive struggles and forced restraint.

The other significant collection of Cavendish essays is *Authorial Conquests: Essays on Genre in the Writings of Margaret Cavendish*. Editors Line Cottegnies and Nancy Weitz claim that the aim of this interdisciplinary collection is to explore her works with her contemporaries and to approach Cavendish's literature as entering into dialogue with a tradition. In part 1, 'Non-Fictional Writings', Emma L.E. Rees, in 'Triply Bound: Genre and the Exilic Self', argues that Cavendish experienced exile in three ways: 'legislatively, politically, and along gender lines'. By manipulating contemporary expectations of genre, Cavendish experimented and played with generic conventions in a complex way to resist and write herself out of this triple exile. In '*Leviathan* and the Lady: Cavendish's Critique of Hobbes in the *Philosophical Letters*', Lisa T. Sarasohn examines how Cavendish used the genre of the philosophical letter to critique other philosophers, particularly Hobbes, whose theories were very similar to yet fundamentally different from her own. Through the genre of philosophical letters, along with her own animistic, vitalistic philosophical system, Cavendish allows the existence of a woman philosopher. Cavendish's engagement with science is also explored in Brandie R. Siegfried's 'Anecdotal and Cabalistic Forms in *Observations upon Experimental Philosophy*'. Siegfried argues that Cavendish mixes three modes of discourse: parody of gendered metaphors, the theatricality of matter borrowed from cabbalistic theories, and the Cartesian deployment of personal anecdote. Her experiment with form demonstrates how rival philosophical systems could yield mutually incompatible accounts of the natural world. In 'Margaret Cavendish's *Life of William*, Plutarch, and Mixed Genre' James Fitzmaurice considers Cavendish's contribution to seventeenth-century biography, arguing that the mixture of genres in her biography was not entirely unusual for that era. Through blending genres, Cavendish is able to establish herself as a serious historian where she creates a parallel between William Cavendish and Caesar, consequently becoming her husband's Plutarch. Cavendish's self-writing is also explored in 'The "Native Tongue" of the "Authoress": The Mythical Structure of Margaret Cavendish's Autobiographical Narrative', where Line Cottegnies explains how Cavendish's autobiography challenges the rhetorical emphasis on memory. This consequently frees the genre of self-writing from subservience to history and collapses historical truth into fiction, allowing her to manipulate the text to write her own self-truth or stabilized, personal myth.

In part 2, 'Imaginative Writings', Hero Chalmers's '"Flattering Division": Margaret Cavendish's Poetics of Variety' places Cavendish in the context of contemporary poetry. Chalmers argues that, in *Poems and Fancies*, Cavendish appropriates a royalist 'poetics of variety' influenced by rhetorical and literary theory as well as verse. Her poetics reflect her natural philosophy, which theorizes that change and diversity are paradoxically the model of order. In 'Romantic Fiction, Moral Anxiety, and Social Capital in Cavendish's "Assaulted and Pursued Chastity"', Nancy Weitz examines Cavendish's understanding of rape and chastity in comparison to that of her contemporaries, arguing that, in *Assaulted and Pursued Chastity* Cavendish participates in the tradition of conduct literature. Yet, through complying with both contradictory conventions of chastity and romance, she creates a pragmatic view of chastity that allows women to achieve social power. In 'Science and Satire: The Lucianic Voice of Margaret Cavendish's *Description of a New World Called the Blazing World*' Sarah Hutton argues that, though *The Blazing World* resembles Bacon's and More's utopias, it is better understood as being modelled on Lucian of Samosata. His science fiction provides a satirical model not only to comically and elegantly critique contemporary philosophy, but to satirize her own science as well. In Alexandra G. Bennett's 'Fantastic Realism: Margaret Cavendish and the Possibilities of Drama', Bennett argues that, rather than using traditional modes, Cavendish deliberately creates a lack of unity in plot construction in her drama, exploiting its disjunctive, mimetic possibilities. This 'generic flexibility' allows Cavendish to portray, comment on and change society, inviting her readers to expand their roles 'on the stage of the world'. Drama is also the focus of Sara Mendelson's article, 'Playing Games with Gender and Genre: The Dramatic Self-Fashioning of Margaret Cavendish'. Mendelson explores how Cavendish understood drama as not only educational, but a site for self-fashioning. Examining Cavendish's drama in relation to her autobiography, Mendelson argues that her plays are part of her autobiographical and 'anti-autobiographical' project which consequently breaks generic rules and destabilizes gender hierarchy. In 'Margaret Cavendish's Drama: An Aesthetic of Fragmentation', Gisele Venet examines the baroque aesthetics in several of Cavendish's plays, arguing that the loss of unified perspectives challenges idealized genres such as pastoral, epic and heroic. Though her plots are fragmented, they depict an idealized, monadic female self that is unified, a conception which anticipates the modern insular self.

This year also saw Katie Whitaker's biography, *Mad Madge: Margaret Cavendish, Duchess of Newcastle, Royalist, Writer and Romantic*, republished from the 2002 edition. This well-researched and detailed account of Cavendish's life initially discusses her family origins, her childhood ambitions, the violence and tragedy that the Cavendish family experienced during the civil war period, and her own adventures fleeing into exile. The biography moves on, not only examining aspects of Cavendish's life such as her informal education, life during the Restoration, public opinions, financial problems and controversies, but further tracing the development of her literary, political and philosophical thought, and often demonstrating how life experiences, cultural influences and political events affected her writings. Whitaker, who has a doctorate in the history of science, aptly explores Cavendish's literary and scientific endeavours in the context of the intellectual and political climate she lived in. In contrast to many twentieth-century biographical understandings of Cavendish, she demonstrates her intellectual correspondences and debates with eminent seventeeth-century thinkers, even establishing the influence she had on some scientists and writers. The Epilogue is particularly illuminating as Whitaker traces the changes in critical opinions of Cavendish, starting with the general seventeenth-century view, where she was not only an established and respected writer but a heroic woman. Perceptions began to alter in the eighteenth century when her work, which was highly censored, was depicted as exemplifying ideal feminine virtue.

Opinions changed once again in the nineteenth century to the unfounded perception of her being an isolated, ridiculed eccentric whose writings never influenced the world around her, a belief that has influenced criticism even today. The biography as a whole is an interesting and highly recommended way for Cavendish scholars to reacquaint themselves with 'Mad Madge'.

In *Women Philosophers of the Seventeenth Century* Jacqueline Broad traces the development of early modern women's philosophical thought. Focusing on women who were critical of Cartesian philosophy, Broad discusses authors such as Elisabeth of Bohemia, Anne Conway, Mary Astell, Damaris Masham and Catherine Trotter Cockburn. Chapter 2 gives a very insightful explanation of Cavendish's philosophical position in response to three key philosophers of her time, Descartes, Thomas Hobbes and Henry More. Broad argues that Cavendish's epistemological position is in some ways shaped by Hobbes and More. Yet Cavendish takes More's method to its logical extreme to critique aspects of mechanism, to refute Cartesian dualism, and to demonstrate the problems with More's own theories. In '"Angry I was, and Reason strook away": Margaret Cavendish and her Lyrical Acts of Rebellion' (in Luis-Martínez and Figueroa-Dorrego, eds., Re-shaping the Genres: Restoriation Women Writers), Maria Isabel Caderon argues that, although many critics have understood Cavendish's contradictions as unintentional, they not only strategically veiled her subversive thought but were also part of her larger project of dismantling and rebelling against classical epistemology and its understanding of reason, fancy, and human and gender hierarchy.

Domesticity and lesbian eroticism are explored in Theodora A. Jankowski's interesting essay 'Good Enough to Eat: The Domestic Economy of Woman–Woman Eroticism in Margaret Cavendish and Andrew Marvell' (in Abate, ed., *Privacy, Domesticity, and Women in Early Modern England*). Jankowski discusses how Cavendish's blazon, which is also a food recipe, radically alters the traditional Petrarchan relationship between the speaker and the desired female into a more egalitarian context. Both Cavendish and Marvell depict enclosed, female communities, demonstrating that restricting women to a private/domestic space does not necessarily deny them the ability to exercise their talents or find pleasure.

The concept of self within Cavendish's writings is explored in Frédéric Regard's edited volume, *Mapping the Self: Space, Identity, Discourse in British Auto/Biography*. Although the volume discusses British biography and autobiography from as early as the early modern period to contemporary self-writings, two articles address Cavendish. In 'Margaret Cavendish and the Landscapes of a Woman's Life', Helen Wilcox focuses on Cavendish's use of place in her autobiography, arguing that the landscape of her life can be used to understand her definition of selfhood. Autobiography becomes the means for Cavendish not only to gain personal control, but to map and explore her invented, singular self. In 'The Garden and the Tower: Pastoral Retreat and Configurations of the Self in the Auto/Biographical Works of Margaret Cavendish and Lucy Hutchinson' Line Cottegnies discusses how, for both Cavendish and Hutchinson, the discourse of the self is founded on special metaphors related to pastoral retirement. Though both demonstrate differing politics and poetics, Cavendish's use of the garden image and Hutchinson's imagining of a tower were both reactions to traumatic crisis.

This year Cavendish's science was discussed in numerous journal articles. In 'Margaret Cavendish as Natural Philosopher: Gender and Early Modern Science' (*Interdisciplinary Science Reviews* 28:iii[2003] 200–8) Denise Tillery explains that, in *Observations*, Cavendish's scientific method relies on reason combined with observations that are personal and connected to the larger social and natural world, opposed to an invasive separation from the object. Cavendish further advocates a plain style that would make science more accessible to readers. In 'Francis Godwin, Henry Neville, Margaret Cavendish, H.G. Wells: Some Utopian Debts' (*ANQ* 16:iii[2003] 12–18), William Poole examines the influence of Francis Godwin's utopia, *The Man in the Moone*, on various authors, including Margaret Cavendish, arguing that the property of stones in her *The Blazing World* is adapted from Godwin's text. In her interesting article 'Romancing Multiplicity: Female Subjectivity and the Body Divisible in Margaret Cavendish's Blazing World' (*EMLS* 9:i[2003]) Geraldine Wagner demonstrates that Cavendish used romance along with materialism to explore female subjectivity, arguing that the relationships between Cavendish's selves create an infinite multiplicity. The self is not stable, but becomes powerful and self-generative when merged with the Other. This idea is further mirrored by the circular structure of the text, making available for her readers, an un-dominated and un-subjected selfhood.

Cavendish was compared to Milton in two journal articles this year. Kathryn Schwarz discusses the radical potentials of chastity in 'Chastity, Militant and Married: Cavendish's Romance, Milton's Masque' (*PMLA* 118:ii[2003] 270–85). She juxtaposes Milton's *A Mask* and Cavendish's *Assaulted and Pursued Chastity* in the context of expectations of female virtue and contemporary feminine conduct manuals. Both authors create chaste female subjects whose chastity paradoxically alters cultural ideologies. Militant chastity becomes a subversive mode of heroism and wilful female determination. Marianne Micros compares *The Blazing World* and *Paradise Lost* in '"A World of my Own": John Milton and Margaret Cavendish's Reflections of Paradise' (*Cithara* 43:i[2003] 3–24). Micros argues that, though Milton and Cavendish demonstrate comparable portrayals of paradise, science and knowledge, Cavendish subverts the hierarchical system on which Eden is based, depicting a highly secular paradise of the mind which challenges patriarchal, conventional beliefs about women and encourages change and growth.

Julie Crawford argues that Cavendish was not a feminist in 'Convents and Pleasures: Margaret Cavendish and the Drama of Property' (*RenD* 32[2003] 177–223), characterizing *The Convent of Pleasure* as a 'self-interested petition' registering complaints of unrecompensed royalist property. The play further advocates the restoration of the privileges and status of the nobility, demonstrating that the aristocracy should be simultaneously loyal to and demanding of the monarch. A contrasting portrayal of Cavendish can be found in James Fitzmaurice, '"The Lotterie": A Transcription of a Manuscript Play Probably by Margaret Cavendish' (*HLQ* 66:i and ii[2003] 155–67), which examines *The Lotterie*, a play probably performed for the king and attributed to William Cavendish. However, it is best understood as being written by his wife

Margaret, who was concerned with gambling and sometimes portrays sympathy towards the lower classes, characteristics that are evident in *The Lotterie*. In 'Using Sex: Margaret Cavendish's *The Lady Contemplation* and the Authorial Fantasy of Class Permanence' (*PCP* 38[2003] 77–98) Erika Mae Olbricht argues that chastity, rather than titles or wealth, is what differentiates Lady Virtue from lower-class female characters. Though she becomes a poor labourer, Olbricht explains that this is a liminal state which reaffirms static class relations. Cavendish's own chastity underwrites her textual authority, allowing gender to be subordinate to class.

Books Reviewed

Abate, Corinne S. ed. *Privacy, Domesticity, and Women in Early Modern England*. Ashgate. [2003] pp. ix + 204. £40 ISBN 0 7546 3043 9.

Becker, Lucinda M. *Death and the Early Modern Englishwoman*. Ashgate. [2003] pp. ix + 226. £45 ISBN 0 7546 3349 7.

Blom, Jos and Frans Blom, eds. *Elizabeth Eveline, II*. The Early Modern Englishwoman: A Facsimile Library of Essential Works—Printed Writings, 1500–1640, ser. 1, pt. 3, vol. v. Ashgate. [2003] pp. xviii + 176. £40 ISBN 0 7546 0444 6.

Brennan, Michael G., and Noel J. Kinnamon. *A Sidney Chronology, 1554–1654*. Palgrave. [2003] pp. xxiii + 342. £60 ISBN 0 3339 6400 4.

Broad, Jacqueline. *Women Philosophers of the Seventeenth Century*. CUP. [2002] pp. x + 191. £40 ISBN 0 5218 1295 X.

Bushnell, Rebecca W. *Green Desire: Imagining Early Modern English Gardens*. CornUP. [2003] pp. x + 198. $29.95 ISBN 0 8014 4143 9.

Clark, Sandra. *Women and Crime in the Street Literature of Early Modern England*. Palgrave. [2003] pp. xi + 233. £50 ISBN 1 4039 0212 7.

Clucas, Stephen, ed. *A Princely Brave Woman: Essays on Margaret Cavendish, Duchess of Newcastle*. Ashgate. [2003] pp. xvi + 285. £45 ISBN 0 7546 0464 0.

Cottegnies, Line, and Nancy Weitz, eds. *Authorial Conquests: Essays on Genre in the Writings of Margaret Cavendish*. FDUP. [2003] pp. 240. $39.50 ISBN 0 8386 3983 6.

Cotterill, Anne. *Digressive Voices in Early Modern English Literature*. OUP. [2003] pp. viii + 260. £65 ISBN 0 1992 6117 2.

Cressy, David. *Society and Culture in Early Modern England*. Variorum Collected Studies Series. Ashgate. [2003] £57.50 ISBN 0 86078 911 X.

Doran, Susan, and Thomas S. Freeman, eds. *The Myth of Elizabeth*. Palgrave Macmillan. [2003] pp. ix + 269. hb. $72 ISBN 0 3339 3084 3.

Evans, Robert C. ed. *An Collins*. The Early Modern Englishwoman: A Facsimile Library of Essential Works—Printed Writings, 1641–1700, ser. 2, pt. 2, vol. i. Ashgate. [2003] pp. xviii + 110. £40 ISBN 0 7546 3093 5.

Ferguson, Margaret W. *Dido's Daughters: Literacy, Gender, and Empire in Early Modern England and France*. UChicP. [2003] pp. xiv + 506. pb $25 ISBN 0 2262 4312 5, hb $65 ISBN 0 2262 4311 7.

Glimp, David. *Increase and Multiply: Governing Cultural Reproduction in Early Modern England*. UMinnP. [2003] pp. xxviii + 230. hb $65.95 ISBN 0 8166 3990 6, pb $21.95 ISBN 0 8166 3991 4.

Gowing, Laura. *Common Bodies: Women, Touch and Power in Seventeenth-Century England*. YaleUP. [2003] pp. ix + 260. £25 ISBN 0 3001 0096 5.

Gutierrez, Nancy A. *'Shall she famish then?': Female Food Refusal in Early Modern England*. Ashgate. [2003] pp. vii + 146. £40 ISBN 1 8401 4240 5.

Habermann, Ina. *Staging Slander and Gender in Early Modern England*. Ashgate. [2003] pp. vii + 202. £45 ISBN 0 7546 3384 5.

James, Susan, ed. *Margaret Cavendish: Political Writings*. CUP. [2003] pp. xxxix + 300. hb £47.50 ISBN 0 5216 3349 4, pb £17.99 ISBN 0 5216 3350 8.

Kallendorf, Hilaire. *Exorcism and Its Texts: Subjectivity in Early Modern Literature of England and Spain*. UTorP. [2003] pp. xix + 327. £48 ISBN 0 8020 8817 1.

Levin, Carole, Jo Eldridge Carney and Debra Barrett-Graves, eds. *'High and Mighty Queens' of Early Modern England: Realities and Representations*. Palgrave Macmillan. [2003] pp. x + 271. $55 ISBN 1 4039 6088 7.

Luis-Martínez, Zenón and Jorge Figueroa-Dorrego, eds. *Re-shaping the Genres: Restoration Women Writers*. Lang. [2003] pp. 303. £29 ISBN 3 9067 6986 0.

Maley, Willy. *Nation, State, and Empire in English Renaissance Literature: Shakespeare to Milton*. Palgrave Macmillan. [2003] pp. xvii + 185. $69 ISBN 0 3336 4077 2.

Mazzola, Elizabeth. *Favorite Sons: The Politics and Poetics of the Sidney Family*. Palgrave Macmillan. [2003] pp. x + 150. £30 ISBN 1 4039 6321 5.

McManus, Clare, ed. *Women and Culture at the Courts of the Stuart Queens*. Palgrave. [2003] pp. xiii + 252. £50 ISBN 1 4039 0260 7.

Netzloff, Mark. *England's Internal Colonies: Class, Capital, and the Literature of Early Modern English Colonialism*. Palgrave Macmillan. [2003] pp. xii + 280. $59.95 ISBN 1 4039 6183 2.

North, Marcy. *The Anonymous Renaissance: Cultures of Discretion in Tudor–Stuart England*. UChicP. [2003] pp. xi + 309. $37.50 ISBN 0 2265 9437 8.

Powers-Beck, Jeffrey, ed. *Elizabeth Major*. The Early Modern Englishwoman: A Facsimile Library of Essential Works—Printed Writings, 1641–1700, ser. 2, pt. 2, vol. vi. Ashgate. [2003] pp. xvi + 240. £47.50 ISBN 0 7546 3098 6.

Raymond, Joad. *Pamphlets and Pamphleteering in Early Modern Britain*. CUP. [2003] pp. xviii + 403. £50 ISBN 0 5218 1901 6.

Rees, Emma L.E. *Margaret Cavendish: Gender, Genre, Exile*. ManUP. [2003] pp. vi + 218. £40 ISBN 0 7190 6072 9.

Regard, Frédéric, ed. *Mapping the Self: Space, Identity, Discourse in British Auto/Biography*. University of Saint-Étienne. [2003] pp. 398. €23 ISBN 2 8627 2269 3.

Rhodes, Neil, Jennifer Richards, and Joseph Marshall, eds. *King James VI and I: Selected Writings*. Ashgate. [2003] pp. xii + 413. £49.50 ISBN 0 7546 0482 9.

Richards, Jennifer, ed. *Early Modern Civil Discourses*. Palgrave Macmillan. [2003] pp. 240. $65 ISBN 1 4039 1736 1.

Semler, L.E., ed. *'Eliza'*. The Early Modern Englishwoman: A Facsimile Library of Essential Works—Printed Writings, 1641–1700, ser. 2, pt. 2, vol. iii. Ashgate. [2003] . £35 ISBN 0 7546 3095 1.

Sheen, Erica, and Lorna Hutson, eds. *Literature, Politics and Law in Renaissance England*. Palgrave Macmillan. [2003] pp. 256. $65 ISBN 0 3339 8399 8.

Sim, Stuart, and David Walker. *The Discourse of Sovereignty, Hobbes to Fielding: The State of Nature and the Nature of the State*. Studies in Early Modern English Literature. Ashgate. [2003] pp. 217. £40 ISBN 0 7546 0455 1.

Suzuki, Mihoko. *Subordinate Subjects: Gender, the Political Nation, and Literary Form in England, 1588–1688*. Ashgate. [2003] pp. x + 330. £45 ISBN 0 7546 0605 8.

Towers, S. Mutchow. *Control of Religious Printing in Early Stuart England*. Boydell. [2003] pp. vii + 304. £45 ISBN 0 8111 5939 7.

Weber, Alan S. ed. *Almanacs*. The Early Modern Englishwoman: A Facsimile Library of Essential Works—Printed Writings, 1641–1700, ser. 2, pt. 1, vol. vi. Ashgate. [2002] pp. xxiv + 290. £47.50 ISBN 0 7546 0215 X.

Whitaker, Katie. *Mad Madge: Margaret Cavendish, Duchess of Newcastle, Royalist, Writer and Romantic*. C&W. [2003] pp. x + 436. £20 ISBN 0 7011 6929 X.

Woodbridge, Linda, and Sharon Beehler, eds. *Women, Violence, and English Renaissance Literature: Essays Honoring Paul Jorgensen*. MRTS. [2003] pp. lix + 446. £36 ISBN 0 8669 8299 X.

Yates, Julian. *Error, Misuse, Failure: Object Lessons from the English Renaissance*. UMinnP. [2003] pp. xx + 250. hb $59.95 ISBN 0 8166 3962 0, pb $19.95 ISBN 0 8166 3961 2.

Zurcher, Amelia A. ed. *Judith Man*. The Early Modern Englishwoman: A Facsimile Library of Essential Works—Printed Writings, 1500–1640, ser. 1, pt. 3, vol. 2. Ashgate. [2003] pp. 176. £40 ISBN 0 7546 0441 1.

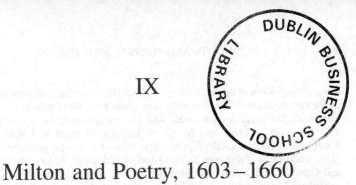

DUBLIN BUSINESS SCHOOL LIBRARY

IX

Milton and Poetry, 1603–1660

KEN SIMPSON, MARGARET KEAN, HOLLY FAITH NELSON, PAUL DYCK AND JOAD RAYMOND

This chapter has five sections: 1. General; 2. Milton; 3. Donne; 4. Herbert; 5. Marvell. Section 1 is by Ken Simpson; section 2 is by Margaret Kean; section 3 is by Holly Faith Nelson; section 4 is by Paul Dyck; section 5 is by Joad Raymond.

1. General

The revised historicisms that pervade the study of early modern poetry can be seen in all forms of publication under review, from self-contained articles and chapters to books, anthologies, and literary histories. Michael Payne and John Hunter's *Renaissance Literature: An Anthology*, part of the Blackwell Anthologies series, reflects one of the contradictions that arises in the practice of historicism by anthologists: the displacement of the author is asserted at the same time as the anthology is organized, for the most part, according to canonical authors presented in chronological order. Women authors, less canonical genres such as ballads and hymns, and non-fiction prose selections are included, but they are overshadowed by the towering presence of canonical authors, texts, and genres. The overwhelming impression created by this anthology is that nothing much has changed in the profession over the last fifty years, despite theoretically informed introductions and annotations provided by the editors. The latest developments in the profession should be reflected in the anthology's principles of organization and selection as well as in its theoretical statements.

If the editors of *Renaissance Literature* could have put into practice the model of literary history developed in David Loewenstein and Janel Mueller's *The Cambridge History of Early Modern English Literature*, a more consistent and useful anthology might have resulted. Loewenstein and Mueller emphasize 'sites of production' rather than authors, diverse voices rather than a single 'grand récit', the integration of text and context rather than the separation of text and background, and multi-national, multi-class perspectives rather than representations of a single, elite culture. These principles lead to the innovative

Year's Work in English Studies, Volume 84 (2005) © The English Association; all rights reserved. For permissions, please email: journals.permissions@oxfordjournals.org

doi: 10.1093/ywes/mai009

and exciting vision of literary history that underlies the organization and selection of the twenty-six essays in the collection, many by leading scholars in the field. There are five main sections and, with the exception of the opening section devoted to the 'Modes and Means of Literary Production, Circulation and Reception', each represents a predictable area of historical periodization from 'The Tudor Era: From the Reformation to Elizabeth I' to 'The Civil War and Commonwealth Era'. Within each section, essays are devoted to 'sites of production' such as 'literature and the court' and 'literature and the church' as well as the theme of 'literature and national identity', providing continuity from one era to another. Historical discontinuities are apparent as well, since 'sites of production' shift throughout the period: 'literature and the church' becomes 'literature and religion' in the civil war period, reproducing the well-known narrative of individualism; London, the household, and the theatre become important sites in the Elizabethan, Stuart and Commonwealth periods but are less dominant in the Tudor era, so essays on these sites are excluded from discussions of the earlier period. The historicist approach, however, has its drawbacks: the editors claim that the emphasis on 'institutional sites' complicates 'our sense of an individual author's agency' but does not 'diminish' it, but this is asserted rather than demonstrated. The arc of history that is presented is over-determined and, once again, I found myself wanting someone to talk about the music of verse and the art of poetry.

Brian Cummings, in *The Literary Culture of the Reformation*, also wants to erase boundaries between text and context, literature and other forms of writing, authorial agency and material conditions, but he takes a postmodern turn that Loewenstein and Mueller are not willing to take, arguing that in their 'entrapment within language' early modern writers are 'no different than us' (p. 14). The Reformation is not a monolithic historical movement but a culture of writing, a literary practice arising out of encounters with the Bible that are 'always already' forms of grammar and material production. In part 1 Cummings argues that Erasmus's literary humanism, especially his close textual analysis of grammar, influenced Luther's theology of grace and habits of reading, showing that Protestant doctrine is embedded in a material, literary process rather than a kind of baggage carried by language and separable from it. Cummings begins the second section by exploring the relationship between grammar, translation, and the vernacular in the debates between More's and Luther's follower, Tyndale, and then discusses Wyatt's penitential psalms as examples of Protestant literature produced in a culture of suspicion and surveillance. Protestant writing gains new confidence and self-consciousness under Edward and Elizabeth, and under the influence of Calvin's 'metaphysics of presence'. Calvin's method, which develops Erasmus's literary humanism to its logical conclusion, is appropriated by logicians, rhetoricians, and grammarians such as Fenner, Granger, Perkins and Fraunce, as well as by poets and critics like Sidney and Greville. Here the tensions between literary power and moral restraint resulting in the plain style of truth in Protestant writing first come to the surface. Part 3 and the Epilogue survey the dynamic legacy of Calvinism, and in some cases, anti-Calvinism, in the poetry of Greville, Southwell, Herbert, Donne and Milton. In each case, an examination of grammar and syntax leads to ambiguity and indeterminacy in the poets' attempts to represent the grammar of grace, which is 'at once invisible trace and dangerous supplement, simultaneously grammatological and illegible' (p. 490). The pursuit of indeterminacy and the sheer density of many discussions, especially those devoted to the fine points of grammar, make this book challenging to read, but the challenge is worth it: Cummings's notion of the literary opens up exciting possibilities for configuring the Reformation as a culture of writing.

Fischlin and Fortier, eds., *Royal Subjects: Essays on the Writings of James VI and I*, collects six essays that contextualize James VI/I's poetry and also includes five essays each on 'Prose, Politics, and Society' and on 'Writing and Religion' respectively. The premise of the collection is that 'monarchic writing … is a neglected literary genre' (p. 40). Peter Herman's '"Best of poets, best of kings": King James VI and the Scene of Monarchic Verse' (pp. 961–103), repeats a great deal of the material found in a previously published essay reviewed in *YWES* (82[2003] 432). The new material on Mary Stuart is too slight to justify the thesis that 'monarchic verse [thus] constituted a recognized subgenre in the early modern period' (p. 70). The next three essays locate James's poetry within the coterie culture of the Scottish court and the 'Castalian band'. In '"The fountain and very being of truth": James VI, Poetic Invention, and National Identity' (pp. 104–23), Carolyn Ives and David J. Parkinson suggest that James's contradictory self-fashionings as king and poet, formed during his adolescence, are reinforced by water images in his poetry, especially images of fountains. Originary and derivative, source and vessel, fixed and masculine but also unstable and feminine, these images influenced Scottish culture and its gendering of power, poetry, and the body. Morna R. Fleming, in 'The *Amatoria* of James VI: Loving by the *Reulis*' (pp. 124–48), shows that the poems of *Amatoria* follow the suggestions in James's *Short Treatise Containing Reulis and Cautelis To Be Observed and Eschewed in Scottis Poesie*. Scottish traditions of versification and persona are used to rewrite Petrarchan conventions, creating a 'new Scots authorized verse' (p. 126). Sarah M. Dunigan's 'Discovering Desire in the *Amatoria* of James VI' (pp. 149–81) claims that the gender of sexual authority oscillates in James's sonnet series and that the 'antifeminism' of 'Satire' should be read as a coterie performance. Simon Wortham argues, in '"Pairt of my taill is yet untolde": James VI and I, *The Phoenix*, and the Royal Gift' (pp. 182–204) that James's 'self-referential and absolute style', as Goldberg put it, is reflected in the king's attitude to gift-giving but also in his gifts of words, in the prefaces of his works and in *The Phoenix*, which eventually return to him. Finally, Curtis Perry, '"If proclamations will not serve": The Late Manuscript Poetry of James I and the Culture of Libel' (pp. 205–32), suggests that James's use of manuscript poetry to quell libels about Buckingham, Charles's wedding plans, and royal favouritism, which were circulating in news books and manuscript miscellanies, inadvertently backfired since, in using the methods of the libellers to counter the libels, he shows his lack of control over them. Perry's reading of 'Off Jacke and Tom' within the context of Jonson's royalist pastoralism, the Spenserians' nostalgic, anti-courtly nationalism, and the growing problem of libel against the state is especially compelling.

Chapters from books on miscellaneous topics are also resolutely historicist, as scholars continue to examine the way in which the material conditions of book production and political ideology inform the writing of poetry. Andrew Lacy's 'Elegies and Commemorative Verse in Honour of Charles the Martyr, 1649–60' (in Peacey, ed., *The Regicides and the Execution of Charles I*, pp. 225–46), explores how poetry commemorating Charles's death contributed to the cult of 'Charles the martyr' and helped create the literary identity of royalism. One of nine essays on Ben Jonson reviewed this year also examines the early modern elegy. In Jonson's 'On My First Son' and 'Eupheme' W. Scott Howard finds evidence of a modern sense of historicity in Jonson's use of writing as consolation. At the same time, Howard's '"Mine own breaking": Resistance, Gender, and Temporality in Seventeenth-Century English Elegies and Jonson's "Eupheme"' (pp. 215–30) engages the gendering of grief, the theme of Vaught, ed., *Grief and Gender, 700–1700*. Grief is the subject of Ernest B. Gilman's 'Plague Writing, 1603: Jonson's "On My First Sonne"' (in Berley, ed., *Reading the Renaissance: Ideas and Idioms from Shakespeare to Milton*, pp. 153–75). Gilman discusses the poem in the context of plague and disease discourses of the period, finding the poem's power in the combination of the speaker's Roman composure and the guilt he feels for surviving the plague and outliving his son.

Jonson is often prominent in studies of the early modern book trade, and this year is no exception. Jonson's observations about the material culture of book production were, almost without exception, anticipated by Martial, according to Joseph Loewenstein's 'Martial, Jonson and the Assertion of Plagiarism' (in Sharpe and Zwicker, eds., *Reading, Society and Politics in Early Modern England*, pp. 275–94). Another essay on the book trade, Kathryn Perry's '"I do it onely for the Printers sake": Commercial Imperatives and Epigrams in the Early Seventeenth Century' (*EnterText* 3[2003] 204–26), examines how animal imagery is used to market collections of epigrams by William Goddard and Henry Parrot and to construct readerships for a genre that was saved from literary disrespect by Jonson. In 'Marketing the Gift: Jonson, Multiple Patronage, and Strategic Exchange' (*Parergon* 20:ii[2003] 135–59), Alison V. Scott argues that Jonson exploits the coexistence of market and gift economies as well as his standing as both a professional writer and a classical author in his dedications of works to multiple patrons, hoping to initiate competition among them for his material benefit.

Three other essays scrutinize details of Jonson's biography. In 'Catholicism, Religion, and Ben Jonson' (*Cithara* 42:ii[2003] 25–34), Richard Harp provides a sketch of how Catholicism influenced his work from 1598 to 1610, but also later in his life when he praised Catholics, Catholic sympathizers, and devotional figures such as the Virgin Mary. The essay doesn't explain in detail why Jonson couldn't praise the same figures and still remain a member of the Church of England. Gabriel Heaton and James Knowles's '"Entertainment Perfect": Ben Jonson and Corporate Hospitality' (*RES* 54[2003] 587–600) examines three songs found in the Cecil papers at Hatfield House. They were written by Jonson for an 'ostentatious display of corporate hospitality' (p. 594) put on by the Merchant Taylors' Company in 1607 for the King, Prince Henry, and others. The attribution sheds light on Jonson's participation in civic rituals early in his career and on the complex patronage relationship between the emergent author, the court, and commercial interests. 'Robert Sidney, "Mr. Johnson", and the Education of William Sidney at Penshurst' (*N&Q* 50[2003] 430–7), by Michael G. Brennan and Noel J. Kinnamon, identifies the poet as the 'Mr. Johnson' mentioned by Robert Sidney in a letter of 25 July 1611, in which he praises his son's tutor at Penshurst. The authors claim that the identification has implications for the dating of some of Jonson's poems, especially 'To Penshurst', which appears to have been written in late 1611 while Jonson resided at the Sidney estate.

The last two essays on Jonson to be reviewed are bibliographical. 'The Final Stages of Printing Ben Jonson's *Works*, 1640–1' (*PBSA* 97[2003] 57–68), by Eugene Giddens, considers the printing history of the third volume of Jonson's *Works*, arguing that *The Sad Shepherd* and *Discoveries* were printed, to a great extent, in 1640 before the legal dispute that interrupted their production, not hastily printed in 1641 as the Simpsons claimed, following W.W. Greg's lead. Martin Butler's 'The Riddle of Jonson's Chronology Revisited' (*Library* 4[2003] 49–63), the most substantial essay of this group, rejects W.W. Greg's thesis that the riddles of Jonson's chronology are part of a 'predictable pattern' based on the poet's use of calendrical dating until around 1620 and legal dating afterward. There is too much evidence of Jonson's inconsistent dating for this explanation to work. Jonson's inconsistency also works against the view of him as an author exerting superhuman control over his texts and as an 'anally retentive personality given to an almost pathological orderliness' (p. 61).

Henry Vaughan is the other author from this period to have several essays devoted to his life and works. In '"A deep but dazzling darkness": Writing Poetry in Extremity' (*Scintilla* 7[2003] 53–61), Myra Schneider narrates how writing poetry was therapeutic in her battle with cancer, and draws parallels with the life and work of Vaughan, who wrote his greatest poetry during times of extremity. According to John Powell Ward, in 'Darkness and Light: Poetry, Religion and the Environment' (*Scintilla* 7[2003] 73–86), our new technological environment calls for new metaphors of darkness and light entwining, also found in Vaughan's poetry. Donald Dickson's 'The Identity of Rebecca Archer Vaughan' (*Scintilla* 7[2003] 129–42) identifies Rebecca Vaughan, wife of Thomas Vaughan, the poet's brother, as the eleventh child of Dr Timothy Archer (1597–1672), rector of Meppershall, Bedfordshire. Dickson shows that Rebecca Vaughan played an important role in alchemical discoveries attributed in the past only to her husband, and that she enjoyed a close, companionate marriage with him. Holly Faith Nelson argues, in 'Gender and Politics in the Writings of Henry Vaughan' (*Scintilla* 7[2003] 99–115), that Henry Vaughan redefines masculinity and femininity as he responds to the masculinist assumptions underlying the civil war. He begins by identifying himself with his father, father-figures like Donne and Jonson, and male communities like the 'Cavaliers', but as the war continued he was forced to interrogate these models of militarism and stoicism and incorporate aspects of femininity—the Holy Spirit, Nature, and the English Church—into his sense of masculinity, especially in *Silex Scintillans*. According to Nelson, while Vaughan's 'spiritual vision' remains primarily masculine, it is feminine enough not to be threatened by maternal power and, therefore, should be applauded for attempting to overcome 'an oppressive masculine nation-state'.

Three essays on little-known works round out this year's offerings. In 'William Morrell's *New England* [1625]: An Invitation To A New Plantation' (*Renfor* 6[2003]), Joanna Moody notes Morrell's delight in the natural paradise of America but also his call for planters to be missionaries in order to convert Native Americans. Joshua Fisher's '"He is turned a ballad-maker": Broadside Appropriations in Early Modern England' (*EMLS* 9[2003]) explores the use of ballads by Richard Corbett and John Suckling to criticize Puritanism. In an essay that goes against the grain of prevailing historicisms, Donald M. Friedman argues, in 'A Caroline Fancy: Carew on Representation' (*JDJ* 21[2003] 151–82) that 'A Fancy' is 'a poem about the writing of a poem about writing' (p. 151) which reveals Carew's radical scepticism about 'the power of signs to communicate' (p. 156).

2. Milton

One prominent trend in the essays for review this year is the contextualization of Milton's epic against the new science of the Restoration period, but we start with the discourses of economics, philosophy and radical religion. Blair Hoxby, *Mammon's Music: Literature and Economics in the Age of Milton*, has provided what seems at first a counter-intuitive approach to Milton, positioning his texts against the commercial revolution of the seventeenth century. His courage in undertaking this task is commendable and the results thoroughly justify his ways. His basic point is that the new economic discourse and methods bring new moral problems for authors and social commentators, and moreover change the language which they have at their disposal. The interdependence of the state and the economy is the richest vein to be tapped in his discussion of Milton's position, but his discussion on the meaning of trade and the importance of labour ranges widely, involving the Hartlib circle, John Denham, John Dryden, Sir William Petty and Bernard Mandeville. The discussion starts with Milton's *Maske* and its engagement with the new economic order, but the majority of Hoxby's text relates to the Restoration moment and the decades that followed. He wishes to argue that Milton had a sophisticated understanding of economic thought and, further, that he understood the logic of economic reasoning. In so doing, Hoxby traces a growing resistance within Milton's late texts to the reality of labouring for a hostile regime rather than the ideal, still extant in the epic, that the liberty of the individual might be promoted through the trading of commodities and ideas. Particularly thought-provoking is Hoxby's work on *Samson Agonistes* as an oppositional discourse on labour which should be read against the Restoration imperative of production and of rebuilding after the Great Fire. He suggests that Milton's Philistine theatre may relate to the new, imposing design for the Royal Exchange, rebuilt as a priority after the Great Fire in order to cement the joint commercial programme of the Stuart Crown and the City of London.

Joshua Scodel, *Excess and the Mean in Early Modern English Literature*, is an exemplary piece of criticism, deeply erudite and subtle in its close readings of numerous early modern texts and genres. At its heart lies the ancient ideal of the virtuous mean, as it was understood and transformed in the early modern period, although parallels are also drawn and connections made with present-day cultural and ethical debates. Milton receives due coverage throughout Scodel's work, but two sections have a specific Miltonic focus. The early works *L'Allegro* and *Il Penseroso* are discussed with reference to Spenser and the development of an English georgic interest in the theme of temperance. A further chapter is dedicated to *Paradise Lost*, '*Paradise Lost*, Pleasurable Restraint, and the Mean of Self-Respect' (pp. 255–84). This is a delightful discourse on the theme of self-restraint and the virtue of self-respect within the epic, including a particularly rich critical reading of the phrase 'modest pride' (*PL* IV.310). Scodel concludes his exploration of the epic by noting that the domestic ideology promoted in England during the late seventeenth and the eighteenth centuries was deeply indebted to Milton's presentation of our first parents. Nicholas McDowell, *The English Radical Imagination: Culture, Religion, and Revolution, 1630–1660*, recognizes that an elite cultural background lies behind many of the central radical writers of the mid-seventeenth century. His lucid and scholarly monograph focuses on figures from the Leveller movement, Ranter writers, and those involved in Quakerism and other sects, and he aims to show how in many instances a humanist education was turned to satiric use by those involved in revolutionary reform. This provides a far more nuanced contemporary context for Milton's radicalism than has previously been available. The tension apparent between humanism and radical Puritanism within Milton's works can now be seen in a wider and more discerning critical context, and McDowell's 'Epilogue: Milton and the Radical Imagination' (pp. 183–92) provides an excellent comparison of Milton's residual ideal of humanist study resulting in political and religious liberty with the more disillusioned view of the efficacy of such an education taken by contemporaries such as John Rogers, Richard Overton, Abiezer Coppe, or Samuel Fisher.

Neil Forsyth's monograph, *The Satanic Epic*, deserves to be singled out for praise. This is a disarmingly polished and engaging presentation on Milton's use of the Satanic tradition in *Paradise Lost*. Forsyth intends to return the devil to his rightful place in the epic, that is centre stage. He explains in a compelling fashion how Satan is intended to be the focus of our attention, not least because humanity needs him in order to be saved. That may seem a contradictory argument, but the necessity of the Devil for human salvation is for Forsyth a mainstay of the epic's theodicy and narration. The subversive thrill of such a contention would in itself produce an attentive audience, but Forsyth is also an accomplished close reader of Milton's poetry and this monograph is rich in insight and balanced analysis. It is bound to become a favourite of students and academics alike, although perhaps unsurprisingly it does lose some of its pace in its final two chapters when the discussion moves to the last two (Satan-free) books of the poem.

There are two other monographs on Milton for review this year. David Gay, *The Endless Kingdom: Milton's Scriptural Society*, takes Milton's late poetry to be the site for a debate over biblical proof-texts. Gay shows how numerous sermons and pamphlets used biblical references to confirm the restoration of the monarchy as an act of divine providence. Milton's late poetry, he argues, controverts such orthodoxy and instead represents the Bible as a radical and oppositional authority, countermanding any contemporary secular attempts to control its meaning. The book of Proverbs, Ecclesiastes, and the Gospels all feature prominently in Gay's explication of Milton's typological strategies, which, he finds, culminate in the reading presented and performed by the messianic figure of Jesus in *Paradise Regained*. Kristin A. Pruitt, *Gender and the Power of Relationship: 'United as one individual Soul' in Paradise Lost*, combines gender studies and theology in its exploration of the full implications of the marriage metaphor in *Paradise Lost*. Pruitt's work is clear and sensitive, alive to the dynamic and redemptive powers of the human relationship within the epic and to the appropriateness of the marriage metaphor to an exploration both of choice and of the nature of divine love within the epic. This is a discursive argument, moving seamlessly from the delights of Edenic conversation to a consideration of the doctrine of the Atonement as a further means of discovering at*one*ness with God. It has much to recommend it, although some additional consideration of the divorce tracts would have been welcome.

Marion Wynne-Davies, *Sidney to Milton, 1580–1660*, is a new student guide to the literature of the early modern period. Unfortunately, it gives little coverage to Milton, offering only a page or so on *Lycidas*, and mentioning the sonnets and prose works only in passing. Space is necessarily at a premium in a guide such as this, and Wynne-Davies has done well to find room to introduce a number of women writers but, given what else is available on the market, few Miltonists will wish to recommend a guide which mentions *Areopagitica* only in its chronology.

A collection of essays concentrating on Milton's engagement with eschatological ideas was published this year: Cummins, ed., *Milton and the Ends of Time*. There is much to be admired in the scholarship of the individual essays here. Juliet Cummins's introduction, '"Those thoughts that wander through Eternity"' (pp. 1–9) offers a brief overview of the volume, while Barbara K. Lewalski, 'Milton and the Millennium' (pp. 13–28), takes a long view of Milton's work. At different political moments Milton's arguments for the timing of the millennium may shift, but Lewalski contends that the idea of the millennium remains bedrock, a constant belief that necessitates prompt reformation in all aspects of civic and personal life. Lewalski calls on a large number of Milton's texts, beginning with the *Nativity Ode*, and including *De Doctrina Christiana*, to explicate her point that the process of liberation and reformation will both precede and be the means to bring about the millennium. Sarah Hutton, 'Mede, Milton, and More: Christ's College Millenarians' (pp. 29–41), finds a general cultural interest in apocalypticism within seventeenth-century England, but is interested particularly in how such patterns of thought respond to specific historical events, for example the Restoration. She notes the collegiate allegiance of the biblical scholar Joseph Mede, and positions both John Milton and the younger Neoplatonist Henry More as two near-contemporary students at Christ's College Cambridge who can both confidently be presumed to have been aware of Mede and his highly influential work, *Clavis Apocalyptica*. The figure of old Damaetas in *Lycidas* may be a reference to the college tutor but, as Hutton notes, it is the other pupil, Henry More, who ultimately helps to publish a Restoration edition of Mede's collected works in 1664. Despite this connection, Hutton finds more divergence from Mede than might be expected in Henry More's own position and contrasts this with the possible debt to Mede found in

Milton's texts, particularly *De Doctrina Christiana* and *Paradise Lost*, with regard to the sequence for the last days. It is Hutton's contention that the Restoration experience leads Henry More away from Mede and into a more muted and quietist expression of millenarian expectations.

Stella P. Revard's contribution to the volume, 'Milton and Millenarianism: From the Nativity Ode to *Paradise Regained*' (pp. 42–81), is a sustained analysis of millenarian hopes across the mid-seventeenth century. Revard first provides an overview on the theologians and commentators, such as John Napier, Thomas Brightman and David Pareus, whose work most influenced English Puritan thought. Then, having established the background, she is ready to tackle the divisions between radicals and others during the revolutionary period of the 1640s, and to place Milton's works within that excited, radical, context. She identifies millenarianism in the 1640s as an issue 'that both defined and separated Puritans, Presbyterians, and the orthodox oldliners of the Church of England' (p. 47), and explains how a threat to conservative values developed with the rise of the Fifth Monarchists and the dissolution of monarchy. After the Restoration, millenarianism indicates dissent, and Revard sees Milton becoming circumspect in his expression of ideas which he had previously promoted openly. However, she argues persuasively that his views had not changed and that there are pervasive indications and hints of a millenarian approach to be found in both *Paradise Lost* and *Paradise Regained*. Her reading of both these poems is, as one would expect, outstandingly fluent and insightful. Malabika Sarkar, 'Astronomical Signs in *Paradise Lost*: Milton, Ophiucus, and the Millennial Debate' (pp. 82–95), provides us with a fascinating addition to our understanding of the use of astronomy within *Paradise Lost*. Sarkar notes the general excitement and exaggerated prophecies surrounding the phenomenon of a comet. Comets can be negative, but the appearance of a new star in the constellation Ophiucus in 1604 was a landmark discovery, quickly interpreted as a celestial sign indicating the immanence of the millennium. However, Sarkar argues, Milton wishes to critique those who misread the signs so spectacularly. Within the epic, he introduces comets in both Book II and Book IV as signs of false hope, directly associated with Satan. William B. Hunter, 'The Millennial Moment: Milton vs. "Milton"' (pp. 96–105), takes the line that Milton is not the author of *De Doctrina Christiana*. He bases this in the main on the fact that the treatise shows no interest in the millennium or in the politics of millenarianism. Such an omission contrasts with Milton's prose writing from the 1640s and 1650s—although Hunter is also challenging the critical assumption of millenarian views before *Lycidas* or in the late poems. In particular, Hunter finds insufficient evidence for interpreting a number of passages in the epic, such as the War in Heaven, as millenarian. The next essay, John T. Shawcross, 'Confusion: The Apocalypse, the Millennium' (pp. 106–19), takes issue with with Hunter. To Shawcross's mind, there is no call for a theological thesis to lay emphasis upon the millennium, given the limited role that the idea plays in the scriptural account of the apocalypse. However, Shawcross does find that *De Doctrina Christiana* has expressed a belief that Christ will reign for a thousand years, and he seeks to clarify the distinction between the millennium and the wider concept of apocalypse. Shawcross maintains that Milton's views remained consistent, although political realities meant that the immanence of the millennium was no longer proclaimed after 1657.

Beverley Sherry, 'John Martin's Apocalyptic Illustrations to *Paradise Lost*' (pp. 123–43), gives a lovely reading of how the Romantic artist John Martin's work responds creatively to Milton's epic. She concentrates on the nuances of light and dark in the mezzotint series produced by Martin, and shows how the illustrator's manipulation of both light and space produce a sympathetic and insightful vision of Miltonic themes of creativity and apocalypse. She wishes to suggest that there is a creative sequence within Martin's work, and a developing response to the themes of the epic poem, and her main point of connection is the artistic revelation of light from darkness, which aptly fits both the illustrator's technique and the impetus of Milton's poetry. This is a sensitive and suggestive essay and it would be rewarding to expand its cross-comparison further. Catherine Gimelli Martin is also interested in a comparative approach in her essay, 'The Enclosed Garden and the Apocalypse: Immanent Versus Transcendent Time in Milton and Marvell' (pp. 144–68). Here she discovers and expands upon the distinct approaches to time and providence in Milton and Marvell in impressive and provocative ways. Juliet Cummins, 'Matter and Apocalyptic Transformations in *Paradise Lost*' (pp. 169–83), considers how Milton's monist philosophy might incorporate descriptions of the apocalypse. Cummins argues for a material continuity between the extant fallen world and the expected apocalyptic universe. Matter is to be refined and sublimated but not annihilated. This makes the fate of the damned all the more intriguing but, for Cummins, the continuity between pre- and post-apocalyptic states of being continues to justify God's ways, meaning that it is humanity's free will and our freely made choices that will determine the individual's fate at the end of time. Claude N. Stulting, Jr., '"New Heav'ns, new Earth": Apocalypse and the Loss of Sacramentality in the Postlapsarian Books of *Paradise Lost*' (pp. 184–201), is a beautifully argued counter-thesis. He finds discontinuities between humanity's prelapsarian and apocalyptic conditions in *Paradise Lost* and detects a failure in the poetic application of Milton's monist theories. For Stulting the prelapsarian world was a sacramental vision of nature which cannot be regained in the poem. Instead, there is a residual emphasis on destruction and disjunction. In conclusion, Stulting suggests that, because the redemption of the entire creation is not a clear possibility in *Paradise Lost*, the success of Milton's entire monist theodicy is in jeopardy.

Ken Simpson, 'The Apocalypse in *Paradise Regained*' (pp. 202–23), reads the brief epic as a critique of the English Reformation and the failure to separate church and state. He equates the wilderness motif with the nonconformist Restoration experience in ways which chime with the essays in *Milton Studies* 42[2002]. Simpson sees Milton as retaining his active political stance, though at a remove from the actions of Fifth Monarchists. His late poetry shows the reader how to bring Christ's kingdom to earth and encourages us to recognize his spiritual rule. Simpson also touches on the importance to Milton of the comet simile as false portent (see also the essay by Sarkar in this volume). Karen L. Edwards, 'Inspiration and Melancholy in *Samson Agonistes*' (pp. 224–40), gives a subtle and fresh reading of the flawed hero in this late poem. She challenges us to consider Samson as a melancholic, and suggests that the projection of such dark instability is a daring representational strategy on Milton's part. Edward is clear to state that Samson is the type not of Christ but of those born afterwards, i.e. those awaiting apocalypse, and in this well-judged and detailed reading of *Samson Agonistes* as a Restoration poem she shows how melancholia might relate to enthusiasm, a controversial and double-edged figuration at the time, interpretable either as self-delusion or inspiration depending upon which side of the ideological divide one stands on. David Loewenstein, 'Afterword: "The time is come"' (pp. 241–9), sums up the findings of the volume, confident that radical millenarianism is not rejected by the later Milton. He identifies *Paradise Lost* Books III, VI and XII as important contexts for engaging with the Miltonic idea of millenarianism, but concentrates on *Poems 1671* as intentionally double-edged, offering alternative responses to this debate—one spectacular, violent and catastrophic, the other a millenarian vision.

Essays in general collections with a Miltonic theme include Margaret Kean, 'Escaping the Lazar-House: States of Damnation in *Paradise Lost*' and Ann Torday Gulden, 'Milton's Eve and Wisdom: the 'Dinner-Party' Scene in *Paradise Lost*' (both in Lausund and Olsen, eds, *Self-Fashioning and Metamorphosis in Early Modern English Literature*, pp. 187–208, 209–19). Kean looks at Milton's consideration of transgression after the Fall through an examination of two decisive passages, namely the transformation of the devils to snakes in Book X and the representation of the lazar-house in Book XI, arguing that both passages are underpinned by an episode in Lucan's *De Bello Civili*. Gulden illuminates the intimate knowledge of the natural order shown by Eve in Eden, arguing that her creative domestic skills should be an education to Adam. Anthony Low, 'The Fall into Subjectivity: Milton's "Paradise Within" and "Abyss of Fears and Horrors"' (in Berley, ed., *Reading the Renaissance*, pp. 205–32), is (like Mary Beth Long below) interested in both transgression and Milton's portrayal of isolation. He discusses the multivalence of the term 'alien' in *Paradise Lost* and links Milton's trope of vertiginous falling to the idea of a solipsistic void of the self. The central argument is that the Fall can be read in terms of self-consciousness, with Milton's narrative encapsulating the idea that, without external assistance, the individual cannot escape the abyss of subjectivity, or, in other words, that without God's grace man will remain locked in despair. Low expands from these points to a more general discussion of the isolation and vulnerability experienced by Milton himself in the Restoration period. Michael Davies is investigating the trope of exile in the 1660s. In his essay, '"Heaven's Fugitives": Exile and Nonconformity in the Restoration' (in Ouditt, ed., *Displaced Persons: Conditions of Exile in European Culture*, pp. 33–53), Davies finds a developed rhetoric of exile to be employed by dissenters and royalists alike. He makes good use of his research on the Baptist Henry Adis, and, having shown that the concept of exile is paradigmatic in this period, he goes on to suggest that *Paradise Lost* offers its readers a model for discriminating between godly and ungodly responses to exile. Ruth Gilbert, 'The Masculine Matrix: Male Births and the Scientific Imagination in Early-Modern England' (in Jowitt and Watt, eds., *The Arts of Seventeenth-Century Science: Representations of the Natural World in European and North American Culture*, pp. 160–76), has a slightly different contemporary context in mind. She discusses Satan as an archetypal new scientific hero testing the boundaries of knowledge and power. Gilbert places this diabolic figuration against a thoughtful re-evaluation of how views of masculine creativity underpin the developing field of early modern science, and she shows how complex the representation of gender and conception is in both Francis Bacon's *Temporis Partus Masculus* and William Harvey's *Exercitationes de generatione animalium*.

We now turn to this year's journals. No new issue of *Milton Studies* has become available for review, so we move directly to *Milton Quarterly* 37[2003]. John K. Hale kicks off with a short manifesto on why a fresh translation of *De Doctrina Christiana* is needed in 'On Translating the *De Doctrina Christiana*' (*MiltonQ* 37:i[2003] 1–10). Although this is a short piece, it is significant, with Hale not only identifying for us some of the deep interpretative cruces embedded in this theological discourse but also asking for responses from other Milton scholars to the task he has in hand. Next, Henry Weinfield, '"With serpent error wand'ring found thir way": Milton's Counterplot Revisited' (*MiltonQ* 37[2003] 11–20), asks again whether the ubiquitous presence of error in the reading process of *Paradise Lost* does not necessarily constitute a counterplot which undermines the received theology and doctrine of the Fall. Ryan J. Stark, 'Cold Styles: On Milton's Critiques of Frigid Rhetoric in *Paradise Lost*' (*MiltonQ* 37[2003] 21–30), offers what turns out to be a delightful excursion through the frozen depths of Hell, as imagined by both Dante and Milton, as he discusses the metaphorical conjunction of cold climes with the frigidity of the heart. He argues that in *Paradise Lost* Milton has identified Satan with the type of arrogance that breeds contempt and which brings a chill to the air, whereas the Creator and divine creativity within the cosmos are associated with heat. This Stark takes to be a matter of both style and ontology, and he suggests a further link to contemporary empiricism as Satan can be identified with cold, detached, quantification. David Reid, 'Milton's Royalism' (*MiltonQ* 37[2003] 31–40), contributes a rich and nuanced discussion of Milton's continued appropriation of, and iconoclastic negotiation with, royalist imagery in *Paradise Lost*. Reid's focus is the description of sunset in Book IV of the epic, where he discovers continued royalist imaginings. This he reads against earlier Caroline aesthetics of the 1630s and 1640s, with particular reference to Milton's own usage in *Comus*. Angelica Duran, 'The Sexual Mathematics of *Paradise Lost*' (*MiltonQ* 37[2003] 55–76), returns us without prejudice to Eve's question about the stars in Book IV of *Paradise Lost*. This is a commendable essay, both for its scientific discussion and for its re-evaluation of gender hierarchies within the epic. Duran promotes *Paradise Lost* as a scientific poem, best read in its Restoration context and against contemporary Royal Society publications. She finds numerous balances within the epic—not least the comparative stance of scientific enquiry over astronomy in Books IV and VIII—but is most interested in re-addressing Eve's position. Duran suggests that, instead of thinking about the question on the night sky as tagged on to Eve's 'sonnet', we regroup and assess Eve's speech in the round. The harmonies inherent in the eighteen-line speech then become apparent, and it is Duran's contention that Eve's construction of the cosmos might profitably be considered against the contemporary development in mathematics leading to calculus. Beverley Sherry, 'A "Paradise Within" Can Never Be "Happier Farr": Reconsidering the Archangel Michael's Consolation in *Paradise Lost*' (*MiltonQ* 37[2003] 77–91), sensibly remarks that Michael's voice is not necessarily to be presumed authorial (or divine) in the promotion of the internalized concept of paradise above all other options. Taking the multi-vocal nature of *Paradise Lost* seriously, Sherry assesses the relative merits of the three available paradisal options, namely Eden, the paradise within and the eternal paradise. Eric LeMay, "To the highth of this great argument": The Plummet of Postmodern Undergraduates from Milton's Early Modern Epic and its Prevention' (*MiltonQ* 37[2003] 92–9), is aware of the degenerate nature of man, and here he offers some practical advice on how to get the current generation of students to read Milton attentively. Mary Beth Long, 'Contextualizing Eve's and Milton's Solitudes in Book 9 of *Paradise Lost*' (*MiltonQ* 37[2003] 100–15), considers Miltonic solitude to be an intriguing but surprisingly under-discussed topic. She offers certain comparisons between Milton and other contemporary writers, such as Katherine Philips, Andrew Marvell and Abraham Cowley, but is most interested in pursuing her view that Adam and Eve have been given differing conceptions of solitude within *Paradise Lost*. She argues that, based on their first experiences, solitude is for Adam equivalent to loneliness, and is a condition in need of remedy; Eve, on the other hand, has retained a more positive memory of her initial solitude. This distinction underpins their disagreement over working patterns at the start of Book IX, but from a wider perspective, throughout Milton's texts, the solitary condition is tied to an inevitable temptation. Daniel Fried, 'Milton and Empiricist Semiotics' (*MiltonQ* 37[2003] 117–38), is an ambitious piece. Fried first shows how Milton's prose locates him with respect to empiricist philosophy and semiotics, tracing a tradition through from Francis Bacon to Thomas Hobbes, John Wilkins and John Locke. He then moves on to argue that, in *Paradise Lost*, Satan's actions highlight both the insights and the dangers of semiotic theory. David A. Harper, '"Perhaps more than enough": The Dangers of Mate-Idolatry in Milton's *Samson Agonistes*' (*MiltonQ* 37[2003] 139–51), focuses on Dalila's idol status and Samson's weakness, and compares these positions with those constructed around the central female figures in *Comus* and *Paradise Lost*. Elisabeth Liebert, 'Rendering "More Equal": Eve's Changing Discourse in *Paradise Lost*' (*MiltonQ* 37[2003] 152–65), discovers changes occurring in Eve's discourse as she becomes aware of the influence of her views on Adam. Liebert reads this movement within the text as pertinent to the question of patriarchal authority and Eve's role within the text. George F. Butler, 'Boccaccio and Milton's "Manlike" Eve: The *Geneologia Deorum Libri* and *Paradise Lost*' (*MiltonQ* 37[2003] 166–71), points out the influence of Boccaccio's text on English Renaissance writers, and the specific allusions in a number of Milton texts, before suggesting that the description of Eve's birth in Book VIII of the epic may be indebted to Boccaccio's description of Pandora. There are two short notes at the close of this issue. Gregory Machacek, 'Right Accent' (*MiltonQ* 37[2003] 172–3), remarks not only on the need for a good memory in *Paradise Lost* but also for correct phrasing, suggesting that Eve's downfall may in part be due to her poor pronunciation. Finally, John K. Hale,

'Breakfast with Milton' (*MiltonQ* 37[2003] 174–5), gives us suggestions for re-creating contemporary early modern fare.

The final issue of *Milton Quarterly* focuses on the Spenserian sexual politics at work in Milton's *A Maske*. Both the critical history and the current essays are clearly introduced by Andrew Escobedo and Beth Quitslund in their introduction, 'Sage and Serious: Milton's Chaste Original' (*MiltonQ* 37[2003] 179–83). William Shullenberger, 'Girl, Interrupted: Spenserian Bondage and Release in Milton's Ludlow *Maske*' (*MiltonQ* 37[2003] 184–204), distinguishes between the chastity of the Lady which is not sufficient to free her from her chair and the free-flowing charity of the river goddess, Sabrina. The essay connects the imprisonment of Milton's Lady with the erotic torment of Amoret in Spenser's *Faerie Queene* and proposes Spenser's complex portrayal of sexual desire as a strong influence upon the young Milton. James W. Broaddus, '"Gums of glutinous heat" in Milton's *Maske* and Spenser's *Faerie Queene*' (*MiltonQ* 37[2003] 205–14), interprets the word 'gum' in terms of Galenic physiology. He is much taken by the connection between Britomart's feelings of sexual frustration in the Garden of Adonis and the Lady's implied erotic arousal which is cooled only through the intercession of Sabrina. Catherine Gimelli Martin, 'The Non-Puritan Ethics, Metaphysics, and Aesthetics of Milton's Spenserian Masque' (*MiltonQ* 37[2003] 215–44), argues strongly that Milton's *Maske* is an Arminian rather than a Puritan text, involving a denial of irresistible grace. She uncovers both Spenserian and Baconian sources for the masque, and argues that the Lady parallels Guyon from the *Faerie Queene* because she too must actively refute temptation and defeat 'Mammon'.

The most significant of the essays on Milton appearing in other journals this year is Barbara K. Lewalski, 'Milton and Idolatry' (*SEL* 43[2003] 213–32). This is a fine description and analysis of Milton's attitude towards idolatry, emphasizing his reverence for human beings as the *imago dei* and therefore the priority given throughout his works to human liberation, first as an internal process and then as a political agenda. Lewalski's discussion ranges widely through Milton's poetry and prose. She clearly defines idolatry as the act of worshipping either a false god or a representation of the true God, and positions Milton's lifelong work as 'a relentless effort to eradicate that disposition [external and/or internal] in his readers' (p. 215). She also makes it clear that alongside the abstract concept of idolatry come specific civic and religious targets depending on the historical moment, for example Laudian ceremony, Stuart monarchy, Catholic acts of worship in the 1670s. The clarity of the discussion here means that this essay will be finding its way onto reading lists very soon. Also pertinent from this volume are essays by Mary C. Fenton, Peter C. Herman and David Reid. Mary C. Fenton, 'Hope, Land Ownership, and Milton's "Paradise Within"' (*SEL* 43[2003] 151–80), knows the changing land laws in mid-seventeenth-century England to be of significance when reading Milton's political tracts, so that for example the question of individual freedom is closely tied to the contemporary debates over land rights in a text such as *Tenure of Kings and Magistrates*. In this essay, Fenton takes the discussion forward to *Paradise Lost*, where she finds a deep divide between notions of faithful stewardship and Satanic acquisition. There is obviously a wider thesis here (and one which would link neatly with

Hoxby's work reviewed above), but Fenton concentrates on what she terms Milton's ontology of hope in the epic: Satan grounds his hopes in material possession, but the converse is the spiritual hope that is held to be achievable through faithful stewardship. Peter C Herman, '*Paradise Lost*, the Miltonic "Or," and the Poetics of Incertitude' (*SEL* 43[2003] 181–211), shows how the epic is composed out of a series of suspended choices, both at the level of syntactical choices and in structural terms relating to the grand cosmic plan. Herman suggests that Milton 'inscribes' (p. 201) incertitude at the heart of *Paradise Lost* and includes a good number of close readings to prove his point. David Reid, on the other hand, is intrigued by the interpretative choices made by one reader of Milton's epic. In 'Thomson's Poetry of Reverie and Milton' (*SEL* 43[2003] 667–82), Reid shows how the later poet selectively adapted and developed ideas from the moral and theological frame of *Paradise Lost*. The creative process in Milton's epic is twofold: a divorcing action and a diffusing process. Reid argues that Thomson is influenced by the latter idea, and that he has developed this understanding of the incorporation of the deity into the creative process not only for his descriptions of nature but as his method of conveying the idea of a divine power behind the appearance of things. This is a careful and insightful piece which does justice to both Milton and Thomson.

The following essays also add to our understanding of the reception of Milton's texts by later poets. William Kolbrener, 'The Jacobite Milton: Strategies of Literary Appropriation and Historiography' (*Clio* 32:ii[2003] 153–76), is intrigued and amused by the ways in which certain Jacobite writers at the start of the eighteenth century approved Milton's War in Heaven as a conservative model. Looking at works by Mary Astell, Charles Leslie and William Baron, as well as some early eighteenth-century anonymous tracts, Kolbrener shows how effective it could be to impose this inherited model on contemporary dissent, allowing the dissenting position to be rejected as diabolic and rebellious and by extension showing Jacobite loyalties to be endorsed by Heaven. In appropriating Milton in this way, Jacobite polemicists might be said to have hoisted him with his own petard, but it is unclear whether they were necessarily aware of what they were doing. However, the work of Elijah Fenton from this same period is more consciously witty, and that is the subject of Juan Christian Pellicer, '*Cerealia* [1706]: Elijah Fenton's Burlesque of Milton and Spenser in Critique of John Philips' (*N&Q* 50[2003] 197–201). Pellicer confirms the attribution of *Cerealia*, a 207-line burlesque poem written in Miltonic blank verse in praise of English beer, to Elijah Fenton. He argues that Fenton would have known far in advance that John Philips was working on a Miltonic poem lauding cider (*Cyder* [1708]) and suggests that this pre-emptive strike is intended as both a parody of Philips and an independent critique and burlesque of the Miltonic style. Rodney Stenning Edgecombe, 'Milton, Gray, and West's 'Monody on the Death of Queen Caroline' (*RES* 54[2003] 386–98), traces the impact of Richard West's *Monody on the Death of Queen Caroline* on Gray's 'Elegy Written in a Country Courtyard', revealing this text by West to be an important step between Milton's elegy, *Lycidas*, and Gray's famous poem. Edgecombe argues successfully that West has taken inspiration from *Lycidas* in securing his ambition to produce a real alternative to the standard Augustan elegy. Both the rhyme scheme and the emotional depth in West's poem make it worthy of a larger audience and suggest that Gray may well have been influenced by this work by his close friend. Adriana Craciun, 'Romantic Satanism and the Rise of Nineteenth-Century Women's Poetry' (*NLH* 34[2003] 699–721), finds women writers to be intrigued by the figuration of Satan and explores this interest in the works of Charlotte Smith, Mary Robinson, Mary Wollstonecraft and Mary Ann Browne, amongst others.

Two essays on Milton appear in *ELR* 33[2003]. William Shullenberger makes a second appearance in this year's entry, again writing on the *Maske*. In 'Tragedy in Translation: The Lady's Echo Song' (*ELR* 33[2003] 403–23) Shullenberger pays close attention to the echo motif within the *Maske*, and he suggests that it becomes a method of translating Ovidian myths based on female subjection into a new form of poetic and ethical responsibility. In the Lady's song itself, Echo gives place to the abstract (feminized) virtues of Faith, Hope and Charity, and Shullenberger reads this as a paradigm for a general act of selective reiteration within Milton's text which translates and thereby reforms its original pretexts. As Shullenberger notes, 'translate' is a key term within the *Maske* referring not only to a linguistic transaction but also to the possibility of apotheosis. This makes the embedded references to the myths of Philomela and Oedipus in the *Maske* all the more resonant, and encourages Shullenberger to suggest that classical myths of lovelornness or self-absorption are actively 'translated' by the Lady into a principle of self-transcendence. Marshall Grossman, 'The Rhetoric of Feminine Priority and the Ethics of Form in *Paradise Lost*' (*ELR* 33[2003] 424–43), is interested in how authors and characters may come to know themselves. He links Milton's narrative of how our first parents come to terms with their own identity in part through their understanding of difference to the ways in which the writer of a text is then transformed into an 'author' by his encounter with that text as its first reader.

The following notes were also published this year. George F. Butler, 'Adamantine Chains in Statius and Milton's Prolusion I' (*N&Q* 50[2003] 177–80), is aware that the phrase *catenis adamantinis* 'adamantine chains' from Prolusion I recurs later in Milton's prose tract, *Doctrine and Discipline of Divorce* and twice in Book I of *Paradise Lost*. The second occurrence of the phrase in the epic is closely linked to the figure of Briareus. Butler thinks it unlikely that Thomas May's translation of Lucan's *De Bello Civili* in 1627 could have influenced Milton's Prolusion I [1628?]. So, instead, he suggests Statius' *Thebaid* as a likely source. As the Briareus connection is also made in Statius, Butler's contention is that this is the correct source text for all of Milton's uses of this phrase. William Poole, 'Milton and Calamy' (*N&Q* 50[2003] 180–3), finds a link between a phrase in Milton's *Areopagitica*, 'the reforming of Reformation itself', and a construction in Edmund Calamy's *Englands Looking-Glasse* [1641]. Poole uses this seemingly minor connection to review the biographical links between the two figures. In so doing, he suggests a possible ironic context for Milton's possible allusion. Given that Calamy had been appointed a licenser of theological books in 1643, it is certainly possible that he would be a target in Milton's attack on pre-publication censorship. Philip Cardinale, 'Satan as Aeneas: An Allusion to Virgil in *Paradise Lost*' (*N&Q* 50[2003] 183), aligns *Paradise Lost* I. 125–6, where Satan is vaunting aloud, 'but racked with deep despair', with the moment early in the *Aeneid* where Aeneas rallies his shipwrecked troops, despite being himself in deep distress (*Aeneid* I. 208–9). Finally, we have Paul Hammond, 'Allusions to Milton, Marvell, and Dryden in an Unpublished Cambridge Prologue' (*N&Q* 50[2003] 193–4). Hammond describes an unpublished miscellany of later seventeenth-century verse, relating mainly to affairs of state, Princeton University Library Taylor Restoration MS 5, focusing his attention on a short prologue seemingly written for performance in Cambridge by a company of London actors. This he publishes in full. It contains references to a sequence of Cambridge poets, including Spenser, Milton, and Marvell, as well as a somewhat catty allusion to Dryden. Hammond is dating the poem to around 1687/8 and therefore wishes to suggest that this previously unknown work allows us to gain a new insight into Whig views (with Cambridge connections) on the eve of the Glorious Revolution. Hammond's essay means we end on a high, but it should be noted that a number of works with 2003 publication dates have either not yet reached this reviewer or have arrived too late for inclusion in the main body of the review. These include Evans, ed. *John Milton: Twentieth Century Perspectives*, a five-volume set of reprinted essays proffering a cross-section of critical essays from the twentieth century; a monograph by Sharon Achinstein, *Literature and Dissent in Milton's England*; and a collection of new essays edited by Mark R. Kelley, Michael Lieb, and John T. Shawcross, *Milton and the Grounds of Contention*. Bibliographical details are given below, and it is hoped to include full reviews of these titles in next year's section.

3. Donne

Publications on Donne this year illuminate his aesthetics, professional life, religious and political sensibility, and literary influence. Cousins and Grace, eds., *Donne and the Resources of Kind*, present nine brief but stimulating essays on Donne's absorption, subversion and transformation of inherited genres. In his introductory essay, 'Donne and the Resources of Kind', Cousins claims that Donne established a transgressive poetic genealogy for himself; the intersection of Ovidian elegy, medieval love literature, Marlovian epyllion and Morean utopian fiction is examined in several of Donne's lyrics to substantiate this claim. Earl Miner, in 'Donne, Decorum, and Truth: Grounds of His Literary Art', reflects on the rewarding tension between decorum and truth in the Donnean lyric, exposing Donne's tendency to violate generic decency to reveal fresh truths that accord with experience if not convention. In 'Mannerist Donne: Showing Art in the Descriptive Verse Epistles and the Elegies', L.E. Semler reads Donne's *Poems* [1633] through the lens of Renaissance rhetoric, poetics and visual art theories, concluding that the descriptive verse epistles and some elegies conform to the *difficultà: facilità* formula characteristic of Italian mannerist art, which celebrated effortless virtuosity and merged affective expressiveness and intense artifice. Heather Dubrow's reprinted essay, 'Donne's Elegies and the Ugly Beauty Tradition', investigates Donne's idiosyncratic application of the ugly beauty tradition in his verse; though obsessed in his ugly beauty poems with mutability, disease, decay and death, themes typical of the genre, Donne diverges from the tradition by deflecting his focus from the ugly beauty to the subject of male rivalry.

In the same volume, 'To "build in sonnets pretty roomes?" Donne and the Renaissance Love Lyric', N.H. Keeble explores Donne's subversion of the lyrical mode in his *Songs and Sonets*, whose metrically jarring and indecorously colloquial poems are neither melodious nor Petrarchan. Finding in the *Songs and Sonets* features of the epigram, epistle, elegy and satire, Keeble concludes that these poems are less lyrical than dramatic, closer to the dramatic monologues of Browning than the subjective lyrics of the Romantics. In 'The Holy Sonnets', F.W. Brownlow suggests that 'La Corona' and the Holy Sonnets are socio-political exercises by which Donne hopes to penetrate courtly circles. Donne's turn to religious verse, he concludes, reflects a modification of court tastes brought on by the accession of James I, and exhibits theatrical self-presentation rather than religious devotion. Marea Mitchell, in 'Gender, Genre, and the Idea of John Donne in the *Anniversaries*', finds in Donne's elegies both a masculine and a metatextual sensibility; the poems, she claims, dissect the female body to foreground the practice of writing poetry and to fashion John Donne the poet. The single essay in the volume on Donne's prose, Eugene Hill's 'Donne the Snake-Handler', examines the intersection of form and substance in Donne's sermon of 25 January 1628 [1629] on Acts 28:6, the day of the Feast of Paul's Conversion. Hill claims that Donne relies upon a serpentine homiletic structure, a Virgilian and biblical voice, and the snake emblem, to interrogate Stuart absolutism. Damian Grace's concluding essay, 'Recent Genre Criticism of the Works of John Donne', briefly examines the application of an appropriately elastic genre criticism to the works of Donne in the 1980s and 1990s.

Four journal articles this year also situate Donne's work within the wider literary tradition. In 'Plato in John Donne's "The Good Morrow"' (*ANQ* 16:i[2003] 20–1), Christopher S. Nassaar argues that Donne creatively reinterprets the Platonic cave allegory in 'The Good Morrow' to absorb his lovers (paradoxically) in the World of Ideas, or, at the very least, to expose them to 'the Platonic Idea of sexual love' (p. 21). In a suggestive, if not always persuasive, comparison of two near contemporaries, Magdalena Kay, in 'The Metaphysical Sonnets of John Donne and Mikolaj Sep Szarzynski: A Comparison' (*EMLS* 9:ii[2003]), identifies similarities in the biographies, syntactical strategies, metaphysical discourse and theological concerns of Donne and Sep; she ultimately contrasts, however, Donne's melodramatic, rhetorical poetics and theological optimism with Sep's laconic poetics and inclination to spiritual despair. Paula Loscocco makes a significant contribution to the debate on the influence of Donne on the Matchless Orinda in 'Inventing the English Sappho: Katherine Philips's Donnean Poetry' (*JEGP* 102[2003] 59–87). Challenging the notion that Philips's Donnean poems stress her royalism, conservatism, lesbianism, and concern with self-display, Loscocco argues that a comprehensive review of her 'Donnean verses discovers a largely (if not entirely) untroubled poetics that alternates purposefully between mysterious privacy and radical expressiveness' (p. 61).

Barbara Ryerse ponders the legacy of Donne in the Victorian period in 'Browning's *Christmas-Eve and Easter Day*: Formal Verse Satire and the Donnean Influence' (*VR* 29:i[2003] 49–69). Ryerse asserts that Browning's double poem *Christmas-Eve and Easter-Day* [1850] was modelled on Donne's good-humoured, intellectually inquisitive *Satyres* on the Christian faith; despite theological and cultural differences in their satirical poems, Donne's *Satyres* provided a structural pattern, and spiritual resource for Browning's expression of religious uncertainty. Finally, in '*Wit*, Pride and the Resurrection: Margaret Edson's Play and John Donne's Poetry' (*Renascence* 55:ii[2003] 163–74), John D. Sykes suggests that the Augustinian theology of 'Hymn to God, My God in My Sicknesse', 'Batter my heart', and 'If poysonous mineralls', provides an essential context for Edson's play, which he reads as a dramatic expression of 'anonymous Christianity' (p. 172). In a sensitive and perceptive reading of the play, Sykes reads *Wit* as a study in grace and redemption, whose optimism is based on the ability of the arrogant protagonist (a Donne scholar) to follow 'the Augustinian trajectory' described in Donne's devotional poems (p. 167).

In recent years, a renewed interest in Donne's life has resulted in a proliferation of works on his private and public identities. *John Donne's Professional Lives*, a noteworthy twelve-chapter volume edited and introduced by David Colclough, participates in this discussion, exploring the range of professional positions assumed by Donne, and the professional discourses upon which he relied. In 'Donne and the Words of the Law', the late Jeremy Maule, to whom the volume is dedicated, argues that Donne's years at the Inns of Court produced a lifelong fascination with the English law, which influenced not merely his vocabulary but the very structure of his thought; Maule demonstrates the validity of this claim in a reading of the twelfth Holy Sonnet as a 'legal pleading' (p. 26). In 'Mr Secretary Donne: The Years with Sir Thomas Egerton', Louis A. Knafla investigates the significance of Donne's position as secretary of the Lord Keeper, situating Donne in 'the legal, political, and religious institutions and culture' of Stuart England (p. 38). In his striking article 'John Donne the Controversialist: The Poet as Political Thinker', Johann P. Sommerville posits that, in the *Pseudo-Martyr*, an altruistic Donne frequently alludes to Catholic source texts to convince his Catholic readers to take the Jacobean oath of allegiance, thereby avoiding unnecessary false martyrdom. Donne's counsel in the *Pseudo-Martyr*, Sommerville observes, echoes that of the Catholic advocates of the oath (William Barret, William Warmington, John Barclay and Thomas Preston). In 'The Profession of Friendship in Donne's Amatory Verse Letters', David Cunningham considers Donne's complex construction of self in his poetic letters of compliment to aristocratic female patrons, which profess devotion in the hopes of furthering professional ambition. In 'Donne and Sir Edward Hoby: Evidence for an Unrecorded Collaboration', Alison Shell argues that Donne either influenced or collaborated with the polemicist Sir Edward Hoby in the composition of his anti-Catholic pamphlets (particularly the dialogic *A curry-combe for a coxe-combe*), which were attacked by the Jesuit John Floyd and by Theophilus Higgons, a Catholic convert. While Shell warns against attributing Hoby's works to Donne, she provides a compelling account of the collaborative nature of authorship in early modern coteries.

In part 2 of *John Donne's Professional Life*, three essays address Donne's religious professions in his role as a preacher at church and at court. In 'Labels, Controversy, and the Language of Inclusion in Donne's Sermons', Jeanne Shami admonishes scholars who attempt to pigeonhole Donne, thereby distorting his religious and political beliefs and ignoring his calculated rejection of divisive vocabularies. The fundamental principles inscribed in the sermons, Shami claims, suggest that Donne redefines controversial terms in such a way as to produce a circumspect, inclusive 'rhetoric of moderation' that fosters 'public tranquility' (p. 145). Mary Morrissey notes, in 'John Donne as a Conventional Paul's Cross Preacher' that Donne modifies the homiletic genre in his Paul's Cross sermons to balance political commentary and moral instruction. Donne did not disingenuously endorse or ruthlessly disparage Jacobean policy in these political sermons, Morrissey insists; rather, he used discretion and decorum to highlight the subject's duty. In 'Donne as Preacher at Court: Precarious "Inthronization"', Peter E. McCullough avers that Donne, appointed chaplain-in-ordinary to James I in February 1615, preached his first court sermon at Greenwich on 30 April 1615, not on 29 April 1616 as earlier speculated. After detailing the preaching schedule and monthly duties of royal chaplains, McCullough argues that Donne's court attendance in the early years of Charles I's reign indicates that he was then favoured by that king; Donne 'offered Charles an exquisitely rare combination of both the churchmanship in which he had been raised … and the more liberal theology he was increasingly willing to endorse' (p. 193), though he fell out of favour in 1627 when his sermons no longer conformed to the Laudian ecclesiastical ideal.

James Cannon, in the third and final section of *John Donne's Professional Lives*, continues to address the politics of Donne's sermons in 'Reverent Donne: The Double Quickening of Lincoln's Inn Chapel'. Cannon finds that Donne's Encaenia sermon of 1623 participates in the debate within the Church of England on church sacrality and concludes that Donne 'unambiguously stated his belief that churches were sacred buildings, made so by the ceremony of consecration as well as the presence of believers' (p. 208). In 'Essaying the Body: Donne, Affliction, and Medicine', Stephen Pender contends that Donne's profound knowledge of medicine and his personal experience of bodily affliction led him to employ a medical semiotics which enabled him 'to confirm embodied experience as one key to knowledge of the soul' (p. 220). The volume concludes with Jessica Martin's 'Izaak Walton and the "Re-Inanimation" of Dr Donne', a brief study in Walton's homiletic clerical biography of Donne. Martin maintains that Walton not only echoes Donnean language in his biography (thereby resurrecting Donne's voice), but also spotlights the few revivifying images in *Deaths Dvell* (rather than the dominant imagery of dissolution) to style Donne an exemplary clerical subject.

The ongoing fascination with Donne's religious leanings has produced some worthwhile studies this year on liturgy, theology and ecclesiology in his works. Jeanne Shami has written a first-rate study of sermon literature in the late Jacobean period in *John Donne and Conformity in Crisis in the Late Jacobean Pulpit*, a distinguished work of literary and historical criticism. Though Shami concentrates on those sermons of Donne written between 1620 and 1625, the volume traces with impressive detail and insight the homiletic discourse of numerous Jacobean preachers, discourse which participated in, and often strove to alter, the course of history. Shami draws attention to the early modern sermon as 'a medium of instruction, debate, propaganda, and polemic' (p. 2); despite James I's *Directions for Preachers*, late Jacobean sermons, Shami proves, responded to, and offered (often unwelcome) advice, on domestic and foreign policy. The anti-Catholic tenor of many of the sermons of the period, sermons frequently dedicated to the subject of suffering and lamentation, reflected widespread anxiety about the king's policies on recusants and his questionable relationship with Catholic nations. In a rhetorical tour de force, Shami presents Donne as the voice of discretion, inclusion, civility and charity in this period of intense crisis, controversy and censorship. Though at times favoured by James I and Charles I, Donne is no 'apologist for absolutism', no mouthpiece of the Jacobean state, says Shami (p. 77). Donne, she insists, is a 'willing conformist' whose sense of vocation compelled him to endorse in his topical sermons an inclusive, flexible, moderate English Church, a middle way ignored by many divisive preachers of the late Jacobean period (p. 75).

John Donne and the Protestant Reformation: New Perspectives, meticulously edited by Mary Arshagouni Papazian, also makes a valuable contribution to current debates on Donne's theological inclinations and identity as an agent of the Stuart Church. The thirteen essays in this cohesive and rigorous scholarly volume challenge past visions of a crypto-Catholic or Arminian Donne, and serve as a primer on Donne's dedication to the Reformed religion. In 'Polemist or Pastor? Donne and Moderate Calvinist Conformity', Daniel W. Doerksen maintains that, despite the doctrinal spectrum in the Stuart Church and notwithstanding Donne's 'points of difference with Calvin' on predestination (p. 21), Donne does not stray sufficiently from the Thirty-Nine Articles to be labelled an Arminian, Laudian, or Catholic sympathizer. However, though a moderate Calvinist conformist, Donne is less interested in theological polemic than in the spiritual well-being of those he pastors. Jeanne Shami agrees that Donne is a moderate Calvinist, exploring his reliance on the discourses of consensus, civility and compromise in his role as prolocutor for the clergy of the province of Canterbury (February 1626). In '"Speaking Openly and Speaking First": John Donne, the Synod of Dort, and the Early Stuart Church', Shami finds that in negotiating ideas in the lower house of clergy and in presenting them to the upper house, Donne, with sobriety and decorum, denounces internal religious divisions and strives for consensus, upholding the doctrines held by the 'temperate' English delegates to the Synod of Dort.

Elena Levy-Navarro and Annette Deschner, in 'Breaking Down the Walls That Divide: Anti-Polemicism in the *Devotions Upon Emergent Occasions*' and 'Reforming Baptism: John Donne and Continental Irenicism' respectively, share Shami's vision of Donne as an agent of reconciliation. Levy-Navarro contends that the anti-polemical Donne is committed to the Reformed faith; however, Donne rejects in the *Devotions* both a rigid dogmatic Calvinism and an avant-garde conformism, promoting instead an inclusive 'broadly defined Reformation faith' (p. 275) which fosters 'a more devout and … quiescent church membership' (p. 274). Deschner situates Donne in the European irenic movement, reading his poetry and prose alongside the works of Grotius, Luther, Zwingli and Franciscus Junius the Elder. Though she considers Donne's support of 'the irenic concept of fundamental articles' in general (p. 295), she attends in particular to his irenic treatment of baptism. Gale H. Carrithers and James D. Hardy, in '"Not upon a Lecture, but a Sermon": Devotional Dynamics of the Donnean Fisher of Men', also conceive of Donne as a moderate Protestant who rejects extreme Calvinism and Catholic legalism in favour of the 'mysteries of love and transcendence' (p. 352), demonstrating as much in their analysis of liturgy, ecclesiology and salvific theology in Donne's double sermon on Matthew 4:18–20.

Three essays in *John Donne and the Protestant Reformation* focus on the theological and literary influences on Donne's works. In 'The Augustinian Donne: How a "Second S. Augustine"?' Papazian insists that Donne espouses Augustine's late anti-Pelagian predestinarian theology as recorded in the *Confessions*, placing him 'squarely in the theological mainstream of the Church of England' (p. 69). In a stimulating essay on Donne's association with European theologians, Jeffrey Johnson, in 'John Donne and Paolo Sarpi: Rendering the Council of Trent', claims that both Donne and Sarpi were dissatisfied with the Council of Trent, condemned papal self-interest, demanded non-sectarian religious reform, and lamented the failure of conciliarism, though Donne did not share Sarpi's particular, localized, private ecclesiology nor his pessimism about human reason. Raymond-Jean Frontain, in 'Donne's Protestant *Paradiso*: The Johannine Vision of the *Second Anniversary*', explores 'Donne's experimentation with Dantean self-presentation' (p. 113). Though both poets were influenced by the apocalyptic prophecy of Revelation, Frontain claims that in the *Second Anniversary* Donne rejects the Dantean visionary prophet—'the passive witness to a divine drama' (p. 113)—in favour of an active Reformed Christian meditator, and supplants the Virgin Mary with Elizabeth Drury, 'a Protestant Everywoman' (p. 123).

Continuing in the same volume, Paul R. Sellin, in a lengthy historical essay, grounded in first-rate archival research, '"Souldiers of one Army": John Donne and the Army of the States General as an International Protestant Crossroads, 1595–1625', discusses Donne's associations with the chief British officers in The Netherlands during and after his military service in the Low Countries. In 'Unmeete Contraryes: The Reformed Subject and the Triangulation of Religious Desire in Donne's *Anniversaries* and *Holy Sonnets*', Catherine Gimelli Martin reads the 'aesthetic instability' and spiritual anxiety of Donne's religious verse through the filter of René Girard's notions of the double bind and religious triangulation (p. 193). Chanita Goodblatt, in 'From "Tav" to the Cross: John Donne's Protestant Exegesis and Polemics', identifies Donne as a third order Hebraist well versed in Jewish literature in translation. Goodblatt suggests that, while Donne relied upon Jewish, Catholic, and Protestant exegesis in his interpretation of the Hebrew Bible, he simultaneously voiced anti-Catholic and anti-Jewish opinions in an attempt to assert a decisively Protestant hermeneutic.

Finally, two essays in *John Donne and the Protestant Reformation* address the link between rhetoric and Protestantism in Donne's works: Brent Nelson's '*Pathopoeia* and the Protestant Form of Donne's *Devotions Upon Emergent Occasions*' and Maria Salenius's 'True Purification: Donne's Art of Rhetoric in Two Candlemas Sermons'. Nelson asserts that Donne employs pathopoeic devices in his sermons and devotions to arouse the emotions of, and generate spiritual growth in, his audience. Relying heavily on hypotyposis, Donne's *Devotions* engender in readers a particularly Protestant experience of fall and redemption, preparing them for spiritual surrender to God. Salenius reads Donne's Candlemas sermons through the filter of Thomas Wilson's *Art of Rhetoric*. Relying upon a Protestant rhetoric, Donne redefines, according to Salenius, 'medieval and Catholic themes' by shifting 'from a medieval framework to a more linguistically oriented view emphasized by the Reformation' (pp. 315, 323).

Volume 21[2002] of the *John Donne Journal: Studies in the Age of Donne* offers four compelling articles on Donne's devotional writings, furthering our sense of the complex ways in which theology, ecclesiology and poetics intersect in his works. Judith H. Anderson, in 'Donne's Tropic Awareness: Metaphor, Metonymy, and *Devotions Upon Emergent Occasions*' (*JDJ* 21[2002] 11–34), situates Donne's use of figurative language in Station XII of the *Devotions* within the broader tropologies of Luther, Zwingli and Calvin. In their diptych 'A Man Is to Himself a Dioclesian: Donne's Rectified Litany' (*JDJ* 21[2002] 35–49) and 'Is There a Future for Donne's "Litany"?' (*JDJ* 21[2002] 51–88), Annabel Patterson and Dayton Haskin respectively seek to revive scholarly interest in 'A Litany'. Patterson maintains that 'A Litany' reveals more about Donne's post-conversion theology than do *La Corona* and the Holy Sonnets, that it is his boldest adaptation of a devotional genre, and that it is nothing less than 'one of the most carefully planned, most intellectual exercises in the history of early modern devotional poetry' (p. 35). Though influenced primarily by the Catholic Litany of the Saints rather than the Reformed Litany of Cranmer, 'A Litany' records Donne's incessant search for a compromise between the Catholic and Reformed religion. In order to provide a culturally and theologically sensitive analysis of 'A Litany', Haskin identifies past misguided readings of the poem, particularly those which interpret it solely in autobiographical terms. He offers a rousing reading of 'A Litany' as a work intent on inspiring reconciliation between the Catholic and Reformed traditions and on promoting an expansive human solidarity. Finally, P.G. Stanwood, in 'The Vision of God in the Sonnets of John Donne and George Herbert' (*JDJ* 21[2002] 89–100), eloquently meditates on the differing spiritualities of Herbert and Donne, highlighting their dissimilar treatment of vocation, the Atonement, prayer and repentance in selected sonnets.

Two other journal articles published this year also seek to situate Donne in the theological spectrum of the early modern English Church. In 'Godly Fear, Sanctification, and Calvinist Theology in the Sermons and "Holy Sonnets" of John Donne' (*SP* 100 [2003] 71–86), Paul Cefalu refutes Richard Strier's reading of Donne's devotional poems as Arminian. Donne does not doubt his salvation in the Holy Sonnets, Cefalu claims, nor does he voice 'a servile fear of unrepentant death and damnation' (p. 73). Donne is merely apprehensive of 'backsliding from his election' (p. 86), which Calvinists deem a reverential or 'filial fear' necessary for regeneration. Jeanne Shami, in '"Trying to Walk on Logs in Water," John Donne, Religion, and the Critical Tradition' (*Ren&R* 25:iv[2001] 81–98), focuses on Donne as the embodiment of ecclesiastical conflicts and his work as the site of intersecting discourses on the national religion of Stuart England. In considering his enigmatic religious beliefs, Shami pays particular attention to the influence of Donne's Catholic heritage on his sacramental theology, an influence which appears to conflict with the anti-Catholicism expressed in several of his works.

Franz Wöhrer, in *Phänomenologie mystischer Erfahrung in der religiösen Lyrik Englands im 17. Jahrhundert*, also seeks to define the spiritual sensibility of Donne, as well as that of other early modern devotional poets. He revisits the subject of Donne's mysticism, reading his works through the filters of the psychology of consciousness, Christian mysticism, Western and Eastern religious thought, and recent studies on mysticism (p. 439). He concludes that the speaker of the Holy Sonnets fails to move beyond the stage of purification, and thus finds himself unable to 'achieve inner peace and loving communion with God' (p. 440).

Although more attention has been paid this year to Donne's devotional poetry and prose, two other journal articles were published on his secular poetry: Raymond-Jean Frontain's 'Donne, Coryate, and the Sesqui-superlative' (*EIRC* 29[2003] 211–24) and Manfred Malzahn's 'The Flea, the Sun, and the Critic: A Communicational Approach to John Donne's Poetry' (*Symbolism* 3[2003] 53–70). In an instructive article on Donne's mock-commendatory poem 'Upon Mr. Thomas Coryats Crudities', Frontain argues that the frustration of Donne's professional ambitions caused him to compose this caustic poetic attack on Coryate's superlative, hyperbolic, Latinate travel narrative. Malzahn applies the communicational theory of Paul Watzlawick et al., as set forth in *The Pragmatics of Human Communication*, to 'The Flea' and 'The Sun Rising'. 'The Flea' does not so much document the lover's attempt to seduce a woman, Malzahn claims, as it details the pathological communication that follows the botched seduction; the schizophrenic voice in 'The Sun Rising' is also seen to produce a dysfunctional interaction. Note should also be made of the reprinting of Nicholas Barker's 1973 essay 'Donne's "Letter to the Lady Carey and Mrs. Essex Riche"' in Barker's *Form and Meaning in the History of the Book: Selected Essays*, an essay that includes a photo-facsimile of the manuscript of Donne's verse epistle.

The works reviewed above reflect the current trend of curbing the uncritical application of theory to Donnean texts. Such is the intent of Berley, ed., *Reading the Renaissance*, dedicated to Edward W. Tayler, which contain four essays on Donne. In 'Reading Donne: Old and New His- and Her-storicisms', Stanley Stewart vigorously attacks new historicist, or 'New-Empsonian', misreadings of Donne's writings (p. 132). Though Stewart's dismissal of contemporary theory as an analytical tool is, at times, reactionary, he rightly exposes the danger of naively applying a postmodern hermeneutic to Renaissance literature. The late Louis L. Martz, in 'Donne's *Anniversaries*: The Powers of the Soul', offers a new reading of the progress of the soul in the *Anniversaries.* In light of Tayler's *Donne's Idea of a Woman: Structure and Meaning in 'The Anniversaries'*, Martz revises his earlier claim that the progress of Elizabeth Drury's spirit follows the order of the Augustinian three powers of the soul as set forth in the Jesuit *Exercises*: memory, will and understanding. Martz now asserts that Donne positions understanding before memory and will in the soul's pilgrimage, a 'Protestant variation upon the Jesuit method' (p. 83). In 'The *Donna Angelicata* of Donne's "Aire and Angels"', Albert C. Labriola performs a witty and original reading of 'Aire and Angels' by drawing attention to the complementary influence of Thomistic, Neoplatonic and Paracelsian thought on the poem. Labriola claims that the angelic object of the speaker's desire, in a process akin to heavenly influxion, is transformed into a bodily *Donna Angelicata* when she scents herself with the essence of this plant. The potent effect of the fragrant woman in 'Aire and Angels', Labriola suggests, is analogous to that of Raphael on Adam in *Paradise Lost*. In 'Male Lesbian Voices: Ronsard, Tyard and Donne Play Sappho', Anne Lake Prescott compares Donne's 'lesbian' voice in 'Sapho to Philænis' to those of the French elegists Pierre de Ronsard and Pontus de Tyard. Prescott maintains that Donne shares with Ronsard an 'imaginative empathy' with lesbian desire, and outdoes Ronsard and Tyard in resisting the impulse to define such desire in masculine courtly terms or to render one of the lovers masculine (p. 121). Though she finds moments of misogyny and cynicism in these pseudo-lesbian poems, Prescott insists that their authors make an effort to transcend a masculine, heterosexual subjectivity.

Finally, an attractive anthology of selections from the poetry and prose of John Donne, compiled, edited and introduced by John Moses, the current dean of St Paul's, was published this year: *One Equal Light: An Anthology of the Writings of John Donne*. The volume includes three sizeable and engaging introductory essays, in which Moses sketches Donne's biography, discusses his roles as poet, propagandist, preacher and dean of St Paul's, and addresses the significance of Donne's oeuvre to modern readers. Eighty per cent of the nearly one thousand quotations cited are taken from Donne's sermons, which speak to Donne's faith, wit, rhetorical aptitude, tropic and stylistic agility, and attentiveness to daily life. The anthology, a practical and informative introduction to Donne's thoughts on the nature and habits of humanity and the divine, resembles an early modern commonplace book, inasmuch as the quotations are placed under sixteen headings and ninety-nine subheadings (ranging from 'The Human Condition' to 'Sexual Desire' and from 'The Desire to Know God' to 'An Infinite Eternity').

4. Herbert

Elizabeth Clarke, in her article 'The Character of a Non-Laudian Country Parson' (*RES* 54[2003] 479–96), examines the circumstances that delayed the first printing of *The Country Parson* until 1652, nineteen years after Herbert's death. She begins with a letter from Sir Robert Cooke (the husband of Herbert's widow) to Sir Robert Harley (a member of the counter-Laudian Committee for Religion) of June 1641 in which the former urges the latter to help get the book to press. Clarke argues that the book was too moderate in 1641 for Laudian censors, but that, ironically, by 1652 its pro-Church of England stance was a probable cause of possible censorship from the anti-royalists, and also made it useful in future decades as a pro-royalist, conformist text under the title *A Priest to the Temple*.

Like Clarke's article, Esther Gilman Richey's 'Herbert's *Temple* and the Liberty of the Subject' (*JEGP* 102:ii[2003] 244–68) locates Herbert's work within a highly specific historical context. Richey argues that Herbert's 'private' poems were an engagement in a very public church dispute, namely, the contest over private prayer between the Laudian John Cosin and the Puritans Henry Burton and William Prynne. In particular, Richey situates *The Temple* between Cosin's *Private Devotions*, which mandated set forms for private prayer, and Burton and Prynne's hostile responses. Herbert, refusing to be 'cozened', reasserts the Reformation devotional subject, who exercises choice in responding to authority, and whose freely chosen subjection provides an example that invites the warring parties into communion.

Ryan Netzley's article '"Take and Taste": Sacramental Physiology, Eucharistic Experience, and George Herbert's *The Temple*' (in Karant-Nunn, ed., *Varieties of Devotion in the Middle Ages and Renaissance*, pp. 179–206) attempts to correct previous efforts to historicize Herbert's eucharistic language. Netzley argues that, in *The Temple*'s eucharistic poems, Herbert differentiates between 'tasting' and 'eating', and that in this difference lies his critique of experience as a ground of the religious life. In particular, Christ invites the speaker to 'taste' because in so doing one has communion without consumption, or taking possession of that which is offered. Netzley critiques Strier, Guibbory, and Schoenfeldt, whose analyses assume that 'one can possess an experience of union', the very possessing under suspicion in *The Temple*.

In a more general contextualization, Francis M. Malpezzi reads Herbert's work within the Church year. 'Herbert's "Grace"' (*Expl* 62:i[2003] 7–9) argues that the poem, which immediately follows 'Whitsunday', refers to the week of Whit Embertide, the ember days (of prayer and fasting) that follow the celebration of Whitsunday. The poem's gardening metaphor, its hortatory tone, and its form all relate it to the particular actions of ember days and to the season of summer.

Lastly, Philipp Wolf, in 'Why Themes Matter: Literary Knowledge and the Thematic Example of Money' (in Louwerse, ed., *Thematics: Interdisciplinary Studies*, pp. 341–52), argues for the existence of 'theme' as the meaning across texts that makes communication possible and allows the identification of particularly 'literary' meaning. As an example of this he examines the theme of money in some poems of Donne and Herbert, discovering there a critique of money that is unavailable within the 'science' of economics.

5. Marvell

The year 2003 may prove a turning-point in the fortunes of Marvell's reputation, much as 1776 seems to have been. Two major new editions have laid the foundations of Marvell criticism for the foreseeable future, and the circumstances are propitious for the poet's increasing importance as a central figure in seventeenth-century studies for the next quarter-century. First, the Yale edition of the prose works in two volumes, produced by a team led by Annabel Patterson, who also supplies the general introduction. Volume 1 (eds Martin Dzelzainis and Patterson), includes *The Rehearsal Transpros'd*, edited by Dzelzainis, and *The Rehearsal Transpros'd: The Second Part* edited by Dzelzainis and Patterson; volume 2 (ed. Patterson, von Maltzahn and Keeble) has *Mr Smirke* and its appended *Short Historical Essay,* edited by Patterson, *An Account of the Growth of Popery*, edited by Nicholas von Maltzahn and *Remarks Upon a Late*

Disingenuous Discourse, edited by N.H. Keeble. In addition, appendices to the first volume include Marvell's first prose work, a translation of a Latin tract about the Swedish cause in 1658; excerpts from Marvell's translation of Suetonius, recently attributed by Patterson (unfortunately the arguments for Marvell's authorship are not included in this volume, and one has to consult *MLQ* 61[2000] 463–80 to see the justice of this attribution); and a satirical mock-speech by the king that may be Marvell's. The edition also bears traces of the input of the late Jeremy Maule, who was to have edited *Mr Smirke*. The volume does not include the letters, for which one still has to turn to volume 2 of Margoliouth's *Poems and Letters of Andrew Marvell*, revised by Pierre Legouis and E.E. Duncan-Jones (Oxford [1971]), though von Maltzahn's ongoing work suggests that a new edition of the correspondence would be welcome. The typography deserves commendation for its clarity and readability, despite a few typos. The edition has a full textual apparatus, but its strengths lie in contextual introductions and expert annotation (the first time any of the prose works has been properly annotated) which are excellent. One can learn a great deal about Restoration politics and religion by reading Marvell's dry interventions. The acuity with which the editors supply nuanced political contexts, and unpick the merits of Marvell's prose and argumentation, reflects the quality of Marvell criticism in recent years as much as it promises future scholarship.

The poetry has also been revisited in *The Poems of Andrew Marvell*, edited by Nigel Smith in the Longman Annotated English Poets series. This contains all the poems of known authorship, plus the more probable texts with uncertain attributions. Once again, though it has a full textual apparatus, the strength of this edition lies in the copious annotation and insightful contextual headnotes. Marvell is a poet of echoes, and Smith's notes supply many suggestions of associations with English, foreign-language and classical poetry and numerous political tracts and newsbooks. Smith embeds Marvell's writing in a dense political culture, the languages of which Marvell sometimes purposefully echoes. This is the first edition of a seventeenth-century poet that undertakes this pamphlet contextualization, in recognition of the powerful critical historicism now regnant in Milton and Marvell studies and elsewhere. It is a tremendous achievement, and often one feels that one is reading the poems anew.

New texts can be found in Nicholas von Maltzahn, 'Andrew Marvell and the Lord Wharton' (*SC* 18[2003] 252–65), which produces three new Marvell documents: two letters to Phillip, fourth Baron Wharton, one from 1668 reporting proceedings in the lower house and another from 1674 discussing marriage negotiations; plus a 1668 address to the king, drafted by Wharton and Marvell, encouraging him to use his prerogative in matters of religious comprehension. The closeness of the relationship between Marvell and Wharton (with his country houses) may contribute to the dating of Marvell's lyrics, especially 'The Garden'. Marvell seems to have been involved in marriage negotiations earlier, as Art Kavanagh shows in 'Andrew Marvell and the Duttons of Sherborne in 1657' (*N&Q* 50[2003] 183–8). This discusses the proceedings in Chancery and the Upper Bench over John Dutton's will, in which Marvell, tutor to John's son William, was a deponent. Kavanagh's new evidence sheds additional light on the relationships between the family, the poet and Cromwell, whose youngest daughter's hand was sought by the Dutton family. Another useful note is Paul Hammond, 'Allusions to Milton, Marvell, and Dryden in an Unpublished Cambridge Prologue' (*N&Q* 50[2003] 193–4), which gives the text of a Princeton University Library manuscript miscellany that mentions the three poets as products of the genius of Cambridge; the former two are commended, implying perhaps Whig sympathies.

Among the most interesting of this year's critical essays is Paul Hammond's very suggestive, though brief, 'Marvell's Pronouns' (*EinC* 53[2003] 219–34). Hammond looks closely at Marvell's pronouns, suggesting that he does not commit himself as a subject of desire in the love poems, instead defining the selves who speak in them through reflections that never really consolidate; that in the retirement poems the poet-figure seems to find a solitary existence within the communities he imagines; and that in the political poems pronouns reflect the fragmented nature of the political community. He concludes: '"I" and "we", the grammar of commitment, did not come easily to Marvell's pen'. Equally wide-ranging is Nigel Smith's 'The Boomerang Theology of Andrew Marvell' (*Ren&R* 25:iv[2001] 139–55). In a brisk excursus through a wide range of Marvell's poetry and prose (this is the only critical article this year to address the prose), Smith suggests that both are characterized by a form of (Continental) libertinism, with which Marvell interrogates religious positions. Just as his poetic form is characterized by a subtle and flexible balance of containment and liberty, his Puritan poetics place contrary religious tendencies at the formal and thematic centre of his writing, and develop his own positions through a striking articulation of others'. In '"A storm of lamentations writ": *Lachrymae Musarum* and Royalist Culture After the Civil War' (*YES* 33[2003] 273–89), John McWilliams discusses *Lachrymae Musarum* [1649], a collection of poems published to commemorate the death of Henry Lord Hastings, which reflects, and tries to reconcile, the conflict between mourning and the articulation of political partisanship. McWilliams concludes with a reading of Marvell's contribution to the volume as a commentary on the nature and role of elegy.

A historically informed approach characterizes almost all of this year's criticism, though not with even success. Alex Garganigo, in 'Mourning the Headless Body Politic: The Regicide Elegies and Marvell's "Horatian Ode"' (*Exemplaria* 15[2003] 509–50), reads a range of royalist elegiac writing from 1649, arguing that it effects a shift in emphasis from the body politic to the natural body of the king. Moving through an account of 'mourning theory', he suggests that this is a symptom of the historical moment, and that the Horatian Ode is produced out of the same moment. Marvell unsuccessfully tries to turn Cromwell into a new symbol of the body politic. The essay is full of interesting material, but confuses the theory of the body politic with that of the king's two bodies, in order to claim that republican culture intellectually failed because it was dependent on royalist culture; it is hard to see what this adds to recent historicized readings of the ode. In 'Marvell's Dialogized Nymph' (*SEL* 43[2003] 137–50), Daniel Jaeckle argues that 'The Nymph Complaining' projects not a unified speaker but a range of social languages—this phrase seems stripped of its linguistic and Pocockian associations and Jaeckle means by it biblical language, simple words, learned and new terms, literary language. The poem is a heteroglossia that suggests the limitations of the female complaint genre in an age of violence, offers a critique of the divisions of the time, and at the same time does not pass judgement but lets these allegedly different languages speak for themselves. Peggy Samuels, in '"The Picture of Little T.C. in a Prospect of Flowers": Marvell's Portrait of a Tender Conscience' (*PLL* 39[2003] 245–80), reads the poem in the context of debates between Presbyterians and Independents, especially in Norwich in 1646–7, suggesting that verbal echoes reveal that the poem is about those who, while perceiving themselves as chaste and using the language of love, would violently impose religious uniformity on others. The poem is a picture of the destructive actions of tender conscience. It is an imaginative reading, and glosses, for example, 'glancing wheels' elegantly, though the loose echoes are not always persuasive, and Marvell was probably overseas when these specific debates took place. For a Picture of Tenuous Criticism, however, we can turn to Peter R. Moore, who, in 'The Irony of Marvell's Horatian Ode' (*ES* 84:i[2003] 33–56), simplistically argues that the Horatian Ode is throughout an ironic attack on Cromwell (because others suffered deeper scars, for example). Though well informed and filled with historical detail, Moore's argument is not sensitive to context, and his gauge of the 'obviously' ironic seems precisely miscalibrated.

Books Reviewed

Achinstein, Sharon. *Literature and Dissent in Milton's England*. CUP. [2003] pp. 314. £45 ISBN 0 5218 1804 4.

Barker, Nicholas. *Form and Meaning in the History of the Book: Selected Essays*. BL. [2003] pp. xiii + 514. £50 ISBN 0 7123 4777 1.

Berley, Marc, ed. *Reading the Renaissance: Ideas and Idioms from Shakespeare to Milton*. DuquesneUP. [2003] pp. 278. $60 ISBN 0 8207 0336 2.

Colclough, David, ed. *John Donne's Professional Lives*. Brewer. [2003] pp. xiii + 272. £50 ISBN 0 8599 1775 4.

Cousins, A.D. and Damian Grace, eds. *Donne and the Resources of Kind*. FDUP. [2002] pp. 150. $35 ISBN 0 8386 3901 1.

Cummings, Brian. *The Literary Culture of the Reformation: Grammar and Grace*. OUP. [2002] pp. xviii + 470. £63 ISBN 0 1981 8735 1.

Cummins, Juliet, ed. *Milton and the Ends of Time*. CUP. [2003] pp. x + 254. £40 ISBN 0 5218 1665 3.

Dzelzainis, Martin, and Annabel Patterson, eds. *The Prose Works of Andrew Marvell*, vol. 1. YaleUP. [2003] pp. liv + 479. $45 ISBN 0 3000 9935 5.

Evans, Martin, ed. *John Milton: Twentieth Century Perspectives*, 5 vols. Routledge. [2003] £425 ISBN 0 4159 4046 X.

Fischlin, Daniel, and Mark Fortier, eds. *Royal Subjects: Essays on the Writings of James VI and I*. WSUP. [2002] pp. 543. $39.95 ISBN 0 8143 2877 6.

Forsyth, Neil,. *The Satanic Epic*. PrincetonUP. [2003] pp. x + 382. hb. £43.95 ISBN 0 6910 9996 0, pb £14.95 ISBN 0 6911 1339 4.

Gay, David,. *The Endless Kingdom: Milton's Scriptural Society*. AUP. [2002] pp. 220. £29.50 ISBN 0 8741 3777 2.

Hoxby, Blair. *Mammon's Music: Literature and Economics in the Age of Milton*. Yale. [2002] pp. xii + 320. £30 ISBN 0 3000 9378 0.

Jowitt, Claire, and Diane Watt, eds. *The Arts of Seventeenth-Century Science: Representations of the Natural World in European and North American Culture*. Ashgate. [2002] pp. xiv + 270. £47.50 ISBN 0 7546 0417 9.
Karant-Nunn, Susan C. ed. *Varieties of Devotion in the Middle Ages and Renaissance*. Brepols. [2003] pp. xv + 213. £69 ISBN 2 5035 1389 1.
Kelley, Mark R., Michael Lieb, and T. John Shawcross, eds. *Milton and the Grounds of Contention*. DuquesneUP. [2003] pp. 352. £48 ISBN 0 8207 0345 1.
Lausund, Olav, and Stein Haugom Olsen, eds. *Self-Fashioning and Metamorphosis in Early Modern English Literature*. Novus. [2003] pp. xx + 260. n.p. ISBN 8 2709 9386 7.
Loewenstein, David, and Janel Mueller, eds. *The Cambridge History of Early Modern Literature*. CUP. [2003] pp. xii + 1038. £100 ISBN 0 5216 3156 4.
Louwerse, Max, and Willie van Peer, eds. *Thematics: Interdisciplinary Studies*. Benjamins. [2002] pp. pp. x + 448. £85 ISBN 1 5881 1107 5.
McDowell, Nicholas. *The English Radical Imagination: Culture, Religion, and Revolution, 1630–1660*. OUP. [2003] pp. ix + 219. £47 ISBN 0 1992 6051 6.
Moses, John, ed. *One Equall Light: An Anthology of the Writings of John Donne*. Eerdmans. [2003] pp. xvi + 352. $28 ISBN 0 8028 2772 1.
Ouditt, Sharon, ed. *Displaced Persons: Conditions of Exile in European Culture*. Ashgate. [2002] pp. xix + 201. £49 ISBN 0 7546 0511 6.
Papazian, Mary Arshagouni, ed. *John Donne and the Protestant Reformation: New Perspectives*. WSUP. [2003] pp. viii + 385. $39.95 ISBN 0 8143 3012 6.
Patterson, Annabel, Nicholas von Maltzahn, and N.H. Keeble, eds. *The Prose Works of Andrew Marvell*. vol. 2. YaleUP. [2003] pp. xx + 493. $45 ISBN 0 3000 9936 3.
Payne, Michael, and John Hunter, eds. *Renaissance Literature: An Anthology*. Blackwell. [2003] pp. xxx + 1161. £19.99 ISBN 0 6311 9898 9.
Peacey, Jason, ed. *The Regicides and the Execution of Charles I*. Palgrave. [2001] pp. x + 294. $72 ISBN 0 3338 0259 4.
Pruitt, Kristin A. *Gender and the Power of Relationship: 'United as One Individual Soul' in Paradise Lost*. DuquesneUP. [2003] pp. xvi + 196. £48.50 ISBN 0 8207 0340 0.
Scodel, Joshua. *Excess and the Mean in Early Modern English Literature*. PrincetonUP. [2002] pp. viii + 367. £41.95 ISBN 0 6910 9028 9.
Shami, Jeanne. *John Donne and Conformity in Crisis in the Late Jacobean Pulpit*. Brewer. [2003] pp. viii + 318. £50 ISBN 0 8599 1789 4.
Sharpe, Kevin, and Steven N. Zwicker, eds. *Reading, Society and Politics in Early Modern England*. CUP. [2003] pp. ix + 363. $70 ISBN 0 5218 2434 6.
Smith, Nigel, ed. *The Poems of Andrew Marvell*. Longman. [2003] pp. xxv + 468. £50.99 ISBN 0 5820 7770 2.
Vaught, Jennifer, ed. *Grief and Gender, 700–1700*. Palgrave. [2003] pp. xiv + 310. pb £15.99 ISBN 0 3122 9381 X.
Wöhrer, Franz. *Phänomenologie mystischer Erfahrung in der religiösen Lyrik Englands im 17. Jahrhundert*. Lang. [2003] pp. 498. £45 ISBN 3 6313 8528 5.
Wynne-Davies, Marion. *Sidney to Milton, 1580–1660*. Palgrave. [2003] pp. xvi +211. hb £45 ISBN 0 3336 9618 2, pb £14.99 ISBN 0 3336 9619 0.

X

The Later Seventeenth Century

SARAH DEWAR-WATSON, LESLEY COOTE, JANE MILLING AND JAMES OGDEN

This chapter has three sections: 1. Poetry; 2. Prose; 3. Drama. Section 1 is by Sarah Dewar-Watson; section 2 is by Lesley Coote; section 3(a) is by Jane Milling; section 3(b) is by James Ogden.

1. Poetry

This has been a somewhat quieter year for Dryden criticism, following the intense activity of the tercentenary period. In '*Lachrymae Musarum* and the Metaphysical Dryden' (*RES* 54[2003] 615–38) Aaron Santesso considers the relation between Dryden's *Upon the Death of the Lord Hastings* and the volume *Lachrymae Musarum* in which it was first published. Santesso argues that Dryden's use of metaphysical imagery in the poem is consistent with, rather than at odds with, his later work. In 'The Delicate Art of Anonymity: The Case of *Absalom and Achitophel*' (*Restoration* 27:ii[2003] 41–60) Randy Robertson explores the connection between anonymity and illegitimacy which is presented in the poem, and discusses how these tropes serve aesthetic and political ends.

A full-length study by Christopher Yu, *Nothing to Admire: The Politics of Poetic Satire from Dryden to Merrill*, takes Dryden as the starting point in a historical survey of satire. Yu devotes his opening chapter, '*Satura Redux*: Dryden and the Augustan Ideal' (pp. 23–48) exclusively to Dryden. In evaluating subversive undercurrents in Dryden's use of the Augustan metaphor, Yu argues that the poet's assumption of the Virgilian persona displaces Charles as the symbolic centre of civilization. The chapter offers a close reading of *MacFlecknoe* and the other satires of the 1680s.

In '"To tune our sorrows and instruct the crowd": The Cultural Work of John Dryden's *Threnodia Augustalis*' (in Cope and Ahrens, eds., *Talking Forward, Talking Back: Critical Dialogues with the Enlightenment*, pp. 133–43), Anna Battigelli considers Dryden's self-presentation in his elegy to Charles. She pays close attention to the doctrine of the king's two bodies in relation to the poem, and argues that Dryden sets out to perform cultural work in officiating in

Year's Work in English Studies, Volume 84 (2005) © The English Association; all rights reserved. For permissions, please email: journals.permissions@oxfordjournals.org

doi: 10.1093/ywes/mai010

a quasi-priestly capacity over the transfer of the crown. In a biographical study of Dryden, David Haley asks 'Was Dryden a "Cryptopapist" in 1681?' (*SECC* 32[2003] 277–96) and poses an enquiry into the origins of Dryden's Catholic sympathies. He reconsiders the evidence that the martyrdom of Dryden's wife's cousin, William Howard, in 1680 was a crucial event in Dryden's conversion, in conjunction with the attack on the poet in Rose Alley in 1679.

Paul Hammond's 'Allusions to Milton, Marvell, and Dryden in an Unpublished Cambridge Prologue' (*N&Q* 50[2003] 193–4) focuses primarily on Dryden. Hammond provides the text of a prologue from a late seventeenth-century manuscript at Princeton University Library, which contains references to a number of poets connected with Cambridge: Spenser, Milton, Cowley and Marvell. Hammond argues that the references to Dryden are muted or ambiguous in tone, and suggests that this provides a clue to the Whig allegiances of the prologue's author at a moment of historical crisis.

One article considers Dryden's response to Jonathan Swift's early poetic efforts. In 'Dryden's "Cousin Swift" Re-Examined' (*SStud* 18[2003] 99–103), Robert M. Philmus discusses the anecdote concerning Dryden's dismissal of Swift's poetic aspirations. Philmus considers the evidence surrounding a possible meeting between the two, and concludes that if such an encounter did take place it was probably in the period 1692–4.

In an article which considers Tom D'Urfey's revisions of his work, Alan Roper's 'Recycling Political Poetry: Tom D'Urfey's *The Progress of Honesty* 1680/1739' (*SEL* 43[2003] 579–603) discusses how D'Urfey changes topical references appropriate to the Popish Plot and the Exclusion Crisis in the original version of the poem to suit the circumstances of its subsequent publication in 1738–9.

This has been a rich year for work in the area of women's writing. In 'Anne Finch's Fair Play' (*MQ* 45[2003] 74–94), Susannah B. Mintz focuses on two poems, *The Apology* and *The Circuit of Apollo*, and discusses ways in which the poet challenges cultural roles assigned to women in the domestic sphere and in the pursuit of cosmetic beauty.

Three articles are devoted to the work of Katherine Philips. In 'Katherine Philips: agent of matchlessness' (*WW* 10[2003] 119–36), Elizabeth M.A. Hodgson considers ways in which Katherine Philips negotiates gender identity in her epithalamia, and how she distinguishes her poetic voice from those of male predecessors in the tradition. Hodgson argues that Philips resists a poetic approach which is self-revealing or straightforwardly biographical in her complex treatment of identity in the poems. Paula Loscocco's 'Inventing the English Sappho: Katherine Philips's Donnean Poetry' (*JEGP* 102[2003] 59–87) offers a study of Katherine Philips's friendship poems. Loscocco challenges the recent critical practice of reading Philips's use of Donnean images according to a narrowly autobiographical template, and instead emphasizes her transformation of them. She argues that Philips frequently departs from Donne's representation of erotic motifs in pursuit of a discourse appropriate to female intimacy. In her article, '"We live by chance, and slip into events": Occasionality and the Manuscript Verse of Katherine Philips' (*ECI* 18[2003] 9–23), Marie-Louise Coolahan considers Philips's preference for manuscript circulation over print publication, and argues that the complex arrangement of the poems in manuscript evades the kind of linear chronological narrative which some recent critics have sought to impose on it.

The year has also seen the production of a new volume, Prescott and Shuttleton, eds., *Women and Poetry, 1660–1750*, which offers a series of articles on individual women poets of the later seventeenth century. In the opening article, 'Aphra Behn (1640?–89): Virginia Woolf and the "Little Gods of Love"' (pp. 17–28), Susan Wiseman looks at the role of Virginia Woolf in the reception of Aphra Behn. Wiseman argues that the two poems which Woolf mentions in her 1928 essay, 'A Room of One's Own' (*A Thousand Martyrs I have made* and *Love in Fantastic Triumph Sat*), are unrepresentative of Behn's oeuvre, and notes a shift in the way the Behn canon has been defined during the last century. David E. Shuttleton considers issues of fame and literary authority in 'Anne Killigrew (1660–85): "…let 'em Rage, and 'gainst a Maide Conspire"' (pp. 29–39), and in particular Killigrew's desire to transcend the pursuit of worldly recognition in favour of prophetic status. The article concludes with a note on Killigrew's paintings.

Also in this collection, Carol Shiner Wilson, in 'Jane Barker (1652–1732): From Galesia to Mrs Goodwife' (pp. 40–9), considers Barker's volume of poetry, *Poetical Recreations* (1688), with special reference to the manuscript edition at Magdalen College, Oxford. Wilson discusses the factors which render Barker a marginalized figure, particularly her unmarried status and her conversion to Roman Catholicism, in a discussion of the role of female agency in the poems. In 'Anne Finch, Countess of Winchilsea (1661–1720): Sorrow into Song' (pp. 60–70), Jane Spencer examines the theme of retirement in Anne Finch's work and her resistance to the satirical mode. Spencer offers a close reading of Finch's most famous poem, *The Spleen*, and assesses its manuscript and print history. Sarah Prescott's article, 'Elizabeth Singer Rowe (1674–1737): Politics, Passion and Play' (pp. 71–8) draws attention to the evidence of Whig sympathies in Singer Rowe's Athenian verse and Philomela poems.

This year has yielded a good range of work on the poetry of Marvell. Several of these articles look in detail at the Horatian Ode. Alex Garganigo, in 'Mourning the Headless Body Politic: The Regicide Elegies and Marvell's "Horatian Ode"' (*Exemplaria* 15[2003] 509–50), considers the metaphor of the body politic in relation to elegiac literature on the death of Charles I. Garganigo combines psychoanalytical mourning theory and close reading to argue that Marvell's poem attempts to figure Cromwell as a substitute for the Caroline body politic.

Paul Hammond, in 'Marvell's Pronouns' (*EIC* 53[2003] 219–34), discusses the ambiguity of personal pronouns, particularly that of the first person, in Marvell's poetry. Commenting on evasions in the role of the speaker in the Horatian Ode, Hammond argues that this is a strategy by which Marvell renders the status of his own political allegiances an enigma. Taking the same poem as its main focus, Peter Moore's 'The Irony of Marvell's Horatian Ode' (*ES* 84:i[2003] 33–56) offers detailed historical context and a close reading of the poem. He examines the relationship between panegyric and irony in the ode, and argues that it stands as anti-Cromwellian polemic, in which Cromwell is figured as a leader more concerned with personal rivals than with the public enemy. Matthew

Harkins's article '"Forward Youth" and Marvell's *An Horatian Ode*' (*Criticism* 45[2003] 343–58) offers a historical reading of the idiom and goes on to consider ways in which relations between youth and maturity are understood by Marvell. Harkins argues that the 'forward youth' of this ode should be identified not with a single, specific figure, but points to Marvell's preoccupation with youth more generally.

Peggy Samuels considers Marvell's adaptation of Petrarchan figures to suit the contemporary political scene in '"The Picture of Little T.C. in a Prospect of Flowers": Marvell's Portrait of Tender Conscience' (*PLL* 39[2003] 245–80). She offers Presbyterian and other appropriations of the vocabulary of tenderness as a context for her reading of the nuanced language of Marvell's poem.

In his article 'Marvell's Dialogized Nymph' (*SEL* 43[2003] 137–50), Daniel Jaeckle examines the complex verbal texture of 'The Nymph Complaining for the Death of her Faun', and its borrowings from legal, military, theological and other discourses. Jaeckle argues that in the nymph Marvell creates a disunified persona as a figure of social disorder. Looking at the biographical context, Art Kavanagh's note 'Andrew Marvell and the Duttons of Sherborne in 1657' (*N&Q* 50[2003] 183–8) discusses the period in which Marvell acted as tutor to William Dutton (1653–6) and the litigation surrounding the legacy of William's uncle, John Dutton, who died in 1656–7. Kavanagh looks at Marvell's deposition in this case and considers the evidence that Marvell was acquainted with members of the family before his appointment as tutor.

In 'Sir Philip Wodehouse's Pantheon of Renaissance Poets' (*SC* 18[2003] 54–60) Paul Hammond plays close attention to a manuscript poem by Sir Philip Wodehouse (1608–81) which appears in both Latin and English versions, in which Wodehouse celebrates Shakespeare, Jonson and a number of Latin humanists while excluding any mention of more recent or contemporary models such as Milton, Cowley or Dryden. Hammond provides a transcript of the poem, which he suggests is evidence of Wodehouse's literary conservatism. An epigram by Wodehouse to Katherine Philips is also briefly discussed.

This year has seen some important publications on the libertine poetry of the period, including one major full-length study, James Grantham Turner's *Schooling Sex: Libertine Literature and Erotic Education in Italy, France, and England 1534–1685*. Turner devotes three chapters of the book to the poetry of the later seventeenth century. He discusses the influence of Chorier on Rochester, and offers the first full critical appraisal of John Oldham's poetic fragments and drafts. He goes on to consider Oldham's response to the emerging tradition and looks at translations of libertine literature and their role in effecting a shift from clandestine modes of reading and writing to the formation of a distinct canon. Turner also considers the contemporary critical reception of Rochester's work by Robert Wolseley, as well as his memorialization by Aphra Behn and Anne Wharton.

In a shorter note on Oldham, 'The Source for John Oldham's "What Joy Without Dear C. Has Life in Store?"' (*N&Q* 50[2003] 192–3), Turner identifies an additional Latin source for the poem, which is alluded to in the manuscript version of the text. He argues that Oldham has used a poem by Mimnermus, published in a parallel-text collection by Hugo Grotius of 1623. In an article which focuses on Rochester, Melissa Pino's 'Devilish Appetites, Doubtful Beauty, and Dull Satisfaction: Rochester's *scorn of ugly ladies (which are very near all)*' (*Restoration* 27:i[2003] 1–21) offers a discussion of Rochester's love lyrics and examines ways in which he manipulates the conventions of erotic poetry.

2. Prose

Considering later seventeenth-century prose as a whole, the publishing 'event' of 2003 has to be Joad Raymond's *Pamphlets and Pamphleteering in Early Modern Britain*, which is at once a survey of, and a searching investigation into, the pamphlet as object, as rhetorical tool and as political weapon in what might be dubbed 'the age of the pamphlet', *c.*1580–*c.*1700.

It is always dangerous to assume that one knows precisely what is meant by a term such as 'pamphlet', and yet this type of assumption is one of the most common mistakes made by scholars. Raymond, therefore, begins by asking the most basic, but most important, of questions: 'What *is* a pamphlet?' This, he says, is a question which would not have received an authoritative answer in 1580, but by 1700 everyone knew. His examination of the pamphlet as object makes the important point that both the term and the object were medieval in origin, and therefore it was originally handwritten. Produced in octavo on one or two sheets of cheap parchment, later paper, pamphlets were relatively cheap. Printing made them even cheaper, and in post-Reformation society the term became, like 'Puritan', one of abuse. It indicated poor authorship with low levels of rhetoric, and therefore of education, at the same time casting a slur on those who read, as well as those who created and peddled, it.

The 1580s, says Raymond, proved a watershed for the pamphlet, and he examines in detail the Martin Marprelate controversy, at the same time evaluating and stressing its importance in the development of the pamphlet as a tool and a weapon in polemical debate. He relates this to the self-consciously plain rhetorical style adopted by Martin and his 'sons', copied by his respondents, and their biting, personalized satire allied to commonsensical syllogisms and simple syntax. This challenged expectations of serious debate on religion and politics, and heavily influenced the development of pamphleteering. Raymond includes a chapter on the production and dissemination of news, charting this from the beginning of sensational news reporting in terms of abnormal birth narratives, to the translated news publications from abroad banned by Charles I, and the use of news publication as a recruitment tool during the civil wars. The advent of *Mercurius Politicus* in 1650 is singled out for particular attention, as is its editor, the tremendously gifted Marchamont Nedham. The survey/analysis continues to the publication of the *Oxford*, later the *London*, *Gazette* (the first true newspaper) in 1665, and the first scientific journal, the Royal Society's *Philosophical Transactions*, also in 1665. The news aspect of this book is both an expansion of, and a complement to, Raymond's earlier book, *Making the News: an Anthology of the Newsbooks of Revolutionary England 1641–1660* (1993).

In another chapter, Raymond addresses the idea of 'the explosion of print' in 1641, and concludes that there is a firm basis for this, although the idea needs to be qualified by the fact that this was an expansion of a phenomenon which was already in evidence, and that it also reflects, to some extent, the collecting activities of George Thomason. Thomason collected no Scottish Covenanting material, and one of the great strengths of Raymond's book is his inclusion of the copious Scottish pamphlet polemic before and during the Bishops' War of 1638. Raymond notes that, although there was less Scottish material than English, its influence south of the border was proportionately greater. He also stresses the European aspects of 'pamphlet wars'. Amsterdam and Leiden were important cities for the printing of Scottish, and of English, material. A central section of the book is concerned with the mechanics of producing pamphlets, the people and the skills involved. Everything, down to the composition of printing ink and the price of paper, is included. One chapter is devoted to women and pamphleteering. This includes not only information on Quaker women and Fifth Monarchist Anna Trapnel, who immediately spring to mind in this respect, but also female political polemicists such as Elizabeth Cellier, who was heavily involved in subversive pamphleteering against the Catholic succession under Charles II. Also included are women, such as Elizabeth Alsop, who were involved in the printing and dissemination of pamphlets. The involvement of women in the use of the printed petition is highlighted, with illustrations of contemporary material.

The fact that this volume is illustrated is a genuine advantage, The examples are judiciously chosen to complement the text, and provide invaluable insight into the materials being discussed. The whole argument is framed within a series of small scenes which vividly bring to life the world and the idea of the pamphlet through a century and a half of its dominance. There is a very full index, but no bibliography, although this may be because the book itself is quite long at 384 pages of text and illustration. Sources are clearly given in the footnotes, so the reader has to find the appropriate section of text in order to track down the reference required. This may be something of a drawback, but the text is such a joy to read that it seems not to matter too much. This is a seminal work, with something for everyone working in this and related fields.

The English Radical Imagination: Culture, Religion and Revolution, 1630–1660 is a monograph based on a D.Phil. thesis by Nicholas McDowell. He begins by citing Thomas Edwards, author of *Gangraena*, and others, for their views that 'illiterate Mechanick persons' should not be allowed to discuss religion, or anything else of import, in the public arena. McDowell investigates the prevailing view (since Christopher Hill) that most, if not all, writers of socially and religiously radical material were of humble origin, and were either uneducated, or did not have the benefit of a university education. He cites examples to demonstrate that it suited radicals to collude in this view, as it cast their opponents as elitist and themselves as bona fide representatives of the poor and oppressed. They also discovered that including 'the middling sort' with the masses ideologically created a much wider readership for their publications. McDowell notes more recent challenges to this perception of radicals as lower-class and uneducated, and proposes to explore these ideas further. He makes the telling observation that John Lilburne's background was wealthier than that of Thomas Hobbes. McDowell's method is to study the works themselves as well as the authors, in order to tease out, by means of references, allusions, style, language and other contextualizing factors, how far the educational background of the writer contributed to that writer's radical prose. This, again, is linked back to the writer's context, to form as complete a view as possible of that individual's perception of 'radicalism'.

McDowell demonstrates how men of radical views, such as William Dell, were part of a movement of 'anti-intellectualization' spreading out *from* the universities, rather than assaulting them from without. There were, says McDowell, many such 'middle-of-the-road' radicals like Dell, who have failed to capture the imagination of modern scholars. He cites the research of Nigel Smith into translations of occult and Neoplatonic texts which circulated in lay culture outside the universities, noting that the translators had to be intellectually educated men. The clergy who preached messages of anti-intellectualization had, by the nature of their calling, to be university educated. William Walwyn, himself a grandson of the bishop of Hereford, was influenced by Montaigne, through Pierre Charron's adaptation of *De la sagesse*, which he had read in Samson Lennard's translation. The work of Richard Overton shows a similar theological background to that of Milton, but best of all is McDowell's interpretation and examination of the Ranter Abiezer Coppe who, although he did not complete his degree, was still a former Oxford undergraduate. A very detailed study of the *Fiery Flying Roll* texts indicates the extent of Coppe's education and intellectual powers, as well as hidden links with his varsity background. His persona of 'holy fool' is linked with Erasmian definitions of Folly, and the influence of Coppe's university study of Hebrew is traced. An interesting and original view of Gerard Winstanley is followed by an investigation of Samuel Fisher, another Hebrew scholar who assumed the anti-intellectual persona of the 'holy fool'.

In his conclusion, McDowell makes the interesting observation that John Milton, the most famous of seventeenth-century radical writers, saw grammar-school boys as the natural heroes of the English republic. There will undoubtedly be more work on this and related subjects from Nicholas McDowell and others, perhaps also on the possible similarities with medieval heresy to which he alludes on two or three occasions. As they stand, these references are 'hostages to fortune', which are not contextualized nearly enough. They could form the basis for future research, though. This little book is packed full of 'gems' of research, and is a must-read for everyone interested in mid-seventeenth-century radicalism.

The next two books for review are collections of essays. The first, Andersen and Sauer, eds., *Books and Readers in Early Modern England: Material Studies*, contains some potentially important and very interesting essays on the book as created object, and as an instrument in the collusive construction of meaning between writer and reader. In 'Books and Scrolls: Navigating the Bible', Peter Stallybrass examines the form and functions of the Bible as codex, and the methodologies employed in reading it. He notes that the idea of continuous reading, i.e. from beginning to end without a break, was an innovation on the part of the Protestants, in opposition to the Catholic process of liturgical reading, which split the Bible into parts, which were then read out of order, and joined together again in the mind as the year went on. The Anglican liturgy also did, and still does, this. Indeed, this was the accepted way of reading in the seventeenth century, Stallybrass points out, when Protestants also took their bibles to sermons, in order to follow the preacher's references. Decontextualized biblical references were praised as a way of refuting authority and countering prosecutors at trials, and Stallybrass cites the trial of Anne Askew as an example. This interesting study has implications for the ordering and reading of many longer seventeenth-century works. Were they read, or intended to be read, from start to finish, and, if they were, how did the writer try to accomplish this?

Anne Hughes's 'Approaches to Presbyterian Print Culture: Thomas Edwards's *Gangraena* as Source and Text', also in Anderson and Sauer, looks at the interchange between the writer's intention and the readers' input in the case of one of the most important, and infamous, sources for radical religion in the 1640s. Surveying previous work on Edwards's book, she poses the question, 'Did this radicalism exist, or was it created by Edwards?' She also examines what *Gangraena* can tell the scholar about the nature of seventeenth-century print culture. The conclusions reveal how a work like this created a diasporic community of readers (rather like modern-day fan club members), who were identified as a group by it, and whose views were then shaped by their reactions to it. The book contributed to the notoriety of those who were presented in it, as well as its author, for whom fame produced more material of a similar kind. *Gangraena* was, in short, like a snowball rolling down a hill, producing its own effects, as well as relating and reacting to them. 'Lego Ego: Reading Seventeenth-Century Books of Epigrams', by Randall Ingram, is really about poetry, but again contributes to the debate about reading, noting how the reader constitutes him/herself while at the same time constructing their own book out of the miscellaneous verses collected in the epigram book. Kathleen Lynch's 'Devotion Bound: A Social History of *The Temple*' is, again, about a book of poetry, but Lynch's work on the significance of binding has implications for books of prose, too. With an ambiguous writer such as Herbert, the publisher's conception of his book's contents is reflected in the nature of the binding. The article invites careful examination of bound editions.

Also in Anderson and Sauer, eds., Sabina A. Baron's 'Licensing Readers, Licensing Authorities in Seventeenth-Century England' concentrates on the work, and the ideology, of the licenser. She examines the work of two different licensers, Georg Weckherlin and John Milton. The detailing of Milton's associations in the London book trade is illuminating as a portrait of London book publishing and selling in general, and the examination of the differing practices of the two men, one a bourgeois bureaucrat working 'by the book' for Charles I and the other a radical thinker adapting his practices in the service of the Commonwealth, provides a telling portrait. This essay can be placed alongside the year's other works on licensing and the book trade, to produce a very illuminating overall picture. 'Preserving the Ephemeral: Reading, Collecting and the Pamphlet Culture of Seventeenth-Century England', by Michael Mendle, should be read alongside Joad Raymond's book (reviewed above). Mendle focuses on the collecting of pamphlets, and the 'why' and the 'how' that lie behind the pamphlet collections of the seventeenth century. He notes the difference between collectors of 1640–60, such as Thomason, who collected items selected by themselves because they recorded events which they deemed to be of great moment, and the collections offered in bundles in the 1670s and 1680s, when collecting had become a hobby. Mendle notes other ways in which the two waves of collecting were similar and different: they were similar in that pamphlets old and new appeared side by side on the stands, but they were different in that the later collectors were collectors in every sense of the word, creating collections according to title, series, etc., while collectors such as Thomason were saving the ephemeral from destruction, in order to preserve the events they contained for the future.

Finally in Anderson and Sauer's collection, Lana Cable's 'Licensing Metaphor: Parker, Marvell and the Debate over Conscience' focuses on the writing and the beliefs, or lack of them, of Samuel Parker, the cleric famously lambasted by Andrew Marvell in his satirical prose work, *The Rehearsal Transpros'd*. What is really interesting in Cable's work is not so much the association with Marvell, but her study of Parker's writings. She examines his attack on language, and particularly his attempts to characterize the use of metaphor as vulgar (in every sense of the word) and impolite. Parker, Cable argues, besides being a time-serving trimmer in matters of religion, attempts to turn religious belief into a matter not of faith, but of civility, or polite manners. This enables him to argue that all such religion exists only in the service of the state, going so far as to argue that laws exist simply in order to be obeyed. In short, this secularized religion not only excludes Dissenters (whose faith is frequently expressed in metaphorical terms), but serves to render all its adherents entirely obedient to the state. Faith should be kept entirely private, not even expressed. Cable demonstrates that, despite his attack on Hobbes, Parker's view of religion works to the same ends, in fact to even more extreme ends, than the Hobbesean one, and its effects would be the same. She also shows how successful Parker's arguments were. In 1669 Parker claimed to be part of an intellectual and social elite, but by 1680 such views were being expressed as part of patriotism. The Church of England had become an example of polite civility, or gentility, rather than a church of militant faith.

The second collection is Merritt, ed., *Imagining Early Modern London: Perceptions and Portrayals of the City from Stow to Strype, 1598–1720*, a book of interdisciplinary essays. As much seventeenth-century prose writing concerns itself with, was printed in, or was published from London (either the metropolis or the 'Great Wen' depending upon one's viewpoint), a book of this kind is contextually invaluable. It is anchored by prose surveys of London, beginning with 1598, the publication date of John Stow's *Survey of London*, and ending with 1720, the date on which John Strype published his edition of Stow's *Survey*. Following Patrick Collinson's first essay, an evaluation of Stow, Merritt analyses later surveys, either editions of Stow or dependent upon his work, in her essay 'The Reshaping of Stow's *Survey*: Munday, Strype and the Protestant City'. She demonstrates how seventeenth- and early eighteenth-century writers and editors such as Anthony Munday, James Howell, Edward Hatton and John Strype 'Protestantized' the Catholic Stow's account, selecting materials appropriate to a more Protestant history, and downplaying some of Stow's pre-Reformation sympathies. They also added significant material more closely related to Protestant concerns, such as almsgiving and civic benefaction, while retaining a spirit of pride in 'their' city. It is an interesting example of editorial processes at work to alter the viewpoint of a work without significantly, if at all, altering the original content. This idea of creating a more Protestant city without affecting civic pride, sense of community or the citizens' self-identification is examined in a narrower framework in a short essay, 'The Arts and Acts of Memorialisation in Early Modern London', by Ian W. Archer. Archer demonstrates how post-Reformation city authorities sought to celebrate and commemorate individual, civic and corporate identities in new ways.

Staying with Merritt, a group of essays concerning London as a series of spaces within a larger space opens with Vanessa Harding's 'City, Capital and Metropolis: the Changing Shape of Seventeenth-Century London', an account of the rapid growth of Stuart London, illustrated by contemporary maps. It is followed by Robert B. Shoemaker's 'Gendered Spaces: Patterns of Mobility and Perceptions of London's Geography, 1660–1750'. This is very illuminating in terms of the environment of Restoration writers. It is, after all, the London of Samuel Pepys. Shoemaker examines the problems caused by physical growth, and asks, 'How did residents in the vastly expanded London after 1660 see themselves in relation to the city?' Growth, mobility, shifting, often seasonal, populations, and the large number of Dissenters made the city too large, and the urban parish too small as a self-defining factor. The answer, Shoemaker concludes, depended upon one's individual outlook, occupation, social status, wealth and cultural attitudes. On the whole, gentlemen and ladies remained close to the western suburban areas, sometimes visiting the city. The city retained its links with artisans and merchants, who were more stable and travelled less, while the urban poor travelled widely in search of work. Most wide-ranging of all were poor females in domestic service, but on the whole women travelled more widely than men in pursuit of shopping and housekeeping. Samuel Pepys, Shoemaker notes, viewed London through the very narrow lens of his personal ambition, only noticing the people and places that were likely to serve it. London, he concludes, was many different places to many different inhabitants, even according to the time of day or night. Mrs Pepys visited Drury Lane for the plays earlier in the day, while her husband visited it after daylight hours for other reasons entirely.

'"To recreate and refresh their dulled spirites in the sweet and wholesome ayre": Green Space and the Growth of the City', by Laura Williams (also in Merritt, ed.), investigates the replacement of Stow's green fields by planned green spaces in the seventeenth century. Williams traces the history of medical reasons for the creation of parks and gardens, and notes their health-giving properties, which were only efficacious if the visitor kept on walking. They were meant to be a retreat and an escape from the threat of excess represented by the city. Royal parks were important in this respect, but Williams also notes the desire for social control, allowing only a privileged elite access to these facilities. Peter Lake's article on society in Stow's London (not relevant to this review) is followed by Tim Harris's 'Perceptions of the Crowd in Later Stuart London', in which he investigates the make-up of the 'mob' and how it was perceived by later seventeenth-century commentators. He notes that London had no professional police force, and that crowd trouble was endemic. Authorities were often forced to negotiate with angry crowds, and to make concessions. Behind this lay the acceptance that the London crowd consisted not entirely of lower-class ne'er-do-wells, but of substantial citizens or their household members, the apprenticed sons of gentlemen and the 'middling' artisan and merchant classes. Care for London's citizens formed part of the patriarchal nature of monarchy, and thus of all government, including the city authorities. Harris relates this to manifestations of crowd power during the Exclusion Crisis.

The final essay from Merritt, '"Making Fire": Conflagration and Religious Controversy in Seventeenth-Century London' by Nigel Smith, features the idea of fire as apocalyptic and prophetic. Unfortunately, the references are not integrated into any overall argument, and the initial use of illustration from film does not offer anything to the sense of the essay. Having said this, its central section is really interesting, being an evaluation of Abiezer Coppe's *Divine Fire-Works* (1657). It is to be regretted that the publishers did not see fit to include a picture, or at least some visual representation, of the associated woodcut, and anyone who has not seen the illustration has to rely solely on Smith's verbal description, good though it is. Illustrations are needed where they are needed, even if they feature erections and nipple-sucking lambs. Equally interesting are Anna Trapnel's visions of 1654, but both of these sections are far too short. Much more could have been made of this, with much greater detail and a deeper investigation of the relationship between them. Taken as a whole, the essay is something of a patchwork, leaving the conclusion somewhat strained.

The style and presentation of the book make it accessible to both scholars and the general reader. Not only is it really well written and good to read for anyone with an interest in early modern London, but the insights which it provides are of tremendous usefulness in contextualizing later seventeenth-century writing.

Now for some articles. 'Allegory, Maps and Modernity' by Peter Crisp (*Mosaic* 36[2003] 49–64) investigates the concept of life as a journey in the light of recent metaphor theory, which relates one metaphor to another. Following the ideas of George Lakoff and Mark Turner, Crisp begins with the themes of 'States are Locations', 'Changes are Movements', 'Purposes are Destinations' and 'Means are Paths', and relates these to John Bunyan's *The Pilgrim's Progress* and E.M. Forster's *The Other Side of the Hedge*. The first, he states, illustrates the metaphorical theme of life as a journey, and the second the theme of history as a journey. Crisp views the Bible as an early example of the 'linearism' of Western tradition (although did the children of Israel not wander round and round for forty years?), and wonders how easily Bunyan's readers understood the idea of 'the straight road'. He does, interestingly, make the point that 'strait' had a different meaning in its New Testament context, and that Bunyan was reinterpreting the term when he spoke of the way as being 'straight'. He notes that Bunyan actually uses the term in both of the understood senses. Using evidence from *The Pilgrim's Progress*, Crisp demonstrates that the progress of the characters cannot have been linear, and that this undermines Bunyan's statement that the way was 'straight'. This contrasts with the 'way' as conceived and presented by Forster, which is one of linear progression, in fact of progress in its wider sense. The only straight way to the Celestial City would be suicide, which (Crisp does not note) Christian himself considers and rules out as an option. The questions raised here are, to a large extent, tackled—and to some extent answered—in N.H. Keeble's article '"To be a pilgrim"', which is reviewed below. Crisp makes an interesting observation in terms of contemporary social conditions, in that there were no good, straight roads in Bunyan's day, and that, given seventeenth-century travelling conditions, he would not have understood William Blake's aversion to straight roads. Metaphor, Crisp notes, is conditioned by experience.

Another perspective on the issues raised by Laura Cable in her essay on Samuel Butler is provided by Sharon Achinstein, in her article '"When civil fury first grew high": Politics and Incivility in Restoration England' (in Richards, ed., *Early Modern Civil Discourses*, pp. 85–98). This study is at once less intensive, and more wide-ranging, than Cable's, as it includes a Dissenting point of view to set alongside those of Samuel Butler and John Dryden. The starting point is that of the secularization of religious belief, and the Anglican establishment's attempt to make the metaphorical, Dissenting, expression of faith appear 'uncivil', 'impolite', and 'lower-class'. Achinstein begins by stressing the extent of the problem for the victorious Anglicans after 1660: as a result of the Act of Uniformity at least 2,000 clergy and lecturers, a staggering one in five of the total clergy, were expelled from their livings for refusal to conform. Many of these were moderate Puritans, who would, and could, have been included in a broader Church settlement. The creation of the 'wild Dissenter prophet' was a tool in a desperate struggle against large sections of the worshipping population. Achinstein produces evidence from Samuel Butler (at this point a reading of Cable's essay is also to be recommended), John Dryden and the Quaker Mary Mollineux. What is stressed—and is of very great interest—in this article, is that Mollineux, on the extreme 'wing' of Dissent, colluded in the idea of the 'wild prophet', which she was able to use for her own purposes. Using this evidence, Achinstein postulates that Dissenters produced ecstatic prophecy as being 'outside the social'. Like Mollineux, they were not 'uncivil' in the sense that they had no idea of collectivity, but they envisaged an alternative society from the orthodox. The collusion of Dissenters, therefore, increased the polarization of Anglicanism and Dissent in the popular imagination during the period immediately following the English civil wars.

The area covered by this article invites much further interdisciplinary study: there must be many other ways of viewing the evidence, and there must, indeed, be much more evidence to consider (perhaps this field is one which invites the creation of a database, or linked databases). The viewpoint of a Quaker woman is very interesting when set against that of two orthodox, 'establishment' males, but what about orthodox women? Is there evidence for their beliefs to set against those of Quaker women, and what factors surround the collection of such evidence? There are many other questions which arise from the materials, and the argument, employed in Achinstein's extremely useful article.

On the subject of licensing, again, there is a relevant article to be found elsewhere. This is by Peter Hind on 'Roger L'Estrange, the Rye House Plot, and the Regulation of Political Discourse in Late-Seventeenth-Century London' (*Library* 3[2003] 3–31). This centres on the so-called 'Rye House Plot' of June 1683, when it was alleged that William, Lord Russell and some associates planned to intercept the royal coach on its way back from Newmarket races near Rye House, and to murder Charles II and his brother James. Given the anxieties generated by the Exclusion Crisis and the insecurity of the succession, this led to

Russell's execution (21 July 1683). Hind's study concentrates on the publishing events surrounding the execution, the fate of a paper handed over by Russell on the scaffold and its subsequent publication history, and the activities of the royal licenser, Roger L'Estrange, as a result of this. The story is a fascinating one, and the issues raised are of great moment for the study of censorship and the press. They provide interesting insights into the nature of society on the eve of the Catholic succession and the Glorious Revolution, at the same time revealing the persistence of issues fought over during the civil wars, not to mention the instability of the restored Stuart monarchy. Hind traces the publication of the 'speech', in the process demonstrating the power of the 'death speech' as a genre, and notes how ambiguity in such a speech could lead to alternative readings. This may not be unexpected, but what is remarkable in this study is the revealed machinations and linguistic gyrations, not to mention exploitation of positions of power by L'Estrange, in order to access, survey and reinterpret physical, bibliographical and linguistic networks of alternative meaning in Stuart London. L'Estrange was spymaster, author, journalist, magistrate, administrator and spin-doctor all rolled into one. This is an alternative view of the licenser in action, which can be profitably set alongside Baron's vignettes of Milton and Weckherlin in action. The contrasts are very telling.

In his article '"Such a general itching after book-learning": Popular Readers of "the most eminent wits"' (*YES* 33[2003] 262–72), Adam Smyth examines another cheap, commercial genre, the printed miscellany. Beginning with the miscellany known as *The Academy of Complements*, he attempts to discover the readership of these (physically) small publications, which sold for 1*s.* 6*d.* or less, and were thus accessible to 'artisan'-class readers. Containing poems, potted histories, court dialogues, model letters, songs, riddles, and extracts from plays, among other miscellaneous items, these frequently claim to originate in court circles. They are, Smyth notes, manuals of etiquette and style, which encourage their readers to make use of these examples within their own social context. Smyth cites evidence that readers did, indeed, do this, but within their own social milieu and according to their own contextualized needs, rather than as vehicles of social mobility. As if realizing the subversive possibilities of their own product, compilers of these miscellanies also reject any idea that the books might feed the social aspirations of their readers, mocking their use by ill-educated, lower-class readers, who are depicted as ridiculous. Thus these books reinforce the status of the social and political elite, while offering it to the general public. They then attempt to control any socially disruptive forces which might be unleashed by this. What is important, says Smyth, is how the book is being read. As Smyth mentions himself in passing, this might also be related to work on other popular genres, such as the chapbook, the ballad collection, the garland (including the 'Robin Hood' garlands).

Returning to the idea of Bunyan and the pilgrimage, this subject is at the heart of N.H. Keeble's article, '"To be a pilgrim": Constructing the Protestant Life in Early Modern England' (in Morris and Roberts, eds., *Pilgrimage: The English Experience from Becket to Bunyan*, pp. 238–56). The volume itself is very interesting in that it approaches the seventeenth century from the medieval period forwards, rather than from the usual Renaissance/early modern standpoint. This is particularly appropriate in the case of Bunyan, the self-confessed avid reader of medieval romance. Keeble looks at why Bunyan and his contemporaries, given the history of Lollardy, and of Protestant resistance to the idea of pilgrimage as ungodly and serving the material interests of a corrupt and venal Roman Church, should embrace the idea of pilgrimage to such an extent that Bunyan's idea of a 'pilgrim's progress' should be readily available, and amenable, to them. The medieval examples used are actually two trial accounts which were published by Reformation editors, John Bale (trial of John Oldcastle, 1416, published 1544) and William Tyndale (trial of William Thorpe, 1407, published 1530), although previous work has demonstrated that this was a point of view which can be gleaned from medieval record.

Keeble demonstrates that the idea of pilgrimage was adapted by Protestants, and by Dissenters, in order to demonstrate their otherworldliness, or unworldliness—in fact, their 'otherness' in a ceremonialist, Anglican world (much as did Mary Mollineux, in Sharon Achinstein's article). The Dissenting concept of pilgrimage was based on Old Testament models. They saw themselves as the children of Israel wandering in the desert, as in Exodus, or as followers of Abram/Abraham, wandering to the Promised Land in Canaan. Keeble points out that many unorthodox Protestants of all kinds, including those who joined the New Model Army, were constantly on the move, or on the march, impelled by the need to preach or prophesy, or to escape persecution. The idea, therefore, frequently had a basis in the realities of life. In addition to this, Keeble takes up the idea of the 'straight road', discussed by Crisp in his article. This, he concludes, is a spiritual conceptualization of the pilgrim's way as being 'strait' or demanding and difficult (the New Testament meaning), and 'straight', or undeviating and uncompromising. This way was also visualized in terms of the race, as in St Paul's letter to the Philippians. Keeble gives full biblical referencing for all of his quotations and ideas. He concludes that these images present the 'pilgrim' as eschewing the way of idleness, in contrast to the ease-loving conformists, who thus forfeit their right to the ultimate prize. Keeble describes the reinterpretation of an old idea which, in the light of other articles reviewed here, can also be seen as fuelling the polarization of Anglicans and Dissenters after the Restoration.

On the subject of *The Pilgrim's Progress* or, more correctly (and why not?) *The Pilgrim's Progress from This World to That Which Is To Come*, a very short but noteworthy contribution to the debate surrounding the book and its publication is made by David Stoker in his article 'William Proctor, Nathaniel Ponder, and the Financing of *Pilgrim's Progress*' (*Library* 4[2003] 64–9). This details the financing of an edition of the book by a stationer named William Proctor, who loaned money to Nathaniel Ponder to finance the printing. By various turns, Stoker demonstrates how Ponder never recovered from lawsuits relating to the pirating of the book, and how some of the rights to legal publication eventually passed into the hands of the 'pirate' himself, one Thomas Braddyll. The details supplied here are intended to supplement other work on the publication of Bunyan's book, but they also provide a fascinating insight into the precarious, and hawkish, world of the late seventeenth- and early eighteenth-century book trade.

An article on a seemingly unrelated subject, but one which touches once again on the history and perception of the book and its contents, is Liliana

Barczyk-Barakonska's '"Never go forth of the limits": Space and Melancholy in Robert Burton's Library Project' (*JES* 33[2003] 213–26). Although Burton may be considered a little early for inclusion in this section of the volume, his *Anatomy of Melancholy*, written in 1621, was influential much later in the century, and is briefly reviewed here in respect of ideas applicable to later seventeenth-century prose writers and bibliophiles, not to mention the ideas and projects of the Royal Society. Burton saw the library as a therapeutic space, a cure for the melancholy condition, a vision mirrored in his own writing, which forms a 'personal library' of extracted quotations. Barczyck-Barakonska notes that Burton speaks of the library in terms of prison, but as a prison which is also a release. The reader in his library may visit the entire world through reading, which is described by Burton as 'seeing'. This act of seeing through reading renders the imagined world 'real', as it captures the world for the reader. In fact, the imagined/real world may be better than the reality it encompasses, as the duplicate becomes more immediate, and more real, than the object it duplicates. Burton also stresses the need for forgetfulness of the world outside the library, the reality which is thereby obliterated. This protects the reader from emotions such as grief, and from suffering and ambition. Even the excitement, and therefore the chaotic disruption, of touching a book is to be avoided. This creation of a new world and forgetting the old, along with other ideas in this article, opens up a whole range of possibilities worthy of exploration.

Another interesting article on the nature and context of prose is Christopher Johnson's 'Intertextuality and Translation: Borges, Browne and Quevedo' (*T&L* 11[2003] 174–94), in which he compares the context and language of Sir Thomas Browne's *Hydriotaphia, Urne Buriall, or A Discourse of the Sepulchrall Urnes lately found in Norfolk* (1658) with its translation by Spanish writer Jorge Luis Borges (1944). Johnson notes Borges's Brownean qualities, which he lists as 'delight in emblematic details', 'copious use of learned allusion and citation', 'digressive rhetoric' and 'love of paradox', but his exploration of Borges's prose and the nature of his translation also reveals many interesting aspects of Browne's writing. Johnson notes that Browne's penchant for citation, paraphrase and learned allusion creates texts which read like palimpsests. That is, the work is Browne's overall, but it retains the imprint of the many different writers whose work he uses as his source material. This is true also of Borges's translation of Browne, which remains overall Borges's work, but is 'infiltrated', as it were, by the voices of Borges's own sources, as well as those of Browne and his sources. Johnson then demonstrates Borges's 'borrowings' from and interpretation of Quevedo, and how this links Borges, Quevedo and Browne in 'an intertextual network'. In his study and evaluation of the details of his theses, Johnson gives an intricate and very useful account of Browne's method and style of writing, which is also a valuable contribution to the field of translation study.

The methodology of scriptural study is highlighted by Joseph M. Levine in 'Matter of Fact in the English Revolution' (*JHI* 64[2003] 317–29). Although the initial assertion that 'the seventeenth century in England saw a succession of religious controversies that absorbed much of the intellectual energy of the period' is a general one, the rest of the study actually focuses on one aspect of these controversies, the extent to which the testimony of the Bible could be said to be 'true', and how this might be demonstrated. Levine cites the efforts of a variety of biblical scholars, including Richard Baxter, Henry Hammond, Brian Walton and William Stillingfleet, to argue the truth of the Bible by 'reasonable' means. Levine notes how Walton's project for an authoritative, polyglot Bible, supported by Cromwell, was disliked by all because of the huge number of textual variations it displayed. He argues that the Bible as an infallible witness to a doctrine's, or an interpretation's veracity was something of a poisoned chalice for Protestant apologists who, having used it as a weapon against the Roman Church during the Reformation, then found it unstable and unreliable in testimony against the spirit-driven sectaries of the civil war and Restoration periods. Given the problem that reasoning scholarship found the Bible—because of its translations, its many versions and the contradictions inherent in its text—less than useful as a polemical tool, these scholars then attempted to use contextualization to prove its worth. They cited historical context, other ancient texts, and the suffering of witnesses as evidence for its essential truth, while acknowledging its instability as a text. In conclusion, Levine stresses the importance of the methodological legacy left by these scholars to historians in general. Seen alongside the orthodox 'secularization' of religious faith as outlined by Achinstein and Cable, it is little wonder that they were so unpopular in their own day.

3. Drama

(a) General

Once again women dramatists have occupied a leading place in the scholarship of the year. In his *History of Irish Theatre* Christopher Morash has a chapter on the seventeenth-century origins of theatre in Ireland, and an inter-chapter on the 1663 performance of Katherine Philips's *Pompey* in Dublin. In the audience for Philips's tragedy were both the duke of Ormonde, the new Lord Lieutenant, and the earl of Ossory, the former leader of the parliamentary forces. As *Pompey* included a description and justification of the judicial murder of its hero, the tragedy risked reviving the trauma of regicide, yet worked towards reconciliation by suggesting that defeat might be glorious, and victory might not be villainous. As a whole the book makes an original and interesting approach to its subject. Irene Burgess's 'Recent Studies' in the Cavendish/Newcastle canon (*ELR* 32[2002] 452–73) will prove useful to anyone studying the plays of Margaret Cavendish, duchess of Newcastle. James Fitzmaurice makes a case, in '*The Lotterie*: A Transcription of a Manuscript Play Probably by Margaret Cavendish' (*HLQ* 66[2003] 155–67), for this playlet to be attributed to Margaret Cavendish, rather than her husband, as it is firmer than he would have been in opposition to lotteries and sympathy with their victims. It was probably performed at court in 1660. The manuscript is now in Nottingham University Library.

In 'The Politics of Adapting Behn's *Oroonoko*' (*CompD* 37[2003] 189–223), Anne Widmayer looks at 'Biyi Bandele's recent stage adaptation for the RSC, and takes him to task for having 'stolen in the second half from two earlier dramatic adaptations of Behn's novel, Thomas Southerne's *Oroonoko: A Tragedy*

(1695) and John Hawkesworth's *Oroonoko* (1759)' (p. 189). She gives detailed examples of the extent of the 'theft', which for her is only acceptable if viewed in the light of seventeenth-century notions of adaptation. Widmayer concludes that the modern adaptation has reduced the complexity of racial viewpoints in Behn's novel, and that 'Bandele unacceptably turns Behn's *Oroonoko* into a twentieth-century anti-slavery tract' (p. 192)—a trend that Hawkesworth had himself begun. The staging of Behn's plays underpins Kate Aughterson's accessible study of *Aphra Behn: The Comedies*, for Palgrave's Analysing Texts series. Aimed squarely at students, with bullet point summaries and suggested work questions, the book launches straight into a discussion of the staging mechanics of *The Rover Part I*, *The Feigned Courtesans* and *The Lucky Chance*. Political context, and a summary of Behn's writing career and of leading critical responses to her work follow in a much smaller part 2. This model allows Aughterson to offer close readings of the dramaturgy of these three comedies, which undergraduate students will find useful.

Aphra Behn and Mary Pix are the subject of four essays in Luis-Martínez and Figueroa-Dorrego's collection *Re-shaping the Genres: Restoration Women Writers*. Pilar Zozaya's 'Representing Women in Restoration England: A Reassessment of Aphra Behn's *The Rover*' reads Angellica and Hellena as symbols of Behn's failure to challenge a woman's 'commodified status in (the) patriarchal system' (p. 120). By contrast, in 'Of Spain, Moors and Women: The Tragedies of Aphra Behn and Mary Pix' Pilar Cuder-Dominguez argues that women playwrights were active in the evolution of the tragic genre. While Behn found that her figures of female agency in *Abdelazar* could only be presented as villainous, Pix's *Conquest of Spain* used female pathos to challenge the social order and as 'a vehicle of female heroicity' (p. 171). Carlos Gómez argues that Pix uses witty, masked and cross-dressed women to offer troubling virtuous female figures in 'Witty Women Masking Gender and Identity: The Comedies of Mary Pix in Context'. Zenón Luis-Martínez looks at Pix's history play *Queen Catharine* and finds much historical inaccuracy, but argues that this is in order to create a powerful, romantic heroine and to reconfigure the genre of the history play itself, in '"Shakespear with enervate voice": Mary Pix's *Queen Catharine* and the Interruption of History'. Margo Collins also explores 'Feminine Conduct and Violence in Mary Pix's She-Tragedies' (*RECTR* 18[2003] 1–16), contrasting the inherently contradictory rhetoric of conduct books, which warn against the violence unleashed by natural feminine passions unfettered by women's weaker reason, with Pix's violent female characters in *Ibrahim* and *The False Friend*. Collins discusses how Pix draws attention to these contradictions through the character of Appamia, whose violence is censured but also presented as necessary to punish the transgression of social norms.

Marcie Frank's *Gender, Theatre, and the Origins of Criticism: From Dryden to Manley*, examines the critical writing of Aphra Behn, Catherine Trotter and Delarivier Manley. Frank offers a clear thesis on the way in which gender inflected and defined the development of literary criticism by charting Dryden's attempt to generate a historical literary tradition, followed by the three female dramatists' critical commentary which echoed, transformed and extended that enterprise. Frank's overarching attempt is to recover the place of theatre in the emergence of literary criticism, the 'retention of traces of this dependence even after it comes into its own', and the shifting 'socio-historical coordinates of the critic', who, particularly when female, contributed to the attempt to ignore the performative features of criticism in order to preserve their critical authority (p. 138).

The works of Behn, Pix and Manley figure widely in Cynthia Lowenthal's lively *Performing Identities on the Restoration Stage*. Lowenthal explores how ideas and categories of identity, which were shifting and evolving in Restoration culture, were played out, created, or redefined on the stage. The centre of her work explores the relationship between bodies, representation and identity, and she looks at the construction and reconstruction of images of masculinity and femininity by playwrights and performers in the playhouse. Using close readings of plays from canonical writers, female writers and lesser-known playwrights, she builds a picture of contesting and contested new identities on and off the stage. Her readings are carefully contextualized against the background of emergent understandings of savage and civilized bodies circulating through Britain's imperial ambitions; of the rise of the economic power of trade; and of redefinitions of female identity, desire and agency through burgeoning print discourses.

Gender issues within Restoration drama are pursued in two further articles in *RECTR*. Candy B.K. Schille is also interested in prescriptions for female conduct in '*Now, Cato*: Addison, Gender, and Cultural Occasion' (*RECTR* 18[2003] 31–43). She reads Addison's women in *Cato* as representing the values of a thriving, imperial trading bourgeoisie, and the play's stoic 'manliness' as 'benevolent self-fashioning for an emergent, colonialist British middle class male' (p. 41). James E. Evans, 'Libertine Gamblers in Late Stuart Comedy' (*RECTR* 18[2003] 17–30), explores the relationship between libertinism and gambling in four rakish comedies. Dryden's *Wild Gallant*, and Horner in Wycherley's *Country Wife* successfully blend gambling and the pursuit of women, while Gayman in Behn's *Luckey Chance* loses his love through gambling, and by the time Centlivre's Valere is engaged in obsessive gaming in *The Gamester*, Evans finds that the libertine figure must renounce gambling most fully to succeed in love. This builds on Evans's earlier work on the theatricality and spectacle of gambling (*SECC* 31[2002] 1–20).

The duke of Buckingham, considered by some as a model libertine of the Restoration, is receiving a new edition of his works. In 'Editing a Nebulous Author' (*Library* 4[2003] 249–77) Robert D. Hume shows how he and Harold Love have solved the problem of editing *Plays, Poems and Miscellaneous Writings* associated with the duke of Buckingham. The duke was not so much their author as variously contributor, adapter, collaborator, composer and inspirer. The editors have 'little idea of how much responsibility Buckingham had' for the six plays, but both *The Chances* and *The Rehearsal* were successful in the theatre and deserve more attention from critics. The duke himself emerges as a more attractive character than biographers have usually suggested. As for other editions, Joseph Arrowsmith's comedy *The Reformation* appeared this year in its first critical modern edition, with a thorough, readable and scholarly introduction by Juan Prieto-Pablos, María José Mora, Manuel Gómez-Lara, and Rafael

Portillo, through the University of Barcelona. The editors of this attractive and usable series preface the work with a detailed analysis of the performance possibilities of the play, and its personal satire. They point out the particular delight that a contemporary audience could take in the mockery of Dryden as the stuffy, conceited English Tutor, who pontificates on playwriting.

P.A. Skantze, in *Stillness in Motion in the 17th Century Theatre*, examines the tension between stillness and motion as philosophical categories in a study of the performance of seventeenth-century theatre. Following close readings of Jonson's *Epicoene* and *The Gypsies Metamorphosed* and Milton's *A Maske*, where metaphors of motion and stillness reflect tensions between authorship and performance, Skantze turns her attention to the theatrical nature of pamphlets during the civil war, in which she echoes much of Susan Wiseman's work. Chapter 4 looks at the staging possibilities of Behn's *The Rover Part I* and *The Feigned Courtesans*, and her final chapter examines how metaphors of stillness and motion are used in Vanbrugh's soliloquies in *The Provok'd Wife* and the debate about marriage prosecuted by Jeremy Collier.

Studies in Restoration theatre history this year have included 'Arthur Bedford's *A Serious Advertisement* (1705) and the Early History of Theatre in Bristol' (*TN* 57[2003] 2–10), in which Judith Milhous and Robert D. Hume give the full text of a tract occasioned by a Bristol performance of Colley Cibber's *The Careless Husband*. It quotes 'Profane and Atheistical Expressions' and its likely author was the Reverend Arthur Bedford, a local vicar who wrote other anti-theatrical works. In 'The Economics of Theatrical Dance in Eighteenth-Century London' (*TJ* 55[2003] 481–508) Judith Milhous finds in the last decade of the seventeenth century the beginnings of theatrical dance as an independent activity, not just something actors—Nell Gwyn, for example—did as a sideline. She also gives Vanbrugh's budget for actors, singers and dancers in the company he planned for the Haymarket theatre. In 'Casting Issues in the Original Production of Purcell's Opera *The Fairy Queen*' (*M&L* 84[2003] 595–607) Michael Burden cites evidence that the roles of Titania and Oberon were taken by juveniles. Among aspects of the opera's construction and performance that were affected, Burden emphasizes the rigid division between spoken and sung sections. In 'Dancing Monkeys at Dorset Garden' (*TN* 57[2003] 119–35) Burden traces the symbolic resonance of the monkey as wild and natural, and suggests that live monkeys may have been used for *The Fairy Queen*'s peculiar 'Monkeys' Dance. In 'A Present for the Ladies' (*M&L* 84[2003] 189–208) Wendy Heller reconsiders the influence of Ovid and Montaigne on Tate and Purcell's *Dido and Aeneas* in the light of Tate's *A Present for the Ladies* (1692). The librettist sought to vindicate Dido by endowing her with stoic virtue; the composer further emphasized her redemption in his setting of her lament.

In 'The Restoration English History Plays of Roger Boyle, Earl of Orrery' (*SEL* 43[2003] 559–77) Tracey E. Tomlinson suggests that, while Boyle knew that Charles II would never be a great military leader, *Henry V* and *The Black Prince* in effect urged him to pursue a more bellicose policy against the French and the Dutch. These plays have been seen as inaugurating heroic drama, and may now be seen as reviving the history play. In 'Confused Identities in Nathaniel Lee's *Nero*'

(*N&Q* 50[2003] 190–2) Anthony W. Butler argues that Sylvius is probably a Roman slave owned by Cyara.

This year London did less than the provinces for Restoration drama, judging mainly by the reviews in *London Theatre Record*. *The Way of the World* (Gatehouse) and *The Provok'd Wife* (Southwark Playhouse) both suffered from ill-advised efforts to shift these plays to today's media world. *The Recruiting Officer* (Garrick, Lichfield) was the first play at this fine new theatre, and was billed as 'the greatest British comedy ever written'. *Venice Preserv'd* (Citizens, Glasgow) was acclaimed as a brilliant production of an impressive play.

(b) Dryden

Studies of Dryden's plays are sometimes temporarily lost in books on broader subjects. For example, David B. Haley's *Dryden and the Problem of Freedom* (*YWES* 78[1999] 412) has a substantial chapter on 'Masterless Men' in the heroic plays, and a brief account of Dryden's intentions in *The Spanish Friar* (of which more later). Blair Hoxby's *Mammon's Music*, a study of commerce and its effects on English writers in 'The Age of Milton', has a section on *Amboyna*, seeing beyond its propaganda for a trade war against the Dutch to its consideration of the possible costs of empire. Marcie Frank's *Gender, Theatre, and the Origins of Criticism* describes Dryden's legacy to Delarivier Manley and other women writers; it included both theoretical essays and theatrical adaptations, notably *Oedipus* (a critique of Sophocles), *All for Love* and *Troilus and Cressida* (critiques of Shakespeare), and *The State of Innocence* (a critique of Milton). Parts of this book derive from earlier essays (*YWES* 74[1995] 268 and 75[1996] 322), but Frank's conclusion is certainly new: Dryden's 'theatricalized bitchiness' has been undervalued in traditional histories of criticism.

This year's essays in the learned journals were not a bad bunch. In '"Transgressing nature's law": Representations of Women and the Adapted Version of *The Tempest*, 1667' (*L&H* 12[2003] 19–40) Barbara A. Murray argues that men were deeply disturbed by the influence of women in Charles II's court, but this adaptation reassured them that women couldn't really play men. The part of Hippolito was taken by a woman, and when he is wounded he is revived by a herbal concoction used for procuring menstruation; hence femaleness and fallibility are 'entertainingly reaffirmed'. You would need all Murray's considerable learning and an odd sense of humour to be so entertained today. In 'John Dryden's *Conquest of Granada* and James Cameron's *Terminator* Films' (*Restoration* 27:ii[2003] 17–40) Victoria Warren focuses on 'the question of hegemonic discourse in relation to the texts' cultural contexts, the exclusions implicit in gender identities, the textual use of cultural narrative, and the principal thematic implications'. Despite some alien dialect this essay arouses interest in some striking parallels between these works and their times. The 'hegemonic discourses' are those of royalism and Reaganism, and the 'thematic implications' are that individuals can prevail against what seems fated.

In 'Judas-Friars of the Popish Plot' (*Clio* 32[2003] 177–203) Anne Gardiner argues that *The Spanish Friar* was intended by Dryden, and apprehended by his readers, as 'subtly pro-Catholic'. Characters represent real people: the deplorable Friar Dominic, both Titus Oates and his henchmen the Dominicans Matthew Clay and Bernard Dennis; the unhappy Gomez, the persecuted Catholics; the would-be usurper Bertran, Shaftesbury; the heroic true heir Torrismond, the duke of York, afterwards James II; the imprisoned Sanchez, Dryden's imprisoned cousin Viscount Stafford. The play suggests that if only the government would repudiate Oates and his Judas-friars, Shaftesbury and James could be reconciled. Gardiner uses her exceptional learning to confirm David Haley's ideas about what Dryden intended, but what audiences apprehended remains debatable; they enjoyed the buffoonery of Leigh as Dominic and Nokes as Gomez, and the play's Catholicism was too subtle for James himself, who in 1686 banned its performance. Haley returns to the play and its context in 'Was Dryden a "Cryptopapist" in 1681?' (*SECC* 32[2003] 277–96). Well, he feared the Whigs would say he was, so in 1680–2 he successively represented himself as Protestant, Tory, and Anglican. Both Gardiner and Haley imply that in calling *The Spanish Friar* 'a Protestant play' Dryden protested too much.

Books Reviewed

Andersen, Jennifer, and Elizabeth Sauer, eds. *Books and Readers in Early Modern England: Material Studies*. UPennP. [2003] pp. 312. hb £39 ISBN 0 8122 3633 5, pb £17.50 ISBN 0 8122 1794 2.

Aughterson, Kate. *Aphra Behn: The Comedies*. Palgrave. [2003] pp. ix + 259. hb £40 ($65) ISBN 0 3339 6321 0, pb £12.99 ($19.95) ISBN 0 3339 6319 9.

Cope, Kevin L., ed. and introd., Rüdiger Ahrens, ed. and epilogue. *Talking Forward, Talking Back: Critical Dialogues with the Enlightenment*. AMS. [2002] pp. xvi + 388. £58.50 ISBN 0 4046 3535 0.

Frank, Marcie. *Gender, Theatre, and the Origins of Criticism: From Dryden to Manley*. CUP. [2003] pp. ix + 175. £40 ISBN 0 5218 1810 9.

Hoxby, Blair. *Mammon's Music*. YaleUP. [2002] pp. xii + 320. £30 ISBN 0 3000 9378 0.

Lowenthal, Cynthia. *Performing Identities on the Restoration Stage*. SIUP. [2002] pp. x + 270. £28.50 ($40) ISBN 0 8093 2462 8.

Luis-Martínez, Zenón, and Jorge Figueroa-Dorrego, eds. *Re-shaping the Genres: Restoration Women Writers*. Lang. [2003] pp. 303. £29 ($53.95) ISBN 3 9067 6986 0.

McDowell, Nicholas. *The English Radical Imagination: Culture, Religion, and Revolution 1630-1660*. OUP. [2003] pp. 219. £45 ISBN 0 1992 6051 6.

Merritt, J.F., ed. *Imagining Early Modern London: Perceptions and Portrayals of the City from Stow to Strype, 1598-1720*. CUP. [2003] pp. 305. £45 ISBN 0 5217 7346 6.

Morash, Christopher. *A History of Irish Theatre, 1600-2000*. CUP. [2002] pp. xvii + 322. £40 ($60) ISBN 0 5216 4117 9.

Morris, Colin, and Peter Roberts, eds. *Pilgrimage: The English Experience from Becket to Bunyan*. CUP. [2003] pp. 235 £45 ISBN 0 5218 0811 1.

Prescott, Sarah, and David E. Shuttleton, eds. *Women and Poetry, 1660-1750*. Palgrave. [2003] pp. xiii + 258. hb £52.50 ISBN 1 4039 0654 8, pb £18.99 ISBN 1 4039 0655 6.

Prieto-Pablos, Juan, María José Mora, Manuel Gómez-Lara and Rafael Portillo, eds. *The Reformation*. by Joseph Arrowsmith. UBarcelona. [2003] pp. 201. £15 ISBN 8 4833 8381 0.

Raymond, Joad. *Pamphlets and Pamphleteering in Early Modern Britain*. Cambridge Studies in Early Modern British History. CUP. [2003] pp. 403. £50 ISBN 0 5218 1901 6.

Richards, Jennifer, ed. *Early Modern Civil Discourses*. Palgrave. [2003] pp. 216. £50 ISBN 1 4039 1736 1.

Skantze, P.A. *Stillness in Motion in the 17th Century Theatre*. Routledge. [2003] pp. 224. £65 ($114.95) ISBN 0 3152 8668 9.

Turner, James Grantham. *Schooling Sex: Libertine Literature and Erotic Education in Italy, France, and England 1534-1685*. OUP. [2003] pp. xxviii + 408. £58 ISBN 0 1992 5426 5.

Yu, Christopher. *Nothing to Admire: The Politics of Poetic Satire from Dryden to Merrill*. OUP. [2003] pp. 219. £30.50 ISBN 0 1951 5530 0.

XI

The Eighteenth Century

GAVIN BUDGE, FREYA JOHNSTON, JAMES A.J. WILSON
AND MARJEAN PURINTON

This chapter has four sections: 1. Prose and General; 2. The Novel; 3. Poetry; 4. Drama. Section 1 is by Gavin Budge; section 2 is by Freya Johnston; section 3 is by James A.J. Wilson; section 4 is by Marjean Purinton.

1. Prose and General

Publications on prose this year were strongly marked by the emergence of approaches based on the history of the book. The significance of the attention paid to libraries, the technology of printing, and the activities of publishers by a number of writers is that it enables a reconceptualization of intellectual history: instead of describing rather nebulous 'ideas' which persist historically without visible means of support, the focus becomes the series of material practices which constitute intellectual life. This shift in emphasis also has implications for how the object of scholarly analysis is conceived. To attend to the materiality of literature is to redirect attention towards figures who may previously have seemed intellectually marginal, but whose role in the transmission and circulation of texts places them at the centre of the intellectual life of their period, when this is understood as praxis.

Justin Champion's *Republican Learning: John Toland and the Crisis of Christian Culture, 1696–1722* employs a focus on the history of the book to argue that the deist Whig publicist John Toland, instead of being the 'second-rate, isolated, marginal and mediocre figure' (p. 253) of standard historical characterizations, was in fact for most of his life a powerfully influential individual through his contacts with the Whig aristocracy and the Hanoverian monarchy. Champion concedes that much of Toland's work is intellectually unimpressive, and sometimes deliberately misleading, but contends that his writing must be seen in the context of his overarching 'cultural project' of undermining 'the political status of clergymen and the "Church" as an independent institution' (p. 4). Champion employs a dialogic model of historical interpretation as a means for understanding Toland, the aim of which

Year's Work in English Studies, Volume 84 (2005) © The English Association; all rights reserved. For permissions, please email: journals.permissions@oxfordjournals.org

doi: 10.1093/ywes/mai011

is to reconstruct how 'the work of making meaning was done in the reception rather than the utterance of speech-acts' (p. 12).

Toland's intellectual and social milieu is explored through examination of the libraries he is known to have used, with Champion arguing that a library in the early eighteenth century was not merely a place where texts were passively consumed (p. 41), but was assembled 'for instrumental purposes rather than mere display' (p. 34) and represented a 'space of sociability' (p. 29). Champion analyses Toland's use of 'scribal publication' (p. 52) as a means of manipulating different audiences, his important role in establishing a canon of English republican theory (p. 97), and his seemingly anomalous engagement with inaccurate and misleading Patristic scholarship, which Champion interprets as a form of what Naomi Klein calls 'cultural jamming' in which 'the distinction between spurious and authentic, and between suppositious and canonical' (p. 201) in the field of biblical scholarship was undermined. Although Champion's argument is hermeneutically sophisticated, this last aspect of it is liable to objections of the same kind that recent 'new historicist' interpretations of supposed Jacobite sympathies in the later Johnson have aroused, in that a dialogic engagement with other texts is presupposed in order to arrive at an interpretation which is not evident from Toland's texts themselves, taken on their own. Champion's 'strong' reading of Toland, in which his every action and publication becomes a purposeful intervention, seems to foreclose the possibility that sometimes Toland might have been genuinely inconsistent or mistaken, an interpretative problem which the book nowhere addresses directly.

Champion's study cites the example of Robert Darnton's work on the history of the clandestine (p. 15), an influence which is also acknowledged by Julie Peakman in her *Mighty Lewd Books: The Development of Pornography in Eighteenth-Century England* (p. 3). Peakman offers a thematic survey of eighteenth-century pornography, drawing on the late nineteenth-century bibliography of erotic literature by the eccentric bibliophile H.S. Ashbee, without attempting a detailed investigation of the trade in obscene books. She is concerned to stress the continuities between pornography and other areas of English eighteenth-century culture, pointing out that there is evidence of a wide readership for obscene literature which includes women (p. 35) and 'the middling sort, with the cheaper material stretching to include the lower classes' (p. 37). Production of pornography increased dramatically, so that by the end of the century England was 'a society awash with erotica' (p. 44), and pornographic genres reflected preoccupations in the culture at large, with 'findings in botany, reproduction and electricity' (p. 67) influencing erotic metaphor: English interest in landscape gardening, for example, was reflected in the production of 'sexual utopias in which landscapes were depicted in the form of a woman's body' (p. 93). Peakman discerns a development in English pornography towards a more privatized 'pornographic world', often accompanied by a 'claustrophobic atmosphere' (p. 8), suggesting that the 'predilection for incest' which appears during the second half of the eighteenth century could be seen as a reaction against 'the increasing importance being placed on family values' (p. 18) which accompanied the Sensibility movement. She emphasizes the important role played in this process by 'anti-Catholic erotica', in which 'depictions of women in submissive victim roles' (p. 193) and an interest in flagellation (p. 166) were significant features. Peakman's account of this material represents an important new context for the study of late eighteenth-century fiction, particularly Gothic novels such as Lewis's *The Monk*, though this is not a context which Peakman herself explores.

Simon Dickie's article 'Hilarity and Pitilessness in the Mid-Eighteenth Century: English Jestbook Humor' (*ECS* 37[2003] 1–22) undertakes a similar kind of thematic survey of non-canonical printed material, but from a more evaluative perspective informed by Disability Studies (p. 5). Dickie notes the popularity and wide diffusion of jestbooks even among 'middle- or upper-class readers' (p. 4), and their consistently callous depiction of the 'deformed and disabled', an attitude which he suggests was entirely compatible with eighteenth-century standards of 'politeness' (p. 5). Dickie considers the possibility that eighteenth-century laughter at physical infirmity might have been a defensive reaction (p. 16), but adduces evidence to show that derision of the disabled was a practice deeply ingrained in eighteenth-century society (pp. 15–16).

Lisa Maruca's article 'Bodies of Type: The Work of Textual Production in English Printers' Manuals' (*ECS* 36[2003] 321–43) represents a kind of scholarship in the history of the book which is more concerned with the way in which the mechanics of textual manufacture are implicated in the production of culturally specific hermeneutic stances. Maruca deploys a theoretically sophisticated reading of a seventeenth-century printer's manual in order to argue that during this period the print worker's 'physical construction of print' is regarded as 'every bit as, if not more, important than the writer who supplies text' (p. 234). She contrasts this with the elimination of the printer worker's body from the language of a mid eighteenth-century printer's manual, which she argues reflects a changed hermeneutic regime in which the author has achieved a condition of 'near theological immanence' (p. 336) which is also reflected in the changed economic and legal status of copyright.

An attention to the ideological implications of textual production is also evident in Urmi Bhowmik's 'Facts and Norms in the Marketplace of Print: John Dunton's *Athenian Mercury*' (*ECS* 36[2003] 345–65), which suggests that the question-and-answer format invented by Dunton's pioneering periodical served a popular cultural need for the reintegration of facts and social norms in the wake of their separation by the discourse of the new science (p. 346). Bhowmik argues that the secularized moral casuistry which was Dunton's staple mimicked the form of scientific argument, in that it 'involved the same dynamic of interaction between universal principles and specific circumstances as that operating in questions about natural science' (p. 359). The periodical thus implicitly provided rhetorical authorization for a discursive sphere in which publication of a personal moral dilemma, through the universalizing mechanism of print, could be equated with its rational and scientific resolution (p. 360).

Bhowmik's fundamental concern with the relationship of print culture to the institutions of modernity is shared by Brycchan Carey in 'William Wilberforce's Sentimental Rhetoric: Parliamentary Reportage and the Abolition Speech of 1789' (*AgeJ* 14[2003] 281–305), though Carey's emphasis differs in that the focus of his investigation is the pre-modern nature of eighteenth-century parliamentary reporting, in which an authorized text is impossible to identify. Drawing on an approach suggested by Dror Wahrman (p. 285), Carey argues that the contemporary scholar, instead of elevating one source such as Cobbett's *Parliamentary History* into a received text, can usefully analyse a number of variant texts of the same speech in order to explore 'the working of rhetoric in the period' (p. 285), and offers as an example varying newspaper reports of Wilberforce's 1789 speech for the abolition of the slave trade, suggesting that the sentimental aspects of Wilberforce's rhetoric are exaggerated in the reports in pro-government papers as a way of neutralizing his more substantive arguments (p. 296).

Helen Braithwaite takes the publishing career of Joseph Johnson as the focus of her monograph *Romanticism, Publishing and Dissent: Joseph Johnson and the Cause of Liberty* (see also Chapter XII, section 1, below). She intends not only to complicate standard characterizations of Johnson as a 'radical publisher' (p. xiii) by illustrating the political range of his publishing commitments, but also to question assumptions about the nature of late eighteenth-century 'radicalism' itself (p. xiv). Through discussion of Johnson's decision not to publish Paine's *Rights of Man*, she illustrates how he differed from 'other more reckless, innately oppositional and fomenting booksellers' (p. 110), and shows that some of his other decisions of the 1790s, such as the dropping of Blake's *The French Revolution* (p. 119) and publishing of Wordsworth's *An Evening Walk* (p. 129), were commercial in nature, rather than being politicized in the manner suggested by some historicist literary critics. Her survey of Johnson's publishing business demonstrates how closely it was entwined with the development of Unitarianism (p. 10), and particularly with the career of Priestley, but she emphasizes the contrast between Johnson's willingness to publish 'even the most controversial and speculative religious works' (p. 110), and the way he avoided identification with specific political causes, such as American independence (p. 42), suggesting that the identification of Johnson and his fellow Unitarians as political 'radicals' has its origin in British counter-revolutionary propaganda rather than historical reality (p. 101), so that 'any reputation he might have as an explicitly "radical" publisher has its roots less in the world of "radical" politics than "radicalized" dissent' (p. 181). Braithwaite comments that 'probably the most over-archingly "radical" and, in many ways, heroic feature of Johnson's career as a bookseller was his scrupulous attempt to conduct his business independently during a period of intense political factionalism and when press-buying and hiring … were commonplace' (p. 168).

Stuart Andrews covers similar historical territory to Braithwaite in his *Unitarian Radicalism: Political Rhetoric, 1770–1814*, which aims to identify 'the continuities in Unitarian rhetoric' (p. 158) before and after the crucial decade of the 1790s, in order to make a case for the continuing political significance of Unitarianism up to the final passing of the Unitarian Relief Bill of 1813 (p. x). Following J.C.D. Clark's emphasis on the continuing importance of religion in eighteenth-century Britain, Andrews is careful to stress that Unitarianism cannot adequately be characterized as a secularizing rationalism (pp. 13–20), and provides a useful overview of the Unitarian theological position. Andrews's exclusive focus on sermons, however, starts to feel somewhat limiting in the latter half of the book, and doesn't adequately address the question he raises as to whether 'anyone [was] still listening after 1800' (p. 158) in the way he might have done had he paid some attention to Unitarian rhetoric in other discursive genres.

Recent critical interest in the category of 'affect' has prompted renewed attention to the other side of the revolution controversy in the shape of the melodramatic rhetoric of Burke's *Reflections on the Revolution in France*. Two important articles, also covered in Chapter XII below, can be briefly mentioned here. Anne Mallory's 'Burke, Boredom and the Theater of Counterrevolution' (*PMLA* 118[2003] 224–38) extends previous critical study of 'the relation between Burke's theatrical style and his counterrevolutionary argument (p. 224) by examining the relationship Burke perceives between the 'revolutionary temperament' (p. 227) and boredom. Elizabeth Samet's 'Spectacular History and the Politics of Theater: Sympathetic Arts in the Shadow of the Bastille' (*PMLA* 118[2003] 1305–19) suggests that an explanation of the theatricality of Burke's rhetoric in the *Reflections* can be found in his assumptions about the moral exemplarity of the theatre; for Burke theatre acts as a 'school of moral sentiments'(p. 1308).

A focus on the affective dimension of eighteenth-century politics also characterizes Barbara Taylor's intellectual biography, *Mary Wollstonecraft and the Feminist Imagination* (also discussed in Chapter XII in relation to Wollstonecraft's fiction). Taylor seeks to rescue Wollstonecraft's thought from the 'presentism of recent interpretations' (p. 10) by reinstating it within the context of her religious beliefs. She argues that the modern critical tendency to secularize Wollstonecraft's ideas obscures the 'utopian thrust' (p. 4) which is essential to their critical force, leading to a 'misrepresentation of her as a bourgeois liberal' (p. 12). The true 'radicalism' (p. 3) of her feminism, Taylor suggests, can only be understood from a perspective that is prepared to acknowledge her vision of 'a female self redeemed by [the] transcendent fantasy' (p. 21) of theism, since the assumption that there can be 'a politics purged of feeling and fantasy is a chimera, a modern myth' (p. 19). Taylor deploys a psychoanalytic vocabulary in order to analyse the affective roots of Wollstonecraft's early contemptuous dismissal of the available models of femininity and her later embrace of domesticity with Godwin, and suggests in conclusion that the dissenting religious tradition gives 1790s radicalism a social dimension which distinguishes it from the 'heroic individualism' (p. 229) of bourgeois liberalism, enabling the later Wollstonecraft to escape from the 'misogyny of the republican civic ideal' (p. 211) and find a model of 'female independence' which 'is not merely compatible with women's domestic obligations, but defined by them' (p. 229).

Anne Stott's biography, *Hannah More: The First Victorian*, similarly attempts to reclaim its subject from a decontextualized modern interpretation, in this case E.P. Thompson's portrayal of her Sunday schools as 'counter-revolutionary institutions imposing an alien value system through "psychological atrocities"' (p. 106). Stott emphasizes the necessarily strategic element in More's engagements with the society of her day, pointing out that as a not particularly wealthy woman More had no special authority over the poor (p. 106) and producing evidence to show that 'the Mendip schools had to work hard at being popular' (p. 115). When considering statements drawn from her letters which emphasize 'the utilitarian aspects of her programme' (p. 120), Stott notes, we need to take into account the people to whom they were written, as it was necessary for More to appeal to the self-interest of local stakeholders (p. 108) in order to win support for the schools; it was only this 'assiduous networking' (p. 240), Stott argues, which enabled More's schools to survive the Blagdon controversy, in which they were accused of social subversion. Stott interprets More's well-known counter-revolutionary tract *Village Politics* as reflecting 'Pittite Whiggism rather than unreconstructed Toryism' (p. 139), suggesting that 'its conservatism is ambiguous and paradoxical' (p. 143) in that the gesture of putting the loyalist case into the mouth of the village blacksmith tacitly acknowledges 'that it was no longer possible to pretend that the mass of the population could be excluded from political debates' (p. 144). Kevin Gilmartin, in 'Study to be Quiet: Hannah More and the Invention of Conservative Culture in Britain' (*ELH* 70[2003] 493–540), protests against the kind of political recuperation of More which Stott's biography represents, claiming that More's tracts 'are clearly driven more by her own aims and desires than by any scrupulous fidelity to the way that individuals in the position of her characters might have thought and felt' (p. 508). He concludes instead that the example of More demonstrates the need for modern interpreters to acknowledge the reformist impulse behind many 'conservative movements during the extended crisis that has been termed Britain's "long counterrevolution"' rather than seeking to assimilate all forms of conservatism during the 1790s to a Burkean position characterized as 'primarily defensive, traditionalist, exclusionary and tied to an organic vision of history and society that resisted wholesale strategies of revision' (p. 501).

A questioning of the Boswellian stereotype of a gruff misogynist has provided the impetus behind much recent work on Samuel Johnson, and Sarah R. Morrison's 'Samuel Johnson, Mr Rambler and Women' (*AgeJ* 14[2003] 23–50) continues this trend, arguing that Johnson's reluctance to emphasize gender difference among the audience for his periodical (p. 26) can be interpreted as a sign that he was 'more conscious of women as an important part of his audience than is generally recognized' since it implies a recognition that 'they partake equally of universal human nature with men' (p. 24). Iona Italia, in 'Johnson as Moralist in *The Rambler*' (*AgeJ* 14[2003] 51–76), shares this characterization of the stylistic features of *The Rambler* as a direct reflection of Johnson's 'anachronistic project' (p. 73) as moralist, highlighting its unusual 'uniformity of tone; its adoption of a person who is a representative figure, rather than an eccentric individual; its focus on the universals of human behaviour rather than current affairs or the fashions and follies beloved of Richard Steele … its didactic tone' (p. 51) as consequences of Johnson's attempt 'to reunite a society which he regarded as deeply divided' (p. 53). Timothy Erwin suggests, in 'Scribblers, Servants and Johnson's *Life of Savage*' (*AgeJ* 14[2003] 99–130), that this concern with social unity underlies Johnson's portrayal of Savage, widely understood as a veiled criticism of Pope's divisive attacks in *The Dunciad* which were based on information supplied by Savage (pp. 102–3).

Johnson's relationships with women also receive some biographical scrutiny. Gay W. Hughes argues, in 'The Estrangement of Hester Thrale and Samuel Johnson: A Revisionist View' (*AgeJ* 14[2003]145–91), that modern biographers have uncritically reproduced the Boswellian view of the cooling off between Johnson and Hester Thrale, tinged as it is with jealousy at her relationship with Johnson (p. 145), and that Thrale's behaviour is understandable as a reaction to the very particular set of circumstances she was left in after her husband's death. In 'Johnson's Poverty: The Uses of Adversity' (*AgeJ* 14[2003] 131–43) Aaron Stavisky suggests that the biographical myth of Johnson's poverty in his early days as a writer has served to cover up his reluctance to visit his mother. Lyle Larsen, meanwhile, in 'Dr Johnson's Friend, the Elegant Topham Beauclerk' (*AgeJ* 14[2003] 221–37), examines Johnson's uncharacteristic friendship with a society figure.

The reception of Johnson also comes in for attention. Michael Bundock, in 'The Making of Johnson's *Prayers and Meditations*' (*AgeJ* 14[2003] 77–97), examines George Strahan's editorial practice in preparing Johnson's spiritual journal for posthumous publication, a book which, surprisingly, influenced Beckett's play *Krapp's Last Tape* (p. 81). Stephen Clarke, in '"Prejudice, Bigotry and Arrogance": Horace Walpole's Abuse of Samuel Johnson' (*AgeJ* 14[2003] 239–57), scrutinizes Walpole's strikingly personal and vindictive comments on Johnson in annotations to his books, while Catherine Dille, in 'Johnson, Hill and the "Good Old Cause": Liberal Interpretation in the Editions of George Birkbeck Hill' (*AgeJ* 14[2003] 193–219), describes the politically liberal nineteenth-century milieu from which Birkbeck Hill's influential scholarly edition of the *Life of Johnson* emerged. Johnson's own reception of Milton is examined in Christine Rees, 'Johnson Reads *Areopagitica*' (*AgeJ* 14[2003] 1–21), in which 'Johnson's unexpected and continued interest in Milton's prose' (p. 3), which it is suggested was an influence on some of the *Rambler* essays on criticism, is explained in terms of his opposition to stage censorship (p. 6).

Some more sustained interpretation of Johnson is offered in Fred Parker's monograph, *Scepticism and Literature: An Essay on Pope, Hume, Sterne and Johnson*, where a reading of *Rasselas* which stresses its 'open-endedness or inconclusiveness' (p. 262) is offered as justification for a characterization of Johnson which portrays him as a thinker similar to Hume, in that he incorporates 'the sceptical awareness of plurality and indeterminacy within the activity of positive inquiry and the articulation of strong perceptions' (p. 2). The book's assimilation of these two very different figures reflects Parker's interpretation of Hume, which centres on the end of Book I of the *Treatise on Human Nature*, where, as Parker puts it, there is a turn 'from sceptical crisis to "the common affairs of life"' (p. 143). Parker omits any discussion of Hume's influential eighteenth-century opponents, the Common Sense philosophers Thomas Reid and James Beattie, who are very much concerned with the implications of scepticism and whose interpretations of Hume bear some resemblance to Parker's own, and as a result the basically Rortyean model of 'scepticism' which Parker employs (p. 4) is liable to the objection that it ignores the historical specificity of the positions adopted by the figures he discusses, tending to reduce 'scepticism' to a purely formal quality of discourse. In particular, Parker largely neglects the role that the issue of religious belief played in eighteenth-century debates about scepticism, so that it might be questioned whether a definition of 'sceptical thinking' which is potentially broad enough to accommodate such unquestionably orthodox divines as Joseph Butler or William Paley is really an adequate tool of analysis.

Such questions about historical method in criticism are, as Jack Lynch shows in *The Age of Elizabeth in the Age of Johnson*, essentially an invention of the eighteenth century. Lynch argues that the eighteenth century had a recognizably modern conception of the period we now call the Renaissance (p. 67), and shows that this was formed remarkably early in the century, being reflected above all in Milton's 'rapid transformation into a vernacular classic' (p. 145) through commentaries and glosses. Lynch suggests that this forms part of the wider project of canon-formation by which eighteenth-century Britain came to articulate its own sense of modernity (p. 143). The crucial role of historical discourse in shaping conceptions of modernity is an issue underlying William Kolbrener's radical reinterpretation of Mary Astell in 'Gendering the Modern: Mary Astellapos;s Feminist Historiography' (*ECent* 44[2003] 1–24), which characterizes both Astell's High Church position and her feminism as aspects of an overarching critique of 'latitudinarian orthodoxy' (p. 2) in which 'the inauthenticity of ... Williamite culture' is understood as indicative of a society 'governed by masculine artifice' (p. 11). Eighteenth-century historiography also comes under scrutiny in Mark Salber Phillips, 'Relocating Inwardness: Historical Distance and the Transition from Enlightenment to Romantic Historiography' (*PMLA* 118:iii[2003] 436–49), whose examination of continuities between the affective aims of eighteenth-century historiography and the radicalization of those aims in Romantic historians, in which 'the historian's own relation to the past' (p. 447) becomes an issue, forms the basis for a more general theory of 'historiographical genres' (p. 428).

The recent historiographical and critical emphasis on eighteenth-century consumer culture is at once continued and modified in Berg and Eger, eds., *Luxury in the Eighteenth Century: Debates, Desires and Delectable Goods*, which seeks to complicate over-simplistic historical narratives of a 'progression from disapprobation to endorsement of luxury' (p. 2) by exploring the contested nature of the concept throughout the eighteenth century. In their introductory essay, 'The Rise and Fall of the Luxury Debates', Berg and Eger argue that the desire for a clear historical narrative leads historians of ideas such as John Sekora to neglect 'satire that is less clearly poised in a position of moral outrage, but rather suggests the complexity and confusion of modern experience' (p. 17), and suggest that Mandeville himself might be interpreted as writing this kind of satire. Edward Hundert's 'Mandeville, Rousseau and the Political Economy of Fantasy' continues this line of argument by suggesting that the aspect of Mandeville's thought that had the most profound influence on Rousseau's 'critique of modernity' (p. 28) was his emphasis on 'how fantasy had become an integral feature of worlds transformed by a surfeit of goods' (p. 29), an emphasis that also accounts for the re-emergence of interest in Mandeville in the twentieth-century society of the spectacle. The ambivalence of the eighteenth century's relationship with luxury is stressed in Michael McKeon's 'Aestheticising the Critique of Luxury: Smollett's *Humphry Clinker*', which draws attention to the way in which the character of Matthew Bramble, often assumed to be a mere mouthpiece for Smollett's own views on luxury (p. 57), is shown to be 'ineluctably mixed ' with 'the things he purports to despise' (p. 63). John Styles further explores this ambivalence in 'Custom or Consumption? Plebeian Fashion in Eighteenth-Century England', in which he argues that the tendency of historians to assume that participation in the fashion market by 'young adult plebeians' is incompatible with 'the commitment to custom that Edward Thompson saw as the principal defence of working people against the rigours of the free market' (p. 104) is mistaken.

A number of the essays in the collection examine the relationship of luxury to eighteenth-century ideas about aesthetics. Annie Richardson, in 'From the Moral Mound to the Material Maze: Hogarth's *Analysis of Beauty*', argues that the 'materialism and apparent "amorality"' of Hogarth's aesthetics, particularly in its emphasis on variety, aligns him with those thinkers who were attempting to 'demoralize' (p. 119) the issue of luxury. John Crowley, in 'From Luxury to Comfort and Back Again: Landscape Architecture and the Cottage in Britain and America', suggests a connection between the picturesque aesthetic and the 'new historical phenomenon of concern about the miserably uncomfortable housing of the mass of the rural population' (p. 141), while Jenny Uglow, in 'Vase Mania', provides a historical account of Wedgwood and Boulton's exploitation of the fashion for vases in 1771–2. The relationship between women and the feminized category of luxury also represents a focus for the collection, with Ros Ballaster's 'Performing Roxane: The Oriental Woman as the Sign of Luxury in Eighteenth-Century Fictions' arguing that the 'class mobility ... and ideological flexibility' of figures of 'orientalised femininity' such as Defoe's Roxana testify to 'the ambivalent attitudes towards luxury in England' (p 166), and Vivien Jones, in 'Luxury, Satire and Prostitute Narratives', drawing attention to the satirical nature and generic self-consciousness of the eighteenth-century 'prostitution narrative' which often makes it function as a commentary on the 'luxury debates' (p. 181). The link between the luxury debate and the literary canon is explored in Elizabeth Eger's 'Luxury, Industry and Charity: Bluestocking Culture Displayed', which suggests that ideas about luxury inform reactions to the embryonic salon culture of Elizabeth Montagu and her fellow Bluestockings.

It is difficult in a review of this kind to do justice to the multifaceted or 'polyphonic' (p. 3) argument of Peter de Bolla's *The Education of the Eye: Painting, Landscape and Architecture in Eighteenth-Century Britain*, an extraordinary study which explores issues in eighteenth-century aesthetics in order to mount a case for an ethics of culture (pp. 216–17) in opposition to the moral emptiness of postmodern irony (p. 165), with more than a nod to Ruskin (p. 153). De Bolla's central theoretical concern is with the cultural phenomenology of looking, an act whereby we enter 'the theatre of visuality... seeing as others see, seeing ourselves as others see us' and so become a 'social subject' (p. 86). This interpretative approach, which is indebted to Adam Smith's account of the 'ideal spectator' in his *Theory of Moral Sentiments* (p. 76), is applied to mid-eighteenth-century visual culture, represented by painting, gardens and architecture and characterized by de Bolla as an induction into 'a public space in which the viewer learned how to look and to be seen, observed, in the activity of looking' (p. 57). De Bolla concludes the book with an extended reading of Adams's building Kedlestone Hall, which he suggests is a concrete embodiment of 'a sociopolitical program that seeks to educate the eye into the fraternity of culture' (pp. 216–17). One of the most impressive features of the book is the fresh agenda it sets for scholarly work on the eighteenth century, in that its critical readings articulate a new kind of cultural politics in which aesthetic interpretation would not be concerned to 'allegorize' cultural artefacts in the manner of much new-historicist criticism, but would represent a quasi-Heideggerian 'way of being with the artwork, being with its knowingness' (p. 13).

2. The Novel

First, an apology: last year's entry failed to include Thomas Keymer, *Sterne, the Moderns, and the Novel* [2002]. This generous and careful study takes a fresh look at one of the most persistent of literary-critical spats. The homage that Russian formalists of the 1920s paid to *Tristram Shandy* as a 'radical revolutionary' in formal terms (p. 22) has endured into our own times: Sterne is often celebrated for his modernity, open-endedness, and intertextuality. Meanwhile, plenty of scholarly endeavour has been spent on asserting, contrariwise, that *Tristram Shandy* is 'not a stranded modern but a wilful Renaissance throwback'—a late addition to the 'learned wit' camp of Rabelais, Burton, and Menippean satire (p. 5). Keymer cheerily concedes that the goal of his study will seem, in this context, 'doubly perverse', for it is to insist that *Tristram Shandy* is neither exclusively forward-looking nor exclusively backward-looking (p. 6). While he often registers the 'learned wit' tradition as it manifests itself in *Tristram Shandy*, Keymer also gives ample space to the novel's prescient, 'disruptive sophistication', seeing a 'creative co-existence' between the two (pp. 6, 26). The great strength of *Sterne, the Moderns, and the Novel* is its scrupulous, lucid analysis of how novelists play with the imagination of their readers. Keymer is especially good at eliciting Sterne's dependence on, and impish reinventions of, numerous major and minor eighteenth-century writers of fiction. And the book's sustained comparison of Sterne's approach to serialization with George Eliot's—a form of publishing caught 'between openness and closure', which gives *Tristram Shandy* much of its improvisatory, modern feel (p. 88)—is as enjoyable as it is illuminating. On the evidence of this study, Keymer is quite right to argue that 'it is worth the effort of imaginatively reconstructing the experience of [Sterne's] first audience, for whom access to *Tristram Shandy* came in five distinct stages of reading, phased over eighty-five months' (p. 85).

For Fred Parker in *Scepticism and Literature: An Essay on Pope, Hume, Sterne, and Johnson*, eighteenth-century thinking about the limits of rationality inherits its shape and complexity from Montaigne's digressive, tolerant, self-sufficient essays—particularly from his musings on the character of Socrates. Parker makes an excellent case for the influence of Montaigne and Locke on the only novelist among his four titular subjects. Without diminishing Sterne's complex intelligence, Parker's fifth chapter manages to explain how the novel subdues all experience to its own singular indeterminacy. The sceptical, freewheeling humour of *Tristram Shandy* seemingly finds its natural opponent in the figure of Walter Shandy, whose 'narrow and overweening rationality' and 'determination to regulate life' are set against the 'joyous spontaneity' and deflection of reality that typify Sterne's narrative from the outset (p. 192). Yet Tristram fails to provide the formulaic conclusion of a comedy—marriage—while even Walter's notions are classed within the novel as sceptical, because they are as eccentric as everyone else's. Like Tristram, Walter has his hobby-horse; the only difference is that Tristram is aware of the fact. Parker argues that widow Wadman, who 'has intentions, and acts accordingly', is the closest *Tristram Shandy* gets to a moral agent; as such, she threatens the contingency and uniqueness that characterize the novel's protagonists (and the fiction itself): 'Their singularity is what they have in common' (p. 210). Like Berkeley and Locke, Sterne erodes the authenticity of generalization in favour of the particular and the individual. But successful communication jeopardizes singularity—hence the 'spectacular failures' of description and narration, as well as the emphasis on modesty, isolation, and self-consciousness throughout *Tristram Shandy* (p. 214).

Christina Lupton, '*Tristram Shandy*, David Hume and Epistemological Fiction' (*P&L* 27[2003] 98–115), covers much of the same terrain as Parker's chapter on Sterne: the 'quandaries of rationality under pressure' and 'the fracturing implications of skepticism' (pp. 98, 99). Lupton diverges from a critical tradition which sees *Tristram Shandy* as solving or resolving the problems of epistemological uncertainty articulated by Locke and Hume. She prefers to think of such uncertainty as the foundation for a productive fictional relationship between 'literature as an object of knowledge' and literary language as 'subjective response' (p. 99).

Christopher Fanning, 'Small Particles of Eloquence: Sterne and the Scriblerian Text' (*MP* 100[2003] 360–92), appears in a special issue of *Modern Philology* (100:iii[2003]), dedicated to 'Early Prose Fiction: Edges and Limits of the Novel'. Fanning summarizes attitudes towards textuality as expressed by classical and Renaissance Menippean satirists, before discussing the relationship to this tradition of Pope and Sterne's *mise-en-page*. Contextualized within the history of the book, *Tristram Shandy* is said to place 'manuscript uniqueness' at odds with 'printed repetition' (p. 392). Originality, it is suggested, lies in each individual copy of the book, rather than in the abstract entity that is *Tristram Shandy* the novel. Robert A. Erickson, 'Fictions of the Heart: Sterne, Law, and the Long Eighteenth Century' (*ECF* 15[2003] 559–82), explores 'the fiction-making powers' of literary and religious authors ranging from Boehme to Wordsworth, and discovers resemblances between Sterne and William Law—chiefly in their 'visionary view of Christianity' (pp. 560, 562). Robert Darby, '"An oblique and slovenly initiation": The Circumcision Episode in *Tristram Shandy*' (*ECLife* 27[2003] 72–84), asks why Sterne made so much of Tristram's childhood encounter with a sash window, and of his parents' failure to attend immediately to his injury. He concludes that it may have something to do with the 1753 campaign against the Jewish Naturalization Act, a campaign which 'emphasized possession of a foreskin as the sign of a "true born Briton"' whose individual property rights had to be respected (p. 74).

The year 2002 saw publication of another door-stopper volume (number 6) in the Florida Edition of the Works of Laurence Sterne: New and Day, eds., *A Sentimental Journey through France and Italy and Continuation of the Bramine's Journal*. The introduction is humanely alert to the treatment of illness, charity, and solitude in both texts; it manages to tease out the distinctive aspects of Sterne's sensibility without coming across as mawkish or stale. Supported by a bewildering wealth of textual appendices, this edition reveals, above all else, Sterne's 'sensitivity to diction and syntax' (p. lvii). Christopher Nagle, 'Sterne, Shelley, and Sensibility's Pleasures of Proximity' (*ELH* 70[2003] 813–45), argues that Shelley's posthumously published essay 'On Love' draws on *A Sentimental Journey*'s brand of quivering, redemptive social communion. Unlike Fred Parker, Nagle perceives in Sterne the reciprocal expression of feeling.

The best book about Jane Austen to have emerged for at least a decade places her in the communicative milieu of Sterne, Johnson, Flaubert, and Beckett. In *Jane Austen and the Morality of Conversation*, Bharat Tandon argues that 'conversation is in Austen less a technique than a constitutive atmosphere of her work' (p. 3). Setting out as a writer at the close of the eighteenth century, Austen testifies to a linguistic and social diffusion that was threatening earlier ideals of conversation 'as a cohesive activity, which not only displayed but materially advanced the refinement of civilization' (p. 12). By the 1780s and 1790s, manuals on female conduct and linguistic practice tended to advance a prescriptive moralism. Against such conservative social demarcation as was on show in, say, Hester Lynch Piozzi's *British Synonymy*, stood radical treatises such as Horne Tooke's *Diversions of Purley*, as well as attacks on female accomplishments. Prescription and radicalism, in Tandon's account, skirt the margins of Austen's writing. Endorsing neither of them, she creates in her novels a form of circumvention: 'refusing to be defined by what confined her', one of Austen's major achievements is 'the ability to make reticence speak' (pp. 64, 35). Tandon variously conceives of the novels as exchanges between characters, between narrators and heroines, between readers and the texts, and between the texts and themselves. Construing Austen's novels as conversations is to revisit and to clarify a sense of their language as vocal and bodily performance—at once personally committed and resistant to a single line of interpretation. Depressing as it is to acknowledge in a review of the latest work on eighteenth-century novels, the real value of this book inheres in its refusal to embrace the latest trends of Austen criticism. Rather, Tandon draws attention to the comedy of manners and to the ethics of fiction—aspects of her writing which have fallen out of favour. Stressing throughout his study the importance of gesture, contingency, furniture, clutter, memory, space, and the complex matter of literary surfaces which are in touch with their depths, Tandon's subtlest and most imaginative engagements are with *Mansfield Park*. His interpretation of this persistently under-rated, puzzling novel as a masterpiece of 'differential narrative' which toys knowingly with melodramatic symbols, connections, and 'narrative watersheds'—only to redirect its reader towards 'apparent troughs or plateaus … the murkier and less conspicuous parts' of the story—is full of moving surprises (pp. 215, 219). Here,

Austen's skill lies in prompting her audience 'to recognize both the psychological suggestiveness of inhabited space, and those instances where a door may simply be a door' (p. 207). Considering Austen as 'a poet of domestic pathology' (p. 229) produces very different readings from those now prevalent in the American academy: Tandon's beautifully written study makes room for his subject's many voices. This book suggests a heartening new direction for Austen criticism, currently bogged down (for the most part) in latent and meretricious readings.

One such reading is presented by William H. Galperin, *The Historical Austen*, a book which aspires by turns to be 'ironic', 'earnest', and 'provocative' (pp. 1, 109), but which succeeds chiefly in being flashy and difficult to understand. This is a shame, as many striking elements of Galperin's lengthy study—Austen's response to theories of the picturesque; the legacy of epistolary writing to free indirect style; Austen's reception history—have the potential, as is shown by Tandon's discussion of the same topics, to illuminate the novels. Part of the problem here is that there is too little quotation from the fictions themselves, and too much glancing, quixotic summary. Galperin begins with the acknowledgement that his subject (like Sterne) has been cast as ahead of and as behind her times. Such viewpoints, he argues, pay insufficient heed to 'more antithetical aspects' of the historical Austen (p. 68), whose writings might be described as resistant to contemporary norms. Reading her novels through other histories—aesthetic, literary, cultural, and social—Galperin endeavours to modify the feminist/conservative figure of Austen perpetuated in literary criticism. Even though he sets out to complicate matters, he could have done so in terms more accessible than those of a 'heterogeneity' which is 'the answerable method to a representational initiative from which the difference or "density" accruable to a world "over time" was largely inseparable' (p. 7).

The young Austen was among the earliest readers of Charlotte Smith's first novel *Emmeline*, which has been reissued in affordable, lively, and attractive form by Broadview Press. Loraine Fletcher's helpful introduction ranges with ease over a number of social, historical, and literary influences on and contexts for Smith's work. The mixed reception of the novel is well represented in one appendix, while the inclusion of Mary Hays's anonymous biographical entry in *British Public Characters* makes it conveniently possible for the reader to discern resemblances between heroine and author.

David Wheeler, 'Jane Austen and the Discourse of Poverty' (*ECN* 3[2003] 243–62) sees Austen's fictional treatment of poor and marginalized characters as poised between a faith in 'traditional feudal relationships' and a consciousness of 'the gentry's deficiency in performing its responsibilities' (pp. 259, 258). Addressing a related topic, Kay Weeks, 'Fielding Looks Down: *Tom Jones* and the Lower Orders' (*ECN* 3[2003] 97–127), concludes that Fielding's 'conflicting sensibilities' (p. 123)—sympathy for the poor, combined with a fear of social mobility—are on show throughout his novelistic career.

It seems to amount to a rule in most quarters, these days, that a text must be cast as transgressive or subversive in order to defend its right to critical analysis or renewed attention. But since so many works are now labelled as such, to be transgressive or subversive no longer seems to indicate something that is genuinely challenging, ground-breaking, or even mildly disconcerting. The latest rediscovered novel to come in for the boundary-crossing treatment is Frances Brooke's *The History of Emily Montague*, her second work of fiction, set chiefly in colonial Canada. Jodi L. Wyett, '"No place where women are of such importance": Female Friendship, Empire, and Utopia in *The History of Emily Montague*' (*ECF* 16[2003] 33–57), reads the book as a daring combination of sentimental fiction with travelogue, a form which 'transgresses many boundaries—generic, geographic, and gendered—in its wide geographical scope, its uneasy negotiation of the colonial economy, and its potentially transgressive utopian possibilities for women' (p. 33). The same critic investigates the same author in 'Of Innocence and Experience: Fame, Fortune, and Women's Intellectual Labor in Frances Brooke's *The Excursion*' (*ECN* 3[2003] 129–56). In a discussion which typifies recent criticism of eighteenth-century novels in its failure to consider literary or stylistic merit, Brooke is said to demonstrate 'a deep ambivalence towards the connection between intellectual labor and economic profit' (p. 129). Ana M. Acosta, 'Hotbeds of Popery: Convents in the English Literary Imagination' (*ECF* 15[2003] 615–42), which figures in a special number of the journal, 'Fiction and Religion' (*ECF* 15:iii–iv[2003]), includes *The History of Emily Montague* as one of a series of female, Richardsonian, and sentimental novels whose central plot device is the abduction or voluntary removal of an English girl to a French convent.

Other articles devoted to 'Fiction and Religion' are, not surprisingly, dominated by the figure of Richardson. John A. Dussinger, '"Stealing in the Great Doctrines of Christianity": Samuel Richardson as a Journalist' (*ECF* 15[2003] 451–506), charts the novelist's parallel careers of printing and anonymous hack-writing. As in his fiction, so in his journalism Richardson was preoccupied by 'the many practical moral concerns facing his contemporaries' (p. 482). Lois Chaber, 'Christian Form and Anti-Feminism in *Clarissa*' (*ECF* 15[2003] 507–38), rehearses the critic's mixed feelings about a 'considerable vein of Christian patriarchal authority' that she has recently discerned in the novel—having previously mistaken it for a feminist manifesto (p. 508). Teri Doerksen, '*Sir Charles Grandison*: The Anglican Family and the Admirable Roman Catholic' (*ECF* 15[2003] 539–58), finds Richardson's last novel remarkable for the positive virtues it bestows on Catholic characters, and for the dream of English 'ascendance over the continent' elaborated at its close (p. 558). Here, Doerksen argues, Richardson presents a vision of England as 'the centre of a new kind of international and inter-religious community' (p. 558).

Other articles in this number include Martin C. Battestin, 'The Critique of Freethinking from Swift to Sterne' (*ECF* 15[2003] 341–420)—a useful survey of heterodox writing and its adversaries—and George Starr, 'Why Defoe Probably Did Not Write *The Apparition of Mrs. Veal*' (*ECF* 15[2003] 421–50). Starr challenges the conventional ascription of this work on the grounds that Defoe did not believe in ghosts (and would therefore be unlikely to make one the central figure in his work). Several Anglican divines mentioned approvingly in *The Apparition* were High Church anti-dissenters and therefore 'anathema to Defoe', who poked fun at two of them in print (p. 421). Srividhya Swaminathan, 'Defoe's Alternative Conduct Manual: Survival Strategies and Female Networks in *Moll Flanders*' (*ECF* 15[2003] 185–206), compares Defoe's fiction with his *Family*

Instructor. Presented as genuine historical accounts, the novels 'may offer the opportunity to illustrate more realistic social conditions than those which [Defoe] creates for the family in his conduct manual … Defoe embeds in each novel a moral lesson that can be read as an extension of the instruction he gives in his conduct manual' (p. 189). In the end, however, Moll's narrative puts survival above ethical instruction, and the novelist vanquishes the moralist. James Cruise, 'Childhood, Play, and the Contexts of *Robinson Crusoe*' (*AgeJ* 14[2003] 259–80), examines the fictional lacuna that is Crusoe's early life 'as constituting a period that is inherently significant with consequences that spur him throughout his adventures' (p. 260). Why then, he asks, 'does Crusoe have no real childhood to report in his narrative life? Were answers as easy as questions' (p. 262). Indeed. Cruise spends the bulk of his article deferring an answer, instead presenting evidence about contemporary developments in child-rearing, even speculating on the contents of a spurious parental 'tea chest' preserving the young Crusoe's toys 'in one of the recesses of the Yorkshire estate' (p. 265). Despite promising us that 'The case I intend to plead' is that Crusoe compensates for his lost childhood 'through play', Cruise is still considering three pages before the end of his essay the conditions that must exist 'Before [Crusoe] can play' (p. 274).

Patricia Brückmann, '"Men, Women and Poles": Samuel Richardson and the Romance of a Stuart Princess' (*ECL* 27[2003] 31–52), is a historical investigation into why Richardson might have chosen 'Clementina' as the name for his Italian heroine in *Sir Charles Grandison*: it summons up the figure of Maria Clementina Sobieska, who later married James Stuart, pretender to the English throne. By the time Richardson was composing *Grandison*, the princess had been abducted on two occasions and repeatedly invoked in Jacobite and Catholic propaganda. Her force in the novel, however, is (Brückmann concludes) 'literary and imaginative, not a sign of instructive allegory' (p. 44). Albert J. Rivero, 'Teaching the Eighteenth-Century Novel: Beginning *Grandison*' (*ECN* 3[2003] 293–301), is a useful overview of interpretative complexities in Richardson, but it offers very few of 'the pedagogical strategies' that are promised at the outset (p. 293).

Jennifer Preston Wilson, '*Clarissa*: The Nation Misruled' (*ECN* 3[2003] 65–96), reads the novel through a series of parallels between family and nation: Mr Harlowe is represented as a tyrannical king, responsible for failures of wit and judgement throughout his clan, while the heroine's closeness to Anna Howe suggests 'an opposing view of how a healthy community might function with wit and judgment in alliance' (p. 68). Building on Scott Paul Gordon, *The Power of the Passive Self in English Literature, 1640–1770* [2002], Heather Zias, 'Who Can Believe? Sentiment vs. Cynicism in Richardson's *Clarissa*' (*ECL* 27[2003] 99–123), examines how the novelist sought to convert suspicious Mandevillian readers into a belief in Clarissa's virtue. Addressing the conceptual problems which underpin natural law theory, Zias asserts that sentimentality or sensibility, far from compelling the audience (as Gordon argues) to side with the heroine, 'really becomes a means for Richardson to avoid the puzzling question: how *does* one believe?' (p. 102).

Kate Loveman, '"Full of improbable lies": *Gulliver's Travels* and Jest Books' (*BJECS* 26[2003]15–26) traces Swift's covert references, especially in

Gulliver's Lilliputian and Brobdingnagian adventures, to 'a veritable genre of coffee-house tall tales' (p. 15). She draws a series of comparisons between the improbabilities rehearsed in jest books from the Restoration to the early eighteenth century and those which govern Swift's fiction, concluding that the ideal reader of *Gulliver's Travels* is synonymous with the ideal participant in a coffee-house exchange or lying contest: 'one who learns the rules of the game, asks questions, and brings [his] own wit to bear on the subject at hand' (p. 24). Catherine Skeen, 'Projecting Fictions: *Gulliver's Travels*, *Jack Connor*, and *John Buncle*' (*MP* 100[2003] 330–59), usefully and deftly traces a series of associations between the plan, project, proposal, or scheme and the Irish novel. Pamphlets on national improvement derived chiefly from Anglican landowners and clergymen—those modest proposers whose elite status was compromised by instability and by their own tendency to take refuge in fantasy and a 'wishful amnesia' about their personal origins and identity (p. 340). Reading *Gulliver's Travels* through the 'lens of Irish projecting' (p. 340) turns out to make sense of many episodes that otherwise appear to be merely whimsical or inconsistent, while Chaigneau's *Jack Connor* 'draws attention to the projecting in all novels' (p. 348). *John Buncle* is less obvious a case study, since its author, unlike Swift and Chaigneau, was not himself a projector. Yet Amory's fiction also sees marginalia displacing plot, thereby translating 'the tensions that lie at the heart of Irish projecting—between what is desirable and what is doable, between vision and reality, between rhetoric and action—into novel form' (p. 359).

Scott Black, 'Trading Sex for Secrets in Haywood's *Love in Excess*' (*ECF* 15[2003] 207–39), is a well-intentioned attempt to see Haywood not only as a '*woman* writer' but also as a 'woman *writer*'—that is to say, as an individual 'who grappled not only with questions of identity but also with issues of form, and who belongs in our histories of the novel because her texts are self-conscious explorations of narrative' (p. 207). The remainder of the article fails to live up to its promising start. Black ends up contending that we should recognize in Haywood the pleasures she contrives for a curious reader: authorial wit and playfulness. Suzan Last, '"The Cabal were at a loss for the author's meaning": Eliza Haywood's *Adventures of Eovaai* as Metasatire' (in Troost, ed., *Eighteenth-Century Women*, pp. 25–46) makes a related pitch for Haywood's parodic and satirical instincts, arguing that the elaborate distancing framework of *Eovaai* mimics and exaggerates the stock techniques of anti-Walpole propaganda.

Robert J. Mayhew, 'Gothic Trajectories: Latitudinarian Theology and the Novels of Ann Radcliffe' (*ECF* 15[2003] 583–613), asserts that Radcliffe's fiction needs to be read in the specific context of latitudinarianism, central to which was 'the belief that natural religion proved the existence of God' (p. 590). Mayhew applies this belief to Radcliffe's descriptions of landscape—usually interpreted without any reference to their theological contours: 'Looking at picturesque and pastoral landscapes, Radcliffe characters were continually led to an appreciation of God's benevolence' (p. 599). Referring chiefly to *The Italian*, Beth Swan, 'Radcliffe's Inquisition and Eighteenth-Century Legal Practice' (*ECN* 3[2003] 195–216), relates late eighteenth-century images of the Bastille to those of the Inquisition, concluding that Radcliffe employs both as a means of reflecting on the practices of English law courts and prisons. Anne H. Stevens,

'Sophia Lee's Illegitimate History' (in Rivero, ed. pp. 263–91), views the Gothic novel *The Recess* as a means of refashioning more conventional histories—such as those of Hume and Robertson—into conjectural, uncertain, and imaginative hybrids. The dependence of fiction on historical narrative is also investigated in Betty A. Schellenberg, 'Making Good Use of History: Sarah Robinson Scott in the Republic of Letters' (in Mostefai and Ingrassia, eds., *Studies in Eighteenth-Century Culture*, pp. 45–92).

R. B. Gill, 'The Author in the Novel: Creating Beckford in *Vathek*' (*ECF* 15[2003] 241–54), sees *Vathek* as a work 'especially in need of a biographical centre to resolve its ambiguities' (p. 242); Beckford employs authorial self-consciousness and creates a number of personae in order to establish 'an aura of sophistication and control' (p. 243). Gill's argument lacks shape, so a reader gains little sense of why Beckford would have shirked direct self-presentation, or indeed whether he is unusual in this.

Besides *Emmeline*, Broadview has produced another excellent novelistic text this year: Walpole's *Castle of Otranto and The Mysterious Mother*, edited by Frederick S. Frank, complete with Walter Scott's 1811 introduction and a variety of contemporary reactions. Marcie Frank, 'Horace Walpole's Family Romances' (*MP* 100[2003] 417–35), is a Foucauldian study of incest in the two works. As a plot device, incest blocks inheritance—but it also points to a broader socio-political context: 'a clash between aristocratic and bourgeois models of the family' (p. 417). In Walpole's fiction and drama, incest overlaps with the genre of romance; this illicit mingling of genres and of family relationships springs, in addition, from an ambivalent sense of authorship. Incest is here construed as 'a crossroads at which questions of authorial position and cultural identity, questions of generic organization and hierarchy, and questions of the status of family relations converge' (p. 418).

Ellen Pollak, *Incest and the English Novel, 1684–1814*, is even more heavily influenced by Foucault; the study is also concerned, up to a point, with the relationship between incest as a topic and the novel 'as a bastard form' (p. 144). 'Significantly', as Pollak asserts, this is the first book-length study of incest in the novel (p. 2)—although that fact may be significant for reasons other than those she assumes. Critics have hitherto construed the possibility (very rarely is it a reality) of taboo familial relations as little more than an incidental or accidental recurrence in eighteenth-century novels. For Pollak, however, as for Frank, the motif of incest in Behn, Defoe, Delarivier Manley, Sarah and Henry Fielding, Burney, and Austen is evidence of a middle-class challenge to the landed aristocracy—a challenge bound up with the language of natural law and liberty, with acts of rebellion against (or reinforcements of) patriarchy and royalism, and with contests between the civil and ecclesiastical courts. She endeavours 'to show how reading some of the more canonical, male-authored versions of the [novel] against their lesser-known counterparts by women works to destabilize conventional binaries that have structured traditional discussions of the genre by exposing the ideological continuities that subtend the differences between, for example, formally closed and open texts, or between representations of male and female protagonists, and between averted and actual or intergenerational and intragenerational incest' (p. 23).

Diane Osland, 'Heart-Picking in *A Simple Story*' (*ECF* 16[2003] 79–101), argues that Elizabeth Inchbald struggles in her fiction with some 'intractable problems' (p. 101) of characterization and narrative device—problems that were later resolved by Austen. Yet *A Simple Story*'s failing in this regard might, according to Osland, also be seen as its merit, 'since it is in the very intractability of her characters that the strength of Inchbald's narrative lies' (p. 101).

Two articles on Wollstonecraft (reviewed in Chapter XII below) can be briefly mentioned here. Diane Long Hoeveler, 'The Tyranny of Sentimental Form: Wollstonecraft's *Mary* and the Gendering of Anxiety' (*ECN* 3[2003] 217–41), argues that Wollstonecraft's variety of feminism, thanks to its semi-reliance on an outdated sensibility, is riddled with contradictions. Gloria Schultz Eastman, 'Method to this Madness: Fragmented Discourse in Mary Wollstonecraft's *Maria*' (in Troost, ed., pp. 295–316), discerns in the 'amalgamation of fragments' that constitutes the novel 'a polyphonic clash of perspectives' (pp. 297, 296). Paradoxically, Wollstonecraft's protagonists discover in the confines of the prison and the madhouse 'a sphere of discursive freedom' (p. 298) in which fractured confession predominates. Andreas Gailus, 'Poetics of Containment: Goethe's *Conversations of German Refugees* and the Crisis of Representation' (*MP* 100[2003] 436–74), makes a similar case for Goethe's cycle of novellas as works that, at a moment of crisis, 'begin to answer … the problem of how to respond within communication to that which exceeds it' (p. 466).

Katherine Binhammer, 'The Persistence of Reading: Governing Female Novel-Reading in *Memoirs of Emma Courtney* and *Memoirs of Modern Philosopher*' (*ECL* 27[2003] 1–22) is preoccupied with the morally improving or disastrous effects of women's fiction in the late eighteenth century: 'If novels were so widely believed to be the evil agents of seduction and myth, why and how did women persist in reading and writing them?' (p. 2). Justine Crump, 'Prescription, Practice, and Eighteenth-Century Women's Reading: The Case of Frances Burney' (in Troost, ed., pp. 99–124), examines Burney's conformity to and divergence from conduct-book recommendations about female reading. In her active interventions in and responses to the classics, Burney 'differs markedly from the moralists' apprehension of the female reader as Locke's *tabula rasa*, a passive surface for the text's inscription' (p. 112). Burney sought not so much to police whatever morally compromising books she may privately have read as to restrict public knowledge of that reading: 'to suggest the expansion of her knowledge into disreputable texts was tantamount to inviting her to a sexual indiscretion' (p. 113).

Virginia H. Cope, 'Evelina's Peculiar Circumstances and Tender Relations' (*ECF* 16[2003] 59–78), pays close and fruitful attention to the origins of the word 'peculiar' as it is applied to Evelina's social status—that of a disowned heiress: 'in the eighteenth century the word clung to its etymological roots in private property' (p. 59). Citing Locke, various conduct manuals, and legal sources, Cope demonstrates that Evelina finally earns her birthright by revealing to her father that she possesses a tender heart, 'proof of which comes, paradoxically, in her unwillingness to demand her legacy … For women like Evelina, "peculiar circumstances" depend upon "tender relations" for their remedy' (p. 61). Jeanine Casler, 'Rakes and Races: Art's Imitation of Life in Frances Burney's *Evelina*'

(*ECN* 3[2003] 157–69), discerns in Burney's youthful novel a surprising level of insight into the isolation of older women. Erik Bond, 'Farewell, Mr. Villars: *Cecilia* and Frances Burney's "Inward Monitor"' (*ECN* 3[2003] 171–93), argues that her second work of fiction constitutes an endeavour to circumvent the limitations of epistolary writing: the figure of a male monitor commenting on female confession is replaced by an emphasis on the heroine's personal 'interpretative skill' (p. 174). Mascha Gemmeke, *Frances Burney and the Female Bildungsroman: An Interpretation of The Wanderer; or, Female Difficulties* is a dutiful, thorough survey of Burney's last novel, paying close attention to its mixture of Gothic, dramatic, and conduct book ingredients with those of the German novel of formation or education. Unlike the conventional *Bildungsroman*, *The Wanderer* precludes direct access to the heroine's thoughts and evolving identity by cloaking Juliet's story in allegory and metaphor—'a device of the gothic novel employed to keep the reader's interest awake, and … to test the reader's capacity for sympathy' (p. 51). Gemmeke sees points of comparison between *The Wanderer*'s loose, episodic structure, concluding in a lesson of uncertain import, and Cervantes' and Lennox's quixotic, picaresque fictions.

Patricia Meyer Spacks began *Privacy: Concealing the Eighteenth-Century Self* in the expectation that it would focus on physical or architectural privacy—on the closet in *Pamela*, for instance—but soon found that '"psychological privacy": the kind … that entails self-protection of a sort not immediately visible to others' (p. 7) was a far more pressing concern for the majority of writers after Richardson. Her thoughtful, wide-ranging work is therefore centrally interested in privacy as an imaginative category—one that expresses a tension between individual and social selves. Novelists who come in for attention include Burney and Richardson (both generously represented), Henry and Sarah Fielding, Lennox, Sterne, Cleland, Goldsmith, and Austen. By focusing on some implications of privacy in this period, Spacks is also able to investigate the link between the rise of the novel and the rise of individualism. *Clarissa*, for instance, is 'energized by its intricate dynamic of privacy and richly revelatory of privacy's ambiguities' (p. 15); *Sense and Sensibility* explores the competing claims of privacy and society; in *The Vicar of Wakefield*, privacy creates stumbling blocks in the plot; in *A Sentimental Journey*, it unmasks character; in *Fanny Hill*, it holds erotic potential. But this is not a book about the novel alone. Nor, since she is dealing with a 'tangle' which is 'itself the subject', does Spacks offer any single-minded interpretations of what privacy might mean (pp. 14–15). Rather, her study is organized according to the different arenas in which privacy, an especially vexed matter for women, might be said to operate: in reading, sensibility, hypocrisy, propriety, conversation, scandalous narrative, and diaries, amongst others. The pleasure of reading novels in private crops up as a matter of concern both within and outside eighteenth-century fiction; imagining other people's secret lives, and experienced in solitude, novels could have consequences in the real world if they encouraged their readers to develop an 'interior independence' (p. 10). The novel's emphasis on sensibility suggests, to Spacks, another way of thinking about privacy. If sensibility entails display, it therefore seems to be opposed to privacy—and yet sensibility is potentially deceptive, concealing the personal opinions of someone apparently wearing them on his or her sleeve. Burney's Camilla, for one, 'proceeds by a series of lurches, alternately hiding and helplessly revealing herself' (p. 65). At the opposite extreme to sensibility, social decorum seemingly announces its possessor's self-control, as well as suggesting the defensive or theatrical ability to deceive: 'Awareness of the dangers of social hypocrisy attended consciousness of its useful possibilities' (p. 89). This book is brimful of insights and argued with panache.

The same cannot be said of Sarah Prescott, *Women, Authorship and Literary Culture, 1690–1740*, a study which aims to restore our sense of non-metropolitan networks of eighteenth-century publishing, and therefore to complicate the standard picture of urban and professional female authorship. Prescott includes discussion of Haywood's, Mary Davys', and Penelope Aubin's (among others') anxious negotiations with the literary marketplace. There is very little textual analysis at work here, and Prescott is wrong to coerce the modesty tropes she discovers in female prefaces and dedications into 'authenticating strategies' that are 'gender specific' (p. 44), since men were just as likely as women to employ them. The book is stalked throughout by a malevolent straw man against whose putative binary endeavours to fix 'women's literary experience into rigid and often oppositional categories' or to construct 'a crude professional/amateur dichotomy' the author sets her own 'significant corrective' (pp. 10, 16, 17). It is hard persuasively or significantly to correct an unnamed source—and what critic would deliberately impose rigid oppositions and crude dichotomies on his or her material? Lisa Wood, *Modes of Discipline: Women, Conservatism, and the Novel after the French Revolution*, makes similarly heavy interpretative weather of anti-revolutionary, didactic fiction published between 1793 and 1815 by Laetitia Hawkins, Jane West, Elizabeth Hamilton, Hannah More, Mary Brunton, and Jane Porter. The paucity of stylistic evaluation, the strong reliance on secondary material, the use of novels as historical evidence of what is 'ideologically effective', and the 'formulaic' nature of the novels themselves (pp. 125, 68) add up to a trying read. Like so many works of recent criticism, *Modes of Discipline* leaves you wondering, first, whether these eighteenth-century novelists are worth reading; second—if their aim was simply to communicate a political, economical, or gender affiliation—why they elected to write in a literary form at all.

The years 2002 and 2003 were good for Smollett. Two further volumes, both concerned with madness and knight-errantry, appeared in the University of Georgia Press's edition of his works: *The Life and Adventures of Sir Launcelot Greaves*, edited by Robert Folkenflik and Barbara Laning Fitzpatrick, and *The History and Adventures of the Renowned Don Quixote*, edited by Martin C. Battestin and O.M. Brack, Jr. Both are beautifully presented, amply annotated, definitive editions. The introduction to *Launcelot Greaves*, featuring discussions of insanity, politics, style, form, characterization, and reception history, is meticulously executed: especially welcome is the section on Anthony Walker's engravings (not all of which faithfully illustrate the novel's action). Equally useful are Martin C. Battestin's appendix, comparing a selection of Francis Hayman's original illustrations with the engraved prints used in *Don Quixote*, and his glossary of Smollett's unfamiliar locutions and obsolete terms. Jeremy Lewis, *Tobias Smollett*, is the first full biography of its subject since Lewis Knapp's

Tobias Smollett: Doctor of Men and Manners was published in 1949. Few general readers now show much interest in Smollett's punitive, rambunctious, Juvenalian strain; even Lewis cursorily discounts much of the fiction. He is chiefly drawn to Smollett as the unflagging, genre-hopping man of eighteenth-century letters: a surgeon turned novelist, playwright, editor, journalist, historian, and reviewer. This new life is an accessible, energetic reformulation of existing materials, adding little to what is already known about Smollett (and the absence of notes is irritating). But what the biography lacks in literary detail and originality it makes up for in its Smollett-like pace, exuberance, and capacity for fellow-feeling.

Fowler and Jackson, eds., *Launching Fanny Hill: Essays on the Novel and its Influence* is divided into three sections which address, respectively, 'Understanding the Text', 'Historical and Cultural Perspectives', and 'Contemporary Manifestations'. Most essays have points to score about patriarchy, gender, economics, and pornography. There is an element of repetition across the book as a whole, as well as a very limited sense of the comic zest of Cleland's fiction—one major reason why it has remained in print to this day. John C. Benyon, '"Traffic in more precious commodities": Sapphic Erotics and Economics in *Memoirs of a Woman of Pleasure*' (pp. 3–23) focuses on the material use of the word 'account' and its cognates, suggesting that Cleland also proffers 'a hidden realm of unaccountability … a female utopia' (p. 22), while Andrew Elfenbein, 'The Management of Desire in *Memoirs of a Woman of Pleasure*' (pp. 27–48), reads *Fanny Hill* as an allegory of the capitalist labour market. Patsy S. Fowler, '"This tail-piece of morality": Phallocentric Reinforcements of Patriarchy in *Memoirs of a Woman of Pleasure*' (pp. 49–80), insists that Cleland's work is 'a traditional pornographic text objectifying women and focusing only on male power and gratification … thereby exalting the power of the phallus' (pp. 29–30). So it is an unfortunate lapse in attention to her own linguistic habits that she describes her essay as one that 'fills' a 'void' (p. 30). Lena Olsson, 'Idealized and Realistic Portrayals of Prostitution in John Cleland's *Memoirs of a Woman of Pleasure*' (pp. 81–101), examines the distinction between fantastic, improbable seraglios and violent, alcohol-riddled bawdy houses. For Marvin D.L. Lansverk in '"Delightful Vistas": Genital Landscapes and Addisonian Aesthetics in Cleland's *Memoirs of a Woman of Pleasure*' (pp. 103–23), the combination of sexual voyeurism with disconcerting references to landscape foregrounds 'the scopophilic pleasures of seeing nature directly' (p. 121) and suggests a pornographic reinterpretation of Mr Spectator's pleasures of imagination. Sylvie Kleiman-Lafon, 'The French Adventures of Fanny Hill' (pp. 127–51), surveys cross-Channel appropriations, duplications, and betrayals of Cleland's paradigmatic heroine. Julie Peakman, 'Initiation, Defloration, and Flagellation: Sexual Propensities in *Memoirs of a Woman of Pleasure*' (pp. 153–72), argues that Cleland is the first British writer to combine in novelistic form various medical, religious, and cultural references common in French erotica of the seventeenth and early eighteenth centuries. Elizabeth Kubek, 'The Man Machine: Horror and the Phallus in *Memoirs of a Woman of Pleasure*' (pp. 173–97), presents a Freudian reading of the uncanny in Cleland, concluding that the sense of disproportion in his novel 'dramatizes the condition of all masculine subjects under modern patriarchy' (p. 179). Misty G. Anderson, 'Mr. Barvile's

Discipline: Habit, Passion, and Methodism in the Eighteenth-Century Imagination' (pp. 199- 220), asserts that 'Methodist discourse' is depicted as a parallel to Fanny's erotic discovery: in both cases, 'for the disciplined self, pain can be turned into pleasure' (p. 218). Jody Greene, 'Arbitrary Tastes and Commonsense Pleasures: Accounting for Taste in Cleland, Hume, and Burke' (pp. 221–65), sees 'the novel of personal development', concluding in marriage, as the most appropriate domain in which to rehearse the dangers and pleasures of sexual experimentation (p. 261). Brian McCord, '"Charming and wholesome literature": *Fanny Hill* and the Legal "Production of Production"' (pp. 267–85), compares eighteenth-century publication and censorship of the novel with its twentieth-century re-publication and censorship in America. The remaining three essays, on 'Contemporary Manifestations', address pedagogical approaches to, and adaptations or rewritings of, the novel. Mark Blackwell, '"It stood an object of terror and delight": Sublime Masculinity and the Aesthetics of Disproportion in John Cleland's *Memoirs of a Woman of Pleasure*' (*ECN* 3[2003] 39–63), focuses on 'three predominant male corporeal styles' (p. 41) within the *Memoirs*, arguing that they embody varieties of social organization and forms of power. Cleland has yet to find a critic who does justice to his style.

The recent growth of studies in the history of the book has generated many new insights into the paratextual apparatus through which eighteenth-century texts identified themselves to their readers; far more attention has focused on *Tristram Shandy*, however, than on any other work of fiction. In *Graphic Design, Print Culture, and the Eighteenth-Century Novel*, Janine Barchas sets out to recover the 'lost visual dynamism' and 'textual body' of the novel as a genre (p. 6). Early eighteenth-century authors and their publishers discovered, in print, a creative resource in its own right. Barchas persuasively asserts that Sterne's manipulations of textual format proved effective in their day thanks to a public that had been trained to interpret visual components as an integral part of any text. In the 1720 s, the use of frontispiece portraiture implied literary authority, generic preoccupations, a cult of celebrity, and commentary on the texts that followed in works by Defoe, Haywood, and others. Crowded title pages were a 'tell-tale sign of an experimental genre', usurping 'all available space as explanatory gloss' (p. 65). The learned addenda of tables, catalogues, synopses, and indexes provided opportunities for extending authorial control, while also laying claim to prestige. Barchas's initial 'panorama of generic form' is more convincing than subsequent discussion of Richardson's and Sarah Fielding's 'experiments with the novel's design' (p. 90). In these later chapters, she begins to exaggerate her claims regarding Richardson's 'involvement with the minutest details of his fiction's visual production': he was not always capable of overseeing such minutiae (p. 116). And she does Henry Fielding a grave disservice by accusing him—inexplicably, in view of his own novelistic experiments with punctuation—of having removed his sister's expressive dashes, hence of deliberately attenuating the effect of *David Simple*. The first half of *Graphic Design, Print Culture, and the Eighteenth-Century Novel* is vivacious, stylish, and convincingly argued; the rest overplays its hand.

3. Poetry

In the conclusion of her study *Women Peasant Poets in Eighteenth-Century England, Scotland, and Germany: Milkmaids on Parnassus*, Susanne Kord asserts that the 'definition of Art as essentially male and bourgeois turned out to be decisively influential in the process of canonization... and still dominates academic discourse today' (p. 241). This statement seems a little less accurate after 2003, a year in which marginalized and non-canonical eighteenth-century poets received unprecedented attention. Critical editions of the poetry of the maidservant Mary Leapor and the mariner William Falconer were published, alongside anthologies of verse by labouring-class poets and about slavery and the slave trade (with several poems by former slaves). There were also various articles concerned with poetry by women or lower-class writers. Scottish authors were particularly well represented, with new books on Burns and Macpherson. A couple of articles went for the full house, dealing with poets who were Scottish, female, *and* lower-class, and one would presumably struggle to be more marginalized than that.

I shall begin, as I would now recommend undergraduates to do, with David Fairer's excellent introduction to the field, *English Poetry of the Eighteenth-Century 1700–1789*. Fairer organizes his history by themes, rather than granting chapters to particular individuals or groups of poets. Although the book is broadly chronological in structure, the period spanned by each chapter is dictated by appropriateness rather than contiguity. Fairer is perceptive as to how certain genres and discourses become 'subsumed' into others as the century progresses (such as the georgic into the topographical poem (p. 209)). Beginning with a chapter entitled 'Between Manuscript and Print', which discusses the literary community and audience of early eighteenth-century England, Fairer proceeds to cover notions of 'politeness'; the concepts of wit and the imagination in the context of the mock-heroic mode; the verse letter; the pastoral and georgic genres; the 'romantic mode' up to 1730; sublimity, nature, and God; the 'recovery' of the English poetic tradition and formation of the canon; the search for 'genuine' voices; political and economic debate as conducted in landscape poetry; and, finally, the theory and practice of sensibility. As with the other publications in this series (Longman Literature in English), the book concludes with a selective general bibliography, and useful potted biographies of the major poets (with individual reading lists). Fairer's assignment of particular poets to particular themes encourages new readings and helps the reader situate them in both their literary and intellectual contexts. A problem that might be thought likely to crop up as a result of this method—an undue concentration upon particular aspects of a poet's writing at the expense of a broader appreciation—does not in practice arise, thanks to Fairer's adept handling: key figures, such as Pope and Swift, are returned to in consecutive chapters, providing a sense of the interrelatedness of the topics, as well as ensuring that poets are not confined within narrow boundaries of interpretation.

Fairer characterizes the eighteenth century as a 'miscellaneous age' (p. x), and he successfully conveys the diversity of period while noting that particular modes such as the 'sentimental' and 'satirical' persist throughout (p. 75). The acknowledgement of these persistent themes helps to caution against adopting the simple critical dichotomies and assumptions that formerly dogged studies of eighteenth-century poetry, while retaining a sense of the shifting emphases over the period. The manner in which the 'romantic mode' is traced through the century while being carefully differentiated from the 'sublime mode' is particularly original and persuasive. This draws attention to another of the book's qualities: despite being an overview presumably intended primarily for undergraduate students, it is no mere digest or summation of the current critical consensus but includes novel readings of standard texts, and materials previously unpublished. A poem by the little-known Isaac Thompson, not reprinted since 1731, is compared with slightly better-known works by Anne Finch and Thomas Parnell, and ultimately with Alexander Pope's famous *Eloisa to Abelard*, the effect of which is not only to allow the reader to see Pope's work in a broader context, but also to allow due voice to the peripheral figures. Fairer admits in his preface that he found it a challenge to integrate women poets into his literary history without consigning them to a separate category, but by and large this integration does not seem awkward when encountered; occasionally one senses an effort to accommodate idiosyncratic poets, but this is not intrusive. Concise and interesting throughout, *English Poetry of the Eighteenth Century* confronts several long-standing perceptions of the era. Fairer criticizes the view that the poets of the mid-century were afraid to find their own voice (p. 148), and argues that what was once characterized as 'the age of Johnson' should more accurately be considered 'the age of Johnsonian resistance to the tastes of his time' (p. 38). Perhaps most importantly, he communicates the strengths of eighteenth-century poetry with a critical enthusiasm that should encourage undergraduates unsure what to look for in the period between Pope and Wordsworth.

Susanne Kord's important study, *Women Peasant Poets*, takes a theoretical approach to the issue of how lower-class women's poetry is valued, and why it has traditionally been excluded from the canon. She opens by stating three assumptions that she believes have dominated literary approaches to the eighteenth century: first, the great writers of the age are male and (mostly) middle-class; this is seen to be related to the 'emancipation of the middle-class artist from seventeenth-century aristocratic patronage'; and these factors, which she claims made 'the new bourgeois art "Art"', resulted in a definition of all 'Art' as being independent 'from social, political, and biographical context', with the 'resulting ability to embody universally *human* values, transcending all specificities of gender and class' (p. 1). Kord contends that the works of peasant poets were not, maybe cannot be, dissociated from the biographical context in which they were written, rendering such poets 'ineligible' for consideration as 'true Artists'. A key factor in this was the role of middle-class patronage, with patrons constructing the biographies of lower-class poets according to the bourgeois aesthetics of their time. Kord states that the purpose of her study, 'rather than attempting to assign an "aesthetic quality" to the writing of lower-class women', is instead to seek to use their 'literature and their reception by male bourgeois readers to question how judgments of "quality" are made in the first place' (p. 13). A range of poets is discussed, with especial attention being paid to the case of the German cowherd Anna Louisa Karsch, and significant commentary devoted to Mary Leapor, Mary Collier, and Ann Yearsley. Like Fairer, Kord appends a selection of short biographies of poets to her work.

Kord adopts the position that aesthetic theory and poetic practice were '*mutually* influential' (p. 2), poetry not simply being criticized within the parameters of contemporary aesthetics, but aesthetic rules changing in response to poetry. This is reasonable enough, and helps inform her theory of reception, in which the 'natural-genius' aesthetic proposed by Edward Young and others is seen to steer patronage. The argument is well supported, as are most of Kord's propositions, with explicit statements of aesthetic approbation by Anna Karsch being cited, and evidence that lower-class poets were to some extent willing to collude in the presentation of themselves as unlettered savantes. Kord illustrates how the biographies of peasant poets were managed, or even falsified, to meet middle-class expectations—the problem being that this form of marketing precluded the poets from disinterested *literary* consideration. The patrons and editors of many lower-class poets used the prefaces and advertisements for collections of poetry in order to emphasize their own charity, making 'the object of publication … in every case, financial rather than literary' (p. 55). Kord argues that the biographical prefaces to volumes of poetry by lower-class women writers serve a 'gatekeeping function that... ultimately precludes all nonbiographical interpretations of the work' (p. 158).

Although largely convincing, *Women Peasant Poets* is not unproblematic. Kord's explicit and outright refusal to offer aesthetic judgements of the poetry she discusses ('which would merely reiterate the very power relations that this project seeks to confront', p. 12), removes the most obvious means of its rehabilitation. Furthermore, her attack on traditional criticism's 'lack of interest in the poet's work and... exclusive emphasis on the poet's life' (p. 158) is blunted by the fact that she precludes herself from such an approach. Kord, having dismantled the framework of aesthetic judgement, does not establish an alternative means of locating value in the poetry she defends. Nevertheless, *Women Peasant Poets* is a significant and provocative contribution to eighteenth-century literary studies that opens up a new channel of criticism.

Margery Palmer McCulloch touches upon some of the same themes as Kord in her article on women, poetry, and song in lowland Scotland (*WW* 10[2003] 453–68). McCulloch surveys the careers of Janet Little, Anna Gordon of Aberdeenshire, Jane Elliot, Alison Cockburn, Isabel Pagan, and Carolina Oliphant. Although McCulloch attempts to reassess Janet Little based on her '*literary* achievement', the pressure to engage with biographical readings soon becomes apparent, as Little's poetry concerning her relationship with Robert Burns takes centre stage. McCulloch notes that it was often educated upper-class women who *composed* the 'traditional' songs of the period, and casts doubt on assignation of *Ca' the Yowes to the Knowes* to Isabel Pagan. Bill Overton attempts to rescue another lower-class Scottish female poet from critical neglect in his long article on Jean Adam (*WW* 10[2003] 425–52). He presents new biographical information about Adam, and considers the organization of her one published collection, *Miscellany Poems*, observing a tension between constraints of faith and social position, and her invention and poetic aspirations. Adam's adeptness with various verse forms and her sense of irony are emphasized, and it is reasonably suggested that her relatively straightforward religious poems may have been composed for use in her school. Overton debates Adam's proposed authorship of the poem 'There's Nae Luck About the House', and concludes that no firm conclusion can be reached on the matter. His assessments generally seem fair, although he rather strengthens Susanne Kord's case against aesthetic valuations of lower-class women poets by remarking that, 'given the moral and doctrinal constraints to which so many of her poems testify, not to mention those of her sex and social position, it was a great achievement on her part to write and publish poetry at all'.

Remaining with lower-class Scottish poets, but switching genders, Matthew Simpson contributes a slightly strange essay concerning Robert Fergusson and globalization (*ECLife* 27[2003] 107–29). Simpson recruits Fergusson as an opponent of globalization, drawing parallels between his resistance to the cosmopolitanism of eighteenth-century Edinburgh (and Britain more widely) and contemporary ecological concerns. His readings of Fergusson are generally observant and alive to the humour of the poetry, but his support for Fergusson's parochialism (although the word is avoided) is problematic. Fergusson's satirical distaste for imported luxuries is employed to present a case for self-sufficiency and the consumption of locally sourced food and drink, but while this back-to-whence-we-came agrarian idyll might be considered palatable enough, Simpson glosses over the more distasteful aspects of a philosophy based on such principles, in particular a prejudice against people who are 'not from these parts' (an attitude to which Fergusson comes close). He also seems to imply that people should restrict themselves to satisfying their 'needs', as servicing their 'wants' would be morally reprehensible, a stance that would seem to demand the denial of fairly fundamental human instincts. Simpson's argument seems rather to emphasize the differences between a rural eighteenth-century society in which a nostalgia for life before international trade could be felt with some validity, and a modern economic environment in which such feelings must be based on a romantic ideal.

Dafydd Moore offers a reconsideration of the Ossian poems in his study *Enlightenment and Romance in James McPherson's 'The Poems of Ossian': Myth, Genre and Cultural Change*. Moore begins by questioning the genre of the poems, unequivocally stated in the titles of the poems themselves as epic. He contends that they may be more profitably discussed according to the terms of romance, in which the 'purity' of the world portrayed 'is in fact guaranteed by the impossibility of realization' (p. 157). This is a bold move. It is also, as Moore himself acknowledges (p. 2), the principal aspect in which his study differs from other recent revisionist work on Macpherson. Whether Macpherson himself recognized his work as owing more to romance than epic is not extensively discussed, but it is made clear that if he were intending to create an ancient Scottish cultural tradition (which Moore agrees to have been one of his motives), then the only viable literary genre in which to do so, according to the primitivist critical dictates of the mid-eighteenth century, was the epic. The eighteenth-century understanding of romance form, as expressed by Macpherson's friend Hugh Blair in particular, 'stood for everything *Ossian* was not, and in particular it was not natural and not native when *Ossian* was predicated on being both these things' (p. 41). It is suggested in addition that there were political reasons why Blair might feel queasy about 'chivalric medievalism', which could be read as Catholic and Stuart in its associations, something that it was necessary to avoid in the *Ossian* poems if they were to have their intended appeal.

The second key strand of Moore's argument, which is related to the central characteristics of the romance mode, is that in the *Ossian* poems an attempt is made to blend heroic civic virtue with polite eighteenth-century sensibility, a blend that Moore regards as impossible and self-defeating. On recognizing Ossian's appeal as a 'man of sympathy and moral sentiment... comes an awareness that the martial side of the story has been rendered redundant, absurdly pointless' (p. 101). This absurdity is persuasively illustrated by Moore. The society that Ossian inhabits is shown to be unsustainable and inherently doomed, as 'the old destroy the young, the past the present' (p. 152). The sentimental and the sublime, which inform the aesthetics of the poetry, are read as analogous to the commercial and the civic, but while the classical sublime and civic virtues are seen as belonging to a discourse of 'effort, difficulty, and vigour', the sentimental and commercial are regarded as belonging to a quite incompatible sphere of affection, sociability, sympathy, and exchange: 'those qualities that make something or someone sublime disqualify them from being sentimental and social' (p. 115). Moore suggests that this was a wider problem for eighteenth-century theorists of the sublime such as Burke and Blair. Although he accepts that the memorialization of this impossible primitive Scottish society has implications for the eighteenth-century political situation in Scotland, Moore is cautious when considering the controversy surrounding *Ossian*'s 'wider cultural politics' (p. 140). He offers a careful analysis of Macpherson's presumed sympathies, and the 'histories of defeat' (p. 163) he creates, without arriving at any over-simplifying conclusions.

Moore's interpretations of the *Ossian* poems are subtle and generally convincing. His appeal to romance theory does open some interesting readings, and challenges generic assumptions previously unquestioned. While he leaves the reader in no doubt as to why Macpherson and Blair would have preferred to cast *Ossian* as an epic, however, its status as a 'romance' is partly dependent upon fairly sophisticated twentieth-century constructions of the term, which encourage a particular interrogation of ideals. This is not to say that such interrogations are not fruitful here, as they clearly are, although expecting such a method of reading from the poems' contemporary audience might be asking a bit much, therefore colouring the interpretation of the text's (historical) political significance.

Another Scot on the receiving end of a reconsideration during 2003 was Robert Burns. Ashgate advertise Walter McGinty's *Robert Burns and Religion* as the 'first extensive treatment of religion in the life of the poet Robert Burns since... 1931', although it should be observed that several more recent, if less specific, accounts have dealt quite admirably with this aspect of Burns's life and poetry, such as Liam McIlvanney's *Burns the Radical: Poetry and Politics in Late Eighteenth-Century Scotland* [2002]. McGinty's book is not especially radical. It portrays Burns as comfortingly moderate in his religious beliefs, if a little antagonistic towards those more fervent than himself.

The first six chapters of McGinty's book consist of a relatively straightforward and unproblematic biographical narrative looking at Burns's gradually evolving attitude to religion and his key beliefs. Burns is portrayed as being attracted to religion 'as a factor capable of helping form "the finer feelings of the heart"' (p. 1). He is said to have regarded religion as 'an aid to the enjoyment of life' (p. 21), and understood the Bible 'as a valuable but not infallible book' (p. 34). Some allusions to biblical texts in the poetry are picked out to demonstrate his awareness of Scripture, and his correspondence is mined to support McGinty's thesis that Burns maintained a thoughtful, slightly unorthodox religious stance that rejected many aspects of Calvinism and tended towards Arminianism. The letters are also used to illustrate Burns's engagement with the ideas and attitudes of many Scots churchmen of his day. McGinty identifies 'three recurring themes' that characterize Burns's religious concerns: first, a belief in the benevolence of God; second, 'a speculation on an existence beyond the grave'; and third, 'an acknowledgement of his own accountability' as opposed to a Calvinist emphasis upon Grace or predestination (p. 55). McGinty is observant as to the implications of the terminology that Burns uses, at one point inserting a table listing all the various descriptive titles used for God in the letters. Most of this section seems reasonable enough, although there are some passages that do not so much analyse Burns's comments as reword them. McGinty also has a slightly disconcerting tendency towards mind-reading, seeming to know exactly what Burns's innermost thoughts were about certain topics despite the lack of any specific evidence—'He appreciated their [John Taylor and John Goldie's] open-minded approach to the [biblical] text and their assertion of the value of the judgement of the individual's own natural understanding' (p. 34). In such instances a small qualification would not go amiss. McGinty occasionally seems to identify his own theological attitudes uncomfortably closely with those of his subject, and in other places he simply offers his own opinions on religion instead. Comments such as 'for many people religion is something that helps them swim against the stream' (p. 11), or 'for those prone to doubt... once doubt sets in they are undone, excluded by the very faith that had initially brought them to a sense of having been saved by God' (p. 95), say more about the author's religious experiences than Burns's (McGinty was formerly a parish minister).

While objections to the first part of the book should not be overstated, its central part is disappointing. It falls short of the standard to be expected of a scholarly publication, yet does not seem to be intended for a general audience. The chapter on William Cowper is better than that on Christopher Smart, but in both instances there is too much judgement of character and an apparent neglect of recent critical and biographical discussions. Cowper's experiences of religion are insensitively contrasted with those of Burns, leading to judgements such as: 'although raised up in a materially poorer home than that of Cowper, Burns probably had the more enriching experience, and in all likelihood emerged from it the better equipped to face the world' (p. 91). McGinty offers novel interpretations of some passages from Smart's *Jubilate Agno*, but admits to having only a 'cursory knowledge' of Smart's work, and suggests that 'the time is surely right for a fuller assessment of the work of a poet that I am sure is worthy of re-evaluation' (p. 139). Given that the most recent work devoted solely to Smart that is cited in the footnotes is Moira Dearnley's *The Poetry of Christopher Smart* [1968], this statement should perhaps have been omitted. Neither chapter is especially pertinent to the discussion of Burns's religious views.

The latter part of *Robert Burns and Religion* returns to Burns himself, with a lengthy discussion of the 'miniature portraits' of the church ministers involved in the heresy charge against the Reverend Dr William McGill of the Auld Kirk of Ayr, as provided in 'The Church of Scotland's Garland—a New Song' (otherwise known as 'The Kirk's Alarm'). McGinty examines each 'portrait' in turn, referring to historical documents and the published writings of those involved in the case to evaluate Burns's often scathing comments. This section is more sure-footed, although McGinty still tends to speak for Burns and to judge character by religious inclination. The book concludes with a study of Burns's poems that reflect the recurrent themes of his religious beliefs. McGinty's analyses of the poems are on the whole considered, and raise some interesting points. Better use is made of contextual sources, and additional support is provided for the religious preferences described in the early part of the book.

The year 2003 also saw the publication of Richard Greene and the late Ann Messenger's critical edition of Mary Leapor, *The Works of Mary Leapor*, a well-presented and informatively annotated single volume consisting of Leapor's extant poetry and her tragic drama, *The Unhappy Father*. The introduction opens with a biography of Leapor, relating what is known of her life and her dealings with the community in which she grew up. While not downplaying the relative provincial isolation in which she developed, it does point to her connections with the wider literary world and her early reading. It mentions the slightly muted early responses to Leapor's poetry, and notes that she was 'both the object of curiosity as a natural genius, as well as the object of sympathy since she died young' (p. xxvi), none of which could be said to contradict Susanne Kord's analysis of women peasant poets being biographically constructed according to the bourgeois aesthetics of the time. Greene observes that Leapor attracted the attention of Samuel Richardson, William Cowper, and Christopher Smart, concurring with Betty Rizzo's opinion that Smart may have written the epitaph to Leapor that accompanied Isaac Hawkins Browne's 1751 edition of her poems. A strong section on twentieth-century engagements with Leapor's poetry summarizes the various arguments concerning feminism, primitivism, and patronage that have been published since Rizzo's pioneering work in the 1980s. Greene takes a sensible, sceptical view of some of the more radical interpretations to have been offered. Given the recent growth of interest in eighteenth-century women poets, and Leapor in particular, this new standard edition should be keenly received.

Another lower-class poet marginalized by traditional academic criticism is William Falconer; William R. Jones makes a strong case for rehabilitating his reputation. His *A Critical Edition of the Poetical Works of William Falconer* is the first edition of the poet for over a century. It provides a good scholarly text of Falconer's most important poem, 'The Shipwreck', with the first [1762] and third [1769] versions printed on facing pages (the textual alterations of the second version are included in the footnotes). A biographical account of Falconer, an extensive discussion of his critical reception, and several critical essays by Jones are included in the introductory material.

Jones's stated aims are to provide reliable copy-texts of the poems; to present Falconer's reworking of his major poem as a 'case-study in the development of a self-made poet of the mid eighteenth century'; to make the poems accessible to the modern reader; and to enable Falconer to 'reassume his modest but unique place in literature' (pp. xiv–xvi). The first three aims have been met, and a good case for the fourth has been made. Although long neglected, Jones shows that Falconer's 'Shipwreck' was received with some enthusiasm by his contemporaries, and that his reputation survived well into the nineteenth century. Lord Byron was particularly impressed by Falconer's evident experience of his subject, as well as excited by his descriptions of the Greek coast, with its concomitant artistic associations (p. 31). With its mixture of didactic precepts and heroic narration, Jones regards 'The Shipwreck' as generically unique, being 'part epic, part Georgic' (p. 76). He uses this evidence to make the case that in the 1760s 'poems over-lapping genre boundaries were more acceptable than is generally believed' (p. 61). Contemporary responses also suggest that Falconer's technical language did not meet with the disapproval that might be expected, given the distaste of critics such as Addison and Johnson for 'terms of art' in poetry. The introduction traces how Falconer, encouraged by the positive initial critical response to the poem, increasingly added and emphasized episodes that looked to exploit fashionable sensibility and emotional responses, while also attempting to harness the poem's popularity in order to encourage naval reform, dwelling less on the Georgic aspects of the sailor's craft as he revised it. Jones's short 'essays' do not interrogate the poems in great depth, but should provide (re)starting points for future considerations of Falconer.

Another field of growing interest in eighteenth-century studies (and broader post-colonial debate) is the history of slavery, the slave trade, and contemporaneous attitudes towards the subject. This interest is served by a new anthology edited by James G. Basker, *Amazing Grace: An Anthology of Poems About Slavery 1660–1810*. Weighing in at over 700 pages, and covering the work of more than 250 poets, this collection sets the standard for any such future venture. Basker's editorial principle is comprehensiveness. He claims to have 'gathered every poem or poetic fragment from the period that brings slavery into view, whether as its main subject, in a single passage or character, or, more glancingly, in bits of allusion or metaphor' (p. xxxiii). A significant minority of the poems in the anthology were written by women, and more than twenty black authors are represented, providing a broad and varied range of voices and biographical experiences. Authors are arranged chronologically according to the date at which their earliest included poem was written (or published, if the composition date is unknown). Brief headnotes summarize each poet's life and any known involvement with the slave trade, as well as highlighting attitudes to slavery expressed or implied in the poems and extracts provided.

Basker is primarily interested in the poems he publishes as historical documents, adopting the view that poetry reflects broader cultural knowledge. He openly admits that, in terms of literary quality, his inclusions vary 'from the sublime to the insufferable' (p. xxxiii). His initial justification for publishing an anthology of verse rather than prose is a bit limp—'the focus on poetry allows greater range'—although he does go on to suggest rather more grandly that poetry 'best enables us to approximate or intimate the unspeakable', making it the preferred medium for expressing the distressing nature of slavery (p. xxxiv). Basker's literary observations are not overly sophisticated, although such observations are clearly not his primary concern. At one point he notes that 'the whole transition from classicism to romanticism could be traced through this poetry' (p. xl), although the material also 'challenges our generalizations and our preconceptions' about neoclassical and Romantic modes (p. xli). Although the frequent use of excerpts rather than complete poems inevitably calls for a certain caution with regard to interpreting texts out of their contexts, Basker does frame his selections with introductory notes, and provides full bibliographical records of his sources for those wishing to pursue them further.

One aspect of the anthology that is worth remarking upon is that it reveals how few eighteenth-century poets or poetasters were prepared to publish verses *defending* slavery or maintaining the status quo (other than through their silence), James Boswell being a noticeable exception. Basker, considering the persistence of slavery in the face of such cultural opposition, touches on the historical issue of whether the poets might have been 'merely an impotent body of social critics' (p. xlvii), but does not consider the more literary angle: whether the poems demonstrate the enlightenment of the poets, or the inappropriateness of poetry as a form for pro-slavery arguments. Basker concludes his introduction by arguing that his anthology adds to the recent revisionist challenge to the late twentieth-century view that English literature was 'complicitous in Empire' (p. xlvii). It is certainly a significant contribution. Most importantly, perhaps, Basker uncovers several obscure or previously unconsidered voices, and reveals their relevance to an important debate in the history of ideas.

As if labouring-class poets had not been demarginalized enough already during 2003, the three-volume anthology *Eighteenth-Century English Labouring-Class Poets 1700–1800* should be enough to make canonical authors fear for their pedestals. Edited by John Goodridge, William Christmas, Bridget Keegan, and Tim Burke, the fifty or so poets included in the anthology are regarded as constituting a 'tradition of writing that was an integral part of the eighteenth-century literary scene' (vol. 1, p. xiii). In his introduction, Goodridge notes many of the same problems attendant upon reading labouring-class poems in non-biographical terms that were also perceived by Susanne Kord. While Kord, however, uses such readings to critique the very possibility of disinterested 'aesthetic' readings, Goodridge sees this project as attempting to allow the 'one thing these writers have rarely been allowed... simply to be *poets*' (p. xiii). Rather than 'sustain the stereotypes', Goodridge hopes to 'recover a richer and more diverse tradition' of labouring-class poetry (p. xiv). The three volumes each deal with a specific chronological period within the eighteenth century: volume 1 covers the period up to 1740, dominated by the paradigmatic Stephen Duck; volume 2 spans the period between 1740 and 1780; the final volume anthologizes the poets of the last couple of decades of the century. Biographical summaries are provided for each poet, along with brief suggestions for further reading. A companion volume covers labouring-class poets of the nineteenth century.

William Christmas, in his introduction to the first volume, posits rising literacy rates (especially amongst the middle-class *market* for poetry), and the accessibility of libraries as the key factors that enabled the proliferation of labouring-class writers in the period, along with the inspirational success of Stephen Duck in acquiring patronage and wealth. Duck is regarded as a 'media event' created by Queen Caroline in her 'ongoing battle with the wits', and Joseph Spence, to support his theory of 'natural genius' (vol. 1, p. xx). Christmas writes of Duck being 'packaged with his poems' and 'commodified for consumption' (p. xx)—themes by now familiar. He does point out, however, that despite the encouragement that Duck incidentally gave to other lower-class poets, not everyone was 'beholden to the Duck media event for his or her entrance into print culture' (p. xxxiii). Bridget Keegan, introducing the second volume, describes the mid-century poets as 'notoriously resistant to handy generalizations' (vol. 2, p. xv), but does draw out five themes that differentiate them from earlier writers and which enable fruitful discussion. Again, the first three of these have been met with before: an aesthetic based on the idea of 'natural genius'; a growing interest in antiquarianism and literary primitivism; and a transformation of modes of patronage (from courtly to middle-class) and avenues of publication. Keegan's fourth theme is that of linguistic and grammatical standardization, and her fifth the impact of religion as a source of literacy and literary influence. She provides a short discussion of each, the impact of religion in particular being well observed. Tim Burke's introduction to the final volume covers some of the same ground as Keegan, but notes in particular the emergence of Robert Burns as the labouring-class tradition's 'first international celebrity' (vol. 3, p. xvii), and suggests that a feeling of guilt at the nation's 'perceived maltreatment of Thomas Chatterton' (p. xvii) stimulated increased attention to poetic talents from non-traditional backgrounds. Burke cautions that the poems of the late eighteenth-century 'tend to resist any resolution into simple binaries', opposing what he sees as the 'tidy but misleading organizations of the tradition' (p. xviii) initiated by Robert Southey in the nineteenth century. Each of the introductions is short, and they do not attempt to summarize all critical opinion, but they do suggest common interpretations and lines of enquiry. The scholarly quality of the anthology should ensure its status as a standard resource for those eighteenth-century labouring-class poets who cannot (yet!) boast their own critical editions. The inclusion of a thematic index should also ensure its usefulness as a reference work for students undertaking more general research in the period.

Attention turns to the poetry of the 1740 s in Sandro Jung's *Poetic Meaning in the Eighteenth-Century Poems of Mark Akenside and William Shenstone*. As noted in the preface by Angus Ross, Jung offers a 'critical discourse firmly fixed on actual poems, rather than convenient and conventional formulas or misleading abstractions'. This is both the strength and weakness of the study. Jung's readings are generally fair, but a reluctance to draw from them extended arguments and conclusions leaves the text feeling a little directionless. While Akenside and Shenstone receive the most attention, Jung keeps an eye on the literary context in which they wrote, with frequent comparisons and digressions to consider the works of William Collins, Joseph Warton, Richard Savage, and other writers seeking new approaches to poetry following the death of Pope. Beginning with an exploration of Akenside's odes, Jung proceeds to consider the influence of Pindar on the mid-century poets, the uses of personification (particularly in Collins), approaches to 'nature poetry', and Akenside's conception of 'health' in relation to Plato and theories of beauty. He concludes with an extended analysis of the poems of Shenstone, paying particular attention to Shenstone's pastoralism and poetic relationship to James Thomson and Edmund Spenser.

Jung's expressed objective is to establish a sense of 'the continuity that has been ignored by thinking [only] of canonical authors and their works', by 'considering those authors that are on the threshold of a new literary tradition or aesthetic emphasis and preference' (p. 3). This approach entails an examination of the ways in which Akenside and Shenstone anticipate some of the criteria of Romanticism, although Jung is appropriately careful to individuate his authors and the aesthetic contexts in which their compositions were produced. Supporting Fairer's observation on Johnsonian resistance to the tastes of his time, Jung argues that Johnson's evaluation of the two poets is inappropriate due to his adherence to notions of 'public poetry' (p. 13). Akenside and Shenstone are characterized as challengers to the 'great Augustans', as they emphasize 'the key principle of Romantic poetry, the imagination' (p. 14). Jung can at times seem a little too rooted in this traditional dichotomy of Augustan versus Romantic. The observations made in the study about personifications, the influence of Plato, and Akenside's peculiar notions of 'health' as influenced by his medical background, are all insightful, and testify to a careful study of the poems and their implications. This care can on occasion, however, result in a reluctance to prioritize a particular reading. Discussing Akenside's ode *To the Evening Star*, Jung's repeated use of the suppositional 'may', while acknowledging the ambivalence of the poem, begins to feel like a reluctance to take sides or draw conclusions (p. 41). This feeling persists throughout the text: there is such comprehensive quotation of secondary criticism that Jung's own voice often ends up being drowned out. His habit of quoting passages of criticism in German, without providing an English translation, is also a little frustrating. Despite these reservations, *Poetic Meaning in the Eighteenth-Century Poems of Mark Akenside and William Shenstone* offers enough new readings and interpretations of mid-century poetry to justify its publication, and it presents a good number of hints and suggestions that might profitably repay further research.

In the canonical corner, Adam Rounce fights something of a rearguard action for Alexander Pope, or possibly doesn't, in his three-volume collection of eighteenth-century critical commentaries, *Alexander Pope and his Critics*. Mid-century critical responses to the poems of Pope have for over a century been used to illustrate a shift in taste from a 'rational' Augustan mode of poetry, to a proto-Romantic poetry of imaginative subjectivity. Arguably, the text most often employed to support this simple narrative of literary history has been Joseph Warton's *Essay on the Genius and Writings of Pope*, with its memorable categorization of English poets into four distinct classes prominently placed in the initial dedication. Rounce sees fit to reprint the *Essay* in its entirety, alongside Warton's *Ranelagh House*, Robert Shiels's 'Life of Alexander Pope', Percival Stockdale's *Inquiry into the Nature, and Genuine Laws of Poetry*, and Joseph Weston's 'Essay on the Superiority of Dryden's Versification over that of Pope, and of the Moderns'. Rounce contends that nineteenth- and twentieth-century critics have been too eager to oversimplify Warton's treatise to fit a teleological narrative, and that Warton's genuine respect for Pope has been conversely downplayed. His introduction asks for a reconsideration of the *Essay*, and argues against the portrayal of Warton as 'a sort of John the Baptist figure' anticipating the 'second coming' of 1798 (p. xxxi).

The text of Warton's *Essay* provided in the first and second volumes of the set is a facsimile reproduction of the fourth edition, published by Dodsley in 1782. A textual appendix in the third volume lists changes from earlier editions. Rounce also appends a useful index to the somewhat sprawling original. The introduction discusses (and seeks to justify) Warton's digressive method, analyses his revisions, and examines the initial reception of the volumes contrasted with later responses, which began to interpret the work as 'a deliberately provocative and controversial thesis' (p. xvii). Rounce notes that most early responses took account of the book as a whole, rather than concentrating predominantly on the dedication, and were broadly favourable, in some cases enthusiastic. There was little immediate outcry at any perceived denigration of the memory of Pope. Samuel Johnson is cited amongst favourable reviewers, even though his later 'Life of Pope' seems to disapprove of the sentiments of the dedication. Rounce also summarizes the debate as to why there was such a delay between publication of the first and second volumes, preferring the simplicity of John Vance's theory, that 'Warton's middle years were fairly devoid of literary ambition' (p. xlvi), to more complex or conspiratorial explanations. In contrast to the respect he shows for Joseph Warton, Rounce is markedly less positive about the writings and opinions of Percival Stockdale, who is portrayed as a resentful literary failure and an undiscriminating admirer of Pope. Be this as it may, the inclusion of Stockdale's response to Warton in the third volume allows a dissenting voice to be heard. It is a little regrettable that, although discussed in the introduction, Owen Ruffhead's *Life of Alexander Pope* could not similarly be squeezed into the collection. All in all, this is a timely reprint, and Rounce's introduction should act as a useful corrective to those inclined to give Warton's *Essay* only a cursory reading.

A twenty-first-century reading of Pope is offered by John Richardson (*JEGP* 102[2003] 486–505), who reinterprets some of the poet's early works, in particular the first version of *The Rape of the Lock*, in the context of the war poetry of the previous decade. Richardson puts forward the plausible argument that *The Rape of the Lock* 'mocks not only the tradition of classical heroic verse that it parodies but also the contemporary heroic of modern generals and the verses that celebrate them'. Pope is constructed as an anti-war poet who sought to distinguish himself from the general throng of scribblers eager to express their adulation for the duke of Marlborough. In *Windsor-Forest*, Pope's decision to celebrate Edward III's conquest of France instead of Marlborough's much more recent defeat of the French is interpreted as a deliberate insult. Tom Jones (*T&L* 12[2003] 263–73) turns his attention to Pope's reading of Plutarch's *Moralia*, suggesting that, despite his unfavourable mention in the *Dunciad*, Philemon Holland was the translator Pope was most apt to turn to for reference to Plutarch, even to the extent of adapting parts of Holland's translation for his own verse. The examples provided make this claim seem pretty incontrovertible. Jones notes, however, that more than one translation of Plutarch was employed in assembling the notes to Pope's edition of Homer. In the latter part of the article, Jones observes the more general influence of Plutarch's philosophical style and approach on Pope, noting how both proceed 'by example, preferring the duplication and variation of specific instances of a vice to an abstract description of its sources, symptoms, and effects'. Ronald Paulson, in a stimulating essay (in Jacobs and Sussman, eds., *Acts of Narrative*, pp. 130–45), reads *The Rape of the Lock* as embodying a Christian Jacobite aesthetics inherently antagonistic to Shaftesbury's classical Platonic Whig aesthetics. This is problematized by Paulson's idea that a Jacobite aesthetics would in fact be a *non*-aesthetics, 'returning the attention from the authority of response, criticism, and taste to the authority of the maker, from the many back to the one'. Although this sophisticated notion is expressed with perhaps disconcerting brevity, it leads into a sensitive and novel reading of the poem in terms of metaphors of the Fall and redemption. Following his meandering train of argument, Paulson turns his attention to Jonathan Swift's rather different aesthetic as he 'rewrites Pope' in his *Progress of Beauty*, then, via John Gay's *Trivia*, to William Hogarth, whose serpentine line of beauty is discussed in terms of an aesthetic correspondence with Eve-like Belinda's 'wanton ringlets'.

Gay's *Trivia* is the subject of an article by Regina Janes (*ELH* 70[2003] 447–63), or at least the passage concerning Doll's bouncing head is. Remarking that 'bouncing heads are rare in literature', Janes explores the relationship between Gay's use of the topos, and Ariosto's in *Orlando Furioso* (which she posits Gay had translated). The macabre absurdity in each instance is taken to figure ideological crises: in Ariosto's case the disjuncture between the courtly romantic mode and the realities of sixteenth-century Italy; in Gay's between a later courtly classical tradition and the 'burgeoning commercial society' that formed his market. Towards the end of the article, Janes draws attention to the unexpectedly real and present danger in 1715 and 1716 of being decollated for political reasons, but unfortunately does not find any political implications for Doll's head, merely a vague 'insecurity in the natural order of things'.

The wit of the Scriblerians was troubling Roger D. Lund during 2003, as his article on epigram and false wit attests (*ECLife* 27[2003] 67–95). Lund observes that, despite critical mistrust, if not outright condemnation, the mischievous epigrammatic turn was 'too deeply implicated in the Augustan mode ever to be successfully proscribed'. He argues that the epigrammatic nature of the heroic couplet, which was so effective for conveying moral wisdom in a memorable way, could approach dangerously closely to the conceits and quibbles that constituted 'false wit'. The Scriblerians themselves, Lund notes, recognized that poetic sublimity and the epigram were incompatible. There is reason for concern then, as 'the hierarchy of poetic forms [was] amenable to being subsumed into higher forms', the epigram into satire, into georgic, into epic, with potentially bathetic outcomes. The essay is well illustrated and draws attention to a genuinely problematic issue in Augustan poetics.

The influence of Milton is the subject of two further articles. David Read looks at James Thomson's Miltonic precedents (*SEL* 43[2003] 667–82), while Rodney

Stenning Edgecombe traces an elegiac line from Milton, via Richard West, to Thomas Gray (*RES* 54[2003] 386–98). Read begins by announcing eighteenth-century poets to be remarkably free from the 'anxiety of influence' once diagnosed as their illness. In a somewhat impressionistic essay, he presents a Thomson who has 'absorbed' Milton and can imitate innovatively and with creativity. Regarding the two key creative principles in *Paradise Lost* as diffusion and division, Read argues that Thomson takes up the former while largely rejecting the latter, his characteristic style of narrative progression being to change or transform things from one form into another, leading to a sense of overwhelming abundance. Thomson is characterized as possessing a 'straying wantoning' reverie derived from his reading of Milton. Edgecombe observes structural similarities between West's *Monody on the Death of Queen Caroline* and Milton's *Lycidas*, and examines the use of private and public voices in the poems, both of which are seen in turn to inform Gray's *Elegy*. West is credited with reclaiming the public ode as a 'vehicle of genuine emotion', enabling Gray to take this form of abstract grief further by mourning humanity in general. In a separate publication (*ANQ* 16[2003] 18–19), Edgecombe proposes an additional source for the epitaph in Gray's *Elegy,* besides those suggested in Roger Lonsdale's edition of *The Poems of Thomas Gray, William Collins, Oliver Goldsmith* [1972]. This is the 'inscription' at the end of Pope's 'To Mr. Addison, Occasioned by his Dialogues on Medals'. While this is feasible, the 'overlap in ethos' that Edgecombe suggests links the two poems seems fairly typically Horatian, and not exactly unique.

Thomas Gray's taste in wallpaper is of moment in Barrett Kalter's article on Gray and the medieval revival (*ELH* 70[2003] 989–1019). Gray's difficulties in finding appropriately Gothic wallpaper are used as a starting point to explore his aesthetics, the broader tastes of his age, and the growing impact of market commodification. Kalter sees the medieval revival as an aesthetic movement that challenged the social changes associated with the market economy while relying on the practices that the new economy made possible to 'recover and reinvent England's cultural heritage'. A history of wallpaper is included, tracing the vogue for particular styles from the sixteenth century onwards. There is also some discussion about the impact of the Ossian poems and how Gray's enthusiasm for authentic antiquarian items confirmed for him the validity of his emotional responses towards them.

Thomas Keymer's discovery of important new evidence about the composition of Christopher Smart's *A Translation of the Psalms of David* (*RES* 54[2003] 52–66) indicates that there is still some possibility of casting further light upon the poet's murky 'mad' years. The little-known William Toldervy, novelist and travel writer, is revealed to have been an enthusiastic supporter of Smart. Keymer also uncovers some notable anticipations of Sterne and Smollett in Toldervy's *The History of Two Orphans*. His most significant find, however, is a 'premature chapter-length puff' for Smart's translation of the Psalms, inserted rather incongruously into Toldervy's novel. This antedates other unambiguous references to Smart's project by six years. Other new discoveries publicized in 2003 were made by Sandro Jung, who unearthed two poems by Anna Seward, assumed to date from the 1760 s or 1770 s (*ANQ* 16[2003] 18–19). The first is interpreted as an explicit confirmation of Seward's homosexuality (it is indeed erotic, if rather conventional). The second poem is a little more sophisticated, employing the topos of the mutability of physical beauty in contrast with the immortalizing power of poetry. Jung opens another article with an anonymous and previously unpublished poem from the 1740 s, *An Address to Fancy*, before moving on to consider the role of 'sweetness' in the poetry of William Collins (*ELN* 41[2003] 36–43). Jung notes that, amongst eighteenth-century poets, the term 'sweet' was theorized most prominently by Collins, who connects it with naturally pleasing appeals to the senses; the aesthetic context of classical Hellenism; poetic inspiration (via the myth of the bees feeding honey to Pindar); simplicity; and 'a whole diversity of poetic ideas'. While Jung is arguably sensible not to restrict Collins's 'sweetness' to a simple aesthetic definition, the reader is left feeling little wiser at the end of the article than at the beginning.

William Cowper's misgivings about critical responses to his poetry is the subject of the final article reviewed here. Priscilla Gilman offers a sensitive account of Cowper's shifting attitudes towards his critics, his fears concerning his reception, and the manner in which he revised his poems in response to reviews (*ELH* 70[2003] 89–115). Describing his concerns as 'truly obsessive', Gilman finds plenty of evidence in Cowper's correspondence to suggest that he was neither able to assume indifference to critical opinion, nor to accommodate it, for any length of time. Gilman interprets this psychologically as a 'constitutional flexibility of self-presentation', which sounds a little generous.

4. Drama

One prevailing theme among this year's publications about eighteenth-century drama addresses matters of the body, sexuality, and the performative nature of identity. Catherine B. Burroughs, in 'British Women Playwrights and the Staging of Female Initiation: Sophia Lee's *The Chapter of Accidents* [1780]' (*ERR* 14:i[2003] 7–16), also discussed in Chapter XII below, perceptively points out that British pornography of the period linked the eroticization of defloration to a heroine who was obsessively preoccupied with virginity, a connection that Lee exploits in her play. At a meta-dramatic level, the preface to *The Chapter of Accidents* includes a self-portrayal of Lee as a victim of theatrical politics, as she distanced herself from her playscript about victimization so that she might emerge virtuous, innocent, virginal in contrast to the fictitious character in her play. Gill Perry, 'Ambiguity and Desire: Metaphors of Sexuality in Late Eighteenth-Century Representation of the Actress' (in Robyn Asleson, ed., *Notorious Muse: The Actress in British Art and Culture 1776–1812*, pp. 57–80), discusses the changing association of the actress with prostitution at the end of the eighteenth century, facilitated by respectable performers such as Sarah Siddons, theatrical biographies of performers, and portraits of stage players. Perry considers the ways in which the struggles for respectable identity and professional recognition revolved around contested notions of femininity and masculinity and how these struggles were mediated through painted representations of actresses.

Contemporary discourses on the actress were often reflected in the portraiture, as Mary Robinson's self-representation illustrates. The portrait was an instrument for promoting her 'feminine' morality while simultaneously capturing her professional 'masculine' status. Cross-dressing was still deployed on the stage in the late eighteenth century, and the spectacle of women dressed like men had a strong commercial appeal capitalized by painters, for example, the portrait of Dorothy Jordan and Frances Abington, in their breeches roles.

In 'Words and Bodies: A Discourse on Male Sexuality in Late Eighteenth-Century English Representational Practices' (*TRI* 18:i[2003] 1–19), Michael Kobialka outlines the idea that as the actor's body and image in the eighteenth century occupied an ambiguous social position and were constantly scrutinized, William Kenrick's *Love in the Suds* and Humphrey Nettle's *Sodom and Onan* place the discourse of sexuality on stage where all the gazes are directed at the same male figure—the homosexual. *Love in the Suds* satirizes Isaac Bickerstaff and David Garrick as homosexuals, and the satire of *Sodom and Onan* indicts Samuel Foote as a sodomite. All three men were recognizable theatre celebrities, highlighting the tensions which existed between an abstract performative body on stage and a living performative body in society and thereby questioning the power of new representational practices (specific to the Industrial Revolution and capitalism as well as medical and legal dispositions) in the codification of morality and in the production of personality types, political control, and normalization of a body. Kobialka convincingly argues that attempts to expose Garrick, Bickerstaff, and Foote point to the campaign to normalize a 'dignified masculinity' (p. 14) for the male body. According to Joyce G. MacDonald in 'Public Wounds: Sexual Bodies and the Origins of State in Nathaniel Lee's *Lucius Janius Brutus*' (*SECC* 32[2003] 229–144), Lee's drama conflates private sexual conduct and the preservation of public order. That the play projects the body as a civic signifier at a critical moment for British sovereign masculinity is significant in Lee's recoding of the Roman myth. While sexual desire threatens to disrupt and destroy the male body, Lucrece's body, on the other hand, is reduced to the status of a 'public wound' (p. 232). MacDonald cogently argues that *Lucius Janius Brutus* interrogates the problem of how to manage the body's sexuality, specifically proper manliness, in such a way as to retain its affiliation with an orderly sovereign body and state, an analogy that it destabilizes in the process of recuperating a rigorously masculine public sphere, a solidarity gained at the expense of the body politic's feminine parts. Titus's death reinforces the subordination of the feminine to the masculine Roman will, a lesson about the power of men and the importance of paternal authority.

Shearer West, 'Body Connoisseurship' (in Robyn Asleson, ed., *Notorious Muse*, pp. 151–70), examines the attention theatre audiences directed towards the bodies of male and female performers. The growing popularity of the breeches role and changes in theatrical fashions meant that the shape of women's bodies was exposed to the audience's gaze and critical commentary. Consequently, 'body connoisseurship' was doubly identified with decorum and propriety as well as voyeurism and desire. The use of detailed physical features intensified following the initiation of public art exhibitions in the 1760 s, and what the public admired in visual art it demanded in performing arts.

An engaging book-length study, Cynthia Lowenthal, *Performing Identities on the Restoration Stage*, examines multiple categories of crisis associated with identity produced by Restoration theatre from 1656 to 1707. The study focuses on plays written by men and women in four sites of analysis in which gender and national identities are featured, at a time when new importance was given to the relationship between the body and identity: unruly European national bodies and British mercantilism, discursive female bodies and representations of female desire, and the regulation of female bodies through acts of sexual assault. John Dryden's *The Indian Emperour* [1665], William Davenant's *The Cruelty of the Spaniards in Peru* [1656], and Aphra Behn's *Widow Ranter* [1689] are dramatic romances of conquest at the heart of Lowenthal's analysis of British imperialism and its efforts to colonize unruly savage bodies. These plays reflect English ambivalence about the New World, the simultaneous attraction to and repulsion from colonial differences, and their love plots, Lowenthal compellingly argues, function as ideological tropes in portraying the intimate relation between seeing and possessing in 'love as conquest' contexts. The contested woman creates the conditions for conquest and acts as the site for displaced European hostility.

Essential 'Englishness' became a necessary complement to British expansionism, and Lowenthal considers the formations and representations of national identities in Behn's *Dutch Lover* [1673], William Wycherley's *Gentleman Dancing-Master* [1673], and Mary Pix's *Adventures in Madrid* [1706]. The bodies of Restoration actresses (especially Elizabeth Barry and Anne Bracegirdle) were read as character representations onstage and as objectified bodies offstage, doubly bound to the male gaze. The visual spectacle of woman onstage was frequently read through extra-theatrical knowledge of offstage private activities, particularly those that brought signs of aristocratic status into question. It is in this context that Lowenthal reads Delarivier Manley's *Royal Mischief* [1696] and Behn's *Rover; or, The Banish'd Cavaliers* [1677]. Both plays demonstrate how Restoration theatre participated in a culture of discourse in which a 'self' separated from the character an actress performed was a sexually available body.

Behn's *Second Part of The Rover* [1681] features a giant and a dwarf, actual Restoration monsters, but Lowenthal's study is more interested in the metaphorical monsters, characters who exceed sanctioned boundaries of gender roles—i.e. the libertine—of Thomas Shadwell's comedies *The Woman-Captain* [1679] and *The Virtuoso* [1676]. These Restoration rape plays suggest that men are naturally violent, thus excusing the 'hero' who is a serial rapist and murderer, a man whose sexual appetite is fed by novelty and adventure. Libertines waste bodies; women's bodies are the object of their insatiable appetite for various sexual pleasures and sexual violence. The women victims of these plays are compelled to narrate their trauma, to exceed their female identity with impulsive and explosive speech. In Pix's *Ibrahim, the Thirteenth Emperour* [1696] and Manley's *Almyna: or, the Arabian Vow* [1707], Lowenthal notes a difference in the portrayal of 'monstrous' women in plays written by women and of monstrous rapists in plays written by men. Pix and Manley create monstrous women who do not prey upon a victim, and they exceed the bounds of femininity only to protect others from violence or injustice. In the Epilogue, Lowenthal looks at the performance of identity in several plays which integrate the four sites of analysis in which *Performing Identities* has been engaged. This interdependence reveals the period's cultural movements from aristocratic to bourgeois economies and towards the feminine as the gendered ideal of behaviour for both sexes. *Performing Identities* contributes significantly to criticism about the long eighteenth century's engagement with colonialism and gender, and how performative and performing identities were shaped by cultural pressures upon the body, its sex, gender and nationality.

The eighteenth-century public consumption of theatrical performers was central to several of this year's works. Heather McPherson, 'Painting, Politics and the Stage in the Age of Caricature' (in Robyn Asleson, ed., *Notorious Muse*, pp. 171–93), shows us that, because the late eighteenth-century was the age of the stage and the age of caricature, it is not surprising to see the theatre, its performers, its playwrights, and its spectacles satirized in caricature painting and printing that became increasingly associated with oppositional politics. The essay looks particularly at depictions of Sarah Siddons and O.P. Riots. Aileen Riberio, 'Costuming the Part: A Discourse of Fashion and Fiction in the Image of the Actress in English, 1776–1812' (in Robyn Asleson, ed., *Notorious Muse*, pp. 104–27), demonstrates how difficult it was for women to perform in historically accurate dress because the female image was conditioned by the period's notions of fashionable body shape, with specific modifications for tragedy and comedy. Portraits of popular actresses of the day illustrate how fashion, including hairstyles, trumped historical accuracy.

Cheryl Wanko, *Roles of Authority: Thespian Biography and Celebrity in Eighteenth-Century Britain*, examines the biographies and autobiographies of actors and actresses emerging during the eighteenth century as contributions to the widespread public attention to performers generated by the period's inchoate consumer culture. Enter the 'celebrity', the personality turned commodity, who, Wanko convincingly argues, by the end of the century achieved in many instances the status of cultural authority. In Britain's market economy, currency is an appropriate metaphor for the celebrity. This development of player biography and performance criticism changed assumptions about acting and the function of drama and theatre in society, and gave audiences unprecedented control over images, knowledge, and expectations of performers, further blurring the boundaries between public and private lives. The stage and the page operated dialogically in promoting star performers, the first stage celebrity being David Garrick.

Roles of Authority first analyses the different claims to authority made by biographies and points to ways in which these reveal something about eighteenth-century claims about sources of authority, particularly the ongoing debate between the ancients and the moderns. Charles Gildon's *The Life of Mr. Thomas Betterton, the Late Eminent Tragedian* [1710] is an example of the gentleman-actor or thespian biography, with its connections to conventional theatre, and demonstrates how the actor's image becomes integrated into popular culture, taking on a public life that is ambivalently linked to the actual private person. *Roles of Authority* next considers how *The Beggar's Opera* encouraged biographies that elevated performers to the status of new social 'heroes' and 'heroines' whose fame was media-generated rather than earned from deeds: for example, *Life of Fenton*, *Memoirs of Macheath*, and *Life of Spiller*. These biographies do not admire their subjects, their narratives often condescending, hostile, and disapproving.

Biographies and autobiographies of actresses reveal the problems particular to the public woman who sought cultural authority and respect for her art. The *Life of Lavinia Beswick, Alias Fenton, Alias Polly Peachum* [1728] depicts the actress as a harlot. Published during Fenton's lifetime, the biography creates a role for the actress in her lived world that makes her gender in the theatrical world acceptable. The result is a text that invites voyeurism. *A Narrative of the Life of Mrs. Charlotte Clarke* [1755] unveils the struggles of the actress's life. The autobiography relates the complex interplay of roles demanded of performing women: stage, textual, and actual. Both texts demonstrate how femininity is a social construction.

Discussing the social construction of masculinity, Wanko reviews three biographies about the actor Barton Booth: one by an anonymous writer published by John Cooper [1733], Benjamin Victor's *Memoirs of the Life of Baron Booth, Esq.* [1733], and one by Theophilus Cibber [1753]. The three biographies negotiate Booth's madness, diagnosing it variously as a consequence of acting, his professional life being devoted to the expressive powers of the body. While Victor publicizes Booth as a dignified, upstanding citizen, Cooper's Booth is a roguish, unstable character. Booth's biographers attempt to demystify his body's physiological secrets as they unveil his performing, play-acting art.

Performers' struggles to achieve 'authorization' required them to reconcile the century's changing concepts of authorship, as Wanko illustrates with the thespian autobiography *An Apology for the Life of Mr. Colley Cibber, Esq.* [1740]. Cibber shifts the importance of the theatre from the playwright to the actor in his autobiography, suggesting that actors should control both the theatre and their textual representation—the authority of self-presentation. Participating in the period's print controversy, *Apology* registered new directions in performance criticism and theatre history, becoming a literary model that other actors replicated.

Roles of Authority looks at the portrayal of performers by those outside the theatrical world: for example the biography of Ann Oldfield, and fictional characters in the period's novels. As the mid-eighteenth-century market was increasingly driven by consumption, biographers became preoccupied with the value of performers, measured by actors' salaries and wills, audience approval and public support. Biographies served to regulate this value, helping the public to evaluate actors as public figures by scrutinizing their real and metaphorical relation to money. This revealing study concludes with an examination of the biographies of David Garrick by Thomas Davies and Arthur Murphy, both published after Garrick's death and instrumental in maintaining his legendary and celebrity stature. Davies presents Garrick as the consummate theatrical professional, while Murphy establishes him as literary authority, one who shaped and reformed Britain's national theatre. Both biographies confirm Garrick as celebrity and cultural authority. By the end of the eighteenth century, performers realized the value of the public attention they received as a result of print culture, and its contributions to their own 'currency' and permanence as figures of authority.

Two studies situate eighteenth-century drama in the period's political struggles. Helen M. Burke, *Riotous Performances: The Struggle for Hegemony in the Irish Theater, 1712–1784*, examines the contested and revolutionary nature of eighteenth-century Irish theatre, its challenging of dominant political ideology with its 'unauthorized' actors' 'riotous performances' and oppositional counter-theatre that resisted emerging bourgeois disciplinary demarcations between page and stage, performers and spectators, Irish Protestant and Irish Catholic. According to Burke, the eighteenth-century Irish theatre was a site where hegemonic struggles occurred, but she expands the field of performance beyond the conventional theatre to include Williamite street theatre, Irish Protestant plays and pamphlets, tavern performances of Irish music, Catholic political tracts, rude folk dramas, Gaelic poems, weavers' riots, and Volunteer parades, for example, in order to reveal it as unstable and dynamic, its disruptive acts opening a space for the Irish Catholic voice from 1712 to 1786. *Riotous Performances* offers us a much-needed analysis of the period's Irish drama and its engagement with Anglo-Irish politics.

Riotous Performances considers Nicholas Rowe's *Tamerlane* in the context of a subversive Irish Protestant imaginary, made visible in the Williamite riot and effigy of 1712 and reified by Rowe's Williamite–Jacobite drama. Burke persuasively asserts that this 'riot' might be regarded as a defining moment in the struggle to create a stage for all of the people of Ireland. The trope of the native Gaelic costuming takes on political and economic meanings staged in official entertainments as well as in the theatres, as exemplified in Thomas Shadwell's government plays. Irish Protestant musical appropriations in the Irish theatre contributed significantly to the revival of Gaelic music and culture as well as the reclamation of the Irish Catholic nation, its dreams and aspirations, as music from John Gay's *The Beggar's Wedding* and *The Beggar's Opera* illustrate.

The Kelly riot of 1745, a conflict that spread from the theatre to Dublin's streets, coffee-houses, the press, the university, and the courts, reproduces the colonial myth of English civility and Irish barbarity in its conclusion, which found Thomas Sheridan innocent of assault and Kelly guilty of making unwanted sexual advances to female performers and of throwing an orange at Sheridan onstage. Sheridan's Theatre Royal, explains Burke, participated in ideological efforts to intimidate and contain Catholics in its portrayal of Catholic characters onstage and its handling of Catholic theatre-goers. Using the 'Gentlemen's Quarrel' as pretext, Charles Lucas staged Irish patriot counter-drama that opened up spaces for the marginalized Irish Catholic subject to speak, but in the pamphlet war following the staging of this counter-drama, Edmund Burke spurned Lucas as a mountebank and associated his drama with clowns (especially Punch), buffoons, and street entertainments. In response, Lucas argued that the British Constitution was applicable to the Irish, staging a pedagogical mini-drama on constitutional theory and practice even as his street theatre undermined Sheridan's control over the stage. The Chapel Street theatre likewise was a site of opposition to Dublin's Theatre Royal during 1748–50, as *Riotous Performances* explores.

During the 1749–50 season, tensions between 'native' and 'foreign' musicians escalated. By the 1753–4 season, the result was the Money-Bill Dispute, a conflict between Irish patriots and English administrators, supported by Sheridan's troop of performers. *Mahomet the Imposter* staged the conflict between Protestant Britain and Catholic France, justifying the imperial presence of the religiously and politically tolerant English. From 1754 to 1779, playwrights, players, and spectators challenged English dominance, creating alternative social and cultural configurations. By 1784, the Dublin playhouse was implicated in the larger revolutionary activities which had been brewing since 1779 (such as the Volunteer street theatre), and the imperial subject was driven from the theatre. Socially diverse audiences resisted government control of the theatre, with John O'Keeffe and Robert Owenson bringing Gaelic artists and culture on to the stage. The Stage Act of 1786 arrested disruptive political performances and the revolution in the Irish theatre.

Daniel O'Quinn, 'Hannah Cowley's *A Day in Turkey* and the Political Efficacy of Charles James Fox' (*ERR* 14:i[2003] 17–30), argues that Hannah Cowley's *A Day in Turkey; or, The Russian Slaves* [1792] criticizes Foxite politics and theorizes the sexual undercurrents of governance through its interjection of the topical and recognizable allusions to political and social news. Cowley's sexualization of politics can be seen in the play's 'Advertisement', where she refers to Edmund Burke as one who sacrificed love for politics. For her caricature of Fox, his sexual practices, and the sexual underpinnings of despotism, Cowley draws on the political features of her Eastern setting. A print by Joseph Dent, *Black Carlo's White Bust, or The Party's Plenipo in Catherine's Closet* [1791], is the source for the character name A La Grecque, the character representing Fox, treason, libertinism, and suspect sexual hybridity, and which, according to O'Quinn, points to Cowley's deployment of sexual deviance in political arguments, a strategy influenced by Burke's *Reflections on the French Revolution*. The character Lauretta figures Mrs Armistead, a courtesan, and Cowley herself, a dramatic gesture that connects women of the theatre with prostitution, to suggest that the female playwright and courtesan inhabit a space necessary to the masculine realm of politics. The metatheatricality of Lauretta's role as playwright/manager points to the possibilities of women in power, modelling the ideal of domestic government that *A Day in Turkey* supports.

Several critical works addressed matters of genre and aesthetics. Victoria Warren, 'Gender and Genre in Susanna Centlivre's *The Gamester* and *The Basset Table*' (*SEL* 43:iii[2003] 605–24), challenges the categorization of Susanna Centlivre's plays as sentimental comedy, arguing that such a label is inaccurate and distorts the plays in three ways: (1) it casts them in an inferior position, one frequently reserved for women writers; (2) it overlooks their dialectic, the tensions and contradictions within them; and (3) it forces them into a preconceived mould, with its expectations of a moral, for example. Warren asserts that the plays might be more accurately identified as 'plays of signification', the connotations of 'play' registering meanings of gaming, acting, and dissimulation. She points out that, during the Restoration, the term 'sentimental' would not have been used to describe these plays. Even so, most of the scenes and characters in the two plays are 'anti-sentimental' and are instead realistic, witty, and satirical. To illustrate this, Warren examines how the incongruities and ambiguities of Centlivre's work undermine assumptions about her plays' reification of moral reform, and gives ample evidence that the reforms they presented were not wholly 'moral' at all, for instance in their affirmation of female independence.

The central role of theatre in early eighteenth-century criticism occupies Marcie Frank, *Gender, Theatre, and the Origins of Criticism: Fry Dryden to Manley*, an enlightening study that provides a historical account of criticism's emergence between 1660 and 1714 by looking at the critical writings of John Dryden and those of women of the following generation whose writings were shaped by his example: Aphra Behn, Catharine Trotter, and Delarivier Manley. Frank argues that Dryden's criticism is historical and theatrical, and she emphasizes the importance of dramatic writing to the early development of criticism by claiming that the production of criticism from 1660 to 1717 was conditioned by its proximity to the stage, with gender and sexuality as its key terms. Frank asserts that late seventeenth- and early eighteenth-century criticism is often depicted as male-gendered because of its disengagement from theatre, and this study seeks to recover its theatrical-female legacy. Theatre was the site of critical discourse in its prologues, epilogues, letters of dedication, and prefatory essays, and the critic's social position bridged the boundaries between court and theatre, patronage and consumerism. Criticism is thus performative, and the theatricality that shapes it Frank terms the 'critical stage' (p. 2), for, as criticism came to be more fully associated with the prose essay, the theatre diminished as a site for its production.

Dryden's *Essay of Dramatick Poesy* [1668] establishes his critical lineage to Shakespeare, as the critic who guarantees Shakespeare's literary transmission. His prefatory essay to *Troilus and Cressida*, 'Grounds of Criticism in Tragedy', situates Shakespeare as the 'universal mind', masculine and patriarchal, privileged and aristocratic. In its staging of literary competition as rivalry between women, Dryden's *All for Love* associates women writers with criticism and creates paradigmatic female literary critics. Behn's criticism appears in prefaces to *The Dutch Lover* [1673] and *The Lucky Chance* [1687], in which she examines writing as a woman in relation to her female audience. She affiliates herself with Shakespeare and with Dryden, her dramatic/critical heritage, but she maintains that writing makes possible imaginative self-translation across gendered lines. In her self-genealogizing, Trotter looks to Behn as well as to Shakespeare and Dryden, even though she does not share Dryden's association of softness with effeminacy. In the prologue of *Love at a Loss: or Most Votes Carry It* [1701], Trotter includes homosocial friendship and female independence as possibilities for women. The prologue to *The Revolution of Sweden* [1706] expands the role of the woman writer to that of social reformer and politician.

Gender, Theatre, and the Origins of Criticism examines Manley's portrayal of Trotter in *The New Atlantis*, as literary criticism and political satire, and in

Manley's theatrical writings, with special consideration of Dryden's influence on them. In the dedicatory letter to *The New Atlantis*, Manley uses Dryden to authorize her voice, but she does so reservedly as she simultaneously affirms and disavows his literary precedent. Manley demonstrates how men and women writers were public figures, and she deploys the term 'character' to confound critical repercussions about women writers' gender. Manley satirically reduces everything to sex to empower her literary and critical authority. For Manley, the theatre is the site for literary and critical authority, and the performance of the actress (e.g. Elizabeth Berry) becomes the basis of her authorial appeal and an example for female spectators/readers. 'To the Reader', which prefaces *The Secret History of Queen Zarah and the Zarazians* [1705], indicates Manley's awareness that the theatre-going audience was becoming a reading public.

Peter Millington, 'The Truro Cordwainer's Play: A "New" Eighteenth-Century Christmas Play' (*Folklore* 114[2003] 53–73), challenges the Cornwall Record Office's identification of location for the eighteenth-century manuscript of a Christmas mummers' play, the 'Mylor' play, and insists that the play is more accurately identified with Truro, particularly its central parish of St Mary's, as the site where the play was performed sometime between 1768 and 1803. Probably performed in the late 1780s, the Truro play is one of the oldest available English folk-play texts. Millington gives a physical description of the manuscript, discusses the probable actors, delineates textual parallels among the sources from which the pastiche play was constructed, and discusses the play's Orientalism.

The first four chapters of Christopher S. Sweeny's seven-chapter Ph.D. dissertation, '"The drama is a haunted ruin": Theatrical Ghosts and the Necromantic Stage' (University of Rochester), consider eighteenth-century drama and study ghosts as vehicles of satire in Henry Fielding's *The Author's Farce* [1730], *Tom Thumb* [1730], and *Pasquin* [1736]. *The Author's Farce* reforms *Hamlet* into a comedy. *Tom Thumb*'s ghost functions as a metaphor for the ambivalence Fielding feels about tragedy. *Pasquin* is an elaborate rehearsal ghost play illustrating the shortcomings of contemporary theatre. Sweeny also claims that the Licensing Act of 1737 had two significant effects on the history of theatre: first, it codified state censorship that eliminated plays with any hint of political satire; second, it singled Fielding out for blame for the need of such censorship. The study superficially examines the role of Shakespeare in eighteenth-century drama, in critics' and theatre-goers' expectations of Shakespearian supernatural, and in David Garrick's portrayal of Shakespearian characters.

One edition of eighteenth-century drama was published this year, in the wake of several editions published in 2001 and 2002. Douglas J. Canfield, gen. ed., *The Broadview Anthology of Restoration and Early Eighteenth-Century Drama*, concise edition, offers us a shorter version of the Broadview anthology by the same title issued in 2002. This collection includes twenty-one representative plays written by twenty-one playwrights from 1660 to 1737, and targets students as its audience. The editors of the plays have modernized spellings and punctuation and omitted dedications and prefaces, theoretical discourses, and lists of players. Arranged chronologically, the plays are annotated, and since readability is the goal of the anthology, the editions make no claim to be definitive texts. The anthology includes a brief introduction which discusses historical contexts in relation to the roles of theatre and drama, distinguishes among Restoration, revolution, and early Georgian drama, and delineates playhouse and staging innovations for each period. The various sub-genres of drama are discussed. Each edition begins with a one-page introduction to the play, and students will find a glossary of period-specific terms at the end of the anthology.

Books Reviewed

Andrews, Stuart. *Unitarian Radicalism: Political Rhetoric, 1770–1814*. Palgrave. [2003] pp. 248. £47.50 ISBN 0 3339 6925 1.

Asleson, Robyn, ed. *Notorious Muse: The Actress in British Art and Culture 1776–1812*. YaleUP. [2003] pp. 240. £40 ISBN 0 3001 0005 1.

Asleson, Robyn, ed. *The Actress in British Art and Culture 1776–1812*. YaleUP. [2003] pp. 209. $70 ISBN 0 3001 0005 1.

Barchas, Janine. *Graphic Design, Print Culture, and the Eighteenth-Century Novel*. CUP. [2003] pp. xvi +296. £45 ISBN 0 5218 1908 3.

Basker, James, ed. *Amazing Grace: An Anthology of Poems About Slavery 1660–1810*. YaleUP. [2003] pp. lvii +721. £35 ($50) ISBN 0 3000 9172 9.

Battestin, Martin C., and O.M. Brack, Jr., eds. *The History and Adventures of the Renowned Don Quixote,* trans. Tobias Smollett. UGeorgiaP. [2003] pp. xlix +942. $100 ISBN 0 8203 2430 2.

Berg, Maxine, and Eger Elizabeth, eds. *Luxury in the Eighteenth Century: Debates, Desires and Delectable Goods*. Palgrave. [2003] pp. 272. £55 ISBN 0 3339 6382 2.

Braithwaite, Helen. *Romanticism, Publishing and Dissent: Joseph Johnson and the Cause of Liberty*. Palgrave. [2003] pp. 264. £47.50 ISBN 0 3339 8394 7.

Burke, Helen M. *Riotous Performances: The Struggle for Hegemony in the Irish Theatre, 1712–1784*. UNDP. [2003] pp. 356. $70 ISBN 0 2680 4015 X.

Canfield, J. Douglas, and gen, eds. *The Broadview Anthology of Restoration and Early Eighteenth-Century British Drama*. Broadview. [2003] pp. 1,033. $39.95 ISBN 1 5511 1581 6.

Champion, Justin. *Republican Learning: John Toland and the Crisis of Christian Culture, 1696–1722*. ManUP. [2003] pp. 272. £47.50 ISBN 0 7190 5714 0.

De Bolla, Peter. *The Education of the Eye: Painting, Landscape and Architecture in Eighteenth-Century Britain*. StanfordUP. [2003] pp. 296, hb $55 ISBN 0 8047 4455 6; pb $21.95 ISBN 0 8047 4800 4.

Fairer, David. *English Poetry of the Eighteenth Century 1700–1789*. Longman. [2003] pp. 304. pb £20.99 ($37.60) ISBN 0 5822 2777 1.

Fletcher, Loraine, ed. *Emmeline* by Charlotte Smith. Broadview. [2003] pp. 520. pb $CAN22.95 ($17.95, £9.99) ISBN 1 5511 1359 7.

Folkenflik, Robert, and Barbara Laning Fitzpatrick, eds. *The Life and Adventures of Sir Launcelot Greaves* by Tobias Smollett. UGeorgiaP. [2002] pp. liv 314. $60 ISBN 0 8203 2307 1.

Fowler, Patsy S., and Alan Jackson, eds. *Launching Fanny Hill: Essays on the Novel and its Influences*. AMS Studies in the Eighteenth Century 41. AMS. [2003] pp. xix +364. $82.50 ISBN 0 4046 3541 5.

Frank, Frederick S., ed. *The Castle of Otranto and the Mysterious Mother* by Horace Walpole. Broadview. [2003] pp. 357. pb $CAN14.95 ($9.95, £5.99) ISBN 1 5511 1304 X.

Frank, Marcie. *Gender, Theatre, and the Origins of Criticism: From Dryden to Manley*. CUP. [2003] pp. 175. $60 ISBN 0 5218 1810 9.

Galperin, William H. *The Historical Austen*. UPennP. [2003] pp. viii +286. $39.95 (£28) ISBN 0 8122 3687 4.

Gemmeke, Mascha. *Frances Burney and the Female Bildungsroman: An Interpretation of The Wanderer; or, Female Difficulties*. Münster Monographs on English Literature, 28. Lang. [2003] pp. 359. €56.50 ISBN 3 6315 2303 3.

Goodridge, John, William Christmas, Bridget Keegan and Tim Burke, eds. *Eighteenth-Century English Labouring-Class Poets 1700–1800*. P&C. [2003] pp. 1,288. £275 ($460) ISBN 1 8519 6758 3, 3 vols.

Greene, Richard, and Ann Messenger, eds. *The Works of Mary Leapor*. OUP. [2003] pp. xlii +358. £89 ($150) ISBN 0 1981 8292 9.

Jacobs, Carol, and Henry Sussman, eds. *Acts of Narrative*. StanfordUP. [2003] pp. 296. hb £40.95 ($60) ISBN 0 8047 4650 8; pb $24.95 ISBN 0 8047 4651 6.

Jones, William R., ed. *A Critical Edition of the Poetical Works of William Falconer*. Mellen. [2003] pp. xvi +518. £84.95 ($139.95) ISBN 0 7734 6766 1.

Jung, Sandro. *Poetic Meaning in the Eighteenth-Century Poems of Mark Akenside and William Shenstone*. Mellen. [2003] pp. iv +265. £69.95 ($109.95) ISBN 0 7734 6963 X.

Keymer, Thomas. *Sterne, the Moderns, and the Novel*. OUP. [2002] pp. xiii +223. £45 ($65) ISBN 0 1992 4592 4.

Kord, Susanne. *Women Peasant Poets in Eighteenth-Century England, Scotland, and Germany: Milkmaids on Parnassus*. Camden House. [2003] pp. xiii +325. £50 ($75) ISBN 1 5711 3268 6.

Lewis, Jeremy. *Tobias Smollett*. Cape. [2003] pp. xix +316. £20 ISBN 0 2240 6151 8.

Lowenthal, Cynthia. *Performing Identities on the Restoration Stage*. SIUP. [2003] pp. 270. $40 ISBN 0 8093 2462 8.

Lynch, Jack. *The Age of Elizabeth in the Age of Johnson*. CUP. [2003] pp. 236. £40 ISBN 0 5218 1907 5.

McGinty, J. Walter. *Robert Burns and Religion*. Ashgate. [2003] pp. vi +281. £45 ($79.95) ISBN 0 7546 3504 X.

Moore, Dafydd. *Enlightenment and Romance in James McPherson's 'The Poems of Ossian': Myth, Genre and Cultural Change*. Ashgate. [2003] pp. ix +187. £40 ($69.95) ISBN 0 7546 0973 1.

Mostefai, Ourida, and Catherine Ingrassia, eds. *Studies in Eighteenth-Century Culture*, vol. 32. JHUP. [2003] pp. xi +385. $40 ISBN 0 8018 7256 1.

New, Melvyn, and W.G. Day, eds. *A Sentimental Journey through France and Italy and Continuation of the Brahmine's Journal: The Text and Notes*. The

Florida Edition of the Works of Laurence Sterne, vol. 6. UFlorP. [2002] pp. lxxii +567. $65 ISBN 0 8130 1771 8.

Parker, Fred. *Scepticism and Literature: An Essay on Pope, Hume, Sterne, and Johnson*. OUP. [2003] pp. x + 290. £50 ISBN 0 1992 5318 8.

Peakman, Julie. *Mighty Lewd Books: The Development of Pornography in Eighteenth-Century England*. Palgrave. [2003] pp. 280. £25 ISBN 1 4039 1500 8.

Pollak, Ellen. *Incest and the English Novel, 1684–1814*. JHUP. [2003] pp. x + 261. $39.95 ISBN 0 8018 7204 9.

Prescott, Sarah. *Women, Authorship and Literary Culture, 1690–1740*. Palgrave. [2003] pp. x + 237. £45 ISBN 1 4039 0323 9.

Rounce, Adam, ed. *Alexander Pope and his Critics*, 3 vols. Routledge. [2003] pp. lxii + 415. (vol. 1), 423 (vol. 2), lxxi +132 (vol. 3). £350 ($695) ISBN 0 4153 0909 3.

Spacks, Patricia Meyer. *Privacy: Concealing the Eighteenth-Century Self*. UChicP. [2003] pp. 242. $36 ISBN 0 2267 6860 0.

Stott, Anne. *Hannah More: The First Victorian*. OUP. [2003] pp. 408. hb £35 ISBN 0 1992 4532 0, pb £20 ISBN 0 1992 7488 6.

Tandon, Bharat. *Jane Austen and the Morality of Conversation*. Nineteenth Century Studies. Anthem. [2003] pp. 208. hb £45 ISBN 1 8433 1101 1, pb £21.95 ISBN 1 8433 1102 X.

Taylor, Barbara. *Mary Wollstonecraft and the Feminist Imagination*. CUP. [2003] pp. 352. hb £45 ISBN 0 521 66144 7, pb £16.99 ISBN 0 5210 0417 9.

Troost, Linda V., ed. *Eighteenth-Century Women: Studies in their Lives, Work, and Culture*. vol. 3. AMS. [2003] pp. x + 355. $94.50 ISBN 0 404 6473 0.

Wanko, Cheryl. *Roles of Authority: Thespian Biography and Celebrity in Eighteenth-Century Britain*. TexasTechUP.[2003] pp. 280. £15 ISBN 0 8967 2499 9.

Wood, Lisa. *Modes of Discipline: Women, Conservatism, and the Novel after the French Revolution*. Bucknell Studies in Eighteenth-Century Literature and Culture. BuckUP/AUP. [2003] pp. 189. $39.50 ISBN 0 8387 5527 5.

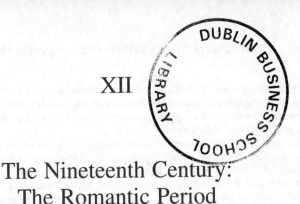

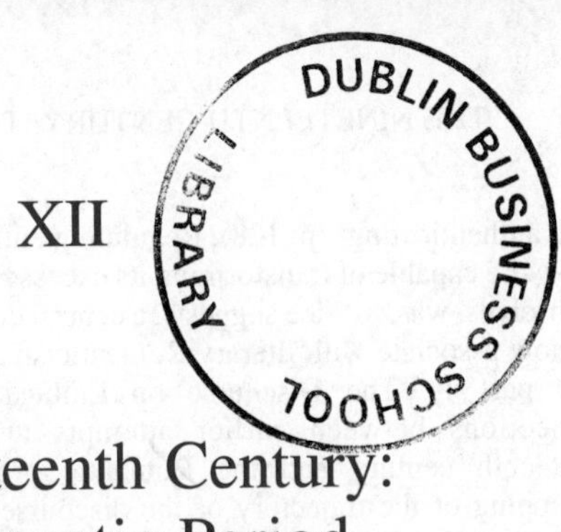
DUBLIN BUSINESS SCHOOL LIBRARY

XII

The Nineteenth Century: The Romantic Period

ORIANNE SMITH, MATTHEW SCOTT, EMMA MASON,
JASON WHITTAKER, FELICITY JAMES,
DANIEL SANJIV ROBERTS AND AMY MUSE

This chapter has seven sections: 1. General; 2. Poetry (excluding Blake and Women Poets); 3. Women Poets; 4. William Blake; 5. Prose Fiction; 6. Non-Fictional Prose; 7. Drama. Section 1 is by Orianne Smith; section 2 is by Matthew Scott; section 3 is by Emma Mason; section 4 is by Jason Whittaker; section 5 is by Felicity James; section 6 is by Daniel Sanjiv Roberts; section 7 is by Amy Muse.

1. General

Jon Mee's book, *Romanticism, Enthusiasm and Regulation: Poetics and the Policing of Culture in the Romantic Period*, is, without a doubt, the most important contribution to general Romantic era studies this year. Mee's illuminating study of the discourse of enthusiasm in the long eighteenth century calls into question the confident assertions by scholars from M.H. Abrams to Shaun Irlam that, by the Romantic period, enthusiasm was purged of its dangerous associations with the religious and political excesses of the civil war sectarians, and safely harnessed to the powers of the imagination. As Mee demonstrates, the process of saving enthusiasm from itself was in fact a much messier business than has been suggested by the assumption of a steady, progressive secularization of enthusiasm during the eighteenth century—a process of rehabilitation that was, according to these scholars and others, effectively completed by William Wordsworth. In the Romantic period, as Mee convincingly argues, the fears generated by the unruly energies of enthusiasm, and identified with the delirium of the crowd, continued to haunt its contemporary critics. Writers such as Robert Southey, Francis Jeffrey, Samuel Coleridge, and Wordsworth continued to be motivated by the anxiety that enthusiasm—even poetic enthusiasm—ran the risk of 'dissolving the very subjectivity it was meant

Year's Work in English Studies, Volume 84 (2005) © The English Association; all rights reserved. For permissions, please email: journals.permissions@oxfordjournals.org

doi: 10.1093/ywes/mai012

to be authenticating' (p. 128). Regulating enthusiasm, and preserving it for those who were capable of transforming its excesses into art without becoming infected themselves, was, as Mee suggests, a central concern of many of the writers whom we now associate with literary Romanticism.

In part 1, 'The Discourse on Enthusiasm', Mee establishes the close connections between earlier attempts at disciplining enthusiasm in the eighteenth century and the Romantic project. A crucial figure in Mee's remapping of the trajectory of the discourse on enthusiasm is the third earl of Shaftesbury, Anthony Ashley Cooper, who identified enthusiasm as a vulgar expression of a universal human desire to transcend the self in order to connect with the spiritual world. Shaftesbury's emphasis on the positive, moral aspects of enthusiasm represented a distinct shift from the Anglican attacks on enthusiasm in the wake of the civil war by writers such as Henry More and Meric Casaubon, who characterized enthusiasm as an infectious disease, or a form of madness. By pathologizing enthusiasm, More and Casaubon had initiated the process of distancing it from its origins as a species of heresy to a generalized mania; Shaftesbury went even further in dislodging enthusiasm from its heretical roots by refusing to abandon it entirely to the crowd. According to Shaftesbury, enthusiasm was a natural outgrowth of human sociability that could be brought back into the pale of polite society by a certain class of men who possessed the regulatory technology of self-fashioning. As Mee notes, Shaftesbury's idea of the disciplining of spiritual agency as central to eighteenth-century notions of civility, and his emphasis on the moral implications of social affections, appealed to Anglicans and Dissenters alike, and had a tremendous influence on poets such as James Thomson and Mark Akenside. Despite Shaftesbury's attempts to reclaim enthusiasm, however, not everyone was convinced that it could ever be wholly rehabilitated. For instance, Frances Hutcheson, who popularized many of Shaftesbury's ideas, substituted the notion of 'benevolence'—a regulated and refined product of sensibility—for the more slippery and potentially dangerous idea of enthusiasm. While David Hume agreed with Shaftesbury regarding the powers of enthusiasm, he remained sceptical, along with Adam Smith, that enthusiasm, or even benevolence, could ever be entirely drained of their associations with the religious and political fervour of the civil war sectarians. Later in the century, Burke explicitly politicized the fear articulated by these moral philosophers in *Reflections on the Revolution in France*. As Mee perceptively notes, Burke's condemnation of the supporters of the French Revolution was, in many respects, a hysterical version of Hume's insistence that the regulation of the passions could not be effectively managed within the individual, but could only come about by conforming to the external pressures of society and the established authority of the Church.

The first half of *Romanticism, Enthusiasm and Regulation* traces the unmooring of enthusiasm from a strictly religious context during the eighteenth century—a movement aided by the valorization of affect and sympathy, and the birth of a poetic tradition that grew out of Shaftesbury's efforts to rehabilitate enthusiasm as an aesthetic and moral principle. Yet, as Mee reminds us in part 2, 'The Poetics of Enthusiasm', enthusiasm never entirely lost its connection with its roots: significantly, the anxieties and aspirations regarding enthusiasm continued to haunt the poetry by writers such as Coleridge, Anna Barbauld, Wordsworth and William Blake, whose work reflected, and reflected on, the urgent need to regulate enthusiasm in the volatile conditions of the Romantic era. Using these four canonical figures as case studies—along with detailed analyses of the debates between John Thelwall and William Godwin, and Leigh Hunt's vociferous attack on religious enthusiasm in *The Folly and Danger of Methodism*—Mee reveals how apocalyptic speculation and millenarianism continued to underwrite the cultural productions of the Romantic era.

The intersection of apocalyptic discourse and literary endeavour in the Romantic period is also the subject of Eric G. Wilson's *The Spiritual History of Ice: Romanticism, Science and the Imagination*. Like Mee, Wilson investigates the continuities between the late eighteenth-century preoccupation with visionary perception and earlier apocalyptic accounts of the world. However, whereas Mee confines his argument to eighteenth-century responses to, and attempts to police, religious and political enthusiasm, Wilson's exploration of the apocalyptic significance of ice in Romantic literature is considerably more ambitious and wide-ranging in scope. As Wilson notes, his book is 'a spiritual history of Western representations of frozen shapes from ancient times to the early nineteenth century, an anatomy of these representations of ice and an apology for a Romantic mode of seeing that ecologically inflects the spiritual history and anatomy of ice' (pp. 2–3). Until the Romantic period, Wilson argues, descriptions of ice in Christian theology and scientific theory tended to focus on its negative value as a potentially evil, cold and impenetrable surface—reducing frozen forms to signifiers of numbness, aloofness, monstrosity, stasis and death. At the end of the eighteenth century, however, research by scientists such as Humphry Davy and James Hutton began to suggest that the study of crystals and glaciers could yield important new information about the laws of electromagnetism and terrestrial transformation. This new perspective on ice as a significant conductor of vital energy brought with it a renewed interest in earlier esoteric texts by Cornelius Agrippa, Nostradamus and Paracelsus, amongst others, who had used crystals to divine the future. In this impressively researched book, Wilson suggests that Romantic writers such as Percy Shelley, Mary Shelley, Byron and Coleridge, as well as other later writers such as the American Transcendentalists and Edgar Allen Poe, drew upon both contemporary science and esoteric texts in their literary representation of crystals, glaciers and the poles. Although Wilson's poetic and semi-mystical treatment of his topic can at times be distracting, at its best *The Spiritual History of Ice* captures the genuine sense of excitement at the end of the eighteenth century regarding the potential of ice as a key to unlock the sacred and secular mysteries of life.

The rich dialogue between the literary and scientific communities in the Romantic era is the focus of an important collection of essays published this year. Heringman, ed., *Romantic Science: The Literary Forms of Natural Science*, makes a significant contribution to our understanding of the dynamic exchange between works of natural history and literature in the eighteenth and nineteenth centuries. Like the studies by Mee and Wilson, this book deliberately resists traditional disciplinary and generic boundaries in a series of essays that explore literature and natural science as interlocking cultural practices in the period roughly between Linnaeus and Charles Darwin. The first three essays reveal the rich commerce and dialogue between the literary and scientific communities. As Catherine E. Ross suggests in '"Twin labourers and heirs of the same hopes": The Professional Rivalry of Humphry Davy and William Wordsworth' (pp. 23–52), this exchange took on an adversarial dimension as poets and scientists often competed for the same audiences. Ross argues persuasively that a rivalry existed between Wordsworth and the much more popular and successful scientist, Davy, as the two men sought to cultivate public identities that hinged on mutually exclusive ideas concerning human nature and the natural world. In 'The Rock Record and Romantic Narratives of the Earth' (pp. 53–84), Heringman investigates the influence of the teleological narrative of the natural world theorized by geologists such as William Smith on Percy Shelley's *Prometheus Unbound*. While the relationship between Smith and Shelley was not as personally charged as the one between Wordsworth and Davy, the differences between Smith and Shelley underscore Heringman's thesis that the 'rock record' functioned as '*both* a literary and a scientific metaphor' (p. 67), and provided a language and an aesthetic that could be appropriated and reinterpreted by Romantic-era poets and natural historians alike. The last essay in this section, Stuart Peterfreund's '"Great frosts and … some very hot summers": Strange Weather, the Last Letters, and the Last Days in Gilbert White's *The Natural History of Selborne*' (pp. 85–110), underscores this point in an intriguing discussion of White's blend of Miltonic imagery and contemporary catastrophic theory in his Edenic portrait of local natural history.

The essays in the second section of *Romantic Science* tease out the sociopolitical and global implications of the contemporary narrative of natural history, focusing on its ability to structure and explain cultural, racial and social difference. Alan Bewell makes a compelling argument in 'Jefferson's Thermometer: Colonial Biogeographical Constructions of the Climate of America' (pp. 111–38) that the late eighteenth-century debate over America as a biological habitat was fuelled by a 'politics of climate' inspired by Buffon's *Natural History*. As Bewell demonstrates, Buffon's biogeographical representation of the New World was rooted in the Enlightenment belief that human beings had a moral imperative to improve upon their surroundings, and that the land itself reflected the level of sophistication of its inhabitants. Not only did Buffon's theory provide a moral justification for colonial expansion, it also, as Bewell astutely notes, influenced Jefferson's attempts to prove that the new republic's climate was significantly improved by the introduction of its superior political and social institutions. In 'Robinson's Earthenware Pot: Science, Aesthetics and the Metaphysics of True Porcelain' (pp. 139–71), Lydia Liu uses Robinson Crusoe's haphazard discovery of a method to create earthenware pots as a point of departure for a rich discussion of British and Continental anxieties regarding the import of Chinese porcelain as an index of the economic rivalries of the time. The third essay in this group, Anne K. Mellor's '*Frankenstein*, Racial Science, and the "Yellow Peril"' (pp. 173–96), focuses more explicitly on the link between scientific theory and racial anxieties. Mellor argues that Mary Shelley appropriates contemporary racial taxonomies in her description of Frankenstein's monster as an Asian type—a description that reveals, according to Mellor, Shelley's sympathy with interracial marriage and her belief in the necessity of racial unity.

The last three essays in this collection articulate the didactic function of botany. In 'Lyrical Strategies, Didactic Intent: Reading the Kitchen Garden Manual' (pp. 199–222), Rachel Crawford argues that 'the aesthetic that emerged from the fascination with the relationship between containment and productivity was influenced by kitchen garden design and plant taxonomy, helped to shape requirements for lyric verse, and naturalized reproduction as the telos of female sexuality' (p. 200). According to Crawford, the fascination with containment of social space, established earlier in the eighteenth century, had a direct influence on the renewed interest in, and elevated status of, lyric poetry at the end of the eighteenth century. Theresa M. Kelley's 'Romantic Exemplarity: Botany and "Material" Culture' (pp. 223–54) reveals how botanical taxonomy provided a template for literary representations of individual difference and dissent in the works of Charlotte Smith and John Clare. Finally, in 'Taxonomical Cures: The Politics of Natural History and Herbalist Medicine in Elizabeth Gaskell's *Mary Barton*' (pp. 255–70), Amy Mae King foregrounds the links between folk medicine and natural history, and suggests the usefulness of the working-class medical tradition, with its emphasis on communal responsibility and selflessness, as a corrective to the false logic of classifying human beings according to social status.

Romantic Science firmly grounds the contemporary narrative of natural history within the context of the social, literary and political tensions of the Romantic era. Another very good book concerned with probing the political implications of the dialogue between literature and other discourses in this period is Charles Mahoney's *Romantics and Renegades: The Poetics of Political Reaction*. Beginning with the accusations of political apostasy levelled by William Hazlitt at Coleridge, Wordsworth and Southey in the fierce border wars between politics, poetry and literary criticism in the early nineteenth century, this study explores the rhetorical instability of apostasy—implying a 'falling-away' or figures 'on a verge'—in a series of close readings of the works of these poets and one of their most vociferous critics. The first chapter does an excellent job of setting up Mahoney's argument in a discussion of the literary and political implications of Leigh Hunt's 1812 trial for libel and his condemnation of the office of Poet Laureate as a position in which a poet, in the capacity of literary sycophant, must inevitably give up his political autonomy. Not coincidentally, as Mahoney notes, it was after Southey's appointment as Poet Laureate in September, 1813 that the term 'apostate' appears in Hunt's diatribes against the poet and his official office. Chapters 2, 3 and 4 (on Coleridge, Wordsworth and Southey, respectively) take a closer look at the ways in which these poets 'fall away' from their earlier, more radical politics. In these chapters Mahoney rehearses the contemporary debate on the subject of the apostasy of these three canonical poets, but the argument here seems less sure-footed, providing an overview of recent scholarship on this subject without adding much in the way of original insight. The brilliance of the last two chapters on Hazlitt, however, more than makes up for this deficit. In his reading of Kemble's *Coriolanus*, Hazlitt wrote: 'The language of poetry naturally falls in with the language of power.'

These words, deftly deployed as an epigraph for chapter 5, alert the reader to the rich discussion that follows. As Mahoney notes, Hazlitt's interpretation of Kemble's *Coriolanus* (both his production and his representation of its hero) dramatizes the very real post-revolutionary difficulty of determining the difference between standing and falling; in the play's vertiginous crossing of standing firm and falling off, moreover, we can recognize and reconsider the complexity of the abiding relations between Romantic politics and Romantic writing (p. 145).

Coriolanus *is* an apostate: turning 'neither to the right or the left', he is nevertheless 'swayed by a single impulse' that causes his spectacular and inevitable fall (p. 147). His failure, ultimately, is a failure of language. As Mahoney persuasively argues, Coriolanus's inability verbally to bridge the gap between his political performance and his ethics is a powerful demonstration of the troubled relationship between politics, poetry and power that Hazlitt sought to articulate in his condemnation of the Romantic poets. Taking the argument even further, the final chapter of *Romantics and Renegades* turns Hazlitt's criticism back on to the critic himself, considering the extent to which Hazlitt himself cannot help falling in with the language of power and is, therefore, equally complicit in the literary-political discourse of crisis signified by Romantic apostasy.

Mahoney's reading of the radical critic Hazlitt as an apostate should remind us to proceed with caution before too quickly assigning the words 'radical' or 'conservative' to Britons at this time. Similarly, Helen Braithwaite's *Romanticism, Publishing and Dissent: Joseph Johnson and the Cause of Liberty* complicates our assumption of the radicalism of the bookseller and publisher Joseph Johnson. Best known today as the publisher of Joseph Priestley, William Blake, Thomas Paine and Mary Wollstonecraft, Johnson was certainly put on trial in 1798 for supposedly publishing a seditious libel. Yet to apply the label 'radical' to him without qualification, Braithwaite suggests, is to present only a partial view of the man, and to ignore the real complexity of political and commercial interactions in the late eighteenth century. His publications also included many far more conservative writers than one might expect—the Sunday school pioneer Sarah Trimmer, for example—and they embraced topics other than politics, notably education and science. Probing all of these aspects of Johnson's career, and teasing out the very different strands of political commitment that comprised Romantic radicalism, Braithwaite offers a vivid, detailed picture of reformist circles in the late eighteenth century. Her study proceeds chronologically, from the dissenting campaigns of the 1770s, through the responses to the American War of Independence and the French Revolution, the war with France, and finally, Johnson's trial, with the emphasis throughout being placed on 'the ideas, the substance, and ethos of *what* Johnson published rather than the detailed technicalities of his role as a bookseller or patron' (p. xiii). Overall, *Romanticism, Publishing and Dissent* is a well-written and illuminating reconstruction of Johnson's professional and political milieux, and the intersection of literature, politics and commerce in the Romantic period.

Another book published this year, Jones, ed., *The Satiric Eye: Forms of Satire in the Romantic Period*, is essential reading for scholars interested in the connections between politics, commerce and literature in this era. Expertly edited by Steven E. Jones, this collection of essays demonstrates the ways in which the traditionally conservative genre of satire was energized by the sociopolitical tensions in England at the end of the eighteenth century, and transformed in Romantic prose, literature and commercial writing into a forum in which high and low culture freely mingled, providing an outlet for biting social commentary and critical reflection on a variety of topical issues. Building on the recent interest in satire of the Romantic period generated by a series of books published over the past decade by Marcus Wood, Gary Dyer and Steven Jones himself, the eleven essays in *The Satiric Eye* provide further evidence of the significant function of Romantic satire as 'a kind of generic Other against which the more canonical works of British Romanticism defined themselves or came to be defined' (p. 173). Although the essays are organized in chronological order, they are also conveniently clustered around general thematic concerns. The best essay of the first group that addresses the topic of what Jones describes as 'taste-making in the public sphere' (p. 8) is Michael Gamer's '"Bell's Poetics": *The Baviad*, The Della Cruscans, and the Book of *The World*' (pp. 31–53). Whereas earlier studies of the Della Cruscan poets by Jerome McGann and Judith Pascoe rightfully defend their importance in the formative years of early Romanticism, Gamer focuses here on the threat these poets posed to literary authority, and argues that William Gifford's *The Baviad* [1790] was written as a direct response to their imminent republication in book form. Previously printed in the pages of *The World*, a popular newspaper published by Peter Bell, the Italianate and self-consciously improvisational poetry of Della Cruscan writers such as Robert Merry and Hannah Cowley was perceived as 'Deliberately consumable and temporary' which was 'perfectly suited to the disposable medium of newsprint' (p. 36). As Gamer perceptively notes, it was Bell's decision to collect these poems and publish them in book format that prompted Gifford's vitriolic response and his attack on 'Bell's poetics' as an affront to both literary taste and the regulatory function of publishers and reviewers.

Gamer's essay is exemplary in its articulation of how Romantic satire was deployed as an effective means of protecting the literary status quo from contamination from below. Similarly, in 'Wordsworth and the Parodic School of Criticism' (pp. 71–97), Nicola Trott explores the complicated relationship between Wordsworth and the reviewers who satirized him, revealing the parallels between the parodic techniques of the 'new school of criticism' and their Augustan forebears. Questionable literary taste is the subject of Marcus Wood's 'Black Bodies and Satiric Limits in the Long Eighteenth Century' (pp. 55–70). In this essay, Wood discusses how, throughout the eighteenth century, both pro-slavery and abolitionist satire reveal white sexual pathologies and evince a hysterical anxiety about the black body. In '"Getting and Spending": The Orientalization of Satire in Romantic London' (pp. 11–29), Tim Fulford discusses how Romantic satirists from Gillray to Byron represented the decadent taste, and the greedy desire for power and money, of contemporary society as a species of Orientalism. These four chapters reveal the way in which Romantic satire was used to contain or expose a perceived threat to the integrity of British society and culture. The following three chapters investigate the didactic strategies behind other forms of Romantic satire, focusing specifically on women and children as authors, readers and characters. Karl Kroeber's 'Jane Austen's *Northanger Abbey*: Self-Reflexive Satire and Biopoetics' (pp. 99–114) probes the satiric self-reflexivity of Austen's novel as an example of the way in which fictional narratives can 'modify those psychic processes through which culture modulates effects upon humankind of biological history' (p. 100). In 'Satirical Birds and Natural Bugs: J. Harris' Chapbooks and the Aesthetic of Children's Literature' (pp. 115–37), Donelle R. Ruwe analyses how Romantic ideology influenced the formation of a canon of children's literature that deliberately suppresses the political and the satirical in its literary representation of the natural, innocent and decidedly non-satirical child. The unique position of Jane Taylor as the only Romantic female poet classified as a satirist illustrates how the political thrust of satirical writing was considered inappropriate for women of the Romantic era, as well as for children. As Stuart Curran points out in 'Jane Taylor's Satire on Satire' (pp. 139–50), even Jane Taylor enlists realistic vernacular and the satiric form in order to point out the disjunction between contemporary society and the world as God intended it to be. Thus the satirical portraits of London society in her *Essays in Rhyme, on Morals and Manners* [1816] are harnessed to a didactic and moral agenda as she seeks to restore 'an interior spirituality that will deny the world its power over the human condition' (p. 150).

The last cluster of essays in *The Satiric Eye* evince what Jones describes as the 'promiscuous opportunism regarding medium and form' (p. 3) characteristic of radical political satire in this era. Gary Dyer's essay, 'Intercepted Letters, Men of Information: Moore's *Twopenny Post-Bag* and *Fudge Family in Paris*' (pp. 151–71) explores Tom Moore's use of the device of the intercepted letter in his topical and political satires as a means of critiquing the culture of surveillance in the Regency period. As Dyer demonstrates, Moore collapses the distinction between popular and literary culture in the fictitious gossipy letters written by and about the royal family. John Strachan's chapter, '"Trimming the *Muse of Satire*": J.R.D. Huggins and the Poetry of Hair-Cutting' (pp. 185–206), also investigates the blend of high and low culture in the satirical puffery engaged in by the irrepressible New York barber Huggins. In 'Verbal Jujitsu: William Hone and the Tactics of Satirical Conflict' (pp. 173–84), Kyle Grimes uses Hone as an example of 'hacker satire'—a radical new form of satire that emerged in the Romantic period as a 'material and intentionally disruptive intervention into the public discourses of the day' (p. 174). Finally, Marilyn Gaull's 'Pantomime as Satire: Mocking the Broken Chain' (pp. 207–24) argues that the Covent Garden pantomimes that flourished during the harsh censorship of the Regency period epitomize the hybrid, ironic, and topical form of writing that was quintessentially Romantic and satirical.

The last chapters in *The Satiric Eye* vividly illustrate the transformation of satire in this period into a new, radicalized generic Other that exerted internal pressure on the increasingly self-conscious construction of literary Romanticism. This nuanced interpretation of the complex relationship between cultural centres and Romantic peripheries is in many ways indebted to the recent interest amongst scholars of Romanticism in Romantic Orientalism. Two books published this year make substantial contributions to our understanding of this subject. Carruthers and Rawes, eds., *English Romanticism and the Celtic World* and Turhan, *The Other Empire: British Romantic Writings about the Ottoman Empire* explore the ways in which Romantic Orientalism worked to shape and solidify the national and cultural identity of England after the mid-eighteenth century. Superbly edited by Gerard Carruthers and Alan Rawes, *English Romanticism and the Celtic World* investigates 'Celticism' as an emergent strain of cultural ethnicity in the literary history of the 'four nations': England, Wales, Scotland and Ireland. Dealing with topics ranging from Welsh antiquarianism, the Ossian controversy, the legend of Madoc, and the bardic tradition to Celtic landscapes and Irish nationalism, this collection articulates the dynamic exchange between the Romantic form and ideas of the 'Celtic' in works by Blake, Byron, Percy Shelley, Wordsworth and Felicia Hemans. Although nineteenth-century appropriations of the Celtic were often aligned with militaristic and imperial aims, as the editors suggest, the interest in Celticism was also driven by a generalized anxiety regarding the integrity of the British nation engendered by the English civil war and the Jacobite rebellions. Thus the mythologization and idealization of Celticism by British Romantic writers was often the product of diverse and sometimes contradictory motives and aspirations.

The first two essays in this collection set the stage for the close readings that follow. An early example of the anxieties about nation formation and empire-building is discussed in Michael J. Franklin's 'Sir William Jones, the Celtic Revival and the Oriental Renaissance' (pp. 20–37), which posits the significance of the Welsh Orientalist Jones in the Romantic reversal of English notions of centre and periphery. In his work as both poet and linguist, as Franklin notes, Jones constructed a myth of origins that brought together the figure of the Druid and the heroic Indian, complicating the question of British superiority in relation to the Middle East, India and the Celtic world. In 'The Critical Response to Ossian's Romantic Bequest' (pp. 38–53), Dafydd R. Moore makes the important point that, although *The Poems of Ossian* were one of the first works of European Romanticism, Macpherson himself has been marginalized in scholarship on the Romantic period—a tendency which, Moore suggests, has larger implications for the power relations established by conventional literary historiography than what Macpherson's contemporaries and near-contemporaries thought about these poems.

Utilizing the theories of Gilles Deleuze and Felix Guattari, David Punter demonstrates, in 'Blake and Gwendolen: Territory, Periphery and the Proper Name' (pp. 54–68), that the Celtic functions in Blake's works as a nostalgic reminder of a 'primal British greatness' as well as a geographical marker of his millennial vision. Therefore, the Celtic nations, although poised 'on the brink of an overwhelming extinction', also function in Blake's poetry as 'the guardians of the guardian, as outer bulwarks of the state' (p. 57) and 'a specific staging post on the route of a diaspora, a point from which a new grouping can be promulgated' (p. 58). The connections between Romantic millennialism and the Celtic world are further developed in Caroline Franklin's 'The Welsh American Dream: Iolo Morganwg, Robert Southey and the Madoc Legend' (pp. 69–84). As Franklin notes, Southey's *Madoc* illustrates how his earlier utopian dreams of setting up a community in America founded on the ideals of Pantisocracy were mapped onto the Madoc legend in this poem and retooled to reflect Southey's transformation from pacifist Jacobin to militant imperialist.

Wordsworth's appropriation of the bardic tradition and druidic power as precursors of the success of Christianity (and his vision of his own significance within this trajectory) are considered in J.R. Watson's 'Wordsworth, North Wales and the Celtic Landscape' (pp. 85–102). Bernard Beatty's 'The Force of "Celtic Memories" in Byron's Thought' (pp. 103–16) and Andrew Nicholson's 'Byron and the "Ariosto of the North"' (pp. 130–50) explore Byron's uneasy yet productive relationship with his Scottish roots and his literary and artistic dialogue with Sir Walter Scott. Murray G.H. Pittock's 'Scott and the British Tourist' (pp. 151–66) offers a brilliant close reading of chapter 22 of *Waverley* to argue for Scott's self-conscious participation in preserving Scotland for tourists as a locus of primitive simplicity that no longer existed yet which continued to exert a sturdy and palpable influence on the construction of British identity in the Romantic period.

The specificity of Scott's Celticism was markedly different from the attempts by many other Romantic writers to apply the lessons of Celtic history and legend more generally to the problems of English colonialism. For instance, as Arthur Bradley argues in 'Shelley, Ireland and Romantic Orientalism' (pp. 117–29), Percy Shelley conflates his constructions of Ireland and the Orient in *Laon and Cythna* in order to 'construct and enact his homogenizing ideology of world reform' (p. 129). Similarly, in 'Felicia Hemans, Byronic Cosmopolitanism and the Ancient Welsh Bards' (pp. 167–81), William D. Brewer establishes the connection between Hemans's bardic ideology and her commitment to international nationalism—a cosmopolitanism that differed from Byron's moral relativity and Shelley's tendency to universalize all religions but which nonetheless takes the example of the ancient bards of Wales 'who base their identity on natural sites and their heroic ancestors' (p. 181) as a model for contemporary Britons and society at large. The final two essays interrogate the fate of the Romantic 'Celticism' in later works. Malcolm Kelsall's '*Luttrell of Arran* and the Romantic Invention of Ireland' (pp. 182–95) points to the critique of Irish nationalism in Charles Lever's *Luttrell of Arran* [1865] as a continuation of the Romantic construction of nationalism which was 'divided between … the old, dying world of Burkean conservatism and Byronic revolt on the one hand, and, on the other, a new world struggling to define selfhood and place' (p. 185). Lever's resistance to idealizing either the past or the present in Celtic Ireland—an ultimately sceptical and ironizing position that Kelsall traces back to Byron's *Don Juan*—is present in the literary productions of contemporary Irish poets as well. As Michael O'Neill demonstrates in 'Contemporary Northern Irish poets and Romantic Poetry' (pp. 196–209), works by poets such as Seamus Heaney self-consciously display a disdain for the abstract idealism of Romanticism while continuing to explore the 'capacity of Romantic poetry to enact and criticize longing and desire' (p. 196). The consistently rigorous scholarship and impressive range of readings in *English Romanticism and the Celtic World* make this book an extraordinarily rich resource for scholars of both Romanticism and Celtic studies.

The second book published this year on the subject of Romantic Orientalism, Filiz Turhan's *The Other Empire: British Romantic Writings about the Ottoman*

Empire, investigates the ways in which the figure of the Turk, the Ottoman empire and the city of Constantinople were cast as powerful counter-images of empire by both conservative and liberal British writers in poetry, novels and travel writing from 1789 to 1846. Building on the work of post-colonial scholars such as Mary Louise Pratt and Homi Bhabha, Turhan focuses on the flexibility of the trope of the Ottoman Other within three broad categories: the Turks' despotic treatment of the Greeks, their economic backwardness, and the institution of the harem. In each case, Turhan points to the fundamental instabilities inherent in these issues, and the difficulties British writers encountered when they attempted to harness these 'slippery signifiers' to their sociopolitical critiques. The analysis of Elizabeth Craven's *A Journey through the Crimea to Constantinople* [1789] in chapter 2 exemplifies these problems. Even though Craven criticizes Turkey's oppression of the minority population, she cannot escape her own subject position as an imperialist when she imagines the British helping the Turks to become more civilized; Craven contrasts the lethargy of Turkey's economy to Britain's commercial successes, but in doing so betrays her own fears as an aristocrat at the increasing power of Britain's mercantile class; finally, she extols the virtues of the harem system in contrast to the limitations placed on British women, yet registers nothing but contempt for the Turkish women she encounters. The chapters that follow (on Byron, the Shelleys and Lady Hester Stanhope) develop Turhan's claim that the appropriation of the Turkish Other, whether used as a foil to praise or to criticize British imperialism, often resulted in textual instability as these writers struggled with their own complicity as British citizens in their attempts to articulate the differences and similarities between Turkey as a disintegrating medieval empire and England's increasingly powerful position as a modern one. Turhan's strict adherence to her three-pronged argument throughout the book, underscored by a tendency to repeat her thesis at the end of each chapter, does occasionally make the argument feel stale and programmatic; however, the excellent contextual material that she provides in addition to the close readings, ranging from the history of the Ottoman empire as it was known to the reading public in England to detailed analyses of the infrastructure of the Turkish government and the institution of the harem, adds a great deal to our understanding of British representations of the Other Empire in this period.

While most of the books published this year in general Romantic studies participate in the movement over the past few decades away from reading Romanticism as a set of cultural and aesthetic concerns in the works of the canonical poets towards a methodology rooted more specifically in tracing the connections between Romantic literature, history and culture, Paul Hamilton's *Metaromanticism: Aesthetics, Literature, Theory* is a notable exception. This study investigates the influence of Continental philosophers such as Schiller and Rousseau on the major British Romantic writers, including Coleridge, William Godwin, the Shelleys, Keats, Walter Scott and others. The argument for the significance of metaromanticism—the ironizing and self-reflexive stance of literary Romanticism in its mobilization of the aesthetic—is, of course, a continuation of the theoretical approach that dominated Romantic studies during the 1980s. However, the introduction here of Jürgen Habermas's theories of 'communicative action' and the public sphere, and Hamilton's attempt to read political discourse through the aesthetic, brings something new and important to the discussion. This book can be read, on the one hand, as a rebuttal of David Simpson's influential argument in *Nationalism and the Revolt Against Theory* (UChicP [1993]), which questioned the influence of German idealism on British Romanticism, and, on the other, as a rebuke to the intensive archival work that has shifted the concentration of Romantic studies from the aesthetic conceits of High Romanticism to a more comprehensive and historically inflected understanding of this period. In contrast to the 'archival decentering of canonical thought prevailing now in Romantic studies', Hamilton's 'reworking of the immanence of Romantic self-critique bids to recover at its center a neglected philosophical archive of a kind' (pp. 2–3). *Metaromanticism* achieves this goal, provoking intriguing questions about the current direction of Romantic criticism and the possibilities for reading with and against the grain of contemporary theory.

Metaromanticism is unique in the field because it eschews the comparative approach of many other studies on this subject by confining itself exclusively to the works of British Romantic writers. The other book published this year on the subject of aesthetics and Romanticism, Justin Clemens's *The Romanticism of Contemporary Theory: Institution, Aesthetics and Nihilism*, takes an entirely different approach. Instead of attempting to prove the historical, transnational influence of German philosophy, Clemens reads contemporary theory through the lens of Romantic aesthetics, arguing that 'contemporary theory is still essentially Romantic—despite all its declarations to the contrary, and despite all its attempts to elude or exceed the limits bequeathed it by Romantic thought' (p. viii). For Clemens, 'Romantic thought' is metaromantic in the sense that Hamilton defines it: a self-reflexive and negative form of writing that continually presses at limits of all kinds, seeking an immanence that it cannot sustain or unselfconsciously enjoy as an end in itself. According to Clemens, it is the aporias of Romantic thinking, specifically the problems of the institution, aesthetics and nihilism, that fuelled the twentieth-century debates regarding the significance and signification of Romanticism and that continue to haunt modern critical thinking. In the first chapter, Clemens discusses how the localization of Romantic philosophy in the university imposed discursive limits on Romantic thought that 'drove it inexorably towards the diagnosis of nihilism'. Dissatisfaction with this account of its institutional difficulties led to the attempt 'to plug the resulting ontological gap by way of recourse to aesthetics' (p. 97). Analysing major texts from Kant through Nietzsche to Jacques Lacan and Alain Badiou among others, Clemens suggests that contemporary theory, either explicitly or (more often) implicitly, continues to circle around the three problems of the university, aesthetics and nihilism without being able to solve them. As Clemens notes, it is the ultimately irresolvable nature of this dilemma—a dilemma that is fundamentally Romantic—that proves the inherent and inescapable Romanticism of contemporary theory. All in all, this is an exemplary and engaging book that makes a compelling argument for the continuities between Romantic ideology and the work of seemingly disparate modern theorists.

Readers interested in the question of the pervasive influence and endurance of Romanticism will be particularly engaged by the eloquent and wide-ranging collection of essays published in 'Afterlives of Romanticism', a special issue of

South Atlantic Quarterly devoted to this subject (*SAQ* 102:i[2003]). Edited by Ian Baucom and Jennifer Kennedy, this collection includes essays by some of the most distinguished Romantic scholars today, including James Chandler, Frances Ferguson and Alan Liu. Using the newspaper in Cowper's *The Task* as a point of departure, Kevis Goodman's 'The Loophole in the Retreat: The Culture of News and the Early Life of Romantic Self-Consciousness' (*SAQ* 102:i[2003] 25–52) complicates the assumption of the distinctiveness of contemporary media culture by revealing its engagement with modes of affect that have typically been perceived as the hallmarks of early Romantic self-consciousness. Thomas Pfau's 'Conjuring History: Lyric Cliché, Conservative Fantasy, and Traumatic Awakening in German Romanticism' (*SAQ* 102:i[2003] 53–92) makes a powerful and convincing argument that, contrary to the much-vaunted theory that German Romanticism was born out of an 'evasion of history', the form of the German Romantic lyric in fact emerged as an affective response to the specific traumatic sociohistorical conditions of the period, and that the Romantic aesthetic mediated, rather than occluded, historical consciousness. In 'Authentic Effects: The Work of Fiction in Romantic Scotland' (*SAQ* 102:i[2003] 93–116), Ian Duncan reads James Hogg's 'outcast text' *Confessions of a Justified Sinner* as paradoxically representing the failure of the career of its author and the failure of literature itself as a transparent medium of social life, while simultaneously asserting the power of aesthetic production. Celeste Langan's 'Pathologies of Communication from Coleridge to Schreber' (*SAQ* 102:i[2003] 117–52) usefully pairs Coleridge's *Christabel* with Daniel Paul Schreber's *Memoirs of My Nervous Illness* to suggest that the latter is an extended meditation on the former, and, more specifically, to argue that Coleridge's metrical experiment did not represent a nostalgia for the oral culture of the ballad, but was instead a purposeful exploration of the question of 'who speaks'. In 'Nonbiological Clock: Literary History against Newtonian Mechanics' (*SAQ* 102:i[2003] 153–77), Wai Chee Dimock explores the parallelism of the literary 'afterlives' of Blake's and Einstein's quarrel with Newton to posit the idea that, like the revolutionary shift that occurred in physics as a result of this debate, Blake's arguments are worth revisiting as a paradigm of resistance, and a diachronic challenge, to normative literary practices. In 'The Colonial Logic of Late Romanticism' (*SAQ* 102:i[2003] 179–214), Srinivas Aravamudan investigates the conceptual stakes of discussing Indian Romanticism, and suggests that the major difference between earlier British and German Romanticism and its revival in the colonial contexts of the late nineteenth- and twentieth-century India is that Indian Romanticism eschewed Romantic-era nostalgia for lost community in favour of revolutionary agendas that attempted to invent both the past and the future. Frances Ferguson's 'The Afterlife of the Romantic Child: Rousseau and Kant Meet Deleuze and Guattari' (*SAQ* 102:i[2003] 215–34) points to the crucial significance of the figure of the child in the liberal tradition inaugurated by Rousseau and Kant as a site for the ongoing debate regarding the limitations of doctrine and belief, the borders between reason and unreason, and as a testing-ground for the regulatory practice of representation. James Chandler's 'About Loss: W.G. Sebald's Romantic Art of Memory' (*SAQ* 102:i[2003] 235–62) delivers an incisive reading of the Romantic preoccupation with elegiac meditation on history and memory in Sebald's novels, and Sebald's indebtedness to the historical novel tradition established by Walter Scott. Finally, Alan Liu's 'Remembering the Spruce Goose: Historicism, Postmodernism, Romanticism' (*SAQ* 102:i[2003] 263–78) makes a persuasive and trenchant argument for the interconnectedness of postmodernism and Romanticism as a viable and instructive alternative to the 'modern versus postmodern' debate.

The present interest in rethinking the relationship between Romantic writers and Romantic historiography, between Romanticism and eighteenth-century literature and culture, and between Romanticism and its afterlives is apparent in special issues of two journals published this year. Although most of the essays chosen for inclusion in *PMLA*'s special issue, 'Imagining History' (*PMLA* 118:iii[2004]), take up subjects well before and after the period between 1789 and 1832, as Tilottama Rajan notes in her introduction, the topic of 'imagining history' has taken on a particular, crucial significance in Romantic studies today. As Rajan points out, Romanticism as a category of study has recently undergone a number of radical changes that present serious challenges to our understanding of Romantic historiography as well as the historical significance of this period. For instance, Romanticism has been folded into the general category of nineteenth-century studies in many English departments and by the academic publishing industry. This reconfiguration elides the significant influence of the French Revolution on the writers we associate with Romanticism, and ignores the first half of the careers of writers such as Wordsworth, Coleridge and Blake. The problem is compounded by the recent shift, as discussed earlier in this chapter, from thinking of Romanticism as what Rajan calls 'a curricular category that made a space for singularity and alterity' (p. 429) to an exploration of other Romanticisms, and an emphasis on the period itself rather than the exceptional cases of six poets. Rajan's nuanced and thoughtful introduction frames 'imagining history' as an issue that necessarily invokes Romanticism, and is highly recommended as essential reading for anyone interested in the problems confronting Romantic-era studies today.

The subject of Romanticism and history is also the focus of a special issue of *European Romantic Review* (*ERR* 14[2003]). The ten essays in this issue, selected from the presentations given at the tenth annual conference of the North American Society for the Study of Romanticism in 2002, reflect on how Romantic writers thought and wrote about history, and how 'history' itself subsequently perceived and reconstructed Romanticism. In 'Fancy's History' (*ERR* 14[2003] 163–76), Julie Carlson offers a psychoanalytical reading of the displacement of fancy in the family romance of the Wollstonecraft–Godwin–Shelley circle. Sophie Thomas probes the Romantic obsession with antiquarianism in 'Assembling History: Fragments and Ruins' (*ERR* 14[2003] 177–86). Tilottama Rajan's 'Spirit's Psychoanalysis: Natural History, the History of Nature, and Romantic Historiography,' situates the emergence of German idealism as a response to the trauma induced by the geologization of time in Romantic natural science (*ERR* 14[2003] 187–96). In '(Re)Zoning the Naïve: Schiller's Construction of Auto-Historiography' (*ERR* 14[2003] 197–203), Mark Algee Hewitt explores Schiller's essay *Über naïve und sentimentalische Dichtung* as a deconstruction of its own aesthetic ideology. Jerrold E. Hogle uses Keats's 'Eve of St. Agnes' as a case study of how the Gothic haunted Romantic historicity in 'The Gothic–Romantic Relationship: Underground Histories in "The Eve of St. Agnes"' (*ERR* 14[2003] 205–23). In 'The Uses and Abuses of Austen's "Absolute Historical Pictures"' (*ERR* 14[2003] 225–31), William Galperin analyses the transformation of Jane Austen's fictions into pedagogical tools in the nineteenth century. The implications of Walter Scott's shift from poetry to prose for representations of national history in the Romantic period and in our own time are discussed in Yoon Sun Lee's 'Time, Money, Sanctuary, and Sociability in Scott's *The Fortunes of Nigel*' (*ERR* 14[2003] 233–8). Julia M. Wright analyses Thomas Moore's parodic critique of the collusion between history-writing and English colonialism in '"The same dull round over again": Colonial History in Moore's *Memoirs of Captain Rock*' (*ERR* 14[2003] 239–49). The pathologization of the figure of the Byronic poet in the Victorian period is addressed in Dino Franco Felluga's 'The Fetish-Logic of Bourgeois Subjectivity, or, the Truth the Romantic Poet Reveals about the Victorian Novel' (*ERR* 14[2003] 251–60). Finally, David L. Clark places De Quincey's reading of Kant's late work within the larger context of Romanticism's excessive need for self-control through self-reflection and the transference of its own excesses in 'We "Other Prussians": Bodies and Pleasures in De Quincey and Late Kant' (*ERR* 14[2003] 261–87).

Two essays published this year in *Studies in Romanticism* (*SiR* 42:i[2003]) conclude this section: Uttara Natarajan's 'The Veil of Familiarity: Romantic Philosophy and the Familiar Essay' (*SiR* 42[2003] 27–44) and Linda M. Austin's 'Children of Childhood: Nostalgia and the Romantic Legacy' (*SiR* 42[2003] 75–98). Natarajan defamiliarizes the Romantic familiar essay, arguing against the critical assumption that the genre of the familiar essay in the Romantic period did not participate in the philosophical concerns of Romantic literature. As Natarajan demonstrates, the aesthetic of the British Romantic essay, like the aesthetic of British Romantic poetry, engaged in a particular form of idealism that blended the British empirical tradition with the German idealist tendency to subordinate the senses to the mind. Austin's essay explores the appropriation of the Romantic concept of childhood in later works in the nineteenth century as the subjective product of individual narration—either an infinitely recessive object of nostalgia or a locus created for a discarded self. Although Wordsworth's mythic child of nature haunted Victorian literature, as Austin notes, a new concept of the 'imitative child' emerged as well: representations of children who functioned as markers of the superiority of the adult world. Ironically, however, what this new un-Wordsworthian and un-nostalgic child shared with the congenitally innocent Romantic child was a necessary reliance on the existence of a corresponding state of adulthood in order to give it meaning. This intriguing insight enables Austin's argument to double back on itself—shedding new light on Romantic as well as Victorian representations of childhood.

2. Poetry (excluding Blake and Women Poets)

Britain in 1803 was a country ill at ease with the Peace of Amiens, its newspapers dominated by scares about the growing fear of invasion from France even as its citizens were finally free to travel there. Two centuries on and the media convulsed first with the threat of war in Iraq and then woke up to its awful reality. Amid this climate, it is perhaps fitting that several exciting general studies of Romantic poetry should have addressed the theme of the country at war. Yet if scholarship within the field gestured in this direction in 2003, it was not overtly dominated by politically engaged historicist studies. There was instead a faintly perceptible turn away from critical approaches circumscribed by a historical determinism tying the production of poetry to the ravages of political tumult. Criticism in 2003 engaged with the intellectual climate of the period's literary history in ways that are alive as much to aesthetic concerns as they are to the lessons of careful social contextualization. Among general surveys, certain trends were discernible. Several critics dealt with the religious climate of the time, addressing radical enthusiasm, the presence of a post-Miltonic idea of evil, and individual conscience. Related to this last topic, there was a reconsideration of the autobiographical self and of the nature of consciousness. Meanwhile, critics addressed themselves to themes as diverse as exploration, Romantic science, satire, the Celtic inheritance, and to the nature of editorial scholarship. This was something of a wonder year for lesser-known poets, with both John Clare and Leigh Hunt taking centre stage, in the latter case preparing the ground for serious biographical reconsideration. Byron too was treated handsomely, while important guidebooks, lives and student-friendly editions emerged for Wordsworth, Coleridge, Shelley and Keats.

Amid this richness, there are a number of general studies that will long remain indispensable to students working within this field, and I should like to discuss these before turning to single-author studies. One book that stands out is Paul Hamilton's *Metaromanticism* (also discussed above in Section 1). This is a startling reconsideration of the ontology of the Romantic aesthetic as it is constructed within an exclusive critical orthodoxy, but its approach is far removed from any McGann-influenced ideological critique. It has implications for the boundaries of this section by flagging up the act of aesthetic privilege that is implicit in any gendered division between Romantic poetry and Romantic women's writing (on account of the latter's necessary exclusion from the terms by which the academy once constructed the former), and moreover Hamilton ends his study with interesting reflections on the ways in which Dorothy Wordsworth is to be distinguished from her brother in that she eschews the absolute moment of transport in her description of the extraordinary. But his is not a book that attacks the aesthetic, wrestling instead with its own inherent paradoxes and implicit contradictions. Hamilton's main contribution to our critical engagement with Romantic poetry lies in two chapters that focus on Keats and Shelley, but his overall argument is articulated through readings of German theory, especially that of Friedrich Schiller. He suggests that the valorization of aesthetic experience—the acknowledgement of its specific difference from the experience of the habitual and indeed the supposed vitality of a temporary transfiguration of the ordinary—characterizes a Romantic aesthetic that is present in the poetry of the period, amid a key awareness both of its own personal limitations and of its removal from political instantiation. As such, Romantic poetry requires neither deconstruction nor ideological analysis of a half-hidden political radicalism (within a new historical model), but rather needs to be read for a lacerating awareness of its own immanent self-critique. The lie of Romantic poetry's promise exists in its affirmation of an elevated, deictic presence that stands in for an absent present, and which is always necessarily privileged above that absence. As such it is always pointing to something that is privileged above its own actual subject; it is almost always about that act of pointing, and is, as such, inherently about itself, about absence. It is in the awareness of this absence that the vitally political nature of the poetry suggests itself, and Hamilton reveals this in particular in his analysis of Shelley, whose ongoing commitment to materialism is shown to be an implicitly political act. Hamilton reads interestingly against the grain, confounding our familiarity with a variety of Romantic texts. The radically driven relationship between Godwin and Coleridge is explored, as is the question of Keats's engagement with cultural critique, a part of the book that grows out of seminal work by Nicholas Roe. In a sense, the chapter on Shelley is exemplary of Hamilton's careful approach. It has long been assumed in Shelley scholarship that there was a turn away from the political committed French materialists who so preoccupied the young poet of *Queen Mab*, as he embraced the Platonic idealism that seems ostensibly to be so central to late poems like *The Triumph of Life*. Hamilton challenges this, carefully decoding that poem, as he reads it alongside *The Defence of Poetry*, and in so doing suggests that it is a work distinctly involved in its own self-critique. His writing is penetrating (though it can be pretty demanding at times) and the implications of Hamilton's argument are incredibly interesting and central to any study of literary aesthetics in this field.

An oddly related exercise, which brings to bear his considerable knowledge of the Romantic and post-Romantic tradition in poetry amid a wider discussion of the emotions in aesthetic experience, is Charles Altieri's *The Particulars of Rapture: An Aesthetics of Affect*. This begins with the slightly jaded apprehension that emotion has long been considered a dirty word in literary-critical analysis (a tenet that we might trace back to the work of Wimsatt and Beardsley for example) but forms part of a larger project exhibited in the work of Philip Fisher, amongst others, which has sought to demonstrate the ways in which an aesthetic analysis of literature can inform the post-Enlightenment division between cognition and feeling, exposing in so doing a sense of the ways in which emotions act as guides to thoughts. Altieri turns with useful effect to Wordsworth's *Tintern Abbey* at the end of his study in order to show how seriously Wordsworth himself takes emotional experience as a guide to inner states of being that cannot be justified rationally, even as they are assumed to be states of consciousness that might be felt universally. He uncovers a rich tradition of writing about the emotions that has been reprised usefully within the philosophical tradition by thinkers such as Martha Nussbaum and the late Richard Wollheim, both of whom have written recently about the centrality of emotion to moral deliberation. In the popular sphere, the key figure in this field, with books on Spinoza and Descartes, is Antonio Damasio, and it is with a rejoinder to his work in the latter field that one of the best general studies of Romantic poetry in 2003 begins. This is John Beer's *Romantic Consciousness*, a book (like Hamilton's) that began life as a series of articles and lectures but which is much more than this in its final state. Beer ranges very widely—from Blake to Tennyson, by way of De Quincey and Mary Shelley—but his central chapter is on Coleridge. This is an extremely fine piece of work that must be required reading for anyone working in the field. Beer builds on his seminal earlier work on Coleridge's interest in supernaturalism and the irrational to fascinating effect, demonstrating the ways in which his conception of imaginative experience diverged from Wordsworth's. Beer's study is keenly informed by a knowledge of early nineteenth-century medicine and science, but it grows out of an engagement with contemporary accounts of consciousness, such as those of Damasio and Penrose, while suggesting that interest in the irrational is central to appreciating modernity's debt to the Romantic period. Nowhere is this so apparent as in the poetry of Coleridge, Keats and Shelley. In a late chapter, Beer presents an enticing division between the rival accounts of being that drove Byron and Shelley, drawing heavily upon *Julian and Maddalo*. He aims to suggest that the dialogue between the two men reproduced that between Coleridge and Wordsworth some years earlier and, although we may be tempted to counter that the later poets were much more obviously divided—Shelley's optimism lying very distant from Byron's ironic detachment—this is nevertheless an intriguing idea.

Another suggestive link between the first and second generations is given in Beer's intelligent chapter on Keats, in which he reads *Lamia* beside *Christabel*. The focus of this chapter is an analysis of Keats's theory of the imagination, and Beer provides striking grounds for considering this alongside Coleridgean thought. Beer's Keats is a poet alive to the many conflicting states of consciousness and is so, at least in part, as a consequence of his medical learning. Beer draws out an interesting sense of the relevance of animal magnetism, brain theory and the work of such Continental scientists as J.F. Blumenbach to British Romanticism. Bearing in mind an allusion of Hallam's to phrenology from *In Memoriam*, it is, I think, relatively easy to sense the kind of intellectual territory (in which poetry reflects the intriguing scientific theories of its time, precisely because it is necessarily concerned with the nature of the conscious mind) that Beer intends to map out. He does so with a delicate lightness of touch. Charles I. Armstrong's *Romantic Organicism: From Idealist Origins to Ambivalent Afterlife* is a very different work but also aims to revisit the question of the influence of German thought on England. This difficult but impressive study traces the growth of theories of organicism in Germany, paying attention to Kant, Fichte and Schelling, before turning in its central chapter to an examination of the idea of organic unity in the work of Wordsworth and Coleridge. When Armstrong looks to the former, it is with a view to examining the growth of the project of *The Recluse* as a work that intends to inscribe a sense of the totality of imaginative apprehension, suggesting that this is something that critics have tended to ignore in their predominant appreciation of one part of Wordsworth's overall achievement, *The Prelude*. Armstrong is strongest in his reading of Wordsworth, displaying a debt to Kenneth Johnston, but he also demonstrates an impressive understanding of Coleridge's Conversation Poems, informing keenly upon his relationship with Southey. The approach that he takes forms part of a wider leaning that we can apprehend in 2003, which considers Continental thought alongside British Romanticism in ways that are productive for both traditions. His final chapters consider I.A. Richards alongside Bataille, before moving on to the work of Gadamer, Blanchot and Derrida.

Interest in Continental philosophy was also notable in an important volume that reconsidered the subject of biography in the period, Bradley and Rawes, eds., *Romantic Biography*. Bradley's own piece sends us back to Paul de Man's Derridean essay 'Shelley Disfigured', but does so in order to reconsider the Shelley–Byron relationship from a post-deconstructive point of view. This is an exciting collection that acknowledges the centrality of autobiography to the period while making us significantly aware of the focus on biographical studies of Romantic poets in the last decade. Jonathan Bate contributes a piece on his own work on John Clare that is interesting to read alongside two other essays, those of Mark Storey on Robert Southey and Kenneth Johnston on Wordsworth, the latter being keenly aware of the waves made by his earlier politicized study of life of the poet. Among a number of interesting essays that deal with Scott and Byron as well as the question of writing Romantic biography within a critical culture that has challenged the very nature of authorship, two essays stand out. These are by Jennifer Wallace and Michael O'Neill. The latter is a beautifully constructed essay on the subject of self-creation in the Romantic period that suggests some of the ways in which poets created their own legacy amid a culture of posterity. It is characteristically impressive. Wallace's contribution looks at Keats and the body and is a delicate work of criticism that bears appropriate comparison with that of Beer discussed earlier.

A work that continues this fascination with the body and which is both impressively historicist and alive to the implications of Romantic science is Paul Youngquist's *Monstrosities: Bodies and British Romanticism*. Youngquist writes with penetrating insight on matters of race and physicality, addressing issues that follow from colonialism, economics and nationalism. Students of Coleridge and Wordsworth will profit from his work, which focuses on subjects as diverse as the Bartholomew Fair festivities and Romantic representations of pregnancy. Youngquist also examines the discourse of the body as it was influenced by the war at the time, and in so doing he engages with a trend in 2003 that is reflected in two other splendid studies, J.R. Watson's *Romanticism and War: A Study of British Romantic Period Writers and the Napoleonic Wars* and Simon Bainbridge's *British Poetry and the Revolutionary and Napoleonic Wars: Visions of Conflict*. In retrospect, it is, I think, astonishing that this subject has not been treated more widely before: both books are very welcome and build on the work of Richard Cronin and Philip Shaw. While they cover similar ground, they approach the subject in rather different ways. Watson's study is an outstanding work of cultural history whose approach is chronological. He is concerned to describe not only the ways in which war emerges as a key theme in the poetry of the central writers of the time (Wordsworth, Coleridge, Byron and Shelley), but also some of the cultural implications for the nation of its being at war for most of the Romantic period. Poets both negotiated the fact of writing about a time of war and helped to produce perceptions of the war itself, conditioning the public's apprehension of its dreadful repercussions. Watson covers the early wars of the 1790s, dealing with the issue of Jacobin rivalries in the period. He uncovers interesting material relating to Thomas Campbell, whose work has been largely ignored in serious scholarship in spite of its enormous popularity at the time. Significantly he then turns to the Convention of Cintra (which notably engaged Wordsworth) and the Peninsular War, before examining the literature relating to Waterloo. The end of the book looks at three writers from the post-Romantic period, whose work nevertheless describes the ravages of the Napoleonic wars as they were later remembered, De Quincey, Ruskin and Hardy. Watson is particularly valuable for the attention that he pays to the poetry of Walter Scott, which is rather neglected outside these studies.

A central chapter of Simon Bainbridge's book, however, also examines Scott, writing sensitively on his most important narrative poems, *The Lady of the Lake, The Lay of the Last Minstrel* and *Marmion*. Bainbridge demonstrates with admirable intelligence the ways in which the culture of warfare was reflected in Scott's poetry. His study gathers together much of the immense public poetry that dealt with the theme of war and constructs an interesting argument about the ways in which the fact of being at war conditioned poets in their role as public spokesmen. Apart from Scott, Bainbridge also directs our attention towards Southey, whose lesser-known work appeared widely in newspapers and periodicals of the time. Central to his study is the creation of a public form of address in the poetry of the time, which stands in discrete opposition to a private mode of confession that has long been seen to define the Romantic period. He folds into this a gendered argument in which the male poets of the period use the theme of war in order to reconceive the act of writing as a male activity distinct from its feminization in the later stages of the eighteenth century. Bainbridge is self-conscious about the fact that his is not a survey of the whole period of the wars with France, as Watson attempts, but is rather a study of particular points of tension, or moments of special historical crisis when the role of the poet became especially charged. It is a fascinating work.

Several important editions in 2003 engaged with the history of the period in a literary context. Marcus Wood's *The Poetry of Slavery* will be indispensable to anyone working on this central issue. His collection is prefaced by a stylish and impressive introduction describing the literature relating to the abolition debates of the late eighteenth and early nineteenth centuries. Wood approaches the subject from a transatlantic angle, ensuring that this is an anthology that contributes to an important and growing trend in scholarship on the Romantic period that examines the literature of the time from an Anglo-American perspective. There are some fascinating selections here. Shelley emerges as a poet concerned with race alongside more obviously public writers such as Southey. In the second half of the anthology, exciting American poets are widely represented. Wheatley, Whittier and Emerson may be well known, but many of the names will be new to most of us. In all, the reader is confronted with a diverse body of writing. Some of it is familiar (Cowper, Coleridge and Blake), but there is a wealth of material by both male and female poets that has been unjustly neglected, and of particular interest is that by writers of colour such as Olaudah Equiano. Wood also contributes an interesting essay on race to Jones, ed., *The Satiric Eye* (discussed above). This is an extremely valuable set of essays that contextualizes the work of a number of important poets within a popular culture that was alive to the various forms of satire. Gary Dyer writes interestingly about

Thomas Moore, while John Strachan builds on his impressive scholarship on Romantic parody to inform us about J.R.D. Huggins, a welcome piece with a transatlantic focus. Not the least of the achievements of this impressive collection is to challenge some of the conventional assumptions about Romanticism's central preoccupations—a fascination with the natural world, the valorization of imaginative experience, and its distance from the Augustan decorum of the eighteenth century. Of course we should no longer buy into a literary history conditioned by neat period divisions, but this collection does a lot to further muddy the waters. Michael Gamer writes strikingly about the Della Cruscans and William Gifford's reaction to them, encouraging us to look again at the transitional period of the 1790s, and Nicola Trott, in a wonderful essay on Wordsworth ranging over the work of Francis Jeffrey and Leigh Hunt, challenges us to think more rigorously about the relationship between the eighteenth-century satirists and their Romantic readers, discovering in the process a serious aesthetic purpose in the parody of the time.

Jeffrey also emerges as a figure of some importance in following the growth of Byron's admiration for Scott as he turned away from the hostility of 'English bards and Scotch reviewers'. Andrew Nicholson outlines this complicated relationship, tracing an interesting literary dialogue between the two men in his contribution to Carruthers and Rawes, eds., *English Romanticism and the Celtic World* (also discussed in Section 1). This is a very wide-ranging collection of essays in which Byron figures quite highly. He is the subject of an interesting biographical essay by Bernard Beatty, which suggests that Scotland remained central to Byron's consciousness as late as *The Island* and *Don Juan*. Meanwhile, *Beppo* appears as an intriguing influence on Felicia Hemans in an essay by William D. Brewer. He details the significance of the Welsh landscape to Hemans and suggests that the mythology surrounding the Welsh bard contributed to Romantic conceptions of poetic genius. His essay is to be read alongside very welcome contributions by Caroline Franklin and J.R. Watson, both of whom address themselves to the literary significance of Wales in the period. Watson confronts the importance of Snowdon in Wordsworth's imaginative life, while Franklin engages with Southey's *Madoc*. The collection ends with a very suggestive piece by Michael O'Neill that ranges widely over the poetry of contemporary Northern Ireland, pointing out a number of Romantic resonances especially in the literary relationship between Wordsworth and Heaney. In sum, this is a heterogeneous but rich collection that challenges a simple construction of 'English' Romanticism, and it goes a long way towards reforming our understanding of the ways in which Romantic period writers thought about notions of national identity.

A very different work, which nevertheless also confronts the issue of nationalism in the period, is Marc Redfield's *The Politics of Aesthetics: Nationalism, Gender, Romanticism*. This is a strikingly intelligent work, which bears comparison with the scholarship of Paul Hamilton discussed above. It is strongly influenced by deconstruction and engages with, amongst others, the work of Paul de Man. Much of Redfield's book lies outside the field of our concern, there being chapters on Fichte, Schiller, Arnold and Friedrich Schlegel. The essence of his argument in these chapters, however, undergirds an impressive thesis about the relationship between aesthetics and politics. Redfield ranges himself against critics who have argued that the aesthetic is an escapist zone in flight from the political. He intends us to reread the history of aesthetic discourse within the modern, eighteenth-century and Romantic tradition focusing on its figurative language in order to suggest some of the ways in which that discourse becomes unconsciously politicized through unpredictable effects of reference. Central to this thesis, Redfield argues, is the figure of the body in aesthetic discourse, and he writes very impressively about the apprehension of idealized beauty in the work of Friedrich Schiller. This enables Redfield to engage closely with the work of Paul de Man and leads him on to the most useful part of the book for the student of British Romanticism, a chapter on Shelley which reads *The Cenci* beside *The Mask of Anarchy* to interesting effect, and which once again revisits some of the implications of 'Shelley Disfigured'. Redfield might be said to participate in a more widespread and welcome trend in Romantic criticism, which gives much-needed consideration to the history of aesthetics, while paying attention to both political and historical evidence. One of the leading figures in this movement is Jon Mee, whose *Romanticism, Enthusiasm and Regulation* is discussed at length in Section 1 above. It is worth while to draw attention once again to the outstanding chapters on the subject of enthusiasm in Coleridge and Wordsworth. In the history of cultural aesthetics, enthusiasm is a fascinating topic, in part because it is such a Janus-faced term. As much as it is suggestive of the divine inspiration of the male Romantic genius, it also describes the fanaticism of the crowd and, as such, it is pregnant with ambiguous religious and political implications, which Mee draws out brilliantly.

A study that takes a very different approach to the influence of Romantic religion on the poets of the time is J. Robert Barth's *Romanticism and Transcendence: Wordsworth, Coleridge, and the Religious Imagination*. Barth argues that high Romantic theories of the imagination such as those of Wordsworth and Coleridge, which place such a stress upon the individual's imaginative capacity to create symbols, are inherently and necessarily religious. The implications of Barth's argument are that any theory of the imagination must be sanctioned by belief in a Christian God, and in this he might be challenged by certain recent scholarship (such as that of Nicholas Halmi), which has suggested that Coleridge's theory of the symbol is not uncomplicatedly Christian. Whether, like the work of the divine Logos, saying that acts of the imagination are religious acts makes them come into being as such readers will have to judge for themselves. At the very least, it rather commits Barth to a strong defence of Wordsworth's revisions to the 1850 *Prelude*, and some readers may demur from this. Nevertheless, in spite of these possible reservations, there is a lot of great learning on display here. At the centre of the book is a series of readings of *The Prelude*, which lead into some reflections on prayer in Coleridge's poetry. The book closes with some suggestive ways of pursuing Barth's thesis about the interrelation of religious and aesthetic experience in twentieth-century thought, and he displays a debt to the thought of both Karl Rahner and George Steiner.

Richard Gravil's richly rewarding monograph, *Wordsworth's Bardic Vocation, 1787–1842*, presents us with much more diverse figure than Barth's, a poet driven by his fascination with the ancient bardic tradition in Great Britain to embrace the many roles of balladist, minstrel, elegist and, later, national bard. This study is, one senses, the product of many years of devoted scholarship, and while one might wonder whether Wordsworth's early interest in druid revelries really fuelled his poetic vocation to quite such an extent, Gravil adduces an enormous amount of evidence to support his case. The book is a remarkable resource on all the periods of Wordsworth's career. It ends with an impressively articulated historical analysis of *Poems Chiefly of Early and Late Years*, and explores the theme of dialogue in *The Excursion*. Meanwhile, at its centre there are chapters that examine an important poem that has been widely ignored, *The White Doe of Rylstone*, and also *Hart-Leap Well*. Gravil writes especially well on the political power of Wordsworth's early poetry in *Salisbury Plain, The Ruined Cottage* and *Lyrical Ballads*, and his range of reference is astonishing. Baron d'Holbach, Dugald Stewart, John Toland and Horne Tooke all make appearances as Gravil decodes the system of nature as it is present in *Tintern Abbey*. Perhaps the most original part of this book is the first, however, in which Gravil describes a culture of antiquarianism in Britain that sought to uncover the pre-Christian past, relating this to a diverse body of Wordsworth's writing, from some of the earliest work such as *An Evening Walk* to his mature vision of the nation in *Ecclesiastical Sonnets* and the *Guide to the Lakes*. Gravil's is certainly one of the most important publications on Wordsworth in recent years. Alongside it, however, is Gill, ed., *The Cambridge Companion to Wordsworth*. This continues the fine traditions of that series, perhaps even outstripping the achievements of the earlier volumes on Keats and Coleridge. The list of contributors makes pretty distinguished reading and together they comprise a group of some of the leading scholars in the field from both sides of the Atlantic. Kenneth Johnston, Lucy Newlyn and James A. Butler examine individual works, while Nicholas Roe, Paul Hamilton, Ralph Pite and editor Stephen Gill himself address central themes within Wordsworth (politics, the concept of Romanticism, nature and philosophy). The troublesome relationship with Coleridge is brilliantly handled by Seamus Perry, and while Nicola Trott sensitively describes the shaping of the poet's career, Susan Wolfson writes acutely about the formal qualities of Wordsworth's poetry. There are other, less obvious articles here too, which will contribute an awful lot to any reader's understanding of Wordsworth's career. The overall standard is very high indeed. Duncan Wu writes expertly about the early poetry before *Lyrical Ballads* and, in an extremely learned essay, Joel Pace opens up the exciting topic of Wordsworth's reception in America, in so doing suggesting the extraordinarily diverse nature of his reading public there. In a related article, 'A Publisher's Politics: *Lyrical Ballads* (Philadelphia, 1802)' (*Symbiosis* 7[2003] 35–55), Pace describes the reception of Wordsworth's *Lyrical Ballads* in post-revolutionary Philadelphia, detailing the circumstances of Wordsworth first American publisher, James Humphries.

A number of important articles on Wordsworth were published in 2003. The work of Marjorie Levinson was the starting point for two rather different pieces by Charles J. Rzepka and Stuart Allen. The former, 'Pictures of the Mind: Iron and Charcoal, "Ouzy" Tides and "Vagrant Dwellers" at Tintern, 1798' (*SiR* 42[2003] 155–85), takes issue with Levinson's influential thesis that Wordsworth transforms and distorts the scene of industrialized Tintern that confronted him on his return there, turning it into a representation of pastoral retreat. Rzepka presents a great deal of new material in order to refute this, and his article is richly accompanied by illustrations of the Wye Valley which suggest what Wordsworth would actually have seen during the walking tour. In a related article, 'From Relics to Remains: Wordsworth's "The Thorn" and the Emergence of Secular History' (*RoN* 31[2003]), Rzepka writes interestingly about Wordsworth's reading of Druid history, valuably read alongside the work of Richard Gravil. Stuart Allen, in 'Wordsworth's Ear and the Politics of Aesthetic Autonomy' (*Romanticism* 9[2003] 37–53), grapples with a different thesis of Levinson's, namely that Wordsworth, in privileging vision above hearing, was a reactionary poet. Allen is a very sensitive reader who goes to great lengths to show that the role of listening in Wordsworth is central to his aesthetic. Sound and feeling, and the ways in which these interrelate in a formal analysis of poetry, form the central subjects for a deeply learned and clever article by J. Mark Smith, '"Unrememberable" Sound in Wordsworth's 1799 Prelude' (*SiR* 42[2003] 501–18). Smith reads Wordsworth's poem as a series of sounds and moods, which together constitute the emotional moment of the work. He is interested in revisiting the classical rhetorical topos of *inventio* as a way of exposing the structure of that poem, using the work of the contemporary philosopher Giorgio Agamben as a lens through which to read Augustine and Aristotle. An interest in emotion is also palpable in Michelle Levy's admirable essay 'The Wordsworths, the Greens, and the Limits of Sympathy' (*SiR* 42[2003] 541–65) in which she turns to the influence of Adam Smith and David Hume upon Wordsworth, illuminating in the process the relationship between the Wordsworths and the orphaned children of a couple, Sarah and George Green, both of whom perished on Langdale Fell in 1808.

Important essays on Wordsworth were also to be found in a special issue of *The Wordsworth Circle* (*WC* 34[2003]), devoted to Wordsworth's 'Second Selves' 1789–2002, and edited by Sally Bushell. These grew out of a conference whose theme was the reception of Wordsworth and the critical and creative responses to his poetry, from those of his contemporaries to the present. There are useful pieces in this collection that address the reading of Wordsworth by Arnold, Browning and Rossetti. Samantha Matthews writes interestingly about Wordsworth's grave and notes its status as a shrine for visitors such as Nathaniel Hawthorne as early as 1855. In a very welcome essay on Wordsworth's relationship with Southey, meanwhile, David Chandler turns his attention to the decline in Southey's critical reputation, finding its origins in Southey's self-constructed image as the 'Lake' writer from Greta Hall, which overcame the international ambitions of his earlier poetical projects. The collection begins with a fine essay by Andrew Bennett, which navigates between two rival critical traditions that he finds in the twentieth century, each of which makes an opposing claim about the centrality of poetic diction and language to Wordsworth. Bennett finds that, although Wordsworth was clearly studied in his composition, he nevertheless presented an image of himself as a poet who composed on the hoof. One very interesting publication from 2003 that is usefully set alongside this collection is *Wordsworth's Poets*, edited by

Duncan Wu. This draws on the extensive research into Wordsworth's reading and his literary influences that Wu has undertaken and, in a very useful introduction, he explains the process of selection for this new volume, which consists of extracts from some of the key poetry (and prose by poets) that Wordsworth endorsed during his lifetime of reading. Wu introduces some important context for each selection in a headnote, and presents the selections in the approximate chronological order in which Wordsworth would have encountered them. It is a very valuable collection and will be vital to students who are interested in exploring Wordsworth's diverse influences, especially from the eighteenth century. This is a subject that Seamus Perry also explores to very interesting effect in his 'Wordsworth's Heroics' (*WC* 34[2003] 65–73), an essay which looks at the influence of Pope and Cowper on Wordsworth, arguing for the importance of an ongoing burlesque tradition.

The most important article to deal with Samuel Taylor Coleridge in 2003 is also by Perry, 'Ordinary Consolation and its Modern Fate' (*ERR* 14[2003] 479–86). This starts out with the reflection that, for late modernity, the idea that imaginative activity can be curative, providing a sense of consolation or solace in the face of the inevitability of death, is horribly *passé*. Perry traces the idea of consolation in Coleridge's thought, paying attention to his account of Wordsworth's poetry as a bringer of health, itself an anticipation of a Victorian tradition exemplified in Mill. The latter part of the article suggests the ways in which Wordsworth's poetics of defamiliarization serve to justify this position by granting a particular vitality to the ordinary, and Perry ends with some reflections on the persistence of this idea in modern poetry. Perry is also the author of an attractive short life, *Samuel Taylor Coleridge*, in the British Library's Writers' Lives series. This is a beautifully illustrated volume containing images from Coleridge's marginalia and notebooks that really serve to give the reader a feeling for the writer and a sense of the wider culture of the time. It should introduce a new audience to Coleridge, presenting them with a short and concise but also rich and witty account, which while its focus is principally on the pre-Highgate period, nevertheless also takes us to the end of Coleridge's life. Two important editions of Coleridge emerged in 2003. The long-awaited Norton Critical Edition of *Coleridge's Poetry and Prose*, edited by Nicholas Halmi, Paul Magnuson and Raimonda Modiano, should now become the standard edition by which all undergraduates approach the study of Coleridge. This has an outstanding selection of the poetry, presented in order of its publication with excellent textual apparatus and useful notes. The edition also includes a valuable and judicious selection of the published and unpublished prose works, a number of letters, and an interesting section of miscellaneous prose, which dips into many of the curious obsessions that preoccupied Coleridge. It contains, moreover, a good deal of useful criticism from the nineteenth and twentieth centuries. David Vallins's admirable edition of Coleridge's writings, *On the Sublime*, is the latest in the important Palgrave series, whose general editor is John Beer. Vallins writes a useful introduction in which he details Coleridge's interest in the sublime from his early political lectures and poems (such as *Religious Musings*) through to the late thoughts on religion. At the heart of the volume are of course Coleridge's writings on literature and the visual arts, and Vallins's fine selection allows us to see exactly how significantly central were his thoughts on the sublime to questions that preoccupied him within the field of aesthetics. Since Coleridge's writing on the sublime is spread so widely through so much of the corpus of his work, it is extremely useful to have everything together in one place. Editing Coleridge is, however, notoriously tricky for this very reason and this forms the subject of an interesting essay by J.C.C. Mays on his experience of producing the poetry for the Bollingen series in Andrew Nash's collection of essays, *Culture of Collected Editions*. Nash also includes an important contribution by Donald H. Reiman, which assess the various different approaches that have been taken to the major Romantic editions of the last quarter-century or so.

If Coleridge was ill served by book-length studies, a number of monographs were published about Byron in 2003. Several revisited old subjects. Byron's putative homosexuality and his interest in sexual politics are re-examined in Abigail F. Keegan's *Byron's Othered Self and Voice: Contextualizing the Homographic Signature*, while the influence of his Calvinist upbringing and his continued attention to the Fall is discussed in Paul D. Barton's *Lord Byron's Religion: A Journey into Despair*. Neither is particularly remarkable or distinguished. Some of the same ground as Barton's is, however, covered in an impressive comparative study, Peter A. Schock's *Romantic Satanism: Myth and the Historical Moment in Blake, Shelley, and Byron*, which deals with the trope of Satanism in Romantic poetry in an admirably novel fashion. Schock contends that the figure of Satan, especially as he is conditioned by Milton's representation in *Paradise Lost*, has long been assumed by critics to exist in the period as a celebrant of private individualism and subjective mental experience. Schock explores the ways in which this myth of Satanic but individual consciousness is conditioned culturally by a nation threatened first by Jacobin revolt and then by war with Napoleon. Much of the book is devoted to a set of readings of Shelley which aim to unpick his ambiguous relationship with Christianity, but the study ends with interesting and welcome readings of two lesser-known works of Byron, *The Vision of Judgment* and *The Deformed Transformed*.

The most original book-length study of Byron in 2003 was Stephen Cheeke's *Byron and Place: History, Translation, Nostalgia*. This is a very fine work, which ranges extremely widely in Byron's work and also unpicks a number of the intellectual and cultural relationships that the poet had over the course of his diverse life, including reference to Sheridan, Elgin, Hobhouse and Murray. Cheeke also writes very interestingly about subjects that have been examined before but never brought together so comprehensively: Orientalism, Philhellenism, Byron's appreciation of Rome, and the influence of Dante. Articulating Cheeke's work is the drive to merge two related influences in recent scholarship (geography and history) into a species of 'geo-historical' criticism, which seeks to examine the ways in which Byron situates himself within specific places and historical moments in his early work, in so doing contributing to a form of self-fashioning, which is to be marked out from the later poetry of his self-imposed Italian exile. This is an extremely impressive thesis, held together by a chronologically arranged set of close biographical readings of the poetry and prose. The book ends with an interesting reflection upon Byron's later nostalgia for the Britain of the Regency period, and Cheeke writes well about the critique of memory and the construction of homesickness.

A sense of nostalgia for a past poetic tradition, and indeed for Byron's efforts at literary self-construction (albeit within a tradition of eighteenth-century satire), also emerges from an interesting study in literary history, Christopher Yu's *Nothing to Admire: The Politics of Poetic Satire from Dryden to Merrill*. This contains an essay on Byron which is structured principally around readings of Beppo and Don Juan. Yu's overarching argument is that there is a diachronic tradition in poetic satire that extends from Restoration England to modern America, and his landing-places are Dryden, Pope, Byron, Auden and Merrill. He aims to suggest that the governing, Horatian principle of satire—the *nil admirari*—contains a discreetly coded critique of political power and valorization of individual freedom that is exhibited in his focal poets. Byron emerges from this context as a more distinctly political poet than we might expect. Two articles in 2003, however, argue the case even more strongly for reading the early Byron (at least) as very much a politically engaged figure, concerned with the public act of writing. These are Tom Mole, 'Byron's "Ode to the Framers of the Frame Bill": The Embarrassment of Industrial Culture' (*KSJ* 52[2003] 111–29) and Andrew Nicholson, 'Napoleon's "Last Act" and Byron's *Ode*' (*Romanticism* 9[2003] 68–81).

A number of articles in 2003 looked at the work of Percy Shelley, and there was one important edition. The latter is *The Major Works*, edited with an introduction and notes by Michael O'Neill and Zachary Leader, which lives up to the high standards of that series and should now become the standard undergraduate edition. It contains a valuable selection of the prose and poetry, including extracts from such lesser-known works as *Laon and Cynthna*, with helpful notes and a lively introduction. It is to be highly recommended. Useful articles on Shelley include Ghislaine McDayter, 'O'er Leaping the Bounds: The Sexing of the Soul in *Epipsychidion*' (*KSJ* 52[2003] 21–9), which draws out some of the implications of that poem's intertextual relationship with Pope's *Eloisa to Abelard*. In the same journal issue, Cian Duffy, 'Revolution or Reaction? Shelley's *Assassins* and the Politics of Necessity' (*KSJ* 52[2003] 77–93), and Fred N. Randel, 'Shelley's Revision of Coleridgean Traditionalism in "Lines Written Among the Euganean Hills"' (*KSJ* 52[2003] 50–76), both explore his literary and intellectual influences. The former examines Shelley's little-known work *Assassins*, and points up its role in conditioning a politically driven theory of the sublime, which is articulated through the influence of both Godwin and Gibbon. Randel meanwhile turns to the rather better trodden ground of the influence of Coleridge's conversation poems on Shelley. Two other impressive articles appeared on Shelley in 2003, both in *Studies in Romanticism*. Stuart Peterfreund's 'The Color Violaceous, or, Chemistry and the Romance Dematerialization: The Subliming of Iodine and Shelley's *Adonais*' (*SiR* 42[2003] 45–54), is characteristically informed by a striking knowledge of the science of the Romantic period and reads Shelley's poetry through this lens. Meanwhile, Forest Pyle, in 'Kindling and Ash: Radical Aestheticism in Keats and Shelley' (*SiR* 42[2003] 427–59), returns us to some of the same ground that was explored in the work of Hamilton and Redfield earlier. Pyle's article is deeply impressive in its grasp of recent Continental theory, and he sets out to explore certain moments of tension in the poetry of Shelley and Keats at which their work explores the nature of aesthetic experience while eschewing a simple escape into art.

The poetry of John Keats was itself served in 2003 by a number of important articles and two books. The first of these, John Strachan's edition *The Poems of John Keats: A Sourcebook* is in the Routledge Guides to Literature series and it contains a selection of important letters and poems alongside critical extracts from both the nineteenth and twentieth centuries. These are given the kind of context that will be useful for undergraduates coming to Keats for the first time. La Cassagnère, ed., *Keats, ou Le Sortilège des mots*, is a collection dealing with the theme of writing and aesthetics in Keats. The contribution of Denis Bonnecase is worth mentioning, returning us as it does to a consideration of the importance of Hazlitt to Keats. For the most part though, these essays are pretty conventional. At the other end of the critical spectrum is Orrin N.C. Wang's splendid piece, 'Coming Attractions: *Lamia* and Cinematic Sensation' (*SiR* 42[2003] 461–500). This reads Keats from a critical perspective that is alive to the history of spectacle in the Romantic period, drawing fascinating parallels between the controlled conditioning of pre-cinematic audiences at the time and the visual dynamics of Keats's poem. Another article to focus on the contemporary theatrical culture and its effects on Keats is Jonathan Mulrooney's excellent 'Keats in the Company of Kean' (*SiR* 42[2003] 227–50). Two pieces that deal with his decline, first critical and then physical, and with the attendant writing that accompanied them, are Grant F. Scott's fine analysis of the poet's earliest biographers, 'Writing Keats's Last Days: Severn, Sharp, and Romantic Biography' (*SiR* 42[2003] 4–26), and Paul Bentley's study of the Blackwood's attacks, 'Caviare from the Count: *Blackwood's* and John Keats's *La Belle Dame Sans Merci*' (*Romanticism* 9[2003] 54–67). The Gothicism of his most obviously related poetry, and the influence of contemporary modes of Gothic writing more generally on Keats, are together explored by Jerrold E. Hogle in 'The Gothic–Romantic Relationship: Underground Histories in "The Eve of St. Agnes"' (*ERR* 14[2003] 205–23), as is noted above. Beth Lau, meanwhile, looks into a different literary relationship, that with Chatterton, in 'Protest, "Nativism" and Impersonation in the Works of Chatterton and Keats' (*SiR* 42[2003] 520–39).

In a short but important book, *Coming of Age as a Poet: Milton, Keats, Eliot, Plath*, which grew out of her James Murray Brown lectures, Helen Vendler explores the development of Keats's sonnet style. Her subject is the development of an individual and recognizable voice in the poets that she examines, and the admirable chapter on Keats goes some way towards demonstrating the extent of his debt to Leigh Hunt in his formative years. Amongst many other subjects, this is key to Nicholas Roe's formative edited collection of essays, *Leigh Hunt: Life, Poetics, Politics*. This work forms part of a renaissance in Hunt studies that also saw the publication of a multi-volume *Selected Writings* in 2003 (discussed below). Among the very fine list of contributors, Roe's own work stands out, inasmuch as he places Hunt in a cultural context from which we can begin to re-envisage his wide-ranging influence in Romantic and Victorian Britain. John Barnard, Jeffrey Cox, Elizabeth Jones and Greg Kucich, meanwhile, all examine aspects of the Cockney culture that conditioned both Hunt's influence on Keats and then the critical attacks suffered by both men. Kim Wheatley examines the critical backlash and, in two outstanding pieces by Jane Stabler and Michael O'Neill respectively, there is a real sense given of the sensitive nature of Hunt's own poetic project.

An influential poet of a very different type who received some attention in 2003 was Robert Bloomfield. Two articles make the case for our considering his contribution to the development of rural themes in Romantic poetry more carefully. They are Bruce Graver's 'Illustrating *The Farmer's Boy*' (*Romanticism* 9[2003] 157–75) and Simon J. White, 'Rural Medicine: Robert Bloomfield's "Good Tidings"' (*Romanticism* 9[2003] 140–55). In retrospect, this work on Bloomfield needs to be set alongside the large amount of attention devoted to the work of John Clare in 2003. Central to this is the magnificent life by Jonathan Bate, *John Clare: A Biography*. This is a stunning achievement which involved both an enormous amount of archival research and a good deal of speculative reconstruction. Not only was there no real precedent for the task that Bate undertook but there also remains effectively no independent evidence for the first twenty-five years of Clare's life. In order to compensate for this absence of material, and in a way as a fortunate consequence of it, Bate makes the first part of the work into a lively, wide-ranging cultural study of the late eighteenth and early nineteenth centuries. He structures his account of Clare's early life around a set of themes that address the geographical and social environment as much as Clare's own erotic entanglements and his early activities as a writer. The well-documented period that follows is focused around Clare's critical discovery and his consequent literary celebrity. These are the years of his greatest sustained creativity, which sadly presage a period of mental instability in which documentary evidence beyond the autobiographical becomes once again fairly unreliable. If the general arc of Clare's life was known before Bate's biography, then nevertheless (and by critical consent) he has done much to transform the reader's understanding of this rather depressing narrative in an extraordinary work of scholarship. Another major study that seeks impressively to transform our appreciation of Clare is Alan Vardy's monograph *John Clare: Politics and Poetry*. He takes issue with what he assumes to be a casual critical *donnée* about Clare, namely that the poet was always an outsider to the London literary scene, patronized as minor, and mistreated by his editors. Vardy instead, while recognizing the extent to which Clare suffered from some of the consequences of historical circumstance, nevertheless aims to suggest that he participated in aesthetic debates of the time, such as those about poetic diction, while remaining active in an examination of his professional relationships and self-conscious about the extent to which the literary marketplace situated him within key social and political questions of the day. Vardy's study, like Bate's brilliant biography, deserves to be widely read for its analysis of the literary world of the 1820s. In passing, both enter into the ongoing critical debate about the virtues of textual primitivism as it has been practised in the Clarendon Press edition of Clare's poetry, and Vardy suggests that the argument for reversing Taylor's interference with the manuscripts does not entirely outweigh the virtues of having an easy reading text. Whatever one feels about this most discussed of Romantic editorial decisions, the completion in 2003 of that edition, and with it the appearance of *John Clare: Poems of the Middle Period, 1822–1837*, edited by Eric Robinson, David Powell and P.M.S. Dawson, makes available at last all the work of that most productive period and with it allows us to reckon with the precise extent of Clare's extraordinary achievement.

3. Women Poets

After an explosion of work on Romantic women poets in the last five years, this year's output is relatively thin, although its quality remains high. While almost everything published this time round was restricted to journals, one monograph does stand out as a focused study of a Romantic woman poet, and for this alone Jacqueline M. Labbe's study of Charlotte Smith deserves substantial praise. *Charlotte Smith: Romanticism, Poetry and the Culture of Gender* is the first serious critical study of Smith's poetry, and addresses the *Elegiac Sonnets* [1784], *The Emigrants* [1793], and *Beachy Head* [1807] amidst some insightful discussion of eighteenth-century conceptions of gender and subjectivity. Labbe begins by thinking about Smith's representation of herself as both a unified female author and a figure inhabiting multiple personae in her poetry: Smith seems to survey the numerous compromised selves available to women in the period while also exploiting the pressures attendant on being a woman poet. Marking out a terrain in which she carefully considers the nature of the sexual and social female subject, Smith encourages her readers to understand and read her work as the product of a woman performing her own sorrows and trials. For Labbe, the endless frontispieces that portray Smith in her books—embattled, weary, but always costumed in a ruffled headdress and filmy collar—give her to the reader as a physical and 'sexed' figure who performs her gender literally, rather than in a Butlerian, psychological sense. By doing so, Smith invites her readers to sympathize with and thus 'rescue' her, appealing to their chivalric impulses at the same time as dramatizing her own alienation amidst social pressures. Instead of confining the subject matter of her poetry to women's work, the domestic, the quotidian and so on, Smith 'plays the gender game' by making her sorrows explicit, forcing the reader to confront the financial difficulties thrown upon her by a roguish husband and fraudulent lawyers. Performing and directing her own persona, then, Smith manipulates gender, genre and selfhood to commodify her own identity while exploding it into a multiplicity of feminized 'I' roles.

Labbe's first chapter, 'The Possibilities of Print', examines the prefaces and illustrations to Smith's poetry to argue that the poet markets an image of herself 'in need', a strategy she then immediately undermines by cementing her literary authority in her notes to the poems. The space offered by these notes allows Smith to occupy a more flexible, self-aware and fluent selfhood that underwrites her feminized helplessness while embedding her numerous poetic identities. Two further chapters on the *Elegiac Sonnets* establish Smith first as a 'Good Mother' writing to support her children and secondly as a woman waiting to be gallantly saved, readings Labbe achieves by recourse to the Kristevan chora. Smith's performative practices are also politicized in the study: chapter 4, 'On the Edge: Politics and the Strictures of Subjectivity in *The Emigrants*', examines the place of gender when poeticizing the masculine machinery of war. Privileging her own trials over those of the emigrants, Smith also deliberately confuses her subject position with theirs, polemically standing against war and in support of revolution in order to question the culture that has oppressed them both.

For Labbe, however, *Beachy Head* remains Smith's most important poem, one that presents a hybrid self, feminine and contemplative, masculine and confident, but always multivocal and self-reflexive. Able to construct such a formally exceptional poem, equipped as it is with detailed notes and a coherently structured plot, this self claims a version of authority grounded in a variety that memorializes itself. The study closes with a brief coda on Smith's poems for children (1804–6) which lightheartedly observe the personal 'sorrows' of the likes of bees and fish. Labbe also suggests here that the 'Romanticism' we traditionally associate with Wordsworth, one based on a poetics of subjectivity, nature, the imagination and the formation of identity, should instead be attributed to Smith, whose innovations Wordsworth colonized and co-opted. Judith Phillips Stanton's *The Collected Letters of Charlotte Smith* makes a welcome companion resource to Labbe's study, printing most of the nearly 500 surviving letters that Smith wrote to publishers, patrons, solicitors, relatives and friends. While many letters were burned by associates concerned by their raw and personal content, Stanton's edition provides a more than adequate history of Smith, including commentaries on her literary patronage, failed marriage, twelve children, health and many changes of residence. The letters, covering Smith's career from 1784 to 1806, also provide extra commentary on the publication of all but two of her novels, as well as exposing her epistolary skill. The edition is also furnished with a good biographical introduction to Smith, a full discussion of Stanton's sources, and a number of useful framing narratives regarding Smith's husband, his will and her relation to his estate.

Smith has also been the subject of several articles this year, each serving to establish her as one of the most significant eighteenth-century poets for current scholarship. In '*Elegiac Sonnets*: Charlotte Smith's Formal Paradoxy' (*PLL* 39:ii[2003] 185–220), Daniel Robinson examines Smith's formal construction of the sonnet through both eighteenth-century conceptions of elegy and the Petrarchan tradition. The *Elegiac Sonnets*, Robinson points out, do not conventionally resonate with the 'elegiac', refusing to lament any particular death and instead producing a more generalized and oppressive funereal mood. This unorthodox use of the elegiac is mirrored by Smith's equally subversive use of Petrarch, whose Laura she vindicates by critiquing the poet's representation of his beloved. Undermining the sonnet's usual role as a vehicle for Christian consolation and poetic immortality, Smith creates a hybrid sonnet, at once erotic and elegiac and so radical in its presentation of love and gender. In 'British Romantic Melancholia: Charlotte Smith's *Elegiac Sonnets*, Medical Discourse and the Problem of Sensibility' (*JES* 33:iii–iv[2003] 237–53), Elizabeth A. Dolan also turns to Smith's elegies but here in relation to contemporary medical conceptions of melancholia. Caught amidst a backlash against the cult of sensibility, the profile of the melancholic was reconfigured by physicians such as

George Cheyne, William Buchan and Thomas Trotter as a highly rational, rather than emotional, literary identity. Yet while such medical definitions successfully marginalized the type of dangerous passion associated with the French Revolution, they also served to define male nervous illness as a marker of sensitivity and intellect, while women were rendered hysterical and excessively emotional. For Dolan, Smith's *Elegiac Sonnets* are a testimony to the poet's brilliant negotiation of the gendered medical and cultural definitions of melancholia, one achieved by a balance of emotion and intellect that undermines both Wertherian feeling and obsessive rationality.

Critics are concerned with Smith's view of society as well as her melancholy aesthetics, and two articles focus on her radical politics: William D. Brewer's 'Charlotte Smith and the American Agrarian Ideal' (*ELN* 40:iv[2003] 51–61) and Toby Ruth Benis's '"A Likely Story": Charlotte Smith's Revolutionary Narratives' (*ERR* 14:iii[2003] 291–306). For Brewer, Smith's *The Young Philosopher* [1798] and *The Letters of a Solitary Wanderer* [1800] both initiate strong attacks on the corrupt eighteenth-century capitalist marketplace. Exploiting individuals, especially women, as economic commodities, capitalism seems inescapable, unhindered even by the French Revolution, and Smith turns to America in her later novels as a space full of democratic potential. Free of European prejudices, America, particularly its rural areas, is painted by Smith as an ideal environment within which to unite people under a banner of benevolence. Brewer shows how Smith's novels explore this in relation to Paine, Wollstonecraft and Burke, thus serving to locate her work within the public debate over the New World. Benis takes a similar line, reading Smith's neglected novel *The Banished Man* [1794] as a commentary on the backlash against the revolution. For Benis, the novel forges a theory of narrative politics by exploring the ambivalence in France and England towards this national crisis, and ultimately suggests that from such political instability new dimensions of literary expression will emerge.

Anna Barbauld continues to attract critical attention, and three astute articles address her poetry this year. Robert W. Jones's fascinating 'Barbauld, Milton and the Idea of Resistance' (*Romanticism* 9:ii[2003] 119–40) explores the formation of Barbauld's early public and poetic identity, one considered 'inferior only to the works of Shakespeare and Milton' by *The Monthly Review* [1773]. Reading the Miltonic allusions and references in 'A Summer Evening's Meditation', 'Corsica', and 'The Invitation', Jones suggests that Barbauld was most drawn to the defeated Puritan Milton of *Paradise Lost*, one rejected by many as a republican washout. Intent on realizing the politics of liberal dissent within this poem, Jones argues, Barbauld was gripped by those images of struggle and resistance in Milton's epic that granted her a religious and political poetic mode 'at once forceful and flexible'. Adelaide Morris also examines the tensions in Barbauld's poetic identity in 'Woman Speaking to Women: Retracing the Feminine in Anna Laetitia Barbauld', but turns to the often fraught question of her feminist politics (*WW* 10:i[2003] 47–72). Avoiding the notion of Barbauld as either submissive to or subversive of an established women's literary tradition, Morris seeks instead to locate her subjectivity in a Pythagorean notion of fluid gender. For Morris, this grants Barbauld a poetic voice capable of irony, clarity and vision which seeks to avoid conflict with either women or men even as it casts light on women's compromised economic status in the literary marketplace. Barbauld was thus able sensually to realize the self beyond its artificial gender definitions, a move that also allowed her access to a male hegemonic literary sphere. Mary Ellen Bellanca turns to Barbauld's relationship with Priestley in 'Science, Animal Sympathy and Anna Barbauld's "The Mouse's Petition"' (*ECS* 37:i[2003] 47–67), an essay that explores her reaction against the scientist's use of live mice in his laboratory. Barbauld, Bellanca reports, delivered her poem, 'The Mouse's Petition', in a mouse-trap to Priestley just after breakfast, humorously domesticating a subject usually confined to the workspace of science while engaging serious issues regarding the treatment of animals. The essay insightfully connects sensibility's valorization of feeling with the promotion of new beliefs that animals experience sensation and pain, and shows how Barbauld used this knowledge to highlight Priestley's betrayal of his usual commitment to fellow-feeling and benevolence.

After some critical neglect in recent years, Dorothy Wordsworth is beginning to attract serious attention once again, and Michelle Levy's 'The Wordsworths, the Greens, and the Limits of Sympathy' (*SiR* 42[2003] 541–63) is an exceptional example of this. The article opens with a discussion of the Wordsworths' negotiation with issues of poverty in relation to their efforts to help the dependents of George and Sarah Green, left orphaned after their parents were caught in a storm in Langdale Fell. Levy eloquently engages with the debate over William's sympathetic identification with the poor by historicizing his social conscience in relation to Dorothy's *Narrative Concerning George and Sarah Green of the Parish of Grasmere addressed to a Friend* [1808]. While Dorothy was an important source for William's poetry on the poor, she was also, Levy shows, an 'acute commentator on his views', questioning his reliance on voluntary action to relieve suffering and reminding him of the limits, rather than the infinite potential, of human sympathy. Patricia Comitini's '"More than half a poet": Vocational Philanthropy and Dorothy Wordsworth's Grasmere Journals' (*ERR* 14:iii[2003] 307–22) is also focused on Dorothy's literary and critical role, and suggests that her characterization as a domestic subject, novice writer, subverted genius or helpmate is one instigated by Dorothy herself. For Comitini, Dorothy's *Grasmere Journal* self-consciously constructs, and then promotes, a kind of gendered 'vocational philanthropy' in which women are encouraged to participate. This manoeuvre enabled Dorothy to inscribe herself in a superior, benevolent, middle-class role within an 'ideology of improvement' wherein she could fix the social conditions of the poor, the Wordsworth home, and William's manuscripts. Pamela Woof's 'Dorothy Wordsworth: Story-Teller' (*WC* 34:ii[2003] 103–10) is a slightly unsophisticated exploration of Dorothy's narrative technique, one Woof claims was based on an ability to 'relate what happened, to tell it how it was'. There is some useful biographical detail here, however, and the reader is granted a sense of the differences between William's and Dorothy's visions of natural phenomena as well as Dorothy's particular fascination with calamity, disaster and catastrophe.

While studies of individual poets continue to govern the field, then, an excellent special edition of *RoN* (29–30[2003]) addressing 'The Transatlantic

Poetess' serves to sharpen our perceptions and definitions of one particular kind of Romantic woman poet. As the guest editor of the collection, Laura Mandell, writes in her introduction, this group of essays seeks to ask why the term 'poetess' is so derogatory, why its associated poetry is rendered 'minor', and how the reader might think about and define a sentimental poetics ('Introduction: The Poetess Tradition'). Tracing the history of the word 'poetess' in both Britain and America, Mandell explores those emotive, shadowy and feminized undertones that have helped shape it into a style of poetry open to men as well as women. She astutely asks why the subjects of much poetess poetry, flowers for example, have not become key disciplinary objects for cultural critics or new historicists. Mandell's answer is more problematic, as she perhaps over-generalizes by suggesting that poetess poetry destabilizes Arnold's distinction between the desire for cultural and for material acquisition by 'consuming' high cultural artefacts and consequently 'celebrating' capitalism. The transatlantic nature of much poetess poetry, however, necessarily politicizes its content, as Mandell points out, and her essay concludes by leading the reader into a fine review of criticism about the poetess published during the last ten years by Peggy Davis, 'Recent Criticism of the Poetess: A Review Essay'. The body of the collection, however, opens with three fascinating essays on Hemans: Nanora Sweet's '"Under the subtle wreath": Louise Bogan, Felicia Hemans, and Petrarchan Poetics'; Jeffrey C. Robinson's 'The Poetics of Expiration: Felicia Hemans'; and Kathleen Lundeen's '"When life becomes art": on Hemans's "Image in Lava"'. Sweet begins with the declaration that the austere modernist Louise Bogan once commented that in a former life she had been 'Felicia Hemans', pointing to their shared relationship to poetry, love and fame. Both poets, Sweet argues, allude to Petrarch's formal innovations and sentimental thematics but then work to complicate them by questioning his constructions of gender and romance. Writing after Hemans, Bogan also found in her predecessor an emotional well from which to draw in a period dependent on the cerebral and masculine. It is also worth mentioning here a second article on Hemans by Sweet, '"The Inseparables": Hemans, the Brownes and the Milan Commission' (*FMLS* 39:ii[2003] 165–77). The article points out that a recently recovered travel journal by Harriet Browne makes reference to a certain 'Colonel Browne', known as the investigator of Queen Caroline in Italy who was nearly assassinated in Milan, but significant here as Hemans's brother. The recovery, Sweet argues, allows us to rethink the 'Milan commission' in the context of the Holy Alliance and British Constitution as well as its impact on the whole of the Browne family and their artistic interests.

Robinson and Lundeen sustain our interest in Hemans, insightfully and thoughtfully attending to her religious lyricism. 'The Poetics of Expiration' executes an outstanding reading of the poet's heaven-centred lyrics, grounded in a meditative 'holy contemplation' in which the poem becomes a process of 'expiration or breathing out' of what 'has been observed in the presence of a god'. Robinson contrasts this 'poetics of expiration' to the high Romantic 'poetics of effusion', one devoted to the immaterial and insubstantial, the other to the material and monumental. Hemans's ostensible 'superficiality' thus becomes a technique for imagining substance just as it threatens to disappear, a 'dying into the moment' that the poet refers to, Robinson argues, as 'holiness'. Lundeen locates an 'unorthodox theology' at the heart of Hemans's 'The Image in Lava' by arguing that the poem presents the immortal aspect of the mother and child not as an interior soul that escaped the body after death, but as an exterior form caught in the ashes of Pompeii. Hemans imbues a sentimental feeling usually associated with excess with an epistemological value by forcing the reader to confront a timeless aesthetic object that is in fact human. Katherine Montwieler rethinks feeling of a different kind in 'Laughing at Love: L.E.L. and the Embellishment of Eros', arguing that Landon forges an erotics of poetess poetry in *The Improvisatrice* into which the reader is clandestinely invited. Depicting thinly veiled pornographic scenes of indulgence in poetic sensibility, Landon, Montwieler contends, encourages readers to engage in an 'onanistic poesaphilia', an experience that reveals her heroines to be more than passive sentimental victims. Indeed, as players in an eroticism that is both 'bookish and solitary', Landon's heroines are proponents of 'safe sex', exposing the opposite alternative—relationships based on control and manipulation—through parody and masquerade. Cynthia Lawford's '"Thou shalt bid thy fair hands rove": L.E.L'.s Wooing of Sex, Pain, Death and the Editor' also focuses on Landon's poetic construction of love by granting authenticity to her heroines' expressions of desire for death. Lawford argues that her discovery regarding Landon's three illegitimate children by William Jerdan validates the fatal passion at the root of her 'early, sexually daring poems', while exposing the poet's reliance on her powerful editor's influence in the literary marketplace.

Still in *RoN* 29–30[2003], Robert Edward Mitchell's '"The soul that dreams it shares the power it feels so well": The Politics of Sympathy in the Abolitionist Verse of Williams and Yearsley' locates abolitionist poetry as a significant site for exploring how late eighteenth-century women's poetry generates sympathy. Reminding us that not all contemporary readers would have immediately identified with the representations of suffering inherent in abolitionist poetry, Mitchell shows how Yearsley and Williams promoted a successful form of reflexive sympathy that lacked the usual self-indulgent element. While both regulated the representation of pain in their poetry, Williams endeavoured to ensure that the reader would identify with the reformer rather than the slaver as Yearsley sought to lay bare the power structures that maintained slavery as an institution. Shelley King's 'Politics, Poetics and Propriety: Reviewing Amelia Opie' tracks the changing nature of Opie's critical reception, one that gradually eroded her early, radical position and recast her as a poet able to reflect, rather than analyse, the feelings of her time. King suggests that this process ensured her canonical marginalization, Victorian critics in particular reading her lyrical presentations of pathos and affect as nostalgic sentiment rather than political commentaries on class and race. In '"Formed with curious skill": Blessington's Negotiation of the "Poetess" in *Flowers of Loveliness*', Ann R. Hawkins pays close attention to Blessington's Byronic attack on the annuals, 'The Stock in Trade of the Modern Poetess', a satirical poem on writers willing to exploit poetess 'stock'. At once relying on and subverting poetess politics, Blessington reinterprets typically sentimental symbols in her poetry to achieve financial success while gently mocking those who made her rich. Her giftbook volume

Flowers of Loveliness [1835] thus presents flowers as both botanical luxuries and lushly pornographic representations of her own female readers.

Wendy Dasler Johnson's 'Reviving Lydia Huntley Sigourney' turns to the 'American Hemans' to portray how she has suffered a predictable fate—in a way that is comparable to Hemans, Sigourney has achieved both fame and censure, both praised and assailed for the maudlin lyricism of her *Moral Pieces in Prose and Verse* [1819]. Where most critics regard Sigourney as an elegist or purveyor of sentimentality, Johnson urges us to read her as a canny ventriloquist of masculine identity and commentator on female education. Annie Finch offers a reassessment of Wheatley in 'Phillis Wheatley and the Sentimental Tradition' by elevating her poetry into an originary manifesto of sentimentality. Constructing a sentimental poetry of intersubjectivity in order to discuss the politics of race and the poetics of oppression, Wheatley works to create a lyric that is rhetorically public even as it allows for a pre-Romantic, sentimental engagement with private emotions such as grief. Patrick H. Vincent's 'Lucretia Davidson in Europe: Female Elegy, Literary Transmission and the Figure of the Romantic Poetess' stays on the subject of grief by exploring the culturally constructed figure of Davidson, who died aged only 16. Reading elegies to Davidson by Robert Southey, Edgar Allen Poe, Marceline Desbordes-Valmore and Karolina Pavlova, Vincent suggests that a problematic ethic of self-sacrifice sits at the heart of the poetess tradition, one that ignores the individuality of the writer to promote a generalized, interchangeable poetess subjectivity. English translations of Desbordes-Valmore's and Pavlova's memorials are usefully reproduced in appendices at the end of the article, indicating these poets' attempts to forge a community of women writers in which the consuming despair of loss might be redressed. Aimée Boutin's accomplished essay, 'Inventing the "Poétesse": New Approaches to French Women Romantic Poets', closes Mandell's collection by opening the poetess debate into the realms of French Romanticism. Boutin confirms the untenable nature of Anne Mellor's distinction between the poetess and female poet by focusing on the grammatically uncertain *poétesse*, a word that embraces meanings connoting both domesticity and social engagement. For example, while Desbordes-Valmore's *Les Pleurs*, *Pauvres fleurs* and *Bouquets et prières* capitalize on conventionally feminine and sentimental themes, they do so in order simultaneously to address public ones such as patriotism and gender codes. Readings of poems by Christine Planté, Amable Tastu, Delphine Gay, Elisa Mercoeur, Louise Colet and Anaïs Ségalas are placed next to diatribes against them by Gaschon de Molènes and Charles Labitte, offering the reader a captivating introduction to a newly developing area of Romantic women's poetry.

Other articles in the field this year include Frank Felsenstein's 'Ann Yearsley and the Politics of Patronage: The Thorp Arch Archive: Part II', an updated discussion of his exploration of Yearsley outlined in the previous *YWES* (*TSWL* 22:i[2003] 13–56), and Ann R. Hawkins's 'Marguerite, Countess of Blessington, and L.E.L.: Evidence of a Friendship' (*ANQ* 16:ii[2003] 27–32). For Hawkins, the dynamic friendship that existed between Blessington and Landon is an important example of the close involvement of nineteenth-century women writers in each other's professional lives. She tracks their relationship through their successive editorships of *Heath's Book of Beauty*, as well as Blessington's role in securing Landon's lucrative editorship of *Fisher's Drawing Room Scrapbook*. The article closes with a reading of Blessington's novel *Victims of Society* [1837], portraying a female heroine under siege from polite London society, an experience with which the sometimes provocative Landon was familiar. As Hawkins argues, this resonance suggests that Blessington understood and sympathized with the difficulties Landon was forced to confront as a woman in the public eye and that 'this understanding translated to an impetus for Blessington's own art'. Kevin Gilmartin's '"Study to be quiet": Hannah More and the Invention of Conservative Culture in Britain' (*ELH* 70:ii[2003] 493–540) turns readers away from More's often discussed work to focus on *History of Tom White the Postilion* [1795] and its sequel, *The Way to Plenty*. Gilmartin argues that *Tom White* provides a 'map' of More's reactionary fiction, typifying her anti-revolutionary fiction in its heterogeneous narrative form (against the dialogue of *Village Politics*) and situated sense of rural virtue. This foundation allows More to construct a moral parable of fall and redemption that serves to give precedence to allegory over social realism and, for Gilmartin, suggests that her object was not the social texture of village life but rather 'the ideological work done upon it by fiction'. Finally, Anne Hartman's 'Doing Things with Poems: Performativity and Cultural Form' (*VP* 41:iv[2003] 481–90) focuses on Hemans's 'Our Daily Paths' to render it a 'performative poem', a text which is understood in terms of the roles and discourses it stages. Written in response to the Common Sense philosopher Dugald Stewart, and headed by a quotation from *Tintern Abbey*, Hemans's poem, Hartman argues, interprets its cultural sources while creating a new cultural experience of this very authority.

4. William Blake

The year 2003 saw a considerable number of books and articles published on Blake. As with previous years, a comprehensive list of publications is included in G.E. Bentley Jr., 'William Blake and his Circle: A Checklist of Publications and Discoveries in 2003' (*Blake* 37:i[2004] 4–35.

Several substantial works of scholarship and criticism in Blake studies came out this year, the first of which, Morton D. Paley's *The Traveller in the Evening: The Last Works of William Blake*, concentrates on those texts (such as *The Ghost of Abel* and Blake's illustrations to Thornton's edition of Virgil's *Pastorals*) that are often neglected. Paley begins his book with the sound proposition that Blake's system was never fixed, and that the last works (which he defines as those begun after the printing of *Jerusalem* or, more accurately, after meeting John Linnell in 1818) saw Blake largely abandoning the complex personal mythology he had developed between the early prophetic books of the 1790s and his final epic, *Jerusalem*.

These late works, then, demonstrate Blake's experimentation with alternative theological and philosophical systems such as Gnosticism. Paley's subsequent chapters on texts such as the Virgil and 'יה and his Two Sons' provide some superb background to these works and will set the scholarly standard for their future discussion. His detailed readings are exhaustive, although—and this is particularly the case with the discussion of the Virgil woodcuts—the overall argument can be overwhelmed by a mass of detail. The chapter on יה (Jah), however, contains marvellous details on the genesis and contexts of this strange engraving that, as Paley observes, 'has given editors of Blake's works some special problems' (p. 89).

Paley turns next to Dante's *Divine Comedy*, the reputation of which, he argues, was beginning to emerge from a low point in its reception during the eighteenth century when Blake began his illustrations. Blake, of course, had been interested in the Dante legend since the 1780s when he produced sketches of Count Ugolino and his sons. With his illustrations of the *Comedy*, however, he was critical of Dante's attempt to yoke together the classical and biblical, the natural and spiritual (a common theme of the later works, points out Paley), yet approached his subject with zest, 'not as a subject for a systematic artistic interpretation but as providing a series of targets of opportunity for visual representation' (p. 172). The final chapter of *Traveller in the Evening* deals with a series of interpretations of the Bible, including *The Everlasting Gospel, The Ghost of Abel*, and the illustrations to *The Book of Job*, all of which demonstrate Blake's belief in the Old and New Testaments as the 'Great Code of Art'. As with the preceding sections of the book, Paley offers a scholarly account of some texts (such as the preliminary drawings to the book of Enoch) which are rarely considered in Blake studies.

The second text on Blake, Joyce H. Townsend, ed., *William Blake: The Painter at Work*, is a collection of essays covering Blake's artistic practices from colour printing to tempura painting. Written mainly by curators and conservationists at Tate Britain, the authors provide a detailed analysis of Blake's practice and the contexts of his art, returning attention to that element of the artist's production that tends to be neglected in favour of engraving and writing. In her introduction, Townsend remarks on the contradictions implicit in Blake's training (which tended towards careful, small-scale work appropriate to engraving) and his ambitions to produce larger, more painterly frescoes.

There is a small section on Blake's engraving techniques, but the majority of the book is devoted to colour printing, watercolours and tempura painting. Unsurprisingly, considering the team of authors, *The Painter at Work* is outstanding on the technical details of Blake's paintings, not merely in terms of their original production but also their conservation, appearance and presentation today. Chapters include discussions of all Blake's major series of paintings, including the biblical tempuras produced for Thomas Butts, and one-off commissions such as *Epitome of James Hervey's 'Meditations among the Tombs'*, as well as the more famous large colour prints on display at Tate Britain. If there is any criticism of this beautifully illustrated and extremely well-presented book, it is perhaps of the paucity of guidance as to current interpretation of the significance of these images. Yet even this is not really a weakness: while such interpretation will always be subject to critical fashions, *The Painter at Work* will long remain an invaluable technical manual for anyone concerned with Blake's visual practice, covering everything from the chemical composition of pigments at the time to the effect of gallery lighting in modern museums. This, of course, is standard fare far anyone studying a painter, but is a useful reminder to the literary academic of the often peculiar nature of the Blakean text.

An important contribution to the historical contexts of those texts is Saree Makdisi's *William Blake and the Impossible History of the 1790s*, in which Makdisi sets out to provide an account of the ways in which Blake's illuminated books explore this 'impossible history', reconsidering them as cultural moments in a history that, as E.P. Thompson points out, requires rewriting. This is not just the history of revolution, but also of modernity itself. Makdisi is right to point out that Blake is often conscripted to a modernity of individual rights to which (in its liberal form) he was often opposed. This is excellently demonstrated in the first chapter on *America* which Makdisi reads as a critique of the bourgeois enlightenment of Washington, Franklin and even Paine. Much of the material is familiar here, particularly from Linebaugh and Rediker's *The Many Headed Hydra*, yet their reappraisal of the appropriation of radical revolt by the newly emergent middle classes was written in 2000, so that even if Makdisi does reiterate some of their basic points, such as the fact that Blake is often critical of the American War of Independence, to do so in 2003 is brave and thoughtful. The critique of a post-Lockean political orthodoxy amongst enlightened radicals is extended to philosophies of the body that combine new historicist contexts with a Foucauldian reading of power and a subtle (or slight) appeal to Deleuzian notions of organization. Tristanne Connolly's *William Blake and the Body* is, not surprisingly, more comprehensive on the subject of Blake's corporeal forms, but Makdisi has some very impressive points to make on the disciplining of the body as a subject of the industrial factory system, often itself celebrated by liberal radicals. Blake, suggests Makdisi, is a privileged observer of this system because 'the art of engraving was in [his] time being transformed by precisely the same principles of production efficiency and the division of labour that were already animating the early factory' (p. 147). The next chapter, on the commodification of the image, is less impressive—drawing on features of the 'new bibliography' that, post-Viscomi, has become so important to Blake studies. Yet Makdisi's discussion of such factors as repetition in the illuminated books which, ironically, frees the reader from 'the determinism of those texts that pretend to be closed and definite' (p. 169) is vague and not a little tedious. He makes good use of Eaves and McGann, but this section of *The Impossible History* is more difficult going. Not surprisingly for the author of *Romantic Imperialism*, chapter 5 on 'Blake and Romantic Imperialism' is an extremely interesting account of Orientalism which draws on the earlier book. The main criticism is that, for a substantial part of the chapter, Makdisi has remarkably little to say about Blake: his comments on Wollstonecraft, Wordsworth and other Romantics are scholarly and thoughtful, but this means that discussion of Blake's most resolutely Oriental text—*The Song of Los*—is far too cursory, particularly as he has many pertinent points to make, for example about 'Blake's tendency to de-exoticize as much as possible... images of otherness' (p. 252), something that Anne Mellor has seen as an indication of Blake's imperialist mentality, but which Makdisi views in a more positive light.

Another interesting work, though not as significant a contribution as the three titles listed above, is John B. Pierce's *The Wond'rous Art: William Blake and Writing*, an attempt to combine post-structuralist readings of Blake's texts with new bibliographical studies into the variant copies of those texts, to offer a grammatological study of writing in a tradition that (he claims) extends back to the late seventeenth century. There are some flaws in the book—using Derrida to destabilize the apocalyptic model offered by Frye and Bloom is itself hardly new, particularly for those who were first introduced to Blake studies in the 1980s, and Pierce points out the important work done by Hilton, Vogler and Damrosch in this area. Nonetheless, Pierce's observation that Blake is being recovered as a prophet of *écriture* via publications such as the Tate Illuminated Blake and the online Blake Archive is a useful one. He is also concerned with the ways in which Blake engages with writing not simply as process but also as illumination via rereading of the past: 'Keeping in mind that Blake is an interpreter of Milton, the Bible, Bunyan, a host of others and also of himself, we can see that his work evinces this dual experience [of simultaneous writing and interpretation]' (p. 14).

The 'wond'rous art' is a phrase from *Jerusalem* that Pierce interprets as referring to the 'two principal functions—mediation and communication' offered by writing (p. 38). In an initial contextual and theoretical section on these 'scenes of writing', we see the ways in which writing could be seen as mediating the divine or, by contrast, as an entirely human and rationalistic progression of civilization that was ultimately democratic and demystifying. These theoretical and contextual chapters of *The Wond'rous Art*, are followed by a section on narrative in which Pierce attempts to outline how tensions operate in narrative between a move towards cohesive completeness and individual elements that disrupt or decay that closure. What we have, then, is a 'torn book', the sacred text deliberately violated as befits the Bible of Hell.

The final part, 'Re-Writing', uses this idea to produce some of Pierce's most sophisticated readings with particular regard to *The Four Zoas* and *Milton* (though, surprisingly, not *Jerusalem*). The problem of studying the manuscript of *Vala or The Four Zoas* is familiar territory, being in part a return to his arguments around narrative experiment in *Flexible Design: Revisionary Poetics in William Blake's Vala or The Four Zoas* [1998]. Central to this argument is an extended application of Foucault's notion of archaeology, mediated through De Quincey's description of the palimpsest in *Suspiria de Profundis* and Derrida's reading of Freud's Mystic Writing Pad. *The Wond'rous Art* concludes by returning to a detail from *The Marriage of Heaven and Hell* where a devil dictates to scribes, part of what Pierce calls 'the Infernal Scriptorium'. The devil dictating as part of this scriptorium, engaged in argument, is intrinsically dialogic rather than monologic: Pierce's comments that he wishes to emphasize this social aspect of writing so as not to detach a theory of writing from historical and social concerns 'as some strands of American deconstruction have appeared to do' (p. 156) are, unfortunately, too little too late. Nonetheless, his attempt to recuperate a theory of Blake's writing from mechanical repetition is a worthy one, and *The Wond'rous Art* provides illumination into some of the minute particulars of Blake's writing.

Other monographs on Blake may be dealt with more briefly. David Weir's *Brahma in the West: William Blake and the Oriental Renaissance*, is a potentially very useful contextualization of Blake's relationship to Oriental (and especially Hindu) religion that is undermined by sometimes rather vague aspirations to combine Hinduism, Hebrew traditions and Neoplatonism into an inspiration for Blake's work. Of course, one can detect this tendency in Blake, and it was certainly a feature of writers such as Joseph Priestley (whose *Comparison of the Institutions of Moses with those of the Hindoos* is dealt with by Weir), but it is also important to recognize that Blake held to the primacy of the Bible, particularly towards the end of his life. Thus, for example, Weir's excellent discussion of the ways in which work by William Jones and others into the antiquity of Vedic texts was challenging the authority of the Hebrew Bible is undermined by the fact that, in *The Descriptive Catalogue* where the most extensive discussion of Hindu religion is be found, Blake inverts this relationship to offer his everlasting gospel as the original for both Greek and Oriental pagan mythologies. *Brahma in the West* contains much good work, especially for those seeking an introduction to the Indic texts available to British writers in the Romantic period, but some of its argument is diluted by the fact that Blake's Orientalism (like that of Edward Said) often stopped at the Middle East.

A very different model of Blake is offered in Nick Rawlinson's *William Blake's Comic Vision*. Despite the Cockney humour of *The Marriage of Heaven and Hell* (as well as occasional pieces such as his attacks on one of Hayley's favourite poets, Klopstock), Blake's humour has rarely been a subject of investigation by writers, and Rawlinson's book is the first full-length study of the various models he employed. Part of the reason for this, suggests Rawlinson, is that Blake critics themselves do not take comedy seriously, but the more innovative argument of this book is to make the case that the comic provides a perfect vehicle for visionary perception, not merely because it mixes the sublime and grotesque but because it is also a removal from the world of the polite. Rawlinson provides several definitions of comedy and the comic (satire, jokes, the carnivalesque), concluding that, while comic vision may begin with debasement and degradation, its ultimate aim is participation in a greater sense of unity. While it is hard to agree entirely with this idealism, Rawlinson's discussion of the different comic modes in Blake's work is generally well done; he does not neglect the contemporary satire of printmakers such as Rowlandson and Gillray, a rich source for Blake's own work which also provided plenty of examples of 'mirth at errors of a foe', but also notes that, although Blake can be (nearly) as satirical as any eighteenth-century artist or writer, he was also very conscious of the limitations of the form.

Peter A. Schock's *Romantic Satanism* (also discussed in Section 2 above) deals, obviously, with the diabolical myths of the two later Romantics as well as Blake, but is good fun as well as being a sophisticated examination of the Satanic trope during the Romantic period. Very significantly, Schock delineates the progression of this trope throughout Blake's works, away from the post-Enlightenment revolutionary devil of *The Marriage of Heaven and Hell* (which Schock reads as a detailed critique of the Johnson circle that Blake was involved with at the beginning of the 1790s) to the more strongly Christian—and in many ways even more revolutionary—attack on Satan as 'the God of this world' in *The Four Zoas*, *Milton* and *Jerusalem*. Schock combines close readings of these texts with a theoretically astute view that is in many ways similar to Pierce's, but less weighed down by the jargon. As he remarks, 'whatever claims are made about the largely esthetic implications of the work of Los and subordination of Orc's revolutionary energy [with regard to those critics who see Blake as adopting a largely apolitical stance in the nineteenth century], Blake's transactions with Satanic myth in the major prophecies confirm that Blake never abandoned his strong pre-Millennial interest in sudden change' (p. 77).

'Four Mighty Ones Are in Every Man': The Development of the Fourfold in Blake is the doctoral dissertation of Dóra Janzer Csikós, and comprises a psychological study of *The Four Zoas*. In many respects, especially as it deals with Freudian and Jungian interpretations of the text, much of this is familiar from the work of writers such as Kerrison Preston and Diana Hume George. There is, however, a discussion of Blake in relation to the depth psychology of Lipót Szondi, which was at least new to me, and which does offer a new perspective on such psychoanalytical studies of Blake's work as an example of the 'analysis of vicissitudes—or simply: fate analysis (commonly known as *Schicksalsanalysis*)' (p. 43). In common with most such studies, Csikós tends to be far too schematic in plotting the Zoas on to specific character types (Steve Clarke's essay on Blake and Locke in *Blake in the Nineties*, for example, is just one of several recent studies to suggest that rigid demarcations between Los and Urizen are problematic), but there is a good summary of critical work on *The Four Zoas*. Derek Pearsall's *William Langland, William Blake, and the Poetry of Hope* is a slender, charming and insubstantial pamphlet on the two writers. Too impressionistic to really offer much insight to the reader (his final assessment of two poets as 'pushed to the margins of the literary canon' (p.18), is simply no longer true, at least for this reader), the book does not attempt any explanation as to Blake's reception of Langland—they merely 'have, for me, come to seem extraordinarily alike' (p. 1). This is not necessarily a problem: using Blake as a lens to read Langland, particularly via the influence of seventeenth-century radicals such as Bunyan, could be an illuminating exercise but *The Poetry of Hope* ultimately does not inspire.

Finally, with regard to book-length studies, Eaves, ed., *The Cambridge Companion to William Blake*, is a new addition to the extensive series of Cambridge Companions to Literature, and this text, with perhaps a couple of exceptions, is an excellent introduction to the study of Blake for the general student. The book is divided into two parts: the first, 'Perspectives', deals with contexts surrounding Blake's life and work, while the second, 'Works', deals with the illuminated books. Aileen Ward's 'William Blake and his Circle' begins the *Companion* with a fair account of Blake's life, though it does not engage with some recent scholarly work on the subject, such as that undertaken by Keri Davies; in addition—and this applies to most of the chapters—recommendations for further reading tend to be a little skimpy. Joseph Viscomi's chapter on the techniques of illuminated printing is a very good summary of the important research he has conducted in texts such as *William Blake and the Idea of The Book* [1993], while David Bindman provides a succinct yet comprehensive outline of Blake's work as a painter and the contexts of British art during the Georgian period. Susan Wolfson does a good job of dealing with the metrical elements of Blake's poetic language, drawing on Hilton, Vogler and Mitchell in particular (though she does not really deal with Angela Esterhammer's discussion of the performative element of Blake's poetry). Saree Makdisi's 'The Political Aesthetic of Blake's Images' is a version of the chapter that appears in *Impossible*

History, while Jon Mee and David Simpson provide useful accounts of Blake's political ideas and relationship to Romanticism respectively. The only essay that falls a little flat is Robert Ryan's 'Blake and Religion', which is vague compared to work on the subcultures of millenarian religions of the 1790s and early 1800s done in recent years. The second, shorter, part of the *Companion* includes contributions by Nelson Hilton (on the early works), Andrew Lincoln (on the prophetic books of the 1790s), Mary Lynn Johnson (on *Milton*), and Robert Essick (on *Jerusalem* and the final works). With a useful glossary and brief bibliography provided by Alexander Gourlay, this final section provides a decent summary of current Blake studies and, as with most of the volumes in the series, will be particularly helpful to undergraduate students or those seeking to brush up on Blake.

Of essays published in *Blake: An Illustrated Quarterly*, the first for 2003 was, as is usual, Robert Essick's round-up of Blakeana in the marketplace for 2002 (*Blake* 36[2003] 116–36). This, as Essick remarks, was meant to be 'the year of *The Grave*', the auction of the original watercolours to Blair's *The Grave*: unfortunately, the book dealer who had valued the watercolours had not been entirely open in his own purchase, and sale of the paintings became entangled in legal proceedings. Despite this rather sorry tale, Essick did note that other Blake drawings (such as a monochrome wash of *The Resurrection*) were commanding high prices. This issue of *Blake* also included a note on 'Erdman's Pagination of *The Four Zoas*' (*Blake* 36[2003] 140–3), renumbering some pages in David Erdman's and Cettina Magno's 1987 facsimile edition of the text, as well as a fascinating snippet on Haydn's notation of the composition of Psalm 100, which was sung by the London charity school children at St Paul's, as depicted in Blake's 'Holy Thursday' poems (*Blake* 36[2003] 137–9).

Blake 37:i[2004] includes Bentley's publication list, as noted above, and two more 'Minute Particulars'. In 'Muir's Facsimiles and the Missing *Visions*' (*Blake* 37[2004] 32–4), David Duff discusses the William Muir facsimile held at the University of Aberdeen, which is particularly interesting as it includes an extra plate showing a detail from 'The Ancient of Days'. Duff proposes that this (or a similar) facsimile is the actual source of the supposed missing Copy Q of *Visions of the Daughters of Albion*. Alexander Gourlay's '"Man on a Drinking Horse": A Print by Thomas Butts, Jr.' (*Blake* 37[2004] 35–6) details the fairly minor print executed by Blake's pupil.

More substantial pieces are to be found in issue ii, with a discussion of 'Encyclopaedic Resistance: Blake, Rees's *Cyclopædia* and the *Laocoön* Separate Plate' by Rosamund Paice (*Blake* 37[2004] 44–62), and Sheila Spector's 'Blake's Graphic Use of Hebrew' (*Blake* 37[2004] 63–79). Paice's article is, in many ways, a complementary text to Morton D. Paley's *Traveller in the Evening*, dealing in this case with the relationship between Blake's separate plate and the engravings he produced for Rees's commercial project, especially the role that Flaxman played in authoring the *Cyclopædia* article on sculpture. Paice offers a compelling (and rather poignant) view of Blake struggling against the tedium and cost-cutting involved in pursuing the 'uninspired copywork' he was meant to produce for the *Cyclopædia*, turning to his own subversive interpretation of the *Laocoön* sculpture in revenge. Sheila Spector's article is a development of some of the ideas developed in her earlier two volumes on Blake and kabbalah, *Glorious Incomprehensible* and *Wonders Divine* [2001]. Noting that 'Hebrew was clearly not a major element of Blake's graphics' (p. 63), she does offer an interesting insight into Blake's experiments with the visual possibilities of the language, for example in *Tiriel Denouncing his Sons and Daughters* or the idiosyncratic *Study of Hebrew Characters in Human Form*, observing that 'it is less a matter of *what* the words mean than *how* the letters signify within the total context of a particular picture or plate' (p. 78).

The final issue of *Blake* for 2003 includes an extended discussion of nine 'Newly Uncovered Blake Drawings in the British Museum' (*Blake* 37[2004] 84–100) by Robert Essick and Rosamund Paice. The drawings, discovered while Essick, Joseph Viscomi and Morris Eaves were shooting transparencies of Blake's works in the Department of Prints and Drawings in the British Museum, are represented as a series of incidental sketches performed by Blake at early stages in his career. As the authors remark, 'None of the sketches presented here will enhance Blake's reputation as an artist' (p. 84), but they are all related to other projects that the artist was engaged on and can be seen as indicating how various designs and iconography evolved. Two 'Minute Particulars': '"Friendship", Love and Sympathy in Blake's *Grave* Illustrations' by Alexander Gourlay (*Blake* 37[2004] 100–4) offers some provisional interpretations (and titles) of the newly discovered drawings to Blair's *The Grave*, while 'A Dutch Bibliophile Edition of *The Marriage of Heaven and Hell* [1928]' by Oskar Wellens (*Blake* 37[2004] 104–7) considers the publication of a limited edition of *The Marriage* produced for the collector's market, indicating the international interest that Blake was starting to attract in the earlier part of the twentieth century.

Of other articles published during 2003, one of the most interesting is Ted Holt's 'Blake's "Elohim" and the Hutchinsonian Fire: Anti-Utopianism and Christian Hebraism in the Work of William Blake' (*Romanticism* 9[2003] 20–36). This is a useful companion piece to Spector's discussion of Blake's graphic use of Hebrew, but contains evidence that Blake was influenced by the Christian Hebraist John Hutchinson, who offered a fascinating anti-Newtonian cosmology that would have been particularly appealing to Blake. A more extensive, if somewhat less focused, discussion of Blake's anti-Newtonian position is the subject of Wai Chee Dimock's 'Nonbiological Clock: Literary History against Newtonian Mechanics' (*SAQ* 102[2003] 153–77), which concentrates on *Milton* and the illustrations to Dante which enable him 'to score a point against Newton and against a nation unified behind Newton' (p. 168). To complete the trilogy of cosmology-inspired papers, David Baulch's 'Time, Narrative, and the Multiverse: Post-Newtonian Narrative in Borges's "The Garden of the Forking Paths" and Blake's *Vala or the Four Zoas*' (*Comparatist* 27[2003] 56–78) offers an entertaining application of quantum mechanics to these two texts. I am always slightly suspicious of the discovery of such theoretical applications when applied retrospectively to such texts (Holt and Dimock concentrate much more on the strong historical contexts of Blake's work), and the notion that Blake somehow discovered Einsteinian cosmology a century before Einstein (implicit in phrases such as 'Blake's proleptically

Einsteinian depiction of a space-time continuum') is simply false. Nonetheless, this is a delightfully thought-provoking example of the ways in which contemporary readings can revitalize our interpretation of Blake.

Two articles in volume 3 of *Angles on the English Speaking World* deal with Blake. The first, by Robert Rix, 'William Blake and the Prophetic Marketplace' (*Angles* 3[2003] 47–61), makes the important, if fairly obvious, point that Blake's apocalyptic imagination needs to be contextualized according to publication trends of the 1790s. Rix has done some excellent work in terms of new historicist readings of Blake, but this particular article, while drawing attention to some original research into texts such as Isaac Eaton's *Extermination, or an Appeal to the People of England on the Present War with France* [1794], feels more cursory. Lene Østermark-Johansen's 'Victorian Angles on Blake: Reading the Artist's Head in the Late Nineteenth Century' (*Angles* 3[2003] 141–64) is a more original piece, examining some of the ways in which representations of Blake (including his life mask and self-portraits) were seized upon by Victorian artists as an interpretative emblem of the artist, using the genre of portraiture to 'suggest this parallel between the image and the life' (p. 146).

Jon Saklofske's 'A Fly in the Ointment: Exploring the Creative Relationship between William Blake and Thomas Gray' (*WI* 19[2003] 166–79) is a straightforward reading of Blake's illustrations to Gray, emphasizing the similarities between the two artists. It does not necessarily offer much that is new to this discussion, but is a useful reminder of how Blake was influenced by much more conventional writings of the eighteenth century. A more innovative piece is Jason Snart's 'Recentering Blake's Marginalia' (*HLQ* 66[2003] 235–53), although such innovation perhaps makes this piece less genuinely useful to the general reader of Blake, dealing as it does with questions of authorship in Blake's annotations to Lavater's *Aphorisms*. Nonetheless, discussion of textual and material issues in those annotations (part of the subject of Snart's Ph.D. thesis) does offer an alternative focus for bibliographical discussion.

'Space, the Body, and the Text in *The Marriage of Heaven and Hell*' by Eynel Ward (*OrbisLit* 58[2003] 253–70) is a wide-ranging phenomenological study of Blake's visionary habitations of space that draws particularly on Merleau-Ponty and Derrida. The article is perhaps a little too vague to offer much of an advance on De Luca's 'A Wall of Words: The Sublime as Text' ([1986], cited by Ward), or a number of texts that deal with the Blakean sublime. Another discussion of space, Bryan Nudelman's 'Spaces of Transformation: Liminality and William Blake's *America: A Prophecy*' (*LJHum* 28[2003] 33–46), could have offered a potentially much more interesting account of space derived from postmodern and post-structuralist theorists of space (such as those of Virilio and de Certeau), but ends up, like Ward's article, somewhat vague. I was intrigued by the appeals to Gadamer and Spariosu at the end, but this was too little too late.

Finally, 2003 saw a great deal of activity on the William Blake Archive (www.blakearchive.org), beginning with the publication of an electronic edition of *Jerusalem*, Copy E, the most magnificent coloured version of Blake's most ambitious prophecy. This was followed by publication of *The* [*First*] *Book of Urizen*, Copy B, the illustrations to Blair's *The Grave* and a version of the chapter on illuminated printing from the *Cambridge Companion*, the main difference being that this edition is illustrated with ninety-five images from the archive. With these additions, particularly a complete version of the colour-printed *Jerusalem*, the William Blake Archive continues to grow into the most important single resource for Blake scholars world-wide.

5. Prose Fiction

The year's work on Romantic fiction continued to challenge and question boundaries, between cultures, readers, genders, and nations. 2003 was marked by particularly strong writing on women authors, and on questions of nationhood, often, as in some excellent discussions of Wollstonecraft, Edgeworth and Sydney Owenson, intricately connected. Scott attracted a good deal of attention, particularly on this issue of national identity; so too did Mary Shelley, although much of this writing revisited classic feminist readings of creativity and reproduction.

Two provocative and lively studies of women writers, both of which worried at the boundaries of the canon, and of criticism, provide us with a good starting point. Adriana Craciun's *Fatal Women of Romanticism* engages with the figure of the 'femme fatale', tracing its importance in the development of Romantic women's writing identities, and placing it in the context of both contemporary and modern feminist debate on the body and sexuality. Particularly of note for this fiction section are her chapters on Mary Lamb and Charlotte Dacre. Craciun evokes Mary Lamb not only as a literal figure of violence, but also, interestingly, as a seriously considered fiction writer, whose literary representations of excluded or absent mothers, as in her children's story 'Elizabeth Villiers; or the Sailor Uncle', may prompt us to 'revise our assumptions about women, violence, and language' (p. 24). In distinct contrast to Sarah Burton's reading of Mary Lamb in *A Double Life*, which, although it minutely details her murderous act and mental illness, pays scant attention to her authorial identity, Craciun fiercely argues for the *writerly* 'possibilities of a female subject of violence', something she sees as often overlooked by modern feminist criticism. Similarly, her discussion of Charlotte Dacre focuses on her 'doctrine of destruction', which Craciun reads as 'strikingly similar to Sade's' (p. 115). The erotic charge of Dacre's descriptions of violence in *The Passions* and *Zofloya* may be read alongside Mary Lamb's family violence: both startlingly 'challenge the notion of a "woman's tradition"' (p. 155), as Craciun herself attempts to do.

The representation of women in the Romantic period was also addressed by Julie Kipp, in her excellent, richly contextualized study, *Romanticism, Maternity, and the Body Politic*: the chapters of particular note for this section are those on Wollstonecraft, Edgeworth and Scott. The mother–child bond, argues Kipp, 'served many writers of the period as a natural marker of the often conflicting interests of the one and the many, the local and the universal' (p. 18). Like Craciun, she is interested by the absences or silences of criticism regarding this point: although the maternal trope in Wollstonecraft's *The Wrongs of Woman, or, Maria* has often been recognized, Kipp argues that the 'more horrific or sublime aspects' of maternity in her work have largely been ignored (p. 77). She suggestively explores these often violent depictions of maternal physicality in the context of Wollstonecraft's concern over the ways in which radical politics or ideologies may be internalized by women. A reading of Jemima's pregnancy, for example, which ends in suffering and abortion, is usefully set alongside Wollstonecraft's views of France, and the way in which its revolutionary ideals are aborted, because conceived in violence. Maternity thus becomes a 'vehicle through which to examine the interpersonal relations governing political bodies' (p. 85); it may also be used, as in Edgeworth's novels, to express doubts over national, as well as political, identity. Kipp focuses particularly on *Ennui*, where the figure of the lower-class Irish wet-nurse, Ellinor O'Donoghoe, allows Edgeworth to question, with a vivid immediacy, the 'material dynamics of power relations in Ireland' (p. 98). These complicated, ambivalent readings of maternity and the body politic also run through *The Heart of Midlothian*, in which, as Kipp persuasively shows, 'Scotland's story is itself a tale of murderous motherhood' (p. 124).

New work on Wollstonecraft's fiction echoed this engagement with issues of female identity and representation. Barbara Taylor's study, *Mary Wollstonecraft and the Feminist Imagination*, sensitively places her fiction in the context of her 'radical imagination' (p. 4), a term, Taylor explains, which refers both to Wollstonecraft's creative consciousness and her intellectual, religious, and political thinking, and also to her often unconscious fantasies and desires. This becomes particularly apposite in her reading of *Maria*, where she unpacks the connections to *A Vindication*, and shows how the novel makes Wollstonecraft's philosophical ideas 'explosively plain', while simultaneously using 'romance as a vehicle to explore the ambiguous role of fantasy in feminine experience' (p. 232). Taylor sees *Maria*, in its appreciation of the 'wrongs of different classes of woman', as moving towards future possibilities for feminism. She see this consciousness of class difference, coupled with the woman/slave analogies running throughout the novel, as courageously, optimistically, offering 'a prefigurative outline of feminist constituencies to come', a 'diverse sorority' (p. 240) which she traces through later feminist readings of Wollstonecraft. Taylor's argument, propelled by her own fast-moving, vigorous prose style, is forceful and spirited. It is interesting to read it alongside Diane Long Hoeveler's 'The Tyranny of Sentimental Form: Wollstonecraft's *Mary* and the Gendering of Anxiety' (*ECN* 3[2003] 217–41), which similarly reads the two novellas as dramatizations of Wollstonecraft's philosophical arguments. However, she takes a more pessimistic view of their outcome, arguing that they put forward a 'form of special pleading', a 'gothic feminism' which fosters feelings of passivity: 'She succeeded in creating a powerful trope—female victimization—but she only half-glimpsed the way out'. In part, for Hoeveler, this is a problem of genre: Wollstonecraft 'still clung to the vestiges of an outmoded Sentimental tradition' (p. 236), but she also sees Wollstonecraft's victimization trope as continuing to exert a dangerous power over subsequent feminist readings. Gloria Schultz Eastman, 'Method to this Madness: Fragmented Discourse in Mary Wollstonecraft's Maria' (in Troost, ed., *Eighteenth-Century Women*, pp. 295–316), also linked ideas of oppression with genre, but her reading of Maria saw the novel's contradictory impulses in a positive light, suggesting that it affords 'a polyphonic clash of perspectives' (p. 296), as it moves between different kinds of discourse and location. Arguing that its fragmentary structure points to liberating 'open-ended possibilities' (p. 296), she suggests that Wollstonecraft's rejection of generic containment is central to her rejection of literal confinement or oppression.

Ideas of genre were similarly questioned in Ryall and Sandbach-Dahlström, eds., *Mary Wollstonecraft's Journey to Scandinavia: Essays*. Building on the work of Mitzi Myers, Mary Poovey, and Mary Favret, this collection reads Wollstonecraft's *Letters Written During a Short Residence in Sweden, Norway, and Denmark* [1796] variously as travel narrative, aesthetic enquiry, and autobiography. Essays by Anka Ryall and Martin Aberg place this reading of her own identity in the context of national representations; Ingrid Kuczynski's contribution, '"Only by the Eye": Visual Perception in Women's Travel Writing in the 1790s', sets Wollstonecraft alongside travel narratives by Hester Lynch Piozzi and Ann Radcliffe to explore the empowerment of the female observer. Similarly, Anne Scott Sorensen, in '"Losing My Breath through my Eyes": Mary Wollstonecraft and the Picturesque', reads her narrative through the framework of contemporary aesthetics of the picturesque, again emphasizing the importance of the visual. Perhaps the most striking essay is John Whale's 'Death in the Face of Nature Itself: Society and Body in Wollstonecraft's *Letters*', which explores, in the context of Rousseau and Kant, the 'complex process of self-definition' (p. 203) going on in the text. Whale emphasizes the generic plurality of the *Letters*, which echoes the conditions under which they were written, 'out of a mixed motive of commerce and romance' (p. 188) and, in a wider sense, questions the nature of the individual.

The intersection between theory and text also informed a lucid and thorough essay by David Collings, 'The Romance of the Impossible: William Godwin in the Empty Place of Reason' (*ELH* 70[2003] 847–74). Mirroring Taylor and Hoeveler in their treatment of Wollstonecraft, Collings sets *Caleb Williams* and *St Leon* alongside Godwin's philosophy, tracing their interconnected patterns of imagery and allusion, and showing how Godwin's narratives explored and tested his ethics. Elsewhere, Julie Carlson read Godwin's history, in his *Life of Chaucer* and *Essay on Sepulchres*, as romance, alongside Wollstonecraft's *The Cave of Fancy: A Tale*, and Mary Shelley's *The Fields of Fancy*. 'Fancy's History' (*ERR* 14[2003] 163–76) places family writing relationships alongside the 'romance revival' of Romanticism to build up a picture of influence across chronological and genre boundaries.

There was plenty of good writing on Scott this year, most of it struggling with questions of nationhood and historical representation. Catherine Jones, in a welcome full-length study, *Literary Memory: Scott's Waverley Novels and the Psychology of Narrative*, sets the novels in a specific, carefully contextualized and historicized philosophical perspective, challenging previous studies such as Alexander Welsh's ahistorically Freudian perspective on the Waverley novels. She seeks to show how Scott's concept of 'literary memory' was formed by both the epistemological arguments of the Scottish Enlightenment, filtered through his eloquent and influential teacher Dugald Stewart, and what she terms the 'folk memory' of ballads, songs and tales passed on by oral tradition. Jones begins by reading Scott's memoirs as a way of understanding this fusion of the philosophical and the folk, a dual inheritance which 'brings together contrasting registers of history, culture and tradition' (p. 23). She then shows how these different registers shape the Waverley novels themselves, which present variants of 'literary memory', testing its boundaries and limits. Thus she provides insightful new readings of, for example, *The Heart of Midlothian* in terms of 'associative memory', and *Saint Ronan's Well* as an example of 'fragmentary memory'. Scott's readings of memory are then set into perspective by her closing survey of later readings of Scott, in the works of Washington Irving, James Fenimore Cooper and Nathaniel Hawthorne, which place Scottish literary memory into a new framework. This wide-ranging book is not only a refreshing new consideration of Scott's works; it also usefully reflects on the relationship of reading, writing, and remembering throughout the nineteenth century.

Three essays in the *Scottish Studies Review* also offered historicized readings of Scott. Stefan Thomas Hall, in 'Awkward Silences in Scott's *Waverley*' (*SSR* 4[2003] 82–97), attempts to voice Scott's unspoken meanings, showing how instances of conversational silence mirror greater narrative absences, such as the battle of Culloden. This technique, he argues, forms part of a larger argument, as Scott points, albeit idealistically, to the soon to be silenced Highland culture. Joan Garden Cooper, in 'Scott's Critique of the English Treason Law in *Waverley*' (*SSR* 4[2003] 17–36), similarly presents Scott as an 'advocate for Scottish national identity', suggesting that his presentation of the insurrection against King George II demonstrates his strong 'belief that English law should not be superimposed onto Scotland' (p. 33). Andrew Lincoln, in 'The Mercenary, the Savage, and the Civilized War: Scott and *A Legend of the Wars of Montrose*' (*SSR* 4[2003] 37–47), also argues for a more complex reading of Scott, appropriately urging us to recognize the ways in which he 'both confronts and reproduces the double thinking that runs through contemporary attitudes to war'. Pointing to the ambiguities and contradictions of the supposedly civilized figure Menteith in *Montrose*, he demonstrates how Scott's narrative works to identify and undermine the persistent desire to humanize the conduct of war.

Similarly, Mike Goode, in 'Dryasdust Antiquarianism and Soppy Masculinity: The Waverley Novels and the Gender of History' (*Rep* 82[2003] 52–86), shows how Scott 'interrogates the cultural legitimacy of various modes through which individuals know the past and live with that knowledge'. Focusing on *The Antiquary*, Goode reads the novel through '"the idea of history" as it develops in Romantic-era Britain' (p. 78), showing how Scott recognizes, and defends, both history and antiquarianism as gendered pursuits. Yoon Sun Lee, in 'Time, Money, Sanctuary, and Sociality in Scott's *The Fortunes of Nigel*' (*ERR* 14[2003] 233–8), also examines the construction of history. Exploring the novel's interwoven images of 'telling'—the telling of time, of money, of fortunes and of stories—Lee uses them to argue, persuasively, that the novel offers 'new configurations of nation, time and sociality' (p. 234). And this attention to national history was echoed by Claire Lamont's 'Scott and Eighteenth-Century Imperialism: India and the Scottish Highlands' (in D'Haen, Liebregts, and Tigges, eds., *Configuring Romanticism: Essays offered to C.C. Barfoot*, pp. 35–51), which focuses on Scott's neglected story 'The Surgeon's Daughter', worth remembering if only for the gruesome end of its villain, ceremoniously crushed beneath an elephant's foot. The Indian setting allows Lamont to set two differing contested spaces alongside one another, and emphasize the way in which 'the imperial story in Scott is fraught with paradoxes' (p. 50).

This movement was echoed by Elizabeth S. Kim, one of several writers on Edgeworth this year, in 'Maria Edgeworth's "The Grateful Negro": A Site for Rewriting Rebellion' (*ECF* 16[2003] 103–26). Like Lamont, she places this little-known story of 1802, dealing with slave rebellion on a plantation, alongside *Belinda*, teasing out parallels between the two colonized spaces of Jamaica and Ireland. If there is, on occasion, a smack of contemporary self-righteousness about Kim's condemnation of Edgeworth's failure to 'question the colonialist system itself, both its existence and moral soundness' (p. 106) this is outweighed by her painstaking readings of the texts themselves, to uncover Edgeworth's 'idealized system of colonizer–colonized relations' (p. 107). Meanwhile, in 'The Bosom of the Bourgeoisie: Edgeworth's *Belinda*' (*ELH* 70[2003] 575–96), Jordana Rosenberg offers a sidelong perspective on class relations. Through close attention to the novel's attitude to wit, she concludes that its aim is not to demonstrate the superiority of Belinda's domestic ethos over the aristocratic debauchery of Lady Delacour, but a more subtle demystification of wit itself.

Like Rosenberg, David Thame, in 'Madness and Therapy in Maria Edgeworth's *Belinda*: Deceived by Appearances' (*BJECS* 26[2003] 271–88), also focused on Edgeworth's manipulation of genre, and the distinction between surface and reality in the novel. However, Thame challenges Rosenberg's assertion that no character in the novel can see clearly: for him, 'recognition of the falsity of surface is essential to moral and mental health' in *Belinda* (p. 272), and also in wider society. Edgeworth's lucid social commentary, in his convincing reading, works to redeem the genre of fiction itself, particularly fiction by and for women, from its previous associations of falsity or irrationality.

Martha Adams Bohrer adopts a pleasingly original approach to these questions of genre in her article 'Tales of Locale: The Natural History of Selborne and Castle Rackrent' (*MP* 100[2003] 393–416), arguing that Edgeworth and Gilbert White both focus on particular environments to create 'tales of locale', which generate 'new, comprehensive, systemic socioeconomic representations of rural places as habitats and locales' (p. 395). Edgeworth's interest in natural history is traced through her association with the Lunar Society, and both she and White are shown to have a methodical approach to observation, using 'scientific form to legitimate provincial knowledge' (p. 404). This allows Edgeworth to portray Irish identity in a new way, focusing not on existing ethical or religious affiliations, but instead on its vivid diversity.

Questions of national and class allegiance were also tackled by Susanne Hagemann in 'Tales of a Nation: Territorial Pragmatism in Elizabeth Grant, Maria Edgeworth, and Sydney Owenson' (*IUR* 33[2003] 263–78). Using Grant's diaries as a way into thinking about representations of Ireland in *Ormond* and *The Wild Irish Girl*, she addresses the way in which the contradictions and conflicts of Irish society may be paralleled by the instability of identity. Edgeworth and Owenson were also paired by Fraser Easton in his article, 'Cosmopolitical Economy: Exchangeable Value and National Development in

Adam Smith and Maria Edgeworth' (*SiR* 42[2003] 99–125). Like Yoon Sun Lee on Scott, Easton notices the importance of the *Wealth of Nations* to a consideration of nationhood, arguing that Smith's ideas 'served as a distinct locus for the theorization of domestic politics and social relations by those writing after 1776' (p. 101). For Edgeworth, as for Owenson, references to Smith allow them to 'defend national character within a cosmopolitical frame of reference' (p. 115), and he interestingly explores the tensions to which this gives rise.

Mary Robinson was represented this year by two useful new Broadview critical editions: *Walsingham*, edited by Julie A. Shaffer, and *The Natural Daughter*, paired with *A Letter to the Women of England* in an edition by Sharon M. Setzer. Shaffer's helpful introductory essay to *Walsingham* unpacks the novel's 'allusive density' (p. 29), and explores Robinson's own exhibitionism, and the wide variety of roles, fictional and performative, she constructed for herself. Setzer, whose edition usefully includes contemporary reviews and excerpts from the *Morning Post*, reads the novel alongside Wollstonecraft to emphasize its status as ideological enquiry.

Meanwhile, an essay by Toby Ruth Benis, '"A likely story": Charlotte Smith's Revolutionary Narratives' (*ERR* 14[2003] 291–306), argued for an understanding of the integral importance of revolution to Smith's novels: in particular, suggests Benis, *The Banished Man*, with its narrative 'privileging of memoranda and fragments', points to wider political instabilities.

Other, lesser-known, women received welcome attention: Andrew Monnickendam's edition of *Clan-Albin: A National Tale* by Christian Isobel Johnstone made this startlingly 'argumentative novel' (p. vi), with its challenging views of nationalism, readily available. Two online issues of *Cardiff Corvey: Reading the Romantic Text* also drew attention to forgotten women writers. First, Michael Page examined 'Mary Meeke's *Something Strange*: The Development of the Novel and the Possibilities of the Imagination', (*Corvey* 11[2003] http://www.cf.ac.uk/encap/corvey/articles/cc11_n01.html). Page's article, though at times prolix, nevertheless valuably questions the neglect of Mary Meeke's popular novels. In the same issue, Franz Potter, in 'Writing for the Spectre of Poverty: Exhuming Sarah Wilkinson's Bluebooks and Novels' (*Corvey* 11[2003] http://www.cf.ac.uk/encap/corvey/articles/cc11_n02.html), again pushed at canonical boundaries, encouraging rereadings of Wilkinson, not least for the insights she affords into the position of women trying to live by the pen. Lisa Hopkins, in her contribution to issue 10, 'Jane C. Loudon's *The Mummy!* Mary Shelley Meets George Orwell, and They Go in a Balloon to Egypt' (*Corvey* 10[2003] http://www.cf.ac.uk/encap/corvey/articles/ cc10_n01.html) not only offers a thoughtful reading of Loudon's novel itself, but also places it in the context of the contemporary reception of *Frankenstein*, suggesting that it forms a 'sensational but ultimately pious corrective to the pessimism and atheism of Mary Shelley'.

Mary Shelley herself had a bumper year. She was finally given her own *Cambridge Companion*, edited by Esther Schor, an attempt to offset the way in which she is so often represented on the undergraduate syllabus by one text alone, and to reconsider her as a figure who moved through upheaval and change 'to produce an oeuvre of bracing intelligence and wide cultural sweep' (p. 2). Schor's introductory words could, indeed, stand for the *Companion* itself, packed with lively and insightful essays from a wide range of perspectives. Anne Mellor's opening essay examines Percy Shelley's revisions and rewritings of *Frankenstein*, and Shelley's own 1831 changes, as a prelude to the different readings offered within the *Companion*. Pamela Clemit works backwards to explore Shelley's own readings of Godwin and Wollstonecraft, and this insight into Shelley's inheritance, familial and intellectual, is nicely answered by Diane Long Hoeveler, who traces the impact of the novel on subsequent feminist studies. Strong essays by Schor and Jay Clayton discuss the novel's cinematic legacy, from James Whale to Spielberg's *AI*. Some of the most exciting aspects of recent Shelley scholarship emerge in the closing sections of the *Companion*. Here Stuart Curran reconsiders the 'radical force' of *Valperga*, Kate Ferguson Ellis rereads *Falkner* as a culmination of Shelley's social critique, and Kari Lokke and Deidre Lynch both offer insights into Shelley's historicism in, respectively, *The Last Man* and *Perkin Warbeck*. Her dramas, *Proserpine* and *Midas*, her letters, and travel writing are all given serious consideration. We glimpse the extent, and the labour, of Shelley's professional writing, as Charlotte Sussman urges us to reconsider her contributions to *The Keepsake* seriously, Susan Wolfson points to her thorough work as an editor, and Greg Kucich, aided by the new Pickering editions, outlines her work as a biographer for Lardner. Tim Morton's closing essay sums up the aims of the *Companion*: Mary Shelley, he argues, should be read both as a contributor to culture at large, in its many varied forms, and as an active cultural critic.

Two good new critical editions of *Frankenstein*, edited by Susan Wolfson and Judith Wilt, provided useful tools for teaching. Wilt's edition, *Making Humans*, pairs the 1818 text of *Frankenstein* with *The Island of Dr. Moreau*, in the context of writing by Darwin, Huxley and Tennyson and reprinted essays from modern critics such as Marilyn Butler and Coral Lansbury. Wolfson's edition, with a particularly stimulating introduction, places the 1818 version in conversation with a wide range of different texts, from Godwin and Wollstonecraft to Dr Spock. *Frankenstein* was also well served by a special edition of the *Romantic Circles Praxis Series*, edited by Jerrold E. Hogle (http://www.rc.umd.edu/praxis/frankenstein/index.html), *Frankenstein's Dream*. This again emphasized the importance of placing the text in dialogue with cultural preoccupations, taking as its focus the hallucinatory sleep into which Victor Frankenstein falls after seeing his creature take its first breaths: in the words of Hogle, this dream, and its subsequent readings, prompt us to 'confront the most basic ways in which Western self-representation has occurred over the last several centuries'. Anne Williams's contribution '"Mummy, possest": Sadism and Sensibility in Shelley's *Frankenstein*', argues that the complexity of Shelley's narrative techniques points to the 'unspeakable anxiety' aroused by the ambiguous 'mummy' figure glimpsed by Frankenstein as he awakes, at once deathly and maternal. This gendered anxiety is also examined in John Rieder's contribution, 'Patriarchal Fantasy and the Fecal Child in Mary Shelley's *Frankenstein* and its Adaptations', a Lacanian reading of traumatic awakenings in the novel. Matthew VanWinkle's essay, 'Mocking Stupendous Mechanisms: Romantic Parody and Frankenstein's Dream', argues against this creative anxiety, attempting to show how Shelley's allusive humour points us towards a non-antagonistic reading of parody in the Romantic era. Although his claim that 'Shelley dispenses a … blend of shudders and chuckles' is strangely off-putting, VanWinkle's is a thoughtful insight into reading practices. All the essays in the collection pay attention to revisions and filmic reanimations of the novel, and Marc Redfield, '*Frankenstein*'s Cinematic Dream', explicitly analyses Whale's *Frankenstein* alongside Shelley's in terms of 'technological manipulation'. Redfield's essay is at times over-written—'Victor is on speed, hooked on and keyed to the temporality of technics'—but may usefully be read alongside the contributions of Schor and Clayton to the *Mary Shelley Companion*.

Three other readings of *Frankenstein* variously considered issues of creativity. Susan Eilenberg's imaginative chapter in Griffin, ed., *Faces of Anonymity*, 'Nothing's Namelessness: Mary Shelley's *Frankenstein*', used its anonymous 1818 publication as a way into considering Shelley's conception of authorial identity, invoking instances of superstition or confusion over names within the text and within the Shelley circle itself. Jonathan Padley, '*Frankenstein* and (Sublime) Creation' (*Romanticism* 9[2003] 196–212), adopted a keenly contemporary viewpoint, examining Shelley's transgressive creativity not only in terms of the sublime, but also alongside debate on genetic manipulation and modification, and Gunther von Hagens's *Body World* exhibition. The issue of creative responsibility was similarly insisted upon by Harriet Hustis in 'Responsible Creativity and the "Modernity" of Mary Shelley's Prometheus' (*SEL* 43[2003] 845–58). Hustis reads Shelley's creative variations on the Prometheus myth alongside a recent study of the psychological effects of unwanted pregnancy. However, in her care to delineate existing critical arguments, from Bloom to Poovey to Mellor, Hustis does not go far enough with her own: no strikingly new readings emerge.

Two readings of *Mathilda* attempted to argue against such psychobiological interpretations. Lauren Gillingham, in 'Romancing Experience: The Seduction of Mary Shelley's *Mathilda*' (*SiR* 42[2003] 251–69), challenging what she calls the repeated 'biographical collapse of author into her text' (p. 252), argued for a new consideration of issues of genre and narrative form in the novel. She was joined by Robert Ready, who in 'Dominion of Demeter: Mary Shelley's *Mathilda*' (*KSJ* 52[2003] 94–110) traced the Proserpine trope within the novel, making a claim, like Gillingham, for Shelley's literary, allusive power. Meanwhile, *The Last Man* attracted a scrupulous historical contextualization by Charlotte Sussman. In '"Islanded in the World": Cultural Memory and Mobility in *The Last Man*' (*PMLA* 118[2003] 286–301) Sussman reads the novel's issues of nation and population through the lens of debates about emigration in the first three decades of the nineteenth century, affording a new perspective on the fragility of identity—national, cultural and literary—within the novel.

6. Non-Fictional Prose

Two major efforts of editorial scholarship this year require to be noted in the area of Romantic non-fictional prose. First, the magisterial edition of Thomas De Quincey's *Works* (general editor Grevel Lindop), earlier noted in *YWES* 81[2002] and 82[2003], has finally (and remarkably quickly, for an edition of this scope) reached completion with volumes 10, 11, 15, 16, and 19–21. These include articles from *Tait's Edinburgh Magazine* and *Blackwood's Edinburgh Magazine* as well as a number of lesser-known journals from 1834 onwards until his last years, as well as his longest unified work, the *Autobiographic Sketches*, which has never been properly presented after De Quincey's own collective edition, *Selections Grave and Gay*. The recovery of accurate texts (distorted in many cases by De Quincey's Victorian editors) with manuscript collations, backed up with an excellent critical apparatus, including detailed introductions, headnotes, and textual and explanatory notes, renders this a major work of scholarship which will undoubtedly define the study of De Quincey in the future. The twenty-first volume contains the index, which seemed, however, disappointingly prone to omissions—in particular recurrent items are patchily covered and the assiduous researches of the explanatory notes are partly lost by inadequate indexing—an unfortunate conclusion to an otherwise massively impressive achievement. Secondly, also from Pickering & Chatto, another work of immense scholarly significance is the *Selected Writings of Leigh Hunt* (general editors Robert Morrison and Michael Eberle-Sinatra). Hunt's authority in the critical scene and his wide-ranging literary efforts (including of course his celebrated essays), have never been properly or comprehensively presented in a critical edition, and this path-breaking collection gives us a comprehensive and representative selection of Hunt's works, collected from their scattered publication across the literary journals that he shaped and edited so influentially in his day. As with the De Quincey edition, the volumes are excellently annotated with fresh and diligent contextual scholarship including introductory material and explanatory notes, making this another landmark edition that is bound to generate a major reassessment of Hunt and his journalistic context. The heartening sight of these meticulously edited volumes of De Quincey and Hunt—both writers so influentially and substantially involved in the literary culture of the day—augurs well for continuing scholarship in the arena of Romantic prose.

Appropriately enough, the emergence of the De Quincey edition has been accompanied by critical scholarship on the opium-eater elsewhere. De Quincey's relation to the empirical tradition is discriminatingly treated by Deanne Westbrook in her article 'Deciphering Oracle: De Quincey's Textual Epistemology' (*WC* 34[2003] 158–71), the first of several engagements we will notice this year between Romantic prose and philosophy. Ranging through De Quincey's vast oeuvre, Westbrook argues persuasively that De Quincey's epistemology emerges through the involutions of his labyrinthine prose as a combination 'not only of empiricism and idealism, but also of aesthetics, rhetoric, metaphysics, and psychology' (p. 169). De Quincey's uneasy and shifting relationship with philosophies from associationism to German idealism, and his invocation of the 'uncanny' and the sublime alongside the familiar and familial subjects of his autobiographical writings, place his work in a dense matrix of influences which challenges interpretative attempts to categorize him philosophically. A more materialist approach to De Quincey is suggested by Daniel O'Quinn in his essay 'Who Owns What: Slavery, Property and Eschatological Compensation in Thomas De Quincey's Opium Writings' (*TSLL* 45[2003] 262–92). Locating De Quincey's subjection as an opium addict—'the accursed chain which fettered' him, as he described it in the *Confessions*—in the context of autobiographical discourses of slavery such as Equiano's *The Interesting Narrative*, O'Quinn suggests that both writers respond in comparable ways to the problem of commodification as experienced in early Romantic culture. De Quincey's confessional writings are examined in relation to his later journalism on the issue of 'West Indian Property', in which he argued against the emancipation of West Indian slaves on the grounds of the sacredness of property (which they constituted in their own bodies). De Quincey's predicament as an autobiographer and metaphysician in the 'Savannah-La-Mar' section of his *Suspiria de Profundis*—that he is unable to lay hold of the present which vanishes 'into a mote of a mote' on account of the infinite divisibility of time—is resolved by the 'Dark Interpreter' who, as O'Quinn argues, reveals the conversion of 'the human present into the property of God' (p. 285). This convenient (and, it may be noted, typically conservative) relegation of property rights to God, in conjunction with De Quincey's racial ideology, results, in O'Quinn's view, in a 'perverse twist' whereby 'having the Dark Interpreter make this argument on the unpresentability of the present is tantamount to making the slave argue against immediate manumission in favour of eschatological emancipation' (p. 286).

The continuity between political and rhetorical strategies is further examined in a couple of rewarding essays on Edmund Burke's theatricality and politics. In 'Spectacular History and the Politics of Theater: Sympathetic Arts in the Shadow of the Bastille' (*PMLA* 118[2003] 1305–19), Elizabeth D. Samet locates the Paine–Burke debate on the theatricality of the French Revolution in a longer eighteenth-century debate inaugurated by Bernard Mandeville and Rousseau on the relationship between sympathy and action. Paine's later incarceration at the hands of the Jacobins provided an ironic enactment in real life of his own argument, as he struggled ineffectually to dramatize his plight for American audiences in order to spur them into action to secure his release. In 'Burke, Boredom, and the Theater of Counterrevolution' (*PMLA* 118[2003] 224–38), Anne Mallory reflects on Burke's *Reflections on the Revolution in France* as an emanation of his ineffectuality and boredom, following on from his unsuccessful impeachment of Warren Hastings. Here 'boredom' is notably an emergent eighteenth-century conception 'characterized by free-floating dissatisfaction and a restless craving for excitement' (p. 225). Burke's characterization of the French as restless and prone to revolution is contrasted with his antithetical vision of England as a utopian economic and political order in which the affections of people are always engaged. Mallory argues that Burke's analysis of the revolution and his sense of theatricality may be seen to emerge from his aesthetic understanding of the sublime and beautiful as appropriate alternatives to 'indolence and inaction', thus positioning the *Reflections* as a hinge between his earlier and later writings, rather than tendentiously reading an incipient conservatism into his earlier works as critics have hitherto tended to do.

While Dorothy Wordsworth's prose is covered this year in Section 3 above, it is worth noting one significant article here, Patricia Comitini's 'More Than Half a Poet: Vocational Philanthropy and Dorothy Wordsworth's *Grasmere Journals*' (*ERR* 14[2003] 307–22). Comitini rewardingly reads the journals as an instance of 'vocational philanthropy', which she defines as 'a special calling to women to "love mankind"'. As she argues, reading them in the context of evangelical influences such as Hannah More and William Wilberforce, it is not the activity of benevolence that we are asked to contemplate but 'the value assigned to the activity as a reified labor of love' that is the true focus of Dorothy Wordsworth's regulatory endeavours.

Following the completion of the editorial project of publishing Coleridge's *Marginalia* in five volumes, a new field of editorial research seems to have opened itself with the marginalia of non-canonical writers claiming critical attention. If the male canonical writers could merit careful textual study right down to the level of their marginalia, why not their non-canonical sisters and brothers? Since such detailed editorial work in the case of Coleridge has indeed brought a degree of complexity and detail of signal importance to scholarship, it behoves us to follow this up with similar work on the hitherto marginalized non-canonical writers. The De Quincey edition, discussed above, includes his marginalia in volume 21, and Bruce Graver similarly offers a study (appropriately enough) of 'Lucy Aikin's Marginalia to *Biographia Literaria*' (*ERR* 14[2003] 323–43) as she recorded these in Sara Coleridge's 1847 edition of the *Biographia*. Aikin's apparently unfavourable attitude to Wordsworth as reported by Crabb Robinson in 1851 is tempered by a far more complex attitude to the poet, as her comments on Coleridge's treatment of Wordsworth in the *Biographia* show. While Aikin had little patience with the transcendental and 'mystical' aspects of Wordsworth's poetry, she found him greatly rewarding as a poet for children, and was favourably receptive to his later, and more neoclassical, poetry as well. With the publication and study of the non-canonical writers' marginal (and other 'ephemeral') writings, a new area of study appears to be opening up in the area of Romantic non-fictional prose.

The sole monograph for review this year is Tim Milnes's ambitious, complex and engaging study, *Knowledge and Indifference in English Romantic Prose*, examining the relationship of Romantic prose writers to the problem of knowledge in the aftermath of Hume's scepticist challenge to philosophy through his strict separation between statements of truth which were epistemic and those of value which were not. This separation clearly provided a challenge to any philosophy which wished to retain a place for statements of value within the epistemic order. Milnes reads Wordsworth, Coleridge and Hazlitt as responding to this challenge in ambivalent and anxious ways, with various consequences for the development of their aesthetic theories and creative writings. After an introduction exposing the deceptive nature of the indifference—or 'indifferentism' as Kant called it in his *Critique of Pure Reason*—displayed by several of the Romantic prose writers to this problem, Milnes's first chapter deals with the legacy of eighteenth-century empiricism for the English Romantics, suggesting that, as the eighteenth century struggled to reconcile its epistemology with an emerging creationist aesthetic, poetry progressively took on the task of communicating 'aspects of experience that philosophy now refused to carry' (p. 68), such as the moments of insight and communion with nature typical of the high Romantic mode. Milnes's second chapter focuses on Wordsworth's critical prose from 1800 to 1815, showing that his earlier empiricist leanings (endeavouring, as he put it in 1800, 'to look steadily at my subject') yielded in time to a greater insistence on the creative powers of the mind and of poetic transcendence, though without entirely letting go of his earlier empiricist epistemology: a discord that reveals itself in an indifference to the problem. As Milnes puts it, Wordsworth 'oscillates between the perspectives of epistemology and indifference, and then again between an indifference that would bring knowledge into a dialectic with being, and an indifference that would *write* it out of existence' (p. 104).

Hazlitt's traditional reputation as a thoroughgoing empiricist among the Romantics has been strongly challenged of late, and Milnes usefully extends this revisionist line in his exposure of Hazlitt's Janus-faced attitude to empiricism throughout his writings. Chapter 3 accordingly probes Hazlitt's philosophical inconsistencies as an aspect of the vexed relationship he bore to empiricism. Although the generalizing nature of abstraction is evidently opposed to the particularizing nature of originality, the two are collapsed within Hazlitt's thinking, a stress fracture that, as Milnes argues, 'represents the predicament of Hazlitt's epistemology in general: there is nothing to determine what degree of power counts as knowledge other than power itself' (p. 142). Two following chapters confront the damaged archangel of Romantic criticism, S.T. Coleridge, who, inspired by the 'giant's hand' of Kant, as Milnes argues, turned from poetry to prose in order to attempt a complete reorientation of philosophy, 'steering it between the Scylla and Charybdis of skeptical empiricism and speculative metaphysics, towards an attempt to understand the *a priori* foundations of experience itself' (p. 145). Coleridge's attempts to found his principles of poetry on the central notions of will and reason exposed him, however, to the regressive nature of such foundations and resulted in the famous failure of his transcendental deduction in the *Biographia Literaria*. Coleridge's later works, from *The Friend* [1818] to *Aids to Reflection* [1825], continue his efforts to harmonize philosophy with religion in a manner that would, as he wrote in the *Philosophical Lectures*, allow philosophy to see 'religion as its end and supplement'. Here Coleridge's foundational epistemology comes into conflict with his Christian insistence on an 'invisible' nature, leaving him in a predicament which may be seen as inevitable, and indeed foreshadowing the confrontations with foundationalism in the work of modern philosophers such as Wittgenstein, Kuhn and Quine. The English Romantics, in this thoughtful study, do not emerge as post-structuralists, delighting playfully in their dilemma, but as troubled and ambivalent thinkers whose apparent indifference concealed a deeper anxiety at the heart of their creative work and critical thought. Milnes's argument, however, is clearly in the high Romantic mode and seems not to engage with the non-canonical Romantics, particularly the women writers, who have now been restored to serious consideration in the period, and whose notions of creativity may have differed notably from their canonical (male) counterparts.

Another significant contribution to the field of non-fictional prose appears in Uttara Natarajan's article 'The Veil of Familiarity: Romantic Philosophy and the Familiar Essay' (*SiR* 42[2003] 27–44; also noticed above) which places the familiar essays of figures such as Hazlitt, Lamb, and Hunt in the philosophical framework of Romantic idealism along with the poetry from which it has been traditionally separated. Against the polarity assumed between

German idealism and British empiricism Natarajan usefully recovers a less antagonistic arena for prose literature of the period, namely British idealism: the recognition, theorized by S.T. Coleridge and Percy Shelley among others, of the ideal as veiled by the familiar—a prose version of the idealist aesthetic long accorded to the Romantic poets. A surprising—and perhaps rather debatable—exception is De Quincey (traditionally placed along with Hazlitt and Lamb) whose work Natarajan places generically in the realm of the autobiographical as opposed to the familiar. In seeking to restore the familiar essay to the arena of Romantic aesthetics Natarajan is wise not to overload her subject with dense theoretical readings of the essays; it has perhaps been their lightness of touch that has paradoxically resulted in the critical marginalization of the Romantic essayists, even if they have always retained a discriminating readership based on pleasure. A final article on the topic of the Romantic familiar essay is Karen Fang's 'Empire, Coleridge, and Charles Lamb's Consumer Imagination' (*SEL* 43[2003] 815–43), which focuses on Lamb's essay on 'Old China' as an entry into a submerged arena of consumerist and imperial awareness in Lamb's work, deriving no doubt from Lamb's own service for the East India Company alongside his journalistic career. This awareness extends into the Elian persona created for the *London Magazine*, which was founded, as Fang reminds us, at the start of 'a new era of optimistic economic expansion' (p. 834). In this richly rewarding context, 'Old China' emerges not as a quaint and unworldly piece dictated by Romantic genius but more appropriately as 'literary chinoiserie for an age shaped by the new imperial industry' (p. 837).

7. Drama

With the publication of Cox and Gamer, eds., *The Broadview Anthology of Romantic Drama*, we finally have the classroom resource necessary for drama to become a regular part of the Romantic literature curriculum. Cox and Gamer's substantive introduction situates the texts in the material conditions of the London playhouses to overcome the division between the 'literary' and the 'theatrical' and showcase the breadth of Romantic dramatic output. Any anthology necessarily determines which plays will become part of the classroom canon; the choice for Baillie, for instance—*Orra*—ensures that it will continue to be one of her most widely read plays, as *De Monfort*, now available in at least three modern paperback editions, has become. The collection leads off with two late eighteenth-century social comedies—Hannah Cowley's *A Bold Stroke for a Husband* and Elizabeth Inchbald's *Every One Has His Fault*—that do not fit neatly into a traditionally Romantic 'mental theatre' category but introduce the era's drama as popular and socially engaged. Percy Shelley and Byron are represented by *The Cenci* and *Sardanapalus*, and Coleridge's *Remorse* appears in its first inexpensive edition. Rounding out the assemblage are stage hits: George Colman the Younger's *Blue-Beard* and *The Quadrupeds of Quedlinburgh*, Matthew Lewis's *Timour the Tartar*, and Thomas John Dibdin's pantomime *Harlequin and Humpo*. While we could quibble over individual inclusions, Cox and Gamer have given us an excellent one-volume introduction to the rich diversity of Romantic drama. Their apparatus also includes an appendix containing contemporary reviews and a glossary of the actors and actresses who starred in these plays.

Innovations in Romantic drama scholarship (and that of the nineteenth century in general) have made clear the need to revise the practice of theatre historiography. Jacky Bratton's *New Readings in Theatre History* will be an important text in this undertaking. It is included in this review for Bratton's excellent critique of the 'grand narrative' of dramatic history established in the 1830s which discounted earlier historiography and began the custom of denigrating the drama of the Romantic era. Using case studies of nineteenth-century theatre Bratton works to theorize and rehistoricize the discipline of theatre history.

European Romantic Review (14[2003]) devoted an issue to 'Romantic Drama: Origins, Permutations, and Legacies'. Framing the collection of articles are Diane Long Hoeveler's introduction, '"Humanizing the Heart", or Romantic Drama and the Civilizing Process' (*ERR* 14[2003] 1–6), which presents the stage—and the series of articles—as a venue for airing conflicts between public and private life, and Alex Dick's 'Romantic Drama and the Performative: A Reassessment' (*ERR* 14[2003] 97–116), which challenges scholars to critically examine our use of the term 'performative' as an ideal for imagined social action that implies an agency beyond theatrical production, a notion he tests in a reading of *Manfred*. The remaining articles in the special edition continue the current scholarly practice (demonstrated in Cox and Gamer's Broadview anthology discussed above) of intermingling analyses of popular and closet drama. Catherine B. Burroughs's 'British Women Playwrights and the Staging of Female Sexual Initiation: Sophia Lee's *The Chapter of Accidents* [1780]' (*ERR* 14[2003] 7–16) examines how Lee's play exercises fantasies of sexual initiation and hymen-restoration and controversially allowed its deflowered heroine to be rewarded rather than suffer. Daniel O'Quinn's 'Hannah Cowley's *A Day in Turkey* and the Political Efficacy of Charles James Fox' (*ERR* 14 [2003] 17–30) is a very interesting study which argues that Cowley's Orientalist play—set during the Russo-Turkish war—dramatizes the famous conflict between Fox and Burke and offers a critique of both Fox's politics and the sexual undercurrents of governance itself. Aileen Forbes, in '"Sympathetic Curiosity" in Joanna Baillie's Theater of the Passions' (*ERR* 14[2003] 31–48), makes a persuasive argument that it is the *performativity* of passion, the 'act of making passion visible' (p. 45) that is considered more authentic than the internal feeling of passion.

Hoeveler is represented again in this issue with 'The Temple of Morality: Thomas Holcroft and the Swerve of Melodrama' (*ERR* 14[2003] 49–64), in which she argues that when Holcroft revised French melodramas for the London stage he caused the genre to swerve towards a Jacobin positioning of the female servant character as moral arbiter in bourgeois society. Edwin Block Jr.'s 'Heinrich von Kleist: "On the Puppet Theater", *The Broken Jug*, and Tensions in the Romantic Theatrical Paradigm' (*ERR* 14[2003] 65–80) reads Kleist's essay and play as illustrating an Enlightenment Romanticism, a tension between Idealism and scientistic rationality. Marjean Purinton's theory of the Techno-Gothic is further developed in 'Staging the Physical: Romantic Science

Theatricalized in T.L. Beddoes's *The Bride's Tragedy*' (*ERR* 14[2003] 81–96) through analysis of how Beddoes positions his audience as anatomist/physician viewing an operating theatre. The issue concludes with Thomas C. Crochunis and Michael Eberle-Sinatra's 'Putting Plays (and More) in Cyberspace: An Overview of the *British Women Playwrights around 1800* Project' (*ERR* 14[2003] 117–32), which explains that the aim of the website is to provide an alternative venue for collective historiographical work. To illustrate this work they present two case studies: a hypermedia archive of Baillie's *De Monfort* and a virtual conference on Hemans's *The Vespers of Palermo*.

Thomas Lovell Beddoes's Jacobean-style tragedy *Death's Jest-Book* is enjoying a comeback, with two editions published this year. Michael Bradshaw's edition (Routledge), based on Beddoes's original text from 1829, is accompanied by an introduction which situates the play and Beddoes within current discourses on gender and queer studies. By contrast, Alan Halsey's edition for the Thomas Lovell Beddoes Society (West House Books) presents Beddoes's revised version (the γ text, edited by H.W. Donner in 1935), along with a more traditional introduction that focuses on thematic issues of death.

Death's Jest-Book allows us another text through which to see the Romantic interest in Jacobean revenge tragedy, which we have been analysing for years in *The Cenci*, a perennially popular work. In an interesting new reading that engages recent scholarship on author–audience relationships, Eric Eisner's '*The Cenci*'s Celebrity' (*Prism(s)* 11[2003] 7–36) argues that the play, which Shelley wrote in hopes of finding fame, contains within itself a reflection on the idea and ethics of celebrity, as Shelley associates himself with Beatrice's mystery and charisma. Stephen Hancock also sees Shelley identifying himself with Beatrice Cenci, in '"Shelley himself in petticoats": Joanna Baillie's *Orra* and Non-Violent Masculinity as Remorse in *The Cenci*' (*RoN* 31[2003]). Hancock's essay seeks to demonstrate Baillie's influence on Shelley: both plays enact violence on women and attempt to create effective non-violence through a passive femininity, though Shelley finds that this strategy fails and that he must masculinize Beatrice and have her enact an unavoidable violence.

As witnessed in Aileen Forbes's article reviewed above, scholars have been establishing Baillie's relationship to other moral philosophers, particularly Adam Smith. Julie Murray's 'Governing Economic Man: Joanna Baillie's Theatre of Utility' (*ELH* 70[2003] 1043–65) argues that *Plays on the Passions* confront and contest the 'psychodynamics of spectatorship' (p. 1043) in Smith's *Theory of Moral Sentiments*, and that *De Monfort* is a critique of a seamless 'Smithean sociability' that reveals the rupture between surface appearance and internal reality. In a similar move, Linda Brigham's 'Aristocratic Monstrosity and Sublime Femininity in *De Monfort*' (*SEL* 43[2003] 701–18) presents Baillie as a theorist of emotions, and compares her *Introductory Discourse* and *De Monfort* with Edmund Burke's theories of the oppositional sublime and beautiful, arguing that Jane De Monfort (especially as played by Sarah Siddons) is complexly both beautiful *and* sublime. Inadvertently neglected in earlier *YWES* were Julie Anderson's 'Spectacular Spectators: Regendering the Male Gaze in Delariviere Manley's *The Royal Mischief* and Joanna Baillie's *Orra*' (*Encult* 3[2001] http://enculturation.gmu.edu/3_2/anderson/index.html), and Deidre Gilbert's 'Joanna Baillie, Passionate Anatomist: *Basil* and its Masquerade' (*RECTR* 16[2001] 42–54), which reveal ways in which Baillie's plays redirect the gaze of male characters and spectators. Finally, demonstrating the range of views on Baillie's work, George E. Haggerty, with 'Psychodrama: Hypertheatricality and Sexual Excess on the Gothic Stage' (*TRI* 28[2003] 20–33), categorizes Baillie's *De Monfort* as Gothic sensationalism alongside Lewis's *The Castle Spectre*, both of which use excessive sexuality to 'expose cracks in normative masculinity' (p. 32).

Complicated sexuality and excess always seem to lead us to Byron, whose drama, particularly the experimental and seemingly modern *Sardanapalus*, continues to attract scholars. Barbara Judson, in 'Tragicomedy, Bisexuality, and Byronism; or, Jokes and their Relation to *Sardanapalus*' (*TSLL* 45[2003] 25–61), calls our attention to the sharply different styles of the play itself (tragicomedy) and its preface (high seriousness) to propose that the play is a kind of joke against conventional tragedy, a libidinous subversion or burlesque of the genre's bourgeois morality. John Gardner, in 'Hobhouse, Cato Street and *Marino Faliero*' (*ByronJ* 31[2003] 23–37), proposes that the pretext of *Marino Faliero* is not only the Cato Street conspiracy (as in David Erdman's argument), but a quarrel between Byron and Hobhouse, and that the play is written, in part, to understand Hobhouse's shift to more radical political behaviour.

The radicalism of Romantic drama is also represented in the *Romantic Circles* electronic edition of Robert Southey's *Wat Tyler*, edited by Matthew Hill and other postgraduate students at the University of Maryland, College Park; the edition includes a scholarly introduction and literary and historical contexts as well as the full text of the dramatic poem with hypertext links that gloss terms and offer commentary.

To conclude with performance research, Judith Page, in '"Hath not a Jew eyes?": Edmund Kean and the Sympathetic Shylock' (*WC* 34[2003] 116–19), argues not just that Kean's Shylock encouraged sympathy with Shakespeare's character and toward Jews in general, but that he gave play-going Jews in London a public voice.

Books Reviewed

Altieri, Charles. *The Particulars of Rapture: An Aesthetics of Affect*. CornUP. [2003] pp. x + 299. £30.50 ($50) ISBN 0 8014 4154 4.

Armstrong, Charles. *Romantic Organicism: From Idealist Origins to Ambivalent Afterlife*. Palgrave. [2003] pp. ix + 272. £47.50 ISBN 1 4039 0475 8.

Bainbridge, Simon. *British Poetry and the Revolutionary and Napoleonic Ward: Visions of Conflict*. OUP. [2003] pp. xii + 259. £52.50 ISBN 0 1981 8758 0.

Barth, J., and S.J. Robert. *Romanticism and Transcendence: Wordsworth, Coleridge, and the Religious Imagination*. UMissP. [2003] pp. xi + 146. £21.50 ISBN 0 8262 1453 3.

Barton, Paul D. *Lord Byron's Religion: A Journey into Despair*. Mellen. [2003] pp. 182. $99.95 ISBN 0 7734 6634 7.

Bate, Jonathan. *John Clare: A Biography*. Picador. [2003] pp. xxi + 648. £9.99 ISBN 0 3303 7126 1.

Beer, John. *Romantic Consciousness: Blake to Mary Shelley*. Palgrave. [2003] pp. xiii + 205. £47.50 ISBN 1 4039 0324 7.

Bradley, Arthur, and Alan Rawes, eds. *Romantic Biography*. Ashgate. [2003] pp. xvii + 202. £42.50 ISBN 0 7546 0993 6.

Bradshaw, Michael, ed. *Death's Jest-Book*. by Thomas Lovell Beddoes. Routledge. [2003] pp. 96. $14.95 ISBN 0 4159 6933 6.

Braithwaite, Helen. *Romanticism, Publishing and Dissent: Joseph Johnson and the Cause of Liberty*. Palgrave. [2002] pp. xiv + 243. £47.50 ISBN 0 3339 8394 7.

Bratton, Jacky. *New Readings in Theatre History*. CUP. [2003] pp. 238. $22 ISBN 0 5217 9463 3.

Burton, Sarah. *A Double Life: A Biography of Charles and Mary Lamb*. Viking. [2003] pp. x + 146. hb £16.99 ISBN 0 6708 9399 4, pb £8.99 ISBN 0 1402 9715 4.

Carruthers, Gerald, and Alan Rawes, eds. *English Romanticism and the Celtic World*. CUP. [2003] pp. x + 265. £40 ISBN 0 5218 1085 X.

Cheeke, Stephen. *Byron and Place: History, Translation, Nostalgia*. Palgrave. [2003] pp. ix + 241. £47.50 ISBN 1 4039 0403 0.

Clemens, Justin. *The Romanticism of Contemporary Theory: Institution, Aesthetics Nihilism*. Ashgate. [2003] pp. xvii + 219. £45 ISBN 0 7546 0875 1.

Cox, Jeffrey N., and Michael Gamer, eds. *The Broadview Anthology of Romantic Drama*. Broadview. [2003] pp. 432. $29.95 ISBN 1 5511 1298 1.

Craciun, Adriana. *Fatal Women of Romanticism*. CUP. [2002] pp. xvi + 328. £45 ISBN 0 5218 1668 8.

Csikós, Dóra Janzer. *'Four Mighty Ones Are in Every Man': The Development of the Fourfold in Blake*. AK. [2003] pp. 135. pb $25 ISBN 9 6305 7936 7.

De Quincey, Thomas, *The Works of Thomas De Quincey*. P&C. [2003]: vol. 10: *Articles from Tait's Edinburgh Magazine, 1834–8,* ed. Alina Clej, pp. xvi + 435; *vol. 11: Articles from Tait's Magazine and Blackwood's Magazine, 1838–41*, ed. Julian North, pp. x + 721; vol. 15: *Articles from Blackwood's Edinburgh Magazine and Tait's Edinburgh Magazine, 1844–46*, ed. Frederick Burwick, pp. x + 754; vol. 16: *Articles from Tait's Edinburgh Magazine, Macphail's Edinburgh Ecclesiastical Journal, The Glasgow Athenaeum Album, The North British Review and Blackwood's Edinburgh Magazine, 1847–49*, ed. Robert Morrison, pp. xviii + 751; vol. 19: *Autobiographic Sketches*, ed. Daniel Sanjiv Roberts, pp. xx + 499; vol. 20: *Prefaces &c. to the Collected Editions, Published Addenda, Marginalia, Manuscript Addenda, Undatable Manuscripts*, ed. Grevel Lindop et al, pp. xv + 509; vol. 21: *Transcripts of Unlocated Manuscripts, Index*, ed. Grevel Lindop, pp. ix + 377. Set £1,650 ($2,775) ISBN 1 8519 6519 X

D'Haen, Theo, Peter Liebregts and Wim Tigges, eds. *Configuring Romanticism: Essays Offered to C.C. Barfoot*. Rodopi. [2003] pp. 314. $67 ISBN 9 0420 1055 X.

Eaves, Morris, ed. *The Cambridge Companion to William Blake*. CUP. [2003] pp. xix + 302. pb £15.99 ISBN 0 5217 8677 0.

Gill, Stephen, ed. *The Cambridge Companion to Wordsworth*. CUP. [2003] pp. 320. £15.99 ISBN 0 5216 4681 2.

Gravil, Richard. *Wordsworth's Bardic Vocation, 1787–1842*. Palgrave. [2003] pp. viii + 310. £47.50 ISBN 0 3335 6283 6.

Griffin, Robert J., ed. *Faces of Anonymity: Anonymous and Pseudonymous Publication, 1600–2000*. Palgrave. [2003] pp. vi + 260. £40 ISBN 0 3122 9530 8.

Halmi, Nicholas, Paul Magnuson and Raimonda Modiano, eds. *Coleridge's Poetry and Prose*. Norton. [2003] pp. 704. £11.95 ISBN 0 3939 7904 0.

Halsey, Alan, ed. *Death's Jest-Book* by. Thomas Lovell Beddoes. West House Books. [2003] pp. 167. $25 ISBN 1 9040 5208 8.

Hamilton, Paul. *Metaromanticism: Aesthetics, Literature, Theory*. UChicP. [2003] pp. vii + 316. £45.50 ISBN 0 2263 1479 0.

Heringman, Noah, ed. *Romantic Science: The Literary Forms of Natural History*. SUNYP. [2003] pp. xiii + 281. £54 ISBN 0 7914 5701 X.

Hunt, Leigh, *The Selected Writings of Leigh Hunt*. P&C. [2003] vol. 1: *Periodical Essays 1805–14*, ed. Greg Kucich and Jeffrey N. Cox, pp. 414; vol. 2: *Periodical Essays 1815–21*, ed. Greg Kucich and Jeffrey N. Cox, pp. 435; vol. 3: *Periodical Essays 1822–38*, ed. Robert Morrison, pp. 449; vol. 4: *Later Literary Essays*, ed. Charles Mahoney, pp. 411. vol. 5: *Poetical Works 1801–21*, ed. John Strachan, pp. 343; vol. 6: *Poetical Works 1822–59*, ed. John Strachan, pp. 354. Set £495 ($840) ISBN 1 8519 6714 1.

Jones, Catherine. *Literary Memory: Scott's Waverley Novels and the Psychology of Narrative*. BuckUP/AUP. [2003] pp. 249. $46 ISBN 0 8387 5539 9.

Jones, Steven E., ed. *The Satiric Eye: Forms of Satire in the Romantic Period*. Palgrave. [2003] pp. 229. £47.50 ISBN 0 3122 9496 4.

Keegan, Abigail F. *Byron's Othered Self and Voice: Conceptualizing the Homographic Signature*. Lang. [2003] pp. x + 162. £40 ISBN 0 8204 6742 1.

Kipp, Julie. *Romanticism, Maternity, and the Body Politic*. CUP. [2003] pp. xiii + 256. £40 ISBN 0 5218 1455 3.

La Cassagnère, Christian, ed. *Keats, ou Le Sortilège des mots*. Lyon. [2003] pp. 254. €18 ISBN 2 7297 0734 4.

Labbe, Jacqueline M. *Charlotte Smith: Romanticism, Poetry and the Culture of Gender*. ManUP. [2003] pp. x + 180. £42.50 ($74.95) ISBN 0 7190 6004 4.

Mahoney, Charles. *Romantics and Renegades: The Poetics of Political Reaction*. Palgrave. [2003] pp. x + 266. £47.50 ISBN 0 3339 6849 2.

Makdisi, Saree. *William Blake and the Impossible History of the 1790s*. UChicP. [2003] pp. 412. hb $59 ISBN 0 2265 0259 7.

Mee, Jon. *Romanticism, Enthusiasm and Regulation: Poetics and the Policing of Culture in Romantic Britain*. OUP. [2003] pp. x + 320. £53 ISBN 0 1981 8757 2.

Milnes, Tim. *Knowledge and Indifference in English Romantic Prose*. CUP. [2003] pp. viii + 278. £45 ($65) ISBN 0 5218 1098 1.

Monnickendam, Andrew, ed. *Clan-Albin: A National Tale*. by Christian Isobel Johnstone. ASLS. [2003] pp. xxi + 598. hb £25 ISBN 0 9488 7752 9, pb £8.95 ISBN 0 9488 7753 7.

Morrison, Lucy, and Staci L. Stone, eds. *A Mary Shelley Encyclopedia*. Greenwood. [2003] pp. xx + 539. $95 ISBN 0 3133 0159 X.

Nash, Andrew, ed. *Culture of Collected Editions*. Palgrave. [2003] pp. 288. £50 ISBN 1 4039 0266 6.

O'Neill, Michael, and Zachary Leader, eds. *Percy Bysshe Shelley: The Major Works*. OUP. [2003] pp. xxviii + 845. £10.99 ISBN 0 1928 1374 9.

Paley, Morton D. *The Traveller in the Evening: The Last Works of William Blake*. OUP. [2003] pp. xiv + 332. hb £50 ISBN 0 1992 5562 8.

Pearsall, Derek. *William Langland, William Blake, and the Poetry of Hope*. WMU. [2003] pp. 22. pb $5 ISBN 1 5804 4043 6.

Perry, Seamus. *Samuel Taylor Coleridge*. BL. [2003] pp. 128. £10.95 ISBN 0 7123 4787 9.

Pierce, John B. *The Wond'rous Art: William Blake and Writing*. FDUP. [2003] pp. 186. hb $39.50 ISBN 0 8386 3938 0.

Rawlinson, Nick. *William Blake's Comic Vision*. Palgrave. [2003] pp. xiii + 292. £42.50 ISBN 0 3337 4565 5.

Redfield, Marc. *The Politics of Aesthetics: Nationalism, Gender, Romanticism*. StanfordUP. [2003] pp. x + 252. £38.95 0 8047 4460 2.

Robinson, Eric, David Powell and P.M.S. Dawson, eds. *John Clare: Poems of the Middle Period*, vol. 5. OUP. [2003] pp. xxxvi + 822. £110 ISBN 0 1981 2386 8.

Roe, Nicholas, ed. *Leigh Hunt: Life, Poetics, Politics*. Routledge. [2003] pp. viii + 253. £55 ISBN 0 4153 0984 0.

Ryall, Anka, and Catherine Sandbach-Dahlström, eds. *Mary Wollstonecraft's Journey to Scandinavia: Essays*. A&W. [2003] pp. 248. $69.50 ISBN 9 1220 2018 7.

Schock, Peter A. *Romantic Satanism: Myth and the Historical Moment in Blake, Shelley, and Byron*. Palgrave. [2003] pp. x + 210. £47.50 ISBN 1 4039 1182 7.

Schor, Esther, ed. *The Cambridge Companion to Mary Shelley*. CUP. [2003] pp. xxi + 289. hb £45 ISBN 0 5218 0984 3, pb £15.99 ISBN 0 5210 0770 4.

Setzer, Sharon M., ed. *A Letter to the Women of England and The Natural Daughter*. by Mary Robinson. [2003] pp. 336. £8.99 ISBN 1 5511 1236 1. Broadview.

Shaffer, Julie A., ed. *Walsingham* by Mary Robinson. Broadview. [2003] pp. 559. £8.99 ISBN 1 5511 1299 X.

Stanton, Judith Phillips. *The Collected Letters of Charlotte Smith*. IndUP. [2003] pp. xlv + 813. £52 ($59.95) ISBN 0 2353 4012 8.

Strachan, John, ed. *The Poems of John Keats: A Sourcebook*. Routledge. [2003] pp. 198. £14.99 ISBN 0 4152 3478 6.

Taylor, Barbara. *Mary Wollstonecraft and the Feminist Imagination*. CUP. [2003] pp. xvi + 331. hb £45 ISBN 0 5216 6144 7, pb £16.99 ISBN 0 5210 0417 9.

Townsend, Joyce H., ed. *William Blake: The Painter at Work*. Tate. [2003] pp. 192. pb £19.99 ISBN 1 8543 7468 0.

Troost, Linda V., ed. *Eighteenth-Century Women: Studies in their Lives, Work, and Culture*, vol. 3. AMS. [2003] pp. x + 355. $94.50 ISBN 0 4046 4703 0.

Turhan, Filiz. *The Other Empire: British Romantic Writings about the Ottoman Empire*. Routledge. [2003] pp. xiii + 202. £50 ISBN 0 4159 6805 4.

Vallins, David, ed. *Coleridge's Writings*, vol. 5: *On the Sublime*. Palgrave. [2003] pp. xiii + 192. £47.50 ISBN 0 3339 7250 3.

Vardy, Alan. *John Clare: Politics and Poetry*. Palgrave. [2003] pp. ix + 221. £47.50 ISBN 0 3339 6617 1.

Vendler, Helen. *Coming of Age as a Poet: Milton, Keats, Eliot, Plath*. HarvardUP. [2003] pp. 174. £12.40 ISBN 0 6740 1024 8.

Watson, J.R. *Romanticism and War: A Study of British Romantic Period Writers and the Napoleonic Wars*. Palgrave. [2003] pp. viii + 254. £47.50 ISBN 0 3338 0176 8.

Weir, David. *Brahma in the West: William Blake and the Oriental Renaissance*. SUNYP. [2003] pp. xiii + 170. pb $17.95 ISBN 0 7914 5818 0.

Wilson, Eric G. *The Spiritual History of Ice: Romanticism, Science, and the Imagination*. Palgrave. [2003] pp. viii + 278. £25 ISBN 0 3122 9299 6.

Wilt, Judith, ed. *Making Humans: Frankenstein and The Island of Dr. Moreau, by Mary Shelley and* H.G. Wells. HoughtonM. [2003] pp. 359. $11.56 ISBN 0 6180 8489 4.

Wolfson, Susan J., ed. *Frankenstein* by Mary Shelley. Longman Cultural Edition. [2003] pp. 384. $8 ISBN 0 3210 9698 3.

Wood, Marcus, ed. *The Poetry of Slavery: An Anglo-American Anthology, 1764–1865*. OUP. [2003] pp. lxi + 704. £74 ISBN 0 1981 8709 2.

Wu, Duncan, ed. *Wordsworth's Poets*. Carcarnet. [2003] pp. 311. £9.95 ISBN 1 8575 4639 3.

Youngquist, Paul. *Monstrosities: Bodies and British Romanticism*. UMinnP. [2003] pp. 224. £42 ISBN 0 8166 3979 5.

Yu, Christopher. *Nothing to Admire: The Politics of Satire from Dryden to Merrill*. OUP. [2003] pp. 219. $49.95 ISBN 0 1951 5530 0.

XIII

The Nineteenth Century: The Victorian Period

WILLIAM BAKER, HALIE CROCKER, KIRSTIE BLAIR, JIM DAVIS AND DAVID FINKELSTEIN

This chapter has four sections: 1. Cultural Studies and Prose; 2. The Novel; 3. Poetry; 4. Drama and Theatre; 5. Periodicals and Publishing History. Sections 1 and 2 are by William Baker and Halie Crocker; section 3 is by Kirstie Blair; section 4 is by Jim Davis; section 5 is by David Finkelstein.

1. Cultural Studies and Prose

(a) General

General works on Victorian culture include *Victorians at Home and Abroad* by Paul Atterbury and Suzanne Fagence Cooper, a wide-ranging study of Victorian culture, attitudes, and achievements. Section 1, 'Royalty and the New Britain', discusses images of Queen Victoria and changing views of the family, education, and political systems. Section 2, 'Visions of the New Britain', focuses on change wrought at least in part by the Great Exhibition in terms of new technologies, leisure, medicine, and public health, among other subjects. Also discussed are new attitudes regarding the ethics of work, death, religion, and changing outlooks on women's roles. In section 3, 'Nature', the authors discuss Victorian opinions about nature and landscape, and section 4, 'Style and Decoration', discusses jewellery, crafts, art, and interior design. Section 5, 'Visions of the World', explores conceptions of East India, the Americas, the Pacific, and Africa. Another interdisciplinary introduction to the study of Victorian literature and culture is Adam C. Roberts, *Victorian Culture and Society: The Essential Glossary*. It contains a selection of over 400 cross-referenced entries covering important events, terms, figures, writers and their works, literary genres, and ideas of the period.

The subject of Clark and Kaiser, eds., *Culture Wars: Secular–Catholic Conflict in Nineteenth-Century Europe*, is the controversy that accompanied the emergence of constitutional nation-states in nineteenth century Europe and its

Year's Work in English Studies, Volume 84 (2005) © The English Association; all rights reserved. For permissions, please email: journals.permissions@oxfordjournals.org

doi: 10.1093/ywes/mai013

effect on social and religious life in terms of education, marriage, public space, and popular perceptions of nationhood. The sixth chapter, by J.P. Perry, provides useful information on the subject of 'Nonconformity, Clericalism and "Englishness": The United Kingdom' (pp. 152–80). A more specific Victorian phenomenon occupies Marlene Tromp in her 'Spirited Sexuality: Sex, Marriage, and Victorian Spiritualism' (*VLC* 31:i[2003] 67–81), which has as its subject the darkened parlour of the séance. Tromp focuses on ways in which the spiritualism phenomenon affected the institution of marriage, as well as its impact on romantic affairs in Victorian social circles. Rod Preece, 'Darwinism, Christianity, and the Great Vivisection Debate' (*JHI* 64:iii[2003] 399–420), discusses the impact on the history of animal ethics of Darwin's theory of evolution in comparison to Christian principles. Preece argues that 'the depth of revulsion in which vivisection was held by prominent Christians … [was] far stronger than those of the most prominent proponents of evolution by natural selection' (p. 419).

Science and technology continue to be subjects of great interest in Victorian studies. In *In Pursuit of Plants: Experiences of Nineteenth and Early Twentieth Century Plant Collectors*, Philip Short provides a very useful survey of writings from the journals and various correspondence of botanists, naturalists, and plant collectors of the nineteenth century. The book is organized by continent, and each extract of writings is introduced by a brief commentary by Short. Katherine Anderson, 'Looking at the Sky: The Visual Context of Victorian Meteorology' (*BJHS* 36:iii[2003] 301–32), looks at Victorian scientific and meteorological representations in the context of the broader visual culture in which they emerged and developed.

A recent issue of *Cahiers Victoriens et Édouardiens* (*CVE* 57[2003]) includes a sampling of papers recently presented at the University of Oporto conference commemorating the 150 years of the Great Exhibition. They include the following: 'The Wonders of Common Things' by Luísa Leal de Faria (*CVE* 57[2003] 171–84); 'A Victorian Looking-Glass: The Art Sector of the Great Exhibition as a Mirror of Mid-Victorian Society' by Isabel Donas Botto (*CVE* 57[2003] 185–96); '"Palaces for the People": A Kind of Utopia?' by Patrick Parrinder (*CVE* 57[2003] 197–210); '"Tell me what you like and I'll tell you what you are": An Overview of the Victorian Political Economy of Art' by Iolanda Freitas Ramos (*CVE* 57[2003] 211–22); and 'The Two Crystal Palaces or the Reception of the Great Exhibition in Portugal' by Fàtima Vieira (*CVE* 57[2003] 223–32).

Stemming the Torrent: Expressions and Control in the Victorian Discourses on Emotions, 1830–1872, by Gesa Stedman, discusses the discourses of emotion and emotional vocabularies of nineteenth-century fiction and non-fiction writers, focusing specifically on the tension between the apparent need to express and control those feelings. Included are discussions of both canonical and non-canonical works, for example Dickens's *Hard Times*, Brontë's *Shirley*, Germaine de Staël's *Corinne*, Sarah Ellis's *The Education of the Heart*, and Darwin's *The Expression of Emotion in Man and Animals*. Stedman also focuses on expressions of emotion and emotional discourses as responses to the political and social issues of the time. Small and Tate, eds., *Literature, Science, Psychoanalysis, 1830–1970: Essays in Honour of Gillian Beer*, is a collection of new essays not unsurprisingly, given that the collection is dedicated to the distinguished work of Gillian Beer, exploring relationships between and among literature, psychoanalysis, and science. They are as follows: 'Darwin's "Second Sun": Alexander von Humbolt and the Genesis of *The Voyage of the Beagle*' by Nigel Leask (pp. 13–36); '"And if it be a pretty woman all the better": Darwin and Sexual Selection' by George Levine (pp. 37–51); 'Ordering Creation, or Maybe Not' by Harriet Ritvo (pp. 52–63); 'Chances Are: Henry Buckle, Thomas Hardy, and the Individual at Risk' by Helen Small (pp. 64–85); 'The Psychology of Childhood in Victorian Literature and Medicine' by Sally Shuttleworth (pp. 86–107); 'A Freudian Curiosity' by Rachel Bowlby (pp. 108–17); 'Freud's Theory of Metaphor: *Beyond the Pleasure Principle*, Nineteenth-Century Science and Figurative Language' by Suzanne Raitt (pp. 118–30); 'On Not Being Able to Sleep' by Jacqueline Rose (pp. 131–44); '"Brownie" Sharpe and the Stuff of Dreams' by Mary Jacobus (pp. 145–59); 'On Not Knowing Why: Memorializing the Light Brigade' by Trudi Tate (pp. 160–80); 'Sounds of the City: Virginia Woolf and Modern Noise' by Kate Flint (pp. 181–94); '"Chloe Liked Olivia": The Woman Scientist, Sex, and Suffrage' by Maroula Joannou (pp. 195–211); 'The Chemistry of Truth and the Literature of Dystopia' by Alison Winter (pp. 212–32); and 'Coming of Age' by E.F. Keller (pp. 233–42). Helen Small's informative introduction (pp. 1–12), in addition to summarizing the contributions, contains a succinct account of the importance and influence of Gillian Beer's contribution to our understanding of Victorian and post-Victorian culture, ideas and literature. The volume concludes with a 'Select Bibliography and Works by Gillian Beer' (pp. 245–8). All the contributions in this scrupulously edited volume are of the highest quality.

Several studies this year focus on the lives and works of important scientific figures. In *The Man Who Changed Everything: The Life of James Clerk Maxwell*, Basil Mahone takes a look at one of the most important, though little known, scientists of modern technology and physical science. James Clerk Maxwell (1831–79) made many important scientific and technological contributions, such as his theory of colour vision (which was used later in the development of colour television), and an understanding of the nature of electromagnetic waves (later used in television, radio, and the mobile phone). The only caveat is that Mahone missed the opportunity to write more upon the impact of Maxwell's work on his literary contemporaries such as George Eliot. Her notebooks used in the writing of *Daniel Deronda*, for instance, contain extracts from Maxwell's 1871 presidential address to the Mathematics and Physics section of the British Association for the Advancement of Science, where Maxwell spoke on theories of ring vortices (see W. Baker, ed., *Some George Eliot Notebooks*, 4 vols. [1976–85], vol. 3, pp. 75, 216). In *Thomas Huxley: Making the 'Man of Science'* Paul White investigates the 'man of science' persona and how Huxley helped define that category. Particularly interesting is White's focus on Huxley's role as a professional scientific practitioner who was also regarded as a moral and religious figure. Also discussed are the ways in which the idea of 'scientific authority' met, merged, and integrated with literary and religious authority in various 'high culture' institutions, including the worlds of print, education, and research. Michael Bulmer's *Francis Galton: Pioneer of Heredity and Biometry* is a biography of the 'father of biometry', Darwin's half-cousin and the statistician whose statistical models on variability and heredity helped lay the foundation for the mathematical explanation of natural selection. Bulmer examines Galton's achievements in their scientific and cultural context. Again, both works would have benefited from more examination of their subjects' impact on the thinking and writing of such literary contemporaries as, for example, Eliot or George Henry Lewes.

Not surprisingly, several works this year investigate women's changing roles in public and private life. Eleanor Gordon and Gwyneth Nair, *Public Lives: Women, Family, and Society in Victorian Britain*, consider the pivotal and diverse roles of women in the creation of middle-class culture and identity. Elaine Freedgood, '"Fine Fingers": Victorian Handmade Lace and Utopian Consumption' (*VS* 45:iv[2003] 625–48), argues that 'Victorian representations of handmade lace are significant in that they succeed in inventing a mode of apparently utopian commodity consumption' (p. 625). Lynn M. Alexander, *Women, Work, and Representation; Needlewomen in Victorian Art and Literature*, draws on various novels, illustrations, and letters to describe the unsuitable working conditions (including long hours, low wages, and the potential for injury) endured by seamstresses. Images of the seamstress became symbols of the afflicted working class and helped to stimulate reform. In *Women's Bodies and Dangerous Trades, 1880–1914*, Carolyn Malone takes a look at the public debate over whether certain types of women's work (for example, the white lead and pottery trades) would cause harm to women's bodies and their ability to reproduce. Malone examines the roles of the numerous politicians, workers, and feminist organizations taking part in this debate and the resulting protective labour legislation and dangerous trades regulations. These debates and the ensuing legislation led to a growing feminist activism. Suzanne Keen, 'Quaker Dress, Sexuality, and the Domestication of Reform in the Victorian Novel' (*VLC* 30:i[2002] 211–36), argues that the 'Quakerish' dress of Dorothea Brooke and Jane Eyre suggests not plainness, but that these two Victorian heroines offer a 'promise of spirited sexuality'. Further, Keen says that their dress reflects 'an admonition about the class-crossing potential of the respectable female contained in it' (p. 211). Gina Marlene Dorré, 'Horses and Corsets: *Black Beauty*, Dress Reform, and the Fashioning of the Victorian Woman' (*VLC* 30:i[2002] 157–78), uses Anna Sewell's *Black Beauty* to argue that the body of the bridled horse also represents the body of the corseted woman. Ann C. Colley, 'Stevenson's Pyjamas' (*VLC* 30:i[2002] 129–55), discusses ways in which clothing can reflect how 'we relate to ourselves, our surroundings, and our mortality' and how this applies to Victorian styles of dress (p. 129). Several other articles in *VLC* 30:i[2002] discuss fashion and clothing during the Victorian period: 'Elegant Amazons: Victorian Riding Habits and the Fashionable Horsewoman' by Alison Matthews David (*VLC* 30:i[2002] 179–210); 'Kashmir Shawls in Mid-Victorian Novels' by Suzanne Daly (*VLC* 30:i[2002] 237–56); 'Fringe' by Elaine Freedgood (*VLC* 30:i[2002] 257–64); 'Cameo Appearances: The Discourse of Jewelry in *Middlemarch*' by Jean Arnold (*VLC* 30:i[2002] 265–88); 'Delightful Coxcombs to Industrious Men: Fashionable Politics in *Cecil* and *Pendennis*' by Claire Nicolay (*VLC* 30:i[2002] 289–304); and 'Dressing Up: Hardy's *Tess of the d'Urbervilles* and Oliphant's *Phoebe Junior*' by Elsie B. Michie (*VLC* 30:i[2002] 305–26).

Children are the subject of several new works. In 'The Psychology of Childhood in Victorian Literature and Medicine' (in Small and Tate, eds., pp. 86–101), Sally Shuttleworth demonstrates how representations of childhood psychology are more prevalent and precisely detailed in both fictional and non-fiction prose (for example, *Jane Eyre* and *Jude the Obscure*) than in any formal body of medical literature at the time. Peter Kirby's *Child Labour in Britain, 1750–1870* is a careful empirical analysis of how social and economic change were linked to child labour in Britain during that period, covering a range of subjects including how Britain went from high numbers of child labourers in 1750 to relatively few by the year 1870. Focusing on child workers aged 10–15, Kirby's thorough examination has as its premise that employment of children was a fundamental part of 'the interaction between households and the labour market' (p. 5). Also discussed are responses to child labour by the state and the types of employment available to children, as well as a useful overview of sources dealing with child labour and difficulties in interpreting the data. Finally, Josephine McDonagh, *Child Murder and British Culture, 1720–1900*, takes a look at references to child murder in a variety of mediums, including fictional works, public debate, and social practices. Included are discussions of, among others, George Eliot, George Egerton, and Thomas Hardy, whose fictional works are placed within their social and cultural contexts. McDonagh also offers analyses of interconnected subjects such as treatment of the poor, birth control, the New Woman debates, and slavery. Similarly, Thorn, ed., *Writing British Infanticide: Child Murder, Gender, and Print, 1722–1859*, has as its subject the unique responses to and transformative effects of writings about child murder in various mediums, from magazines and pamphlets to newspaper accounts and professional journals.

In another area of interest, Simon Cordery, *British Friendly Societies, 1750–1914*, considers the role of these self-help organizations in working-class life in terms of social status and the 'culture of respectability'. Cordery also discusses political activism within Friendly Societies. Also on the subject of self-help and reform is Ann Baltz Rodrick's 'The Importance of Being an Earnest Improver: Class, Caste, and Self-Help in Mid-Victorian England' (*VLC* 29:i[2001] 39–50). Michelle Allen, 'From Cesspool to Sewer: Sanitary Reform and the Rhetoric of Resistance, 1848–80' (*VLC* 30:ii[2002] 383–402), takes a look at the various discourses of resistance to sanitary reform, arguing that the privileging of 'cleanliness' is a part of the Western historical progress narrative. Drawing on important literary figures (for example, Dickens, Gissing, Martineau, and Trollope), as well as other well-known social reform writers of the time period, Lauren M.E. Goodlad, in *Victorian Literature and the Victorian State: Character and Governance in a Liberal Society*, argues that Michel Foucault's analysis of modern power in *Discipline and Punish* applies more to the Continent than to Britain. Goodlad contends that Foucault's model of social power is more Franco-oriented, while his later essays concerning liberalism are more helpful in understanding the British state in the nineteenth century. W.M.M. Phillips, *Nightmares of Anarchy: Language and Cultural Change, 1870–1914*, considers examples of anarchist rhetoric in the United States and Britain beginning in the late nineteenth century. Drawing on discourses of anarchy in canonical and non-canonical fiction, journalism, and academic writing, Phillips looks particularly at the figure of the anarchist as a symbol of social change, also exploring links between perceptions of anarchy in relation to degeneracy, revolution, and the mob. Christopher Lane's *Hatred and Civility: The Antisocial Life in Victorian England* challenges romantic stereotypes of Victorians as being pious, earnest, socially ethical philanthropists, focusing instead on examples of snobbery, misanthropy, hypocrisy, and anti-social behaviour in a variety of fiction and non-fiction sources.

A few works this year deal with issues related to place, poverty and the urban landscape. Stephen Wade, *In My Own Shire: Region and Belonging in British Writing, 1840–1970*, discusses regionalism and various Victorian writers' perceptions of place and community, highlighting the tension between urban metropolitan centres and the more rural, regional peripheries. Wade also discusses political and social contexts of the regional novel beginning to emerge in the early nineteenth century, as well as the surrounding literary and print cultures. In *Capital Offenses: Geographies of Class and Crime in Victorian London* Simon Joyce examines most illuminatingly representations of London geography and urban landscapes in novels, journalism, poetry, and social commentary, exploring in particular the often conflicting connections between criminality and the urban landscape in the writings of Dickens, Stevenson, Mayhew, Doyle, and Wilde. Joyce focuses on the shift in fictional representations from attention to the criminals of Newgate and urban slums to privileged criminals such as Dorian Gray and Dr Jekyll.

Art and music continue to be growing fields of interest in Victorian studies. Linda M. Lewis, *Germaine de Staël, George Sand, and the Victorian Woman as Artist,* discusses how Staël's *Corinne* and Sand's *Consuelo* embody aspects of the female genius artist figure, a guiding myth which is later found in Victorian 'English artist-as-heroine' narratives by George Eliot, Elizabeth Barrett Browning, Geraldine Jewsbury and Mrs Humphry Ward. Lewis shows how elements of the myths of Sybil, Sophia, Psyche, Medusa, and Athena are embodied in these two female protagonists and discusses ways in which later female artist characters who must choose between love and art inherit them. Samuel Lyndon Gladden, 'Passages: The Long and Difficult Death of the Victorian Era, 1893–1945' (*VIJ* 31[2003] 41–56), discusses negative space, 'the pleasures and potentials of openings' in the artistic works of Charles Rennie Mackintosh, Aubrey Beardsley, Charles Rickett, Oscar Wilde, and Richard Wagner (p. 41).

In John M. Picker's thoughtful, important, pioneering and erudite monograph *Victorian Soundscapes,* the author considers the role of silence and sound (music, noise, echo, and voice) in literary and scientific writings in conjunction with the development of Victorian self-awareness. Picker draws on the writings of a number of important figures, such as Babbage, Dickens, Eliot and Stoker, to explore the 'aural dimensions' of Victorian culture. To be highly commended is Picker's use of source materials found in comparatively neglected archives such as those of Thomas Alva Edison in Edison, New Jersey. Another significant addition to our knowledge is Helen Groth's *Victorian Photography and Literary Nostalgia*, which thoroughly investigates the idea of 'arrested time' and the role of photographic illustration in the works of nineteenth-century poets, as well as the sense of nostalgia inspired by these poets in Victorian photographers.

Charles Villiers Stanford: Man and Musician by Jeremy Dibble is a biography of the well-known composer of the late nineteenth century known especially for his church music, written for the Anglican liturgy, as well as for his symphonies and choral works. Villiers is also notable for his interest in the advancement of British music in a variety of roles, including composer, musician, and professor. In *The House of Novello: The Practice and Policy of a Victorian Music Publisher, 1829–1866*, Victoria Cooper discusses, among other subjects, the business practices, methods of acquisition, editorial techniques, and financial records of entrepreneur Vincent Novello in order to trace the nineteenth-century growth and development of the music publishing house business. Examining the music of choirs, singers, symphonies, ballads, music halls, and film scores, Jeffrey Richards, *Imperialism and Music*, investigates ways in which music was used to reinforce, underpin, and dramatize British imperialist ideology. Richards draws on a comprehensive range of materials.

Several other works this year are influenced by post-colonial theory. Burton, ed., *After the Imperial Turn: Thinking With and Through the Nation*, is a collection of interdisciplinary essays assessing primarily British imperialism from a variety of cultural and postcolonial perspectives (see also Section 2(*b*) below). Frederick N. Bohrer, *Orientalism and Visual Culture: Imagining Mesopotamia in Nineteenth-Century Europe*, discusses the visual culture surrounding Mesopotamian archaeological discoveries and their reception in England, France, and Germany. Analysing various forms of art in the nineteenth century (including painting, illustrations in magazines, sculpture, jewellery, poetry, and museum displays), Bohrer discusses exoticism and representations of Assyria in terms of nationality, class, and gender. Ann C. Colley, 'Colonies of Memory' (*VLC* 31:ii[2003] 405–27), looks at the role of missionaries in the South Seas in the nineteenth century, pointing out that, while they were partially responsible for the islanders' loss of traditions, these missionaries also helped to preserve and gather artefacts which were important to anthropologists studying Polynesian culture. Janet C. Myers, also drawing on primary prose documentation in 'Performing the Voyage Out: Victorian Emigration and the Class Dynamics of Displacement' (*VLC* 29:i[2001] 129–46), takes a look at the ways in which emigration and 'matrimonial colonization' allowed single middle-class women to avoid poverty.

In 'The Adventures of Geography: Women Writers Un-Map and Re-Map Imperialism' (*VN* 103[2003] 20–7), Megan A. Norcia takes a look at imperial ideologies embedded in children's geography primers. Don Randall, 'Autumn 1857: The Making of the Indian "Mutiny"' (*VLC* 31:i[2003] 3–18), assesses various sermons and public discourses occurring on the national fast-day declared by Queen Victoria, focusing on how these discourses helped to inform public opinion about the mutiny and national imperial mythologies. The subject of M. van Wyk Smith's 'The Boers and the Anglo-Boer War (1899–1902) in the Twentieth-Century Moral Imaginary' (*VLC* 31:ii[2003] 429–46) is a series of letters written from Rhodesia and published in the *Daily Graphic* by Lord Randolph Churchill on the subject of the 'idle' and 'uneducated' Boer farmer. These were later published as *Men, Mines and Animals in South Africa* [1892]. Several other works this year are influenced by postcolonial theory. Laura E. Franey, *Victorian Travel Writing and Imperial Violence: British Writing on Africa, 1855–1902*, analyses elements of imperial violence in the writings of, among others, Henry M. Stanley, Samuel Baker, Mary Kingsley, Olive Schreiner and Joseph Conrad. George Olakunle's 'The "Native" Missionary, The African Novel, and In-Between' (*Novel* 36:i[2002] 5–25), draws on Victorian material, in particular the writings of S.A. Crowther, who wrote *The Gospel on the Banks of the Niger* [1859] and *Journals and Notices of the Native Missionaries Accompanying the Niger Expedition of 1857–59.*

The projected eight-volume *Nineteenth-Century Travels, Explorations and Empires: Writings From the Era of Imperial Consolidation, 1835–1910* (general editor Peter J. Kitson) provides a useful collection of primary writings on the subject of travel and exploration during a time of great expansion in the Victorian era. The first four volumes now available are as follows: volume 1, *North and South Poles*, edited by Peter J. Kitson; volume 2, *North America*, edited by William Baker; volume 3, *India*, edited by Indira Ghose; and volume 4, *The Far East*, edited by Susan Schoenbauer Thurin. Each of the volumes, in addition to the general editor's general introduction, contains informative introductory overviews written by the individual editors. These are followed by the reprinted extracts, each of which is prefaced by an extensive biographical and contextual introduction. These are followed by items for further reading and useful explanatory textual notes. The first volume contains fifteen reprinted pieces chronologically ranging from John Balleny's 'Discoveries in the Antarctic Ocean, in February 1839' as communicated by Charles Enderby to the *Journal of the Royal Geographical Society of London* [1839], to Robert Edwin Peary's *Nearest the Pole. A Narrative of the Polar Expedition of the Peary Arctic Club in the S.S. Roosevelt, 1905–1906*, [published in London in 1907]. There are twenty-five extracts in William Baker's volume focusing on North America. They include Sir Charles Lyell's *A Second Visit to the United States of North America* [published in 1849] recounting his 1845–6 travels along the North Atlantic sea coast and the Mississippi hinterland. The second volume concludes with extracts from Alfred Russell Wallace's *My Life: A Record of Events and Opinions* [1908], and his 1886–7 American tour. Indira Ghose extracts ten passages on travels to India, beginning with Alexander Barnes's travels between 1831 and 1833 [first published in 1834]. This volume concludes with Wilfrid Scawen Blunt's *India Under Ripon: A Private Diary* [1909]. Susan Schoenbauer Thurin's *The Far East* contains five extracts focusing on China and five on Japan. In short, there is much to interest students of nineteenth-century literature and culture in these very worthwhile volumes.

Another valuable addition to the developing study of travel writing is Jennifer Speake's three-volume *The Literature of Travel and Exploration: An Encyclopedia*. Entries by nearly 300 contributors from thirty-five countries are by no means confined to nineteenth-century prose. However, there are most helpful essays with detailed primary and secondary bibliographies on such diverse and neglected figures as Samuel White Baker [1821–93], Isabella Lucy Bird [1837–1904], Wilfrid Scawen Blunt [1840–1922] and Lady Anne Blunt [1837–1917], and, to mention just one other writer of relevance to the present section, Alexander William Kinglake [1809–91]. Jennifer Schacker, *National Dreams: The Remaking of Fairy Tales in Nineteenth-Century England*, considers several critically neglected fairy and folk tales and their relationship to foreign culture, national identity, modernity, popular culture, and the nature of 'Englishness'. Along with an introduction, notes on publishing history, story texts, and illustrations, are chapters on the following subjects: 'The Household Tales in the Household Library: Edgar Taylor's *German Popular Stories*'; 'Everything Is in the Telling: T. Crofton Croker's *Fairy Legends and Traditions of the South of Ireland*'; 'Otherness and Otherworldliness: Edward W. Lane's *Arabian Nights*'; 'The Dreams of the Younger Brother: George Webbe Dasent's *Popular Tales from the Norse*'; and 'Conclusion: Dreams'.

Sexuality is the focus of several interesting new studies. John Patrick Pattinson, 'The Man Who Was Walter' (*VLC* 30:i[2002] 19–40), makes a case for the identity of the author of *My Secret Life*, the anonymously written erotic memoir of the mid-Victorian period. Ellen Bayuk Rosenman's *Unauthorized Pleasures: Accounts of Victorian Erotic Experience* draws on a wide range of sources such as diaries, letters, medical literature and popular novels to explore erotic narratives, many of which defy traditional representations of the strait-laced Victorian. Among the subjects discussed are the erotic epic *My Secret Life* and the 'spermatorrhea panic' an imagined middle-class disease exemplified by male sexual anxiety. Angelique Richardson, *Love and Eugenics in the Late Nineteenth Century: Rational Reproduction and the New Woman*, explores expressions of selective breeding in fiction and the popular press. Richardson focuses particularly on the 'New Woman' and 'social purity feminist' writers such as Sarah Grand and Ellice Hopkins, who supported eugenics as a means of reinforcing the middle-class morality of the British race. On the other hand, Marcus Wood's *Slavery, Empathy and Pornography* discusses sentimental and pornographic perspectives on slavery in the works of various Victorian writers. Jonathan Taylor, *Mastery and Slavery in Victorian Writing*, also treats images of servitude in the works of various writers such as Carlyle, Dickens, Collins and Eliot. Depictions of figures such as the musician, the slaveholder, the butler, and 'the Jew' are examined in some detail.

This year's work in Victorian studies is also marked by the continuation of a growing interest in writing and publishing. Bradley Deane, *The Making of the Victorian Novelist: Anxieties of Authorship in the Mass Market*, describes changing perceptions of the novel-writing profession from the Romantic period through the late nineteenth century. According to Deane, the change occurred in several phases, starting with the struggle to legitimize novel-writing as a profession and culminating in a confrontation between the classics and mass-market fiction. Deane focuses on Scott, Dickens, Collins, Henry James, Gaskell and Eliot. Included are discussions of the growth of serial fiction and periodical presses and their impact on novel-writing. Christoph Lindner, *Fictions of Commodity Culture: From the Victorian to the Postmodern*, explores representations of consumerism in the Victorian period and on, as well as the ways in which they anticipate contemporary consumer culture. (see also discussions of Gaskell, Thackeray, and Trollope in Section 2(*b*) below). In *The Copyrights: Intellectual Property and the Literary Imagination*, Paul K. Saint-Amour considers literary composition in terms of changing perceptions of production, consumption, and private property in a time of increased public awareness of intellectual property law. The 'counterdiscourses' of Victorian and modernist writers (primarily Oscar Wilde and James Joyce) dealt with, and in some ways confronted, intellectual property law, making freedom of expression a part of the public domain and a commodity in and of itself. In his contentious *Dead From the Waist Down: Scholars and Scholarship in Literature and the Popular Imagination,* A.D. Nuttall traces the changing popular perception of intellectuals and literary scholars, from Faustian magicians to figures of sexual impotence and death. Nuttall's study focuses on three figures: the classical scholar Isaac Casaubon (1559–1614), Mr Casaubon in *Middlemarch*, and Mark Pattison, the Lincoln College rector on whom Eliot's character is thought to have been based. In doing so Nuttall, somewhat surprisingly for an astute critic and scholar, ignores recent studies. In general his well-written book would have benefited from a more thorough checking of previous critical and scholarly discourse.

Two essays on the subject of transnational study and the possibilities for and problems inherent in cross-cultural study of the nineteenth century are Sharon Marcus's 'Same Difference? Transnationalism, Comparative Literature, and Victorian Studies' (*VS* 45:iv[2003] 677–86) and Irene Tucker's 'International Whiggery' (*VS* 45:iv[2003] 687–98). Duncan Andrew Campbell, *English Public Opinion and the American Civil War,* examines English attitudes and opinions about the Civil War, arguing against the popular view that progressives sided with the North and conservatives with the South. Chapman and Stabler, eds., *Unfolding the South: Nineteenth-Century British Women Writers and Artists in Italy*, is a collection of essays on Anglo-Italian relations during the Victorian and Romantic periods examining the complex relationships between women, the Italian peninsula, and art. Included are discussions of George Eliot and Vernon Lee, among others. Leslie Williams, *Daniel O'Connell, the British Press, and the Irish Famine: Killing Remarks* looks at newspaper accounts and illustrated journals to investigate the role of the British press in shaping Britain's response to the Irish famine. According to Williams, reporters and cartoonists covering the famine drew on a 'metropolitan mentality'—particularly in their negative response to Daniel O'Connell—that allowed public opinion and governmental responses to distance themselves from the tragedy. Included in this thoughtfully researched study are analyses of reporting on the Irish famine in journals such as *The Times*, the *Observer*, *Punch*, the *Morning Chronicle*, and the *Illustrated London News*.

In '"The Ineffaceable Curse of Cain": Race, Miscegenation, and the Victorian Staging of Irishness' (*VLC* 29:ii[2001] 383–96), Scott Boltwood focuses on the Irish melodrama *The Colleen Bawn* to examine 'the dynamic resonance of English ethnography within Irish culture by using Victorian theories of Celtic racial character to inform a reading of a seminal dramatic portrayal of the Irish' (p. 383). Emily Allen, 'Culinary Exhibition: Victorian Wedding Cakes and Royal

Spectacle' (*VS* 45:iii[2003] 457–84), discusses ideological rituals that were associated with Victorian weddings, focusing particularly on how readers viewing the royal cake in print performed acts of consumption, thus participating in 'dramas of national affiliation' (p. 459). David Sonstroem looks at 'Teeth in Victorian Art' (*VLC* 29:ii[2001] 351–82), exploring reasons why Victorians 'checked the impulse to show their teeth' (p. 351). He misses documentation from George Eliot's letters in which she laments more than once how painful her teeth are. Ruth Hoberman, 'In Quest of Museal Aura: Turn of the Century Narratives about Museum-Displayed Objects' (*VLC* 31:ii[2003] 467–82), explores depictions of museum settings in novels, short stories, and journal articles, arguing that such accounts present museum objects as decommodified and decontextualized for the detached viewer. Kieran Dolin, 'The Transfiguration of Caroline Norton' (*VLC* 30:ii[2002] 503–27), discusses visual representations of poet and law reformer Caroline Norton, who, according to Dolin, illustrates the contradictory imperatives of modesty for women and the necessity of theatrical display for the purpose of commercial success. Janice Carlisle, 'The Smell of Class: British Novels of the 1860s' (*VLC* 29:i[2001] 1–20), discusses conventional scents like that of dried roses in contrast to other scents such as tallow, and their connections to class in Victorian novels. Also of interest is 'Madame Rachel's Enamel: Fatal Secrets of Victorian Sensational Mirrors' by Laurence Talairach-Vielmas (*WCSJ* 6[2003] 3–18).

Reviews of critical work in cultural studies are as follows: *The Victorian Parlour*, by Thad Logan, reviewed by Johanna M. Smith (*VPR* 36:iii[2003] 281–3); *Literature, Money and the Market: From Trollope to Amis*, by Paul Delany, reviewed by Jim Barloon (*VPR* 36:iv[2003] 375–6); *Ornamentalism: How the British Saw their Empire*, by David Cannadine, reviewed by Ian Christopher Fletcher (*VS* 45:iii[2003] 532–3); *Love & Death: Art in the Age of Queen Victoria*, edited by Angus Trumble, reviewed by Susan P. Casteras (*VPR* 36:iv[2003] 378–81); *Orphan Texts: Victorian Orphans, Culture and Empire*, by Laura Peters, reviewed by Hugh Cunningham (*VS* 45:iv[2003] 737–8); *The Brother–Sister Culture in Nineteenth-Century Literature: From Austen to Woolf*, by Valerie Sanders, reviewed by Leila S. May (*VS* 45:iv[2003] 738–9); *Women and Literature in Britain, 1800–1900*, edited by Joanne Shattock, reviewed by Deirdre d'Albertis (*VS* 45:iv[2003] 742–3); *Divine Feminine: Theosophy and Feminism in England*, by Joy Dixon, reviewed by Sandra Stanley Holton (*VS* 45:iv[2003] 746–7); *Governing Pleasures: Pornography and Social Change in England, 1815–1914*, by Lisa Z. Sigel, reviewed by Ross G. Forman (*VS* 45:iv[2003] 777–81); *Men in Wonderland: The Lost Girlhood of the Victorian Gentleman*, by Catherine Robson, reviewed by Deirdre David (*VS* 45:ii[2003] 375–6); *The Spectacle of Intimacy: A Public Life for the Victorian Family*, by Karen Chase and Michael Levenson, reviewed by Margaret Homans (*VS* 45:ii[2003] 377–8).

Other review listings for cultural studies are as follows: *Men in Wonderland: The Lost Girlhood of the Victorian Gentleman*, by Catherine Robson, reviewed by Patricia Pulham (*ELT* 46:iv[2003] 412–15); *Joyce and the Victorians*, by Tracey Teets Schwartze (*VS* 45:iii[2003] 538–40); *The Victorian Illustrated Book*, edited by Richard Maxwell, reviewed by Wendell V. Harris (*ELT* 46:iv[2003]

415–19); *A Companion to the Victorian Novel*, edited by William Baker and Kenneth Womack, reviewed by Sally Mitchell (*ELT* 46:iv[2003] 419); *The Victorians and the Visual Imagination*, by Kate Flint, reviewed by Susan P. Casteras (*VS* 45:ii[2003] 355–6); and *Women and British Aestheticism*, edited by Talia Schaffer and Kathy Alexis Psomiades, and *The Forgotten Female Aesthetes: Literary Culture in Late-Victorian England*, by Talia Schaffer, both reviewed by Angelique Richardson (*VS* 45:ii[2003] 370–3). Frederick S. Roden's 'Gender and Religion in Recent Victorian Studies Publications' (*VLC* 31:i[2003] 393–403) provides an excellent and succinct review of recent 'scholarly work in religious studies and contemporary theories of gender' (p. 393).

(b) Prose

The 'Family Bible with Notes' is the subject of Mary Wilson Carpenter's extensive *Imperial Bibles, Domestic Bodies: Women, Sexuality, and Religion in the Victorian Market*. First produced in the eighteenth century and aimed at the family, the serially published Family Bible was an important part of the emerging culture of commercial religious goods and publications. Elaborate depictions of the 'domestic angel' made the Victorian woman, who was already an important new consumer in the marketplace, a profitable commodity and augmented family social status and national identity. Carpenter also includes readings of literary writings by Charlotte Brontë, George Eliot, and Elizabeth Barrett Browning. Carpenter is certainly exploring interesting and relatively unexplored terrain. Several other articles on prose this year have religion as their subject: 'Protestants against the Jewish and Catholic Family, *c.*1829–60' by Miriam Elizabeth Burstein (*VLC* 31:i[2003] 333–58); '"Popish Legends and Bible Truths": English Protestant Identity in Catherine Sinclair's *Beatrice*' by Gabrielle Ceraldi (*VLC* 31:i[2003] 359–73); and 'Prophecy and Anti-Popery in Victorian London: John Cumming Reconsidered' by Robert H. Ellison and Carol Marie Engelhardt (*VLC* 31:i[2003] 373–93). A final article on prose which discusses religion and gender is Julie Melnyk's '"Mighty Victims": Women Writers and the Feminization of Christ' (*VLC* 31:i[2003] 131–58).

Several works discuss aestheticism and the Pre-Raphaelite movement. Latham, ed., *Haunted Texts: Studies in Pre-Raphaelitism*, comprises ten essays by contributors considering a range of subjects relating to Pre-Raphaelitism and/or the Decadent movement, including paintings, prose writings, decorative arts, poetry and illustrations. George C. Schoolfield's *A Baedecker of Decadence: Charting of Literary Fashion, 1884–1927* takes account of a range of turn-of-the-century writers, including Wilde, Huysmans, and Stoker, as well as Thomas Mann, Halldór Kiljan Laxness, and August Strindberg. Included in this study are translations, excerpts, and synopses, along with commentary and analysis on each of the thirty-two works of international literary decadence from Europe, Scandinavia, Australia, the United States, and the British Isles. Schoolfield focuses on motifs, themes, and intellectual links between and amongst the various strains of decadence, offering coverage of some well-known works such as *The Picture of Dorian Gray*, as well as other more obscure writings until now not translated into English. In a complex and sophisticated analysis, 'Painting Memory' (*TPr* 17:iii[2003] 527–42), Kate Flint 'develops the Victorian fascination with the ways in which one visualizes, in the mind's eye, what is in fact invisible'. She argues, drawing upon John Everett Millais' *Dew-Drenched Furze* and John Byam Shaw's *Boer War*, amongst other examples, that increasingly artists 'moved away from evoking times and places … and tried to invoke the condition of memory in the responses of the spectator' (p. 613).

Angela Thirlwell's biography of *William and Lucy: The Other Rossettis* discusses two important, but often ignored, figures of the Pre-Raphaelite movement. William was a sibling of Christina and Dante Gabriel, and Lucy Madox Brown was the daughter of Ford Madox Brown. Including various unpublished sources and visual material, Thirlwell details a passionate and tragic relationship (Lucy died when she was only 50), and also traces their separate careers; William was a radical author, poet, critic, and taxman, while Lucy was an artist and biographer of Mary Shelley. Pointing out that nearly one-third of John Addington Symonds's autobiography remains unpublished, Sarah J. Heidt, '"Let JAS words stand": Publishing John Addington Symonds's Desires' (*VS* 46:i[2003] 7–32), investigates the nature of self-disclosure in Symonds's memoir, along with its various sociocultural contexts and the unique processes, questions, and problems associated with editing and publishing autobiographical accounts. Julie F. Codell, *The Victorian Artist: Artists' Lifewritings in Britain, ca. 1870–1910*, assesses the growing popularity of biographical writings on artists beginning in the late nineteenth century. Codell discusses various genres of biographies on the life of the artist, as well as ways in which the new body of literature affected notions of economic exchange and national identity. J. Mordaunt Crook, *The Architect's Secret: Victorian Critics and the Image of Gravity*, investigates four critics of the Victorian period—George Atchison, Benjamin Webb, Beresford Hope, and Coventry Patmore—and their writings on architecture.

Margaret Belcher collects the letters of designer, architect, and ecclesiologist A.W.N Pugin in the second in a series of five volumes, *The Collected Letters of A.W.N. Pugin*, volume 2: *1843–1845*. As well as being valuable to the study of architecture, religious history, and the Gothic revival, Pugin's letters draw attention to important public events of the time. For example, this volume highlights his involvement in rebuilding the Houses of Parliament, as well as the publication of his *Glossary of Ecclesiastical Ornament and Costume*. Oxford University Press continue the high production standards set by the first volume briefly noticed in *YWES* (82[2003] 562). Belcher's editing is thorough, with accompanying documentation and helpful footnotes. There are four illustrative full-page plates and figures, plus an index to the first two volumes. When it is completed, Belcher's edition will be a most significant contribution to our knowledge of Pugin, and of Victorian Britain, worthy to stand alongside other monuments such as the editions of Dickens's or George Eliot's letters. The Pugin Society has published Pugin's *Contrasts* and *The True Principles of Pointed or Christian Architecture*. As Timothy Brittain-Catlain points out in his informative introduction, *Contrasts* aroused controversy 'in the national and professional press during the course of 1837'. Pugin's revisions and additions to 'its later edition of 1841' reflect the 'enormous changes' undergone since its publication five years previously (p. iv). *True Principles* also was published in 1841 and both are 'presented as authentic facsimiles, allowing the reader an unprecedented opportunity to enjoy the writing of an architect in the full flower of his creativity within a single volume' (p. vii).

G. Singh, 'Q.D. Leavis and the Novel' (*ES* 4[2003] 335–71), looks at the writings of Q.D. Leavis, whose critical readings of the novel extended beyond the range of those covered by her husband, F.R. Leavis. Q.D. Leavis still reads well and has fascinating insights into Dickens, Mrs Oliphant, George Eliot and many other writers. Singh's essay rightly draws attention to an incisive and distinctive voice whose prose and opinions stand up very well to the test of time. Matt Carter, *T.H. Green and the Development of Ethical Socialism*, explores works of ethical socialism and their applications to politics, tracing the work of R.H. Tawney to T.H. Green and the British idealists. Harrison, ed., *Henry Sidgwick*, is a collection of essays published to coincide with the centenary of the death of this important Victorian scholar. The essays are as follows: 'My Roles and their Duties: Sidgwick as Philosopher, Professor and Public Moralist' by Stefan Collini; 'Ethics, Utilitarianism, and Positive Boredom' by Jonathan Rée; 'Three Methods and a Dualism' by John Skorupski; 'Sidgwick on Practical Reason' by Onora O'Neill; 'The Sanctions of Utilitarianism' by Ross Harrison; and 'Sanctions in Bentham, Mill, and Sidgwick' by Roger Crisp.

Ian Christopher Fletcher, 'Double Meanings: Nation and Empire in the Edwardian Era' (in Burton, ed., pp. 246–59), contrasts Lord Milner's *The Nation and the Empire*, Mohandas K. Gandhi's *Hind Swaraj*, and J.E. Casely Hayford's *Ethiopia Unbound* in order to 'suggest some of the ways imperialists and nationalists deployed contested, and appropriated notions of nation and empire' (p. 246). Fletcher also includes discussion of the controversy surrounding Erskine Childers's *The Framework of Home Rule* to illustrate imperialistic metropolitan politics and the 'whiteness' of Irish nationalism. Lyn Innes, *A History of Black and Asian Writing in Britain, 1700–2000,* offers an extended analysis of Asian and black writings in Britain which, though popular in their time, are often neglected today. Using a good deal of new archival material, Innes's study includes narratives, letters, and other writings of immigrants and slaves beginning in the mid-eighteenth century, and includes detailed discussion of the 'vigorous and fertile interaction between black, Asian and white intellectuals and communities'.

New in Arnold studies is Bernard Bergonzi's well-written *A Victorian Wanderer: The Life of Thomas Arnold the Younger*, a well-researched biography of Matthew Arnold's younger brother Thomas, who thought of himself as a wanderer in both spiritual and geographical terms. Thomas Arnold spent much of his life travelling, living, and working outside England. Bergonzi highlights time spent in New Zealand, Tasmania, and Dublin, as well as Thomas's dealings with notable Victorian figures, such as John Henry Newman, Lewis Carroll, Lord Acton, Gerard Manley Hopkins, Wordsworth, and Arthur Hugh Clough. The sixteen illustrations accompanying the text, largely Victorian photographs of Arnold, his family and their contemporaries provide a moving glimpse of actual physical appearance. Tom Arnold's photograph taken in the 1890s reveals his still striking visage.

New in Carlyle studies is 'Communities in Mourning: Making Capital Out of Loss in Carlyle's *Past and Present* and *Heroes*', by Daniela Garofalo (*TSLL* 45:iii

[2003] 293–310), in which the author argues that Carlyle 'represents leaders perpetually marked by social failure … [his] failure to become visible to the public actually constitutes a powerful form of charismatic seduction that relies on invisibility, absence, and mourning' (p. 293). 'The Anatomy of Bigotry: Carlyle, Ruskin, Slavery, and a New Language of Race', a chapter in Marcus Wood's *Slavery, Empathy and Pornography*, discusses Ruskin's and Carlyle's perspectives on slavery, which Wood argues were racist. Rainer Emig, 'Eccentricity Begins at Home: Carlyle's Centrality in Victorian Thought' (*TPr* 17:ii[2003] 379–90), presents a thoughtful study of Carlyle as a controversial and contradictory eccentric. Eccentricity, however, Emig argues, is not a 'marginal phenomenon' but a 'crucial mechanism with which Western culture has been negotiating its dynamic margins while retaining confidence in an imaginary center since the seventeenth century'. Vanessa L. Ryan, 'The Unreliable Editor: Carlyle's *Sartor Resartus* and the Art of Biography' (*RES* 54[2003] 287–307), argues that 'the relationship between the Editor's Heuschrecke's Teufelsdröckh in *Sartor Resartus* strongly resembles the relationship between Croker's Boswell's Johnson' (p. 287). Roger Swift, 'Thomas Carlyle, Chartism, and the Irish in Early Victorian England' (*VLC* 29:i[2001] 67–84), explores Carlyle's negative depictions of the 'crowds of miserable Irish' who 'darken all our towns' in his famous *Chartism* pamphlet.

The Carlyle Studies Annual for the year 2003 (number 20) includes the following essays: 'The Carlyle–Dickens Traffic: Slavery in the Americas' by Jude V. Nixon (pp. 27–58); 'The Road Not Taken? Points of Intersection and Deflection in Carlyle and the American Transcendentalists' by Margaret Rundle (pp. 59–72); 'Literary Portraits: Carlyle Among the Americans' by Sheila McIntosh (pp. 73–81); and '"A mixture of yea and nay"': D.H. Lawrence, his *Last Poems*, and the Presence of Thomas Carlyle' by Brent E. Kinser (pp. 82–104). Reviews of critical work on Thomas Carlyle included: *The Simple Story of My Own First Love*, by Jane Welsh Carlyle (edited by Kenneth J. Fielding and Ian Campbell, with Aileen Christianson), reviewed by Mary B. Werner (*CStA* 20[2003] 105–7); and *The Victorian Internet: The Remarkable Story of the Telegraph and the Nineteenth Century's On-Line Pioneers*, by Tom Standage, reviewed by Alex Nalbach (*CStA* 20[2003] 108–12).

Cohen and Wakeling, eds., *Lewis Carroll and his Illustrators: Collaborations and Correspondence, 1865–1898*, comprises letters written by Carroll to his illustrators and prospective illustrators, including John Tenniel, Henry Holiday, Arthur Burdett Frost, Harry Furniss, and Emily Gertrude Thomson. The letters effectively illuminate Carroll's detailed knowledge of the publishing process. Included are sketches by Carroll alongside illustrators' versions of sketches, allowing for a unique look at their origin and development. *Dreaming in Pictures: The Photography of Lewis Carroll*, by Douglas R. Nickel, is reviewed by Jennifer Green-Lewis (*VS* 45:iv[2003] 729–30). Diane Waggoner's 'Seeing Photographs in Comfort: The Social Uses of Lewis Carroll's Photograph Albums' (*PULC* 62:iii[Spring 2003] 403–33) is accompanied by sixteen fascinating black and white illustrations, including many photographs. Waggoner draws upon many unpublished materials from the Helmut Gernsheim collection in the Harry Ransom Humanities Center at the University of Texas, and from the Morris

L. Parrish Collection of Victorian Novelists at Princeton. Her article is followed by Charlie Lovett's account of 'Philip Conklin Blackburn: An Underappreciated Lewis Carroll Scholar' (*PULC* 62:iii[Spring 2003] 434–50). Blackburn [1907–63], a 'research bibliographer at Goodspeed's Book Shop' gave up book collecting to become an Episcopalian priest. His 500-item Carroll collection had been formed by 1939, and remained in family hands until the mid-1990s.

Frances Power Cobbe [1822–1904] is the subject of an extensive biography by Sally Mitchell, published in 2004, to be reviewed in the next *YWES*. Janet L. Larson's 'Where is the Woman in this Text? Frances Power Cobbe's "Voices in Broken Lights"' (*VLC* 31:i[2003] 99–129) concentrates on Cobbe's *Broken Lights* [1864]. This 'put the case against an infallible Revelation' and was 'her main contribution to the mid-Victorian Bible wars'. It 'went through at least eight editions' (p. 99). Of course the impact of Darwin's thought may well have been an underlying reason for such biblical controversies amongst the Victorians. Darwin's *The Origin of Species; and The Voyage of the Beagle* reprints together the first edition of the former and the second edition of the latter, along with an introduction by Richard Dawkins and glossary and historical sketch by Darwin. Nigel Leask's extensively documented, 'Darwin's "Second Sun": Alexander von Humboldt and the Genesis of *The Voyage of the Beagle*' (in Small and Tate, eds., pp. 13–36) considers the influence on Darwin of von Humboldt's writings on the South American tropics. Leask recounts that 'Darwin was "a little disappointed" when he met the great man himself … finding him unduly garrulous' (p. 36). In '"And If It Be a Pretty Woman All the Better"—Darwin and Sexual Selection' (in Small and Tate, eds., pp. 37–51), George Levine looks at Darwin's *Descent of Man and Sexual Selection in Relation to Sex*, focusing on how some of Darwin's 'Victorian' attitudes about sexuality and gender, actually helped—instead of acting as a barrier to—our understanding of female sexual choice.

In November 1822, Robert FitzRoy [1805–65] was made commander of the *Beagle*, a survey ship operating along the shores of Patagonia, Terra del Fuego, Chile and Peru. From 1843, for three years, FitzRoy was governor of New Zealand. In 1854 he became of head of the Meteorological Department of the Board of Trade. Just over ten years later, the by then vice-admiral committed suicide. His most famous passenger on the *Beagle* was Charles Darwin. FitzRoy's fascinating life is the subject of a most informative biography by John and Mary Gribbin, who draw upon the collected primary materials in their *FitzRoy: The Remarkable Story of Darwin's Captain and the Invention of the Weather Forecast*. FitzRoy is revealed as a complex personality of great personal integrity. Harriet Ritvo, 'Ordering Creation, or Maybe Not' (in Small and Tate, eds., pp. 52–63), discusses Darwin and problems associated with the creation of taxonomies. Michael Bulmer's *Francis Galton: Pioneer of Heredity and Biometry* is a biography of the 'father of biometry' Darwin's half-cousin and the statistician whose statistical models on variability and heredity helped lay the foundation for the mathematical explanation for natural selection. Bulmer examines Galton's achievements in their scientific and cultural contexts, although he doesn't fully examine their impact upon late Victorian writing.

Published to coincide with the William Morris exhibition at the Huntington (which recently acquired a major Morris collection), Waggoner, ed., *'The Beauty of Life': William Morris and the Art of Design*, is a lavishly illustrated collection of Morris's designs and decorative arts. Essays by Pat Kirkham, Gillian Naylor, Edward R. Bosley, and editor Waggoner cover the range of Morris's achievements (along with those of his firm Morris & Company), Morris's life, and the history of design. Two other articles in Morris studies are also of interest: Giles E.M. Gasper's 'Kenneth Grahame's *The Wind in the Willows* and William Morris's Old Norse Translations' (*N&Q* 248[2003] 323–4) and Nicholas Frankel's 'The Ecology of Decoration: Design and Environment in the Writings of William Morris' (*JPRAS* 12[2003] 58–85).

Ian Ker, *The Catholic Revival in English Literature, 1845–1961: Newman, Hopkins, Chesterton, Greene, Waugh*, discusses how Catholicism influenced these five important writers of the literary Catholic revival and the relationships between their theologies and writings. Ker offers an analysis of Newman's essay 'Catholic Literature in the English Tongue, 1854–8', in which Newman discusses the lack of significant Catholic contributions to post-medieval English literature, which he said was largely Protestant. Françoise Petiard-Lianos, '"Rival Brothers"? Cardinal John Henry Newman and his Brother Francis William Newman ' (*CVE* 57[2003] 135–52), explores the strained relationship between Newman and his brother Francis (who was once even better known among the Victorian intelligentsia than Newman himself), especially in terms of their growing theological differences. William Shuter's essay 'Pater, Wilde, Douglas and the Impact of "Greats"' (*ELT* 46:iii[2003] 279–95) is discussed under Wilde in the next section. Also of interest in Pater studies this year is Lene Østermark-Johansen's 'Serpentine Rivers and Serpentine Thought: Flux and Movement in Walter Pater's Leonardo Essay' (*VLC* 30:ii[2002] 455–82).

Published to coincide with the Rossetti exhibition at the Van Gogh Museum in Amsterdam, *Dante Gabriel Rossetti*, by Julian Treuherz, Elizabeth Prettejohn, and Edwin Becker, is a beautifully illustrated book covering the range of Rossetti's life and works. Along with 190 illustrations (most of which are in colour), essays by the authors include the following: 'The Most Startlingly Original Living' by Treuherz, in which the author discusses Rossetti's role in founding the Pre-Raphaelites, his selection of themes from the Middle Ages, and his drawings of his wife; 'Beautiful Women With Floral Adjuncts', by Elizabeth Prettejohn, an analysis of images of women in the works of Rossetti; and 'Sensual Eroticism or Empty Tranquillity', by Edwin Becker, in which Becker discusses Rossetti's reputation around 1900, as well as his impact on nineteenth- and twentieth-century art. Debra N. Mancoff's well-illustrated 'Seeing Mrs. Morris: Photographs of Jane Morris from the Collection of Dante Gabriel Rossetti' (*PULC* 62:iii[Spring 2001] 376–402) illuminates both the Rossetti and the William and Jane Morris families. Although the publishers Thoemmes Press were unresponsive to a request for a review copy, brief mention should be made of their four-volume *Prose Works of Christina Rossetti*, introduced by Maria Keating.

Brendan Fleming, in a welcome essay, focuses on a neglected writer. His '"Balzac and the Land League": A "New" Article by George Moore' (*ELT*

46:iv[2003] 356–64) argues that 'the section of Moore's essay which concerns *Les Payans* is based upon the arguments of "Balzac and the Land League"' (p. 356). New from Francis O'Gorman is '"To see the finger of god in the dimensions of the pyramid": A New Context For Ruskin's *The Ethics of the Dust*' (*MLR* 98:iii[2003] 563–73), which discusses Ruskin's collection of lectures on crystallography [1866]. Katherine Anderson's 'Looking at the Sky: The Visual Context of Victorian Meteorology' (*BJHS* 36:iii[2003] 301–32), includes some discussion of Ruskin in her examination of Victorian scientific and meteorological representations in the context of the broader visual culture in which they emerged. Alexandra K. Wettlaufer, *In the Mind's Eye: The Visual Impulse in Diderot, Baudelaire and Ruskin,* explores the relationship between literature and visual art and the development of art criticism as a genre in France and Britain from 1750 to 1900. Included are discussions of 'Ruskin and the Language of Images' 'Ruskin's Moving Images: The Politics and the Poetics of the Paragone' and 'Diderot, Baudelaire, Ruskin: Envisioning Visionaries'. Also of interest is David Amigoni's 'Gothic Choirs and Gothic Fictions: Habitus, Moral Space and Identity in the Autobiographies of Ruskin and Newman' (in Regard, ed. *Mapping the Self: Space, Identity, Discourse in British Auto/Biography*, pp. 231–46). Daniels and Brandwood, eds., *Ruskin and Architecture*, contains, in addition to an introduction by Michael Brooks ('Ruskinisms', pp. 13–24), eleven essays assessing Ruskin's architectural achievement and legacy. There are contributions by Gill Chitty, Peter Howell, Geoffrey Tyack, Brian Hanson, Chris Brooks, Malcolm Hardman, Rosemary Hill, Michael Hall, Aileen Reid, Paul Snell, and Richard MacCormac.

Omitted from discussion in last year's *YWES* review of 2002 publications was *The Dictionary of Nineteenth-Century British Philosophers*. The general editors W.J. Mander and Alan P. F. Sell have compiled two volumes comprising 'more than 600 entries by 160 authors' (p. vii). Alphabetically arranged entries begin with four paragraphs on the life and writing of Edwin Abbott [1838–1926]. They conclude with four paragraphs on Thomas Young [1773–1829]. Entries are followed by primary bibliographies and secondary readings. Eight of Abbott's works, for instance, are listed, and only two concerning him. Entries are uneven in quality and length and inclusion is patchy: Elizabeth Barrett Browning and Robert Browning are included, Thomas Hardy and George Meredith excluded. The great logician and Kantian scholar James Joseph Sylvester [1814–97] is omitted. On the other hand there are welcome entries for William Cyples [1831–82], Clement Mansfield Ingleby [1823–86], George Croom Robertson [1842–92] and William Henry Stanley Monck [1838–1915]. Henry Sidgwick [1838–1900] and William Whewell [1794–1866] are two of the most extensive entries. The index includes names of people, but not of movements such as Positivism or Utilitarianism. Inclusions are eclectic and the volumes could well be retitled *The Dictionary of Nineteenth-Century British Intellectual History* or *Thinkers* or *Non-Fiction Prose Writers*.

Before moving to reviews of critical work in prose which have come to our attention, mention should be made of an online resource, the *Routledge*

Encyclopedia of Philosophy, edited by Edward Craig and available at <www.rep.routledge.com>. Entries appearing in 2003 include William Baker on George Henry Lewes and Samuel Butler. Also to be noted is a welcome and extensive article by Robert L. Carneiro and Robert G. Perrin, 'Herbert Spencer's *Principles of Sociology*: A Centennial Retrospective and Appraisal' (*Annals of Science* 59:iii[2002] 221–61). Carneiro and Perrin describe Spencer's book, first published in 1870–2, and assess its impact on academic sociology and anthropology since Spencer's death in 1903. A fascinating and informative exchange of letters forms the main text of Damien Atkinson's scrupulously edited *The Correspondence of John Stephen Farmer and W.E. Henley on their Slang Dictionary, 1890–1904*. Atkinson's excellent edition of *The Selected Letters of W.E. Henley* was noted in *YWES* 81[2002], 690. As Linda K. Hughes shrewdly observes in her preface, the correspondence 'reminds us that in the shadow of the *OED* another major reference work took shape that paralleled while exposing the limits (and ideological bias) of the *OED*'. Farmer and Henley's *Slang and its Analogues* [1890–1904] 'printed the "naughty bits" and specialized slang that the *OED* censored in the interests of decorum' (p. xiii). Atkinson's edition includes a bibliography of John Stephen Farmer (pp. 151–4), a detailed index and an 'Index of Correspondence' (pp. 155–6).

J.B. Schneewind, reviewing Mander and Sell's volumes (*VS* 45:iii[2003] 563–6), makes judicious observations about the strengths and weaknesses of their *Dictionary of Nineteenth-Century British Philosophers*. Reviews of other critical work in prose are as follows: *The Sensation Novel and the Victorian Family Magazine*, by Deborah Wynne, reviewed by the late Barbara Quinn Schmidt (*VPR* 36:iii[2003] 279–80); *Victorian Women's Magazines: An Anthology*, edited by Margaret Beetham and Kay Boardman, reviewed by Larry K. Uffelman (*VPR* 36:iii[2003] 285–6); *Print in Transition, 1850–1910: Studies in Media and book History*, by Laurel Brake, reviewed by Margaret D. Stetz (*VPR* 36:iii[2003] 283–4); *Macmillan: A Publishing Tradition*, edited by Elizabeth James, reviewed by Rosemary T. Van Arsdel (*VPR* 36:iii[2003] 287–8); *'Storm and Struggle': The Life and Death of Francis Adams*, by Meg Tasker, reviewed by Richard Duvall (*VPR* 36:i[2003] 78–9); *Negotiating India in the Nineteenth-Century Media*, edited by David Finkelstein and Douglas M. Peers, reviewed by Richard D. Fulton (*VPR* 36:i[2003] 80–1); *Literary Magazines and British Romanticism*, by Mark Parker, reviewed by Robert Morrison (*VPR* 36:i[2003] 84–5); *Women of the Press in Nineteenth-Century Britain*, by Barbara Onslow, reviewed by Lillian Nayder (*VPR* 36:i[2003] 86–7); *Jack the Ripper and the London Press*, by Perry Curtis, Jr., reviewed by Lydia Murdoch (*VS* 45:iv[2003] 760–1); *Florence Fenwick Miller: Victorian Feminist, Journalist, and Educator*, by Rosemary T. Van Arsdel, reviewed by I.A. Flammang (*VS* 45:iv[2003] 744–5); *The Theological and Ethical Writings of Frances Power Cobbe, 1822–1904*, by Sandra J. Peacock, reviewed by Barbara Caine (*VS* 45:iv[2003] 748–9); *The Rescue of Romanticism: Walter Pater and John Ruskin*, by Kenneth Daley, reviewed by Linda M. Austin (*VPR* 36:ii[2003] 182–3); and *'Victorian Sensation': The Extraordinary Publication, Reception, and Secret Authorship of Vestiges of the Natural History of Creation*, by Simon J. Knell, reviewed by Virginia Zimmerman (*VS* 45:ii[2003] 344–5).

2. The Novel

(a) General

In a thoughtful new study, *Victorian Detective Fiction and the Nature of Evidence: The Scientific Investigations of Poe, Dickens, and Doyle*, Lawrence Frank explores ways in which detective fiction responded to various scientific writings by, for example, Darwin, Lyell, Huxley, and Tyndall. According to Frank, the genre helped to promote a secular world-view. To paraphrase, he traces the history of the genre using a model with foundations in the *Origin of Species*, and reads it as a kind of postmodern historiography. A plethora of texts are found in Cox, ed., *The Oxford Book of Victorian Detective Stories*, comprising thirty-one short stories by Braddon, Dickens, Collins, and Doyle, as well as lesser-known Victorian crime and detective writers, such as J.S. Le Fanu, Mrs Henry Wood, M.P. Shiel, Baroness Orczy, Sax Rohmer, and Robert Barr.

Caroline Levine's *The Serious Pleasures of Suspense: Victorian Realism and Narrative Doubt* looks at the role of suspense in a variety of Victorian fictional genres (not just mystery, Gothic, and detective fiction) and claims that the suspension of judgement is important in understanding the emerging approach to knowledge known as realism. Arguing that such texts are not merely conservative, Levine shows how scepticism and the experience of doubt helped train readers to understand the epistemology of science. Joseph A Kestner, *Sherlock's Sisters: The British Female Detective, 1864–1913*, takes a look at female detective figures in Victorian and Edwardian fiction and shows how they are empowered politically, socially, institutionally, and professionally in both official and unofficial investigative capacities. According to Kestner, important cultural and social issues (such as suffragism and emerging notions of the New Woman) are emphasized as female detective characters investigate a host of crimes—such as embezzlement, fraud, and sexual harassment—which are committed by both male and female perpetrators. Included are incisive discussions of the works of several lesser-known authors, such as Beatrice Heron-Maxwell, Emmuska Orczy, L.T. Meade, Catherine Pirkis, Fergus Hume, Grant Allen, and Richard Marsh, along with a few works by writers such as Collins and Braddon. There is most welcome attention to the fiction of Leonard Merrick [1864–1939], whose *Mr. Bazalgette's Agent* [published in 1888] has as its central figure a female detective. Kestner writes appropriately that Merrick's 'importance to detective literature has scarcely been recognized. His value to the study of the female detective in British literature is decisive albeit stupefyingly neglected' (p. 33). Kestner's study is a most important one, not least for his intelligent probing of texts and authors hitherto neglected by literary scholars, historians and critics. Susan Cannon Harris, 'Pathological Possibilities: Contagion and Empire in Doyle's Sherlock Holmes Stories' (*VLC* 31:ii[2003] 447–66), discusses the notion of the 'strange pathological possibilities' of sickness in the East which could not be treated by the general practitioner.

The subject of Françoise Dupeyron-Lafay's 'Fatal Women: Sirens, Monsters and Criminals in Victorian Fiction' (*CVE* 57[2003] 55–66) is the criminal female character in the works of Collins, Braddon, and Haggard. Dupeyron-Lafay discusses how, although these female monsters or 'sirens' are not conventionally ugly, the authors depend on other strategies (paintings, symbolism, and allusion, for example) to depict their inner corruption.

Two studies rather riddled with critical jargon include Lisa Rodensky's *The Crime in Mind: Criminal Responsibility and the Victorian Novel* and Upamanyu Pablo Mukherjee, *Crime and Empire: The Colony in Nineteenth-Century Fictions of Crime*. Rodensky focuses on how Victorian legal fiction depicts the interior life of its characters, thus challenging and confirming notions of criminal responsibility. She considers novels by Dickens, Eliot, and Hardy, alongside noted legal historians of the time. In spite of some rather dense prose, Rodensky has valuable and thoughtful things to say about the relationship between Victorian criminal law and fiction. She is particularly good on *Middlemarch* and *Daniel Deronda*. Mukherjee demonstrates the ways in which the rhetoric of crime in British narratives about India was used to understand and rule the empire. Simon Cooke's 'Dangerous Subversives: The Role of Painters in Sensational Fiction' (*VIJ* 31[2003] 157–72), assesses the mysterious, subversive, and sometimes dangerous painter figure in the works of Collins, Braddon, Reade, and Le Fanu, among others. Patricia Pulham, 'The Castrato and the Cry in Vernon Lee's Wicked Voices' (*VLC* 30:ii[2002] 421–38), explores the role of art, specifically the operatic voice, in Lee's supernatural short stories.

Hoeveler and Heller, eds., *Approaches to Teaching Gothic Fiction: The British and American Traditions*, in the generally useful MLA series on approaches to teaching, includes sections on materials (including references and background sources, critical approaches, and aids to teaching) and approaches to teaching the background to Gothic (definitions, philosophy, and ideology). Sections are devoted to the British Victorian Gothic and American Victorian Gothic traditions, and guidelines for teaching the Gothic in specific classroom settings (for example, in interdisciplinary contexts, role-playing, and in the incorporation of film adaptations) are provided. To give a specific instance from this volume, Tricia Lootens's 'Fear of Furniture: Commodity Gothicism and the Teaching of Victorian Literature' explores links between Gothic objects and their creation, consumerism, and the politics of race, gender, and empire.

Smith and Hughes, eds., *Empire and the Gothic: The Politics of Genre*, investigates connections between postcolonial theories and the Gothic, illustrating ways in which contemporary writers such as Salman Rushdie and Arundhati Roy make use of various Gothic elements, as well as applying postcolonial theories to writers such as Stoker and Haggard. Linda Dryden, *The Modern Gothic and Literary Doubles: Stevenson, Wilde and Wells*, shows how traditional rural scenes of the Victorian Gothic were relocated to the city in the late nineteenth century, and how perceptions of London shaped the encounters and transformations of the new modern, metropolitan Gothic. The subject of Peter K. Garrett's highly intelligent *Gothic Reflections: Narrative Force in Nineteenth-Century Fiction* is Gothic self-consciousness and modern narrative theory. Included are provocative interrelated readings of Poe, Walpole, Hogg, Shelley,

Stevenson, Stoker, Dickens, Eliot, and James. Cox and Gilbert, eds., *The Oxford Book of Victorian Ghost Stories*, comprises thirty-five ghost stories by Gaskell, Collins, Charles Dickens, Doyle, and Stevenson, as well as lesser-known Victorian writers, for example Mrs Craik, J.S. Le Fanu, Rhoda Broughton, and Charlotte Riddell. Also included are source notes and a useful chronology of ghost story collections from 1850 to 1910. Sally Harris, 'Spiritual Warnings: The Ghost Stories of Joseph Sheridan Le Fanu' (*VIJ* 31[2003] 9–41), discusses representations of spiritual forces, particularly elements of Catholicism, in Le Fanu's ghost stories. Also of interest is Terry W. Thompson's '"A sense of something lost": The Unlived Jamesian Life in Algernon Blackwood's "The Tryst"' (*PLL* 39:iv[2003] 366–74).

Yael Halevi-Wise, *Interactive Fictions: Scenes of Storytelling in the Novel*, investigates the role of dramatic storytelling moments in various novels, from Cervantes' *Don Quixote* to more contemporary novels, such as *Like Water for Chocolate* by Laura Esquivel. Some discussion of Victorian novels (Austen's *Northanger Abbey* and Dickens's *Little Dorritt*) is included. Halevi-Wise emphasizes storytelling events in which characters participate in debates over how to tell a story in such a way that it conforms appropriately to their social category or aesthetic expectations. Examining the division between highbrow and popular culture, Sean Latham looks at the figure of the snob in *'Am I a Snob?': Modernism and the Novel.* Looking at the works of Thackeray, Wilde, Woolf, Joyce and Dorothy L. Sayers, Latham shows how the snob figure evolved from a rather vulgar social climber into an arbiter of cultural taste. Laura Fasick, *Professional Men and Domesticity in the Mid-Victorian Novel*, explores the tension between the stern work ethic advocated by Carlyle and domestic values which were seen as gentler and more 'feminine'. Presenting critical readings on a range of novels (including *Great Expectations, Wives and Daughters, Pendennis,* and *Two Years Ago*), Fasick's study illustrates how these works were influenced by Carlyle's theories of work and intellectual vocation.

Amy M. King's critically imaginative study *Bloom: The Botanical Vernacular in the English Novel* explores ways in which the language of botany and the natural sciences contributed to sexualized representations of maturation and marriage in nineteenth-century courtship novels. Focusing particularly on images and metaphors of the 'blooming girl', King's study includes useful discussion of novels by, among others, Austen, Eliot, and James. Patricia Menon, *Austen, Eliot, Charlotte Brontë, and the Mentor-Lover*, explores and compares mentor-lover figures in the works of the three novelists, analysing the varying degrees of power, love, and judgement manifested by each. Menon also discusses how, through their authorship, the novelists themselves become mentor-lovers.

Ayres, ed., *Silent Voices: Forgotten Novels by Victorian Women Writers*, contains ten interesting and scholarly essays on unknown or neglected Victorian female novelists, including, among others, Grace Aguilar, Charlotte Elizabeth Tonna, Catherine Crowe, Annie E. Holdsworth, Flora Annie Steel, Ella Hepworth Dixon, Sarah Grand, and Anne Thackeray. Liana F. Piehler, *Spatial Dynamics and Female Development in Victorian Art and Novels: Creating a Woman's Space,* looks at the creative use of space in novels by female writers and Victorian paintings. Included are chapters on, amongst others, 'Windows to Women's

Worlds, Portals to their Imaginations: Visual Female Spaces in Victorian Art'; 'Charlotte Brontë's *Villette*: Spatial Composition/Topography as Discovery and Narrative'; 'Elizabeth Gaskell's *Wives and Daughters*: Micro/Macro-cosmic Visions'; 'George Eliot's *Middlemarch*: Dorothea Brooke's Visionary Spaces'; and 'Anita Brookner's *Hotel du Lac*: A Twentieth-Century Epilogue to a Nineteenth-Century Discussion'.

Sarah Anne Browne, *Devoted Sisters: Representations of the Sister Relationship in Nineteenth-Century British and American Literature*, takes a look at depictions of sisters and their appeal to Victorian readers. When presented as rivals, depictions of sisters can be read as sites of struggle, according to Browne, whose study includes a range of canonical and non-canonical fiction (American and British), such as *Sense and Sensibility*, *The Woman in White*, *Little Women*, and *Middlemarch*, along with novels by Dinah Mulock Craik and Catharine Sedgwick. Browne concludes with an examination of the 'Deceased Wife's Sister Act', a law which made invalid all marriages to a deceased wife's sister after a certain date, and a chapter entitled 'The Double Taboo: Lesbian Incest in the Nineteenth Century'.

Daphne M. Kutzer's thoughtful study *Beatrix Potter: Writing in Code* examines Potter's writings in the context of her personal life, as well as the cultural and social milieu of her time. Kutzer argues that although Potter [1866–1943] led a restricted life that was typical of many Victorian women, she was able to express her opinions on politics, class, and social issues in a codified way in her children's fiction, her other writings and her art. Many of these opinions, according to Kutzer, are related to her struggle against and longing for escape from the constraints of the home and domesticity. Kutzer has a most interesting reading of *The Tale of Peter Rabbit* [1901]. In *Fiction, Famine, and the Rise of Economics in Victorian Britain and Ireland*, Gordon Bigelow analyses the writings of Elizabeth Gaskell and Charles Dickens—along with other forms of social discourse, such as newspaper accounts, pamphlets and travel narratives—on the subject of the Irish famine from 1845 to 1852. Bigelow argues that the formal study of economics drew significantly from literary concepts and the language of subjectivity, which gave rise to a new kind of economic theory based on the individual consumer, rather than a more systematized form of capitalism. The subject of Michael Flavin's *Gambling in the Nineteenth-Century English Novel: 'A Leprosy Is O'er the Land'* is how Disraeli, Thackeray, Dickens, Hardy, Eliot, Trollope, and George Moore use gambling scenes as tropes for character development. Flavin also includes an interesting discussion about perceived similarities between marriage and gambling, although he misses opportunities to investigate sources used by his writers.

Nicholas Dames, *Amnesiac Selves: Nostalgia, Forgetting, and British Fiction, 1810–1870,* uses a range of Victorian theories of the mind to explore the part novels played in transmuting remembering into something secure, sentimental and communal, rather than something based on the individual. Gavriel Reisner, *The Death-Ego and the Vital Self: Romances of Desire in Literature and Psychoanalysis*, looks at expressions of desire and anti-desire in the fictional narratives of psychoanalytical writings. Reisner's study includes readings of *Wuthering Heights*, and *Jane Eyre*. Also of interest is Paul Goetsch's *The Oral and the Written in Nineteenth-Century British Fiction*, which, as the title indicates, uses selected texts to explore the interrelation between the spoken and the written.

Klein, ed., *Fictions of the Sea: Critical Perspectives on the Ocean in British Literature and Culture*, is a collection of twelve original essays by various scholars about representations of and references to the sea in literature and history. Of interest to Victorian scholars are the following: 'The Sea is History: Historicizing the Homeric Sea in Victorian Passages' by Tobias Döring, which discusses Prime Minister Gladstone and historian Froude (pp. 121–40); '"As I wuz a-rolling down the Highway one morn": Fictions of the 19th-Century English Sailortown' by Valerie Burton (pp. 141–56); and 'Cabin'd Yet Unconfined: Heroic Masculinity in English Seafaring Novels' by Susan Bassnett (pp. 176–87), which includes discussion of novels by Captain Marryatt.

Reviews of critical work on the Victorian novel which have come to our attention are as follows: *The Illustrated London News (1842–1901); The Graphic (1869–1901): Indexes to Fiction, Victorian Research Guides, 29*, compiled by Graham Law, reviewed by Richard Fulton (*VPR* 36:iii[2003] 267–8); *A Companion to the Victorian Novel*, edited by William Baker and Kenneth Womack, reviewed by Solveig C. Robinson (*VPR* 36:iii[2003] 277–9); *The Sensation Novel and the Victorian Family Magazine*, by Deborah Wynne, reviewed by Barbara Quinn Schmidt (*VPR* 36:iii[2003] 279–80); *Chartist Fiction*, vol. 2: *Ernest Jones, Woman's Wrongs*, edited by Ian Haywood, reviewed by Constance Harsh (*VPR* 36:i[2003] 82–3); *Passion and Pathology in Victorian Fiction*, by Jane Wood, reviewed by Athena Vrettos (*VS* 45:iv[2003] 735–6); *In Another Country: Colonialism, Culture, and the English Novel in India*, by Priya Joshi, reviewed by Leah Price (*VS* 45:ii[2003] 333–4); *Rereading the Imperial Romance: British Imperialism and South African Resistance in Haggard, Schreiner, and Plaatje*, by Laura Chrisman, reviewed by Wendy R. Katz (*VS* 45:ii[2003] 336–7); and *Hidden Hands: Working-Class Women and Victorian Social-Problem Fiction*, by Patricia E. Johnson, reviewed by Kelly J. Mays (*VS* 45:ii[2003] 363–4).

(b) Individual Authors

Stephen James Carver's *The Life and Works of the Lancashire Novelist William Harrison Ainsworth, 1850–1882* is a welcome and important contribution to scholarship on the prolific Gothic novelist whose works were largely neglected until recently, but which were highly regarded in their time. Carver's carefully researched study includes discussion of Ainsworth's relationships with important figures of the day (Scott, Dickens, Thackeray, and Bulwer-Lytton to name a few) and his career as a fiction writer for horror magazines, as well as many of his most important novels, including, among others, *Rookwood*, *Jack Sheppard, Guy Fawkes, The Tower of London, A Tale of the Plague and the Fire, Windsor Castle, Sir John Chiverton,* and *The Lancashire Witches.* Also included are passages from his correspondence and journalism, as well as extensive primary and secondary bibliographies.

There are three Braddon items this year. Jennifer S. Kushnier, 'Educating Boys To Be Queer: Braddon's *Lady Audley's Secret*' (*VLC* 30:i[2002] 61–76), discusses homosocial depictions of detective Robert Audley and their connection to Eton College. Also of interest is Andrew Mangham's 'Hysterical Fictions: Mid-Nineteenth-Century Medical Constructions of Hysteria and the Fiction of Mary Elizabeth Braddon' (*WCSJ* 6[2003] 35–52). Mangham draws on nineteenth-century medical treatises and journals in order to illuminate Braddon's work, in particular *Eleanor's Victory* [1863] and *John Marchmont's Legacy* [1863]. A new edition of Braddon's *The Trail of the Serpent* [1861] from the Modern Library is edited by Chris Willis (who died in November 2004 at a tragically young age), and includes an introduction by Sarah Waters.

The most important contribution to Brontë studies for many years is Christine Alexander and Margaret Smith's *The Oxford Companion to the Brontës*, which comprises over 2,000 alphabetically arranged entries about the Brontës' lives and works. Written by nine expert authorities, and of a high quality overall, entries cover a variety of subjects pertaining to Anne, Emily, and Charlotte Brontë, as well as to their father and brother. Also included are maps, a chronology, cross-references, illustrations, bibliography, and a section devoted to dialect and obsolete words. An important source, this reference work will have a major impact on subsequent Brontë scholarship and criticism. Lisa Paddock and Carl Rollyson's *The Brontës A to Z* somewhat pales by comparison with Alexander and Smith's splendid volume. However, it includes maps, bibliography, chronology and illustrations, as well as over 500 alphabetically arranged entries on characters, major and minor works, family members, friends, other publications, pseudonyms, and other Brontë-related subjects. Some entries on major works include synopses and publication histories.

Angela Hague, *Fiction, Intuition, and Creativity: Studies in Brontë, James, Woolf, and Lessing*, takes a look at ways in which the creative process and intuitive consciousness inform the content and form of fiction. Hague contends that intuition forms the basis of content in *Villette* and *Jane Eyre* by empowering the female protagonists with modes of perception. Carol A Bock, 'Authorship, the Brontës, and *Fraser's Magazine*: "Coming Forward" as an Author in early Victorian England' (*VLC* 29:ii[2001] 241–66), explores the Brontës' situation in the history of authorship in connection with *Fraser's Magazine*. Antonia Losano, 'The Professionalization of the Woman Artist in Anne Brontë's *The Tenant of Wildfell Hall*' (*NCL* 58:i[2003] 1–41), discusses the character of Helen Graham and the historical and narratological implications of her role as an artist. On a related subject, Robert D. Butterworth, 'The Professional Adrift in the Victorian Novel: (1) *Agnes Grey*' (*VN* 104[2003] 13–16), focuses on the uncertain professional role of the governess, discussing how, while depictions of work in mines and factories in Victorian fiction often show physical danger, the professional working world in *Agnes Grey* is fraught with a different kind of danger—one that is psychological. In 'Instructive Sufficiency: Re-reading the Governess through *Agnes Grey*' (*VLC* 29:i[2001] 85–108), Dara Rossman Regaignon argues that the figure of the governess 'disturbed the early Victorians not only because she blurred the boundary between the separate spheres, but also because she dramatized the potentially illimitable effects of education' (p. 85). A chapter by Jana Gohrisch in Drexler, ed., *Nice Work? Critical Perspectives on the Changing Nature of Labour, Leisure, and Unemployment in Britain*, entitled 'Emotion Work in Anne Brontë's *Agnes Grey*', discusses that novel (pp. 63–82).

Jennifer M. Stolpa, 'Preaching to the Clergy: Anne Brontë's *Agnes Grey* as a Treatise on Sermon Style and Delivery' (*VLC* 31:i[2003] 225–40), shows how Anne challenges the assumptions of institutionalized Christianity, particularly in terms of the sermon, which was almost exclusively a male genre at that time.

Patricia Menon, *Austen, Eliot, Charlotte Brontë, and the Mentor-Lover*, is introduced above: explores and compares representations of mentor-lover figures in the works of the three novelists, analysing the varying degrees of power, love, and judgement manifested by each. Menon also discusses how, through authorship, the novelists themselves become mentor-lovers of interest to Charlotte Brontë scholars are chapters 3 and 4: '"Slave of a fixed and dominant idea": Charlotte Brontë's Early Writings—Preliminaries or Precursors?' (pp. 80–97) and '"Should we try to counteract this influence?": *Jane Eyre*, *Shirley and Villette*' (pp. 98–128). Janis McLarren Caldwell, 'Conflict and Revelation: Literalization in the Novels of Charlotte Brontë' (*VLC* 31:ii[2003] 483–99), explores tensions between the artistic qualities and the confessional, autobiographical nature of Brontë's fiction. Marcus Wood, 'Canons to the Right of Them, Canons to the Left of Them: *Mansfield Park*, *Jane Eyre*, and Memorial Subversions of Slavery' (a chapter in his *Slavery, Empathy and Pornography*) discusses the exploitation of women in *Jane Eyre* and *Mansfield Park.* Kate E. Brown, 'Catastrophe and the City: Charlotte Brontë as Urban Novelist' (*NCL* 57:iii[2002] 350–80), looks at the figure of the governess in Gothic spaces of urban confinement in *Villette*. Also of interest is a chapter by Rosemary D. Babcock in Knapp and Womack, eds., *Reading the Family Dance: Family Systems Therapy and Literary Studies*, entitled 'The Enigmatic Jane Eyre: A Differentiation Story Without Family in Charlotte Brontë's *Jane Eyre*' (pp. 46–70). Kathleen Vejvoda, 'Idolatry in *Jane Eyre*' (*VLC* 31:i[2003] 241–62), explores the dialectical marriage and identity idolatry plots and the ways in which the novel was shaped by Catholicism. Jeffrey Cass's 'Miltonic Orientalism: Jane Eyre and the Two Dalilas' (*DSA* 33[2003] 191–214) is an intertextual study of *Jane Eyre* and *Samson Agonistes*. Cass challenges previous critics who have claimed that Milton is an author 'against whom many women writers struggle to find their voices' proposing a much more complex relationship between Brontë and Milton (p. 191). Laura Haigwood's '*Jane Eyre*, Eros and Evangelicalism' (*VN* 104[2003] 4–12), focuses on the subversiveness of the novel's evangelical rhetoric and how it empowers Jane in her quest for spiritual and sexual fulfilment. Warren Edminster, 'Fairies and Feminism: Recurrent Patterns in Chaucer's "The Wife of Bath's Tale" and Brontë's *Jane Eyre*' (*VN* 104[2003] 22–8), explores similarities between the two works in their use of fairies to represent the female characters' struggle for independence.

Philip Rogers, 'Tory Brontë: *Shirley* and the "Man"' (*NCL* 58:ii[2003] 141–75), focuses on Charlotte Brontë's depiction of Robert Moore to argue that *Shirley* conforms to more conservative Tory politics, though many critics (including Elizabeth Gaskell, one of Charlotte's biographers) highlight liberal, feminist aspects of her novels. In '*Shirley*: Reflections on Marrying Moores' (*VLC* 30:i[2003] 1–17), Judith Wilt reflects that at the heart of the novel *Shirley* lies a 'metaphysical question, the fusion, the confusion, of "hollow" with "more"' (p. 1). Lawrence J. Starzyk, 'Charlotte Brontë's *The Professor:*

The Appropriation of Images' (*JNT* 33:ii[2003] 143–62), takes a look at visual images and portraits in the novel to show how they are used to shape the professor's identity. William A. Cohen, 'Material Interiority in Charlotte Brontë's *The Professor*' (*NCL* 57:iii[2003] 443–76), suggests that the character of the professor reflects a fantasy of male embodiment for Brontë, one that raises interesting questions about human interiority and 'the strangeness of the idea of being inside any body at all' (p. 445). Jennifer Ruth, 'Between Labor and Capital: Charlotte Brontë's Professional Professor' (*VS* 45:ii[2003] 279–303), investigates the price of intellectual labour in the novel and its positioning in relation to the market. Mention should be made of a new Victorian fiction written in the early years of the twenty-first century, Emma Brown's *Claire Boylan and Charlotte Brontë*, a highly readable metanarrative based on a Charlotte Brontë idea.

Emma Mason's '"Some God of wild enthusiast's dreams": Emily Brontë's Religious Enthusiasm' (*VLC* 31:i[2003] 263–76), interestingly focuses on 'Brontë's fascination with enthusiasm as a device through which she could validate her rendering of passion in a literary society that deemed the power of her work masculine, unnatural, and strange' (p. 264). A new Norton edition of *Wuthering Heights* (*Wuthering Heights: The 1847 text, Backgrounds and Criticisms*, edited by Richard J. Dunn, is based on the first edition and collated with several modern editions. New explanatory notes are included, along with reviews, chronology, select bibliography, prose and poetry selections, and five critical essays by noted Brontë scholars. Another new edition of *Wuthering Heights*, edited by Linda H. Peterson, is a revised critical edition from the Case Studies in Contemporary Criticism series, and is again based on the 1847 text. The second edition includes a revised introduction and glossary, critical essays (two of which are new), a bibliography, and a sampling of contemporary responses to the novel.

A new biography by Leslie Mitchell, *Bulwer Lytton: The Rise and Fall of a Victorian Man of Letters,* focuses on narrating the life of this prolific, well-known and important, but critically neglected, writer, marking the 200th anniversary of his birth. Gabriel Finkelstein's well-documented 'M. du Bois-Reymond Goes to Paris' (*BJHS* 36:iii[2003] 261–300) discusses references to scientist and electrophysiologist Emile du Bois-Reymond in Bulwer Lytton's *A Strange Story*.

We hope that Bulwer Lytton will share a critical fate similar to that of Wilkie Collins. Gradually, interest in Collins is reawakening from a lengthy fallow period of critical and scholarly neglect. This resurrection is exemplified by the publication of Maria K. Bachman and Don Richard Cox's *Reality's Dark Light: The Sensational Wilkie Collins*, a collection of fourteen essays focusing on the grotesque and radical elements of Collins's fiction—for example, his depictions of doppelgängers and vengeful heroines. The articles include the following: 'Introduction: The Real Wilkie Collins' by Maria K. Bachman and Don Richard Cox; 'Fatal Newness: *Basil*, Art, and the Origins of Sensation Fiction' by Tom Dolin and Lucy Dougan; 'Framed and Hung: Collins and the Economic Beauty of the Manly Artist' by Dennis Denisoff; '"Bolder with her lover in the dark": Collins and Disabled Women's Sexuality' by Martha Stoddard Holmes; 'Chemical Seductions: Exoticism, Toxicology, and the Female Poisoner in *Armadale* and *The Legacy of Cain*' by Piya Pal-Lapinski; 'Marian's Moustache:

Bearded Ladies, Hermaphrodites, and Intersexual Collage in *The Woman in White*' by Richard Collins; 'The Crystal Palace, Imperialism, and the "Struggle for Existence": Victorian Evolutionary Discourse in Collins's *The Woman in White*' by Gabrielle Ceraldi; 'Fosco Lives!' by A.D. Hutter; 'Outlandish English Subjects in *The Moonstone*' by Timothy L. Carens; '"Blue like me": Collins, Poor *Miss Finch*, and the Construction of Racial Identity' by Lillian Nayder; 'Plain Faces, Weird Cases: Domesticating the Law in Collins's *The Law and the Lady* and the Trial of Madeleine Smith' by Karin Jacobson; 'Collins, Race, and Slavery' by Audrey Fisch; 'Yesterday's Sensations: Modes of Publication and Narrative Form in Collins's Late Novels' by Graham Law; and 'Afterword: Masterpiece Theatre and Ezra Jennings's Hair; Some Reflections on Where We've Been and Where We're Going in Collins Studies' by Tamar Heller. The University of Tennessee Press has done justice to the subject in producing a fine and well-indexed volume in the ongoing Tennessee Studies in Literature series. As Maria Bachman and Don Richard Cox note in the conclusion of their introduction to the volume, 'clearly Wilkie Collins, in his determined pursuit of Reality's dark light, has much to teach us in the twenty-first century about the intricacies of life in the nineteenth' (p. xxv).

Carolyn W. de la L. Oulton's *Literature and Religion in Mid-Victorian England* is an excellent account focusing on the subtleties of the liberal Christian beliefs of Dickens and Collins. Discussions of George Eliot and John Henry Newman are also included by way of contrast. As Norman Vance notes in an incisive review of Oulton's study, 'she has performed a valuable service for students of Dickens and Collins by demonstrating that there is a serious and sustained engagement with religious matters in their work'. However Oulton is unfortunately 'less effective in her handling of religious ecclesiastical contexts' (*WCSJ* 6[2003] 60–1). Zlata Antonova's dissertation, written for Cherepovets State University in Russia, 'The Third Period of Creative Work of Wilkie Collins', demonstrates that interest in Collins's life and work is not confined to English-speaking countries. According to Kirsten Hüttner's summary, included by the Wilkie Collins Society with the *Wilkie Collins Society Journal* 2003 issue, Antonova discusses Collins's evolution and development as a writer through his three major periods, focusing particularly on the third period, during which time he wrote *Man and Wife* [1870] and *The Law and the Lady* [1875]. Hüttner notes that Antonova's 'perspective from the background of Russian scholarship certainly adds new insights to existing Western criticism' (p. 4).

Michael Hollington, 'Eros and Thanatos in *Iolani* and "The Captain and the Nymph"' (*CVE* 57[2003] 99–114), offers an analysis of Collins's first novel *Iolani* and compares it to a later story, 'The Captain and the Nymph', which has the same 'South Seas Gothic' setting. Both stories emphasize the eros/thanatos binary, but, as Hollington shows, the latter work demonstrates a higher degree of technical skill and a more controlled handling of 'exotic' material. Allan W. Atlas, 'Wilkie Collins, Mr. Vanstone, and the Case of Beethoven's "No Name" Symphony' (*DSA* 33[2003] 215–38), makes the case that the symphony mentioned at the beginning of *No Name* [1864] is Beethoven's Seventh Symphony. Atlas's essay is a necessary corrective one to the perception that Collins was somewhat hostile to classical music.

Maria K. Bachmanand Don Richard Cox's welcome new edition of Collins's *Blind Love* includes the following appendices: 'Reaction to the Death of Wilkie Collins' (three of these are reprinted); six 'Contemporary Reviews of Collins's Work'; 'Horace Pym's Notes on the Von Scheurer Case'; three 'Newspaper Accounts of the Insurance Trial' drawn on by Collins for the novel; 'The Prologue to "Iris", 1887'; 'Excerpts from Collins's Plans for *Blind Love*: The Synopsis'; 'The Irish Question'; and 'The Duties of a Lady's Maid'. Collins's final novel, left unfinished at his death and completed by Walter Besant, is of especial interest, not least because of its setting. It takes place against the backdrop of the Irish Land War in the early years of the 1880s. One of its central protagonists is a member of an Irish secret society. Bachman and Cox interestingly use as their copy-text the 1890 Chatto & Windus three-volume edition, in other words, the first book edition rather than the serialized version in *The Illustrated London News*. Of particular interest is their use of portions of the hitherto unpublished Collins short novel 'Iris', which was incorporated into *Blind Love*.

Also new in Collins studies is Patricia Pulham's 'Textual/Sexual Masquerades: Reading the Body in *The Law and the Lady*' (*WCSJ* 6[2003] 19–34). Pulham's focus is on 'textual and sexual masquerades' (p. 33) in an essay aiming 'to explore the textual and sexual worlds [which] revolve around the issue of a masquerade' (p. 19). *The Moonstone* is the focus of two articles. William Baker's 'Wilkie Collins's Notes for *The Moonstone*' (*VIJ* 31[2003] 187–205) publishes for the first time, with extensive annotation, seventeen separate items relating to *The Moonstone* now in the Parrish Collection at Princeton University Library. Baker's 'Wilkie Collins in the Parrish Collection' (*PULC* 62:iii[Spring 2001] 501–18] appeared in 2003 in the issue of the *Princeton University Library Chronicle* 'dedicated to the memory of Alexander James Dallas Wainwright (1917–2000), who was for fifty-two years curator of the Morris L. Parrish Collection of Victorian Novelists at Firestone Library' (p. 347). Replete with illustrations from the collection, Baker's 'review of the Wilkie Collins treasures in the Parrish Collection merely skims the surface of an exceedingly rich and diverse repository' (p. 518). David J. Holmes's introduction ('The Constant Curator') to the Wainwright dedicatory issue (*PULC* 62:iii[Spring 2001] 347–60) provides a fascinating glimpse into its subject's life, personality and acquisition policies. Stephen Ferguson, Curator of Rare Books at Princeton, and a former colleague of Wainwright, introduces a [1951] speech of his on 'The Morris L. Parrish Collection of Victorian Novelists'. This gives a detailed and clear account of the formation and history of the 'donated collection' over which, to use David J. Holmes's words, 'Alec was the ideal caretaker' (p. 360). Finally, in this rich harvest of materials on Collins and others mention should be made of James R. Simmons's suggestive '"Read the name … that I have written inside": Onomastics and Wilkie Collins's *The Moonstone*' (*ELN* 41:i[2003] 69–75).

Two new articles this year discuss Marie Corelli's *A Romance of Two Worlds*. In one, Jill Galvan, 'Christians, Infidels, and Women's Channelling in the Writings of Marie Corelli' (*VLC* 31:i[2003] 83–98), investigates the role of technology and spiritualism in the novel. In the second, J. Jeffrey Franklin, 'The Counter-Invasion of Britain by Buddhism in Marie Corelli's *A Romance of Two*

Worlds and H. Rider Haggard's *Ayesha: The Return of She*' (*VLC* 31:i[2003] 19–42), assesses the emergence of Buddhist themes in British literary discourse beginning in the 1860s, focusing particularly on the ways in which Eastern themes were interwoven with images of Christianity and empire. Franklin then goes on to describe what he sees as a discursive contest in *A Romance of Two Worlds* and *Ayesha: The Return of She*. The author best known for *John Halifax Gentleman* [1856], Dinah Craik is the subject of Margaret Sherry Rich's description of *Dinah Craik's Library Catalog* (*PULC* 62:iii[Spring 2001] 568–70). Sherry Rich briefly describes 'her library catalog, a handwritten 332-page alphabetical list of her books' acquired in 1998 by Princeton University Library (p. 568).

There were many new contributions in Dickens studies this year. Ralph Pite and John Mullan's *Lives of Victorian Literary Figs.: Eliot, Dickens and Tennyson* reproduces selections of useful biographical materials (letters, memoirs, conversations, anecdotes, essays, and so forth) drawn primarily from sources that are otherwise difficult to access. Volume 2, *Charles Dickens*, is edited by Corinna Russell. The volume contains, in addition to a detailed introduction concerning the responses to Dickens by his contemporaries, twenty-eight selections. Some, such as those by George Sala and Sir Arthur Helps, are obituary notices. Each selection has an informative headnote placing the extract in a biographical, historical and literary context. Russell's helpful volume includes a bibliography, a chronology and notes. New from the Authors in Context series (general editor Patricia Ingham) is *Charles Dickens* by Andrew Sanders, an examination of Dickens's work in relation to the Victorian period and to the present. Included in this well-written study are chapters devoted to Dickens's life, Victorian politics, religion, and science, along with suggestions for further readings, notes, illustrations, and sections devoted to websites and film and television adaptations. A useful new guide by John L. Drew, *Dickens the Journalist,* considers the canon of Dickens's journalistic writings, including his sketches, reviews, reports, satires, and essays, focusing especially on his work as a journalist apart from his career as a novelist. Catherine Waters, '"Trading in Death": Contested Commodities in *Household Words*' (*VPR* 36:iv[2003] 313–31), considers connections between the emerging commodity culture and Dickens's writings about bodies and funerals in *Household Words*.

Drawing on the ideas of Walter Benjamin, Graham Smith, in *Dickens and the Dream of Cinema*, argues that the 'proto-filmic' nature of the language and structure in Dickens's fiction played an important role in the anticipation and emergence of cinema. Smith focuses on Dickens's interest in panorama and railway travel, as well as on the role of the city (London and Paris, in particular), as metaphors for human consciousness. John Glavin's *Dickens on Screen* is a collection of essays by various experts on film adaptations of Dickens's novels, as well as related subjects, including Gerhard Joseph's 'Dickens, Psychoanalysis and Film: A Roundtable'; John O. Jordan's '*Great Expectations* on Australian Television'; Robert M. Polhemus's 'Screen Memories in Dickens and Woody Allen'; John Romano's 'Writing After Dickens: The Television Writer's Art'; Steve J. Wurzler's '*David Copperfield* [1935] and the U.S. Curriculum'; and Margaret Rippy's 'Orson Welles and Charles Dickens, 1938–41'. *Rereading the City/Rereading Dickens: Representation, the Novel, and Urban Realism*, by

Efraim Sicher, is an extensive study of Dickens's urban realism and its connection to the railway, prison, sanitation, and other urban systems and discourses. Elizabeth A. Campbell, *Fortune's Wheel: Dickens and the Iconography of Women's Time*, examines fictional and iconographical images of wheels, which came to be powerful symbols of England's industrial progress and modernity. In the works of Dickens, Campbell focuses on depictions where the 'masculine' industrial wheel is fused with the feminine goddess Fortune, a reflection of Dickens's pessimistic perception of time and fate. Thompson, ed., *The Literal Imagination: Selected Essays* comprises previously uncollected essays by the late Ian Watt and includes an essay of interest to Dickens scholars, 'Oral Dickens' (pp. 171–93).

Jay Clayton, *Charles Dickens in Cyberspace: The Afterlife of the Nineteenth Century in Postmodern Culture*, compares literary and scientific elements of nineteenth-century and contemporary American culture, for example linking Frankenstein's creature with cyborgs, in order to demonstrate parallels that share a sometimes curious, submerged logic. Clayton's discussion encompasses a diverse range of nineteenth-century and contemporary figures, such as Charles Dickens, Thomas Hardy, Ada Lovelace, Joseph Paxton, and Mary Shelley, along with late twentieth-century critics and creative writers, including Hélène Cixous, Salman Rushdie, Ridley Scott, Susan Sontag, and Tom Stoppard, and focusing particularly on a common investment in what Clayton perceives as the blending of science and the arts in a predisciplinary atmosphere that often disregarded intellectual boundaries. In *Dickens's Fiction: Tapestries of Conscience*, Stanley Friedman examines Dickens's use of certain literary techniques such as repetition and paradox in order to make his fiction more intricate and to provide moral guidance to his readers. Paul Goetsch, '"The Horror! The Horror!" Last Words from Dickens to Conrad' (*ZAA* 51:ii[2003] 168–85), considers the significance of last words in deathbed scenes in the works of the Brontës, Dickens, Eliot, Gaskell, Gissing, and Hardy. Goetsch argues that, in the later Victorian and early modern periods, the final words of dying characters undermine earlier, more conventional representations of such scenes. Also of interest is Luisa Carrer's 'Trieste's Early Role in the Italian Reception of Charles Dickens' (*MLR* 98:i[2003] 1–10), which provides new evidence that Dickens's work was available in translation in Italy half a century earlier than has been presumed.

The subject of Lara Kriegel's 'The Pudding and the Palace: Labor, Print Culture, and Imperial Britain in 1851' (in Burton, ed., pp. 230–45) is a short tale about a Christmas pudding published in *Household Words* just six months before the Great Exhibition. In this tale, mercantile commodities of various nations are intended to represent their place of origin, and Kriegel insightfully compares this representation to the Great Exhibition of 1851 with its seeming 'encapsulations of the globe' (p. 231). Robert Tracy, 'Lighthousekeeping: *Bleak House* and the Crystal Palace' (*DSA* 33[2003] 25–54), investigates the role of Esther as a cataloguer of social ills and one who guides the reader into the presence of the darker voice of the other narrator. According to Tracy, one of Esther's roles is to remind readers of the need for social progress that is comparable to the technological progress of the Great Exhibition. In 'Glass Windows: The View from *Bleak House*' (*DSA* 33[2003] 55–86), Katherine Williams considers windows as actual characters in the novel, whose role it is to provide boundaries and limitations, as well as light and vision.

In a follow up to *Post-Romantic Consciousness*, John Beer, *Post-Romantic Consciousness: Dickens to Plath*, devotes discussion to Dickens's internal struggle 'between a consciously affectionate and benevolent view of the world' and his 'unconscious attraction to the criminal and violent' in *The Mystery of Edwin Drood.* Beer argues this was one reason it was left unfinished (p. x). Christophe Gelly, 'Charles Dickens's *The Mystery of Edwin Drood*: An Unfinished Novel, A Novel to be Continued' (*CVE* 57[2003] 67–82), speculates that, by positioning Jasper as the supposed guilty party, Dickens may have wished to eventually surprise readers who had discarded that solution as too obvious. Gelly also discusses *L'Affaire D,* a humorous Italian sequel to Dickens's unfinished work. Hyungji Park, '"Going to wake up Egypt": Exhibiting Empire in *Edwin Drood*' (*VLC* 30:ii[2002] 529–50), looks at 'Egypt-gazing' in the novel and how displays of Egypt became a form of visual commodity in the West.

Oxford World's Classics's *Barnaby Rudge*, edited by Clive Hurst, is based on the 1841 edition originally published in forty-two weekly numbers in *Master Humphrey's Clock.* Collated against the manuscript, extant proofs, the Philadelphia edition, and three later corrupt editions which were not systematically revised by Dickens, this new edition also includes an introduction by Iain McCalman and Jon Mee, as well as a bibliography, chronology, appendices on sources, and explanatory notes. John Bowen is the editor of a rival edition of *Barnaby Rudge* published by Penguin. This too has as its copy-text the 1841 edition, and includes original illustrations, appendices, a map of London at the time of the Gordon Riots, the preface to the 1868 edition, and an introduction by Bowen.

Elaine Freedgood, 'Realism, Fetishism, and Genocide: "Negro Head" Tobacco in and around *Great Expectations*' (*Novel* 36:i[2002] 26–41), argues that, in *Great Expectations*, 'there is a particularly overwhelming horror that cannot be named but only encoded fetishistically in the most apparently negligible of details' (p. 26). Bernard N. Schilling's *The Rain of Years: Great Expectations and the World of Dickens* is a collection primarily of impressions and interpretations of the novel's characters, themes, and images. Marielle Seichepine, 'Frustration of the Victorian Woman and Time: Miss Havisham and Mrs. Transome' (*CVE* 57[2003] 153–70), discusses these two characters in terms of the burden of past unfulfilled desires and their experiences of time.

In 'Conviction in Writing: Crime, Confession, and the Written Word in *Great Expectations*' (*DSA* 33[2003] 87–108), Monique R. Morgan writes that the guilt associated with writing and the forgiveness associated with speech are 'thematic links … rooted in nineteenth-century confession law, and *Great Expectations* provides an alternative to recent accounts of the status of testimony in Victorian legal practice and Victorian fiction' (p. 87). In 'A Rabelaisian View from Todgers's Backside, Or "Partly Spiritual, Partly Spiritous" in *Martin Chuzzlewit*' (*DSA* 33[2003] 1–24), Mark M. Hennelly Jr. considers the role of carnivalesque motifs, focusing especially on the novel's preface and the American chapters. Tamara Ketabgian, '"Melancholy mad elephants": Affect and the Animal

Machine in *Hard Times*' (*VS* 45:iv[2003] 649–76), discusses how powerful emotional forces such as anger and violence are aligned with images of machines and animals in the novel. Jennifer Gribble, 'Why the Good Samaritan Was a Bad Economist: Dickens' Parable for *Hard Times*' (*L&T* 18:iv[2003] 427–41), explores the tension between utilitarian self-interest and Christian altruism in the novel.

Daniel P. Scoggin, 'A Speculative Resurrection: Death, Money, and the Vampiric Economy of *Our Mutual Friend*' (*VLC* 30:i[2002] 99–128), argues that 'the attempt to respond to death-in-life by a fiction of life-in-death culminates in the Harmon–Rokesmith deception at the heart of the plot of *Our Mutual Friend*' (p. 101). In '*David Copperfield* and the Pursuit of Happiness' (*VS* 46:i[2003] 69–96), Annette R. Federico assesses Dickens's writings about his restlessness and pursuit of happiness in his own journals and their connection to *David Copperfield*. New from the Norton Annotated series is *The Annotated Christmas Carol: A Christmas Carol in Prose*. Edited by Michael Hearn, it is the first edition of Dickens's popular Christmas story to include the original along with his Public Reading Text. Original illustrations by John Leech are accompanied by other contemporary images, such as photographs and drawings related to Dickens and *A Christmas Carol*. Included are literary and historical annotations and an introduction on the story's creation and publication by Hearn. Also in Dickens studies are the following articles of interest: Natalie Bell Cole's '"Attached to life again": The "Queer Beauty" of Convalescence in *Bleak House*' (*VN* 103[2003] 17–19); Ellen Miller Casey's '"Boz has got the town by the ear": Dickens and the *Athenaeum* Critics' (*DSA* 33[2003] 159–90); Gareth Cordery's 'Public Houses: Spatial Instabilities in *Sketches by Boz* and *Oliver Twist* (Part One)' (*DQu* 20:i[2003] 3–13); Galia Ofek's '"Tie her up by the hair": Dickens's Retelling of the Medusa and Rapunzel Myths' (*DQu* 20:iii[2003] 184–99); Toshikatsu Murayama's 'A Professional Contest over the Body: Quackery and Respectable Medicine in *Martin Chuzzlewit*' (*VLC* 30:ii[2002] 403–20), and Lauren M.E. Goodlad's '"Is there a pastor in the house?" Sanitary Reform, Professionalism, and Philanthropy in Dickens's Mid-Century Fiction' (*VIJ* 31:ii[2003] 525–53).

Reviews of critical work that we have encountered on Dickens include: *Unequal Partners: Charles Dickens, Wilkie Collins, and Victorian Authorship*, by Lillian Nayder, reviewed by Robert L. Patten (*VPR* 36:iii[2003] 273–4); *The Cambridge Companion to Charles Dickens*, edited by John O. Jordan, reviewed by George J. Worth (*VPR* 36:iii[2003] 294–5); *Dickens's Villains: Melodrama, Character, Popular Culture*, by Juliet John, reviewed by John Bowen (*VS* 45:ii[2003] 352–3); *The Rain of Years: Great Expectations and the World of Dickens*, by Bernard N. Schilling, and *Dickens's Great Expectations: Misnar's Pavilion Versus Cinderella*, by Jerome Meckier, both reviewed by John Glavin (*VS* 45:iii[2003] 542–44).

The sole contribution to George du Maurier scholarship and criticism is Sarah Gracombe's 'Converting Trilby: Du Maurier on Englishness, Jewishness, and Culture' (*NCL* 58:i[2003] 75–107), which discusses the 'opposing conversion strategies' in Trilby, and how they relate to 'Englishness' (p. 75), especially in terms of consumption of novels and food.

There is a profusion of work on George Eliot reflecting a diversity of perspectives. Margaret Harris, 'George Eliot: Elegies and Eulogies' (*GER* 34[2003] 28–42), discusses characteristics of the eleven obituaries and poems dedicated to Eliot on her death, exploring various similarities and differences among them. Ralph Pite and John Mullan's *Lives of Victorian Literary Figs.: Eliot, Dickens and Tennyson* reproduces selections of useful biographical materials (letters, memoirs, conversations, anecdotes, essays, and so forth), including primary sources that are otherwise difficult to access. The first volume, devoted to George Eliot, is edited by Gail Marshall. In addition to an extensive introduction, bibliography and chronology, it contains the reprints of twenty items focusing on the life of George Eliot. As Gail Marshall observes, 'in her works Eliot is fascinated by acts of remembrance, and by memory and the workings of history more generally' (p. xx). Not inappropriately her selection begins with the 1871 preface to the first edition of Alexander Main's *Wise, Witty and Tender Sayings in Prose and Verse, selected from the Works of George Eliot*. Her concluding tribute reprints Virginia Woolf's centenary essay on George Eliot from the *TLS* (20 November 1919). Each passage is prefaced by Marshall's detailed headnote and there are also helpful notes to the passages. An addition to 'Intelex Humanities Databases Full-Text Scholarly Editions' is William Baker's *The Notebooks and Library of George Eliot* in their Women Writers Collection. These make available in CD-ROM format his *An Edition of the Carl H. Pforzheimer Library's George Eliot Holograph Notebooks, Mss 707–711* [1976–85]; *George Eliot—George Henry Lewes, an Annotated Catalogue of their Books at Doctor William's Library* [1977] and *The Libraries of George Eliot and George Henry Lewes* [1981]. A.G. van den Broek's review in *GE-GHLS* (46–7[September 2004] 123–5) notes that 'the CD is ... a very welcome addition to anyone interested in Eliot's notebooks and personal library' (p. 125).

Robert Sawyer's interesting *Victorian Appropriations of Shakespeare: George Eliot, A.C. Swinburne, Robert Browning, and Charles Dickens*, argues that, although references to Shakespeare are usually thought to be conservative, Shakespeare can also be appropriated by marginal groups, thus making multiple readings possible, depending on the context. While references to Shakespeare in works by Charles Dickens and Robert Browning may promote conservative values and interpretations, in works by George Eliot and A.C. Swinburne, they may be used to subvert traditional, conservative ideas and interpretations. Anna K. Nardo's *George Eliot's Dialogue with John Milton* is an extensive, well-written intertextual exploration of Milton's influence on Eliot's beliefs and works. Mike Edwards's *George Eliot: The Novels* consists of two sections, the first of which includes analysis of Eliot's novels in terms of several thematic categories (beginnings, characters, relationships, society, morality, and conclusions). Part 2 provides information on contexts and critical receptions of Eliot, including overviews of important critical approaches to Eliot by Barbara Hardy, Michael Wheeler, and Kate Flint. Patricia Menon's *Austen, Eliot, Charlotte Brontë, and the Mentor-Lover* is discussed above. Of interest to Eliot scholars are chapters 5 and 6: 'George Eliot and "The clerical sex": From *Scenes of Clerical Life* to *Middlemarch*' (pp. 129–62) and '"Worth nine-tenths of the sermons"? The Author as Mentor-Lover in *Daniel Deronda*' (pp. 163–87).

Brenda McKay's exceedingly thorough *George Eliot and Victorian Attitudes to Racial Diversity, Colonialism, Darwinism, Class, Gender, and Jewish Culture and Prophecy* defends Eliot against critics such as Edward Said. McKay scrupulously acknowledges her indebtedness to previous scholars and critics who have laboured to explicate her subject's deep engagement with ethnicity and has produced a valuable monograph. Nancy Henry's 'George Eliot and the Colonies' (*VLC* 29:ii[2001] 413–33), explores *Impressions of Theophrastus Such* in her analysis of Eliot's views on colonization, emphasizing that critics should more often consider 'non-fictional as well as fictional discourses in their generalizations about discursive formations and imperialist ideologies' (p. 430). Alicia Carroll's *Dark Smiles: Race and Desire in George Eliot* applies postcolonial theory to several poems and novels by Eliot. Carroll's book suffers somewhat from too much application of theoretical critical terminology, which detracts from some sound insights. The subject of George Scott Christian's 'Comic George Eliot' (*GER* 34[2003] 21–7) is the role of comic theory in Eliot's realist aesthetic. Michael Carnigan, 'Analogical Reasoning in Victorian Historical Epistemology' (*JHI* 64:iii[2003] 445–64), discusses Eliot's historical epistemology and how it exemplifies her opposition to objectivist tendencies in historical writing. Bernard J. Paris, *Rereading George Eliot: Changing Responses to her Experiments in Life*, traces his own changing personal and psychological responses to Eliot over the years. Paris's book focuses on two novels, *Middlemarch* and *Daniel Deronda*, and the all-pervasive impact of his 'fortuitous reading of Karen Horney' (p. x) upon his literary responses. Probably Paris's *Rereading George Eliot* will have less impact than his outstanding earlier intertextual study *Experiments in Life: George Eliot's Quest for Values* [1965]. More than thirty years on, Paris repudiates this work—a great pity. The subject of Charles LaPorte's 'George Eliot, the Poetess as Prophet' (*VLC* 31:i[2003] 159–80), is Eliot's ambivalence about being associated with 'feminine writing'. LaPorte makes out an interesting case for a reassessment of some of George Eliot's neglected poems. Delia Da Sousa Correa, *George Eliot, Music, and Victorian Culture*, investigates musical references in Eliot's writings, as well as other related subjects, such as female musicianship, Eliot's friendship with Wagner, and connections between scientific theory and music. The focus is on *Mill on the Floss* and *Daniel Deronda.*

Seth Lerer, '*Middlemarch* and Julius Charles Hare' (*Neophil* 87[2003] 653–64), explores the possible influence of the once highly regarded and influential scholar Julius Charles Hare (author of *Guesses at Truth*) on Eliot's *Middlemarch*, and especially on the characterization of Casaubon. Lerer's *Error and the Academic Self: The Scholarly Imagination, Medieval to Modern*, an exploration of the role of mistakes, misquotations, and other errors in the development of academic writing, also includes discussion of *Middlemarch* in a chapter entitled 'My Casaubon: The Novel of Scholarship and Victorian Philology'. In a largely derivative '*Daniel Deronda* Then and Now' (*Jewish Quarterly*188 [2002/3] 61–6), Samantha Ellis discusses the development of Eliot's fascination with Judaism, considering especially the binary divide between Jewish and Gentile themes and characters in the novel. Omer-Sherman Ranan, '"Thy people are my people": Emma Lazarus, *Daniel Deronda*, and the Ambivalence of Jewish

Modernity' (*JMJS* 1:i[2002] 49–72) assesses the influence of Eliot on Lazarus. Louise Penner, '"Unmapped Country": Uncovering Hidden Wounds in *Daniel Deronda*' (*VLC* 30:i[2002] 77–98), explores questions of identity and the function of the mind and memory in the novel, specifically with regard to Gwendolen and Daniel. Grace Kehler, 'Opera in the Family: Eliot's *Daniel Deronda*' (*VIJ* 31[2003] 109–56), discusses the social status of the prima donna, focusing particularly on the interactions between Daniel Deronda and the three singers in the novel. Kehler argues that 'theatre and family mutually conditioned one another's ideas of merit, although the dialogue between them remained wary' (p. 110). Nancy Anne Marck, 'Narrative Transference and Female Narcissism: The Social Message of *Adam Bede*' (*SEL* 35:iv[2003] 447–70), discusses the characterization of Hetty Sorrel in terms of a specific type of female egoism which works to support the eventual moral regeneration of the 'male-centered community'. Marielle Seichepine, 'Frustration of the Victorian Woman and Time: Miss Havisham and Mrs. Transome' (*CVE* 57[2003] 153–70), is discussed above in relation to Dickens.

An item of interest not picked up earlier is Randall L. Beebe's 'George Eliot and Emil Lehmann: The Translator Translated' (*SN* 72[2000] 63–74). Drawing on archival materials largely unavailable to previous scholars, Beebe illuminates Eliot and Lewes's relationship with Lehmann, the German translator of *Felix Holt* and *Middlemarch*. Beebe's findings 'help piece together some gaps in Eliot's biography concerning how Lehmann came to translate Eliot' (p. 63). Eliot's essays in the *Westminster Review* receive attention in David Goslee's 'Ethical Discord and Resolution in George Eliot's Essays' (*PS* 25:iii[2002] 58–81). The value of Goslee's analysis is somewhat weakened by his insistence on relating the 'reviewing persona' to her fictional heroines such as Maggie Tulliver and Dorothea Brooke. More on Eliot's 'effort to salvage Christian morality while jettisoning Christian theology' (p. 58) in the *Westminster Review* would be welcome. Hina Nazar's 'Philosophy in the Bedroom: *Middlemarch* and the Scandal of Sympathy' (*YJC* 15:ii[2002] 293–314) distinguishes between 'sympathy and egoism' in order to show that 'Dorothea's myopic adornment of individuals is symbolic of the abstraction built into love, and abstraction embodied in a feeling for concrete others' (p. 310).

The following articles are also of interest: 'Property Morality in *The Mill on the Floss*' by Eric Levy (*VIJ* 31[2003] 173–86); 'George Eliot and Misquotation' by Robert MacFarlane (*GEGHLS* 44–5[2003] 2–11); 'Charles Waldstein Waits upon George Eliot' by Margaret Harris and Christopher Stray (*GEGHLS* 44–5[2003] 12–25); 'George Eliot's Borrowing from Dante: A List of Sources' by Andrew Thompson (*GEGHLS* 44–5[2003] 26–74); and 'Art into Life, Life into Art: *Middlemarch* and George Eliot's Letters, with Special Reference to Jane Senior' by Barbara Hardy (*GEGHLS* 44–5[2003] 75–96). MacFarlane's is a brilliantly argued disquisition based on the startling proposition that 'Eliot's misquotations are everywhere apparent, although they have never previously been remarked upon' (p. 3). Margaret Harris and Christopher Stray explicate a name in George Eliot's diary for Sunday, 18 January 1880: amongst the callers was a certain 'Dr. Waldstein'. Born in New York in March 1856 and dying in March 1927, Waldstein, a prolific writer 'was a strange mixture of conflicting qualities' (p. 22) whose diaries shed much light upon himself and the great writer whom he called upon. Harris and Stray are to be congratulated for a remarkable piece of sleuthing. Andrew Thompson's lengthy and erudite article enumerates and comments on George Eliot's borrowings from Dante: 'Eliot was as much steeped in Dante as she was in Homer and the classical world, and the list can provide us with some starting points for exploration of Eliot's relationship with the Florentine poet' (p. 31). In her article the distinguished George Eliot critic Barbara Hardy brings her shrewd critical insights to bear upon *Middlemarch*, its author's letters and her correspondence with Jane Senior. Hardy has perceptive observations to make on 'the prose of George Eliot, fictional and non-fictional' (p. 95).

New in Elizabeth Gaskell studies is Chapple and Shelston, eds., *Further Letters of Mrs. Gaskell*. Like its 2000 hardback counterpart (*YWES* 81[2002] 712), *Further Letters* includes letters to correspondents such as Florence Nightingale, Harriet Martineau, and John Ruskin, along with helpful editorial apparatus. The new 2003 paperback, however, includes six new letters, one of which was written to Gaskell's good friend Eliza Peterson and includes remarks about the press coverage of the Crimean War. Amy Mae King, 'Taxonomical Cures; the Politics of Natural History and Herbalist Medicine in Elizabeth Gaskell's *Mary Barton*' (in Heringman, ed., *Romantic Science: The Literary Forms of Natural History*, pp. 255–70) identifies Alice Wilson's vocation as not simply that of a washerwoman, but of a herbalist. This is evidence, according to King, of the 'lingering vernacular medical tradition in the nineteenth century', and in making this identification King emphasizes 'the importance of this medical epistemology to novelistic representations of social ills. In *Mary Barton*, the physical ills that Alice's herbalist medicine intends to cure are extended to the "remedies" for social ills by one important bridge: a cure for what I will call the "ills of perception" that the taxonomical basis of natural history implicitly suggests' (p. 256).

Roland Végs, '*Mary Barton* and the Dissembled Dialogue' (*JNT* 33:ii[2003] 163–83), looks at examples of doubling and disguise in the novel to examine how social dialogue defines the role of fiction as overtly political. Further, Végs writes that Gaskell 'presents the poetics of dissembled dialogue as a means of effective political action' but that the conflation of aesthetics and politics in the novel results in a suspension of political judgement (p. 165). Liam Corley, in 'The Imperial Addiction of *Mary Barton*' (*GSJ* 17[2003] 1–11), argues that Mary Barton presents a 'critique of the imperial addictions and assumptions which increasingly characterized early Victorian descriptions of economic and political normalcy' (p. 1). Mitsuharu Matsuoka, 'Gaskell's Strategies of Silence in *The Half Brothers*' (*GSJ* 17[2003] 50–8), considers the role of silence in Gaskell's short stories and novels and the ways silence is used to convey the characters' feelings, especially in connection to love.

Christoph Lindner's *Fictions of Commodity Culture* (also noticed above), includes a chapter on Gaskell ('Down and Out in Gaskell's Industrial Novels') in which Lindner somewhat ingeniously argues that Gaskell's representation of production in a newly industrialized city prefigures the Irvine Welsh film *Trainspotting*. In '"Charming and Sane": School Editions of *Cranford* in

America, 1905–14' (*VS* 45:iv[2003] 597–624), Thomas Recchio discusses themes and pedagogical uses of Gaskell's *Cranford*, which was once considered a classic in American classrooms to the extent that nine editions were produced between 1905 and 1914. Alan Shelston, 'From *Cranford* to *The Country of the Pointed Firs*: Elizabeth Gaskell's American Publication and the Work of Sarah Orne Jewett' (*GSJ* 17[2003] 77–91), traces the history of Gaskell's publications in the United States, their reception and popularity there, and her influence on American writer Sarah Orne Jewett. Also new in Gaskell studies are the following: Natalka Freeland's '*Ruth*'s Perverse Economies: Women, Hoarding, and Expenditure' (*ELH* 70:i[2003] 197–221); Louise Henson's 'History, Science and Social Change: Elizabeth Gaskell's 'Evolutionary' Narratives' (*GSJ* 17[2003] 12–33); Lorna Huett's 'Commodity and Collectivity: *Cranford* in the Context of *Household Words*' (*GSJ* 17[2003] 34–49); Tonya Moutray McArtur's '"Unwed Orders": Religious Communities for Women in the Works of Elizabeth Gaskell' (*GSJ* 17[2003] 59–76); and Larry K. Uffleman's 'From "Martha Preston" to "Half a Life-Time Ago": Elizabeth Gaskell Rewrites a Story' (*GSJ* 17[2003] 92–103).

Simon James's *Unsettled Accounts: Money and Narrative in the Novels of George Gissing* is a thorough, well-written examination of the power of capital and its influence on art, love, virtue, and other facets of daily life in Gissing's fiction. James most usefully places Gissing's works (primarily *The Odd Women* and *New Grub Street*) alongside the fictions of other Victorian writers (for example Charles Dickens) whose work also often reflects a preoccupation with commodity and its hold on the material world. Lewis Moore, 'George Gissing and Morley Roberts: The Life of Writing in Late-Victorian England' (*GissingJ* 34:iv[2003] 34–46), discusses depictions of struggling artists in Gissing's *New Grub Street*, as well as in *The Private Life of Henry Maitland* [1912], which was written by Gissing's friend Street Morley Roberts and is based on Gissing's life as a writer.

John Spiers reports on the recent Gissing Centenary conference in London in 'An Event, *and* History: The Gissing Centenary Conference' (*GissingJ* 34:iv[2003] 1–4). In 'From "Phoebe's Fortune" to "Phoebe" by courtesy of George Bentley, *Temple's Bar* Hatchet Man' (*GissingJ* 34:iv[2003] 15–34), Barbara Rawlinson discusses the publication of Gissing's short story 'Phoebe' in 1884. Also new in Gissing studies are the following articles of interest: Robin Woolven's 'George Gissing's London Residences (1877–91)' (*GissingJ* 34:iv[2003] 5–15); Ralph Pordzik's 'Narrating the Ecstatic Moment: George Gissing and the Beginnings of the Modern Short Story' (*ArAA* 28:ii[2003] 349–62); Robert D. Butterworth's 'The Professional Adrift in the Victorian Novel (2): *New Grub Street*' (*VN* 104[2003] 17–21); and Eitan Bar-Yosef's '"Let me die with the Philistines": Gissing's Suicidal Realism' (*LIT* 14:iii[2003] 185–204).

New in H. Rider Haggard studies is John D. Coates's 'The "Spiritual Quest" in Rider Haggard's *She* and *Ayesha*' (*CVE* 57[2003] 33–54), a discussion of the role of Haggard's spiritual views in his fiction, focusing especially on his exploration of contradictions within the teachings of occultist Madame Blavatsky. J. Jeffrey Franklin, 'The Counter-Invasion of Britain by Buddhism in Marie Corelli's *A Romance of Two Worlds* and H. Rider Haggard's *Ayesha: The Return of She*'

(*VLC* 31:i[2003] 19–42), is discussed above under Corelli. Many of Rider Haggard's best-known stories about Allan Quatermain are regularly reprinted; now collected together for the first time in *Hunter Quatermain's Story: The Uncollected Adventures of Allan Quatermain,* edited by Peter Haining, are lesser-known works (five short stories and a novella), as follows: 'Hunter Quatermain's Story'; 'Long Odds'; 'A Tale of Three Lions'; 'Magepa the Buck'; 'Zigali the Wizard'; and *Allan's Wife*. Haining also includes a chronology and an introduction providing a useful overview of Haggard's life, career, and works.

New from the Authors in Context series is Patricia Ingham's *Thomas Hardy*, an examination of Hardy's work read in the context of his own time, as well as in relation to the present. Included are clearly written chapters devoted to biography, social issues, women and society, religion, class, and science—along with a chronology, suggestions for further reading, notes, illustrations, and sections devoted to websites and film and television adaptations. *The Complete Critical Guide to Thomas Hardy* by Geoffrey Harvey also provides an introduction to Hardy's life and works, highlighting important aspects of recent criticism, as well as supplying a commentary on the cultural and social contexts of his writings.

Simon Gattrell, *Thomas Hardy's Vision of Wessex*, provides a comprehensive and thorough account of the evolving stages of Hardy's vision of Wessex, as well as the internal and external forces driving his gradual changes in perception. The website with which Gattrell's study is associated, <www.english.uga.edu/wessex>, includes extensive information about almost all the revisions Hardy made to aspects of Wessex in his fiction. Also included on the website are further secondary materials and endnotes. David Musselwhite, *Social Transformations in Hardy's Tragic Novels: Megamachines and Phantasms*, utilizes the theoretical frameworks of Deleuze and Guattari to offer new readings of four tragic novels: *The Return of the Native*, *The Mayor of Casterbridge*, *Tess of the d'Urbervilles*, and *Jude the Obscure*.

In *Thomas Hardy and the Survivals of Time*, Andrew D. Radford explores Hardy's artistic responses to the burgeoning Victorian sciences of geology, archaeology, and anthropology to show in turn how they are assimilated into his imaginative works. Of particular interest is Radford's discussion of the extent to which popular periodicals helped to shape Hardy's understanding of science, as well as how these periodicals contributed to a growing body of non-specialist scientific discourses. Bharat Tandon, '"… among the Ruins": Narrative Archaeology in *The Mayor of Casterbridge*' (*SEL* 35:iv[2003] 471–89), explores Hardy's recurrent interest in time, architecture, and archaeology, writing that Hardy's 'interest in wreckage is not only architectural: as is shown by these overlaps of vocabulary, physical ruins become cognate with emotional fractures within the metaphorical density of his language, which picks over and analyzes wreckage and remnants as if they were archaeological discoveries' (p. 472).

In *Knowledge and Survival in the Novels of Thomas Hardy*, Jane Mattison focuses on depictions of traditional wisdom and skills of rural life and discusses how they conflicted with the Industrial Revolution's new, more scientific, brand of knowledge. T.R. Wright's *Hardy and his Readers* is a most welcome biographical account of Hardy as viewed by actual reviewers and readers, as well as an analysis of the 'implied readers' of the novels. Helen Small, 'Chances Are: Henry Buckle, Thomas Hardy, and the Individual at Risk' (in Small and Tate, eds., pp. 64–85), explores notions of chance, probability, and ethics in Hardy's *The Return of the Native* and Henry Buckle's *The History of Civilisation in England*. William A. Davis's *Thomas Hardy and the Law: Legal Presences in Hardy's Life and Fiction* discusses the influence on Hardy's fiction of his legal experience and research. William Leung, '"The difference between old and new": The Tragic Premise of *The Mayor of Casterbridge*' (*L&A* 13:ii[2003] 31–56), focuses on formal and thematic tragic elements in the novel.

In 'Seminal Gothic Dissemination in Hardy's Writings' (*VLC* 29:ii[2001] 451–67), Brigitte Hervoche-Bertho argues that 'the diffusion of Gothic motifs in the whole of Hardy's literary production is something both intentional and fruitful' (p. 451). Satoshi Nishimura's 'Thomas Hardy and the Language of the Inanimate' (*SEL* 43:iv[2003] 897–912) discusses Hardy's use of pathetic fallacy in his fiction and poetry, and the role of personification in general as an essential element of language and knowledge. Oliver Lovesey, 'Reconstructing Tess' (*SEL* 43:iv[2003] 913–39), argues cogently that the novel attempts to resolve Angel Clare's apostasy through a 'sexualized reconstruction of the resurrection and particularly through the reconstruction of Tess's virginity' (p. 913). Also new in Hardy studies are the following articles of interest: John Holder's 'The Reverend Caddell Holder: Brother-in-Law of Thomas Hardy' (*THJ* 19:iii[2003] 45–6); Patrick Roper's 'The Hardys and their Wimborne House "Lanherne"' (*THJ* 19:iii[2003] 67–9); Birgit Plietzsch's 'Hardy's First Experiences with American Publishers' (*THJ* 19:ii[2003] 42–4); Shanta Dutta's 'Hardy and his Mayor: A Gendering of Critical Responses' (*THJ* 19:ii[2003] 33–40); and Nathalie Oussaid's 'A Reading of *Wessex Tales*' (*THJ* 19:ii[2003] 25–32). A new edition of Hardy's first novel, *Desperate Remedies* by Patricia Ingham is based on the first three-volume edition of 1871. Also included are a select bibliography, notes, chronology, and an introduction by Ingham. Also of interest in Hardy studies are John Stock Clarke and Graham Law's 'More Light on the Serial Publication of *Tess of the D'Urbervilles*' (*RES* 54[2003] 94–101); Martin Ray's 'Hardy's "The Catching Ballet of the Wedding Clothes": A Source' (*N&Q* 248:iii[2003] 319–20); and *Thomas Hardy A to Z: The Essential Reference to his Life and Work* by Sarah Bird Wright, reviewed by Philip V. Allingham (*VPR* 36:iv[2003] 373–4).

It was yet again unfortunately a very thin year for Charles Kingsley studies. Laura Fasick, 'Christian Manliness and Fatherhood in Charles Kingsley's Writings' (*VN* 104[2003] 1–2), discusses the roles of biological and priestly fathers, concluding that, 'when forced to confront the implications of his own theory, it appears that Kingsley decides the best father is a mother after all' (p. 1). Also of interest is Evan M. Gottlieb's 'Charles Kingsley, the Romantic Legacy, and the Unmaking of the Working-Class Intellectual' (*VLC* 29:i[2001] 51–66).

Phillip Mallett's biography *Rudyard Kipling: A Literary Life* covers influences on Kipling's writings, his family background and work as a journalist and travel writer, his role as laureate of empire, and his shifting reputation and relationship with the literary world. Mallet also discusses Kipling's friendships with Cecil Rhodes (a vocal opponent to Irish Home Rule), King George V (for whom

Kipling was a speech writer), and his cousin Stanley Baldwin. Steward, ed., *Kipling's America: Travel Letters, 1889–1895*, consists of articles Kipling wrote for the *Pioneer* while in west India (later revised and abridged in *From Sea to Sea* in 1899), as well as the syndicated articles he published in England and America (later collected and published in *Letters of Travel* in 1920). Along with reproductions of the original printed versions, Steward includes annotations and a thoughtful introduction. In 'Kipling and the Motoring Diaries' (*KJ* 77:cccvi[2003] 12–28), Meryl Macdonald Bendle (one of Kipling's first cousins once removed) discusses his 'Motoring Diaries' a record of his travels by automobile. John McBratney, *Imperial Subjects, Imperial Space: Rudyard Kipling's Fiction of the Native-Born,* discusses the subject of racial identity and foreign-born Britons during the late Victorian and the Edwardian periods. According to McBratney, the native-born is adept at playing both these roles because he is neither exclusively British nor exclusively 'native'.

While much Kipling criticism focused on race, John Kucich's interesting 'Sadomasochism and the Magical Group: Kipling's Middle-Class Imperialism' (*VS* 46:i[2003] 33–68), focuses attention on social class, arguing that social determination, modes of control and order in Kipling's works are 'organized around sadomasochistic psychological and cultural logic' (p. 34). Jane Hotchkiss, 'The Jungle of Eden: Kipling, Wolf Boys, and the Colonial Imagination' (*VLC* 29:ii[2001] 435–49), takes a look at the figure of the 'wild child' as embodied by Mowgli in *The Jungle Book*. William B. Dillingham, 'Sorrow and the Redemptive Role of Fate: Kipling's "On Greenhow Hill"' (*PLL* 39:i[2003] 3–21), draws attention to this somewhat critically neglected story by Kipling in order to investigate the role of grief and the dual nature of fate in Kipling's system of beliefs, especially in terms of his relationship to Christianity. George Engle, '"Excellent herbs had our fathers of old"' (*KJ* 77:306[2003] 34–49), discusses the historical and literary figure Nicholas Culpeper, a seventeenth-century doctor and author of *Culpeper's Herbal* who is characterized in Kipling's story 'A Doctor's Medicine' (*Rewards and Fairies* [1910]). Also of interest in Kipling studies are the following: 'Comments on "The Bull that Thought"' by Jean Maler (adapted by Max Rives) (*KJ* 77:cccvi[2003] 9–11); 'Kipling in Bohemia' by Tom Pinney (*KJ* 77:cccvi[2003] 29–33); 'Music, Kipling and Musicians' by Brian J.H. Mattinson (*KJ* 77:cccviii[2003] 33–4); 'Kipling's Comic and Serious Verse' by Christie Davies (*KJ* 77:cccviii [2003] 34–54); 'John Henry Chilcote Brooking' by Ian Whiteman (*KJ* 77:cccviii [2003] 55–8); 'A Short Walk on the Wilde Side: Kipling's First Impressions of Japan' by Harry Ricketts (*PNR* 29:vi.152[2003] 7–10); 'Artist of Empire: Kipling and *Kim*' by Clara Claiborne Park (*HudR* 54:iii[2003] 537–61); and 'The Savage City: Locating Colonial Modernity' by Alan Johnson (*NCC* 25:iv[2003] 315–32);

Elizabeth Bradburn, 'The Metaphorical Space of Meredith's *Diana of the Crossways*' (*SEL* 43:iv[2003] 877–96), provides a fresh reading of Meredith's 1885 novel using the cognitive theories of George Lakoff, Mark Johnson, and Mark Turner. Bradburn focuses on the novel's network of interrelated martial, musical, and gastronomic metaphors. Again it is the only item we have encountered on Meredith's novels. This neglect of a major Victorian writer is a sad reflection on the state of scholarship and criticism. Margaret Oliphant, on the other hand, has fared better. *Hester*, first published in three volumes by Macmillan in 1883, is now available in Oxford's World Classics. Edited with an informative introduction and notes by Philip Davis and Brian Nellist, this excellent study of complicated psychological relationships and 'financial and sexual risk-taking' (to cite from the blurb), is most welcome. There is one item only to report on George Moore. Joellen Masters examines elements of sensation melodrama in '"A great part to play": Gender, Genre, and Literary Fame in George Moore's *A Mummer's Wife*' (*VLC* 29:ii[2001] 285–301).

Rose Lovell-Smith, 'Science and Religion in the Feminist *Fin-de-Siècle* and a New Reading of Olive Schreiner's *From Man to Man*' (*VLC* 29:ii[2001] 303–26), explores the blending of science and religion by many turn-of-the-century feminists in an attempt to 'reconcile the world-views of Darwinism and religious belief' (p. 303). In doing so, Lovell-Smith offers a fresh reading of Schreiner's novel as one that 'presents a world outside of religious belief' (p. 320). John Kucich, 'Olive Schreiner, Masochism, and Omnipotence: Strategies of a Preoedipal Politics' (*Novel* 36:i[2002] 79–109), discusses Schreiner's writings in terms of the pre-Oedipal and masochistic fantasy dynamics that underlie her colonial and political writings. Gerard Carruthers, 'Remaking Romantic Scotland: Lockhart's Biographies of Burns and Scott' (in Bradley and Rawes, eds. *Romantic Biography*, pp. 93–108), includes an interesting, mostly favourable assessment of John Gibson Lockhart's *Memoirs of Sir Walter Scott* [1837–8].

Cheryl A. Wilson's 'The Victorian Woman Reader in May Sinclair's *Mary Olivier*: Self-Stimulation, Intellectual Freedom, and Escape' (*ELT* 46:iv[2003] 365–81), shows how Sinclair rewrites the Victorian female reader so that the act of reading becomes overtly political. Gabrielle Ceraldi's '"Popish legends and Bible truths": English Protestant Identity in Catherine Sinclair's *Beatrice*' (*VIJ* 31:i[2003] 359–72) examines *Beatrice* [1852] as 'one of the most popular of the so-called Papal Aggression novels (p. 361). Jason Marc Harris, 'Robert Louis Stevenson: Folklore and Imperialism' (*ELT* 46:iv[2003] 382–99), demonstrates ways in which Stevenson's use of folkloric and literary traditions challenges conventional notions of British empire and literary culture. Also of interest in Stevenson studies is Katherine Linehan's 'Two Unpublished Letters from Robert Louis Stevenson to Thomas Russell Sullivan' (*N&Q* 248:iii[2003] 320–3). Stevenson's *The Beach of Falesá* is included with Conrad's *Heart of Darkness* and Kipling's *The Man Who Would Be King* in a New Riverside Edition *Fictions of Empire*, edited by John Kucich and accompanied by appropriate critical and contextual materials.

New in Bram Stoker studies is Carol A. Senf's *Science and Social Science in Bram Stoker's Fiction,* an exploration of depictions of science and technology in the works of Stoker, and how they are blended with other supernatural, fantasy, and Gothic elements. Patricia McKee, 'Racialization, Capitalism and Aesthetics in Stoker's *Dracula*' (*Novel* 36:i[2002] 42–60), discusses depictions of modernized whiteness and how they acquire 'regenerative powers' (p. 42) when coupled with capitalistic production. Philip Holden, 'Castle, Coffin, Stomach: *Dracula* and the Banality of the Occult' (*VLC* 29:ii[2001] 469–85), examines the roles of the self, the occult, and the Victorian social environment in *Dracula.*

Thackeray studies again are not flourishing, if the paucity of publication is a reliable guide. Drawing on correspondence, diaries, memoirs, later biographical accounts, and memoirs written about Thackeray by his contemporaries, Edgar F. Harden, *A William Makepeace Thackeray Chronology,* provides a detailed account of Thackeray's life, writings, and career. Christoph Lindner's *Fictions of Commodity Culture* includes a chapter on Thackeray, 'Thackeray's Gourmand: Carnivals of Consumption in *Vanity Fair*', in which Lindner presents an analysis of the character Jos Sedley and how he embodies the obsession with commodities and consumer seduction. Also of interest in Thackeray studies are Francis A. Burkle-Young's 'Thackeray's "Transparent" German Pun' (*N&Q* 248:iii[2003] 315–18) and Daniel P. Deneau's 'Rhetorical Punctuation in Vanity Fair?' (*VN* 104[2003] 29–1). A welcome reissue from the AMS Press is *The Two Thackerays*: Carol Hanbery MacKay provides a critical introduction and Peter L. Shillingsburg and Julia Maxey a bibliographical introduction to Anne Thackeray Ritchie's *Centenary Biographical Introduction to the Works of William Makepeace Thackeray*. Although expensive, the two-volume reprint is a salutary reminder of the fact that Thackeray wished no official biography of him to be written, and of the important role in his legacy played by his daughter Anne Thackeray Ritchie.

A supplement to Michael Sadleir's standard bibliography, *Trollope: A Bibliography*, is provided by Walter E Smith's *Anthony Trollope; A Bibliography of his First American Editions, 1858–84, with Photographic Reproductions of Bindings and Titlepages*. The supplement describes each of the American editions and discusses the publishing history of each. Also included are appendices detailing minor writings and illustrated editions. In his 'Anthony Trollope in America: A Brief Survey of the Publication History' (*PULC* 62:iii[Spring 2001] 479–500), Walter E. Smith succinctly surveys Trollope's publishing history in America. Smith notes that, 'without international copyright law, any work published in England could be pirated by American publishers' (p. 481). Well illustrated by photographs of a carte-de-visite of Trollope, title pages and illustrations for his novels now in the Parrish and other collections at Princeton, Smith's article serves as a prelude to his important bibliography, described above. Lindner's *Fictions of Commodity Culture* also includes a chapter on Trollope, 'Trollope's Material Girl: Gender and Capitalism in The Eustace Diamonds', which argues that 'Trollope's novel of mercenary female duplicity examines, challenges, and manipulates commodity culture's economic constructions of the feminine' (p. 65). Nicholas Dames, 'Trollope and the Career: Vocational Trajectories and the Management of Ambition' (*VS* 45:ii[2003] 247–78), shows the connection between certain instances in Trollope's fiction of 'making one's way' and the emergence of the idea of a career during the Victorian period.

A recent issue of *Cahiers Victoriens et Edouardiens* [October 2003] is entitled 'Studies in Anthony Trollope' and includes several articles of interest. The late Ruth ApRoberts, in 'Historicizing Trollope' (*CVE* 58[2003] 17–34), discusses Trollope in terms of realism, his 'up-to-date' (p. 17) representations of contemporary Victorian life. Laurent Bury's 'Trollopian Gothic' (*CVE* 58[2003] 35–46) focuses on Gothic elements in two lesser-known novels, *Nina*

Balatka and *Linda Tressel*. The subject of Jacqueline Fromonot's 'On the Right to Tell Lies from Benevolent Motives: Trollope's Contribution to the Debate in *Dr Thorne*' (*CVE* 58[2003] 47–56) is how Trollope negotiates truthfulness and its limitations in *Dr Thorne*. In '*The Way We Live Now*, or Trollope in *Vanity Fair*' (*CVE* 58[2003]71–80), Alain Jumeau discusses similarities between *The Way We Live Now* and Thackeray's *Vanity Fair*. Margaret Markwick, in 'The Diocese as Circus' (*CVE* 58[2003] 71–80), explores Trollope's presentation of clerical life in *The Barchester Chronicles*. In '*Castle Richmond*, the Famine, and the Critics' (*CVE* 58[2003] 81–90), Jane Nardine examines the narrator's comments on the potato famine of 1845–51 in *Castle Richmond,* concluding that no distinct authorial view emerges on that subject. Picton Hervé, 'Trollope and Tractarianism' (*CVE* 58[2003] 91–104), discusses the nature and scope of Trollope's Tractarianism, focusing in particular on *The Last Chronicle* and *The Claverings*. In 'Rachel Ray: The Story of a Modern Mother/Daughter Relationship' (*CVE* 58[2003] 105–16), Brigitte Schoubrenner explores 'Trollope's dual attitude to women' (p. 14). Donald Stone, 'Trollope for the 21st Century: *He Knew He Was Right*' (*CVE* 58[2003] 117–28), compares Eliot's *Middlemarch* to one of Trollope's later novels, *He Knew He Was Right*, which is a 'multi-layered depiction of nineteenth-century in the midst of change' (p. 14).

J. Jeffrey Franklin's 'Anthony Trollope Meets Pierre Bourdieu: The Conversion of Capital as Plot in the Mid-Victorian British Novel' (*VLC* 31:ii[2003] 501–21) focuses on examples of capital being exchanged in *The Last Chronicle of Barset* to show how these exchanges reflect an understanding of human interactions and what they say about the cultural work of the Victorian novel. A welcome new edition of *Phineas Redux* is edited by Gregg A. Hecimovich and is based on the two volumes publication by Chapman & Hall [1874]. This new edition includes original illustrations by Frank Holl, which originally accompanied the serially published edition in *The Graphic* [1873–4], along with an introduction by Hecimovich, a chronology, and notes.

In 'Knowing Too Much and Never Enough: Knowledge and Moral Capital in Frances Trollope's *Life and Adventure of Michael Armstrong, the Factory Boy*' (*Novel* 36:i[2002] 61–78), Carolyn Betensky discusses the degree to which various middle-class characters, as well as some middle-class Victorian readers, are aware of the 'real condition' (p. 78) of the poor. Susan M. Griffin, 'Revising the Popish Plot: Frances Trollope's *The Abbess* and *Father Eustace*' (*VLC* 31:i[2003] 359–72), offers a reading of Frances Trollope's two novels and their critique of and engagement with Roman Catholicism. Griffin also shows how she draws on the shape of the Gothic genre and anti-Catholic literature to explore gender identity issues.

In 'Around the World Without a Gaze: Englishness and the Press in Jules Verne' (*VPR* 36:ii[2003] 135–52), Peter W. Sinnema examines depictions of 'Englishness' and masculinity in *Around the World*. Gisela Argyle, in 'Mrs. Humphry Ward's Fictional Experiments in the Woman Question' (*SEL* 43:iv[2003] 939–58), provides a new reading of Ward's fiction and opposing interpretations of her work and views. While some critics have labelled her 'anti-feminist', others have called her a 'New Woman' novelist. In accordance with Hans Robert Jauss's theories on the aesthetics of reception, Argyle proposes the study of five of Ward's novels as a literary series for a more nuanced understanding of moral problems at work within her writing. This, according to Jauss, happens when the author's works are considered within a serial context.

The year 2003 saw a number of items of interest to Wilde scholars, including the unabridged account of the first of Oscar Wilde's three trials [1895], which is edited and introduced by Wilde's grandson, Merlin Holland. While other accounts of Wilde's trial have been censored, distorted, or incomplete, *The Real Trial of Oscar Wilde: The First Uncensored Manuscript of the Trial of Oscar Wilde Vs. John Douglass (Marquess of Queensberry, 1895)*, includes heretofore unpublished passages of cross-examination and extensive notes and commentary accompanying the text. Philip E. Smith II, 'Wilde in the Bodleian, 1878–81' (*ELT* 46:iii[2003] 279–95), provides more details of Wilde's borrowings from the Bodleian while in Oxford. William Shuter, 'Pater, Wilde, Douglas and the Impact of "Greats"' (*ELT* 46:iii[2003] 279–95), discusses the degree to which each of the three Oxford men was influenced by their study of the Greats in the ambitious school of Literae Humaniores. New from the Authors in Context series is *Oscar Wilde* by John Sloan. Included are a chronology, illustrations, and comprehensive index, along with chapters on 'The Life of Oscar Wilde', 'The Fabric of Society', 'The Literary Scene', 'Wilde and Social Issues', 'Wilde and Intellectual Issues', and 'Recontextualizing Wilde'. Horst Schroeder's useful *Additions and Corrections to Richard Ellmann's Oscar Wilde* provides over a thousand annotations correcting mistakes, errors, faulty references, and misquotations in Ellmann's 1987 biography.

Tame Passions of Wilde: The Styles of Manageable Desire, by Jeff Nunokawa, explores notions of compulsion, desire, and modern sexuality as related to Wilde and Victorian culture in general. In 'Erotic Bafflement and the Lesson of Oscar Wilde' (*Genre* 35:ii[2003] 309–30), Kevin Ohi discusses 'the paradoxical pedagogy of De Profundis'. Neil McKenna's biography, *The Secret Life of Oscar Wilde*, focuses primarily on Wilde's sexuality and its influence on his work. John-Charles Duffy, 'Gay-Related Themes in the Fairy Tales of Oscar Wilde' (*VLC* 29:ii[2001] 327–49), centres on homosexual themes in *The Happy Prince and Other Tales* (Wilde's first book) and *A House of Pomegranates*. Nils Clausson, '"Culture and Corruption"; Paterian Self-Development Versus Gothic Degeneration in Oscar Wilde's *The Picture of Dorian Gray*' (*PLL* 39:iv[2003] 339–64), shows how the novel's meaning or interpretation often depend on how critics classify it in terms of genre. Also of interest are Keane, ed., *Oscar Wilde: The Man, his Writings, and his World*, a collection of essays that were revised after their presentation at a Hofstra University conference in 2000, and Simon Joyce's lively 'Sexual Politics and the Aesthetics of Crime: Oscar Wilde in the Nineties' (*ELH* 69:ii[2002] 501–23).

Bristow, ed., *Wilde Writings: Contextual Conditions*, comprises thirteen original essays exploring Wilde's works, their textual history and cultural contexts. The essays are as follows: 'Wilde's World: Oscar Wilde and Theatrical Journalism in the 1880s' by John Stokes; ''The Soul of Man under Socialism': A (Con)Textual History' by Josephine M. Guy; 'Love-Letter, Spiritual

Autobiography, or Prison Writing? Identity and Value in *De Profundis*' by Ian Small; 'Wilde's Exquisite Pain' by Ellis Hanson; 'Wilde Man: Masculinity, Feminism, and *A Woman of No Importance*' by Kerry Powell; 'Wilde, and How To Be Modern: or, Bags of Red Gold' by Peter Raby; 'Master Wood's Profession: Wilde and the Subculture of Homosexual Blackmail in the Victorian Theatre' by Laurence Senelick; 'Wilde's *The Woman's World* and the Culture of Aesthetic Philanthropy' by Diana Maltz; 'The Origins of the Aesthetic Novel: Ouida, Wilde, and the Popular Romance' by Talia Schaffer; 'Oscar Wilde, New Women, and the Rhetoric of Effeminacy' by Lisa Hamilton; 'Oscar Wilde and Jesus Christ' by Stephen Arata; 'Oscar Wilde's Legacies to *Clarion* and the *New Age* Socialist Aestheticism' by Ann Ardis; and '*Salomé* in China: The Aesthetic Art of Dying' by Xiaoyi Zhou.

Last, and by no means least, it is pleasant to record a first-rate research article on a neglected writer, Charlotte Mary Yonge [1823–1901]. Ellen Jordan, in 'Charlotte M. Yonge, Woman of Letters' (*PULC* 62:iii[Spring 2001] 451–78) draws on 'almost two hundred letters by Charlotte Yonge in the Parrish Collection, as well as several addressed to her' (p. 455). These demonstrate that Yonge 'was driven to write her novels and tales by an abundant literary imagination'. Further, she 'believed that her writing committed her to a public role as, to quote her own words "a sort of instrument for popularizing Church Views"' (p. 454). The extracts from the Yonge letters cited by Jordan reveal that a scholarly edition is long overdue and would make an important contribution of our understanding of Yonge, Victorian life and letters, and 'the careers carved out by the women who devoted their lives to the profession of letters' (p. 478). Yonge is also the subject of Gavin Budge's 'Realism and Typology in Charlotte M. Yonge's *The Heir of Redclyffe*' (*VLC* 31:i[2003] 193–223).

3. Poetry

In his review article on Matthew Arnold (*VP* 41[2003] 364–76), Clinton Machann concludes by printing a chart showing the decline of database entries on the major Victorian poets since the 1960s: the most marked decline is in works on Arnold, but Tennyson and Browning also suffer. The decline is, of course, partly offset by the significant rise of work on Barrett Browning and Christina Rossetti. Machann's gloom about the future of Arnold's poetry may be justified in the light of the relative paucity of articles and monographs on him in the last few years, but to argue for the decline of work on the major Victorian poets is not a clinching argument for the decay of Victorian poetry studies given the massive expansion of this subject, and the subsequent focus on minor poets and on poetry read in relation to other discourses, rather than single-author studies. Judging from this year's work, the shape of the field is certainly changing: Christina Rossetti emerges as the most discussed poet, with the Brownings close behind, and the most significant interventions are probably not monographs but the two special issues of *Victorian Poetry*, one on poetry and science and one on the future of the field, both of which mix the canonical and the unfamiliar in their selected articles.

To begin with the latter, edited by Linda Hughes, twenty-six essays by critics in the field (mainly younger critics, primarily but not solely based in the USA) attempt to assess how the study of nineteenth-century poetry could be conceived and refigured for the new millennium. Designed, according to the introduction, as a 'casebook of collective brainstorming' (*VP* 41[2003] 459–64), the essays present reflections or starting points rather than detailed discussion. Erik Gray's 'A Bounded Field: Situating Victorian Poetry in the Literary Landscape' (*VP* 41[2003] 465–72) takes Michael Field as an example of how critics 'seem to be more interested in learning how our poets relate to each other than how they relate to other periods of literature or art' (p. 467), suggesting that limiting discussion to 'Victorian' poetry does the poets themselves a disservice, and that critics might now move towards a wider view. Lee O'Brien's 'Reading/Writing the Forgotten: The Poetry of Mary Boddington' (*VP* 41[2003] 473–81) offers a slightly different perspective by arguing that it is important to study women's poetry as a separate category, but that closer attention should be paid to intertextual and ideological readings rather than biographical, historical and social context. Next, Anne Hartman's 'Doing Things with Poems: Performativity and Cultural Form' (*VP* 41[2003] 481–90) discusses the idealist/materialist impasse in Victorian studies and traces a shift towards considering performativity, poems constituting and producing what they describe (a topic dealt with in detail by E. Warwick Slinn's study, discussed below). She analyses Hemans's 'Our Daily Paths' as a representative example. Dino Felluga turns to genre in 'Novel Poetry: Transgressing the Law of Genre' (*VP* 41[2003] 490–9), arguing that nineteenth-century novels need to be read in part as responses to poetry, and vice versa, and that cross-generic forms (like the verse novel) deserve further discussion. He suggests that such works might additionally challenge concepts of genre in themselves. Monique Morgan's 'Productive Convergences, Producing Converts' (*VP* 41[2003] 500–4) takes a similar line to Gray's piece, arguing that the significance of Victorian poetry will not be recognized unless it is discussed in relation to poetry from other periods. Her argument also relates to Felluga's in that she argues that narrative theory should be incorporated into this discussion.

In the succeeding essay, 'Why Clough? Why Now?' (*VP* 41[2003] 504–12), Vanessa Ryan considers why Clough is becoming popular again (relatively speaking), and suggests that interest in his work might indicate a 'reconciliation between cultural criticism and a renewed formalist approach' (p. 505). Stephanie Kuduk, in 'Victorian Poetry as Victorian Studies' (*VP* 41[2003] 513–18), follows this up, exploring the importance of approaches which combine formalism and interdisciplinary study. Charles LaPorte, 'Post-Romantic Ideologies and Victorian Poetic Practice, or, the Future of Criticism at the Present Time' (*VP* 41[2003] 519–25), discusses how the ideology (in terms of criticism published in periodicals etc.) and practice of poetry have been curiously separated—celebrating the databases and online resources which make new and productive conjunctions between these possible, and which democratize the field by offering access to previously obscure texts. Andrew Stauffer, in 'Victorian Paperwork' (*VP* 41[2003] 526–31), argues that continued editorial work and bibliographical and textual criticism are vital in producing new interpretations of Victorian poetry. Ana Vadillo's 'A Note Upon the "Liquid Crystal Screen" and Victorian Poetry' (*VP* 41[2003] 531–6), relates to this, discussing how technology and the internet have altered our idea of the shape of the field. Margaret Linley, 'Conjuring the Spirit: Victorian Poetry, Culture and Technology' (*VP* 41[2003] 536–44), shifts to an analysis of Victorian technology and its intersection with poetry, using Tennyson as an example, and then suggesting directions for research in terms of the relation between gender and nineteenth-century technologies. William McKelvy's 'In the Valley of the Shadow of Books' (*VP* 41[2003] 544–52) gives an interesting account of the literary economy which produced changed contexts for reading and discussing poetry, new and complex 'landscapes of readerships' (p. 550). Following this, Robert Sulcer, 'Budgets and Brownings: The Function of Poetry at the Present Time' (*VP* 41[2003] 552–9), discusses the material context of the US college classroom, noting that if Victorian poetry will survive, it will survive through teaching, and that more work could be done on how to teach poetry in current educational institutions.

Foucault's influence is the next to be reconsidered, as Lee Behlman, in 'From Ancient to Victorian Cultural Studies: Assessing Foucault' (*VP* 41[2003] 559–69), suggests that his work remains crucial, but critics now need to move away from a narrow canon of Foucauldian texts. This is followed by James Najarian's 'Canonicity, Marginality and the Celebration of the Minor' (*VP* 41[2003] 570–5), in which he points out that 'marginal' poets are still seldom discussed, and suggests that attention to the 'minor' as a category might raise interesting questions of originality. Marion Thain then returns to women's poetry, in 'What Kind of a Critical Category is "Women's Poetry"?' (*VP* 41[2003] 575–84), discussing the usefulness of this classification and the need to examine the haunting figure of the 'poetess' more closely, and Katharine McGowran succeeds this with another assessment of fin-de-siècle women's poetics and the female aesthetic, 'Rereading Women's Poetry at the Turn of the Century' (*VP* 41[2003] 584–9). Jason Rudy next takes spasmodic poetry as a focus in his valuable discussion of the return of formalism to Victorian poetry in 'On Cultural Neoformalism, Spasmodic Poetry, and the Victorian Ballad' (*VP* 41[2003] 590–6). Two pieces then focus on Victorian poetry and modernity: in 'Whither, Whether, Woolf: Victorian Poetry and *A Room of One's Own*' (*VP* 41[2003] 596–603), Cornelia Pearsall considers Woolf's response to Victorian poets and poetry, while Ivan Keilkramp's 'Victorian Poetry's Modernity' (*VP* 41[2003] 603–11) questions whether bringing nineteenth-century works into discussions of European modernity might alter our perceptions of them. After this, the volume turns to Victorian poetry and the arts—Helen Groth examines the role of poetry in the development of Victorian visual culture and its relation to photography, with Barrett Browning as a key example, in 'Consigned to Sepia: Remembering Victorian Poetry' (*VP* 41[2003] 611–20), and Michele Martinez, in 'Women Poets and the Sister Arts in Nineteenth-Century England' (*VP* 41[2003] 621–8), considers the significance of Victorian women painters and sculptors for studies of Hemans and many others. Another context which has attracted much recent interest—ecology and the environment—is briefly explored by Nicholas Frankel in 'The Ecology of Victorian Poetry' (*VP* 41[2003] 629–35), before the final pair of essays turns to the aftermath of 9/11 and its possible implications for poetry studies. Rebecca Stern suggests the service of scholarship which draws attention to the 'small moments and subtle nuances' (p. 641) of poems, and draws on her experience of finding comfort in reading *In Memoriam*. John Picker also finds echoes of Tennysonian rhetoric in memorializations of 9/11, and suggests that this might hint at the possibilities of Victorian poetry outside the academy, a future which might be more important than its function within it.

Taken together, these essays give valuable insight into the directions in which the field might be moving, though the individualistic and overlapping approach does not provide the same kind of systematic and quietly polemical reassessment that last year's *Blackwell's Companion to Victorian Poetry* offered. If these essays are representative of the work of younger scholars, the two most notable points are first, the continued focus on women poets, who provide examples and case studies in a significant number of the essays, and secondly, a general sense of agreement about the renewed importance of form—indicated not only by the arguments presented, but also by the detailed close readings used to support them in many essays. Given the widespread lack of discussions of form in many of the monographs or other studies reviewed here in the last few years this is interesting, suggesting that a change might still be to come. An emphasis on the need to situate Victorian poetry in wider contexts is also reiterated throughout the volume, whether in relation to other genres within the period, to other disciplines or arts, or to other periods. All these critics strongly agree that poetry should not be discussed as separate category unto itself. In addition, there is a high level of agreement on the need to broaden the canon still further: the spasmodic poets (the subject of a forthcoming special edition of *VP*), working-class poetry and religious poetry are mentioned as examples of missing categories by several authors. In fact, this is where this collection most obviously seems deficient: given the number of publications on Victorian poetry and religion in the last two years, many of which are reviewed below, this volume might already be out of date in its lack of any consideration of religious poetry. Class and politics, in the specific sense of Victorian party politics, are also little discussed, and national identity/foreignness, another interest of recent criticism (witness the material on Italy discussed below) is similarly largely absent. More broadly, while there is some angst here about the problems facing Victorian poetry in the classroom and on the jobs market, there is less consideration of the constraints imposed by academic publishing—is the noted decline in monographs in the field due to a decline in academic interest, or to a perception that they are unlikely to be read and hence unlikely to be accepted for publication? Perhaps this is a topic of more immediate urgency to British scholars, but the issue still seems to beg discussion. It would also have been interesting to know whether a collection of essays like this could have appeared anywhere other than in the one journal devoted to the field: there is clearly a sense of preaching to the converted in these essays, which thus inevitably re-enact the problem of restricting Victorian poetry scholarship to a narrow field and readership. Nonetheless, this is an important intervention and raises many possibilities for the development of the subject in the twenty-first century.

VP further enhanced its status as the leading forum for debate about the future of the field with the long-awaited special issue on Victorian poetry and science. The editors, Sally Shuttleworth and Gowan Dawson, suggest that one of the aims of this volume is to expand the field of science and literature to include a more diverse range of poetic responses, and fringe as well as mainstream sciences. On both counts the collection is successful. The first essay, Rowena Fowler's 'Blougram's Wager, Guido's Odds: Browning, Chance and Probability' (*VP* 41[2003] 11–28) is an excellent and thought-provoking account of probability theory and chance as it relates to Browning's poems. Fowler discusses the nineteenth-century context in which probability became important, and describes Browning's interest in exploring the wager, the gamble, the chance encounter or event, in relation to the speakers of his poems and their propensity to hedge their bets or weigh up different possibilities. This piece seems to offer a way of reading Victorian poetry more widely, beyond its specific focus. Anna Henchman then offers a reading of Tennyson in relation to astronomy, '"The Globe we groan in": Astronomical Distance and Stellar Decay in *In Memoriam*' (*VP* 41[2003] 29–45): while less original than the first essay, Henchman's study of how Tennyson saw and used the stars is detailed and scholarly. Alison Chapman's '"A poet never sees a ghost": Photography and Trance in Tennyson's *Enoch Arden* and Julia Margaret Cameron's Photography' (*VP* 41[2003] 47–72) sets up a complex relation between gender, photography, spectrality and Tennyson's 'optical aesthetics' (p. 47). The theoretical links here aren't entirely clear, but this is nonetheless a very suggestive piece, and Chapman's readings of visuality in *Enoch Arden* and in Cameron's photographs are excellent. Erika Behrisch then turns to the forgotten and fragmented poetry left by Arctic explorers, in '"Far as the eye can reach": Scientific Exploration and Explorers' Poetry in the Arctic, 1832–52' (*VP* 41[2003] 73–91). Science, in her argument, worked both for and against poetry: scientific emphasis on detail encouraged a poetic vision, but scientific discourse also attempted to excise the poetic by requiring rigorously objective accounts. Personal responses to the experience of the Arctic and the stance of detached, neutral observation required for official accounts often collide in these poems. In the next essay, 'Crowd Management: Matthew Arnold and the Science of Society', by Gage McWeeny (*VP* 41[2003] 93–111), Arnold's criticism is read as in part constituent of the new social sciences emerging in the nineteenth century. McWeeny suggests that Arnold sees the crowd not simply as threatening and terrifying, but as a potential tool for social ordering, and, in drawing attention to the crowded streets in Arnold's poems, suggests news ways of reading the classic Arnoldian despairing subjectivity.

Gowan Dawson also focuses on Victorian criticism in 'Intrinsic Earthliness: Science, Materialism and the Fleshly School of Poetry' (*VP* 41[2003] 113–29), discussing Pater's introduction to D.G. Rossetti's poems and its transformation of materialism (a charge often laid against Rossetti) into something ethereal and pure. By situating the materialist debate across Victorian science, literature and culture, Dawson demonstrates the ambiguity of 'materialism' and its potential for appropriation in different contexts. Continuing this focus on the literature of the 1860s, Jonathan Smith's 'Une Fleur du Mal? Swinburne's "The Sundew" and Darwin's *Insectivorous Plants*' (*VP* 41[2003] 131–50) concentrates on a less well known poem from *Poems and Ballads*, noting that the poem became controversial when it was 'swept into discussions of the ethical, philosophical and cultural implications of Darwin's work' (p. 141), given that Darwin devoted much of his book on carnivorous plants to the sundew. This article provides a very good example of a specific case in which scientific investigation impinged on the interpretation of poetry. Finally, Marion Thain adds to her work on late Victorian women writers in '"Scientific Wooing": Constance Naden's Marriage of Science and Poetry' (*VP* 41[2003] 151–69), in which she studies Naden's poem in the light of her scientific publications and her philosophical 'Hylo-Idealism'.

E. Warwick Slinn produced the only generalist monograph on Victorian poetry this year, with *Victorian Poetry as Cultural Critique: The Politics of Performative Language*. This book takes its impetus from the concept of performativity: Slinn argues that 'deliberately conceived performative language', a characteristic of nineteenth-century poetry, can focus attention on contested discourses and theories and thus 'enact a form of cultural critique' (p. 7) by revealing and obliquely commenting upon their actions within culture. This is not an entirely original argument, and seems fairly self-evident when considering the dramatic monologue, but Slinn presents it with conviction and manages, here as in his other works, neatly to integrate his close readings of poetry with attention to context and with broader theoretical concerns—reading Barrett Browning in relation to Hegel, for instance, or Browning and Kristeva together. Materialism versus idealism is also a key theme throughout the book, a conflict which Slinn sees in almost every poem he analyses. *Victorian Poetry as Cultural Critique*, read in relation to 'Whither Victorian Poetry?', is very much of the moment. The book is structured around close readings of five poems, suggesting an adherence to formalist analysis, and the poems selected all reflect current critical concerns: 'The Bishop Orders his Tomb at St Praxed's Church' with religion; 'The Runaway Slave at Pilgrim's Point' with race and gender; Clough's *Dipsychus* with materialism; D.G. Rossetti's 'Jenny' with masculinity and economics, and Webster's 'The Castaway' with sexual politics. The concerns in each poem, of course, also overlap, meaning that the book reflects more broadly on questions of power, agency and cultural context in the dramatic monologue. 'The Bishop Orders His Tomb' is read as a 'failed performative' (p. 38), and Slinn examines how the speaker confuses the categories of material and spiritual. His succeeding reading of Barrett Browning resonates with Marjorie Stone's recent work (discussed below), by placing theoretical discussion within a historical framework and considering the material circumstances of the poem's publication. The reading of Clough in the next chapter is very good, focusing more clearly on Dipsychus' struggle with idealism, as opposed to the material world in which he is embedded, and associating this nicely with the hybrid form and shifting construction of the poem itself. The paired readings of 'Jenny' and 'The Castaway' are also fine, studying how the speaker of 'Jenny' idealizes and objectifies Jenny in order to deny his own material desires, and how Eulalie in Webster's poem, like Barrett Browning's slave, gives us a sense of 'what it is to see the self-acclaimed male centre from the female margin' (p. 161). Slinn is alert to the political implications of reading these poems—in their nineteenth-century contexts as well as at the present time—and always aware of their complexity and ambiguity. His readings are not presented as definitive, but they do offer inclusive discussions of a number of concerns loosely linked by concepts of performativity, and would be good introductions to these poems for students.

Another monograph which dealt extensively with Victorian poetry was Helen Groth's *Victorian Photography and Literary Nostalgia*. Groth's book is notable because, unlike many generalist studies of Victorian culture, it concentrates largely on poetic examples rather than drawing on prose or the novel. Her argument places the development of photography and the debates surrounding it in the context of a kind of cultural nostalgia, conveyed in poetry collections and illustrated volumes, such as the Tennyson edition which featured Julia Margaret Cameron's photographs. She also studies photographs of poets and assesses their function in the marketing of poetry. Individual chapters consider Barrett Browning's 'self-consciously modern visual poetics' (p. 115), particularly in *Casa Guidi Windows*, and Tennyson in relation to Cameron. Groth's work is remarkably topical (see the articles on *Casa Guidi Windows* described below) and offers a rich study of a newly important area.

Women's poetry was once again an important topic this year, both in the works described above and in a number of articles. The most significant publication was Alison Chapman's edited collection of essays on Victorian women's poetry for the 2003 edition of Essays and Studies. In her introduction Chapman notes that, despite the recent attention to women poets, more remains to be done, particularly on poets who published in periodicals and magazines, often anonymously, and on working-class and non-English poets. The first essay in the collection, Patricia Pulham's '"Jewels—delights—perfect loves": Victorian Women Poets and the Annuals' (pp. 9–31), discusses the feminization of publishing in the annuals, and considers the 'latent eroticism' (p. 15) associated with this form, a sensuality inherent in both poems and pictures. This sensuality, Pulham suggests, is both revisionary in its association with a Sapphic gaze (since women are describing women), and reactionary in that it reinscribes woman as the object rather than subject of poetry. Marjorie Stone continues this attention to publication circumstances in 'Elizabeth Barrett Browning and the Garrisonians: "The Runaway Slave at Pilgrim's Point", the Boston Female Anti-Slavery Society, and Abolitionist Discourse in the *Liberty Bell*' (pp. 33–55). Stone's work on Barrett Browning's anti-slavery poems is always illuminating, and this essay, in setting 'The Runaway Slave' firmly in its mid-nineteenth century contexts, is no exception. Stone discusses how the poem reflects the rhetoric and debates of Boston abolitionists, studies other publications in the *Liberty Bell*, and considers the compositional history of the poem itself. Barrett Browning is also significant, though not the primary focus, in the next essay, Chapman's 'The Expatriate Poetess: Nationhood, Poetics and Politics' (pp. 57–77). Chapman examines women's poetry of the Risorgimento and links this to the poetess, arguing that the Anglocentric figure created by poetess discourse is predicated on an attachment to foreignness. Writers such as Barrett Browning and the circle of expatriates in Italy, she suggests, exploit this disjunction. This is an effective reconsideration of both poetic nationalisms and the poetess tradition.

Glennis Byron, in 'Rethinking the Dramatic Monologue: Victorian Women Poets and Social Critique' (pp. 79–98), suggests that women writers did not necessarily conceptualize this form differently, but that they did differ in that they focused on the monologue as social critique, targeting the system rather than the speaker. This is an excellent essay, with very good readings of Hemans and others, useful for students or critics studying the dramatic monologue as well as those with particular interests in women's poetry. Michele Martinez, in 'Christina Rossetti's Petrarcha', next discusses Christina Rossetti's early essay on Petrarch and assesses how her knowledge of his works and of biographical controversies surrounding him might have shaped her early poems, particularly 'Memory' (pp. 99–121). Mathilde Blind is the subject of the next essay, '"A still and mute-born vision": Locating Mathilde Blind's Reproductive Poetics', by Susan Brown (pp. 122–44). Brown considers Blind's poem on the Scottish clearances, *The Heather on Fire*, and argues that her poetic preoccupation with reproduction mirrors tensions between the natural and the social in this poem, besides relating the political events in it to wider evolutionary processes. Natalie Houston's 'Towards a New History: Fin-de-Siècle Women Poets and the Sonnet' (pp. 145–64) examines poems by Blind, Michael Field and Rosamund Marriott Watson in relation to the sonnet genre and its cultural meanings in the late nineteenth century. Through a valuable discussion of the sonnet in general, she concludes that gender is less important than genre for this particular form. To conclude the volume, Joseph Bristow's 'Reassessing Margaret Veley's Poetry: The Value of *Harper's* Transatlantic Spirit' (pp. 165–94) opens with the nagging question of how to assign value to minor women's poetry beyond the mere fact of its existence, and then argues that tracing publication histories and outlets might help, in that we can see more clearly the ways in which a poet might have been esteemed in her lifetime. His discussion of Veley is detailed, enlightening—and entertaining in its account of the alleged channelling of Veley's voice by a later spiritualist. Overall, this is an impressive collection, in which established scholars revisit key themes in the field.

Among those women poets not covered below as individuals, George Eliot received some attention this year. June Syke Szirotny, in 'George Eliot's *Spanish Gypsy*: The Spanish–Moorish Motif' (*ANQ* 16[2003] 36–45), explores parallels between Eliot's poem and other works of the period, including Heine's *Almansor*, Bulwer-Lytton's *Leila*, Corneille's *Le Cid* and Lewes's tragedy *The Noble Heart*. She persuasively suggests that these writers and others inspired Eliot's interest in the Spanish–Moorish wars, and notes ways in which Eliot revises her sources. In the special issue of *VLC* on literature and religion, Charles LaPorte, 'George Eliot, the Poetess as Prophet' (*VLC* 31:i[2003] 159–80) discusses Eliot's interaction with the 'poetess' tradition, and her interest in links between the biblical prophetess and the woman poet. This is a significant account of Eliot's engagement with the tradition of women's poetry and poetics in the period. The same issue contains Robert P. Fletcher's '"Convent Thoughts": Augusta Webster and the Body Politics of the Victorian Cloister' (*VLC* 31:i[2003] 295–314), in which he discusses how Webster confuses both traditional associations between women and the body, and spirituality and bodilessness (p. 301), primarily focusing on her dramatic monologue 'Sister Annunciata'. Tonya Moutray McArthur, 'The Cloistered Pen: Penetration and Conception in Eliza Keary's "Christine and Mary: A Correspondence"' (*VLC* 31:i[2003] 315–32), looks at Eliza Keary, again discussing how her epistolary poem 'Christine and Mary' undoes gendered bodily categories, particularly in its depiction of Mary's sensual relation to Christ. Both articles help to draw attention to relatively neglected religious poems.

Mathilde Blind was the subject of one article, James Diedrick's 'A Pioneering Female Aesthete: Mathilde Blind in *The Dark Blue*' (*VPR* 36[2003] 210–41). He discusses Blind's association with this short-lived progressive journal and analyses her published work there in relation to the politics and aesthetics espoused by the journal, tracing significant connections between her texts and work by Swinburne, Morris, and others. Alice Meynell was studied in relation to concepts of poetic identity in Kathleen Anderson's '"I make the whole world answer to my art": Alice Meynell's Poetic Identity' (*VP* 41[2003] 259–75). Anderson argues that Meynell's obsessed speakers present the world as a reflection of their poetic genius, and considers how her religious poems construct an idea of Mary as the poet and Christ himself as a poem. Working-class poetry was revisited by Florence Boos in 'The "Queen" of the "Far-Famed Penny Post": "The Factory Girl Poet" and her Audience' (*WW* 10[2003] 503–26), which examines the interaction between Ellen Johnston, her editor, and her readers in the pages of the *Penny Post*. This important article views Johnston in relation to the material and historical circumstances in which her poems were published. Boos also discusses working-class women's poetry more broadly in '"Nurs'd up amongst the scenes I have describ'd": Political Resonances in the Poetry of Working-Class Women' (in Krueger, ed. *Functions of Victorian Culture at the Present Time*, pp. 137–56). She sets out four ways of reading these writers, moving from the explicitly political (e.g. Janet Hamilton's poems on Italian liberation) to more personal verse, embodying or obliquely referencing political issues, and finally to rarely preserved forms of oral verse. Elsewhere, a blind west of Ireland poet of the 1840s, Frances Browne, is discussed by Thomas McLean in 'Arms and the Circassian Woman: Frances Browne's "The Star of Atteghai"' (*VP* 41[2003] 295–318). Browne's poem, set in nineteenth-century Circassia, is read by McLean in relation to contemporary historical events, and as a reflection on troubled nationalisms with potential relevance to Browne's Irishness. His biographical account of Browne and his discussion of her poem point towards an undeservedly neglected poet, and are compelling in their implication that Browne merits more sustained attention. Charlotte Mew's collected poems and selected prose, edited by Val Warner, also became available again in a second edition from Carcanet's imprint, Fyfield Books.

In terms of other minor poets, Kirstie Blair's 'John Keble and the Rhythm of Faith' (*EIC* 53[2003] 129–50) assesses how metrical patterns in *The Christian Year* might contribute to the underlying affective power of the poem, in terms of shaping and directing the reader's faith. Coventry Patmore was discussed by Ernest Fontana in 'Patmore, Pascal and Astronomy' (*VP* 41[2003] 277–86), in relation to astronomical references. Fontana argues that Patmore used Herschel's work to counteract Pascal's 'astronomy of dread' (p. 277), and uses a valuable and perceptive reading of 'The Two Deserts' to demonstrate this. His essay would fit well with Henchman's study of Tennyson and astronomy (discussed above). George Meredith's *Modern Love* was discussed in a special issue of *SIL* on forgery, where Natalie Houston, in 'Affecting Authenticity: *Sonnets from the Portuguese* and *Modern Love*' (*SIL* 35[2002] 99–122), considers how Barrett

Browning and Meredith used language and form to stage the sonnet as authentic, private, colloquial and personal, while recognizing that rewriting the Renaissance sonnet sequence was itself an affected move, a deliberate performance. Like Houston's work on the sonnet in general, this is finely nuanced and wholly convincing.

The study of 1890s poetry received a boost with the publication of Ernest Dowson's *Collected Poems*, edited by R.K.R. Thornton and Caroline Dowson. The introduction inevitably has to defend Dowson from insinuations of drug and alcohol abuse and a sexualized interest in young girls: the editors argue that what Dowson saw and worshipped in girls was a desexualized innocence, and that accusations of his promiscuity and decadent behaviour were heavily exaggerated. The poems themselves, including unpublished work and Dowson's many translations from or versions of French poems, are interesting to read in the context of 1890s writing, though there are no real surprises here in terms of assessing Dowson's poetic merit. His 'Pierrot: A Dramatic Phantasy' is perhaps particularly good to have in print, casting light on the theatrical practices of the 1890s and how these intersected with poetry. Notes to the poems are detailed and give full information on sources and manuscripts. Arthur Symons's *Selected Writings*, edited by Roger Holdsworth and first published in 1974, were also reissued, again adding to the Victorian poetry made available by Fyfield.

In relation to Victorian poetry criticism, Isobel Armstrong provided a brief and fascinating evaluation of changes in the position of Victorian poetry within the academy, surveying her own career in the field and the educational doctrines which shaped the perception of nineteenth-century poetry in post-war Britain (*JVC* 8[2003] 292–304). Anthony Kearney also contributed a discussion of nineteenth-century poetry and twentieth-century criticism, in 'Confusing the Issue? A.C. Bradley's Theory of Poetry and its Contexts' (*VP* 31[2003] 245–57), in which he considers the implications of Bradley's inaugural lecture as Oxford Professor of Poetry, and how his idealist views influenced the study of literature as a discipline.

Turning to individual authors, relatively little work was published on Matthew Arnold this year. Perhaps the most significant piece was Daniel Kline's '"Unhackneyed thoughts and winged words": Arnold, Locke and the Similes of *Sohrab and Rustum*' (*VP* 41[2003] 173–96). Kline discusses the ways in which Arnold's reading of Locke in 1850 might have added a 'linguistic dimension' to his recurring themes of loneliness and isolation, but then suggests that by the mid-1850s Arnold was moving away from this towards a new ideal of communication and understanding, in which Locke's work also featured. Kline's analysis of epic similes as tools to produce more accurate readerly understanding, in Lockean terms, is excellent. In 'Matthew Arnold's "Rugby Chapel" and Thomas Arnold's Travel Journals' (*ELN* 40[2003] 61–73), Francis O'Gorman uses Thomas Arnold's unpublished travel journals to argue credibly that he saw travel as a moral and educational necessity, and hence that Matthew Arnold's imagery of journeying in 'Rugby Chapel' should be taken literally as well as metaphorically. Robert Carballo's 'Intellectual Anguish and the Quest for Harmony in *Empedocles on Etna*: Arnold's Foregrounding of Modern Existentialism' (*CVE* 57[2003] 23–32), as the title suggests, argues that Arnold's poem anticipates key existential questions and is thus a departure from Romantic idealism. *Wordsworth Circle* contained Samuel Baker's 'Wordsworth, Arnold, and the Maritime Matrix of Culture' (*WC* 34[2003] 24–9), which suggests that both poets used maritime imagery to convey an ethics of insularity, to envisage shaping the self in relation to the aqueous and shifting nature of culture and poetry.

Three articles appeared on the Brontës' poetry. Julie Pfeiffer, 'John Milton's Influence on the Inspired Poetry of Charlotte Brontë (*BS* 28[2003] 37–45), adds to our knowledge of Milton's influence on Charlotte Brontë by tracing his presence in her poems, in terms of allusion but also general patterns of invocation and imagery of darkness versus divine light and grace. Cosetta Veronese, in 'Patterns of Doubleness in Emily Brontë's Poetic World' (*BS* 28[2003] 47–56), suggests that Emily Brontë's possible interest in German dialectics might contribute to the dichotomies and doublings found throughout her work. Emma Mason returns to the theme of Emily Brontë as enthusiast in '"Some God of wild enthusiast's dreams": Emily Brontë's Religious Enthusiasm' (*VLC* 31:i[2003] 263–78). She discusses the importance of Methodism in Brontë's Yorkshire, and argues persuasively that the wild desires of Brontë's writing have their roots in the religious enthusiasm and revivalist rhetoric of the dissenting evangelical movement.

The Brownings received a great deal of attention in 2003 and 2004, with a lengthy biography of Robert Browning, Iain Finlayson's *Robert Browning: A Private Life* (HarperCollins [2004]), which will be reviewed next year, a critical study of Barrett Browning, and Mary Sanders Pollock's study of the two poets together, *Elizabeth Barrett and Robert Browning: A Creative Partnership*. Pollock begins by arguing that the two poets did not 'influence' each other in a straightforward sense, and that we should escape from paradigms which see their marriage as either nurturing or stifling to one or the other's poetic gift. Rather, her preferred term for their partnership is 'collaboration', and she sees the two poets as enabling one another's development, as Browning becomes more aware of his readership and Barrett develops a new poetic idiom. Pollock works with a conversational model drawn from Bakhtin, in which the poets move from dialectic to dialogue, creating together 'a dialogic space in which new ideas and meanings could emerge' (p. 64). In effect, however, this book discusses the two poets separately, devoting chapters to Barrett's early development and then Browning's early poems, *Men and Women* and then *Aurora Leigh*, and so forth, meaning that the dialogue between the poets is not always clear. Pollock does, however, present refreshing readings of some neglected poems—her discussion of the tensions and complexities of Browning's *Saul* is particularly good, and her account of *Christmas-Eve* in relation to Menippean satire is also enlightening. In fact, for this reader, her commentary on Browning stood out more than the sections on Barrett Browning, which focused chiefly on *Sonnets from the Portuguese* and *Aurora Leigh*. Pollock is slightly dismissive about Barrett's ballads and early poems, and suggests that her 'strident political poetry' contrasts with 'some of her most nearly perfect poems' (p. 205), although she does make intriguing comparisons between *Casa Guidi Windows* and *Sordello*. The chief problem with this book is that it includes relatively little discussion of the form or language of the poems, meaning that difficult and ambiguous passages are described in very general and inadequate terms. On 'O lyric love', to take one instance, Pollock observes that 'These beautiful lines were an essential part of Browning's grieving. Naturally, so soon after her death, he would remember his wife in a rush of blood, wings and fire' (p. 206). What is 'natural' about this? To see these lines and others purely as a commentary on the Browning's marriage is reductive, and Pollock's judgement of poems as beautiful or perfect needs more defence and explication. Ultimately this discussion of the Brownings' lives and works seems considerably less subtle than Daniel Karlin's study of their courtship correspondence, or other work in this field. There are also some factual errors: Swinburne was not aged 19 in the 1890s, Hemans's name is misspelt (and her work is somewhat cursorily dismissed), and in one case two sentences in a paragraph seem to be in the wrong order (p. 63). These are minor mistakes, but they do undermine confidence in the work to some extent.

Simon Avery and Rebecca Stott's *Elizabeth Barrett Browning* is a more significant publication, not only because it is clearly intended for the student market and would be an ideal set text for courses on Barrett Browning's poetry, but because it provides an excellent overview, both general and detailed, of recent critical interest in her poetry (plus a useful bibliography and timeline). The book roughly moves chronologically, from Barrett's early life and formative writings to *Aurora Leigh* and her last poems. All major works are covered, including a particularly welcome chapter on *Casa Guidi Windows*, which explains Barrett Browning's engagement with politics clearly and coherently. Chapters are divided between the two contributors and, loosely speaking, Avery's pieces are more concerned with setting the poems in their particular political and historical contexts, while Stott's take a broader look at concerns with gender, genre and religion. While this separate authoring of chapters sometimes involves overlap and can seem disjunctive, it does serve to highlight the diversity of possible responses to Barrett Browning's work, and ensures that no one approach is uppermost. Given Barrett Browning's increasing presence on undergraduate Victorian literature courses, this is a timely and valuable study: an excellent introduction to Barrett Browning's poetry for those encountering it for the first time, as well as a book that could be used by critics.

Barrett Browning and Italy was a key theme this year. Chapman and Stabler, eds., *Unfolding the South*, is a absorbing and indispensable book for anyone interested in expatriate communities, attitudes towards foreignness, Italian politics of the period, or simply women's writing. Taking *Corinne* as a starting point, the editors suggest that Italy functioned as a space of indeterminacy and negotiation for nineteenth-century women, offering a vision of subversive sexuality combined with political and artistic engagement. The number of writers whose work is briefly discussed in the introduction, including Emma Lazarus, Adah Isaacs Menken, Janet Hamilton, A. Mary F. Robinson and Michael Field, not to mention the obvious suspect, Elizabeth Barrett Browning, suggests from the outset the scope and extent of women's interest in Italy. While the book as a whole would be useful for anyone working on these or other poets, I will consider here only the three chapters which specifically deal with poetry, all of which are on Barrett Browning. The first, Richard Cronin's '*Casa Guidi*

Windows: Elizabeth Barrett Browning, Italy and the Poetry of Citizenship' (pp. 35–50) is largely drawn from his recent book *Romantic Victorians*, reviewed last year. It brilliantly argues that *Casa Guidi Windows* functions as a poem about the nature of citizenship, concluding that Barrett Browning's trope of watching from the window points towards the 'true citizen, at once separate from the state and joined to it' (p. 50). Isobel Armstrong's succeeding essay, '*Casa Guidi Windows*: Spectacle and Politics in 1851' (pp. 51–69), also focuses largely on the window trope, but her argument concentrates on the 'poetics of the window', how the act of looking itself, an act bound up with Barrett Browning's imagery of light, perspective and glass, might be of vital importance in the poem. She concludes that the 'proliferation of optical signs' forces the subject to choose between them, and eventually 'to discard outworn symbol and commit to new images' (p. 69). In another excellent piece, Alison Chapman then turns to a wider consideration of how Barrett Browning's spiritualism might relate to her politics, showing how her disillusion with Sophia Eckley's spiritual gifts was associated with disillusion at the peace of Villafranca, and positing that the sense of 'risorgimento' (rising or resurrection) could be imaginatively linked with the resurrection of the dead in a séance. Dante himself, Chapman notes, supposedly arose to crown Barrett Browning with a poetic wreath ('Risorgimenti: Spiritualism, Politics and Elizabeth Barrett Browning', pp. 70–89). These three essays suggest the multiple perspectives from which Barrett Browning's involvement with Italy could be viewed.

Elsewhere, Chapman published another article on Barrett Browning and Italy, '"In our own blood drenched the pen": Italy and Sensibility in Elizabeth Barrett Browning's *Last Poems* (1862)' (*WW* 10[2003] 269–86). She sees a change in Barrett Browning's response to Italy between 1846 and 1862, arguing that the last poems radically combine extremes of sensibility with commentary on Italian politics, reimagining the role of the woman poet in the process. Michele Martinez takes up her own suggestions in the *VP* special issue, and considers Barrett Browning in Italy through an account of her friendship with the expatriate sculptress Harriet Hosmer in 'Sister Arts and Artists: Elizabeth Barrett Browning's *Aurora Leigh* and the Life of Harriet Hosmer' (*FMLS* 39[2003] 214–26). Her fine article suggests that the focus on sculpture at key moments in *Aurora Leigh* may invoke Hosmer's work, and that Hosmer may in part have served as a model for Aurora. Martinez also considers Barrett Browning's attitudes towards sculpture in relation to Frances Power Cobbe's similar comments. Another significant article, published too late to be included last year, appeared in *VLC*: Linda Shires' 'Elizabeth Barrett Browning: Cross-Dwelling and the Reworking of Female Poetic Identity' (*VLC* 30:i[2002] 41–59). Shires borrows the notion of 'cross-dwelling' to describe how Barrett Browning could inhabit dual identities—wife and mother as opposed to poetess, for instance—adopting masculine and feminine styles alternately and deploying different impulses and attitudes at different times. Shires' reading is convincing, and presents an intriguing means of conceptualizing Barrett Browning's disparate poetic personae. In *VP*, Margaret Morlier's 'The Hero and the Sage: Elizabeth Barrett's Sonnets "To George Sand" in Victorian Context' (*VP* 41[2003] 319–32) discusses representations of Sand in the press at the time when Barrett was writing. Morlier argues that Barrett draws on the rhetoric of journalistic pieces, as well as using sustained historical, biblical and literary allusion to re-vision Sand's heroism and celebrate her feminine poetics. Barrett Browning's influence on Emily Dickinson is re-examined by Ann Swyderski in 'Dickinson's Enchantment: The Barrett Browning Fascicles' (*Symbiosis* 7[2003] 76–98), which investigates Dickinson's complex interaction with Barrett Browning by studying the fascicle in which Dickinson collected her elegies and other poems about the older poet. Also worth noting, in conclusion, is the reprinting of Barrett Browning's *Selected Poems*, ed. Malcolm Hicks (first published 1983), again by the Fyfield Books imprint.

Nick De Marco published a short study this year, *Robert Browning's The Ring and the Book: A Critical Appraisal*. De Marco considers the poem through two major strands: its historicism and its questions about truth in language. The first part argues that Browning is effectively a new historicist and that reading his poem through new historicist methodologies reveals something about Browning's own methods. De Marco revisits the evidence for Browning's deviation from historical fact and retells the historical story behind the poem using the new evidence accumulated in Italian archives. His conclusion that Browning was deliberately questioning categories of historical fidelity is not new, but this part is a good summary of where criticism stands on Browning and historicism and would be helpful to anyone encountering the poem for the first time. Likewise, the second half of the book essentially reworks familiar critical debates about the relation between language and truth in the poem. De Marco works towards the notion of truth as process, created somewhere between the flawed language of the poem and the reader's understanding of it. Again, this is a helpful account, and while some sections, such as De Marco's detailed discussion of the structure of the poem and his plot summaries, might seem unnecessary to a Browning scholar, this brief study would be useful for students.

Joseph Phelan reconsidered the biographical controversy over the Brownings' alleged mixed-race origins in 'Ethnology and Biography: The Case of the Brownings' (*Biography* 26[2003] 261–82). This wide-ranging article is of general interest to anyone concerned with race and ethnicity in the period as Phelan demonstrates convincingly that virtually every nineteenth-century celebrity was suspected of dubious racial origins. He concludes that biographies that reiterate these claims, such as Julia Markus's *Dared and Done*, are very questionable in their adoption of Victorian assumptions about the racial implications of various character traits. Phelan also published another fine article on Robert Browning, 'Robert Browning and Colonialism' (*JVC* 8[2003] 80–107). He situates Browning in the 1830s and 1840s in the group of young men known as 'The Colloquials', and notes that many of these acquaintances went on to become powerful in colonial settings. In studying Browning's *The Return of the Druses* and other poems, including 'Through the Metidja to Abd-el-Kadr – 1842', he argues that the poet used discourses of Orientalism but recognized that the colonial project was problematic and potentially flawed, at times presenting a strongly anti-colonial stance. Again, this is a useful article not just for Browning scholars but in the wider context of colonial and postcolonial studies. Another significant article on Browning appeared in *Essays in*

Criticism: Matthew Reynolds' 'Browning and Translationese' (*EIC* 53[2003] 97–128). Reynolds studies extracts from *Balaustion's Adventure*, *Agamemnon* and *The Ring and the Book* to analyse what he describes as the 'double tongue' of translationese, the way in which Browning's translations, or poems based on writings in another language, bear traces of that other language behind their English. He is particularly good on this sense of strangeness in *The Ring and the Book*, where Browning's awkward phrasing often points to his Italian original. One more essay on translation, Kathleen Riley's 'Browning's Versions: Robert Browning, Greek Tragedy and the Victorian Translation Debate' (*L&A* 13[2003] 51–70), considers Browning's translation of *Herakles* in the light of contemporary debates over the appropriate methodology and objectives for translators of Greek and Latin texts.

Browning and religion was a favoured topic this year, with the publication of a series of papers from the Golden Jubilee Conference, held in 2001 at the Armstrong Browning Library, in *Studies in Browning and his Circle*, edited by Mairi C. Rennie and Kathleen Miller. The essays printed here are variable in quality, some presenting relatively straightforward accounts of issues in Browning's poetry while others offer significant contributions to a revaluation of Browning as a religious poet and thinker. The volume opens with Ashby Crowder's 'Re-viewing Robert Browning as a Christian Poet' (*SBHC* 25[2003] 7–23), which discusses the reception history of Browning's work in his lifetime and after, and points out that nineteenth-century contemporaries had no difficulty in perceiving him as a spiritual guide. The next essay, Rowena Fowler's 'Bishop Blougram and the Probability of God' (*SBHC* 25[2003] 24–35), is a shorter version of an article published in *VP* and discussed above. Michael di Massa also concentrates on this poem in 'Bishop Blougram and "Brother Newman": Catholic Undercurrents in "Bishop Blougram's Apology"' (*SBHC* 25[2003] 36–48), in which he persuasively argues that Browning's poem could be read as a specific debate about whether an intelligent man could subscribe to Catholic doctrine, as well as a general debate about the plausibility of faith. He suggests that 'Bishop Blougram' could potentially be read from a Catholic perspective.

Daniel Karlin's 'A Life in the Desert: Browning, Moses and St John' (*SBHC* 25[2003] 49–71), is a dense and richly allusive piece about Browning's representation of biblically inspired desert spaces. Through a series of clever close readings of passages from *Sordello*, 'One Word More' and 'A Death in the Desert', Karlin argues that Browning moves from viewing Moses, the divinely inspired leader, as a model for the poet, to the more conflicted image of St John. Following this, Rieko Suzuki's 'Recovering the Female Voice: The "Sad Dishevelled Ghost" in Browning's *Sordello*' (*SBHC* 25[2003] 72–85) also considers *Sordello*, but from the perspective of Browning's treatment of the muse in this poem. Browning's earthly, unattractive muse invites feminist meditation on the muse figure and points towards his focus on real, palpable lives rather than romantic clichés. Two short articles then focus on Browning among the philosophers. Rodica Silvia Stan's 'The Enigma of Self' (*SBHC* 25[2003] 86–93) presents some preliminary comparisons between Browning's poetics and Nietzsche's philosophy, while Shigeko Kurobane's 'Browning, an Existential Feminist' (*SBHC* 25[2003] 94–100) sets Browning in relation to

Kierkegaard—the second Victorian poet to be compared to him this year—and argues that *The Ring in the Book* has a strongly feminist agenda in privileging Pompilia's speech. Michael Meredith's succeeding article turns to historical research, presenting new information from Arezzo about the originals of Browning's characters in *The Ring and the Book* (*SBHC* 25[2003] 101–16). Next, Rose Williams, in 'Browning's View of Aging' (*SBHC* 25[2003] 117–23), and Joseph Dupras, in 'Marking Time in "How it Strikes a Contemporary"' (*SBHC* 25[2003] 124–33), present discursive and speculative considerations of 'Rabbi Ben Ezra' and 'How it Strikes'. Finally, Britta Martens adds to Karlin's account of Browning's biblical typology by discussing his use of David and Moses as types for the poet in 'The Poet and Christ: Robert Browning's Self-Conceptualization Through Biblical Typology Revisited' (*SBHC* 25[2003] 134–42), and Herbert Tucker, in 'Robert Browning's Message for Our Time' (*SBHC* 25[2003] 143–61), concludes the volume with a lively argument that Browning should be read less as a pioneering, proto-modernist, avant-garde writer, and more as '*the* poet of the emergent entrepreneurial-management class' (p. 147), a poet who believed in truth and in the importance of the messages he sought to convey through poetry. Tucker supplies a fitting conclusion to a volume which ranges widely in its discussion of Browning's lasting significance, particularly in relation to his thought on and depiction of religious ideas.

'A Death in the Desert' featured again in *VP* in 'Two Interpolated Speeches in Robert Browning's "A Death in the Desert"' (*VP* 41[2003] 333–47), in which Robert Inglesfield, like Karlin and Martens, considers its function in relation to the crisis of faith in the 1860s, studying the repeated use of interpolated questions and sceptical voices as Browning's means of responding to this crisis. This is an intricate argument, alert to Browning's many allusions to religious texts and contexts. Browning and religion also appears in Andrew Tate's '"He Himself with his human air": Browning Writes the Body of Christ' (*NCC* 25[2003] 39–53), where he discusses 'Christmas-Eve' as a rereading of Paul's description of the Church as the body of Christ. Browning, Tate demonstrates, sets the claims of the dissenting chapel in a wider context and both questions and celebrates the concept of 'church' and his own place in it.

The chapter on Browning in Robert Sawyer's *Victorian Appropriations of Shakespeare* contains a useful discussion of Browning's drama and its relation to Shakespearian acting, and also devotes considerable space to a reading of 'Caliban on Setebos'. Sawyer's argument that Browning appropriates Shakespeare's cultural authority does not seem particularly original, but his discussion of how Browning himself came to be constructed as Shakespearian is interesting, especially in tracing links between the Browning Society and the New Shakespeare Society. A darker aspect of the links between Browning and Shakespeare, however, might be found in *SLI*'s special issue on forgery, which contained C.D. Blanton's 'Impostures: Robert Browning and the Poetics of Forgery' (*SLI* 35 [2002] 1–25). Blanton discusses how Browning (as well as Shakespeare) was a target for Wise and Foreman's forgeries in the late Victorian period, and suggests that this is interesting in that Browning's own writings seem to 'slyly authorize' these forgeries by meditating on the authenticity of texts. Blanton also briefly discusses Barrett Browning's *Sonnets* in this respect.

In 'Browning's Apology: Robert Browning, William Wordsworth, and William Knight' (*RES* 54[2003] 220–37), John H. Baker studies Browning's correspondence with William Knight, the founder of the Wordsworth Society, and uses this to explore Browning's changing attitude towards Wordsworth, particularly with reference to the poems he selected as personal favourites when Knight consulted him about an edition he was preparing. As Baker notes, Browning's selection implies a greater interest in Wordsworth's writings on humanity than in those on nature, and suggests his admiration of the realism contained within Romanticism. Nathan Cervo continued his close readings of Victorian poetry by analysing the imagery of lines 48–52 of 'Andrea del Sarto' (*Expl* 61[2003] 11–13); discussing the importance of the name Anselm (related to that St Anselm who put forward an 'ontological' argument for God's existence) in 'The Bishop Orders his Tomb at St Praxed's Church' (*Expl* 61[2003] 204–6), and, in 'Browning's "Soliloquy of the Spanish Cloister"' (*Expl* 61[2003] 81–4), identifying a particular text in Galatians which could have twenty-nine different heretical readings.

Shirley Chew's edition of Clough's *Selected Poems* (first published 1987) is back in print from Fyfield Books, making these poems more widely available through this relatively cheap edition. It is a pity, however, that the bibliographical information in this volume has not been updated to take account of more recent work. With the exception of Slinn's chapter, and Vanessa Ryan's essay, discussed above, though, very little work actually appeared this year. Howard Jacobson's brief piece, 'Some Quotations in Arthur Hugh Clough's Verse' (*ANQ* 16[2003] 41–2), which notes without comment several examples of Clough's borrowing from Greek and Latin missed by Mulhauser in his standard edition of the poems, was the only article I found. Michael Field, somewhat similarly, had a strong presence in *VP*'s 'Whither Victorian Poetry?' collection, but just one article appeared on Bradley and Cooper this year, Holly A. Laird's 'The Coauthored Pseudonym: Two Women Named Michael Field' (in Griffin, ed., *The Faces of Anonymity: Anonymous and Pseudonymous Publications from the Sixteenth to the Twentieth Century*, pp. 193–210). Laird argues that the name 'Michael Field' needs to be examined further in terms of its personal and cultural allusions, as an 'expression' of these poets, and suggests that 'Michael Field' and its various connotations serves as one example of their repeated imagining of pairs and paired worlds.

Thomas Hardy scholars may want to consult Andrew Radford's *Thomas Hardy and the Survivals of Time* and Geoffrey Harvey's *The Complete Critical Guide to Thomas Hardy*, both covered earlier in this chapter, for material relevant to the poems. In terms of articles, Jon Roberts's 'Mortal Projections: Thomas Hardy's Dissolving Views of God' (*VLC* 31:i[2003] 43–66) investigates references to God in Hardy's poetry. Martin Bidney, in 'War of the Winds: Shelley, Hardy and Harold Bloom' (*VP* 41[2003] 229–44), discusses Bloom's defensiveness about Shelley's influence on Hardy, and suggests an alternative reading of this influence in which Hardy's response might be more parodic and playful than Bloom suggests. The article acts as a valuable corrective to some of Bloom's statements, and also contains a fine reading of Hardy's 'The Wind's Prophecy'. The *Thomas Hardy Journal* prints a lecture by Merryn Williams on *The Dynasts*, in which he discusses the poem in relation to war poetry and other commentaries on the Napoleonic era, and suggests that it anticipated the poetry of the First World War (*THJ* 19[2003] 39–53). Ronald Butler examines the metre of 'At the Altar-Rail' and 'Over the Coffin' in detail (*THJ* 19[2003] 61–4), and Peter Coxon finds a possible source for the word 'stalk' in 'In Time of "The Breaking of Nations"' in James Beattie (*THJ* 19[2003] 45–7). Martin Ray's note on a source for 'The Catching Ballet of the Wedding Shoes', published in *N&Q*, is also reprinted here (*THJ* 19[2003] 53–4; *N&Q* 50[2003] 319–20). Nathan Cervo also supplies a brief note on a Hardy poem, 'Hardy's "The Impercipient"' (*Expl* 61[2003] 92–4) in which he discusses the significance of the title change, from 'The Agnostic' to 'The Impercipient'.

As usual, Hopkins featured in a number of articles, and this year also saw the publication of Jill Muller's *Gerard Manley Hopkins and Victorian Catholicism*—the second monograph published on Hopkins and religion in two years. Muller suggests that critics have been reluctant to explore Hopkins's Victorian Catholic identity. She points out that English Catholicism was itself a divided party, and that Hopkins's allegiance to various factions was more complex and ambiguous than has been discussed, arguing that concentration on Newman's influence, for instance, obscures Hopkins's interest in the Ultramontane position of more extreme and floridly emotional Catholics, such as Manning and Frederick Faber. This is a useful discussion, though Muller perhaps overlooks the need to defend her use of the term 'Catholic' as opposed to 'Roman Catholic', given the debate within Victorian Christianity about precisely this distinction—the Tractarians, who led the way in viewing themselves as 'Catholic' but not 'Roman', are largely absent here, apart from the obvious converts to Roman Catholicism. Muller suggests, convincingly, that Hopkins considered his early poems part of an effort to become a specifically Catholic poet, addressed primarily to an 'imagined audience of his Catholic contemporaries' (p. 4), and incorporating both political and religious concerns of particular interest to this party. Her analysis of Hopkins's early poems and of *The Wreck of the Deutschland* in relation to his conversion does sometimes stray into reading poetry as autobiography (though she notes the dangers of this). Succeeding chapters trace Hopkins's growing disillusionment, which Muller reads in relation to a turn towards nature and away from theology. She suggests that his vision of nature, inspired by Scotus, was 'singularly ill-timed' (p. 79) in relation to wider currents in Catholicism, and that his optimism about reconciling faith, science and nature was uncharacteristic of the views of his contemporaries. Her discussion of Hopkins's years in Ireland is equally sensitive to his place within a Catholic context, reading his poems with particular attention to eschatological concerns of this period. Again, this is an illuminating reading which persuasively sees the poems as commentaries on specifically Catholic concerns. The focus on this context does mean that the poems themselves are studied in less detail, and with emphasis on content rather than language or form, but on the whole this is an admirable book in the ways in which it reconstructs a precise sectarian atmosphere for Hopkins's poems.

John Parham offered another take on Hopkins and ecology, in 'Green Man Hopkins: Gerard Manley Hopkins and Victorian Ecological Criticism' (*NCC* 25[2003] 257–76). Parham sets Hopkins in the context of the debate over the terms 'ecology' and 'environment', and suggests that his poetry should be seen as part of a wider Victorian understanding of ecological concepts: poems like 'Inversnaid', he argues, demonstrate an innate understanding of ecosystem and should not simply be read as environmental or preservationist. Hopkins and homosexuality is revisited by Dennis Sobolev, whose 'Hopkins's "Bellbright Bodies": The Dialectics of Desire in his Writings' (*TSLL* 45[2003] 114–40) is a balanced yet strongly argued account of critical interest in Hopkins's alleged homoerotic tendencies, proposing a more subtle, nuanced and historicized reading of his attraction to men. Ernest Fontana, in 'Thomas Meyrick, Jesuit Madness, and Hopkins' (*VN* 104[2003] 31–3), considers whether the career of Meyrick, who described how he was committed to an asylum against his will in *My Imprisonings* [1880], might have affected Hopkins's fear of insanity in his sonnets.

In *Hopkins Quarterly* Michelle Faubert, 'A Kierkegaardian Reading of Hopkins' "Terrible Sonnets"' (*HQ* 30[2003] 3–30), considers the relation between Hopkins and Kierkegaard in terms of their shared individualism and disdain for Hegel, usefully examining how Kierkegaard's notion that faith develops from and rests upon dread might be evident in the language of Hopkins's sonnets. Sarah Winters, in 'Heavenly Bodies in "The Windhover"' (*HQ* 30[2003] 31–44), suggests that Hopkins's falcon may be associated with a flaming meteor and with the fiery dove of Pentecost, and Arnd Bohm revisits the relations between 'Binsey Poplars' and Cowper's 'The Poplar-Field', considering how the former serves to challenge the latter, in 'William Cowper's "The Poplar-Field" and Hopkins' "Binsey Poplars": The Politics of Pastoral' (*HQ* 30[2003] 45–58).

Following this, Bernadette Waterman Ward, 'Hopkins on Warfare: "The war within"' (*HQ* 30[2003] 72–82), discusses how Hopkins's enthusiasm for the military—partly inspired by Ruskin's *Unto This Last*—inspires imagery in his poems and encourages presentations of Christ as a soldier, and how he moves towards perceiving warfare as relevant to his poetic vocation in terms of it requiring courage, fortitude and strength. Peter Groves, 'Gerard Among the Puseyites: New Light from Old Archives on Hopkins' Undergraduate Religion' (*HQ* 30[2003] 83–97), then examines some new sources from Pusey House in Oxford, including lecture notes by Liddon and the records of the 'Brotherhood of the Holy Trinity', an undergraduate group Hopkins considered joining, which shed light on the culture of Oxford during Hopkins's undergraduate days. Finally, Frederick W. Schlatter, 'Hopkins' Dublin Critic, Joseph Darlington, SJ' (*HQ* 30[2003] 98–126), discusses the career of Joseph Darlington, an unreliable source for anecdotes on Hopkins, but an interesting historical (and literary, given his appearance in Joyce's work) figure in his own right. Also in this volume, the editors of *HQ* print two translations of Hopkins's poems into French, from an award-winning collection by Bruno Gaurier.

Christina Rossetti, as noted at the start of this section, was much discussed this year and last. Three full-length monographs, Lorraine Kooistra's *Christina Rossetti and Illustration* [2002], Lynda Palazzo's *Christina Rossetti's Feminist Theology* [2002] and Mary Arseneau's *Recovering Christina Rossetti: Female Community and Incarnational Poetics* [2004, reviewed next year] have appeared on her within two years, as well as numerous articles. Judging from these works, Rossetti and religion is emerging as a key area of interest, although discussion is still focused more on her early poems ('Goblin Market' in particular continues to attract significant attention) than on the devotional works. The exception is Palazzo's study of Rossetti in relation to feminist theological concepts, which pays considerable attention to the devotional prose works and Rossetti's other religious publications, including *Annus Domini*, *Called to Be Saints*, *Letter and Spirit* and *Time Flies*. Less space is spent on the poetry in this volume, with only one chapter focusing on Rossetti's poems and, what seems stranger, little sustained discussion of her religious verse. Palazzo seeks to demonstrate that, far from placidly accepting Tractarian theological principles, and indeed Christian principles in general, Rossetti actively questioned and challenged her faith, particularly in relation to its treatment of women. This is certainly an important argument, but it is hampered here precisely by Palazzo's firmness in asserting it. Any suggestion that Rossetti might have felt something other than outrage, anger and alienation at the Church's attitude towards women is excised, leaving a somewhat one-sided impression of Anglicanism, and Tractarianism in particular, as ruthlessly and deliberately repressive and misogynistic. The subtlety of recent work on women and Victorian religion, such as Cynthia Scheinberg's *Women's Poetry and Religion in Victorian England: Jewish Identity and Christian Culture* [2002], which suggests that religion might have provided an enabling as well as a disabling framework for women writers, is missing here. At times, indeed, Palazzo unconsciously seems to be restating anti-Tractarian or anti-Catholic rhetoric of the nineteenth century—as when she suggests that Pusey's belief in self-mortification and fasting might have led to the death of several women in one of his sisterhoods. The effect is to present a rather caricatured view of both High Church Christianity and Rossetti's stake in it, in which her writings are read solely to support Palazzo's account of her theological beliefs. In relation to the poems, this seems reductive, though the chapters on prose writings do make a convincing case for Rossetti's sensitivity to gender issues in her religious writing and show how she radically reinterprets biblical texts. The feminist theology which Palazzo uses as a framework fits well here, and sheds new light on these neglected texts.

Lorraine Kooistra's *Christina Rossetti and Illustration*, missed last year, covers some similar ground in its examination of the interaction between text and picture in some of Rossetti's religious writings. Kooistra's fascinating study of the materiality of Rossetti's published texts, their afterlife in the twentieth century, and the relation between image and text more generally in her work, will be of use to all Rossetti scholars as well as Victorian poetry scholars, bibliographers and book historians. Illustrations, Kooistra argues, can be read typologically and analogically in Rossetti's works, carrying symbolic force, so that texts like 'Goblin Market' and *The Prince's Progress* 'may be looked on as modified emblem books for a Victorian audience accustomed to symbolic interpretation' (p. 66). She describes Rossetti's own illustrations to her books and her possible interest in an artistic career, before situating her published works in the context of Pre-Raphaelite-inspired illustrators: Arthur Hughes, Dante Gabriel Rossetti and Frederick Sandys, among others. Kooistra's discussion of how their illustrations reflect upon Rossetti's text—and vice versa, given that she also altered her text to fit the images in the case of Hughes's *Sing-Song*—is sensitive and interesting, and her case for how illustrations affected the marketing and readership of Rossetti's works is compelling. She suggests, for instance, that 'Goblin Market' came to be perceived as a work for children, *Playboy* illustrations notwithstanding, because it was often presented as an illustrated edition. Likewise, later chapters are good on Rossetti's involvement with the Society for Promoting Christian Knowledge and its subsequent marketing of a saintlike image of her as devotional writer. The final chapters also discuss Rossetti's published works in terms of the rare book market, and Kooistra concludes with a brief examination of Rossetti's afterlife on the web. While there are one or two minor factual errors here, and some points where the focus on illustration means that the language of Rossetti's poems is little discussed (surely 'Goblin Market' was partly perceived as children's literature owing to its form and language as well as presentation and marketing?), this is an outstanding book on Victorian illustrations. It is also, in keeping with the topic, well produced and lavishly illustrated throughout.

One of the most important articles this year, for this reader, was Herbert Tucker's 'Rossetti's Goblin Marketing: Sweet to Tongue and Sound to Ear' (*Rep* 82[2003] 117–33), which succeeds in presenting a new and convincing reading of a poem which can seem over-analysed by criticism. In a brilliant and entertaining exposition, Tucker adds the discourse of advertising to current discussions of 'Goblin Market' in relation to economics and consumerism, and shows how Laura falls for the hype of the goblin men while Lizzie exposes the strategies which underpin their mercantilism. Alongside this runs Tucker's discussion of the orality of the poem, the way in which the reader might interpret by ear as well as eye. Articles on Rossetti also appeared in several other journals. In *SEL*, Scott Rogers's 'Re-reading Sisterhood in Christina Rossetti's "Noble Sisters" and "Sister Maude"' (*SEL* 43[2003] 859–75) revisits Rossetti's interest in the Highgate Penitentiary in relation to her attitude towards communities of women. His convincing argument is that these sister poems are marked by aggression and competitiveness, possibly springing from Rossetti's reconsideration of models of sisterhood in the light of her experiences at Highgate. Mary Arseneau's 'Recovering Female Community: Frances, Maria and Christina Rossetti' (*JPRS* 12[2003] 17–38), takes a more positive view of Rossetti's investment in sisterhood, persuasively arguing for the importance of reconstructing Rossetti's domestic community and examining how she influenced and was influenced by the work of sisters and mother. In the same journal, Debra L. Cumberland, 'Modelling God, Modelling Resistance' (*JPRS* 12[2003] 39–58), argues that understanding Rossetti's modelling might help in appreciating her view of Christian faith as performative, enacted. Diane d'Amico's 'Christina Rossetti's Last Poem: "Sleep, at Last" or "Heaven Overarches"?' (*VN* 103[2003] 11–16) discusses why William Michael Rossetti might have wished to select the peaceful 'Sleeping at Last' as Rossetti's final poem, rather than the overtly Christian 'Heaven Overarches'. Mary Lane-Evans presents a brief reading of 'After Death', suggesting that the speaker is a girl imagining a staged deathbed scene: her reading is marred by the misspelling of Rossetti's name throughout (*Expl* 61[2003] 17–19). John Woolford furthers our awareness of Victorian poetic responses to Romanticism in 'Robert Browning, Christina Rossetti and the Wordsworthian Scene of Writing' (*WC* 34[2003] 30–4). He discusses revisions of Wordsworth by the Brownings and Rossetti, primarily focusing on how the latter undertakes 'a difficult remix of the Romantic poem, reaching back through others who were doing the same' (p. 33).

A new edition of Dante Gabriel Rossetti's *Collected Poetry and Prose*, edited by Jerome McGann, came out from Yale UP in 2003. This edition, based on the 'Reading Text' section of the Rossetti Archive, provides what McGann describes as a 'reader's edition' of Rossetti, presenting his key writings in one volume. The editorial apparatus is brief, presumably because so much more information can be found in the online archive, but does include significant explanatory notes which occasionally offer a theoretical or critical perspective on a poem besides providing relevant historical information. The inclusion of the prose, such as 'Hand and Soul', and of Rossetti's translations from Dante, make this a well-rounded collection which would be very useful for those who would prefer to use a book rather than the database for reading and teaching Rossetti.

Andrew M. Stauffer contributed two articles on D.G. Rossetti this year, both based on research conducted in the Huntington Library. In 'The Lost Pamphlet Version of Dante Gabriel Rossetti's "The Stealthy School of Criticism"' (*VP* 41[2003] 197–227) he describes the original version of Rossetti's rejoinder to Buchanan, assessing differences in tone and style between this and the final version, and reprinting the pamphlet in full. Stauffer's 'Notes and Documents: Five Letters from D.G. Rossetti to John Payne' (*HLQ* 66[2003] 177–89) prints some unpublished letters between Rossetti and the poet and translator. In *JPRS*, the one article on D.G. Rossetti, D.M.R. Bentley's 'Love for Love: Dante Gabriel Rossetti's *Bocca Baciata* and "The Song of the Bower"' (*JPRS* 12[2003] 5–16), considers how both painting and poem rest on Shelley's *Peter Bell the Third* and play on sensual and sexual connotations. Bentley also wrote on 'Mary Philadelphia Merrifield's Edition of Cennino Cennini's *Il Libro dell'Arte* and Dante Gabriel Rossetti's "Hand and Soul"' (*ELN* 40[2003] 49–58), discussing the importance of Merrifield's translation for Rossetti's early 'manifesto' on the artistic life. Clive Wilmer's 'Maundering Medievalism: Dante Gabriel Rossetti and William Morris's Poetry' (*PNR* 29[2003] 69–73) traces the course of Rossetti and Morris's friendship and the links between their paintings and poems, ending with a consideration of how they both allied the medieval to the modern. Missed last year, Jessica Feldman's chapter on Rossetti in her *Victorian Modernism: Pragmatism and the Varieties of Aesthetic Experience* also argues for Rossetti's 'modernism', presenting an intriguing case for the relation between his 'sentimental domesticity' and his paintings and poetry (p. 66). In fitting Rossetti into her broader argument about art and pragmatism (defined in terms of openness, pluralism, geniality and inclusiveness), she disagrees with critics who emphasize darkness, despair or incipient insanity in his works and concentrates on the positive ways in which he might be described as feminized, associated with the domestic and everyday, and with the 'arrangement' (an important word for Feldman) of objects and spaces. While this is an intriguing reading, it doesn't quite work, lacking full theorization and detailed discussion of the relation between domestic and aesthetic spaces, and not entirely integrating this point with the related comments on Rossetti and sentimentalism. Although it primarily concentrates on Rossetti's paintings, Julian Treuherz, Elizabeth Prettejohn, and Edwin Becker's *Dante Gabriel Rossetti* (reviewed earlier in this chapter) may also be of interest to poetry scholars.

Two good articles dealt with the sensationalism—in bodily and literary terms—of Swinburne's poetry. Catherine Maxwell, in 'Swinburne: Style, Sympathy and Sadomasochism' (*JPRS* 12[2003] 86–96), describes how form can contribute to the 'pleasurable violence' (p. 89) of Swinburne's poems, and can aid the spread of dangerous sexual sympathies. This is an intelligent and highly suggestive article, excellent at analysing the power of Swinburne's verse. Equally good is Heather Seagroatt's 'Swinburne Separates the Men from the Girls: Sensationalism in *Poems and Ballads*' (*VLC* 30:i[2002] 41–59). She discusses how the discourse of sensationalism was not restricted to the novel in the 1860s, but fed into poetry as well: *Poems and Ballads* shares a vocabulary of physical pleasures and pains and the ambiguous depiction of aberrant sexuality with sensation fiction. The article is slightly less plausible on how the sensation craze related to Swinburne's anxieties about readership, but does argue well that his poems were not restrictively aimed at a circle of young male readers. Malcolm Hardman links Swinburne and Hopkins in 'Faithful to the Greek? Swinburnian Patterning (Hopkinsian Dapple)' (*YES* 32[2002] 19–35). He suggests that Swinburne and Hopkins shared an interest in the Greek sense of 'the dappled', an important concept in terms of patterning. Hardman traces this through classical writing and then suggests that, while Hopkins reinvents the concept for Christianity, Swinburne finds it unfeasible. This is a difficult but rewarding essay, again paying valuable attention to the detail of language, structure and rhythm in Swinburne's work. Sawyer's chapter on Swinburne and Shakespeare in his *Victorian Appropriations of Shakespeare* presents a radical Swinburne, deploying Shakespeare to promote his own sexual and political agendas. Sawyer's close attention to Swinburne's *A Study of Shakespeare* [1880] and the critical response to it sheds new light on his stance as a critic. Terry L. Meyers, 'A Note on Swinburne and Whitman' (*WWR* 21[2003] 38–9), adds a note to her earlier discussion of Swinburne and Whitman, using new evidence from Arthur Munby's diaries to suggest that Swinburne was already distancing himself from Whitman by the late 1860s. A brief article on Swinburne from *VP*, Francis O'Gorman's '"Death lies dead": The Allusive Texture of Swinburne's "The Forsaken Garden"' (*VP* 41[2003] 348–52), concludes this year's work on Swinburne. O'Gorman argues that the unrecognized theological context and biblical allusions of this poem indicate Swinburne's incorporation of the sacred in the secular.

Tennyson was the subject of one monograph, J. Timothy Lovelace's *The Artistry and Tradition of Tennyson's Battle Poetry*. Lovelace's book, like Jill Muller's (discussed above), is published in the 'outstanding dissertations' series, and its status as a dissertation does seem to show in its repeated reiteration of the central point, leaving little room for ambiguity, and in particular in the time spent on refuting other critical ideas and summarizing their comments (or lack of them) on Tennyson's poems of war and battle. Lovelace argues that readers have found these poems uncomfortable because they have failed to be alert to the heroic background—taken from classical literature and from mythological epics, such as the Irish *Tain*—of Tennyson's poems, which he reads here in terms of an emphasis on the hero and his battle fury, the role of the bard, and the concept of chivalry. He defends Tennyson's less popular poems, such as the 1852 calls to arms, and provides a rare discussion of his early war poetry and his poems on legendary and historical battles. The Tennyson in this book certainly emerges as more obsessed with war and battle than most studies would suggest, as Lovelace attempts to reinsert these poems into the Tennyson canon. His comments on the Edison recordings of Tennyson's readings also stress that he deliberately chose to read poems associated with war. Lovelace is particularly interesting on Tennyson's translations from the *Iliad* and the Anglo-Saxon *Battle of Brunanburh*, reading these poems carefully and with attention to detail to show how they support heroic themes. Closing chapters on *Maud* and *Idylls of the King* then apply the concepts laid out earlier to two of Tennyson's best-known poems. Lovelace compares the speaker of *Maud*, again, to a wrathful hero, but suggests that 'The main region of [Tennyson's] song is not an external but an internal battlefield, where the hero's great exploit is the recovery of his sanity' (p. 119). This reading is illuminating, but of necessity it focuses on a narrow aspect of the poem: it is a pity that there is little discussion of the Crimean War itself, and virtually no commentary on other war poetry of this period. This lack of contemporary context leaves the reader wondering how anomalous or otherwise Tennyson's attitudes to war poetry might have been, and whether he could have been as much influenced by his contemporaries as by his reading of classical epic. Patmore's warmongering, for instance, Sydney Dobell's sonnets on the Crimea, the foundation of the National Rifle Corps (which included many poets and artists)—this kind of historical and literary context seems oddly absent from the book as a whole. Finally, Lovelace analyses the *Idylls* and their attempt to control and harness destructive passions in the service of chivalry. Again, while he considers much criticism, it would have been interesting to see how recent discussions of this epic in relation to empire could have fed into this work. In short, as a book on Tennyson's engagement with classical ideals of war and heroism, and with a tradition of battle poetry, *The Artistry and Tradition of Tennyson's Battle Poetry* is successful, but it lacks the wider scope which might have made it relevant in relation to broader Victorian cultural and literary attitudes.

Another significant publication on Tennyson was volume 3 of the *Lives of Victorian Literary Figures* (p. 70) series from Pickering & Chatto. This collection, edited by Matthew Bevis, is a significant addition to the contemporary reviews collected in the Critical Heritage series, and is a valuable source of biographical and critical information on Tennyson. Bevis's introduction describes Tennyson's celebrity status in his age, and usefully surveys varying biographical accounts from both the nineteenth and twentieth centuries. He also notes the entertainment value of Tennyson's reported statements and conversations, whether these are deliberately shocking, surprising or amusing. The book is arranged in loosely chronological order and includes not only well-known accounts of Tennyson, from the *Memoir* or the letters of famous contemporaries, but also more obscure sources and—helpfully—a selection of images of the poet.

The fine introductions to each selection set them in context and give frameworks for interpretation. This is an enjoyable and extremely useful collection, which should become indispensable not only to critics and students but to Tennyson fans.

Missed last year, Matthew Curr's *The Consolation of Otherness: The Male Love Elegy in Milton, Gray and Tennyson* [2002], although not wholly original, and at times more celebratory than critical in its presentation of a queer reading of Tennyson, is interesting in that it relates *In Memoriam* to a tradition of elegies for male love-objects exemplified by Gray and Milton. In *Tennyson Research Bulletin* Robert Douglas-Fairhurst published an article on 'Young Tennyson and "Old Fitz"' (*TRB* 8[2003] 69–84), largely drawn from his *Victorian Afterlives* (Oxford [2002], reviewed last year). This wide-ranging and allusive piece discusses Tennyson and FitzGerald's shared attraction to the past, their interest in memory, and suggests that the cooling off in their friendship might have been the result of FitzGerald's preference for remembering and missing friends rather than seeing them. The next piece in this volume, 'Tennyson and the Figure of Christ' (*TRB* 8[2003] 85–100), by Valerie Purton, reads Hallam as Christ in *In Memoriam*, and Prince Albert's representation as a Christ-like figure in Tennyson's poems and contemporary culture, through Lacanian concepts of the ideal Other and the shift from the Symbolic to the Imaginary. John Crompton's succeeding piece, 'Haunts of Coot and Tern: Tennyson's Birds' (*TRB* 8[2003] 101–10), in sharp contrast to this theoretical study, is a light and entertaining account of birds and birdsong in Tennyson's poems, mainly concentrating on the accuracy or otherwise of his descriptions. Terry Meyers, in 'Several Letters by Tennyson and his Family' (*TRB* 8[2003] 111–17), then prints several unpublished letters, mainly short notes about appointments and so forth, and discusses one longer previously published letter about the attempt to nominate Tennyson as Rector of Glasgow. Matthew Bevis gives a fine description of the new manuscript of 'Roses on the Terrace' purchased by the Tennyson Research Centre, assessing how the changes Tennyson made slightly alter the focus of the poem (*TRB* 8[2003] 118–20). Finally, Robin Brumby, in 'Touching (upon) the Tsarina's Thigh: Versions of Events on the "Pembroke Castle"' (*TRB* 8[2003] 121–6), discusses the varying accounts of Tennyson's cruise on the *Pembroke Castle* and encounter with a Russian royal in 1883, and Cammy Thomas considers 'The Charge of the Heavy Brigade' in relation to Tennyson's wistful interest in soldiering in 'Old Poet, Old Soldier' (*TRB* 8[2003] 127–32).

Roger Ebbatson's *Tennyson's English Idylls: History, Narrative, Art*, one of the Tennyson Society's Occasional Papers, examines the radical conservatism of the *English Idylls*, contributing a nuanced discussion to the relatively scant literature on these poems. His account draws on recent work on gender and class, and on Derrida's *Specters of Marx*, to suggest that these poems might be more subversive than their speakers know, as well as more strange and ambiguous than has been recognized. Tennyson's relation to Australian poetry, partly explored last year in a special issue of *VP*, recurs in Louise d'Arcens, 'Antipodean Idylls: An Early Australian Translation of Tennyson's Medievalism' (in Ingham and Warren, eds., *Postcolonial Moves: Medieval Through Modern*, pp. 237–56). D'Arcens considers how John Woolley, first professor of medieval language and literature in Sydney, adapted the *Idylls* to his discussions of colonial identity, using them to convey ideals of chivalry and civic action in a colonial setting. *Symbiosis* contained another interesting article on Tennyson's reception abroad, this time in the USA, Richard Gravil's 'Emily Dickinson (and Walt Whitman): The Escape from "Locksley Hall"' (*Symbiosis* 7[2003] 56–75). Gravil persuasively argues that Tennyson's influence on Dickinson, as on Whitman, has been neglected, and provides excellent readings of the half-heard linguistic and metrical echoes of Tennyson in Dickinson's verse. Finally, besides the essays on Tennyson in *VP*'s special issue on poetry and science, Jane Wright, in 'A Reflection on Fiction and Art in "The Lady of Shalott"' (*VP* 41[2003] 287–90), briefly attends to inwardness and outwardness in 'The Lady of Shalott' through a subtle discussion of the line 'Out flew the web and floated wide'.

To conclude with Wilde, *Wildean* has two articles on his poetry. Peter Vernier's '"Poem-Sites" at Magdalen: Oscar Wilde' (*Wildean* 23[2003] 38–43) is an account of the particular views, rooms, and so on which may have inspired poems Wilde wrote at college, and Tully Atkinson's '*The Sphinx*: Wilde's Decadent Poem and its Place in Fin-de-Siècle Letters' (*Wildean* 23[2003] 44–54), while mainly a summary of critical views on this poem, argues that it deserves to be seen as a key decadent text.

4. Drama and Theatre

Several publications during 2003 demonstrated overlaps and continuities between drama and theatre in the Romantic and Victorian periods. Roy, ed., *Theatre in Europe: A Documentary History 1789–1860*, devotes only limited space to the British theatre of the Victorian era, but (like Edward Ziter's *The Orient on the Victorian Stage* reviewed below) reminds us just how essential it is to view theatre in the nineteenth century as a continuum. The British section, compiled by Victor Emeljanow, carries separate entries on theatre, the law and management practices; playhouses; repertoires, taste and audiences; actors and acting; and stage presentation. Emeljanow suggests that during the period examined theatre audiences and speculators contended with old and new orthodoxies, reconfiguring both the nature of theatre-going and the financial management of theatres. The period also saw the rise of melodrama and the converging influence of Romanticism and realism on theatrical representation. The first section of the book usefully provides extracts from the Theatre Regulation Act 1843 and from documents in the Public Record Office to demonstrate the state of British theatre in the wake of the report of the Select Committee on Dramatic Literature in 1832 and the subsequent enactment of legislation. Some of the extracts relating to melodrama, playwriting and audiences take us into the Victorian period—Samuel Phelps's management at Sadler's Wells theatre is particularly well represented—but there is little reference to playhouses or acting and staging practices after Queen Victoria's accession. Overall, this collection of documents is an interesting anthology of excerpts from books, manuscripts and periodicals, but does not really fuse into a coherent documentary history of the theatre in the period. Nevertheless, Emeljanow's selection provides a very readable cross-section of documents, and the inclusion of less accessible and less familiar material from the Public Record Office and periodicals is to be welcomed.

Ziter's *The Orient on the Victorian Stage* considers how changing interpretations of space in nineteenth-century Europe and developments in academic disciplines such as geography and anthropology impacted on the theatre's representation of the Orient. He argues that Europe's picture of the East and the constitution of the modern colonial imagination were enhanced by Orientalist staging in the nineteenth century. Drawing particularly, but not exclusively, on the work of Edward Said and Michel Foucault on space, Ziter grounds his work in a wealth of contemporary discourses. A proportion of his book looks at the development of the geographic imagination as demonstrated in panoramas and exhibition halls, as well as in theatres, in the early part of the century, and at the environments built during and after the Great Exhibition of 1851 for the purpose of ethnographic display. While Ziter's discussion of theatrical representation looks initially at adaptations of Byron's Oriental romances and Kean's exotic performances, his final two chapters examine the performance of authenticity in Fitzball's *Azael the Prodigal* (Drury Lane [1851]) and Byron's *Sardanapalus* (Princess's [1853]) and the late Victorian theatre's development of 'a new geographic mode of representation by combining exotic and colonial imagery with new scenic methods for representing space' (p. 18), especially through the 1885 melodramas *Khartoum* (William Muskerry and John Jourdain, at Sanger's) and *Human Nature* (Henry Pettit and August Harris, at Drury Lane). The staging of the biblical environments of Judea, Memphis and Nineveh in *Azael* and *Sardanapalus* is contextualized in relationship to the developing museum culture of the time, while the contemporary political implications of representing such spectacular and often decadent civilizations are also emphasized. Towards the end of the century, however, the celebration of imperialism and of imperial structures was more prominent in productions such as *Khartoum* and *Human Nature*, which 'repeatedly pitted European morality and armaments against the savagery and primitive technology of colonized peoples' (p. 166). Ziter argues that new staging practices reinforced audience confidence in the accuracy of the geographies on display, and develops an interesting discussion of the staging of colonial wars in non-realistic forms such as the Drury Lane pantomimes. Overall, his book is a fascinating addition to studies of Orientalism in the theatre, particularly through his emphasis on the changing meanings and interpretations of theatrical space, and his contextual references to developments in ethnography and geography and the development of the museum in the nineteenth century.

The sensations associated with Orientalist pantomime and melodrama are also touched on in Michael Diamond's *Victorian Sensation or the Spectacular, the Shocking and the Scandalous in Nineteenth Century Britain*. This book provides a populist account of sensation melodrama and adds nothing new to our knowledge or understanding of the sensational plays of Dion Boucicault or the Drury Lane melodramas of Augustus Harris. A subsequent chapter on 'Stars of Entertainment', which includes reference to Ada Isaacs Menken in *Mazeppa*, E.A. Sothern as Dundreary in *Our American Cousin*, Henry Irving and Eleanora Duse, revisits familiar territory.

The career of Samuel Beazley, theatrical architect and playwright, documented in Gorel Garlick, *To Serve the Purpose of the Drama: The Theatre Designs and Plays of Samuel Beazley 1786–1851,* falls mainly outside the Victorian period, but Beazley's association into the Victorian period with such theatres as the Adelphi and Drury Lane, as architect and dramatist, are briefly mentioned. Also largely outside the scope of this section but of enormous significance for our future interpretation of Victorian theatre is Jacky Bratton's *New Readings in Theatre History*, which interrogates the way in which British theatre history came to be written in the first place. Divided into two sections, the book provides an overview of current issues in theatre historiography and a series of carefully argued case studies. Closely analysing the gestation of theatre reform through the Select Committee on Dramatic Literature in 1832 and the elitist agenda of many of the reformers, Bratton's study provides an essential introduction to the complex cultural situation out of which Victorian theatre emerged.

This elitism was particularly manifest in the Victorian appropriation of Shakespeare, as Julia Swindells demonstrates in her essay in the first volume of Marshall and Poole, eds., *Victorian Shakespeare*, which concentrates on *Theatre, Drama and Performance* and ranges across such topics as genre and gender, national identity and authenticity, and the political and the pictorial. The political background for the Victorian perception of Shakespeare in the theatre is set by Kate Newey and Swindells in essays that look at the pre-Victorian period. Newey shows how the talismanic invocation of Shakespeare by minor theatres in south London provides the possibility of an alternative interpretation of Shakespeare's cultural significance, while Swindells demonstrates the cultural iconicity of Shakespeare as used by the Select Committee on Dramatic Literature and those it interviewed in 1832, anticipating the appropriation of Shakespeare as a bastion of Victorian high culture. According to Richard Schoch there was a backlash against this appropriation in the many burlesque representations of Shakespeare throughout the Victorian period. Concentrating on burlesques of *The Colleen Bawn* and *Hamlet*, Schoch shows how the burlesquing of Shakespeare confounded genre stereotyping, while relying for its impact on an intense and well-informed knowledge of both Shakespeare and contemporary theatre practice among burlesque audiences. Inga-Stina Ewbank reveals confusion over the fluidity of genre in Shakespeare in some European countries, while revealing that the comedies, although considered more British, were as popular in Europe as the tragedies. European dramatists such as Ibsen, however, were more easily assimilated into English theatre when, as Sara Jan shows us, his historical drama *The Pretenders* was presented with the lavish staging synonymous with spectacular Shakespeare.

Many of the essays emphasize the significance of Victorian Shakespeare in the assertion of national identity. Not only is the appropriation of Shakespeare in support of Englishness, Britishness and empire evoked, but also the distinctive perceptions of Shakespeare current in Europe and North America. Lisa Merrill, Jane Moody and Inga-Stina Ewbank take us provocatively through the ways in which American and European performances of Shakespeare demonstrated different aspects of national identity and also released Shakespeare from some of the moribund conventions imposed on him by the Victorian age. Ewbank's account of Shakespearian performance in Denmark, Germany and France indicates just how nationally defined were nineteenth-century productions of Shakespeare, while Moody's analysis of the xenophobic English response to European performers of Shakespeare helps us understand how limiting contemporary English notions of psychology and decorum were when applied to the performance of Shakespeare. Merrill's equation of North American Shakespeare with an emergent national identity is superbly contextualized and makes a very convincing case for the impact of Forrest and Booth not only on Shakespearian interpretation but also on North American self-perception. Of particular interest in Merrill's essay is the combination of masculinity and homoeroticism she finds present in North American Shakespeare and the changing perceptions of appropriate gendered behaviour which she finds embedded in the performances of Forrest and Booth. Gender representation as a dominant issue also emerges in Richard Foulkes's essay, which argues that the popularity of *As You Like It* on the English stage from 1871 to 1911 depended on two contradictory factors: that Rosalind as a role enabled a full display of the female figure in the Ganymede scenes, while in her male assumption she also reflected the desire of women to take greater control over their lives in the era of the New Woman and the suffragette movement.

The pictorial representation of Shakespeare receives appropriate attention. Peter Holland's account of illustrated Victorian texts of Shakespeare is less about the representation of Shakespeare in the theatre and more about the performative potential implicit in illustrations of Shakespeare's plays. John Stokes's discussion of Wilde and Shakespeare draws heavily on the pictorial impact of Shakespeare, in portraiture as well as performance, particularly through his discussion of Ellen Terry's Lady Macbeth costume, depicted by John Singer Sargent in his famous portrait of Terry in the Irving *Macbeth*. Wilde's witty comment about Lady Macbeth 'shopping in Byzantium' is the starting point for an essay that acknowledges the homoerotic nature of Wilde's engagement with Shakespeare, while also charting a change in emphasis from Shakespeare as theatre artist and aesthete to a perception him as an author whose intentions could only be realized objectively through theatrical performance. Additionally, Jean Chiotha discusses the competing philosophies informing the spectacular Shakespearian productions of Beerbohm Tree (whose production values anticipate those of filmed Shakespeare) and the minimalist attempts at authentic Elizabethan staging by William Poel.

The second volume, *Literature and Culture*, has less to say about drama and theatre, but several essays are worth mentioning. Diana E. Henderson traces the influence of *Othello* on the plot of Sir Walter Scott's *Kenilworth*, as well as the novel's anachronistic depiction of Shakespeare. While the novel situates Shakespeare on the borders between art and business, aesthetics and politics, stage adaptations simplified both the novel's themes and its *Othello*-like plot. Scott erases blackness from the Othello story, a tendency also prevalent on the stage, as witnessed in Kean's representation of an Arabic and Europeanized rather than black Moor. (Ira Aldridge, the black American actor, was less acceptable as Othello to English audiences at this time precisely on account of his colour.) John Glavin traces this development from black to tawny to blanched, suggesting that in general nineteenth-century English actors were unable to cross the 'colour line'. He argues that Trevelyan, the protagonist of Trollope's *He Knew He Was Right*, is 'a blanched Othello', and that Trollope's relocation of the Othello story to nineteenth-century colonial enterprise makes him 'the play's most capable reader' in the Victorian period (p. 44). Juliet Johns uses an essay on *Hamlet* to demonstrate how Dickens refused identification with the artist as disengaged thinker. Although *Hamlet* is the play most frequently referred to by Dickens, his 'novelistic allusions to *Hamlet* invariably violate the illusion that Hamlet is Everyman' (p. 58). Thus *Hamlet* is used as a negative point of reference in *Great Expectations*. For Dickens 'excessive introspection is no substitute for socially constructive action' (p. 58).

Shakespeare was often the focus of Victorian burlesque, as Richard Schoch has revealed not only in his essay in *Victorian Shakespeare*, but also in his monograph *Not Shakespeare* [2002]. He broadens his investigation of burlesque in his new anthology, *Victorian Theatrical Burlesques*, which comprises burlesques of four prominent nineteenth-century melodramas and of Wilde's society drama *Lady Windermere's Fan*. The melodrama burlesques all date from the 1860s: three, *Miss Eily O'Connor* [1861], *1863; or the Sensations of the Past Season* [1863], and *The Corsican 'Brothers'; or, the Troublesome Twins* [1869], are by H.J. Byron, one of the most prolific and outstanding burlesque authors of the mid-Victorian period. The first two are highly topical parodies of *The Colleen Bawn* and *Lady Audley's Secret*, while the third was prompted by Irving's revival of Boucicault's famous melodrama. F.C. Burnand's *The Very Latest Edition of Black-Eyed Susan* [1869] attests to the fact that Jerrold's original nautical melodrama still had currency of sorts forty years after its first performance. Charles H.E. Brookfield and James Glover's parody of Wilde, *The Poet and the Puppets* [1892], represents a later period and a different sort of drama. In his excellent introduction, Schoch teaches us to read burlesques as dialogues with the material they parody, and as documents rather than texts for revival. This does not mean that he is insensitive to their potential in performance, but that his emphasis is on their historical and cultural significance. Schoch suggests that we should look beyond parody to see burlesques as a critique of dramatic form—seeing them not as adaptations, but rather as representations or interpretations of their sources. He discusses both the topicality and punning of Victorian burlesque and the extent to which these qualities were enhanced by the highly energized and disciplined prowess of its performers. His comments on burlesque audiences—who might have constituted them and the 'knowingness' required to comprehend burlesque—are also enlightening. He divides spectators into the 'competent' and 'incompetent', and implies that a high degree of competency would be required to unravel the multiple points of reference contained in Victorian burlesque. He suggests it appealed particularly to young professional men around town, in particular the 'swells' and the 'fast' young men who were often also parodied in the burlesques. Burlesque was often profligate, transgressive and questioning of the values associated with legitimate culture. Its use of innuendo and cross-dressing further enhanced its potential to subvert. And, while the texts of some burlesques were censored by the Lord Chamberlain's Office, the offending references were often restored in performance.

Each burlesque in the anthology is preceded by a short and informative introduction, often highlighting the particular objects parodied, especially stage convention and performance. There are also copious footnotes to explain contemporary allusions and some of the more obscure punning, as well as a list of the most representative Victorian burlesques. Despite the sharpness of their satire, the burlesques also impress with their general benignity of tone. There is affection, as well as scorn, for the excesses of melodrama: indeed, if burlesque eventually helped sound the death knell of popular melodrama through relentless ridicule, it also kept it alive through this very obsession. While these plays are invariably ephemeral, they also tell us much about contemporary attitudes and opinions, as well as implying the existence of a partially submerged alternative culture. Burlesque, as Schoch so engagingly reveals, survives as a form of critical discourse, sometimes radical, sometimes conservative, but always with the power to destabilize Victorian culture.

In a lean year for articles on Victorian drama and theatre, even in specialist periodicals, only two are worthy of specific note. Victor Emejanow's 'The Events of June 1848: The "Monte Cristo" Riots and the Politics of Protest' (*NTQ* 9:i[2003] 23–32) considers the notorious Monte Cristo riots, when protests at French performances of Dumas' *The Count of Monte Cristo* in London were orchestrated by English actors for very specifically protectionist reasons at a time when the dissent generated by the Chartist movement was creating civil unrest. Emeljanow suggests that the dissatisfaction expressed by protesters in the Drury Lane auditorium reflected not just the immediate concerns of the acting profession, but also the political and social uncertainties in the community at large. Heidi J. Holder 's 'Outcast London on the Victorian and Edwardian stage' (*THStud* 13[2003] 49–64) comprehensively surveys the depiction of London in both West End and East End melodrama, as well as in the work of later, more socially orientated dramatists. The presentation of London life on stage reflected prevailing contemporary 'urban' theories. This was true of Victorian melodrama, which presented London in spectacular but hyper-realistic settings, offset by the formulaic nature and fantasy happy endings of the genre. The unsettled class status of many of the protagonists reflected contemporary uncertainties over the gulf between the rich and poor, while many of the plays of 'outcast London' mingled dispossession and spectacle by grounding their characters in multiple locations across London. The metropolis was ambiguously depicted as threatening, as a marker of boundaries and as an image of boundless possibilities. Holder refers to the 'unmooring of identity' (p. 56) in many of these plays, and to the anxiety manifest in critical responses to East End melodramas which 'attempted to appropriate the power to define' (p. 58), taken for granted as right in the West End theatre. Holder suggests that, while these plays tended to resolve the problems faced by their protagonists, the dramas of new socially committed writers such as Shaw, Galsworthy, Granville-Barker and Cicely Hamilton were less benign. Hamilton's *Diana of Dobson's* [1908], for instance, challenged and unsettled its audiences by showing there was no easy formula for dealing with life in London or easy alleviation for the misery of the poor.

5. Periodicals and Publishing

Over the past decade, book and library historians have begun releasing works that have benefited from dedicated research into the business archives and papers of significant nineteenth-century British publishing and printing companies. Several works published this year highlight what can be done with material currently to hand.

Vizetelly & Compan(ies): *A Complex Tale of Victorian Printing and Publishing*, published by the University of Toronto Press to accompany an exhibition held in Toronto in 2003, focuses on the history of the London publishing firms developed by James and Henry Vizetelly between 1838 and 1890. Inevitably, as the introduction notes, the business of reconstructing the internal history of small and specialized firms such as those run by the Vizetellys depends greatly on success in excavating primary evidence from archival and printed sources. With the Vizetellys, the matter is made difficult by the fact that little exists in the way of publishing correspondence or business material. The contributors to this volume have therefore sought to shed light on the brothers' activities by means of external published sources such as trade journals, catalogues and advertisements, newspaper clippings, legal records and the unreliable memoirs of Henry Vizetelly [1820–94], written late in his life. The results point out both what can be achieved through diligent analysis of printed sources, and what we miss when valuable business records are dispersed or lost to view. In covering the history of the Vizetelly firms, this short volume does as well as can be expected in face of a dearth of primary evidence. The most successful pieces, such as Richard Landon's short study of Henry Vizetelly's prosecution for obscenity in 1888 and 1889 (for publishing in translation the works of Émile Zola), provide useful historical and cultural contexts for weighing up the place of the firm in its niche markets. Other pieces cover the firm's activities through providing catalogues of publication lists and dates, noting the brothers' changing addresses of operation and summarizing the few facts known about their business history. As the authors themselves admit, more remains to be done on related topics, such as exploring the firm's lists in the context of the British reception (often hostile) of French 'naturalist' fiction in the late nineteenth century, or examining the fortunes of small, specialist firms in the wake of changing *fin-de-siècle* literary and business interests and practices.

Alexis Weedon approaches the business of Victorian publishing from a quantitatively richer perspective in *Victorian Publishing: The Economics of Book Production for a Mass Market, 1836–1916*. The work benefits from Weedon's many years of research into the business of book production, and is a bonanza find for those needing well-defined and researched details of trends in British book production for the eighty years covered in this survey. From statistical charts on book production costs to appendices covering the value of book exports to the US and British colonies, and from charts comparing the increase in book manufacturing with the growth of English and Welsh literary rates to tables ranking outputs of British publishing centres, the work overflows with facts and figures. Such material is much needed, and we should be grateful that individuals like Weedon undertake such endeavours on behalf of the less statistically inclined amongst us. The work is somewhat inconsistent, though, veering from sections that read like 'how to' guides for undergraduate or postgraduate students seeking entry into quantitative archival research, to densely packed sections exploring general trends and costs in Victorian book production, to sophisticated, informed sections that demonstrate how statistics can be used to track fluctuations in business activity, confirming that while most areas of British industry may have suffered during what economists have described as a period of extended depression between 1873 and 1896, the British book trade actually grew steadily in size and importance (buttressed mainly by colonial exports). The details are impressive, the scholarship obvious. Having said that, what is clear is that the premise of this work is one that deliberately seeks to distance itself from the type of work we have begun to see emerging in book history circles. Weedon claims her perspective is not that of the literary, social or book historian, but rather of 'the student of publishing economics' (p. 3). It is an important distinction, since in saying this Weedon seeks to deflect what will inevitably be a criticism of this work: that its statistical and sociometric basis can overwhelm the reader more used to the contextual, social history approach now increasingly favoured in studies on print culture activity.

Other perspectives being applied in the area of book history are the concerns of two important survey pieces which Victorianists are encouraged to find: Joan Shelley Rubin's 'What is the History of the History of the Books?' (*JAmH* 90[2003] 555–75) and Harold Love's 'Early Modern Print Culture: Assessing the Models' (*Parergon* 30[2003] 45–64). Their general reviews of contemporary approaches to studying the business of publishing and print culture are inflected within US and eighteenth-century studies perspectives respectively, but both also reach into the nineteenth century for relevant examples, and offer important insights worthy of attention.

How an author's active participation in the production process could complicate publishing matters is the theme of Clare Imholtz's 'The History of Lewis Carroll's *The Game of Logic*' (*PBSA* 97[2003] 183–214). After much travail, in early 1887 Macmillan published C.L. Dodgson's (Lewis Carroll's) combination of game and book, *The Game of Logic*. The production process was dogged by Dodgson's frequent corrections, and his insistence on having the printing undertaken by a local printer who was unequal to the task. Imholtz reconstructs the history of the book's publication from extant correspondence, diary entries and corrected proof copies, concluding that Dodgson's exacting intrusions were partially responsible for the difficulties Macmillan had in bringing the printed text to fruition.

James Raven tackles the complex issue of late eighteenth- and early nineteenth-century anonymous and pseudonymous fiction in 'The Anonymous Novel in Britain and Ireland, 1750–1830' (in Griffin, ed., *Faces of Anonymity*, pp. 141–67). Raven analyses statistical information gathered over several years of individual and collaborative research, presenting the reader with some startling conclusions about the proliferation of anonymous publications during the early nineteenth century. Among his many revisionist conclusions is that, after 1800, a surge in admitted rather than anonymous female authorship can be attributed to the promotion of a certain model of femininity within an expanding literary marketplace, thus encouraging entry for women authors in a manner not considered previously, and at the expense of male authors, who were often compelled to adopt anonymity to avoid classification within such literary spheres.

Anonymity is also a feature of Susan Eilenberg's study of Mary Shelley's production of *Frankenstein*, 'Nothing's Namelessness: Mary Shelley's *Frankenstein*' (in Griffin, ed., pp. 167–92). Eilenberg studies the paratextual structure of the novel, as well as Mary Shelley's assumption of anonymity and her eventual claiming of authorship, and locates this within a reading of the novel's main character (Frankenstein), and his battle for recognition and against anonymity. The argument is at times overstretched, but the concept is an interesting one.

David McKitterick's most recent book, *Print, Manuscript and the Search for Order, 1450–1830*, deals mainly with rebutting the common presumption that the arrival and development of print production in the late fifteenth century quickly overthrew cultural communication patterns associated with manuscript culture. McKitterick argues against this view, suggesting that a vigorous manuscript culture existed even into the nineteenth century, with all its attendant qualities of inconstancy, fluidity and diversity.

The link between orality and text is also explored in Stephen Orgel's *Imagining Shakespeare: A History of Texts and Visions*, or to be more accurate, the tension between text and performance. Orgel links performance to visual and textual representations of Shakespeare's plays from the seventeenth century to the present. Of interest to Victorian scholars is his tracing of the effect of stage performances, such as those enacted in the nineteenth century by the lauded actors Charles Kean, Henry Irving and Ellen Terry, on subsequent illustrations in reprints of Shakespeare's work. In this case, dramatic poses culled from contemporary performance practice were often reproduced to accompany and illustrate key moments in such texts, creating visual keys as to how Victorians conceived 'correct' and 'authentic' stage interpretations of Shakespeare. Orgel argues persuasively that such linked analysis of text and illustration helps provide insight into how popular Shakespearian texts were regarded and received historically.

During the Victorian period the railway bookstall retailer W.H. Smith emerged, along with Charles Mudie and his commercial library, as one of the main distributors and retailers of texts in Britain. The 'Subscription Library of W.H. Smith' (begun in 1860), became a main source of texts for commuters, and both Mudie and W.H. Smith to a great extent shaped the reading habits of a large portion of Britain's literate classes in the second half of the nineteenth century. In '"A larger outlay than any return": The Library of W.H. Smith & Son, 1860–73' (*PubH* 54[2003] 67–93), Stephen Colclough uses unpublished W.H. Smith records to demonstrate how the firm's directors originally envisaged the subscription library as a marketing tool to promote their railway bookstall concessions. The result was that, contrary to popular belief, the library incurred significant losses in its first five years of existence (between 1860 and 1865), and was only able to recoup its initial investment through periodic sales of redundant stock at reduced prices, with a profound effect on the manner in which other general second-hand book trade sectors distributed and retailed texts.

John Plunkett looks at another Victorian phenomenon in 'A Media Monarchy? Queen Victoria and the Radical Press, 1837–1901' (*MedHis* 9[2003] 3–18). The reign of Victoria coincided with a dramatic rise in print culture activity in Britain, from the development of a daily press to the establishment of weekly, monthly, quarterly and illustrated periodicals. Plunkett analyses media reports and the mass reproduction of Victoria's image through comic cartoons, satirical drawings and general illustrations to demonstrate how her cultural positioning changed over the decades of her reign. The piece comes from his book-length study on the subject, *Queen Victoria: First Media Monarch*, which draws on a wide range of media and periodical sources to look at five interlocking themes: 'civic publicness'; visual portrayals of the monarch; photographic reproductions of the royal family; contemporary political and social media constructions of the queen's image; and media reporting of royal activities. The result is a fascinating study of the relationship between royalty and nineteenth-century media culture.

While Queen Victoria's image was one mainly constructed by media sources, there are other Victorian examples of individuals consciously forging public assessments of value through invisible networks of contacts and well-placed media sources. One such vehicle was the controlled publication of collected editions of authors' works. One of the key examples of a limited, collected edition whose issue helped enshrine the reputation of its subject was the Edinburgh edition of *The Works of Robert Louis Stevenson*, published in late 1894, and covered in Andrew Nash's carefully etched piece '"The dead should be protected from their own carelessness": The Collected Editions of Robert Louis Stevenson' (in Nash, ed., *The Culture of Collected Editions*, pp. 111–27). Nash examines the production of the edition, and in particular the manner in which its authority was undermined by family wrangling and control over subsequent publishing ventures exploiting Stevenson's work after his death in 1894. The success of these editions inspired emulation by other authors such as Henry James and Thomas Hardy, a subject aptly and succinctly covered in the same essay collection by Simon Gatrell in 'The Collected Editions of Hardy, James, and Meredith, with Some Concluding Thoughts on the Desirability of a Taxonomy of the Book' (in Nash, ed., pp. 80–94). A third piece in the collection of relevance to Victorian interests is J.C.C. Mays's survey of the nineteenth-century antecedents to the Bollingen Collected Coleridge series begun in 1962, 'The Life in Death of Editorial Exchange: The Bollingen Collected Coleridge' (in Nash, ed., pp. 183–200).

George Smythe—charismatic Conservative MP for Canterbury in 1841, model for several of Disraeli's political novels, and implicated in a major social scandal of the late 1840s that ruined his political career and reputation—is another example of a successful mediator of image and public assessments of political matters. His association with the *Morning Chronicle* as one of its two principal leader writers between 1848 and 1852 is the subject of Mary S. Millar's in-depth and useful piece '"Very like assassination": George Smythe's Journalism in the *Morning Chronicle*' (*VPR* 36[2003] 242–60). His enthusiasm for his journalistic work belied his position in the upper echelons of society, with his initial foreign correspondence from the French capital during the 1848 revolution giving way to strongly worded leader work verging on character assassinations of some of the leading politicians of the day. Millar shows how Smythe's journalism was employed as useful propaganda in influencing political manoeuvrings within the Conservative Party.

The Morning Chronicle equally features in Tom Mole's 'Byron's "Ode to the Framers of the Frame Bill": The Embarrassment of Industrial Culture' (*KSJ* 52[2003] 111–29). Most commentators tend to ignore Byron's political ode, issued in the wake of a government bill making it a capital offence to destroy weaving frames (a response to contemporary civil disturbance amongst Midland weavers), and published eight days before his reputation-making *Childe Harold's Pilgrimage*. Mole makes the case for reassessing its value in light of contemporary political concerns. Also of interest is Mole's comparison of its anti-industrial message with the production process by which the poem became public—the development, for example of the Koenig steam press, adopted around the time of Byron's ascendancy to iconic status, revolutionized the manner in which literary producers like Byron were to reach the marketplace. Revolutions in the industrialized production of texts empowered commentators such as Byron to turn their material rapidly from manuscript to print. Byron would be urged to 'write by steam', as a friend noted (p. 128), and in doing so become a beneficiary of the industrial revolution he criticizes in the ode.

Politics is also the theme of David Morphet's 'Political Comment in the *Quarterly Review* after Croker: Gladstone, Salisbury, and Jennings' (*VPR* 36[2003] 109–34). For this piece, Morphet draws on the more than fifty articles contributed between 1856 and 1892 by three significant political figures (William Ewart Gladstone, Lord Robert Cecil, and Louis Jennings), to shed light on the *Quarterly Review*'s political stance before and after the great Reform Bill of 1867. Morphet offers a useful analysis of several key articles by these three essayist/politicians, suggesting that they reflect interesting transitional points in their political thinking. In Gladstone's case, we see a shift from a Tory to a Liberal stance; Louis Jennings consciously positioned himself as a champion of the Tory cause, while Lord Cecil (later Lord Salisbury) set out a robust, Tory intellectual agenda that was to prove a vital aspect of his political thinking.

Politics, literature and journalism mix in John Drew's *Dickens the Journalist* (also briefly reviewed in Section 2 above). Drew draws on research conducted both as a postdoctoral fellow and as an editor on the Dent Uniform Edition of Dickens's journalism for this in-depth study of Dickens's forty-year career in the media as contributor, editor and 'conductor'. Drew argues that Dickens's press and periodical work was unique and remarkable, part of his all-consuming passion and energy for work, a 'remarkable combination of writing and business skills, special interests, and journalistic innovations' (p. 178). His mastery of shorthand, essential for processing material during his period as parliamentary and elections reporter for the *Mirror of Parliament*, the *Morning Chronicle* and the *Evening Chronicle*, his editorial and organizational skills, and his seamless ability to intertwine and reuse his political and literary journalism in his fiction, distinguish Dickens from his contemporaries. Drew does an excellent job of drawing our attention to the strengths, successes and weaknesses of Dickens's journalistic output.

Heather Street offers another interestingly written case study from a different arena in 'Military Influence in Late Victorian and Edwardian Popular Media:

The Case of Frederick Roberts' (*JVC* 8[2003] 231–56). Through astute use of archival material in London and Edinburgh, she outlines how General Frederick Roberts used personal friendships and media contacts with individuals such as William Blackwood (of *Blackwood's Magazine*), Charles Frederick Moberley Bell (managing editor of the *London Times*), Charles a Court Repington (military correspondent on *The Times* from 1903 to 1918) and Alfred Harmsworth (proprietor of the *Daily Mail*) to direct and shape information about himself and his military activities, as well as to funnel material supporting his views about the military and its interests. From the 1870s to his death in 1914 Roberts sought to use the popular media to his own advantage, contributing material to various journals, passing on personal commentary and confidential information for others to shape and 'spin' into articles and media material favourable to his views, and using the press as a forum to counter the views of other powerful, similarly media-minded military rivals such as Sir Garnet Wolseley and General Kitchener. Street offers particularly astute analysis of how Roberts, learning important lessons in media management, managed to reshape initially negative media images of himself into positive, celebratory and heroic portrayals, particularly after successful military campaigns in Kandahar and South Africa in the 1880s and 1890s. The essay brings to focus relatively unexplored links between Victorian media culture and military personnel use of popular media sources to advance their own interests and agendas.

Attempts to increase the visibility of one's work were not confined to the military and political sphere. The nineteenth century also saw authors turn to multiple markets to augment their income and improve their public profile. Among those they turned to for help were newspaper syndication organizations such as Tillotson's Fiction Bureau. In 'Trollope and the Newspapers' (*MedHis* 9[2003] 47–62), Graham Law studies this phenomenon in detail, providing new evidence on the syndication of Trollope's 1878 novel *Ayala's Angel* in the provincial newspapers the *People's Friend*, the *Western Weekly News* and the *Wakefield and West Riding Herald* between 1881 and 1883. The range of publications the work appeared in illustrates how Trollope's work was recycled to service different regional outlets, in this case covering Scotland, Cornwall and other parts of England.

Syndication in regional papers also features in Graham Law and John Stock Clarke's 'More Light on the Serial Publication of *Tess of the D'Urbervilles*' (*RES* 54[2003] 94–101). They report the discovery of previously unknown serializations in 1891 of Thomas Hardy's classic novel, found in this case in the provincial newspapers the *Nottinghamshire Guardian* and the *Birmingham Weekly*. The serializations, arranged through the efforts of Hardy's literary agent A.P. Watt, demonstrate interesting textual variations that shed light on the material provided by Hardy in late 1890 to the *Graphic* (where it was originally serialized). Law and Clarke use this short case study to highlight the commercial value to authors of syndication in the regional press, and to argue for more study of this overlooked aspect of Victorian publishing history.

In line with this is T.R. Wright's insightful study *Hardy and his Readers*. Wright draws on recent work on readership and reading reception, particularly that connected with the field of book history studies, and pauses to reflect on the varying audiences who read and at times influenced the production and consumption of Hardy's novels during his lifetime. Reiterating a point brought out but not always supported by previous critics, Wright suggests, through close analysis of archival evidence, reviews and other sources, that not until the 1920s, when Hardy passed into the literary canon as a worthy giant of English literature, did he reach audiences beyond the middle and upper classes. Wright's work was published too soon to have benefited from Graham Law's recent investigations into British newspaper syndication, which suggest that Hardy's appearance in provincial newspapers may indeed have been noted by a mass readership drawn from the late nineteenth-century working and labouring classes. However, Wright's studies of the general cultural, social and material issues surrounding the appearance of each of Hardy's novels are on the whole well designed and convincing.

Getting one's work published was not always an easy thing, particularly if your work went against contemporary literary trends. Andrew van der Vlies tracks the tortuous trail to publication of one such case in 'The Editorial Empire: The Fiction of "Greater Britain", and the Early Readers of Olive Schreiner's *The Story of an African Farm*' (*Text* 15[2003] 237–60). The novel, set in South Africa and containing an unconventional plot line including loss of religious faith, illegitimacy and rejection of conventional marriage, was turned down by five major British publishers before being accepted and published by Chapman & Hall in 1882. It would become a commercial success, published in at least thirty-five editions before and after the author's death in 1920, and a cornerstone of South African literary history. Van der Vlies, although he does not acknowledge it, utilizes an approach to the textual history of Schreiner's work informed by Robert Darnton's 'communication circuit', drawing on readers' reports, Schreiner's letters, contemporary media reviews and other external sources to study the progress of the work from production through to reception. The study is by no means exhaustive, as van der Vlies acknowledges, but proves a useful starting point for reassessing Schreiner's work within a book history context.

In 'Robbery Under Arms: The Colonial Market, Imperial Publishers, and the Demise of the Three-Decker Novel' (*Book History* 6[2003] 127–46), Paul Eggert turns attention to another cornerstone of colonial literature; in this case the 'three-decker' Australian set *Robbery Under Arms* by 'Rolf Boldrewood' (the pseudonym of the New South Wales magistrate Thomas Alexander Browne). The novel, first issued in London by Remington in 1888, achieved classic status following its republication in 1889 by Macmillan as part of its Colonial Library: over 500,000 copies would be sold in the next fifty years, and it would continue to be reprinted throughout the 1950s and 1960s. Eggert does an excellent job of using the book's production history to demonstrate the links between British publishers, colonial booksellers and colonial market demands. More importantly, he argues that evidence such as can be found in Browne's publishing history illustrates how the colonial markets played a previously unacknowledged role in hastening the demise of the three-volume novel: the huge increase in profits generated by cheap colonial library series such as the one pioneered by Macmillan played a considerable part in the decision by British publishers and the British retail trade to discard the 'three-decker' novel in 1894.

The colonial market was also a site of pioneering work by British emigrants in book and periodical press activity. The role of the Scots in establishing nineteenth-century book and periodical publishing centres in New Zealand, for example, is the subject of David Finkelstein's '"Jack's as good as his master": Scots and Print Culture in New Zealand, 1860–1900' (*Book History* 6[2003] 95–108). Over 330 newspapers were started by British emigrants between 1860 and 1890: all relied on imported expertise and machinery, much of which was provided by Scottish-trained staff and Scottish-based firms. The piece offers examples of Scots enterprise and innovation in New Zealand's print culture between 1860 and 1900, also illustrating how expertise refined in colonial settings was in turn re-exported back to Scotland with the return of significant print culture specialists to their homeland.

'Brits abroad' is the theme of 'Around the World without a Gaze: Englishness and the Press in Jules Verne' (*VPR* 36[2003] 135–52), Peter Sinnema's study of Jules Verne's construction of the English character in *Around the World in Eighty Days*. Sinnema's original take on this is to view Verne's representation of Phineas Fogg through his reading of and reaction to English newspapers and periodicals, offering a close textual reading of Verne's work in the process.

The imperial theme is continued in three comparative studies of nineteenth-century periodical discourse in Britain, Canada and Australia, published in *Épilogue*. How the media shaped middle-class ideology and exported it to Canada and Australia links pieces by Linda E. Connors, Mary Lu MacDonald and Elizabeth Morrison, forming a neat triangulation of international print culture activity. Connors's piece, 'Creating a Usable Past: The Role of the *Quarterly Review* in Shaping a National Identity for its Provincial Readers, 1820s–1850s' (*Épilogue* 13[2003] 11–20), discusses John Gibson Lockhart's editorship of the *Quarterly Review*, arguing that under his direction the journal subscribed to an ideological view of Britishness that was conservative, hierarchical, anti-French, and capable of drawing in Tories from the margins towards the centre of mid-Victorian political life. Mary Lu MacDonald's 'The Export/Import Trade in Ideas: The Role of United Kingdom Periodicals in Shaping Canadian Political and Social, as well as Literary Discourses in the Middle of the Nineteenth Century' (*Épilogue* 13[2003] 21–8), focuses on the recirculation of British periodical material on Canada within the pages of journals and newspapers published or imported into upper and lower Canada during the political crises between 1836 and 1840. Selective editing and quotation from such sources were used by different political factions to buttress their own arguments in favour of or against the ultimately unsuccessful rebellion against the Crown in 1837 and 1838. In 'A Fourth Estate Down Under: How Newspapers in the British Mould Dominated Colonial Australian Print Culture, Maintained Imperial Ties, and Fostered National Consciousness' (*Épilogue* 13[2003] 29–40), Elizabeth Morrison covers the development of the nineteenth-century Australian newspaper press, illustrating how such productions, geared towards the developing British settlements, at first modelled themselves on British press examples. Their role in political and social discourse, initially conceived as upholding the essential Britishness of Australian society, would shift in time to positions espousing proto-nationalist conceptions of Australian identity as distinct, yet still participating within a 'supra-national, imperial, Greater British identity' (p. 37). A useful introductory piece by Connors, MacDonald, and Morrison, 'The Periodicals and Newspapers of Nineteenth-Century Britain and its Empire: Three Case Studies in "Being British"' (*Épilogue* 13[2003] 1–10) precedes the authors' individual essays, summarizing the major shifts in nineteenth-century British print and periodical production.

Print culture, empire, and the Great Exhibition of 1851 intertwine in Lara Kriegel's 'The Pudding and the Palace: Labor, Print Culture, and Imperial Britain in 1851' (in Burton, ed., *After the Imperial Turn*, pp. 230–45). Kriegel usefully examines the form in which imperial goods were transmuted in print, focusing on texts produced both for and in response to the great Crystal Palace exhibition (organized by Prince Albert and Henry Cole). She draws particular attention to how articles in contemporary journals, trade catalogues and exhibition texts anthropomorphized foreign commodities to 'speak' in ways that reflected and evoked figures of English, imperial and foreign labour, bringing the empire to life for a British reading audience. Images produced often confirmed particular stereotypes of imperial workers; they also challenged received notions of Englishness, and were used to question issues related to mechanization, industry, the division of labour and the destruction of artisanal craftsmanship.

Troy Gregory draws our attention to early Victorian representations of sport, and in particular to Robert Smith Surtees' editorship and comic contributions between 1831 and 1836 to the short-lived *New Sporting Magazine*, in his award-winning contribution, 'Mr. Jorrock's Lost Sporting Magazine' (*VPR* 36[2003] 331–50). The essay draws on close textual analysis of the articles submitted to the periodical to suggest that the material demonstrated a comic value and strength of style that were ahead of their time, and which were only replicated when Surtees began contributing material to *Punch* from 1841 onwards.

Similar study of less well-known Victorian writers and their periodical production continues apace. In 'A Pioneering Female Aesthete: Mathilde Blind in *The Dark Blue*' (*VPR* 36[2003] 210–41), also discussed in Section 3 above, James Diedrick plunders the pages of the short lived avant-garde journal *The Dark Blue* [1871–3] to analyse contributions by the poet and essayist Mathilde Blind. He traces her connections with the aesthetic movement of the 1870s and 1880s, linking that to the themes subsequently expounded in her prose and verse contributions to *The Dark Blue*. He concludes that the five pieces she contributed are worthy of reappraisal, given their significance in establishing her literary credentials as a pioneering aesthete and laying the foundations of a long and successful literary career.

Anne Humpherys turns our attention to another short-lived periodical with radical tendencies in 'The Journal That Did: Form and Content in *The Adult* (1897–9)' (*MedHis* 9[2003] 63–78). The Legitimation League was a radical organization founded in 1893 in Leeds, initially dedicated to securing equal rights, and in particular inheritance rights, for children born out of wedlock. With the move of the League to London, between 1897 and 1899 it published a monthly periodical, *The Adult*, whose major theme was the advocacy of partnerships outside marriage. The periodical (and the organization), was shut down in 1899 because of its associations with Havelock Ellis and his controversial *Studies in the Psychology of Sex*, published by the same firm that brought out *The Adult*. Other reasons for its suppression were the concerns of the British authorities over the social threat seemingly posed by anarchist and radical groups such as the Legitimation League. The agenda established by the organization and its journal, however, was to resonate in the decades that followed.

Cheap periodical publications is the subject of Valerie Gray's 'Charles Knight and the Society for the Diffusion of Useful Knowledge: A Special Relationship (1827–46)' (*PubH* 53[2003] 23–74). From 1827 to 1846 Charles Knight was the main publisher of journals and books commissioned and supported by the Society for the Diffusion of Useful Knowledge (SDUK). The aim of the SDUK, founded in the mid-1820s by a group of liberal philanthropists, was to encourage adult working-class education. To this end it set up Mechanics' Institutes and other local centres of learning, and financed the production of inexpensive periodicals and texts. Among those Knight was personally responsible for producing were the *Penny Magazine*, the *Penny Cyclopaedia*, and the *British Almanac*. Through his association with the SDUK, Knight was able to raise his publishing business from a state of near bankruptcy in 1826 to respectable profitability. Knight's role in securing success for SDUK's publications deserves further attention from cultural historians.

Emily Lorraine de Montluzin corrects some authorial attributions in, and some misconceptions about, the editorial reign of John Gifford at the *Anti-Jacobin Review* (begun in 1798) during the first decade of the nineteenth century, in her article 'The *Anti-Jacobin* Revisited: Newly Identified Contributions to the *Anti-Jacobin Review* during the Editorial Regime of John Gifford, 1798–1806' (*Library*, 7th series 4[2003] 278–302). Using internal periodical production evidence and previously overlooked secondary sources, de Montluzin argues that, contrary to popular belief, John Gifford ceased editorial duties on the *Review* not on his death in 1818, but much earlier, in 1806. Her article usefully identifies authorship of over a hundred articles published in the *Review*'s pages in its first eight years of existence. Similar bibliographical corrections and additions for items relating to *Bentley's Miscellany*, *Blackwood's Magazine*, *British and Foreign Review*, *Edinburgh Review*, *Fraser's Magazine*, *Monthly Chronicle*, *Tait's Edinburgh Magazine* and the *Temple Bar* are included in Eileen Curran's annual summary piece, '*The Wellesley Index*: Additions and Corrections' (*VPR* 36[2003] 351–63).

A similar focus on the early nineteenth century informs Wheatley, ed., *Romantic Periodicals and Print Culture*. The starting point is the material to be found in the ephemeral pages of early nineteenth-century literary journals and periodicals such as *Blackwood's*, the *Edinburgh Review*, the *London Magazine* and the *New Monthly Magazine*, among others. Issues covered in this compact volume include gender identities, male reviewers' appraisals of popular and until recently non-canonical women writers, politics, and the public shaping and reinforcement of literary reputations. The collection features the following contributions: Kim Wheatley's introduction (pp. 1–18); Adriana Craciun, 'Mary Robinson, the *Monthly Magazine*, and the Free Press' (pp. 19–40); Andrea Bradley, 'Correcting Mrs. Opies' Powers: The *Edinburgh* Review of Amelie

Opie's *Poems* [1802]' (pp. 41–61); Mark Schoenfield, 'Novel Marriages, Romantic Labor, and the Quarterly Press' (pp. 62–83); Boonie J. Gunzenhauser, 'Reading the Rhetoric of Resistance in William Cobbett's *Two-Penny Trash*' (pp. 84–101); Lisa Niles, '"May the married be single, and the single happy": *Blackwood's*, the *Maga* for the Single Man' (pp. 102–21); David Higgins, '*Blackwood's Edinburgh Magazine* and the Construction of Wordsworth's Genius' (pp. 122–36); Peter J. Manning, 'Detaching Lamb's Thoughts' (pp. 137–46); Nanora Sweet, 'The *New Monthly Magazine* and the Liberalism of the 1820s' (pp. 147–62).

Helen Small studies two giants of Victorian periodical production in 'Liberal Editing in the *Fortnightly Review* and the *Nineteenth Century*' (*PubH* 53[2003] 75–96). Both the *Fortnightly Review* and the *Nineteenth Century* were ranked amongst the most influential periodical spaces for late nineteenth-century liberal thought and debate on issues related to science, literature, politics and religion. The *Fortnightly*, begun in 1865, was for many years distinguished for its support of scientific debate. In 1877 James Thomas Knowles founded the *Nineteenth Century*, which quickly became the *Fortnightly*'s closest liberal-minded periodical rival. Both journals have tended to be lumped together. A close inspection of the financial and economic pressures faced by their respective editors, however, demonstrates significant divergences in editorial policy. In the case of John Morley, editor of the *Fortnightly* from 1866 to 1882, budgetary restraints and close monitoring by his publishers Chapman & Hall led to significant interference and shaping of periodical content. The resulting friction directly led to Morley's resignation as editor in 1882 (contrary to published accounts on the matter). James Knowles, on the other hand, had a freer hand in shaping the *Nineteenth Century*, having started it with his own capital. His relationship with the journal's publisher James Virtue was more flexible and less fraught as a result. Knowles was therefore able to run the journal on a more structured, diverse and financially independent platform than Morley, shaping editorial content as he chose.

How Victorian periodicals were used to promote public health reform is at the heart of Clare Horrocks's 'The Personification of "Father Thames": Reconsidering the Role of the Victorian Periodical Press in the "Verbal and Visual Campaign" for Public Health Reform' (*VPR* 36[2003] 2–19). Horrocks draws on both visual and textual examples from *Punch* and *Household Words* to demonstrate how such journals shaped popular representations between 1848 and 1858 of the River Thames—using the rhetorical and visual representation of the river as an old and unhealthy father figure to create a vivid image subsequently employed for reforming purposes. At the same time, Horrocks corrects and challenges particular readings of this image by such figures as Asa Briggs and Richard Altick.

In contrast, death, or rather its increasing commercialization in Victorian society, is explored in Catherine Waters, '"Trading in Death": Contested Commodities in *Household Words*' (*VPR* 36[2003] 313–30). Waters examines material in Dickens's edited weekly throughout the 1850s, concentrating on essays and articles covering the commercial development of the Victorian funeral, the growth of privatized cemeteries, and 'body snatching and the commodification of corpses' (p. 314). She concludes that the trade in death, and its increasing marketability as a social commodity, receives ambivalent treatment in the pages of *Household Words*, representing 'a process of contested commodification that registers a number of mid-Victorian anxieties about the appropriate scope of the market' (p. 326).

Relatively little focused attention has been paid to how political conflict was systematically represented and shaped in the illustrated periodicals of the late nineteenth century. In 'Conflictual Imaginaries: Victorian Illustrated Periodicals and the Franco-Prussian War (1870–1)' (*VPR* 36[2003] 41–58), Michèle Martin offers a short case study of visual representations of the Franco-Prussian war of 1870–1 in the four major British illustrated periodicals of the period—the *Illustrated London News*, *Graphic*, *Penny Illustrated Paper* and *Illustrated Times*. Martin digs up interesting representations of the war, and notes (with some surprise), that the stances taken in the journals varied widely, from pro-French (*Penny Illustrated Paper* and *Illustrated Times*) to pro-Prussian (*Illustrated London News* and the *Graphic*). These stances changed and shifted as the war progressed and concluded, and Martin uses the shifts to argue for closer attention to be paid to the manner in which such journals offered varying but nevertheless important visual commentary on political issues of the period.

Staying with the matter of illustrations, in 'War Cartooned/Cartoon War: Matt Morgan and the American Civil War in *Fun* and *Frank Leslie's Illustrated Newspaper*' (*VPR* 36[2003] 153–81) Christopher Kent offers an articulate and interesting comparative piece on the visual representations of the American Civil War of 1860–4 as found in the satirical London journal *Fun* (rival to *Punch*) and the US-based *Frank Leslie's Illustrated Newspaper*. The results range from puzzlement, parody and caricature to hero-worship and political critique. Kent also contrasts some of the compositions provided to *Fun* by Matthew Morgan with those submitted by Thomas Nast to *Frank Leslie's Illustrated Newspaper*.

In *Imperial Persuaders: Images of Africa and Asia in British Advertising*, Anandi Ramamurthy pays close textual attention to images of colonial subjects in advertisements of the late nineteenth and early twentieth centuries. It will be of particular value to Victorian periodical scholars with an interest in following her focus on material featured in such illustrated journals as *The Graphic*, *Punch* and the *Illustrated London News*. Ramamurthy's book has an overt political agenda which may provoke strong reactions—namely, to outline the racist and imperialist ideology underpinning such early advertising material. Among her targets are soap, cocoa, tea and tobacco advertisements, with chapters on each and copious illustrations to accompany the close textual and visual analysis of contemporary advertising imagery and copy.

In *Manliness and the Boys' Story Paper in Britain: A Cultural History, 1855–1940*, Kelly Boyd focuses on masculinity and gender issues in her close readings of boys' story papers and magazines prior to the advent of the comic book. The title of the book makes clear that this is a work combining textual analysis with cultural studies-inflected argumentation. Boyd tackles soundly issues such as the readership of these magazines, details briefly the history of those who created and contributed to such journals, and moves on to explicate the formulas underpinning much of the material produced for them. She also outlines how a longitudinal study of such material clearly indicates a shift in representations of masculinity and hero-worship, figures that responded to contemporary shifts in society and class structures.

From the same publisher comes a similar study of masculinity and heroism in Edwardian mass print, in this case Glenn Wilkinson's *Depictions and Images of War in Edwardian Newspapers, 1899–1914*. This is a short and competent study focusing particularly on the militarist and sporting imagery that marked British newspaper representations of war activities during this period (most notably the 'Boer' wars and the Russo-Japanese war of 1902). The work does not focus on 'news values' or the development of pre-First World War reportage systems per se, but rather examines the language, imagery and metaphors employed in supporting particular cultural and social values associated with military activity in this period.

In contrast, Chandrika Kaul's *Reporting the Raj: The British Press and India, c.1880–1922* very much links the management of news and 'information flow' with case studies on contemporary reportage of key, flashpoint moments in British–Indian relations during the late Victorian and Edwardian periods. Kaul offers interesting and useful material on the role of press barons such as Lord Northcliffe in shaping the policies, stances and reporting infrastructure of British overseas press representatives, and effectively combines political and MedHis agendas in this very readable work.

For a complementary study, readers would do well to turn to Simon J. Potter's *News and the British World: The Emergence of an Imperial Press System*. This is a carefully researched history of the development from 1876 to 1922 of a press network linking Britain, Canada, New Zealand, Australia and South Africa. With the development of overseas cable connections between Britain and its far-flung possessions, the processing of news and information speeded up in a manner enabling the development of an imperial press system. The challenges and successes of such a system are ably and carefully delineated, and the book is worth reading.

To what extent the image of 'new journalism', as articulated by Matthew Arnold and W.T. Stead in the 1880s, was a victim of hyperbole or was a genuine revolution in journalistic discourse is an issue tackled in Kate Campbell's densely written 'W.E. Gladstone, W.T. Stead, Matthew Arnold and a New Journalism: Cultural Politics in the 1880s' (*VPR* 36[2003] 20–40). Campbell offers a complex reading of the rise of new journalism—a bombastic, reformist journalism emphasizing human interest, and practised by larger-than-life individuals such as W.T. Stead—intriguingly linking its journalistic innovations to a similar theatricality and public-orientated mode of political discourse employed by William Gladstone and other popular liberals at key electoral moments such as the 1880 general election. The piece is worth decoding for what it has to say about the manner in which periodical press mediations shaped and transformed the political field of the late nineteenth century.

Periodical production could also transform those emerging from the private sphere. Kate Kelman draws attention to the remarkable 'awakening of woman' that occurred in the drawing rooms of polite Edinburgh society in the latter third of the nineteenth century in '"Self Culture": The Educative Reading Pursuits of the Ladies of Edinburgh, 1865–85' (*VPR* 36[2003] 59–75). The Ladies' Edinburgh Debating Society, founded as a reading group whose focus included discussing and debating books and current issues, quickly expanded its remit to include the writing, editing and publication of a monthly journal. Kelman skilfully draws from archival records and written sources to demonstrate how the act of reading, producing and consuming print culture played a significant role in shifting those who participated from private to public spheres of action. Those involved in the debating society, their media skills honed at first in private and then more publicly, would become leading figures in Scottish public life, particularly in the field of education, founding institutes of higher education, schools and medical centres. Their actions, Kelman argues, were a direct result of the training and skills honed at first in a private sphere orientated towards print culture.

Books Reviewed

Alexander, Christine, and Margaret Smith. *The Oxford Companion to the Brontës*. OUP. [2003] pp. 544. $95 ISBN 0 1986 6218 1.

Alexander, Lynn M. *Women, Work, and Representation: Needlewomen in Victorian Art and Literature*. OhioUP. [2003] pp. viii +257. $44 ISBN 0 8214 1493 3.

Atkinson, Damian, ed. *The Correspondence of John Stephen Farmer and W.E. Henley on their Slang Dictionary, 1890–1904. Mellen*. [2003] pp. xxxiii +164. $109.95 ISBN 0 7734 6612 6.

Atterbury, Paul, and Suzanne Fagence Cooper. *Victorians at Home and Abroad*. Abrams. [2003] pp. 96. $16.95 ISBN 0 8109 6573 9.

Avery, Simon, and Rebecca Stott. *Elizabeth Barrett Browning*. Longman. [2003] pp. 264. ($32) ISBN 0 5824 0470 3.

Ayres, Brenda, ed. *Silent Voices: Forgotten Novels by Victorian Women Writers*. Praeger. [2003] pp. 272. $69.95 ISBN 0 3133 2462 X.

Bachman, Maria K., and Don Richard Cox, eds. *Blind Love by Wilkie Collins*. Broadview. [2003] pp. 350. $16.95 ISBN 1 5511 1447 X.

Bachman, Maria K., and Don Richard Cox, eds. *Reality's Dark Light: The Sensational Wilkie Collins*. UTennP. [2003] pp. 386. $40 ISBN 1 5723 3274 3.

Baker, William, ed. *The Notebooks and Library of George Eliot. Past Masters: The Women Writers Collection*. CD-ROM Intelex Corporation. [2003] . $200 ISBN 1 5708 5427 0.

Beer, John. *Post-Romantic Consciousness: Dickens to Plath*. Palgrave. [2003] pp. 216. $65 ISBN 1 4039 0518 5.

Belcher, Margaret, ed. *The Collected Letters of A.W.N. Pugin*, vol. 2: 1843–1845. OUP. [2003] pp. 448. $135 ISBN 0 1992 5586 5.

Bergonzi, Bernard, '*A Victorian Wanderer: The Life of Thomas Arnold the Younger*' OUP. [2003] pp. 288. $39.95 ISBN 0 1992 5741 8.

Bevis, Matthew, ed. *Lives of Victorian Literary Figures,* 3 vols.; vol. 3.: Alfred, Lord Tennyson, P&C. [2003] pp. xxxix +504. £275 ($440) ISBN 1 8519 6759 1.

Bigelow, Gordon. *Fiction, Famine, and the Rise of Economics in Victorian Britain and Ireland*. CUP. [2003] pp. 242. £45 ISBN 0 5218 2848 1.

Bohrer, Frederick N. *Orientalism and Visual Culture: Imagining Mesopotamia in Nineteenth-Century Europe*. CUP. [2003] pp. 398. $90 ISBN 0 5218 0657 7.

Bowen, John, ed. *Barnaby Rudge by Charles Dickens*. Penguin. [2003] pp. 744. $11 ISBN 0 1404 3728 2.

Boyd, Kelly. *Manliness and the Boys' Story Paper in Britain: A Cultural History, 1855–1940*. Palgrave. [2003] pp. x + 274. £50 ISBN 0 3336 4172 8.

Bradley, Arthur, and Alan Rawes, eds. *Romantic Biography*. Ashgate. [2003] pp. xvii +202. £? ISBN 0 7546 0993 6.

Bratton, Jacky. *New Readings in Theatre History*. CUP. [2003] pp. xi +238. hb £40 ISBN 0 5217 9121 9, pb £16.99 ISBN 0 5217 9463 3.

Bristow, Joseph, ed. *Wilde Writings: Contextual Conditions*. UTorP. [2003] pp. 312. $63 ISBN 0 8020 3532 9.

Brittain-Catlin, Timothy. introd. *Contrasts and The True Principles of Pointed or Christian Architecture by A.W.N. Pugin*. Spire Books in association with the Pugin Society. [2003] pp. 190. £33.95 ISBN 0 9543 6154 7.

Brown, Emma. *Claire Boylan and Charlotte Brontë*. Little Brown. [2003] pp. 435. $25.95 ISBN 0 3167 2547 1.

Browne, Sarah-Anne. *Devoted Sisters: Representations of the Sister Relationship in Nineteenth-Century British and American Literature*. Ashgate. [2003] pp. 177. $64 ISBN 0 7546 0478 0.

Bulmer, Michael. *Francis Galton: Pioneer of Heredity and Biometry*. JHUP. [2003] pp. 352. $45 ISBN 0 8018 7403 3.

Burton, Antoinette, ed. '*After the Imperial Turn: Thinking With and Through the Nation*'. DukeUP. [2003] pp. 369. hb $79.95 ISBN 0 8223 3106 3, pb $23.95 ISBN 0 8223 3142 X.

Campbell, Duncan Andrew. *English Public Opinion and the American Civil War*. Boydell. [2003] pp. 274. $70 ISBN 0 8619 3263 3.

Campbell, Elizabeth A. *Fortune's Wheel: Dickens and the Iconography of Women's Time*. OhioUP. [2003] pp. xxiii +253. $42.95 ISBN 0 8214 1514 X.

Carpenter, Mary Wilson, '*Imperial Bibles, Domestic Bodies: Women, Sexuality, and Religion in the Victorian Market*'. OhioUP. [2003] pp. xxii +206. $39.95 ISBN 0 8214 1515 8.

Carroll, Alicia. *Dark Smiles: Race and Desire in George Eliot*. OhioUP. [2003] pp. 208. $39.95 ISBN 0 8214 1441 0.

Carter, Matt. *T.H. Green and the Development of Ethical Socialism*. Imprint. [2003] pp. 230. £25 ISBN 0 9078 4532 0.

Carver, Stephen James. *The Life and Works of the Lancashire Novelist William Harrison Ainsworth, 1850–1882*. Mellen. [2003] pp. 490. $129.95 ISBN 0 7734 6633 9.

Chapman, Alison, ed. *Victorian Women Poets*. Boydell & Brewer (Essays and Studies). [2003] pp. viii +206. £30 ($50) ISBN 0 8599 1787 8.

Chapman, Alison, and Jane Stabler, eds. *Unfolding the South: Nineteenth-Century British Women Writers and Artists in Italy*. ManUP. [2003] pp. x + 246. £47.50 ($74.95) ISBN 0 7190 6130 X.

Chapple, John, and Alan Shelston, eds. *Further Letters of Mrs. Gaskell*. ManUP. [2003] pp. 368. $24.95 ISBN 0 7190 6771 5.

Chew, Shirley, ed. *Arthur Hugh Clough: Selected Poems*. 7. Carcanet. [2003] pp. 240. £9.95 ($12.95) ISBN 1 8575 4718 7.

Clark, Christopher, and Wolfram Kaiser, eds. *Culture Wars: Secular–Catholic Conflict in Nineteenth-Century Europe*. CUP. [2003] pp. 376. $70 ISBN 0 5218 0997 5.

Clayton, Jay. *Charles Dickens in Cyberspace: The Afterlife of the Nineteenth Century in Postmodern Culture*. OUP. [2003] pp. 270. $35 ISBN 0 1951 6051 7.

Codell, Julie F. *The Victorian Artist: Artists' Lifewritings in Britain, ca. 1870–1910*. CUP. [2003] pp. xvi +376. $85 ISBN 0 5218 1757 9.

Cohen, Morton N., and Edward Wakeling, eds. *Lewis Carroll and his Illustrators: Collaborations and Correspondence, 1865–1898*. CornellUP. [2003] pp. 349. $36.95 ISBN 0 8014 4148 X.

Cooper, Victoria. *The House of Novello: The Practice and Policy of a Victorian Music Publisher, 1829–1866*. Ashgate. [2003] pp. 224. $79.94 ISBN 0 7546 0088 2.

Cordery, Simon. *British Friendly Societies, 1750–1914*. Palgrave. [2002] pp. 230. $65 ISBN 0 3339 9031 5.

Cox, Michael, ed. *The Oxford Book of Victorian Detective Stories*. OUP. [2003] pp. 606. £9.99 ISBN 0 1928 0448 0.

Cox, Michael, and R.A. Gilbert, eds. *The Oxford Book of Victorian Ghost Stories*. OUP. [2003] pp. 497. $17.95 ISBN 0 1928 0447 2.

Craig, Edward, ed. *Routledge Encyclopedia of Philosophy* (online). [2003] <www.rep.routledge.com>.

Crook, J. Mordaunt. *The Architect's Secret: Victorian Critics and the Image of Gravity*. Murray. [2003] pp. 224. $36.58 ISBN 0 7195 6057 8.

Curr, Matthew. *The Consolation of Otherness: The Male Love Elegy in Milton, Gray and Tennyson*. McFarland. [2002] pp. 176. £21.95 ($32) ISBN 0 7864 1239 9.

Da Sousa Correa, Delia. *George Eliot, Music, and Victorian Culture*. Palgrave. [2003] pp. 272. $70 ISBN 0 3339 9757 3.

Dames, Nicholas. *Amnesiac Selves: Nostalgia, Forgetting, and British Fiction, 1810–1870*. OUP. [2003] pp. 308. $24.95 ISBN 0 1951 4357 4.

Daniels, Rebecca, and Geoffrey Brandwood, eds. *Ruskin and Architecture*. Spire Books in association with the Victorian Society. [2003] pp. 382. £32.95 ISBN 0 9543 6151 2.

Darwin, Charles. *The Origin of Species; and, The Voyage of the Beagle*. Knopf. [2003] pp. 972. $30 ISBN 1 4000 4127 9.

Davis, Philip, and Brian Nellist, eds. *Hester by Margaret Oliphant*. WC, OUP. [2003] pp. 544. £7.99 ISBN 1 1928 0411 1.

Davis, William A. *Thomas Hardy and the Law: Legal Presences in Hardy's Life and Fiction*. UDelP. [2003] pp. 199. $39.95 ISBN 0 8741 3798 5.

De la L. Oulton, Carolyn W. *Literature and Religion in Mid-Victorian England*. Palgrave. [2003] pp. 265. $69.95 ISBN 0 3339 9337 3.

De Marco, Nick. *Robert Browning's The Ring and the Book: A Critical Appraisal*. Edizioni Campus (Pescara). [2003] pp. 135. €14 ISBN 8 8874 1321 5.

Deane, Bradley. *The Making of the Victorian Novelist: Anxieties of Authorship in the Mass Market*. Routledge. [2003] pp. 192. $65 ISBN 0 4159 4020 6.

Diamond, Michael. *Victorian Sensation or the Spectacular: The Shocking and the Scandalous in Nineteenth-Century Britain*. Anthem. [2003] pp. 328. £24.95 ISBN 1 8433 1076 7.

Dibble, Jeremy. *Charles Villiers Stanford: Man and Musician*. OUP. [2003] pp. 450. $110 ISBN 0 1981 6383 5.

Drew, John L. *Dickens the Journalist*. Palgrave. [2003] pp. viii +255. £45 ($60.95) ISBN 0 3339 8773 X.

Drexler, Peter, ed. *Nice Work? Critical Perspectives on the Changing Nature of Labour, Leisure, and Unemployment in Britain*. Wissenschaftlicher Verlag Trier. [2002] pp. 164. £19.50 ISBN 3 8847 6556 6.

Dryden, Linda. *The Modern Gothic and Literary Doubles: Stevenson, Wilde and Wells*. Palgrave. [2003] pp. 240. $65 ISBN 1 4039 0510 X.

Dunn, Richard J., ed. *Wuthering Heights by Emily Brontë*. Norton. [2003] pp. 432. $12.10 ISBN 0 3939 7889 3.

Ebbatson, Roger. *Tennyson's English Idylls: History, Narrative, Art*. Tennyson Society Occasional Papers. [2003] pp. 32. £3 ISBN 0 9019 5860 3.

Edwards, Mike. *George Eliot: The Novels*. Palgrave. [2003] pp. 213. hb $59.95 ISBN 1 4039 0056 6, pb $18.95 ISBN 1 4039 0057 4.

Fasick, Laura, *Professional Men and Domesticity in the Mid-Victorian Novel*. Mellen. [2003] pp. 199. $109.95 ISBN 0 7734 6716 5.

Feldman, Jessica R. *Victorian Modernism: Pragmatism and the Varieties of Aesthetic Experience*. CUP. [2002] pp. xiii +261. £45 ($60) ISBN 0 5218 1581 9.

Flavin, Michael. *Gambling in the Nineteenth-Century English Novel: 'A Leprosy is O'er the Land'*. SussexAP. [2003] pp. 254. $69.50 ISBN 1 9039 0018 2.

Franey, Laura E. *Victorian Travel Writing and Imperial Violence: British Writing on Africa, 1855–1902*. Palgrave. [2003] pp. 256. $65 ISBN 1 4039 0508 8.

Frank, Lawrence. *Victorian Detective Fiction and the Nature of Evidence: The Scientific Investigations of Poe, Dickens, and Doyle*. Palgrave. [2003] pp. 272. $69.95 ISBN 1 4039 1139 8.

Friedman, Stanley. *Dickens's Fiction: Tapestries of Conscience*. AMS. [2003] $72.50 ISBN 0 4046 4460 0.

Garlick, Gorel. *To Serve the Purpose of the Drama: The Theatre Designs and Plays of Samuel Beazley 1786–1851*. STR. [2003] pp. iv +220. £16 ISBN 0 8543 0073 2.

Garrett, Peter K. *Gothic Reflections: Narrative Force in Nineteenth-Century Fiction*. CornUP. [2003] pp. 232. hb $45 ISBN 0 8014 4156 0, pb $19.95 ISBN 0 8014 8888 5.

Gattrell, Simon. *Thomas Hardy's Vision of Wessex*. Palgrave. [2003] pp. 288. $69.95 ISBN 0 3337 4834 4.

Glavin, John, ed. *Dickens on Screen*. CUP. [2003] pp. 225. £47.50 ISBN 0 5218 0652 6.

Goetsch, Paul. *The Oral and the Written in Nineteenth-Century British Fiction*. Lang. [2003] pp. viii +234. $33.95 ISBN 3 6315 0674 0.

Goodlad, Lauren M.E. *Victorian Literature and the Victorian State: Character and Governance in a Liberal Society*. JHUP. [2003] pp. 280. $45 ISBN 0 8018 6963 3.

Gordon, Eleanor, and Gwyneth Nair. *Public Lives: Women, Family, and Society in Victorian Britain*. YaleUP. [2003] pp. 304. $45 ISBN 0 3001 0220 8.

Gribbin, John, and Mary Gribbin. *FitzRoy: The Remarkable Story of Darwin's Captain and the Invention of the Weather Forecast*. YaleUP. [2003] pp. 336. £7.99 ISBN 0 3001 0361 1.

Griffin, Robert J., ed. *The Faces of Anonymity: Anonymous and Pseudonymous Publications from the Sixteenth to the Twentieth Century*. Palgrave. [2003] pp. xi + 250. £40 ($65) ISBN 0 3122 9530 8.

Groth, Helen. *Victorian Photography and Literary Nostalgia*. OUP. [2003] pp. 280. £47 ($72) ISBN 0 1992 5624 1.

Hague, Angela. *Fiction, Intuition, and Creativity: Studies in Brontë, James, Woolf, and Lessing*. CUAP. [2003] pp. 344. $59.95 ISBN 0 8132 1314 2.

Haining, Peter, ed. *Hunter Quatermain's Story: The Uncollected Adventures of Allan Quatermain by H. Rider Haggard*. Owen. [2003] pp. 256. $26.95 ISBN 0 7206 1182 2.

Halevi-Wise, Yael. *Interactive Fictions: Scenes of Storytelling in the Novel*. Praeger. [2003] pp. 216. $68.95 ISBN 0 3133 2007 1.

Harden, Edgar F. *A William Makepeace Thackeray Chronology*. Palgrave. [2003] pp. 228. $65 ISBN 1 4039 0301 8.

Harrison, Ross, ed. *Henry Sidgwick*. BA. [2002] pp. 110. $30 ISBN 0 1972 6249 X.

Harvey, Geoffrey. *The Complete Critical Guide to Thomas Hardy*. Routledge. [2003] pp. xii + 228. $75 ISBN 0 4152 3492 1.

Hearn, Michael Patrick, ed. *The Annotated Christmas Carol: A Christmas Carol in Prose*. Norton. [2003] pp. 288. $29.95 ISBN 0 3930 5158 7.

Hecimovich, Gregg A., ed. *Phineas Redux by Anthony Trollope*. Penguin. [2003] pp. 768. $11 ISBN 0 1404 3762 2.

Heringman, Noah, ed. *Romantic Science: The Literary Forms of Natural History*. SUNY. [2003] pp. 352. hb $86.50 ISBN 0 7914 5702 8, pb $29.95 ISBN 0 7914 5701 X.

Hicks, Malcolm, ed. *Elizabeth Barrett Browning: Selected Poems*. Carcanet. [2003] pp. 119. £9.95 ($12.95) ISBN 1 8575 4700 4.

Hoeveler, Diane Long, and Tamar Heller, eds. *Approaches to Teaching Gothic Fiction: The British and American Traditions*. MLA. [2003] pp. 324. hb $37.50 ISBN 0 8735 2906 5, pb $19.75 ISBN 0 8735 2907 3.

Holdsworth, Roger, ed. *Arthur Symons: Selected Writings*. Carcanet. [2003] pp. 98. £9.95 ($12.95) ISBN 1 8575 4727 8.

Holland, Merlin, '*The Real Trial of Oscar Wilde: The First Uncensored Manuscript of the Trial of Oscar Wilde vs. John Douglass (Marquess of Queensberry, 1895)*' FE. [2003] pp. 384. $27.95 ISBN 0 0071 5664 2.

Hurst, Clive, ed. *Barnaby Rudge by Charles Dickens*. OUP. [2003] pp. 768. £6.99 ISBN 0 1928 4056 8.

Ingham, Patricia. *Thomas Hardy*. OUP. [2003] pp. 263. $9.95 ISBN 0 1928 3980 2.

Ingham, Patricia, ed. *Desperate Remedies by Thomas Hardy*. OUP. [2003] pp. 263. $12.95 ISBN 0 1928 4070 3.

Ingham, Patricia, and Michelle R. Warren, eds. *Postcolonial Moves: Medieval Through Modern*. Palgrave. [2003] pp. x + 264. £40 ($60) ISBN 1 4039 6073 9.

Innes, Lyn. *A History of Black and Asian Writing in Britain, 1700–2000*, CUP. [2002] pp. 330. $60 ISBN 0 5216 4327 9.

James, Simon. *Unsettled Accounts: Money and Narrative in the Novels of George Gissing*. Anthem. [2003] pp. 304. $75 ISBN 1 8433 1107 0.

Joyce, Simon. *Capital Offenses: Geographies of Class and Crime in Victorian London*. UPVirginia. [2003] pp. 267. $39.95 ISBN 0 8139 2180 5.

Kaul, Chandrika. *Reporting the Raj: The British Press and India, c.1880–1922*. ManUP. [2003] pp. xvii +302. pb £16.99 ISBN 0 7190 6176 8.

Keane, Robert, ed. *Oscar Wilde: The Man, his Writings, and his World*. AMS. [2003] pp. 278. $76.50 ISBN 0 4046 4462 7.

Ker, Ian. *The Catholic Revival in English Literature, 1845–1961: Newman, Hopkins, Chesterton, Greene, Waugh*. UNDP. [2003] pp. 248. $60 ISBN 0 2680 3879 1.

Kestner, Joseph. *Sherlock's Sisters: The British Female Detective, 1864–1913*. Ashgate. [2003] pp. 254. $79.95 ISBN 0 7546 0481 0.

King, Amy M. *Bloom: The Botanical Vernacular in the English Novel*. OUP. [2003] pp. 265. $49.95 ISBN 0 1951 6151 3.

Kirby, Peter. *Child Labour in Britain, 1750–1870*. Palgrave. [2003] pp. 224. $24.95 ISBN 0 3336 7194 5.

Kitson, Peter, gen, ed. *Nineteenth-Century Travels, Explorations and Empires: Writings from the Era of Imperial Consolidation, 1835–1910*. vols. 1–4. P&C. [2003] pp. 1,880. £350 ISBN 1 8519 6760 5.

Klein, Bernhard, ed. *Fictions of the Sea: Critical Perspectives on the Ocean in British Literature and Culture*. Ashgate. [2003] pp. 244. $74.95 ISBN 0 7546 0620 1.

Knapp, John V., and Kenneth Womack, eds. *Reading the Family Dance: Family Systems Therapy and Literary Studies*. UDelP. [2003] pp. 333. $55 ISBN 0 8741 3823 X.

Kooistra, Lorraine. *Christina Rossetti and Illustration*. OhioUP. [2002] pp. xvi +332. £37.50 ($55) ISBN 0 8214 1454 2.

Krueger, Christine L., ed. *Functions of Victorian Culture at the Present Time*. OhioUP. [2002] pp. xx +195. £30.95 ($44.95) ISBN 0 8214 1460 7.

Kucich, John, ed. *Fictions of Empire: Heart of Darkness by Joseph Conrad; The Man Who Would Be King by Rudyard Kipling; The Beach of Falesá by Robert Louis Stevenson*. New Riverside. HoughtonM. [2003] pp. 421. $11.56 ISBN 0 6180 8488 6.

Kutzer, Daphne M. *Beatrix Potter: Writing in Code*. Routledge. [2003] pp. 192. $90.95 ISBN 0 4159 4352 3.

Lane, Christopher. *Hatred and Civility: The Antisocial Life in Victorian England*. ColUP. [2003] pp. 224. $27.40 ISBN 0 2311 3064 3.

Latham, David, ed. *Haunted Texts: Studies in Pre-Raphaelitism*. UTorP. [2003] pp. 336. $55 ISBN 0 8020 3662 7.

Latham, Sean. *'Am I a Snob?': Modernism and the Novel*. CornUP. [2003] pp. 240. $19.95 ISBN 0 8014 8841 9.

Lerer, Seth. *Error and the Academic Self: The Scholarly Imagination, Medieval to Modern*. ColUP. [2002] pp. 388. $24 ISBN 0 2311 2373 6.

Levine, Caroline. *The Serious Pleasures of Suspense: Victorian Realism and Narrative Doubt*. UPVirginoia. [2003] pp. 256. $39.50 ISBN 0 8139 2217 8.

Lewis, Linda M. *Germaine de Staël, George Sand, and the Victorian Woman as Artist*. UMissP. [2003] pp. 278 + bibliography and index. $24.95 ISBN 0 8262 1455 X.

Lindner, Christoph. *Fictions of Commodity Culture: From the Victorian to the Postmodern*. Ashgate. [2003] pp. 199. $69.95 ISBN 0 7546 3483 3.

Lovelace, J. Timothy. *The Artistry and Tradition of Tennyson's Battle Poetry*. Routledge. [2003] pp. 187. £45 ($79.95) ISBN 0 4159 6763 5.

Mahone, Basil. *The Man Who Changed Everything: The Life of James Clerk Maxwell*. Wiley. [2003] pp. 254. £18.99 ISBN 0 4708 6088 X.

Mallett, Phillip. *Rudyard Kipling: A Literary Life*. Palgrave. [2003] pp. 256. $49.95 ISBN 0 3335 5720 4.

Malone, Carolyn. *Women's Bodies and Dangerous Trades, 1880–1914*. RHS. [2003] pp. 184. $75 ISBN 0 8619 3264 1.

Mander, W.J., and Alan P.F. Sells, gen. eds. *The Dictionary of Nineteenth-Century British Philosophers*. 2 vols. Thoemmes. [2002] pp. 1,280. £350 ISBN 1 8550 6955 5.

Marshall, Gail, and Adrian Poole, eds. *Victorian Shakespeare,* vol. 1: *Theatre, Drama and Performance*. Palgrave Macmillan. [2003] pp. xvi +213. £50 ISBN 1 4039 1116 9.

Marshall, Gail, and Adrian Poole, eds. *Victorian Shakespeare,* vol. 2: *Literature and Culture*. Palgrave. [2003] xvi +213. £50 ISBN 1 4039 1117 7.

Mattison, Jane, *Knowledge and Survival in the Novels of Thomas Hardy*. LundU. [2002] pp. 423. $73 ISBN 9 1974 0230 3.

McBratney, John. *Imperial Subjects, Imperial Space: Rudyard Kipling's Fiction of the Native-Born*. OhioUP. [2003] pp. 224. $54.95 ISBN 0 8142 0909 2.

McDonagh, Josephine. *Child Murder and British Culture, 1720–1900*. CUP. [2003] pp. 292. $65 ISBN 0 5217 8193 0.

McGann, Jerome, ed. *Dante Gabriel Rossetti: Collected Poetry and Prose*. YaleUP. [2003] pp. xxix +424. hb $45 ISBN 0 3000 9801 4, pb $24 ISBN 0 3000 9802 2.

McKay, Brenda. *George Eliot and Victorian Attitudes to Racial Diversity, Colonialism, Darwinism, Class, Gender, and Jewish Culture and Prophecy*. Mellen. [2003] pp. 597. $149.95 ISBN 0 7734 6621 5.

McKenna, Neil. *The Secret Life of Oscar Wilde*. Century. [2003] pp. 564. £20 ISBN 0 7126 6986 8.

McKitterick, David. *Print, Manuscript and the Search for Order, 1450–1830*. CUP. [2003] pp. xv +311. £45 ISBN 0 5218 2690 X.

Menon, Patricia. *Austen, Eliot, Charlotte Brontë, and the Mentor-Lover*. Palgrave. [2003] pp. 240. $65 ISBN 1 4039 0259 3.

Mitchell, Leslie. *Bulwer Lytton: The Rise and Fall of a Victorian Man of Letters*. H&L. [2003] pp. 320. $34.95 ISBN 1 8528 5423 5.

Mukherjee, Upamanyu Pablo. *Crime and Empire: The Colony in Nineteenth-Century Fictions of Crime*. OUP. [2003] pp. 340. $65 ISBN 0 1992 6105 9.

Muller, Jill. *Gerard Manley Hopkins and Victorian Catholicism*. Routledge. [2003] pp. xiii + 185. £50 ($126) ISBN 0 4159 6707 4.

Musselwhite, David. *Social Transformations in Hardy's Tragic Novels: Megamachines and Phantasms*. Palgrave. [2003] pp. 240. $65 ISBN 1 4039 1662 4.

Nardo, Anna K. *George Eliot's Dialogue with John Milton*. UMissp. [2003] pp. xiv + 278. $39.95 ISBN 0 8262 1465 7.

Nash, Andrew, ed. *The Culture of Collected Editions*. Palgrave. [2003] pp. xii + 274. £50 ISBN 1 4039 0266 6.

Nunokawa, Jeff. *Tame Passions of Wilde: The Styles of Manageable Desire*. PrincetonUP. [2003] pp. 176. hb $57.50 ISBN 0 6911 1379 3, pb $18.95 ISBN 0 6911 1380 7.

Nuttall, A.D. *Dead From the Waist Down: Scholars and Scholarship in Literature and the Popular Imagination*. YaleUP. [2003] pp. 240. $26 ISBN 0 3000 9840 5.

Orgel, Stephen. *Imagining Shakespeare: A History of Texts and Visions*. Palgrave. [2003] pp. xvi + 172. £25 ISBN 1 4039 1177 0.

Paddock, Lisa, and Carl Rollyson. *The Brontës A to Z*. FOF. [2003] pp. 252 + xvii. $65 ISBN 0 8160 4302 7.

Palazzo, Lynda. *Christina Rossetti's Feminist Theology*. Palgrave. [2002] pp. xiv + 165. £40 ($60) ISBN 0 3339 2033 3.

Paris, Bernard J. *Rereading George Eliot: Changing Responses to her Experiments in Life*. SUNY. [2003] pp. 224. $57.50 ISBN 0 7914 5833 4.

Peterson, Linda H., ed. *Wuthering Heights by Emily Brontë*. St Martin's. [2003] pp. 532. $11.95 ISBN 0 3122 5686 8.

Phillips, W.M.M. *Nightmares of Anarchy: Language and Cultural Change, 1870–1914*. BuckUP. [2003] pp. 240. $47.50 ISBN 0 8387 5525 9.

Picker, John M. *Victorian Soundscapes*. OUP. [2003] pp. 220. $74 ISBN 0 1951 5190 9.

Piehler, Liana F. *Spatial Dynamics and Female Development in Victorian Art and Novels: Creating a Woman's Space*. Lang. [2003] pp. 178. $58.95 ISBN 0 8204 6201 2.

Pite, Ralph, and John Mullan, gen. eds. *Lives of Victorian Literary Figures: Eliot, Dickens and Tennyson*. P&C. [2003] pp. 1,200. $460 ISBN 1 8519 6759 1.

Plunkett, John. *Queen Victoria: First Media Monarch*. OUP. [2003] pp. x + 256. £19.99 ISBN 0 1992 5392 7.

Pollock, Mary Sanders. *Elizabeth Barrett and Robert Browning: A Creative Partnership*. Ashgate. [2003] pp. 248. £45 ($79.95) ISBN 0 7546 3328 4.

Potter, Simon. *News and the British World: The Emergence of an Imperial Press System, 1876–1922*. Clarendon. [2003] pp. xiii + 246. £50 ISBN 0 1992 6512 7.

Radford, Andrew D. *Thomas Hardy and the Survivals of Time*. Ashgate. [2003] pp. 272. $69.95 ISBN 0 7546 0778 X.

Ramamurthy, Anandi, *Imperial Persuaders: Images of Africa and Asia in British Advertising*. Studies in Imperialism. ManUP. [2003] pp. xv + 234. pb £16.99 ISBN 0 7190 6379 5.

Regard, Frédéric, ed. *Mapping the Self: Space, Identity, Discourse in British Auto/Biography*. USE. [2003] pp. 398. £? ISBN 2 8627 2269 3.

Reisner, Gavriel. *The Death-Ego and the Vital Self: Romances of Desire in Literature and Psychoanalysis*. FDUP. [2003] pp. 277. $55 ISBN 0 8386 3921 6.

Richards, Jeffrey. *Imperialism and Music*. ManUP. [2003] pp. 544. $32 ISBN 0 7190 6143 1.

Richardson, Angelique. *Love and Eugenics in the Late Nineteenth Century: Rational Reproduction and the New Woman*. OUP. [2003] pp. 250. $75 ISBN 0 1981 8700 9.

Ritchie, Anne Thackeray. *The Two Thackerays*. 2 vols. AMS Press. [2003] pp. 830. $215 ISBN 0 4046 1483 3.

Roberts, Adam C. *Victorian Culture and Society: The Essential Glossary*. Arnold. [2003] pp. 256. $74 ISBN 0 3408 0761 X.

Rodensky, Lisa. *The Crime in Mind: Criminal Responsibility and the Victorian Novel*. OUP. [2003] pp. 275. $72 ISBN 0 1951 5073 2.

Rosenman, Ellen Bayuk. *Unauthorized Pleasures: Accounts of Victorian Erotic Experience*. CornUP. [2003] pp. 231. $18.95 ISBN 0 8014 8856 7.

Rossetti, Christina. *Prose Works of Christina Rossetti* introd. Maria Keaton. 4 vols. Thoemmes/UChicP. [2003] pp. 1,600. $445 ISBN 1 8437 1075 7.

Roy, Donald, ed. *Theatre in Europe: A Documentary History. Romantic and Revolutionary Theatre, 1789–1860*. CUP. [2003] pp. xxv +558. £90 ISBN 0 5212 5080 3.

Saint-Amour, Paul K. *The Copyrights: Intellectual Property and the Literary Imagination*. CornUP. [2003] pp. 281. $35 ISBN 0 8014 4077 7.

Sanders, Andrew. *Charles Dickens*. OUP. [2003] pp. 234. $9.95 ISBN 0 1928 4048 7.

Sawyer, Robert. *Victorian Appropriations of Shakespeare: George Eliot, A.C. Swinburne, Robert Browning, and Charles Dickens*. AUP. [2003] pp. 176. £25 ($38.50) ISBN 0 8386 3970 4.

Schacker, Jennifer. *National Dreams: The Remaking of Fairy Tales in Nineteenth-Century England*. UPennP. [2003] pp. 198. $39.95 ISBN 0 8122 3697 1.

Schilling, Bernard. *The Rain of Years: Great Expectations and the World of Dickens*. URP. [2001] pp. 120. $24.95 ISBN 1 5804 6100 X.

Schoch, Richard W., ed. *Victorian Theatrical Burlesques*. Ashgate. [2003] pp. xlvi +255. £47.50 ISBN 0 7546 3362 4.

Schoolfield, George C. *A Baedecker of Decadence: Charting of Literary Fashion, 1884–1927*. 2. YaleUP. [2003] pp. 416. $45 ISBN 0 3000 4714 2.

Schroeder, Horst. *Additions and Corrections to Richard Ellmann's Oscar Wilde*. Schroeder. [2003] pp. 82 ISBN 3 0001 1696 6.

Senf, Carol A. *Science and Social Science in Bram Stoker's Fiction*. Greenwood. [2002] pp. xii +158. $59.95 ISBN 0 3133 1203 6.

Short, Philip. *In Pursuit of Plants: Experiences of Nineteenth and Early Twentieth Century Plant Collectors*. UWAP. [2003] pp. 352. $45 ISBN 1 8762 6898 0.

Sicher, Efraim. *Rereading the City/Rereading Dickens: Representation, the Novel, and Urban Realism*. AMS. [2003] pp. 427. $87.50 ISBN 0 4046 4459 7.

Slinn, E. Warwick. *Victorian Poetry as Cultural Critique: The Politics of Performative Language*. UPVirginia. [2003] pp. 224. £26.95 ($39.50) ISBN 0 8139 2166 X.

Sloan, John. *Oscar Wilde*. OUP. [2003] pp. 225. $9.95 ISBN 0 1928 4064 9.

Small, Helen, and Trudi Tate, eds. *Literature, Science, Psychoanalysis, 1830–1970: Essays in Honour of Gillian Beer*. OUP. [2003] pp. 320. $74 ISBN 0 1992 6667 0.

Smith, Andrew, and William Hughes, eds. *Empire and the Gothic: The Politics of Genre*. Palgrave. [2003] pp. xiv +248. $62 ISBN 0 3339 8405 6.

Smith, Graham. *Dickens and the Dream of Cinema*. ManUP. [2003] pp. 240. £14.99 ISBN 0 7190 5563 6.

Smith, Walter E. *Anthony Trollope: A Bibliography of his First American Editions 1858–1884, with Photographic Reproductions of Bindings and Titlepages*. Heritage. [2003] pp. xxiii +301. $95 ISBN 0 9665 3621 5.

Speake, Jennifer, ed. *The Literature of Travel and Exploration: An Encyclopedia*. 3 vols. Routledge. [2003] pp. 1,520. $495 ISBN 1 5795 8247 8.

Stedman, Gesa. *Stemming the Torrent: Expressions and Control in the Victorian Discourses on Emotions, 1830–1872*. Ashgate. [2002] pp. 266. $79 ISBN 0 7546 0643 0.

Steward, D.H., ed. *Kipling's America: Travel Letters, 1889–1895*. ELT. [2003] pp. 386. $40 ISBN 0 9443 1817 7.

Taylor, Jonathan. *Mastery and Slavery in Victorian Writing*. Palgrave. [2003] pp. x + 229. $52.50 ISBN 0 3339 9312 8.

Thirlwell, Angela. *William and Lucy: The Other Rossettis*. YaleUP. [2003] pp. 352. $45 ISBN 0 3001 0200 3.

Thompson, Bruce, ed. *The Literal Imagination: Selected Essays by Ian Watt*. SPSS. [2002] pp. 300. $22.95 ISBN 0 9306 6425 6.

Thorn, Jennifer, ed. *Writing British Infanticide: Child Murder, Gender, and Print, 1722–1859*. UDelP. [2003] pp. 296. $52.50 ISBN 0 8741 3819 1.

Thornton, R.K.R., with Caroline Dowson, eds. *The Collected Poems of Ernest Dowson*. BirminghamUP. [2003] pp. xxvi +270. £19.95 ($37) ISBN 1 9024 5947 4.

Treuherz, Julian, Elizabeth Prettejohn, and Edwin Becker. *Dante Gabriel Rossetti*. T&H. [2003] pp. 247. $45 ISBN 0 5000 9316 4.

Vizetelly & Compan(ies). *A Complex Tale of Victorian Printing and Publishing*. Exhibition catalogue, with essays by Marie Elena Korey, Yannick Portebois, Dorothy E. Speirs and Richard Landon. Thomas Fisher Rare Books Library. UTorP. [2003] pp. 140. $CAN20 ISBN 0 7727 6044 6.

Wade, Stephen. *In My Own Shire: Region and Belonging in British Writing, 1840–1970*. Praeger. [2003] pp. 192. $63.95 ISBN 0 3133 2182 5.

Waggoner, Diane, ed. *'The Beauty of Life': William Morris and the Art of Design*. T&H. [2003] pp. 176. $27.50 ISBN 0 5002 8434 2.

Warner, Val, ed. *Charlotte Mew: Collected Poems and Selected Prose*. Carcanet. [2003] pp. 124. $15.95 ISBN 1 8575 4706 3.

Weedon, Alexis. *Victorian Publishing: The Economics of Book Production for a Mass Market, 1836–1916*. Ashgate. [2003] pp. xvi +212. £45 ISBN 0 7546 3527 9.

Wettlaufer, Alexandra K. *In the Mind's Eye: The Visual Impulse in Diderot, Baudelaire and Ruskin*. Rodopi. [2003] pp. 310. $66 ISBN 9 0420 1035 5.

Wheatley, Kim, ed. *Romantic Periodicals and Print Culture*. Cass. [2003] pp. ix + 173. pb £18.99 ISBN 0 7146 8437 6.

White, Paul. *Thomas Huxley: Making the 'Man of Science'*. CUP. [2003] pp. 222. $60 ISBN 0 5216 4019 9.

Wilkinson, Glenn. *Depictions and Images of War in Edwardian Newspapers, 1899–1914*. Palgrave. [2003] pp. xiv + 185. £45 ISBN 0 3337 1743 0.

Williams, Leslie. *Daniel O'Connell, the British Press, and the Irish Famine: Killing Remarks*. Ashgate. [2003] pp. 402. $79.95 ISBN 0 7546 0553 1.

Willis, Chris, ed. *The Trail of the Serpent by Mary Elizabeth Braddon*. Modern Library. [2003] pp. 462. $13.95 ISBN 0 8129 6678 3.

Wood, Marcus. *Slavery, Empathy and Pornography*. OUP. [2002] pp. 478. $35 ISBN 0 1981 8720 3.

Wright, T.R. *Hardy and his Readers*. Palgrave. [2003] pp. x + 241. £45 ($65) ISBN 0 3339 6260 5.

Ziter, Edward. *The Orient on the Victorian Stage*. CUP. [2003] pp. ix + 235. £45 ISBN 0 5218 1829 X.

XIV

Modern Literature

JULIAN COWLEY, COLIN GRAHAM, CHRIS HOPKINS, ANNE FOGARTY, BETHAN JONES, NANCY PAXTON, JOHN BRANNIGAN, STEVE NICHOLSON, ALEKS SIERZ AND JO GILL

This chapter has seven sections: 1. General; 2. Pre-1945 Fiction; 3. Post-1945 Fiction; 4. Pre-1950 Drama; 5. Post-1950 Drama; 6. Pre-1950 Poetry; 7. Post-1950 Poetry. Section 1(*a*) is by Julian Cowley; section 1(*b*) is by Colin Graham; section 2(*a*) is by Chris Hopkins; section 2(*b*) is by Anne Fogarty; section 2(*c*) is by Bethan Jones; section 2(*d*) is by Nancy Paxton; section 3 is by John Brannigan; section 4 is by Steve Nicholson; section 5 is by Aleks Sierz; section 6 is by Jo Gill; section 7 is by John Brannigan. The sections on the English novel 1900–1930 and on Irish poetry have been omitted this year; 2003 publications in these areas will be covered in *YWES* 85.

1. General

(a) British

David Ellison casts himself as Virgil to his readers' Dante in prefatory remarks to *Ethics and Aesthetics in European Modernist Literature*. He also suggests that his book can be read either as 'literary-historical chronology' or for its 'structural musicality' (p. xi). That degree of compositional self-awareness is appropriate for a shrewd and sophisticated critical project, which insists that modernism 'cannot be studied independently of its figuration in the uncanny' (p. 53), figuration that manifests both fear and desire. Ellison argues that the uncanny has become the sublime for our age and takes Freud's 'Das Unheimliche' as a key text for his trajectory into reading twentieth-century literature. That essay and the Hoffman tale that underlies it are used to illuminate theoretical difficulties of framing the aesthetic within the ethical. Preliminary to this he explores the delineation and interplay of aesthetic and ethical spheres in Kant and Kierkegaard. The second part of the book addresses potent foregrounding of the aesthetic in late Romantic work by Baudelaire, Wagner, and Nietzsche; Alain-Fournier's *Le Grand*

Year's Work in English Studies, Volume 84 (2005) © The English Association; all rights reserved. For permissions, please email: journals.permissions@oxfordjournals.org

doi: 10.1093/ywes/mai014

Meaulnes is situated at a crucial point of transition between fading Romanticism and burgeoning modernism, and 'the narrative emergence of uncanniness as territory' (p. 133) is charted in fiction by Proust, Kafka, Conrad, Gide, and Woolf. The uncanny is identified as radical otherness that carries these representative modernist texts beyond 'formal symmetries and moral certainties' (p. 134). An Epilogue brings Kafka and Blanchot into suggestive proximity.

Paul Sheehan's *Modernism, Narrative and Humanism* shows modernist novels by Conrad, Lawrence, Woolf, and Beckett engaged in exploration of 'the modalities of the inhuman' (pp. 22–3) in order to evade familiar narrative constraints and to escape the grip of Victorian liberalism's humanistic discourse. *Lord Jim* and *Nostromo* are read in relation to Schopenhauer's philosophy to elucidate Conrad's sense of a mechanistic relationship between human beings and the world. Lawrence's literary aesthetic is juxtaposed with Heidegger's phenomenology in order to clarify the nature of the novelist's 'agonistic antihumanism' (p. 120) and his enduring fascination with issues of transcendence. Woolf's 'metamorphic ahumanism' (p. 149) in *Mrs Dalloway* and *To the Lighthouse* is found to undo the assumptions and aspirations of the *Bildungsroman* and the *Künstlerroman* traditions. Struggle between the animal and the mechanical is declared to offer a 'minimal, *performative* affirmation' (p. 179) in Beckett's fiction. In the course of these studies Sheehan charts 'loss of the conditions necessary for narratability' (p. 182). A 'postnarrative' orientation is then identified in the writings of Levinas and Foucault.

Fiction should locate itself 'not in the moment that passes, nor in the decision that lasts, but in the intuition that lingers', where 'perceptual totality' may be achieved (p. 1). Ramifications of that tenet, shared by Pater, James, Hardy, Proust, Conrad, Woolf, and Ford, are examined critically and richly by Jesse Matz in *Literary Impressionism and Modernist Aesthetics*. The impression hovers between feeling and thought, an aesthetic aspiration, although Matz is alert to its changing philosophical status from Hume to Derrida. The visual arts are mentioned only in passing, but subtle evaluation of the viability and significance of inter-art relationships is implied throughout and is at times addressed explicitly. Sexuality, gender, race or class concerns are brought to bear on texts including *Marius the Epicurean*, *Heart of Darkness*, *Mrs Dalloway*, and *The Good Soldier*. Matz shows the development of modernist assumptions and priorities in the aesthetic successes of impressionist fiction; he also shows the failure of this array of associated literary orientations to bear the burden of the writers' various socio-cultural desires and expectations.

Darwin's cousin Francis Galton formulated the basis for the study of eugenics in the late nineteenth century. Donald J. Childs investigates Galton's legacy in *Modernism and Eugenics*, discovering interest in this science of purported race improvement in writing by Woolf, Eliot, and Yeats. Childs finds that 'the eugenical opinion that surrounded Woolf seems to have converged in her own mind on the question of abortion' (p. 35). *Mrs Dalloway* is read for other indications, and a 'eugenical logic of inheritance' (p. 58), enabling conception of a woman-centred literary tradition, is detected in *A Room of One's Own*. Eliot's scholarly attraction to biology and heredity is shown to have precipitated a eugenicist position in his views on breeding and birthrate, in his personal conduct within marriage, and in allusions to prostitution and sexually transmitted disease in *The Waste Land*. Childs suggests that Yeats's interest in eugenics arose long before it found overt expression in his writings of the 1930s. Yeats's membership of the Eugenics Society and his undergoing a theoretically sexually rejuvenating Steinach operation are both touched upon. His plays are examined for their concern with heredity and degeneration, stimulated by his reading of Allan Eastlake's *The Oneida Community*. The concluding chapter gauges the impact on Yeats of Auguste Forel's book *The Sexual Question*.

A meeting in January 1939 between Freud and Leonard and Virginia Woolf provides a starting point for Kylie Valentine's *Psychoanalysis, Psychiatry and Modern Literature*, a study of disciplinary interrelatedness, exploring connections between scientific and artistic understanding of behaviour and personality. HD's account of her session of analysis with Freud in 1933 is taken as a key intersection of literary modernism and psychoanalysis. A chapter surveys aspects of the psychoanalytic and physicalist strands of psychiatry in Britain during the inter-war years. Valentine argues that 'modernist literature introduces a new recognition of the sexed production of madness and feminist analysis of this production' (p. 101). She looks at representations of Virginia Woolf's life and work, including her own deliberate translations of 'cultural and clinical representations of madness circulating through the modernist field' (p. 142). A broader view of 'modernist madness' that examines their diaries as well as their fiction is offered through an account of Antonia White and Emily Holmes Coleman (p. 163).

Thormählen, ed., *Rethinking Modernism*, is the outcome of a research project testing the term 'modernism' within sceptical perspectives. Vincent Sherry finds loss of confidence in rational language during the Great War to have been an enabling factor for Eliot, Pound, and Woolf. David Trotter tracks the will-to-abstraction in writings of Wyndham Lewis and Hulme and finds it 'a psychopathology of expertise' (p. 36). Lennart Nyberg discerns in the professionalization of poetry a route of continuity from Romanticism to modernism. Jewel Spears Brooker brings Levinas's critique of modernist aesthetics to bear on Eliot and Pound's use of language. Marianne Thormählen's own contribution provocatively finds academic posterity culpable of generating a false gulf between Georgian traditionalists and modernist experimentalism. Claude Rawson interrogates contrived primitivism connecting Eliot with Conrad's Kurtz. Lars-Håkan Svensson takes stock of 'intricate transformations of classical poems' (p. 128) by Pound and HD. Michael Bell takes D.H. Lawrence as a test case for the meaning of modernism, a writer who critiques that category while simultaneously being revealed in its light. Derek Attridge looks for ways to reconcile his taste for both *Ulysses* and Norwegian writer Sigrid Undset's novel *Kristin Lavransdatter*. Edna Longley stringently interrogates assumptions concerning Anglo-American modernism in the light of selected Irish poetic practices from Yeats to Ciaran Carson. Stan Smith traces some of Eliot's roles in authorizing the status of 'modernism' between 1920 and 1940. Christopher Innes weighs that term critically in the balance of theatrical productions by Yeats, Eliot, and Beckett, and Erik Hedling situates it within the history of academic study of film. Stefan Holander witnesses

Wallace Stevens suspended between modernist and postmodernist categories, and Gunilla Florby evaluates the contributions of Frederic Jameson and Linda Hutcheon to postmodernist debate. The editor appends a useful bibliography.

Pound's observation 'It can't all be in one language' and Walter Benjamin's 'Translation is a mode' (p. v) are used by Steven G. Yao as epigraphs to his *Translation and the Languages of Modernism*. This study acknowledges that 'feats of translation not only accompanied and helped to give rise to, but sometimes even themselves constituted, some of the most significant Modernist literary achievements in English' (p. 3). Yao posits a programme of cultural renewal performed within a coherent Anglo-American modernist agenda reliant in part upon translations that granted access to the past and other cultures yet were in themselves a generative writing practice. Gender and sexual politics are addressed in chapters on Pound's departures from translation orthodoxy in *Cathay* and *Homage to Sextus Propertius* and on HD's poetic liaisons with classical Greek texts. Yeats as translator is considered in the context of Irish cultural politics. Pound's interest in Confucianism is scrutinized for its political implications. *Finnegans Wake* is read as a kind of monumental culmination of modernist engagement with translation as a literary mode. Robert Lowell and Louis and Celia Zukofsky are viewed as inheritors of modernism's radical approaches, translating in ways that decouple absolutely 'the linguistic and literary dimensions of the practice' (p. 21). Heaney's *Beowulf* features briefly in Yao's concluding remarks.

In *Modernist Fiction, Cosmopolitanism and the Politics of Community*, Jessica Berman argues that community should be viewed as a narrative process and sets out 'to demonstrate modernism's historical and political engagement with the dual question of community and cosmopolitanism' (p. 4). Her critical attention, finely honed through sensitive encounters with promoters of a wide yet pertinent range of theoretical positions, is directed to texts by James, Proust, Woolf, and Stein. James is read within a nexus of ideas concerning cosmopolitanism and femininity that arose in the American popular press at the end of the nineteenth century. A contemporary discourse of Jewish identity is used to disclose 'a coherent politics of marginality' (p. 4) within *A la recherche du temps perdu*. An 'anti-fascist, feminist model of community' (p. 5) is found in *Orlando* and *The Waves* when they are scrutinized in the light of a comparable model embodied by the British Women's Co-operative Guild. Nomadic and polyvocal subjectivities are discerned, connected intimately with particularities of topography and physical movement, in radical narratives by Stein written at a time when geographical study was undergoing fundamental change away from the descriptive. Berman affirms the pivotal importance of gender issues in the dynamics of community, and contends that 'modernist fiction challenges our ability to restrict social identity to civic consensus or the public politics of recognition' (p, 27).

Beckett's *Waiting for Godot* provides an unexpected starting point for Sarah Cole's *Modernism, Male Friendship, and the First World War*. The play is used to shed initial light on the value assigned to male intimacy by preceding generations, and on the fragility of such friendship. Texts of *fin-de-siècle* Hellenism are then used to read the male body and homoerotic desire, culminating in the reassessment of Forster as an interrogator of narrative containment and a theorizer of modernity. A chapter on Conrad's fiction finds a crisis that entangles literary authority and male comradeship within a profoundly troubled imperial discourse. Another traces a breakdown of faith in comradeship as registered in war poetry and as appropriated in writings of the post-war period by figures such as Vera Brittain, Eliot, and Woolf. The concluding chapter takes Lawrence's representation of friendless masculinity as focal point for extensive and detailed discussion of the social and political problems besetting Britain in the wake of the war.

'On or about the year 1913 the idea of progress changed' (p. 1); Louise Blakeney Williams adapts Woolf's famous statement concerning human nature to match her concern with cyclic views of the past in *Modernism and the Ideology of History*. Ford, Pound, Hulme, Yeats, and D.H. Lawrence are treated as a group loosely affiliated around cyclical conceptions of history arrived at following dalliance with medievalism and progressive notions. Williams offers a broad overview of contemporary political problems and illustrates the radically conservative reaction of these writers before outlining the emergence for each of a stabilizing sense of cyclic historical patterning. A chapter examines the influence of Asian aesthetics, philosophy and social organization; another assesses the impact of various strands of post-impressionist visual art. The advent of the cyclical historical model is identified in the Vorticist alliance, Yeats's *A Vision*, and the structure of Ford's *The Good Soldier* and Lawrence's *The Rainbow*. Its consolidation is witnessed in the context of the Great War and its traumatized aftermath. In her Conclusion Williams makes her own fundamental tenet explicit, asserting that 'cyclic views of history are realistic and optimistic' (p. 212).

Lisa Colletta's *Dark Humor and Social Satire in the Modern British Novel* examines early twentieth-century novelists whose fiction imposes kinds of comedic order upon a world perceived in characteristically modernist terms as chaotic and bereft of intrinsic value. She argues that there are continuities of concern and shared perspectives between innovative writers such as Woolf and formally more cautious makers of darkly humorous narratives such as Ivy Compton-Burnett, Evelyn Waugh, Anthony Powell, or Aldous Huxley. In order to underline affinities between comedy and modernism, as well as postmodernism, Colletta cites Jean-François Lyotard's suggestion that humour says that there is no single point of view that can be considered correct. Her first chapter examines the terms of a move away from the corrective critique of folly and injustice to a kind of resilient resignation. Later chapters look at Woolf's use in *Mrs Dalloway* of 'comedic strategies to confront the pain and oppression of her historical moment' (p. 57), the gloomy domestic stasis of Compton-Burnett's *A House and its Head*, Waugh's comedy of senseless activity in *Vile Bodies*, and the grim understatement of Anthony Powell's first novel *Afternoon Men*. All represent, Colletta claims, 'the triumph of narcissism' (p. 35), counteracting continuous threats to the individual self from accumulated social pressures or random and meaningless occurrences.

Georgian Bloomsbury is the third and concluding volume of S.P. Rosenbaum's account of the early literary history of the Bloomsbury Group, addressing the period between Roger Fry's initial post-impressionist exhibition and the outbreak of the First World War. It is indeed a 'literary history'—emphasis falls squarely upon the work rather than the personalities involved. The setting and the cast need little introduction so Rosenbaum is able to concentrate on description and comparison of indicative writings. Clive Bell's *Art* is considered as the first of Bloomsbury's manifestos and as a volume of literary post-impressionist polemics. Rosenbaum examines the authorial problems that beset Forster as he struggled to write *Maurice* and his unfinished, fragmentary novel *Arctic Summer*. Strachey's development as a writer is traced through the pages of his *Landmarks in French Literature*. Desmond McCarthy is the central figure in a chapter devoted to Georgian literary journalism. Woolf's *The Voyage Out* is read in terms of Bloomsbury preoccupations, and its critical reception is scrutinized. Leonard Woolf's awareness of an uneasy relationship between his Jewishness and Bloomsbury values is considered in the light of his novel *The Wise Virgins*. Rosenbaum affirms consistency between the old Bloomsbury of these pre-war years and the esteemed productions of the later Bloomsbury.

'What Whistler and Ruskin have most in common', proposes Lesley Higgins in her intelligently polemical *The Modernist Cult of Ugliness*, 'is a masculinist need to exercise control over a category of value that is for them wholly, disturbingly feminized' (p. 30). Strident in their aftermath, she argues, came the masculinist modernism of Pound and Wyndham Lewis. A homophobic turn against Pater is indicated through writings by Lewis and Eliot. Marinetti is included among those proclaiming 'the inadequacy of conventional beauty in a modernized world' (p. 158) and competing to produce and extol ugliness as a measure of masculine difference. American poetry furnishes material for the last third of the book, with the gendered topography of the modern city providing a critical focus that discloses male poets handling alienation and metaphysical discomfiture while women poets work towards self-definition after situating themselves in constructive relation to life-affirming, non-urban landscapes. Higgins's basic assertion is that 'transformative reading practices are what the heterogeneous "conditions" of modern literature demand' (p. 230).

Peter Brooker's *Modernity and Metropolis* offers glimpses of Pound and Eliot in London, and Langston Hughes and his associates in Harlem, before following less well worn paths through the ethnicities of contemporary Britishness, as evidenced in literature by Kureishi, Rushdie, and Zadie Smith, the reimagination of London by Iain Sinclair and others, and urban mapping practised by the likes of Paul Auster, Sarah Schulman, and William Gibson. Brooker is alert to disjunction between modernism and modernity, and also addresses continuities and breaks between modernist and postmodernist assumptions and practices. Films as well as written texts are drawn into his probing of urban formations, the metropolis repeatedly fabricated anew in imagination and so capable, he argues, of sustaining and invigorating critical culture.

The basic thesis of Peter Barry's *Contemporary British Poetry and the City* is that 'contemporary poetry is in trouble' (p. 3) and that any serious rescue attempt requires the re-establishment of a vital connection between poets and experience of the urban. Various approaches to writing the inner city are examined through carefully focused studies of poems by Ken Edwards, Barry MacSweeney,

John Barnie, Peter Reading, and Ken Smith. Birmingham poet Roy Fisher is for Barry 'a kind of laureate of the urban-prosaic', 'the quintessential city poet' (p. 9), and he is allocated a chapter to himself. Other chapters look at the London epics of Iain Sinclair, Allen Fisher, and Aidan Dun, and at significant poets of Hull and Liverpool. Ciaran Carson, Edwin Morgan, and W.N. Herbert are read as poets of post-industrial urban decline. Barry touches upon the work of Deryn Rees-Jones and Denise Riley, but he expresses regret at the limited attention he is able to pay in this book to women poets. Still, his study offers helpfully attentive readings of writers who have registered 'the urban trauma and dislocation of our times' (p. 242).

Lynn Wells examines six prominent instances of British self-referential fiction in *Allegories of Telling*: John Fowles's *The French Lieutenant's Woman*, Angela Carter's *The Infernal Desire Machines of Doctor Hoffman*, Graham Swift's *Waterland*, A.S. Byatt's *Possession: A Romance*, and Salman Rushdie's *Midnight's Children* and *The Satanic Verses*. All are shown in the light of appropriate theory to be at once overtly metafictional and profoundly connected to the world beyond the text. Particular attention is paid to each novel's concern for the reader's role, involvement with intertextuality and literary tradition, and engagement with the nexus of history, representation, and narrative. Wells's analysis makes effective use of notions of textual seduction, derived from critic Ross Chambers, and, as her chosen title suggests, she draws throughout upon Paul de Man's insight that 'any narrative is primarily the allegory of its own reading' (quoted on page 1). The concluding chapter suggests that, although Pat Barker's historical fiction appears to restore primacy to straightforward realist narrative techniques, her novels are designed to prompt some reflection upon the problematic nature of fictional reconstructions of the past.

Beer and Bennett, eds., *Special Relationships: Anglo-American Affinities and Antagonisms 1854–1936*, includes Janet Beer and Ann Heilmann's collaborative essay '"If I Were A Man": Charlotte Perkins Gilman, Sarah Grand and the Sexual Education of Girls'. Fiction and theoretical or polemical texts by these two authors are cited to show their promotion within a maternalist perspective of feminist sex education contrary to prevailing moral and medical orthodoxy. Katherine Joslin contributes '"Embattled Tendencies": Wharton, Woolf and the Nature of Modernism', exploring nuances in the tempered antipathy between those two writers. Joslin argues that the nature of modernism 'is not a radical shift from traditional to experimental literary forms but rather a sharp dialogue, here a transatlantic dialogue, over literary possibilities' (p. 204). Indeed, she suggests, modernism actually comes into being through such 'passionate disagreement over form and content' (p. 219). Avril Horner and Sue Zlosnik identify the tense co-presence of T.S. Eliot's high cultural authority and a Gothic legacy in Waugh's *A Handful of Dust* and Barnes's *Nightwood*. Kate Fullbrook looks into the friendship of Gertrude Stein and Alfred North Whitehead and perceives a marked degree of intellectual harmony between them, chiming even in their conceptions of genius.

Charles E. Gannon's *Rumors of War and Infernal Machines* is subtitled 'Technomilitary Agenda-Setting in American and British Speculative Fiction'. The book investigates an exchange between future-war fiction and political entities in Victorian and Edwardian Britain and in the USA through and beyond the Cold War. In early chapters Gannon skilfully deploys a range of discursive materials to discuss and analyse fictional anticipations of a technologically enabled 'Great War'; William Le Queux's novelistic exploitation of Edwardian fears concerning imminent invasion; literary premonitions and promotions of the tank, the submarine, and the aeroplane; and Wells's more remotely futuristic projections, including atomic weaponry. He then addresses America's rise to superpower status accompanied by literary imagining of nuclear destruction, death rays, cyborg soldiers, and starship troopers.

Meek and Watson, eds., *Coming of Age in Children's Literature* opens with Watson's musings on the theme of maturation and the history of biographical continuity in fictional writing. He claims that 'in Defoe's fiction lie the origins of children's fiction' (p. 5), and he finds a significant subsequent line of descent from Alcott's *Little Women*. Through a series of leaps he reaches 'post-modernism' and concludes with mention of Philippa Pearce, Cynthia Voigt, and Jan Mark, the writers addressed in the three chapters that follow. Meek writes on Pearce and Mark, Watson on Voigt. In each case the emphasis falls upon representation of critical moments in a child's intellectual and emotional development, closely related to specific texts. Watson affirms that 'maturation—like reading these novels—is collaborative and exploratory' (p. 121).

Hazel Bell, a freelance indexer and formerly editor of the journal of the Society of Indexers, has made an index for A.S. Byatt's serial quartet of novels which the author has found an illuminating map of the workings of her own mind. Byatt furnishes, in turn, a characteristically astute foreword for Bell, ed., *Indexers and Indexes in Fact and Fiction*, declaring that 'a good index is a work of art and science, order and chance, delight and usefulness' (p. 16). Bell's introductory note very briefly addresses the history of indexes and their compilers. Examples then follow, excerpts from indexes, isolated and glossed to shed light on their character and enhance their capacity to divert and entertain. Factual instances start with St Augustine, then Robert Burton. Twentieth-century entries include Shaw, Norman Douglas, musicologist Donald Tovey, and Julian Barnes. The section on fiction and verses with indexes starts with *The Dunciad* and includes Woolf's *Orlando*, Nabokov's *Pale Fire*, George Perec's *Life: A User's Manual*, Malcolm Bradbury's *My Strange Quest for Mensonge*, Lucy Ellmann's *Sweet Desserts*, and J.G. Ballard's *War Fever*. A third section cites indexers within fiction by writers including Angela Thirkell, Barbara Pym, Graham Swift, and Penelope Lively. As well as providing plenty to amuse, Bell's selection is particularly effective in disclosing political or otherwise satirical barbs lurking within ostensibly functional listings.

(b) Irish

In recent years Irish literary studies have merrily crested the waves of commemoration. Scholarly activities to mark the bicentenary of the Act of Union of 1801 set off a minor commemoration industry in 2001, following the success of the 200th anniversary of the 1798 rebellion. While 2003 was yet another bicentenary (of Robert Emmet's rebellion, which had some literary connections), the year 2003 was primarily marked by a sense of preparation for

2004. Being both the 100th anniversary of the establishment of the Abbey Theatre and a hundred years since the 1904 setting of the events in Joyce's *Ulysses*, 2004 was a more purely literary anniversary than its immediate predecessors. The year 2003 was, thankfully, more than merely a warm-up act for the year to follow. Commemorations these days bring their own ready-made controversies, since no one likes to be seen celebrating the past too naively. In the case of the Irish Literary Revival this has meant that existing 'orthodox' narratives of the Revival were bound to be challenged by new modes of reading and new scholarly interests. This was certainly long overdue. The Revival's critical reception has been bound too closely to its own self-image. Scholarship in 2003 saw some of the micro-narratives of the Revival period recovered. Inevitably, it was also a year in which new readings of the Revival, a period of cataclysmic change in Ireland, were inflected by the very different changes which Ireland underwent in the final decade of the twentieth century and the first years of the current century.

The special issue of *Irish University Review* (*IUR* 33:i[2003]), 'New Perspectives on the Irish Literary Revival', delivers on its editor's promise to provide 'a new type of literary history of the Revival'. As Margaret Kelleher notes in her introduction (*IUR* 33:i[2003] vii–xii), 'The materialist and historicist approaches employed here recover the history of ideas and beliefs, institutions and movements, periodicals and publishers, while also restoring long-neglected individuals … to attention' (p. xi). So Eve Patten, for example, writes with her customary authority and clarity on 'Ireland's "Two Cultures" Debate: Victorian Science and the Literary Revival' (*IUR* 33:i[2003] 1–13), showing that the origins of the Revival, which often seems to have arrived at a moment of *fin-de-siècle* airiness, are in fact entwined, in their reaction against Victorianism, with the scientific culture which late Victorian Ireland was trying to embrace. Patten notes the rift in Revival discourse around science (which was understood in the crudest of forms by those 'opposed' to it). John Eglinton's evocative notion that the 'kinematograph', for example, '*is*' the poetry of an age of science was, as Patten notes, swiftly knocked back by Yeats and Æ, who were intent on a spiritual rather than materialist trajectory for the Revival's future. Patten suggests that this version of the Revival has contributed to a general marginalization of science as part of Irish culture in the twentieth century. In the same issue of *IUR* Nicholas Allen's essay 'States of Mind: Science, Culture and the Irish Intellectual Revival, 1900–30' (*IUR* 33:i[2003] 150–64) suggests a slightly less allergic relationship between science and the Revival than that described in Patten's essay. Allen ranges over literary and cultural controversies of the Revival and sees scientific interest as widespread in the period and as something 'mutually accessible', and, in that sense, sees science as a refuge from the sundered cultural forms of affiliation which the Revival promoted.

Nicholas Allen's book on George Russell, *George Russell (Æ) and the New Ireland, 1905–30*, was also published in 2003. Russell's varied intellectual life is covered in fine detail by Allen, and the Russell who emerges from the book is forward-thinking and often visionary, and this in much more positive ways than he is usually given credit for. Rather than a fey mystic, Allen's Russell is primarily an activist, involved in editing journals and organizing the co-operative agriculture movement, as well as imagining an alternative future. Allen's overarching argument is that the received view of the Revival is restrictive and too 'literary'. He argues that: 'Irish writing in the late nineteenth and twentieth centuries was … a literature committed to the moment, part of a cultural fabric that held writing to be one expression of minds that could also be consumed with agriculture, art, co-operation, education and, sometimes, revolution'. Leeann Lane's contribution to *IUR*, '"It is in the cottages and farmers' houses that the nation is born": Æ's *Irish Homestead* and the Cultural Revival' (*IUR* 33:i[2003] 165–81), similarly examines the cultural dynamics of Æ's involvement in the Co-operative movement.

P.J. Mathews's *Revival: The Abbey Theatre, Sinn Féin, the Gaelic League and the Co-operative Movement* covers similar ground in that it is interested in binding back together the separated strands indicated in the book's title. Underlying the book is a conviction which is slightly different to some of this year's other contributors on Revival revisions (and an essay by Mathews is also included in the special issue of *IUR*: 33:i[2003] 99–116). Mathews appears to be reliant on the notion that the Revival has appeared in critical discourse as 'a duplicitous Ascendancy project' (as Richard Kirkland, quoting Robbie Meredith, calls it—see Kirkland's essay discussed below). Mathews sets out to show that the Revival was not, after all, Ascendancy leadership of the benighted people (or 'people-nation' as he bizarrely describes it, or them). But, for this reader at least, this book is disappointingly vague in its arguments and at times banal (to set out to 'prove' 'that, between 1899 and 1905, Ireland was rapidly evolving and mutating both politically and culturally in all kinds of interesting ways' is to set out to prove the undeniable). The book is at its best when animated by its central conviction, though this continually collapses along the way, such as when the reactionary D.P. Moran is described as a 'pragmatist'. Mathews claims to be carrying out a 'materialist' reading of the period; his method seems much more to be a series of reactions against sometimes misconstrued straw men.

At the end of the book Mathews suggests that the Revival as he has discussed it may have much to teach us about Ireland in the globalized twenty-first century. It's not clear what these lessons are, and given the decoupling of EU farm subsidies it is hard to see the Co-operative movement as much of a runner in the current climate. Shaun Richards's '"The outpouring of a morbid, unhealthy mind": The Critical Condition of Synge and McDonagh' (*IUR* 33:i[2003] 201–14) makes a series of concrete textual, thematic, and theatrical connections across the two periods, seeing Martin McDonagh as a complex inheritor of the work (and reception) of Synge. In its way Richards's essay is as provocative in making us rethink our post-Revival legacy as anything published this year.

The Revival's lost textures and submerged politics are rediscovered from many angles in recent scholarship. Selina Guinness, in her article '"Protestant Magic Reappraised": Evangelicalism, Dissent, and Theosophy' (*IUR* 33:i[2003] 14–27), also in the special issue of *Irish University Review*, examines what she quotes Roy Foster as describing as the 'Southern Californian aspect' of Yeats and the Revival more generally. The sometimes outlandish and shifting versions of spiritualism explored by Yeats, Æ, and others as part of the Revival have been described by Foster as a form of 'Protestant Magic', that is, broadly speaking, as a search for a transcendent spiritual belief in the years after Victorian science and evolutionary theory had buffeted traditional Christianity. Guinness pursues and revises Foster's thesis, noting that theosophy (the most influentially global of the cultic pursuits of the Revivalists) had a peculiar complexion (being dominated by northern Protestant converts) and a particular, and nationalist, political complexion in Ireland. Guinness writes that the Dublin Lodge of the Irish theosophical movement 'seems to have offered the Ulster Protestant a new liberty of conscience, and a new way of expressing dissent from an intellectual climate constrained by sectarianism, while remaining vulnerable to the sectarian stereotyping it sought to renounce'. Susan Johnston Graf's article in *Irish Studies Review*, 'Heterodox Religions in Ireland: Theosophy, the Hermetic Society, and the Castle of Heroes' (*ISR* 11:i[2003] 51–9) has similar interests, beginning with the premise that 'discussion of the function of religion in relation to the Irish Literary Renaissance of the late nineteenth and early twentieth centuries usually amounts to a consideration of Protestantism and Catholicism'. It might be argued, in further support of Graf's thesis, that Irish literary criticism has in fact shied away from discussing such basic doctrinal-political differences in any sustained way. As Graf points out, Yeats and Æ, as the main examples, are often referred to as 'Protestant', a label that both assumes a kind of genetically inherited ideology and hides the complex politics of their theosophical and hermetic 'conversions'. Graf usefully outlines the contours of some of the better-known activities of Yeats and his circle in relation to theosophy and its offshoots, though her article's reliance on already published sources in a field which is still largely hidden in the archives slightly hampers its capacity to say something new. There remains much to be discovered and discussed in this strand of Revival revisionism.

The theosophical movement in the Revival period, as Graf and Guinness both point out, had a strongly northern bias to it, and one of the ways in which new narratives of the Revival are beginning to appear is in a critical-historical interest in the regional variation in revivalism which occurred in the northern counties of Ireland, both before and after partition. Richard Kirkland, who has been working in this area for some years now, contributes to the special issue of *IUR* with 'Dialogues of Despair: National Cultural Discourse and the Revival in the North of Ireland, 1900–1920' (*IUR* 33:i[2003] 64–78), a typically well-researched, perceptive, and often amusing piece of scholarship which centres on the career of Cathal O'Byrne, but also sketches out some of the more tellingly offbeat activities of northern revivalists of various hues. Magazines, theatrical performances, 'midgets' dancing Highland reels, and cultural festivals which merge into music hall are sprinkled throughout Kirkland's narrative, constructing a story which sees these elements as bound together by their essential hopelessness, their inability to 'revive' a national(ist) culture in the north, or more pertinently, to prevent partition. Catherine Morris is, like Kirkland, Mary Burgess (see below), and several others, currently engaged in excavating the northern Revival, and in 'Becoming Irish? Alice Milligan and the Revival' (*IUR* 33:i[2003] 79–98) Morris makes a crusading attempt to rescue the not entirely tarnished reputation of Milligan as both writer and politico. While full of interest, Morris's essay serves largely as an introduction to Milligan's writing and thought, and it is to be hoped that her work can engage more fully with Milligan in the future. Morris published another essay on Milligan in 2003, 'In the Enemy's Camp: Alice Milligan and *Fin de Siècle* Belfast' (in Allen and Kelly, eds., *The Cities of Belfast*; discussed further below), which further sketches out the picture.

Morris pays little attention to Milligan's status as yet another 'minor' female writer of the Revival, perhaps because Milligan makes little of the issue herself. Moynagh Sullivan, again in *IUR*, reveals what can be done with conceptually alert close reading in the recuperation of lost writers. Many of the excellent essays in the special issue take a necessarily broad-brush approach to cultural history, raising as many questions about the 'true' story of the Revival as they answer. Sullivan's essay, '"I am not yet delivered of the past": The Poetry of Blanaid Salkeld' (*IUR* 33:i[2003] 182–200), reads Salkeld's poetry, rarely discussed otherwise and only recently available through the *Field Day Anthology of Irish Women's Writing: Irish Women's Writing and Traditions* [2002], in ways that are detailed, informed, and alive to nuance. Sullivan places Salkeld's work at the 'axis on which modernism, nationalism and feminism' (p. 183) coincide, and simple and obvious as this may seem, that combination of an awareness of an international artistic context and a cultural politics beyond national identity means that Sullivan's critique is refreshingly different from many of the other contributors to the special issue.

Finally on this issue of *IUR*, it should be noted that the other essays are of an equally high standard, making this one of the best and most coherent special issues of an Irish journal for some time. The issue also contains excellent essays by Clare Hutton, on 'Joyce and the Institutions of Revivalism' (*IUR* 33:i[2003] 117–32); Brian Ó Conchubhair, on 'The Gaelic Font Controversy: The Gaelic League's (Post-Colonial) Crux' (*IUR* 33:i[2003] 46–63); Eamonn Hughes, on '"The fact of me-ness": Autobiographical Writing in the Revival Period' (*IUR* 33:i[2003] 28–45); and Ben Levitas's 'Plumbing the Depths: Irish Realism and the Working Class from Shaw to O'Casey' (*IUR* 33:i[2003] 133–49).

Georg Grote's *Anglo-Irish Theatre and the Formation of a Nationalist Political Culture Between 1890 and 1930* was one of several Revival-related books published by the Edwin Mellen Press in 2003. Grote's book covers well-trodden ground and does not have much original to add to existing scholarship or interpretation of the texts its covers. It is ambitiously broad in the number of texts it examines, and it does trace several consistent themes through Revival writing. One of these is the much-discussed figure of Ireland as a female symbol—Grote begins with Standish O'Grady's Kathleen and sees it develop into Yeats's *Cathleen ni Houlihan* and beyond. Grote, and indeed P.J. Mathews, share the consistent mistake of naming Yeats's and Lady Gregory's play as *Kathleen Ni Houlihan*, and Grote makes the further error of not recognizing the recently established co-authorship of the play, something which, to say the least, should further complicate its reception.

Eibhear Walshe's edition of Teresa Deevy's plays *Selected Plays of Irish Playwright Teresa Deevy, 1894–1963* was also published by Edwin Mellen in 2003. Deevy, after several rejections, became an Abbey playwright with *Reapers* in 1930. Walshe quotes a marvellously choice extract from Joseph Holloway's diary describing the play: 'Some of the characters attacked religion and others the republicans and so the prejudice of the [Abbey Theatre] Directors was appeased and a bad play accepted … One hoped against hope that something would come along to redeem it but alas nothing did—the young woman who wrote it is stone deaf.' Not very encouraging perhaps, but Holloway's irascible opinion should never be taken as authoritative, and Walshe's edition of Deevy's plays is a welcome addition to the published canon of Irish drama. Jerry Nolan has edited *The Tulira Trilogy of Edward Martyn (1859–1923), Irish Symbolist Dramatist*, also published by Edwin Mellen. Martyn was central to the early years of the Irish theatre which evolved into the Abbey, though by 1904 he had been sidelined from the main movement. Perhaps as a result, his plays have received little attention, and Jerry Nolan has been crusading in Martyn's cause for some time. Here he chooses three of his plays, *The Heather Field* (by far the best known of his works because it was performed along with Yeats's *The Countess Cathleen* in the first season of the Irish Literary Theatre in 1899), *Maeve*, from the following year, and the little known *An Enchanted Sea*, a play which should perhaps remain a historical curiosity. 'The Tulira Trilogy' is a title of Nolan's own invention and it might easily have been altered to include Martyn's later play *The Dream Physician*, which has a dig at his cousin George Moore (described, oddly as a 'friend' by Nolan), and would at least allow Martyn retrospective revenge for the comic version of him which stalks the pages of Moore's *Hail and Farewell.* Like Walshe's Deevy edition, it is useful to have some of Martyn's plays in print again.

Looking beyond the Revival, Paul Delaney is one of the most exciting of a generation of new critics in Irish studies. His essay '"A Marginal Footnote": O'Faolain, the Subaltern, and the Travellers' (*ISR* 11:ii[2003] 155–64) takes further his interest in Travellers and Traveller culture. Delaney is keenly aware of the ethical imperative to acknowledge the ways in which Travellers have been excluded from definitions of Ireland and Irish culture. In addition he is alive to the ways in which this exclusion can, when examined, prise open the neat closures of Irish literary identity. In this essay he discusses how Traveller culture might be understood through the Gramscian-derived notion of the subaltern (filtered through the Indian Subaltern Studies project). In reading several short stories by Sean O'Faolain, however, Delaney finds little new conceptual ground: 'Traveller characters were … prefigured in a characteristically stereotypical fashion.' Whether it is worth constructing a theoretical framework to reveal such deadening disappointment and predictability is a moot point. Nevertheless, Delaney is one of few critics writing today who take the issue of minority identities in Ireland as a serious topic.

Elsewhere in *Irish Studies Review* in 2003, Lynda Prescott discusses 'The Indian Connection in J.G. Farrell's *Troubles*' (*ISR* 11:ii[2003] 165–73) and moves towards a conviction in 'Farrell's awareness of the textuality of history' as part of his 'global theme of empire'. Eóin Flannery, in 'Reading in the Light of *Reading in the Dark*' (*ISR* 11:i[2003] 71–80), presents a persuasive argument that the power of Seamus Deane's novel lies in its engagement with the silences which inhabit ideology, while recognizing that a 'community demands a system of legitimation or an index by which its communal heritage and belief system can be verified'.

Comparative colonial possibilities are at the heart of Irene Boada-Montagut's *Women Write Back: Contemporary Irish and Catalan Short Stories in Colonial*

Context. Boada-Montagut explores short stories by Anne Devlin, Edna O'Brien, Eilísh Ní Duibhne, and Julia O'Faolain, amongst many others, and it is good to see a book which tries to forward a comparative and conceptual agenda at the same time. Also important for recent Irish women's literary production is Imelda Foley's enjoyable *The Girls in the Big Picture: Gender in Contemporary Ulster Theatre*, which, typically for the year, begins with the Ulster Literary Theatre as an alternative to the Dublin-based Literary Revival. The bulk of the book is made up of chapters on Charabanc, Marie Jones, Christina Reid, and Anne Devlin. The final chapter, on Frank McGuinness, is provocative but, despite the author's protestations, still looks a little out of place. Also on recent northern drama, Bernard McKenna's *Rupture, Representation, and the Fashioning of Identity in Drama from the North of Ireland, 1969–1994* is a densely referenced, well argued, and intelligent book.

The New Voices in Irish Criticism conferences continue to generate interest and fresh perspectives in Irish literary studies. In 2003 the proceedings of the fourth conference were published as, simply, Dillane and Kelly, eds., *New Voices in Irish Criticism 4*. As ever, the contents are diverse and short, giving snapshots of work in progress. There is an encouraging amount of work being done on female writers: for example, Marisa Glaser's 'Dethroning the Goddess, Crowning the Woman: Eva Gore-Booth and Augusta Gregory's Mythic Heroines'; Leontia Flynn's 'The Life of the Author: Medbh McGuckian and her Critics'; and Jenny McDonnell's 'Making her own History: Katherine Mansfield's Revolutions'. There are also signs that the 'new' Ireland is beginning to make an impact, at last, on the ways in which Irish literature and culture is being read. Jason King's essay, 'Biographies of Displacement: Irish Refugee Narrative in Historical and Contemporary Perspective', and Patrick Lonergan's 'Recent Irish Theatre: The Impact of Globalisation' are cases in point. Overall, *New Voices in Irish Criticism 4* maintains the diversity and quality of its predecessors.

Other essay collections published in 2003 include Böss and Maher, eds., *Engaging Modernity: Reading Irish Politics, Culture and Literature at the Turn of the Century*. The book is effectively the conference proceedings of a European Federation of Centres and Associations of Irish Studies conference in Aarhus, and the collection, despite its promising title, reads very much as a set of conference papers. While most of the papers could, *de facto*, be said to engage with modernity, reading the essays on literary topics reinforces the fact that modernity is sometimes a catch-all term. That said, there are good contributions here, including Clare Wallace, 'Versions and Reversions: The New Old Story and Contemporary Irish Drama', and Heidi Hansson, 'Writing the Interspace: Emily Lawless's Geographical Imagination', on another female writer made minor by the Revival (some essays from this collection are also reviewed in section 5 below). In Conroy, ed., *Cross-Cultural Travel: Papers from the Royal Irish Academy International Symposium on Literature and Travel*, Barbara Schaff examines literary views of Ireland from Germany ('A Lost World: Ireland in Contemporary German Travel Writing'), and along the way discusses Heinrich Böll and Barbara Krause. Also looking at Ireland internationally is Kuch and Robson, eds., *Irelands in the Asia-Pacific*, a very full volume of conference proceedings of high quality, including many which discuss the cultural and literary connections between Ireland and Australia. Finally Allen and Kelly, eds., *The Cities of Belfast*, is a collection of essays celebrating, mourning and being bewildered by the city. On literary topics the collection includes Catherine Morris's essay on Alice Milligan (noted above) and Mary Burgess's 'Belfast Carnivalesque: The Satires of Gerald MacNamara', another uncovering of the buried northern Revival. Alan Gillis contributes the excellent 'Ciaran Carson: Beyond Belfast'. Terence Brown's 'Let's Go To Graceland: The Drama of Stewart Parker' is exemplary for its critical intelligence, while Aaron Kelly's '*Terror*-torial Imperatives: Belfast and Eoin MacNamee's *Resurrection Man*' confirms again that Kelly is one of the sharpest young critics currently writing in Irish studies.

2. Pre-1945 Fiction

(a) The English Novel, 1930–1945

The essays in the substantial collection *And In Our Time: Vision, Revision and British Writing of the 1930s*, edited by Anthony Shuttleworth, revisit the texts and critical traditions from the period up until 1940. As Shuttleworth's introduction acknowledges, the 1930s as a literary period have been re-examined a number of times during the last two decades, but he argues that in many ways the period nevertheless remains 'marginalised' (p. 11) and that its literature and culture have still not been accorded the kind of attention they merit (p. 11). More fundamentally, he suggests that the operations of this marginalization can give us insights into the ways in which dominant mappings of twentieth-century literary and cultural history obscure, suppress, or confuse particular kinds of issue. Shuttleworth takes as a starting point Frank Kermode's description of the 1930s as 'that critical decade in politics and art, which tried to face the problems … which we comfortably push out of sight and out of mind' (quoted p. 11). In short, the period is worth studying both for itself and because its problems are still highly relevant: 'the very attributes that have contributed to this neglect, and have made the texts of the thirties an awkward, unwieldy, body of work should now be understood as sources of the period's true importance for current critical debate' (p. 11). The essays in the collection very much fulfil this statement of the book's aims, dealing with the actual variety of 1930s writing and with how (and why) assumptions and distortions in the remembering of the period have had an impact not just on that decade but on surrounding conceptions of modernism, realism, postmodernism, gender, and politics.

Three of the eleven essays deal partially with poetry (in each case considered alongside novels), but there is a focus on prose works, including criticism and other non-fiction works as well as novels. Patrick Deane discusses the neglected interchange between Christian texts, groups and ideals, and leftists in the period in his '"Building the Just City Now": Exchanges between English Literature, Socialism and Christianity in the 1930s', drawing on a rich variety of forgotten debate. Christopher Pawling explores Terry Eagleton's commentaries on and relationships to interwar British Marxist criticism (especially that of Caudwell and West) in his work between the 1970s and the 1990s. Pawling argues persuasively that Caudwell and West's work had strengths which were obscured by the attitudes of later Marxist critics such as Eagleton, who regarded it as flawed by 'humanism'. Pawling points to a shift in Eagleton's views in more recent work, and draws attention to the contemporary value of some 1930s Marxist approaches in strengthening 'those areas of critical theory which offer the most systematic … alternatives to the vagaries of an autotelic postmodernism' (p. 48).

Kristin Bluemel, in 'Not Waving or Drowning: Refusing Critical Options, Rewriting Literary History', explores how the standard oppositions of modernism/postmodernism, pre-war/post-war, domestic novel/war novel have shaped conceptions of 1930s writing to the particular detriment of understanding how women writers of the 1930s and 1940s functioned. Bluemel discusses the work of Stevie Smith (including her novels, a number of poems, and her 'prose-poem' 'Surrounded by Children') as an example of how these oppositions work and of how they might be recast to tell somewhat 'different narratives' of the literature of the twentieth century. Laura Severin also discusses Stevie Smith in '"Disinvolve, Dissociate": Stevie Smith and the Politics of Passive Experiment', focusing on the development in Smith's writing—especially her novels, *Novel on Yellow Paper* and *Over the Frontier*—of a particular feminine politics of 'passivity', of a refusal to join groups which, even when apparently oppositional, are drawn into already existing hierarchical definitions. Smith's stance is illustrated concisely in a striking quotation from *Over the Frontier* when her protagonist Pompey asserts: 'No, I am not interested to concentrate upon politics, fascism or communism, or upon any groupismus whatever; I am not interested to centre my thoughts in anything so frivolous as these variations upon a theme that is so banal … so suspect in its origin' (quoted p. 143). Severin points out that we need to understand that this is not simply a 'humanist' rejection of politics, but a specific intervention in the political discourses of the time: 'Reinserting women writers into the traditional canon of 1930s literature requires a careful remapping of the decade's political conversations, since these women's voices reconfigure the dialogue, challenging our very notions of what counts as political work' (p. 144).

In a related vein, Lisa Colletta examines 'The Dark Domestic Fiction of Ivy Compton-Burnett', offering new insights into Compton-Burnett's understanding of power and politics through her fictions about families, and her use of humour as a way of dealing with what she regards as the inevitably resulting traumas. Looking closely at *A House and its Head* [1935], Colleta concludes that, partly through the use of her own kind of gallows humour, Compton-Burnett's 'fiction speaks directly to the changes in British cultural life after World War I and unflinchingly confronts the fractured ideals of domestic family life, responsible uses of authority and power, and religious morality' (p. 113). Phyllis Lassner discusses two novelists who were undoubtedly important writers and public figures, but whose work has certainly not been as widely discussed as its contemporary influence might merit, in her essay '"On the Point of a Journey": Storm Jameson, Phyllis Bottome, and the Novel of Women's Political Psychology'. Noting both writers' dismay at the quality of progressive change European social democracy in the 1930s seemed able to deliver, as well as their reservations (at the least) about Soviet communism, Lassner argues that

'Jameson's 1934–36 *Mirror in Darkness* trilogy and Bottome's 1934 novel, *Private Worlds*, are dramatic interventions in what they define as an abusive marriage between British inter-war power politics and prevailing psychological theories of masculine power and feminine subordination' (p. 116). Moreover, Lassner argues that as part of this intervention both authors, partly through critiquing contemporary psychological theories of gender, reject the given idea of an 'aesthetic opposition' (p. 116) between politically committed realism and the interior dramas of modernism.

Chris Hopkins, in 'Leftists and Thrillers: The Politics of a Thirties Sub-Genre', notes that by 1940 it was reckoned that a quarter of all novels published in Britain could be described as 'thrillers' and in the light of this examines 'how Marxist critics of the 1930s responded to this extremely popular kind of writing, how they thought about the politics of the genre, and how some left writers responded to this cultural debate in their work' (p. 147). The essay discusses the attitudes of speakers at the 1934 Soviet Writers Congress to the sub-genre, and of other Marxist critics, including Georg Lukács, Christopher Caudwell, Philip Henderson, and Alick West, concluding that there was general hostility to what was seen as an escapist form which actively drew attention away from the understanding of reality. A few critics, including, half-willingly, Caudwell and, more fully, West, did suggest at least the possibility of radical understandings for the thriller. The second part of the essay goes on to discuss the ways in which, in parallel to this critical debate, creative writers such as Eric Ambler and Graham Greene developed in their fiction radical uses of the thriller to understand the contradictions of contemporary conditions of actuality. Andy Croft, in a distinctly original essay, tests against more specific evidence the commanding-seeming statement Orwell made in 1940 that 'Between 1935 and 1939 … the central stream of English literature was more or less under Communist control' (quoted p. 163). Croft opens out the implications of a document preserved among the papers of Randall Swingler which details plans for Communist Party of Great Britain literary activism under the heading 'Ralph Fox (Writers') Group of the C.P.G.B.'. Croft argues that Orwell's implication that there was a conspiracy to penetrate Britain's literary institutions was not well founded: the writers' group document strongly suggests that, in these terms, 'before the Second World War, the Party's cultural organization was extremely haphazard and *ad hoc*' (p. 165). On the other hand, the writers' group document draws attention to cultural activism of a more open kind, drawing on popular support and engagement with a broad range of art and culture, and Croft traces both the activities to which this group specifically contributed and those that developed in the lines along which they were thinking. Thus the essay traces the history of such committed arts projects as *Left Review*, the Left Book Club Writers and Readers Group, the 'Key Books' series, the Left Song Book, the revival of Handel's suitably critical oratorio *Belshazzar*, and the Music and the People Festival. The discussion of the extent of left musical activity is particularly welcome, since many literary critical accounts, at least, tend to neglect the important collaborations of the period across the arts. The specific tracking down of the facts is a suitable corrective to Orwell's apparently indisputable observation about the Communist Party and literature in the latter part of the 1930s.

In a wide-ranging essay which relates the 1930s productively to the longer perspectives of Enlightenment thought, and Scottish Enlightenment thought in particular, John Fordham discusses relations and contradictions between Enlightenment rejections of superstition and modernism's interest in myth. Fordham's essay, 'The Revolution of the Scots Word: Modernism, Myth and Nationhood in Gibbon and MacDiarmid', argues that, in the development of their work in poetry and the novel during the 1930s, Grassic Gibbon and Hugh MacDiarmid, by drawing on modernist mythopoeia, participated in a political discourse particular to Scotland: 'the revolution of the Scots word is an intervention in a relatively stabilized English collective, confident in its nationalist supremacy. But it is only a means to an end and eventually the mythic must be rejected as a dominant force, in favour of a new materialist collective' (p. 201).

Anthony Shuttleworth suggests a striking re-evaluation of George Orwell, as a figure through whom the 1930s are now often principally remembered. His essay 'The Real George Orwell: Dis-simulation in *Homage to Catalonia* and *Coming Up for Air*' argues for an Orwell whose understandings of reality as revealed through his writing were much more complex than either his supporters or his enemies have allowed. Building on the insights of Richard Rorty, Shuttleworth argues persuasively that 'these texts of the thirties suggest that Orwell values the "window pane" text not because he believes that some unmediated idea of truth is "out there" to be bumped into, but rather because of the *absence* of any such unmediated truth. Equally, inspection of these texts reveals crucial alternatives to the sense of political impotence that haunts *Nineteen Eighty-Four*, alternatives which can be understood as one of the most valuable of the legacies of Orwell's work in the period' (p. 206).

The final essay in the volume is Kristin Hammet's 'Remembering the Thirties: Christina Stead's *For Love Alone* and *I'm Dying Laughing*', which offers an appropriate conclusion to the book's concerns with remembering and revising. The essay looks at two of the novels that the Australian 'Thirties novelist' Christina Stead wrote in later life about the 1930s, when she lived and worked in Europe. Both novels, one published in 1944, the other in 1986, drew on unpublished material which she had written during the 1930s. Hammet suggests interestingly how the time of publication of these two novels has impacted on how they are remembered, and traces through them Stead's reflections on several dimensions of her relation to politics and writing: 'together with her analysis of the ambivalent relations between the female writer and the conventionally masculine realm of revolutionary politics and between the empire and colony in *For Love Alone*, it [*I'm Dying Laughing*] offers a provocative contribution to our understanding of the processes of remembering and rewriting the thirties' (p. 238).

Maud Ellmann's *Elizabeth Bowen: The Shadow Across the Page* joins a number of distinguished but chronologically quite separate studies of Bowen's work. Ellmann notes that there has been a resurgence of critical interest in Bowen's writing since the 1990s, particularly enabled by 'the development of feminist criticism, Irish studies, and reassessments of the cultural impact of World War II' (p. xi). She observes similarities between Bowen and a number of predecessors and contemporaries: Henry James, E.M. Forster, James Joyce,

Patrick Hamilton, Graham Greene, Evelyn Waugh, and Virginia Woolf (one could, of course, add more names to this list of influences and comparators). But Ellmann feels that the strangeness of Bowen's work has in no sense yet been accounted for: 'yet Bowen is stranger than her rivals: ethically, psychologically, stylistically, her fiction constantly takes our categories by surprise' (p. xi). Ellmann sets out to extend current approaches to Bowen which predominantly contextualize her experiments with the novel in terms of national histories and gender identities, but her most individual angle is her attempt to tease out 'Bowen's strangeness through close readings informed by psychoanalytic and deconstructive methods of interpretation', together with her discussion of Bowen's 'hallucinatory treatment of objects, particularly furniture and telephones' (p. xi). Ellmann also acknowledges what a number of other critics have noted in their own ways—that Bowen's writing often 'pre-empts and in some cases confounds the literary theories brought to bear upon it' (p. xi). Thus, though the study clearly tries to interpret the 'dream-work' of Bowen's texts, it is always aware that 'Bowen's writing leads the reader up the garden path by inviting yet exceeding psychoanalytic scrutiny' (p. 3). Nevertheless, a psychoanalytic approach reveals much, as for example in this observation on the sexual dynamics in many of Bowen's novels, including *The Hotel* and *A World of Love*: 'While Bowen avoids Freud's gender stereotypes, she shares his intuition that a third person is required to create a circuit of desire. Operating as both an obstruction and a conduit between lovers, this shadowy third holds couples together precisely by disrupting their duality, diverting two-way love into a three-way relay system' (p. 72). Overall, the study takes up what seems a positive invitation to psychoanalytic interpretation in much of Bowen's writing, both fictional and critical; 'the aesthetic', writes Bowen in 1946, 'is nothing but a return to images that will allow nothing to take their place; the aesthetic is nothing but an attempt to disguise and glorify the enforced return' ('Out of a Book'; quoted by Ellmann, p. 2).

Stephen E. Tabachnik's *Fiercer Than Tigers: The Life and Works of Rex Warner* is undoubtedly the fullest biographical treatment of this important figure from the 1930s, and gives much detail of his life which is not to be found elsewhere (Tabachnik was one of Rex Warner's doctoral students at the university of Connecticut, when Warner taught in the US in the post-war period). Tabachnik states the book's aims clearly: it sets out to be 'a life and works … I have tried to write a straightforward, accurate story based on eyewitness testimony (including my own), literary and historical documentation, and Warner's texts themselves' (p. 4). In literary-critical terms, this is not as sophisticated a study as N.H. Reeve's monograph on Warner's fiction (*The Novels of Rex Warner* [1989]), but it is valuable in being, as the introduction says, the first full-length biography of Warner, and it is based on extensive and careful work on his papers and other relevant sources. The last section of the book's last chapter gives a useful account of Warner's current reputation and concludes that, in addition to his post-war influence as a very well regarded translator of a number of classical authors for the Penguin Classics series, he should be 'viewed as an important, if not major, twentieth-century novelist. *The Wild Goose Chase* and *The Professor* are historically important and still readable, and he produced at least one minor classic, *The Aerodrome*, which remains perennially relevant' (p. 434).

Several articles and notes on Orwell discuss him in association with a literary predecessor. Jeffrey Meyers, in 'Orwell's Debt to Somerset Maugham' (*NConL* 33:i[2003] 8–12), starts by quoting Orwell's 'Autobiographical Note, 1940': 'the modern writer who has influenced me most is Somerset Maugham, whom I admire immensely for his power of telling a story straightforwardly and without frills' (p. 8). The note continues by citing parallels between texts by Maugham and Orwell, and also by referring to some parallels in their lives and circumstances. Some of the instances seemed more persuasive than others—echoes between phrases in Maugham's *The Summing Up* and Orwell's 'Such. Such were the Joys', and between the plots more broadly of Maugham's story 'Force of Circumstance' and Orwell's first novel *Burmese Days*, are convincing, while other parallels (for example between their approaches to autobiography; p. 12) seem less self-evident and could be regarded as coincidental rather than clear signs of influence. Meyers also published a short article, 'Orwell on Writing' (*NewC* 22:ii[2003] 27–33), which usefully traces Orwell's comments on writing, but does not really link these observations together into a thesis. Anna Vaninskaya's essay, 'Janus-Faced Fictions: Socialism as Utopia and Dystopia in William Morris and George Orwell' (*UtopSt* 14:ii[2003] 83–98) does not try to argue that Morris is a direct influence on Orwell (though there are curious parallels between their life and work), but rather that they can both be usefully seen as belonging to a particular English 'romantic-socialist' tradition: 'Morris shares with Orwell a certain valuation of tradition and the national past … of individuality within an equalitarian community … their outlook is libertarian and semi-anarchistic … characterized by an intense aversion to elitism, hierarchical state centralization, and worship of the machine. Each opposes a utopian vision of decentralized democratic community to the evils of rationalist utilitarianism, bureaucracy, and industrial regimentation' (p. 84). The essay is very careful in the way in which it associates its two authors and various of their texts: the striking similarities (as well as contrasts) between *News from Nowhere* and *Coming Up For Air*, and between *A Dream of John Bull* and *Animal Farm* are carefully weighed. Overall, the essay offers an illuminating insight into some continuities between the debates about the nature of a possible socialist England from the 1880s until the 1930s. Peter Henry, in a related way, examines relationships between the writings of Dostoevsky and Graham Greene in 'Dostoevskian Echoes in the Novels of Graham Greene' (*Dostoevsky Studies* 6[2002] 119–33). Though some direct influences are evidenced, the significance of some of the parallels drawn between the two authors remains tenuous.

In 'Ressentiment, the Superego, and Totalitarianism: George Orwell's *1984* [*sic*]' (*Cardozo Law Review* 24:iii[2003] 1099–1130), Sinkwan Cheng examines the nature of totalitarianism by bringing to bear philosophical and psychoanalytic conceptions of 'bad conscience', 'introjection', and 'internalization' as developed in the thought of Nietzsche, Freud, and Lacan, and through ideas about absolute truth developed during the French Revolution. This heady-sounding mixture is in fact carefully deployed in the article, and does much to illuminate the workings of the State in Oceania (and in actual historical totalitarian states), and to help us to understand the intensity of the relationship between Winston Smith and O'Brien, between power and its subjects: 'for the Party to "have power" all it needs is its subjects' consent and acknowledgement that it does "have power"'. The Party's strength is its weakness, for it fears contact with any reality which might bring contradiction: it is an idealist force which must never allow it ideals to be testable. Hence 'the mind is the be all and end all of real power for the Party' (p. 1118), and the Party 'is constantly forging memory because it cannot face life as it was and as it is' (p. 1115).

Kristin Bluemel explores an astounding gap in Orwell's response to totalitarianism in 'St. George and the Holocaust' (*LIT* 14[2003] 119–47). As she states near the beginning of her article: 'Orwell did not himself write about the Holocaust' (p. 120), yet he made numerous brief references to Jewish issues and to Zionism, and provided a number of Jewish historians of the Holocaust with an understanding of modernity which they felt helped them to understand that 'characteristically modern phenomenon' (Zygmunt Bauman, quoted by Bluemel, p. 120). Bluemel examines the (often passing) comments which Orwell made on the Jews, the places where he might be expected to refer to the Holocaust and does not, the differences in his attitudes towards Indians and Jews, and the tradition of 'habitual anti-Semitism' (p. 121) of which Orwell may only have been able to achieve partial consciousness. The essay is a sustained and important attempt to understand a blind-spot in Orwell's own sense of the modern world: 'The contradictory intellectual and emotional responses we see in Orwell's writing about Indians, Englishmen, and Jews testify to the deeply personal, psychological level at which he can be described as an important writer of twentieth-century modernity … These internal conflicts, extreme and unresolved, require us to name the political and moral costs, as well as benefits of accepting him as a guide through the crises of mid-century modernity. Near blindness to the Holocaust is one of the costs; bold criticism of racial injustice in India is one of the benefits' (p. 139).

(b) James Joyce

Some of the signal contributions to Joyce studies in 2003 lie in the realms of biography and cultural studies. Carol Loeb Shloss's *Lucia Joyce: To Dance in the Wake* is an impassioned, richly documented and provocative exercise in historical reclamation. In piecing together the troubled story of Joyce's daughter, Shloss aligns herself with the expanded scope and experimental tendencies of much current biography that fastens on marginal lives. In her introduction, she weighs up the difficulties facing the biographer of Lucia Joyce, including the suppression of the bulk of her correspondence and the skewed portraits of her disseminated by Maria Jolas, among others. Shloss's objectives in producing this work are as a consequence manifold, at once documentary and investigative. In addition, the biography attempts an imaginative reconstruction of the emotional, sexual, and psychological problems and experiences that shaped Lucia as an individual. In this latter endeavour, speculative and exacting analysis of the Joyce household and of the management of Lucia's supposed mental illness—a diagnosis which Shloss firmly refutes—yields uncomfortable insights. The most absorbing facets of this biography, however, are the account of Lucia's quest to become an artist in her own right in her pursuit of her career as a dancer and the depiction of the extraordinary creative symbiosis that linked father and daughter. Shloss's central proposition is that Joyce and Lucia were jointly involved in 'modernism's battle for new, unfettered ways of thinking and feeling' (p. 418), but that paternal artistry was ultimately to win through at the expense of daughterly desire. She also winningly demonstrates that *Finnegans Wake* encrypts the terrible spiritual and personal costs of Joyce's literary vocation as well as the devastating and undying bonds of affection that bound him to Lucia. The thesis that Lucia is the secret subject of her father's final, radical fictional experiment is not a novel one. But Shloss's ardently defended argument that she is simultaneously its audience and its active co-creator adduces important contexts for understanding the psychosexual and imaginative energies imbuing *Finnegans Wake* that challenge our attempts to view it at a remove or to laud it simply as the product of self-contained male genius.

James Joyce, Sexuality and Social Purity, by Katherine Mullin, also opens up startling new dimensions of Joyce's texts. This original and revealing study examines the manner in which nineteenth- and twentieth-century social purity crusades not only inflected but also constituted essential subtexts and instigating moments for his writings and, indeed, for modernism in general. Mullin's argument is that Joyce consciously took on the role of *agent provocateur* and resisted being reduced to a hapless victim of censorship and of prudish moral standards. Her investigation demonstrates how archival research can persuasively reconstruct the often seemingly irretrievable materialist conditions informing early twentieth-century culture, and exemplifies how such lines of enquiry may revivify and ground Joyce studies in fresh and convincing ways. Mullin marries such historical commentary with elucidations of Joyce's works which demonstrate that social purity is a 'silent presence' (p. 15) in their margins. The contexts she evokes yield fresh insights into well-known texts. Thus, she indicates that 'the queer old josser' in 'An Encounter' may be a parody of child-protecting social purists with their much-advertised predilection for flagellation, and that 'Eveline' symbolically captures contemporary anxieties about the white slave trade. Likewise, discussion of contemporary sexological and educational debates about the policing of masculinity adds to our understanding of *A Portrait of the Artist as Young Man*, while the cross-connection of 'Nausicaa' with the new vogue for the mutoscope and the voyeuristic pornography that it promoted allows Gerty McDowell to emerge not just as a put-upon romantic heroine but as a knowing participant in the commodification of sexuality in early modernity.

R. Brandon Kershner, in his editorial introduction to a collection of essays on *Cultural Studies of James Joyce*, provides an adept overview of the emergence of this field of critical enquiry and the way in which it has modified and widened our readings of Joyce. Kershner contends that, while definitions of cultural studies must remain necessarily 'unfinalizable' (p. 9), its ruling precepts are that cultural practices are embedded in social relations and systems of power and that texts are part of networks of meaning rather than inert objects which we subject to critical scrutiny. Beyond this, the unifying thread of the essays in this collection is the quest to locate the historical specificities of Joyce's works. That such overall goals encourage diversity rather than the mouthing of critical commonplaces is borne out by the variety of approaches adopted in the individual contributions. Paul K. Saint-Amour's elegant and densely argued essay, 'Over Assemblage: *Ulysses* and the *Boîte-en-Valise* from Above', utilizes Marcel Duchamp's so-called portable museum assemblages and the emergence of the airborne 'look-down' view in advertising to explicate the competing vectors and vertiginous conflicts of scale in *Ulysses* as it alternates between gigantism and minutiae, exteriorized distance and interiorized proximity, containment and encyclopedic excess. The effect of his wide-ranging meditation is to see Joyce's work not as determined by the knowing insights culled from cultural studies but as rendered increasingly inscrutable by our attempts to encompass it. Other essays, such as Valérie Bénéjam's exploration of the aesthetic debates sparked off by the Venus of Praxiteles, R. Brandon Kershner's investigation of the politics of professorial appointments in University College Dublin, Thomas Jackson Rice's study of the 'gramophony' of *Ulysses* and Joyce's preoccupation with the audio potential of the text, and Tracey Teets Schwarze's probing of Joycean versions of the madwoman in the light of contemporary discourses about hysteria maintain a similarly flexible and playful approach to the texts they examine. Two further chapters by Cheryl Herr and Garry Leonard exemplify the urge of cultural studies not just to provide object lessons in how texts might be interwoven with given material contexts, but to generate synoptic theories capable of elucidating aspects of Irish society. Looking at the impact of the suppression of the Irish language, Herr speculates that what she terms 'schizophrenesis' might be used to evaluate the tendency of Anglophone Irish writers to use syntax and expression in a divided way to denote meaning while also gesturing at occluded values and lost systems. In a similarly rigorous theoretical exploration, Garry Leonard contends that commodity fetishism operates in a distinctive way in 'semi-colonial' communities and that the relationship between self and object often seems especially fragile in Joyce. In short, this fifteenth volume of European Joyce Studies proves that this series continues to foster provocative and innovative approaches to Joyce and Irish culture in general.

Although Joycean texts undoubtedly court psychoanalytical interpretation, the means by which such readings might be effected and contoured still remain a matter of debate. Two interrelated applications of Freudian and post-Freudian theory to Joyce—Jean Kimball's *Joyce and the Early Freudians: A Synchronic Dialogue of Texts* and David Cotter's *James Joyce and the Perverse Ideal*—indicate how engagements of this kind permit searching accounts of his work. Kimball's study sets out, as she declares, less to use psychoanalysis as an aid for assessing Joyce's characters than to posit the writings of Freud, Ernest Jones, and Otto Rank, amongst many others, as vital intertexts for his fictions. Her juxtaposition of a rich array of early texts in the field of psychoanalysis with *Ulysses* provides the occasion for delicately balanced readings that reveal layers of allusiveness that have hitherto been overlooked. Historical congruence, as she indicates, allows multiple levels of signification to swim into focus. Overall, her claim is that the case histories newly spawned by psychoanalysis and many of the key early essays in this burgeoning field were adapted, echoed, or reworked by Joyce. Thus, she contends that Joyce possibly drew upon Freud's 'Leonardo da Vinci and a Memory of his Childhood' in crafting aspects of the intertwined psychology of both Stephen Dedalus and Bloom. In reviewing 'Scylla and Charybdis', she argues that its concerns with primordial conflicts between father and son and the quest for a self-fathering selfhood have been filtered through Ernest Jones's theories about *Hamlet* and Otto Rank's *The Myth of the Birth of the Hero*. Likewise, she discerns the influence of the Jungian dualism of the 'loving and terrible mother' on the portrait of Stephen's mother in *Ulysses*, particularly in her incarnation in 'Circe'. Interestingly, too, she traces how Joyce may have dispersed or even transposed aspects of his own psychology in *Ulysses*, through the motif of the treacherous brother and the figuration of jealousy and of father–daughter incest. A final chapter suggests that Joyce incoporates aspects of the drama of Oedipus into his work, thereby complicating the relations between the family triad of father, son, and mother depicted in Homer's *Odyssey*. For Kimball, the operations of intertextuality ultimately realize themselves at an unconscious level and via subterranean layers of identification. Hence, she arrives at the paradoxical conclusion that Joyce, despite his overt denial of Freudian influence, composes a text suffused with an eclectic mix of psychoanalytic theory and allusion.

David Cotter is less cautious in his findings in *James Joyce and the Perverse Ideal*. Also, unlike Kimball, he is at pains to demonstrate that the predominant patterns of sexual perversion in *Ulysses* might be seen within a coherent and overarching frame and that they gesture at the radicalism of Joyce's reconsideration of subjectivity. Drawing on notions of selfhood and masochism proposed in particular by Gilles Deleuze and Félix Guattari, he maintains that Joyce's portrayal of varying manifestations of sexual masochism in both Stephen and, above all, Bloom, such as flagellomania, cuckoldry, and rituals of shame and enforced feminization, are not merely embellishments but evidence of a deep-seated engagement with this subject on the author's part. Contrary, however, to the traditional Freudian interpretation which might see such symptomology as denoting psychic disorder, Cotter, referencing the radical views of Deleuze, holds that masochism in Joyce ultimately serves liberty in that it dismantles 'the inauthentic interests of the socially constructed self' (p. 20) and, moreover, permits the emergence of a psychic dualism or multiplicity. In a combative epilogue to his dissection of motifs of masochism in *Ulysses*, he holds further that criticism has too readily accepted the 'wholeness and self-completion' of this text. Although this admonition seems overstated, Cotter's hypothesis that in Joyce the self 'is spurious, paradoxical, parodic and subversive' (p. 221) is convincingly upheld throughout.

Tim Conley's *Joyces Mistakes: Problems of Intention, Irony, and Interpretation* and Sean P. Murphy's *James Joyce and Victims: Reading the Logic of Exclusion* both cast their net widely, with varying results. Conley's volume is a loose set of meditations on Joyce's aesthetics of error which views his deployment of mistakes, misquotations, misprision, and linguistic and syntactic confusion as at once intentional and involuntary. Peculiarly, despite his recognition that error is an inescapable feature of Joycean textuality, Conley devotes much space to the detection of mistakes in critics and editors of Joyce. Sean P. Murphy's examination of the figure of the victim in Joyce's writings is a more satisfactory, if sometimes schematic, study. Situating his investigation in a Marxist framework, he sets out to look at the logic of victimage in Joyce's texts. Although he holds that *Dubliners* exposes how the Irish accept and collude with the colonial condition and consequently their own subjugation, he sees subsequent works as disrupting the binary logic of power regimes and opening up ways in which entrapment might be eluded. Placing Joyce's texts in a continuum, Murphy argues that they become increasingly capable of enunciating resistance and of imagining forms of empowering agency for the Irish subaltern. By this token, *Finnegans Wake* slips the bearings of imperial power systems and subverts the confining myths and social conditions that produce victims. Even though this account of the successive instalments of the Joycean oeuvre has cogency and an appealing logic, it assumes too readily that they conform to a neat progression. Moreover, agency and colonialism are presupposed to be incompatible while the historical contingencies and ideological conflicts that continue to haunt the *Wake* are ignored.

Both Nicholas Miller, in *Modernism, Ireland and the Erotics of Memory*, and Paul K. Saint-Amour, in *The Copywrights: Intellectual Property and the Literary Imagination*, weave Joyce into accounts of the aesthetics and politics of modernism. Miller's study belongs with the growing body of work devoted to the topic of cultural memory. In his theoretical reflections, he treats of the links between memory, desire, and subjectivity and puts forward the view that *Finnegans Wake*, in foregrounding our subjective investment in recreations of the past, troubles conventional notions of history that see it in terms of objective knowledge. In keeping with these propositions, he interprets 'Nightlessons' as disrupting the customary goal of education—the formal acquisition of knowledge—by concentrating instead on 'desire and its vicissitudes' (p. 167). Further, he argues that *Finnegans Wake* depicts history not as memory but as remembering, and in so doing reveals that the historical subject is never bounded but rather extended and dispersed across time. In sum, Miller suggestively outlines how Joyce thematizes a radical 'erotics of memory' (p. 186) in which the past is recycled and reworked and never simply reducible to rational narrative.

Paul K. Saint-Amour, in his penetrating and original investigation, considers how modernist texts 'register a self-awareness about their status as literary property' (p. 13) and produce a metadiscourse that mirrors and engages with those aspects of copyright law that dominated public debates in the early twentieth century. *Ulysses*, for Saint-Amour, is a paradigmatic example of a text that exhibits proprietary self-consciousness. In an illuminating discussion of 'Oxen of the Sun', he refutes the view propounded by Mark Osteen that this episode limns a portrait of its author as a plunderer of copyrights. Rather than deeming this section to be the by-product of Joyce's resourceful plagiarization of the English literary canon, Saint-Amour contends that it should more appropriately be seen as testing the boundaries between fair use and infringement. In at once copying and also changing and parodying the source texts with which he operates, Joyce, in fact, upholds the rights of the public domain. However, simultaneously, in the dexterous argument that Saint-Amour evolves, the deep structures of 'Oxen' consistently destabilize legal definitions of authorship and copyright and blur the boundaries between original and copy and between matter and manner. Saint-Amour's poised and thought-provoking discussion indicates how cultural materialist and theoretical analysis might combine to show how the historical and legal conditions of publication are not merely an extraneous set of circumstances but embedded aspects of the imaginative processes of the text itself. *Ulysses*, as he points out, usefully intervenes in the constricting legal regimes that increasingly complicate and even obstruct our access to modern literature and also incubates oppositional strategies by which they might be countered.

Techné: James Joyce, Hypertext and Technology, by Louis Armand, is a landmark volume as it is the first attempt to consider the interconnections between the poetics of Joyce's work and the concepts of technology and hypertextuality that it at once encodes and invites. Utilizing the Derridean notion of solicitation, Armand's primary claim is that Joyce's writings can be said to 'solicit hypertext' (p. xi) because of their reliance on non-sequential writing and their deliberate presentation of themselves as textual apparatuses or machines. Further, their overt instigation of genetic critical investigation also invites hypertextual production. Armand's method in this volume is to engage with a wide range of theorists who have considered the machinic design and nature of *Finnegans Wake*, thereby generating a conceptual vocabulary as well as an interlocking series of reflections that allow the hypertextual aspects of this text to be pinpointed. Crucial to his attempt to reconceive *Finnegans Wake* is the insistence that it must not be thought of as a physical object or as having any of the commonplace attributes of the book, such as linearity, boundedness, and fixity. As he notes in his discussion of the ideas of Danis Rose, the hypertextuality of Joyce's 'work in progress' is 'not founded upon an empirical logistics, but on a textual condition' (p. 39). Indeed, Armand's own elicitation of a theory of Joycean hypertextuality might also be claimed to mimic the notion of *techné* that he supports in its deferral of totalizing statements and generation of a gridwork of substitute terms. Hence, he proffers accounts of virtuality, textual machines, vicociclometry, surface kinetics, and Borromean knots, and probes notions of the acrostic and the transversal in order to provide a basis for understanding of *Finnegans Wake* as a 'textual edifice... always *in medias res*'. Armand's exacting and erudite treatment of Joycean hypertextuality makes significant demands on its readers but rewardingly illuminates a vital set of concerns that will increasingly impact on our understanding of Joyce in future years.

In her introduction to *Suspicious Readings of Joyce's Dubliners*, Margot Norris provides a judicious summary of the collection's critical reception. She notes that, although it was at one point dismissed as juvenilia, the final decades of the twentieth century saw an upsurge of interest in it, issuing in numerous single-author books, compendia of critical essays, and special issues of journals. Norris traces her own fascination with Joyce's stories to her discovery that they supply keys to motifs in *Finnegans Wake* or feature as distant echoes in its surreal scenes. Her present monograph sets out to consolidate such findings by reading *Dubliners* through a Wakean lens. This altered optics regards it as 'much more wild and strange and defamiliarized' (p. 6) than has ordinarily been assumed. In pursuing such consciously unsettling interpretations, Norris also notes the degree to which this text faces us with numerous critical challenges that cannot readily be resolved, including the problem of its silences and ellipses, the quandary of placing the narrative voices and of adjudicating on the unreliability of many of the tellers of the tales. The methodology that she proposes in the light of such framing questions derives from the hermeneutics of suspicion, enunciated by Paul Ricœur. The reader she posits needs to practise resistance and to question the slippages, gaps, and even the prompts that the texts afford us. In part, too, this wariness extends to the received views of these stories that tend to blind us to aspects of them.

Norris has previously been known for the acuity of her interpretations of *Finnegans Wake* and her discerning application of the tenets of post-structuralism. Although such interpretative strategies are still in evidence here, this volume represents a departure from her previous work to the degree that it yokes the attentiveness to moments of undecidability within the text to ethical issues. In her careful ruminations on her methodology, she invokes Joyce's much-cited declaration that *Dubliners* was intended, in part, as a moral history of his country. As a consequence, she contends, all of the stories toy with moral perspectives and enjoin ethical readings upon us. This, however, is not to say that they urge us to partisanship or reductionism. Rather, it is her view that the stories demand that we involve ourselves in the moral dilemmas that they unfold and that we learn to discriminate between the various alternative versions of things that are overtly represented and also occluded. In some ways, as Norris's speculative analyses evince, this ethical role forces the reader to become a kind of storyteller, pursuing permutations and outcomes that the plotlines of Joyce's tales eschew.

In the suspicious readings proposed in this volume, Norris approaches the stories with forensic deliberation. She sifts them for interpretative clues but also wrestles with the false leads that they put in our way. Many of the analyses, in addition, deliberately fasten on marginal features and figures or attempt to articulate the unspoken dimensions of the texts. Thus, a discussion of guilt and innocence in 'The Sisters' focuses on the seemingly peripheral roles of the titular characters and speculates that they are potentially 'more sinister, incriminated, and tragic' (p. 27) than has customarily been presumed. The reading of 'Eveline', by contrast, questions the belief that she is simply a victim caught in a melodramatic scenario of seduction and draws attention to the extent to which the narrative foregrounds her rational concerns rather than her romantic delusions. In interpreting 'Counterparts', Norris alerts us to the way in which the narrative deliberately belittles Farrington and refuses to allow us to engage with his pain and humiliation, while her probing of 'Clay' demonstrates that its focalization through the limited point of view of Maria operates to mask and falsify the actual misery of her existence. Norris's perspicacious and challenging exegesis of 'The Dead', highlighting its muffled feminist subtexts, which concludes this collection has already become one of the most frequently cited rereadings of this text in recent years. In similar fashion, the interlocking series of essays in *Suspicious Readings of Joyce's Dubliners* constitutes a magisterial and provocative reassessment that lastingly alters the ways in which we decipher a collection of short stories that had seemingly been domesticated and mastered by previous criticism.

Milesi, ed., *James Joyce and the Difference of Language*, has the overall aim of scrutinizing the experimentalism of Joyce's literary language. The contributors to this collection are at once concerned with explicating the radical poetics of

Joyce's works and with delving into the linguistic properties and quirks that distinguish them. In his elaborate and astute introduction Laurent Milesi examines Joyce's attitude to language and contends that he evolves a 'regional internationalism' (p. 4) as a response to his sense of alienation from his mother tongue. He further claims that he strategically deploys the creolization and foreignization of English in order to achieve linguistic decolonization. As Milesi succinctly avers, for Joyce 'politics … first and foremost materializes as style' (p. 13). This insight is examined from various vantage points by the essays in this volume. Fritz Senn, in a close consideration of Joycean syntax in *Ulysses*, notes the manner in which it often suspends the rules of grammar and delights in aberrational constructions that prevent ease of comprehension. Similarly, Derek Attridge, focusing on the initial chapter of *A Portrait of the Artist as a Young Man*, highlights Stephen's defamiliarized view of words and his inability to apprehend them simply in conventional or commonsensical ways. This intense lexical attention, Attridge argues, recedes in later sections of Joyce's *Bildungsroman* but reasserts itself as the matrix of *Finnegans Wake*. Other contributors adduce various intertexts in order to elucidate aspects of Joycean textuality: Lucia Boldrini looks at how Dante's account of post-Babelian language in *De Vulgari Eloquentia* informs the conflict between debased expression and the sublimity of art in *Finnegans Wake*, while Marie-Dominique Garnier draws on the notion of the plateau, formulated by Gilles Deleuze and Félix Guattari, to act as the basis for her microreading of 'Calypso'. Strikingly different formulations of the utopian aspects of Joyce's aesthetic are put forward in several of the chapters. Thomas Docherty sees Joyce as a post-Romantic who, although recognizing that the loss of experience and immediacy are the preconditions of the modern, nonetheless strives to recreate a pristine connection to the world through language. Ellen Carol Jones, by contrast, directs attention to the way in which colonial dispossession allows Joyce to reconceive literary history in 'Oxen of the Sun' as a 'redismembering' (p. 154) and as a space of possibility as well as of containment. Patrick McGee makes the bold claim that '*Finnegans Wake* is one of the most ethical books ever written' (p. 179) because it insists that desire can never be relinquished and that the abject facets of the self need to be embraced rather than denied. In sum, the diversity of the individual engagements is the strength of this collection that does not seek to impose a false unity or to foreclose on a topic that demands numerous different responses.

Two further, well-stocked, collections of essays directed at the classroom, Wollaeger, ed., *James Joyce's A Portrait of the Artist as a Young Man: A Casebook*, and Emig, ed., *Ulysses: James Joyce*, also encourage a lively pluralism. Both volumes reprint previously published work that has acquired a critical currency and also aim at showcasing a diversity of critical opinion. Mark A. Wollaeger's anthology juxtaposes articles from several different decades, by Hugh Kenner, Maud Ellmann, and Joseph Valente amongst others, and thus tracks the shifts in debates and methodologies. Rainer Emig's collection, by contrast, unites essays from a single era, the 1990s, but is at pains to foreground the variety of approaches adopted by critics such as Mark Osteen, Enda Duffy,

Adam Woodruff, and Eva Plonowska Ziarek rather than the existence of a unifying framework or of an underlying consensus.

(c) D.H. Lawrence

Publications on D.H. Lawrence in 2003 were predictably diverse, ranging from densely argued theoretical explorations, close textual readings, and studies of influence to more personal, biographically driven studies. The first three books reviewed here identify and explore a specific instance of ideological, literary, or philosophical assimilation, exploring anarchism, the influence of Italian Futurism, and Darwinism as reflected within Lawrence's works. The fourth book considered contrasts methodologically, adopting a close-reading approach to examine evolving drafts of works composed within the late period of Lawrence's life, while the fifth offers an intertextual and specifically Derridean analysis of Lawrence's poetic discourse. Texts by Philip Callow and Leslie Williamson are subsequently discussed: both authors emphasize the significance of their personal response to Lawrence, issuing in a full-scale biography and a pamphlet incorporating a number of original poems.

In *Naked Liberty and the World of Desire: Elements of Anarchism in the Work of D.H. Lawrence*, Simon Casey is careful to clarify his aim: 'I believe that the links between Lawrence and philosophical anarchism are deep and substantial and that reading Lawrence within the context of this tradition will significantly enhance our understanding of his work as a whole' (p. 3); he also claims that the focus of his work 'is directed not by the question of possible influence but by analogy' (p. 12). Thus, for the most part, he considers 'parallels' and 'consistencies' (though he does discuss possible direct and indirect influences in his introduction).

Such analogies are problematized first by 'anarchism' being a wide-ranging concept (wider and narrower definitions appear through the text), and secondly by Lawrence's work not having 'any single, coherent ideological perspective … [while it] is often fraught with self-contradiction' (p. 109). So essentially we are presented with a comparison between central elements of anarchism and general tendencies within Lawrence's writing. This is, however, combined with highly specific, detailed analysis of the views of, for instance, Stirnen, Bakunin, and Godwin, and equally meticulous and perceptive analysis of Lawrence's fiction and non-fiction.

Postulated similarities include the desired abolition of all structures of authority and control, and the assertion that the role of the state should be to support, not dominate, individuals; the view that an ideal society should be small and contain no external laws, only the internal 'higher' laws of human nature; the belief that freedom of the individual is contingent upon the freedom of all other members of society; and the conviction that marriage should constitute a 'natural', not legal, relationship. Casey's ideas are presented in the context of critical views which are often in conflict with his own, and he is forced to confront instances of self-contradiction in Lawrence's writing. Yet it is impossible not to be struck by the degree of similarity between Lawrence's thought and anarchism, convincingly established within Casey's study.

Andrew Harrison's *D.H. Lawrence and Italian Futurism: A Study of Influence* contextualizes Lawrence's development with reference to Italian Futurism, proceeding from the belief that his 'engagement with the Futurist manifestos was decisive in the innovation of his own style, and the movement away from the realism of his early fiction and that of his literary models' (pp. xviii–xix). Marinetti's Futurism in particular acted as a focus of ideas for Lawrence in rejecting, yet engaging productively with, dead tradition—yet (as Harrison notes) this intertextual engagement has received insufficient, or too narrowly focused, critical coverage. As Harrison's book is also a study of influence in more general terms, he engages with Harold Bloom's theory of the anxiety of influence, and with Paul de Man's review in which he argues that Bloom confuses psychological and linguistic modes of influence. According to de Man, it is necessary to discard a wealth of external circumstantial detail in order to generate an antithetical textual criticism. Harrison engages with such terminology and, where appropriate, adopts such reading strategies.

The first chapter provides a detailed analysis of Lawrence's engagement with the 'Edwardian novelists' (a phrase Virginia Woolf used for Bennett, Wells, and Galsworthy), comparing Lawrence's reaction to their 'outmoded form of realism' with that of Woolf. For Lawrence, this rejection of a tradition that had underpinned his work up to *Sons and Lovers* is shown to be highly significant in his move towards a concept of the self which is not confined by social restraints, but which could be realized in an asocial context—and would necessitate a new kind of fiction.

Chapter 2 begins a critique of Lawrence as envisaged at the interface between Futurism and Naturalism (and the author clarifies the similarities and differences between the two movements). Harrison is cautious and astute in distinguishing between views which Lawrence happened to have in common with, for instance, Marinetti, and those he actually adopted from reading his work. Yet he claims Lawrence *was* influenced both by his readings of the Futurists and by the Naturalist writers, in particular Zola, 'as they were mediated through Futurism' (p. 35).

Chapters 3 and 4 trace in depth these dichotomous influences through *The Rainbow* and *Women in Love* in particular (and several shorter works as well), arguing that they were never finally reconciled in these texts. The analysis of additions to the final draft of *The Rainbow* gives insight into the way Lawrence integrated his new metaphysics into earlier material. Futurism and Naturalism are said to operate in complex ways in *Women in Love*, and the 'futuristic drive towards new forms of articulation is set against a disintegrative naturalistic fatalism' (p. 181). Perhaps the most obvious manifestation of this is the juxtaposition of Gerald's (Zolaesque) steady progress towards tragic destruction with the futuristic vocabulary and 'impersonality' that give rise to hope for Birkin and Ursula.

The final chapter is entitled '"Futurism long before Futurism found paint": The Allusions to Italian Futurism in *Studies in Classic American Literature*', identifying in these essays a Futurist 'dual rhythm' and other significantly analogous traits. Overall, this book has been aptly described as a vital contextualizing study that recovers Lawrence as a fully historicized figure.

Ronald Granofsky's *D.H. Lawrence and Survival: Darwinism in the Fiction of the Transitional Period* is a compellingly argued and meticulously researched comparison between two *prima facie* quite different writers, Lawrence and Charles Darwin. Referring to 'Worthen's remark that there is little trace of Darwin in Lawrence's writing in spite of the novelist's early enthusiasm for the evolutionists' (p. 42), Granofsky wonders why this subject has not aroused much critical interest and argues that there is a largely unconscious but highly significant influence. He accepts a common division between the 'marriage' novels (up to *Women in Love* in 1920) and the 'leadership' novels (from *Kangaroo* in 1923). He argues that the 'transitional' intervening works were 'a catalyst that transformed a writer of exploratory, experimental and significant fiction into one who produced mediocre writing at best, and, at worst, strident, preachy and just plain poor work' (p. 4). Such value judgements abound, though it might be possible to question or reject these while still being persuaded of a Darwinian influence (the latter, according to Granofsky, being largely responsible for the alleged deterioration).

The fact that the transitional period entailed the reworking of several earlier short stories into novellas provides Granofsky with a Darwinian model in which Lawrence is engaged in masterminding the evolution of his writing. Lawrence is said to use narrative strategies to express his changing ideology by, for example, 'culling the weakest members of his conceptual herd in order to strengthen the whole … and setting up characters who are sent through the alembic of a narratological survival-of-the-fittest test in order to distil the character traits he approved of' (p. 7). Clearly, the choice of terminology underlines the argument in favour of a Darwinian influence. Similarly, Lawrence's concern for a 'better' society is seen to be, at the very least, analogous to Darwinian movement towards a 'better' (in this case physically stronger) society as a result of natural selection.

The other important issue is the degree to which Darwinian concepts infiltrate parts of the fictional texts. Chapters analysing the 'Ladybird' novellas ('The Ladybird', 'The Fox', and 'The Captain's Doll'), *The Lost Girl*, *Aaron's Rod*, and the *England My England* short stories provide detailed and persuasive cases of Lawrence's use of 'food and illness', 'confinement and survival', and 'death and survival'. Granofsky's analyses are based on the distinction between an upper level of authorial intention and a 'lower', subliminal, system of imagery which he argues points to the evolutionary concepts. In general, this is a thought-provoking study, not least because of its insightful exploration of Lawrence's complex views on the body and man's relation to nature, through reference to Darwinian theory.

In his preface to *Reading Late Lawrence,* Neil Reeve explains that his concern is with Lawrence's compositional process as evident in frequent revisions of his own writings. In fact, he accuses the latter of an 'almost wilful open-endedness' (p. vii), only to be 'closed' (if at all) by the demands of publishing and monetary survival. However, the author also sees in Lawrence an opposite trend, namely a desire to find the 'inevitable destination' that was somehow latent in his work, so that there is 'a registration in the very manner of his work of the unresolved dispute within him between the traveller and the settler' (p. viii).

The comparatively neglected works studied are those written after Lawrence's final return to Europe in the autumn of 1925, and include 'Glad Ghosts', 'In Love',

'The Blue Moccasins', 'Sun', 'The Lovely Lady', 'Mother and Daughter', and the three *Lady Chatterley* novels. Regarding his method, Reeve says he is 'trying to follow the little undercurrents and stirring of implication as they feed in and out of the larger flow', following 'the phantom imprints, as it were, left by Lawrence's first thoughts upon the thoughts that replace them' (p. ix). Later, in his discussion of 'Glad Ghosts', he claims as most stimulating the 'registration by the writing of the trouble its author seems to have had with it' (p. 22).

Perhaps the most obvious mark of quality in this book is the excellent analysis of specific revisions made in the evolution of given stories, but each chapter evidences a particularly effective combination of these localized insights with more general material concerning the development of Lawrence's style and thought. It is obvious that Lawrence is much occupied, for example, with issues of inheritance and lineage, with age and ageing, with death, and with the functioning of the body—though Reeve's central concern is with how these ideas change in the late writings.

It is impossible to do more here than mention a few instances of Reeve's analysis. In the comparison of two versions of a passage from 'In Love' he stresses stylistic differences, the second version being 'more slippery and mercurial … a vigorous example of the later style', also alluding to 'its restless uprooting of itself in obedience to sudden inner promptings' (p. 2). Again, he shows how two apparently simple changes of tense in 'Sun' function as a 'near-systematic suppression of elements in the original story that had pointed in directions he no longer wished to follow' (pp. 70–1). Finally, in a comparison of the *Lady Chatterley* versions, he brings out, for example, changes in the handling of Constance's meeting with Parkin's daughter Connie, and shows how these are indicative of the hardening in Lawrence's view of how people react to the suffering of others. These examples provide a mere glimpse of the kind of intricate analysis that characterizes this engrossing and highly successful book.

Amit Chaudhuri's *D.H. Lawrence and 'Difference'* is one of only a few full-length monographs on Lawrence's poetry to date. Chaudhuri establishes his premise by alluding to previous evaluations of Lawrence's poetry: accounts that have tended either to be unjustifiably derogatory or to rely on the selection of a few masterpieces, to the exclusion of a broader sense of Lawrence's poetic discourse. Chaudhuri adopts an entirely different approach to the perceived inadequacies inherent in Lawrence's poems, arguing that a true response necessitates an imaginative leap of faith, demanding a strategy that is 'participatory' rather than focused or localized. His concern is with Lawrence's poetic discourse in its entirety, and in order to address it he adopts intertextual—and specifically Derridean—methods in order to articulate his interpretations.

While chapter 1 begins with an interpretation of three poems elucidated through an intertextual approach that prioritizes the meaning of each poem individually, the book tends to employ the term 'intertextuality' in a different sense thereafter. While Chaudhuri rejects Derrida's method of 'deconstruction', which (like new criticism) tends to uphold the sense of a poem enclosed within its own rigid frame, he adopts Derrida's concept of 'trace', suggesting that a signifier or image contains within itself the hint of its multiple usages elsewhere. Thus, a poem may be situated within its poetic discourse or linguistic field. Later,

Chaudhuri employs the Derridean term 'grammatology', which he labels as a method of creating a 'non-logocentric language' (p. 5), devoid of centre, hierarchy, and linearity. This mirrors Lawrence's language used within his poetic discourse, and harbours a political dimension that is crucial to the author's own reading of Lawrence.

Chaudhuri does not adopt a chronological or developmental approach here, choosing instead to focus on clusters of poems, informed through reference to other works by Lawrence, such as his literary criticism and non-fiction. He also brings into play Lawrence's writings on foreign cultures, such as *Mornings in Mexico* and *Etruscan Places*, exploring cultural 'difference' as well as the 'difference' inherent in Lawrence's poetic discourse. He contextualizes his own position as a postcolonial reader of Lawrence in his conclusion. This book is wide-ranging in its literary, political, and theoretical insights, serving as an invaluable addition to the rare books focusing on an undervalued genre within Lawrence's writing.

In *Body of Truth: D.H. Lawrence, the Nomadic Years, 1919–1930*, Philip Callow describes the three-volume Cambridge biography as 'definitive' (p. 289), yet asserts that his response to Lawrence's work inspired him to write his own account. Callow argues that what Lawrence says of his poetry is true of all his work, namely it 'needs the penumbra of its own time and place and circumstance to make it full and whole' (p. 287). He establishes the premise that Lawrence's work is, in many subtle, intricate, fluctuating, and difficult ways, so rooted in his world that surely no single biography can define it once and for all.

Perhaps the fact that Callow is a novelist and a biographer (of five other writers and artists) is significant. Although the lack of scholarly apparatus providing precise and verifiable references may be disquieting (and some kind of chronology would have been useful), the book must be judged ultimately according to whether or not this particular act of literary creativity has selected and presented material so that Lawrence's writings can be better understood in the context of his life.

Callow makes perceptive use of those features of Lawrence's works that correlate interestingly with the biographical context. Occasionally, there seems to be an abrupt transition between the literary analysis and what seems to be less significant information, but in general the absorbing nature of the book is a reflection of an integrated whole. In the last few chapters especially, the measure of Callow's success is the poignancy of Lawrence's involvement with the Etruscans' treatment of death and the composition of late works such as 'Hymns in a Man's Life', *Apocalypse*, and *Last Poems*, seen in the context of his slow struggle against failing physical strength. If the book may justifiably be described as a 'Body of Truth', its truth must be identified as instinctive rather than scholarly, located in the creative 'act of attention' with which its author engages with a revered subject.

An interesting contrast to strictly academic research, Leslie Williamson's booklet *D.H. Lawrence and the Country He Loved* is based on personal memories of the 1920s when he was a young boy. The title on the first page is 'D.H. Lawrence and Eastwood', followed, in parenthesis, by 'where it all went wrong'.

This is indicative of the author's style, which tends to be colloquial, and sometimes derogatory.

The main body of the pamphlet consists of a number of Williamson's own poems, the majority juxtaposed with short anecdotal prose passages. Many of the poems, including 'The Story of Coal', 'Coal Belt', 'Willey Water', and 'Garsington And All That', engage explicitly with Lawrentian contexts. Others, such as 'Eastwood Then and Now', 'A Toast to Lawrence and Frieda', 'The Prodigal Son', and 'Looking Back', either evoke Lawrence as a protagonist or present the poem from his perspective. Thematically and linguistically the poetry does at times reveal Lawrence's influence, exemplified in the journey into the past through recollection described in 'A Collection from Grandad' (reminiscent of Lawrence's 'Piano'), and the mother kissing the 'cold dead lips' of her collier son in 'Coal Ghosts'. At times, the poems slide into cliché, most often when they are inhibited by an un-Lawrentian propensity to rhyme. Generally, however, they are extreme vivid, employing language that is at once direct and imbued with startling images in an effective evocation of past and present scenes.

Having discussed a number of monographs on Lawrence I will move on to edited works. It seems apposite to begin with a fresh addition to the prestigious Cambridge University Press edition of Lawrence's letters and works before proceeding to a collection of articles edited by the renowned Lawrentians Keith Cushman and Earl G. Ingersoll. I will then discuss a book on modernist writers, incorporating a chapter on Lawrence and focusing on issues of gender, before considering Keith Sagar's new and welcome edition of Lawrence's painting.

Greenspan, Vasey, and Worthen, eds., *Studies in Classic American Literature*, bears the literal and figurative stamp of the CUP edition of Lawrence's letters and literary works. Literally, it bears the trademark Lawrentian phoenix; figuratively, its scholarly comprehensiveness locates it unmistakably within this invaluable series. For a volume whose content attests to an inevitable, innate complexity it is extremely well organized and easy to negotiate. It also contains some exciting material hitherto unavailable within the public domain, such as the 'intermediate' version of the 'Whitman' essay, in which Lawrence places his American precursor alongside Dante and Shakespeare in status, and offers his most blatant and physiological elucidation of Whitmanesque manly love.

It is fascinating to chart the development of the *SCAL* essays between 1917 and 1923, considering their radical ideological and stylistic shifts. The editors also provide a clear indication of Lawrence's intention for the collection at various stages. Initially there were fifteen items intended for the book, all of which were revised on various occasions. Two essays were discarded; others were expanded and split into two distinct essays. Although the editors assert that it would be impossible to establish a clear textual history due to the number of lost items, they do identify five stages within the process of textual evolution. A helpful textual diagram indicates the status and variants of the extant and lost manuscripts of each essay, while the introduction locates these texts through reference to letters and other biographical sources.

The main section of the volume is split into three parts, each providing a distinct version of the *SCAL* book: the 'Final Version [1923]'; 'First Version [1918–19]'; and 'Intermediate Version [1919]'. Additional material is incorporated within appendices, which contain 'Reading Notes for *The Scarlet Letter* [1917]'; two versions of a foreword to the book (1920 and 1922); 'Other TS Versions of Nathaniel Hawthorne's *Blithedale Romance* [1920–1]'; and two further drafts of the 'Whitman' essay (1921–2 and 1922). The explanatory notes that follow are detailed, perceptive, and illuminating, while, in addition to the usual textual apparatus there is a full variorum apparatus focusing on manuscript and typescript variants, revealing the extent to which this edition has proved a scholarly *tour de force*.

Cushman and Ingersoll, eds., *D.H. Lawrence: New Worlds*, proceeds from the view that 'the beginning of the twenty-first century offers an opportunity for reappraisal of the major modernist writers' (p. 17). The material incorporated here is indicative of a diversity of approaches (though there is a sense of chronological progression through Lawrence's career after the first four essays), and reflects the increasing 'internationalization' of Lawrence studies. The book's title engages with Lawrence's discovery of 'new worlds' in Australia, Mexico, and New Mexico, while there is also an emphasis on the situating of Lawrence within the context of postmodern theory—a phenomenon that the editors identify as relatively new.

The collection incorporates studies of several of the major novels: 'The Life of the Son/Sun and the Death of the Mother in *Sons and Lovers*' by Gavriel Reisner; 'Metaphor in *Women in Love*' by Kyoko Kay Kondo; '*Kangaroo* and the Narrative of Contingency' by Neil Roberts; '"Demonish maturity": Identity, Consumption, and the Discourse of Species in *The Plumed Serpent*' by Carrie Rohman; 'Mexican Cypresses: Multiculturalism in Lawrence's "Novel of America"' by Virginia Hyde; and 'Deconstructing Myth in *Lady Chatterley's Lover*' by Ginette Katz-Roy. John Worthen creates an original and illuminating revaluation of the play *David* in 'Lawrence's Theater of the Southwest', while Laurie McCollum offers an interesting new reading of (arguably) Lawrence's most controversial story in 'Ritual Sacrifice in "The Woman Who Rode Away": A Girardian Reading'. Characteristically, Holly Laird's contribution, 'Records of Pain and Hope Now Spent: Elegy and Expenditure in *Amores*', focuses on Lawrence as poet, while Jack Stewart approaches the literature of travel from a tropological perspective, focusing on Lawrence's use of metonymy in his essay 'Movement, Space, and Rhetoric in Lawrence's Travel Writing'.

Of the remaining four contributions, those placed at the forefront of the collection, Michael Squires's 'Lawrence and the Calculus of Change' offers an 'unusual overview of Lawrence's fiction' (p. 18). Judith Ruderman discusses 'Englishness' and 'Jewishness' in her article 'An "Englishman at heart?": Lawrence and the National Identity Debates', while Keith Cushman and Peter Preston explore representations of Lawrence in fiction and the visual arts. In 'Lawrence and Knud Merrild: New Materials, New Perspectives', Cushman examines the Danish painter's portraits of Lawrence, while in '"I am in a novel": Lawrence in Recent British Fiction', Preston traces allusions to Lawrence and his works within contemporary fiction.

The collection remains true to its alleged diversity, not least in its wide frame of reference and plethora of contextualizing theories and debates. Authors draw on the writings of Lacan, Georges Bataille, René Girard, Derrida, Marianne Torgovnick, and Paul Ricœur. Approaches such as postcolonialism and cultural materialism combine to reveal the 'vital, complex, multi-faceted, original, provocative Lawrence' (p. 20) to which the editors lay claim.

James J. Miracky's *Regenerating the Novel: Gender and Genre in Woolf, Forster, Sinclair and Lawrence* is a lucidly written and particularly well-structured work that would be of great value to students of modernist literature. It opens with a short preface and ends with a one-paragraph, generalizing conclusion, but each chapter, devoted to a specific novelist, is divided into sections and has its own introduction. There are notes on the four chapters at the end of the book and an ample bibliography.

Miracky argues that, 'Given the interrelatedness of gender and genre in the history and theory of the novel, it is no wonder that the early twentieth century, considered a time of "gender crisis" and instability, ushered in a period of contestation over the form of the novel that was often articulated in gendered terms' (p. xii). The novelists Virginia Woolf, E.M. Forster, May Sinclair, and D.H. Lawrence, though in many ways distinct, are all said to 'both regenerate and "regenderate" the form of the novel to suit their particular aims' (p. xiii).

Central to the argument is his revelation of the ways in which Lawrence uses gender-related terms and metaphors to illuminate the shortcomings of both modern society and literature of the nineteenth and twentieth centuries. For example, 'Lawrence uses the language and imagery of emasculation to explain the impotence of modern man in a feminized self-conscious society' (p. 118), while condemning feminine tendencies and praising masculine qualities in his assessment of the nineteenth-century realist novel. Miracky identifies Lawrence's principal aim as the desire to 'revitalize' the novel, seeing it as a 'unique medium by which, if it is written properly, the emptiness of culture can be challenged and the spirit of humanity can be revivified, through the revelation of "true and vivid relationships"' (p. 133).

There are some partial truths articulated here, occasioned by the sheer complexity and ambiguity inherent in Lawrence's shifting views on gender roles. Also, there are moments in which Miracky covers old ground, evident (for example) in his argument that, although Lawrence's ideal is articulated in terms of equitable heterosexual relationships characterized by phallic consciousness, his work always has, at the very least, homoerotic or misogynistic overtones: 'Even on his deathbed Lawrence's inclusive vision is undermined by a one-sided phallic reality' (p. 145). Yet this is, in general, an interesting study, situating Lawrence in the context of his contemporaneous fiction-writers and provoking fruitful contrasts and connections.

Sagar, ed., *D.H. Lawrence's Paintings*, presents a comprehensive display of Lawrence's visual art. It contains colour reproductions of high quality, interspersed with much information about Lawrence's life, his views on art, and his literature. His engagement with art is charted from the early meticulous copying of others' work to the prolific period during the years prior to his death, culminating in the infamous display of a number of paintings at the Warren Street Gallery in 1929, during which thirteen of the paintings were confiscated as a consequence of their alleged obscenity.

Lawrence's writing is shown to have some affinity with his art: for instance in employing painterly description and colour symbolism. More significant, however, is the way that writing composed near the creation of a painting provides an indication of Lawrence's intent. For instance, *Flight Back into Paradise*, *Throwing Back the Apple*, and *Dance Sketch* are seen as 'part of the same programme as *Lady Chatterley's Lover* and the poem "Paradise Re-entered"' (p. 43), while *Dandelions* reflects a reaction to the enforced expurgation of Lawrence's most notorious novel, and *Resurrection* is related to *The Escaped Cock*.

Some deficiencies in technique, especially pertaining to anatomy, are explained in terms of a refusal to accept the 'tyranny of the eye over the imagination' (for example, comparatively small heads in paintings reflect a reaction to the modern European 'living from the head'). Sagar asserts that Lawrence refused to work from models or photographs, even for the ostensible portrait *Contadini*, citing Lawrence's contention that 'the picture must all come out of the artist's inside... It is an image as it lives in the consciousness, alive like a vision, but unknown' (p. 52).

Nowhere does Sagar claim that Lawrence has mastery over his technique, though he does praise certain paintings: *Boccaccio Story* is 'so wholly successful' while *Red Willow Trees* is an 'accomplished picture'. He incorporates the perspective articulated by the novelist Rhys Davies (a friend of Lawrence's), who believed that because of the Lawrentian intensity in his paintings 'the technical errors seemed not to matter; almost because of the errors they achieved a barbaric aliveness' (p. 64).

As well as an extensive commentary on the paintings, Sagar includes three essays expressing Lawrence's views on art and creativity: 'Making Pictures', 'Pictures on the Walls' and 'Introduction to these Paintings' (for the Mandrake edition). The resulting juxtaposition of theory and practice reflects interestingly on Lawrence as artist and non-fiction writer, in the context of a book that incorporates a wider range of paintings than any previous edition, including some hitherto unpublished material.

In the foreword to the 2002–3 issue of the (British) *Journal of the D.H. Lawrence Society*, the editor Bethan Jones indicates that the embodied articles employ a plethora of diverse methodologies, adopting interdisciplinary, intertextual, topographical, historicist, and linguistic approaches to Lawrence's writing.

In the opening article, 'The Thinker as Poet (On Dissolving the Genre Distinction Between Philosophy and Literature)' (*JDHLS* [2002–3] 7–19) Stephen Alexander interrogates the implications of breaking down barriers between the two related disciplines of poetry (or poetic fiction) and philosophy. He indicates ways in which both Lawrence and Nietzsche explore the role of poet as thinker, a hybrid visionary with potential to create the bright possibility of a new dawn in a nihilistic modern era.

The subsequent essays are biographically orientated, focusing on fiction arising from Lawrence's travels. In 'Rananim Glimpsed: Lawrence in Taos' (*JDHLS* [2002–3] 20–40) Amitav Banerjee provides a detailed account of Lawrence's twenty-month stay in New Mexico and its portrayal in both fiction and non-fiction: he identifies this period as one of the most fruitful and productive of Lawrence's literary career. In 'D.H. Lawrence and Norman Douglas: The Enthralling Attraction of Southern Italy' (*JDHLS* [2002–3] 41–99) Nick Ceramella combines his own intuitive knowledge and understanding as a native of the Calabrian region of Italy with an account of Norman Douglas' journey as portrayed in the travel book *Old Calabria*. In the second part of his article he turns to Lawrence's *Sea and Sardinia*, indicating comparisons and contrasts with Douglas's method of evoking landscapes and the customs of native inhabitants. In 'Nottingham Canal and *The Rainbow*' (*JDHLS* [2002–3] 100–6) Ronald Morris interrogates the dichotomy of fact and fiction, using historicist research to illuminate aspects of the novel.

George Hyde, in an article that must merit a prize for its quirky title—'Suave Loins, Venison Pasties and Other Tasty Nonsense: The Unacceptable Face of Lawrence' (*JDHLS* [2002–3] 107–22)—adopts an intertextual methodology in order to analyse the controversial, oft-maligned language of specific passages in *Women in Love*, through reference to texts as diverse as Genesis and Freud's *Dora* case history. Finally, Stephen Adams's intertextual piece, 'Drowning Ishmael: D.H. Lawrence and Herman Melville's *Moby-Dick*' (*JDHLS* [2002–3] 123–7) is founded on an original and enlightening piece of scholarship. He explains Lawrence's curious omission of any allusion to Ishmael's survival at the end of *Moby-Dick* as the consequence of a printing error within the 1851 text edited by Richard Bentley, in which the epilogue is omitted.

The other journal articles reviewed below have been grouped according to the Lawrence texts discussed, with an initial focus on *Women in Love* and a subsequent emphasis on *Kangaroo*, before moving on to a consideration of Lawrence's poetry and travel writing. It seems appropriate, however, to precede the discussion of two novels engaging (implicitly or explicitly) with the impact of the First World War on society with an article directly on this subject.

In 'Lawrence and the Great War' (*Neophil* 87:i[2003] 153–70) Jae-Kyung Koh identifies this social and political cataclysm as a 'watershed in Lawrence's life' (p. 162), examining the author's response to the event as reflected in correspondence, fiction, and non-fiction. He proceeds from the standpoint that Lawrence perceived the outbreak of war as arising from the repression and distortion of instinctive urges and desires endemic in the Christian era, with its emphasis on selflessness, altruism, and servitude. Koh briefly introduces the Lamarckian concept of 'inheritance of acquired characteristics' into his argument regarding the way in which the disciplining and restraint of the senses and ego were perpetuated during the Christian centuries in Europe. Koh examines Lawrence's bitter detestation of war and his proffered alternatives—from conventional socialism and anarchic individualism to the concept of 'Rananim'—subsequently indicating how the censorship of *The Rainbow* led to Lawrence's deep-seated disillusionment with England and his determination to escape. Ultimately, though, the war was envisaged as potentially apocalyptic—a paradigm of the dichotomy of creation and destruction that Lawrence hoped might issue in a 'new heaven and new earth'—hence the optimism in the relationship between Connie and Mellors in the post-war novel *Lady Chatterley's Lover*. This article, though a little repetitive, incorporates a good deal of useful material; it serves as a productive addition to the existing explorations of this key period in Lawrence's life and works, combining literary and cultural studies analysis.

In 'Ontological Incoherence in *Women in Love*' (*CollL* 30:iv[2003] 156–65) Erik Levy both engages with and extends insights derived from the work of the prominent Lawrentians Michael Bell and Jack Stewart. Proceeding from a consideration of the ontological incoherence arising from the discontinuities within the Cartesian mind–body split, he argues that, in *Women in Love*, Lawrence both *insists* on this incoherence and offers a reinterpretation of the Cartesian view. He goes on to link the 'problem of incoherence' to the 'problem of time' (p. 159), subsequently introducing Henri Bergson's *Creative Evolution* and the principle of 'duration' as a means of illuminating and clarifying crucial preoccupations within Lawrence's novel. Levy sees Lawrence as both enacting and reversing the uni-directional principle of 'duration' in his depiction of creation and destruction, progression and devolution. The final part of the article focuses on Birkin and the 'opposition between finality and creativity' (p. 163) inherent in his motivation and desires, with a concluding emphasis on Lawrence's affirmation of the ontological principle of 'eternal creative mystery'. The article is admirable in the way that it deals very lucidly and concisely with complex philosophical issues, providing new insight into aspects of this novel that have been much explored.

Anne E. Fernald's '"Out of it": Alienation and Coercion in D.H. Lawrence' (*MFS* 49:ii[2003] 183–203) is a spirited piece whose energy is entirely concomitant with its subject. Fernald establishes the interdependence of coercion and alienation—of 'fighting and being out of it' (p. 185)—indicating that both issue in the kind of responsiveness and alert engagement that are the antithesis of conformity and bored conservatism. Fernald examines the provocative prose of *Fantasia of the Unconscious*, focusing on its abrasive language, which challenges the reader, inciting them to fight back. She considers the purpose underlying the unformed and disordered argument generated by Lawrence's 'brilliant and self-indulgent' writing (p. 192), and the inadequacy of reason or 'understanding' in responding to it. Neither does she shirk the most controversial and unpalatable parts of this non-fictional work, examining anti-Semitic sentiment as an aspect of the brutal honesty characteristic of the author. Equally, the article engages with *Women in Love* as a dramatization of the kinds of provocative exchange discussed in relation to the non-fiction. She also locates her key terms (coercion and alienation) in the wider context of modernism, alluding to Eliot, Yeats, and Conrad in order to highlight distinctions and shed light on Lawrence's unique method. Overall, this is a highly compelling and persuasive piece.

The next two articles focus on Lawrence's Australian fiction. Philip Skelton's '"A slobbery affair" and "stinking mongrelism": Individualism, Postmodernity and D.H. Lawrence's *Kangaroo*' (*ES* 84:vi[2003] 545–57) emphasizes the relevance of this novel's social critique to a contemporary world 'that is straitened as ever between the Scylla and Charybdis of the material reality of imperialism and the rhetorical seductiveness of individualism' (p. 557). Part I establishes the socio-political premise for the investigation, and examines

Somers's conflict between the individual as 'alone ... with the dark God' and the opposing demand for a 'communion in power'. Part II discusses Somers as rootless, restless prototype of postmodernity, examining an individualism which is fragmented and relativistic. Part III brings two precursive novels—*The Rainbow* and *Women in Love*—into the equation, discussing social and political hierarchies and, specifically, the novels' representation of aristocratic architecture, which Skelton contrasts with the scorn for the aristocratic concern with legitimate lineal descent articulated in *Kangaroo*. This article offers an interesting perspective on the role of individualism within both modernist and postmodern contexts.

In 'The Dutch–Australian connection: Willem Siebenhaar, D.H. Lawrence, *Max Havelaar* and *Kangaroo*' (*ALS* 21:i[2003] 3–19) Paul Eggert examines the unlikely connection between Lawrence and a 'high-minded idealist and theosophist ... an anarchist who knew and corresponded with the leading militant Dutch socialist-anarchist, Ferdinand Domela Nieuwenhuis' (p. 3). Eggert tells the story of Siebenhaar's migration to Perth in 1891, discussing his political affiliations and his writings, while also evaluating the significance of his works in various genres: notably his poetry collection *Dorothea*, two major translations, historical essays, editorial work, and reviews. Yet Eggert's most crucial contribution in terms of Lawrence studies is his attempt to establish the significance of Lawrence's discussions with Siebenhaar and his reading, in particular, of the *Max Havelaar* translation (for which Lawrence wrote an introduction). He argues that such encounters operated as a fundamental influence on the 'Nightmare' chapter of *Kangaroo*—and, more crucially, provided the impetus for the writing of the novel in its entirety. Thus Eggert sheds new light on one of the 'great curiosities of *Kangaroo*' (p. 13), and in so doing allows a fascinating Dutch–Australian connection to be revealed and scrutinized.

The next 'pair' of articles, by Keith Sagar and Roger Simmonds respectively, engage with Lawrence as poet. In 'Lawrence's Debt to Whitman' (*Symbiosis* 7:i[2003] 99–117) Sagar supplements the pre-existing criticism and scholarship on this subject with a fresh and incisive discussion. Lawrence, Sagar asserts, *became* a great poet—he would not have been one had he died before 1920—and the essence of his greatness lies in the immeasurable influence of the precursive American free-verse poet, Walt Whitman. Sagar examines the way in which Lawrence's initial skirmishes with Whitman (as early as 1908) gave rise to poetic glimpses of greatness, yet culminated only in a 'false dawn' (represented by the early poems in *Look! We Have Come Through!*), petering out during the war period. He then goes on to discuss the reinvigoration of Lawrence's poetry through the later, more mature, engagement with Whitman (from 1918), as evidenced in the burgeoning *Birds, Beasts and Flowers* collection and beyond. Sagar's article is candid and forthright, unafraid to label a weak stanza a 'dog's dinner', and equally unafraid to afford the highest accolade to Lawrence's poetry at its best. He cites copious examples to illustrate his interpretation of the poetry, while also examining the evolving 'Whitman' essay in *Studies in Classic American Literature* and 'Poetry of the Present', discussing Lawrence's misreadings of Whitman in conjunction with the acknowledgements of profound indebtedness.

In 'The Poem as Novel: Lawrence's *Pansies* and Bakhtin's Theory of the Novel' (*ES* 84:ii[2003] 119–44) Roger Simmonds offers a new and perceptive reading of a book of poetry often dismissed too lightly by critics. Indicating ways in which critics have 'normalized' or misrepresented these poems through subjective and misguided selection, Simmonds indicates their fundamental value, describing ways in which they depart from (for instance) 'poetic' characteristics as defined by the Russian formalists. In their frequently complex and estranging use of ordinary language, the *Pansies* poems subvert expectation, departing from established conventions of the poetic genre and venturing into new territory. An analysis of 'Money-Madness' reveals the way in which poems embody multiple discourses, conflicting voices and languages which undercut and undermine each other, sometimes through self-mockery and subversive laughter—thus acquiring characteristics Bakhtin has applied to the novel, asserting that they are absent from the monologism of poetic style. Though unnecessarily stringent in satirizing and condemning the approaches of notable scholars early on, the essay is refreshing in focusing on a collection that rarely receives enough attention. It is extremely convincing in its analysis and the conclusions drawn.

M.B. Mencher's 'Lawrence and Sex' (*ES* 84:iv[2003] 347–54) aims to evade the potential pitfall of creating another account that will 'rehash a very old story' (p. 347) by indicating the limitations of previous writings on this topic, characterized, among other things, by 'embarrassed evasion' (p. 347). This article itself is curiously and paradoxically evasive, never talking in detail about frank (or otherwise) portrayals of sexuality in Lawrence's texts. Instead, Mencher uses this subject as a pretext for an essentially intertextual method, placing Lawrence alongside a vast range of precursors and contemporaries—ranging from Shelley and Dickens to Dylan Thomas—in order to establish both his shortcomings and his immense significance. This account feels energized, vivid, and spontaneous rather than scholarly and tightly focused; its ultimate aim seems to be to celebrate the 'mysterious engaging warmth' (p. 354) that is identified as the 'touchstone of [Lawrence's] ultimate value to us as a writer' (p. 354).

Rosemary Sullivan's 'A Trip to Tarquinia with D.H. Lawrence' (*Brick* 72[2003] 55–9) identifies and celebrates some of the same characteristics in Lawrence as the previous article. It is an unashamedly personal account, describing a visit to the Etruscan tombs, triggered by the chance acquisition of a copy of Lawrence's *Etruscan Places* in Siena. The article offers a humorous and compelling evocation of the tribulations and frustrations experienced during a number of thwarted attempts to locate the tombs, followed by a moment of delight on finding the tombs echoing Lawrence's own. The account reminds the reader of crucial aspects of Lawrence's response to the Etruscans, such as his rewriting of history in charting the overthrow of the Etruscans by the 'vicious' Romans—and his thoroughly Lawrentian recreation of the Etruscans as the idealized embodiment of his life principle. Most poignantly perhaps, Sullivan reminds us of the proximity of Lawrence's journey to the tombs to the rapid worsening of his precarious health, so that, during this visit, 'Lawrence was rehearsing his own death with equanimity' (p. 59).

In 'The Cambridge Edition of D.H. Lawrence's *Letters*' (*ES* 84:iii[2003] 231–8) Amitav Banerjee celebrates the exemplary scholarship evident in a project (begun in 1979 by James T. Boulton) that has been invaluable in providing us with 'a cohesive self-portrait of the *living* artist' (p. 238). He situates the project within the developing continuum of correspondence published since shortly after the author's death, indicating the extent of the editorial achievement through describing the comprehensiveness of the embodied material, while also touching on the crucial role of introductory material and copious annotation. Banerjee is keen to link letters to Lawrence's fiction, indicating how the 'jottings' of 'inchoate thoughts' in the correspondence provide us with real insight into the workings of Lawrence's mind, while also equipping us with an understanding of crucial concepts that we can bring to bear on other works. This article effectively illustrates the significance of this wealth of epistolary material, while celebrating a recently completed project that will remain a fundamental landmark in the history of D.H. Lawrence scholarship.

Finally, in 'The Date of Birth of D.H. Lawrence's Father' (*N&Q* 50:iii[2003] 327–8) John Worthen challenges the assumption held by biographers that Arthur Lawrence was born on 18 June 1846, formulating a persuasive argument for the alternative birth date of 26 February 1848. Worthen describes how information within the Lawrence family birthday book points to the revised date, suggesting that the Arthur Lawrence who became D.H. Lawrence's father was given the name of a recently deceased elder sibling, taking the place of the dead child in the official records. Worthen does not offer his evidence as conclusive, but the brief entry is convincing and provides a useful emendation to assumptions made regarding the Lawrence family biography.

(d) Virginia Woolf

Among the many books published about Virginia Woolf this year, Melba Cuddy-Kean's *Virginia Woolf, the Intellectual, and the Public Sphere* ranks as one of the most distinguished. Cuddy-Kean, who will be well known for earlier important essays on Woolf (in *PMLA* 105:ii [1990] 273–85, and in Pamela Caughie, ed., *Virginia Woolf in the Age of Mechanical Reproduction*, Garland [2000]), invites her readers in this volume to rethink many critical clichés and presumptions about Woolf's class and political affiliation. In this original, judicious, theoretically informed, and fair-minded study, Cuddy-Kean surveys more than 500 essays and reviews written by Woolf, and locates her very precisely in her culture and historical moment when 'the achievement of universal franchise, the extension of adult education to the working class and to women, and the rise of mass publishing all added urgency to the need to foster accessible cultural education' (p. 1). Rejecting both the 'older image of Woolf as elitist or "aloof" and more recent accusations that she was an aesthetic capitalist bent on acquiring cultural and economic power through self-commodification' (p. 2), Cuddy-Kean argues instead that Woolf's 'common reader' offers a 'model of active, self-reflexive reading' that is more democratic and empowering than many of Woolf's critics have recognized (p. 1).

Cuddy-Kean describes Woolf's pedagogical practices as a teacher in the adult education program at Morley College between 1905 and 1907, and explains how they informed her writing as an essayist, noting that she continued to write reviews even after her financial success as a novelist alleviated the need to supplement her income. Faced with students who 'lacked the exposure to intellectual culture that she herself had', Woolf preferred discussions rather than lecturing since she regarded the latter as an 'obsolete custom which not merely wastes time and temper but incites the most debased of human passions—vanity, ostentation, self-assertion and the desire to convert' (quoted p. 96). Cuddy-Kean shows how Woolf's anti-authoritarian pedagogy shaped her writing style and rhetorical strategies in *A Room of One's Own* and *Three Guineas*, a point Teresa Winterhalter similarly makes, using a Bakhtinian vocabulary, to describe Woolf's construction of voices and modes of argumentation in 'What Else Can I Do But Write: Discursive Disruption and the Ethics of Style in Virginia Woolf's *Three Guineas*' (*Hypatia* 18:iv[2003] 236–57).

Showing that Woolf rejected the models of the reader as student and buyer, Cuddy-Kean argues that Woolf invented another alternative, the 'common reader' as 'eater' (p. 68). Despite her bluestocking reputation, Woolf wrote essays designed to encourage all people to think, read, and write critically. Her preferred educational site was the library rather than the lecture hall. Recognizing the 'struggles of working-class people, particularly working-class women', and their 'long, historic effort to make themselves articulate' (p. 106), Woolf expressed delight in a diary entry when she found tea stains and lipstick on a copy of *A Common Reader* in the Lewes Library, seeing them as signs of 'everyday use' (p. 113). While some readers may find Cuddy-Kean's argument that the university is no longer the opponent that it was for Woolf to be a bit overly optimistic, or may dispute her contention that the field of English studies has moved beyond the need to adopt an obscure vocabulary that blocks ordinary readers' access to specialized knowledge, few will doubt that she has succeeded in following Woolf's example as an eloquent proponent of 'individual democratic highbrowism' (p. 196).

Sean Latham, in his witty, stylishly designed volume '*Am I a Snob? Modernism and the Novel*, comes to different conclusions about Woolf's role as a public intellectual in his exploration of her reputation as a self-confessed 'snob'. Latham's objective is to analyse how modernity transformed the Victorian figure of the snob, and he offers a brief history, beginning with the figures created by Thackeray and Wilde and ending with those described by Virginia Woolf and Dorothy Sayers, with interesting asides on Aldous Huxley and George Orwell. Latham devotes two chapters to Woolf, noting that she had the audacity to pose the question frankly in her essay 'Am I a Snob?', though he does not speculate on her unwillingness to publish the essay in her lifetime. Latham offers fairly predictable observations on *To the Lighthouse* and *Orlando* as well as on Woolf's better-known essays, but he barely mentions her most obvious example of a snob, Mrs Dalloway. Deferring to Pierre Bourdieu's definition of 'cultural capital', Latham assumes, apparently, that it was the financial success of *Orlando* and *The Years* that tempted Woolf to take the snob's pose, claiming that she sought refuge in what he calls her 'privileged' position as outsider only after she had 'passed through the gauntlet of fame and sampled the pleasures of snobbery' (p. 117), though Brenda Silver offers a more nuanced consideration of Woolf's response to fame in *Virginia Woolf: Icon* (UChicP [1999]). While Latham's study is historically organized, it treats the history of authorship in England over more than a century with telescopic ease, dating, for example, the creation of a 'mass market' readership to Thackeray's time and citing, in support, E.P. Thompson's classic study which he transforms, in a telling error, into *The Rise of the English Ruling Class* (p. 14). Latham also neglects the role of language and accent in his discussion of the colonial-born Thackeray and the Irish Wilde, so in discussions of Woolf he ignores her lack of a 'gentleman's education' and the gendered restraints of the literary marketplace, not to mention how her assessment of capitalism, especially after the collapse of Ramsay MacDonald's Labour government in 1931, encouraged her greater political engagement, as demonstrated in earlier studies by Jane Marcus, Melba Cuddy-Kean, Naomi Black, and Anna Snaith, as well as in Janet McVicker's 'Six Essays on London Life: A History of Dispersal, Part 1' (*WstA* 9[2003] 143–65), published this year.

Patricia Laurence also addresses the complex relationship between race, nationality, and modernity in her ambitious study, *Lily Briscoe's Chinese Eyes: Bloomsbury, Modernism, and China*. One of the most original and valuable contributions of this study is Laurence's reconstruction of Julian Bell's little-known work as a teacher of modern English literature at Wuhan University in China from 1934 to 1937, which she considers in the larger context of the renewed interest in Chinese culture expressed by many members of the Bloomsbury Group. Laurence's well-documented, innovative study traces the two-way exchange between English modernists and Chinese writers in the Crescent Moon Group, often nicknamed the 'Chinese Bloomsbury Group', and so delineates what she terms the multiple and 'evolving international modernisms' (p. 359) of the first three decades of the twentieth century in order to interrogate the unexamined nationalism that has previously restricted the modernist canon. Drawing primarily on postmodern theory, Laurence's study is driven by her self-confessed desire to promote a greater recognition of the importance of 'place' (p. 4), and in response to Fredric Jameson's call to always 'historicize'. She presents a fresh, creatively organized, though sometimes startlingly ahistorical, composite portrait of the individual feelings of members of the Bloomsbury and Crescent Moon groups, noting that individuals in both groups have been vilified as 'decadent', 'snobbish', or 'dangerously hybrid' (p. 31).

Certainly, Julian Bell could have been identified as epitomizing the sexual exploitation that was one of the disciplining forces in British imperialism, but Laurence avoids simple judgements, presenting instead a thoughtful, complex analysis of his 'performance of Englishness' during his stint as a professor at Wuhan University, where he lectured on Woolf's *To the Lighthouse* and other modernist texts. Laurence admits that Julian Bell had 'little linguistic or cultural preparation' (p. 8) for this work, acknowledges the elite social networks that made it possible, and recognizes the Boxer Indemnity funds that subsidized his travel and teaching in China. She attempts to counter the image of Bell as 'the imperialist predator freely ranging in another's space' (p. 9) by outlining his warm relationships with his students and his scandalous affair with the writer Ling Shuhua, wife of the dean who hired him. What makes her study so enduringly valuable is that it presents the results of Laurence's original archival research, including her recovery of Bell's China photo album and Ling Shuhua's 'friendship scroll' and manuscripts, though unfortunately not her lost letters to

Bell. She also describes the rest of Ling Shuhua's story by outlining her subsequent travel to study in England, her relationship with Vanessa Bell after Julian's death in 1937, and her moving correspondence with Virginia Woolf, from 1937 to 1941, as they both struggled to come to terms with Julian's death and voice their resistance to gender subordination, war, and fascism. Encouraged by Woolf to write her autobiography in English, Ling Shuhua later completed *Ancient Melodies*, which was published in 1953 by the Hogarth Press.

Another important contribution of this study is Laurence's analysis of the Bloomsbury Group's interest in Chinese art and culture. She describes G.L. Dickinson's travels in China, offers a reading of his satirical 'Letters from John Chinaman' [1901], and outlines his warm relationships with several of Chinese students, including Xu Zhimo. She similarly explores Roger Fry's interest in the formal qualities of Chinese sculpture and offers an analysis of Lytton Strachey's little-known play *Son of Heaven*, lavishly produced at Scala in 1928, with sets by Duncan Grant and music by William Walton. She shows how Bloomsbury's openness about homosexuality appealed to some of the writers in the Crescent Moon Group, noting, for example, that Forster shared the unpublished manuscript of *Maurice* with Xiao Xian, and describes how Chinese traditions of cross-dressing and gender impersonation reinforced Bloomsbury's interest in Chinese opera and court traditions in the 1920s. Laurence is less willing, however, to acknowledge the underlying racism that clearly coexisted with this interest, or indeed to discuss the larger political and economic inequalities that structured East–West relations but remain largely outside the frame of her study. The organizing metaphor of this study is, of course, a reference to Lily Briscoe's 'Chinese eyes', and the volume concludes with an illuminating reading of Woolf's *To the Lighthouse*. Lily's concern with rhythm and 'line' in her painting as well as in the ecstatic 'dissolution' of self that she experiences as she completes it, Laurence argues, demonstrates Woolf's understanding of the formal conventions of Chinese art, since she invites readers of her experimental novels to take the position assigned to viewers of a Chinese landscape painting and 'imagine what's left out' (p. 387).

Jane Garrity's *Step-Daughters of England: British Women Modernists and the National Imaginary* offers a more historically based analysis of the relationship between gender, sexuality, race, and nationalism. Garrity focuses on what she calls a 'period of national crisis in Britain', roughly from 1915 to 1938, and her title, echoing Woolf's comment that English women remained 'step-daughters' in England, even after they won the vote, signals Woolf's centrality to her project. Garrity compares experimental novels by Virginia Woolf, Dorothy Richardson, Sylvia Townsend Warner, and Mary Butts, placing them in a cultural context that is chronologically precise, and extraordinarily well documented. Demonstrating how each writer struggled to reimagine women's roles as citizens, mothers, and racialized symbols of motherhood in the 1920s and 1930s, Garrity draws on an enormous range of cultural material to show how each writer responded to 'women's participation in the war effort, the sex-reform movement, new marital ideals, public discourse on homosexuality, debates about birth control and eugenics, the emergence of film, psychoanalysis, and the rise of feminism and mass culture' (p. 4). In brilliantly organized arguments informed by her expansive reading of feminist, postmodern and postcolonial theory, Garrity demonstrates how British modernist women's responses to war, empire, race, and sexuality differed from those of their more famous male contemporaries (p. 13).

Like several other important studies published this year, Garrity's volume includes an original and important reading of *The Waves* that incorporates Julia Kristeva's more recent theories of the pre-Oedipal mother, abjection, and the 'foreigner within' to argue that Percival embodies the maternal in this text. Woolf's six characters are, despite their differing gendered education and cultural conditioning, 'infantilized', she argues, when they recall Percival. Demonstrating a residual classism, racism, and 'imperialist nostalgia' in the language of Louis, Susan, and Ginny, Garrity reveals similar patterns in the story-telling of Neville, Rhoda, and Bernard and explains how the Elvedon episode encodes a 'motif of conquest', in a reading which will, no doubt, prompt controversy. Lisa Low, for example, in 'Feminist Elegy/Feminist Prophecy: Lycidas, *The Waves*, Kristeva, Cixous' (*WStA* 9[2003] 221–42), comes to different conclusions when she considers Woolf's framing narrative and 'prophetic' narrative voice, elements that Garrity excludes from her discussion. Nonetheless, overall Garrity's study is so clearly organized, so scrupulously documented, and so eloquently written that her contribution to Woolf scholarship and to a more complete understanding of British modernism will be widely recognized.

Holly Henry, in *Virginia Woolf and the Discourse of Science: The Aesthetics of Astronomy*, considers what Woolf's lifelong interest in astronomy added to her thinking and her creative process. Henry's volume complements and extends previous studies of Woolf's scientific interests, for example by Gillian Beer [1996], Susan Squier [1994], Ann Banfield [2000], and Jane Goldman, in her chapter on the solar eclipse in *The Feminist Aesthetics of Virginia Woolf* [1998]. Henry demonstrates how Woolf's interest in contemporary astronomy led her to recognize the profound 'rescaling' of the universe made possible by the new telescopes in the 1920s and 1930s, and explains how the 'new physics' deepened her understanding of the epistemological implications of humankind's place in this expanded universe. Unlike Michael Wentworth, who in *Einstein's Wake: Relativity, Metaphor, and Modernist Literature* (OUP [2001]) glosses Woolf's famous reference to the 'shower of innumerable atoms' in 'The Modern Novel' as an image of modern consumer culture (p. 109), Henry takes Woolf's interest in astronomy more seriously, showing that it shaped her characterization of Katharine Hilbery in *Night and Day*, Mr Clutterbuck in *Jacob's Room*, Eleanor and Sara in *The Years*, and even Mrs McNab in *To the Lighthouse*. In an interesting chapter on *The Waves*, Henry notes that Woolf mentions James Jeans's books in diary entries while she was writing the novel, and shows how the debate surrounding Jeans's *The Mysterious Universe* [1930] may have prompted her to describe Bernard as aspiring to become a mathematician as well as a poet, to see outside as well as inside the 'universe' that he imagines. As Henry explains, 'The images of "far-flung galaxies" reprinted in Jeans's texts afforded Woolf a wide-angled vision that allowed the possibility of positioning her characters against the infinite vistas of the universe' (p. 66). Drawing on her original archival research on James Jeans and Edwin Hubble as well as on popular newspaper accounts of the rescaling of the universe in the period, Henry suggests how

Woolf's interests in astronomy enhanced her 'global vision' and 'anti-war politics' (p. 47), which Henry's attentive readings of 'The Searchlight', *Three Guineas*, and *Between the Acts* convincingly demonstrate.

Christopher Reed's landmark study, *Bloomsbury Rooms: Modernism, Subculture, and Domesticity*, offers an interdisciplinary perspective on the Bloomsbury Group that could truly revolutionize scholarship on Virginia Woolf. This ambitious, beautifully designed, and lavishly illustrated volume refers to an enormous range of art and writing produced by all the members of the Bloomsbury Group, from the founding of the Omega workshop in 1913 through the 1930s, and compares their paintings, murals, sculptures, and interior designs not only with the works and theories of other British modernists including Wyndham Lewis, Ezra Pound, and T.S. Eliot, but also with modernist artists and writers in Germany, France, Italy, Spain, and the United States. Reed's book is a pleasure to read, not least because he avoids the hectoring tone and self-righteousness that have sometimes disfigured previous studies. It also provides meticulous documentation, reflecting his discriminating reading of virtually all the novels, letters, journals, and essays of major figures in the Bloomsbury Group, his extensive knowledge of the scholarship on them, and his sophisticated application of feminist, cultural, materialist, postmodern, and queer theories.

Reed makes four points particularly relevant to controversies that have persisted for many years in Woolf studies. First, though his primary aim in this study is to compare Duncan Grant's and Vanessa Bell's artistic development, his analysis of their changing responses to Roger Fry's 'primitivism' invites comparison with Woolf's representations of Otherness, a topic recently much debated. Reed's study is particularly powerful because of the brilliantly observed analysis of the visual elements of the paintings and interior designs that it contains. When seen through his eyes, familiar canvases like Grant's *Queen of Sheba* [1912] or Bell's *Studland Beach* [1911–12] and *The Tub* [1917–18] become luminous with new meaning. In discussing the murals, interior designs, and lesser-known paintings of the 1920s and 1930s, Reed illustrates how Fry's ideas about the 'primitive' found expression in the deliberate 'awkwardness' and roughness of Grant's and Bell's designs as well as in their use of 'vibrant color, active gesture, and unabashed eroticism' (p. 139), again offering another register to assess Woolf's use of colour and form in her novels.

Second, Reed directly challenges the often unexamined assumption that British modernism, like other modernisms, was positioned in opposition to the home and domesticity. He argues that Bloomsbury artists and writers rejected the modernist aesthetics of the machine, showing that Roger Fry, Duncan Grant, and Vanessa Bell dedicated themselves, instead, to recuperating the domestic by 'creating conditions of domesticity outside mainstream definitions of home and family' (p. 7). Reed's analysis thus invites a rethinking of the links between the class and gender and the sexual and political identities of various members of the Bloomsbury Group. Reed disputes the often repeated claim that the group escaped the rigours of city life during the Great War by retreating to 'the comfort of its country seat' (p. 183). Pointing out that Vanessa Bell was instrumental in 'turning Bloomsbury against the war', Reed argues that Bell and Grant's decision to move to the countryside in Sussex was a defensive response to the threat of conscription and an assertion of their pacifism. Far from offering a life of luxurious domestic comfort, the dilapidated farmhouse at Charleston where Bell, Grant, and David Garnett moved in October 1916 provided uncomfortable shelter, at best, for men who 'worked six days a week as manual laborers' and where Vanessa Bell raised two young sons and later an infant daughter in relative isolation with few modern conveniences, though admittedly with some paid domestic help. The interior designs at Charleston illustrate this 'aesthetic of pleasure hard won from privation' (p. 190). Reed's analysis invites a reconsideration of Woolf's relation to the domestic as well.

Third, Reed challenges long-standing assumptions about the apolitical stance of members of the Bloomsbury Group by noting that they 'stuck together', unlike many other avant-garde coalitions, and remained at the 'center of political activism' (p. 7) for more than two decades through their 'anti-authoritarian individualism', their pacifism, and their redefinition of the domestic and the family. Disputing Raymond Williams's widely accepted view that the Bloomsbury Group was an apolitical and class-bound 'social formation', Reed contends that the group can be better understood as a 'subculture' that 'made a belief in individualistic dissent a principle for collaboration' (p. 14). In charting the post-war aesthetics and politics of the Bloomsbury Group, Reed demonstrates the increasing importance of writers, noting especially Leonard and Virginia Woolf's growing prominence. He contrasts Bloomsbury's post-war modernism with that, for example, of Wyndham Lewis, who has been identified in recent influential studies as the 'paradigmatic modernist' who gave up painting altogether and endorsed the model of the writer as 'a single genius/leader who would re-impose stability on the flux of post-war culture' (p. 226). The artists and writers of the Bloomsbury Group, on the other hand, resisted this 'superman' model, regarding the 'principles of humanistic individualism' as providing the best grounding for 'challenges to the ideologies of competitive laissez-faire capitalism and nationalist militarism' (p. 226) as well as fascism.

Finally, by illustrating how the Omega workshop, established in 1913, produced art that displayed its founders' 'commitment to cooperative, anonymous production', principles that were at odds with the marketing tactics adopted by the most successful interior designers, artists, and writers after the Great War (p. 123), Reed offers a new perspective on Bloomsbury's relationship to the consumer capitalism of post-war Britain. He asserts that members of the Bloomsbury Group publicly resisted the 'ideal of stable heterosexual coupledom' through their unconventional marriages and their enthusiastic participation in what he calls the 'sexual subcultures' of the 1920s. He considers not only the domestic spaces they designed for themselves but also their delight in masquerade and the aesthetics of a kind of 'camp' that was 'only legible to some but not all of its audience' (p. 241). Reed places Woolf's uncharacteristic, and by now notorious, decision to allow her photographs to appear in *Vogue* in this context. Anyone who has visited Charleston Farmhouse will see Bell and Grant's domestic decorations with new eyes after reading Christopher Reed's illuminating book.

Maggie Humm also explores Woolf's complex relationship with visual culture in her theoretically sophisticated *Modernist Women and Visual Cultures: Virginia*

Woolf, Vanessa Bell, Photography and Cinema. Unlike Reed, Humm uses gender as her principle of selection, arguing that, 'in their cinema writing and domestic photography, modernist women explore gender issues in perhaps a freer way than in their better known works' (p. 4). Humm illustrates this claim well in her chapter comparing Woolf's writing about the cinema with that of Dorothy Richardson, Bryher, HD, Colette, Janet Flanner, Adrienne Monnier, and Gertrude Stein, suggesting how they variously recognized film as offering a space yet unmapped by language, a borderland more amenable, as Woolf explained, to 'a kind of psychic montage' that could expose the 'archaic processes' of human consciousness.

Humm's most original contribution to Woolf scholarship may prove to be her elegant synthesis of feminist psychoanalytic theory in her discussion of Woolf's and Bell's photograph albums. Demonstrating how Bracha Lichtenberg Ettinger's concept of the 'matriaxial gaze' can be seen at work in these photographs, Humm traces the dynamics of a 'female imaginary' whose aim is to recover 'a lost maternal object' (p. 8), especially evident in the poignant photographs Virginia Stephen took and developed of her mother's empty chair and later those of her friends similarly posed in 'comfy chairs'. Humm's point that Woolf's albums show her 'repression of chronological narrative' (p. 38) and anticipate her innovative representation of time in her mature fiction is less persuasive since she overlooks the possibility that other hands might have rearranged the photographs since Woolf's death. Likewise, in discussing Woolf's staging and selection of the photographs for *Orlando*, Humm defensively obfuscates the erotic appeal of the snapshots Woolf included of Angelica Garnett as Sasha by asserting that they are 'invitational rather than voyeuristic' (p. 55). Her analysis of Vanessa Bell's more orderly and chronologically arranged photograph albums is more clearly problematic. Although she admits that her photographs of Bell's children are more obviously 'erotic', she evades the more troubling implications of what could be seen as the paedophilic appeal especially of the shots of Bell's naked sons. Christopher Reed, by contrast, argues that these photographs express Bell's artistic interest in the spontaneous gesture and her rejection of Victorian sentimental idealization of children. Perhaps because Humm's book includes a considerable amount of previously published material, it seems to lack a dynamic, overarching argument, leaving room for others to explore the provocative angles it offers on Woolf's views of privacy, sexuality, and the artistic uses of photography and the cinema in modern culture.

Helen Southworth's *The Intersecting Realities and Fictions of Virginia Woolf and Colette* invites comparison with previous studies, by Mary Ann Caws and Nicola Luckhurst, of Woolf's reception in France. In this attractively illustrated, fast-paced introductory survey, Southworth identifies 'parallels' in the lives and writings of both novelists. Though Woolf and Colette never met, Southworth argues that Woolf's relationship with Vita Sackville-West and the Paris-based lesbian salon culture of the 1920s and 1930s provided a social network that connected them, allowing, for example, Gisèle Freund to obtain permission to photograph both Woolf and Colette in 1939. Southworth thus establishes a biographical rationale for her study and cites Woolf's comments in her diary about Colette's *Sido* and *Duo* to show Woolf's appreciation for her style and 'racy' French. Admitting that there is less direct evidence that Colette read Woolf's novels, Southworth contends, nonetheless, that she knew of Woolf's *A Room of One's Own*, and identifies formal evidence to show that *Le Pur et l'impur* can be read as a 'sequel' to it. Identifying the gaps in both texts and noting how the censorship of Radclyffe Hall's *The Well of Loneliness* haunted Woolf's text, a point established some time ago by Jane Marcus in *Virginia Woolf and the Languages of the Patriarchy* (IndUP [1987]), Southworth argues that both authors used voyages to organize their narratives and to explore the advantages that outsiders enjoyed. Although her comparison of Woolf's description of the famous meals at Oxbridge and Fernham with Charlotte's two visits to a Paris opium den in *Le Pur et l'impur* seems strained, Southworth's discussion of parallels between Woolf's theory of the 'androgynous mind' and Colette's 'hermaphrodisme mental' (p. 55) is provocative. While Southworth asserts that Woolf and Colette interrogated 'questions of gender and sexual difference via a questioning of space' (p. 73) and invented new hybrid genres that blend features of the novel, autobiography, memoir, and letter, she presents only the briefest discussions of Woolf's major novels and ignores considerable evidence of Woolf's representation of lesbian desire throughout her career as well as more than two decades of scholarship on this subject. Georgia Johnston's 'The Politics of Retrospective Space in Virginia Woolf's Memoir "A Sketch of the Past"', Elizabeth Hirsch's 'Writing as Spatial Historiography: Woolf's *Roger Fry* and the National Identity' (both in Regard, ed., *Mapping the Self: Space, Identity, Discourse in British Auto-Biography*), Andelys Wood's 'Walking the Web in the Lost London of Mrs. Dalloway' (*Mosaic* 36:ii[2003] 19–32), and Kathryn Simpson's wonderful 'Queer Fish: Woolf's Writing of Desire between Women in *The Voyage Out* and *Mrs. Dalloway*' (*WStA* 9[2003] 55–82) are just four notable studies published this year that explore these themes. Southworth's study, which also invites comparison with Diane McGee's *Writing the Meal: Dinner in the Fiction of Early Twentieth-Century Women Writers* (Toronto [2001]) will, nonetheless, serve as a springboard for further consideration of Woolf's and Colette's writing because of her sensitive translations of well-chosen passages from Colette's novels.

With well over a hundred articles and reviews published on Woolf this year in periodicals, there are far too many to note individually, though several not already mentioned merit particular attention. Returning to the vexed topic of Woolf's autobiographical writing, Alex Zwerdling, in 'Mastering the Memoir: Woolf and the Family Legacy' (*Mo/Mo* 10:i[2003] 165–88), provides a clear, chronologically organized, and theoretically informed analysis of Woolf's ongoing efforts to find an autobiographical form that accommodated present and past versions of the self. Zwerdling offers evidence that Woolf's 'Sketch of the Past' is only a partial draft of a longer autobiographical essay that she planned, but he argues nonetheless that it is 'less inhibited and self-censoring than any of her earlier experiments in life-writing' (p. 185). Anna Snaith's 'Stray Guineas: Virginia Woolf and the Fawcett Library' (*L&H* 12:ii[2003] 16–35) challenges 'obsolete' assumptions about Woolf's apolitical stance through its well-documented analysis of the 'wealth of archival material' and unpublished letters by Woolf that lay untouched for sixty years (p. 16) until Snaith found them in the collections of what is now the Fawcett Library. Snaith shows Woolf's unequivocal support for this library, originally established by the London and National Society for Women's Service, renamed the Fawcett Library in 1938, and suggests how it reveals her commitment to preserving the history of women's suffrage and providing a comfortable space where working women and 'outsiders' of any class could meet to educate themselves and each other. Merry Pawlowski, co-editor with Vara Neverow of the electronic archive *Woolf's Reading Notes for Three Guineas*, considers the creative uses of this new type of archive, and thus identifies reasons for renewed interest in Woolf's later writing, in her 'Exposing Masculine Spectacle: Virginia Woolf's Newspaper Clippings for *Three Guineas* as a Cultural History' (*WStA* 9[2003] 167–92). Jane Lilienfeld, Jeffrey Oxford, and Lisa Low, who edited the supplement to the *Woolf Studies Annual*, as well as Mark Hussey who agreed to publish it, deserve commendation for assembling such a distinguished collection of essays.

This review would not be complete without mention of Mark Wollaeger's splendid 'The Woolfs in the Jungle: Intertextuality, Sexuality and the Emergence of Female Modernism in *The Voyage Out*' (*MLQ* 64:i[2003] 33–69). Suggesting how Woolf's marriage deepened her 'ambivalence toward powerful male authorities', Wollaeger cites shocking descriptions of male violence directed at women from Leonard Woolf's *The Village in the Jungle* and argues that she 'had to think past her husband' to get to Joseph Conrad in order to finish *The Voyage Out*. Returning to Woolf's much-discussed revisions to three interlocking scenes: Rachel's engagement, Helen Ambrose's mysteriously violent response, and the subsequent visit to the native village, Wollaeger synthesizes several models of 'female modernism' in his demonstration of how the novel reveals what he calls a 'compromise formation' that expresses Woolf's reservations about the 'phallic maternal'.

3. Post-1945 Fiction

One of the most stimulating and innovative books published this year is James Proctor's study of black British writing and culture, *Dwelling Places: Postwar Black British Writing*. Proctor argues that insufficient attention has been paid to the ways in which black literary and cultural production has been preoccupied with the spatial and with territorial locations. As a corrective to this deficiency his book offers a provocative and brilliant analysis of the dwelling-places and contact zones of black settlement. Proctor is admirably lucid on the shifting politics of black cultural production, and the shifting social and political contexts in which black settlement has been represented more broadly. He also pays due attention to the ways in which writers like Stuart Hall and Paul Gilroy have theorized the particular cultural conditions enabling and problematizing the term 'black British'. In the conclusion he also examines the politics of recent attempts to celebrate, and construct heritage narratives about, the early post-war pioneers of black settlement in Britain. The book's chapters, 'Dwelling Places', 'The Street', 'Suburbia', and 'The North', roughly correspond to an expanding landscape of black cultural representation, from an early focus on London and housing, to later loci around suburban, middle-class life and cities outside London with substantial portions of black and Asian settlement, such as Bradford. Proctor uses posters, museum exhibitions, films, and newspaper reports to develop his analysis, as well as detailed explorations of some literary texts. The argument, although compelling, sometimes lacks breadth. In the chapter on the 1950s, for example, Sam Selvon's *The Lonely Londoners* and George Lamming's *The Emigrants* bear the weight of Proctor's analysis. Proctor is well aware that there are other examples of texts in which settlement and dwelling are major preoccupations—Andrew Salkey's *Escape to an Autumn Pavement* and E.R. Braithwaite's *To Sir, With Love* are two examples which would have benefited from more extensive treatment. V.S. Naipaul's *The Enigma of Arrival* surely deserved greater consideration than the short paragraph in which it is mentioned, but is also dismissed simply as too disdainful of tourists for Proctor's particular focus. Victor Headley's *Yardie*, again clearly a crucial text in black British literary production, is not even mentioned. At times the parameters of Proctor's study appear too constrictive, but probably my criticism here is that Proctor doesn't appear to have the space to explore fully the ramifications of his analysis. A longer treatment, with a greater range of texts studied, would be very desirable, but this criticism seems churlish when Proctor has done such valuable and impressive work in explaining the significance of place in black British writing and culture, and in arguing for the centrality of black British landscapes to a fuller understanding of post-war British culture.

Dowson, ed., *Women's Writing, 1945–1960: After the Deluge*, deserves special praise as a collection which devotes attention to a long neglected and much misunderstood period of women's writing. Jane Dowson's introduction, along with essays by Elizabeth Maslen, Linden Peach, and Diana Wallace, provide valuable insights into this post-war period for women's writing generally. Dowson indicates the ways in which the work represented in the volume builds upon recent scholarship, and argues that the essays 'record the rich texture of women's writing in the postwar period' (p. 13). Maslen provides a commanding overview of feminism during the period, and the problems faced by women writers in addressing feminist contexts. Peach's essay examines the flourishing of women's crime writing in the period, and argues that women writers are using the genre to 'engage not only with the performative nature of femininity but the unravelling of traditional notions of masculinity' (p. 51). Wallace surveys a rich vein of historical fiction by women writers, and argues that the historical novel 'offered a form into which they could retreat and under cover of which they could express and explore subversive ideas which might otherwise have been regarded as unfeminine, or even unpatriotic' (p. 132). There are two essays on poetry—Alice Entwistle on Denise Levertov, and Jane Dowson on Elizabeth Jennings, Kathleen Raine and Stevie Smith (reviewed in section 6 below), and one on drama, Yvonne Mitchell's *The Same Sky*, by Claire Tylee. The bulk of the volume, however, is devoted to fiction writers. There are important and valuable essays on Elizabeth Bowen (Briggs; Sceats), and the early work of Doris Lessing (Fullbrook; Watkins), Iris Murdoch (Grimshaw) and Muriel Spark (Sceats), but perhaps the real treat of this volume is the attention given to relatively neglected, yet enormously popular, novelists of the time: Nancy Mitford (Joannou), Elizabeth Taylor (Brannigan), Barbara Pym (Hanson), Rosemary Sutcliff, Mary

Renault, and Cecil Woodham Smith (Bell), and Agatha Christie (Peach). How women writers responded to the effects of the war is one dominant social theme, obviously, but other preoccupations include domesticity, conservatism, gender and cross-gender identities, sexual politics, class and racial differences, and genre. In each of these essays, an important process of reassessment and recontextualization is taking place. Joannou, for example, addresses the ways in which Mitford was writing an ironic and comic version of the romance. Hanson explores the influence of anthropology on Pym's 'laying bare' of structures of society in her fiction, and Pym emerges a more complex novelist from this perspective. To single out essays in this manner is, of course, problematic, especially given the strengths of the collection as a whole. *Women's Writing, 1945–1960* is a much-needed and superbly accomplished collection of essays which does much to reassess and revalue women's writing of this period.

Rewriting Scotland: Welsh, McLean, Warner, Banks, Galloway and Kennedy, by Cristie L. March, is an introductory survey of the ways in which, in the 1990s, these six writers charted new understandings of Scottishness. The book is aimed at those readers who might be unfamiliar with contemporary Scottish writing and with literary theory, with a view to providing accessible guides to the writings and their social, cultural, and political contexts. James Kelman and Alasdair Gray are figured as the precursors of contemporary Scottish writing, but March is particularly concerned with the ways in which her chosen writers are extending and developing their work in new, sometimes agonistic, directions. A preoccupation with youth culture, and the blurring of both gender and genre boundaries, is common to many of the writings March discusses. Her study is written in an accessible and lucid style, and she surveys a wider range of lesser-known contemporary writers in the conclusion. She concludes that 'the availability of "non-traditional" styles and issues has moved Scottish literature out of easy classifications of parochialism and rusticity, and instead into an increasingly mainstream, multinational readership' (p. 165).

Nine essays are collected in Lea and Schoene, eds., *Posting the Male: Masculinities in Post-War and Contemporary British Literature*. The collection derives from a conference on representations of masculinity in the twentieth century held at Liverpool John Moores University in 2000, but is clearly more narrowly focused than the conference. The editors are somewhat idealistic in heralding the beginning of the twenty-first century as a time when 'both men and women dream of a new, pluralist and categorically disorderly gender order' (p. 8), and they propose that the collection aims to 'capture and document this historical moment at which masculinity ... has once and for all lost its traditional transparency as the incontestable biological essence of unadulterated manly being and instead become visible as a performative gender construct, and a rather frail and fraudulent one to boot' (p. 9). There is something of the manifesto about the introduction, perhaps appropriate given the still fledgling position of contemporary men's studies in the academy, but the editors succeed in situating the essays that follow in suitable academic and social contexts. Where the editors really deserve praise is in the selection of nine diverse, illuminating, and stimulating essays. Susan Brook's essay on the 'angry young men' trawls through the usual critique of *Look Back in Anger* before embarking on a thoughtful and insightful consideration of the fascination of the new left with the kinds of masculinity celebrated in the angry young writings of the 1950s. Richard Hornsey's exploration of reading practices and sexual deviancy surrounding the *Lady Chatterley's Lover* trial and Joe Orton and Kenneth Halliwell's conviction for stealing and vandalizing library books in the early 1960s is strikingly original and brilliant. Gill Plain examines the return of the 'hard man' in Scottish crime fiction, while Neil McMillan studies masculinity across a broader range of contemporary Scottish writing. Emma Parker's essay pushes recent critical approaches to Graham Swift's *Last Orders* a little further by arguing that the novel 'exposes the limits of English masculinity' (p. 90). Rhiannon Davies makes a similar argument in relation to Ian McEwan's *Enduring Love*. Antony Rowland comments on the current state of the concept of 'patriarchy' in critical discourses before discussing Carol Ann Duffy's 'Psychopath'. Irene Rose argues that Jackie Kay's *Trumpet* 'stands as an epitaph to monolithic masculinity' (p. 156), while Emma Liggins's essay, which concludes the collection, situates Alan Hollinghurst's fiction in relation to contemporary critical theories of gay sexualities, most notably Alan Sinfield's argument that we are 'entering the period of the post-gay' (p. 159). One outstanding achievement of the collection is that each of the essays displays an admirably lucid and reflexive awareness of the complexities of contemporary masculinity studies.

Janis E. Haswell has published a new study of the writings of Paul Scott, entitled *Paul Scott's Philosophy of Place(s): The Fiction of Relationality*. As the title indicates, Haswell does not simply apply cultural theories of space and place to Scott's fiction, but argues that Scott was ahead of much recent postcolonial and postmodern theory in his fictional exploration of the meanings of space. In particular, Haswell argues that, in his deployment of multiple narrative perspectives and juxtaposition of seemingly contrasting identities and places, Scott reimagines the relationship between self and place on several levels: as physical location, embedded space, interior space, and moral space. The moral and political contexts in which Haswell places Scott are fascinating. Scott was determined to explore with unerring candour the complex legacy of imperialism, and the ideologies underpinning it, at a time when 'England seemed obdurately resolved to ignore the past and allow its former empire to disappear' (p. 67). As a result, she argues, 'Scott's novels were themselves marginalized by the artistic, cultural and political mood of the 1950s through 1970s'. There is no better explanation of Scott's curiously liminal position in the post-war literary canon, and Haswell proves to be an astute and persuasive reader of Scott as a post-imperial iconoclast, engaging the reader in a moral dialogue on the meanings of England's imperial past, its human costs, and the lasting impact of India on England. But Scott emerges from Haswell's study not as a postcolonial firebrand, but as a profoundly moral novelist, whose understanding of the complex moral terrain of imperialism, and its legacy even in his own beliefs and assumptions, finds perfect form in novels in which we can follow 'the lived and fluid dynamic of the relationality of singular selves in formation, and in the still-continuing story of the British in relation to India' (pp. 265–6).

A selection of key interviews with Iris Murdoch has been edited and collected by Gillian Dooley, entitled *From a Tiny Corner in the House of Fiction: Conversations with Iris Murdoch*. The interviewers include Harold Hobson, Frank Kermode, Christopher Bigsby, and Jonathan Miller, among many others, and range widely in depth and length, but the selections have been chosen prudently and reveal much about Murdoch's writings, and indeed the personality of the writer herself. She chafes against Harold Hobson's dismay at the 'extraordinary idea' of allowing women into gentlemen's clubs in the opening interview, for example, while equally expressing discomfort at the prospect of being bracketed off as a woman writer in the interview with Sheila Hale. She has decided opinions on many subjects, but she responds to most interviewers with a keen and generous intelligence, and modesty about her own work. Many of the extracts are short, but those of some length reveal Murdoch's enjoyment of dialogue, and passion in particular for literary and philosophical enquiry. In her introduction Dooley charts Murdoch's habits as an interviewee, and her changing sense of literary tastes and influences. Murdoch has interesting things to say on a wide range of literature, as well as answering questions about moral philosophies, and as Dooley observes is often led only by skilful interviewers to talk about her own writings in some depth. Dooley's selection of interviews makes more accessible an interesting range of enquiries into Murdoch's writings, and is arranged so as to show the changing shape of her life and career.

Angela Carter's writings for radio, film, and television are the subjects of Charlotte Crofts's *'Anagrams of Desire'*. Crofts surveys the considerable body of critical discussion of Carter's fiction to discover that her writings for communications media are relatively neglected. The book addresses in particular those of Carter's media writings which were performed and broadcast, and in which Carter herself was involved. The degree of Carter's collaboration in broadcast media leads Crofts to consider the implications of this for the notion of authorship in her work, which links neatly with the chapter on Carter's radio 'biographemes' on Richard Dadd and Ronald Firbank. Although a number of recent studies of Carter have privileged her work as a novelist, Crofts makes a good case here for maintaining a fuller sense of Carter as a writer and intellectual, who was, as is evidenced in her fiction as much as in the writings Crofts discusses, fascinated by the cinema and the radio, and more broadly in their potential as vehicles of cultural criticism. An important dimension to Crofts's study is her consideration of Carter's ventures into communications media from feminist perspectives, and her attentiveness to the ways in which Carter wished to experiment with the medium in which she worked. In particular, Carter is shown to have 'enacted' her interest in blurring the boundaries between high and popular culture in her media writings, and pursued her fascination with narrative and the oral tradition through the radio and cinema. Crofts advances a convincing argument that the neglect of Carter's media writings may have more to do with the conservative practices of 'traditional English studies', than with the significance of these writings *per se*, and that 'Carter studies' may have to engage more closely with cultural and media studies in order to assess the range of Carter's interests as a writer more fully.

Robert Fraser is well placed to write the first book-length critical study of Ben Okri. His short study, published in the excellent Writers and their Work series, builds on his long friendship with Okri to explain the life and work of the award-winning Nigerian novelist and poet. It abounds with insights from Fraser's recollections of their friendship, and provides an affectionate portrait of Okri's upbringing in war-torn Nigeria and his time as a student and writer in England. This familiarity with his subject might hamper the critical task of assessing Okri's literary achievements, but Fraser's treatment of Okri's life and work succeeds in balancing the sense of intimacy which illuminates Okri's personality with a subtle and detailed analysis of his work. Fraser effectively situates Okri within two traditions—a Nigerian literary tradition of Christopher Ikigbo, Chinua Achebe, Wole Soyinka, and, more recently, Ken Saro Wiwa, and an English literary tradition of Shakespeare, Blake, Dickens, T.S. Eliot, and James Joyce. That the latter is a specifically 'English' tradition, however, is always complicated by the uses to which Okri puts these influences: 'Shakespeare', Okri is quoted as saying, 'is an African writer' (p. 102). Okri's comments on literature and politics are frequently quoted in the book, including the injunction that Fraser was not to turn him into a 'post-anything'. Fraser studiously avoids any serious contemplation of how such terms as 'postcolonial', 'postmodern', or 'magic realist' might apply to Okri. In fact, one of the few weaknesses in the book is that the possible significance of such terms is dismissed rather too glibly. Fraser's achievement, however, is to trace the narrative innovations, aesthetic idealism, and subliminally utopian project of Okri's work with precision and aplomb.

Also published in the Writers and their Work series is Matthew Pateman's *Julian Barnes*. Pateman concentrates on the novels published under Barnes's own name, and thus excludes the short stories, journalism, and translations, as well as the four novels published under the pseudonym, Dan Kavanagh. This focus allows Pateman to trace the development of a number of themes from *Metroland* through to *Love, etc.*, including ideas of history, identity, truth, and science. Barnes emerges from Pateman's study like one of his characters, to borrow a phrase Pateman repeats, 'trying to find new certainties in a moral vacuum' (p. 89). Barnes is thus championed as a kind of moral explorer, standing on the cusp of 'failed pieties' and the 'platitudinous relativism of postmodern culture' (p. 3). It is clear, however, that he offers no answers, but rather sets up the dilemmas for his readers to resolve, as Pateman shows most plainly in his analysis of *The Porcupine*. Pateman is most convincing when he argues that Barnes's ingenuity is in the ways in which he ties particular narratives to formal innovations. His defence of Barnes's formal experimentation in *The History of the World in $10\frac{1}{2}$ Chapters* is based on this argument, claiming that the 'novel enacts its own critique at the level of the failure of art' (p. 73). At the same time, Pateman demonstrates why *England, England* simply does not succeed, even in Barnes's own terms, although he is perhaps a little harsh in declaring the novel 'a rather predictable, and even tired, piece of work' (p. 73). Pateman's study perhaps suffers a little from the brevity required by the series in which it is published. The chapters are all a little too short, too cursory. It is not, of course, the first critical book published on Barnes, and Merritt Moseley's book [1997] is a better critical companion, but for a short introduction Pateman's book offers an interesting reading of Barnes's novels, and provides concise explanations of his significance as a contemporary British novelist.

There has been a growing field of Harry Potter studies since 1999, which I have ignored up to now, but which on volume alone, will probably require a separate section in *YWES* if it continues to grow. Four books were published on Harry Potter or J.K. Rowling this year, and on the evidence they supply a centre for Harry Potter studies is surely nearing completion somewhere. *J.K. Rowling: A Biography* by Connie Ann Kirk is not the first biography of its subject—Marc Shapiro and Sean Smith have published mass-market books which partially fulfilled this brief, although not without controversy. Kirk's biography is also not an authorized or scholarly biography, neither of which has yet been published on Rowling, who is, in any case, reputedly shy of biographical interest. Kirk's book is designed principally for high school students, and provides a lively account of Rowling's life, adverting at several points to inconsistencies in what is known of Rowling and the limitations of biography as an art. Information for the book is largely gleaned from already published sources, including television profiles as well as books and articles, so there is nothing particularly new presented here. But Kirk writes lucidly and accessibly, and explains the controversies, criticisms, and popularity of the Potter books with admirable sensitivity to the needs of her readers. Her biography also contains useful appendices of Rowling's awards, readings, chronology, and a good bibliography.

Greenwood Press has published Kirk's biography, and it is another Greenwood imprint, Praeger, which has published a collection entitled *Reading Harry Potter: Critical Essays*, edited by Giselle Liza Anatol. Anatol's introduction raises some vital questions about the Harry Potter phenomenon, and what it reveals about publishing, reading, the status of children's literature as a genre, and critical and theoretical approaches to popular texts. The collection is divided into three parts. The first part includes five essays exploring theories of child development and learning through the Harry Potter novels, and all of which address in various ways moral, psychological or behavioural perspectives on Potter. Part 2 examines the literary influences and historical contexts of the novels. Four essays place the Potter books in relation to boarding-school stories, fairy-tales, anti-slavery histories, and wizard technology. The third part is concerned with moral and social values, and five essays address moral complexity, legal concepts, and ethnic, social, and gender identities. The three parts are not sufficiently distinguished, which is to say that there were several essays which might have been included in another part of the volume, but in general the essays collected here take their subject seriously. The lasting impression from reading all of the essays included in this collection is that the Potter novels are not just new materials co-opted to show off particular critical and theoretical approaches, but emerge from critical analysis as richer, more complex and dense texts.

The section divisions in Heilman, ed., *Harry Potter's World: Multidisciplinary Critical Perspectives*, work better than those of Anatol's collection. Under the heading 'Cultural Studies Perspectives', three essays explore the phenomenal success of the novels, particularly relating to the fan mania, commercial contexts, and accusations that the novels are harmful to children. Part 2 takes up reader-response and interpretative perspectives, and pursues issues relating to the implied and actual readers of the novels. The third part, on literary perspectives, investigates generic and paradigmatic approaches, while the fourth and final part of the book includes five essays examining critical and sociological perspectives on home and family, education and schooling, gender relations, social inclusion and exclusion, and notions of agency and civic leadership. The collection as a whole is attentive to the ways in which the novels are now a crucial part of social and cultural identity formation, and have been read and interpreted in very different ways and contexts. The editor is concerned in particular with the idea that *Harry Potter* represents a multinational corporate product with huge implications for social authority, but which, as literature, is amenable to various kinds of reading experience and various processes of identity construction: 'we can talk back to *Harry Potter*' (p. 9).

Another collection of academic studies of Harry Potter, entitled *The Ivory Tower and Harry Potter: Perspectives on a Literary Phenomenon*, edited by Lana A. Whited, was the first of its kind, published in October 2002. It is also the most substantial volume, including sixteen essays divided into seven sections. Whited provides a survey of the measures of success and controversy which marked the four Harry Potter novels published by 2002, including a polite wrangle she entered herself with one of Rowling's agents about the proposed title for the volume, which was to be, in self-conscious mimicry of the novels' titles, 'Harry Potter and the Ivory Tower', but which would, it was feared, mislead 7- or 8-year-olds into buying the book in the expectation that it was another instalment of the series. Such absurdities flow from the huge commercial business which Rowling and her creations have become. The essays in this collection admirably see through the mists of commercial success and controversies about copyright and censorship to examine both the implications of the Potter craze, and, more importantly, the meanings and values of the novels themselves. A considerable number are concerned with exploring the precursors and generic traditions to which we might relate the novels—stories of wizardry, boarding-school education, epic heroes, folklore, and fairy-tales. A number of contributors also tackle the problems of translating the novels, not just between two languages, but also within English between disparate cultures. There is a strong showing from cultural studies perspectives again, spurred by the popularity of the series, and also some essays on social, moral, and political contexts. All told, these three collections of essays indicate a significant and rapidly growing community of scholars engaging in Potter studies, and there is already a sizeable bibliography of critical sources upon which Potter scholars can draw. The similarities between the three collections begs the question about whether the subject merits quite so much scholarly attention, but this is a charge which could be levelled at other fields of literary scholarly enquiry.

Modesty forbids me to say anything more about the publication of my survey study of post-war writing than to give notice of its existence: *Orwell to the Present: Literature in England, 1945–2000* by John Brannigan has been published at an affordable price and with an attractive cover.

4. Pre-1950 Drama

Despite a gradually increasing body of scholarly work, this continues to be an under-researched area which will benefit both from continuing empirical and archive-based research and from more theoretical approaches—something which is reflected in the year's publications.

David Rabey begins *English Drama Since 1940* by declaring his intention to concentrate on what he designates 'important instances of fictional drama which interrogates the conventional notions of social consensus'. Probably inevitably, he concentrates primarily on the post-1950 (especially post-1956) period, but there are some useful discussions (and one or two revelations) of earlier material in the opening chapter. Despite the recent tendency to question and complicate assumptions about the overarching significance of 1956 as the watershed of the post-war period, we are still waiting for detailed explorations of the post-war decade; Rabey claims that theatre was faced with the task of having 'to win back an audience in the face of a passive consumerist consensus', but he produces little or no evidence to support this view, and it is one which is not necessarily reflected when one reads the confident and upbeat predictions of many of the theatre magazines of the late 1940s. He reminds us that theatre in Britain after the war was dominated by actors rather than by playwrights (that is probably true, though it is an assumption which might nevertheless be worth further interrogation at some point), but he offers some interesting perspectives on Eliot, Fry, and MacNeice, and briefer references to Priestley and O'Casey. However, his insertion of Anne Ridler's *The Shadow Factory*—performed as part of the Mercury Theatre's 1945 season of 'New Plays by Poets'—is particularly welcome. Ridler's allegory depicts a factory director who is seeking to exert social control over all elements of his workers' lives in the name of efficiency. He incorporates celebration and art as key elements in his project to manipulate and manage consent, and, according to Rabey, the play anticipates not only Orwell's *Nineteen Eighty-Four* but much later texts such as Howard Barker's *Scenes from an Execution*. Elsewhere, Rabey also seeks to re-establish John Whiting as a dramatist of lasting significance, and one whose work leads directly into the following decades. In particular, his *Conditions of Agreement* is said, through situation, plot, and its 'neo-Jacobean sense of the grotesque and macabre' to prefigure both *The Birthday Party* and the writing of Angela Carter. Though written in 1948, the play was not performed until the mid-1960s.

Rabey's discussion of Eliot and Fry draws attention to the fact that performances of their early work frequently relied 'on the unpredictable and often uneven abilities of *ad hoc* amateur companies', and he also notes 'the ready access of amateurs to a public space'. It is certainly the case that for the first half of the twentieth century—and beyond—the non-professional theatre was an important setting and context for the performance of original work of different kinds. After all, in the politically significant year of 1926, the government published a 250-page report detailing dramatic activity up and down the country, as manifested in villages, towns, factories, churches, prisons, and so on. Drama, as practised at such levels, was identified as having the potential to introduce an 'element of healing and of reconciliation into the warring elements in our national life'. And yet with a few notable exceptions (such as Mick Wallis and his work on pageants), the study of non-professional theatre of the period has not featured much in academic research. This near absence is challenged by Claire Cochrane in 'The Contaminated Audience: Researching Amateur Theatre in Wales before 1939' (*NTQ* 19:ii[2003] 169–76). Citing Edward Said, Cochrane argues persuasively that in going beyond the dominating discourse, the (theatre) historian must not only recover the oppositional but the multiple voices of the past—including those which may have colluded with the dominant voice. Specifically, she suggests that the experiences and expectations of those attending (and, presumably, participating in) amateur performances have been filtered out by most historians, leading 'to the virtual silencing of half a century of extensive theatrical activity'. Cochrane notes the contrast between the exasperated failure of the professional Welsh National Theatre players to attract audiences in its tours of the 1930s and the extensive amateur activity simultaneously occurring through the Eisteddfod, with its festivals, amateur competitions, large audiences, and lengthy adjudications of prizes. But she properly rejects the temptation of a 'univocal reading' which might find here a 'defiant resistance to cultural colonialism', in favour of something much less straightforward, and reminds us that 'Imperialism best achieves its objectives in colonized territories not by direct oppression but through negotiated mutual interests.' However, although Cochrane unearths some tantalizing fragments of empirical research (how wonderful to discover that in 1927 the aristocratic English owner of a castle in North Wales commissioned Komisarjesky to stage a vast amateur production of a Welsh translation of Ibsen's *The Pretenders* at the Holyhead Eisteddfod), her primary project here is to hypothesize and theorize on the cultural significance of the practices rather than to paint the details which might be squeezed out of what she describes as 'the desultory, inadequate, hard-to-access records'. In so far as such records yield us much information, they seem to be more about audiences and reception than about performances or performers.

If Cochrane's article might leave some readers wishing for further insights into the detail of practice, frustrations will surely surface in relation to Geoff Davidson's intriguingly entitled 'Twentieth Century Choices; or, What Did They See from the Stalls, Circle and Gallery? II—Derek Kenward' (*TN* 57:i [2003] 25–71). Kenward was evidently an avid theatre-goer for fifty years from the mid-1940s onwards, and passed his collection of 350 or so programmes to Davidson, but, disappointingly, the collection on its own yields very little other than the most basic factual data, and the majority of this article (nearly forty pages) is taken up with a listing of performances attended, venues, dates, and (occasionally) one or two brief details. Certainly, it is interesting to know that in 1944 ENSA were playing Ben Travers in Algiers, J.B. Priestley in Naples, and Thornton Wilder, Noel Coward, Terence Rattigan, and Patrick Hamilton at Caserta. But one longs to hear something—anything—more about what it was audiences were actually seeing from the stalls, circle, and gallery, and how they responded to it.

In his attempt to revive interest in the work and ideas of John Whiting, David Rabey quotes the dramatist's very modern-sounding declaration that 'The purpose of art is to raise doubt: the purpose of entertainment is to reassure.'

The distinction is one that looks back towards the beginning as well as forwards towards the end (and beyond) of the twentieth century. In 'Shakespeare in the Age of Mechanical Reproduction: Cultural Discourse and the Film of Tree's "Henry VIII"' (*NTQ* 19:iv[2003] 352–65), Cary DiPietro examines the 'general recognition' by dramatists and practitioners of the early twentieth century that theatre was in crisis, and the contest to take possession of it was waged by intellectuals and the middle classes who sought to define it as an art rather than as a commercial business. As so often, the treatment of Shakespeare can be used as an appropriate indicator: in the blue corner, the old-fashioned, money-making, spectacularly lavish approach of Herbert Tree, a product of the actor-manager and capitalist system; in the pink, the 'art for art's sake', or 'art for social enlightenment and social education' approach to theatre-making of Craig, Archer, Granville Barker, Shaw, and Ervine. But DiPietro argues that, in their anxiety that 'the aesthetic of beauty' was losing out to the 'horrible contagion of commonness', and that theatre was being driven by commercialism to follow cinema and target 'a largely unintelligent and undiscerning growing mass audience', those who insisted that art must not be sullied by trade were guilty not only of romanticism, but perhaps of something worse. While 'cautious to suggest' a link with the fascistic impulse, DiPietro finds that, in 'the rhetoric of nationalism, the demand for an elite leadership, the predilection for tragedy and violence and the emphasis upon genius' we may discover the existence of 'some deeper, darker anxiety underneath the idealism of these writers'. It is a provocative argument, well made, and it requires engagement. Barker and Shaw are accused of having sought 'to infuse mass culture with the precepts of traditional high art'. One suspects that they—and some later practitioners—would have owned up to that without embarrassment.

Meanwhile, in 'GBS & the BBC: "Saint Joan", 1929' (*TN* 57:i [2003] 11–24), L.W. Conolly examines a specific moment from Shaw's twenty-five-year-long relationship with another growing medium, the radio. The relationship had begun in 1924 with Shaw playing all the roles, and singing, in a production of one of his short plays, and continued with his contributions to debates on 'What Is Coming' and on 'The Menace of the Leisured Woman'. Conolly draws primarily on the BBC archives to reconstruct some of the debates that took place within the BBC (and with Shaw) about casting, and about whether his three-hour play should be cut to fit the normal two-hour evening time slot (Shaw would probably not have given approval for this), permitted to disrupt the schedules (the producer was against having it interrupted by news bulletins and the shipping forecast), broadcast on a Sunday afternoon (unacceptable because Sundays were reserved for church services and serious music), or split over two evenings. The last of these routes was chosen, but even then objections were raised that it would finish after midnight ('as a general rule, people should not be encouraged to sit up till all hours, but we feel that one special occasion will not hurt them'). Conolly makes no attempt to extrapolate or theorize from what is a straightforward piece of detailed empirical research; but even though it offers no profound insights and probably does little or nothing to change our basic view of Shaw, the BBC, or the period, a window is opened which allows us a glimpse of something we hadn't previously seen—and in a period still full of boarded-up and forgotten windows that is a worthwhile achievement.

Shaw also features in Georg Grote's *Anglo-Irish Theatre and the Formation of a Nationalist Political Culture Between 1890 and 1930*, a book which sets out to investigate the connections between street and stage, and whether it is possible to trace the influence of dramatic texts and their stage performances in the active struggle for Irish independence. Grote's first sentence unequivocally announces that 'Writing in itself is a political act', and his final chapter takes as its title a line from Yeats's 1938 retrospective poem 'Man and the Echo': 'Did that play send out certain men the English shot?' On one level, the book deals with material and stages (in both senses) with which we may feel we already have some familiarity—the emergency of the Abbey Theatre, Shaw and Wilde as exiles, Lady Gregory, Synge, and O'Casey. But Grote aims to go beyond the surely indisputable claim that political ideas (and actions) were broadly influenced and shaped by Anglo-Irish writers, and to see whether it is possible to be more precise about the connections and the creation of an Irish identity. What responsibility, asks Grote, must a writer be expected to take for the public impact of what he or she creates? He points out that historians have reconstructed in minute detail the actual events of Easter 1916, 'but it still needs to be explained why these people were there if it was obvious that a military success against the British army was out of the question'. Grote seeks to go further still, sidestepping any problems associated with identifying authorial intention, and seeking to incorporate biographical research 'to address the question "*Why* did he write the play that sent out certain men the English shot?"'. He also seeks to identify why the medium of theatrical performance could have become so influential, and thus answer the question '*How* did that play send out certain men the English shot?' These are ambitious and not unproblematic aims, but though they are perhaps impossible to fulfil, the book certainly raises important questions.

There are some obvious links between Grote's work and Paul Murphy's 'J.M. Synge and the Pitfalls of National Consciousness' (*TRI* 28:ii[2003] 125–42). Murphy identifies the physical battle before 1922 as 'predicated on an ideological war of representations over how Ireland was to be constituted as a cultural and political entity'. He argues that the theatre was the primary site of this struggle (which took place not only between the colonized and the external colonizer, but also between different factions within Ireland) 'to the extent that venues such as the Abbey Theatre seemed as much a theatre in the militaristic sense as … in the primarily aesthetic sense'. Framed partly by Lacanian concepts and language, the core of Murphy's article centres on Synge's depiction of the peasant, contesting the recently expressed claims of those who have attempted to incorporate Synge as a radical and socialist agent of the process of decolonization. For Murphy, Synge (along with Yeats and Lady Gregory) is essentially and inevitably tied to his roots in the landed colonial elite, given to 'constructing the peasantry as fantasy objects' in ways which allow him to retain contempt for the new middle classes and, in effect, to defend aristocratic values. In this reading, *The Playboy of the Western World* represents 'the peak of Synge's investment of the peasant with aristocratic qualities' and a betrayal of the actual peasant society which was being forcibly destroyed: 'famine, eviction, military oppression and landlordism, the characteristic facts of late nineteenth-century Irish rural existence for the peasantry are almost entirely repressed features of the text'. While Synge may have been reading key socialist and Marxist texts, these, says Murphy, are not reflected in the construction of his on-stage world, which prefers rather to 'fetishize the miserable lifestyle of wandering tramps and indulge in their social exclusion'. Murphy's argument is a powerful contribution to a continuing debate, and it seems unlikely that this will be the last word.

A different example of Irish theatre-writing is the subject of Kirsten Shepherd Barr's 'Reconsidering Joyce's *Exiles* in its Theatrical Context' (*TRI* 28:ii[2003] 169–80). Shepherd Barr argues that *Exiles* (written in 1915 but not performed in England until 1926) has been largely dismissed and overlooked by scholars because it lacks the innovation and experimentation associated with its author's approach to prose writing. Only rarely has it been approached by critics as a text for the theatre—something, suggests the writer, which tends to indicate 'the marginalization of theatrical performance in the historiography of modernism'. Shepherd Barr's aim here is to locate the play in relation to the European theatre with which Joyce was involved—he had, for example, translated Hauptmann into English and Synge into Italian, and was also familiar with Jarry and with avant-garde practices. But more links are identified here to Maeterlinck and the French symbolist theatre of the late nineteenth century, to Ibsen and, perhaps most illuminatingly, to some of the early (and less comic) Wilde and even to Pinero. However, it is actually the connections to the writing of Harold Pinter (which became apparent when Pinter directed Joyce's play with great success at the start of the 1970s) which most demands an academic reappraisal of *Exiles*: 'Theatre reviewers of *Exiles* have been documenting for decades what critics and scholars of Joyce have refused to acknowledge, that "Joyce was struggling towards a new kind of theatre", at whose centre lie "ambiguity and stylized silences … Wrapped in a method of pronounced pauses and silences".'

Beyond the specific case of *Exiles*, Shepherd Barr is keen to challenge a long-standing critical reluctance (arising from 'entrenched anti-theatrical prejudice') to foreground drama in the analysis of modernism and artistic innovation in the early part of the twentieth century. But at the risk of siding with the elitist philosophies identified by DiPietro (above), one feels bound to point out that the British professional theatre did tend instinctively to resist rather than welcome innovation—especially if it came from abroad. One of the most obvious gatekeepers (but by no means the only one) was the Lord Chamberlain in his role as stage censor, a role considered in two publications this year. Paul Marshall's 'The Lord Chamberlain and the Containment of Americanization in the British Theatre of the 1920s' (*NTQ* 19:iv[2003] 381–94) uses five case studies to examine some of the strategies employed to resist any challenge to those values identified as quintessentially English. Rather surprisingly, Marshall finds that 'despite the personal prejudices of the "establishment", respect for the creative skill of an author might hold sway', and cites the licensing by the Lord Chamberlain's Office of Eugene O'Neill's *Anna Christie*. He even suggests that 'the Lord Chamberlain was acutely aware of the pressure he was under not to suppress genuine talent'. It's slightly hard to know how this squares with prolonged refusals to license *Miss Julie* or plays by Shaw, Ibsen, Pirandello, and Cocteau (to name but a few), though there was certainly a perceived need to try and avoid exposing the Office to critical ridicule by rejecting something which had achieved 'classic status'. But Marshall's detailed work is welcome, and he is surely right to note that 'behind the façade that the Office was acting fairly towards foreign drama there was the desire that the British view of "taste" should prevail'.

There is, of course, an individual file of reports, correspondence, and memoranda from the Lord Chamberlain's Office for every single play submitted for a licence (as all plays seeking public performance had to be) between 1911 and 1968. With anything up to a thousand scripts a year submitted (the licence covered amateur as well as professional work) that makes a lot of files, and the strength of Steve Nicholson's *The Censorship of British Drama 1900–1968* arises largely from the fact that its author can claim to be the first person to have read through all of those files. So far, only the first of three intended volumes has been published, taking the story up to 1932; even then it is apparent that Nicholson has had to be selective in the stories and examples he gives—and even in the areas on which he focuses. Nevertheless, the use of quite extensive quotations from the correspondence files gives more than a flavour of primary documentation and may even allow the reader to notice points other than those to which the author is specifically drawing attention. In the context of looking at some of the crudely racist dramas of the period, Nicholson makes the case that in order to understand the (often unspoken) values informing any censorship, it is necessary to look at what *is* as well as what *isn't* allowed, and he also seeks to challenge the assumption that the Lord Chamberlain represented an extreme position of repression, showing that he frequently fended off campaigns and demands (for example from the Public Morality Council) that he should be considerably more draconian and less liberal. Perhaps what is most remarkable today is the evidence of the power attributed to theatre to influence its audiences. Also striking are some of the less overt manifestations of censorship which flourished; in theory it was only plays written since 1843 which were susceptible to the Lord Chamberlain's control, but an MP speaking in 1913 pointed out that he had to go to Germany to see an uncensored version of *Romeo and Juliet*, and Vienna to see any version at all of *Measure for Measure*. It was not that the censor would intervene directly, but rather that 'because of the whole sense of restriction that the Censor has brought about, managers themselves when they are considering the production of a Shakespeare play have to emasculate the whole force of the drama'.

Finally, it would not be right to end this review without reference to the republication, following her death in 2002, of Joan Littlewood's autobiography, now simply entitled *Joan's Book: The Autobiography of Joan Littlewood*. Originally published in 1994, there are no apparent alterations other than the addition of a foreword by a former working associate and friend, and a series of extracts from reviews of the original publication. Of course, most of the book concentrates on the period after 1950, but given that there is still a relative dearth of material about the theatre of the 1940s, Littlewood's memories here are still important—even if we can't always rely on their accuracy. Indeed, in 'Closing Joan's Book: Some Personal Footnotes' (*NTQ* 19:ii[2003] 99–108) another former working colleague, Clive Barker, describes the book, not unadmiringly, as 'an ingenious work of eighteenth-century romantic fiction'. But insightful (and enjoyable) though Barker's memories of working with Littlewood are, they relate exclusively to the period after he joined Theatre Workshop in 1955, and are therefore beyond the scope of this review.

5. Post-1950 Drama

Nine books on individual playwrights tackle important figures such as Samuel Beckett, Brian Friel, David Hare, Sean O'Casey, and Joe Orton. There is also a book by David Rabey which offers an overview of the period, plus monographs on feminist playwrights, black women playwrights, and political playwrights. Seven more books examine, sometimes superficially, diverse aspects of recent drama history, and two reference works are also considered.

Playwrights are probably no better judges of their own work than academics: many admit that the creative process is a mystery, and some are genuinely surprised by the interpretations that their work evokes. Nevertheless, playwrights have the advantage of a close proximity to their creations, and—especially after the experience of collaborating with a sympathetic director—can often reveal much of interest about the imaginary world of their plays. A new series of books from Faber both offers a commentary on major writers and gives them the space to tell their story in their own words. The first four titles—on Sean O'Casey, Samuel Beckett, Brian Friel, and David Hare—resembles a panorama of some eighty years of English-language drama, from O'Casey's *The Shadow of a Gunman* [1923] to Hare's *The Breath of Life* [2002]. The series has a distinctive format, with each expert offering a short biographical essay on the playwright, followed by some economic, social and political background to the plays, and then quoting at length from interviews, culled from newspapers or specially undertaken for this series, with them and their collaborators (usually directors and actors). Smart chronologies and brief annotated bibliographies give the books a student-friendly feel, and they are generally readable, accessible and jargon-free.

The best is Richard Boon's *About Hare*, not only because Hare has been interviewed frequently, but also because he has contributed his own polemical articles to newspapers and magazines. This enables Boon to neatly chart Hare's career, and offer a simple introduction to post-war British economics, society, and politics—the main themes of Hare's most important work. Boon shows how Hare evolved from being a fringe agitprop writer into a mainstream moral playwright, and gives a sympathetic account of his work, which has appeared on all kinds of stages (from touring venues to the National Theatre and West End), as well as on television and film. Boon weaves together extracts from Hare's interviews and essays, and includes new interviews with actors such as Bill Nighy and Lia Williams and with other theatre-makers such as designer Vicki Mortimer and director Richard Eyre. Occasionally, Boon's predilection for politics is misleading, as when his analysis of *Skylight* [1995] emphasizes the politics of the two main characters but ignores the play's emotional core, Tom's betrayal of

Kyra's trust. But, minor quibbles apart, this is a really excellent introduction to Hare's work.

In such a series, John Fletcher's *About Beckett* might have suffered from one major drawback—his subject's legendary reluctance to give interviews and his unwillingness to explain the meaning of his work. In fact, it is remarkable how often—despite the myth of his incommunicability—the Nobel prizewinner did talk to journalists and admirers, and Fletcher has collected some fascinating material, including recollections by novelist Edna O'Brien and art critic Charles Juliet. This is followed by an interesting section on Beckett as a director and by a collection of extracts from more familiar interviews with Beckett's collaborators, such as director Peter Hall and actors Billy Whitelaw and Jack MacGowran. But, more than any other volume in the series, this one expects the reader to already know Beckett's work. In his introduction, Fletcher sets the plays in the context of current debates about modernism and postmodernism, but he has also plagiarized the first fifty-five pages of his own *Beckett*, a Faber Critical Guide published in 2000, and he ignores Mel Gussow's important collection of interviews with other Beckettians.

In Tony Coult's engaging *About Friel*, the writer is quoted as saying that class politics are 'the qualifying decor but not the core' (p. 66) of his work. Yet, as Coult ably shows, his best plays—which include *Volunteers* [1975], *Translations* [1980], and *Dancing at Lughnasa* [1990]—marry the personal and the political in an imaginative and often provocative way. Despite this account's high-speed beginning, with a dash through Irish history from prehistory to the Irish Free State in just fifteen pages, Coult's summary of Friel's working life is measured, detailed, and revealing. But while Friel emerges as a humane and committed writer who is sceptical of extremists on all sides, Coult's attitude is sometimes annoyingly biased. Readers of his book are reminded on several occasions that the British once colonized Ireland, but IRA crimes are rarely mentioned. In one place (p. 53), Friel is quoted as saying that thirteen people were shot by the British army on Bloody Sunday in 1972, but in another (p. 48) Coult exaggerates the number to seventeen. Still, despite such minor lapses, this is a clear and intelligent reading of an important author.

Finally, Victoria Stewart's *About O'Casey* is a mixed success. The first part is an exemplary collection of newspaper interviews, in which O'Casey's personality, with his characteristic mix of pugnacity and whimsy, comes across very well. But, in the second part, Stewart's choice of interviewees—with the exception of those with his daughter Shivaun O'Casey and actress Dearbhla Molloy—is not very inspiring, and there is too little about the role in O'Casey's career of the Abbey and Gate theatres in Dublin. However, the strong point of the whole series, which at its best lives up to its subtitle of 'The Playwright and the Work', is the distinctive voices of the writers themselves, and the way these are reflected in their plays. The main weakness is the superficial accounts of the economic, social, and political background, and the assumption that most readers will already be familiar with the work of the playwrights.

As always, the Beckett industry has been productive. Although John Haynes and James Knowlson's *Images of Beckett* has been marketed mainly as a picture book, its chief delight is the text by Knowlson, in which he restates in his usual clear and succinct way the main outlines of Beckett's character and work. In three new essays, dealing with Beckett the man, his use of imagery from art, and his directing, Knowlson summarizes the insights of his long career as Beckett's friend and explicator. As ever, he writes in an appealingly accessible style. For example, on the suggestive power of religious imagery in Beckett's work, he says, 'These frequently hidden or half-hidden echoes of religious paintings (or writings) suggest far more than they state, weaving complex patterns of the explicit and the implicit' (p. 67). Occasionally, the essays are also revealing on a personal level: 'As someone who (to my acute embarrassment) found himself bursting into tears at a dress rehearsal of *Footfalls*, I find the notion of Beckett as an arid, inhuman formalist extremely difficult to accept' (p. 95). John Haynes's superb black and white photographs include the familiar pictures of Beckett from 1973, plus a series of useful production shots dating from the 1970s to the 1990s. Particularly useful are reproductions of some of the artworks considered in the text.

The illustrated approach to Beckett is also exemplified by Enoch Brater's *The Essential Samuel Beckett*, a biography aimed mainly at the general reader and which includes 122 photographs, mainly of various productions of his plays. Especially interesting is the picture which shows how actress Billie Whitelaw's head was held firm during the Royal Court's 1973 production of *Not I* (p. 111), and some rare photographs of Beckett's later works will interest experts as well as beginners. As an introduction to Beckett's work, this has the virtues of clarity, comprehensiveness, and empathy. Brater emphasizes the Irishness of Beckett's writing and the relationships between Beckett's novels and his work for theatre, radio, and film. For example, after Beckett missed hearing the BBC broadcast of his radio play *All That Fall*, he asked the broadcaster for a tape of it: 'The next week, he writes again, this time requesting a manual on how to operate a tape-recorder' (p. 90). Such is the background of *Krapp's Last Tape*. Brater's interpretations may not be especially original, yet he not only captures the essence of Beckett's style, but also convincingly and sympathetically conveys an impression of his imaginative world. Originally published in 1989 as *Why Beckett*, this is a really fine, stylishly written introduction to the playwright.

A more specialized approach to Beckett's work is exemplified by two important publications. First, the annual *Samuel Beckett Today/Aujourd'hui*, edited by Marius Buning and colleagues, is subtitled *'Three Dialogues' Revisited* and the first half contains conference papers from the 2002 conference on *Three Dialogues with George Duthuit* which was held at the South Bank University in London. Led by Steve Barfield ('The Resources of Unrepresentability: A Lacanian Glimpse of Beckett's *Three Dialogues*', pp. 15–28), contributors are David Cunningham, Andrew Gibson, David A. Hatch, Lois Oppenheim, Jeremy Parrott, and Philip Tew. Ten other articles, including one on the Beckett on Film project by this reviewer, represent a sample of papers from two other conferences, 'Beckett and Modern Theatre' at Westminster University, and 'ReReading Beckett's Late Drama: Aesthetics, Representation, Performance' at Royal Holloway, University of London. Secondly, Daniel Albright's *Beckett and Aesthetics* is a profound and challenging work which looks at the writer's lifelong struggle with artistic media and technological means of expression: 'This book argues that Beckett's whole canon is intimately engaged with technological problems' (p. 1). It charts his progress through various attempts to wrestle with aesthetic media, 'his extraordinary dotting on technique' (p. 3). Starting with an account of Beckett's engagement with surrealism, Albright goes on to examine his use and subversion of theatre conventions, then his assault on radio, film, and television, before exploring his attitude to music, a subject that Albright is an expert on. All in all, this is a readable, succinct, and thought-provoking study.

A satisfying volume of essays about Joe Orton, *Joe Orton: A Casebook*, edited by Francesca Coppa, covers both his work and his life. In her introduction Coppa points out that Orton has become a figure of fascination, with 'nearly as many plays written about Orton as Orton himself wrote' (p. 2), and that the popular image of the writer was a joint creation of Orton and his long-term lover Kenneth Halliwell: 'Together, the two men created "Joe Orton," the figure who swaggers through London' (p. 3). The essays are all very good, and the most substantial ones include John Bull on the relationship between Orton and Oscar Wilde ('"What the Butler Did See": Joe Orton and Oscar Wilde', pp. 45–60); Alan Sinfield on Orton's place in the broad sweep of new wave drama after 1956 ('Is There a Queer Tradition, and Is Orton In It?' pp. 85–94); and David Van Leer's meticulous deconstruction of the misunderstandings and clichés about the relationship between Orton and Halliwell ('Saint Joe: Orton as Homosexual Rebel', pp. 109–39). The collection's climax is a provocative essay by Simon Shepherd ('A Coloured Girl Reading Proust', pp. 141–54), which briefly but thoughtfully revisits his engagement with the writer and the work, especially in the wake of his own seminal book, *Because We're Queers* [1989]. Finally, there is a transcript (pp. 155–66) of Coppa's revealing discussion with Leonie Orton, the playwright's youngest sister and caretaker of his estate, and actor John Alderton, who starred in the National Theatre's 1995 production of *What the Butler Saw*.

The most extensive new survey of post-war British drama is David Rabey's *English Drama Since 1940*, a comprehensive sweep that starts with Rodney Ackland and Terence Rattigan, covers the new wave of the late 1950s, then comedy from the 1960s to the 1990s, political drama of the 1970s and 1980s, and 'New Expressionism', and ends with the new writers of the 1990s. Beckett and Pinter share a chapter, and Edward Bond and Howard Barker get one each. Added to this, there are useful chronologies, mini-biographies, and an annotated bibliography. So although writing a book about drama in the Literature in English series clearly poses several problems of definition—do you include American, Australian, Scottish, Welsh, or Irish playwrights?—Rabey manages to steer a zig-zag course between frantically mentioning everything superficially and engaging in depth with the most important writers, as well as including one chapter on Irish writing. His range of knowledge is impressive and his own preferences are clear: he rates Edward Bond, David Rudkin, and Howard Barker highly, proving once again that their status in the academy is in inverse proportion to their popularity with theatre-goers. Rabey's mission is to give an account of 'the most conspicuous and confrontational emergences of interrogatory drama since the English Renaissance' and suggests that interrogatory drama 'offers an erotic (usually nocturnal) dialogue between *dayenglish* and *nightenglish*, between different liberties, of inclusion and distinction, of containment and transgression'

(p. 3), although these categories only surface occasionally in his account. Even so, despite a writing style that is dense and occasionally frustratingly opaque, this is an original introductory survey.

Three monographs from the Cambridge Studies in Modern Theatre series cover important aspects of recent drama. *Contemporary Black and Asian Women Playwrights in Britain* by Gabriele Griffin is the first monograph to examine plays by British black and Asian women. Griffin sensibly seeks to rescue plays by writers such as Tanika Gupta, Winsome Pinnock, Maya Chowdhry, Meera Syal, and Zindika from the clichés of postcolonial or intercultural theory, pointing out correctly that 'the work itself is produced by writers who do not necessarily view themselves as "other" within Britain and who are now claiming their place at the table of British high culture. Their points of reference—in theatrical terms—are thus not the rituals, performances, or theatre works that are prevalent in the West Indies, parts of Africa, India, or Pakistan, but those of contemporary British theatre' (p. 9). Using Avtar Brah's theory of 'diaspora space', she gives a stimulating and richly nuanced account of how black and Asian female playwrights have imagined individual and community history in the past quarter-century. Her subordinate themes include arranged marriage, sexploitation, and lesbian sexuality, and she takes into account an impressively wide range of writers, including Paulette Randall, Pat Cumper, and Dolly Dhingra as well as Jacqueline Rudet, Amrit Wilson, Valerie Mason-John, and Kara Miller. In general, her approach focuses on the text, and there are few details of where the plays were performed or what they actually looked like on stage—for example, she ignores the usual practice of quoting from first-night reviews. Occasionally, Griffin shows her ignorance of theatre practice, as when she uses the fact that Winsome Pinnock's *Mules* had a cast of only three to play twelve roles as an example of the invisibility of black actors (p. 240), when actually the play was commissioned by Clean Break Theatre Company, which has a small budget and always specifies a maximum of three actors. So although this is a carefully written, thoroughly researched account of a subject too often ignored by theatre academics, it suffers from a tendency to be uncritical of its subject, and often fails to grapple with the ideas of the plays it so lucidly describes.

A similar verdict could be delivered on Elaine Aston's monograph, *Feminist Views on the English Stage: Women Playwrights, 1990–2000*, which challenges the crass idea that the 1990s were a post-feminist decade by looking at a range of women playwrights, from Sarah Kane to Caryl Churchill, and includes a substantial discussion of the more recent work of Sarah Daniels, Rebecca Prichard, Judy Upton, Bryony Lavery, Phyllis Nagy, Winsome Pinnock, and Timberlake Wertenbaker. Her readings are appreciative, and she ranges widely, often using theory to elucidate and deepen her understanding of the work. The trouble is that Aston's ideological standpoint tends to narrow her point of view to a bland 1980s feminism, which rejects all 1990s theories from Judith Butler to 'power feminism' (pp. 6–8). Women writers are consistently seen as victims of marginalization, which is ironic given that, as this book abundantly testifies, the 1990s saw an explosion of female talent, much of which appeared at mainstream venues. So while Aston is surely right to criticize the dominance of laddish drama in the mid-1990s, her account of women's writing is un-celebratory and occasionally patronizing. For example, whenever a woman behaves badly, as in the case of Sarah Kane, Aston claims that she is 'exploiting the image that she had been given that was not of her choosing' (p. 80). A simpler explanation, and a less ideological one, is that Kane deliberately chose her own unfeminist image. It is hard to see how Aston's intellectual stance—which complacently repeats the formulations of the past—could challenge or stimulate the student of today, and what is missing from this study is the pungent whiff of criticism: every play by every woman seems to carry equal value, and if Aston prefers any one work to any other she conceals the fact very well. On a more personal note, although she is aware that *In-Yer-Face Theatre* [2001], written by this reviewer, includes some of the same writers and plays, she consistently ignores it in her footnotes—surely not because its author is a man?

Michael Patterson's monograph on political theatre is a workmanlike but rather old-fashioned volume which covers, at times apologetically, the usual suspects in British post-war political theatre: Arnold Wesker's *Roots*, John Arden's *Serjeant Musgrave's Dance*, Trevor Griffiths's *Comedians*, Howard Barker's *Stripwell*, Howard Brenton's *The Churchill Play*, John McGrath's *The Cheviot, the Stag and the Black, Black Oil*, David Hare's *Fanshen*, Edward Bond's *Lear*, and Caryl Churchill's *Cloud Nine*. Although political theatre is conservatively defined as 'a kind of theatre that not only depicts social interaction and political events but implies the possibility of radical change on socialist lines' (pp. 3–4), Patterson includes apposite maxims from thinkers such as Gotthold Lessing in his introductory discussion. Here, he sets out to 'discover a wide range of strategies of political theatre' (p. 6) and his theoretical overview contrasts social realism—which he points out is a misnomer 'since the plots and character depictions were highly idealized' (p. 14)—with agitprop, before focusing the discussion on the interventionist and reflectionist strands of political drama. This sound summary is followed by case studies which offer detailed readings of each chosen play, with background on the writers and the social and political context. Unfortunately, few of these readings take into account any of the actual productions of the plays, so there is a bloodless feel to the whole exercise. Ironically, just as this book was published, a new wave of political theatre—led by David Hare's *The Permanent Way* [2003] and *Stuff Happens* [2004]—has arisen in the wake of 11 September and the 'War on Terror'. Since many examples of new political drama are either verbatim drama or scabrous satire, it is rather sad to read Patterson's final hope that it would be 'desirable' if any new wave would 'draw on the work of a group of remarkable playwrights of the last century' (p. 179). Of course, this is precisely what the current new wave is not doing.

Although most theatre critics do a good job as consumer pundits, few are worth rereading after their ink has dried. Exceptions, of course, include Kenneth Tynan, legendary critic of the *Evening Standard* and *Observer* and dramaturg at Laurence Olivier's National Theatre in the 1960s. At a time when most of his work is out of print, interest has focused on his private life: his second wife, Kathleen, published a biography [1987] and his letters [1994], and his first wife, Elaine Dundy, published her memoirs [2001]. His diaries, edited by John Lahr, also came out in 2001. Now Dominic Shellard, who has already written about Tynan's arch-rival, Harold Hobson of *The Sunday Times*, argues that Tynan's career as a theatre critic from 1952 to 1963 'encapsulates his brilliance' (p. viii) and concentrates on this part of his life. Of course, Tynan was a literary phenomenon in his own right, but was he actually any good as a critic? He may have been triumphantly right about John Osborne, greeting *Look Back in Anger* as the 'best young play of its decade' (p. 162), but he was wrong about Rodney Ackland's *The Pink Room*, Tennessee Williams's *Cat on a Hot Tin Roof*, Beckett's *Endgame*, Ionesco's *The Lesson*, Pinter's *The Birthday Party*, and so on. Even when he was right, his rhetoric had an unpleasant taste. When he declared that 'I doubt if I could love anyone who did not wish to see *Look Back in Anger*' (p. 162), the daring of the phrase almost blinds you to its sheer narcissism. Nevertheless, Shellard records some good anecdotes and the first half of the book is engrossing. The second is more superficial and much sadder. Tynan's provocative use of 'fuck' on television was a cultural milestone, but his record as dramaturg was poor, his *Oh! Calcutta!* sex revue was limp, and his final years were spent in failure. Despite this, Shellard's book is all hagiographic applause and very little reflection. Tynanophiles will enjoy it, but more critical spirits might see it as a squandered opportunity.

Artistic directors can also give insights into the work of writers. In the 2003 reissue of *Joan's Book*, Joan Littlewood's 1994 autobiography, there is plenty of material on the theatre practice of her Theatre Workshop at the Theatre Royal Stratford East, where she premiered writers such as Shelagh Delaney and Brendan Behan, although not before she had beaten their work into shape. As Peter Rankin remarks in his new foreword, when Littlewood fought 'tooth and nail with her editors' on this book 'I liked to imagine these scenes affording amusement to the writers whose work she completely rewrote' (p. xxxiii). Vigorously written, full of lively insights, *Joan's Book* is an important source which illuminates a colourful and provocative career. By contrast, Richard Eyre, who headed the National Theatre from 1987 to 1997, writes in a more restrained and reflective style. His diaries are full of his characteristic shyness, his struggles with failing self-confidence, and his abashed reactions to criticism. The high points of his decade at the helm—David Hare's trilogy, Tom Stoppard's *Arcadia*, Alan Bennett's *The Madness of George III*—jostle with vaguely amusing celebrity anecdotes. There is also some information about Patrick Marber's *Closer* and Martin McDonagh's *The Cripple of Inishmaan*, although Eyre's record of staging young writers was not good.

In 2003 the National had a hit with Nicholas Wright's two-play adaptation of Philip Pullman's *His Dark Materials* trilogy. In Robert Butler's *The Art of Darkness* there is a lot of material about how this adaptation was realized through the rehearsal process, as well as some interesting information both about Philip Pullman (pp. 27–43) and Nicholas Wright (pp. 64–6), plus a few wry comments on the difficulties of adapting imaginative literature (pp. 6–8). There is also some material on the writing process, plus a lot of background and showbiz anecdotes, in actor Martin Jarvis's *Broadway Jeeves?*, a diary account of Alan Ayckbourn and Andrew Lloyd Webber's musical *By Jeeves*, which opened in New York in 2001. Books about individual authors rather than productions offer greater depth, and these include *Spike Milligan*, a new and readable biography by Humphrey Carpenter. Milligan's surreal and humorous scripts for *The Goon Show* were immensely popular among radio listeners in the 1950s and early 1960s, and Carpenter—using material from Milligan's correspondence with the BBC—outlines the writer's unsettled relationship with his employers, gives some insight into his influences (more Lewis Carroll than Eugène Ionesco) and suggests that he might well have a claim to be one of the era's Angry Young Men (p. 147). There is a fair amount of detail about Milligan's working practices and his relationships with his co-writers. But although it is easy to see why Carpenter concentrates on *The Goon Show*—which ran for six months a year for most of a decade, had an audience of millions, and whose gleeful zaniness soon became part of the national fabric—this tends to bias the book heavily towards one decade of Milligan's fifty-year career.

On a much less parochial scale, Svich, ed., *Trans-Global Readings: Crossing Theatrical Boundaries*, is an up-to-date collection of pieces by and about theatre artists of all kinds which provides something of a forum on new technologies, intercultural collaborations, and interdisciplinary work. For example, the Scottish writer David Greig talks about his experimental work for the group Suspect Culture from 1990 onwards (pp. 157–61), while director Nick Philippou talks to Caridad Svich about his work with ATC, including the staging of two of Mark Ravenhill's plays, *Faust Is Dead* and *Handbag*, as well as the work of young writer Michael Wynne (pp. 167–71). Experienced playwright Tanika Gupta (pp 99–104) and new talent Joanna Laurens (pp. 126–30), who writes in an unusual poetic style, are also included among many performance artists and American theatre-makers.

A century of Irish playwriting is briefly considered in Christopher Fitz-Simon's centenary celebration of the Abbey Theatre, 'Ireland's National Theatre'. This is mainly a lavishly produced picture book, with some superb production shots, but it includes brief information on post-war writers who have made an important contribution to British theatre, such as Sebastian Barry, Brendan Behan, Marina Carr, Brian Friel, Frank McGuinness, Gary Mitchell, and Billy Roche. The book ends with a useful list of productions, covering 1904–2003. Elsewhere, in Böss and Maher, eds., *Engaging Modernity* (also reviewed in section 1(*b*) above), there are good chapters by Clare Wallace on 1990s playwrights in the context of social change ('Versions and Reversions: The New Old Story and Contemporary Irish Drama', pp. 112–20) and Michael Lachmann on British-born Martin McDonagh's *Leenane Trilogy* ('Happy in Exile? Martin McDonagh's "Leenane Trilogy"', pp. 194–206).

There are also two updates on established reference works. The third edition of Trevor R. Griffiths's *The Theatre Guide* includes more than 500 entries on the most important playwrights performed today, as opposed to those who feature in histories of drama but are rarely staged. Griffiths ranges from Greek poets to the latest British playwrights such as Leo Butler or Zinnie Harris, with plenty of names from all over the world and from each historical period. Although the absence of a bibliography is a handicap, this remains a sound reference book. Another work of reference, *The World of Theatre*, edited by Ian Herbert and Nicole Leclercq, covers theatre from all over the world and has brief chapters on England, written by Peter Hepple (pp. 323–7), on Scotland, by Mark Fisher (pp. 328–33), and on Wales by David Adams and Hazel Walford Davies (pp. 333–7). Both volumes are well illustrated with production photographs.

As regards drama journals, the big news is the relaunch of *Contemporary Theatre Review* under its new editors David Bradby and Maria Delgado, whose first issue (*ConTR* 13:i[Feb. 2003]) is entitled 'Playwrights, Politics, Performance' and succeeds in injecting a welcome dose of politics into the study of today's drama. The issue has the following contributions: Mary Luckhurst, 'Political Point-Scoring: Martin Crimp's *Attempts on her Life*' (*ConTR* 13:i[2003] 47–60); Dan Rebellato '"And I will reach out my hand with a kind of infinite slowness and say the perfect thing": The Utopian Theatre of Suspect Culture' (*ConTR* 13:i[2003] 61–80); Caridad Svich, 'Commerce and Morality in the Theatre of Mark Ravenhill' (*ConTR* 13:i[2003] 81–6); and Graham Saunders, '"Just a word on a page and there is the drama": Sarah Kane's Theatrical Legacy' (*ConTR* 13:i[2003] 97–110); plus a personal view of John McGrath's achievements by Nadine Holdsworth, 'Remembering John McGrath' (*ConTR* 13:i[2003] 111–14). A contribution by this reviewer is an ambitious if not entirely successful attempt to put new writing for theatre in a wider social context: Aleks Sierz, '"Art flourishes in times of struggle": Creativity, Funding and New Writing' (*ConTR* 13:i[2003] 33–46). But the least successful article is Vera Gottlieb's lead piece, 'Theatre Today: The "New Realism"' (*ConTR* 13:i[2003] 5–14), which attempts to show how drama responds to the changing post-9/11 world. Her argument, however, would be more impressive if her strong opinions were backed with reliable facts. For example, in a footnote (p. 13) on black and Asian British playwrights, she includes the white Rebecca Prichard (misspelt as Pritchard) and misses out Roy Williams and Tanika Gupta, two prolific writers whose work has been seen at the National Theatre and other high-profile venues. Subsequent issues of *ConTR* include interesting articles, such as Nadine Holdsworth, 'Travelling Across Borders: Re-imagining the Nation and Nationalism in Contemporary Scottish Theatre' (*ConTR* 13:ii[2003] 25–40), on David Greig and Stephen Greenhorn; Janelle Reinelt and Gerald Hewitt, '*The Prisoner's Dilemma*: Game Theory, Conflict Resolution and the New Europe' (*ConTR* 13:ii[2003] 41–56), on David Edgar; and John Ginman on the Out of Joint company's contribution to new writing: 'Out of Joint: Max Stafford Clark and "The Temper of our Time"' (*ConTR* 13:iii[2003] 16–25).

Another journal, *Modern Drama*, continues to offer interesting and important work. In the summer issue Carina Bartleet's 'Sarah Daniels' Hysteria Plays: Re-presentations of Madness in *Ripen Our Darkness* and *Head-Rot Holiday*' (*MD* [2003] 241–60) gives a clear and engaging account of Sarah Daniels's use of images of mental illness in two of her plays, analysing them from the perspective of Jean-Martin Charcot as well as Elin Diamond. In the autumn issue are Camilla Stephens, '"The Future of Old Trinidad": The Performance of National Cultural Identity in Two Plays by Derek Walcott' (*MD* [2003] 450–69), on Derek Walcott's *Beef, No Chicken* and *The Last Carnival*; Maria Germanou, 'Brian Friel and the Scene of Writing: Reading *Give Me Your Answer, Do!*' (*MD* [2003] 470–81); and Lisa Sternlieb and Nancy Selleck, '"What is carnal embrace?" Learning to Converse in Stoppard's *Arcadia*' (*MD* [2003] 482–502). In the *European Journal of English Studies*, there is an appreciative article by Heiner

Zimmermann on Martin Crimp's masterpiece, 'Images of Women in Martin Crimp's *Attempts on her Life*' (*EJES* [2003] 69–85), and in *New Theatre Quarterly* there is my report on the 'In-Yer-Face? British Drama in the 1990s' conference in 2002 (Aleks Sierz, 'In-Yer-Face in Bristol' (*NTQ* 73[2003] 90–1)), and 'Closing Joan's Book: Some Personal Footnotes' (*NTQ* 74[2003] 99–107), an appreciation of the role of Joan Littlewood by Clive Barker, a Theatre Workshop veteran. The next issue includes an interesting article by playwright Alan Plater, 'Learning the Facts of Life: Forty Years as a TV Dramatist' (*NTQ* 75[2003] 203–13), in which he tells the following anecdote, which seems to sum up much about the timidity of much recent new writing for the British stage: 'A friend of mine took three young actors to see the revival of Caryl Churchill's play *Top Girls*, and they were staggered to realize you could have an exciting play about politics. They hadn't realized such a thing was possible' (pp. 212–13). At a time when so many new plays are naturalistic accounts of 'me and my mates', and much political theatre takes the form of edited verbatim extracts, it is good to remember that drama doesn't have to be so limited.

6. Pre-1950 Poetry

Studies of the work of T.S. Eliot have dominated 2003's list. The year opened with a special issue of the journal *Modernism/Modernity* ('Eliot and Anti-Semitism: The Ongoing Debate', *Mo/Mo* 10:i[2003]), and this was closely followed by a new edition, with a new preface and afterword, of Anthony Julius's *T.S. Eliot, Anti-Semitism and Literary Form* 1995. Turning first to the articles in *Mo/Mo*, the special issue is kick-started by Ronald Schuchard's fleet-footed essay 'Burbank with a Baedeker, Eliot with a Cigar: American Intellectuals, Anti-Semitism, and the Idea of Culture' (*Mo/Mo* 10:i[2003] 1–26). Schuchard's primary aim is to take Eliot's pre-First World War sojourn in Europe as a biographical and historical context and to trace Eliot's 'definition and defense of culture in relation to some American intellectuals with opposing ideas' (p. 2). His secondary aim is rather broader: 'to address the widespread assumption that [Eliot's] writings are anti-Semitic'. Schuchard sees anti-Semitic elements in certain of Eliot's poems as features of his much more comprehensive assessment of the plight of modern Europe and, by extension, of the failure of humanism. In support of his recuperation of Eliot, Schuchard cites recently discovered correspondence between Eliot and Horace M. Kallen (a 'Jewish social philosopher and Zionist', p. 4), arguing that Eliot's target is not Jews, but 'free-thinkers' of any race and religion.

The ripostes to Schuchard's essay which follow in this *Mo/Mo* special issue are various and, problematically, each is persuasive in its own terms. David Bromwich's 'A Response to Ronald Schuchard' (*Mo/Mo* 10:i[2003] 27–31) carefully delineates Eliot's tripartite view of Jews and, although he concedes that Eliot 'practiced better than he preached' (p. 28), retains profound reservations about his perception and representation of Jewishness. Ronald Bush's 'Response' (*Mo/Mo* 10:i[2003] 33–6) leapfrogs Schuchard and goes back to Anthony Julius—the 'catalyst' to appropriate one of Eliot's own terms—for this whole debate. Bush's rhetoric is legalistic, but he closes without insisting on judgement and by recognizing ambivalence. Denis Donoghue's essay (*Mo/Mo* 10:i[2003] 37–9), one of the briefest and the most personal in the journal, is also, perhaps, the most valuable in its polemical and frank appraisal of the situation. Other 'Responses' by James Longenbach (*Mo/Mo* 10:i[2003] 49–50) and Marjorie Perloff (*Mo/Mo* 10:i[2003] 51–6) follow, as do responses to 'Responses', as it were, from Schuchard—'My Reply: Eliot and the Foregone Conclusions' (*Mo/Mo* 10:i[2003] 57–70)—and from Anthony Julius himself (*Mo/Mo* 10:i[2003] 41–7).

Turning now to the new edition of Julius's *T.S. Eliot: Anti-Semitism and Literary Form*, mentioned above, we find Julius developing his original argument (that it is important that we recognize Eliot's anti-Semitism and the fact that he did not only 'reflect the anti-Semitism of his time, he contributed to it', p. xiii) and rebutting hostile responses to its original appearance. There is a Möbius Strip-like effect to all this, with Julius's 'Postscript: Fourteen Propositions Responding to Critics' citing both Schuchard's *Mo/Mo* essay and his own riposte in the same journal.

T.S. Eliot also dominates the *Journal of Modern Literature*'s special double issue on 'Modern Poets' (*JML* 27:i/ii[2003]). In 'Death by Gramophone' (*JML* 27:i/ii[2003] 1–13), Sebastian D.G. Knowles turns to a theme also discussed by Juan A. Suárez in a recent issue of *New Literary History* (reviewed in *YWES* 82[2003] 706). Knowles traces the simultaneous rise of the gramophone and of modernism and the persistent importance of the former to the latter as the contradictory embodiment of lifelessness *and* progress. Drawing on the work of a range of modernist writers, he focuses in particular on Eliot's rejection of the gramophone as a signifier of the mechanization of humanity and of the death of traditional values. Also in this issue of *JML*, Loretta Johnson's 'T.S. Eliot's Bawdy Verse: Lulu, Bolo and More Ties' (*JML* 27:i/ii[2003] 14–25) reads Eliot's early bawdy verse in terms of what it reveals about his persistent interest in the 'spirit and the body' and 'thought and feeling in poetry' (p. 14). Johnson summarizes critical responses to the work, offers likely sources for some of the fragments, and provides a close reading of selected passages. Saman Gupta's brief but illuminating essay 'In Search of Genius: T.S. Eliot as Publisher' (*JML* 27:i/ii[2003] 26–35) cites unpublished rejection letters from Eliot, written in his role as editor at Faber & Faber, and asks what these reveal, first about Eliot's editorial perspective, and second about his own practice as a writer.

Also in this issue, Ronald Schuchard (see above) continues his diligent analysis of Eliot's poetic career. In 'Did Eliot Know Hulme?' (*JML* 27:i/ii[2003] 63–9) he turns to the long-standing question of whether Eliot and T.E. Hulme knew each other personally in London in or around 1916 (that is, before Hulme's death in the First World War). Schuchard's view, arrived at after many years of study and the archetypal serendipitous archival find, is that they did know each other—although as his conclusion is based on interpretation and corroboration, this argument looks likely to run and run.

Nancy D. Hargrove's 'T.S. Eliot and Popular Entertainment in Paris, 1910–11' (*JPC* 36:iii[2003] 547–88) complements David Chinitz's essay on Eliot and the 'lively arts' (reviewed in *YWES* 82[2004] 706). Hargrove focuses on Eliot's encounter during his year in Paris with various light entertainment spectacles (from melodramatic detective plays to cabaret acts, circuses, music hall, and cinema) and suggests that this context informs many of his poems. In some cases the connections she asserts seem tenuous (that the foggy settings of Sherlock Holmes-inspired detective plays, which Eliot may or may not have seen, provide the setting for 'The Love Song of J. Alfred Prufrock'). In other cases, particularly that of the music hall, the connections are more convincing, and Hargrove performs a valuable service in identifying shows and artists active in Paris during Eliot's stay.

Claudia Milstead's thorough and interesting essay, 'Echoes of Krishna and Arjuna in Eliot's "Dry Salvages" and "Little Gidding"' (*ELN* 40:iii[2003] 62–76) recaps critical readings of the relationship between *Four Quartets* and the *Bhagavad Gita*, but then takes the connection rather further. She suggests that Krishna emerges as the 'familiar compound ghost' in section II of the latter and that the voice of Eliot's narrator represents Arjuna. Milstead sees here a model for the notes of 'simultaneous engagement and selfless detachment' (p. 69) in *Four Quartets* and specifically for the profound 'non-attachment' of 'Little Gidding'.

In his self-consciously and therefore rather tiresomely witty essay, 'Thoughts after Margate: Alternative Readings of *The Waste Land* lines 300–2' (*PNR* 29:v[2003] 10–13), Raymond Tallis speculates about the status of and relationship between 'Nothing' and 'nothing' in 'On Margate Sands | I can connect | Nothing with nothing', and suggests that Eliot's very ability to articulate this problem undermines its existence: 'rushing back [from Margate] to report the end of all sorts of things is not quite the same as being able to connect nothing with nothing' (p. 11). Brian Southam's 'A Possible New Source for *The Waste Land*, lines 1–18' (*N&Q* 50:iii[2003] 330–2) suggests the influence of the work of the Spanish poet Gabriel Ferrater on the opening lines of Eliot's poem. Mike Pincombe's contribution to the same issue of *N&Q*, entitled '"Gloomy Orion": Eliot, Marlowe, Virgil' (*N&Q* 50:iii[2003] 329–30), extends a point Brian Southam has made elsewhere about the Virgilian source of 'Gloomy Orion' in Eliot's 'Sweeney Among the Nightingales'. Pincombe cites Marlowe's *Dido, Queen of Carthage* as another potential source.

Christina Hauck's 'Abortion and the Individual Talent' (*ELH* 70:i[2003] 223–66) is a lucid and compelling essay which takes as its starting point the episode described by Peter Ackroyd in his biography in which Eliot annotates a page from the *Midwives' Gazette* in order to draw attention to '"various forms of vaginal discharge"' (p. 223, citing Ackroyd pp. 150–1). Hauck argues that Eliot's use of these and other metaphors of abortion, menstruation, and similar signifies a self-reflexive anxiety about the non-viability of his own poetry and of modernism. Hauck traces the multiple and at times contradictory images of fertility, birth, contraception, and abortion in Eliot's poetry, offering a fine contribution to our reading of his work and life and its social and ethical context.

In 'T.S. Eliot and Poetic Confession' (*L&T* 17:i[2003] 1–16), Dennis Brown traces interwoven strands of psychological and spiritual questioning in Eliot's work, from the early poetry to the late play *The Cocktail Party*. Brown's point is that Eliot engages his reader in these complementary voyages. Although he briefly cites Foucault's model of confession, he does not develop Foucault's point about the reader's role in its successful realization (nor Leigh Gilmore's argument that there is a triangulation of penitent, text, and confessor; a point which would sustain Brown's own thesis about the importance to Eliot of the poem as 'aesthetic artefact', p. 2). Nevertheless, he offers a persuasive and original reading of 'Ash-Wednesday' as a song of mourning, and of *Four Quartets* as a self-conscious account/confession of the difficulties of self- (and poetic) interpretation. Also looking in more abstract terms at Eliot's poetry, David Rosen, in 'T.S. Eliot and the Lost Youth of Modern Poetry' (*MLQ* 64:iv[2003] 473–94), reads the work—and specifically its representations of youth and age—in the context of lingering *fin-de-siècle* anxieties about voice and imagination, or about the role and responsibility of the poet. Ultimately, he attempts to recuperate Eliot's own defiantly maintained sense of the importance of the individual imagination—a sense which he returned to at the end of his career, even in the light of modernist denial and his own early insistence on the primacy of a neutral, impersonal consciousness.

In 'New Light on *The Sacred Wood*' (*RES* 54[2003] 497–515), a welcome and persuasive essay on Eliot's criticism, Peter White outlines Eliot's own intention that *The Sacred Wood* should read as a coherent whole rather than a collection of disparate essays, but contends that the opposite effect is achieved. Specifically, he identifies a difference in tone between earlier and later sections of the book, indicative of a significant shift in Eliot's views as the book neared completion. The implication of this, as White shows, is that Matthew Arnold—the villain of the opening sections—has been unjustly vilified, Eliot's real target being Edmund Gosse.

Finally, two recent books include Eliot in their argument: Colin Falck's *American and British Verse in the Twentieth Century: The Poetry that Matters* (Ashgate) of which I have not yet seen a review copy, and Helen Vendler's perceptive and precise *Coming of Age as a Poet*. Vendler dedicates the central chapter of her book to tracing Eliot's emergence as a poet of real distinction and influence. This succinct but wide-ranging book, which began life as the James Murray Brown Lectures at the University of Aberdeen, looks to the early work of a number of poets (Milton, Keats, Eliot, Plath) in order to understand their individual quests for a personal style, for a voice or voices, and for a place in the world. In the case of Eliot, Vendler argues, early ideas, influences, anxieties, and experiments come to fruition in what she sees as his first mature work, 'The Love Song of J. Alfred Prufrock'.

W.H. Auden's poetry stimulated a number of excellent commentaries in the period under review. Joseph Epstein's 'Vin Audenaire' (*HudR* 56:i[2003] 57–72) is a pacy and affectionate overview of Auden's life and writing. It offers a valuable reminder of what his prolonged stay in America meant to his work. Although Epstein is treading familiar ground in his appraisal of the relative worth of Auden's earlier (pre-American) and later (post-American) poems, he does argue—largely against the grain—that the earlier poems are less politically credible and therefore less successful. In '"September 1, 1939" Revisited: Or, Poetry, Politics, and the Idea of the Public' (*ALH* 15:iii[2003] 533–59), Stephen Burt contemplates the media appropriation and mass popularity of Auden's eponymous poem in the US in the days after 9/11. Burt takes the resurgence of interest in the poem as symptom of, and paradoxically a response or solution to, a crisis of confidence in contemporary poetry and its place in public life. But he also raises the possibility that such expectations might be misplaced, might misrepresent what poetry can and should do in the world. It is precisely this uncertainty about the competing claims of rhetoric and justice that, he suggests, lie at the heart of Auden's own ambivalence about the poem.

William J. Hyde's fluent and intriguing essay, 'The Fall of Icarus: A Note on Ovid, Brueghel, and Auden's "Expensive Delicate Ship"' (*ELN* 41:ii[2003] 66–71), considers the relationship between Auden's well-known 1940 poem 'Musée des Beaux Arts', Ovid's tale of Icarus and Daedelus, and Brueghel's *Landscape with the Fall of Icarus*. In each rendering of the myth, attention is paid to the onlookers' inability or unwillingness to engage with the tragic events before them. Hyde, in common with others, reads this as a commentary on modernism's (or, for Auden, humanity's) disengagement. But, in a final twist, Hyde shares a personal anecdote about a delayed 1959 voyage out of New York by ocean liner. The ship was late into port on this occasion because it had—albeit ineffectually—attempted to rescue a 'person overboard'. The attitude of the resigned onlookers in Auden's poem is, this example suggests, 'neither universal nor inevitable' (p. 70). In 'Auden's Stormy Fens', a brief note on Auden (*N&Q* 50:iii[2003] 338), Derek Roper suggests a little-known fenland mystery novel by Richard Keverne (*Carteret's Cure* [1926]) as a source for Auden's 1930 poem 'Consider this and in our time'.

Edward Thomas is the subject of '"Leaving Town" and "Swedes": Edward Thomas and Amen-Hotep' (*N&Q* 50:iii[2003] 325–7). Here David Gill and Caroline Gill detect a source for Thomas's poem 'Swedes' (written in January 1915) in his own essay of 1906, 'Leaving Town', which in turn was influenced by a number of well-known Egyptian excavations of the period. David Gervais's '"Cock Crow": Why Edward Thomas Isn't Thomas Hardy' (*PNR* 30:ii[2003] 38–40) discusses Edward Thomas's genealogy and his successors, demurring from any too-ready association of Edward Thomas with Thomas Hardy (and thereby ultimately with Philip Larkin). Instead, he emphasizes stylistic or prosodic differences between Thomas and Hardy and proposes a similarity between Thomas's simplicity of focus and rejection of over-ornate emotion and, say, T.S. Eliot's use of the 'object correlative'. In this respect, like others (see, for example, Clive Wilmer's earlier *Poetry Nation Review* article, reviewed in *YWES* 82[2003] 705), he emphasizes the rewards of reading Thomas as a proto-modernist.

Peter Howarth also touches on Edward Thomas in his discussion of 'The Simplicity of W.H. Davies' (*ELT* 46:ii[2003] 155–74). In this lucid account of the apparent—but in fact beguiling—'simplicity' of W.H. Davies's poetry, Howarth takes his cue from Thomas's reading of the poet's work and suggests that this 'simplicity' is a function of 'dissonance' and 'authorial lack of control' rather than 'purity of origin' (p. 157). In this respect it anticipates, and has much in common with, early modernist poetics. Similarly, Archie Burnett, in 'Silence and Allusion in Housman' (*EIC* 53:ii[2003] 151–73), reconsiders 'surface simplicities' (p. 151) in A.E. Housman's work. He points to a far more complex, allusive, and elusive quality in the poetry—its paradoxically plangent silences which, he suggests, both mimic and allow release from the poet's own famous taciturnity. Burnett points, too, to Housman's appropriation of voices, and specifically voices of the past, as a way of finding his own; an insight which one might also extend to T.S. Eliot. Housman is also one of the subjects of Christopher Ricks's *Allusion to the Poets* (OUP [2002]). Regrettably, a review copy has not been received.

Poetry Nation Review continues to bring together an eclectic, illuminating, and usually entertaining mixture of essays. A sequence of articles in successive editions of the journal traces the origins of the Apocalyptic movement in poetry and takes issue with its habitual dismissal by critics and commentators. These articles attempt to re-establish the parameters of the movement and to recuperate some of its key figures, including Dylan Thomas. James Keery's essays 'The Burning Baby and the Bathwater I' (*PNR* 29:iv[2003] 58–62), 'II' (*PNR* 29:v[2003] 49–54), and 'III' (*PNR* 29:vi[2003] 57–62) discuss the grounds for considering Dylan Thomas as an Apocalyptic poet (a question to which Andrew Lycett fleetingly returns in his biography of Thomas, discussed below). The *PNR* series culminates with two essays on the newly discovered Apocalyptic archive and the draft of the original manifesto. Giles Goodland's 'John Goodland and the Apocalyptic Movement: Notes from the Son of a Literary Footnote' (*PNR* 30:ii[2003] 22–5) presents previously unknown papers documenting the origins of the movement. Goodland junior describes his father's reticence about his involvement, and reproduces what appears to be the original or *ur*-text of the better-known, although on this evidence inferior, 'Apocalyptic Manifesto' of 1942. James Keery's concluding companion piece 'The Burning Baby and the Bathwater IV' (*PNR* 30:ii[2003] 26–32) contextualizes and comments on this newly discovered Goodland archive.

In '"Unworthy of a serious song"? Modern Love Poetry and its Critics' (*CQ* 32:i[2003] 1–25), Tim Hancock surveys the state and status of love poetry, indicting modernists (Eliot) and others (Riding and Graves' *Survey of Modernist Poetry* [1927]) for devaluing the form in favour of an aesthetics of impersonality. This is a persuasive point, although only if one accepts at face value the rhetoric of these poets' public pronouncements on the issue, and only if one takes a rather conventional view of the characteristics of love poetry. One might equally argue that the failure or absence or disappointment of love (physical, spiritual, cerebral) is Eliot's major preoccupation. Hancock is right, though, to explain the rejection of, say, D.H. Lawrence's love poems in terms of a general distaste for the personal and the confessional (a distaste which arguably persists). His closing comments on parallels between Thomas Hardy's 'Poems of 1912–1913' and Ted Hughes's *Birthday Letters* are well judged.

A pleasing feature of Hancock's essay, as of a number of others under review this year (for example, Stephen Burt on Auden and David Gervais on Edward Thomas, both reviewed above), is the way in which it glances across and between poets and periods. Tim Kendall proceeds in a similar way in 'Keith Douglas and Self-Elegy' (*EIC* 53:iv[2003] 366–83). Kendall opens with a survey of contradictory readings of Rupert Brooke's 'The Soldier' (specifically of the opening line 'If I should die...', with the emphasis on the multiple possible inflections of 'should'), and then moves on to discuss a similar tension in Keith Douglas's Second World War poetry between what one *must* and what one would *rather not* do. Kendall then broadens his range again to consider these and other poets (Christina Rossetti, Hardy, Auden) in terms of elegy and self-elegy. In every case it is the engagement or dialogue with the reader which is regarded as significant. What does the reader expect of the poet? What does the poet need or demand of the reader?

This breadth of focus and willingness to look across received poetic, personal, and chronological boundaries is also to be found in a number of books published recently. Robert Crawford's *The Modern Poet* considers the productive relationship between poetry and academia (or between writing and studying poetry) since the eighteenth century. This should, more properly, be understood as a genealogy of poetry as the object of academic enquiry, and of what we now recognize as the 'modern poet'. Crawford mentions Arnold, Auden, and Eliot—looking in particular at what we might call their 'push me–pull you' relationship with their readers—and concludes by considering other more recent, and now frequently taught, names. *The Modern Poet* is a polemical, engaging, and original read. John Lucas's *Starting to Explain: Essays on Twentieth-Century British and Irish Poetry* (Trent), which I regret that I have not seen, also promises broad and exciting coverage, ranging from Hardy, Robert Graves, Sylvia Townsend Warner, and Edward Thomas through to contemporary poets.

Another important book which, although published in 2001, has only recently come to my attention is Marjorie Perloff's *21st-Century Modernism: The 'New' Poetics* (part of Blackwell's 'Manifestos' series). Perloff argues that it is only with the clarifying perspective of time that one can at last see the true legacy, indeed the completion, of modernist endeavours. The avant-garde poetries of Eliot, Gertrude Stein, and others, particularly their rigorous rethinking of language, form, and subjectivity, come to fruition, she suggests, only in the work of a twenty-first-century generation of poets (all of them North American: Charles Bernstein, Susan Howe, et al.). An interesting question, albeit one beyond the parameters of Perloff's book, is what the legacy has been for British and other poets. This is a stimulating read, though, and one which attempts to reshuffle the pack of great poets and to rethink accepted lines of influence.

Essays in Dowson, ed., *Women's Writing, 1945–1960: After the Deluge*, cover several periods and genres. Dowson's own contribution '"There is a sweetness in willing surrender"? Self-Loss and Renewal in the Poetry of Elizabeth Jennings, Kathleen Raine and Stevie Smith' (pp. 217–32) discusses the 'spiritual aesthetic' (p. 218) which she identifies in the work of these poets. Dowson describes this as a dimension in which 'sensation and representation', or emotion and actuality, coexist (p. 219). She shows how an aesthetics of impersonality (deriving from Eliot) begins to give way in writing by women of the mid-century to a more consciously personal and self-expressive voice. In Stevie Smith, though, as Dowson concedes, the trajectory is complex. For Smith, the personal and the self-expressive are insufficient and it is the inadequacy or failure of these which are her concerns.

Taking a different perspective on this period, Andrew Thacker's *Moving Through Modernity: Space and Geography in Modernism* is a wide-ranging and accessible book which resists reading modernism in the context of temporality, or historical change, and reads it instead in terms of geography, movement, *spatial* change. As his extensive research and copious notes indicate, this is not an entirely novel preoccupation. Nevertheless Thacker is stimulating and thorough on spatial motifs in modernist literature, and specifically on what this distinct way of reading modernism tells us about subjectivity, perception, and aesthetics. Gender, too, is at issue as Thacker explains in his chapter on imagist poetics. Given this, it is to be regretted that the book concentrates on the male vision of the metropolis (seeing women as the object of the male gaze) while acknowledging only in a note the different and intriguing ways in which women in imagism located themselves geographically and generically.

I noted in last year's review the abundance of biographies. This year has seen far fewer of note. Phillip Mallett's *Rudyard Kipling: A Literary Life* perceptively establishes the biographical and historical background to the emergence of Kipling's *The Years Between* [1903]. It also identifies a stark disjunction between the tone and voice of these poems (bombastic and keen, as T.S. Eliot commented in his *Athenaeum* review, to 'impose on you an idea', p. 176) and those of Georgian and modernist poetries. Finally, Andrew Lycett's biography, *Dylan Thomas: A New Life*, seems to start rather slowly. However, as the story develops and one reaches the most intriguing, notorious, and contested episodes, the careful groundwork is fully vindicated. The biography fully and sensitively traces the immense complexity and variety of Thomas's experience such that the catastrophic finale is portrayed (in an appropriately contradictory way) as both the inevitable *terminus ad quem* of the life *and* as merely one part of a much bigger and richer whole. What remains unexplained—what is, perhaps, inexplicable given the chaotic frustrations of the life—is quite how and when and why Thomas wrote the poems by which we know him. How did he create this poetry? What did it mean to him? We are left, again, with what is surely a mistaken impression that the poetry simply happened to Dylan Thomas, like some terrible accident.

7. Post-1950 Poetry

Edwin Morgan: Inventions of Modernity, by Colin Nicholson, is the first book-length study of the poet's work. Morgan's place as a major experimental poet in of modern times is established here, as Nicholson surveys his contribution to the new Apocalyptic movement of the 1940s, his engagement with surrealism as a liberatory aesthetics throughout his work, his use of Vladimir Mayakovsky's futurist techniques in his own poetry, his gay poetry which emerged from the 1960s onwards, and his attraction to science fiction motifs and imagery. Throughout the book Nicholson draws attention to Morgan's commitment to socialist ideals and to the cultural politics of Scottish independence. Rooted in Glasgow, Morgan emerges from this study as a generous, outgoing internationalist, whose translations and poetry alike are profound examinations of transnational and transcultural human relations. He is also situated superbly in relation to the dominant modernist aesthetic of the post-war period, as a poet who transforms and reconstructs that modernism, while at the same time transcending a postmodernism rapidly being exhausted in the twenty-first century. Nicholson analyses and situates each phase of Morgan's poetic career carefully and perceptively, locating influences and sources, and identifying the dominant motifs and recurrent themes of his work. The book concludes appropriately with an autobiographical sequence of poems by Morgan, 'Pieces of Me', published here for the first time.

Michelis and Rowlandf, eds., *The Poetry of Carol Ann Duffy: 'Choosing Tough Words'*, the first book-length collection of essays on Duffy's work, sets itself the bold task of explaining her popularity, situating her work in relation to national identity, feminism, and gender issues, and charting her career to date. The editors begin the introduction by remarking on the controversies she has stirred as a poet, and her 'naughtiness' in using deliberately whimsical rhymes to undercut poetic seriousness. They proceed to mark out the development of her career, her experiments with poetic form, her key influences (Philip Larkin emerges as an interesting precursor), and her engagement with identity politics. The nine essays included in the volume are substantial and rich studies of various aspects of her work. Neil Roberts compares the aesthetic of impersonality in the work of Duffy and T.S. Eliot, arguing that Duffy learns from Eliot and shares many of his poetic effects, although ultimately the effect of impersonality is achieved in different ways by each poet. Jeffrey Wainwright explores Duffy's reworking of Ovid's *Metamorphoses* in her collection, *The World's Wife*. Antony Rowland charts the shift in the representation of masculinity in Duffy's work, between the amorous note of *Standing Female Nude* to the more abrasive and dismissive treatment in *The World's Wife*. Angelica Michelis studies gender and national identity in Duffy's work, particularly the ways in which national identity is founded on exclusion and marginalization. Avril Horner argues that Duffy wittily exposes the fallacies of Western metaphysics. Jane Thomas argues that the discourse of gender is at the heart of Duffy's concerns, and that she is preoccupied with iteration and repetition in linguistic performances of gender. Stan Smith's essay follows on neatly by exploring how Duffy's poetry accurately exemplifies Derrida's concept of *différance*. Michael Wood's essay is on translation as a literal and metaphorical act in Duffy's work. The final essay in the collection, by Eva Müller-Zettermann, examines Duffy's popular and postmodern poems for children.

Christopher Morgan has published the first book-length study of the complete poems of R.S. Thomas, *R.S. Thomas: Identity, Environment, and Deity*. The subtitle indicates the tripartite concerns of the book, with Thomas's exploration of the meanings of identity (personal, national, religious), his deep concern with the natural world, not just as a revelation of spirituality, but also as a wild and violent place, and his search through the meanings and problems of a spiritual life. There are important and revealing chapters in the book on Thomas's use of poetry as a form of autobiographical probing, on comparisons between Thomas and Ted Hughes for their depictions of the darker side of nature, and on Thomas's preoccupation with the schism between religion and science. Morgan's concluding chapters are perhaps the most interesting, in which he argues that Thomas expands from his 'religious poetry' of the early period to a wider understanding of what constitutes experience of the divine. This Morgan describes as Thomas's reconfiguring of theology, 'his insistence on the central validity and importance of individual spiritual experience, both as absence and presence' (p. 147). Morgan is also attentive to the ways in which Thomas works with language, and is particularly concerned with the problem of writing in one language while wanting to speak in another. Morgan terms this biculturalism, and argues that it runs deep through Thomas's twenty-seven-volume oeuvre. The book also includes a helpful bibliography of Thomas's publications and criticism of his work, as well as further reading on the broader areas touched on in Morgan's arguments.

Rodopi's Studies in Literature series continues to publish exciting and worthy collections of essays on major and under-appreciated writers. The latest offering is Barfoot and Healey, eds., *'My Rebellious and Imperfect Eye': Observing Geoffrey Grigson*. The collection includes reflections and critical explorations of the achievements and breathtaking range of Grigson's work as a poet, anthologist, critic, and broadcaster, by Tom Paulin, Anthony Thwaite, Philip Hobsbaum, Peter Levi, and many others. The editors quote G.S. Fraser's assessment that Grigson was 'one of the most important figures in the history of English taste in our time, the history of taste in painting, and in the sense of landscape and history, as well as of taste in poetry' (p. 2), and that judgement stands fairly well with the examination of his life's work in these essays. There are too many essays to review each carefully and attentively, but mention of their range might help to elucidate the breadth of the approaches and appreciations included here. Grigson's love of botany is explored by Tess Darwin; Peter Levi examines his fascination with prehistoric art; Glyn Pursglove surveys his astounding achievements as a prolific anthologist; and some contributors argue for his distinctive merit as an anthologist of Romanticism. Stuart Sillars writes about Grigson's attributes as an art critic; James McGonigal considers the difficulties of teaching Grigson's poetry; R.M. Healey examines the work Grigson did as a BBC broadcaster. John Mole argues that Grigson's strengths and foibles as a critical observer and ardent reviewer can be found in his two 'notebooks', *Notes from an Odd Country* and *The Private Art*. Seamus Perry explores Grigson's writings on Romanticism. Jeremy Hooker writes about the problems in designating Grigson an 'English' writer. In one of his two essays in the collection, C.C. Barfoot does a good job of explaining what is distinctive about Grigson as a poet, and why he was relatively unappreciated when he died in 1980 (going beyond the obvious problem posed by his acerbic reviews of many of his contemporaries). In his second essay Barfoot writes about Grigson's love poems, particularly 'Legenda', and finds there seventeenth-century affinities. Peter Scupham likewise returns to Grigson's reputation and reassesses the poetry. Philip Hobsbaum studies the importance of Auden for Grigson, while Francis Scarfe revisits Grigson in the 1930s. The range of responses to Grigson's work in this collection, and the depth of reflection on his achievements, makes this an invaluable, monumental reassessment of his significance—for poetry, certainly, but also more widely in English literature and culture in the twentieth century. The collection also includes a helpful bibliography of Grigson's many publications, arranged chronologically, alphabetically, and by category.

I have no doubt that Dana Gioia is correct in his assertion that American readers are largely ignorant of much contemporary British poetry. Gioia's *Barrier of a Common Language: An American Looks at Contemporary British Poetry* is a slim selection of his essays and reviews on a handful of British poets, based on the implicit claim that Gioia is one of the few Americans interested in poetry in what he calls 'the Mother country'. Gioia's reviews are interesting, eloquent pieces, which sparkle with insights and intelligent observations about particular poets and collections. As a 'look' at contemporary British poetry, however, it is (perhaps inevitably) eccentric and glancing at best. The title essay reviews two anthologies published in the 1980s: the infamous Motion and Morrison collection, and the Michael Schmidt anthology from Carcanet. Gioia proceeds to introduce James Fenton and Charles Causley to American readers, to survey Larkin's life and work in his review of Motion's biography, and to dissect brilliantly the problem with Wendy Cope, before offering short pieces on Ted Hughes, Kingsley Amis, Tony Connor, Dick Davis, Thom Gunn, and Charles Tomlinson. The final two pieces in the book are reviews of Anthony Burgess's verse novel *Byrne* and Donald Davie's *The Poet in the Imaginary Museum*. Gioia's preference for rhyme and metre is apparent throughout, and his admiration particularly for Cope, Causley, and Larkin might be read as indicative of what he feels Americans might learn from British poets, namely that 'understanding what currently fashionable ideas they ignore challenges our own aesthetic assumptions' (p. xii). One can't help but feel sometimes in this selection that Gioia views British poetry as a kind of literary exoticism, a better-read version of the American readers he bemoans.

Juvenilia Press, which aims to recover and publish for pedagogical and research purposes the early work of renowned authors, has published an edition of Philip Larkin's *Incidents from Phippy's Schooldays*, written when he was at secondary school. *Phippy* has been carefully edited by Brenda Allen and James Acheson, based on the typescript contained in the Brynmor Jones Library at the University of Hull. The story itself is a parody of the genre of schoolboy adventures, and the editors pinpoint the influences of Thomas Hughes and P.G. Wodehouse in particular. Hugh Minden Philipson ('Phippy') attends a public school before going to Oxford and then on to a dull career as a schoolmaster. The story is part prose, part drama, and takes the form of hastily drawn scenes from Phippy's early life. It is possible that Larkin intended to write a much fuller treatment, and that the typescript consists of brief sketches to be filled out later. On the other hand, it may also be an experiment in comedy, impersonation, and social satire, not intended for publication. It is primarily of interest to Larkin scholars, I would suggest, for these experiments, and for its satirical observations on Larkin's schooldays. Here we find Larkin playing with particular voices and caricatures, and although *Phippy* is not an autobiographical work (or not meant to be), it is full of Larkin's characteristic self-deprecating humour, and his witty observations on the nuances of English social life. With regard to this edition, the text is presented with admirable clarity and with comic illustrations by Rodney Fitzgerald. The annotations are provided as endnotes, and serve to explain Larkin's references to life in 1930s Britain, his private jokes, and the objects of his satirical and parodic humour.

Books Reviewed

Albright, Daniel. *Beckett and Aesthetics*. CUP. [2003] pp. 175. £40 ISBN 0 5218 2908 9.

Allen, Nicholas. *George Russell (Æ) and the New Ireland, 1905–30*. FCP. [2003] pp. 267. £45 ISBN 1 8518 2691 2.

Allen, Nicholas, and Aaron Kelly, eds. *The Cities of Belfast*. FCP. [2003] pp. 252. £39.95 ISBN 1 8518 2771 4.

Anatol, Giselle Liza, ed. *Reading Harry Potter: Critical Essays*. Praeger. [2003] pp. xxv +217. £22.99 ISBN 0 3133 2067 5.

Armand, Louis. *Techné: James Joyce, Hypertext and Technology*. Karolinum/CharlesUP. [2003] pp. xiii +228. pb $11.09 ISBN 8 0246 0391 8.

Aston, Elaine. *Feminist Views on the English Stage: Women Playwrights 1990–2000*. CUP. [2003] pp. 228. £45 ISBN 0 5218 0003 X.

Barfoot, C.C., and R.M. Healey, eds. *'My Rebellious and Imperfect Eye': Observing Geoffrey Grigson*. DQR Studies in Literature 33. Rodopi. [2002] pp. xiii +305. €60 ISBN 9 0420 1358 3.

Barry, Peter. *Contemporary British Poetry and the City*. MUP. [2000] pp. x + 260. pb £15.99 ISBN 0 7190 5594 6.

Beer, Janet, and Bridget Bennett, eds. *Special Relationships: Anglo-American Affinities and Antagonisms 1854–1936*. MUP. [2002] pp. x + 266. pb £16.99 ISBN 0 7190 5818 X.

Bell, Hazel, ed. *Indexers and Indexes in Fact and Fiction*. UTorP. [2001] pp. 160. pb $24.95 ISBN 0 8020 8494 X.

Berman, Jessica. *Modernist Fiction, Cosmopolitanism, and the Politics of Community*. CUP. [2001] pp. x + 242. £45 ISBN 0 5218 0589 9.

Boada-Montagut, Irene. *Women Write Back: Contemporary Irish and Catalan Short Stories in Colonial Context*. IAP. [2003] pp. viii +207. £35 ISBN 0 7165 2749 9.

Boon, Richard. *About Hare*. Faber. [2003] pp. xxviii +241. pb £8.99 ISBN 0 5712 1429 0.

Böss, Michael, and Eamon Maher, eds. *Engaging Modernity: Reading Irish Politics, Culture and Literature at the Turn of the Century*. Veritas. [2003] pp. 234. pb £14.95 ISBN 1 8539 0642 5.

Brannigan, John. *Orwell to the Present: Literature in England, 1945–2000*. Palgrave. [2003] pp. x + 244. £15.99 ISBN 0 3336 9617 4.

Brater, Enoch. *The Essential Samuel Beckett: An Illustrated Biography*. T&H. [2003] pp. 138. pb £10.95 ISBN 0 5002 8411 3.

Brooker, Peter. *Modernity and Metropolis: Writing, Film and Urban Formations*. Palgrave. [2002] pp. ix +230. £50 ISBN 0 3338 0168 7.

Buning, Marius, Matthijs Engelberts, Sjef Houppermans and Danièle de Ruyter-Tognotti, eds. *'Three Dialogues' Revisited. Samuel Beckett Today/Aujourd'hui*. 13. Rodopi. [2003] pp. 278. €35 ISBN 9 0420 0808 3.

Butler, Robert. *The Art of Darkness: Staging the Philip Pullman Trilogy*. National Theatre/Oberon. [2003] pp. 120. pb £12.99 ISBN 1 8400 2414 3.

Callow, Philip. *Body of Truth: D.H. Lawrence, the Nomadic Years, 1919–1930*. Ivan R. Dee. [2003] pp. xvi +303. £20.50 ISBN 1 5666 3494 6.

Carpenter, Humphrey. *Spike Milligan: The Biography*. Hodder. [2003] pp. 352. £20 ISBN 0 3408 2611 8.

Casey, Simon. *Naked Liberty and the World of Desire: Elements of Anarchism in the Work of D.H. Lawrence*. Routledge. [2003] pp. xv + 143. £45 ISBN 0 4159 6592 6.

Chaudhuri, Amit. *D.H. Lawrence and 'Difference'*. Clarendon. [2003] pp. xii + 226. £20 ISBN 0 1992 6052 4.

Childs, Donald J. *Modernism and Eugenics: Woolf, Eliot, Yeats, and the Culture of Degeneration*. CUP. [2001] pp. vii + 266. £45 ISBN 0 5218 0601 1.

Cole, Sarah. *Modernism, Male Friendship, and the First World War*. CUP. [2003] pp. vii + 297. £45 ISBN 0 5218 1923 7.

Colletta, Lisa. *Dark Humor and Social Satire in the Modern British Novel*. Palgrave. [2003] pp. 154. £35 ISBN 1 4039 6365 7.

Conley, Tim. *Joyces Mistakes: Problems of Intention, Irony, and Interpretation*. UTorP. [2003] pp. xii + 192. $53 (£32) ISBN 0 8020 8755 8.

Conroy, Jane, ed. *Cross-Cultural Travel: Papers from the Royal Irish Academy International Symposium on Literature and Travel*. Lang. [2003] pp. xxii + 549. £59 ISBN 0 8204 6930 0.

Coppa, Francesca, ed. *Joe Orton: A Casebook*. Routledge. [2003] pp. 170. £60 ISBN 0 8153 3627 6.

Cotter, David. *James Joyce and the Perverse Ideal. Studies in Major Literary Authors: Outstanding Dissertations*. Routledge. [2003] pp. xi + 256. £60 ISBN 0 4159 6786 4.

Coult, Tony. *About Friel*. Faber. [2003] pp. xvi + 237. pb £8.99 ISBN 0 5712 0164 4.

Crawford, Robert. *The Modern Poet*. OUP. [2001] pp. vi + 296. £45 ISBN 0 1981 8677 0.

Crofts, Charlotte. *'Anagrams of Desire': Angela Carter's Writings for Radio, Film and Television*. MUP. [2003] pp. vii + 215. £15.99 ISBN 0 7190 5724 8.

Cuddy-Keane, Melba. *Virginia Woolf, The Intellectual and the Public Sphere*. CUP. [2003] pp. 248. $60 ISBN 0 5218 2867 8.

Cushman, Keith, and Earl G. Ingersoll, eds. *D.H. Lawrence: New Worlds*. FDUP. [2003] pp. 281. £39.95 ISBN 0 8386 3981 X.

Dillane, Fionnuala, and Ronan Kelly, eds. *New Voices in Irish Criticism 4*. FCP. [2003] pp. 228. £45 ISBN 1 8518 2734 X.

Dooley, Gillian, ed. *From a Tiny Corner in the House of Fiction: Conversations with Iris Murdoch*. USCP. [2003] pp. xxx + 267. £25.50 ISBN 1 5700 3499 0.

Dowson, Jane, ed. *Women's Writing, 1945–1960: After the Deluge*. Palgrave. [2003] pp. xxii + 239. pb £45 ISBN 1 4039 1309 9.

Ellison, David. *Ethics and Aesthetics in European Modernist Literature: From the Sublime to the Uncanny*. CUP. [2001] pp. xiv + 290. £42.50 ISBN 0 5218 0680 1.

Ellmann, Maud. *Elizabeth Bowen: The Shadow Across the Page*. EdinUP. [2003] pp. xiv + 241. £45 ISBN 0 7486 1702 7.

Emig, Rainer, ed. *Ulysses: James Joyce*. New Casebooks. Palgrave. [2003] pp. ix + 223. pb £14.99 ISBN 0 3335 4605 9.

Eyre, Richard. *National Service: Diary of a Decade*. Bloomsbury. [2003] pp. 422. £18.99 ISBN 0 7475 6589 9.

Fitz-Simon, Christopher. *The Abbey Theatre*. T&H. [2003] pp. 203. £16.95 ISBN 0 5002 8426 1.

Fletcher, John. *About Beckett*. Faber. [2003] pp. xiv +220. pb £8.99 ISBN 0 5712 0124 5.

Foley, Imelda. *The Girls in the Big Picture: Gender in Contemporary Ulster Theatre*. Blackstaff. [2003] pp. viii +170. pb £12.99 ISBN 0 8564 0715 1.

Fraser, Robert. *Ben Okri*. Northcote, WTW. [2002] pp. xviii + 121. £10.99 ISBN 0 7463 0993 7.

Gannon, Charles E. *Rumors of War and Infernal Machines: Technomilitary Agenda-Setting in American and British Speculative Fiction*. LiverUP. [2003] pp. 311. hb £50 ISBN 0 8532 3698 4, pb £20 ISBN 0 8532 3708 5.

Garrity, Jane. *Step-Daughters of England: British Women Modernists and the National Imaginary*. ManUP. [2003] pp. 349. hb £47.50 ISBN 0 7190 6163 6, pb £15.99 ISBN 0 7190 6164 4.

Gioia, Dana. *Barrier of a Common Language: An American Looks at Contemporary British Poetry*. UMichP. [2003] pp. xii +106. $16.95 ISBN 0 4720 6582 3.

Granofsky, Ronald. *D.H. Lawrence and Survival: Darwinism in the Fiction of the Transitional Period*. McG-QUP. [2003] pp. xi +212. £61 ISBN 0 7735 2544 0.

Greenspan, Ezra, Lindeth Vasey, and John Worthen, eds. *Studies in Classic American Literature*. CUP. [2003] pp. 712. £80 ISBN 0 5215 5016 5.

Griffin, Gabriele. *Contemporary Black and Asian Women Playwrights in Britain*. CUP. [2003] pp. 284. £45 ISBN 0 5218 1725 0.

Griffiths, Trevor R. *The Theatre Guide: A Comprehensive A–Z of the World's Best Plays and Playwrights*. A&C Black. [2003] pp. viii +375. £19.99 ISBN 0 7136 6171 2.

Grote, Georg. *Anglo-Irish Theatre and the Formation of a Nationalist Political Culture between 1890 and 1930*. Mellen. [2003] pp. xi +241. £69.95 ISBN 0 7734 6811 0.

Harrison, Andrew. *D.H. Lawrence and Italian Futurism: A Study of Influence*. Rodopi. [2003] pp. xxvi +235. £37.44 ISBN 9 0420 1195 5.

Haswell, Janice. *Paul Scott's Philosophy of Place(s): The Fiction of Relationality*. Studies in Twentieth-Century British Literature. Lang. [2002] pp. xii + 280. £41 ISBN 0 8204 5679 9.

Haynes, John, and James Knowlson. *Images of Beckett*. CUP. [2003] pp. 154. £20 ISBN 0 5218 2258 0.

Heilman, Elizabeth E., ed. *Harry Potter's World: Multidisciplinary Critical Perspectives*. Routledge. [2003] pp. ix +308. £16.99 ISBN 0 4159 3374 9.

Henry, Holly. *Virginia Woolf and the Discourse of Science: The Aesthetics of Astronomy*. CUP. [2003] pp. 208. £40 ISBN 0 5218 1297 6.

Herbert, Ian, and Nicole Leclercq, eds. *The World of Theatre, 2003 edition*. Routledge. [2003] pp. ix +388. £60 ISBN 0 4153 0621 3.

Higgins, Lesley. *The Modernist Cult of Ugliness: Aesthetic and Gender Politics*. Palgrave. [2002] pp. xiii +312. £45 ISBN 0 3122 4037 6.

Humm, Maggie. *Modernist Women and Visual Cultures: Virginia Woolf, Vanessa Bell, Photography and Cinema*. EdinUP. [2002] pp. 244. £25 ISBN 0 7486 1683 7.

Jarvis, Martin. *Broadway Jeeves? The Diary of a Theatrical Adventure*. Methuen. [2003] pp. 290. £16.99 ISBN 0 4137 7331 0.

Julius, Anthony. *T.S. Eliot, Anti-Semitism and Literary Form*, 2nd edn. Thames & Hudson. [2003] pp. 360. £16.95 ISBN 0 5002 8280 3.

Kershner, R. Brandon, ed. *Cultural Studies of James Joyce*. European Joyce Studies 15. Rodopi. [2003] pp. 215. €55 ($74) ISBN 9 0420 0996 9.

Kimball, Jean. *Joyce and the Early Freudians: A Synchronic Dialogue of Texts*. UFlorP. [2003] pp. xviii +240. $55 ISBN 0 8130 2619 9.

Kirk, Connie Ann. *J.K. Rowling: A Biography*. Greenwood. [2003] pp. xiii +143. £16.99 ISBN 0 3133 2205 8.

Kuch, Peter, and Robson Julie-Ann, eds. *Irelands in the Asia-Pacific*. Smythe. [2003] pp. xvii +489. £45 ISBN 0 8614 0414 9.

Larkin, Philip. *Incidents from Phippy's Schooldays*, ed. Brenda Allen and James Acheson, illus. Rodney Fitzgerald. Juvenilia Press. [2002] pp. xxii +55. $10 ISBN 0 9688 2830 2.

Latham, Sean. *'Am I a Snob?' Modernism and the Novel*. CornUP. [2003] pp. 240. hb £98.93 ISBN 0 8014 4022 X, pb £11.50 ISBN 0 8014 8841 9.

Laurence, Patricia. *Lily Briscoe's Chinese Eyes: Bloomsbury, Modernism, and China*. USCP. [2003] pp. 488. £44.50 ISBN 1 5700 3505 9.

Lea, Daniel, and Berthold Schoene, eds. *Posting the Male: Masculinities in Post-War and Contemporary British Literature*. Genus. Rodopi. [2003] pp. 171. €38 ISBN 9 0420 0976 4.

Littlewood, Joan. *Joan's Book: The Autobiography of Joan Littlewood*. Methuen. [2003] pp. xxxiii +779. pb £12.99 ISBN 0 4137 7318 3.

Lycett, Andrew. *Dylan Thomas: A New Life*. W&N. [2003] pp. xiv +434. £20 ISBN 0 2976 0793 6.

Mallett, Phillip. *Rudyard Kipling: A Literary Life*. Palgrave. [2003] pp. x + 223. pb £14.99 ISBN 0 3335 5721 2.

March, Cristie L. *Rewriting Scotland: Welsh, McLean, Warner, Banks, Galloway and Kennedy*. MUP. [2002] pp. xi +179. £14.99 ISBN 0 7190 6033 8.

Mathews, P.J. *Revival: The Abbey Theatre, Sinn Féin, the Gaelic League and the Co-operative Movement*. CorkUP. [2003] pp. viii +208. pb. £19.95 ISBN 1 8591 8365 4.

Matz, Jesse. *Literary Impressionism and Modernist Aesthetics*. CUP. [2001] pp. ix +278. £45 ISBN 0 5218 0352 7.

McKenna, Bernard. *Rupture, Representation, and the Fashioning of Identity in Drama from the North of Ireland, 1969–1994*. Praeger. [2003] pp. 207. £34.99 ISBN 0 3133 2029 2.

Meek, Margaret, and Victor Watson, eds. *Coming of Age in Children's Literature*. Contemporary Classics of Children's Literature. Continuum. [2003] pp. 197. £55 ISBN 0 8264 5842 4.

Michelis, Angelica, and Antony Rowland, eds. *The Poetry of Carol Ann Duffy: 'Choosing Tough Words'*. MUP. [2003] pp. x + 212. £14.99 ISBN 0 7190 6301 9.

Milesi, Laurent, ed. *James Joyce and the Difference of Language*. CUP. [2003] pp. xiii +232. £45 ISBN 0 5216 2337 5.

Miller, Nicholas Andrew. *Modernism, Ireland and the Erotics of Memory*. CUP. [2002] pp. xi +226. £45 ISBN 0 5218 1583 5.

Miracky, James J. *Regenerating the Novel: Gender and Genre in Woolf, Forster, Sinclair and Lawrence*. Routledge. [2003] pp. xiii +178. £45 ISBN 0 4159 4205 5.

Morgan, Christopher. *R.S. Thomas: Identity, Environment, Deity*. MUP. [2003] pp. x + 209. £40 ISBN 0 7190 6248 9.

Mullin, Katherine. *James Joyce, Sexuality and Social Purity*. CUP. [2003] pp. xi +224. £40 ISBN 0 5218 2751 5.

Murphy, Sean P. *James Joyce and Victims: Reading the Logic of Exclusion*. FDUP. [2003] pp. 192. $41.50 ISBN 0 8386 3950 X.

Nicholson, Colin. *Edwin Morgan: Inventions of Modernity*. MUP. [2002] pp. viii +216. £40 ISBN 0 7190 6360 4.

Nicholson, Steve. *The Censorship of British Drama 1900–1968,* vol. 1: *1900–1932*. UExeP. [2003] pp. 352. £39.50 ISBN 0 8598 9638 2.

Nolan, Jerry, ed. *The Tulira Trilogy of Edward Martyn (1859–1923: Irish Symbolist Dramatist*. Mellen. [2003] pp. xi +202. £69.95 ISBN 0 7734 6709 2.

Norris, Margot. *Suspicious Readings of Joyce's Dubliners*. UPennP. [2003] pp. viii +279. $49.95 (£32.50) ISBN 0 8122 3739 0.

Pateman, Matthew. *Julian Barnes*. Northcote, WTW. [2002] pp. xi +106. £10.99 ISBN 0 7463 0978 3.

Patterson, Michael. *Strategies of Political Theatre: Post-War British Playwrights*. CUP. [2003] pp. xviii +222. £45 ISBN 0 5212 5855 3.

Perloff, Marjorie. *21st-Century Modernism: The 'New' Poetics*. Blackwell. [2002] pp. ix +222. pb £14.99 ISBN 0 6312 1970 6.

Proctor, James. *Dwelling Places: Postwar Black British Writing*. MUP. [2003] pp. viii +224. £14.99 ISBN 0 7190 6054 0.

Rabey, David Ian. *English Drama Since 1940*. Longman. [2003] pp. xii +243. pb. £20.99 £?? ISBN 0 5824 2372 4.

Reed, Christopher. *Bloomsbury Rooms: Modernism, Subculture, and Domesticity*. YaleUP. [2003] pp. 315. £25 ISBN 0 3001 0248 8.

Reeve, N.H. *Reading Late Lawrence*. Palgrave. [2003] pp. xii +178. £45 ISBN 1 4039 1596 2.

Regard, Frederic, ed. *Mapping the Self: Space, Identity, Discourse in British Auto-Biography*. University of Saint-Etienne. [2003] pp. 398. ISBN 2 8627 2269 3.

Rosenbaum, S.P. *The Early Literary History of the Bloomsbury Group,* vol. 3: *Georgian Bloomsbury*. Palgrave. [2003] pp. xii +253. £50 ISBN 0 3334 5824 9.

Sagar, Keith, ed. *D.H. Lawrence's Paintings*. Chaucer Press. [2003] pp. 106. £25 ISBN 1 9044 4917 4.

Saint-Amour, Paul K. *The Copywrights: Intellectual Property and the Literary Imagination*. CornUP. [2003] pp. xiii +304. $35 ISBN 0 8014 4077 7.

Sheehan, Paul. *Modernism, Narrative and Humanism*. CUP. [2002] pp. xiii +234. £45 ISBN 0 5218 1457 X.
Shellard, Dominic. *Kenneth Tynan: A Life*. YaleUP. [2003] pp. x + 377. £25 ISBN 0 3000 9919 3.
Shloss, Carol Loeb. *Lucia Joyce: To Dance in the Wake*. FS&G. [2003] pp. 560. pb £20 ISBN 0 3741 9424 6.
Shuttleworth, Anthony, ed. *And In Our Time: Vision, Revision, and British Writing of the 1930s*. AUP. [2003] pp. 252. $44.50 ISBN 0 8387 5518 6.
Southworth, Helen. *The Intersecting Realities and Fictions of Virginia Woolf and Colette*. OSUP. [2003] pp. xii +240. hb $59.95 ISBN 0 8142 0964 5, pb $22.95 ISBN 0 8142 5136 6.
Stewart, Victoria. *About O'Casey*. Faber. [2003] pp. 142. pb £8.99 ISBN 0 5712 0159 8.
Svich, Caridad, ed. *Trans-Global Readings: Crossing Theatrical Boundaries*. MUP. [2003] pp. 206. pb £14.99 ISBN 0 7190 6325 6.
Tabachnik, Stephen E. *Fiercer Than Tigers: The Life and Works of Rex Warner*. UMichP. [2003] pp. iv +522. $37.95 ISBN 0 8701 3552 X.
Thacker, Andrew. *Moving Through Modernity: Space and Geography in Modernism*. ManUP. [2003] pp. ix +245. £45 ISBN 0 7190 5309 9.
Thormählen, Marianne, ed. *Rethinking Modernism*. Palgrave. [2003] pp. xiv +276. £50 ISBN 1 4039 1180 0.
Valentine, Kylie. *Psychoanalysis, Psychiatry and Modernist Literature*. Palgrave. [2003] pp. viii +224. £47.50 ISBN 1 4039 0061 2.
Vendler, Helen. *Coming of Age as a Poet: Milton, Keats, Eliot, Plath*. HarvardUP. [2003] pp. 174. £15.50 ISBN 0 6740 1024 8.
Walshe, Eibhear, ed. *Selected Plays of Irish Playwright Teresa Deevy, 1894–1963*. Mellen. [2003] pp. xii +252. £69.95 ISBN 0 7734 6635 5.
Wells, Lynn. *Allegories of Telling: Self-Referential Narrative in Contemporary British Fiction*. Rodopi. [2003] pp. 182. €38 ($42) ISBN 9 0420 1114 9.
Whited, Lana A., ed. *The Ivory Tower and Harry Potter: Perspectives on a Literary Phenomenon*. UMissP. [2002] pp. x + 408. £30.50 ISBN 0 8262 1443 6.
Williams, Louise Blakeney. *Modernism and the Ideology of History: Literature, Politics, and the Past*. CUP. [2002] pp. ix +265. £45 ISBN 0 5218 1499 5.
Williamson, Leslie. *D.H. Lawrence and the Country He Loved*. Poetry Monthly Press. [2003] pp. 32. £2.50 ISBN 1 9030 3152 4.
Wollaeger, Mark A., ed. *James Joyce's A Portrait of the Artist as a Young Man: A Casebook*. OUPAm. [2003] pp. xii +360. hb $49.95 ISBN 0 1951 5075 9, pb $19.95 ISBN 0 1951 5076 7.
Yao, Steven G. *Translation and the Languages of Modernism: Gender, Politics, Language*. Palgrave. [2002] pp. xii +291. £40 ISBN 0 3122 9519 7.

DUBLIN BUSINESS SCHOOL LIBRARY

XV

American Literature to 1900

HENRY CLARIDGE, ANNE-MARIE FORD AND THERESA SAXON

This chapter has three sections: 1 General; 2 American Literature to 1830; 3 American Literature, 1830–1900. Sections 1 and 2 are by Henry Claridge; section 3 is by Anne-Marie Ford and Theresa Saxon.

1. General

Current bibliographical listings for books in the field and period continue to be available quarterly in the 'Book Reviews' and 'Brief Mentions' sections of *American Literature*. The index to *American Literature*, published annually in the December issue, usefully lists the books reviewed over the year in a way that serves as a bibliographical resource. Annually the *Modern Language Association International Bibliography* provides an exhaustive bibliography of books, articles, review essays, notes and dissertations that is indispensable. *American Literary Scholarship: An Annual, 2001*, a narrative bibliography under the editorship of Gary Scharnhorst, casts its informed and attentive eye over the year's critical and scholarly writings: the editor and his contributors have an increasingly difficult job to do, given the sheer magnitude of the scholarship they are expected to review. *ALS* remains the best and most thorough narrative bibliography in the field. The Spring 2003 issue of *American Literary History* is substantially devoted to general and theoretical questions in the writing of American literary history. 'A Cambridge Literary History of the US Forum' gathers together brief papers by Robert von Hallberg, Eric J. Sundquist, Susan Mizruchi and Werner Sollors, amongst others, which address the difficulties of constructing cogent literary-historical accounts of what were deemed, so Sacvan Bercovitch tells us in his introduction, the 'most problematic areas' of poetry and ethnicity. In a similar vein of concern with issues of broader cultural history, the Winter 2003 issue of the journal presents a 'Forum of Alan Trachtenberg's *The Incorporation of America*' that brings together essays on the impact, and influence, of Trachtenberg's 1982 book on the methodologies of American studies.

Year's Work in English Studies, Volume 84 (2005) © The English Association; all rights reserved. For permissions, please email: journals.permissions@oxfordjournals.org

doi: 10.1093/ywes/mai015

2. American Literature to 1830

The December issue of *American Literature* offers two important essays on Native American writing: Annette Kolodny's 'Fictions of American Prehistory: Indians, Archaeology, and National Origin Myths' (*AL* 75[2003] 693–721) explores the extent to which 'the fictions of prehistory offer a rich—and virtually untouched—field for the literary historian' and 'an especially rich field for those interested in national origins myths and their implications for Native peoples'; Michael A. Elliott's 'Coyote Comes to the *Norton*: Indigenous Oral Narrative and American Literary History' (*AL* 73[2003] 723–49) considers the implications of the inclusion in the fifth edition of *The Norton Anthology of American Literature* [1998] of Clatsop Chinook's 'Coyote Establishes Fishing Taboos', a story first published by the anthropologist Franz Boas in *Chinook Texts* [1894]. Elliot argues that the appearance of the text in the anthology 'exemplifies the recent victories of those advocating a pluralistic, multicultural approach to American literary history—an advocacy now so familiar that its arguments have become, in a word, canonical.' *Early American Literature* devotes a special section of its third issue of the year to 'The Indian Mission': Kristina Bross in her introduction, '"Come over and help us": Reading Mission Literature' (*EAL* 38[2003] 395–400) introduces the essays gathered here by remarking that, although all three essays 'are focused on New England, all of them understand that region and its literary production as only a part of "the complicated contestation of global imperial agendas and creolized cultures"'; David Thomson addresses the fashioning of a 'vibrant, autonomous, indigenous Puritanism' in 'The Antinomian Crisis: Prelude to Puritan Missions' (*EAL* 38[2003] 401–35); in 'The Praying Indian Speeches as Texts of Massachusetts Oral Culture' (*EAL* 38[2003] 437–67) Craig White investigates Algonquian oral traditions in colonial Massachusetts as evidence of a 'cultural narrative that engagingly differs from that of the mission'; and in 'The Ambivalent Uses of Roger Williams's *A Key Into the Language of America*' (*EAL* 38[2003] 469–94) J. Patrick Cesarini focuses on that 'charged moment in 1643, when the reality of New England's mission seemed at last to catch up with its transatlantic rhetoric, but when, at the same time, the mission encountered its most resourceful competitor in Roger Williams, arguably the best known of New England's troubling exiles'. The essays here offer that characteristically high level of exposition and scholarship that we associate with *EAL*, and, as so often with essays in this journal, each comes with an invaluable bibliography of works cited.

Ed White's 'Captaine Smith, Colonial Novelist' (*AL* 75[2003] 487–513) is an attempt to rewrite the history of the American novel (White takes William Hill Brown's *The Power of Sympathy* [1789] as its starting point) by asserting that 'John Smith, colonizer of Virginia, was a colonial novelist, and that his *The Generall Historie of Virginia, New England, and the Summer Isles* [1624] and *The True Travels, Adventures and Observations of Captaine John Smith* [1630] are best understood as innovative works at the dawn of novelistic prose'. White's argument proceeds in part by purely literary analysis that seeks to locate the literary and fictional qualities of Smith's prose, in part by challenging 'the Eurocentric tale of the continental and metropolitan origins of modernity' and locating modernity, instead, in a 'New World encounter between European and native Americans that was decisive for modern consciousness'. 'Mapping the Gift Path: Exchange and Rivalry in John Smith's *A True Relation*' (*AmLH* 15[2003] 655–82), by William Boelhower, explores Smith's importance as a cartographer, arguing that, although the map appended to his autobiographical letter of 1608, *A True Relation of Such Occurrences and Accidents of Noate as Hath Happened in Virginia*... 'is rudimentary and sketchy, an understanding of its relation to the text is essential if we hope to appreciate the kind of narrative we are dealing with but also the complex process of self-fashioning that Smith rather flamboyantly invested in'. This is a valuable essay, particularly for its analysis of the performative levels of Smith's writings, but it would be more instructive if a copy of the Smith/Zuniga map that was sent with Smith's letter were included in the text. Andrew Newman's 'Captive on the Literacy Frontier: Mary Rowlandson, James Smith, and Charles Johnston' (*EAL* 38[2003] 31–65) argues that the 'literacy frontier', the area of contact 'between cultures with widespread literacy and those with little or no exposure to reading and writing', can be used as a way of understanding the formation of cultural self-definition and that the captivity narratives, in particular, show how their authors 'employed literacy to insulate themselves from the circumstances of their captivities and to attenuate their cultural alienation'.

John C. Shields, *The American Aeneas: Classical Origins of the American Self*, is an important study. The book's subtitle indicates something of the 'conventional wisdom' it seeks to challenge: most accounts of the origins of the American self locate them in Adamic myths of man in the New World or Puritan teleologies of 'mission' and 'errand'. Shields argues that an equally strong (perhaps, in fact, a greater) claim can be made for America's sense of national and cultural identity as having evolved from classical tradition, here, particularly, the image of Aeneas as a sailor who founds a new civilization. He seeks to show that 'both the largely spiritual Adamic discourse and the largely secular classical discourse crossed over from Europe', and that 'The peculiar blending of classical and biblical mythoi on the American strand constitutes the American cultural self.' The thesis drives him through an impressive body of material, and he finds evidence of a Virgilian narrative in the poetry of Anne Bradstreet, Edward Taylor, and Phillis Wheatley (on whom Shields has written elsewhere), in Cotton Mather's *Magnalia*, and in the addresses and orations of George Washington, who, for Shields, 'incorporates into American consciousness the American Way, or pietas revised, as the American national identity'. Later chapters take the debate into the nineteenth century, notably the writings of Hawthorne and Melville, and the concluding chapter, 'America's Classical Origins Besieged', considers the broader theoretical implications of his 'restatement' of the case for the recovery of America's classical origins, arguing, particularly, that the 'American canon, however it may be changed as the result of recovering classical discourse, has always been linked to ancient classical texts ... just as it has always owed an immense debt to the Bible'. This is an immensely learned and informed book whose importance extends into areas beyond those that one would normally associate with the study of early American literature, for it invites its readers to rethink the imagery and vocabulary of 'Americanness'.

Where Shields discusses matters that are religious in character, for example in his conception of Washington as a 'purveyor of pietas', he seems to be in territory occupied some forty years ago by Robert Bellah, whose writings on American 'Civil Religion' did much to explain the coherence of American national symbols and images when juxtaposed with the pluralistic and multicultural origins of the American people. Shields doesn't present his book as offering a 'strong thesis' comparable to that of Bellah, but, reading it, one senses that, digested into essay form, Shields's argument might end up as 'required reading'. The book is perhaps over-long, but it would be churlish to pursue this criticism, given that what we have here is unquestionably a major work of scholarship.

Beyond Shields's book I have seen little on seventeenth- and eighteenth-century poetry this year that is worthy of note. Jane Donahue Eberwein's '"His wayes disgrac'd are grac'd": Edward Taylor's *Metrical History of Christianity* as Puritan Narrative' (*EAL* 38[2003] 339–64) is an important essay on one of the 'least available, least read, and least admired' of Taylor's poetic productions. Eberwein addresses central, first-order questions about Puritan verse by way of an analysis of Taylor's 'sense of poetic vocation' and what it tells us, more generally, about Puritan poetics, showing persuasively how *A Metrical History* can both inform and be informed by our understanding of Cotton Mather's *Magnalia* as an exercise of spiritual discipline. Colin Wells's *The Devil & Doctor Dwight: Satire and Theology in the Early American Republic* offers both an annotated text and a scholarly analysis of Dwight's *The Triumph of Infidelity* [1788], a rather ponderous poem in heroic couplets that warns us against the temptations of carnal love and social glamour. Wells concedes that the poem is little read nowadays, and his informed and meticulous account of Dwight's political and theological allusions serves, to some extent, to make the poem more 'accessible', but the real barrier for the reader is that the poem is simply not very good. This said, on a more general level Wells's book considerably enlarges what we know about Augustan satire in the New World. The georgic poem is the subject of Jim Egan's 'The "Long'd-for Aera" of an "Other Race": Climate, Identity, and James Grainger's *The Sugar-Cane*' (*EAL* 38[2003] 189–212), which reads Grainger's 1764 poem in four books for its 'British-American' construction of a new imperial identity through the determining character of climate. Vincent Carretta's 'Who Was Francis Williams?' (*EAL* 38[2003] 213–37), in the same issue of *EAL*, seeks to identify Francis Williams, 'a free black in Jamaica who wrote poetry in Latin during the eighteenth century'. Carretta's essay reprints, in colour, an anonymous portrait in oil of Williams, done *circa* 1740, which shows its subject in his library in Spanish Town, Jamaica. Carretta's essay uncovers some important and intriguing facts, about Williams's life (notably his wealth and his power in Jamaica) as well as suggesting that the portrait of Williams is one of the many caricatures done of him. 'Susanna Wright's "The Grove": A Philosophic Exchange with James Logan' (*EAL* 38[2003] 239–55), by Catherine La Courreye Blecki and Lorett Treese, presents, as an appendix, a text of Wright's 'The Grove', a poem of 127 lines in heroic couplets, that they read for its anti-pastoral sentiments. This is very minor poetry by a Quaker woman who befriended James Logan, the Philadelphia Quaker who contributed much to the early classification of the flora and fauna of the American colonies, and Benjamin Franklin, but the essay enhances our understanding of Quaker culture in the New World.

Interest in what might be called the 'gastronomic culture' of early America surfaces in Mark McWilliams's 'Distant Tables: Food and the Novel in Early America' (*EAL* 38[2003] 365–93), where both poetry and fiction are mined for what they tell us about the 'popular debate over the proper cuisine for a new nation'. McWilliams stresses the notion of 'republican simplicity' as a way of explaining the emphasis on wholesomeness and simplicity in both the food eaten and its preparation, in early American cookbooks and in the fiction of James Fenimore Cooper, Lydia Maria Child, and Catharine Maria Sedgwick: 'The heart of republican simplicity', he writes, 'lies in the rejection (or at least suspicion) of luxury as associated with aristocracy by birth', and this, he concludes, speaks to larger matters that are bound up with 'the progress of American society since its founding as a European frontier'. In 'Farmer versus Lawyer: Crèvecoeur's *Letters* and the Liberal Subject' (*EAL* 38[2003] 257–79), David J. Carlson argues that *Letters from an American Farmer* 'continues to strike a key-note in the national mythology of the United States: it advances the ideas that liberal legal and political institutions provide the best mechanisms for effacing ethnic differences and producing a cohesive society of individual citizens'. In Carlson's reading the *Letters* are dehistoricized by any attempt to read them through what he calls 'an American Studies paradigm', and he seeks to reassert the importance of biographical and historical readings that are informed by the 'deeper ideological issues and debates of the period' in which Crèvecoeur wrote. This essay is important for its understanding of the legal and philosophical levels on which the *Letters* can be read, as well as for its broader account of the image of the American farmer that Crèvecoeur projects.

3. American Literature, 1830–1900

Robert E. Abrams's *Landscapes and Ideology in American Renaissance Literature: Topographies of Skepticism* ponders cultural constructs. In this evocative study, Abrams contends that mid-nineteenth-century writers, from Henry Thoreau to Margaret Fuller, are deeply influenced by both a sense of place and its instability. Place is perceived through the lens of maps, ideas of nature, styles of painting, and other cultural frameworks that can contradict one another or change dramatically over time. Divided into two parts, Abrams's study begins by examining the writings of Hawthorne, Thoreau and Melville. In Hawthorne's literary revisiting of colonial New England in *The Scarlet Letter*, Abrams locates a landscape of bewilderment, while he identifies Thoreau's desire to take his readers into a destabilized space. The Thoreauvian landscape, at its most radical, he argues, proves too mutable, given to sudden transitions in terms of how it is seen and experienced. Melville's *Moby-Dick* and *The Confidence-Man* take Abrams on a voyage of exploration with which he concludes part 1. The second half of his book considers Indian removal, slavery and class, and focuses on Margaret Fuller's *Summer on the Lakes*, where she documents her travels into freshly incorporated US territory and her meetings with Native Americans, who remain, for her and for us, largely eclipsed. The power of negative space is explored, too, in the writings of Frederick Douglass, who recounts his experiences as a slave. American enslavement denied inclusion and citizenship to the African American, replacing home with homelessness and a confused sense of place. Such alienation is further explored in Rebecca Harding Davis's *Life in the Iron Mills*, where she leads the reader into a slum world. This space is one of decay and decrepitude, removed from the landscape of economic privilege. Notes, bibliography and some fascinating black and white prints of the American landscape complete this compelling study of place and placelessness.

In *A Sense of Things: The Object Matter of American Literature* Bill Brown seeks to uncover the depths of America's ambivalent love affair with things. This captivating study explores the roots of American's relationship with possessions, and considers how crucial the role of novels has been in making 'things' not a solution to problems, but problems in their own right. Brown considers the work of such authors as Mark Twain, Frank Norris, Sarah Orne Jewett and Henry James to investigate why and how objects are seen to encode meaning. Why and how, these writers ask, do we use objects to create meaning, to make or remake ourselves, to organize our anxieties and affections, to sublimate our fears, and to shape our wildest dreams? This intelligent and probing study offers a remarkable new way to think about materialism. In chapter 1, entitled 'The Tyranny of Things', Brown focuses in particular on Twain's *The Prince and the Pauper*, and ponders the power of the Great Seal as a symbol of the British monarchy, so central to the plot of the novel. In 'The Nature of Things', the second chapter, he reads Norris as the American novelist who most scientifically depicts humankind as thing, while 'Regional Artifacts' explores the writings of regionalist Sarah Orne Jewett. The final chapter, 'The Decoration of Houses', examines the writings of such authors as Henry James and Edith Wharton, and is illustrated with black and white images of works by John Singer Sargent. Provocatively, Brown examines the power of material culture to possess and define Americans. Compellingly told, this study is fresh and illuminating, with fine illustrations and notes for further investigation of this wide-ranging and absorbing subject.

In *Domestic Abolitionism and Juvenile Literature, 1830–1865*, Deborah C. De Rosa explores the ways in which women writers accessed the literary through the conventional. Embracing the social ideology of a woman's sphere, writers turned to juvenile literature as the means of creating an acceptable public space. They chose not only to write for a juvenile audience, but also to speak through fictional representations of the child. This enabled women writers to attempt to influence readers for their moral good. The convergence of discourses about women, children, and slavery in juvenile literature during the early and mid-nineteenth century is the central preoccupation of this study. As such, it complicates our understanding of women's literary production and reveals the political culture enmeshed within the domestic. Quite simply, argues De Rosa, becoming domestic abolitionists allowed women authors to develop a discourse which enabled them to negotiate both personal views and cultural imperatives. The study is divided into four sections: 'Domestic Abolitionists and their Publishers'; 'Sentimentalised Victims and Abolitionists Tears'; 'The Abolitionist Mother-Historian'; and 'Juvenile Abolitionists'. Detailed notes and bibliography, together with black and white plates, make up this collection of materials, which enhances our understanding of racial and gendered constructs in women's literary production.

Peter K. Garrett's *Gothic Reflections: Narrative Force in Nineteenth-Century Fiction* is a fascinating study of the subversive power of Gothicism. The book is divided into three sections, entitled 'The Force of a Frame', 'Monster Stories' and 'The Language of Destiny'. In a series of readings ranging between Horace Walpole, the Romantics and Victorians, and Henry James, Garrett probes the tensions inherent in the Gothic form, revealing the plight of the isolated individual. He opens a new case for the importance of Edgar Allan Poe and also, in 'Monster Stories', offers a close textual analysis of *Frankenstein*, *Dr Jekyll and Mr Hyde* and *Dracula*. Garrett explores the relationship between Gothic and the canonical writings of Charles Dickens, George Eliot and Henry James. The novels of these writers develop similar tensions to the Gothic, he asserts, by introducing Gothic motifs and effects into their more realistic social and psychological representations. Locating both Gothic and other Victorian fiction in a larger literary and cultural field, Garrett argues that the oppositions usually posed between them are actually at work within both. By offering alternative versions of its stories, he insists, nineteenth-century Gothic fiction repeatedly reflects on narrative force and the power exerted by both writers and readers.

In *Whitewashing America: Material Culture and Race in the Antebellum Imagination* Bridget T. Heneghan considers how material goods shaped antebellum notions of race, class, gender and purity. From the Revolutionary War to the Civil War, Heneghan records, American consumers increasingly sought white-coloured goods. White consumers surrounded themselves with refined domestic items, visual reminders of who they were, equating the wealth, discipline and purity of such items with their own whiteness. Clothing, paint, dinnerware, gravestones and buildings staked a visual claim of superiority, she argues, in contrast to the items belonging to lower-class neighbours and household servants. Developing this argument, Heneghan, in the first chapter, 'White Goods and the Construction of Race in Antebellum America', considers the manner in which racial divisions were exacerbated through material possessions and, in chapter 2, 'Class Consideration and the Refinement of Whiteness', further explores the principle of segregation through social status. Such white middle-class pretensions are, unsurprisingly, mocked in the writings of Frederick Douglass and Harriet Jacobs. But Heneghan also explores the work of James Fenimore Cooper, Harriet Beecher Stowe, Nathaniel Hawthorne, Edgar Allan Poe and Herman Melville to understand the way in which they negotiated a complex agenda of domesticity, the body politic and privilege. Whiteness in terms of femininity and cleanliness are further discussed in this examination of material culture and racial difference and detailed notes complete a compelling study.

John D. Kerkering's *The Poetics of National and Racial Identity in Nineteenth-Century American Literature* examines the literary history of racial and national identity. Kerkering argues that writers such as W.E.B. Du Bois, Sidney Lanier, and William Gilmore Simms used poetic effects to assert the distinctive quality of specific groups in a varied social landscape. The book is divided into two distinct sections: 'The Poetics of National Identity' and 'The Poetics of Racial Identity'. The first section examines aspects of nationhood and the spirit of place in the work of such diverse writers as Simms and Hawthorne, while the second explores the musicality of language as a signifier of racial identity. Kerkering discusses this patterning in works ranging from the poetry of Walt Whitman to the music of Antonin Dvorak. Reprints of posters and of sheet music enhance this section, in which the blending of music and language create a poetic experience. This musical theme is developed in the final chapter of the study, 'Blood Will Tell', where the author examines the rhythmic language employed by African American preachers, with its deeply seductive quality. Perhaps the major difficulty of this book lies in its wide-ranging observations, in terms of place and time. This reduces the focus of the text and, ultimately, its strength. Nevertheless, this is an exciting study, in terms of the power of sound; it will prompt further investigation.

In *The Syntax of Class: Writing Inequality in Nineteenth-Century America* Amy Schrager Lang is preoccupied with considering the way in which people classify and separate themselves, but through language rather than possessions. The book explores the literary expression of classification that occupied public discourse in the mid-nineteenth century. It focuses on a group of novels written, like most books, by middle-class city dwellers, in this case by American men and women living, almost without exception, in the urban north-east. Their particularity lies in the fact that they tell stories of people who are not themselves members of the middle class. In 'Home, in the Better Sense', Lang discusses texts such as Susan Warner's *The Wide, Wide World,* Maria Cummins's *The Lamplighter* and Nathaniel Hawthorne's *The House of the Seven Gables*. Chapter 2 contemplates colour, class and community in 'Orphaned in America', through such novels as Frank Webb's *The Garies and their Friends* and Harriet Wilson's *Our Nig*. In 'Women Workers, and the Limits of Literary Language', Lang is preoccupied with the writings of Rebecca Harding Davis, Elizabeth Stuart Phelps and Harriet Beecher Stowe. She concludes her study by investigating social inequalities in Charles Loring Brace's *The Dangerous Classes of New York* and Louisa May Alcott's *Work*. She interrogates throughout the deeply felt nineteenth-century American longing for a fictional home, in which inequalities were erased and class struggles averted. Lang reflects that, in reality, it was to remain a vision to be struggled over and for. The texts discussed in this study include a number of 'rediscovered' writings which illuminate our understanding of mid-nineteenth-century America and the language of class inherent in writings of the period.

Joycelyn Moody's *Sentimental Confessions: Spiritual Narratives of Nineteenth-Century African American Women* traces the ways in which these women appropriated white-sanctioned literary conventions and used them to create an area in which to voice their protests against racism and patriarchy. Early black holy women autobiographers documented their personal and national history from an unusual vantage point, and *Sentimental Confessions* examines the writings of some of these women: Martha Stewart, Jarena Lee, Zilpha Elaw, Nancy Prince, Mattie J. Jackson and Julia Foote. Moody argues for an appreciation of their work because, not in spite of, the fact that they were holy texts. Martha Stewart's essays blend themes of Christian evangelism, literary sentimentalism, and black nationalism; Jarena Lee and Zilpha Elaw, two of Stewart's contemporaries, were itinerant ministers living and preaching in the antebellum north-eastern United States. Their spiritual autobiographies express a 'theology of suffering', a form amenable to the reconstruction of African American women's particular experiences, sacred and secular. In 1850 a very different form of autobiography, *A Narrative of the Life and Travels of Mrs Nancy Prince*, was published. It offers sharp insights into the class, caste, religious, and national differences between black women in different parts of the African diaspora. The writings of Mattie Jackson, however, have more in common with those of Martha Stewart, embracing, as they do, a theology of survival, of resistance and defiance. Moody's deliberations on the literary production of Julia Foote demonstrate African Americans' readiness for civil rights and social equity. Nineteenth-century black holy women's narratives portray elements of women whose religiosity places them, Moody argues, as diviners, as mediums. Detailed notes and bibliography complete this groundbreaking study of evangelism and sentimentalism in the writings of these spiritual women.

Although camp is generally associated with the English *fin de siècle*, argues Mike Perkovich, in *Nature Boys: Camp Discourse in American Literature from Whitman to Wharton*, there was also evidence of camp discourse in American letters of the nineteenth century, in Civil War accounts, writings concerning mining camps, tall tales, and parodies, and it was also to be seen in realist fiction. Perkovich defines camp discourse within a critical evaluation of previous writers on the subject of campness, such as Susan Sontag's association of the term with 'pop' culture, arguing that, while camp has come to be regarded as something glib, superficial and playful, the term has also historically constituted a threat to the compulsory heterosexuality of official culture. Perkovich contends that the homosexual figure that emerged in the late nineteenth century finds its prototype in the sign system of campness to be found in the writings of Walt Whitman, Bret Harte, Ambrose Bierce, Mark Twain, Charles Warren Stoddard, Frank Norris and Edith Wharton, as much as, or even more than, in the medical, legal and educational discourses that Michel Foucault locates as central to the production of homosexual identity. Focusing on predominantly canonical writers and/or texts that are not necessarily considered to be 'queer', Perkovich intends to show how camp discourse entered America's mainstream culture through some surprising mediums, in its contribution to the construction of homosexuality, constituting a subversive element to compulsory heterosexuality.

Susan M. Ryan's *The Grammar of Good Intentions: Race and the Antebellum Culture of Benevolence* is also preoccupied with aspects of language and identity. It explores, however, the power of cultural values in considering the practice of benevolence. Drawing on both cultural and literary texts, Ryan traces the way in which those working and writing within social reform movements helped confirm racial and class ideologies. Categories were sought in order to define identity more thoroughly, something Ryan investigates through readings of Herman Melville's *The Confidence Man*, Frederick Douglass's *My Bondage and My Freedom*, and Harriet Beecher Stowe's *Uncle Tom's Cabin*. She also considers the reports of charity societies, African American and Native American newspapers, travel writing, juvenile fiction, cartoons, and sermons, and explores dialogues between different literary forms while debating the ways in which society felt good intentions should be expressed and enacted. *The Grammar of Good Intentions* effectively breaks down rigid boundaries between the private and public spheres and challenges traditional notions of male and female activities. In demonstrating benevolence as a central social concern which excited much discussion and disagreement, Ryan reframes the practice of good works in antebellum America. The first chapter, 'Benevolent Violence', considers Indian removal; this is succeeded by 'Misgivings', which elaborates on duplicity and need in Melville's late fiction. Ryan continues to focus on Melville's writings as she contemplates 'The Racial Politics of Self-Reliance'. This naturally leads to a discussion of Emerson and Transcendentalism, before moving on to consider the self-reliance of African Americans, through the works of Douglass. 'Pedagogies of Emancipation' examines the end of slavery as a crucial moment in the American culture of benevolence. The antislavery novels of Stowe are central to a discussion on 'Charity Begins at Home', where *Uncle Tom's Cabin* and *Dred* are examined in detail. The concluding chapter is ironically entitled 'Save Us from Our Friends', and considers free African Americans and the culture of benevolence, in its shifting representations. The book includes black and white reproductions of posters, cartoons and literary illustrations, which make an effective contribution to the images evoked in the text, through an ongoing dialogue. An epilogue and detailed notes complete this absorbing work.

Hearts of Darkness: Wellsprings of a Southern Literary Tradition, by Bertram Wyatt-Brown, is a beautifully crafted study that explores the defining role of melancholy in southern literature. Wyatt-Brown traces the origins of this pervasive mood in 'Alienation and Art', in which he analyses Edgar Allan Poe's 'The Raven'. Identifying a close association between creativity and psychological distress, Wyatt-Brown explores the works of writers as diverse as William Gilmore Simms, Mark Twain, Constance Fenimore Woolson, Sidney Lanier and Ellen Glasgow. In so doing, he develops original insights into the lives and creative impulses of both major and more obscure writers. Deeply marked by high death rates following the Civil War, and the experience of bitter defeat, white southerners imposed a climate of parochial pride and, consequently, stifling conventions of masculinity. Many writers experienced a conscious or unconscious alienation from the prevailing social currents, and they expressed emotional turmoil in and through their writing. Wyatt-Brown contends, however, that the southern tradition of literary penetration of pain, despair and suffering was far from a male preserve. He makes a convincing case for the existence of a deep sense of depression embedded in the literary production of Woolson, Glasgow, Kate Chopin and Willa Cather, as the southern tradition evolved into modernist alienation. This is a powerful exploration of a significant southern literary tradition.

Kris Fresonke's *West of Emerson: The Design of Manifest Destiny* aims to produces an account of manifest destiny as a product of a theological—notably Christian—lineage, which underpins how America appeared to Americans in the nineteenth century, through an analysis of what are referred to as exploration narratives, alongside the nature writings of Ralph Waldo Emerson and Henry

David Thoreau. Fresonke, rather than recapitulating accounts of the generic category of exploration narratives, or regurgitating critical assessments of Transcendentalism, has focused on the way in which Jacksonian exploration fed into the works of Emerson and Thoreau. In other words, Fresonke's focus is on how images of the Far West contributed to the Romantic classics of 'Nature' and *Walden*, relocating both texts as informed by a particularly Western form of political parody and forms of resistance, while at the same time pointing out the critical problems with speaking about American writing as specifically regional. Accounts of travelling through America from Lewis and Clarke and Zebulon Pike, supported by useful illustrations of travel in America, set out the main terms of Fresonke's analysis of the exploration narrative as an essentially conservative form, which serves to consolidate what is assumed to be already known. Fresonke's account of the quasi-sacred approach of Americans to America in the nineteenth century is enthusiastic as well as informed, and constitutes a lively read for the general student of American studies and a useful addition to the critical debates that surround Emerson, Thoreau and the writing of nature. David M. Robinson has compiled a selection of essays, under the title *The Spiritual Emerson: Essential Writings*, in celebration of the 200th anniversary of the birth, in 1803, of one of America's most influential essayists. Robinson's comprehensive collection intends to highlight Ralph Waldo Emerson's significance as a leading figure in spiritual thinking, illustrating how his early religious upbringing and time in the ministry contributed towards shaping his later ideas, as expressed in essays such as 'Nature' [1836], 'The Divinity School Address' [1838], 'Self-Reliance', 'Compensation', 'The Over-Soul', and 'Circle' [all published in 1841—a busy year], to later essays such as 'The Fugitive Slave Law' [1854], 'Worship' [1860], and 'Essential Principles of Religion' [1862]. Situating Emerson as unfulfilled by traditional religious attitudes and codes, Robinson maps the essayist's developing spiritual ideas, examining his thinking regarding nature and the soul, his dealings with loss, and the expression of a more persevering belief in the authority and influence of moral and ethical thinking that would be available to all. This book constitutes a significant contribution to critical debates surrounding Emerson as a religious writer and, in a useful introductory essay, Robinson provides an interesting and informative guide for emerging as well as established Emerson scholars. Although the image of Emerson as a confident advocate and living ideal of self-reliance has been somewhat tarnished by critical accounts of the past few decades, this still appears to be the enduring impression. Kenneth S. Sacks's *Understanding Emerson: 'The American Scholar' and his Struggle for Self-Reliance* participates in debates that call this prevailing vision of Emerson into question. Focusing specifically on the 'The American Scholar' oration, Sacks examines a variety of contemporary resources, from correspondence and diaries—much of which has been previously unexamined—looking at Emerson in the process of clarifying his ideas and principles. Sacks's account of the 'American Scholar' is primarily biographical, examining the dilemma faced by Emerson's Transcendental philosophy in giving this oration at Harvard, the seat of Unitarianism. Ultimately, argues Sacks, the event was one which thrust Emerson into a more invigorated awareness of social justice and participation in formulating a role for the intellectual in America, a role which continues to resonate in the twenty-first century. Usefully including the complete text of 'The American Scholar', Sacks's text is written in an accessible manner, which would appeal to a wide audience as well as constituting a significant addition to biographical accounts of one of America's most important nineteenth-century scholars.

Henry James's investigation into male identity forms the subject of Leland S. Person's *Henry James and the Suspense of Masculinity*, which draws on theoretical terms of feminist criticism, men's studies and gay and queer readings, focusing particularly on the ways in which the Master subverted and challenged conventional categories of masculinity and heterosexuality. Engaging in an account of the proliferation of classifications of gender and sexuality in the later nineteenth and early twentieth centuries, Person argues that James took advantage of emergent taxonomic confusions, investigating and experimenting with a series of non-conventional gendered and sexual configurations. Arguing that critical attempts to locate the writer within a single sexual identity should be superseded by an account of the writer's moulding of his male characters, Person points out that James's own sexual identity should be regarded as a form of narrative, an aesthetic category. Through his examination of some of James's canonical novels, notably *Roderick Hudson*, *The American*, *The Portrait of a Lady*, *The Bostonians*, *The Ambassadors* and *The Golden Bowl*, Person contends that James employs a form of metaphorical language that engages with the construction and deconstruction of a series of male characters, whose potential male subjectivity is ultimately deferred in an assessment of pluralized gendered and sexual identity. Person's text is rigorous and detailed, and will be a significant resource for the dedicated scholar of Henry James.

In '"Every one to his trade": *Mardi*, Literary Form, and Professional Ideology' (*AL* 75:ii[2003] 305–34), John Evelev examines Herman Melville's third publication, the first to be acknowledged by Melville himself as a work of fiction, as marking a pivotal episode in his writing career, signifying his commitment to becoming a professional writer. Drawing on the infamously fragmentary and digressive framework of the novel, Evelev further contends that *Mardi* indicates how the idea of professional authorship itself underwent changes at this time. The novel is shown to be charting shifts in antebellum understandings of authorship, as well as to be investigating the ideological fragmentations and contradictions which were fundamental to the formation of middle-class identity in the urban arena of America's northern cities. Referring to William Charvat's account of *The Profession of Authorship in America* [1968], Evelev assesses the complicated context of developing forms of professional identities in the emerging market culture of the urban environment that, he argues, is reflected in the contradictory symbolism of *Mardi*. This, in turn, reveals much about the problems of the ideology of specialization and automation, and exposes the inherent contradictions in such aspects of professional identities, as either part of a self-interested class movement, or an attempt to improve or reform American society. Focusing on Melville's volume of Civil War poetry, *Battle-Pieces and Aspects of the War*, Deak Nabers, in 'Victory of Law: Melville and Reconstruction' (*AL* 75:i[2003] 1–39) sets out to examine the collection's response to political and legal issues, chiefly addressing the interest expressed by the poems and the prose 'Supplement' to contemporaneous debates regarding the legal grounds on which the Civil War was fought, and also the way in which reconstruction was to be legitimated. While acknowledging that previous critical approaches to Melville's Civil War poetry have addressed its political dimensions, Nabers sets out to focus more fully on the way in which the collection exposes the contradictions inherent in the political and legal implications of reconstruction. Situating Melville's writing within the context of debates surrounding secession and slavery as criminal acts, assessing the seemingly incompatible projects of emancipation and union between politically divided North and South, Nabers argues that Melville's *Battle-Pieces*, although offering no solution to the contradiction, usefully demonstrates an awareness of the instrumental power of the law in the project of reconstruction, but at the same time offers a recognition that such a project would problematically negate a political agenda for the South.

The opening section of Lawrence Frank's *Victorian Detective Fiction and the Nature of Evidence: The Scientific Investigation of Poe, Dickens, and Doyle*, published in Palgrave's Studies in Nineteenth-Century Writing and Culture, a series of monographs that aims to represent research on literary works from the time of the Napoleonic Wars to the *fin de siècle*, will be of particular interest to students of American literature, based as it is on the detective writing of Edgar Allan Poe. This section consists of two chapters, one focusing on 'The Murders in the Rue Morgue' and the other dealing with 'The Gold-Bug'. Franks contextualizes Poe's detective fiction in a consideration of scientific controversies of the period, notably those which surrounded the nebular hypothesis of Pierre Simon Laplace, which was one of several naturalistic theories regarding the emergence of the galaxies which were precursors to the big bang theories of twentieth-century science. The section on Poe considers the significance of the nebular hypothesis in the action of the short stories and as contributing to the problematization of historical knowledge, in an account that looks at issues of epistemology and narratology, drawing attention to Poe's awareness of current scientific disputes and the vagaries of chance in the world-view of the tales. Frank's text is a useful analysis of detective fiction and a good general guide to scientific debates taking place across the Atlantic throughout the nineteenth century and leading into the twentieth. In 'Absolute Poe: His System of Transcendental Racism' (*AL* 74:iv[2003] 751–82), Maurice S. Lee argues that Edgar Allan Poe has been portrayed, in recent critical debates, as a somewhat divided figure: on the one hand embedded in the material discourses of his contemporary world, on the other, divorced from the metaphysics of that world. However, Lee contends, from his reading of 'Metzengerstein' [1832], a more persistently historical Poe emerges, who partakes of his era's political and cultural moment but also draws on available ideas to theorize the world in which he lives, a world inevitably torn by issues of slavery and race. Tracing Poe's divergent urges for metaphysical unity and assertions of racial difference, Lee argues that ultimately Poe can be regarded as a writer who strategically enacts his prejudicial metaphysics of race rather than being tormented by repressed racial fears.

In Damon-Bach and Clements, eds., *Catharine Maria Sedgwick: Critical Perspectives*, Sedgwick's wide-ranging literary production is explored alongside nineteenth-century reviews and new critical essays on her work. The collection illuminates Sedgwick's skilful use of rhetoric, her reform activities, and her role in shaping the nation's literature, and begins with a celebratory foreword by Mary Kelley. Sedgwick and her place in literary history is described in Carolyn L. Karcher's essay, followed by Melissa J. Homestead's exploration of Sedgwick's anonymous publications and the anxiety they signalled, in terms of female literary production. Clements then focuses on *A New-England Tale* and Damon-Bach considers '*Redwood*'s Revisionary Heroines', before 'The Rhetoric of Catharine Sedgwick's *Hope Leslie* is scrutinized by Judith Fetterley, and Patricia Larson Kalayjian considers 'Disinterest as Moral Corrective in *Clarence*'s Cultural Critique'. An excerpt from Sedgwick's 'Unfinished Antislavery Manuscript' introduces Karen Woods Weierman's deliberation on Sedgwick's work as a precursor to Harriet Beecher Stowe's antislavery texts, while Robert Daly ponders 'Mischief, Insanity, Memetics, and Agency in *The Linwoods*', and John Austin discusses 'Sedgwick's *Tales and Sketches* of 1835'. Social and political aspects of this extraordinary woman are contemplated in Sondra Smith Gales's essay on 'Sedgwick's American Poor', Charlene Avallone's 'Catharine Sedgwick and the "Art" of Conversation', and Jennifer Banks's writing on Sedgwick's prison work. In exploring Sedgwick's *Letters from Abroad to Kindred at Home*, Brigitte Bailey discusses the experience of witnessing and the need to place the spectacle of otherness within American ideology. Political issues of gender inform Sedgwick's *Married or Single?* through which Deborah Gussman examines Sedgwick's feminist perspective. This is further debated in the politics of resistance by Susan K. Harris, as she probes the social and historical moment of Sedgwick's most important writings. This fascinating collection concludes with an essay by Dana Nelson which reflects upon Sedgwick's centrality to the current study of nineteenth-century literature. Detailed notes complete this study.

Regula Giovani, in *'I Believe I Shall Die an Impenetrable Secret': The Writings of Elizabeth Barstow Stoddard*, also focuses on the literary production of a nineteenth-century woman writer. A contemporary of Julia Ward Howe, Stoddard was born in 1823, and sought literary success in a highly original voice of her own. Stoddard began her career as a journalist, writing bi-monthly letters for the *Daily Alta California*. Married to the poet Richard Henry Stoddard, she also wrote poems and short stories, often published in the important journals of the day. Stoddard's greatest achievement, however, was her novels, the first of which, *The Morgesons*, was published in 1862. Stoddard's self-willed writing shows confidence in her creation of a heroine whose very nature explores individual isolation—a theme more important to Stoddard than reform and women's rights. Giovani discusses Stoddard's subsequent novel, *Two Men*, in which, as before, she writes of women who are strong, independent and, in many ways, autonomous, and she also renders a sense of the isolated consciousness. Neither of Stoddard's books achieved popular success, and she experienced increasing tension between her artistic vision and her desire for recognition. Her final novel, *Temple House*, she considered her best, but, like the others, it failed to excite public attention. One of the reasons, perhaps, is that Stoddard's writing, particularly in her last two books, explores the inner lives of her characters in a fascinating psychological form considerably ahead of her time. Giovani's exploration of this unorthodox writer, whose work seemed fated to die with her, reveals a brilliant and original author, whose writing demands rediscovery. The study includes some of Stoddard's poems and extracts from her prose, as well as brief biographical details and a bibliography.

McClure Smith and Weinaur, eds., *American Culture, Canons, and the Case of Elizabeth Stoddard*, also proclaims the importance of this writer, who has been virtually excluded from literary memory. Seeking reasons for this, the book explores Stoddard's life and works in three parts: 'The Writer, the Canon, and the Protocols of Print'; 'Gender, Selfhood, and the Discourse of Domesticity'; and 'Race, Reconstruction, and American Citizenship'. McClure Smith examines Stoddard's relationship to the canon of nineteenth-century American women's poetry, and Margaret A. Amstutz explores Stoddard's significant contributions as a journalist to the *Daily Alta California*. In 'Haunting the House of Print' Paul Crumbley contrasts Stoddard's 'Collected by a Valetudinarian' with Constance Fenimore Cooper's 'Miss Grief', since both texts concern themselves with characters who never appear. This reflection upon identity and absence is developed in Julia Stern's exploration of Stoddard's heroine Cassandra in *The Morgesons*. Framing her sense of self by considering her sensual and desiring nature, Cassandra is a character entirely different from those created by most of Stoddard's contemporaries. Only Emily Dickinson's poetry offers such examples of eroticism and self-possession and, like Stoddard, Dickinson is also obsessed with appetite and starvation. Susanna Ryan's essay argues that the figure of the self-starving woman in their texts points to a larger, culturally and historically specific set of discourses that signify a particularly gendered relation to the self. Jaime Osterman Alves concludes the second part of this study by exploring Stoddard's interrogations of domesticity in her short stories, published in *Harper's New Monthly Magazine*. She reveals the manner in which Stoddard's writings disrupt the conventional, thus exposing the tyranny of the cult of domesticity. The final part of this book dwells on the riddle of national identity, explored in Stoddard's *Two Men*. Here Jennifer Putzi discusses the way in which national and familial identity are intertwined, suggesting that Stoddard sees social change as a positive force, necessary for a nation to thrive. Lisa Radinovsky, meanwhile, explores the dynamics of race in the novel, investigating representations of miscegenation and incest. In the final chapter of this study, 'Reconstructing *Temple House*', Weinauer debates Stoddard's last book, in which she deploys Gothic tropes to interrogate freedom and unity. An afterword by Lawrence Buell offers a scholarly consideration of Stoddard's writing and calls for her retrieval and re-evaluation. Both the recent studies of Stoddard's work reviewed in these pages are convincing in their support of Buell's view that Stoddard is one of the most important woman writers of her age.

Schwartz, ed., *Baptist Faith in Action: The Private Writings of Maria Baker Taylor, 1813–1895*, brings into print the writings of a strong-minded plantation mistress, who spent her life in South Carolina and Florida. The granddaughter of Richard Furman, South Carolina's foremost nineteenth-century Baptist minister, Taylor was a well-educated and sophisticated member of South Carolina's planter class and, unsurprisingly, a fervent Baptist. Notable for its geographical and temporal breadth, this collection of letters, diary entries, essays, and poems affords an unmatched view of the life of a woman living on the South's interior frontier during the nineteenth century. Born in Sumter County, South Carolina, Maria Baker married John Morgandoller Taylor in 1834. Reading voraciously, as she reared and educated an ever-growing family, Taylor also wrote a vast number of letters and diary entries, as well as occasionally publishing anonymous articles in Baptist publications. The writings document the spiritual life of an evangelical Baptist woman and explore the impact of the American Civil War on her world. Her day-to-day experiences are fascinating in that they offer images dramatically different from the stereotypical view of southern plantation life. This careful interweaving of primary texts and commentary is a valuable addition to our understanding of time and place, and includes detailed notes and some fine black and white photographs. Schwartz also offers a contextual biography of Taylor, with clear information on the extensive cast of characters populating her writings and changing locales.

Valarie H. Ziegler's *Diva Julia: The Public Romance and Private Agony of Julia Ward Howe* investigates a woman writer's quest for autonomy. Already a published author when she married Samuel Gridley Howe, at the age of 23, Julia Ward Howe is perhaps best remembered as the writer of the 'Battle Hymn of the Republic'. This biography is an intelligent investigation of her ambitions, at odds with those of her husband, who desired that she confine herself to the domestic realm. This view was, of course, reflected in the social and cultural values of the time and Howe desired respectability every bit as much as she longed for autonomy. Despite the literary ambition which drove her, Howe was in many ways an extremely conventional woman; hence she was constantly at war with herself. In adopting a career as a reformer, therefore, she sought to champion traditional ideas yet, in her peace activism, she offered some radical notions. Her theory was that women were superior to men, because the female was naturally nurturing while men were aggressive; this, she felt, legitimized her public role. However, Howe recognized the demands of a conventional domestic role in her longing for respectability; as a result, her personal life was represented in a positive manner, both by Howe and by her children. Once Howe's public reputation was established it became easier for her to rewrite the tumultuous experiences of her domestic life, especially after her husband's death in 1876. Nevertheless, private papers record the discrepancies between the ideal public picture and the reality. Ziegler's study examines the troubled gender dynamics that Howe negotiated as a nineteenth-century American woman writer and reformer. It also offers a glimpse of the careful rewriting and editing the Howe family participated in when narrating their mother's private and public life. In their reworking of Howe's life, she achieved what she most desired: autonomy and respectability. In addition to notes and a bibliography there are several photographs of Howe and her family.

Astrid Galbraith, in *New England as Poetic Landscape: Henry David Thoreau and Robert Frost*, volume 39 in Peter Lang's Trierer Studien zur Literatur series, looks at the way in which New England performed as a site of inspiration for the poetry of both Thoreau and Frost, arguing that the traditions and habits as well as the countryside of the region played their part in stimulating the poetic imagination of both writers. Galbraith further contends that the rural arena of New England contributed to the developing individualism of the two writers, informing their shared disdain for state controls and institutions, invigorating a form of poetic proto-ecology. Galbraith's book is predominantly comparative, examining the affinities between the two poets, but it also takes the individual nuances of each, in its consideration of common themes and background, while assessing the extent of Thoreau's influence on the writing of Frost. An accessible account, this text would be a useful guide for the general reader of American studies, as well as being of interest to scholars of Thoreau and Frost.

The latest edition from the Library of America's American Poet's Project, which sets out to offer a compact library of American poetry, *Walt Whitman: Selected Poems*, is edited by Harold Bloom, who also provides a useful introductory essay which examines the development of *Leaves of Grass* and makes available to the reader some psychoanalytical insights into reading Whitman's poetry. An invaluable index of titles and first lines makes this a good introductory guide for readers unfamiliar with, or wishing to refresh their awareness of, Whitman's poetry.

Books Reviewed

Abrams, Robert E. *Landscapes and Ideology in American Renaissance Literature: Topographies of Skepticism*. CUP. [2003] pp. 178. £40 ($60) ISBN 0 5218 3064 8.

Bloom, Harold, ed. *Walt Whitman: Selected Poems*. American Poets Project. LAm. [2003] pp. xxxi +224. £10.99 ISBN 1 9310 8232 4.

Brown, Bill. *A Sense of Things: The Object Matter of American Literature*. UChicP. [2003] pp. 246. £22.50 ISBN 0 2260 7628 8.

Damon-Bach, Lucinda, and Victoria Clements, eds. *Catharine Maria Sedgwick: Critical Perspectives*. NortheasternU. [2003] pp. 328 + xxxix. £28.50 ($40) ISBN 1 5555 3548 8.

De Rosa, Deborah C. *Domestic Abolitionism and Juvenile Literature, 1830–1865*. SUNYP. [2003] pp. 224. hb £36 ISBN 0 7914 5825 3, pb £11 ISBN 0 7914 5826 1.

Frank, Lawrence. *Victorian Detective Fiction and the Nature of Evidence: The Scientific Investigation of Poe, Dickens, and Doyle*. Palgrave Macmillan [2003] pp. xii +250. £45 ISBN 1 4039 1139 8.

Fresonke, Kris. *West of Emerson: The Design of Manifest Destiny*. UCalP. [2003] pp. xii +204. £32.50 ISBN 0 5202 2509 0.

Galbraith, Astrid. *New England as Poetic Landscape: Henry David Thoreau and Robert Frost*. Trierer Studien zur Literatur 39. Lang. [2003] pp. 153. pb £23 ISBN 3 6315 0575 2.

Garrett, Peter K. *Gothic Reflections: Narrative Force in Nineteenth-Century Fiction*. CornUP. [2003] pp. 232. £11.50 ISBN 0 8014 8888 5.

Giovani, Regula. *'I Believe I Shall Die an Impenetrable Secret': The Writings of Elizabeth Barstow Stoddard*. Lang. [2003] pp. 261. £27 ISBN 3 9067 7041 9.

Heneghan, Bridget T. *Whitewashing America: Material Culture and Race in the Antebellum Imagination*. UMP. [2003] pp. xxvii +204. £45 ($65) ISBN 1 5780 6585 2.

Kerkering, John D. *The Poetics of National and Racial Identity in Nineteenth-Century American Literature*. CUP. [2003] pp. 366. £45 ($65) ISBN 0 5218 3114 8.

Lang, Amy Schrager. *The Syntax of Class: Writing Inequality in Nineteenth-Century America*. PrincetonUP. [2003] pp. 168. £32.50 ($45) ISBN 0 6911 1389 0.

McClure Smith, Robert, and Ellen Weinaur, eds. *American Culture, Canons, and the Case of Elizabeth Stoddard*. UAlaP. [2003] pp. 295. £28.95 ISBN 0 8173 1313 3.

Moody, Joycelyn. *Sentimental Confessions: Spiritual Narratives of Nineteenth-Century African American Women*. UGeoP. [2003] pp. 216. £14.50 ISBN 0 8203 2574 0.

Perkovich, Mike. *Nature Boys: Camp Discourse in American Literature from Whitman to Wharton*. Lang. [2003] pp. ix +182. £40 ISBN 0 8204 6173 3.

Person, Leland S. *Henry James and the Suspense of Masculinity*. UPennP. [2003] pp. 208. £27 ISBN 0 8122 3725 0.

Robinson, David M., ed. *The Spiritual Emerson: Essential Writings*. Beacon. [2003] pp. xiii +266. pb $15 ISBN 0 8070 7719 4.

Ryan, Susan M. *The Grammar of Good Intentions: Race and the Antebellum Culture of Benevolence*. CornUP. [2003] pp. 272. £24.50 ISBN 0 8014 3955 8.

Sacks, Kenneth S. *Understanding Emerson: 'The American Schola' and his Struggle for Self-Reliance*. PrincetonUP. [2003] pp. xiv +202. £18.95 ISBN 0 6910 9982 0.

Scharnhorst, Gary, ed. *American Literary Scholarship: An Annual, 2001*. DukeUP. [2003] pp. xxii +558. £59 ISSN 0065 9142.

Schwartz, Kathryn Carlisle, ed. *Baptist Faith in Action: The Private Writings of Maria Baker Taylor*. USCP. [2003] pp. 400. £30.50 ISBN 1 5700 3497 4.

Shields, John C. *The American Aeneas: Classical Origins of the American Self*. UTennP. [2001] pp. xiv +432. $45 ISBN 1 5723 3132 1.

Wells, Colin. *The Devil & Doctor Dwight: Satire and Theology in the Early American Republic*. UNCP. [2002] pp. x + 254. $49.95 ISBN 0 8078 2715 0.

Wyatt-Brown, Bertram. *Hearts of Darkness: Wellsprings of a Southern Literary Tradition*. LSUP. [2003] pp. 236. hp £45.95 ISBN 0 8071 2822 8, pb £19.50 ISBN 0 8071 2844 9.

Ziegler, Valarie H. *Diva Julia: The Public Romance and Private Agony of Julia Ward Howe*. Continuum. [2003] pp. 228. £13 ($24) ISBN 1 5633 8418 3.

XVI

American Literature: The Twentieth Century

LACY RUMSEY, STEPHEN McVEIGH, ELIZABETH NOLAN, SARAH MACLACHLAN, RACHEL VAN DUYVENBODE, LUIGI FIDANZA, STEVEN PRICE AND A. ROBERT LEE

This chapter has five sections: 1. Poetry; 2. Fiction 1900–1945; 3. Fiction since 1945; 4. Drama; 5. Native, Asian American, Latino/a and General Ethnic Writing. Section 1 is by Lacy Rumsey; section 2 is by Stephen McVeigh and Elizabeth Nolan; section 3 is by Sarah MacLachlan, Rachel van Duyvenbode and Luigi Fidanza; section 4 is by Steven Price; section 5 is by A. Robert Lee. Alan Rice's section on African American literature was unavoidably postponed this year; his section next year will cover material published in both 2003 and 2004.

1. Poetry

The year was rich in new editions of major poets. Particularly welcome was the publication by New Directions of Ezra Pound's *The Pisan Cantos*, edited by Richard Sieburth. This is the first time since 1948 that Pound's famously controversial text has received publication separate from the other cantos, and it is a pleasure to see such reputedly specialist material presented attractively and cheaply, with the kind of relationship between price and critical apparatus typically reserved for classic fiction. The text, familiar to readers of the Faber and New Directions editions, contains no surprises; the extensive endnotes, however, include some material which will be new to many readers, even those familiar with Carroll F. Terrell's *Companion to the 'Cantos' of Ezra Pound* (UCalP [1980]). Sieburth contributes a useful introduction, albeit one whose adoption of a biographical framework might be taken to suggest that the *Pisan Cantos* are primarily to be read through the perspective of Pound's life—which is, one might think, the perspective from which the poetry will need at some point to escape if its value is to be dispassionately assessed. Overall, the edition is a near-ideal one for students. Teachers will want to continue to refer to Carroll Terrell for the broader range of references (and interpretations) that he provides, but will not

Year's Work in English Studies, Volume 84 (2005) © The English Association; all rights reserved. For permissions, please email: journals.permissions@oxfordjournals.org

doi: 10.1093/ywes/mai016

want to be without it. If the volume can bring the *Pisan Cantos* to the wide readership that the work's reputation demands, and if criticism can then build into its assessment of the poetry the responses of that wider readership, it will have performed an invaluable service.

Sieburth is also the editor of the Library of America's new edition of Pound's *Poems and Translations*, which contains all of Pound's published poetry except the *Cantos*, as well as the poems of 'Hilda's Book' and the 'San Trovaso Notebook', and virtually all of Pound's published translations, including the Confucian prose texts. There is no introduction, but, as usual with this series, the texts are reliable, clearly set out, and followed by a restrained but helpful chronology and notes. These are clear and to the point, even if, as in other works reviewed here, foreign-language names have not been adequately checked—'La Dorotea' becomes 'La Doreata', for example. A book-by-book listing of the contents of each of Pound's volumes is also provided. For those readers used to the pocket-sized intimacy of a *Personae* or a *Translations*, the volume comes as a defamiliarizing and salutary shock: the sheer extent of Pound's lyric output, and its presentation within a canon-making series, will oblige many to reconsider how it now reads page by page.

Robert Lowell: Collected Poems, edited by Frank Bidart and David Gewanter, is a massive book, but its mass is largely accounted for by the bulk of Lowell's poetry, the clear and comprehensive presentation of which is clearly this attractive volume's primary goal, and one in which it wholly succeeds. The notes, which identify allusions, set out poems' publishing history, and cross-reference some of Lowell's subjects to his discussions of them elsewhere, notably in the *Collected Prose*, are informed, precise and helpful; the critical and introductory material is brief and to the point. Most important in a collection of the arch-reviser Lowell, of course, are the editorial decisions, and Bidart and Gewanter's are sensitive and explicit, and at times grounded, as Bidart states in his introduction, in a personal assessment of poetic value. Since the edition does not aim to be a variorum, only 'interesting' variants are included; variations in spelling are not corrected, as, since Bidart correctly points out, 'after-dinner' and 'after dinner' and 'afterdinner' are each different rhythmically, and in the few cases where the editors depart from the final published version of the text Bidart makes their motives clear, as in the case of Lowell's suppression of a stanza division in 'Night Sweat', a suppression which Bidart and Gewanter allow themselves to overrule here. The principal regret which some readers may have will be the suppression of *Notebook* in favour of the later versions of that volume's poems found in *To Lizzie and Harriet* and *History*; one hopes that the earlier volume will remain in print.

Grace Schulman's edition of *The Poems of Marianne Moore*, on the other hand, leaves the reader slightly confused as to the detail of its editorial principles, which are nowhere set out, though they are at bottom probably very close to Bidart and Gewanter's. The edition, which is based on chronological order, reconstructs the original sequences in which poems received first magazine publication, yet in general (but not always) prints the final versions of them. Moreover, Schulman chooses not to print in sequence the famously reduced version of 'Poetry' included in the body of the 1967 *Complete Poems*—a version about which Schulman notes the 'devastation' it caused in 'many readers'—preferring instead the longer version that Moore placed in the notes to that volume, where Moore hoped that 'the serious reader may look it up'. As with Bidart, one can respect the editor's right to correct what she or he considers to be flagrant errors of taste on the poet's part, but this may be a step too far, since it will force on readers new to Moore exactly the process of disappointment that Schulman describes: would it not be preferable to discover the poem at its most concentrated, and then encounter the extra lines as a glorious bonus, rather than the other way around? These caveats do not distract from the fact that, in the unprecedented range of Moore's poems—many previously uncollected—that it makes available, and in its underlying chronological order, the volume is a rich and important one.

The Correspondence of William Carlos Williams and Louis Zukofsky, edited by Barry Ahearn, has a great deal to offer admirers of either poet. Rich in literary-historical information, permitting the reader to gauge the efforts made by Williams to see Zukofsky respected and published, but also how at times—notably during the 1930s—there is tension between the two, the volume also contains a certain amount of biographical material, particularly on Williams's side: the older poet is notably more discursive about his family life, and indeed about Zukofsky's. The correspondence's greatest interest, however, is in the many moments of critical insight it contains: there are heady moments of close reading (and high-handed dismissal) of other poets' work—Williams on Pound, for example, and Zukofsky on Oscar Williams, whose ubiquity had been worrying his namesake—as well, of course, as multiple insights into Williams's and Zukofsky's own poetry. The correspondence regarding Zukofsky's 'A Marriage Song for Florence and Harry' constitutes an exemplary critical exchange: Williams complains of the poem's obscurity but discerns a Herrick-like music within it; Zukofsky responds by explaining his syntactic reticence, confirming the Herrick connection, and expatiating on how he hopes his cadences will be read. In general, however, as Ahearn notes in his excellent introduction, the critical traffic flows the other way, with Zukofsky much the more confident in his ability to understand and improve upon the other's work. Particularly valuable in illustrating this is the volume's third appendix, which recounts the suggestions and alterations made by Zukofsky concerning Williams's *The Wedge*.

Finally, *Conversations with Gwendolyn Brooks*, edited by Gloria Wade Gayles, contains interviews conducted with Brooks between 1964—a Studs Terkel piece—and 1994. For many readers, the volume's primary interest will be in Brooks's discussion of her relationship to black political activism, and in particular to her radicalization after 1967. Also suggestive are Brooks's theoretical observations on poetry, and especially its reception; there is acute discussion, for example, of the readerly freedoms afforded by reading, as opposed to listening to, a poem. At such points the reader regrets that Brooks's interviewers seem on the whole to have been willingly distracted from such nuts-and-bolts questions of poetics, as such insights are rarely given space for development or detailed discussion.

Looming large among the year's collective publications in the field is *The Cambridge History of American Literature*, volume 5: *Poetry and Criticism,*

1900–1950, whose general editor is Sacvan Bercovitch. The volume falls into three main parts: 'Modernist Lyric in the Culture of Capital', by Frank Lentricchia and Andrew DuBois, which includes chapters on anthologies and their audience, and on Frost, Stevens, Eliot, and Pound; 'Poetry in the Machine Age', by Irene Ramalho Santos, which includes chapters on Stein, Williams, H.D., Moore, Crane, and Hughes; and 'Literary Criticism', by William E. Cain, which will not be considered here.

Though attributed to Frank Lentricchia and Andrew DuBois, the first part is an only slightly re-edited version of Lentricchia's *Modernist Quartet* (CUP [1994]), a work originally commissioned as a contribution to this volume. The many excellencies (and occasional weaknesses) of Lentricchia's work are too well known to need rehearsing here; the chapter on T.S. Eliot, in particular, remains as fresh as ever, and makes an excellent early port of call for any student of his poetry. New in this version of the text are a reordering of some material, the correction of some minor errors, and an epilogue on the fate of the modernist artist. It is perhaps a pity that more has not been made of the opportunity to pay renewed attention to the specificity of the publication context; in a work such as this—whose readers, as Robert von Hallberg noted in volume 8 [1995], are likely to have 'more curiosity than knowledge'—the chapter on Pound should surely make at least some mention of *Cathay*; some of that chapter's more tendentious interpretations would, likewise, need careful contextualization for the non-specialist reader really to find them useful.

The second section, despite bearing a Lentricchia-esque title, is a conventional set of single-author studies, in which Ramalho Santos has clearly taken great care to find the right mode of address for her readership. The opening to the chapter on Williams, for example, expertly winnows out from a long quotation from the poet the points and questions that most require development, and then provides that development lucidly and instructively. Some of the conclusions offered could be disputed, and at times one finds oneself wishing for more of a sense of the fierce debate that has surrounded these authors, but on the whole this is an important job done well.

Some criticisms must, however, be made of the production standards of this volume. There are too many errors of spelling (some, to be fair, inherited from *Modernist Quartet*): it seems remarkable that such names as de Gourmont and d'Aubigné cannot be got right; ditto Louis Zukofsky, who becomes Zukovsky on several occasions, some of them, furthermore, absent from the index. I also notice a falling-off in paper quality as compared to earlier volumes in the series; the pages are less pleasant to the eye and hand, and, in the copy stocked in my institution's library, are already starting to yellow. For £75 one hopes for better.

Férez Kuri, ed., *Brion Gysin: Tuning In to the Multimedia Age*, is the first publication devoted to this British-born artist, naturalized American in 1946, whose invention of 'permutated poems', based on a cut-up approach to text, famously influenced William Burroughs in his composition of *The Naked Lunch*. Beautifully produced, rich in reproductions of Gysin's paintings and, to a lesser extent, of the original printings of his permutated poems, the volume will clearly become the primary resource for anyone interested in Gysin's work. Whether it will make new converts is a different matter. Reminiscences and essays (including texts by Burroughs and Gregory Corso) convey some of the fascination that Gysin exerts, but despite repeated assertions of his creative importance do not convince the non-aligned reader—at least in so far as the poems are concerned. The essay most directly concerned with Gysin's poetry, Nicholas Zurbrugg's 'Letting the Mice In: Brion Gysin's Multimedia Poetics', is a useful compilation of original quotations, and makes some suggestive (if blunt) comparisons between Gysin and Roland Barthes, but Zurbrugg's choice of a largely narrative approach prevents the development of any real analysis, and this is largely true throughout the volume.

Cook, ed., *From the Center of Tradition: Critical Perspectives on Linda Hogan*, is the first volume devoted to the Chickasaw poet and novelist. Most of the contributors concentrate on the novels; two essays, Jennifer Love's 'Rhetorics of Truth Telling in Linda Hogan's *Savings*' and Ernest Smith's '"The Inside of Lies and History": Linda Hogan's Poetry of Conscience', do discuss the poetry in depth, and make claims for it which seem accurate representations both of the poetry's ambitions and of the ways it is typically read. One notes a tendency for the bibliographies in this collection to contain citations of Hogan's own work, and perhaps one or two theoretical texts, but little evidence of an engagement with earlier poetic traditions.

Romana Huk's collection *Assembling Alternatives: Reading Postmodern Poetries Transnationally* is a rich, admirable and necessary attempt, based on a conference held in 1996 at the University of New Hampshire, to set up a sense of dialogue between American avant-garde poets and critics and those from different Anglophone cultures. Language and post-Language practices are here revealed to be more nuanced, various and period-specific than either advocates or critics might suspect. The contributions are uneven; some pieces are too ready to express their author's sense of heroic embattlement, but others are informed and thoughtful, particularly those—such as Keith Tuma's 'Slobbering Distance: American, British, and Irish Exploratory Poetries in a Global Era'—that place American avant-garde practice in direct contact with non-American models. Much comparative material can also be gleaned from the analyses of British, Irish, Australian and Canadian poetries presented here by figures such Alison Mark, Peter Middleton, cris cheek, Trevor Joyce and John Wilkinson. Most immediately useful to critics and researchers in American poetry, however, will probably be Steve Evans's survey of recent writing, 'The American Avant-Garde after 1989: Notes Towards a History'. Evans is an acute reader of poetry, and readers will be grateful for the lines of approach sketched in his opening overview, which, as well as giving ample bibliographical information, theorizes the renewed importance of George Oppen as an example to contemporary American poets as evidence of a 'refusal to subordinate the social to the linguistic' which distinguishes contemporary avant-garde writers from their immediate predecessors. Evans's readings of six poets—Kevin Davies, Lisa Jarnot, Bill Luoma, Rod Smith, Lee Ann Brown and Jennifer Moxley—include ample argument and quotation, and the variety of contemporary American and Canadian styles is made very visible. The volume is also notable for its inclusion of David Marriott's bracing attack, on psychoanalytical and political grounds, on the model of reading implicit in Language poetry ('Signs Taken for Signifiers: Language Writing, Fetishism and Disavowal').

Another set of conference proceedings, Delville and Pagnoulle, eds., *Sound as Sense: Contemporary US Poetry &/In Music*, is slightly less successful in establishing a sense of dialogue between its contributors, who write on subjects as various as rock lyrics, Heidegger, and contemporary French opera, and on a wide range of late twentieth-century poets, including Robert Creeley, Clark Coolidge, Harryette Mullen and Hilda Morley. As Tim Woods points out very helpfully in one of the articles collected here ('"Art Tracking Music": Louis Zukofsky's Po/Ethics of Music'), the musicality of language has often been considered as a means to make of it a counter-discourse to reason and referentiality, and this counter-discursive status underlies several of the pieces collected here. Only some, however, analyse how such a counter-discourse might function in detail. One such is Richard Quinn's 'Black Power, Black Arts, and the Ethic of the Ensemble', which provides a powerful argument linking the political implications of jazz improvisation with the formal strategies of Amiri Baraka, as well as a full and very useful bibliography. Other articles bring poetry and music into informative dialogue: these include Antoine Cazé's study of contemporary French composer Pascal Dusapin's settings of Gertrude Stein ('"Pas de Deux": Dusapin Sings/Stein to be Sung') and Erik Ullman's account of how his own compositional practice takes inspiration from the poetry of Charles Olson ('Olson and Musical Composition'). If not all participants avoid what the editors themselves identify as the danger of their project, 'a merely metaphorical use of music', the volume remains, nonetheless, a useful contribution to the field.

A final work born of conference proceedings is Ferguson, ed., *Jarrell, Bishop, Lowell, & Co.* As well as sections devoted to each of the three poets named in the title, the volume begins with an overview of 'The Middle Generation', featuring accounts of the personal and poetic relations between a group of poets whom Edward Hirsch, in his essay '"One Life, One Writing!": The Middle Generation', suggests contemporary readers now find a 'more approachable and vulnerable group of democratic masters' than are to be found among the earlier poets of modernism. Hirsch's passionate account of the pleasure to be found in these poets, and of their 'simple commitment to the humanly flawed' is a high point of this volume, and is complemented by group studies by Steven Gould Axelrod, 'Gwendolyn Brooks and the Middle Generation', Thomas Travisano, 'Reflecting Randall Jarrell in the Bishop/Lowell Letters', and Jeredith Merrin, whose 'Randall Jarrell and Elizabeth Bishop: "The Same Planet"' contains some particularly acute moments. Also valuable in its exposure of some of the mechanics and dynamics of this generation of poets is Diederik Oostdijk's '"Not like an editor at all": Karl Shapiro at *Poetry* Magazine'. This section is much the strongest in the book; those devoted to single-poet studies reflect too closely the limited ambitions set out in Ferguson's preface, which promises that 'the biographical and psychological sources of the poetry having been so exhaustively probed', the contributors to this volume 'look beyond these to the poets' reflections of ... social constructions'; that the focus might ever be on the poem as poem, to be read and lived with on its own terms, is clearly not to be countenanced. Other ways of reading poetry are recalled by Elise Partridge's closing piece, '"But we must notice": Lowell's Harvard Classes on Berryman, Bishop, and Jarrell'.

Robert H. Deutsch and John N. Serio, eds., *The Poetry of Delmore Schwartz* (WSSoc) and Marina Camboni, ed., *H.D.'s Poetry: 'The Meanings That Words Hide'* (AMS) were not received in time for the preparation of this review.

Turning now to single-authored studies, William Patrick Jeffs's *Feminism, Manhood, and Homosexuality: Intersections in Psychoanalysis and American Poetry* contains chapters on Ginsberg and Rich, as well as on Emerson, Whitman and Dickinson. The work has an old-fashioned feel to it: its careful and humane readings in the different poets build to a conclusion that looks to the construction of a freer and less unequal world. The work's lack of a developed set of tools for either literary or theoretical analysis is, however, limiting; the discussion of Ginsberg, for example, is largely a narrative of his career, with brief discussion of the most thematically germane poems. Though the book could teach a new reader much about the poets discussed, and might well encourage a library browser to pick up them up and give them a try, it has relatively little to offer the specialist in American poetry.

Merrill Cole's *The Other Orpheus: A Poetics of Modern Homosexuality* is a much more ambitious work, whose author states that he aims to reconnect prosody and aesthetics with political literary enquiry, with the broader goal of 'a rehabilitation of the concepts of affect and imagination'. This way of putting things suggests that Cole's profoundest allegiances are political and ideological ones—elsewhere he states, with a peremptoriness to which the reader must become accustomed, that his work avoids 'the ideological implications of chronological order'—and such is indeed the case. Yet these allegiances are energized and complicated by Cole's repeated return to the aesthetic. The study is thus unusual in its movements across generic and disciplinary boundaries. At ease with popular culture—the book begins, rather disconcertingly, with an account of artistic, academic and journalistic responses to the murder of Matthew Shepard—it is careful to distinguish between aspects of that culture that are and are not worthy of serious enquiry, and though focusing primarily on American poets (the early Eliot and Crane), the work contains two chapters on Rimbaud, and it makes excellent use of the writings of Leo Bersani, best known as a critic of French literature. The chapter on Crane is particularly notable for its ability to draw on what Cole sees as the distinctive methodological advances achieved by queer studies, while resisting the 'rigid opposition between historical reality and art' which Cole identified as the risk of such methods. Its close readings in the detail of Crane's poetry examine sexual, political and linguistic-formal elements with equal attentiveness.

Colin Falck's *American and British Verse in the Twentieth Century: The Poetry that Matters* is an unabashedly polemical work. Describing Romantic philosophy and poetry as 'unsuperseded', and his own work as a footnote to Wordsworth's 1802 preface, Falck argues that the literature must 'convey a sense of lived experience ... along with a degree of insight into an underlying order that that experience or life reveals'. He sees much twentieth-century British and American poetry as having abandoned this mission in favour of a highbrow intellectualism that has little to offer most of its potential readers. Few readers will be wholly out of sympathy with Falck's account; his passion for lived complexity and the 'singing line' is infectious, and his readings of the twentieth-century poets whose work he respects—including Williams, Jeffers, Plath and Millay—can be warm and insightful. His critiques, however, are less attractive: dismissing Robert Creeley by relineating one of his weaker poems to 'improve' it is an old and not particularly illuminating tactic in the absence of any sustained reflection on the nature of line-break, and it is surely negligent to dismiss Olson's poetry, and that of all those he influenced, simply on account of the weakness of his theories of breath. Most regrettable, however, is the loose structure of the book, which integrates previously published and unpublished material in what feels like a meander through Falck's favourites and bugbears, and generates a distinct lack of theoretical intensity; one rarely has the sense that Falck is willing to engage in detail with the ramifications of a particular question, let alone with possible objections to his position.

Kim Fortuny's *Elizabeth Bishop: The Art of Travel* attempts to reconcile political and aesthetic approaches to the poet. It does so via two chapters devoted to overview and general discussion—to what Fortuny calls Bishop's 'social aesthetic', and to 'The Ethics of Travel'—and three devoted to extended accounts of three of Bishop's great longer poems, 'Over 2,000 Illustrations and a Complete Concordance', 'Questions of Travel', and 'Crusoe in England'. Fortuny quickly demonstrates her abilities as a close reader in the first chapter's account of the much-maligned 'Manuelzinho', and her critical acumen in several extremely acute perceptions, suggesting, for example, that the complexity of Bishop's poetry is linked to the demands which it makes on its lyrical subject, demands that may be overlooked because of the 'seemingly seamless texture of the language'. The subsequent readings are, however, slightly lacking in focus, and the prosodic analyses which they include not always reliable. A full engagement with major Bishop critics such as Costello and Travisano is also wanting, and the bibliography is heavily weighted towards work published in the 1990s.

Joon-Hwan Kim's *Out of the 'Western Box': Towards a Multicultural Poetics in the Poetry of Ezra Pound and Charles Olson* seeks to rectify what the author sees as a critical failure to distinguish Olson's poetic practice from that of Pound. For Kim, both poets 'searched for the Other outside the imperial discourse of the West', but whereas Pound sought to make room for the other within a 'closed poetic discourse', Olson attempted a radical opening-up of the working principles of poetic discourse. The author is well versed in the theoretical and critical literature surrounding these questions and these poets, but this study attempts too massive a synthesis; its accounts of Eliot and Cleanth Brooks as representations of the 'Unity' in opposition to which Pound represents 'Diversity', for example, are schematic. Whether Pound can genuinely be identified with a 'multicultural poetics' remains unclear, and the author's method is better adapted to Olson.

Two other notable studies must be mentioned. Paul Wadden's *The Rhetoric of Self in Robert Bly and Adrienne Rich: Doubling and the Holotropic Urge* represents a scrupulous attempt to provide a nuanced view of both the poetry chosen for discussion and the conceptual framework within which it is addressed. Drawing, with reservations, on a Jungian vocabulary, Wadden shows how in both poets the use of doubles in key texts represents an attempt to rethink and refashion the self. The discussion intersects very productively with the specificities of the two poets, most notably in its tracing of the use and subsequent disappearance of male doubles in Rich's work. Wadden also suggests that the work of both poets provides a necessary complication of post-structuralist notions of the self. The closing chapter is devoted to the pedagogical potential of Bly's and Rich's work within the teaching of student composition.

Finally, Mark Bauer's *This Composite Voice: The Role of W.B. Yeats in James Merrill's Poetry* is a sensitive, erudite and theoretically nuanced monograph. Providing multiple close readings in Merrill's early poetry, as well as in *The Changing Light at Sandover*, and drawing in particular on Yeats's *A Vision* as a source-text for Merrill, Bauer shows how Merrill's initially vexed relationship with Yeats's example gradually eases, becoming in Merrill's later poetry a significant source of authority and power. Some of the close readings, such as that comparing 'Sailing to Byzantium' with Merrill's 'About the Phoenix', are very good indeed, and extensive use is made of Merrill's annotated personal copies of Yeats's works. Like Wadden's work, the study also includes a sustained critical engagement with its chosen critical tools, in this case Harold Bloom's model of poetic influence, which Bauer finds productive but limiting.

Other single-authored studies requested but not received include Bonnie Costello, *Shifting Ground: Reinventing Landscape in Modern American Poetry* (HarvardUP), Tim Dayton, *Muriel Rukeyser's 'The Book of the Dead'* (UMissP), Elisabeth A. Frost, *The Feminist Avant-Garde in American Poetry* (UIowaP), Nick Halpern, *Everyday and Prophetic: The Poetry of Lowell, Ammons, Merrill, and Rich* (UWiscP), Daniel Kane, *All Poets Welcome: The Lower East Side Poetry Scene in the 1960s* (UCalP) and Rod Philips, *Michael McClure* (BoiseSUP); and, among reference material, Christopher Beach, *The Cambridge Introduction to Twentieth-Century American Poetry* (CUP) and Emmanuel S. Nelson, *Contemporary Gay American Poets and Playwrights: An A-to-Z Guide* (Greenwood); likewise Elizabeth Gregory, ed., *The Critical Response to Marianne Moore* (Praeger). We hope to discuss a selection in next year's volume.

In a slightly lean year for journal articles, two publications stand out. The Spring 2003 number of *American Literary History* is devoted to two panel discussions organized by Sacvan Bercovitch in 2001 among contributors to the *Cambridge History of American Literature*, focusing on what Bercovitch, as the general editor of that work, identifies as the two most regularly problematic fields within it: poetry and ethnicity (in 'Problems in the Writing of American Literary History: The Examples of Poetry and Ethnicity' (*AmLH* 15[2003] 1–3)). The poetry panel includes five contributions, and its discussions constitute an illuminating intervention in the field. Barbara Packer, 'Two Histories Contending' (*AmLH* 15[2003] 4–6), identifies two poles within debate about how to write literary history: the historical determinism of a Taine, and the contrasting approach of 'critical idealists' such as Robert von Hallberg, author of the *Cambridge History*'s section on poetry since 1945. For critics such as von Hallberg, Packer argues, the critic is a kind of museum curator, a presenter of perfect specimens. In distinguishing the two approaches, Packer makes the unusual—and startlingly direct—point that different critical methods may fit the professional needs of specialists in different eras: 'Like fastidious shoppers at an upscale supermarket examining a pile of identically sized peaches, historians of twentieth-century American poetry forget the plight of their colleagues in earlier eras, rummaging through bushels of packinghouse culls at sad local groceries'.

The lines of allegiance suggested by Packer's argument are borne out by the other contributions: Shira Wolosky's 'The Claims of Rhetoric: Toward a Historical Poetics (1820–1900)' (*AmLH* 15[2003] 14–21) argues for and exemplifies an approach to the American poem that is grounded in history and culture, while those contributors whose field of expertise is the twentieth century all mount a more or less sustained defence of evaluation. Robert von Hallberg, in 'Literary History and the Evaluation of Poetry' (*AmLH* 15[2003] 7–13), contributes a defence of his *Cambridge History* piece that is explicitly and articulately grounded in his scepticism regarding the ultimate value of historical enquiry within criticism: 'The best poems resist not only the erosion of memory but also absorption by other discourses', and 'what one says historically about poems is not going to be what makes them poems rather than some other form of discourse'. Arguing that poets, not critics, make literary history, von Hallberg makes persuasive use of examples as diverse as Paul Celan and Bob Dylan; this brief piece constitutes an important reference point for future discussion of the relationship of evaluation and criticism.

Other contributors make similar points in different ways. Andrew DuBois, 'Historical Impasse and the Modern Lyric Poem' (*AmLH* 15[2003] 22–6), notes what DuBois sees as 'an almost Pavlovian' reflex against evaluative criticism of poetry, and indeed against all criticism that is not explicitly historical in ambition. Ascribing this reflex to a 'cultural shorthand' and 'slippage' that sees formalism as necessarily ahistorical, the ahistorical as equivalent to the universal, and the universal as 'actually ideological imperialism', DuBois echoes Packer in arguing for the need for a range of critical methods to be drawn on in responding to poetry of different periods: if post-war American poetry is particularly suited to evaluative 'sifting' (the term is von Hallberg's), earlier periods require a different approach. Finally, Alan Filreis's contribution to the debate, 'Tests of Poetry' (*AmLH* 15[2003] 27–34), recalls a *Sewanee Review* piece of 1948 by Vivienne Koch, which preferred Louis Zukofsky's 'A Test of Poetry' to the literary histories published by E.M.W Tillyard in that decade on the grounds that it 'enunciate[d] some principles of judgment', and goes on to locate what he sees as the historical-cultural orientation of much contemporary nineteenth-century scholarship as indicative of a 'latent anti-modernism'.

American Literary History's Summer issue also contains an important study: Bonnie Costello's 'Elizabeth Bishop's Impersonal Personal' (*AmLH* 15[2003] 334–66). Costello argues powerfully against readings of Bishop that absorb the lyric speaker into the biographical author, and proposes that voice and identity be decoupled, with the voice of each poem interrogated for the historical rhetorics and discourses of which it is the site. The study includes dense, extended analysis of one of Bishop's most discussed poems, 'Crusoe in England', arguing persuasively that the poem combines a compelling personal voice with a set of preoccupations much wider than can be resolved within any individual; hence its, and the poem's, continuing power to hold readers. An instructive complement to the approach to Bishop taken in Costello's article can be found in Steven Gould Axelrod, 'Elizabeth Bishop and Containment Policy' (*AL* 75[2003] 843–67). After a long biographical overview of Bishop's arm's-length relationship to Cold War politics, Axelrod reads 'View of the Capitol from the Library of Congress'—a poem which, as he neatly puts it, 'refuses to salute'—as a manifestation of a subversive relationship to a Cold War lexicon (Axelrod interrogates, in particular, the use of the word 'intervenes') and, following Camille Roman, as a covert expression of Bishop's lesbianism.

Like *American Literary History*, the *Journal of Modern Literature* published an excellent range of articles in the field in 2003. J.T. Barbarese's 'Theology for Atheists: Reading Ammons' (*JML* 26:iii–iv[2003] 73–83) provides an attractive account, based on close reading, of Ammons's negotiations of self and nature, and of the 'enthusiastic ambivalence' onto which these negotiations give. The article also contains an illuminating aside on what Barbarese considers to be the basic structural principle of Ammons's lyrics, 'a series of precepts mated to corresponding examples'. *JML*'s Fall 2003 number is devoted to modern poetry, much of it American. Joanna Gill's '"My Sweeney, Mr Eliot": Anne Sexton and the "Impersonal Theory of Poetry"' (*JML* 27:i[2003] 36–56) seeks to nuance the familiar opposition between modernist impersonality and the self-revelation by which confessional poetry is defined. This opposition, which has recently been challenged by accounts of the place of personality in Eliot, is for Gill too dependent, in Sexton's case, on a naive identification of the 'Anne' and 'I' of her work with the poet herself. Reading Sexton's 'Hurry Up Please It's Time' against its model, *The Waste Land*, Gill shows how Sexton uses multiple personae and allusiveness in a dialectic of personal and impersonal voices. David Sanders's 'Frost's *North of Boston*: Its Language, its People and its Poet' (*JML* 27:i[2003] 70–8) provides an expert and highly readable overview of Frost's ambitions—descriptive, dramatic, moral and prosodic—in preparing his second volume of poems. Sanders's emphasis on the relationship between Frost's technical and moral goals, and on differences in this respect between Frost and Wordsworth, Emerson, and Pound, is valuable.

Pound himself receives considerable attention from contributors to this number of *JML*. Feng Lan's 'Ezra Pound/Ming Mao: A Liberal Disciple of Confucius' (*JML* 27:i[2003] 79–89) performs a service to Pound scholarship by providing the first reading of an article on Confucianism submitted by Pound to *The Egoist* in 1914, although published under the name 'M.M'; the chain of reasoning by which Feng Lan connects 'M.M' to Pound is itself a pleasure. 1914 is a much earlier date than is customary for the identification of the beginning of Pound's interest in Confucianism, and Feng Lan argues that the connections in Pound's thought between Confucianism, aesthetic individualism, and the construction of a counter-discourse to Christianity are already fully in place in the *Egoist* article. Massimo Bacigalupo, 'America in Ezra Pound's Posthumous Cantos' (*JML* 27:i[2003] 90–8), explains the rationale of his Milan edition of selections of Pound's unpublished fragments (*Canti postumi*, Mondadori [2002]), and provides descriptions of some of the material contained therein. Janine Utell's 'Virtue in Scraps, Mysterium in Fragments: Robert Graves, Hugh Kenner, and Ezra Pound'

(*JML* 27:i[2003] 99–104) uses Pound and Kenner to critique what Utell sees as the attempt by Graves and Laura Riding to 'foster the annihilation of history'.

Other poets to be considered in this number include the pleasing and unusual pairing of Elizabeth Bishop and Allen Ginsberg. Jonathan Ellis's '"A Curious Cat": Elizabeth Bishop and the Spanish Civil War' (*JML* 27:i[2003] 137–48) seeks to defend Bishop from accusations of political aloofness during and after her 1936 visit to Spain. Ellis's argument may not convince all readers—it seems not quite to convince Ellis himself—but his emphasis on Bishop's admiration of Shelley, his use of (and extensive quotation from) an unpublished poem ('In A Room: Seville 1936'), his scepticism regarding a criticism that has 'fallen in love with a tragic life', and his quizzical but passionate involvement with Bishop's poetry, are all welcome. Justin Quinn's 'Coteries, Landscape and the Sublime in Allen Ginsberg' (*JML* 27:i[2003] 193–206) seeks to rehabilitate the sublime as a literary-critical category, via a concentration on 'sublimes that are not naive in the sense that Emerson's is'. For Quinn, Ginsberg's early poetry socializes and familiarizes the sublime via its creation of a coterie of friends and fellow visionaries. The subsequent development of Quinn's argument is very valuable in its tracing of a development and change in Ginsberg's poetics. He argues that the willingness of 'Kaddish' to distinguish sanity from insanity provides evidence of the poet's successful identification of 'the difficulty which is inherent to Beat culture, the difficulty of recognition and distinction', and that the newly detailed descriptions of landscape to be found in 'Wichita Vortex Sutra' are part of an attempt on Ginsberg's part to refine his poetic sublime in order to make it resistant to charges of antinomianism, such as were levelled at Ginsberg by Norman Podhoretz. A final appeal for more critical attention to be paid to the non-naive sublime of a Ginsberg, a Pinsky, a Clampitt or a Jorie Graham, completes this subtle and invigorating piece. This issue of *JML*also includes articles on Wallace Stevens: Ann Mikkelsen, '"Fat! Fat! Fat! Fat!"—Wallace Stevens's Figurations of Masculinity' (*JML* 27:i[2003] 105–21), and Lisa Goldfarb, "Pure Rhetoric of a Language Without Words": Stevens's Musical Creation of Belief in "Credences of Summer" (*JML* 27:i[2003] 122–36); Marianne Moore: Alison Rieke, '"Plunder" or "Accessibility to Experience": Consumer Culture and Marianne Moore's Modernist Self-Fashioning' (*JML* 27:i[2003] 149–70); and Sylvia Plath: John Gordon's brief but illuminating 'Being Sylvia Being Ted Being Dylan: Plath's "The Snowman on the Moor" (*JML* 27:i[2003] 188–92).

Modernism/Modernity published two interesting articles on less-studied poets. John Timberman Newcomb's 'The Footprint of the Twentieth Century: American Skyscrapers and Modernist Poems' (*Mo/Mo* 10[2003] 97–125) discusses relatively little-known poems by Teasdale, Ridge, Benét, and poets published in *The Liberator* and *The Masses*, linking them to the complex of symbolic values connecting skyscrapers to modernity. The article constitutes a useful historical account, particularly in its steady focus on poems about the Metropolitan Life Tower, even if not all readers will share the author's conviction that in 'a postmodern academic climate' such poems 'should [be taken] as seriously as the poems of Pound, Eliot, Stevens or Moore'. Donna K. Hollenberg, '"History as I desired it": Ekphrasis as Postmodern Witness in Denise Levertov's Late Poetry' (*Mo/Mo* 10[2003] 519–37), provides a careful and sensitive account of

Levertov's use of painting and painters (notably Anselm Kiefer, Chaim Soutine and Emmanuel de Witte) as vectors of humanist, and subsequently of Catholic, values, and in particular as symbols of a maintained 'faith in human possibility'.

Other notable articles published this year include Chris Beyers's 'Louis Zukofsky in Kentucky in History' (*CollL* 30:iv[2003] 71–88), which brings detailed local knowledge to bear on what Beyers calls 'the Kentucky theme' in *A*. Though identifying everything from Zukofsky's awareness of the poverty in the town of Hazard, Eastern Kentucky (*A* 14) to the national attention given to Kentucky chair-maker Chester Cornett in 1965 (*A* 18), Beyers draws larger conclusions from his research. He suggests that the Kentuckyan theme reveals an 'inviolable individualism' within Zukofsky's politics, and that, though the meanings of many references in *A* may remain unknown, that does not mean that they are unknowable, so that accounts of the poem that depend on its inscrutability are premature. Bringing a different variety of specialist expertise to bear, David W. Clippinger, 'The Prophetic Gaze of Orpheus: Charting New Lands in Small Poetry Journals' (*AmPer* 13[2003] 105–16), focuses on a single journal, *Maps*, which appeared from 1966 to 1974, and notes its eclecticism, which for Clippinger distinguishes it both from traditional poetry journals, represented by *Poetry*, and the more tightly focused innovation of radical anthologies such as those edited and co-edited by Donald Allen.

2. Fiction 1900–1945

In terms of critical focus very little changed in 2003. William Faulkner continued to dominate both book and journal studies, followed by Ernest Hemingway and F. Scott Fitzgerald. It is good to see, though, a number of other novelists making an appearance in studies this year, notable amongst them Theodore Dreiser and Owen Wister in books, and Sinclair Lewis, Dashiell Hammett, and Jack London in articles and papers.

William Faulkner received a variety of book-length considerations in 2003. The proceedings of the 2000 Faulkner and Yoknapatawpha conference, *Faulkner in the Twenty-First Century*, edited by Robert W. Hamblin and Ann J. Abadie, provides the usual excellent range of perspectives on the state of Faulkner criticism. The conference from which the essays emerge, in its twenty-seventh year, asked whether there is anything left to say about Faulkner and his works. The first five essays represent new approaches or current trends; the later ones offer fresh ways of thinking about long-standing Faulkner topics. In some ways the first half is the most interesting. Theresa M. Towner offers an interrogation of canonicity, of the traditional classifications of Faulkner's works as 'major' and 'minor', and seeks to move away from Faulkner's so-called major phase of 1929–42 and explore the more neglected of his characters, to examine 'the central marginality or marginal centrality … in Faulkner's novels'. In line with one of the more apparent trends in Faulkner criticism in journals this year, there are two essays offering postcolonial perspectives. Deborah N. Cohn highlights Faulkner's works' relevance to the 'other south' of postcolonial Latin America. She explores the influence Faulkner had on Spanish authors from 1930 to the present and makes the point that recognition of Faulkner's utility among Spanish Americans has only recently created a reciprocal North American response, a situation she believes will be at the forefront of Faulkner studies in the twenty-first century. Annette Trefzer offers a different postcolonial perspective by exploring Faulkner's contradictory treatment of Indians in the short stories *Red Leaves* and *Lo!*, and details Faulkner's use of not simply binary opposition but mimicry 'to produce an uncomfortable doubleness that blurs any clear hierarchical distinctions' within a wider discussion of the politics of ethnicity. All in all, this is a significant work and one which suggests that Faulkner will continue to occupy scholars for a long time to come.

In *Balancing the Books: Faulkner, Morrison and the Economies of Slavery*, Erik Dussere argues that the writers' engagement with the past 'is enabled by an engagement with the economics of slavery'. He suggests that both writers construct novels around the 'enduring, fractured memory of slavery' and that this encounter is frequently couched in the language of the marketplace. Taking the idea that, primarily, slavery represented the attempt to transform people into monetary value, he suggests that 'this attempt was the initial act in an ongoing process by which cultural traditions of race in America have been figured through concepts such as debt and repayment, exchange and accounting, property and the market'. From this perspective, Dussere interrogates the 'figures'. Through analysis of such perspectives as the ledger as a form of written history, history as debt, and the regulation of 'blood', Dussere provides a fascinating and convincing set of connections.

Helen Oakley, in *The Recontextualisation of William Faulkner in Latin American Fiction and Culture*, relates the novelist's work to a number of authors and texts in Latin American literature, specifically to Maria Luisa Bomball's *A Rose for Emily*, Juan Carlos Onetti's *La Novia Robada* and *Tan Triste Como Ella*, and Juan Rulfo's *Pedro Paramo*. At one level, Oakley's book offers a comparative literary analysis situated within the broader context of relations between the US and Latin America. As such she examines the cultural contexts of Argentina in the 1930s, Argentina and Uruguay in the 1940s and 1950s, and Mexico in the 1950s. At another level the book addresses the 'labyrinth' of perspectives, interactions and reciprocal exchanges between Faulkner and Latin American writing.

On William Faulkner by Eudora Welty is a fascinating anthology, a collection of speeches, lectures, writing and musings on Faulkner by his literary neighbour. As the introduction makes clear, they did not have a direct relationship, but each was aware of the other's work. The book in its entirety presents Welty as one of Faulkner's 'most astute critics', 'ever Faulkner's apologist, admirer and defender'. The material in the collection is wide-ranging, entertaining and illuminating, from comedic pieces such as the previously unpublished caricature of Faulkner, through reviews of his works and even an odd postcard written to Welty, praising her work although seemingly attributing Zora Neale Hurston's *Gilded Six Bits* to her in the process.

Faulkner's works receive a large amount of attention in journals this year. Two articles have as their focus Faulkner's Snopes trilogy. Owen Robinson in 'Interested Parties and Theorems to Prove: Narrative and Identity in Faulkner's

Snopes Trilogy' (*SLJ* 36:i[2003] 58–73) discusses the different narrative approaches employed by Faulkner in *The Hamlet*, *The Town*, and *The Mansion*. He indicates that, while *The Hamlet* is delivered by an authorial voice with contributions of others, most notably V.K. Ratliff, *The Town* is entirely constructed from first-person accounts of Ratliff, Charles Mallison and Gavin Stevens. In *The Mansion* these three figures feature prominently but are joined by an authorial voice in certain sections of the story: most importantly for Robinson, the sections featuring Mink and Linda Snopes, who themselves are never given a narrative voice of their own. For Robinson, these narrative set-ups have very distinct effects on the material they deal with. So, he argues, the authorial voice with contributions means 'we observe Ratliff and the chorus reading Flem Snopes, but our own necessary uncertainty with regard to reading them reminds us of the doubt at every level from writer to character to reader'. The narrative device of *The Town* seeks to keep the reader at arm's length. *The Mansion*, Robinson suggests, represents a merging of the two styles, which offers a balance but also develops some of the possibilities of such narrative techniques. He argues that in each case what we are presented with are the possibilities and problems of reading, of considering the 'spaces between character, event and perspective'.

In 'Tradition and Change in William Faulkner's Snopes Trilogy' (*McNR* 41:ii[2003] 26–40), Earl G. Ingersoll argues that Faulkner's fiction has a long-standing concern with the relationship between tradition and its 'other', change. He seeks to demonstrate this by employing Jacques Derrida's reading of Plato's *Phaedrus* and its enquiry into the relationship between speaking and writing as representing the old order and its modernization. He argues that, even though he is 'so often (mis)read simplistically as a cultural conservative, Faulkner may be more interested in representing a rich complexity in the conflict between tradition and change'.

In '"Liable to be anything": The Creation of Joe Christmas in Faulkner's *Light in August*' (*JAmS* 37:i[2003] 119–33), Owen Robinson argues that, because of the complexity of his role and presence in the novel and, more widely, Yoknapatawpha, Christmas 'suggests himself strongly as a means of considering the personal manifestations of the county's sprawling networks of readings and writing as a theoretical mass'. The paper explores Christmas as means of comprehending the 'analagous nature of the writing and reading to be found within Yoknapatawpha with that of the series of novels in which the county is sited'. For Robinson, Christmas is the archetypal Yoknapatawphan: 'he is a southern chronotope who throws into focus the infinite heteroglossia that works to construct him'.

In '"Memory believes before knowing remembers": Faulkner, Canetti and Survival' (*PLL* 39:iii[2003] 316–34), Jeffrey J. Folks offers a comparison of the works of Faulkner and Bulgarian novelist Elias Canetti, a contemporary of Faulkner's (though there is no evidence of mutual influence). Folks argues that, despite their differing cultural, political and intellectual backgrounds, both writers have similar concerns and, more importantly, arrived at strikingly similar conclusions concerning mankind and its propensity for violence. Folks suggests that both men used their art to search for ways to transform social existence, with its implicit fear of persecution and violence, into a more enlightened and compassionate condition: 'like Canetti, William Faulkner spent a lifetime engaged in an effort to uncover the hidden realities of power, instinct and fear within human society, and to encourage humanity to transcend these destructive instincts through self-knowledge and acts of courage'.

Thomas Argiro, in '"As though we were kin": Faulkner's Black-Italian Chiasmus' (*MELUS* 28:iii[2003] 111–32), sets about investigating certain elements of Faulkner's biography from a very particular vantage point as a means of gaining insight into his writing. He argues that, although Faulkner never publicly acknowledged his mulatto or 'shadow' kin, he 'persistently created fictional figures whose lives are made problematical by racial and social contradictions similar to those present within his own family'. Argiro discusses Faulkner's use of 'an unexpected route' through representations that feature Italian Americans. He sees Faulkner employing a strategy for dealing with ambiguous racial identity that sees the identities of blacks and Italian Americans being assimilated and reversed in a 'signifying arrangement involving both displacement and substitution'. In all of this, Argiro throws light on a writer who is attempting to negotiate the problems he believes he carries because of family secrets and his public role as a writer confronting racial politics. His solution, according to Argiro, 'an anxious literary surrogacy with Italian Americans covertly enabling Faulkner's confession of his unspoken kinship with African-Americans'.

In '"What else could a southern gentleman do?": Quentin Compson, Rhett Butler and Miscegenation' (*SLJ* 35:ii[2003] 41–63), Ben Railton analyses Margaret Mitchell's *Gone With the Wind* and *Absalom, Absalom!*, and specifically the supporting characters of Compson and Butler as representative of the writers' personal understanding and attitudes towards the role of race in the southern past. Railton argues that the novels, published in the same year [1936], epitomize two key tendencies, of southern thought and issues of race in the past, that were heading towards conflict at precisely this moment. Mitchell, he argues, presents the reconstruction in such a way as to reinforce the tradition of hatred and exclusion that was a part of the established historical tradition, and this endorsement helped spread such ideas to a new and larger generation of Americans. Faulkner on the other hand is not given enough credit for the 'complex understanding of the issue of race in southern life' in *Absalom, Absalom!* The tortured prose that he described becomes for him evidence of the confrontation between Faulkner and layers of myth and evasion in not only the southern consciousness but also (and in a similar vein to Argiro and his focus on Faulkner's 'shadow' kin) his own.

In 'Southern Postcoloniality and the Improbability of Filipino-American Postcoloniality: Faulkner's *Absalom, Absalom!* and Hagedorn's *Dogeaters*' (*MissQ* 57:i[2003] 41–54), Sarita See outlines the problems Filipino Americans face in staking a claim to US postcolonial identity. The problems, she suggests, issue from the Philippine–American war's fate in American history: 'one of forgetting both by colonizers and the colonized'. See offers a number of contexts (historical, legal and literary) in which she explores the reasons for these problems. She uses Faulkner's novel in relation to Jessica Hagedorn's *Dogeaters*, as texts that are 'masterful experiments with narrative … in the distortion of sequence [that] use multiple narrators and perspectives, texts that loudly say something about history, memory, and the particular pressures that history comes to bear upon the children of war', to argue that 'Lost Cause nostalgia in its past and present forms—the insistence on the South as an occupied region—constitutes a major site for postcolonial discourse in the U.S.' From this argument, See asks the question, 'Who is inside and outside America?' That is, while US postcolonial discourse remains fixated on the 'Occupied South', the Filipino Americans will remain outside that discourse.

In 'The Political Economy of Southern Race: *Go Down, Moses*, Spatial Equality and the Color Line' (*MissQ* 57:i[2003] 55–64), Hosam Aboul-Ela argues that analysis of the literature of the Americas, a burgeoning trend within the discussion of literature in American studies, has not been sufficiently concerned to highlight spatial inequalities in the hemisphere. The paper advocates an awareness of the difficulties in simply discussing a North American writer in relation to a South American writer: 'it may not be enough, in other words, for us to speak as though the entire hemisphere has one history, one culture, and one literature, when the history and culture of the southern half of the hemisphere are so clearly marked by neo-colonial domination, while the history and culture of the United States have become a history of empire'. Aboul-Ela sees in *Go Down, Moses* a novel that gives primacy to such spatial inequalities and may provide a model for the discussion of the literature of the Americas.

Ernest Hemingway was the subject of a great deal of criticism in 2003. A comprehensive collection of essays exploring *The Sun Also Rises*, two themed anthologies of his writings, and a reference guide to *A Farewell to Arms* constitute the book-length studies. Linda Wagner-Martin, one of the foremost Hemingway scholars, has, in *Ernest Hemingway's The Sun Also Rises: A Casebook* produced an edited collection of the finest calibre interrogating every aspect of Hemingway's first novel. It brings together essays from a broad timeframe—1958–2000—and this scope is a key feature of the stated aim of the book: 'to create a montage, a palimpsest of ideas that may help to give *The Sun Also Rises* a life relevant to the twenty-first century'. One of the strengths of the book is the way in which it offers a view of the evolution of critical perspectives on the novel. The essays cover all the major themes (sexuality, gender, race, Lost Generation), and this is an immensely satisfying collection.

Wagner-Martin has also produced a magnificent resource in *Ernest Hemingway's A Farewell to Arms: A Reference Guide*. The stated aims of the book are straightforward: it is 'aimed at describing the way the novel has achieved its audience, as well as helping readers understand Hemingway's important book from a variety of perspectives'. The book is, however, more than that. This is not a dry, academic crib sheet for the novel; it is exhaustive, without being prescriptive in its provision of a range of contexts into which the novel can be placed (biographical, historical, literary, cultural). Add to that a realistic bibliography and Wagner-Martin has produced a text that will be of use to academics, students and the general reader alike.

Hemingway on Hunting, which received its paperback release in 2003, provides a comprehensive sampling of the author's writings (short stories, extracts from the novels, journalism, letters) that deal with one of his greatest passions. From a biographical introduction, written by Sean Hemingway, the anthology presents in roughly chronological structure the writings that illuminate Hemingway's relationship with the sport, and, of crucial importance, its place within his work. Framing the intentions of the whole is the excerpt from *Death in the Afternoon*, which articulates Hemingway's unusual perspective on the meaning of hunting and killing: 'Killing cleanly and in a way which gives you aesthetic pleasure and pride has always been one of the greatest enjoyments of the human race.' Sean Hemingway is concerned with trying to convey through the collection a multitude of perspectives that he sees in his grandfather's writing: 'not only the process of hunting, the actions leading up to the kill, but as many different dimensions as possible: the country, the weather, the element of chance, the hunter's thoughts, and … the perspective of the hunted'. Much of the material can be readily found elsewhere, although there are some pieces that have not been previously collected, specifically in the section on Hemingway's journalism.

Given its focus on killing, albeit killing wildlife, *Hemingway on Hunting* makes a neat companion piece to the second anthology, *Hemingway on War*, again edited by Sean Hemingway. If the subject matter of the first collection to some extent explains elements of Hemingway, this collection details a concern that in many ways created him in the first instance. The anthology is structured in much the same way, with an introductory biographical chapter that locates Hemingway and his war experiences, and then offers selections of his writing, arranged around specific wars and conflicts. Given his position as a witness to many of the major conflicts of the first of half of the twentieth century, there is in Hemingway's oeuvre much to collect, and it is to the merit of the volume that it is full, varied and resonant. The editor makes his selection from Hemingway's journalism and fiction, and a number of things emerge. First, we see a figure who is engaged with a host of political contexts, and informed and knowledgeable about a range of historical, social and cultural contexts. Secondly, we see a writer who is not merely trying to capture the experience of war by reporting it, but trying to gain and subsequently project a psychological representation of war's effects on an individual, personal level. Of note in these regards are the selections made from *Ken* magazine which present a series of harrowing images that go beyond mere reportage of a context, beyond that with which Hemingway is normally associated. The collection does not offer any new material, although some pieces are certainly more obscure. The first short story in the anthology, *The Mercenaries*, is one such example. Written by a very young Hemingway, and described as 'undistinguished' by the editor, the story does make for an excellent starting point for an exploration of Hemingway's interaction with war. As a text for Hemingway scholars, this is a useful one-stop resource, but its appeal is wider than that: this is a valuable text for anyone interested in America and war.

Articles, essays and papers dealing with Hemingway and his writings predominantly fell into two distinct categories this year: those dealing with issues of gender and sexuality and those that approach his work from a biographical direction. Scott Donaldson, in 'The Averted Gaze in Hemingway's Fiction' (*SR* 111:i[2003] 128–51), explores the form and function of scopophilia in the author's writings. He argues that there are few examples in Hemingway's novels of the traditional masculine gaze that would suggest male dominance, and that this is initially counter-intuitive. That is, that the absence of the degrading male gaze may seem odd given Hemingway's public macho persona. Donaldson makes the distinction here between Hemingway as a public figure and Hemingway as writer. From this perspective, Donaldson proceeds to offer a series of close readings and biographical vignettes that illustrate the centrality of looking in Hemingway's writing, and how that motif evolved. In so doing, Donaldson presents the averted gaze as a major vehicle for emotions and feeling, a subtextual motif that corresponds not only with the iceberg style, but also Hemingway's self-professed aversion to 'writing love'. The range of Hemingway's fiction that Donaldson analyses is broad, though *The Sun Also Rises* and Hemingway's short fiction provide specific focus. This is an interesting article that opens up a fascinating element of Hemingway's tendency.

Richard Fantina in his challenging and contentious 'Hemingway's Masochism, Sodomy, and the Dominant Woman' (*Hemingway Review* 23:i[2003] 84–105) also begins by making a distinction between Hemingway the writer and Hemingway the public persona, and seeks to locate Hemingway's work within recent debate in gender theory that deals with masculine sexuality and masochism. Fantina suggests that masochism has been falsely connected to homosexuality and/or femininity in contemporary criticism. He sees in Hemingway an indication of 'a masochistic sensibility coexisting with his cult of traditional masculinity'. Although he recognizes that this is diametrically opposed to his public persona, he argues that Hemingway's writing embodies 'diverse models of masculinity [which] may be his greatest legacy.' Fantina proceeds to illustrate how Hemingway's work 'dethrones' the male phallus and celebrates sodomy performed on the man by the woman. This sodomy is revealed in direct fashion, as in *The Garden of Eden*, or through metaphor, usually in relation to a gun or rifle and its nearness to the male. In all of this, his concern is male penetration, such that a gunshot wound contains the necessary sexual allusion. Fantina takes examples from characters such as Brett Ashley, Margot Macomber, Helen and Miss Mary, but he suggests that Catherine Bourne in *The Garden of Eden*is an accumulation of these concerns.

Continuing the gender/sexuality theme, Marc Hewson, in '"The Real Story of Ernest Hemingway": Cixous, Gender and *A Farewell to Arms*' (*Hemingway Review* 22:ii[2003] 51–62), explores a way of reading the novel as detailing Hemingway's dissatisfaction with cultural definitions of gender. Working with Hélène Cixous's definition of bisexuality (that 'all people are innately both masculine and feminine', but that Western culture has privileged masculinity and created a hierarchy of gender in which the masculine value is positive and the feminine negative), he suggests that *A Farewell to Arms* is a 'nascent—if unconscious—example of Cixous' *écriture feminine*'. Hewson argues that, although the early parts of the novel see Frederick Henry trying to work within a traditional masculine narrative, increasingly it presents such constructions being undone. Hewson extends his analysis to look in detail at the central relationship between Henry and Catherine Barkley. In it he sees a similar dynamic: once Henry is removed from the combat situation, the relationship moves from masculine concepts of proprietorship and commodification to a clearer, equal love. Hewson is careful to note that this reading is not infallible, and presents several counter-arguments, but the essay does highlight some very interesting connections between Hemingway and Cixous's ideas, and illuminates Hemingway's concerns with gender and his attempts to come to terms with them.

In relation to the biographical trend in Hemingway criticism this year, Sean O'Rourke, in 'Who Was with Pascin at the Dome?' (*JML* 26:ii[2003] 160–3), discusses a moment in *A Moveable Feast* where Hemingway recounts meeting the painter Jules Pascin at the Dome in Paris in 1925. He argues that on the surface it is 'a banal piece of writing', but that, if scrutinized more closely, the episode actually dramatizes what O'Rourke sees as the key themes of the book: 'industry and idleness, poverty and affluence, innocence and corruption'. In a meticulous deconstruction of the episode, O'Rourke effectively answers questions such as why Hemingway would devote a chapter to 'a 2nd rate artist and man about town': 'the chapter's subject is Hemingway and not Pascin'. Hemingway, he argues, uses Pascin to portray himself as hard-working and a devoted family man. O'Rourke concludes that the scene is a composite: Hemingway did not meet Pascin in 1925, but, regardless, the scene illuminates Hemingway's purpose.

This ability of Hemingway to fictionalize real events effectively also lies at the heart of Matthew Stewart's '"It was all a pleasant business": The Historical Context of *On the Quai at Smyrna*' (*Hemingway Review* 23:i[2003] 58–71). By exploring the specifics of the event itself, and the process by which Hemingway would have learned of them, Stewart offers an insightful reading of the story. At the heart of the essay is an attempt to understand and account for its remarkable and puzzling narrator. In his search for answers, he offers historical and diplomatic contextualization of the event and biographical detail that he believes will help the reader to form a better sense of the whole. He concludes that the tone of the narrator can be explained: 'his mind has been working overtime to overcome the self-disgust engendered by an enforced and prolonged powerlessness'. Stewart gives a fascinating combination of perspectives that provide illumination on an ambiguous story.

John Leonard, in '*The Garden of Eden*: A Question of Dates' (*Hemingway Review* 22:ii[2003] 63–85), provides an insight into the vexed issue of when the novel was produced. Biographers and critics have proposed a wide variety of conflicting dates for its composition, ranging from 1946 to 1958. Leonard, through an examination of dates written in the margins of Hemingway's manuscripts, argues that chapters 13 to 35 were written between 20 May and 11 September 1957. He proceeds to overlay these dates on events in Hemingway's life, aiming to establish *The Garden of Eden* as a 'fully achieved narrative written very late in the life of a great American author'. The article is a comprehensive and valuable piece of primary research.

Paul Quick, in 'Hemingway's *A Way You'll Never Be* and Nick Adams' Search for Identity' (*Hemingway Review* 22:ii[2003] 30–44), also focuses closely on one story and makes use of biographical information in its analysis. The essay explores Nick's crisis of self in the wake of his wounding. Quick argues that Adams has returned to the site of the wounding to affirm his sense of self, but is continually confronted with obstacles. Beginning with an interrogation of the purpose of his visit and subsequently analysing the two hallucinations, Quick explores issues and symbols such as cowardice and the yellow house, the repeated questioning of Adams's identity, and issues of post-traumatic stress. Quick's handling of chronological issues is somewhat contrived, something that he recognizes. However, this paper offers an interesting perspective on a traditionally undervalued story.

In '*Hills Like White Elephants*: The Jilting of Jig' (*Hemingway Review* 23:i[2003] 72–83), Nilofer Hashmi explores one of Hemingway's most acclaimed but also most divisive stories. Nilofer sets out to determine why it is that critics have been able to read the story in so many different ways. The ambiguous ending leads Nilofer to discuss three existing versions of the end of the novel: 'the girl will have the abortion … and stay with the man; the girl will have the abortion and leave the man; or the girl will not have the abortion having won the man over to her point of view'. Crucially, he proceeds to add a fourth: that the girl will have the abortion, expecting to stay with the man, but will be abandoned once the operation has been performed. In an authoritative interrogation of existing perspectives Nilofer persuasively argues for his fourth way.

Suzanne del Gizzo, in 'Going Home: Hemingway, Primitivism and Identity' (*MFS* 49:iii[2003] 496–523), offers an authoritative look at the way in which white writers use racial difference to construct white identity. Looking at Hemingway's African safaris, she suggests that while his race changes express his longing for authenticity and origins, they ultimately point to the hybridity and performativity of identity. She argues that the primitive is a theme that exerted a powerful influence over Hemingway at every stage of his development and that he continued to return to it even after its cultural moment was over. Trying to unravel what the primitive actually connotes for Hemingway, she suggests that initially he 'exploited assumptions about the primitive, specifically its resonance in Anglo-American culture with physicality and authenticity, to cultivate and fuel his public persona', but 'ultimately it was his engagement and identification with primitive cultures that allowed him to distance himself from that persona and articulate a profound self-critique'. She presents Hemingway as not simply an observer of different cultures but one who wishes to identify with them, one who sought through rites and feats to become one of them. Del Gizzo, by tracking these themes through his life and work, from Native Americans through the Paris years, from Africa to his unfinished works, concludes that Hemingway's concern with the primitive is not simply about being authentic, but acts as a means for rewriting the self.

F. Scott Fitzgerald was relatively neglected this year, although a number of book-length studies published in 2003 were unavailable for review: Ronald Berman, *Fitzgerald—Wilson—Hemingway: Language and Experience* [UAlaP]; Harold Bloom, ed., *F. Scott Fitzgerald's The Great Gatsby* [ChelseaH]; Jackson R. Bryer, Ruth Prigozy and Milton R. Stern, eds., *F. Scott Fitzgerald in the Twenty-First Century: Centennial Essays* [UAlaP]; and Bernard R. Tanner, *F. Scott Fitzgerald's Odyssey: A Reader's Guide to the Gospel in The Great Gatsby* [R&L]. Of note is *Conversations with F. Scott Fitzgerald*, edited by Matthew J. Bruccoli and Judith S. Baughman. The anthology collects thirty-seven interviews spanning 1920–39. As noted in the introduction, these are not traditional interviews; indeed only one, a three-part interview that appeared in the *St. Paul Daily News* in 1922, fits the description readily. The rest are reports that use quotes from Fitzgerald. The real interest generated by these pieces emerges from the insight into Fitzgerald's public image, the lack of savvy he displays in his dealings with the media, and consequently the way in which he did not receive the same respect as his contemporaries. Weighed against the revival in the post-war period of his literary merit, and his current place in American literature, the reports in the collection are fascinating.

In 'Fitzgerald's French' (*TCL* 49:i[2003] 123–30), Michael Hollington discusses the fascination the novelist had with the French language as a vehicle not only for dreams but also for issues of class and social pretension. Hollington describes Fitzgerald's childhood years in St Paul, Minnesota, a city that was originally French Canadian, where he was surrounded by French names. From this basis, Hollington discusses the way in which French 'became for him a language of dream expressing fantasies and glamour, elegance, sexual conquest and upward mobility—even if all these were equally understood by his daytime consciousness as pretensions offering apt targets for social satire'. Hollington also suggests that failure to speak French well becomes a symptom, in *Tender Is the Night* in particular, of the modernist preoccupation with decline and dissolution.

In 'White Skin, White Mask: Passing, Posing and Performing in *The Great Gatsby*' (*MFS* 49:iii[2003] 443–68), Meredith Goldsmith reads the novel against post-First World War African American identity formation. Specifically, she argues that Gatsby's parties miniaturize the process of identity formation that characterizes the novel as a whole. Goldsmith, by identifying the racial analogies with which the characters describe the scandal of Jay Gatsby's success, points to the ways in which 'racial miscegenation and immigrant ethnic assimilation provide models of identity formation and upward mobility more easily comprehensible than the amalgam of commerce, love and ambition underlying Gatsby's rise'. In all of this Goldsmith is pointing to a gap in the narration of white working-class masculinity, one that reveals an interdependence of such working-class identity with African American and ethnic models, and consequently exposes 'an alternative genealogy for the man who remains, in Maxwell Perkins's words, "more or less a mystery"'.

There was a body of material this year dealing with the less prominent novelists of this period. Theodore Dreiser has two books worthy of mention. First, the Library of America has produced a fine edition of *An American Tragedy* with illuminating notes by Thomas P. Riggio. The other book is Newlin, ed., *A Theodore Dreiser Encyclopedia*, which attempts to synthesize the vast body of material written by and about the author into a wide-ranging single reference volume. Made up from contributions by well-established Dreiser scholars as well as newer academics, this volume is an essential resource, with a comprehensive and nuanced bibliography and the benefit of being not only academically rigorous but also lively and engaging.

It is welcome to see among the more renowned names a book discussing a novelist, and specifically a novel, that tends to be overlooked. In Graulich and Tatum, eds., *Reading 'The Virginian' in the New West*, the contributors seek to offer readings that challenge the traditional conception of Owen Wister's novel.

The collection, published to commemorate the novel's centennial, challenges the traditional view that the novel is notable because it inaugurated the generic Western. By applying a range of theoretical perspectives to the novel, the contributors illuminate a variety of themes and issues. Graulich suggests in the introduction that Wister and the novel are often dismissed on the grounds of racism, misogyny, imperialism and elitism, and the collection does not necessarily try to rectify these criticisms. Rather, it seeks to illustrate how the novel has functioned and continues to function as a social text, whose interpretation evolves with the historical and cultural context. As such the writers illuminate and account for the novel's continuing relevance. The eleven essays which make up the collection foreground the theory a little too heavily at times, leaving textual analysis sometimes unsatisfactorily underdeveloped (there is no attempt for example to broaden findings in relation to Wister's other works). The collection is varied, illuminating and engaging. The stated aim is to give readers the opportunity to think differently about Wister and *The Virginian*, and in that they have been eminently successful.

In 'Before the White Negro: Sin and Salvation in *Kingsblood Royal*' (*AmLH* 15[2003] 311–33), Jennifer Delton seeks to rescue Sinclair Lewis's novel from the charge that it fails to have any impact upon the issue of race relations in the US by arguing that it extends a critique of American society to notions of whiteness and blackness and sin and salvation, overturning the traditional pairings of these concepts. The piece offers a broad sense of the novel's fit historically and socially, and provides a detailed reading of the story itself. Delton suggests that 'in the pages of *Kingsblood Royal* two previously separate phenomena converged: "the African-American struggle for justice … and white cultural anxieties about purpose and salvation in modern, capitalist America"'. For Delton the contradiction between 'white anti-racism, which promised whites a way out of the consequences of material abundance, and black civil rights, which promised blacks a way to partake of the benefits of this abundance' has, by keeping open a door for salvation and grace, 'save[d] white America from itself'.

In 'From Modernity's Detection to Modernist Detectives: Narrative Vision in the Work of Allan Pinkerton and Dashiell Hammett' (*MFS* 49:iv[2003] 629–59), Christopher T. Raczkowski offers a fascinating and insightful comparison of Pinkerton's post-Civil War memoirs and the prohibition era detective fiction of ex-Pinkerton detective Dashiell Hammett. He suggests that between the works of the two men there is a critical shift in how vision is constructed: visual-oriented enlightenment, as Raczkowski suggests, being a source of disillusionment for modernism. He presents Pinkerton's memoirs as representative of a type of vision that makes 'crime and criminals visible to the state'. In that sense the detective has a 'rational, scientific, technocratic gaze … [and is] an instrument of American political and economic modernity'. Hammett, he argues, refuses this 'epistemological priority of vision' and from this perspective transforms the character of the detective into a 'literary modernist agent for the critique of modernity'.

In '"No ties except blood": Class, Race, and Jack London's American Plague' (*PLL* 39:iv[2003] 390–430), David Raney argues that *The Scarlet Plague* offers a literary version of the issue of twentieth-century immigration and national identity. He suggests that London had long been interested in germs and infection, and that it appears as a theme in several of his works. Raney discusses the arrival of such terms in historical, social and literary contexts and the way in which they became representative of issues such as class and race. He discusses *The Scarlet Plague*'s opening sequence as indicative of London's tendency. The image of the decrepit railroad, a symbol of man's ascendancy, now overrun by nature, offers an immediate suggestion of man's place having been reclaimed by nature; but this attack on the natural order, Raney argues, was constructed 'only so that nature's royalty, the Anglo-Saxon, can reinstate it'. In 'Rethinking Authorship: Jack London and the Motion Picture Industry' (*AL* 75:i[2003] 91–117), Marsha Orgeron discusses London's relationship with cinema, and specifically the willingness he demonstrated in selling himself, his 'brand' name, while in the process rejecting 'the sacred status of the single author'. Although his cinematic dealings, as Orgeron describes them, were not terribly successful, he remained to the end optimistic that motion pictures offered a future for him. In London, Orgeron presents a writer who foreshadows the many other writers who would experience a similar fate and attempt to make their name and fortune by adapting their work to and working in Hollywood.

The substantial, four-volume *Willa Cather: Critical Assessments*, edited by Guy Reynolds, provides a rich resource for Cather scholars this year. The collection forms part of a series which aims to 'offer students and researchers authoritative overviews of the often discouraging mass of critical material on significant writers', and to make accessible, 'difficult to locate and out-of-print' documents. Volume 1, *Memoirs and Recollections: General Responses and Critical Overviews*, includes the reminiscences of close personal acquaintances of Willa Cather, including Edith Lewis and Yehudi Menuhin, together with a range of critical responses to her writings from Lionel Trilling, V.L. Parrington, and Carl Van Doren, amongst others, which chart developments in Cather studies from the 1920s to the 1960s. Volume 2, *Critical Reviews and Intertextualities*, contains reviews of individual Cather works dating from 1913 to 1950, and essays on her connections with writers such as Edgar Allan Poe and Walt Whitman. In volume 3, *Essays on Specific Works*, Reynolds brings together the critical assessments of notable Cather scholars including Sharon O'Brien, Hermione Lee, and Cynthia Griffin Wolff. Volume 4, *New Approaches to Willa Cather*, is organized according to the multiplicity of readings and interpretations Cather's writing has generated. This section includes writings from Susan J. Rosowski on Cather and the literature of place, Sandra Gilbert and Susan Gubar on Cather and gender studies, and Paul Borgman on Cather and religion. This collection is an invaluable resource for Cather scholars, providing an impressive survey of the changing responses to the writer and her work throughout the twentieth century.

In Perry and Weaks, eds., *The History of Southern Women's Literature*, published but not reviewed last year, Willa Cather's work is considered in a regional context, as part of a broad survey of female-authored literature from the southern states. With contributions from notable scholars including Helen Taylor, Elizabeth Fox-Genovese, Linda Wagner-Martin, and Anne Goodwyn Jones, this comprehensive text identifies traditions, and traces developments in southern women's writings from the antebellum era to the present day. In addition to addressing issues of evolving genre and form, the volume brings together critical interpretations of the work of a great diversity of writers—Harriet Jacobs, Mary Chestnut, Kate Chopin, Ellen Glasgow, Katherine Anne Porter, and Zora Neale Hurston amongst them—whose writings are informed by a distinctly southern culture. In her appraisal of *Sapphira and the Slave Girl*, which she describes as Cather's 'only southern novel', Elizabeth Jane Harrison discusses the author's rejection and revision of 'the masculine "pastoral impulse"—to feminize the landscape and objectify women characters'. Cather's 'alternative female pastoral', she notes, 'undermine[s] the mythic construction of the southern garden', enabling the 'psychological development of a woman protagonist' and the creation of 'autonomous female characters'.

Two articles take as their theme the unspoken Native American presence in Willa Cather's writings. In 'The Enclosure of America: Civilization and Confinement in Willa Cather's *O Pioneers!*' (*AL* 75:ii[2003] 275–304), Melissa Ryan considers Cather's 'latent ambivalence toward the pioneering enterprise'. Exploring the tensions in the novel between the freedom of the unbound space and the boundaries imposed as that space is 'civilized', she identifies a subtext of anxiety about the displacement and confinement to reservations of the indigenous population. Identifying numerous Native American resonances as, for example, in the fantasy figure of Alexandra Bergson's recurring vision, Ryan asserts that this anxiety 'constitutes the most deeply disavowed layer of meaning embedded in Cather's complex motif of enclosure'. In '"Fragmentary and Inconclusive" Violence: National History and Literary Form in *The Professor's House*' (*AL* 75:iii[2003] 571–600), Sarah Wilson reads the 1925 novel as Willa Cather's 'historicist critique of nostalgia', and as a commentary on the construction of national identity through an appropriation of Native American artefacts. Paying particular attention to the fragmentary form of the text, she identifies the 'stand alone' narration of the archaeological recovery, sale and ownership of ancient relics as 'formal witness to Cather's discomfort with, and ambivalence about, the colonial gaze at work in the building of national histories'. Ancient American relics and artefacts also figure in María Carla Sánchez's 'Immovable: Willa Cather's Logic of Art and Place' (*WAL* 32:ii[2003] 117–30). Citing Walter Benjamin's theory that 'even the most perfect reproduction of a work of art is lacking in one element: its presence in time and space, its unique existence at the place where it happens to be', Sánchez interrogates Cather's association of particular aesthetic cultures with specific regions and the 'loss of meaning' which accompanies 'reproduction, substitution and, most of all, movement'. In an essay which interprets the novel *Death Comes for the Archbishop* as a lament for the 'pillaging of southwestern artifacts', Sánchez claims that, for Willa Cather, 'Just as carved images detached from Catholic churches in New Mexico may not signify what they should or could, in Chicago, Robert Browning poems become pathetic when recited by a lush in a frontier bar.'

In 'Willa Cather's Reluctant New Woman Pioneer' (*GPQ* 23:ii[2003] 161–73), Reginald Dyck argues that in Alexandra Bergson, the single, independent, 'entrepreneurial' female protagonist of the 1913 novel *O Pioneers!*, Willa Cather creates a contradictory and ambiguous version of the 'New Woman'. The article discusses the way in which the rapid industrialization and urbanization of the period generated a demand for nostalgic literary representations of pioneer life, connecting this with Cather's interrogation of the options available to women as a result of the new cultural conditions, options which are figured in terms of both opportunity and personal loss: 'Alexandra is emblematic of the struggle the United States faced at the turn of the twentieth century in reconciling its rural, pioneer past with the cultural transformations inherent in the urban New Woman and the industrialism from which she emerged.' Janis P. Stout takes an original approach to Cather's writings this year, focusing not on her extensively debated prose works, but on her lesser-known poetry. In 'Willa Cather's Poetry and the Object(s) of Art' (*ALR* 35:ii[2003] 159–74), Stout notes that Cather wrote poetry throughout her life, and that it was an activity which provided her with 'a vehicle for her prolonged engagement with the nature of art and the artist and the social function of the artist's work'. Tracing Cather's poetic maturation, she identifies a move away from early 'Arcadian artifice' to 'a celebration of the commonplace', a development which Stout claims is reflected in the author's prose fiction. In a consideration of the poem 'Poor Marty', which is 'a tribute to the daily work of the humble household servant in the kitchen', the essay identifies 'the linkage of art with home, or dailiness' as Cather's central and most important literary theme.

In Henderson, ed., *Seers and Judges: American Literature as Political Philosophy*, published but not reviewed last year, Christine Dunn Henderson applies the work of Alexis de Tocqueville to the writings of Willa Cather. Responding to the social theorist's comments on the derivative nature of American literature and the absence in the nation of a distinctive literary voice, she identifies Cather, along with Mark Twain, Ernest Hemingway and F. Scott Fitzgerald, as a particularly 'American' artist. Henderson describes *The Song of the Lark* as a 'decidedly American novel', pointing out that the 'individualism', 'independence' and 'self-determinism' demonstrated by Thea Kronborg, the novel's central protagonist, 'correspond to Tocqueville's observations about the American character'. She notes that both Cather and de Tocqueville are critical of such 'democratic individualism', de Tocqueville concentrating on its 'harmful effects on American politics, Cather focusing on its 'deleterious effects upon human beings'. Despina Korovessis's contribution, '*The House of Mirth*: Edith Wharton's Critique of American Society', examines *The House of Mirth* through a de Tocquevillian lens, and claims to engage a 'previously unexplored aspect' of the text. There is, however, much that is familiar in this discussion of a society debased by its preoccupation with materialism and a heroine ruined by her desire for wealth.

Cather and Wharton also share space in *Civil Wars: American Novelists and Manners 1880–1940*, by Susan Goodman, a study that also treats the work of William Dean Howells, Henry James, Ellen Glasgow and Jessie Fauset. Tracing the relationship between manners and American fiction around the start of the twentieth century, Goodman identifies the emphasis on manners as a 'defining quality' in American letters. While acknowledging that Willa Cather is not 'a novelist of manners in the traditional sense', her discussions of *The Professor's House*, *Shadows on the Rock* and *Sapphira and the Slave Girl* suggest that Cather repeatedly 'arrests a moment in history and tests her characters against accepted standards of conduct' and that the author's 'understanding of manners is tied to her brand of "regionalism"'. Across the body of her fiction, Goodman notes, Cather demonstrates a 'continued interest in social boundaries'. Unlike Cather, Wharton is discussed in terms of the 'traditional' novelist of manners. Drawing on Wharton's long association and deep affinity with the customs, practices and traditions of Europe, Goodman examines *The Decoration of Houses*, *The Valley of Decision* and *The Age of Innocence* to consider the way in which Wharton uses manners as 'cultural indicators' in her critique of modern American society. The keen interest in architecture and interior design that infuses her work, together with her frequent association of people and place, human character and architecture, are interpreted as Wharton's attribution of a 'spatial dimension to manners'.

In the *Student Companion to Edith Wharton*, part of the Greenwood Press Student Companions to Classic Writers series, Melissa McFarland Pennell offers an introduction to Wharton's life and work, 'designed to meet the needs of students and general readers'. Following the series template, Pennell includes an informative biographical chapter and one which provides a general overview of Edith Wharton's writings, together with a consideration of her contributions to the short story, travel writing, the novel of manners, and the Gothic. Subsequent chapters address a selection of individual works: *The House of Mirth* [1905], *Ethan Frome* [1911], *Summer* [1917] and *The Age of Innocence* [1920], each divided into headed sub-sections which pay attention to issues of setting, plot, character, theme, and symbol. While the layout suggests a standard, rudimentary study guide, the *Companion* distinguishes itself through the inclusion of 'alternative reading' sections that introduce a range of critical approaches and interpretations to encourage independent, analytical understandings of the work. With reference to Foucault and Bakhtin, Pennell discusses *The House of Mirth* in the context of new historicist criticism; she offers a Marxist reading of *Ethan Frome*, and applies feminist literary theory to *Summer*. These accessible elementary-level engagements with critical interpretation are supported by an extensive bibliography. The volume offers a basic but effective introduction to Wharton studies.

This year saw the publication of a valuable contribution to the Norton Critical Edition series: Wharton's *The Age of Innocence*, edited by Candace Waid. In addition to the scholarly annotations to the novel and an informative introduction, Waid includes an extensive range of documents, maps, photographs, and illustrations, which effectively situate the text within social, cultural, and historical frameworks. In bringing together a rich variety of material contemporary with the novel's late nineteenth-century setting, the 'Background and Contexts' and 'Sources' sections provide an illuminating picture of the economic climate, attitudes to marriage and divorce, changing social etiquette and mores, and the lifestyles of the leisure-class, old New York 'aristocracy'. Particularly worthy of note are the extracts from an 1888 newspaper interview with Ward McAllister, 'the recognized master of protocol', and the recipes for 'Roman Punch' from *The Encyclopedia of Practical Cookery*. Waid's selection of critical approaches to the novel is divided into 'Reviews' and 'Modern Criticism'. The former includes early responses from prominent figures in America and Britain, including the frequently reproduced 'Our Literary

Aristocrat' by Vernon L. Parrington. The latter reprints extracts from important studies of Wharton's work, for example, '*The Age of Innocence* as Bildungsroman', from Cynthia Griffin Wolff's *A Feast of Words: The Triumph of Edith Wharton*, as well as including several new essays written specifically for this edition. In '"To read these pages is to live again": The Historical Accuracy of *The Age of Innocence*', Julia Ehrhardt explores the 'extraordinary number, depth, and breadth of the historical references' in the novel and the controversy and debate that ensued as, post-publication, Wharton responded to her critics' 'petty' preoccupation with minor textual inaccuracies. Jennifer Rae Greeson offers a consideration of the composition of the novel, and the careful 'creative process' in which Wharton engaged, discussing the three plot outlines of *The Age of Innocence* housed in the Beinecke Library at Yale University. Further contributions to this section include an examination of Martin Scorsese's 1993 cinematic adaptation of the novel and an essay giving prominence to issues of race, reading Ellen Olenska as a 'dark heroine'. This authoritative edition also includes a comprehensive bibliography of Wharton criticism.

Carol J. Singley makes a significant contribution to Wharton scholarship this year, editing both *Edith Wharton's The House of Mirth: A Casebook*, and *A Historical Guide to Edith Wharton*. In the casebook Singley provides an introduction to the novel and its critical reception, reproduces Wharton's introduction to the 1936 edition of *The House of Mirth*, and includes extracts from the author's autobiography, *A Backward Glance*. She also reprints eleven essays which will be very familiar to scholars of Wharton but which are, nonetheless, important studies and offer a range of critical approaches to the novel. Included here are Elaine Showalter's 'The Death of the Lady (Novelist): Wharton's *House of Mirth*', which draws comparisons between Wharton's narrative and Kate Chopin's *The Awakening*, both identified by Showalter as examples of 'the novel of the woman of thirty'; and 'Debasing Exchange: Edith Wharton's *The House of Mirth*', by Wai Chee Dimock, which explores the significance of economics and market forces in the text. The work of notable Wharton scholars Shari Benstock, Amy Kaplan, and Cynthia Griffin Wolff is also represented in this study, which provides a useful resource for students new to the novel.

The *Historical Guide*—'historical' in the sense that it places Wharton and her work within the literary, political and social contexts of a particular cultural moment between Victorianism and modernity—brings together a series of new essays written specifically for the volume. Shari Benstock contributes 'A Brief Biography' of Edith Wharton. Ranging widely across Wharton's fiction (*The Age of Innocence*, *The House of Mirth*, *The Custom of The Country*, *Ethan Frome*, *The Mother's Recompense*), Martha Banta considers the author's use, particularly of women's fashions, but also of domestic interiors, architectural styles, modes of transport and communications, as 'important markers by which she traced shifts in the social habitus occupied by her fictional characters in the final decades of the nineteenth century and the first three decades of the twentieth century'. Focusing on the 1913 novel *The Custom of the Country*, Cecelia Tichi examines the influence of Darwinian theory on Wharton's writing, and Dale M. Bauer discusses Wharton's complex portrayals of female sexuality, suggesting that, for her female characters, sexual expression is frequently substituted by drug addiction. Through an examination of *The House of Mirth*, *The Fruit of the Tree* and *Ethan Frome*, Bauer argues that 'Wharton's ambivalence about modern sexuality surfaces in her social critique of alienation, which she understood not as repression or absence of passion, but as passion misdirected toward objects and ideas, or, worse, as passion degraded to desire-driven consumerism.' The volume also contains an illustrated chronology of Wharton's life and work, and includes contributions from Nancy Bentley on 'Wharton, Travel, and Modernity' and Linda Costanzo Cahir on cinematic adaptations of the author's writings, and a comprehensive 'Bibliographic Essay' from Clare Colquitt.

Two essays in Papke, ed., *Twisted from the Ordinary: Essays on American Literary Naturalism*, are devoted to Edith Wharton. Donna M. Campbell explores the literary relationship between *The House of Mirth* [1905] and David Graham Phillips's *Susan Lenox: Her Fall and Rise* [1917], a novel for which Wharton expressed particular admiration. Describing the later novel as both 'a retrospective commentary' and 'a dark mirror version' of *The House of Mirth*, Campbell draws parallels of plot, characterization, and language, including the 'language of Darwinian thought', between the two naturalistic narratives. In *Susan Lenox*, she claims, Edith Wharton found a 'vindication' of her own literary vision and social critique. In '"Hunting for the Real": Responses to Art in Edith Wharton's *Custom of The Country*', Lilian R. Furst draws on the work of Walter Benjamin to explore the novel's preoccupation with the authentic work of art. Discussing the naturalistic struggle for survival in which the old social order is pitted against the new money 'invader', she notes that differences are articulated primarily through 'divergent attitudes toward works of art'.

In 'Property and Identity in *The Custom of the Country*' (*MFS* 49:iv[2003] 687–713), Ticien Marie Sassoubre argues that, although Wharton's novel is most often interpreted in semi-autobiographical terms, as a narrative about divorce or the patriarchal oppression of women, it can also be read as 'a novel about the changing property relations and the ways in which those property relations are constitutive of personal identity'. Discussing Wharton's articulation of the commodification of human attributes, she figures Undine Spragg, the novel's protagonist, as, 'a creature of new market conditions', who is willing 'to exchange sex for status and her child for cash' as a reflection of 'Wharton's concern that the collapse of stable property relations precipitates a failure of interpersonal relationships'. *The Custom of the Country* also features in Debora Clarke, 'Women on Wheels: "A threat at yesterday's order of things"' (*ArQ* 59:iv[2003] 103–36), which considers the way in which 'women's access to the automobile … profoundly transformed American culture and helped to shape twentieth-century American literature'. Clarke offers a fascinating insight into the carefully managed marketing campaigns employed by companies such as Ford, which sought to negate cultural anxieties about the greater freedoms afforded to women by 'auto-mobility', by positioning them as consumers while at the same time presenting them within traditionally domestic roles. She goes on to offer a reading of *The Custom of the Country* in which Undine Spragg 'like the motor-car, seems to represent the new age of automobility—rapacious and unfeeling, highlighting the tension between old and new and, increasingly between men and women'.

Anne M. Fields', '"Years hence of these scenes": Wharton's *The Spark* and World War I' (*EWhR* 19:ii[2003] 1–9), argues that despite the novella's nineteenth-century setting, its many references to time and change identify it as 'a part of Wharton's World War I corpus', informed by the author's anxiety about writing, as a woman, in the male-dominated arena of war. She makes connections between this text and the body of Wharton's war writings in terms of their shared 'sense of the incommunicable' and 'motifs of interrupted expression'. An essay worthy of note this year is '"This isn't exactly a ghost story": Edith Wharton and Parodic Gothic' (*JAmS* 37:ii[2003] 269–87), in which Janet Beer and Avril Horner discuss Wharton's 'indebtedness' to, but also her 'independence' from, previous practitioners of the Gothic mode, including the Brontës, Hawthorne, Stevenson and Le Fanu. The introduction of 'parody'—defined as 'a literary mode that, whilst engaging with a target text or genre, exhibits a keen sense of the comic, an acute awareness of intertextuality and an engagement with the idea of metafiction'—is identified as the feature that distinguishes Wharton's Gothic from its precursors. Considering the short stories 'Miss Mary Pask' [1926], 'Bewitched' [1926] and 'All Souls' [1937], and making connections between these narratives and texts such as *Wuthering Heights* and *The Scarlet Letter*, the essay examines Edith Wharton's skilful appropriation and manipulation of the genre, including her excessive and humorous use of 'Gothic clichés'. Beer and Horner note that Wharton's shift into parodic mode 'most often occurs when the sexual appetite of women' is at the heart of the narrative. They argue that, rather than being 'subversive in the classic Gothic sense' of taboo-breaking and challenges to legitimacy, in her ghost stories Wharton 'uses comedy and the idea of the supernatural to unsettle conventional values and beliefs'. Also considering Wharton's writing in the context of Gothic fiction this year is Kathy Justice Gentile's contribution to Hoeveler and Heller, eds., *Approaches to Teaching Gothic Fiction: The British and American Traditions.* Discussing Wharton's short stories 'The Lady's Maid's Bell' [1904] and 'The Pomegranate Seed' [1931], alongside others by Sarah Orne Jewett, Mary Wilkins Freeman and Charlotte Perkins Gilman, Gentile offers strategies for teaching the writings which she describes as 'supernaturalized commentaries on gendered fin de siècle anxieties'. The essay also includes a brief discussion of Gilman's best-known short story, 'The Yellow Wall-paper'.

Studies of the work of Charlotte Perkins Gilman continue to concentrate on analysis of this particular story, and two publications this year take as their focus pedagogical approaches to the text. Weinstock, ed., *The Pedagogical Wallpaper: Teaching Charlotte Perkins Gilman's 'The Yellow Wall-paper'*, offers a range of strategies for utilizing the text, as a teaching tool, including Formalist, Existentialist, Genre, Reader Response, and Dialogic approaches. Aimed at a secondary and early-stage undergraduate studentship, the volume includes contributions from educators who offer both critical appraisals of the text and ideas for practical classroom application. Many contributors suggest lists of questions for classroom discussion; some offer reflection on learning outcomes and a consideration of student responses. Janet Gebhart Auten advocates encouraging students to engage with the text through the production of what she calls a 'sequential-response' journal, their 'initial impressions' and 'emotional responses' recorded as they read. Jim O'Loughlin recommends dividing the student group, having one half read Gilman's text alongside Poe's 'The Fall of the House of Usher', while the others read it in conversation with Steinam's 'Ruth's Song', a practice which, he testifies, stimulates vigorous debate about generic convention and expectation. Debra K. Peterson introduces the innovative concept of student interaction with the characters and setting of 'The Yellow Wall-paper' through the medium of computer technology and virtual space, although to appreciate this strategy fully the less computer literate will first have to negotiate explanations of 'MOO' or 'Multi User Domain, Object-Oriented Spaces'. Some contributions are, perhaps inevitably, less useful than others, providing rather rigid and prescriptive lesson plans which lack the flexibility for adaptation. In the main, however, this text provides a useful pedagogical tool.

In Knight and Davis, eds., *Approaches to Teaching Gilman's 'The Yellow Wall-Paper' and Herland*, a contribution to an established series, Denise D. Knight and Cynthia J. Davies bring together strategies for teaching 'The Yellow Wall-paper' as well as a range of approaches to Gilman's 1915 utopian novel *Herland*. Highlights of this volume include Carol Farley Kessler and Priscilla Ferguson Clement's 'Using Role-Playing in Teaching "The Yellow Wall-paper"', which seeks, through dramatization of the text, to broaden students' understanding of 'male and female gender-role expectations' at the time of the story's composition in 1892, and an essay by Lisa Ganobcsik-Williams which suggests that Gilman's problematic treatment of race and ethnicity in the novel is 'more complex than simple bigotry', identifying her racist sentiments as a part of her social evolutionary theory in which some races were positioned at a more advanced stage of progression than others. A useful contribution from Cynthia J. Davis considers Gilman's short story in the context of American literary realism and naturalism. The volume also contains a section offering approaches to teaching a wider range of Gilman's writings. Notable amongst these is Michelle N. McEvoy's examination of the way in which Gilman employs a variety of forms and genres, including utopian novels, short stories, Gothic writings, journalism, sociological studies and poetry, as vehicles to promote her socialist reform agenda. Gilman's socialist vision is also the subject of Jennifer Hudak, 'The "Social Inventor": Charlotte Perkins Gilman and the (Re)Production of Perfection' (*WS* 32:iv [2003] 455–77), which examines the influence of 'the discourses of evolution and eugenics' on the utopian novel *Herland*. This essay discusses the ways in which Gilman's writings were shaped by scientific and evolutionary theories, most particularly those of 'reformer-Darwinist' Lester F. Ward.

3. Fiction since 1945

In *Inventing Orders: An Essay and Critique on 20th Century American Literature (1950–2000)* Aaron Sultanik presents a wide-ranging, chronological survey of individual texts such as *Invisible Man*, *The Catcher in the Rye*, *Lolita*, the stories of John Cheever, *Catch-22*, *Herzog*, *The Crying of Lot 49*, *Slaughterhouse-Five*, *Gravity's Rainbow*, *In Cold Blood*, *The Armies of the Night*, *The Bluest Eye*,

The Color Purple, the stories of Raymond Carver, John Updike's *Rabbit* tetralogy, *Love Medicine* and *Beloved*. These are grouped into three styles/periods (existential realism, radical realism and postmodern realism) which constitute the second part of his study, 'Defending Orders'. Part 1, 'Inventing Orders', provides a rationale for his grouping of the texts in relation to these specific categories of realism. Sultanik asserts that his 'study of literary craft' provides a 'streamlined critical vocabulary' which revisits the notion that 'text is context'.

Anthony Arthur's collection of essays about notorious feuds between American writers, *Literary Feuds: A Century of Celebrated Quarrels—from Mark Twain to Tom Wolfe*, provides a humorous and enjoyable supplement to existing biographical scholarship of American writers. In his preface, Arthur makes a bid for the reappraisal of literary feuds as vehicles through which the 'social and intellectual history' of the twentieth century is made visible. However, his rationale for the reflexive power of literary feuds does not seem to be borne out in the course of the study. His anecdotal discussions of literary quarrels include analysis of the relationships between Edmund Wilson and Vladimir Nabokov, Lillian Hellman and Mary McCarthy, and Truman Capote and Gore Vidal. Though compelling, the collection is clearly orientated towards a popular readership, although the final chapter on John Updike and Tom Wolfe shows scholarly application by virtue of original correspondence between the Arthur and these warring writers.

Kimberly A. Freeman's *Love, American Style: Divorce and the American Novel, 1881–1976* examines how the marriage plot and its dissolution remains central to studies of the American novel. Freeman's book locates a shared symbology of divorce in the works of William Dean Howells, Edith Wharton, Mary McCarthy and John Updike, and argues that divorce functions as an ambivalent emblem of American 'personality'. *Love, American Style* demonstrates that the idea of divorce constitutes a resolutely American commitment to individual liberty, self-reinvention and social duty and, moreover, that the social and literary practices of divorce lend themselves to the development of ideas of American modernity. Of special interest to this section are chapters 4 and 5, which discuss the work of Mary McCarthy and John Updike. In these chapters, Freeman analyses selected texts such as McCarthy's *A Charmed Life* [1955] and *The Group* [1963], and Updike's *Marry Me: A Romance* [1976]. Freeman's comments about the presence of divorce registered on the level of form seem particularly innovative, and the author makes a compelling case for the reading of McCarthy's use of the figure of divorce as a mode of questioning the limits of realist representation. Similarly, Freeman argues that Updike's structuring of divorce collapses the polarities between realist and romance forms. Overall, this study is a welcome contribution to the field and illuminates the scripting power of the sign of divorce as a tool for literary and cultural forms of representation.

In Strehle and Carden, eds., *Doubled Plots: Romance and History*, the theoretical and textual work of the romance plot is subjected to critical re-examination. In the introduction to the edition, the authors argue that the narrative of love ventriloquizes cultural values that naturalize patriarchal models of gender while the narrative also critiques the ideology of the heterosexual romance.

Doubled Plots foregrounds the interaction of history and romance by deploying a wide variety of applications of the terms of history, text and desire. Equally, the collection showcases productive crossings of genre, period and literary field, illustrated by the wide treatment of popular, canonical and ethnic romance novels. Of particular interest to this section are the essays by Mary Paniccia Carden, Stephanie Burley and Charles H. Hinnant, which attend to the form and function of the contemporary American romance. Carden's essay, entitled 'Making Love, Making History: (Anti)Romance in Alice McDermott's *At Weddings and Wakes* and *Charming Billy*', identifies an epistemology of romance in McDermott's popular 1992 and 1998 novels, and shows how the equation of romance and history is put under pressure by the failure of the promise of the heterosexual union. In a different vein, Stephanie Burley turns her attention to the 'problem' of subterranean homoeroticism in popular Harlequin romances. Her article, 'What's a Nice Girl Like You Doing Reading a Book Like This?: Homoerotic Reading and Popular Romance', explores how discursive apparatuses prevent romance readers from seeing themselves as homoerotic subjects. Burley's essay adopts a 'queer reading' strategy to manifest the instabilities inherent in theorizing reading practices, and concludes her article with an appeal for critics to inspect anew the counter-discursive effects of the embedded homoerotic narrative. Similarly, Charles H. Hinnant's focus, in 'Desire and the Marketplace: A Reading of Kathleen Woodiwiss's *The Flame and the Flower*', rests upon a broad analysis of the dynamics of reading. Structured around a discussion of Woodiwiss's seminal 1972 novel, Hinnant explores the relationship between romance writing and economic fields of production. Equally, Hinnant's article shows the symbiotic rapport between the contemporary American romance and the formation of modern, liberal market ideologies.

While *Love, American Style* and *Doubled Plots* aim to provide fresh readings of the occluded forms of romance writing, Clare L. Taylor's *Women, Writing, and Fetishism 1890–1950: Female Cross-Gendering* claims to reformulate the 'concept of fetishism as both a sexual practice for women and textual practice for modernist women writers'. Conceived as a corrective to existing psychoanalytical models of female fetishism, this study reformulates Freudian fetishism to suggest that 'female cross-gendering' enhances the sexual body/self of the female author and/or protagonist. Taylor examines the work of Sarah Grand, Radclyffe Hall, H.D., Djuna Barnes and Anaïs Nin, but it is her extended treatment of the relationship between Barnes and Nin that reveals the full force of Taylor's innovative and meticulous scholarship. In chapter 5 Taylor links her treatment of Barnes to readings of Nin's diaries and fictional works. Her extended analysis of the *House of Incest* and *Cities of the Interior* series reveal the author's adept transition between paratextual and literary play, and Taylor's close attention to matters of form and viewpoint produces original readings of Nin's work. Although decidedly modernist in its focus, Taylor's book addresses explicitly the contemporary author's debt to the fictional and critical writings of Barnes and Nin. Taylor notes in her afterword that the exploration of the '"dark unconscious" of fetishistic desire', manifest in the work of Nin and Barnes, demonstrates that these authors set the standard for subsequent writers' adoption of the model of fetishistic cross-gendering as textual practice.

Taylor's agile manoeuvrings between theory, text and context can be seen to complement a similar methodological position adopted by Michael T. Gilmore in his study of the 'quest for legibility' in American culture. In *Surface and Depth: The Quest for Legibility in American Culture*, Gilmore straddles the twin disciplines of psychoanalysis and literary studies by illuminating the persistent American fascination with regimes of visibility and the vexed relationship between writing and seeing. *Surface and Depth* engages a heterogeneous range of literary works including foundational documents of the American republic, studies of film, psychoanalytical theory and the canonical writings of Edgar Allan Poe, Nathaniel Hawthorne, Herman Melville, Henry James, F. Scott Fitzgerald and Ernest Hemingway. In chapter 7 Gilmore addresses the forms of obscuration, silence and illegibility in the contemporary works of Ralph Ellison and Philip Roth and underscores the salience of race as an operative dynamic structuring the discourse of legibility. In this chapter, Gilmore demonstrates how the signs of race and ethnicity denote the refusal of ideas of transparency, textual and otherwise, and appeals to critics to address their oversights surrounding discourses of social class within American literature and culture. Gilmore's study of the leitmotifs of occularity in a diverse range of American texts exemplifies the rise in popularity of reading strategies that produce 'border' crossings between literary fields and historical periods.

Two notable pieces of scholarship in the field underscore this evident methodological turn, yet their inclusion in this section for review constitutes in itself a trespassing of boundaries. Madsen, ed., *Beyond the Borders: American Literature and Post-Colonial Theory* and James A. Snead's *Racist Traces and Other Writings* have been selected for review in this section because of their appeal to critics to analyse the cross-fertilization of influences that complicate the facile separation of ethnic and unmarked (i.e. white) American writing. *Beyond the Borders* brings together a diverse range of essays concerned with the redirection of current theories of postcoloniality to the study of American literature. Of particular importance to critics of contemporary American literature is Deborah L. Madsen's introduction to the collection, 'American Literature and Post-Colonial Theory', which traces the implications of the theoretical work of postcolonialism and, in turn, probes the contours of American canon-building. In the process of examining texts beyond the geographical borders of 'America', *Beyond the Border* demonstrates the peculiar tendency of multiethnic literatures to naturalize and reinscribe 'inherited concepts of American cultural identity as being equivalent with the United States'. In other words, Madsen makes the case for the presence of a shared symbology associated with the place of the 'United States' and the idea or identity of the 'American' functioning in both ethnic and canonical (white-authored) American literatures. Madsen's call to examine the identificatory criteria of American literature is taken up in the book's final essay by Geraldine Stoneham: 'U.S. and US: American Literature of Immigration and Assimilation'. Stoneham's article attempts to move beyond the signs of race and ethnicity to probe the opposition between mainstream and marginal American literatures. She opens her analysis with an exploration of the 'condition of otherness' in white European American narratives and shows how the myth of autonomy and individuation constitutes a more productive analytical tool through which to explore ideas of Americanness than paradigms of race, class and language. Her efforts to blur the boundaries between literary fields, though inadvertently reverting to problematic definitions of the universal, serve as a useful reminder of what is at stake in our adoption of reading methodologies and curriculum selection.

Palgrave's publication of the collected essays and fictional works of James A. Snead, Keeling, MacCabe and West, eds., *Racist Traces and Other Writings: European Pedigrees/African Contagions*, is a worthy tribute to Snead's exceptional contribution to the study of German, English, and African American literature, film studies and critical theory. Kara Keeling's introduction to the book underscores how Snead 'rejected the idea that African American intellectuals must confine themselves to studying only Black culture and he repudiated the notion that Black culture could itself be adequately understood in isolation'. The nine essays collected in the volume demonstrate Snead's intellectual commitment to the convergence of philosophical traditions and the mutuality of European and black cultural thought. Echoing Madsen's appeal to reconsider the borders between marginal and mainstream American literatures to inspect for their points of continuity and difference, Snead's work challenges the easy separation between black and white literary and theoretical traditions. Reading Snead's work again, one is struck by his prescient call to read against the grain and to open up literary works, such as those of William Faulkner and Herman Melville, and cultural texts such as basketball, MTV, and film to the rigours of deconstructionist theory and cross-disciplinary analysis. This collection of his seminal critical essays, including 'On Repetition in Black Culture' and 'Litotes and Chiasmus: Cloaking Tropes in *Absalom, Absalom!*', and five short stories, finally makes Snead's work widely available and is indispensable reading for scholars of American literature.

Amy Hungerford's treatment of the work of personification in postwar literature argues that 'the conflation of texts and persons has…been crucial to postmodern understandings of both nuclear holocaust and ethnic holocaust'. Further, in *The Holocaust of Texts: Genocide, Literature and Personification*, Hungerford connects strategies of textual and cultural personification to the ascendance of the theoretical work of New Criticism and Multiculturalism, which privileges the centrality of ethnic identity and authorship to formulations of human subjectivity. *The Holocaust of Texts* moves from an exploration of the disembodied text in Sylvia Plath's work to a focus on the political and cultural uses of personified texts in Ray Bradbury's 1953 novel *Fahrenheit 451* and the work of nuclear analyst Herman Kahn and philosopher Jacques Derrida. In Chapter 3, Hungerford poses questions about memory and modes of identification in *Schindler's List*, Art Spiegelman's work and the U.S. Holocaust Memorial and then moves, in Chapter 4, to a study of the communication of traumatic experience enacted by Binjamin Wilkomirski's *Fragments* [1996]. In Chapter 5, Hungerford turns her attention to the work of Philip Roth and Saul Bellow, arguing that these authors present an alternative way of thinking about the relationship between persons and texts. Hungerford shows that Roth and Bellow make space for forms of identification that are not determined by history; moreover, framed by the fulcrum of performativity, Roth and Bellow liberate their characters' identities from the binds of race, ethnicity and past history. In her conclusion, Hungerford expands on the ethnical problems posed by conflating texts and persons by invoking the powerful and essential function of recognizing alterity: 'I argue that justice requires us to be able to recognize the otherness of other persons, an otherness that is belied by an understanding of literature based on the mechanisms of identification'.

Michael Davidson's *Guys Like Us: Citing Masculinity in Cold War Poetics* is an important contribution to the mechanics of 'compulsory heterosexuality' in poetic/artistic communities and a marker of the growing influence of masculinity studies on literary criticism this year. Davidson examines citations of normative masculinity in the context of post war consensus seen, for example, in David Riesman's *The Lonely Crowd*. The centre of Davidson's argument is that the potentially subversive masculinities of poetic/artistic communities are subject to similar processes as the performative citationality of normative masculinity of larger Cold War anxieties about gender and subversion. In chapter 3, 'The Lady from Shanghai: California Orientalism and "Guys Like Us"', Davidson submits Kenneth Rexroth, Gary Snyder and Jack Kerouac to the charge of 'orientalizing' the west as a strategy of normalizing beat masculinity. Of particular interest is Chapter 6, 'Definitive Haircuts: Female Masculinity in Elizabeth Bishop and Sylvia Plath', where Davidson argues that masculinity is made more legible and visible when removed from the male body.

In *Male Sexuality Under Surveillance: The Office in American Literature* Graham Thompson makes interesting connections between public discussions of the Clinton–Lewinsky scandal, the issue of homosexuality in the military, and the Iraq conflict to suggest that they are similarly informed by a number of assumptions about masculinity, sexuality, and power whose historical development can be mapped in American literary representations of the office. It is Thompson's contention that 'literary representations of the office ... lay witness to many of the demands, constraints, and contradictions implicit in the formation' of a normative male heterosexual identity in the wider culture. Thompson discusses the traditionally male space of the office as an arena of desire, in which, drawing on the work of Eve Kosofsky Sedgwick, male–male relationships take place in a 'continuum' between the homosocial and the homosexual which must be policed by the rigid separation of the heterosexual and the homosexual, a disruption of Sedgwick's 'continuum' based upon a comparison between the invisibility or 'naturalness' of the heterosexual male body and the visibility of the homosexual body, a distinction which gives rise to a culture of surveillance. As a space in which male sexuality and masculine identity can be understood as in a perpetual crisis of definition, Thompson's literary offices of the mid-nineteenth and late twentieth centuries are connected by their importance as visual regimes 'at that moment in Western culture when the epistemological nature of society is changing, when, in Michel Foucault's terms, surveillance and disciplinary society as epitomized in Bentham's Panopticon are rearranging the organization of power relations'. Thompson's study is divided into three sections. 'Managing Desire' begins in the 1830s with a discussion of the work of Herman Melville, William Dean Howells and Sinclair Lewis, focused on the ways that representations of male friendship speak of the fluidity of masculinities of the late nineteenth and early twentieth centuries (presenting possibilities for the consideration of a 'continuum' of male sexuality) which are nevertheless closed down. 'Postwar Unsettlement' discusses structural changes in office work from the end of the Second World War to the 1970s as they are treated in the work of Sloan Wilson and Joseph Heller, changes which cause anxieties manifested as a fear of feminization. The final section, 'A Word for Windows', a discussion of the work of Nicholson Baker and Douglas Coupland, informed by recent developments in queer theory, suggests that positive male experiences of the contemporary breakdown of traditional office structures due to changing work patterns speak of an escape from constraining masculinist discourses reliant on an economy of surveillance. This is a theoretically informed and compelling intervention in the burgeoning cross-over field of literary criticism and masculinity studies.

Marilyn C. Wesley's *Violent Adventure: Contemporary Fiction by American Men* challenges the popular assumption that violent contemporary American fiction reinforces the male violence dramatized by, for example, the Columbine school shooting, September 11, boxing and gang warfare. Wesley questions the contradictory popular impulses which condemn violent behaviour and its representation on the one hand, while celebrating the kinds of violence promoted by Hollywood in masculine coming-of-age narratives on the other. She argues that recent fiction by writers such as Tobias Wolff, Pinckney Benedict, Richard Ford, Cormac McCarthy, Thom Jones, Tim O'Brien, Ernest Gaines, Walter Mosley, Russell Banks and Don DeLillo is engaged in the revision of narratives of 'violent adventure' which are central to conventional constructions of a powerful, white American masculinity. For Wesley, the revision of traditional genres by these writers, such as the Western, detective fiction and war stories, challenges popular assumptions about the significance of violence for masculine identity. However, while she recognizes that part of the appeal of narratives of male violence lies in the ways that their repetition reinforces a sense of male power, she does not consider the possibility that contemporary revisions may also function in the same way, reinforcing male violence in a stylistic, if not thematic, way.

In *Unsettling the Literary West: Authenticity and Authorship*, Nathaniel Lewis explores another literary arena for the representation of masculinity to focus on the ways in which it essentializes its subject matter as outside cultural construction. This is a wide-ranging, theoretically informed and innovative critical contribution to the emergent field of 'New West' criticism. Lewis's starting point is that 'the very struggle over authenticity … [is] perhaps the only "true" condition of the western cultural imagination'. It is Lewis's contention that writers and critics of Western literature privilege a connection between the West and the 'real' at the expense of an attention to textuality, and he attempts to reroute discussion back to stylistic designs and cultural and canonical contexts. For Lewis, Western literature is conceived as merely a historical record, and he points to the lack of theoretical critical approaches to the area, suggesting that this is the result of conceptions of the West as 'pure' space outside the demands of contemporary culture. For Lewis, 'treating western literature as simulation rather than representation redirects our attention from history and place to text or screen;

makes the connection between language and reality not only suspect but playfully unnecessary; and helps us to project and finally glimpse a previously *invisible* history of western literature'. It is Lewis's claim that such an unsettling of traditional approaches to Western literature reveals an unsettling body of writing which might be seen as postmodern writing *par excellence*, whose 'banality, reliability, and repetitive imitations cloak its extraordinary achievement: the production of a hyperreal West'. Lewis discusses a wide historical range of writers, but of particular interest in this section are the final chapters 'Coming Out of the Country: Environmental Constructivism in Western Nature Writing', which discusses the work of Terry Tempest Williams and Gary Snyder, and 'Inside Out in the Postmodern West', which references writers such as Nathanael West, Thomas Pynchon, Hunter S. Thompson, E.L. Doctorow, Vikram Seth, Cormac McCarthy, E. Annie Proulx, Jonathan Franzen and T. Coraghessan Boyle, while focusing on Native American writers and providing a substantial discussion of Vladimir Nabokov's interest in the West. Also published in this field is Lyons, ed., *Literature of the American West: A Cultural Approach*, an anthology of writing on the American West. This is intended as a teaching aid and no new scholarship is presented. There have been a number of publications in the field of ecocriticism, often related to studies of the West. Dana Phillips's *The Truth of Ecology: Nature, Culture and Literature in America* represents an attempt to redefine ecocriticism from a theoretical perspective. Here, Phillips negotiates tensions between literary and scientific realism, of experience and representation and theory and practice of nature writing. Of interest to this section is Phillips's examination of Annie Dillard's *Pilgrim at Tinker Creek* [1974]. Not received for review was *Practical Ecocriticism: Literature, Biology and the Environment* by Glen A. Love.

Continuing the attention to gendered literary spaces, Nancy Gerber, in *Portrait of the Mother-Artist: Class and Creativity in Contemporary American Fiction*, considers the ways that interactions between class, race and motherhood are dramatized in relation to the figure of the mother-artist in contemporary women's writing. Gerber sketches how creative explorations of motherhood at the margins produce a distinct literary tradition from an inter-subjective perspective to subvert Western understandings of creativity, subjectivity and authorship. She discusses the works of Gwendolyn Brooks, Tillie Olsen, Cynthia Ozick and Edwidge Danticat in relation to the topics of domesticity, silence, history and memory.

General studies of postmodern fiction are in short supply this year, while single-author journal articles and monographs (below) continue to appear steadily. In *The Myth of the Descent to the Underworld in Postmodern Literature*, Evans Lansing Smith charts the use of archetypal images and ancient texts in a focused and highly specific study of postmodern literature which sees the underworld as metaphor for that which lies beneath the surface. For Smith the repeated occurrence of myths of the underworld (or 'necrotypes') in postmodern texts speaks of a connection back to the modernist texts of Eliot, Joyce and Pound, in which postmodern adaptations are unconvincingly envisaged as markers of continuity with the past. Of interest in this section are chapters on Ken Kesey, Thomas Pynchon and Robert Coover.

Studies of popular fiction seem similarly thin this year, with the exception of *Doubled Plots* (above) and *The Trash Phenomenon: Contemporary Literature, Popular Culture and the Making of the American Century*, in which Stacey Olster considers the ways in which popular culture is integrated into contemporary literature as part of a consideration of the role of the popular in processes of nation-building. Olster is interested in how contemporary writers subvert the nationalist designs integral to popular cultural texts. The study initially discusses how the works of Gore Vidal, John Updike and Larry Beinhart are concerned with the role of mass media in the rise of US dominance in the twentieth century, before moving on to discuss literary considerations of the imperial influence of American popular culture in England, Argentina and Japan. Olster concludes in the US with a consideration of treatments of media spectacle in post-1963 literature, in texts such as Don DeLillo's *Libra*, as they variously respond to such spectacles as unifying devices.

The publication of journal articles and single-author monographs on the post-1945 period showed a steady decline in 2003. *American Literature* has a proliferation of articles about early American literature, with Susan Mizruchi's article entitled '*Lolita* in History' (*AL* 73:iii[2003] 629–52) being the exception that proves the rule. Her article traces the references to historical events that haunt Nabokov's novel, and Mizruchi identifies the embedded historical subtexts of the Holocaust and American consumer culture that reveal the 'novel's larger perspective on the moral questions it raises'. The first volume of 2003's *American Literary History* was devoted to the study of ethnicity, poetry and multiculturalism, emerging out of the Cambridge Literary History of the US forum in May 2001. The subsequent parts of volume 15 show a similar decline in the number of articles published on post-1945 American literature. However, of notable interest was Jennifer Dalton's article, 'Before the White Negro: Sin and Salvation in *Kingsblood Royal*' (*AmLH* 15[2003] 311–29). Dalton's discussion of Sinclair Lewis's 1947 best-seller notes how this novel constitutes both a radical critique of white racism and the inability to transcend the logic of racial difference. Dalton links her analysis of racial passing to current studies of whiteness and, further, argues that ideas of American nationalism in the post-war period were inextricably tied to ideas of racial whiteness, consumerism and suburbanization.

An article on Burroughs, Oliver Harris's *William Burroughs and the Secret of Fascination*, reappraises his novels from the perspective of his biography. Harris places Burroughs's work in the productive correspondence of the other beat writers. This is a significant addition to the body of work on Burroughs and is illustrative of 'beat' literary community. Sid Sondergaard's 'Unable to Queer the Deal: William S. Burroughs's Negotiations with "Eugene Allerton"' (*Crit* 44:ii[2003] 144–56) follows Harris's methodology of locating explication in Burroughs's biography. Sondergaard examines how the pressures of Burroughs's successful antecedents may have influenced his writing. Situating the writing of *Queer* just after the accidental shooting of his wife, Sondergaard argues for the representation of guilt in the novel. The Lee/Allerton–Burroughs/Marber relationship is represented in capitalist terms, with Lee/Burroughs as the consumer. The importance of biography is continued in Susanne Vees-Guiani's 'Diagnosing Billy Pilgrim: A Psychiatric Approach to Kurt Vonnegut's

Slaughterhouse-Five' (*Crit* 44:ii[2003] 175–84). Vees-Guiani emphasizes Vonnegut's war experience of the bombing of Dresden to contextualize Billy Pilgrim's schizophrenic temporal existence. Vonnegut's writing is seen as part of a therapeutic approach to post-traumatic stress disorder. Biography is also the key to Brendan Nicholls's article 'The Melting Pot that Boiled Over: Racial Fetishism and the *Lingua Franca* of Jack Kerouac's Fiction' (*MFS* 49:iii[2003] 524–49). Here, Nicholls argues that Kerouac 'attempts to map his marginal identity—as a French Canadian ethnic minority—onto the American landscape by masking him in the racial attributes of African Americans, Mexicans, and Native Americans'. In a careful Freudian reading of Kerouac's fetishization of his mother's bathrobe, Nicholls argues that America is figured as a castrating and castrated 'dark woman'. He sees this as part of a larger mythology of self, enacted through 'the Duluoz Legend'. Andrea Levine's 'The (Jewish) White Negro: Norman Mailer's Racial Bodies' (*MELUS* 28:ii[2003] 59–81) reassesses Mailer's essay in terms of a remasculinization of the Jewish male body. This depends on a dissociation of the Jewish male from the feminine and history.

An interesting range of articles and a few single-author monographs continue to appear on writers in the post-1970 period, particularly in relation to the topic of postmodernity. Two significant single-author studies which seek to expand the boundaries of postmodern criticism are David Cowart's *Don DeLillo: The Physics of Language* and Christopher Palmer's *Philip K. Dick: Exhilaration and Terror of the Postmodern*. Cowart charts DeLillo's rise as a major contemporary American author, discussing each of his twelve novels. His wide-ranging study makes connections between DeLillo's work and a host of other writers and thinkers such as Walt Whitman, Ludwig Wittgenstein, Martin Heidegger, Sigmund Freud, Jacques Lacan, Jacques Derrida, Ernest Hemingway, James Joyce and T.S. Eliot, as well as considering the ways in which DeLillo's work interacts with the fields of post-structuralism and postmodernism, which are more usually the focus of attention in DeLillo criticism. Cowart's overarching attention is on DeLillo's use of language, and he argues that it is this aspect of his work which provides the key to understanding his engagement with postmodernism, but also his resonance with the work of earlier writers and critics. Palmer discusses the work of Philip K. Dick in relation to its simultaneous excitement about the possibilities of postmodern transformations and fears about the loss of ethical certainties those possibilities gesture towards. This dual focus is discussed as a marker of Dick's historical position at the intersection between humanism and postmodernism, and Palmer suggests that the ongoing, unresolvable clash between these discourses informs Dick's work.

A range of sophisticated journal articles appeared in relation to postmodern writers. In 'Literary Narrative and Information Culture: Garbage, Waste, and Residue in the Work of E.L. Doctorow' (*Crit* 44:iii[2003] 501–35), Michael Wutz extends postmodern discussions of waste as a symptom of the modes of production of late capitalism to suggest that the trope of garbage is extended in relation to narrative function in the works of E.L. Doctorow. Wutz suggests that for Doctorow waste becomes a metaphor for marginal or residual knowledge, 'a domain that is outside the boundaries of received disciplinary practices as well as the contemporary media landscape' yet which is central to the understanding of culture. Within this context, Wutz argues that dirt and dust in Doctorow's works function as metaphors for the role of print narrative in an electronic age. In 'Wrong Numbers: The Endless Fiction of Auster and Deleuze and Guattari and ...' (*Crit* 44:ii[2003] 213–24) Robert Briggs discusses Gilles Deleuze and Félix Guattari's rethinking of the book in relation to the concept of the rhizome, a metaphor which suggests that the book is without subject or object, having multiple connections within and without itself which nullify endings and beginnings. Such a position informs Briggs's argument that Paul Auster's *The New York Trilogy* is not so much focused on the ways in which meaning is conveyed or refused by a text but how it makes connections beyond itself. Briggs points out that not only is each part of the trilogy incomplete, but that the trilogy is a trilogy is a fiction, in that each part does not complete a whole and gestures more widely towards the entire range of Auster's texts. Timothy Melley's 'Postmodern Amnesia: Trauma and Forgetting in Tim O'Brien's *In the Lake of the Woods*' (*Crit* 44:i[2003] 106–31) sketches a contemporary American cultural climate of traumatic amnesia which speaks of the instability of the liberal subject: 'they operate on a profound sense of self-division—a sense that one's experience can be secret even to oneself'. Melley connects this crisis of subjectivity to a crisis of historiography—the idea that it is no longer possible to ground historical narratives securely leads to dangerous forms of collective forgetting. Amnesia in O'Brien's text is discussed as an important trope through which the correlation between failures of individual memory and failures in representing the historical past, as they relate to postmodern theories of subjectivity and history, can be evaluated—the traumatic personal event compares with the 'real' of history and, as O'Brien's text illustrates, both are inaccessible: the traumatic must remain hidden in order for it to function as an 'authentic' space which is outside contaminated or flawed narratives.

Copestake, ed., *American Postmodernity: Essays on the Recent Fiction of Thomas Pynchon*, signals a renewed interest in Pynchon this year, particularly in relation to the reassessment of *The Crying of Lot 49* and the ways that *Vineland* and *Mason & Dixon* mark a shift in his earlier concerns. Essays consider the ways in which Pynchon's ethical strategies evolve in relation to notions of postmodernity, discussing his work in relation to Marshall McLuhan's account of mass media and the 'decentring of the subject' (David Seed, 'Media Systems in *The Crying of Lot 49*'); ethics: David Dickson, 'Pynchon's *Vineland* and "That fundamental agreement in what is good and proper": What Happens When We Need to Change It?', and David Thoreen, 'In which "Acts have Consequences": Ideas of Moral Order in the Qualified Postmodernism of Pynchon's Recent Fiction'; metafiction: Francisco Collado Rodríguez, '*Mason & Dixon*, Historiographic Metafiction and the Unstable Reconciliation of Opposites'; science: William B. Millard, 'Delineations of Madness and Science: *Mason & Dixon*, Pynchonian Space and the Snovian Disjunction', and Ian D. Copestake, '"Off the deep end again": Sea-Consciousness and Insanity in *The Crying of Lot 49* and *Mason & Dixon*; hybridity: Martin Saar and Christian Skirke, '"The realm of velocity and spleen": Reading Hybrid Life in *Mason & Dixon*'; American comic traditions: John Heon, 'Surveying the Punchline: Jokes and their Relation to the American Racial Unconscious/Conscience in *Mason & Dixon* and the Liner

Notes to *Spiked!*'; and mapmaking and representation: Robert L. McLaughlin, 'Surveying, Mapmaking, and Representation'.

The desire to update Pynchon criticism continues in journal articles. In 'Japan, Creative Masochism, and Transnationality in *Vineland*' (*Crit* 44:iv[2003] 371–88) Terry Caesar and Takashi Aso attempt to explain the presence of Japan in Pynchon's text by restoring its specificity as a national space, an attention neglected in Pynchon criticism. Caesar and Aso employ the concept of masochism as a metaphor for Japan's cultural dependence on the US, exploring the ways in which transnational exchange in Vineland subverts that dependence; hence, 'creative masochism' is a reference to Pynchon's representation of in-between spaces which are the site of the untranslatable. In 'Pynchon in Popular Magazines' (*Crit* 44:iv[2003] 389–404) John K. Young argues for the importance of recontextualizing Pynchon's work in relation to the popular magazines of the mid-1960s, such as Esquire and Cavalier, which were the site for much of its original publication. It is Young's contention that only by understanding the textual history of Pynchon's work can we appreciate his position within popular media, as well as his responses to the consumer culture through which he developed his initial authorial image. The further significance of Young's argument is forcefully demonstrated by a discussion of the public visibility of Toni Morrison in relation to Pynchon's (more recent) invisibility. Young suggests that an uncritical acceptance of Pynchon's status as a genius recluse, detached from specific contexts of production, allows an ongoing assumption that the work of white, male authors represents universal concerns. In 'Pynchon's Ghosts' (*Crit* 44:ii[2003] 250–74) Daniel Punday takes as his starting point the idea that ghosts provide alternatives to official accounts of history in Pynchon's work, suggesting that in Pynchon's later texts, particularly *Mason & Dixon*, the focus has shifted from the demands of the haunted to the responsibilities of the haunted, a transformation linked to his changing ethical approach to the past. Punday argues that Pynchon's recent work engages with the notion that our debt to the past is one of mourning, as part of a process of responsible involvement.

The continued popularity of Cormac McCarthy is demonstrated again this year and the following three articles provide welcome theoretical interventions in the field. In 'The Flawed Design: American Imperialism in N. Scott Momaday's *House Made of Dawn* and Cormac McCarthy's *Blood Meridian*' (*Crit* 45:i[2003] 3–24), Christopher Douglas compares the ways in which Momaday and McCarthy attend to migrations and colonizations in the south-west as part of their interrogation of Western modernity as it relates to white imperialism, considering both as postcolonial critiques. In 'Dis(re)membered Bodies: Cormac McCarthy's Border Fiction' (*MFS* 49:i[2003] 155–80) Mark A. Eaton references debates about McCarthy's regional affiliations as a writer (which necessarily connect him to canonical southern or Western writers) to suggest that he might be more productively considered alongside Chicano and Latin American writers as part of the emerging genre of post-nationalist fiction, a move which in turn allows reflection upon the changing concerns of the Western and southern literary traditions. In 'The Dawning of the Age of Aquarius: Abjection, Identity, and the Carnivalesque in Cormac McCarthy's *Suttree*' (*Crit* 44:iv[2003] 664–96),

J. Douglas Canfield opens with a surprising reference to Adorno which situates *Suttree* as a text which demonstrates the post-Holocaust impossibility of meaning. The varied concerns of the article, informed by the work of Julia Kristeva and Mikhail Bahktin, are perhaps best summed up by the statement that McCarthy 'respond[s] to modern abjection by indulging in a nostalgia for Bakhtin's holistic vision of the folk humor of the middle ages' without providing any sense of transcendence or truth, only an unfailing attempt to present a 'new, albeit sometimes comic, dawning to balance against the abject evening redness of the west'. In '"Everything a hunter and everything hunted': Schopenhauer and Cormac McCarthy's *Blood Meridian*' (*Crit* 45:i[2003] 25–33) Dwight Eddins extends some of the familiar and rather tired concerns of existing McCarthy criticism, arguing that McCarthy's engagement with the 'onto-epistemological problematic' is a marker of his sophistication and stature as a worthy successor to Joyce, Faulkner, Mann and Pynchon. McCarthy is discussed in relation to the work of Arthur Schopenhauer.

Studies of women writers were in surprisingly short supply this year. Paul Christian Jones's article on Anne Tyler is a welcome exception and its attention to post-feminism may explain this shortage. In 'A Re-awakening: Anne Tyler's Postfeminist Edna Pontellier in *Ladder of Years*' (*Crit* 44:iii[2003] 271–83), Jones assesses critical reception of Tyler's work as part of a feminist backlash to suggest that *Ladder of Years* is actually a post-feminist revision of Kate Chopin's *The Awakening*, 'one that posits a feminist trajectory for women that does not necessitate a complete flight from the domestic sphere'. Jones outlines definitions of post-feminism to suggest that Tyler's work is most usefully viewed as presenting a 'form of feminism adapted to a postmodern age' in which feminism evolves in relation to uncertainty, ambiguity and pluralism. For Jones, Anne Tyler's post-feminism lies in her presentation of a protagonist empowered within a transformed homespace. It may well be that the established tradition of reading women's writing in relation to feminist frameworks in this section has led to a difficulty in engaging with such texts in a 'post-feminist era'. Perhaps the evolution of feminist concerns as they relate to notions of post-feminism has yet to be sufficiently developed for new frameworks of literary criticism to emerge. Nancy Gerber's study of the mother-artist, above, provides a welcome return to feminist concerns, which nevertheless feels rather dated. A writer who continues to attract interest is Barbara Kingsolver, whose work engages the fields of postcolonial studies and ecocriticism as part of a feminist critique. In 'The Africa of Two Western Women Writers: Barbara Kingsolver and Margaret Laurence' (*Crit* 44:iii[2003] 284–94), Kimberly A. Koza discusses the ways in which the lack of African voices in Kingsolver's *The Poisonwood Bible* is part of a critique of American arrogance, connections between feminism and critiques of colonization being made via the narrative of the female members of the American family. Koza compares Kingsolver's focus on the American burden of guilt for colonization in which Africa is a background for essentially American concerns to Canadian writer Margaret Laurence's work, which foregrounds African voices. Koza suggests that Kingsolver draws attention to the complicity of the women in the text (who are nevertheless subject to white, male colonial authority) to ask American readers to revise their understanding of their own responsibilities.

An interesting article which focuses on the self-conscious treatment of whiteness as a constructed identity (a growing area of enquiry in literary studies, introduced above in John K. Young's article on Pynchon, Deborah Madsen's collection, and James Snead's collected writings) is Heather J. Hicks, 'On Whiteness in T. Coraghessan Boyle's *The Tortilla Curtain*' (*Crit* 45:i[2003] 43–64), which seeks to understand Boyle's text as a comment on white, suburban, middle-class group identity in America which 'can be understood to point in directions that critical race studies might take in its interrogation of whiteness'.

Finally, an interesting publication, *Eudora Welty on William Faulkner*, draws on Welty's admiration for Faulkner. Reproduced are Faulkner's postcard encouraging Welty, extracts from Welty's review of *Intruder in the Dust* and speeches from the presentation of the Gold Medal for Fiction presented to Faulkner in 1962 and the Southern Literary Festival in 1965. The volume is concluded by Noel Polk's essay, 'Welty and Faulkner and the Southern Literary Tradition', which puts the collection into context.

The following titles published in 2003 were unavailable for review: Kim Loudermilk, *Fictional Feminism: Representing Feminism in American Bestsellers* (Routledge); Gene D. Phillips, *Creatures of Darkness: Raymond Chandler, Detective Fiction and Film Noir* (UPKen); Roland Walter, *Narrative Identities: Intercultural In-Betweens in the Americas* (Lang); and Jeffrey Weinstock, *Spectral America: Phantoms and the National Imagination* (UWiscP).

4. Drama

(a) General

Publications in the field of American drama display two continuing trends: criticism of drama is increasingly being displaced by interdisciplinary studies of theatre, and work on individual playwrights is diminishing in favour of studies of groups of authors and historical analyses.

For example, discussion of even the most seminal African American playwrights is highly compressed in Errol G. Hill and James V. Hatch's *A History of African American Theatre*. This is slightly disappointing, because many of the most accessible surveys of the drama—for example, Samuel A. Hay's *African American Theatre: An Historical and Critical Analysis* (CUP [1994])—have glaring deficiencies. Nevertheless, given the authors' self-imposed restrictions, and the vast range of the material, one could not reasonably ask for much more from this remarkable study. Hill and Hatch largely restrict their scope to North America, and focus on drama, although they also provide selective coverage of relevant developments in musical theatre and dance, including of course minstrelsy as well as vaudeville and cabaret acts. They have also resisted any temptation to theorize such phenomena as minstrelsy and blackface, and the treatment of individual plays and playwrights is strictly subsumed within the larger narrative, but what a narrative it is: despite the 600-odd pages (over a hundred of which are devoted to notes, bibliography and index), the book rattles along, with an astonishing breadth of detail and a seamless fluency in the style. This will be the standard reference work for years to come.

No other book published this year can hope to match Hill and Hatch for range. Instead, a remarkable number of studies focus on particular periods and developments within American drama. While few radically alter the familiar narrative arc of twentieth-century American drama, almost all add new detail, unfamiliar primary material, or distinctive connections. There is little to surprise in John H. Houchin's *Censorship of the American Theatre in the Twentieth Century*: in this account, conservative social forces implement censorship in order to restrain the expression of ideas that threaten to subvert an established order. Houchin begins by establishing the history of censorship prior to the twentieth century before exploring the period from 1900 to 1930, in which the concern was primarily with sex; later, censorship was more rigorously focused on attempts to muzzle politically subversive theatre. The final two chapters explore sex as a metaphor for political and social radicalism. All of the topics one would expect to encounter are surveyed in detail: Mae West, the Federal Theatre Project, the House Un-American Activities Committee, the Living Theatre and Off-Off-Broadway, and the 'Culture Wars' post-1972, culminating in the coalition of conservative, anti-federal politicians and Christian fundamentalists that drove the New Right's attack on the National Endowment for the Arts, for example in its response to the growing number of 1980s plays about AIDS. For the most part it is a familiar and increasingly depressing story, and although Houchin has no particularly new angle, that is because the issues have never been more starkly or bleakly apparent. The book combines magisterial scope with lucid and convincing detail.

One can piece together a standard chronological history of American drama of the twentieth century from the several studies published this year that concentrate on a particular development within the field. Cheryl Black's *The Women of Provincetown, 1915–1922* takes a fresh look at what is widely regarded as the century's first significant advance, the establishment of the Provincetown Players. Black aims to offer a different approach and emphasis than previous studies have provided by focusing on the achievements of women in all aspects of the Players' work. Of fifty-one dramatists who wrote for the Players, sixteen were women, who were involved in writing over a third of the plays that emerged. Susan Glaspell, of course, is a key figure in the chapter on writing, but Black places her in a broader context and discusses the recurrent concerns of female playwrights, many of whom Black regards as feminist in their often critical views of marriage, their creation of heroic female characters, their avoidance of female stereotyping, and their pacifist politics. One would have welcomed a longer chapter, but Black is specifically concerned to argue for the centrality of women in all aspects of production, including managing, performing, stage-directing, and designing. She also argues for the feminist politics of contemporary Greenwich Village as an influence as important as the European aesthetics that the Players are widely credited with importing. Not surprisingly, Black also interweaves biographical information on the women working in Provincetown with their theatrical achievements. Although the study bears some traces of the doctoral dissertation from which it is drawn, it is a timely and well-researched contribution to the growing field of literature both on the Provincetown Players and on female dramatists working in the early decades of the twentieth century.

The papers in Gewirtz and Kolb, eds., *Experimenters, Rebels, and Disparate Voices: The Theatre of the 1920s Celebrates American Diversity*, are derived from a conference held at Hofstra University in 1994. Unusual contributions include several pieces on set design, a discussion of African American theatre critics, an account of Howard University's 1920s drama programme, and a short account of Chinese dramatists. The pieces on playwrights can be broadly grouped under three headings: several welcome contributions looking at the work of John Howard Lawson; African American playwrights; and women dramatists (almost inevitably, Sophie Treadwell and Susan Glaspell). Particularly noteworthy among these is Kornelia Tancheva's argument that Treadwell's *Machinal* was successful precisely because it was not seen as a feminist play. A very useful contribution to deixis and other semiotic systems within theatre studies generally is Beverly Bronson Smith's 'They Knew What They Wanted: American Theatre's Use of Nonverbal Communication Codes to Marginalize Non-Native Characters in the 1920s'. The origins of most of the papers are all too apparent, however; although the collection of conference proceedings is a useful means of circulating work in progress, the reprinted conference paper as an individual item is usually just too brief and provisional to be rewarding in published form.

Barry B. Witham's *The Federal Theatre Project: A Case Study* begins by making the same kind of observation that Houchin's book on censorship compels: 'Imagine a new play on Broadway in 1985 subsidized by the United States Congress urging support for the Contra movement in Nicaragua.' Insert your own, post-2004 're-election' analogy here. Like Houchin, Witham finds little to overturn received views of his subject, but he does approach the FTP from a different angle and unearths substantial new primary material by presenting a case study of the unit in Seattle. In so doing, he moves beyond the familiar, cherry-picked successes of the FTP to ask questions about 'the *thousands* of other productions' across the States. He gives a detailed analysis of the establishment of the unit, its research activities, the Negro unit and racial tensions, the Living Newspapers, the Children's Theatre, and several productions, before coming to a balanced set of conclusions about the Seattle unit and, at least by implication, the FTP generally. It never satisfactorily defined its audience, or found a way to reconcile ambivalent demands: committed and relevant theatre with the box office, populism with legitimization, centralization and professionalism with outreach and local interest. Unlike the many accounts of marginalized topics that feel compelled to argue for an unwarranted quality and centrality, Witham accepts that 'the quality of the work was not consistently professional' and often 'painfully amateurish', although there were some successes, most notably the work produced by the Negro unit. Despite the failure of the federal government actively to combat racism, 'the Negro Repertory Theatre was the centerpiece of the Seattle unit and symptomatic of what was fundamentally forward looking and decent about the whole New Deal enterprise'. As for the suspicions of many conservatives that the FTP had been infiltrated by subversives, Witham finds little evidence of communist activity, and indeed identifies many in the Seattle programme who were actively opposed to the radical left.

Dennis G. Jerz, *Technology in American Drama, 1920–1950: Soul and Society in the Age of the Machine*, argues that in this period bookended by the two world wars the obsession with technological progress at once glorifies and demystifies the machine because of its increasing ubiquity in everyday domestic life. 'Over three decades, dramatists illustrate three distinct stages in the individual's responses to the machine: first, self-destructive hostility; second, socialized acceptance; and finally, a full, deeply intimate integration.' Jerz illustrates this argument in a chronological sequence of chapters, each of which explores two or three plays in detail. At the start of the 1920s, O'Neill's *The Hairy Ape* and Elmer Rice's *The Adding Machine* expressionistically dramatize apparent polarities: the alienated individual and mechanization, nature and technology. The climax of such plays tends to present a grimly ironic fusion that becomes explicit at the end of the decade in O'Neill's *Dynamo*, Rice's *The Subway* and Sophie Treadwell's *Machinal*, which express a profound horror in the recognition that, far from being our polar opposite, the machine 'is, in the eyes of the protagonists, a conduit of power, inspiration, and even love—but only at the cost of one's soul'. During the Depression era the benefits of mechanization became more apparent, and the drama revolved around ownership, as plays such as Clifford Odets's *Waiting for Lefty*, the Federal Theatre Project's *Altars of Steel* and Clare Booth Luce's *O, Pyramids* debated industrialization and the related issues of regionalism and class, and explored the conflict between unionized labour and capital. By the 1940s technology had become domesticated, and '[t]he internally complex characters of Wilder, Miller, and Williams are not silhouetted against a technological background but are instead knitted into a richly developed technological context' in which 'these dramatists hold the characters (and audience members) morally accountable for their own failures'. Throughout, Jerz inscribes these plays within an informed analysis of the dialectic of theatrical representation and industrial change, while his fascinating but regrettably and needlessly highly compressed introduction provides some fascinating perspectives on the broader cultural meanings of technological change. This is a fine, suggestive study of an important topic that could easily have been developed at greater length.

The most significant theoretical development in this field is to be found in Bruce McConachie's remarkable *American Theater in the Culture of the Cold War: Producing and Contesting Containment, 1947–1962*. In focusing on the issue of spectatorial pleasure, and by tracing this to ways of seeing that have been pre-formed by 'presemiotic' changes in the dominant culture, McConachie enters territory that is more familiar in film than in theatre studies, which seem largely to have assumed that affective pleasure is a result of immediate engagement with the unfolding performance. McConachie feels that the usual arguments advanced to explain changes in American theatre and drama after the Second World War—military victory, the rise of the Cold War superpowers, economic advance, and the internal struggle against dissent and subversion—are inadequate. Instead he develops an approach via cognitive psychology that strongly recalls some recent developments in the misleadingly entitled 'post-theory' in film studies, associated for example with the work of Noël Carroll and David Bordwell. McConachie draws extensively on psychological studies of 'containment', whereby the spectator perceives phenomena via an 'image schema' that creates the perception of an image as having an inside, an outside, and a boundary, and relates this to the period's dominant ideology, the 'containment liberalism' exemplified in the National Security Act of 1947. (From this point of view the book works well alongside John H. Houchin's study of censorship, reviewed above.) McConachie studies some of the major plays of the period in terms of three primary examples of different forms of containment: the narcissistic 'Empty Boys' of plays like George Axelrod's *The Seven Year Itch*; 'Family Circles', including the empathetic mother in plays like William Inge's *The Dark at the Top of the Stairs*; and the passive 'Fragmented Hero'. He argues that Arthur Miller presents heroes who resist this fragmentation, but 'at the price of demonizing female sexuality'. For McConachie, a second major development to account for spectatorial pleasure is to be found in the formative influence of technological change, notably in the fields of photography and audiophony. For example, he suggests that the popularity of radio drama moved audience tastes away from realism and towards allegory and abstraction: radio privileges the mental over the material, makes distant things seem close, and (in an important commentary on the use of the word 'compulsion', often used uncritically to indicate the protagonist's assertive individuality) removes the sense of will. This aspect of McConachie's superb study usefully complements Jerz's account of technology and the American stage, above.

Much more straightforward is David A. Crespy's *Off-Off Broadway Explosion: How Provocative Playwrights of the 1960s Ignited a New American Theater*. This is a work of cultural and biographical history rather than dramatic criticism (although it touches on a large number of plays), a narrative account enlivened by extensive research, many photographs, interviews with many of the key figures, and a prefatory endorsement from Edward Albee. Although there is little in the way of contextualizing material—no lengthy introductory accounts of the state of Broadway in the 1950s, for example, although the sense of radical change and renewal explodes from practically every page—this is at the very least an essential addition to the more sober accounts of the period in the standard histories.

Several other studies were published that take a theoretical or thematic, rather than historical, approach. Of these, unquestionably the most important is David Savran's *A Queer Sort of Materialism: Recontextualizing American Theater*. This is a diverse collection of essays, including 'Ambivalence, Utopia, and a Queer Sort of Materialism', the indispensable study of Tony Kushner's *Angels in America*, most of which are previously published, albeit sometimes in different form. There is not space here to summarize Savran's remarkably diversity of material and critical thinking that ranges from an occasionally gleefully unreconstructed Marxism to queer theory, abjection, and musings about the trains of thought provoked by walking along the beach on Fire Island. Savran is interested in 'the troublemakers—the ghost, closeted lesbian, masochist, drag king, anticolonist, or angry white male—who, because they are both present and absent, are never offered to the unobstructed gaze of the spectator'. Many of the pieces, such as the Kushner essay or the discussion of 'middlebrow anxiety', already have the feeling of standard critical analyses. Despite the complexity and sometimes even the abstruseness of the approach, Savran is nevertheless repeatedly trenchant, illuminating, even blunt: one has to cheer a critic who, without resorting to the crude populism of Terry Eagleton's recent work, states frankly that 'postmodernism ... represents less a momentous epistemological shift than it does an attempt to divert attention away from increasingly uneven patterns of capital accumulation and economic development toward the cultural and the social'.

Two studies this year focus on the relationship between classical theatre and the contemporary American stage. In *Drawing Upon the Past: Classical Theatre in the Contemporary American Theatre*, Robert J. Andreach explores intertextual connections between classical theatre and a large range of plays by contemporary dramatists: A.R. Gurney, Tina Howe, Edward Albee, Charles Ludlam, Harry Kondoleon, Richard Foreman, P.J. Gibson, Adrienne Kennedy, David Rabe, Charles Mee, Ellen McLaughlin, John Guare, Eric Overmyer and David Greenspan. As this list suggests, the book includes extensive consideration of both canonical and non-canonical works, and of playwrights who affirm the primacy of the verbal element in theatre as well as those drawn more to plastic experimentation. The organization of the book is somewhat problematic. Andreach divides it into three sections: the first two essentially deal with comedy and tragedy, while the third and final section, 'which consists of a single chapter, examines three plays, each for the self primarily actualized, although it is practically impossible to keep the three selves separate'. This gives a good indication of Andreach's unsympathetic and sometimes baffling prose style, as well as suggesting that the concerns of the book are somewhat compromised by layering the classical/contemporary discussion on top of what apparently remains Andreach's primary concern, the presentation of self. There is also a certain grim inevitability about the approach to each play, as in the discussion of Albee's *The Zoo Story*, which jumps in a paragraph from recognizing that 'Jerry's description of the dog and description of the hag indicate that he understands the significance of the epic descent' to finding in this an illustration of 'an initiatory death' that then invokes an enumeration of a large number of examples from Dante and classical literature, none of which particularly aids in the understanding of the play. In short, Andreach's problem is that confronted by all studies that make a single element central to the reading of genre: they inescapably privilege similarity over difference at the expense of engaging with recalcitrant detail. This, and the style, make the book a dull and unrewarding read.

A related but more focused study is Kevin J. Wetmore Junior's *Black Dionysus: Greek Tragedy and African American Theatre*, which examines how Greek tragedy has been used to explore African American identity. To this end, he makes a threefold distinction between 'Black Orpheus' (which is Eurocentric, the African American being read metaphorically in terms of the European), 'Black Athena' (the Afrocentric assumption that considers the Greek model to have been derived from Afro-Asiatic origins, a view questioned by Wetmore in a fascinating discussion), and 'Black Dionysus' (which 'us[es] Greek material metaphorically, but presents the material in a counter-hegemonic, subversive manner … to critique the dominant culture using its own material'). A lengthy chapter explores the presentation of Greek drama on the African American stage and discusses aspects of production, including non-traditional casting, and the effects of the transcultural insertion of elements from one culture into another. This chapter contains analysis of works by Adrienne Kennedy, Lee Breuer and Rita Dove, while the next focuses specifically on productions of *Medea*; a final chapter discusses the Caribbean. It is unfortunate that the introduction to the book is somewhat declamatory and excessively self-conscious about terminology, because otherwise this is a lucid and engaging account.

Konstantinos Blatanis's *Popular Culture Icons in Contemporary American Drama* surveys Hollywood, rock music, television and pulp fiction, before looking at the West and the figure of the cowboy. The book presses all of the likelier theoretical buttons, including Jean Baudrillard and Fredric Jameson, and covers a range of playwrights including Thomas Babe, John Guare, Len Jenkin, Adrienne Kennedy, Arthur Kopit, Michael McClure, Terrence McNally, Stephen Metcalfe, Marsha Norman and Jean-Claude Van Itallie. This is an impressively diverse range of playwrights, but in the final analysis the book rather suffers for it, perhaps because Shepard, who remains the dominant figure here, has been the subject of more detailed analyses along similar lines that dig deeper into the relationships between text and performance, the canonical author and popular culture, and modernism and postmodernism. Finally, Jenckes, ed., *New Readings in American Drama: Something's Happening Here*, is a collection of nineteen essays on various dramatists and topics, all of which have been previously published in *American Drama* and therefore previously reviewed in *YWES*. The selection is judicious, and in keeping with the interests of the parent journal the essays are focused more on drama than on theatre.

(b) Individual Playwrights

Two excellent essays provide illuminating historical contexts for Eugene O'Neill's work. In a superbly original discussion, Tamsen Wolff, in '"Eugenic O'Neill" and the Secrets of *Strange Interlude*' (*TJ* 55[2003] 215–34), explains the contemporary popularity yet subsequent critical dismissal of O'Neill's problematic play of 1928 by historicizing its melodramatic anxieties about heredity in the context of a debate surrounding eugenics at the time of its first production. Eugenics provided O'Neill with a framework for exploring relations between past and present, visibility and spectatorship, and linear causality. Wolff's exceptionally thorough research convincingly supports her suggestion that, 'Given the flawed forces of heredity in O'Neill's play, arguably audiences were looking to theatre as much to contradict as to uphold the vision of linear causality that the eugenics movement asserted … eugenics fed both desires and anxieties about what would be transmitted to a postwar generation. At the same time, in drawing on the phenomenon of eugenics and exploiting its inherent tensions, O'Neill began to rethink the shape and effect of drama.' Equally good is Patrick J. Chura, '"Vital Contact": Eugene O'Neill and the Working Class' (*TCL* 49[2003] 520–46), which historicizes the youthful O'Neill's many attempts to adopt working-class signifiers within the context of 'vital contact', wherein 1910s well-heeled liberals and radicals would attempt to acquire an invigorating masculinity—or, for women, 'a surrogate maternal function'—by means of cross-class contact. Chura traces O'Neill's engagement with this idea through the early plays up to *The Hairy Ape* [1922], which he analyses at illuminating length, concluding that, for O'Neill, this process was ultimately, and typically, marked by disillusionment: 'By the time O'Neill began writing *Long Day's Journey into Night* in 1939, he seems to have understood not only the ineluctable harm of cross-class interventions ... but also a potentially injurious oversimplification underlying his own youthful and adventure-driven "vital contact".'

Lawrence Dugan, 'The Tyrone Anthology: Authority in the Last Act of *Long Day's Journey into Night*' (*CompD* 37[2003] 379–95), argues that the play in effect concludes twice: the dramatic problems and questions have been resolved by the end of Act III, while the battle of quotations in Act IV 'is an essential element in understanding who speaks with most authority in the play, in discovering who is right and who wrong in its extended argument'. Dugan analyses both the quotations and the contents of both of the bookcases on the stage: 'The first is a repository of authors quoted by Janie and Edmund, holding an analytic, fragmented modern romanticism, while the other bookcase represents Tyrone's older, broader tradition, one that seems well-integrated.' Tyrone, however, lacks philosophy, and, 'a bad Catholic, is left holding the banner of a perverse Whig version of history as understood by a romantic', while his flawed sons are nevertheless 'not without a sense of intellectual confidence'. Mary, on the other hand, is 'spiritually impotent' and 'not sincere'.

Christopher J. Herr's *Clifford Odets and American Political Theatre* is a rare book-length study of the playwright who, after O'Neill, was arguably the most important playwright of the 1930s, and certainly the most important new playwright. Herr provides much useful information about Odets, and the substantial, central chapter on 'the marketplace in Odets' Group plays' is a valuable critical analysis of the writer's best work. If there is a certain sense of disappointment after reading Herr's book, it is perhaps because Praeger's new 'Lives of the Theatre' series may have placed constraints on the writing, so that the book oscillates between social, critical and biographical analysis within such a short span (around 150 pages minus the chronology and bibliography) that it cannot do justice to all or any of these topics. There may, however, be a problem with Odets himself as subject. The outlines of the life are sufficiently well known, and in any case fall into a somewhat predictable career arc: the son of an immigrant, coming of age during the 1920s and joining Harold Clurman's Group Theatre in time to become its most important playwright as the Depression bit, his radical politics soon becoming unacceptable to a conservative Cold War mentality, and his work in the theatre losing out to the more commercial interests of Hollywood as his star waned. Paradoxically, although Odets is one of those playwrights whose work seems inextricable from the life, one hardly needs the biography, because he is so easily inscribed within other, larger theatrical and social movements of the period: the immigrant experience, the Depression, the Group Theatre and the Federal Theatre Project, he Second World War, the HUAC hearings, the familiar standoff between Broadway and Hollywood. Consequently, Herr's solid study would have benefited from a still closer critical engagement with the plays.

Philip C. Kolin, ed., *The Undiscovered Country: The Later Plays of Tennessee Williams* (Lang [2002]), will be reviewed next time. In 'Williams's *The Demolition Downtown*' (*Expl* 62:i[2003] 39–41), Kolin intriguingly notes that the apocalyptic elements of this one-act play of 1971, including its 'futuristic and revolutionary America' and subtitle *Count Ten in Arabic—and Try to Run*, invite comparison to our own joyous times. Reclaiming the piece for Williams's oft-overlooked radicalism, Kolin aptly describes it as the playwright's 'political comedy of terror'. Brian Sutton, 'Williams's *The Glass Menagerie* and Uhry's *The Last Night of Ballyhoo*' (*Expl* 61:iii[2003] 172–4), notes that, although the two works are completely unrelated by theme or idea, Alfred Uhry's play 'almost entirely replicates some of *The Glass Menagerie*'s characters and the relationships among them. It also replicates the earlier play's closing image and its political and social setting', even though the influence appears to have been, in a word that has acquired unfortunate connotations in Britain in the wake of the Hutton inquiry, 'subconscious'.

Martin Gottfried's substantial new biography, *Arthur Miller: His Life and Work* (Da Capo [2003]) will be reviewed next time. Several essays appeared on Miller, mostly devoted to *Death of a Salesman*. Terry W. Thompson, 'The Ironic Hercules Reference in *Death of a Salesman*' (*ELN* 40:iv[2003] 73–7), observes that when Willy tells Biff he is 'Like a young God, Hercules—something like that', he characteristically does not realize that he is accurately both predicting his son's failure and implying his own inadequacies as a father. In 'Miller's *Death of a Salesman*' (*Expl* 60:iii[2002] 162–3), Thompson notes similar ironies in Willy's comparison of his sons to 'Adonises'. James E. Walton, '*Death of a Salesman*'s Willy Loman and *Fences*'s Troy Maxson: Pursuers of the Elusive American Dream' (*CLAJ* 47:i[2003] 55–65), takes a very familiar comparison between these plays of Arthur Miller and August Wilson, respectively, but turns it on its head by insisting that 'Troy Maxson caught more hell *every* day of his life than Willy Loman ever saw'. A quick-off-the-mark Jeffrey D. Mason offers, in 'Arthur Miller's Ironic Resurrection' (*TJ* 55[2003] 657–77), a close reading of Miller's 2002 play *Resurrection Blues*, bookending the analysis with an argument that the play illustrates a shift in Miller away from the seemingly committed (and yet, Mason suggests, equivocal) activism of his earlier work towards a position in which 'irony is the essential mode … The *sine qua non* of activism is not just conviction, but faith in one's convictions and in the potential for action to realize them. Miller's detailed vision of his characters' weaknesses leaves him too cynical to find a resolution to the problems they create.' Miller's own short speech 'Unlocking the Secrets of Cultures' (printed in *TDR* 47:i[2003] 5–7) offers something of a footnote to his *Salesman in Beijing* by reflecting on the playwright's experiences of Japanese productions on his work and concluding that 'beneath the varieties of different etiquettes, social communication, local habits and conventions, there is a common humanity, a reassurance, but only up to a point'.

American Drama for 2003 is a special double issue devoted to the work of Arthur Laurents. It features excerpts from two of Laurents's plays (*My Good Name* [1996] and *Jolson Sings Again* [1999]), and celebratory remarks by Stephen Sondheim and David Saint. These pieces aside, the entire double issue is the work of Gabriel Miller. The most substantial of these pieces are 'The Meaning of the Moon: The Plays of Arthur Laurents' (*AmDram* 12:i–ii[2003] 9–51), which offers a critical overview of Laurents's work for the stage as a whole, and 'An Interview with Arthur Laurents' (*AmDram* 12:i–ii[2003] 57–110), an exceptionally revealing discussion in which Laurents discusses his life and work and makes trenchant observations about productions of many plays by himself and others. The remainder of the issue contains three further interviews, with 'Nicholas Martin on Directing Arthur Laurents' (*AmDram* 12:i–ii[2003] 140–60), 'Andre Bishop on the Intelligent Craft of Arthur Laurents' (*AmDram* 12:i–ii[2003] 161–74), which contains discussion about the potential for future productions at the Lincoln Center, and 'Bernadette Peters on *Gypsy*' (*AmDram* 12:i–ii[2003] 175–83). In all, this is a full and engaging collection that, with some revision and additional critical material, could easily have made a book.

After a lengthy period in which almost nothing of note was published about Edward Albee, he is now receiving extensive attention, largely in the wake of *Three Tall Women*; one can expect this trend to continue after his brilliant *The Goat; or, Who Is Sylvia?* [2002]. That play appeared too late to receive more than a passing mention by the author as a work in progress in Mann, ed., *Edward Albee: A Casebook*. This is a collection of all-new material, including the editor's wide-ranging discussion with the playwright that largely restates views Albee has expressed many times before but includes the fascinating observation that the ending of *Three Tall Women* was modelled on the fugue at the end of *Don Giovanni*. Anne Paolucci's 'Edward Albee: A Retrospective (and Beyond)' is a celebratory survey that represents an overview of both Albee's career and the critical stance of this doyenne of Albee studies, rehearsing again her Pirandellian analysis and including an unusually extensive discussion and defence of *The Man Who Had Three Arms*. Two pieces consider the plays from the director's point of view, with Rakesh H. Solom discussing Albee's own work as director via a well-documented study of a 1978–9 production of *Box* and *Quotations from Chairman Mao Tse-Tung*, and Lawrence Sacharow's first-hand account of directing *Three Tall Women*. Not surprisingly, this 1994 play, which saw Albee's return to popular and critical acclaim, is the most extensively analysed work in the collection. Mann's '*Three Tall Women*: Return to the Muses' examines the autobiographical genesis of the play and compares it to other later-life autobiographical pieces such as O'Neill's *Long Day's Journey into Night* and Williams's *Something Cloudy, Something Clear*. Lincoln Konkle's study of *Who's Afraid of Virginia Woolf?*, which presents Albee as an American Jeremiah, covers similar ground to that trodden previously by this critic in 'American Jeremiah: Edward Albee as Judgment Day Prophet in *The Lady from Dubuque*' (*AmDram* 7:i[1997] 30–49). Ronald F. Rapin takes a different approach to this problematic play in his contribution to the *Casebook*, '*The Lady from Dubuque*: Into the Labyrinth', although the piece is rather too brief to make much headway with the self-reflexive complexities of the piece. Emily Rosenbaum's 'A Demystified Mystique: *All Over* and the Cult of True Womanhood' is equally short, although more interesting in anchoring the play in various nineteenth- and twentieth-century constructions of womanhood and femininity. Konkle, Rosenbaum and, indeed, Albee himself demonstrate one strand of criticism of this playwright that finds his recurrent concerns to be rooted deep in the foundational stories and structures of America. A different strand, represented to some extent by Rapin but more extensively in this collection by Lisa M. Siefker Bailey, Robert F. Gross and Norma Jenckes, locates those concerns somewhat later, at the boundaries of modernism and postmodernism. Bailey's 'Absurdly American: Rediscovering the Representation of Violence in *The Zoo Story*' occupies largely familiar territory in tracing the violence of this play to the Cold War anxieties of 1950s America, and the invocation of a Derridean *différance* looks a little forced. The neologism in the title of Gross's 'Like Father, Like Son: The Ciphermale in *A Delicate Balance* and *Malcolm*' refers to that recurrent figure in Albee's work, the 'characterological blank', 'male protagonists who exhibit a pronounced passivity that arises from loss'. This well-researched and solidly theorized discussion persuasively roots the plays 'in the dynamics of gender and sexuality in mid-'60s American culture', and argues that 'In place of in-depth psychological portraiture, the ciphermale is a collage of impulses, both diffident and passionate, that cannot be explained by references to a psychological case history.' In 'Postmodernist Tensions in Albee's Recent Plays', Norma Jenckes argues that *Marriage Play*, *Fragments* and *Three Tall Women* explore the tensions between postmodernist self-ironizing and modernist sincerity, with Albee ultimately remaining 'a high modernist' with 'a nostalgia for meaning' who 'cannot abandon the search for truth'. That seems right, and in general the *Casebook* offers both a solid introduction for those with little prior knowledge of this important playwright as well as some stimulating discussion for the expert. Several of the essays are too short to be particularly useful, however, and at just 150 pages the book cannot possibly do justice to the range and depth of Albee's work. The inadequately short critical book is another depressingly notable feature of current publishing trends, as is the unavoidable observation that $114.95, like $80 billion, doesn't go very far these days.

Rana Nayar's *Edward Albee: Towards a Typology of Relationships* categorizes the interpersonal relationships in Albee's plays as variously 'circular' (rigid and without exit), 'dialectical' (when violence, but with the possibility of synthesis and growth, becomes the only possibility), symptomatic' (pathologically one-sided), 'symbiotic' (sado-masochistic and over-dependent), 'transformative' (a regenerative relationship between autonomous subjects) and 'abstract' (existentialist, metaphysical and ontological; the category is to a large extent defined by contrast with the preceding five 'concrete' kinds of relationship). Although the book captures to some extent the variety of relationships in Albee's work, it rapidly becomes tedious, partly because it is unconvincingly schematic but also because of its wholesale and largely unsubstantiated dismissal of much previous criticism, combined, at times, with a dangerously naive swallowing of some complacent right-wing humbug. For example, Nayar claims that 'All those critics who choose to talk about Albee's concern with problems other than that of human relationships somehow miss the point that he was, first and foremost, a humanist … A great majority of Albee critics have chosen to ignore the fact that it is the problematics of relationships that gives to the diverse body of his work, a sense of coherence as well as continuity.' Who are these critics who have somehow missed Albee's obvious humanism and the functions of relationships in his work? And is Nayar suggesting that it would be idiotic to write about anything other than relationships? Is it in any way helpful to cite approvingly Paul Johnson's description of the 1960s as the 'decade of illusion' when, in the following sentence, Nayar notes that 'This was the period marked with anti-war protests, urban riots, rise of Black power and democratic explosion'? Aside from the critical myopia and often imperfect English, there are some alarming errors: *The Man Who Had Three Arms*, which dates from 1982, becomes '*Man with Three Arms* [1989]', and it is simply not true that this play and *Lolita* 'not only dazzled the audiences across America, but also received rave reviews from the theatre critics'; in fact, those plays represent the nadir of Albee's critical reception. Sam Shepard becomes 'Sam Shepherd', and Gareth Lloyd Evans becomes 'Gerath Llyod Evans', which will distress the Welsh. Frank Ardolino, in 'Nugent and Thurber's *The Male Animal* and Albee's *Who's Afraid of Virginia Woolf?*' (*Expl* 61:ii[2003] 112–14) uses the fact that both Albee's work and Elliot Nugent and James Thurber's play allude to the nursery rhyme 'Who's Afraid of the Big Bad Wolf?' to identify a few further connections.

Lotta M. Löfgren, 'Clay and Clara: Baraka's *Dutchman*, Kennedy's *The Owl Answers*, and the Black Arts Movement' (*MD* 46[2003] 424–49), reads Adrienne Kennedy's play of 1965 as a response to Amiri Baraka's foundational play of the previous year. Löfgren situates this dialogue within a broader context in which Kennedy, initially marginalized by Baraka and other members of the Black Arts Movement for her supposed 'double consciousness', in fact represents a more fertile engagement with issues of race and sexual identity than does the monologic revolutionary voice espoused by the movement in the 1960s. 'For Kennedy, monologism is the true horror', and in Löfgren's supple analysis this is already revealed in the character of Lula in *Dutchman*, who 'is white and black, male and female, real and mythic. In fact, she mitigates Baraka's misogyny in fascinating ways.' Similarly, Jacqueline Wood, in 'Weight of the Mask: Parody and the Heritage of Minstrelsy in Adrienne Kennedy's *Funnyhouse of a Negro*' (*JDTC* 17:ii[2003] 5–24), argues for the 'duality' of Kennedy's work, in this case by analysing the parody of minstrelsy, and specifically blackface, via Henry Louis Gates's work on 'Signifyin', where 'Signifyin' is itself seen as a black hermeneutics of the parodic performance'. This is by now quite a familiar approach, although it remains productive, and in this essay provides a solid theoretical foundation for Wood's argument, which again resembles Löfgren's in presenting Kennedy as a playwright who 'at the end of the twentieth and the beginning of the twenty-first century is finally beginning to receive credit for the complex manner in which she views and has always viewed American race politics'.

Laurin Porter, *Orphans' Home: The Voice and Vision of Horton Foote*, explores the nine-play *Orphans' Home Cycle*, written in the 1970s. Porter makes the comparison to O'Neill that is inevitable not only because each wrote a major cycle but because Porter sees Foote's major theme as being the very O'Neillian preoccupation with time and the relation between past and present, although for Porter this is also inflected through a Faulknerian southern accent, this southernness, particularly in the approach to place and family, being the major broader context in which porter Places Foote's work. This aside, the discussion is rather embedded, Foote's uniqueness being taken somewhat for granted. Porter shares her subject's humanist interest in why some people's lives work out and others don't, in why people are the way they are, in the relationships between individual and family. She makes some useful core observations: unlike O'Neill's rather frantic and unconvincing attempts to capture demotic speech, Foote's characters 'all sound the same' and can speak only the language their culture makes available; his language 'seems to disappear', and the plots have a kind of Chekhovian inactivity. The structure of both the plays and of Porter's book is underpinned by an awareness of leitmotifs, parallel characters, and 'parallel and inverted episodes', a strategy that Porter then expands to show how individual plays within the cycle are paired. This is the latest of a number of book-length studies that have been devoted to the previously neglected Texan, although Porter, like others, runs the risk of contributing to his marginalization by continuing to position him as a figure geographically and aesthetically at the edge of American drama.

David K. Sauer and Janice A. Sauer, *David Mamet: A Research and Production Sourcebook*, is, like other volumes in this series, an invaluable resource. Beginning with a primary bibliography and selected shorter pieces and interviews, the Sauers proceed to an annotated bibliography of criticism, with sections on each of the plays, followed by a consideration of texts treating multiple works, before returning to listings of dissertations, film scholarship, and bibliographical work. It is a little disappointing that the work on film does not receive any annotation or commentary. This produces some strange distortions: for example, only the shortish section on plays in Gay Brewer's *David Mamet and Film: Illusion/Disillusion in a Wounded Land* (McFarland [1992]) receives any comment, with the bulk of the book being passed over in silence. This is probably due to the restrictions imposed by the series format, but in Mamet's case it is unfortunate. This caveat aside, the book is highly illuminating. A fairly meaty paragraph is devoted to each article, within which there is usually sufficiently lucid description or extensive quotation to give a reasonable flavour of the piece, and a remarkably, and often almost invisibly, dry wit informs much of the commentary. At least, I think it does.

Two essays commenting on Mamet's films were published elsewhere. For Mike Digou, examples of 'Hitchcock's MacGuffin in the Works of David Mamet' (*LFQ* 31:iv[2003] 270–5) include the coin in *American Buffalo*, the 'leads' in *Glengarry Glen Ross*, the 'process' in *The Spanish Prisoner*, and the bribe paid to Gino in *Things Change*. This list collapses a number of important distinctions, and in a curious discussion of *The Spanish Prisoner* Digou seems to miss his own point: 'Mamet's lack of humor results in the occurrence of short, abrupt, incomplete, cliché-ridden sentences in the discussions about the MacGuffin. Carried on for some length, a scene of this type becomes difficult to follow, and suggests that Mamet and his characters have no idea what the Process is.' Three and a half pages are devoted to Mamet in Brian Woolland, 'Tricksters, Hucksters and Suckers: Jonsonian Cinema' (in Woolland, ed. *Jonsonians: Living Traditions*, pp. 203–28). The comparison to Jonson has been made before, but in small space Woolland nevertheless establishes a number of important points: that Mamet's view of characterization resembles Jonsonian Humours; that in

House of Games 'Ford's desire to take unrealistic control of the world around her places her in the strange company of Sejanus, Fitzdotterel and Morose'; that both dramatists are interested in 'the commodification of human exchange' and 'use the confidence trick as a dramatic device to reveal self-delusion'; and, most trenchantly of all, that Mamet's dislike of Method acting and psychological characterization 'is also revealing of a thoroughly Jonsonian tendency to want total control of his texts', and 'contrasts with the openness of the texts themselves … Given the nature of his dialogue, which is often clipped, elliptical and self-reflexively performative, this is a deep—and profoundly Jonsonian—contradiction.'

Fesmire, ed., *Beth Henley: A Casebook*, provides the first substantial study of the works of a playwright who is largely known for a single play, *Crimes of the Heart*, first produced in 1979. Although, as one would expect, many of the contributions argue that this unfairly distorts and limits Henley's achievement, it is a gnawing obsession that ultimately defines the collection. Only one of the seven contributions, Gene A. Plunka's 'Existential Despair and the Modern Neurosis: Beth Henley's *Crimes of the Heart*', is devoted to this play, although Linda Rohrer Paige's essay looks at its film adaptation alongside that of *The Miss Firecracker Contest*. Several pieces broaden the understanding of Henley's work by placing her in the context of southern literature. In 'Lessons from the Past: Loss and Redemption in the Early Plays of Beth Henley', Larry G. Mapp briefly relates the themes of family, culture and the loss of community in six of Henley's plays to the work of writers such as William Faulkner, Kate Chopin and Zora Neale Hurston, while Gary Richards's 'Moving Beyond Mississippi: Beth Henley and the Anxieties of Postsouthernness' more expansively sees the plays of the 1990s as engaging parodically with notions of southernness in order to escape from its confining constructions. One of the supposedly dominant modes of 'southern' writing, the grotesque, is the subject of Miriam M. Chirico's '"Dancing on the edge of a cliff": Images of the Grotesque in the Plays of Beth Henley'. Chirico notes that although the grotesque is more prominent in the later plays it has been there from the beginning, contributing to one of this books primary aims: to argue for Henley as a more experimental and less realistic writer than is commonly assumed. Similarly, Chirico, like Richards, is concerned to take Henley beyond the constricting boundaries of southernness, although this runs the risk of collapsing important distinctions, as when she suggests that the grotesque engages with 'a portion of the human condition'. Again, Rebecca King's '*The Lucky Spot* as Immanent Critique' seeks to distance Henley from the southern label, this time by intriguingly reading this play's critique of familial relationships and, in King's view, of liberalism more generally, through a lens that relates its presentation of liberalism and capitalism to the ideas of Thomas Hobbes and John Locke. Karen L. Laughlin likewise argues for a radical feminism in Henley in 'Abundance or Excess? Beth Henley's Postmodern Romance of the True West', which compares *Abundance* [1989] to Sam Shepard's *True West*. Given the concerted attempts by the contributors to present Henley as a more radical playwright, politically and formally, than has generally been perceived, it is bizarre that in her introduction Fesmire admits that 'I always think of her in conjunction with songwriter and singer Christopher Cross, who burst upon the music scene at about the same time Henley achieved her first success in 1979. Cross's first album … was one of the most celebrated debut albums of all time … Just as many music fans consider *Rendezvous* [1992], or even *Walking in Avalon* [1998], to be Christopher Cross's best work, taking his music in new directions, many of Henley's later plays are rich texts for discerning critics.' On the contrary, no real music fan would have any album by Christopher Cross anywhere on the premises, and in making the comparison Fesmire unintentionally reinforces the one view of Henley that the *Casebook* is specifically designed to repudiate: that she, like Cross, is a one-hit non-wonder.

In 'Been There, Done That: Paving the Way for *The Vagina Monologues*' (*MD* 46[2003] 404–23), Shelly Scott discusses the performance history and reception of Eve Ensler's play before situating it in the context of its forerunners in the feminist theatres of the 1970s. Scott ponders the implications of the fact that 'This sense of isolation and struggle for survival is an updated version of what the consciousness-raising groups of the seventies targeted', concluding ambivalently that 'history is repeating itself in a watered-down way'.

5. Native, Asian American, Latino/a and General Ethnic Writing

Not a little boldly, Robert Dale Parker's *The Invention of Native American Literature* takes on the thorny perennial of what actually is meant by Native writing. Careful about his own ideological positioning, and at a lively turn of pace, he tries to think through which bearings best apply. Does Native writing encompass each and every work by writers of Native heritage? What, with due recognition of the slipperiness of all literary-cultural category, has that body of writing most invented? The upshot is nothing if not engaging: revisionist readings of John Joseph Mathews's Osage-centred *Sundown*[1934] and D'Arcy McNickle's Salish-Flathead world of *The Surrounded*[1936] as fictions of 'restless young men'; a rethinking of how Native oral story works in written or video form and with case-analysis of the poetry and narratives of Ray Young Bear, Leslie Marmon Silko and Thomas King; and an epilogue taken up with ongoing issues of canonicity and representativeness from John Rollin Ridge through to Elizabeth Cook-Lynn. Parker's own contextual savvy, which draws upon African American and Latino/a debate as well as a Native literary-critical roster of Robert Warrior, Craig Womack and others, serves him well. He rightly sees his orientation as deriving from critical multiculturalism, readings alert to the width and hybridity of recent Native American literature yet keenly centred in the imaginative specificities of his chosen texts. It makes for an agreeably bracing critique.

Elvira Pulitano's *Towards A Native Critical Theory*, the work of a Swiss-based Italian scholar whose doctoral work was done under the supervision of Louis Owens, does important service in mapping the body of Native-generated literary theory. Using a spectrum of Paula Gunn Allen, Robert Warrior, Craig Womack, Greg Sarris, Louis Owens and Gerald Vizenor, she delineates the span of comparative approaches and typologies. Her account thus turns on 'gynocentrism' in Allen as a Native-feminist analogy with Alice Walker's

African American womanism; Native 'red-stick' viewpoint in Warrior and Womack—a kind of cultural-separatist ethos in whose name Elizabeth Cook-Lynn is also invoked; dialogism, and other hybridities of form, as the refraction of mixedblood Native lives in the fiction of Sarris and Owens; and the trickster aesthetic of Gerald Vizenor as the pathway, in his best-known signature phrase, into a 'postindian' sense of history. In eschewing non-Native scholarship like that, say, of Arnold Krupat, Karl Kroeber or Brian Swann, Pulitano runs a certain risk of too exclusivist or hermetic a focus, the closed in-house comparison of the one 'Native' track as against the other. But the returns are not to be denied. As Native writing emerges ever more into visibility, and with it the quickening cross-ply of debate about appropriate critical theory and etiquette, she offers a keen, elucidatory survey of ideological workings.

Breinig, ed., *Imaginary (Re-)Locations: Tradition, Modernity, and the Market in Contemporary Native American Literature and Culture*, bears witness to the ongoing German interest in Native culture. Based on a University of Erlangen-Nürnberg conference in 2000, this essay collection amounts to an inviting round of creative and interpretative work. The former includes a sheaf of poems by the White Earth Anishinaabe poet Kimberley Blaeser (especially 'Family Tree' as a memory-gallery of dynastic voice); a Haida grandfather story by Jeane Coburn Breinig (unrelated to the editor) together with a brief but vivid memoir of potatoes, flowers and raven myth by her mother Julie Coburn; 'The Powwow Committee', a wry if fond swipe at community politics by the First Nations Peigan writer Emma Lee Warrior; and extracts by the Anishinaabe authors Gerald Vizenor (including a scene from his 'postindian' novel *Chancers*) and Gordon Henry, author of *The Light People* [1994].

The critical contributions begin with a rich, carefully detailed anatomy by Breinig of 'identity positions' and what he terms 'transdifference' in, and behind, Native texts, whether oral-trickster or scriptural, from Leslie Marmon Silko to Gerald Vizenor. It sets a rallying note for the pieces to follow. These include James Ruppert on Native narratives of urban residence from Scott Momaday's *House Made of Dawn* [1968] to Louise Erdrich's poem 'Jacklight' and Gerald Vizenor's short film *Harold of Orange*; Klaus Lösch on imaginary and historic homelands in Momaday's *Ancient Child* [1989], Silko's *Almanac of the Dead*[1991] and Vizenor's *The Heirs of Columbus* [1991]; Arnold Krupat on three modes of deconstructing Native writing which he terms nationalist, indigenist and cosmopolitan; Hartwig Isernhagen on 'the identity of discourse' in Silko's *Gardens in the Dunes* [1999]; and, one of the collection's best-managed pieces, Brigitte Georgi-Findlay on the case for thinking the late Louis Owens's fiction and critical work as 'mixedblood' in its literary fashioning as in the life-issues which most drew his interests as a writer.

Rader and Gould, eds., *Speak To Me Words: Essays on Contemporary Indian Poetry*, brings together fifteen essays, a conspectus both general and particular of names and kinds from across the Native verse roster. Contributions, notably, include Eric Gary Anderson on the relevance or otherwise of received Western genre when applied to Native poetry; Daniel Heath Justice on the life-into-literature trope of weaving in the Cherokee poet Marilou Awiakta; Susan Berry Brill de Ramirez in a shrewdly comparative account of the oral as written in the poetry of Awiaka, Kimberley Blaeser (Anishianaabe) and Marilyn Dumont (Métis); Patricia Clark Smith on family as both division and refuge in poets like Marnie Walsh (Dakota) and nila northSun (Soshone-Chippewa); Dean Rader in a spirited account of 'lyric epic' as manifested in the poetry of Luci Tapahonso (Navajo), Simon Ortiz (Acoma) and Linda Hogan (Chickasaw); Paula Gunn Allen (Laguna-Sioux) on the bardic tradition in Native women's poetry; and the late Elaine A. Janner on Paula Gunn Allen's own evolving poetic style from the more abstract early poetry to the tough, circumstantial verse of a collection like *Life is a Fatal Disease* [1997]. There are two discursive pieces by leading poets: Carter Revard (Osage) in a series of paired comparisons (Simon Ortiz with Wallace Stevens for instance), in which healing acts as fulcrum, and Simon Ortiz, in an autobiographical essay, on song, dance and language as they shape his own and other Native poetry. The collection includes a useful primary and secondary bibliography.

Brian Holloway offers scrupulous scholarship in his *Interpreting the Legacy: John Neihardt and 'Black Elk Speaks'*, a full, due account of the collaboration between the Nebraska-based writer and journalist and the Oglala Lakota healer from Pine Ridge reservation, South Dakota, which has become a landmark of Native autobiography. Holloway documents the critical reception of the work, the various manuscript drafts and histories and Neihardt and Black Elk as interviewees in the wake of their joint text. Using recent theory-work on autobiography, he concludes with a number of apposite pathways into both the spirituality and the narrative shaping of the *Black Elk Speaks*. This, overall, makes for genuinely careful annotation and scholarship.

SAIL (15:i[2003]) devotes a complete issue to the Osage-born Carter Revard, the first-ever Native American Rhodes Scholar and the poet and writer of *Ponca War Dancers* [1980], *Cowboys and Indians*, *Christmas Shopping* [1992] and *An Eagle Nation* [1993], the essay collection *Family Matters, Tribal Affairs* [1998] and the subtle, mixed-genre memoir *Winning the Dust Bowl* [2001]. This timely celebration of his considerable body of work includes the printed version of Revard's 'Some Notes on Native American Literature' (*SAIL* 15:i[2003] 1–15), a consideration of literary genres, the role of anthologies and the environmental politics of fossil fuel and alternative forms of energy; the poem 'Transformations' (*SAIL* 15:i[2003] 16–21) on recent Anglo-US warmongering and its implications; and a short interview given to Janet M. McAdams mainly on form and measure in poetry. Critical accounts of his writing include Ellen Arnold on the operative seams of image in Revard's verse (*SAIL* 15:i[2003] 32–9); Lauren Stuart Mullen on his use of song allusion throughout the poetry (*SAIL* 15:i[2003] 53–9); Suzanne Evertsen Lundquist on Osage and related other Oklahoma ethnography as it enters Revard's different texts (*SAIL* 15:i[2003] 67–73); a number of online exchanges as to Revard's general standing and achievement (*SAIL* 15:i[2003] 109–41); and a selective but greatly helpful Revard bibliography (*SAIL* 15:i[2003] 142–9).

In 'Louise Erdrich's Lulu Nanapush: A Modern-Day Wife of Bath?' (*SAIL* 15:i[2003] 92–103) Peter Beidler engages in a lively speculation as to the Chaucer–Erdrich connection. On offer is a shrewdly turned source-analysis, the overlapping similarities which give grounds for aligning Lulu Nanapush

Morrissey Lamartine of Erdrich's *Tales of Burning Love* and her other fiction with Chaucer's Alisoun, the Wife of Bath, whether in the form of their respective forms of sexual initiation or their shared gapped teeth. Beidler returns to Erdrich's imaginative world in '"In the Old Language": A Glossary of Ojibwe Words, Phrases, and Sentences in Louise Erdrich's Novels' (*AICRJ*27:iii[2003] 53–70), a brief reprise of Erdrich's use of Ojibway terminology in her fiction. Typically he alights on usage such as *daashkikaa* ('cracked apart') as a key locution in *The Antelope Wife*. A listing of relevant Ojibway language dictionaries is also given. For Julie Tharp in 'Windigo Ways: Eating and Excess in Louise Erdrich's *The Antelope Wife*' (*AICRJ*27:iv[2003] 117–31), the windigo, defined as 'a cannibalistic monster set loose by human greed, envy, and jealousy', serves as one of the determining metaphors at work in the novel. In a narrative which begins with a US cavalry attack on a sleeping Indian encampment and continues its timeline through to modern-day Minneapolis, food becomes the very trope of survival, a way of sustaining Ojibway dynasty in all its tribal and mixedblood turns against odds and time. As Tharp convincingly demonstrates, male and female cooks proliferate in the novel, with Erdrich's deployment of nutrition reference and imagery necessary shaping tropes in her overall story.

Patrice Hollrah's '"The men in the bar feared her": The Power of Ayah in Leslie Marmon Silko's "Lullaby"' (*SAIL*15:ii[2003] 1–38) develops a careful and extensive reading of the story 'Lullaby' that was first published as a separate entity and then incorporated into *Storyteller* [1981]. Ayah's internal soliloquy, it is suggested, opens from her personal situation into a more inclusive dispensation of Navaho gender relations, matrilineal power, the complexities of *hozho* or balance, alcoholism, the role of tribal ritual and healing, and spider-woman as figured in Ayah herself. It makes for an informed, well-taken reading.

SAIL(15:iii–iv[2003]) offers a joint issue on Latino/a and Native literary intersections and hybridities not only of subject-matter but expressive form. The coverage does good duty in dealing with the comparative resort to myth within English, Spanish and Native-language texts, and different kinds of code-switching and humour. A key name which recurs as reference-point is that of the leading Chicana feminist Gloria Anzaldúa, especially in issues of *mestizaje*. For Molly McGlennen in 'Adjusting the Margins: Locating Identity in the Poetry of Diane Glancy' (*SAIL*15:iii–iv[2003] 128–46), Glancy's (to date) thirteen poetry collections act as an ongoing imaginative site of mixedblood experience and memory. Highlighting Glancy's Cherokee, German–English heritage and Arkansas backcountry roots, she builds an informative map of 'borderline' legacy as it operates in the poetry, typically in compositions like 'Iron Woman' and 'The Revenant'. A helpfully comparative essay is Shawna Thorp's 'Re-asserting the World: The Convergence of Mythic and Modern Realities in Enactment Narratives' (*SAIL*15:iii–iv[2003] 147–67). She addresses the interaction of tribal-indigenous myths of the supernatural with modernity in Silko's *Ceremony* [1977] and Louis Owens's *Nightland*[1996] in a close, well-observed examination of culture-specific Pueblo and Cherokee literary forms as against some amorphous pan-Indian allusion in the two novels.

Lee Schweninger's 'Claiming Europe: Native American Literary Responses to the Old World' (*AICRJ* 27:ii[2003] 61–76) offers a nice reversal of the usual

European and Euro-American 'discovery' accounts of Native America. Using Native authorship like Carter Revard's 'Report of the Nation: Claiming Europe' [1983], Gerald Vizenor's *The Heirs of Columbus*[1991], James Welch's *The Heartsong of Charging Elk* [2000], Leslie Marmon Silko's *Gardens in the Dunes* [1999] and Louise Erdrich's *The Master Butcher's Singing Club*[2002], Schweniger emphasizes the reverse-Atlantic reference within Native writing. In showing how each text uses a compendium of European reference, history and myth, he suggests a timely redress: Native America's vision of Europe seen both as endemic to its own modern cultural identity and, as it were, geography the other way round. *AIQ* for 2003 is currently not available; it will be covered in next year's *YWES*.

Patti Duncan's *Tell This Silence: Asian American Women Writers and the Politics of Speech* can be said to take up where King-Kok Cheung's *Articulate Silences: Hisaye Yamamoto, Maxine Hong Kingston, Joy Kogawa* [1993] left off. Using texts which span Maxine Hong Kingston to Meena Alexander, the issue, for Duncan, centres on the 'multiple meanings of silence', the different styles through which Asian American women's texts address the cultural and gender politics both of being silenced and the liberation of articulating, and so commandeering, that silence. To this end she offers strong, pertinent readings of the energies of 'counter-discourse' in Mitsuye Yamada's *Camp Notes* [1976], Joy Kogawa's *Obasan* [1981], Theresa Hak Kyung Cha's *Dictée* [1982], Nora Okja Keller's *Comfort Woman* [1997] and Anchee Min's *Red Azalea* [1994]. This account is assiduously grounded in queer and feminist theory as it holds for 'liberative' writing, the refusal, as Duncan construes it, of Asian women writers to allow themselves to be situated at the margin or to 'participate in their own erasure'.

The contribution of Winnifred Eaton Reeve, an author Chinese British by birth and US and Canadian Japanese by pseudonym, to Asian American writing has increasingly won recognition, not least in the implications of the persona she invented for herself as Onoto Watanna. Jean Lee Cole's *The Literary Voices of Winnifred Eaton: Redefining Ethnicity and Authenticity* adds greatly to the ongoing process of reappraisal. This is an exploration of the masks, the voices, which operate inside Eaton's fiction, and which contributed greatly to her success as an American popular writer. Ethnicity, in more than an obvious sense of setting or character, actually plays little central role in her work; but in Cole's account, the sixteen or so novels inaugurated with *Miss Numè of Japan* [1899] and the plethora of short stories and different Hollywood scenarios and film scripts, come at it more obliquely. The Asian and other ethnic legacy which would seem to enter a novel like *A Japanese Blossom*[1906], or conversely seem wholly absent, as in her last novel, *His Royal Nibs* [1925], in fact gets displaced into a deliberate run of invented 'authorial personae'. These, intriguingly, Cole enumerates (and explores) as Eaton 'the flighty girl-author, a member of the urbane New York literati, booster of Japan, scrappy Hollywood screenwriter and arbiter of Canadian culture'.

Foster, Stewart and Fenkl, eds., *Century of The Tiger: One Hundred Years of Korean Culture in America, 1903–2003*, with texts and visual materials under the auspices of the Centennial Committee of Korean Immigration to the United

States, offers a handsome anthology of writing and art forged in the historical wake of the SS *Gaelic*'s landing in Honolulu with the first Korean immigrants in January 1903. The literary extracts include sequences from Younghill Kang's pioneer Korea-to-America autobiographical fictions *The Grass Roof*[1931] and *East Goes West* [1937], Kim Ronyoung's memory novel of Korean Los Angeles *Clay Walls*[1986], Richard Kim's intimate autobiography *Lost Names* [1988] and Mary Paik Lee's rare, affecting emigrant story *Quiet Odyssey* [1990], together with selective storytelling and poetry by Gary Pak, Don Lee, Sue Kwock Kim, Walter Lew and Chang-rae Lee. These, together with the volume's gloss paper, art work and calligraphy, are set out within an evolving chronological frame, five chapters spanning Korean history in brief through to an American history of New Arrivals, sojourners and settlers, and Koreans and Korean Americans. *Century of The Tiger* does timely good service as a compendium of word and visual image, its selections engaging both mind and eye.

Kim and Kang, eds., *Echoes Upon Echoes: New Korean American Writings*, makes for an apt follow-up, forty or so names brought together as a live current of contemporary literary work. Born, for the most part, in the 1970s, the contributors confirm a post-immigrant Korean America whether taken up or not with its own cultural hybridity. The span runs from Stephanie Uys's poetry of the Asian female body ('one country's | landscape shifting into another') to Dennis Kim's poetry of childbirth ('the yellow pages | of your skin), the inclusions each situated under the editors' six headings of arrival, return, dwelling, crossing, descent and flight. Strengths inevitably differ, but the well-titled *Echoes Upon Echoes* offers proof certain of the wide, ongoing flow by which Korean American word and imagining continues to find its measure. Less consequential is Dorothy M. Hong's primly titled *Tales From a Korean Maiden in America*, a slender folder of stories and journalism often in flawed English and not a little reflective of her own Korean-Christian shock at American moral licence.

Judith Oster's *Crossing Culture: Creating Identity in Chinese and Jewish American Literature* has a worthy enough aim, the overlap of two prime ethnic American literary traditions to do with migration, identity, community, inter-language and bi-culturism. The chosen texts are mainly of an autobiographical kind, factual and fictive, and span Anzia Yezierska to Philip Roth, Amy Tan to Frank Chin. Under related thematic headings such as 'Mirrors and Mirroring', 'Language and Self', and 'Family, and Education', Oster manages a number of shrewd explicatory and comparative readings. If, at times, there is a touch of the classroom manner in her tendency to put configurations of theme ahead of individual imaginative fashioning of the texts, the span-like the approach of the book is generously conceived. Huang, ed., *Asian American Short Story Writers: An A-To-Z Guide*, does more solid expository service, fifty or so entries ranging from the Filipino American novelist Peter Bacho to the Chinese American poet John Yau. An appropriate short primary and critical bibliography accompanies each entry.

A number of studies tangential to Asian American writing, but not to a cultural studies perspective, have come to hand. Although Gregory B. Lee's *Chinas Unlimited: Making the Imaginaries of China and Chineseness* mainly addresses the way China has been figured in the politics and popular culture of the UK—radio, newspapers, comedy, Liverpool as diasporic immigrant city—it offers a number of enlightening comparisons with the USA. Kim, Machida and Mizota, eds., *Fresh Talk Daring Gazes: Conversations on American Art*, offers a run of intriguing, original and handsomely illustrated annotations from paintings, installations, cartoon work, photography and line drawing by current artists of US Asian descent.

In Lee and Wong, eds., *Asian America.Net: Ethnicity, Nationalism, and Cyberspace*, Rachel C. Lee and Sau-ling Cynthia Wong bring together thirteen interdisciplinary essays dealing in how 'internet technology' has both attracted, and in turn imaged, Asian America, whether Vietnam as the first televized war, 'Oriental' Asian women and sexuality, Filipino Catholics and US Hindus, or the persisting stereotype of Asian Americans as cyber-nerds. For Kandice Chuh in *Imagine Otherwise: On Asian American Critique* the issue is Asian American studies as a field, a discipline. What paradigms, whether social, literary, legal, or cultural, best apply? Has not the field been too readily fashioned in the image of Euro-American studies? If there is not a collective Asian American discourse, how best to disinter the understanding of the one heritage-specific and interior cultural identity from another? For Chuh the corrective pathway lies in the study of comparative difference, from community history to individual forms of gender, from creative and authorial subjectivity to the larger expressive politics of transnationalism.

AmasJ (29:i[2003]) assigns its whole issue to 'Vietnamese Americans: Diaspora and Dimensions'. The span includes migrancy, employment, gender, the classroom syllabus—its inclusions and omissions, health issues, and generational change. Section V, 'Finding Voice', offers a short but vivid anthology of literary work: Isabelle Thuy Pelaud's analysis of Andrew X. Pham's *Catfish and Mandala: A Two Wheeled Voyage through the Landscape and Memory of Vietnam*[1999] as 'the Vietnamese American story most read in North America'; the visual artist Viet Le's poem 'I Sleep in Your Old Bed'; the memoirs of a Vietnamese Pennsylvanian resident like Brandy Liên Worral and the Houston-based chaplain Phúc Luu; and Michelle Janette's greatly useful overview and bibliography of Vietnamese American literature from 1963 to 1994. *AmasJ*(29:iii[2003]) in kind tackles Korean America: population studies, Korean settlement in China and Japan, the Korean War and the US, and an excavatory analysis by Seiwoong Oh (*AmasJ* 29.iii[2003] 43–55) of Philip Jaisoln Haisu's novella *James* [1921] as the likely first Korean American literary text. Oh makes a convincing argument for associating Haisu with the founding literary figure and generation of Younghill Kang. Although it contains no especially literary considerations the issue offers a wide-ranging overview of Asian American studies as an emergent, and anything but uncontentious, academic discipline in which a number of well-known scholars (among them the *Amerasia Journal*'s long-time editor Russell C. Leong, Glenn K. Omatsu, Arif Dirlik, Yen le Espiritu and David Palumbo-Liu) speak both to the present state of play and to prospective next stages.

In taking its title from Tomás Rivera's classic episode 'When We Arrive' in his bilingual ...*Y no se lo tragó la tierra / And the Earth Did Not Devour Him* [1971], José F. Aranda Jr.'s *When We Arrive: A New Literary History of Mexican*

America proposes 'a renarration of American literary history from the vantage point of Chicano/a studies'. The results are lively to a fault: identity issues as dramatized in literature from Lucha Corpi's *Eulogy for a Brown Angel*[1992] to the polemical texts of Richard Rodriguez and Gloria Anzaldúa; the dialectic of US multicultural and Anglo literary canon; the historic legacy of writers and scholars such as the nineteenth-century María Amparo Ruiz de Burton and early twentieth-century Américo Paredes; and a run of at first unlikely comparisons, such as the Puritan Michael Wigglesworth with Lorna Dee Cervantes as Chicana contemporary. Aranda's point, throughout, is well targeted: has there not been a huge and all too readily unregarded overlap in issues of community, dream, persecution or migrancy between Anglo and Hispanic literary-cultural traditions? Why, under US literary auspices, name the one tradition a mainstream and the other a minority? If American literature is indeed to be thought coeval, and inextricably multicultural, then appropriate taxonomies need to come into the reckoning: Aranda's account takes a bold, genuinely engaging step in that direction.

Maria Antònia Oliver-Rotger, a Catalan scholar, takes her working cue in *Battlegrounds and Crossroads: Social and Imaginary Space in Writings by Chicanas* from Gloria Anzaldúa's much circulated notion of borderlands: US literary terrain as one, despite conventional categories, *sin fronteras*. This leads directly into a full, closely annotated account of the writings of Ana Castillo, Sandra Cisneros, Pat Mora, Cherrié Moraga and Helena Viramontes, with an emphasis within their work on the treatment of gender and power relations and what Oliver-Rotger, a little abstractly, terms the 'multiplicity of communal struggles and predicaments'. Each writer, on this reading, is to be credited with an adversary stance, their authorship engaged in the rite of passage against patriarchal order. The upshot, it has to be said, is procedural, a somewhat dogged feminist-ideological and would-be postcolonial set of readings of 'real and imaginary borderlands' as, hardly a surprise, 'not necessarily fixed or stable'. The footfalls of a doctoral thesis lie within hearing.

The sixteen contributors to Dick, ed., *A Poet's Truth: Conversations with Latino/Latina Poets*, bring to bear a formidable line of Latino/a literary achievement: Miguel Algarín, Martín Espada, Sandra María Esteves, Victor Hernández Cruz, Carolina Hospital and Carlos Medina (a joint interview), Demetria Martínez, Pat Mora, Judith Ortiz Cofer, Ricardo Pau-Llosa, Gustavo Pérez Firmat, Leroy Quintana, Aleida Rodriguez, Luis Rodriguez, Benjamin Alire Sáenz and Virgil Suárez. The editor's questioning nicely responds to each poet's career (as against the one template for all) to invoke birth and upbringing, the role of Spanish alongside English, and the aims and effects of their respective bodies of poetry. The accompanying introduction, with its notation of the Chicano and the US Puerto Rican and Cuban literary spectrum, the photographs, and selective lists of publications, give an added particularity and cross-reference to a timely, and highly useful, volume.

In his interview with Bruce Dick, Gustavo Pérez Firmat speaks as a Cuban American author of 'life on the hyphen', a first-hand, lived US biculturism also reflected in his 1994 volume *Life on the Hyphen: The Cuban-American Way*. It points directly to his new discursive work, again teasingly entitled, *Tongue Ties:*

Logo-Eroticism in Anglo-Hispanic Literature. Firmat displays all his well-known agility as poet, novelist and critic in his ruminations on bilingualism, the difference between US English and Cuban Spanish literary traditions and, in a typical show of relish, 'the 'knots of language and sexuality'. He brings an amply informed literary perspective to bear, from George Santayana to Richard Rodriguez, from Guillermo Cabrera Infante and the neglected Calvert Casey to the role of *I Love Lucy*in US Cuban cultural figurations. More personally he speaks of hearing Spanish as feminine, English as masculine; the challenging interplay of spoken and written idiom; and the use of English and Spanish as a nexus in his own poetry and fiction in the exploration of being Cuban in America. This is a wonderfully provocative foray into two American languages as cultural kin, and yet divided, and the cross-ply implications for a writer and critic born into, and happily—indeed, often exhilaratedly—called to the making of literary texts from each.

Aldama, ed., *Arturo Islas: The Uncollected Works*, does considerable service: the recovery, and compilation, of stories, poetry, lectures and reviews by the important Chicano author of *The Rain God*[1984] as a saga-novel of Tex-Mex dynasty and the matriarch Mama Chona. The creative work included reflects Islas's charged, mixed-fortune life, especially his early medical setbacks. The observations on José Antonio Villarreal, Oscar Zeta Acosta and Rudolfo A. Anaya, as much as the creative work, retain their edge. As a Latino and gay author (he died of AIDS in 1991), Islas both offers a figure of contrast and comparison with John Rechy or Richard Rodriguez while, in his own literary right and for reasons this collection underscores, occupying a considerable status within the still larger spectrum of Chicano authorship and beyond.

In 'The Politics of Blood: Miscegenation and Phobias of Contagion in Alejandro Morales's *The Red Doll Plagues*' (*Aztlán*28:i[2003] 39–73), Miguel López explores the tropes of blood, disease and *mestizaje* as ways of entering Morales' 1992 novel. His assiduous reading yields good results: the novel's critique of how 'interracial blood relations' and 'cultural hybridization' have been shadowed in denigratory images of bodily infection. He emphasizes the differences of cultural perception in Morales' portraits of Los Angeles and Mexico City, two major Latino cities for which *mestizaje* holds important, but revealingly contrasting, value.

MELUS (28:ii[2003]) gives its whole issue to 'Haunted by History', multicultural writings in which memory, the past as its own ongoing imaginative present, has taken on new forms of literary and narrative imagining. In 'Representing History in Amy Tan's *The Kitchen God's Wife*' (*MELUS*28:ii[2003] 9–30), Bella Adams considers whether the sexual rape of Weili in the novel does, or does not, mirror the larger Japanese military rape of Nanking. Bryn Gribben, in 'The Mother That Won't Reflect Back: Situating Psychoanalysis in the Japanese Mother in *No-No Boy*' (*MELUS*28:ii[2003] 31–46), explores dislocation as shaping dynamic in John Okada's landmark novel, most centrally the impact of the breakdown and death of Mrs Yamada on her already greatly self-divided *Nisei* son Ichiro in his wartime protest at the internment of Japanese Americans. Erika T. Lin, in 'Mona on the Phone: The Performative Body and Racial Identity in *Mona in the Promised Land*' (*MELUS*

28:ii[2003] 47–57), gives lively exploration to the function of body imagery in Gish Jen's 1996 novel. Mona's own evolving body is seen as the interwoven site of cultural, religious and sexual signature.

Brewster E. Fitz's 'Undermining Narrative Stereotypes in Simon Ortiz's "The Killing of a State Cop"' (*MELUS*28:ii[2003] 105–20) both compares Ortiz's story with its other incarnation in Leslie Marmon Silko's 'Tony's Story' in *Storyteller*, and looks to how Ortiz circles his version in ambiguity to undermine any all too customary Indian Killer stereotype. Teresa Derrickson's '"Cold/Hot, English/Spanish": The Puerto Rican Divide in Judith Ortiz Cofer's *Silent Dancing*' (*MELUS*28:ii[2003] 121–37) sets out, with considerable acuity, the bicultural perspective of Ortiz's autobiography. She explores each of several kinds of border in play, the two languages, the mother–daughter relationship, and the island–mainland dialectic as contained within the text's single yet always elusively plural narrative self. To good effect she quotes Cofer's own pronouncement: 'There is not just one reality to being a Puerto Rican writer.' Interviews with the Chicana poet Pat Mora (*MELUS*28:ii[2003] 139–50), the Cuban American writer Beatriz Rivera (*MELUS*28:ii[2003] 151–62), and the essayist Richard Rodriguez as 'public intellectual' (*MELUS* 28:ii[2003] 165–77), who observes that 'my sexual coming out was parallel to my writing career', add human weight and interest to this *MELUS* issue.

Multicultural critique can look to a number of new publications. Fludernik, ed., *Diaspora and Multiculturalism: Common Traditions and New Developments*, operates across a broad front: Europe, Asia, Africa, the Caribbean and the USA. Inclusions look to British and American Jewish diaspora writing (Ursula Zeller, Bryan Cheyette and Beate Neumeier), Feroza Jussawalla in a lively piece on cultural rights and the US–Mexican border, Vera Alexander on M.G. Vassanji's *No New Land* [1991] as a novel of Afro-Indian passage from Kenya to Canada; Ulfied Reichardt on the role and visibility of diaspora memory in the poetry of Derek Walcott, Kamau Brathwaite and Linton Kwesi Johnson; and, of great relevance to a Europe obliged to understand its own cultural postcoloniality, Sandra Hesterman on German-Turkish diaspora in the writings of Zafer Şenocak and Feridun Zaimoğlu.

Blank, ed., *Rediscovering America: The Making of Multicultural America, 1900–2000*, seeks to make up for the usual omissions, the oversights or deliberate exclusions, in any number of US cultural histories. In an inspired series of entries—writing to photography, politics to science, film to dance, and with a due emphasis on the contributions to the American national narrative of women, migrants, dissidents and artists of every stripe—it supplies a necessary reference volume. Appropriate recognition is given to each and all of the voices that make up the US's multicultural tradition, whether white-ethnic, African American, Native, Asian American or Latino/a, which are set within an informative and unfolding timeline of both US and world events. The entries, drawn from recognized expertise, come over succinctly and to the point, helped not a little by the user-friendly overall layout.

A. Robert Lee's *Multicultural American Literature: Comparative Black, Native, Latino/a and Asian American Fictions*, an American Book Award Winner from the Before Columbus Foundation, offers a species of *compte rendu* of US multicultural fiction. Using 'fiction' in the inclusive sense of Jorge Luis Borges's *ficciones*, and from an opening prospectus of 'America and the Multicultural Word: Legacies, Maps, Vistas, Theory', its ten chapters situate authorship and texts within a context of US history, politics, popular culture, visual and media activity, and, of necessity, the debates about pluralism in ethnicity, region, gender and language. The book opens with a re-estimation of Ralph Ellison, Scott Momaday, Rudolfo Anaya and Maxine Hong Kingston as landmark names, explores a broad swath of multicultural autobiography as its own kind of fiction, and analyses and contextualizes each of the four relevant traditions (African American, Native, Latino/a and Asian American). The ensuing coverage takes close bearings on the imagining of comparative sites (Indian Country, Black City, Borderland and the like); on literary fictions which explore island America as both literal and figural geography from Hawaii to Cuba; on the postmodern turn in multicultural fiction in Ishmael Reed, Gerald Vizenor, Ana Castillo, Maxine Hong Kingston and Theresa Hak Kyung Cha; and on the construction and ideological and literary implications of American 'fictions of whiteness'. Naturally enough the fond author, the present reviewer, hopes it will become a standard critique.

Books Reviewed

Ahearn, Barry, ed. *The Correspondence of William Carlos Williams and Louis Zukofsky*. WesleyanUP. [2003] pp. xxiv +576. £44.50 ($65) ISBN 0 8195 6490 7.

Aldama, Frederick Luis, ed. *Arturo Islas: The Uncollected Works*. Arte Público. [2003] pp. xli +246. $16.95 ISBN 1 5588 5368 5.

Andreach, Robert J. *Drawing Upon the Past: Classical Theatre in the Contemporary American Theatre*. Lang. [2003] pp. 236. $64.95 ISBN 0 8204 6356 6.

Aranda, José F., Jr. *When We Arrive: A New Literary History of Mexican America*. UArizP. [2003] pp. xxvii +256. $40 ISBN 0 8165 2141 7.

Arthur, Anthony. *Literary Feuds: A Century of Celebrated Quarrels—from Mark Twain to Tom Wolfe*. ?. [200] pp.? £? ISBN?

Bauer, Mark. *This Composite Voice: The Role of W.B. Yeats in James Merrill's Poetry*. Routledge. [2003] pp. xviii +272. £60 ISBN 0 4159 6637 X.

Bercovitch, Sacvan, ed. *The Cambridge History of American Literature*, vol. 5: *Poetry and Criticism, 1900–1950*. CUP. [2003] pp. viii +624. £75 ($130) ISBN 0 5213 0109 2.

Bidart, Frank, and David Gewanter, eds. *Robert Lowell: Collected Poems*. FS&G. [2003] pp. xviii +1,186. $45 ISBN 0 3741 2617 8.

Black, Cheryl. *The Women of Provincetown, 1915–1922*. UAlaP. [2003] pp. 245. $29.95 ISBN 0 8173 1112 2.

Blank, Carla, ed. *Rediscovering America: The Making of Multicultural America, 1900–2000*. Three Rivers Press. [2003] pp. xiv +479. $18 ISBN 0 6098 0784 6.

Blatanis, Konstantinos. *Popular Culture Icons in Contemporary American Drama*. AUP. [2003] pp. 195. $39.50 ISBN 0 8386 4008 7.

Breinig, Helmbrecht, ed. *Imaginary (Re-)Locations: Tradition, Modernity, and the Market in Contemporary Native American Literature and Culture*. Stauffenburg. [2003] pp. 297. €39 ISBN 3 8605 7747 6.

Bruccoli, Matthew J., and Judith S. Baughman, eds. *Conversations with F. Scott Fitzgerald*. UMP. [2003] pp. 133. pb $18 ISBN 1 5780 6605 0.

Chuh, Kandice. *Imagine Otherwise: On Asian Americanist Critique*. DukeUP. [2003] pp. xii +215. $19.95 ISBN 0 8223 3140 3.

Cole, Jean Lee. *The Literary Voices of Winnifred Eaton: Redefining Ethnicity and Authenticity*. RutgersUP. [2003] pp. xiii +224. $24 ISBN 0 8135 3087 3.

Cole, Merrill. *The Other Orpheus: A Poetics of Modern Homosexuality*. Routledge. [2003] pp. xii +186. £50 ISBN 0 4159 6705 8.

Cook, Barbara J., ed. *From the Center of Tradition: Critical Perspectives on Linda Hogan*. UPColorado. [2003] pp. x + 198. pb £13.99 ($19.95) ISBN 0 8708 1738 8.

Copestake, Ian D., ed. *American Postmodernity: Essays on the Recent Fiction of Thomas Pynchon*. ?. [2003] pp.? £? ISBN?

Cowart, David. *Don DeLillo: The Physics of Language*. ?. [2002] pp. ? £? ISBN?

Crespy, David A. *Off-Off Broadway Explosion: How Provocative Playwrights of the 1960s Ignited a New American Theater*. Back Stage. [2003] pp. 192. pb $19.95 ISBN 0 8230 8832 4.

Delville, Michel, and Christine Pagnoulle, eds. *Sound As Sense: Contemporary US Poetry &/In Music*. Lang. [2003] pp. 196. pb £16 ISBN 0 8204 6610 7.

Dick, Bruce Allen, ed. *A Poet's Truth: Conversations with Latino/Latina Poets*. UArizP. [2003] pp. 230. $17.95 ISBN 0 8165 2276 6.

Dreiser, Theodore. *An American Tragedy*. LAm. [2003] pp. 972. $40 ISBN 1 9310 8231 6.

Duncan, Patti. *Tell This Silence: Asian American Women Writers and the Politics of Speech*. UIowaP. [2003] pp. xvi +274. $34.95 ISBN 0 8774 5856 1.

Dussere, Erik. *Balancing the Books: Faulkner, Morrison and the Economics of Slavery*. Routledge. [2003] pp. 161. $69.95 ISBN 0 4159 4298 5.

Falck, Colin. *American and British Verse in the Twentieth Century: The Poetry that Matters*. Ashgate. [2003] pp. xiv +254. £47.50 ($79.95) ISBN 0 7546 3424 8.

Férez Kuri, José, ed. *Brion Gysin: Tuning In To the Multimedia Age*. T&H/Edmonton Art Gallery. [2003] pp. 240. pb £29.95 ($44.95) ISBN 0 5002 8438 5.

Ferguson, Suzanne, ed. *Jarrell, Bishop, Lowell, & Co*. UTennP. [2003] pp. xxxii +336. $38 ISBN 1 5723 3229 8.

Fesmire, Julia A., ed. *Beth Henley: A Casebook*. Routledge. [2002] pp. 173. $95.95 ISBN 0 8153 3878 3.

Firmat, Gustavo Pérez. *Tongue Ties: Logo-Eroticism in Anglo-Hispanic Literature*. Palgrave. [2003] pp. 195. $26.95 ISBN 1 4039 6288 X.

Fludernik, Monika, ed. *Diaspora and Multiculturalism: Common Traditions and New Developments*. Rodopi. [2003] pp. xxxviii +391. $65 (€50) ISBN 9 0420 0906 3.

Fortuny, Kim. *Elizabeth Bishop: The Art of Travel*. UPColorado. [2003] pp. xiv +122. $45 ISBN 0 8708 1741 8.

Foster, Jenny Ryun, Frank Stewart and Heinz Insu Fenkl, eds. *Century of the Tiger: One Hundred Years of Korean Culture in America, 1903–2003*. UHawaiiP. [2003] pp. 256. $24.95 ISBN 0 8248 2644 2.

Freeman, Kimberly A. *Love, American Style: Divorce and the American Novel, 1881–1976*. [2003] pp. ? £? ISBN?

Gayles, Gloria Wade, ed. *Conversations with Gwendolyn Brooks*. UPMissip. [2003] pp. xx + 168. hb $46 ISBN 1 5780 6574 7, pb $18 ISBN 1 5780 6575 5.

Gerber, Nancy. *Portrait of the Mother-Artist: Class and Creativity in Contemporary American Fiction*. ?. [2003] pp. ? £? ISBN?

Gewirtz, Arthur, and James J. Kolb, eds. *Experimenters, Rebels, and Disparate Voices: The Theatre of the 1920s Celebrates American Diversity*. Praeger. [2003] pp. xvii + 196. $59.85 ISBN 0 3133 2466 2.

Gilmore, Michael T. *Surface and Depth: The Quest for Legibility in American Culture*. ?. [2003] pp. ? £? ISBN?

Goodman, Susan. *Civil Wars: American Novelists and Manners 1880–1940*. JHUP. [2003] pp. xvii + 198. £28.50 ISBN 0 8018 6824 6.

Graulich, Melody, and Stephen Tatum, eds. *Reading 'The Virginian' in the New West*. UNebP. [2003] pp. 300. pb $39.95 ISBN 0 8032 7104 2.

Hamblin, Robert W., and Ann J. Abadie, eds. *Faulkner in the Twenty-First Century*. UMP. [2003] pp. 177. $45 ISBN 1 5780 6513 5.

Hemingway, Sean, ed. *Hemingway on Hunting*. Scribner. [2003] pp. 344 (hb) 296 (pb). hb $27.50 ISBN 0 7432 4326 9, pb $14 ISBN 0 7432 2529 5.

Hemingway, Sean, ed. *Hemingway on War*. Scribner. [2003] pp. 344. $27.50 ISBN 0 7432 4326 9.

Henderson, Christine Dunn, ed. *Seers and Judges: American Literature as Political Philosophy*. Lexington. [2002] pp. xvi + 170. £50 ISBN 0 7391 0319 9.

Herr, Christopher J. *Clifford Odets and American Political Theatre*. Praeger. [2003] pp. 177. $49.95 ISBN 0 3133 1594 9.

Hill, Errol G., and James V. Hatch. *A History of African American Theatre*. CUP. [2003] pp. 608. $130 ISBN 0 5216 2443 6.

Hoeveler, Diane Long, and Tamar Heller, eds. *Approaches to Teaching Gothic Fiction: The British and American Traditions*. MLA. [2003] pp. xiv + 310. pb £18.50 ISBN 0 8735 2907 3.

Holloway, Brian. *Interpreting The Legacy: John Neilhardt and 'Black Elk Speaks'*. UPColorado. [2003] pp. 220. $27.95 ISBN 0 8708 1679 9.

Hong, Dorothy M. *Tales From a Korean Maiden in America*. iUniverse. [2003] pp. viii + 55. $8.99 ISBN 0 5952 8390 X.

Houchin, John H. *Censorship of the American Theatre in the Twentieth Century*. CUP. [2003] pp. 332. $75 ISBN 0 5218 1819 2.

Huang, Guiyou, ed. *Asian American Short Story Writers: An A-to-Z Guide*. Greenwood. [2003] pp. xxxii + 358. $61.50 ISBN 0 3132 29 5.

Huk, Romana. *Assembling Alternatives: Reading Postmodern Poetries Transnationally*. WesleyanUP. [2003] pp. xii + 412. hb $70 ISBN 0 8195 6539 3, pb $24.95 ISBN 0 8195 6540 7.

Jeffs, William Patrick. *Feminism, Manhood, and Homosexuality: Intersections in Psychoanalysis and American Poetry*. Lang. [2003] pp. 172. £38 ($57.95) ISBN 0 8204 1999 0.

Jenckes, Norma, ed. *New Readings in American Drama: Something's Happening Here*. Lang. [2002] pp. 286. pb $29.95 ISBN 0 8204 5589 X.

Jerz, Dennis G. *Technology in American Drama, 1920–1950: Soul and Society in the Age of the Machine*. Greenwood. [2003] pp. 167. $61.95 ISBN 0 3133 2172 8.

Keeling, Kara, Colin MacCabe and Cornel West, eds. *Racist Traces and Other Writings: European Pedigrees/African Contagions* by James A. Snead. Palgrave. [2003] pp.? £? ISBN?

Kim, Elaine H., and Laura Hyun Yi Kang, eds. *Echoes Upon Echoes: New Korean American Writings*. Asian American Writers's Workshop/TempleUP. [2003] pp. 296. $19.95 ISBN 1 8898 7613 5.

Kim, Elaine H., Margo Machida and Sharon Mizota, eds. *Fresh Talk Daring Gazes: Conversations on Asian American Art*. UCalP. [2003] pp. xxiii +210. £26.95 ISBN 0 5202 3535 5.

Kim, Joon-Wan. *Out of the 'Western Box': Towards a Multicultural Poetics in the Poetry of Ezra Pound and Charles Olson*. Lang. [2003] pp. xvi +264. £46 ISBN 0 8204 3768 9.

Knight, Denise D., and Cynthia J. Davis, eds. *Approaches to Teaching Gilman's 'The Yellow Wall-Paper' and 'Herland'*. MLA. [2003] pp. xvii +198. pb £18.50 ISBN 0 8735 2901 4.

Lee, A. Robert. *Multicultural American Literature: Comparative Black, Native, Latino/a Asian American Fictions*. EdinUP. [2003] pp. x + 307. £19.95 ISBN 0 7486 1227 0. Also UMP: hb $50 ISBN 1 5780 6644 1, pb $20 ISBN 1 5780 6645 X.

Lee, Gregory B. *Chinas Unlimited: Making the Imaginaries of China and Chineseness*. Routledge/UHawaiiP. [2003] pp. xi +121. £61 ISBN 0 8248 2680 9.

Lee, Rachel C., and Sau-ling Cynthia Wong, eds. *Asian America. Net: Ethnicity, Nationalism, and Cyberspace*. Routledge. [2003] pp. xxxv +316. £16.99 ISBN 0 4159 6560 8.

Lewis, Nathaniel. *Unsettling the Literary West: Authenticity and Authorship.*.?. [2003] pp. ? £?ISBN?

Lyons, Greg, ed. *Literature of the American West: A Cultural Approach*,?. [2003] pp.? £?ISBN?

Madsen, Deborah L., ed. *Beyond the Borders: American Literature and Post-Colonial Theory*.?. [2003] pp.? £? ISBN?

Mann, Bruce J., ed. *Edward Albee: A Casebook*. Routledge. [2003] pp. xiii +150. $114.95 ISBN 0 8153 3165 7.

Manzanas, Ana María, and Jesús Benito, eds. *Intercultural Mediations: Hybridity and Mimesis in American Literatures*. LitVerlag. [2003] pp. 224. €29.50 ISBN 3 8258 6738 2.

McConachie, Bruce. *American Theater in the Culture of the Cold War: Producing and Contesting Containment, 1947–1962*. UIowaP. [2003] pp. xiv +347. $49.95 ISBN 0 8774 5862 6.

Nayar, Rana. *Edward Albee: Towards a Typology of Relationships*. Prestige. [2003] pp. 256. $33.30 ISBN 8 1755 1140 0.

Newlin, Keith, ed. *A Theodore Dreiser Encyclopedia*. Greenwood. [2003] pp. 431. $99.95 ISBN 0 3133 1680 5.

Oakley, Helen. *The Recontextualisation of William Faulkner in Latin American Fiction and Cultur*. Mellen. [2003] pp. 223. $109.95 ISBN 0 7734 7013 1.

Olivier-Rotger, Maria Antònia. *Battlegrounds and Crossroads: Social and Imaginary Space in Writing by Chicanas*. Rodopi. [2003] pp. 408. $104. €80 ISBN 9 0201 196 3.

Olster, Stacey. *The Trash Phenomenon: Contemporary Literature, Popular Culture and the Making of the American Century*.?. [2003] pp. ?£? ISBN?

Oster, Judith. *Crossing Cultures: Creating Identity in Chinese and Jewish American Literature*. UMissP. [2003] pp. xi +283. $47.50 ISBN 0 8262 1486 X.

Palmer, Christopher. *Philip K. Dick: Exhilaration and Terror of the Postmodern*.?. [2003] pp. ? £? ISBN?

Papke, Mary E. ed. *Twisted from the Ordinary: Essays on American Literary Naturalism*. UTennP. [2003] pp. xiv +416. $42 ISBN 1 5723 3223 9.

Parker, Robert Dale. *The Invention of Native American Literature*. CornUP. [2003] pp. xi +244. $19.95 ISBN 0 8014 4067 X.

Pennell, Melissa McFarland. *Student Companion to Edith Wharton*. Greenwood. [2003] pp. xiii +186. £22.99 ISBN 0 3133 1715 1.

Perry, Carolyn, and Mary Louise Weaks, eds. *The History of Southern Women's Literature*. LSUP. [2002] pp. xvii +689. £37.50 ISBN 0 8071 2753 1.

Phillips, Dana. *The Truth of Ecology: Nature, Culture and Literature in America*. ?. [2003] pp. ? £? ISBN?

Porter, Laurin. *Orphans' Home: The Voice and Vision of Horton Foote*. LSUP. [2003] pp. 233. hb £38.50 ISBN 0 8071 2845 7, pb £17.50 ISBN 0 8071 2879 1.

Pulitano, Elvira. *Towards A Native American Critical Theory*. UNebP. [2003] pp. xii +233. $50 ISBN 0 8032 3737 5.

Rader, Dean, and Janice Gould, eds. *Speak To Me Words: Essays on Contemporary American Indian Poetry*. UArizP. [2003] pp. x + 295. $24.95 ISBN 0 8165 2349 5.

Reynolds, Guy, ed. *Willa Cather: Critical Assessments*. Helm. [2003] pp. xix +2,039. £375 ISBN 1 8734 0338 0.

Sauer, David K., and Janice A. Sauer. *David Mamet: A Research and Production Sourcebook*. Praeger. [2003] pp. 382. $75 ISBN 0 3133 1836 0.

Savran, David. *A Queer Sort of Materialism: Recontextualizing American Theater*. UMichP. [2003] pp. xii +234. hb $55 ISBN 0 4720 9836 5, pb $22.95 ISBN 0 4720 6836 9.

Schulman, Grace, ed. *The Poems of Marianne Moore*. Viking. [2003] pp. xxx +450. $40 ISBN 0 6700 3198 4.

Sieburth, Richard, ed. *The Pisan Cantos* by Ezra Pound. ND. [2003] pp. xliv +162. pb $13.95 ISBN 0 8112 1558 X.

Sieburth, Richard, ed. *Poems and Translations* by Ezra Pound. LAm. [2003] pp. xxiv +1370. $45 ISBN 1 9310 8241 3.

Singley, Carol, J. ed. *Edith Wharton's The House of Mirth: A Casebook*. OUP. [2003] pp. viii +337. £37.99 ISBN 0 1951 5602 1.

Singley, Carol J., ed. *A Historical Guide to Edith Wharton*. OUP. [2003] pp. x + 302. pb £12.99 ISBN 0 1951 3591 1.

Smith, Evans Lansing. *The Myth of the Descent to the Underworld in Postmodern Literature*?. [2003] pp. ? £? ISBN?

Strehle, Susan, and Mary Paniccia Carden, eds. *Doubled Plots: Romance and History*.?. [2003] pp.? £? ISBN?

Sultanik, Aaron. *Inventing Orders: An Essay and Critique on 20th Century American Literature (1950–2000)*.?. [2003] pp.? £? ISBN?

Taylor, Clare L. *Women, Writing, and Fetishism 1890–1950: Female Cross-Gendering*.?. [2003] pp. ? £? ISBN?

Thompson, Graham. *Male Sexuality Under Surveillance: The Office in American Literature*?. [2003] pp. ? £? ISBN?

Wadden, Paul. *The Rhetoric of Self in Robert Bly and Adrienne Rich: Doubling and the Holotropic Urge*. Lang. [2003] pp. x + 162. £38 ISBN 0 8204 6241 1.

Wagner-Martin, Linda, ed. *Ernest Hemingway's The Sun Also Rises: A Casebook*. OUP. [2002] pp. 189. $59.24 ISBN 0 1951 4573 9.

Wagner-Martin, Linda. *Ernest Hemingway's A Farewell to Arms: A Reference Guide*. Greenwood. [2003] pp. 172. $55 ISBN 0 3133 1702 X.

Waid, Candace, ed. *The Age of Innocence* by Edith Wharton. NCE. Norton. [2003] pp. xx +523. pb £8.99 ISBN 0 3939 6794 8.

Weinstock, Jeffrey Andrew, ed. *The Pedagogical Wallpaper: Teaching Charlotte Perkins Gilman's 'The Yellow Wall-paper'*. Lang. [2003] pp. viii +162. £18 ISBN 0 8204 6305 1.

Welty, Eudora. *On William Faulkner*. UMP. [2003] pp. 96. $25 ISBN 1 5780 6570 4.

Wesley, Marilyn C. *Violent Adventure: Contemporary Fiction by American Men*?. [2003] pp. ? £? ISBN?

Wetmore, Kevin J., Jr. *Black Dionysus: Greek Tragedy and African American Theatre*. McFarland. [2003] pp. 262. pb $35 ISBN 0 7864 1545 2.

Witham, Barry B. *The Federal Theatre Project: A Case Study*. CUP. [2003] pp. 190. $70 ISBN 0 5318 2259 9.

Woolland, Brian, ed. *Jonsonians: Living Traditions*. Ashgate. [2003] pp. 246. £47.50 ISBN 0 7546 0610 4.

XVII

New Literatures

LEIGH DALE, CHRIS TIFFIN, RICHARD LANE,
CHESTER ST. H. MILLS, ALEX TICKELL AND NELSON WATTIE

This chapter has five sections: 1. Australia; 2. Canada; 3. The Caribbean; 4. India; 5. New Zealand and the South Pacific. Section 1 is by Leigh Dale and Chris Tiffin; section 2 is by Richard Lane; section 3 is by Chester St. H. Mills; section 4 is by Alex Tickell; section 5 is by Nelson Wattie.

1. Australia

(a) General

Considering the criticism of Australian literature for 2003 one is struck by the disjunction between the prevailing interest in indigenous and Asian Australian writing, and the tendency in the media to portray indigenous peoples and Asians, especially refugees, as almost demonic forces who are intrinsically and fatally threatening to the social polity. Most critics at some point in their work address this disparity: a scathing aside about Prime Minister John Howard is almost *de rigueur* for anyone going into print in 2003, or perhaps just irresistible. Part of the reason for this scholarly interest was the continuation of the 'History Wars', a debate about the veracity of historians' accounts of massacres of Aborigines during colonization. Keith Windschuttle's provocative interrogation of the methods and motivations of leading Australian historians, notably Lyndall Ryan, in his *The Fabrication of Aboriginal History* (Macleay) provoked a range of responses. Prominent among these was *The History Wars* (MelbourneUP), edited by Stuart Macintyre and Anna Clark. The debate continues into 2004 with Macintyre's further collection *Historian's Conscience: Thirteen Historians on the Ethics of History* (MelbourneUP). The decade so far has also seen an upsurge in discussion of Australian Asian literature. In 2003 earlier writers such as Mena Abdullah came back into view, interest in established writers such as Yasmine Gooneratne and Ouyang Yu has been consolidated, and the work of more recently published authors such as Chandani Lokuge, Chitra Fernando, Adib Khan and Christopher Cyrill gained critical attention, some for the first time. Much of this

Year's Work in English Studies, Volume 84 (2005) © The English Association; all rights reserved. For permissions, please email: journals.permissions@oxfordjournals.org

doi: 10.1093/ywes/mai017

work, creative and critical, seems to be an explicit (not to say angry) reaction to the isolationist foreign policy pursued by the Howard federal government.

Impinging on the field is the state of publishing, with criticism of Australian literature now as likely to find a home with a European house like Rodopi or Peter Lang as it is to find one within the country. Aside from journal publishing, which is constantly imperilled—see Laurie Hergenhan's 'The Struggles of the Little Magazines' (*Quadrant* 47:vii–viii[2003] 84–5) on the demise of the journal, *Imago*—only half the books discussed here have managed to find an Australian publisher. There are perhaps some positives in this for those who find international outlets for their work, such as Tseen-Ling Khoo. Khoo's *Banana Bending: Asian-Australian and Asian-Canadian Literature* takes nation, community and 'the gendered self' (p. 1) as the vectors of its discussion of diasporic writing. While claiming the increasing visibility, diversity and influence of Asian Australian cultural production in the later decades of the twentieth century, Khoo suggests nevertheless that various Asian Australian communities have been relatively slow to mobilize politically. The study discusses literary texts, historical events, critical debates and government policy in extended detail, describing the terms and the complexities that inhere in the positioning of Asian Australian and Asian Canadian writers and communities. Further chapters consider masculinity in relation to patriotism and military conflict, women's writing, and the relationship between community and ethnicity. The study is a landmark one, but its great strength—its theoretical eclecticism and the range of its topics—also means that the discussion is sometimes a little too accommodating of other (implicitly contradictory) views to gain its own momentum.

A third concern, with identity, authenticity and hoaxes, is evident. This interest in identity crises has been spurred by the publication of Peter Carey's *My Life as a Fake* in 2003, a novel which revisits the Ern Malley hoax of the 1940s. The Malley case has been revived in the public consciousness because it has been the touchstone for heated debates about numerous cases of ambiguous identity or authorship in the 1990s and beyond. Pertinent critical discussions include Tom Thompson's 'A Comment on Mort and Malley' (*Southerly* 63:ii[2003] 96–102), in which Thompson shows that Stewart and McAuley's 'Ern Malley' hoax was preceded by the creation of another phantom poet, 'Mort Brandish', who was published in the Melbourne journal *A Comment*. Philip Morrissey, in 'Stalking Aboriginal Culture: The Wanda Koolmatrie Affair' (*AuFS* 18[2003] 299–307), revisits the 1996 hoax in which a white man posed as an Aboriginal woman, partly to record his own peripheral role in the matter, and partly to raise (if not fully explore) its wider implications. Whiteness (and its interconnection with gender, sexuality and empire) is a growing concern, and is the focus of Angela Woollacott's essay on Mary Gaunt, 'Creating the White Colonial Woman' (in Teo and White, eds., *Cultural History in Australia*, pp. 186–200). Although generally more concerned with questions of historical method and Australian culture than with literature per se, this volume has a number of contributors whose work is frequently of interest to literary critics, among them Ann Curthoys, Tom Griffiths, Marilyn Lake, Jan Kociumbas, Greg Dening and Joy Damousi.

Overviews of the field are offered in the several bibliographies that appear annually in *Australian Literary Studies* (*ALS* 21[2004] 379–95) and the *Journal of Commonwealth Literature* (at time of writing yet to appear for 2003). The *ALS* bibliography is organized by writer, and is preceded by a useful 'general' section; we are indebted to it. These compilations are increasingly supplemented and even supplanted by the powerful electronic databases, *AustLit*, *ABELL* and *MLA*; of these, *AustLit* is to be preferred for its comprehensiveness. Carol Hetherington's 'Setting the Record Straight: Bibliography and Australian Literature' (*ALS* 21[2003] 198–208) considers the history of literary bibliography in Australia before detailing the conceptual framework *AustLit* uses to identify and catalogue an individual work and its versions. It is a helpful guide for researchers and students. *Westerly* publishes annual review essays on fiction, poetry and non-fiction for the year ending 30 June, and separate discussions of poetry, fiction and non-fiction for the first and the second half of 2003 can be found in *Westerly* 48[2003] and 49[2004] respectively. Faye Christenberry compiled her seventh annual survey, 'A Bibliography of Australian Literature and Criticism Published in North America: 2001–2002' (*Antipodes* 17[2003] 79–81). Louise Poland's 'An Enduring Record: Aboriginal Publishing in Australia 1988–1998' (*AuS* 16:ii[2001] 83–110) offers a careful chronicle of publishers, prizes, individual publications and significant events such as the launch in 1994 *The Encyclopaedia of Aboriginal Australia* on CD. Brian Taylor concluded his three-part bibliographical survey, 'Australian English: A Neglected Area of Australiana Collecting?' (*Biblionews* 28[2003] 3–22).

Of particular interest in the journals this year was the special issue of *Southerly* on translation, edited by Vivian Smith (63:i[2003]). Two points are strikingly illustrated in this collection. The first is that, when it comes to translation, the devil is very much in the detail, so that most of the articles are in part case studies of problems experienced by the authors in making translations. Secondly, these days translation in Australia is an export as well as an import process: there are articles on translating Les Murray into Danish, Patrick White into Greek and Nicholas Jose into Chinese. A new cultural and critical quarterly appeared, the *Griffith Review*, with issues being concerned mainly with political and polemical themes. The launch was discussed by Julianne Schultz, Frank Moorhouse and Geraldine Doogue in *Sydney Papers* (15:iii–iv[2003] 64–74). The year saw the passing of Clem Christesen, founding editor of *Meanjin* from 1940 to 1974, and winner of the A.A. Phillips Prize (given by ASAL) for his outstanding contribution to Australian literary scholarship. The infrequently awarded prize was given in 2003 to Elizabeth Webby, holder of the Chair of Australian Literature at Sydney University, for 'her distinguished and foundational role in developing the scholarly infrastructure for the study of Australian literature'. Laurie Duggan's *Mangroves* was the winner of the 2003 ASAL Gold Medal, while the winner of the Walter McRae Russell Award for the best book of literary scholarship published in 2002–3 went to Sylvia Lawson's *How Simone de Beauvoir Died in Australia* (UNSW [2002]). The Miles Franklin Award was won by Alex Miller for *Journey to the Stone Country*, the other short-listed novels being Andrea Goldsmith's *The Prosperous Thief*, Sonya Hartnett's *Of a Boy*, Dorothy Porter's *Wild Surmise*, Thomas Keneally's *An Angel in Australia* and Kate Jennings's *Moral Hazard*. Jennings's discussion of the reception of *Moral Hazard*, 'Advertisements for Myself', registers pleased puzzlement about being labelled a 'business novelist' (*Sydney Papers* 15:i[2003] 176–91).

Several papers address the state of literary criticism, or pursue themes of general interest. Ken Goodwin, 'A Metahistory of Commonwealth National Literatures' (in Bennett et al., eds., *Resistance and Reconciliation*, pp. 130–51), makes a magisterial sweep through literary historiography, mainly Australian, connecting the writing of national(ist) literary histories with the nineteenth-century fashion for nationalist celebration. Robert Dixon's balanced 'Australian Literature and Post-Colonialism' (*AUMLA* 100[2003] 108–21) traces the history of the relationship between Australian literary studies and postcolonial studies. John Hawke's 'Australian Literary Criticism: An International Approach' (*Salt* 15[2002] 71–100) was part of a special issue of *Salt* entitled 'An ABC of Theory and Praxis'. The essay is mainly historical, concerning itself with the literary criticism of A.G. Stephens and Christopher Brennan, and exploring the nature and extent of the influence of various international movements, including symbolism, on their work. Robyn Walton's 'Utopian and Dystopian Impulses in Australia' (*Overland* 173[2003] 5–20) provides a catalogue history of Australian utopian and dystopian works, suggestively and elegantly relating them to the cultural fashions that inflected them. One of the more innovative contributions to scholarship in 2003 was J.M. Arthur's *The Default Country: A Lexical Cartography of Twentieth-Century Australia*. Making imaginative and sustained use of a wide range of literary and popular writings, Arthur charts non-indigenous Australians' changing views of the land during the twentieth century. She presents a passionate and detailed argument about the ways in which colonialist values and assumptions are sedimented into Australian English—its vocabulary, its positives and pejoratives, and its sheer range of adjectives to describe the activities of colonization. Henrike Wenzel's *Geschichte erzählen: Untersuchungen zur Behandlung von Geschichte und nationaler Identität in australischer Gegenwartsliteratur*—('To Tell History: Studies on the Treatment of History and National Identity in Contemporary Australian Literature'; not sighted) was published in the Anglophone Literaturen series (Lit 2003).

The identity debates mentioned earlier receive sustained attention by indigenous critics in two major publications, one a monograph and the other an edited collection. Anita M. Heiss's *Dhuuluu-Yala = To Talk Straight: Publishing Indigenous Literature*, a revised Ph.D. dissertation, considers in detail the publishing of Aboriginal writing. The book has sections on each of authorship, editing and publishing, and readership, followed by two chapters on First Nations literature in Canada and Maori literature in New Zealand respectively. Heiss considers the ongoing debates about the identification of writers who have claimed or have been thought to be Aboriginal, and is firmly in favour of deferring to the authority of local communities in determining the answers to these questions. Also considered are key terms, Heiss emphatically rejecting the usage of 'postcolonial'—which she takes to mean 'after colonialism'—to describe Aboriginal cultures. Chapters in section 2 consider the history of publishing, with brief discussions of major publishing houses (including Magabala, the Institute of Aboriginal Development Press in Alice

Springs and the Aboriginal Studies Press in Canberra), while a longer chapter on debates over editing practice includes interesting accounts by Aboriginal writers such as Jackie Huggins and Melissa Lucashenko of their experiences of being edited by white and by indigenous editors. The book pays considerable attention to broader institutional aspects of writing such as property rights, marketing and distribution of books, reviewing, and the mentoring of Aboriginal writers. In the main, Heiss's study combines advocacy and analysis while developing and drawing on an extraordinarily wide range of sources, notably interviews with key writers and publishers.

The theme of self-determination in questions of identity and cultural production is likewise prominent in the collection Grossman, ed., *Blacklines: Contemporary Critical Writing by Indigenous Australians*, which includes fourteen pieces by indigenous literary and cultural critics and historians. Most of these articles have been published previously (albeit in different forms) and so, as its introduction notes, the collection is useful in making available materials that have only appeared in academic journals or specialist publications. Section introductions by scholars such as Aileen Moreton-Robinson and Marcia Langton helpfully situate the essays. Most of the contributors are well known to an academic audience, although the final one is by a younger scholar, Sonja Kurtzer. Her '*Wandering Girl*: Who Defines "Authenticity" in Aboriginal Literature?' considers issues that Kurtzer has addressed in thoughtful and sophisticated ways in her 'Is She or Isn't She? Roberta Sykes and "Authentic" Aboriginality' (*Overland* 171[2003] 50–6). Cheryl Taylor's 'Constructing Aboriginality: Archibald Meston's Literary Journalism, 1870–1924' (*JASAL* 2[2003] 121–39) likewise considers representations of indigenous peoples in popular and policy domains. Taylor points to the sheer volume of Meston's writings as evidence for her argument that, as 'Protector' of Aborigines in the southern part of Queensland from 1896 to 1904, Meston played a leading role in developing the views of the non-indigenous population of the 'nature and habits' of the Aboriginal inhabitants of the state. In discussions of children's literature too there was a sustained interest in Aboriginal identities and white displacement, following on from Clare Bradford's influential *Reading Race: Aboriginality in Australian Children's Literature*. Brooke Collins-Gearing's discussion of 'Non-Indigenous Dreaming in Historical Writing for Children' (*JAS* 76[2003] 65–76, 235–6) finds a number of types of exploitation of Aboriginal lore by white writers, over two centuries. Rosemary Ross Johnston's 'Summer Holidays and Landscapes of Fear' (*CCL* 109–10[2003] 87–104) compares Australian and Canadian writing for children, and includes discussion of John Marsden's extraordinarily popular *Tomorrow When the War Began*.

Notwithstanding the strong objections of Aboriginal writers to the term, the stock of postcolonial criticism—with postcolonial taken to mean an ongoing engagement with the effects and attitudes of colonialism—remained strong in Australian literary studies, with the publication of numerous papers on Australian writers and writing. Four separate collections of conference papers are considered here. Bierbaum, Harrex and Hosking, eds., *The Regenerative Spirit*, Volume 1: *Polarities of Home and Away, Encounters and Diasporas, in Post-colonial Literatures* is the first in a two-volume collection—the second published in

2004—which commemorates the life and work of Anna Rutherford. Rutherford, who passed away in 2000, was a critic, publisher, mentor and teacher of postcolonial literatures who spent her long and influential career at the University of Aarhus in Denmark. Reflecting her personal and professional significance, Rutherford is also the dedicatee of vanden Driesen and Nandan, eds., *Austral-Asian Encounters: From Literature and Women's Studies to Politics and Tourism*, and Bennett et al., eds., *Resistance and Reconciliation*. The fourth of the postcolonial collections is Sankaran, Leong and Patke, eds., *Complicities: Connections and Divisions*. In their brief but stimulating general introduction to this volume (pp. 13–17), the editors define and defend their use of the term 'complicity', suggesting that relationships between Asian and Pacific nations are characterized by the tension between economic forces, which 'compel the networking nations to put aside and indeed gloss over their cultural differences, while on the other hand, cultural differences lead them to consistently devise points of resistance that thwart or hinder efforts at affiliation' (p. 14). They suggest three ways in which 'complicity' characterizes the position of writers in these complex and volatile relationships: choice of language; authorial positioning (in terms of cultural and political values); and audience—'the writing is split about whom it speaks to, and why' (p. 15). Bruce Bennett's quite strongly personal piece 'Singapore and Australia: Collaborators' briefly outlines his commitment to a highly localized postcolonial politics—his preferred term is 'region'—before considering the role and the impact of the long-running collaboration between the National University of Singapore and the University of Western Australia, in conducting symposia on the literature of the Asia Pacific (pp. 27–42).

Reflecting their origins as conference papers from the twelfth triennial ACLALS conference held in Canberra in 2001, Bennett et al.'s *Resistance and Reconciliation* includes relatively few pieces that are concerned exclusively with Australian literature. However, many touch on issues highly pertinent to the field, the most stimulating of which are those by Stephen Slemon, J.M. Coetzee and Chris Prentice. Slemon, in his examination of the trope of 'The Return of the Native' that includes Thomas Hardy's novel of that name, as well as media representations of two controversies (in southern Africa and in Canada) over the repatriation of the bodily remains of indigenous people, argues that there must be a coalition between critics concerned with globalization and critics concerned with (post)colonialism. He concludes with the assertion that 'the real work of both resistance and reconciliation requires coalition, and requires complex voicing' (p. 13). A very different approach to the theme of 'reconciliation and resistance' is taken by Coetzee, whose move to Australia was followed by his receipt of the Nobel Prize for literature in 2003. (Some institutions of Australian literature have moved quickly to claim the novelist, with his most recent book *Elizabeth Costello* having been shortlisted for the 2004 Miles Franklin Prize. Bibliographers, trembling, are moving rather more slowly.) Coetzee's contribution takes up the broad question of the nature and purpose of the teaching of literature, in a creative piece with a surprisingly overt pedagogical purpose for critics and teachers of literature working in Australian universities. One character declares that the humanities are dead, killed by the 'reason' that is said to underpin the Enlightenment; her sister, Elizabeth Costello, muses that the 'core discipline' of modern Australian universities (or at least those in Melbourne, where she lives!) is 'moneymaking' (p. 23). Costello asserts that 'If the humanities want to survive … it is those energies and that craving for guidance [in perplexity; in how to live our lives] which they must respond to: a craving that is, in the end, a quest for salvation' (p. 25).

Chris Prentice, in her 'Reconciliation and Cultural (In)difference' (pp. 168–86), states that her purpose 'is not to oppose either reconciliation or the modes of indigenous empowerment under modernity, but to critique the closures of national teleology and culture-as-image presumed in much reconciliation discourse' (p. 182). Making an argument informed by post-structuralist and psychoanalytic theory, Prentice suggests that the unity of nation on which the desire for 'reconciliation' is premised needs to be interrogated, and contends that the concept of reconciliation 'tends towards a neutralisation of the stakes of cultural encounter' (p. 172). She points out that reconciliation as a process presumes specific notions of cultural identity and cultural difference, as well as the desirability of a unified nation. Commencing with a discussion of landscape poetry and two canonical works, Keri Hulme's *the bone people* and Sally Morgan's *My Place*, Prentice suggests reconciliation features in these texts as a teleology, an ultimate truth and longing that fantasizes the union of colonist and landscape, 'settler and history, indigene and history' (p. 172). In addressing nation, discourses of reconciliation gather all peoples and cultures but there is the danger that 'when groups are positioned along the same scale of values, within the same law, judgments of lack or excess, identity or difference, may be made' (p. 178). On this basis, Prentice contends that it is critical that 'The political efficacy of certain postcolonial form(ul)ations of indigeneity … remain subject to a critique which would prevent their reification into identity-images' (p. 181). This is essential because, once brought within the rubric of the national, a process that frequently also involves the commodification of some art forms and even lifestyles, Aboriginal and Maori cultures each become subject to policy management (pp. 176 and 181 respectively).

Austral-Asian Encounters is at once the most dispersed and the most focused of the collections: dispersed in terms of disciplinary approach, with essays on science, social anthropology and politics as well as literature; focused in its concentration on Australian–Asian connections. The book includes personal tributes to Judith Wright (by Jennifer Strauss) and A.D. Hope (by Satendra Nandan), and five sections of concern here: 'Indian Commentaries on Australian Literature', 'On Asian-Australian Writing', 'On Aboriginal Writing in English', 'On Australian Writing on India' and 'Theorizing the Shared Postcolonial Space'. In two of the collections, *The Regenerative Spirit* and *Resistance and Reconciliation*, there is a focus on fiction, and these essays are discussed below. Exceptions include Sue Hosking's reflection on the re-publication—for the first time under his own name—of Ngarrindjeri man David Unaipon's *Legendary Tales of the Australian Aborigines*, and the ethical and political issues that collection, editing and re-publication present for contemporary readers (in Bierbaum, Harrex, and Hosking, eds., pp. 6–13). Perhaps disappointingly, almost none of the papers in the four collections works comparatively: notwithstanding claims made by editors, the tendency is to place discussions of writers, Australian and other, within the same covers of a volume, rather than for individual critics to use thematic or other sustained side-by-side comparison in a single essay or chapter. Thus the 'comparative' element of these books is implicit and occasional rather than explicit and sustained. Nevertheless each collection, taken as a whole, may be read as usefully repositioning Australian literature within postcolonial, transnational, global and Asian contexts.

Whereas 'place', considered in historical, ontological and psychological terms, was once a major theme in Australian literary criticism, this is now being 'replaced' to a certain extent by discussions which take environmentalist philosophies and politics as their motivating force. This movement is being driven by academics including Ruth Blair, Kate Rigby and Mark Tredinnick. Tredinnick's *A Place on Earth: An Anthology of Nature Writing from Australia and North America* (UNSW) is a useful resource for those developing undergraduate courses in this field, while Andrew Taylor, at Edith Cowan University, is behind the launching of a soon to be seen journal, *Landscapes*. An offshoot of this interest is a set of critical projects on gardens, gardening and gardeners by Helen Tiffin, Susan K. Martin and Katie Holmes, among others. Martin's 'Gardening and the Cultivation of Australian National Space: The Writings of Ethel Turner' (*AuFS* 18[2003] 285–98) argues that the colonial garden offered an alternative space to the anti-human bush of the *Bulletin* orthodoxy. This feminized, liminal space produced an alternative set of perceptions of Australia, and alternative myths. The argument is illustrated from two of Ethel Turner's less well-known novels, *The Ungardeners* and *Flower o' the Pine*. Anne Brewster melds discussions of landscape and indigenous politics in 'The Beach as "Dreaming Place": Reconciliation, the Past and the Zone of Intersubjectivity in Indigenous Literature' (*NLitsR* 40[2003] 33–41). Further mention of this theme occurs in the poetry section.

The focus on indigenous and Asian Australian writing has perhaps meant that questions of gender and sexuality are less prominent, important exceptions including Christine Boman's '"Let's Get Her": Masculinities and Sexual Violence in Contemporary Australian Drama and its Film Adaptations' (*JAS* 76[2003] 127–35, 246–7). Boman's title comes from the chilling last words of the film *The Boys*, which fictionalizes the lead-up to the horrific murder of Sydney woman Anita Cobby in February 1986. Peter Mitchell's 'Wishing for Political Dominance: Representations of History and Community in *Queer Theory*' (*ALS* 21[2003] 189–97) brings a Marxist perspective to the historicization of the gay and lesbian movement in Australia in the 1960s and 1970s, with the aim of critiquing the version of liberationist history offered by Annamarie Jagose in her *Queer Theory* (MelbourneUP). Caroline Webb's 'Forming Feminism: Structure and Ideology in *Charades* [by Janette Turner Hospital] and "The Djinn in the Nightingale's Eye" [by A.S. Byatt]' (*Hecate* 29:i[2003] 132–41) argues that both authors develop methods of complex, multi-branched narrative that are characteristic of 'female story'.

Feminism is to the fore in discussions of publishing history, which in 2003 included three articles on feminist presses. The best of these is Louise Poland's 'The Devil and the Angel? Australia's Feminist Presses and the Multinational Agenda' (*Hecate* 29:ii[2003] 123–39), which combines a survey of presses of the last two decades with a discussion of how purpose-driven publishing can accommodate itself to global publishing economics. Poland also published 'Out of Type: Bessie Mitchell (Guthrie) and Viking Press (1939–44)' (*Hecate* 29:i[2003] 19–33). Diane Brown and Maryanne Lynch's 'Creating a Space: Sybylla Feminist Press, 1988–2003' (*Hecate* 29:ii[2003] 285–96) gives a detailed chronicle of a significant Melbourne feminist publisher. Periodical publishing received attention in Kerryn Goldsworthy's 'The Oily Ratbag and the Recycled Waratah: Early Years of *ABR*' (*ABR* 250[2003] 23–4). Goldsworthy finds that, 250 issues later, *ABR* is still true to the journal's original aims laid down in 1961. Also with a historical theme was Caroline V. Jones's misleadingly titled essay, 'The Influence of Angus and Robertson on Colonial Knowledge' (*JRAHS* 89:i[2003] 26–37). Jones actually argues that the publisher George Robertson (not the publishing firm Angus and Robertson), acting as agent for the Public Library, the university, and prominent collectors such as D.S. Mitchell, exerted considerable influence on which books became available in the colony.

(b) Fiction and Autobiography

Paul Genoni, in 'Tampa Proof? Australian Fiction 2002–2003' (*Westerly* 48[2003] 159–74), fears a growing timidity in recent Australian fiction, much of which he finds accomplished but lightweight. Honourable exceptions include Thomas Keneally's *The Tyrant's Novel* and Gail Jones's *Black Mirror*. A similar concern is explored by Delia Falconer in 'Historical Novels' (*EST* 13:ii[2003] 31–4). Falconer weighs the thesis that a recent fashion for historical fiction is an evasion of the problems of the contemporary. She rejects this view, arguing that there is nothing 'easy' in writing about the past, and that it offers a perspective from which to critique the present. Contrastingly, Lisa M. Fiander's essay, 'Writing in "A Fairy Story Landscape"', argues that the prevalence of the fairy tale in contemporary Australian fiction is a tangible legacy of the alienation from the land of white colonists (*JASAL* 2[2003] 157–65). Measured in terms of critical attention it is clear that Mudrooroo/Colin Johnson and Peter Carey remain the most prominent Australian writers of fiction, nationally and internationally. The second edition of Bruce Woodcock's *Peter Carey* adds chapters on *Jack Maggs* and *True History of the Kelly Gang* without disturbing the book's conclusions. Elizabeth Francesca Ho, by some bold steps of logic, reads Carey's mesmerism motif in *Jack Maggs* as a response to the current federal government's failure to achieve reconciliation in her 'Peter Carey's *Jack Maggs* and the Trauma of Convictism' (*Antipodes* 17[2003] 124–32). Cliff Lobe's 'Reading the "Remembered World"' (*Mosaic* 35:iv[2002] 17–34) considers 'carceral architecture and cultural mnemonics' in *Illywhacker*, while *Jack Maggs* is considered in Robert Sirabian's 'Writing Nineteenth-Century Fiction in the Twentieth Century' (*POMPA* [2002] 53–60). Françoise Kral, in 'Re-Surfacing through Palimpsests: A (False) Quest for Repossession in the Works of Mudrooroo and Alexis Wright' (*Com* 25:i[2002] 7–14), finds palimpsests in Mudrooroo's *Dr Wooreddy's Prescription for Enduring the Ending of the World* and Alexis Wright's *Plains of Promise*, both in the landscape and on the bodies of the characters. She argues, further, that the concept of palimpsest should be extended to include the layers of reference and allusion in such texts. Sheila Collingwood-Whittick, in 'Re-presenting the Australian Aborigines: Challenging Colonial Discourse through Autoethnography' (*WLWE* 38:ii[2000] 110–31), proposes 'autoethnography' as the appropriate term for recent Aboriginal life-writing, and retells the history of white abuse of Aborigines. Collingwood-Whittick also uses the concept of autoethnography in a discussion of the narratology of *My Place* in 'Sally Morgan's *My Place*: Exposing the (Ab)original "Text" Behind Whitefellas' History' (*Com* 25:i[2002] 41–58).

Essays in Bennett et al., eds., *Resistance and Reconciliation*, show a heavy concentration on indigenous peoples and histories. Dorothy Lane's discussion of Carey's representation of the collusion between religiosity and imperialism (pp. 114–29) begins by noting the convergence of certain tropes—notably dominion, conversion and cultivation—in capitalist, colonialist and missionary discourses of the nineteenth century. Lane considers the refiguring of those tropes by Carey in *Oscar and Lucinda* and by Mudrooroo in *Dr Wooreddy's Prescription for Enduring the Ending of the World*. In doing so, she offers a rare demonstration of the usefulness of considering the intersection of Christianity and colonialism outside of the confines of the recently fashionable investigation of missionary narratives. Kay Schaffer writes on Stolen Generation testimony (pp. 47–62), Stella Borg Barthet on David Malouf's *Conversations at Curnow Creek* (pp. 265–77), Santosh Sareen on Ruby Langford's *Don't Take Your Love to Town* (pp. 278–87), and Lisa Slater on Kim Scott's novel *Benang* (pp. 358–70). In her discussion of the HREOC report, *Bringing Them Home*, Schaffer argues for the significance of personal testimony and, especially, the power not only of narrative but of *being listened to* in the process of reconciliation. Her 'Legitimating the Personal Voice' considers personal testimony as it is present in Morgan's *My Place* and in Glenyse Ward's *Unna You Fullas*. An Aboriginal novelist whose work received critical attention for the first time, Vivienne Cleven, has gone on to publish her highly regarded second novel *Her Sister's Eye*. Alison Ravenscroft returns to Cleven's very funny debut work *Bitin' Back*—about an outback rugby league hero who decides that he is Jean Rhys and wants to dress as a woman, told from the perspective of his perplexed mother—in '"Curled up like a skinny black question mark": The Irreducibility of Gender and Race in Vivienne Cleven's *Bitin' Back*', an article that considers the intersections of gender and race (*AuFS* 18[2003] 187–98).

The most focused of the edited collections published in 2003 is Annalisa Oboe, ed., *Mongrel Signatures: Reflections on the Work of Mudrooroo*, which has contributions from twelve scholars from Australia, Italy, Denmark and Canada—indeed the relative absence of Australian and, especially, indigenous critics is perhaps indicative of the volatility in critical readings and assessments of work by Mudrooroo/Colin Johnson in Australia, although the final contribution to the book is Ruby Langford Ginibi's 'Sharing Stories with Mudrooroo' (pp. 225–31). While contributors tend to reject attempts to essentialize Aboriginal identity, none except Langford Ginibi engages with calls from members of Aboriginal communities that Mudrooroo should either prove or renounce his Aboriginality. But the implications of Langford Ginibi's essay, in which she emphatically asserts Mudrooroo's Aboriginality on the basis of the nature and impact of his writing, are more or less ignored by other writers. That problem aside, Annalisa

Oboe offers a well-informed introduction to debates about Mudrooroo's biography and the critical reception of his work (pp. vii–xxi). However, in her deployment of the arguments of post-structuralist theory, which emphasize the indeterminacy of identity, she might be seen as avoiding rather than interrogating both the political debates that surround identification in Australia and the striking contradictions between Mudrooroo's fiction, which is usually read as problematizing naming and identity, and his criticism, which seems inclined to fix and essentialize Aboriginal identity in terms of racial descent. This contradiction between Mudrooroo's fiction and his literary criticism *is* addressed at some length by Adam Shoemaker in 'Mudrooroo and the Curse of Authenticity' (pp. 1–23), and by Maggie Nolan. Shoemaker, in recounting the author's own investigations of his ancestry, casts doubt on the view that Mudrooroo's grandfather was African American, making it puzzling that Cassandra Pybus's contribution on the African diaspora in Australia (pp. 25–41) should immediately follow. The remaining pieces are more or less unified in being concerned with the ways in which Mudrooroo's fiction engages, at a literary or textual level, with colonialism. The more challenging of these contributions are Wendy Pearson's '"I, the Undying": The Vampire of Subjectivity and the Aboriginal "I"' (pp. 185–202) and Nolan's 'Identity Crises and Orphaned Rewritings' (pp. 107–28). Pearson takes up questions of gender and sexuality in interrogating the twin tropes of the virus and the vampire, concluding that the survival of the protagonist in Mudrooroo's *The Undying* is 'quite markedly not the survival of a "pure" Aboriginal, but of a remarkable form of hybridity, one which is not only black *and* white, but living *and* dead' (p. 197). Nolan, after outlining the origin of Freud's discussion of identification in 'colonial and oedipal modes' (p. 119; see pp. 109–11), suggests that Mudrooroo's fiction, particularly *Master of the Ghost Dreaming*, offers models for rethinking notions and practices of identification in Australia. Both Pearson and Nolan use subtle and suggestive readings of Mudrooroo's fiction as the basis for intervention in the debate about indigeneity and identity.

Makarand Paranjape's paper in *Resistance and Reconciliation* explores the double ambivalence that characterizes his subject—Australian attitudes to Asia and Asian accounts of Australia—in writing by Asian Australian writers including Mena Abdullah and Chandani Lokuge (in Bennett et al., eds., pp. 288–307). Paranjape broadens his comparative scope further in a second essay which considers Abdullah's work: 'Triple Ambivalence: Australia, Canada and South Asia in the Diasporic Imagination' (*ACS* 20:ii[2002] 81–113). *Austral-Asian Encounters* initiates critical discussion of Christopher Cyrill. Eugenie Pinto's 'Christopher Cyrill's *Hymns for the Drowning*' (in vanden Driesen and Nandan, eds., pp. 397–407) reads the novel as a 'cultural odyssey'. See also in the same volume K.T. Sunitha and R. Ramachandra's 'The Mandala of the Return: Narration and Identity in Cyrill's *The Ganges and its Tributaries*' (pp. 422–9). Wenche Ommundsen's 'Too Close to Home: Evelyn Lau, Ouyang Yu and the Performing Self' (*NLitsR* 40[2003] 42–56) offers a lucid consideration of the way in which these two writers relate writing and sex. Even more interesting is the framing of the essay, which observes that positivist attempts to escape racial stereotypes often create other stereotypes, and that the way out of this might be through some form of self-performance. Shirley Tucker analyses the ways in which Asian Australian women writers engage with creative and critical understandings of the Australian landscape in 'The Great Southern Land' (*ALS* 21[2003] 178–88). Tucker considers the ways in which writers like Mena Abdullah, Dewi Anggraeni, Yasmine Gooneratne and Simone Lazaroo refigure metaphors of landscape to engage with the stereotype of the 'Asian' (woman) as threat to Australia, and demonstrates that their engagement with critical traditions (including Judith Wright's *Preoccupations in Australian Poetry* and the work of G.A. Wilkes) is highly self-conscious and deliberately polemical. Ouyang Yu, in 'Lawson, Gunn and the "White Chinaman": A Look at How Chinese are Made White in Henry Lawson and Mrs Aeneas Gunn's Writings' (*LiNQ* 30:ii[2003] 10–23), argues that the positive portrayals of Chinese by these two writers are limited because the virtues allowed to the characters are invariably those of a servant, and do not support claims that the writers were atypically tolerant.

Similar findings are made in several essays on Australian writers who have journeyed to or lived in various parts of Asia and the near north. John McLaren's 'Nationalism and Imperialism: Australia's Ambivalent Relationship to Papua New Guinea and the Pacific Islands' (in Sankaran, Leong, and Patke, eds., pp. 53–63) surveys Australian literary responses to Papua New Guinea, ranging from the short stories of Louis Becke and an unpublished diary by Stephen Murray-Smith to the writing of James McAuley and Randolph Stow. He claims that colonialist attitudes towards Papua New Guinea have gone largely unacknowledged, but that the country continues to be influenced by its Australian connections. Rick Hosking's article on John Lang (in Bierbaum, Harrex, and Hosking, eds., pp. 45–56) urges attention to the Australian-born writer (1816–64), who moved to India in 1842 and after a sojourn in London remained in India until his death. In developing a reading of Lang's *The Wetherbys, or Chapters of Indian Experience* [1853], Hosking notes intriguing details of Lang's life and career as a novelist and journalist—after his wife left him he became itinerant, sometimes dressing as a woman in his travels. Hosking concludes that, although he was 'the native-born grandson-of-a-Jewish-convict, a "currency lad"', his writing 'still participates in the dominant and hegemonic communal dream of empire, and by so doing he reveals the complex bonds that in the nineteenth century connected Britain, India and Australia' (p. 53). The same book, along with Lang's slightly later *Wanderings in India, and Other Sketches of Life in Hindoostan* [1859], is the subject of a paper by Adrian Mitchell (in vanden Driesen and Nandan, eds., pp. 305–16). Intriguingly, both Mitchell and Hosking make comparative reference to Henry Kingsley, although the discussion is not fully developed in either case. Mitchell speculates on the ways in which Lang's Australian background might have informed his writing in distinctive ways. Another 'Australian' writer recuperated in this volume is Hugh Atkinson, whose novel *The Pink and the Brown* [1957] is considered by Ralph J. Crane in terms of its negotiation of social and racial difference between English and Indian in India (pp. 115–28).

Very different in tenor is Noel Henricksen's *Island and Otherland: Christopher Koch and his Books*, in being uncomplicatedly laudatory in its view of its subject. Nevertheless, this biographical and critical work contains a wealth of contextual information on Koch and his novels. Henricksen seems to aim to defend Koch from the criticism—and the neglect—that followed the novelist's attack on literary critics and their methods during his acceptance speech for the 1996 Miles Franklin Award (for *Highways to a War*). However, Koch's comments are not really engaged with explicitly or at length, although Henricksen does reprint an extract from the speech (pp. 286–7). Koch's work is also the subject of essays by Bruce Bennett and Chad Habel. Bennett's 'A Family Closeness? Australia, India, Indonesia' commences with a quotation from Koch in which the novelist declares his view that Australians will experience 'family closeness' only with those cultures which are part of the 'Indo-European zone', such as India and Indonesia (in Bierbaum, Harrex, and Hosking, eds., pp. 57–67). Bennett juxtaposes this view with that of Stephen Fitzgerald, who declared (in 1977) that by the early twenty-first century 'the predominant influences on Australian cultural and economic life would be China and Japan' (p. 57). Bennett uses these contrasting assertions as the basis for readings of Yasmine Gooneratne's *Masterpiece*, Dewi Anggraeni's *Stories of Indian Pacific* and *Neighbourhood Tales*, and Safina Uberoi's film *My Mother India*. Habel's 'Koch: From Dis to Boeotia' (in Bierbaum, Harrex, and Hosking, eds., pp. 84–90) develops a postcolonial reading of Koch's most recent novel *Out of Ireland*, while Ioana Petrescu wrestles with some of the same problems that are considered by critics of Koch and his work in her study of Garry Disher, 'Before Postcolonialism' (in Bierbaum, Harrex, and Hosking, eds., pp. 77–83). She suggests that theories of postcolonialism, postmodernism and deconstruction should not be brought to bear on Disher's work because it is 'situated … in a different time and space to that occupied by postcolonialism; it is written in good faith and with a deep commitment to humane values' (p. 81). David Malouf's writing is placed within a postcolonial framework by K. Radha, who compares the protagonist of *Remembering Babylon* with the eponymous hero of Arun Joshi's novel *The Strange Case of Billy Biswas* (in vanden Driesen and Nandan, eds., pp. 156–63), and by R. Kamala, who considers the anti-hero theme in *Johnno* (in vanden Driesen and Nandan, eds., pp. 164–70). Elsewhere Malouf's libretti were discussed by Stephen Benson in 'David Malouf's Moments Musicaux' (*JCL* 38:i[2003] 5–21), and translating his novels into Italian was considered by Franca Cavagnoli (*Southerly* 63:i[2003] 73–8). In a fresh and compelling discussion, Benson ranges quickly across musical references in Malouf's poetry and fiction to come to a theory of the relationship between libretto and music, and to offer a reading of two of Malouf's four libretti. Cavagnoli stresses the importance of replicating sound as well as meaning, even in prose translation.

The centrality of colonialism is maintained in Susan K. Martin's discussion of body-snatching in her 'Getting a Head: Dismembering and Remembering in Robert Drewe's *The Savage Crows*' (*ALS* 21[2003] 54–66). Drewe's novel considers the theft and dismemberment of William Lanney, said to be the last Tasmanian Aboriginal man, by a scientific establishment eager to feed on his corpse. With occasional reference to *Dr Wooreddy's Prescription for Enduring the Ending of the World* by Mudrooroo, and engaging with a previous reading of Drewe's novel by Penny van Toorn, Martin contends that *The Savage Crows* is less successful than *Wooreddy* in evading the colonialist empiricism that it ostensibly seeks to contest. She concludes that 'the beheading of Lanney, and the scattering of his body parts, operate in the novel to represent a final and irremediable fracturing and dispersal of the Aboriginal social body' (p. 64). Tasmania is also foregrounded in Jesse Shipway's 'Wishing for Modernity: Temporality and Desire in *Gould's Book of Fish*' (*ALS* 21[2003] 43–53). This novel's author, Richard Flanagan, has played a leading role in debates in Tasmania, notably on environmental issues, which have a stronger potency in Tasmania than perhaps in any other part of Australia. However, Shipway contends that the pervasiveness and power of the state's self-image as the place that was 'left behind' is too great for Flanagan to resist: 'Flanagan's desire for an alternative modernity for Tasmania, with all its condensations and displacements of Tasmania's "real" passage to the present, cannot quite escape a repetition of the story of the Island's mediocre, "actual" modernisation' (p. 52). Influenced, one suspects, by Fredric Jameson's visit to Tasmania as keynote speaker for the 'What's Left of Theory?' conference in 2001, Shipway makes use of Jameson's writings on modernity to frame his argument.

Especially well served by critics in 2003 was Marcus Clarke, with three essays of high quality by Andrew McCann and Ian Henderson. Henderson's 'Treating Dora in *His Natural Life*' (*ALS* 21[2003] 67–80) aims 'to cast new light on Clarke's literary aesthetic, and on his philosophy, by examining the treatment of his heroine in the context of the middle-class Victorian market for popular books' (p. 67). His argument hinges on a rich and intelligent use of the term 'treatment', taken as referring both to literary representation and to the events which assail Dora throughout the novel, particularly as they are transformed between the serial and the book versions of the novel. McCann's 'Textual Phantasmagoria: Marcus Clarke, Light Literature and the Colonial Uncanny' (*ALS* 21[2003] 137–50) draws attention to the significance of 'the colonial production of the supernatural and the fantastic in the textual phantasmagoria' (p. 147) and the ways in which these tropes and that body of writing contributed to the formation of the colonial subject. McCann emphasizes that these literary forms, precisely because they entertain, 'have an efficacy that completely belies their contemporary status as ephemeral' (p. 149). In a highly original and insightful article, he demonstrates the ways in which various kinds of writing by Clarke embodied the tension between the supernatural and the secular, the spectacular and the quotidian, in the service of the colonialist psyche, as indigenous cultures are exploited 'as a reserve of uncanny affect' (p. 148). McCann turns even more explicitly to colonial history and violence against Aboriginal peoples in his subtle and forceful piece, 'The Savage Metropolis: Animism, Aesthetics and the Pleasures of a Vanished Race' (*TPr* 17[2003] 317–33).

Other canonical works to receive attention included Xavier Herbert's *Poor Fellow My Country*, Patrick White's *Voss*, and Joseph Furphy's *Such Is Life*. The briefest of these was Damien Barlow's 'Un/Making Sexuality: *Such Is Life* and the Observant Queer Reader' (*ALS* 21[2003] 166–77), which directs readers' attention to several moments in Furphy's novel which complicate or unsettle identifications of gender and sexuality. His lively exploration of cross-dressing in colonial Australia—unforgettable in its discussion of the complications of horses' names and their positionings—sheds new light on *Such Is Life*. More extensive is

Judith L. Tabron's discussion of White's *Voss* in her *Postcolonial Literature from Three Continents: Tutuola, H.D., Ellison and White*. After outlining the main issues in Australian literary history Tabron engages with prior readings of White's novel by Simon During, Peter Knox-Shaw, Ken Goodwin, Leonie Kramer and Ingmar Björksten. Special disdain is reserved for David Tacey, whose interpretation is dismissed as 'completely unconvincing' (p. 183). Tabron argues that *Voss* is White's most influential novel, although she is also critical of its representation of indigenous peoples on the grounds that they are used as symbols of primitivism. This tendency is explained as reflecting White's affinities with modernism: 'there is some indication that he is aware of the tradition predating him of treating the Aborigines as part of the local fauna; he partly falls prey to that tradition but also attempts to revitalize it for his own purposes' (p. 198).

Sean Monahan also centralizes the representation of indigenous peoples in his well-received study *A Long and Winding Road: Xavier Herbert's Literary Journey*. A committed advocate for Herbert—'the primary motivation [for the book] was a desire to enter the lists on behalf of *Poor Fellow My Country*'—but nevertheless clear-eyed about his subject's appalling sexism, Monahan says, 'The secondary motivation was an interest in finding explanations for the strangeness of Herbert's total output' (p. 3), two major novels, *Capricornia* and *Poor Fellow My Country*, separated by thirty years. Using Northrop Frye's taxonomy, Monahan argues that Herbert's longest novel has been undervalued because it has been read as a romance and as a novel, rather than as what Frye terms 'an anatomy'. In Frye's terms, anatomy is characterized by 'its didacticism, its lengthy intellectual discussions, its willingness to digress from the narrative in order to explore ideas, and its connection with satire and the comedy of humours' (pp. 7–8). After an extended discussion (over five chapters) of aspects of Herbert and his writing which pays attention to Herbert's representation of Aboriginal characters, his literary style and use of character, and psychoanalysis, Monahan devotes a further five chapters to *Poor Fellow My Country*. Monahan's main interest is in what he argues is the central problem that the novel addresses: 'that the dominance of white culture in Australia has made it impossible for Aboriginals to "be what they are proud of being". Instead they are presented with two choices, both unpalatable: assimilate and accept the cultural values of the white invaders or remain in squalor and poverty on the edges of white society' (p. 200). 'The final sign of how deeply rooted colonial attitudes are in Australia is the fact that their fiercest critic [in the novel] is himself tainted by them' (p. 224). Monahan suggests that *Poor Fellow My Country* has special relevance in contemporary Australia, a 'nation that supports the mean-spirited refugee and social welfare policies of a government like John Howard's' (p. 231).

Another mid-century writer to gain considerable attention was Christina Stead. Heather Stewart's 'Feminism and Male Chauvinism in the Writings of Christina Stead' (*Hecate* 29:ii[2003] 113–22) argues for the writer's feminist credentials despite Stead's own caution about the label, and prints an unpublished piece by Stead on rebellious women. Essays on Stead published in *JASAL* derive from papers presented at the 2002 ASAL conference, on a day commemorating the centenary of Christina Stead's birth. Margaret Harris's introduction to the journal issue, 'Christina Stead at 100', provides a comprehensive and judicious survey of Stead criticism, situating the contributions within and against existing views of the writer and her work (*JASAL* 2[2003] 5–12). She pays special tribute to the work of R.G. (Ron) Geering, Stead's literary executor, in compiling *Ocean of Story*, a collection of Stead's sketches and stories, many previously unpublished, and *I'm Dying Laughing*. Harris notes in passing that Geering's edition of *I'm Dying Laughing* is now the most frequently discussed of Stead's novels. Judith Kegan Gardiner's essay on Stead's critical reception in the United States, 'Christina Stead and the Synecdochic Scam: *The Little Hotel*', gives insight into the carelessness with which Australian writers can be treated. Her advocacy of the significance of *The Little Hotel* is developed through a detailed and sympathetic reading, from which she concludes that Stead was aiming to show that 'small swindles' are 'part of the whole system of inhumane individualism fostered by capitalism' (pp. 22–3). Brigid Rooney, in 'Crossing the Rubicon: Abjection and Revolution in Christina Stead's *I'm Dying Laughing*' (*JASAL* 2[2003] 29–39) deploys Julia Kristeva's notion of the abject, as developed in *The Powers of Horror*, to read *I'm Dying Laughing*, giving much of her attention to the character Emily Wilkes. In contrast, Susan Sheridan, in 'Christina Stead's Last Book: The Novel and the Bestseller' (*JASAL* 2[2003] 41–52) develops a reading of the same novel that is grounded in the political context in which it was written. Sheridan considers Stead's own views, as expressed in letters, of the people on which Wilkes and Stephen Howard are based, as well as the difficulties of the writing profession which Stead and her husband Bill Blake encountered. Michael Ackland's stated intention in 'Whatever Happened to Coppelius? Antecedents and Design in Christina Stead's *The Salzburg Tales*' (*JASAL* 2[2003] 53–60) is to recuperate this neglected early collection. Nicole Moore, in 'The Totally Incredible Obscenity of *Letty Fox*' (*JASAL* 2[2003] 67–79) considers the public debates and bureaucratic processes entailed in the banning in Australia of *Letty Fox*, a book that she describes as a 'blazingly critical portrait of the American bourgeoisie, the family and the marriage market' (p. 67). Susan Lever's 'Christina Stead's Workshop in the Novel: How To Write a "Novel of Strife"' (*JASAL* 2[2003] 81–91) considers the nature of Stead's communism and of her feminism, contending that 'it is possible to read Stead's novels as the work of a liberal individualist, or an unconscious feminist, despite her apparent communism' (p. 81). Two brief commentaries discuss Stead in relation to China and to Japan respectively. Another major event of the Cairns ASAL conference was the delivery of the Dorothy Green Memorial Lecture by Delys Bird, whose paper on Elizabeth Jolley's *George's Wife* trilogy in relation to epistolary traditions is published as 'Gertrude and Elizabeth: Letters, Lives and Fictions' (*JASAL* 2[2003] 105–19).

Along with the focus on Stead, left-wing politics is to the fore in books mainly concerned with Melbourne radicalism: a collection of essays on Frank Hardy, and John McLaren's *Free Radicals: On the Left in Postwar Melbourne*. McLaren appraises the lives and activism of Stephen Murray-Smith, Ian Turner and Ken Gott, three sometime members of the Communist Party who met while studying at Melbourne University, and who inaugurated and sustained the journal *Overland*. Adams and Lee, eds., *Frank Hardy and the Literature of Commitment*, signals by its title an engagement with Susan Lever's study *A Question of Commitment: Australian Literature in the Twenty Years after the War* [1989], although the engagement is not made explicit. The best of the twelve articles on Hardy are by John McLaren, Carole Ferrier, and David Carter, each of whom considers in careful and scholarly detail the relationship between writing and politics. In 'Bad Tempered Democrats, Biased Australians: Socialist Realism, *Overland* and the Australian Legend' (pp. 53–69), McLaren considers Hardy's relationship to debates about socialist realism and cultural nationalism, particularly as they were played out in (and around) the journal *Overland* in the late 1950s and early 1960s. Drawing on manuscript and published materials, he asserts that polemic about 'the Australian tradition' preceded by many years the interrogations of the 1970s by writers such as Humphrey McQueen, Anne Summers and John Docker. Equally judicious is Carole Ferrier's engaging discussion of literary politics in the writing and lives of Jean Devanny and Dorothy Hewett. In '"These Girls Are On the Right Track"' (pp. 71–87) Ferrier brings an eye for witty quotation, notably of misogynist ranting, to support her assertions regarding the problematic relationship between women writers and party politics. Tempting as it is to borrow the more hilarious (not to say lurid) of these remarks, readers are better directed to Ferrier's original to appreciate their context. More solemn in tone is David Carter's 'The Story of Our Epoch, a Hero of Our Time: The Communist Novelist in Postwar Australia' (pp. 89–111), which scrutinizes the nuances of communist literary and political discourses between the 1930s and 1950s, moving into a reading of Judah Waten's *Time of Conflict* [1961]. Carter aims to demonstrate that the novel, although flawed, is of interest to critics because it is successful in 'domesticating and naturalising the narrative of communism' (p. 110), suggesting that this is why the book was well received by certain groups of readers within the party. The collection reprints some early work on Hardy, including John Frow's 'Who Shot Frank Hardy? Intertextuality and Textual Politics' ([1982]; pp. 137–58), Hardy's reply ([1994]; pp. 247–50), and an updated version of Dave Nadel's 'key' to *Power Without Glory* (pp. 251–73). Other contributions include an evocative discussion of 'the stranger' by Cathy Greenfield and Peter Williams (pp. 171–83), and a meditation on the complex relationship between class and masculinity (that almost seems to be interrupted by its focus on Hardy) by Nathan Hollier (pp. 221–36). Also in the volume are two essays on Katharine Prichard, by Delys Bird (pp. 185–97) and Cath Ellis (pp. 199–219). Likewise of interest in terms of the history of leftist politics is Nicholas Hasluck's *The Legal Labyrinth: The Kisch Case and Other Reflections*, on one of Australia's most celebrated legal controversies.

In closing this section, we should note some significant work on writers likely to move (back) into view in coming years, including Deborah Jordan's essay on Nettie Palmer, 'Palmer's Present: Gender and the National Community in 1934' (*Hecate* 29:ii[2003] 99–112). Carole Ferrier and Maryanne Dever are preparing the complete correspondence between Nettie Palmer and Vance Palmer, which extends from 1909 to 1959. Roger Averill's interview with Randolph Stow (*NLitsR* 39[2003] 89–103) not only adds some details to the biographical basis of Stow's Sussex novels, but supplements them with relevant fragments of unpublished verse. Paul Eggert discusses the relationship between little-known

Western Australian writer Willem Siebenhaar and D.H. Lawrence, in his 'The Dutch–Australian Connection' (*ALS* 21[2003] 3–19). Eggert casts new light on the origins of Lawrence's novel *Kangaroo*. Thea Astley was the subject of little critical work, with more likely to come following her death in 2004, and the sessions devoted to her writing at the 2004 ASAL conference held in Sydney. Susan Sheridan's 'Thea Astley: A Woman among the Satirists of Post-War Modernity' (*AuFS* 18[2003] 261–71) argues that Astley's first four novels show her to be a satirical modernist sharing a masculinist anti-suburban stance with Patrick White and others. Only later did she develop a more feminist position.

Popular writing began to receive increased attention, marked by the fact that authors Frank Clune, Gwen Meredith, Elizabeth O'Connor, and Colin Simpson appear in the *ALS* bibliography for the first time. Cheryl Taylor's 'Gender and Race Relations in Elizabeth O'Connor's Northern Homesteads' (*ALS* 21[2003] 20–31) proposes that O'Connor's seven novels consolidate a colonialist view of the northern Queensland landscape and its societies. Lyn Jacobs covers similar ground in 'Homelands vs "The Tropics": Crossing the Line' (*JASAL* 2[2003] 167–78), a survey of the literature of the tropics by writers including Astley, Inez Baranay, Janette Turner Hospital, Gerard Lee, Eva Sallis, Trevor Shearston, Eric Wilmot and Alexis Wright.

(c) Poetry

The year was a strong one for poetry itself rather than criticism, seeing collected or selected poems by Laurie Duggan (*Mangroves*), John Kinsella (*Peripheral Light: New Poems*), Geoff Page (*Drumming on Water*) and John Tranter (*Studio Moon*) and, posthumously, *Gwen Harwood*: *Collected Poems 1943–1995*. Also appearing were several anthologies: Peter Craven's *The Best Australian Poems*, Martin Duwell and Bronwyn Lea's *The Best Australian Poetry 2003*, and Geoff Page's *The Indigo Book of Modern Australian Sonnets*. Readers will be pleased to learn that the collected works of Judith Wright and Mary Gilmore are in preparation. David McCooey reviewed the year's (and 2002's) poetry in 'Always Disappearing' (*Westerly* 48[2003] 74–84), developing an idea from Laurie Duggan that poetry inevitably memorializes its own lost self. As well as Duggan's *Mangroves*, McCooey finds Sudesh Mishra's *Diaspora and the Difficult Art of Dying* particularly accomplished.

One of two major critical studies on poetry this year was Eleonore Wildburger's *Politics, Power and Poetry: An Intercultural Perspective on Aboriginal Identity in Black Australian Poetry*, in which the author asserts that her main concern, inspired by Foucault, is 'the interrelationship between knowledge and colonial power relations' (p. 45). Wildburger's readings are framed in terms set by Aboriginal communities, while her reading practice is drawn from Antony Easthope's *Literary into Cultural Studies* (p. 105). The author is attentive to indigenous protocols in research, and cites the work not only of indigenous intellectuals but of institutional bodies which have established terms for enquiry by non-indigenous academics. Clearly writing for a European and non-specialist audience, Wildburger includes discussions of terminology, cultural history, theoretical approach and identity politics, with a further chapter outlining indigenous literature in English (including oral literatures) before embarking on brief discussions of the work of nine poets: Lisa Bellear, Graeme Dixon, Eve Mumewa Doreen Fesl, Lionel Fogarty, Anita Heiss, Eva Johnson, Roberta Sykes, Maureen Watson and Errol West. Also from Europe was Antonella Riem Natale's 'Women and the Sacred Partnership in Tales of the Aboriginal Dreamtime: "Goonur the Woman Doctor"' (in Natale and Albarea, eds. *The Art of Partnership: Essays on Literature, Culture, Language and Education Towards a Cooperative Paradigm*, pp. 47–65). Indigenous cultures are discussed in letters between two of Australia's foremost poets, Judith Wright and Les Murray, published as 'Correspondence' (*Southerly* 63:i[2003] 162–80) with annotations by Brigid Rooney. The letters, written between 1980 and 1983, show the writers' contrasting positions on the then contemporary debate about the value of a treaty between Aboriginal and non-Aboriginal Australians.

The second monograph was Anne Whitehead's *Bluestocking in Patagonia* whose dust-jacket subtitle, *Mary Gilmore's Quest for Love and Utopia at the World's End*, indicates the approach. Whitehead's informative if rather dramatic subtitle does not, unfortunately, appear on the book's title page, meaning that it had been entirely removed from the hardbound copy examined for this review. Atmospheric detail is provided by the author's account of her own travels in the southern part of the Americas, 'in the footsteps of Gilmore', and Whitehead is able to spend 300 pages discussing what William Wilde, in his biography *Courage a Grace*, covers in little more than a chapter. However, the tendency to take Gilmore's own accounts at face value, and to set aside contradictory evidence, means that *Bluestocking in Patagonia* is unlikely to supplant other accounts of the colonies in South America, or of Gilmore's life and work. At the opposite end of the spectrum is Peter Kirkpatrick's difficult but rewarding 'The Wanderer and the *Flâneur*: Christopher Brennan as Modernist' (*Southerly* 63:ii[2003] 63–77). Kirkpatrick uses Homer and Baudelaire to argue that the Wanderer's quest is essentially modernist, even if stylistically the poem remains a Victorian piece. C.T. Indra discusses Lee Cataldi's (unpublished) Indian poems (in vanden Driesen and Nandan, eds., pp. 138–48). Indra shows an intense appreciation of Cataldi's empathy and sympathy for the poor and the oppressed, if not always for her Marxist politics. Bindu N. and Rashmi Talwar are likewise admiring of the humanity evident in the poetry of Judith Rodriguez, in their discussion of the trope of 'the mirror' in her work (in vanden Driesen and Nandan, eds., pp. 149–55). John Kinsella maintained his prolific output, including a lyrical and suggestive effusion entitled 'Landscape Poetry?' (*Coppertales* 9[2003] 78–84). The same subject was considered by Gary Clark in his 'Rethinking Literary Ecology: Social Ecology, Anarchism and the Poetry of John Kinsella' (*Antipodes* 17[2003] 13–20), and 'History and Ecology: The Poetry of Les Murray and Gary Snyder' (*Isle* 10:i[2003] 27–53). Marjorie Perloff considered '"Vocable Scriptsigns": Differential Poetics in Kenneth Goldsmith's *Fidget* and John Kinsella's *Kangaroo Virus*' (in Roberts and Allison, eds., *Poetry and Contemporary Culture: The Question of Value*, pp. 21–43).

James McAuley continues to loom large, perhaps because his life and writing other than poetry offer scope for harnessing and interrogating a range of theoretical approaches. Some half-dozen articles on his work appeared. Among the more substantive of these are Ken Goodwin's 'James McAuley as

Hymn-Writer' (*ACR* 80[2003] 131–44) and Cassandra Pybus's 'The Black Swan of Trespass: James McAuley and the Ern Malley Hoax' (*Brick* 70[2003] 140–9). The relationship between McAuley and New Guinea is considered by Tony Hughes d'Aeth in 'Old Walls and New: The Australian Poet in the Asia-Pacific' (in Sankaran, Leong, and Patke, eds., pp. 65–76), in which d'Aeth follows Robert Dixon in centralizing New Guinea in the narrative of the development of McAuley's views on politics and culture. D'Aeth suggests that McAuley's view of colonialism was characterized by 'projection', as he became frustrated not so much by colonialism as by its failure. Somewhat sharper in its analysis than some of the other essays in this collection, d'Aeth's contribution comes from a larger study on 'the relationship between land, friendship and creativity in Australia' under the rubric of 'Kinships'. He includes comments on the poetry of Henry Lawson, James McAuley, Harold Stewart and Oodgeroo Noonuccal, as their work pertains to this theme. Equally complicated is the relationship between Australia's 'literary' and its popular poetic traditions. Something of this problem is canvassed in William Hatherell's forensic study 'Some Versions of Manifold: Brisbane and the "Myth" of John Manifold' (*ALS* 21[2003] 151–65), which focuses on the different dimensions of Manifold's life and reputation: 'the scion of the Victorian squattocracy and Cambridge graduate who became a dogmatic and active communist' (p. 151). A significant dimension of Hatherell's argument is his reading of the conflicting representations of Manifold by former associates who reconsider their reverence for Manifold, among them fellow poets Rodney Hall, Judith Rodriguez, David Malouf and Thomas Shapcott. Of these, Rodriguez is said to be the writer most sympathetic to Manifold and his politics.

(d) Drama

Marc Maufort's comparative volume *Transgressive Itineraries: Postcolonial Hybridizations of Dramatic Realism* and Schafer and Bradley Smith, eds., *Playing Australia: Australian Theatre and the International Stage* are the major critical publications in Australian drama for 2003. Maufort begins—perhaps somewhat idiosyncratically—by framing his arguments about Australian, Canadian and New Zealand drama in terms of the ways in which dramatists 'respond' to the work of American playwright Eugene O'Neill. The Australian author who is the focus of this argument is Louis Nowra, to whom a very large proportion of the long first chapter is devoted. There is a brief discussion of Tes Lyssiotis's *A White Sports Coat*, and a half-chapter on dramatic works which centralize Aboriginal characters: *The Dreamers* by Jack Davis, Eva Johnson's *Murras*, the musical *Bran Nue Dae*, Wesley Enoch and Deborah Mailman's *The 7 Stages of Grieving*, Leah Purcell's one-woman show *Box the Pony* and Jane Harrison's *Stolen*. Notwithstanding his use of a postcolonial vocabulary that valorizes 'hybridity' above all else, Maufort's discussion of these works occasionally shows the residue of an older critical lexicon informed by Eurocentric values. More hard-edged are the contributions to Schafer and Bradley Smith's *Playing Australia*, which range in scope from discussions of wire walkers and Tap Dogs to cricket, Gilbert Murray and an interview with Cate Blanchett. A number of essays, including the opening one, Helen Gilbert's 'Millennial Blues: Racism, Nationalism and the Legacy of Empire' (pp. 12–28), focus on questions of race and, especially, whiteness. Gilbert, in a provocative comparison of Randolph Bedford's 1909 production *White Australia (or the Empty North)* and *After the Ball*, a work by Australia's most popular contemporary dramatist David Williamson, argues that Australia remains trapped by the yoking together of racism and nationalism, a situation which theatre and theatre criticism should work to change. Elizabeth Schafer goes some way towards addressing this issue in her article, 'Reconciliation Shakespeare? Aboriginal Presence in Australian Shakespeare Production' (pp. 63–78), on the work of Aboriginal actors in Australian productions of plays by Shakespeare. The final piece, Susan Bradley Smith's 'Rhetoric, Reconciliation and Other National Pastimes: Showcasing Contemporary Australian Theatre in London' (pp. 195–211), again draws attention to the centrality of racial difference and racial inequality. Essays by Katherine Newey on May Holt (pp. 93–107), by Elizabeth Schafer on Gilbert Murray and Haddon Chambers (pp. 108–25) and by Susan Bradley Smith on Inez Bensusan (pp. 126–41) are recuperative, in terms of aiming to make better known the careers of Australians who worked and had success as playwrights and actors in Britain. Notwithstanding this aim, each of these critics offers an informative and nuanced account of the cultural affiliations of her subject, in a generally very strong collection. Taking a lighter approach was Delyse Ryan, in '"Does all Melbourne smell like this?": The Colonial Metropolis in *Marvellous Melbourne*' (*ALS* 21[2003] 81–91). Ryan considers this unusually popular play of 1889—the title of which was meant ironically—and its affinities with the sensationalist European literature of urban underworlds and the theatrical and literary conventions of its time. A contemporary dramatist whose work received extended discussion for the first time is Hannie Rayson, who is interviewed by Denise Varney (*ADS* 42[2003] 146–60). Varnie's 'Hannie Rayson's Life after George: Theatrical Intervention and Public Intellectual Discourse' (*ADS* 42[2003] 161–76) puts the case for Rayson being considered a public intellectual.

2. Canada

(a) General

An idiosyncratic but significant addition to reference work in Canada is the revised and enlarged third edition of *Peel's Bibliography of the Canadian Prairies to 1953*, edited by Ernie B. Ingles and N. Merrill Distad. Entries follow the historical 'date of activity' that the bibliographical materials refer to (not the date of publication); consequently, the indexes prove crucial for tracking items of interest. The bibliography has 7,429 entries, a considerable expansion of the previous edition. The 'Biography of Bruce Peel' is invaluable for understanding the genesis of the bibliography and Peel's positive and productive role in the development of the University of Alberta's research libraries. Beginning life as 'a card file of western Canadian titles', and developing into a bibliography focusing on the Prairie Provinces, Peel's ten-year project was finally published in 1956, with a supplement in 1963, and a second edition in 1973. Peel had been working on a supplement to the second edition when approached by the University of

Toronto Press for a third edition; a long-term illness brought this work to a halt. Peel died in 1998. The work of the third edition was taken over by Ernie B. Ingles and N. Merrill Distad; new features include renumbered entries (with a conversion table) and a new index of works in languages other than English. Reliance on online library catalogues facilitated the task of expanding the bibliography, but the accuracy and general reliability of online catalogues may need some further consideration. The 'sample entry explained' is a useful and important feature given the idiosyncratic nature of the text's organization; the author index has biographical notes, which are invaluable for researchers. Illustrations are placed throughout the book, with high-quality colour reproductions of the 'Canada West' map covers, showing a paradisiacal land of bounteous farming and ensuing prosperity awaiting new immigrants. Opening the book at random at page 274, entries range from Georges d'Ussel's *Rapport sur l'agriculture dans l'ouest canadien* [1908] to documents from the Wetaskiwin Board of Trade, the Winnipeg Development and Industrial Bureau, and the House of Commons, Ottawa. Cultural diversity is represented by entries on the poets William Talbot Allison and Robert Thompson Anderson, as well as a text called *Blackfoot hymns* [1909] from the Crowfoot Indian Residential School in Cluny, Alta. Even more obscure items include a high school souvenir from Wetaskiwin, Alberta, and a fête programme for the Société Saint Jean-Baptiste in Winnipeg. The montage effect created by this eclectic constellation of bibliographical entries is reminiscent of Walter Benjamin's *The Arcades Project* [trans. 1999], where myriad textual entries are juxtaposed, creating remarkable contrasts and intertextual interpretations. With Peel's, these juxtapositions serve to map the Canadian prairies in a similar montage form. Peel's own choices concerning precisely which materials made it into his bibliography lead necessarily to the construction of metaphorical prairie borders.

E.D. Blodgett, in *Five-Part Invention: A History of Literary History in Canada*, examines the borders of nationhood as composed by Canada's diverse literary history. The 'five parts' that make up this literary history are English Canada, French Canada, First Nations communities, Inuit communities, and immigrant communities. The introduction is a sophisticated critique of the shift away from the study of literary history in the humanities, which has come about with the turn to more theoretical and ideological methodologies. However, Blodgett also draws upon and synthesizes the most relevant concepts from such contemporary theoretical approaches to reinvigorate and reassess the history of literary history in Canada. The introduction ends with a chronological list of literary histories of Canada (with bibliographical information), which is a useful resource for scholars. Blodgett takes a chronological approach in the ten insightful chapters that follow the introduction, covering such topics as borders (1874–1920), the nation as discourse (1924–46) and the search for agency (1948–65). Quebec is the focus in chapter 4 (1967–9) and history as salvation in chapter 5 (1973–83). *La Vie littéraire au Québec* [1991], edited by Maurice Lemire and Denis Saint-Jacques, is the focus of chapter 6, and multicultural and postcolonial models of literary history make an appearance in chapter 7 (1968–93), where Blodgett comments insightfully that 'The paradox for First Nations people, Inuit, and immigrants whose native language is not English, is that if access to agency appears offered by English, it carries a high cultural price' (p. 230). Europeans looking in, and Canadians representing literary history for those outside of the country, are the subjects of chapters 8 and 9, entitled respectively 'Canada as Alterity: The View from Europe, 1895–1961' and 'Canada by Canadians for Europeans, 1974–1989'. Finally, in 'Afterthoughts, Models, Possibilities', Blodgett re-examines the *Bildungsroman* model used in the book, as well as ways of developing and respecting a 'plurality of memories'.

A late arrival that brings another perspective to the literary history of Canada is James Doyle, *Progressive Heritage: The Evolution of a Politically Radical Literary Tradition in Canada*. Rejecting oversimplified criticism of Marxist literature, Doyle re-examines Marxist literary history to reassess previous harsh critical comments (notably from Frye) and foreground otherwise obscure authors. Doyle argues that the 'close identification of Marxist-inspired literary activity with the 1930s is not an exclusively Canadian tendency. The same inclination is typical of scholarly studies of the much more abundant radical literary heritage of the United States' (p. 6). Chapters on the 1940s, the 1950s, 'After Stalinism', and the 'New Left' support Doyle's thesis by a charting of hitherto unexplored or ignored literary materials. Another late arrival is Katarina Leandoer, *From Colonial Expression to Export Commodity: English-Canadian Literature in Canada and Sweden, 1945–1999*. Leandoer's study is wide-ranging and historically comprehensive, beginning with postwar Canadian literature, the colonial heritage, and the search for a national literature in chapter 1, exploring Canadian cultural nationalism and the role of governmental interventions in chapter 2, and then moving on to Canadian literature as an export commodity in the third chapter. Chapter 4 in effect begins again, with survey and analysis of the 200 years of Canadian writing in Sweden, with chapter 5 analysing the critical reception of Canadian literature from a Swedish perspective. The book concludes with discussion of English Canadian literature as a 'multicultural commodity' in the 1990s, and also prints three appendices concerning Swedish translations of Canadian literature and critical receptions.

The critical dominance and impact of Northrop Frye upon literary history continue to be subjects of study: four essays in O'Grady and Ning, eds., *Northrop Frye: Eastern and Western Perspectives*, have a Canadian focus. An accessible, compact overview is provided by Wang Ning, 'Northrop Frye and Cultural Studies', while the short 'Frye and Canada' section of the collection offers literary-critical readings. Sandra Djwa, '"Canadian Angles of Vision": Northrop Frye, Carl Klinck, and the *Literary History of Canada*', examines the genesis of the *Literary History of Canada* [1965], beginning with Carl Klinck listening to a paper delivered by Frye at the English Institute of Columbia University in 1956. Djwa points out the collaborative nature of the *Literary History* project, and compares the Canadian endeavour with the team-based production of the *Literary History of the United States* [1956]; she also charts the intellectual framework provided by Frye's authoritative literary-critical output. Myth and symbol informed Frye's work thoroughly, influencing an entire 'generation of poets, critics, and readers in Canada' (p. 111), as Thomas Willard puts it in 'Gone Primitive: The Critic in Canada'. Willard also traces the influence of James George Frazer (1854–1941) and Oswald Spengler (1880–1936) on Frye's thinking. Rejecting the reading of Atwood's novel *Cat's Eye* [1988] as a *Bildungsroman* or *Kunstlerroman*, James Steele, 'Margaret Atwood's *Cat Eye*: New Feminism or Old Comedy?', explores the novel's underlying narrative pattern or 'mythos', to use Frye's term. Steele argues that *Cat's Eye* is fundamentally a 'satirically comic story' (p. 121). The combined force of the literary essays in *Northrop Frye: Eastern and Western Perspectives* reveals that Frye's insights into literary structures remain valid today.

Laura Moss answers the question 'Is Canada Postcolonial?' via an edited collection of essays, some of which emerged from the 2000 University of Manitoba conference with the same title. Twenty-two essays, with a preface and afterword, make up *Is Canada Postcolonial? Unsettling Canadian Literature*. The collection is usefully organized into four parts: 'Questioning Canadian Postcolonialism'; 'Postcolonial Methodologies'; 'Is Canadian Literature Postcolonial?'; and 'Meditations on the Question'. Moss notes that the collection is 'driven by a shared concern with the place of Canadian literature in ever-evolving literary theories and the place of Canada in theories and practices of nationalism, postnationalism, and postcolonialism' (p. vi). In her introduction, 'Is Canada Postcolonial? Introducing the Question', Moss contextualizes the collection via pedagogy and the diverse responses to an already heterogenous field of study. In part 1, George Elliott Clarke, 'What Was Canada?', explores the US–Canadian relationship and the ethnically hybrid state of Canada via the ground of 'political criteria'. Neil Besner, 'What Resides in the Question "Is Canada Postcolonial?"?', situates his response theoretically and ontologically, suggesting a replacement set of questions that 'might inquire whether postcolonialism is a methodology; a condition; or a development, chronological or otherwise' (p. 41). 'It depends' is the 'expected Canadian response' (p. 49) explored by Diana Brydon, in 'Canada and Postcolonialism: Questions, Inventories, and Futures', while Donna Palmateer Pennee, in 'Looking Elsewhere for Answers to the Postcolonial Question: From Literary Studies to State Policy in Canada', examines 'the role of national literatures in the literary studies curriculum' (p. 78). Turning to part 2, Susan Gingell, 'The Absence of Seaming, or How I Almost Despair of Dancing: How Postcolonial Are Canada's Literary Institutions and Critical Practices?', takes a playful approach to the institutionalization of postcolonial studies in Canada, while asking seriously how significantly the dominance of postcolonial theory has helped marginalized peoples. The rejection of specifically postcolonial theoretical discourses by Canada's First Peoples informs the pedagogical dilemma explored by Judith Leggatt in 'Native Writing, Academic Theory: Post-Colonialism across the Cultural Divide'. Leggatt provides a useful definition: 'I conceive of post-colonialism as a process, an ongoing attempt to find means of cross-cultural communication that escape the repressive hierarchies of colonial encounters' (p. 111). The commodification of the Other is the subject of Mridula Nath Chakraborty's 'Nostalgic Narratives and the Otherness Industry', while Chelva Kanaganayakam, in 'Cool Dots and a Hybrid Scarborough: Multiculturalism as Canadian Myth', completes the second part of the collection with analysis of a film about immigration, called *Just a Little Red Dot* [1997]. The literary focus of part 3 begins with a study of what has been called Canada's first novel, Francis

Brooke's *The History of Emily Montague* [1769], alongside other writings from this period; Pam Perkins, 'Imagining Eighteenth-Century Quebec: British Literature and Colonial Rhetoric', discusses ways in which texts produced by one colonial power replacing another can be inadvertently self-undermining. Beginnings and originary texts are explored in diverse but related ways by the following: Douglas Ivison, '"I too am a Canadian": John Richardson's *The Canadian Brothers* as Postcolonial Narrative'; Cecily Devereux, 'Are We There Yet? Reading the "Post-Colonial" and *The Imperialist* in Canada'; and Barbara S. Bruce, 'Figures of Collection and (Post)Colonial Processes in Major John Richardson's *Wacousta* and Thomas King's *Truth and Bright Water*'. A significant contribution to theories of auto/biographical writing and collaboration is Manina Jones's '*Stolen Life*? Reading through Two I's in Postcolonial Autobiography', where Yvonne Johnson's and Rudy Wiebe's co-written *Stolen Life: The Journey of a Cree Woman* [1998] is regarded as a positive instance of cross-cultural communication and expression. Five literary-critical essays that examine concepts of home and divergent immigrant identities complete this part of the collection: Karen E. Macfarlane, '"A place to stand on": (Post)colonial Identity in *The Diviners* and "The Rain Child"'; Amy Kroeker, 'A "Place" through Language: Postcolonial Implications of Mennonite/s Writing in Western Canada'; Jim Zucchero, 'What's Immigration Got to Do with It? Postcolonialism and Shifting Notions of Exile in Nino Ricci's Italian-Canadians'; and Marie Vautier, 'Religion, Postcolonial Side-by-Sidedness, *la Transculture*'; and Robert Budde, 'After Postcolonialism: Migrant Lines and the Politics of Form in Fred Wah, M. Nourbese Philip, and Roy Miki'. Four significant critics provide short meditations on the question in the final part of the collection: Len Findlay, 'Is Canada a Postcolonial Country?'; Terry Goldie, 'Answering the Questions'; Victor J. Ramraj, 'Answering the Answers, Asking More Questions'; and Stephen Slemon, 'Afterword'. The collection as a whole is challenging and explores a wide range of pedagogical issues that confront teachers of postcolonial studies.

A special issue of *Canadian Literature* covers literature and war. In her editorial, Susan Fisher, 'The Study of War' (*CanL* 179[2003] 10–14), analyses the stained glass religious tableaux in Vancouver's Canadian Memorial United Church, and the encoded messages about war, and the ways in which narratives of 'discovery and conquest' clearly have more enduring power for the nation as a whole. Fisher also surveys the foregrounding of war literature for school students in the early to mid twentieth century, noting the effacement of Canadian war narratives from anthologies in the 1960s onwards. She ponders why there has been this effacement of Canadian involvement in war, as well as the ongoing relevance for war narratives in the teaching of citizenship. The editorial is followed by a piece from Her Excellency Adrienne Clarkson, the Governor General of Canada, 'Eulogy for Canada's Unknown Soldier' (*CanL* 179[2003] 15–18). Jonathan F. Vance, 'The Soldier as Novelist: Literature, History, and the Great War' (*CanL* 179[2003] 22–37), examines the competing claims for ownership and interpretative control of narratives of war, describing the backlash against what were perceived to be 'anti-war' texts; intriguingly, it is the 'anti-war' texts that were most despised by veterans that have now become a staple of student history and war literature courses. Judy Brown focuses on the issues involved in writing about war for younger people in '"How the World Burns": Adults Writing War for Children' (*CanL* 179[2003] 39–54), where she argues that history textbooks and reference books for children generally fail to engage successfully in representing war for children, whereas children's fiction does productively explore from an experiential perspective the impact of war on the young. Theodore Goossen, in 'Writing the Pacific War in the Twenty-First Century: Dennis Bock, Rui Umezawa, and Kerri Sakamoto' (*CanL* 179[2003] 56–71), asks why Canadian novelists should suddenly turn to writing about the Pacific war almost sixty years after it ended. After examination of three recent novels, Dennis Bock's *The Ash Garden* [2001], Rui Umezawa's *The Truth about Death and Dying* [2002], and Kerri Sakamoto's *One Hundred Million Hearts* [2003], Goossen takes a biographical approach to ponder the relationship between those who experienced the Pacific war and those who are only now attempting to recover memories and stories. Lucy Maud Montgomery's war novel is reassessed and in many respects recuperated by Amy Tector in 'A Righteous War? L.M. Montgomery's Depiction of the First World War in *Rilla of Ingleside*' (*CanL* 179[2003] 72–86). Instead of being regarded as a 'chauvinistic tract' (quoting Margery Fee and Ruth Cawker), Tector argues that Montgomery's novel 'explores sacrifice, wartime idealism, feminism, the development of a Canadian literature, and the emergence of a Canadian identity' (p. 73). With its focus on the 'home front', Tector's essay reveals that the impact of war on the domestic community created opportunities for women in Canada as well as England, as well as a space of subtle but subversive critique. The special issue is concluded with the wartime stories of an intriguing character from colonial British Columbia, Princess Peggy Abkhazi, in Laurie McNeill, 'Performing Genres: Peggy Abkhazi's *A Curious Cage* and Diaries of War' (*CanL* 179[2003] 89–105). A complex interplay of forces that are revealed in *A Curious Cage* include class constraints, audience, generic restrictions, and the concerns of an internee who shouldn't be keeping a diary in the first place. McNeill does an excellent job of providing biographical and historical background, and casts a critical eye at a text republished in 2002 as part of a barrage of publicity to accompany a conservation campaign (to protect Abkhazi's garden).

(b) Fiction

Fiction is well served by David Lucking with a wide-ranging critical study, *The Serpent's Part: Narrating the Self in Canadian Literature*. Lucking provocatively argues that 'naming' is a central existential act in much Canadian fiction, forging a family resemblance of identity formation. The first chapter, 'Rampant with Memory: History and Identity in Canadian Literature', is an overview of Lucking's thesis, with emphasis on the ways in which the past is 'dredged' for meanings that will serve the present; subsequent chapters explore in detail works by Susanna Moodie, Howard O'Hagan, Jack Hodgins, George Bowering, Robertson Davies, Margaret Atwood and Timothy Findley.

Scholars of Carol Shields's work will be delighted by the collection edited by Edward Eden and Dee Goertz, *Carol Shields, Narrative Hunger, and the Possibilities of Fiction*, especially the annotated bibliography of Shields's work, compiled and annotated by Faye Hammill. The first section of the collection is a talk delivered by Shields in 1996 at her Alma Mater, Hanover College, 'Narrative Hunger and the Overflowing Cupboard'. The second section, 'The "Precious Oxygen of Permission": Shields's Experiments with Narrative Form', has five essays. Beginning with an analysis of narrative as 'a medium of perception' in Shields's work, Sarah Gamble also sensitively reveals the postmodern aspects of the novels in 'Filling the Creative Void: Narrative Dilemmas in *Small Ceremonies*, the *Happenstance* Novels, and *Swann*'. Postmodern self-reflexivity is the subject of Faye Hammill, '*The Republic of Love* and Popular Romance'. Shields's parody and subversion of the romance genre is also a serious attempt to reveal how the genre handles issues of love and sexuality, and how it has been stripped of meaning over time. Repetition and the impact of rereading romances are the themes of Dianne Osland, '*The Stone Diaries*, *Jane Eyre*, and the Burden of Romance', while the 'meta-biographical', or literature that comments on auto/biographical genres, is the subject of Wendy Roy, 'Autobiography as Critical Practice in *The Stone Diaries*'. Melissa Pope Eden, '"The subjunctive mode of one's self": Carol Shields's Biography of Jane Austen', asks if Shields is a postmodern, feminist biographer. The third section of the collection, 'To "Shorten the distance between what is privately felt and universally known": Reaching beyond the Word', has four essays, the first of which continues the exploration of auto/biography. Chiara Briganti, 'Fat, Nail Clippings, Body Parts, or the Story of Where I Have Been: Carol Shields and Auto/Biography', argues that there is a shift from an originary maternal body in Shields's auto/biographical writing towards a grounded 'telling of a woman's life in the inescapable corporeality of the mother tongue' (p. 176). Lisa Johnson, '"She enlarges on the available materials": A Postmodernism of Resistance in *The Stone Diaries*', argues for a recuperative account of postmodernism, enabling a reading of *The Stone Diaries* which leads to awareness of strategies of resistance and transformation. Agency and subjectivity, in Johnson's reading, replace the nihilism of the postmodern assemblage, as theorized by Deleuze and others. Dee Goertz, 'Treading the Maze of *Larry's Party*', rereads the symbol of the maze as fundamentally connecting and generating meaning, agreeing with Lisa Johnson's reading of a recuperative postmodernism. Kathy Barbour, 'The Swann who Laid the Golden Egg: A Cautionary Tale of Deconstructionist Cannibalism in *Swann*', takes a creative approach to the either/or question of how deliberately playful Shields is as a writer, given her knowledge of postmodern and post-structuralist theories. The collection ends with Faye Hammill, 'Carol Shields: An Annotated Bibliography', listing primary, secondary, and film materials. The collection has been edited and written in such a way that connections between the essays are established and highlighted, and where the contributors take different theoretical positions their reasons for doing so are also clearly articulated.

Ethel Wilson gets substantial critical treatment in a new biography by David Stouck, *Ethel Wilson: A Critical Biography*. Narrating the story of a writing life, by chapter 7 the biography becomes focused on literary production and reception, starting with the nineteen-year history of Wilson's *The Innocent Traveller* [1949]. Stouck reviews the critical reception upon publication of the novel, discusses the novel's style and 'sophisticated ironies', and then reviews and summarizes more recent criticism, including postcolonial analysis. Chapter 8 steps backward in time to cover the publication of *Hetty Dorval* [1947], which Wilson wrote in 1945; Stouck performs some interesting analysis of editorial and stylistic issues during the novel's production, and notes the divided reception of the book upon publication. A similar format is used by Stouck for coverage of *The Equations of Love* [1952] in chapter 9, before he moves on to consider Wilson's role as 'the doyenne of British Columbia writers' (p. 164) in chapter 10, with fascinating material concerning her professional relationship with Earle Birney and 'her detractor and adversary' (p. 168), the influential critic William Arthur Deacon. The literary-critical format returns for chapter 11, considering the period of *Swamp Angel* [published in 1954]; chapter 12 covers *Love and Salt Water* [1956], and chapter 13 *Mrs Golightly and Other Stories* [1961], followed by a chapter on Wilson as a 'grande dame' (p. 257), before finishing with Wilson's widowhood and death. Stouck's literary biography is balanced, fair and compassionate; he engages in criticisms of the shortcomings of Wilson's work as much as he produces critical praise. A key feature is the way in which Stouck situates Wilson as an author ahead of her time, more in tune with the current international scope of Canadian writing than the nationalist demands of an earlier phase of Canadian literature criticism. Stouck's biography will be useful for students, researchers, and those simply interested in learning more about the life and works of Ethel Wilson.

Two-thirds of Caroline Rosenthal's *Narrative Deconstructions of Gender in Works by Audrey Thomas, Daphne Marlatt, and Louise Erdrich* cover major Canadian authors. Rosenthal explores the relationships between 'gender identity formation' and narrative through close reading of her three authors. A useful chapter is 'Framing Theories', where Rosenthal covers the critical territory that informs her literary readings; sections are devoted to identity, gender, and gender and narrative. An awareness of Canadian theory is clear, especially with the brief discussion of the shift from *écriture féminine* to the Canadian emphasis upon *écriture au féminine* or writing in the feminine, which replaces the psychoanalytical with a deconstructive approach. Audrey Thomas's *Intertidal Life* [1984] is read as 'dismembering the corporeality of language' (p. 32) and remapping identity through textual space; Daphne Marlatt's *Ana Historic* [1988] is explored for signs of an unruly 'monstrous' (p. 68) and transgressive lesbian identity, which is regarded as preparatory for alternative future identities. The thematic of trickster writing pervades Rosenthal's study, but it is in a co-authored text that trickster receives the most engaging treatment, Arnold E. Davidson, Priscilla L. Walton and Jennifer Andrews, *Border Crossings: Thomas King's Cultural Inversions*. Given the growing international recognition of the significance of First Nations writing, this well-researched and clearly written book is a highly significant and timely publication in the field. Thomas King's hybrid identity is in itself one of the main 'border crossings', and the book therefore covers American and Canadian indigenous culture and writing. In the introduction the authors cover King's biography, his dissertation 'Inventing the Indian: White Images, Native Oral Literature, and Contemporary Native Writers' (University of Utah [1986]), his edited collection of First Nations writing, *All My*

Relations: An Anthology of Contemporary Canadian Native Fiction [1990], and his groundbreaking essay 'Godzilla vs. Post-Colonial' [1990]; also covered in some depth is the theoretical concept of 'in-betweenness' as it relates to border construction and crossing. Comedy is a key aspect of King's Native writing, and the authors devote two chapters to its study: 'Comic Contexts' and 'Comic Inversions'. Gerald Vizenor's notion of a 'trickster discourse' is used to explain and recover the powerful scatological humour of King's writing, as well as close analysis of the blending of comic and tragic modes in Native writing in general. King's playful and subversive parodies of canonical literatures are discussed in the third chapter, 'Genre Crossings', and his powerful forays into other artistic forms are the subject of chapter 4, 'Comedy, Politics, and Audio and Visual Media', with reproduction of some of King's photographs. Notions of nation and race have two chapters devoted to them, 5, 'Humouring Race and Nationality', and 6, 'The Comic Dimensions of Gender, Race, and Nation: King's Contestatory Narratives'; the authors argue that King deconstructs hierarchical gender and racial conventions, producing indigenous counter-narratives. The book ends with a study of King's 'Comic Intertextualities', countering the usual cross-literary intertextual study of King with an intratextual study that reveals that much of his 'intertextuality' refers playfully to his own published works. Readers who are interested in critical materials on a particular publication by King will not be disappointed; key novels and stories are covered in depth in various places, making the book suitable for teaching and research. The rejection of the 'postcolonial' approach by King is respected by the authors, but they also suggest that there is some theoretical border-crossing occurring which leads to an awareness of other key postcolonial ideas and theories that intersect with King's indigenous concerns.

Relatively recent work by Margaret Atwood (from the 1980s and 1990s) is the subject of Wilson, ed., *Margaret Atwood's Textual Assassinations: Recent Poetry and Fiction* (articles on poetry and poetics are reviewed below). Atwood's generic boundary-blurring, or crossings, dominate the essays in the collection. Mary K. Kirtz, '(Dis)unified Field Theories: The Clarendon Lectures Seen through (a) *Cat's Eye*', writes thematic plot summaries of key Atwood texts as reread and articulated in Atwood's own Oxford University Clarendon Lectures delivered in 1991. Atwood's resistance to criticism leads her to playfully undermine reader's expectations; Carol L. Beran, 'Strangers within the Gates: Margaret Atwood's *Wilderness Tips*', examines the ten stories that can be grouped according to 'particular currently fashionable literary theories' (p. 75), revealing how Atwood employs ambiguity and contradiction to create a literature that recognizes otherness, rather than conforming to predetermined literary theories. Atwood's staging of national identity is the subject of Coral Ann Howells, '*The Robber Bride*; or, Who Is a True Canadian?'. Utilizing Homi Bhabha's notion of a 'discourse of nation', Howells identifies *The Robber Bride* as a postcolonial novel where subjectivity is fundamentally perceived as constituted through difference. Unlike the ghostly immigrant identity of Zenia in *The Robber Bride*, the protagonist of *Alias Grace*, Grace Marks, has a more substantial historical existence. Nonetheless, her story is told via multiple genres that are patched together, as many critics have noted, including Sharon R. Wilson,

'Quilting as Narrative Art: Metafictional Construction in *Alias Grace*', with the additional observation that Atwood's postmodern and metafictional turn coincides with a move towards archival documentation. Atwood's love of the Gothic is the subject of Karen F. Stein, 'A Left-Handed Story: *The Blind Assassin*', where the identically named novels-within-novels are analysed for their social and ideological critiques. Narrative theory continues with a second essay by Karen F. Stein, 'Talking Back to Bluebeard: Atwood's Fictional Storytellers', where the possibly redemptive female-centred knowledge of others is revealed to be articulated mainly through Atwood's first-person narrators. Novels are the focus of two theoretically astute journal essays on Atwood: Roxanne J. Fand, 'Margaret Atwood's *The Robber Bride*: The Dialogic Moral of a Nietzschean Fairy Tale' (*Crit* 45:i[2003] 65–81), and Jennifer A. Wagner-Lawlor, 'From Irony to Affiliation in Margaret Atwood's *The Handmaid's Tale*' (*Crit* 45:i[2003] 83–96). Drawing on Bakhtin's theories of dialogism, Fand also reads Woolf's seminal 'The Mark on the Wall' [1917] and Atwood's 'The Page' [1983] as instances of open dialogic subjectivity, leading Fand to a rejection of the Freudian and Lacanian models of intrasubjectivity in favour of intersubjective models that are used to read *The Robber Bride*. Wagner-Lawlor draws on Linda Hutcheon's and Richard Rorty's work on irony to re-examine the entire issue of irony, agency and power relations in Atwood's science fiction novel *The Handmaid's Tale*, where to 'affiliate oneself ironicaly [*sic*] is to accept contingency; it is also to accept that one's affiliative choices must always be reviewed and revaluated' (p. 93).

Wide-ranging essays appeared on Michael Ondaatje: Carmen Concilio, 'The Discourse of Resistance and the "War Machine" in David Malouf's *The Conversations at Curlow Creek* and Michael Ondaatje's *The Real Works of Billy the Kid*' (*ES* [2003] 69–81); Vernon Provencal, 'The Story of Candaules in Herodotus and *The English Patient*' (*CML* 23:i[2003] 49–64); David L. Kranz, '*The English Patient*: Critics, Audiences, and the Quality of Fidelity' (*LFQ* 31:ii[2003] 99–110); Monika Fludernik, 'Chronology, Time, Tense and Experientiality in Narrative' (*L&L* 12:ii[2003] 117–34); and Gordon Bölling, 'Metafiction In Michael Ondaatje's Historical Novel *In the Skin of a Lion*' (*Symbolism* 3[2003] 215–53). Concilio's comparative approach to outlaw figures in Australian and Canadian writing is productive and illuminating; she reads the outlaws in Malouf's and Ondaatje's works as 'nomads' in Deleuze's sense, disrupting realism and classical biography. Provencal reveals an intriguing web of connecting texts, all of which adopt the Candaules story from Herodotus, including Robertson Davies's *Fifth Business* [1970] and Iris Murdoch's *The Severed Head* [1961]; Provencal notes that the Candaules story 'appears in *The English Patient* as a historical archetype that gives rise to recurring psychological patterns that beget historical consequences' (p. 57). Kranz covers an area of ongoing study and speculation with the question of text-to-film adaptation; after reviewing the critical field in this area, he turns to an intriguing experiment surveying readers and viewers of text and film versions of *The English Patient*, concluding that 'the collective audience' agree that the film version is essentially faithful to the text, contradicting individual academic critical views, and essentially revealing similarities with Ondaatje's own position on the film version of his novel. Fludernik's essay uses *The English Patient* as a case study in a much larger narratological study of tense acquiring a 'literary function'; she foregrounds the 'oddity' of literary tense-usage, and her observations concerning Ondaatje's novel are particularly useful for disentangling the anachronisms expressed therein. Metafictional writing strategies in Ondaatje's novel *In the Skin of a Lion* [1987] are the subject of Bölling's in-depth study; he argues that the working-class perspective of the novel does not offer another totalizing history precisely because of the metafictional process of revealing history to be a construct. Turning to the Pacific northwest, two essays by Richard J. Lane, 'Reclaiming Maps and Metaphors: Canadian First Nations and Narratives of Place' (in Madsen, ed., *Beyond the Borders: American Literature and Post-Colonial Theory*), and 'Performing Gender: First Nations, Feminism, and Trickster Writing in Eden Robinson's *Monkey Beach*' (*HJEAS* 9:i[2003] 161–71), address issues of cultural reclamation and the role of postcolonial theory and practice in Haisla First Nations author Eden Robinson. Robinson has been recognized as an important new voice in Canadian literature, reworking Eurocentric genres from a Native perspective; Lane builds on this general argument with focus on gender performance in Robinson's work. A related essay is Deena Rymhs, 'A Residential School Memoir: Basil Johnston's *Indian School Days*' (*CanL* 178[2003] 58–70). Rymhs notes how Johnston's book is quietly subversive of official accounts of the residential schools, yet has at times been ignored by critics because of this. In a close reading of the text, Rymhs reveals how Johnston's failure to follow the expected script concerning residential schools is in itself a mode of resistance and difference; Johnston thus celebrates instances of community and solidarity in the middle of his ongoing trial. Problematizing claims to postcolonialism in Urquhart's work is Cynthia Sugars's fascinating essay 'Haunted by (a Lack of) Postcolonial Ghosts: Settler Nationalism in Jane Urquhart's *Away*' (*ECW* 79[2003] 1–32), which also looks at the contradictions inherent in searching for 'new' Canadian ghosts. Two essays in the same volume of *Essays on Canadian Writing* engage in cultural recovery and dynamic memorialization: Pilar Cuder-Domínguez, 'African Canadian Writing and the Narration(s) of Slavery' (*ECW* 79[2003] 55–75) and George Elliott Clarke, 'Inking BC in Black and Blue' (*ECW* 79[2003] 76–82). Cuder-Domínguez examines the contested spaces of African Canadian literature, but also finds critical agreement that history writing is an important but 'challenging' task for black Canadian writers (p. 56). George Elliott Clarke is encouraged by the response to his two-volume anthology on 'Africadian' black Nova Scotian writing, [1991–2], in the form of Wayde Compton's anthology of black British Columbian literature and orature in 2002; Clarke critically compares and contrasts these two significant, groundbreaking anthologies.

Brief but informative notes on fiction include Corey Thompson, 'Alistair MacLeod's "To everything there is a season": An Allegorical Second Coming' (*NConL* 33:ii[2003] 2–3) and Tim Lehnert, 'Mordecai's Version' (*AntigR* 135[2003] 94–7). Thompson identifies the allegorical meaning of MacLeod's story by comparing phrases that parallel biblical texts announcing the conditions and results of Christ's Second Coming; Lehnert examines narrative tense to argue for a more language-based criticism of Richler's works. Significant new essays on

Margaret Laurence include John C. Eustace, 'African Interests: White Liberalism and Resistance in Margaret Laurence's "Pure Diamond Man"' (*IFR* 30:i–ii[2003] 20–6), Brenda Beckman-Long, 'The Narratee as Confessor in Margaret Laurence's *The Fire-Dwellers*' (*L&T* 17:ii[2003] 113–26), and a critical review article by Wendy Roy, 'Metaphors of Dualism in Margaret Laurence's Writings' (*ECW* 79[2003] 41–6). Eustace ponders a key issue in postcolonial studies, that of mediating the language and culture of the Other, in this case Laurence's writings about Africa; rather than attacking Laurence, Eustace shows that it was her own disaffection and recognition of a 'neocolonial agency' in her writing that led her to stop writing about Africa, even though she had won recognition and approval from writers such as Chinua Achebe. Laurence's short story 'The Pure Diamond Man' [1963] is read as a sophisticated, self-reflexive recognition of 'neocolonial agency'. It is precisely this sophisticated awareness of the colonial situation that Roy finds lacking in her in-depth review of David Lucking, *Ancestors and Gods: Margaret Laurence and the Dialectics of Identity* [2002]; Roy argues, *contra* Lucking, that Laurence not only portrays well the complexities of colonial encounter in her fiction, but also raises awareness of gender difference and historical and cultural specificities. Gendered 'confessions' in *The Fire-Dwellers* are regarded as spiritual exercises by Beckman-Long; the confessional genre becomes polyphonic in Laurence's treatment of it, with an underlying spirituality leading to 'self-perception'. Critics are increasingly turning to complex theoretical approaches to analyse fiction. Neal Bruss, 'Anne Michaels' *Fugitive Pieces*, Object Relations, Internalization, and the Development of Discourse' (*Reader* 48[2003] 20–50), is an extended exploration of 'object relations psychology' in the construction of a discourse; Bruss's essay serves as a thoughtful and useful applied introduction to object relations, taking a chronological and literary-critical approach. Literary production is the theme of Mary Eagleton, 'Carol Shields and Pierre Bourdieu: Reading *Swann*' (*Crit* 44:iii[2003] 313–28), who also argues that 'Bourdieu has been underrepresented in Anglo-American literary thinking' (p. 313). Eagleton devotes a section of her essay to key terms from Bourdieu, with the focus on 'field' and 'habitus', before moving on to her extended analysis. The essay should be of interest to a wide range of literary critics, especially given Eagleton's insights into feminist literary and social history. Two types of narrative 'logic' are revealed by Tamas Benyei to be at work in Richler's novel, in 'What the Raven Said: Genealogy and Subjectivity in Mordecai Richler's *Solomon Gursky Was Here*' (*Com* 25:ii[2003] 95–111), a linear 'generational' narrative and one of repetition, leading to 'anecdotal organization'. Benyei situates Richler in an extensive network of fiction to ponder the ways in which *Solomon Gursky Was Here* [1989] interrogates 'the coherence and stability of the genealogically conceived subject' (p. 96); Benyei's reading is rich and insightful, especially with his discussion of the raven, regarded as an overdetermined and 'ambiguous trope' (p. 109).

(c) Poetry and Drama

Margaret Atwood's poetry is well served by Wilson, ed., *Margaret Atwood's Textual Assassinations: Recent Poetry and Fiction* (prose fiction essays are reviewed above). Reingard M. Nischik, 'Murder in the Dark: Margaret Atwood's Inverse Poetics of Intertextual Minuteness', examines the 'small-large dichotomy' as a structuring device for Atwood's poetics, being revealed in her poetry, prose, and visual materials such as her cartoons. Atwood's more recent 'hybrid genre' of short texts that are 'hard to categorize' and which have 'few real ancestors in Canadian literature' (p. 5) is discussed as 'a radical contribution to the development of genre hybridization' (p. 6), i.e. the introduction of the Baudelairean prose poem into Canadian literature. Nischik expands upon Atwood's critique and recoding of Baudelaire's patriarchal perspective through exceptionally close reading of her poetry. Atwood's prose poems are correctly treated as hybrid forms, called 'flash fiction' by Sharon R. Wilson in 'Fiction Flashes: Genre and Intertexts in *Good Bones*'. Wilson notes that others have called these 'fiction flashes' 'short short stories', 'sudden fiction', 'lyrical prose poems' and 'lyric paragraphs', but all of these names also recognize in one way or another the essential act in Atwood's work of the crossing of generic boundaries. Ending a related sequence of poetry volumes, *Interlunar* [1984] is regarded by Shannon Hengen, in 'Strange Visions: Atwood's *Interlunar* and Technopoetics', as having more significance than it has previously been accorded. Through examination of contrasting imagery, Hengen reveals that any dominant perspective on the natural world is perceived by Atwood to be destructive, and thus Atwood critiques technology and a static poetic, where, as Donna Harraway argues, the nature/culture opposition has 'broken down' (p. 52). A dynamic poetic can emerge from one in which the trickster figure plays a key role. Kathryn Van Spanckeren, 'Humanizing the Fox: Atwood's Poetic Tricksters and *Morning in the Burned House*', argues that the trickster is more dominant in Atwood's poems, especially revealed in Atwood's subversion of generic conventions. Atwood's poetry makes a brief appearance in Youngmin Kim, 'The Experimental Spirit in Canadian Poetry: Margaret Atwood, Eli Mandel, George Bowering, and the Experimental Poets Thereafter' (*JELL* 49:iii[2003] 755–79). Kim regards the 'fragmented' Canadian culture of the 1970s to be reflected in the shift to experimental poetic form, basing this argument on some solid theoretical analysis following Paul de Man's concept of 'duplication' as reworked by Linda Hutcheon. Kim examines the 'duplication of human existence and language' in the works of Atwood and Mandel and the 'internal multiplication of poetic forms and contents' in Bowering and Kroetsch, and concludes by exploring 'external multiplication' in a large number of other Canadian poets. A very different approach is taken with extended focus on one poem utilizing 'text world theory', in Ernestine Lahey, 'Seeing the Forest for the Trees in Al Purdy's "Trees at the Arctic Circle"' (*Bell* 1[2003] 73–83). Lahey's summary of 'text world theory' is excellent, and perfectly suited for teaching purposes, especially as it includes the modifications of Paul Werth's 'cognitive theory of discourse' as put forward by Joanna Gavins; the reading of Purdy's 'Arctic Circle' that follows examines landscape, the poetic persona's attitude, and an analysis of the advantages of using 'text world theory' within a Canadian context. To write of nature as grounded, or as transcended, characterizes the poetic struggle explored through highly detailed and imaginative close readings in Lance La Rocque, 'Breathing

Books, Deranged Bodies: Reading and Writing Landscapes in the Poetry of Harry Thurston' (*Isle* 10:i[2003] 115–35).

A special issue of *Canadian Literature* will delight readers of Anne Carson's poetry; in his editorial, 'Five Fairly Short Talks on Anne Carson' (*CanL* 176[2003] 6–10), Kevin McNeilly creatively explores some etymological clues to Carson's elusive and labyrinthine poetic; he follows this with an interview, 'Gifts and Questions: An Interview with Anne Carson' (*CanL* 176[2003] 12–27). Beginning with poetic alienation, and poetic impertinence, Robert Stanton, '"I am writing this to be as wrong as possible to you": Anne Carson's Errancy' (*CanL* 176[2003] 28–43), looks at the chiasmus of the critical and poetic in Carson's work. A hypercritical review by David Solway is deconstructed at length in Ian Rae, 'Anne Carson and the Solway Hoaxes' (*CanL* 176[2003] 45–65), while the elegiac mode is the subject of Tanis MacDonald, 'The Pilgrim and the Riddle: Father–Daughter Kinship in Anne Carson's "The Anthropology of Water"' (*CanL* 176[2003] 67–83). The intertextual complexities of Carson's self-confessed debt to Celan are explored in Andre Furlani, 'Reading Paul Celan with Anne Carson: "What kind of withness would that be?"' (*CanL* 176[2003] 84–104); through close reading of Carson's poetry, Furlani elucidates the subtleties of Carson's 'encounter' with Celan, where the term 'encounter' is perceived as a conceptual and creative tool.

A truly collaborative, internationally produced collection contributes significantly to drama research: Grace and Glaap, eds., *Performing National Identities: International Perspectives on Contemporary Canadian Theatre*. Eighteen essays and an introduction, as well as illustrations of theatrical performances, are organized in three parts: playwrights and their works; productions and reception; and movements and issues. As the editors note, the collection 'brings together scholars, theatre practitioners, translators, editors, and reviewers from Canada and many other countries in what we believe is a benchmark exploration and celebration of contemporary Canadian drama' (p. 13). Part 1 opens with Susan Bennett, 'Performing Lives: Linda Griffiths and Other Famous Women', a study of performative feminist life-writing via three female 'public personae' in Linda Griffith's work: Margaret Trudeau in *Maggie & Pierre* [1980], Wallis Simpson in *The Duchess* [1998] and Gwendolyn MacEwan in *Alien Creature* [1999]. Martin Bowman, 'Michel Tremblay in Scots: Celebration and Rehabilitation', narrates the fascinating story of the translation of Tremblay's plays, notably *Les Belles-Soeurs* into the Scots vernacular of *The Guid Sisters*, which then went on to gain considerable international acclaim. Sherrill Grace, 'Imagining Canada: Sharon Pollock's *Walsh* and *Fair Liberty's Call*', addresses the twin poles of history and theatre in Pollock's work, arguing that her staging of history is highly complex and leads to the possibility of political intervention. Marc Maufort, '"Some kind of transition place between Heaven and Hell": George Walker's Aesthetics of Hybridity in Heaven', utilizes the theories of Homi Bhabha to explore Walker's aesthetics of transgression. John Thieme, 'A Different "Othello Music": Djanet Sear's *Harlem Duet*', continues his project of exploring the relationships between canonical 'pre-texts' and post-colonial 'con-texts', the latter interrogating the former. The interweaving of monologic and dialogic performance creates a 'complex emotional geography' in Jerry

Wasserman, 'Joan MacLeod and the Geography of the Imagination'. Part 2 contains seven essays that explore in diverse ways the international reception of Canadian theatre: Albert-Reiner Glaap, 'Canadian Plays on a German Stage: A Production of Michel Marc Bouchard's *Le Chemin des passes-dangereuses*'; Jen Harvie, 'The Alarming/Boring Binary Logic of Reviewing English-Canadian Drama in Britain'; Colin Hicks, 'Imagination Import: Reception and Perception of the Theatre of Quebec in the United Kingdom'; Erin Hurley, 'Theatre as National Export: On Being and Passing in the United States'; Yoshinari Minami, 'Canadian Plays on the Japanese Stage'; Péter Szaffkó, 'The Story of Morris Panych's *7 Stories* in Hungary: A Documentary Production Analysis'; and Cynthia Zimmerman, 'Maintaining the Alternative: An Interview with Urjo Kareda'. The essays in part 2 form an archive of international production and reception issues and are a significant resource, especially given the extensive bibliographical materials, for the study of Canadian theatre outside of the country. Part 3 presents more critical perspectives, beginning with Alan Filewood, 'Naming the Movement: Recapitalizing Popular Theatre', an astute deconstructive approach to theatrical 'movements', revealing their discursive and ideological formations and deformations. The importance of First Nations cultural remembrance and healing, especially with the ongoing impact of the residential school system, is the subject of Ric Knowles, 'The Heart of its Women: Rape, Residential Schools, and Re-Membering'. First Nations ritual and performance form the crucial interpretative framework of Richard J. Lane, 'Performing History: The Reconstruction of Gender and Race in British Columbian Drama'; playwrights covered include George Ryga, Sharon Pollock, Margaret Hollingsworth, Marie Clements, and the practitioners who form Headlines Theatre. First Nations continue to be the focus with Mark Shackleton, 'Can Weesageechak Keep Dancing? The Importance of Trickster Figures in the Work of Native Earth Dramatists, 1986–2000', and the collection is completed with Joanne Tompkins, 'Yellow Fever, Yellow Claw, Yellow Peril: Performing the Fantasy of the "Asian-Canadian"'.

British Columbia theatre is well served by a special issue of *B.C. Studies*, guest-edited by Jerry Wasserman. Six articles are published, with their origins in the second BC theatre conference, 'Staging the Pacific Province', held at the University of British Columbia in 2001. James Hoffman, 'Shedding the Colonial Past: Rethinking British Columbia Theatre' (*BCS* 137[2003] 5–45), reviews the history of BC theatre and BC theatre criticism, suggesting that comprehensive theatre histories are themselves a rarity in Canada. Arguing that the structures and experiences of the dominant Eurocentric proscenium theatre are mimetic of 'the colonized/colonizer relationship' (p. 8), Hoffman goes on to suggest that more contemporary postcolonial perspectives and theatre practices in British Columbia embrace a more diverse and dynamic range of performance styles. Hoffman suggests that 'intercultural' performance activities need more study, and that a more theoretical discourse (especially postcolonial theory) needs to be adopted by the critics; true to his word, he performs a lengthy postcolonial analysis of BC theatre, ending with a summary of the work of specialist critics in the area, such as Malcolm Page, Jerry Wasserman, Celeste Derksen, Laurie Ricou and Richard J. Lane. The list of references is extensive and serves as a research bibliography.

Leading historian of British Columbia, Jean Barman, examines the first BC playwright to have been professionally staged, in '"Vancouver's First Playwright": Constance Lindsay Skinner and *The Birthright*' (*BCS* 137[2003] 47–62). Barman draws on the Constance Lindsay Skinner Papers in the Manuscript and Archives Division of the New York Public Library to develop a strong argument for backdating the emergence of a professional BC theatre, with a play that deals with issues of ethnicity and hybridity. The fascinating story of an innovative and influential home theatre in the British Columbia interior is told by Patrick O'Neill in 'Carroll Aikins's Experiments in Playwriting' (*BCS* 137[2003] 65–91), which also contains reproductions of detailed and useful performance photographs. Metadramatic forms offer another way of exploring BC's theatre history, utilized by George Belliveau in 'Investigating British Columbia's Past: *The Komagata Maru Incident* and *The Hope Slide* as Historiographic Metadrama' (*BCS* 137[2003] 93–106). A critically significant essay completes the special issue, Sherrill Grace, 'From Emily Carr to Joy Coghill … and Back: Writing the Self in *Song of This Place*' (*BCS* 137[2003] 109–30). Beginning with Carr's resistance to biography, Grace argues that only one outstanding play version of Carr's life, Joy Coghill's *Song of This Place* [1987], merits close analysis; using theories of auto/biography, Grace suggests that only theatre gets beyond being 'about' Carr to actually performing Carr's subjectivity through an act of auto/biographical identification.

Marc Maufort's comparative book-length study of Australasian and Canadian postcolonial theatre, *Transgressive Itineraries* (also discussed above) contains substantial critical material on Canadian drama. After an introductory critical overview, Maufort's first chapter on staging the Other in mainstream dramaturgies opens with Judith Thompson, explored as a magic realist. Plays are analysed with insight and attention to detail, and this is the case throughout the book. Thompson is followed by George Walker and his 'aesthetic of hybridity'. Societal transformation, driven by multiculturalism, is the subject of Maufort's second chapter, where he explores performative representations of ethnic minorities, beginning with Argentinian Canadian playwright Guillermo Verdecchia, and following with sections on African Canadian and Asian Canadian playwrights, with emphasis on Djanet Sears, Betty Quan and Marty Chan. The third and final chapter of the book covers leading First Nations and Aboriginal dramatists, beginning with a section on 'trickster transgressions'. First Nations playwrights covered are Tomson Highway, Daniel David Moses, and Drew Hayden Taylor. Maufort's accessible close readings of the plays, and his adoption of a clearly articulated postcolonial discourse, make this book suitable for undergraduate teaching, and for researchers in need of an introductory text.

Canadian Theatre Review 113 is devoted to Urjo Kareda (1944–2001), the artistic director of Tarragon Theatre and theatre critic for the *Toronto Star*. The essays offer critical assessment and personal reflection. Essays on Tarragon are Robin Breon's 'Tarragon Flavoured Memories' (*CTR* 113[2003] 5–7), and Michael McKinnie's interview with Kareda's successor Richard Rose, 'Legacies: Richard Rose's Vision of Tarragon Theatre' (*CTR* 113[2003] 29–33). Journalist Martin Knelman shares his 'Messages from Urjo' (*CTR* 113[2003] 8–10), while Denis Johnston discusses the historical impact of 'Our Man at the *Star*' (*CTR*

113[2003] 19–22). Kareda's impact upon a wide range of theatrical forms and key playwrights is explored in three essays: Judith Thompson, '"It's my birthday forever now": Urjo Kareda and Me' (*CTR* 113[2003] 11–14); Judith Rudakoff, 'Urjo Kareda and Emerging Playwrights: Seeding the Field, Cultivating the Roots' (*CTR* 113[2003] 15–18); and Grace Kehler, 'The Language of Emotion: Urjo Kareda's Opera Criticism' (*CTR* 113[2003] 23–8). The script is 'The Good Life' by Daniel Brooks (*CTR* 113[2003] 34–68).

A two-part issue of *CTR*, originating in a Stratford, Ontario, festival and conference in 2002, celebrates Canadian plays and playwrights. In his editorial (*CTR* 114[2003] 3–5), Ric Knowles writes about the irony of holding the festival/ conference at Stratford, Ontario, when so little support for Canadian plays or playwrights has been forthcoming from the Stratford stage. In his second editorial (*CTR* 115[2003] 3–4), Knowles explains how the two-part special issue is divided between historical, literary and canonical plays and issues (*CTR* 114), and developmental, experimental, political and 'the new' in Canadian plays (*CTR* 115).

CTR 114 opens with a celebration of the fiftieth anniversary of both the Frederic Wood theatre in Vancouver, and the Stratford Festival, in Jerry Wasserman, 'Where Were You in '52? Canadian Theatre on the Eve of Stratford' (*CTR* 114[2003] 6–10). The tensions between colonial culture and indigenous cultures as expressed theatrically are the subject of Ellen Mackay, 'Fantasies of Origin: Staging the Birth of the Canadian Stage' (*CTR* 114[2003] 11–15), while Michael McKinnie utilizes an economic model to discuss the origins of the Canadian stage in his 'Canadian Theatre, the State, and Industrial Development' (*CTR* 114[2003] 16–20). Anne Nothof describes three productions in a useful piece of historical research, 'Ironic Images: Sharon Pollock's Stratford Productions' (*CTR* 114[2003] 21–5), followed by an interview between Sherrill Grace and Sharon Pollock, 'How Passionate Are You? An Interview with Sharon Pollock' (*CTR* 114[2003] 26–32). Close analyses of plays by Judith Thompson and Wendy Lill are offered in Claudia Barnett, 'Judith Thompson's Ghosts' (*CTR* 114[2003] 33–7) and in Jacqueline Petropoulos, 'Language and Racism: Wendy Lill's *The Occupation of Heather Rose*' (*CTR* 114[2003] 38–41). East coast theatre and economics are the subjects of Bruce Barton's essay 'Wrestling with Regionalism in Atlantic Canada: The Playwrights Atlantic Resource Centre' (*CTR* 114[2003] 42–6). A panel transcript completes the critical material, George Elliot Clarke (chair), Bill Glassco, Conni Massing, Jason Sherman and Judith Thompson, 'Turning an Elephant into a Microphone: A Conversation on Translation and Adaptation' (*CTR* 114[2003] 47–53). The script is by Timothy Findley, 'Shadows: A One-Act Play' (*CTR* 114[2003] 54–71).

The second part of the special issue opens with Joanne Tompkins, 'Canadian Theatre and Monuments' (*CTR* 115[2003] 5–11), where she discusses counter-monuments and performance, focusing on three plays 'that open dialogues with monumental images of the nation' (p. 5). Innovative Newfoundland theatre is the subject of Denyse Lynde, '*Icycle*: New Languages' (*CTR* 115[2003] 12–16); Deborah Porter explores innovations in textual form in her 'Adapting Fiction for the Stage: Necessary Angel's *Coming Through Slaughter*' (*CTR* 115[2003] 17–20). The transcript of a panel made up of Alisa Palmer (chair), Sally Han, Lise

Ann Johnson, D.D. Kugler, and Paul Thompson on 'New Play Development' follows (*CTR* 115[2003] 21–5). Turning once more to a historical survey, Kevin Longfield describes the late flowering of Canadian playwrights in Manitoba, 'MAPping New Play Development in Manitoba' (*CTR* 115[2003] 29–34). Juxtaposed with Thompson's account of theatre project development is an account of an alternative, indigenous creative process called the 'Four Directions', which is explained by Shannon Hengen in 'The De-Ba-Jeh-Mu-Jig Method: Making Stories' (*CTR* 115[2003] 35–8); Hengen's article is an important one for critics exploring the production of indigenous art-forms and concepts within Canada. Alternative methods of performing social and political differences are explored by Kirsty Johnson in 'Playwriting Madness: New Play and Playwright Development at Toronto's Workman Theatre Project' (*CTR* 115[2003] 39–42), as also by the panel transcript on 'The Politics and Business of Playwriting', with Angela Rebeiro (chair), Wendy Lill, Yvette Nolan, Jason Sherman and Guillermo Verdecchia (*CTR* 115[2003] 43–6), and by the panel transcript on 'Politics and Plays', with Ric Knowles (chair), Sky Gilbert, Joan MacLeod, Rahul Varma and Jean Yoon (*CTR* 115[2003] 52–6). An essay that will intrigue scholars and fans of Tomson Highway's work is Gerhard Hauck, 'Roses on the Rez: Chronicle of a Failure?' (*CTR* 115[2003] 47–51). Hauck follows the long period of the play's development (the third in Highway's projected seven-play 'Rez' cycle), up to, and following, the amateur student production in 2000 at the University of Toronto; Highway's comments are interwoven with critical reviews and analyses concerning the project, as well as a thoughtful list of points for discussion concerning the obstacles to a full-scale professional performance of the play. Another intriguing and well-argued essay is Catherine Graham, 'The Audience-Driven Aesthetic of Recent Canadian Political Plays' (*CTR* 115[2003] 57–61); Graham's observations concerning performance–audience relationships have wide historical scope and are critically insightful. The final critical essay is Aida Jordão, 'Playwriting in Canadian Popular Theatre: Developing Plays with Actors and Non-Actors' (*CTR* 115[2003] 62–5). The scripts are 'Eternal Hydra' by Anton Piatigorsky (*CTR* 115[2003] 66–87) and 'High-Gravel-Blind' by Paul Dunn (*CTR* 115[2003] 88–110). In summary, this two-part special issue of *CTR* provides a diverse series of essays that explore the myths of Canada's theatrical origins, and contemporary realities and practices. Critics often bemoan the lack of critical texts covering Canadian theatre, yet *CTR* continues to produce outstandingly high-quality critical materials; this two-part special issue contributes significantly to this output.

A highly innovative image-based volume of *CTR* examines 'Recent Portfolios: Six Photographers and the Performing Arts', edited by Michael Cooper and Harry Lane. Each portfolio has a brief introductory biography, followed by images: David Cooper (*CTR* 116[2003] 4–11), Michael Cooper (*CTR* 116[2003] 12–19), Ken Kam (*CTR* 116[2003] 20–7), Trudie Lee (*CTR* 116[2003] 28–35), Yves Renaud (*CTR* 116[2003] 36–43), and Cyyla Von Tiedemann (*CTR* 116[2003] 44–51). Harry Lane follows the portfolios with his 'Afterword: The Uses of Theatrical Photographs' (*CTR* 116[2003] 54–6), which provides a condensed survey of photographic theory and discussion of the use of photographic theatre images. Daniel David Moses completes this innovative issue with 'A Small Essay on the Largeness of Light' (*CTR* 116[2003] 57). The script is by Camyar Chai, 'The Asylum of the Universe (A Fool's Ode to History)' (*CTR* 116[2003] 58–88).

3. The Caribbean

(a) General

For the past fifty years, the literary theme of Caribbean writers has been one of innocence, exile, resistance, and a struggle for identity. All of these ideas, about which these authors write, are also centred on race, class, gender, and language. It is clear from the works reviewed that these issues and ideas remain constant and troubling to the people of the Caribbean. Whether these people are Dutch-, English-, French-, or Spanish-speaking, the imperial paradigm imposed by the colonizer on the displaced or on the enslaved naturally results in trauma that continues for generations. The oppression will never be forgotten! Thus, writing about our past and our present is a way to vitiate or expel the pre-colonial demons of exile, slavery, and resistance so that a catharsis can take place, and the healing can begin. The writers discussed in the following pages discuss this trauma of oppression, exile, language, and resistance, and they use the works of well-known Caribbean poets, novelists, and authors to tell their stories.

(b) Dissertations

Georgene Bess Montgomery's dissertation, 'Ifa as a Paradigm for the Interpretation of Caribbean and African-American Literature', tries to find some commonality between the African American experience and the Caribbean literary experience. She thus uses Ifa—'an ancient African spiritual system'—to establish the link and shape her work. Of the four works Bess Montgomery considers, those of Edouard Glissant (Martinique), *The Ripening*, and Merle Collins (Grenada), *Angel,* are the Caribbean examples she examines. The ideas she posits may be laudable, but one wonders if two Caribbean sources are sufficient to revisit a theme that has been overworked.

The dissertation '"Kingston 21": Diaspora, Migrancy and Caribbean Literature', by Kezia Page, might suggest to Bess Montgomery that the Caribbean can no longer be described as a postmodern rootless space without a centre where its peoples look to Africa as 'home'. Few have gone back to stay. That's why 'Kingston 21' becomes relevant to the ideology of today. Page's dissertation dispels the Ifa paradigm and asks us to consider 'the material constraints on movement to the Caribbean experience at home and in Diaspora'. 'Indeed', argues Page, 'the Caribbean region because of its history of colonialism and imperialism presents interesting models of creolization. The region boasts four major language groups as well as an array of Creoles and dialects. The immigration of East Indian and Chinese laborers, merchants and trades people further diversified the African, European and what little aboriginal presence remained in the region. In this sense our Caribbean seas have touched and are touched by the shores of the world' (p. 5).

Paula Catherine Makris, in her dissertation *Colonial Education and Cultural Inheritance: Caribbean Literature and the Classes*, posits what everybody knows as a given: that 'Caribbean writers have no long-standing literary or cultural background, aside from the English model provided by their colonial education'. Makris does support the thematic ideas of Caribbean writers espoused by Cynthia James, 'innocence, exile, and a history of hurt, all revolving around a quest for identity', when she writes that 'colonial education has often produced a sense of alienation in its students, who become increasingly aware of the fracture in their cultural and linguistic identity'. Much Caribbean literature, continues Makris, 'reflects this struggle, as its writers self-consciously come to terms with the educational forces that helped to shape them both culturally and linguistically' (p. 1).

Roberto Strongman's 'Allegorical I/Lands: Personal and National Development in Caribbean Autobiographical Writing', also makes a strong case for what is already well known: that 'despite the existence of … works prior to the 1950s, the absence of a large literary corpus and established literary traditions does not allow the formation of any real Caribbean canons before that date' (p. 5).

(c) Edited Collections

Christian Mair has a section in the work he has edited, *The Politics of English as a World Language: New Horizons in Postcolonial Cultural Studies*, called 'The Caribbean Diaspora and the African Diaspora in North America and Britain'. Three of the five essays here discuss the postcolonial literature of the Caribbean. Hubert Devonish writes on 'Language Advocacy and "Conquest": Diglossia in the "Anglophone" Caribbean', where he makes a case for the varieties of (English) language and their use. He uses Ferguson's work as his reference, and German-speaking Switzerland and Haiti as his examples. Devonish maintains that the Swiss Germans accepted 'an external norm—German—as the language of writing and formal interaction, while French in Haiti 'owes its status and function to colonial imposition', which Devonish now calls 'conquest diglossia' (p. 158). Other parts of his article discuss the Caribbean Lexicography Project and about the Creole language becoming invisible, besides making a few references to himself.

The second essay, by Hazel Simmons-McDonald, 'Decolonizing English: The Caribbean Counter-Thrust', argues that indeed several varieties of English coexist in the Caribbean, and that the debate about their place and function in the development of Caribbean peoples is manifold. Simmons-McDonald discusses and explores the 'changing attitudes to [the] varieties of English and tries to develop a 'critical language pedagogy for the region'.

In one of the two footnotes of the very carefully framed third essay by Fiona Darroch, 'Re-Reading the Religious Bodies of Postcolonial Literature', she argues that her essay refers to 'the English translation of the Bible which has often been used to perpetuate colonial violence'. The common misconception, argues Darroch, is that religion or, more specifically, 'religious bodies', are 'devoid of power'. 'If this be the case', she maintains, 'how can Ella in Erna Brodber's *Myal* or Beloved in Toni Morrison's *Beloved* be understood … ?' (p. 204). Darroch proposes a new postcolonial agenda where she demonstrates that religious bodies are powerful and appeal to Western imperialism.

Huk, ed., *Assembling Alternatives: Reading Postmodern Poetries Transnationally*, is separated into three parts: 'International Inflections/Histories/Comparisons', 'Intranational Divides and Intracultural Differences', and 'In Practice/Polemics'. One essay in part 2 has something to do with the Caribbean: M. NourbeSe Philip's 'Interview with an Empire' is a mock-interview that discusses her Tobagonian origins, her removal to Canada, her writings as a Caribbean artist, and her view of the world.

(d) Literary Criticism

Tobias Döring's *Caribbean–English Passages: Intertextuality in a Postcolonial Tradition,* uses Walcott's Nobel Prize acceptance speech in 1993 as a pivot to suggest that linguistic shifts and cultural mysteries have shaped the culture and history of the peoples in the Caribbean. He maintains that *Caribbean–English Passages* should be read with the idea of 'intertextuality' in mind. Döring retells Walcott's story of a visit to a Hindu ceremony in Trinidad. At the end of the ceremony, parts of the body of a gigantic Hindu god are burnt in effigy. What comes to mind at that time to Walcott is 'Shelley's sonnet on the fallen statue of Ozymandias and his empire, that "colossal wreck" in its empty desert' (p. 1). Döring goes on to suggest that the admixture of British literature and the cultural heritage of the English-speaking Caribbean peoples can be both 'enabling and restrictive', and 'reflect transatlantic alliances' instead of a cultural identity. His work is a prolix discussion replete with first-person pronouns and possessive adjectives, with lengthy notes and an extensive bibliography. His research extends from 1976 to 2000 with sprinklings of references from Conrad's *Heart of Darkness*, Doyle's *The Lost World*, and Forster's *A Passage to India*, to demonstrate how 'twentieth-century passages' function as catalysts for maintaining power. In his second chapter Döring then launches into an analysis of Grainger's 1764 poem 'West Indian Georgic' and suggests that it 'merits close attention and more careful reading, because it gives a highly interesting example of the effects of cultural contact zones and provides a challenge to rethink the historical narrative of identity under colonialism' (p. 54). Perhaps by now Döring has read Gregory Alles's essay 'The Greeks in the Caribbean: Reflections on Derek Walcott, Homer, and Syncretism' (*Reflections/Reflexions Historiques* 27:iii[2001] 425–52], or Marian Aquilar's 'Decolonizing the Tongue: Reading Speech and Aphasia in the Work of Michelle Cliff' (*L&P* 47:i–ii[2001] 94–108), or 'Decolonizing the Mind: The Politics of Language in African Literature' (Portsmouth: Heinemann [1994]) by Ngugi wa Thiong'o, and will see his work in a different light.

While Döring considers linguistic shifts and cultural migrations from a deconstructive point of view, Joy Mahabir, in her *Miraculous Weapons: Revolutionary Ideology in Caribbean Culture,* argues that the constant and incessant struggle for freedom is contained in the 'work of progressive Caribbean novelists, poets, visual artists, musicians, and Carnivalists who have shaped a field of anti-colonial and anti-capitalist cultural resistance' (p. 1). Mahabir further maintains that slave revolts, rebellions against indentureship, revolutions, and the struggles for independence are the dynamics intrinsic to Caribbean culture that developed after the Haitian Revolution. She thus attempts to examine Caribbean culture by creating a new body out of the writings, paintings, music, and visual arts of Caribbean artists. 'Even more compelling reasons to examine these forms together are their historical coeval emergence, and their ideological cohesiveness' (p. 2). Mahabir uses the argument of Amilcar Cabral that 'the affirmation of repressed cultural forms by the colonized becomes a form of resistance against colonialism on the level of culture'. She would argue that such modes of resistance are more likely in India and Africa, where there is a written and spoken body of native languages, but 'this is not exactly the case in the Caribbean … since the original languages of the enslaved and indentured have been creolized as part of a complex process … to ensure the retention of these languages' (p. 6). She then explores the various areas of literature, music and art in her work to show their intertextuality for protest and revolution.

Cynthia James approaches Caribbean literature from a different direction. She argues, in *The Maroon Narrative: Caribbean Literature in English across Boundaries, Ethnicities, and Centuries*, that the novel is 'the main Caribbean narrative genre', and that she will chart 'a continuum of narratives and a dialogue among narratives from the beginning of fictional writing about the Caribbean in the eighteenth century through the twentieth century'. James laboriously gives the reader a potpourri of information on Caribbean literature before delivering the meat in her book. It is on page 11 that she makes the point that the word 'maroon' represents a member of a group of people of African descent, as well as a group of people marooned on an island. Here she traces the origin of the word and establishes her argument. 'As the [*OED*] citations show', she states, '"*maroon*" in both senses of African runaway and white flotsam economic adventurer bears persistent and intertwined associations with the Caribbean. The non-European maroon is most commonly the resistant maroon, while the European is the shipwrecked-adventurer-turned-imperial-master' (p. 11). It is at this juncture that *The Maroon Narrative* begins to take shape.

William T. Gifford's *Narrative and the Nature of Worldview in the Clare Savage Novels of Michelle Cliff* expands on what he purports to be the *Weltanschauung* of Michelle Cliff and the characters in her Clare Savage novels: *Abeng* and *No Telephone to Heaven.* It is an *explication de texte* of the two works and suitable for high-school students.

In *Clear Word and Third Sight: Folk Groundings and Diasporic Consciousness in African Caribbean Writing,* Catherine John revives the perennial issues of negritude in African diaspora discourse. She sets out her premise in a lengthy introduction invoking the 'negritude legacy of Aimé Césaire and Léopold Senghor' that was explored in 1956 at the First International Conference of Negro Artists and Writers, in Paris. John focuses on the diaspora. She considers black females writing in the diaspora (after asking 'who are Black women?'), and discusses the critical reactions to 'Afro-Caribbean women's writing'. Finally, John discusses writers of the French Caribbean—French Guyana, Martinique, and Guadeloupe—all with a focus on negritude or 'postnegritude theory of creolization' in mind.

The theme that seems to be evolving this year is manifested in Branche, ed., *Lo que teníamos que tener: raza y revolución en Nicolás Guillén* ('What We Had To Have: Race and Revolution in [the Works of] Nicolás Guillén), which celebrates the centenary of Nicolás Guillén, the Cuban poet. Jerome Branche, who wrote the introduction, captures the ideas central to Joy Mahabir's work previously discussed. He states that 'the two threads central to Guillén's extensive theme seem to be brilliantly wrapped up in one of his celebrated works, i.e., the racial question with all its complexities and social ramifications, and the question of revolution: profound, provocative as it was then, and continues to be now' (p. 7; my translation). Although many of the contributors are from the English-speaking Caribbean countries, they have written this homage to Guillén in Spanish.

The second edition of Bruce King's *V.S. Naipaul* is an updated rendition following Naipaul's winning the Nobel Prize. King's text includes discussion of his recent novels and his two books on Islam, along with other 'interpretative' material. The work is biographical and objective. King does not attempt to praise or vilify Naipaul: he sets out his life, his arrogance, his works, and his world-view in a readable manner without dispelling any ideas one may have about the Nobel laureate.

Ula Taylor, in *The Veiled Garvey: The Life and Times of Amy Jacques Garvey*, writes an impressive biography of Garvey from her birth, her schooling in Jamaica, and her marriage to Marcus Garvey to her total involvement in the Universal Negro Improvement Association (UNIA) in New York City, and her uncanny ability to destabilize 'masculinist discourse, offering a glimpse into the range and scope of feminism possible during the 1920s and a model of women as political beings who could change the world'. Taylor's book is almost complete. It includes the relationship of Amy and Marcus, the birth of their children, estrangement, the dissolution of the Black Star Line, his arrest in the United States for fraud, and his expulsion from the US. But it does not include Amy's relationship with her sister Ethlin Jacques, who was the psychological outlet for Amy's angst, and who played an important role in her adult life with Marcus Garvey. Perhaps that account will wait for another day.

Amy Jacques Garvey's fifty-four years of political activism and her call for the empowerment of Caribbean woman do not go unheeded in Denise de Caires Narain's *Contemporary Caribbean Women's Poetry: Making Style*. Narain suggests that the Caribbean literary landscape has been dominated by men who have been recognized as the 'founding fathers of West Indian literary tradition'. But women have entered this literary landscape, have altered this tradition, and have made 'a much bigger impact in establishing Caribbean women's writing as a recognizable category of literature'. Narain's book focuses on Caribbean women's poetry. She explores the impact of gender on this genre in an attempt to create a critical discourse on what she calls the 'exclusive focus on women's fiction'. Narain begins with the poetry of Una Marson and Phyllis Shand Allfrey, who should be given the title of 'founding mothers'. Solid biographies of the poets follow. The book also includes a detailed discussion of the poetry of Louise Bennett, Valerie Bloom, Jean 'Binta' Breeze, Merle Collins, Amryl Johnson, and many other female poets.

Jean Goulbourne's *Woman Song* is a poetic compilation that is somewhat reminiscent of a New Orleans jazz funeral in its tone and linguistic style. There is a dirge-like quality to the work as it celebrates women as mothers. The work suggests a movement from traditional English to Jamaican patois. Its pieces are quiet and demure, yet commanding.

4. India

(a) General

This year is marked by a reinvestigation and expansion of the canon of Indian literature in English through the publication of several new literary-historical surveys, some of which readdress important areas of critical consideration, in particular the early phases of Indian writing in English in the nineteenth century. The most accessible of these new works is Mehrotra, ed., *A History of Indian Literature in English*. In his introduction Arvind Krishna Mehrotra is careful to locate his project in a tradition of literary-historical surveys stretching back through William Walsh's *Indian Literature in English* [1990] and M.K. Naik's *A History of Indian Literature in English* [1982] to K.R. Srinivasa Iyengar's pioneering *Indian Writing in English* [1972]. Unlike those of his predecessors, though, Mehrotra's history comprises specially commissioned essays on single authors, literary movements, and political contexts, a feature that gives the text an admirable sense of both focus and range. Edited with the non-specialist reader in mind and illustrated throughout, *A History of Indian Literature in English* includes sections on key authors (R.K. Narayan, V.S. Naipaul, Salman Rushdie) but also incorporates 'omnibus' chapters covering significant periods in the development of fiction such as the 1930s and 1980s, and the evolution in drama and poetry since independence.

The edition's real strength, however, is the way in which it recuperates Indian English poetry and prose traditions of the nineteenth century, in chapter sections on Henry Derozio and Michael Madhusudhan Dutt, the Dutt family, and the early novel, as well as hosting some good author studies such as Pankaj Mishra's piece on R.K. Narayan. It also gives considerable emphasis to traditions of reformist and political prose, and in Sunil Khilnani's probing section on Gandhi and Nehru the relevance of political prose styles in the development of the nationalist novel is revealed. As always, there will be readers who find omissions and inconsistencies in a work of this type, and the fact that none of the single-author sections features women writers (Anita Desai and Attia Hosain spring to mind) is a significant oversight. Mehrotra also hints in his preface that other chapters were commissioned—on the art-historian Ananda Coomaraswamy, small-press publications and the historian as author—but failed to make it into the first edition. Nevertheless, this is a collection that manages to be both imaginative in its mapping of Indian English literary history and authoritative in its excellent, informed sense of the field. It will be particularly appreciated by undergraduate students of Indian literature and does a great deal to correct assumptions that Indian writing in English is a largely contemporary, postcolonial genre.

A new anthology of Indian English poetry and prose, *Away: The Indian Writer as Expatriate*, Amitava Kumar's collection of 'expatriate' Indian writing, is similarly expansive in its formal and historical selection, and incorporates journalistic, autobiographical accounts of Britain in the late nineteenth century by Dean Mahomed, Sunity Devee, and Tagore, as well as the metropolitan experiences of nationalists such as Gandhi, Nehru, and Sarojini Naidu. Attentive to the creative paradoxes faced by diasporic Indian writers, Kumar claims that his anthology pays homage to 'the enormous richness, and pain, of displacement and loss' entailed in 'the ordinary experience of migration'. While he notes the expectations of representation (or representativeness) that often burden the Indian writer abroad, Kumar also argues that 'often, more than their writing about India, it is the portraits of the lands in which they now live, portraits drawn by discerning outsiders, which [are] … the greatest achievements of the desi writer' (p. xvii). As well as selections from Mulk Raj Anand's *Conversations in Bloomsbury* and an account by R.K. Narayan of his American experience, *Away* includes A.K. Ramanujan's wonderful poem 'Some Indian Uses of History on a Rainy Day', lively essays by Bharati Mukherjee, Hanif Kureishi and Pankaj Mishra, and excerpts from the fictions of Amit Chaudhuri, Anita Desai and Meera Syal.

Compared with the texts reviewed above, B.R. Agrawal and M.P. Sinha's *Major Trends in Post-Independence Indian Fiction* is less willing to question the boundaries of the Indian English literary canon, or stray into new areas of critical enquiry. Thematically structured around issues such as 'Social Conditions, Economic Problems, Political Trends', *Major Trends* addresses all the significant Indian authors of the postcolonial era, but tends to be under-theorized and, for all its contextual mooring, strangely unwilling to discuss how Indian literature in English reflects the material and political circumstances of its production. The scope of the project is ambitious, and Agrawal and Sinha provide a lively review of their subject, but readers in search of a sophisticated critical assessment of literary 'trends' should look elsewhere. Another overview of contemporary Indian writing is Khatri, ed., *Indian Literature in English: Critical Discourses*, which includes essays on Shoba Dé's fiction and Nissim Ezekiel's *Latter Day Psalms*, the nationalist fictions of K.S. Venkataramani and the drama of Girish Karnad. For an academic critical collection, many of the essays lack sufficient critical depth, although some, such as Jaya Prasad's 'Arundhati Roy and her Concern for the Environment in her Novel and in her Essays', take an original perspective on their subject matter.

The most ambitious literary-historical survey published this year is Pollock, ed., *Literary Cultures in History: Reconstructions from South Asia*, which goes far beyond the monolingual focus of the texts already mentioned in an overview of the major literary cultures of the subcontinent, and includes sections from key translators and critics such as Frances Pritchett on 'History, Performances, and Masters' in Urdu writing, Sudipta Kaviraj on 'The Two Histories of Bengali Literary Culture' and Harish Trivedi on 'Hindi and the Nation'. *Literary Cultures in History* also includes sections on Sanskrit and Persian, and an essay by Vinay Dharwadker on 'The Historical Formation of Indian-English Literature'. In some ways, Dharwadker's schematic essay is as much a careful mapping of the historical 'contact zones' (after Mary Louise Pratt's use of the term), through which English was disseminated in the subcontinent, as it is a literary-historical survey. The emergence of Indian English culture is plotted across the zones of 'employment', 'marriage and the family', 'religious conversion' and 'friendship', and, like some of the sections in Mehrotra's texts, Dharwadker's perspective gives an admirable sense of the long history of Indian English, and includes commentaries on Dean Mahomed's *Travels* as well as the poetry of Henry Derozio and Michael Madhusudan Dutt. Dharwadker's critical methodology is less instructive as his subject material widens and becomes more complex in the postcolonial period, but in other ways it reveals interesting aspects of cross-cultural relationships largely ignored in critical work, a history of collaboration that, as Dharwadker points out, in 'its actuality appears to contradict the bleak perspectives on East–West friendship that have been thematised in British as well as Indian writing about India in the twentieth century' (p. 216).

The complexities of English as a postcolonial lingua franca are also addressed in Mair, ed., *The Politics of English as a World Language*, published as part of the Rodopi Cross/Cultures series. This text includes a section on the politics of English in the Indian subcontinent, although two of the main discussions of literary/linguistic politics, by D.C.R.A. Goonetilleke and Rajiva Wijesinha, concentrate on Sri Lanka. (Goonetilleke also reviews J.G. Farrell's fiction in 'J.G. Farrell's Indian Works: His Majesty's Subjects?', *MAS* 37:ii[2003] 407–27, in which he engages with Farrell's 'crypto-racism'.) The mapping of colonial and postcolonial linguistic contact zones by Dharwadker and the critics in Mair's collection takes a more local form in a compelling literary-historical essay, Sisir Kumar Das's 'Sahibs and Memsahibs' (*NLitsR* 39[2003] 5–25), which reverses the traditional direction of the Orientalist gaze by looking at the representation of Europeans in a range of Indian prose and poetry from the eighteenth and nineteenth centuries. Covering narratives in a number of India's state languages, and recalling some of A.K. Ramanujan's discussions of translation, Das's essay is as much about linguistic trans-creation as it is about forms of literary critique and collaboration.

In June this year Susan Sontag's essay 'The World as India—Translation as a Passport within the Community of Literature' (*TLS* 5228[13 June 2003] 13–15) sparked off an impassioned response from Harish Trivedi on the letters pages of the *TLS.* In her essay Sontag claims that the main opposition to Hindi as a national language came from India's Muslim community, and goes on to illustrate her reading of Friedrich Schleiermacher's concept of 'inauthentic' market-driven translation (from his 1812 essay 'On Different Methods of Translation') by making reference to India's burgeoning call-centre industry, in which Indian graduates work night shifts and adopt American English names and accents for their Western clients. Trivedi, in his reply (*TLS* 5230[27 June 2003] 17), takes issue with Sontag's political description of Hindi, pointing out that the main linguistic opposition has come from Tamil groups. He also criticizes Sontag's characterization of a happy generation of 'cyber-coolies', pointing out that the rates of pay in Indian call-centres are exploitative and conditions stressful. Trivedi's letter elicited further varied responses about 'cyber-coolies' from Indian correspondents in subsequent editions of the *TLS.*

The importance of translation as creative precursor of Indian English fiction, and as a metaphor for wider processes of cultural negotiation, is emphasized in several critical essays this year. One of the most interesting is Anjali Nerlekar's discussion of the linguistic conflict apparent in A.K. Ramanujan's translation of his maternal linguistic inheritance of Tamil and Kannada, and the Anglophone linguistic culture that he associated with his father. As Nerlekar argues, in 'Of Mothers and Other Things: The Sources of A.K. Ramanujan's Poetry' (*Wasafiri* 38[2003] 49–54), English, for Ramanujan, seemed to fit the hegemonic linguistic slot of a 'great tradition' vacated by Sanskrit. Indian writing in translation—this time the work of the prolific Oriya writer Gopinath Mohanty—is also analysed in Kirstin W. Shand and Himansu Mohapatra's 'Reading the Figure of the Body in Gopinath Mohanty's *High Tide Ebb Tide*' (*Wasafiri* 39[2003] 35–8). Other critical discussions of translation as a metaphor for colonial cultural negotiation are summarized in the 'fiction' section of this review.

Postmodern Indian English Literature, by Bijay Kumar Das, includes sections on 'postmodern' Indian poetry, fiction, short stories, drama and autobiography, although there is only a limited discussion of the critical choice of the term 'postmodern'. In general, Das uses the category as a temporal (rather than philosophical or aesthetic) one, and states that we can 'divide Indian English Literature from 1930s to the end of the 20th century into two phases: modernist and postmodernist, the former beginning with Raja Rao's *Kanthapura* (1938), the latter beginning with Salman Rushdie's *Midnight's Children* (1981)' (p. 2). Questions about texts that might complicate this bold literary-historical division or about the cultural politics of Indian modernism/postmodernism are left unanswered, and debates about the efficacy of terms such as the postmodern and the postcolonial by other Indian critics such as Aijaz Ahmad and Meenakshi Mukherjee are largely ignored.

Das does expand the conventional purview of Indian English literature by including a section on autobiography, however, and an interesting development this year has been a greater openness to political prose and life-writing as a literary genre worthy of study. Alongside Sunil Khilnani's analysis of the literary influence of Gandhi's and Nehru's prose on Indian English fiction (in Mehrotra, ed., mentioned above), one of the best examples of this new critical attention to Indian nationalist prose is Anna Guttman's essay, 'Compromise and Contradiction in Jawaharlal Nehru's Multicultural Nation-State: Constructing National History in *The Discovery of India*' (*Clio* 32:iii[2003] 263–84). Attentive to the selective historical archaeologies of Nehru's famous vision of Indian identity, Guttman examines Nehru's strategic use of ancient sites of the Indus valley civilizations at Mohenjodaro and Harappa as precursors of his (secular, socialist) vision of India's postcolonial future. These myths of national belonging are contrasted with other events such as the 1857 Mutiny, represented in Nehru's historical narrative as a lesson on the perils of communal conflict. In contrast, Ian Christian Fletcher's paper, 'Double Meanings: Nation and Empire in the Edwardian Era' (in Burton, ed., *After the Imperial Turn: Thinking With and Through the Nation*), looks at Gandhi's *Hind Swaraj* as a text that appropriates the 'floating signifiers' of nation and empire in new and complex ways.

Intersections between literature and an emergent Indian nationalist politics are also investigated in '"The Best of Brahmans": India Reading Emerson Reading India' (*NCP* 30[2003] 337–68), in which Alan Hodder discusses both the Orientalist influences in Ralph Waldo Emerson's work and the complex political reappropriation of Emerson by nationalist activists in the late nineteenth century.

The connection between American Transcendentalism and Indian political thought is more often noted in Mohandas Gandhi's reading of Thoreau (especially the latter's writing on civil disobedience), but in his essay Hodder traces a more involved network of two-way influence and intercommunication between Emerson and figures such as P.C. Majumdar and Swami Vivekenanda, both of whom lectured in the United States. Emerson's 'perennialist' (p. 364) readings of India, and 'certain forms of orientalist logic' were effectively appropriated 'by Asian peoples themselves as a mode of resistance to colonial domination' (p. 340).

More contemporary political developments were discussed this year by the venerable writer and journalist Khushwant Singh in his collection of essays *The End of India*, a title that signals Singh's sense of outrage at the political objectives of the Hindu right and the communal massacres in Gujarat in 2002. Some of the essays incorporate journalistic material gathered in the 1970s, but this does not diminish Singh's forceful denunciation of the 'enduring and damaging' evils of communal hatred. As well as providing a historical review of communal politics, and personal reflections on events such as the Babri Masjid/Ramjanmabhumi incident, Singh also prescribes a return to a solidly Nehruvian secular politics. The rise of communal politics in India and the personal impact of civil violence are also the subject of two important essays, 'The Ghosts of Mrs Gandhi' and 'The Fundamentalist Challenge', reprinted in Amitav Ghosh's collected prose pieces *The Imam and the Indian*. For students of Ghosh's fiction this collection has been especially welcome because it includes 'The Slave of MS H.6', an essay which formed the basis for the subplot of social-anthropological research in Ghosh's *In an Antique Land.*

Studies of Indian English drama were less in evidence this year. Both Bijay Kumar Das's monograph and C.L. Khatri's collection (reviewed above) contain discussion of playwrights such as Girish Karnad, but the only major text on drama available for review was Yadav and Prasad, eds., *Studies in Indian Drama in English*, which contains papers on the drama of Girish Karnad and Vijay Tendulkar, amongst others, and also includes essays on 'Aurobindo as Playwright' and Tagore's *Chitra* and *The Post Office.* Amar Nath Prasad has also edited a collection of essays on Indian women novelists (discussed in the fiction section below), which includes a critical work by Jai Shanker Jha on Mahasweta Devi's play *Mother of 1084.*

(b) Fiction

This section reviews criticism of prose fiction, but readers should also refer to Section 4(*a*) above for work that examines and anthologizes fiction alongside other forms. Taken as a whole, the monographs and journal articles published this year revealed the continuing, steady engagement with key concerns in contemporary Indian literature in English, such as writing and gender, the literary expression of diasporic, culturally hybrid and 'partial' postcolonial identities, and also some newer areas such as the debate over marketing and literary cosmopolitanism. The critical field has also widened to encompass more writing by authors belonging to marginalized constituencies within India, such as

Eurasians, and has taken in previously overlooked genres such as postcolonial science fiction.

With fiction by South Asian women achieving increasing international recognition and acclaim, Indian women's writing has generated a substantial level of critical attention this year, and several monographs and collections of interviews have been published. One of the most eclectic of these is Philippa Kafka's *On the Outside Looking In(dian)*, which analyses a broad range of authors from Krupabhai Sattianadhan to Sunetra Gupta. Arranged in topic-based sections covering issues such as *purdah*, child marriage, expatriation and domestic violence, Kafka provides an overview of key thematic and political concerns in Indian women's literature and frames these against relevant issues within Indian feminism. There are, however, strange omissions in Kafka's sometimes over-synoptical work and, although a large section deals with subaltern groups such as *adivasi* or tribals, neither Arundhati Roy nor the eco-feminist commentator Vandana Shiva are accorded more than reference in a footnote. What Kafka loses in critical breadth she gains in her sense of historical context, and the monograph works well as a reference text, especially in its treatment of lesser-known activists and writers such as Rokeya Sakhawat Hossain.

Perhaps the most interesting monograph on Indian women's writing to appear this year is Antoinette Burton's *Dwelling in the Archive: Women Writing House, Home and History in Late Colonial India*, a carefully historicized comparative study of Janaki Majumdar, Cornelia Sorabji and Attia Hosain. Burton's subjects all wrote on the (familial) margins of the national movement and her work is a major contribution to the understanding of how Indian woman's fiction and life-writings have operated as both supplement and challenge to the standard archives of national historiography. As Burton states: 'If ... imagining home is as political an act as imagining the nation, the archival sources I am interested in calling "history" demonstrate how a certain class of Indian women tried to manage the political implications of the past by putting their own narratives within the realm of public memory' (p. 30). Burton's interest in different forms of cultural-historical archive is also evident in her compelling essay on memory and state violence in Michael Ondaatje's *Anil's Ghost*, 'Archive of Bones: *Anil's Ghost* and the Ends of History' (*JCL* 38:i[2003] 39–56).

Joel Kuortti's *Tense Past, Tense Present: Women Writing in English* follows his earlier *Indian Women's Writing in English* (see *YWES* 82[2003]) and provides useful contextual background for students and readers of Shashi Deshpande, Shama Futehully, Githa Hariharan, Anuradha Marwah-Roy and Mina Singh. Prefaced by an introductory essay on Indian feminism, the book includes personal interviews with each of these authors as well as excerpts of works such as Deshpande's *Small Remedies* and Hariharan's *On the Way to Paradise*. Prasad, ed., *New Light on Indian Women Novelists in English,* includes a large number of contributions—of variable quality—on contemporary Indian women's fiction, from the work of Nayantara Sahgal, Anita Desai and Shashi Deshpande to Mahasweta Devi, Arundhati Roy and Jhumpa Lahiri. The essays are short, allowing the editor to include twenty-three in the collection, but also preventing individual contributors from developing their critical ideas at any substantial length. Noteworthy essays include Jai Shanker Jha's brief study of Mahasweta

Devi's *Mother of 1084* (see above), and R.S. Sharma and S.B. Talwar's 'Architectonics in *The God of Small Things*', which looks at the time-scheme of Roy's novel and compares it with temporal structures in Faulkner's writing.

Another major critical concern this year has been the theorizing of writing from the South Asian diaspora, and one of the most wide-ranging literary-critical studies of diasporic fiction to appear is Fludernik, ed., *Diaspora and Multiculturalism: Common Traditions and New Developments*. Divided into a theoretical introduction, a section on the Jewish diaspora and a larger section on postcolonial diasporas and 'multiculturalisms at play', the collection includes an essay by Vera Alexander on 'Postponed Arrivals: The Afro-Asian Diaspora and M.G. Vassanji's *No New Land*', Makarand Paranjape's 'Writing Across Boundaries: South Asian Diasporas and Homelands' and Monika Fludernik's 'Imagined Communities as Imaginary Homelands: The South Asian Diaspora in Fiction', which engages with the work of Hanif Kureishi, Meena Alexander, Meera Syal, Shauna Singh Baldwin and Chitra Bannerjee Divakaruni among others. For Fludernik, these are writers who anticipate the possibilities of a new diaspora-consciousness by exploring the ties of community and the freedoms of diversity without the nostalgia for 'home' that features so strongly in traditional models of diaspora literature.

The issues discussed in *Diaspora and Multiculturalism* are at the heart of Monica Ali's *Brick Lane*, one of the literary triumphs of this year, and the subject of Sukhdev Sandhu's grudging review 'Come Hungry, Leave Edgy' (*LRB* 25:xix[2003] 13). Much of Sandhu's review is taken up with a cultural history of London's immigrant East End, and he describes Ali's *Brick Lane* as 'a patchy but promising first novel, strongly indebted to its black and Asian literary antecedents, more interested in character than in language, or even from the area from which it derives its name, a series of set pieces waiting to be dramatized into a feel good Sunday-night serial on BBC1'. Sandhu's interest in the cultural palimpsest of postcolonial London is evident in his own work *London Calling: How Black and Asian Writers Imagined a City* (HarperCollins), which deals, in part, with aspects of Kureishi's and Rushdie's fiction.

Diasporic identities and diaspora as the basis of critical categorization form the subject of Heike Härting's comparative essay 'Diasporic Cross-Currents in Michael Ondaatje's *Anil's Ghost*, and Anita Rau Badami's *The Hero's Walk*' (*SCL* 28:i[2003] 43–70). In her reading, Härting balances the 'largely ahistoric' diaspora consciousness that constitutes 'Anil's nomadic identity, cultural relativism and political failure' (p. 44) with Rau Badami's fashioning of 'pattern of disapora identification—rather than identity—around moments of stillness and disruption that generate new forms of communal and individual autonomy' (p. 44). Härting is particularly astute in her discussion of the way concepts of cultural hybridity and the 'triumphalist rhetoric of dissident post-nationalism connected with them' evoke 'forms of nomadism that are, paradoxically, intrinsic to modernity' (p. 48). Other writers of the South Asian diaspora in Canada, such as Rohinton Mistry, have also been the subject of critical interest this year, notably in Peter Morey's searching essay, 'Running Repairs: Corruption, Community and Duty in Rohinton Mistry's *Family Matters*' (*JCL* 38:ii[2003] 59–75).

In Morey's paper the focus is Mistry's ancestral Parsi community and faith, and how problems of political accommodation are conveyed through images of corporeal corruption and familial sacrifice in *Family Matters*. Morey's essay is acute in its reading of the cultural-historical specificity of the Parsi community, and sensitive to Mistry's subtle memorialization of its declining presence in contemporary Bombay. Another author, Farrukh Dhondy, who has roots in the Indian Parsi community but is better known for his novel of Asian British metropolitan life in the 1980s, *Bombay Duck*, is interviewed by Martina Ghosh-Schellhorn in *Anglistik* (14:i[2003] 52–5), and attacks the political orthodoxies of some forms of postcolonial diaspora studies, arguing that 'the diaspora identity seems to want to found itself on a destructive view of the colonial past [which] distorts history and is basically dishonest' (p. 53).

The ongoing critical interest in the partial identities and cultural-political negotiations occasioned by various diasporic experiences in contemporary Indian English fiction is complemented by a continuing critical elaboration on forms of cultural hybridity—especially when hybridity (as both a disabling metaphor in colonial discourse and a falsely enabling theoretical figure in *post* colonial thought) has seemed to contradict the 'lived experience' of actual trans-cultural groups. These issues are drawn out in two essays on the representation of Eurasians or 'Anglo-Indians' in Indian literature in English; Glenn D'Cruz's 'My Two Left Feet: The Problem of Anglo-Indian Stereotypes in Post-Independence Indo-English Fiction' (*JCL* 38:ii[2003] 105–23), and Loretta Mijares's '"You are an Anglo-Indian?": Eurasians and Hybridity and Cosmopolitanism in Salman Rushdie's *Midnight's Children*' (*JCL* 38:ii[2003] 125–45). Drawing on his own experience as an Anglo-Indian, D'Cruz's article responds to the need, voiced at the Fourth International Anglo-Indian Reunion, to 'correct' the essentializing image of Anglo-Indians in fiction. While questioning the possibility (or likelihood) of this correction, D'Cruz considers the Anglo-Indian as a 'marker of racial and cultural hybridity in Kipling, Salman Rushdie and Allan Sealy'.

Mijares's essay makes a similar point, questioning the tendency within postcolonial theory to rely on ahistorical, decontextualized concepts of hybridity, and ignoring the political particularities of the 'half-caste' in India. Quoting Pheng Cheah's work on transnationalism, Mijares argues that within postcolonial studies the intellectual currency of ideas of linguistic freedom and cultural flux has led to a 'general theory of transformative agency [that] inevitably exaggerates the role of signification and cultural representation in the functioning of socio-political life and its institutions'. For both D'Cruz and Mijares, I. Allan Sealy's work—especially *The Trotter Nama*—is seen as the richest, most complex representation of the need for a formal reinterpretation of Eurasians in new literary modes. However, D'Cruz also warns us that, while 'the *Trotter Nama*… brings together a series of discourses on history, hybridity and modernity which makes it possible for an alternative postcolonial Anglo-Indian identity to be articulated', the text never allows this identity to be wholly 'authenticated' (p. 118). Mijares continues her engagement with Sealy's work in another essay 'The Fetishism of the Original: Anglo-Indian History and Literature in I. Allan Sealy's *The Trotter Nama*'.

While critics such as D'Cruz and Mijares recontextualize postcolonialism's investment in hybridity, a writer who is often held responsible for the formulation of a hybrid aesthetics within the contemporary Indian novel in English, Salman Rushdie, continues to garner some searching critical attention. In her important book, *Home Truths: Fictions of the South Asian Diaspora in Britain* [2002], Susheila Nasta uses Rushdie's collection of short stories, *East, West*, to illustrate the complexity of its author's metamorphic, migrant self-fashioning. Rushdie's post-*fatwa* foray into the short story has also been the subject of a journal article by Antje M. Rauwerda, who traces the diasporic preoccupations and migrant tropes in '*East, West*: Rushdie's Writing Home' (*South Asian Review* 24:ii[2003] 133–48). Rushdie's post-*fatwa* novel, *The Moor's Last Sigh*, with its central ekphrastic motif of the layered, over-painted portrait of Aurora Zogoiby, is the subject of Jung Su's 'Inscribing the Palimpsest: Politics of Hybridity in *The Moor's Last Sigh*' (*Concentric* 29:i[2003] 199–226). For Jung Su, hybridity in Rushdie's novel is occurs in three dimensions: the central palimpsest motif, hybrid characterization and forms of historical postcolonial layering in Indian culture.

As a feted member of the English literary establishment, Rushdie also features in two surveys of contemporary British fiction: Philip Tew's *The Contemporary British Novel*, and Richard Lane, Rod Mengham and Philip Tew's *Contemporary British Fiction.* In the former, Rushdie is discussed alongside Wilson Harris, Zadie Smith, Hanif Kureishi and Jeanette Winterson as part of a wider thematic survey of 'Multiplicities and Hybridity', and it is only *The Satanic Verses* and Rushdie's first collection of essays, *Imaginary Homelands*, that are covered. Rather more comprehensive is Stephen Baker's essay 'Salman Rushdie: History, Self and the Fiction of Truth', included in the 'Cultural Hybridity' section of Lane, Mengham and Tew's *Contemporary British Fiction.* Here, focusing on *Midnight's Children,* Baker examines the way in which narrative authority is continually undermined in the novel and, consequently, how the 'contingency of all truths, selves and histories' (p. 155) is both a condition of loss and a precondition of art's 'groundless' capacity to 'rethink, recreate, reimagine' (p. 156) in Rushdie's fiction.

Taking a view of Rushdie's *Shame* that considers the cultural contexts of his Pakistan novel more carefully than usual, Hima Raza, in 'Unravelling *Sharam*: Narrativisation as a Political Act in Salman Rushdie's *Shame*' (*Wasafiri* 39[Summer 2003] 55–61) provides a compelling, culturally sensitive and informed reading of the *Mohajir* or immigrant community in Pakistan in the post-independence period, focusing on the way the mohajir's stubborn adherence to a historical narrative of unbelonging questions the boundaries of nationalist identity. Given the importance of a *mohajir* discourse in contemporary Urdu writing, and the paradoxical angle that Pakistan's history gives to concepts of migration and trans-nationalism, Raza's essay is a valuable contribution to understanding the nuances of a localized (rather than a universalizing) migrant aesthetics in Rushdie's *Shame.* Sukeshi Kamra examines the existential and psychological damage caused by the cataclysmic migrations and displacements of Partition in her article 'Ruptured Histories: Literature on the Partition (India, 1947)' (*Kunapipi* 25:ii[2003] 108–26). Dealing with the representation of space and spatial practice as a largely ignored 'naturalised' aspect of Partition writings, Kamra covers a number of key authors in translation such as Ashfaq Ahmad, Ismat Chugtai, Suraiya Qasim and Sadat Hasan Manto. Kamra draws on Henri Lefebvre's work on space to examine the repercussions of national splitting on community spaces in her texts such as the neighbourhood or *mohalla*, and traces the liminal spaces created by Partition.

The other Indian novelist in English who received a noticeable amount of critical attention this year was Amitav Ghosh, whose work was celebrated in two important collections of critical essays: Bose, ed., *Amitav Ghosh: Critical Perspectives* and Khair, ed., *Amitav Ghosh: A Critical Companion.* Bose's *Critical Perspectives* is divided into two main sections, 'Critical Readings' and 'Pedagogy', and provides informative discussions of all Ghosh's fiction to date, and some of his prose works. It includes Kavita Daiya's 'No Home But in Memory', a discussion of globalization and nationalism in *The Circle of Reason* and *The Shadow Lines*, and Vanita Chandra's complementary piece, 'Suppressed Memory and Forgetting: History and Nationalism in *The Shadow Lines*'. The critical focus on Ghosh's challenge to nationalist claims to selfhood and belonging is maintained in Neelam Srivastava's 'Fictions of Nationhood in Amitav Ghosh's *The Shadow Lines*', and nuanced in Shirley Chew's 'Texts and Worlds in *In an Antique Land*', in which Chew develops a persuasive reading of the subtle interaction between abstraction and locatedness and of the narrative interplay between 'the mediaeval and the modern' (p. 111) in Ghosh's genre-crossing semi-autobiographical work, and shows how he excavates a history of cultural accomodations in his text whilst also 'rooting them somewhere in the actual' (p. 114). The 'pedagogical' section of Bose's collection comprises a 'Students' Colloquium on Studying *The Shadow Lines*' and an essay by Meenakshi Malhotra on 'Gender, Nation, History: Some Observations on Teaching *The Shadow Lines*'. The text also includes an interview recorded by Neluka Silva and Alex Tickell with Amitav Ghosh in 1997, reprinted from the journal *Kunapipi.*

Like Bose's *Critical Perspectives*, Tabish Khair's *Critical Companion* contains a number of excellent essays on Ghosh's major fiction, amongst them Claire Chambers's 'Historicizing Scientific Reason in Amitav Ghosh's *The Circle of Reason*', which outlines the discursive role played by concepts of scientific rationality in Ghosh's first novel. Padmini Mongia makes connections between Ghosh's *In an Antique Land* and the work of anthropologists such as James Clifford, in 'Medieval Travel in Postcolonial Times: Amitav Ghosh's *In an Antique Land*', arguing that 'the shift in the epistemological position of the traveller is also the shift that has marked anthropology and other human sciences in the past two decades'. Khair includes an essay by Leela Gandhi '"A Choice of Histories": Ghosh vs. Hegel in *In an Antique Land*', which is reproduced in a volume of the *New Literatures Review* (see below). Khair's own contribution questions the extent and representation of subaltern agency in *The Calcutta Chromosome*, and the text also includes a short essay by Amitav Ghosh on one of his heroes, the writer and film-maker Satyajit Ray. Students of Ghosh's oeuvre will also find the extensive general bibliography compiled by Khair very useful.

In critical journals published in 2003 we might have expected Ghosh's *The Glass Palace* to have attracted most comment, but more attention is reserved for earlier works such as his colonial science fiction *The Calcutta Chromosome* and *In an Antique Land*. In *The Calcutta Chromosome* Ghosh taps into a tradition of Bengali science fiction popularized by figures such as Satyajit Ray, and Claire Chambers draws out these links, and the other medical-historical contexts of the novel, in her searching essay 'Postcolonial Science Fiction: Amitav Ghosh's *The Calcutta Chromosome*' (*JCL* 38:i[2003] 57–72). For Chambers, Ghosh's imaginative recuperation of the history of Ronald Ross's research on malaria is significant because it suspends Western discourses of individualistic discovery and scientific mastery by reading the narrative of colonial medical discovery as a literal 'science fiction'. As Chambers points out, Ghosh's novel also poses intriguing questions about the mediation of scientific knowledge as an aspect of cultural encounter and cross-cultural negotiation.

Writing from an anthropological perspective, Diane M. Nelson looks at the same novel in her essay, 'A Social Science Fiction of Fevers, Delirium and Discovery: *The Calcutta Chromosome*, the Colonial Laboratory, and the Postcolonial New Human' (*SFS* 30:ii[2003] 246–66). Drawing on Donna Haraway's famous work on the cyborg, Nelson argues—in what some might consider a utopian vein—that colonial science fiction 'gives us technologies to work on the new human emerging from the tropics … from alchemical networkings and interventions in the germline to immune-systems defenses and forms of reproduction that circumvent the Darwinian bottleneck of heterosexuality' (p. 249). Nelson's research field, political and ethnic violence in Guatemala, gives her an intriguing angle on the connection between colonialism, science and the military, themes that she draws out in her reading of the 'troops and tropes' in Ghosh's science fiction.

More generally, the politics of Ghosh's fiction and fictional historiography is the subject of two journal articles, Leela Gandhi's '"A Choice of Histories": Ghosh vs. Hegel in *In an Antique Land*' (*NLitsR* 40[2003] 17–32), and Anshuman Mondal's 'Allegories of Identity: "Postmodern" Anxiety and Postcolonial Ambivalence in Amitav Ghosh's *In an Antique Land* and *The Shadow Lines*' (*JCL* 38:iii[2003] 19–37). In a pastiche of the kind of fantastic historical juxtaposition we might find in *The Calcutta Chromosome*, Gandhi introduces her essay—which appears in Khair's collection as well—by imagining a meeting between G.W.F. Hegel and Amitav Ghosh at a tea-stall outside Delhi University. Making reference to the literal master–slave relationship of Bomma and Ben Yiju in the text, which Ghosh interprets as devotional rather than coercive, Gandhi reads *In an Antique Land* as a counter-discourse to Hegel's master–slave paradigm. Ghosh's challenge to Hegelian historiography, argues Gandhi, is routed through both French post-structuralism and the Subaltern Studies project, and these disciplinary affiliations and influences are also the subject of Anshuman Mondal's essay.

Looking at Ghosh's earlier work, *The Shadow Lines*, as well as *In an Antique Land*, Mondal discusses how Ghosh's identity politics can be read as a mediation of postcolonial and postmodern identity politics. Revisiting the debate inaugurated by Ian Adam and Helen Tiffin in their critical collection *Past the*

Last Post: Theorising Post-Colonialism and Post-Modernism, Mondal contends that 'modernity' is a curiously unstable concept in Ghosh's thinking—something that is both 'desired and detested'. For Mondal this theoretical ambivalence shapes works such as *In an Antique Land*, because it not only informs its author's values (which are humanist and secular, and thereby the product of modernity), but also provides the basis for Ghosh's work as an ongoing critique of certain epistemological and political offshoots of Western modernity, such as nationalist historiography and the political primacy of the nation-state. Like Gandhi, Mondal also makes links between Ghosh's debt to the Subaltern Studies collective and more general forms of radical uncertainty that underlie the postmodern.

Arundhati Roy's polemical contributions to the anti-war and anti-globalization debates and her energetic support of environmental pressure-groups in India kept her in the public eye a great deal this year. Roy describes her political journalism as a continuation of the politics of her first novel, *The God of Small Things*, but it is still her fiction that attracts most critical study. A noteworthy exception is Rashmi Varma's 'Developing Fictions: The Tribal in the New Indian Writing in English' (in Kumar, ed., *World Bank Literature*), which sets up a comparative discussion of Roy's essay on the Narmada Dam project, 'The Greater Common Good', and Sohaila Abdulali's 1998 novel *The Madwoman of Jogare*. Responding to Gayatri Spivak's 1994 essay, 'How to Teach a Culturally Different Book', Varma argues 'against Spivak's assertion of "the erasure of the tribal" in the service of a cosmopolitan identity in contemporary Indian Literature in English' and instead makes the point that 'recent writing from India … has in fact recuperated the figure of the tribal, constructed it anew, and mapped onto it new anxieties and desires about the future of Indian identity in a globalising world economy'.

Unfortunately, Varma does not sustain a theoretical engagement with Spivak after the first page, and therefore the possibility that the contemporary Indian English 'recuperation' of the tribal might involve new and more complex modes of 'erasure', as well as forms of representational emancipation, remains unexplored. This said, Varma is highly attentive to the way in which Roy constructs the rural communities of the Narmada valley, using 'the classic anthropological gesture that displaces the time of the Other onto some prehistoric moment' while simultaneously rejecting easy political dyads such as modernity/tradition or romantic assumptions that 'tribals' embody a 'superior environmental consciousness' (the kind of manoeuvre, incidentally, that recalls Spivak's discussion of 'catachrestic' theoretical usage). Varma's essay is revealing in its gesture towards the more complex modes through which *adivasi* groups have been politically co-opted in contemporary India, as both a strangely cosmopolitan sign in the cultural discourses of elite liberal identity and a key figure in debates about 'reconversion' amongst the Hindu right.

Roy's only fiction to date generates a number of critical readings. In an article entitled 'Of Gods and Gods and Men: A Thematic Study of Arundhati Roy's *The God of Small Things*' (*JIWE* 31:ii[2003] 66–7), M.K. Naik explores the antinomies of 'big and small things' and the collision between individual lives and larger religious, social and cultural forces in Roy's writing. Naik goes on to claim that some of the central characters in the novel are compromised by their own desires, and argues that the narrative is almost a parable of libidinous excess. In a more extensive comparative article, 'Configuring the Dynamics of Dispossession in Rohinton Mistry's *A Fine Balance* and Arundhati Roy's *The God of Small Things*' (*NZJAS* 5:ii[2003] 56–76), Doreen D'Cruz advances a cogent reading of caste in what must surely be the two most important Indian English fictional treatments of the subject since Mulk Raj Anand's *Untouchable*. D'Cruz's reading reviews the cultural history of 'pollution' as an aspect of the *dharmashastras*, and carefully delineates the politics and representation of untouchability in both novels.

Other commentators have concentrated on some of the theoretical issues raised by the sophisticated marketing and international commercial success of Roy's novel. In his *The Postcolonial Exotic* Graham Huggan sees both Rushdie and Roy as writers who self-consciously anticipate the exotic predilections of their Western readers by developing a strategic '*meta*-exoticism' (p. 77). In Roy's writing this involves tropes 'designed to trap the unwary reader into complicity with the Orientalisms of which the novel so hauntingly relates'. In '*The God of Small Things:* Arundhati Roy's Postcolonial Cosmopolitanism' (*JCL* 38:i[2003] 73–89), Alex Tickell builds on this reading, and examines contiguities between Roy's literary presentation of split or hybrid subjectivities and the presiding concerns of postcolonial theory. However, he also asks how far we can read images of doubled audiences (of Kathakali drama) in the novel as ironic, reflexive references to the predicament of the 'cosmopolitan' South Asian writer.

The issue of how 'representative' Indian English fiction is, or how (often non-resident, 'cosmopolitan') South Asian novelists working in English can claim the same cultural credentials as authors writing in the subcontinent's other major languages, is a perennial concern. John C. Hawley delineates the most recent, and vehement, exchanges in this debate in 'Can the Cosmopolitan Speak? The Question of Indian Novelists' Authenticity' (*South Asian Review* 24:ii[2003] 26–39), in which he looks at the controversy surrounding Vikram Chandra's now famous attack on 'India's cultural commissars' published in the March 2000 *Boston Review*. Hawley provides an informative summary of key issues and covers a number of other writers implicated in the fracas, including Salman Rushdie and Vikram Seth, concluding that 'like it or not, marketing decisions will … [increasingly] determine the outcome of these cultural battles, and a growing consciousness of global citizenship (if the concept makes any sense) may eventually obviate a good many of these skirmishes' (p. 36).

Hawley ends his article by endorsing Rajeswari Sunder Rajan's claim that the disputes over cosmopolitan writing might be ameliorated by 'a good vibrant translation industry … that would bring [Indian] regional writers the visibility they deserve'. In an article on translation, 'Towards an Indian Theory of Translation' (*Wasafiri* 40[2003] 27–30), Shibani Phukan considers what this might mean in terms of the linguistic history of the subcontinent and the 'plurality of practices informing translation activities in pre-colonial India' (p. 27). Thus, while acknowledging and tracking the disciplinary history of colonial translation, Phukan also argues for a recognition of the different cultural models of 'transcreative' translation that inform translation in India today.

Translation is also the concern of Makarand Paranjape, a critic who has often defended a critical politics sympathetic to forms of nativist identification. In his '"Home and Away": Colonialism and Alter*Nativity* in India' (*NLitsR* 40[2003] 116–31), Paranjape argues that modern Indian culture, which he tends to collapse into a history of Hindu reformers and politicians, is characterized by a continual translation between home and 'away'; modernity and tradition; the scientific and the spiritual. Referring to Tagore's *Gora and Ghare Baire*, Paranjape distinguishes his version of cultural 'double vision' from similar models proposed by 'postcolonial' critics, stating that '[unlike] Bhabha's hybridity [which] lacks the ambition or the possibility of being rendered into a national or civilisational space … this other was not a hybrid, not some kind of mongrel inbetweenness, but a third world without the pejorative associations of that term' (p. 129). In a different essay, 'The Reluctant Guru: R.K. Narayan's *The Guide*' (*South Asian Review* 24:ii[2003] 170–85), Paranjape examines what he calls R.K. Narayan's 'non-assertive traditionalism' in a comparable vein, and argues for an understanding of Narayan's fictional microcosm of Malgudi as a model for India's engagement with modernity'.

In an eloquent essay in Hogan and Pandit, eds., *Rabindranath Tagore: Universality and Tradition*, Ashis Nandy discusses Tagore in terms of violence and creativity in the context of the late twentieth century. For Nandy, Tagore is exemplary in the way that he 'spoke out against the violence built into India's traditional social order, but also sensed that violence was being overtaken in scale and range by the new violence' of twentieth-century modernity. As a necessary part of recognizing Tagore's importance as an Indian intellectual who 'journeyed' from the universalism of the European Enlightenment to 'an alternative universalism more rooted in non-Western traditions', Nandy argues that Tagore must be freed from his iconic position in Bengali culture so that he can be 'recontextualized' according to the needs of a new generation of readers. Hogan and Pandit's collection, which is a welcome contribution to Tagore scholarship, also includes a study of Tagore's nationalism by Manju Radhakrishnan and Debasmita Roychowdhury, a comparative examination of Tagore's *Gora* and Kipling's *Kim* by Jaya Mehta, and essays on *The Home and the World*, and Tagore's fiction and the cinema of Satyajit Ray.

5. New Zealand and the South Pacific

BSANZB 25:i–ii[2001] is a special issue in memory of D.F. McKenzie, who may well be the most distinguished scholar ever associated with New Zealand. It is bracketed by two tributes to McKenzie. In the editorial Ian Morrison outlines McKenzie's academic career and 'awe-inspiring' publication history: groundbreaking books and articles which have led international bibliographers to reassess their discipline in terms of methodology and its very meaning. His influence continues in vast projects involving numerous scholars from many countries that will long be the source of publications and new ideas. In 'Don McKenzie: Books, Libraries and Scholarship' (*BSANZB* 25:i–ii[2001] 165–6), J.E. Traue offers a personal memoir and tribute. In general, the special issue contains articles more appropriately covered in the bibliographical section of *YWES*, covering as they do some part of the huge range of McKenzie's own interests, but their relationship to New Zealand studies is a *cantus firmus* underlying their more general application. Of direct relevance to New Zealand studies are the following articles: Sydney Shep, 'Book History and the Practice of Material Culture: The Example of Wai-te-Ata Press' (*BSANZB* 25:i–ii[2001] 3–7), which surveys the history of the press founded by McKenzie at Victoria University of Wellington; J.E. Traue, 'Two Histories of the Book in New Zealand' (*BSANZB* 25:i–ii[2001]8–16), which takes two essays by T.M. Hocken as the starting-point for a survey of the history of printing in the country; Noel Waite, 'Printer's Proof: The Dunedin Master Printers' Association, 1889–1894' (*BSANZB* 25:i–ii[2001] 17–41), which provides a very detailed account of that institution with special focus on Coupland Harding, one of McKenzie's 'discoveries'; and Roderick Cave, 'John Buckland Wright: Engraver and Book Illustrator' (*BSANZB* 25:i–ii[2001] 50–66), which examines the case of a New Zealander whose career, like McKenzie's, carried him to Britain, Europe and the United States. Other articles in the special issue, though focusing on topics of more general relevance, nonetheless make reference to New Zealand and McKenzie.

Another richly informative survey of McKenzie's contribution to bibliographical and New Zealand studies is by Keith Maslen: 'Donald Francis McKenzie 1932–1999: A Tribute' (*BSANZB* 23:i[1999–2000] 3–10).

For many years now, Lawrence Jones, author of a wide range of essays on aspects of New Zealand literary history, has been working towards a major study of 'modern' New Zealand literature. This is usually held to begin in the 1920s with the poems of R.A.K. Mason, but Jones has long asserted a fourfold history of 'phases'—early colonial, late colonial, provincial and post-provincial—in the history he attempts to overview, and his 'provincial' period sets in with the publication of *Phoenix* and the related social event of the 'Queen Street riots', both of which occurred in 1932. This is consequently the year he has chosen for the beginning of his study. In his newest book and elsewhere (e.g. *Barbed Wire and Mirrors: Essays on New Zealand Prose* [1987]), Jones likes to present his work as an act of 'public self-education', and so immensely has his topic grown in his own mind and in the research he and others have conducted during the book's gestation that he has found it necessary to divide his historical study into two volumes. The first of these, *Picking Up the Traces: The Making of a New Zealand Literary Culture 1932–1945*, was published in 2003. It is a densely argued and researched text of 430 pages plus bibliographical material and index. Since he assures us that the subsequent period is even more complex than this one, we may expect a thousand-page study of New Zealand literature since 1932 to eventuate once the two volumes are complete. This is far and away the largest—and most thorough—study of the country's literature ever undertaken by a single hand.

Jones's approach is not empirically based on the literature itself but begins with the ideas and the social context underlying literary production. This means that he foregrounds the theoretical and critical works of the writers he deals with, while their poems, novels and plays, though often analysed in some detail, have a second-rank position in his narrative. It also means that there are valuable summaries of the sometimes opaque ideas of Cresswell, Curnow and others. Although the emphasis on ideas creates a cart-before-the-horse feel to much of the book, it also adds greatly to its overall coherence, so that Jones is able to present an essentially chronological study in the form of a theoretical argument. This makes certain demands on the reader, which some may not be prepared to respond to. This would be to their own loss, since the study has great virtues. One of them is its (apparent?) comprehensiveness; another is the original research Jones has conducted in archives and libraries, bringing much unpublished material to light; yet another is the way in which phenomena that may seem isolated are shown to be part of a broad pattern. Whether that pattern is invented by the historian or pre-exists in his material is likely to be the question that will occupy future students who engage with this book. In either case it offers a wide range of insights into the way writers were conducting their business during the thirteen years it covers. I, for one, intend to go back and read it again before I make a more detailed judgement of it. If nothing else, it is a monumental and deeply honest achievement, and a conscientious reader can learn much from it.

John Thomson has provided his customary annual overview of recent literary publications and a full bibliography in the *Journal of Commonwealth Literature* (*JCL* 38:iv[2003] 83–100). In the New Zealand fiction of 2002 he finds, again and again, that the characterization is too weak to give life to otherwise interesting and unusual ideas. In Charlotte Randall's *Within the Kiss*, for example, he responds to the allusions to Byron and Goethe more strongly than to the characters they are intended to illustrate. In Christine Johnston's *The Shark Bell,* 'the author's characters struggle to breathe under the weight of significance imposed on them' (p. 85). And so it goes on with similar comments on other novels, with Alan Duff's *Jake's Long Shadow* coming in for a particularly strong judgement about the way sociology outweighs characterization and even language—Thomson writes of the characters' 'deformed English' (p. 86). For him, even the characters in Stephanie Johnson's prizewinning *The Shag Incident* (which others find extremely skilful) do not 'carry quite enough (weight)' (p. 87). More generous accounts are given of novels by Lloyd Jones and Damien Wilkins and short stories by Owen Marshall, Elizabeth Smither and Fiona Kidman. In poetry, Thomson notes the widespread thematic emphasis on family life: James Brown, Rachel Bush, Janet Charman and Bob Orr have all written of childhood and parenthood. More detached, and more appealing to Thomson, is the stance of Chris Price in *Husk.* A glance at the bibliography is interesting for showing what Thomson did *not* consider worthy of critical discussion in the accompanying essay. Books of poetry by Tony Beyer, Stephanie de Montalk, Rob Jackaman, Cilla McQueen, Chris Orsman, Robert Sullivan and Albert Wendt, as well as works of fiction by Graham Billing, Tim Corballis, Peter Hawes, David Hill, Paula Morris, Renee, Mark Richards, Elspeth Sandys, Tina Shaw and Paul Harris, are all passed over in silence, even though these names regularly cause a stir in the reading community.

In the essay 'Cultural Transformations: New Zealand Literary and Cultural Studies' (*AUMLA* 100[2003] 134–46), Chris Prentice gives a critical survey of the development of New Zealand studies in New Zealand universities from the 1970s, when such studies were gradually professionalized, through the 1980s, when they were integrated with broader postcolonial studies and the range of courses was expanded to include generic and thematic structures as well as historical ones, to the 1990s, when this work was consolidated, and inter-university (including international) work became the norm, due partly to publications in major journals and even more to encounters at a series of conferences. Prentice concludes by suggesting that the 'way ahead' is to focus on 'cultural studies' rather than literary studies in the more restricted sense. This will have the virtue of coping more adequately with the growing multicultural reality of the country.

Meanwhile a vigorous debate erupted around a short essay by Patrick Evans, 'The Baby Factory' (*NZListener* [16 August 2003] 29–30), where he argued that the youngest generation of New Zealand writers has been over-influenced by creative writing courses, especially that of Bill Manhire in Wellington, with the result that writing has been 'commodified'—turned into a product for international consumption. He notes in particular that certain young writers no longer set their novels in New Zealand and, worse, to achieve international recognition they choose to use 'polite and well-behaved' rather than vigorous and critical attitudes. A flurry of anxious letters in later issues of *Listener* were brought to a head by Damien Wilkins (*Booknotes* 143[2003] 3). He argued that the writers of the 'Manhire School' in fact have virtually no common characteristics and that the attempt to write 'to the limit' is illustrated by the effort to go beyond national assumptions. No doubt Wilkins was concerned because his own novels have tended to be of the kind Evans abhors. In 'Who Are We Writing For?' in the Christmas supplement of *New Zealand Books* (13:v[2003] 2), Chris Else tries to bring in a note of reasonable balance. After summarizing the various arguments, he argues that novelists should 'confront life', and if they do that, the locality of the setting is of little importance. He does believe, however, that New Zealand writers deserve and would benefit from a broader New Zealand readership, and he proposes that literary politics should take that as its aim.

While for writers of Maori identity there is a painful divide between traditional and modern aspects of their culture, for New Zealanders of European ancestry there is a no less painful divide between the awareness of ancestral origin and the realities of the lived life. At one extreme end of this spectrum are nationalistic assertions that the European background is of no significance: New Zealand is all. At the other extreme end is the New Zealander's 'return' to Britain, almost comically blind in the case of, say Alan Mulgan, and acutely, painfully aware in the case of Fleur Adcock. In 'Fleur Adcock: Ambivalent Expatriate, 1964–1974' (*JNZL* 21[2003] 54–72), Janet Wilson examines this case. After five years as an infant in New Zealand, Adcock was taken to Britain by her parents for a large part of her childhood. Her adolescence and early adulthood, including marriage, were spent in New Zealand, where she wrote her first published poems. But even before her return to Britain in 1963, Adcock never wrote of specific New Zealand localities. In this she implicitly challenged the ideology of the elder, nationalistic poet Allen Curnow. Other members of the group she was attached to—the 'Wellington Group'—also challenged Curnow, yet wrote vividly of New Zealand landscapes and urban life. In Britain, Adcock became a part of 'The Group':

London poets whose concerns were remote from those of New Zealand writers. She forged a British identity and came to be accepted there as one of the poets on the local scene; yet she was never quite forgotten in New Zealand—though often resented—and was awarded an OBE for services to New Zealand literature in 1996. The 'ambivalence' is therefore as much in how she is perceived by her peers as in her own work, but Wilson is able to point to some pivotal poems where the ambivalence is sharply felt and structured into complex verse. It must be said, however, that if 'ambivalence' implies equal pressures in two directions, then the word is not well applied to Adcock, who leans much more towards Britain than New Zealand, without quite losing the colonial connection.

A lively and even skittish assessment of Charles Brasch was written by David Eggleton for *NZListener* ([9 August 2003] 34–5) to celebrate the fact that the Brasch papers have become available to scholars in the Hocken Library, Dunedin. If Eggleton's views are typical, Brasch has lost favour with younger writers. Once viewed as an austere but admirable master, he is treated here as so obsessed with English and international standards that he was unable to respond in a living way to the New Zealand that surrounded him. His poems are described as fustian pastiche of Eliot and other modernists. Eggleton is generous, however, in acknowledging Brasch's undoubted skills as editor of the key journal of its time, *Landfall*, and as a benefactor to artists and writers less financially privileged than himself.

There could scarcely be a contrast greater than that between the sophisticated, elegant, affluent Brasch and the direct, grassroots, impoverished Geoff Cochrane—and yet Cochrane is more likely than Brasch to care nothing for life in New Zealand. Unlike most New Zealand writers, he has never left the country and, unlike them, he is indifferent to it. In an illuminating interview with Damien Wilkins (in *Sport* 31[2003] 3–31) he claims, 'I'm an international poet.' Although it is not simple to distil an 'essence' from the interview, the accumulation of direct comments on many things—alcoholism, sex, film, music, living alone, depression, writing and publishing, and more—adds up to the portrait of an interesting writer and personality. He believes, with some justice, that he has been neglected by the media and the literary establishment, but he sees that as a form of liberation: since nobody cares, he can do whatever he likes. He sees his poetry as the result of a need to 'make something' (p. 16), which could well have been directed towards painting or, indeed, anything at all. Underlying much of what he says is a negativity symptomatic of depression, but the urge to turn even that into a creative gesture overrides anything melancholic. To summarize his attitude he quotes Kingsley Amis to the effect that 'there is no point to existence, but there is a point to art' (p. 31).

The case of D'Arcy Cresswell has been largely ignored by recent historians and critics. After his rather surprising acceptance in the anthologies of Allen Curnow in the 1940s his reputation went downhill, so far down indeed as to be subterranean by now. An essay by John Newton, 'Poetry and other Marvels: D'Arcy Cresswell on his Own Terms' (*JNZL* 21[2003] 14–31), succeeds in making him a more interesting figure than his reputation might suggest, but makes no real effort to make him out to be a 'good' poet. The interest begins in a question of definition: 'Was Cresswell a *gay* writer?' (p. 14). But in the course of the article the question of the colonial's status in a class-ridden London environment becomes almost as central. The two themes are inseparable: Cresswell is shown to have 'lorded it sexually' over domestic servants and to have been lorded over in a mirror-image way by upper-class English homosexuals, notably Edward Marsh (pp. 18–25). The literary question behind this sociological concern is: how are we to read D'Arcy Cresswell? Newton shows that his most prominent readers, from the English Marsh to the Christchurch-based Rhodes, can only tolerate his style if they see it as amusing: Cresswell is a figure of fun. But the writer himself was utterly humourless in his insistence that he was a deadly serious theoretician of poetics and should be compared with Plato, Montaigne and Plutarch. The apparently self-mocking title of the autobiographical *Present without Leave* (London [1939]) was provided by the publisher against the author's resistance. A sense of comedy in the reader or listener contrasting with earnest argument in the writer or performer is almost a definition of 'Camp' and Newton concludes by relating Cresswell to Susan Sontag's term 'failed seriousness' in her classic 'Notes on Camp' (pp. 30–1). It may or may not be unfair to say that there is more of interest in Newton's article than in the collected works of D'Arcy Cresswell.

Alfred Domett, the nineteenth-century author of the massive poetic epic *Ranolf and Amohia*, is more frequently mentioned in literary histories than actually read. In 1990 Patrick Evans commented in *The Penguin History of New Zealand Literature* that, 'like a stranded whale, the poem lies rotting on the beach of New Zealand literature, an embarrassment that no one knows what to do with' (p. 43). In her article 'Alfred Domett, Robert Browning and a Dream of Two Lives' (*JNZL* 21[2003] 32–53), Jane Stafford does us the service of providing a twenty-first-century version of what to do with it. She traces Domett's background in the Robert Browning circle and his adventures in New Zealand with some sound scholarship. Interestingly she compares *Ranolf and Amohia* to Browning's *Sordello*: both are virtually unreadable and both are set in imagined versions of real places, New Zealand and Italy respectively. But it is her conclusion that is of greatest interest. She locates Domett's poem in a place she calls 'Maoriland', a constructed 'archaic space' securely surrounded by European, and specifically London culture. Stafford and Mark Williams have written of this 'Maoriland' before, seeing it as an invented country bearing no more than a fleeting resemblance to historical reality, and there is some danger that they will themselves construct a place of no reality, too readily confused with the 'Maoriland' of the Sydney *Bulletin* and its acolytes. But the essential fact that Domett, for all his thirty years in New Zealand, was part of an English poetic culture, his exotic New Zealand no more real than Browning's exotic Italy, is a point worth making. Browning himself is quoted as saying of *Sordello* that 'the historical decoration was purposely of no more importance than a background requires; and my stress lay in the incidents in the development of the soul: little else is worth study' (p. 49). Similarly, Domett, whose attitude to the real Maori in his political life was dismissive and patronizing, merely uses them as fictional constructs in an English poetico-philosophical discourse.

With 'Beyond the Myth: Janet Frame Unframed' (*JNZL* 21[2003] 122–39), Ruth Brown has attempted an essay in cultural analysis. The graceless and ungracious pun in the title is unfortunately a signal of the essayist's attitude. Her attention is on the formation of literary reputation in Britain and in New Zealand. To examine this topic she implicitly believes that she must maintain a considerable moral and intellectual distance from the writer and the writing: neither Janet Frame as a creative personality nor her novels, stories, poems and autobiographies as literary artefacts are illuminated by this approach. The focus on reviewers and journalistic purveyors of reputation even implies a certain distaste for engaging with the writer and her work. Brown leaves that engagement to others, whom she then rather coolly quotes and expounds, even here evading the question of the value of their work in favour of assessing their assumed motivations. The result is an essay without taste—its flavour diminished by refrigeration.

No New Zealand writer has been more closely studied and edited recently than 'Robin Hyde' (Iris Wilkinson). Perhaps none has been so prolific, especially considering the shortness of her life: her literary production covered only fifteen years. On the whole, her fiction is available in good editions, extensive selections of her journalism have been authoritatively reprinted, and there is a vast biographical study by Derek Challis (*The Book of Iris* [2002]), but until 2003 there was no totally reliable or comprehensive edition of her most important output, namely her poems. This gap has now been filled by Michele Leggott's truly splendid edition, *Young Knowledge: The Poems of Robin Hyde*. Beautifully presented by Auckland University Press and meticulously edited and annotated, this is both a landmark and a benchmark in the history of poetry editing in New Zealand. Many of the poems were completely inaccessible to any but determined scholars in research libraries, and even the best-known, oft-anthologized pieces have never before undergone such rigorous textual analysis to provide versions that can be viewed as definitive.

In some degree the edition is associated with Challis's biography, which was itself based on research conducted by Gloria Rawlinson and extended by Challis. Challis and Rawlinson were also planning a 'Collected Poems', a natural by-product of the biography, since only detailed research into the poetry could permit the biography to be accurate. The editorial work, however, was left incomplete, although Rawlinson left a chronological collection of 500 poems, which are now in Auckland University's Manuscripts and Archives. There is a complementary collection, overlapping with the Auckland one, among J.H.E. Schroder's papers in the Alexander Turnbull Library, Wellington. Leggott has now reorganized this material, focusing on manuscripts while referring to the book publications only in the second instance. The poems are organized into five chronological sections and thematically within the sections.

The entire process is completely transparent, due to the exemplary introduction, a detailed chronology, and a very extensive bibliography. Anyone who uses this material diligently can quickly see how the poems relate to each other, sometimes across years, and how they relate to phases of the poet's life and developing thought. Greater depth on all these aspects is provided by a truly innovative instrument: in a section of the website of the New Zealand Electronic Poetry Centre, www.nzepc.auckland.ac.nz/authors/hyde, there are introductory notes to each section of the book and details of textual variants and explanatory notes for each of the poems. This material, which would have been delivered on paper in variorum editions of the past, can be constantly corrected, updated and complemented by the editor and her team of assistants so that the reader is always sure of having the most recent scholarship available at the click of a mouse. Together, the beautiful book and the totally reliable online information comprise the finest editorial work any New Zealand poet has enjoyed.

Of the many biographies of writers which have appeared in recent years, Terry Sturm's *An Unsettled Spirit: The Life and Frontier Fiction of Edith Lyttleton (G.B. Lancaster)* is among the most competent. Sturm, a leading scholar of New Zealand literature with a special interest in 'popular fiction', here turns the full range of his skills on a figure who has been largely forgotten. His book can be read as an attempt to draw attention to 'G.B. Lancaster', perhaps to resurrect her reputation and to make a case for her as a writer worthy of both close and extensive reading. It can also be read simply as a fascinating narration because his subject has great interest in herself. Furthermore, the narration indirectly casts a great deal of light on attitudes towards writers, especially women writers, in the puritanical generations of 'early' New Zealand—at least up to the 1930s and 1940s. Like other women, Edith Lyttleton (1873–1945) chose to publish under a pseudonym and, by using initials, to conceal or at least obfuscate her gender. Her twelve long novels and 250 stories often told of a very masculine world—the pioneer world of farming, forestry and mining in New Zealand, Australia and Canada—and many reviewers assumed that they were written by a man. She was born in Tasmania and moved with her family to a large Canterbury property when she was 6. There she grew up, but as an adult she travelled very widely, especially in Europe and North America, and her fiction has many settings.

In her lifetime she was both popular and respected. Her stories appeared in most of the prestigious English-language papers and magazines, and her novels were eagerly awaited and most went through numerous reprintings. And yet she remained something of a mystery to her readers—this was in the years before mandatory publicity tours. As long as her mother lived, and she lived for a very long time, Edith had to conceal her authorship as a matter of family policy, for writing was not considered to be a 'respectable' occupation, and she had to hide from her family that she was working for hours at home and later as a fully professional, full-time writer. In spite of opposition from family and a patronizing attitude in the literary world, she wrote confidently and prolifically. She had an assured place on bestseller lists. Sturm explores these attitudes in detail and also examines her writing as a vigorous outgrowth of empire. He is deeply aware of cultural and literary politics, but he is especially sensitive to Lyttleton as an individual. He quotes extensively from her letters, and this strategy creates an in-depth portrait of a multifaceted personality. As narration, as literary history, and as human portraiture this is an outstanding book.

Len Lye's biographer, Roger Horrocks, has written a short account of Lye's poetry: 'My Word, My World' (*Landfall* 205[2003] 179–84). He makes a good argument for placing him at the beginning of experimental verse, alongside R.A.K. Mason and A.R.D. Fairburn. Lye's expatriate life did not prevent him from drawing on New Zealand landscapes, implicitly, when creating his fantastic prose poems. Horrocks suggests that Lye should be part of an anthology of New Zealand experimental poetry, but one could also ask why he is absent from more general anthologies of New Zealand verse.

The mature stories of Katherine Mansfield have, often enough, been compared to Impressionist painting: the capturing of a moment before it flees, with its dazzle and shimmering impermanence. To my knowledge, a comparison with Fauvist painting has not been tried before Angela Smith's essay, 'Katherine Mansfield and *Rhythm*' (*JNZL* 21[2003] 102–21). The comparison brings a new emphasis to aspects of the story, such as 'outline' and the broad surface in one place and the absence of colour in another. At the same time, Smith draws on the philosophy of Bergson, who was the impulse behind Middleton Murry's journal *Rhythm*, to make a more convincing portrayal of Mansfield's use of time than that provided by the comparison with Impressionism. Bergson contrasted two kinds of time, which he labelled 'time' and 'duration'. While time is measured by the clock, duration is measured by the rhythms of the human body. By combining Fauvist vision with Bergsonian ideas Smith is able to achieve original interpretations of the stories Mansfield published in *Rhythm*, especially 'The Woman at the Store' and 'How Pearl Button Was Kidnapped'. In the latter, for example, Pearl Button is removed by her captors from a world where 'time' dominates into one pervaded by 'duration'. At the same time there is a 'literary equivalent of the characteristic traits of Fauvist painting: sharply defining lines round figures or aspects of the landscape; a rhythmical design, paint applied thickly in places and sparsely, or leaving the canvas bare, in others; an emphasis on mobility; a thematic concern with the empowerment of any restricted person, including of course women' (p. 116). Finally Smith applies these analytical techniques to an insightful reading of 'The Daughters of the Late Colonel'.

In 2003 Rachel Barrowman brought out her keenly anticipated biography of R.A.K. Mason, who is sometimes seen as the first modern New Zealand poet, writing in a rigorous, haunted, melancholic and erudite manner quite unlike any of his Victorian and Edwardian predecessors. In some fine analyses of Mason's poems, Barrowman makes it clear, nonetheless, that he was indebted to the Georgians, and especially to Housman. Unlike some local biographers, she does not shy away from serious discussion of his writing, and is very strong on its relationships to the classics. Although working outside academe (like Barrowman herself), Mason was a fine Latin scholar and the story of his education, which never loosened his working-class connections, is very well told. Barrowman is the author of a study of left-wing politics and art in New Zealand and is well placed to explore Mason's active connections with the trade union movement and the Communist Party. Her detailed study makes it more or less clear—a sense of mystery remains—why Mason started so strongly and then ceased writing for many years. The local environment was not welcoming to his political stance, and his political friends and associates had little interest in his poetry. Although his work was always respected, it was never loved or even taken seriously by his workmates. Mason bridged the gap by writing agit-prop drama and engaging in left-wing theatre, but this never brought the same recognition as his poetry. In his later years, partly with the help of the Burns Fellowship, he returned to writing more lyrical poetry and also tried his hand at poetic drama in Scottish dialect—a quixotic undertaking on the face of it, and never really successful. The account of his closing years is distressing, as this vigorous man grew mentally and physically gross and filled with a sense of failure. But Barrowman's style is as Mason would want, truthful and unsentimental. Mason has been captured by the nationalists in literary history but was never a nationalist himself, rejecting interpretations of his verse that tried to tie it down to its locality. With enormous intelligence he set out to create strong, uncompromising verse about the deepest verities of human life, and Barrowman has done him and us a service by examining the biographical background to this endeavour.

Two more biographical studies cover the generation that flourished in the 1930s and 1940s. One is a broad-brush study of five literary lives—John Mulgan, Dan Davin, James Bertram, Geoffrey Cox and Ian Milner—with excursions into many more; the other is a tightly focused work on one of them, John Mulgan, while inevitably drawing the others into the line of vision as well.

James McNeish has written a dramatic story, or rather a series of stories, in *Dance of the Peacocks: New Zealanders in Exile in the Time of Hitler and Mao Tse Tung*. With the exception of John Mulgan, all of his five protagonists were recipients of Rhodes Fellowships, and in the eyes of his contemporaries Mulgan should also have been of their number. McNeish uses this as the cement for his book, but it is only in the early chapters that it really works. As the five lives continue, they diverge more and more, and by the second half of the book there is really no structural principle that can hold it together. From a purist viewpoint, this is damning, but from the point of view of 'a jolly good read' McNeish provides a great deal of entertainment and information. All five men retained a relationship with New Zealand, with various degrees of tenuousness, while living exciting and dramatic international lives. Two of them—Mulgan and Davin—are central to New Zealand literary history, but it is stretching things a little to include the others, even though they are writers—journalists and memoirists—in a broader sense. There are others who might have been included, notably Robin Hyde, who also travelled extensively—like Bertram she had experience of China that was vital to her work. Even though the Rhodes Scholarship connection does not apply to her, her life is a natural companion to the others. Was she overlooked because of her gender? In fact she does find mention here and there, as does Charles Brasch, who was presumably excluded from the pantheon because he is a less exciting figure. In short, there are holes in this book that a critic could drive a herd of elephants through. In spite of that it is an enjoyable volume, and an enriching one. Interconnections are shown that more focused studies fail to point up, and the style of the writing has the tone of a novel, drawing the reader into the locations and events in a more vivid manner than most biographies can do.

In contrast, Vincent O'Sullivan's biography of John Mulgan, *Long Journey to the Border*, is more conventional, more disciplined, and more reliable. As a literary biography it has a paradoxical feature: it demonstrates that this author of an iconic New Zealand novel, and the son of a man devoted to the art of fiction, was actually more interested in other things. Even as a student of literature, an editor of literary magazines and an assistant to the mighty Oxford University Press, his mind was elsewhere. He was conscious of the huge political events and social changes taking place in the world around them and wanted to be a significant part of them. In the end he fought as a brilliant partisan with Greek guerrilla fighters against German occupation. O'Sullivan presents this paradox in an honest yet restrained manner. The excitement of the story he tells never leads him—as it does McNeish—into extravagant rhetorical flourishes or startling imagery. He simply presents the facts as he has found them. Inevitably—as in all biographies—there are gaps between them that call out for interpretation. With cool detachment, O'Sullivan leaves those interpretations in the reader's hands. There are moments in Mulgan's life, notably the Rhodes Scholarship debacle and his ultimate suicide, that have always seemed mysterious. O'Sullivan makes no attempt to solve the mysteries. He even creates another: was Mulgan a homosexual? Rather than answer such questions, he leaves them open. Although there is a fundamental honesty in such an approach, there is also some frustration for the reader because, even though evidence is presented, it never seems to be quite enough to provide grounds for a clear answer. The most useful function of the book, no doubt, is to provide a context for the novel *Man Alone*, although even here O'Sullivan plays a tantalizing game, suggesting that it is not really a very good book, nor worthy of its iconic status, while Mulgan's brief memoir or long essay *Report on Experience* is given a more positive evaluation.

Stuart Murray's essay, 'John Mulgan at the Clarendon Press' (*JNZL* 21[2003] 73–82), has been made virtually redundant by O'Sullivan's biography of Mulgan. Murray has little to say that we cannot read or infer from O'Sullivan's book. His account of the conflict revolving around Auden's *Oxford Book of Light Verse* [1938], when Mulgan was embroiled in a controversy with the Delegates of the Press, is a little more detailed than in O'Sullivan. Murray's attempt to provide a background to the conditions under which *Man Alone* was written is, however, of little merit in comparison with the much broader context O'Sullivan is able to provide in a book-length study.

Bill Pearson is a vaguely acknowledged yet frequently ignored ancestor in the New Zealand literary canon. Some reasons for this semi-neglect can be gleaned from Jeffrey Paparoa Holman's very personal obituary article, 'Under-Read, Underwritten, Undercover: William Harrison (Bill) Pearson, 1922–2002' (*Landfall* 205[2003] 152–7). One reason is that his one fine novel, *Coal Flat* [1963], was already out of date when it appeared. Its heavy realistic style, refusing to acknowledge the claims of fantasy, and almost those of imagination, was an echo of the 'Sargeson School' of the 1930s and 1940s. This was partly because of the long gestation of the novel—by the time it was completed its day had virtually passed. Holman reveals that it was also due to Pearson's conservative reading habits—he read nothing of postwar fiction, and his 'Cold War Anti-Americanism' blinded him to the experiments of Updike, say, or Heller. Even more problematic was Pearson's homosexuality at a time when this was both scorned and illegal. This led him to revise and rewrite his novel again and again— hence the long gestation period. In the revisions he eliminated the homosexual passions of his protagonist, leaving 'a somewhat bloodless ideologue, a mouthpiece for laudable intentions, but really a product of Pearson's self-mutilation' (p. 156). This suggests a flaw at the heart of what is otherwise a quite powerful book, and a sense of this 'absence' must surely limit readers' appreciation. Sadly, this inability to present his own sexuality in fiction is a major reason for his silence as a novelist once *Coal Flat* had been completed. Pearson devoted himself to left-wing causes and Polynesian writing, and made a worthy contribution to their dissemination, but the loss of the novelist's creativity must, as Holman acknowledges, be a major factor contributing to his being 'under-read'.

The death of Bill Sewell also prompted a re-evaluation, in *NZB*, which he had co-edited for five years. In *NZB* 13:i[2003] 3–4, Brian Turner asks why Sewell has been neglected by anthologists, and answers his own question with the comment, 'Perhaps it's because his poetry has never been tricksy [*sic*], etiolated, fey or plumped. Mostly his work is pared down, direct, lyrically restrained (but often deftly lyrical for all that), terse, acerbic. ... His poems, one should say, are clearly the work of a candid, serious-minded writer perturbed about matters of grave human concern' (p. 3). On this basis, Turner goes on to assess Sewell's poems, concentrating on his balance between the political and the private and especially on his unpretentious but (usually) extremely effective language.

Mary Taylor, novelist, letter-writer, friend of Charlotte Brontë and emigrant to New Zealand, is not unknown. Joan Stevens and other scholars of colonial women's lives have explored and presented her writings. It is still of interest to see them reconsidered in Bekki Cardwell's '"Living as I do in 2 places at once": The Inscription of Displacement in the Writing of Mary Taylor' (*JNZL* 21[2003] 147–64). Taylor's descriptions of a woman's life in early Wellington are of great historical interest. Cardwell makes no original contribution in terms of ideas or interpretation but she does present the material in a lively way and with awareness of recent postcolonial debates. As the subtitle suggests, she also brings fashionable terminology to bear on the subject, which has the effect of making it appear more relevant to current interests.

As a minor literary curiosity, Kirsti Bohata and Roger Robinson have unearthed a successor to Julius Vogel's utopian novel *Anno Domini 2000, or, Woman's Destiny* [1899] and have presented their finding in 'Vogel in Wales: *Anno Domini 2000*, "Lady Gwen" and the Federated Empire' (*JNZL* 21[2003] 140–6). The incomplete novel, 'Lady Gwen, or, The Days That Are To Be. By a Welsh Nationalist', was published in the journal *Cymru Fydd* in 1890–91. The anonymous author directly acknowledges that it is based on Vogel's vision of a federated British empire. Bohata and Robinson argue rather pugnaciously for its historical significance, but it is surely no more than a second-level text in the movement for 'Imperial Federation', more fully documented and discussed by Keith Sinclair. Bibliographers will be pleased at the discovery, but the literary and socio-political value of the fragment is not great.

Worthy of note in Pacific studies, and neglected in earlier surveys, is a bibliography, 'Creative Writing by Solomon Islanders Listed in Chronological Order', compiled by Julian Treadaway (*Mana* 13:i[2001] 143–7).

A broad study of Anglophone Polynesian poetry was presented as an essay-review of a new anthology, itself an important contribution to Pacific literature: Wendt, Whaitiri and Sullivan, eds., *Whetu Moana: Contemporary Polynesian Poems in English*. The review was 'Ocean-Going Craft: The Writing of Contemporary Polynesia' (*Landfall* 206[2003] 21–38) by Philip Armstrong. His central thesis is that despite the huge diversity of background cultures subsumed under the term 'Polynesian', the anthology and the literatures it represents are not a 'confused babble. Rather, the reader gains a clear sense of a complex conversation, a structure of shared experiences and concerns' (p. 21). The ocean that divides them is also a powerful factor the varied cultures share, and the act of trans-oceanic travel is a symbol of the network of interconnections between individuals and peoples. The English language also has an ambivalent character in these poems: it is the language of colonization and also the language binding the work of multi-lingual authors. Like the ocean itself, the language can divide or unite and care must be taken to ensure that it does the latter. The poems are *waka*, a means of transport between the islands. As the Polynesian cultures regroup, they 'possess related, but distinct, experiences of home and of its loss, of birth and death, of the negotiation between origins and destination' (p. 28). Armstrong makes a stimulating—but not entirely valid—distinction between the 'linear' travel of the colonizers and a back-and-forth ethos in the colonized cultures. The migrants from Britain have a 'one-way ticket' but the Polynesians as they travel use 'two-way ticket(s)'. The persistent belief among European New Zealanders that they 'have no history' in the islands stands in contrast to the Polynesian sense of tradition and of the closeness of ancestors. This black and white distinction is a useful crutch but ultimately untrue, since genealogy—the search for ancestors—is a passion among European New Zealanders, and awareness of history has grown exponentially, as the voyages of young people to Gallipoli and the immense popularity of Michael King's *Penguin History of New Zealand* [2003] testify. Nonetheless Armstrong's concept of an 'alternative history' based on 'ancient routes' as a contrast to industrial globalization deserves further exploration. Another distinction he points to could also be a path for further research and speculation: 'There are plenty of poems about identity: angry resistance to definition by outsiders, celebrations of ancestries, laments about sundered kinships and repressed histories. But there are no rhapsodies to the deep self, no soul searching expeditions into the dark heart of the psyche' (p. 37). The Polynesian concept of identity is communal; that of the European is individual: such distinctions are, I fear, simplistic, but they can be used as a basis for more differentiated studies. Armstrong goes some way along the path of more sophisticated study by discussing in some detail the idea of ancestry—which includes gods and the natural world—as presented in these poems, and further by discussing the 'decolonisation of the body'—the celebration of physical difference—in a writer like Sia Figiel. In short, Philip Armstrong offers some stimulation to thought that deserves close attention by those who wish to examine more deeply the distinctions implicit in the literatures of the Pacific.

Pacific literature in English, even when written by indigenous people, owes much to the works of Melville and Stevenson, who created images of colonized Polynesia that have proven to be pervasive. Either as models or as outsiders in need of correction, they have been starting points for a wide range of opinions, images and counter-images. For the sake of historical perspective it is therefore necessary to return to them again and again. Now Roger Robinson has collected, in *Robert Louis Stevenson: His Best Pacific Writings*, what, as the title indicates, he rather contentiously calls the 'best' of Stevenson's autobiographical and fictional writing about the Pacific area. Extracts from longer works predominate, but there are also complete short stories, notably 'The Bottle Imp' and 'The

Beach of Falesá'. As a guide to readers Robinson has written introductions and connecting texts. His own prose is fluent and often mellifluous, but that cannot seal over some rather large cracks in the information provided. Furthermore the guidance provided is often insistent to the point of being polemical. Robinson's enthusiasm for Stevenson is infectious—he becomes so involved that he refers to as 'Fanny' the woman Stevenson himself calls 'Mrs Stevenson'—which is no doubt of value in arousing the interest of students and beginners, but it also tends to run away with him so that he insists that the reader must read as he does, adopting a sometimes tiresomely overbearing tone. It is in keeping with this enthusiastic insistence that superlatives are used more widely than just in the book's title: 'The Beach at Falesá' is said to be 'one of the most finely crafted works of narratorial art in English fiction' (p. 176). It is impossible to confirm or refute such a sweeping statement without writing at length on the subject. Its purpose seems to be to make the reader duly respectful before starting out on the story itself. In general, the placing of such comments as introductions seems to insist that the reader must agree with the editor's assessment—or else.

The commentary is interpretative rather than informative, so that students might look in vain for explanations they require. For example, the focus on the Pacific means that Stevenson's Scottish and European vocabulary and references are usually left unexplained. On page 25 I was puzzled by the phrase 'the sleeping space divided off by an endlong coaming'. My *Shorter Oxford* tells me that 'coaming' is from 'dialect' and 'slang'. Other terms used by Stevenson are from the language of seamen, and again it is too much to expect student readers to cope with these without some assistance. In place of such practical information Robinson offers us polemical interpretation. Furthermore, extraction from a longer work often and inevitably means that the writer refers back to a part of his text that is not in the excerpt, and this is precisely where annotation would be most useful. For example on pages 34–5 there are references to a Dr Turner and a Mr Whalon. The broader context of the original text would explain these; in the extract an editor's note would be most helpful. Most problematic about the presentation is that it is often unclear to the uninformed (i.e. to the readers most in need of a selected edition in the first place) precisely how the various extracts relate to each other. The bibliographical information is too skimpy for the reader to locate the sources of each extract. Since the arrangement is thematic rather than chronological the vitally important question of *when* a passage was written—before or after some other passage—remains unanswered.

On the whole, the strengths of this book are Stevenson's. He writes of Pacific places and people with acute observation, cultural awareness, and a ready sympathy. He is curious about the cultural life of Polynesia before the European invasion and finds enough remnants of it to paint a lively and convincing picture. But he is without sentimentality and is also accepting of the culture arising from the blend of Polynesia and Europe. At his best, Robinson characterizes this writing well, as in his comment, 'Time and again Stevenson surprises his reader, goes under first impressions and interweaves anecdote, character, dialogue and drama into his descriptions, always the lively and engaging travel writer rather than anthropologist.' The question remains: is it the editor's task to pre-empt the reader's assessment or rather to guide the reader through the potential difficulties of the text?

The comprehensive bibliography at the back of Paul Sharrad's *Albert Wendt and Pacific Literature: Circling the Void* is a model of the kind of information that is lacking in Robinson's book. Indeed it provides an invaluable service to all students of Pacific literature. Sharrad uses it as the basis of a wide-ranging study of this most central Polynesian writer—Albert Wendt, the poet, novelist, playwright, essayist and university professor—who has done more than any other individual to create a vision of what literature in the Pacific might be. Sharrad's skills as a presenter are admirable, and they are at their best in the chapters and passages of his book that deal with Wendt's theoretical ideas about the relationship between literature and society. He is able to summarize, muster and clarify the concepts in a way that makes them seem more coherent and comprehensible when one returns to Wendt's own writing, and this is a service that must be acknowledged. Sharrad's skills as an analyst and critic are less notable, at least in this book, so that even in the chapters on individual works it is exposition rather than commentary that is of greatest value. Of course he does more than merely summarize plots: he tells us of the biographical and broader social background that provides a context for these works of literature. But he does little to interpret them, and his evaluations seem to be based on the assumption that closeness to biography and social reality is a sufficient virtue in itself. If this were so, one might ask why Wendt does not confine himself to essay-writing. The creative function of fiction and its aesthetic features deserve more attention than they are given here. Nevertheless, this is a solid, dependable book and its bibliographical qualities are of a very high order. Nobody who reads it need fear that any work of Wendt's has been neglected, and the same goes for the reviews and critical essays that have been devoted to them, which are conscientiously reviewed in this volume.

We need ask no more of it than that, since its stated purpose is to make 'an attempt to help readers "do their homework" and produced informed readings of Pacific writing' (p. 20). Note the broad application of the last phrase. While focusing on Albert Wendt, Paul Sharrad has the whole pattern of Pacific literature in mind, as his subtitle suggests. Because Wendt is so central and because he has inspired many who came after him, he provides a good springboard for a leap into the wider ocean. Many other important writers are mentioned in passing: not all, however. The implication that Wendt was the 'first' Pacific writer is not quite accurate either. He would be sure to acknowledge the influence of writers who came into the Pacific from the outside—Stevenson, Melville and others—even if the 'influence' is often a matter of setting up a force to resist. And the pivotal influence of Alistair Campbell, who shifted in his poetry from an outsider's to an insider's view of Polynesia, demonstrating in his own person the direction that was to be taken, has often been gracefully acknowledged by Wendt. The absence of Campbell from Sharrad's book is the one major gap in a study that otherwise provides a very useful introduction to the field.

Books Reviewed

Adams, Paul, and Lee Christopher, eds. *Frank Hardy and the Literature of Commitment*. VP. [2003] pp. 291. pb $A39.95 ISBN 0 9580 7941 2.

Agrawal, B.R., and M.P. Sinha. *Major Trends in Post-Independence Indian English Fiction*. Atlantic. [2003] pp. vi +278. Rs550 ISBN 8 1269 0294 9.

Arthur, J.M. *The Default Country: A Lexical Cartography of Twentieth-Century Australia*. UNSW. [2003] pp. 216. pb $A39.95 ISBN 0 8684 0542 6.

Barrowman, Rachel. *Mason: The Life of R.A.K. Mason*. VictUP. [2003] pp. 455. pb $NZ49.95 ISBN 0 8647 3463 8.

Bennett, Bruce, Susan Cowan, Jacqueline Lo, Satendra Nandan, and Jen Webb, eds. *Resistance and Reconciliation: Writing in the Commonwealth*. ACLALS. [2003] pp. xvii +396. pb $A25 ISBN 0 6464 2112 3.

Bess Montgomery, Georgene. 'Ifa as a Paradigm for the Interpretation of Caribbean and African-American Literature'. Dissertation, University of Maryland, College Park. [2002]. DA 3078242.

Bierbaum, Nina, Syd Harrex, and Sue Hosking, eds. *The Regenerative Spirit*, Vol. 1: *Polarities of Home and Away, Encounters and Diasporas, in Post-colonial Literatures*. Lythrum. [2003] pp. x + 220. pb $A29.95 ISBN 0 9751 2602 4.

Blodgett, E.D. *Five-Part Invention: A History of Literary History in Canada*. UTorP. [2003] pp. 371. $65 ISBN 0 8020 4801 3.

Bose, Brinda, ed. *Amitav Ghosh: Critical Perspectives*. PencraftI. [2003] pp. 221. £28.50 ISBN 8 1857 5352 0.

Branche, Jerome, ed. *Lo que teníamos que tener: raza y revolución en Nicolás Guillén*. Instituto Internacional de Literatura Iberoamericana. [2003] pp. vi +275. $27 ISBN 1 9307 4411 0.

Braziel, Jana Evans, and Anita Mannur, eds. *Theorising Diaspora: A Reader*. Blackwell. [2003] pp. ix +345. hb £55, ISBN 0 6312 3391 1 pb £16.99 ISBN 0 6312 3392 X.

Burton, Antoinette. *Dwelling in the Archive: Women Writing House, Home and History in Late Colonial India*. OUP. [2003] pp. x + 202. pb £13.50 ISBN 0 1951 4425 2.

Burton, Antoinette, ed. *After the Imperial Turn: Thinking With and Through the Nation*. DukeUP. [2003] pp. 369. £18.95 ISBN 0 8223 3106 3.

Das, Bijay Kumar. *Postmodern Indian English Literature*. Atlantic. [2003] pp. 162. Rs500 ISBN 8 1269 0258 2.

Davidson, Arnold E., Priscilla L. Walton, and Jennifer Andrews. *Border Crossings: Thomas King's Cultural Inversions*. UTorP. [2003] pp. 223. $35 ISBN 0 8020 4134 5.

Döring, Tobias. *Caribbean–English Passages: Intertextuality in a Postcolonial Tradition*. Routledge. [2003] pp. vii +236. $105 ISBN 0 4152 5584 8.

Doyle, James. *Progressive Heritage: The Evolution of a Politically Radical Literary Tradition in Canada*. WLUP. [2002] pp. 322. $29.95 ISBN 0 8892 0397 0.

Eden, Edward, and Dee Goertz, eds. *Carol Shields, Narrative Hunger, and the Possibilities of Fiction*. UTorP. [2003] pp. 323. $60 ISBN 0 8020 3660 0.

Fludernik, Monika, ed. *Diaspora and Multiculturalism: Common Traditions and New Developments*. Rodopi. [2003] pp. xxxviii +391. hb €115 ($144) ISBN 9 0420 0916 0, pb €50 ($63) ISBN 9 0420 0906 3.

Ghosh, Amitav. *The Imam and the Indian: Prose Pieces*. Ravi Dayal. [2002] pp. xiv +361. Rs495 ISBN 8 1753 0047 7.

Gifford, William T. *Narrative and the Nature of Worldview in the Clare Savage Novels of Michelle Cliff*. Lang. [2003] pp. vii +130. $55 ISBN 0 8204 4591 6.

Goulbourne, Jean. *Woman Song*. Peepal Tree. [2002] pp. vi +48. $13 ISBN 1 9007 1503 1.

Grace, Sherrill, and Albert-Reiner Glaap, eds. *Performing National Identities: International Perspectives on Contemporary Canadian Theatre*. Talonbooks. [2003] pp. 320. $19.95 ISBN 0 8892 2475 7.

Grossman, Michele, ed. *Blacklines: Contemporary Critical Writing by Indigenous Australians*. MelbourneUP. [2003] pp. xiii +244. pb $A34.95 ISBN 0 5228 5069 3.

Hasluck, Nicholas. *The Legal Labyrinth: The Kisch Case and Other Reflections*. Freshwater Bay Press. [2003] pp. 253. $A24.95 ISBN 1 7400 8240 0.

Heiss, Anita M. *Dhuuluu-Yala = To Talk Straight: Publishing Indigenous Literature*. AStP [2003] pp. ix +318. pb $A34.95 ISBN 0 8557 5444 3.

Henricksen, Noel. *Island and Otherland: Christopher Koch and his Books*. Educare. [2003] pp. 356. $A29.95 ISBN 1 7405 1272 3.

Hogan, Patrick Colm, and Lalita Pandit, eds. *Rabindranath Tagore: Universality and Tradition*. FDUP. [2003] pp. 297. £35.95 ISBN 0 8386 3980 1.

Huggan, Graham. *The Postcolonial Exotic: Marketing the Margins*. Routledge. [2001] pp. xvi +328. hb £65 ISBN 0 4152 5033 1, pb £17.99 ISBN 0 4152 5034 X.

Huk, Romana, ed. *Assembling Alternatives: Reading Postmodern Poetries Transnationally*. WesleyanUP. [2003] pp. ix +412. $25 ISBN 0 8195 6539 3.

Ingles, Ernie B., and N. Merrill Distad, eds. *Peel's Bibliography of the Canadian Prairies to 1953*. UTorP. [2003] pp. 900. $80 ISBN 0 8020 4825 0.

James, Cynthia. *The Maroon Narrative: Caribbean Literature in English across Boundaries, Ethnicities, and Centuries*. Heinemann. [2003] pp. vii +134. $62 ISBN 0 3250 7099 7.

John, Catherine A. *Clear Word and Third Sight: Folk Groundings and Diasporic Consciousness in African Caribbean Writing*. DukeUP. [2003] pp. vii +241. $75 ISBN 0 8223 3232 9.

Jones, Lawrence. *Picking Up the Traces: The Making of a New Zealand Literary Culture 1932–1945*. VictUP. [2003] pp. 520. $NZ49.95 ISBN 0 8647 3455 7.

Kafka, Philippa. *On the Outside Looking In(dian): Indian Women Writers at Home and Abroad*. Lang. [2003] pp. xii +223. £22.56 ISBN 0 8204 5812 0.

Khair, Tabish, ed. *Amitav Ghosh: A Critical Companion*. Permanent Black. [2003] pp. vii +185. Rs500 ISBN 8 1782 4074 2.

Khatri, C.L., ed. *Indian Literature in English: Critical Discourses*. Book Enclave. [2003] pp. viii +248. Rs480 ISBN 8 1815 2021 1.

Khoo, Tseen-Ling. *Banana-Bending: Asian-Australian and Asian-Canadian Literatures*. HongKongUP/McG–QUP. [2003] pp. viii +223. pb $HK235 ($CAN65) ISBN 9 6220 9630 1.

King, Bruce. *V.S. Naipaul*. Palgrave. [2003] pp. ix +230. $60 ISBN 1 4039 0455 3.

Kumar, Amitava, ed. *Away: The Indian Writer as an Expatriate*. Routledge. [2003] pp. xxvi +386. hb £55 ISBN 0 4159 6896 8, pb £13.99 ISBN 0 4159 6897 6.

Kumar, Amitava, ed. *World Bank Literature*. UMinnP. [2003] pp. xxxiii +307. £16 ISBN 0 8166 3836 5.

Kuortti Joel. *Tense Past, Tense Present: Women Writing in English*. Stree. [2003] pp. 235. Rs450 ISBN 8 1856 0458 4.

Lane, Richard J., Rod Mengham, and Philip Tew. *Contemporary British Fiction*. Polity. [2003] pp. x + 276. hb £50 ISBN 0 7456 2866 4, pb £15.99 ISBN 0 7456 2867 2.

Leandoer, Katarina. *From Colonial Expression to Export Commodity: English-Canadian Literature in Canada and Sweden, 1945–1999*. Uppsala. [2002] pp. 273. $51.50 ISBN 9 1554 5237 X.

Leggott, Michele, ed. *Young Knowledge: The Poems of Robin Hyde*. AucklandUP. [2003] pp. xvi +399. pb $NZ49.99 ISBN 1 8694 0298 7.

Lucking, David. *The Serpent's Part: Narrating The Self in Canadian Literature*. Lang. [2003] pp. 211. £26 ISBN 3 0391 0039 4.

Madsen Deborah L., ed. *Beyond the Borders: American Literature and Post-Colonial Theory*. Pluto. [2003] pp. 272. hb $80 ISBN 0 7453 2046 5, pb $24.95 ISBN 0 7453 2045 7.

Mahabir, Joy A.I. *Miraculous Weapons: Revolutionary Ideology in Caribbean Culture*. Routledge. [2003] pp. vii +167. $59 ISBN 0 8204 6155 5.

Makris, Paula Catherine. 'Colonial Education and Cultural Inheritance: Caribbean Literature and the Classics'. Dissertation. Case Western Reserve University. [2002]. DA 3058354.

Mair, Christian, ed. *The Politics of English as a World Language: New Horizons in Postcolonial Cultural Studies*. Rodopi. [2003] pp. ix +497. $131 (£35) ISBN 9 0420 0876 8.

Maufort, Marc. *Transgressive Itineraries: Postcolonial Hybridizations of Dramatic Realism*. Lang. [2003] pp. 250. pb €29.90 (£20) ISBN 9 0520 1178 8.

McLaren, John. *Free Radicals: On the Left in Postwar Melbourne*. ASP. [2003] pp. xi +386. $A39.95 ISBN 1 7409 7025 X.

McNeish, James. *Dance of the Peacocks: New Zealanders in Exile in the Time of Hitler and Mao Tse Tung*. RandomH. [2003] pp. 480. pb $NZ29.95 ISBN 1 8694 1564 7.

Mehrotra, Arvind Krishna, ed. *A History of Indian Literature in English*. Hurst. [2003] pp. xxii +406. hb £45 ISBN 1 8506 5680 0, pb £17.50 ISBN 1 8506 5681 9.

Monahan, Sean. *A Long and Winding Road: Xavier Herbert's Literary Journey*. UWAP. [2003] pp. xi +322. $A38.95 ISBN 1 8762 6893 X.

Moss, Laura, ed. *Is Canada Postcolonial? Unsettling Canadian Literature*. WLUP. [2003] pp. 368. $34.95 ISBN 0 8892 0416 0.

Narain, Denise deCaires. *Contemporary Caribbean Women's Poetry: Making Style*. Routledge. [2002] pp. vii +260. $105 ISBN 0 4153 4060 8.

Nasta, Susheila. *Home Truths: Fictions of the South Asian Diaspora in Britain*. Palgrave. [2002] pp. xi +305. £52.50 ISBN 0 3336 7005 1.

Natale, Antonella Riem, and Roberto, Albarea, eds. *The Art of Partnership: Essays on Literature, Culture, Language and Education Towards a Cooperative Paradigm*. Actions of the International Convention of Studies, Udine, 14–15 June 2002. [2003] pp. 224. €15 ISBN 1 7400 8240 0.

Oboe, Annalisa, ed. *Mongrel Signatures: Reflections on the Work of Mudrooroo*. Rodopi. [2003] pp. xxi +236. hb €60 ISBN 9 0420 0964 8, pb €26 ISBN 9 0420 0974 8.

O'Grady, Jean, and Wang Ning, eds. *Northrop Frye: Eastern and Western Perspectives*. UTorP. [2003] pp. 183. $53 ISBN 0 8020 3720 8.

O'Sullivan, Vincent. *Long Journey to the Border: A Life of John Mulgan*. Penguin. [2003] pp. 368. pb $NZ45.95 ISBN 0 1430 1871 X.

Page, Kezia, '"Kingston 21": Diaspora, Migrancy and Caribbean Literature'. Dissertation. University of Miami. [2002] DA 3071266.

Pollock, Sheldon, ed. *Literary Cultures in History: Reconstructions from South Asia*. UCalP. [2003] pp. xxix +1,066. £51.95 ISBN 0 5202 2821 9.

Prasad, Amar Nath, ed. *New Light on Indian Women Novelists in English*. Sarup. [2003] pp. xiii +220. Rs400 ISBN 8 1762 5367 7.

Roberts, Andrew Michael, and Jonathan Allison, eds. *Poetry and Contemporary Culture: The Question of Values*. EdinUP. [2003] pp. 240. $76 ISBN 0 7486 1137 1.

Robinson, Roger, ed. *Robert Louis Stevenson: His Best Pacific Writings*. Streamline. [2003] pp. 320. pb $NZ34.95 ISBN 0 9582 1062 4.

Rosenthal, Caroline. *Narrative Deconstructions of Gender in Works by Audrey Thomas, Daphne Marlatt, and Louise Erdrich*. CamdenH. [2003] 193. $60 ISBN 1 5711 3267 8.

Sandhu, Sukhdev. *London Calling: How Black and Asian Writers Imagined a City*. HC. [2003] pp. 498. £20 ISBN 0 0025 7182 X.

Sankaran, Chitra, Liew-Geok Leong, and Rajeev S. Patke, eds. *Complicities: Connections and Divisions. Perspectives on Literatures and Cultures of the Asia-Pacific Region*. Lang. [2003] pp. 361. $54.95 ISBN 3 9067 7048 6.

Schafer, Elizabeth, and Susan Bradley Smith, eds. *Playing Australia: Australian Theatre and the International Stage*. Rodopi. [2003] pp. ix +230 + 13 plates. pb €50 ISBN 9 0420 0817 2.

Sharrad, Paul. *Albert Wendt and Pacific Literature: Circling the Void*. AucklandUP. [2003] pp. xvi +296. pb $NZ44.99 ISBN 1 8694 0303 7.

Singh, Khushwant. *The End of India*. Penguin. [2003] pp. 163. pb £7.99 ISBN 0 1430 2994 0.

Stouck, David. *Ethel Wilson: A Critical Biography*. UTorP. [2003] pp. 353. $50 ISBN 0 8020 8741 8.

Strongman Roberto. 'Allegorical I/Lands: Personal and National Development in Caribbean Autobiographical Writing'. Dissertation. University of California, San Diego. [2003] DA 3090454.

Sturm, Terry. *An Unsettled Spirit: The Life and Frontier Fiction of Edith Lyttleton (G.B. Lancaster)*. AucklandUP. [2003] pp. xii +308. pb $NZ44.99 ISBN 1 8694 0294 4.

Tabron, Judith L. *Postcolonial Literature from Three Continents: Tuotola, H.D., Ellison, and White*. Lang. [2003] pp. xii +234. £42 ISBN 0 8204 5238 6.

Taylor, Ula Yvette. *The Veiled Garvey: The Life and Times of Amy Jacques Garvey*. UNCP. [2003] pp. ix +310. $19 ISBN 0 8078 5386 0.

Teo, Hsu-Ming, and Richard White, eds. *Cultural History in Australia*. UNSW. [2003] pp. 288. pb $A39.95 ISBN 0 8684 0589 2.

Tew, Philip. *The Contemporary British Novel*. Continuum. [2003] pp. xv +205. hb £55 ISBN 0 8264 7349 0, pb £14.99 ISBN 0 8264 7350 4.

vanden Driesen, Cynthia, and Satendra Nandan, eds. *Austral-Asian Encounters: From Literature and Women's Studies to Politics and Tourism*. PrestigeB. [2003] pp. 440. $35 ISBN 8 1755 1131 1.

Wendt, Albert, Reina Whaitiri, and Robert Sullivan, eds. *Whetu Moana: Contemporary Polynesian Poems in English*. AucklandUP. [2003] pp. 288. $NZ44 ISBN 1 8694 0 273 1.

Whitehead, Anne. *Bluestocking in Patagonia: Mary Gilmore's Quest for Love and Utopia at the World's End*. Profile. [2003] pp. 312. £14.99 ISBN 1 8619 7504 X.

Wildburger, Eleonore. *Politics, Power and Poetry: An Intercultural Perspective on Aboriginal Identity in Black Australian Poetry*. Stauffenburg. [2003] pp. 208. €40 ISBN 3 8605 7319 5.

Wilson, Sharon Rose. *Margaret Atwood's Textual Assassinations: Recent Poetry and Fiction*. OSUP. [2003] pp. 200. $44.95 ISBN 0 8142 0929 7, CD-ROM $9.95 ISBN 0 8142 9012 4.

Woodcock, Bruce. *Peter Carey*. 2nd edn. ManUP. [2003] pp. x + 223. pb £11.99 ISBN 0 7190 6798 7.

Yadav, Saryug, and Prasad Amar Nath, eds. *Studies in Indian Drama in English*. Prakash. [2003] pp. 197. Rs150 ISBN 8 1797 7081 8.

XVIII

Bibliography and Textual Criticism

WILLIAM BAKER AND PAUL WEBB

This year's work in bibliography and textual criticism begins on a sad note. In the last survey we commented that 'a journal that still fortunately survives even in the electronic age is the *Bulletin of Bibliography*' (*YWES* 83[2003] 1031). It is with regret that we record the demise of this important journal of enumerative bibliography, which came into existence in 1897. Its death may owe something to the death of its editor, Bernard F. McTigue. In recent years, the Greenwood Publishing Group had taken over the journal from Faxon, who published it for many years. For more than a century the *Bulletin of Bibliography* was an important source of checklists recording the output of many writers. In many instances it still remains the definitive repository of record for scholars and librarians, and its contributions were annually included in the *Bibliographic Index* published since 1937. Given the essential and ephemeral nature of bibliographical checklists put out on the world-wide web and their lack of any overall authoritative control, the passing of this refereed journal constitutes a serious loss for scholarship. It is only to be hoped that it will be quickly be resurrected. Currently its disappearance it is just one further illustration of the destruction of information which is taking place at the present time.

The Papers of the Bibliographical Society of America appear quarterly and maintains its tradition of publishing articles and reviews of the highest standard. Staffan Fogelmark's 'The Anonymous Rome 1522 "Chrysoloras": A Newly Discovered Greek Press' (*PBSA* 97[2003] 5–42), examines the 1522 printing in Rome of Chrysoloras' *Erotemata*. Vernon Guy Dickson widens 'our understanding of Ralph Crane as a scrivener and editor (a mediator) of Shakespeare's works' (p. 44) in his 'What "I Will": Mediating Subjects; Or, Ralph Crane and the Folio's *Tempest*' (*PBSA* 97[2003] 43–56). His article concludes with an appendix of 'The Folio Plays, in Folio Order, Correlated by Compositor' (pp. 53–6). A similar area is explored in Eugene Giddens's 'The Final Stage of Printing Ben Jonson's "Works", 1640–1' (*PBSA* 97[2003] 57–68). Giddens focuses upon the printing of the Folio of *The Sad Shepherd, 1640–1641*. Maximillian E. Novak's '"A Narrative of the Proceedings in France": Reattributing a De-Attributed Work by Defoe' (*PBSA* 97[2003] 69–80) again addresses the very complicated issue of attributing work to Defoe and takes issue

Year's Work in English Studies, Volume 84 (2005) © The English Association; all rights reserved. For permissions, please email: journals.permissions@oxfordjournals.org

doi: 10.1093/ywes/mai018

with conclusions in P.N. Furbank and W.R. Owen's *Defoe De-Attributions* [1994]. In 'Bibliographical Notes' Keith Arbour addresses the problem of 'Where Was John Davenport's 1669 Massachusetts Election Sermon Printed?' (*PBSA* 97[2003] 81–7) and concludes that 'Davenport's election sermon ([London]: Printed [by John Darby?] in the Year, 1670) should be struck from early American imprints lists' (p. 87). Arthur Sherbo's 'From the 1818 Sale Catalogue of the Greater Portion of the Library of the Late Edmond Malone, Esq.' (*PBSA* 97[2003] 89–91) contains extracts from 'a number items of interest to book collectors and bibliophiles' (p. 89). J.D. Fleeman's two-volume *A Bibliography of the Works of Samuel Johnson* is the subject of an extensive review essay by Shef Rogers (*PBSA* 97[2003] 93–8). Rogers concludes that the 'bibliography now becomes a fundamental part of Johnsonian scholarship and will require the collective efforts of all Johnsonians to enrich the legacy that David Fleeman has left us' (p. 98). To return to articles, Mari Agata's 'Stop-Press Variants in the Gutenberg Bible: The First Report of the Collation' (*PBSA* 97[2003] 139–65) contains twenty-two illustrations taken from a copy of the Gutenberg at Keio University Library and Cambridge University Library. She concludes that her collation 'proves the usefulness of applying digital technology … especially as regards the detection of … subtle stop-press variants'. A further 'twenty stop-press variants were detected on thirteen pages of the same setting, which had previously assumed to be identical'. Such evidence might well provide 'a further clue to a reconstruction of the practices' in the Gutenberg Bible 'printing house' (pp. 163, 165). Joseph A. Dane's 'Note of Some Fifteenth-Century Types of Johannes Koelhoff' (*PBSA* 97[2003] 167–82) is illustrated with four examples from the Henry E. Huntington Library. 'Koelhoff was active as a printer in Cologne from 1472 to 1492 and is generally considered essential to histories of early printing techniques and book production' (p. 167). The next article moves forward to the nineteenth-century. Clare Imholtz, in 'The History of Lewis Carroll's *The Game of Logic*' (*PBSA* 97[2003] 183–213), examines the 1886 edition, which was suppressed by Dodgson. Five illustrations accompanying add to a fascinating history of the book which provides 'further insight into Dodgson at work' (p. 211). There are two appendices: 'Changes Marked by Dodgson in the 1886 Proof Copy' and 'Title-Pages—Detailed Changes'—a comparison of four title pages utilizing Dodgson's ink corrections (pp. 212–13). An earlier nineteenth-century publication is the preoccupation of Walter Sauer's 'A Classic Is Born: The "Childhood" of *Struwwelpeter*' (*PBSA* 97[2003] 215–63). Sauer's article considers *Struwwelpeter*'s 'genesis and early publication history' first published in Frankfort in 1845 (pp. 215–16). Replete with eight sets of multiple illustrations from title pages, covers, and various other images, plus an appendix on 'The Evolution of the "*Struwwelpeter* Canon" 1845–7' (p. 261), Sauer's is an extensive description of 'the most popular and influential German children's book ever written' (p. 262).

Seth Lerer's 'Medieval Literature and Early Modern Readers: Cambridge University Library Sel. 5.51–5.63' (*PBSA* 97[2003] 311–32) examines 'a group of quartos now identified by their shelf-marks' now at Cambridge University Library (p. 311). Lerer's 'purpose … is to describe the contents … to identify … earliest known owners and readers, and to explain the literary and historical context for … [the] assembly and reception' of the Quartos (p. 312). There is an appendix on annotation in the volumes (pp. 330–2). Lerer argues that the 'texts, though printed in the early sixteenth-century, were assembled in the later sixteenth-century, and that their generic, thematic, and authorial associations contribute to our understanding of recusant reading tastes in post-Reformation England' (p. 312). Chiaki Hanabusa, in 'Shared Printing in Robert Wilson's *The Cobbler's Prophecy* (1594)' (*PBSA* 97[2003] 333–49), investigates the printing habits of John Danter, the late sixteenth-century London printer. Using three illustrations drawn from copies at the Huntington Library and the Bodleian Library, Hanabusa provides evidence for shared printings. In an appendix there is a 'List of Identified Types in Books Printed by Thomas Scarlet' (p. 349), a fellow printer of Danter. Jason P. Rosenblatt's 'Ink and Vinegar: The Authorship of *A Survay of That Foolish, Seditious, Scandalous, Prophane Libell, The Protestation Protested*' (*PBSA* 97[2003] 351–65) 'argues that Peter Heylyn rather than Joseph Hall is the author of the vicious anonymous pamphlet' published in London in 1641 (p. 351). A regular contributor to *PBSA*, Arthur Sherbo, in his 'From *Bibliotheca Boswelliana*: The Sale Catalogue of the Library of James Boswell, the Younger' (*PBSA* 97[2003] 367–78), adds to our knowledge of the younger Boswell. Sherbo provides evidence for 'some future student of the history of the history of Shakespeare studies' who might 'wish to learn more about the life of the Boswell–Malone 1821 *Shakespeare*' (p. 378). Sherbo's essay is followed by Jeffrey P. Barton's most welcome and timely review essay on the occasion of the production of John F. Barber's *The Brautigan Bibliography: Bibliographic Information Focusing on the Works of Richard Brautigan*. (http://www.eaze.net/~jfbarber/brautigan/index.html) (*PBSA* 97[2003] 379–86). Barton considers the ramifications of online bibliographic endeavour and offers 'modest proposals for web-site content in the hope that they can provide a basis for future discussion and evaluation of bibliographic resources' (p. 385). There is much to think about in Barton's essay and his analysis does suggest valuable 'general yardsticks, or standards, which may help us evaluate *any* online bibliographic resource' (p. 384). This essay should be on all graduate research methods lists as essential reading.

Paul F. Gehl's address to the Bibliographical Society of America on 24 January 2003 is printed as his 'Religion and Politics in the Market for Books: The Jesuits and their Rivals' (*PBSA* 97[2003] 435–60). Four illustrations accompany Gehl's research, which focuses on the work of Manuel Alvares (1526–83), whose grammar became a standard text in Jesuit colleges and 'the symbol of an educational system' (p. 458). There are fifteen illustrations, none of which, unfortunately, are in colour, accompanying Jean Lee Cole's 'Coloring Books: The Forms of Turn-of-the-Century American Literature' (*PBSA* 97[2003] 461–93). Cole's focus is on the production of 'three non white writers [who] made their debut in the American mainstream market' at the close of the nineteenth century: 'the African-American writers Paul Laurence Dunbar (1872–1906) and Charles Chesnutt (1858–1932), and the half-Chinese, half-English, Canadian-born Winnifred Eaton (1875–1954), writing under the pseudonym Onoto Watanna' (p. 461). Clare Hutton's 'Chapters of Moral History: Failing to Publish *Dubliners*' (*PBSA* 97[2003] 495–519) draws upon James Joyce's correspondence with his publisher Grant Richards in order to examine the publishing history of *Dubliners* and the hostile reaction to it in Dublin. Margaret Meserve's 'Patronage and Propaganda at the First Paris Press: Guillaume Fichet and the First Edition of Bessarion's *Orations against the Turks*' (*PBSA* 97[2003] 521–88) is an extensive consideration of the publication of Cardinal Bessarion's activities. There are thirteen illustrations and four appendices. These include: 'Description and Analysis of the *Orations*' (pp. 570–2); 'Fichet's Correspondence, Prefatory Letters and Related Events' (pp. 572–4); 'Known Copies of Bessarion's *Orations* Produced by Fichet' (pp. 575–86); and 'Manuscript Corrections Inserted After Printing' followed by 'Correction Groups by Individual Copy' (pp. 587–8). This is followed by a review essay in which David L. Vander Meulen considers John Bidwell's *Fine Papers at the Oxford University Press*, published in 1999 (*PBSA* 97[2003] 589–95). Vander Meulen concludes that 'the outcome is a book that contributes to the history of papermaking, printing, and publishing and that also provides a model for how such study might be carried out' (p. 595).

In another review essay James E. May discusses the implications of Kenneth E. Carpenter's *The Dissemination of the* Wealth of Nations *in French and in France, 1776–1843* (*PBSA* 97[2003] 596–602). Each issue of the *PBSA* contains book reviews, short unsigned notices, written by the editor Trevor Howard-Hill and in most instances a listing of 'Publications Received'. The fourth issue contains the annual reports of the Bibliographical Society of America, and there is an index to the volume.

The latest volume of *Studies in Bibliography* (54[2003]) has a 2001 dating on its title page, and on the verso, its imprint page, a 2003 copyright. The extensive opening essay contains G. Thomas Tanselle's 'Textual Criticism at the Millennium' (*SB* 54[2003] 1–80). In line with his other recent surveys this one also contains extensive documentation. Tanselle remarks in his opening paragraph that 'for the first time the majority of writings on textual matters expressed a lack of interest in, often active disapproval of, approaching texts as the products of individual creators'. He continues: 'it promoted instead the forms of texts that emerged from the social process leading to public distribution, forms that were therefore accessible to readers' (pp. 1–2). The 118-footnote documentation to Tanselle's essay is replete with bibliographical information, although some of the observations have a Leavisian quality to them, especially if one becomes the victim of Tanselle's negativity. Some recent textual critics receive more attention than others, and not always in a favourable manner. The criticism of David Greetham and especially his *Theories of the Text* [1999] seems at times unnecessarily lengthy. Perhaps there is an implicit compliment here in that Tanselle needs to spend so much time on Greetham's apparent limitations (see pp. 52–60). Tanselle concludes his extensive reflections on a positive note concerning the fate of textual criticism and critics. His last sentence reads: 'Their multifarious, unceasing efforts, which can never be more than tentative, exemplify the richest kind of experience that readers can have' (p. 80). To the present reviewers this seems to border on being too enthusiastic.

James McLaverty, 'David Foxon, Humanist Bibliographer' (*SB* 54[2003] 81–113), is a tribute, with a largely enumerative bibliographical listing of publications ranging from 1953 to 1991 (pp. 110–13), of the late David Foxon

(1923–2001). McLaverty, surveying Foxon's life and career, writes: 'the trajectory of David Foxon's life was from a family background of provincial non-conformity, through public school, war-time intelligence, and Magdalen College, Oxford, to the British Museum Library, and finally to university teaching at Queen's Ontario and Oxford' (p. 84). Fascinating is the account of Foxon's activities at Bletchley as a cryptologist, and his subsequent 'transfer to Japanese intelligence ... after the fall of Italy' (p. 86). The account of Foxon's bibliographical achievement is comprehensive. McClaverty writes 'Foxon's legacy lies not only in the great resource of his catalogue [*English Verse, 1701–1750*] and in the stories he uncovered of Pope and Wise and their machinations, but also in the possibility of future discoveries by the application of the same humane curiosity and technical know-how' (p. 109). Michael Hancher, '*Littera scripta manet*: Blackstone and Electronic Text' (*SB* 54[2003] 115–32), is a somewhat complicated examination of the complexities of the concepts discussed in William Blackstone's *Commentaries on the Laws of England* [1765–9] and their application to modern textual reconstruction and in particular the electronic text. Hancher's observations are followed by another G. Thomas Tanselle contribution, in this instance the brief 'Thoughts on the Authenticity of Electronic Texts' (*SB* 54[2003] 133–6). Paul J. Klemp's 'John Manningham's Diary and a Lost Whit-Sunday Sermon by Lancelot Andrewes' (*SB* 54[2003] 137–55) compares, contrasts, and comments upon the significance of two documents: a diary maintained at the Middle Temple by John Manningham (*c*.1575–1622) and Lancelot Andrewes's 'Lost Whit-Sunday Sermon' preached on 23 May 1602 at Westminster (p. 137). Jill Farringdon, in 'A Funerall Elegye ... not ... *by* W.S.' (*SB* 54[2003] 157–72), returns to the thorny subject of Donald W. Foster's findings in his *Elegy by W.S.: A Study in Attribution* [1989], a work challenged by Brian Vickers at length in his *Counterfeiting Shakespeare* [2002]. Farringdon considers Foster's arguments and subsequent work attributing the authorship of *Elegye* to John Ford. She concludes that 'cusum analysis has shown Shakespeare to be extremely unlikely as author of *A Funerall Elegye* and supports the consensus that John Ford is the likely author (though not of its Dedication)' (p. 172). In other words, she comes down on the side of Vickers: she observes that 'Foster's subsequent acceptance of Ford's likely authorship was reported in the *New York Times*, 26 June, 2002. p. E3' (p. 158 n. 6). Martin C. Battestin's 'Fielding's Contributions to *The Comedian* (1732)' (*SB* 54[2003] 173–89) reconsiders the authorship of a political essay defending the Walpole administration against the attacks of Opposition writers and a verse epistle praising the painter John Ellys. In addition to publishing an annotated version of both (pp. 176–84: 186–9), Battestin quite convincingly quotes 'from the evidence presented' and demonstrates that both 'are by Fielding' (p. 186). William McCarthy, in 'What Did Anna Barbauld Do To Samuel Richardson's Correspondence? A Study of her Editing' (*SB* 54[2003] 91–223), draws upon materials now in the Foster Collection at the Victoria and Albert Museum in order to discuss the complicated relationships between Samuel Richardson, the six-volume 1804 edition of his *Correspondence* [1804], and his biographer Anna Letitia Barbauld. There are three appendices: 'The Manuscript Counterparts of Texts in *Correspondence: Summary of Collations*' (pp. 208–18); 'Manuscripts

Marked by Barbauld but not Printed' (pp. 219–22); and reflections upon 'The Richardson–Edward Young Correspondence' (pp. 222–3)—in other words the twenty letters of Young to Richardson found in the second volume of the *Correspondence* and the 149 Young to Richardson letters which appeared in *The Monthly Magazine* from 1813 to 1819. Marcus Walsh's 'Form and Function in the English Eighteenth-Century Literary Edition: The Case of Edward Capell' (*SB* 54[2003] 225–41) is accompanied by fourteen full-page plates largely taken from Capell's *Prolusions* [1760], Capell's 1768 edition of Shakespeare, and other Capell texts. Walsh's essay discusses 'the highly individual editorial work of Edward Capell', and is concerned with 'the "bibliographical codes" of Capell's works of English editorial scholarship: matters of volume, format, and makeup, the relations among texts and paratexts, styling and *mise en page*' (p. 226). R. Carter Hailey, in '"This instance will not do": George Steevens and the Revision(s) of Johnson's *Dictionary*' (*SB* 54[2003] 243–64), assesses 'the changes Steevens introduced in seeing the successive editions' of Johnson's *Dictionary* [1773] 'through the press' (p. 264). In their 'Two New Pamphlets by William Godwin: A Case of Computer-Assisted Authorship Attribution' (*SB* 54[2003] 265–84), Pamela Clemit and David Woolls draw upon contemporary technology to assess Godwin's role in the publication of two pamphlets, the first published in 1788 and the second published in 1789. The article is replete with some rather complex illustrative figures and tables and an appendix with a 'List of Codes and Word Counts and All Texts Used in the Computer Analysis'. There is also a listing of references (pp. 282–4). Clemit and Woolls conclude that the 'two pamphlets … are important editions to the canon of Godwin's works' (p. 281).

David Chandler provides 'A Bibliographical History of Thomas Howes' *Critical Observations* (1776–1807) and his Dispute with Joseph Priestley' (*SB* 54[2003] 285–95). This is a consideration of 'a daunting bibliographical problem' (p. 285). The problem is one of authorship and the relationship between Thomas Howes (*c.*1728–1814) and his main opponent, Joseph Priestley. Chandler's account concludes with a detailed 'Synopsis of the Publishing History of *Critical Observations*' (pp. 294–5). Andrew M. Stauffer's brief 'The First Publication of Byron's "Touch the Po"' (*SB* 54[2003] 297–300) is an account of the activities of Thomas Medwin and 'enacts an editorial theory that respects the deep connections of poetry and biography for readers of Byron' (p. 300). Roger Osborne's 'Joseph Conrad's *Under Western Eyes*: The Serials and First Editions' (*SB* 54[2003] 301–16) examines the American texts of Conrad to demonstrate 'how much instability lies behind the printed text familiar to most readers' (p. 301). The final contribution to this issue of *Studies in Bibliography* is Arthur Sherbo's 'Unrecorded Writing by G.K. Chesterton, H.G. Wells, Padraic Colum, Mary Colum, T.S. Eliot, George Bernard Shaw, and William Butler Yeats' (*SB* 54[2003] 317–23). Through his burrowing into esoteric journals once again we are indebted to Arthur Sherbo for adding to the bibliographical record. In this instance we have two items not recorded in Gallop's *T.S. Eliot: A Bibliography* [1969], items not recorded in Dan E. Laurence's *Bernard Shaw: A Bibliography* [1982] or its 2000 supplement, or in Allan Wade's *A Bibliography of the Writings of W.B. Yeats* [1968] or Jochum's additions [1978]. There are also considerable additions to John Sullivan's *G.K. Chesterton: A Bibliography* [1958] and to J.R. Hammond's *Herbert George Wells: An Annotated Bibliography* [1977]. Sherbo adds considerably to Allen Denson's Padraic Colum checklist published in 1967 in the *Dublin Magazine*.

The Library: The Transactions of the Bibliographical Society continues to include fascinating material. In addition to regular extensive reviews, it includes 'Some New Light on the Early Career of William Thynne, Chief Clerk of the Kitchen of Henry VIII and Editor of Chaucer' by Robert Costomiris (*Library* 7th series[2003] 3–15). Costomiris's article throws light on the early editing and printing of Chaucer. Richard Rex's 'Redating Henry VIII's *A Glass of the Truthe*' (*Library* 7th series[2003] 16–27) illuminates the history of 'a dialogue published in support of Henry VIII's case for a divorce from his first wife, Catherine of Aragon' (p. 16). Peter J. Lucas illuminates seventeenth-century Anglo-Saxon printing in his 'From Politics to Practicalities: Printing Anglo-Saxon in the Context of Seventeenth-Century Scholarship' (*Library* 7th series[2003] 28–48). Martin Butler's 'The Riddle of Jonson's *Chronology Revisited*' (*Library* 7th series[2003] 49–63) considers some of the many riddles in Jonson's chronology and takes issue with W.W. Greg's article of the same name published in *The Library* in 1996. Butler includes an appendix, 'Dates in the Jonson Canon' (pp. 61–3). Butler's 'analysis suggests that [Jonson] was genuinely inconsistent in his habits, and that Greg's attempt to find a predictable pattern was flawed' (pp. 60–1). David Stoker's 'William Proctor, Nathaniel Ponder, and the Financing of *Pilgrim's Progress*' (*Library* 7th series[2003] 64–9) draws upon a ledger found amongst 'the manuscripts of the Beauchamp-Proctor family in the Norfolk Record Office' (p. 64). This ledger illuminates the activities of William Proctor, a London stationer, who was active in the very early years of the eighteenth century. Orietta Da Rold's 'The Quiring System in Cambridge University Library MS Dd.4.24 of Chaucer's *Canterbury Tales*' (*Library* 7th series[2003] 107–28) is a most detailed analysis, including the study of watermarks and paper. There are three appendices specifically analysing the quiring system. Liudmila V. Charipova's 'Latin Books and the Orthodox Church in Ruthenia: Two Catalogues of Books Purchased by Peter Mohyla in 1632 and 1633′ (*Library* 7th series[2003] 129–49) explores an area of book history often neglected by Anglo-American scholars.

The late Peter Isaac and Tanya Schmoller, in 'a revised version of a paper read to the Bibliographical Society on 19 November 2002′, 'Letters from a Newspaper Man in Prison' (*Library* 7th series[2003] 150–67), draw upon materials deposited in the Sheffield City archives to illuminate the publishing activities and problems encountered by James Montgomery (1771–1854). Montgomery owned and edited *The Iris*, 'Sheffield's leading local newspaper during dangerous times for publishers' (p. 150). His newspaper was regarded as too radical. 'In January 1793 [Montgomery] was indicted for selling Tom Paine's *Rights of Man* and was sentenced to imprisonment for eighteen months' (p. 155). Isaac and Schmoller print extracts from the letters Montgomery sent from prison and also throw light on Montgomery's publishing and other activities. This article is followed by obituaries of two important bibliographers and book historians. Graham Shaw writes movingly on 'Barry Bloomfield (1931–2002)' (*Library* 7th series[2003]

168–70), 'who died suddenly on 26 February 2002' and who 'achieved equal distinction as both librarian and bibliographer, and remarkably in totally unrelated fields: in Asian studies as the Director of the United Kingdom's most important library collections, and in modern English literary studies as the bibliographer of Auden and Larkin' (p. 168). Barry McKay's tribute to 'Peter Isaac (1921–2002)' (*Library* 7th series[2003] 171–2) is as moving as Graham Shaw's tribute to Barry Bloomfield. McKay writes that Isaac 'held a distinguished and honored place among historians of the book in Great Britain' (p. 171). His achievement is essentially twofold. First was his 'life-long passion for the work of William Bulmer', the late eighteenth- and early nineteenth-century printer. Second was his 'significant contribution to the study of the provincial book trade' (p. 172). Erik Kwakkel, in 'A New Type of Book for a New Type of Reader: The Emergence of Paper in Vernacular Book Production' (*Library* 7th series[2003] 219–48), is a well-illustrated discussion of 'one of the most remarkable Middle Dutch manuscripts that survive from the fourteenth century' today to be found at the convent of St John's in Bruges (p. 219). Kwakkel uses this manuscript as the foundation for a discussion of 'our understanding of the scribes who first started to use paper for vernacular books' (p. 227). Robert D. Hume's 'Editing a Nebulous Author: The Case of the Duke of Buckingham' (*Library* 7th series[2003] 249–77) raises issues relating to 'a concept of authorship radically foreign to the assumptions most of us bring to literary texts' (p. 272). In 'The *Anti-Jacobin* Revisited: Newly Identified Contributions to the *Anti-Jacobin Review* during the Editorial Regime of John Gifford, 1798–1806' (*Library* 7th series[2003] 278–302), El de Montluzin draws upon 'the British Library's annotated volumes' of the *Anti-Jacobin Review* 'to identify the authors of over one hundred additional anonymous, pseudo-anonymous, or incompletely signed items appearing in volumes 7–25' (pp. 278–9). The article also adds to our knowledge of the activities of John Gifford, who served as its first editor. Linne R. Mooney and Lister M. Matheson, 'The Beryn Scribe and his Texts: Evidence for Multiple-Copy Production of Manuscripts in Fifteenth-Century England' (*Library* 7th series[2003] 347–70), is a detailed analysis of 'the Duke of Northumberland's manuscript of Chaucer's *Canterbury Tales*, Alnwick Castle, MS 455′ (p. 347). Isabelle Pingree's 'A Catalogue of the Bindings of the Fifteenth-Century Bookbinder Called the Rood and Hunt Binder' (*Library* 7th series[2003] 370–401) 'lists twenty-six bindings, the twenty-three printed books in question ranging in date from 1473 to 1483′ and 'emphasizes the structurally and decorative features of the Rood and Hunt binders work' (p. 375). Arlen Blyum's 'George Orwell in the Soviet Union: A Documentary Chronicle on the Centenary of his Birth' (*Library* 7th series[2003] 402–16) is a translation from the Russian. As the translator I.P. Foote indicates in a note, Professor Arlen Blyum of the St Petersburg Academy of Culture, gained access in the 1990s to the archives of Glavlit (the Soviet censorship authority). The article consists largely of documents 'mostly held in the Russian State Archive of Literature and Arts' (p. 402) and illuminates the reception of Orwell in Russia. Bloom concludes that 'the Party—not an invented but a real one—"thrust its hand" into the heritage of a great English writer in an attempt to make him non-existent' (p. 416). David Paisley, in a review article on 'German Book Fair Catalogues' (*Library* 7th series[2003] 417–27), uses the publication of facsimile volumes of fair catalogues to assess the importance of book fairs held in Frankfurt and Leipzig between 1564 and 1600. It would be remiss to conclude this annual evaluation of *The Library* without drawing attention to its most useful and regular enumeration of 'Recent Periodicals' in the field of bibliography and book history and its listings of 'Books Received'.

The Antiquarian Book Monthly Review is going through various name changes. In its 2003 incarnation it became *The Antiquarian Book Review* (*ABR*). The February 2003 issue—in addition to the usual auction, catalogue and book reviews, glossy advertisements from various booksellers and page on the 'shop of the month' (p. 74), listing of book fairs, and useful web directory containing book dealers' websites and auction websites—includes several items of interest to readers of *YWES*. Geoffrey Barne, in 'Dark Angel' (*ABR* 30:ii[2003] 24–8), examines Byron's fugitive pieces to find the man behind the myth. Barne's is the first of several pieces on Byron, and is followed by Peter Cochran's 'Unreel' (*ABR* 30:ii[2003] 31) examining 'the shocking portrayal of Byron [which] has overlooked one minor detail—his poetry' (p. 31). Christine Kenyon-Jones in 'Man's Best Friend' (*ABR* 30:ii[2003] 32–4) considers 'Byron's canine passions, including his close relationship with his appropriately named dog "Boatswain".' This article is accompanied by an illustration of Byron's 'grandiose monument' to Boatswain (p. 34). Adam Douglas writes on 'Rebel Rebel', which has the subtitle 'The Poet Percy Bysshe Shelley Lived Fast and Furiously' (*ABR* 30:ii[2003] 36–40). One whole page of Douglas's article is taken up with Alfred Clint's portrait of Shelley. 'Mad About the Boy' (*ABR* 30:ii[2003] 42–3) consists of an account of 'Fiona McCarthy's lifelong passion for Byron [which] led her to write his definitive biography, as she tells Hugo Worthy'. One page is take up with the reproduction of 'A Portrait of the Young Lord Byron from the collection of Geoffrey Bond' (p. 43). McCarthy observes that 'Byron's yearnings toward adolescent boys rather undermines his own heartthrob image' (p. 42). The March 2003 issue opens with Hugo Worthy's 'Breaking the Waves' (*ABR* 30:iii[2003] 6–7), which is an account of an Edward Ardizzone exhibition. Elizabeth Crawford, 'Talkin 'Bout a Revolution' (*ABR* 30:iii[2003] 21–5), is a well-illustrated account of suffragette materials, including fascinating ephemera. The physicality of books, including endpapers which reproduce fabrics, are the subject of Nicola Beauman's 'Wings of Desire' (*ABR* 30:iii[2003] 26–30). Beauman focuses on 'the neglected passions of women's writing' (p. 27). Replete with fascinating illustrations of decorative endpapers, Beauman's article focuses upon her own publishing house, Persephone Books. Her output differs from 'other high-quality paperbacks in having endpapers reproducing fabrics that are the same date and the same mood as the book' (p. 30). Lucy Harris in her *Medieval Women* (*ABR* 30:iii[2003] 32–6) looks at 'the plight of Anglo-Saxon women as seen through books' (p. 32). Lindsay Schapiro, in 'A Woman's Work' (*ABR* 30:iii[2003] 38–42), looks at the 'Woman's Library' started by Millicent Fawcett in Westminster (London). Margaret Lane Ford's 'Private Passions' (*ABR* 30:iii[2003] 44–8) assesses the collection of Count Oswald von Seilern und Aspang (1901–67) which is 'rich in incunabula, but also boasts valuable medieval and renaissance manuscripts and printed books of the 16th to 18th centuries' (p. 44). Christie's London auction house offered a selection of highlights from the collection on 26 March 2003.

Hugo Worthy, in 'Turkish Delight' (*ABR* 30:iii[2003] 50–2), provides a taste of some of the wonders from the great collection of Asian art focusing on the Islamic world put together in the late twentieth century by Nasser David Kahili. Some of Kahili's collection was on exhibit in 2003. Worthy's review opens with a double-spread illustration from 'A Copy of al-Bukhari's *Sahih* dated 9 Zilhicce 935 (4 August 1529)' (pp. 50–1). Stewart A. Baldwin, in 'Books That Aren't' (*ABR* 30:iv[2003] 6–7), considers the collecting of books that have no individual pages. This issue also contains regular features, including William Reese's 'Letter from America' (p. 10), Ed Maggs's sometimes outrageous 'From the Tea Room' (p. 12), James Morton's 'Reflections in Word' (p. 14), Sandra Hindman's 'Unscripted' (p. 16), which contains an interesting profile of the Norwegian collector of medieval materials Martin Schøyen, and Brian Lake's provocative 'A View from the Lake' (p. 18). The fascination with collecting anything relating to Horatio Nelson preoccupies Hugo Worthy in 'The Perfect Storm' (*ABR* 30:iv[2003] 20–3). John B. Hattendorf, in 'The Englishman Abroad' (*ABR* 30:iv[2003] 24–8), 'charts the emergence of the maritime book from its earliest origins in the 15th century' (p. 24). Norman Fiering, in 'Deep Impact' (*ABR* 30:iv[2003] 30–3), takes us on an all-too-brief survey of the great John Carter Brown Library in Providence, Rhode Island. James Morton, in 'Comic Relief' (*ABR* 30:iv[2003] 35–6), surveys the collection of showbusiness memorabilia collected by the late Bob Monkhouse.

Illustrated articles are becoming the feature of *ABR*. Matthew Walpole's 'Through a Glass Darkly' (*ABR* 30:iv[2003] 38–41) is no exception. His journey 'into the medieval masterpiece that is Cheetham's Library' (p. 38) is accompanied by fascinating photograph of the Long Library that 'contains many of the masterpieces of the collection' (pp. 38–9). Pieter VanDer Merwe, in 'New Horizons' (*ABR* 30:iv[2003] 42–6), looks into the library of the Greenwich National Maritime Museum; the article is illustrated by a photographic vista of the museum,. In 'Flower Girls' (*ABR* 30:v[2003] 22–5) Maureen Lazarus looks at the way in which women have been largely ignored in the history of botanical illustration. Judith M. Taylor, in 'Gardens in the Gold Rush' (*ABR* 30:v[2003] 6–28), reviews items on California's horticulture, focusing on San Francisco. Sara Waterson, in 'The Italian Garden' (*ABR* 30:v[2003] 30–4), draws upon 'books celebrating famous Baroque gardens' (p. 34). Todd Longstaffe-Gowan, in 'At Play in the Fields of the Lords' (*ABR* 30:v[2003] 36–9), looks at books on Hampton Court. Hugo Worthy, in 'The Book and the Brotherhood' (*ABR* 30:v[2003] 40–4), considers the Lindisfarne Gospels. Sixteenth-century horticulture books are the subject of Mathew Walpole's 'The Apple of My Eye' (*ABR* 30:v[2003] 46–9). Robert Watson, in 'The Man with the Midas Touch' (*ABR* 30:vi[2003] 20–5), considers the James Bond collecting phenomenon. In 'The People's Prospero' (*ABR* 30:vi[2003] 26–8) Leo Burley 'talks to literary Lord Melvin Bragg about writing, broadcasting and his love affair with books' (p. 27). Hugo Worthy, in 'Powerhouse' (*ABR* 30:vi[2003] 30–2), considers the library at the House of Commons. D.J. Taylor, in 'The Road to 1984' (*ABR* 30:vi[2003] 34–6), considers the genesis of Orwell's great novel. Philippe Garner's 'A Photographic Alchemist' (*ABR* 30:vi[2003] 47–50) records a meeting with Paul Caffell, who is concerned with the platinum print. This article is fully documented with black and white illustrations. Peter Barber's 'Spy Games' (*ABR* 30:vi[2003] 52–6) 'tracks the covert world of maps from their earliest origins to today' (p. 53).

ABR for July 2003 is an issue devoted to sport in which Hugo Worthy's 'A Green and Pleasant Land' (*ABR* 30:vii[2003] 20–2) uncovers some of the treasures to be found at the MCC library at Lord's cricket ground, and Jeremy Mailes all too briefly, in 'Bowled Over' (*ABR* 30:vii[2003] 23–4), assesses cricket bibliophilia. The interesting and rather neglected area of books on tennis is the subject of Karen Cass's 'Smashing into History' (*ABR* 30:vii[2003] 26–9), which focuses upon the Kenneth Ritchie Library at Wimbledon. The British Library's recent purchase of the *Charleston Bulletin* containing material by Virginia Woolf and Julian and Quentin Bell is the subject of Peter Robin's report, 'A More Human Form of Woolf' (*ABR* 30:vii[2003] 30–1). In 'House of Leeds' (*ABR* 30:vii[2003] 32–3) Hugo Worthy all too briefly reviews Iris Murdoch's marginalia found in books in her library. The Bridgeman Collection is the subject of Emma Lewis's 'Lady Oracle' (*ABR* 30:vii[2003] 34–7). Golf bibliophilia is investigated by Peter Robins in 'Here Comes the Bogeyman' (*ABR* 30:vii[2003] 38–42). In the August /September 2003 issue of *ABR*, Vita Sackville-West's gardening journalism is the focus for Peter Robin's 'Friend of the Earth' (*ABR* 30:viii–ix[2003] 6–7) which is based on a visit to the new newsroom archive at the *Guardian* newspapers. Ed Maggs's 'Nothing Like a Dame' (*ABR* 30:viii–ix[2003] 24–6) considers the book-collecting of Barry Humphries. Slave literature is the subject of Hugo Worthy's 'Unchained Melody' (*ABR* 30:vii–ix[2003] 28–32), which is essentially a review of James Basker's *Amazing Grace: An Anthology of Poems About Slavery, 1660–1810* [2003]. The work of the crusading Victorian journalist W.T. Stead is the subject of Darren Lazarus's 'Victorian Crusader' (*ABR* 30:viii–ix[2003] 34–6). Naomi Grayn, in 'Testament of Experience' (*ABR* 30:viii–ix[2003] 38–41), examines some of the samples to be found in the Wiener Library in London. Ephemera concerns Amoret Tanner in 'Tea & Biscuits' (*ABR* 30:viii–ix[2003] 44–5).

The Booker Literary Prize is the main theme for the October issue and contains 'Booked!' (*ABR* 30:x[2003] 20–3), on the subject Cathy Courtney's meeting with Martyn Goff, who was the chairman of the Booker Prize for many years. Angela James, in 'Binding the Booker' (*ABR* 30:x[2003] 26–8), considers the special binding which goes into the design of the Booker Prize books. Hugo Worthy's 'Whispering Judges' (*ABR* 30:x[2003] 30–2) is a discussion with John Carey, the 2003 chair of the Booker Prize panel, and Lisa Jardine, who chaired the 2002 panel of judges, which also talks about 'books and book collecting' (p. 33). Chiara Nikolany, in 'Masters of the Art' (*ABR* 30:x[2003] 34–9), considers picture books and whether they are 'just for kids' (p. 35). Mathew Walpole's 'Spanish Gold' (*ABR* 30:x[2003] 40–1) examines the treasures of the vault of the cathedral of Toledo. Frank Herrmann, in 'The Miffy Man' (*ABR* 30:x[2003] 42–5), meets the creator of Miffy, the Dutch graphic artist Dick Bruna.

The November 2003 issue includes Chris Wright's 'An American Tome of Chinese Stone' (*ABR* 30:xi[2003] 6–7), which considers Heber Bishop's two-volume *Investigations and Studies in Jade* [1906]. Renaissance manuscripts and a visit to the Getty Museum in Los Angeles are the subject of Hugo Worthy's

'The Reflective Life' (*ABR* 30:xi[2003] 8–22). The bibliography of Mao's 'Little Red Book' is the subject of Oliver HanLei's 'How Read Is the Little Red Book?' (*ABR* 30:xi[2003] 24–6). Dylan Thomas is the subject of two articles. In the first, 'Dylan in the Docks' (*ABR* 30:xi[2003] 28–30), 'Andrew Lycett, the New Biographer of Dylan Thomas, speaks to Kate Templeton and pronounces judgment on the poet's life and work' (p. 28). This is followed by Jeff Towns, 'Collecting Dylan Thomas' (*ABR* 30:xi[2003] 31). Heath Robinson is the subject of the 'Many Shades of the Penman' (*ABR* 30:xi[2003] 36–9), in which Alex Capon 'meets Geoffrey Beare, the curator of the new Heath Robinson exhibition' (p. 36). Jorge Louis Borges is the subject 'Argentina Alight' by David Hume (*ABR* 30:xi[2003] 40–3). Books about the Napoleonic Wars preoccupy Mathew Walpole's 'Urban Warfare' (*ABR* 30:xi[2003] 44–7). Pip Brooking, in 'University Challenge' (*ABR* 30:xi[2003] 48–9), is concerned with the arguments between Christ Church College, Oxford, and Nippon Dental University in Tokyo 'over a stolen Vasalias'. Overall this run of the *ABR* follows a recent pattern of sacrificing quality and depth and range of analysis for illustrative and glossy features. No doubt the thinking behind this is to sell more copies on English news-stands. However the short regular features containing auction and fair reviews and the auction diary are most useful.

Another important journal, which continues to impress with the diversity and quality of its contents and contains important obituaries sometimes reprinted from newspaper sources such as *The Independent*, is *The Book Collector*. Volume 52[2003] includes David Gilson, 'Jane Austen and Europe' (*BC* 52:i[2003] 31–45) and David Vaisey, 'Overtravelled with the Librarie Businesse' (*BC* 52:i[2003] 46–57). In this issue there are obituaries, four of which come from the pen of Nicholas Barker and are reprinted from *The Independent*. Barker writes on the bookseller Charles Traylen (1905–2002) (*BC* 52:i[2003] 104–5). As Barker points out, 'respect was never a word in [Traylen's] vocabulary, nor was history' (p. 104). There are some interesting anecdotes about London sales room activities in the post-war period and some fine writing with not inapposite comparisons with the great cricketer Jack Hobbs, who scored 696 runs in the year before Traylen's birth! Barker writes a much more extensive obituary of John Fuggles (1949–2002), who died far too young. Fuggles was the National Trust library adviser. He moved to the British Library in 1975 to continue the Trust's work investigating private libraries and 'became Secretary of the Friends of the National Libraries as well' (p. 108). Barker's account of Fuggles's last years makes sad reading (*BC* 52:i[2003] 105–9). John Dreyfus (1918–2002) was a very distinguished typographer who was 'much concerned with the design of Cambridge University Press books' (p. 111). In 1954 he succeeded the great Stanley Morrison as 'the Press's typographical adviser' and played a major hand in the 1963 'great "Printing and the Mind of Man" exhibition, staged at Olympia and the British Museum'. The 1968–73 period saw Dreyfus serving as president of the Association Typographique Internationale. In 1976 he 'organized the printing historical society's conference to celebrate the quincentenary of Caxton … becoming its president in 1991' (p. 112). Barker also writes on the Oxford-based bookseller Robert Clark (1951–2003), who specialized in seventeenth- and eighteenth-century English literature and theology. Other obituaries include

Jennie Renton writing on the Edinburgh-based seller of second-hand books Marjorie McNaughtan (1911–2002) (*BC* 52:i[2003] 109–10). G. Thomas Tanselle writes on Harrison Hayford (1916–2001), the great Melville collector and scholar who taught at Northwestern University for forty-three years (*BC* 52:i[2003] 114–17). Nico Israel (1919–2002) is the subject of an obituary by Kenneth Nebenzahl: 'Israel entered the antiquarian book business with his older brother Max after the Second World War, and in 1950 established his own premises … For over fifty-five years Nico practiced the fair dealing that became his hallmark' (p. 117). He 'sustained two parallel careers simultaneously in the book world. In addition to his role as one of the great rare book dealers of his time, he also became an important speciality publisher' (p. 118). His special area of publication was cartography.

The *Book Collector* 52:ii[2003] contains three articles of interest to readers of *YWES*. The opening, unattributed, essay focuses on 'The Medieval Libraries of Britain' (*BC* 52:ii[2003] 51–170). In effect it is an extensive review article of the Corpus of British Medieval Library Catalogues series sponsored by the British Academy. The first volume was published in 1990, and 2002 saw the project reaching its tenth volume. The review article has some caveats about the series which are worthy of consideration, the most serious being 'the correlation of the "Corpus" data' with Neil Ker's *Medieval Libraries of Great Britain* (p. 169). Gregory V. Jones and Jane E. Brown write on the subject of 'Victorian Binding Designer WR: William Ralston (1841–1911), not William Harry Rogers' (*BC* 52:ii[2003] 171–98). Their fascinating entangling of what Ralston and Rogers actually bound is followed by a 'List of WR Binding Designs' (pp. 183–6). Eleven black and white illustrative figures of covered designs, and a signed photograph of William Ralston, accompany the article (pp. 187–98). Lord Wardington, in part 1 of 'Sir Robert Dudley and the *Arcano del Mare*, 1646–8 and 1661' (*BC* 52:ii[2003] 199–211), discusses 'one of the greatest atlases of the world and one of the most complex ever produced' (p. 199). Wardington's article is accompanied by two rather sumptuous coloured illustrations of a 1759 binding now at the Reading University Library (pp. 218–19). Obituaries in this issue are of two important American figures. The first, by Nicholas Barker, focuses on Walter Pforzheimer (1914–2002), the distinguished American intelligence officer and book collector who was 'one of the founders of what is now the Central Intelligence Agency (CIA)' (p. 256). Clearly more needs to be revealed about Pforzheimer's joint intelligence and book-buying activities. The other obituary is of Hanni Kraus, wife of the great Hans Kraus, who was 'the dominant New York bookseller from the 1950s to the 1980s' (p. 258).

The *Book Collector* 52:iii[2003] also contains several articles of interest. The opening, unattributed, piece, 'The Stationers' Company' (*BC* 52:iii[2003] 295–316), is partially a review essay of *The Stationers' Company: A History of the Later Years, 1800–2000*, edited by Robin Myers and published in 2001 by the Worshipful Company of Stationers and Newspaper Makers. The essay focuses on the pre-1800 period and contains a lively discussion of the development of the medieval guilds of London into the modern livery companies of the present. Scholars and others will find a richly detailed discussion concerning not only the evolution of the Stationer's Company, but pertinent sources that chronicle the company's history. There then follows the second part of 'Sir Robert Dudley and the *Arcano del Mare*, 1646–8 and 1661' (*BC* 52:iii[2003] 317–55), which exhaustively details the order of engraved plates in the six books of the first edition of the *Arcano del Mare* followed by an extensive description of the second volume. The article concludes with a tabulation of differences of copies in six locations (pp. 352–5). Nicolas Barker's 'Notes on the Origins of the Second-Hand Book Trade' (*BC* 52:iii[2003] 356–70) was originally delivered at the conference 'Markets for Books and Manuscripts: The Trade in Antiquarian Materials Past and Present', held in September 1989. Barker focuses upon books from 'well-documented' libraries (p. 363) from the late fifteenth and mid-seventeenth centuries. He also focuses upon the activities of Humfrey Wanley, the early eighteenth-century bibliophile. Barker ends with the observations that 'human nature' changes little over the centuries and that 'the books you want are not to be had … the price of old books is far too high and, worse, going up' (p. 370). All in all, Barker's essay is both salutary and shrewd. It is followed by most detailed and helpful 'News and Comment' and 'Exhibitions and Catalogues' sections (*BC* 52:i[2003] 373–98; 399–415).

The *Book Collector* (*BC* 52:iv[2003]) leads with an essay based on a review of Margaret M. Smith's *The Title-Page: Its Early Development, 1460–1510* [2000] (*BC* 52:iv[2003] 447–58). G. Thomas Tanselle's 'Fifty Years On: Bibliography Then and Now' (*BC* 52:iv[2003] 459–70) is a reflection upon changes in the world of bibliography in the past half-century. Its immediate occasion is the celebration of fifty years of publication of *The Book Collector*. Tanselle is the doyen of contemporary bibliographical historians and appositely concludes that 'the world of bibliography, like all other worlds, has changed during the past half-century. But *The Book Collector* has maintained its reassuring presence (full of continuities—in editorship, in tone, even in its Monotype typography)' (p. 470). William H. Sherman's 'Rather Soiled by Use: Attitudes toward Readers' Marks' (*BC* 52:iv[2003] 471–90) is a revised and extended version of an essay previously published in Sabrina Alcorn Baron's *The Reader Revealed* (Folger [2001]). Sherman concentrates on reader marks in Renaissance books and is concerned primarily with the complex question of 'how to read marginalia' (p. 490). Humour is always welcome, and 'Christmas Catalogue No. 10' (*BC* 52:iv[2003] 491–527) continues *The Book Collector*'s tradition of publishing selective curiosities and observations from dealers' catalogues, many of which have been sent in by its readers.

Nicolas Barker's 'Arthur Edward Wrigley (1865–1952), Author of *A Book-Hunter's Yesterdays*' (*BC* 52:iv[2003] 529–36) discusses the author of an article which was reprinted from the *Times Literary Supplement* in the 1952 initial issues of *The Book Collector*. Barker's essay is followed by 'News and Comment' (*BC* 52:iv[2003] 537–68) and 'Exhibitions and Catalogues' (*BC* 52:iv[2003] 569–72), and after the regular Books Received listing (*BC* 52:iv[2003] 573–4) there are obituaries reprinted from the *Independent*. These tributes are to John Brett-Smith, Mary, Viscountess Eccles, Brooke Crutchley and Leo Barnard (*BC* 52:iv[2003] 575–84). There are, of course, as usual in *The Book Collector*, book reviews.

James E. May's *East-Central Intelligencer: The Newsletter (with directory) of the East-Central/American Society for Eighteenth Century Studies* continues to produce items of interest. The contents of *ECIntell* 17:i[2003] include the editor's review of the first volume of Raven and Forster's *The English Novel 1770–1829*, followed by James E. May's '[Eighteenth-Century] Rare Books, Listed and Acquired, 1999–2002' (*ECIntell* 17:ii[2003] 32–45). Issue 17:ii[2003] opens with Sayre Greenfield's report of 'The EC/ASECS Annual Meeting, October 2003' (*ECIntell* 17:ii[2003] 1–3), followed by Daniel J. Slive's 'Eighteenth-Century Resources in the UCLA Department of Special Collections: A Survey' (*ECIntell* 17:ii[2003] 3–8). Sylvia Kasey Marks writes on 'Holy Living and Holy Dying in British Fiction for Young People, 1672–1839' (*ECIntell* 17:ii[2003] 8–14), and Lisa Rosner reflects on 'Lisa's Travels into Several Remote Sites of the Internet (Tendered with Due Respect to Mr. Swift)' (*ECIntell* 17:ii[2003] 14–15). Rosner's is a short recounting of her 'adventures in some of the most useful [web]sites devoted to 18th century subjects' (p. 14). Linda Troost's 'The Pedagogue's Post' (*ECIntell* 17:ii[2003] 16–17) is an account of a semester teaching an undergraduate course in 'Studies in the Restoration and Eighteenth Century' at Washington and Jefferson College. There are also book reviews (pp. 17–35) and various items on fellowships and contests and an interesting account of recent publications, including a briefly annotated section of 'Recent Studies on the History of the Book as a Physical Object: Including Binding, Paper and Papermaking, Printing, and Typography (Part 2)' (*ECIntell* 17:ii[2003] 55–9).

Probably the most important item in the 2003 volume is James Wooley's contribution, 'First-Line Indexes of English Verse, 1650–1800: A Checklist' (*ECIntell* 17:iii[2003] 1–10). This most valuable guide is divided into 'Indexes to Manuscript Verse' (pp. 2–4) and 'Indexes to Printed Verse (or Printed and Manuscript Verse Combined)' (pp. 4–10). A Swiss author is the focus of the following entry. Éva Pósfay's 'Isabelle de Montolieu (1751–1832) and her Readers' (*ECIntell* 17:iii[2003] 10–13) concentrates on the 'novelist, translator and adapter' (p. 10). Sylvia Kasey Marks, 'From Fielding to Sherwood: Setting a Good Example' (*ECIntell* 17:ii[2003] 13–21), focuses on fiction for young people and contains extensive footnotes on juvenile fiction (pp. 19–21). Hermann J. Real's 'Archimedes in Laputa, III, V, IX' (*ECIntell* 17:ii[2003] 21–4) is an explication of Swift. Michael Ritterson reflects on 'The Lessing Society and *Lessing Yearbook*' (*ECIntell* 17:iii[2003] 25–7). James E. May judiciously reflects upon book reviewing today in a valuable essay entitled 'The Spectator, No. 22' (*ECIntell* 17:ii[2003] 27–32). May concludes: 'if one wants to avoid any negative reviews, he or she need only work on Elizabeth Carter's translations of Epictetus' (p. 32). Mark Vareschi's 'E-Enacting the E-Enlightenment: How Electronic Classrooms Make the Private Act of Scholarship into Public Performance' (*ECIntell* 17:iii[2003] 32–5) assesses the impact of 'the addition of an online component' to eighteenth-century British literature undergraduate classes (p. 32). John Greene focuses upon 'Two Important Contributions to Theatre History by William J. Burling' (*ECIntell* 17:iii[2003] 35–7). In addition to detailed reviews and miscellaneous notes, this third issue concludes with a listing of fellowships and forthcoming meetings, and an informative 'Tools, as Publications and Websites' (*ECIntell* 17:iii[2003] 75–7).

The *Journal of Scholarly Publishing*, published by the University of Toronto Press on behalf of the North American University Publishers, continues to include contributions of considerable relevance to *YWES* readers. The January 2003 issue opens with recommendations by a distinguished group from the MLA, including Judith Ryan, Idelber Avelar, Jennifer Fleissner, David E. Lashmet, J. Hillis Miller, Karen H. Pike, John Sitter and Lynne Tatlock, 'The Future of Scholarly Publishing: MLA Ad Hoc Committee on the Future of Scholarly Publishing' (*JScholP* 34:ii[2003] 65–82). In addition to a most useful listing of 'Works Cited and Selected Bibliography' (pp. 80–2), there are recommendations for English departments, university libraries, publishers, and university administrators. In this examination of 'the current state of academic publishing in the fields of languages and literatures' (p. 65), the committee 'has come to understand that there is no ready or simple solution to the current crisis' (p. 77); however, it does make recommendations. This salutary document is followed by an article reflecting the comprehensive and eclectic nature of the *Journal of Scholarly Publishing*. David Henige's 'The Power of Pink: Graphical Display as Imposed Epistemology' (*JScholP* 34:ii[2003] 83–100) examines graphics, which 'are often found to distort the very image they seek to convey'. Henige argues that, consequently, 'authors have a special obligation to ensure that their data are arrayed in the most conscientious ways possible, Conversely, readers must be cautious in accepting more readily as true that which is couched by graphic rather than verbal discourse' (p. 83). Also of interest is James Hartley's all too brief 'Single Authors Are Not Alone: Colleagues Often Help' (*JScholP* 34:ii[2003] 108–13). Hartley reports on 'the number of times single, pairs, and groups of three or more authors acknowledge the help of colleagues and/or referees in their published papers'. He concludes that his 'results indicate that significantly more single authors acknowledge the help of others than do pairs who, in turn, do so more than larger groups. However, there were no significant differences between the number of acknowledgments made to referees by the three groups' (p. 108). This provides fuel for thought, especially amongst colleagues under pressure in British university departments to display evidence of productivity in the rankings game.

William J. Pesce's keynote address to the 2003 annual conference of the Association of American Publishers, and Professional and Scholarly Publishers, leads the April 2003 issue (*JScholP* 34:iii[2003] 129–39). Pesce, currently president and chief executive officer of John Wiley & Sons, reflects upon the 'extraordinary period of change … customer-led and technology-enabled' (p. 130) experienced by publishers. He takes comfort in a citation from Oliver Wendell Holmes: 'I find the great thing in this world is not so much where we stand, as in what direction we are moving. To reach the port of heaven, we must sail sometimes with the wind and sometimes against it. But, we must sail, and not drift, nor lie at anchor' (p. 139). A topic of perennial concern preoccupies Peter Givler, executive director of the Association of American University Presses, in his 'What Good is Copyright?' (*JScholP* 34:iii[2003] 140–5). William W. Savage Jr.'s 'Times Ain't Now Nothin' Like They Used To Be' (*JScholP* 34:iii[2003] 146–52) reflects upon 'the doctoral dissertation, never the most felicitous of literary forms [which] is nowadays worse than ever'. For Savage the situation is 'exacerbated by the economics of scholarly publishing'. In addition to the pressures of graduate programmes and the job market, Savage 'does not see change looming on the horizon' (p. 146). He writes from an American perspective and that of an American university-based historian. His strictures have considerable relevance to the state of affairs in departments of English in the UK and elsewhere. Changes in the American publishing industry are reflected in Charles H. E. Ault's detailed review of Richard E. Abel and Lyman W. Newlin, eds., *Scholarly Publishing: Books, Journals, Publishers, and Libraries in the Twentieth Century* [2002] (*JScholP* 34:iii[2003] 165–76).

The July 2003 issue opens with 'Looking Back on the Future History of the "Book": The Council of Editors of Learned Journals Keynote Addresses MLA Convention 2002′ by two most distinguished literary scholars and editors, David Greetham and George Bornstein. Their observations have been edited and introduced by Michael Cornett. Greetham, in 'What Is a "Book"? Some Post-Foucauldian Ruminations (a Prolegomenon)' (*JScholP* 34:iv[2003] 182–97)—a title no doubt deliberately chosen to amuse reviewers—ruminates upon many issues including the relation of the physicality of the book to electronic possibilities. He also ruminates 'in the bibliographic mode on Foucault's prescription for ''an author'' (p. 192). There is also much food for thought in George Bornstein's 'Pages, Pixels, and the Profession' (*JScholP* 34:iv[2003] 197–207), a consideration of the implications of 'the intellectual prospects of adding electronic media to our print culture'. For Bornstein this seems 'vast and encouraging' (p. 206). Hazel K. Bell's pithy 'In Others' Words' (*JScholP* 34:iv[2003] 208–13) considers 'how necessary it may be for writers to give the origin of quotations they use, with regard to the likelihood of readers' recognizing them'. Apart from the legal and moral rights of authors to acknowledgement Bell discusses 'the pleasure that may be derived from discovering the source for oneself' (p. 208). Her quotations extend from Thackeray's *The Rose and the Ring* to Angela Thirkell's profuse quotations in her novels and 'the exquisite pleasures of unaided discovery of sources, echoes, parallels' in A.S. Byatt's *Possession* (p. 211). The topical subject of plagiarism concerns William W. Savage Jr. in his 'My Favourite Plagiarist: Some Reflections of an Offended Party' (*JScholP* 34:iv[2003] 214–20). Interestingly Savage 'calls into question the validity of copyright law, the commitment of scholarly publishers to the protection of academic work, and the determination of university administrators to preserve standards of integrity among faculty' (p. 214). The editing of 'a modern progressive feminist journal' is the concern of Batya Weinbaum and Monique Morrison in their 'Bridging Matriarchal Order and Patriarchal Culture in a State Institution: The Evolving *Femspec* Kitchen on the Eighteenth Floor' (*JScholP* 34:iv[2003] 221–35). Malcolm Litchfield, director of Ohio State University Press, makes some hard-hitting observations in his 'Reading the Agenda of the 2003 Annual AAUP [American Association of University Presses] Directors' Meeting to Discover What's Wrong with the University Press Publishing' (*JScholP* 34:iv[2003] 249–53). The issue concludes with an index to volume 34 (pp. 255–60).

Volume 35 (October 2003) opens with observations from the new editor of the journal, Tom Radko, 'The Journal of Scholarly Publishing: Continuing and Enhancing the Tradition' (*JScholP* 35:i[2003] 1–3). Four members of the Fordham University School of Business—Albert N. Greco, Walter F. O'Connor,

Sharon P. Smith, and Robert M. Wharton—discuss 'The Price of University Press Books, 1989–2000' (*JScholP* 35:i[2003] 4–39). Replete with fifteen tables, the article analyses 'the decision-making process at university presses for determining suggested retail prices of books and evaluate[s] the effects of pricing strategies on the financial vitality of the presses' (p. 4). Although restricted to North America, this article contains fascinating information, including 'a preliminary investigation into the buying habits of academics' (p. 23). Further, the research reveals that university presses lost potential revenue rather than gaining it in their apparent refusal to hike prices, unlike commercial houses (see p. 19). William W. Savage, in his 'Scribble, Scribble, Toil and Trouble: Forced Productivity in the Modern University' (*JScholP* 35:i[2003] 40–6) (given the frequency of Savage's contributions to the journal this is somewhat ironically titled), argues that 'emphasis on book publication as the sole evidence of faculty productivity has led to a variety of unhappy consequences for those pressured to write books and for scholarly presses expected to issue them, principally panic and pandemonium' (p. 40). Ronald W. Tobin's 'The Commensality of Book Reviewing' (*JScholP* 35:i[2003] 47–51) revisits a neglected and important subject. Tobin, who has 'served as the extra-mural consultant for the Research Assessment Exercise (REA) 2000 for French Departments in the British Isles' has now 'more sympathy for those who publish with vanity presses' (p. 51). Thomas E. Hecker's 'The Twilight of Digitalization Is Now' (*JScholP* 35:i[2003] 52–62) argues that the 'transition from a paper-based knowledge system to an electronically based system ... is not sustainable' and that 'constraints on energy resources and other necessary resources will arrest digitalization in the not-distant future'. Hence for Hecker, 'archives in physical formats, not digitalized archives, are essential to preserve the scholarly record' (p. 52).

Book History (6[2003]), edited by Ezra Greenspan and Jonathan Rose, maintains the high standard set by previous volumes. It includes Edward Jacob's detailed 'Eighteenth-Century British Circulating Libraries and Cultural Book History' (*BoH* 6[2003] 1–22), which argues that 'circulating library catalogs show us the lived culture surrounding eighteenth-century British books' in ways that *The English Novel 1770–1829: A Bibliographical Survey of Prose Fiction Published in the British Isles* (TEN) and other resources cannot (p. 17). Jacob's argument is thoughtful, well-documented and enlightening. Anindita Ghosh's 'An Uncertain "Coming of the Book": Early Print Cultures in Colonial India' (*BoH* 6[2003] 23–55) places the Euro-centred study of the history of the book in a wider geographical and historical context by contrasting it with the history of the book in colonial India, focusing on nineteenth-century Bengal. Ghosh argues that 'print in nineteenth-century Bengal was not used and engineered by dominant power groups alone ... Most important, Bengali readers as consumers of print engaged with it as subjects and agents, capable of affecting its impact, thickening the modernity narrative and exposing its internal tensions' (p. 48). Replete with 118 footnotes and drawing on a wide range of documentation based on readings in nineteenth-century journals published in India, Ghosh's is an important pioneering study of a relatively neglected area of publishing history. Lisa Spiro's 'Reading with a Tender Rapture: Reveries of a Bachelor and the Rhetoric of

Detached Intimacy' (*BoH* 6[2003] 57–93) focuses on depictions of the American family in nineteenth-century American literature with a special focus on Emily Dickinson and Donald Grant Mitchell. Mitchell's *Reveries of a Bachelor* [1850], one of the most popular American works of the 1850s, 'offers a rich opportunity to study detached intimacy, since it focuses on fantasy and uses a rhetorical strategy that simultaneously invites readers' participation and pushes them away' (p. 61) Spiro's essay is illustrated with four figures, including the very suggestive one of Donald Grant Mitchell's leering bachelor narrator from his *The Lorgnette* [1850].

David Finkelstein's rather brief 'Jack's as Good as his Master: Scots and Print Culture in New Zealand, 1860–1900' (*BoH* 6[2003] 95–107) deals with an important subject, namely the impact of nineteenth-century Scottish immigration on New Zealand culture. His 'essay offers some insight into what the trained Scottish printer in particular might have found on his arrival' in New Zealand 'and the role Scots and their expertise in printing and publishing played in encouraging regional identities and the establishment of an infrastructure for print cultural activity in the first century of New Zealand's Pakeha (white) colonization' (p. 96). This important and huge subject is treated in a rather perfunctory manner, perhaps owing to a paucity of evidence, although Finkelstein does draw on contemporary letters and memoirs. Clearly this is the beginning of a subject which, curiously, does not seem to have received a great deal of attention, although New Zealand has produced many distinguished bibliographers and book historians of Scottish antecedence. In 'Japan and the Internationalization of the Serial Fiction Market' (*BoH* 6[2003] 109–25) Graham Law and Norimasa Morita examine the *roman-feuilleton*, which 'has a long history in Japan, perhaps even lengthier than in France its country of origin' (p. 109). They pay special attention to 'the systematic practice of serializing new fiction, not in independent installments or literary magazines but in the columns of newspapers' (p. 111). This fascinating and informative essay is accompanied by illustrations, including photographs, with examples of works of four Japanese translators/adapters of Western fiction during the Meiji Period (p. 118). Paul Eggert's 'Robbery Under Arms: The Colonial Market, Imperial Publishers, and the Demise of the Three-Decker Novel' (*BoH* 6[2003] 127–46) 'offers a case-study of the production history of a late Victorian novel by a colonial author, published in London by the firm of Remington in three volumes in 1888': *Robbery Under Arms* by 'Rolf Boldrewood'. This was the pseudonym used by Thomas Alexander Browne (1826–1915), a New South Wales magistrate (p. 127). Based on his case-study, Eggert draws a fascinating conclusion relating 'the demise of the three-decker form' to the growth in the colonial publishing trade (p. 141). Jason Camlot's 'Early Talking Books: Spoken Recordings and Recitation Anthologies, 1880–1920' (*BoH* 6[2003] 147–73) uses Thomas Edison's 1878 print speculations on 'the practical significance of his invention of a sound recording device or talking machine' (p. 147) as the foundation for a discussion of 'the ways in which all books can be said to talk' (p. 151). In addition to examining 'early spoken recordings', Camlot concludes that their examination reveals 'much about the modes of aesthetic experience produced by particular performative manifestations of literature, and can serve to remind us that reading a book is never a simple or quiet activity, but always a technologically informed and culturally rehearsed practice' (p. 168).

Andrew Nash, in 'A Publisher's Reader on the Verge of Modernity: The Case of Frank Swinnerton' (*BoH* 6[2003] 175–195), takes as his main focus Swinnerton's activity as reader for Chatto & Windus between the years 1909 and 1926, when 'he played a major role in helping to transform that firm into one of the most important literary publishers of the 1920s' (p. 175). Nash draws upon the Chatto & Windus archive held on deposit in Reading University Library and cites from Swinnerton's reader's reports. He places Swinnerton's activities as a reader in the historical context of other readers' activities and concerns and of the situation of the fortunes of Chatto & Windus. British publishing activity of the early years of the twentieth century is implicitly placed in perspective by the subject of the next essay, in which David Shneer draws upon the Russian State Archive for Social and Political Research, and other hitherto previously inaccessible archives, in his 'Who Owns the Means of Cultural Production? The Soviet Yiddish Publishing Industry of the 1920s' (*BoH* 6[2003] 197–226). This begins with a fascinating story of 'the midnight theft of reams of paper that had been earmarked for producing state-sponsored Yiddish books' from the Yiddish publishing warehouse in central Moscow. Shneer examines the activities of publishing houses during a revolutionary period of transition and compares 'quantitatively and qualitatively, the production of Soviet Jewish culture … [with] that of other ethnic minorities in the Soviet Union' (p. 219). Somewhat ironically given certain perceptions of F.R. Leavis, safer and calmer waters are negotiated in Ross Alloway's 'Selling the Great Tradition: Resistance and Conformity in the Publishing Practices of F.R. Leavis' (*BoH* 6[2003] 227–50). Alloway examines 'the circumstances in which Leavis's texts and his reputation were produced and disseminated' and observes that 'a close examination of Leavis's publishing history raises a number of pertinent questions, not least why a critic famously opposed to the twentieth-century book market was so effective in its manipulation' (p. 227). Alloway's analysis draws upon the Leavis papers at Reading and Cambridge university libraries. Rebecca Rego Barry, in 'The Neo-Classics: (Re)Publishing the "Great Books" in the United States in the 1990s' (*BoH* 6[2003] 251–75), considers the reprinting of classics in the Modern Library and other series, such as Penguin Classic paperbacks, in the last decade of the twentieth century. This issue of *Book History* concludes with Hortensia Calvo's 'The State of the Discipline, the Politics of Print: The Historiography of the Book in Early Spanish America' (*BoH* 6[2003] 277–305). Calvo's contribution concludes with the comment that 'much has yet to be explored with respect to the impact of books and printing on the social, cultural, and economic life of early Spanish America' (p. 296).

Students of bibliographical and textual criticism will find the following of interest in *Textual Practice* 17[2003]. Michael Gardiner's '"British Territory": Irvine Welsh in English and Japanese' (*TPr* 17[2003] 101–17) examines the implications of the export of the work of Irving Welsh during the late 1990s and its consequences, especially in terms of perceptions of 'Standard English' (p. 115). Melissa Mohr's 'Defining Dirt: Three Early Modern Views of Obscenity' (*TPr* 17[2003] 253–75) draws on the works of John Florio [published in 1598], Thomas Elyot [published in 1591], and George Puttenham [published in 1589] in order to examine the operation of bad language in the period. The relationship between a popular print culture and the destruction of an indigenous culture within the context of nineteenth-century Australia is the subject of Andrew McCann's 'The Savage Metropolis: Animism, Aesthetics and the Pleasures of a Vanished Race' (*TPr* 17[2003] 317–33). The focus of McCann's often opaque essay is the writing of Marcus Clarke, Henry Kendall and George Gordon McCrae during the 1860s. *Textual Practice* contains extensive book reviews. It must be confessed, however, that the present reviewers find the journal exceedingly dense stylistically. It is replete with interest in many areas, but we do wish its contributors would write more clearly and with less use of sometimes very complicated terminology.

Text: An Interdisciplinary Annual of Textual Studies 15[2003] contains sixteen essays and studies, six review essays, and seven reviews. Eight of the essays and studies in this issue are 'expanded versions of papers delivered at the 'Re-marking the Text' conference, held at the School of English, University of St Andrews, Scotland, in July 2001. The first essay in volume 15 is Barbara Oberg's Presidential Address delivered to the Society for Textual Scholarship on 20 April, 2001 and entitled 'Decoding an American Icon: The Textuality of Thomas Jefferson' (*Txt* 15[2003] 1–17). Oberg rightly draws attention to Jefferson's textual legacy. She pays particular attention to the three texts known to be extant of his first inaugural address upon becoming President of the United States on 4 March 1801. A totally different concern and subject is reflected in Ronald Broude's 'Composition, Performance, and Text in Solo Music of the French Baroque' (*Txt* 15[2003] 19–49). Broude's is a rather wordy disquisition on 'the relationships among composition, performance and text obtaining in French Baroque solo music' (p. 48). Broude draws, amongst others, from the work of François Couperin and Jacques Champion Dechambonnières. David Leon Higdon's 'The Concordance: Mere Index or Needful Census' (*Txt* 15[2003] 51–68) is a reflection upon the significance and usefulness of the concordance. The essay is, 'in part, an exercise in self-criticism', and a reflection on the experience of having made 'four concordance volumes'. After having constructed concordances to Joseph Conrad's novels and two novels by Henry James, Higdon 'did not fully know how to "use" them and had not had to answer a number of hard questions about them'. There appear to be today 'three central problems with literary concordances'. First, present-day ones seem to be 'marginalized from critical uses in ways the originating concordances were not'. Secondly, 'key information is often omitted'. Thirdly, 'one cannot be confident of an audience' (p. 55). Higdon's discussion ranges from scriptural concordances compiled in the sixteenth century through computer-generated concordances. He embraces discussions by Trevor H. Howard-Hill and Steven M. Parrish. Higdon's thoughtful reflections conclude with a listing of items which he feels should be offered in an introduction to a concordance. He is also somewhat envious of 'the concordance work of the future' (pp. 67–8).

Neil Fraistat and Steven E. Jones, 'Immersive Textuality: The Editing of Virtual Spaces' (*Txt* 15[2003] 69–82), consists of the reflections of 'editors of electronic archives and editions' on the implications of 'editing protocols and their differences from those in traditional textual editions' (p. 69). Fraistat and Jones assert that 'the historically dominant physique and technique of literary works, the technology of the codex book, is fundamentally a spatial matter' (p. 75). They conclude their reflections with the belief 'that computer-mediated editorial environments offer intriguing possibilities for editions of all kinds' (p. 82). Clearly the authors are excited by the web environment, and their considerations reflect some of their enthusiasm. Of course only time will tell whether with them this is only a passing phase, and indeed whether technology itself will make their thoughts redundant. A.S.G. Edwards, 'The Text of John Trevisa's Translation of Bartholomaeus Anglicus *De Proprietatibus Rerum*' (*Txt* 15[2003] 83–96), is a consideration of the Clarendon Press's three-volume text of John Trevisa's Middle English translation. The first two volumes were published in 1975, and the third in 1988. Edwards 'was involved in the editing of [the] first two volumes', but he 'did not contribute to the third volume of textual commentary' and did not feel 'able to continue to work on this edition'. His essay contains 'some attempt to set out the views on the editing of Trevisa's work' that led him to that position (p. 84). Daniel E. O'Sullivan's 'Text and Melody in Early Trouvère Song: The Example of Chrétien de Troyes's "D'Amors qui m'a tolu a moi"' (*Txt* 15[2003] 97–119) questions 'how closely literary scholars are committed to the belief that texts and melody are co-essential components of the lyric, for interpretation of Trouvere's song that integrates words and melody, while not entirely absent, remains sparse'. Instead O'Sullivan, in a reading of 'D'Amors qui m'a tolu a moi', offers 'an analytical model that integrates text and music and interpretation'. O'Sullivan's intention is 'to show how such readings enrich our understanding of the Trouvere art' (p. 97). This is a complex discussion with an appendix containing text and music followed by four extensive 'Bibliographical Notes' (pp. 111–19). Adrian Armstrong's 'Versification on the Page in Jean Molinet's *Art de rhétorique*: From the Aesthetic to the Utilitarian' (*Txt* 15[2003] 121–39) focuses upon the output of Jean Molinea, 'the profilic poet and chronicler of the fifteenth-century Burgundian Netherlands' (p. 121). Molinea's literary career, Armstrong tell us, 'lasted from the early 1460s until his death in 1507' (p. 122). Armstrong focuses largely on Molinea's *Art de rhétorique*, 'a manual of versification composed in or shortly before 1492' (p. 121). Following a detailed analysis of three manuscript transmissions of the *Art de rhétorique* and a consideration of the prosody and its printed forms, Armstrong concludes that 'Molinet's manual is a microcosm of its contemporary literary world' (p. 139). John Jowett explores, in 'Henry Chettle, "Your old Compositor"' (*Txt* 15[2003] 141–61), 'some aspects of' Henry Chettle's 'mediation between the printed trade and literary authorship' (p. 141). Chettle was active as a pamphlet writer and agent for stationers in the 1590s. He is better known for his printing activities and participation in the 'publication of the first edition of Romeo and Juliet in 1597' (p. 145). Jowett's article is somewhat marred by excursions into postmodern literary theory relating to 'the idea of the absent author'. Apart from this, he illuminates well the publishing activities of the 1590s. The activities 'of female printers, publishers, and booksellers' during the hundred years between 1550 and 1650 concern Helen Smith in her '"Print[ing] your royal father off": Early Modern Female Stationers and the Gendering of the British

Book Trades' (*Txt* 15[2003] 163–86). Three of the five illustrations accompanying Smith's contribution contain maps of the British Isles, and, in one instance, northern Europe, illustrating the 'geographical location of female stationers' or a 'provincial distribution network' (pp. 169–70, 172).

Danielle Clarke 'Nostalgia, Anachronism, and the Editing of Early Modern Women's Texts' (*Txt* 15[2003] 187–209), focuses on 'the political, textual, and methodological problems found in the editing of these texts' (pp. 187–8). H.T.M. van Vliet considers the reception of Emily Dickinson in the Netherlands and translations of the great poet into Dutch in 'The Introduction of Emily Dickinson in Holland and the Goals of Editing' (*Txt* 15[2003] 211–36). The author focuses specifically upon a proposed 'scholarly edition of the Dickinson translations by Vestdijk' (p. 229), who was born in 1898 and died in 1971. Vestdijk became 'one of the most important Dutch writers of the twentieth century' (p. 212) and in 1932 wrote an essay on Emily Dickinson. It is this essay and its manuscript which preoccupies a good deal of van Vliet's attention. Andrew van der Vlies, 'The Editorial Empire: The Fiction of "Greater Britain," and the Early Readers of Olive Schreiner's *The Story of an African Farm*' (*Txt* 15[2003] 237–60), discusses the earliest reception of Schreiner's novel [published in 1883]. Of particular interest is 'a series of letters written by Schreiner to the critic Philip Kent, between February and December 1883' (p. 241), in which Schreiner discusses her difficulties in finding a publisher for her novel. Chris Jones, '"One can emend a mutilated text": Auden's *The Orators* and the old English Exeter Book' (*Txt* 15[2003] 261–75), focuses on Auden's use of 'several poems from [the] problematic Old English miscellany as sources for sections of his work *The Orators*' (p. 262). Dirk Van Hulle's 'Words and Works: Transtextual Nominalism and Beckett's "Missing Word"' (*Txt* 15[2003] 278–90) focuses upon Beckett's later writings in order to comment on 'the controversy between editorial realists and textual nominalists' (p. 279). Van Hulle considers different versions of *Waiting for Godot* in order to observe that 'a crucial aspect of Beckett's poetics ... is essentially a poetics of process rather than an aesthetics of the finished product' (p. 288). Damian Judge Rollison, in his 'The Poem on the Page: Graphical Prosody in Postmodern American Poetry' (*Txt* 15[2003] 291–303), uses examples from Clark Coolidge and Robert Duncan. Rollison's aim is to comment upon 'certain types of signification—such as relative type size and the deployment of inter- and intra-linear white space'; these 'permit finer distinctions, as between chapter and initial page and body' (p. 292). Although Rollison's examples are rather limited, his reflections still raise fascinating issues concerning the significance of words on the page and their visual representation.

Translation and its electronic representation is the concern of Manuel Portela's 'Untranslations and Transcreations' (*Txt* 15[2003] 305–20). His focus is the work of the Brazilian poets Augusto de Campos and Geraldo Campos. Two of the review essays focus upon the significance of the recent work of David Greetham. Paul Eggert's 'These Post-Philological Days ...' (*Txt* 15[2003] 323–36) considers in extensive detail Greetham' *Theories of the Text* [1999]. Eggert finds the work to be brilliant, restless, endlessly curious'. For Eggert 'it is the last word for the editorial theory of the 1990s' (p. 336). Marta Werner, in her '"Post-Everything". David Greetham's Textual Transmissions: Essays Toward the Construction of a Bibliography' (*Txt* 15[2003] 337–49), also finds Greetham's work to be 'provocative, illuminous, and often maddening'. Greetham's 'essays on textuality describe the end of textual criticism while enacting the endlessness of that endgame' (p. 348). It is instructive to compare Eggert's and Werner's responses to Greetham with that of G. Thomas Tanselle whose strictures, as we have commented, in *SB* 54, are exceedingly negative. In 'The Hermeneutic Value of Material Texts', a review essay on George Bornstein's *Material Modernism: The Politics of the Page* [2001] (*Txt* 15[2003] 350–60), Nicholas Frankel considers Bornstein's book to be 'one of the fullest extensions of textual theory to the practical domains of literary criticism in recent years' (p. 360). Recent work on Oscar Wilde is the subject of David Holdeman in 'Wilde's Textual Masks', a review essay on *The Complete Works of Oscar Wilde*, volume 1: *Poems and Poems Prose* [2000], edited by Bobby Fong and Karl Beckson (*Txt* 15[2003] 361–71). W. Speed Hill's 'The Texts of Edmund Spenser's *The Faerie Queene*: Greg Redivivus?' (*Txt* 15[2003] 372–84) considers *The Faerie Queene* [2001], edited by A.C. Hamilton, Hiroshi Yamashita and Toshiyuki Suzuki, and *A Textual Companion to the Faerie Queene 1590* [1993], edited by Hiroshi Yamashita et al. H.T.M. Van Vliet, in 'New Standards in German Editing' (*Txt* 15[2003] 437–54), reviews two recent editions of works by Georg BǓchner, who died in 1837 at the age of 23. In addition to these review essays there are some lengthy reviews. Of particular interest are those by Wesley Raabe on Susan Hockey, 'Electronic Texts in the Humanities', and Dale Kramer's consideration of Martin Ray's *Thomas Hardy: A Textual Study of the Short Stories* [1997] (*Txt* 15[2003] 406–12).

The *Bibliographical Society of Australia and New Zealand Bulletin* 27[2003] begins with Ray Choate's 'Art: Genius and Madness in the Making and Keeping of Books' (*BSANZB* 27[2003] 1–2), an account of 'the [eight] papers presented Adelaide Conference of the Bibliographic Society of Australia and New Zealand in September 2001'. The theme was 'passion—or mania—in the world of books and bibliography' (p. 1). Wallace Kirsop's 'Boulard's Syndrome' (*BSANZB* 27[2003] 3–13) is an account of 'one of the most extraordinary figures in the annals of bibliomania' (p. 4) Antoine Marie-Henri Boulard (1754–1825). Boulard, a Parisian notary according to a translation published in London in 1893 of Octave Uzanne's *The Book-Hunter in Paris: Studies Among the Bookstalls and the Quays*, 'bought books by the metre … by the acre!' (p. 5). He also managed to publish various volumes and prefaces. K.K. Ruthven, in his 'From Imaginary Libraries to Ficto-Bibliography' (*BSANZB* 27[2003] 14–27), is concerned 'not with isolated instances of imaginary books but with their aggregation into satirical catalogues for the amusement of learned readers' (p. 15). Ruthven concludes sagely that 'the library catalogue is a dream of order imposed on the human imagination, whose operations are anarchic, and whose hybrid products frequently question the adequacy of any taxonomical system designed to contain them' (p. 27). Robyn Holmes, in 'Between the Sheets: Two Centuries of Australian Sheet Music' (*BSANZB* 27[2003] 28–33), draws on sheet music now at the National Library of Australia at Canberra where she is Curator of Music. Maureen Pritchard's 'Christine Macgregor's Illustrated Private Press Books' (*BSANZB* 27[2003] 34–47) considers the work of Christine Margaret Macgregor

(1890–1974), an active illustrated private press collector in both Australia and Britain, where she spent some time. Pritchard's article is a fascinating account of the migrations of books. J. McI. Emmerson's 'Dan Fleming and John Evelyn: Two Seventeenth Century Book Collectors' (*BSANZB* 27[2003] 48–61) is an account of the library of Dan Fleming (1633–1701), whose library was finally dispersed at Christie's at London in 1969. At the Christie's sale 'there were about 900 volumes, all printed before 1701 and all in plain contemporary bindings of calf or sheep, usually with handwritten paper labels' and largely 'in excellent condition' (p. 48). J. McI. Emmerson's concern is with Fleming's and Evelyn's book ordering on the shelf systems, or in other words, the attempt to maintain order in their collections. Patricia Holt, in '"It's enough to drive a bloke mad": Norman Lindsay's *Art and Literature*' (*BSANZB* 27[2003] 62–81), considers the reception of Lindsay's illustrations in Australia. Marcie Muir's 'The History of Prince Lee Boo' (*BSANZB* 27[2003] 82–90) discusses 'the publishing history of the story Prince Lee Boo, a young South Pacific Islander who in 1784 travelled on an East India Company packet to England where he was feted by London society but died of smallpox a few months later' (p. 1). Susan Woodburn's 'Making Books for God: Mission Printing in the Pacific Islands and Australia' (*BSANZB* 27[2003] 91–106) studies the intricacies of mission printing in exceedingly remote areas of the world, such as the Pacific Islands, in the very early nineteenth century. Patrick Spedding adds 'A Note on the Ornament Usage of Henry Woodfall' (*BSANZB* 27[2003] 109–16). Woodfall (1719–47) was a London printer, and Spedding adds to the listing of ornaments described in Richard Goulden's *The Ornament Stock of Henry Woodfall*. This issue of *BZANZB* concludes with reviews by Chris Tiffin, B.J. McMullin and Ian Morrison (*BSANZB* 27[2003] 117–25).

The 2002 edition of *Library History* includes two items of interest that were overlooked in last year's *YWES*. These include Peter H. Reid's 'Proto-Bibliophiles Amongst the English Aristocracy, 1500–1700' (*LH* 18[2002] 25–38), a narration concerning the early history of aristocratic book-collecting in Great Britain during the sixteenth and seventeenth centuries. Reid's contribution points clearly to the relationship between the rise of aristocratic bibliophilia and the interplay of its adherents with the royal court and the Church. Also of considerable interest is Mark Purcell's 'Warfare and Collection-Building: The Faro Raid of 1596' (*LH* 18[2002]), a highly informative account of the presence in the Bodleian Library of a number of Portuguese books dealing with the Faro and Cadiz raids of 1596 by the earl of Essex, the donor of the books. Purcell's article is interesting for the insights it provides regarding the importation of books into England during the sixteenth and seventeenth centuries and how the English binding trade profited from favourable protectionist measures in effect at the time. The July 2002 issue of *LH* contains several items of interest. Library settings in palatial houses in Victorian fiction, for instance in novels by Wilkie Collins, George Eliot and others, have been neglected. An article which throws some light on them is Jennifer Ciro's 'Country House Libraries in the Nineteenth Century' (*LH* 18[2002] 89–98). Ciro points out that nineteenth-century aristocrats maintained substantial libraries in their country houses; these frequently existed for a multitude of social reasons rather than for reading. She argues that 'the social life of the aristocrat library changed completely during the course of the century, from male sanctuary to public reception room' (p. 89). Her instances are drawn from the sixth duke of Devonshire's libraries at Chatsworth, the library at Wherstead, in Suffolk and elsewhere. Clearly, so much of importance transpires in library settings in fiction that more examination of actual Victorian country house libraries can only be useful for students of literature. Chris Baggs, '"Librarianship's a fraud—that's clear: for Africa I'll volunteer": Public Libraries and the Boer War' (*LH* 18[2002] 99–115), illuminates the background to a not forgotten imperial venture with profound consequences. Baggs's focus is 'the response—or lack of response—to the Boer War from public libraries in Great Britain' (p. 99). The growth of public libraries in twentieth-century provincial England is the subject of Dave Muddiman's 'The Public Library in an Age of Inclusion: Edward Sydney, Harold Jolliffe and the Rise and Fall of Library Extension, 1927–1972' (*LH* 18[2002] 117–30). Muddiman draws particular attention to the social inclusiveness of libraries in Leyton and Swindon, and to their social significance as a place for reading groups, dramatic productions, discussion groups, lectures on all types of topics, poetry readings, and so on.

The November 2002 issue of *LH* focuses on country house libraries. Mark Purcell's 'The Country House Library Reassess'd: Or, Did the "Country House Library" Ever Really Exist?' (*LH* 18[2002] 157–74) reveals that 'in reality surprisingly little work has actually been done' on what a country house library actually is, many of them being entirely mythical (p. 157). Purcell draws from the diversity of historical periods and sources to demonstrate that 'the very construct of the "country house library" is an artificial genre, one which often comes dangerously close to being a way of analyzing a library without having to know anything about its contents' (p. 171). This article, and its extensive documentation running to sixty-eight footnotes, is an important document for literary scholars concerned with what actually resides in terms of reading material within the English country house. A similar theme is pursued in Simon Jervis's 'The English Country House Library: An Architectural History' (*LH* 18[2002] 175–90). As its title suggests, Jervis's article, which begins with Henry VIII, is the examination of the architectural history of the English private library. He observes that, 'in the eighteenth century, the library often appears as a counterpoint to the chapel, a more popular choice than awarding a central position to the library'. With the Gothic influence and its ramifications, 'library rooms become more sociable and are often used to display portraits and sculpture. In Victorian times, the library was often a family living room' (p. 175). This article is again well documented, in this instance with 138 footnotes. A specific library is the subject of David Adshead's '"A Noble Musæum of Books": A View of the Interior of the Harleian Library at Wimpole Hall?' (*LH* 18[2002] 191–206). Adshead examines the various locations of the Harleian Library, which moved from London to Wimpole Hall in Cambridgeshire during the second decade of the eighteenth century. His focus is on the paintings and busts that adorn the libraries. Adshead makes particular use of Harley's 1742 sale catalogue of the collection of the late Edward, earl of Oxford. The article is particularly well documented and his footnotes are a rich source of information on the eighteenth-century history of the book.

Elizabeth Quarmby Lawrence, in her '"There is no describing the library": The Parkers of Saltram and their Books' (*LH* 18[2002] 207–14), examines 'when a country house book collection becomes a library'. She makes the distinction 'between a purposeful library and a random collection of books' (p. 207). Her examples are taken specifically from the library at Saltram House near Plymouth in Devon. This house belonged to the Parker family, local landed gentry, from the early eighteenth century until being transferred to the National Trust in 1957. Another library which remained in the hands of a family, in this instance the Bankes family, is the subject of Yvonne Lewis's 'Sir Ralph Bankes (1631–77) and the Origins of the Library at Kingston Hall' (*LH* 18[2002] 215–23). The library at Kingston Hall in Dorset was developed by Sir Ralph Bankes in the seventeenth century; he built up a collection of 'around 2,000 volumes, of which about one half are still extant' (p. 215).

Peter Hoare's 'The Perils of Provenance: Serial Ownership, Bookplates, and Obfuscation at Belton House' (*LH* 18[2002] 225–34) describes the Belton House Lincolnshire Library developed over a period of 'more than 300 years by successive members of the related Brownlow and Cust families. Most of the books survive and include many French and Italian works. Inscriptions and bookplates reveal that over 150 family members contributed to the collection' (p. 225). Hugh Meller's 'Knightshayes Court: Reconstructing a Victorian Library Room' (*LH* 18[2002] 235–8) is an all too brief account accompanied by two photographs of 'the original Victorian library room at Knightshayes Court in Devon which was restored in the 1980s after being removed thirty years earlier' (p. 235). Felicity Stimpson's '"Servant's Reading": An Examination of the Servants' Library at Cragside' (*LH* 18[2002] 3–11) uses the establishment, during the last decade of the nineteenth century, of a servants' library at Cragside in Northumberland, as evidence: 'such libraries are rare but can add to our understanding of contemporary reading practices' (p. 3). For instance, although the servants mainly had popular novels, the housekeeper's room had biographies and volumes by, amongst others, Trollope and Thackeray. The Servants Hall had bound sets of periodicals, including for instance *Good Words* for 1886. Stimpson shrewdly observes that 'The servants library at Cragside epitomizes the problems of trying to recreate reading history and much must remain supposition' (p. 9). Elizabeth Quarmby Lawrence's 'Researching Historic Library Buildings in the British Isles: Problems and Ways Forward' (*LH* 18[2002] 39–54) is a report commissioned by the committee of the British Library History Group, which 'has always been enthusiastic of the recording and preservation of libraries as physical entities' (p. 39) especially in an age of the destruction and disintegration of libraries and their buildings. Lawrence's report has four appendices: 'A Bibliography of General Sources for the Study of Historic Library Buildings, to 1945'; 'Historic Library Building to 1945: Websites'; 'Historic Library Buildings of Scotland: Data Collection'; and 'Historic Library Buildings of Scotland: Type of Library'.

The July 2003 issue of *LH* includes Michelle Johansen's 'A Fault-Line in Library History: Charles Goss, the Society of Public Librarians, and "the Battle of the Books" in the Late Nineteenth Century' (*LH* 19[2003] 75–91). In addition to outlining the professional life of Goss, 'librarian at London's Bishopsgate

Institute from 1897 until 1941', who amongst other activities was engaged in a bibliography of the writings of George Jacob Holyoake, the neglected Victorian radical and freethinker, this article deals with an important topic. Johansen raises the whole question of the control of libraries and the hitherto relatively unexamined subject of 'the inevitably narrow and partial interest of the Library Association' (p. 75)—the controlling professional library organization. Paul Sturges, 'Great City Libraries of Britain: Their History from a European Perspective' (*LH* 19[2003] 93–111), brings a different set of perspectives to bear upon attitudes to great British city libraries such as Manchester, Liverpool, Sheffield and Birmingham, as well as Leeds. Although Sturges grounds his article in the nineteenth-century creation of these libraries, a great deal of his focus is on late twentieth-century developments. A similar difference of perspective is the focus of Peter Vodosek's 'Transatlantic Perspectives: German Views of American Libraries and Vice Versa' (*LH* 19[2003] 113–18). Mark Purcell's 'The Private Library in Seventeenth- and Eighteenth-Century Surrey' (*LH* 19[2003] 119–27) returns to the subject of private libraries in country house settings in England. His particular focus is the library at Ham House, the home of the first duke of Lauderdale, which developed in the late seventeenth century. Eric Glasgow's 'Two Public Libraries in Victorian Liverpool' (*LH* 19[2003] 129–41) has as its focus 'two different libraries in nineteenth-century Liverpool: the Athenaeum … and the public library' (p. 129). On the other hand, Susie West's 'An Overlooked Inventory for Blickling Hall, Norfolk' (*LH* 19[2003] 143–5) draws upon archival sources to examine a seventeenth-century library.

In the November 2003 issue of *LH* contributions include Ruth Clayton's 'Masses or Classes? The Question of Community in the Foundation of Gladstone's Library' (*LH* 19[2003] 163–72). The focus of Clayton's article is the foundation of a politician's library created and built during the last two decades of the nineteenth century. A totally different walk of life is the concern of Peter Hoare's 'The Operatives' Libraries of Nottingham: A Radical Community's Own Initiative' (*LH* 19[2003] 173–84). Libraries north of the border occupy K.A. Manley in his 'Scottish Circulating and Subscription Libraries as Community Libraries' (*LH* 19[2003] 185–94). Manley focuses on Alan Ramsey's library in Edinburgh, which provided the model for other commercial circulating libraries in Scotland. His article concludes with a rather humorous and informative poem containing some of the contents of 'the Dalkeith Subscription Library, founded in 1798′ (p. 193). A county is the subject of Bob Duckett's historically based 'From Village Hall to Global Village: Community Libraries in England's Largest County' (*LH* 19[2003] 195–209). Duckett has a section entitled 'Before 1850: Where Did the Brontës Borrow Books?' (pp. 196–7). A specific town and its library provisions, or rather the lack of them, preoccupies Gordon Armstrong in his 'Libraries in Burnley, 1900, and the Absence of a Public Library' (*LH* 19[2003] 211–25).

Publishing History 53[2003] includes three lengthy articles. The first, Jeroen Salman, 'Peddling in the Past: Dutch Itinerant Bookselling in a European Perspective' (*PubH* 53[2003] 5–21), considers the 'important function of itinerant booksellers' who, for instance, acted 'as distributors of cheap print in seventeenth-century England' (p. 5). Salmon's emphasis is on the role played by

Dutch pedlars. There is some fascinating information here in need of elaboration. One would like to know, for instance, more on the activities of 'the street-seller Mathijs van Mordechay Cohen who bought his pornographic books in 1768 not in a bookshop but at the home of a bookbinder in the Pijlsteeg in Amsterdam' (p. 15). Valerie Gray's 'Charles Knight and the Society for the Diffusion of Useful Knowledge: A Special Relationship (1827–46)' (*PubH* 53[2003] 23–74), replete with a 152 footnotes, draws insightfully upon archival material in the SDUK Collection at University College London. Perhaps Valerie Gray will extend this article and her previous work on the SDUK to write the history of this influential nineteenth-century institution. Helen Small's 'Liberal Editing in the *Fortnightly Review* and the *Nineteenth Century*' (*PubH* 53[2003] 75–96) is a well-written analysis of the differences and similarities between these two important journals. She focuses upon the roles of the two respective editors, John Morley with the *Fortnightly*, and James Thomas Knowles with the *Nineteenth Century*. Small shrewdly observes that 'many of the claims' of her paper 'would, of course, hold true for any periodical or journal. Any editor's intellectual freedom will always be constrained by the presence of those others who have an interest in, and a degree of influence over, the way a periodical takes shape.' However, Small writes, 'such constraints were peculiarly over-determined in the context of late-Victorian liberalism' (p. 93).

Three extensive contributions form the contents of the fifty-fourth issue of *Publishing History*. The first, John Issitt's 'A Network for Radical and Political Education in the 1790s' (*PubH* 54[2003] 5–18), focuses, with illustrations, upon the record of the meeting of the Society of Constitutional Information, held on Friday, 29 June 1792. The records of the meeting are found today in the Treasury Solicitor's Papers at the Public Record Office (Document TS 11/962) (pp. 7–8). The document is reproduced in Issitt's article (pp. 9–11). The meeting concerned the drafting of a letter, 'the number of copies to be sent, the names of the people to receive them and the means by which they should be sent (p. 8). The letter was written by Tom Paine. Issitt discusses its distribution and concludes that 'the letter' played some, probably small, part in developing the political consciousness of the emerging working classes' (p. 17). An entirely different facet of publishing history is documented in the next article, by Phil Parkinson, who examines 'A Language Peculiar to the Word of God: The Anglican Liturgy in the Maori Language' (*PubH* 54[2003] 19–65). The 112 footnotes to this article show Parkinson drawing upon early nineteenth-century New Zealand materials, including those printed in the Maori language. His work 'describes the creation of the Maori translation of the Book of Common Prayer—the primary liturgical service book of the Maori Anglican Communion' (p. 19). This was begun in 1820 and initially 'completed' in 1841. Parkinson's is an important and fascinating insight into the history of the printed book in the early history of New Zealand. The concluding article in this issue of *Publishing History* returns to the 'Mother Country'. Stephen Colclough's '"A larger outlay than any return": The Library of W.H. Smith & Son, 1860–73' (*PubH* 54[2003] 67–93) draws on the archives of W.H. Smith to illuminate its library, which 'rapidly established itself as a major resource for Victorian readers' (p. 89). Drawing on exploitation of the railway system and the consequent opportunities for cheaper transportation, the Smiths were able to compete very favourably with other commercial libraries such as that operated by Charles Mudie. Colclough's article interestingly contains figures illustrating Smith's 'Subscription Library Rates' for December 1862 (p. 74) and 'Library Accounts for W.H. Smith & Son, 1 July 1860–31 December 1865' (pp. 80–1).

Moving from serials to monographic publications and essay collections, a number of notable works related to Shakespearian studies were published in 2003. In *As You Like It, Much Ado About Nothing, and Twelfth Night, or, What you will: an annotated bibliography of Shakespeare studies, 1673–2001*, Marilyn L. Williamson annotates upwards of 300 sources dealing with three of Shakespeare's middle comedies. Her effort updates previous work and is divided into five sections. The first focuses upon 'the most basic editions in general references', the second focuses upon the three comedies collectively, and the remaining sections focus on each of the three comedies. The second to fifth sections are subdivided by type of work, for example criticism, and include 'adaptations' and pedagogy. The arrangement is alphabetical within the subsections and the entries are arranged numerically. There are cross-references and the annotations are evaluative. All in all, this is a most useful addition to the bibliography of writings about the three plays. In *The Shakespeare First Folio: The History of the Book*, volume 2: *A New Worldwide Census of First Folios*, Anthony James West has assembled a work that will serve as a valuable reference tool regarding the number of known First Folios of Shakespeare's work scattered in their diverse locations. West's labours also provide a wonderful point of departure for future Shakespearian scholars and researchers.

The latest work by Stephen Orgel, a most distinguished Shakespearian scholar, *Imagining Shakespeare: A History of Texts and Visions*, is primarily concerned with Shakespearian texts. For Orgel, 'Shakespeare never conceived, or even re-conceived, his plays as texts to be read. They were scripts, not books; the only readers were the performers, and the function of the script was to be realized on the stage' (p. 1). Drawing upon his extensive knowledge of Shakespearian critical editions, myth, performance history and other elements, Orgel's book covers many areas of concern. For example, in his chapter on *The Merchant of Venice*, he analyses the different ways of perceiving Shylock on the stage, as well as differing critical perceptions of Shylock. The book is accompanied by detailed illustrations of actors and art associated with Shakespeare and Shakespearian performance.

Perhaps one of the most important books to appear for many years is Andrew Murphy's *Shakespeare in Print: A History and Chronology of Shakespeare Publishing*. Murphy attempts nothing less than the first-ever comprehensive chronology of the publishing of Shakespeare. His book is divided into two parts. The first deals with the 'text', and, in eleven chapters plus a conclusion, Murphy takes us on a voyage of description from the early quartos to the later twentieth century. His introduction places the accompanying history within its context and his conclusion deals with 'twenty-first-century Shakespeares'. The second part of Murphy's monograph consist of an appendix, with an introduction and an extensive hundred-page 'Chronological Appendix' containing the bibliographical details of all single-text Shakespeare editions up to 1709. Following this chronological documentation there are five indexes breaking the data in the appendix down by play/poem title, by series title, by editor, by publisher, and by place (excluding London). Murphy transforms what could be dull description into something highly readable. An example of his style appears in the opening sentence of his acknowledgements, where he writes: 'All books incur debts, but a book such as *Shakespeare in Print* acquires creditors at a rate of profligacy that would shame a drunken gambler' (p. ix).

Topics dealing with the history of the book, book-collecting, incunabula, book cover design, printing, and textual scholarship are well represented this year. In *Collecting Prints and Drawings in Europe c.1500–1750*, editors Christopher Baker, Caroline Elam and Genevieve Warwick have brought together twelve essays from different perspectives on 'some of the principle themes and individuals involved in the history of collecting works on paper in Renaissance and Early Modern Europe, as well as unifying research on prints and drawings' (p. iii). Of special interest to scholars of seventeenth-century English literature is Jeremy Wood's 'Nicholas Lanier (1588–1666) and the Origins of Drawing Collecting in Stuart England'. The volume is accompanied with black and white illustrations. Another compilation of essays dealing with collecting is Nash, ed., *The Culture of Collected Editions*, based on a conference held at the Institute of English Studies, School of Advanced Study, University of London in July 2001. The overall quality of the fifteen contributions is exceedingly high and the content is of importance to readers of *YWES*. Following Andrew Nash's introduction, 'The Culture of Collected Editions: Authorship, Reputation, and the Canon' (pp. 1–18), the book is divided into two parts. The first part, 'Authorial and Cultural Perspectives', consists of eight contributions: Ian Donaldson's 'Collecting Ben Jonson' (pp. 19–31); Peter Lindenbaum's 'Dividing and Conquering Milton' (pp. 32–48); James McLaverty's '"For who so fond as youthful bards of fame?" Pope's *Works* of 1717' (pp. 49–68); Michael Anesko's '"Notes Towards the Redefinition of Culture"' (pp. 69–79); Simon Gatrell's 'The Collected Editions of Hardy, James, and Meredith, with Some Concluding Thoughts on the Desirability of a Taxonomy of the Book' (pp. 80–94); Philip Horne's 'Henry James and the Cultural Frame of the *New York Edition*' (pp. 95–110); Andrew Nash's second contribution, '"The dead should be protected from their own carelessness": The Collected Editions of Robert Louis Stevenson' (pp. 111–27); and Warwick Gould's 'Contested Districts: Synge's Textual Self' (pp. 128–56). The second part. 'Editorial and Managerial Perspectives', consists of seven contributions: Grace Ioppolo's '"Much they ought not to have attempted": Editors of Collected Editions of Shakespeare from the Eighteenth to the Twentieth Centuries' (pp. 157–71); Andrew Murphy's 'Shakespeare Goes to College: Oxford and Cambridge Collected Editions' (pp. 172–82); J.C.C. Mays's 'The Life in Death of Editorial Exchange: The Bollingen Collected Coleridge' (pp. 183–200); Donald H. Reiman's 'Romantic Collected Editions: Varieties of Editorial Experience' (pp. 201–17); Peter Davison's 'An Editorial Assessment of *The Complete Works of George Orwell*' (pp. 218–36); Mathew J. Bruccoli's 'What Bowers Wrought: An Assessment of the Center for Editions of American Authors' (pp. 237–44); and Jerome J. McGann's 'Textonics: Literary and Cultural Studies in a Quantum World' (pp. 245–60). These distinguished contributors make this an important collection of essays encompassing diverse Anglo-American literatures and editing issues from the Renaissance to the present world of projected electronic/digital texts. Indeed, in the final essay Jerome J. McGann assesses the whole business of the advent of electronic media and their implications for editors and scholars.

Graphic Design, Print Culture and the Eighteenth-Century Novel by Janine Barchas synthesizes traditional bibliographical approaches with book history and literary criticism. The focus of attention is Samuel Richardson, and especially *Clarissa*, with its use of a musical score, and printers' ornaments suggesting the passage of time. Discussion also includes the subject of punctuation in Sarah Fielding's *David Simple*. Barchas' book is well illustrated and almost convinces the reader that 'accidentals' have more substantive importance than has hitherto has been acknowledged. In *Victorian Decorated Trade Bindings, 1830–1880: A Descriptive Bibliography*, Edmund M.B. King has completed an important and exhaustively researched and detailed work regarding the evolution of book cover design in Victorian England. Over 750 book items are discussed and indexed, and King's work will serve as a much-heralded reference source for students and professional researchers of publishing practices and habits in the Victorian era. Steven Roger Fischer, in *A History of Reading*, is concerned with the evolution from ancient times to the present day of reading habits and patterns. In seven chapters, beginning with reading before the papyrus through to the present electronic world, Fischer explores what it means to read. In his preface he observes: 'Writing is expression, reading impression. Writing is public, reading personal. Writing is limited, reading open-ended. Writing freezes the moment. Reading is forever' (p. 8). In *Marketing Modernism between the Two World Wars*, Catherine Turner examines the marketing strategies of five major publishing houses during the 1920s and 1930s and provides insight into how works of literary fiction were mass-produced and marketed to mainstream America. The publishing houses profiled range from small firms to large corporate entities, and Turner's highly readable work demonstrates the emergence of a mass consumer market for literature, reflecting the changes evident in American culture and society between the two world wars. Turner's is an interesting and perhaps timely piece in the light of the ongoing consolidation of the publishing industry into ever larger disparate corporate entities.

In Jensen, ed., *Incunabula and their Readers: Printing, Selling and Using Books in the Fifteenth Century*, eleven original and informative essays have been assembled, each originally presented as papers at a conference of the same name held at the University of London's Senate House to celebrate the Gutenberg Year of 2000. While diverse in their specific content, the essays contained in this work all address important aspects related to the development of the book in the fifteenth century. A wide range of methodologies is evident in these pieces, demonstrating the interdisciplinary nature of studies related to the book and publishing in general. Included are eight colour plates, a notes section, and an index. In *The Pleasures of Bibliophily. Fifty Years of The Book Collector: An Anthology*, editor Nicolas Barker has culled the best essays from the last fifty years that have appeared in *The Book Collector* and has assembled a very impressive collection. A significant number of the selections deal with specific books, authors, and related topics. Barker, who has edited *The Book Collector* since 1965, has a second contribution to this year's *YWES* in his *Form and Meaning in the History of the Book*, a wonderful example of his wide-ranging interests and expertise. In this edition of selected essays, topics covered include books and texts, typography and early printing, the history of the book, bookselling, the forgery of manuscripts, and books and people. The volume marks Nicolas Barker's seventieth birthday, and demonstrates well the range and depth of his extensive bibliophilic interests and scholarship.

Philip H. Young's *The Printed Homer: A 3,000 Year Publishing and Translation History of the Iliad and the Odyssey* is divided into two sections. In the first Young considers such issues as the identity of Homer, the creation of the Homeric text, and its history through the centuries. The second portion of the work is an extensive, chronologically based listing of all known printed editions of the Homeric texts. Young begins with a Greek/Latin version of 'The Battle of the Frogs and Mice' which appeared in the early years of the fifteenth century; he concludes with the English translation of the *Iliad* which Oxford University Press published in 2000. The seven appendices list printings by author or translator, printings by printer or publisher, place where printed, and first printings in the vernacular languages. Clearly Young's volume is of use for students of English literature, and his application of computer technology makes it even more relevant.

The seventeenth and latest volumes to be published of R.C. Alston's bibliographical exploration of writings on English, *A Bibliography of the English Language from the Invention of Printing to the Year 1800: A Systematic Record of Writings on English, and on Other Languages in English Based on the Collections of the Principal Libraries of the World* focuses on botany, horticulture, and agriculture. As Alston explains in his introduction, 'This volume is not a bibliography of the history of botany in England, but seeks to identify all works published between 1525 and 1800 in which the names of plants in English are provided, either in the body of the text or in an index. It omits works written wholly in Latin' (p. vii). The first volume contains bibliographical descriptions and an extensive index of authors, translators, editors and illustrators. The second volume contains facsimiles of title pages. In *The Meaning of Everything: The Story of the Oxford English Dictionary*, Simon Winchester presents the progress of the *OED* from its inception to its vaulted ascendancy as one of the premier sources regarding the meaning and use of the English language. In presenting his work, Winchester provides the reader with intriguing glimpses of the individuals associated with its development, including James Murray, although greater emphasis is placed on the early years of the *OED* and scanter attention is devoted to its later years of development. While not a thick book, it does contain some quality photographs and includes a six-page index to assist the reader in navigating its pages. Overall, a nice addition to the corpus of literature associated with both nineteenth-century England and the field of lexicography. Another useful general reference source of interest is Levinson, ed., *The Oxford Handbook of Aesthetics*. Under Jerrold Levinson's shrewd guidance and direction, forty-eight essays have been assembled to assist students and academics working in the field of philosophical aesthetics, with the overall structure of the work divided into three main parts. Part 1 deals mainly with chapters devoted to issues such as expression, fiction, and aesthetic experience. Part 2 deals with these as they intersect with specific art forms such as music, film, or dance. Part 3 deals largely with interdisciplinary issues, those fields of enquiry that focus on the relations between aesthetics and other disciplines. The chapters vary in length, with an average of 8,500 words for each entry. While much of the content is heavily Anglo-American in nature, readers will find a wealth of valuable material in its pages. Each chapter concludes with a list of cross-references to chapters and items of similar interest in the handbook, providing a seamless quality that assists the reader in getting the most out of this excellent and valuable work.

Roger Schonfeld's *JSTOR: A History* is an important history of a recent highly trumped development which may or may not stand the test of time. JSTOR, underwritten by the Andrew W. Mellon Foundation, is the attempt to give electronic access to journals. It developed from its infancy in 1993 to two years later emerging as an independent organization. The president of the Andrew W. Mellon Foundation, William G. Bowen, believed that enormous amounts of physical space could be saved in university libraries in North America by the creation of a very reliable and high-quality digital archive. Roger C. Schonfeld writes in his introduction: 'Publicly available since 1997, JSTOR has digitized the backfiles of about three hundred academic journals, as far back as 1665 in one case, and distributes them online to libraries around the world' (p. xvi). His history of this development is fascinating and 'worth telling as the case of a well-managed non-profit' tale (p. xix). There is an 'Epilogue' on the 'lessons learned', and an appendix updated to 31 December 2001 lists all journals in the arts and sciences and in general science and business whose full text is accessible through JSTOR. Many more are now available. Of course, JSTOR is important for contemporary literary researchers and students. What a historian of *YWES* will think of the whole idea in even a decade or two's time, the present writers can only speculate. The sceptics amongst us may argue that JSTOR is a current and passing fad, especially given the enormous degree of mutability involved in anything electronic—indeed, in life itself.

It is appropriate after JSTOR to consider Joseph Loewenstein's historically based monograph, *The Author's Due: Printing and the Prehistory of Copyright*. Loewenstein's work is nothing short of a history of intellectual property. His study begins with the law of intellectual property; amongst the phenomena considered are 'changes in industrial organization characteristic of early modern economic practice [that] can be seen with particular clarity of the early history of the book trade' (p. 22). Following an extensive introductory chapter encompassing theories of authorship and discussion of Foucault's theories, Loewenstein moves into the implications of an industrial dispute 'within the Stationers' Company arising in the late 1570s'. Loewenstein begins with this as he regards it as 'a watershed in the history of English intellectual property' (p. 23). He then examines the Elizabethan book trade, monopolies, and the development of 'the interplay of economic policy and ideological control in the early European book trade'. The focus is upon England and the sixteenth and seventeenth centuries. In his final chapter, entitled 'Authentic Reproductions', Loewenstein, as his subheadings suggest, writes on 'Shakespeare and international copyright;

modernist technologies of reproduction and the institutional history of the book; the Wise forgeries' (p. vii). All in all then, these two books, Schonfeld on *JSTOR* and Loewenstein on *Printing and the Prehistory of Copyright*, provide much food for thought within the context of recent developments generated by the implications of electronic technology.

Similar concerns underpin David McKitterick's *Print, Manuscript and the Search for Order, 1450–1830*, which reconsiders assumptions underlying perspectives on the printing revolution of the early modern period. The book is a 'considerably expanded version of the Lyell lectures in Bibliography, delivered at the Oxford University in May 2000' (p. ix). Placing the electronic implications for bibliography—such as scanned images—in perspective, McKitterick emphasizes the importance of original printed documents for the investigation of the processes of manufacture, of the materials involved, of typography, of design method, and of the habits of workmen and their masters within the actual printing house. His deeply learned study negotiates the areas of the actual printed text and their electronic reproduction. He also draws attention to late-nineteenth century perceptions concerning ways in which the early printed book was used. It is salutary to be reminded that notions of the early printed book were the product of a historical construct—a late nineteenth-century construct. Well illustrated with materials from Oxford and Cambridge college and university libraries, McKitterick's is an important monograph.

There are two titles of interest for readers interested in illustration and its relationship to books and bibliographies. In *The Life and Works of Alfred Bestall, Illustrator of Rupert Bear*, with a foreword by Sir Paul McCartney, Caroline G. Bott has produced an original and unique item documenting the work and life of Alfred Bestall (1892–1986). Drawing heavily on sources such as Bestall's diaries and sketches, as well as letters, photographs and archival materials, Bott provides a detailed portrait that admirers of Bestall's work will greatly appreciate. The book is divided into five chapters, each corresponding to significant periods of Bestall's life and work. Included are sample materials from Bestall's sketchbooks and a listing of his artwork. In *Edward Ardizzone: A Bibliographic Commentary*, Brian Alderson has provided a wonderfully produced account of Ardizzone's work, which included illustrating over 200 books and pamphlets prior to his death in 1979. Alderson's commentary includes material related to Ardizzone's work involving dust-jackets, his commercial work and other ephemera, his periodical contributions, war art, posters, prints, and bookplates. The Bibliographic Commentary includes over seventy black and white illustrations.

In *Justice Denoted: The Legal Thriller in America, British, and Continental Courtroom Literature* Terry White has compiled a unique, slightly eccentric, but interesting book covering the legal thriller genre. Items discussed by White include mostly novels, with some short-story collections, teleplays, and cinematic adaptations. Overall, this is a unique contribution, which should definitely please its intended audience and a fine example of bibliography devoted to genre literature. British and American crime fiction from the eighteenth century to the end of the twentieth are the subject of Priestman, ed., *The Cambridge Companion to Crime Fiction*. Regarding authors profiled, readers will find the expected names of Arthur Conan Doyle, Raymond Chandler, and Agatha Christie, but other lesser-known authors are also represented, including those whose work represents the thriller and spy genres. The *Companion* contains fourteen essay contributions that represent an eclectic grouping of topics from respected international specialists. Overall, this *Cambridge Companion* will serve as a valuable reference source to students and professional researchers alike.

Another item touching upon fictionalized legal works is Treadwell, ed., *The Bulldog Drummond Encyclopedia*, with forewords by Andrew Drummond, Calthrop McNeile, and F.I. 'Jock' Fairlie. Treadwell's industrious efforts have produced a volume that, in exacting detail, describes the characters and stories of the much-beloved Bulldog Drummond. Treadwell's work serves as a wonderful example of a piece of 'niche scholarship', the result being a most useful book devoted to a fictional character whose exploits endured beyond his original creator (Herman Cyril McNeile) and entertained many between the two world wars until exiting the stage during the 1950s as new themes and characters, principally James Bond, came to dominate the printed word and feature films. Genre literature is further explored in James and Mendlesohn, eds., *The Cambridge Companion to Science Fiction*. Divided into three sections, James and Mendlesohn's work consists of twenty original essays composed by scholars and practitioners. Issues include the origins and inception of the genre, its historical development, and the methodologies used to critique the field as it grows in both popularity and acceptance as a scholarly field of research. The largest section of the *Companion* deals with the various themes and sub-genres of science fiction.

Items devoted to the subject of national literatures were well represented this year. The subject of American writers and scholarship is highlighted in several works, including the well-respected *American Literary Scholarship: An Annual 2001*. Edited by Gary Scharnhorst, a role he has distinguished himself in for the last ten years, the edition for 2001 is divided into three main sections, and has twenty-one contributions, including one by Scharnhorst concerning 'General Reference Works'. Useful indexes related to author and subject assist the reader in using this perennial and valued publication. Another perennial source related to archival scholarship and the bibliographical analysis of American literature is Bryer and Kopley, eds., *Resources for American Literary Study*, volume 28. This current edition includes thirty-one valuable essays and a very useful comprehensive index to volumes 1–27, compiled by Heather Moreland of the University of Maryland. Serafin, ed., *The Continuum Encyclopedia of American Literature*, contains brief entries related to American writers, poets, literary critics and playwrights, among other topics. Entries consist of evaluative narratives of varying lengths and include limited bibliographies devoted to further readings. Unfortunately, this particular work lacks a title index and this limits its usefulness, particularly for the general reader and undergraduate student.

The topic of contemporary gay authors, both well-known and lesser-known talents, is the subject of Nelson, ed., *Contemporary Gay American Poets and Playwrights: An A-to-Z Guide*, published by Greenwood. The work includes sixty-two entries, each with a standard structure consisting of sections devoted to biography, major works, themes, and critical reception, and concluding with useful bibliographies to assist in further reading and research. An original and laudatory example of scholarship is provided in Sibyl E. Moses, *African American Women Writers in New Jersey, 1836–2000: A Biographical Dictionary and Bibliographic Guide*. Moses' work is groundbreaking as it documents the lives and work of over a hundred African American women writers native to New Jersey. Historically she covers the period from 1836 to 2000. In addition to chronicling the biographical and bibliographical detail of the women she profiles, Moses also included material related to reports and articles authored by her subjects, as well as excerpts from their work. Photographs are included for most of her subjects, as well as two appendices which delineate the geographical distribution of her subjects by genre and city and town of residence. Moses' work represents scholarship at its best and will serve as a valuable tool not only for the cultural history of New Jersey and US women's history, but also as an example to be emulated for similar topics and themes.

In *A Companion to the Regional Literatures of America*, editor Charles L. Crow has compiled thirty original essays that add to this popular and growing field of enquiry and research. The book is arranged in three main sections: the 'History and Theory of Regionalism in the United States', a discussion of the theories used in discussing American regional literary issues; 'Mapping Regions', the largest section of the book, which discusses regional literatures based on geography; and 'Some Regional Masters', a discussion of recognized masters who have made an enduring and lasting impression in the field, such as Bret Harte, Mark Twain, Willa Cather and Wallace Stegner. A useful index is also included. In *Gertrude Stein: The Language That Rises, 1923–1934*, Ulla E. Dydo, with assistance from William Rice, has written a work that extensively examines Stein's letters, notebooks, and manuscripts with the purpose of reviewing Stein's literary output during what is often considered her most productive period as an author. Stein scholars and professional researchers will find Dydo's work a welcome addition to existing scholarship.

Huang, ed., *Asian American Short Story Writers: An A-to-Z Guide*, published by Greenwood Press, discusses the work of forty-five Asian American authors. Each entry is divided into sections dealing with biography, major works, themes, and critical reception, and has useful bibliographies subdivided into works about and by the authors profiled. In *American Literature and the Culture of Reprinting, 1834–1853*, Meredith L. McGill has assembled a thorough and interesting work dealing with such diverse issues as copyright law, plagiarism, writer–reader relations, unauthorized reprints, and the desire to establish a unique and original American literary culture. Although it is largely a historical work, McGill employs methods of research commonly associated with bibliography as well as a number of other disciplines. Under the editorship of Gregg Camfield, Oxford University Press has published *The Oxford Companion to Mark Twain*, a highly informative, valuable and useful work containing over 300 compelling and original essays as well as entries arranged in an A–Z format. This work is also lavishly illustrated, including reproductions of early facsimile pages and selections from Twain's novels, as well as an eight-page photo essay chronicling the most important events of Twain's long, productive and sometimes tragic life.

In *1000 Years of English Literature: A Treasury of Literary Manuscripts*, Chris Fletcher, Curator of Library Manuscripts at the British Library has compiled, with the assistance of Roger Evans and Sally Brown, an impressive and valuable resource for scholars and students of English literature. Arranged chronologically, it describes manuscripts of the works of around eighty of the greatest British and Irish writers which are now at the British Library, beginning with *Beowulf* and concluding with Ted Hughes. The book is subdivided into periods, and chapter headings include 'Early and Medieval', 'Renaissance and Restoration', 'The Eighteenth Century', 'The Nineteenth Century' and 'The Twentieth Century'. A useful index is included, as well as a short suggested further readings section. *1000 Years of English Literature* is lavishly illustrated. Catherine Lynette Innes's *A History of Black and Asian Writing in Britain* is a pioneering effort to chronicle the output of forgotten authors whose work was often popular in its contemporary setting. Relying heavily on archival sources, Innes argues that many 'non-white' authors represented a challenge to British ideological and cultural norms, and that their work has multicultural importance, as well as abundant interest for cultural and literary historians. A detailed bibliography and index are included in this important work.

Robert J. Griffin, ed., *The Faces of Anonymity: Anonymous and Pseudonymous Publications from the Sixteenth Century to the Twentieth Century*, is an interesting and highly original piece of scholarship. In ten chapters Griffin has assembled a series of provocative and original essays that deal with the issue of anonymous publication in England from the Elizabethan age up to the present. Each essay has an extensive notes section, and the work also contains a useful index. An interesting and little-known aspect of British literature is the topic of Eugenia R. Vera's *The British Book Trade and Spanish American Independence: Education and Knowledge Transmission in Transcontinental Perspective*. Vera considers the export of books from Britain to Spanish America and discusses aspects of how these books helped shape cultures, customs, and identities in the New World. Her work should pique the interest of not only book lovers and bibliophiles, but also book historians and scholars whose major area of research concerns cultural and social history throughout Latin America. Included in this fine and highly original work are three appendices dealing with the Spanish publication of the Ackerman publishing house, the dominant exporter of British books to the New World. The book also contains a bibliography and a useful index. Frank Shovlin's *The Irish Literary Periodical 1923–1958* is a long overdue study focusing on six important Irish literary magazines: *The Irish Statesman* [1923–30], *The Dublin Magazine* [1923–58], *Ireland To-Day* [1936–8], *The Bell* [1940–54], *Envoy* [1949–51] and *Rann* [1948–53]. In addition, Shovlin's study concludes 'with a survey of the literary journal's progress in Ireland up to the end of the twentieth century' (p. 4). The selected journals are examples of a neglected genre which made an important contribution to literary and cultural history at a difficult time 'for writers who wished to remain in Ireland and stay true to their art' (p. 3). Shovlin's analysis is thorough, well documented, and well written. His is an important contribution to scholarship on the literary periodical and to the history of the book in Ireland and in general.

Welsh writing for English readers is discussed in detail in Thomas, ed., *A Guide to Welsh Literature: Welsh Writing in English*, published by the University of Wales Press. Under M. Wynn Thomas's editorship, ten essays have been assembled that trace and analyse the rise, growth, and development of Welsh literature from the Middle Ages to the present day. The latest publication in *The Collected Works of James Hogg* made its appearance in 2003 as represented by *In Altrive Tales: Collected among the Peasantry of Scotland and from Foreign Adventurers*, edited by Gillian Hughes. This latest addition to this ongoing series contains much useful material, including notes relating to the text, a hyphenation list, a glossary, an index and three illustrations. Australian subjects are represented in several publications, the first being Sellick, ed., *Venus in Transit: Australia's Women Travellers, 1788–1930*. In this interesting work, Douglas R.G. Sellick has brought together original accounts of twenty female travellers, presenting their experiences as representative of the British fascination with antipodean travel. The accounts presented range from early colonial times to modern Australia. In a work whose subject is one of the most respected contemporary writers, Bruce Woodcock has revised and brought out the second edition of his earlier bibliography, *Peter Carey*, devoted to the Australian-born writer who has resided for some time in the United States. Woodcock's work is divided into sections listing Carey's fiction, non-fiction, screenplays, uncollected works, manuscripts, interviews and profiles, video material, websites, criticism, and general articles and essays on Carey. Woodcock's latest edition is highly recommended as a mandatory purchase regarding the still flourishing career of this most important author. In *A Companion to Catalan Literature*, Arthur Terry illuminates an important and distinctive body of work little known outside Catalonia. Terry's book is divided into six sections: 'Medieval and Early Renaissance', 'Decadence and Enlightenment', 'The Nineteenth Century', 'The Twentieth Century', 'The Present' and an 'Epilogue'. A select bibliography is included, as well as an index related to English translations which English-speaking readers will find helpful and useful. Terry focuses primarily on major writers, and places each within their relevant historical and social context, and his research efforts have produced a work that will serve as a valuable resource on an otherwise obscure but vital literary tradition.

For those interested in the intersection of bibliographical and textual studies with the subject of religion, there are three items of particular interest. The first of these is McKendrick and O'Sullivan, eds., *The Bible As Book: The Transmission of the Greek Text*. This publication represents the final title in a five volume series published by Oak Knoll Press and the British Library devoted to the art and science of textual criticism of the Greek Bible. Examples of topics covered in the sixteen essays contained in the work include the relationship between Jewish scribal culture and Christian writing practices, and the discovery of Greek biblical texts in the Judaean desert. In *The Book of Hebrew Script: History, Palaeography, Script Styles, Calligraphy and Design*, Ada Yardeni delineates the development of the Hebrew script, starting in the eighth century. This valuable work includes over 480 illustrations regarding the design of Hebrew letters. Bruschi and Biller, eds., *Texts and the Repression of Medieval Heresy*, examines the substance and intent of texts used to co-ordinate and implement the Inquisition. The efforts of editors Caterina Bruschi and Peter Biller provide a richly historical survey of the central role these texts played in helping shape and guide the course of the Inquisition, and the eleven essays in the work represent a significant contribution to textual studies.

We conclude this year's review with two items. *The Eighteenth Century: A Current Bibliography*, under the general editorship of Jim Springer Borck and Steven R. Price, 'lists significant books, articles, and reviews published during 1993 together with some from preceding years' (p. v). The annotations are thorough. The problem is, people in the field have waited ten years for it to appear! On a more positive note, Colin G.C. Tite, in *The Early Records of Sir Robert Cotton' s Library: Formation, Cataloguing and Use* is well illustrated, and a thorough and important piece of scholarship. Indeed, British Library Publications, under its sagacious head, David Way, continues to produce in splendid volumes seminal works which will stand the test of time. 'About 270 distinct records of loans, acquisitions and, occasionally, of other matters relating to the library are printed and edited' in Tite's volume (p. 3). There are three indexes: 'Index of Printed Books' (pp. 275–6), 'Index of Names' (pp. 277–93), and 'Index of Manuscripts Cited' (pp. 294–7).

Books Reviewed

Alderson, Brian. *Edward Ardizzone: A Bibliographic Commentary*. OakK. [2003] pp. 292. $75 ISBN1 5845 6103 3.

Alston, R.C. *A Bibliography of the English Language from the Invention of Printing to the Year 1800: A Systematic Record of Writings on English, and on Other Languages in English Based on the Collections of the Principal Libraries of the World,* Leeds [England] printed for the author E.J. Arnold 2 vols. [2003] ISBN 0 9022 9608, 0 9022 9611 6.

Baker, Christopher, Caroline Elam and Genevieve Warwick, eds. *Collecting Prints and Drawings in Europe, c.1500–1750*. Ashgate. [2003] pp. xxvii +225. $80 ISBN 0 7546 0037 8.

Barchas, Janine. *Graphic Design, Print Culture, and the Eighteenth-Century Novel*. CUP. [2003] pp. 296. $60 ISBN 0 5218 1908 3.

Barker, Nicolas. *Form and Meaning in the History of the Book*. BL. [2003] pp. xiii +514. £50 ISBN 0 7123 4777 1.

Barker, Nicolas, ed. *The Pleasures of Bibliophily. Fifty Years of The Book Collector: An Anthology*. OakK. [2003] pp. 320 + 50 b/w illustrations. $59.95 ISBN 5845 6097 5.

Borck, Jim Springer, and Steven R. Price, gen. eds. *The Eighteenth Century: A Current Bibliography*. Ns 19 [for 1993], part II, sections V–VI. AMS. [2003] pp. 475. $94.75 ISBN 0 4046 2194 5.

Bott, Caroline G. *The Life and Works of Alfred Bestall, Illustrator of Rupert Bear*. Foreword by Sir Paul McCartney. Bloomsbury. [2003] pp. xiii +338 + 32 pp. plates. £20 ISBN 0 7475 7336 0.

Bruschi, Caterina, and Peter Biller, eds. *Texts and the Repression of Medieval Heresy*. York Medieval Press. [2003] pp. xvii +256. $90 ISBN 1 9031 5310 7.

Bryer, Jackson R., and Kopley Richard. *Resources for American Literary Study*, 28. AMS. [2003] pp. vii +317. $89.50 ISBN 0 4046 4628 X.

Camfield, Gregg. *The Oxford Companion to Mark Twain*. OUP. [2003] pp. xxi +767 + 8 pp. plates. $65 ISBN 0 1951 0710 1.

Crow, Charles L., ed. *A Companion to the Regional Literatures of America*. Blackwell. [2003] pp. xvi +606. $131.65 ISBN 0 6312 2631 1.

Dydo, Ulla E., with William Rice. *Gertrude Stein: The Language That Rises, 1923–1934*. NorthwesternUP. [2003] pp. xvi +686. $49.95 ISBN 0 8101 1919 6.

Fischer, Steven Roger. *A History of Reading*. Reaktion. [2003] pp. 240. £19.95 ISBN1 8618 9160 1.

Fletcher, Chris. *1000 Years of English Literature: A Treasury of Literary Manuscripts*. BL. [2003] pp. 191. $51.65 ISBN 0 7123 4814 X.

Griffin, Robert J., ed. *Faces of Anonymity: Anonymous and Pseudonymous Publications from the Sixteenth to the Twentieth Century*. Palgrave. [2003] pp. xi +260. $65 ISBN 0 3122 9530 8.

Huang, Guiyou. *Asian American Short Story Writers: An A-to-Z Guide*. Greenwood. [2003] pp. 359. $94.95 ISBN 0 3133 2229 5.

Hogg, James. *Altrive Tales: Collected among the Peasantry of Scotland and from Foreign Adventurers by the Ettrick Shepherd*, ed. by Gillian Hughes. EdinUP. [2003] pp. lvxii +293. $60 ISBN 0 7486 1893 7.

Innes, Catherine Lynette. *A History of Black and Asian Writing in Britain*. CUP. [2002] pp. xxi +308. $80.06 ISBN 0 5216 4327 9.

James, Edward, and Farah Mendlesohn, eds. *The Cambridge Companion to Science Fiction*. CUP. [2003] pp. xxvii +295. $65 ISBN 0 5218 1626 2.

Jensen, Kristian, ed. *Incunabula and their Readers: Printing, Selling and Using Books in the Fifteenth Century*. UTorP. [2003] pp. x + 291. $75 ISBN 0 7123 4769 0.

King, Edmund M.B. *Victorian Decorated Trade Bindings, 1830–1880: A Descriptive Bibliography*. OakK. [2003] pp. xxiii +324. $98 ISBN 1 5845 6095 9.

Levinson, Jerrold. *The Oxford Handbook of Aesthetics*. OUP. [2003] pp. xv +821. $75 ISBN 0 1982 5025 8.

Loewenstein, Joseph. *The Author's Due: Printing and the Prehistory of Copyright*. UChicP. [2003] pp. x + 349. $50 ISBN 0 2264 9040 8.

McGill, Meredith L. *American Literature and the Culture of Reprinting, 1834–1853*. UPennP. [2003] pp. 364. $39.95 ISBN 0 8122 3698 X.

McKendrick, Scot, and Orlaith O'Sullivan. *The Bible as Book: The Transmission of the Greek Text*. U of Chicago Press. [2003] pp. 252. $60 ISBN 1 5845 6082 7.

McKitterick, David. *Print, Manuscript and the Search for Order, 1450–1830*. CUP. [2003] pp. 360. $75 ISBN 0 5218 2690 X.

Moses, Sibyl E. *African American Women Writers in New Jersey, 1836–2000: A Biographical Dictionary and Bibliographic Guide*. RutgersUP. [2003] pp. xx +231. $60 ISBN 0 8135 3183 7.

Murphy, Andrew. *Shakespeare in Print: A History and Chronology of Shakespeare Publishing*. CUP. [2003] pp. xiii +503. $75 ISBN 0 5217 7104 8.

DUBLIN BUSINESS SCHOOL LIBRARY

Nash, Andrew, ed. *The Culture of Collected Editions*. Palgrave. [2003] pp. xii +274 + 4 pp. plates. $69.95 ISBN 1 4039 0266 6.

Nelson, Emmanuel S., ed. *Contemporary Gay American Poets and Playwrights: An A-to-Z Guide*. Greenwood. [2003] pp. 475. $99.95 ISBN 0 3133 2232 5.

Orgel, Stephen. *Imagining Shakespeare: A History of Texts and Visions*. Palgrave. [2003] pp. 172. $26.95 ISBN 1 4039 1177 0.

Priestman, Martin, ed. *The Cambridge Companion to Crime Fiction*. CUP. [2003] pp. xvii +287. £45 ISBN 0 5218 0399 3.

Scharnhorst, Gary, ed. *American Literary Scholarship: An Annual 2001*. DukeUP. [2003] pp. xx + 588. $60 ISSN 0065 9142.

Schonfeld, Roger C. *JSTOR: A History*. PrincetonUP. [2003] pp. xxxiv +412. $37.95 ISBN 0 6911 1531 1.

Sellick, Douglas R.G., ed. *Venus in Transit: Australia's Women Travellers, 1788–1930*. Freemantle Arts Centre Press. [2003] pp. 364. $24.95 ISBN 1 8636 8394 1.

Serafin, Steven, ed. *The Continuum Encyclopedia of American Literature*. Continuum. [2003] pp. 1,305. $49.95 ISBN 0 8264 1517 2.

Shovlin, Frank. *The Irish Literary Periodical 1923–1958*. OUP. [2003] $110 ISBN 0 1992 6739 1.

Terry, Arthur. *A Companion to Catalan Literature*. B&B. [2003] pp. viii +172. $70 ISBN 1 8556 6089 X.

Thomas, M. Wynn, ed. *A Guide to Welsh Literature: Welsh Writing in English*, vol. 7. UWalesP. [2003] pp. 348. £14.99 ISBN 0 7083 1679 4.

Tite, Colin G.C. *The Early Records of Sir Robert Cotton's Library: Formation, Cataloguing, and Use*. BL. [2003] pp. xviii +297. £60 ISBN 0 7123 4824 7.

Treadwell, Lawrence P. Jr. *The Bulldog Drummond Encyclopedia*. Forewords Andrew Drummond, Calthrop McNeile, and F.I. 'Jock' Fairlie. McFarland. [2001] pp. 223. $45 ISBN 0 7864 0769 7.

Turner, Catherine. *Marketing Modernism between the Two World Wars*. UMassP. [2003] pp. 280. $39.95 ISBN 1 5584 9376 X.

Vera, Eugenia Roldán. *The British Book Trade and Spanish American Independence: Education and Knowledge Transmission in Transcontinental Perspective*. Ashgate. [2003] pp. xiv +287. $94.95 ISBN 0 7546 3278 4.

West, Anthony J. *The Shakespeare First Folio. The History of the Book*, vol. 2. *A New Worldwide Census of First Folios*. OUP. [2003] pp. 308. $200 0 1981 8768 8.

White, Terry. *Justice Denoted: The Legal Thriller in American, British, and Continental Courtroom Literature*. Foreword Michael A. Kahn. Praeger. [2003] pp. xxv +560. £61.50 ISBN 0 3133 0301 0.

Williamson, Marilyn L. *As You Like It, Much Ado About Nothing, and Twelfth Night, or, What You Will: An Annotated Bibliography of Shakespeare Studies, 1673–2001*. Pegasus. [2003] $9.95 ISBN 1 8898 1835 6.

Winchester, Simon. *The Meaning of Everything: The Story of the Oxford English Dictionary*. OUP. [2003] pp. xxii +271. $25 ISBN 0 1986 0702 4.

Woodcock, Bruce. *Peter Carey*. 2nd edn. ManUP. [2003] pp. x + 223. $21.95 ISBN 0 7190 6798 7.

Yardeni, Ada. *The Book of Hebrew Script: History, Palaeography, Script Styles, Calligraphy and Design*. OakK. [2003] pp. 365. $69.95 ISBN 1 5845 6087 8.

Young, Philip H. *The Printed Homer: A 3,000 Year Publishing and Translation History of the Iliad and the Odyssey*. McFarland. [2003] $75 ISBN 0 7864 1550 9.

Index I. Critics

Notes

(1) Material which has not been seen by contributors is not indexed.
(2) Authors such as J.M. Coetzee, who are both authors of criticism and subjects of discussion, are listed in whichever index is appropriate for each reference.
(3) Contributors to multi-authored works, all of whom may not be mentioned in the text, are listed with the name of the first author in brackets

DUBLIN BUSINESS SCHOOL
LIBRARY

Index II. Authors and Subjects Treated

Notes

(1) Material which has not been seen by contributors is not indexed.
(2) Authors such as J.M. Coetzee, who are both authors of criticism and subjects of discussion, are listed in whichever index is appropriate for each reference.
(3) Author entries have subdivisions listed in the following order:
  (a) author's relationship with other authors
  (b) author's relationship with other subjects
  (c) author's characteristics
  (d) author's works (listed alphabetically)
(4) A page reference in **bold** represents a main entry for that particular subject.